WHITAKER'S CONCISE ALMANACK
2005

A & C BLACK

LONDON

AN

Almanack

For the Year of Our Lord

2005

ESTABLISHED 1868

BY

JOSEPH WHITAKER, FSA

CONTAINING AN ACCOUNT OF THE

ASTRONOMICAL AND OTHER PHENOMENA

AND

A vast Amount of INFORMATION respecting the
GOVERNMENT, FINANCES, POPULATION,
COMMERCE, and GENERAL STATISTICS of
the various Nations of the WORLD
with an INDEX containing
nearly 10,000
References

LONDON

OFFICE: 37 SOHO SQUARE
LONDON W1D 3QZ

The traditional design of the title page for Whitaker's Almanack which has appeared in each edition since 1868

WHITAKER'S CONCISE ALMANACK
2005

A & C BLACK

LONDON

A & C BLACK (PUBLISHERS) LTD
37 Soho Square, London W1D 3QZ

Whitaker's Almanack published annually since 1868
© 137th edition A & C Black (Publishers) Ltd 2004

CONCISE EDITION
Paperback 0-7136-6996-9

STANDARD EDITION
Hardback 0-7136-6995-0

Designed by: Fiona Pike
Jacket photographs: © Corbis
Typeset in the EU by: RefineCatch Ltd,
  Bungay, Suffolk, Great Britain
Printed and bound in the EU by: William Clowes,
  Beccles, Suffolk, Great Britain

The publishers make no representation, express or implied, with regard to the accuracy of the information contained in this book and cannot accept legal responsibility for any errors or omissions that take place.

Crown copyright material is reproduced with the permission of the Controller of Her Majesty's Stationery Office.

Whitaker's is a Registered trade mark of J. Whitaker and Sons Ltd, Registered Trade Mark Nos. (UK) 1322125/09; 13422126/16 and 1322127/41; (EU) 19960401/09, 16, 41, licensed for use by A & C Black (Publishers) Ltd.

A CIP catalogue record for this book is available from the British Library.

EDITORIAL STAFF
Editor-in-Chief: Lauren Simpson
Editor: Inna Ward
Editorial team: Ruth Northey; Anna Collishaw; Luke Block

INDEX
Colin Izat, Fiona Smith – IndX Ltd

CONTENTS

6

TIME AND SPACE

PREFACE

TO THE 137TH ANNUAL EDITION

Welcome to the 2005 edition of *Whitaker's Concise Almanack*. Since the research and updating of this edition commenced, much has taken place on the global stage. The Madrid bombings in March 2004 indicate that the campaign against terror is far from over and allegations that US and UK troops tortured prisoners of war in Iraq caused widespread controversy during April and May. At home we countenanced higher-than-ever turnouts for the Mayoral, London Assembly and European elections and saw interest rates steadily increase following a 40-year low.

If there is one thing certain in the media it's that today's top stories rapidly become yesterday's news. No sooner do we finish reading a newspaper or watching a news broadcast when some other story develops to capture our attention. In such a fast-paced world, *Whitaker's Almanack* is invaluable because it summarises recent newsworthy events, outlines governmental and infrastructural developments and keeps one appraised of who's who and what's what in the UK today while, at the same time, providing a unique, historical record for the future.

It is of vital importance that a reference book like *Whitaker's Concise Almanack* goes further than merely reporting headline news. By providing such information as who runs our public offices, how our water and energy industries operate, how much it costs to send a child to an independent school and how our national health system works, *Whitaker's Concise Almanack* gives a real insight into exactly which people, institutions and processes keep modern Britain's cogs turning. And, lest we forget, *Whitaker's Concise Almanack*'s value as an all-round reference tool is enhanced by the inclusion of such stalwart sections as tidal data, astronomy and calendars.

As our world changes, it is important that *Whitaker's Concise Almanack* evolves accordingly, and we included a readership survey in last year's edition to build a picture of what readers want from *Whitaker's Concise Almanack* in the future. I'd like to take this opportunity to thank all those who took the time to fill in our questionnaire. We received some constructive feedback which will help us ensure that *Whitaker's Concise Almanack* continues to improve year on year and that new content is added to give the publication a contemporary feel.

It was particularly refreshing to see from the results that over 90% of readers either 'liked' or 'strongly liked' the new page design. Other interesting findings included:

- The most frequently read sections are Government and Parliament
- The least frequently read sections are Astronomy and Peerage

This edition includes comprehensive coverage of the European Parliament and London Assembly and Mayoral elections, and included for the first time in *Whitaker's Concise Almanack* is a section on historic and tourist sites in London.

As always, this edition has been fully updated using only the most authoritative sources. Each year literally hundreds of people and organisations assist in the updating of *Whitaker's Concise Almanack*. Without such help and support, *Whitaker's Concise Almanack* would be but a shadow of its current form. To all of you, many thanks.

Lauren Simpson
Editor-in-Chief

Whitaker's Almanack
A & C Black Publishers Ltd
37 Soho Square
London
W1D 3QZ

Email: whitakers@acblack.com
Web: www.whitakersalmanack.com

THE YEAR 2005

CHRONOLOGICAL CYCLES AND ERAS

Dominical Letter	B
Golden Number (Lunar Cycle)	XI
Julian Period	6718
Roman Indiction	13
Solar Cycle	26

	Beginning
Japanese year Heisei 17	1 January
Chinese year of the Chicken or Rooster	9 February
Regnal year 54	6 February
Hindu new year	9 April
Indian (Saka) year 1927	9 April
Muslim year AH 1426	10 February
Sikh new year	14 March
Jewish year AM 5766	4 October
Roman year 2758 AUC	

RELIGIOUS CALENDARS

CHRISTIAN

Epiphany	6 January
Presentation of Christ in the Temple	2 February
Ash Wednesday	9 February
Maundy Thursday	24 March
The Annunciation	25 March
Good Friday	25 March
Easter Day (western churches)	27 March
Easter Day (Eastern Orthodox)	1 May
Rogation Sunday	1 May
Ascension Day	5 May
Pentecost (Whit Sunday)	15 May
Trinity Sunday	22 May
Corpus Christi	26 May
All Saints' Day	1 November
Advent Sunday	27 November
Christmas Day	25 December

HINDU

Makara Sankranti	14 January
Vasant Panchami (Sarasvati-puja)	13 February
Mahashivaratri	8 March
Holi	25 March
Chaitra (Hindu new year)	9 April
Ramanavami	18 April
Raksha-bandhan	19 August
Janmashtami	26 August
Ganesh Chaturthi, first day	7 September
Ganesh festival, last day	17 September
Durga-puja	4 October
Navaratri festival, first day	4 October
Sarasvati-puja	10 October
Dasara	12 October
Diwali, first day	30 October
Diwali, last day	3 November

JEWISH

Purim	25 March
Passover, first day	24 April
Feast of Weeks, first day	13 June
Jewish new year, first day	4 October
Yom Kippur (Day of Atonement)	13 October
Feast of Tabernacles, first day	18 October
Chanucah, first day	26 December

MUSLIM

Muslim new year	10 February
Ramadan, first day	4 October

SIKH

Birthday of Guru Gobind Singh Ji	5 January
Baisakhi Mela (Sikh new year)	14 March
Martyrdom of Guru Arjan Dev Ji	16 June
Birthday of Guru Nanak Dev Ji	15 November
Martyrdom of Guru Tegh Bahadur Ji	24 November

CIVIL CALENDAR

Accession of Queen Elizabeth II	6 February
Duke of York's birthday	19 February
St David's Day	1 March
Earl of Wessex birthday	10 March
Commonwealth Day	14 March
St Patrick's Day	17 March
Birthday of Queen Elizabeth II	21 April
St George's Day	23 April
Europe Day	9 May
Coronation of Queen Elizabeth II	2 June
Duke of Edinburgh's birthday	10 June
The Queen's Official Birthday	11 June
Princess Royal's birthday	15 August
Lord Mayor's Day	12 November
Remembrance Sunday	13 November
Prince of Wales's birthday	14 November
Wedding Day of Queen Elizabeth II	20 November
St Andrew's Day	30 November

LEGAL CALENDAR

LAW TERMS

Hilary Term	11 January to 23 March
Easter Term	5 April to 27 May
Trinity Term	7 June to 29 July
Michaelmas Term	1 October to 21 December

QUARTER DAYS

England, Wales and Northern Ireland

Lady	25 March
Midsummer	24 June
Michaelmas	29 September
Christmas	25 December

TERM DAYS

Scotland

Candlemas	28 February
Whitsunday	28 May
Lammas	28 August
Martinmas	28 November
Removal Terms	28 May, 28 November

2005

JANUARY							FEBRUARY						MARCH					
Sunday	2	9	16	23	30		Sunday		6	13	20	27	Sunday		6	13	20	27
Monday	3	10	17	24	31		Monday		7	14	21	28	Monday		7	14	21	28
Tuesday	4	11	18	25			Tuesday	1	8	15	22		Tuesday	1	8	15	22	29
Wednesday	5	12	19	26			Wednesday	2	9	16	23		Wednesday	2	9	16	23	30
Thursday	6	13	20	27			Thursday	3	10	17	24		Thursday	3	10	17	24	31
Friday	7	14	21	28			Friday	4	11	18	25		Friday	4	11	18	25	
Saturday	1	8	15	22	29		Saturday	5	12	19	26		Saturday	5	12	19	26	

APRIL							MAY						JUNE					
Sunday	3	10	17	24			Sunday	1	8	15	22	29	Sunday		5	12	19	26
Monday	4	11	18	25			Monday	2	9	16	23	30	Monday		6	13	20	27
Tuesday	5	12	19	26			Tuesday	3	10	17	24	31	Tuesday		7	14	21	28
Wednesday	6	13	20	27			Wednesday	4	11	18	25		Wednesday	1	8	15	22	29
Thursday	7	14	21	28			Thursday	5	12	19	26		Thursday	2	9	16	23	30
Friday	1	8	15	22	29		Friday	6	13	20	27		Friday	3	10	17	24	
Saturday	2	9	16	23	30		Saturday	7	14	21	28		Saturday	4	11	18	25	

JULY							AUGUST						SEPTEMBER					
Sunday	3	10	17	24	31		Sunday		7	14	21	28	Sunday		4	11	18	25
Monday	4	11	18	25			Monday	1	8	15	22	29	Monday		5	12	19	26
Tuesday	5	12	19	26			Tuesday	2	9	16	23	30	Tuesday		6	13	20	27
Wednesday	6	13	20	27			Wednesday	3	10	17	24	31	Wednesday		7	14	21	28
Thursday	7	14	21	28			Thursday	4	11	18	25		Thursday	1	8	15	22	29
Friday	1	8	15	22	29		Friday	5	12	19	26		Friday	2	9	16	23	30
Saturday	2	9	16	23	30		Saturday	6	13	20	27		Saturday	3	10	17	24	

OCTOBER							NOVEMBER						DECEMBER					
Sunday	2	9	16	23	30		Sunday		6	13	20	27	Sunday		4	11	18	25
Monday	3	10	17	24	31		Monday		7	14	21	28	Monday		5	12	19	26
Tuesday	4	11	18	25			Tuesday	1	8	15	22	29	Tuesday		6	13	20	27
Wednesday	5	12	19	26			Wednesday	2	9	16	23	30	Wednesday		7	14	21	28
Thursday	6	13	20	27			Thursday	3	10	17	24		Thursday	1	8	15	22	29
Friday	7	14	21	28			Friday	4	11	18	25		Friday	2	9	16	23	30
Saturday	1	8	15	22	29		Saturday	5	12	19	26		Saturday	3	10	17	24	31

PUBLIC HOLIDAYS	England and Wales	Scotland	Northern Ireland
New Year	†3 January	3, 4 January	†3 January
St Patrick's Day	–	–	‡17 March
*Good Friday	25 March	25 March	25 March
Easter Monday	28 March	–	28 March
Early May	†2 May	2 May	†2 May
Spring	30 May	†30 May	30 May
Battle of the Boyne	–	–	‡12 July
Summer	29 August	1 August	29 August
*Christmas	25, 26 December	25, †26 December	25, 26 December
	27 taken in lieu	27 taken in lieu	27 taken in lieu

*In England, Wales and Northern Ireland, Christmas Day and Good Friday are common law holidays
In the Channel Islands, Liberation Day is a bank and public holiday
† Subject to royal proclamation
‡ Subject to proclamation by the Secretary of State for Northern Ireland

2006

JANUARY
Sunday	1	8	15	22	29
Monday	2	9	16	23	30
Tuesday	3	10	17	24	31
Wednesday	4	11	18	25	
Thursday	5	12	19	26	
Friday	6	13	20	27	
Saturday	7	14	21	28	

FEBRUARY
Sunday		5	12	19	26
Monday		6	13	20	27
Tuesday		7	14	21	28
Wednesday	1	8	15	22	
Thursday	2	9	16	23	
Friday	3	10	17	24	
Saturday	4	11	18	25	

MARCH
Sunday		5	12	19	26
Monday		6	13	20	27
Tuesday		7	14	21	28
Wednesday	1	8	15	22	29
Thursday	2	9	16	23	30
Friday	3	10	17	24	31
Saturday	4	11	18	25	

APRIL
Sunday		2	9	16	23	30
Monday		3	10	17	24	
Tuesday		4	11	18	25	
Wednesday		5	12	19	26	
Thursday		6	13	20	27	
Friday		7	14	21	28	
Saturday	1	8	15	22	29	

MAY
Sunday		7	14	21	28
Monday	1	8	15	22	29
Tuesday	2	9	16	23	30
Wednesday	3	10	17	24	31
Thursday	4	11	18	25	
Friday	5	12	19	26	
Saturday	6	13	20	27	

JUNE
Sunday		4	11	18	25
Monday		5	12	19	26
Tuesday		6	13	20	27
Wednesday		7	14	21	28
Thursday	1	8	15	22	29
Friday	2	9	16	23	30
Saturday	3	10	17	24	

JULY
Sunday		2	9	16	23	30
Monday		3	10	17	24	31
Tuesday		4	11	18	25	
Wednesday		5	12	19	26	
Thursday		6	13	20	27	
Friday		7	14	21	28	
Saturday	1	8	15	22	29	

AUGUST
Sunday		6	13	20	27
Monday		7	14	21	28
Tuesday	1	8	15	22	29
Wednesday	2	9	16	23	30
Thursday	3	10	17	24	31
Friday	4	11	18	25	
Saturday	5	12	19	26	

SEPTEMBER
Sunday		3	10	17	24
Monday		4	11	18	25
Tuesday		5	12	19	26
Wednesday		6	13	20	27
Thursday		7	14	21	28
Friday	1	8	15	22	29
Saturday	2	9	16	23	30

OCTOBER
Sunday	1	8	15	22	29
Monday	2	9	16	23	30
Tuesday	3	10	17	24	31
Wednesday	4	11	18	25	
Thursday	5	12	19	26	
Friday	6	13	20	27	
Saturday	7	14	21	28	

NOVEMBER
Sunday		5	12	19	26
Monday		6	13	20	27
Tuesday		7	14	21	28
Wednesday	1	8	15	22	29
Thursday	2	9	16	23	30
Friday	3	10	17	24	
Saturday	4	11	18	25	

DECEMBER
Sunday		3	10	17	24	31
Monday		4	11	18	25	
Tuesday		5	12	19	26	
Wednesday		6	13	20	27	
Thursday		7	14	21	28	
Friday	1	8	15	22	29	
Saturday	2	9	16	23	30	

PUBLIC HOLIDAYS

	England and Wales	Scotland	Northern Ireland
New Year	†2 January	2, 3 January	†2 January
St Patrick's Day	–	–	‡17 March
*Good Friday	14 April	14 April	14 April
Easter Monday	17 April	–	17 April
Early May	†1 May	1 May	†1 May
Spring	29 May	†29 May	29 May
Battle of the Boyne	–	–	‡12 July
Summer	28 August	7 August	28 August
*Christmas	25, 26 December	25, †26 December	25, 26 December

*In England, Wales and Northern Ireland, Christmas Day and Good Friday are common law holidays
In the Channel Islands, Liberation Day is a bank and public holiday
† Subject to royal proclamation
‡ Subject to proclamation by the Secretary of State for Northern Ireland

FORTHCOMING EVENTS

*Provisional dates
†Venue not confirmed

JANUARY
6–16   Schroders London Boat Show, Excel,
           London Docklands
15–30   London International Mime Festival
19–23   London Art Fair, Business Design
           Centre, London

FEBRUARY
9   Chinese New Year Celebrations,
           London
11–13   Labour Party Spring Conference,
           Newcastle/Gateshead
26–6 March Bath Literature Festival

MARCH
2–28   Ideal Home Exhibition, Earls Court,
           London
3   World Book Day
10–13   Crufts Dog Show, NEC, Birmingham
10–13   Liberal Democrat Party Spring
           Conference, Newcastle/
           Gateshead
11–20   National Science Week
13–15   London Book Fair, London Olympia

APRIL
April–October Pitlochry Festival Theatre season
21–24   Chelsea Art Fair, Chelsea Old Town
           Hall

MAY
19–28 August   Glyndebourne Festival Opera season
20–5 June Bath International Music Festival
24–28   Chelsea Flower Show, Royal
           Hospital, Chelsea
27–5 June The Hay Festival, Hay-on-Wye,
           Hereford
May–September Chichester Festival Theatre season,
           Tayside

JUNE
June–August   Royal Academy of Arts Summer
           Exhibition
10–26   The Aldeburgh Festival of Music and
           the Arts
11   Trooping the Colour, Horseguards
           Parade, London

JULY
1–17   Cheltenham International Festival of
           Music
3–6   The Royal Show, National
           Agricultural Centre, Stoneleigh
           Park
5–10   Hampton Court Palace Flower Show,
           Surrey
8–17   York Early Music Festival
8–24   Buxton Festival, Derbyshire
Mid-July   The Welsh Proms, St David's Hall,
           Cardiff
15–10 September BBC Promenade Concerts, Royal
           Albert Hall, London

20–24   RHS Flower Show, Tatton Park,
           Cheshire
30–6 August   Royal National Eisteddfod of Wales,
           Meifod, Powys

AUGUST
5–27   Edinburgh Military Tattoo,
           Edinburgh Castle
6–12   Three Choirs Festival, Worcester
14–4 September Edinburgh International Festival
23–25   Wisley Flower Show, RHS Garden,
           Wisley
28–29   Notting Hill Carnival, Notting Hill,
           London
27–29   Town and Country Festival, National
           Agricultural Centre, Stoneleigh
           Park

SEPTEMBER
2–6 November   Blackpool Illuminations, Promenade
3   Braemar Royal Highland Gathering,
           Aberdeenshire
September TUC Annual Congress
16–25   Southampton Boat Show, Mayflower
           Park, Southampton
18–22   Liberal Democrat Party Autumn
           Conference, Bournemouth
25–29   Labour Party Conference, Brighton

OCTOBER
3–6   Conservative Party Conference,
           Blackpool
6   National Poetry Day
October–January Turner Prize Exhibition
*20 October–4 London Film Festival, NFT and other
November   venues

NOVEMBER
6   London to Brighton Veteran Car Run
12   Lord Mayor's Procession and Show,
           City of London
18–27   Huddersfield Contemporary Music
           Festival
28–29   CBI Annual Conference

SPORTS EVENTS

FEBRUARY
13–20   Snooker: Masters, Wembley
           Conference Centre
5   Rugby Union: Six Nations
           Championship, France v. Scotland,
           Stade de France
5   Rugby Union: Six Nations
           Championship, Wales v. England,
           Millennium Stadium, Cardiff
6   Rugby Union: Six Nations
           Championship, Italy v. Ireland,
           Stadio Faliminio, Rome
12   Rugby Union: Six Nations
           Championship, Italy v. Wales,
           Stadio Faliminio, Rome
12   Rugby Union: Six Nations
           Championship, Scotland v.
           Ireland, Murrayfield

13	Rugby Union: Six Nations Championship, England v. France, Twickenham	14–17	Golf: The Open Championship, St Andrews Golf Club
26	Rugby Union: Six Nations Championship, Scotland v. Italy, Murrayfield	14–23	Shooting: NRA Imperial Meeting, Bisley Camp, Surrey
26	Rugby Union: Six Nations Championship, France v. Wales, Stade de France	28–31	Golf: The Women's British Open, Royal Birkdale Golf Club, Southport
27	Rugby Union: Six Nations Championship, Ireland v. England, Lansdowne Road	30–6 August	Sailing: Cowes Week, Isle of Wight

MARCH

AUGUST

12	Rugby Union: Six Nations Championship, Ireland v. France, Lansdowne Road	7	Sailing: The Rolex Fastnet Race
12	Rugby Union: Six Nations Championship, England v. Italy, Twickenham	27	Rugby League: Challenge Cup Final, Millennium Stadium, Cardiff

SEPTEMBER

13	Rugby Union: Six Nations Championship, Scotland v. Wales, Murrayfield	1–4	Burghley Horse Trials, Burghley Park, Lincolnshire
19	Rugby Union: Six Nations Championship, Italy v. France, Stadio Faliminio, Rome	9–11	Golf: The Solheim Cup, Indiana, USA

OCTOBER

19	Rugby Union: Six Nations Championship, Wales v. Ireland, Millennium Stadium, Cardiff	12–16	Horse of the Year Show, NEC, Birmingham

HORSE RACING

19	Rugby Union: Six Nations Championship, England v. Scotland, Twickenham	26 March	Lincoln Handicap, Doncaster
27	Oxford and Cambridge Boat Race, Putney to Mortlake, London	7–9 April	Grand National, Aintree, Liverpool
		30 April	Two Thousand Guineas, Newmarket
		1 May	One Thousand Guineas, Newmarket

APRIL

16–2 May	Snooker: Embassy World Championship, Crucible Theatre, Sheffield	3 June	The Oaks, Epsom
		3 June	Coronation Cup, Epsom
		4 June	The Derby, Epsom
17	Athletics: Flora London Marathon	14–18 June	Royal Ascot
		22 July	King George VI and Queen Elizabeth Diamond Stakes

MAY

5–8	Badminton Horse Trials, Badminton	9 September	St Leger, Doncaster
8	Welsh FA Cup Final†	29 September–1 October	Cambridgeshire Meeting, Newmarket
12–15	Royal Windsor Horse Show, Home Park, Windsor	13–15 October	Champions Meeting, Newmarket
21	The FA Cup Final, Millennium Stadium, Cardiff		

CRICKET

28	Scottish FA Cup Final, Hampden Park, Glasgow	*Npower Test Match Series*	
28–10 June	TT Motorcycle Races, Isle of Man	26–30 May	England v. Bangladesh, 1st, Lord's
30–4 June	British Amateur Golf Championship, Royal Birkdale/Southport and Ainsdale Golf Clubs	3–7 June	England v. Bangladesh, 2nd, Durham
		21–25 July	England v. Australia, 1st, Lord's
		4–8 August	England v. Australia, 2nd, Edgbaston
		11–15 August	England v. Australia, 3rd, Old Trafford, Manchester

JUNE

20–3 July	Tennis: Wimbledon Championship, All England Lawn Tennis Club, Wimbledon	25–29 August	England v. Australia, 4th, Trent Bridge, Nottingham
29–3 July	Rowing: Henley Royal Regatta, Henley-on-Thames	8–12 September	England v. Australia, 5th, The Oval

JULY

		NatWest Series	
		16 June	England v. Bangladesh, The Oval
		18 June	Australia v. Bangladesh, Cardiff
*3	British Formula 1 Grand Prix, Silverstone, Northants	19 June	England v. Australia, Bristol
9–17	Sailing: The Admiral's Cup	21 June	England v. Bangladesh, Trent Bridge, Nottingham
		25 June	Australia v. Bangladesh, Old Trafford, Manchester
		28 June	England v. Australia, Edgbaston
		30 June	Australia v. Bangladesh, Canterbury
		2 July	The Final, Lord's

CENTENARIES OF 2005

1305
23 August   William Wallace, died

1405
14 February Timur, Mongol monarch and conqueror, died
18 October   Pope Pius II, born

1505
27 October   Ivan III, also known as Ivan the Great, died

1605
13 April   Boris Godunov, tsar of Russia 1598–1605, died

1705
17 January   John Ray, naturalist, died
13 July   Titus Oates, Anglican priest, fabricated the Popish Plot in 1678, died
17 November Ninon de l'Enclos, French courtesan, died

1805
27 January   Samuel Palmer, painter, born
2 April   Hans Christian Andersen, novelist and writer of fairy tales, born
9 May   Johann von Schiller, dramatist, died
28 May   Luigi Boccherini, composer, died
21 October   Lord Horatio Nelson, naval commander, died
23 October   John Bartlett, lexicographer, born

1905
2 January   Sir Michael Tippett, composer, born
21 January   Christian Dior, dress designer and couturier, born
18 March   Robert Donat, actor, born
24 March   Jules Verne, writer, died
26 April   Jean Vigo, film director, born
15 May   Joseph Cotten, actor, born
16 May   Henry Fonda, film actor, born
16 May   H. E. Bates, novelist and playwright and short story writer born
21 June   Jean-Paul Sartre, writer, born
25 July   Elias Canetti, novelist and playwright; won Nobel Prize for Literature in 1981, born
5 September Arthur Koestler, political refugee and prisoner, born
18 September Agnes de Mille, dancer and choreographer, born
18 September Greta Garbo, film actress, born
19 September Thomas Barnardo, founder of the Barnardo's children's homes, died
15 October   Sir Charles Snow, novelist, born
23 October   Felix Bloch, physicist, Nobel prize winner 1952, born
21 December Anthony Powell, writer, born
24 December Howard Hughes, industrialist, pilot, film producer, born
31 December Jule Styne, composer, born

THE UNITED KINGDOM

THE UK IN FIGURES

The United Kingdom comprises Great Britain (England, Wales and Scotland) and Northern Ireland. The Isle of Man and the Channel Islands are Crown dependencies with their own legislative systems, and not a part of the United Kingdom.

POPULATION

The first official census of population in England, Wales and Scotland was taken in 1801 and a census has been taken every ten years since, except in 1941 when there was no census because of war. The last official census in the United Kingdom was taken on 29 April 2001 and the next is due in April 2011.

The first official census of population in Ireland was taken in 1841. However, all figures given below refer only to the area which is now Northern Ireland. Figures for Northern Ireland in 1921 and 1931 are estimates based on the censuses taken in 1926 and 1937 respectively.

Estimates of the population of England before 1801, calculated from the number of baptisms, burials and marriages, are:

1570	4,160,221	1670	5,773,646
1600	4,811,718	1700	6,045,008
1630	5,600,517	1750	6,517,035

For further details see www.statistics.gov.uk

CENSUS RESULTS 1801–2001

Thousands	United Kingdom			England and Wales			Scotland			Northern Ireland		
	Total	Male	Female	Total	Male	Female	Total	Male	Female	Total	Male	Female
1801	—	—	—	8,893	4,255	4,638	1,608	739	869	—	—	—
1811	13,368	6,368	7,000	10,165	4,874	5,291	1,806	826	980	—	—	—
1821	15,472	7,498	7,974	12,000	5,850	6,150	2,092	983	1,109	—	—	—
1831	17,835	8,647	9,188	13,897	6,771	7,126	2,364	1,114	1,250	—	—	—
1841	20,183	9,819	10,364	15,914	7,778	8,137	2,620	1,242	1,378	1,649	800	849
1851	22,259	10,855	11,404	17,928	8,781	9,146	2,889	1,376	1,513	1,443	698	745
1861	24,525	11,894	12,631	20,066	9,776	10,290	3,062	1,450	1,612	1,396	668	728
1871	27,431	13,309	14,122	22,712	11,059	11,653	3,360	1,603	1,757	1,359	647	712
1881	31,015	15,060	15,955	25,974	12,640	13,335	3,736	1,799	1,936	1,305	621	684
1891	34,264	16,593	17,671	29,003	14,060	14,942	4,026	1,943	2,083	1,236	590	646
1901	38,237	18,492	19,745	32,528	15,729	16,799	4,472	2,174	2,298	1,237	590	647
1911	42,082	20,357	21,725	36,070	17,446	18,625	4,761	2,309	2,452	1,251	603	648
1921	44,027	21,033	22,994	37,887	18,075	19,811	4,882	2,348	2,535	1,258	610	648
1931	46,038	22,060	23,978	39,952	19,133	20,819	4,843	2,326	2,517	1,243	601	642
1951	50,225	24,118	26,107	43,758	21,016	22,742	5,096	2,434	2,662	1,371	668	703
1961	52,709	25,481	27,228	46,105	22,304	23,801	5,179	2,483	2,697	1,425	694	731
1971	55,515	26,952	28,562	48,750	23,683	25,067	5,229	2,515	2,714	1,536	755	781
1981	55,848	27,104	28,742	49,155	23,873	25,281	5,131	2,466	2,664	*1,533	750	783
1991	56,467	27,344	29,123	49,890	24,182	25,707	4,999	2,392	2,607	1,578	769	809
2001	58,789	28,581	30,208	52,042	25,327	26,715	5,062	2,432	2,630	1,685	821	864

* Figure includes 44,500 non-enumerated persons
Source: ONS – Census Reports (Crown copyright)

RESIDENT POPULATION: 2002 ESTIMATES AND FUTURE PROJECTIONS (MID-YEAR)

Thousands	United Kingdom			England and Wales			Scotland			Northern Ireland		
	Total	Male	Female	Total	Male	Female	Total	Male	Female	Total	Male	Female
2002	59,229	28,911	30,318	52,478	25,651	26,827	5,055	2,432	2,623	1,697	829	868
2006	59,995	29,329	30,666	53,252	26,071	27,181	5,022	2,417	2,605	1,720	841	880
2011	61,022	29,853	31,169	54,287	26,600	27,687	4,984	2,398	2,586	1,751	855	896
2021	63,239	30,897	32,342	56,517	27,661	28,856	4,911	2,354	2,557	1,811	882	929
2026	64,178	31,297	32,880	57,492	28,088	29,404	4,854	2,319	2,535	1,831	890	941

Source: The Stationery Office – Annual Abstract of Statistics 2004 (Crown copyright)

ISLANDS: CENSUS RESULTS 1901–2001

	Isle of Man			Jersey			*Guernsey		
	Total	Male	Female	Total	Male	Female	Total	Male	Female
1901	54,752	25,496	29,256	52,576	23,940	28,636	40,446	19,652	20,794
1911	52,016	23,937	28,079	51,898	24,014	27,884	41,858	20,661	21,197
1921	60,284	27,329	32,955	49,701	22,438	27,263	38,315	18,246	20,069
1931	49,308	22,443	26,865	50,462	23,424	27,038	40,643	19,659	20,984
1951	55,123	25,749	29,464	57,296	27,282	30,014	43,652	21,221	22,431
1961	48,151	22,060	26,091	57,200	27,200	30,000	45,068	21,671	23,397
1971	56,289	26,461	29,828	72,532	35,423	37,109	51,458	24,792	26,666
1981	64,679	30,901	33,778	77,000	37,000	40,000	53,313	25,701	27,612
1991	69,788	33,693	36,095	84,082	40,862	43,220	58,867	28,297	30,570
2001	76,315	37,372	38,943	87,186	42,485	44,701	59,807	29,138	30,669

* Population of Guernsey, Herm, Jethou and Lithou.
Figures for 1901–71 record all persons present on census night; census figures for 1981–2001 record all persons resident in the islands on census night. The 2001 population census also recorded the population of Alderney as 2,294 and an informal census of Sark gave its population as 591.
Source: Census 2001 (Crown copyright).

RESIDENT POPULATION

BY AGE AND SEX 2002

	Thousands	
Age Range	Males	Females
Under 1	338	322
1–4	1,406	1,341
5–9	1,885	1,795
10–14	2,002	1,903
15–19	1,926	1,826
20–29	3,685	3,703
30–44	6,681	6,795
45–59	5,597	5,704
60–64	1,413	1,475
65–74	2,325	2,640
75–84	1,337	2,004
85+	315	810

Source: The Stationery Office – Annual Abstract of Statistics 2004 (Crown copyright)

BY ETHNIC GROUP AVERAGE SPRING 2002–WINTER 2002/3

Ethnic group	Estimated population (thousands)
White	
British*	51,010
Other*	1,946
Mixed	
White and Black Caribbean	234
White and Black African	72
White and Asian	129
Other Mixed	74
Asian	
Indian	1,016
Pakistani	718
Bangladeshi	273
Other Asian	302
Black	
Black Caribbean	584
Black African	541
Black Other	59
Chinese	199
Other	458
All†	59,330

*Data excludes Northern Ireland as detailed level ethnicity questions are not asked of the White group in Northern Ireland.
†Includes ethnic group not stated.
Source: The Stationery Office – Annual Abstract of Statistics 2004 (Crown copyright).

IMMIGRATION

ACCEPTANCE FOR SETTLEMENT IN THE UK BY NATIONALITY

Region	Number of persons	
	2001	2002
Europe*	13,990	11,740
Americas: total	11,975	11,680
USA	4,385	4,355
Canada	1,320	1,300
Africa: total	31,925	39,165
Asia: total	44,155	46,585
Indian sub-continent	23,020	24,665
Middle East	4,830	5,345
Oceania: total	5,455	6,250
British Overseas Citizens	520	330
Stateless	390	215
All nationalities	108,410	115,965

* Excluding European Economic Area nationals
Source: The Stationery Office – Annual Abstract of Statistics 2004 (Crown copyright)

BIRTHS

2002

	Live births	Male	Female	Birth rate*
United Kingdom	669,000	343,000	327,000	11.3
England and Wales	596,000	306,000	290,000	11.4
Scotland	5,000	26,000	25,000	10.1
Northern Ireland	2,000	11,000	11,000	12.6

*Live births per 1,000 population
Source: The Stationery Office – Annual Abstract of Statistics 2004 (Crown copyright)

LEGAL ABORTIONS

	1997	2002
England and Wales	170,145	175,569
Scotland	12,109	11,594

Source: The Stationery Office – Annual Abstract of Statistics 2004 (Crown copyright)

DEATHS

2002

Males	Deaths	Death Rate*
United Kingdom	287,837	10.0
England and Wales	253,144	
Scotland	27,743	
Northern Ireland	6,950	
Females		
United Kingdom	318,379	10.5
England and Wales	280,383	
Scotland	30,360	
Northern Ireland	7,636	

* Death rate per 1,000 population
Source: The Stationery Office – *Annual Abstract of Statistics 2004*
(Crown copyright).

INFANT MORTALITY 2002
Deaths of infants under 1 year of age per 1,000 live births

	Number
United Kingdom	5.2
England and Wales	5.2
Scotland	5.3
Northern Ireland	4.7

Source: The Stationery Office – *Annual Abstract of Statistics 2004*
(Crown copyright).

MARRIAGE AND DIVORCE

2002

	Marriages	Divorces
United Kingdom	286,129*	160,726
England and Wales	249,227*	147,735
Scotland	29,826	10,826
Northern Ireland	7,599	2,165

* 2001 Figures
Source: The Stationery Office – *Annual Abstract of Statistics 2004*
(Crown copyright).

HOUSEHOLDS

BY TYPE OF HOUSEHOLD AND FAMILY IN GREAT
BRITAIN 2003
Percentages

One Person	
Under state pension age	15
Over state pension age	14
Two or more unrelated adults	8
One family households	
Couple	
No children	28
1–2 dependent children	18
3 or more dependent children	4
Non-dependent children only	6
Lone parent	
Dependent children	5
Non-dependent children only	3
Multi-family households	1

Source: The Stationery Office – *Social Trends 2004*
(Crown copyright).

HOUSEHOLDS BY SIZE 2003
Percentages

One person	29
Two people	35
Three people	15
Four people	14
Five people	5
Six or more people	2
All households (=100%) *(millions)*	24.5
Average household size (number of people)	2.4

Source: The Stationery Office – *Social Trends 2004*
(Crown copyright).

PERCENTAGE OF DEPENDENT CHILDREN LIVING IN
DIFFERENT FAMILY TYPES (GREAT BRITAIN)

	1992	2001	2003
Couple families			
1 child	18	17	17
2 children	39	38	37
3 or more children	27	25	24
Lone mother families			
1 child	4	6	6
2 children	5	7	8
3 or more children	4	5	6
Lone father families			
1 child	1	1	2
2 or more children	1	1	1

Source: The Stationery Office – *Social Trends 2004*
(Crown copyright).

ADULTS LIVING WITH THEIR PARENTS BY AGE AND
GENDER (ENGLAND)
Percentages

	1991	2002	2003
Males			
20–24	50	56	56
25–29	19	20	21
30–34	9	8	8
Females			
20–24	32	37	37
25–29	9	10	10
30–34	5	2	3

Source: The Stationery Office – *Social Trends 2004*
(Crown copyright).

UK HOUSEHOLDS WITH INTERNET ACCESS BY
HOUSEHOLD TYPE
Percentages

	1998/9	2002/3
One person		
Over state pension age	1	7
Under state pension age	8	36
Couple without children		
Over state pension age	2	21
Under state pension age	14	55
All other adults without children	16	57
Lone parent	5	35
Couple with children	16	69
All other adults with children	20	52

Source: The Stationery Office – *Social Trends 2004*
(Crown copyright).

TENURE BY TYPE OF ACCOMODATION 2001 (ENGLAND AND WALES)
Percentages

	House or Bungalow Detached	Semi-detached	Terraced	Flat or Maisonette Purpose-built	Other
Owner-occupied					
Owned outright	35	35	22	6	2
Owned with mortgage	27	36	29	5	3
Shared ownership	6	34	33	21	5
Rented from social sector					
Council	4	31	26	37	3
Other	3	23	26	40	8
Rented privately					
Private landlord or letting agency	9	17	28	20	25
Employer of a household member	22	31	20	11	16
Relative or friend of a household member	14	26	34	13	13
Other	18	23	19	19	20
Living rent free	19	28	20	23	10
All tenures	23	32	26	13	5

Source: The Stationery Office – *Social Trends 2004* (Crown copyright).

HEALTH

DEATHS ANALYSED BY CAUSE 2002

	England and Wales	Scotland	N. Ireland
TOTAL DEATHS	533,527	58,103	14,586
Deaths from natural causes	515,262	55,689	13,949
Certain infectious and parasitic diseases	4,330	651	134
Intestinal infectious diseases	847	96	11
Respiratory & other tuberculosis	443	52	10
Meningococcal infection	115	13	7
Viral hepatitis	170	13	0
AIDS (HIV – disease)	198	33	3
Neoplasms	140,174	15,391	3,766
Malignant neoplasms	136,777	15,051	3,652
Malignant neoplasm of oesophagus	6,330	763	163
Malignant neoplasm of stomach	5,588	621	164
Malignant neoplasm of colon	9,504	975	270
Malignant neoplasm of rectum and anus	3,907	384	90
Malignant neoplasm of pancreas	6,142	562	194
Malignant neoplasm of trachea, bronchus and lung	28,806	4,039	802
Malignant neoplasm of skin	1,480	132	38
Malignant neoplasm of breast	11,557	1,110	278
Malignant neoplasm of cervix uteri	1,001	100	25
Malignant neoplasm of prostate	8,973	775	193
Leukaemia	3,911	330	93
Diseases of blood and blood-forming organs and certain disorders involving the immune mechanism	1,086	122	24
Endocrine, nutritional and metabolic diseases	7,897	902	238
Diabetes mellitus	6,192	676	187
Mental and behavioural disorders	14,444	2,446	411
Vascular and unspecified dementia	12,753	1,763	329
Alcohol abuse	435	339	74
Drug dependence and non-dependent abuse of drugs	882	294	6
Diseases of the nervous system and sense organs	14,796	1,317	531
Meningitis (including meningococcal)	173	6	5
Alzheimer's disease	4,771	388	246
Diseases of the circulatory system	209,433	22,688	5,729
Ischaemic heart diseases	102,833	11,692	2,948
Cerebrovascular diseases	59,068	6,722	1,573

Diseases of the respiratory system	69,900	6,806	1,883
Influenza	38	6	1
Pneumonia	32,631	2,466	951
Bronchitis, emphysema and other chronic obstructive pulmonary diseases	24,159	2,840	553
Asthma	1,264	131	36
Diseases of the digestive system	24,124	3,153	581
Gastric and duodenal ulcer	3,746	308	62
Chronic liver disease	5,376	1,128	166
Diseases of the skin and subcutaneous tissue	1,470	118	21
Diseases of the musculo-skeletal system and connective tissue	4,647	384	90
Rheumatoid arthritis and juvenile arthritis	966	133	21
Osteoporosis	1,605	59	19
Diseases of the genito-urinary system	8,452	1,013	333
Diseases of the kidney and ureter	4,072	627	246
Complications of pregnancy, childbirth and the puerperium	34	5	1
Certain conditions originating in the perinatal period (excluding neonatals)	208	155	62
Congenital malformations, deformations and chromasomal abnormalities (excluding neonatals)	1,233	168	53
Congenital malformations of the nervous system	127	31	7
Congenital malformations of the circulatory system	541	60	17
Symptons, signs and abnormal findings not classified elsewhere	13,034	370	92
Senility without mention of psychosis (old age)	11,645	191	63
Sudden infant death syndrome	137	32	0
Deaths from external causes	16,139	2,414	637
All accidents	10,382	1,315	424
Land transport accidents	2,929	321	144
Accidental falls	2,509	668	60
Accidental poisonings	814	37	30
Suicide and intentional self-harm	3,269	636	162
Homicide and assault	373	118	27
Event of undetermined intent	1,754	263	21

Source: The Stationery Office – Annual Abstract of Statistics 2004 (Crown copyright).

NOTIFICATIONS OF INFECTIONS DISEASES (UK)

	2001	2002
Measles	2,661	3,675
Mumps	3,433	2,333
Rubella	1,782	2,002
Whooping cough	1,059	1,051
Scarlet fever	2,320	2,749
Dysentery	1,495	1,167
Food poisoning	95,752	81,562
Typhoid and paratyphoid fevers	254	183
Hepatitis	4,419	5,035
Tuberculosis	7,204	7,239
Malaria	1,118	866

Source: The Stationery Office – Annual Abstract of Statistics 2004 (Crown copyright).

HIGH BLOOD PRESSURE BY AGE AND GENDER 2001 (ENGLAND)

Percentages

	16–44	45–54	55–64	65–74	75+	All 16+
Males†						
Treated	1	6	15	20	20	8
Untreated	19	32	37	41	42	29
Females						
Treated	1	6	13	23	28	9
Untreated	8	24	33	41	44	22

Source: The Stationery Office – Social Trends 2004 (Crown copyright)

ADULTS EXCEEDING BENCHMARKS* OF ALCOHOL BY AGE AND GENDER 2001–2 (GREAT BRITAIN)

Percentages

	Males	Females
16–24	49	39
25–44	46	30
45–64	36	19
65+	18	5
All 16+	39	22

* On heaviest drinking day in the last week. Current Department of Health advice is that consumption of between three and four units a day for men and between 2 and 3 units a day for women should not lead to significant health risks. A unit of alcohol is 8 grams by weight or 10ml by volume of pure alcohol, i.e. the amount contained in half a pint of ordinary strength beer or lager, a single pub measure of spirits or a small glass of ordinary strength wine.

Source: The Stationery Office – Social Trends 2004 (Crown copyright)

PREVALENCE OF DRUG MISUSE BY YOUNG ADULTS* BY DRUG CATEGORY AND GENDER 2001–2 (ENGLAND AND WALES)
Percentages

	Males	Females
Cannabis	33	21
Amphetamines	7	3
Ecstasy	9	4
Magic mushrooms or LSD	3	1
Cocaine	7	2
All Class 'A' drugs†	12	5
Any drug	35	24

* aged 16–24 years
† includes heroin, cocaine (powder and 'crack'), ecstasy, magic mushrooms, LSD and unprescribed use of methadone.
Source: The Stationery Office – *Social Trends 2004*
(Crown copyright)

BODY MASS* BY GENDER 2001 (ENGLAND)
Percentages

	Males	Females
Underweight	4	6
Desirable	28	38
Overweight	47	33
Obese	21	23

* The Body Mass Index (BMI) standardised weight for height and is calculated as weight (kg)/height (m)^2. Underweight is defined as a BMI of 20 or less, desirable 20–25, overweight 25–30 and obese over 30.
Source: The Stationery Office – *Social Trends 2003*
(Crown copyright)

AVERAGE DAILY PORTIONS OF FRUIT AND VEGETABLES CONSUMED* BY AGE AND GENDER 2000–1 (GREAT BRITAIN)
Percentages

	Average number of portions per day				
	None	0–1	1–3	3–5	5+
Males					
19–24	6	32	57	5	0
25–34	1	26	49	17	7
35–49	0	14	45	27	14
50–64	1	6	38	31	24
All males 19–64	1	17	46	23	13
Females					
19–24	2	34	47	13	4
25–34	1	18	52	20	9
35–49	1	15	45	22	17
50–64	0	7	37	34	22
All females 19–64	1	15	45	24	15

* The Department of Health recommends that a healthy diet should included a least five portions of a variety of fruit and vegetables (excluding potatoes) a day. All fruit juice, baked beans and other pulses are counted as one portion.
Source: The Stationery Office – *Social Trends 2004*
(Crown Copyright)

THE NATIONAL FLAG

The national flag of the United Kingdom is the Union Flag, generally known as the Union Jack.

The Union Flag is a combination of the cross of St George, patron saint of England, the cross of St Andrew, patron saint of Scotland, and a cross similar to that of St Patrick, patron saint of Ireland.

Cross of St George: cross Gules in a field Argent (red cross on a white ground)

Cross of St Andrew: saltire Argent in a field Azure (white diagonal cross on a blue ground)

Cross of St Patrick: saltire Gules in a field Argent (red diagonal cross on a white ground)

The Union Flag was first introduced in 1606 after the union of the kingdoms of England and Scotland under one sovereign. The cross of St Patrick was added in 1801 after the union of Great Britain and Ireland.

FLYING THE UNION FLAG

The correct orientation of the Union Flag when flying is with the broader diagonal band of white uppermost in the hoist (i.e. near the pole) and the narrower diagonal band of white uppermost in the fly (i.e. furthest from the pole).

It is the practice to fly the Union Flag daily on some customs houses. In all other cases, flags are flown on government buildings by command of The Queen. It is now customary for the Union Flag to be flown at Buckingham Palace, Windsor Castle and Sandringham when The Queen is not in residence.

The flying of the Union Flag on public buildings is decided by the Department for Culture, Media and Sport at The Queen's command. On the days appointed, the Union Flag is flown on government buildings in the United Kingdom from 8 a.m. to sunset.

FLAGS AT HALF-MAST

Flags are flown at half-mast (i.e. two-thirds up between the top and bottom of the flagstaff) on the following occasions:

(a) From the announcement of the death up to the funeral of the Sovereign, except on Proclamation Day, when flags are hoisted right up from 11 a.m. to sunset
(b) The funerals of members of the royal family, subject to special commands from The Queen in each case
(c) The funerals of foreign rulers, subject to special commands from The Queen in each case
(d) The funerals of prime ministers and ex-prime ministers of the UK, subject to special commands from The Queen in each case
(e) Other occasions by special command of The Queen

On occasions when days for flying flags coincide with days for flying flags at half-mast, the following rules are observed. Flags are flown:

(a) although a member of the royal family, or a near relative of the royal family, may be lying dead, unless special commands are received from The Queen to the contrary
(b) although it may be the day of the funeral of a foreign ruler

If the body of a very distinguished subject is lying at a government office, the flag may fly at half-mast on that office until the body has left (provided it is a day on which the flag would fly) and then the flag is to be hoisted right up. On all other government buildings the flag will fly as usual.

THE ROYAL STANDARD

The Royal Standard is hoisted only when The Queen is actually present in the building, and never when Her Majesty is passing in procession.

DAYS FOR FLYING FLAGS

Birthday of The Countess of Wessex	20 January
The Queen's Accession	6 February
Birthday of The Duke of York	19 February
*St David's Day (in Wales only)	1 March
Birthday of The Earl of Wessex	10 March
**Commonwealth Day (2005)	14 March
Birthday of The Queen	21 April
*St George's Day (in England only)	23 April
†Europe Day	9 May
Coronation Day	2 June
Birthday of The Duke of Edinburgh	10 June
The Queen's Official Birthday (2005)	11 June
Birthday of The Princess Royal	15 August
Remembrance Sunday (2005)	13 November
Birthday of The Prince of Wales	14 November
The Queen's Wedding Day	20 November
*St Andrew's Day (in Scotland only)	30 November
‡The opening of Parliament by The Queen	
‡The prorogation of Parliament by The Queen	

* Where a building has two or more flagstaffs, the appropriate national flag may be flown in addition to the Union Flag, but not in a superior position
** Commonwealth Day is always the second Monday in March
† The Union Flag should fly alongside the European flag. On government buildings that have only one flagpole, the Union Flag should take precedence
‡ Flags are flown whether or not The Queen performs the ceremony in person. Flags are flown only in the Greater London area

ROYAL FAMILY

THE SOVEREIGN

ELIZABETH II, by the Grace of God, of the United Kingdom of Great Britain and Northern Ireland and of her other Realms and Territories Queen, Head of the Commonwealth, Defender of the Faith
Her Majesty Elizabeth Alexandra Mary of Windsor, elder daughter of King George VI and of HM Queen Elizabeth the Queen Mother
Born 21 April 1926, at 17 Bruton Street, London W1
Ascended the throne 6 February 1952
Crowned 2 June 1953, at Westminster Abbey
Married 20 November 1947, in Westminster Abbey, HRH The Prince Philip, Duke of Edinburgh
Official residences: Buckingham Palace, London SW1A 1AA; Windsor Castle, Berks; Palace of Holyroodhouse, Edinburgh
Private residences: Sandringham, Norfolk; Balmoral Castle, Aberdeenshire

HUSBAND OF THE QUEEN

HRH THE PRINCE PHILIP, DUKE OF EDINBURGH, KG, KT, OM, GBE, AC, QSO, PC, Ranger of Windsor Park
Born 10 June 1921, son of Prince and Princess Andrew of Greece and Denmark, naturalised a British subject 1947, created Duke of Edinburgh, Earl of Merioneth and Baron Greenwich 1947

CHILDREN OF THE QUEEN

HRH THE PRINCE OF WALES (Prince Charles Philip Arthur George), KG, KT, GCB, OM and Great Master of the Order of the Bath, AK, QSO, PC, ADC(P)
Born 14 November 1948, created Prince of Wales and Earl of Chester 1958, succeeded as Duke of Cornwall, Duke of Rothesay, Earl of Carrick and Baron Renfrew, Lord of the Isles and Great Steward of Scotland 1952
Married 29 July 1981 Lady Diana Frances Spencer (Diana, Princess of Wales (1961–97), youngest daughter of the 8th Earl Spencer and the Hon. Mrs Shand Kydd), marriage dissolved 1996
Issue:
(1)   HRH Prince William of Wales (Prince William Arthur Philip Louis), *born* 21 June 1982
(2)   HRH Prince Henry of Wales (Prince Henry Charles Albert David), *born* 15 September 1984
Residences of the Prince of Wales: Clarence House, London SW1A 1BA; Highgrove, Doughton, Tetbury, Glos GL8 8TN; Birkhall, Ballater, Aberdeenshire

HRH THE PRINCESS ROYAL (Princess Anne Elizabeth Alice Louise), KG, GCVO
Born 15 August 1950, declared The Princess Royal 1987
Married (1) 14 November 1973 Captain Mark Anthony Peter Phillips, CVO (*born* 22 September 1948), marriage dissolved 1992; (2) 12 December 1992 Captain Timothy James Hamilton Laurence, MVO, RN (*born* 1 March 1955)
Issue:
(1)   Peter Mark Andrew Phillips, *born* 15 November 1977

(2)   Zara Anne Elizabeth Phillips, *born* 15 May 1981
Residence: Gatcombe Park, Minchinhampton, Glos GL6 9AT

HRH THE DUKE OF YORK (Prince Andrew Albert Christian Edward), KCVO, ADC(P)
Born 19 February 1960, created Duke of York, Earl of Inverness and Baron Killyleagh 1986
Married 23 July 1986 Sarah Margaret Ferguson, now Sarah, Duchess of York (*born* 15 October 1959, younger daughter of Major Ronald Ferguson and Mrs Hector Barrantes), marriage dissolved 1996
Issue:
(1)   HRH Princess Beatrice of York (Princess Beatrice Elizabeth Mary), *born* 8 August 1988
(2)   HRH Princess Eugenie of York (Princess Eugenie Victoria Helena), *born* 23 March 1990
Residences: Buckingham Palace, London SW1A 1AA; Sunninghill Park, Ascot, Berks SL5 7TH

HRH THE EARL OF WESSEX (Prince Edward Antony Richard Louis), KCVO
Born 10 March 1964, created Earl of Wessex, Viscount Severn 1999
Married 19 June 1999 Sophie Helen Rhys-Jones, now HRH The Countess of Wessex (*born* 20 January 1965, daughter of Mr and Mrs Christopher Rhys-Jones)
Issue:
(1)   Lady Louise Windsor (Louise Alice Elizabeth), *born* 8 November 2003
Residence: Bagshot Park, Bagshot, Surrey GU19 5HS

NEPHEW OF THE QUEEN

DAVID ALBERT CHARLES ARMSTRONG-JONES, VISCOUNT LINLEY, *born* 3 November 1961, *married* 8 October 1993 the Hon. Serena Stanhope, and has issue, Hon. Charles Patrick Inigo Armstrong-Jones, *born* 1 July 1999; Hon. Margarita Elizabeth Alleyne Armstrong-Jones, *born* 14 May 2002

NIECE OF THE QUEEN

LADY SARAH CHATTO (Sarah Frances Elizabeth), *born* 1 May 1964, *married* 14 July 1994 Daniel Chatto, and has issue, Samuel David Benedict Chatto, *born* 28 July 1996; Arthur Robert Nathaniel Chatto, *born* 5 February 1999
Residence: Kensington Palace, London W8 4PU

AUNT OF THE QUEEN

HRH PRINCESS ALICE, DUCHESS OF GLOUCESTER (Alice Christabel), GCB, CI, GCVO, GBE, Grand Cordon of Al Kamal
Born 25 December 1901, third daughter of the 7th Duke of Buccleuch and Queensberry
Married 6 November 1935 (as Lady Alice Montagu-Douglas-Scott) Prince Henry, Duke of Gloucester, third son of King George V
Residence: Kensington Palace, London W8 4PU

COUSINS OF THE QUEEN

HRH THE DUKE OF GLOUCESTER (Prince Richard Alexander Walter George), KG, GCVO, Grand Prior of the Order of St John of Jerusalem
Born 26 August 1944
Married 8 July 1972 Birgitte Eva van Deurs, now HRH The Duchess of Gloucester, GCVO (*born* 20 June 1946, daughter of Asger Henriksen and Vivian van Deurs)
Issue:
(1) Earl of Ulster (Alexander Patrick Gregers Richard), *born* 24 October 1974 *married* 22 June 2002 Dr Claire Booth
(2) Lady Davina Lewis (Davina Elizabeth Alice Benedikte), *born* 19 November 1977 *married* 31 July 2004 Gary Lewis
(3) Lady Rose Windsor (Rose Victoria Birgitte Louise), *born* 1 March 1980
Residence: Kensington Palace, London W8 4PU

HRH THE DUKE OF KENT (Prince Edward George Nicholas Paul Patrick), KG, GCMG, GCVO, ADC(P)
Born 9 October 1935
Married 8 June 1961 Katharine Lucy Mary Worsley, now HRH The Duchess of Kent, GCVO (*born* 22 February 1933, daughter of Sir William Worsley, Bt.)
Issue:
(1) Earl of St Andrews (George Philip Nicholas), *born* 26 June 1962, *married* 9 January 1988 Sylvana Tomaselli, and has issue, Baron Downpatrick, (Edward Edmund Maximilian George) *born* 2 December 1988; Lady Marina-Charlotte Windsor (Marina-Charlotte Alexandra Katharine Helen), *born* 30 September 1992; Lady Amelia Windsor (Amelia Sophia Theodora Mary Margaret) *born* 24 August 1995
(2) Lady Helen Taylor (Helen Marina Lucy), *born* 28 April 1964, *married* 18 July 1992 Timothy Taylor, and has issue, Columbus George Donald Taylor, *born* 6 August 1994; Cassius Edward Taylor, *born* 26 December 1996; daughter Eloise Olivia Katharine Taylor, *born* 3 March 2003
(3) Lord Nicholas Windsor (Nicholas Charles Edward Jonathan), *born* 25 July 1970
Residence: Wren House, Palace Green, London W8 4PY

HRH PRINCESS ALEXANDRA, THE HON. LADY OGILVY (Princess Alexandra Helen Elizabeth Olga Christabel), KG, GCVO
Born 25 December 1936
Married 24 April 1963 The Rt. Hon. Sir Angus Ogilvy, KCVO (*born* 14 September 1928, second son of 12th Earl of Airlie)
Issue:
(1) James Robert Bruce Ogilvy, *born* 29 February 1964, *married* 30 July 1988 Julia Rawlinson, and has issue, Flora Alexandra Ogilvy, *born* 15 December 1994; Alexander Charles Ogilvy, *born* 12 November 1996
(2) Marina Victoria Alexandra, Mrs Mowatt, *born* 31 July 1966, *married* 2 February 1990 Paul Mowatt (marriage dissolved 1997), and has issue, Zenouska May Mowatt, *born* 26 May 1990; Christian Alexander Mowatt, *born* 4 June 1993
Residence: Thatched House Lodge, Richmond Park, Surrey TW10 5HP

HRH PRINCE MICHAEL OF KENT (Prince Michael George Charles Franklin), GCVO
Born 4 July 1942
Married 30 June 1978 Baroness Marie-Christine Agnes Hedwig Ida von Reibnitz, now HRH Princess Michael of Kent (*born* 15 January 1945, daughter of Baron Gunther von Reibnitz)
Issue:
(1) Lord Frederick Windsor (Frederick Michael George David Louis), *born* 6 April 1979
(2) Lady Gabriella Windsor (Gabriella Marina Alexandra Ophelia), *born* 23 April 1981
Residences: Kensington Palace, London W8 4PU; Nether Lypiatt Manor, Stroud, Glos GL6 7LS

ORDER OF SUCCESSION

1	HRH The Prince of Wales
2	HRH Prince William of Wales
3	HRH Prince Henry of Wales
4	HRH The Duke of York
5	HRH Princess Beatrice of York
6	HRH Princess Eugenie of York
7	HRH The Earl of Wessex
8	Lady Louise Windsor
9	HRH The Princess Royal
10	Peter Phillips
11	Zara Phillips
12	Viscount Linley
13	Hon. Charles Armstrong-Jones
14	Hon. Margarita Armstrong-Jones
15	Lady Sarah Chatto
16	Samuel Chatto
17	Arthur Chatto
18	HRH The Duke of Gloucester
19	Earl of Ulster
20	Lady Davina Lewis
21	Lady Rose Windsor
22	HRH The Duke of Kent
23	Lady Marina-Charlotte Windsor
24	Lady Amelia Windsor
25	Lady Helen Taylor
26	Columbus Taylor
27	Cassius Taylor
28	Eloise Taylor
29	Lord Frederick Windsor
30	Lady Gabriella Windsor
31	HRH Princess Alexandra, the Hon. Lady Ogilvy
32	James Ogilvy
33	Alexander Ogilvy
34	Flora Ogilvy
35	Marina, Mrs Paul Mowatt
36	Christian Mowatt
37	Zenouska Mowatt

HRH Prince Michael of Kent, and The Earl of St Andrews both lost the right of succession to the throne through marriage to a Roman Catholic. Lord Nicholas Windsor renounced his rights to the throne on converting to Roman Catholicism in 2001 and Baron Downpatrick in 2003. Any children remain in succession provided that they are in communion with the Church of England.

PRIVATE SECRETARIES TO THE ROYAL FAMILY

THE QUEEN

Office: Buckingham Palace, London SW1A 1AA
T 020-7930 4832
W www.royal.gov.uk
Private Secretary to The Queen, The Rt. Hon. Sir Robin Janvrin, KCB, KCVO

PRINCE PHILIP, THE DUKE OF EDINBURGH

Office: Buckingham Palace, London SW1A 1AA
T 020-7930 4832
Private Secretary, Brig. Sir Miles Hunt-Davis, KCVO, CBE

THE PRINCE OF WALES

Office: Clarence House, London SW1A 1BA
T 020-7930 4832
Private Secretary, Sir Michael Peat, KCVO

THE DUKE OF YORK

Office: Buckingham Palace, London SW1A 1AA
T 020-7930 4832
Private Secretary, Alistair Watson

THE EARL AND COUNTESS OF WESSEX

Office: Bagshot Park, Surrey GU19 5PJ
T 01276-707040
Private Secretary, Brig. J. Smedley

THE PRINCESS ROYAL

Office: Buckingham Palace, London SW1A 1AA
T 020-7930 4832
Private Secretary, Capt. N. P. Wright, LVO, RN

PRINCESS ALICE, DUCHESS OF GLOUCESTER AND THE DUKE OF GLOUCESTER

Office: Kensington Palace, London W8 4PU
T 020-7368 1000
Private Secretary, Sqn Ldr Lyn Johnson, MVO

THE DUKE OF KENT

Office: St James's Palace, London, SW1A 1BQ
T 020-7930 4872
Private Secretary, N. Adamson, LVO, OBE

THE DUCHESS OF KENT

Office: Wren House, Palace Green, London, W8 4PY
T 020-7937 2730
Personal Secretary, Miss V. Utley

PRINCE AND PRINCESS MICHAEL OF KENT

Office: Kensington Palace, London W8 4PU
T 020-7938 3519
Private Secretary, N. Chance

PRINCESS ALEXANDRA, THE HON. LADY OGILVY

Office: Buckingham Palace, London SW1A 1AA
T 020-7024 4270
Private Secretary, Col. Richard Macfarlane

ROYAL HOUSEHOLD

PRIVATE SECRETARY'S OFFICE
The Private Secretary, assisted by the two Assistant Private Secretaries, is responsible for:

- Informing and advising The Queen on constitutional, governmental and political matters in the UK, her other Realms and the wider Commonwealth, including communications with the Prime Minister and Government Departments
- Organising The Queen's domestic and overseas official programme, including the Presentation of Credentials by incoming foreign ambassadors from overseas countries
- The Queen's speeches and messages, The Queen's patronage, The Queen's photographs and official presents, portraits of The Queen and dedications and congratulatory messages
- Communications in connection with the role of the Royal Family and other members of the Royal Family and their households
- Dealing with correspondence to The Queen from members of the public
- Organising and co-ordinating Royal travel through the Royal Travel Office
- Co-ordinating and initiating research to support engagements by members of the Royal Family through the Co-ordination and Research Unit

The Private Secretary is also responsible for communications and media affairs. The Press Secretary is in charge of Buckingham Palace Press Office and reports to the Private Secretary. Assisted by the Deputy Press Secretary and three Assistant Press Secretaries, the Press Secretary is responsible for:

- Developing communications strategies to enhance the public understanding of the role of the Monarchy, including an education strategy, encompassing website development and other multi-media initiatives
- Briefing the British and international media on the role and duties of The Queen and issues relating to the royal family
- Responding to media enquiries
- Arranging media facilities in the United Kingdom and overseas to support royal functions and engagements
- The management of the Royal website

The Private Secretary is Keeper of the Royal Archives and is responsible for the care of the records of the Sovereign and the Royal Household from previous reigns. These papers are preserved in the Royal Archives at Windsor, where they are managed by the Registrar, reporting to the Assistant Keeper, and made available for historical research. As Keeper, it is the Private Secretary's responsibility to ensure the proper management of the records of the present reign with a view to their transfer to the archives as and when appropriate. The Private Secretary is an ex officio trustee of the Royal Collection Trust.

PRIVY PURSE AND TREASURER'S OFFICE
The Keeper of the Privy Purse and Treasurer to The Queen is responsible for:

- The Queen's Civil List, which is the money paid from the Government's Consolidated Fund to meet official expenditure relating to The Queen's duties as Head of State and Head of the Commonwealth
- Through the Director of Personnel, the identification, planning and management of personnel policy across the Household, the administration of all pension schemes provided for the Household and Private Estates employees, and the allocation of employee and pensioner housing
- Information technology systems for the Household
- Internal audit services
- Health and safety
- All insurance matters
- The Privy Purse, which is mainly financed by the net income of the Duchy of Lancaster, and which meets both official expenditure incurred by The Queen as Sovereign and private expenditure
- Liaison with other Members of the Royal Family and their Households on financial matters
- The Queen's private estates at Sandringham and Balmoral, The Queen's Racing Establishment and the Royal Studs and liaison with the Ascot Authority
- The Home Park at Windsor and liaison with the Crown Estate Commissioners concerning the Home Park and the Great Park at Windsor
- The Royal Philatelic Collection, which is managed by the Keeper of the Royal Philatelic Collection
- Administrative aspects of the Military Knights of Windsor and the Royal Almonry
- Administration of the Royal Victorian Order, of which the Keeper of the Privy Purse is Secretary, Long and Faithful Service Medals, and the Queen's Cups, Medals and Prizes, and policy on Commemorative Medals

The Keeper of the Privy purse is one of three Royal Trustees (in respect of his responsibilities for the Civil List) and is Receiver General of the Duchy of Lancaster and a member of the Duchy's Council. The Keeper of the Privy Purse is also responsible for property services for the Occupied Royal Palaces in England, which comprise Buckingham Palace, St James's Palace and Clarence House, Marlborough House Mews, the residential, office and general areas of Kensington Palace, Windsor Castle and related areas and buildings, Frogmore House, and Hampton Court Mews and Paddocks. The costs of property services for the Occupied Royal Palaces are met from a Grant-in-aid from the Department for Culture, Media and Sport. The Director of Property Services, assisted by the Deputy Treasurer has day-to-day responsibility for the Royal Household's Property Section, which is responsible for:

- Fire safety issues
- Repairs and refurbishment of buildings and new buildings work

- Utilities and telecommunications
- Putting up stages, tents and other work in connection with ceremonial occasions and official functions

The Property Section is also responsible, in effect on a sub-contract basis from the Department for Culture, Media and Sport, for the maintenance of Marlborough House. The Keeper of the Privy Purse also oversees Royal Communications and Information expenditure, which is met from the Property Services Grant-in-aid. The Keeper of the Privy Purse is responsible for the financial aspects of Royal Travel, which are overseen on a day-to-day basis by the Deputy Treasurer. The costs of official Royal Travel by aeroplane and train are met from a Grant-in-aid provided by the Department for Transport. The Keeper of the Privy Purse is an ex officio trustee of the Royal Collection Trust and is also chairman of its trading subsidiary Royal Collection Enterprises Limited. He is also an ex officio trustee of the Historic Royal Palaces Trust. The Queen's Civil List and the Grants-in-aid for property services and Royal Travel are provided by the Government in return for the surrender by the Sovereign of the net surplus from the Crown Estate and other hereditary revenues.
Keeper of the Privy Purse, Alan Reid

MASTER OF THE HOUSEHOLD'S DEPARTMENT
The Master of the Household is responsible for the staff and domestic arrangements at Buckingham Palace, Windsor Castle and the Palace of Holyroodhouse and at Balmoral Castle and Sandringham House when The Queen is in residence. These arrangements include:

- The provision of meals for The Queen and other members of the Royal Family, their guests and Royal Household employees
- Service by liveried staff at meals, receptions and other events
- Travel arrangements for employees and the movement of baggage between the Royal residences
- Cleaning and laundry
- Furnishings and the internal decorative appearance of the Occupied Royal Palaces in collaboration with the Director of the Royal Collection
- Liaison with the Royalty and Diplomatic Protection Department of the Metropolitan Police concerning security procedures at the Occupied Royal Palaces

The Master of the Household is responsible for The Queen's official entertaining, both at home and overseas, including preparation of guest lists, invitations and seating plans, and overseeing aspects of The Queen's private entertaining.
Master of the Household, Vice Adm. Tom Blackburn, KCVO, CB, LVO

LORD CHAMBERLAIN'S OFFICE
The Comptroller of the Lord Chamberlain's Office is responsible for:

- The organisation of all ceremonial engagements
- Garden Parties at Buckingham Palace and Palace at Holyroodhouse (except for catering and tents)
- The Crown Jewels, which are part of the Royal Collection, when they are in use on state occasions
- Co-ordination of the arrangements for The Queen to be represented at funerals and memorial services and at the arrival and departure of visiting Heads of State
- Advising on matters of precedence, style and titles, dress, flying of flags, gun salutes, mourning and other ceremonial questions

- Supervising the applications from tradesmen for Royal Warrants of Appointment
- Advising on the commercial use of royal emblems and contemporary royal photographs
- The Ecclesiastical Household, the Medical Household, the Body Guards and certain ceremonial appointments such as Gentlemen Ushers and Pages of Honour
- The Lords in Waiting, who represent The Queen on various occasions and escort the visiting Head of State during incoming state visits
- The Queen's Bargemaster and Watermen and The Queen's Swans

The Comptroller is also responsible for the Royal Mews, assisted by the Crown Equerry, who has day-to-day responsibility for:

- The provision of carriage processions for the State Opening of Parliament, State Visits, Trooping of the Colour, Royal Ascot, the Garter Ceremony, the Thistle Service, the Presentation of credentials to The Queen by incoming foreign Ambassadors and High Commissioners, and other state and ceremonial occasions
- The provision of chauffeur-driven cars
- Co-ordinating the travelling and transport arrangements by road in respect of The Queen's official engagements
- Supervision and administration of the Royal Mews at Buckingham Palace, Windsor Castle, Hampton Court and the Palace of Holyroodhouse

The Comptroller, Lord Chamberlain's Office also has overall responsibility for the Marshal of the Diplomatic Corps and the Secretary of the Central Chancery of the Orders of Knighthood.

Comptroller of the Lord Chamberlain's Office, Lt. Col. Sir Malcolm Ross, KCVO, OBE

ROYAL COLLECTION DEPARTMENT

The Royal Collection, which contains a large number of works of art of all kinds, is held by The Queen as Sovereign in trust for her successors and the nation and is not owned by her as an individual. The administration, conservation and presentation of the Royal Collection are funded by the Royal Collection Trust solely from income from visitors to Windsor Castle, Buckingham Palace and the Palace of Holyroodhouse in Edinburgh. The Royal Collection Trust is chaired by the Prince of Wales. The Lord Chamberlain, the Private Secretary and the Keeper of the Privy Purse are ex officio trustees and there are three external trustees appointed by The Queen. The Director of the Royal Collection is responsible for:

- The administration and custodial control of the Royal Collection in all royal residences
- The care, display, conservation and restoration of items in the Collection
- Initiating and assisting research into the Collection and publishing catalogues and books on the Collection
- Making the Collection accessible to the public by display in places open to the public (including the unoccupied palaces), The Queen's Gallery at Buckingham Palace and the Queen's Gallery at the Palace of Holyroodhouse, by travelling exhibitions organised by museums and galleries in the United Kingdom and abroad
- Educating and informing the public about the Collection

The Director of the Royal Collection, who is at present also the Surveyor of The Queen's Works of Art, is assisted by the Surveyor of the Queen's Pictures, the Royal Librarian, the Deputy Surveyor of The Queen's Works of Art, the Managing Director, Royal Collection Enterprises, and the Finance Director, Royal Collection.

The Surveyor of the Queen's Pictures is responsible for pictures and miniatures, the Royal Librarian is responsible for all the books, manuscripts, coins and medals, insignia and works of art on paper including the watercolours, prints and drawings in the Print Room at Windsor Castle, and the Surveyor of the Queen's Works of art is responsible for furniture, ceramics and the other decorative arts in the Collection. The Director of the Royal Collection has overall responsibility for the trading activities that fund the Royal Collection Department. These are administered by Royal Collection Enterprises Limited, the trading subsidiary of The Royal Collection Trust, which is run by the Managing Director, Royal Collection Enterprises. The company, whose chairman is the Keeper of the Privy Purse, is responsible for:

- Managing access by the public to Windsor Castle (including Frogmore House), Buckingham Palace (including the Royal Mews and The Queen's Gallery) and the Palace of Holyroodhouse
- Running shops at each location
- Managing the images and intellectual property rights of the Royal Collection

The Director of the Royal Collection is also an ex officio trustee of the Historic Royal Palaces Trust.

ROYAL SALUTES

ENGLAND

The basic Royal Salute is 21 rounds with 41 rounds fired at Hyde Park because it is a Royal park. At the Tower of London 62 rounds are fired on Royal anniversaries (21 plus a further 20 because the Tower is a Royal Palace and a further 21 'for the City of London'). Gun salutes occur on the following Royal anniversaries:

- Accession Day
- The Queen's birthday
- Coronation Day
- The birthday of the Duke of Edinburgh
- The Queen's official birthday
- State Opening of Parliament

Gun salutes also occur when Parliament is prorogued by the Sovereign, on Royal births and when a visiting Head of State meets the Sovereign in London, Windsor or Edinburgh.

In London, salutes are fired at Hyde Park and The Tower of London although on some occasions (State visits, State Opening of Parliament and The Queen's Birthday Parade) Green Park is used instead.

Constable of the Royal Palace and Fortress of London, Gen. Sir Roger Wheeler, GCB, CBE

Lieutenant of the Tower of London, Lt.-Gen. Sir Hew Pike, KCB, MBE, DSO

Resident Governor and Keeper of the Jewel House, Maj.-Gen.
Geoffrey Field, CB, OBE
Master Gunner of St James's Park, Gen. Sir Alex Harley,
KBE, CB
Master Gunner within the Tower, Col. George Clarke, TD

SCOTLAND
Royal salutes are authorised at Edinburgh Castle and
Stirling Castle, although in practice Edinburgh Castle is
the only operating saluting station in Scotland.
A salute of 21 guns is fired on the following occasions:

– the anniversaries of the birth, accession and
coronation of the Sovereign

– the anniversary of the birth of HRH Prince Philip,
Duke of Edinburgh

A salute of 21 guns is fired in Edinburgh on the
occasion of the opening of the General Assembly of the
Church of Scotland. A salute of 21 guns may also be fired
in Edinburgh on the arrival of HM The Queen or a
member of the royal family who is a Royal Highness on
an official visit.

Other Military saluting stations are at Cardiff and Belfast.

ROYAL FINANCES

FUNDING

CIVIL LIST
The Civil List dates back to the late 17th century. It was
originally used by the sovereign to supplement hereditary
revenues for paying the salaries of judges, ambassadors
and other government officers as well as the expenses of
the royal household. In 1760 on the accession of George
III it was decided that the Civil List would be provided by
Parliament to cover all relevant expenditure in return for
the King surrendering the hereditary revenues of the
Crown. At that time Parliament undertook to pay the
salaries of judges, ambassadors, etc. In 1831 Parliament
agreed also to meet the costs of the royal palaces in return
for a reduction in the Civil List. Each sovereign has agreed
to continue this arrangement.

The Civil List paid to The Queen is charged on the
Consolidated Fund. Until 1972, the amount of money
allocated annually under the Civil List was set for the
duration of a reign. The system was then altered to a fixed
annual payment for ten years but from 1975 high
inflation made an annual review necessary. The system of
payments reverted to the practice of a fixed annual
payment of £7.9m for ten years from 1 January 1991. In
2001 the payments were further fixed until 31 December
2010. In June 2002 the annual accounts for the Civil List
were published for the first time and are to continue to be
published annually instead of at 10 yearly intervals.

The Civil List Acts provide for other members of the
royal family to receive parliamentary annuities from
government funds to meet the expenses of carrying out
their official duties. Since 1975 The Queen has
reimbursed the Treasury for the annuities paid to the
Duke of Gloucester, the Duke of Kent and Princess
Alexandra. Since 1993 The Queen has reimbursed all the
annuities except those paid to herself, the late Queen
Elizabeth the Queen Mother and the Duke of Edinburgh.

The Prince of Wales does not receive a parliamentary
annuity. He derives his income from the revenues of the
Duchy of Cornwall and these monies meet the official and
private expenses of the Prince of Wales and his family.
The annual payments for the years 2001–11:

The Queen	£7,900,000
The Duke of Edinburgh	359,000
*The Duke of York	249,000
*The Earl of Wessex	141,000
*The Princess Royal	228,000
*Princess Alice, Duchess of Gloucester	87,000
*The Duke and Duchess of Gloucester	175,000
*The Duke and Duchess of Kent	236,000
*Princess Alexandra	225,000
	9,600,000
*Refunded to the Treasury	1,341,000
Total	8,259,000

GRANTS-IN-AID
The royal household receives grants-in-aid from two
government departments to meet various official expenses.
The Department for Culture, Media and Sport provides
grant-in-aid to pay for the upkeep of English occupied
royal palaces, the maintenance of Marlborough House
and to meet the cost of royal media and information
services. The Royal Travel grant-in-aid is provided by the
Department for Transport to meet the cost of official royal
travel by air and rail, using mainly aircraft from 32 (The
Royal) Squadron, chartered commercial aircraft for major
overseas state visits and the Royal Train.

Grants-in-aid voted by Parliament 2003–4:
Property Services, Royal Communications
and Information and Maintenance of
Marlborough House   £15,300,000 *(£16,050,000)**
Royal Travel   £5,942,000 *(£4,762,000)**
* Amount in parentheses is the total spent.

THE PRIVY PURSE
The funds received by the Privy Purse pay for official
expenses incurred by The Queen as head of state and for
some of The Queen's private expenditure. The revenues of
the Duchy of Lancaster are the principal source of income
for the Privy Purse.

FUNDING
The Queen's personal income derives mostly from
investments, and is used to meet private expenditure.

EXPENDITURE MET BY GOVERNMENT
DEPARTMENTS AND THE CROWN ESTATE
Administration of Honours
Equerries and orderlies
Maintenance of the Palace of Holyroodhouse
State visits to and by the Queen and Liaison with the
Diplomatic Corps
Ceremonial occasions
Maintenance of Home Park, Windsor Castle

TAXATION

The sovereign is not legally liable to pay income tax or capital gains tax. After income tax was reintroduced in 1842, some income tax was paid voluntarily by the sovereign but over a long period these payments were phased out. In 1992 The Queen offered to pay tax on a voluntary basis from 6 April 1993, and the Prince of Wales offered to pay tax on a voluntary basis on his income from the Duchy of Cornwall. (He was already taxed in all other respects.)

The main provisions for The Queen and the Prince of Wales to pay tax, set out in a Memorandum of Understanding on Royal Taxation presented to Parliament on 11 February 1993, are that The Queen will pay income tax and capital gains tax in respect of her private income and assets, and on the proportion of the income and capital gains of the Privy Purse used for private purposes. Inheritance tax will be paid on The Queen's assets, except for those which pass to the next sovereign, whether automatically or by gift or bequest. The Prince of Wales will pay income tax on income from the Duchy of Cornwall used for private purposes.

The Prince of Wales has confirmed that he intends to pay tax on the same basis following his accession to the throne. Other members of the royal family are subject to tax as for any taxpayer.

MILITARY RANKS AND TITLES

THE QUEEN

ROYAL NAVY
Lord High Admiral of the United Kingdom

ARMY
Colonel-in-Chief
   The Life Guards; The Blues and Royals (Royal Horse Guards and 1st Dragoons); The Royal Scots Dragoon Guards (Carabiniers and Greys); The Queen's Royal Lancers; Royal Tank Regiment; Corps of Royal Engineers; Grenadier Guards; Coldstream Guards; Scots Guards; Irish Guards; Welsh Guards; The Royal Welch Fusiliers; The Queen's Lancashire Regiment; The Argyll and Sutherland Highlanders (Princess Louise's); The Royal Green Jackets; Adjutant General's Corps; The Royal Mercian and Lancastrian Yeomanry; The Governor General's Horse Guards (of Canada); The King's Own Calgary Regiment (Royal Canadian Armoured Corps); Canadian Forces Military Engineers Branch; Royal 22e Regiment (of Canada); Governor General's Foot Guards (of Canada); The Canadian Grenadier Guards; Le Regiment de la Chaudiere (of Canada); 2nd Battalion Royal New Brunswick Regiment (North Shore); The 48th Highlanders of Canada; The Argyll and Sutherland Highlanders of Canada (Princess Louise's); The Calgary Highlanders; Royal Australian Engineers; Royal Australian Infantry Corps; Royal Australian Army Ordnance Corps; Royal Australian Army Nursing Corps; The Corps of Royal New Zealand Engineers; Royal New Zealand Infantry Regiment; The Malawi Rifles; The Royal Malta Artillery

Affiliated Colonel-in-Chief
   The Queen's Gurkha Engineers

Captain General
   Royal Regiment of Artillery; The Honourable Artillery Company; Combined Cadet Force; Royal Regiment of Canadian Artillery; Royal Regiment of Australian Artillery; Royal Regiment of New Zealand Artillery; Royal New Zealand Armoured Corps

Patron
   Royal Army Chaplains' Department

ROYAL AIR FORCE
Air Commodore-in-Chief
   Royal Auxiliary Air Force; Royal Air Force Regiment; Air Reserve of Canada; Royal Australian Air Force Reserve; Territorial Air Force (of New Zealand)

Commandant-in-Chief
   Royal Air Force College, Cranwell

Royal Hon. Air Commodore
   Royal Air Force Marham; 603 (City of Edinburgh) Squadron Royal Auxiliary Air Force

HRH THE PRINCE PHILIP, DUKE OF EDINBURGH

ROYAL NAVY
Admiral of the Fleet
Admiral of the Fleet, Royal Australian Navy
Admiral of the Fleet, Royal New Zealand Navy
Admiral of the Royal Canadian Sea Cadets

ROYAL MARINES
Captain General, Royal Marines

ARMY
Field Marshal
Field Marshal, Australian Military Forces
Field Marshal, New Zealand Army

Colonel-in-Chief
   The Queen's Royal Hussars (Queen's Own and Royal Irish); The Royal Gloucestershire, Berkshire and Wiltshire Regiment; The Highlanders (Seaforth, Gordons and Camerons); Corps of Royal Electrical and Mechanical Engineers; Intelligence Corps; Army Cadet Force Association; The Royal Canadian Regiment; Royal Hamilton Light Infantry (Wentworth Regiment of Canada); The Cameron Highlanders of Ottawa; The Queen's Own Cameron Highlanders of Canada; The Seaforth Highlanders of Canada; The Royal Canadian Army Cadets; The Royal Australian Corps of Electrical and Mechanical Engineers; The Australian Army Cadet Corps

Colonel
Grenadier Guards

Royal Hon. Colonel
City of Edinburgh University Officers' Training Corps;
The Trinidad and Tobago Regiment

Member
Honourable Artillery Company

ROYAL AIR FORCE
Marshal of the Royal Air Force
Marshal of the Royal Australian Air Force
Marshal of the Royal New Zealand Air Force

Air Commodore-in-Chief
Air Training Corps; Royal Canadian Air Cadets

Royal Hon. Air Commodore
Royal Air Force Kinloss

HRH THE PRINCE OF WALES

ROYAL NAVY
Vice Admiral

ARMY
Lieutenant-General

Colonel-in-Chief
The Royal Dragoon Guards; The Cheshire (22nd)
Regiment; The Royal Regiment of Wales (24th/41st
Foot); The Parachute Regiment; The Royal Gurkha
Rifles; Army Air Corps; The Royal Canadian Dragoons;
Lord Strathcona's Horse (Royal Canadians); Royal
Regiment of Canada (10th Royal Grenadiers); Royal
Winnipeg Rifles; Royal Australian Armoured Corps;
The Royal Pacific Islands Regiment; 1st The Queen's
Dragoon Guards; The Black Watch (Royal Highland
Regiment); The King's Regiment

Deputy Colonel-in-Chief
The Highlanders (Seaforth, Gordons and Camerons)

Colonel
Welsh Guards

Royal Hon. Colonel
The Queen's Own Yeomanry

ROYAL AIR FORCE
Air Marshal

Hon. Air Commodore
Royal Air Force Valley

Air Commodore-in-Chief
Royal New Zealand Air Force

Colonel-in-Chief
Air Reserve Group of Air Command (of Canada)

HRH THE DUKE OF YORK

ROYAL NAVY
Admiral of the Sea Cadet Corps

ARMY
Colonel-in-Chief
The Staffordshire Regiment (The Prince of Wales's);
The Royal Irish Regiment (27th (Inniskilling), 83rd,
87th and The Ulster Defence Regiment); 9th/12th
Royal Lancers; The Royal Highland Fusiliers; Small
Arms School Corps; The Queen's York Rangers (First
Americans); Royal New Zealand Army Logistics
Regiment

ROYAL AIR FORCE
Royal Hon. Air Commodore
Royal Air Force Lossiemouth

HRH THE EARL OF WESSEX

ARMY
Colonel-in-Chief
Hastings and Prince Edward Regiment; Saskatchewan
Dragoons
Royal Hon. Colonel
Royal Wessex Yeomanry

HRH THE PRINCESS ROYAL

ROYAL NAVY
Rear Admiral Chief Commandant for Women in the Royal Navy

ARMY
Colonel-in-Chief
The King's Royal Hussars; Royal Corps of Signals;
Royal Logistic Corps; The Worcestershire and
Sherwood Foresters Regiment (29th/45th Foot); The
Royal Scots (The Royal Regiment); The Royal Army
Veterinary Corps; 8th Canadian Hussars (Princess
Louise's); Royal Newfoundland Regiment; Canadian
Forces Communications and Electronics Branch; The
Grey and Simcoe Foresters (Royal Canadian Armoured
Corps); The Royal Regina Rifle Regiment; Canadian
Forces Medical Branch; Royal Australian Corps of
Signals; Royal New Zealand Corps of Signals; Royal
New Zealand Nursing Corps

Affiliated Colonel-in-Chief
The Queen's Gurkha Signals; The Queen's Own
Gurkha Transport Regiment

Colonel
The Blues and Royals (Royal Horse Guards and 1st
Dragoons)

Royal Hon. Colonel
University of London Officers' Training Corps

Commandant
First Aid Nursing Yeomanry (Princess Royal's
Volunteer Corps)

ROYAL AIR FORCE
Royal Hon. Air Commodore
Royal Air Force Lyneham; University of London Air
Squadron

HRH PRINCESS ALICE, DUCHESS OF GLOUCESTER

ARMY
Colonel-in-Chief
The King's Own Scottish Borderers; The Royal Anglian Regiment; Royal Australian Corps of Transport

Deputy Colonel-in-Chief
The King's Royal Hussars

ROYAL AIR FORCE
Air Chief Marshal

Air Chief Commandant
Women, Royal Air Force

HRH THE DUKE OF GLOUCESTER

ARMY
Deputy Colonel-in-Chief
The Royal Gloucestershire, Berkshire and Wiltshire Regiment; The Royal Logistic Corps

Royal Hon. Colonel
Royal Monmouthshire Royal Engineers (Militia)

ROYAL AIR FORCE
Hon. Air Marshal

Royal Hon. Air Commodore
Royal Air Force Odiham; No 501 (County of Gloucester) Squadron Royal Auxiliary Air Force

HRH THE DUCHESS OF GLOUCESTER

ARMY
Colonel-in-Chief
Royal Army Dental Corps; Royal Australian Army Educational Corps; Royal New Zealand Army Educational Corps

Deputy Colonel-in-Chief
Adjutant-General's Corps

HRH THE DUKE OF KENT

ARMY
Field Marshal

Colonel-in-Chief
The Royal Regiment of Fusiliers; The Devonshire and Dorset Regiment; Lorne Scots (Peel, Dufferin and Hamilton Regiment)

Deputy Colonel-in-Chief
The Royal Scots Dragoon Guards (Carabiniers and Greys)

Colonel
Scots Guards

ROYAL AIR FORCE
Hon. Air Chief Marshal

Royal Hon. Air Commodore
Royal Air Force Leuchars

HRH THE DUCHESS OF KENT

ARMY
Hon. Major-General

Colonel-in-Chief
The Prince of Wales's Own Regiment of Yorkshire

Deputy Colonel-in-Chief
The Royal Dragoon Guards; Adjutant-General's Corps; The Royal Logistic Corps

HRH PRINCE MICHAEL OF KENT

ROYAL NAVY
Hon. Commodore Royal Naval Reserve

ARMY
Major (retd), The Royal Hussars (Prince of Wales's Own)

Colonel-in-Chief
Essex and Kent Scottish Regiment (Ontario)

ROYAL AIR FORCE
Royal Hon. Air Commodore
RAF Benson

HRH PRINCESS ALEXANDRA, THE HON. LADY OGILVY

ROYAL NAVY
Patron
Queen Alexandra's Royal Naval Nursing Service

ARMY
Colonel-in-Chief
The King's Own Royal Border Regiment; The Light Infantry; The Queen's Own Rifles of Canada; The Canadian Scottish Regiment (Princess Mary's)

Deputy Colonel-in-Chief
The Queen's Royal Lancers

Royal Hon. Colonel
The Royal Yeomanry

ROYAL AIR FORCE
Patron and Air Chief Commandant
Princess Mary's Royal Air Force Nursing Service

Royal Hon. Air Commodore
Royal Air Force Cottesmore

THE HOUSE OF WINDSOR

King George V assumed by royal proclamation (17 July 1917) for his House and family, as well as for all descendants in the male line of Queen Victoria who are subjects of these realms, the name of Windsor.

KING GEORGE V
(George Frederick Ernest Albert), second son of King Edward VII, *born* 3 June 1865; *married* 6 July 1893 HSH Princess Victoria Mary Augusta Louise Olga Pauline Claudine Agnes of Teck (Queen Mary, *born* 26 May 1867; *died* 24 March 1953); *succeeded* to the throne 6 May 1910; *died* 20 January 1936. *Issue:*

1. HRH PRINCE EDWARD Albert Christian George Andrew Patrick David, *born* 23 June 1894, *succeeded* to the throne as King Edward VIII, 20 January 1936; *abdicated* 11 December 1936; created *Duke of Windsor* 1937; *married* 3 June 1937, Mrs Wallis Simpson (Her Grace The Duchess of Windsor, *born* 19 June 1896; *died* 24 April 1986), *died* 28 May 1972

2. HRH PRINCE ALBERT Frederick Arthur George, *born* 14 December 1895, *created* Duke of York 1920; *married* 26 April 1923, Lady Elizabeth Bowes-Lyon, youngest daughter of the 14th Earl of Strathmore and Kinghorne (HM Queen Elizabeth the Queen Mother, *born* 4 August 1900; *died* 30 March 2002), *succeeded* to the throne as King George VI, 11 December 1936; *died* 6 February 1952, having had issue

3. HRH PRINCESS (Victoria Alexandra Alice) MARY, *born* 25 April 1897, *created* Princess Royal 1932; *married* 28 February 1922, Viscount Lascelles, later the 6th Earl of Harewood (1882–1947), *died* 28 March 1965. *Issue:*
(1) George Henry Hubert Lascelles, 7th Earl of Harewood, KBE, *born* 7 February 1923; *married* (1) 1949, Maria

(Marion) Stein (marriage dissolved 1967); *issue, (a)* David Henry George, Viscount Lascelles, *born* 1950; *(b)* James Edward, *born* 1953; *(c)* (Robert) Jeremy Hugh, *born* 1955; (2) 1967, Mrs Patricia Tuckwell; *issue, (d)* Mark Hubert, *born* 1964
(2) Gerald David Lascelles (1924–98), *married* (1) 1952, Miss Angela Dowding (marriage dissolved 1978); *issue, (a)* Henry Ulick, *born* 1953; (2) 1978, Mrs Elizabeth Colvin; *issue, (b)* Martin David, *born* 1962

4. HRH PRINCE HENRY William Frederick Albert, *born* 31 March 1900, *created* Duke of Gloucester, Earl of Ulster and Baron Culloden 1928, *married* 6 November 1935, Lady Alice Christabel Montagu-Douglas-Scott, daughter of the 7th Duke of Buccleuch (HRH Princess Alice, Duchess of Gloucester); *died* 10 June 1974. *Issue:*
(1) HRH Prince William Henry Andrew Frederick, *born* 18 December 1941; *accidentally killed* 28 August 1972
(2) HRH Prince Richard Alexander Walter George (HRH The Duke of Gloucester)

5. HRH PRINCE GEORGE Edward Alexander Edmund, *born* 20 December 1902, *created* Duke of Kent, Earl of St Andrews and Baron Downpatrick 1934, *married* 29 November 1934, HRH Princess Marina of Greece and Denmark (*born* 30 November, 1906; *died* 27 August 1968); *killed on active service,* 25 August 1942. *Issue:*
(1) HRH Prince Edward George Nicholas Paul Patrick (HRH The Duke of Kent)
(2) HRH Princess Alexandra Helen Elizabeth Olga Christabel (HRH Princess Alexandra, the Hon. Lady Ogilvy)
(3) HRH Prince Michael George Charles Franklin (HRH Prince Michael of Kent)

6. HRH PRINCE JOHN Charles Francis, *born* 12 July 1905; *died* 18 January 1919

DESCENDANTS OF QUEEN VICTORIA

QUEEN VICTORIA
(Alexandrina Victoria), *born* 24 May 1819; *succeeded* to the throne 20 June 1837; *married* 10 February 1840 (Francis) Albert Augustus Charles Emmanuel, Duke of Saxony, Prince of Saxe-Coburg and Gotha (HRH Albert, Prince Consort, *born* 26 August 1819, *died* 14 December 1861); *died* 22 January 1901. *Issue:*

1. HRH PRINCESS VICTORIA Adelaide Mary Louisa (Princess Royal) (1840–1901), *m.* 1858, Friedrich III (1831–88), German Emperor March–June 1888. *Issue:*
(1) HIM Wilhelm II (1859–1941), German Emperor 1888–1918, *m.* (1) 1881 Princess Augusta Victoria of Schleswig-Holstein-Sonderburg-Augustenburg (1858–1921); (2) 1922 Princess Hermine of Reuss (1887–1947). *Issue:*
(a) Prince Wilhelm (1882–1951), *Crown Prince* 1888–1918, *m.* 1905 Duchess Cecilie of Mecklenburg-Schwerin; *issue:* Prince Wilhelm (1906–40); Prince Louis Ferdinand (1907–94), *m.* 1938 Grand Duchess Kira; Prince Hubertus (1909–50); Prince Friedrich Georg (1911–66); Princess Alexandrine Irene (1915–80); Princess Cecilie (1917–75)

(b) Prince Eitel-Friedrich (1883–1942), *m.* 1906 Duchess Sophie of Oldenburg (marriage dissolved 1926)
(c) Prince Adalbert (1884–1948), *m.* 1914 Princess Adelheid of Saxe-Meiningen; *issue:* Princess Victoria Marina (1917–81); Prince Wilhelm Victor (1919–89)
(d) Prince August Wilhelm (1887–1949), *m.* 1908 Princess Alexandra of Schleswig-Holstein-Sonderburg-Glücksburg (marriage dissolved 1920); *issue:* Prince Alexander (1912–85)
(e) Prince Oskar (1888–1958), *m.* 1914 Countess von Ruppin; *issue:* Prince Oskar (1915–39); Prince Burchard (1917–88); Princess Herzeleide (1918–89); Prince Wilhelm-Karl (*b.* 1922)
(f) Prince Joachim (1890–1920), *m.* 1916 Princess Marie of Anhalt; *issue:* Prince (Karl) Franz Joseph (1916–75), and has issue
(g) Princess Viktoria Luise (1892–1980), *m.* 1913 Ernst, Duke of Brunswick 1913–18 (1887–1953); *issue:* Prince Ernst (1914–87); Prince Georg (*b.* 1915), *m.* 1946 Princess Sophie of Greece and has issue (two sons, one daughter); Princess Frederika (1917–81), *m.* 1938 Paul I, King of the

Hellenes; Prince Christian (1919–81); Prince Welf Heinrich (1923–97)
(2) Princess Charlotte (1860–1919), m. 1878 Bernhard, Duke of Saxe-Meiningen 1914 (1851–1928). Issue: Princess Feodora (1879–1945), m. 1898 Prince Heinrich XXX of Reuss
(3) Prince Heinrich (1862–1929), m. 1888 Princess Irene of Hesse. Issue:
  (a) Prince Waldemar (1889–1945), m. Princess Calixta Agnes of Lippe
  (b) Prince Sigismund (1896–1978), m. 1919 Princess Charlotte of Saxe-Altenburg; issue: Princess Barbara (1920–94); Prince Alfred (b. 1924)
  (c) Prince Heinrich (1900–4)
(4) Prince Sigismund (1864–6)
(5) Princess Victoria (1866–1929), m. (1) 1890, Prince Adolf of Schaumburg-Lippe (1859–1916); (2) 1927, Alexander Zubkov (1900–36)
(6) Prince Waldemar (1868–79)
(7) Princess Sophie (1870–1932), m. 1889 Constantine I (1868–1923), King of the Hellenes 1913–17, 1920–3. Issue:
  (a) George II (1890–1947), King of the Hellenes 1923–4 and 1935–47, m. 1921 Princess Elisabeth of Roumania (marriage dissolved 1935)
  (b) Alexander I (1893–1920), King of the Hellenes 1917–20, m. 1919 Aspasia Manos; issue: Princess Alexandra (1921–93), m. 1944 King Petar II of Yugoslavia
  (c) Princess Helena (1896–1982), m. 1921 King Carol of Roumania, (marriage dissolved 1928)
  (d) Paul I (1901–64), King of the Hellenes 1947–64, m. 1938 Princess Frederika of Brunswick; issue: King Constantine II (b. 1940), m. 1964 Princess Anne-Marie of Denmark, and has issue (three sons, two daughters); Princess Sophie (b. 1938), m. 1962 Juan Carlos I of Spain; Princess Irene (b. 1942)
  (e) Princess Irene (1904–74), m. 1939 4th Duke of Aosta; issue: Prince Amedeo, 5th Duke of Aosta (b. 1943)
  (f) Princess Katherine (Lady Katherine Brandram) (b. 1913), m. 1947 Major R. C. A. Brandram, MC, TD; issue: R. Paul G. A. Brandram (b. 1948)
(8) Princess Margarethe (1872–1954), m. 1893 Prince Friedrich Karl of Hesse (1868–1940). Issue:
  (a) Prince Friedrich Wilhelm (1893–1916)
  (b) Prince Maximilian (1894–1914)
  (c) Prince Philipp (1896–1980), m. 1925 Princess Mafalda of Italy; issue: Prince Moritz (b. 1926); Prince Heinrich (1927–99); Prince Otto (1937–98); Princess Elisabeth (b. 1940)
  (d) Prince Wolfgang (1896–1989), m. (1) 1924 Princess Marie Alexandra of Baden; (2) 1948 Ottilie Möller
  (e) Prince Richard (1901–69)
  (f) Prince Christoph (1901–43), m. 1930 Princess Sophie of Greece (see below) and has issue (two sons, three daughters)

2. HRH PRINCE ALBERT EDWARD (HM KING EDWARD VII), b. 9 November 1841, m. 1863 HRH Princess Alexandra of Denmark (1844–1925), succeeded to the throne 22 January 1901, d. 6 May 1910. Issue:
(1) Albert Victor, Duke of Clarence and Avondale (1864–92)
(2) George (HM KING GEORGE V) (1865–1936)
(3) Louise (1867–1931) Princess Royal 1905–31, m. 1889 1st Duke of Fife (1849–1912). Issue:

  (a) Princess Alexandra, Duchess of Fife (1891–1959), m. 1913 Prince Arthur of Connaught (b) Princess Maud (1893–1945), m. 1923 11th Earl of Southesk (1893–1992); issue: The Duke of Fife (b. 1929)
(4) Victoria (1868–1935)
(5) Maud (1869–1938), m. 1896 Prince Carl of Denmark (1872–1957), later King Haakon VII of Norway 1905–57. Issue:
  (a) Olav V (1903–91), King of Norway 1957–91, m. 1929 Princess Märtha of Sweden (1901–54); issue: Princess Ragnhild (b. 1930); Princess Astrid (b. 1932); Harald V, King of Norway (b. 1937)
(6) Alexander (6–7 April 1871)

3. HRH PRINCESS ALICE Maud Mary (1843–78), m. 1862 Prince Ludwig (1837–92), Grand Duke of Hesse 1877–92. Issue:
(1) Victoria (1863–1950), m. 1884 Admiral of the Fleet Prince Louis of Battenberg (1854–1921), cr. 1st Marquess of Milford Haven 1917. Issue:
  (a) Alice (1885–1969), m. 1903 Prince Andrew of Greece (1882–1944); issue: Princess Margarita (1905–81), m. 1931 Prince Gottfried of Hohenlohe-Langenburg (see below); Princess Theodora (1906–69), m. Prince Berthold of Baden (1906–63) and has issue (two sons, one daughter); Princess Cecilie (1911–37), m. George, Grand Duke of Hesse (see below); Princess Sophie (1914–2001), m. (1) 1930 Prince Christoph of Hesse (see above); (2) 1946 Prince Georg of Hanover; Prince Philip, Duke of Edinburgh (b. 1921)
  (b) Louise (1889–1965), m. 1923 Gustaf VI Adolf (1882–1973), King of Sweden 1950–73
  (c) George, 2nd Marquess of Milford Haven (1892–1938), m. 1916 Countess Nadejda, daughter of Grand Duke Michael of Russia; issue: Lady Tatiana (1917–88); David Michael, 3rd Marquess (1919–70)
  (d) Louis, 1st Earl Mountbatten of Burma (1900–79), m. 1922 Edwina Ashley, daughter of Lord Mount Temple; issue: Patricia, Countess Mountbatten of Burma (b. 1924), Pamela (b. 1929)
(2) Elizabeth (1864–1918), m. 1884 Grand Duke Sergius of Russia (1857–1905)
(3) Irene (1866–1953), m. 1888 Prince Heinrich of Prussia (4) Ernst Ludwig (1868–1937), Grand Duke of Hesse 1892–1918, m. (1) 1894 Princess Victoria Melita of Saxe-Coburg (see below) (marriage dissolved 1901); (2) 1905 Princess Eleonore of Solms-Hohensolmslich. Issue:
  (a) Princess Elizabeth (1895–1903)
  (b) George, Hereditary Grand Duke of Hesse (1906–37), m. Princess Cecilie of Greece (see above), and had issue, two sons, accidentally killed with parents, 1937
  (c) Ludwig, Prince of Hesse (1908–68), m. 1937 Margaret, daughter of 1st Lord Geddes
(5) Frederick William (1870–3)
(6) Alix (Tsaritsa of Russia) (1872–1918), m. 1894 Nicholas II (1868–1918) Tsar of All the Russias 1894–1917, assassinated 16 July 1918. Issue:
  (a) Grand Duchess Olga (1895–1918)
  (b) Grand Duchess Tatiana (1897–1918)
  (c) Grand Duchess Marie (1899–1918)
  (d) Grand Duchess Anastasia (1901–18)
  (e) Alexis, Tsarevich of Russia (1904–18)
(7) Marie (1874–8)

4. HRH PRINCE ALFRED Ernest Albert, Duke of

Edinburgh, *Admiral of the Fleet* (1844–1900), *m.* 1874 Grand Duchess Marie Alexandrovna of Russia (1853–1920); succeeded as Duke of Saxe-Coburg and Gotha 22 August 1893. *Issue:*
(1) Alfred, Prince of Saxe-Coburg (1874–99)
(2) Marie (1875–1938), *m.* 1893 Ferdinand (1865–1927), King of Roumania 1914–27. *Issue:*
  (a) Carol II (1893–1953), King of Roumania 1930–40, *m.* (2) 1921 Princess Helena of Greece (*see* above) (marriage dissolved 1928); *issue:* Michael (*b.* 1921), King of Roumania 1927–30, 1940–7, *m.* 1948 Princess Anne of Bourbon-Parma, and has issue (five daughters)
  (b) Elisabeth (1894–1956), *m.* 1921 George II, King of the Hellenes
  (c) Marie (1900–61), *m.* 1922 Alexander (1888–1934), King of Yugoslavia 1921–34; *issue:* Petar II (1923–70), King of Yugoslavia 1934–45, *m.* 1944 Princess Alexandra of Greece (*see* above) and has issue (Crown Prince Alexander, *b.* 1945); Prince Tomislav (1928–2000), *m.* (1) 1957 Princess Margarita of Baden (daughter of Princess Theodora of Greece and Prince Berthold of Baden, *see* above); (2) 1982 Linda Bonney; and has issue (three sons, one daughter); Prince Andrej (1929–90), *m.* (1) 1956 Princess Christina of Hesse (daughter of Prince Christoph of Hesse and Princess Sophie of Greece, *see* above); (2) 1963 Princess Kira-Melita of Leiningen (*see* below); and has issue (three sons, two daughters)
  (d) Prince Nicolas (1903–78)
  (e) Princess Ileana (1909–91), *m.* (1) 1931 Archduke Anton of Austria; (2) 1954 Dr Stefan Issarescu; *issue:* Archduke Stefan (1932–98); Archduchess Maria Ileana (1933–59); Archduchess Alexandra (*b.* 1935); Archduke Dominic (*b.* 1937); Archduchess Maria Magdalena (*b.* 1939); Archduchess Elisabeth (*b.* 1942)
  (f) Prince Mircea (1913–16)
(3) Victoria Melita (1876–1936), *m.* (1) 1894 Grand Duke Ernst Ludwig of Hesse (*see* above) (marriage dissolved 1901); (2) 1905 the Grand Duke Kirill of Russia (1876–1938). *Issue:*
  (a) Marie Kirillovna (1907–51), *m.* 1925 Prince Friedrich Karl of Leiningen; *issue:* Prince Emich (1926–91); Prince Karl (1928–90); Princess Kira-Melita (*b.* 1930), *m.* Prince Andrej of Yugoslavia (*see* above); Princess Margarita (1932–96); Princess Mechtilde (*b.* 1936); Prince Friedrich (1938–98)
  (b) Kira Kirillovna (1909–67), *m.* 1938 Prince Louis Ferdinand of Prussia; *issue:* Prince Friedrich Wilhelm (*b.* 1939); Prince Michael (*b.* 1940); Princess Marie (*b.* 1942); Princess Kira (*b.* 1943); Prince Louis Ferdinand (1944–77); Prince Christian (*b.* 1946); Princess Xenia (1949–92)
  (c) Vladimir Kirillovich (1917–92), *m.* 1948 Princess Leonida Bagration-Mukhransky; *issue:* Grand Duchess Maria (*b.* 1953), and has issue
(4) Alexandra (1878–1942), *m.* 1896 Ernst, Prince of Hohenlohe Langenburg. *Issue:*
  (a) Gottfried (1897–1960), *m.* 1931 Princess Margarita of Greece (*see* above); *issue:* Prince Kraft (1935–2004), Princess Beatrice (1936–97), Prince Georg Andreas (*b.* 1938), Prince Ruprecht (1944–76); Prince Albrecht (1944–92)
  (b) Maria (1899–1967), *m.* 1916 Prince Friedrich of Schleswig-Holstein-Sonderburg-Glücksburg; *issue:* Prince Peter (1922–80); Princess Marie (1927–2000)

  (c) Princess Alexandra (1901–63)
  (d) Princess Irma (1902–86)
(5) Princess Beatrice (1884–1966), *m.* 1909 Alfonso of Orleans, Infante of Spain. *Issue:*
  (a) Prince Alvaro (1910–97), *m.* 1937 Carla Parodi-Delfino; *issue:* Doña Gerarda (*b.* 1939); Don Alonso (1941–75); Doña Beatriz (*b.* 1943); Don Alvaro (*b.* 1947)
  (b) Prince Alonso (1912–36)
  (c) Prince Ataulfo (1913–74)

5. HRH PRINCESS HELENA Augusta Victoria (1846–1923), *m.* 1866 Prince Christian of Schleswig-Holstein-Sonderburg-Augustenburg (1831–1917). *Issue:*
(1) Prince Christian Victor (1867–1900)
(2) Prince Albert (1869–1931), Duke of Schleswig-Holstein 1921–31
(3) Princess Helena (1870–1948)
(4) Princess Marie Louise (1872–1956), *m.* 1891 Prince Aribert of Anhalt (marriage dissolved 1900)
(5) Prince Harold (12–20 May 1876)

6. HRH PRINCESS LOUISE Caroline Alberta (1848–1939), *m.* 1871 the Marquess of Lorne, afterwards 9th Duke of Argyll (1845–1914); without issue

7. HRH PRINCE ARTHUR William Patrick Albert, Duke of Connaught, *Field Marshal* (1850–1942), *m.* 1879 Princess Louisa of Prussia (1860–1917). *Issue:*
(1) Margaret (1882–1920), *m.* 1905 Crown Prince Gustaf Adolf (1882–1973), afterwards King of Sweden 1950–73. *Issue:*
  (a) Gustaf Adolf, Duke of Västerbotten (1906–47), *m.* 1932 Princess Sibylla of Saxe-Coburg-Gotha (*see* below); *issue:* Princess Margaretha (*b.* 1934); Princess Birgitta (*b.* 1937); Princess Désirée (*b.* 1938); Princess Christina (*b.* 1943); Carl XVI Gustaf, King of Sweden (*b.* 1946)
  (b) Count Sigvard Bernadotte (1907–2002), *m.* (1) 1934 Erika Patzeck; (2) 1943 Sonja Robbert; (3) 1961 Marianne Lindberg; *issue:* Count Michael (*b.* 1944)
  (c) Princess Ingrid (Queen Mother of Denmark) (1910–2000), *m.* 1935 Frederick IX (1899–1972), King of Denmark 1947–72; *issue:* Margrethe II, Queen of Denmark (*b.* 1940); Princess Benedikte (*b.* 1944); Princess Anne-Marie (*b.* 1946), *m.* 1964 Constantine II of Greece
  (d) Prince Bertil, Duke of Halland (1912–97), *m.* 1976 Mrs Lilian Craig
  (e) Count Carl Bernadotte (*b.* 1916), *m.* (1) 1946 Mrs Kerstin Johnson; (2) 1988 Countess Gunnila Bussler
(2) Arthur (1883–1938), *m.* 1913 HH the Duchess of Fife *Issue:*
Alastair Arthur, 2nd Duke of Connaught (1914–43)
(3) (Victoria) Patricia (1886–1974), *m.* 1919 Adm. Hon. Sir Alexander Ramsay. *Issue:*
  (a) Alexander Ramsay of Mar (1919–2000), *m.* 1956 Hon. Flora Fraser (Lady Saltoun)

8. HRH PRINCE LEOPOLD George Duncan Albert, Duke of Albany (1853–84), *m.* 1882 Princess Helena of Waldeck (1861–1922). *Issue:*
(1) Alice (1883–1981), *m.* 1904 Prince Alexander of Teck (1874–1957), *cr.* 1st Earl of Athlone 1917. *Issue:*
  (a) Lady May (1906–94), *m.* 1931 Sir Henry Abel-Smith, KCMG, KCVO, DSO; *issue:* Anne (*b.* 1932); Richard (*b.* 1933); Elizabeth (*b.* 1936)

(b) Rupert, Viscount Trematon (1907–28)
(c) Prince Maurice (March–September 1910)
(2) Charles Edward (1884–1954), Duke of Albany 1884 until title suspended 1917, Duke of Saxe-Coburg-Gotha 1900–18, *m.* 1905 Princess Victoria Adelheid of Schleswig-Holstein-Sonderburg-Glücksburg. *Issue:*
(a) Prince Johann Leopold (1906–72), and has issue
(b) Princess Sibylla (1908–72), *m.* 1932 Prince Gustav Adolf of Sweden (*see* above)
(c) Prince Dietmar Hubertus (1909–43)
(d) Princess Caroline (1912–83), and has issue
(e) Prince Friedrich Josias (1918–98), and has issue

9. HRH PRINCESS BEATRICE Mary Victoria Feodore (1857–1944), *m.* 1885 Prince Henry of Battenberg (1858–96). *Issue:*
(1) Alexander, 1st Marquess of Carisbrooke (1886–1960), *m.* 1917 Lady Irene Denison. *Issue:*

Lady Iris Mountbatten (1920–82), *m.*; *issue:* Robin A. Bryan (*b.* 1957)
(2) Victoria Eugénie (1887–1969), *m.* 1906 Alfonso XIII (1886–1941) King of Spain 1886–1931. *Issue:*
(a) Prince Alfonso (1907–38)
(b) Prince Jaime (1908–75), and has issue
(c) Princess Beatriz (1909–2002), and has issue
(d) Princess Maria (1911–96), and has issue
(e) Prince Juan (1913–93), Count of Barcelona; *issue:* Princess Maria (*b.* 1936); Juan Carlos I, King of Spain (*b.* 1938), *m.* 1962 Princess Sophie of Greece and has issue (one son, two daughters); Princess Margarita (*b.* 1939)
(f) Prince Gonzalo (1914–34)
(3) Major Lord Leopold Mountbatten (1889–1922)
(4) Maurice (1891–1914), died of wounds received in action

KINGS AND QUEENS

ENGLISH KINGS AND QUEENS 927 TO 1603

HOUSES OF CERDIC AND DENMARK

Reign

927–939 ÆTHELSTAN
Son of Edward the Elder, by Ecgwynn, and grandson of Alfred
Acceded to Wessex and Mercia c.924, established direct rule over Northumbria 927, effectively creating the Kingdom of England
Reigned 15 years

939–946 EDMUND I
Born 921, son of Edward the Elder, by Eadgifu
Married (1) Ælfgifu (2) Æthelflæd
Killed aged 25, *reigned* 6 years

946–955 EADRED
Son of Edward the Elder, by Eadgifu
Reigned 9 years

955–959 EADWIG
Born before 943, son of Edmund and Ælfgifu
Married Ælfgifu
Reigned 3 years

959–975 EDGAR I
Born 943, son of Edmund and Ælfgifu
Married (1) Æthelflæd (2) Wulfthryth (3) Ælfthryth
Died aged 32, *reigned* 15 years

975–978 EDWARD I (the Martyr)
Born c.962, son of Edgar and Æthelflæd
Assassinated aged c.16, *reigned* 2 years

978–1016 ÆTHELRED (the Unready)
Born c.968/969, son of Edgar and Ælfthryth
Married (1) Ælfgifu (2) Emma, daughter of Richard I, Count of Normandy
1013–14 dispossessed of kingdom by Swegn Forkbeard (King of Denmark 987–1014)
Died aged c.47, *reigned* 38 years

1016 EDMUND II (Ironside)
Born before 993, son of Æthelred and Ælfgifu
Married Ealdgyth
Died aged over 23, *reigned* 7 months (April–November)

1016–1035 CNUT (Canute)
Born c.995, son of Swegn Forkbeard, King of Denmark, and Gunhild
Married (1) Ælfgifu (2) Emma, widow of Æthelred the Unready
Gained submission of West Saxons 1015, Northumbrians 1016, Mercia 1016, King of all England after Edmund's death
King of Denmark 1019–35, King of Norway 1028–35
Died aged c.40, *reigned* 19 years

1035–1040 HAROLD I (Harefoot)
Born c.1016/17, son of Cnut and Ælfgifu
Married Ælfgifu
1035 recognised as regent for himself and his brother Harthacnut; 1037 recognised as king
Died aged c.23, *reigned* 4 years

1040–1042 HARTHACNUT
Born c.1018, son of Cnut and Emma
Titular king of Denmark from 1028
Acknowledged King of England 1035–7 with Harold I as regent; effective king after Harold's death
Died aged c.24, *reigned* 2 years

1042–1066 EDWARD II (the Confessor)
Born between 1002 and 1005, son of Æthelred the Unready and Emma
Married Eadgyth, daughter of Godwine, Earl of Wessex
Died aged over 60, *reigned* 23 years

1066 HAROLD II (Godwinesson)
Born c.1020, son of Godwine, Earl of Wessex, and Gytha
Married (1) Eadgyth (2) Ealdgyth
Killed in battle aged c.46, *reigned* 10 months (January – October)

THE HOUSE OF NORMANDY

1066–1087 WILLIAM I (the Conqueror)
Born 1027/8, son of Robert I, Duke of Normandy; obtained the Crown by conquest
Married Matilda, daughter of Baldwin, Count of Flanders
Died aged c.60, *reigned* 20 years

1087–1100 WILLIAM II (Rufus)
Born between 1056 and 1060, third son of William I; succeeded his father in England only
Killed aged c.40, *reigned* 12 years

1100–1135   HENRY I (Beauclerk)
Born 1068, fourth son of William I
Married (1) Edith or Matilda, daughter of
Malcolm III of Scotland (2) Adela, daughter
of Godfrey, Count of Louvain
Died aged 67, *reigned* 35 years

1135–1154   STEPHEN
Born not later than 1100, third son of
Adela, daughter of William I, and Stephen,
Count of Blois
Married Matilda, daughter of Eustace,
Count of Boulogne
1141 (February – November) held captive
by adherents of Matilda, daughter of
Henry I, who contested the crown until
1153
Died aged over 53, *reigned* 18 years

THE HOUSE OF ANJOU (PLANTAGENETS)

1154–1189   HENRY II (Curtmantle)
Born 1133, son of Matilda, daughter of
Henry I, and Geoffrey, Count of Anjou
Married Eleanor, daughter of William, Duke
of Aquitaine, and divorced queen of Louis
VII of France
Died aged 56, *reigned* 34 years

1189–1199   RICHARD I (Coeur de Lion)
Born 1157, third son of Henry II
Married Berengaria, daughter of Sancho VI,
King of Navarre
Died aged 42, *reigned* 9 years

1199–1216   JOHN (Lackland)
Born 1167, fifth son of Henry II
Married (1) Isabella or Avisa, daughter of
William, Earl of Gloucester (divorced) (2)
Isabella, daughter of Aymer, Count of
Angoulême
Died aged 48, *reigned* 17 years

1216–1272   HENRY III
Born 1207, son of John and Isabella of
Angoulême
Married Eleanor, daughter of Raymond,
Count of Provence
Died aged 65, *reigned* 56 years

1272–1307   EDWARD I (Longshanks)
Born 1239, eldest son of Henry III
Married (1) Eleanor, daughter of Ferdinand
III, King of Castile (2) Margaret, daughter
of Philip III of France
Died aged 68, *reigned* 34 years

1307–1327   EDWARD II
Born 1284, eldest surviving son of Edward I
and Eleanor
Married Isabella, daughter of Philip IV of
France
Deposed January 1327, *killed* September
1327 aged 43, *reigned* 19 years

1327–1377   EDWARD III
Born 1312, eldest son of Edward II
Married Philippa, daughter of William,
Count of Hainault
Died aged 64, *reigned* 50 years

1377–1399   RICHARD II
Born 1367, son of Edward (the Black
Prince), eldest son of Edward III
Married (1) Anne, daughter of Emperor
Charles IV (2) Isabelle, daughter of Charles
VI of France
Deposed September 1399, *killed* February
1400 aged 33, *reigned* 22 years

THE HOUSE OF LANCASTER

1399–1413   HENRY IV
Born 1366, son of John of Gaunt, fourth son
of Edward III, and Blanche, daughter of
Henry, Duke of Lancaster
Married (1) Mary, daughter of Humphrey,
Earl of Hereford (2) Joan, daughter of
Charles, King of Navarre, and widow of
John, Duke of Brittany
Died aged c.47, *reigned* 13 years

1413–1422   HENRY V
Born 1387, eldest surviving son of Henry
IV and Mary
Married Catherine, daughter of Charles VI
of France
Died aged 34, *reigned* 9 years

1422–1471   HENRY VI
Born 1421, son of Henry V
Married Margaret, daughter of René, Duke
of Anjou and Count of Provence
Deposed March 1461, *restored* October
1470
Deposed April 1471, *killed* May 1471 aged
49, *reigned* 39 years

THE HOUSE OF YORK

1461–1483   EDWARD IV
Born 1442, eldest son of Richard of York
(grandson of Edmund, fifth son of Edward
III, and son of Anne, great-granddaughter
of Lionel, third son of Edward III)
Married Elizabeth Woodville, daughter of
Richard, Lord Rivers, and widow of Sir
John Grey
Acceded March 1461, *deposed* October
1470, *restored* April 1471
Died aged 40, *reigned* 21 years

1483   EDWARD V
Born 1470, eldest son of Edward IV
Deposed June 1483, *died* probably July –
September 1483, aged 12, *reigned* 2 months
(April – June)

1483–1485   RICHARD III
Born 1452, fourth son of Richard of
York
Married Anne Neville, daughter of Richard,
Earl of Warwick, and widow of Edward,
Prince of Wales, son of Henry VI
Killed in battle aged 32, *reigned* 2 years

THE HOUSE OF TUDOR

1485–1509   HENRY VII
Born 1457, son of Margaret Beaufort (great-
granddaughter of John of Gaunt, fourth son
of Edward III) and Edmund Tudor, Earl of
Richmond
Married Elizabeth, daughter of Edward IV
Died aged 52, *reigned* 23 years

1509–1547   HENRY VIII
Born 1491, second son of Henry VII
Married (1) Catherine, daughter of
Ferdinand II, King of Aragon, and widow
of his elder brother Arthur (divorced) (2)
Anne, daughter of Sir Thomas Boleyn
(executed) (3) Jane, daughter of Sir John
Seymour (died in childbirth) (4) Anne,
daughter of John, Duke of Cleves (divorced)
(5) Catherine Howard, niece of the Duke of
Norfolk (executed) (6) Catherine, daughter
of Sir Thomas Parr and widow of Lord
Latimer
Died aged 55, *reigned* 37 years

1547–1553   EDWARD VI
Born 1537, son of Henry VIII and Jane
Seymour
Died aged 15, reigned 6 years

1553   JANE
Born 1537, daughter of Frances (daughter
of Mary Tudor, the younger daughter of
Henry VII) and Henry Grey, Duke of
Suffolk
Married Lord Guildford Dudley, son of the
Duke of Northumberland
Deposed July 1553, executed February 1554
aged 16, reigned 14 days

1553–1558   MARY I
Born 1516, daughter of Henry VIII and
Catherine of Aragon
married Philip II of Spain
Died aged 42, reigned 5 years

1558–1603   ELIZABETH I
Born 1533, daughter of Henry VIII and
Anne Boleyn
Died aged 69, reigned 44 years

BRITISH KINGS AND QUEENS SINCE 1603

THE HOUSE OF STUART
Reign

1603–1625   JAMES I (VI OF SCOTLAND)
Born 1566, son of Mary, Queen of Scots
(granddaughter of Margaret Tudor, elder
daughter of Henry VII), and Henry Stewart,
Lord Darnley
Married Anne, daughter of Frederick II of
Denmark
Died aged 58, reigned 22 years

1625–1649   CHARLES I
Born 1600, second son of James I
Married Henrietta Maria, daughter of Henry
IV of France
Executed 1649 aged 48, reigned 23 years

COMMONWEALTH DECLARED 19 May
1649
1649–53 Government by a council of state
1653–8 Oliver Cromwell, Lord Protector
1658–9 Richard Cromwell, Lord Protector

1660–1685   CHARLES II
Born 1630, eldest son of Charles I
Married Catherine, daughter of John IV of
Portugal
Died aged 54, reigned 24 years

1685–1688   JAMES II (VII OF SCOTLAND)
Born 1633, second son of Charles I
Married (1) Lady Anne Hyde, daughter of
Edward, Earl of Clarendon (2) Mary,
daughter of Alphonso, Duke of Modena
Reign ended with flight from kingdom
December 1688
Died 1701 aged 67, reigned 3 years

INTERREGNUM
11 December 1688 to 12 February 1689

1689–1702   WILLIAM III
Born 1650, son of William II, Prince of
Orange, and Mary Stuart, daughter of
Charles I
Married Mary, elder daughter of James II
Died aged 51, reigned 13 years

1689–1694   MARY II
Born 1662, elder daughter of James II and
Anne
Died aged 32, reigned 5 years

1702–1714   ANNE
Born 1665, younger daughter of James II
and Anne
Married Prince George of Denmark, son of
Frederick III of Denmark
Died aged 49, reigned 12 years

THE HOUSE OF HANOVER

1714–1727   GEORGE I (Elector of Hanover)
Born 1660, son of Sophia (daughter of
Frederick, Elector Palatine, and Elizabeth
Stuart, daughter of James I) and Ernest
Augustus, Elector of Hanover
Married Sophia Dorothea, daughter of
George William, Duke of Lüneburg-Celle
Died aged 67, reigned 12 years

1727–1760   GEORGE II
Born 1683, son of George I
Married Caroline, daughter of John
Frederick, Margrave of Brandenburg-
Anspach
Died aged 76, reigned 33 years

1760–1820   GEORGE III
Born 1738, son of Frederick, eldest son of
George II
Married Charlotte, daughter of Charles
Louis, Duke of Mecklenburg-Strelitz
Died aged 81, reigned 59 years

REGENCY 1811–20
Prince of Wales regent owing to the insanity
of George III

1820–1830   GEORGE IV
Born 1762, eldest son of George III
Married Caroline, daughter of Charles,
Duke of Brunswick-Wolfenbüttel
Died aged 67, reigned 10 years

1830–1837   WILLIAM IV
Born 1765, third son of George III
Married Adelaide, daughter of George,
Duke of Saxe-Meiningen
Died aged 71, reigned 7 years

1837–1901   VICTORIA
Born 1819, daughter of Edward, fourth son
of George III
Married Prince Albert of Saxe-Coburg and
Gotha
Died aged 81, reigned 63 years

THE HOUSE OF SAXE-COBURG AND GOTHA

1901–1910   EDWARD VII
Born 1841, eldest son of Victoria and Albert
Married Alexandra, daughter of Christian
IX of Denmark
Died aged 68, reigned 9 years

THE HOUSE OF WINDSOR

1910–1936   GEORGE V
Born 1865, second son of Edward VII
Married Victoria Mary, daughter of Francis,
Duke of Teck
Died aged 70, reigned 25 years

1936   EDWARD VIII
Born 1894, eldest son of George V
Married (1937) Mrs Wallis Simpson
Abdicated 1936, died 1972 aged 77, reigned
10 months (20 January to 11 December)

1936–1952 GEORGE VI
Born 1895, second son of George V
Married Lady Elizabeth Bowes-Lyon,
daughter of 14th Earl of Strathmore and
Kinghorne
Died aged 56, reigned 15 years

1952– ELIZABETH II
Born 1926, elder daughter of George VI
Married Philip, son of Prince Andrew of
Greece

KINGS AND QUEENS OF SCOTS 1016 TO 1603

Reign

1016–1034 MALCOLM II
Born c.954, son of Kenneth II
Acceded to Alba 1005, secured Lothian
c.1016, obtained Strathclyde for his
grandson Duncan c.1016, thus reigning
over an area approximately the same as that
governed by later rulers of Scotland
Died aged c.80, reigned 18 years

THE HOUSE OF ATHOLL

1034–1040 DUNCAN I
Son of Bethoc, daughter of Malcolm II, and
Crinan, Mormaer of Atholl
Married a cousin of Siward, Earl of
Northumbria
Reigned 5 years

1040–1057 MACBETH
Born c.1005, son of a daughter of Malcolm
II and Finlaec, Mormaer of Moray
Married Gruoch, granddaughter of Kenneth
III
Killed aged c.52, reigned 17 years

1057–1058 LULACH
Born c.1032, son of Gillacomgan, Mormaer
of Moray, and Gruoch (and stepson of
Macbeth)
Died aged c.26, reigned 7 months (August –
March)

1058–1093 MALCOLM III (Canmore)
Born c.1031, elder son of Duncan I
Married (1) Ingibiorg (2) Margaret (St
Margaret), granddaughter of Edmund II of
England
Killed in battle aged c.62, reigned 35 years

1093–1097 DONALD III BÁN
Born c.1033, second son of Duncan I
deposed May 1094, restored November
1094, deposed October 1097, reigned 3 years

1094 DUNCAN II
Born c.1060, elder son of Malcolm III and
Ingibiorg
Married Octreda of Dunbar
Killed aged c.34, reigned 6 months (May–
November)

1097–1107 EDGAR
Born c.1074, second son of Malcolm III and
Margaret
Died aged c.32, reigned 9 years

1107–1124 ALEXANDER I (The Fierce)
Born c.1077, fifth son of Malcolm III and
Margaret
Married Sybilla, illegitimate daughter of
Henry I of England
Died aged c.47, reigned 17 years

1124–1153 DAVID I (The Saint)
Born c.1085, sixth son of Malcolm III and
Margaret

Married Matilda, daughter of Waltheof, Earl
of Huntingdon
Died aged c.68, reigned 29 years

1153–1165 MALCOLM IV (The Maiden)
Born c.1141, son of Henry, Earl of
Huntingdon, second son of David I
Died aged c.24, reigned 12 years

1165–1214 WILLIAM I (The Lion)
Born c.1142, brother of Malcolm IV
Married Ermengarde, daughter of Richard,
Viscount of Beaumont
Died aged c.72, reigned 49 years

1214–1249 ALEXANDER II
Born 1198, son of William I
Married (1) Joan, daughter of John, King
of England (2) Marie, daughter of Ingelram
de Coucy
Died aged 50, reigned 34 years

1249–1286 ALEXANDER III
Born 1241, son of Alexander II and Marie
Married (1) Margaret, daughter of Henry III
of England (2) Yolande, daughter of the
Count of Dreux
Killed accidentally aged 44, reigned 36 years

1286–1290 MARGARET (The Maid of Norway)
Born 1283, daughter of Margaret (daughter
of Alexander III) and Eric II of Norway
Died aged 7, reigned 4 years

FIRST INTERREGNUM 1290–2
Throne disputed by 13 competitors. Crown
awarded to John Balliol by adjudication of
Edward I of England

THE HOUSE OF BALLIOL

1292–1296 JOHN (Balliol)
Born c.1250, son of Dervorguilla, great-
great-granddaughter of David I, and John
de Balliol
Married Isabella, daughter of John, Earl of
Surrey
Abdicated 1296, died 1313 aged c.63,
reigned 3 years

SECOND INTERREGNUM 1296–1306
Edward I of England declared John Balliol
to have forfeited the throne for contumacy
in 1296 and took the government of
Scotland into his own hands

THE HOUSE OF BRUCE

1306–1329 ROBERT I (Bruce)
Born 1274, son of Robert Bruce and
Marjorie, countess of Carrick, and great-
grandson of the second daughter of David,
Earl of Huntingdon, brother of William I
Married (1) Isabella, daughter of Donald,
Earl of Mar (2) Elizabeth, daughter of
Richard, Earl of Ulster
Died aged 54, reigned 23 years

1329–1371 DAVID II
Born 1324, son of Robert I and Elizabeth
Married (1) Joanna, daughter of Edward II
of England (2) Margaret Drummond,
widow of Sir John Logie (divorced)
Died aged 46, reigned 41 years
1332 Edward Balliol, son of John Balliol,
crowned King of Scots September, expelled
December
1333–6 Edward Balliol restored as King of
Scots

THE HOUSE OF STEWART

1371–1390   ROBERT II (Stewart)
Born 1316, son of Marjorie (daughter of Robert I) and Walter, High Steward of Scotland
Married (1) Elizabeth, daughter of Sir Robert Mure of Rowallan (2) Euphemia, daughter of Hugh, Earl of Ross
Died aged 74, *reigned* 19 years

1390–1406   ROBERT III
*Born c.*1337, son of Robert II and Elizabeth
Married Annabella, daughter of Sir John Drummond of Stobhall
Died aged *c.*69, *reigned* 16 years

1406–1437   JAMES I
Born 1394, son of Robert III
Married Joan Beaufort, daughter of John, Earl of Somerset
Assassinated aged 42, *reigned* 30 years

1437–1460   JAMES II
Born 1430, son of James I
Married Mary, daughter of Arnold, Duke of Gueldres
Killed accidentally aged 29, *reigned* 23 years

1460–1488   JAMES III
Born 1452, son of James II
Married Margaret, daughter of Christian I of Denmark
Assassinated aged 36, *reigned* 27 years

1488–1513   JAMES IV
Born 1473, son of James III
Married Margaret Tudor, daughter of Henry VII of England
Killed in battle aged 40, *reigned* 25 years

1513–1542   JAMES V
Born 1512, son of James IV
Married (1) Madeleine, daughter of Francis I of France (2) Mary of Lorraine, daughter of the Duc de Guise
Died aged 30, *reigned* 29 years

1542–1567   MARY
Born 1542, daughter of James V and Mary
Married (1) the Dauphin, afterwards Francis II of France (2) Henry Stewart, Lord Darnley (3) James Hepburn, Earl of Bothwell
Abdicated 1567, prisoner in England from 1568, *executed* 1587, *reigned* 24 years

1567–1625   JAMES VI (and I of England)
Born 1566, son of Mary, Queen of Scots, and Henry, Lord Darnley
Acceded 1567 to the Scottish throne, *reigned* 58 years
Succeeded 1603 to the English throne, so joining the English and Scottish crowns in one person. The two kingdoms remained distinct until 1707 when the parliaments of the kingdoms became conjoined

WELSH SOVEREIGNS AND PRINCES

The title Prince of Wales is borne after individual conferment and is not inherited at birth, though some Princes have been declared and styled Prince of Wales but never formally so created (*s.*). The title was conferred on Prince Charles by The Queen on 26 July 1958. He was invested at Caernarvon on 1 July 1969.

INDEPENDENT PRINCES AD 844 TO 1282

844–878	Rhodri the Great
878–916	Anarawd, son of Rhodri
916–950	Hywel Dda, the Good
950–979	Iago ab Idwal (or Ieuaf)
979–985	Hywel ab Ieuaf, the Bad
985–986	Cadwallon, his brother
986–999	Maredudd ab Owain ap Hywel Dda
999–1008	Cynan ap Hywel ab Ieuaf
1018–1023	Llywelyn ap Seisyll
1023–1039	Iago ab Idwal ap Meurig
1039–1063	Gruffydd ap Llywelyn ap Seisyll
1063–1075	Bleddyn ap Cynfyn
1075–1081	Trahaern ap Caradog
1081–1137	Gruffydd ap Cynan ab Iago
1137–1170	Owain Gwynedd
1170–1194	Dafydd ab Owain Gwynedd
1194–1240	Llywelyn Fawr, the Great
1240–1246	Dafydd ap Llywelyn
1246–1282	Llywelyn ap Gruffydd ap Llywelyn

ENGLISH PRINCES SINCE 1301

1301	Edward (Edward II)
1343	Edward the Black Prince, son of Edward III
1376	Richard (Richard II), son of the Black Prince
1399	Henry of Monmouth (Henry V)
1454	Edward of Westminster, son of Henry VI
1471	Edward of Westminster (Edward V)
1483	Edward, son of Richard III (*d.* 1484)
1489	Arthur Tudor, son of Henry VII
1504	Henry Tudor (Henry VIII)
1610	Henry Stuart, son of James I (*d.* 1612)
1616	Charles Stuart (Charles I)
*c.*1638 (*s.*)	Charles Stuart (Charles II)
1688 (*s.*)	James Francis Edward Stuart (The Old Pretender), son of James II (*d.* 1766)
1714	George Augustus (George II)
1729	Frederick Lewis, son of George II (*d.* 1751)
1751	George William Frederick (George III)
1762	George Augustus Frederick (George IV)
1841	Albert Edward (Edward VII)
1901	George (George V)
1910	Edward (Edward VIII)
1958	Charles, son of Elizabeth II

PRINCESSES ROYAL

The style Princess Royal is conferred at the Sovereign's discretion on his or her eldest daughter. It is an honorary title, held for life, and cannot be inherited or passed on. It was first conferred on Princess Mary, daughter of Charles I, in approximately 1642.

*c.*1642	Princess Mary (1631–60), daughter of Charles I
1727	Princess Anne (1709–59), daughter of George II
1766	Princess Charlotte (1766–1828), daughter of George III
1840	Princess Victoria (1840–1901), daughter of Victoria
1905	Princess Louise (1867–1931), daughter of Edward VII
1932	Princess Mary (1897–1965), daughter of George V
1987	Princess Anne (b. 1950), daughter of Elizabeth II

PRECEDENCE

ENGLAND AND WALES

The Sovereign
The Prince Philip, Duke of
  Edinburgh
The Prince of Wales
The Sovereign's younger sons
The Sovereign's grandsons
The Sovereign's cousins
Archbishop of Canterbury
Lord High Chancellor
Archbishop of York
The Prime Minister
Lord President of the Council
Speaker of the House of Commons
Lord Privy Seal
Ambassadors and High
  Commissioners
Lord Great Chamberlain
Earl Marshal
Lord Chamberlain of the Household
Lord Steward of the Household
Master of the Horse
Dukes, according to their patent of
  creation:
(1) of England
(2) of Scotland
(3) of Great Britain
(4) of Ireland
(5) those created since the Union
Eldest sons of Dukes of the Blood
  Royal
Marquesses, according to their patent
  of creation:
(1) of England
(2) of Scotland
(3) of Great Britain
(4) of Ireland
(5) those created since the Union
Dukes' eldest sons
Earls, according to their patent of
  creation:
(1) of England
(2) of Scotland
(3) of Great Britain
(4) of Ireland
(5) those created since the Union
Younger sons of Dukes of Blood Royal
Marquesses' eldest sons
Dukes' younger sons
Viscounts, according to their patent of
  creation:
(1) of England
(2) of Scotland
(3) of Great Britain
(4) of Ireland
(5) those created since the Union
Earls' eldest sons
Marquesses' younger sons
Bishop of London
Bishop of Durham
Bishop of Winchester
Other English Diocesan Bishops
  according to seniority of
  consecration
Suffragan Bishops, according to
  seniority of consecration
Secretaries of State, if of the degree of
  a Baron
Barons, according to their patent of
  creation:

(1) of England
(2) of Scotland
(3) of Great Britain
(4) of Ireland
(5) those created since the Union,
  including Life Barons
Treasurer of the Household
Comptroller of the Household
Vice-Chamberlain of the Household
Secretaries of State under the degree of
  Baron
Viscounts' eldest sons
Earls' younger sons
Barons' eldest sons
Knights of the Garter
Privy Counsellors
Chancellor of the Exchequer
Chancellor of the Duchy of Lancaster
Lord Chief Justice of England
Master of the Rolls
President of the Family Division
Vice-Chancellor
Lords Justices of Appeal, according to
  seniority of appointment
Judges of the High Court, according
  to seniority of appointment
Viscounts' younger sons
Barons' younger sons
Sons of Life Peers and Lords of Appeal
  in Ordinary
Baronets, according to date of patent
Knights of the Thistle
Knights Grand Cross of the Bath
Knights Grand Commanders of the
  Star of India
Knights Grand Cross of St Michael
  and St George
Knights Grand Commanders of the
  Indian Empire
Knights Grand Cross of the Royal
  Victorian Order
Knights Grand Cross of the British
  Empire
Knights Commanders of the Bath
Knights Commanders of the Star of
  India
Knights Commanders of St Michael
  and St George
Knights Commanders of the Indian
  Empire
Knights Commanders of the Royal
  Victorian Order
Knights Commanders of the British
  Empire
Knights Bachelor
Vice-Chancellor of the County
  Palatine of Lancaster
Circuit Judges who held office as
  Official Referees to Supreme Court
  (immediately before 1 January
  1972)
Recorder of London
Recorders of Liverpool and
  Manchester, according to priority of
  appointment
Common Serjeant
Circuit Judges who held office
  immediately before 1 January
  1972, according to priority of
  appointment
Other Circuit Judges according to

priority or order of their respective
  appointments
Companions of the Bath
Companions of the Star of India
Companions of St Michael and St
  George
Companions of the Indian Empire
Commanders of the Royal Victorian
  Order
Commanders of the British Empire
Companions of the Distinguished
  Service Order
Lieutenants of the Royal Victorian
  Order
Officers of the British Empire
Companions of the Imperial Service
  Order
Eldest sons of younger sons of Peers
Baronets' eldest sons
Eldest sons of Knights, in the same
  order as their fathers
Members of the Royal Victorian
  Order
Members of the British Empire
Younger sons of Baronets
Younger sons of Knights, in the same
  order as their fathers
Esquires
Gentlemen

SCOTLAND

The Sovereign
The Prince Philip, Duke of Edinburgh
The Lord High Commissioner to the
  General Assembly of the Church of
  Scotland (while that Assembly is
  sitting)
The Duke of Rothesay (eldest son of
  the Sovereign)
The Sovereign's younger sons
Grandsons of the Sovereign
The Sovereign's cousins
Lord-Lieutenants
Lord Provosts of Cities being ex-officio
  Lord-Lieutenants of those Cities
  during their term of office
Sheriffs Principal, successively, within
  their own localities and during
  holding of office
Lord Chancellor of Great Britain
Moderator of the General Assembly of
  the Church of Scotland
Keeper of the Great Seal of Scotland
  (the First Minister)
The Presiding Officer
The Secretary of State for Scotland
Hereditary High Constable of
  Scotland
Hereditary Master of the Household in
  Scotland
Dukes, in same order as in England
Eldest sons of Dukes of the Blood
  Royal
Marquesses, as in England
Eldest sons of Dukes
Earls, as in England
Younger sons of Dukes of Blood
  Royal
Eldest sons of Marquesses

Dukes' younger sons
Lord Justice General
Lord Clerk Register
Lord Advocate
The Advocate-General
Lord Justice Clerk
Viscounts, as in England
Eldest sons of Earls
Marquesses' younger sons
Lord-Barons, as in England
Eldest sons of Viscounts
Earls' younger sons
Lord-Barons' eldest sons
Knights of the Garter
Knights of the Thistle
Privy Counsellors
Senators of College of Justice (Lords of
    Session)
Viscounts' younger sons
Lord-Barons' younger sons
Baronets
Knights Grand Cross and Knights
    Grand Commanders of Orders, as
    in England
Knights Commanders of Orders, as in
    England
Solicitor-General for Scotland
Lord Lyon King of Arms
Sheriffs Principal, when not within
    own county
Knights Bachelor
Sheriffs
Companions of Orders, as in England
Commanders of the Royal Victorian
    Order
Commanders of the British Empire
Companions of the Distinguished
    Service Order
Lieutenants of the Royal Victorian
    Order
Officers of the British Empire
Companions of the Imperial Service
    Order
Eldest sons of younger sons of Peers
Eldest sons of Baronets
Eldest sons of Knights, as in England
Members of the Royal Victorian Order
Members of the British Empire
Baronets' younger sons
Knights' younger sons
Esquires
Gentlemen

WOMEN

Women take the same rank as their husbands or as their brothers; but the daughter of a peer marrying a commoner retains her title as Lady or Honourable. Daughters of peers rank next immediately after the wives of their elder brothers, and before their younger brothers' wives. Daughters of peers marrying peers of lower degree take the same order of precedence as that of their husbands; thus the daughter of a Duke marrying a Baron becomes of the rank of Baroness only, while her sisters married to commoners retain their rank and take precedence of the Baroness. Merely official rank on the husband's part does not give any similar precedence to the wife.

Peeresses in their own right take the same precedence as peers of the same rank, i.e. from their date of creation.

LOCAL PRECEDENCE
Scotland
The Lord Provosts of the city districts of Aberdeen, Dundee, Edinburgh and Glasgow are Lord Lieutenants for those districts *ex officio* and take precedence as such.

FORMS OF ADDRESS

It is only possible to cover here the forms of address for peers, baronets and knights, their wife and children, and Privy Counsellors. Greater detail should be sought in one of the publications devoted to the subject.

Both formal and social forms of address are given where usage differs; nowadays, the social form is generally preferred to the formal, which increasingly is used only for official documents and on very formal occasions.

F_ represents forename
S_ represents surname

BARON – *Envelope (formal),* The Right Hon. Lord _; *(social),* The Lord _. *Letter (formal),* My Lord; *(social),* Dear Lord _. *Spoken,* Lord _.
BARON'S WIFE – *Envelope (formal),* The Right Hon. Lady _; *(social),* The Lady _. *Letter (formal),* My Lady; *(social),* Dear Lady _. *Spoken,* Lady _.
BARON'S CHILDREN – *Envelope,* The Hon. F_ S_. *Letter,* Dear Mr/Miss/Mrs S_. *Spoken,* Mr/Miss/Mrs S_.
BARONESS IN OWN RIGHT – *Envelope,* may be addressed in same way as a Baron's wife or, if she prefers *(formal),* The Right Hon. the Baroness _; *(social),* The Baroness _. Otherwise as for a Baron's wife.
BARONET – *Envelope,* Sir F_ S_, Bt. *Letter (formal),* Dear Sir; *(social),* Dear Sir F_. *Spoken,* Sir F_.
BARONET'S WIFE – *Envelope,* Lady S_. *Letter (formal),* Dear Madam; *(social),* Dear Lady S_. *Spoken,* Lady S_.
COUNTESS IN OWN RIGHT – As for an Earl's wife.
COURTESY TITLES – The heir apparent to a Duke, Marquess or Earl uses the highest of his father's other titles as a courtesy title. (For a list, *see* the Peerage section.) The holder of a courtesy title is not styled The Most Hon. or The Right Hon., and in correspondence 'The' is omitted before the title. The heir apparent to a Scottish title may use the title 'Master' (*see* below).
DAME – *Envelope,* Dame F_ S_, followed by appropriate post-nominal letters. *Letter (formal),* Dear Madam; *(social),* Dear Dame F_. *Spoken,* Dame F_.
DUKE – *Envelope (formal),* His Grace the Duke of _; *(social),* The Duke of _. *Letter (formal),* My Lord Duke; *(social),* Dear Duke. *Spoken (formal),* Your Grace; *(social),* Duke.
DUKE'S WIFE – *Envelope (formal),* Her Grace the Duchess of _; *(social),* The Duchess of _. *Letter (formal),* Dear Madam; *(social),* Dear Duchess. *Spoken,* Duchess.
DUKE'S ELDEST SON – *see* Courtesy titles.
DUKE'S YOUNGER SONS – *Envelope,* Lord F_ S_. *Letter (formal),* My Lord; *(social),* Dear Lord F_. *Spoken (formal),* My Lord; *(social),* Lord F_.
DUKE'S DAUGHTER – *Envelope,* Lady F_ S_. *Letter (formal),* Dear Madam; *(social),* Dear Lady F_. *Spoken,* Lady F_.
EARL – *Envelope (formal),* The Right Hon. the Earl (of) _; *(social),* The Earl (of) _. *Letter (formal),* My Lord; *(social),* Dear Lord _. *Spoken (formal),* My Lord; *(social),* Lord _.
EARL'S WIFE – *Envelope (formal),* The Right Hon. the Countess (of) _; *(social),* The Countess (of) _. *Letter (formal),* Madam; *(social),* Lady _. *Spoken (formal),* Madam; *(social),* Lady _.

EARL'S CHILDREN – *Eldest son, see* Courtesy titles. *Younger sons,* The Hon. F_ S_ (for forms of address, *see* Baron's children). *Daughters,* Lady F_ S_ (for forms of address, *see* Duke's daughter).
KNIGHT (BACHELOR) – *Envelope,* Sir F_ S_. *Letter (formal),* Dear Sir; *(social),* Dear Sir F_. *Spoken,* Sir F_.
KNIGHT (ORDERS OF CHIVALRY) – *Envelope,* Sir F_ S_, followed by appropriate post-nominal letters. Otherwise as for Knight Bachelor.
KNIGHT'S WIFE – As for Baronet's wife.
LIFE PEER – As for Baron/Baroness in own right.
LIFE PEER'S WIFE – As for Baron's wife.
LIFE PEER'S CHILDREN – As for Baron's children.
MARQUESS – *Envelope (formal),* The Most Hon. the Marquess of _; *(social),* The Marquess of _. *Letter (formal),* My Lord; *(social),* Dear Lord _. *Spoken (formal),* My Lord; *(social),* Lord _.
MARQUESS'S WIFE – *Envelope (formal),* The Most Hon. the Marchioness of _; *(social),* The Marchioness of _. *Letter (formal),* Madam; *(social),* Dear Lady _. *Spoken,* Lady _.
MARQUESS'S CHILDREN – *Eldest son, see* Courtesy titles. *Younger sons,* Lord F_ S_ (for forms of address, *see* Duke's younger sons). *Daughters,* Lady F_ S_ (for forms of address, *see* Duke's daughter).
MASTER – The title is used by the heir apparent to a Scottish peerage, though usually the heir apparent to a Duke, Marquess or Earl uses his courtesy title rather than 'Master'. *Envelope,* The Master of _. *Letter (formal),* Dear Sir; *(social),* Dear Master of _. *Spoken (formal),* Master, or Sir; *(social),* Master, or Mr S_.
MASTER'S WIFE – Addressed as for the wife of the appropriate peerage style, otherwise as Mrs S_.
PRIVY COUNSELLOR – *Envelope,* The Right (or Rt.) Hon. F_ S_. *Letter,* Dear Mr/Miss/Mrs S_. *Spoken,* Mr/Miss/ Mrs S_. It is incorrect to use the letters PC after the name in conjunction with the prefix The Right Hon., unless the Privy Counsellor is a peer below the rank of Marquess and so is styled The Right Hon. because of his rank. In this case only, the post-nominal letters may be used in conjunction with the prefix The Right Hon.
VISCOUNT – *Envelope (formal),* The Right Hon. the Viscount _; *(social),* The Viscount _. *Letter (formal),* My Lord; *(social),* Dear Lord _. *Spoken,* Lord _.
VISCOUNT'S WIFE – *Envelope (formal),* The Right Hon. the Viscountess _; *(social),* The Viscountess _. *Letter (formal),* Madam; *(social),* Dear Lady _. *Spoken,* Lady _.
VISCOUNT'S CHILDREN – As for Baron's children.

THE PEERAGE

The rules which govern the creation and succession of peerages are extremely complicated. There are, technically, five separate peerages, the Peerage of England, of Scotland, of Ireland, of Great Britain, and of the United Kingdom. The Peerage of Great Britain dates from 1707 when an Act of Union combined the two kingdoms of England and Scotland and separate peerages were discontinued. The Peerage of the United Kingdom dates from 1801 when Great Britain and Ireland were combined under an Act of Union. Some Scottish peers have received additional peerages of Great Britain or of the United Kingdom since 1707, and some Irish peers additional peerages of the United Kingdom since 1801.

The Peerage of Ireland was not entirely discontinued from 1801 but holders of Irish peerages, whether pre-dating or created subsequent to the Union of 1801, were not entitled to sit in the House of Lords if they had no additional English, Scottish, Great Britain or United Kingdom peerage. However, they are eligible for election to the House of Commons and to vote in parliamentary elections. An Irish peer holding a peerage of a lower grade which enabled him to sit in the House of Lords was introduced there by the title which enabled him to sit, though for all other purposes he was known by his higher title.

In the Peerage of Scotland there is no rank of Baron; the equivalent rank is Lord of Parliament, abbreviated to 'Lord' (the female equivalent is 'Lady'). All peers of England, Scotland, Great Britain or the United Kingdom who are 21 years or over, and of British, Irish or Commonwealth nationality were entitled to sit in the House of Lords until the House of Lords Act 1999, when hereditary peers lost the right to sit. Ninety-two hereditaries including the two Royal Office Holders, The Earl Marshal and the Lord Great Chamberlain, were allowed to remain, pending further reform. In the listings which follow, these peers are indicated by **.

HEREDITARY WOMEN PEERS

Most hereditary peerages pass on death to the nearest male heir, but there are exceptions, and several are held by women.

A woman peer in her own right retains her title after marriage, and if her husband's rank is the superior she is designated by the two titles jointly, the inferior one second. Her hereditary claim still holds good in spite of any marriage whether higher or lower. No rank held by a woman can confer any title or even precedence upon her husband but the rank of a hereditary woman peer in her own right is inherited by her eldest son (or in some cases daughter).

After the Peerage Act 1963, hereditary women peers in their own right were entitled to sit in the House of Lords, subject to the same qualifications as men, until the House of Lords Act 1999.

LIFE PEERS

Since 1876 non-hereditary or life peerages have been conferred on certain eminent judges to enable the judicial functions of the House of Lords to be carried out. These Lords are known as Lords of Appeal or law lords. In 2004, Baroness Hale of Richmond became the first female law lord.

Since 1958 life peerages have been conferred upon distinguished men and women from all walks of life, giving them seats in the House of Lords in the degree of Baron or Baroness. They are addressed in the same way as hereditary Lords and Barons, and their children have similar courtesy titles.

PEERAGES EXTINCT SINCE THE LAST EDITION

LIFE PEERAGES: Blake (cr. 1971); Brigstocke (cr. 1990); Bullock (cr. 1976); Constantine of Stanmore (cr. 1981); Diamond (cr. 1970); Dormand of Easington (cr. 1987); Gallacher (cr. 1982); Geraint (cr. 1992); Gibson (cr. 1975); Greene of Harrow Weald (cr. 1974); Hill-Norton (cr. 1979); Hardy of Wath (cr. 1997); Hobhouse of Woodborough (cr. 1998); Islwyn (cr. 1997); Jenkins of Putney (cr. 1981); Keith of Castleacre (cr. 1980); Murray of Epping Forest (cr. 1985); Pike (cr. 1974); Rayne (cr. 1976); Richardson (cr. 1979); Scanlon (cr. 1979); Walker of Doncaster (cr. 1997); Wallace of Coslany (cr. 1974); Wigoder (cr. 1974)

DISCLAIMER OF PEERAGES

The Peerage Act 1963 enables peers to disclaim their peerages for life. Peers alive in 1963 could disclaim within twelve months after the passing of the Act (31 July 1963); a person subsequently succeeding to a peerage may disclaim within 12 months (one month if an MP) after the date of succession, or of reaching 21, if later. The disclaimer is irrevocable but does not affect the descent of the peerage after the disclaimant's death, and children of a disclaimed peer may, if they wish, retain their precedence and any courtesy titles and styles borne as children of a peer. The disclaimer permitted the disclaimant to sit in the House of Commons if elected as an MP. As the House of Lords Act 1999 removed hereditary peers from the House of Lords, they are now entitled to sit in the House of Commons without having to disclaim their titles.

The following peerages are currently disclaimed:

EARLDOMS: Durham (1970); Selkirk (1994)
VISCOUNTCIES: Stansgate (1963)
BARONIES: Merthyr (1977); Reith (1972); Sanderson of Ayot (1971)

PEERS WHO ARE MINORS (i.e. under 21 years of age)
EARLS: Craven (b. 1989)
VISCOUNTS: Selby (b. 1993)

CONTRACTIONS AND SYMBOLS

S.	Scottish title
I.	Irish title
**	Hereditary peer remaining in the House of Lords for a transitional period
o	there is no 'of' in the title
b.	Born
s.	Succeeded
m.	Married
w.	widower or widow
M.	Minor
†	heir not ascertained at time of going to press

HEREDITARY PEERS

PEERS OF THE BLOOD ROYAL

Style, His Royal Highness The Duke of _/His Royal Highness the Earl of_
Style of address (formal) May it please your Royal Highness; *(informal)* Sir

Created	Title, order of succession, name, etc.	Heir
	Dukes	
1947	*Edinburgh* (1st), HRH The Prince Philip, Duke of Edinburgh	The Prince of Wales §
1337	*Cornwall,* Charles, Prince of Wales, *s.* 1952	‡
1398 S.	*Rothesay,* Charles, Prince of Wales, *s.* 1952	‡
1986	*York* (1st), The Prince Andrew, Duke of York	None
1999	*Wessex* (1st), The Prince Edward, Earl of Wessex	None
1928	*Gloucester* (2nd), Prince Richard, Duke of Gloucester, *s.* 1974	Earl of Ulster
1934	*Kent* (2nd), Prince Edward, Duke of Kent, *s.* 1942	Earl of St Andrews

§ In June 1999, Buckingham Palace revealed that the current Earl of Wessex will succeed to the Dukedom of Edinburgh after the title has returned to the crown. The Prince of Wales will only be able to confer the Dukedom on the Earl of Wessex when he succeeds his mother as King.
‡ The title is held by the Sovereign's eldest son from the moment of his birth or the Sovereign's accession.

DUKES

Coronet, Eight strawberry leaves
Style, His Grace the Duke of _
Wife's style, Her Grace the Duchess of _
Eldest son's style, Takes his father's second title as a courtesy title
Younger sons' style, 'Lord' before forename and family name
Daughters' style, 'Lady' before forename and family name
For forms of address, *see* page 43

Created	Title, order of succession, name, etc.	Heir
1868 I.	*Abercorn (5th),* James Hamilton, KG, *b.* 1934, *s.* 1979, *m., Lord Steward*	Marquess of Hamilton, *b.* 1969
1701 S.	*Argyll (13th),* Torquhil Ian Campbell, *b.* 1968, *s.* 2001	Lord Colin I. C., *b.* 1946
1703 S.	*Atholl (11th),* John Murray, *b.* 1929, *s.* 1996, *m.*	Marquis of Tullibardine, *b.* 1960
1682	*Beaufort (11th),* David Robert Somerset, *b.* 1928, *s.* 1984, *w.*	Marquess of Worcester, *b.* 1952
1694	*Bedford (15th),* Andrew Ian Henry Russell, *b.* 1962, *s.* 2003, *m.*	Lord Robin L. H. R., *b.* 1963
1663 S.	*Buccleuch (9th) and Queensberry (11th) (S. 1684),* Walter Francis John Montagu Douglas Scott, KT, VRD, *b.* 1923, *s.* 1973, *m.*	Earl of Dalkeith, KBE, *b.* 1954
1694	*Devonshire (12th),* Peregrine Andrew Morny Cavendish, *b.* 1944, *s.* 2004, *m.*	Marquess of Hartington, *b.* 1969
1900	*Fife (3rd),* James George Alexander Bannerman Carnegie, *b.* 1929, *s.* 1959	Earl of Southesk, *b.* 1961
1675	*Grafton (11th),* Hugh Denis Charles FitzRoy, KG, *b.* 1919, *s.* 1970, *m.*	Earl of Euston, *b.* 1947
1643 S.	*Hamilton (15th) and Brandon (12th) (1711),* Angus Alan Douglas Douglas-Hamilton, *b.* 1938, *s.* 1973 *Premier Peer of Scotland*	Marquis of Douglas and Clydesdale, *b.* 1978
1766 I.	*Leinster (8th),* Gerald FitzGerald, *b.* 1914, *s.* 1976, *m. Premier Duke and Marquess of Ireland*	Marquess of Kildare, *b.* 1948
1719	*Manchester (13th),* Alexander Charles David Drogo Montagu, *b.* 1962, *s.* 2002, *m.*	Viscount Mandeville, *b.* 1993
1702	*Marlborough (11th),* John George Vanderbilt Henry Spencer-Churchill, *b.* 1926, *s.* 1972, *m.*	Marquess of Blandford, *b.* 1955
1707 S.	** *Montrose (8th),* James Graham, *b.* 1935, *s.* 1992, *m.*	Marquis of Graham, *b.* 1973
1483	** *Norfolk (18th),* Edward Wiliam Fitzalan-Howard, *b.* 1956, *s.* 2002, *m. Premier Duke and Earl Marshal*	Earl of Arundel and Surrey, *b.* 1987
1766	*Northumberland (12th),* Ralph George Algernon Percy, *b.* 1956, *s.* 1995, *m.*	Earl Percy, *b.* 1984
1675	*Richmond (10th) and Gordon (5th) (1876)* Charles Henry Gordon Lennox, *b.* 1929, *s.* 1989, *m.*	Earl of March and Kinrara, *b.* 1955

Created	Title, order of succession, name, etc.	Heir
1707 S.	Roxburghe (10th), Guy David Innes-Ker, b. 1954, s. 1974, m. Premier Baronet of Scotland	Marquis of Bowmont and Cessford, b. 1981
1703	Rutland (11th), David Charles Robert Manners, b. 1959, s. 1999, m.	Marquess of Granby, b. 1999
1684	St Albans (14th), Murray de Vere Beauclerk, b. 1939, s. 1988, m.	Earl of Burford, b. 1965
1547	Somerset (19th), John Michael Edward Seymour, b. 1952, s. 1984, m.	Lord Seymour, b. 1982
1833	Sutherland (7th), Francis Ronald Egerton, b. 1940, s. 2000, m.	Marquess of Stafford, b. 1975
1814	Wellington (8th), Arthur Valerian Wellesley, KG, LVO, OBE, MC, b. 1915, s. 1972, m.	Marquess of Douro, b. 1945
1874	Westminster (6th), Gerald Cavendish Grosvenor, KG, OBE, b. 1951, s. 1979, m.	Earl Grosvenor, b. 1991

MARQUESSES

Coronet, Four strawberry leaves alternating with four silver balls
Style, The Most Hon. the Marquess (of) _ . In Scotland the spelling 'Marquis' is preferred for pre-Union creations
Wife's style, The Most Hon. the Marchioness (of) _
Eldest son's style, Takes his father's second title as a courtesy title
Younger sons' style, 'Lord' before forename and family name
Daughters' style, 'Lady' before forename and family name
For forms of address, see page 43

Created	Title, order of succession, name, etc.	Heir
1916	Aberdeen and Temair (7th), Alexander George Gordon, b. 1955, s. 2002, m.	Earl of Haddo, b. 1983
1876	Abergavenny (6th) and 10th Earl, Abergavenny, 1784, Christopher George Charles Nevill, b. 1955, s. 2000, m.	To Earldom only, David M. R. N., b. 1941
1821	Ailesbury (8th), Michael Sidney Cedric Brudenell-Bruce, b. 1926, s. 1974	Earl of Cardigan, b. 1952
1831	Ailsa (8th), Archibald Angus Charles Kennedy, b. 1956, s. 1994	Lord David Kennedy, b. 1958
1815	Anglesey (7th), George Charles Henry Victor Paget, b. 1922, s. 1947, m.	Earl of Uxbridge, b. 1950
1789	Bath (7th), Alexander George Thynn, b. 1932, s. 1992, m.	Viscount Weymouth, b. 1974
1826	Bristol (8th), Frederick William Augustus Hervey, b. 1979, s. 1999	Timothy H. H., b. 1960
1796	Bute (7th), John Colum Crichton-Stuart, b. 1958, s. 1993, m.	Lord Mount Stuart, b. 1989
1812	° Camden (6th), David George Edward Henry Pratt, b. 1930, s. 1983	Earl of Brecknock, b. 1965
1815	** Cholmondeley (7th), David George Philip Cholmondeley, b. 1960, s. 1990, Lord Great Chamberlain	Charles G. C., b. 1959
1816	° Conyngham (7th) , Frederick William Henry Francis Conyngham, b. 1924, s. 1974, m.	Earl of Mount Charles, b. 1951
1791 I.	Donegall (7th), Dermot Richard Claud Chichester, LVO, b. 1916, s. 1975, w.	Earl of Belfast, b. 1952
1789 I.	Downshire (9th), (Arthur Francis) Nicholas Wills Hill, b. 1959, s. 2003, m.	Earl of Hillsborough, b. 1996
1801 I.	Ely (8th), Charles John Tottenham, b. 1913, s. 1969, w.	Viscount Loftus, b. 1943
1801	Exeter (8th), (William) Michael Anthony Cecil, b. 1935, s. 1988, m.	Lord Burghley, b. 1970
1800 I.	Headfort (6th), Thomas Geoffrey Charles Michael Taylour, b. 1932, s. 1960, m.	Earl of Bective, b. 1959
1793	Hertford (9th), Henry Jocelyn Seymour, b. 1958, s. 1997, m.	Earl of Yarmouth, b. 1993
1599 S.	Huntly (13th), Granville Charles Gomer Gordon, b. 1944, s. 1987, m. Premier Marquess of Scotland	Earl of Aboyne, b. 1973
1784	Lansdowne (9th), Charles Maurice Mercer Nairne Petty-Fitzmaurice, b. 1941, s. 1999, m.	Earl of Shelburne, b. 1970
1902	Linlithgow (4th), Adrian John Charles Hope, b. 1946, s. 1987, m.	Earl of Hopetoun, b. 1969
1816 I.	Londonderry (9th), Alexander Charles Robert Vane-Tempest-Stewart, b. 1937, s. 1955, m.	Viscount Castlereagh, b. 1972
1701 S.	Lothian (12th), Peter Francis Walter Kerr, KCVO, b. 1922, s. 1940, m.	Earl of Ancram, PC, MP, b. 1945
1917	Milford Haven (4th), George Ivar Louis Mountbatten, b. 1961, s. 1970, m.	Earl of Medina, b. 1991
1838	Normanby (5th), Constantine Edmund Walter Phipps, b. 1954, s. 1994, m.	Earl of Mulgrave, b. 1994

Created	Title, order of succession, name, etc.	Heir
1812	*Northampton (7th)*, Spencer Douglas David Compton, *b.* 1946, *s.* 1978, *m.*	Earl Compton, *b.* 1973
1682 S.	*Queensberry (12th)*, David Harrington Angus Douglas, *b.* 1929, *s.* 1954	Viscount Drumlanrig, *b.* 1967
1926	*Reading (4th)*, Simon Charles Henry Rufus Isaacs, *b.* 1942, *s.* 1980, *m.*	Viscount Erleigh, *b.* 1986
1789	*Salisbury (7th) and Baron Gascoyne-Cecil (life peerage, 1999)*, Robert Michael James Gascoyne-Cecil, PC, *b.* 1946, *s.* 2003, *m.*	Viscount Cranborne, *b.* 1970
1800 I.	*Sligo (11th)*, Jeremy Ulick Browne, *b.* 1939, *s.* 1991, *m.*	Sebastian U. B., *b.* 1964
1787	° *Townshend (7th)*, George John Patrick Dominic Townshend, *b.* 1916, *s.* 1921, *w.*	Viscount Raynham, *b.* 1945
1694 S.	*Tweeddale (13th)*, Edward Douglas John Hay, *b.* 1947, *s.* 1979	Lord Charles D. M. H., *b.* 1947
1789 I.	*Waterford (8th)*, John Hubert de la Poer Beresford, *b.* 1933, *s.* 1934, *m.*	Earl of Tyrone, *b.* 1958
1551	*Winchester (18th)*, Nigel George Paulet, *b.* 1941, *s.* 1968, *m. Premier Marquess of England*	Earl of Wiltshire, *b.* 1969
1892	*Zetland (4th)*, Lawrence Mark Dundas, *b.* 1937, *s.* 1989, *m.*	Earl of Ronaldshay, *b.* 1965

EARLS

Coronet, Eight silver balls on stalks alternating with eight gold strawberry leaves
Style, The Right Hon. the Earl (of) _
Wife's style, The Right Hon. the Countess (of) _
Eldest son's style, Takes his father's second title as a courtesy title
Younger sons' style, 'The Hon.' before forename and family name
Daughters' style, 'Lady' before forename and family name
For forms of address, *see* page 43

Created	Title, order of succession, name, etc.	Heir
1639 S.	*Airlie (13th)*, David George Coke Patrick Ogilvy, KT, GCVO, PC, Royal Victorian Chain, *b.* 1926, *s.* 1968, *m.*	Lord Ogilvy, *b.* 1958
1696	*Albemarle (10th)*, Rufus Arnold Alexis Keppel, *b.* 1965, *s.* 1979, *m.*	Crispian W. J. K., *b.* 1948
1952	° *Alexander of Tunis (2nd)*, Shane William Desmond Alexander, *b.* 1935, *s.* 1969, *m.*	Hon. Brian J. A., *b.* 1939
1662	*Annandale and Hartfell (11th)*, Patrick Andrew Wentworth Hope Johnstone, *b.* 1941, *s.* 1983, *m.* claim established 1985	Lord Johnstone, *b.* 1971
1789	° *Annesley (11th)*, Philip Harrison Annesley, *b.* 1927, *s.* 2001, *m.*	*Hon.* Michael R. A., *b.* 1933
1785	*Antrim (9th)*, Alexander Randal Mark McDonnell, *b.* 1935, *s.* 1977, *m.*	Viscount Dunluce, *b.* 1967
1762	** *Arran (9th)*, Arthur Desmond Colquhoun Gore, *b.* 1938, *s.* 1983, *m.*	Paul A. G., CMG, CVO, *b.* 1921
1955	° ** *Attlee (3rd)*, John Richard Attlee, *b.* 1956, *s.* 1991, *m.*	None
1714	*Aylesford (11th)*, Charles Ian Finch-Knightley, *b.* 1918, *s.* 1958, *w.*	Lord Guernsey, *b.* 1947
1937	° ** *Baldwin of Bewdley (4th)*, Edward Alfred Alexander Baldwin, *b.* 1938, *s.* 1976, *w.*	Viscount Corvedale, *b.* 1973
1922	*Balfour (5th)*, Roderick Francis Arthur Balfour, *b.* 1948, *s.* 2003, *m.*	Charles G. Y. B., *b.* 1951
1772	° *Bathurst (8th)*, Henry Allen John Bathurst, *b.* 1927, *s.* 1943, *m.*	Lord Apsley, *b.* 1961
1919	° *Beatty (3rd)*, David Beatty, *b.* 1946, *s.* 1972, *m.*	Viscount Borodale, *b.* 1973
1797	*Belmore (8th)*, John Armar Lowry-Corry, *b.* 1951, *s.* 1960, *m.*	Viscount Corry, *b.* 1985
1739 I.	*Bessborough (12th)*, Myles Fitzhugh Longfield Ponsonby, *b.* 1941, *s.* 2002, *m.*	Viscount Duncannon, *b.* 1974
1815	*Bradford (7th)*, Richard Thomas Orlando Bridgeman, *b.* 1947, *s.* 1981, *m.*	Viscount Newport, *b.* 1980
1469	*Buchan (17th)*, Malcolm Harry Erskine, *b.* 1930, *s.* 1984, *m.*	Lord Cardross, *b.* 1960
1746	*Buckinghamshire (10th)*, (George) Miles Hobart-Hampden, *b.* 1944, *s.* 1983, *m.*	Sir John Hobart, Bt., *b.* 1945
1800	° *Cadogan (8th)*, Charles Gerald John Cadogan, *b.* 1937, *s.* 1997, *m.*	Viscount Chelsea, *b.* 1966
1878	° *Cairns (6th)*, Simon Dallas Cairns, CVO, CBE, *b.* 1939, *s.* 1989, *m.*	Viscount Garmoyle, *b.* 1965
1455	** *Caithness (20th)*, Malcolm Ian Sinclair, PC, *b.* 1948, *s.* 1965, *w.*	Lord Berriedale, *b.* 1981
1800	*Caledon (7th)*, Nicholas James Alexander, *b.* 1955, *s.* 1980, *m.*	Viscount Alexander, *b.* 1990
1661	*Carlisle (13th)*, George William Beaumont Howard, *b.* 1949, *s.* 1994	Hon. Philip C. W. H., *b.* 1963
1793	*Carnarvon (8th)*, George Reginald Oliver Molyneux Herbert, *b.* 1956, *s.* 2001, *m.*	Lord Porchester, *b.* 1992
1748 I.	*Carrick (10th)*, David James Theobald Somerset Butler, *b.* 1953, *s.* 1992, *m.*	Viscount Ikerrin, *b.* 1975

Created	Title, order of succession, name, etc.	Heir
1800 I.	° Castle Stewart (8th), Arthur Patrick Avondale Stuart, b. 1928, s. 1961, w.	Viscount Stuart, b. 1953
1814	° Cathcart (7th), Charles Alan Andrew Cathcart, b. 1952, s. 1999, m.	Lord Greenock, b. 1986
1647 I.	Cavan, The 12th Earl died in 1988.	†Roger C. Lambart, b. 1944
1827	° Cawdor (7th), Colin Robert Vaughan Campbell, b. 1962, s. 1993, m.	Viscount Emlyn, b. 1998
1801	Chichester (9th), John Nicholas Pelham, b. 1944, s. 1944, m.	Richard A. H. P., b. 1952
1803 I.	Clancarty (9th), Nicholas Power Richard Le Poer Trench, b. 1952, s. 1995	None
1776 I.	Clanwilliam (7th), John Herbert Meade, b. 1919, s. 1989, w.	Lord Gillford, b. 1960
1776	Clarendon (7th), George Frederick Laurence Hyde Villiers, b. 1933, s. 1955, m.	Lord Hyde, b. 1976
1620 I.	Cork and Orrery (15th), John Richard Boyle, b. 1945, s. 2003, m.	Viscount Dungarvan, b. 1978
1850	Cottenham (9th), Mark John Henry Pepys, b. 1983, s. 2000	Hon. Sam R. P., b. 1986
1762 I.	** Courtown (9th), James Patrick Montagu Burgoyne Winthrop Stopford, b. 1954, s. 1975, m.	Viscount Stopford, b. 1988
1697	Coventry (13th), Victor Gerald Coventry, b. 1917, s. 2004, m.	George W. C., b. 1939
1857	° Cowley (7th), Garret Graham Wellesley, b. 1934, s. 1975, m.	Viscount Dangan, b. 1965
1892	Cranbrook (5th), Gathorne Gathorne-Hardy, b. 1933, s. 1978, m.	Lord Medway, b. 1968
1801 M.	Craven (9th), Benjamin Robert Joseph Craven, b. 1989, s. 1990	Rupert J. E. C., b. 1926
1398 S.	Crawford (29th) and Balcarres (12th) (S. 1651) and Baron Balniel (life peerage, 1974), Robert Alexander Lindsay, KT, GCVO, PC, b. 1927, s. 1975, m. Premier Earl on Union Roll	Lord Balniel, b. 1958
1861	Cromartie (5th), John Ruaridh Blunt Grant Mackenzie, b. 1948, s. 1989, m.	Viscount Tarbat, b. 1987
1901	Cromer (4th), Evelyn Rowland Esmond Baring, b. 1946, s. 1991, m.	Viscount Errington, b. 1994
1633 S.	Dalhousie (17th), James Hubert Ramsay, b. 1948, s. 1999, m.	Lord Ramsay, b. 1981
1725 I.	Darnley (11th), Adam Ivo Stuart Bligh, b. 1941, s. 1980, m.	Lord Clifton, b. 1968
1711	Dartmouth (10th), William Legge, b. 1949, s. 1997	Hon. Rupert L., b. 1951
1761	° De La Warr (11th), William Herbrand Sackville, b. 1948, s. 1988, m.	Lord Buckhurst, b. 1979
1622	Denbigh (12th) and Desmond (11th) (I. 1622), Alexander Stephen Rudolph Feilding, b. 1970, s. 1995, m.	William D. F., b. 1939
1485	Derby (19th), Edward Richard William Stanley, b. 1962, s. 1994, m.	Lord Stanley, b. 1998
1553	Devon (18th), Hugh Rupert Courtenay, b. 1942, s. 1998, m.	Lord Courtenay, b. 1975
1800 I.	Donoughmore (8th), Richard Michael John Hely-Hutchinson, b. 1927, s. 1981, w.	Viscount Suirdale, b. 1952
1661 I.	Drogheda (12th), Henry Dermot Ponsonby Moore, b. 1937, s. 1989, m.	Viscount Moore, b. 1983
1837	Ducie (7th), David Leslie Moreton, b. 1951, s. 1991, m.	Lord Moreton, b. 1981
1860	Dudley (4th), William Humble David Ward, b. 1920, s. 1969, m.	Viscount Ednam, b. 1947
1660 S.	** Dundee (12th), Alexander Henry Scrymgeour, b. 1949, s. 1983, m.	Lord Scrymgeour, b. 1982
1669 S.	Dundonald (15th), Iain Alexander Douglas Blair Cochrane, b. 1961, s. 1986, m.	Lord Cochrane, b. 1991
1686 S.	Dunmore (12th), Malcolm Kenneth Murray, b. 1946, s. 1995, m.	Hon. Geoffrey C. M., b. 1949
1822 I.	Dunraven and Mount-Earl (7th), Thady Windham Thomas Wyndham-Quin, b. 1939, s. 1965, m.	None
1833	Durham (6th), Antony Claud Frederick Lambton, b. 1922, s. 1970, m., Disclaimed for life 1970	Hon. Edward R. L. (Baron Durham), b. 1961
1837	Effingham (7th), David Mowbray Algernon Howard, b. 1939, s. 1996, m.	Lord Howard of Effingham, b. 1971
1507 S.	Eglinton (18th) and Winton (9th) (S. 1600), Archibald George Montgomerie, b. 1939, s. 1966, m.	Lord Montgomerie, b. 1966
1733 I.	Egmont (12th), Thomas Frederick Gerald Perceval, b. 1934, s. 2001, m.	Hon. Donald W. P., b. 1954
1821	Eldon (5th), John Joseph Nicholas Scott, b. 1937, s. 1976, m.	Viscount Encombe, b. 1962
1633 S.	Elgin (11th) and Kincardine (15th) (S. 1647), Andrew Douglas Alexander Thomas Bruce, KT, b. 1924, s. 1968, m.	Lord Bruce, b. 1961
1789 I.	Enniskillen (7th), Andrew John Galbraith Cole, b. 1942, s. 1989, m.	Arthur G. C., b. 1920
1789 I.	Erne (6th), Henry George Victor John Crichton, b. 1937, s. 1940, m.	Viscount Crichton, b. 1971
1452 S.	** Erroll (24th), Merlin Sereld Victor Gilbert Hay, b. 1948, s. 1978, m. Hereditary Lord High Constable and Knight Marischal of Scotland	Lord Hay, b. 1984
1661	Essex (10th), Robert Edward de Vere Capell, b. 1920, s. 1981, m.	Viscount Malden, b. 1944
1711	° ** Ferrers (13th), Robert Washington Shirley, PC, b. 1929, s. 1954, m.	Viscount Tamworth, b. 1952
1789	° Fortescue (8th), Charles Hugh Richard Fortescue, b. 1951, s. 1993, m.	Hon. Martin D. F., b. 1924
1841	Gainsborough (5th), Anthony Gerard Edward Noel, b. 1923, s. 1927, m.	Viscount Campden, b. 1950
1623 S.	Galloway (13th), Randolph Keith Reginald Stewart, b. 1928, s. 1978, w.	Andrew C. S., b. 1949

Created	Title, order of succession, name, etc.	Heir
1703 S.	Glasgow (10th), Patrick Robin Archibald Boyle, b. 1939, s. 1984, m.	Viscount of Kelburn, b. 1978
1806 I.	Gosford (7th), Charles David Nicholas Alexander John Sparrow Acheson, b. 1942, s. 1966, m.	Hon. Patrick B. V. M. A., b. 1915
1945	Gowrie (2nd), Alexander Patrick Greysteil Hore-Ruthven, PC, b. 1939, s. 1955, m.	Viscount Ruthven of Canberra, b. 1964
1684 I.	Granard (10th), Peter Arthur Edward Hastings Forbes, b. 1957, s. 1992, m.	Viscount Forbes, b. 1981
1833	° Granville (6th), Granville George Fergus Leveson-Gower, b. 1959, s. 1996, m.	Lord Leveson, b. 1999
1806	° Grey (6th), Richard Fleming George Charles Grey, b. 1939, s. 1963, m.	Philip K. G., b. 1940
1752	Guilford (10th), Piers Edward Brownlow North, b. 1971, s. 1999, m.	Lord North, b. 2002
1619	Haddington (13th), John George Baillie-Hamilton, b. 1941, s. 1986, m.	Lord Binning, b. 1985
1919	° Haig (2nd), George Alexander Eugene Douglas Haig, OBE, b. 1918, s. 1928, m.	Viscount Dawick, b. 1961
1944	Halifax (3rd), Charles Edward Peter Neil Wood, b. 1944, s. 1980, m.	Lord Irwin, b. 1977
1898	Halsbury (4th), Adam Edward Giffard, b. 1934, s. 2000, m.	None
1754	Hardwicke (10th), Joseph Philip Sebastian Yorke, b. 1971, s. 1974	Charles E. Y., b. 1951
1812	Harewood (7th), George Henry Hubert Lascelles, KBE, b. 1923, s. 1947, m.	Viscount Lascelles, b. 1950
1742	Harrington (11th), William Henry Leicester Stanhope, b. 1922, s. 1929, m.	Viscount Petersham, b. 1945
1809	Harrowby (7th), Dudley Danvers Granville Coutts Ryder, TD, b. 1922, s. 1987, m.	Viscount Sandon, b. 1951
1605	** Home (15th), David Alexander Cospatrick Douglas-Home, CVO, CBE, b. 1943, s. 1995, m.	Lord Dunglass, b. 1987
1821	° ** Howe (7th), Frederick Richard Penn Curzon, b. 1951, s. 1984, m.	Viscount Curzon, b. 1994
1529	Huntingdon (16th), William Edward Robin Hood Hastings Bass, LVO, b. 1948, s. 1990, m.	Hon. Simon A. R. H. H. B., b. 1950
1885	Iddesleigh (5th), John Stafford Northcote, b. 1957, s. 2004, m.	Viscount St Cyres, b. 1985
1756	Ilchester (9th), Maurice Vivian de Touffreville Fox-Strangways, b. 1920, s. 1970, m.	Hon. Raymond G. F.-S., b. 1921
1929	Inchcape (4th), (Kenneth) Peter (Lyle) Mackay, b. 1943, s. 1994, m.	Viscount Glenapp, b. 1979
1919	Iveagh (4th), Arthur Edward Rory Guinness, b. 1969, s. 1992	Hon. Rory M. B. G., b. 1974
1925	° Jellicoe (2nd) and Baron Jellicoe of Southampton (life peerage, 1999), George Patrick John Rushworth Jellicoe, KBE, DSO, MC, PC, b. 1918, s. 1935, m.	Viscount Brocas, b. 1950
1697	Jersey (10th), George Francis William Child Villiers, b. 1976, s. 1998 m.	Hon. Jamie C. V., b. 1994
1822 I.	Kilmorey (6th), Richard Francis Needham, PC, b. 1942, s. 1977, m., (does not use title)	Viscount Newry and Mourne, b. 1966
1866	Kimberley (5th), John Armine Wodehouse, b. 1951, s. 2002, m.	Lord Wodehouse, b. 1978
1768 I.	Kingston (12th), Robert Charles Henry King-Tenison, b. 1969, s. 2002, m.	Viscount Kingsborough, b. 2000
1633 S.	Kinnoull (15th), Arthur William George Patrick Hay, b. 1935, s. 1938, m.	Viscount Dupplin, b. 1962
1677 S.	Kintore (13th), Michael Canning William John Keith, b. 1939, s. 1989, m.	Lord Inverurie, b. 1976
1914	° Kitchener of Khartoum (3rd), Henry Herbert Kitchener, TD, b. 1919, s. 1937	None
1624	Lauderdale (17th), Patrick Francis Maitland, b. 1911, s. 1968, w.	Viscount Maitland, b. 1937
1837	Leicester (7th), Edward Douglas Coke, b. 1936, s. 1994, m.	Viscount Coke, b. 1965
1641 S.	Leven (14th) and Melville (13th) (S. 1690), Alexander Robert Leslie Melville, b. 1924, s. 1947, m.	Lord Balgonie, b. 1954
1831	Lichfield (5th), Thomas Patrick John Anson, b. 1939, s. 1960	Viscount Anson, b. 1978
1803 I.	Limerick (7th), Edmund Christopher Pery, b. 1963, s. 2003, m.	Viscount Glentworth, b. 1991
1572	Lincoln (19th), Robert Edward Fiennes-Clinton, b. 1972, s. 2001	Hon. William R. F.-C., b. 1980
1633 S.	** Lindsay (16th), James Randolph Lindesay-Bethune, b. 1955, s. 1989, m.	Viscount Garnock, b. 1990
1626	Lindsey (14th) and Abingdon (9th) (1682), Richard Henry Rupert Bertie, b. 1931, s. 1963, m.	Lord Norreys, b. 1958
1776 I.	Lisburne (8th), John David Malet Vaughan, b. 1918, s. 1965, m.	Viscount Vaughan, b. 1945
1822 I.	** Listowel (6th), Francis Michael Hare, b. 1964, s. 1997, m.	Hon. Timothy P. H., b. 1966
1905	** Liverpool (5th), Edward Peter Bertram Savile Foljambe, b. 1944, s. 1969, m.	Viscount Hawkesbury, b. 1972
1945	° Lloyd George of Dwyfor (3rd), Owen Lloyd George, b. 1924, s. 1968, m.	Viscount Gwynedd, b. 1951

Created	Title, order of succession, name, etc.	Heir
1785 I.	*Longford (8th)*, Thomas Frank Dermot Pakenham, *b.* 1933, *s.* 2001, *m.*	Hon. Edward M. P., *b.* 1970
1807	*Lonsdale (7th)*, James Hugh William Lowther, *b.* 1922, *s.* 1953, *m.*	Viscount Lowther, *b.* 1949
1633 S.	*Loudoun (14th)*, Michael Edward Abney-Hastings, *b.* 1942, *s.* 2002, *m.*	Lord Mauchline, *b.* 1974
1838	*Lovelace (5th)*, Peter Axel William Locke King, *b.* 1951, *s.* 1964, *m.*	None
1795 I.	*Lucan (7th)*, Richard John Bingham, *b.* 1934, *s.* 1964, *m.* (missing since 8 November 1974)	Lord Bingham, *b.* 1967
1880	*Lytton (5th)*, John Peter Michael Scawen Lytton, *b.* 1950, *s.* 1985, *m.*	Viscount Knebworth, *b.* 1989
1721	*Macclesfield (9th)*, Richard Timothy George Mansfield Parker, *b.* 1943, *s.* 1992, *m.*	Hon. J. David G. P., *b.* 1945
1800	*Malmesbury (7th)*, James Carleton Harris, *b.* 1946, *s.* 2000, *m.*	Viscount FitzHarris, *b.* 1970
1776	*Mansfield and Mansfield (8th) (1792)*, William David Mungo James Murray, *b.* 1930, *s.* 1971, *m.*	Viscount Stormont, *b.* 1956
1565 S.	*Mar (14th) and Kellie (16th) (S. 1616) and Baron Erkine of Alloa Tower (life peerage, 2000)*, James Thorne Erskine, *b.* 1949, *s.* 1994, *m.*	Hon. Alexander D. E., *b.* 1952
1785 I.	*Mayo (10th)*, Terence Patrick Bourke, *b.* 1929, *s.* 1962	Lord Naas, *b.* 1953
1627 I.	*Meath (15th)*, John Anthony Brabazon, *b.* 1941, *s.* 1998, *m.*	Lord Ardee, *b.* 1977
1766	*Mexborough (8th)*, John Christopher George Savile, *b.* 1931, *s.* 1980, *m.*	Viscount Pollington, *b.* 1959
1813	*Minto (6th)*, Gilbert Edward George Lariston Elliot-Murray-Kynynmound, OBE, *b.* 1928, *s.* 1975, *m.*	Viscount Melgund, *b.* 1953
1562 S.	*Moray (20th)*, Douglas John Moray Stuart, *b.* 1928, *s.* 1974, *m.*	Lord Doune, *b.* 1966
1815	*Morley (6th)*, John St Aubyn Parker, KCVO, *b.* 1923, *s.* 1962, *m.*	Viscount Boringdon, *b.* 1956
1458	*Morton (22nd)*, John Charles Sholto Douglas, *b.* 1927, *s.* 1976, *m.*	Lord Aberdour, *b.* 1952
1789	*Mount Edgcumbe (8th)*, Robert Charles Edgcumbe, *b.* 1939, *s.* 1982	Piers V. E., *b.* 1946
1805	° *Nelson (9th)*, Peter John Horatio Nelson, *b.* 1941, *s.* 1981, *m.*	Viscount Merton, *b.* 1971
1660 S.	*Newburgh (12th)*, Don Filippo Giambattista Camillo Francesco Aldo Maria Rospigliosi, *b.* 1942, *s.* 1986, *m.*	Princess Donna Benedetta F. M. R., *b.* 1974
1827 I.	*Norbury (7th)*, Richard James Graham-Toler, *b.* 1967, *s.* 2000	None
1806 I.	*Normanton (6th)*, Shaun James Christian Welbore Ellis Agar, *b.* 1945, *s.* 1967, *m.*	Viscount Somerton, *b.* 1982
1647 S.	** *Northesk (14th)*, David John MacRae Carnegie, *b.* 1954, *s.* 1994, *m.*	Patrick C. C., *b.* 1940
1801	** *Onslow (7th)*, Michael William Coplestone Dillon Onslow, *b.* 1938, *s.* 1971, *m.*	Viscount Cranley, *b.* 1967
1696 S.	*Orkney (9th)*, (Oliver) Peter St John, *b.* 1938, *s.* 1998, *m.*	Viscount Kirkwall, *b.* 1969
1328 I.	*Ormonde and Ossory (I. 1527)*, The 25th/18th Earl (7th Marquess) died in 1988	†Viscount Mountgarret *b.* 1961 (*see* that title)
1925	*Oxford and Asquith (2nd)*, Julian Edward George Asquith, KCMG, *b.* 1916, *s.* 1928, *w.*	Viscount Asquith, OBE, *b.* 1952
1929	° ** *Peel (3rd)*, William James Robert Peel, *b.* 1947, *s.* 1969, *m.*	Viscount Clanfield, *b.* 1976
1551	*Pembroke (18th) and Montgomery (15th) (1605)*, William Alexander Sidney Herbert, *b.* 1978, *s.* 2003	Earl of Carnarvon *b.* 1956 (*see* that title)
1605	*Perth (18th)*, John Eric Drummond, *b.* 1935, *s.* 2002, *m.*	Viscount Strathallan, *b.* 1965
1905	*Plymouth (3rd)*, Other Robert Ivor Windsor-Clive, *b.* 1923, *s.* 1943, *m.*	Viscount Windsor, *b.* 1951
1785	*Portarlington (7th)*, George Lionel Yuill Seymour Dawson-Damer, *b.* 1938, *s.* 1959, *m.*	Viscount Carlow, *b.* 1965
1689	*Portland (12th)*, Count Timothy Charles Robert Noel Bentinck, *b.* 1953, *s.* 1997, *m.*	Viscount Woodstock, *b.* 1984
1743	*Portsmouth (10th)*, Quentin Gerard Carew Wallop, *b.* 1954, *s.* 1984, *m.*	Viscount Lymington, *b.* 1981
1804	*Powis (8th)*, John George Herbert, *b.* 1952, *s.* 1993, *m.*	Viscount Clive, *b.* 1979
1765	*Radnor (8th)*, Jacob Pleydell-Bouverie, *b.* 1927, *s.* 1968, *w.*	Viscount Folkestone, *b.* 1955
1831 I.	*Ranfurly (7th)*, Gerald Françoys Needham Knox, *b.* 1929, *s.* 1988, *m.*	Viscount Northland, *b.* 1957
1771	*Roden (10th)*, Robert John Jocelyn, *b.* 1938, *s.* 1993, *m.*	Viscount Jocelyn, *b.* 1989
1801	*Romney (8th)*, Julian Charles Marsham, *b.* 1948, *s.* 2004, *m.*	Hon. David C. M., *b.* 1977
1703 S.	*Rosebery (7th)*, Neil Archibald Primrose, *b.* 1929, *s.* 1974, *m.*	Lord Dalmeny, *b.* 1967
1806 I.	*Rosse (7th)*, William Brendan Parsons, *b.* 1936, *s.* 1979, *m.*	Lord Oxmantown, *b.* 1969
1801	** *Rosslyn (7th)*, Peter St Clair-Erskine, *b.* 1958, *s.* 1977, *m.*	Lord Loughborough, *b.* 1986
1457 S.	*Rothes (21st)*, Ian Lionel Malcolm Leslie, *b.* 1932, *s.* 1975, *m.*	Lord Leslie, *b.* 1958
1861	° ** *Russell (5th)*, Conrad Sebastian Robert Russell, *b.* 1937, *s.* 1987, *m.*	Viscount Amberley, *b.* 1968
1915	° *St Aldwyn (3rd)*, Michael Henry Hicks Beach, *b.* 1950, *s.* 1992, *m.*	Hon. David S. H. B., *b.* 1955
1815	*St Germans (10th)*, Peregrine Nicholas Eliot, *b.* 1941, *s.* 1988	Lord Eliot, *b.* 1966
1660	** *Sandwich (11th)*, John Edward Hollister Montagu, *b.* 1943, *s.* 1995, *m.*	Viscount Hinchingbrooke, *b.* 1969
1690	*Scarbrough (13th)*, Richard Osbert Lumley, *b.* 1973, *s.* 2004	Hon. Thomas H. L., *b.* 1980

Created	Title, order of succession, name, etc.	Heir
1701 S.	Seafield (13th), Ian Derek Francis Ogilvie-Grant, b. 1939, s. 1969, m.	Viscount Reidhaven, b. 1963
1882 **	Selborne (4th), John Roundell Palmer, KBE, b. 1940, s. 1971, m.	Viscount Wolmer, b. 1971
1646 S.	Selkirk, Disclaimed for life 1994 (see Lord Selkirk of Douglas, page 70)	Hon. John A. D.-H., b. 1978
1672	Shaftesbury (10th), Anthony Ashley-Cooper, b. 1938, s. 1961, m.	Lord Ashley, b. 1977
1756 I.	Shannon (9th), Richard Bentinck Boyle, b. 1924, s. 1963	Viscount Boyle, b. 1960
1442 **	Shrewsbury and Waterford (22nd), Charles Henry John Benedict Crofton Chetwynd Chetwynd-Talbot, b. 1952, s. 1980, m. Premier Earl of England and Ireland	Viscount Ingestre, b. 1978
1961	Snowdon (1st) and Baron Armstrong-Jones (life peerage, 1999), Antony Charles Robert Armstrong-Jones, GCVO, b. 1930, m.	Viscount Linley, b. 1961
1765 °	Spencer (9th), Charles Edward Maurice Spencer, b. 1964, s. 1992, m.	Viscount Althorp, b. 1994
1703 S.	Stair (14th), John David James Dalrymple, b. 1961, s. 1996	Hon. David H. D., b. 1963
1984	Stockton (2nd), Alexander Daniel Alan Macmillan, MEP, b. 1943, s. 1986, m.	Viscount Macmillan of Ovenden, b. 1974
1821	Stradbroke (6th), Robert Keith Rous, b. 1937, s. 1983, m.	Viscount Dunwich, b. 1961
1847	Strafford (8th), Thomas Edmund Byng, b. 1936, s. 1984, m.	Viscount Enfield, b. 1964
1606 S.	Strathmore and Kinghorne (18th) (S. 1677), Michael Fergus Bowes Lyon, b. 1957, s. 1987, m.	Lord Glamis, b. 1986
1603	Suffolk (21st) and Berkshire (14th) (1626), Michael John James George Robert Howard, b. 1935, s. 1941, m.	Viscount Andover, b. 1974
1955	Swinton (2nd), David Yarburgh Cunliffe-Lister, b. 1937, s. 1972, m.	Hon. Nicholas J. C.-L., b. 1939
1714	Tankerville (10th), Peter Grey Bennet, b. 1956, s. 1980	Revd the Hon. George A. G. B., b. 1925
1822 °	Temple of Stowe (8th), (Walter) Grenville Algernon Temple-Gore-Langton, b. 1924, s. 1988, m.	Lord Langton, b. 1955
1815	Verulam (7th), John Duncan Grimston, b. 1951, s. 1973, m.	Viscount Grimston, b. 1978
1729 °	Waldegrave (13th), James Sherbrooke Waldegrave, b. 1940, s. 1995, m.	Viscount Chewton, b. 1986
1759	Warwick (9th) and Brooke (9th) (1746), Guy David Greville, b. 1957, s. 1996, m.	Lord Brooke, b. 1982
1633 S.	Wemyss (12th) and March (8th), Francis David Charteris, KT, b. 1912, s. 1937, m.	Lord Neidpath, b. 1948
1621 I.	Westmeath (13th), William Anthony Nugent, b. 1928, s. 1971, m.	Hon. Sean C. W. N., b. 1965
1624	Westmorland (16th), Anthony David Francis Henry Fane, b. 1951, s. 1993, m.	Hon. Harry St C. F., b. 1953
1876	Wharncliffe (5th), Richard Alan Montagu Stuart Wortley, b. 1953, s. 1987, m.	Viscount Carlton, b. 1980
1801	Wilton (8th), Francis Egerton Grosvenor, b. 1934, s. 1999, m.	Viscount Grey de Wilton, b. 1959
1628	Winchilsea (17th) and Nottingham (12th) (1681), Daniel James Hatfield Finch Hatton, b. 1967, s. 1999, m.	Viscount Maidstone, b. 1998
1766 °	Winterton (8th), (Donald) David Turnour, b. 1943, s. 1991, m.	Robert C. T., b. 1950
1956	Woolton (3rd), Simon Frederick Marquis, b. 1958, s. 1969, m.	None
1837	Yarborough (8th), Charles John Pelham, b. 1963, s. 1991, m.	Lord Worsley, b. 1990

COUNTESSES IN THEIR OWN RIGHT

Style, The Right Hon. the Countess (of) _
Husband, Untitled
Children's style, As for children of an Earl
For forms of address, see page 43

Created	Title, order of succession, name, etc.	Heir
1643 S.	Dysart (12th in line), Katherine Grant of Rothiemurchus, b. 1918, s. 2003	Lord Huntingtower, b. 1946
c.1115 S. **	Mar (31st in line), Margaret of Mar, b. 1940, s. 1975, m. Premier Earldom of Scotland	Mistress of Mar, b. 1963
1947 °	Mountbatten of Burma (2nd in line), Patricia Edwina Victoria Knatchbull, CBE, b. 1924, s. 1979, m.	Lord Romsey, b. 1947
c..1235 S.	Sutherland (24th in line), Elizabeth Millicent Sutherland, b. 1921, s. 1963, m.	Lord Strathnaver, b. 1947

VISCOUNTS

Coronet, Sixteen silver balls
Style, The Right Hon. the Viscount _
Wife's style, The Right Hon. the Viscountess _
Children's style, 'The Hon.' before forename and family name
In Scotland, the heir apparent to a Viscount may be styled 'The Master of _ (title of peer)'
For forms of address, *see* page 43

Created	*Title, order of succession, name, etc.*	*Heir*
1945	*Addison (4th),* William Matthew Wand Addison, *b.* 1945, *s.* 1992, *m.*	Hon. Paul W. A., *b.* 1973
1946	*Alanbrooke (3rd),* Alan Victor Harold Brooke, *b.* 1932, *s.* 1972	None
1919	** *Allenby (3rd),* Lt.-Col. Michael Jaffray Hynman Allenby, *b.* 1931, *s.* 1984, *m.*	Hon. Henry J. H. A., *b.* 1968
1911	*Allendale (4th),* Wentworth Peter Ismay Beaumont, *b.* 1948, *s.* 2002, *m.*	Hon. Wentworth A. I. B., *b.* 1979
1642 S.	*Arbuthnott (16th),* John Campbell Arbuthnott, KT, CBE, DSC, *b.* 1924, *s.* 1966, *m.*	Master of Arbuthnott, *b.* 1950
1751 I.	*Ashbrook (11th),* Michael Llowarch Warburton Flower, *b.* 1935, *s.* 1995, *m.*	Hon. Rowland F. W. F., *b.* 1975
1917	** *Astor (4th),* William Waldorf Astor, *b.* 1951, *s.* 1966, *m.*	Hon. William W. A., *b.* 1979
1781 I.	*Bangor (8th),* William Maxwell David Ward, *b.* 1948, *s.* 1993, *m.*	Hon. E. Nicholas W., *b.* 1953
1925	*Bearsted (5th),* Nicholas Alan Samuel, *b.* 1950, *s.* 1996, *m.*	Hon. Harry R. S., *b.* 1988
1963	*Blakenham (2nd),* Michael John Hare, *b.* 1938, *s.* 1982, *m.*	Hon. Caspar J. H., *b.* 1972
1935	** *Bledisloe (3rd),* Christopher Hiley Ludlow Bathurst, QC, *b.* 1934, *s.* 1979	Hon. Rupert E. L. B., *b.* 1964
1712	*Bolingbroke (7th) and St John (8th) (1716),* Kenneth Oliver Musgrave St John, *b.* 1927, *s.* 1974	Hon. Henry F. St J., *b.* 1957
1960	*Boyd of Merton (2nd),* Simon Donald Rupert Neville Lennox-Boyd, *b.* 1939, *s.* 1983, *m.*	Hon. Benjamin A. L.-B., *b.* 1964
1717 I.	*Boyne (11th),* Gustavus Michael Stucley Hamilton-Russell, *b.* 1965, *s.* 1995, *m.*	Hon. Gustavus A. E. H.-R., *b.* 1999
1929	*Brentford (4th),* Crispin William Joynson-Hicks, *b.* 1933, *s.* 1983, *m.*	Hon. Paul W. J.-H., *b.* 1971
1929	** *Bridgeman (3rd),* Robin John Orlando Bridgeman, *b.* 1930, *s.* 1982, *m.*	Hon. Luke R. O. B., *b.* 1971
1868	*Bridport (4th) and 7th Duke, Bronte in Sicily, 1799,* Alexander Nelson Hood, *b.* 1948, *s.* 1969, *m.*	Hon. Peregrine A. N. H., *b.* 1974
1952	** *Brookeborough (3rd),* Alan Henry Brooke, *b.* 1952, *s.* 1987, *m.*	Hon. Christopher A. B., *b.* 1954
1933	*Buckmaster (3rd),* Martin Stanley Buckmaster, OBE, *b.* 1921, *s.* 1974	Adrian C. B., *b.* 1949
1939	*Caldecote (3rd),* Piers James Hampden Inskip, *b.* 1947, *s.* 1999, *m.*	Hon. Thomas J. H. I., *b.* 1985
1941	*Camrose (4th),* Adrian Michael Berry, *b.* 1937, *s.* 2001, *m.*	Hon. Jonathan W. B., *b.* 1970
1954	*Chandos (3rd) and Baron Lyttelton of Aldershot (life peerage, 2000),* Thomas Orlando Lyttelton, *b.* 1953, *s.* 1980, *m.*	Hon. Oliver A. L., *b.* 1986
1665 I.	*Charlemont (15th),* John Dodd Caulfeild, *b.* 1966, *s.* 2001, *m.*	Hon. Shane A. C., *b.* 1996
1921	*Chelmsford (4th) and UK Baron Chelmsford, 1858,* Frederic Corin Piers Thesiger, *b.* 1962, *s.* 1999	To Barony only, Roderic M. D. T. *b.* 1915
1717 I.	*Chetwynd (10th),* Adam Richard John Casson Chetwynd, *b.* 1935, *s.* 1965, *m.*	Hon. Adam D. C., *b.* 1969
1911	*Chilston (4th),* Alastair George Akers-Douglas, *b.* 1946, *s.* 1982, *m.*	Hon. Oliver I. A.-D., *b.* 1973
1902	*Churchill (3rd) and 5th UK Baron Churchill, 1815,* Victor George Spencer, *b.* 1934, *s.* 1973	To Barony only, Richard H. R. S., *b.* 1926
1718	*Cobham (11th),* John William Leonard Lyttelton, *b.* 1943, *s.* 1977, *m.*	Hon. Christopher C. L., *b.* 1947
1902	** *Colville of Culross (4th),* John Mark Alexander Colville, QC, *b.* 1933, *s.* 1945, *m.*	Master of Colville, *b.* 1959
1826	*Combermere (6th),* Thomas Robert Wellington Stapleton-Cotton, *b.* 1969, *s.* 2000	Hon. David P. D. S.-C., *b.* 1932
1917	*Cowdray (4th),* Michael Orlando Weetman Pearson, *b.* 1944, *s.* 1995, *m.*	Hon. Peregrine J. D. P., *b.* 1994
1927	** *Craigavon (3rd),* Janric Fraser Craig, *b.* 1944, *s.* 1974	None
1886	*Cross (3rd),* Assheton Henry Cross, *b.* 1920, *s.* 1932	None
1943	*Daventry (4th),* James Edward FitzRoy Newdegate, *b.* 1960, *s.* 2000, *m.*	Hon. Humphrey J. F. N., *b.* 1995

Created	Title, order of succession, name, etc.	Heir
1937	Davidson (2nd), John Andrew Davidson, b. 1928, s. 1970, m.	Hon. Malcolm W. M. D., b. 1934
1956	De L'Isle (2nd), Philip John Algernon Sidney, MBE, b. 1945, s. 1991, m.	Hon. Philip W. E. S., b. 1985
1776 I.	De Vesci (7th), Thomas Eustace Vesey, b. 1955, s. 1983, m.	Hon. Oliver I. V., b. 1991
1917	Devonport (3rd), Terence Kearley, b. 1944, s. 1973	Chester D. H. K., b. 1932
1964	Dilhorne (2nd), John Mervyn Manningham-Buller, b. 1932, s. 1980, m.	Hon. James E. M.-B., b. 1956
1622 I.	Dillon (22nd), Henry Benedict Charles Dillon, b. 1973, s. 1982	Hon. Richard A. L. D., b. 1948
1785 I.	Doneraile (10th), Richard Allen St Leger, b. 1946, s. 1983, m.	Hon. Nathaniel W. R. St J. St L., b. 1971
1680 I.	Downe (12th), Richard Henry Dawnay, b. 1967, s. 2002	Thomas P. D., b. 1978
1959	Dunrossil (3rd), Andrew William Reginald Morrison, b. 1953, s. 2000, m.	Hon. Callum A. B. M., b. 1994
1964	Eccles (2nd), John Dawson Eccles, CBE, b. 1931, s. 1999, m.	Hon. William D. E., b. 1960
1897	Esher (5th), Christopher Gordon Baliol Brett, b. 1936, s. 2004, m.	Hon. Matthew C. A. B., b. 1963
1816	Exmouth (10th), Paul Edward Pellew, b. 1940, s. 1970, m.	Hon. Edward F. P., b. 1978
1620 S. **	Falkland (15th), Lucius Edward William Plantagenet Cary, b. 1935, s. 1984, m. Premier Scottish Viscount on the Roll	Master of Falkland, b. 1963
1720	Falmouth (9th), George Hugh Boscawen, b. 1919, s. 1962, m.	Hon. Evelyn A. H. B., b. 1955
1720 I.	Gage (8th), (Henry) Nicolas Gage, b. 1934, s. 1993, m.	Hon. Henry W. G., b. 1975
1727 I.	Galway (12th), George Rupert Monckton-Arundell, b. 1922, s. 1980, m.	Hon. J. Philip M., b. 1952
1478 I.	Gormanston (17th), 1868, Jenico Nicholas Dudley Preston, b. 1939, s. 1940, w. Premier Viscount of Ireland	Hon. Jenico F. T. P., b. 1974
1816 I.	Gort (9th), Foley Robert Standish Prendergast Vereker, b. 1951, s. 1995, m.	Hon. Robert F. P. V., b. 1993
1900 **	Goschen (4th), Giles John Harry Goschen, b. 1965, s. 1977, m.	Hon. Alexander J. E. G., b. 2001
1849	Gough (5th), Shane Hugh Maryon Gough, b. 1941, s. 1951	None
1929	Hailsham (3rd), Douglas Martin Hogg, PC, QC, MP, b. 1945, s. 2001, m.	Hon. Quintin J. N. M. H., b. 1973
1891	Hambleden (4th), William Herbert Smith, b. 1930, s. 1948, m.	Hon. William H. B. S., b. 1955
1884	Hampden (6th), Anthony David Brand, b. 1937, s. 1975, m.	Hon. Francis A. B., b. 1970
1936	Hanworth (3rd), David Stephen Geoffrey Pollock, b. 1946, s. 1996, m.	Hon. Richard C. S. P., b. 1951
1791 I.	Harberton (11th), Henry Robert Pomeroy, b. 1958, s. 2004, m.	Hon. Patrick C. P., b. 1995
1846	Hardinge (7th), Andrew Hartland Hardinge, b. 1960, s. 2004, m.	Hon. Thomas H. de M. H., b. 1993
1791 I.	Hawarden (9th), (Robert) Connan Wyndham Leslie Maude, b. 1961, s. 1991, m.	Hon. Varian J. C. E. M., b. 1997
1960	Head (2nd), Richard Antony Head, b. 1937, s. 1983, m.	Hon. Henry J. H., b. 1980
1550	Hereford (19th), Charles Robin De Bohun Devereux, b. 1975, s. 2004, m. Premier Viscount of England	Hon. Edward M. de B. D., b. 1977
1842	Hill (9th), Peter David Raymond Charles Clegg-Hill, b. 1945, s. 2003	Paul A. R. C.-H., b. 1979
1796	Hood (8th), Henry Lyttleton Alexander Hood, b. 1958, s. 1999, m.	Hon. Archibald L. S. H., b. 1993
1956	Ingleby (2nd), Martin Raymond Peake, b. 1926, s. 1966, w.	None
1945	Kemsley (3rd), Richard Gomer Berry, b. 1951, s. 1999, m.	Hon. Luke G. B., b. 1998
1911	Knollys (3rd), David Francis Dudley Knollys, b. 1931, s. 1966, m.	Hon. Patrick N. M. K., b. 1962
1895	Knutsford (6th), Michael Holland-Hibbert, b. 1926, s. 1986, m.	Hon. Henry T. H.-H., b. 1959
1954	Leathers (3rd), Christopher Graeme Leathers, b. 1941, s. 1996, m.	Hon. James F. L., b. 1969
1781 I.	Lifford (9th), (Edward) James Wingfield Hewitt, b. 1949, s. 1987, m.	Hon. James T. W. H., b. 1979
1921	Long (4th), Richard Gerard Long, CBE, b. 1929, s. 1967, m.	Hon. James R. L., b. 1960
1957	Mackintosh of Halifax (3rd), (John) Clive Mackintosh, b. 1958, s. 1980, m.	Hon. Thomas H. G. M., b. 1985
1955	Malvern (3rd), Ashley Kevin Godfrey Huggins, b. 1949, s. 1978	Hon. M. James H., b. 1928
1945	Marchwood (3rd), David George Staveley Penny, b. 1936, s. 1979, w.	Hon. Peter G. W. P., b. 1965
1942	Margesson (2nd), Francis Vere Hampden Margesson, b. 1922, s. 1965, m.	Capt. Hon. Richard F. D. M., b. 1960
1660 I.	Massereene (14th), John David Clotworthy Whyte-Melville Foster Skeffington, b. 1940, s. 1992, m.	Hon. Charles J. C. W.-M. F. S., b. 1973
1802	Melville (9th), Robert David Ross Dundas, b. 1937, s. 1971, m.	Hon. Robert H. K. D., b. 1984
1916	Mersey (4th), Richard Maurice Clive Bigham, b. 1934, s. 1979, m.	Master of Nairne, b. 1966
1717 I.	Midleton (12th), Alan Henry Brodrick, b. 1949, s. 1988, m.	Hon. Ashley R. B., b. 1980
1962	Mills (3rd), Christopher Philip Roger Mills, b. 1956, s. 1988, m.	None
1716 I.	Molesworth (12th), Robert Bysse Kelham Molesworth, b. 1959, s. 1997	Hon. William J. C. M., b. 1960
1801 I.	Monck (7th), Charles Stanley Monck, b. 1953, s. 1982. Does not use title	Hon. George S. M., b. 1957

Created	Title, order of succession, name, etc.	Heir
1957	*Monckton of Brenchley (2nd)*, Maj.-Gen. Gilbert Walter Riversdale Monckton, CB, OBE, MC, *b.* 1915, *s.* 1965, *m.*	Hon. Christopher W. M., *b.* 1952
1946	*Montgomery of Alamein (2nd)*, David Bernard Montgomery, CBE, *b.* 1928, *s.* 1976, *m.*	Hon. Henry D. M., *b.* 1954
1550 I.	*Mountgarret (18th)*, Piers James Richard Butler, *b.* 1961, *s.* 2004, *m.*	Hon. Edmund H. R. B., *b.* 1962
1952	*Norwich (2nd)*, John Julius Cooper, CVO, *b.* 1929, *s.* 1954, *m.*	Hon. Jason C. D. B. C., *b.* 1959
1651 S.	*Oxfuird (14th)*, Ian Arthur Alexander Makgill, *b.* 1969, *s.* 2003	Hon. Robert E. G. M., *b.* 1969
1873	*Portman (10th)*, Christopher Edward Berkeley Portman, *b.* 1958, *s.* 1999, *m.*	Hon. Luke O. B. P., *b.* 1984
1743 I.	*Powerscourt (10th)*, Mervyn Niall Wingfield, *b.* 1935, *s.* 1973, *m.*	Hon. Mervyn A. W., *b.* 1963
1900	*Ridley (4th)*, Matthew White Ridley, KG, GCVO, TD, *b.* 1925, *s.* 1964, *m.*	Hon. Matthew W. R., *b.* 1958
1960	*Rochdale (2nd)*, St John Durival Kemp, *b.* 1938, *s.* 1993, *m.*	Hon. Jonathan H. D. K., *b.* 1961
1919	*Rothermere (4th)*, (Harold) Jonathan Esmond Vere Harmsworth, *b.* 1967, *s.* 1998, *m.*	Hon. Vere R. J. H. H., *b.* 1994
1937	*Runciman of Doxford (3rd)*, Walter Garrison Runciman (Garry), CBE, *b.* 1934, *s.* 1989, *m.*	Hon. David W. R., *b.* 1967
1918	*St Davids (3rd)*, Colwyn Jestyn John Philipps, *b.* 1939, *s.* 1991, *m.*	Hon. Rhodri C. P., *b.* 1966
1801	*St Vincent (7th)*, Ronald George James Jervis, *b.* 1905, *s.* 1940, *m.*	Hon. Edward R. J. J., *b.* 1951
1937	*Samuel (3rd)*, David Herbert Samuel, OBE, PHD, *b.* 1922, *s.* 1978, *m.*	Hon. Dan J. S., *b.* 1925
1911	*Scarsdale (4th)*, Peter Ghislain Nathaniel Curzon, *b.* 1949, *s.* 2000, *m.*	Hon. David J. N. C., *b.* 1958
1905 M.	*Selby (6th)*, Christopher Rolf Thomas Gully, *b.* 1993, *s.* 2001	Hon. (James) Edward H. G. G., *b.* 1945
1805	*Sidmouth (7th)*, John Tonge Anthony Pellew Addington, *b.* 1914, *s.* 1976, *m.*	Hon. Jeremy F. A., *b.* 1947
1940	** *Simon (3rd)*, Jan David Simon, *b.* 1940, *s.* 1993, *m.*	None
1960	** *Slim (2nd)*, John Douglas Slim, OBE, *b.* 1927, *s.* 1970, *m.*	Hon. Mark W. R. S., *b.* 1960
1954	*Soulbury (2nd)*, James Herwald Ramsbotham, *b.* 1915, *s.* 1971, *w.*	Hon. Sir Peter E. R., GCMG, GCVO, *b.* 1919
1776 I.	*Southwell (7th)*, Pyers Anthony Joseph Southwell, *b.* 1930, *s.* 1960, *m.*	Hon. Richard A. P. S., *b.* 1956
1942	*Stansgate*, Anthony Neil Wedgwood Benn, *b.* 1925, *s.* 1960, *w.* Disclaimed for life 1963.	Stephen M. W. B., *b.* 1951
1959	*Stuart of Findhorn (3rd)*, James Dominic Stuart, *b.* 1948, *s.* 1999, *m.*	Hon. Andrew M. S., *b.* 1957
1957	** *Tenby (3rd)*, William Lloyd George, *b.* 1927, *s.* 1983, *m.*	Hon. Timothy H. G. L. G., *b.* 1962
1952	*Thurso (3rd)*, John Archibald Sinclair, MP, *b.* 1953, *s.* 1995, *m.*	Hon. James A. R. S., *b.* 1984
1721	*Torrington (11th)*, Timothy Howard St George Byng, *b.* 1943, *s.* 1961, *m.*	John L. B., MC, *b.* 1919
1936	*Trenchard (3rd)*, Hugh Trenchard, *b.* 1951, *s.* 1987, *m.*	Hon. Alexander T. T., *b.* 1978
1921	** *Ullswater (2nd)*, Nicholas James Christopher Lowther, PC, LVO, *b.* 1942, *s.* 1949, *m.*	Hon. Benjamin J. L., *b.* 1975
1621 I.	*Valentia (15th)*, Richard John Dighton Annesley, *b.* 1929, *s.* 1983, *m.*	Hon. Francis W. D. A., *b.* 1959
1952	** *Waverley (3rd)*, John Desmond Forbes Anderson, *b.* 1949, *s.* 1990	Hon. Forbes A. R. A., *b.* 1996
1938	*Weir (3rd)*, William Kenneth James Weir, *b.* 1933, *s.* 1975, *m.*	Hon. James W. H. W., *b.* 1965
1918	*Wimborne (4th)*, Ivor Mervyn Vigors Guest, *b.* 1968, *s.* 1993	Hon. Julien J. G., *b.* 1945
1923	*Younger of Leckie (5th)*, James Edward George Younger, *b.* 1955, *s.* 2003, *m.*	Hon. Alexander W. G. Y., *b.* 1993

BARONS/LORDS

Coronet, Six silver balls
Style, The Right Hon. the Lord _ . In the Peerage of Scotland there is no rank of Baron; the equivalent rank is Lord of
Parliament (*see* page 44) and Scottish peers should always be styled 'Lord', never 'Baron'
Wife's style, The Right Hon. the Lady _
Children's style, 'The Hon.' before forename and family name
In Scotland, the heir apparent to a Lord may be styled 'The Master of _ (title of peer)'
For forms of address, *see* page 43

Created	Title, order of succession, name, etc.	Heir
1911	*Aberconway (4th)*, (Henry) Charles McLaren, *b.* 1948, *s.* 2003, *m.*	Hon. Charles S. M., *b.* 1984
1873	** *Aberdare (4th)*, Morys George Lyndhurst Bruce, KBE, PC *b.* 1919, *s.* 1957, *m.*	Hon. Alastair J. L. B., *b.* 1947
1835	*Abinger (9th)*, James Harry Scarlett, *b.* 1959, *s.* 2002, *m.*	Hon. Peter R. S., *b.* 1961
1869	*Acton (4th) and Acton of Bridgnorth (life peerage, 2000)*, Richard Gerald Lyon-Dalberg-Acton, *b.* 1941, *s.* 1989, *m.*	Hon. John C. F. H. L.-D.-A., *b.* 1966
1887	** *Addington (6th)*, Dominic Bryce Hubbard, *b.* 1963, *s.* 1982	Hon. Michael W. L. H., *b.* 1965
1896	*Aldenham (6th) and Hunsdon of Hunsdon (4th) (1923)*, Vicary Tyser Gibbs, *b.* 1948, *s.* 1986, *m.*	Hon. Humphrey W. F. G., *b.* 1989
1962	*Aldington (2nd)*, Charles Harold Stuart Low, *b.* 1948, *s.* 2000, *m.*	Hon. Philip T. A. L., *b.* 1990
1945	*Altrincham (3rd)*, Anthony Ulick David Dundas Grigg, *b.* 1934, *s.* 2001, *m.*	Hon. (Edward) Sebastian G., *b.* 1965
1929	*Alvingham (2nd)*, Maj.-Gen. Robert Guy Eardley Yerburgh, CBE, *b.* 1926, *s.* 1955, *m.*	Capt. Hon. Robert R. G. Y., *b.* 1956
1892	*Amherst of Hackney (4th)*, William Hugh Amherst Cecil, *b.* 1940, *s.* 1980, *m.*	Hon. H. William A. C., *b.* 1968
1881	** *Ampthill (4th)*, Geoffrey Denis Erskine Russell, CBE, PC, *b.* 1921, *s.* 1973	Hon. David W. E. R., *b.* 1947
1947	*Amwell (3rd)*, Keith Norman Montague, *b.* 1943, *s.* 1990, *m.*	Hon. Ian K. M., *b.* 1973
1863	*Annaly (6th)*, Luke Richard White, *b.* 1954, *s.* 1990, *m.*	Hon. Luke H. W., *b.* 1990
1885	*Ashbourne (4th)*, Edward Barry Greynville Gibson, *b.* 1933, *s.* 1983, *m.*	Hon. Edward C. d'O. G., *b.* 1967
1835	*Ashburton (7th)*, John Francis Harcourt Baring, KG, KCVO, *b.* 1928, *s.* 1991, *m.*	Hon. Mark F. R. B., *b.* 1958
1892	*Ashcombe (4th)*, Henry Edward Cubitt, *b.* 1924, *s.* 1962, *m.*	Mark E. C., *b.* 1964
1911	*Ashton of Hyde (3rd)*, Thomas John Ashton, TD, *b.* 1926, *s.* 1983, *m.*	Hon. Thomas H. A., *b.* 1958
1800 I.	*Ashtown (7th)*, Nigel Clive Crosby Trench, KCMG, *b.* 1916, *s.* 1990, *m.*	Hon. Roderick N. G. T., *b.* 1944
1956	** *Astor of Hever (3rd)*, John Jacob Astor, *b.* 1946, *s.* 1984, *m.*	Hon. Charles G. J. A., *b.* 1990
1789 I.	*Auckland (10th) and Auckland (10th) (1793)*, Robert Ian Burnard Eden, *b.* 1962, *s.* 1997, *m.*	Hon. Ronald J. E., *b.* 1931
1313	*Audley*, Barony in abeyance between three co-heiresses since 1997	
1900	** *Avebury (4th)*, Eric Reginald Lubbock, *b.* 1928, *s.* 1971, *m.*	Hon. Lyulph A. J. L., *b.* 1954
1718 I.	*Aylmer (13th)*, Michael Anthony Aylmer, *b.* 1923, *s.* 1982, *m.*	Hon. A. Julian A., *b.* 1951
1929	*Baden-Powell (3rd)*, Robert Crause Baden-Powell, *b.* 1936, *s.* 1962, *m.*	Hon. David M. B.-P., *b.* 1940
1780	*Bagot (10th)*, (Charles Hugh) Shaun Bagot, *b.* 1944, *s.* 2001, *m.*	Richard C. V. B., *b.* 1941
1953	*Baillieu (3rd)*, James William Latham Baillieu, *b.* 1950, *s.* 1973, *m.*	Hon. Robert L. B., *b.* 1979
1607 S.	*Balfour of Burleigh (8th)*, Robert Bruce, *b.* 1927, *s.* 1967, *m.*	Hon. Victoria B., *b.* 1973
1945	*Balfour of Inchrye (2nd)*, Ian Balfour, *b.* 1924, *s.* 1988, *m.*	None
1924	*Banbury of Southam (3rd)*, Charles William Banbury, *b.* 1953, *s.* 1981, *m.*	None
1698	*Barnard (11th)*, Harry John Neville Vane, TD, *b.* 1923, *s.* 1964	Hon. Henry F. C. V., *b.* 1959
1887	*Basing (5th)*, Neil Lutley Sclater-Booth, *b.* 1939, *s.* 1983, *m.*	Hon. Stuart W. S.-B., *b.* 1969
1917	*Beaverbrook (3rd)*, Maxwell William Humphrey Aitken, *b.* 1951, *s.* 1985, *m.*	Hon. Maxwell F. A., *b.* 1977
1647 S.	*Belhaven and Stenton (13th)*, Robert Anthony Carmichael Hamilton, *b.* 1927, *s.* 1961, *m.*	Master of Belhaven, *b.* 1953
1848 I.	*Bellew (7th)*, James Bryan Bellew, *b.* 1920, *s.* 1981, *w.*	Hon. Bryan E. B., *b.* 1943
1856	*Belper (5th)*, Richard Henry Strutt, *b.* 1941, *s.* 1999, *m.*	Hon. Michael H. S., *b.* 1969
1938	*Belstead (2nd) and Ganzoni (life peerage, 1999)*, John Julian Ganzoni, PC, *b.* 1932, *s.* 1958	None

Created	Title, order of succession, name, etc.	Heir
1421	*Berkeley (18th) and Gueterbock (life peerage, 2000)*, Anthony Fitzhardinge Gueterbock, OBE, *b.* 1939, *s.* 1992, *m.*	Hon. Thomas F. G., *b.* 1969
1922	*Bethell (4th)*, Nicholas William Bethell, MEP, *b.* 1938, *s.* 1967, *m.*	Hon. James N. B., *b.* 1967
1938	*Bicester (3rd)*, Angus Edward Vivian Smith, *b.* 1932, *s.* 1968	Hugh C. V. S., *b.* 1934
1903	*Biddulph (5th)*, (Anthony) Nicholas Colin Maitland Biddulph, *b.* 1959, *s.* 1988, *m.*	Hon. Robert J. M. B., *b.* 1994
1938	*Birdwood (3rd)*, Mark William Ogilvie Birdwood, *b.* 1938, *s.* 1962, *m.*	None
1958	*Birkett (2nd)*, Michael Birkett, *b.* 1929, *s.* 1962, *w.*	Hon. Thomas B., *b.* 1982
1907	*Blyth (4th)*, Anthony Audley Rupert Blyth, *b.* 1931, *s.* 1977, *m.*	Hon. James A. I. B., *b.* 1970
1797	*Bolton (8th)*, Harry Algar Nigel Orde-Powlett, *b.* 1954, *s.* 2001, *m.*	Hon. Thomas O.-P., *b.* 1979
1452 S.	*Borthwick (24th)*, John Hugh Borthwick, *b.* 1940, *s.* 1996, *m.*	Hon. James H. A. B. of Glengelt, *b.* 1940
1922	*Borwick (4th)*, James Hugh Myles Borwick, MC, *b.* 1917, *s.* 1961, *m.*	(Geoffrey Robert) James B., *b.* 1955
1761	*Boston (10th)*, Timothy George Frank Boteler Irby, *b.* 1939, *s.* 1978, *m.*	Hon. George W. E. B. I., *b.* 1971
1942	** *Brabazon of Tara (3rd)*, Ivon Anthony Moore-Brabazon, *b.* 1946, *s.* 1974, *m.*	Hon. Benjamin R. M.-B., *b.* 1983
1880	*Brabourne (7th)*, John Ulick Knatchbull, CBE, *b.* 1924, *s.* 1943, *m.*	Lord Romsey, *b.* 1947
1925	*Bradbury (3rd)*, John Bradbury, *b.* 1940, *s.* 1994, *m.*	Hon. John B., *b.* 1973
1962	*Brain (2nd)*, Christopher Langdon Brain, *b.* 1926, *s.* 1966, *m.*	Hon. Michael C. B., *b.* 1928
1938	*Brassey of Apethorpe (3rd)*, David Henry Brassey, OBE, *b.* 1932, *s.* 1967, *m.*	Hon. Edward B., *b.* 1964
1788	*Braybrooke (10th)*, Robin Henry Charles Neville, *b.* 1932, *s.* 1990, *m.*	George N., *b.* 1943
1957	** *Bridges (2nd)*, Thomas Edward Bridges, GCMG, *b.* 1927, *s.* 1969, *m.*	Hon. Mark T. B., *b.* 1954
1945	*Broadbridge (4th)*, Martin Hugh Broadbridge, *b.* 1929, *s.* 2000, *m.*	Hon. Richard J. M. B., *b.* 1959
1933	*Brocket (3rd)*, Charles Ronald George Nall-Cain, *b.* 1952, *s.* 1967, *m.*	Hon. Alexander C. C. N.-C., *b.* 1984
1860	** *Brougham and Vaux (5th)*, Michael John Brougham, CBE, *b.* 1938, *s.* 1967	Hon. Charles W. B., *b.* 1971
1945	*Broughshane (3rd)*, (William) Kensington Davison, DSO, DFC, *b.* 1914, *s.* 1995	None
1776	*Brownlow (7th)*, Edward John Peregrine Cust, *b.* 1936, *s.* 1978, *m.*	Hon. Peregrine E. Q. C., *b.* 1974
1942	*Bruntisfield (2nd)*, John Robert Warrender, OBE, MC, TD, *b.* 1921, *s.* 1993, *m.*	Hon. Michael J. V. W., *b.* 1949
1950	*Burden (3rd)*, Andrew Philip Burden, *b.* 1959, *s.* 1995	Hon. Fraser W. E. B., *b.* 1964
1529	*Burgh (8th)*, (Alexander) Gregory Disney Leith, *b.* 1958, *s.* 2001, *m.*	Hon. Alexander J. S. L., *b.* 1986
1903	** *Burnham (6th)*, Hugh John Frederick Lawson, *b.* 1931, *s.* 1993, *m.*	Hon. Harry F. A. L., *b.* 1968
1897	*Burton (3rd)*, Michael Evan Victor Baillie, *b.* 1924, *s.* 1962, *m.*	Hon. Evan M. R. B., *b.* 1949
1643	*Byron (13th)*, Robert James Byron, *b.* 1950, *s.* 1989, *m.*	Hon. Charles R. G. B., *b.* 1990
1937	*Cadman (3rd)*, John Anthony Cadman, *b.* 1938, *s.* 1966, *m.*	Hon. Nicholas A. J. C., *b.* 1977
1945	*Calverley (3rd)*, Charles Rodney Muff, *b.* 1946, *s.* 1971, *m.*	Hon. Jonathan E. M., *b.* 1975
1383	*Camoys (7th)*, (Ralph) Thomas Campion George Sherman Stonor, GCVO, PC, *b.* 1940, *s.* 1976, *m.*	Hon. R. William R. T. S., *b.* 1974
1715 I.	*Carbery (11th)*, Peter Ralfe Harrington Evans-Freke, *b.* 1920, *s.* 1970, *m.*	Hon. Michael P. E.-F., *b.* 1942
1834 I.	*Carew (7th) and Carew (7th) (1838)*, Patrick Thomas Conolly-Carew, *b.* 1938, *s.* 1994, *m.*	Hon. William P. C.-C., *b.* 1973
1916	*Carnock (4th)*, David Henry Arthur Nicolson, *b.* 1920, *s.* 1982	Nigel N., MBE, *b.* 1917
1796 I.	*Carrington (6th) and Carrington (6th) (1797) and Carington of Upton (life peerage, 1999)*, Peter Alexander Rupert Carington, KG, GCMG, CH, MC, PC, *b.* 1919, *s.* 1938, *m.*	Hon. Rupert F. J. C., *b.* 1948
1812	*Castlemaine (8th)*, Roland Thomas John Handcock, MBE, *b.* 1943, *s.* 1973, *m.*	Hon. Ronan M. E. H., *b.* 1989
1936	*Catto (3rd)*, Innes Gordon Catto, *b.* 1950, *s.* 2001, *m.*	Hon. Alexander G. C., *b.* 1952
1918	*Cawley (4th)*, John Francis Cawley, *b.* 1946, *s.* 2001, *m.*	Hon. William R. H. C., *b.* 1981
1937	*Chatfield (2nd)*, Ernle David Lewis Chatfield, *b.* 1917, *s.* 1967, *m.*	None
1858	*Chesham (6th)*, Nicholas Charles Cavendish, *b.* 1941, *s.* 1989, *m.*	Hon. Charles G. C. C., *b.* 1974
1945	*Chetwode (2nd)*, Philip Chetwode, *b.* 1937, *s.* 1950, *m.*	Hon. Roger C., *b.* 1968
1945	** *Chorley (2nd)*, Roger Richard Edward Chorley, *b.* 1930, *s.* 1978, *m.*	Hon. Nicholas R. D. C., *b.* 1966
1858	*Churston (5th)*, John Francis Yarde-Buller, *b.* 1934, *s.* 1991, *m.*	Hon. Benjamin F. A. Y.-B., *b.* 1974
1946	*Citrine (3rd)*, Ronald Eric Citrine, *b.* 1919, *s.* 1997, *m.* Does not use title	None
1800	*Clanmorris (8th)*, Simon John Ward Bingham, *b.* 1937, *s.* 1988, *m.*	Robert D. de B. B., *b.* 1942

Created	Title, order of succession, name, etc.	Heir
1672	*Clifford of Chudleigh (14th)*, Thomas Hugh Clifford, *b.* 1948, *s.* 1988, *m.*	Hon. Alexander T. H. C., *b.* 1985
1299	*Clinton (22nd)*, Gerard Nevile Mark Fane Trefusis, *b.* 1934, *s.* 1965, *m.*	Hon. Charles P. R. F. T., *b.* 1962
1955	*Clitheroe (2nd)*, Ralph John Assheton, *b.* 1929, *s.* 1984, *m.*	Hon. Ralph C. A., *b.* 1962
1919	*Clwyd (3rd)*, (John) Anthony Roberts, *b.* 1935, *s.* 1987, *m.*	Hon. J. Murray R., *b.* 1971
1948	*Clydesmuir (3rd)*, David Ronald Colville, *b.* 1949, *s.* 1996, *m.*	Hon. Richard C., *b.* 1980
1960	** *Cobbold (2nd)*, David Antony Fromanteel Lytton Cobbold, *b.* 1937, *s.* 1987, *m.*	Hon. Henry F. L. C., *b.* 1962
1919	*Cochrane of Cults (4th)*, (Ralph Henry) Vere Cochrane, *b.* 1926, *s.* 1990, *m.*	Hon. Thomas H. V. C., *b.* 1957
1954	*Coleraine (2nd)*, (James) Martin (Bonar) Law, *b.* 1931, *s.* 1980, *m.*	Hon. James P. B. L., *b.* 1975
1873	*Coleridge (5th)*, William Duke Coleridge, *b.* 1937, *s.* 1984, *m.*	Hon. James D. C., *b.* 1967
1946	*Colgrain (3rd)*, David Colin Campbell, *b.* 1920, *s.* 1973, *m.*	Hon. Alastair C. L. C., *b.* 1951
1917	** *Colwyn (3rd)*, (Ian) Anthony Hamilton-Smith, CBE, *b.* 1942, *s.* 1966, *m.*	Hon. Craig P. H.-S., *b.* 1968
1956	*Colyton (2nd)*, Alisdair John Munro Hopkinson, *b.* 1958, *s.* 1996, *m.*	Hon. James P. M. H., *b.* 1983
1841	*Congleton (8th)*, Christopher Patrick Parnell, *b.* 1930, *s.* 1967, *m.*	Hon. John P. C. P., *b.* 1959
1927	*Cornwallis (3rd)*, Fiennes Neil Wykeham Cornwallis, OBE, *b.* 1921, *s.* 1982, *m.*	Hon. F. W. Jeremy C., *b.* 1946
1874	*Cottesloe (5th)*, Cdr. John Tapling Fremantle, *b.* 1927, *s.* 1994, *m.*	Hon. Thomas F. H. F., *b.* 1966
1929	*Craigmyle (4th)*, Thomas Columba Shaw, *b.* 1960, *s.* 1998, *m.*	Hon. Alexander F. S., *b.* 1988
1899	*Cranworth (3rd)*, Philip Bertram Gurdon, *b.* 1940, *s.* 1964, *w.*	Hon. Sacha W. R. G., *b.* 1970
1959	** *Crathorne (2nd)*, Charles James Dugdale, *b.* 1939, *s.* 1977, *m.*	Hon. Thomas A. J. D., *b.* 1977
1892	*Crawshaw (5th)*, David Gerald Brooks, *b.* 1934, *s.* 1997, *m.*	Hon. John P. B., *b.* 1938
1940	*Croft (3rd)*, Bernard William Henry Page Croft, *b.* 1949, *s.* 1997, *m.*	None
1797 I.	*Crofton (7th)*, Guy Patrick Gilbert Crofton, *b.* 1951, *s.* 1989, *m.*	Hon. E. Harry P. C., *b.* 1988
1375	*Cromwell (7th)*, Godfrey John Bewicke-Copley, *b.* 1960, *s.* 1982, *m.*	Hon. David G. B.-C., *b.* 1997
1947	*Crook (3rd)*, Robert Douglas Edwin Crook, *b.* 1955, *s.* 2001, *m.*	Hon. Matthew R. C., *b.* 1990
1920	*Cullen of Ashbourne (3rd)*, Edmund Willoughby Marsham Cokayne, *b.* 1916, *s.* 2000, *w.*	(Hon.) John O'B. M. C., *b.* 1920
1914	*Cunliffe (3rd)*, Roger Cunliffe, *b.* 1932, *s.* 1963, *m.*	Hon. Henry C., *b.* 1962
1927	*Daresbury (4th)*, Peter Gilbert Greenall, *b.* 1953, *s.* 1996, *m.*	Hon. Thomas E. G., *b.* 1984
1924	*Darling (3rd)*, (Robert) Julian Henry Darling, *b.* 1944, *s.* 2003, *m.*	Hon. Robert J. C. D., *b.* 1972
1946	*Darwen (3rd)*, Roger Michael Davies, *b.* 1938, *s.* 1988, *m.*	Hon. Paul D., *b.* 1962
1932	*Davies (3rd)*, David Davies, *b.* 1940, *s.* 1944, *m.*	Hon. David D. D., *b.* 1975
1812 I.	*Decies (7th)*, Marcus Hugh Tristram de la Poer Beresford, *b.* 1948, *s.* 1992, *m.*	Hon. Robert M. D. de la P. B., *b.* 1988
1299	*de Clifford (27th)*, John Edward Southwell Russell, *b.* 1928, *s.* 1982, *m.*	Hon. William S. R., *b.* 1930
1851	*De Freyne (7th)*, Francis Arthur John French, *b.* 1927, *s.* 1935, *m.*	Hon. Fulke C. A. J. F., *b.* 1957
1821	*Delamere (5th)*, Hugh George Cholmondeley, *b.* 1934, *s.* 1979, *m.*	Hon. Thomas P. G. C., *b.* 1968
1838	*de Mauley (7th)*, Rupert Charles Ponsonby, *b.* 1957, *s.* 2002, *m.*	Ashley G. P., *b.* 1959
1937	** *Denham (2nd)*, Bertram Stanley Mitford Bowyer, KBE, PC, *b.* 1927, *s.* 1948, *m.*	Hon. Richard G. G. B., *b.* 1959
1834	*Denman (5th)*, Charles Spencer Denman, CBE, MC, TD, *b.* 1916, *s.* 1971, *w.*	Hon. Richard T. S. D., *b.* 1946
1885	*Deramore (6th)*, Richard Arthur de Yarburgh-Bateson, *b.* 1911, *s.* 1964, *m.*	None
1887	*De Ramsey (4th)*, John Ailwyn Fellowes, *b.* 1942, *s.* 1993, *m.*	Hon. Freddie J. F., *b.* 1978
1264	*de Ros (28th)*, Peter Trevor Maxwell, *b.* 1958, *s.* 1983, *m.* Premier Baron of England	Hon. Finbar J. M., *b.* 1988
1881	*Derwent (5th)*, Robin Evelyn Leo Vanden-Bempde-Johnstone, LVO, *b.* 1930, *s.* 1986, *m.*	Hon. Francis P. H. V.-B.-J., *b.* 1965
1831	*de Saumarez (7th)*, Eric Douglas Saumarez, *b.* 1956, *s.* 1991, *m.*	Hon. Victor T. S., *b.* 1956
1910	*de Villiers (4th)*, Alexander Charles de Villiers, *b.* 1940, *s.* 2001, *m.*	None
1930	*Dickinson (2nd)*, Richard Clavering Hyett Dickinson, *b.* 1926, *s.* 1943, *m.*	Hon. Martin H. D., *b.* 1961
1620 I.	*Digby (12th) and Digby (5th) (1765)*, Edward Henry Kenelm Digby, KCVO, *b.* 1924, *s.* 1964, *m.*	Hon. Henry N. K. D., *b.* 1954
1615	*Dormer (17th)*, Geoffrey Henry Dormer, *b.* 1920, *s.* 1995, *m.*	Hon. William R. D., *b.* 1960
1943	*Dowding (3rd)*, Piers Hugh Tremenheere Dowding, *b.* 1948, *s.* 1992	Hon. Mark D. J. D., *b.* 1949
1439	*Dudley (15th)*, Jim Anthony Hill Wallace, *b.* 1930, *s.* 2002, *m.*	Hon. Jeremy W. G. W., *b.* 1964
1800 I.	*Dufferin and Clandeboye*, The 10th Baron died in 1991.	†Sir John Blackwood, Bt., *b.* 1944
1929	*Dulverton (3rd)*, (Gilbert) Michael Hamilton Wills, *b.* 1944, *s.* 1992	Hon. Robert A. H. W., *b.* 1983
1800 I.	*Dunalley (7th)*, Henry Francis Cornelius Prittie, *b.* 1948, *s.* 1992, *m.*	Hon. Joel H. P., *b.* 1981
1324 I.	*Dunboyne (29th)*, John Fitzwalter Butler, *b.* 1951, *s.* 2004, *m.*	Hon. Richard P. T. B., *b.* 1983

Created	Title, order of succession, name, etc.	Heir
1892	Dunleath (6th), Brian Henry Mulholland, b. 1950, s. 1997, m.	Hon. Andrew H. M., b. 1981
1439 I.	Dunsany (20th), Edward John Carlos Plunkett, b. 1939, s. 1999, m.	Hon. Randal P., b. 1983
1780	Dynevor (9th), Richard Charles Uryan Rhys, b. 1935, s. 1962	Hon. Hugo G. U. R., b. 1966
1963	Egremont (2nd) and Leconfield (7th) (1859), John Max Henry Scawen Wyndham, b. 1948, s. 1972, m.	Hon. George R. V. W., b. 1983
1643	Elibank (14th), Alan D'Ardis Erskine-Murray, b. 1923, s. 1973, w.	Master of Elibank, b. 1964
1802	Ellenborough (8th), Richard Edward Cecil Law, b. 1926, s. 1945, m.	Maj. Hon. Rupert E. H. L., b. 1955
1509 S.	Elphinstone (19th) and Elphinstone (5th) (1885), Alexander Mountstuart Elphinstone, b. 1980, s. 1994	Hon. Angus J. E., b. 1982
1934	** Elton (2nd), Rodney Elton, TD, b. 1930, s. 1973, m.	Hon. Edward P. E., b. 1966
1627 S.	Fairfax of Cameron (14th), Nicholas John Albert Fairfax, b. 1956, s. 1964, m.	Hon. Edward N. T. F., b. 1984
1961	Fairhaven (3rd), Ailwyn Henry George Broughton, b. 1936, s. 1973, m.	Maj. Hon. James H. A. B., b. 1963
1916	Faringdon (3rd), Charles Michael Henderson, b. 1937, s. 1977, m.	Hon. James H. H., b. 1961
1756	Farnham (13th), Simon Kenlis Maxwell, b. 1933, s. 2001, m.	Hon. Robin S. M., b. 1965
1856	Fermoy (6th), Patrick Maurice Burke Roche, b. 1967, s. 1984, m.	Hon. E. Hugh B. R., b. 1972
1826	Feversham (6th), Charles Antony Peter Duncombe, b. 1945, s. 1963, m.	Hon. Jasper O. S. D., b. 1968
1798 I.	ffrench (8th), Robuck John Peter Charles Mario ffrench, b. 1956, s. 1986, m.	Hon. John C. M. J. F. ff., b. 1928
1909	Fisher (3rd), John Vavasseur Fisher, DSC, b. 1921, s. 1955, m.	Hon. Patrick V. F., b. 1953
1295	Fitzwalter (21st), (Fitzwalter) Brook Plumptre, b. 1914, s. 1953, m.	Hon. Julian B. P., b. 1952
1776	Foley (8th), Adrian Gerald Foley, b. 1923, s. 1927, m.	Hon. Thomas H. F., b. 1961
1445	Forbes (22nd), Nigel Ivan Forbes, KBE, b. 1918, s. 1953, m. Premier Lord of Scotland	Master of Forbes, b. 1946
1821	Forester (9th), Charles Richard George Weld-Forester, b. 1975, s. 2003, m.	Wolstan W. W.-F., b. 1941
1922	Forres (4th), Alastair Stephen Grant Williamson, b. 1946, s. 1978, m.	Hon. George A. M. W., b. 1972
1917	Forteviot (4th), John James Evelyn Dewar, b. 1938, s. 1993, w.	Hon. Alexander J. E. D., b. 1971
1951	** Freyberg (3rd), Valerian Bernard Freyberg, b. 1970, s. 1993	None
1917	Gainford (3rd), Joseph Edward Pease, b. 1921, s. 1971, m.	Hon. George P., b. 1926
1818	Garvagh (5th), (Alexander Leopold Ivor) George Canning, b. 1920, s. 1956, m.	Hon. Spencer G. S. de R. C., b. 1953
1942	** Geddes (3rd), Euan Michael Ross Geddes, b. 1937, s. 1975, m.	Hon. James G. N. G., b. 1969
1876	Gerard (5th), Anthony Robert Hugo Gerard, b. 1949, s. 1992, m.	Hon. Rupert B. C. G., b. 1981
1824	Gifford (6th), Anthony Maurice Gifford, b. 1940, s. 1961, m.	Hon. Thomas A. G., b. 1967
1917	Gisborough (3rd), Thomas Richard John Long Chaloner, b. 1927, s. 1951, m.	Hon. T. Peregrine L. C., b. 1961
1960	Gladwyn (2nd), Miles Alvery Gladwyn Jebb, b. 1930, s. 1996	None
1899	Glanusk (5th), Christopher Russell Bailey, b. 1942, s. 1997, m.	Hon. Charles H. B., b. 1976
1918	** Glenarthur (4th), Simon Mark Arthur, b. 1944, s. 1976, m.	Hon. Edward A. A., b. 1973
1911	Glenconner (3rd), Colin Christopher Paget Tennant, b. 1926, s. 1983, m.	Cody C. E. T., b. 1994
1964	Glendevon (2nd), Julian John Somerset Hope, b. 1950, s. 1996	Hon. Jonathan C. H., b. 1952
1922	Glendyne (3rd), Robert Nivison, b. 1926, s. 1967, m.	Hon. John N., b. 1960
1939	** Glentoran (3rd), (Thomas) Robin (Valerian) Dixon, CBE, b. 1935, s. 1995, m.	Hon. Daniel G. D., b. 1959
1909	Gorell (4th), Timothy John Radcliffe Barnes, b. 1927, s. 1963, m.	Hon. Ronald A. H. B., b. 1931
1953	** Grantchester (3rd), Christopher John Suenson-Taylor, b. 1951, s. 1995, m.	Hon. Jesse D. S.-T., b. 1977
1782	Grantley (8th), Richard William Brinsley Norton, b. 1956, s. 1995	Hon. Francis J. H. N., b. 1960
1794 I.	Graves (10th), Timothy Evelyn Graves, b. 1960, s. 2002	None
1445 S.	Gray (23rd), Andrew Godfrey Diarmid Stuart Campbell-Gray, b. 1964, s. 2003, m.	Master of Gray, b. 1996
1950	Greenhill (3rd), Malcolm Greenhill, b. 1924, s. 1989	None
1927	** Greenway (4th), Ambrose Charles Drexel Greenway, b. 1941, s. 1975, m.	Hon. Nigel. P. G., b. 1944
1902	Grenfell (3rd) and Grenfell of Kilvey (life peerage, 2000), Julian Pascoe Francis St Leger Grenfell, b. 1935, s. 1976, m.	Francis P. J. G., b. 1938
1944	Gretton (4th), John Lysander Gretton, b. 1975, s. 1989	None
1397	Grey of Codnor (6th), Richard Henry Cornwall-Legh, b. 1936, s. 1996, m.	Hon. Richard S. C. C.-L., b. 1976
1955	Gridley (3rd), Richard David Arnold Gridley, b. 1956, s. 1996, m.	Hon. Carl R. G., b. 1981
1964	Grimston of Westbury (3rd), Robert John Sylvester Grimston, b. 1951, s. 2003, m.	Hon. Gerald C. W. G., b. 1953

Created	Title, order of succession, name, etc.	Heir
1886	*Grimthorpe (5th)*, Edward John Beckett, *b.* 1954, *s.* 2003, *m.*	Hon. Harry M. B., *b.* 1993
1945	*Hacking (3rd)*, Douglas David Hacking, *b.* 1938, *s.* 1971, *m.*	Hon. Douglas F. H., *b.* 1968
1950	*Haden-Guest (5th)*, Christopher Haden-Guest, *b.* 1948, *s.* 1996, *m.*	Hon. Nicholas H.-G., *b.* 1951
1886	*Hamilton of Dalzell (4th)*, James Leslie Hamilton, *b.* 1938, *s.* 1990, *m.*	Hon. Gavin G. H., *b.* 1968
1874	*Hampton (7th)*, John Humphrey Arnott Pakington, *b.* 1964, *s.* 2003, *m.*	None
1939	*Hankey (3rd)*, Donald Robin Alers Hankey, *b.* 1938, *s.* 1996, *m.*	Hon. Alexander M. A. H., *b.* 1947
1958	*Harding of Petherton (2nd)*, John Charles Harding, *b.* 1928, *s.* 1989, *m.*	Hon. William A. J. H., *b.* 1969
1910	*Hardinge of Penshurst (4th)*, Julian Alexander Hardinge, *b.* 1945, *s.* 1997	Hon. Hugh F. H., *b.* 1948
1876	*Harlech (6th)*, Francis David Ormsby-Gore, *b.* 1954, *s.* 1985, *m.*	Hon. Jasset D. C. O.-G., *b.* 1986
1939	*Harmsworth (3rd)*, Thomas Harold Raymond Harmsworth, *b.* 1939, *s.* 1990, *m.*	Hon. Dominic M. E. H., *b.* 1973
1815	*Harris (8th)*, Anthony Harris, *b.* 1942, *s.* 1996, *m.*	Anthony J. T. H., *b.* 1915
1954	*Harvey of Tasburgh (2nd)*, Peter Charles Oliver Harvey, *b.* 1921, *s.* 1968, *w.*	Charles J. G. H., *b.* 1951
1295	*Hastings (22nd)*, Edward Delaval Henry Astley, *b.* 1912, *s.* 1956, *m.*	Hon. Delaval T. H. A., *b.* 1960
1835	*Hatherton (8th)*, Edward Charles Littleton, *b.* 1950, *s.* 1985, *m.*	Hon. Thomas E. L., *b.* 1977
1776	*Hawke (11th)*, Edward George Hawke, TD, *b.* 1950, *s.* 1992, *m.*	Hon. William M. T. H., *b.* 1995
1927	*Hayter (4th)*, George William Michael Chubb, *b.* 1943, *s.* 2003, *m.*	Hon. Thomas F. F. C., *b.* 1986
1945	*Hazlerigg (3rd)*, Arthur Grey Hazlerigg, *b.* 1951, *s.* 2002, *m.*	Hon. Arthur W. G. H., *b.* 1987
1943	*Hemingford (3rd)*, (Dennis) Nicholas Herbert, *b.* 1934, *s.* 1982, *m.*	Hon. Christopher D. C. H., *b.* 1973
1906	*Hemphill (5th)*, Peter Patrick Fitzroy Martyn Martyn-Hemphill, *b.* 1928, *s.* 1957, *m.*	Hon. Charles A. M. M.-H., *b.* 1954
1799 I.	** *Henley (8th) and Northington (6th) (1885)*, Oliver Michael Robert Eden, *b.* 1953, *s.* 1977, *m.*	Hon. John W. O. E., *b.* 1988
1800 I.	*Henniker (9th) and Hertsmere (5th) (1866)*, Mark Ian Philip Chandos Henniker-Major, *b.* 1947, *s.* 2004, *m.*	Hon. Frederick J. C. H.-M., *b.* 1983
1461	*Herbert (19th)*, David John Seyfried, *b.* 1952, *s.* 2002, *m.*	Hon. Oliver R. S. H., *b.* 1976
1886	*Herschell (3rd)*, Rognvald Richard Farrer Herschell, *b.* 1923, *s.* 1929, *m.*	None
1935	*Hesketh (3rd)*, Thomas Alexander Fermor-Hesketh, KBE, PC, *b.* 1950, *s.* 1955, *m.*	Hon. Frederick H. F.-H., *b.* 1988
1828	*Heytesbury (6th)*, Francis William Holmes à Court, *b.* 1931, *s.* 1971, *m.*	Hon. James W. H. à. C., *b.* 1967
1886	*Hindlip (6th)*, Charles Henry Allsopp, *b.* 1940, *s.* 1993, *m.*	Hon. Henry W. A., *b.* 1973
1950	*Hives (3rd)*, Matthew Peter Hives, *b.* 1971, *s.* 1997	Hon. Michael B. H., *b.* 1926
1912	*Hollenden (4th)*, Ian Hampden Hope-Morley, *b.* 1946, *s.* 1999, *m.*	Hon. Edward H.-M., *b.* 1981
1897	*Holm Patrick (4th)*, Hans James David Hamilton, *b.* 1955, *s.* 1991, *m.*	Hon. Ion H. J. H., *b.* 1956
1797 I.	*Hotham (8th)*, Henry Durand Hotham, *b.* 1940, *s.* 1967, *m.*	Hon. William B. H., *b.* 1972
1881	*Hothfield (6th)*, Anthony Charles Sackville Tufton, *b.* 1939, *s.* 1991, *m.*	Hon. William S. T., *b.* 1977
1930	*Howard of Penrith (3rd)*, Philip Esme Howard, *b.* 1945, *s.* 1999, *m.*	Hon. Thomas Philip H., *b.* 1974
1960	*Howick of Glendale (2nd)*, Charles Evelyn Baring, *b.* 1937, *s.* 1973, *m.*	Hon. David E. C. B., *b.* 1975
1796 I.	*Huntingfield (7th)*, Joshua Charles Vanneck, *b.* 1954, *s.* 1994, *m.*	Hon. Gerard C. A. V., *b.* 1985
1866	** *Hylton (5th)*, Raymond Hervey Jolliffe, *b.* 1932, *s.* 1967, *m.*	Hon. William H. M. J., *b.* 1967
1933	*Iliffe (3rd)*, Robert Peter Richard Iliffe, *b.* 1944, *s.* 1996, *m.*	Hon. Edward R. I., *b.* 1968
1543 I.	*Inchiquin (18th)*, Conor Myles John O'Brien, *b.* 1943, *s.* 1982, *m.*	Conor J. A. O'B., *b.* 1952
1962	*Inchyra (2nd)*, Robert Charles Reneke Hoyer Millar, *b.* 1935, *s.* 1989, *m.*	Hon. C. James C. H. M., *b.* 1962
1964	** *Inglewood (2nd)*, (William) Richard Fletcher-Vane, MEP, *b.* 1951, *s.* 1989, *m.*	Hon. Henry W. F. F.-V., *b.* 1990
1919	*Inverforth (4th)*, Andrew Peter Weir, *b.* 1966, *s.* 1982	Hon. John V. W., *b.* 1935
1941	*Ironside (2nd)*, Edmund Oslac Ironside, *b.* 1924, *s.* 1959, *m.*	Hon. Charles E. G. I., *b.* 1956
1952	*Jeffreys (3rd)*, Christopher Henry Mark Jeffreys, *b.* 1957, *s.* 1986, *m.*	Hon. Arthur M. H. J., *b.* 1989
1906	*Joicey (5th)*, James Michael Joicey, *b.* 1953, *s.* 1993, *m.*	Hon. William J. J., *b.* 1990
1937	*Kenilworth (4th)*, (John) Randle Siddeley, *b.* 1954, *s.* 1981, *m.*	Hon. William R. J. S., *b.* 1992
1935	*Kennet (2nd)*, Wayland Hilton Young, *b.* 1923, *s.* 1960, *m.*	Hon. W. A. Thoby Y., *b.* 1957
1776 I.	*Kensington (8th) and Kensington (5th) (1886)*, Hugh Ivor Edwardes, *b.* 1933, *s.* 1981, *m.*	Hon. W. Owen A. E., *b.* 1964
1951	*Kenswood (2nd)*, John Michael Howard Whitfield, *b.* 1930, *s.* 1963, *m.*	Hon. Michael C. W., *b.* 1955
1788	*Kenyon (6th)*, Lloyd Tyrell-Kenyon, *b.* 1947, *s.* 1993, *m.*	Hon. Lloyd N. T.-K., *b.* 1972
1947	*Kershaw (4th)*, Edward John Kershaw, *b.* 1936, *s.* 1962, *m.*	Hon. John C. E. K., *b.* 1971
1943	*Keyes (2nd)*, Roger George Bowlby Keyes, *b.* 1919, *s.* 1945, *w.*	Hon. Charles W. P. K., *b.* 1951

Created	Title, order of succession, name, etc.	Heir
1909	Kilbracken (3rd), John Raymond Godley, DSC, b. 1920, s. 1950	Hon. Christopher J. G., b. 1945
1900	Killanin (4th), (George) Redmond Fitzpatrick Morris, b. 1947, s. 1999, m.	Hon. Luke M. G. M., b. 1975
1943	Killearn (3rd), Victor Miles George Aldous Lampson, b. 1941, s. 1996, m.	Hon. Miles H. M. L., b. 1977
1789 I.	Kilmaine (7th), John David Henry Browne, b. 1948, s. 1978, m.	Hon. John F. S. B., b. 1983
1831	Kilmarnock (7th), Alastair Ivor Gilbert Boyd, b. 1927, s. 1975, m.	Hon. Robin J. B., b. 1941
1941	Kindersley (3rd), Robert Hugh Molesworth Kindersley, b. 1929, s. 1976, m.	Hon. Rupert J. M. K., b. 1955
1223 I.	Kingsale (35th), John de Courcy, b. 1941, s. 1969, Premier Baron of Ireland	Nevinson M. de C., b. 1958
1902	Kinross (5th), Christopher Patrick Balfour, b. 1949, s. 1985, m.	Hon. Alan I. B., b. 1978
1951	Kirkwood (3rd), David Harvie Kirkwood, PHD, b. 1931, s. 1970, m.	Hon. James S. K., b. 1937
1800 I.	Langford (9th), Col. Geoffrey Alexander Rowley-Conwy, OBE, b. 1912, s. 1953, m.	Hon. Owain G. R.-C., b. 1958
1942	Latham (2nd), Dominic Charles Latham, b. 1954, s. 1970	Anthony M. L., b. 1954
1431	Latymer (9th), Crispin James Alan Nevill Money-Coutts, b. 1955, s. 2003, m.	Hon. Drummond W. T. M.-C., b. 1986
1869	Lawrence (5th), David John Downer Lawrence, b. 1937, s. 1968	None
1947	Layton (3rd), Geoffrey Michael Layton, b. 1947, s. 1989, m.	Hon. David L., b. 1914
1839	Leigh (6th), Christopher Dudley Piers Leigh, b. 1960, s. 2003, m.	Hon. Rupert D. L., b. 1994
1962	Leighton of St Mellons (3rd), Robert William Henry Leighton Seager, b. 1955, s. 1998	Hon. Simon J. L. S., b. 1957
1797	Lilford (7th), George Vernon Powys, b. 1931, s. 1949, m.	Hon. Mark V. P., b. 1975
1945	Lindsay of Birker (3rd), James Francis Lindsay, b. 1945, s. 1994, m.	Alexander S. L., b. 1940
1758 I.	Lisle (9th), (John) Nicholas Geoffrey Lysaght, b. 1960, s. 2003	Hon. David J. L., b. 1963
1850	Londesborough (9th), Richard John Denison, b. 1959, s. 1968, m.	Hon. James F. D., b. 1990
1541 I.	Louth (16th), Otway Michael James Oliver Plunkett, b. 1929, s. 1950, m.	Hon. Jonathan O. P., b. 1952
1458 S.	Lovat (16th) and Lovat (5th) (1837), Simon Fraser, b. 1977, s. 1995	Hon. Jack F., b. 1984
1946	Lucas of Chilworth (3rd), Simon William Lucas, b. 1957, s. 2001, m.	Hon. John R. M. L., b. 1995
1663	** Lucas (11th) and Dingwall (14th) (S. 1609), Ralph Matthew Palmer, b. 1951, s. 1991	Hon. Lewis E. P., b. 1987
1929	** Luke (3rd), Arthur Charles St John Lawson-Johnston, b. 1933, s. 1996, m.	Hon. Ian J. St J. L.-J., b. 1963
1914	** Lyell (3rd), Charles Lyell, b. 1939, s. 1943	None
1859	Lyveden (7th), Jack Leslie Vernon, b. 1938, s. 1999, m.	Hon. Colin R. V., b. 1967
1959	MacAndrew (3rd), Christopher Anthony Colin MacAndrew, b. 1945, s. 1989, m.	Hon. Oliver C. J. M., b. 1983
1776 I.	Macdonald (8th), Godfrey James Macdonald of Macdonald, b. 1947, s. 1970, m.	Hon. Godfrey E. H. T. M., b. 1982
1937	McGowan (4th), Harry John Charles McGowan, b. 1971, s. 2003, m.	Hon. Dominic J. W. McG., b. 1951
1922	Maclay (3rd), Joseph Paton Maclay, b. 1942, s. 1969, m.	Hon. Joseph P. M., b. 1977
1955	McNair (3rd), Duncan James McNair, b. 1947, s. 1989, m.	Hon. William S. A. M., b. 1958
1951	Macpherson of Drumochter (2nd), (James) Gordon Macpherson, b. 1924, s. 1965, m.	Hon. James A. M., b. 1979
1937	** Mancroft (3rd), Benjamin Lloyd Stormont Mancroft, b. 1957, s. 1987, m.	Hon. Arthur L. S. M., b. 1995
1807	Manners (5th), John Robert Cecil Manners, b. 1923, s. 1972, w.	Hon. John H. R. M., b. 1956
1922	Manton (4th), Miles Ronald Marcus Watson, b. 1958, s. 2003, m.	Hon. Thomas N. C. D. W., b. 1985
1908	Marchamley (4th), William Francis Whiteley, b. 1968, s. 1994	None
1964	Margadale (3rd), Alastair John Morrison, b. 1958, s. 2003, m.	Hon. Declan J. M., b. 1993
1961	Marks of Broughton (3rd), Simon Richard Marks, b. 1950, s. 1998, m.	Hon. Michael M., b. 1989
1964	Martonmere (2nd), John Stephen Robinson, b. 1963, s. 1989	David A. R., b. 1965
1776 I.	Massy (10th), David Hamon Somerset Massy, b. 1947, s. 1995	Hon. John H. M., b. 1950
1935	May (3rd), Michael St John May, b. 1931, s. 1950, m.	Hon. Jasper B. St J. M., b. 1965
1928	Melchett (4th), Peter Robert Henry Mond, b. 1948, s. 1973	None
1925	Merrivale (3rd), Jack Henry Edmond Duke, b. 1917, s. 1951, w.	Hon. Derek J. P. D., b. 1948
1911	Merthyr, Trevor Oswin Lewis, CBE, b. 1935, s. 1977, m.	Disclaimed for life 1977. David T. L., b. 1977
1919	Meston (3rd), James Meston, b. 1950, s. 1984, m.	Hon. Thomas J. D. M., b. 1977
1838	** Methuen (7th), Robert Alexander Holt Methuen, b. 1931, s. 1994, m.	James P. A. M.-C., b. 1952
1711	Middleton (12th), (Digby) Michael Godfrey John Willoughby, MC, b. 1921, s. 1970	Hon. Michael C. J. W., b. 1948
1939	Milford (4th), Guy Wogan Philipps, b. 1961, s. 1999, m.	Hon. Archie S. P., b. 1997

Created	Title, order of succession, name, etc.	Heir
1933	*Milne (2nd)*, George Douglass Milne, TD, *b.* 1909, *s.* 1948, *m.*	Hon. George A. M., *b.* 1941
1951	*Milner of Leeds (3rd)*, Richard James Milner, *b.* 1959, *s.* 2003, *m.*	None
1947	*Milverton (2nd)*, Revd Fraser Arthur Richard Richards, *b.* 1930, *s.* 1978, *m.*	Hon. Michael H. R., *b.* 1936
1873	*Moncreiff (6th)*, Rhoderick Harry Wellwood Moncreiff, *b.* 1954, *s.* 2002, *m.*	Hon. Harry J. W. M., *b.* 1986
1884	*Monk Bretton (3rd)*, John Charles Dodson, *b.* 1924, *s.* 1933, *m.*	Hon. Christopher M. D., *b.* 1958
1885	*Monkswell (5th)*, Gerard Collier, *b.* 1947, *s.* 1984, *m.*	Hon. James A. C., *b.* 1977
1728	** *Monson (11th)*, John Monson, *b.* 1932, *s.* 1958, *m.*	Hon. Nicholas J. M., *b.* 1955
1885	** *Montagu of Beaulieu (3rd)*, Edward John Barrington Douglas-Scott-Montagu, *b.* 1926, *s.* 1929, *m.*	Hon. Ralph D.-S.-M., *b.* 1961
1839	*Monteagle of Brandon (6th)*, Gerald Spring Rice, *b.* 1926, *s.* 1946, *m.*	Hon. Charles J. S. R., *b.* 1953
1943	** *Moran (2nd)*, (Richard) John (McMoran) Wilson, KCMG, *b.* 1924, *s.* 1977, *m.*	Hon. James M. W., *b.* 1952
1918	*Morris (3rd)*, Michael David Morris, *b.* 1937, *s.* 1975, *m.*	Hon. Thomas A. S. M., *b.* 1982
1950	*Morris of Kenwood (2nd)*, Philip Geoffrey Morris, *b.* 1928, *s.* 1954, *m.*	Hon. Jonathan D. M., *b.* 1968
1831	*Mostyn (6th)*, Llewellyn Roger Lloyd-Mostyn, *b.* 1948, *s.* 2000, *m.*	Hon. Gregory P. R. L.-M., *b.* 1984
1933	*Mottistone (4th)*, David Peter Seely, CBE, *b.* 1920, *s.* 1966, *m.*	Hon. Peter J. P. S., *b.* 1949
1945	*Mountevans (3rd)*, Edward Patrick Broke Evans, *b.* 1943, *s.* 1974, *m.*	Hon. Jeffrey de C. R. E., *b.* 1948
1283	** *Mowbray (26th), Segrave (27th) (1295) and Stourton (23rd) (1448)*, Charles Edward Stourton, CBE, *b.* 1923, *s.* 1965, *m.*	Hon. Edward W. S. S., *b.* 1953
1932	*Moyne (3rd)*, Jonathan Bryan Guinness, *b.* 1930, *s.* 1992, *m.*	Hon. Jasper J. R. G., *b.* 1954
1929	** *Moynihan (4th)*, Colin Berkeley Moynihan, *b.* 1955, *s.* 1997, *m.*	Hon. Nicholas E. B. M., *b.* 1994
1781 I.	*Muskerry (9th)*, Robert Fitzmaurice Deane, *b.* 1948, *s.* 1988, *m.*	Hon. Jonathan F. D., *b.* 1986
1627 S.	*Napier (14th) and Ettrick (5th) (1872)*, Francis Nigel Napier, KCVO, *b.* 1930, *s.* 1954, *m.*	Master of Napier, *b.* 1962
1868	*Napier of Magdala (6th)*, Robert Alan Napier, *b.* 1940, *s.* 1987, *m.*	Hon. James R. N., *b.* 1966
1940	*Nathan (2nd)*, Roger Carol Michael Nathan, *b.* 1922, *s.* 1963, *m.*	Hon. Rupert H. B. N., *b.* 1957
1960	*Nelson of Stafford (3rd)*, Henry Roy George Nelson, *b.* 1943, *s.* 1995, *m.*	Hon. Alistair W. H. N., *b.* 1973
1959	*Netherthorpe (3rd)*, James Frederick Turner, *b.* 1964, *s.* 1982, *m.*	Hon. Andrew J. E. T., *b.* 1993
1946	*Newall (2nd)*, Francis Storer Eaton Newall, *b.* 1930, *s.* 1963, *m.*	Hon. Richard H. E. N., *b.* 1961
1776 I.	*Newborough (8th)*, Robert Vaughan Wynn, *b.* 1949, *s.* 1998, *m.*	Hon. Charles H. R. W., *b.* 1923
1892	*Newton (5th)*, Richard Thomas Legh, *b.* 1950, *s.* 1992, *m.*	Hon. Piers R. L., *b.* 1979
1930	*Noel-Buxton (3rd)*, Martin Connal Noel-Buxton, *b.* 1940, *s.* 1980, *m.*	Hon. Charles C. N.-B., *b.* 1975
1957	*Norrie (2nd)*, (George) Willoughby Moke Norrie, *b.* 1936, *s.* 1977, *m.*	Hon. Mark W. J. N., *b.* 1972
1884	** *Northbourne (5th)*, Christopher George Walter James, *b.* 1926, *s.* 1982, *m.*	Hon. Charles W. H. J., *b.* 1960
1866	** *Northbrook (6th)*, Francis Thomas Baring, *b.* 1954, *s.* 1990, *m.*	To the Baronetcy, Peter B., *b.* 1939
1878	*Norton (8th)*, James Nigel Arden Adderley, *b.* 1947, *s.* 1993, *m.*	Hon. Edward J. A. A., *b.* 1982
1906	*Nunburnholme (6th)*, Stephen Charles Wilson, *b.* 1973, *s.* 2000	Hon. David M. W., *b.* 1954
1950	*Ogmore (2nd)*, Gwilym Rees Rees-Williams, *b.* 1931, *s.* 1976, *m.*	Hon. Morgan R.-W., *b.* 1937
1870	*O'Hagan (4th)*, Charles Towneley Strachey, *b.* 1945, *s.* 1961	Hon. Richard T. S., *b.* 1950
1868	*O'Neill (4th)*, Raymond Arthur Clanaboy O'Neill, TD, *b.* 1933, *s.* 1944, *m.*	Hon. Shane S. C. O'N., *b.* 1965
1836 I.	*Oranmore and Browne (5th) and Mereworth (3rd) (1926)*, Dominick Geoffrey Thomas Browne, *b.* 1929, *s.* 2002	Hon. Martin M. D. B., *b.* 1931
1933	** *Palmer (4th)*, Adrian Bailie Nottage Palmer, *b.* 1951, *s.* 1990, *m.*	Hon. Hugo B. R. P., *b.* 1980
1914	*Parmoor (4th)*, (Frederick Alfred) Milo Cripps, *b.* 1929, *s.* 1977	Michael L. S. C., *b.* 1942
1937	*Pender (3rd)*, John Willoughby Denison-Pender, *b.* 1933, *s.* 1965, *m.*	Hon. Henry J. R. D.-P., *b.* 1968
1866	*Penrhyn (7th)*, Simon Douglas-Pennant, *b.* 1938, *s.* 2003, *m.*	Hon. Edward S. D.-P., *b.* 1966
1603	*Petre (18th)*, John Patrick Lionel Petre, *b.* 1942, *s.* 1989, *m.*	Hon. Dominic W. P., *b.* 1966
1918	*Phillimore (5th)*, Francis Stephen Phillimore, *b.* 1944, *s.* 1994, *m.*	Hon. Tristan A. S. P., *b.* 1977
1945	*Piercy (3rd)*, James William Piercy, *b.* 1946, *s.* 1981	Hon. Mark E. P. P., *b.* 1953
1827	*Plunket (8th)*, Robin Rathmore Plunket, *b.* 1925, *s.* 1975, *m.*	Hon. Shaun A. F. S. P., *b.* 1931
1831	*Poltimore (7th)*, Mark Coplestone Bampfylde, *b.* 1957, *s.* 1978, *m.*	Hon. Henry A. W. B., *b.* 1985
1690 S.	*Polwarth (10th)*, Henry Alexander Hepburne-Scott, TD, *b.* 1916, *s.* 1944, *m.*	Master of Polwarth, *b.* 1947
1930	*Ponsonby of Shulbrede (4th) and Ponsonby of Roehampton (life peerage, 2000)*, Frederick Matthew Thomas Ponsonby, *b.* 1958, *s.* 1990	None
1958	*Poole (2nd)*, David Charles Poole, *b.* 1945, *s.* 1993, *m.*	Hon. Oliver J. P., *b.* 1972

Created	Title, order of succession, name, etc.	Heir
1852	Raglan (5th), FitzRoy John Somerset, b. 1927, s. 1964	Hon. Geoffrey S., b. 1932
1932	Rankeillour (4th), Peter St Thomas More Henry Hope, b. 1935, s. 1967	Michael R. H., b. 1940
1953	Rathcavan (3rd), Hugh Detmar Torrens O'Neill, b. 1939, s. 1994, m.	Hon. François H. N. O'N., b. 1984
1916	Rathcreedan (3rd), Christopher John Norton, b. 1949, s. 1990, m.	Hon. Adam G. N., b. 1952
1868	Rathdonnell (5th), Thomas Benjamin McClintock-Bunbury, b. 1938, s. 1959, m.	Hon. William L. M.-B., b. 1966
1911	Ravensdale (3rd), Nicholas Mosley, MC, b. 1923, s. 1966, m.	Hon. Shaun N. M., b. 1949
1821	Ravensworth (9th), Thomas Arthur Hamish Liddell, b. 1954, s. 2004, m.	Hon. Henry A. T. L., b. 1987
1821	Rayleigh (6th), John Gerald Strutt, b. 1960, s. 1988, m.	Hon. John F. S., b. 1993
1937	** Rea (3rd), John Nicolas Rea, MD, b. 1928, s. 1981, m.	Hon. Matthew J. R., b. 1956
1628 S.	** Reay (14th), Hugh William Mackay, b. 1937, s. 1963, m.	Master of Reay, b. 1965
1902	Redesdale (6th) and Mitford (life peerage 2000), Rupert Bertram Mitford, b. 1967, s. 1991, m.	Hon. Bertram D. M., b. 2000
1940	Reith, Christopher John Reith, b. 1928, s. 1971, m. Disclaimed for life 1972.	Hon. James H. J. R., b. 1971
1928	Remnant (3rd), James Wogan Remnant, CVO, b. 1930, s. 1967, m.	Hon. Philip J. R., b. 1954
1806	Rendlesham (9th), Charles William Brooke Thellusson, b. 1954, s. 1999, m.	Hon. Peter R. T., b. 1920
1933	Rennell (3rd), (John Adrian) Tremayne Rodd, b. 1935, s. 1978, m.	Hon. James R. D. T. R., b. 1978
1964	Renwick (2nd), Harry Andrew Renwick, b. 1935, s. 1973, m.	Hon. Robert J. R., b. 1966
1885	Revelstoke (6th), James Cecil Baring, b. 1938, s. 2003, m.	Hon. Alexander R. B., b. 1970
1905	Ritchie of Dundee (5th), (Harold) Malcolm Ritchie, b. 1919, s. 1978, m.	Hon. C. Rupert R. R., b. 1958
1935	Riverdale (3rd), Anthony Robert Balfour, b. 1960, s. 1998	Hon. David R. B., b. 1938
1961	Robertson of Oakridge (2nd), William Ronald Robertson, b. 1930, s. 1974, m.	Hon. William B. E. R., b. 1975
1938	Roborough (3rd), Henry Massey Lopes, b. 1940, s. 1992, m.	Hon. Massey J. H. L., b. 1969
1931	Rochester (2nd), Foster Charles Lowry Lamb, b. 1916, s. 1955, w.	Hon. David C. L., b. 1944
1934	Rockley (3rd), James Hugh Cecil, b. 1934, s. 1976, m.	Hon. Anthony R. C., b. 1961
1782	Rodney (10th), George Brydges Rodney, b. 1953, s. 1992, m.	Hon. John G. B. R., b. 1999
1651 S.	Rollo (14th) and Dunning (5th) (1869), David Eric Howard Rollo, b. 1943, s. 1997, m.	Master of Rollo, b. 1972
1959	Rootes (3rd), Nicholas Geoffrey Rootes, b. 1951, s. 1992, m.	William B. R., b. 1944
1796 I.	Rossmore (7th) and Rossmore (6th) (1838), William Warner Westenra, b. 1931, s. 1958, m.	Hon. Benedict W. W., b. 1983
1939	** Rotherwick (3rd), (Herbert) Robin Cayzer, b. 1954, s. 1996, m.	Hon. H. Robin C., b. 1989
1885	Rothschild (4th), (Nathaniel Charles) Jacob Rothschild, OM, GBE, b. 1936, s. 1990, m.	Hon. Nathaniel P. V. J. R., b. 1971
1911	Rowallan (4th), John Polson Cameron Corbett, b. 1947, s. 1993	Hon. Jason W. P. C. C., b. 1972
1947	Rugby (3rd), Robert Charles Maffey, b. 1951, s. 1990, m.	Hon. Timothy J. H. M., b. 1975
1919	Russell of Liverpool (3rd), Simon Gordon Jared Russell, b. 1952, s. 1981, m.	Hon. Edward C. S. R., b. 1985
1876	Sackville (7th), Robert Bertrand Sackville-West, b. 1958, s. 2004, m.	Hon. Arthur S.-W., b. 2000
1964	St Helens (2nd), Richard Francis Hughes-Young, b. 1945, s. 1980, m.	Hon. Henry T. H.-Y., b. 1986
1559	** St John of Bletso (21st), Anthony Tudor St John, b. 1957, s. 1978, m.	Hon. Oliver B. St J., b. 1995
1887	St Levan (4th), John Francis Arthur St Aubyn, DSC, b. 1919, s. 1978, w.	Hon. O. Piers St. A., b. 1920
1885	St Oswald (6th), Charles Rowland Andrew Winn, b. 1959, s. 1999, m.	Hon. Rowland C. S. H. W., b. 1986
1960	Sanderson of Ayot, Alan Lindsay Sanderson, b. 1931, s. 1971, m. Disclaimed for life 1971.	Hon. Michael S., b. 1959
1945	Sandford (2nd), Revd John Cyril Edmondson, DSC, b. 1920, s. 1959, m.	Hon. James J. M. E., b. 1949
1871	Sandhurst (6th), Guy Rees John Mansfield, b. 1949, s. 2002, m.	Hon. Edward J. M., b. 1982
1802	Sandys (7th), Richard Michael Oliver Hill, b. 1931, s. 1961, m.	The Marquess of Downshire
1888	Savile (3rd), George Halifax Lumley-Savile, b. 1919, s. 1931	John A. T. L-S., b. 1947
1447	Saye and Sele (21st), Nathaniel Thomas Allen Fiennes, b. 1920, s. 1968, m.	Hon. Martin G. F., b. 1961
1826	Seaford (6th), Colin Humphrey Felton Ellis, b. 1946, s. 1999, m.	Hon. Benjamin F. T. E., b. 1976
1932	** Selsdon (3rd), Malcolm McEacharn Mitchell-Thomson, b. 1937, s. 1963, m.	Hon. Callum M. M. M.-T., b. 1969
1489 S.	Sempill (21st), James William Stuart Whitemore Sempill, b. 1949, s. 1995, m.	Master of Sempill, b. 1979
1916	Shaughnessy (4th), Michael James Shaughnessy, b. 1946, s. 2003	Charles, G. P. S., b. 1955
1946	Shepherd (3rd), Graham George Shepherd, b. 1949, s. 2001, m.	Hon. Patrick M. S.
1964	Sherfield (2nd), Christopher James Makins, b. 1942, s. 1996, m.	Hon. Dwight W. M., b. 1951
1902	Shuttleworth (5th), Charles Geoffrey Nicholas Kay-Shuttleworth, b. 1948, s. 1975, m.	Hon. Thomas E. K.-S., b. 1976

Created	Title, order of succession, name, etc.	Heir
1950	Silkin (3rd), Christopher Lewis Silkin, b. 1947, s. 2001	Rory L. S., b. 1954
1963	Silsoe (2nd), David Malcolm Trustram Eve b. 1930, s. 1976, m.	Hon. Simon R. T. E., b. 1966
1947	Simon of Wythenshawe (3rd), Matthew Simon, b. 1955, s. 2002	Martin S., b. 1944
1449 S.	Sinclair (18th), Matthew Murray Kennedy St Clair, b. 1968, s. 2004	Malcolm A. J. St C., b. 1927
1957	Sinclair of Cleeve (3rd), John Lawrence Robert Sinclair, b. 1953, s. 1985	None
1919	Sinha (6th), Arup Kumar Sinha, b. 1966, s. 1999	Hon. Dilip K. S., b. 1967
1828	** Skelmersdale (7th), Roger Bootle-Wilbraham, b. 1945, s. 1973, m.	Hon. Andrew B.-W., b. 1977
1916	Somerleyton (3rd), Savile William Francis Crossley, GCVO, b. 1928, s. 1959, m.	Hon. Hugh F. S. C., b. 1971
1784	Somers (9th), Philip Sebastian Somers Cocks, b. 1948, s. 1995	Alan B. C., b. 1930
1780	Southampton (6th), Charles James FitzRoy, b. 1928, s. 1989, m.	Hon. Edward C. F., b. 1955
1959	Spens (4th), Patrick Nathaniel George Spens, b. 1968, s. 2001, m.	Hon. Peter L. S., b. 2000
1640	Stafford (15th), Francis Melfort William Fitzherbert, b. 1954, s. 1986, m.	Hon. Benjamin J. B. F., b. 1983
1938	Stamp (4th), Trevor Charles Bosworth Stamp, MD, b. 1935, s. 1987, m.	Hon. Nicholas C. T. S., b. 1978
1839	Stanley of Alderley (8th), Sheffield (8th) (I. 1738) and Eddisbury (7th) (1848), Thomas Henry Oliver Stanley, b. 1927, s. 1971, m.	Hon. Richard O. S., b. 1956
1318	** Strabolgi (11th), David Montague de Burgh Kenworthy, b. 1914, s. 1953, m.	Andrew D. W. K., b. 1967
1954	Strang (2nd), Colin Strang, b. 1922, s. 1978, m.	None
1955	Strathalmond (3rd), William Roberton Fraser, b. 1947, s. 1976, m.	Hon. William G. F., b. 1976
1936	Strathcarron (2nd), David William Anthony Blyth Macpherson, b. 1924, s. 1937, m.	Hon. Ian D. P. M., b. 1949
1955	** Strathclyde (2nd), Thomas Galloway Dunlop du Roy de Blicquy Galbraith, PC, b. 1960, s. 1985, m.	Hon. Charles W. du R. de B. G., b. 1962
1900	Strathcona and Mount Royal (4th), Donald Euan Palmer Howard, b. 1923, s. 1959, m.	Hon. D. Alexander S. H., b. 1961
1836	Stratheden (6th) and Campbell (6th) (1841), Donald Campbell, b. 1934, s. 1987, m.	Hon. David A. C., b. 1963
1884	Strathspey (6th), James Patrick Trevor Grant of Grant, b. 1943, s. 1992, m.	Hon. Michael P. F. G., b. 1953
1838	Sudeley (7th), Merlin Charles Sainthill Hanbury-Tracy, b. 1939, s. 1941	D. Andrew J. H.-T., b. 1928
1786	Suffield (11th), Anthony Philip Harbord-Hamond, MC, b. 1922, s. 1951, w.	Hon. Charles A. A. H.-H., b. 1953
1893	Swansea (4th), John Hussey Hamilton Vivian, b. 1925, s. 1934, m.	Hon. Richard A. H. V., b. 1957
1907	Swaythling (5th), Charles Edgar Samuel Montagu, b. 1954, s. 1998, m.	Hon. Anthony T. S. M., b. 1931
1919	** Swinfen (3rd), Roger Mynors Swinfen Eady, b. 1938, s. 1977, m.	Hon. Charles R. P. S. E., b. 1971
1935	Sysonby (3rd), John Frederick Ponsonby, b. 1945, s. 1956	None
1831 I.	Talbot of Malahide (10th), Reginald John Richard Arundell, b. 1931, s. 1987, m.	Hon. Richard J. T. A., b. 1957
1946	Tedder (3rd), Robin John Tedder, b. 1955, s. 1994, m.	Hon. Benjamin J. T., b. 1985
1884	Tennyson (5th), Cdr. Mark Aubrey Tennyson, DSC, b. 1920, s. 1991, m.	David H. A. T., b. 1960
1918	Terrington (6th), Christopher Richard James Woodhouse, MB, b. 1946, s. 2001, m.	Hon. Jack H. L. W., b. 1978
1940	Teviot (2nd), Charles John Kerr, b. 1934, s. 1968, m.	Hon. Charles R. K., b. 1971
1616	Teynham (20th), John Christopher Ingham Roper-Curzon, b. 1928, s. 1972, m.	Hon. David J. H. I. R.-C., b. 1965
1964	Thomson of Fleet (2nd), Kenneth Roy Thomson, b. 1923, s. 1976, m.	Hon. David K. R. T., b. 1957
1792	Thurlow (8th), Francis Edward Hovell-Thurlow-Cumming-Bruce, KCMG, b. 1912, s. 1971, w.	Hon. Roualeyn R. H.-T.-C.-B., b. 1952
1876	Tollemache (5th), Timothy John Edward Tollemache, b. 1939, s. 1975, m.	Hon. Edward J. H. T., b. 1976
1564 S.	Torphichen (15th), James Andrew Douglas Sandilands, b. 1946, s. 1975, m.	Robert P. S., b. 1950
1947	** Trefgarne (2nd), David Garro Trefgarne, PC, b. 1941, s. 1960, m.	Hon. George G. T., b. 1970
1921	Trevethin (4th) and Oaksey (2nd) (1947), John Geoffrey Tristram Lawrence, OBE, b. 1929, s. 1971, m.	Hon. Patrick J. T. L., b. 1960
1880	Trevor (5th), Marke Charles Hill-Trevor, b. 1970, s. 1997, m.	Hon. Iain R. H.-T., b. 1971
1461 I.	Trimlestown (21st), Raymond Charles Barnewall, b. 1930, s. 1997	None
1940	Tryon (3rd), Anthony George Merrik Tryon, b. 1940, s. 1976	Hon. Charles G. B. T., b. 1976
1935	Tweedsmuir (3rd), William de l'Aigle Buchan, b. 1916, s. 1996, m.	Hon. John W. H. de l'A. B., b. 1950
1523	Vaux of Harrowden (11th), Anthony William Gilbey, b. 1940, s. 2002, m.	Hon. Richard H. G. G., b. 1965
1800 I.	Ventry (8th), Andrew Wesley Daubeny de Moleyns, b. 1943, s. 1987, m.	Hon. Francis W. D. de M., b. 1965
1762	Vernon (11th), Anthony William Vernon-Harcourt, b. 1939, s. 2000, m.	Hon. Simon A. V.-H., b. 1969

Created	Title, order of succession, name, etc.	Heir
1922	Vestey (3rd), Samuel George Armstrong Vestey, b. 1941, s. 1954, m.	Hon. William G. V., b. 1983
1841	Vivian (7th), Charles Crespigny Hussey Vivian, b. 1966, s. 2004	Hon. Victor A. R. B. V., b. 1940
1934	Wakehurst (3rd), (John) Christopher Loder, b. 1925, s. 1970, m.	Hon. Timothy W. L., b. 1958
1723	** Walpole (10th) and Walpole of Wolterton (8th) (1756), Robert Horatio Walpole, b. 1938, s. 1989, m.	Hon. Jonathan R. H. W., b. 1967
1780	Walsingham (9th), John de Grey, MC, b. 1925, s. 1965, m.	Hon. Robert de. G., b. 1969
1936	Wardington (2nd), Christopher Henry Beaumont Pease, b. 1924, s. 1950, m.	Hon. William S. P., b. 1925
1792 I.	Waterpark (7th), Frederick Caryll Philip Cavendish, b. 1926, s. 1948, m.	Hon. Roderick A. C., b. 1959
1942	Wedgwood (4th), Piers Anthony Weymouth Wedgwood, b. 1954, s. 1970, m.	John W., b. 1919
1861	Westbury (6th), Richard Nicholas Bethell, MBE, b. 1950, s. 2001, m.	Hon. Alexander B., b. 1986
1944	Westwood (3rd), (William) Gavin Westwood, b. 1944, s. 1991, m.	Hon. W. Fergus W., b. 1972
1544/5	Wharton (12th), Myles Christopher David Robertson, b. 1964, s. 2000, m.	Hon. Christopher J. R., b. 1969
1935	Wigram (2nd), (George) Neville (Clive) Wigram, MC, b. 1915, s. 1960, w.	Maj. Hon. Andrew F. C. W., b. 1949
1491	** Willoughby de Broke (21st), Leopold David Verney, b. 1938, s. 1986, m.	Hon. Rupert G. V., b. 1966
1946	Wilson (2nd), Patrick Maitland Wilson, b. 1915, s. 1964, w.	None
1937	Windlesham (3rd) and Hennesy (life peerage, 1999), David James George Hennessy, CVO, PC, b. 1932, s. 1962, w.	Hon. James R. H., b. 1968
1951	Wise (2nd), John Clayton Wise, b. 1923, s. 1968, m.	Hon. Christopher J. C. W., b. 1949
1869	Wolverton (7th), Christopher Richard Glyn, b. 1938, s. 1988	Hon. Andrew J. G., b. 1943
1928	Wraxall (3rd), Eustace Hubert Beilby Gibbs, KCVO, CMG, b. 1929, s. 2001, w.	Hon. Anthony H. G., b. 1958
1915	Wrenbury (3rd), Revd John Burton Buckley, b. 1927, s. 1940, m.	Hon. William E. B., b. 1966
1838	Wrottesley (6th), Clifton Hugh Lancelot de Verdon Wrottesley, b. 1968, s. 1977, m.	Hon. Stephen J. W., b. 1955
1829	Wynford (9th), John Philip Robert Best, b. 1950, s. 2002, m.	Hon. Harry R. F. B., b. 1987
1308	Zouche (18th), James Assheton Frankland, b. 1943, s. 1965, m.	Hon. William T. A. F., b. 1984

BARONESSES/LADIES IN THEIR OWN RIGHT

Style, The Right Hon. the Lady _ , or The Right Hon. the Baroness _ , according to her preference. Either style may be used, except in the case of Scottish titles (indicated by S.), which are not baronies (see page 44) and whose holders are always addressed as Lady
Husband, Untitled
Children's style, As for children of a Baron
For forms of address, see page 43

Created	Title, order of succession, name, etc.	Heir
1664	Arlington, Jennifer Jane Forwood, b. 1939, s. 1999, w. Title called out of abeyance 1999	Hon. Patrick J. D. F., b. 1967
1455	Berners (16th), Pamela Vivien Kirkham, b. 1929, s. 1995, m.	Hon. Rupert W. T. K., b. 1953
1529	Braye (8th), Mary Penelope Aubrey-Fletcher, b. 1941, s. 1985, m.	Two co-heiresses
1321	Dacre (27th), Rachel Leila Douglas-Home, b. 1929, s. 1970, w.	Hon. James T. A. D.-H., b. 1952
1332	** Darcy de Knayth (18th), Davina Marcia Ingrams, DBE, b. 1938, s. 1943, w.	Hon. Caspar D. I., b. 1962
1490 S.	Herries of Terregles (14th), Anne Elizabeth Fitzalan-Howard, b. 1938, s. 1975, w.	Lady Mary Mumford, b. 1940
1597	Howard de Walden (10th), Mary Hazel Caridwen Czernin, b. 1935, s. 2004, m. Title called out of abeyance 2004	Hon. Peter J. J. C., b. 1966
1602 S.	Kinloss (12th), Beatrice Mary Grenville Freeman-Grenville, b. 1922, s. 1944, m.	Master of Kinloss, b. 1953
1445 S.	** Saltoun (20th), Flora Marjory Fraser, b. 1930, s. 1979, w.	Hon. Katharine I. M. I. F., b. 1957
1628	** Strange (16th), (Jean) Cherry Drummond of Megginch, b. 1928, s. 1986, m.	Hon. Adam H. D. of M., b. 1953
1313	Willoughby de Eresby (27th), (Nancy) Jane Marie Heathcote-Drummond-Willoughby, b. 1934, s. 1983	Two co-heiresses

LIFE PEERS

NEW LIFE PEERAGES *1 September 2003 to 31 August 2004:*

Sir David Alliance, CBE; Prof. Sir (Sushantha) Kumar Bhattacharyya, CBE; Jane Bonham Carter; Prof. Sir Alec (Nigel) Broers; Sir Simon Denis Brown, PC; Sir Ewen (James Hanning) Cameron; Sir Robert Douglas Carswell, PC; Patrick Robert Carter; Nicola Jane Chapman; Paul Rudd Drayson; Dr Frances Gertrude Claire D'Souza, CMG; Hugh John Maxwell Dykes; Kishwer Falkner; Sir Timothy Garden, KCB; Sir Edward (Alan John) George, GBE, PC; Prof. Anthony Giddens; Philip Gould; Revd. Dr Leslie John Griffiths; Dame Brenda Marjorie Hale, DBE, PC; Garry Richard Rushby Hart; Dr Edward Haughey; Alan Robert Haworth; Ruth Beatrice Henig; Greville Patrick Charles Howard; CBE; Sir Harold Stanley Kalms; Sir John (Olav) Kerr; Irvine Alan Stewart Laidlaw; Alexander Park Leitch; Margaret Josephine McDonagh; William David McKenzie; John Alston Maxton; Delyth Jane Morgan; Patricia Morris, OBE; Elaine Murphy; Dame Julia (Babette Sarah) Neuberger, DBE; Margaret Theresa Prosser, OBE; Dr. Diljit Singh Rana, MBE; Revd. John Roger Roberts; Richard Andrew Rosser; Edward Rowlands, CBE; Janet Anne Royall; Peter Charles Snape; Leonard Steinberg; David Maxim Triesman; Dr Peter Derek Truscott; Denis Tunnicliffe, CBE; Sir Iain Vallance; Margaret Mary Wall; Sir Anthony Young; Prof. Margaret Omolola Young, OBE

CREATED UNDER THE APPELLATE JURISDICTION ACT 1876 (AS AMENDED)

BARONS
Created

1986   *Ackner,* Desmond James Conrad Ackner, PC,
       b. 1920, *m.*
1980   *Bridge of Harwich,* Nigel Cyprian Bridge, PC,
       b. 1917, *m.*
1982   *Brightman,* John Anson, Brightman PC,
       b. 1911, *m.*
2004   *Brown of Eaton-under-Heywood,* Simon Denis
       Brown, PC, *b.* 1937, *m. Lord of Appeal in
       Ordinary*
1991   *Browne-Wilkinson,* Nicolas Christopher Henry
       Browne-Wilkinson, PC, *b.* 1930, *m.*
2004   *Carswell,* Robert Douglas Carswell, PC, *b.* 1934,
       m. Lord of Appeal in Ordinary
1996   *Clyde,* James John Clyde, PC, *b.* 1932, *m.*
1986   *Goff of Chieveley,* Robert Lionel Archibald Goff,
       PC, *b.* 1926, *m.*
1985   *Griffiths,* (William) Hugh Griffiths, MC, PC,
       b. 1923, *m.*
1995   *Hoffmann,* Leonard Hubert Hoffmann, PC,
       b. 1934, *m. Lord of Appeal in Ordinary*
1997   *Hutton,* (James) Brian (Edward) Hutton, PC,
       b. 1931, *m.*
1988   *Jauncey of Tullichettle,* Charles Eliot Jauncey, PC,
       b. 1925, *m.*
1979   *Lane,* Geoffrey Dawson Lane, AFC, PC,
       b. 1918, *m.*
1993   *Lloyd of Berwick,* Anthony John Leslie Lloyd,
       PC, *b.* 1929, *m.*
1998   *Millett,* Peter Julian Millett, PC, *b.* 1932, *m.*

1992   *Mustill,* Michael John Mustill, PC, *b.* 1931, *m.*
1994   *Nicholls of Birkenhead,* Donald James Nicholls,
       PC, *b.* 1933, *m. Second Senior Lord of Appeal
       in Ordinary*
1994   *Nolan,* Michael Patrick Nolan, PC, *b.* 1928, *m.*
1986   *Oliver of Aylmerton,* Peter Raymond Oliver, PC,
       b. 1921, *m.*
1999   *Phillips of Worth Matravers,* Nicholas Addison
       Phillips, b. 1938, *m. Master of the Rolls*
1997   *Saville of Newdigate,* Mark Oliver Saville, PC,
       b. 1936, *m. Lord of Appeal in Ordinary*
1977   *Scarman,* Leslie George Scarman, OBE, PC,
       b. 1911, *m.*
1992   *Slynn of Hadley,* Gordon Slynn, PC, *b.* 1930, *m.*
1995   *Steyn,* Johan van Zyl Steyn, PC, *b.* 1932, *m. Lord
       of Appeal in Ordinary*
1982   *Templeman,* Sydney William Templeman, MBE,
       PC, *b.* 1920, *m.*
1992   *Woolf,* Harry Kenneth Woolf, PC, *b.* 1933, *m.
       Lord Chief Justice of England and Wales*

BARONESSES
2004   *Hale of Richmond,* Brenda Marjorie Hale, DBE,
       PC, *b.* 1945, *m., Lord of Appeal in Ordinary*

CREATED UNDER THE LIFE PEERAGES ACT 1958

* Hereditary peer who has been granted a life peerage. For further details, please refer to the Hereditary Peers section, pages 44–64. For example, life peer *Balniel* can be found under his hereditary title *Earl of Crawford and Balcarres.*

BARONS
Created

2000   **Acton of Bridgnorth,* Lord Acton, *b.* 1941, *m.*
       (see Hereditary Peers)
2001   *Adebowale,* Victor Olufemi Adebowale, CBE,
       b. 1962
1998   *Ahmed,* Nazir Ahmed, *b.* 1957, *m.*
1996   *Alderdice,* John Thomas Alderdice, *b.* 1955, *m.*
1988   *Alexander of Weedon,* Robert Scott Alexander,
       QC, *b.* 1936, *m.*
1976   *Allen of Abbeydale,* Philip Allen, GCB,
       b. 1912, *w.*
1998   *Alli,* Waheed Alli, *b.* 1964
2004   *Alliance,* David Alliance, GBE, *b.* 1932
1997   *Alton of Liverpool,* David Patrick Paul Alton,
       b. 1951, *m.*
1992   *Archer of Sandwell,* Peter Kingsley Archer, PC,
       QC, *b.* 1926, *m.*
1992   *Archer of Weston-super-Mare,* Jeffrey Howard
       Archer, *b.* 1940, *m.*
1988   *Armstrong of Ilminster,* Robert Temple
       Armstrong, GCB, CVO, *b.* 1927, *m.*
1999   **Armstrong-Jones,* Earl of Snowdon, GCVO,
       b. 1930, *m.* (see Hereditary Peers)
2000   *Ashcroft,* Michael Anthony Ashcroft, KCMG,
2001   *Ashdown of Norton-sub-Hamdon,* Jeremy John
       Durham (Paddy) Ashdown, KBE, PC,
       b. 1941, *m.*
1992   *Ashley of Stoke,* Jack Ashley, CH, PC, *b.* 1922, *w.*
1993   *Attenborough,* Richard Samuel Attenborough,
       CBE, *b.* 1923, *m.*
1998   *Bach,* William Stephen Goulden Bach,
       b. 1946, *m.*
1997   *Bagri,* Raj Kumar Bagri, CBE, *b.* 1930, *m.*

1997   *Baker of Dorking*, Kenneth Wilfred Baker, CH,
PC, *b. 1934, m.*

2004   *Ballyedmond*, Dr Edward Haughey, OBE,
b. 1944, m.

1974   **Balniel*, The Earl of Crawford and Balcarres,
b. 1927, m. (see Hereditary Peers)

1974   *Barber*, Anthony Perrinott Lysberg Barber, TD,
PC, *b. 1920, m.*

1992   *Barber of Tewkesbury*, Derek Coates Barber,
b. 1918, m.

1983   *Barnett*, Joel Barnett, PC, *b. 1923, m.*

1997   *Bassam of Brighton*, (John) Steven Bassam,
b. 1953

1967   *Beaumont of Whitley*, Revd Timothy Wentworth
Beaumont, *b. 1928, m.*

1998   *Bell*, Timothy John Leigh Bell, *b. 1941, m.*

2000   *Bernstein of Craigweil*, Alexander Bernstein,
b. 1936, m.

2001   *Best*, Richard Stuart Best, OBE, *b. 1945, m.*

2001   *Bhatia*, Amirali Alibhai Bhatia, OBE, *b. 1932, m.*

2004   *Bhattacharyya*, Prof. (Sushantha) Kumar
Bhattacharyya, CBE *b. 1932, m.*

1997   *Biffen*, (William) John Biffen, PC, *b. 1930, m.*

1996   *Bingham of Cornhill*, Thomas Henry Bingham,
PC, *b. 1933, m. Senior Lord of Appeal in
Ordinary*

2000   *Birt*, John Francis Hodgess Birt, *b. 1944, m.*

2001   *Black of Crossharbour*, Conrad Moffat Black,
OC, PC, *b. 1944, m.*

1997   *Blackwell*, Norman Roy Blackwell, *b. 1952, m.*

1994   *Blaker*, Peter Allan Renshaw Blaker, KCMG, PC,
b. 1922, m.

1978   *Blease*, William John Blease, *b. 1914, m.*

1995   *Blyth of Rowington*, James Blyth, *b. 1940, m.*

1996   *Borrie*, Gordon Johnson Borrie, QC, *b. 1931, m.*

1976   *Boston of Faversham*, Terence George Boston,
QC, *b. 1930, m.*

1996   *Bowness*, Peter Spencer Bowness, CBE,
b. 1943, m.

2003   *Boyce*, Michael Boyce, GCB, OBE, *b. 1943*

1999   *Bradshaw*, William Peter Bradshaw, *b. 1936, m.*

1998   *Bragg*, Melvyn Bragg, *b. 1939, m.*

1987   *Bramall*, Edwin Noel Westby Bramall, KG, GCB,
OBE, MC, *b. 1923, m.*

2000   *Brennan*, Daniel Joseph Brennan, QC,
b. 1942, m.

1999   *Brett*, William Henry Brett, *b. 1942, m.*

1976   *Briggs*, Asa Briggs, FBA, *b. 1921, m.*

2000   *Brittan of Spennithorne*, Leon Brittan, PC, QC,
b. 1939, m.

2004   *Broers*, Prof. Alec (Nigel) Broers, *b. 1938, m.*

1997   *Brooke of Alverthorpe*, Clive Brooke, *b. 1942, m.*

2001   *Brooke of Sutton Mandeville*, Peter Leonard
Brooke, CH, PC, *b. 1934, m.*

1998   *Brookman*, David Keith Brookman, *b. 1937, m.*

1979   *Brooks of Tremorfa*, John Edward Brooks,
b. 1927, m.

2001   *Browne of Madingley*, Edmund John Phillip
Browne, *b. 1948*

1974   *Bruce of Donington*, Donald William Trevor
Bruce, *b. 1912, m.*

1997   *Burlison*, Thomas Henry Burlison, *b. 1936, m.*

1998   *Burns*, Terence Burns, GCB, *b. 1944, m.*

1998   *Butler of Brockwell*, (Frederick Edward) Robin
Butler, KG, GCB, CVO, *b. 1938, m.*

1978   *Buxton of Alsa*, Aubrey Leland Oakes Buxton,
KCVO, MC, *b. 1918, m.*

1987   *Callaghan of Cardiff*, (Leonard) James
Callaghan, KG, PC, *b. 1912, m.*

2004   *Cameron of Dillington*, Ewen (James Hanning)
Cameron, *b. 1949, m.*

1984   *Cameron of Lochbroom*, Kenneth John Cameron,
PC, *b. 1931, m.*

1981   *Campbell of Alloway*, Alan Robertson Campbell,
QC, *b. 1917, m.*

1974   *Campbell of Croy*, Gordon Thomas Calthrop
Campbell, MC, PC, *b. 1921, m.*

2001   *Campbell-Savours*, Dale Norman Campbell-
Savours, *b. 1943, m.*

2002   *Carey of Clifton*, Rt. Revd George Leonard
Carey, PC, *b. 1935, m.*

1999   **Carington of Upton*, Lord Carrington, GCMG,
b. 1919, m. (see Hereditary Peers)

1999   *Carlile of Berriew*, Alexander Charles Carlile,
QC, *b. 1948, m.*

1987   *Carlisle of Bucklow*, Mark Carlisle, QC, PC,
b. 1929, m.

1975   *Carr of Hadley*, (Leonard) Robert Carr, PC,
b. 1916, m.

1987   *Carter*, Denis Victor Carter, PC, *b. 1932, m.*

2004   *Carter of Coles*, Patrick Robert Carter,
b. 1946, m.

1990   *Cavendish of Furness*, (Richard) Hugh Cavendish,
b. 1941, m.

1996   *Chadlington*, Peter Selwyn Gummer, *b. 1942, m.*

1964   *Chalfont*, (Alun) Arthur Gwynne Jones, OBE,
MC, PC, *b. 1919, m.*

2001   *Chan*, Michael Chew Koon Chan, MBE,
b. 1940, m.

1985   *Chapple*, Francis (Frank) Joseph Chapple,
b. 1921, w.

1987   *Chilver*, (Amos) Henry Chilver, FRS, FREng,
b. 1926, m.

1977   *Chitnis*, Pratap Chidamber Chitnis, *b. 1936, m.*

1998   *Christopher*, Anthony Martin Grosvenor
Christopher, CBE, *b. 1925, m.*

1992   *Clark of Kempston*, William Gibson Haig Clark,
PC, *b. 1917, m.*

2001   *Clark of Windermere*, David George Clark, PC,
PHD, *b. 1939, m.*

1998   *Clarke of Hampstead*, Anthony James Clarke,
CBE, *b. 1932, m.*

1998   *Clement-Jones*, Timothy Francis Clement-Jones,
CBE, *b. 1949, m.*

1990   *Clinton-Davis*, Stanley Clinton Clinton-Davis,
PC, *b. 1928, m.*

1978   *Cockfield*, (Francis) Arthur Cockfield, PC,
b. 1916, w.

2000   *Coe*, Sebastian Newbold Coe, OBE, *b. 1956, m.*

2001   *Condon*, Paul Leslie Condon, QPM, *m.*

1992   *Cooke of Islandreagh*, Victor Alexander Cooke,
OBE, *b. 1920, m.*

1996   *Cooke of Thorndon*, Robin Brunskill Cooke,
KBE, PC, PHD, *b. 1926, m.*

1997   *Cope of Berkeley*, John Ambrose Cope, PC,
b. 1937, m.

2001   *Corbett of Castle Vale*, Robin Corbett,
b. 1933, m.

1991   *Craig of Radley*, David Brownrigg Craig, GCB,
OBE, *b. 1929, m.*

1987   *Crickhowell*, (Roger) Nicholas Edwards, PC,
b. 1934, m.

1978   *Croham*, Douglas Albert Vivian Allen, GCB,
b. 1917, w.

2003 *Cullen,* William Douglas Cullen, PC, *b.* 1935, *m.*
Lord Justice General of Scotland and Lord
President of the Court of Session

1995 *Cuckney,* John Graham Cuckney, *b.* 1925, *w.*

1996 *Currie of Marylebone,* David Anthony Currie,
b. 1946, *m.*

1993 *Dahrendorf,* Ralf Dahrendorf, KBE, PHD, DPHIL,
FBA, *b.* 1929, *m.*

1997 *Davies of Coity,* (David) Garfield Davies, CBE,
b. 1935, *m.*

1997 *Davies of Oldham,* Bryan Davies, *b.* 1939, *m.*

1993 *Dean of Harptree,* (Arthur) Paul Dean, PC,
b. 1924, *m.*

1998 *Dearing,* Ronald Ernest Dearing, *b.* 1930, *m.*

1986 *Deedes,* William Francis Deedes, KBE MC, PC,
b. 1913, *w.*

1991 *Desai,* Prof. Meghnad Jagdishchandra Desai,
PHD, *b.* 1940, *m.*

1997 *Dholakia,* Navnit Dholakia, OBE, *b.* 1937, *m.*

1997 *Dixon,* Donald Dixon, PC, *b.* 1929, *m.*

1993 *Dixon-Smith,* Robert William Dixon-Smith,
b. 1934, *m.*

1988 *Donaldson of Lymington,* John Francis
Donaldson, PC, *b.* 1920, *m.*

1985 *Donoughue,* Bernard Donoughue, DPHIL,
b. 1934

2004 *Drayson,* Paul Rudd Drayson, *b.* 1960, *m.*

1994 *Dubs,* Alfred Dubs, *b.* 1932, *m.*

2004 *Dykes,* Hugh John Maxwell Dykes, *b.* 1939, *m.*

1995 *Eames,* Robert Henry Alexander Eames, PHD,
b. 1937, *m.*

1992 *Eatwell,* John Leonard Eatwell, PHD, *b.* 1945, *m.*

1983 *Eden of Winton,* John Benedict Eden, PC,
b. 1925, *m.*

1999 *Elder,* Thomas Murray Elder, *b.* 1950

1992 *Elis-Thomas,* Dafydd Elis Elis-Thomas,
b. 1946, *m.*

1985 *Elliott of Morpeth,* Robert William Elliott,
b. 1920, *m.*

1981 *Elystan-Morgan,* Dafydd Elystan Elystan-
Morgan, *b.* 1932, *m.*

2000 **Erskine of Alloa Tower,* Earl of Mar and Kellie,
b. 1949, *m.* (*see* Hereditary Peers)

1997 *Evans of Parkside,* John Evans, *b.* 1930, *m.*

2000 *Evans of Temple Guiting,* Matthew Evans, CBE,
b. 1941, *m.*

1998 *Evans of Watford,* David Charles Evans,
b. 1942, *m.*

1992 *Ewing of Kirkford,* Harry Ewing, *b.* 1931, *m.*

1983 *Ezra,* Derek Ezra, MBE, *b.* 1919, *m.*

1997 *Falconer of Thoroton,* Charles Leslie Falconer,
QC, *b.* 1951, *m.*

1999 *Faulkner of Worcester,* Richard Oliver Faulkner,
b. 1946, *m.*

2001 *Fearn,* Ronald Cyril Fearn, OBE, *b.* 1931, *m.*

1996 *Feldman,* Basil Feldman, *b.* 1926, *m.*

1999 *Fellowes,* Robert Fellowes, GCB, GCVO, PC,
b. 1941, *m.*

1999 *Filkin,* David Geoffrey Nigel Filkin, CBE,
b. 1944

1983 *Fitt,* Gerard Fitt, *b.* 1926, *w.*

1979 *Flowers,* Brian Hilton Flowers, FRS, *b.* 1924, *m.*

1999 *Forsyth of Drumlean,* Michael Bruce Forsyth,
b. 1954, *m.*

1982 *Forte,* Charles Forte, *b.* 1908, *m.*

1999 *Foster of Thames Bank,* Norman Robert Foster,
OM, *b.* 1935, *m.*

2001 *Fowler,* (Peter) Norman Fowler, PC, *b.* 1938, *m.*

1989 *Fraser of Carmyllie,* Peter Lovat Fraser, PC, QC,
b. 1945, *m.*

1997 *Freeman,* Roger Norman Freeman, PC,
b. 1942, *m.*

2000 *Fyfe of Fairfield,* George Lennox Fyfe,
b. 1941, *m.*

1999 **Ganzoni,* Lord Belstead, PC, *b.* 1932, (*see*
Hereditary Peers)

2004 *Garden,* Timothy Garden, KCB, *b.* 1939, *m.*

1997 *Garel-Jones,* (William Armand) Thomas Tristan
Garel-Jones, PC, *b.* 1941, *m.*

1999 **Gascoyne-Cecil,* The Marquess of Salisbury, PC ,
b. 1946, *m.* (see Hereditary Peers)

1999 *Gavron,* Robert Gavron, CBE, *b.* 1930, *m.*

2004 *George,* Edward (Alan John) George, GBE, PC,
b. 1938, *m.*

2004 *Giddens,* Prof. Anthony Giddens, *b.* 1938, *m.*

1997 *Gilbert,* John William Gilbert, PC, PHD,
b. 1927, *m.*

1992 *Gilmour of Craigmillar,* Ian Hedworth John
Little Gilmour, PC, *b.* 1926, *m.*

1977 *Glenamara,* Edward Watson Short, CH, PC,
b. 1912, *m.*

1999 *Goldsmith,* Peter Henry Goldsmith, QC,
b. 1950, *m.*

1997 *Goodhart,* William Howard Goodhart, QC,
b. 1933, *m.*

1997 *Gordon of Strathblane,* James Stuart Gordon,
CBE, *b.* 1936, *m.*

2004 *Gould of Brookwood,* Philip Gould *b.* 1950 *m.*

1999 *Grabiner,* Anthony Stephen Grabiner, QC,
b. 1945, *m.*

1983 *Graham of Edmonton,* (Thomas) Edward
Graham, *b.* 1925, *m.*

1983 *Gray of Contin,* James (Hamish) Hector Northey
Gray, PC, *b.* 1927, *m.*

2000 *Greaves,* Anthony Robert Greaves, *b.* 1942, *m.*

1975 *Gregson,* John Gregson, *b.* 1924

2000 **Grenfell of Kilvey,* Lord Grenfell, *b.* 1935, *m.*
(*see* Hereditary Peers)

2004 *Griffiths of Burry Port,* Revd. Dr Leslie John
Griffiths, *b.* 1942, *m.*

1991 *Griffiths of Fforestfach,* Brian Griffiths,
b. 1941, *m.*

2001 *Grocott,* Bruce Joseph Grocott, PC, *b.* 1940, *m.*

2000 **Gueterbock,* Lord Berkley, OBE, *b.* 1939, *m.* (*see*
Hereditary Peers)

2000 *Guthrie of Craigiebank,* Charles Ronald
Llewelyn Guthrie, GCB, LVO, OBE, *b.* 1938, *m.*

1995 *Habgood,* Rt. Revd John Stapylton Habgood, PC,
PHD, *b.* 1927, *m.*

2001 *Hannay of Chiswick,* David Hugh Alexander
Hannay, GCMG, CH, *b.* 1935, *m.*

1998 *Hanningfield,* Paul Edward Winston White,
b. 1940

1983 *Hanson,* James Edward Hanson, *b.* 1922, *w.*

1997 *Hardie,* Andrew Rutherford Hardie, QC, PC,
b. 1946, *m.*

1998 *Harris of Haringey,* (Jonathan) Toby Harris,
b. 1953, *m.*

1979 *Harris of High Cross,* Ralph Harris, *b.* 1924, *m.*

1996 *Harris of Peckham,* Philip Charles Harris,
b. 1942, *m.*

1999 *Harrison,* Lyndon Henry Arthur Harrison,
b. 1947, *m.*

2004 *Hart of Chilton,* Garry Richard Rushby Hart,
b. 1940, *m.*

1993 *Haskel,* Simon Haskel, *b.* 1934, *m.*

1998   *Haskins,* Christopher Robin Haskins, *b.* 1937, *m.*

1997   *Hattersley,* Roy Sidney George Hattersley, PC,
    b. 1932, *m.*

2004   *Haworth,* Alan Robert Haworth, *b.* 1948, *m.*

1992   *Hayhoe,* Bernard John (Barney) Hayhoe, PC,
    b. 1925, *m.*

1992   *Healey,* Denis Winston Healey, CH, MBE, PC,
    b. 1917, *m.*

1999   *Hennessey,* Lord Windlesham, CVO, *b.* 1932, *m.*
    (*see* Hereditary Peers)

2001   *Heseltine,* Michael Ray Dibdin Heseltine, CH,
    PC, *b.* 1933, *m.*

1997   *Higgins,* Terence Langley Higgins, KBE, PC,
    b. 1928, *m.*

2000   *Hodgson of Astley Abbotts,* Robin Granville
    Hodgson, CBE, *b.* 1942, *m.*

1997   *Hogg of Cumbernauld,* Norman Hogg,
    b. 1938, *m.*

1991   *Hollick,* Clive Richard Hollick, *b.* 1945, *m.*

1990   *Holme of Cheltenham,* Richard Gordon Holme,
    CBE, *b.* 1936, *m.*

1979   *Hooson,* (Hugh) Emlyn Hooson, QC, *b.* 1925, *m.*

1995   *Hope of Craighead,* (James Arthur) David Hope,
    PC, *b.* 1938, *m. Lord of Appeal in Ordinary*

2004   *Howard of Rising,* Greville Patrick Charles
    Howard, *b.* 1941, *m.*

1992   *Howe of Aberavon,* (Richard Edward) Geoffrey
    Howe, CH, PC, QC, *b.* 1926, *m.*

1997   *Howell of Guildford,* David Arthur Russell
    Howell, PC, *b.* 1936, *m.*

1978   *Howie of Troon,* William Howie, *b.* 1924, *m.*

1997   *Hoyle,* (Eric) Douglas Harvey Hoyle, *b.* 1930, *w.*

1997   *Hughes of Woodside,* Robert Hughes, *b.* 1932, *m.*

2000   *Hunt of Chesterton,* Julian Charles Roland Hunt,
    CBE, *b.* 1941, *m.*

1997   *Hunt of Kings Heath,* Philip Alexander Hunt,
    OBE, *b.* 1949, *m.*

1980   *Hunt of Tanworth,* John Joseph Benedict Hunt,
    GCB, *b.* 1919, *m.*

1997   *Hunt of Wirral,* David James Fletcher Hunt,
    MBE, PC, *b.* 1942, *m.*

1997   *Hurd of Westwell,* Douglas Richard Hurd, CH,
    CBE, PC, *b.* 1930, *m.*

1996   *Hussey of North Bradley,* Marmaduke James
    Hussey, *b.* 1923, *m.*

1978   *Hutchinson of Lullington,* Jeremy Nicolas
    Hutchinson, QC, *b.* 1915, *m.*

1999   *Imbert,* Peter Michael Imbert, QPM, *b.* 1933, *m.*

1997   *Inge,* Peter Anthony Inge, KG, GCB, *b.* 1935, *m.*

1987   *Irvine of Lairg,* Alexander Andrew Mackay
    Irvine, PC, QC, *b.* 1940, *m.*

1997   *Jacobs,* (David) Anthony Jacobs, *b.* 1931, *m.*

1997   *Janner of Braunstone,* Greville Ewan Janner, QC,
    b. 1928, *w.*

1999   *Jellicoe of Southampton,* Earl Jellicoe, KBE,
    b. 1918, *w.* (*see* Hereditary Peers)

1987   *Jenkin of Roding,* (Charles) Patrick (Fleeming)
    Jenkin, PC, *b.* 1926, *m.*

2000   *Joffe,* Joel Goodman Joffe, CBE, *b.* 1932, *m.*

2001   *Jones,* (Stephen) Barry Jones, *b.* 1937, *m.*

1997   *Jopling,* (Thomas) Michael Jopling, PC,
    b. 1930, *m.*

2000   *Jordan,* William Brian Jordan, CBE, *b.* 1936, *m.*

1991   *Judd,* Frank Ashcroft Judd, *b.* 1935, *m.*

2004   *Kalms,* Harold Stanley Kalms, *b.* 1931 *m.*

1997   *Kelvedon,* (Henry) Paul Guinness Channon, PC,
    b. 1935, *m.*

2004   *Kerr of Kinlochard,* John (Olav) Kerr, GCMG,
    b. 1942, *m.*

2001   *Kilclooney,* John David Taylor, PC (NI),
    b. 1937, *m.*

1996   *Kilpatrick of Kincraig,* Robert Kilpatrick, CBE,
    b. 1926, *m.*

1985   *Kimball,* Marcus Richard Kimball, *b.* 1928, *m.*

2001   *King of Bridgwater,* Thomas Jeremy King, CH,
    PC, *b.* 1933, *m.*

1983   *King of Wartnaby,* John Leonard King,
    b. 1918, *m.*

1999   *King of West Bromwich,* Tarsem King, *b.* 1937

1993   *Kingsdown,* Robert (Robin) Leigh-Pemberton,
    KG, PC, *b.* 1927, *m.*

1994   *Kingsland,* Christopher James Prout, TD, PC,
    QC, *b.* 1942

1999   *Kirkham,* Graham Kirkham, *b.* 1944, *m.*

1975   *Kirkhill,* John Farquharson Smith, *b.* 1930, *m.*

1987   *Knights,* Philip Douglas Knights, CBE, QPM,
    b. 1920, *m.*

2004   *Laidlaw,* Irvine Alan Stewart Laidlaw,
    b. 1942, *m.*

1991   *Laing of Dunphail,* Hector Laing, *b.* 1923, *m.*

1999   *Laird,* John Dunn Laird, *b.* 1944, *m.*

1998   *Laming,* (William) Herbert Laming, CBE,
    b. 1936, *m.*

1998   *Lamont of Lerwick,* Norman Stewart Hughson
    Lamont, PC, *b.* 1942, *m.*

1990   *Lane of Horsell,* Peter Stewart Lane, *b.* 1925, *w.*

1997   *Lang of Monkton,* Ian Bruce Lang, PC,
    b. 1940, *m.*

1992   *Lawson of Blaby,* Nigel Lawson, PC, *b.* 1932, *m.*

2000   *Layard,* Peter Richard Grenville Layard,
    b. 1934, *m.*

1999   *Lea of Crondall,* David Edward Lea, OBE,
    b. 1937

2004   *Leitch,* Alexander Park Leitch, *b.* 1947, *m.*

1993   *Lester of Herne Hill,* Anthony Paul Lester, QC,
    b. 1936, *m.*

1997   *Levene of Portsoken,* Peter Keith Levene, KBE,
    b. 1941, *m.*

1997   *Levy,* Michael Abraham Levy, *b.* 1944, *m.*

1989   *Lewis of Newnham,* Jack Lewis, FRS, *b.* 1928, *m.*

1999   *Lipsey,* David Lawrence Lipsey, *b.* 1948, *m.*

2001   *Livsey of Talgarth,* Richard Arthur Lloyd Livsey,
    CBE, *b.* 1935, *m.*

1997   *Lloyd-Webber,* Andrew Lloyd Webber,
    b. 1948, *m.*

1997   *Lofthouse of Pontefract,* Geoffrey Lofthouse,
    b. 1925, *w.*

2000   *Luce,* Richard Napier Luce, GCVO, PC,
    b. 1936, *m.*

2000   *Lyttleton of Aldershot,* The Viscount Chandos,
    b. 1953, *m.* (*see* Hereditary Peers)

1984   *McAlpine of West Green,* (Robert) Alistair
    McAlpine, *b.* 1942, *m.*

1988   *Macaulay of Bragar,* Donald Macaulay, QC,
    b. 1933, *m.*

1975   *McCarthy,* William Edward John McCarthy,
    DPHIL, *b.* 1925, *m.*

1976   *McCluskey,* John Herbert McCluskey,
    b. 1929, *m.*

1989   *McColl of Dulwich,* Ian McColl, CBE, FRCS,
    FRCSE, *b.* 1933, *m.*

1998   *Macdonald of Tradeston,* Angus John
    Macdonald, CBE, *b.* 1940, *m.*

1991   *Macfarlane of Bearsden,* Norman Somerville
    Macfarlane, KT, FRSE, *b.* 1926, *m.*

2001	*MacGregor of Pulham Market,* John Roddick Russell MacGregor, CBE, PC, *b.* 1937, *m.*	2000	*Oakeshott of Seagrove Bay,* Matthew Alan Oakeshott, *b.* 1947, *m.*
1982	*McIntosh of Haringey,* Andrew Robert McIntosh, *b.* 1933, *m.*	1997	*Orme,* Stanley Orme, PC, *b.* 1923, *m.*
		2001	*Ouseley,* Herman George Ouseley, *b.* 1945, *m.*
1979	*Mackay of Clashfern,* James Peter Hymers Mackay, KT, PC, FRSE, *b.* 1927, *m.*	1992	*Owen,* David Anthony Llewellyn Owen, CH, PC, *b.* 1938, *m.*
1995	*Mackay of Drumadoon,* Donald Sage Mackay, PC, *b.* 1946, *m.*	1999	*Oxburgh,* Ernest Ronald Oxburgh, KBE, FRS, PHD, *b.* 1934, *m.*
2004	*McKenzie of Luton,* William David McKenzie, *b.* 1946, *m.*	1991	*Palumbo,* Peter Garth Palumbo, *b.* 1935, *m.*
1999	*Mackenzie of Culkein,* Hector Uisdean MacKenzie, *b.* 1940	2000	*Parekh,* Bhikhu Chhotalal Parekh, *b.* 1935, *m.*
1998	*Mackenzie of Framwellgate,* Brian Mackenzie, OBE, *b.* 1943, *m.*	1992	*Parkinson,* Cecil Edward Parkinson, PC, *b.* 1931, *m.*
1974	*Mackie of Benshie,* George Yull Mackie, CBE, DSO, DFC, *b.* 1919, *m.*	1975	*Parry,* Gordon Samuel David Parry, *b.* 1925, *m.*
1996	*MacLaurin of Knebworth,* Ian Charter MacLaurin, *b.* 1937, *m.*	1999	*Patel,* Narendra Babubhai Patel, *b.* 1938
		2000	*Patel of Blackburn,* Adam Hafejee Patel, *b.* 1940
2001	*Maclennon of Rogart,* Robert Adam Ross Maclennan, PC, *b.* 1936, *m.*	1997	*Patten,* John Haggitt Charles Patten, PC, *b.* 1945, *m.*
1995	*McNally,* Tom McNally, *b.* 1943, *m.*	1996	*Paul,* Swraj Paul, *b.* 1931, *m.*
2001	*Maginnis of Drumglass,* Kenneth Wiggins Maginnis, *b.* 1938, *m.*	1990	*Pearson of Rannoch,* Malcolm Everard MacLaren Pearson, *b.* 1942, *m.*
1991	*Marlesford,* Mark Shuldham Schreiber, *b.* 1931, *m.*	2001	*Pendry,* Thomas Pendry, *b.* 1934, *m.*
		1987	*Peston,* Maurice Harry Peston, *b.* 1931, *m.*
1981	*Marsh,* Richard William Marsh, PC, *b.* 1928, *m.*	1983	*Peyton of Yeovil,* John Wynne William Peyton, PC, *b.* 1919, *m.*
1998	*Marshall of Knightsbridge,* Colin Marsh Marshall, *b.* 1933, *m.*	1998	*Phillips of Sudbury,* Andrew Wyndham Phillips, OBE, *b.* 1939, *m.*
1987	*Mason of Barnsley,* Roy Mason, PC, *b.* 1924, *m.*	1996	*Pilkington of Oxenford,* Revd Canon Peter Pilkington, *b.* 1933, *w.*
2004	*Maxton,* John Alston Maxton, *b.* 1936, *m.*		
2001	*May of Oxford,* Robert McCredie May, OM, *b.* 1936, *m.*	1992	*Plant of Highfield,* Prof. Raymond Plant, PHD, *b.* 1945, *m.*
1997	*Mayhew of Twysden,* Patrick Barnabas Burke Mayhew, QC, PC, *b.* 1929, *m.*	1987	*Plumb,* (Charles) Henry Plumb, *b.* 1925, *m.*
		1981	*Plummer of St Marylebone,* (Arthur) Desmond (Herne) Plummer, TD, *b.* 1914, *m.*
1992	*Merlyn-Rees,* Merlyn Merlyn-Rees, PC, *b.* 1920, *m.*	2000	**Ponsonby of Roehampton,* Lord Ponsonby of Shulbrede, *b.* 1958 (*see* Hereditary Peers)
1978	*Mishcon,* Victor Mishcon, QC, *b.* 1915, *m.*	2000	*Powell of Bayswater,* Charles David Powell, KCMG, *b.* 1941
2000	*Mitchell,* Parry Andrew Mitchell, *b.* 1943		
2000	**Mitford,* Lord Redesdale, *b.* 1967, *m.* (*see* Hereditary Peers)	1987	*Prior,* James Michael Leathes Prior, PC, *b.* 1927, *m.*
1997	*Molyneaux of Killead,* James Henry Molyneaux, KBE, PC, *b.* 1920	1982	*Prys-Davies,* Gwilym Prys Prys-Davies, *b.* 1923, *m.*
1997	*Monro of Langholm,* Hector Seymour Peter Monro, AE, PC, *b.* 1922, *m.*	1997	*Puttnam,* David Terence Puttnam, CBE, *b.* 1941, *m.*
1992	*Moore of Lower Marsh,* John Edward Michael Moore, PC, *b.* 1937, *m.*	1987	*Pym,* Francis Leslie Pym, MC, PC, *b.* 1922, *m.*
		1982	*Quinton,* Anthony Meredith Quinton, FBA, *b.* 1925, *m.*
1986	*Moore of Wolvercote,* Philip Brian Cecil Moore, GCB, GCVO, CMG, PC, *b.* 1921, *m.*	1994	*Quirk,* Prof. (Charles) Randolph Quirk, CBE, FBA, *b.* 1920, *m.*
2000	*Morgan,* Kenneth Owen Morgan, *b.* 1934, *m.*	2001	*Radice,* Giles Heneage Radice, PC, *b.* 1936
2001	*Morris of Aberavon,* John Morris, KG, QC, *b.* 1931, *m.*	2004	*Rana,* Dr Diljit Singh Rana, MBE, *b.* 1938, *m.*
1997	*Morris of Manchester,* Alfred Morris, PC, *b.* 1928, *m.*	1997	*Randall of St Budeaux,* Stuart Jeffrey Randall, *b.* 1938, *m.*
2001	*Moser,* Claus Adolf Moser, KCB, CBE, *b.* 1922, *m.*	1978	*Rawlinson of Ewell,* Peter Anthony Grayson Rawlinson, PC, QC, *b.* 1919, *m.*
1979	*Murton of Lindisfarne,* (Henry) Oscar Murton, OBE, TD, PC, *b.* 1914, *m.*	1997	*Razzall,* (Edward) Timothy Razzall, CBE, *b.* 1943, *m.*
1997	*Naseby,* Michael Wolfgang Laurence Morris, PC, *b.* 1936, *m.*	1987	*Rees,* Peter Wynford Innes Rees, PC, QC, *b.* 1926, *m.*
1997	*Neill of Bladen,* (Francis) Patrick Neill, QC, *b.* 1926, *m.*	1988	*Rees-Mogg,* William Rees-Mogg, *b.* 1928, *m.*
		1991	*Renfrew of Kaimsthorn,* (Andrew) Colin Renfrew, FBA, *b.* 1937, *m.*
1997	*Newby,* Richard Mark Newby, OBE, *b.* 1953, *m.*		
1997	*Newton of Braintree,* Antony Harold Newton, OBE, PC, *b.* 1937, *m.*	1999	*Rennard,* Christopher John Rennard, MBE, *b.* 1960
1994	*Nickson,* David Wigley Nickson, KBE, FRSE, *b.* 1929, *m.*	1979	*Renton,* David Lockhart-Mure Renton, KBE, TD, PC, QC, *b.* 1908, *w.*
1975	*Northfield,* (William) Donald Chapman, *b.* 1923	1997	*Renton of Mount Harry,* (Ronald) Timothy Renton, PC, *b.* 1932, *m.*
1998	*Norton of Louth,* Philip Norton, *b.* 1951		

1997	Renwick of Clifton, Robin William Renwick, KCMG, b. 1937, m.
1990	Richard, Ivor Seward Richard, PC, QC, b. 1932, m.
1983	Richardson of Duntisbourne, Gordon William Humphreys Richardson, KG, MBE, TD, PC, b. 1915, m.
1992	Rix, Brian Norman Roger Rix, CBE, b. 1924, m.
2004	Roberts of Llandudno, Revd John Roger Roberts, b. 1935, m.
1997	Roberts of Conwy, (Ieuan) Wyn (Pritchard) Roberts, PC, b. 1930, m.
1999	Robertson of Port Ellen, George Islay MacNeill Robertson, PC, b. 1946, m.
1992	Rodger of Earlsferry, Alan Ferguson Rodger, PC, QC, FBA, b. 1944, Lord of Appeal in Ordinary
1992	Rodgers of Quarry Bank, William Thomas Rodgers, PC, b. 1928, m.
1999	Rogan, Dennis Robert David Rogan, b. 1942, m.
1996	Rogers of Riverside, Richard George Rogers, RA, RIBA, b. 1933, m.
1977	Roll of Ipsden, Eric Roll, KCMG, CB, b. 1907, w.
2001	Rooker, Jeffrey William Rooker, PC, b. 1941, m.
2000	Roper, John Francis Hodgess Roper, b. 1935, m.
2004	Rosser, Richard Andrew Rosser, b. 1944, m.
2004	Rowlands, Edward Rowlands, CBE, b. 1940, m.
1997	Russell-Johnston, (David) Russell Russell-Johnston, b. 1932, m.
1997	Ryder of Wensum, Richard Andrew Ryder, OBE, PC, b. 1949, m.
1996	Saatchi, Maurice Saatchi, b. 1946, m.
1989	Sainsbury of Preston Candover, John Davan Sainsbury, KG, b. 1927, m.
1997	Sainsbury of Turville, David John Sainsbury, b. 1940, m.
1987	St John of Fawsley, Norman Antony Francis St John-Stevas, PC, b. 1929
1997	Sandberg, Michael Graham Ruddock Sandberg, CBE, b. 1927, m.
1985	Sanderson of Bowden, Charles Russell Sanderson, b. 1933, m.
1998	Sawyer, Lawrence (Tom) Sawyer, b. 1943
2000	Scott of Foscote, Richard Rashleigh Folliott Scott, PC, b. 1934, m. Lord of Appeal in Ordinary
1997	Selkirk of Douglas, James Alexander Douglas-Hamilton, MSP, PC, QC, b. 1942, m.
1996	Sewel, John Buttifant Sewel, CBE, b. 1946
1999	Sharman, Colin Morven Sharman, OBE, b. 1943, m.
1994	Shaw of Northstead, Michael Norman Shaw, b. 1920, m.
2001	Sheldon, Robert Edward Sheldon, PC, b. 1923, m.
1994	Sheppard of Didgemere, Allan John George Sheppard, KCVO, b. 1932, m.
1998	Sheppard of Liverpool, David Stuart Sheppard, b. 1929, m.
2000	Shutt of Greetland, David Trevor Shutt, OBE, b. 1942
1971	Simon of Glaisdale, Jocelyn Edward Salis Simon, PC, b. 1911, m.
1997	Simon of Highbury, David Alec Gwyn Simon, CBE, b. 1939, m.
1997	Simpson of Dunkeld, George Simpson, b. 1942, m.
1991	Skidelsky, Robert Jacob Alexander Skidelsky, DPHIL, b. 1939, m.
1997	Smith of Clifton, Trevor Arthur Smith, b. 1937, m.
1999	Smith of Leigh, Peter Richard Charles Smith, b. 1945, m.
2004	Snape, Peter Charles Snape, b. 1942
1990	Soulsby of Swaffham Prior, Ernest Jackson Lawson Soulsby, PHD, b. 1926, m.
1983	Stallard, Albert William Stallard, b. 1921, m.
1997	Steel of Aikwood, David Martin Scott Steel, PC, KBE, MSP, b. 1938, m.
2004	Steinberg, Leonard Steinberg, b. 1936
1991	Sterling of Plaistow, Jeffrey Maurice Sterling, GCVO, CBE, b. 1934, m.
1987	Stevens of Ludgate, David Robert Stevens, b. 1936, m.
1999	Stevenson of Coddenham, Henry Dennistoun Stevenson, CBE, b. 1945, m.
1992	Stewartby, (Bernard Harold) Ian (Halley) Stewart, RD, PC, FBA, FRSE, b. 1935, m.
1983	Stoddart of Swindon, David Leonard Stoddart, b. 1926, m.
1969	Stokes, Donald Gresham Stokes, TD, FENG, b. 1914, w.
1997	Stone of Blackheath, Andrew Zelig Stone, b. 1942, m.
2001	Sutherland of Houndwood, Stewart Ross Sutherland, KT, b. 1941, m.
1971	Tanlaw, Simon Brooke Mackay, b. 1934, m.
1996	Taverne, Dick Taverne, QC, b. 1928, m.
1978	Taylor of Blackburn, Thomas Taylor, CBE, b. 1929, m.
1996	Taylor of Warwick, John David Beckett Taylor, b. 1952, m.
1992	Tebbit, Norman Beresford Tebbit, CH, PC, b. 1931, m.
2001	Temple-Morris, Peter Temple-Morris, b. 1938, m.
1996	Thomas of Gresford, Donald Martin Thomas, OBE, QC, b. 1937, m.
1987	Thomas of Gwydir, Peter John Mitchell Thomas, PC, QC, b. 1920, w.
1997	Thomas of Macclesfield, Terence James Thomas, CBE, b. 1937, m.
1981	Thomas of Swynnerton, Hugh Swynnerton Thomas, b. 1931, m.
1977	Thomson of Monifieth, George Morgan Thomson, KT, PC, b. 1921, m.
1990	Tombs, Francis Leonard Tombs, FENG, b. 1924, m.
1998	Tomlinson, John Edward Tomlinson, MEP, b. 1939
1994	Tope, Graham Norman Tope, CBE, b. 1943, m.
1981	Tordoff, Geoffrey Johnson Tordoff, b. 1928, m.
2004	Triesman, David Maxim Triesman, b. 1943
1999	Trotman, Alexander Trotman, b. 1933
2004	Truscott, Dr Peter Derek Truscott, b. 1959 m.
1993	Tugendhat, Christopher Samuel Tugendhat, b. 1937, m.
2004	Tunnicliffe, Denis Tunnicliffe, CBE, b. 1943, m.
2000	Turnberg, Leslie Arnold Turnberg, MD, b. 1934, m.
2004	Vallance of Tummel, Iain (David Thomas) Vallance, b. 1943, m.
1990	Varley, Eric Graham Varley, PC, b. 1932, m.
1996	Vincent of Coleshill, Richard Frederick Vincent, GBE, KCB, DSO, b. 1931, m.
1985	Vinson, Nigel Vinson, LVO, b. 1931, m.

1990   *Waddington,* David Charles Waddington, GCVO, PC, QC, *b.* 1929, *m.*
1990   *Wade of Chorlton,* (William) Oulton Wade, *b.* 1932, *m.*
1992   *Wakeham,* John Wakeham, PC, *b.* 1932, *m.*
1999   *Waldegrave of North Hill,* William Arthur Waldegrave, PC, *b.* 1946, *m.*
2003   *Walker of Gestingthorpe,* Robert Walker, PC, *b.* 1938, *m. Lord of Appeal in Ordinary*
1992   *Walker of Worcester,* Peter Edward Walker, MBE, PC, *b.* 1932, *m.*
1995   *Wallace of Saltaire,* William John Lawrence Wallace, PHD, *b.* 1941, *m.*
1989   *Walton of Detchant,* John Nicholas Walton, TD, FRCP, *b.* 1922, *m.*
1998   *Warner,* Norman Reginald Warner, *b.* 1940, *m.*
1997   *Watson of Invergowrie,* Michael Goodall Watson, MSP, *b.* 1949, *m.*
1999   *Watson of Richmond,* Alan John Watson, CBE, *b.* 1941, *m.*
1992   *Weatherill,* (Bruce) Bernard Weatherill, PC, *b.* 1920, *m.*
1977   *Wedderburn of Charlton,* (Kenneth) William Wedderburn, FBA, QC, *b.* 1927, *m.*
1976   *Weidenfeld,* (Arthur) George Weidenfeld, *b.* 1919, *m.*
1978   *Whaddon,* (John) Derek Page, *b.* 1927, *m.*
1996   *Whitty,* John Lawrence (Larry) Whitty, *b.* 1943, *m.*
1985   *Williams of Elvel,* Charles Cuthbert Powell Williams, CBE, *b.* 1933, *m.*
1999   *Williamson of Horton,* David (Francis) Williamson, GCMG, CB, *b.* 1934, *m.*
2002   *Wilson of Dinton,* Richard Thomas James Wilson, GCB, *b.* 1942, *m.*
1992   *Wilson of Tillyorn,* David Clive Wilson, KT, GCMG, PHD, *b.* 1935, *m.*
1995   *Winston,* Robert Maurice Lipson Winston, FRCOG, *b.* 1940, *m.*
1985   *Wolfson,* Leonard Gordon Wolfson, *b.* 1927, *m.*
1991   *Wolfson of Sunningdale,* David Wolfson, *b.* 1935, *m.*
1999   *Woolmer of Leeds,* Kenneth John Woolmer, *b.* 1940, *m.*
1994   *Wright of Richmond,* Patrick Richard Henry Wright, CGMG, *b.* 1931, *m.*
2004   *Young of Norwood Green,* Anthony (Ian) Young, *b.* 1942, *m.*
1984   *Young of Graffham,* David Ivor Young, PC, *b.* 1932, *m.*

BARONESSES
Created
1997   *Amos,* Valerie Ann Amos, *b.* 1954
2000   *Andrews,* Elizabeth Kay Andrews, OBE, *b.* 1943, *m.*
1996   *Anelay of St Johns,* Joyce Anne Anelay, DBE, *b.* 1947, *m.*
1999   *Ashton of Upholland,* Catherine Margaret Ashton, *b.* 1956, *m.*
1999   *Barker,* Elizabeth Jean Barker, *b.* 1961
2000   *Billingham,* Angela Theodora Billingham, DPHIL, *b.* 1939, *w.*
1987   *Blackstone,* Tessa Ann Vosper Blackstone, PHD, *b.* 1942
1987   *Blatch,* Emily May Blatch, CBE, PC, *b.* 1937, *m.*
1999   *Blood,* May Blood, MBE, *b.* 1938

2000   *Boothroyd,* Betty Boothroyd, PC, *b.* 1929
2004   *Bonham-Carter of Yarnbury,* Jane Bonham Carter, *b.* 1957, *w.*
1998   *Buscombe,* Peta Jane Buscombe, *b.* 1954, *m.*
1996   *Byford,* Hazel Byford, DBE, *b.* 1941, *m.*
1982   *Carnegy of Lour,* Elizabeth Patricia Carnegy of Lour, *b.* 1925
1992   *Chalker of Wallasey,* Lynda Chalker, PC, *b.* 1942, *m.*
2004   *Chapman of Leeds,* Nicola Jane Chapman, *b.* 1961
2000   *Cohen of Pimlico,* Janet Cohen, *b.* 1940, *m.*
1982   *Cox,* Caroline Anne Cox, *b.* 1937, *m.*
1998   *Crawley,* Christine Mary Crawley, MEP, *b.* 1950, *m.*
1990   *Cumberlege,* Julia Frances Cumberlege, CBE, *b.* 1943, *m.*
1978   *David,* Nora Ratcliff David, *b.* 1913, *w.*
1993   *Dean of Thornton-le-Fylde,* Brenda Dean, PC, *b.* 1943, *m.*
1974   *Delacourt-Smith of Alteryn,* Margaret Rosalind Delacourt-Smith, *b.* 1916, *m.*
2004   *D'Souza,* Dr Frances Gertrude Claire D'Souza, CMG, *b.* 1944 *m.*
1990   *Dunn,* Lydia Selina Dunn, DBE, *b.* 1940, *m.*
1990   *Eccles of Moulton,* Diana Catherine Eccles, *b.* 1933, *m.*
1972   *Elles,* Diana Louie Elles, *b.* 1921, *m.*
1997   *Emerton,* Audrey Caroline Emerton, DBE, *b.* 1935
1974   *Falkender,* Marcia Matilda Falkender, CBE, *b.* 1932
2004   *Falkner of Margravine,* Kishwer Falkner, *b.* 1955, *m.*
1994   *Farrington of Ribbleton,* Josephine Farrington, *b.* 1940, *m.*
2001   *Finlay of Llandaff,* Ilora Gillian Finlay, *b.* 1949, *m.*
1974   *Fisher of Rednal,* Doris Mary Gertrude Fisher, *b.* 1919, *w.*
1990   *Flather,* Shreela Flather, *m.*
1997   *Fookes,* Janet Evelyn Fookes, DBE, *b.* 1936
1999   *Gale,* Anita Gale, *b.* 1940
1981   *Gardner of Parkes,* (Rachel) Trixie (Anne) Gardner, *b.* 1927, *m.*
2000   *Gibson of Market Rasen,* Anne Gibson, OBE, *b.* 1940, *m.*
2001   *Golding,* Llinos Golding, *b.* 1933, *m.*
1998   *Goudie,* Mary Teresa Goudie, *b.* 1946, *m.*
1993   *Gould of Potternewton,* Joyce Brenda Gould, *b.* 1932, *m.*
2001   *Greenfield,* Susan Adele Greenfield, CBE, *b.* 1950, *m.*
2000   *Greengross,* Sally Ralea Greengross, OBE, *b.* 1935, *m.*
1991   *Hamwee,* Sally Rachel Hamwee, *b.* 1947
1999   *Hanham,* Joan Brownlow Hanham, CBE, *b.* 1939, *m.*
1999   *Harris of Richmond,* Angela Felicity Harris, *b.* 1944
1996   *Hayman,* Helene Valerie Hayman, PC, *b.* 1949, *m.*
2004   *Henig,* Ruth Beatrice Henig, CBE, *b.* 1943, *m.*
1991   *Hilton of Eggardon,* Jennifer Hilton, QPM, *b.* 1936
1995   *Hogg,* Sarah Elizabeth Mary Hogg, *b.* 1946, *m.*
1990   *Hollis of Heigham,* Patricia Lesley Hollis, DPHIL, *b.* 1941, *m.*

1985   *Hooper,* Gloria Dorothy Hooper, CMG, *b.* 1939
2001   *Howarth of Breckland,* Valerie Georgina Howarth, OBE, *b.* 1940
2001   *Howe of Idlicote,* Elspeth Rosamond Morton Howe, CBE, *b.* 1932, *m.*
1999   *Howells of St Davids,* Rosalind Patricia-Anne Howells, *b.* 1931, *m.*
1991   *James of Holland Park,* Phyllis Dorothy White (P. D. James), OBE, *b.* 1920, *w.*
1992   *Jay of Paddington,* Margaret Ann Jay, PC, *b.* 1939, *m.*
1979   *Jeger,* Lena May Jeger, *b.* 1915, *w.*
1997   *Kennedy of the Shaws,* Helena Ann Kennedy, QC, *b.* 1950, *m.*
1997   *Knight of Collingtree,* (Joan Christabel) Jill Knight, DBE, *b.* 1927, *w.*
1997   *Linklater of Butterstone,* Veronica Linklater, *b.* 1943, *m.*
1996   *Lloyd of Highbury,* Prof. June Kathleen Lloyd, DBE, FRCP, FRCPE, FRCGP, *b.* 1928
1978   *Lockwood,* Betty Lockwood, *b.* 1924, *w.*
1997   *Ludford,* Sarah Ann Ludford, MEP, *b.* 1951
2004   *McDonagh,* Margaret Josephine McDonagh
1979   *McFarlane of Llandaff,* Jean Kennedy McFarlane, *b.* 1926
1999   *McIntosh of Hudnall,* Genista Mary McIntosh, *b.* 1946
1997   *Maddock,* Diana Margaret Maddock, *b.* 1945, *m.*
1991   *Mallalieu,* Ann Mallalieu, QC, *b.* 1945, *m.*
1970   *Masham of Ilton,* Susan Lilian Primrose Cunliffe-Lister, *b.* 1935, *m.*
1999   *Massey of Darwen,* Doreen Elizabeth Massey, *b.* 1938, *m.*
2001   *Michie of Gallanach,* Janet Ray Michie, *b.* 1934, *m.*
1998   *Miller of Chilthorne Domer,* Susan Elizabeth Miller, *b.* 1954
1993   *Miller of Hendon,* Doreen Miller, MBE, *b.* 1933, *m.*
2004   *Morgan of Drefelin,* Delyth Jane Morgan *b.* 1961, *m.*
2001   *Morgan of Huyton,* Sally Morgan, *b.* 1959, *m.*
2004   *Morris of Bolton,* Patricia Morris, OBE, *b.* 1953
2004   *Murphy,* Elaine Murphy, *b.* 1947, *m.*
2004   *Neuberger,* Rabbi Julia (Babette Sarah), DBE, *b.* 1950, *m.*
1997   *Nicholson of Winterbourne,* Emma Harriet Nicholson, MEP, *b.* 1941, *m.*
1982   *Nicol,* Olive Mary Wendy Nicol, *b.* 1923, *m.*
2000   *Noakes,* Shiela Valerie Masters, DBE, *b.* 1949, *m.*
2000   *Northover,* Lindsay Patricia Granshaw, *b.* 1954
1991   *O'Cathain,* Detta O'Cathain, OBE, *b.* 1938, *m.*
1999   *O'Neill of Bengarve,* Onora Sylvia O'Neill, CBE, PHD, *b.* 1941
1989   *Oppenheim-Barnes,* Sally Oppenheim-Barnes, PC, *b.* 1930, *m.*
1990   *Park of Monmouth,* Daphne Margaret Sybil Désirée Park, CMG, OBE, *b.* 1921

1991   *Perry of Southwark,* Pauline Perry, *b.* 1931, *m.*
1997   *Pitkeathley,* Jill Elizabeth Pitkeathley, OBE, *b.* 1940
1981   *Platt of Writtle,* Beryl Catherine Platt, CBE, FENG, *b.* 1923, *m.*
1999   *Prashar,* Usha Kumari Prashar, CBE, *b.* 1948, *m.*
2004   *Prosser,* Margaret Theresa Prosser, OBE, *b.* 1937
1996   *Ramsay of Cartvale,* Margaret Mildred (Meta) Ramsay, *b.* 1936
1994   *Rawlings,* Patricia Elizabeth Rawlings, *b.* 1939
1997   *Rendell of Babergh,* Ruth Barbara Rendell, CBE, *b.* 1930, *m.*
1998   *Richardson of Calow,* Kathleen Margaret Richardson, OBE, *b.* 1938, *m.*
2004   *Royall of Blaisdon,* Janet Anne Royall, *b.* 1955, *m.*
1997   *Scotland of Asthal,* Patricia Janet Scotland, QC, *b.* 1955, *m.*
2000   *Scott of Needham Market,* Rosalind Carol Scott, *b.* 1957
1991   *Seccombe,* Joan Anna Dalziel Seccombe, DBE, *b.* 1930, *m.*
1998   *Sharp of Guildford,* Margaret Lucy Sharp, *b.* 1938, *m.*
1973   *Sharples,* Pamela Sharples, *b.* 1923, *m.*
1995   *Smith of Gilmorehill,* Elizabeth Margaret Smith, *b.* 1940, *w.*
1999   *Stern,* Vivien Helen Stern, CBE, *b.* 1941
1996   *Symons of Vernham Dean,* Elizabeth Conway Symons, *b.* 1951
1992   *Thatcher,* Margaret Hilda Thatcher, KG, OM, PC, FRS, *b.* 1925, *w.*
1994   *Thomas of Walliswood,* Susan Petronella Thomas, OBE, *b.* 1935, *m.*
1998   *Thornton,* (Dorothea) Glenys Thornton, *b.* 1952, *m.*
1980   *Trumpington,* Jean Alys Barker, PC, *b.* 1922, *w.*
1985   *Turner of Camden,* Muriel Winifred Turner, *b.* 1927, *m.*
1998   *Uddin,* Manzila Pola Uddin, *b.* 1959, *m.*
2004   *Wall of New Barnet,* Margaret Mary Wall, *b.* 1941, *m.*
2000   *Walmsley,* Joan Margaret Walmsley, *b.* 1943
1985   *Warnock,* Helen Mary Warnock, DBE, *b.* 1924, *w.*
1999   *Warwick of Undercliffe,* Diana Mary Warwick, *b.* 1945, *m.*
1999   *Whitaker,* Janet Alison Whitaker, *b.* 1936
1996   *Wilcox,* Judith Ann Wilcox, *b.* 1940, *w.*
1999   *Wilkins,* Rosalie Catherine Wilkins, *b.* 1946
1993   *Williams of Crosby,* Shirley Vivien Teresa Brittain Williams, PC, *b.* 1930, *m.*
2004   *Young of Hornsey,* Prof. Margaret Omolola Young, OBE, *b.* 1951, *m.*
1997   *Young of Old Scone,* Barbara Scott Young, *b.* 1948

LORDS SPIRITUAL

The Lords Spiritual are the Archbishops of Canterbury and York and 24 diocesan bishops of the Church of England. The Bishops of London, Durham and Winchester always have seats in the House of Lords; the other 21 seats are filled by the remaining diocesan bishops in order of seniority. The Bishop of Sodor and Man and the Bishop of Gibraltar are not eligible to sit in the House of Lords.

ARCHBISHOPS

Style, The Most Revd and Right Hon. the Lord
  Archbishop of _
Addressed as Archbishop, or Your Grace

INTRODUCED TO HOUSE OF LORDS

2003   Canterbury (104th), Rowan Douglas Williams, PC, DPHIL, b. 1950, m., cons. 1992, elected 2002
1990   York (96th), David Michael Hope, KCVO, PC, DPHIL, LLD, b. 1940, cons. 1985, elected 1985, trans. 1995

BISHOPS

Style, The Right Revd the Lord Bishop of _
Addressed as My Lord
Elected date of confirmation as diocesan bishop

INTRODUCED TO HOUSE OF LORDS
(as at 31 August 2004)

1996   London (132nd), Richard John Carew Chartres, b. 1947, m., cons. 1992, elected 1995
2003   Durham (71st), Nicholas Thomas Wright, DPHIL, b. 1948, m., cons. 2003, elected 2003
1996   Winchester (96th), Michael Charles Scott-Joynt, b. 1943, m., cons. 1987, elected 1995
1993   Oxford (41st), Richard Douglas Harries, b. 1936, m., cons. 1987, elected 1987
1997   Southwark (9th), Thomas Frederick Butler, b. 1940, m., cons. 1985, elected 1991, trans. 1998
1997   Manchester (11th), Nigel Simeon McCulloch, b. 1942, m., cons. 1986, elected 1992, trans. 2002
1998   Salisbury (77th), David Staffurth Stancliffe, b. 1942, m., cons. 1993, elected 1993
1999   Rochester (106th), Michael James Nazir-Ali, PHD, b. 1949, m., cons. 1984, elected 1994
1999   Chelmsford (9th) John Warren Gladwin, b. 1942, m., cons. 1994, elected 1994, trans. 2003
1999   Portsmouth (8th), Kenneth William Stevenson, b. 1949, m., cons. 1995, elected 1995
1999   Derby (6th), Jonathan Sansbury Bailey, b. 1940, m., cons. 1992, elected 1995

1999   St Albans (9th), Christopher William Herbert, b. 1944, m., cons. 1995, elected 1995
2001   Peterborough (37th), Ian Cundy, b. 1945, m., cons. 1992, elected 1996
2001   Chester (40th), Peter Robert Forster, PHD, b. 1950, cons. 1996, elected 1996
2002   St Edmundsbury and Ipswich (9th), (John Hubert) Richard Lewis, b. 1943, m., cons. 1992, elected 1997
2002   Truro (14th), William Ind, b. 1942, m., cons. 1987, elected 1997
2002   Worcester (112th), Peter Stephen Maurice Selby, b. 1941, cons. 1984, elected 1997
2003   Newcastle (11th), (John) Martin Wharton, b. 1944, m., cons. 1992, elected 1997
2003   Sheffield (6th), John Nicholls, b. 1943, m., cons. 1990, elected 1997
2003   Coventry (8th), Colin J. Bennetts, b. 1940, m., cons. 1994, elected 1998
2003   Liverpool (7th), James Jones, b. 1948, m., cons. 1994, elected 1998
2003   Leicester (6th), Timothy John Stevens, b. 1946, m., cons. 1995, elected 1999
2004   Southwell (10th), George Henry Cassidy, b. 1942, m., cons. 1999, elected 1999
2004   Norwich (71st), Graham R. James, b. 1951, m., cons. 1993, elected 1999

BISHOPS AWAITING SEATS, in order of seniority
(as at 31 August 2004)
Exeter (70th), Michael L. Langrish, b. 1946, m., cons. 1993, elected 2000
Ripon and Leeds (12th), John R. Packer, b. 1946, m., cons. 1996, elected 2000
Ely (68th) Dr. Anthony Russell, b. 1943, m., cons. 1988, elected 2000
Carlisle (65th) Graham Dow, b. 1942, m., cons. 1985, elected 2000
Chichester (102nd) John Hind, b. 1945, cons. 1991, elected 2001
Lincoln (71st) Dr John Saxbee, b. 1946, cons. 1994, elected 2001
Bath & Wells (77th) Peter Price, b. 1944, m., cons. 1997, elected 2002
Birmingham (8th) Dr John Tucker Mugabi Sentamu, PHD, b. 1949, m., cons. 1996, elected 2002
Bradford (9th) David James, b. 1945, cons.1998, elected 2002
Wakefield (12th) Stephen G. Platten, b. 1947, m., cons. 2003, elected 2003
Bristol (55th) Michael A. Hill, b. 1947, m., cons. 1998, elected 2003
Lichfield (98th) Jonathan Gledhill, b. 1949, m., cons. 1996, elected 2003
Blackburn (8th) Nicholas Reade, b. 1946, m., cons. 2004, elected 2004
Hereford (104th), Anthony Martin Priddis, b. 1948, m., cons. 1996, elected 2004
Gloucester (40th) Michael Francis Perham, b. 1947, m., cons. 2004, elected 2004
Guildford (9th) vacant

COURTESY TITLES

From this list it will be seen that, for example, the Marquess of Blandford is heir to the Dukedom of Marlborough, and Viscount Amberley to the Earldom of Russell. Titles of second heirs (when in use) are also given, and the courtesy title of the father of a second heir is indicated by * e.g. Earl of Mornington, eldest son of *Marquess of Douro

For forms of address, see page 43

MARQUESSES
*Blandford –
  Marlborough, D.
Bowmont and Cessford –
  Roxburghe, D.
Douglas and Clydesdale –
  Hamilton, D.
*Douro – Wellington, D.
Graham – Montrose, D.
Hamilton – Abercorn, D.
Hartington – Devonshire,
  D.
Kildare – Leinster, D.
Stafford – Sutherland, D.
Tullibardine – Atholl, D.
*Worcester – Beaufort, D.

EARLS
Aboyne – Huntly, M.
Ancram – Lothian, M.
Arundel and Surrey –
  Norfolk, D.
*Bective – Headfort, M.
*Belfast – Donegall, M.
Brecknock – Camden, M.
Burford – St Albans, D.
*Cardigan – Ailesbury, M.
Compton – Northampton,
  M.
*Dalkeith – Buccleuch, D.
*Euston – Grafton, D.
Glamorgan – *Worcester,
  M.
Grosvenor – Westminster,
  D.
Haddo – Aberdeen and
  Temair, M.
Hillsborough – Downshire,
  M.
Hopetoun – Linlithgow, M.
March and Kinrara –
  Richmond, D.
Medina – Milford Haven,
  M.
*Mount Charles –
  Conyngham, M.
Mornington – *Douro, M.
Mulgrave – Normanby, M.
Percy – Northumberland,
  D.
Ronaldshay – Zetland, M.
*St Andrews – Kent, D.
Shelburne – Lansdowne,
  M.
*Southesk – Fife, D.
Sunderland – *Blandford,
  M.

*Tyrone – Waterford, M.
Ulster – Gloucester, D.
*Uxbridge – Anglesey, M.
Wiltshire – Winchester, M.
Yarmouth – Hertford, M.

VISCOUNTS
Alexander – Caledon, E.
Althorp – Spencer, E.
Amberley – Russell, E.
Andover – Suffolk and
  Berkshire, E.
Anson – Lichfield, E.
Asquith – Oxford and
  Asquith, E.
Boringdon – Morley, E.
Borodale – Beatty, E.
Boyle – Shannon, E.
Brocas – Jellicoe, E.
Campden – Gainsborough,
  E.
Carlow – Portarlington, E.
Carlton – Wharncliffe, E.
Castlereagh – Londonderry,
  M.
Chelsea – Cadogan, E.
Chewton – Waldegrave, E.
Chichester – *Belfast, E.
Clanfield – Peel, E.
Clive – Powis, E.
Coke – Leicester, E.
Corry – Belmore, E.
Corvedale – Baldwin of
  Bewdley, E.
Cranborne – Salisbury, M.
Cranley – Onslow, E.
Crichton – Erne, E.
Curzon – Howe, E.
Dangan – Cowley, E.
Dawick – Haig, E.
Drumlanrig – Queensberry,
  M.
Duncannon – Bessborough,
  E.
Dungarvan – Cork and
  Orrery, E.
Dunluce – Antrim, E.
Dunwich – Stradbroke, E.
Dupplin – Kinnoull, E.
Ednam – Dudley, E.
Emlyn – Cawdor, E
Encombe – Eldon, E.
Enfield – Strafford, E.
Erleigh – Reading, M.
Errington – Cromer, E.
FitzHarris – Malmesbury,
  E.

Folkestone – Radnor, E.
Forbes – Granard, E.
Garmoyle – Cairns, E.
Garnock – Lindsay, E.
Glenapp – Inchcape, E.
Glentworth – Limerick, E.
Grey de Wilton – Wilton,
  E.
Grimstone – Verulam, E.
Gwynedd – Lloyd George
  of Dwyfor, E.
Hawkesbury – Liverpool,
  E.
Hinchingbrooke –
  Sandwich, E.
Ikerrin – Carrick, E.
Ingestre – Shrewsbury, E.
Ipswich – *Euston, E.
Jocelyn – Roden, E.
Kelburn – Glasgow, E.
Kingsborough – Kingston,
  E.
Kirkwall – Orkney, E.
Knebworth – Lytton, E.
Lascelles – Harewood, E.
Linley – Snowdon, E.
Loftus – Ely, M.
Lowther – Lonsdale, E.
Lymington – Portsmouth,
  E.
Macmillan of Ovenden –
  Stockton, E.
Maidstone – Winchilsea, E
Maitland – Lauderdale, E.
Malden – Essex, E.
Mandeville – Manchester,
  D.
Melgund – Minto, E.
Merton – Nelson, E.
Moore – Drogheda, E.
Newport – Bradford, E.
Northland – Ranfurly, E
Newry and Mourne –
  Kilmorey, E.
Petersham – Harrington, E.
Pollington – Mexborough,
  E
Raynham – Townshend,
  M.
Reidhaven – Seafield, E.
Ruthven of Canberra –
  Gowrie, E.
St Cyres – Iddesleigh, E.
Sandon – Harrowby, E.
Savernake – *Cardigan, E.
Slane – *Mount Charles, E.
Somerton – Normanton, E.
Stopford – Courtown, E.
Stormont – Mansfield, E.
Strathallan – Perth, E.
Stuart – Castle Stewart, E.
Suirdale – Donoughmore,
  E.
Tamworth – Ferrers, E.
Tarbat – Cromartie, E.
Vaughan – Lisburne, E.

Weymouth – Bath, M.
Windsor – Plymouth, E.
Wolmer – Selborne, E.
Woodstock – Portland, E.

BARONS (LORDS)
Aberdour – Morton, E.
Apsley – Bathurst, E.
Ardee – Meath, E.
Ashley – Shaftesbury, E.
Balgonie – Leven and
  Melville, E.
Balniel – Crawford and
  Balcarres, E.
Berriedale – Caithness, E.
Bingham – Lucan, E.
Binning – Haddington, E.
Brooke – Warwick, E.
Bruce – Elgin, E.
Buckhurst – De La Warr, E
Burghley – Exeter, M.
Cardross – Buchan, E.
Carnegie – *Southesk, E.
Clifton – Darnley, E.
Cochrane – Dundonald, E.
Courtenay – Devon, E.
Dalmeny – Rosebery, E.
Doune – Moray, E.
Downpatrick – *St
  Andrews, E.
Dunglass – Home, E.
Eliot – St Germans, E.
Eskdail – *Dalkeith, E.
Formartine – *Haddo, E.
Gillford – Clanwilliam, E.
Glamis – Strathmore, E.
Greenock – Cathcart, E.
Guernsey – Aylesford, E.
Hay – Erroll, E.
Howard of Effingham –
  Effingham, E.
Huntingtower – Dysart, C.
Hyde – Clarendon, E.
Inverurie – Kintore, E.
Irwin – Halifax, E.
Johnstone – Annandale and
  Hartfell, E.
Kenlis – *Bective, E.
Langton – Temple of
  Stowe, E.
La Poer – *Tyrone, E.
Leslie – Rothes, E.
Leveson – Granville, E
Loughborough – Rosslyn,
  E.
Mauchline – Loudoun, C.
Medway – Cranbrook, E.
Montgomerie – Eglinton
  and Winton, E.
Moreton – Ducie, E.
Mount Stuart – Bute, M
Naas – Mayo, E.
Neidpath – Wemyss and
  March, E.
Norreys – Lindsey and
  Abingdon, E.

North – *Guilford, E.*
Ogilvy – *Airlie, E.*
Oxmantown – *Rosse, E.*
Paget de Beaudesert –
*Uxbridge, E.

Porchester – *Carnarvon, E.*
Ramsay – *Dalhousie, E.*
Romsey – *Mountbatten of
Burma, C.*
Scrymgeour – *Dundee, E.*

Seymour – *Somerset, D.*
Stanley – *Derby, E.*
Strathnaver – *Sutherland,
C.*

Wodehouse – *Kimberley,
E.*
Worsley – *Yarborough, E.*

PEERS' SURNAMES WHICH DIFFER FROM THEIR TITLES

The following symbols indicate the rank of the peer holding each title:

C.   Countess
D.   Duke
E.   Earl
M.   Marquess
V.   Viscount
*   Life Peer

Where no designation is given, the title is that of an hereditary Baron or Baroness

Abney-Hastings – *Loudoun, C.*
Acheson – *Gosford, E.*
Adderley – *Norton*
Addington – *Sidmouth, V.*
Adebowale – *A. of Thornes**
Agar – *Normanton, E.*
Aitken – *Beaverbrook*
Akers-Douglas – *Chilston, V.*
Alexander – *A. of Tunis, E.*
Alexander – *A. of Weedon**
Alexander – *Caledon, E.*
Allen – *A. of Abbeydale**
Allen – *Croham**
Allsopp – *Hindlip*
Alton – *A. of Liverpool**
Anderson – *Waverley, V.*
Anelay – *A. of St Johns**
Annesley – *Valentia, V.*
Anson – *Lichfield, E.*
Archer – *A. of Sandwell**
Archer – *A. of Weston-super-Mare**
Armstrong – *A. of Ilminster**
Armstrong-Jones – *Snowdon, E.*
Arthur – *Glenarthur*
Arundell – *Talbot of Malahide*
Ashdown – *A. of Norton-sub-Hamdon**
Ashley – *A. of Stoke**
Ashley-Cooper – *Shaftesbury, E.*
Ashton – *A. of Hyde*
Ashton – *A. of Upholland**
Asquith – *Oxford and Asquith, E.*
Assheton – *Clitheroe*
Astley – *Hastings*
Astor – *A. of Hever*

Aubrey-Fletcher – *Braye*
Bailey – *Glanusk*
Baillie – *Burton*
Baillie Hamilton – *Haddington, E.*
Baker – *B. of Dorking**
Baldwin – *B. of Bewdley, E.*
Balfour – *B. of Inchrye*
Balfour – *Kinross*
Balfour – *Riverdale*
Bampfylde – *Poltimore*
Banbury – *B. of Southam*
Barber – *B. of Tewkesbury**
Baring – *Ashburton*
Baring – *Cromer, E.*
Baring – *Howick of Glendale*
Baring – *Northbrook*
Baring – *Revelstoke*
Barker – *Trumpington**
Barnes – *Gorell*
Barnewall – *Trimlestown*
Bassam – *B. of Brighton**
Bathurst – *Bledisloe, V.*
Beauclerk – *St Albans, D.*
Beaumont – *Allendale, V.*
Beaumont – *B. of Whitley**
Beckett – *Grimthorpe*
Benn – *Stansgate, V.*
Bennet – *Tankerville, E.*
Bentinck – *Portland, E.*
Beresford – *Decies*
Beresford – *Waterford, M.*
Bernstein – *B. of Craigweil**
Berry – *Camrose, V.*
Berry – *Kemsley, V.*
Bertie – *Lindsey, E.*
Best – *Wynford*
Bethell – *Westbury*
Bewicke-Copley – *Cromwell*
Bigham – *Mersey, V.*
Bingham – *B. of Cornhill**
Bingham – *Clanmorris*
Bingham – *Lucan, E.*
Black – *B. of Crossharbour**
Bligh – *Darnley, E.*
Blyth – *B. of Rowington**
Bonham Carter – *B.-C. of Yarnbury**
Bootle-Wilbraham – *Skelmersdale*
Boscawen – *Falmouth, V.*
Boston – *B. of Faversham**

Bourke – *Mayo, E.*
Bowes Lyon – *Strathmore, E.*
Bowyer – *Denham*
Boyd – *Kilmarnock*
Boyle – *Cork and Orrery, E.*
Boyle – *Glasgow, E.*
Boyle – *Shannon, E.*
Brabazon – *Meath, E.*
Brand – *Hampden, V.*
Brassey – *B. of Apethorpe*
Brett – *Esher, V.*
Bridge – *B. of Harwich**
Bridgeman – *Bradford, E.*
Brittan – *B. of Spennithorne**
Brodrick – *Midleton, V.*
Brooke – *Alanbrooke, V.*
Brooke – *B. of Alverthorpe**
Brooke – *Brookeborough, V.*
Brooke – *B. of Sutton Mandeville**
Brooks – *B. of Tremorfa**
Brooks – *Crawshaw*
Brougham – *Brougham and Vaux*
Broughton – *Fairhaven*
Brown – *B. of Eaton-under-Heywood**
Browne – *Kilmaine*
Browne – *B. of Madingley**
Browne – *Oranmore and Browne*
Browne – *Sligo, M.*
Bruce – *Aberdare*
Bruce – *Balfour of Burleigh*
Bruce – *B. of Donington**
Bruce – *Elgin and Kincardine, E.*
Brudenell-Bruce – *Ailesbury, M.*
Buchan – *Tweedsmuir*
Buckley – *Wrenbury*
Butler – *B. of Brockwell**
Butler – *Carrick, E.*
Butler – *Dunboyne*
Butler – *Mountgarret, V.*
Buxton – *B. of Alsa**
Byng – *Strafford, E.*
Byng – *Torrington, V.*
Callaghan – *C. of Cardiff**
Cambell-Savours – *C.-S. of Allerdale**

Cameron – *C. of Dillington**
Cameron – *C. of Lochbroom**
Campbell – *Argyll, D.*
Campbell – *C. of Alloway**
Campbell – *C. of Croy**
Campbell – *Cawdor, E.*
Campbell – *Colgrain*
Campbell – *Stratheden and Campbell*
Campbell-Gray – *Gray*
Canning – *Garvagh*
Capell – *Essex, E.*
Carey – *C. of Clifton**
Carington – *Carrington*
Carlisle – *C. of Berriew**
Carlisle – *C. of Bucklow**
Carnegie – *Fife, D.*
Carnegie – *Northesk, E.*
Carr – *C. of Hadley**
Carter – *C. of Coles**
Cary – *Falkland, V.*
Caulfeild – *Charlemont, V.*
Cavendish – *C. of Furness**
Cavendish – *Chesham*
Cavendish – *Devonshire, D.*
Cavendish – *Waterpark*
Cayzer – *Rotherwick*
Cecil – *Amherst of Hackney*
Cecil – *Exeter, M.*
Cecil – *Rockley*
Czernin – *Howard de Walden*
Chalker – *C. of Wallasey**
Chaloner – *Gisborough*
Channon – *Kelvedon**
Chapman – *C. of Leeds**
Chapman – *Northfield**
Charteris – *Wemyss and March, E.*
Chetwynd-Talbot – *Shrewsbury, E.*
Chichester – *Donegall, M.*
Child Villiers – *Jersey, E.*
Cholmondeley – *Delamere*
Chubb – *Hayter*
Clark – *C. of Kempston**
Clarke – *C. of Hampstead**
Clegg-Hill – *Hill, V.*
Clifford – *C. of Chudleigh*
Cochrane – *C. of Cults*
Cochrane – *Dundonald, E.*
Cocks – *Somers*
Cohen – *C. of Pimlico**

Cokayne – *Cullen of Ashbourne*
Coke – *Leicester, E.*
Cole – *Enniskillen, E.*
Collier – *Monkswell*
Colville – *Clydesmuir*
Colville – *C. of Culross, V.*
Compton – *Northampton, M.*
Condon – *C. of Langdon Green**
Conolly-Carew – *Carew*
Cooke – *C. of Islandreagh**
Cooke – *C. of Thorndon**
Cooper – *Norwich, V*
Cope – *C. of Berkeley**
Corbett – *C. of Castle Vale*.*
Corbett – *Rowallan*
Cornwall-Leigh – *Grey of Condor*
Courtenay – *Devon, E.*
Craig – *C. of Radley**
Craig – *Craigavon, V.*
Crichton – *Erne, E.*
Crichton-Stuart – *Bute, M.*
Cripps – *Parmoor*
Crossley – *Somerleyton*
Cubitt – *Ashcombe*
Cunliffe-Lister – *Masham of Ilton**
Cunliffe-Lister – *Swinton, E.*
Currie – *C. of Marylebone**
Curzon – *Howe, E.*
Curzon – *Scarsdale, V.*
Cust – *Brownlow*
Dalrymple – *Stair, E.*
Daubeny de Moleyns – *Ventry*
Davies – *D. of Coity**
Davies – *Darwen*
Davies – *D. of Oldham**
Davison – *Broughshane*
Dawnay – *Downe, V.*
Dawson-Damer – *Portarlington, E.*
Dean – *D. of Harptree**
Dean – *D. of Thornton-le-Fylde**
Deane – *Muskerry*
de Courcy – *Kingsale*
de Grey – *Walsingham*
Delacourt-Smith – *Delacourt Smith of Alteryn**
Denison – *Londesborough*
Denison-Pender – *Pender*
Devereux – *Hereford, V.*
Dewar – *Forteviot*
De Yarburgh-Bateson – *Deramore*
Dixon – *Glentoran*
Dodson – *Monk Bretton*
Donaldson – *D. of Lymington**
Douglas – *Morton, E.*
Douglas – *Queensberry, M.*

Douglas-Hamilton – *Hamilton, D.*
Douglas-Hamilton – *Selkirk, E.*
Douglas-Hamilton – *Selkirk of Douglas**
Douglas-Home – *Dacre*
Douglas-Home – *Home, E.*
Douglas-Pennant – *Penrhyn*
Douglas-Scott-Montagu – *Montagu of Beaulieu*
Drummond – *Perth, E.*
Drummond of Megginch – *Strange*
Dugdale – *Crathorne*
Duke – *Merrivale*
Duncombe – *Feversham*
Dundas – *Melville, V.*
Dundas – *Zetland, M.*
Eady – *Swinfen*
Eccles – *E. of Moulton**
Eden – *Auckland*
Eden – *E. of Winton**
Eden – *Henley*
Edgcumbe – *Mount Edgcumbe, E.*
Edmondson – *Sandford*
Edwardes – *Kensington*
Edwards – *Crickhowell**
Egerton – *Sutherland, D.*
Eliot – *St Germans, E.*
Elliott – *E. of Morpeth**
Elliot-Murray-Kynyn-mound – *Minto, E.*
Ellis – *Seaford*
Erskine – *Buchan, E.*
Erskine – *Mar and Kellie, E.*
Erskine-Murray – *Elibank*
Evans – *E. of Parkside**
Evans – *E. of Temple Guiting**
Evans – *E. of Watford**
Evans – *Mountevans*
Evans-Freke – *Carbery*
Eve – *Silsoe*
Ewing – *E. of Kirkford**
Fairfax – *F. of Cameron*
Falconer – *F. of Thoroton**
Falkner – *F. of Margravine**
Fane – *Westmorland, E.*
Farrington – *F. of Ribbleton**
Faulkner – *F. of Worcester**
Fearn – *F. of Southport**
Feilding – *Denbigh, E.*
Felton – *Seaford*
Fellowes – *De Ramsey*
Fermor-Hesketh – *Hesketh*
Fiennes – *Saye and Sele*
Fiennes-Clinton – *Lincoln, E.*
Finch Hatton – *Winchilsea, E.*
Finch-Knightley – *Aylesford, E.*

Finlay – *F. of Llandaff**
Fisher – *F. of Rednal**
Fitzalan-Howard – *Herries of Terregles*
Fitzalan-Howard – *Norfolk, D.*
FitzGerald – *Leinster, D.*
Fitzherbert – *Stafford*
FitzRoy – *Grafton, D.*
FitzRoy – *Southampton*
FitzRoy Newdegate – *Daventry, V.*
Fletcher-Vane – *Inglewood*
Flower – *Ashbrook, V.*
Foljambe – *Liverpool, E.*
Forbes – *Granard, E*
Forsyth – *F. of Drumlean*.*
Forwood – *Arlington*
Foster – *F. of Thames Bank**
Fowler – *F. of Sutton Caulfield**
Fox-Strangways – *Ilchester, E.*
Frankland – *Zouche*
Fraser – *F. of Carmyllie**
Fraser – *F. of Kilmorack**
Fraser – *Lovat*
Fraser – *Saltoun*
Fraser – *Strathalmond*
Freeman-Grenville – *Kinloss*
Fremantle – *Cottesloe*
French – *De Freyne*
Fyfe – *F. of Fairfield**
Galbraith – *Strathclyde*
Ganzoni – *Belstead*
Gardner – *G. of Parkes**
Gascoyne-Cecil – *M. of Salisbury**
Gathorne-Hardy – *Cranbrook, E.*
Gibbs – *Aldenham*
Gibbs – *Wraxall*
Gibson – *Ashbourne*
Gibson – *G. of Market Rasen**
Giffard – *Halsbury, E.*
Gilbey – *Vaux of Harrowden*
Gilmour – *G. of Craigmillar**
Glyn – *Wolverton*
Godley – *Kilbracken*
Goff – *G. of Chieveley**
Golding – *G. of Newcastle-under-Lyme**
Gordon – *Aberdeen, M.*
Gordon – *G. of Strathblane**
Gordon – *Huntly, M.*
Gordon Lennox – *Richmond, D.*
Gore – *Arran, E.*
Gould – *G. of Brookwood**
Gould – *G. of Potternewton**

Graham – *G. of Edmonton**
Graham – *Montrose, D.*
Graham-Toler – *Norbury, E.*
Granshaw – *Northover**
Grant of Grant – *Strathspey*
Grant of Rothiemurchus – *Dysart, C.*
Granville – *G. of Eye**
Gray – *G. of Contin**
Greenall – *Daresbury*
Greville – *Warwick, E.*
Griffiths – *G. of Burry Port**
Griffiths – *G. of Fforestfach**
Grigg – *Altrincham*
Grimston – *G. of Westbury*
Grimston – *Verulam, E.*
Grosvenor – *Westminster, D.*
Grosvenor – *Wilton and Ebury, E*
Guest – *Wimborne, V*
Gueterbock – *Berkeley*
Guinness – *Iveagh, E.*
Guinness – *Moyne*
Gully – *Selby, V.*
Gummer – *Chadlington**
Gurdon – *Cranworth*
Guthrie – *G. of Craigiebank**
Gwynne Jones – *Chalfont**
Hale – *H. of Richmond**
Hamilton – *Abercorn, D.*
Hamilton – *Belhaven and Stenton*
Hamilton – *H. of Dalzell*
Hamilton – *Holm Patrick*
Hamilton-Russell – *Boyne, V.*
Hamilton-Smith – *Colwyn*
Hanbury-Tracy – *Sudeley*
Handcock – *Castlemaine*
Hannay – *H. of Chiswick**
Harbord-Hamond – *Suffield*
Harding – *H. of Petherton*
Hardinge – *H. of Penshurst*
Hare – *Blakenham, V.*
Hare – *Listowel, E.*
Harmsworth – *Rothermere, V.*
Harris – *H. of Haringey**
Harris – *H. of High Cross**
Harris – *H. of Peckham**
Harris – *H. of Richmond**
Harris – *Malmesbury, E.*
Hart – *H. of Chilton**
Harvey – *H. of Tasburgh*
Hastings Bass – *Huntingdon, E.*
Haughey – *Ballyedmond**
Hay – *Erroll, E.*
Hay – *Kinnoull, E.*
Hay – *Tweeddale, M.*

Heathcote-Drummond-
Willoughby –
Willoughby de Eresby
Hely-Hutchinson –
Donoughmore, E.
Henderson – Faringdon
Hennessy – Windlesham
Henniker-Major –
Henniker
Hepburne-Scott –
Polwarth
Herbert – Carnarvon, E.
Herbert – Hemingford
Herbert – Pembroke, E.
Herbert – Powis, E.
Hervey – Bristol, M.
Heseltine – H. of
Thenford*
Hewitt – Lifford, V.
Hicks Beach – St Aldwyn,
E.
Hill – Downshire, M.
Hill – Sandys
Hill-Trevor – Trevor
Hilton – H. of Eggardon*
Hobart-Hampden –
Buckinghamshire, E.
Hodgson – H. of Astley
Abbotts*
Hogg – Hailsham, V.
Hogg – H. of
Cumbernauld*
Holland-Hibbert –
Knutsford, V.
Hollis – H. of Heigham*
Holme – H. of
Cheltenham*
Holmes à Court –
Heytesbury
Hood – Bridport, V.
Hope – Glendevon
Hope – H. of Craighead*
Hope – Linlithgow, M.
Hope – Rankeillour
Hope Johnstone –
Annandale and Hartfell,
E.
Hope-Morley – Hollenden
Hopkinson – Colyton
Hore Ruthven – Gowrie,
Hovell-Thurlow-
Cumming-Bruce –
Thurlow
Howard – Carlisle, E.
Howard – Effingham, E.
Howard – H. of Penrith
Howard – H. of Rising*
Howard – Strathcona
Howard – Suffolk and
Berkshire, E.
Howarth – H. of
Breckland*
Howe – H. of Aberavon*
Howe – H. of Idlicote*
Howell – H. of Guildford*
Howells – H. of St. Davids*
Howie – H. of Troon*

Hubbard – Addington
Huggins – Malvern, V.
Hughes – H. of Woodside*
Hughes-Young – St Helens
Hunt – H. of Chesterton*
Hunt – H. of Kings Heath*
Hunt – H. of Tanworth*
Hunt – H. of Wirral*
Hurd – H. of Westwell*
Hussey – H. of North
Bradley*
Hutchinson – H. of
Lullington*
Ingrams – Darcy de Knayth
Innes-Ker – Roxburghe, D.
Inskip – Caldecote, V.
Irby – Boston
Irvine – I. of Lairg*
Isaacs – Reading, M.
James – J. of Holland
Park*
James – Northbourne
Janner – J. of Braunstone*
Jauncey – J. of Tullichettle*
Jay – J. of Paddington*
Jebb – Gladwyn
Jenkin – J. of Roding*
Jervis – St Vincent, V.
Jocelyn – Roden, E.
Jolliffe – Hylton
Jones – J. of Deeside*
Joynson-Hicks – Brentford,
V.
Kay-Shuttleworth –
Shuttleworth
Kearley – Devonport,
V.
Keith – Kintore, E.
Kemp – Rochdale, V.
Kennedy – Ailsa, M
Kennedy – K. of the
Shaws*.
Kenworthy – Strabolgi
Keppel – Albemarle, E.
Kerr – K. of Kinlochard*
Kerr – Lothian, M.
Kerr – Teviot
Kilpatrick – K. of
Kincraig*
King – Lovelace, E.
King – K. of Wartnaby*
King – K. of West
Bromwich*
King-Tenison – Kingston,
E.
Kirkham – Berners
Kitchener – K. of
Khartoum, E.
Knatchbull – Brabourne
Knatchbull – Mountbatten
of Burma, C.
Knight – K. of Collingtree*
Knox – Ranfurly, E.
Laing – L. of Dunphail*
Lamb – Rochester
Lambton – Durham, E.
Lamont – L. of Lerwick*
Lampson – Killearn

Lane – L. of Horsell*
Lang – L. of Monkton*
Lascelles – Harewood, E.
Law – Coleraine
Law – Ellenborough
Lawrence – Trevethin and
Oaksey
Lawson – Burnham
Lawson – L. of Blaby*
Lawson-Johnston – Luke
Lea – L. of Crondall*
Legge – Dartmouth, E.
Legh – Grey of Codnor
Legh – Newton
Leigh-Pemberton –
Kingsdown*
Leith – Burgh
Lennox-Boyd – Boyd of
Merton, V.
Le Poer Trench –
Clancarty, E.
Leslie – Rothes, E.
Leslie Melville – Leven and
Melville, E.
Lester – L. of Herne Hill*
Levene – L. of Portsoken*
Leveson-Gower –
Granville, E.
Lewis – L. of Newnham*
Lewis – Merthyr
Liddell – Ravensworth
Lindesay-Bethune –
Lindsay, E.
Lindsay – Crawford, E.
Lindsay – L. of Birker
Linklater – L. of
Butterstone*
Littleton – Hatherton
Lloyd – L. of Berwick*
Lloyd – L. of Highbury*
Lloyd George – Lloyd
George of Dwyfor, E.
Lloyd George – Tenby, V.
Lloyd-Mostyn – Mostyn
Loder – Wakehurst
Lofthouse – L. of
Pontefract*
Lopes – Roborough
Lour – Carneggy of Lour*
Low – Aldington
Lowry-Corry – Belmore, E.
Lowther – Lonsdale, E.
Lowther – Ullswater, V.
Lubbock – Avebury
Lucas – L. of Chilworth
Lumley – Scarbrough, E.
Lumley-Savile – Savile
Lyon-Dalberg-Acton –
Acton
Lysaght – Lisle
Lyttelton – Chandos, V.
Lyttelton – Cobham, V.
Lytton Cobbold – Cobbold
McAlpine – M. of West
Green*
Macaulay – M. of Bragar*
McClintock-Bunbury –
Rathdonnell

McColl – M. of Dulwich*
Macdonald – M. of
Tradeston*
McDonnell – Antrim, E.
Macfarlane – M. of
Bearsden*
McFarlane – M. of
Llandaff*
MacGregor – M. of
Pulham Market*
McIntosh – M. of
Haringey*
McIntosh – M. of
Hudnall*
McKenzie – M. of Luton*
Mackay – Inchcape, E.
Mackay – M. of Clashfern*
Mackay – M. of
Drumadoon*
Mackay – Reay
Mackay – Tanlaw*
MacKenzie – M. of
Culkein*
MacKenzie – M. of
Framwellgate*
Mackenzie – Cromartie, E.
Mackie – M. of Benshie*
Mackintosh – M. of
Halifax, V.
McLaren – Aberconway
MacLaurin – M. of
Knebworth*
MacLennan – M. of
Rogart*
Macmillan – Stockton, E.
Macpherson – M. of
Drumochter
Macpherson – Strathcarron
Maffey – Rugby
Maginnis – M. of
Drumglass*
Maitland – Lauderdale, E.
Makgill – Oxfuird, V.
Makins – Sherfield
Manners – Rutland, D.
Manningham-Buller –
Dilhorne, V.
Mansfield – Sandhurst
Marks – M. of Broughton
Marquis – Woolton, E.
Marshall – M. of
Knightsbridge*
Marsham – Romney, E.
Martyn-Hemphill –
Hemphill
Mason – M. of Barnsley*
Massey – M. of Darwen*
Masters – Noakes*
Maude – Hawarden, V.
Maxwell – de Ros
Maxwell – Farnham
May – M. of Oxford*
Mayhew – M. of
Twysden*
Meade – Clanwilliam, E.
Mercer Nairne Petty-
Fitzmaurice –
Lansdowne, M.

Slynn – *S. of Hadley**
Smith – *Bicester*
Smith – *Hambleden, V.*
Smith – *Kirkhill**
Smith – *S. of Clifton**
Smith – *S. of Gilmorehill**
Smith – *S. of Leigh**
Somerset – *Beaufort, D.*
Somerset – *Raglan*
Soulsby – *S. of Swaffham Prior**
Spencer – *Churchill, V.*
Spencer-Churchill – *Marlborough, D.*
Spring Rice – *Monteagle of Brandon*
Stanhope – *Harrington, E.*
Stanley – *Derby, E.*
Stanley – *Stanley of Alderley and Sheffield*
Stapleton-Cotton – *Combermere, V.*
Steel – *S. of Aikwood**
Sterling – *S. of Plaistow**
Stevens – *S. of Ludgate**
Stevenson – *S. of Coddenham**
Stewart – *Galloway, E.*
Stewart – *Stewartby**
Stoddart – *S. of Swindon**
Stone – *S. of Blackheath**
Stonor – *Camoys*
Stopford – *Courtown, E.*
Stourton – *Mowbray*
Strachey – *O'Hagan*
Strutt – *Belper*
Strutt – *Rayleigh*
Stuart – *Castle Stewart, E.*
Stuart – *Moray, E.*
Stuart – *S. of Findhorn, V.*
Suenson-Taylor – *Grantchester*

Sutherland – *S. of Houndwood**
Symons – *S. of Vernham Dean**
Taylor – *Kilclooney**
Taylor – *T. of Blackburn**
Taylor – *T. of Warwick**
Taylour – *Headfort, M.*
Temple-Gore-Langton – *Temple of Stowe, E*
Temple-Morris – *Temple-Morris of Llandaff**
Tennant – *Glenconner*
Thellusson – *Rendlesham*
Thesiger – *Chelmsford, V.*
Thomas – *T. of Gresford**
Thomas – *T. of Gwydir**
Thomas – *T. of Macclesfield**
Thomas – *T. of Swynnerton**
Thomas – *T. of Walliswood**
Thomson – *T. of Fleet*
Thomson – *T. of Monifieth**
Thynn – *Bath, M.*
Tottenham – *Ely, M.*
Trefusis – *Clinton*
Trench – *Ashtown*
Tufton – *Hothfield*
Turner – *Netherthorpe*
Turner – *T. of Camden**
Turnour – *Winterton, E.*
Tyrell-Kenyon – *Kenyon*
Vanden-Bempde-John-stone – *Derwent*
Vane – *Barnard*
Vane-Tempest-Stewart – *Londonderry, M.*
Vanneck – *Huntingfield*
Vaughan – *Lisburne, E.*

Vereker – *Gort, V.*
Verney – *Willoughby de Broke*
Vernon – *Lyveden*
Vesey – *De Vesci, V.*
Villiers – *Clarendon, E.*
Vincent – *V. of Coleshill**
Vivian – *Swansea*
Wade – *W. of Chorlton**
Waldegrave – *W. of North Hill**
Walker – *W. of Gestingthorpe**
Walker – *W. of Worcester**
Wall – *W. of New Barnett**
Wallace – *Dudley*
Wallace – *W. of Saltaire**
Wallace – *W. of Tummel**
Wallop – *Portsmouth, E.*
Walton – *W. of Detchant**
Ward – *Bangor, V.*
Ward – *Dudley, E.*
Warrender – *Bruntisfield*
Warwick – *W. of Undercliffe**
Watson – *W. of Invergowrie**
Watson – *Manton*
Watson – *W. of Richmond**
Webber – *Lloyd-Webber**
Wedderburn – *W. of Charlton**
Weir – *Inverforth*
Weld-Forester – *Forester*
Wellesley – *Cowley, E.*
Wellesley – *Wellington, D.*
Westenra – *Rossmore*
White – *Annaly*
White – *Hanningfield**
Whiteley – *Marchamley*
Whitfield – *Kenswood*

Vereker – *Gort, V.*

Williams – *W. of Crosby**
Williams – *W. of Elve**
Williamson – *Forres*
Williamson – *W. of Horton**
Willoughby – *Middleton*
Wills – *Dulverton*
Wilson – *Moran*
Wilson – *Nunburnholme*
Wilson – *W. of Dinton**
Wilson – *W. of Tillyorn**
Windsor – *Gloucester, D.*
Windsor – *Kent, D.*
Windsor-Clive – *Plymouth, E.*
Wingfield – *Powerscourt, V.*
Winn – *St Oswald*
Wodehouse – *Kimberley, E.*
Wolfson – *W. of Sunningdale**
Wood – *Halifax, E.*
Woodhouse – *Terrington*
Woolmer – *W. of Leeds**
Wright – *W. of Richmond**
Wyndham – *Egremont and Leconfield*
Wyndham-Quin – *Dunraven, E.*
Wynn – *Newborough*
Yarde-Buller – *Churston*
Yerburgh – *Alvingham*
Yorke – *Hardwicke, E.*
Young – *Kennet*
Young – *Y. of Graffham**
Young – *Y. of Hornsey**
Young – *Y. of Norwood Green**
Young – *Y. of Old Scone**
Younger – *Y. of Leckie, V.*

ORDERS OF CHIVALRY

THE MOST NOBLE ORDER OF THE GARTER (1348)

KG
Ribbon, Blue
Motto, Honi soit qui mal y pense
(Shame on him who thinks evil of it)

The number of Knights Companions is limited to 24

SOVEREIGN OF THE ORDER
The Queen

LADIES OF THE ORDER
HRH The Princess Royal, 1994
HRH Princess Alexandra, The Hon.
 Lady Ogilvy, 2003

ROYAL KNIGHTS
HRH The Prince Philip, Duke of
 Edinburgh, 1947
HRH The Prince of Wales, 1958
HRH The Duke of Kent, 1985
HRH The Duke of Gloucester, 1997

EXTRA KNIGHTS COMPANIONS AND LADIES
Grand Duke Jean of Luxembourg,
 1972
HM The Queen of Denmark, 1979
HM The King of Sweden, 1983
HM The King of Spain, 1988
HM The Queen of the Netherlands,
 1989
HIM The Emperor of Japan, 1998
HM The King of Norway, 2001

KNIGHTS AND LADY COMPANIONS
The Duke of Grafton, 1976
The Lord Richardson of
 Duntisbourne, 1983
The Lord Carrington, 1985
The Lord Callaghan of Cardiff,
 1987
The Duke of Wellington, 1990
Field Marshal the Lord Bramall,
 1990
Sir Edward Heath, 1992
The Viscount Ridley, 1992
The Lord Sainsbury of Preston
 Candover, 1992
The Lord Ashburton, 1994
The Lord Kingsdown, 1994
Sir Ninian Stephen, 1994
The Baroness Thatcher, 1995
Sir Edmund Hillary, 1995
Sir Timothy Colman, 1996
The Duke of Abercorn, 1999
Sir William Gladstone, 1999
Field Marshal The Lord Inge, 2001

Sir Anthony Acland, 2001
The Duke of Westminster, 2003
The Lord Butler of Brockwell, 2003
The Lord Morris of Aberavon, 2003
Prelate, The Bishop of Winchester

Chancellor, The Lord Carrington, KG,
 GCMG, CH, MC
Register, The Dean of Windsor
Garter King of Arms, P. Gwynn-Jones,
 CVO
Gentleman Usher of the Black Rod, Lt.-
 Gen. Sir Michael Willcocks, KCB
Secretary, P. L. Dickinson

THE MOST ANCIENT AND MOST NOBLE ORDER OF THE THISTLE (REVIVED 1687)

KT
Ribbon, Green
Motto, Nemo me impune lacessit
(No one provokes me with impunity)

The number of Members is limited to
16

SOVEREIGN OF THE ORDER
The Queen

LADY OF THE THISTLE
HRH The Princess Royal, 2000

ROYAL KNIGHTS
HRH The Prince Philip, Duke of
 Edinburgh, 1952
HRH The Prince of Wales, Duke of
 Rothesay, 1977

KNIGHTS AND LADIES
The Earl of Wemyss and March,
 1966
The Duke of Buccleuch and
 Queensberry, 1978
The Earl of Elgin and Kincardine,
 1981
The Lord Thomson of Monifieth,
 1981
The Earl of Airlie, 1985
Sir Iain Tennant, 1986
The Viscount of Arbuthnott, 1996
The Earl of Crawford and Balcarres,
 1996
Lady Marion Fraser, 1996
The Lord Macfarlane of Bearsden,
 1996
The Lord Mackay of Clashfern,
 1997
The Lord Wilson of Tillyorn, 2000

The Lord Sutherland of Houndwood,
 2002
Sir Eric Anderson, 2002

Chancellor, The Duke of Buccleuch
 and Queensberry, KT, VRD
Dean, The Very Revd G. I.
 Macmillan, CVO
Secretary and Lord Lyon King of Arms,
 R. O. Blair, LVO, WS
Usher of the Green Rod, Rear-Adm.
 C. H. Layman, CB, DSO, LVO

THE MOST HONOURABLE ORDER OF THE BATH (1725)

GCB *Military*   GCE *Civil*

GCB   Knight (or Dame) Grand
       Cross
KCB   Knight Commander
DCB   Dame Commander
CB   Companion

Ribbon, Crimson
Motto, Tria juncta in uno
(Three joined in one)

Remodelled 1815, and enlarged
many times since. The Order is
divided into civil and military
divisions. Women became eligible for
the Order from 1 January 1971.

THE SOVEREIGN

GREAT MASTER AND FIRST OR
PRINCIPAL KNIGHT GRAND CROSS
HRH The Prince of Wales, KG, KT,
 GCB, OM

Dean of the Order, The Dean of
 Westminster
Bath King of Arms, Gen. Sir Brian
 Kenny, GCB, CBE
Registrar and Secretary, Air Vice-
 Marshal Sir Richard Peirse, KCVO,
 CB
Genealogist, P. Gwynn-Jones, CVO
Gentleman Usher of the Scarlet Rod,
 Rear-Adm. I. R. Henderson, CB,
 CBE
Deputy Secretary, The Secretary of the
 Central Chancery of the Orders of
 Knighthood
Chancery, Central Chancery of the
 Orders of Knighthood, St James's
 Palace, London SW1A 1BH

THE ORDER OF MERIT (1902)

OM *Military*   OM *Civil*

OM
Ribbon, Blue and crimson

This Order is designed as a special distinction for eminent men and women without conferring a knighthood upon them. The Order is limited in numbers to 24, with the addition of foreign honorary members.

THE SOVEREIGN
HRH The Prince Philip, Duke of Edinburgh, 1968
Revd Prof. Owen Chadwick, KBE, 1983
Sir Andrew Huxley, 1983
Dr Frederick Sanger, 1986
Dame Cicely Saunders, 1989
The Baroness Thatcher, 1990
Dame Joan Sutherland, 1991
Sir Michael Atiyah, 1992
Lucian Freud, 1993
Sir Aaron Klug, 1995
The Lord Foster of Thames Bank, 1997
Sir Denis Rooke, 1997
Sir James Black, 2000
Sir Anthony Caro, 2000
Prof. Sir Roger Penrose, 2000
Sir Tom Stoppard, 2000
HRH The Prince of Wales, 2002
The Lord May of Oxford, 2002
The Lord Rothschild, 2002

Honorary Member, Nelson Mandela, 1995

Secretary and Registrar, The Lord Fellowes, GCB, GCVO, PC, QSO
Chancery, Central Chancery of the Orders of Knighthood, St James's Palace, London SW1A 1BH

THE MOST DISTINGUISHED ORDER OF ST MICHAEL AND ST GEORGE (1818)

GCMG   KCMG

GCMG   Knight (or Dame) Grand Cross
KCMG   Knight Commander
DCMG   Dame Commander
CMG   Companion

Ribbon, Saxon blue, with scarlet centre
Motto, Auspicium melioris aevi *(Token of a better age)*

THE SOVEREIGN

GRAND MASTER
HRH The Duke of Kent, KG, GCMG, GCVO, ADC

Prelate, The Rt. Revd Simon Barrington-Ward, KCMG
Chancellor, Sir Antony Acland, KG, GCMG, GCVO
Secretary, The Permanent Under-Secretary of State at the Foreign and Commonwealth Office and Head of the Diplomatic Service
Registrar, Lord Wilson of Tillyorn, KT, GCMG
King of Arms, Sir Ewen Fergusson, GCMG, GCVO
Gentleman Usher of the Blue Rod, Sir Anthony Figgis, KCVO, CMG
Dean, The Dean of St Paul's
Deputy Secretary, The Secretary of the Central Chancery of the Orders of Knighthood
Chancery, Central Chancery of the Orders of Knighthood, St James's Palace, London SW1A 1BH

THE MOST EMINENT ORDER OF THE INDIAN EMPIRE (1878)

GCIE   Knight Grand Commander
KCIE   Knight Commander
CIE   Companion

Ribbon, Imperial purple
Motto, Imperatricis auspiciis *(Under the auspices of the Empress)*

THE SOVEREIGN
Registrar, The Secretary of the Central Chancery of the Orders of Knighthood
No conferments have been made since 1947

THE IMPERIAL ORDER OF THE CROWN OF INDIA (1877) FOR LADIES

CI
Badge, the royal cipher in jewels within an oval, surmounted by an heraldic crown and attached to a bow of light blue watered ribbon, edged white

The honour does not confer any rank or title upon the recipient

No conferments have been made since 1947

HM The Queen, 1947
HRH Princess Alice, Duchess of Gloucester, 1937

THE ROYAL VICTORIAN ORDER (1896)

GCVO   KCVO

GCVO   Knight or Dame Grand Cross
KCVO   Knight Commander
DCVO   Dame Commander
CVO   Commander
LVO   Lieutenant
MVO   Member

Ribbon, Blue, with red and white edges
Motto, Victoria

THE SOVEREIGN

Chancellor, The Lord Chamberlain
Secretary, The Keeper of the Privy Purse
Registrar, The Secretary of the Central Chancery of the Orders of Knighthood
Chaplain, The Chaplain of the Queen's Chapel of the Savoy
Hon. Genealogist, D. H. B. Chesshyre, LVO

THE MOST EXCELLENT ORDER OF THE BRITISH EMPIRE (1917)

GBE   KBE

The Order was divided into military and civil divisions in December 1918

GBE   Knight or Dame Grand Cross
KBE   Knight Commander
DBE   Dame Commander
CBE   Commander
OBE   Officer
MBE   Member

Ribbon, Rose pink edged with pearl grey with vertical pearl stripe in centre (military division); without vertical pearl stripe (civil division)
Motto, For God and the Empire

THE SOVEREIGN

GRAND MASTER
HRH The Prince Philip, Duke of
Edinburgh, KG, KT, OM, GBE, PC

Prelate, The Bishop of London
King of Arms, Air Chief Marshal Sir
Patrick Hine, GCB, GBE
Registrar, The Secretary of the
Central Chancery of the Orders of
Knighthood
Secretary, The Secretary of the
Cabinet and Head of the Home
Civil Service
Dean, The Dean of St Paul's
Gentleman Usher of the Purple Rod, Sir
Alexander Michael Graham, GBE,
DCL
Chancery, Central Chancery of the
Orders of Knighthood, St James's
Palace, London SW1A 1BH

ORDER OF THE COMPANIONS OF HONOUR (1917)

CH

Ribbon, Carmine, with gold edges

This Order consists of one class only
and carries with it no title. The
number of awards is limited to 65
(excluding honorary members).

Anthony, Rt. Hon. John, 1981
Ashley of Stoke, The Lord, 1975
Attenborough, Sir David, 1995
Baker, Dame Janet, 1993
Baker of Dorking, The Lord, 1992
Birtwistle, Sir Harrison, 2000
Brenner, Sydney, 1986
Brook, Peter, 1998
Brooke of Sutton Mandeville, The
Lord, 1992
Carrington, The Lord, 1983
Christie, Sir George, 2001
Davis, Sir Colin, 2001
De Chastelain, Gen. John, 1999
Doll, Prof. Sir Richard, 1995
Fraser, Rt. Hon. Malcolm, 1977
Freud, Lucian, 1983
Glenamara, The Lord, 1976
Hamilton, Richard, 1999

Hannay of Chiswick, The Lord,
2003
Hawking, Prof. Stephen, 1989
Healey, The Lord, 1979
Heseltine, The Lord, 1997
Hobsbawm, Prof. Eric, 1998
Hockney, David, 1997
Hodgkin, Sir Howard, 2002
Howard, Sir Michael, 2002
Howe of Aberavon, The Lord,
1996
Hurd of Westwell, The Lord, 1995
Jones, James, 1977
King of Bridgewater, The Lord,
1992
Lange, Rt. Hon. David, 1989
Lessing, Doris, 1999
Lovelock, James, 2002
McKenzie, Prof. Dan Peter, 2003
MacKerras, Sir Charles, 2003
Mahon, Sir Denis, 2002
Major, Rt. Hon. John, 1998
Owen, The Lord, 1994
Patten, Rt. Hon. Christopher, 1997
Pinter, Harold, 2002
Riley, Bridget, 1998
Sanger, Frederick, 1981
Scofield, Paul, 2000
Smith, Sir John, 1993
Somare, Rt. Hon. Sir Michael, 1978
Talboys, Rt. Hon. Sir Brian, 1981
Tebbit, The Lord, 1987
Varah, Revd Dr Chad, 1999

Honorary Members, Lee Kuan Yew,
1970; Prof. Amartya Sen, 2000;
Bernard Haitink, 2002
Secretary and Registrar, The Secretary
of the Central Chancery of the
Orders of Knighthood

THE DISTINGUISHED SERVICE ORDER (1886)

DSO

Ribbon, Red, with blue edges

Bestowed in recognition of especial
services in action of commissioned
officers in the Navy, Army and Royal
Air Force and (since 1942)
Mercantile Marine. The members are
Companions only. A Bar may be
awarded for any additional act of
service.

THE IMPERIAL SERVICE ORDER (1902)

ISO

Ribbon, Crimson, with blue centre

Appointment as Companion of this
Order is open to members of the
Civil Services whose eligibility is
determined by the grade they hold.
The Order consists of The Sovereign
and Companions to a number not
exceeding 1,900, of whom 1,300
may belong to the Home Civil
Services and 600 to Overseas Civil
Services. The then Prime Minister
announced in March 1993 that he
would make no further
recommendations for appointments
to the Order.

Secretary, The Secretary of the
Cabinet and Head of the Home
Civil Service
Registrar, The Secretary of the
Central Chancery of the Orders of
Knighthood

THE ROYAL VICTORIAN CHAIN (1902)

It confers no precedence on its
holders

HM THE QUEEN

HM The King of Thailand, 1960
HM King Zahir Shah of Afghanistan,
1971
HM The Queen of Denmark, 1974
HM The King of Sweden, 1975
HM The Queen of the Netherlands,
1982
Gen. Antonio Eanes, 1985
HM The King of Spain, 1986
HM The King of Saudi Arabia, 1987
Dr Richard von Weizsäcker, 1992
HM The King of Norway, 1994
The Earl of Airlie, 1997
The Rt. Revd and Rt. Hon. Lord
Carey of Clifton, 2002

BARONETAGE AND KNIGHTAGE

BARONETS

Style, 'Sir' before forename and surname, followed by 'Bt.'
Wife's style, 'Lady' followed by surname
For forms of address, *see* page 43

There are five different creations of baronetcies: Baronets of England (creations dating from 1611); Baronets of Ireland (creations dating from 1619); Baronets of Scotland or Nova Scotia (creations dating from 1625); Baronets of Great Britain (creations after the Act of Union 1707 which combined the kingdoms of England and Scotland); and Baronets of the United Kingdom (creations after the union of Great Britain and Ireland in 1801).

Badge of Baronets of the   *Badge of Baronets*
United Kingdom   *of Nova Scotia*

Badge of Ulster

The patent of creation limits the destination of a baronetcy, usually to male descendants of the first baronet, although special remainders allow the baronetcy to pass, if the male issue of sons fail, to the male issue of daughters of the first baronet. In the case of baronetcies of Scotland or Nova Scotia, a special remainder of 'heirs male and of tailzie' allows the baronetcy to descend to heirs general, including women. There are four existing Scottish baronets with such a remainder.

The Official Roll of the Baronetage is kept at the Department for Constitutional Affairs by the Registrar of the Baronetage. Anyone who considers that he is entitled to be entered on the Roll may petition the Crown through the Lord Chancellor. Every person succeeding to a baronetcy must exhibit proofs of succession to the Lord Chancellor. A person whose name is not entered on the Official Roll will not be addressed or mentioned by the title of baronet in any official document, nor will he be accorded precedence as a baronet.

BARONETCIES EXTINCT SINCE THE LAST EDITION
de Montmorency (cr. I.1631); Colyer-Fergusson (cr. 1866); Lewthwaite (cr. 1927)

Registrar of the Baronetage, Andrew McDonald
Assistant Registrar, Steven Johnson
Office, Department for Constitutional Affairs, Constitutional Policy Division, 6th Floor, Selborne House, 54 Victoria Street, London SW1E 6QW
T 020-7210 8564

KNIGHTS

Style, 'Sir' before forename and surname, followed by appropriate post-nominal initials if a Knight Grand Cross, Knight Grand Commander or Knight Commander
Wife's style, 'Lady' followed by surname
For forms of address, *see* page 43

The prefix 'Sir' is not used by knights who are clerics of the Church of England, who do not receive the accolade. Their wives are entitled to precedence as the wife of a knight but not to the style of 'Lady'.

ORDERS OF KNIGHTHOOD
Knight Grand Cross, Knight Grand Commander, and Knight Commander are the higher classes of the Orders of Chivalry (*see* page 80). Honorary knighthoods of these Orders may be conferred on men who are citizens of countries of which The Queen is not head of state. As a rule, the prefix 'Sir' is not used by honorary knights.

KNIGHTS BACHELOR

The Knights Bachelor do not constitute a Royal Order, but comprise the surviving representation of the ancient State Orders of Knighthood. The Register of Knights Bachelor, instituted by James I in the 17th century, lapsed, and in 1908 a voluntary association under the title of The Society of Knights (now The Imperial Society of Knights Bachelor by Royal Command) was formed with the primary objects of continuing the various registers dating from 1257 and obtaining the uniform registration of every created Knight Bachelor. In 1926 a design for a badge to be worn by Knights Bachelor was approved and adopted; in 1974 a neck badge and miniature were added.

Knight Principal, Sir Richard Gaskell
Prelate, Rt. Revd and Rt. Hon. The Bishop of London
Registrar, Sir Robert Balchin, DL
Hon. Treasurer, Sir Paul Judge
Clerk to the Council, R. L. Jenkins, LVO, TD
Office, 21 Old Buildings, Lincoln's Inn, London WC2A 3UJ

LIST OF BARONETS AND KNIGHTS

Revised to 31 August 2004
Peers are not included in this list
†   Not registered on the Official Roll of the Baronetage at the time of going to press
( )   The date of creation of the baronetcy is given in parenthesis
I   Baronet of Ireland
NS   Baronet of Nova Scotia
S   Baronet of Scotland

A full entry in italic type indicates that the recipient of a knighthood died during the year in which the honour was conferred. The name is included for purposes of record.

Abbott, Sir Albert Francis, Kt., CBE
Abbott, *Adm.* Sir Peter Charles, GBE, KCB
Abdy, Sir Valentine Robert Duff, Bt. (1850)
Acheson, *Prof.* Sir (Ernest) Donald, KBE
Ackers, Sir James George, Kt.
Ackers-Jones, Sir David, KBE, CMG
Ackroyd, Sir Timothy Robert Whyte, Bt. (1956)
Acland, Sir Antony Arthur, KG, GCMG, GCVO
Acland, *Lt.-Col.* Sir (Christopher) Guy (Dyke), Bt., MVO (1890)
Acland, Sir John Dyke, Bt. (1644)
Acland, *Maj.-Gen.* Sir John Hugh Bevil, KCB, CBE
Adam, Sir Christopher Eric Forbes, Bt. (1917)
Adam, Sir Kenneth Hugo, Kt., OBE
Adams, Sir William James, KCMG
Adsetts, Sir William Norman, Kt., OBE
Adye, Sir John Anthony, KCMG
Aga Khan IV, HH Prince Karim, KBE
Agnew, Sir Crispin Hamlyn, Bt. (S. 1629)
Agnew, Sir John Keith, Bt. (1895)
Agnew, Sir Rudolph Ion Joseph, Kt.
Agnew-Somerville, Sir Quentin Charles Somerville, Bt. (1957)
Aiken, *Air Chief Marshal* Sir John Alexander Carlisle, KCB
Aikens, *Hon.* Sir Richard John Pearson, Kt.
†Ainsworth, Sir Anthony Thomas Hugh, Bt. (1916)
Aird, *Capt.* Sir Alastair Sturgis, GCVO
Aird, Sir (George) John, Bt. (1901)
Airy, *Maj.-Gen.* Sir Christopher John, KCVO, CBE
Aitchison, Sir Charles Walter de Lancey, Bt. (1938)
Akehurst, *Gen.* Sir John Bryan, KCB, CBE
Alberti, *Prof.* Sir Kurt George Matthew Mayer, Kt.
Albu, Sir George, Bt. (1912)
Alcock, *Air Chief Marshal* Sir (Robert James) Michael, GCB, KBE
Aldous, *Rt. Hon.* Sir William, Kt.
Alexander, Sir Charles Gundry, Bt. (1945)
Alexander, Sir Douglas, Bt. (1921)
Allen, *Prof.* Sir Geoffrey, Kt., PHD, FRS
Allen, Sir John Derek, Kt., CBE
Allen, *Hon.* Sir Peter Austin Philip Jermyn, Kt.
Allen, Sir Thomas Boaz, Kt., CBE
Allen, *Hon.* Sir William Clifford, KCMG, MP
Allen, Sir William Guilford, Kt.
Alleyne, Sir George Allanmoore Ogarren, Kt.
Alleyne, *Revd* John Olpherts Campbell, Bt. (1769)
Allinson, Sir (Walter) Leonard, KCVO, CMG
Alliott, *Hon.* Sir John Downes, Kt.

Allison, *Air Chief Marshal* Sir John Shakespeare, KCB, CBE
Althaus, Sir Nigel Frederick, Kt.
Alun-Jones, Sir (John) Derek, Kt.
Ambo, *Rt. Revd* George, KBE
Amet, *Hon.* Sir Arnold Karibone, Kt.
Amory, Sir Ian Heathcoat, Bt. (1874)
Anderson, Sir John Anthony, KBE
Anderson, *Maj.-Gen.* Sir John Evelyn, KBE
Anderson, Sir John Muir, Kt., CMG
Anderson, Sir Leith Reinsford Steven, Kt., CBE
Anderson, *Vice-Adm.* Sir Neil Dudley, KBE, CB
Anderson, Sir (William) Eric Kinloch, KT
Anderson, *Prof.* Sir (William) Ferguson, Kt., OBE
Anderton, Sir (Cyril) James, Kt., CBE, QPM
Andrew, Sir Robert John, KCB
Andrews, Sir Derek Henry, KCB, CBE
Andrews, *Hon.* Sir Dormer George, Kt.
Angus, Sir Michael Richardson, Kt.
Annesley, Sir Hugh Norman, Kt., QPM
Anson, *Vice-Adm.* Sir Edward Rosebery, KCB
Anson, Sir John, KCB
Anson, *Rear-Adm.* Sir Peter, Bt., CB (1831)
Anstruther, Sir Ian Fife Campbell, Bt., (S. 1694)
Anstruther-Gough-Calthorpe, Sir Euan Hamilton, Bt. (1929)
Antico, Sir Tristan Venus, Kt.
Antrobus, Sir Edward Philip, Bt. (1815)
Appleyard, Sir Leonard Vincent, KCMG
Appleyard, Sir Raymond Kenelm, KBE
Arbib, Sir Martyn, Kt.
Arbuthnot, Sir Keith Robert Charles, Bt. (1823)
Arbuthnot, Sir William Reierson, Bt. (1964)
Arbuthnott, *Prof.* Sir John Peebles, Kt., PHD, FRSE
Archdale, *Capt.* Sir Edward Folmer, Bt., DSC, RN (1928)
Arculus, Sir Ronald, KCMG, KCVO
Armitage, *Air Chief Marshal* Sir Michael John, KCB, CBE
Armour, *Prof.* Sir James, Kt., CBE
Armstrong, Sir Christopher John Edmund Stuart, Bt., MBE (1841)
Armstrong, Sir Patrick John, Kt., CBE
Armstrong, Sir Richard, Kt., CBE
Armytage, Sir John Martin, Bt. (1738)
Arnold, *Rt. Hon.* Sir John Lewis, Kt.
Arnold, Sir Malcolm Henry, Kt., CBE
Arnold, Sir Thomas Richard, Kt.
Arnott, Sir Alexander John Maxwell, Bt. (1896)
Arrindell, Sir Clement Athelston, GCMG, GCVO, QC
Arthur, Sir Gavyn Farr, Kt.

Arthur, *Lt.-Gen.* Sir (John) Norman Stewart, KCB
Arthur, Sir Michael Anthony, KCMG
Arthur, Sir Stephen John, Bt. (1841)
Ash, *Prof.* Sir Eric Albert, Kt., CBE, FRS, FRENG
Ashburnham, Sir James Fleetwood, Bt. (1661)
Ashley, Sir Bernard Albert, Kt.
Ashmore, *Admiral of the Fleet* Sir Edward Beckwith, GCB, DSC
Aske, Sir Robert John Bingham, Bt. (1922)
Askew, Sir Bryan, Kt.
Asscher, *Prof.* Sir (Adolf) William, Kt., MD, FRCP
Astill, *Hon.* Sir Michael John, Kt.
Astley-Cooper, Sir Alexander Paston, Bt. (1821)
Aston, Sir Harold George, Kt., CBE
Astwood, *Hon.* Sir James Rufus, KBE
Atcherley, Sir Harold Winter, Kt.
Atiyah, Sir Michael Francis, Kt., OM, PHD, FRS
Atkins, *Rt. Hon.* Sir Robert James, Kt.
Atkinson, *Prof.* Sir Anthony Barnes, Kt.
Atkinson, *Air Marshal* Sir David William, KBE
Atkinson, Sir Frederick John, KCB
Atkinson, Sir John Alexander, KCB, DFC
Atkinson, Sir Robert, Kt., DSC, FRENG
Atopare, Sir Sailas, GCMG
Attenborough, Sir David Frederick, Kt., CH, CVO, CBE, FRS
Aubrey-Fletcher, Sir Henry Egerton, Bt. (1782)
Audland, Sir Christopher John, KCMG
Audley, Sir George Bernard, Kt.
Augier, *Prof.* Sir Fitz-Roy Richard, Kt.
Auld, *Rt. Hon.* Sir Robin Ernest, Kt.
Austin, Sir Anthony Leonard, Bt. (1894)
Austin, *Vice-Adm.* Sir Peter Murray, KCB
Austin, *Air Marshal* Sir Roger Mark, KCB, AFC
Austen-Smith, *Air Marshal* Sir Roy David, KBE, CB, CVO, DFC
Avei, Sir Moi, KBE
Axford, Sir William Ian, Kt.
Ayckbourn, Sir Alan, Kt., CBE
Aykroyd, Sir James Alexander Frederic, Bt. (1929)
Aykroyd, Sir William Miles, Bt., MC (1920)
Aylmer, Sir Richard John, Bt. (I. 1622)
Bacha, Sir Bhinod, Kt., CMG
Backhouse, Sir Jonathan Roger, Bt. (1901)
Bacon, Sir Nicholas Hickman Ponsonby, Bt. *Premier Baronet of England* (1611 and 1627)
Bacon, Sir Sidney Charles, Kt., CB, FRENG
Baddeley, Sir John Wolsey Beresford, Bt. (1922)

Baddiley, *Prof.* Sir James, Kt., PHD, DSC, FRS, FRSE

Badge, Sir Peter Gilmour Noto, Kt.

Baer, Sir Jack Mervyn Frank, Kt.

Bagge, Sir (John) Jeremy Picton, Bt. (1867)

Bagnall, *Air Chief Marshal* Sir Anthony, GBE, KCB

Bailey, Sir Alan Marshall, KCB

Bailey, Sir Brian Harry, Kt., OBE

Bailey, Sir Derrick Thomas Louis, Bt., DFC (1919)

Bailey, Sir John Bilsland, KCB

Bailey, Sir Richard John, Kt., CBE

Bailey, Sir Stanley Ernest, Kt., CBE, QPM

Bailhache, Sir Philip Martin, Kt.

Baillie, Sir Adrian Louis, Bt. (1823)

Bain, *Prof.* Sir George Sayers, Kt.

Baird, Sir Charles William Stuart, Bt. (1809)

†Baird, Sir James Andrew Gardiner, Bt. (S. 1695)

Baird, *Lt.-Gen.* Sir James Parlane, KBE, MD

Baird, *Air Marshal* Sir John Alexander, KBE

Baird, *Vice-Adm.* Sir Thomas Henry Eustace, KCB

Bairsto, *Air Marshal* Sir Peter Edward, KBE, CB

Baker, Sir Bryan William, Kt.

Baker, *Prof.* Sir John Hamilton, Kt., QC

Baker, *Rt. Hon.* Sir (Thomas) Scott (Gillespie), Kt.

Balchin, Sir Robert George Alexander, Kt.

Balderstone, Sir James Schofield, Kt.

Baldwin, *Prof.* Sir Jack Edward, Kt., FRS

Baldwin, Sir Peter Robert, KCB

Ball, *Air Marshal* Sir Alfred Henry Wynne, KCB, DSO, DFC

Ball, Sir Christopher John Elinger, Kt.

Ball, Sir Richard Bentley, Bt. (1911)

Ball, *Prof.* Sir Robert James, Kt., PHD

Ballantyne, *Dr* Sir Frederick Nathaniel, GCMG

Bamford, Sir Anthony Paul, Kt.

Band, *Adm.* Sir Jonathon, KCB

Banham, Sir John Michael Middlecott, Kt.

Bannerman, Sir David Gordon, Bt., OBE (S. 1682)

Bannister, Sir Roger Gilbert, Kt., CBE, DM, FRCP

Barber, Sir (Thomas) David, Bt. (1960)

Barbour, *Very Revd* Robert Alexander Stewart, KCVO, MC

Barclay, Sir Colville Herbert Sanford, Bt. (S. 1668)

Barclay, Sir David Rowat, Kt.

Barclay, Sir Frederick Hugh, Kt.

Barclay, Sir Peter Maurice, Kt., CBE

Barder, Sir Brian Leon, KCMG

Baring, Sir John Francis, Bt. (1911)

Barker, Sir Colin, Kt.

Barker, *Hon.* Sir (Richard) Ian, Kt.

Barlow, Sir Christopher Hilaro, Bt. (1803)

Barlow, Sir Frank, Kt., CBE

Barlow, Sir (George) William, Kt., FRENG

†Barlow, Sir James Alan, Bt. (1902)

Barlow, Sir John Kemp, Bt. (1907)

Barnard, Sir Joseph Brian, Kt.

Barnes, *The Most Revd.* Brian James, KBE

Barnes, Sir (James) David (Francis), Kt., CBE

Barnes, Sir Kenneth, KCB

Barnewall, Sir Reginald Robert, Bt. (I. 1623)

Baron, Sir Thomas, Kt., CBE

Barraclough, *Air Chief Marshal* Sir John, KCB, CBE, DFC, AFC

Barran, Sir John Napoleon Ruthven, Bt. (1895)

Barratt, Sir Lawrence Arthur, Kt.

Barratt, Sir Richard Stanley, Kt., CBE, QPM

Barratt-Boyes, Sir Brian Gerald, KBE

Barrett, Sir Stephen Jeremy, KCMG

Barrett-Lennard, *Revd* Hugh Dacre, Bt. (1801)

Barrington, Sir Benjamin, Bt. (1831)

Barrington, Sir Nicholas John, KCMG, CVO

Barrington-Ward, *Rt. Revd* Simon, KCMG

Barron, Sir Donald James, Kt.

Barrow, *Capt.* Sir Richard John Uniacke, Bt. (1835)

Barry, Sir (Lawrence) Edward (Anthony Tress), Bt. (1899)

Barter, Sir Peter Leslie Charles, Kt., OBE

†Bartlett, Sir Andrew Alan, Bt. (1913)

Barttelot, *Col.* Sir Brian Walter de Stopham, Bt., OBE (1875)

Batchelor, Sir Ivor Ralph Campbell, Kt., CBE

Bate, Sir David Lindsay, KBE

Bates, Sir Alan Arthur, Kt., CBE

Bates, Sir Geoffrey Voltelin, Bt., MC (1880)

Bates, Sir Malcolm Rowland, Kt.

Bates, Sir Richard Dawson Hoult, Bt. (1937)

Bateson, *Prof.* Sir Patrick, Kt.

Batho, Sir Peter Ghislain, Bt. (1928)

Bathurst, *Admiral of the Fleet* Sir (David) Benjamin, GCB

Bathurst, Sir Maurice Edward, Kt., CMG, CBE, QC

Batten, Sir John Charles, KCVO

Battersby, Prof. Sir Alan Rushton, Kt., FRS

Battishill, Sir Anthony Michael William, GCB

Baxendell, Sir Peter Brian, Kt., CBE, FRENG

Bayliss, Sir Richard Ian Samuel, KCVO, MD, FRCP

Bayne, Sir Nicholas Peter, KCMG

Baynes, Sir John Christopher Malcolm, Bt. (1801)

Bazley, Sir Thomas John Sebastian, Bt. (1869)

Beach, *Gen.* Sir (William Gerald) Hugh, GBE, KCB, MC

Beache, *Hon.* Sir Vincent Ian, KCMG

Beale, *Lt.-Gen.* Sir Peter John, KBE, FRCP

Beament, Sir James William Longman, Kt., SCD, FRS

Beamish, Sir Adrian John, KCMG

Beaumont, *Capt.* the Hon. Sir (Edward) Nicholas (Canning), KCVO

Beaumont, Sir George (Howland Francis), Bt. (1661)

Beaumont, Sir Richard Ashton, KCMG, OBE

Beaumont-Dark, Sir Anthony Michael, Kt.

Beatson, *Hon.* Sir Jack, Kt.

Beavis, *Air Chief Marshal* Sir Michael Gordon, KCB, CBE, AFC

Beck, Sir Edgar Philip, Kt.

Beckett, Sir Richard Gervase, Bt., QC (1921)

Beckett, Sir Terence Norman, KBE, FRENG

Beckwith, Sir John Lionel, Kt., CBE

Bedser, Sir Alec Victor, Kt., CBE

Beecham, Sir Jeremy Hugh, Kt.

Beecham, Sir John Stratford Roland, Bt. (1914)

Beetham, *Marshal of the Royal Air Force* Sir Michael James, GCB, CBE, DFC, AFC

Beevor, Sir Thomas Agnew, Bt. (1784)

Beldam, *Rt. Hon.* Sir (Alexander) Roy (Asplan), Kt.

Belich, Sir James, Kt.

Bell, Sir Brian Ernest, KBE

Bell, Sir David Charles Maurice, Kt.

Bell, Sir John Lowthian, Bt. (1885)

Bell, *Prof.* Sir Peter Robert Frank, Kt.

Bell, *Hon.* Sir Rodger, Kt.

Bell, Sir Stuart, Kt.

Bellamy, *Hon.* Sir Christopher William, Kt.

Bellingham, Sir Anthony Edward Norman, Bt. (1796)

Bender, Sir Brian Geoffrey, KCB

Bengough, *Col.* Sir Piers, KCVO, OBE

Benn, Sir (James) Jonathan, Bt. (1914)

Bennett, *Air Vice-Marshal* Sir Erik Peter, KBE, CB

Bennett, *Hon.* Sir Hugh Peter Derwyn, Kt.

Bennett, *Gen.* Sir Phillip Harvey, KBE, DSO

Bennett, Sir Richard Rodney, Kt., CBE

Bennett, Sir Ronald Wilfrid Murdoch, Bt. (1929)

Benson, Sir Christopher John, Kt.

Benyon, Sir William Richard, Kt.

Beresford, Sir (Alexander) Paul, Kt., MP

Beresford-Peirse, Sir Henry Grant de la Poer, Bt. (1814)

Berghuser, *Hon.* Sir Eric, Kt., MBE

Beringer, *Prof.* Sir John Evelyn, Kt., CBE

Berman, Sir Franklin Delow, KCMG

Berners-Lee, Sir Timothy John, KBE
Bernard, Sir Dallas Edmund, Bt. (1954)
Bernstein, Sir Howard, Kt.
Berney, Sir Julian Reedham Stuart, Bt. (1620)
Berridge, *Prof.* Sir Michael John, Kt., FRS
Berrill, Sir Kenneth Ernest, GBE, KCB
Berriman, Sir David, Kt.
Berry, *Prof.* Sir Colin Leonard, Kt., FRCPath.
Berry, *Prof.* Sir Michael Victor, Kt., FRS
Berthon, *Vice-Adm.* Sir Stephen Ferrier, KCB
Berthoud, Sir Martin Seymour, KCVO, CMG
Best, Sir Richard Radford, KCVO, CBE
Best-Shaw, Sir John Michael Robert, Bt. (1665)
Bethune, *Hon.* Sir (Walter) Angus, Kt.
Bett, Sir Michael, Kt., CBE
Bevan, Sir Martyn Evan Evans, Bt. (1958)
Bevan, Sir Nicolas, Kt., CB
Bevan, Sir Timothy Hugh, Kt.
Beverley, *Lt.-Gen.* Sir Henry York La Roche, KCB, OBE, RM
Bibby, Sir Michael James, Bt. (1959)
Bichard, Sir Michael George, KCB
Bickersteth, *Rt. Revd* John Monier, KCVO
Biddulph, Sir Ian D'Olier, Bt. (1664)
Bide, Sir Austin Ernest, Kt.
Bidwell, Sir Hugh Charles Philip, GBE
Biggam, Sir Robin Adair, Kt.
Biggs, Sir Norman Paris, Kt.
Bilas, Sir Angmai Simon, Kt., OBE
Billière, *Gen.* Sir Peter Edgar de la Cour de la, KCB, KBE, DSO, MC
Bingham, *Hon.* Sir Eardley Max, Kt.
Birch, Sir John Allan, KCVO, CMG
Birch, Sir Roger, Kt., CBE, QPM
Bird, Sir Richard Geoffrey Chapman, Bt. (1922)
Birkin, Sir John Christian William, Bt. (1905)
Birkin, Sir (John) Derek, Kt., TD
Birkmyre, Sir James, Bt. (1921)
Birrell, Sir James Drake, Kt.
Birtwistle, Sir Harrison, Kt., CH
Bischoff, Sir Winfried Franz Wilhelm, Kt.
Bishop, Sir Frederick Arthur, Kt., CB, CVO
Bishop, Sir Michael David, Kt., CBE
Bisson, *Rt. Hon.* Sir Gordon Ellis, Kt.
Bjelke-Petersen, Sir Johannes, KCMG
Black, Sir James Whyte, Kt., OM, FRCP, FRS
Black, *Adm.* Sir (John) Jeremy, GBE, KCB, DSO
Black, Sir Robert David, Bt. (1922)
Blackburn, *Vice-Adm.* Sir David Anthony James, KCVO, CB, LVO
Blackburne, *Hon.* Sir William Anthony, Kt.
Blacker, *Gen.* Sir (Anthony Stephen) Jeremy, KCB, CBE

Blackett, Sir Hugh Francis, Bt. (1673)
Blackham, *Vice-Adm.* Sir Jeremy Joe, KCB
Blacklock, *Surgeon Capt. Prof.* Sir Norman James, KCVO, OBE
Blackman, Sir Frank Milton, KCVO, OBE
Blackwood, Sir John Francis, Bt. (1814)
Blair, *Lt.-Gen.* Sir Chandos, KCVO, OBE, MC
Blair, Sir Edward Thomas Hunter, Bt. (1786)
Blair, Sir Ian Warwick, Kt., QPM
Blake, Sir Alfred Lapthorn, KCVO, MC
Blake, Sir Francis Michael, Bt. (1907)
Blake, Sir Peter Thomas, Kt., CBE
Blake, Sir (Thomas) Richard (Valentine), Bt. (I. 1622)
Blaker, Sir John, Bt. (1919)
Blakiston, Sir Ferguson Arthur James, Bt. (1763)
Blanch, Sir Malcolm, KCVO
Bland, Sir (Francis) Christopher (Buchan), Kt.
Bland, *Lt.-Col.* Sir Simon Claud Michael, KCVO
Blank, Sir Maurice Victor, Kt.
Blatherwick, Sir David Elliott Spiby, KCMG, OBE
Blelloch, Sir John Nial Henderson, KCB
Blennerhassett, Sir (Marmaduke) Adrian Francis William, Bt. (1809)
Blewitt, *Maj.* Sir Shane Gabriel Basil, GCVO
Blofeld, *Hon.* Sir John Christopher Calthorpe, Kt.
Blois, Sir Charles Nicholas Gervase, Bt. (1686)
Blom-Cooper, Sir Louis Jacques, Kt., QC
Blomefield, Sir Thomas Charles Peregrine, Bt. (1807)
Bloomfield, Sir Kenneth Percy, KCB
Blount, Sir Walter Edward Alpin, Bt., DSC (1642)
Blundell, Sir Thomas Leon, Kt., FRS
Blunden, Sir George, Kt.
Blunden, Sir Philip Overington, Bt. (I. 1766)
Blunt, Sir David Richard Reginald Harvey, Bt. (1720)
Blyth, Sir Charles (Chay), Kt., CBE, BEM
Boardman, *Prof.* Sir John, Kt., FSA, FBA
Bodey, *Hon.* Sir David Roderick Lessiter, Kt.
Bodmer, Sir Walter Fred, Kt., PHD, FRS
Body, Sir Richard Bernard Frank Stewart, Kt., MP
Bogan, Sir Nagora, KBE
Boileau, Sir Guy (Francis), Bt. (1838)
Boles, Sir Jeremy John Fortescue, Bt. (1922)
Boles, Sir John Dennis, Kt., MBE
Bolland, Sir Edwin, KCMG

Bollers, *Hon.* Sir Harold Brodie Smith, Kt.
Bolt, *Air Marshal* Sir Richard Bruce, KBE, CB, DFC, AFC
Bolton, Sir Frederic Bernard, Kt., MC
Bona, Sir Kina, KBE
Bonallack, Sir Michael Francis, Kt., OBE
Bond, Sir John Reginald Hartnell, Kt.
Bond, Sir Kenneth Raymond Boyden, Kt.
Bond, *Prof.* Sir Michael Richard, Kt., FRCPsych., FRCPGlas., FRCSE
Bondi, *Prof.* Sir Hermann, KCB, FRS
Bone, Sir Roger Bridgland, KCMG
Bonfield, Sir Peter Leahy, Kt., CBE, FRENG
Bonham, *Maj.* Sir Antony Lionel Thomas, Bt. (1852)
Bonington, Sir Christian John Storey, Kt., CBE
Bonsall, Sir Arthur Wilfred, KCMG, CBE
Bonsor, Sir Nicholas Cosmo, Bt. (1925)
Boolell, Sir Satcam, Kt.
Boord, Sir Nicolas John Charles, Bt. (1896)
Boorman, *Lt.-Gen.* Sir Derek, KCB
Booth, Sir Christopher Charles, Kt., MD, FRCP
Booth, Sir Douglas Allen, Bt. (1916)
Booth, Sir Gordon, KCMG, CVO
Boothby, Sir Brooke Charles, Bt. (1660)
Bore, Sir Albert, Kt.
Boreel, Sir Stephan Gerard, Bt. (1645)
†Borthwick, Sir Anthony Thomas, Bt. (1908)
Borysiewicz, *Prof.* Sir Leszek Krzysztof, Kt.
Bossom, *Hon.* Sir Clive, Bt. (1953)
Boswell, *Lt.-Gen.* Sir Alexander Crawford Simpson, KCB, CBE
Bosworth, Sir Neville Bruce Alfred, Kt., CBE
Booth, Sir Clive, Kt.
Bottoms, *Prof.* Sir Anthony Edward, Kt.
Bottomley, Sir James Reginald Alfred, KCMG
Boughey, Sir John George Fletcher Bt. (1798)
Boulton, Sir Clifford John, GCB
Boulton, Sir William Whytehead, Bt., CBE, TD (1944)
Bourn, Sir John Bryant, KCB
Bowater, Sir Euan David Vansittart, Bt. (1939)
Bowater, Sir (John) Vansittart, Bt. (1914)
Bowden, Sir Andrew, Kt., MBE
Bowden, Sir Nicholas Richard, Bt. (1915)
Bowen, Sir Geoffrey Fraser, Kt.
Bowen, Sir Mark Edward Mortimer, Bt. (1921)
Bowett, *Prof.* Sir Derek William, Kt., CBE, QC, FBA
†Bowlby, Sir Richard Peregrine Longstaff, Bt. (1923)

Bowman, Sir Edwin Geoffrey, KCB
Bowman, Sir Jeffery Haverstock, Kt.
Bowman-Shaw, Sir (George) Neville, Kt.
Bowness, Sir Alan, Kt., CBE
Bowyer-Smyth, Sir Thomas Weyland, Bt. (1661)
Boyce, Sir Graham Hugh, KCMG
Boyce, Sir Robert Charles Leslie, Bt. (1952)
Boyd, Sir Alexander Walter, Bt. (1916)
Boyd, Sir John Dixon Iklé, KCMG
Boyd, Prof. Sir Robert David Hugh, Kt.
Boyd-Carpenter, Sir (Marsom) Henry, KCVO
Boyd-Carpenter, Lt.-Gen. Hon. Sir Thomas Patrick John, KBE
Boyle, Sir Stephen Gurney, Bt. (1904)
Boynton, Sir John Keyworth, Kt., MC
Boyson, Rt. Hon. Sir Rhodes, Kt.
Brabham, Sir John Arthur, Kt., OBE
Bracewell-Smith, Sir Charles, Bt. (1947)
Bradbeer, Sir John Derek Richardson, Kt., OBE, TD
Bradford, Sir Edward Alexander Slade, Bt. (1902)
Bradshaw, Sir Kenneth Anthony, KCB
Brady, Prof. Sir John Michael Kt. FRS
Braithwaite, Sir (Joseph) Franklin Madders, Kt.
Braithwaite, Rt. Hon. Sir Nicholas Alexander, Kt., OBE
Braithwaite, Sir Rodric Quentin, GCMG
Bramley, Prof. Sir Paul Anthony, Kt.
Branson, Sir Richard Charles Nicholas, Kt.
Bratza, Hon. Sir Nicolas Dušan, Kt.
Breckenridge, Prof. Sir Alasdair Muir, Kt. CBE
Brennan, Hon. Sir (Francis) Gerard, KBE
Brett, Sir Charles Edward Bainbridge, Kt., CBE
Brickwood, Sir Basil Greame, Bt. (1927)
Bridges, Hon. Sir Phillip Rodney, Kt., CMG
Brierley, Sir Ronald Alfred, Kt.
Bright, Sir Graham Frank James, Kt.
Bright, Sir Keith, Kt.
Brigstocke, Adm. Sir John Richard, KCB
Brinckman, Sir Theodore George Roderick, Bt. (1831)
†Brisco, Sir Campbell Howard, Bt. (1782)
Briscoe, Sir Brian Anthony, Kt.
Briscoe, Sir John Geoffrey James, Bt. (1910)
Brittan, Sir Samuel, Kt.
Britton, Sir Edward Louis, Kt., CBE
†Broadbent, Sir Andrew George, Bt. (1893)
Broadbent, Sir Richard John, KCB
Brocklebank, Sir Aubrey Thomas, Bt. (1885)
Brodie, Sir Benjamin David Ross, Bt. (1834)

Brodie-Hall, Sir Laurence Charles, Kt., AO, CMG
Bromhead, Sir John Desmond Gonville, Bt. (1806)
Bromley, Sir Michael Roger, KBE
Bromley, Sir Rupert Charles, Bt. (1757)
Brook, Prof. Sir Richard John, Kt. OBE
†Brooke, Sir Alistair Weston, Bt. (1919)
Brooke, Sir Francis George Windham, Bt. (1903)
Brooke, Rt. Hon. Sir Henry, Kt.
Brooke, Sir (Richard) David Christopher, Bt. (1662)
Brooking, Sir Trevor David, Kt., CBE
Brooks, Sir Timothy Gerald Martin, KCVO
Brooksbank, Sir (Edward) Nicholas, Bt. (1919)
Broomfield, Sir Nigel Hugh Robert Allen, KCMG
†Broughton, Sir David Delves, Bt. (1661)
Broun, Sir William Windsor, Bt. (S. 1686)
Brown, Sir (Austen) Patrick, KCB
Brown, Adm. Sir Brian Thomas, KCB, CBE
Brown, Sir (Cyril) Maxwell Palmer, KCB, CMG
Brown, Sir David, Kt.
Brown, Vice-Adm. Sir David Worthington, KCB
Brown, Sir Douglas Denison, Kt.
Brown, Hon. Sir Douglas Dunlop, Kt.
Brown, Sir George Francis Richmond, Bt. (1863)
Brown, Sir George Noel, Kt.
Brown, Sir Mervyn, KCMG, OBE
Brown, Sir Peter Randolph, Kt.
Brown, Rt. Hon. Sir Stephen, GBE
Brown, Sir Stephen David Reid, KCVO
Browne, Sir Nicholas Walker, KBE, CMG
Brownrigg, Sir Nicholas (Gawen), Bt. (1816)
Browse, Prof. Sir Norman Leslie, Kt., MD, FRCS
Bruce, Sir (Francis) Michael Ian, Bt. (S. 1628)
Bruce, Sir Hervey James Hugh, Bt. (1804)
Bruce-Gardner, Sir Robert Henry, Bt. (1945)
Bruce-Lockhart, Sir Alexander John (Sandy), Kt., OBE
Buckworth-Herne-Soame, Sir Charles John, Bt. (1697)
Brunner, Sir John Henry Kilian, Bt. (1895)
Brunton, Sir (Edward Francis) Lauder, Bt. (1908)
Brunton, Sir Gordon Charles, Kt.
Bryan, Sir Arthur, Kt.
Bryan, Sir Paul Elmore Oliver, Kt., DSO, MC
Bryson, Adm. Sir Lindsay Sutherland, KCB, FRENG

Buchan-Hepburn, Sir John Alastair Trant Kidd, Bt. (1815)
Buchanan, Sir Andrew George, Bt. (1878)
Buchanan, Vice-Adm. Sir Peter William, KBE
Buchanan, Sir (Ranald) Dennis, Kt., MBE
Buchanan, Sir Robert Wilson (Robin), Kt.
Buchanan-Jardine, Maj. Sir (Andrew) Rupert (John), Bt., MC (1885)
Buckland, Sir Ross, Kt.
Buckley, Sir Michael Sidney, Kt.
Buckley, Lt.-Cdr. Sir (Peter) Richard, KCVO
Buckley, Hon. Sir Roger John, Kt.
Budd, Sir Alan Peter, Kt.
Budd, Sir Colin Richard, KCMG
Bull, Sir George Jeffrey, Kt.
Bull, Sir Simeon George, Bt. (1922)
Bullard, Sir Julian Leonard, GCMG
Bultin, Sir Bato, Kt., MBE
Bunbury, Sir Michael William, Bt. (1681)
Bunch, Sir Austin Wyeth, Kt., CBE
Bunyard, Sir Robert Sidney, Kt., CBE, QPM
Burbidge, Sir Herbert Dudley, (1916)
Burden, Sir Anthony Thomas, Kt., QPM
Burdett, Sir Savile Aylmer, Bt. (1665)
Burgen, Sir Arnold Stanley Vincent, Kt., FRS
Burgess, Gen. Sir Edward Arthur, KCB, OBE
Burgess, Sir (Joseph) Stuart, Kt., CBE, PHD, FRSC
Burgh, Sir John Charles, KCMG, CB
Burke, Sir James Stanley Gilbert, Bt. (I. 1797)
Burke, Sir (Thomas) Kerry, Kt.
Burley, Sir Victor George, Kt., CBE
Burnell-Nugent, Vice-Adm. Sir James Michael, KCB, CBE, ADC
Burnet, Sir James William Alexander (Sir Alastair Burnet), Kt.
Burnett, Air Chief Marshal Sir Brian Kenyon, GCB, DFC, AFC
Burnett, Sir Charles David, Bt., (1913)
Burnett, Sir John Harrison, Kt.
Burnett, Sir Walter John, Kt.
Burney, Sir Nigel Dennistoun, Bt. (1921)
Burns, Sir (Robert) Andrew, KCMG
Burnton, Hon. Sir Stanley Jeffrey, Kt.
Burrell, Sir John Raymond, Bt. (1774)
Burridge, Air Chief Marshal Sir Brian Kevin, KCB, CBE, ADC
Burston, Sir Samuel Gerald Wood, Kt., OBE
Burt, Sir Peter Alexander, Kt.
Burton, Sir Carlisle Archibald, Kt., OBE
Burton, Sir George Vernon Kennedy, Kt., CBE

Burton, *Lt.-Gen.* Sir Edmund Fortescue Gerard, KBE

Burton, Sir Graham Stuart, KCMG

Burton, *Hon.* Sir Michael John, Kt.

Burton, Sir Michael St Edmund, KCVO, CMG

Bush, *Adm.* Sir John Fitzroy Duyland, GCB, DSC

Butler, *Rt. Hon.* Sir Adam Courtauld, Kt.

Butler, *Hon.* Sir Arlington Griffith, KCMG

Butler, Sir Michael Dacres, GCMG

Butler, Sir (Reginald) Michael (Thomas), Bt. (1922)

Butler, Sir Percy James, Kt., CBE, DL

Butler, *Hon.* Sir Richard Clive, Kt.

Butler, Sir Richard Pierce, Bt. (1628)

Butter, *Maj.* Sir David Henry, KCVO, MC

Butterfield, *Hon.* Sir Alexander Neil Logie, Kt.

Butterfill, Sir John Valentine, Kt., MP

Buxton, Sir Jocelyn Charles Roden, Bt. (1840)

Buxton, *Rt. Hon.* Sir Richard Joseph, Kt.

Buzzard, Sir Anthony Farquhar, Bt. (1929)

Byatt, Sir Hugh Campbell, KCVO, CMG

Byatt, Sir Ian Charles Rayner, Kt.

Byford, Sir Lawrence, Kt., CBE, QPM

Byron, Sir Charles Michael Dennis, Kt.

†Cable-Alexander, Sir Patrick Desmond William, Bt. (1809)

Cadbury, Sir (George) Adrian (Hayhurst), Kt.

Cadbury, Sir (Nicholas) Dominic, Kt.

Cadogan, *Prof.* Sir John Ivan George, Kt., CBE, FRS, FRSE

Cahn, Sir Albert Jonas, Bt. (1934)

Cain, Sir Henry Edney Conrad, Kt.

Caine, Sir Michael (Maurice Micklewhite), Kt., CBE

Caines, Sir John, KCB

Calderwood, Sir Robert, Kt.

Caldwell, Sir Edward George, KCB

Callan, Sir Ivan Roy, KCVO, CMG

Callaway, *Prof.* Sir Frank Adams, Kt., CMG, OBE

Calman, *Prof.* Sir Kenneth Charles, KCB, MD, FRCP, FRCS, FRSE

Calne, *Prof.* Sir Roy Yorke, Kt., FRS

Calvert-Smith, Sir David, Kt., QC

Cameron, Sir Hugh Roy Graham, Kt., QPM

Campbell, Sir Alan Hugh, GCMG

Campbell, *Prof.* Sir Colin Murray, Kt.

Campbell, *Prof.* Sir Donald, Kt., CBE, FRCS, FRCPGlas.

Campbell, Sir Ian Tofts, Kt., CBE, VRD

Campbell, Sir Ilay Mark, Bt. (1808)

Campbell, Sir James Alexander Moffat Bain, Bt. (S. 1668)

Campbell, Sir Lachlan Philip Kemeys, Bt. (1815)

†Campbell, Sir Roderick Duncan Hamilton, Bt. (1831)

Campbell, Sir Robin Auchinbreck, Bt. (S. 1628)

Campbell, *Rt. Hon.* Sir Walter Menzies, Kt., CBE, QC, MP

Campbell, *Rt. Hon.* Sir William Anthony, Kt.

Campbell-Orde, Sir John Alexander, Bt. (1790)

†Carden, Sir Christopher Robert, Bt. (1887)

Carden, Sir John Craven, Bt. (I. 1787)

Carew, Sir Rivers Verain, Bt. (1661)

Carey, Sir de Vic Graham, Kt.

Carey, Sir Peter Willoughby, GCB

Carleton-Smith, *Maj.-Gen.* Sir Michael Edward, Kt., CBE

Carlisle, Sir James Beethoven, GCMG

Carlisle, Sir John Michael, Kt.

Carlisle, Sir Kenneth Melville, Kt.

Carnegie, *Lt.-Gen.* Sir Robin Macdonald, KCB, OBE

Carnegie, Sir Roderick Howard, Kt.

Carnwath, *Rt. Hon.* Sir Robert John Anderson, Kt., CVO

Caro, Sir Anthony Alfred, Kt., OM, CBE

Carr, Sir (Albert) Raymond (Maillard), Kt.

Carr-Ellison, *Col.* Sir Ralph Harry, KCVO, TD

Carrick, *Hon.* Sir John Leslie, KCMG

Carrick, Sir Roger John, KCMG, LVO

Carruthers, Sir Ian James, Kt., OBE

Carsberg, *Prof.* Sir Bryan Victor, Kt.

Carter, *Prof.* Sir David Craig, Kt., FRCSE, FRCSGlas., FRCPE

Carter, Sir John, Kt., QC

Carter, Sir John Alexander, Kt.

Carter, Sir John Gordon Thomas, Kt.

Carter, Sir Philip David, Kt., CBE

Carter, Sir Richard Henry Alwyn, Kt.

Cartland, Sir George Barrington, Kt., CMG

Cartledge, Sir Bryan George, KCMG

Cary, Sir Roger Hugh, Bt. (1955)

Casey, *Rt. Hon.* Sir Maurice Eugene, Kt.

Cash, Sir Gerald Christopher, GCMG, GCVO, OBE

Cass, Sir Geoffrey Arthur, Kt.

Cassel, Sir Timothy Felix Harold, Bt. (1920)

Cassels, Sir John Seton, Kt., CB

Cassels, *Adm.* Sir Simon Alastair Cassillis, KCB, CBE

Cassidi, *Adm.* Sir (Arthur) Desmond, GCB

Castell, Sir William Martin, Kt.

Cater, Sir Jack, KBE

Catford, Sir (John) Robin, KCVO, CBE

Catherwood, Sir (Henry) Frederick (Ross), Kt.

Catling, Sir Richard Charles, Kt., CMG, OBE

Catto, *Prof.* Sir Graeme Robertson Dawson, Kt.

Cave, Sir John Charles, Bt. (1896)

Cave-Browne-Cave, Sir Robert, Bt. (1641)

Cayley, Sir Digby William David, Bt. (1661)

Cayzer, Sir James Arthur, Bt. (1904)

Cazalet, *Hon.* Sir Edward Stephen, Kt.

Cazalet, Sir Peter Grenville, Kt.

Cecil, *Rear-Adm.* Sir (Oswald) Nigel Amherst, KBE, CB

Chadwick, *Revd Prof.* Henry, KBE

Chadwick, *Rt. Hon.* Sir John Murray, Kt., ED

Chadwick, Sir Joshua Kenneth Burton, Bt. (1935)

Chadwick, *Revd Prof.* (William) Owen, OM, KBE, FBA

Chadwyck-Healey, Sir Charles Edward, Bt. (1919)

Chalmers, Sir Iain Geoffrey, Kt.

Chalmers, Sir Neil Robert, Kt.

Chalstrey, Sir (Leonard) John, Kt., MD, FRCS

Chan, *Rt. Hon.* Sir Julius, GCMG, KBE

Chance, Sir (George) Jeremy ffolliott, Bt. (1900)

Chandler, Sir Colin Michael, Kt.

Chandler, Sir Geoffrey, Kt., CBE

Chantler, *Prof.* Sir Cyril, Kt., MD, FRCP

Chaplin, Sir Malcolm Hilbery, Kt., CBE

Chapman, Sir David Robert Macgowan, Bt. (1958)

Chapman, Sir George Alan, Kt.

Chapman, Sir Sidney Brookes, Kt., MP

Chapple, *Field Marshal* Sir John Lyon, GCB, CBE

Charles, *Hon.* Sir Arthur William Hessin, Kt.

Charles, Sir George Frederick Lawrence, KCMG, CBE

Charlton, Sir Robert (Bobby), Kt., CBE

Charnley, Sir (William) John, Kt., CB, FRENG

Chataway, *Rt. Hon.* Sir Christopher, Kt.

Chatfield, Sir John Freeman, Kt., CBE

Chaytor, Sir George Reginald, Bt. (1831)

Checketts, *Sqn. Ldr.* Sir David John, KCVO

Checkland, Sir Michael, Kt.

Cheshire, *Air Chief Marshal* Sir John Anthony, KBE, CB

Chessells, Sir Arthur David (Tim), Kt.

Chesterton, Sir Oliver Sidney, Kt., MC

Chetwood, Sir Clifford Jack, Kt.

Chetwynd, Sir Arthur Ralph Talbot, Bt. (1795)

Cheyne, Sir Joseph Lister Watson, Bt., OBE (1908)

Chichester, Sir (Edward) John, Bt. (1641)

Chichester-Clark, Sir Robin, Kt.

Chilcot, Sir John Anthony, GCB

Child, Sir (Coles John) Jeremy, Bt. (1919)

Chilton, *Brig.* Sir Frederick Oliver, Kt., CBE, DSO

Chilwell, *Hon.* Sir Muir Fitzherbert, Kt.

Chinn, Sir Trevor Edwin, Kt., CVO

Chipperfield, Sir Geoffrey Howes, KCB

Chisholm, Sir John Alexander Raymond, Kt., FRENG

Chitty, Sir Thomas Willes, Bt. (1924)

Cholmeley, Sir Hugh John Frederick Sebastian, Bt. (1806)

Chow, Sir Chung Kong, Kt.

Chow, Sir Henry Francis, Kt., OBE

Christie, Sir George William Langham, Kt., CH

Christie, Sir William, Kt., MBE

Christopher, Sir Duncan Robin Carmichael, KBE, CMG

Chung, Sir Sze-yuen, GBE, FRENG

Clark, Sir Francis Drake, Bt. (1886)

Clark, Sir John Arnold, Kt.

Clark, Sir Jonathan George, Bt. (1917)

Clark, Sir Robert Anthony, Kt., DSC

Clark, Sir Terence Joseph, KBE, CMG, CVO

Clark, Sir Thomas Edwin, Kt.

Clarke, *Rt. Hon.* Sir Anthony Peter, Kt.

Clarke, Sir Arthur Charles, Kt., CBE

Clarke, Sir (Charles Mansfield) Tobias, Bt. (1831)

Clarke, *Hon.* Sir David Clive, Kt.

Clarke, Sir Ellis Emmanuel Innocent, GCMG

Clarke, Sir Jonathan Dennis, Kt.

Clarke, *Maj.* Sir Peter Cecil, KCVO

Clarke, Sir Robert Cyril, Kt.

Clarke, Sir Rupert William John, Bt., MBE (1882)

Clay, Sir Richard Henry, Bt. (1841)

Clayton, Sir David Robert, Bt. (1732)

Cleaver, Sir Anthony Brian, Kt.

Clementi, Sir David Cecil, Kt.

Cleminson, Sir James Arnold Stacey, KBE, MC

Clerk, Sir Robert Maxwell, Bt., OBE (1679)

Clerke, Sir John Edward Longueville, Bt. (1660)

Clifford, Sir Roger Joseph, Bt. (1887)

Clifford, Sir Timothy Peter Plint, Kt.

Clothier, Sir Cecil Montacute, KCB, QC

Clucas, Sir Kenneth Henry, KCB

Clutterbuck, *Vice-Adm.* Sir David Granville, KBE, CB

Coates, Sir Anthony Robert Milnes, Bt. (1911)

Coates, Sir David Frederick Charlton, Bt. (1921)

Coats, Sir Alastair Francis Stuart, Bt. (1905)

Coats, Sir William David, Kt.

Cobham, Sir Michael John, Kt., CBE

Cochrane, Sir (Henry) Marc (Sursock), Bt. (1903)

Cockburn, Sir John Elliot, Bt. (S. 1671)

Cockburn-Campbell, Sir Alexander Thomas, Bt. (1821)

Cockshaw, Sir Alan, Kt., FRENG

Codrington, Sir Simon Francis Bethell, Bt. (1876)

Codrington, Sir William Alexander, Bt. (1721)

Coghill, Sir Patrick Kendal Farley, Bt. (1778)

Coghlin, *Hon.* Sir Patrick, Kt.

Cohen, Sir Edward, Kt.

Cohen, Sir Ivor Harold, Kt., CBE, TD

Cohen, *Prof.* Sir Philip, Kt., PHD, FRS

Cohen, Sir Ronald, Kt.

Cole, Sir (Robert) William, Kt.

Coleridge, *Hon.* Sir Paul James Duke, Kt.

Coles, Sir (Arthur) John, GCMG

Colfox, Sir (William) John, Bt. (1939)

Collett, Sir Christopher, GBE

Collett, Sir Ian Seymour, Bt. (1934)

Collins, *Hon.* Sir Andrew David, Kt.

Collins, Sir Bryan Thomas Alfred, Kt., OBE, QFSM

Collins, Sir John Alexander, Kt.

Collins, Sir Kenneth Darlingston, Kt.

Collins, *Hon.* Sir Lawrence Antony, Kt.

Collum, Sir Hugh Robert, Kt.

Collyear, Sir John Gowen, Kt.

Colman, *Hon.* Sir Anthony David, Kt.

Colman, Sir Michael Jeremiah, Bt. (1907)

Colman, Sir Timothy, KG

Colquhoun of Luss, Sir Ivar Iain, Bt. (1786)

Colt, Sir Edward William Dutton, Bt. (1694)

Colthurst, Sir Charles St John, Bt. (1744)

Coltman, Sir (Arthur) Leycester Scott, KBE, CMG

Colvin, Sir Howard Montagu, Kt., CVO, CBE, FBA

Compton, *Rt. Hon.* Sir John George Melvin, KCMG

Conant, Sir John Ernest Michael, Bt. (1954)

Connell, *Hon.* Sir Michael Bryan, Kt.

Connery, Sir Sean, Kt.

Connor, Sir William Joseph, Kt.

Conran, Sir Terence Orby, Kt.

Cons, *Hon.* Sir Derek, Kt.

Constantinou, Sir Georkios, Kt., OBE

Cook, Sir Christopher Wymondham Rayner Herbert, Bt. (1886)

Cooke, *Col.* Sir David William Perceval, Bt. (1661)

Cooke, Sir Howard Felix Hanlan, GCMG, GCVO

Cooke, *Hon.* Sir Jeremy Lionel, Kt.

Cooke, *Prof.* Sir Ronald Urwick, Kt.

Cooksey, Sir David James Scott, Kt.

Cooper, *Gen.* Sir George Leslie Conroy, GCB, MC

Cooper, Sir Henry, Kt.

Cooper, Sir Richard Powell, Bt. (1905)

Cooper, Sir Robert George, Kt., CBE

Cooper, *Maj.-Gen.* Sir Simon Christie, GCVO

Cooper, Sir William Daniel Charles, Bt. (1863)

Coote, Sir Christopher John, Bt., *Premier Baronet of Ireland* (I. 1621)

Copas, *Most Revd* Virgil, KBE, DD

Copisarow, Sir Alcon Charles, Kt.

Corbett, *Maj.-Gen.* Sir Robert John Swan, KCVO, CB

Corby, Sir (Frederick) Brian, Kt.

Cordy-Simpson, *Lt.-Gen.* Sir Roderick Alexander, KBE, CB

Corfield, *Rt. Hon.* Sir Frederick Vernon, Kt.

Corfield, Sir Kenneth George, Kt., FRENG

Corley, Sir Kenneth Sholl Ferrand, Kt.

Cormack, Sir Patrick Thomas, Kt., MP

Corness, Sir Colin Ross, Kt.

Cornforth, Sir John Warcup, Kt., CBE, DPHIL, FRS

Corry, Sir James Michael, Bt. (1885)

Cortazzi, Sir (Henry Arthur) Hugh, GCMG

Cory, Sir (Clinton Charles) Donald, Bt. (1919)

Cory-Wright, Sir Richard Michael, Bt. (1903)

Cossons, Sir Neil, Kt., OBE

†Cotter, Sir Patrick Laurence Delaval Bt. (I. 1763)

Cotterell, Sir John Henry Geers, Bt. (1805)

Cotton, *Hon.* Sir Robert Carrington, KCMG

Cotton, Sir William Frederick, Kt., CBE

Cottrell, Sir Alan Howard, Kt., PHD, FRS, FRENG

†Cotts, Sir Richard Crichton Mitchell, Bt. (1921)

Couper, Sir James George, Bt. (1841)

Court, *Hon.* Sir Charles Walter Michael, KCMG, OBE

Courtenay, Sir Thomas Daniel, Kt.

Cousins, *Air Chief Marshal* Sir David, KCB, AFC

Coville, *Air Marshal* Sir Christopher Charles Cotton, KCB

Cowan, *Gen.* Sir Samuel, KCB, CBE

Coward, *Vice-Adm.* Sir John Francis, KCB, DSO

Cowen, *Rt. Hon. Prof.* Sir Zelman, GCMG, GCVO

Cowie, Sir Thomas (Tom), Kt., OBE

Cowper-Coles, Sir Sherard Louis, KCMG, LVO

Cowperthwaite, Sir John James, KBE, CMG

Cox, Sir Alan George, Kt., CBE

Cox, *Prof.* Sir David Roxbee, Kt.

Cox, Sir Geoffrey Sandford, Kt., CBE

Cox, *Vice-Adm.* Sir John Michael Holland, KCB

Cradock, *Rt. Hon.* Sir Percy, GCMG

Craft, *Prof.* Sir Alan William, Kt.

Craig, Sir (Albert) James (Macqueen), GCMG

Craig-Cooper, Sir (Frederick Howard) Michael, Kt., CBE, TD

Crane, *Hon.* Sir Peter Francis, Kt.

Crane, *Prof.* Sir Peter Robert, Kt.

Craufurd, Sir Robert James, Bt. (1781)

Craven, Sir John Anthony, Kt.

Crawford, *Prof.* Sir Frederick William, Kt., FRENG

Crawley-Boevey, Sir Thomas Michael Blake, Bt. (1784)

Crew, Sir (Michael) Edward, Kt., QPM

Cresswell, *Hon.* Sir Peter John, Kt.

Crichton-Brown, Sir Robert, KCMG, CBE, TD

Crick, *Prof.* Sir Bernard, Kt.

Crill, Sir Peter Leslie, KBE

Crisp, Sir Edmund Nigel Ramsay, KCB

Crisp, Sir (John) Peter, Bt. (1913)

†Critchett, Sir Charles George Montague, Bt. (1908)

Crockett, Sir Andrew Duncan, Kt.

Croft, Sir Owen Glendower, Bt. (1671)

Croft, Sir Thomas Stephen Hutton, Bt. (1818)

†Crofton, Sir Hugh Denis, Bt. (1801)

Crofton, *Prof.* Sir John Wenman, Kt.

†Crofton, Sir Julian Malby, Bt. (1838)

Crompton, Sir Dan, Kt., CBE, QPM

Crossland, *Prof.* Sir Bernard, Kt., CBE, FRENG

Crossley, Sir Julian Charles, Bt. (1909)

Crowe, Sir Brian Lee, KCMG

Cruthers, Sir James Winter, Kt.

Cubbon, Sir Brian Crossland, GCB

Cubitt, Sir Hugh Guy, Kt., CBE

Cullen, Sir (Edward) John, Kt., FRENG

Culme-Seymour, Sir Michael Patrick, Bt. (1809)

Culpin, Sir Robert Paul, Kt.

Cummins, Sir Michael John Austin, Kt.

Cunliffe, Sir David Ellis, Bt. (1759)

Cunliffe-Owen, Sir Hugo Dudley, Bt. (1920)

Cunningham, *Lt.-Gen.* Sir Hugh Patrick, KBE

Cunynghame, Sir Andrew David Francis, Bt. (S. 1702)

†Currie, Sir Donald Scott, Bt. (1847)

Curry, Sir Donald Thomas Younger, Kt., CBE

Curtain, Sir Michael, KBE

Curtis, Sir Barry John, Kt.

Curtis, *Hon.* Sir Richard Herbert, Kt.

Curtis, Sir William Peter, Bt. (1802)

Curtiss, *Air Marshal* Sir John Bagot, KCB, KBE

Curwen, Sir Christopher Keith, KCMG

Cuschieri, *Prof.* Sir Alfred, Kt.

Cutler, Sir Charles Benjamin, KBE, ED

Dacie, *Prof.* Sir John Vivian, Kt., MD, FRS

Dain, Sir David John Michael, KCVO

Dales, Sir Richard Nigel, KCVO

Dalrymple-Hay, Sir James Brian, Bt. (1798)

Dalrymple-White, *Wg Cdr.* Sir Henry Arthur, Bt., DFC (1926)

Dalton, Sir Alan Nugent Goring, Kt., CBE

Dalton, *Vice-Adm.* Sir Geoffrey Thomas James Oliver, KCB

Dalyell, Sir Tam (Thomas), Bt., MP (NS 1685)

Daniel, Sir John Sagar, Kt., DSc

Dannatt, *Lt.-Gen.* Sir Francis Richard, KCB, CBE

Darby, Sir Peter Howard, Kt., CBE, QFSM

Darell, Sir Jeffrey Lionel, Bt., MC (1795)

Darling, Sir Clifford, GCVO

Darrington, Sir Michael John, Kt.

Dasgupta, *Prof.* Sir Partha Sarathi, Kt.

†Dashwood, Sir Edward John Francis, Bt., *Premier Baronet of Great Britain* (1707)

Dashwood, Sir Richard James, Bt. (1684)

Daunt, Sir Timothy Lewis Achilles, KCMG

Davenport-Handley, Sir David John, Kt., OBE

David, Sir Jean Marc, Kt., CBE, QC

David, *His Hon.* Sir Robin (Robert) Daniel George, Kt.,

Davidson, Sir Robert James, Kt., FRENG

Davies, Sir Alan Seymour, Kt.

Davies, *Hon.* Sir (Alfred William) Michael, Kt.

Davies, Sir (Charles) Noel, Kt.

Davies, *Prof.* Sir David Evan Naughton, Kt., CBE, FRS, FRENG

Davies, *Hon.* Sir (David Herbert) Mervyn, Kt., MC, TD

Davies, Sir David John, Kt.

Davies, Sir Frank John, Kt., CBE

Davies, *Prof.* Sir Graeme John, Kt., FRENG

Davies, Sir John Howard, Kt.

Davies, Sir John Michael, KCB

Davies, *Vice-Adm.* Sir Lancelot Richard Bell, KBE

Davies, Sir Peter Maxwell, Kt., CBE

Davies, Sir Rhys Everson, Kt., QC

Davis, Sir Andrew Frank, Kt., CBE

Davis, Sir Colin Rex, Kt., CH, CBE

Davis, Sir Crispin Henry Lamert, Kt.

Davis, Sir (Ernest) Howard, Kt., CMG, OBE

Davis, Sir John Gilbert, Bt. (1946)

Davis, *Hon.* Sir Nigel Anthony Lambert, Kt.

Davis, Sir Peter John, Kt.

Davis, *Hon.* Sir Thomas Robert Alexander Harries, KBE

Davis-Goff, Sir Robert (William), Bt. (1905)

Davison, *Rt. Hon.* Sir Ronald Keith, GBE, CMG

Davson, Sir Christopher Michael Edward, Bt. (1927)

Dawanincura, Sir John Norbert, Kt., OBE

Dawbarn, Sir Simon Yelverton, KCVO, CMG

Dawson, *Hon.* Sir Daryl Michael, KBE, CB

Dawson, Sir Hugh Michael Trevor, Bt. (1920)

Dawtry, Sir Alan (Graham), Kt., CBE, TD

Day, Sir Derek Malcolm, KCMG

Day, *Air Chief Marshal* Sir John Romney, KCB, OBE, ADC

Day, Sir (Judson) Graham, Kt.

Day, Sir Michael John, Kt., OBE

Day, Sir Simon James, Kt.

Deakin, Sir (Frederick) William (Dampier), Kt., DSO

Deane, *Hon.* Sir William Patrick, KBE

Dear, Sir Geoffrey James, Kt., QPM

Dearlove, Sir Richard Billing, KCMG, OBE

de Bellaigue, Sir Geoffrey, GCVO

†Debenham, Sir Thomas Adam, Bt. (1931)

de Deney, Sir Geoffrey Ivor, KCVO

de Hoghton, Sir (Richard) Bernard (Cuthbert), Bt. (1611)

De la Bère, Sir Cameron, Bt. (1953)

de la Rue, Sir Andrew George Ilay, Bt. (1898)

Dellow, Sir John Albert, Kt., CBE

Delves, *Lt.-Gen.* Sir Cedric Norman George, KBE

Denholm, Sir John Ferguson (Ian), Kt., CBE

Denison-Smith, *Lt.-Gen.* Sir Anthony Arthur, KBE

Denman, Sir (George) Roy, KCB, CMG

Denny, Sir Anthony Coningham de Waltham, Bt. (I. 1782)

Denny, Sir Charles Alistair Maurice, Bt. (1913)

Denton, *Prof.* Sir Eric James, Kt., CBE, FRS

Derbyshire, Sir Andrew George, Kt.

Derham, Sir Peter John, Kt.

de Trafford, Sir Dermot Humphrey, Bt. (1841)

Deverell, *Gen.* Sir John Freegard, KCB, OBE

Devesi, Sir Baddeley, GCMG, GCVO

De Ville, Sir Harold Godfrey Oscar, Kt., CBE

Devitt, Sir James Hugh Thomas, Bt. (1916)

de Waal, Sir (Constant Henrik) Henry, KCB, QC

Dewey, Sir Anthony Hugh, Bt. (1917)

Dewhurst, *Prof.* Sir (Christopher) John, Kt.

De Witt, Sir Ronald Wayne, Kt.

Dhenin, *Air Marshal* Sir Geoffrey Howard, KBE, AFC, GM, MD

Dhrangadhra, HH the Maharaja Raj Saheb of, KCIE

Dibela, *Hon.* Sir Kingsford, GCMG

Dick-Lauder, Sir Piers Robert, Bt. (S. 1690)

Dickinson, Sir Harold Herbert, Kt.

Dickinson, Sir Samuel Benson, Kt.

Dilke, Sir Charles John Wentworth, Bt. (1862)

Dillwyn-Venables-Llewelyn, Sir John Michael, Bt. (1890)

Dixon, Sir Jeremy, Kt.

Dixon, Sir Jonathan Mark, Bt. (1919)

Djanogly, Sir Harry Ari Simon, Kt., CBE

Dobson, *Vice-Adm.* Sir David Stuart, KBE

Dodds, Sir Ralph Jordan, Bt. (1964)

Dodds-Parker, Sir (Arthur) Douglas, Kt.

Doll, *Prof.* Sir (William) Richard (Shaboe), Kt., CH, OBE, FRS, DM, MD, DSC

Dollery, Sir Colin Terence, Kt.

Don-Wauchope, Sir Roger (Hamilton), Bt. (S. 1667)

Donald, Sir Alan Ewen, KCMG

Donald, *Air Marshal* Sir John George, KBE

Donaldson, *Prof.* Sir Liam Joseph, Kt.

Donne, *Hon.* Sir Gaven John, KBE

Donne, Sir John Christopher, Kt.

Donnelly, Sir Joseph Brian, KBE, CMG

Dookun, Sir Dewoonarain, Kt.

Dorey, Sir Graham Martyn, Kt.

Dorman, Sir Philip Henry Keppel, Bt. (1923)

Doughty, Sir Graham Martin, Kt.

Doughty, Sir William Roland, Kt.

Douglas, *Hon.* Sir Roger Owen, Kt.

Dover, *Prof.* Sir Kenneth James, Kt., DLitt, FBA, FRSE

Dowell, Sir Anthony James, Kt., CBE

Dowling, Sir Robert, Kt.

Down, Sir Alastair Frederick, Kt., OBE, MC, TD

Downes, Sir Edward Thomas, Kt., CBE

Downey, Sir Gordon Stanley, KCB

Downs, Sir Diarmuid, Kt., CBE, FRENG

Downward, *Maj.-Gen.* Sir Peter Aldcroft, KCVO, CB, DSO, DFC

Downward, Sir William Atkinson, Kt.

Dowson, Sir Philip Manning, Kt., CBE, PRA

Doyle, Sir Reginald Derek Henry, Kt., CBE

D'Oyly, Sir Hadley Gregory Bt. (1663)

Drake, *Hon.* Sir (Frederick) Maurice, Kt., DFC

Drewry, *Lt.-Gen.* Sir Christopher Francis, KCB, QC

Drinkwater, Sir John Muir, Kt., QC

Driver, Sir Eric William, Kt.

Drummond, Sir John Richard Gray, Kt., CBE

Drury, Sir (Victor William) Michael, Kt., OBE

Dryden, Sir John Stephen Gyles, Bt. (1733 and 1795)

du Cann, *Rt. Hon.* Sir Edward Dillon Lott, KBE

†Duckworth, Sir Edward Richard Dyce, Bt. (1909)

du Cros, Sir Claude Philip Arthur Mallet, Bt. (1916)

Dudley-Williams, Sir Alastair Edgcumbe James, Bt. (1964)

Duff-Gordon, Sir Andrew Cosmo Lewis, Bt. (1813)

Duffell, *Lt.-Gen.* Sir Peter Royson, KCB, CBE, MC

Duffy, Sir (Albert) (Edward) Patrick, Kt., PHD

Dugdale, Sir William Stratford, Bt., MC (1936)

Duggin, Sir Thomas Joseph, Kt.

Dummett, *Prof.* Sir Michael Anthony Eardley, Kt., FBA

Dunbar, Sir Archibald Ranulph, Bt. (S. 1700)

Dunbar, Sir Robert Drummond Cospatrick, Bt. (S. 1698)

Dunbar, Sir James Michael, Bt. (S. 1694)

Dunbar of Hempriggs, Sir Richard Francis, Bt. (S. 1706)

Dunbar-Nasmith, *Prof.* Sir James Duncan, Kt., CBE

Duncan, Sir James Blair, Kt.

Dunlop, Sir Thomas, Bt. (1916)

Dunn, *Air Marshal* Sir Eric Clive, KBE, CB, BEM

Dunn, *Rt. Hon.* Sir Robin Horace Walford, Kt., MC

Dunne, Sir Thomas Raymond, KCVO

Dunning, Sir Simon William Patrick, Bt. (1930)

Dunnington-Jefferson, Sir Mervyn Stewart, Bt. (1958)

Dunstan, *Lt.-Gen.* Sir Donald Beaumont, KBE, CB

Dunt, *Vice-Adm.* Sir John Hugh, KCB

Duntze, Sir Daniel Evans Bt. (1774)

Dupre, Sir Tumun, Kt., MBE

Dupree, Sir Peter, Bt. (1921)

Durand, Sir Edward Alan Christopher David Percy, Bt. (1892)

Durant, Sir (Robert) Anthony (Bevis), Kt.

Durham, Sir Kenneth, Kt.

Durie, Sir David Robert Campbell, KCMG

Durrant, Sir William Alexander Estridge, Bt. (1784)

Duthie, *Prof.* Sir Herbert Livingston, Kt.

Duthie, Sir Robert Grieve (Robin), Kt., CBE

Dwyer, Sir Joseph Anthony, Kt.

Dyke, Sir David William Hart, Bt. (1677)

Dyson, *Rt. Hon.* Sir John Anthony, Kt.

Eady, *Hon.* Sir David, Kt.

Eardley-Wilmot, Sir Michael John Assheton, Bt. (1821)

Earle, Sir (Hardman) George (Algernon), Bt. (1869)

Easton, Sir Robert William Simpson, Kt., CBE

Eaton, *Adm.* Sir Kenneth John, GBE, KCB

Eberle, *Adm.* Sir James Henry Fuller, GCB

Ebrahim, Sir (Mahomed) Currimbhoy, Bt. (1910)

Echlin, Sir Norman David Fenton, Bt. (I. 1721)

Eckersley, Sir Donald Payze, Kt., OBE

Edge, *Capt.* Sir (Philip) Malcolm, KCVO

†Edge, Sir William, Bt. (1937)

Edmonstone, Sir Archibald Bruce Charles, Bt. (1774)

Edward, Sir David Alexander Ogilvy, KCMG

Edwardes, Sir Michael Owen, Kt.

Edwards, Sir Christopher John Churchill, Bt. (1866)

Edwards, Sir Llewellyn Roy, Kt.

Edwards, *Prof.* Sir Samuel Frederick, Kt., FRS

†Edwards-Moss, Sir David John, Bt. (1868)

Egan, Sir John Leopold, Kt.

Egerton, Sir Stephen Loftus, KCMG

Eichelbaum, *Rt. Hon.* Sir Thomas, GBE

Elias, *Hon.* Sir Patrick, Kt.

Eliott of Stobs, Sir Charles Joseph Alexander, Bt. (S. 1666)

Ellerton, Sir Geoffrey James, Kt., CMG, MBE

Elliot, Sir Gerald Henry, Kt.

Elliott, Sir Clive Christopher Hugh, Bt. (1917)

Elliott, Sir David Murray, KCMG, CB

Elliott, *Prof.* Sir John Huxtable, Kt., FBA

Elliott, Sir Randal Forbes, KBE

Elliott, *Prof.* Sir Roger James, Kt., FRS

Ellis, Sir Ronald, Kt., FRENG

Elphinstone, Sir John, Bt. (S. 1701)

Elphinstone, Sir John Howard Main, Bt. (1816)

Elsmore, Sir Lloyd, Kt., OBE

Elton, Sir Arnold, Kt., CBE

Elton, Sir Charles Abraham Grierson, Bt. (1717)

Elton, Sir Leslie, Kt.

Elwes, Sir Jeremy Vernon, Kt., CBE

Elwood, Sir Brian George Conway, Kt., CBE

Elworthy, Sir Peter Herbert, Kt.

Elworthy, *Air Cdre. Hon.* Sir Timothy Charles, KCVO, CBE

Emery, *Rt. Hon.* Sir Peter Frank Hannibal, Kt., MP

Empey, Sir Reginald Norman Morgan, Kt., OBE

Enderby, *Prof.* Sir John Edwin, Kt. CBE, FRS

Engle, Sir George Lawrence Jose, KCB, QC

English, Sir Terence Alexander Hawthorne, KBE, FRCS

Epstein, *Prof.* Sir (Michael) Anthony, Kt., CBE, FRS

Errington, *Col.* Sir Geoffrey Frederick, Bt., OBE (1963)

Errington, Sir Lancelot, KCB

Erskine, Sir (Thomas) David, Bt. (1821)

Erskine-Hill, Sir Alexander Rodger, Bt. (1945)

Esmonde, Sir Thomas Francis Grattan, Bt. (I. 1629)

Espie, Sir Frank Fletcher, Kt., OBE

Esplen, Sir John Graham, Bt. (1921)

Essenhigh, *Adm.* Sir Nigel Richard, GCB

Etherton, *Hon.* Sir Terence Michael Elkan Barnet, Kt.

Evans, Sir Anthony Adney, Bt. (1920)

Fraser, *Gen.* Sir David William, GCB, OBE
Fraser, Sir Iain Michael Duncan, Bt. (1943)
Fraser, Sir (James) Campbell, Kt.
Fraser, Sir James Murdo, KBE
Fraser, Sir William Kerr, GCB
Frayling, *Prof.* Sir Christopher John, Kt.
Frederick, Sir Christopher St John, Bt. (1723)
Freedman, *Prof.* Sir Lawrence David, KCMG, CBE
Freeland, Sir John Redvers, KCMG
Freeman, Sir James Robin, Bt. (1945)
Freer, *Air Chief Marshal* Sir Robert William George, GBE, KCB
French, *Air Marshal* Sir Joseph Charles, KCB, CBE
Frere, *Vice-Adm.* Sir Richard Tobias, KCB
Fretwell, Sir (Major) John (Emsley), GCMG
Freud, Sir Clement Raphael, Kt.
Friend *Prof.* Sir Richard Henry, Kt.
Froggatt, Sir Leslie Trevor, Kt.
Froggatt, Sir Peter, Kt.
Frossard, Sir Charles Keith, KBE
Frost, Sir David Paradine, Kt., OBE
Fry, Sir Peter Derek, Kt.
Fulford, *Hon.* Sir Adrian Bruce, Kt.
Fuller, Sir James Henry Fleetwood, Bt. (1910)
Fuller, *Hon.* Sir John Bryan Munro, Kt.
Furness, Sir Stephen Roberts, Bt. (1913)
Gadsden, Sir Peter Drury Haggerston, GBE, FRENG
Gage, *Hon.* Sir William Marcus, Kt.
Gains, Sir John Christopher, Kt.
Gainsford, Sir Ian Derek, Kt., DDS
Gaius, *Rt. Revd* Saimon, KBE
Galsworthy, Sir Anthony Charles, KCMG
Galway, Sir James, Kt., OBE
Gam, *Rt. Revd* Sir Getake, KBE
Gamble, Sir David Hugh Norman, Bt. (1897)
Gambon, Sir Michael John, Kt., CBE
Gardiner, Sir John Eliot, Kt., CBE
Gardner, Sir Roy Alan, Kt.
Garland, *Hon.* Sir Patrick Neville, Kt.
Garland, *Hon.* Sir Ransley Victor, KBE
Garlick, Sir John, KCB
Garner, Sir Anthony Stuart, Kt.
Garnett, *Adm.* Sir Ian David Graham, KCB
Garnier, *Rear-Adm.* Sir John, KCVO, CBE
Garrard, Sir David Eardley, Kt.
Garrett, Sir Anthony Peter, Kt., CBE
Garrick, Sir Ronald, Kt., CBE, FRENG
Garrioch, Sir (William) Henry, Kt.
Garrod, *Lt.-Gen.* Sir (John) Martin Carruthers, KCB, OBE
Garthwaite, Sir (William) Mark (Charles), Bt. (1919)
Gaskell, Sir Richard Kennedy Harvey, Kt.

Geno, Sir Makena Viora, KBE
Gent, Sir Christopher Charles, Kt.
George, Sir Arthur Thomas, Kt.
George, *Prof.* Sir Charles Frederick, MD, FRCP
George, Sir Richard William, Kt., CVO
Gerken, *Vice-Adm.* Sir Robert William Frank, KCB, CBE
Gershon, Sir Peter Oliver, Kt., CBE
Gethin, Sir Richard Joseph St Lawrence, Bt. (I. 1665)
Ghurburrun, Sir Rabindrah, Kt.
Gibb, Sir Francis Ross (Frank), Kt., CBE, FRENG
Gibbings, Sir Peter Walter, Kt.
Gibbons, Sir (John) David, KBE
Gibbons, Sir William Edward Doran, Bt. (1752)
Gibbs, *Rt. Hon.* Sir Harry Talbot, GCMG, KBE
Gibbs, *Hon.* Sir Richard John Hedley, Kt.
Gibbs, Sir Roger Geoffrey, Kt.
Gibbs, *Field Marshal* Sir Roland Christopher, GCB, CBE, DSO, MC
†Gibson, *Revd* Christopher Herbert, Bt. (1931)
Gibson, Sir Ian, Kt., CBE
Gibson, *Rt. Hon.* Sir Peter Leslie, Kt.
Gibson-Craig-Carmichael, Sir David Peter William, Bt. (S. 1702 and 1831)
Giddings, *Air Marshal* Sir (Kenneth Charles) Michael, KCB, OBE, DFC, AFC
Giffard, Sir (Charles) Sydney (Rycroft), KCMG
Gilbart-Denham, *Lt.-Col.* Sir Seymour Vivian, KCVO
Gilbert, *Air Chief Marshal* Sir Joseph Alfred, KCB, CBE
Gilbert, Sir Martin John, Kt., CBE
†Gilbey, Sir Walter Gavin, Bt. (1893)
Gill, Sir Anthony Keith, Kt.
Gill, Sir Arthur Benjamin Norman, Kt., CBE
Gillam, Sir Patrick John, Kt.
Gillen, *Hon.* Sir John de Winter, Kt.
Gillett, Sir Robin Danvers Penrose, Bt., GBE, RD (1959)
Gilmour, Sir John Edward, Bt., DSO, TD (1897)
Gina, Sir Lloyd Maepeza, KBE
Gingell, *Air Chief Marshal* Sir John, GBE, KCB, KCVO
Girolami, Sir Paul, Kt.
Girvan, *Hon.* Sir (Frederick) Paul, Kt.
Gladstone, Sir (Erskine) William, Bt., KG (1846)
Glenn, Sir (Joseph Robert) Archibald, Kt., OBE
Glidewell, *Rt. Hon.* Sir Iain Derek Laing, Kt.
Glover, Sir Victor Joseph Patrick, Kt.
Glyn, Sir Richard Lindsay, Bt. (1759 and 1800)
Goavea, Sir Sinaka Vakai, KBE
Gobbo, Sir James Augustine, Kt., AC
Godber, Sir George Edward, GCB, DM
Goldberg, *Prof.* Sir Abraham, Kt., MD, DSC, FRCP

Goldberg, *Prof.* Sir David Paul Brandes, Kt.
Goldman, Sir Samuel, KCB
Goldring, *Hon.* Sir John Bernard, Kt.
Gomersall, Sir Stephen John, KCMG
Gonsalves-Sabola, *Hon.* Sir Joaquim Claudino, Kt
†Gooch, Sir Miles Peter, Bt. (1866)
Gooch, Sir Timothy Robert, Bt., MBE (1746)
Goodall, Sir (Arthur) David Saunders, GCMG
Goodall, *Air Marshal* Sir Roderick Harvey, KBE, CB, AFC
Goode, *Prof.* Sir Royston Miles, Kt., CBE, QC
Goodenough, Sir Anthony Michael, KCMG
Goodenough, Sir William McLernon, Bt. (1943)
Goodhart, Sir Philip Carter, Kt.
Goodhart, Sir Robert Anthony Gordon, Bt. (1911)
Goodhew, Sir Victor Henry, Kt.
Goodison, Sir Alan Clowes, KCMG
Goodison, Sir Nicholas Proctor, Kt.
Goodlad, *Rt. Hon.* Sir Alastair Robertson, KCMG
Goodman, Sir Patrick Ledger, Kt., CBE
Goodson, Sir Mark Weston Lassam, Bt. (1922)
Goodwin, Sir Frederick, KBE
Goodwin, Sir Frederick Anderson, Kt.
Goodwin, Sir Matthew Dean, Kt., CBE
†Goold, Sir George William, Bt. (1801)
Gordon, Sir Charles Addison Somerville Snowden, KCB
Gordon, Sir Gerald Henry, Kt., CBE, QC
Gordon, Sir Keith Lyndell, Kt., CMG
Gordon, Sir Robert James, Bt. (S. 1706)
Gordon, Sir Sidney Samuel, Kt., CBE
Gordon-Cumming, Sir Alexander Penrose, Bt. (1804)
Gordon Lennox, Lord Nicholas Charles, KCMG, KCVO
†Gore, Sir Nigel Hugh St George, Bt. (I. 1622)
Gore-Booth, *Hon.* Sir David Alwyn, KCMG, KCVO
Gore-Booth, Sir Josslyn Henry Robert, Bt. (I. 1760)
Gorham, Sir Richard Masters, Kt., CBE, DFC
Goring, Sir William Burton Nigel, Bt. (1627)
Gorman, Sir John Reginald, Kt., CVO, CBE, MC
Gorst, Sir John Michael, Kt.
Goschen, Sir (Edward) Alexander, Bt. (1916)
Gosling, Sir (Frederick) Donald, KCVO
Goswell, Sir Brian Lawrence, Kt.
Gough, Sir Charles Brandon, Kt.
Goulden, Sir (Peter) John, GCMG
Goulding, Sir Marrack Irvine, KCMG

Goulding, Sir (William) Lingard Walter, Bt. (1904)

Gourlay, *Gen.* Sir (Basil) Ian (Spencer), KCB, OBE, MC, RM

Gourlay, Sir Simon Alexander, Kt.

Govan, Sir Lawrence Herbert, Kt.

Gow, *Gen.* Sir (James) Michael, GCB

Gowans, Sir James Learmonth, Kt., CBE, FRCP, FRS

†Graaff, Sir David de Villiers, Bt. (1911)

Grabham, Sir Anthony Henry, Kt.

Graham, Sir Alexander Michael, GBE

Graham, Sir James Bellingham, Bt. (1662)

Graham, Sir James Fergus Surtees, Bt. (1783)

Graham, Sir James Thompson, Kt., CMG

Graham, Sir John Alexander Noble, Bt., GCMG (1906)

Graham, Sir John Alistair, Kt.

Graham, Sir John Moodie, Bt. (1964)

Graham, Sir Norman William, Kt., CB

Graham, Sir Peter, KCB, QC

Graham, Sir Peter Alfred, Kt., OBE

Graham, *Lt.-Gen.* Sir Peter Walter, KCB, CBE

†Graham, Sir Ralph Stuart, Bt. (1629)

Graham-Moon, Sir Peter Wilfred Giles, Bt. (1855)

Graham-Smith, *Prof.* Sir Francis, Kt.

Grant, Sir Archibald, Bt. (S. 1705)

Grant, Sir Clifford, Kt.

Grant, Sir (John) Anthony, Kt.

Grant, Sir Patrick Alexander Benedict, Bt. (S. 1688)

Grant, *Lt.-Gen.* Sir Scott Carnegie, KCB

Grant-Suttie, Sir James Edward, Bt. (S. 1702)

Granville-Chapman, *Lt.-Gen.* Sir Timothy John, KCB, CBE

Gratton-Bellew, Sir Henry Charles, Bt. (1838)

Gray, *Hon.* Sir Charles Anthony St John, Kt.

Gray, *Prof.* Sir Denis John Pereira, Kt., OBE, FRCGP

Gray, Sir John Archibald Browne, Kt., SCD, FRS

Gray, *Lt.-Gen.* Sir Michael Stuart, KCB, OBE

Gray, Sir Robert McDowall (Robin), Kt.

Gray, Sir William Hume, Bt. (1917)

Graydon, *Air Chief Marshal* Sir Michael James, GCB, CBE

Grayson, Sir Jeremy Brian Vincent Harrington, Bt. (1922)

Green, Sir Allan David, KCB, QC

Green, Sir Andrew Fleming, KCMG

†Green, Sir Edward Patrick Lycett, Bt. (1886)

Green, Sir Gregory David, KCMG

Green, *Hon.* Sir Guy Stephen Montague, KBE

Green, Sir Kenneth, Kt.

Green, Sir Owen Whitley, Kt.

Green-Price, Sir Robert John, Bt. (1874)

Greenaway, Sir John Michael Burdick, Bt. (1933)

Greenbury, Sir Richard, Kt.

Greener, Sir Anthony Armitage, Kt.

Greengross, Sir Alan David, Kt.

Greening, *Rear-Adm.* Sir Paul Woollven, GCVO

Greenstock, Sir Jeremy Quentin, GCMG

Greenwell, Sir Edward Bernard, Bt. (1906)

Gregson, Sir Peter Lewis, GCB

Greig, Sir (Henry Louis) Carron, KCVO, CBE

Grenside, Sir John Peter, Kt., CBE

Grey, Sir Anthony Dysart, Bt. (1814)

Grey-Egerton, Sir (Philip) John (Caledon), Bt. (1617)

Grierson, Sir Michael John Bewes, Bt. (S. 1685)

Grierson, Sir Ronald Hugh, Kt.

Griffin, *Maj.* Sir (Arthur) John (Stewart), KCVO

Griffiths, Sir Eldon Wylie, Kt.

Grigson, *Hon.* Sir Geoffrey Douglas, Kt.

Grimshaw, Sir Nicholas Thomas, Kt., CBE

Grimwade, Sir Andrew Sheppard, Kt., CBE

Grindrod, *Most Revd* John Basil Rowland, KBE

Grinstead, Sir Stanley Gordon, Kt.

Grose, *Vice-Adm.* Sir Alan, KBE

Gross, *Hon.* Sir Peter Henry, Kt.

Grossart, Sir Angus McFarlane McLeod, Kt., CBE

Grotrian, Sir Philip Christian Brent, Bt. (1934)

Grove, Sir Charles Gerald, Bt. (1874)

Grove, Sir Edmund Frank, KCVO

Grugeon, Sir John Drury, Kt.

Guinness, Sir Howard Christian Sheldon, Kt., VRD

Guinness, Sir John Ralph Sidney, Kt., CB

Guinness, Sir Kenelm Ernest Lee, Bt. (1867)

Guise, Sir John Grant, Bt. (1783)

Gull, Sir Rupert William Cameron, Bt. (1872)

Gumbs, Sir Emile Rudolph, Kt.

Gun-Munro, Sir Sydney Douglas, GCMG, MBE

Gunn, Sir Robert Norman, Kt.

†Gunning, Sir Charles Theodore, Bt. (1778)

Gunston, Sir John Wellesley, Bt. (1938)

Gurdon, *Prof.* Sir John Bertrand, Kt., DPHIL, FRS

Guthrie, Sir Malcolm Connop, Bt. (1936)

Guy, *Gen.* Sir Roland Kelvin, GCB, CBE, DSO

Haddacks, *Vice-Adm.* Sir Paul Kenneth, KCB

Hadfield, Sir Ronald, Kt., QPM

Hadlee, Sir Richard John, Kt., MBE

Hagart-Alexander, Sir Claud, Bt. (1886)

Hague, *Prof.* Sir Douglas Chalmers, Kt., CBE

Halberg, Sir Murray Gordon, Kt., MBE

Hall, Sir Basil Brodribb, KCB, MC, TD

Hall, *Prof.* Sir David Michael Baldock, Kt.

Hall, Sir Ernest, Kt., OBE

Hall, Sir Graham Joseph, Kt.

Hall, Sir Iain Robert, Kt.

Hall, Sir (Frederick) John (Frank), Bt. (1923)

Hall, Sir John, Kt.

Hall, Sir John Bernard, Bt. (1919)

†Hall, Sir John Douglas Hoste, Bt. (S. 1687)

Hall, Sir Peter Edward, KBE, CMG

Hall, *Prof.* Sir Peter Geoffrey, Kt., FBA

Hall, Sir Peter Reginald Frederick, Kt., CBE

Hall, Sir Robert de Zouche, KCMG

Halliday, *Vice-Adm.* Sir Roy William, KBE, DSC

Halpern, Sir Ralph Mark, Kt.

Halsey, *Revd* John Walter Brooke, Bt. (1920)

Halstead, Sir Ronald, Kt., CBE

Hambling, Sir (Herbert) Hugh, Bt. (1924)

Hamer, *Hon.* Sir Rupert James, KCMG, ED

Hamilton, Sir Andrew Caradoc, Bt. (S. 1646)

Hamilton, *Rt. Hon.* Sir Archibald Gavin, Kt., MP

Hamilton, Sir Edward Sydney, Bt. (1776 and 1819)

Hamilton, Sir James Arnot, KCB, MBE, FRENG

Hamilton-Dalrymple, *Maj.* Sir Hew Fleetwood, Bt., GCVO (S. 1697)

Hamilton-Spencer-Smith, Sir John, Bt. (1804)

Hammick, Sir Stephen George, Bt. (1834)

Hammond, Sir Anthony Hilgrove, KCB, QC

Hampel, Sir Ronald Claus, Kt.

Hampson, Sir Stuart, Kt.

Hampton, Sir (Leslie) Geoffrey, Kt.

Hanbury-Tenison, Sir Richard, KCVO

Hancock, Sir David John Stowell, KCB

Hand, *Most Revd* Geoffrey David, KBE

Hanham, Sir Michael William, Bt., DFC (1667)

Hanley, *Rt. Hon.* Sir Jeremy James, KCMG

Hanmer, Sir John Wyndham Edward, Bt. (1774)

Hannam, Sir John Gordon, Kt.

Hanson, Sir (Charles) Rupert (Patrick), Bt. (1918)

Hanson, Sir John Gilbert, KCMG, CBE

Harcourt-Smith, *Air Chief Marshal* Sir David, GBE, KCB, DFC

Hardie, Sir Douglas Fleming, Kt., CBE

Hardie Boys, *Rt. Hon.* Sir Michael, GCMG

Harding, Sir George William, KCMG, CVO

Harding, *Marshal of the Royal Air Force* Sir Peter Robin, GCB

Harding, Sir Roy Pollard, Kt., CBE

Hardy, Sir David William, Kt.

Hardy, Sir James Gilbert, Kt., OBE

Hardy, Sir Richard Charles Chandos, Bt. (1876)

Hare, Sir David, Kt., FRSL

Hare, Sir Nicholas Patrick, Bt. (1818)

Harford, Sir (John) Timothy, Bt. (1934)

Hargroves, *Brig.* Sir Robert Louis, Kt., CBE

Harington, *Gen.* Sir Charles Henry Pepys, GCB, CBE, DSO, MC

Harington, Sir Nicholas John, Bt. (1611)

Harland, *Air Marshal* Sir Reginald Edward Wynyard, KBE, CB

Harley, *Gen.* Sir Alexander George Hamilton, KBE, CB

Harman, *Gen.* Sir Jack Wentworth, GCB, OBE, MC

Harman, *Hon.* Sir Jeremiah LeRoy, Kt.

Harman, Sir John Andrew, Kt.

Harmsworth, Sir Hildebrand Harold, Bt. (1922)

Harper, Sir Ewan William, Kt. CBE

Harper, *Prof.* Sir Peter Stanley, Kt., CBE

Harris, *Prof.* Sir Henry, Kt., FRCP, FRCPath., FRS

Harris, Sir Jack Wolfred Ashford, Bt. (1932)

Harris, *Air Marshal* Sir John Hulme, KCB, CBE

Harris, *Prof.* Sir Martin Best, Kt., CBE

Harris, Sir Thomas George, KBE, CMG

Harris, Sir William Gordon, KBE, CB, FRENG

Harrison, Sir David, Kt., CBE, FRENG

Harrison, Sir Ernest Thomas, Kt., OBE

Harrison, *Surgeon Vice-Adm.* Sir John Albert Bews, KBE

Harrison, *Hon.* Sir (John) Richard, Kt., ED

Harrison, *Hon.* Sir Michael Guy Vicat, Kt.

Harrison, Sir Michael James Harwood, Bt. (1961)

Harrison, Sir (Robert) Colin, Bt. (1922)

Harrison, Sir Terence, Kt., FREng

Harrop, Sir Peter John, KCB

Hart, Sir Graham Allan, KCB

Hart, *Hon.* Sir Michael Christopher Campbell, Kt.

Hartwell, Sir (Francis) Anthony Charles Peter, Bt. (1805)

Harvey, Sir Charles Richard Musgrave, Bt. (1933)

Harvey-Jones, Sir John Henry, Kt., MBE

Harvie, Sir John Smith, Kt., CBE

Harvie-Watt, Sir James, Bt. (1945)

Haselhurst, *Rt. Hon.* Sir Alan Gordon Barraclough, Kt., MP

Haskard, Sir Cosmo Dugal Patrick Thomas, KCMG, MBE

Haslam, *Rear-Adm.* Sir David William, KBE, CB

Hassett, *Gen.* Sir Francis George, KBE, CB, DSO, LVO

Hastings, Sir Max Macdonald, Kt.

Hastings, Sir Stephen Lewis Edmonstone, Kt., MC

Hatch, Sir David Edwin, Kt., CBE

Hatter, Sir Maurice, Kt.

Havelock-Allan, Sir (Anthony) Mark David, Bt. (1858)

Hawkins, Sir Richard Caesar, Bt. (1778)

Hawley, Sir Donald Frederick, KCMG, MBE

†Hawley, Sir Henry Nicholas, Bt. (1795)

Haworth, Sir Philip, Bt. (1911)

Hawthorne, *Prof.* Sir William Rede, Kt., CBE, SCD, FRS, FRENG

Hay, Sir David Osborne, Kt., CBE, DSO

Hay, Sir David Russell, Kt., CBE, FRCP, MD

Hay, Sir Hamish Grenfell, Kt.

Hay, Sir John Erroll Audley, Bt. (S. 1663)

†Hay, Sir Ronald Frederick Hamilton, Bt. (S. 1703)

Hayes, Sir Brian, Kt., CBE, QPM

Hayes, Sir Brian David, GCB

Hayman-Joyce, *Lt.-Gen.* Sir Robert John, KCB, CBE

Hayward, Sir Anthony William Byrd, Kt.

Hayward, Sir Jack Arnold, Kt., OBE

Haywood, Sir Harold, KCVO, OBE

Head, Sir Francis David Somerville, Bt. (1838)

Heap, Sir Peter William, KCMG

Heap, *Prof.* Sir Robert Brian, Kt., CBE, FRS

Hearne, Sir Graham James, Kt., CBE

Heath, *Rt. Hon.* Sir Edward Richard George, KG, MBE

Heath, Sir Mark Evelyn, KCVO, CMG

Heathcote, *Brig.* Sir Gilbert Simon, Bt., CBE (1733)

Heathcote, Sir Michael Perryman, Bt. (1733)

Heatley, Sir Peter, Kt., CBE

Hedley, *Hon.* Sir Mark, Kt.

Heiser, Sir Terence Michael, GCB

Henao, Revd Ravu, Kt., OBE

Henderson, Sir Denys Hartley, Kt.

Henderson, Sir (John) Nicholas, GCMG, KCVO

Henley, Sir Douglas Owen, KCB

Hennessy, Sir James Patrick Ivan, KBE, CMG

†Henniker, Sir Adrian Chandos, Bt. (1813)

Henniker-Heaton, Sir Yvo Robert, Bt. (1912)

Henriques, *Hon.* Sir Richard Henry Quixano, Kt.

Henry, *Rt. Hon.* Sir Denis Robert Maurice, Kt.

Henry, *Hon.* Sir Geoffrey Arama, KBE

†Henry, Sir Patrick Denis, Bt. (1923)

Henry, *Hon.* Sir Trevor Ernest, Kt.

Henshaw, Sir David George, Kt.

Hepple, *Prof.* Sir Bob Alexander, Kt.

Herbecq, Sir John Edward, KCB

Herbert, *Adm.* Sir Peter Geoffrey Marshall, KCB, OBE

Herbert, Sir Walter William, Kt.

Hermon, Sir John Charles, Kt., OBE, QPM

Heron, Sir Conrad Frederick, KCB, OBE

Heron, Sir Michael Gilbert, Kt.

Heron-Maxwell, Sir Nigel Mellor, Bt. (S. 1683)

Hervey, Sir Roger Blaise Ramsay, KCVO, CMG

Hervey-Bathurst, Sir Frederick John Charles Gordon, Bt. (1818)

Heseltine, *Rt. Hon.* Sir William Frederick Payne, GCB, GCVO

Hetherington, Sir Thomas Chalmers, KCB, CBE, TD, QC

Hewetson, Sir Christopher Raynor, Kt., TD

Hewett, Sir Richard Mark John, Bt. (1813)

Hewitt, Sir (Cyrus) Lenox (Simson), Kt., OBE

Hewitt, Sir Nicholas Charles Joseph, Bt. (1921)

Heygate, Sir Richard John Gage, Bt. (1831)

Heywood, Sir Peter, Bt. (1838)

Hezlet, *Vice-Adm.* Sir Arthur Richard, KBE, CB, DSO, DSC

Hibbert, Sir Jack, KCB

Hickey, Sir Justin, Kt.

Hickman, Sir (Richard) Glenn, Bt. (1903)

Hicks, Sir Robert, Kt.

Hidden, *Hon.* Sir Anthony Brian, Kt.

Hielscher, Sir Leo Arthur, Kt.

Higgins, *Hon.* Sir Malachy Joseph, Kt.

Higginson, Sir Gordon Robert, Kt., PHD, FRENG

Higgs, Sir Derek Alan, Kt.

Hill, Sir Arthur Alfred, Kt., CBE

Hill, Sir Brian John, Kt.

Hill, Sir James Frederick, Bt. (1917)

Hill, Sir John McGregor, Kt., PHD, FRENG

Hill, Sir John Alfred Rowley, Bt. (S. 1779)

Hill, *Vice-Adm.* Sir Robert Charles Finch, KBE, FRENG

Hill-Norton, *Vice-Adm. Hon.* Sir Nicholas John, KCB

Hill-Wood, Sir Samuel Thomas, Bt. (1921)

Hillary, Sir Edmund, KG, KBE

Hillhouse, Sir (Robert) Russell, KCB

Hills, Sir Graham John, Kt.

Hine, *Air Chief Marshal* Sir Patrick Bardon, GCB, GBE

Hirsch, *Prof.* Sir Peter Bernhard, Kt., PHD, FRS

Hirst, *Rt. Hon.* Sir David Cozens-Hardy, Kt.

Hirst, Sir Michael William, Kt.

Hoare, *Prof.* Sir Charles Anthony Richard, Kt., FRS

†Hoare, Sir David John, Bt. (1786)

Hoare, Sir Timothy Edward Charles, Bt., OBE (I. 1784)

Hobart, Sir John Vere, Bt. (1914)

Hobbs, *Maj.-Gen.* Sir Michael Frederick, KCVO, CBE

Hobday, Sir Gordon Ivan, Kt.

Hobhouse, Sir Charles John Spinney, Bt. (1812)

†Hodge, Sir Andrew Rowland, Bt. (1921)

Hodge, Sir James William, KCVO, CMG

Hodges, *Air Chief Marshal* Sir Lewis MacDonald, KCB, CBE, DSO, DFC

Hodgkin, Sir (Gordon) Howard (Eliot), Kt., CH, CBE

Hodgkinson, Sir Michael Stewart, Kt.

Hodgkinson, *Air Chief Marshal* Sir (William) Derek, KCB, CBE, DFC, AFC

Hodgson, Sir Maurice Arthur Eric, Kt., FRENG

Hodson, Sir Michael Robin Adderley, Bt. (I. 1789)

Hoffenberg, *Prof.* Sir Raymond, KBE

Hogg, Sir Christopher Anthony, Kt.

†Hogg, Sir Piers Michael James, Bt. (1846)

Holcroft, Sir Peter George Culcheth, Bt. (1921)

Holderness, Sir Martin William, Bt. (1920)

Holden, Sir Edward, Bt. (1893)

Holden, Sir John David, Bt. (1919)

Holden-Brown, Sir Derrick, Kt.

Holder, Sir John Henry, Bt. (1898)

Holdgate, Sir Martin Wyatt, Kt., CB, PHD

Holdsworth, Sir (George) Trevor, Kt., CVO

Holland, *Hon.* Sir Alan Douglas, Kt.

Holland, *Hon.* Sir Christopher John, Kt.

Holland, Sir Clifton Vaughan, Kt.

Holland, Sir Geoffrey, KCB

Holland, Sir John Anthony, Kt.

Holland, Sir Kenneth Lawrence, Kt., CBE, QFSM

Holland, Sir Philip Welsby, Kt.

Holliday, *Prof.* Sir Frederick George Thomas, Kt., CBE, FRSE

Hollings, *Hon.* Sir (Alfred) Kenneth, Kt., MC

Hollom, Sir Jasper Quintus, KBE

Holloway, *Hon.* Sir Barry Blyth, KBE

Holm, Sir Carl Henry, Kt., OBE

Holm, Sir Ian (Ian Holm Cuthbert), Kt., CBE

Holman, *Hon.* Sir (Edward) James, Kt.

Holmes, *Prof.* Sir Frank Wakefield, Kt.

Holmes, Sir John Eaton, GCVO, KBE, CMG

Holmes-Sellors, Sir Patrick John, KCVO

Holroyd, *Air Marshal* Sir Frank Martyn, KBE, CB

Holt, *Prof.* Sir James Clarke, Kt.

Holt, Sir Michael, Kt., CBE

Home, Sir William Dundas, Bt. (S. 1671)

Honeycombe, *Prof.* Sir Robert William Kerr, Kt., FRS, FRENG

Honywood, Sir Filmer Courtenay William, Bt. (1660)

Hood, Sir Harold Joseph, Bt., TD (1922)

Hookway, Sir Harry Thurston, Kt.

Hooper, *Hon.* Sir Anthony, Kt.

Hope, Sir Colin Frederick Newton, Kt.

Hope, *Rt. Revd and Rt. Hon.* David Michael, KCVO

Hope, Sir John Carl Alexander, Bt. (S. 1628)

Hope-Dunbar, Sir David, Bt. (S. 1664)

Hopkin, Sir (William Aylsham) Bryan, Kt., CBE

Hopkins, Sir Anthony Philip, Kt., CBE

Hopkins, Sir Michael John, Kt., CBE, RA, RIBA

Hopwood, *Prof.* Sir David Alan, Kt., FRS

Hordern, *Rt. Hon.* Sir Peter Maudslay, Kt.

Horlick, *Vice-Adm.* Sir Edwin John, KBE, FRENG

Horlick, Sir James Cunliffe William, Bt. (1914)

Horlock, *Prof.* Sir John Harold, Kt., FRS, FRENG

Horn, *Prof.* Sir Gabriel, Kt., FRS

Horn-Smith, Sir Julian Michael, Kt.

Hornby, Sir Derek Peter, Kt.

Hornby, Sir Simon Michael, Kt.

Horne, Sir Alan Gray Antony, Bt. (1929)

Horne, *Dr* Sir Alistair Allan, CBE

Horsbrugh-Porter, Sir John Simon, Bt. (1902)

Horsfall, Sir John Musgrave, Bt., MC, TD (1909)

†Hort, Sir Andrew Edwin Fenton, Bt. (1767)

Horton, Sir Robert Baynes, Kt.

Hosker, Sir Gerald Albery, KCB, QC

Hoskyns, Sir Benedict Leigh, Bt. (1676)

Hoskyns, Sir John Austin Hungerford Leigh, Kt.

Hotung, Sir Joseph Edward, Kt.

Houghton, Sir John Theodore, Kt., CBE, FRS

Houldsworth, Sir Richard Thomas Reginald, Bt. (1887)

Hourston, Sir Gordon Minto, Kt.

House, *Lt.-Gen.* Sir David George, GCB, KCVO, CBE, MC

Houssemayne du Boulay, Sir Roger William, KCVO, CMG

Houstoun-Boswall, Sir (Thomas) Alford, Bt. (1836)

Howard, Sir David Howarth Seymour, Bt. (1955)

Howard, *Prof.* Sir Michael Eliot, Kt., CH, CBE, MC

Howard-Dobson, *Gen.* Sir Patrick John, GCB

Howard-Lawson, Sir John Philip, Bt. (1841)

Howell, Sir Ralph Frederic, Kt.

Howells, Sir Eric Waldo Benjamin, Kt., CBE

Howes, Sir Christopher Kingston, KCVO, CB

Howlett, *Gen.* Sir Geoffrey Hugh Whitby, KBE, MC

Huggins, *Hon.* Sir Alan Armstrong, Kt.

Hugh-Jones, Sir Wynn Normington, Kt., LVO

Hugh-Smith, Sir Andrew Colin, Kt.

Hughes, *Hon.* Sir Anthony Philip Gilson, Kt.

Hughes, Hon. Sir Davis, Kt.

Hughes, Sir Jack William, Kt.

Hughes, Sir Thomas Collingwood, Bt. (1773)

Hughes, Sir Trevor Poulton, KCB

Hughes-Morgan, *His Hon. Maj.-Gen.* Sir David John, Bt., CB, CBE (1925)

Hull, *Prof.* Sir David, Kt.

Hulse, Sir Edward Jeremy Westrow, Bt. (1739)

Hum, Sir Christopher Owen, KCMG

Hume, Sir Alan Blyth, Kt., CB

Hunt, Sir John Leonard, Kt.

Hunt, *Adm.* Sir Nicholas John Streynsham, GCB, LVO

Hunt, *Hon.* Sir Patrick James, Kt.

Hunt, Sir Rex Masterman, Kt., CMG

Hunt-Davis, *Brig.* Sir Miles Garth, KCVO, CBE

Hunter, Sir Alistair John, KCMG

Hunter, *Prof.* Sir Laurence Colvin, Kt., CBE, FRSE

Huntington-Whiteley, Sir Hugo Baldwin, Bt. (1918)

Hurn, Sir (Francis) Roger, Kt.

Hurrell, Sir Anthony Gerald, KCVO, CMG

Hurst, Sir Geoffrey Charles, Kt., MBE

Husbands, Sir Clifford Straugh, GCMG

Hutchinson, *Hon.* Sir Ross, Kt., DFC

Hutchison, Sir James Colville, Bt. (1956)

Hutchison, *Rt. Hon.* Sir Michael, Kt.

Hutchison, Sir Robert, Bt. (1939)

Hutt, Sir Dexter Walter, Kt.

Huxley, *Prof.* Sir Andrew Fielding, Kt., OM, FRS

Huxtable, *Gen.* Sir Charles Richard, KCB, CBE

Ibbs, Sir (John) Robin, KBE

Imbert-Terry, Sir Michael Edward Stanley, Bt. (1917)

Imray, Sir Colin Henry, KBE, CMG

Ingham, Sir Bernard, Kt.

Ingilby, Sir Thomas Colvin William, Bt. (1866)

Inglefield-Watson, Sir John Forbes, Bt. (1895)

Inglis, Sir Brian Scott, Kt.

Inglis of Glencorse, Sir Roderick John, Bt. (S. 1703)

Ingram, Sir James Herbert Charles, Bt. (1893)
Ingram, Sir John Henderson, Kt., CBE
Inkin, Sir Geoffrey David, Kt., OBE
†Innes, Sir David Charles Kenneth Gordon, Bt. (NS 1686)
Innes of Edingight, Sir Malcolm Rognvald, KCVO
Innes, Sir Peter Alexander Berowald, Bt. (S. 1628)
Irvine, Sir Donald Hamilton, Kt., CBE, MD, FRCGP
Irving, *Prof.* Sir Miles Horsfall, Kt., MD, FRCS, FRCSE
Irwin, *Lt.-Gen.* Sir Alistair Stuart Hastings, KCB, CBE
Isaacs, Sir Jeremy Israel, Kt.
Isham, Sir Ian Vere Gyles, Bt. (1627)
Jack, *Hon.* Sir Alieu Sulayman, Kt.
Jack, Sir David, Kt., CBE, FRS, FRSE
Jack, Sir David Emmanuel, GCMG, MBE
Jack, *Hon.* Sir Raymond Evan, Kt.
Jackling, Sir Roger Tustin, KCB, CBE
Jackson, Sir Barry Trevor, Kt.
Jackson, Sir Kenneth Joseph, Kt.
Jackson, *Gen.* Sir Michael David, KCB, CBE
Jackson, Sir Michael Roland, Bt. (1902)
Jackson, Sir Nicholas Fane St George, Bt. (1913)
Jackson, Sir Keith Arnold, Bt. (1815)
Jackson, *Hon.* Sir Rupert Matthew, Kt.
†Jackson, Sir (William) Roland Cedric, Bt. (1869)
Jacob, *Hon.* Sir Robert Raphael Hayim (Robin), Kt.
Jacobi, Sir Derek George, Kt., CBE
Jacobi, *Dr* Sir James Edward, Kt., OBE
Jacobs, Sir Cecil Albert, Kt., CBE
Jacobs, *Hon.* Sir Kenneth Sydney, KBE
Jacomb, Sir Martin Wakefield, Kt.
Jaffray, Sir William Otho, Bt. (1892)
Jagger, Sir Michael Philip, Kt.
James, Sir Cynlais Morgan, KCMG
James, Sir Jeffrey Russell, KBE
James, Sir John Nigel Courtenay, KCVO, CBE
James, Sir Stanislaus Anthony, GCMG, OBE
Jamieson, *Air Marshal* Sir David Ewan, KBE, CB
Jansen, Sir Ross Malcolm, KBE
Janvrin, *Rt. Hon.* Sir Robin Berry, KCB, KCVO
Jardine of Applegirth, Sir Alexander Maule, Bt. (S. 1672)
Jardine, Sir Andrew Colin Douglas, Bt. (1916)
Jarman, *Prof.* Sir Brian, Kt., OBE
Jarratt, Sir Alexander Anthony, Kt., CB
Jarvis, Sir Gordon Ronald, Kt.
Jawara, *Hon.* Sir Dawda Kairaba, Kt.
Jay, Sir Antony Rupert, Kt., CVO
Jay, Sir Michael Hastings, KCMG
Jeewoolall, Sir Ramesh, Kt.

Jefferson, Sir George Rowland, Kt., CBE, FRENG
Jeffreys, *Prof.* Sir Alec John, Kt., FRS
Jeffries, *Hon.* Sir John Francis, Kt.
Jehangir, Sir Cowasji, Bt. (1908)
Jejeebhoy, Sir Jamsetjee, Bt. (1857)
Jenkins, Sir Brian Garton, GBE
Jenkins, Sir Elgar Spencer, Kt., OBE
Jenkins, Sir James Christopher, KCB, QC
Jenkins, Sir Michael Nicholas Howard, Kt., OBE
Jenkins, Sir Michael Romilly Heald, KCMG
Jenkins, Sir Simon, Kt.
Jenkinson, Sir John Banks, Bt. (1661)
Jenks, Sir Maurice Arthur Brian, Bt. (1932)
Jenner, *Air Marshal* Sir Timothy LVO, KCB
Jennings, Sir John Southwood, Kt., CBE, FRSE
Jennings, Sir Peter Neville Wake, Kt., CVO
Jephcott, Sir Neil Welbourn, Bt. (1962)
Jessel, Sir Charles John, Bt. (1883)
Jewkes, Sir Gordon Wesley, KCMG
Job, Sir Peter James Denton, Kt.
John, Sir David Glyndwr, KCMG
John, Sir Elton Hercules (Reginald Kenneth Dwight), Kt., CBE
Johns, *Air Chief Marshal* Sir Richard Edward, GCB, CBE, LVO
Johnson, Sir Colpoys Guy, Bt. (1755)
Johnson, *Gen.* Sir Garry Dene, KCB, OBE, MC
Johnson, Sir John Rodney, KCMG
†Johnson, Sir Patrick Eliot, Bt. (1818)
Johnson, *Hon.* Sir Robert Lionel, Kt.
Johnson, Sir Vassel Godfrey, Kt., CBE
Johnson-Ferguson, Sir Ian Edward, Bt. (1906)
Johnston, Sir John Baines, GCMG, KCVO
Johnston, *Lt.-Col.* Sir John Frederick Dame, GCVO, MC
Johnston, *Lt.-Gen.* Sir Maurice Robert, KCB, OBE
Johnston, Sir Thomas Alexander, Bt. (S. 1626)
Johnstone, Sir Geoffrey Adams Dinwiddie, KCMG
Johnstone, Sir (George) Richard Douglas, Bt. (S. 1700)
Johnstone, Sir (John) Raymond, Kt., CBE
Jolliffe, Sir Anthony Stuart, GBE
Jolly, Sir Aurthur Richard, KCMG
Jonas, Sir John Peter Jens, Kt., CBE
Jones, *Gen.* Sir (Charles) Edward Webb, KCB, CBE
Jones, *Air Marshal* Sir Edward Gordon, KCB, CBE, DSO, DFC
Jones, Sir Harry George, Kt., CBE
Jones, Sir John Francis, Kt.
Jones, Sir Keith Stephen, Kt.
Jones, Sir Lyndon, Kt.
Jones, Sir (Owen) Trevor, Kt.
Jones, Sir Richard Anthony Lloyd, KCB

Jones, Sir Robert Edward, Kt.
Jones, Sir Simon Warley Frederick Benton, Bt. (1919)
†Joseph, *Hon.* Sir James Samuel, Bt. (1943)
Jowitt, *Hon.* Sir Edwin Frank, Kt.
Judge, *Rt. Hon.* Sir Igor, Kt.
Judge, Sir Paul Rupert, Kt.
Jugnauth, *Rt. Hon.* Sir Aneerood, KCMG
Jungius, *Vice-Adm.* Sir James George, KBE
Kaberry, *Hon.* Sir Christopher Donald, Bt. (1960)
Kakaraya, Sir Pato, KBE
Kalo, Sir Kwamala, Kt., MBE
Kan Yuet-Keung, Sir, GBE
Kapi, *Hon.* Sir Mari, Kt., CBE
Kaputin, Sir John Rumet, KBE, CMG
Kaufman, *Rt. Hon.* Sir Gerald Bernard, Kt., MP
Kausimae, Sir David Nanau, KBE
Kavali, Sir Thomas, Kt., OBE
Kawharu, *Prof.* Sir Ian Hugh, Kt.
Kay, *Prof.* Sir Andrew Watt, Kt.
Kay, *Hon.* Sir Maurice Ralph, Kt., PC
Kaye, Sir Paul Henry Gordon, Bt. (1923)
Keane, Sir Richard Michael, Bt. (1801)
Kearney, *Hon.* Sir William John Francis, Kt., CBE
Keeble, Sir (Herbert Ben) Curtis, GCMG
Keegan, Sir John Desmond Patrick, Kt., OBE
Keene, *Rt. Hon.* Sir David Wolfe, Kt.
Keith, *Hon.* Sir Brian Richard, Kt.
Keith, *Prof.* Sir James, KBE
†Kellett, Sir Stanley Charles, Bt. (1801)
Kelly, Sir Christopher William, KCB
Kelly, Sir David Robert Corbett, Kt., CBE
Kelly, *Rt. Hon.* Sir (John William) Basil, Kt.
Kemakeza, Sir Allan, Kt.
Kemball, *Air Marshal* Sir (Richard) John, KCB, CBE
Kemp, Sir (Edward) Peter, KCB
Kemp-Welch, Sir John, Kt.
Kenilorea, *Rt. Hon.* Sir Peter, KBE
Kennaway, Sir John Lawrence, Bt. (1791)
Kennedy, Sir Francis, KCMG, CBE
Kennedy, *Hon.* Sir Ian Alexander, Kt.
Kennedy, *Prof.* Sir Ian McColl, Kt.
Kennedy, Sir Ludovic Henry Coverley, Kt.
†Kennedy, Sir Michael Edward, Bt., (1836)
Kennedy, *Rt. Hon.* Sir Paul Joseph Morrow, Kt.
Kennedy, *Air Chief Marshal* Sir Thomas Lawrie, GCB, AFC
Kennedy-Good, Sir John, KBE
Kenny, Sir Anthony John Patrick, Kt. DPHIL, LITT, FBA
Kenny, *Gen.* Sir Brian Leslie Graham, GCB, CBE
Kentridge, Sir Sydney Woolf, KCMG, QC

Kenyon, Sir George Henry, Kt.
Kermode, Sir (John) Frank, Kt., FBA
Kermode, Sir Ronald Graham Quale, KBE
Kerr, *Hon.* Sir Brian Francis, Kt.
Kerr, *Adm.* Sir John Beverley, GCB
Kerry, Sir Michael James, KCB, QC
Kershaw, *Prof.* Sir Ian, Kt.
Kershaw, Sir (John) Anthony, Kt., MC
Keswick, Sir John Chippendale Lindley, Kt.
Kevau, *Prof.* Sir Isi Henao, Kt., CBE
Kikau, *Ratu* Sir Jone Latianara, KBE
Killen, *Hon.* Sir Denis James, KCMG
Kimber, Sir Charles Dixon, Bt. (1904)
King, *Prof.* Sir David Anthony, Kt., FRS
King, Sir John Christopher, Bt. (1888)
King, *Vice-Adm.* Sir Norman Ross Dutton, KBE
King, Sir Wayne Alexander, Bt. (1815)
Kingman, *Prof.* Sir John Frank Charles, Kt., FRS
Kingsland, Sir Richard, Kt., CBE, DFC
Kingsley, Sir Ben, Kt.
Kinloch, Sir David, Bt. (S. 1686)
Kinloch, Sir David Oliphant, Bt. (1873)
Kipalan, Sir Albert, Kt.
Kirkpatrick, Sir Ivone Elliott, Bt. (S. 1685)
Kirkwood, *Hon.* Sir Andrew Tristram Hammett, Kt.
Kirkwood, Sir Archibald Johnstone, Kt., MP
Kiszely, *Lt.-Gen.* Sir John Panton, KCB, MC
Kitcatt, Sir Peter Julian, Kt., CB
Kitson, *Gen.* Sir Frank Edward, GBE, KCB, MC
Kitson, Sir Timothy Peter Geoffrey, Kt.
Kleinwort, Sir Richard Drake, Bt. (1909)
Klug, Sir Aaron, Kt., OM
Kneller, Sir Alister Arthur, Kt.
Knight, Sir Harold Murray, KBE, DSC
Knight, *Air Chief Marshal* Sir Michael William Patrick, KCB, AFC
†Knill, Sir Thomas John Pugin Bartholomew, Bt. (1893)
Knowles, Sir Charles Francis, Bt. (1765)
Knowles, Sir Durward Randolph, Kt., OBE
Knowles, Sir Richard Marchant, Kt.
Knox, Sir David Laidlaw, Kt.
Knox, *Hon.* Sir John Leonard, Kt.
Knox, *Hon.* Sir William Edward, Kt.
Knox-Johnston, Sir William Robert Patrick (Sir Robin), Kt., CBE, RD
Koraea, Sir Thomas, Kt.
Kornberg, *Prof.* Sir Hans Leo, Kt., DSC, SCD, PHD, FRS
Korowi, Sir Wiwa, GCMG
Krebs, *Prof.* Sir John Richard, Kt., DPHIL, FRS

Kroto, *Prof.* Sir Harold Walter, Kt., FRS
Kulukundis, Sir Elias George (Eddie), Kt., OBE
Kurongku, *Most Revd* Peter, KBE
Lachmann, *Prof.* Sir Peter Julius, Kt.
Lacon, Sir Edmund Vere, Bt. (1818)
Lacy, Sir Patrick Brian Finucane, Bt. (1921)
Lacy, Sir John Trend, Kt., CBE
Laddie, *Hon.* Sir Hugh Ian Lang, Kt.
Laidlaw, Sir Christopher Charles Fraser, Kt.
Laing, Sir (John) Martin (Kirby), Kt., CBE
Laing, Sir (John) Maurice, Kt.
Laing, Sir (William) Kirby, Kt., FRENG
Laird, Sir Gavin Harry, Kt., CBE
Lake, Sir (Atwell) Graham, Bt. (1711)
Laker, Sir Frederick Alfred, Kt.
Lakin, Sir Michael, Bt. (1909)
Laking, Sir George Robert, KCMG
Lamb, Sir Albert Thomas, KBE, CMG, DFC
Lambert, Sir Anthony Edward, KCMG
Lambert, Sir John Henry, KCVO, CMG
†Lambert, Sir Peter John Biddulph, Bt. (1711)
Lampl, Sir Frank William, Kt.
Lampl, Sir Peter, Kt., OBE
Lamport, Sir Stephen Mark Jeffrey, KCVO
Landale, Sir David William Neil, KCVO
Landau, Sir Dennis Marcus, Kt.
Lander, Sir Stephen James, KCB
Lane, Prof. Sir David Philip, Kt.
†Langham, Sir John Stephen, Bt. (1660)
Langlands, Sir Robert Alan, Kt.
Langley, *Hon.* Sir Gordon Julian Hugh, Kt.
Langley, *Maj.-Gen.* Sir Henry Desmond Allen, KCVO, MBE
Langrishe, Sir James Hercules, Bt. (I. 1777)
Lankester, Sir Timothy Patrick, KCB
Lapli, Sir John Ini, GCMG
Lapun, *Hon.* Sir Paul, Kt.
Larcom, Sir (Charles) Christopher Royde, Bt. (1868)
Large, Sir Andrew McLeod Brooks, Kt.
Large, Sir Peter, Kt., CBE
Latham, *Rt. Hon.* Sir David Nicholas Ramsey, Kt.
Latham, Sir Michael Anthony, Kt.
Latham, Sir Richard Thomas Paul, Bt. (1919)
Latimer, Sir (Courtenay) Robert, Kt., CBE
Latimer, Sir Graham Stanley, KBE
Latour-Adrien, *Hon.* Sir Maurice, Kt.
Laughton, Sir Anthony Seymour, Kt.
Laurence, Sir Peter Harold, KCMG, MC
Laurie, Sir Robert Bayley Emilius, Bt. (1834)
Lauterpacht, Sir Elihu, Kt., CBE, QC

Lauti, *Rt. Hon.* Sir Toaripi, GCMG
Lavan, *Hon.* Sir John Martin, Kt.
Law, *Adm.* Sir Horace Rochfort, GCB, OBE, DSC
Lawes, Sir (John) Michael Bennet, Bt. (1882)
Lawler, Sir Peter James, Kt., OBE
†Lawrence, Sir Clive Wyndham, Bt. (1906)
Lawrence, Sir Henry Peter, Bt. (1858)
Lawrence, Sir Ivan John, Kt., QC
Lawrence, Sir John Patrick Grosvenor, Kt., CBE
Lawrence, Sir William Fettiplace, Bt. (1867)
Lawrence-Jones, Sir Christopher, Bt. (1831)
Laws, *Rt. Hon.* Sir John Grant McKenzie, Kt.
Lawson, Sir Christopher Donald, Kt.
Lawson, Sir Charles John Patrick, Bt. (1900)
Lawson, *Gen.* Sir Richard George, KCB, DSO, OBE
Lawson-Tancred, Sir Henry, Bt. (1662)
Layard, *Adm.* Sir Michael Henry Gordon, KCB, CBE
Lea, *Vice-Adm.* Sir John Stuart Crosbie, KBE
Lea, Sir Thomas William, Bt. (1892)
Leach, *Admiral of the Fleet* Sir Henry Conyers, GCB
Leahy, Sir Daniel Joseph, Kt.
Leahy, Sir John Henry Gladstone, KCMG
Leahy, Sir Terence Patrick, Kt.
Learmont, *Gen.* Sir John Hartley, KCB, CBE
Leather, Sir Edwin Hartley Cameron, KCMG, KCVO
Leaver, Sir Christopher, GBE
Le Bailly, *Vice-Adm.* Sir Louis Edward Stewart Holland, KBE, CB
Le Cheminant, *Air Chief Marshal* Sir Peter de Lacey, GBE, KCB, DFC
Lechmere, Sir Reginald Anthony Hungerford, Bt. (1818)
Ledger, Sir Philip Stevens, Kt., CBE, FRSE
Lee, Sir Arthur James, KBE, MC
Lee, *Brig.* Sir Leonard Henry, Kt., CBE
Lee, Sir Quo-wei, Kt., CBE
Leeds, Sir Christopher Anthony, Bt. (1812)
Lees, Sir David Bryan, Kt.
Lees, Sir Thomas Edward, Bt. (1897)
Lees, Sir Thomas Harcourt Ivor, Bt. (1804)
Lees, Sir (William) Antony Clare, Bt. (1937)
Le Fanu, *Maj.* Sir (George) Victor (Sheridan), KCVO
le Fleming, Sir David Kelland, Bt. (1705)
Legard, Sir Charles Thomas, Bt. (1660)
Legg, Sir Thomas Stuart, KCB, QC
Leggatt, *Rt. Hon.* Sir Andrew Peter, Kt.
Leggatt, Sir Hugh Frank John, Kt.

Leggett, *Prof.* Sir Anthony James, KBE

Leigh, Sir Geoffrey Norman, Kt.

Leigh, Sir Richard Henry, Bt. (1918)

Leighton, Sir Michael John Bryan, Bt. (1693)

Leitch, Sir George, KCB, OBE

Leith-Buchanan, Sir Charles Alexander James, Bt. (1775)

Le Marchant, Sir Francis Arthur, Bt. (1841)

Leng, *Gen.* Sir Peter John Hall, KCB, MBE, MC

Lennox-Boyd, The Hon. Sir Mark Alexander, Kt.

Leon, Sir John Ronald, Bt. (1911)

Leonard, *Rt. Revd Monsignor* and *Rt. Hon.* Graham Douglas, KCVO

Lepping, Sir George Geria Dennis, GCMG, MBE

Le Quesne, Sir (John) Godfray, Kt., QC

Lee-Steere, Sir Ernest Henry, KBE

Leslie, Sir Colin Alan Bettridge, Kt.

Leslie, Sir John Norman Ide, Bt. (1876)

Leslie, Sir Peter Evelyn, Kt.

Lester, Sir James Theodore, Kt.

Lethbridge, Sir Thomas Periam Hector Noel, Bt. (1804)

Lever, Sir Jeremy Frederick, KCMG, QC

Lever, Sir Paul, KCMG

Lever, Sir (Tresham) Christopher Arthur Lindsay, Bt. (1911)

Leveson, *Hon.* Sir Brian Henry, Kt.

Levey, Sir Michael Vincent, Kt., LVO

Levine, Sir Montague Bernard, Kt.

Levinge, Sir Richard George Robin, Bt. (I. 1704)

Lewinton, Sir Christopher, Kt.

Lewis, Sir David Courtenay Mansel, KCVO

Lewis, Sir John Anthony, Kt., OBE

Lewis, Sir Terence Murray, Kt., OBE, GM, QPM

Lewison, *Hon.* Sir Kim Martin Jordan, Kt.

Ley, Sir Ian Francis, Bt. (1905)

Li, Sir Ka-Shing, KBE

Lickiss, Sir Michael Gillam, Kt.

Liddington, Sir Bruce, Kt.

Liggins, *Prof.* Sir Graham Collingwood, Kt., CBE, FRS

Lightman, *Hon.* Sir Gavin Anthony, Kt.

Lighton, Sir Thomas Hamilton, Bt. (I. 1791)

Likierman, *Prof.* Sir John Andrew, Kt.

Lilleyman, *Prof.* Sir John Stuart, Kt.

Limon, Sir Donald William, KCB

Linacre, Sir (John) Gordon (Seymour), Kt., CBE, AFC, DFM

Lindop, Sir Norman, Kt.

Lindsay, Sir James Harvey Kincaid Stewart, Kt.

Lindsay, *Hon.* Sir John Edmund Frederic, Kt.

†Lindsay, Sir James Martin Evelyn, Bt., (1962)

†Lindsay-Hogg, Sir Michael Edward, Bt. (1905)

Lipton, Sir Stuart Anthony, Kt.

Lipworth, Sir (Maurice) Sydney, Kt.

Lister-Kaye, Sir John Phillip Lister, Bt. (1812)

Liston-Foulis, Sir Ian Primrose, Bt. (S. 1634)

Lithgow, Sir William James, Bt. (1925)

Little, *Most Revd* Thomas Francis, KBE

Littler, Sir (James) Geoffrey, KCB

Llewellyn, Sir David St Vincent, Bt. (1922)

Llewellyn-Smith, *Prof.* Sir Christopher Hubert, Kt.

Lloyd, *Prof.* Sir Geoffrey Ernest Richard, Kt., FBA

Lloyd, Sir Ian Stewart, Kt.

Lloyd, Sir Nicholas Markley, Kt.

Lloyd, *Rt. Hon.* Sir Peter Robert Cable, Kt., MP

Lloyd, Sir Richard Ernest Butler, Bt. (1960)

Lloyd, *Hon.* Sir Timothy Andrew Wigram, Kt.

Lloyd-Hughes, Sir Trevor Denby, Kt.

Lloyd-Jones, Sir (Peter) Hugh (Jefford), Kt.

Loane, *Most Revd* Marcus Lawrence, KBE

Lobo, Sir Rogerio Hyndman, Kt., CBE

†Loder, Sir Edmund Jeune, Bt. (1887)

Logan, Sir David Brian Carleton, KCMG

Logan, Sir Donald Arthur, KCMG

Logan, Sir Raymond Douglas, Kt.

Lokoloko, Sir Tore, GCMG, GCVO, OBE

Longmore, *Rt. Hon.* Sir Andrew Centlivres, Kt.

Loram, *Vice-Adm.* Sir David Anning, KCB, CVO

Lord, Sir Michael Nicholson, Kt.

Lorimer, Sir (Thomas) Desmond, Kt.

Los, *Hon.* Sir Kubulan, Kt., CBE

Loughran, Sir Gerald Finbar, KCB

Lovell, Sir (Alfred Charles) Bernard, Kt., OBE, FRS

Lovelock, Sir Douglas Arthur, KCB

Loveridge, Sir John Warren, Kt.

Lovill, Sir John Roger, Kt., CBE

Lowe, *Air Chief Marshal* Sir Douglas Charles, GCB, DFC, AFC

Lowe, Sir Frank Budge, Kt.

Lowe, Sir Thomas William Gordon, Bt. (1918)

Lowson, Sir Ian Patrick, Bt. (1951)

Lowther, *Col.* Sir Charles Douglas, Bt. (1824)

Lowther, Sir John Luke, KCVO, CBE

Loyd, Sir Francis Alfred, KCMG, OBE

Loyd, Sir Julian St John, KCVO

Lu, Sir Tseng Chi, Kt.

Lucas, *Prof.* Sir Colin Renshaw, Kt.

Lucas, Sir Thomas Edward, Bt. (1887)

Lucas-Tooth, Sir (Hugh) John, Bt. (1920)

Lucy, Sir Edmund John William

Hugh Cameron-Ramsay-Fairfax, Bt. (1836)

Luddington, Sir Donald Collin Cumyn, KBE, CMG, CVO

Lumsden, Sir David James, Kt.

Lush, *Hon.* Sir George Hermann, Kt.

Lushington, Sir John Richard Castleman, Bt. (1791)

Luttrell, *Col.* Sir Geoffrey Walter Fownes, KCVO, MC

Lyell, *Rt. Hon.* Sir Nicholas Walter, Kt., MP

Lygo, *Adm.* Sir Raymond Derek, KCB

Lyle, Sir Gavin Archibald, Bt. (1929)

Lynch-Blosse, *Capt.* Sir Richard Hely, Bt. (1622)

Lynch-Robinson, Sir Dominick Christopher, Bt. (1920)

Lyne, Sir Roderic Michael John, KBE, CMG

Lyons, Sir Edward Houghton, Kt.

Lyons, Sir James Reginald, Kt.

Lyons, Sir John, Kt.

Lyons, Sir Michael Thomas, Kt.

McAlpine, Sir William Hepburn, Bt. (1918)

Macara, Sir Alexander Wiseman, Kt., FRCP, FRCGP

†Macara, Sir Hugh Kenneth, Bt. (1911)

McAvoy, Sir (Francis) Joseph, Kt., CBE

McCaffrey, Sir Thomas Daniel, Kt.

McCallum, Sir Donald Murdo, Kt., CBE, FRENG

McCamley, Sir Graham Edward, KBE

McCartney, Sir (James) Paul, Kt., MBE

Macartney, Sir John Barrington, Bt. (I. 1799)

McClintock, Sir Eric Paul, Kt.

McColl, Sir Colin Hugh Verel, KCMG

McCollum, *Rt. Hon.* Sir William, Kt.

McCombe, *Hon.* Sir Richard George Bramwell, Kt.

McConnell, Sir Robert Shean, Bt. (1900)

McCorkell, *Col.* Sir Michael William, KCVO, OBE, TD

MacCormac, Sir Richard Cornelius, Kt., CBE

MacCormick, *Prof.* Sir Donald Neil, Kt., MEP, QC

†McCowan, Sir David William, Bt. (1934)

McCullough, *Hon.* Sir (Iain) Charles (Robert), Kt.

MacDermott, *Rt. Hon.* Sir John Clarke, Kt.

McDermott, Sir (Lawrence) Emmet, KBE

Macdonald of Sleat, Sir Ian Godfrey Bosville, Bt. (S. 1625)

Macdonald, Sir Kenneth Carmichael, KCB

McDonald, Sir Trevor, Kt., OBE

McDowell, Sir Eric Wallace, Kt., CBE

Mace, *Lt.-Gen.* Sir John Airth, KBE, CB

McEwen, Sir John Roderick Hugh, Bt. (1953)

McFarland, Sir John Talbot, Bt. (1914)

MacFarlane, *Prof.* Sir Alistair George James, Kt., CBE, FRS

Macfarlane, Sir (David) Neil, Kt.

Macfarlane, Sir George Gray, Kt., CB, FRENG

McFarlane, Sir Ian, Kt.

McGeoch, *Vice-Adm.* Sir Ian Lachlan Mackay, KCB, DSO, DSC

McGrath, Sir Brian Henry, GCVO

Macgregor, Sir Edwin Robert, Bt. (1828)

McGregor, Sir Ian Alexander, Kt., CBE

McGregor, Sir James David, Kt., OBE

MacGregor of MacGregor, Sir Malcolm Gregor Charles, Bt. (1795)

McGrigor, *Capt.* Sir Charles Edward, Bt. (1831)

McIntosh, Sir Neil William David, Kt., CBE

McIntosh, Sir Ronald Robert Duncan, KCB

McIntyre, Sir Donald Conroy, Kt., CBE

McIntyre, Sir Meredith Alister, Kt.

Mackay, *Hon.* Sir Colin Crichton, Kt.

MacKay, *Prof.* Sir Donald Iain, Kt.

MacKay, Sir Francis Henry, Kt.

McKay, Sir John Andrew, Kt., CBE

McKay, Sir William Robert, KCB

Mackay-Dick, *Maj.-Gen.* Sir Iain Charles, KCVO, MBE

Mackechnie, Sir Alistair John, Kt.

McKee, *Maj.* Sir (William) Cecil, Kt., ERD

McKellen, Sir Ian Murray, Kt., CBE

Mackenzie, Sir (James William) Guy, Bt. (1890)

Mackenzie, *Gen.* Sir Jeremy John George, GCB, OBE

†Mackenzie, Sir Peter Douglas, Bt. (S. 1673)

†Mackenzie, Sir Roderick McQuhae, Bt. (S. 1703)

McKenzie, Sir Roy Allan, KBE

Mackerras, Sir (Alan) Charles (MacLaurin), Kt., CH, CBE

Mackeson, Sir Rupert Henry, Bt. (1954)

McKillop, Sir Thomas Fulton Wilson, Kt.

McKinnon, Sir James, Kt.

McKinnon, *Hon.* Sir Stuart Neil, Kt.

Mackintosh, Sir Cameron Anthony, Kt.

Mackworth, Sir Digby (John), Bt. (1776)

McLaren, Sir Robin John Taylor, KCMG

McLaughlin, *Hon.* Mr Justice, Sir Richard, Kt.

Maclean of Dunconnell, Sir Charles Edward, Bt. (1957)

Maclean, Sir Donald Og Grant, Kt.

Maclean, Sir Lachlan Hector Charles, Bt. (NS 1631)

Maclean, Sir Murdo, Kt.

McLeod, Sir Charles Henry, Bt. (1925)

MacLeod, Sir (John) Maxwell Norman, Bt. (1924)

Macleod, Sir (Nathaniel William) Hamish, KBE

McLintock, Sir (Charles) Alan, Kt.

McLintock, Sir Michael William, Bt. (1934)

Maclure, Sir John Robert Spencer, Bt. (1898)

McMahon, Sir Brian Patrick, Bt. (1817)

McMahon, Sir Christopher William, Kt.

McMaster, Sir Brian John, Kt., CBE

Macmillan, Sir (Alexander McGregor) Graham, Kt.

MacMillan, *Lt.-Gen.* Sir John Richard Alexander, KCB, CBE

McMullin, *Rt. Hon.* Sir Duncan Wallace, Kt.

McMurtry, Sir David, Kt., CBE

Macnaghten, Sir Patrick Alexander, Bt. (1836)

McNair-Wilson, Sir Patrick Michael Ernest David, Kt.

McNamara, *Air Chief Marshal* Sir Neville Patrick, KBE

Macnaughton, *Prof.* Sir Malcolm Campbell, Kt.

McNee, Sir David Blackstock, Kt., QPM

McNulty, Sir (Robert William) Roy, Kt., CBE

MacPhail, Sir Bruce Dugald, Kt.

Macpherson, Sir Ronald Thomas Steward (Tommy), CBE, MC, TD

Macpherson of Cluny, *Hon.* Sir William Alan, Kt., TD

McQuarrie, Sir Albert, Kt.

MacRae, Sir (Alastair) Christopher (Donald Summerhayes), KCMG

Macready, Sir Nevil John Wilfrid, Bt. (1923)

MacSween, *Prof.* Sir Roderick Norman McIver, Kt.

Mactaggart, Sir John Auld, Bt. (1938)

Macwhinnie, Sir Gordon Menzies, Kt., CBE

McWilliam, Sir Michael Douglas, KCMG

McWilliams, Sir Francis, GBE

Madden, Sir David Christopher Andrew, KCMG

Madden, Sir Peter John, Bt. (1919)

Maddox, Sir John Royden, Kt.

Madel, Sir (William) David, Kt., MP

Magnus, Sir Laurence Henry Philip, Bt. (1917)

Mahon, Sir (John) Denis, Kt., CH, CBE

Mahon, Sir William Walter, Bt. (1819)

Maiden, Sir Colin James, Kt., DPHIL

Main, Sir Peter Tester, Kt., ERD

Maingard de la Ville ès Offrans, Sir Louis Pierre René, Kt., CBE

Maini, *Prof.* Sir Ravinder Nath, Kt.

Maino, Sir Charles, KBE

†Maitland, Sir Charles Alexander, Bt. (1818)

Maitland, Sir Donald James Dundas, GCMG, OBE

Malbon, *Vice-Adm.* Sir Fabian Michael, KBE

Malcolm, Sir James William Thomas Alexander, Bt. (S. 1665)

Malet, Sir Harry Douglas St Lo, Bt. (1791)

Mallaby, Sir Christopher Leslie George, GCMG, GCVO

Mallet, Sir William George, GCMG, CBE

Mallick, *Prof.* Sir Netar Prakash, Kt.

Mallinson, Sir William James, Bt. (1935)

Malpas, Sir Robert, Kt., CBE

Mamo, Sir Anthony Joseph, Kt., OBE

Mance, *Rt. Hon.* Sir Jonathan Hugh, Kt.

Mancham, Sir James Richard Marie, KBE

Manchester, Sir William Maxwell, KBE

Mander, Sir Charles Marcus, Bt. (1911)

Manduell, Sir John, Kt., CBE

Mann, *Hon.* Sir George Anthony, Kt.

Mann, *Rt. Revd* Michael Ashley, KCVO

Mann, Sir Rupert Edward, Bt. (1905)

Manning, Sir David Geoffrey, KCMG

Mansel, Sir Philip, Bt. (1622)

Mansfield, *Vice-Adm.* Sir (Edward) Gerard (Napier), KBE, CVO

Mansfield, *Prof.* Sir Peter, Kt.

Mantell, *Rt. Hon.* Sir Charles Barrie Knight, Kt.

Manton, Sir Edwin Alfred Grenville, Kt.

Manuella, Sir Tulaga, GCMG, MBE

Manzie, Sir (Andrew) Gordon, KCB

Margetson, Sir John William Denys, KCMG

Mark, Sir Robert, GBE

Markham, Sir Charles John, Bt. (1911)

Marling, Sir Charles William Somerset, Bt. (1882)

Marmot, *Prof.* Sir Michael Gideon, Kt.

Marr, Sir Leslie Lynn, Bt. (1919)

Marriner, Sir Neville, Kt., CBE

†Marsden, Sir Simon Neville Llewelyn, Bt. (1924)

Marsh, *Prof.* Sir John Stanley, Kt., CBE

Marshall, Sir Arthur Gregory George, Kt., OBE

Marshall, Sir Denis Alfred, Kt.

Marshall, *Prof.* Sir (Oshley) Roy, Kt., CBE

Marshall, Sir Peter Harold Reginald, KCMG

Marshall, Sir (Robert) Michael, Kt.

Martin, Sir Clive Haydon, Kt., OBE

Martin, Sir George Henry, Kt., CBE

Martin, *Vice-Adm.* Sir John Edward Ludgate, KCB, DSC

Martin, *Prof.* Sir Laurence Woodward, Kt.

Martin, Sir (Robert) Bruce, Kt., QC

Marychurch, Sir Peter Harvey, KCMG

Masefield, Sir Charles Beech Gordon, Kt.

Masefield, Sir Peter Gordon, Kt.

Mason, *Hon.* Sir Anthony Frank, KBE

Mason, Sir (Basil) John, Kt., CB, DSC, FRS

Mason, *Prof.* Sir David Kean, Kt., CBE

Mason, Sir Frederick Cecil, KCVO, CMG

Mason, Sir Gordon Charles, Kt., OBE

Mason, Sir John Charles Moir, KCMG

Mason, Sir John Peter, Kt., CBE

Mason, Sir Peter James, KBE

Mason, *Prof.* Sir Ronald, KCB, FRS

Massy-Greene, Sir (John) Brian, Kt.

Matane, Sir Paulias Nguna, Kt., CMG, OBE

Mather, Sir (David) Carol (Macdonell), Kt., MC

Mathers, Sir Robert William, Kt.

Matheson of Matheson, Sir Fergus John, Bt. (1882)

Mathewson, Sir George Ross, Kt., CBE, PHD, FRSE

Matthews, Sir Peter Alec, Kt.

Matthews, Sir Terence Hedley, Kt., OBE

Maud, *The Hon.* Sir Humphrey John Hamilton, KCMG

Maughan, Sir Deryck, Kt.

Mawer, Sir Philip John Courtney, Kt.

Mawhinney, *Rt. Hon.* Sir Brian Stanley, Kt., MP

Maxwell, Sir Michael Eustace George, Bt. (S. 1681)

Maxwell-Hyslop, Sir Robert John (Robin), Kt.

Maxwell-Scott, Sir Dominic James, Bt. (1642)

May, *Rt. Hon.* Sir Anthony Tristram Kenneth, Kt.

May, Sir Richard George, Kt.

Mayhew-Sanders, Sir John Reynolds, Kt.

Maynard, *Hon.* Sir Clement Travelyan, Kt.

Mayne, *Very Revd* Michael Clement Otway, KCVO

Meadow, *Prof.* Sir (Samuel) Roy, Kt., FRCP, FRCPE

Medlycott, Sir Mervyn Tregonwell, Bt. (1808)

Megarry, *Rt. Hon.* Sir Robert Edgar, Kt., FBA

Meldrum, Sir Graham, Kt., CBE, QFSM

Melhuish, Sir Michael Ramsay, KBE, CMG

Mellon, Sir James, KCMG

Melmoth, Sir Graham John, Kt.

Menter, Sir James Woodham, Kt., PHD, SCD, FRS

Merifield, Sir Anthony James, KCVO, CB

Meyer, Sir Anthony John Charles, Bt. (1910)

Meyer, Sir Christopher John Rome, KCMG

Meyjes, Sir Richard Anthony, Kt.

†Meyrick, Sir Timothy Thomas Charlton, Bt. (1880)

Miakwe, *Hon.* Sir Akepa, KBE

Michael, Sir Duncan, Kt.

Michael, Sir Peter Colin, Kt., CBE

Middleton, Sir John Maxwell, Kt.

Middleton, Sir Peter Edward, GCB

Miers, Sir (Henry) David Alastair Capel, KBE, CMG

Milbank, Sir Anthony Frederick, Bt. (1882)

Milborne-Swinnerton-Pilkington, Sir Thomas Henry, Bt. (S. 1635)

Milburn, Sir Anthony Rupert, Bt. (1905)

Miles, Sir Peter Tremayne, KCVO

Miles, Sir William Napier Maurice, Bt. (1859)

Millais, Sir Geoffrey Richard Everett, Bt. (1885)

Millar, Sir Oliver Nicholas, GCVO, FBA

Millard, Sir Guy Elwin, KCMG, CVO

Miller, Sir Albert Joel, KCMG, MVO, MBE, QPM, CPM

Miller, Sir Donald John, Kt., FRSE, FRENG

Miller, Sir Harry Holmes, Bt. (1705)

Miller, Sir Hilary Duppa (Hal), Kt.

Miller, *Lt.-Col.* Sir John Mansel, GCVO, DSO, MC

Miller, Sir Jonathan Wolfe, Kt., CBE

Miller, Sir Peter North, Kt.

Miller, Sir Robin Robert William, Kt.

Miller, Sir Ronald Andrew Baird, Kt., CBE

Miller of Glenlee, Sir Stephen William Macdonald, Bt. (1788)

Mills, *Vice-Adm.* Sir Charles Piercy, KCB, CBE, DSC

Mills, Sir Ian, Kt.

Mills, Sir Frank, KCVO, CMG

Mills, Sir John Lewis Ernest Watts, Kt., CBE

Mills, Sir Peter Frederick Leighton, Bt. (1921)

Milman, Sir David Patrick, Bt. (1800)

Milne, Sir John Drummond, Kt.

Milne-Watson, Sir Andrew Michael, Bt. (1937)

Milner, Sir Timothy William Lycett, Bt. (1717)

Milton-Thompson, *Surgeon Vice-Adm.* Sir Godfrey James, KBE

Mirrlees, *Prof.* Sir James Alexander, Kt., FBA

Mitchell, Sir David Bower, Kt.

Mitchell, Sir Derek Jack, KCB, CVO

Mitchell, *Rt. Hon.* Sir James FitzAllen, KCMG

Mitchell, *Very Revd* Patrick Reynolds, KCVO

Mitchell, *Hon.* Sir Stephen George, Kt.

Mitting, *Hon.* Sir John Edward, Kt.

Moate, Sir Roger Denis, Kt.

Mobbs, Sir (Gerald) Nigel, Kt.

Moberly, Sir Patrick Hamilton, KCMG

Moffat, Sir Brian Scott, Kt., OBE

Moffat, *Lt.-Gen.* Sir (William) Cameron, KBE

Mogg, Sir John Frederick, KCMG

Moir, Sir Christopher Ernest, Bt. (1916)

†Molesworth-St Aubyn, Sir William, Bt. (1689)

†Molony, Sir Thomas Desmond, Bt. (1925)

Monck, Sir Nicholas Jeremy, KCB

Money-Coutts, Sir David Burdett, KCVO

Montagu, Sir Nicholas Lionel John, KCB

Montagu-Pollock, Sir Giles Hampden, Bt. (1872)

Montague-Browne, Sir Anthony Arthur Duncan, KCMG, CBE, DFC

Montgomery, Sir (Basil Henry) David, Bt. (1801)

Montgomery, Sir (William) Fergus, Kt.

Montgomery-Cuninghame, Sir John Christopher Foggo, Bt. (NS 1672)

Moody-Stuart, Sir Mark, KCMG

Moollan, Sir Abdool Hamid Adam, Kt.

Moollan, *Hon.* Sir Cassam (Ismael), Kt.

†Moon, Sir Roger, Bt. (1887)

Moore, *Most Revd* Desmond Charles, KBE

Moore, Sir Francis Thomas, Kt.

Moore, *Maj.-Gen.* Sir (John) Jeremy, KCB, OBE, MC

Moore, Sir John Michael, KCVO, CB, DSC

Moore, *Vice Adm.* Sir Michael Antony Claës, KBE, LVO

Moore, *Prof.* Sir Norman Winfrid, Bt. (1919)

Moore, Sir Patrick Alfred Caldwell, Kt., CBE

Moore, Sir Patrick William Eisdell, Kt., OBE

Moore, Sir Roger George, KBE

Moore, Sir William Roger Clotworthy, Bt., TD (1932)

Moore-Bick, *Hon.* Sir Martin James, Kt.

Moores, Sir Peter, Kt., CBE

Morauta, Sir Mekere, Kt.

Mordaunt, Sir Richard Nigel Charles, Bt. (1611)

Moreton, Sir John Oscar, KCMG, KCVO, MC

Morgan, *Vice-Adm.* Sir Charles Christopher, KBE

Morgan, Sir Graham, Kt.

Morgan, Sir John Albert Leigh, KCMG

Morgan-Giles, *Rear-Adm.* Sir Morgan Charles, Kt., DSO, OBE, GM

Morison, *Hon.* Sir Thomas Richard Atkin, Kt.

Morland, *Hon.* Sir Michael, Kt.

Morland, Sir Robert Kenelm, Kt.

Morpeth, Sir Douglas Spottiswoode, Kt., TD

†Morris, Sir Allan Lindsay, Bt. (1806)

Morris, *Air Marshal* Sir Arnold Alec, KBE, CB

Morris, Sir Derek James, Kt.

Morris, Sir (James) Richard (Samuel), Kt., CBE

Morris, Sir Keith Elliot Hedley, KBE, CMG
Morris, *Prof.* Sir Peter John, Kt.
Morris, Sir Trefor Alfred, Kt., CBE, QPM
Morris, Sir William, Kt.
Morris, *Very Revd* William James, KCVO
Morrison, Sir (Alexander) Fraser, Kt., CBE
Morrison, *Hon.* Sir Charles Andrew, Kt.
Morrison, Sir Howard Leslie, Kt., OBE
Morrison, Sir Kenneth Duncan, Kt., CBE
Morrison-Bell, Sir William Hollin Dayrell, Bt. (1905)
Morrison-Low, Sir James Richard, Bt. (1908)
Morritt, *Rt. Hon.* Sir (Robert) Andrew, Kt., CVO
Morrow, Sir Ian Thomas, Kt.
Morse, Sir Christopher Jeremy, KCMG
Mortimer, Sir John Clifford, Kt., CBE, QC
Morton, *Adm.* Sir Anthony Storrs, GBE, KCB
Moseley, Sir George Walker, KCB
Moses, *Hon.* Sir Alan George, Kt.
Moss, Sir David Joseph, KCVO, CMG
Moss, Sir Stirling Craufurd, Kt., OBE
Mostyn, *Gen.* Sir (Joseph) David Frederick, KCB, CBE
Mostyn, Sir William Basil John, Bt. (1670)
Mott, Sir John Harmer, Bt. (1930)
Mottram, Sir Richard Clive, KCB
†Mount, Sir (William Robert) Ferdinand, Bt. (1921)
Mountain, Sir Denis Mortimer, Bt. (1922)
Mountfield, Sir Robin, KCB
Mowbray, Sir John, Kt.
Mowbray, Sir John Robert, Bt. (1880)
Muir, Sir Laurence Macdonald, Kt.
†Muir, Sir Richard James Kay, Bt. (1892)
Muir-Mackenzie, Sir Alexander Alwyne Henry Charles Brinton, Bt. (1805)
Mulcahy, Sir Geoffrey John, Kt.
Mullens, *Lt.-Gen.* Sir Anthony Richard Guy, KCB, OBE
Mummery, *Rt. Hon.* Sir John Frank, Kt.
Munby, *Hon.* Sir James Lawrence, Kt.
Munn, Sir James, Kt., OBE
Munro, Sir Alan Gordon, KCMG
†Munro, Sir Kenneth Arnold William, Bt. (S. 1634)
†Munro, Sir Keith Gordon, Bt. (1825)
Muria, *Hon.* Sir Gilbert John Baptist, Kt.
Murphy, Sir Leslie Frederick, Kt.
Murray, *Rt. Hon.* Sir Donald Bruce, Kt.
Murray, Sir James, KCMG
Murray, *Prof.* Sir Kenneth, Kt.

Murray, Sir Nigel Andrew Digby, Bt. (S. 1628)
Murray, Sir Patrick Ian Keith, Bt. (S. 1673)
†Murray, Sir Rowland William, Bt. (S. 1630)
Mursell, Sir Peter, Kt., MBE
Musgrave, Sir Christopher John Shane, Bt. (1782)
Musgrave, Sir Christopher Patrick Charles, Bt. (1611)
Musson, *Gen.* Sir Geoffrey Randolph Dixon, GCB, CBE, DSO
Myers, Sir Philip Alan, Kt., OBE, QPM
Myers, *Prof.* Sir Rupert Horace, KBE
Mynors, Sir Richard Baskerville, Bt. (1964)
Naipaul, Sir Vidiadhar Surajprasad, Kt.
Nairn, Sir Michael, Bt. (1904)
Nairne, *Rt. Hon.* Sir Patrick Dalmahoy, GCB, MC
Naish, Sir (Charles) David, Kt.
Nall, Sir Edward William Joseph Bt. (1954)
Namaliu, *Rt. Hon.* Sir Rabbie Langanai, KCMG
†Napier, Sir Charles Joseph, Bt. (1867)
Napier, Sir John Archibald Lennox, Bt. (S. 1627)
Napier, Sir Oliver John, Kt.
Naylor-Leyland, Sir Philip Vyvyan, Bt. (1895)
Neal, Sir Eric James, Kt., CVO
Neal, Sir Leonard Francis, Kt., CBE
Neale, Sir Gerrard Anthony, Kt.
Neave, Sir Paul Arundell, Bt. (1795)
Neill, *Rt. Hon.* Sir Brian Thomas, Kt.
Neill, Sir (James) Hugh, KCVO, CBE, TD
†Nelson, Sir Jamie Charles Vernon Hope, Bt. (1912)
Nelson, *Hon.* Sir Robert Franklyn, Kt.
Neuberger, *Hon.* Sir David Edmond, Kt., PC
Neubert, Sir Michael John, Kt.
Neville, Sir Roger Albert Gartside, Kt.
New, *Maj.-Gen.* Sir Laurence Anthony Wallis, Kt., CB, CBE
Newall, Sir Paul Henry, Kt., TD
Newby, *Prof.* Sir Howard Joseph, Kt., CBE
Newington, Sir Michael John, KCMG
Newman, Sir Francis Hugh Cecil, Bt. (1912)
Newman, Sir Geoffrey Robert, Bt. (1836)
Newman, *Hon.* Sir George Michael, Kt.
Newman, Sir Kenneth Leslie, GBE, QPM
Newman, *Vice-Adm.* Sir Roy Thomas, KCB
Newsam, Sir Peter Anthony, Kt.
†Newson-Smith, Sir Peter Frank Graham, Bt. (1944)
Newton, Sir (Charles) Wilfred, Kt., CBE

Newton, Sir (Harry) Michael (Rex), Bt. (1900)
Newton, Sir Kenneth Garnar, Bt., OBE, TD (1924)
Ngata, Sir Henare Kohere, KBE
Nichol, Sir Duncan Kirkbride, Kt., CBE
Nicholas, Sir David, Kt., CBE
Nicholas, Sir John William, KCVO, CMG
Nicholls, *Air Marshal* Sir John Moreton, KCB, CBE, DFC, AFC
Nicholls, Sir Nigel Hamilton, KCVO, CBE
Nichols, Sir Richard Everard, Kt.
Nicholson, Sir Bryan Hubert, Kt.
†Nicholson, Sir Charles Christian, Bt. (1912)
Nicholson, *Rt. Hon.* Sir Michael, Kt.
Nicholson, Sir Paul Douglas, Kt.
Nicholson, Sir Robin Buchanan, Kt., PHD, FRS, FRENG
Nicoll, Sir William, KCMG
Nightingale, Sir Charles Manners Gamaliel, Bt. (1628)
Nixon, Sir Simon Michael Christopher, Bt. (1906)
Nixon, Sir Edwin Ronald, Kt., CBE
Noble, Sir David Brunel, Bt. (1902)
Noble, Sir Iain Andrew, Bt., OBE (1923)
Nombri, Sir Joseph Karl, Kt., ISO, BEM
Noon, Sir Gulam Kaderbhoy, Kt., MBE
Norman, Sir Arthur Gordon, KBE, DFC
Norman, Sir Mark Annesley, Bt. (1915)
Norman, Sir Robert Henry, Kt., OBE
Norman, Sir Ronald, Kt., OBE
Norrington, Sir Roger Arthur Carver, Kt., CBE
Norris, Sir Eric George, KCMG
Norriss, Air Marshal Sir Peter Coulson, KBE, CB, AFC
North, Sir Peter Machin, Kt., CBE, QC, DCL, FBA
North, Sir Thomas Lindsay, Kt.
North, Sir (William) Jonathan (Frederick), Bt. (1920)
Norton-Griffiths, Sir John, Bt. (1922)
Nossal, Sir Gustav Joseph Victor, Kt., CBE
Nott, *Rt. Hon.* Sir John William Frederic, KCB
Nourse, *Rt. Hon.* Sir Martin Charles, Kt.
Nugent, Sir John Edwin Lavallin, Bt. (I. 1795)
Nugent, Sir Robin George Colborne, Bt. (1806)
†Nugent, Sir (Walter) Richard Middleton, Bt. (1831)
Nunn, Sir Trevor Robert, Kt., CBE
Nunneley, Sir Charles Kenneth Roylance, Kt.
Nursaw, Sir James, KCB, QC
Nurse, Sir Paul Maxime, Kt.
Nuttall, Sir Nicholas Keith Lillington, Bt. (1922)

Nutting, Sir John Grenfell, Bt., QC (1903)

Oakeley, Sir John Digby Atholl, Bt. (1790)

Oakes, Sir Christopher, Bt. (1939)

Oakshott, Hon. Sir Anthony Hendrie, Bt. (1959)

Oates, Sir Thomas, Kt., CMG, OBE

O'Brien, Sir Frederick William Fitzgerald, Kt.

O'Brien, Sir Richard, Kt., DSO, MC

O'Brien, Sir Timothy John, Bt. (1849)

O'Brien, *Adm.* Sir William Donough, KCB, DSC

O'Connell, Sir Bernard, Kt.

O'Connell, Sir Maurice James Donagh MacCarthy, Bt. (1869)

O'Dea, Sir Patrick Jerad, KCVO

Odell, Sir Stanley John, Kt.

Odgers, Sir Graeme David William, Kt.

O'Donnell, Sir Christopher John, Kt.

O'Dowd, Sir David Joseph, Kt., CBE, QPM

Ogden, Sir Robert, Kt., CBE

Ogilvy, *Rt. Hon.* Sir Angus James Bruce, KCVO

Ogilvy, Sir Francis Gilbert Arthur, Bt. (S. 1626)

Ogilvy-Wedderburn, Sir Andrew John Alexander, Bt. (1803)

Ognall, *Hon.* Sir Harry Henry, Kt.

Ohlson, Sir Brian Eric Christopher, Bt. (1920)

Oldham, *Dr* Sir John, Kt., OBE

Oliver, Sir James Michael Yorrick, Kt.

O'Loghlen, Sir Colman Michael, Bt. (1838)

Olver, Sir Stephen John Linley, KBE, CMG

Omand, Sir David Bruce, GCB

O'Nions, Prof. Sir Robert Keith, Kt., FRS, PHD

Ondaatje, Sir Christopher, Kt., CBE

Onslow, Sir John Roger Wilmot, Bt. (1797)

Oppenheimer, Sir Michael Bernard Grenville, Bt. (1921)

O'Regan, *Dr* Sir Stephen Gerard (Tipene), Kt.

O'Reilly, Sir Anthony John Francis, Kt.

Orr, Sir David Alexander, Kt., MC

Orr, Sir John, Kt., OBE

Orr-Ewing, Sir (Alistair) Simon, Bt. (1963)

Orr-Ewing, Sir Archibald Donald, Bt. (1886)

Osborn, Sir John Holbrook, Kt.

Osborn, Sir Richard Henry Danvers, Bt. (1662)

Osborne, Sir Peter George, Bt. (I. 1629)

Osmond, Sir Douglas, Kt., CBE

Osmotherly, Sir Edward Benjamin Crofton, Kt., CB

O'Sullevan, Sir Peter John, Kt., CBE

Oswald, *Admiral of the Fleet* Sir (John) Julian Robertson, GCB

Oswald, Sir (William Richard) Michael, KCVO

Otton, Sir Geoffrey John, KCB

Otton, *Rt. Hon.* Sir Philip Howard, Kt.

Oulton, Sir Antony Derek Maxwell, GCB, QC

Ouseley, *Hon.* Sir Brian Walter, Kt.

Outram, Sir Alan James, Bt. (1858)

Owen, Sir Geoffrey, Kt.

Owen, *Hon.* Sir John Arthur Dalziel, Kt.

Owen, *Hon.* Sir Robert Michael, Kt.

Pakenham, *Hon.* Sir Michael Aiden, KBE, CMG

Packer, Sir Richard John, KCB

Page, Sir (Arthur) John, Kt.

Page, Sir Frederick William, Kt., CBE, FRENG

Page, Sir John Joseph Joffre, Kt., OBE

Paget, Sir Julian Tolver, Bt., CVO (1871)

Paget, Sir Richard Herbert, Bt. (1886)

Pain, *Lt.-Gen.* Sir (Horace) Rollo (Squarey), KCB, MC

Paine, Sir Christopher Hammon, Kt., FRCP, FRCR

Palin, *Air Chief Marshal* Sir Roger Hewlett, KCB, MBE

Palliser, *Rt. Hon.* Sir (Arthur) Michael, GCMG

Palmar, Sir Derek James, Kt.

Palmer, Sir (Charles) Mark, Bt. (1886)

Palmer, Sir Geoffrey Christopher John, Bt. (1660)

Palmer, *Rt. Hon.* Sir Geoffrey Winston Russell, KCMG

Palmer, Sir John Edward Somerset, Bt. (1791)

Palmer, *Maj.-Gen.* Sir (Joseph) Michael, KCVO

Palmer, Sir Reginald Oswald, GCMG, MBE

Pantlin, Sir Dick Hurst, Kt., CBE

Paolozzi, Sir Eduardo Luigi, Kt., CBE, RA

Parbo, Sir Arvi Hillar, Kt.

Park, *Hon.* Sir Andrew Edward Wilson, Kt.

Parker, Sir Alan William, Kt., CBE

Parker, Sir Eric Wilson, Kt.

Parker, *Rt. Hon.* Sir Jonathan Frederic, Kt.

Parker, *Maj.* Sir Michael John, KCVO, CBE

Parker, Sir Richard (William) Hyde, Bt. (1681)

Parker, *Rt. Hon.* Sir Roger Jocelyn, Kt.

Parker, Sir (Thomas) John, Kt.

Parker, *Vice-Adm.* Sir (Wilfred) John, KBE, CB, DSC

Parker, Sir William Peter Brian, Bt. (1844)

Parkes, Sir Edward Walter, Kt., FRENG

Parry, Sir Emyr Jones, KCMG

Parry-Evans, *Air Chief Marshal* Sir David, GCB, CBE

Parsons, Sir John Christopher, KCVO

Parsons, Sir (John) Michael, Kt.

Parsons, Sir Richard Edmund (Clement Fownes), KCMG

Partridge, Sir Michael John Anthony, KCB

Pascoe, *Gen.* Sir Robert Alan, KCB, MBE

†Pasley, Sir Robert Killigrew Sabine, Bt. (1794)

Paston-Bedingfeld, *Capt.* Sir Edmund George Felix, Bt. (1661)

Paterson, Sir Dennis Craig, Kt.

Patnick, Sir (Cyril) Irvine, Kt., OBE

Patten, *Hon.* Mr Justice, Sir Nicholas John, Kt.

Pattie, *Rt. Hon.* Sir Geoffrey Edwin, Kt.

Pattinson, Sir (William) Derek, Kt.

Pattison, *Prof.* Sir John Ridley, Kt., DM, FRCPath.

Pattullo, Sir (David) Bruce, Kt., CBE

Pauncefort-Duncombe, Sir Philip Digby, Bt. (1859)

Payne, Sir Norman John, Kt., CBE, FRENG

Payne-Gallwey, Sir Philip Frankland, Bt. (1812)

Peach, Sir Leonard Harry, Kt.

Peacock, *Prof.* Sir Alan Turner, Kt., DSC

Pearce, Sir (Daniel Norton) Idris, Kt., CBE, TD

Pearse, Sir Brian Gerald, Kt.

Pearson, Sir Francis Nicholas Fraser, Bt. (1964)

Pearson, *Gen.* Sir Thomas Cecil Hook, KCB, CBE, DSO

Peart, *Prof.* Sir William Stanley, Kt., MD, FRS

Pease, Sir (Alfred) Vincent, Bt. (1882)

Pease, Sir Richard Thorn, Bt. (1920)

Peat, Sir Gerrard Charles, KCVO

Peat, Sir Michael Charles Gerrard, KCVO

Peck, Sir Edward Heywood, GCMG

Peckham, *Prof.* Sir Michael John, Kt.

Peek, *Vice-Adm.* Sir Richard Innes, KBE, CB, DSC

† Peek, Sir Richard Grenville, Bt. (1874)

Peel, Sir John Harold, KCVO

Peirse, *Air Vice-Marshal* Sir Richard Charles Fairfax, KCVO, CB

Pelgen, Sir Harry Friedrich, Kt., MBE

Peliza, Sir Robert John, KBE, ED

Pelly, Sir Richard John, Bt. (1840)

Pemberton, Sir Francis Wingate William, Kt., CBE

Pendry, *Prof.* Sir John Brian, Kt.

Penrose, *Prof.* Sir Roger, Kt., OM, FRS

Penry-Davey, *Hon.* Sir David Herbert, Kt.

Pereira, Sir (Herbert) Charles, Kt., DSC, FRS

Perowne, *Vice-Adm.* Sir James Francis, KBE

Perring, Sir John Raymond, Bt. (1963)

Perris, Sir David (Arthur), Kt., MBE

Perry, Sir David Howard, KCB

Perry, Sir (David) Norman, Kt., MBE

Perry, Sir Michael Sydney, GBE

Pervez, Sir Mohammed Anwar, Kt., OBE

Pestell, Sir John Richard, KCVO

Peters, *Prof.* Sir David Keith, Kt., FRCP

Petersen, Sir Jeffrey Charles, KCMG

Peterson, Sir Christopher Matthew, Kt., CBE, TD

†Petit, Sir Jehangir, Bt. (1890)

Peto, Sir Henry George Morton, Bt. (1855)

Peto, Sir Michael Henry Basil, Bt. (1927)

Peto, *Prof.* Sir Richard, Kt., FRS

Petrie, Sir Peter Charles, Bt., CMG (1918)

Pettigrew, Sir Russell Hilton, Kt.

Pettit, Sir Daniel Eric Arthur, Kt.

Pettitt, Sir Dennis, Kt.

Philips, *Prof.* Sir Cyril Henry, Kt.

Philipson-Stow, Sir Christopher, Bt., DFC (1907)

Phillips, Sir Fred Albert, Kt., CVO

Phillips, Sir (Gerald) Hayden, GCB

Phillips, Sir Henry Ellis Isidore, Kt., CMG, MBE

Phillips, Sir John David, Kt., QPM

Phillips, Sir Peter John, Kt., OBE

Phillips, Sir Robin Francis, Bt. (1912)

Phillis, Sir Robert Weston, Kt.

Pickard, Sir (John) Michael, Kt.

Pickthorn, Sir James Francis Mann, Bt. (1959)

Pidgeon, Sir John Allan Stewart, Kt.

†Piers, Sir James Desmond, Bt. (I. 1661)

Piggott-Brown, Sir William Brian, Bt. (1903)

Pigot, Sir George Hugh, Bt. (1764)

Pigott, *Lt.-Gen.* Sir Anthony David, KCB, CBE

Pigott, Sir Berkeley Henry Sebastian, Bt. (1808)

Pike, *Lt.-Gen.* Sir Hew William Royston, KCB, DSO, MBE

Pike, Sir Michael Edmund, KCVO, CMG

Pike, Sir Philip Ernest Housden, Kt., QC

Pilditch, Sir Richard Edward, Bt. (1929)

Pile, Sir Frederick Devereux, Bt., MC (1900)

Pill, *Rt. Hon.* Sir Malcolm Thomas, Kt.

Pilling, Sir Joseph Grant, KCB

Pinker, Sir George Douglas, KCVO

Pinsent, Sir Christopher Roy, Bt. (1938)

Pippard, *Prof.* Sir (Alfred) Brian, Kt., FRS

Pitakaka, Sir Moses Puibangara, GCMG

Pitcher, Sir Desmond Henry, Kt.

Pitchers, *Hon.* Sir Christopher (John), Kt.

Pitchford, *Hon.* Sir Christopher John, Kt.

Pitman, Sir Brian Ivor, Kt.

Pitoi, Sir Sere, Kt., CBE

Pitt, Sir Harry Raymond, Kt., PHD, FRS

Pitts, Sir Cyril Alfred, Kt.

Plastow, Sir David Arnold Stuart, Kt.

Platt, Sir Harold Grant, Kt.

Platt, Sir Martin Philip, Bt. (1959)

Pledger, *Air Chief Marshal* Sir Malcolm David, KCB, OBE, AFC

Plumbly, Sir Derek John, KCMG

Pogo, *Most Revd.* Ellison Leslie, KBE

Pohai, Sir Timothy, Kt., MBE

Pole, Sir (John) Richard (Walter Reginald) Carew, Bt. (1628)

Pole, Sir Peter Van Notten, Bt. (1791)

Polkinghorne, *Revd Canon* John Charlton, KBE, FRS

Pollard, Sir Charles, Kt.

†Pollen, Sir Richard John Hungerford, Bt. (1795)

Pollock, Sir George Frederick, Bt. (1866)

Pollock, *Admiral of the Fleet* Sir Michael Patrick, GCB, LVO, DSC

Ponsonby, Sir Ashley Charles Gibbs, Bt., KCVO, MC (1956)

Poole, *Hon.* Sir David Anthony, Kt.

Poore, Sir Herbert Edward, Bt. (1795)

Pope, Sir Joseph Albert, Kt., DSC, PHD

Popplewell, *Hon.* Sir Oliver Bury, Kt.

†Porritt, Sir Jonathon Espie, Bt. (1963)

Portal, Sir Jonathan Francis, Bt. (1901)

Porter, Sir Leslie, Kt.

Porter, Sir Robert Wilson, Kt., PC (NI)

Posnett, Sir Richard Neil, KBE, CMG

Potter, *Rt. Hon.* Sir Mark Howard, Kt.

Potter, *Maj.-Gen.* Sir (Wilfrid) John, KBE, CB

Potts, *Hon.* Sir Francis Humphrey, Kt.

Pound, Sir John David, Bt. (1905)

Povey, Sir Keith, Kt., QPM

Powell, Sir Nicholas Folliott Douglas, Bt. (1897)

Powell, Sir Richard Royle, GCB, KBE, CMG

Power, Sir Alastair John Cecil, Bt. (1924)

Power, *Hon.* Sir Noel Plunkett, Kt.

Prance, *Prof.* Sir Ghillean Tolmie, Kt., FRS

Prendergast, Sir (Walter) Kieran, KCVO, CMG

Prentice, *Hon.* Sir William Thomas, Kt., MBE

Prescott, Sir Mark, Bt. (1938)

†Preston, Sir Philip Charles Henry Hulton, Bt. (1815)

Prevost, Sir Christopher Gerald, Bt. (1805)

Price, Sir David Ernest Campbell, Kt.

Price, Sir Francis Caradoc Rose, Bt. (1815)

Price, Sir Frank Leslie, Kt.

Price, Sir Norman Charles, KCB

Prickett, *Air Chief Marshal* Sir Thomas Other, KCB, DSO, DFC

Prideaux, Sir Humphrey Povah Treverbian, Kt., OBE

†Primrose, Sir John Ure, Bt. (1903)

Prince-Smith, Sir (William) Richard, Bt. (1911)

Pringle, *Air Marshal* Sir Charles Norman Seton, KBE, FRENG

Pringle, *Hon.* Sir John Kenneth, Kt.

Pringle, *Lt.-Gen.* Sir Steuart (Robert), Bt., KCB, RM (S. 1683)

Pritchard, Sir Neil, KCMG

Prichard-Jones, Sir John, Bt. (1910)

†Proby, Sir William Henry, Bt. (1952)

Proctor-Beauchamp, Sir Christopher Radstock, Bt. (1745)

Prosser, Sir Ian Maurice Gray, Kt.

Pryke, Sir Christopher Dudley, Bt. (1926)

Puapua, *Rt. Hon.* Sir Tomasi, GCMG, KBE

Pugh, Sir Idwal Vaughan, KCB

Pumfrey, *Hon.* Sir Nicholas Richard, Kt.

Pumphrey, Sir (John) Laurence, KCMG

Purves, Sir William, Kt., CBE, DSO

Purvis, *Vice-Adm.* Sir Neville, KCB

Quan, Sir Henry (Francis), KBE

Quicke, Sir John Godolphin, Kt., CBE

Quigley, Sir (William) George (Henry), Kt., CB, PHD

Quilliam, *Hon.* Sir (James) Peter, Kt.

Quilter, Sir Anthony Raymond Leopold Cuthbert, Bt. (1897)

Quinlan, Sir Michael Edward, GCB

Quinton, Sir James Grand, Kt.

Radcliffe, Sir Sebastian Everard, Bt. (1813)

Radda, *Prof.* Sir George Karoly, Kt., CBE, FRS

Rae, *Hon.* Sir Wallace Alexander Ramsay, Kt.

Raeburn, Sir Michael Edward Norman, Bt. (1923)

Raikes, *Vice-Adm.* Sir Iwan Geoffrey, KCB, CBE, DSC

Raison, *Rt. Hon.* Sir Timothy Hugh Francis, Kt.

Ralli, Sir Godfrey Victor, Bt., TD (1912)

Ramdanee, Sir Mookteswar Baboolall Kailash, Kt.

Ramphal, Sir Shridath Surendranath, GCMG

Ramphul, Sir Baalkhristna, Kt.

Ramphul, Sir Indurduth, Kt.

Ramsay, Sir Alexander William Burnett, Bt. (1806)

Ramsay, Sir Allan John (Hepple), KBE, CMG

Ramsbotham, *Gen.* Sir David John, GCB, CBE

Ramsbotham, *Hon.* Sir Peter Edward, GCMG, GCVO

Ramsden, Sir John Charles Josslyn, Bt. (1689)

Randle, *Prof.* Sir Philip John, Kt.

Rankin, Sir Ian Niall, Bt. (1898)

Rasch, Sir Simon Anthony Carne, Bt. (1903)

Rashleigh, Sir Richard Harry, Bt. (1831)

Ratford, Sir David John Edward, KCMG, CVO

Rattee, *Hon.* Sir Donald Keith, Kt.

Rattle, Sir Simon Dennis, Kt., CBE

Rawlins, *Surgeon Vice-Adm.* Sir John Stuart Pepys, KBE

Rawlins, *Prof.* Sir Michael David, Kt., FRCP, FRCPED

Rawlinson, Sir Anthony Henry John, Bt. (1891)

Read, *Air Marshal* Sir Charles Frederick, KBE, CB, DFC, AFC

Read, Sir John Emms, Kt.

†Reade, Sir Kenneth Ray, Bt. (1661)

Reardon-Smith, Sir (William) Antony (John), Bt. (1920)

Reay, *Lt.-Gen.* Sir (Hubert) Alan John, KBE

Redgrave, *Maj.-Gen.* Sir Roy Michael Frederick, KBE, MC

Redgrave, Sir Steven Geoffrey, Kt., CBE

Redmayne, Sir Nicholas, Bt. (1964)

Redwood, Sir Peter Boverton, Bt. (1911)

Reece, Sir Charles Hugh, Kt.

Rees, Sir David Allan, Kt., PHD, DSC, FRS

Rees, *Prof.* Sir Martin John, Kt., FRS

Reeve, Sir Anthony, KCMG, KCVO

Reeves, *Most Revd* Paul Alfred, GCMG, GCVO

Reffell, *Adm.* Sir Derek Roy, KCB

Refshauge, *Maj.-Gen.* Sir William Dudley, Kt., CBE

Reid, Sir Alexander James, Bt. (1897)

Reid, Sir (Harold) Martin (Smith), KBE, CMG

Reid, Sir Hugh, Bt. (1922)

Reid, Sir Norman Robert, Kt.

Reid, Sir Robert Paul, Kt.

Reid, Sir William Kennedy, KCB

Reiher, Sir Frederick Bernard Carl, KBE, OMB

Reilly, *Lt.-Gen.* Sir Jeremy Calcott, KCB, DSO

Renals, Sir Stanley, Bt. (1895)

Renouf, Sir Clement William Bailey, Kt.

Renshaw, Sir John David Bine, Bt. (1903)

Renwick, Sir Richard Eustace, Bt. (1921)

Reporter, Sir Shapoor Ardeshirji, KBE

Reynolds, Sir David James, Bt. (1923)

Reynolds, Sir Peter William John, Kt., CBE

Rhodes, Sir John Christopher Douglas, Bt. (1919)

Rhodes, Sir Peregrine Alexander, KCMG

Rice, *Maj.-Gen.* Sir Desmond Hind Garrett, KCVO, CBE

Rice, Sir Timothy Miles Bindon, Kt.

Richard, Sir Cliff, Kt., OBE

Richards, Sir Brian Mansel, Kt., CBE, PHD

Richards, *Hon.* Sir David Anthony Stewart, Kt.

Richards, Sir Francis Neville, KCMG, CVO

Richards, *Lt.-Gen.* Sir John Charles Chisholm, KCB, KCVO, RM

Richards, Sir Rex Edward, Kt., DSC, FRS

Richards, *Hon.* Sir Stephen Price, Kt.

Richardson, Sir Anthony Lewis, Bt. (1924)

Richardson, *Rt. Hon.* Sir Ivor Lloyd Morgan, Kt.

Richardson, Sir (John) Eric, Kt., CBE

Richardson, *Lt.-Gen.* Sir Robert Francis, KCB, CVO, CBE

Richardson, Sir Thomas Legh, KCMG

Richardson-Bunbury, Sir (Richard David) Michael, Bt. (I. 1787)

Richmond, *Prof.* Sir Mark Henry, Kt., FRS

Ricketts, Sir Robert Cornwallis Gerald St Leger, Bt. (1828)

Riddell, Sir John Charles Buchanan, Bt., CVO (S. 1628)

Ridley, Sir Adam (Nicholas), Kt.

Ridley, Sir Michael Kershaw, KCVO

Rigby, Sir Anthony John, Bt. (1929)

Rigby, Sir Peter, Kt.

Rimer, *Hon.* Sir Colin Percy Farquharson, Kt.

†Ripley, Sir William Hugh, Bt. (1880)

Risk, Sir Thomas Neilson, Kt.

Ritako, Sir Thomas Baha, Kt., MBE

†Rivett-Carnac, Sir Miles James, Bt. (1836)

Rix, *Rt. Hon.* Sir Bernard Anthony, Kt.

Rix, Sir John, Kt., MBE, FRENG

Robati, Sir Pupuke, KBE

Robb, Sir John Weddell, Kt.

Roberts, *Hon.* Sir Denys Tudor Emil, KBE,

Roberts, Sir Derek Harry, Kt., CBE, FRS, FRENG

Roberts, *Prof.* Sir Edward Adam, KCMG

Roberts, Sir (Edward Fergus) Sidney, Kt., CBE

Roberts, *Prof.* Sir Gareth Gwyn, Kt., FRS

Roberts, Sir Gilbert Howland Rookehurst, Bt. (1809)

Roberts, Sir Hugh Ashley, KCVO

Roberts, Sir Ivor Anthony, KCMG

Roberts, Sir Samuel, Bt. (1919)

Roberts, Sir William James Denby, Bt. (1909)

Robertson, Sir Lewis, Kt., CBE, FRSE

Robins, Sir Ralph Harry, Kt., FRENG

Robinson, Sir Albert Edward Phineas, Kt.

†Robinson, Sir Christopher Philipse, Bt. (1854)

Robinson, Sir Gerrard Jude, Kt.

Robinson, Sir Ian, Kt.

Robinson, Sir John James Michael Laud, Bt. (1660)

Robinson, *Dr* Sir Kenneth, Kt.

Robinson, Sir Wilfred Henry Frederick, Bt. (1908)

Robson, *Prof.* Sir James Gordon, Kt., CBE

Robson, Sir John Adam, KCMG

Robson, Sir Stephen Arthur, Kt., CB

Robson, Sir Robert William, Kt., CBE

Roch, *Rt. Hon.* Sir John Ormond, Kt.

Roche, Sir David O'Grady, Bt. (1838)

Roche, Sir Henry John, Kt.

Rodgers, Sir (Andrew) Piers (Wingate Aikin-Sneath), Bt. (1964)

Rodley, *Prof.* Sir Nigel, KBE

Rodrigues, Sir Alberto Maria, Kt., CBE, ED

Rogers, Sir Frank Jarvis, Kt.

Rogers, *Air Chief Marshal* Sir John Robson, KCB, CBE

Rooke, Sir Denis Eric, Kt., OM, CBE, FRS, FRENG

Ropner, Sir John Bruce Woollacott, Bt. (1952)

†Ropner, Sir Robert Clinton, Bt. (1904)

Rose, *Rt. Hon.* Sir Christopher Dudley Roger, Kt.

Rose, Sir Clive Martin, GCMG

Rose, Sir David Lancaster, Bt. (1874)

Rose, *Gen.* Sir (Hugh) Michael, KCB, CBE, DSO, QGM

Rose, Sir John Edward Victor, Kt.

Rose, Sir Julian Day, Bt. (1872 and 1909)

Ross, *Maj.* Sir Andrew Charles Paterson, Bt. (1960)

Ross, *Lt.-Gen.* Sir Robert Jeremy, KCB, OBE

Ross, *Lt.-Col.* Sir Walter Hugh Malcolm, KCVO, OBE

Rossi, Sir Hugh Alexis Louis, Kt.

Rotblat, *Prof.* Sir Joseph, KCMG, CBE, FRS

Roth, *Prof.* Sir Martin, Kt., MD, FRCP

Rothschild, Sir Evelyn Robert Adrian de, Kt.

Rougier, *Hon.* Sir Richard George, Kt.

Rowe, *Rear-Adm.* Sir Patrick Barton, KCVO, CBE

Rowe-Beddoe, Sir David Sydney, Kt.

Rowe-Ham, Sir David Kenneth, GBE

Rowland, Sir (John) David, Kt.

Rowlands, *Air Marshal* Sir John Samuel, GC, KBE

Rowley, Sir Charles Robert, Bt. (1836) (1786)

Rowling, Sir John Reginald, Kt.

Rowlinson, *Prof.* Sir John Shipley, Kt., FRS

Royce, *Hon.* Sir Roger John, Kt.

Royden, Sir Christopher John, Bt. (1905)

Rudd, Sir (Anthony) Nigel (Russell), Kt.

Rudge, Sir Alan Walter, Kt., CBE, FRS

Rugge-Price, Sir James Keith Peter, Bt. (1804)

Ruggles-Brise, Sir John Archibald, Bt., CB, OBE, TD (1935)

Rumbold, Sir Henry John Sebastian, Bt. (1779)

Runchorelal, Sir (Udayan) Chinubhai Madhowlal, Bt. (1913)

Rusby, *Vice-Adm.* Sir Cameron, KCB, LVO

†Russell, Sir (Arthur) Mervyn, Bt. (1812)

Russell, Sir Charles Dominic, Bt. (1916)

Smith, Sir Andrew Thomas, Bt. (1897)
Smith, Sir Christopher Sydney Winwood, Bt. (1809)
Smith, *Prof.* Sir Colin Stansfield, Kt., CBE
Smith, Sir Cyril, Kt., MBE
Smith, *Prof.* Sir David Cecil, Kt., FRS
Smith, Sir David Iser, KCVO
Smith, Sir Dudley (Gordon), Kt.
Smith, *Prof.* Sir Eric Brian, Kt., PHD
Smith, Sir Geoffrey Johnson, Kt., MP
Smith, Sir John Alfred, Kt., QPM
Smith, Sir John Lindsay Eric, Kt., CH, CBE
Smith, Sir Joseph William Grenville, Kt.
Smith, Sir Leslie Edward George, Kt.
Smith, Sir Michael John Llewellyn, KCVO, CMG
Smith, Sir (Norman) Brian, Kt., CBE, PHD
Smith, Sir Paul Brierley, Kt., CBE
Smith, *Hon.* Sir Peter (Winston), Kt.
Smith, Sir Robert Courtney, Kt., CBE
Smith, Sir Robert Haldane, Kt
Smith, Sir Robert Hill, Bt., MP (1945)
Smith, *Gen.* Sir Rupert Anthony, KCB, DSO, OBE, QGM
Smith-Dodsworth, Sir John Christopher, Bt. (1784)
Smith-Gordon, Sir (Lionel) Eldred (Peter), Bt. (1838)
Smith-Marriott, Sir Hugh Cavendish, Bt. (1774)
Smithers, Sir Peter Henry Berry Otway, Kt., VRD, DPHIL
Smyth, Sir Timothy John, Bt. (1955)
Soakimori, Sir Frederick Pa-Nukuanca, KBE, CPM
Sobers, Sir Garfield St Auburn, Kt.
Solomon, Sir Harry, Kt.
Somare, *Rt. Hon.* Sir Michael Thomas, GCMG, CH
Somerville, *Brig.* Sir John Nicholas, Kt., CBE
Sorrell, Sir Martin Stuart, Kt.
Soulsby, Sir Peter Alfred, Kt.
Soutar, *Air Marshal* Sir Charles John Williamson, KBE
South, Sir Arthur, Kt.
Southby, Sir John Richard Bilbe, Bt. (1937)
Southern, *Prof.* Sir Edwin Mellor, Kt.
Southgate, Sir Colin Grieve, Kt.
Southgate, Sir William David, Kt.
Southward, Sir Leonard Bingley, Kt., OBE
Southward, *Dr* Sir Nigel Ralph, KCVO
Southwood, *Prof.* Sir (Thomas) Richard (Edmund), Kt., FRS
Souyave, *Hon.* Sir (Louis) Georges, Kt.
Sowrey, *Air Marshal* Sir Frederick Beresford, KCB, CBE, AFC
Sparkes, Sir Robert Lyndley, Kt.
Sparrow, Sir John, Kt.
Spearman, Sir Alexander Young Richard Mainwaring, Bt. (1840)
Spedding, *Prof.* Sir Colin Raymond William, Kt., CBE

Speed, Sir (Herbert) Keith, Kt., RD
Speelman, Sir Cornelis Jacob, Bt. (1686)
Speight, *Hon.* Sir Graham Davies, Kt.
Spencer, Sir Derek Harold, Kt., QC
Spencer, *Vice-Adm.* Sir Peter, KCB
Spencer-Nairn, Sir Robert Arnold, Bt. (1933)
Spicer, Sir James Wilton, Kt.
Spicer, Sir Nicholas Adrian Albert, Bt., MB (1906)
Spicer, Sir (William) Michael Hardy, Kt., MP
Spiers, Sir Donald Maurice, Kt., CB, TD
Spooner, Sir James Douglas, Kt.
Spratt, *Col.* Sir Greville Douglas, GBE, TD
Spring, Sir Dryden Thomas, Kt.
Squire, *Air Chief Marshal* Sir Peter Ted, GCB, DFC, AFC, ADC
Stainton, Sir (John) Ross, Kt., CBE
Stamer, Sir (Lovelace) Anthony, Bt. (1809)
Standard, Sir Kenneth Livingstone, Kt., MD
Stanhope, *Adm.* Sir Mark, KCB, OBE
Stanier, Sir Beville Douglas, Bt. (1917)
Stanier, *Field Marshal* Sir John Wilfred, GCB, MBE
Stanley, *Rt. Hon.* Sir John Paul, Kt., MP
Staples, Sir Richard Molesworth, Bt. (I. 1628)
Stark, Sir Andrew Alexander Steel, KCMG, CVO
Starkey, Sir John Philip, Bt. (1935)
Staughton, *Rt. Hon.* Sir Christopher Stephen Thomas Jonathan Thayer, Kt.
Staveley, Sir John Malfroy, KBE, MC
Stear, *Air Chief Marshal* Sir Michael James Douglas, KCB, CBE
Steel, *Hon.* Sir David William, Kt.
Steer, Sir Alan William, Kt.
Stephen, *Rt. Hon.* Sir Ninian Martin, KG, GCMG, GCVO, KBE
Stephens, Sir (Edwin) Barrie, Kt.
Stephenson, Sir Henry Upton, Bt. (1936)
Stern, *Prof.* Sir Nicholas Herbert, Kt.
Sternberg, Sir Sigmund, Kt.
Stevens, Sir Jocelyn Edward Greville, Kt., CVO
Stevens, Sir John, Kt.
Stevens, Sir Laurence Houghton, Kt., CBE
Stevenson, Sir Simpson, Kt.
Stewart, Sir Alan, KBE
Stewart, Sir Alan d'Arcy, Bt. (I. 1623)
Stewart, Sir Brian John, Kt., CBE
Stewart, Sir David James Henderson, Bt. (1957)
Stewart, Sir David John Christopher, Bt. (1803)
Stewart, Sir Edward Jackson, Kt.
Stewart, Sir James Douglas, Kt.
Stewart, Sir James Moray, KCB
Stewart, Sir (John) Simon (Watson), Bt. (1920)
Stewart, Sir John Young, Kt., OBE

Stewart, *Lt.-Col.* Sir Robert Christie, KCVO, CBE, TD
Stewart, Sir Robertson Huntly, Kt., CBE
Stewart, Sir Robin Alastair, Bt. (1960)
Stewart, *Prof.* Sir William Duncan Paterson, Kt., FRS, FRSE
Stewart-Clark, Sir John, Bt., MEP (1918)
Stewart-Richardson, Sir Simon Alaisdair, Bt. (S. 1630)
Stewart-Wilson, *Lt.-Col.* Sir Blair Aubyn, KCVO
Stibbon, *Gen.* Sir John James, KCB, OBE
Stirling, Sir Alexander John Dickson, KBE, CMG
Stirling, Sir Angus Duncan Aeneas, Kt.
Stirling-Hamilton, Sir Malcolm William Bruce, Bt. (S. 1673)
Stirrup, *Air Chief Marshal* Sir Graham Eric, KCB, AFC
Stockdale, Sir Thomas Minshull, Bt. (1960)
Stoddart, *Wg Cdr.* Sir Kenneth Maxwell, KCVO, AE
Stoker, *Prof.* Sir Michael George Parke, Kt., CBE, FRCP, FRS, FRSE
Stones, Sir William Frederick, Kt., OBE
Stonhouse, *Revd* Michael Philip, Bt. (1628 and 1670)
Stonor, *Air Marshal* Sir Thomas Henry, KCB
Stoppard, Sir Thomas, Kt., OM, CBE
Storey, *Hon.* Sir Richard, Bt., CBE (1960)
Stothard, Sir Peter Michael, Kt.
Stott, Sir Adrian George Ellingham, Bt. (1920)
Stoute, Sir Michael Ronald, Kt.
Stowe, Sir Kenneth Ronald, GCB, CVO
Stracey, Sir John Simon, Bt. (1818)
Strachan, Sir Curtis Victor, Kt., CVO
Strachey, Sir Charles, Bt. (1801)
Strang Steel, Sir (Fiennes) Michael, Bt. (1938)
Strawson, *Prof.* Sir Peter Frederick, Kt., FBA
Street, *Hon.* Sir Laurence Whistler, KCMG
Streeton, Sir Terence George, KBE, CMG
Strickland-Constable, Sir Frederic, Bt. (1641)
Stringer, Sir Donald Edgar, Kt., CBE
Stringer, Sir Howard, Kt.
Strong, Sir Roy Colin, Kt., PHD, FSA
Stronge, Sir James Anselan Maxwell, Bt. (1803)
Stroud, *Prof.* Sir (Charles) Eric, Kt., FRCP
Stuart, Sir James Keith, Kt.
Stuart, Sir Kenneth Lamonte, Kt.
†Stuart, Sir Phillip Luttrell, Bt. (1660)
†Stuart-Forbes, Sir William Daniel, Bt. (S. 1626)

Stuart-Menteth, Sir James Wallace, Bt. (1838)
Stuart-Paul, *Air Marshal* Sir Ronald Ian, KBE
Stuart-Smith, *Rt. Hon.* Sir Murray, Kt.
Stuart-White, *Hon.* Sir Christopher Stuart, Kt.
Stubbs, Sir William Hamilton, Kt., PHD
Stucley, *Lt.* Sir Hugh George Coplestone Bampfylde, Bt. (1859)
Studd, Sir Edward Fairfax, Bt. (1929)
Studholme, Sir Henry William, Bt. (1956)
†Style, Sir William Frederick, Bt. (1627)
Sugar, Sir Alan Michael, Kt.
Sullivan, *Hon.* Sir Jeremy Mirth, Kt.
Sullivan, Sir Richard Arthur, Bt. (1804)
Sulston, Sir John Edward, Kt.
Sumner, *Hon.* Sir Christopher John, Kt.
Sutherland, Sir John Brewer, Bt. (1921)
Sutherland, Sir William George MacKenzie, Kt.
Sutton, Sir Frederick Walter, Kt., OBE
Sutton, *Air Marshal* Sir John Matthias Dobson, KCB
Sutton, Sir Richard Lexington, Bt. (1772)
Swaffield, Sir James Chesebrough, Kt., CBE, RD
Swaine, Sir John Joseph, Kt., CBE
Swan, Sir Conrad Marshall John Fisher, KCVO, PHD
Swan, Sir John William David, KBE
Swann, Sir Michael Christopher, Bt., TD (1906)
Swartz, *Hon.* Sir Reginald William Colin, KBE, ED
Sweeney, Sir George, Kt.
Sweeting, *Prof.* Sir Martin Nicholas, Kt., OBE, FRS
Sweetnam, Sir (David) Rodney, KCVO, CBE, FRCS
Swinburn, *Lt.-Gen.* Sir Richard Hull, KCB
Swinnerton-Dyer, *Prof.* Sir (Henry) Peter (Francis), Bt., KBE, FRS (1678)
Swinton, *Maj.-Gen.* Sir John, KCVO, OBE
Swire, Sir Adrian Christopher, Kt.
Swire, Sir John Anthony, Kt., CBE
Sykes, Sir David Michael, Bt. (1921)
Sykes, Sir Francis John Badcock, Bt. (1781)
Sykes, Sir Hugh Ridley, Kt.
Sykes, *Prof.* Sir (Malcolm) Keith, Kt.
Sykes, Sir Richard, Kt.
Sykes, Sir Tatton Christopher Mark, Bt. (1783)
Symington, *Prof.* Sir Thomas, Kt., MD, FRSE
Symons, *Vice-Adm.* Sir Patrick Jeremy, KBE
Synge, Sir Robert Carson, Bt. (1801)
Synnott, Sir Hilary Nicholas Hugh, KCMG

Tait, *Adm.* Sir (Allan) Gordon, KCB, DSC
Talboys, *Rt. Hon.* Sir Brian Edward, CH, KCB
Tangaroa, *Hon.* Sir Tangoroa, Kt., MBE
Tapps-Gervis-Meyrick, Sir George Christopher Cadafael, Bt. (1791)
Tapsell, Sir Peter Hannay Bailey, Kt., MP
Tate, Sir (Henry) Saxon, Bt. (1898)
Tavaiqia, *Ratu* Sir Josaia, KBE
Tavare, Sir John, Kt., CBE
Tavener, *Prof.* Sir John Kenneth, Kt.
Taylor, Sir (Arthur) Godfrey, Kt.
Taylor, Sir Cyril Julian Hebden, GBE
Taylor, Sir Edward Macmillan (Teddy), Kt., MP
Taylor, *Rt. Revd* John Bernard, KCVO
Taylor, *Dr.* Sir John Michael, Kt., OBE
Taylor, Sir Nicholas Richard Stuart, Bt. (1917)
Taylor, *Prof.* Sir William, Kt., CBE
Taylor, Sir William George, Kt.
Teagle, *Vice-Adm.* Sir Somerford Francis, KBE
Tebbit, Sir Donald Claude, GCMG
Tebbit, Sir Kevin Reginald, KCB, CMG
Telford, Sir Robert, Kt., CBE, FRENG
Temple, *Prof.* Sir John Graham, Kt.
Temple, *Maj.* Sir Richard Anthony Purbeck, Bt., MC (1876)
Templeton, Sir John Marks, Kt.
Tennant, Sir Anthony John, Kt.
Tennant, *Capt.* Sir Iain Mark, Kt.
Tennyson-D'Eyncourt, Sir Mark Gervais, Bt. (1930)
Terry, *Air Marshal* Sir Colin George, KBE, CB
Terry, *Air Chief Marshal* Sir Peter David George, GCB, AFC
Thatcher, Sir Mark, Bt. (1990)
Thomas, Sir David John Godfrey, Bt. (1694)
Thomas, Sir Derek Morison David, KCMG
Thomas, Sir Jeremy Cashel, KCMG
Thomas, Sir (John) Alan, Kt.
Thomas, *Prof.* Sir John Meurig, Kt., FRS
Thomas, Sir Keith Vivian, Kt.
Thomas, Sir Philip Lloyd, KCVO, CMG
Thomas, Sir Quentin Jeremy, Kt., CB
Thomas, Sir Robert Evan, Kt.
Thomas, *Hon.* Sir Roger John Laugharne, Kt.
Thomas, *Hon.* Sir Swinton Barclay, Kt.
Thomas, Sir William James Cooper, Bt., TD (1919)
Thomas, Sir (William) Michael (Marsh), Bt. (1918)
Thompson, Sir Christopher Peile, Bt. (1890)
Thompson, Sir Clive Malcolm, Kt.
Thompson, Sir David Albert, KCMG
Thompson, Sir Donald, Kt.
Thompson, Sir Gilbert Williamson, Kt., OBE

Thompson, *Prof.* Sir Michael Warwick, Kt., DSC
Thompson, Sir Nicholas Annesley, Bt. (1963)
Thompson, Sir Nigel Cooper, KCMG, CBE
Thompson, Sir Paul Anthony, Bt. (1963)
Thompson, Sir Peter Anthony, Kt.
Thompson, *Dr* Sir Richard Paul Hepworth, KCVO
Thompson, Sir Thomas d'Eyncourt John, Bt. (1806)
Thomson, Sir (Frederick Douglas) David, Bt. (1929)
Thomson, Sir John Adam, GCMG
Thomson, Sir John (Ian) Sutherland, KBE, CMG
Thomson, Sir Mark Wilfrid Home, Bt. (1925)
Thomson, Sir Thomas James, Kt., CBE, FRCP
Thorn, Sir John Samuel, Kt., OBE
Thorne, Sir Neil Gordon, Kt., OBE, TD
Thornton, Sir (George) Malcolm, Kt.
Thornton, Sir Peter Eustace, KCB
Thornton, Sir Richard Eustace, KCVO, OBE
†Thorold, Sir (Anthony) Oliver, Bt. (1642)
Thorpe, *Rt. Hon.* Sir Mathew Alexander, Kt.
Thouron, Sir John Rupert Hunt, KBE
Thwaites, Sir Bryan, Kt., PHD
Tickell, Sir Crispin Charles Cervantes, GCMG, KCVO
Tikaram, Sir Moti, KBE
Tilt, Sir Robin Richard, Kt.
Tiltman, Sir John Hessell, KCVO
Timmins, *Col.* Sir John Bradford, KCVO, OBE, TD
Tims, Sir Michael David, KCVO
Tindle, Sir Ray Stanley, Kt., CBE
Tippet, *Vice-Adm.* Sir Anthony Sanders, KCB
Tirvengadum, Sir Harry Krishnan, Kt.
Tod, *Vice-Adm.* Sir Jonathan James Richard, KCB, CBE
Todd, *Prof.* Sir David, Kt., CBE
Todd, Sir Ian Pelham, KBE, FRCS
Tollemache, Sir Lyonel Humphry John, Bt. (1793)
Tololo, Sir Alkan, KBE
Tomkins, Sir Edward Emile, GCMG, CVO
Tomkys, Sir (William) Roger, KCMG
Tomlinson, *Prof.* Sir Bernard Evans, Kt., CBE
Tomlinson, *Hon.* Sir Stephen Miles, Kt.
Tooley, Sir John, Kt.
ToRobert, Sir Henry Thomas, KBE
Torry, Sir Peter James, KCMG
Tory, Sir Geofroy William, KCMG
Touche, Sir Anthony George, Bt. (1920)
Touche, Sir Rodney Gordon, Bt. (1962)
Toulson, *Hon.* Sir Roger Grenfell, Kt.
Tovadek, Sir Martin, Kt. CMG

Tovey, Sir Brian John Maynard, KCMG

ToVue, Sir Ronald, Kt., OBE

Towneley, Sir Simon Peter Edmund Cosmo William, KCVO

Townsend, Sir Cyril David, Kt.

Traill, Sir Alan Towers, GBE

Trant, *Gen.* Sir Richard Brooking, KCB

Treacher, *Adm.* Sir John Devereux, KCB

Treacy, *Hon.* Sir Colman Maurice, Kt.

Treitel, *Prof.* Sir Guenter Heinz, Kt., FBA, QC

Trench, Sir Peter Edward, Kt., CBE, TD

Trescowthick, Sir Donald Henry, KBE

†Trevelyan, Sir Edward (Norman), Bt. (1662)

Trevelyan, Sir Geoffrey Washington, Bt. (1874)

Trezise, Sir Kenneth Bruce, Kt., OBE

Trippier, Sir David Austin, Kt., RD

Tritton, Sir Anthony John Ernest, Bt. (1905)

Trollope, Sir Anthony Simon, Bt. (1642)

Trotman-Dickenson, Sir Aubrey Fiennes, Kt.

Trotter, Sir Neville Guthrie, Kt.

Trotter, Sir Ronald Ramsay, Kt.

Troubridge, Sir Thomas Richard, Bt. (1799)

Troup, *Vice-Adm.* Sir (John) Anthony (Rose), KCB, DSC

Trousdell, *Lt.-Gen.* Sir Philip Charles Cornwallis, KBE, CB

Truscott, Sir George James Irving, Bt. (1909)

Tsang, Sir Donald Yam-keun, KBE

Tuck, Sir Bruce Adolph Reginald, Bt. (1910)

Tucker, *Hon.* Sir Richard Howard, Kt.

Tuckey, *Rt. Hon.* Sir Simon Lane, Kt.

Tugendhat, *Hon.* Sir Michael George, Kt.

Tuita, Sir Mariano Kelesimalefo, KBE

Tuite, Sir Christopher Hugh, Bt., PHD (1622)

Tuivaga, Sir Timoci Uluiburotu, Kt.

Tully, Sir William Mark, KBE

Tupper, Sir Charles Hibbert, Bt. (1888)

Turbott, Sir Ian Graham, Kt., CMG, CVO

Turing, Sir John Dermot, Bt. (S. 1638)

Turnbull, Sir Andrew, KCB, CVO

Turner, Sir Colin William Carstairs, Kt., CBE, DFC

Turner, *Hon.* Sir Michael John, Kt.

Turnquest, Sir Orville Alton, GCMG, QC

Tusa, Sir John, Kt.

Tuti, *Revd* Dudley, KBE

Tweedie, *Prof.* Sir David Philip, Kt.

Tyree, Sir (Alfred) William, Kt., OBE

Tyrwhitt, Sir Reginald Thomas Newman, Bt. (1919)

Unsworth, *Hon.* Sir Edgar Ignatius Godfrey, Kt., CMG

Unwin, Sir (James) Brian, KCB

Ure, Sir John Burns, KCMG, LVO

Urquhart, Sir Brian Edward, KCMG, MBE

Urwick, Sir Alan Bedford, KCVO, CMG

Usher, Sir Andrew John, Bt. (1899)

Utting, Sir William Benjamin, Kt., CB

Vai, Sir Mea, Kt., CBE, ISO

Vallat, Sir Francis Aimé, GBE, KCMG, QC

Vallings, *Vice-Adm.* Sir George Montague Francis, KCB

Vanderfelt, Sir Robin Victor, KBE

Vane, Sir John Robert, Kt., DPHIL, DSC, FRS

Vardy, Sir Peter, Kt.Vasquez, Sir Alfred Joseph, Kt., CBE, QC

Vassar-Smith, Sir John Rathbone, Bt. (1917)

Vavasour, Sir Eric Michael Joseph Marmaduke, Bt. (1828)

Veale, Sir Alan John Ralph, Kt., FRENG

Venner, Sir Kenneth Dwight Vincent, KBE

Vereker, Sir John Michael Medlicott, KCB

†Verney, Sir John Sebastian, Bt. (1946)

Verney, *Hon.* Sir Lawrence John, Kt., TD

†Verney, Sir Edmund Ralph, Bt. (1818)

Vernon, Sir Nigel John Douglas, Bt. (1914)

Vernon, Sir (William) Michael, Kt.

Vestey, Sir (John) Derek, Bt. (1921)

Vickers, *Lt.-Gen.* Sir Richard Maurice Hilton, KCB, CVO, OBE

Vincent, Sir William Percy Maxwell, Bt. (1936)

Vineall, Sir Anthony John Patrick, Kt.

Vinelott, *Hon.* Sir John Evelyn, Kt.

Vines, Sir William Joshua, Kt., CMG

von Schramek, Sir Eric Emil, Kt.

†Vyvyan, Sir Ralph Ferrers Alexander, Bt. (1645)

Wade-Gery, Sir Robert Lucian, KCMG, KCVO

Waine, *Rt. Revd* John, KCVO

Waite, *Rt. Hon.* Sir John Douglas, Kt.

Wake, Sir Hereward, Bt., MC (1621)

Wakefield, Sir (Edward) Humphry (Tyrell), Bt. (1962)

Wakefield, Sir Norman Edward, Kt.

Wakefield, Sir Peter George Arthur, KBE, CMG

Wakeford, Sir Geoffrey Michael Montgomery, Kt., OBE

Wakeford, *Air Marshal* Sir Richard Gordon, KCB, OBE, LVO, AFC

Wakeley, Sir John Cecil Nicholson, Bt., FRCS (1952)

†Wakeman, Sir Edward Offley Bertram, Bt. (1828)

Wakerley, *Hon.* Sir Richard MacLennon, Kt.

Wales, Sir Robert Andrew, Kt.

Waley-Cohen, Sir Stephen Harry, Bt. (1961)

Walford, Sir Christopher Rupert, Kt.

Walker, Sir Alfred Cecil, Kt.

Walker, *Gen.* Sir Antony Kenneth Frederick, KCB

Walker, Sir Baldwin Patrick, Bt. (1856)

Walker, Sir David Alan, Kt.

Walker, Sir Harold Berners, KCMG

Walker, *Maj.* Sir Hugh Ronald, Bt. (1906)

Walker, Sir James Graham, Kt., MBE

Walker, Sir John Ernest, Kt., DPHIL, FRS

Walker, *Air Marshal* Sir John Robert, KCB, CBE, AFC

Walker, *Gen.* Sir Michael John Dawson, GCB, CMG, CBE, ADC

Walker, Sir Miles Rawstron, Kt., CBE

Walker, Sir Patrick Jeremy, KCB

Walker, Sir Rodney Myerscough, Kt.

Walker, *Hon.* Sir Timothy Edward, Kt.

Walker, Sir Victor Stewart Heron, Bt. (1868)

Walker-Okeover, Andrew Peter Monro, Bt. (1886)

Walker-Smith, Sir John Jonah, Bt. (1960)

Wall, Sir John Anthony, Kt., CBE

Wall, Sir (John) Stephen, GCMG, LVO

Wall, *Hon.* Sir Nicholas Peter Rathbone, Kt., PC

Wall, Sir Robert William, Kt., OBE

Wallace, *Lt.-Gen.* Sir Christopher Brooke Quentin, KBE

Wallace, *Prof.* David James, Kt., CBE

Wallace, Sir Ian James, Kt., CBE

Waller, *Rt. Hon.* Sir (George) Mark, Kt.

Waller, Sir Robert William, Bt. (I. 1780)

Wallis, Sir Peter Gordon, KCVO

Wallis, Sir Timothy William, Kt.

Walmsley, *Vice-Adm.* Sir Robert, KCB

†Walsham, Sir Timothy John, Bt. (1831)

Walters, *Prof.* Sir Alan Arthur, Kt.

Walters, Sir Dennis Murray, Kt., MBE

Walters, Sir Frederick Donald, Kt.

Walters, Sir Peter Ingram, Kt.

Walters, Sir Roger Talbot, KBE, FRIBA

Wamiri, Sir Akapite, KBE

Wan, Sir Wamp, Kt., MBE

Ward, *Rt. Hon.* Sir Alan Hylton, Kt.

Ward, Sir John Devereux, Kt., CBE

Ward, *Prof.* Sir John MacQueen, Kt., CBE

Ward, Sir Joseph James Laffey, Bt. (1911)

Ward, Sir Timothy James, Kt.

Wardale, Sir Geoffrey Charles, KCB

Wardlaw, Sir Henry (John), Bt. (S. 1631)

Waring, Sir (Alfred) Holburt, Bt. (1935)

Warmington, Sir David Marshall, Bt. (1908)

Warner, Sir (Edward Courtenay) Henry, Bt. (1910)

Warner, *Prof.* Sir Frederick Edward, Kt., FRS, FRENG

Warner, Sir Gerald Chierici, KCMG

Warner, *Hon.* Sir Jean-Pierre Frank Eugene, Kt.

Warren, Sir (Frederick) Miles, KBE

Warren, Sir Kenneth Robin, Kt.

†Warren, Sir Michael Blackley, Bt. (1784)

Wass, Sir Douglas William Gretton, GCB

Waterhouse, *Hon.* Sir Ronald Gough, GBE

Waterlow, Sir Christopher Rupert, Bt. (1873)

Waterlow, Sir (James) Gerard, Bt. (1930)

Waters, *Gen.* Sir (Charles) John, GCB, CBE

Waters, Sir (Thomas) Neil (Morris), Kt.

Wates, Sir Christopher Stephen, Kt.

Watkins, *Rt. Hon.* Sir Tasker, VC, GBE

Watson, Sir Bruce Dunstan, Kt.

Watson, *Prof.* Sir David John, Kt., PHD

Watson, Sir (James) Andrew, Bt. (1866)

Watson, *Vice-Adm.* Sir Philip Alexander, KBE, LVO

Watson, Sir Ronald Matthew, Kt., CBE

Watt, *Lt.-Gen.* Sir Charles Redmond, KCVO, CBE

Watt, *Surgeon Vice-Adm.* Sir James, KBE, FRCS

Watts, Sir John Augustus Fitzroy, KCMG, CBE

Watts, Sir Arthur Desmond, KCMG

Watts, Sir Philip Beverley, KCMG

Weatherall, *Prof.* Sir David John, Kt., FRS

Weatherall, *Vice-Adm.* Sir James Lamb, KCVO, KBE

Weatherstone, Sir Dennis, KBE

Weatherup, *Hon.* Sir Ronald Eccles, Kt.

Webb, *Prof.* Sir Adrian Leonard, Kt.

Webb, Sir Thomas Langley, Kt.

Webb-Carter, *Gen.* Sir Evelyn John, KCVO, OBE

Webster, *Very Revd* Alan Brunskill, KCVO

Webster, *Vice-Adm.* Sir John Morrison, KCB

Webster, *Hon.* Sir Peter Edlin, Kt.

Wedgwood, Sir (Hugo) Martin, Bt. (1942)

Weekes, Sir Everton DeCourcey, KCMG, OBE

Weinberg, Sir Mark Aubrey, Kt.

Weir, Sir Michael Scott, KCMG

Weir, *Hon.* Sir Reginald George, Kt.

Weir, Sir Roderick Bignell, Kt.

Welby, Sir (Richard) Bruno Gregory, Bt. (1801)

Welch, Sir John Reader, Bt. (1957)

Weldon, Sir Anthony William, Bt. (I. 1723)

Weller, Sir Arthur Burton, Kt., CBE

Wellings, Sir Jack Alfred, Kt., CBE

†Wells, Sir Christopher Charles, Bt. (1944)

Wells, Sir John Julius, Kt.

Wells, Sir William Henry Weston, Kt., FRICS

West, *Adm.* Sir Alan William John, GCB, DSC, ADC

Westbrook, Sir Neil Gowanloch, Kt., CBE

Westmacott, Sir Peter John, KCMG

Weston, Sir Michael Charles Swift, KCMG, CVO

Weston, Sir (Philip) John, KCMG

Whalen, Sir Geoffrey Henry, Kt., CBE

Wheeler, Sir Harry Anthony, Kt., OBE

Wheeler, *Air Chief Marshal* Sir (Henry) Neil (George), GCB, CBE, DSO, DFC, AFC

Wheeler, *Rt. Hon.* Sir John Daniel, Kt.

Wheeler, Sir John Hieron, Bt. (1920)

Wheeler, *Gen.* Sir Roger Neil, GCB, CBE

Wheeler-Booth, Sir Michael Addison John, KCB

Wheler, Sir Edward Woodford, Bt. (1660)

Whishaw, Sir Charles Percival Law, Kt.

Whitaker, Sir John James Ingham (Jack), Bt. (1936)

White, *Prof.* Sir Christopher John, Kt., CVO

White, Sir Christopher Robert Meadows, Bt. (1937)

White, Sir David Harry, Kt.

White, *Hon.* Sir Frank John, Kt.

White, Sir George Stanley James, Bt. (1904)

White, *Adm.* Sir Hugo Moresby, GCB, CBE

White, *Hon.* Sir John Charles, Kt., MBE

White, Sir John Woolmer, Bt. (1922)

White, Sir Lynton Stuart, Kt., MBE, TD

White, Sir Nicholas Peter Archibald, Bt. (1802)

White, *Adm.* Sir Peter, GBE

White, Sir Willard Wentworth, Kt., CBE

Whitehead, Sir John Stainton, GCMG, CVO

Whitehead, Sir Rowland John Rathbone, Bt. (1889)

Whiteley, *Gen.* Sir Peter John Frederick, GCB, OBE, RM

Whitfield, Sir William, Kt., CBE

Whitmore, Sir Clive Anthony, GCB, CVO

Whitmore, Sir John Henry Douglas, Bt. (1954)

Whitney, Sir Raymond William, Kt., OBE, MP

Whitson, Sir Keith Roderick, Kt.

Wickerson, Sir John Michael, Kt.

Wicks, Sir Nigel Leonard, GCB, CVO, CBE

†Wigan, Sir Michael Iain, Bt. (1898)

Wiggin, Sir Alfred William (Jerry), Kt., TD

†Wiggin, Sir Charles Rupert John, Bt. (1892)

†Wigram, Sir John Woolmore, Bt. (1805)

Wilbraham, Sir Richard Baker, Bt. (1776)

Wiles, *Prof.* Sir Andrew John, KBE

Wilford, Sir (Kenneth) Michael, GCMG

Wilkes, *Prof.* Sir Maurice Vincent, Kt.

Wilkes, *Gen.* Sir Michael John, KCB, CBE

Wilkinson, Sir (David) Graham (Brook) Bt. (1941)

Wilkinson, *Prof.* Sir Denys Haigh, Kt., FRS

Wilkinson, Sir Philip William, Kt.

Willcocks, Sir David Valentine, Kt., CBE, MC

Willcocks, *Lt.-Gen.* Sir Michael Alan, KCB

Williams, Sir Alwyn, Kt., PHD, FRS, FRSE

Williams, Sir Arthur Dennis Pitt, Kt.

Williams, Sir (Arthur) Gareth Ludovic Emrys Rhys, Bt. (1918)

Williams, *Prof.* Sir Bruce Rodda, KBE

Williams, Sir Charles Othniel, Kt.

Williams, Sir Daniel Charles, GCMG, QC

Williams, *Adm.* Sir David, GCB

Williams, *Prof.* Sir David Glyndwr Tudor, Kt.

Williams, Sir David Innes, Kt.

Williams, Sir David Reeve, Kt., CBE

Williams, *Hon.* Sir Denys Ambrose, KCMG

Williams, Sir Donald Mark, Bt. (1866)

Williams, *Prof.* Sir (Edward) Dillwyn, Kt., FRCP

Williams, Sir Francis Owen Garbett, Kt., CBE

Williams, *Prof.* Sir Glanmor, Kt., CBE, FBA

Williams, Sir (John) Kyffin, Kt., OBE, DL, RA

Williams, Sir (Lawrence) Hugh, Bt. (1798)

Williams, Sir Leonard, KBE, CB

Williams, Sir Osmond, Bt., MC (1909)

Williams, Sir Peter Michael, Kt.

Williams, Sir (Robert) Philip Nathaniel, Bt. (1915)

Williams, Sir Robin Philip, Bt. (1953)

Williams, Sir (William) Maxwell (Harries), Kt.

Williams-Bulkeley, Sir Richard Thomas, Bt. (1661)

Williams-Wynn, Sir David Watkin, Bt. (1688)

Williamson, *Marshal of the Royal Air Force* Sir Keith Alec, GCB, AFC

Williamson, Sir Robert Brian, Kt., CBE

Willink, Sir Charles William, Bt. (1957)

Willis, *Vice-Adm.* Sir (Guido) James, KBE

Willis, *Air Chief Marshal* Sir John Frederick, GBE, KCB

Willison, *Lt.-Gen.* Sir David John, KCB, OBE, MC

Wills, Sir David James Vernon, Bt. (1923)

Wills, Sir David Seton, Bt. (1904)
Wilmot, Sir David, Kt., QPM
Wilmot, Sir Henry Robert, Bt. (1759)
Wilsey, *Gen.* Sir John Finlay Willasey,
GCB, CBE
Wilshaw, Sir Michael, Kt.
Wilson, *Prof.* Sir Alan Geoffrey, Kt.
Wilson, *Lt.-Gen.* Sir (Alexander)
James, KBE, MC
Wilson, Sir Anthony, Kt.
Wilson, *Vice-Adm.* Sir Barry Nigel,
KCB
Wilson, *Prof.* Sir Colin Alexander St
John, Kt., RA, FRIBA
Wilson, Sir David, Bt. (1920)
Wilson, Sir David Mackenzie, Kt.
Wilson, Sir James William Douglas,
Bt. (1906)
Wilson, *Brig.* Sir Mathew John
Anthony, Bt., OBE, MC (1874)
Wilson, *Hon.* Sir Nicholas Allan Roy,
Kt.
Wilson, Sir Robert Peter, KCMG
Wilson, *Air Chief Marshal* Sir
(Ronald) Andrew (Fellowes), KCB,
AFC
Wilson, *Hon.* Sir Ronald Darling,
KBE, CMG
Wilton, Sir (Arthur) John, KCMG,
KCVO, MC
Wingate, *Capt.* Sir Miles Buckley,
KCVO
Winkley, Sir David Ross, Kt.
Winnington, Sir Anthony Edward,
Bt. (1755)
Winship, Sir Peter James Joseph, Kt.,
CBE
Winskill, *Air Cdre* Sir Archibald
Little, KCVO, CBE, DFC
Winter, *Dr* Sir Gregory Winter, Kt.,
CBE
Winterton, Sir Nicholas Raymond,
Kt.
Winton, Sir Nicholas George, Kt.,
MBE
Wisdom, Sir Norman, Kt., OBE
Wiseman, Sir John William, Bt.
(1628)
Wolfendale, *Prof.* Sir Arnold
Whittaker, Kt., FRS
Wolfson, Sir Brian Gordon, Kt.
Wolseley, Sir Charles Garnet Richard
Mark, Bt. (1628)
†Wolseley, Sir James Douglas, Bt.
(I. 1745)
†Wombell, Sir George Philip
Frederick, Bt. (1778)
Womersley, Sir Peter John Walter, Bt.
(1945)
Woo, Sir Leo Joseph, Kt.

Woo, Sir Po-Shing, Kt.
Wood, Sir Alan Marshall Muir, Kt.,
FRS, FRENG
Wood, Sir Andrew Marley, GCMG
Wood, Sir Anthony John Page, Bt.
(1837)
Wood, Sir Ian Clark, Kt., CBE
Wood, *Hon.* Sir John Kember, Kt.,
MC
Wood, Sir Martin Francis, Kt., OBE
Wood, Sir Michael Charles, KCMG
Wood, *Hon.* Sir Roderic Lionel James,
Kt.
Wood, Sir Russell Dillon, KCVO,
VRD
Wood, Sir William Alan, KCVO, CB
Woodard, *Rear Adm.* Sir Robert
Nathaniel, KCVO
Woodcock, Sir John, Kt., CBE, QPM
Woodhead, *Vice-Adm.* Sir (Anthony)
Peter, KCB
Woodhouse, *Rt. Hon.* Sir (Arthur)
Owen, KBE, DSC
Wooding, Sir Norman Samuel, Kt.,
CBE
Woodroffe, *Most Revd* George
Cuthbert Manning, KBE
Woods, Sir Robert Kynnersley, Kt.,
CBE
Woodward, *Hon.* Sir (Albert) Edward,
Kt., OBE
Woodward, Sir Clive Ronald, Kt.,
OBE
Woodward, *Adm.* Sir John Forster,
GBE, KCB
Worsley, *Gen.* Sir Richard Edward,
GCB, OBE
Worsley, Sir (William) Marcus (John),
Bt. (1838)
Worsthorne, Sir Peregrine Gerard,
Kt.
Wratten, *Air Chief Marshal* Sir
William John, GBE, CB, AFC
Wraxall, Sir Charles Frederick
Lascelles, Bt. (1813)
Wrey, Sir George Richard Bourchier,
Bt. (1628)
Wrigglesworth, Sir Ian William, Kt.
Wright, Sir Allan Frederick, KBE
Wright, Sir David John, GCMG, LVO
Wright, Sir Denis Arthur Hepworth,
GCMG
Wright, Sir Edward Maitland, Kt.,
DPHIL, LLD, DSC, FRSE
Wright, *Hon.* Sir (John) Michael, Kt.
Wright, Sir (John) Oliver, GCMG,
GCVO, DSC
Wright, Sir Paul Hervé Giraud,
KCMG, OBE
Wright, Sir Peter Robert, Kt., CBE

Wright, *Air Marshal* Sir Robert
Alfred, KBE, AFC
Wrightson, Sir Charles Mark
Garmondsway, Bt. (1900)
Wrigley, *Prof.* Sir Edward Anthony
(Sir Tony), Kt., PHD, PBA
Wrixon-Becher, Sir John William
Michael, Bt. (1831)
Wu, Sir Gordon Ying Sheung,
KCMG
Wyldbore-Smith, *Maj.-Gen.* Sir
(Francis) Brian, Kt., CB, DSO, OBE
Yacoub, *Prof.* Sir Magdi Habib, Kt.,
FRCS
Yaki, Sir Roy, KBE
Yang, *Hon.* Sir Ti Liang, Kt.
Yapp, Sir Stanley Graham, Kt.
Yardley, Sir David Charles Miller, Kt.,
LLD
Yarrow, Sir Eric Grant, Bt., MBE
(1916)
Yellowlees, Sir Henry, KCB
Yocklunn, Sir John (Soong Chung),
KCVO
Yoo Foo, Sir (François) Henri, Kt.
Young, Sir Brian Walter Mark, Kt.
Young, Sir Colville Norbert, GCMG,
MBE
Young, Sir Dennis Charles, KCMG
Young, *Rt. Hon.* Sir George Samuel
Knatchbull, Bt., MP (1813)
Young, *Hon.* Sir Harold William,
KCMG
Young, Sir Jimmy Leslie Ronald, Kt.,
CBE
Young, Sir John Kenyon Roe, Bt.
(1821)
Young, *Hon.* Sir John McIntosh,
KCMG
Young, Sir John Robertson, GCMG
Young, Sir Leslie Clarence, Kt., CBE
Young, Sir Nicholas Charles, Kt.
Young, Sir Richard Dilworth, Kt.
Young, Sir Robin Urquhart, KCB
Young, Sir Roger William, Kt.
Young, Sir Stephen Stewart
Templeton, Bt. (1945)
Young, Sir William Neil, Bt. (1769)
Younger, Sir Julian William Richard,
Bt. (1911)
Yuwi, Sir Matiabe, KBE
Zeeman, *Prof.* Sir (Erik) Christopher,
Kt., FRS
Zissman, Sir Bernard Philip, Kt.
Zochonis, Sir John Basil, Kt.
Zoleveke, Sir Gideon Pitabose, KBE
Zunz, Sir Gerhard Jacob (Jack), Kt.,
FRENG
Zurenuoc, Sir Zibang, KBE

THE ORDER OF ST JOHN

THE MOST VENERABLE ORDER OF THE HOSPITAL OF ST JOHN OF JERUSALEM (1888)

GCStJ	Bailiff/Dame Grand Cross
KStJ	Knight of Justice/Grace
DStJ	Dame of Justice/Grace
CStJ	Commander
OstJ	Officer
SBStJ	Serving Brother
SSStJ	Serving Sister
EsqStJ	Esquire

Mottoes, Pro Fide *and* Pro Utilitate Hominum

The Order of St John, founded in the early 12th century in Jerusalem, was a religious order with a particular duty to care for the sick. In Britain the Order was dissolved by Henry VIII in 1540 but the British branch was revived in the early 19th century. The branch was not accepted by the Grand Magistracy of the Order in Rome but its search for a role in the tradition of the Hospitallers led to the founding of the St John Ambulance Association in 1877 and later the St John Ambulance Brigade; in 1882 the St John Ophthalmic Hospital was founded in Jerusalem. A royal charter was granted in 1888 establishing the British Order of St John as a British Order of Chivalry with the Sovereign as its head. Since October 1999, a separate Priory of England and the Islands has governed the Order of England, the Channel Islands and the Isle of Man, with a Commandery in Northern Ireland.

The whole Order world-wide is now governed by a Grand Council including the representatives of all 8 Priories (England, Scotland, Wales, South Africa, New Zealand, Canada, Australia and the United States). There are also branches in about 30 other countries, mostly in the Commonwealth. Apart from the St John Ambulance Foundation, the Order is also responsible for the Jerusalem Eye Hospital.

Admission to the Order is conferred in recognition of service, usually in St John Ambulance or the Eye Hospital. Membership does not confer any rank, style, title or precedence on a recipient.

SOVEREIGN HEAD OF THE ORDER
HM The Queen

GRAND PRIOR
HRH The Duke of Gloucester, KD, GCVO

Lord Prior, Eric Barry
Prelate, The Rt Revd John Waine, KCVO
Deputy Lord Prior: Prof. Anthony Mellows, OBE, TD
Sub Prior, Mr John Strachan
Secretary General, Rear-Adm. Andrew Gough, CB
Headquarters, Priory House, 25 St John's Lane, London ECM 4PP

DAMES

DAMES GRAND CROSS AND DAMES COMMANDERS

Style, 'Dame' before forename and surname, followed by appropriate post-nominal initials. Where such an award is made to a lady already in possession of a higher title, the appropriate initials follow her name
Husband, Untitled
For forms of address, *see* page 43

Dame Grand Cross and Dame Commander are the higher classes for women of the Order of the Bath, the Order of St Michael and St George, the Royal Victorian Order, and the Order of the British Empire. Dames Grand Cross rank after the wives of Baronets and before the wives of Knights Grand Cross. Dames Commanders rank after the wives of Knights Grand Cross and before the wives of Knights Commanders.

Honorary Dames Commanders may be conferred on women who are citizens of countries of which The Queen is not head of state.

LIST OF DAMES
Revised to 31 August 2004

Women peers in their own right and life peers are not included in this list. Female members of the royal family are not included in this list; details of the orders they hold can be found within the Royal Family section.

If a dame has a double barrelled or hyphenated surname, she is listed under the first element of the name.

A full entry in italic type indicates that the recipient of an honour died during the year in which the honour was conferred. The name is included for the purposes of record.

Abaijah, Dame Josephine, DBE
Abel Smith, Lady, DCVO
Abergavenny, The Marchioness of, DCVO
Airlie, The Countess of, DCVO
Albemarle, The Countess of, DBE
Allen, *Prof.* Dame Ingrid Victoria, DBE
Anderson, *Brig. Hon.* Dame Mary Mackenzie (Mrs Pihl), DBE
Andrews, Dame Julie, DBE
Anglesey, The Marchioness of, DBE
Anson, Lady (Elizabeth Audrey), DBE
Anstee, Dame Margaret Joan, DCMG
Arden, *Rt. Hon.* Dame Mary Howarth (Mrs Mance), DBE
Atkins, Dame Eileen, DBE
Bainbridge, Dame Beryl, DBE
Baker, Dame Janet Abbott (Mrs Shelley), CH, DBE
Ballin, Dame Reubina Ann, DBE
Baron, *Hon.* Dame Florence Jacqueline, DBE
Barrow, Dame Jocelyn Anita (Mrs Downer), DBE
Barstow, Dame Josephine Clare (Mrs Anderson), DBE
Bassey, Dame Shirley, DBE
Beaurepaire, Dame Beryl Edith, DBE
Beer, *Prof.* Dame Gillian Patricia Kempster, DBE, FBA
Bergquist, *Prof.* Dame Patricia Rose, DBE
Bewley, Dame Beulah Rosemary, DBE

Bibby, Dame Enid, DBE
Black, *Hon.* Dame Jill Margaret, DBE
Blackadder, Dame Elizabeth Violet, DBE
Blaize, Dame Venetia Ursula, DBE
Blaxland, Dame Helen Frances, DBE
Booth, *Hon.* Dame Margaret Myfanwy Wood, DBE
Bowtell, Dame Ann Elizabeth, DCB
Boyd, Dame Vivienne Myra, DBE
Barbour, Dame Margaret (Mrs Ash), DBE
Bracewell, *Hon.* Dame Joyanne Winifred (Mrs Copeland), DBE
Brain, Dame Margaret Anne (Mrs Wheeler), DBE
Bridges, Dame Mary Patricia, DBE
Brittan, Dame Diana (Lady Brittan of Spennithorne), DBE
Browne, Lady Moyra Blanche Madeleine, DBE
Browne-Evans, Dame Lois Marie, DBE
Buckland, Dame Yvonne Helen Elaine, DBE
Burslem, Dame Alexandra Vivien, DBE
Butler-Sloss, *Rt. Hon.* Dame (Ann) Elizabeth (Oldfield), DBE
Buttfield, Dame Nancy Eileen, DBE
Byatt, Dame Antonia Susan, DBE, FRSL
Bynoe, Dame Hilda Louisa, DBE
Caldicott, Dame Fiona, DBE, FRCP, FRCPsych.
Campbell-Preston, Dame Frances Olivia, DCVO
Cartwright, Dame Silvia Rose, DBE
Charles, Dame (Mary) Eugenia, DBE
Clark, *Prof.* Dame Jill MacLeod, DBE
Clark, *Prof.* Dame (Margaret) June, DBE, PHD
Clay, Dame Marie Mildred, DBE
Clayton, Dame Barbara Evelyn (Mrs Klyne), DBE
Collarbone, Dame Patricia, DBE
Corsar, *The Hon.* Dame Mary Drummond, DBE
Coward, Dame Pamela Sarah, DBE
Cox, Dame Laura Mary (The Hon. Mrs Justice), DBE
Cropper, Dame Hilary Mary, DBE
Davies, Dame Wendy Patricia, DBE
Davis, Dame Karlene Cecile, DBE
Daws, Dame Joyce Margaretta, DBE
Dawson, *Prof.* Dame Sandra Jane Noble, DBE
Deech, Dame Ruth Lynn, DBE
Dell, Dame Miriam Patricia, DBE
Dench, Dame Judith Olivia (Mrs Williams), DBE
Descartes, Dame Marie Selipha Sesenne, DBE, BEM
Devonshire, The Duchess of, DCVO
Digby, Lady, DBE
Docherty, Dame Jacqueline, DBE
Duffield, Dame Vivien Louise, DBE
Dumont, Dame Ivy Leona, DCMG
Dyche, Dame Rachael Mary, DBE
Elcoat, Dame Catherine Elizabeth, DBE
Ellison, Dame Jill, DBE
Else, Dame Jean, DBE
Engel, Dame Pauline Frances (Sister Pauline Engel), DBE
Esteve-Coll, Dame Elizabeth Anne Loosemore, DBE
Evans, Dame Anne Elizabeth Jane, DBE
Evans, Dame Madeline Glynne Dervel, DBE, CMG
Evison, Dame Helen June Patricia, DBE
Fenner, Dame Peggy Edith, DBE
Fielding, Dame Pauline, DBE
Fort, Dame Maeve Geraldine, DCMG, DCVO

Fraser, Dame Dorothy Rita, DBE
Friend, Dame Phyllis Muriel, DBE
Fritchie, Dame Irene Tordoff (Dame Rennie Fritchie), DBE
Frost, Dame Phyllis Irene, DBE
Fry, Dame Margaret Louise, DBE
Gallagher, Dame Monica Josephine, DBE
Gardiner, Dame Helen Louisa, DBE, MVO
Giles, *Air Comdt.* Dame Pauline (Mrs Parsons), DBE, RRC
Glen-Haig, Dame Mary Alison, DBE
Gloster, *Hon.* Dame Elisabeth (Mrs Brodie), DBE
Glover, Dame Audrey Frances, DBE, CMG
Goodall, *Dr* Dame (Valerie) Jane, DBE
Goodman, Dame Barbara, DBE
Gordon, Dame Minita Elmira, GCMG, GCVO
Gordon, *Hon.* Dame Pamela Felicity, DBE
Gow, Dame Jane Elizabeth (Mrs Whiteley), DBE
Grafton, The Duchess of, GCVO
Grant, Dame Mavis, DBE
Green, Dame Pauline, DBE
Grey, Dame Beryl Elizabeth (Mrs Svenson), DBE
Grimthorpe, The Lady, DCVO
Guilfoyle, Dame Margaret Georgina Constance, DBE
Guthardt, *Revd Dr* Dame Phyllis Myra, DBE
Hallett, *Hon.* Dame Heather Carol, DBE
Harbison, Dame Joan Irene, DBE
Harper, Dame Elizabeth Margaret Way, DBE
Harris, Lady Pauline, DBE
Hedley-Miller, Dame Mary Elizabeth, DCVO, CB
Heilbron, *Hon.* Dame Rose, DBE
Herbison, Dame Jean Marjory, DBE, CMG
Hercus, *Hon.* Dame (Margaret) Ann, DCMG
Higgins, *Prof.* Dame Julia Stretton, DBE, FRS
Higgins, *Prof.* Dame Rosalyn, DBE, QC
Hill, *Air Cdre* Dame Felicity Barbara, DBE
Hine, Dame Deirdre Joan, DBE, FRCP
Hodgson, Dame Patricia Anne, DBE
Hogg, *Hon.* Dame Mary Claire (Mrs Koops), DBE
Hollows, Dame Sharon, DBE
Hoodless, Dame Elisabeth Anne, DBE
Hufton, *Prof.* Dame Olwen, DBE
Hussey, Dame Susan Katharine (Lady Hussey of North
    Bradley), DCVO
Hutton, Dame Deirdre Mary, DBE
Imison, Dame Tamsyn, DBE
Isaacs, Dame Albertha Madeline, DBE
James, Dame Naomi Christine (Mrs Haythorne), DBE
Jenkins, Dame (Mary) Jennifer (Lady Jenkins of Hillhead),
    DBE
Johnson, *Prof.* Dame Louise Napier, DBE, FRS
Jones, Dame Gwyneth (Mrs Haberfeld-Jones), DBE
Keegan, Dame Geraldine Mary Marcella, DBE
Kekedo, Dame Rosalina Violet, DBE
Kelleher, Dame Joan, DBE
Kellett-Bowman, Dame (Mary) Elaine, DBE
Kelly, Dame Lorna May Boreland, DBE
Kershaw, Dame Janet Elizabeth Murray (Dame Betty),
    DBE
Kettlewell, *Comdt.* Dame Marion Mildred, DBE
King, Dame Thea, DBE
Kirby, Dame Georgina Kamiria, DBE
Kramer, *Prof.* Dame Leonie Judith, DBE
Laine, Dame Cleo (Clementine) Dinah (Mrs Dankworth),
    DBE
Lamb, Dame Dawn Ruth, DBE
Legge-Schwarzkopf, Dame Elisabeth Friederike Marie
    Olga, DBE
Lewis, Dame Edna Leofrida (Lady Lewis), DBE
Lott, Dame Felicity Ann Emwhyla (Mrs Woolf), DBE

Louisy, Dame (Calliopa) Pearlette, GCMG
Lympany, Dame Moura, DBE
Lynn, Dame Vera (Mrs Lewis), DBE
McDonald, Dame Mavis, DCB
Mackinnon, Dame (Una) Patricia, DBE
McLaren, Dame Anne Laura, DBE, FRCOG, FRS
Macmillan of Ovenden, Katharine, Viscountess, DBE
Mayhew, Dame Judith, DBE
Major, Dame Malvina Lorraine (Mrs Fleming), DBE
Major, Dame Norma Christina Elizabeth, DBE
Markova, Dame Alicia, DBE
Metge, *Dr* Dame (Alice) Joan, DBE
Middleton, Dame Elaine Madoline, DCMG, MBE
Mills, Dame Barbara Jean Lyon, DBE, QC
Mirren, Dame Helen, DBE
Moores, Dame Yvonne, DBE
Morgan, *Dr* Dame Gillian Margaret, DBE
Morrison, *Hon.* Dame Mary Anne, DCVO
Muirhead, Dame Lorna Elizabeth Fox, DBE
Muldoon, Lady Thea Dale, DBE, QSO
Mumford, Lady Mary Katharine, DCVO
Munro, Dame Alison, DBE
Murdoch, Dame Elisabeth Joy, DBE
Murray, Dame (Alice) Rosemary, DBE, DPHIL
Neville, Dame Elizabeth, DBE, QPM
Neville-Jones, Dame (Lilian) Pauline, DCMG
Ogilvie, Dame Bridget Margaret, DBE, PHD, DSC
Oliver, Dame Gillian Frances, DBE
Ollerenshaw, Dame Kathleen Mary, DBE, DPHIL
Oxenbury, Dame Shirley Anne, DBE
Park, Dame Merle Florence (Mrs Bloch), DBE
Paterson, Dame Betty Fraser Ross, DBE
Pauffley, *Hon.* Dame Anna Evelyn Hamilton, DBE
Penhaligon, Dame Annette (Mrs Egerton), DBE
Peters, Dame Mary Elizabeth, DBE
Platt, Dame Denise, DBE
Plowright, Dame Joan Ann, DBE
Polak, *Prof.* Dame Julia Margaret, DBE
Poole, Dame Avril Anne Barker, DBE
Porter, Dame Shirley (Lady Porter), DBE
Powell, Dame Sally Ann Vickers, DBE
Prendergast, Dame Simone Ruth, DBE
Prentice, Dame Winifred Eva, DBE
Price, Dame Margaret Berenice, DBE
Purves, Dame Daphne Helen, DBE
Quinn, Dame Sheila Margaret Imelda, DBE
Rafferty, *Hon.* Dame Anne Judith, DBE
Rawson, *Prof.* Dame Jessica Mary, DBE
Rees, *Prof.* Dame Lesley Howard, DBE
Reeves, Dame Helen May, DBE
Richardson, Dame Mary, DBE
Riddelsdell, Dame Mildred, DCB, CBE
Ridley, Dame (Mildred) Betty, DBE
Ridsdale, Dame Victoire Evelyn Patricia (Lady Ridsdale),
    DBE
Rigg, Dame Diana, DBE
Rimington, Dame Stella, DCB
Ritterman, Dame Janet, DBE
Roberts, Dame Jane Elisabeth, DBE
Robins, Dame Ruth Laura, DBE
Robottom, Dame Marlene, DBE
Roddick, Dame Anita Lucia, DBE
Roe, Dame Marion Audrey, DBE
Roe, Dame Raigh Edith, DBE
Ronson, Dame Gail, DBE
Rothschild, Hon. Dame Miriam Louisa, DBE, FRS
Rue, Dame (Elsie) Rosemary, DBE
Rumbold, *Rt. Hon.* Dame Angela Claire Rosemary, DBE

Runciman of Doxford, The Viscountess, DBE
Salas, Dame Margaret Laurence, DBE
Salmond, *Prof.* Dame Mary Anne, DBE
Saunders, Dame Cicely Mary Strode, OM, DBE, FRCP
Sawyer, *Hon.* Dame Joan Augusta, DBE
Scardino, Dame Marjorie, DBE
Scott, Dame Catherine Margaret (Mrs Denton), DBE
Seward, Dame Margaret Helen Elizabeth, DBE
Shirley, Dame Stephanie, DBE
Shovelton, Dame Helena, DBE
Sibley, Dame Antoinette (Mrs Corbett), DBE
Smieton, Dame Mary Guillan, DBE
Smith, Dame Dela, DBE
Smith, *Rt. Hon.* Dame Janet Hilary (Mrs Mathieson), DBE
Smith, Dame Margaret Natalie (Maggie) (Mrs Cross), DBE
Smith, Dame Margot, DBE
Soames, Lady Mary, DBE
Southgate, *Prof.* Dame Lesley Jill, DBE
Spark, Dame Muriel Sarah, DBE
Spencer, Dame Rosemary Jane, DCMG
Steel, *Hon.* Dame (Anne) Heather (Mrs Beattie), DBE
Strachan, Dame Valerie Patricia Marie, DCB
Strathern, *Prof.* Dame Anne Marilyn, DBE
Sutherland, Dame Joan (Mrs Bonynge), OM, DBE
Sutherland, Dame Veronica Evelyn, DBE, CMG
Symmonds, Dame Olga Patricia, DBE
Taylor, Dame Elizabeth, DBE

Taylor, Dame Meg, DBE
Te Atairangikaahu, Te Arikinui, Dame, DBE
Te Kanawa, Dame Kiri Janette, DBE
Thomas, Dame Maureen Elizabeth (Lady Thomas), DBE
Thorneycroft, Lady Carla, DBE
Tinson, Dame Sue, DBE
Tizard, Dame Catherine Anne, GCMG, GCVO, DBE
Tokiel, Dame Rosa, DBE
Trotter, Dame Janet Olive, DBE
Turner-Warwick, Dame Margaret Elizabeth Harvey, DBE,
    FRCP, FRCPED
Uprichard, Dame Mary Elizabeth, DBE
Varley, Dame Joan Fleetwood, DBE
Wagner, Dame Gillian Mary Millicent (Lady Wagner),
    DBE
Wall, Dame (Alice) Anne, (Mrs Michael Wall), DCVO
Wallis, Dame Sheila Ann, DBE
Warburton, Dame Anne Marion, DCVO, CMG
Waterhouse, Dame Rachel Elizabeth, DBE, PHD
Webb, *Prof.* Dame Patricia, DBE
Weir, Dame Gillian Constance (Mrs Phelps), DBE
Weller, Dame Rita, DBE
Weston, Dame Margaret Kate, DBE
Wheldon, Dame Juliet Louise, DCB, QC
Wilson-Barnett, *Prof.* Dame Jenifer, DBE
Winstone, Dame Dorothy Gertrude, DBE, CMG
Wong Yick-ming, Dame Rosanna, DBE

DECORATIONS AND MEDALS

PRINCIPAL DECORATIONS AND MEDALS
In order of wear

VICTORIA CROSS (VC), 1856 (*see* below)
GEORGE CROSS (GC), 1940 (*see* below)

BRITISH ORDERS OF KNIGHTHOOD (*see* Orders of Chivalry)
BARONET'S BADGE
KNIGHT BACHELOR'S BADGE

INDIAN ORDER OF MERIT (MILITARY)

DECORATIONS
Conspicuous Gallantry Cross (CGC), 1995
Royal Red Cross Class I (RRC), 1883
Distinguished Service Cross (DSC), 1914. For all ranks for actions at sea
Military Cross (MC), December 1914. For all ranks for actions on land
Distinguished Flying Cross (DFC), 1918. For all ranks for acts of gallantry when flying in active operations against the enemy
Air Force Cross (AFC), 1918. For all ranks for acts of courage when flying, although not in active operations against the enemy
Royal Red Cross Class II (ARRC)
Order of British India
Kaisar-i-Hind Medal
Order of St John

MEDALS FOR GALLANTRY AND DISTINGUISHED CONDUCT
Union of South Africa Queen's Medal for Bravery, in Gold
Distinguished Conduct Medal (DCM), 1854
Conspicuous Gallantry Medal (CGM), 1874
Conspicuous Gallantry Medal (Flying)
George Medal (GM), 1940
Queen's Police Medal for Gallantry
Queen's Fire Service Medal for Gallantry
Royal West African Frontier Force Distinguished Conduct Medal
King's African Rifles Distinguished Conduct Medal
Indian Distinguished Service Medal
Union of South Africa Queen's Medal for Bravery, in Silver
Distinguished Service Medal (DSM), 1914
Military Medal (MM), 1916
Distinguished Flying Medal (DFM), 1918
Air Force Medal (AFM)
Constabulary Medal (Ireland)
Medal for Saving Life at Sea (Sea Gallantry Medal)
Indian Order of Merit (Civil)
Indian Police Medal for Gallantry
Ceylon Police Medal for Gallantry
Sierra Leone Police Medal for Gallantry
Sierra Leone Fire Brigades Medal for Gallantry
Colonial Police Medal for Gallantry (CPM)
Queen's Gallantry Medal (QGM), 1974
Royal Victorian Medal (RVM), Gold, Silver and Bronze
British Empire Medal (BEM)

Canada Medal
Queen's Police Medal for Distinguished Service (QPM)
Queen's Fire Service Medal for Distinguished Service (QFSM)
Queen's Volunteer Reserves Medal
Queen's Medal for Chiefs

CAMPAIGN MEDALS AND STARS
Including authorised United Nations, European Community/Union and North Atlantic Treaty Organisation medals (in order of date of campaign for which awarded)

POLAR MEDALS (in order of date)

IMPERIAL SERVICE MEDAL

POLICE MEDALS FOR VALUABLE SERVICE
Indian Police Medal for Meritorious Service
Ceylon Police Medal for Merit
Sierra Leone Police Medal for Meritorious Service
Sierra Leone Fire Brigades Medal for Meritorious Service
Colonial Police Medal for Meritorious Service

BADGE OF HONOUR

JUBILEE, CORONATION AND DURBAR MEDALS
King George V, King George VI, Queen Elizabeth II and Long and Faithful Service Medals

EFFICIENCY AND LONG SERVICE DECORATIONS AND MEDALS
Medal for Meritorious Service
Accumulated Campaign Service Medal
The Medal for Long Service and Good Conduct (Military)
Naval Long Service and Good Conduct Medal
Medal for Meritorious Service (Royal Navy 1918–28)
Indian Long Service and Good Conduct Medal
Indian Meritorious Service Medal
Royal Marines Meritorious Service Medal (1849–1947)
Royal Air Force Meritorious Service Medal (1918–1928)
Royal Air Force Long Service and Good Conduct Medal
Medal for Long Service and Good Conduct (Ulster Defence Regiment)
Indian Long Service and Good Conduct Medal
Royal West African Frontier Force Long Service and Good Conduct Medal
Royal Sierra Leone Military Forces Long Service and Good Conduct Medal
King's African Rifles and Long Service and Good Conduct Medal
Indian Meritorious Service Medal
Police Long Service and Good Conduct Medal
Fire Brigade Long Service and Good Conduct Medal
African Police Medal for Meritorious Service
Royal Canadian Mounted Police Long Service Medal
Ceylon Police Long Service Medal
Ceylon Fire Services Long Service Medal
Sierra Leone Police Long Service Medal
Colonial Police Long Service Medal
Sierra Leone Fire Brigades Long Service Medal
Mauritius Police Long Service and Good Conduct Medal

*Mauritius Fire Services Long Service and Good Conduct
Medal*
*Mauritius Prisons Service Long Service and Good Conduct
Medal*
Colonial Fire Brigades Long Service Medal
Colonial Prison Service Medal
Hong Kong Disciplined Services Medal
Army Emergency Reserve Decoration (ERD)
Volunteer Officers' Decoration (VD)
Volunteer Long Service Medal
Volunteer Officers' Decoration (for India and the Colonies)
Volunteer Long Service Medal (for India and the Colonies)
Colonial Auxiliary Forces Officers' Decoration
Colonial Auxiliary Forces Long Service Medal
Medal for Good Shooting (Naval)
Militia Long Service Medal
Imperial Yeomanry Long Service Medal
Territorial Decoration (TD), 1908
Ceylon Armed Services Long Service Medal
Efficiency Decoration (ED)
Territorial Efficiency Medal
Efficiency Medal
Special Reserve Long Service and Good Conduct Medal
Decoration for Officers of the Royal Navy Reserve (RD),
1910
Decoration for Officers of the Royal Naval Volunteer Reserve
(VRD)
Royal Naval Reserve Long Service and Good Conduct Medal
*Royal Naval Volunteer Reserve Long Service and Good
Conduct Medal*
*Royal Naval Auxiliary Sick Berth Reserve Long Service and
Good Conduct Medal*
Royal Fleet Reserve Long Service and Good Conduct Medal
*Royal Naval Wireless Auxiliary Reserve Long Service and
Good Conduct Medal*
Royal Naval Auxiliary Service Medal
Air Efficiency Award (AE), 1942
Volunteer Reserves Service Medal
Ulster Defence Regiment Medal
Northern Ireland Home Service Medal
Queen's Medal (for Champion Shots of the RN and RM)
Queen's Medal (for Champion Shots of the New Zealand
Naval Forces)
Queen's Medal (for Champion Shots in the Military
Forces)
Queen's Medal (for Champion Shots of the Air Forces)
Cadet Forces Medal, 1950
Coastguard Auxiliary Service Long Service Medal
Special Constabulary Long Service Medal
Canadian Forces Decoration
Royal Observer Corps Medal
Civil Defence Long Service Medal
*Ambulance Service (Emergency Duties) Long Service and
Good Conduct Medal*
Royal Fleet Auxiliary Service Medal Rhodesia Medal
Royal Ulster Constabulary Service Medal
Northern Ireland Prison Service Medal
Union of South Africa Commemoration Medal
Indian Independence Medal
Pakistan Medal
Ceylon Armed Services Inauguration Medal
Ceylon Police Independence Medal (1948)
Sierra Leone Independence Medal
Jamaica Independence Medal
Uganda Independence Medal
Malawi Independence Medal
Fiji Independence Medal
Papua New Guinea Independence Medal

Solomon Islands Independence Medal
Service Medal of the Order of St John
Badge of the Order of the League of Mercy
Voluntary Medical Service Medal (1932)
Women's Voluntary Service Medal
South African Medal for War Services
Colonial Special Constabulary Medal

HONORARY MEMBERSHIP OF COMMONWEALTH
ORDERS

OTHER COMMONWEALTH MEMBERS' ORDERS,
DECORATIONS AND MEDALS

FOREIGN ORDERS

FOREIGN DECORATIONS

FOREIGN MEDALS

THE VICTORIA CROSS (1856)
FOR CONSPICUOUS BRAVERY

VC

Ribbon, Crimson, for all Services (until 1918 it was blue
for the Royal Navy)

Instituted on 29 January 1856, the Victoria Cross was
awarded retrospectively to 1854, the first being held by
Lt. C. D. Lucas, RN, for bravery in the Baltic Sea on 21
June 1854 (gazetted 24 February 1857). The first 62
Crosses were presented by Queen Victoria in Hyde Park,
London, on 26 June 1857.
The Victoria Cross is worn before all other decorations,
on the left breast, and consists of a cross-pattée of bronze,
one-and-a-half inches in diameter, with the Royal Crown
surmounted by a lion in the centre, and beneath there is
the inscription *For Valour*. Holders of the VC receive a
tax-free annuity of £1,300, irrespective of need or other
conditions. In 1911, the right to receive the Cross was
extended to Indian soldiers, and in 1920 to matrons,
sisters and nurses, and the staff of the Nursing Services
and other services pertaining to hospitals and nursing,
and to civilians of either sex regularly or temporarily
under the orders, direction or supervision of the naval,
military, or air forces of the Crown.

SURVIVING RECIPIENTS OF THE VICTORIA CROSS
as at August 2004

Annand, *Capt.* R. W. (Durham Light Infantry)
1940 *World War*
Bhan Bhagta Gurung, *Havildar* (2nd Gurkha Rifles)
1945 *World War*
Cruickshank, *Flt. Lt.* J. A. (RAFVR)
1944 *World War*
Fraser, *Lt.-Cdr.* I. E., DSC (RNR)
1945 *World War*
Kenna, *Pte.* E. (Australian Military Forces, 2/4th (NSW))
1945 *World War*
Lachhiman Gurung, *Havildar* (8th Gurkha Rifles)
1945 *World War*

Norton, *Capt.* G. R., MM (South African Forces, Kaffrarian Rifles)
1944 *World War*
Payne, *WO* K., DSC (USA) (Australian Army Training Team)
1969 *Vietnam*
Rambahadur Limbu, *Capt.*, MVO (10th Princess Mary's Gurkha Rifles)
1965 *Sarawak*
Smith, *Sgt.* E. A., CD (Seaforth Highlanders of Canada)
1944 *World War*
Speakman-Pitts, *Sgt.* W. (Black Watch, attached KOSB)
1951 *Korea*
Tulbahadur Pun, *Lt.* (6th Gurkha Rifles)
1944 *World War*
Umrao Singh, *Sub Major* (Royal Indian Artillery)
1944 *World War*
Watkins, *Maj. Rt. Hon.* Sir Tasker, GBE (Welch Regiment)
1944 *World War*
Wilson, *Lt.-Col.* E. C. T. (East Surrey Regiment)
1940 *World War*

THE GEORGE CROSS (1940)
FOR GALLANTRY

GC

Ribbon, Dark blue, threaded through a bar adorned with laurel leaves
Instituted 24 September 1940 (with amendments, 3 November 1942)

The George Cross is worn before all other decorations (except the VC) on the left breast (when worn by a woman it may be worn on the left shoulder from a ribbon of the same width and colour fashioned into a bow). It consists of a plain silver cross with four equal limbs, the cross having in the centre a circular medallion bearing a design showing St George and the Dragon. The inscription *For Gallantry* appears round the medallion and in the angle of each limb of the cross is the Royal cypher 'G VI' forming a circle concentric with the medallion. The reverse is plain and bears the name of the recipient and the date of the award. The cross is suspended by a ring from a bar adorned with laurel leaves on dark blue ribbon one-and-a-half inches wide.

The cross is intended primarily for civilians; awards to the fighting services are confined to actions for which purely military honours are not normally granted. It is awarded only for acts of the greatest heroism or of the most conspicuous courage in circumstances of extreme danger. From 1 April 1965, holders of the Cross have received a tax-free annuity, which is now £1,300. The cross has twice been awarded collectively rather than to an individual: to Malta (1942) and the Royal Ulster Constabulary (1999).

The royal warrant which ordained that the grant of the Empire Gallantry Medal should cease authorised holders of that medal to return it to the Central Chancery of the Orders of Knighthood and to receive in exchange the George Cross. A similar provision applied to posthumous awards of the Empire Gallantry Medal made after the outbreak of war in 1939. In October 1971 all surviving holders of the Albert Medal and the Edward Medal exchanged those decorations for the George Cross.

SURVIVING RECIPIENTS OF THE GEORGE CROSS
as at August 2004

If the recipient originally received the Empire Gallantry Medal (EGM), the Albert Medal (AM) or the Edward Medal (EM), this is indicated by the initials in parenthesis.

Archer, *Col.* B. S. T., GC, OBE, ERD, 1941
Bamford, J., GC, 1952
Beaton, J., GC, CVO, 1974
Bridge, *Lt.-Cdr.* J., GC, GM and bar, 1944
Butson, *Lt.-Col.* A. R. C., GC, CD, MD (AM), 1948
Bywater, R. A. S., GC, GM, 1944
Errington, H., GC, 1941
Farrow, K., GC (AM), 1948
Finney, Trooper C., GC, 2003
Flintoff, H. H., GC (EM), 1944
Gledhill, A. J., GC, 1967
Gregson, J. S., GC (AM), 1943
Johnson, *WO1* (*SSM*) B., GC, 1990
Kinne, D. G., GC, 1954
Lowe, A. R., GC (AM), 1949
Lynch, J., GC, BEM (AM), 1948
Pratt, M. K., GC, 1978
Purves, Mrs M., GC (AM), 1949
Raweng, Awang anak, GC, 1951
Riley, G., GC (AM), 1944
Rowlands, *Air Marshal* Sir John, GC, KBE, 1943
Stevens, H. W., GC, 1958
Styles, *Lt.-Col.* S. G., GC, 1972
Walker, C., GC, 1972
Walker, C. H., GC (AM), 1942
Walton, E. W. K., GC (AM), DSO, 1948
Wilcox, C., GC (EM), 1949
Wooding, E. A., GC (AM), 1945

CHIEFS OF CLANS IN SCOTLAND

Only chiefs of whole Names or Clans are included, except certain special instances (marked *) who, though not chiefs of a whole name, were or are for some reason (e.g. the Macdonald forfeiture) independent. Under decision (*Campbell-Gray*, 1950) a bearer of a 'double or triple-barrelled' surname cannot be held chief of a part of such.

THE ROYAL HOUSE: HM THE QUEEN

AGNEW: Sir Crispin Agnew of Lochnaw, Bt., QC, 6 Palmerston Road, Edinburgh EH9 1TN

ANSTRUTHER: Sir Ian Fife Campbell Anstruther, Bt., Barlavington, Petworth, West Sussex GU28 0LG

ARBUTHNOTT: The Viscount of Arbuthnott, KT, CBE, DSC, Arbuthnott House, Kincardineshire AB30 1PA

BANNERMAN: Sir David Bannerman of Elsick, Bt., 3 St George's Road, St Margaret's, Twickenham, TW1 1QS

BARCLAY: Peter C. Barclay of Towie Barclay and of that Ilk, 69 Oakwood Court, Abbotsbury Road, London W14 8JF

BORTHWICK: The Lord Borthwick, Crookston, Heriot, Midlothian EH38 5YS

BOYD: The Lord Kilmarnock, MBE, 194 Regent's Park Road, London NW1 8XP

BOYLE: The Earl of Glasgow, Fairlie, Ayrshire KA29 0BE

BRODIE: Alexander Brodie of Brodie, 1 rue de Regrattier, Paris 75004

BROUN OF COLSTOUN: Sir William Broun of Colstoun, Bt., 2–4 Reed Street, Cremorne, NSW 2090, Australia

BRUCE: The Earl of Elgin and Kincardine, KT, Broomhall, Dunfermline, Fife KY11 3DU

BUCHAN: David Buchan of Auchmacoy, Auchmacoy House, Ellon, Aberdeenshire

BURNETT: J. C. A. Burnett of Leys, Crathes Castle, Banchory, Kincardineshire

CAMERON: Donald Cameron of Lochiel, Achnacarry, Spean Bridge, Inverness-shire

CAMPBELL: The Duke of Argyll, Inveraray, Argyll PA32 8XF

CARMICHAEL: Richard Carmichael of Carmichael, Thankerton, Biggar, Lanarkshire

CARNEGIE: The Duke of Fife, Elsick House, Stonehaven, Kincardineshire AB3 2NT

CATHCART: The Earl Cathcart, 18 Smith Terrace, London SW3 4DL

CHARTERIS: The Earl of Wemyss and March, KT, Gosford House, East Lothian EH32 0PX

CLAN CHATTAN: K. Mackintosh of Clan Chattan, Fairburn, Felixburg, Zimbabwe

CHISHOLM: Hamish Chisholm of Chisholm *(The Chisholm)*, Elmpine, Beck Row, Bury St Edmunds, IP28 8BT

COCHRANE: The Earl of Dundonald, Lochnell Castle, Ledaig, Argyllshire

COLQUHOUN: Sir Ivar Colquhoun of Luss, Bt., Camstraddan, Luss, Dunbartonshire G83 8NX

CRANSTOUN: David Cranstoun of that Ilk, Corehouse, Lanark

CUMMING: Sir Alastair Cumming of Altyre, Bt., Altyre, Forres, Moray

DARROCH: Capt. Duncan Darroch of Gourock, The Red House, Camberley, Surrey

DAVIDSON: Alister Davidson of Davidston, 21 Winscombe Street, Takapuna, Auckland, New Zealand

DEWAR: Michael Dewar of that Ilk and Vogrie, Rectory Farm House, Charlton Musgrove, Wincanton BA9 8ET

DRUMMOND: The Earl of Perth, Stobhall, Perth PH2 6DR

DUNBAR: Sir James Dunbar of Mochrum, Bt., 211 Gardenville Drive, Yorktown, Va 23693, USA

DUNDAS: David Dundas of Dundas, 3 Crane Close, Tokai 7945, Cape Town, South Africa

DURIE: Andrew Durie of Durie, CBE, Finnich Malise, Croftamie, Stirlingshire G63 0HA

ELIOTT: Mrs Margaret Eliott of Redheugh, Redheugh, Newcastleton, Roxburghshire

ERSKINE: The Earl of Mar and Kellie, Erskine House, Kirk Wynd, Alloa, Clackmannan FK10 4JF

FARQUHARSON: Capt. A. Farquharson of Invercauld, MC, Invercauld, Braemar, Aberdeenshire AB35 5TT

FERGUSSON: Sir Charles Fergusson of Kilkerran, Bt., Kilkerran, Maybole, Ayrshire

FORBES: The Lord Forbes, KBE, Balforbes, Alford, Aberdeenshire AB33 8DR

FORSYTH: Alistair Forsyth of that Ilk, Annfield Park, PO Box 175, Boyup Brook, Western Australia 6244

FRASER: The Lady Saltoun, Aberdeenshire AB35 5YB

*FRASER (OF LOVAT): The Lord Lovat, Beaufort Lodge, Beauly, Inverness-shire IV4 7AZ

GAYRE: R. Gayre of Gayre and Nigg, Minard Castle, Minard, Inverary, Argyll PA32 8YB

GORDON: The Marquess of Huntly, Aboyne Castle, Aberdeenshire AB34 5JP

GRAHAM: The Duke of Montrose, Drymen, Stirlingshire

GRANT: The Lord Strathspey, The School House, Lochbuie, Mull, Argyllshire PA62 6AA

GRIERSON: Sir Michael Grierson of Lag, Bt., 40C Palace Road, London SW2 3NJ

GUTHRIE: Alexander Guthrie of Guthrie, 22 William Street, Shenton Park, Perth, Western Australia

HAIG: The Earl Haig, OBE, Melrose, Roxburghshire TD6 9DP

HALDANE: Martin Haldane of Gleneagles, Gleneagles, Auchterarder, Perthshire

HANNAY: David Hannay of Kirkdale and of that Ilk, Kirkdale, Carsluith, Dumfriesshire, DG8 7EA

HAY: The Earl of Erroll, Woodbury Hall, Sandy, Beds

HENDERSON: John Henderson of Fordell, 7 Owen Street, Toowoomba, Queensland, Australia

HUNTER: Pauline Hunter of Hunterston, Plover's Ridge, Lon Crecrist, Trearddur Bay, Anglesey LL65 2AZ

IRVINE OF DRUM: David Irvine of Drum, Holly Leaf Cottage, Banchory, Aberdeenshire AB31 4BR

JARDINE: Sir Alexander Jardine of Applegirth, Bt., Ash House, Thwaites, Millom, Cumbria LA18 5HY

JOHNSTONE: The Earl of Annandale and Hartfell, Raehills, Lockerbie, Dumfriesshire

KEITH: The Earl of Kintore, The Stables, Keith Hall, Inverurie, Aberdeenshire AB51 0LD

KENNEDY: The Marquess of Ailsa, Cassillis House, Ayrshire

KERR: The Marquess of Lothian, KCVO, Ferniehurst Castle, Jedburgh, Roxburghshire TN8 6NX

KINCAID: Arabella Kincaid of Kincaid, Wood Farm, Caynton, Newport, Shropshire TF10 8NF

LAMONT: Peter Lamont of that Ilk, 40 Breakfast Road, Marayong, New South Wales, Australia

LEASK: Madam Leask of Leask, c/o 53 St Nicholas Street, Thetford IP24 1BG

LENNOX: Edward Lennox of that Ilk, Tods Top Farm, Downton on the Rock, Ludlow, Shropshire

LESLIE: The Earl of Rothes, Salisbury, Wilts SP5 1LX

LINDSAY: The Earl of Crawford and Balcarres, KT, GCVO, PC, Balcarres, Colinsburgh, Fife

LIVINGSTONE OF MACLEA: Alastair Livingstone of Bachuil, Bachuil, Isle of Lismore, Argyll PA34 5UL

LOCKHART: Angus Lockhart of the Lee, Newholme, Dunsyre, Lanark

LUMSDEN: Gillem Lumsden of that Ilk and Blanerne, Stapely Howe, Hoe Benham, Newbury, Berks

MACALESTER: William St J. McAlester of Loup and Kennox, 27 Durnham Road, Christchurch BH23 7ND

MACARTHUR; John MacArthur of that Ilk, Castle Kennedy House, Castle Kennedy, Stranraer, Wigtownshire DG9 8SJ

MCBAIN: J. H. McBain of McBain, 7025 North Finger Rock Place, Tucson, Arizona 85718, USA

MACDONALD: The Lord Macdonald (The Macdonald of Macdonald), Kinloch Lodge, Sleat, Isle of Skye

*MACDONALD OF CLANRANALD: Ranald Macdonald of Clanranald, Mornish House, Killin, Perthshire FK21 8TX

*MACDONALD OF SLEAT (CLAN HUSTEAIN): Sir Ian Macdonald of Sleat, Bt., Thorpe Hall, Driffield YO25 0JE

*MACDONELL OF GLENGARRY: Ranald MacDonell of Glengarry, 74 Haverhill Road, London SW12 0HB

MACDOUGALL: Morag MacDougall of MacDougall, Dunollie Castle, Oban, Argyll, PA34 5TT

MACDOWALL: Fergus Macdowall of Garthland, 16 Rowe Road, Ottawa, Ontario K29 2ZS

MACGREGOR: Sir Malcolm MacGregor of MacGregor, Bt., Irvine House, Canonbie, Dumfriesshire DG14 0XF

MACINTYRE: Donald MacIntyre of Glenoe, 41 Temescal Terrace, San Francisco, California, USA

MACKAY: The Lord Reay, 98 Oakley Street, London SW3

MACKENZIE: The Earl of Cromartie, Castle Leod, Strathpeffer, Ross-shire IV14 9AA

MACKINNON: Anne Mackinnon of Mackinnon, 3 Anson Way, Bridgewater, Somerset TA6 3TB

MACKINTOSH: John Mackintosh of Mackintosh (The Mackintosh of Mackintosh), Moy Hall, Inverness IV13 7YQ

MACLACHLAN: Euan MacLachlan of MacLachlan, Castle Lachlan, Strathlachlan, Strachur, Argyll PA27 8BU

MACLAREN: Donald MacLaren of MacLaren and Achleskine, Achleskine, Kirkton, Lochearnhead

MACLEAN: The Hon. Sir Lachlan Maclean of Duart, Bt., CVO, Arngask House, Glenfarg, Perthshire PH2 9QA

MACLENNAN: Ruaraidh MacLennan of MacLennan, Oldmill, Dores, Inverness-shire IV2 6R

MACLEOD: John MacLeod of MacLeod, Dunvegan Castle, Isle of Skye

MACMILLAN: George MacMillan of MacMillan, Finlaystone, Langbank, Renfrewshire

MACNAB: J. C. Macnab of Macnab (The Macnab), Leuchars Castle Farmhouse, Leuchars, Fife KY16 0EY

MACNAGHTEN: Sir Patrick Macnaghten of Macnaghten and Dundarave, Bt., Dundarave, Bushmills, Co. Antrim

MACNEACAIL: John Macneacail of Macneacail and Scorrybreac, PO Box 1172, Ballina, NSW 2478, Australia

MACNEIL OF BARRA: Ian Macneil of Barra (The Macneil of Barra), 95/6 Grange Loan, Edinburgh

MACPHERSON: The Hon. Sir William Macpherson of Cluny, TD, Newton Castle, Blairgowrie, Perthshire

MACTAVISH: E. S. Dugald MacTavish of Dunardry, 3049 Vine Lane, Sebring, Florida 33870, USA

MACTHOMAS: Andrew MacThomas of Finegand, 25 Bradbourne Street, London SW6 3TF

MAITLAND: The Earl of Lauderdale, 12 St Vincent Street, Edinburgh

MAKGILL: The Viscount of Oxfuird, 28B Prince of Wales Mansions, Prince of Wales Drive, London SW11 4BQ

MALCOLM (MACCALLUM): Robin N. L. Malcolm of Poltalloch, Duntrune Castle, Lochgilphead, Argyll

MAR: The Countess of Mar, Great Witley, Worcs WR6 6JB

MARJORIBANKS: Andrew Marjoribanks of that Ilk, 10 Newark Street, Greenock

MATHESON: Maj. Sir Fergus Matheson of Matheson, Bt., Old Rectory, Hedenham, Bungay, Suffolk NR35 2LD

MENZIES: David Menzies of Menzies, RMB 1220, Collie, Western Australia 6225

MOFFAT: Madam Moffat of that Ilk, St Jasual, Bullocks Farm Lane, Wheeler End Common, High Wycombe

MONCREIFFE: The Hon. Peregrine Moncreiffe of that Ilk, Easter Moncreiffe, Bridge of Earn, Perthshire

MONTGOMERIE: The Earl of Eglinton and Winton, Balhomie, Cargill, Perth PH2 6DS

MORRISON: Dr Iain Morrison of Ruchdi, Magnolia Cottage, The Street, Walberton, Sussex

MUNRO: Hector Munro of Foulis, Foulis Castle, Evanton, Ross-shire IV16 9UX

MURRAY: The Duke of Atholl, Blair Castle, Perthshire

NESBITT (or NISBET): Mark Nesbitt of that Ilk, 114 Cambridge Road, Teddington, Middlesex TW11 8DJ

NICOLSON: The Lord Carnock, 90 Whitehall Court, London SW1A 2EL

OGILVY: The Earl of Airlie, KT, GCVO, PC, Cortachy Castle, Kirriemuir, Angus

OLIPHANT: Richard Oliphant of that Ilk, 1B Kylerhea, Breaknish, Isle of Skye IV42 8NH

RAMSAY: The Earl of Dalhousie, Brechin Castle, Angus DD7 6SH

RATTRAY: James Rattray of Rattray, Rattray, Perthshire

RIDDELL: Sir John Riddell of Riddell, CB, CVO, Hepple, Morpeth, Northumberland

ROBERTSON: Alexander Robertson of Struan (Struan-Robertson), The Breach Farm, Goudhurst Road, Kent

ROLLO: The Lord Rollo, Pitcairns, Dunning, Perthshire

ROSE: Miss Elizabeth Rose of Kilravock, Kilravock Castle, Croy, Inverness

ROSS: David Ross of that Ilk and Balnagowan, Shandwick, Perth Road, Stanley, Perthshire

RUTHVEN: The Earl of Gowrie, PC, 34 King Street, Covent Garden, London WC2

SCOTT: The Duke of Buccleuch and Queensberry, KT, VRD, Bowhill, Selkirk

SCRYMGEOUR: The Earl of Dundee, Cupar, Fife

SEMPILL: The Lord Sempill, Edinburgh, EH6 8AE

SHAW: John Shaw of Tordarroch, East Craig an Ron, 22 Academy Mead, Fortrose IV10 8TW

SINCLAIR: The Earl of Caithness, 137 Claxton Grove, London W6 8HB

SKENE: Danus Skene of Skene, Orwell House, Manse Road, Milnathort, Fife KY13 9YQ

STIRLING: Fraser Stirling of Cader, 44A Oakley Street, London SW3 5HA

STRANGE: Maj. Timothy Strange of Balcaskie, Little Holme, Porton Road, Amesbury, Wilts

SUTHERLAND: The Countess of Sutherland, House of Tongue, Brora, Sutherland

SWINTON: John Swinton of that Ilk, Alberta, Canada

TROTTER: Alexander Trotter of Mortonhall, Charterhall, Duns, Berwickshire

URQUHART: Kenneth Urquhart of Urquhart, 507 Jefferson Park Avenue, Jefferson, New Orleans, La. 70121, USA

WALLACE: Ian Wallace of that Ilk, 5 Lennox Street, Edinburgh EH4 1QB

WEDDERBURN OF THAT ILK: The Master of Dundee, Birkhill, Cupar, Fife

WEMYSS: David Wemyss of that Ilk, Invermay, Perthshire

THE PRIVY COUNCIL

The Sovereign in Council, or Privy Council, was the chief source of executive power until the system of Cabinet government developed in the 18th century. Now the Privy Council's main functions are to advise the Sovereign and to exercise its own statutory responsibilities independent of the Sovereign in Council.

Membership of the Privy Council is automatic upon appointment to certain government and judicial positions in the United Kingdom, e.g. Cabinet ministers must be Privy Counsellors and are sworn in on first assuming office. Membership is also accorded by The Queen to eminent people in the UK and independent countries of the Commonwealth of which Her Majesty is Queen, on the recommendation of the British Prime Minister. Membership of the Council is retained for life, except for very occasional removals.

The administrative functions of the Privy Council are carried out by the Privy Council Office under the direction of the President of the Council, who is always a member of the Cabinet.

President of the Council, The Rt. Hon. Baroness Amos
Clerk of the Council, A. Galloway

MEMBERS *as at August 2004*

HRH The Duke of Edinburgh, 1951
HRH The Prince of Wales, 1977

Aberdare, Lord, 1974
Ackner, Lord, 1980
Airlie, Earl of, 1984
Aldous, Sir William, 1995
Alebua, Ezekiel, 1988
Amos, Baroness, 2003
Ampthill, Lord, 1995
Ancram, Michael, 1996
Anderson, Donald, 2000
Anthony, Douglas, 1971
Arbuthnot, James, 1998
Archer of Sandwell, Lord, 1977
Arden, Dame Mary, 2000
Armstrong, Hilary, 1999
Arnold, Sir John, 1979
Arthur, *Hon.* Owen, 1995
Ashdown of Norton-sub-Hamdon, Lord, 1989
Ashley of Stoke, Lord, 1979
Atkins, Sir Robert, 1995
Auld, Sir Robin, 1995
Baker, Sir Thomas, 2002
Baker of Dorking, Lord, 1984

Barber, Lord, 1963
Barnett, Lord, 1975
Barron, Kevin, 2001
Battle, John, 2002
Beckett, Margaret, 1993
Beith, Alan, 1992
Beldam, Sir Roy, 1989
Belstead, Lord, 1983 (also known as Lord Ganzoni)
Benn, Anthony, 1964
Benn, Hilary, 2003
Biffen, Lord, 1979
Bingham of Cornhill, Lord, 1986
Birch, William, 1992
Bisson, Sir Gordon, 1987
Blackstone, Baroness, 2001
Blair, Tony, 1994
Blaker, Lord, 1983
Blanchard, Peter, 1998
Blatch, Baroness, 1993
Blunkett, David, 1997
Boateng, Paul, 1999
Bolger, James, 1991
Booth, Albert, 1976
Boothroyd, Baroness, 1992
Boscawen, *Hon.* Robert, 1992
Bottomley, Virginia, 1992
Boyd, Colin, 2000
Boyson, Sir Rhodes, 1987
Bradley, Keith, 2001
Brathwaite, Sir Nicholas, 1991
Bridge of Harwich, Lord, 1975
Brightman, Lord, 1979
Brittan of Spennithorne, Lord, 1981
Brook, Sir Henry, 1996
Brooke of Sutton Mandeville, Lord, 1988
Brown, Gordon, 1996
Brown, Nicholas, 1997
Brown, Sir Stephen, 1983
Brown of Eaton-under-Heywood, Lord, 1992
Browne-Wilkinson, Lord, 1983
Butler, Sir Adam, 1984
Butler of Brockwell, Lord, 2004
Butler-Sloss, Dame Elizabeth, 1988
Buxton, Sir Richard, 1997
Byers, Stephen, 1998
Caborn, Richard, 1999
Caithness, Earl of, 1990
Callaghan of Cardiff, Lord, 1964
Cameron of Lochbroom, Lord, 1984
Camoys, Lord, 1997
Campbell of Croy, Lord, 1970
Campbell, Sir Walter Menzies, 1999
Campbell, Sir William, 1999
Canterbury, The Archbishop of, 2002
Carey of Clifton, Lord, 1991
Carlisle of Bucklow, Lord, 1979
Carnwath, Sir Robert, 2002
Carr of Hadley, Lord, 1963
Carrington, Lord, 1959 (also known as Lord Carrington of Upton)
Carswell, Lord, 1993
Carter, Lord, 1997
Casey, Sir Maurice, 1986
Chadwick, Sir John, 1997

Chalfont, Lord, 1964
Chalker of Wallasey, Baroness, 1987
Chan, Sir Julius, 1981
Chataway, Sir Christopher, 1970
Chilcot, Sir John, 2004
Christie, Perry, 2004
Clark of Windermere, Lord, 1997
Clark, Helen, 1990
Clark of Kempston, Lord, 1990
Clarke, Sir Anthony, 1998
Clarke, Charles, 2001
Clarke, Kenneth, 1984
Clarke, Thomas, 1997
Clinton-Davis, Lord, 1998
Clyde, Lord, 1996
Cockfield, Lord, 1982
Colman, Fraser, 1986
Compton, Sir John, 1983
Cook, Robin, 1996
Cooke of Thorndon, Lord, 1977
Cope of Berkeley, Lord, 1988
Corfield, Sir Frederick, 1970
Corston, Jean, 2003
Cosgrove, Lady, 2003
Coulsfield, Lord, 2000
Cowen, Sir Zelman, 1981
Cradock, Sir Percy, 1993
Crawford and Balcarres, Earl of, 1972
Creech, *Hon.* Wyatt, 1999
Crickhowell, Lord, 1979
Croom-Johnson, Sir David, 1984
Cullen, *Hon.* Lord, 1997
Cunningham, Jack, 1993
Curry, David, 1996
Darling, Alistair, 1997
Davies, Denzil, 1978
Davies, Ronald, 1997
Davis, David, 1997
Davis, Terence, 1999
Davison, Sir Ronald, 1978
Dean of Harptree, Lord, 1991
Dean of Thornton-le-Fylde, Baroness, 1998
Deedes, Lord, 1962
Denham, John, 2000
Denham, Lord, 1981
Dixon, Lord, 1996
Dobson, Frank, 1997
Donaldson of Lymington, Lord, 1979
Dorrell, Stephen, 1994
du Cann, Sir Edward, 1964
Duncan Smith, Iain, 2001
Dunn, Sir Robin, 1980
Dyson, Sir John, 2001
East, Paul, 1998
Eden of Winton, Lord, 1972
Eggar, Timothy, 1995
Eichelaum, Sir Thomas, 1989
Elias, *Hon.* Dame, Sian, 1999
Emery, Sir Peter, 1993
Esquivel, Manuel, 1986
Evans, Sir Anthony, 1992
Eveleigh, Sir Edward, 1977
Falconer of Thoroton, Lord, 2003
Farquharson, Sir Donald, 1989
Fellowes, Lord, 1990
Ferrers, Earl, 1982

Palliser, Sir Michael, 1983
Palmer, Sir Geoffrey, 1986
Parker, Sir Jonathan, 2000
Parker, Sir Roger, 1983
Parkinson, Lord, 1981
Patten, Christopher, 1989
Patten, Lord, 1990
Patterson, Percival, 1993
Pattie, Sir Geoffrey, 1987
Pendry, Lord, 2000
Penrose, Lord, 2000
Peters, Winston, 1998
Peyton of Yeovil, Lord, 1970
Phillips of Worth Matravers, Lord, 1995
Pill, Sir Malcolm, 1995
Pindling, Sir Lynden, 1976
Portillo, Michael, 1992
Potter, Sir Mark, 1996
Prescott, John, 1994
Price, George, 1982
Primarolo, Dawn, 2002
Prior, Lord, 1970
Prosser, Lord, 2000
Puapua, Sir Tomasi, 1982
Pym, Lord, 1970
Quin, Ms Joyce, 1998
Radice, Lord, 1999
Raison, Sir Timothy, 1982
Ramsden, James, 1963
Rawlinson of Ewell, Lord, 1964
Raynsford, Nick, 2001
Redwood, John, 1993
Rees, Lord, 1983
Reid, John, 1998
Renton, Lord, 1962
Renton of Mount Harry, Lord, 1989
Richard, Lord, 1993
Richardson, Sir Ivor, 1978
Richardson of Duntisbourne, Lord, 1976
Rix, Sir Bernard, 2000
Roberts of Conwy, Lord, 1991
Robertson of Port Ellen, Lord, 1997
Roch, Sir John, 1993
Rodger of Earlsferry, Lord, 1992
Rodgers of Quarry Bank, Lord, 1975
Rooker, Lord, 1999
Rose, Sir Christopher, 1992

Ross, *Hon.* Lord, 1985
Rumbold, Dame Angela, 1991
Ryder of Wensum, Lord, 1990
Sainsbury, Sir Timothy, 1992
St John of Fawsley, Lord, 1979
Salisbury, Marquess of, 1994
Sandiford, Erskine, 1989
Saville of Newdigate, Lord, 1994
Scarman, Lord, 1973
Schiemann, Sir Konrad, 1995
Scotland of Asthal, Baroness, 2001
Scott, Sir Nicholas, 1989
Scott of Foscote, Lord, 1991
Seaga, Edward, 1981
Sedley, Sir Stephen, 1999
Selkirk of Douglas, Lord, 1996
Shearer, Hugh, 1969
Sheldon, Lord, 1977
Shephard, Gillian, 1992
Shipley, Jennifer, 1998
Short, Clare, 1997
Simmonds, Kennedy, 1984
Simon of Glaisdale, Lord, 1961
Sinclair, Ian, 1977
Slade, Sir Christopher, 1982
Slynn of Hadley, Lord, 1992
Smith, Andrew, 1997
Smith, Christopher, 1997
Smith, Dame Janet, 2002
Smith, Jacqueline, 2003
Somare, Sir Michael, 1977
Spellar, John, 2001
Stanley, Sir John, 1984
Staughton, Sir Christopher, 1988
Steel of Aikwood, Lord, 1977
Stephen, Sir Ninian, 1979
Stewartby, Lord, 1989
Steyn, Lord, 1992
Strang, Gavin, 1997
Strathclyde, Lord, 1995
Straw, Jack, 1997
Stuart-Smith, Sir Murray, 1988
Sutherland, Lord, 2000
Symons of Vernham Dean, Baroness, 2001
Talboys, Sir Brian, 1977
Taylor, Ann, 1997
Tebbit, Lord, 1981
Templeman, Lord, 1978

Thatcher, Baroness, 1970
Thomas, Edmund, 1996
Thomas of Gwydir, Lord, 1964
Thomas, Sir Roger, 2003
Thomas, Sir Swinton, 1994
Thomson of Monifieth, Lord, 1966
Thorpe, Jeremy, 1967
Thorpe, Sir Matthew, 1995
Tipping, Andrew, 1998
Tizard, Robert, 1986
Trefgarne, Lord, 1989
Trimble, David, 1997
Trumpington, Baroness, 1992
Tuckey, Sir Simon, 1998
Ullswater, Viscount, 1994
Upton, Simon, 1999
Varley, Lord, 1974
Waddington, Lord, 1987
Waite, Sir John, 1993
Wakeham, Lord, 1983
Waldegrave of North Hill, Lord, 1990
Walker of Gestingthorpe, Lord, 1997
Walker of Worcester, Lord, 1970
Wall, Lord, 2004
Wallace, James, 2000
Waller, Sir Mark, 1996
Ward, Sir Alan, 1995
Watkins, Sir Tasker, 1980
Weatherill, Lord, 1980
Wheeler, Sir John, 1993
Widdecombe, Ann, 1997
Wigley, Dafydd, 1997
Williams, Alan, 1977
Williams of Crosby, Baroness, 1974
Wilson, Brian, 2003
Windlesham, Lord, 1973 (also known as Lord Hennessy)
Winti, Paias, 1987
Withers, Reginald, 1977
Woodhouse, Sir Owen, 1974
Woolf, Lord, 1986
Wylie, *Hon.* Lord, 1970
York, The Archbishop of, 1991
Young, Sir George, 1993
Young of Graffham, Lord, 1984
Zacca, Edward, 1992

THE PRIVY COUNCIL OF NORTHERN IRELAND

The Privy Council of Northern Ireland had responsibilities in Northern Ireland similar to those of the Privy Council in Great Britain until the Northern Ireland Act 1974 instituted direct rule and a UK Cabinet minister became responsible for the functions previously exercised by the Northern Ireland government.

Membership of the Privy Council of Northern Ireland is retained for life. Since the Northern Ireland Constitution Act 1973 no further appointments have been made. The postnominal initials PC (NI) are used to differentiate its members from those of the Privy Council.

MEMBERS *as at August 2004*

Bailie, Robin, 1971
Bleakley, David, 1971
Craig, William, 1963
Dobson, John, 1969
Kelly, Sir Basil, 1969
Kilclooney, Lord, 1970
Kirk, Herbert, 1962
Long, William, 1966
McIvor, Basil, 1971
Porter, Sir Robert, 1969

PARLIAMENT

The United Kingdom constitution is not contained in any single document but has evolved over time, formed partly by statute, partly by common law and partly by convention. A constitutional monarchy, the United Kingdom is governed by Ministers of the Crown in the name of the Sovereign, who is head both of the state and of the government.

The organs of government are the legislature (Parliament), the executive and the judiciary. The executive consists of HM Government (Cabinet and other Ministers), government departments, local authorities (see Local Government, Government Departments and Public Offices). The judiciary (see Law Courts and Offices) pronounces on the law, both written and unwritten, interprets statutes and is responsible for the enforcement of the law; the judiciary is independent of both the legislature and the executive.

THE MONARCHY

The Sovereign personifies the state and is, in law, an integral part of the legislature, head of the executive, head of the judiciary, commander-in-chief of all armed forces of the Crown and 'Supreme Governor' of the Church of England. The seat of the monarchy is in the United Kingdom. In the Channel Islands and the Isle of Man, which are Crown dependencies, the Sovereign is represented by a Lieutenant-Governor. In the member states of the Commonwealth of which the Sovereign is head of state, her representative is a Governor-General; in UK dependencies the Sovereign is usually represented by a Governor, who is responsible to the British Government.

Although in practice the powers of the monarchy are now very limited, restricted mainly to the advisory and ceremonial, there are important acts of government which require the participation of the Sovereign. These include summoning, proroguing and dissolving Parliament, giving royal assent to bills passed by Parliament, appointing important office-holders, e.g. government ministers, judges, bishops and governors, conferring peerages, knighthoods and other honours, and granting pardon to a person wrongly convicted of a crime. The Sovereign appoints the Prime Minister; by convention this office is held by the leader of the political party which enjoys, or can secure, a majority of votes in the House of Commons. In international affairs the Sovereign as head of state has the power to declare war and make peace, to recognise foreign states and governments, to conclude treaties and to annex or cede territory. However, as the Sovereign entrusts executive power to Ministers of the Crown and acts on the advice of her Ministers, which she cannot ignore, royal prerogative powers are in practice exercised by Ministers, who are responsible to Parliament.

Ministerial responsibility does not diminish the Sovereign's importance to the smooth working of government. She holds meetings of the Privy Council (see below), gives audiences to her Ministers and other officials at home and overseas, receives accounts of Cabinet decisions, reads dispatches and signs state papers; she must be informed and consulted on every aspect of national life; and she must show complete impartiality.

COUNSELLORS OF STATE

In the event of the Sovereign's absence abroad, it is necessary to appoint Counsellors of State under letters patent to carry out the chief functions of the Monarch, including the holding of Privy Councils and giving royal assent to acts passed by Parliament. The normal procedure is to appoint as Counsellors three or four members of the royal family among those remaining in the UK.

In the event of the Sovereign on accession being under the age of 18 years, or at any time unavailable incapacitated by infirmity of mind or body for the performance of the royal functions, provision is made for a regency.

THE PRIVY COUNCIL

The Sovereign in Council, or Privy Council, was the chief source of executive power until the system of Cabinet government developed. Its main function is to advise the Sovereign to approve Orders in Council and to advise on the issue of royal proclamations. The Council's own statutory responsibilities (independent of the powers of the Sovereign in Council) include powers of supervision over the registering bodies for the medical and allied professions. A full Council is summoned only on the death of the Sovereign or when the Sovereign announces his or her intention to marry. (For a full list of Privy Counsellors, see The Privy Council section.)

There are a number of advisory Privy Council committees, whose meetings the Sovereign does not attend. Some are prerogative committees, such as those dealing with legislative matters submitted by the legislatures of the Channel Islands and the Isle of Man or with applications for charters of incorporation; and some are provided for by statute, e.g. those for the universities of Oxford and Cambridge and the Scottish universities.

The Judicial Committee of the Privy Council is the court of final appeal from courts of the UK dependencies, courts of independent Commonwealth countries which have retained the right of appeal and courts of the Channel Islands and the Isle of Man.

It also has certain jurisdiction within the United Kingdom, the most important of which is that it is the court of final appeal for 'devolution issues,' i.e. issues as to the legal competences and functions of the legislative and executive authorities established in Scotland, Wales and Northern Ireland by the devolution legislation of 1998.

The Committee is composed of Privy Counsellors who hold, or have held, high judicial office, although usually only three or five hear each case.

Administrative work is carried out by the Privy Council Office under the direction of the Lord President of the Council, a Cabinet Minister.

PARLIAMENT

Parliament is the supreme law-making authority and can legislate for the UK as a whole or for any parts of it separately (the Channel Islands and the Isle of Man are Crown dependencies and not part of the UK). The main functions of Parliament are to pass laws, to provide (by voting taxation) the means of carrying on the work of government and to scrutinise government policy and administration, particularly proposals for expenditure. International treaties and agreements are by custom presented to Parliament before ratification.

Parliament emerged during the late 13th and early 14th centuries. The officers of the King's household and the King's judges were the nucleus of early Parliaments, joined by such ecclesiastical and lay magnates as the King might summon to form a prototype 'House of Lords', and occasionally by the knights of the shires, burgesses and proctors of the lower clergy. By the end of Edward III's reign a 'House of Commons' was beginning to appear; the first known Speaker was elected in 1377.

Parliamentary procedure is based on custom and precedent, partly formulated in the Standing Orders of both Houses of Parliament, and each House has the right to control its own internal proceedings and to commit for contempt. The system of debate in the two Houses is similar; when a motion has been moved, the Speaker proposes the question as the subject of a debate. Members speak from wherever they have been sitting. Questions are decided by a vote on a simple majority. Draft legislation is introduced, in either House, as a bill. Bills can be introduced by a Government Minister or a private Member, but in practice the majority of bills which become law are introduced by the Government. To become law, a bill must be passed by each House (for parliamentary stages, see Bill, page 130) and then sent to the Sovereign for the royal assent, after which it becomes an Act of Parliament.

Proceedings of both Houses are public, except on extremely rare occasions. The minutes (called *Votes and Proceedings in the Commons*, and *Minutes of Proceedings in the Lords*) and the speeches (*The Official Report of Parliamentary Debates*, Hansard) are published daily. Proceedings are also recorded for transmission on radio and television and stored in the Parliamentary Recording Unit before transfer to the National Sound Archive. Television cameras have been allowed into the House of Lords since 1985 and into the House of Commons since 1989; committee meetings may also be televised.

By the Parliament Act of 1911, the maximum duration of a Parliament is five years (if not previously dissolved), the term being reckoned from the date given on the writs for the new Parliament. The maximum life has been prolonged by legislation in such rare circumstances as the two world wars (31 January 1911 to 25 November 1918; 26 November 1935 to 15 June 1945). Dissolution and writs for a general election are ordered by the Sovereign on the advice of the Prime Minister. The life of a Parliament is divided into sessions, usually of one year in length, beginning and ending most often in October or November.

DEVOLUTION

The Scottish Parliament has legislative power over all devolved matters, i.e. matters not reserved to Westminster or otherwise outside its powers. The National Assembly for Wales has power to make secondary legislation in the areas where executive functions have been transferred to it. The Northern Ireland Assembly has legislative authority in the fields previously administered by the Northern Ireland departments. The Assembly was suspended in October 2002 and dissolved in April 2003. For further information, *see* the Regional Government section.

THE HOUSE OF LORDS
London SW1A 0PW
T 020-7219 3000 Information Office 020-7219 3107
E hlinfo@parliament.uk
W www.parliament.uk

The House of Lords is the second chamber, or 'Upper House' of the UK's bi-cameral parliament. Until the beginning of the twentieth century, the House of Lords had considerable power, being able to veto any bill submitted to it by the House of Commons. Today the main functions of the House of Lords are to revise legislation, to act as a check on the Government, to provide a forum of independent expertise and to act as a final court of appeal.

The House of Lords has a number of Select Committees. Some relate to the internal affairs of the House – such as its management and administration – while others carry out important investigative work on matters of public interest. There are four main areas of work – Europe, Science, the Economy and the Constitution. House of Lords investigative committees look at broader issues and do not mirror Government Departments as do Select Committees in the Commons.

The House of Lords has judicial powers as the ultimate court of appeal for courts in Great Britain and Northern Ireland, except for criminal cases in Scotland. These powers are exercised by the Lords of Appeal in Ordinary (the Law Lords) (*see* Law Courts and Officers section). On 12 June 2003 the Government announced reforms affecting the role of the Lord Chancellor as a judge and Speaker of the House of Lords and establishing a separate Supreme Court (*see* Government Departments section).

Members of the House of Lords comprise life peers created under the Life Peerages Act 1958, 92 hereditary peers under the House of Lords Act 1999 and Lords of Appeal in Ordinary, i.e. Law Lords, under the Appellate Jurisdiction Act 1876. The Archbishops of Canterbury and York, the Bishops of London, Durham and Winchester, and the 21 senior diocesan bishops of the Church of England are also members.

The House of Lords Act provides for 90 elected hereditary peers to remain in the House of Lords until longer-term reform of the House has been carried out. Elections for each of the party groups and crossbenches were held in October and November 1999; 42 Conservative, 28 crossbench, three Liberal Democrat and two Labour. Fifteen office holders were elected by the Whole House. Two Hereditary Peers, the Earl Marshal and the Lord Great Chamberlain are also members.

Peers are disqualified from sitting in the House if they are:
- aliens, i.e. any peer who is not a British citizen, a Commonwealth citizen (under the British Nationality Act 1981) or a citizen of the Republic of Ireland
- under the age of 21
- undischarged bankrupts or, in Scotland, those whose estate is sequestered
- convicted of treason

Bishops retire at the age of 70 and cease to be members of the house at that time.

Peers who do not wish to attend sittings of the House of Lords may apply for Leave of Absence for the duration of a Parliament.

Members of the House of Lords are unpaid but are entitled to allowances for attendance at sittings of the House. The daily maxima are £128.00 for overnight subsistence, £64.00 for day subsistence and incidental travel, and £53.50 for secretarial costs (as at August 2004).

COMPOSITION *as at 1 August 2004*

Archbishops and Bishops, 26
Life peers under the Appellate Jurisdiction Act 1876, 29 (1 woman)
Life peers under the Life Peerages Act 1958, 567 (120 women)
Peers under the House of Lords Act 1999, 92 (4 women)
Total 714

STATE OF THE PARTIES *as at 1 August 2004**

Conservative, 206
Labour, 191
Liberal Democrats, 66
Crossbench, 179
Archbishops and Bishops, 26
Other, 35**
Total: 703
* Excluding 11 peers on leave of absence from the House
** Includes 24 newly created Life Peers who had not been introduced as at 1 July 2004

OFFICERS

The House is presided over by the Lord Chancellor, who is *ex officio* Speaker of the House. (On 12 June 2003 the Government announced proposals to end the role of the Lord Chancellor as a judge and Speaker of the House of Lords, *see* description of Lord Chancellor's role below and Government Departments section).

A panel of deputy Speakers is appointed by Royal Commission. The first deputy Speaker is the Chairman of Committees, appointed at the beginning of each session, who is a salaried officer of the House. He takes the chair when the whole House is in Committee and in some select committees. He is assisted by a panel of deputy chairmen, headed by the salaried Principal Deputy Chairman of Committees, who is also chairman of the European Communities Committee of the House.

The Clerk of the Parliaments is the Accounting Officer and the chief permanent official responsible for the administration of the House. The Gentleman Usher of the Black Rod is responsible for security and other services and also has royal duties as secretary to the Lord Great Chamberlain.

Secretary of State for Constitutional Affairs and Lord Chancellor (The Lord Chancellor's salary is paid by the Department for Constitutional Affairs and no salary is claimed as Lord Chancellor or Speaker of the House of Lords), The Rt. Hon. Lord Falconer of Thoroton, QC
Private Secretary, Mrs S. Albon
Chairman of Committees (£77,220), The Lord Brabazon of Tara
Principal Deputy Chairman of Committees (£72,243), The Lord Grenfell

HOUSE OF LORDS MANAGEMENT BOARD
Staff are placed in the following pay bands according to their level of responsibility and taking account of other factors such as experience and marketability.

Judicial Group 4	£150,878
Senior Band 3	£90,867–£129,352
Senior Band 2	£73,762–£119,303
Senior Band 1A	£62,004–£100,061
Senior Band 1	£53,541–£89,156
Band A1	£45,911–£65,533
Band A2	£37,861–£54,219

Clerk of the Parliaments (Judicial Group 4), P. D. G. Hayter, LVO
Clerk Assistant (Senior Band 3), M. G. Pownall
Reading Clerk and Clerk of the Journals (Senior Band 2), D. R. Beamish
Clerk of the Committees and Clerk of the Overseas Office (Senior Band 2), Dr R. H. Walters
Principal Finance Officer (Senior Band 1A), E. C. Ollard
Head of Human Resources (Senior Band 1A), Dr F. P. Tudor
Clerk of the Judicial Office and Registrar of Lords Interests (Senior Band 1A), B. P. Keith
Librarian (Senior Band 1A), D. L. Jones
Clerk of Public and Private Bill Office and Examiner of Petitions for Private Bills in the House of Lords (Senior Band 1), T. V. Mohan
Editor of the Official Report (Senior Band 1), Miss J. A. Bradshaw
Clerk of the Records (Senior Band 1), S. K. Ellison
Financial Adviser (Senior Band 1), M. J. Barram
Accountant (Senior Band 1), A. D. Underwood
Director of Public Information (Band A1), Miss M. L. Morgan
Counsel to the Chairman of Committees (Senior Band 2), D. W. Saunders, CB; A. Roberts
Second Counsel to the Chairman of Committees (Senior Band 2), Dr C. S. Kerse, CB
Legal Adviser to the Human Rights Committee (Senior Band 2), M. Hunt
Clerk of the Procedure Committee (Senior Band 1), M. E. Ollard
Clerks of Select Committees (Senior Band 1), S. P. Burton; J. A. Vaughan

DEPARTMENT OF THE GENTLEMAN USHER OF THE BLACK ROD
Gentleman Usher of the Black Rod and Serjeant-at-Arms (Senior Band 2), Lt.-Gen. Sir Michael Willcocks, KCB
Yeoman Usher of the Black Rod and Deputy Serjeant-at-Arms (Band A2), Brig. H. D. C. Duncan, MBE

SELECT COMMITTEES
The main House of Lords select committees, as at June 2004, are as follows:
European Union – Chair, The Lord Grenfell; *Clerk*, S. Burton
European Union – Sub-committees:
  A *(Economic and Financial Affairs and International Trade)* – Chair, The Lord Radice; *Clerk*, J. Brooke
  B *(Internal Market)* – Chair, The Lord Woolmer of Leeds; *Clerk*, P. Wogan
  C *(Foreign Affairs, Defence and Development Policy)* – Chair, The Lord Bowness; *Clerk*, A. Nelson
  D *(Agriculture and the Environment)* – Chair, The Lord Renton of Mount Harry; *Clerk*, N. Besly

E *(Law and Institutions)* – *Chair*, The Lord Scott of
Foscote; *Clerk*, S. Todd
F *(Home Affairs)* – *Chair*, The Baroness Harris of
Richmond; *Clerk*, T. Rawsthorne
G *(Social and Consumer Affairs)* – *Chair*, The Lord
Williamson of Horton; *Clerk*, G. Baker
Constitution Committee – *Chair*, The Lord Norton of
Louth; *Clerk*, I. Mackley
Delegated Powers and Regulatory Reform – *Chair*, The Lord
Dahrendorf; *Clerk*, C. Salmon
Economic Affairs – *Chair*, The Lord Peston; *Clerk*, R.
Graham-Harrison
Science and Technology – *Chair*, The Lord Oxburgh,
FRCOG; *Clerk*, Dr C. S. Johnson
I – *Chair*, The Lord Mitchell; *Clerk*, M. Collon
II – *Chair*, The Lord Oxburgh; *Clerk*, Dr C. S. Johnson
Human Rights Joint Committee – *Chair*, Jean Corston, MP;
Lords Clerk, N. Besly
House of Lords Reform Joint Committee – *Chair*, Dr Jack
Cunningham, MP; *Lords Clerk*, D. Beamish

THE HOUSE OF COMMONS
London SW1A 0AA
T 020-7219 3000
Information Office 020-7219 4272
Forthcoming business 020-7219 5532
E hcinfo@parliament.uk
W www.parliament.uk

The members of the House of Commons are elected by
universal adult suffrage. For electoral purposes, the United
Kingdom is divided into constituencies, each of which
returns one member to the House of Commons, the
member being the candidate who obtains the largest
number of votes cast in the constituency. To ensure
equitable representation, the four Boundary Commissions
keep constituency boundaries under review and
recommend any redistribution of seats which may seem
necessary because of population movements, etc. The
number of seats was raised to 640 in 1945, reduced to
625 in 1948, and subsequently rose to 630 in 1955, 635
in 1970, 650 in 1983, 651 in 1992 and 659 in 1997. Of
the present 659 seats, there are 529 for England, 40 for
Wales, 72 for Scotland and 18 for Northern Ireland. The
number of Scottish MPs at Westminster is likely to be cut
by approximately 12 by 2007.

An electoral reform commission headed by Lord
Jenkins of Hillhead proposed in October 1998 that the
'first-past-the-post' system of electing members of the
House of Commons should be replaced by an alternative
vote top-up system, under which 80–85 per cent of MPs
would be elected by an alternative vote method and the
remaining 15–20 per cent by an open-list system of
proportional representation.

ELECTIONS
Elections are by secret ballot, each elector casting one
vote; voting is not compulsory. For entitlement to vote in
parliamentary elections, *see* Legal Notes section. When a
seat becomes vacant between general elections, a by-
election is held.

British subjects and citizens of the Irish Republic can
stand for election as Members of Parliament (MPs)
provided they are 21 or over and not subject to
disqualification. Those disqualified from sitting in the
House include:
– undischarged bankrupts
– people sentenced to more than one year's imprisonment

– members of the House of Lords (but hereditary peers
not sitting in the Lords are eligible)
– holders of certain offices listed in the House of
Commons Disqualification Act 1975, e.g. members of
the judiciary, civil service, regular armed forces, police
forces, some local government officers and some
members of public corporations and government
commissions.

A candidate does not require any party backing but his or
her nomination for election must be supported by the
signatures of ten people registered in the constituency. A
candidate must also deposit with the returning officer
£500, which is forfeit if the candidate does not receive
more than 5 per cent of the votes cast. All election
expenses at a general election, except the candidate's
personal expenses, are subject to a statutory limit of
£5,483, plus 4.6 pence for each elector in a borough
constituency or 6.2 pence for each elector in a county
constituency. These figures are due to be updated before
the next General Election.

See pages 137–181 for an alphabetical list of MPs,
results of the last general election and results of by-
elections since the general election.

STATE OF THE PARTIES *as at 1 August 2004*
Conservative, 163 (14 women)
Labour, 407 (94 women)
Liberal Democrats, 55 (6 women)
Plaid Cymru, 4
Scottish National Party, 5 (1 woman)
Sinn Fein (have not taken their seats), 4 (1 woman)
Social Democratic Labour, 3
Democratic Unionist Party, 6 (1 woman)
Ulster Unionist, 5 (1 woman)
Independent, 3
The Speaker and three Deputy Speakers, 4 (1 woman)
Total, 659 (119 women)

BUSINESS
The week's business of the House is outlined each
Thursday by the Leader of the House, after consultation
between the Chief Government Whip and the Chief
Opposition Whip. A quarter to a third of the time will be
taken up by the Government's legislative programme and
the rest by other business. As a rule, bills likely to raise
political controversy are introduced in the Commons
before going on to the Lords, and the Commons claims
exclusive control in respect of national taxation and
expenditure. Bills such as the Finance Bill, which
imposes taxation, and the Consolidated Fund Bills,
which authorise expenditure, must begin in the
Commons. A bill of which the financial provisions are
subsidiary may begin in the Lords; and the Commons
may waive its rights in regard to Lords' amendments
affecting finance.

The Commons has a public register of MPs' financial
and certain other interests; this is published annually as a
House of Commons paper. Members must also disclose
any relevant financial interest or benefit in a matter before
the House when taking part in a debate, in certain other
proceedings of the House, or in consultations with other
MPs, with Ministers or with civil servants.

MEMBERS' PAY AND ALLOWANCES
Since 1911 members of the House of Commons have
received salary payments; facilities for free travel were
introduced in 1924. Annual salary rates since 1911 are as
follows:

1911	£400	1985 Jan	£16,904
1931	360	1986 Jan	17,702
1934	380	1987 Jan	18,500
1935	400	1988 Jan	22,548
1937	600	1989 Jan	24,107
1946	1,000	1990 Jan	26,701
1954	1,250	1991 Jan	28,970
1957	1,750	1992 Jan	30,854
1964	3,250	1994 Jan	31,687
1972 Jan	4,500	1995 Jan	33,189
1975 June	5,750	1996 Jan	34,085
1976 June	6,062	1996 July	43,000
1977 July	6,270	1997 April	43,860
1978 June	6,897	1998 April	45,066
1979 June	9,450	1999 April	47,008
1980 June	11,750	2000 April	48,371
1981 June	13,950	2001 April	49,822
1982 June	14,510	2002 April	55,118
1983 June	15,308	2003 April	56,358
1984 Jan	16,106	2004 April	57,485

In 1969 MPs were granted an allowance for secretarial and research expenses, revised in July 2001. From April 2004 Members receive an Incidental Expenses Provision (£19,325) and a staffing allowance (between £66,458 and £77,534).

Since 1972 MPs have been able to claim reimbursement for the additional cost of staying overnight away from their main residence while on parliamentary business; this is known as the Additional Costs Allowance and from April 2004 is £20,902 a year.

Members of staff who are paid out of the allowances can benefit from a sum not exceeding 10 per cent of their gross salary which is paid into the Portcullis Pension Plan. This sum comes from a central budget.

MEMBERS' PENSIONS

Pension arrangements for MPs were first introduced in 1964. The arrangements currently provide a pension of one-fiftieth of salary for each year of pensionable service with a maximum of two-thirds of salary at age 65. Pension is payable normally at age 65, for men and women, or on later retirement. Pensions may be paid earlier, e.g. on retirement due to ill health or at age 60 after 20 years' service. The widow/widower of a former MP receives a pension of five-eighths of the late MP's pension. Pensions are index-linked. Members currently contribute six or nine per cent of salary to the pension fund; there is an Exchequer contribution, currently 24 per cent of an MPs salary.

The House of Commons Members' Fund provides for annual or lump sum grants to ex-MPs, their widows or widowers, and children whose incomes are below certain limits or who are experiencing severe hardship. Members contribute £24 a year and the Exchequer £215,000 a year to the fund.

HOUSE OF COMMONS PAY BANDS

Staff are placed in the following Senior Civil Service pay bands. These pay bands apply to the most senior staff in departments and agencies.

Pay Band 1	£53,451–£112,248
Pay Band 2	£73,762–£155,008
Pay Band 3	£90,867–£192,424
* 2003 Pay Bands	

OFFICERS AND OFFICIALS

The House of Commons is presided over by the Speaker, who has considerable powers to maintain order in the House. A Deputy Speaker, called the Chairman of Ways and Means, and two Deputy Chairmen may preside over sittings of the House of Commons; they are elected by the House, and, like the Speaker, neither speak nor vote other than in their official capacity.

The staff of the House are employed by a Commission chaired by the Speaker. The heads of the six House of Commons departments are permanent officers of the House, not MPs. The Clerk of the House is the principal adviser to the Speaker on the privileges and procedures of the House, the conduct of the business of the House, and committees. The Serjeant-at-Arms is responsible for security, ceremonial, and for accommodation in the Commons part of the Palace of Westminster.

Speaker (£130,347), The Rt. Hon. Michael J. Martin, MP (Glasgow Springburn)

Chairman of Ways and Means (£95,281), Sir Alan Haselhurst, MP (Saffron Walden)

First Deputy Chairman of Ways and Means (£90,703), Sylvia Heal, MP (Halesowen and Rowley Regis)

Second Deputy Chairman of Ways and Means (£90,703), Sir Michael Lord, MP (Suffolk Central and Ipswich North)

OFFICES OF THE SPEAKER AND CHAIRMAN OF WAYS AND MEANS

Speaker's Secretary (*£60,788–£98,099), R. K. Daw

Chaplain to the Speaker, Revd Canon R. Wright

Secretary to the Chairman of Ways and Means (£39,302–£53,600), J. Whatley

DEPARTMENT OF THE CLERK OF THE HOUSE

Clerk of the House of Commons (*£143,258), R. B. Sands

Clerk Assistant (*£89,085–£126,816), D. G. Millar

Clerk of Committees (*£89,085–£126,816), G. Cubie, CB

Clerk of Legislation (*£89,085–£126,816), Dr M. R. Jack

Principal Clerks (*£72,316–£116,964)

Table Office, Ms H. E. Irwin

Journals, W. A. Proctor

Principal Clerk and Deputy Head of Committee Office, R. W. G. Wilson

Principal Clerks (*£60,788–£98,099)

Overseas Office, Ms J. Sharpe

Bills, F. A. Cranmer

Clerk of Domestic Committees/Secretary to the Commission, R. J. Rogers

Select Committees, D. L. Natzler; D. W. N. Doig

Delegated Legislation, L. C. Laurence Smyth

Deputy Principal Clerks (*£52,403–£87,408), Dr C. R. M. Ward; A. Sandall; A. R. Kennon; S. J. Patrick; D. J. Gerhold; C. J. Poyser; D. F. Harrison; S. J. Priestley; A. H. Doherty; P. A. Evans; R. I. S. Phillips; Dr R. G. James; D. R. Lloyd; B. M. Hutton; J. S. Benger, DPHIL; Ms E. C. Samson; N. P. Walker; Mrs E. J. Flood; C. G. Lee; C. D. Stanton; Miss L. M. Gardner; F. J. Reid; C. A. Shaw; P. G. Moon; T. W. P. Healey; Mrs S. A. R. Davies; Mrs J. N. St J. Mulley; M. Hennessy; P. Aylett

Senior Clerks (*£34,979–£50,770), M. Clark; J. D. Whatley; K. C. Fox; J. D. W. Rhys; Mrs E. S. Hunt; Miss S. McGlashan; Mrs C. Oxborough;T. Goldsmith; H. A. Yardley; Ms K. Emms; N. P. Wright; M. Hillyard; J. H. Davies; M. P. Atkins; S. Mark; T. Jarvis; G.K. Clarke; G. F. J. Farrar; J. Patterson; C. Porro; M. Etherton; Ms C. A. Littleboy; Miss T. S. Garralty; Miss F. McLean; R. C. A.

Cooke; J. Gearson; G. McKee; D. Bates; Ms L. Spiers;
I. Rogers; D. H. Griffiths ; D. Lees; A. Kidner; T. Byrne;
Sir Edward Osmotherly; P. Harborne
Examiners of Petitions for Private Bills, F. A. Cranmer;
T. Mohan
Registrar of Members' Interests (*£53,534–£87,598), Ms A.
Barry
Taxing Officer, F. A. Cranmer

VOTE OFFICE
Deliverer of the Vote (£53,451–£112,248), J. F. Collins
Deputy Deliverers of the Vote (*£34,979–£50,770), O. B. T.
Sweeney *(Parliamentary)*; R. Brook *(Development)*; Ms J.
Pitt *(Production)*; A. Powell *(Systems)*

LEGAL SERVICES OFFICE
Speaker's Counsel and Head of Legal Services Office
(£73,762–£155,008), J. E. G. Vaux
Counsel for European Legislation (£73,762–£155,008),
M. Carpenter
Counsel for Legislation, A. D. Preston
Assistant Counsel (£53,451–£112,248), A. Akbar;
P. Brooksbank

DEPARTMENT OF THE SERJEANT-AT-ARMS
Serjeant-at-Arms (£73,762–£155,008), M. J. A.
Cummins
Deputy Serjeant-at-Arms (£53,451–£112,248), R. M.
Morton
Assistant Serjeants-at-Arms, P. A. J. Wright; J. M. Robertson;
M. Harvey

DEPARTMENT OF THE LIBRARY
Librarian (£73,762–£119,303), Miss P. J. Baines
Directors (£53,451–£89,156), K. G. Cuninghame
(Resources); R. Clements *(Research Services)*; Miss E. M.
McInnes *(PIMS Project Director)*; B. Twigger
(Parliamentary and Reference Services); E. Wood
(Information Services)
Heads of Sections (£47,667–£64,989), Dr C. Pond;
Mrs C. Andrews; Ms F. Whittle; Ms D. Clark;
C. Barclay; Mrs C. Gillie; Ms P. J. Strickland;
R. Cracknell; P. Ryan T. Edmonds; B. Morgan
Senior Library Clerks (£39,302–£53,600), A. Seely; Ms F.
Poole; Ms J. Lourie; D. Webb; Ms A. Thorp; Ms L.
Conway; P. Ward; Ms S. Broadbridge; P. Bowers;
T. Youngs; V. Miller; C. Sear; O. Gay; R. Kelly; Ms I.
White; Ms H. Holden; K. Parry; Ms B. Brevitt; Ms D.
Gore; Ms E. Downing; S. McGinnes; Ms J. Roll;
S. Kennedy; T. Jarret; Ms W. Wilson

DEPARTMENT OF FINANCE AND ADMINISTRATION
Director of Finance and Administration (£73,762–
£119,303), A. J. Walker
Director of Operations (£62,004–£100,061), A. A.
Cameron
Director of Human Resource Management (£53,451–
£89,156) Ms S. Craig
Director of Finance Policy (£53,451–£89,156),
C. Ridley
Director of Internal Review Services (£47,667–£64,989),
R. Russell

DEPARTMENT OF THE OFFICIAL REPORT
Editor, W. G. Garland (£73,762–£155,008)
Deputy Editors (£53,451–£112,248), V. A. Widgery; Miss
L. Sutherland; Ms C. Fogarty

REFRESHMENT DEPARTMENT
Director of Catering Services (£62,004–£100,061), Mrs S.
Harrison
Catering Operations Manager (Outbuildings) (£39,302–
£53,600), Ms D. Herd
*Food and Beverage Operations Manager, Palace of
Westminster* (£39,302–£53,600), R. Gibbs
Executive Chef (£34,979–£50,770), D. Dorricott
Business Development Manager (£34,797–£50,770), Mrs J.
Rissen
Retail Manager (£34,979–£57,770), Mrs M. DeSouza
Human Resources and Development Manager (£39,302–
£53,600), J. van den Broek

SELECT COMMITTEES
The more significant committees, as at 1 August 2004:

DEPARTMENTAL COMMITTEES
Accommodation and Works – Chair, Derek Conway, MP;
Clerk, Tim Jarvis
Administration – Chair, Mrs M. Roe, MP; Clerk, Tim
Jarvis
Constitutional Affairs – Chair, The Rt. Hon. Alan Beith,
MP; Clerk, Roger Phillips
Culture, Media and Sport – Chair, The Rt. Hon. Gerald
Kaufman, MP; Clerks, Fergus Reid; Olivia Davidson
Defence – Chair, The Rt. Hon. Bruce George, MP; Clerks,
Steven Mark; Mark Hutton
Education and Skills – Chair, Barry Sheerman, MP, Clerks,
David Lloyd; Susan Griffiths
Environment, Food and Rural Affairs – Chair, The Rt. Hon.
Michael Jack, MP; Acting Clerk, Fiona McLean
Foreign Affairs – Chair, The Rt. Hon. Donald Anderson,
MP; Clerks, Steve Priestley; Geoffrey Farrar
Health – Chair, David Hinchliffe, MP; Clerks, Dr John
Benger; Keith Neary
Home Affairs – Chair, The Rt. Hon. John Denham, MP;
Clerks, Dr Robin James; Mark Etherton
Information – Chair, Robert Key, MP; Clerk, Gordon
Clarke
International Development – Chair, Tony Baldry, MP;
Clerks, Alistair Doherty; Sarah Hartwell
Northern Ireland Affairs – Chair, Michael Mates, MP;
Clerk, Dr John Patterson
*Office of the Deputy Prime Minister: Housing, Planning,
Local Government and the Regions* – Chair, Andrew
Bennett, MP; Clerks, Kate Emms; Libby Preston
Scottish Affairs – Chair, Mrs I. Adams, MP; Clerk, Mike
Clark
Trade and Industry – Chair, Martin O'Neill, MP; Clerks,
Mrs Elizabeth Flood; David Lees
Transport – Chair, Gwyneth Dunwoody, MP; Clerks, Eve
Samson; David Bates
Treasury – Chair, The Rt. Hon. John McFall, MP; Clerks,
Crispin Poyser; Alex Kidner
Welsh Affairs – Chair, Martyn Jones, MP; Clerk, James
Davies
Work and Pensions – Chair, Sir Archy Kirkwood, MP;
Clerks, Phillip Moon; Mick Hillyard

NON-DEPARTMENTAL COMMITTEES
Environmental Audit – Chair, Peter Ainsworth, MP; Clerks,
Mike Hennessy; Lynne Spiers
European Scrutiny – Chair, Jimmy Hood, MP; Clerks,
Dorian Gerhold; Jane Fox
Finance and Services – Chair, Sir Stuart Bell, MP; Clerks,
Robert Rogers; Shona McGlashan
House of Lords Reform (Joint Committee) – Chair, The Rt.

Hon. Jack Cunningham, MP; *Clerks,* Malcolm Jack;
David Beamish
Human Rights (Joint Committee) – Chair, The Rt.
Hon. Jean Corston, MP; *Clerks,* Paul Evans; Nicolas
Besly
Intelligence and Security (Cabinet Office) – Chair, The Rt.
Hon. Ann Taylor, MP; *Clerks,* Alistair Corbett;
Martin Sterling
Modernisation of the House of Commons – Chair, The Rt.
Hon. Peter Hain, MP; *Clerks,* George Cubie; Tom
Healey
Procedure – Chair, Sir Nicholas Winterton, MP; *Clerks,*
Simon Patrick; Jenny McCullough
Public Accounts – Chair, Edward Leigh, MP; *Clerk,* Nick
Wright
Public Administration – Chair, Tony Wright, MP; *Clerks,*
Phillip Aylett; Clive Porro
Regulatory Reform – Chair, Peter Pike, MP; *Clerk,* Martyn
Atkins
Science and Technology – Chair, Dr Ian Gibson, MP; *Clerks,*
Chris Shaw; Emily Commander
Statutory Instruments (Joint Committee) – Chair, David
Tredinnick, MP; *Clerks,* Martyn Atkins; Anna Murphy

PARLIAMENTARY INFORMATION

The following is a short glossary of aspects of the work of
Parliament. Unless otherwise stated, references are to
House of Commons procedures.

BILL – Proposed legislation is termed a bill. The stages
of a public bill (for private bills, *see* page 131) in the House
of Commons are as follows:
First Reading: This stage merely constitutes an order to
have the bill printed.
Second Reading: The debate on the principles of the bill.
Committee Stage: The detailed examination of a bill, clause
by clause. In most cases this takes place in a standing
committee, or the whole House may act as a committee. A
special standing committee may take evidence before
embarking on detailed scrutiny of the bill. Very rarely, a
bill may be examined by a select committee.
Report Stage: Detailed review of a bill as amended in
committee.
Third Reading: Final debate on a bill. Public bills go
through the same stages in the House of Lords, except that
in almost all cases the committee stage is taken in
committee of the whole House.
A bill may start in either House, and has to pass
through both Houses to become law. Both Houses have to
agree the same text of a bill, so that the amendments made
by the second House are then considered in the
originating House, and if not agreed, sent back to
themselves amended, until agreement is reached.
CHILTERN HUNDREDS – A nominal office of profit
under the Crown, the acceptance of which requires an
MP to vacate his/her seat. The Manor of Northstead is
similar. These are the only means by which an MP may
resign.
CONSOLIDATED FUND BILL – A bill to authorise issue
of money to maintain Government services. The bill is
dealt with without debate.
EARLY DAY MOTION – A motion put on the notice
paper by an MP without in general the real prospect of its
being debated. Such motions are expressions of back-
bench opinion.
FATHER OF THE HOUSE – The Member whose
continuous service in the House of Commons is the

longest. The present Father of the House is the Rt. Hon.
Tam Dalyell.
HOURS OF MEETING – The House of Commons
normally meets on Tuesdays, Wednesdays and Thursdays
at 11.30 a.m., Mondays at 2.30 p.m. and some Fridays at
9.30 a.m. There are ten Fridays without sittings in each
session. (*See also* Westminster Hall Sittings, below.) The
House of Lords normally meets at 2.30 p.m. Monday to
Wednesday and at 3 p.m. on Thursday. In the latter part of
the session, the House of Lords sometimes sits on Fridays
at 11 a.m.
LEADER OF THE OPPOSITION – In 1937 the office of
Leader of the Opposition was recognised and a salary was
assigned to the post. Since April 2003 this has been
£121,840 (including parliamentary salary of £56,358).
The present leader of the Opposition is Michael
Howard.
THE LORD CHANCELLOR – The Lord High
Chancellor of Great Britain is (*ex officio*) the Speaker of
the House of Lords. Unlike the Speaker of the House of
Commons, he is a member of the Government, takes part
in debates and votes in divisions. He has none of the
powers to maintain order that the Speaker in the
Commons has, these powers being exercised in the Lords
by the House as a whole. The Lord Chancellor sits in the
Lords on one of the Woolsacks, couches covered with red
cloth and stuffed with wool. If he wishes to address the
House in any way except formally as Speaker, he leaves
the Woolsack.
On 12 June 2003 the Prime Minister announced the
creation of the Department for Constitutional Affairs,
which will incorporate most of the responsibilities of the
Lord Chancellor's department. The post of Lord
Chancellor and the Department of the Lord Chancellor
will eventually be abolished. Other changes announced
include the replacement of the law lords with a Supreme
Court as the final court of appeal, and the creation of a
new Judicial Appointments Commission.
The current Lord Chancellor is Lord Falconer of
Thoroton who will continue in the post until his powers
are transferred to his new post of Secretary of State for
Constitutional Affairs. Lord Falconer currently operates as
a conventional Cabinet Minister and head of department,
and is located together with his permanent secretary and
departmental officials in the offices of the Lord
Chancellor's department. For further information on the
new Department for Constitutional Affairs *see* the
Government section.
NORTHERN IRELAND GRAND COMMITTEE – The
Northern Ireland Grand Committee consists of all MPs
representing constituencies in Northern Ireland, together
with not more than 25 other MPs nominated by the
Committee of Selection. The business of the committee
includes questions, short debates, ministerial statements,
bills, legislative proposals and other matters relating
exclusively to Northern Ireland, and delegated legislation.
The Northern Ireland Affairs Committee is one of the
departmental select committees, empowered to examine
the expenditure, administration and policy of the
Northern Ireland Office and the administration and
expenditure of the Crown Solicitor's Office.
OPPOSITION DAY – A day on which the topic for
debate is chosen by the Opposition. There are 20 such
days in a normal session. On 17 days, subjects are
chosen by the Leader of the Opposition; on the
remaining three days by the leader of the next largest
opposition party.
PARLIAMENT ACTS 1911 AND 1949 – Under these

Acts, bills may become law without the consent of the Lords, though the House of Lords has the power to delay a public bill for 13 months from its first second reading in the House of Commons.

PRIME MINISTER'S QUESTIONS – The Prime Minister answers questions from 12.00 to 12.30 p.m. on Wednesdays.

PRIVATE BILL – A bill promoted by a body or an individual to give powers additional to, or in conflict with, the general law, and to which a special procedure applies to enable people affected to object.

PRIVATE MEMBER'S BILL – A public bill promoted by a Member who is not a member of the Government.

PRIVATE NOTICE QUESTION – A question adjudged of urgent importance on submission to the Speaker (in the Lords, the Leader of the House), answered at the end of oral questions, usually at 3.30 p.m.

PRIVILEGE – The following are covered by the privilege of Parliament:
(i) freedom of speech in parliamentary proceedings
(iii) the printing and publishing of anything relating to the proceedings of the two Houses is subject to privilege
(iv) each House is the guardian of its dignity and may punish any insult to the House as a whole

QUESTION TIME – Oral questions are answered by Ministers in the Commons from 2.30 to 3.30 p.m. Monday to Wednesday and 11.30 a.m. to 12.30 p.m. on Thursdays. Questions are also taken at the start of the Lords sittings, with a daily limit of four oral questions.

ROYAL ASSENT – The royal assent is signified by letters patent to such bills and measures as have passed both Houses of Parliament (or bills which have been passed under the Parliament Acts 1911 and 1949). The Sovereign has not given royal assent in person since 1854. On occasion, for instance in the prorogation of Parliament, royal assent may be pronounced to the two Houses by Lords Commissioners. More usually royal assent is notified to each House sitting separately in accordance with the Royal Assent Act 1967. The old French formulae for royal assent are then endorsed on the acts by the Clerk of the Parliaments.

The power to withhold assent resides with the Sovereign but has not been exercised in the UK since 1707.

SELECT COMMITTEES – Consisting usually of ten to fifteen members of all parties, select committees are a means used by both Houses in order to investigate certain matters.

Most select committees in the House of Commons are tied to departments: each committee investigates matters within a government department's remit. There are other select committees dealing with public accounts (i.e. the spending by the Government of money voted by Parliament) and European legislation, and also domestic committees dealing, for example, with privilege and procedure. Major select committees usually take evidence in public; their evidence and reports are published by The Stationery Office. House of Commons select committees are reconstituted after a general election. For main committees, see page 129.

The principal select committee in the House of Lords is that on the European Communities, which has, at present, six sub-committees dealing with all areas of Community policy. The House of Lords also has a select committee on science and technology, which appoints sub-committees to deal with specific subjects, and a select committee on delegated powers and deregulation. For committees, see page 126. In addition, ad hoc select committees have been set up from time to time to investigate specific subjects. There are also some joint committees of the two Houses, e.g. the committees on statutory instruments and on parliamentary privilege.

THE SPEAKER – The Speaker of the House of Commons is the spokesman and chairman of the Chamber. He or she is elected by the House at the beginning of each Parliament or when the previous Speaker retires or dies. The Speaker neither speaks in debates nor votes in divisions except when the voting is equal.

VACANT SEATS – When a vacancy occurs in the House of Commons during a session of Parliament, the writ for the by-election is moved by a Whip of the party to which the member whose seat has been vacated belonged. If the House is in recess, the Speaker can issue a warrant for a writ, should two members certify to him that a seat is vacant.

WELSH AFFAIRS COMMITTEE – The Welsh Affairs Committee, one of the departmental select committees, was empowered to examine the expenditure, administration and policy of the Welsh Office. Following devolution, the role of the select committee has been questioned. If it continues, it will be concerned with the role and responsibilities of the relevant Secretary of State and on occasion the policy of the UK departments as it affects Wales.

WESTMINSTER HALL SITTINGS – Following a report by the Modernisation of the House of Commons Select Committee, the Commons decided in May 1999 to set up a second debating forum. It is known as 'Westminster Hall' and sittings are in the Grand Committee Room on Tuesdays from 10 a.m. to 1 p.m., Wednesdays from 9.30 a.m. to 2 p.m. and Thursdays from 2.30 p.m. for up to three hours. Sittings will be open to the public at the times indicated.

WHIPS – In order to secure the attendance of Members of a particular party in Parliament, particularly on the occasion of an important vote, Whips (originally known as 'Whippers-in') are appointed. The written appeal or circular letter issued by them is also known as a 'whip', its urgency being denoted by the number of times it is underlined. Failure to respond to a three-line whip is tantamount in the Commons to secession (at any rate temporarily) from the party. Whips are provided with office accommodation in both Houses, and Government and some Opposition Whips receive salaries from public funds.

PARLIAMENTARY EDUCATION UNIT
Norman Shaw Building (North), London SW1A 2TT
T 020-7219 2105
E edunit@parliament.uk
W www.explore.parliament.uk

GOVERNMENT OFFICE

The Government is the body of Ministers responsible for the administration of national affairs, determining policy and introducing into Parliament any legislation necessary to give effect to government policy. The majority of Ministers are members of the House of Commons but members of the House of Lords or of neither House may also hold ministerial responsibility. The Lord Chancellor is always a member of the House of Lords. The Prime Minister is, by current convention, always a member of the House of Commons.

THE PRIME MINISTER

The office of Prime Minister, which had been in existence for nearly 200 years, was officially recognised in 1905 and its holder was granted a place in the table of precedence. The Prime Minister, by tradition also First Lord of the Treasury and Minister for the Civil Service, is appointed by the Sovereign and is usually the leader of the party which enjoys, or can secure, a majority in the House of Commons. Other Ministers are appointed by the Sovereign on the recommendation of the Prime Minister, who also allocates functions amongst Ministers and has the power to obtain their resignation or dismissal individually.

The Prime Minister informs the Sovereign of state and political matters, advises on the dissolution of Parliament, and makes recommendations for important Crown-appointments, the award of honours, etc.

As the chairman of Cabinet meetings and leader of a political party, the Prime Minister is responsible for translating party policy into government activity. As leader of the Government, the Prime Minister is responsible to Parliament and to the electorate for the policies and their implementation.

The Prime Minister also represents the nation in international affairs, e.g. summit conferences.

THE CABINET

The Cabinet developed during the 18th century as an inner committee of the Privy Council, which was the chief source of executive power until that time. The Cabinet is composed of about 20 Ministers chosen by the Prime Minister, usually the heads of government departments (generally known as Secretaries of State unless they have a special title, e.g. Chancellor of the Exchequer), the leaders of the two Houses of Parliament, and the holders of various traditional offices.

The Cabinet's functions are the final determination of policy, control of government and co-ordination of government departments. The exercise of its functions is dependent upon enjoying majority support in the House of Commons. Cabinet meetings are held in private, taking place once or twice a week during parliamentary sittings and less often during a recess. Proceedings are confidential, the members being bound by their oath as Privy Counsellors not to disclose information about the proceedings.

The convention of collective responsibility means that the Cabinet acts unanimously even when Cabinet Ministers do not all agree on a subject. The policies of departmental Ministers must be consistent with the policies of the Government as a whole, and once the Government's policy has been decided, each Minister is expected to support it or resign.

The convention of ministerial responsibility holds a Minister, as the political head of his or her department, accountable to Parliament for the department's work. Departmental Ministers usually decide all matters within their responsibility, although on matters of political importance they normally consult their colleagues collectively. A decision by a departmental Minister is binding on the Government as a whole.

POLITICAL PARTIES

Before the reign of William and Mary the principal officers of state were chosen by and were responsible to the Sovereign alone and not to Parliament or the nation at large. Such officers acted sometimes in concert with one another but more often independently, and the fall of one did not, of necessity, involve that of others, although all were liable to be dismissed at any moment.

In 1693 the Earl of Sunderland recommended to William III the advisability of selecting a ministry from the political party which enjoyed a majority in the House of Commons and the first united ministry was drawn in 1696 from the Whigs, to which party the King owed his throne. This group became known as the Junto and was regarded with suspicion as a novelty in the political life of the nation, being a small section meeting in secret apart from the main body of Ministers. It may be regarded as the forerunner of the Cabinet and in the course of time it led to the establishment of the principle of joint responsibility of Ministers, so that internal disagreement caused a change of personnel or resignation of the whole body of Ministers.

The accession of George I, who was unfamiliar with the English language, led to a disinclination on the part of the Sovereign to preside at meetings of his Ministers and caused the appearance of a Prime Minister, a position first acquired by Robert Walpole in 1721 and retained by him without interruption for 20 years and 326 days.

DEVELOPMENT OF PARTIES

In 1828 the Whigs became known as Liberals, a name originally given to it by its opponents to imply laxity of principles, but gradually accepted by the party to indicate its claim to be pioneers and champions of political reform and progressive legislation. In 1861 a Liberal Registration Association was founded and Liberal Associations became widespread. In 1877 a National Liberal Federation was formed, with headquarters in London. The Liberal Party was in power for long periods during the second half of the 19th-century and for several years during the first quarter of the 20th-century, but after a split in the party the numbers elected were small from 1931. In 1988, a majority of the Liberals agreed on a merger with the Social Democratic Party under the title Social and Liberal Democrats; since 1989 they have been known as Liberal Democrats. A minority continue separately as Liberal Party.

Soon after the change from Whig to Liberal the Tory Party became known as Conservative, a name believed to have been invented by John Wilson Croker in 1830 and to have been generally adopted about the time of the passing of the Reform Act of 1832 to indicate that the preservation of national institutions was the leading principle of the party. After the Home Rule crisis of 1886 the dissentient Liberals entered into a compact with the Conservatives, under which the latter undertook not to contest their seats, but a separate Liberal Unionist organisation was maintained until 1912, when it was united with the Conservatives.

Labour candidates for Parliament made their first appearance at the general election of 1892, when there were 27 standing as Labour or Liberal-Labour. In 1900 the Labour Representation Committee was set up in order to establish a distinct Labour group in Parliament, with its own whips, its own policy, and a readiness to co-operate with any party which might be engaged in promoting legislation in the direct interest of labour. In 1906 the LRC became known as the Labour Party.

The Council for Social Democracy was announced by four former Labour Cabinet Ministers in January 1981 and in March 1981 the Social Democratic Party was launched. Later that year the SDP and the Liberal Party formed an electoral alliance. In 1988 a majority of the SDP agreed on a merger with the Liberal Party but a minority continued as a separate party under the SDP title. In 1990 it was decided to wind up the party organisation and its three sitting MPs were known as independent social democrats. None were returned at the 1992 general election.

Plaid Cymru was founded in 1926 to provide an independent political voice for Wales and to campaign for self-government in Wales.

The Scottish National Party was founded in 1934 to campaign for independence for Scotland.

The Social Democratic and Labour Party was founded in 1970, emerging from the civil rights movement of the 1960s, with the aim of promoting reform, reconciliation and partnership across the sectarian divide in Northern Ireland and of opposing violence from any quarter.

The Democratic Unionist Party was founded in 1971 to resist moves by the Ulster Unionist Party which were considered a threat to the Union. Its aim is to maintain Northern Ireland as an integral part of the UK.

The Ulster Unionist Council first met formally in 1905. Its objectives are to maintain Northern Ireland as an integral part of the UK and to promote the aims of the Ulster Unionist Party.

GOVERNMENT AND OPPOSITION

The government of the day is formed by the party which wins the largest number of seats in the House of Commons at a general election, or which has the support of a majority of members in the House of Commons. By tradition, the leader of the majority party is asked by the Sovereign to form a government, while the largest minority party becomes the official Opposition with its own leader and a 'Shadow Cabinet.' Leaders of Government and Opposition sit on the front benches of the Commons with their supporters (the back-benchers) sitting behind them.

FINANCIAL SUPPORT

Financial support for Opposition parties in the House of Commons was introduced in 1975 and is commonly known as Short Money, after Edward Short, the Leader of the House at that time, who introduced the scheme. Short money allocation for 2004–5 is:

Conservative	£3,666,801.46
Liberal Democrats	£1,244,855.74
Plaid Cymru	£74,087.32
SNP	£119,875.41
SDLP	£58,416.99
Democratic Unionists	£84,812.59
Ulster Unionists	£101,576.31

A specific allocation for the Leader of the Opposition's office was introduced in April 1999 and has been set at £563,448.50 for the years 2004–5.

Financial support for Opposition parties in the House

of Lords was introduced in 1996 and is commonly known as Cranborne Money.

The parties included here are those with MPs sitting in the House of Commons in the present Parliament.

CONSERVATIVE PARTY

Conservative Central Office, 32 Smith Square, London SW1P 3HH
T 020-7222 9000 F 020-7222 1135
E ccoffice@conservatives.com
W www.conservatives.com

SHADOW CABINET *as at September 2004*
Leader of the Opposition, The Rt. Hon. Michael Howard, QC, MP
Deputy Leader and Secretary of State for International Affairs, The Rt. Hon. Michael Ancram, QC, MP
Chancellor of the Exchequer, The Rt. Hon. Oliver Letwin, MP
Secretary of State for Home Affairs, The Rt. Hon. David Davis, MP
Party Chairmen, Dr Liam Fox, MP; Lord Maurice Saatchi, MP
Chief Whip, The Rt. Hon. David Maclean, MP
Secretary of State for Defence, Hon. Nicholas Soames, MP
Secretary of State for Deregulation, The Rt. Hon. John Redwood, MP
Secretary of State for Education, Tim Collins, MP
Secretary of State for Environment and Transport, The Rt. Hon. Tim Yeo, MP
Secretary of State for the Family, The Rt. Hon. Theresa May, MP
Secretary of State for Health, Andrew Lansley, MP
Leader in the House of Lords, The Rt. Hon. Lord Strathclyde
Secretary of State for Local and Devolved Government Affairs, Caroline Spelman, MP
Secretary of State for Work and Pensions, David Willetts, MP

SCOTTISH CONSERVATIVE AND UNIONIST PARTY

83 Princes Street, Edinburgh EH2 2ER
T 0131-247 6890 F 0131-247 6891
E central.office@scottishtories.org.uk
W www.scottishtories.org.uk
Chairman, David Mitchell, CBE
Deputy Chairman, Mrs M. Goodman
Hon. Treasurer, Mrs J. Slater
Campaigns and Operations, Mark McInnes

LABOUR PARTY

16 Old Queen Street, London SW1H 9HP
T 0870-590 0200 F 020-7802 1234
E info@new.labour.org.uk
W www.labour.org.uk
Parliamentary Party Leader, The Rt. Hon. Tony Blair, MP
Deputy Party Leader, The Rt. Hon. John Prescott, MP
Leader in the Lords, The Rt. Hon. Baroness Amos
Chair, The Rt. Hon. Ian McCartney, MP
General Secretary, Matt Carter
General Secretary, Scottish Labour Party, L. Quinn

LIBERAL DEMOCRATS

4 Cowley Street, London SW1P 3NB
T 020-7222 7999 F 020-7799 2170
E info@libdems.org.uk
W www.libdems.org.uk
President, Lord Dholakia
Hon. Treasurer, Reg Clark
Chief Executive, Lord Chris Rennard
Parliamentary Party Leader, The Rt. Hon. Charles Kennedy, MP
Leader in the House of Commons, Paul Tyler, MP
Leader in the Lords, Baroness Williams of Grosby

LIBERAL DEMOCRAT SPOKESMEN
as at July 2004
Deputy Leader and Foreign Secretary, The Rt. Hon. Menzies Campbell, QC, MP
Chancellor, Dr Vincent Cable, MP
Culture, Media and Sport , Don Foster, MP
Defence, Paul Keetch, MP
Education and Skills, Phil Willis, MP
Environment, Norman Baker, MP
Food and Rural Affairs, Andrew George, MP
Foreign Affairs, Michael Moore, MP
Health, Paul Burstow, MP
Home Affairs, Mark Oaten, MP
International Development, Tom Brake, MP
Office of the Deputy Prime Minister, Edward Davey, MP
Scotland and Transport, John Thurso, MP
Spokesperson for London, Simon Hughes, MP
Trade and Industry, Malcolm Bruce, MP
Treasury, David Laws, MP
Wales and Northern Ireland, Lembit Opik, MP
Women and Older People, Sandra Gidley, MP
Work and Pensions, Prof. Steve Webb, MP
Chair of the Parliamentary Party, Matthew Taylor, MP
Chair of Campaigns and Communications Committee, Lord Razzall

LIBERAL DEMOCRAT WHIPS
House of Lords, The Lord Roper of Thorney Island
House of Commons, Andrew Stunell, MP *(Chief Whip)*

SCOTTISH LIBERAL DEMOCRATS

4 Clifton Terrace, Edinburgh EH12 5DR
T 0131-337 2314 F 0131-337 3566
E administration@scotlibdems.org.uk
W www.scotlibdems.org.uk
Party President, Malcolm Bruce, MP
Party Leader, Jim Wallace, MSP
Convener, Judy Hayman
Vice-Convener, Keith Raffan, MSP; Karen Freel; Robert Brown
Treasurer, Douglas Herbison
Chief of Staff, Dr Derek Barrie

WELSH LIBERAL DEMOCRATS
Bay View House, 102 Bute Street, Cardiff CF10 5AD
T 029-2031 3400 F 029-2031 3401
E ldwales@cix.co.uk
W www.welshlibdems.org.uk
Party President, Rob Humphreys
Party Leader, Lembit Opik, MP
Chairman, Rob Humphreys
Treasurer, Phylip Hobson
Secretary, vacant
Administrative Officer, Abigail Hughes
Chief Executive, Chris Lines

PLAID CYMRU – THE PARTY OF WALES
18 Park Grove, Cardiff CF10 3BN
T 029-2064 6000 F 029-2064 6001
E post@plaidcymru.org
W www.plaidcymru.org
Party President, Dafydd Iwan
Chairman, John Dixon
Hon. Treasurer, Jeff Canning
Chief Executive/General Secretary, Dafydd Trystan

SCOTTISH NATIONAL PARTY
107 McDonald Road, Edinburgh EH7 4NW
T 0131-525 8900 F 0131-525 8901
E snp.hq@snp.org W www.snp.org
Parliamentary Party Leader, Alex Salmond, MSP
Chief Whip, Bruce Crawford, MSP
National Convener, Alex Salmond, MSP
Senior Vice-Convener, Nicola Sturgeon, MSP
National Treasurer, Jim Mather, MSP
National Secretary, Alasdair Allan
Chief Executive, Peter Murrell

NORTHERN IRELAND DEMOCRATIC UNIONIST PARTY
91 Dundela Avenue, Belfast BT4 3BU
T 028-9047 1155 F 028-9047 1797
E info@dup.org.uk W www.dup2win.com
Parliamentary Party Leader, Ian Paisley, MP, MEP, MLA
Deputy Leader, Peter Robinson, MP, MLA
Chairman, Maurice Morrow, MLA
Chief Executive, Allan Ewart
Hon. Treasurer, Gregory Campbell, MP, MLA
Party Secretary, Nigel Dodds, MP, MLA

SINN FEIN
53 Falls Road, Belfast BT12 4PD
T 028-9022 3000 F 028-9022 3001
E sfadmin@eircom.net W www.sinnfein.ie
Party President, Gerry Adams, MP, MLA
Vice-President, Pat Doherty, MP, MLA
Chief Negotiator, Martin McGuinness, MP, MLA
General Secretary, Robbie Smyth

SOCIAL DEMOCRATIC AND LABOUR PARTY
121 Ormeau Road, Belfast BT7 1SH
T 028-9024 7700 F 028-9023 6699
E sdlp@indigo.ie W www.sdlp.ie
Parliamentary Party Leader, Mark Durkan, MLA
Deputy Leader, Dr Alasdair McDonnell, MLA
Chief Whip, John Dallat, MLA
Chairperson, Patricia Lewsley, MLA
Hon. Treasurer, Berna McIvor
General Secretary, Geraldine Cosgrove

ULSTER UNIONIST PARTY
429 Holywood Road, Belfast BT4 2LN
T 028-9076 5500 F 028-9076 9419
E uup@uup.org W www.uup.org
Party Leader, The Rt. Hon. David Trimble, MP
Chief Whip, Ald. Roy Beggs, MP

ULSTER UNIONIST COUNCIL
President, Lord Rogan of Lower Iveagh
Leader, The Rt. Hon. David Trimble, MP, MLA
Chairman of the Executive Committee, James Cooper
Hon. Treasurer, Jack Allen, OBE
Vice-Chairman, David Campbell
Vice-Presidents, Lord Maginnis of Drumglass; Jim Nicholson, MEP; Cllr. Jim Rodgers, OBE; Mrs May Steele, MBE
Hon. Secretaries, Mrs Joan Carson; Cllr. Danny Kennedy, MLA; Cllr. Michael McGimpsey, MLA; Dermot Nesbitt, MLA
Assistant Honorary Treasurer, Edward Keown

SPEAKERS OF THE COMMONS

This list comprises Speakers of the House of Commons since 1708. The date of appointment given is the day on which the Speaker was first elected by the House of Commons. The appointment requires royal approbation before it is confirmed and this is usually given within a few days. The present Speaker is the 156th.

PARLIAMENT OF GREAT BRITAIN

Sir Richard Onslow *(Lord Onslow)*, 16 November 1708
William Bromley, 25 November 1710
Sir Thomas Hanmer, 16 February 1714
Spencer Compton *(Earl of Wilmington)*, 17 March 1715
Arthur Onslow, 23 January 1728
Sir John Cust, 3 November 1761
Sir Fletcher Norton *(Lord Grantley)*, 22 January 1770
Charles Cornwall, 31 October 1780
Hon. William Grenville *(Lord Grenville)*, 5 January 1789
Henry Addington *(Viscount Sidmouth)*, 8 June 1789

PARLIAMENT OF THE UNITED KINGDOM

Sir John Mitford *(Lord Redesdale)*, 11 February 1801
Charles Abbot *(Lord Colchester)*, 10 February 1802
Charles Manners-Sutton *(Viscount Canterbury)*, 2 June 1817
James Abercromby *(Lord Dunfermline)*, 19 February 1835
Charles Shaw-Lefevre *(Viscount Eversley)*, 27 May 1839
J. Evelyn Denison *(Viscount Ossington)*, 30 April 1857
Sir Henry Brand *(Viscount Hampden)*, 9 February 1872
Arthur Wellesley Peel *(Viscount Peel)*, 26 February 1884
William Gully *(Viscount Selby)*, 10 April 1895
James Lowther *(Viscount Ullswater)*, 8 June 1905
John Whitley, 27 April 1921
Hon. Edward Fitzroy, 20 June 1928
Douglas Clifton-Brown *(Viscount Ruffside)*, 9 March 1943
William Morrison *(Viscount Dunrossil)*, 31 October 1951
Sir Harry Hylton-Foster, 20 October 1959
Horace King *(Lord Maybray-King)*, 26 October 1965
Selwyn Lloyd *(Lord Selwyn-Lloyd)*, 12 January 1971
George Thomas *(Viscount Tonypandy)*, 2 February 1976
Bernard Weatherill *(Lord Weatherill)*, 15 June 1983
Betty Boothroyd, 27 April 1992
Michael Martin, 23 October 2000

MEMBERS OF PARLIAMENT *as at 1 September 2004*

*Abbott, Ms Diane (*b.* 1953) *Lab., Hackney North and Stoke Newington,* Maj. 13,651

*Adams, Gerard (Gerry) (*b.* 1948) *SF, Belfast West,* Maj. 19,342

*Adams, Mrs K. Irene, JP (*b.* 1948) *Lab., Paisley North,* Maj. 9,321

*Ainger, Nicholas R. (*b.* 1949) *Lab., Carmarthen West and Pembrokeshire South,* Maj. 4,538

*Ainsworth, Peter M. (*b.* 1956) *C., Surrey East,* Maj. 13,203

*Ainsworth, Robert W. (*b.* 1952) *Lab., Coventry North East,* Maj. 15,751

*Alexander, Douglas G. (*b.* 1967) *Lab., Paisley South,* Maj. 11,910

Allan, Richard B. (*b.* 1966) *LD, Sheffield Hallam,* Maj. 9,347

*Allen, Graham W. (*b.* 1953) *Lab., Nottingham North,* Maj. 12,240

*Amess, David A. A. (*b.* 1952) *C., Southend West,* Maj. 7,941

*Ancram, Rt. Hon. Michael A. F. J. K. (Earl of Ancram) (*b.* 1945) *C., Devizes,* Maj. 11,896

*Anderson, Rt. Hon. Donald (*b.* 1939) *Lab., Swansea East,* Maj. 16,148

*Anderson, Mrs Janet (*b.* 1949) *Lab., Rossendale and Darwen,* Maj. 5,223

*Arbuthnot, Rt. Hon. James N. (*b.* 1952) *C., Hampshire North East,* Maj. 13,257

*Armstrong, Rt. Hon. Hilary J. (*b.* 1945) *Lab., Durham North West,* Maj. 16,333

Atherton, Ms Candy K. (*b.* 1955) *Lab., Falmouth and Camborne,* Maj. 4,527

Atkins, Ms Charlotte (*b.* 1950) *Lab., Staffordshire Moorlands,* Maj. 5,838

*Atkinson, David A. (*b.* 1940) *C., Bournemouth East,* Maj. 3,434

*Atkinson, Peter L. (*b.* 1943) *C., Hexham,* Maj. 2,529

*Austin, John E. (*b.* 1944) *Lab., Erith and Thamesmead,* Maj. 11,167

Bacon, Richard (*b.* 1962) *C., Norfolk South,* Maj. 6,893

*Bailey, Adrian (*b.* 1945) *Lab. Co-op., West Bromwich West,* Maj. 11,355

Baird, Vera (*b.* 1950) *Lab., Redcar,* Maj. 13,443

*Baker, Norman (*b.* 1957) *LD, Lewes,* Maj. 9,710

*Baldry, Anthony B. (*b.* 1950) *C., Banbury,* Maj. 5,219

*Banks, Anthony L. (*b.* 1943) *Lab., West Ham,* Maj. 15,645

Barker, Gregory (*b.* 1966) *C., Bexhill and Battle,* Maj. 10,503

*Barnes, Harold (*b.* 1936) *Lab., Derbyshire North East,* Maj. 12,258

Baron, John (*b.* 1959) *C., Billericay,* Maj. 5,013

Barrett, John (*b.* 1954) *LD, Edinburgh West,* Maj. 7,589

*Barron, Rt. Hon. Kevin J. (*b.* 1946) *Lab., Rother Valley,* Maj. 14,882

*Battle, John D. (*b.* 1951) *Lab., Leeds West,* Maj. 14,935

*Bayley, Hugh (*b.* 1952) *Lab., City of York,* Maj. 13,779

Beard, Nigel C. (*b.* 1936) *Lab., Bexleyheath and Crayford,* Maj. 1,472

*Beckett, Rt. Hon. Margaret (*b.* 1943) *Lab., Derby South,* Maj. 13,855

Begg, Ms Anne (*b.* 1955) *Lab., Aberdeen South,* Maj. 4,388

*Beggs, Roy (*b.* 1936) *UUP, Antrim East,* Maj. 128

*Beith, Rt. Hon. Alan J. (*b.* 1943) *LD, Berwick upon Tweed,* Maj. 8,458

*Bell, Stuart (*b.* 1938) *Lab., Middlesbrough,* Maj. 16,330

Bellingham, Henry (*b.* 1955) *Lab., Norfolk North West,* Maj. 3,485

*Benn, Hilary J. (*b.* 1953) *Lab., Leeds Central,* Maj. 14,381

*Bennett, Andrew F. (*b.* 1939) *Lab., Denton and Reddish,* Maj. 15,330

*Benton, Joseph E. (*b.* 1933) *Lab., Bootle,* Maj. 19,043

Bercow, John S. (*b.* 1963) *C., Buckingham,* Maj. 13,325

*Beresford, Sir Paul (*b.* 1946) *C., Mole Valley,* Maj. 10,153

*Berry, Dr Roger (*b.* 1948) *Lab., Kingswood,* Maj. 13,962

*Best, Harold (*b.* 1939) *Lab., Leeds North West,* Maj. 5,236

*Betts, Clive J. C. (*b.* 1950) *Lab., Sheffield Attercliffe,* Maj. 18,844

Blackman, Ms Elizabeth M. (*b.* 1949) *Lab., Erewash,* Maj. 6,932

*Blair, Rt. Hon. Tony C. L. (*b.* 1953) *Lab., Sedgefield,* Maj. 17,713

Blears, Hazel A. (*b.* 1956) *Lab., Salford,* Maj. 11,012

Blizzard, Robert J. (*b.* 1950) *Lab., Waveney,* Maj. 8,553

*Blunkett, Rt. Hon. David (*b.* 1947) *Lab., Sheffield Brightside,* Maj. 17,049

*Blunt, Crispin J. R. (*b.* 1960) *C., Reigate,* Maj. 8,025

*Boateng, Rt. Hon. Paul Y. (*b.* 1951) *Lab., Brent South,* Maj. 17,380

Borrow, David S. (*b.* 1952) *Lab., Ribble South,* Maj. 3,792

*Boswell, Timothy E. (*b.* 1942) *C., Daventry,* Maj. 9,649

*Bottomley, Peter J. (*b.* 1944) *C., Worthing West,* Maj. 9,037

*Bottomley, Rt. Hon. Virginia H. B. M. (*b.* 1948) *C., Surrey South West,* Maj. 861

*Bradley, Rt. Hon. Keith (*b.* 1950) *Lab., Manchester Withington,* Maj. 11,524

Bradley, Peter C. S. (*b.* 1953) *Lab., The Wrekin,* Maj. 3,587

Bradshaw, Benjamin P. J. (*b.* 1960) *Lab., Exeter,* Maj. 11,759

*Brady, Graham (*b.* 1967) *C., Altrincham and Sale West,* Maj. 2,941

Brake, Thomas A. (*b.* 1962) *LD, Carshalton and Wallington,* Maj. 4,547

*Brazier, Julian W. H., TD (*b.* 1953) *C., Canterbury,* Maj. 2,069

Breed, Colin E. (*b.* 1947) *LD, Cornwall South East,* Maj. 5,375

Brennan, Kevin (*b.* 1959) *Lab., Cardiff West,* Maj. 11,321

Brooke, Annette (*b.* 1947) *LD, Dorset Mid and Poole North,* Maj. 384

*Brown, Rt. Hon. J. Gordon, PHD (*b.* 1951) *Lab., Dunfermline East,* Maj. 15,063

*Brown, Rt. Hon. Nicholas H. (*b.* 1950) *Lab., Newcastle upon Tyne East and Wallsend,* Maj. 14,223

Brown, Russell L. (*b.* 1951) *Lab., Dumfries,* Maj. 8,834

Browne, Desmond (*b.* 1952) *Lab., Kilmarnock and Loudoun,* Maj. 10,334

*Browning, Mrs Angela F. (*b.* 1946) *C., Tiverton and Honiton,* Maj. 6,284

*Bruce, Malcolm G. (*b.* 1944) *LD, Gordon,* Maj. 7,879

Bryant, Chris (*b.* 1962) *Lab., Rhondda,* Maj. 16,047

Buck, Ms Karen P. (*b.* 1958) *Lab., Regent's Park and Kensington North,* Maj. 10,266

*Burden, Richard H. (*b.* 1954) *Lab., Birmingham Northfield,* Maj. 7,798

*Davidson, Ian G. (b. 1950) Lab. Co-op., Glasgow Pollok, Maj. 11,268

*Davies, Rt. Hon. D. J. Denzil (b. 1938) Lab., Llanelli, Maj. 6,403

Davies, Geraint R. (b. 1960) Lab., Croydon Central, Maj. 3,984

*Davies, J. Quentin (b. 1944) C., Grantham and Stamford, Maj. 4,518

*Davis, Rt. Hon. David M. (b. 1948) C., Haltemprice and Howden, Maj. 1,903

Dawson, T. Hilton (b. 1953) Lab., Lancaster and Wyre, Maj. 481

Dean, Ms Janet E. A. (b. 1949) Lab., Burton, Maj. 4,849

*Denham, Rt. Hon. John Y. (b. 1953) Lab., Southampton Itchen, Maj. 11,223

*Dhanda, Parmjit (b. 1971) Lab., Gloucester, Maj. 3,880

*Dismore, Andrew H. (b. 1954) Lab., Hendon, Maj. 7,417

Djanogly, Jonathan (b. 1965) C., Huntingdon, Maj. 12,792

Dobbin, James (b. 1941) Lab. Co-op., Heywood and Middleton, Maj. 11,670

*Dobson, Rt. Hon. Frank G. (b. 1940) Lab., Holborn and St Pancras, Maj. 11,175

Dodds, Nigel, MLA (b. 1958) DUP, Belfast North, Maj. 6,387

Doherty, Pat (b. 1945) SF, Tyrone West, Maj. 5,040

Donaldson, Jeffrey M. (b. 1962) UUP, Lagan Valley, Maj. 18,342

*Donohoe, Brian H. (b. 1948) Lab., Cunninghame South, Maj. 11,230

Doran, Frank (b. 1949) Lab., Aberdeen Central, Maj. 6,646

*Dorrell, Rt. Hon. Stephen J. (b. 1952) C., Charnwood, Maj. 7,739

Doughty, Sue (b. 1955) LD, Guildford, Maj. 538

*Dowd, James P. (b. 1951) Lab., Lewisham West, Maj. 11,920

Drew, David E. (b. 1952) Lab. Co-op., Stroud, Maj. 5,039

Drown, Ms Julia K. (b. 1962) Lab., Swindon South, Maj. 7,341

*Duncan, Alan J. C. (b. 1957) C., Rutland and Melton, Maj. 8,612

Duncan, Peter (b. 1965) C., Galloway and Upper Nithsdale, Maj. 74

*Duncan Smith, G. Iain (b. 1954) C., Chingford and Woodford Green, Maj. 5,487

*Dunwoody, Hon. Mrs Gwyneth P. (b. 1930) Lab., Crewe and Nantwich, Maj. 9,906

*Eagle, Ms Angela (b. 1961) Lab., Wallasey, Maj. 12,276

Eagle, Ms Maria (b. 1961) Lab., Liverpool Garston, Maj. 12,494

Edwards, Huw W. E. (b. 1953) Lab., Monmouth, Maj. 384

Efford, Clive S. (b. 1958) Lab., Eltham, Maj. 6,996

*Ellman, Mrs Louise J. (b. 1945) Lab. Co-op., Liverpool Riverside, Maj. 13,950

*Ennis, Jeffrey (b. 1952) Lab., Barnsley East and Mexborough, Maj. 16,789

*Etherington, William (b. 1941) Lab., Sunderland North, Maj. 13,354

*Evans, Nigel M. (b. 1957) C., Ribble Valley, Maj. 11,238

Ewing, Annabelle (b. 1960) SNP, Perth, Maj. 48

*Fabricant, Michael L. D. (b. 1950) C., Lichfield, Maj. 4,426

*Fallon, Michael C. (b. 1952) C., Sevenoaks, Maj. 10,154

Farrelly, Paul (b. 1962) Lab., Newcastle under Lyme, Maj. 9,986

*Field, Rt. Hon. Frank (b. 1942) Lab., Birkenhead, Maj. 15,591

*Field, Mark (b. 1934) C., Cities of London and Westminster, Maj. 4,499

*Fisher, Mark (b. 1944) Lab., Stoke-on-Trent Central, Maj. 11,845

*Fitzpatrick, James (b. 1952) Lab., Poplar and Canning Town, Maj. 14,104

*Fitzsimons, Mrs Lorna (b. 1967) Lab., Rochdale, Maj. 5,655

*Flight, Howard E. (b. 1948) C., Arundel and South Downs, Maj. 13,704

*Flint, Ms Caroline L. (b. 1961) Lab., Don Valley, Maj. 9,520

Flook, Adrian (b. 1963) C., Taunton, Maj. 235

*Flynn, Paul P. (b. 1935) Lab., Newport West, Maj. 9,304

Follett, Ms D. Barbara (b. 1942) Lab., Stevenage, Maj. 8,566

*Forth, Rt. Hon. Eric (b. 1944) C., Bromley and Chislehurst, Maj. 9,037

*Foster, Rt. Hon. Derek (b. 1937) Lab., Bishop Auckland, Maj. 13,926

*Foster, Donald M. E. (b. 1947) LD, Bath, Maj. 9,894

Foster, Michael (b. 1963) Lab., Worcester, Maj. 5,766

*Foster, Michael J. (b. 1946) Lab., Hastings and Rye, Maj. 4,308

*Foulkes, Rt. Hon. George (b. 1942) Lab. Co-op., Carrick, Cumnock and Doon Valley, Maj. 14,856

*Fox, Dr Liam (b. 1961) C., Woodspring, Maj. 8,798

Francis, Dr David Hywel (b. 1946) Lab., Aberavon, Maj. 16,108

Francois, Mark, PHD (b. 1965) C., Rayleigh, Maj. 8,290

*Gale, Roger J. (b. 1943) C., Thanet North, Maj. 6,650

*Galloway, George (b. 1954) Ind. Lab., Glasgow Kelvin, Maj. 7,260

*Gapes, Michael J. (b. 1952) Lab. Co-op., Ilford South, Maj. 13,997

Gardiner, Barry S. (b. 1957) Lab., Brent North, Maj. 10,205

*Garnier, Edward H., QC (b. 1952) C., Harborough, Maj. 5,252

George, Andrew H. (b. 1958) LD, St Ives, Maj. 10,053

*George, Rt. Hon. Bruce T. (b. 1942) Lab., Walsall South, Maj. 9,931

*Gerrard, Neil F. (b. 1942) Lab., Walthamstow, Maj. 15,181

*Gibb, Nicholas J. (b. 1960) C., Bognor Regis and Littlehampton, Maj. 5,643

*Gibson, Dr Ian (b. 1938) Lab., Norwich North, Maj. 5,863

*Gidley, Sandra (b. 1957) LD, Romsey, Maj. 2,370

Gildernew, Michelle (b. 1970) SF, Fermanagh and South Tyrone, Maj. 53

Gill, Parmjit Singh (b. 1966) LD, Leicester South, Maj. 1,654

*Gillan, Mrs Cheryl E. K. (b. 1952) C., Chesham and Amersham, Maj. 11,882

Gilroy, Mrs Linda (b. 1949) Lab. Co-op., Plymouth Sutton, Maj. 7,517

*Godsiff, Roger D. (b. 1946) Lab., Birmingham Sparkbrook and Small Heath, Maj. 16,246

Goggins, Paul G. (b. 1953) Lab., Wythenshawe and Sale East, Maj. 12,608

Goodman, Paul (b. 1960) C., Wycombe, Maj. 3,168

Gray, James W. (b. 1954) C., Wiltshire North, Maj. 3,878

Grayling, Chris (b. 1962) C., Epsom and Ewell, Maj. 10,080

Green, Damian H. (b. 1956) C., Ashford, Maj. 7,359

Green, Matthew (b. 1970) LD, Ludlow, Maj. 1,630

*Greenway, John R. (b. 1946) C., Ryedale, Maj. 4,875

*Grieve, Dominic C. R. (*b.* 1956) *C., Beaconsfield,* Maj. 11,065
*Griffiths, Ms Jane P. (*b.* 1954) *Lab., Reading East,* Maj. 5,588
*Griffiths, Nigel (*b.* 1955) *Lab., Edinburgh South,* Maj. 5,499
*Griffiths, Winston J. (*b.* 1943) *Lab., Bridgend,* Maj. 10,045
Grogan, John T. (*b.* 1961) *Lab., Selby,* Maj. 2,138
*Gummer, Rt. Hon. John S. (*b.* 1939) *C., Suffolk Coastal,* Maj. 4,326
*Hague, Rt. Hon. William J. (*b.* 1961) *C., Richmond,* Maj. 16,319
*Hain, Rt. Hon. Peter G. (*b.* 1950) *Lab., Neath,* Maj. 14,816
*Hall, Michael T. (*b.* 1952) *Lab., Weaver Vale,* Maj. 9,637
Hall, Patrick (*b.* 1951) *Lab., Bedford,* Maj. 6,157
Hamilton, David (*b.* 1950) *Lab., Midlothian,* Maj. 9,014
*Hamilton, Fabian (*b.* 1955) *Lab., Leeds North East,* Maj. 7,089
Hammond, Philip (*b.* 1955) *C., Runnymede and Weybridge,* Maj. 8,360
*Hancock, Michael T., CBE (*b.* 1946) *LD, Portsmouth South,* Maj. 6,094
*Hanson, David G. (*b.* 1957) *Lab., Delyn,* Maj. 8,065
*Harman, Rt. Hon. Harriet, QC (*b.* 1950) *Lab., Camberwell and Peckham,* Maj. 14,123
*Harris, Dr Evan (*b.* 1965) *LD, Oxford West and Abingdon,* Maj. 9,185
Harris, Tom (*b.* 1964) *Lab., Glasgow Cathcart,* Maj. 10,816
*Harvey, Nicholas B. (*b.* 1961) *LD, Devon North,* Maj. 2,984
*Haselhurst, Rt. Hon. Sir Alan (*b.* 1937) *C., Saffron Walden,* Maj. 12,004
Havard, Dai (*b.* 1949) *Lab., Merthyr Tydfil and Rhymney,* Maj. 14,923
Hawkins, Nick (*b.* 1957) *C., Surrey Heath,* Maj. 10,819
Hayes, John H. (*b.* 1958) *C., South Holland and the Deepings,* Maj. 11,099
*Heal, Mrs Sylvia L. (*b.* 1942) *Lab., Halesowen and Rowley Regis,* Maj. 7,359
*Heald, Oliver (*b.* 1954) *C., Hertfordshire North East,* Maj. 3,444
Healey, John (*b.* 1960) *Lab., Wentworth,* Maj. 16,449
Heath, David W., CBE (*b.* 1954) *LD, Somerton and Frome,* Maj. 668
*Heathcoat-Amory, Rt. Hon. David P. (*b.* 1949) *C., Wells,* Maj. 2,796
*Henderson, Douglas J. (*b.* 1949) *Lab., Newcastle upon Tyne North,* Maj. 14,450
Henderson, Ivan J. (*b.* 1958) *Lab., Harwich,* Maj. 2,596
*Hendrick, Mark (*b.* 1958) *Lab.Co-op., Preston,* Maj. 12,268
Hendry, Charles (*b.* 1959) *C., Wealden,* Maj. 13,772
Hepburn, Stephen (*b.* 1959) *Lab., Jarrow,* Maj. 17,595
*Heppell, John (*b.* 1948) *Lab., Nottingham East,* Maj. 10,320
Hermon, Lady Sylvia (*b.* 1956) *UUP, Down North,* Maj. 7,324
Hesford, Stephen (*b.* 1957) *Lab., Wirral West,* Maj. 4,035
Hewitt, Rt. Hon. Patricia H. (*b.* 1948) *Lab., Leicester West,* Maj. 9,639
Heyes, David (*b.* 1946) *Lab., Ashton under Lyne,* Maj. 15,518
*Hill, Rt. Hon. Keith T. (*b.* 1943) *Lab., Streatham,* Maj. 14,270
*Hinchliffe, David M. (*b.* 1948) *Lab., Wakefield,* Maj. 7,954

Hoban, Mark (*b.* 1964) *C., Fareham,* Maj. 7,009
*Hodge, Rt. Hon. Mrs Margaret E., MBE (*b.* 1944) *Lab., Barking,* Maj. 9,534
*Hoey, Ms Catharine (Kate) L. (*b.* 1946) *Lab., Vauxhall,* Maj. 13,018
*Hogg, Rt. Hon. Douglas M., QC (*b.* 1945) *C., Sleaford and North Hykeham,* Maj. 8,622
Holmes, Paul (*b.* 1957) *LD, Chesterfield,* Maj. 2,586
*Hood, James (*b.* 1948) *Lab., Clydesdale,* Maj. 7,794
*Hoon, Rt. Hon. Geoffrey W. (*b.* 1953) *Lab., Ashfield,* Maj. 13,268
Hope, Philip I. (*b.* 1955) *Lab. Co-op., Corby,* Maj. 5,700
Hopkins, Kelvin P. (*b.* 1941) *Lab., Luton North,* Maj. 9,977
*Horam, John R. (*b.* 1939) *C., Orpington,* Maj. 269
*Howard, Rt. Hon. Michael, QC (*b.* 1941) *C., Folkestone and Hythe,* Maj. 5,907
*Howarth, Rt. Hon. Alan, CBE (*b.* 1944) *Lab., Newport East,* Maj. 9,874
*Howarth, George E. (*b.* 1949) *Lab., Knowsley North and Sefton East,* Maj. 18,927
Howarth, J. Gerald D. (*b.* 1947) *C., Aldershot,* Maj. 6,564
*Howells, Dr Kim S., PHD (*b.* 1946) *Lab., Pontypridd,* Maj. 17,684
Hoyle, Lindsay H. (*b.* 1957) *Lab., Chorley,* Maj. 8,444
*Hughes, Rt. Hon. Beverley J. (*b.* 1950) *Lab., Stretford and Urmston,* Maj. 13,239
*Hughes, Kevin M. (*b.* 1952) *Lab., Doncaster North,* Maj. 15,187
*Hughes, Simon H. W. (*b.* 1951) *LD, Southwark North and Bermondsey,* Maj. 9,632
Humble, Mrs Jovanka (Joan) (*b.* 1951) *Lab., Blackpool North and Fleetwood,* Maj. 5,721
*Hume, John, MEP (*b.* 1937) *SDLP, Foyle,* Maj. 11,550
*Hunter, Andrew R. F. (*b.* 1943) *Ind. C., Basingstoke,* Maj. 880
Hurst, Alan A. (*b.* 1945) *Lab., Braintree,* Maj. 358
*Hutton, Rt. Hon. John M. P. (*b.* 1955) *Lab., Barrow and Furness,* Maj. 9,889
Iddon, Dr Brian (*b.* 1940) *Lab., Bolton South East,* Maj. 12,871
*Illsley, Eric E. (*b.* 1955) *Lab., Barnsley Central,* Maj. 15,130
*Ingram, Rt. Hon. Adam P. (*b.* 1947) *Lab., East Kilbride,* Maj. 12,755
*Irranca-Davies, Huw (*b.* 1963) *Lab., Ogmore,* Maj. 5,721
*Jack, Rt. Hon. J. Michael (*b.* 1946) *C., Fylde,* Maj. 9,610
*Jackson, Ms Glenda M., CBE (*b.* 1936) *Lab., Hampstead and Highgate,* Maj. 7,876
*Jackson, Mrs Helen M. (*b.* 1939) *Lab., Sheffield Hillsborough,* Maj. 14,569
*Jackson, Robert V. (*b.* 1946) *C., Wantage,* Maj. 5,600
*Jamieson, David C. (*b.* 1947) *Lab., Plymouth Devonport,* Maj. 13,033
*Jenkin, Bernard C. (*b.* 1959) *C., Essex North,* Maj. 7,186
*Jenkins, Brian D. (*b.* 1942) *Lab., Tamworth,* Maj. 4,598
*Johnson, Rt. Hon. Alan A. (*b.* 1950) *Lab., Kingston upon Hull West and Hessle,* Maj. 10,951
Johnson, Boris (*b.* 1964) *C., Henley,* Maj. 8,458
Johnson, Ms Melanie J. (*b.* 1955) *Lab., Welwyn Hatfield,* Maj. 1,196
Jones, Ms Helen M. (*b.* 1954) *Lab., Warrington North,* Maj. 15,156
*Jones, Jonathan O. (*b.* 1954) *Lab. Co-op., Cardiff Central,* Maj. 659
Jones, Kevan (*b.* 1964) *Lab., Durham North,* Maj. 18,683

*Jones, Dr Lynne M., PHD (b. 1951) Lab., Birmingham Selly Oak, Maj. 10,339

*Jones, Martyn D. (b. 1947) Lab., Clwyd South, Maj. 8,898

*Jones, Nigel D. (b. 1948) LD, Cheltenham, Maj. 5,255

*Jowell, Rt. Hon. Tessa J. H. D. (b. 1947) Lab., Dulwich and West Norwood, Maj. 12,310

*Joyce, Eric (b. 1960) Lab., Falkirk West, Maj. 8,532

*Kaufman, Rt. Hon. Sir Gerald B. (b. 1930) Lab., Manchester Gorton, Maj. 11,304

Keeble, Ms Sally C. (b. 1951) Lab., Northampton North, Maj. 7,893

*Keen, D. Alan (b. 1937) Lab. Co-op., Feltham and Heston, Maj. 12,657

Keen, Mrs Ann L. (b. 1948) Lab. Co-op., Brentford and Isleworth, Maj. 10,318

*Keetch, Paul S. (b. 1961) LD, Hereford, Maj. 968

*Kelly, Ms Ruth M. (b. 1968) Lab., Bolton West, Maj. 5,518

*Kemp, Fraser (b. 1958) Lab., Houghton and Washington East, Maj. 19,818

*Kennedy, Rt. Hon. Charles P. (b. 1959) LD, Ross, Skye and Inverness West, Maj. 12,952

*Kennedy, Rt. Hon. Jane E. (b. 1958) Lab., Liverpool Wavertree, Maj. 12,319

*Key, S. Robert (b. 1945) C., Salisbury, Maj. 8,703

*Khabra, Piara S. (b. 1922) Lab., Ealing Southall, Maj. 13,683

*Kidney, David N. (b. 1955) Lab., Stafford, Maj. 5,032

*Kilfoyle, Peter (b. 1946) Lab., Liverpool Walton, Maj. 17,996

King, Andrew (b. 1948) Lab., Rugby and Kenilworth, Maj. 2,877

*King, Ms Oona T. (b. 1967) Lab., Bethnal Green and Bow, Maj. 10,057

*Kirkbride, Miss Julie (b. 1960) C., Bromsgrove, Maj. 8,138

*Kirkwood, Archibald J. (b. 1946) LD, Roxburgh and Berwickshire, Maj. 7,511

*Knight, Rt. Hon. Greg (b. 1949) C., Yorkshire East, Maj. 4,682

Knight, Jim (b. 1965) Lab., Dorset South, Maj. 153

*Kumar, Dr Ashok (b. 1956) Lab., Middlesbrough South and Cleveland East, Maj. 9,351

*Ladyman, Dr Stephen J. (b. 1952) Lab., Thanet South, Maj. 1,792

Laing, Mrs Eleanor F. (b. 1958) C., Epping Forest, Maj. 8,426

*Lait, Ms Jacqueline A. H. (b. 1947) C., Beckenham, Maj. 4,959

Lamb, Norman (b. 1957) LD, Norfolk North, Maj. 483

*Lammy, David (b. 1972) Lab., Tottenham, Maj. 16,916

*Lansley, Andrew D., CBE (b. 1956) C., Cambridgeshire South, Maj. 8,403

*Lawrence, Mrs Jacqueline R. (b. 1948) Lab., Preseli Pembrokeshire, Maj. 2,946

Laws, David (b. 1965) LD, Yeovil, Maj. 3,928

*Laxton, Robert (b. 1944) Lab., Derby North, Maj. 6,982

Lazarowicz, Mark (b. 1953) Lab., Edinburgh North and Leith, Maj. 8,817

*Leigh, Edward J. E. (b. 1950) C., Gainsborough, Maj. 8,071

*Lepper, David (b. 1945) Lab. Co-op., Brighton Pavilion, Maj. 9,643

Leslie, Christopher M. (b. 1972) Lab., Shipley, Maj. 1,428

Letwin, Rt. Hon. Oliver (b. 1956) C., Dorset West, Maj. 1,414

*Levitt, Tom (b. 1954) Lab., High Peak, Maj. 4,489

*Lewis, Ivan (b. 1967) Lab., Bury South, Maj. 12,772

*Lewis, Dr Julian M. (b. 1951) C., New Forest East, Maj. 3,829

*Lewis, Terence (b. 1935) Lab., Worsley, Maj. 11,787

*Liddell, Rt. Hon. Helen (b. 1950) Lab., Airdrie and Shotts, Maj. 12,340

Liddell-Grainger, Ian (b. 1959) C., Bridgwater, Maj. 4,987

*Lidington, David R., PHD (b. 1956) C., Aylesbury, Maj. 10,009

*Lilley, Rt. Hon. Peter B. (b. 1943) C., Hitchin and Harpenden, Maj. 6,663

Linton, J. Martin (b. 1944) Lab., Battersea, Maj. 5,053

*Lloyd, Anthony J. (b. 1950) Lab., Manchester Central, Maj. 13,742

*Llwyd, Elfyn (b. 1951) PC, Meirionnydd nant Conwy, Maj. 5,684

*Lord, Sir Michael N. (b. 1938) C., Suffolk Central and Ipswich North, Maj. 3,469

*Loughton, Timothy P. (b. 1962) C., Worthing East and Shoreham, Maj. 6,139

*Love, Andrew (b. 1949) Lab. Co-op., Edmonton, Maj. 9,772

Lucas, Ian (b. 1960) Lab., Wrexham, Maj. 9,188

*Luff, Peter J. (b. 1955) C., Worcestershire Mid, Maj. 10,627

Luke, Iain (b. 1951) Lab., Dundee East, Maj. 4,475

Lyons, John (b. 1950) Lab., Strathkelvin and Bearsden, Maj. 11,717

*McAvoy, Thomas M. (b. 1943) Lab. Co-op., Glasgow Rutherglen, Maj. 12,625

*McCabe, Stephen J. (b. 1955) Lab., Birmingham Hall Green, Maj. 6,648

*McCafferty, Ms Christine (b. 1945) Lab., Calder Valley, Maj. 3,094

*McCartney, Rt. Hon. Ian (b. 1951) Lab., Makerfield, Maj. 17,750

*McDonagh, Ms Siobhain A. (b. 1960) Lab., Mitcham and Morden, Maj. 13,785

*MacDonald, Calum A., PHD (b. 1956) Lab., Western Isles, Maj. 1,074

McDonnell, John M. (b. 1951) Lab., Hayes and Harlington, Maj. 13,466

*MacDougall, John (b. 1947) Lab., Fife Central, Maj. 10,075

*McFall, Rt. Hon. John (b. 1944) Lab. Co-op., Dumbarton, Maj. 9,575

*McGrady, Edward K. (b. 1935) SDLP, Down South, Maj. 13,858

McGuinness, Martin (b. 1950) SF, Ulster Mid, Maj. 9,953

McGuire, Mrs Anne (b. 1949) Lab., Stirling, Maj. 6,274

*McIntosh, Miss Anne C. B. (b. 1954) C., Vale of York, Maj. 12,517

McIsaac, Ms Shona (b. 1960) Lab., Cleethorpes, Maj. 5,620

*Mackay, Rt. Hon. Andrew J. (b. 1949) C., Bracknell, Maj. 6,713

McKechin, Ann (b. 1961) Lab., Glasgow Maryhill, Maj. 9,888

McKenna, Ms Rosemary, CBE (b. 1941) Lab., Cumbernauld and Kilsyth, Maj. 7,520

*Mackinlay, Andrew S. (b. 1949) Lab., Thurrock, Maj. 9,997

*Maclean, Rt. Hon. David J. (b. 1953) C., Penrith and the Border, Maj. 14,677

*McLoughlin, Patrick A. (b. 1957) C., Derbyshire West, Maj. 7,370

*McNamara, J. Kevin (*b.* 1934) *Lab., Hull North,* Maj. 10,721

*McNulty, Anthony J. (*b.* 1958) *Lab., Harrow East,* Maj. 11,124

*MacShane, Dr Denis, PHD (*b.* 1948) *Lab., Rotherham,* Maj. 13,077

Mactaggart, Ms Fiona M. (*b.* 1953) *Lab., Slough,* Maj. 12,508

*McWalter, Tony (*b.* 1945) *Lab. Co-op., Hemel Hempstead,* Maj. 3,742

*McWilliam, John D. (*b.* 1941) *Lab., Blaydon,* Maj. 7,809

Mahmood, Khalid (*b.* 1961) *Lab., Birmingham Perry Barr,* Maj. 8,753

*Mahon, Mrs Alice (*b.* 1937) *Lab., Halifax,* Maj. 6,129

Malins, Humfrey J., CBE (*b.* 1945) *C., Woking,* Maj. 6,759

*Mallaber, Ms C. Judith (*b.* 1951) *Lab., Amber Valley,* Maj. 7,227

*Mallon, Seamus (*b.* 1936) *SDLP, Newry and Armagh,* Maj. 3,575

†*Mandelson, Rt. Hon. Peter B. (*b.* 1953) *Lab., Hartlepool,* Maj. 14,571

Mann, John (*b.* 1960) *Lab., Bassetlaw,* Maj. 9,748

*Maples, John C. (*b.* 1943) *C., Stratford-upon-Avon,* Maj. 11,802

Marris, Robert (*b.* 1955) *Lab., Wolverhampton South West,* Maj. 3,487

*Marsden, Gordon (*b.* 1953) *Lab., Blackpool South,* Maj. 8,262

*Marsden, Paul W. B. (*b.* 1968) *Lab., Shrewsbury and Atcham,* Maj. 3,579

*Marshall, David, PHD (*b.* 1941) *Lab., Glasgow Shettleston,* Maj. 9,818

*Marshall-Andrews, Robert G., QC (*b.* 1944) *Lab., Medway,* Maj. 3,780

*Martin, Rt. Hon. Michael J. (*b.* 1945) *The Speaker, Glasgow Springburn,* Maj. 11,378

*Martlew, Eric A. (*b.* 1949) *Lab., Carlisle,* Maj. 5,702

*Mates, Rt. Hon. Michael J. (*b.* 1934) *C., Hampshire East,* Maj. 8,890

*Maude, Rt. Hon. Francis A. A. (*b.* 1953) *C., Horsham,* Maj. 13,666

*Mawhinney, Rt. Hon. Sir Brian, PHD (*b.* 1940) *C., Cambridgeshire North West,* Maj. 8,101

*May, Rt. Hon. Theresa M. (*b.* 1956) *C., Maidenhead,* Maj. 3,284

*Meacher, Rt. Hon. Michael H. (*b.* 1939) *Lab., Oldham West and Royton,* Maj. 13,365

*Meale, J. Alan (*b.* 1949) *Lab., Mansfield,* Maj. 11,038

Mercer, Patrick, OBE (*b.* 1956) *C., Newark,* Maj. 4,073

*Merron, Ms Gillian J. (*b.* 1959) *Lab., Lincoln,* Maj. 8,420

*Michael, Rt. Hon. Alun E. (*b.* 1943) *Lab. Co-op., Cardiff South and Penarth,* Maj. 12,287

*Milburn, Rt. Hon. Alan (*b.* 1958) *Lab., Darlington,* Maj. 9,529

Miliband, David (*b.* 1966) *Lab., South Shields,* Maj. 14,090

*Miller, Andrew P. (*b.* 1949) *Lab., Ellesmere Port and Neston,* Maj. 10,861

Mitchell, Andrew (*b.* 1956) *C., Sutton Coldfield,* Maj. 10,104

*Mitchell, Austin V., DPHIL (*b.* 1934) *Lab., Great Grimsby,* Maj. 11,484

*Moffatt, Mrs Laura J. (*b.* 1954) *Lab., Crawley,* Maj. 6,770

*Mole, Chris (*b.* 1958) *Lab., Ipswich,* Maj. 4,087

*Moonie, Dr Lewis (*b.* 1947) *Lab. Co-op., Kirkcaldy,* Maj. 8,963

*Moore, Michael (*b.* 1965) *LD, Tweeddale, Ettrick and Lauderdale,* Maj. 5,157

*Moran, Ms Margaret (*b.* 1955) *Lab., Luton South,* Maj. 10,133

Morgan, Ms Julie (*b.* 1944) *Lab., Cardiff North,* Maj. 6,165

*Morley, Elliot A. (*b.* 1952) *Lab., Scunthorpe,* Maj. 10,372

*Morris, Rt. Hon. Estelle (*b.* 1952) *Lab., Birmingham Yardley,* Maj. 2,578

*Moss, Malcolm D. (*b.* 1943) *C., Cambridgeshire North East,* Maj. 6,373

Mountford, Ms Kali C. J. (*b.* 1954) *Lab., Colne Valley,* Maj. 4,639

*Mudie, George E. (*b.* 1945) *Lab., Leeds East,* Maj. 12,643

*Mullin, Christopher J. (*b.* 1947) *Lab., Sunderland South,* Maj. 13,667

Munn, Meg (*b.* 1959) *Lab. Co-op., Sheffield Heeley,* Maj. 11,704

Murphy, Denis (*b.* 1948) *Lab., Wansbeck,* Maj. 13,101

Murphy, Jim (*b.* 1967) *Lab., Eastwood,* Maj. 9,141

*Murphy, Rt. Hon. Paul P. (*b.* 1948) *Lab., Torfaen,* Maj. 16,280

Murrison, Andrew (*b.* 1961) *C., Westbury,* Maj. 5,294

Naysmith, Dr J. Douglas (*b.* 1941) *Lab. Co-op., Bristol North West,* Maj. 11,087

Norman, Archibald J. (*b.* 1954) *C., Tunbridge Wells,* Maj. 9,730

Norris, Dan (*b.* 1960) *Lab., Wansdyke,* Maj. 5,113

*Oaten, Mark (*b.* 1964) *LD, Winchester,* Maj. 9,634

*O'Brien, Michael (*b.* 1954) *Lab., Warwickshire North,* Maj. 9,639

*O'Brien, Stephen (*b.* 1957) *C., Eddisbury,* Maj. 4,568

*O'Brien, William (*b.* 1929) *Lab., Normanton,* Maj. 9,937

*O'Hara, Edward (*b.* 1937) *Lab., Knowsley South,* Maj. 21,316

*Olner, William J. (*b.* 1942) *Lab., Nuneaton,* Maj. 7,535

*O'Neill, Martin J. (*b.* 1945) *Lab., Ochil,* Maj. 5,349

Öpik, Lembit (*b.* 1965) *LD, Montgomeryshire,* Maj. 6,234

*Organ, Ms Diana M. (*b.* 1952) *Lab., Forest of Dean,* Maj. 2,049

Osborne, George (*b.* 1971) *C., Tatton,* Maj. 8,611

Osborne, Mrs Sandra C. (*b.* 1956) *Lab., Ayr,* Maj. 2,545

*Ottaway, Richard G. J. (*b.* 1945) *C., Croydon South,* Maj. 8,697

*Owen, Albert (*b.* 1960) *Lab., Ynys Môn,* Maj. 800

*Page, Richard L. (*b.* 1941) *C., Hertfordshire South West,* Maj. 8,181

*Paice, James E. T. (*b.* 1949) *C., Cambridgeshire South East,* Maj. 8,990

*Paisley, Revd Ian R. K., MEP (*b.* 1926) *DUP, Antrim North,* Maj. 14,224

Palmer, Dr Nicholas D. (*b.* 1950) *Lab., Broxtowe,* Maj. 5,873

*Paterson, Owen W. (*b.* 1956) *C., Shropshire North,* Maj. 6,241

*Pearson, Ian P., PHD (*b.* 1959) *Lab., Dudley South,* Maj. 6,817

*Perham, Ms Linda (*b.* 1947) *Lab., Ilford North,* Maj. 2,115

Picking, Anne (*b.* 1958) *Lab., East Lothian,* Maj. 10,830

*Pickles, Eric J. (*b.* 1952) *C., Brentwood and Ongar,* Maj. 2,821

*Pickthall, Colin (*b.* 1944) *Lab., Lancashire West,* Maj. 9,643

*Pike, Peter L. (b. 1937) Lab., Burnley, Maj. 10,498
*Plaskitt, James A. (b. 1954) Lab., Warwick and Leamington, Maj. 5,953
Pollard, Kerry P. (b. 1944) Lab., St Albans, Maj. 4,466
*Pond, Christopher R. (b. 1952) Lab., Gravesham, Maj. 4,862
*Pope, Gregory J. (b. 1960) Lab., Hyndburn, Maj. 8,219
*Portillo, Rt. Hon. Michael (b. 1953) C., Kensington and Chelsea, Maj. 8,771
Pound, Stephen P. (b. 1948) Lab., Ealing North, Maj. 11,837
*Prentice, Ms Bridget T. (b. 1952) Lab., Lewisham East, Maj. 8,959
*Prentice, Gordon (b. 1951) Lab., Pendle, Maj. 4,275
*Prescott, Rt. Hon. John L. (b. 1938) Lab., Hull East, Maj. 15,325
Price, Adam (b. 1968) PC, Carmarthen East and Dinefwr, Maj. 2,590
*Primarolo, Rt. Hon. Dawn (b. 1954) Lab., Bristol South, Maj. 14,181
*Prisk, Mark (b. 1962) C., Hertford and Stortford, Maj. 5,603
*Prosser, Gwynfor M. (b. 1943) Lab., Dover, Maj. 5,199
Pugh, Dr John (b. 1949) LD, Southport, Maj. 3,007
*Purchase, Kenneth (b. 1939) Lab. Co-op., Wolverhampton North East, Maj. 9,965
Purnell, James (b. 1970) Lab., Stalybridge and Hyde, Maj. 8,859
*Quin, Rt. Hon. Joyce G. (b. 1944) Lab., Gateshead East and Washington West, Maj. 17,904
*Quinn, Lawrence W. (b. 1956) Lab., Scarborough and Whitby, Maj. 3,585
*Rammell, William E. (b. 1959) Lab., Harlow, Maj. 5,228
*Randall, A. John (b. 1955) C., Uxbridge, Maj. 2,098
Rapson, Sydney N. J. (b. 1942) Lab., Portsmouth North, Maj. 5,134
*Raynsford, Rt. Hon. W. R. N. (Nick) (b. 1945) Lab., Greenwich and Woolwich, Maj. 13,433
*Redwood, Rt. Hon. John A., DPHIL (b. 1951) C., Wokingham, Maj. 5,994
Reed, Andrew J. (b. 1964) Lab., Loughborough, Maj. 6,378
Reid, Alan (b. 1954) LD, Argyll and Bute, Maj. 1,653
*Reid, Rt. Hon. John, PHD (b. 1947) Lab., Hamilton North and Bellshill, Maj. 13,561
*Rendel, David D. (b. 1949) LD, Newbury, Maj. 2,415
*Robathan, Andrew R. G. (b. 1951) C., Blaby, Maj. 6,209
Robertson, Angus (b. 1969) SNP, Moray, Maj. 1,744
Robertson, Hugh (b. 1962) C., Faversham and Mid Kent, Maj. 4,183
*Robertson, John (b. 1952) Lab., Glasgow Anniesland, Maj. 11,054
Robertson, Laurence A. (b. 1958) C., Tewkesbury, Maj. 8,663
*Robinson, Geoffrey (b. 1938) Lab., Coventry North West, Maj. 10,874
Robinson, Iris, MLA (b. 1949) DUP, Strangford, Maj. 1,110
*Robinson, Peter D. (b. 1948) DUP, Belfast East, Maj. 7,117
*Roche, Mrs Barbara M. R. (b. 1954) Lab., Hornsey and Wood Green, Maj. 10,614
*Roe, Dame Marion A., DBE (b. 1936) C., Broxbourne, Maj. 8,993
*Rooney, Terence H. (b. 1950) Lab., Bradford North, Maj. 8,969

Rosindell, Andrew (b. 1966) C., Romford, Maj. 5,977
*Ross, Ernest (b. 1942) Lab., Dundee West, Maj. 6,800
*Roy, Frank (b. 1958) Lab., Motherwell and Wishaw, Maj. 10,956
*Ruane, Christopher S. (b. 1958) Lab., Vale of Clwyd, Maj. 5,761
*Ruddock, Mrs Joan M. (b. 1943) Lab., Lewisham Deptford, Maj. 15,293
Ruffley, David L. (b. 1962) C., Bury St Edmunds, Maj. 2,503
Russell, Ms Christine M. (b. 1945) Lab., City of Chester, Maj. 6,894
*Russell, Robert E. (b. 1946) LD, Colchester, Maj. 5,553
*Ryan, Ms Joan M. (b. 1955) Lab., Enfield North, Maj. 2,291
*Salmond, Alexander E. A. (b. 1954) SNP, Banff and Buchan, Maj. 10,503
Salter, Martin J. (b. 1954) Lab., Reading West, Maj. 8,849
*Sanders, Adrian M. (b. 1959) LD, Torbay, Maj. 6,708
*Sarwar, Mohammad (b. 1952) Lab., Glasgow Govan, Maj. 6,400
*Savidge, Malcolm K. (b. 1946) Lab., Aberdeen North, Maj. 4,449
*Sawford, Philip A. (b. 1950) Lab., Kettering, Maj. 665
*Sayeed, Jonathan (b. 1948) C., Bedfordshire Mid, Maj. 8,066
*Sedgemore, Brian C. J. (b. 1937) Lab., Hackney South and Shoreditch, Maj. 15,049
Selous, Andrew (b. 1962) C., Bedfordshire South West, Maj. 776
*Shaw, Jonathan R. (b. 1966) Lab., Chatham and Aylesford, Maj. 4,340
*Sheerman, Barry J. (b. 1940) Lab. Co-op., Huddersfield, Maj. 10,046
*Shephard, Rt. Hon. Gillian P. (b. 1940) C., Norfolk South West, Maj. 9,366
*Shepherd, Richard C. S. (b. 1942) C., Aldridge-Brownhills, Maj. 3,768
Sheridan, Jim (b. 1952) Lab., Renfrewshire West, Maj. 8,575
*Shipley, Ms Debra A. (b. 1957) Lab., Stourbridge, Maj. 3,812
*Short, Rt. Hon. Clare (b. 1946) Lab., Birmingham Ladywood, Maj. 18,143
Simmonds, Mark (b. 1964) C., Boston and Skegness, Maj. 515
Simon, Siôn (b. 1969) Lab., Birmingham Erdington, Maj. 9,962
*Simpson, Alan J. (b. 1948) Lab., Nottingham South, Maj. 9,989
*Simpson, Keith (b. 1949) C., Norfolk Mid, Maj. 4,562
Singh, Marsha (b. 1954) Lab., Bradford West, Maj. 4,165
*Skinner, Dennis E. (b. 1932) Lab., Bolsover, Maj. 18,777
*Smith, Rt. Hon. Andrew D. (b. 1951) Lab., Oxford East, Maj. 10,344
*Smith, Ms Angela E. (b. 1959) Lab. Co-op., Basildon, Maj. 7,738
*Smith, Rt. Hon. Christopher R., PHD (b. 1951) Lab., Islington South and Finsbury, Maj. 7,280
*Smith, Ms Geraldine (b. 1961) Lab., Morecambe and Lunesdale, Maj. 5,092
*Smith, Rt. Hon. Jacqui (b. 1962) Lab., Redditch, Maj. 2,484
*Smith, John W. P. (b. 1951) Lab., Vale of Glamorgan, Maj. 4,700
*Smith, Llewellyn T. (b. 1944) Lab., Blaenau Gwent, Maj. 19,313

*Smith, Sir Robert, Bt. (b. 1958) LD, Aberdeenshire West and Kincardine, Maj. 4,821

*Smyth, Revd W. Martin (b. 1931) UUP, Belfast South, Maj. 5,399

*Soames, Hon. A. Nicholas W. (b. 1948) C., Sussex Mid, Maj. 6,898

*Soley, Clive S. (b. 1939) Lab., Ealing, Acton and Shepherd's Bush, Maj. 10,789

Southworth, Ms Helen M. (b. 1956) Lab., Warrington South, Maj. 7,387

*Spellar, Rt. Hon. John F. (b. 1947) Lab., Warley, Maj. 11,850

Spelman, Mrs Caroline A. (b. 1958) C., Meriden, Maj. 3,784

*Spicer, Sir Michael (b. 1943) C., Worcestershire West, Maj. 5,374

Spink, Dr Robert (b. 1948) C., Castle Point, Maj. 985

*Spring, Richard J. G. (b. 1946) C., Suffolk West, Maj. 4,295

*Squire, Ms Rachel A. (b. 1954) Lab., Dunfermline West, Maj. 10,980

*Stanley, Rt. Hon. Sir John (b. 1942) C., Tonbridge and Malling, Maj. 8,250

Starkey, Dr Phyllis M. (b. 1947) Lab., Milton Keynes South West, Maj. 6,978

*Steen, Anthony (b. 1939) C., Totnes, Maj. 3,597

*Steinberg, Gerald N. (b. 1945) Lab., City of Durham, Maj. 13,441

*Stevenson, George W. (b. 1938) Lab., Stoke-on-Trent South, Maj. 10,489

*Stewart, David J. (b. 1956) Lab., Inverness East, Nairn and Lochaber, Maj. 4,716

*Stewart, Ian (b. 1950) Lab., Eccles, Maj. 14,528

*Stinchcombe, Paul D. (b. 1962) Lab., Wellingborough, Maj. 2,355

*Stoate, Dr Howard G. A. (b. 1954) Lab., Dartford, Maj. 3,306

*Strang, Rt. Hon. Dr Gavin (b. 1943) Lab., Edinburgh East and Musselburgh, Maj. 12,168

*Straw, Rt. Hon. J. W. (Jack) (b. 1946) Lab., Blackburn, Maj. 9,249

*Streeter, Gary N. (b. 1955) C., Devon South West, Maj. 7,144

*Stringer, Graham E. (b. 1950) Lab., Manchester Blackley, Maj. 14,464

*Stuart, Mrs Gisela G. (b. 1955) Lab., Birmingham Edgbaston, Maj. 4,698

*Stunell, Andrew (b. 1942) LD, Hazel Grove, Maj. 8,435

*Sutcliffe, Gerard (b. 1953) Lab., Bradford South, Maj. 9,662

Swayne, Desmond A. (b. 1956) C., New Forest West, Maj. 13,191

Swire, Hugo (b. 1959) C., Devon East, Maj. 8,195

*Syms, Robert A. R. (b. 1956) C., Poole, Maj. 7,166

Tami, Mark (b. 1963) Lab., Alyn and Deeside, Maj. 9,222

*Tapsell, Sir Peter (b. 1930) C., Louth and Horncastle, Maj. 7,554

*Taylor, Rt. Hon. Ann (b. 1947) Lab., Dewsbury, Maj. 7,449

*Taylor, Ms Dari J. (b. 1944) Lab., Stockton South, Maj. 9,086

Taylor, David L. (b. 1946) Lab. Co-op., Leicestershire North West, Maj. 8,157

*Taylor, Sir Edward (Teddy) (b. 1937) C., Rochford and Southend East, Maj. 7,034

*Taylor, Ian C., MBE (b. 1945) C., Esher and Walton, Maj. 11,538

*Taylor, John M. (b. 1941) C., Solihull, Maj. 9,407

*Taylor, Matthew O. J. (b. 1963) LD, Truro and St Austell, Maj. 8,065

Taylor, Dr Richard (b. 1935) KHHC, Wyre Forest, Maj. 17,630

Teather, Sarah (b. 1974) LD, Brent East, Maj. 1,118

Thomas, Gareth (b. 1954) Lab., Clwyd West, Maj. 1,115

*Thomas, Gareth R. (b. 1967) Lab., Harrow West, Maj. 6,156

*Thomas, Simon (b. 1963) PC, Ceredigion, Maj. 3,944

*Thurso, John (b. 1953) LD, Caithness, Sutherland and Easter Ross, Maj. 2,744

*Timms, Stephen C. (b. 1955) Lab., East Ham, Maj. 21,032

*Tipping, S. P. (Paddy) (b. 1949) Lab., Sherwood, Maj. 9,373

Todd, Mark W. (b. 1954) Lab., Derbyshire South, Maj. 7,851

Tonge, Dr Jennifer L. (b. 1941) LD, Richmond Park, Maj. 4,964

*Touhig, J. Donnelly (Don) (b. 1947) Lab. Co-op., Islwyn, Maj. 15,309

*Tredinnick, David A. S. (b. 1950) C., Bosworth, Maj. 2,280

*Trend, Hon. Michael St J., CBE (b. 1952) C., Windsor, Maj. 8,889

*Trickett, Jon H. (b. 1950) Lab., Hemsworth, Maj. 15,636

*Trimble, Rt. Hon. W. David (b. 1944) UUP, Upper Bann, Maj. 2,058

Truswell, Paul A. (b. 1955) Lab., Pudsey, Maj. 5,626

Turner, Andrew (b. 1953) C., Isle of Wight, Maj. 2,826

*Turner, Dennis (b. 1942) Lab. Co-op., Wolverhampton South East, Maj. 12,464

Turner, Dr Desmond S. (b. 1939) Lab., Brighton Kemptown, Maj. 4,922

*Turner, Neil (b. 1945) Lab., Wigan, Maj. 13,743

*Twigg, J. Derek (b. 1959) Lab., Halton, Maj. 17,428

*Twigg, Stephen (b. 1966) Lab., Enfield Southgate, Maj. 5,546

*Tyler, Paul A., CBE (b. 1941) LD, Cornwall North, Maj. 9,832

*Tynan, Bill (b. 1940) Lab., Hamilton South, Maj. 10,775

*Tyrie, Andrew G. (b. 1957) C., Chichester, Maj. 11,355

*Vaz, N. Keith A. S. (b. 1956) Lab., Leicester East, Maj. 13,422

*Viggers, Peter J. (b. 1938) C., Gosport, Maj. 2,621

*Vis, Dr R. J. (Rudi) (b. 1941) Lab., Finchley and Golders Green, Maj. 3,716

*Walley, Ms Joan L. (b. 1949) Lab., Stoke-on-Trent North, Maj. 11,784

*Walter, Robert J. (b. 1948) C., Dorset North, Maj. 3,797

*Ward, Ms Claire M. (b. 1972) Lab., Watford, Maj. 5,555

*Wareing, Robert N. (b. 1930) Lab., Liverpool West Derby, Maj. 15,853

*Waterson, Nigel C. (b. 1950) C., Eastbourne, Maj. 2,154

Watkinson, Angela (b. 1941) C., Upminster, Maj. 1,241

*Watson, Tom (b. 1967) Lab., West Bromwich East, Maj. 9,763

Watts, David L. (b. 1951) Lab., St Helens North, Maj. 15,901

Webb, Prof. Steven J. (b. 1965) LD, Northavon, Maj. 9,877

Weir, Michael (b. 1957) SNP, Angus, Maj. 3,611

White, Brian A. R. (b. 1957) Lab., Milton Keynes North East, Maj. 1,829

*Whitehead, Dr Alan P. V. (b. 1950) Lab., Southampton Test, Maj. 11,207

*Whittingdale, John F. L., OBE (b. 1959) C., Maldon and Chelmsford East, Maj. 8,462

*Wicks, Malcolm H. (b. 1947) Lab., Croydon North, Maj. 16,858
*Widdecombe, Rt. Hon. Ann N. (b. 1947) C., Maidstone and the Weald, Maj. 10,318
Wiggin, Bill (b. 1966) C., Leominster, Maj. 10,367
*Wilkinson, John A. D. (b. 1940) C., Ruislip-Northwood, Maj. 7,537
*Willetts, David L. (b. 1956) C., Havant, Maj. 4,207
*Williams, Rt. Hon. Alan J. (b. 1930) Lab., Swansea West, Maj. 9,550
*Williams, Betty (b. 1944) Lab., Conwy, Maj. 6,219
Williams, Hywel (b. 1953) PC, Caernarfon, Maj. 3,511
Williams, Roger (b. 1948) LD, Brecon and Radnorshire, Maj. 751
*Willis, G. Philip (b. 1941) LD, Harrogate and Knaresborough, Maj. 8,845
Wills, Michael D. (b. 1952) Lab., Swindon North, Maj. 8,105
*Wilshire, David (b. 1943) C., Spelthorne, Maj. 3,262
*Wilson, Rt. Hon. Brian D. H. (b. 1948) Lab., Cunninghame North, Maj. 8,398
*Winnick, David J. (b. 1933) Lab., Walsall North, Maj. 9,391
*Winterton, Mrs J. Ann (b. 1941) C., Congleton, Maj. 7,134
*Winterton, Sir Nicholas R. (b. 1938) C., Macclesfield, Maj. 7,200

Winterton, Ms Rosalie (b. 1958) Lab., Doncaster Central, Maj. 11,999
Wishart, Peter (b. 1962) SNP, Tayside North, Maj. 3,283
*Wood, Michael R. (b. 1946) Lab., Batley and Spen, Maj. 5,064
Woodward, Shaun (b. 1958) Lab., St Helens South, Maj. 8,985
*Woolas, Philip J. (b. 1959) Lab., Oldham East and Saddleworth, Maj. 2,726
*Worthington, Anthony (b. 1941) Lab., Clydebank and Milngavie, Maj. 10,724
*Wray, James (b. 1938) Lab., Glasgow Baillieston, Maj. 9,839
Wright, Anthony D., DPHIL (b. 1954) Lab., Great Yarmouth, Maj. 4,564
*Wright, Dr Anthony W. (b. 1948) Lab., Cannock Chase, Maj. 10,704
Wright, David (b. 1967) Lab., Telford, Maj. 8,383
*Wyatt, Derek M. (b. 1949) Lab., Sittingbourne and Sheppey, Maj. 3,509
*Yeo, Timothy S. K. (b. 1945) C., Suffolk South, Maj. 5,081
*Young, Rt. Hon. Sir George, Bt. (b. 1941) C., Hampshire North West, Maj. 12,009
Younger-Ross, Richard (b. 1953) LD, Teignbridge, Maj. 3,011

*Sitting MP
† A by-election for Hartlepool was held on 30 September 2004 following the resignation of Peter Mandelson. See Stop Press.
For by-elections since 2001 see page 181

GENERAL ELECTION STATISTICS

PARLIAMENTS SINCE 1970

Assembled	Dissolved	yr	m.	d.
29 June 1970	8 February 1974	3	7	10
6 March 1974	20 September 1974	0	6	14
22 October 1974	7 April 1979	4	5	16
9 May 1979	13 May 1983	4	0	4
15 June 1983	18 May 1987	3	11	3
17 June 1987	16 March 1992	4	8	28
27 April 1992	8 April 1997	4	11	12
7 May 1997	14 May 2001	4	0	7
13 June 2001				

GENERAL ELECTION TURNOUT

	2001	1997
England	59.4	71.4
Wales	61.6	73.5
Scotland	58.2	71.3
Northern Ireland	68.0	67.1

VOTES CAST 1997 AND 2001

	1997	2001
Conservative	9,600,940	8,357,622
Labour	13,517,911	10,724,895
Liberal Democrats	5,243,440	4,812,833
Scottish Nationalist	622,260	464,305
Plaid Cymru	161,030	195,892
N. Ireland parties	780,920	635,735
Others	1,361,701	1,177,516
Total	31,287,702	26,368,798

PARLIAMENTARY CONSTITUENCIES AS AT 7 JUNE 2001

The results of voting in each parliamentary division at the general election of 7 June 2001 are given below. The majority in the 1997 general election and any by-election between 1997 and 2001, is given below the 2001 result.

Key
*Sitting MP
†Previously MP in another seat
E. Electorate
T. Turnout

Abbreviations

AL	Asian League
Alliance	Alliance
Anti-Corrupt	Anti-Corruption Forum
BNP	British National Party
Bean	New Millennium Bean
CPA	Christian Peoples Alliance
Ch. D.	Christian Democrat
Choice	People's Choice
Comm.	Communist Party
Community	Independent Community Candidate Empowering Change
C.	Conservative
Country	Countryside Party
Customer	Direct Customer Service Party
Def Welfare	Defend the Welfare State Against Blairism
DUP	Democratic Unionist Party
EIP	English Independence Party
Elvis	Church of the Militant Elvis Party
Ext. Club	Extinction Club
FDP	Fancy Dress Party
Free	Freedom Party
Green	Green Party
Grey	Grey Party
Ind.	Independent
Ind. UU	Independent United Unionist
Ind. Vote	Independent – Vote for Yourself Party
IOW	Isle of Wight Party
JLD P	John Lillburne Democratic Party
JP	Justice Party
KHHC	Kidderminster Hospital and Health Concern
Lab.	Labour
Lab. Co-op	Labour and Co-operative
LCA	Legalise Cannabis Alliance
LD	Liberal Democrat
LP	Liberated Party
Left All	All Left Alliance
Lib.	Liberal
Loony	Monster Raving Loony Party
Low Excise	Lower Excise Duty Party
Marxist	Marxist Party
Meb. Ker.	Mebyon Kernow
Muslim	Muslim Party
NBP	New Britain Party
NF	National Front
NI Unionist	Northern Ireland Unionist
NI WC	Northern Ireland Women's Coalition
PC	Plaid Cymru
PF	Pathfinders
PJP	People's Justice Party
PUP	Progressive Unionist Party
Pacifist	Pacifist for Peace, Justice, Cooperation, Environment
Pensioner	Pensioner Coalition
Pro Euro C	Pro Euro Conservative Party
ProLife	ProLife Alliance
Prog Dem	Progress Democratic Party Members Decide Policy
Qari	Qari
R & R Loony	Rock & Roll Loony Party
RP	Rate Payer
Ref. UK	Reform UK
Reform	Reform 2000
Res. Motor	Motor Residents and Motorists of Great Britain
SDLP	Social Democratic and Labour Party
SF	Sinn Fein
SNP	Scottish National Party
SSP	Scottish Socialist Party
Scot. Ref.	Scottish Freedom Referendum Party
Scot. U.	Scottish Unionist
Soc.	Socialist Party
Soc. All.	Socialist Alliance
Soc. Alt.	Socialist Alternative Party
Soc. Lab.	Socialist Labour Party
Socialist	Socialist
Speaker	The Speaker
Stuck	Stuckist
Sunrise	Chairman of Sunrise Radio
Tatton	Tatton Group Independent
Third	Third Way
Truth	Truth Party
UK Ind.	UK Independence Party
UKU	United Kingdom Unionist
UUP	Ulster Unionist Party
Unrep.	Unrepresented People's Party
WSA	Welsh Socialist Alliance
Wessex Reg.	Wessex Regionalist
WFLOE	Women for Life on Earth
Women's Co.	Women's Coalition
WP	Workers' Party
WRP	Workers' Revolutionary Party
Wrestling	Jam Wrestling Party

ENGLAND

ALDERSHOT
E. 78,262 T. 45,315 (57.90%)   C. hold
*Gerald Howarth, C.   19,106
Adrian Collett, LD   12,542
Luke Akehurst, Lab.   11,391
Derek Rumsey, UK Ind.   797
Adam Stacey, Green   630
Arthur Pendragon, Ind.   459
Alan Hope, Loony   390
C. majority 6,564 (14.49%)
1.13% swing LD to C.
(1997: C. maj. 6,621 (12.22%))

ALDRIDGE-BROWNHILLS
E. 62,388 T. 37,810 (60.60%)   C. hold
*Richard Shepherd, C.   18,974
Ian Geary, Lab.   15,206
Mrs Monica Howes, LD   3,251
John Rothery, Soc. All.   379
C. majority 3,768 (9.97%)
2.26% swing Lab. to C.
(1997: C. maj. 2,526 (5.44%))

ALTRINCHAM & SALE WEST
E. 71,820 T. 43,568 (60.66%)   C. hold
*Graham Brady, C.   20,113
Ms Janet Baugh, Lab.   17,172
Christopher Gaskell, LD   6,283
C. majority 2,941 (6.75%)
1.92% swing Lab. to C.
(1997: C. maj. 1,505 (2.91%))

AMBER VALLEY
E. 73,798 T. 44,513 (60.32%) Lab. hold
*Ms Judy Mallaber, Lab.   23,101
Ms Gillian Shaw, C.   15,874
Ms Kate Smith, LD   5,538
Lab. majority 7,227 (16.24%)
2.49% swing Lab. to C.
(1997: Lab. maj. 11,613 (21.21%))

ARUNDEL & SOUTH DOWNS
E. 70,956 T. 45,889 (64.67%)   C. hold
*Howard Flight, C.   23,969
Derek Deedman, LD   10,265
Charles Taylor, Lab.   9,488
Robert Perrin, UK Ind.   2,167
C. majority 13,704 (29.86%)
1.26% swing LD to C.
(1997: C. maj. 14,035 (27.34%))

ASHFIELD
E. 73,428 T. 39,350 (53.59%) Lab. hold
*Rt. Hon. G. Hoon, Lab.   22,875
Julian Leigh, C.   9,607
Bill Smith, LD   4,428
Melvin Harby, Ind.   1,471
George Watson, Soc. All.   589
Ms Katrina Howse, Soc. Lab.   380
Lab. majority 13,268 (33.72%)
5.60% swing Lab. to C.
(1997: Lab. maj. 22,728 (44.91%))

ASHFORD
E. 76,699 T. 47,937 (62.50%)   C. hold
*Damien Green, C.   22,739
John Adams, Lab.   15,380
Keith Fitchett, LD   7,236
Richard Boden, Green   1,353
David Waller, UK Ind.   1,229
C. majority 7,359 (15.35%)
2.84% swing Lab. to C.
(1997: C. maj. 5,355 (9.68%))

ASHTON UNDER LYNE
E. 72,820 T. 35,764 (49.11%) Lab. hold
David Heyes, Lab.   22,340
Tim Charlesworth, C.   6,822
Mrs Kate Fletcher, LD   4,237
Roger Woods, BNP   1,617
Nigel Rolland, Green   748
Lab. majority 15,518 (43.39%)
2.59% swing Lab. to C.
(1997: Lab. maj. 22,965 (48.57%))

AYLESBURY
E. 80,002 T. 49,087 (61.36%)   C. hold
*David Lidington, C.   23,230
Peter Jones, LD   13,221
Keith White, Lab.   11,388
Justin Harper, UK Ind.   1,248
C. majority 10,009 (20.39%)
2.88% swing LD to C.
(1997: C. maj. 8,419 (14.63%))

BANBURY
E. 83,392 T. 51,515 (61.77%)   C. hold
*Tony Baldry, C.   23,271
Leslie Sibley, Lab.   18,052
Tony Worgan, LD   8,216
Bev Cotton, Green   1,281
Stephen Harris, UK Ind.   695
C. majority 5,219 (10.13%)
1.02% swing Lab. to C.
(1997: C. maj. 4,737 (8.10%))

BARKING
E. 55,229 T. 25,126 (45.49%) Lab. hold
*Mrs Margaret Hodge, Lab.   15,302
Mike Weatherley, C.   5,768
Anura Keppetipola, LD   2,450
Mark Toleman, BNP   1,606
Lab. majority 9,534 (37.94%)
5.14% swing Lab. to C.
(1997: Lab. maj. 15,896 (48.22%))

BARNSLEY CENTRAL
E. 60,086 T. 27,543 (45.84%) Lab. hold
*Eric Illsley, Lab.   19,181
Alan Hartley, LD   4,051
Ian McCord, C.   3,608
Henry Rajch, Soc. All.   703
Lab. majority 15,130 (54.93%)
6.26% swing Lab. to LD
(1997: Lab. maj. 24,501 (67.15%))

BARNSLEY EAST & MEXBOROUGH
E. 65,655 T. 32,509 (49.51%) Lab. hold
*Jeff Ennis, Lab.   21,945
Mrs Sharron Brook, LD   5,156
Matthew Offord, C.   4,024
Terry Robinson, Soc. Lab.   722
George Savage, UK Ind.   662
Lab. majority 16,789 (51.64%)
5.57% swing Lab. to LD
(1997: Lab. maj. 26,763 (61.76%))

BARNSLEY WEST & PENISTONE
E. 65,291 T. 34,564 (52.94%) Lab. hold
*Michael Clapham, Lab.   20,244
William Rowe, C.   7,892
Miles Crompton, LD   6,428
Lab. majority 12,352 (35.74%)
2.59% swing Lab. to C.
(1997: Lab. maj. 17,267 (40.91%))

BARROW & FURNESS
E. 64,746 T. 39,020 (60.27%) Lab. hold
*Rt. Hon. J. Hutton, Lab.   21,724
James Airey, C.   11,835
Barry Rabone, LD   4,750
John Smith, UK Ind.   711
Lab. majority 9,889 (25.34%)
2.36% swing Lab. to C.
(1997: Lab. maj. 14,497 (30.06%))

BASILDON
E. 74,121 T. 40,875 (55.15%)
                             Lab. Co-op hold
*Ms Angela Smith, Lab. Co-op   21,551
Dominic Schofield, C.   13,813
Ms Jane Smithard, LD   3,691
Frank Mallon, C.   1,397
Dick Duane, Soc. All.   423
Lab. Co-op majority 7,738 (18.93%)
3.04% swing Lab. Co-op to C.
(1997: Lab. maj. 13,280 (25.02%))

BASINGSTOKE
E. 79,110 T. 47,995 (60.67%)   C. hold
*Andrew Hunter, C.   20,490
Jon Hartley, Lab.   19,610
Steve Sollitt, LD   6,693
Mrs Kim-Elisbeth Graham, UK Ind. 1,202
C. majority 880 (1.83%)
1.18% swing C. to Lab.
(1997: C. maj. 2,397 (4.19%))

BASSETLAW
E. 68,302 T. 38,895 (56.95%) Lab. hold
John Mann, Lab.   21,506
Mrs Alison Holley, C.   11,758
Neil Taylor, LD   4,942
Kevin Meloy, Soc. Lab.   689
Lab. majority 9,748 (25.06%)
5.68% swing Lab. to C.
(1997: Lab. maj 17,460 (36.43%))

BATH
E. 71,372 T. 46,296 (64.87%)   LD hold
*Don Foster, LD   23,372
Ashley Fox, C.   13,478
Ms Marilyn Hawkings, Lab.   7,269
Mike Boulton, Green   1,469
Andrew Tettenborn, UK Ind.   708
LD majority 9,894 (21.37%)
2.06% swing C. to LD
(1997: LD maj. 9,319 (17.26%))

BATLEY & SPEN
E. 63,665 T. 38,542 (60.54%) Lab. hold
*Mike Wood Lab.   19,224
Mrs Elizabeth Peacock C.   14,160
Ms Kath Pinnock, LD   3,989
Clive Lord, Green   595
Allen Burton, UK Ind.   574
Lab. majority 5,064 (13.14%)
0.03% swing C. to Lab.
(1997: Lab. maj. 6,141 (13.08%))

BATTERSEA
E. 67,495 T. 36,804 (54.53%) Lab. hold
*Martin Linton, Lab.   18,498
Mrs Lucy Shersby, C.   13,445
Ms Siobhan Vitelli, LD   4,450
Thomas Barber, Ind.   411
Lab. majority 5,053 (13.73%)
1.21% swing C. to Lab.
(1997: Lab. maj. 5,360 (11.31%))

BEACONSFIELD
E. 68,378 T. 42,044 (61.49%)   C. hold
*Dominic Grieve, C.   22,233
Stephen Lathrope, Lab.   9,168
Stephen Lloyd, LD   9,017
Andrew Moffatt, UK Ind.   1,626
C. majority 13,065 (31.07%)
0.95% swing Lab. to C.
(1997: C. maj. 13,987 (27.86%))

BECKENHAM
E. 72,241 T. 45,562 (63.07%)   C. hold
*Mrs Jacqui Lait, C.   20,618
Richard Watts, Lab.   15,659
Alex Feakes, LD   7,308
Ms Karen Moran, Green   961
Christopher Pratt, UK Ind.   782
Rif Winfield, Lib.   234
C. majority 4,959 (10.88%)
0.89% swing Lab. to C.
(1997 Nov. by-election: C. maj. 1,227
(3.85%); (1997: C. maj. 4,953 (9.11%))

BEDFORD
E. 67,763 T. 40,579 (59.88%) Lab. hold
*Patrick Hall, Lab.   19,454
Mrs Nicky Attenborough, C.   13,297
Michael Headley, LD   6,425
Dr Richard Rawlins, Ind.   973
Mrs Jennifer Lo Bianco, UK Ind.   430
Lab. majority 6,157 (15.17%)
0.89% swing Lab. to C.
(1997: Lab. maj. 8,300 (16.96%))

BEDFORDSHIRE MID
E. 70,594 T. 46,638 (66.07%)   C. hold
*Jonathan Sayeed, C.   22,109
James Valentine, Lab.   14,043
Graham Mabbutt, LD   9,205
Christopher Laurence, UK Ind.   1,281
C. majority 8,066 (17.29%)
1.89% swing Lab. to C.
(1997: C. maj. 7,090 (13.51%))

BEDFORDSHIRE NORTH EAST
E. 69,451 T. 45,246 (65.15%)   C. hold
Alastair Burt, C.   22,586
Philip Ross, Lab.   14,009
Dan Rogerson, LD   7,409
Ms Ros Hill, UK Ind.   1,242
C. majority 8,577 (18.96%)
3.64% swing Lab. to C.
(1997: C. maj. 5,883 (11.68%))

BEDFORDSHIRE SOUTH WEST
E. 72,126 T. 43,854 (60.80%)   C. hold
Andrew Selous, C.   18,477
Andrew Date, Lab.   17,701
Martin Pantling, LD   6,473
Tom Wise, UK Ind.   1,203
C. majority 776 (1.77%)
0.76% swing Lab. to C.
(1997: C. maj. 132 (0.24%))

BERWICK-UPON-TWEED
E. 56,918 T. 36,308 (63.79%)   LD hold
*Rt. Hon. A. Beith, LD   18,651
Glen Sanderson, C.   10,193
Martin Walker, Lab.   6,435
John Pearson, UK Ind.   1,029
LD majority 8,458 (23.30%)
0.94% swing C. to LD
(1997: LD maj. 8,042 (19.24%))

BETHNAL GREEN & BOW
E. 79,192 T. 38,470 (48.58%) Lab. hold
*Ms Oona King, Lab.   19,380
Shahagir Faruk, C.   9,323
Ms Janet Ludlow, LD   5,946
Ms Anna Bragga, Green   1,666
Michael Davidson, BNP   1,267
Dennis Delderfield, NBP   888
Lab. majority 10,057 (26.14%)
0.44% swing C. to Lab.
(1997: Lab. maj. 11,285 (25.26%))

BEVERLEY & HOLDERNESS
E. 75,146 T. 46,375 (61.71%)   C. hold
*James Cran, C.   19,168
Ms Pippa Langford, Lab.   18,387
Stewart Willie, LD   7,356
Stephen Wallis, UK Ind.   1,464
C. majority 781 (1.68%)
0.08% swing Lab. to C.
(1997: C. maj. 811 (1.53%))

BEXHILL & BATTLE
E. 69,010 T. 44,783 (64.89%)   C. hold
Greg Barker, C.   21,555
Stephen Hardy, LD   11,052
Ms Anne Moore-Williams, Lab.   8,702
Nigel Farage, UK Ind.   3,474
C. majority 10,503 (23.45%)
0.40% swing LD to C.
(1997: C. maj. 11,100 (22.66%))

BEXLEYHEATH & CRAYFORD
E. 63,580 T. 40,378 (63.51%) Lab. hold
*Nigel Beard, Lab.   17,593
David Evennett, C.   16,121
Nickolas O'Hare, LD   4,476
Colin Smith, BNP   1,408
John Dunford, UK Ind.   780
Lab. majority 1,472 (3.65%)
1.72% swing Lab. to C.
(1997: Lab. maj. 3,415 (7.08%))

BILLERICAY
E. 78,528 T. 45,598 (58.07%)   C. hold
John Baron, C.   21,608
Ms Amanda Campbell, Lab.   16,595
Frank Bellard, LD   6,323
Nick Yeomans, UK Ind.   1,072
C. majority 5,013 (10.99%)
4.27% swing Lab. to C.
(1997: C. maj. 1,356 (2.45%))

BIRKENHEAD
E. 60,726 T. 28,967 (47.70%) Lab. hold
*Rt. Hon. F. Field, Lab.   20,418
Brian Stewart, C.   4,827
Roy Wood, LD   3,722
Lab. majority 15,591 (53.82%)
0.86% swing Lab. to C.
(1997: Lab. maj. 21,843 (55.55%))

BIRMINGHAM EDGBASTON
E. 67,405 T. 37,749 (56.00%) Lab. hold
*Ms Gisela Stuart, Lab.   18,517
Nigel Hastilow, C.   13,819
Ms Nicola Davies, LD   4,528
John Gretton, Pro Euro C   454
Sam Brackenbury, Soc. Lab.   431
Lab. majority 4,698 (12.45%)
1.23% swing C. to Lab.
(1997: Lab. maj. 4,842 (9.99%))

BIRMINGHAM ERDINGTON
E. 65,668 T. 30,604 (46.60%) Lab. hold
Sion Llewelyn Simon, Lab.   17,375
Oliver Lodge, C.   7,413
Ms Sandra Johnson, LD   3,602
Michael Shore, NF   681
Steve Goddard, Soc. All.   669
Mark Nattrass, UK Ind.   521
Ms Judith Sambrook-Marshall,   343
   Soc. Lab.
Lab. majority 9,962 (32.55%)
0.62% swing C. to Lab.
(1997: Lab. maj. 12,657 (31.32%))

BIRMINGHAM HALL GREEN
E. 57,563 T. 33,084 (57.47%) Lab. hold
*Stephen McCabe, Lab.   18,049
Punjab Singh, LD   11,401
Chris White, C.   2,926
Peter Johnson, UK Ind.   708
Lab. majority 6,648 (20.09%)
0.02% swing Lab. to C.
(1997: Lab. maj. 8,420 (20.14%))

BIRMINGHAM HODGE HILL
E. 55,254 T. 26,465 (47.90%) Lab. hold
*Rt. Hon. T. Davis, Lab.   16,901
Mrs Debbie Lewis, C.   5,283
Alistair Dow, LD   2,147
Lee Windridge, BNP   889
Parwez Hussain, PJP   561
Dennis Cridge, Soc. Lab.   284
Harvey Vivian, UK Ind.   275
Ayub Khan, Muslim   125
Lab. majority 11,618 (43.90%)
1.16% swing C. to Lab.
(1997: Lab. maj. 14,200 (41.58%))

BIRMINGHAM LADYWOOD
E. 71,113 T. 31,493 (44.29%) Lab. hold
*Rt. Hon. Ms C. Short, Lab.   21,694
Benjamin Prentice, C.   3,551
Mahmood Chaudhry, LD   2,586
Allah Ditta, PJP   2,112
Surinder Virdee, Soc. Lab.   443
Mahmood Hussain, Muslim   432
James Caffery, ProLife   392
Dr Anneliese Nattrass, UK Ind.   283
Lab. majority 18,143 (57.61%)
1.59% swing Lab. to C.
(1997: Lab. maj. 23,082 (60.78%))

BIRMINGHAM NORTHFIELD
E. 55,922 T. 29,534 (52.81%) Lab. hold
*Richard Burden, Lab.   16,528
Nils Purser, C.   8,730
Trevor Sword, LD   3,322
Stephen Rogers, UK Ind.   550
Clive Walder, Soc. All.   193
Zane Carpenter, Soc. Lab.   151
Andrew Chaffer, Comm.   60
Lab. majority 7,798 (26.40%)
1.53% swing Lab. to C.
(1997: Lab. maj. 11,443 (29.46%))

BIRMINGHAM PERRY BARR
E. 71,121 T. 37,417 (52.61%) Lab. hold
Khalid Mahmood, Lab.   17,415
David Binns, C.   8,662
Jon Hunt, LD   8,566
Avtar Singh Jouh, Soc. Lab.   1,544
Ms Caroline Johnson, Soc. All.   465
Ms Natalya Nattrass, UK Ind.   352
Michael Roche, Marxist   221
Robert Davidson, Muslim   192
Lab. majority 8,753 (23.39%)
8.96% swing Lab. to C.
(1997: Lab. maj. 18,957 (41.32%))

BIRMINGHAM SELLY OAK
E. 71,237 T. 40,100 (56.29%) Lab. hold
*Dr Lynne Jones, Lab.   21,015
Ken Hardeman, C.   10,676
David Osborne, LD   6,532
Barney Smith, Green   1,309
Mrs Beryl Williams, UK Ind.   568
Lab. majority 10,339 (25.78%)
1.04% swing Lab. to C.
(1997: Lab. maj. 14,088 (27.87%))

BIRMINGHAM SPARKBROOK &
SMALL HEATH
E. 74,358 T. 36,647 (49.28%) Lab. hold
*Roger Godsiff, Lab.   21,087
Qassim Afzal, LD   4,841
Shafaq Hussain, PJP   4,770
Iftkhar Hussain, C.   3,948
Gul Mohammed, Ind.   662
Wayne Vincent, UK Ind.   634
Abdul Aziz, Muslim   401
Salman Mirza, Soc. All.   304
Lab. majority 16,246 (44.33%))
5.31% swing Lab. to C.
(1997: Lab. maj. 19,526 (46.76%))

BIRMINGHAM YARDLEY
E. 52,444 T. 30,013 (57.23%) Lab. hold
*Rt. Hon. Ms E. Morris, Lab. 14,085
John Hemming, LD   11,507
Barrie Roberts, C.   3,941
Alan Ware, UK Ind.   329
Colin Wren, Soc. Lab.   151
Lab. majority 2,578 (8.59%)
2.74% swing Lab. to LD
(1997: Lab. maj. 5,315 (14.07%))

BISHOP AUCKLAND
E. 67,377 T. 38,559 (57.23%) Lab. hold
*Rt. Hon. D. Foster, Lab.   22,680
Mrs Fiona McNish, C.   8,754
Chris Foote-Wood, LD   6,073
Carl Bennett, Green   1,052
Lab. majority 13,926 (36.12%)
4.85% swing Lab. to C.
(1997: Lab. maj. 21,064 (45.82%))

BLABY
E. 73,907 T. 47,642 (64.46%) C. hold
*Andrew Robathan, C.   22,104
David Morgan, Lab.   15,895
Geoff Welsh, LD   8,286
Edward Scott, BNP   1,357
C. majority 6,209 (13.03%)
0.48% swing Lab. to C.
(1997: C. maj. 6,474 (12.08%))

BLACKBURN
E. 72,621 T. 40,484 (55.75%) Lab. hold
*Rt. Hon. J. Straw, Lab.   21,808
John Cotton, C.   12,559
Imtiaz Patel, LD   3,264
Mrs Dorothy Baxter, UK Ind.   1,185
Paul Morris, Ind.   577
Terence Cullen, Soc. Lab.   559
Frederick Nichol, Socialist   532
Lab. majority 9,249 (22.85%)
3.79% swing Lab. to C.
(1997: Lab. maj. 14,451 (30.43%))

BLACKPOOL NORTH & FLEETWOOD
E. 74,456 T. 42,581 (57.19%) Lab. hold
*Ms Joan Humble, Lab.   21,610
Alan Vincent, C.   15,889
Steven Bate, LD   4,132
Colin Porter, UK Ind.   950
Lab. majority 5,721 (13.44%)
1.60% swing Lab. to C.
(1997: Lab. maj. 8,946 (16.64%))

BLACKPOOL SOUTH
E. 74,311 T. 38,792 (52.20%) Lab. hold
*Gordon Marsden, Lab.   21,060
David Morris, C.   12,798
Ms Doreen Holt, LD   4,115
Mrs Val Cowell, UK Ind.   819
Lab. majority 8,262 (21.30%)
0.67% swing Lab. to C.
(1997: Lab. maj. 11,616 (22.63%))

BLAYDON
E. 64,574 T. 37,086 (57.43%) Lab. hold
*John McWilliam, Lab.   20,340
Peter Maughan, LD   12,531
Mark Watson, C.   4,215
Lab. majority 7,809 (21.06%)
7.55% swing Lab. to LD
(1997: Lab. maj. 16,605 (36.16%))

BLYTH VALLEY
E. 63,274 T. 34,550 (54.60%) Lab. hold
*Ronnie Campbell, Lab.   20,627
Jeff Reid, LD   8,439
Wayne Daley, C.   5,484
Lab. majority 12,188 (35.28%)
3.24% swing Lab. to LD
(1997: Lab. maj. 17,736 (41.75%))

BOGNOR REGIS & LITTLEHAMPTON
E. 66,903 T. 38,968 (58.25%) C. hold
*Nick Gibb, C.   17,602
George O'Neill, Lab.   11,959
Ms Pamela Peskett, LD   6,846
George Stride, UK Ind.   1,779
Ms Lilias Rider Haggard Cheyne, 782
    Green
C. majority 5,643 (14.48%)
0.64% swing C. to Lab.
(1997: C. maj. 7,321 (15.76%))

BOLSOVER
E. 67,537 T. 38,271 (56.67%) Lab. hold
*Dennis Skinner, Lab.   26,249
Simon Massey, C.   7,472
Ms Marie Bradley, LD   4,550
Lab. majority 18,777 (49.06%)
4.10% swing Lab. to C.
(1997: Lab. maj. 27,149 (57.26%))

BOLTON NORTH EAST
E. 69,514 T. 38,950 (56.03%) Lab. hold
*David Crausby, Lab.   21,166
Michael Winstanley, C.   12,744
Tim Perkins, LD   4,004
Kenneth McIvor, Green   629
Ms Lynne Lowe, Soc. Lab.   407
Lab. majority 8,422 (21.62%)
2.06% swing Lab. to C.
(1997: Lab. maj. 12,669 (25.74%))

BOLTON SOUTH EAST
E. 68,140 T. 34,154 (50.12%) Lab. hold
*Dr Brian Iddon, Lab.   21,129
Haroon Rashid, C.   8,258
Frank Harasiwka, LD   3,941
Dr William John Kelly, Soc. Lab. 826
Lab. majority 12,871 (37.69%)
5.74% swing Lab. to C.
(1997: Lab. maj. 21,311 (49.16%))

BOLTON WEST
E. 66,033 T. 41,214 (62.41%) Lab. hold
*Ms Ruth Kelly, Lab.   19,381
James Stevens, C.   13,863
Ms Barbara Ronson, LD   7,573
David Toomer, Soc. All.   397
Lab. majority 5,518 (13.39%)
0.50% swing Lab. to C.
(1997: Lab. maj. 7,072 (14.39%))

BOOTLE
E. 56,320 T. 27,594 (49.00%) Lab. hold
*Joe Benton, Lab.   21,400
Jim Murray, LD   2,357
Miss Judith Symes, C.   2,194
Dave Flynn, Soc. Lab.   971
Peter Glover, Soc. All.   672
Lab. majority 19,043 (69.01%)
4.05% swing Lab. to LD
(1997: Lab. maj. 28,421 (74.36%))

BOSTON & SKEGNESS
E. 69,010 T. 40,313 (58.42%) C. hold
Mark Simmonds, C.   17,298
Ms Elaine Bird, Lab.   16,783
Duncan Moffatt, LD   4,994
Cyril Wakefield, UK Ind.   717
Martin Harrison, Green   521
C. majority 515 (1.28%)
0.06% swing C. to Lab.
(1997: C. maj. 647 (1.39%))

BOSWORTH
E. 69,992 T. 45,106 (64.44%) C. hold
*David Tredinnick, C.   20,030
Andrew Furlong, Lab.   17,750
Jon Ellis, LD   7,326
C. majority 2,280 (5.05%)
1.54% swing Lab. to C.
(1997: C. maj. 1,027 (1.97%))

BOURNEMOUTH EAST
E. 60,454 T. 35,799 (59.22%) C. hold
*David Atkinson, C.   15,501
Andrew Garratt, LD   12,067
Paul Nicholson, Lab.   7,107
George Chamberlaine, UK Ind. 1,124
C. majority 3,434 (9.59%)
0.21% swing C. to LD
(1997: C. maj. 4,346 (10.01%))

BOURNEMOUTH WEST
E. 62,038 T. 33,648 (54.24%)   C. hold
*John Butterfill, C.   14,417
David Stokes, Lab.   9,699
Ms Fiona Hornby, LD   8,468
Mrs Cynthia Blake, UK Ind.   1,064
C. majority 4,718 (14.02%)
1.54% swing C. to Lab.
(1997: C. maj. 5,710 (13.90%))

BRACKNELL
E. 81,118 T. 49,225 (60.68%)   C. hold
*Rt. Hon. A. Mackay, C.   22,962
Ms Janet Keene, Lab.   16,249
Ray Earwicker, LD   8,424
Lawrence Boxall, UK Ind.   1,266
Ms Dominica Roberts, (ProLife)   324
C. majority 6,713 (13.64%)
1.97% swing C. to Lab.
(1997: C. maj. 10,387 (17.58%))

BRADFORD NORTH
E. 66,454 T. 35,017 (52.69%)   Lab. hold
*Terry Rooney, Lab.   17,419
Zahid Iqbal, C.   8,450
David Ward, LD   6,924
John Brayshaw, BNP   1,613
Steven Schofield, Green   611
Lab. majority 8,969 (25.61%)
2.44% swing Lab. to C.
(1997: Lab. maj. 12,770 (30.49%))

BRADFORD SOUTH
E. 68,450 T. 35,137 (51.33%)   Lab. hold
*Gerry Sutcliffe, Lab.   19,603
Graham Tennyson, C.   9,941
Alexander Wilson-Fletcher, LD   3,717
Peter North, UK Ind.   783
Tony Kelly, Soc. Lab.   571
Ateeq Siddique, Soc. All.   302
George Riseborough, DefWelfare   220
Lab. majority 9,662 (27.50%)
0.61% swing Lab. to C.
(1997: Lab. maj. 12,936 (28.71%))

BRADFORD WEST
E. 71,620 T. 38,370 (53.57%)   Lab. hold
*Marsha Singh, Lab.   18,401
Mohammed Riaz, C.   14,236
John Robinson, Green   2,672
Abdul Rauf Khan, LD   2,437
Imran Hussain, UK Ind.   427
Farhan Khokhar, AL   197
Lab. majority 4,165 (10.85%)
1.17% swing C. to Lab.
(1997: Lab. maj. 3,877 (8.51%))

BRAINTREE
E. 79,157 T. 50,315 (63.56%)   Lab. hold
*Alan Hurst, Lab.   21,123
Brooks Newmark, C.   20,765
Peter Turner, LD   5,664
James Abbott, Green   1,241
Michael Nolan, LCA   774
Charles Cole, UK Ind.   748
Lab. majority 358 (0.71%)
0.95% swing Lab. to C.
(1997: Lab. maj. 1,451 (2.61%))

BRENT EAST
E. 58,095 T. 28,992 (49.90%)   Lab. hold
Paul Daisley, Lab.   18,325
David Gauke, C.   5,278
Ms Nowsheen Bhatti, LD   3,065
Ms Simone Aspis, Green   1,361
Ms Sarah Macken, ProLife   392
Ms Iris Cremer, Soc. Lab.   383
Ashwin Tanna, UK Ind.   188
Lab. majority 13,047 (45.00%)
0.01% swing Lab. to C.
(1997: Lab. maj. 15,882 (45.03%))

BRENT NORTH
E. 58,789 T. 33,939 (57.73%)   Lab. hold
*Barry Gardiner, Lab.   20,149
Philip Allott, C.   9,944
Paul Lorber, LD   3,846
Lab. majority 10,205 (30.07%)
9.77% swing C. to Lab.
(1997: Lab. maj. 4,019 (10.53%))

BRENT SOUTH
E. 55,891 T. 28,637 (51.24%)   Lab. hold
*Rt. Hon. P. Boateng, Lab.   20,984
Carupiah Selvarajah, C.   3,604
Havard Hughes, LD   3,098
Mick McDonnell, Soc. All.   491
Thomas Mac Stiofain, Res. Motor   460
Lab. majority 17,380 (60.69%)
1.81% swing C. to Lab.
(1997: Lab. maj. 19,691 (57.08%))

BRENTFORD & ISLEWORTH
E. 84,049 T. 44,514 (52.96%)   Lab. hold
*Ms Ann Keen, Lab.   23,275
Tim Mack, C.   12,957
Gareth Hartwell, LD   5,994
Nic Ferriday, Green   1,324
Gerald Ingram, UK Ind.   412
Danny Faith, Soc. All.   408
Asa Khaira, Ind.   144
Lab. majority 10,318 (23.18%)
1.26% swing Lab. to C.
(1997: Lab. maj. 14,424 (25.70%))

BRENTWOOD & ONGAR
E. 64,695 T. 43,542 (67.30%)   C. hold
*Eric Pickles, C.   16,558
†Martin Bell, Ind Bell   13,737
David Kendall, LD   6,772
Ms Diana Johnson, Lab.   5,505
Ken Gulleford, UK Ind.   611
Peter Pryke, Ind.   239
David Bishop, Elvis   68
Tony Appleton, Ind.   52
C. majority 2,821 (6.48%)
(1997: C. maj. 9,690 (19.10%))

BRIDGWATER
E. 74,079 T. 47,847 (64.59%)   C. hold
Ian Liddell-Grainger, C.   19,354
Ian Thorn, LD   14,367
William Monteith, Lab.   12,803
Ms Vicky Gardner, UK Ind.   1,323
C. majority 4,987 (10.42%)
3.57% swing LD to C.
(1997: C. maj. 1,796 (3.28%))

BRIGG & GOOLE
E. 63,536 T. 41,054 (64.62%)   Lab. hold
*Ian Cawsey, Lab.   20,066
Don Stewart, C.   16,105
David Nolan, LD   3,796
Godfrey Bloom, UK Ind.   688
Michael Kenny, Soc. Lab.   399
Lab. majority 3,961 (9.65%)
2.00% swing Lab. to C.
(1997: Lab. maj. 6,389 (13.65%))

BRIGHTON KEMPTOWN
E. 67,621 T. 39,203 (57.97%)   Lab. hold
*Dr Desmond Turner, Lab.   18,745
Geoffrey Theobald, C.   13,823
Ms Jan Marshall, LD   4,064
Hugh Miller, Green   1,290
Dr James Chamberlain-Webber,   543
    UK Ind.
John McLeod, Soc. Lab.   364
Dave Dobbs, Free   227
Ms Elaine Cook, ProLife   147
Lab. majority 4,922 (12.56%)
2.45% swing C. to Lab.
(1997: Lab. maj. 3,534 (7.66%))

BRIGHTON PAVILION
E. 69,200 T. 40,723 (58.85%)
                              Lab. Co-op hold
*David Lepper, Lab. Co-op   19,846
David Gold, C.   10,203
Ms Ruth Berry, LD   5,348
Keith Taylor, Green   3,806
Ian Fyvie, Soc. Lab.   573
Bob Dobbs, Free   409
Stuart Hutchin, UK Ind.   361
Ms Marie Paragallo, ProLife   177
Lab. Co-op majority 9,643
    (23.68%)
1.63% swing Lab. Co-op to C.
(1997: Lab. maj. 13,181 (26.93%))

BRISTOL EAST
E. 70,279 T. 40,334 (57.39%)   Lab. hold
*Ms Jean Corston, Lab.   22,180
Jack Lo-Presti, C.   8,788
Brian Niblett, LD   6,915
Geoff Collard, Green   1,110
Roger Marsh, UK Ind.   572
Mike Langley, Soc. Lab.   438
Andy Pryor, Soc. All.   331
Lab. majority 13,392 (33.20%)
0.16% swing Lab. to C.
(1997: Lab. maj. 16,159 (33.52%))

BRISTOL NORTH WEST
E. 76,756 T. 46,692 (60.83%)
                              Lab. Co-op hold
*Doug Naysmith, Lab. Co-op   24,436
Charles Hansard, C.   13,349
Peter Tyzack, LD   7,387
Miss Diane Carr, UK Ind.   1,149
Vince Horrigan, Soc. Lab.   371
Lab. Co-op majority 11,087 (23.74%)
1.57% swing C. to Lab. Co-op
(1997: Lab. maj. 11,382 (20.60%))

BRISTOL SOUTH
E. 72,490 T. 40,970 (56.52%) Lab. hold
*Ms Dawn Primarolo, Lab.   23,299
Richard Eddy, C.   9,118
James Main, LD   6,078
Glenn Vowles, Green   1,233
Brian Drummond, Soc. All.   496
Chris Prasad, UK Ind.   496
Giles Shorter, Soc. Lab.   250
Lab. majority 14,181 (34.61%)
2.08% swing Lab. to C.
(1997: Lab. maj. 19,328 (38.77%))

BRISTOL WEST
E. 84,821 T. 55,665 (65.63%) Lab. hold
*Ms Valerie Davey, Lab.   20,505
Stephen Williams, LD   16,079
Mrs Pamela Chesters, C.   16,040
John Devaney, Green   1,961
Bernard Kennedy, Soc. Lab.   590
Simon Muir, UK Ind.   490
Lab. majority 4,426 (7.95%)
0.37% swing LD to Lab.
(1997: Lab. maj. 1,493 (2.38%))

BROMLEY & CHISLEHURST
E. 68,763 T. 43,231 (62.87%)   C. hold
*Rt. Hon. E. Forth, C.   21,412
Ms Sue Polydorou, Lab.   12,375
Geoff Payne, LD   8,180
Rob Bryant, UK Ind.   1,264
C. majority 9,037 (20.90%)
0.09% swing C. to Lab.
(1997: C. maj. 11,118 (21.08%))

BROMSGROVE
E. 68,115 T. 45,684 (67.07%)   C. hold
*Miss Julie Kirkbride, C.   23,640
Peter McDonald, Lab.   15,502
Mrs Margaret Rowley, LD   5,430
Ian Gregory, UK Ind.   1,112
C. majority 8,138 (17.81%)
4.22% swing Lab. to C.
(1997: C. maj. 4,895 (9.38%))

BROXBOURNE
E. 68,982 T. 37,845 (54.86%)   C. hold
*Mrs Marion Roe, C.   20,487
David Prendergast, Lab.   11,494
Ms Julia Davies, LD   4,158
Martin Harvey, UK Ind.   858
John Cope, BNP   848
C. majority 8,993 (23.76%)
4.80% swing Lab. to C.
(1997: C. maj. 6,653 (14.16%))

BROXTOWE
E. 73,675 T. 49,004 (66.51%) Lab. hold
*Nick Palmer, Lab.   23,836
Mrs Pauline Latham, C.   17,963
David Watts, LD   7,205
Lab. majority 5,873 (11.98%)
1.20% swing C. to Lab.
(1997: Lab. maj. 5,575 (9.59%))

BUCKINGHAM
E. 65,270 T. 45,272 (69.36%)   C. hold
*John Bercow, C.   24,296
Mark Seddon, Lab.   10,971
Ms Isobel Wilson, LD   9,037
Christopher Silcock, UK Ind.   968
C. majority 13,325 (29.43%)
2.18% swing Lab. to C.
(1997: C. maj. 12,386 (25.08%))

BURNLEY
E. 66,393 T. 36,884 (55.55%) Lab. hold
*Peter Pike, Lab.   18,195
Robert Frost, C.   7,697
Paul Wright, LD   5,975
Steven Smith, BNP   4,151
Richard Buttrey, UK Ind.   866
Lab. majority 10,498 (28.46%)
4.62% swing Lab. to C.
(1997: Lab. maj. 17,062 (37.71%))

BURTON
E. 75,194 T. 46,457 (61.78%) Lab. hold
*Ms Janet Dean, Lab.   22,783
Mrs Maggie Punyer, C.   17,934
David Fletcher, LD   4,468
Ian Crompton, UK Ind.   984
John Taylor, ProLife   288
Lab. majority 4,849 (10.44%)
0.59% swing Lab. to C.
(1997: Lab. Maj. 6,330 (11.62%))

BURY NORTH
E. 71,108 T. 44,788 (62.99%) Lab. hold
*David Chaytor, Lab.   22,945
John Walsh, C.   16,413
Bryn Hackley, LD   5,430
Lab. majority 6,532 (14.58%)
0.15% swing C. to Lab.
(1997: Lab. maj. 7,866 (14.29%))

BURY SOUTH
E. 67,276 T. 39,539 (58.77%) Lab. hold
*Ivan Lewis, Lab.   23,406
Mrs Nicola Le Page, C.   10,634
Tim Pickstone, LD   5,499
Lab. majority 12,772 (32.30%)
3.80% swing C. to Lab.
(1997: Lab. maj. 12,433 (24.70%))

BURY ST EDMUNDS
E. 76,146 T. 50,257 (66.00%)   C. hold
*David Ruffley, C.   21,850
Mark Ereira, Lab.   19,347
Richard Williams, LD   6,998
John Howlett, UK Ind.   831
Mike Brundle, Ind.   651
Michael Benwell, Soc. Lab.   580
C. majority 2,503 (4.98%)
2.16% swing Lab. to C.
(1997: C. maj. 368 (0.66%))

CALDER VALLEY
E. 75,298 T. 47,425 (62.98%) Lab. hold
*Mrs Christine McCafferty, Lab. 20,244
Mrs Sue Robson-Catling, C.   17,150
Michael Taylor, LD   7,596
Steve Hutton, Green   1,034
John Nunn, UK Ind.   729
Philip Lockwood, LCA   672
Lab. majority 3,094 (6.52%)
2.27% swing Lab. to C.
(1997: Lab. maj. 6,255 (11.07%))

CAMBERWELL & PECKHAM
E. 53,694 T. 25,104 (46.75%) Lab. hold
*Rt. Hon. Ms H. Harman, Lab.   17,473
Donnachadh McCarthy, LD   3,350
Jonathan Morgan, C.   2,740
Storm Poorun, Green   805
John Mulrenan, Soc. All.   478
Robert Adams, Soc. Lab.   188
Frank Sweeney, WRP   70
Lab. majority 14,123 (56.26%)
0.91% swing Lab. to LD
(1997: Lab. maj. 16,351 (57.43%))

CAMBRIDGE
E. 70,663 T. 42,836 (60.62%) Lab. hold
*Ms Anne Campbell, Lab.   19,316
David Howarth, LD   10,737
Graham Stuart, C.   9,829
Stephen Lawrence, Green   1,413
Howard Senter, Soc. All.   716
Len Baynes, UK Ind.   532
Ms Clare Underwood, ProLife   232
Ms Margaret Courtney, WRP   61
Lab. majority 8,579 (20.03%)
8.64% swing Lab. to LD
(1997: Lab. maj. 14,137 (27.54%))

CAMBRIDGESHIRE NORTH EAST
E. 79,891 T. 48,051 (60.15%)   C. hold
*Malcolm Moss, C.   23,132
Dil Owen, Lab.   16,759
Richard Renaut, LD   6,733
John Stevens, UK Ind.   1,189
Tony Hoey, ProLife   238
C. majority 6,373 (13.26%)
2.03% swing Lab. to C.
(1997: C. maj. 5,101 (9.20%))

CAMBRIDGESHIRE NORTH WEST
E. 70,569 T. 43,956 (62.29%)   C. hold
*Rt. Hon. Sir B. Mawhinney, C. 21,895
Ms Anthea Cox, Lab.   13,794
Alastair Taylor, LD   6,957
Barry Hudson, UK Ind.   881
David Hall, Ind.   429
C. majority 8,101 (18.43%)
1.27% swing Lab. to C.
(1997: C. maj. 7,754 (15.88%))

CAMBRIDGESHIRE SOUTH
E. 72,095 T. 48,341 (67.05%)   C. hold
*Andrew Lansley, C.   21,387
Ms Amanda Taylor, LD   12,984
Dr Joan Herbert, Lab.   11,737
Simon Saggers, Green   1,182
Mrs Helene Davies, UK Ind.   875
Ms Beata Klepacka, ProLife   176
C. majority 8,403 (17.38%)
0.58% swing LD to C.
(1997: C. maj. 8,712 (16.23%))

CAMBRIDGESHIRE SOUTH EAST
E. 81,663 T. 51,886 (63.54%)   C. hold
*James Paice, C.   22,927
Ms Sal Brinton, LD   13,937
Andrew Inchley, Lab.   13,714
Neil Scarr, UK Ind.   1,308
C. majority 8,990 (17.33%)
0.27% swing C. to LD
(1997: C. maj. 9,349 (16.46%))

CANNOCK CHASE
E. 73,423 T. 41,064 (55.93%) Lab. hold
*Dr Tony Wright, Lab.   23,049
Gavin Smithers, C.   12,345
Stewart Reynolds, LD   5,670
Lab. majority 10,704 (26.07%)
0.79% swing Lab. to C.
(1997: Lab. maj. 14,478 (27.65%))

CANTERBURY
E. 74,159 T. 45,132 (60.86%)   C. hold
*Julian Brazier, C.   18,711
Ms Emily Thornberry, Lab.   16,642
Peter Wales, LD   8,056
Ms Hazel Dawe, Green   920
Ms Lisa Moore, UK Ind.   803
C. majority 2,069 (4.58%)
1.37% swing C. to Lab.
(1997: C. maj. 3,964 (7.33%))

CARLISLE
E. 58,811 T. 34,909 (59.36%) Lab. hold
*Eric Martlew, Lab.   17,856
Mike Mitchelson, C.   12,154
John Guest, LD   4,076
Colin Paisley, LCA   554
Paul Wilcox, Soc. All.   269
Lab. majority 5,702 (16.33%)
6.04% swing Lab. to C.
(1997: Lab. maj. 12,390 (28.41%))

CARSHALTON & WALLINGTON
E. 67,337 T. 40,612 (60.31%) LD hold
*Tom Brake, LD   18,289
Ken Andrew, C.   13,742
Ms Margaret Cooper, Lab.   7,466
Simon Dixon, Green   614
Martin Haley, UK Ind.   501
LD majority 4,547 (11.20%)
3.26% swing C. to LD
(1997: LD maj. 2,267 (4.68%))

CASTLE POINT
E. 68,108 T. 39,763 (58.38%) C. gain
Dr Robert Spink, C.   17,738
*Ms Christine Butler, Lab.   16,753
Billy Boulton, LD   3,116
Ron Hurrell, UK Ind.   1,273
Douglas Roberts, Ind.   663
Nik Searle, Truth   220
C. majority 985 (2.48%)
2.39% swing Lab. to C.
(1997: Lab. maj. 1,116 (2.30%))

CHARNWOOD
E. 74,836 T. 48,265 (64.49%) C. hold
*Rt. Hon. S. Dorrell, C.   23,283
Sean Sheahan, Lab.   15,544
Ms Susan King, LD   7,835
Jamie Bye, UK Ind.   1,603
C. majority 7,739 (16.03%)
2.77% swing Lab. to C.
(1997: C. maj. 5,900 (10.50%))

CHATHAM & AYLESFORD
E. 69,759 T. 39,735 (56.96%) Lab. hold
*Jonathan Shaw, Lab.   19,180
Sean Holden, C.   14,840
David Lettington, LD   4,705
Gregory Knopp, UK Ind.   1,010
Lab. majority 4,340 (10.92%)
2.62% swing C. to Lab.
(1997: Lab. maj. 2,790 (5.68%))

CHEADLE
E. 69,002 T. 43,606 (63.20%) LD gain
Ms Patsy Calton, LD   18,477
*Stephen Day, C.   18,444
Howard Dawber, Lab.   6,086
Vincent Cavanagh, UK Ind.   599
LD majority, 33 (0.08%)
3.07% swing C. to LD
(1997: C. maj. 3,189 (6.07%))

CHELMSFORD WEST
E. 78,291 T. 48,143 (61.49%) C. hold
*Simon Burns, C.   20,446
Adrian Longden, Lab.   14,185
Stephen Robinson, LD   11,197
Mrs Eleanor Burgess, Green   837
Ken Wedon, UK Ind.   785
Christopher Philbin, LCA   693
C. majority 6,261 (13.01%)
0.62% swing C. to Lab.
(1997: C. maj. 6,691 (11.42%))

CHELTENHAM
E. 67,563 T. 41,835 (61.92%) LD hold
*Nigel Jones, LD   19,970
Rob Garnham, C.   14,715
Andy Erlam, Lab.   5,041
Keith Bessant, Green   735
Dancing Ken Hanks, Loony   513
Jim Carver, UK Ind.   482
Anthony Gates, ProLife   272
Roger Everest, Ind.   107
LD majority 5,255 (12.56%)
0.32% swing LD to C.
(1997: LD maj. 6,645 (13.21%))

CHESHAM & AMERSHAM
E. 70,021 T. 45,283 (64.67%) C. hold
*Mrs Cheryl Gillan, C.   22,867
John Ford, LD   10,985
Ken Hulme, Lab.   8,497
Ian Harvey, UK Ind.   1,367
Nick Wilkins, Green   1,114
Ms Gillian Duval, ProLife   453
C. majority 11,882 (26.24%)
0.16% swing C. to LD
(1997: C. maj. 13,859 (26.55%))

CHESTER, CITY OF
E. 70,382 T. 44,877 (63.76%) Lab. hold
*Ms Christine Russell, Lab.   21,760
David Jones, C.   14,866
Tony Dawson, LD   6,589
Allan Weddell, UK Ind.   899
George Rogers, Ind.   763
Lab. majority 6,894 (15.36%)
1.70% swing Lab. to C.
(1997: Lab. maj. 10,553 (18.76%))

CHESTERFIELD
E. 73,252 T. 44,441 (60.67%) LD gain
Paul Holmes, LD   21,249
Reg Race, Lab.   18,663
Simon Hitchcock, C.   3,613
Ms Jeannie Robinson, Soc. All.   437
Bill Harrison, Soc. Lab.   295
Christopher Rawson, Ind.   184
LD majority 2,586 (5.82%)
8.53% swing Lab. to LD
(1997: Lab. maj. 5,775 (11.24%))

CHICHESTER
E. 77,703 T. 49,512 (63.72%) C. hold
*Andrew Tyrie, C.   23,320
Ms Lynne Ravenscroft, LD   11,965
Ms Celia Barlow, Lab.   10,627
Douglas Denny, UK Ind.   2,308
Gavin Graham, Green   1,292
C. majority 11,355 (22.93%)
2.74% swing LD to C.
(1997: C. maj. 9,734 (17.45%))

CHINGFORD & WOODFORD GREEN
E. 63,252 T. 36,982 (58.47%) C. hold
*Iain Duncan Smith, C.   17,834
Ms Jessica Webb, Lab.   12,347
John Beanse, LD   5,739
Ms Jean Griffin, BNP   1,062
C. majority 5,487 (14.84%)
0.99% swing Lab. to C.
(1997: C. maj. 5,714 (12.85%))

CHIPPING BARNET
E. 70,217 T. 42,456 (60.46%) C. hold
*Sir Sydney Chapman, C.   19,702
Damien Welfare, Lab.   17,001
Sean Hooker, LD   5,753
C. majority 2,701 (6.36%)
2.14% swing Lab. to C.
(1997: C. maj. 1,035 (2.09%))

CHORLEY
E. 77,036 T. 47,952 (62.25%) Lab. hold
*Lindsay Hoyle, Lab.   25,088
Peter Booth, C.   6,644
Stephen Fenn, LD   5,372
Graham Frost, UK Ind.   848
Lab. majority 18,444 (17.61%)
0.25% swing C. to Lab.
(1997: Lab. maj. 9,870 (17.10%))

CHRISTCHURCH
E. 73,503 T. 49,567 (67.44%) C. hold
*Christopher Chope, C.   27,306
Ms Dorothy Webb, LD   13,762
Ms Judith Begg, Lab.   7,506
Ms Margaret Strange, UK Ind.   993
C. majority 13,544 (27.32%)
11.74% swing LD to C.
(1997: C. maj. 2,165 (3.85%))

CITIES OF LONDON &
WESTMINSTER
E. 71,935 T. 33,975 (47.23%) C. hold
Mark Field, C.   15,737
Michael Katz, Lab.   11,238
Martin Horwood, LD   5,218
Hugo Charlton, Green   1,318
Colin Merton, UK Ind.   464
C. majority 4,499 (13.24%)
0.54% swing Lab. to C.
(1997: C. maj. 4,881 (12.16%))

CLEETHORPES
E. 68,392 T. 42,418 (62.02%) Lab. hold
*Ms Shona McIsaac, Lab.   21,032
Stephen Howd, C.   15,412
Gordon Smith, LD   5,080
Ms Janet Hatton, UK Ind.   894
Lab. majority 5,620 (13.25%)
2.47% swing Lab. to C.
(1997: Lab. maj. 9,176 (18.18%))

COLCHESTER
E. 78,955 T. 43,736 (55.39%) LD hold
*Bob Russell, LD   18,627
Kevin Bentley, C.   13,074
Chris Fegan, Lab.   10,925
Roger Lord, UK Ind.   631
Leonard Overy-Owen, Grey   479
LD maj 5,553 (12.70%)
4.83% swing C. to LD
(1997: LD maj. 1,581 (3.04%))

COLNE VALLEY
E. 74,192 T. 46,987 (63.33%) Lab. hold
*Ms Kali Mountford, Lab.   18,967
Philip Davies, C.   14,328
Gordon Beever, LD   11,694
Richard Plunkett, Green   1,081
Dr Arthur Quarmby, UK Ind.   917
Lab. majority 4,639 (9.87%)
0.65% swing C. to Lab.
(1997: Lab. maj. 4,840 (8.58%))

CONGLETON
E. 71,941 T. 45,083 (62.67%)   C. hold
*Mrs Ann Winterton, C.   20,872
John Flanagan, Lab.   13,738
David Lloyd-Griffiths, LD   9,719
Bill Young, UK Ind.   754
C. majority 7,134 (15.82%)
1.08% swing Lab. to C.
(1997: C. maj. 6,130 (11.48%))

COPELAND
E. 53,526 T. 34,750 (64.92%) Lab. hold
*Rt. Hon. Dr J. Cunningham, Lab. 17,991
Mike Graham, C.   13,027
Mark Gayler, LD   3,732
Lab. majority 4,964 (14.28%)
7.30% swing Lab. to C.
(1997: Lab. maj. 11,944 (28.89%))

CORBY
E. 72,304 T. 47,222 (65.31%)
                        Lab. Co-op hold
*Phil Hope, Lab. Co-op   23,283
Andrew Griffith, C.   17,583
Kevin Scudder, LD   4,751
Ian Gillman, UK Ind.   855
Andrew Dickson, Soc. Lab.   750
Lab. Co-op majority 5,700 (12.07%)
4.95% swing Lab. Co-op to C.
(1997: Lab. maj. 11,860 (21.98%))

CORNWALL NORTH
E. 84,662 T. 53,983 (63.76%) LD hold
*Paul Tyler, LD   28,082
John Weller, C.   18,250
Mike Goodman, Lab.   5,257
Steve Protz, UK Ind.   2,394
LD majority 9,832 (18.21%)
2.79% swing LD to C.
(1997: LD maj. 13,933 (23.79%))

CORNWALL SOUTH EAST
E. 79,090 T. 51,753 (65.44%) LD hold
*Colin Breed, LD   23,756
Ashley Gray, C.   18,381
Bill Stevens, Lab.   6,429
Graham Palmer, UK Ind.   1,978
Dr Ken George, Meb. Ker.   1,209
LD majority 5,375 (10.39%)
0.45% swing LD to C.
(1997: LD maj. 6,480 (11.28%))

COTSWOLD
E. 68,154 T. 45,981 (67.47%)   C. hold
*Geoffrey Clifton-Brown, C.   23,133
Ms Angela Lawrence, LD   11,150
Richard Wilkins, Lab.   10,383
Mrs Jill Stopps, UK Ind.   1,315
C. majority 11,983 (26.06%)
1.33% swing LD to C.
(1997: C. maj. 11,965 (23.41%))

COVENTRY NORTH EAST
E. 73,998 T. 37,265 (50.36%) Lab. hold
Bob Ainsworth, Lab.   22,739
Gordon Bell, C.   6,988
Geoffrey Sewards, LD   4,163
Dave Nellist, Soc. All.   2,638
Edward Sheppard, BNP   737
Lab. majority 15,751 (42.27%)
2.34% swing Lab. to C.
(1997: Lab. maj. 22,569 (46.94%))

COVENTRY NORTH WEST
E. 76,652 T. 42,551 (55.51%) Lab. hold
*Geoffrey Robinson, Lab.   21,892
Andrew Fairburn, C.   11,018
Napier Penlington, LD   5,832
Ms Christine Oddy, Ind.   3,159
Mark Benson, UK Ind.   650
Lab. majority 10,874 (25.56%)
2.50% swing Lab. to C.
(1997: Lab. maj. 16,601 (30.56%))

COVENTRY SOUTH
E. 72,527 T. 40,096 (55.28%) Lab. hold
*Jim Cunningham, Lab.   20,125
Ms Heather Wheeler, C.   11,846
Vincent McKee, LD   5,672
Rob Windsor, Soc. All.   1,475
Ms Irene Rogers, Ind.   564
Timothy Logan, Soc. Lab.   414
Lab. majority 8,279 (20.65%)
0.61% swing Lab. to C.
(1997: Lab. maj. 10,953 (21.86%))

CRAWLEY
E. 71,626 T. 39,522 (55.18%) Lab. hold
*Ms Laura Moffatt, Lab.   19,488
Henry Smith, C.   12,718
Ms Linda Seekings, LD   5,009
Brian Galloway, UK Ind.   1,137
Ms Claire Staniford, Loony   388
Arshad Khan, JP   271
Karl Stewart, Soc. Lab.   260
Ms Muriel Hirsch, Soc. All.   251
Lab. majority 6,770 (17.13%)
3.05% swing Lab. to C.
(1997: Lab. maj. 11,707 (23.22%))

CREWE & NANTWICH
E. 69,040 T. 41,547 (60.18%) Lab. hold
*Mrs Gwyneth Dunwoody, Lab. 22,556
Donald Potter, C.   12,650
David Cannon, LD   5,595
Roger Croston, UK Ind.   746
Lab. majority 9,906 (23.84%)
3.69% swing Lab. to C.
(1997: Lab. maj. 15,798 (31.22%))

CROSBY
E. 57,375 T. 36,866 (64.25%) Lab. hold
*Ms Claire Curtis-Thomas, Lab. 20,327
Robert Collinson, C.   11,974
Tim Drake, LD   4,084
Mark Holt, Soc. Lab.   481
Lab. majority 8,353 (22.66%)
3.19% swing C. to Lab.
(1997: Lab. maj. 7,182 (16.27%))

CROYDON CENTRAL
E. 77,567 T. 45,860 (59.12%) Lab. hold
*Geraint Davies, Lab.   21,643
David Congdon, C.   17,659
Paul Booth, LD   5,156
James Feisenberger, UK Ind.   545
Ms Lynda Miller, BNP   449
John Cartwright, Loony   408
Lab. majority 3,984 (8.69%)
0.85% swing C. to Lab.
(1997: Lab. maj. 3,897 (6.99%))

CROYDON NORTH
E. 76,600 T. 41,882 (54.68%) Lab. hold
*Malcolm Wicks, Lab.   26,610
Simon Allison, C.   9,752
Ms Sandra Lawman, LD   4,375
Alan Smith, UK Ind.   606
Don Madgwick, Soc. All.   539
Lab. majority 16,858 (40.25%)
2.63% swing C. to Lab.
(1997: Lab. maj. 18,398 (35.00%))

CROYDON SOUTH
E. 73,402 T. 45,060 (61.39%)   C. hold
*Richard Ottaway, C.   22,169
Gerry Ryan, Lab.   13,472
Ms Anne Gallop, LD   8,226
Mrs Kathleen Garner, UK Ind.   998
Mark Samuel, Choice   195
C. majority 8,697 (19.30%)
1.35% swing C. to Lab.
(1997: C. maj. 11,930 (22.01%))

DAGENHAM
E. 59,340 T. 27,580 (46.48%) Lab. hold
Jon Cruddas, Lab.   15,784
Michael White, C.   7,091
Adrian Gee-Turner, LD   2,820
David Hill, BNP   1,378
Berlyne Hamilton, Soc. All.   262
Robert Siggins, Soc. Lab.   245
Lab. majority 8,693 (31.52%)
7.82% swing Lab. to C.
(1997: Lab. maj. 17,054 (47.16%))

DARLINGTON
E. 64,328 T. 40,754 (63.35%) Lab. hold
*Rt. Hon. A. Milburn, Lab.   22,479
Tony Richmond, C.   12,950
Robert Adamson, LD   4,358
Alan Docherty, Soc. All.   469
Craig Platt, Ind.   269
Ms Amanda Rose, Soc. Lab.   229
Lab. majority 9,529 (23.38%)
4.94% swing Lab. to C.
(1997: Lab. maj. 16,025 (33.27%))

DARTFORD
E. 72,258 T. 44,740 (61.92%) Lab. hold
*Howard Stoate, Lab.   21,466
Bob Dunn, C.   18,160
Graham Morgan, LD   3,781
Mark Croucher, UK Ind.   989
Keith Davenport, FDP   344
Lab. majority 3,306 (7.39%)
0.47% swing Lab. to C.
(1997: Lab. maj. 4,328 (8.32%))

DAVENTRY
E. 86,537 T. 56,684 (65.50%)   C. hold
*Tim Boswell, C.   27,911
Kevin Quigley, Lab.   18,262
Jamie Calder, LD   9,130
Peter Baden, UK Ind.   1,381
C. majority 9,649 (17.02%)
2.54% swing Lab. to C.
(1997: C. maj. 7,378 (11.95%))

DENTON & REDDISH
E. 69,236 T. 33,593 (48.52%) Lab. hold
*Andrew Bennett, Lab.   21,913
Paul Newman, C.   6,583
Roger Fletcher, LD   4,152
Alan Cadwallender, UK Ind.   945
Lab. majority 15,330 (45.63%)
0.78% swing C. to Lab.
(1997: Lab. maj. 20,311 (44.08%))

DERBY NORTH
E. 76,489 T. 44,054 (57.60%) Lab. hold
*Bob Laxton, Lab.   22,415
Barrie Holden, C.   15,433
Robert Charlesworth, LD   6,206
Lab. majority 6,982 (15.85%)
1.53% swing Lab. to C.
(1997: Lab. maj. 10,615 (18.91%))

DERBY SOUTH
E. 77,366 T. 43,075 (55.68%) Lab. hold
*Rt. Hon. Mrs M. Beckett, Lab.   24,310
Simon Spencer, C.   10,455
Anders Hanson, LD   8,310
Lab. majority 13,855 (32.16%)
0.54% swing C. to Lab.
(1997: Lab. maj. 16,106 (31.08%))

DERBYSHIRE NORTH EAST
E. 71,527 T. 42,124 (58.89%) Lab. hold
*Harry Barnes, Lab.   23,437
James Hollingsworth, C.   11,179
Mark Higginbottom, LD   7,508
Lab. majority 12,258 (29.10%)
3.08% swing Lab. to C.
(1997: Lab. maj. 18,321 (35.25%))

DERBYSHIRE SOUTH
E. 81,010 T. 51,945 (64.12%) Lab. hold
*Mark Todd, Lab.   26,338
James Hakewill, C.   18,487
Russell Eagling, LD   5,233
John Blunt, UK Ind.   1,074
Paul Liversuch, Soc. Lab.   564
James Taylor, Ind.   249
Lab. majority 7,851 (15.11%)
4.09% swing Lab. to C.
(1997: Lab. maj. 13,967 (23.29%))

DERBYSHIRE WEST
E. 75,067 T. 50,589 (67.39%) C. hold
*Patrick McLoughlin, C.   24,280
Stephen Clamp, Lab.   16,910
Jeremy Beckett, LD   7,922
Stuart Bavester, UK Ind.   672
Nick Delves, Loony   472
Robert Goodall, Ind.   333
C. majority 7,370 (14.57%)
2.99% swing Lab. to C.
(1997: C. maj. 4,885 (8.59%))

DEVIZES
E. 83,655 T. 53,249 (63.65%) C. hold
*Rt. Hon. M. Ancram, C.   25,159
Jim Thorpe, Lab.   13,263
Ms Helen Frances, LD   11,756
Alan Wood, UK Ind.   1,521
Ludovic Kennedy, Ind.   1,078
Ms Vanessa Potter, Loony   472
C. majority 11,896 (22.34%)
1.88% swing Lab. to C.
(1997: C. maj. 9,782 (16.29%))

DEVON EAST
E. 70,278 T. 47,837 (68.07%) C. hold
Hugo Swire, C   22,681
Tim Dumper, LD   14,486
Phil Starr, Lab.   7,974
David Wilson, UK Ind.   2,696
C. majority 8,195 (17.13%)
1.44% swing LD to C.
(1997: C. maj. 7,489 (14.25%))

DEVON NORTH
E. 72,100 T. 49,254 (68.31%) LD hold
*Nick Harvey, LD   21,784
Clive Allen, C.   18,800
Ms Viv Gale, Lab.   4,995
Roger Knapman, UK Ind.   2,484
Tony Bown, Green   1,191
LD majority 2,984 (6.06%)
2.61% swing LD to C.
(1997: LD maj. 6,181 (11.27%))

DEVON SOUTH WEST
E. 70,922 T. 46,904 (66.13%) C. hold
*Gary Streeter, C.   21,970
Christopher Mavin, Lab.   14,826
Phil Hutty, LD   8,616
Roger Bullock, UK Ind.   1,492
C. majority 7,144 (15.23%)
0.58% swing Lab. to C.
(1997: C. maj. 7,433 (14.07%))

DEVON WEST & TORRIDGE
E. 78,976 T. 55,684 (70.51%) LD hold
*John Burnett, LD   23,474
Geoffrey Cox, C.   22,280
David Brenton, Lab.   5,959
Bob Edwards, UK Ind.   2,674
Martin Quinn, Green   1,297
LD majority 1,194 (2.14%)
0.58% swing LD to C.
(1997: LD maj. 1,957 (3.31%))

DEWSBURY
E. 62,344 T. 36,651 (58.79%) Lab. hold
*Rt. Hon. Mrs A. Taylor, Lab.   18,524
Robert Cole, C.   11,075
Ian Cuthbertson, LD   4,382
Russell Smith, BNP   1,632
Ms Brenda Smithson, Green   560
David Peace, UK Ind.   478
Lab. majority 7,449 (20.32%)
0.50% swing C. to Lab.
(1997: Lab. maj. 8,323 (19.33%))

DON VALLEY
E. 66,244 T. 36,630 (55.30%) Lab. hold
*Ms Caroline Flint, Lab.   20,009
James Browne, C.   10,489
Phillip Smith, LD   4,089
Tony Wilde, Ind.   800
David Cooper, UK Ind.   777
Nigel Ball, Soc. Lab.   466
Lab. majority 9,520 (25.99%)
3.84% swing Lab. to C.
(1997: Lab. maj. 14,659 (33.66%))

DONCASTER CENTRAL
E. 65,087 T. 33,902 (52.09%) Lab. hold
*Ms Rosie Winterton, Lab.   20,034
Gary Meggitt, C.   8,035
Michael Southcombe, LD   4,390
David Gordon, UK Ind.   926
Ms Janet Terry, Soc. All.   517
Lab. majority 11,999 (35.39%)
2.85% swing Lab. to C.
(1997: Lab. maj. 17,856 (41.10%))

DONCASTER NORTH
E. 62,124 T. 31,363 (50.48%) Lab. hold
*Kevin Hughes, Lab.   19,788
Mrs Anita Kapoor, C.   4,601
Colin Ross, LD   3,323
Martin Williams, Ind.   2,926
John Wallis, UK Ind.   725
Lab. majority 15,187 (48.42%)
3.28% swing Lab. to C.
(1997: Lab. maj. 21,937 (54.99%))

DORSET MID & POOLE NORTH
E. 66,675 T. 43,718 (65.57%) LD gain
Ms Annette Brooke, LD   18,358
*Christopher Fraser, C.   17,974
James Selby-Bennett, Lab.   6,765
Jeff Mager, UK Ind.   621
LD majority 384 (0.88%)
1.11% swing C. to LD
(1997: C. maj. 681 (1.34%))

DORSET NORTH
E. 72,140 T. 47,821 (66.29%) C. hold
*Robert Walter, C.   22,314
Miss Emily Gasson, LD   18,517
Mark Wareham, Lab.   5,334
Peter Jenkins, UK Ind.   1,019
Joseph Duthie, Low Excise   391
Mrs Cora Bone, Ind.   246
C. majority 3,797 (7.94%)
1.36% swing LD to C.
(1997: C. maj. 2,746 (5.23%))

DORSET SOUTH
E. 69,233 T. 45,345 (65.50%) Lab. gain
Jim Knight, Lab.   19,027
*Ian Cameron Bruce, C.   18,874
Andrew Canning, LD   6,531
Laurence Moss, UK Ind.   913
Lab. majority 153 (0.34%)
0.25% swing C. to Lab.
(1997: C. maj. 77 (0.16%))

DORSET WEST
E. 74,016 T. 49,571 (66.97%) C. hold
*Oliver Letwin, C.   22,126
Simon Green, LD   20,712
Richard Hyde, Lab.   6,733
C. majority 1,414 (2.85%)
0.29% swing C. to LD
(1997: C. maj. 1,840 (3.44%))

DOVER
E. 69,025 T. 44,960 (65.14%) Lab. hold
*Gwyn Prosser, Lab.   21,943
Paul Watkins, C.   16,744
Antony Hook, LD   5,131
Lee Speakman, UK Ind.   1,142
Lab. majority 5,199 (11.56%)
5.05% swing Lab. to C.
(1997: Lab. maj. 11,739 (21.66%))

DUDLEY NORTH
E. 68,964 T. 38,564 (55.92%) Lab. hold
*Ross Cranston, Lab.   20,095
Andrew Griffiths, C.   13,295
Richard Burt, LD   3,352
Simon Darby, BNP   1,822
Lab. majority 6,800 (17.63%)
1.08% swing Lab. to C.
(1997: Lab. maj. 9,457 (19.79%))

DUDLEY SOUTH
E. 65,578 T. 36,344 (55.42%) Lab. hold
*Ian Pearson, Lab.   18,109
Jason Sugarman, C.   11,292
Ms Lorely Burt, LD   5,421
John Westwood, UK Ind.   859
Ms Angela Thompson Soc. All.   663
Lab. majority 6,817 (18.76%)
4.22% swing Lab. to C.
(1997: Lab. maj. 13,027 (27.19%))

DULWICH & WEST NORWOOD
E. 70,497 T. 38,247 (54.25%) Lab. hold
*Rt. Hon. Ms T. Jowell, Lab.   20,999
Nick Vineall, C.   8,689
Ms Caroline Pidgeon, LD   5,806
Ms Jenny Jones, Green   1,914
Brian Kelly, Soc. All.   839
Lab. majority 12,310 (32.19%)
2.29% swing Lab. to C.
(1997: Lab. maj. 16,769 (36.76%))

DURHAM NORTH
E. 67,610 T. 38,568 (57.04%) Lab. hold
Kevan Jones, Lab.   25,920
Matthew Palmer, C.   7,237
Ms Carole Field, LD   5,411
Lab. majority 18,683 (48.44%)
3.65% swing Lab. to C.
(1997: Lab. maj. 26,299 (55.75%))

DURHAM NORTH WEST
E. 67,062 T. 39,226 (58.49%) Lab. hold
*Rt. Hon. Ms H. Armstrong, Lab. 24,526
William Clouston, C.   8,193
Alan Ord, LD   5,846
Ms Joan Hartnell, Soc. Lab.   661
Lab. majority 16,333 (41.64%)
5.90% swing Lab. to C.
(1997: Lab. maj. 24,754 (53.44%))

DURHAM, CITY OF
E. 69,633 T. 41,486 (59.58%) Lab. hold
*Gerry Steinberg, Lab.   23,254
Ms Carol Woods, LD   9,813
Nick Cartmell, C.   7,167
Mrs Chris Williamson, UK Ind.   1,252
Lab. majority 13,441 (32.40%)
7.82% swing Lab. to LD
(1997: Lab. maj. 22,504 (45.80%))

EALING ACTON & SHEPHERD'S
BUSH
E. 70,697 T. 37,201 (52.62%) Lab. hold
*Clive Soley, Lab.   20,144
Miss Justine Greening, C.   9,355
Martin Tod, LD   6,171
Nick Grant, Soc. All.   529
Andrew Lawrie, UK Ind.   476
Carlos Rule, Soc.   301
Ms Rebecca Ng, ProLife   225
Lab. majority 10,789 (29.00%)
1.77% swing C. to Lab.
(1997: Lab. maj. 15,647 (32.55%))

EALING NORTH
E. 77,524 T. 44,957 (57.99%) Lab. hold
*Stephen Pound, Lab.   25,022
Charles Walker, C.   13,185
Francesco Fruzza, LD   5,043
Ms Astra Seibe, Green   1,039
Daniel Moss, UK Ind.   668
Lab. majority 11,837 (26.33%)
4.94% swing C. to Lab.
(1997: Lab. maj. 9,160 (16.44%))

EALING SOUTHALL
E. 82,373 T. 46,828 (56.85%) Lab. hold
*Piara Khabra, Lab.   22,239
Daniel Kawczynski, C.   8,556
Avtar Lit, Sunrise   5,764
Baldev Sharma, LD   4,680
Ms Jane Cook, Green   2,119
Salvinder Dhillon, Community   1,214
Mushtaq Choudhry, Ind.   1,166
Harpal Brar, Soc,. Lab.   921
Mohammed Bhutta, Qari   169
Lab. majority 13,683 (29.22%)
5.00% swing Lab. to C.
(1997: Lab. maj. 21,423 (39.21%))

EASINGTON
E. 61,532 T. 33,010 (53.65%) Lab. hold
*John Cummings, Lab.   25,360
Philip Lovel, C.   3,411
Christopher Ord, LD   3,408
Dave Robinson, Soc. Lab.   831
Lab. majority 21,949 (66.49%)
2.57% swing Lab. to C.
(1997: Lab. maj. 30,012 (71.64%))

EAST HAM
E. 71,255 T. 37,277 (52.31%) Lab. hold
*Stephen Timms, Lab.   27,241
Peter Campbell, C.   6,209
Ms Bridget Fox, LD   2,600
Rod Finlayson, Soc. Lab.   783
Ms Johinda Pandhal, UK Ind.   444
Lab. majority 21,032 (56.42%)
3.95% swing C. to Lab.
(1997: Lab. maj. 19,358 (48.53%))

EASTBOURNE
E. 73,784 T. 44,770 (60.68%)   C. hold
*Nigel Waterson, C.   19,738
Chris Berry, LD   17,584
Ms Gillian Roles, Lab.   5,967
Barry Jones, UK Ind.   907
Ms Theresia Williamson, Lib.   574
C. majority 2,154 (4.81%)
0.51% swing LD to C.
(1997: C. maj. 1,994 (3.79%))

EASTLEIGH
E. 74,603 T. 47,573 (63.77%)   LD hold
*David Chidgey, LD   19,360
Conor Burns, C.   16,302
Sam Jaffa, Lab.   10,426
Stephen Challis, UK Ind.   849
Ms Martha Lyn, Green   636
LD majority 3,058 (6.43%)
2.54% swing C. to LD
(1997: LD maj. 754 (1.35%))

ECCLES
E. 68,764 T. 33,182 (48.25%) Lab. hold
*Ian Stewart, Lab.   21,395
Peter Caillard, C.   6,867
Bob Boyd, LD   4,920
Lab. majority 14,528 (43.78%)
2.09% swing Lab. to C.
(1997: Lab. maj. 21,916 (47.96%))

EDDISBURY
E. 69,181 T. 44,387 (64.16%)   C. hold
*Stephen O'Brien, C.   20,556
Bill Eyres, Lab.   15,988
Paul Roberts, LD   6,975
David Carson, UK Ind.   868
C. majority 4,568 (10.29%)
3.95% swing Lab. to C.
1999 Jul. by-election: C. maj. 1,606
(1997: C. maj. 1,185 (2.39%))

EDMONTON
E. 62,294 T. 34,774 (55.82%)
                          Lab. Co-op hold
*Andy Love, Lab. Co-op   20,481
David Burrowes, C.   10,709
Douglas Taylor, LD   2,438
Miss Gwyneth Rolph, UK Ind.   406
Erol Basarik, Reform   344
Howard Medwell, Soc. All.   296
Dr Ram Saxena, Ind.   100
Lab. Co-op majority 9,772
(28.10%)
0.97% swing Lab. Co-op to C.
(1997: Lab. maj. 13,472 (30.04%))

ELLESMERE PORT & NESTON
E. 68,147 T. 41,528 (60.94%) Lab. hold
*Andrew Miller, Lab.   22,964
Gareth Williams, C.   12,103
Stuart Kelly, LD   4,828
Henry Crocker, UK Ind.   824
Geoff Nicholls, Green   809
Lab. majority 10,861 (26.15%)
2.18% swing Lab. to C.
(1997: Lab. maj. 16,036 (30.51%))

ELMET
E. 70,041 T. 45,937 (65.59%) Lab. hold
*Colin Burgon, Lab.   22,038
Andrew Millard, C.   17,867
Ms Madeleine Kirk, LD   5,001
Andrew Spence, UK Ind.   1,031
Lab. majority 4,171 (9.08%)
3.57% swing Lab. to C.
(1997: Lab. maj. 8,779 (16.22%))

ELTHAM
E. 57,519 T. 33,792 (58.75%) Lab. hold
*Clive Efford, Lab.   17,855
Mrs Sharon Massey, C.   10,859
Martin Morris, LD   4,121
Terry Jones, UK Ind.   706
Andrew Graham, Ind.   251
Lab. majority 6,996 (20.70%)
1.37% swing Lab. to C.
(1997: Lab. maj. 10,182 (23.45%))

ENFIELD NORTH
E. 67,756 T. 38,143 (56.29%) Lab. hold
*Ms Joan Ryan, Lab.   17,888
Nick De Bois, C.   15,597
Ms Hilary Leighter, LD   3,355
Ramon Johns, BNP   605
Brian Hall, UK Ind.   247
Michael Akerman, ProLife   241
Richard Course, Ind.   210
Lab. majority 2,291 (6.01%)
4.15% swing Lab. to C.
(1997: Lab. maj. 6,822 (14.31%))

ENFIELD SOUTHGATE
E. 66,418 T. 41,908 (63.10%) Lab. hold
*Stephen Twigg, Lab.   21,727
John Flack, C.   16,181
Wayne Hoban, LD   2,935
Ms Elaine Graham-Leigh, Green   662
Roy Freshwater, UK Ind.   298
Andrew Malakouna, Ind.   105
Lab. majority 5,546 (13.23%)
5.08% swing C. to Lab.
(1997: Lab. maj. 1,433 (3.08%))

EPPING FOREST
E. 72,645 T. 42,414 (58.39%)   C. hold
*Mrs Eleanor Laing, C.   20,833
Christopher Naylor, Lab.   12,407
Michael Heavens, LD   7,884
Andrew Smith, UK Ind.   1,290
C. majority 8,426 (19.87%)
4.98% swing Lab. to C.
(1997: C. maj. 5,252 (9.91%))

EPSOM & EWELL
E. 74,266 T. 46,643 (62.81%)   C. hold
Chris Grayling, C.   22,430
Charles Mansell, Lab.   12,350
John Vincent, LD   10,316
G. Webster-Gardiner, UK Ind.   1,547
C. majority 10,080 (21.61%)
0.17% swing Lab. to C.
(1997: C. maj. 11,525 (21.27%))

EREWASH
E. 78,484 T. 48,596 (61.92%)   Lab. hold
*Ms Liz Blackman, Lab.   23,915
Gregor MacGregor, C.   16,983
Martin Garnett, LD   5,586
Ms Louise Smith, UK Ind.   692
Steven Belshaw, BNP   591
R U Seerius, Loony   428
Peter Waldock, Soc. Lab.   401
Lab. majority 6,932 (14.26%)
0.44% swing Lab. to C.
(1997: Lab. maj. 9,135 (15.14%))

ERITH & THAMESMEAD
E. 66,371 T. 33,351 (50.25%)   Lab. hold
*John Austin, Lab.   19,769
Mark Brooks, C.   8,602
James Kempton, LD   3,800
Hardev Dhillon, Soc. Lab.   1,180
Lab. majority 11,167 (33.48%)
4.21% swing Lab. to C.
(1997: Lab. maj. 17,424 (41.90%))

ESHER & WALTON
E. 73,541 T. 45,531 (61.91%)   C. hold
*Ian Taylor, C.   22,296
Joe McGowan, Lab.   10,758
Mark Marsh, LD   10,241
Bernard Collignon, UK Ind.   2,236
C. majority 11,538 (25.34%)
0.86% swing Lab. to C.
(1997: C. maj. 14,528 (27.07%))

ESSEX NORTH
E. 71,680 T. 44,944 (62.70%)   C. hold
*Bernard Jenkin, C.   21,325
Philip Hawkins, Lab.   14,139
Trevor Ellis, LD   7,867
George Curtis, UK Ind.   1,613
C. majority 7,186 (15.99%)
2.65% swing Lab. to C.
(1997: C. maj. 5,476 (10.69%))

EXETER
E. 81,942 T. 52,616 (64.21%)   Lab. hold
*Ben Bradshaw, Lab.   26,194
Mrs Anne Jobson, C.   14,435
Richard Copus, LD   6,512
David Morrish, Lib.   2,596
Paul Edwards, Green   1,240
John Stuart, UK Ind.   1,109
Francis Choules, Soc. All.   530
Lab. majority 11,759 (22.35%)
1.71% swing C. to Lab.
(1997: Lab. maj. 11,705 (18.92%))

FALMOUTH & CAMBORNE
E. 72,833 T. 46,820 (64.28%)   Lab. hold
*Ms Candy Atherton, Lab.   18,532
Nick Serpell, C.   14,005
Julian Brazil, LD   11,453
John Browne, UK Ind.   1,328
Ms Hilda Wasley, Meb. Ker.   853
Paul Holmes, Lib.   649
Lab. majority 4,527 (9.67%)
2.33% swing C. to Lab.
(1997: Lab. maj. 2,688 (5.01%))

FAREHAM
E. 72,678 T. 45,447 (62.53%)   C. hold
Mark Hoban, C.   21,389
James Carr, Lab.   14,380
Hugh Pritchard, LD   8,503
William O'Brien, UK Ind.   1,175
C. majority 7,009 (15.42%)
2.21% swing C. to Lab.
(1997: C. maj. 10,358 (19.85%))

FAVERSHAM & KENT MID
E. 67,995 T. 41,051 (60.37%)   C. hold
Hugh Robertson, C.   18,739
Grahame Birchall, Lab.   14,556
Mike Sole, LD   5,529
Jim Gascoyne, UK Ind.   828
Ms Penny Kemp, Green   799
Norman Davidson, R & R Loony   600
C. majority 4,183 (10.19%)
0.89% swing Lab. to C.
(1997: C. maj. 4,173 (8.41%))

FELTHAM & HESTON
E. 73,229 T. 36,177 (49.40%)
                          Lab. Co-op hold
*Alan Keen, Lab. Co-op   21,406
Mrs Liz Mammatt, C.   8,749
Andy Darley, LD   4,998
Surinder Cheema, Soc. Lab.   651
Warwick Prachar, Ind.   204
Asa Khaira, Ind.   169
Lab. Co-op majority 12,657 (34.99%)
1.11% swing C. to Lab. Co-op
(1997: Lab. maj. 15,273 (32.76%))

FINCHLEY & GOLDERS GREEN
E. 76,175 T. 43,675 (57.34%)   Lab. hold
*Rudi Vis, Lab.   20,205
John Marshall, C.   16,489
Ms Sarah Teather, LD   5,266
Ms Miranda Dunn, Green   1,385
John de Roeck, UK Ind.   330
Lab. majority 3,716 (8.51%)
1.08% swing C. to Lab.
(1997: Lab. maj. 3,189 (6.34%))

FOLKESTONE & HYTHE
E. 71,503 T. 45,855 (64.13%)   C. hold
*Rt. Hon. M. Howard, C.   20,645
Peter Carroll, LD   14,738
Albert Catterall, Lab.   9,260
John Baker, UK Ind.   1,212
C. majority 5,907 (12.88%)
0.36% swing LD to C.
(1997: C. maj. 6,332 (12.17%))

FOREST OF DEAN
E. 66,240 T. 44,607 (67.34%)   Lab. hold
*Ms Diana Organ, Lab.   19,350
Mark Harper, C.   17,301
David Gayler, LD   5,762
Simon Pickering, Green   1,254
Allen Prout, UK Ind.   661
Gerald Morgan, Ind.   279
Lab. majority 2,049 (4.59%)
4.02% swing Lab. to C.
(1997: Lab. maj. 6,343 (12.64%))

FYLDE
E. 72,207 T. 44,737 (61.96%)   C. hold
*Rt. Hon. M. Jack, C.   23,383
John Stockton, Lab.   13,773
John Begg, LD   6,599
Mrs Lesley Brown, UK Ind.   982
C. majority 9,610 (21.48%)
2.13% swing Lab. to C.
(1997: C. maj. 8,963 (17.22%))

GAINSBOROUGH
E. 65,871 T. 42,319 (64.25%)   C. hold
*Edward Leigh, C.   19,555
Alan Rhodes, Lab.   11,484
Steve Taylor, LD   11,280
C. majority 8,071 (19.07%)
2.39% swing Lab. to C.
(1997: C. maj. 6,826 (14.29%))

GATESHEAD EAST & WASHINGTON
WEST
E. 64,041 T. 33,615 (52.49%)   Lab. hold
*Rt. Hon. Ms J. Quin, Lab.   22,903
Ron Beadle, LD   4,999
Ms Elizabeth Campbell, C.   4,970
Martin Rouse, UK Ind.   743
Lab. majority 17,904 (53.26%)
4.04% swing Lab. to LD
(1997: Lab. maj. 24,950 (57.92%))

GEDLING
E. 68,540 T. 43,816 (63.93%)   Lab. hold
*Vernon Coaker, Lab.   22,383
Jonathan Bullock, C.   16,785
Tony Gillam, LD   4,648
Lab. majority 5,598 (12.78%)
2.74% swing C. to Lab.
(1997: Lab. maj. 3,802 (7.29%))

GILLINGHAM
E. 70,898 T. 42,212 (59.54%)   Lab. hold
*Paul Clark, Lab.   18,782
Tim Butcher, C.   16,510
Jonathan Hunt, LD   5,755
Tony Scholefield, UK Ind.   933
Wynford Vaughan, Soc. All.   232
Lab. majority 2,272 (5.38%)
0.74% swing to Lab.
(1997: Lab. maj. 1,980 (3.91%))

GLOUCESTER
E. 81,144 T. 48,223 (59.43%)   Lab. hold
Parmjit Dhanda, Lab.   22,067
Paul James, C.   18,187
Tim Bullamore, LD   6,875
Terry Lines, UK Ind.   822
Stewart Smyth, Soc. All.   272
Lab. majority 3,880 (8.05%)
3.11% swing Lab. to C.
(1997: Lab. maj. 8,259 (14.26%))

GOSPORT
E. 69,626 T. 39,789 (57.15%)   C. hold
*Peter Viggers, C.   17,364
Richard Williams, Lab.   14,743
Roger Roberts, LD   6,011
John Bowles, UK Ind.   1,162
Kevin Chetwynd, Soc. Lab.   509
C. majority 2,621 (6.59%)
3.18% swing C. to Lab.
(1997: C. maj. 6,258 (12.94%))

GRANTHAM & STAMFORD
E. 74,459 T. 46,289 (62.17%)   C. hold
*Quentin Davies, C.   21,329
John Robinson, Lab.   16,811
Ms Jane Carr, LD   6,665
Miss Marilyn Swain, UK Ind.   1,484
C. majority 4,518 (9.76%)
2.34% swing Lab. to C.
(1997: C. maj. 2,692 (5.08%))

GRAVESHAM
E. 69,590 T. 43,639 (62.71%)   Lab. hold
*Chris Pond, Lab.   21,773
Jacques Arnold, C.   16,911
Bruce Parmenter, LD   4,031
William Jenner, UK Ind.   924
Lab. majority 4,862 (11.14%)
0.15% swing C. to Lab.
(1997: Lab. maj. 5,779 (10.85%))

GREAT GRIMSBY
E. 63,157 T. 33,017 (52.28%)   Lab. hold
*Austin Mitchell, Lab.   19,118
James Cousins, C.   7,634
Andrew de Freitas, LD   6,265
Lab. majority 11,484 (34.78%)
1.46% swing lab. to C.
(1997: Lab. maj. 16,244 (37.70%))

GREAT YARMOUTH
E. 69,131 T. 40,366 (58.39%)   Lab. hold
*Tony Wright, Lab.   20,344
Charles Reynolds, C.   15,780
Maurice Leeke, LD   3,392
Bertie Poole, UK Ind.   850
Lab. majority 4,564 (11.31%)
3.21% swing Lab. to C.
(1997: Lab. maj. 8,668 (17.73%))

GREENWICH & WOOLWICH
E. 62,530 T. 32,536 (52.03%)   Lab. hold
*Rt. Hon. N. Raynsford, Lab.   19,691
Richard Forsdyke, C.   6,258
Russell Pyne, LD   5,082
Stan Gain, UK Ind.   672
Miss Kirstie Paton, Soc. All.   481
Ms Margaret Sharkey, Soc. Lab.   352
Lab. majority 13,433 (41.29%)
1.79% swing Lab. to C.
(1997: Lab. maj. 18,128 (44.87%))

GUILDFORD
E. 76,046 T. 47,842 (62.91%)   LD gain
Ms Sue Doughty, LD   20,358
*Nick St Aubyn, C.   19,820
Ms Joyce Still, Lab.   6,558
Ms Sonya Porter, UK Ind.   736
John Morris, Pacifist   370
LD majority 538 (1.12%)
4.77% swing C. to LD
(1997: C. maj. 4,791 (8.41%))

HACKNEY NORTH & STOKE
NEWINGTON
E. 60,444 T. 29,621 (49.01%)   Lab. hold
*Ms Diane Abbott, Lab.   18,081
Mrs Pauline Dye, C.   4,430
Ms Meral Ece, LD   4,170
Chit Yen Chong, Green   2,184
Sukant Chandan, Soc. Lab.   756
Lab. majority 13,651 (46.09%)
0.74% swing Lab. to C.
(1997: Lab. maj. 15,627 (47.57%))

HACKNEY SOUTH & SHOREDITCH
E. 63,990 T. 30,347 (47.42%)   Lab. hold
*Brian Sedgemore, Lab.   19,471
Tony Vickers, LD   4,422
Paul White, C.   4,180
Ms Cecilia Prosper, Soc. All.   1,401
Saim Kokshal, Reform   471
Ivan Beavis, Comm.   259
William Rogers, WRP   143
Lab. majority 15,049 (49.59%)
2.60% swing LD to Lab.
(1997: Lab. maj. 14,980 (44.39%))

HALESOWEN & ROWLEY REGIS
E. 65,683 T. 39,274 (59.79%)   Lab. hold
*Ms Sylvia Heal, Lab.   20,804
Les Jones, C.   13,445
Patrick Harley, LD   4,089
Alan Sheath, UK Ind.   936
Lab. majority 7,359 (18.74%)
1.23% swing Lab. to C.
(1997: Lab. maj. 10,337 (21.20%))

HALIFAX
E. 69,870 T. 40,390 (57.81%)   Lab. hold
*Ms Alice Mahon, Lab.   19,800
James Walsh, C.   13,671
John Durkin, LD   5,878
Mrs Helen Martinek, UK Ind.   1,041
Lab. majority 6,129 (15.17%)
3.50% swing Lab. to C.
(1997: Lab. maj. 11,212 (22.18%))

HALTEMPRICE & HOWDEN
E. 67,055 T. 43,928 (65.51%)   C. hold
*Rt. Hon. D. Davis, C.   18,994
John Neal, LD   17,091
Leslie Howell, Lab.   6,898
Ms Joanne Robinson, UK Ind.   945
C. majority 1,903 (4.33%)
5.41% swing C. to LD
(1997: C. maj. 7,514 (15.16%))

HALTON
E. 63,673 T. 34,470 (54.14%)   Lab. hold
*Derek Twigg, Lab.   23,841
Chris Davenport, C.   6,413
Peter Walker, LD   4,216
Lab. majority 17,428 (50.56%)
1.33% swing Lab. to C.
(1997: Lab. maj. 23,650 (53.22%))

HAMMERSMITH & FULHAM
E. 79,302 T. 44,700 (56.37%)   Lab. hold
*Iain Coleman, Lab.   19,801
Matthew Carrington, C.   17,786
Jon Burden, LD   5,294
Daniel Lopez Dias, Green   1,444
Gerald Roberts, UK Ind.   375
Lab. majority 2,015 (4.51%)
1.30% swing Lab. to C.
(1997: Lab. maj. 3,842 (7.11%))

HAMPSHIRE EAST
E. 78,802 T. 50,289 (63.82%)   C. hold
*Michael Mates, C.   23,950
Robert Booker, LD   15,060
Ms Barbara Burfoot, Lab.   9,866
Stephen Coles, UK Ind.   1,413
C. majority 8,890 (17.68%)
1.13% swing C. to LD
(1997: C. maj. 11,590 (19.93%))

HAMPSHIRE NORTH EAST
E. 71,323 T. 43,947 (61.62%)   C. hold
*Rt. Hon. J. Arbuthnot, C.   23,379
Mike Plummer, LD   10,122
Barry Jones, Lab.   8,744
Graham Mellstrom, UK Ind.   1,702
C. majority 13,257 (30.17%)
1.00% swing LD to C.
(1997: C. maj. 14,398 (28.17%))

HAMPSHIRE NORTH WEST
E. 76,359 T. 48,631 (63.69%)   C. hold
*Rt. Hon. Sir G. Young, C.   24,374
Mick Mumford, Lab.   12,365
Alex Bentley, LD   10,329
Stanley Oram, UK Ind.   1,563
C. majority 12,009 (24.69%)
1.53% swing Lab. to C.
(1997: C. maj. 11,551 (21.13%))

HAMPSTEAD & HIGHGATE
E. 65,309 T. 35,407 (54.21%)   Lab. hold
*Ms Glenda Jackson, Lab.   16,601
Andrew Mennear, C.   8,725
Jonathan Simpson, LD   7,273
Andrew Cornwell, Green   1,654
Ms Helen Cooper, Soc. All.   559
Thomas McDermott, UK Ind.   316
Ms Sister Xnunoftheabove, Ind.   144
Ms Mary Teale, ProLife   92
Amos Klein, Ind.   43
Lab. majority 7,876 (22.24%)
3.96% swing Lab. to C.
(1997: Lab. maj. 13,284 (30.17%))

HARBOROUGH
E. 73,300 T. 46,427 (63.34%)   C. hold
*Edward Garnier, C.   20,748
Ms Jill Hope, LD   15,496
Raj Jethwa, Lab.   9,271
David Knight, UK Ind.   912
C. majority 5,252 (11.31%)
0.49% swing C. to LD
(1997: C. maj. 6,524 (12.30%))

HARLOW
E. 67,074 T. 40,115 (59.81%)   Lab. hold
*Bill Rammell, Lab.   19,169
Robert Halfon, C.   13,941
Ms Lorna Spenceley, LD   5,381
Tony Bennett, UK Ind.   1,223
John Hobbs, Soc. All.   401
Lab. majority 5,228 (13.03%)
4.48% swing Lab. to C.
(1997: Lab. maj. 10,514 (21.99%))

HARROGATE & KNARESBOROUGH
E. 65,185 T. 42,179 (64.71%)   LD hold
*Phil Willis, LD   23,445
Andrew Jones, C.   14,600
Alastair MacDonald, Lab.   3,101
Bill Brown, UK Ind.   761
John Cornforth, ProLife   272
LD majority 8,845 (20.97%)
3.94% swing C. to LD
(1997: LD maj. 6,236 (13.09%))

HARROW EAST
E. 81,575 T. 48,077 (58.94%)   Lab. hold
*Tony McNulty, Lab.   26,590
Peter Wilding, C.   15,466
George Kershaw, LD   6,021
Lab. majority 11,124 (23.14%)
3.02% swing C. to Lab.
(1997: Lab. maj. 9,738 (17.09%))

HARROW WEST
E. 73,505 T. 46,648 (63.46%)   Lab. hold
*Gareth Thomas, Lab.   23,142
Danny Finkelstein, C.   16,986
Christopher Noyce, LD   5,995
Peter Kefford, UK Ind.   525
Lab. majority 6,156 (13.20%)
5.42% swing C. to Lab.
(1997: Lab. maj. 1,240 (2.36%))

HARTLEPOOL
E. 67,652 T. 38,051 (56.25%)   Lab. hold
*Rt. Hon. P. Mandelson, Lab.   22,506
Gus Robinson, C.   7,935
Nigel Boddy, LD   5,717
Arthur Scargill, Soc. Lab.   912
Ian Cameron, Ind.   557
John Booth, Ind.   424
Lab. majority 14,571 (38.29%)
0.54% swing Lab. to C.
(1997: Lab. maj. 17,508 (39.38%))

HARWICH
E. 77,539 T. 48,115 (62.05%)   Lab. hold
*Ivan Henderson, Lab.   21,951
Ian Sproat, C.   19,355
Peter Wilcock, LD   4,099
Tony Finnegan-Butler, UK Ind.   2,463
Clive Lawrance, Ind.   247
Lab. majority 2,596 (5.40%)
1.56% swing C. to Lab.
(1997: Lab. maj. 1,216 (2.28%))

HASTINGS & RYE
E. 70,632 T. 41,218 (58.36%)   Lab. hold
*Michael Foster, Lab.   19,402
Mark Coote, C.   15,094
Graem Peters, LD   4,266
Alan Coomber, UK Ind.   911
Ms Sally Phillips, Green   721
Mrs Gillian Bargery, Ind.   486
John Ord-Clarke, Loony   198
Brett McLean, R & R Loony   140
Lab. majority 4,308 (10.45%)
2.62% swing C. to Lab.
(1997: Lab. maj. 2,560 (5.21%))

HAVANT
E. 70,246 T. 40,437 (57.56%)   C. hold
*David Willetts, C.   17,769
Peter Guthrie, Lab.   13,562
Ms Helena Cole, LD   7,508
Kevin Jacks, Green   793
Tim Cuell, UK Ind.   561
Roy Stanley, Ind.   244
C. majority 4,207 (10.40%)
1.34% swing Lab. to C.
(1997: C. maj. 3,729 (7.72%))

HAYES & HARLINGTON
E. 57,561 T. 32,403 (56.29%)   Lab. hold
*John McDonnell, Lab.   21,279
Robert McLean, C.   7,813
Ms Nahid Boethe, LD   1,958
Gary Burch, BNP   705
Wally Kennedy, Soc. Alt.   648
Lab. majority 13,466 (41.56%)
3.39% swing C. to Lab.
(1997: Lab. maj. 14,291 (34.78%))

HAZEL GROVE
E. 65,107 T. 38,478 (59.10%)   LD hold
*Andrew Stunell, LD   20,020
Ms Nadine Bargery, C.   11,585
Martin Miller, Lab.   6,230
Gerald Price, UK Ind.   643
LD majority 8,435 (21.92%)
1.01% swing LD to C.
(1997: LD maj. 11,814 (23.95%))

HEMEL HEMPSTEAD
E. 72,086 T. 45,833 (63.58%)
                          Lab. Co-op hold
*Tony McWalter, Lab. Co-op   21,389
Paul Ivey, C.   17,647
Neil Stuart, LD   5,877
Barry Newton, UK Ind.   920
Lab.Co-opmajority 3,742 (8.16%)
0.78% swing C. to Lab. Co-op
(1997: Lab. maj. 3,636 (6.60%))

HEMSWORTH
E. 67,948 T. 35,227 (51.84%)   Lab. hold
*Jon Trickett, Lab.   23,036
Mrs Elizabeth Truss, C.   7,400
Ed Waller, LD   3,990
Paul Turek, Soc. Lab.   801
Lab. majority 15,636 (44.39%)
4.19% swing Lab. to C.
(1997: Lab. maj. 23,992 (52.76%))

HENDON
E. 78,212 T. 40,851 (52.23%)   Lab. hold
*Andrew Dismore, Lab.   21,432
Richard Evans, C.   14,015
Wayne Casey, LD   4,724
Craig Crosbie, UK Ind.   409
Ms Stella Taylor, WRP   164
Michael Stewart, Prog Dem   107
Lab. majority 7,417 (18.16%)
2.93% swing C. to Lab.
(1997: Lab. maj. 6,155 (12.30%))

HENLEY
E. 69,081 T. 44,401 (64.27%)   C. hold
Boris Johnson, C.   20,466
Ms Catherine Bearder, LD   12,008
Ms Janet Mathews, Lab.   9,367
Philip Collings, UK Ind.   1,413
Oliver Tickell, Green   1,147
C. majority 8,458 (19.05%)
1.31% swing C. to LD
(1997: C. maj. 11,167 (21.66%))

HEREFORD
E. 70,305 T. 44,624 (63.47%)   LD hold
*Paul Keetch, LD   18,244
Mrs Virginia Taylor, C.   17,276
David Hallam, Lab.   6,739
Clive Easton, UK Ind.   1,184
David Gillett, Green   1,181
LD majority 968 (2.17%)
5.24% swing LD to C.
(1997: LD maj. 6,648 (12.65%))

HERTFORD & STORTFORD
E. 75,141 T. 47,176 (62.78%)   C. hold
Mark Prisk, C.   21,074
Simon Speller, Lab.   15,471
Ms Mione Gold Spink, LD   9,388
Stuart Rising, UK Ind.   1,243
C. majority 5,603 (11.88%)
0.37% swing C. to Lab.
(1997: C. maj. 6,885 (12.62%))

HERTFORDSHIRE NORTH EAST
E. 68,790 T. 44,645 (64.90%)   C. hold
*Oliver Heald, C.   19,695
Ivan Gibbons, Lab.   16,251
Ms Alison Kingman, LD   7,686
Michael Virgo, UK Ind.   1,013
C. majority 3,444 (7.71%)
0.89% swing Lab. to C.
(1997: C. maj. 3,088 (5.94%))

HERTFORDSHIRE SOUTH WEST
E. 73,367 T. 47,269 (64.43%)   C. hold
*Richard Page, C.   20,933
Graham Dale, Lab.   12,752
Ed Featherstone, LD   12,431
Colin Dale-Mills, UK Ind.   847
Ms Julia Goffin, ProLife   306
C. majority 8,181 (17.31%)
0.39% swing C. to Lab.
(1997: C. maj. 10,021 (18.08%))

HERTSMERE
E. 68,780 T. 41,505 (60.34%)   C. hold
*James Clappison, C.   19,855
Ms Hilary Broderick, Lab.   14,953
Paul Thompson, LD   6,300
James Dry, Soc. Lab.   397
C. majority 4,902 (11.81%)
2.85% swing to C.
(1997: C. maj. 3,075 (6.11%))

HEXHAM
E. 59,807 T. 42,413 (70.92%)   C. hold
*Peter Atkinson, C.   18,917
Paul Brannen, Lab.   16,388
Philip Latham, LD   6,380
Alan Patterson, UK Ind.   728
C. majority 2,529 (5.96%)
2.74% swing Lab. to C.
(1997: C. maj. 222 (0.49%))

HEYWOOD & MIDDLETON
E. 73,005 T. 38,779 (53.12%)
                          Lab. Co-op hold
*Jim Dobbin, Lab. Co-op   22,377
Mrs Marilyn Hopkins, C.   10,707
Ian Greenhalgh, LD   4,329
Philip Burke, Lib.   1,021
Ms Christine West, Ch. D.   345
Lab. Co-op majority 11,670 (30.09%)
2.30% swing Lab. Co-op to C.
(1997: Lab. maj. 17,542 (34.70%))

HIGH PEAK
E. 73,774 T. 48,114 (65.22%) Lab. hold
*Tom Levitt, Lab.   22,430
Simon Chapman, C.   17,941
Peter Ashenden, LD   7,743
Lab. majority 4,489 (9.33%)
3.03% swing Lab. to C.
(1997: Lab. maj. 8,791 (15.38%))

HITCHIN & HARPENDEN
E. 67,196 T. 44,924 (66.86%) C. hold
*Rt. Hon. P. Lilley, C.   21,271
Alan Amos, Lab.   14,608
John Murphy, LD   8,076
John Saunders, UK Ind.   606
Peter Rigby, Ind.   363
C. majority 6,663 (14.83%)
1.06% swing Lab. to C.
(1997: C. maj. 6,671 (12.72%))

HOLBORN & ST PANCRAS
E. 62,813 T. 31,129 (49.56%) Lab. hold
*Rt. Hon. F. Dobson, Lab.   16,770
Nathaniel Green, C.   5,595
Mrs Roseanne Serelli, C.   5,258
Rob Whitley, Green   1,875
Ms Candy Udwin, Soc. All.   971
Joti Brar, Soc. Lab.   359
Magnus Nielsen, UK Ind.   301
Lab. majority 11,175 (35.90%)
8.31% swing Lab. to LD
(1997: Lab. maj. 17,903 (47.11%))

HORNCHURCH
E. 61,008 T. 35,557 (58.28%) Lab. hold
*John Cryer, Lab.   16,514
Robin Squire, C.   15,032
Ms Sarah Lea, LD   2,928
Lawrence Webb, UK Ind.   893
Mr David Durant, Third   190
Lab. majority 1,482 (4.17%)
4.38% swing Lab. to C.
(1997: Lab. maj. 5,680 (12.93%))

HORNSEY & WOOD GREEN
E. 75,967 T. 44,063 (58.00%) Lab. hold
*Ms Barbara Roche, Lab.   21,967
Ms Lynne Featherstone, LD   11,353
Jason Hollands, C.   6,921
Ms Jayne Forbes, Green   2,228
Ms Louise Christian, Soc. All.   1,106
Ms Ella Rule, Soc. Lab.   294
Erdil Ataman, Reform   194
Lab. majority 10,614 (24.09%)
13.21% swing Lab. to LD
(1997: Lab. maj. 20,499 (39.82%))

HORSHAM
E. 79,604 T. 50,770 (63.78%) C. hold
*Rt. Hon. F. Maude, C.   26,134
Hubert Carr, LD   12,468
Ms Janet Sully, Lab.   10,267
Hugo Miller, UK Ind.   1,472
Jim Duggan, Ind.   429
C. majority 13,666 (26.92%)
0.46% swing LD to C.
(1997: C. maj. 14,862 (26.00%))

HOUGHTON & WASHINGTON EAST
E. 67,946 T. 33,641 (49.51%) Lab. hold
*Fraser Kemp, Lab.   24,628
Tony Devenish, C.   4,810
Richard Ormerod, LD   4,203
Lab. majority 19,818 (58.91%)
2.29% swing Lab. to C.
(1997: Lab. maj. 26,555 (63.49%))

HOVE
E. 70,889 T. 41,988 (59.23%) Lab. hold
*Ivor Caplin, Lab.   19,253
Mrs Jenny Langston, C.   16,082
Harold de Souza, LD   3,823
Ms Anthea Ballam, Green   1,369
Andy Richards, Soc. All.   531
Richard Franklin, UK Ind.   358
Nigel Donovan, Lib.   316
Simon Dobbshead, Free   196
Thomas Major, Ind.   60
Lab. majority 3,171 (7.55%)
0.34% swing Lab. to C.
(1997: Lab. maj. 3,959 (8.23%))

HUDDERSFIELD
E. 64,349 T. 35,383 (54.99%)
                          Lab. Co-op hold
*Barry Sheerman, Lab. Co-op   18,840
Paul Baverstock, C.   8,794
Neil Bentley, LD   5,300
John Phillips, Green   1,254
Mrs Judith Longman, UK Ind.   613
Graham Hellawell, Soc. All.   374
George Randall, Soc. Lab.   208
Lab. Co-op majority 10,046 (28.39%)
3.59% swing Lab. Co-op to C.
(1997: Lab. maj. 15,848 (35.57%))

HULL EAST
E. 66,473 T. 30,875 (46.45%) Lab. hold
*Rt. Hon. J. Prescott, Lab.   19,938
Ms Jo Swinson, LD   4,613
Ms Sandip Verma, C.   4,276
Ms Jeanette Jenkinson, UK Ind.   1,218
Ms Linda Muir, Soc. Lab.   830
Lab. majority 15,325 (49.64%)
5.94% swing Lab. to LD
(1997: Lab. maj. 23,318 (57.60%))

HULL NORTH
E. 63,022 T. 28,633 (45.43%) Lab. hold
*Kevin McNamara, Lab.   16,364
Ms Simone Butterworth, LD   5,643
Paul Charlson, C.   4,902
Ms Tineka Robinson, UK Ind.   655
Roger Smith, Soc. All.   490
Carl Wagner, LCA   478
Christopher Veasey, Ind.   101
Lab. majority 10,721 (37.44%)
6.89% swing Lab. to LD
(1997: Lab. maj. 19,705 (50.79%))

HULL WEST & HESSLE
E. 63,077 T. 28,916 (45.84%) Lab. hold
*Alan Johnson, Lab.   16,880
John Sharp, C.   5,929
Ms Angela Wastling, LD   4,364
John Cornforth, UK Ind.   878
David Harris, Ind.   512
David Skinner, Soc. Lab.   353
Lab. majority 10,951 (37.87%)
1.38% swing Lab. to C.
(1997: Lab. maj. 15,525 (40.48%))

HUNTINGDON
E. 78,604 T. 49,089 (62.45%) C. hold
Jonathan Djanogly, C.   24,507
Michael Pope, LD   11,715
Takki Sulaiman, Lab.   11,211
Derek Norman, UK Ind.   1,656
C. majority 12,792 (26.06%)
7.26% swing C. to LD
(1997: C. maj. 18,140 (31.84%))

HYNDBURN
E. 66,445 T. 38,243 (57.56%) Lab. hold
*Greg Pope, Lab.   20,900
Peter Britcliffe, C.   12,681
Bill Greene, LD   3,680
John Tomlin, UK Ind.   982
Lab. majority 8,219 (21.49%)
1.11% swing Lab. to C.
(1997: Lab. maj. 11,448 (23.71%))

ILFORD NORTH
E. 68,893 T. 40,234 (58.40%) Lab. hold
*Ms Linda Perham, Lab.   18,428
Vivian Bendall, C.   16,313
Gavin Stollar, LD   4,717
Martin Levin, UK Ind.   776
Lab. majority 2,115 (5.26%)
0.67% swing Lab. to C.
(1997: Lab. maj. 3,224 (6.60%))

ILFORD SOUTH
E. 76,025 T. 41,295 (54.32%)
                          Lab. Co-op hold
*Mike Gapes, Lab. Co-op   24,619
Suresh Kuma, C.   10,622
Ralph Scott, LD   4,647
Harun Khan, UK Ind.   1,407
Lab. Co-op majority 13,997 (33.90%)
2.75% swing C. to Lab. Co-op
(1997: Lab. maj. 14,200 (28.39%))

IPSWICH
E. 68,198 T. 38,873 (57.00%) Lab. hold
*Jamie Cann, Lab.   19,952
Edward Wild, C.   11,871
Terry Gilbert, LD   5,904
William Vinyard, UK Ind.   624
Peter Leach, Soc. All.   305
Shaun Gratton, Soc. Lab.   217
Lab. majority 8,081 (20.79%)
0.40% swing Lab. to C.
(1997: Lab. maj. 10,439 (21.58%))

ISLE OF WIGHT
E. 106,305 T. 63,482 (59.72%) C. gain
Andrew Turner, C.   25,223
*Dr Peter Brand, LD   22,397
Ms Deborah Gardiner, Lab.   9,676
David Lott, UK Ind.   2,106
David Holmes, Ind.   1,423
Paul Scivier, Green   1,279
Philip Murray, IOW   1,164
James Spensley, Soc. Lab.   214
C. majority 2,826 (4.45%)
6.61% swing LD to C.
(1997: LD maj. 6,406 (8.76%))

ISLINGTON NORTH
E. 61,970 T. 30,216 (48.76%) Lab. hold
*Jeremy Corbyn, Lab.   18,699
Ms Laura Willoughby, LD   5,741
Neil Rands, C.   3,249
Chris Ashby, Green   1,876
Steve Cook, Soc. Lab.   512
Emine Hassan, Reform   139
Lab. majority 12,958 (42.88%)
6.38% swing Lab. to LD
(1997: Lab. maj. 19,955 (55.64%))

ISLINGTON SOUTH & FINSBURY
E. 59,515 T. 28,206 (47.39%) Lab. hold
*Rt. Hon. C. Smith, Lab.   15,217
Keith Sharp, LD   7,937
Mrs Nicky Morgan, C.   3,860
Ms Janine Booth, Soc. All.   817
Thomas McCarthy, Ind.   267
Charles Thomson, Stuck   108
Lab. majority 7,280 (25.81%)
7.71% swing Lab. to LD
(1997: Lab. maj. 14,563 (41.24%))

JARROW
E. 63,172 T. 34,479 (54.58%) Lab. hold
*Stephen Hepburn, Lab.   22,777
James Selby, LD   5,182
Donald Wood, C.   5,056
Alan Badger, UK Ind.   716
Alan Le Blond, Ind.   391
John Bissett, Soc.   357
Lab. majority 17,595 (51.03%)
1.37% swing Lab. to LD
(1997: Lab. maj. 21,933 (49.91%))

KEIGHLEY
E. 68,349 T. 43,333 (63.40%) Lab. hold
*Ms Ann Cryer, Lab.   20,888
Simon Cooke, C.   16,883
Mike Doyle, LD   4,722
Michael Cassidy, UK Ind.   840
Lab. majority 4,005 (9.24%)
2.30% swing Lab. to C.
(1997: Lab. maj. 7,132 (13.85%))

KENSINGTON & CHELSEA
E. 62,007 T. 28,038 (45.22%) C. hold
*Rt. Hon. M. Portillo, C.   15,270
Simon Stanley, Lab.   6,499
Ms Kishwer Falkner, LD   4,416
Ms Julia Stephenson, Green   1,158
Nicholas Hockney, UK Ind.   416
Ms Josephine Quintavalle, ProLife   179
Ginger Crab, Wrestling   100
C. majority 8,771 (31.28%)
2.81% swing Lab. to C.
(1999 Nov. by-election: C. maj. 6,706
(34.37%); 1997: C. maj. 9,519 (25.66%))

KETTERING
E. 79,697 T. 53,752 (67.45%) Lab. hold
*Philip Sawford, Lab.   24,034
Philip Hollobone, C.   23,369
Roger Aron, LD   5,469
Barry Mahoney, UK Ind.   880
Lab. majority 665 (1.24%)
0.45% swing Lab. to C.
(1997: Lab. Maj. 189 (0.33%))

KINGSTON & SURBITON
E. 72,687 T. 49,093 (67.54%) LD hold
*Edward Davey, LD   29,542
David Shaw, C.   13,866
Phil Woodford ,Lab.   4,302
Chris Spruce, Green   572
Miss Amy Burns, UK Ind.   438
John Hayball, Soc. All.   319
Jeremy Middleton, Unrep.   54
LD majority 15,676 (31.93%)
15.92% swing C. to LD
(1997: LD maj. 56 (0.10%))

KINGSWOOD
E. 80,531 T. 52,676 (65.41%) Lab. hold
*Dr Roger Berry, Lab.   28,903
Robert Marven, C.   14,941
Christopher Greenfield, LD   7,747
David Smith, UK Ind.   1,085
Lab. majority 13,962 (26.51%)
1.35% swing C. to Lab.
(1997: Lab. Maj. 14,253 (23.80%))

KNOWSLEY NORTH & SEFTON EAST
E. 70,781 T. 37,517 (53.00%) Lab. hold
*George Howarth, Lab.   25,035
Keith Chapman, C.   6,108
Richard Roberts, LD   5,173
Ron Waugh, Soc. Lab.   574
Thomas Rossiter, Ind.   356
David Jones, Ind.   271
Lab. majority 18,927 (50.45%)
1.08% swing Lab. to C.
(1997: Lab. maj. 26,147 (52.61%))

KNOWSLEY SOUTH
E. 70,681 T. 36,590 (51.77%) Lab. hold
*Eddie O'Hara, Lab.   26,071
David Smithson, LD   4,755
Paul Jemetta, C.   4,250
Alan Fogg, Soc. Lab.   1,068
Ms Mona McNee, Ind.   446
Lab. majority 21,316 (58.26%)
5.27% swing Lab. to LD
(1997: Lab. maj. 30,708 (64.53%))

LANCASHIRE WEST
E. 72,858 T. 42,971 (58.98%) Lab. hold
*Colin Pickthall, Lab.   23,404
Jeremy Myers, C.   13,761
John Thornton, LD   4,966
David Hill, Ind.   523
David Braid, Ind.   317
Lab. majority 9,643 (22.44%)
4.42% swing Lab. to C.
(1997: Lab. maj. 17,119 (31.28%))

LANCASTER & WYRE
E. 78,964 T. 52,350 (66.30%) Lab. hold
*Hilton Dawson, Lab.   22,556
Steve Barclay, C.   22,075
Ms Liz Scott, LD   5,383
Prof John Whitelegg, Green   1,595
Dr John Whittaker, UK Ind.   741
Lab. majority 481 (0.92%)
0.64% swing Lab. to C.
(1997: Lab. maj. 1,295 (2.20%))

LEEDS CENTRAL
E. 65,497 T. 27,306 (41.69%) Lab. hold
*Hilary Benn, Lab.   18,277
Miss Victoria Richmond, C.   3,896
Stewart Arnold, LD   3,607
David Burgess, UK Ind.   775
Steve Johnson, Soc. All.   751
Lab. majority 14,381 (52.67%)
1.62% swing Lab. to C.
(1999 Jun. by-election: Lab. maj.
2,293 (17.39%); 1997: Lab. maj.
20,689 (55.90%))

LEEDS EAST
E. 56,400 T. 29,055 (51.52%) Lab. hold
*George Mudie, Lab.   18,290
Barry Anderson, C.   5,647
Brian Jennings, LD   3,923
Raymond Northgreaves, UK Ind.   634
Mark King, Soc. Lab.   419
Peter Socrates, Ind.   142
Lab. majority 12,643 (43.51%)
2.64% swing Lab. to C.
(1997: Lab. maj. 17,466 (48.80%))

LEEDS NORTH EAST
E. 73,773 T. 39,773 (62.03%) Lab. hold
*Fabian Hamilton, Lab.   19,540
Owain Rhys, C.   12,451
Jonathan Brown, LD   6,325
Ms Celia Foote, Left All   770
Jeffrey Miles, UK Ind.   382
Colin Muir, Soc. Lab.   173
Mohammed Zaman, Ind.   132
Lab. majority 7,089 (17.82%)
1.27% swing C. to Lab.
(1997: Lab. maj. 6,959 (15.29%))

LEEDS NORTH WEST
E. 72,945 T. 42,451 (58.20%) Lab. hold
*Harold Best, Lab.   17,794
Adam Pritchard, C.   12,558
David Hall-Matthews, LD   11,431
Simon Jones, UK Ind.   668
Lab. majority 5,236 (12.33%)
2.27% swing C. to Lab.
(1997: Lab. maj. 3,844 (7.79%))

LEEDS WEST
E. 64,218 T. 32,094 (49.98%) Lab. hold
*John Battle, Lab.   19,943
Kris Hopkins, C.   5,008
Darren Finlay, LD   3,350
David Blackburn, Green   2,573
William Finley, UK Ind.   758
Noel Nowosielski, Lib.   462
Lab. majority 14,935 (46.54%)
1.31% swing Lab. to C.
(1997: Lab. maj. 19,771 (49.16%))

LEICESTER EAST
E. 65,527 T. 40,661 (62.05%) Lab. hold
*Keith Vaz, Lab.   23,402
John Mugglestone, C.   9,960
Ms Harpinder Athwal, LD   4,989
Dave Roberts, Soc. Lab.   837
Clive Potter, BNP   772
Shirley Bennett, Ind.   701
Lab. majority 13,442 (33.06%)
4.22% swing Lab. to C.
(1997: Lab. maj. 18,422 (41.49%))

LEICESTER SOUTH
E. 72,671 T. 42,142 (57.99%) Lab. hold
*Jim Marshall, Lab.   22,958
Richard Hoile, C.   9,715
Parmjit Singh Gill, LD   7,243
Ms Margaret Layton, Green   1,217
Arnold Gardner, Soc. Lab.   676
Kirti Ladwa, UK Ind.   333
Lab. majority 13,243 (31.42%)
1.43% swing Lab. to C.
(1997: Lab. maj. 16,493 (34.28%))

LEICESTER WEST
E. 65,267 T. 33,219 (50.90%) Lab. hold
*Rt. Hon. Ms P. Hewitt, Lab.   18,014
Chris Shaw, C.   8,375
Andrew Vincent, LD   5,085
Matthew Gough, Green   1,074
Sean Kirkpatrick, Soc. Lab.   350
Steve Score, Soc. All.   321
Lab. majority 9,639 (29.02%)
1.21% swing Lab. to C.
(1997: Lab. maj. 12,864 (31.44%))

LEICESTERSHIRE NORTH WEST
E. 68,414 T. 45,009 (65.79%)
                          Lab. Co-op hold
*David Taylor, Lab. Co-op   23,431
Nick Weston, C.   15,274
Charlie Fraser-Fleming, LD   4,651
William Nattrass, UK Ind.   1,021
Robert Nettleton, Ind.   632
Lab. Co-op majority 8,157 (18.12%)
3.64% swing Lab. Co-op to C.
(1997: Lab. maj. 13,219 (25.41%))

LEIGH
E. 71,054 T. 35,298 (49.68%) Lab. hold
Andrew Burnham, Lab.   22,783
Andrew Oxley, C.   6,421
Ray Atkins, LD   4,524
William Kelly, Soc. Lab.   820
Chris Best, UK Ind.   750
Lab. majority 16,362 (46.35%)
3.50% swing Lab. to C.
(1997: Lab. maj. 24,496 (53.35%))

LEOMINSTER
E. 68,695 T. 46,729 (68.02%)   C. gain
Bill Wiggin, C.   22,879
Ms Celia Downie, LD   12,512
Stephen Hart, Lab.   7,872
Ms Pippa Bennett, Green   1,690
Christopher Kingsley, UK Ind.   1,590
John Haycock, Ind.   186
C. majority 10,367 (22.19%)
2.35% swing LD to C.
(1997: C. maj. 8,835 (17.48%))

LEWES
E. 66,332 T. 45,433 (68.49%)   LD hold
*Norman Baker, LD   25,588
Simon Sinnatt, C.   15,878
Paul Richards, Lab.   3,317
John Harvey, UK Ind.   650
LD majority 9,710 (21.37%)
9.36% swing C. to LD
(1997: LD maj. 1,300 (2.65%))

LEWISHAM DEPTFORD
E. 62,869 T. 29,107 (46.30%) Lab. hold
*Joan Ruddock, Lab.   18,915
Ms Cordelia McCartney, C.   3,622
Andrew Wiseman, LD   3,409
Darren Johnson, Green   1,901
Ian Page, Soc. All.   1,260
Lab. majority 15,293 (52.54%)
1.78% swing Lab. to C.
(1997: Lab. maj. 18,878 (56.11%))

LEWISHAM EAST
E. 58,302 T. 30,040 (51.52%) Lab. hold
*Ms Bridget Prentice, Lab.   16,116
David McInnes, C.   7,157
David Buxton, LD   4,937
Barry Roberts, BNP   1,005
Ms Jean Kysow, Soc. All.   464
Maurice Link, UK Ind.   361
Lab. majority 8,959 (29.82%)
1.30% swing Lab. to C.
(1997: Lab. maj. 12,127 (32.42%))

LEWISHAM WEST
E. 60,947 T. 30,815 (50.56%) Lab. hold
*Jim Dowd, Lab.   18,816
Gary Johnson, C.   6,896
Richard Thomas, LD   4,146
Frederick Pearson, UK Ind.   485
Nick Long, Ind.   472
Lab. majority 11,920 (38.68%)
0.25% swing C. to Lab.
(1997: Lab. maj. 14,337 (38.19%))

LEYTON & WANSTEAD
E. 61,549 T. 33,718 (54.78%) Lab. hold
*Harry Cohen, Lab.   19,558
Edward Heckels, C.   6,654
Alex Wilcock, LD   5,389
Ashley Gunstock, Green   1,030
Ms Sally Labern, Soc. All.   709
M. Skaife D'Ingerthorp, UK Ind.   378
Lab. majority 12,904 (38.27%)
0.17% swing Lab. to C.
(1997: Lab. maj. 15,186 (38.62%))

LICHFIELD
E. 63,794 T. 41,680 (65.34%)   C. hold
*Michael Fabricant, C.   20,480
Martin Machray, Lab.   16,054
Phillip Bennion, LD   4,462
John Phazey, UK Ind.   684
C. majority 4,426 (10.62%)
5.06% swing Lab. to C.
(1997: C. maj. 238 (0.49%))

LINCOLN
E. 66,299 T. 37,125 (56.00%) Lab. hold
*Ms Gillian Merron, Lab.   20,003
Mrs Christine Talbot, C.   11,583
Ms Lisa Gabriel, LD   4,703
Roger Doughty, UK Ind.   836
Lab. majority 8,420 (22.68%)
0.61% swing Lab. to C.
(1997: Lab. maj. 11,130 (23.91%))

LIVERPOOL GARSTON
E. 65,094 T. 32,651 (50.16%) Lab. hold
*Ms Maria Eagle, Lab.   20,043
Ms Paula Keaveney, LD   7,549
Miss Helen Sutton, C.   5,059
Lab. majority 12,494 (38.27%)
2.05% swing Lab. to LD
(1997: Lab. maj. 18,417 (42.36%))

LIVERPOOL RIVERSIDE
E. 74,827 T. 25,503 (34.08%)
                          Lab. Co-op hold
*Ms Louise Ellman, Lab. Co-op   18,201
Richard Marbrow, LD   4,251
Miss Judith Edwards, C.   2,142
Ms Cathy Wilson, Soc. All.   909
Lab. Co-op majority 13,950 (54.70%)
1.23% swing Lab. Co-op to LD
(1997: Lab. maj. 21,799 (57.16%))

LIVERPOOL WALTON
E. 66,237 T. 28,458 (42.96%) Lab. hold
*Peter Kilfoyle, Lab.   22,143
Kiron Reid, LD   4,147
Stephen Horgan, C.   1,726
Paul Forrest, UK Ind.   442
Lab. majority 17,996 (63.24%)
2.00% swing Lab. to LD
(1997: Lab. maj. 27,038 (67.24%))

LIVERPOOL WAVERTREE
E. 72,555 T. 32,138 (44.29%) Lab. hold
*Ms Jane Kennedy, Lab.   20,155
Christopher Newby, LD   7,836
Geoffrey Allen, C.   3,091
Michael Lane, Soc. Lab.   359
Mark O'Brien, Soc. All.   349
Neil Miney, UK Ind.   348
Lab. majority 12,319 (38.33%)
2.29% swing Lab. to LD
(1997: Lab. maj. 19,701 (42.91%))

LIVERPOOL WEST DERBY
E. 67,921 T. 30,907 (45.50%) Lab. hold
*Robert Wareing, Lab.   20,454
Steve Radford, Lib.   4,601
Patrick Moloney, LD   3,366
Bill Clare, C.   2,486
Lab. majority 15,853 (51.29%)
5.15% swing Lab. to Lib.
(1997: Lab. maj. 25,965 (61.59%))

LOUGHBOROUGH
E. 70,077 T. 44,254 (63.15%)
                          Lab. Co-op hold
*Andy Reed, Lab. Co-op   22,016
Neil Lyon, C.   15,638
Ms Julie Simons, LD   5,667
John Bigger, UK Ind.   933
Lab. Co-op majority 6,378 (14.41%)
1.75% swing C. to Lab. Co-op
(1997: Lab. maj. 5,712 (10.91%))

LOUTH & HORNCASTLE
E. 71,556 T. 44,460 (62.13%)   C. hold
*Sir Peter Tapsell, C.   21,543
David Bolland, Lab.   13,989
Ms Fiona Martin, LD   8,928
C. majority 7,554 (16.99%)
1.59% swing Lab. to C.
(1997: C. maj. 6,900 (13.81%))

LUDLOW
E. 63,053 T. 43,124 (68.39%)   LD gain
Matthew Green, LD   18,620
Martin Taylor-Smith, C.   16,990
Nigel Knowles, Lab.   5,785
Jim Gaffney, Green   871
Phil Gutteridge, UK Ind.   858
LD majority 1,630 (3.78%)
8.27% swing C. to LD
(1997: C. maj. 5,909 (12.77%))

LUTON NORTH
E. 65,998 T. 39,126 (59.28%) Lab. hold
*Kelvin Hopkins, Lab.   22,187
Mrs Amanda Sater, C.   12,210
Dr Bob Hoyle, LD   3,795
Colin Brown, UK Ind.   934
Lab. majority 9,977 (25.50%)
2.58% swing C. to Lab.
(1997: Lab. maj. 9,626 (20.34%))

LUTON SOUTH
E. 68,985 T. 39,351 (57.04%) Lab. hold
*Ms Margaret Moran, Lab.   21,719
Gordon Henderson, C.   11,586
Rabi Martins, LD   4,292
Marc Scheimann, Green   798
Charles Lawman, UK Ind.   578
Joe Hearne, Soc. All.   271
Robert Bolton, WRP   107
Lab. majority 10,133 (25.75%)
1.13% swing C. to Lab.
(1997: Lab. maj. 11,319 (23.49%))

MACCLESFIELD
E. 73,123 T. 45,585 (62.34%)   C. hold
*Nicholas Winterton, C.   22,284
Stephen Carter, Lab.   15,084
Mike Flynn, LD   8,217
C. majority 7,200 (15.79%)
0.09% swing C. to Lab.
(1997: C. maj. 8,654 (15.97%))

MAIDENHEAD
E. 68,130 T. 43,318 (63.58%)   C. hold
*Mrs Theresa May, C.   19,506
Ms Kathryn Newbound, LD   16,222
John O'Farrell, Lab.   6,577
Dr Denis Cooper, UK Ind.   741
Lloyd Clarke, Loony   272
C. majority 3,284 (7.58%)
7.98% swing C. to LD
(1997: C. maj. 11,981 (23.54%))

MAIDSTONE & THE WEALD
E. 74,002 T. 45,577 (61.59%)   C. hold
*Rt. Hon. Miss A. Widdecombe,   22,621
  C.
Mark Davis, Lab.   12,303
Ms Allison Wainman, LD   9,064
John Botting, UK Ind.   978
Neil Hunt, Ind.   611
C. majority 10,318 (22.64%)
2.36% swing Lab. to C.
(1997: C. maj. 9,603 (17.91%))

MAKERFIELD
E. 68,457 T. 34,856 (50.92%) Lab. hold
*Rt. Hon. Ian McCartney, Lab.   23,879
Mrs Jane Brooks, C.   6,129
David Crowther, LD   3,990
Malcolm Jones, Soc. All.   858
Lab. majority 17,750 (50.92%)
3.61% swing Lab. to C.
(1997: Lab. maj. 26,177 (58.15%))

MALDON & CHELMSFORD EAST
E. 69,201 T. 44,100 (63.73%)   C. hold
*John Whittingdale, C.   21,719
Russell Kennedy, Lab.   13,257
Ms Jane Jackson, LD   7,002
Geoffrey Harris, UK Ind.   1,135
Walter Schwarz, Green   987
C. majority 8,462 (19.19%)
0.37% swing C. to Lab.
(1997: C. maj. 10,039 (19.92%))

MANCHESTER BLACKLEY
E. 59,111 T. 26,523 (44.87%) Lab. hold
*Graham Stringer, Lab.   18,285
Lance Stanbury, C.   3,821
Gary Riding, LD   3,015
Kevin Barr, Soc. Lab.   485
Ms Karen Reissmann, Soc. All.   461
Aziz Bhatti, Anti-Corrupt   456
Lab. majority 14,464 (54.53%)
0.13% swing Lab. to C.
(1997: Lab. maj. 19,588 (54.79%))

MANCHESTER CENTRAL
E. 66,268 T. 25,928 (39.13%) Lab. hold
*Tony Lloyd, Lab.   17,812
Philip Hobson, LD   4,070
Aaron Powell, C.   2,328
Ms Vanessa Hall, Green   1,018
Ron Sinclair, Soc. Lab.   484
Ms Terrenia Brosnan, ProLife   216
Lab. majority 13,742 (53.00%)
2.84% swing Lab. to LD
(1997: Lab. maj. 19,682 (58.69%))

MANCHESTER GORTON
E. 63,834 T. 27,229 (42.66%) Lab. hold
*Rt. Hon. G. Kaufman, Lab.   17,099
Ms Jackie Pearcey, LD   5,795
Christopher Causer, C.   2,705
Bruce Bingham, Green   835
Rashid Bhatti, UK Ind.   462
Ms Kirsty Muir, Soc. Lab.   333
Lab. majority 11,304 (41.51%)
3.12% swing Lab. to LD
(1997: Lab. maj. 17,342 (47.76%))

MANCHESTER WITHINGTON
E. 67,480 T. 35,050 (51.94%) Lab. hold
*Rt. Hon. K. Bradley, Lab.   19,239
Ms Yasmin Zalzala, LD   7,715
Julian Samways, C.   5,349
Ms Michelle Valentine, Green   1,539
John Clegg, Soc. All.   1,208
Lab. majority 11,524 (32.88%)
7.53% swing Lab. to LD
(1997: Lab. maj. 18,581 (42.20%))

MANSFIELD
E. 66,748 T. 36,852 (55.21%) Lab. hold
*Alan Meale, Lab.   21,050
William Wellesley, C.   10,012
Tim Hill, LD   5,790
Lab. majority 11,038 (29.95%)
6.65% swing Lab. to C.
(1997: Lab. maj. 20,518 (43.26%))

MEDWAY
E. 64,930 T. 38,610 (59.46%) Lab. hold
*Robert Marshall-Andrews, Lab. 18,914
Mark Reckless, C.   15,134
Geoffrey Juby, LD   3,604
Ms Nikki Sinclaire, UK Ind.   958
Lab. majority 3,780 (9.79%)
1.08% swing Lab. to C.
(1997: Lab. maj. 5,354 (11.96%))

MERIDEN
E. 74,439 T. 44,559 (59.86%)   C. hold
*Mrs Caroline Spelman, C.   21,246
Ms Christine Shawcroft, Lab.   17,462
Nigel Hicks, LD   4,941
Richard Adams, UK Ind.   910
C. majority 3,784 (8.49%)
3.71% swing Lab. to C.
(1997: C. maj. 582 (1.07%))

MIDDLESBROUGH
E. 67,659 T. 33,717 (49.83%) Lab. hold
*Stuart Bell, Lab.   22,783
Alex Finn, C.   6,453
Keith Miller, LD   3,512
Geoff Kerr-Morgan, Soc. All.   577
Kai Andersen, Soc. Lab.   392
Lab. majority 16,330 (48.43%)
2.92% swing Lab. to C.
(1997: Lab. maj. 25,018 (54.28%))

MIDDLESBROUGH SOUTH &
CLEVELAND EAST
E. 71,485 T. 43,991 (61.54%) Lab. hold
*Dr Ashok Kumar, Lab.   24,321
Mrs Barbara Harpham, C.   14,970
Ms Linda Parrish, LD   4,700
Lab. majority 9,351 (21.26%)
0.73% swing C. to Lab.
(1997: Lab. maj. 10,607 (19.79%))

MILTON KEYNES NORTH EAST
E. 75,526 T. 47,094 (62.35%) Lab. hold
*Brian White, Lab.   19,761
Mrs Marion Rix, C.   17,932
David Yeoward, LD   8,375
Michael Phillips, UK Ind.   1,026
Lab. majority 1,829 (3.88%)
1.71% swing C. to Lab.
(1997: Lab. maj. 240 (0.47%))

MILTON KEYNES SOUTH WEST
E. 76,607 T. 45,384 (59.24%) Lab. hold
*Dr Phyllis Starkey, Lab.   22,484
Iain Stewart, C.   15,506
Nazar Mohammad, LD   4,828
Alan Francis, Green   957
Clive Davies, UK Ind.   848
Patrick Denning, LCA   500
Dave Bradbury, Soc. All.   261
Lab. majority 6,978 (15.38%)
2.45% swing Lab. to C.
(1997: Lab. maj. 10,292 (20.28%))

MITCHAM & MORDEN
E. 65,671 T. 37,961 (57.80%) Lab. hold
*Ms Siobhain McDonagh, Lab.   22,936
Harry Stokes, C.   9,151
Nicholas Harris, LD   3,820
Tom Walsh, Green   926
John Tyndall, BNP   642
Adrian Roberts, UK Ind.   486
Lab. majority 13,785 (36.31%)
3.83% swing Lab. to C.
(1997: Lab. maj. 13,741 (28.66%))

MOLE VALLEY
E. 67,770 T. 47,072 (69.46%)   C. hold
*Sir Paul Beresford, C.   23,790
Ms Celia Savage, LD   13,637
Dan Redford, Lab.   7,837
Ron Walters, UK Ind.   1,333
William Newton, ProLife   475
C. majority 10,153 (21.57%)
1.41% swing LD to C.
(1997: C. maj. 10,221 (18.74%))

MORECAMBE & LUNESDALE
E. 68,607 T. 41,655 (60.72%) Lab. hold
*Ms Geraldine Smith, Lab.   20,646
David Nuttall, C.   15,554
Chris Cotton, LD   3,817
Gregg Beaman, UK Ind.   935
Ms Cherith Adams, Green   703
Lab. majority 5,092 (12.22%)
0.05% swing C. to Lab.
(1997: Lab. maj. 5,965 (12.12%))

MORLEY & ROTHWELL
E. 71,815 T. 38,442 (53.53%) Lab. hold
Colin Challen, Lab.   21,919
David Schofield, C.   9,829
Stewart Golton, LD   5,446
John Bardsley, UK Ind.   1,248
Lab. majority 12,090 (31.45%)
0.35% swing Lab. to C.
(1997: Lab. maj. 14,750 (32.14%))

NEW FOREST EAST
E. 66,767 T. 42,178 (63.17%)   C. hold
*Dr Julian Lewis, C.   17,902
Brian Dash, LD   14,073
Alan Goodfellow, Lab.   9,141
William Howe, UK Ind.   1,062
C. majority 3,829 (9.08%)
0.78% swing C. to LD
(1997: C. maj. 5,215 (10.63%))

NEW FOREST WEST
E. 67,806 T. 44,087 (65.02%)   C. hold
*Desmond Swayne, C.   24,575
Mike Bignell, LD   11,384
Ms Crada Onuegbu, Lab.   6,481
Michael Clark, UK Ind.   1,647
C. majority 13,191 (29.92%)
3.57% swing LD to C.
(1997: C. maj. 11,332 (22.78%))

NEWARK
E. 71,089 T. 45,147 (63.51%)   C. gain
Patrick Mercer, C.   20,983
*Ms Fiona Jones, Lab.   16,910
David Harding-Price, LD   5,970
Donald Haxby, Ind.   822
Ian Thomson, Soc. All.   462
C. majority 4,073 (9.02%)
7.41% swing Lab. to C.
(1997: Lab. maj. 3,016 (5.80%))

NEWBURY
E. 75,490 T. 50,807 (67.30%)   LD hold
*David Rendel, LD   24,507
Richard Benyon, C.   22,092
Steve Billcliffe, Lab.   3,523
Ms Delphine Gray-Fisk, UK Ind.   685
LD majority 2,415 (4.75%)
5.16% swing LD to C.
(1997: LD maj. 8,517 (15.08%)

NEWCASTLE UPON TYNE CENTRAL
E. 67,970 T. 34,870 (51.30%) Lab. hold
*Jim Cousins, Lab.   19,169
Stephen Psallidas, LD   7,564
Aidan Ruff, C.   7,414
Gordon Potts, Soc. Lab.   723
Lab. majority 11,605 (33.28%)
5.44% swing Lab. to LD
(1997: Lab. maj. 16,480 (35.75%))

NEWCASTLE UPON TYNE EAST &
WALLSEND
E. 61,494 T. 32,694 (53.17%) Lab. hold
*Rt. Hon. N. Brown, Lab.   20,642
David Ord, LD   6,419
Tim Troman, C.   3,873
Andrew Gray, Green   651
Dr Harash Narang, Ind.   563
Ms Blanch Carpenter, Soc. Lab.   420
Martin Levy, Comm.   126
Lab. majority 14,223 (43.50%)
8.53% swing Lab. to LD
(1997: Lab. maj. 23,811 (57.25%))

NEWCASTLE UPON TYNE NORTH
E. 63,208 T. 36,368 (57.54%) Lab. hold
*Doug Henderson, Lab.   21,874
Phillip Smith, C.   7,424
Graham Soult, LD   7,070
Lab. majority 14,450 (39.73%)
1.50% swing Lab. to C.
(1997: Lab. maj. 19,332 (42.74%))

NEWCASTLE-UNDER-LYME
E. 65,739 T. 38,674 (58.83%) Lab. hold
Paul Farrelly, Lab.   20,650
Mike Flynn, C.   10,664
Jerry Roodhouse, LD   5,993
Robert Fyson, Ind.   773
Paul Godfrey, UK Ind.   594
Lab. majority 9,986 (25.82%)
4.60% swing Lab. to C.
(1997: Lab. maj. 17,206 (35.02%))

NORFOLK MID
E. 74,911 T. 52,548 (70.15%)   C. hold
*Keith Simpson, C.   23,519
Daniel Zeichner, Lab.   18,957
Ms V. Clifford-Jackson, LD   7,621
John Agnew, UK Ind.   1,333
Peter Reeve, Green   1,118
C. majority 4,562 (8.68%)
3.18% swing Lab. to C.
(1997: C. maj. 1,336 (2.33%))

NORFOLK NORTH
E. 80,061 T. 56,220 (70.22%)   LD gain
Norman Lamb, LD   23,978
*David Prior, C.   23,495
Michael Gates, Lab.   7,490
Mike Sheridan, Green   649
Paul Simison, UK Ind.   608
LD majority 483 (0.86%)
1.53% swing C. to LD
(1997: C. maj. 1,293 (2.20%))

NORFOLK NORTH WEST
E. 77,387 T. 51,203 (66.16%)   C. gain
Henry Bellingham, C.   24,846
*Dr George Turner, Lab.   21,361
Dr Ian Mack, LD   4,292
Ian Durrant, UK Ind.   704
C. majority 3,485 (6.81%)
4.57% swing Lab. to C.
(1997: Lab. maj. 1,339 (2.33%))

NORFOLK SOUTH
E. 82,710 T. 55,929 (67.62%)   C. hold
Richard Bacon, C.   23,589
Dr Anne Lee, LD   16,696
Mark Wells, Lab.   13,719
Ms Stephanie Ross-Wagenknecht, 1,069
  Green
Joseph Neal, UK Ind.   856
C. majority 6,893 (12.32%)
0.22% swing LD to C.
(1997: C. maj. 7,378 (11.88%))

NORFOLK SOUTH WEST
E. 83,903 T. 52,949 (63.11%)   C. hold
*Rt. Hon. Mrs G. Shephard, C.   27,633
Ms Anne Hanson, Lab.   18,267
Gordon Dean, LD   5,681
Ian Smith, UK Ind.   1,368
C. majority 9,366 (17.69%)
6.75% swing Lab. to C.
(1997: C. maj. 2,464 (4.19%))

NORMANTON
E. 65,392 T. 34,155 (52.23%) Lab. hold
*William O'Brien, Lab.   19,152
Graham Smith, C.   9,215
Stephen Pearson, LD   4,990
Mick Appleyard, Soc. Lab.   798
Lab. majority 9,937 (29.09%)
3.93% swing Lab. to C.
(1997: Lab. maj. 15,893 (36.96%))

NORTHAMPTON NORTH
E. 74,124 T. 41,494 (55.98%) Lab. hold
*Ms Sally Keeble, Lab.   20,507
John Whelan, C.   12,614
Richard Church, LD   7,363
Dusan Torbica, UK Ind.   596
Gordon White, Soc. All.   414
Lab. majority 7,893 (19.02%)
0.16% swing Lab. to C.
(1997: Lab. maj. 10,000 (19.34%))

NORTHAMPTON SOUTH
E. 85,271 T. 51,029 (59.84%) Lab. hold
*Tony Clarke, Lab.   21,882
Shailesh Vara, C.   20,997
Andrew Simpson, LD   6,355
Derek Clark, UK Ind.   1,237
Miss Tina Harvey, LP   362
Ms Clare Johnson, ProLife   196
Lab. majority 885 (1.73%)
0.22% swing C. to Lab.
(1997: Lab. maj. 744 (1.30%))

NORTHAVON
E. 78,841 T. 55,758 (70.72%)   LD hold
*Steve Webb, LD   29,217
Dr Carrie Ruxton, C.   19,340
Robert Hall, Lab.   6,450
Mrs Carmen Carver, UK Ind.   751
LD majority 9,877 (17.71%)
7.15% swing C. to LD
(1997: LD maj. 2,137 (3.42%))

NORWICH NORTH
E. 74,911 T. 45,614 (60.89%) Lab. hold
*Dr Ian Gibson, Lab.   21,624
Ms Kay Mason, C.   15,761
Ms Moira Toye, LD   6,750
Robert Tinch, Green   797
Guy Cheyney, UK Ind.   471
Michael Betts, Ind.   211
Lab. majority 5,863 (12.85%)
2.17% swing Lab. to C.
(1997: Lab. maj. 9,470 (17.20%))

NORWICH SOUTH
E. 65,792 T. 42,592 (64.74%) Lab. hold
*Rt. Hon. C. Clarke, Lab.   19,367
Andrew French , C.   10,551
Andrew Aalders-Dunthorne, LD   9,640
Adrian Holmes, Green   1,434
Alun Buffrey, LCA   620
Edward Manningham, Soc. All.   507
Tarquin Mills, UK Ind.   473
Lab. majority 8,816 (20.70%)
3.67% swing Lab. to C.
(1997: Lab. maj. 14,239 (28.03%))

NOTTINGHAM EAST
E. 65,339 T. 29,731 (45.50%) Lab. hold
*John Heppell, Lab.   17,530
Richard Allan, C.   7,210
Tim Ball, LD   3,874
Pete Radcliff, Soc. All.   1,117
Lab. majority 10,320 (34.71%)
2.04% swing Lab. to C.
(1997: Lab. maj. 15,419 (38.80%))

NOTTINGHAM NORTH
E. 64,281 T. 30,042 (46.74%) Lab. hold
*Graham Allen, Lab.   19,392
Martin Wright, C.   7,152
Rob Lee, LD   3,177
Andrew Botham, Soc. Lab.   321
Lab. majority 12,240 (40.74%)
2.34% swing Lab. to C.
(1997: Lab. maj. 18,801 (45.42%))

NOTTINGHAM SOUTH
E. 73,049 T. 36,605 (50.11%) Lab. hold
*Alan Simpson, Lab.   19,949
Mrs Wendy Manning, C.   9,960
Kevin Mulloy, LD   6,064
David Bartrop, UK Ind.   632
Lab. majority 9,989 (27.29%)
0.13% swing Lab. to C.
(1997: Lab. maj. 13,364 (27.55%))

NUNEATON
E. 72,101 T. 43,312 (60.07%) Lab. hold
*Bill Olner, Lab.   22,577
Mark Lancaster, C.   15,042
Tony Ferguson, LD   4,820
Brian James, UK Ind.   873
Lab. majority 7,535 (17.40%)
3.95% swing Lab. to C.
(1997: Lab. maj. 13,540 (25.30%))

OLD BEXLEY & SIDCUP
E. 67,841 T. 42,133 (62.11%)   C. hold
Derek Conway, C.   19,130
Jim Dickson, Lab.   15,785
Ms Belinda Ford, LD   5,792
Mrs Janice Cronin, UK Ind.   1,426
C. majority 3,345 (7.94%)
0.49% swing Lab. to C.
(1997: C. maj. 3,569 (6.95%))

OLDHAM EAST & SADDLEWORTH
E. 74,511 T. 45,420 (60.96%) Lab. hold
*Phil Woolas, Lab.   17,537
Howard Sykes, LD   14,811
Craig Heeley, C.   7,304
Michael Treacy, BNP   5,091
Ms Barbara Little, UK Ind.   677
Lab. majority 2,726 (6.00%)
0.13% swing Lab. to LD
(1997: Lab. maj. 3,389 (6.26%))

OLDHAM WEST & ROYTON
E. 69,409 T. 39,962 (57.57%) Lab. hold
*Rt. Hon. M. Meacher, Lab.   20,441
Duncan Reed, C.   7,076
Nick Griffin, BNP   6,552
Marc Ramsbottom, LD   4,975
David Roney, Green   918
Lab. majority 13,365 (33.44%)
0.99% swing Lab. to C.
(1997: Lab. maj. 16,201 (35.42%))

ORPINGTON
E. 74,423 T. 50,912 (68.41%)   C. hold
*John Horam, C.   22,334
Chris Maines, LD   22,065
Chris Purnell, Lab.   5,517
John Youles, UK Ind.   996
C. majority 269 (0.53%)
2.19% swing C. to LD
(1997: C. maj. 2,952 (4.91%))

OXFORD EAST
E. 74,421 T. 39,848 (53.54%) Lab. hold
*Rt. Hon. A. Smith, Lab.   19,681
Steve Goddard, LD   9,337
Ms Cheryl Potter, C.   7,446
Pritam Singh, Green   1,501
John Lister, Soc. All.   708
Peter Gardner, UK Ind.   570
Fahim Ahmed, Soc. Lab.   274
Ms Linda Hodge, ProLife   254
Pathmanathan Mylvaganan, Ind.   77
Lab. majority 10,344 (25.96%)
8.08% swing Lab. to LD
(1997: Lab. maj. 16,665 (34.81%))

OXFORD WEST & ABINGDON
E. 79,915 T. 51,568 (64.53%)   LD hold
*Dr Evan Harris, LD   24,670
Ed Matts, C.   15,485
Ms Gillian Kirk, Lab.   9,114
Mike Woodin, Green   1,423
Marcus Watney, UK Ind.   451
Ms Sigrid Shreeve, Ind.   332
Robert Twigger, Ext. Club   93
LD majority 9,185 (17.81%)
3.77% swing C. to LD
(1997: LD maj. 6,285 (10.27%))

PENDLE
E. 62,870 T. 39,732 (63.20%) Lab. hold
*Gordon Prentice, Lab.   17,729
Rasjid Skinner, C.   13,454
David Whipp, LD   5,479
Christian Jackson, BNP   1,976
Graham Cannon, UK Ind.   1,094
Lab. majority 4,275 (10.76%)
6.13% swing Lab. to C.
(1997: Lab. maj. 10,824 (23.02%))

PENRITH & THE BORDER
E. 67,776 T. 44,249 (65.29%)   C. hold
*Rt. Hon. D. Maclean, C.   24,302
Kenneth Geyve Walker, LD   9,625
Michael Boaden, Lab.   8,177
Thomas Lowther, UK Ind.   938
Mark Gibson, LCA   870
John Moffat, Ind.   337
C. majority 14,677 (33.17%)
6.13% swing LD to C.
(1997: C. maj. 10,233 (20.90%))

PETERBOROUGH
E. 64,918 T. 39,812 (61.33%) Lab. hold
*Mrs Helen Brinton, Lab.   17,975
Stewart Jackson, C.   15,121
Nick Sandford, LD   5,761
Julian Fairweather, UK Ind.   955
Lab. majority 2,854 (7.17%)
3.98% swing Lab. to C.
(1997: Lab. maj. 7,323 (15.12%))

PLYMOUTH DEVONPORT
E. 73,666 T. 41,719 (56.63%) Lab. hold
*David Jamieson, Lab.   24,322
John Glen, C.   11,289
Keith Baldry, LD   4,513
Michael Parker, UK Ind.   958
Tony Staunton, Soc. All.   334
Rob Hawkins, Soc. Lab.   303
Lab. majority 13,033 (31.24%)
2.73% swing Lab. to C.
(1997: Lab. maj. 19,067 (36.70%))

PLYMOUTH SUTTON
E. 68,438 T. 39,073 (57.09%)
                             Lab. Co-op hold
*Mrs Linda Gilroy, Lab. Co-op   19,827
Oliver Colvile, C.   12,310
Alan Connett, LD   5,605
Alan Whitton, UK Ind.   970
Henry Leary, Soc. Lab.   361
Lab. Co-op majority 7,517 (19.24%)
0.29% swing Lab. Co-op to C.
(1997: Lab. maj. 9,440 (19.81%))

PONTEFRACT & CASTLEFORD
E. 63,181 T. 31,391 (49.68%) Lab. hold
*Ms Yvette Cooper, Lab.   21,890
Ms Pamela Singleton, C.   5,512
Wesley Paxton, LD   2,315
John Burdon, UK Ind.   739
Trevor Bolderson, Soc. Lab.   605
John Gill, Soc. All.   330
Lab. majority 16,378 (52.17%)
4.99% swing Lab. to C.
(1997: Lab. maj. 25,725 (62.15%))

POOLE
E. 64,644 T. 39,233 (60.69%)   C. hold
*Robert Syms, C.   17,710
David Watt, Lab.   10,544
Nick Westbrook, LD   10,011
John Bass, UK Ind.   968
C. majority 7,166 (18.27%)
1.15% swing C. to Lab.
(1997: C. maj. 5,298 (11.32%))

POPLAR & CANNING TOWN
E. 75,173 T. 34,108 (45.37%) Lab. hold
*Jim Fitzpatrick, Lab.   20,862
Robert Marr, C.   6,758
Ms Alexi Sugden, LD   3,795
Paul Borg, BNP   1,743
Dr Kambiz Boomla, Soc. All.   950
Lab. majority 14,104 (41.35%)
3.41% swing Lab. to C.
(1997: Lab. maj. 18,915 (48.17%))

PORTSMOUTH NORTH
E. 64,256 T. 36,866 (57.37%) Lab. hold
*Syd Rapson, Lab.   18,676
Chris Day, C.   13,542
Darren Sanders, LD   3,795
William McCabe, UK Ind.   559
Brian Bundy, Ind.   294
Lab. majority 5,134 (13.93%)
2.19% swing C. to Lab.
(1997: Lab. maj. 4,323 (9.55%))

PORTSMOUTH SOUTH
E. 77,095 T. 39,215 (50.87%)   LD hold
*Mike Hancock, LD   17,490
Philip Warr, C.   11,396
Graham Heaney, Lab.   9,361
John Molyneux, Soc. All.   647
Michael Tarrant, UK Ind.   321
LD majority 6,094 (15.54%)
3.58% swing C. to LD
(1997: LD maj. 4,327 (8.37%))

PRESTON
E. 72,077 T. 36,041 (50.00%)
                             Lab. Co-op hold
*Mark Hendrick, Lab. Co-op   20,540
Graham O'Hare, C.   8,272
Bill Chadwick, LD   4,746
Bilal Patel, Ind.   1,241
Richard Merrick, Green   1,019
The Rev David Braid, Ind.   223
Lab. Co-op majority 12,268 (34.04%)
2.41% swing Lab. Co-op to C.
(2000 Nov. by-election: Lab. maj.
4,426)
(1997: Lab. majority 18,680
(38.86%))

PUDSEY
E. 71,405 T. 45,175 (63.27%) Lab. hold
*Paul Truswell, Lab.   21,717
John Procter, C.   16,091
Stephen Boddy, LD   6,423
David Sewards, UK Ind.   944
Lab. majority 5,626 (12.45%)
0.34% swing C. to Lab.
(1997: Lab. maj. 6,207 (11.77%))

PUTNEY
E. 60,643 T. 34,254 (56.48%) Lab. hold
*Tony Colman, Lab.   15,911
Michael Simpson, C.   13,140
Tony Burrett, LD   4,671
Ms Pat Wild, UK Ind.   347
Ms Yvonne Windsor, ProLife   185
Lab. majority 2,771 (8.09%)
0.66% swing C. to Lab.
(1997: Lab. maj. 2,976 (6.76%))

RAYLEIGH
E. 70,073 T. 42,773 (61.04%)   C. hold
Mark Francois, C.   21,434
Paul Clark, Lab.   13,144
Geoff Williams, LD   6,614
Colin Morgan, UK Ind.   1,581
C. majority 8,290 (19.38%)
0.72% swing C. to Lab.
(1997: C. maj. 10,684 (20.83%))

READING EAST
E. 74,637 T. 43,618 (58.44%) Lab. hold
*Ms Jane Griffiths, Lab.   19,531
Barry Tanswell, C.   13,943
Tom Dobrashian, LD   8,078
Ms Miriam Kennett, Green   1,053
Miss Amy Thornton, UK Ind.   525
Darren Williams, Soc. All.   394
Peter Hammerson, Ind.   94
Lab. majority 5,588 (12.81%)
2.63% swing C. to Lab.
(1997: Lab. maj. 3,795 (7.55%))

READING WEST
E. 71,688 T. 41,986 (58.57%) Lab. hold
*Martin Salter, Lab.   22,300
Stephen Reid, C.   13,451
Ms Polly Martin, LD   5,387
David Black, UK Ind.   848
Lab. maj 8,849 (21.08%)
7.44% swing C. to Lab.
(1997: Lab. maj. 2,997 (6.20%))

REDCAR
E. 66,179 T. 38,198 (57.72%) Lab. hold
Ms Vera Baird, Lab.   23,026
Chris Main, C.   9,583
Stan Wilson, LD   4,817
John Taylor, Soc. Lab.   772
Lab. majority 13,443 (35.19%)
4.53% swing Lab. to C.
(1997: Lab. maj. 21,664 (44.25%))

REDDITCH
E. 62,543 T. 37,032 (59.21%) Lab. hold
*Ms Jacqui Smith, Lab.   16,899
Mrs Karen Lumley, C.   14,415
Michael Ashall, LD   3,808
George Flynn, UK Ind.   1,259
Richard Armstrong, Green   651
Lab. majority 2,484 (6.71%)
3.49% swing Lab. to C.
(1997: Lab. maj. 6,125 (13.69%))

REGENT'S PARK & KENSINGTON
NORTH
E. 75,886 T. 37,052 (48.83%) Lab. hold
*Ms Karen Buck, Lab.   20,247
Peter Wilson, C.   9,981
David Boyle, LD   4,669
Dr Paul Miller, Green   1,268
China Mieville, Soc. All.   459
Alan Crisp, UK Ind.   354
Ms Charlotte Regan, Ind.   74
Lab. majority 10,266 (27.71%)
1.63% swing Lab. to C.
(1997: Lab. maj. 14,657 (30.96%))

REIGATE
E. 65,023 T. 39,474 (60.71%)   C. hold
*Crispin Blunt, C.   18,875
Simon Charleton, Lab.   10,850
Ms Jane Kulka, LD   8,330
Stephen Smith, UK Ind.   1,062
Harold Green, Ref. UK   357
C. majority 8,025 (20.33%)
2.13% swing Lab. to C.
(1997: C. maj. 7,741 (16.07%))

RIBBLE SOUTH (SOUTH RIBBLE)
E. 73,794 T. 46,130 (62.51%) Lab. hold
*David Borrow, Lab.   21,386
Adrian Owens, C.   17,594
Mark Alcock, LD   7,150
Lab. majority 3,792 (8.22%)
0.49% swing Lab. to C.
(1997: Lab. maj. 5,084 (9.20%))

RIBBLE VALLEY
E. 74,319 T. 49,171 (66.16%)   C. hold
*Nigel Evans, C.   25,308
Mike Carr, LD   14,070
Marcus Johnstone, Lab.   9,793
C. majority 11,238 (22.85%)
5.63% swing LD to C.
(1997: C. maj. 6,640 (11.60%))

RICHMOND (YORKS)
E. 65,360 T. 44,034 (67.37%)   C. hold
*Rt. Hon. W. Hague, C.   25,951
Ms Fay Tinnion, Lab.   9,632
Edward Forth, LD   7,890
Mrs Melodie Staniforth, Loony   561
C. majority 16,319 (37.06%)
8.00% swing Lab. to C.
(1997: C. maj. 10,051 (21.05%))

RICHMOND PARK
E. 72,663 T. 49,151 (67.64%)   LD hold
*Dr Jenny Tonge, LD   23,444
Tom Harris, C.   18,480
Barry Langford, Lab.   5,541
James Page, Green   1,223
Peter St John Howe, UK Ind.   348
Raymond Perrin, Ind.   115
LD majority 4,964 (10.10%)
2.45% swing C. to LD
(1997: LD maj. 2,951 (5.19%))

ROCHDALE
E. 69,506 T. 39,412 (56.70%) Lab. hold
*Ms Lorna Fitzsimons, Lab.   19,406
Paul Rowen, LD   13,751
Ms Elaina Cohen, C.   5,274
Nick Harvey, Green   728
Mohammed Salim, Ind.   253
Lab. majority 5,655 (14.35%)
2.45% swing LD to Lab.
(1997: Lab. maj. 4,545 (9.45%))

ROCHFORD & SOUTHEND EAST
E. 69,991 T. 37,452 (53.51%)   C. hold
*Sir Teddy Taylor, C.   20,058
Chris Dandridge, Lab.   13,024
Stephen Newton, LD   2,780
Adrian Hedges, Green   990
Brian Lynch, Lib.   600
C. majority 7,034 (18.78%)
4.86% swing Lab. to C.
(1997: C. maj. 4,225 (9.07%))

ROMFORD
E. 59,893 T. 35,701 (59.61%)   C. gain
Andrew Rosindell, C.   18,931
*Ms Eileen Gordon, Lab.   12,954
Nigel Meyer, LD   2,869
Stephen Ward, UK Ind.   533
Frank McAllister, BNP   414
C. majority 5,977 (16.74%)
9.14% swing Lab. to C.
(1997: Lab. maj. 649 (1.54%))

ROMSEY
E. 70,584 T. 48,459 (68.65%)   LD hold
*Mrs Sandra Gidley, LD   22,756
Paul Raynes, C.   20,386
Stephen Roberts, Lab.   3,986
Anthony McCabe, UK Ind.   730
Derrick Large, LCA   601
LD majority 2,370 (4.89%)
10.73% swing C. to LD
(2000 May by-election: LD maj. 3,311
(8.55%); 1997: C. maj. 8,585 (16.56%))

ROSSENDALE & DARWEN
E. 70,280 T. 41,358 (58.85%) Lab. hold
*Ms Janet Anderson, Lab.   20,251
George Lee, C.   15,028
Brian Dunning, LD   6,079
Lab. majority 5,223 (12.63%)
4.38% swing Lab. to C.
(1997: Lab. maj. 10,949 (21.38%))

ROTHER VALLEY
E. 69,174 T. 36,803 (53.20%) Lab. hold
*Rt. Hon. K. Barron, Lab.   22,851
James Duddridge, C.   7,969
Ms Win Knight, LD   4,603
David Cutts, UK Ind.   1,380
Lab. majority 14,882 (40.44%)
5.22% swing Lab. to C.
(1997: Lab. maj. 23,485 (50.88%))

ROTHERHAM
E. 57,931 T. 29,354 (50.67%) Lab. hold
*Denis MacShane, Lab.   18,759
Richard Powell, C.   5,682
Charles Hall, LD   3,117
Peter Griffith, UK Ind.   730
Dick Penycate, Green   577
Ms Freda Smith, Soc. All.   352
Geoffrey Bartholomew, JLDP   137
Lab. majority 13,077 (44.55%)
6.24% swing Lab. to C.
(1997: Lab. maj. 21,469 (57.02%))

RUGBY & KENILWORTH
E. 79,764 T. 53,796 (67.44%) Lab. hold
*Andy King, Lab.   24,221
David Martin, C.   21,344
Ms Gwen Fairweather, LD   7,444
Paul Garratt, UK Ind.   787
Lab. maj 2,877 (5.35%)
2.27% swing C. to Lab.
(1997: Lab. maj. 495 (0.81%))

RUISLIP-NORTHWOOD
E. 60,788 T. 37,141 (61.10%) C. hold
*John Wilkinson, C.   18,115
Ms Gillian Travis, Lab.   10,578
Mike Cox, LD   7,177
Graham Lee, Green   724
Ian Edward, BNP   547
C. majority 7,537 (20.29%)
1.46% swing Lab. to C.
(1997: C. maj. 7,794 (17.38%))

RUNNYMEDE & WEYBRIDGE
E. 75,569 T. 42,426 (56.14%) C. hold
*Philip Hammond, C.   20,646
Ms Jane Briginshaw, Lab.   12,286
Chris Bushill, LD   6,924
Christopher Browne, UK Ind.   1,332
Charles Gilman, Green   1,238
C. majority 8,360 (19.70%)
0.27% swing Lab. to C.
(1997: C. maj. 9,875 (19.16%))

RUSHCLIFFE
E. 81,839 T. 54,446 (66.53%) C. hold
*Rt. Hon. K. Clarke, C.   25,869
Paul Fallon, Lab.   18,512
Jeremy Hargreaves, LD   7,395
Ken Browne, UK Ind.   1,434
Ashley Baxter, Green   1,236
C. majority 7,357 (13.51%)
2.69% swing Lab. to C.
(1997: C. maj. 5,055 (8.14%))

RUTLAND & MELTON
E. 72,448 T. 47,056 (64.95%) C. hold
*Alan Duncan, C.   22,621
Matthew O'Callaghan, Lab.   14,009
Kim Lee, LD   8,386
Peter Baker, UK Ind.   1,223
Christopher Davies, Green   817
C. majority 8,612 (18.30%)
0.76% swing Lab. to C.
(1997: C. maj. 8,836 (16.78%))

RYEDALE
E. 66,543 T. 43,899 (65.97%) C. hold
*John Greenway, C.   20,711
Keith Orrell, LD   15,836
David Ellis, Lab.   6,470
Stephen Feaster, UK Ind.   882
C. majority 4,875 (11.11%)
0.37% swing LD to C.
(1997: C. maj. 5,058 (10.37%))

SAFFRON WALDEN
E. 76,724 T. 50,040 (65.22%) C. hold
*Rt. Hon. Sir A. Haselhurst, C.   24,485
Mrs E. Tealby-Watson, LD   12,481
Ms Tania Rogers, Lab.   11,305
Richard Glover, UK Ind.   1,769
C. majority 12,004 (23.99%)
2.73% swing LD to C.
(1997: C. maj. 10,573 (18.53%))

SALFORD
E. 54,152 T. 22,514 (41.58%) Lab. hold
*Ms Hazel Blears, Lab.   14,649
Norman Owen, LD   3,637
Chris King, C.   3,446
Peter Grant, Soc. All.   414
Ms Hazel Wallace, Ind.   216
Roy Masterson, Ind.   152
Lab. majority 11,012 (48.91%)
4.89% swing Lab. to LD
(1997: Lab. maj. 17,069 (51.53%))

SALISBURY
E. 80,538 T. 52,603 (65.31%) C. hold
*Robert Key, C.   24,527
Ms Yvonne Emmerson-Peirce, LD   15,824
Ms Sue Mallory, Lab.   9,199
Malcolm Wood, UK Ind.   1,958
Hamish Soutar, Green   1,095
C. majority 8,703 (16.54%)
2.88% swing LD to C.
(1997: C. maj. 6,276 (10.78%))

SCARBOROUGH & WHITBY
E. 75,213 T. 47,523 (63.18%) Lab. hold
*Lawrie Quinn, Lab.   22,426
John Sykes, C.   18,841
Tom Pearce, LD   3,977
Jonathan Dixon, Green   1,049
John Jacob, UK Ind.   970
Ms Theresa Murray, ProLife   260
Lab. maj 3,585 (7.54%)
0.94% swing Lab. to C.
(1997: Lab. maj. 5,124 (9.43%))

SCUNTHORPE
E. 59,689 T. 33,625 (56.33%) Lab. hold
*Elliot Morley, Lab.   20,096
Bernard Theobald, C.   9,724
Bob Tress, LD   3,156
John Cliff, UK Ind.   347
David Patterson, Ind.   302
Lab. majority 10,372 (30.85%)
1.62% swing Lab. to C.
(1997: Lab. maj. 14,173 (34.09%))

SEDGEFIELD
E. 64,925 T. 40,258 (62.01%) Lab. hold
*Rt. Hon. T. Blair, Lab.   26,110
Douglas Carswell, C.   8,397
Andrew Duffield, LD   3,624
Andrew Spence, UK Ind.   974
Brian Gibson, Soc. Lab.   518
Christopher Driver, R & R Loony   375
Ms Helen John, WFLOE   260
Lab. majority 17,713 (44.00%)
4.69% swing Lab. to C.
(1997: Lab. maj. 25,143 (53.37%))

SELBY
E. 77,924 T. 50,272 (64.51%) Lab. hold
*John Grogan, Lab.   22,652
Michael Mitchell, C.   20,514
Jeremy Wilcock, LD   5,569
Ms Helen Kenwright, Green   902
Bob Lewis, UK Ind.   635
Lab. majority 2,138 (4.25%)
1.28% swing Lab. to C.
(1997: Lab. maj. 3,836 (6.81%))

SEVENOAKS
E. 66,648 T. 42,614 (63.94%) C. hold
*Michael Fallon, C.   21,052
Ms Caroline Humphreys, Lab.   10,898
Clive Gray, LD   9,214
Mrs Lisa Hawkins, UK Ind.   1,155
Mark Ellis, PF   295
C. majority 10,154 (23.83%)
1.48% swing Lab. to C.
(1997: C. maj. 10,461 (20.86%))

SHEFFIELD ATTERCLIFFE
E. 68,386 T. 35,824 (52.38%) Lab. hold
*Clive Betts, Lab.   24,287
John Perry, C.   5,443
Ms Gail Smith, LD   5,092
Ms Pauline Arnott, UK Ind.   1,002
Lab. majority 18,844 (52.60%)
1.69% swing C. to Lab.
(1997: Lab. maj. 21,818 (49.23%))

SHEFFIELD BRIGHTSIDE
E. 54,711 T. 25,552 (46.70%) Lab. hold
*Rt. Hon. D. Blunkett, Lab.   19,650
Matthew Wilson, C.   2,601
Ms Alison Firth, LD   2,238
Brian Wilson, Soc. All.   361
Robert Morris, Soc. Lab.   354
Mark Suter, UK Ind.   348
Lab. majority 17,049 (66.72%)
0.81% swing C. to Lab.
(1997: Lab. maj. 19,954 (58.92%))

SHEFFIELD CENTRAL
E. 62,018 T. 30,069 (48.48%) Lab. hold
Rt. Hon. R. Caborn, Lab.   18,477
Ali Qadar, LD   5,933
Miss Noelle Brelsford, C.   3,289
Bernard Little, Green   1,008
Nick Riley, Soc. All.   754
David Hadfield, Soc. Lab.   289
Ms Charlotte Schofield, UK Ind.   257
Michael Driver, WRP   62
Lab. majority 12,544 (41.72%)
2.36% swing Lab. to LD
(1997: Lab. maj. 16,906 (46.43%))

SHEFFIELD HALLAM
E. 60,288 T. 38,246 (63.44%) LD hold
*Richard Allan, LD   21,203
John Harthman, C.   11,856
Ms Gillian Furniss, Lab.   4,758
Leslie Arnott, UK Ind.   429
LD majority 9,347 (24.44%)
3.12% swing C. to LD
(1997: LD maj. 8,271 (18.19%))

SHEFFIELD HEELEY
E. 62,758 T. 34,139 (54.40%) Lab. hold
Ms Meg Munn, Lab.   19,452
David Willis, LD   7,748
Ms Carolyn Abbott, C.   4,864
Rob Unwin, Green   774
Brian Fischer, Soc. Lab.   667
David Dunn, UK Ind.   634
Lab. majority 11,704 (34.28%)
2.60% swing Lab. to LD
(1997: Lab. maj. 17,078 (39.48%))

SHEFFIELD HILLSBOROUGH
E. 75,097 T. 42,536 (56.64%) Lab. hold
*Ms Helen Jackson, Lab.   24,170
John Commons, LD   9,601
Graham King, C.   7,801
Peter Webb, UK Ind.   964
Lab. majority 14,569 (34.25%)
1.62% swing LD to Lab.
(1997: Lab. maj. 16,451 (31.02%))

SHERWOOD
E. 75,670 T. 45,900 (60.66%) Lab. hold
*Paddy Tipping, Lab.   24,900
Brandon Lewis, C.   15,527
Peter Harris, LD   5,473
Lab. majority 9,373 (20.42%)
4.66% swing Lab. to C.
(1997: Lab. maj. 16,812 (29.74%))

SHIPLEY
E. 69,577 T. 46,020 (66.14%) Lab. hold
*Christopher Leslie, Lab.   20,243
David Senior, C.   18,815
Ms Helen Wright, LD   4,996
Martin Love, Green   1,386
Walter Whitacker, UK Ind.   580
Lab. majority 1,428 (3.10%)
1.28% swing Lab. to C.
(1997: Lab. maj. 2,996 (5.67%))

SHREWSBURY & ATCHAM
E. 74,964 T. 49,909 (66.58%) Lab. hold
*Paul Marsden, Lab.   22,253
Miss Anthea McIntyre, C.   18,674
Jonathan Rule, LD   6,173
Henry Curteis, UK Ind.   1,620
Ms Emma Bullard, Green   931
James Gollins, Ind.   258
Lab. majority 3,579 (7.17%)
2.08% swing C. to Lab.
(1997: Lab. maj. 1,670 (3.02%))

SHROPSHIRE NORTH
E. 73,716 T. 46,520 (63.11%) C. hold
*Owen Paterson, C.   22,631
Michael Ion, Lab.   16,390
Ben Jephcott, LD   5,945
David Trevanion, UK Ind.   1,165
Russell Maxfield, Ind.   389
C. majority 6,241 (13.42%)
4.58% swing Lab. to C.
(1997: C. maj. 2,195 (4.26%))

SITTINGBOURNE & SHEPPEY
E. 65,825 T. 37,858 (57.51%) Lab. hold
*Derek Wyatt, Lab.   17,340
Adrian Lee, C.   13,831
Ms Elvie Lowe, LD   5,353
Michael Young, R & R Loony   673
Robert Oakley, UK Ind.   661
Lab. majority 3,509 (9.27%)
2.54% swing C. to Lab.
(1997: Lab. maj. 1,929 (4.18%))

SKIPTON & RIPON
E. 75,201 T. 49,126 (65.33%) C. hold
*Rt. Hon. D. Curry, C.   25,736
Bernard Bateman, LD   12,806
Michael Dugher, Lab.   8,543
Mrs Nancy Holdsworth, UK Ind.   2,041
C. majority 12,930 (26.32%)
2.47% swing LD to C.
(1997: C. maj. 11,620 (21.38%))

SLEAFORD & NORTH HYKEHAM
E. 74,561 T. 48,719 (65.34%) C. hold
*Rt. D. Hogg, C.   24,190
Ms Elizabeth Donnelly, Lab.   15,568
Robert Arbon, LD   7,894
Michael Ward-Barrow, UK Ind.   1,067
C. majority 8,622 (17.70%)
4.03% swing Lab. to C.
(1997: C. maj. 5,123 (9.64%))

SLOUGH
E. 72,429 T. 38,998 (53.84%) Lab. hold
*Ms Fiona Mactaggart, Lab.   22,718
Mrs Diana Coad, C.   10,210
Keith Kerr, LD   4,109
Michael Haines, Ind.   859
John Lane, UK Ind.   738
Choudry Nazir, Ind.   364
Lab. majority 12,508 (32.07%)
2.34% swing C. to Lab.
(1997: Lab. maj. 13,071 (27.39%))

SOLIHULL
E. 77,094 T. 48,271 (62.61%) C. hold
*John Taylor, C.   21,935
Ms Jo Byron, LD   12,528
Brendan O'Brien, Lab.   12,373
Andy Moore, UK Ind.   1,061
Ms Stephanie Pyne, ProLife   374
C. majority 9,407 (19.49%)
0.07% swing LD to C.
(1997: C. maj. 11,397 (19.35%))

SOMERTON & FROME
E. 74,991 T. 52,684 (70.25%) LD hold
*David Heath, LD   22,983
Jonathan Marland, C.   22,315
Andrew Perkins, Lab.   6,113
Peter Bridgwood, UK Ind.   919
Ms Jean Pollock, Lib.   354
LD majority 668 (1.27%)
0.52% swing C. to LD
(1997: LD maj. 130 (0.23%))

SOUTH HOLLAND & THE DEEPINGS
E. 73,880 T. 46,202 (62.54%) C. hold
*John Hayes, C.   25,611
Graham Walker, Lab.   14,512
Ms Grace Hill, LD   4,761
Malcolm Charlesworth, UK Ind.   1,318
C. majority 11,099 (24.02%)
4.04% swing Lab. to C.
(1997: C. maj. 7,991 (15.94%))

SOUTH SHIELDS
E. 61,802 T. 30,448 (49.27%) Lab. hold
David Miliband, Lab.   19,230
Miss Joanna Gardner, C.   5,140
Marshall Grainger, LD   5,127
Alan Hardy, UK Ind.   689
Roger Nettleship, Ind.   262
Lab. majority 14,090 (46.28%)
5.28% swing Lab. to C.
(1997: Lab. maj. 22,153 (56.84%))

SOUTHAMPTON ITCHEN
E. 76,603 T. 41,373 (54.01%) Lab. hold
*Rt. Hon. J. Denham, Lab.   22,553
Mrs Caroline Nokes, C.   11,330
Mark Cooper, LD   6,195
Kim Rose, UK Ind.   829
Gavin Marsh, Soc. All.   241
Michael Holmes, Soc. Lab.   225
Lab. majority 11,223 (27.13%)
0.37% swing C. to Lab.
(1997: Lab. maj. 14,209 (26.38%))

SOUTHAMPTON TEST
E. 73,893 T. 41,575 (56.26%) Lab. hold
*Alan Whitehead, Lab.   21,824
Richard Gueterbock, C.   10,617
John Shaw, LD   7,522
Garry Rankin-Moore, UK Ind.   792
Mark Abel, Soc. All.   442
Paramjit Bahia, Soc. Lab.   378
Lab. majority 11,207 (26.96%)
0.43% swing C. to Lab.
(1997: Lab. maj. 13,684 (26.10%))

SOUTHEND WEST
E. 64,116 T. 37,375 (58.29%) C. hold
*David Amess, C.   17,313
Paul Fisher, Lab.   9,372
Richard de Ste Croix, LD   9,319
Brian Lee, UK Ind.   1,371
C. majority 7,941 (21.25%)
2.64% swing Lab. to C.
(1997: C. maj. 2,615 (5.62%))

SOUTHPORT
E. 70,785 T. 41,153 (58.14%) LD hold
John Pugh, LD   18,011
Laurence Jones, C.   15,004
Paul Brant, Lab.   6,816
David Green, Lib.   767
Gerry Kelley, UK Ind.   555
LD majority 3,007 (7.31%)
2.44% swing LD to C.
(1997: LD maj. 6,160 (12.18%))

SOUTHWARK NORTH &
BERMONDSEY
E. 73,527 T. 36,862 (50.13%) LD hold
*Simon Hughes, LD   20,991
Kingsley Abrams, Lab.   11,359
Ewan Wallace, C.   2,800
Ms Ruth Jenkins, Green   752
Ms Lianne Shore, NF   612
Rob McWhirter, UK Ind.   271
John Davies, Ind.   77
LD majority 9,632 (26.13%)
8.91% swing Lab. to LD
(1997: LD maj. 3,387 (8.30%))

SPELTHORNE
E. 68,731 T. 41,794 (60.81%) C. hold
*David Wilshire, C.   18,851
Andrew Shaw, Lab.   15,589
Martin Rimmer, LD   6,156
Richard Squire, UK Ind.   1,198
C. majority 3,262 (7.80%)
0.56% swing Lab. to C.
(1997: C. maj. 3,473 (6.69%))

ST ALBANS
E. 66,040 T. 43,761 (66.26%) Lab. hold
*Kerry Pollard, Lab.   19,889
Charles Elphicke, C.   15,423
Nick Rijke, LD   7,847
Christopher Sherwin, UK Ind.   602
Lab. majority 4,466 (10.21%)
0.71% swing C. to Lab.
(1997: Lab. maj. 4,459 (8.78%))

ST HELENS NORTH
E. 70,545 T. 37,601 (53.30%) Lab. hold
Dave Watts, Lab.   22,977
Simon Pearce, C.   7,076
John Beirne, LD   6,609
Stephen Whatham, Soc. Lab.   939
Lab. majority 15,901 (42.29%)
2.64% swing Lab. to C.
(1997: Lab. maj. 23,417 (47.57%))

ST HELENS SOUTH
E. 65,122 T. 33,804 (51.91%) Lab. hold
†Shaun Woodward, Lab.   16,799
Brian Spencer, LD   7,814
Dr Lee Rotherham, C.   4,675
Neil Thompson, Soc. All.   2,325
Mike Perry, Soc. Lab.   1,504
Bryan Slater, UK Ind.   336
Michael Murphy, Ind.   271
David Braid, Ind.   80
Lab. majority 8,985 (26.58%)
14.33% swing Lab. to LD
(1997: Lab. maj. 23,739 (53.63%))

ST IVES
E. 74,256 T. 49,266 (66.35%) LD hold
*Andrew George, LD   25,413
Miss Joanna Richardson, C.   15,360
William Morris, Lab.   6,567
Mick Faulkner, UK Ind.   1,926
LD majority 10,053 (20.41%)
3.55% swing C. to LD
(1997: LD maj. 7,170 (13.30%))

STAFFORD
E. 67,934 T. 44,366 (65.31%) Lab. hold
*David Kidney, Lab.   21,285
Philip Cochrane, C.   16,253
Ms Jeanne Pinkerton, LD   4,205
Earl of Bradford, UK Ind.   2,315
Michael Hames, R & R Loony   308
Lab. maj 5,032 (11.34%)
1.50% swing C. to Lab.
(1997: Lab. maj. 4,314 (8.34%))

STAFFORDSHIRE MOORLANDS
E. 66,760 T. 42,658 (63.90%) Lab. hold
*Ms Charlotte Atkins, Lab.   20,904
Marcus Hayes, C.   15,066
John Redfern, LD   5,928
Paul Gilbert, UK Ind.   760
Lab. maj 5,838 (13.69%)
2.99% swing Lab. to C.
(1997: Lab. maj. 10,049 (19.66%))

STAFFORDSHIRE SOUTH
E. 69,925 T. 42,180 (60.32%) C. hold
*Sir Patrick Cormack, C.   21,295
Paul Kalinauckas, Lab.   14,414
Ms Jo Harrison, LD   4,891
Mike Lynch, UK Ind.   1,580
C. majority 6,881 (16.31%)
0.51% swing Lab. to C.
(1997: C. maj. 7,821 (15.30%))

STALYBRIDGE & HYDE
E. 66,265 T. 32,046 (48.36%) Lab. hold
James Purnell, Lab.   17,781
Andrew Reid, C.   8,922
Brendon Jones, LD   4,327
Frank Bennett, UK Ind.   1,016
Lab. majority 8,859 (27.64%)
3.36% swing Lab. to C.
(1997: Lab. maj. 14,806 (34.36%))

STEVENAGE
E. 69,203 T. 42,453 (61.35%) Lab. hold
*Ms Barbara Follett, Lab.   22,025
Graeme Quar, C.   13,459
Harry Davies, LD   6,027
Steve Glennon, Soc. All.   449
Antal Losonczi, Ind.   320
Ms Sarah Bell, ProLife   173
Lab. majority 8,566 (20.18%)
1.18% swing Lab. to C.
(1997: Lab. maj. 11,582 (22.54%))

STOCKPORT
E. 66,397 T. 35,383 (53.29%) Lab. hold
*Ms Ann Coffey, Lab.   20,731
John Allen, C.   9,162
Mark Hunter, LD   5,490
Lab. majority 11,569 (32.70%)
3.91% swing Lab. to C.
(1997: Lab. maj. 18,912 (40.52%))

STOCKTON NORTH
E. 65,192 T. 35,427 (54.34%) Lab. hold
*Frank Cook, Lab.   22,470
Ms Amanda Vigar, C.   7,823
Ms Mary Wallace, LD   4,208
Bill Wennington, Green   926
Lab. majority 14,647 (41.34%)
3.34% swing Lab. to C.
(1997: Lab. maj. 21,357 (48.02%))

STOCKTON SOUTH
E. 71,026 T. 44,209 (62.24%) Lab. hold
*Ms Dari Taylor, Lab.   23,414
Tim Devlin, C.   14,328
Mrs Suzanne Fletcher, LD   6,012
Lawrie Coombes, Soc. All.   455
Lab. majority 9,086 (20.55%)
0.84% swing Lab. to C.
(1997: Lab. maj. 11,585 (22.23%))

STOKE-ON-TRENT CENTRAL
E. 59,750 T. 28,300 (47.36%) Lab. hold
*Mark Fisher, Lab.   17,170
Ms Jill Clark, C.   5,325
Gavin Webb, LD   4,148
Richard Wise, Ind.   1,657
Lab. majority 11,845 (41.86%)
3.83% swing Lab. to C.
(1997: Lab. maj. 19,924 (49.51%))

STOKE-ON-TRENT NORTH
E. 57,998 T. 30,115 (51.92%) Lab. hold
*Ms Joan Walley, Lab.   17,460
Benjamin Browning, C.   5,676
Henry Jebb, LD   3,580
Lee Wanger, Ind.   3,399
Lab. maj 11,784 (39.13%)
2.92% swing Lab. to C.
(1997: Lab. maj. 17,392 (44.98%))

STOKE-ON-TRENT SOUTH
E. 70,032 T. 36,028 (51.45%) Lab. hold
*George Stevenson, Lab.   19,366
Philip Bastiman, C.   8,877
Christopher Coleman, LD   4,724
Adrian Knapper, Ind.   1,703
Steven Batkin, BNP   1,358
Lab. majority 10,489 (29.11%)
5.23% swing Lab. to C.
(1997: Lab. maj. 18,303 (39.58%))

STONE
E. 68,847 T. 45,642 (66.29%) C. hold
*William Cash, C.   22,395
John Palfreyman, Lab.   16,359
Brendan McKeown, LD   6,888
C. majority 6,036 (13.22%)
3.01% swing Lab. to C.
(1997: C. maj. 3,818 (7.20%))

STOURBRIDGE
E. 64,610 T. 39,924 (61.79%) Lab. hold
*Ms Debra Shipley, Lab.   18,823
Stephen Eyre, C.   15,011
Chris Bramall, LD   4,833
John Knotts, UK Ind.   763
Mick Atherton, Soc. Lab.   494
Lab. majority 3,812 (9.55%)
0.91% swing Lab. to C.
(1997: Lab. maj. 5,645 (11.36%))

STRATFORD-ON-AVON
E. 85,241 T. 54,914 (64.42%) C. hold
*John Maples, C.   27,606
Dr Susan Juned, LD   15,804
Mushtaq Hussain, Lab.   9,164
Ronald Mole, UK Ind.   1,184
Mick Davies, Green   1,156
C. majority 11,802 (21.49%)
0.61% swing C. to LD
(1997: C. maj. 14,106 (22.72%))

STREATHAM
E. 76,021 T. 36,998 (48.67%) Lab. hold
*Keith Hill, Lab.   21,041
Roger O'Brien, LD   6,771
Stephen Hocking, C.   6,639
Mohammed Sajid, Green   1,641
Greg Tucker, Soc. All.   906
Lab. majority 14,270 (38.57%)
5.33% swing Lab. to LD
(1997: Lab. maj. 18,423 (41.04%))

STRETFORD & URMSTON
E. 70,924 T. 38,973 (54.95%) Lab. hold
*Ms Beverley Hughes, Lab.   23,804
Jonathan Mackie, C.   10,565
John Bridges, LD   3,891
Ms Katie Price, Ind.   713
Lab. majority 13,239 (33.97%)
2.98% swing C. to Lab.
(1997: Lab. maj. 13,640 (28.01%))

STROUD
E. 78,878 T. 55,175 (69.95%)
                             Lab. Co-op hold
*David Drew, Lab. Co-op   25,685
Neil Carmichael, C.   20,646
Ms Janice Beasley, LD   6,036
Kevin Cranston, Green   1,913
Adrian Blake, UK Ind.   895
Lab. Co-op majority 5,039 (9.13%)
2.24% swing C. to Lab. Co-op
(1997: Lab. maj. 2,910 (4.66%))

SUFFOLK CENTRAL & IPSWICH
NORTH
E. 74,200 T. 47,104 (63.48%) C. hold
*Michael Lord, C.   20,924
Ms Carole Jones, Lab.   17,455
Mrs Ann Elvin, LD   7,593
Jonathan Wright, UK Ind.   1,132
C. majority 3,469 (7.36%)
0.33% swing Lab. to C.
(1997: C. maj. 3,538 (6.70%))

SUFFOLK COASTAL
E. 75,963 T. 50,407 (66.36%) C. hold
*Rt. Hon. J. Gummer, C.   21,847
Nigel Gardner, Lab.   17,521
Tony Schur, LD   9,192
Michael Burn, UK Ind.   1,847
C. majority 4,326 (8.58%)
1.40% swing Lab. to C.
(1997: C. maj. 3,254 (5.79%))

SUFFOLK SOUTH
E. 68,408 T. 45,293 (66.21%) C. hold
*Tim Yeo, C.   18,748
Marc Young, Lab.   13,667
Mrs Tessa Munt, LD   11,296
Derek Allen, UK Ind.   1,582
C. majority 5,081 (11.22%)
1.59% swing Lab. to C.
(1997: C. maj. 4,175 (8.03%))

SUFFOLK WEST
E. 71,220 T. 42,445 (59.60%)   C. hold
*Richard Spring, C.   20,201
Michael Jeffreys, Lab.   15,906
Robin Martlew, LD   5,017
Will Burrows, UK Ind.   1,321
C. majority 4,295 (10.12%)
3.16% swing Lab. to C.
(1997: C. maj. 1,867 (3.80%))

SUNDERLAND NORTH
E. 60,846 T. 29,820 (49.01%) Lab. hold
*Bill Etherington, Lab.   18,685
Michael Harris, C.   5,331
John Lennox, LD   3,599
Neil Herron, Ind.   1,518
David Guynan, BNP   687
Lab. majority 13,354 (44.78%)
3.38% swing Lab. to C.
(1997: Lab. maj. 19,697 (51.55%))

SUNDERLAND SOUTH
E. 64,577 T. 31,187 (48.29%) Lab. hold
*Chris Mullin, Lab.   19,921
Jim Boyd, C.   6,254
Mark Greenfield, LD   3,675
Joseph Dobbie, BNP   576
Joseph Moore, UK Ind.   470
Ms Rosalyn Warner, Loony   291
Lab. maj 13,667 (43.82%)
2.68% swing Lab. to C.
(1997: Lab. maj. 19,638 (49.18%))

SURREY EAST
E. 75,049 T. 47,049 (62.69%)   C. hold
*Peter Ainsworth, C.   24,706
Jeremy Pursehouse, LD   11,503
Ms Jo Tanner, Lab.   8,994
Anthony Stone, UK Ind.   1,846
C. majority 13,203 (28.06%)
0.23% swing LD to C.
(1997: C. maj. 15,093 (27.61%))

SURREY HEATH
E. 75,858 T. 45,102 (59.46%)   C. hold
*Nicholas Hawkins, C.   22,401
Mark Lelliott, LD   11,582
James Norman, Lab.   9,640
Nigel Hunt, UK Ind.   1,479
C. majority 10,819 (23.99%)
2.89% swing C. to LD
(1997: C. maj. 16,287 (29.76%))

SURREY SOUTH WEST
E. 74,127 T. 49,592 (66.90%)   C. hold
*Rt. Hon. Mrs V. Bottomley, C.   22,462
Simon Cordon, LD   21,601
Martin Whelton, Lab.   4,321
Timothy Clark, UK Ind.   1,208
C. majority 861 (1.74%)
1.52% swing C. to LD
(1997: C. maj. 2,694 (4.77%))

SUSSEX MID
E. 70,632 T. 45,822 (64.87%)   C. hold
*Nicholas Soames, C.   21,150
Ms Lesley Wilkins, LD   14,252
Paul Mitchell, Lab.   8,693
Petrina Holsworth, UK Ind.   1,126
Peter Berry, Loony   601
C. majority 6,898 (15.05%)
1.12% swing LD to C.
(1997: C. maj. 6,854 (12.82%))

SUTTON & CHEAM
E. 63,648 T. 39,723 (62.41%)   LD hold
*Paul Burstow, LD   19,382
Lady Olga Maitland, C.   15,078
Ms Lisa Homan, Lab.   5,263
LD majority 4,304 (10.84%)
3.19% swing C. to LD
(1997: LD maj. 2,097 (4.45%))

SUTTON COLDFIELD
E. 71,856 T. 43,452 (60.47%)   C. hold
Andrew Mitchell, C.   21,909
Robert Pocock, Lab.   11,805
Martin Turner, LD   8,268
Mike Nattrass, UK Ind.   1,186
Ian Robinson, Ind.   284
C. majority 10,104 (23.25%)
2.58% swing C. to Lab.
(1997: C. maj. 14,885 (28.41%))

SWINDON NORTH
E. 69,335 T. 42,328 (61.05%) Lab. hold
*Michael Wills, Lab.   22,371
Nick Martin, C.   14,266
David Nation, LD   4,891
Brian Lloyd, UK Ind.   800
Lab. majority 8,105 (19.15%)
1.61% swing C. to Lab.
(1997: Lab. maj. 7,688 (15.93%))

SWINDON SOUTH
E. 71,080 T. 43,384 (61.04%) Lab. hold
*Ms Julia Drown, Lab.   22,260
Simon Coombs, C.   14,919
Geoff Brewer, LD   5,165
Mrs Vicki Sharp, UK Ind.   713
Roly Gillard, R & R Loony   327
Lab. majority 7,341 (16.92%)
2.94% swing C. to Lab.
(1997: Lab. maj. 5,645 (11.04%))

TAMWORTH
E. 69,596 T. 40,250 (57.83%) Lab. hold
*Brian Jenkins, Lab.   19,722
Ms Luise Gunter, C.   15,124
Ms Jennifer Pinkett, LD   4,721
Paul Sootheran, UK Ind.   683
Lab. majority 4,598 (11.42%)
1.81% swing Lab. to C.
(1997: Lab. maj. 7,496 (15.04%))

TATTON
E. 64,954 T. 41,278 (63.55%)   C. gain
George Osborne, C.   19,860
Steve Conquest, Lab.   11,249
Mike Ash, LD   7,685
Mark Sheppard, UK Ind.   769
Peter Sharratt, Ind.   734
Mrs Viviane Allinson, Tatton   505
John Batchelor, Ind.   322
Jonathan Boyd Hunt, Ind.   154
C. majority 8,611 (20.86%)
(1997: Ind. maj. 11,077 (22.70%))

TAUNTON
E. 81,651 T. 55,225 (67.64%)   C. gain
Adrian Flook, C.   23,033
*Mrs Jackie Ballard, LD   22,798
Andrew Govier, Lab.   8,254
Michael Canton, UK Ind.   1,140
C. majority 235 (0.43%)
2.21% swing LD to C.
(1997: LD maj. 2,443 (4.00%))

TEIGNBRIDGE
E. 85,533 T. 59,310 (69.34%)   LD gain
Richard Younger-Ross, LD   26,343
*Patrick Nicholls, C.   23,332
Christopher Bain, Lab.   7,366
Paul Viscount Exmouth, UK Ind.   2,269
LD majority 3,011 (5.08%)
2.76% swing C. to LD
(1997: C. maj. 281 (0.45%))

TELFORD
E. 59,486 T. 30,875 (51.90%) Lab. hold
David Wright, Lab.   16,854
Andrew Henderson, C.   8,471
Ms Sally Wiggin, LD   3,983
Ms Nicola Brookes, UK Ind.   1,098
Mike Jeffries, Soc. All.   469
Lab. majority 8,383 (27.15%)
1.63% swing Lab. to C.
(1997: Lab. maj. 11,290 (30.42%))

TEWKESBURY
E. 70,276 T. 45,195 (64.31%)   C. hold
*Laurence Robertson, C.   20,830
Keir Dhillon, Lab.   12,167
Stephen Martin, LD   11,863
Charles Vernall, Ind.   335
C. majority 8,663 (19.17%)
0.19% swing C. to Lab.
(1997: C. maj. 9,234 (17.71%))

THANET NORTH
E. 70,581 T. 41,868 (59.32%)   C. hold
*Roger Gale, C.   21,050
James Stewart Laing, Lab.   14,400
Seth Proctor, LD   4,603
John Moore, UK Ind.   980
David Shortt, Ind.   440
Thomas Holmes, NF   395
C. majority 6,650 (15.88%)
5.12% swing Lab. to C.
(1997: C. maj. 2,766 (5.65%))

THANET SOUTH
E. 61,462 T. 39,431 (64.16%) Lab. hold
*Dr Stephen Ladyman, Lab.   18,002
Mark Macgregor, C.   16,210
Guy Voizey, LD   3,706
William Baldwin, Ind.   770
Terry Eccott, UK Ind.   501
Bernard Franklin, NF   242
Lab. majority 1,792 (4.54%)
0.92% swing Lab. to C.
(1997: Lab. maj. 2,878 (6.39%))

THURROCK
E. 76,524 T. 37,362 (48.82%) Lab. hold
*Andrew Mackinlay, Lab.   21,121
Mike Penning, C.   11,124
John Lathan, LD   3,846
Christopher Sheppard, UK Ind.   1,271
Lab. majority 9,997 (26.76%)
4.90% swing Lab. to C.
(1997: Lab. maj. 17,256 (36.55%))

TIVERTON & HONITON
E. 80,646 T. 55,784 (69.17%)   C. hold
*Mrs Angela Browning, C.   26,258
Jim Barnard, LD   19,974
Ms Isabel Owen, Lab.   6,647
Alan Langmaid, UK Ind.   1,281
Matthew Burgess, Green   1,030
Mrs Jennifer Roach, Lib.   594
C. majority 6,284 (11.26%)
4.23% swing LD to C.
(1997: C. maj. 1,653 (2.80%))

TONBRIDGE & MALLING
E. 65,939 T. 42,436 (64.36%) C. hold
*Rt. Hon. Sir J. Stanley, C. 20,956
Ms Victoria Hayman, Lab. 12,706
Ms Merilyn Canet, LD 7,605
Ms Lynn Croucher, UK Ind. 1,169
C. majority 8,250 (19.44%)
0.67% swing C. to Lab.
(1997: C. maj. 10,230 (20.78%))

TOOTING
E. 68,447 T. 37,591 (54.92%) Lab. hold
*Tom Cox, Lab. 20,332
Alexander Nicoll, C. 9,932
Simon James, LD 5,583
Matthew Ledbury, Green 1,744
Lab. majority 10,400 (27.67%)
2.45% swing Lab. to C.
(1997: Lab. maj. 15,011 (32.56%))

TORBAY
E. 72,409 T. 47,569 (65.69%) LD hold
*Adrian Sanders, LD 24,015
Christian Sweeting, C. 17,307
John McKay, Lab. 4,484
Graham Booth, UK Ind. 1,512
Ms Pam Neale, Ind. 251
LD majority 6,708 (14.10%)
7.04% swing C. to LD
(1997: LD maj. 12 (0.02%))

TOTNES
E. 72,548 T. 49,246 (67.88%) C. hold
*Anthony Steen, C. 21,914
Ms Rachel Oliver, LD 18,317
Thomas Wildy, Lab. 6,005
Craig Mackinlay, UK Ind. 3,010
C. majority 3,597 (7.30%)
2.84% swing LD to C.
(1997: C. maj. 877 (1.63%))

TOTTENHAM
E. 65,567 T. 31,601 (48.20%) Lab. hold
*David Lammy, Lab. 21,317
Ms Uma Fernandes, C. 4,401
Ms Meher Khan, LD 3,008
Peter Budge, Green 1,443
Weyman Bennett, Soc. All. 1,162
Unver Shefki, Reform 270
Lab. maj 16,916 (53.53%)
0.03% swing Lab. to C.
(2000 Jun. by-election: Lab. maj.
5,646 (34.39%); 1997: Lab. Maj.
20,200 (53.58%))

TRURO & ST AUSTELL
E. 79,219 T. 50,295 (63.49%) LD hold
*Matthew Taylor, LD 24,296
Tim Bonner, C. 16,231
David Phillips, Lab. 6,889
James Wonnacott, UK Ind. 1,664
Conan Jenkin, Meb. Ker. 1,137
John Lee, Ind. 78
LD majority 8,065 (16.04%)
3.00% swing LD to C.
(1997: LD maj. 12,501 (22.03%))

TUNBRIDGE WELLS
E. 64,534 T. 40,201 (62.29%) C. hold
*Archie Norman, C. 19,643
Keith Brown, LD 9,913
Ian Carvell, Lab. 9,332
Victor Webb, UK Ind. 1,313
C. majority 9,730 (24.20%)
4.34% swing LD to C.
(1997: C. maj. 7,506 (15.52%))

TWICKENHAM
E. 74,135 T. 49,938 (67.36%) LD hold
*Dr Vincent Cable, LD 24,344
Nick Longworth, C. 16,689
Dean Rogers, Lab. 6,903
Ms Judy Maciejowska, Green 1,423
Ray Hollebone, UK Ind. 579
LD majority 7,655 (15.33%)
3.98% swing C. to LD
(1997: LD maj. 4,281 (7.36%))

TYNE BRIDGE
E. 58,900 T. 26,032 (44.20%) Lab. hold
*David Clelland, Lab. 18,345
James Cook, C. 3,456
Jonathan Wallace, LD 3,213
James Fitzpatrick, Soc. Lab. 533
Samuel Robson, Soc. All. 485
Lab. majority 14,889 (57.19%)
4.27% swing Lab. to C.
(1997: Lab. maj. 22,906 (65.73%))

TYNEMOUTH
E. 65,184 T. 43,903 (67.35%) Lab. hold
*Alan Campbell, Lab. 23,364
Karl Poulsen, C. 14,686
Ms Penny Reid, LD 5,108
Michael Rollings, UK Ind. 745
Lab. majority 8,678 (19.77%)
1.14% swing Lab. to C.
(1997: Lab. maj. 11,273 (22.04%))

TYNESIDE NORTH
E. 64,914 T. 37,569 (57.88%) Lab. hold
*Rt. Hon. S. Byers, Lab. 26,127
Mark Ruffell, C. 5,459
Simon Reed, LD 4,649
Alan Taylor, UK Ind. 770
Pete Burnett, Soc. All. 324
Ken Capstick, Soc. Lab. 240
Lab. majority 20,668 (55.01%)
2.02% swing Lab. to C.
(1997: Lab. maj. 26,643 (59.05%))

UPMINSTER
E. 56,829 T. 33,851 (59.57%) C. gain
Mrs Angela Watkinson, C. 15,410
*Keith Darvill, Lab. 14,169
Peter Truesdale, LD 3,183
Terry Murray, UK Ind. 1,089
C. majority 1,241 (3.67%)
5.18% swing Lab. to C.
(1997: Lab. maj. 2,770 (6.70%))

UXBRIDGE
E. 58,066 T. 33,418 (57.55%) C. hold
*John Randall, C. 15,751
David Salisbury-Jones, Lab. 13,653
Ms Catherine Royce, LD 3,426
Paul Cannons, UK Ind. 588
C. majority 2,098 (6.28%)
2.26% swing Lab. to C.
(1997 Jul. by-election: C. maj.
3,766 (11.82%); 1997: C. maj.
724 (1.75%))

VALE OF YORK
E. 73,335 T. 48,490 (66.12%) C. hold
*Miss Anne McIntosh, C. 25,033
Christopher Jukes, Lab. 12,516
Greg Stone, LD 9,799
Peter Thornber, UK Ind. 1,142
C. majority 12,517 (25.81%)
3.78% swing Lab. to C.
(1997: C. maj. 9,721 (18.25%))

VAUXHALL
E. 74,474 T. 33,392 (44.84%) Lab. hold
*Ms Kate Hoey, Lab. 19,738
Anthony Bottrall, LD 6,720
Gareth Compton, C. 4,489
Shane Collins, Green 1,485
Ms Theresa Bennett, Soc. All. 853
Martin Boyd, Ind. 107
Lab. majority 13,018 (38.99%)
4.39% swing Lab. to LD
(1997: Lab. maj. 18,660 (47.77%))

WAKEFIELD
E. 75,750 T. 41,254 (54.46%) Lab. hold
*David Hinchcliffe, Lab. 20,592
Mrs Thelma Karran, C. 12,638
Douglas Dale, LD 5,097
Ms Sarah Greenwood, Green 1,075
Ms Janice Cannon, UK Ind. 677
Abdul Aziz, Soc. Lab. 634
Mick Griffiths, Soc. All. 541
Lab. majority 7,954 (19.28%)
4.82% swing Lab. to C.
(1997: Lab. maj. 14,604 (28.93%))

WALLASEY
E. 64,889 T. 37,346 (57.55%) Lab. hold
*Ms Angela Eagle, Lab. 22,718
Mrs Lesley Rennie, C. 10,442
Peter Reisdorf, LD 4,186
Lab. majority 12,276 (32.87%)
3.92% swing Lab. to C.
(1997: Lab. maj. 19,074 (40.72%))

WALSALL NORTH
E. 66,020 T. 32,312 (48.94%) Lab. hold
*David Winnick, Lab. 18,779
Melvin Pitt, C. 9,388
Michael Heap, LD 2,923
Mrs Jenny Mayo, UK Ind. 812
Dave Church, Soc. All. 410
Lab. majority 9,391 (29.06%)
(1997: Lab. maj. 12,588 (29.07%))

WALSALL SOUTH
E. 62,657 T. 34,899 (55.70%) Lab. hold
*Rt. Hon. B. George, Lab. 20,574
Mike Bird, C. 10,643
Bill Tomlinson, LD 2,365
Derek Bennett, UK Ind. 974
Peter Smith, Soc. All. 343
Lab. majority 9,931 (28.46%)
1.15% swing C. to Lab.
(1997: Lab. maj. 11,312 (26.16%))

WALTHAMSTOW
E. 64,403 T. 34,429 (53.46%) Lab. hold
*Neil Gerrard, Lab. 21,402
Nick Boys Smith, C. 6,221
Peter Dunphy, LD 5,024
Simon Donovan, Soc. Alt. 806
William Phillips, BNP 389
Ms Gerda Mayer, UK Ind. 298
Ms Barbara Duffy, ProLife 289
Lab. majority 15,181 (44.09%)
0.64% swing C. to Lab.
(1997: Lab. maj. 17,149 (42.81%))

WANSBECK
E. 62,989 T. 37,419 (59.41%) Lab. hold
*Denis Murphy, Lab.   21,617
Alan Thompson, LD   8,516
Mrs Rachael Lake, C.   4,774
Michael Kirkup, Ind.   1,076
Dr Nic Best, Green   954
Gavin Attwell, UK Ind.   482
Lab. majority 13,101 (35.01%)
7.25% swing Lab. to LD
(1997: Lab. maj. 22,367 (49.52%))

WANSDYKE
E. 70,728 T. 49,047 (69.35%) Lab. hold
*Dan Norris, Lab.   22,706
Chris Watt, C.   17,593
Ms Gail Coleshill, LD   7,135
Francis Hayden, Green   958
Peter Sandell, UK Ind.   655
Lab. majority 5,113 (10.42%)
0.83% swing C. to Lab.
(1997: Lab. maj. 4,799 (8.77%))

WANTAGE
E. 76,129 T. 49,129 (64.53%) C. hold
*Robert Jackson, C.   19,475
Stephen Beer, Lab.   13,875
Neil Fawcett, LD   13,776
David Brooks-Saxl, Green   1,062
Count Nichola Tolstoy, UK Ind.   941
C. majority 5,600 (11.40%)
0.31% swing Lab. to C.
(1997: C. maj. 6,039 (10.77%))

WARLEY
E. 58,071 T. 31,415 (54.10%) Lab. hold
*Rt. Hon. J. Spellar, Lab.   19,007
Mark Pritchard, C.   7,157
Ron Cockings, LD   3,315
Harbhajan Dardi, Soc. Lab.   1,936
Lab. majority 11,850 (37.72%)
1.00% swing Lab. to C.
(1997: Lab. maj. 15,451 (39.73%))

WARRINGTON NORTH
E. 72,445 T. 38,910 (53.71%) Lab. hold
*Ms Helen Jones, Lab.   24,026
James Usher, C.   8,870
Roy Smith, LD   5,232
Jack Kirkham, UK Ind.   782
Lab. majority 15,156 (38.95%)
0.43% swing C. to Lab.
(1997: Lab. maj. 19,527 (38.10%))

WARRINGTON SOUTH
E. 74,283 T. 45,487 (61.23%) Lab. hold
*Ms Helen Southworth, Lab.   22,409
Ms Caroline Mosley, C.   15,022
Roger Barlow, LD   7,419
Mrs Joan Kelley, UK Ind.   637
Lab. majority 7,387 (16.24%)
1.69% swing Lab. to C.
(1997: Lab. maj. 10,807 (19.62%))

WARWICK & LEAMINGTON
E. 81,405 T. 53,539 (65.77%) Lab. hold
*James Plaskitt, Lab.   26,108
David Campbell Bannerman, C.   20,155
Ms Linda Forbes, LD   5,964
Ms Clare Kime, Soc. All.   664
Greville Warwick, UK Ind.   648
Lab. majority 5,953 (11.12%)
2.73% swing C. to Lab.
(1997: Lab. maj. 3,398 (5.65%))

WARWICKSHIRE NORTH
E. 73,828 T. 44,409 (60.15%) Lab. hold
*Mike O'Brien, Lab.   24,023
Geoff Parsons, C.   14,384
William Powell, LD   5,052
John Flynn, UK Ind.   950
Lab. majority 9,639 (21.71%)
2.76% swing Lab. to C.
(1997: Lab. maj. 14,767 (27.23%))

WATFORD
E. 75,724 T. 46,372 (61.24%) Lab. hold
*Ms Claire Ward, Lab.   20,992
Michael McManus, C.   15,437
Duncan Hames, LD   8,088
Ms Denise Kingsley, Green   900
Edmund Stewart-Mole, UK Ind.   535
Jon Berry, Soc. All.   420
Lab. majority 5,555 (11.98%)
0.75% swing C. to Lab.
(1997: Lab. maj. 5,792 (10.48%))

WAVENEY
E. 76,585 T. 47,167 (61.59%) Lab. hold
*Bob Blizzard, Lab.   23,914
Lee Scott, C.   15,361
David Young, LD   5,370
Brian Aylett, UK Ind.   1,097
Graham Elliot, Green   983
Rupert Mallin, Soc. All.   442
Lab. majority 8,553 (18.13%)
1.93% swing Lab. to C.
(1997: Lab. maj. 12,453 (21.99%))

WEALDEN
E. 83,066 T. 52,756 (63.51%) C. hold
Charles Hendry, C.   26,279
Steve Murphy, LD   12,507
Ms Kathy Fordham, Lab.   10,705
Keith Riddle, UK Ind.   1,539
Julian Salmon, Green   1,273
Cyril Thornton, Pensioner   453
C. majority 13,772 (26.11%)
1.03% swing LD to C.
(1997: C. maj. 14,204 (24.04%))

WEAVER VALE
E. 68,236 T. 39,271 (57.55%) Lab. hold
*Mike Hall, Lab.   20,611
Carl Cross, C.   10,974
Nigel Griffiths, LD   5,643
Michael Cooksley, Ind.   1,484
Jim Bradshaw, UK Ind.   559
Lab. majority 9,637 (24.54%)
1.65% swing C. to Lab.
(1997: Lab. maj. 13,448 (27.84%))

WELLINGBOROUGH
E. 77,389 T. 51,006 (65.91%) Lab. hold
*Paul Stinchcombe, Lab.   23,867
Peter Bone, C.   21,512
Peter Gaskell, LD   4,763
Anthony Ellwood, UK Ind.   864
Lab. majority 2,355 (4.62%)
2.14% swing C. to Lab.
(1997: Lab. maj. 187 (0.33%))

WELLS
E. 74,189 T. 51,314 (69.17%) C. hold
*Rt. Hon. D. Heathcoat-Amory, C. 22,462
Graham Oakes, LD   19,666
Andy Merryfield, Lab.   7,915
Steve Reed, UK Ind.   1,104
Colin Bex, Wessex Reg.   167
C. majority 2,796 (5.45%)
2.25% swing LD to C.
(1997: C. maj. 528 (0.94%))

WELWYN HATFIELD
E. 67,004 T. 42,821 (63.91%) Lab. hold
*Ms Melanie Johnson, Lab.   18,484
Grant Shapps, C.   17,288
Daniel Cooke, LD   6,021
Malcolm Biggs, UK Ind.   798
Ms Fiona Pinto, ProLife   230
Lab. majority 1,196 (2.79%)
3.89% swing Lab. to C.
(1997: Lab. maj. 5,595 (10.57%))

WENTWORTH
E. 64,033 T. 33,778 (52.75%) Lab. hold
*John Healey, Lab.   22,798
Mike Roberts, C.   6,349
David Wildgoose, LD   3,652
John Wilkinson, UK Ind.   979
Lab. majority 16,449 (48.70%)
4.32% swing Lab. to C.
(1997: Lab. maj. 23,959 (57.34%))

WEST BROMWICH EAST
E. 61,198 T. 32,664 (53.37%) Lab. hold
Tom Watson, Lab.   18,250
David MacFarlane, C.   8,487
Ian Garrett, LD   4,507
Steven Grey, UK Ind.   835
Sheera Johal, Soc. Lab.   585
Lab. majority 9,763 (29.89%)
1.43% swing Lab. to C.
(1997: Lab. maj. 13,584 (32.74%))

WEST BROMWICH WEST
E. 66,777 T. 31,840 (47.68%)
                        Lab. Co-op hold
*Adrian Bailey, Lab. Co-op   19,352
Mrs Karen Bissell, C.   7,997
Mrs Sadie Smith, LD   2,168
John Salvage, BNP   1,428
Kevin Walker, UK Ind.   499
Baghwant Singh, Soc. Lab.   396
Lab. Co-op majority 11,355
                        (35.66%)
(2000 Nov. by-election: Lab. maj.
3,232 (17.12%); 1997: Speaker
maj. 15,423 (42.03%))

WEST HAM
E. 59,828 T. 29,273 (48.93%) Lab. hold
*Tony Banks, Lab.   20,449
Syed Kamall, C.   4,804
Paul Fox, LD   2,166
Ms Jackie Chandler Oatts, Green   1,197
Gerard Batten, UK Ind.   657
Lab. majority 15,645 (53.45%)
2.24% swing Lab. to C.
(1997: Lab. maj. 19,494 (57.92%))

WESTBURY
E. 75,911 T. 50,628 (66.69%) C. hold
Dr Andrew Murrison, C.   21,299
David Vigar, LD   16,005
Ms Sarah Cardy, Lab.   10,847
Charles Booth-Jones, UK Ind.   1,261
Bob Gledhill, Green   1,216
C. majority 5,294 (10.46%)
0.12% swing C. to LD
(1997: C. maj. 6,068 (10.69%))

WESTMORLAND & LONSDALE
E. 70,637 T. 47,903 (67.82%)   C. hold
*Tim Collins, C.   22,486
Tim Farron, LD   19,339
John Bateson, Lab.   5,234
Robert Gibson, UK Ind.   552
Tim Bell, Ind.   292
C. majority 3,147 (6.57%)
1.17% swing C. to LD
(1997: C. maj. 4,521 (8.90%))

WESTON-SUPER-MARE
E. 74,343 T. 46,680 (62.79%)   LD hold
*Brian Cotter, LD   18,424
John Penrose, C.   18,086
Derek Kraft, Lab.   9,235
Bill Lukins, UK Ind.   650
John Peverelle, Ind.   206
Richard Sibley, Ind.   79
LD majority 338 (0.72%)
0.83% swing LD to C.
(1997: LD maj. 1,274 (2.39%))

WIGAN
E. 64,040 T. 33,591 (52.45%)   Lab. hold
*Neil Turner, Lab.   20,739
Mark Page, C.   6,996
Trevor Beswick, LD   4,970
Dave Lowe, Soc. All.   886
Lab. majority 13,743 (40.91%)
5.38% swing Lab. to C.
(1999 Sept. by-election: Lab. maj
6,729)
(1997: Lab. maj. 22,643 (51.67%))

WILTSHIRE NORTH
E. 79,524 T. 52,948 (66.58%)   C. hold
*James Gray, C.   24,090
Hugh Pym, LD   20,212
Ms Jo Garton, Lab.   7,556
Neil Dowdney, UK Ind.   1,090
C. majority 3,878 (7.32%)
0.67% swing LD to C.
(1997: C. maj. 3,475 (5.99%))

WIMBLEDON
E. 63,930 T. 41,109 (64.30%)   Lab. hold
*Roger Casale, Lab.   18,806
Stephen Hammond, C.   15,062
Martin Pierce, LD   5,341
Rajeev Thacker, Green   1,007
Roger Glencross, CPA   479
Ms Mariana Bell, UK Ind.   414
Lab. majority 3,744 (9.11%)
1.47% swing C. to Lab.
(1997: Lab. maj. 2,980 (6.17%))

WINCHESTER
E. 81,852 T. 59,158 (72.27%)   LD hold
*Mark Oaten, LD   32,282
Andrew Hayes, C.   22,648
Stephen Wyeth, Lab.   3,498
Ms Joan Martin, UK Ind.   664
Ms Henrietta Rouse, Wessex Reg.   66
LD majority 9,634 (16.29%)
8.14% swing LD to C.
(1997 Nov. by-election: LD maj
21,556 (39.64%))
(1997: LD maj. 2 (0.00%))

WINDSOR
E. 69,136 T. 42,110 (60.91%)   C. hold
*Michael Trend, C.   19,900
Nick Pinfield, LD   11,011
Mark Muller, Lab.   10,137
John Fagan, UK Ind.   1,062
C. majority 8,889 (21.11%)
0.79% swing LD to C.
(1997: C. maj. 9,917 (19.53%))

WIRRAL SOUTH
E. 60,653 T. 39,818 (65.65%)   Lab. hold
*Ben Chapman, Lab.   18,890
Anthony Millard, C.   13,841
Phillip Gilchrist, LD   7,087
Lab. majority 5,049 (12.68%)
0.94% swing Lab. to C.
(1997: Lab. maj. 7,004 (14.56%))

WIRRAL WEST
E. 62,294 T. 40,475 (64.97%)   Lab. hold
*Stephen Hesford, Lab.   19,105
Chris Lynch, C.   15,070
Simon Holbrook, LD   6,300
Lab. majority 4,035 (9.97%)
2.06% swing C. to Lab.
(1997: Lab. maj. 2,738 (5.84%))

WITNEY
E. 74,624 T. 49,203 (65.93%)   C. gain
David Cameron, C.   22,153
Michael Bartlet, Lab.   14,180
Gareth Epps, LD   10,000
Mark Stevenson, Green   1,100
Barry Beadle, Ind.   1,003
Kenneth Dukes, UK Ind.   767
C. majority 7,973 (16.20%)
1.87% swing Lab. to C.
(1997: C. maj. 7,028 (12.46%))

WOKING
E. 71,163 T. 42,910 (60.30%)   C. hold
*Humfrey Malins, C.   19,747
Alan Hilliar, LD   12,988
Sabir Hussain, Lab.   8,714
Michael Harvey, UK Ind.   1,461
C. majority 6,759 (15.75%)
2.30% swing LD to C.
(1997: C. maj. 5,678 (11.15%))

WOKINGHAM
E. 68,430 T. 43,848 (64.08%)   C. hold
*Rt. Hon. J. Redwood, C.   20,216
Dr Royce Longton, LD   14,222
Matthew Syed, Lab.   7,633
Franklin Carstairs, UK Ind.   897
Peter "Top Cat" Owen, Loony   880
C. majority 5,994 (13.67%)
2.51% swing C. to LD
(1997: C. maj. 9,365 (18.69%))

WOLVERHAMPTON NORTH EAST
E. 60,486 T. 31,494 (52.07%)
                          Lab. Co-op hold
*Ken Purchase, Lab. Co-op   18,984
Ms Maria Miller, C.   9,019
Steven Bourne, LD   2,494
Thomas McCartney, UK Ind.   997
Lab. Co-op majority 9,965
(31.64%)
0.14% swing C. to Lab. Co-op
(1997: Lab. maj. 12,987 (31.37%))

WOLVERHAMPTON SOUTH EAST
E. 53,931 T. 27,297 (50.61%)
                          Lab. Co-op hold
*Dennis Turner, Lab. Co-op   18,409
Adrian Pepper, C.   5,945
Peter Wild, LD   2,389
James Barry, NF   554
Lab. Co-op majority 12,464
(45.66%)
1.04% swing C. to Lab. Co-op
(1997: Lab. maj. 15,182 (43.58%))

WOLVERHAMPTON SOUTH WEST
E. 67,171 T. 40,897 (60.88%)   Lab. hold
Robert Marris, Lab.   19,735
David Chambers, C.   16,248
Mike Dixon, LD   3,425
Ms Wendy Walker, Green   805
Doug Hope, UK Ind.   684
Lab. majority 3,487 (8.53%)
0.97% swing Lab. to C.
(1997: Lab. maj. 5,118 (10.46%))

WOODSPRING
E. 71,023 T. 48,758 (68.65%)   C. hold
*Dr Liam Fox, C.   21,297
Chanel Stevens, Lab.   12,499
Colin Eldridge, LD   11,816
David Shopland, Ind.   1,412
Dr Richard Lawson, Green   1,282
Fraser Crean, UK Ind.   452
C. majority 8,798 (18.04%)
2.86% swing C. to Lab.
(1997: C. maj. 7,734 (14.08%))

WORCESTER
E. 71,255 T. 44,210 (62.04%)   Lab. hold
*Michael Foster, Lab.   21,478
Richard Adams, C.   15,712
Paul Chandler, LD   5,578
Richard Chamings, UK Ind.   1,442
Lab. majority 5,766 (13.04%)
0.67% swing Lab. to C.
(1997: Lab. maj. 7,425 (14.38%))

WORCESTERSHIRE MID
E. 71,985 T. 44,897 (62.37%)   C. hold
*Peter Luff, C.   22,937
David Bannister, Lab.   12,310
R. Woodthorpe-Browne, LD   8,420
Tony Eaves, UK Ind.   1,230
C. majority 10,627 (23.67%)
2.57% swing Lab. to C.
(1997: C. maj. 9,412 (18.52%))

WORCESTERSHIRE WEST
E. 66,769 T. 44,807 (67.11%)   C. hold
*Sir Michael Spicer, C.   20,597
Mike Hadley, LD   15,223
Waquar Azmi, Lab.   6,275
Ian Morris, UK Ind.   1,574
Malcolm Victory, Green   1,138
C. majority 5,374 (11.99%)
2.10% swing LD to C.
(1997: C. maj. 3,846 (7.80%))

WORKINGTON
E. 65,965 T. 41,822 (63.40%)   Lab. hold
Tony Cunningham, Lab.   23,209
Tim Stoddart, C.   12,359
Ian Francis, LD   5,214
John Peacock, LCA   1,040
Lab. majority 10,850 (25.94%)
6.93% swing Lab. to C.
(1997: Lab. maj. 19,656 (39.81%))

WORSLEY
E. 69,300 T. 35,363 (51.03%) Lab. hold
*Terry Lewis, Lab.   20,193
Tobias Ellwood, C.   8,406
Robert Bleakley, LD   6,188
Ms Dorothy Entwistle, Soc. Lab.   576
Lab. majority 11,787 (33.33%)
2.30% swing Lab. to C.
(1997: Lab. maj. 17,741 (37.93%))

WORTHING EAST & SHOREHAM
E. 71,890 T. 43,068 (59.91%) C. hold
*Tim Loughton, C.   18,608
Daniel Yates, Lab.   12,469
Paul Elgood, LD   9,876
Jim McCulloch, UK Ind.   1,195
Christopher Baldwin, LCA   920
C. majority 6,139 (14.25%)
1.14% swing C. to Lab.
(1997: C. maj. 5,098 (9.89%))

WORTHING WEST
E. 72,419 T. 43,209 (59.67%) C. hold
*Peter Bottomley, C.   20,508
James Walsh, LD   11,471
Alan Butcher, Lab.   9,270
Tim Cross, UK Ind.   1,960
C. majority 9,037 (20.91%)
2.96% swing LD to C.
(1997: C. maj. 7,713 (15.00%))

WREKIN, THE
E. 65,837 T. 41,490 (63.02%) Lab. hold
*Peter Bradley, Lab.   19,532
Jacob Rees-Mogg, C.   15,945
Ian Jenkins, LD   4,738
Denis Brookes, UK Ind.   1,275
Lab. majority 3,587 (8.65%)
0.98% swing C. to Lab.
(1997: Lab. maj. 3,025 (6.69%))

WYCOMBE
E. 74,647 T. 44,974 (60.25%) C. hold
Paul Goodman, C.   19,064
Chauhdry Shafique, Lab.   15,896
Ms Dee Tomlin, LD   7,658
Christopher Cooke, UK Ind.   1,059
John Laker, Green   1,057
David Fitton, Ind.   240
C. majority 3,168 (7.04%)
1.26% swing Lab. to C.
(1997: C. maj. 2,370 (4.53%))

WYRE FOREST
E. 72,152 T. 49,062 (68.00%) KHHC
                                            gain
Dr Richard Taylor, KHHC   28,487
*David Lock, Lab.   10,857
Mark Simpson, C.   9,350
James Millington, UK Ind.   368
KHHC majority 17,630 (35.93%)
(1997: Lab. maj. 6,946 (12.62%))

WYTHENSHAWE & SALE EAST
E. 72,127 T. 35,055 (48.60%) Lab. hold
*Paul Goggins, Lab.   21,032
Mrs Susan Fildes, C.   8,424
Ms Vanessa Tucker, LD   4,320
Lance Crookes, Green   869
Fred Shaw, Soc. Lab.   410
Lab. majority 12,608 (35.97%)
1.49% swing C. to Lab.
(1997: Lab. maj. 15,019 (32.99%))

YEOVIL
E. 75,977 T. 48,132 (63.35%) LD hold
David Laws, LD   21,266
Marco Forgione, C.   17,338
Joe Conway, Lab.   7,077
Neil Boxall, UK Ind.   1,131
Alex Begg, Green   786
Tony Prior, Lib.   534
LD majority 3,928 (8.16%)
6.47% swing LD to C.
(1997: LD maj. 11,403 (21.10%))

YORK, CITY OF
E. 80,431 T. 47,980 (59.65%) Lab. hold
*Hugh Bayley, Lab.   25,072
Michael McIntyre, C.   11,293
Andrew Waller, LD   8,519
Bill Shaw, Green   1,465
Frank Ormston, Soc. All.   674
Richard Bate, UK Ind.   576
Graham Cambridge, Loony   381
Lab. majority 13,779 (28.72%)
3.23% swing Lab. to C.
(1997: Lab. maj. 20,523 (35.17%))

YORKSHIRE EAST
E. 72,342 T. 43,314 (59.87%) C. hold
Rt. Hon. G. Knight, C.   19,861
Ms Tracey Simpson-Laing, Lab.   15,179
Ms Mary-Rose Hardy, LD   6,300
Trevor Pearson, UK Ind.   1,661
Paul Dessoy, Ind.   313
C. majority 4,682 (10.81%)
1.99% swing Lab. to C.
(1997: C. maj. 3,337 (6.82%))

WALES

ABERAVON
E. 49,660 T. 30,190 (60.79%) Lab. hold
Hywel Francis, Lab.   19,063
Ms Lisa Turnbull, PC   2,955
Chris Davies, LD   2,933
Ali Miraj, C.   2,296
Andrew Tutton, RP   1,960
Captain Beany, Bean   727
Mr Martin Chapman, Soc. All.   256
Lab. majority 16,108 (53.36%)
6.08% swing Lab. to PC
(1997: Lab. maj. 21,571 (59.98%))

ALYN & DEESIDE
E. 60,478 T. 35,421 (58.57%) Lab. hold
Mark Tami, Lab.   18,525
Mark Isherwood, C.   9,303
Derek Burnham, LD   4,585
Richard Coombs, PC   1,182
Klaus Armstrong-Braun, Green   881
William Crawford, UK Ind.   481
Max Cooksey, Ind.   253
Glyn Davies, Comm.   211
Lab. majority 9,222 (26.04%)
6.53% swing Lab. to C.
(1997: Lab. maj. 16,403 (39.10%))

BLAENAU GWENT
E. 53,353 T. 31,725 (59.46%) Lab. hold
*Llew Smith, Lab.   22,855
Adam Rykala, PC   3,542
Edward Townsend, LD   2,945
Huw Williams, C.   2,383
Lab. majority 19,313 (60.88%)
6.68% swing Lab. to PC
(1997: Lab. maj. 28,035 (70.74%))

BRECON & RADNORSHIRE
E. 52,247 T. 37,516 (71.81%) LD hold
Roger Williams, LD   13,824
Dr Felix Aubel, C.   13,073
Huw Irranca-Davis, Lab.   8,024
Brynach Parri, PC   1,301
Ian Mitchell, Ind.   762
Mrs Elizabeth Phillips, UK Ind.   452
Robert Nicholson, Ind.   80
LD majority 751 (2.00%)
4.94% swing LD to C.
(1997: LD maj. 5,097 (11.89%))

BRIDGEND
E. 61,496 T. 37,004 (60.17%) Lab. hold
*Win Griffiths, Lab.   19,422
Ms Tania Brisby, C.   9,377
Ms Jean Barraclough, LD   5,330
Ms Monica Mahoney, PC   2,652
Ms Sara Jeremy, ProLife   223
Lab. majority 10,045 (27.15%)
4.05% swing Lab. to C.
(1997: Lab. maj. 15,248 (35.24%))

CAERNARFON
E. 47,354 T. 29,053 (61.35%) PC hold
Hywel Williams, PC   12,894
Martin Eaglestone, Lab.   9,383
Ms Bronwen Naish, C.   4,403
Melab Owain, LD   1,823
Ifor Lloyd, UK Ind.   550
PC majority 3,511 (12.08%)
4.75% swing PC to Lab
(1997: PC maj. 7,449 (21.59%))

CAERPHILLY
E. 67,593 T. 38,831 (57.45%) Lab. hold
Wayne David, Lab.   22,597
Lindsay Whittle, PC   8,172
David Simmonds, C.   4,413
Rob Roffe, LD   3,649
Lab. majority 14,425 (37.15%)
10.49% swing Lab. to PC
(1997: Lab. maj. 25,839 (57.08%))

CARDIFF CENTRAL
E. 59,785 T. 34,842 (58.28%)
                              Lab. Co-op hold
*Jon Owen Jones, Lab. Co-op   13,451
Ms Jenny Willott, LD   12,792
Gregory Walker, C.   5,537
Richard Grigg, PC   1,680
Stephen Bartley, Green   661
Julian Goss, Soc. All.   283
Frank Hughes, UK Ind.   221
Ms Madeleine Jeremy, ProLife   217
Lab. Co-op majority 659 (1.89%)
8.43% swing Lab. Co-op to LD
(1997: Lab. maj. 7,923 (18.75%))

CARDIFF NORTH
E. 62,634 T. 43,240 (69.04%) Lab. hold
*Ms Julie Morgan, Lab.   19,845
Alastair Watson, C.   13,680
John Dixon, LD   6,631
Sion Jobbins, PC   2,471
Don Hulston, UK Ind.   613
Lab. majority 6,165 (14.26%)
1.25% swing Lab. to C.
(1997: Lab. maj. 8,126 (16.76%))

CARDIFF SOUTH & PENARTH   -
E. 62,125 T. 35,751 (57.55%)
                              Lab. Co-op hold
*Rt. Hon. A. Michael, Lab. Co-op 20,094
Ms Maureen Kelly Owen, C.   7,807
Dr Rodney Berman, LD   4,572
Ms Lila Haines, PC   1,983
Justin Callan, UK Ind.   501
Dave Bartlett, Soc. All.   427
Ms Anne Savoury, ProLife   367
Lab. Co-op majority 12,287 (34.37%)
0.81% swing C. to Lab. Co-op
(1997: Lab. maj. 13,881 (32.74%))

CARDIFF WEST
E. 58,348 T. 34,083 (58.41%) Lab. hold
Kevin Brennan, Lab.   18,594
Andrew Davies, C.   7,273
Ms Jacqui Gasson, LD   4,458
Delme Bowen, PC   3,296
Ms Joyce Jenking, UK Ind.   462
Lab. majority 11,321 (33.22%)
2.79% swing Lab. to C.
(1997: Lab. maj. 15,628 (38.80%))

CARMARTHEN EAST & DINEFWR
E. 54,035 T. 38,053 (70.42%) PC gain
Adam Price, PC   16,130
*Alan Williams, Lab.   13,540
David N Thomas, C.   4,912
Doiran Evans, LD   2,815
Mike Squires, UK Ind.   656
PC majority 2,590 (6.81%)
7.54% swing Lab. to PC
(1997: Lab. maj. 3,450 (8.27%))

CARMARTHEN WEST &
PEMBROKESHIRE SOUTH
E. 56,518 T. 36,916 (65.32%) Lab. hold
*Nick Ainger, Lab.   15,349
Robert Wilson, C.   10,811
Llyr Hughes Griffiths, PC   6,893
William Jeremy, LD   3,248
Ian Phillips, UK Ind.   537
Nick Turner, Customer   78
Lab. majority 4,538 (12.29%)
5.14% swing Lab. to C.
(1997: Lab. maj. 9,621 (22.57%))

CEREDIGION
E. 56,118 T. 34,606 (61.67%) PC hold
*Simon Thomas, PC   13,241
Mark Williams, LD   9,297
Paul Davies, C.   6,730
David Grace, Lab.   5,338
PC majority 3,944 (11.40%)
6.89% swing PC to LD
(2000 Feb. by-election: PC maj. 4,948
(19.74%); 1997: PC maj. 6,961
(17.33%))

CLWYD SOUTH
E. 53,680 T. 33,496 (62.40%) Lab. hold
*Martyn Jones, Lab.   17,217
Tom Biggins, C.   8,319
Dyfed Edwards, PC   3,982
David Griffiths, LD   3,426
Mrs Edwina Theunissen, UK Ind.   552
Lab. majority 8,898 (26.56%)
4.25% swing Lab. to C.
(1997: Lab. maj. 13,810 (35.07%))

CLWYD WEST
E. 53,960 T. 34,600 (64.12%) Lab. hold
*Gareth Thomas, Lab.   13,426
Jimmy James, C.   12,311
Elfed Williams, PC   4,453
Ms Bobbie Feeley, LD   3,934
Matthew Guest, UK Ind.   476
Lab. majority 1,115 (3.22%)
0.68% swing Lab. to C.
(1997: Lab. maj. 1,848 (4.59%))

CONWY
E. 54,751 T. 34,366 (62.77%) Lab. hold
*Mrs Betty Williams, Lab.   14,366
David Logan, C.   8,147
Ms Vicky Macdonald, LD   5,800
Ms Ann Owen, PC   5,665
Alan Barham, UK Ind.   388
Lab. majority 6,219 (18.10%)
3.66% swing C. to Lab
(1997: Lab. maj. 1,596 (3.84%))

CYNON VALLEY
E. 48,591 T. 26,958 (55.48%) Lab. hold
*Ms Ann Clwyd, Lab.   17,685
Steven Cornelius, PC   4,687
Ian Parry, LD   2,541
Julian Waters, C.   2,045
Lab. majority 12,998 (48.22%)
5.44% swing Lab. to PC
(1997: Lab. maj. 19,755 (59.10%))

DELYN
E. 54,732 T. 34,636 (63.28%) Lab. hold
*David Hanson, Lab.   17,825
Paul Brierley, C.   9,220
Tudor Jones, LD   5,329
Paul Rowlinson, PC   2,262
Lab. majority 8,605 (24.84%)
2.29% swing Lab. to C.
(1997: Lab. maj. 11,693 (29.42%))

GOWER
E. 58,943 T. 37,353 (63.37%) Lab. hold
*Martin Caton, Lab.   17,676
John Bushell, C.   10,281
Ms Sheila Waye, LD   4,507
Ms Sian Caiach, PC   3,865
Ms Tina Shrewsbury, Green   607
Darran Hickery, Soc. Lab.   417
Lab. majority 7,395 (19.80%)
5.11% swing Lab. to C.
(1997: Lab. maj. 13,007 (30.02%))

ISLWYN
E. 51,230 T. 31,691 (61.86%)
                              Lab. Co-op hold
*Don Touhig, Lab. Co-op   19,505
Kevin Etheridge, LD   4,196
Leigh Thomas, PC   3,767
Philip Howells, C.   2,543
Paul Taylor, Ind.   1,263
Ms Mary Millington, Soc. Lab.   417
Lab. Co-op majority 15,309 (48.31%)
8.71% swing Lab. Co-op to LD
(1997: Lab. maj. 23,931 (65.73%))

LLANELLI
E. 58,148 T. 36,198 (62.25%) Lab. hold
*Rt. Hon. D. Davies, Lab.   17,586
Dyfan Jones, PC   11,183
Simon Hayes, C.   3,442
Ken Rees, LD   3,065
Ms Jan Cliff, Green   515
John Willock, Soc. Lab.   407
Lab. majority 6,403 (17.69%)
10.62% swing Lab. to PC
(1997: Lab. maj. 16,039 (38.92%))

MEIRIONNYDD NANT CONWY
E. 33,175 T. 21,068 (63.51%) PC hold
*Elfyn Llwyd, PC   10,459
Ms Denise Idris Jones, Lab.   4,775
Ms Lisa Francis, C.   3,962
Dafydd Raw-Rees, LD   1,872
PC majority 5,684 (26.98%)
0.36% swing PC to Lab.
(1997: PC maj. 6,805 (27.69%))

MERTHYR TYDFIL & RHYMNEY
E. 55,368 T. 31,684 (57.22%) Lab. hold
Dai Havard, Lab.   19,574
Robert Hughes, PC   4,651
Keith Rogers, LD   2,385
Richard Cuming, C.   2,272
Jeff Edwards, Ind.   1,936
Ken Evans, Soc. Lab.   692
Anthony Lewis, ProLife   174
Lab. majority 14,923 (47.10%)
11.80% swing Lab. to PC
(1997: Lab. maj. 27,086 (69.20%))

MONMOUTH
E. 62,202 T. 44,462 (71.48%) Lab. hold
*Huw Edwards, Lab.   19,021
Roger Evans, C.   18,637
Neil Parker, LD   5,080
Marc Hubbard, PC   1,068
David Rowlands, UK Ind.   656
Lab. majority 384 (0.86%)
3.83% swing Lab. to C.
(1997: Lab. maj. 4,178 (8.52%))

MONTGOMERYSHIRE
E. 44,243 T. 28,983 (65.51%) LD hold
*Lembit Opik, LD   14,319
David Jones, C.   8,085
Paul Davies, Lab.   3,443
David Senior, PC   1,969
David William Rowlands, UK Ind.   786
Miss Ruth Davies, ProLife   210
Reg Taylor, Ind.   171
LD majority 6,234 (21.51%)
0.88% swing C. to LD
(1997: LD maj. 6,303 (19.74%))

NEATH
E. 56,107 T. 35,020 (62.42%) Lab. hold
*Rt. Hon. P. Hain, Lab.	21,253
Alun Llywelyn, PC	6,437
David Davies, LD	3,335
David Devine, C.	3,310
Huw Pudner, Soc. All.	483
Gerardo Brienza, ProLife	202

Lab. majority 14,816 (42.31%)
11.56% swing Lab. to PC
(1997: Lab. maj. 26,741 (64.84%))

NEWPORT EAST
E. 56,118 T. 31,282 (55.74%) Lab. hold
*Rt. Hon. A. Howarth, Lab.	17,120
Ian Oakley, C.	7,246
Alistair Cameron, LD	4,394
Madoc Batcup, PC	1,519
Ms Liz Screen, Soc. Lab.	420
Neal Reynolds, UK Ind.	410
Robert Griffiths, Comm.	173

Lab. majority 9,874 (31.56%)
2.36% swing Lab. to C.
(1997: Lab. maj. 13,523 (36.29%))

NEWPORT WEST
E. 59,742 T. 35,063 (58.69%) Lab. hold
*Paul Flynn, Lab.	18,489
Dr William Morgan, C.	9,185
Ms Veronica Watkins, LD	4,095
Anthony Salkeld, PC	2,510
Hugh Moelwyn-Hughes, UK Ind.	506
Terry Cavill, BNP	278

Lab. majority 9,304 (26.54%)
4.81% swing Lab. to C.
(1997: Lab. maj. 14,537 (36.16%))

OGMORE
E. 52,185 T. 30,353 (58.16%) Lab. hold
*Sir Ray Powell, Lab.	18,833
Ms Angela Pulman, PC	4,259
Ian Lewis, LD	3,878
Richard Hill, C.	3,383

Lab. majority 14,574 (48.02%)
9.46% swing Lab. to PC
(1997: Lab. maj. 24,447 (64.22%))

PONTYPRIDD
E. 66,105 T. 38,309 (57.95%) Lab. hold
*Dr Kim Howells, Lab.	22,963
Bleddyn Hancock, PC	5,279
Ms Prudence Dailey, C.	5,096
Eric Brooke, LD	4,152
Ms Sue Warry, UK Ind.	603
Joseph Biddulph, ProLife	216

Lab. majority 17,684 (46.16%)
5.61% swing Lab. to PC
(1997: Lab. maj. 23,129 (50.44%))

PRESELI PEMBROKESHIRE
E. 54,283 T. 36,777 (67.75%) Lab. hold
*Ms Jackie Lawrence, Lab.	15,206
Stephen Crabb, C.	12,260
Rhys Sinnet, PC	4,658
Alexander Dauncey, LD	3,882
Ms Trish Bowen, Soc. Lab.	452
Hugh Jones, UK Ind.	319

Lab. majority 2,946 (8.01%)
6.29% swing Lab. to C.
(1997: Lab. maj. 8,736 (20.60%))

RHONDDA
E. 56,059 T. 34,002 (60.65%) Lab. hold
Chris Bryant, Lab.	23,230
Ms Leanne Wood, PC	7,183
Peter Hobbins, C.	1,557
Gavin Cox, LD	1,525
Glyndwr Summers, Ind.	507

Lab. majority 16,047 (47.19%)
6.95% swing Lab. to PC
(1997: Lab. maj. 24,931 (61.09%))

SWANSEA EAST
E. 57,273 T. 30,072 (52.51%) Lab. hold
*Rt. Hon. D. Anderson, Lab.	19,612
John Ball, PC	3,464
Robert Speht, LD	3,064
Paul Morris, C.	3,026
Tony Young, Green	463
Tim Jenkins, UK Ind.	443

Lab. majority 16,148 (53.70%)
9.15% swing Lab. to PC
(1997: Lab. maj. 25,569 (66.12%))

SWANSEA WEST
E. 57,074 T. 32,100 (56.24%) Lab. hold
*Rt. Hon. A. Williams, Lab.	15,644
Ms Margaret Harper, C.	6,094
Mike Day, LD	5,313
Ian Titherington, PC	3,404
Richard Lewis, UK Ind.	653
Martyn Shrewsbury, Green	626
Alec Thraves, Soc. All.	366

Lab. majority 9,550 (29.75%)
2.99% swing Lab. to C.
(1997: Lab. maj. 14,459 (35.73%))

TORFAEN
E. 61,110 T. 35,242 (57.67%) Lab. hold
*Rt. Hon. P. Murphy, Lab.	21,883
Jason Evans, C.	5,603
Alan Masters, LD	3,936
Stephen Smith, PC	2,720
Mrs Brenda Vipass, UK Ind.	657
Steve Bell, Soc. All.	443

Lab. majority 16,280 (46.19%)
5.27% swing Lab. to C.
(1997: Lab. maj. 24,536 (56.74%))

VALE OF CLWYD
E. 51,247 T. 32,346 (63.12%) Lab. hold
*Chris Ruane, Lab.	16,179
Brendan Murphy, C.	10,418
Graham Rees, LD	3,058
John Penri Williams, PC	2,300
William Campbell, UK Ind.	391

Lab. majority 5,761 (17.81%)
2.54% swing Lab. to C.
(1997: Lab. maj. 8,955 (22.89%))

VALE OF GLAMORGAN
E. 67,071 T. 45,184 (67.37%) Lab. hold
*John Smith, Lab.	20,524
Lady Susan Inkin, C.	15,824
Dewi Smith, LD	5,521
Chris Franks, PC	2,867
Niall Warry, UK Ind.	448

Lab. majority 4,700 (10.40%)
4.57% swing Lab. to C.
(1997: Lab. maj. 10,532 (19.54%))

WREXHAM
E. 50,465 T. 30,048 (59.54%) Lab. hold
Ian Lucas, Lab.	15,934
Ms Felicity Elphick, C.	6,746
Ron Davies, LD	5,153
Malcolm Evans, PC	1,783
Mrs Jane Brookes, UK Ind.	432

Lab. majority 9,188 (30.58%)
0.86% swing Lab. to C.
(1997: Lab. maj. 11,762 (32.30%))

YNYS MON
E. 53,117 T. 34,018 (64.04%) Lab. gain
Albert Owen, Lab.	11,906
Eilian Williams, PC	11,106
Albie Fox, C.	7,653
Nick Bennett, LD	2,772
Francis Wykes, UK Ind.	359
Ms Nona Donald, Ind.	222

Lab. majority 800 (2.35%)
4.28% swing PC to Lab
(1997: PC maj. 2,481 (6.21%))

SCOTLAND

ABERDEEN CENTRAL
E. 50,098 T. 26,429 (52.75%) Lab. hold
*Frank Doran, Lab.   12,025
Wayne Gault, SNP   5,379
Ms Eleanor Anderson, LD   4,547
Stewart Whyte, C.   3,761
Andy Cumbers, SSP   717
Lab. majority 6,646 (25.15%)
4.24% swing Lab. to SNP
(1997: Lab. maj. 10,801 (30.32%))

ABERDEEN NORTH
E. 52,746 T. 30,357 (57.55%) Lab. hold
*Malcolm Savidge, Lab.   13,157
Dr Allan Alasdair, SNP   8,708
Jim Donaldson, LD   4,991
Richard Cowling, C.   3,047
Ms Shona Forman, SSP   454
Lab. majority 4,449 (14.66%)
5.70% swing Lab. to SNP
(1997: Lab. maj. 10,010 (26.06%))

ABERDEEN SOUTH
E. 58,907 T. 36,890 (62.62%) Lab. hold
*Ms Anne Begg, Lab.   14,696
Ian Yuill, LD   10,308
Moray Macdonald, C.   7,098
Ian Angus, SNP   4,293
David Watt, SSP   495
Lab. majority 4,388 (11.89%)
2.13% swing LD to Lab.
(1997: Lab. maj. 3,365 (7.64%))

ABERDEENSHIRE WEST & KINCARDINE
E. 61,180 T. 37,914 (61.97%) LD hold
*Sir Robert Smith, LD   16,507
Tom Kerr, C.   11,686
Kevin Hutchens, Lab.   4,669
John Green, SNP   4,634
Alan Manley, SSP   418
LD majority 4,821 (12.72%)
3.28% swing C. to LD
(1997: LD maj. 2,662 (6.16%))

AIRDRIE & SHOTTS
E. 58,349 T. 31,736 (54.39%) Lab. hold
*Rt. Hon. Ms H. Liddell, Lab.   18,478
Ms Alison Lindsay, SNP   6,138
John Love, LD   2,376
Gordon McIntosh, C.   1,960
Ms Mary Dempsey, Scot. U.   1,439
Kenny McGuigan, SSP   1,171
Chris Herriot, Soc. Lab.   174
Lab. majority 12,340 (38.88%)
0.73% swing SNP to Lab.
(1997: Lab. maj. 15,412 (37.42%))

ANGUS
E. 59,004 T. 35,013 (59.34%) SNP hold
Michael Weir, SNP   12,347
Marcus Booth, C.   8,736
Ian McFatridge, Lab.   8,183
Peter Nield, LD   5,015
Bruce Wallace, SSP   732
SNP majority 3,611 (10.31%)
6.67% swing SNP to C.
(1997: SNP maj. 10,189 (23.66%))

ARGYLL & BUTE
E. 49,175 T. 30,957 (62.95%) LD hold
Alan Reid, LD   9,245
Hugh Raven, Lab.   7,592
David Petrie, C.   6,436
Ms Agnes Samuel, SNP   6,433
Des Divers, SSP   1,251
LD majority 1,653 (5.34%)
9.60% swing LD to Lab.
(1997: LD maj. 6,081 (17.03%))

AYR
E. 55,630 T. 38,560 (69.32%) Lab. hold
*Ms Sandra Osborne, Lab.   16,801
Phil Gallie, C.   14,256
Jim Mather, SNP   4,621
Stuart Ritchie, LD   2,089
James Stewart, SSP   692
Joseph Smith, UK Ind.   101
Lab. majority 2,545 (6.60%)
4.01% swing Lab. to C.
(1997: Lab. maj. 6,543 (14.62%))

BANFF & BUCHAN
E. 56,496 T. 30,806 (54.53%) SNP hold
*Alex Salmond, SNP   16,710
Alexander Wallace, C.   6,207
Edward Harris, Lab.   4,363
Douglas Herbison, LD   2,769
Ms Alice Rowan, SSP   447
Eric Davidson, UK Ind.   310
SNP majority 10,503 (34.09%)
1.06% swing C. to SNP
(1997: SNP maj. 12,845 (31.97%))

CAITHNESS, SUTHERLAND & EASTER ROSS
E. 41,225 T. 24,867 (60.32%) LD hold
Viscount Thurso, LD   9,041
Michael Meighan, Lab.   6,297
John Macadam, SNP   5,273
Robert Rowantree, C.   3,513
Ms Karn Mabon, SSP   544
Gordon Campbell, Ind.   199
LD majority 2,744 (11.03%)
1.64% swing Lab. to LD
(1997: LD maj. 2,259 (7.75%))

CARRICK, CUMNOCK & DOON VALLEY
E. 64,919 T. 40,107 (61.78%)
                              Lab. Co-op hold
*George Foulkes, Lab. Co-op   22,174
Gordon Miller, C.   7,318
Tom Wilson, SNP   6,258
Ms Amy Rogers, LD   2,932
Ms Amanda McFarlane, SSP   1,058
James McDaid, Soc. Lab.   367
Lab. Co-op majority 14,856 (37.04%)
2.90% swing Lab. Co-op to C.
(1997: Lab. maj. 21,062 (42.84%))

CLYDEBANK & MILNGAVIE
E. 52,534 T. 32,491 (61.85%) Lab. hold
*Tony Worthington, Lab.   17,249
Jim Yuill, SNP   6,525
Rod Ackland, LD   3,909
Dr Catherine Pickering, C.   3,514
Ms Dawn Brennan, SSP   1,294
Lab. majority 10,724 (33.01%)
0.54% swing Lab. to SNP
(1997: Lab. maj. 13,320 (34.08%))

CLYDESDALE
E. 64,423 T. 38,222 (59.33%) Lab. hold
*Jimmy Hood, Lab.   17,822
Jim Wright, SNP   10,028
Kevin Newton, C.   5,034
Ms Moira Craig, LD   4,111
Paul Cockshott, SSP   974
Donald MacKay, UK Ind.   253
Lab. majority 7,794 (20.39%)
5.01% swing Lab. to SNP
(1997: Lab. maj. 13,809 (30.41%))

COATBRIDGE & CHRYSTON
E. 52,178 T. 30,311 (58.09%) Lab. hold
*Rt. Hon. T. Clarke, Lab.   19,807
Peter Kearney, SNP   4,493
Alistair Tough, LD   2,293
Patrick Ross-Taylor, C.   2,171
Ms Lynne Sheridan, SSP   1,547
Lab. majority 15,314 (50.52%)
0.39% swing Lab. to SNP
(1997: Lab. maj. 19,295 (51.30%))

CUMBERNAULD & KILSYTH
E. 49,739 T. 29,699 (59.71%) Lab. hold
*Ms Rosemary McKenna, Lab.   16,144
David McGlashan, SNP   8,624
John O'Donnell, LD   1,934
Ms Alison Ross, C.   1,460
Kenny McEwan, SSP   1,287
Thomas Taylor, Scot. Ref.   250
Lab. majority 7,520 (25.32%)
2.78% swing Lab. to SNP
(1997: Lab. maj. 11,128 (30.89%))

CUNNINGHAME NORTH
E. 54,993 T. 33,816 (61.49%) Lab. hold
*Brian Wilson, Lab.   15,571
Campbell Martin, SNP   7,173
Richard Wilkinson, C.   6,666
Ross Chmiel, LD   3,060
Sean Scott, SSP   964
Ms Louise McDaid, Soc. Lab.   382
Lab. majority 8,398 (24.83%)
3.51% swing Lab. to SNP
(1997: Lab. maj. 11,039 (26.84%))

CUNNINGHAME SOUTH
E. 49,982 T. 28,009 (56.04%) Lab. hold
*Brian Donohoe, Lab.   16,424
Bill Kidd, SNP   5,194
Mrs Pam Paterson, C.   2,682
John Boyd, LD   2,094
Ms Rosemary Byrne, SSP   1,233
Bobby Cochrane, Soc. Lab.   382
Lab. majority 11,230 (40.09%)
0.93% swing Lab. to SNP
(1997: Lab. maj. 14,869 (41.95%))

DUMBARTON
E. 56,267 T. 33,994 (60.42%)
                              Lab. Co-op hold
*John McFall, Lab. Co-op   16,151
Iain Robertson, SNP   6,576
Eric Thompson, LD   5,265
Peter Ramsay, C.   4,648
Les Robertson, SSP   1,354
Lab. Co-op majority 9,575 (28.17%)
0.89% swing SNP to Lab. Co-op
(1997: Lab. maj. 10,883 (26.38%))

DUMFRIES
E. 62,931 T. 42,586 (67.67%) Lab. hold
*Russell Brow, Lab. 20,830
John Charteris, C. 11,996
John Ross Scott, LD 4,955
Gerry Fisher, SNP 4,103
John Dennis, SSP 702
Lab. majority 8,834 (20.74%)
0.64% swing C. to Lab.
(1997: Lab. maj. 9,643 (19.47%))

DUNDEE EAST
E. 56,535 T. 32,358 (57.24%) Lab. hold
Iain Luke, Lab. 14,635
Stewart Hosie, SNP 10,160
Alan Donnelly, C. 3,900
Raymond Lawrie, LD 2,784
Harvey Duke, SSP 879
Lab. majority 4,475 (13.83%)
5.38% swing Lab. to SNP
(1997: Lab. maj. 9,961 (24.58%))

DUNDEE WEST
E. 53,760 T. 29,242 (54.39%) Lab. hold
*Ernie Ross, Lab. 14,787
Gordon Archer, SNP 7,987
Ian Hail, C. 2,656
Ms Elizabeth Dick, LD 2,620
Jim McFarlane, SSP 1,192
Lab. majority 6,800 (23.25%)
3.65% swing Lab. to SNP
(1997: Lab. maj. 11,859 (30.56%))

DUNFERMLINE EAST
E. 52,811 T. 30,086 (56.97%) Lab. hold
*Rt. Hon. G. Brown, Lab. 19,487
John Mellon, SNP 4,424
Stuart Randall, C. 2,838
John Mainland, LD 2,281
Andy Jackson, SSP 770
Tom Dunsmore, UK Ind. 286
Lab. majority 15,063 (50.07%)
0.60% swing Lab. to SNP
(1997: Lab. maj. 18,751 (51.26%))

DUNFERMLINE WEST
E. 54,293 T. 30,975 (57.05%) Lab. hold
*Ms Rachel Squire, Lab. 16,370
Brian Goodall, SNP 5,390
Russell McPhate, LD 4,832
James Mackie, C. 3,166
Ms Kate Stewart, SSP 746
Alastair Harper, UK Ind. 471
Lab. majority 10,980 (35.45%)
0.77% swing SNP to Lab.
(1997: Lab. maj. 12,354 (33.91%))

EAST KILBRIDE
E. 66,572 T. 41,690 (62.62%) Lab. hold
*Rt. Hon. A. Ingram, Lab. 22,205
Archie Buchanan, SNP 9,450
Ewan Hawthorn, LD 4,278
Mrs Margaret McCulloch, C. 4,238
David Stevenson, SSP 1,519
Lab. majority 12,755 (30.59%)
2.52% swing Lab. to SNP
(1997: Lab. maj. 17,384 (35.63%))

EAST LOTHIAN
E. 58,987 T. 36,871 (62.51%) Lab. hold
Mrs Anne Picking, Lab. 17,407
Hamish Mair, C. 6,577
Ms Judy Hayman, LD 6,506
Ms Hilary Brown, SNP 5,381
Derrick White, SSP 624
Jake Herriot, Soc. Lab. 376
Lab. majority 10,830 (29.37%)
1.68% swing Lab. to C.
(1997: Lab. maj. 14,221 (32.74%))

EASTWOOD
E. 68,378 T. 48,368 (70.74%) Lab. hold
*Jim Murphy, Lab. 23,036
Raymond Robertson, C. 13,895
Allan Steele, LD 6,239
Stewart Maxwell, SNP 4,137
Peter Murray, SSP 814
Dr Manar Tayan, Ind. 247
Lab. majority 9,141 (18.90%)
6.35% swing C. to Lab.
(1997: Lab. maj. 3,236 (6.19%))

EDINBURGH CENTRAL
E. 66,089 T. 34,390 (52.04%) Lab. hold
*Rt. Hon. A. Darling, Lab. 14,495
Andrew Myles, LD 6,353
Alastair Orr, C. 5,643
Dr Ian McKee, SNP 4,832
Graeme Farmer, Green 1,809
Kevin Williamson, SSP 1,258
Lab. majority 8,142 (23.68%)
5.15% swing Lab. to LD
(1997: Lab. maj. 11,070 (25.90%))

EDINBURGH EAST & MUSSELBURGH
E. 59,241 T. 34,454 (58.16%) Lab. hold
*Rt. Hon. Dr G. Strang, Lab. 18,124
Rob Munn, SNP 5,956
Gary Peacock, LD 4,981
Peter Finnie, C. 3,906
Derek Durkin, SSP 1,487
Lab. majority 12,168 (35.32%)
0.41% swing SNP to Lab.
(1997: Lab. maj. 14,530 (34.50%))

EDINBURGH NORTH & LEITH
E. 62,475 T. 33,234 (53.20%) Lab. hold
Mark Lazarowicz, Lab. 15,271
Sebastian Tombs, LD 6,454
Ms Kaukab Stewart, SNP 5,290
Iain Mitchell, C. 4,626
Ms Catriona Grant, SSP 1,334
Don Jacobsen, Soc. Lab. 259
Lab. majority 8,817 (26.53%)
3.67% swing Lab. to LD
(1997: Lab. maj. 10,978 (26.81%))

EDINBURGH PENTLANDS
E. 59,841 T. 38,932 (65.06%) Lab. hold
*Dr Lynda Clark, Lab. 15,797
Sir Malcolm Rifkind, C. 14,055
David Walker, LD 4,210
Stewart Gibb, SNP 4,210
James Mearns, SSP 555
William McMurdo, UK Ind. 105
Lab. majority 1,742 (4.47%)
3.08% swing Lab. to C.
(1997: Lab. maj. 4,862 (10.63%))

EDINBURGH SOUTH
E. 64,012 T. 37,166 (58.06%) Lab. hold
*Nigel Griffiths, Lab. 15,671
Ms Marilyne MacLaren, LD 10,172
Geoffrey Buchan, C. 6,172
Ms Heather Williams, SNP 3,683
Colin Fox, SSP 933
Ms Linda Hendry, LCA 535
Lab. majority 5,499 (14.80%)
7.19% swing Lab. to LD
(1997: Lab. maj. 11,452 (25.54%))

EDINBURGH WEST
E. 61,895 T. 39,478 (63.78%) LD hold
John Barrett, LD 16,719
Ms Elspeth Alexandra, Lab. 9,130
Iain Whyte, C. 8,894
Alyn Smith, SNP 4,047
Bill Scott, SSP 688
LD majority 7,589 (19.22%)
2.59% swing LD to Lab.
(1997: LD maj. 7,253 (15.22%))

FALKIRK EAST
E. 57,633 T. 33,702 (58.48%) Lab. hold
*Michael Connarty, Lab. 18,536
Ms Isabel Hutton, SNP 7,824
Bill Stevenson, C. 3,252
Ms Karen Utting, LD 2,992
Tony Weir, SSP 725
Raymond Stead, Soc. Lab. 373
Lab. majority 10,712 (31.78%)
0.20% swing Lab. to SNP
(1997: Lab. maj. 13,385 (32.18%))

FALKIRK WEST
E. 53,583 T. 30,891 (57.65%) Lab. hold
*Eric Joyce, Lab. 16,022
David Kerr, SNP 7,490
Simon Murray, C. 2,321
Hugh O'Donnell, LD 2,203
William Buchanan, Ind. 1,464
Ms Mhairi McAlpine, SSP 707
Hugh Lynch, Ind. 490
Ronnie Forbes, Soc. Lab. 194
Lab. majority 8,532 (27.62%)
4.15% swing Lab. to SNP
(2000 Dec. by-election: Lab. maj.
705 (3.61%))
(1997: Lab. maj. 13,783 (35.92%))

FIFE CENTRAL
E. 59,597 T. 32,512 (54.55%) Lab. hold
John MacDougall, Lab. 18,310
David Alexander, SNP 8,235
Ms Elizabeth Riches, LD 2,775
Jeremy Balfour, C. 2,351
Ms Morag Balfour, SSP 841
Lab. majority 10,075 (30.99%)
1.33% swing Lab. to SNP
(1997: Lab. maj. 13,713 (33.64%))

FIFE NORTH EAST
E. 61,900 T. 34,692 (56.05%) LD hold
*Rt. Hon. M. Campbell, LD 17,926
Mike Scott-Hayward, C. 8,190
Ms Claire Brennan, Lab. 3,950
Ms Kris Murray-Browne, SNP 3,596
Keith White, SSP 610
Mrs Leslie Von Goetz, LCA 420
LD majority 9,736 (28.06%)
1.66% swing C. to LD
(1997: LD maj. 10,356 (24.75%))

GALLOWAY & UPPER NITHSDALE
E. 52,756 T. 35,914 (68.08%)   C. gain
Peter Duncan, C.   12,222
Malcolm Fleming, SNP   12,148
Thomas Sloan, Lab.   7,258
Neil Wallace, LD   3,698
Andy Harvey, SSP   588
C. majority 74 (0.21%)
6.80% swing SNP to C.
(1997: SNP maj. 5,624 (13.39%))

GLASGOW ANNIESLAND
E. 53,290 T. 26,722 (50.14%) Lab. hold
*John Robertson, Lab.   15,102
Grant Thoms, SNP   4,048
Christopher McGinty, LD   3,244
Stewart Connell, C.   2,651
Charlie McCarthy, SSP   1,486
MsKatherineMcGavigan,Soc.Lab.   191
Lab. majority 11,054 (41.37%)
1.68% swing Lab. to SNP
(2000 Nov. by-election: Lab. maj.
   6,337 (31.35%))
(1997: Lab. maj. 15,154 (44.73%))

GLASGOW BAILLIESTON
E. 49,268 T. 23,261 (47.21%) Lab. hold
*Jimmy Wray, Lab.   14,200
Lachlan McNeill, SNP   4,361
David Comrie, C.   1,580
Jim McVicar, SSP   1,569
Charles Dundas, LD   1,551
Lab. majority 9,839 (42.30%)
2.15% swing Lab. to SNP
(1997: Lab. maj. 14,840 (46.59%))

GLASGOW CATHCART
E. 52,094 T. 27,386 (52.57%) Lab. hold
Tom Harris, Lab.   14,902
Mrs Josephine Docherty, SNP   4,086
Richard Cook, C.   3,662
Tom Henery, LD   3,006
Ronnie Stevenson, SSP   1,730
Lab. majority 10,816 (39.49%)
1.80% swing SNP to Lab.
(1997: Lab. maj. 12,245 (35.90%))

GLASGOW GOVAN
E. 54,068 T. 25,284 (46.76%) Lab. hold
*Mohammad Sarwar, Lab.   12,464
Ms Karen Neary, SNP   6,064
Bob Stewart, LD   2,815
Mark Menzies, C.   2,167
Willie McGartland, SSP   1,531
John Foster, Comm.   174
Badar Mirza, Ind.   69
Lab. majority 6,400 (25.31%)
8.14% swing SNP to Lab.
(1997: Lab. maj. 2,914 (9.04%))

GLASGOW KELVIN
E. 61,534 T. 26,802 (43.56%) Lab. hold
*George Galloway, Lab.   12,014
Ms Tamsin Mayberry, LD   4,754
Frank Rankin, SNP   4,513
Miss Davina Rankin, C.   2,388
Ms Heather Ritchie, SSP   1,847
Tim Shand, Green   1,286
Lab. majority 7,260 (27.09%)
4.85% swing Lab. to LD
(1997: Lab. maj. 9,665 (29.60%))

GLASGOW MARYHILL
E. 55,431 T. 22,231 (40.11%) Lab. hold
Ms Ann McKechin, Lab.   13,420
Alex Dingwall, SNP   3,532
Stuart Callison, LD   2,372
Gordon Scott, SSP   1,745
Gawain Towler, C.   1,162
Lab. majority 9,888 (44.48%)
1.76% swing Lab. to SNP
(1997: Lab. maj. 14,264 (47.99%))

GLASGOW POLLOK
E. 49,201 T. 25,277 (51.37%)
                        Lab. Co-op hold
*Ian Davidson, Lab. Co-op   15,497
David Ritchie, SNP   4,229
Keith Baldssara, SSP   2,522
Ms Isabel Nelson, LD   1,612
Rory O'Brien, C.   1,417
Lab. Co-op majority 11,268
   (44.58%)
1.27% swing SNP to Lab. Co-op

GLASGOW RUTHERGLEN
E. 51,855 T. 29,213 (56.34%)
                        Lab. Co-op hold
*Tommy McAvoy, Lab. Co-op   16,760
Ms Anne McLaughlin, SNP   4,135
David Jackson, LD   3,689
Malcolm Macaskill, C.   3,301
Bill Bonnar, SSP   1,328
Lab. Co-op majority 12,625 (43.22%)
0.48% swing SNP to Lab. Co-op
(1997: Lab. maj. 15,007 (42.25%))

GLASGOW SHETTLESTON
E. 51,557 T. 20,465 (39.69%) Lab. hold
*David Marshall, Lab.   13,235
Jim Byrne, SNP   3,417
Ms Rosie Kane, SSP   1,396
Lewis Hutton, LD   1,105
Campbell Murdoch, C.   1,082
Murdo Ritchie, Soc. Lab.   230
Lab. majority 9,818 (47.97%)
5.60% swing Lab. to SNP
(1997: Lab. maj. 15,868 (59.18%))

GLASGOW SPRINGBURN
E. 55,192 T. 24,104 (43.67%)
                            Speaker hold
*Rt. Hon. M. Martin, Speaker   16,053
Sandy Bain, SNP   4,675
Ms Carolyn Leckie, SSP   1,879
Daniel Houston, Scot. U.   1,289
Richard Silvester, Ind.   208
Speaker majority 11,378 (47.20%)
(1997: Lab. maj. 17,326 (54.87%))

GORDON
E. 59,996 T. 35,001 (58.34%) LD hold
*Malcolm Bruce, LD   15,928
Mrs Nanette Milne, C.   8,049
Mrs Rhona Kemp, SNP   5,760
Ellis Thorpe, Lab.   4,730
John Sangster, SSP   534
LD majority 7,879 (22.51%)
2.97% swing C. to LD
(1997: LD maj. 6,997 (16.57%))

GREENOCK & INVERCLYDE
E. 47,884 T. 28,419 (59.35%) Lab. hold
David Cairns, Lab.   14,929
Chic Brodie, LD   5,039
Andrew Murie, SNP   4,248
Alistair Haw, C.   3,000
Davey Landels, SSP   1,203
Lab. majority 9,890 (34.80%)
3.77% swing Lab. to LD
(1997: Lab. maj. 13,040 (37.59%))

HAMILTON NORTH & BELLSHILL
E. 53,539 T. 30,404 (56.79%) Lab. hold
*Rt. Hon. Dr J. Reid, Lab.   18,786
Chris Stephens, SNP   5,225
Bill Frain Bell, C.   2,649
Keith Legg, LD   2,360
Ms Shareen Blackall, SSP   1,189
Steve Mayes, Soc. Lab.   195
Lab. majority 13,561 (44.60%)
0.16% swing Lab. to SNP
(1997: Lab. maj. 17,067 (44.92%))

HAMILTON SOUTH
E. 46,665 T. 26,750 (57.32%) Lab. hold
*Bill Tynan, Lab.   15,965
John Wilson, SNP   5,190
John Oswald, LD   2,381
Neil Richardson, C.   1,876
Ms Gena Mitchell, SSP   1,187
Ms Janice Murdoch, UK Ind.   151
Lab. majority 10,775 (40.28%)
3.85% swing Lab. to SNP
1999 Sep. by-election: Lab. maj
   556 (2.86%)
(1997: Lab. maj. 15,878 (47.98%))

INVERNESS EAST, NAIRN &
LOCHABER
E. 67,139 T. 42,461 (63.24%) Lab. hold
*David Stewart, Lab.   15,605
Angus MacNeil, SNP   10,889
Ms Patsy Kenton, LD   9,420
Richard Jenkins, C.   5,653
Steve Arnott, SSP   894
Lab. majority 4,716 (11.11%)
3.10% swing SNP to Lab.
(1997: Lab. maj. 2,339 (4.90%))

KILMARNOCK & LOUDOUN
E. 61,049 T. 37,665 (61.70%) Lab. hold
*Des Browne, Lab.   19,926
John Brady, SNP   9,592
Donald Reece, C.   3,943
John Stewart, LD   3,177
Jason Muir, SSP   1,027
Lab. majority 10,334 (27.44%)
6.07% swing SNP to Lab.
(1997: Lab. maj. 7,256 (15.30%))

KIRKCALDY
E. 51,559 T. 28,157 (54.61%)
                        Lab. Co-op hold
*Dr Lewis Moonie, Lab. Co-op   15,227
Ms Shirley-Anne Somerville, SNP   6,264
Scott Campbell, C.   3,013
Andrew Weston, LD   2,849
Dougie Kinnear, SSP   804
Lab. Co-op majority 8,963 (31.83%)
0.60% swing SNP to Lab. Co-op
(1997: Lab. maj. 10,710 (30.63%))

LINLITHGOW
E. 54,599 T. 31,655 (57.98%) Lab. hold
*Tam Dalyell, Lab.   17,207
Jim Sibbald, SNP   8,078
Gordon Lindhurst, C.   2,836
Martin Oliver, LD   2,628
Eddie Cornoch, SSP   695
Ms Helen Cronin, R & R Loony   211
Lab. majority 9,129 (28.84%)
0.75% swing SNP to Lab.
(1997: Lab. maj. 10,838 (27.33%))

LIVINGSTON
E. 64,850 T. 36,033 (55.56%) Lab. hold
*Rt. Hon. R. Cook, Lab.   19,108
Graham Sutherland, SNP   8,492
Gordon Mackenzie, LD   3,969
Ian Mowat, C.   2,995
Ms Wendy Milne, SSP   1,110
Robert Kingdon, UK Ind.   359
Lab. majority 10,616 (29.46%)
1.02% swing SNP to Lab.
(1997: Lab. maj. 11,747 (27.43%))

MIDLOTHIAN
E. 48,625 T. 28,724 (59.07%) Lab. hold
David Hamilton, Lab.   15,145
Ian Goldie, SNP   6,131
Ms Jacqueline Bell, LD   3,686
Robin Traquair, C.   2,748
Bob Goupillot, SSP   837
Terence Holden, ProLife   177
Lab. majority 9,014 (31.38%)
1.69% swing SNP to Lab.
(1997: Lab. maj. 9,870 (28.00%))

MORAY
E. 58,008 T. 33,223 (57.27%) SNP hold
Angus Robertson, SNP   10,076
Mrs Catriona Munro, Lab.   8,332
Frank Spencer-Nairn, C.   7,677
Ms Linda Gorn, LD   5,224
Ms Norma Anderson, SSP   821
Bill Jappy, Ind.   802
Nigel Kenyon, UK Ind.   291
SNP majority 1,744 (5.25%)
8.25% swing SNP to Lab.
(1997: SNP maj. 5,566 (14.00%))

MOTHERWELL & WISHAW
E. 52,418 T. 29,673 (56.61%) Lab. hold
*Frank Roy, Lab.   16,681
Jim McGuigan, SNP   5,725
Mark Nolan, C.   3,155
Iain Brown, LD   2,791
Stephen Smellie, SSP   1,260
Ms Claire Watt, Soc. Lab.   61
Lab. majority 10,956 (36.92%)
1.00% swing SNP to Lab.
(1997: Lab. maj. 12,791 (34.93%))

OCHIL
E. 57,554 T. 35,303 (61.34%) Lab. hold
*Martin O'Neill, Lab.   16,004
Keith Brown, SNP   10,655
Alasdair Campbell, C.   4,235
Paul Edie, LD   3,253
Ms Pauline Thompson, SSP   751
Flash Gordon Approaching,
Loony   405
Lab. majority 5,349 (15.15%)
2.26% swing SNP to Lab.
(1997: Lab. maj. 4,652 (10.63%))

ORKNEY & SHETLAND
E. 31,909 T. 16,733 (52.44%) LD hold
Alistair Carmichael, LD   6,919
Robert Mochrie, Lab.   3,444
John Firth, C.   3,121
John Mowat, SNP   2,473
Peter Andrews, SSP   776
LD majority 3,475 (20.77%)
6.48% swing LD to Lab.
(1997: LD maj. 6,968 (33.72%))

PAISLEY NORTH
E. 47,994 T. 27,153 (56.58%) Lab. hold
*Ms Irene Adams, Lab.   15,058
George Adam, SNP   5,737
Ms Jane Hook, LD   2,709
Craig Stevenson, C.   2,404
Jim Halfpenny, SSP   982
Robert Graham, ProLife   263
Lab. majority 9,321 (34.33%)
1.61% swing Lab. to SNP
(1997: Lab. maj. 12,814 (37.54%))

PAISLEY SOUTH
E. 53,351 T. 30,536 (57.24%) Lab. hold
*Douglas Alexander, Lab.   17,830
Brian Lawson, SNP   5,920
Brian O'Malley, LD   3,178
Andrew Cossar, C.   2,301
Ms Frances Curran, SSP   835
Ms Patricia Graham, ProLife   346
Terence O'Donnell, Ind.   126
Lab. majority 11,910 (39.00%)
2.44% swing SNP to Lab.
(1997 Nov. by-election: Lab. maj.
2,731)
(1997: Lab. maj. 12,750 (34.13%))

PERTH
E. 61,497 T. 37,816 (61.49%) SNP hold
Ms Annabelle Ewing, SNP   11,237
Miss Elizabeth Smith, C.   11,189
Ms Marion Dingwall, Lab.   9,638
Ms Vicki Harris, LD   4,853
Frank Byrne, SSP   899
SNP majority 48 (0.13%)
3.46% swing SNP to C.
(1997: SNP maj. 3,141 (7.05%))

RENFREWSHIRE WEST
E. 52,889 T. 33,497 (63.33%) Lab. gain
James Sheridan, Lab.   15,720
Ms Carol Puthucheary, SNP   7,145
David Sharpe, C.   5,522
Ms Clare Hamblen, LD   4,185
Ms Arlene Nunnery, SSP   925
Lab. majority 8,575 (25.60%)
2.77% swing SNP to Lab.
(1997: Lab. maj. 7,979 (20.05%))

ROSS, SKYE & INVERNESS WEST
E. 56,522 T. 34,812 (61.59%) LD hold
*Rt. Hon. C. Kennedy, LD   18,832
Donald Crichton, Lab.   5,880
Ms Jean Urquhart, SNP   4,901
Angus Laing, C.   3,096
Dr Eleanor Scott, Green   699
Stuart Topp, SSP   683
Philip Anderson, UK Ind.   456
James Crawford, Country   265
LD majority 12,952 (37.21%)
13.57% swing Lab. to LD
(1997: LD maj. 4,019 (10.06%))

ROXBURGH & BERWICKSHIRE
E. 47,059 T. 28,797 (61.19%) LD hold
*Archy Kirkwood, LD   14,044
George Turnbull, C.   6,533
Ms C. Maxwell-Stuart, Lab.   4,498
Roderick Campbell, SNP   2,806
Ms Amanda Millar, SSP   463
Peter Neilson, UK Ind.   453
LD majority 7,511 (26.08%)
1.73% swing C. to LD
(1997: LD maj. 7,906 (22.63%))

STIRLING
E. 53,097 T. 35,930 (67.67%) Lab. hold
*Ms Anne McGuire, Lab.   15,175
Geoff Mawdsley, C.   8,901
Ms Fiona Macaulay, SNP   5,877
Clive Freeman, LD   4,208
Dr Clarke Mullen, SSP   1,012
Mark Ruskell, Green   757
Lab. majority 6,274 (17.46%)
1.27% swing C. to Lab.
(1997: Lab. maj. 6,411 (14.93%))

STRATHKELVIN & BEARSDEN
E. 62,729 T. 41,486 (66.14%) Lab. hold
John Lyons, Lab.   19,250
Gordon Macdonald, LD   7,533
Calum Smith, SNP   6,675
Murray Roxburgh, C.   6,635
Willie Telfer, SSP   1,393
Lab. majority 11,717 (28.24%)
7.44% swing Lab. to LD
(1997: Lab. maj. 16,292 (32.77%))

TAYSIDE NORTH
E. 61,645 T. 38,517 (62.48%) SNP hold
Peter Wishart, SNP   15,441
Murdo Fraser, C.   12,158
Thomas Docherty, Lab.   5,715
Ms Julia Robertson, LD   4,363
Ms Rosie Adams, SSP   620
Ms Tina MacDonald, Ind.   220
SNP majority 3,283 (8.52%)
0.30% swing SNP to C.
(1997: SNP maj. 4,160 (9.13%))

TWEEDDALE, ETTRICK &
LAUDERDALE
E. 51,966 T. 33,217 (63.92%) LD hold
*Michael Moore, LD   14,035
Keith Geddes, Lab.   8,878
Andrew Brocklehurst, C.   5,118
Richard Thomson, SNP   4,108
Norman Lockhart, SSP   695
John Hein, Lib.   383
LD majority 5,157 (15.53%)
5.86% swing Lab. to LD
(1997: LD maj. 1,489 (3.81%))

WESTERN ISLES
E. 21,807 T. 13,159 (60.34%) Lab. hold
*Calum MacDonald, Lab.   5,924
Alasdair Nicholson, SNP   4,850
Douglas Taylor, C.   1,250
John Horne, LD   849
Ms Joanne Telfer, SSP   286
Lab. maj 1,074 (8.16%)
7.02% swing Lab. to SNP
(1997: Lab. maj. 3,576 (22.20%))

NORTHERN IRELAND

ANTRIM EAST
E. 60,897 T. 36,000 (59.12%)UUP hold

*Roy Beggs, UUP	13,101
Sammy Wilson, DUP	12,973
John Mathews, Alliance	4,483
Danny O'Connor, SDLP	2,641
Robert Mason, Ind.	1,092
Ms Jeanette Graffin, SF	903
Alan Greer, C.	807

UUP majority 128 (0.36%)
9.48% swing UUP to DUP
(1997: UUP maj. 6,389 (18.60%))

ANTRIM NORTH
E. 74,451 T. 49,217 (66.11%)DUP hold

*Revd Ian Paisley, DUP	24,539
Lexie Scott, UUP	10,315
Sean Farren, SDLP	8,283
John Kelly, SF	4,822
Miss Jayne Dunlop, Alliance	1,258

DUP majority 14,224 (28.90%)
3.01% swing UUP to DUP
(1997: DUP maj. 10,574 (22.89%))

ANTRIM SOUTH
E. 70,651 T. 44,158 (62.50%)UUP gain

David Burnside, UUP	16,366
*Revd Robert McCrea, DUP	15,355
Sean McKee, SDLP	5,336
Martin Meehan, SF	4,160
David Ford, Alliance	1,969
Norman Boyd, NI Unionist	972

UUP majority 1,011 (2.29%)
10.21% swing UUP to DUP
(2000 Sep. by-election: DUP maj. 822)
(1997: UUP maj. 16,611 (41.33%))

BELFAST EAST
E. 58,455 T. 36,829 (63.00%)DUP hold

*Peter Robinson, DUP	15,667
Tim Lemon, UUP	8,550
Dr David Alderdice, Alliance	5,832
David Ervine, PUP	3,669
Joe O'Donnell, SF	1,237
Ms Ciara Farren, SDLP	880
Terry Dick, C.	800
Joe Bell, WP	123
Rainbow George Weiss, Ind. Vote	71

DUP majority 7,117 (19.32%)
1.01% swing UUP to DUP
(1997: DUP maj. 6,754 (17.30%))

BELFAST NORTH
E. 60,941 T. 40,932 (67.17%)DUP gain

Nigel Dodds, DUP	16,718
Gerry Kelly, SF	10,331
Alban Maginness, SDLP	8,592
*Cecil Walker, UUP	4,904
Ms Marcella Delaney, WP	253
Rainbow George Weiss, Ind. Vote	134

DUP maj 6,387 (15.60%)
(1997: UUP maj. 13,024 (31.42%))

BELFAST SOUTH
E. 59,436 T. 37,952 (63.85%)UUP hold

*Revd M. Smyth, UUP	17,008
Dr Alasdair McDonnell, SDLP	11,609
Prof Monica McWilliams, Women's Co.	2,968
Alex Maskey, SF	2,894
Ms Geraldine Rice, Alliance	2,042
Ms Dawn Purvis, PUP	1,112
Paddy Lynn, WP	204
Rainbow George Weiss, Ind. Vote	115

UUP majority 5,399 (14.23%)
1.29% swing SDLP to UUP
(1997: UUP maj. 4,600 (11.65%))

BELFAST WEST
E. 59,617 T. 40,982 (68.74%)   SF hold

*Gerry Adams, SF	27,096
Alex Attwood, SDLP	7,754
The Revd Eric Smyth, DUP	2,641
Chris McGimpsey, UUP	2,541
John Lowry, WP	736
Mr David Kerr, Third	116
Rainbow George Weiss, Ind. Vote	98

SF majority 19,342 (47.20%)
14.98% swing SDLP to SF
(1997: SF maj. 7,909 (17.24%))

DOWN NORTH
E. 63,212 T. 37,189 (58.83%)UUP gain

Lady Sylvia Hermon, UUP	20,833
*Robert McCartney, UKU	13,509
Ms Marietta Farrell, SDLP	1,275
Julian Robertson, C.	815
Chris Carter, Ind.	444
Eamon McConvey, SF	313

UUP majority 7,324 (19.69%)
11.83% swing UKU to UUP
(1997: UKU maj. 1,449 (3.96%))

DOWN SOUTH
E. 73,519 T. 52,074 (70.83%)
SDLP hold

*Eddie McGrady, SDLP	24,136
Mick Murphy, SF	10,278
Dermot Nesbitt, UUP	9,173
Jim Wells, DUP	7,802
Ms Betty Campbell, Alliance	685

SDLP majority 13,858 (26.61%)
7.97% swing SDLP to SF
(1997: SDLP maj. 9,933 (20.08%))

FERMANAGH & SOUTH TYRONE
E. 66,640 T. 51,974 (77.99%)   SF gain

Ms Michelle Gildernew, SF	17,739
James Cooper, UUP	17,686
Tommy Gallagher, SDLP	9,706
Jim Dixon, Ind. UU	6,843

SF majority 53 (0.10%)
14.22% swing UUP to SF
(1997: UUP maj. 13,688 (28.34%))

FOYLE
E. 70,943 T. 48,879 (68.90%)
SDLP hold

*John Hume, SDLP	24,538
Mitchel McLaughlin, SF	12,988
William Hay, DUP	7,414
Andrew Davidson, UUP	3,360
Colm Cavanagh, Alliance	579

SDLP majority 11,550 (23.63%)
2.47% swing SDLP to SF
(1997: SDLP maj. 13,664 (28.57%))

LAGAN VALLEY
E. 72,671 T. 45,941 (63.22%)UUP hold

*Jeffrey Donaldson, UUP	25,966
Seamus Close, Alliance	7,624
Edwin Poots, DUP	6,164
Ms Patricia Lewsley, SDLP	3,462
Paul Butler, SF	2,725

UUP majority 18,342 (39.93%)
0.86% swing Alliance to UUP
(1997: UUP maj. 16,925 (38.20%))

LONDONDERRY EAST
E. 60,276 T. 39,869 (66.14%)DUP gain

Gregory Campbell, DUP	12,813
*William Ross, UUP	10,912
John Dallat, SDLP	8,298
Francie Brolly, SF	6,221
Mrs Yvonne Boyle, Alliance	1,625

DUP maj 1,901 (4.77%)
7.36% swing UUP to DUP
(1997: UUP maj. 3,794 (9.95%))

NEWRY & ARMAGH
E. 72,466 T. 55,621 (76.75%)   SDLP hold

*Seamus Mallon, SDLP	20,784
Conor Murphy, SF	17,209
Paul Berry, DUP	10,795
Mrs Sylvia McRoberts, UUP	6,833

SDLP majority 3,575 (6.43%)
7.75% swing SDLP to SF
(1997: SDLP maj. 4,889 (9.17%))

STRANGFORD
E. 72,192 T. 43,254 (59.92%)DUP hold

Mrs Iris Robinson, DUP	18,532
*David McNarry, UUP	17,422
Kieran McCarthy, Alliance	2,902
Danny McCarthy, SDLP	2,646
Liam Johnstone, SF	930
Cedric Wilson, NI Unionist	822

DUP majority 1,110 (2.57%)
8.32% swing UUP to DUP
(1997: UUP maj. 5,852 (14.07%))

TYRONE WEST
E. 60,739 T. 48,530 (79.90%)   SF gain

Pat Doherty, SF	19,814
*William Thompson, UUP	14,774
Ms Brid Rodgers, SDLP	13,942

SF majority 5,040 (10.39%)
7.05% swing UUP to SF
(1997: UUP maj. 1,161 (2.51%))

ULSTER MID
E. 61,390 T. 49,936 (81.34%)   SF hold

*Martin McGuinness, SF	25,502
Ian McCrea, DUP	15,549
Ms Eilis Haughey, SDLP	8,376
Francie Donnelly, WP	509

SF majority 9,953 (19.93%)
8.11% swing DUP to SF
(1997: SF maj. 1,883 (3.71%))

UPPER BANN
E. 72,574 T. 51,036 (70.32%)UUP hold

*Rt. Hon. D. Trimble, UUP	17,095
David Simpson, DUP	15,037
Dr Dara O'Hagan, SF	10,770
Ms Dolores Kelly, SDLP	7,607
Tom French, WP	527

UUP majority 2,058 (4.03%)
14.05% swing UUP to DUP
(1997: UUP maj. 9,252 (19.36%))

BY-ELECTIONS SINCE THE 2001 GENERAL ELECTION

BIRMINGHAM HODGE HILL
(15 July 2004)
E. 53,940 T. 37.9%

Liam Byrne, Lab.	7,451
Nicola Davies, LD	6,991
Stephen Eyre, C.	3,543
John Rees, Respect	1,282
James Starkey, NF	805
Mark Wheatley, EDP	277
James Hargreaves, OCV	90
Lab. majority	460

LEICESTER SOUTH
(15 July 2004)
E. 72,514 T. 40.6%

Parmjit Singh Gill, LD	10,274
Peter Soulsby, Lab.	8,620
Chris Heaton-Harris, C.	5,796
Yvonne Ridley, Respect	3,724
David Roberts, Soc. Lab.	263
RU Seerious, Loony	225
Patrick Kennedy, Ind.	204
Paul Lord, Ind.	186
Mark Benson, Ind.	55
Jiten Bardwaj, Ind.	36
Alan Barrett, Ind.	25
LD majority	1,654

BRENT EAST
(18 September 2003)
E. 57,778 T. 36.2%

Sarah Teather, LD	8,158
Robert Evans, Lab.	7,040
Uma Fernandes, C.	3,368
Noel Lynch, Green	638
Brian Butterworth, Soc. All.	361
Khidori Fawzi Ibrahim, Public Services Not War	219
Winston McKenzie, Ind.	197
Kelly McBride, Ind.	189
Harold Immanuel, Ind. Lab.	188
Brian Hall, UK Ind.	140
Iris Cremer, Soc. Lab.	111
Neil Walsh, Ind.	101
Alan Howling Lord Hope, Loony	59
Aaron Barschack, No Description	37
Jiten Bardwaj, No Description	35
Rainbow George Weiss, www.xat.org.	11
LD majority	1,118

OGMORE
(14 February 2002)
E. 52,209 T. 35.2%

Huw Irranca-Davies, Lab.	9,548
Bleddyn Hancock, PC	3,827
Veronica Watkins, LD	1,608
Guto Bebb, C.	1,377
Christopher Herriot, Soc. Lab.	1,152
Jonathan Spink, Green	250
Jeff Hurford, WSA	205
Leslie Edwards, Loony	187
Captain Beany, Bean	122
Revd David Braid, Ind.	100
Lab. majority	5,721

IPSWICH
(22 November 2001)
E. 68,244 T. 40.2%

Chris Mole, Lab.	11,881
Paul West, C.	7,794
Ms Tessa Munt, LD	6,146
Dave Cooper, CPA	581
Jonathan Wright, UK Ind.	276
Tony Slade, Green	255
John Ramirez, LCA	236
Peter Leech, Soc. All.	152
Nicholas Winskill, EIP	84
Lab. majority	4,087

A by-election for Hartlepool was held on 30 September 2004 following the resignation of Peter Mandelson. *See* Stop Press.

PRIME MINISTERS

Over the centuries there has been some variation in the determination of the dates of appointment of Prime Ministers. Where possible, the date given is that on which a new Prime Minister kissed the Sovereign's hands and accepted the commission to form a ministry. However, until the middle of the 19th century the dating of a commission or transfer of seals could be the date of taking office. Where the composition of the Government changed, e.g. became a coalition, but the Prime Minister remained the same, the date of the change of government is given.

YEAR APPOINTED

1721	Sir Robert Walpole, Whig
1742	The Earl of Wilmington, Whig
1743	Henry Pelham, Whig
1754	The Duke of Newcastle, Whig
1756	The Duke of Devonshire, Whig
1757	The Duke of Newcastle, Whig
1762	The Earl of Bute, Tory
1763	George Grenville, Whig
1765	The Marquess of Rockingham, Whig
1766	The Earl of Chatham, Whig
1767	The Duke of Grafton, Whig
1770	Lord North, Tory
1782 March	The Marquess of Rockingham, Whig
1782 July	The Earl of Shelburne, Whig
1783 April	The Duke of Portland, Coalition
1783 Dec.	William Pitt, Tory
1801	Henry Addington, Tory
1804	William Pitt, Tory
1806	The Lord Grenville, Whig
1807	The Duke of Portland, Tory
1809	Spencer Perceval, Tory
1812	The Earl of Liverpool, Tory
1827 April	George Canning, Tory
1827 Aug.	Viscount Goderich, Tory
1828	The Duke of Wellington, Tory
1830	The Earl Grey, Whig
1834 July	The Viscount Melbourne, Whig
1834 Nov.	The Duke of Wellington, Tory
1834 Dec.	Sir Robert Peel, Tory
1835	The Viscount of Melbourne, Whig
1841	Sir Robert Peel, Tory
1846	Lord John Russell (later The Earl Russell), Whig
1852 Feb.	The Earl of Derby, Tory
1852 Dec.	The Earl of Aberdeen, Peelite
1855	The Viscount Palmerston, Liberal
1858	The Earl of Derby, Conservative
1859	The Viscount Palmerston, Liberal
1865	The Earl Russell, Liberal
1866	The Earl of Derby, Conservative
1868 Feb.	Benjamin Disraeli, Conservative
1868 Dec.	William Gladstone, Liberal
1874	Benjamin Disraeli, Conservative
1880	William Gladstone, Liberal
1885	The Marquess of Salisbury, Conservative
1886 Feb.	William Gladstone, Liberal
1886 July	The Marquess of Salisbury, Conservative
1892	William Gladstone, Liberal
1894	The Earl of Rosebery, Liberal
1895	The Marquess of Salisbury, Conservative
1902	Arthur Balfour, Conservative
1905	Sir Henry Campbell-Bannerman, Liberal
1908	Herbert Asquith, Liberal
1915	Herbert Asquith, Coalition
1916	David Lloyd-George, Coalition
1922	Andrew Bonar Law, Conservative
1923	Stanley Baldwin, Conservative
1924 Jan.	Ramsay MacDonald, Labour
1924 Nov.	Stanley Baldwin, Conservative
1929	Ramsay MacDonald, Labour
1931	Ramsay MacDonald, Coalition
1935	Stanley Baldwin, Coalition
1937	Neville Chamberlain, Coalition
1940	Winston Churchill, Coalition
1945 May	Winston Churchill, Conservative
1945 July	Clement Attlee, Labour
1951	Sir Winston Churchill, Conservative
1955	Sir Anthony Eden, Conservative
1957	Harold Macmillan, Conservative
1963	Sir Alec Douglas-Home, Conservative
1964	Harold Wilson, Labour
1970	Edward Heath, Conservative
1974	Harold Wilson, Labour
1976	James Callaghan, Labour
1979	Margaret Thatcher, Conservative
1990	John Major, Conservative
1997	Anthony Blair, Labour

LEADERS OF THE OPPOSITION

The office of Leader of the Opposition was officially recognised in 1937 and a salary was assigned to the post.

YEAR APPOINTED

1916	Herbert Asquith, Liberal
1918	William Adamson, Labour
1921	John Clynes, Labour
1922	Ramsay MacDonald, Labour (leader of official Opposition)
1924	Stanley Baldwin, Conservative
1929	Stanley Baldwin, Conservative
1931	Arthur Henderson, Labour (leader of Labour Opposition)
1931	George Lansbury, Labour
1935	Clement Attlee, Labour
1945	Clement Attlee, Labour
1945	Winston Churchill, Conservative
1951	Clement Attlee, Labour
1955	Hugh Gaitskell, Labour
1963	Harold Wilson, Labour
1965	Edward Heath, Conservative
1974	Edward Heath, Conservative
1970	Harold Wilson, Labour
1975	Margaret Thatcher, Conservative
1979	James Callaghan, Labour
1980	Michael Foot, Labour
1983	Neil Kinnock, Labour
1992	John Smith, Labour
1994	Anthony Blair, Labour
1997	William Hague, Conservative
2001	Iain Duncan Smith, Conservative
2003	Michael Howard, Conservative

THE GOVERNMENT

THE CABINET AS AT 10 SEPTEMBER 2004

Prime Minister, First Lord of the Treasury and Minister for the Civil Service
The Rt. Hon. Tony Blair, MP (since May 1997)
Deputy Prime Minister and First Secretary of State
The Rt. Hon. John Prescott, MP, *Deputy Prime Minister* (since May 1997) and *First Secretary of State* (since June 2001)
Chancellor of the Exchequer
The Rt. Hon. Gordon Brown, MP (since May 1997)
Leader of the House of Commons, Lord Privy Seal and Secretary of State for Wales
The Rt. Hon. Peter Hain, MP (since June 2003)
Secretary of State for Constitutional Affairs and Lord Chancellor
The Rt. Hon. The Lord Falconer of Thoroton, QC (since June 2003)
Secretary of State for Foreign and Commonwealth Affairs
The Rt. Hon. Jack Straw, MP (since June 2001)
Secretary of State for the Home Department
The Rt. Hon. David Blunkett, MP (since June 2001)
Secretary of State for Environment, Food and Rural Affairs
The Rt. Hon. Margaret Beckett, MP (since June 2001)
Secretary of State for International Development (since October 2003)
The Rt. Hon. Hilary Benn, MP
Secretary of State for Transport (since May 2002) *and Secretary of State for Scotland* (since June 2003)
The Rt. Hon. Alistair Darling, MP
Secretary of State for Health
The Rt. Hon. John Reid, MP (since June 2003)
Secretary of State for Northern Ireland
The Rt. Hon. Paul Murphy (since October 2002)
Secretary of State for Defence
The Rt. Hon. Geoff Hoon, MP (since October 1999)
Secretary of State for Work and Pensions
The Rt. Hon. Alan Johnson, MP (since September 2004)
Leader of the House of Lords and Lord President of the Council (since October 2003)
The Rt. Hon. Baroness Amos
Secretary of State for Trade and Industry
The Rt. Hon. Patricia Hewitt, MP (since June 2001)
Secretary of State for Education and Skills
The Rt. Hon. Charles Clarke, MP (since October 2002)
Secretary of State for Culture, Media and Sport
The Rt. Hon. Tessa Jowell, MP (since June 2001)
Parliamentary Secretary to the Treasury (Chief Whip)
The Rt. Hon. Hilary Armstrong, MP (since June 2001)
Minister Without Portfolio and Party Chair
The Rt. Hon. Ian McCartney, MP (since June 2003)
Chief Secretary to the Treasury
The Rt. Hon. Paul Boateng, MP (since May 2002)

The Minister of State at the Department for Work and Pensions with responsibility for Work, and the Government Chief Whip in the House of Lords attend Cabinet meetings although they are not members of the Cabinet.

LAW OFFICERS

Attorney-General
The Rt. Hon. Lord Goldsmith, QC (since June 2001)
Lord Advocate
Colin Boyd, QC (since February 2000)
Solicitor-General
The Rt. Hon. Harriet Harman, MP QC (since June 2001)
Solicitor-General for Scotland
Mrs Elish Angiolini, QC (since November 2001)
Advocate-General for Scotland
Dr Lynda Clark, QC, MP (since May 1999)

MINISTERS OF STATE

Cabinet Office
The Rt. Hon. Alan Milburn, MP *(Chancellor of the Duchy of Lancaster)*
Ruth Kelly, MP *(Cabinet Office)*
Culture, Media and Sport
The Rt. Hon. Richard Caborn, MP *(Sport and Tourism)*
The Rt. Hon. Estelle Morris, MP *(Arts)*
Defence
The Rt. Hon. Adam Ingram, MP *(Armed Forces)*
Office of the Deputy Prime Minister
The Rt. Hon. Keith Hill, MP *(Housing and Planning)*
The Rt. Hon. Nick Raynsford, MP *(Local Government and the Regions)*
The Rt. Hon. Lord Rooker *(Regeneration and Regional Development)*
Education and Skills
David Miliband, MP *(School Standards)*
The Rt. Hon. Margaret Hodge, MBE, MP *(Children)*
Dr Kim Howells, MP *(Universities)*
Environment, Food and Rural Affairs
Elliot Morley, MP *(Environment and Agri-Environment)*
The Rt. Hon. Alun Michael, MP *(Rural Affairs)*
Foreign and Commonwealth Office
Dr Denis MacShane, MP *(Europe)*
The Rt. Hon. The Baroness Symons of Vernham Dean *(Middle East)*
Douglas Alexander, MP *(Trade)*
Health
The Rt. Hon. John Hutton, MP
Rosie Winterton, MP
Home Office
The Rt. Hon. Baroness Scotland of Asthal, QC *(Criminal Justice System and Law Reform)*
Hazel Blears, MP *(Crime Reduction, Policing and Community Safety)*
Des Browne, MP *(Citizenship, Immigration and Counter-Terrorism)*
Northern Ireland Office
The Rt. Hon. John Spellar, MP
Trade and Industry
Mike O'Brien, MP *(E-Commerce, Energy and Competitiveness)*
Douglas Alexander, MP *(Trade)*
The Rt. Hon. Jacqui Smith, MP *(Industry and the Regions* and *Deputy Minister for Women)*

Transport
Tony McNulty, MP
Treasury
The Rt. Hon. Dawn Primarolo, MP *(Paymaster-General)*
Stephen Timms, MP *(Financial Secretary)*
John Healey, MP *(Economic Secretary)*
Work and Pensions
The Rt. Hon. Jane Kennedy, MP *(Work)*
Malcolm Wicks, MP *(Pensions)*

UNDER-SECRETARIES OF STATE

Constitutional Affairs
Baroness Ashton of Upholland
David Lammy, MP
Christopher Leslie, MP
Anne McGuire, MP *(Scotland)*
Don Touhig, MP *(Wales)*
Culture, Media and Sport
The Rt. Hon. Lord McIntosh of Haringey *(Media and Heritage)*
Defence
Ivor Caplin, MP *(Veterans)*
The Lord Bach *(Defence Procurement)*
Office of the Deputy Prime Minister
Yvette Cooper, MP
Phil Hope, MP
Education and Skills
The Lord Filkin, CBE
Ivan Lewis, MP *(Skills and Vocational Education)*
Stephen Twigg, MP *(Schools)*
Environment, Food and Rural Affairs
Ben Bradshaw, MP *(Nature, Conservation and Fisheries)*
The Lord Whitty of Camberwell *(Food, Farming and Sustainable Energy)*
Foreign and Commonwealth Office
Bill Rammell, MP
Chris Mullin, MP
Health
Melanie Johnson, MP
Lord Warner of Brockley
Dr Stephen Ladyman, MP
Home Office
Paul Goggins, MP *(Correctional Services and Reducing Re-offending)*
Caroline Flint, MP *(Anti-Drugs Co-ordination, Reducing Organised Crime and International and European Issues)*
Fiona Mactaggart, MP *(Race Equality, Community Policy and Civil Renewal)*
International Development
Gareth Thomas, MP
Northern Ireland Office
Barry Gardiner, MP
Ian Pearson, MP
Angela Smith, MP

Trade and Industry
The Lord Sainsbury of Turville, KG *(Science and Innovation)*
Gerry Sutcliffe, MP *(Employment Relations, Competition and Consumers)*
Nigel Griffiths, MP *(Small Business)*
Transport
David Jamieson, MP
Charlotte Atkins, MP
Work and Pensions
The Rt. Hon. The Baroness Hollis of Heigham *(Lords)*
Chris Pond, MP
Ms Maria Eagle, MP *(Disabled People)*

GOVERNMENT WHIPS

HOUSE OF LORDS
Captain of the Honourable Corps of the Gentlemen-at-Arms (Chief Whip)
The Rt. Hon. The Lord Grocott
Captain of The Queen's Bodyguard of the Yeomen of the Guard (Deputy Chief Whip)
The Lord Davies of Oldham
Lords-in-Waiting
The Lord Evans of Temple Guiting
The Lord Bassam of Brighton
The Lord Triesman
Baronesses-in-Waiting
The Baroness Farrington of Ribbleton
The Baroness Andrews, OBE
The Baroness Crawley

HOUSE OF COMMONS
Parliamentary Secretary to the Treasury (Chief Whip)
The Rt. Hon. Hilary Armstrong, MP
Treasurer of HM Household (Deputy Chief Whip)
Bob Ainsworth, MP
Comptroller of HM Household
The Rt. Hon. Thomas McAvoy, MP
Vice-Chamberlain of HM Household
Jim Fitzpatrick, MP
Lords Commissioners of HM Treasury
John Heppell, MP; Nick Ainger, MP; Jim Murphy, MP; Joan Ryan, MP; Derek Twigg, MP
Assistant Whips
Fraser Kemp, MP; Charlotte Atkins, MP; Paul Clark, MP; Vernon Coaker, MP; Gillian Merron, MP; Margaret Moran, MP; Bridget Prentice, MP; Tom Watson, MP

GOVERNMENT DEPARTMENTS

THE CIVIL SERVICE

Under the Next Steps programme, launched in 1988, many semi-autonomous executive agencies were established to carry out much of the work of the Civil Service. Executive agencies operate within a framework set by the responsible minister which specifies policies, objectives and available resources. All executive agencies are set annual performance targets by their Minister. Each agency has a chief executive, who is responsible for the day-to-day operations of the agency and who is accountable to the minister for the use of resources and for meeting the agency's targets. The minister accounts to Parliament for the work of the agency. Nearly 80 per cent of civil servants now work in executive agencies. In April 2003 there were about 542,770 permanent civil servants.

The Senior Civil Service was created in 1996 and on 1 April 2002 comprised 4,020 staff from Permanent Secretary to the former Grade 5 level, including all agency chief executives. All Government departments and executive agencies are now responsible for their own pay and grading systems for civil servants outside the Senior Civil Service.

SALARIES 2004–5

MINISTERIAL SALARIES *from 1 April 2004*
Ministers who are Members of the House of Commons receive a parliamentary salary (£57,485) in addition to their ministerial salary.

Prime Minister	£121,437
Cabinet minister (Commons)	£72,862
Cabinet minister (Lords)	£98,899
Minister of State (Commons)	£37,796
Minister of State (Lords)	£77,220
Parliamentary Under-Secretary (Commons)	£28,688
Parliamentary Under-Secretary (Lords)	£67,255

SPECIAL ADVISERS' SALARIES *from 1 April 2004*
Special advisers to Government Ministers are paid out of public funds; their salaries are negotiated individually, but are usually in the range £36,347 to £96,213.

CIVIL SERVICE SALARIES *from 1 April 2004*
Senior Civil Servants

Permanent Secretary	£121,100–£256,550
Band 3	£90,867–£192,424
Band 2	£73,762–£155,008
Band 1A	£62,004–£122,938
Band 1	£53,451–£112,248

Staff are placed in pay bands according to their level of responsibility and taking account of other factors such as experience and marketability. Movement within and between bands is based on performance. Following the delegation of responsibility for pay and grading to Government departments and agencies from 1 April 1996, it is no longer possible to show service-wide pay rates for staff outside the Senior Civil Service.

GOVERNMENT DEPARTMENTS

CABINET OFFICE
70 Whitehall, London SW1A 2AS
Switchboard 020-7276 3000 T 020-7276 1234
W www.cabinet-office.gov.uk

The Cabinet Office has four main roles: to support the Prime Minister in leading the Government; to support the Government in transacting its business; to lead and support the reform and delivery programme and to co-ordinate security and intelligence. The Department is headed by the Chancellor of the Duchy of Lancaster and has one Minister of State. The Cabinet Office has two Executive Agencies: The Government Car and Despatch Agency (GCDA) and the Central Office of Information (COI Communications) which is a department in its own right and operates as a Trading Fund.

Prime Minister and Minister for the Civil Service,
The Rt. Hon. Tony Blair, MP
Principal Private Secretary to the Prime Minister and Head of Policy Directorate, Ivan Rogers
Chancellor of the Duchy of Lancaster, The Rt. Hon. Alan Milburn, MP
Parliamentary Private Secretary, Kevin Brennan, MP
Principal Private Secretary, Tony Sampson
Assistant Private Secretaries, Helen Gahir; Michelle Duncan
Minister for the Cabinet Office, Ruth Kelly, MP
Private Secretary, Georgia Hutchinson
Secretary of the Cabinet and Head of the Home Civil Service, Sir Andrew Turnbull, KCB, CVO
Principal Private Secretary, Penny Ciniewicz
Private Secretary, Sue Pither
Assistant Private Secretaries, Rebecca Mupita; Jeanne Bilbrough
Security and Intelligence Co-ordinator and Permanent Secretary, Sir David Omand, GCB
Principal Private Secretary, Dominic Fagan
Private Secretary, Lisa Harlow
Minister without Portfolio and Party Chair, The Rt. Hon. Ian McCartney, MP
Parliamentary Private Secretary, Gareth Thomas, MP

CEREMONIAL SECRETARIAT
Great Smith Street, London SW1P 3BQ
T 020-7276 2777
Ceremonial Officer, Mrs Gay Catto

CIVIL CONTINGENCIES SECRETARIAT
10 Great George Street, London SW1P 3AE
Head, Susan Scholefield, CMG

DEFENCE AND OVERSEAS AFFAIRS SECRETARIAT
Prime Minister's Foreign Policy Adviser and Head of Secretariat, Sir Nigel Sheinwald, KCMG
Deputy Head, Desmond Bowen, CMG

ECONOMIC AND DOMESTIC SECRETARIAT
Director, Paul Britton, CB
Deputy Head, Robin Fellgett

EUROPEAN SECRETARIAT
Prime Minister's European Policy Adviser and Head of Secretariat, Kim Darroch, CMG
Deputy Head, Katrina Williams

INTELLIGENCE AND SECURITY SECRETARIAT
Director, Security and Intelligence, Chris Wright
Chief of the Assessments Staff, Tim Dowse

OFFICE OF THE COMMISSIONER FOR PUBLIC APPOINTMENTS (OCPA)
35 Great Smith Street, London SW1P 3BQ
T 020-7276 2625
The Commissioner for Public Appointments is responsible for monitoring, regulating and providing advice to departments on 12,000 ministerial appointments to public bodies. The Commissioner publishes a Code of Practice, guidance for departments and an annual report. The Commissioner can investigate complaints about the way in which appointments were made or applicants treated.
Commissioner for Public Appointments, Dame Rennie Fritchie, DBE
Senior Policy Adviser, Alistair Howie
Secretary to the Commissioner and Head of the Office, Jim Barron

OFFICE OF THE CIVIL SERVICE COMMISSIONERS (OCSC)
35 Great Smith Street, London SW1P 3BQ
T 020-7276 2615
The independent Civil Service Commissioners are the custodians of the principle of selection on merit by fair and open competition; they publish a Recruitment Code and audit departments' and agencies' performance against it. When the most senior posts are opened to people from outside the Service, the Commissioners normally chair the recruitment process. The Commissioners also act as an independent appeals body under the Civil Service Code.
First Commissioner, Baroness Usha Prashar, CBE
Commissioners (part-time), D. Bell; P. Bounds; J. Boyle; Ms B. Curtis; Ms S. Forbes, CBE; Dame Rennie Fritchie, DBE; Prof. E. Gallagher, CBE; H. Hamill, CB; G. Lemos, CMG; A. MacDonald, CB; G. Maddrell; Dr M. Semple, OBE
Secretary to the Commissioners and Head of the Office, Jim Barron

REGULATORY IMPACT UNIT (RIU)
22 Whitehall, London SW1A 2WH
T 020-7276 2193
The Regulatory Impact Unit (RIU) works with other Government departments, agencies and regulators to help ensure that regulations are fair and effective, and helps reduce bureaucracy. The RIU also examines the impact on the voluntary sector, charities and the public sector and supports the work of the Better Regulation Task Force.
Director, Simon Virley
Deputy Directors, M. Courtney; Ms J. Cruickshank; I. Morfett; Ms K. Hill; Dr P. Rushbrook; P. Clarke

THE PRIME MINISTER'S DELIVERY UNIT
1 Horse Guards Road, London SW1A 2HQ
T 020-7270 5811
The Prime Minister's Delivery Unit was established in June 2001. Its main role is to ensure the delivery of the Prime Minister's top priority outcomes in the public services sector by 2005. The Unit reports to the Prime Minister through the Head of the Civil Service and the Minister for the Cabinet Office. Following the Spending Review 2002 the Delivery Unit now shares responsibility with the Treasury for the joint Public Service Agreement (PSA) target to improve public services by working with departments to help them meet their PSA targets consistently with the fiscal rules. The Unit's work is carried out by a team of around 40 people drawn from the public and private sectors. The Unit also draws on the expertise of a wider group of Associates with experience of successful delivery in the public, private and voluntary sectors.
Prime Minister's Chief Adviser on Delivery, Prof. Michael Barber
Deputy Directors, William Jordan; Peter Thomas

E-GOVERNMENT UNIT
Stockley House, 130 Wilton Road, Victoria, London SW1V 1LQ
T 020-7276 3283
The e-Government Unit works with departments to efficiently deliver public services by joining up electronic government services with the needs of customers. It also provides sponsorship of Information Assurance. The e-Government Unit takes on the work previously undertaken by the Office of the e-Envoy.
Head of e-Government, Ian Watmore

STRATEGY UNIT (SU)
Admiralty Arch, The Mall, London SW1A 2WH
T 020-7277 1881
The Strategy Unit (SU) is the result of a merger of the Performance and Innovation Unit (PIU) and the Prime Minister's Forward Strategy Unit (PMFSU). The Strategy Unit carries out long-term strategic reviews and policy analysis which can take several forms: reviews of major areas of policy; studies of cross-cutting policy issues; and strategic audit. The Unit undertakes work on a wide range of policy areas, including: e-commerce; rural policy; modernising central government; the future of the Post Office; recovery of criminal assets; adoption; resource productivity; workforce development; ethnic minorities; GM crops and alcohol misuse.
Executive Director, Jamie Rentoul
Deputy Directors, S. Aldridge; Ms P. Greer; Ms C. Laing

THE PRIME MINISTER'S OFFICE OF PUBLIC SERVICES REFORM
22 Whitehall, London SW1A 2WH
T 020-7276 3600
W www.pm-gov.uk/opsr
To strengthen the Government's ability to improve public services, the Prime Minister established the Office of Public Services Reform in 2001, based within the Cabinet Office. The Unit reports directly to the Prime Minister through the Cabinet Secretary. Its role is to advise and work with the Prime Minister and departments in order to implement the following four principles of reform and deliver customer-focused public services. The principles of reform are: to provide standards within a framework of clear accountability; to give local leaders responsibility and accountability for delivery; to meet the diversity of customer needs, to reduce bureaucracy and to offer greater incentives and rewards for staff; and to provide different ways for users to receive services.

The Unit works on local service projects within health, education, the criminal justice system and local government. It also leads work on understanding customers.

Prime Minister's Adviser on Public Services Reform, Dr Wendy Thomson

CENTRAL SPONSOR FOR INFORMATION ASSURANCE (CSIA)
Stockley House, 130 Wilton Road, London SW1V 1LQ
T 020-7276 3267
The CSIA was established on 1 April 2003 to assure the Government that risks to the national information infrastructure are managed appropriately. It works with partners in the public and private sectors, as well as its international counterparts, to help safeguard the nation's IT and telecommunications services.
Director, Dr Steve Marsh

CORPORATE DEVELOPMENT GROUP (CDG)
Admiralty Arch, The Mall, London SW1A 2WH
T 020-7276 1566 F 020-7276 1404
Director-General, Ms A. Perkins, CB
Directors, David Spencer; Anne-Marie Lawlor; Tim Kemp; Richard Furlong

GOVERNMENT INFORMATION AND COMMUNICATION SERVICE (GICS)
10 Great George St, London SW1P 3AE
T 020-7276 5090
The Office of the Head of the Government Information and Communication Service is responsible for the standards of the service provided by the GICS to Whitehall departments and their agencies. It supports the Head of the Civil Service's work and provides guidance on the strategic development of the GICS, its professional practice, recruitment and promotion. Its focus is on cross-departmental communication and management of central GICS units.
Deputy Head of GICS (Corporate and HR Strategy), Ms S. Jenkins
Director of GICS Development Centre, T. Dunmore
Director of Operations, Ms L. Salisbury
Head of GICS Operating Unit, Ms C. McCall
Director, Media Monitoring Unit, Ms E. Thwaites
Head of Government News Network, R. Haslam
Regional Director, Eastern, Ms M. Basham, 2nd Floor, Block A1, Westbrook Centre, Milton Road, Cambridge CB4 1YG
Regional Director, East Midlands, P. Smith, The Belgrave Centre, Talbot Street, Nottingham NG1 5GG
Regional Director, West Midlands, B. Garner, Five Ways House, Islington Row, Middleway, Edgbaston, Birmingham B15 1SH
Regional Director, North East, C. Child, Wellbar House, Gallowgate, Newcastle upon Tyne NE1 4TB
Regional Director, North West, Ms E. Jones, Sunley Tower, Piccadilly Plaza, Manchester M1 4BE
Regional Director, London and South East, Ms V. Burdon, Hercules Road, London SE1 7DU
Regional Director, South West, P. Whitbread, The Pithay, Bristol BS1 2PB
Regional Director, Yorkshire and the Humber, Ms W. Miller, City House, New Station Street, Leeds LS1 4JG

CORPORATE MANAGEMENT
Managing Director Accounting Officer, Colin Balmer
Director of Finance, Jerry Page
Director, Business Development, John Sweetman

Director, Human Resources, Claudette Francis
Deputy Director, Histories and Records, Tessa Stirling
Deputy Director, Infrastructure, Eric Hepburn

HER MAJESTY'S STATIONERY OFFICE
St Clements House, 2–16 Colegate, Norwich NR3 1BQ
T 01603-621000
Controller, Carol Tullo

COMMUNICATION GROUP
70 Whitehall, London SW1A 2AS
T 020-7270 3000
Advises on presentation of departmental policy and activity. Handles media and public relations activities other than recruitment publicity and advertising.
Director of Communication, Melanie Leech
Head of News, John Bretherton

EXECUTIVE AGENCIES
GOVERNMENT CAR AND DESPATCH AGENCY
46 Ponton Road, London SW8 5AX
T 020-7217 3839 F 020-7217 3840
The Agency provides secure transport and mail distribution to Government and the public sector.
Chief Executive, N. Matheson

COI COMMUNICATIONS
Hercules Road, London SE1 7DU
T 020-7928 2345 F 020-7928 5037
COI Communications (The Central Office of Information) is a Government agency which offers consultancy, procurement and project management services to central Government. Administrative responsibility for the COI rests with the Minister for the Cabinet Office.
Chief Executive, A. Bishop
Deputy Chief Executive, P. Buchanan
Senior Personal Secretary, Mrs I. MacMull

MANAGEMENT BOARD
Members, I. Hamilton; Mrs S. Whetton; G. Beasant; A. Wade; Ms E. Lochhead
Secretary, Mrs I. MacMull

PRIME MINISTER'S OFFICE
10 Downing Street, London SW1A 2AA
T 020-7270 3000 F 020-7925 0918
W www.number-10.gov.uk
Prime Minister, The Rt. Hon Tony Blair, MP
Chief of Staff, Jonathan Powell
Principal Private Secretary and Head of Policy Directorate, Ivan Rogers
Parliamentary Private Secretary, David Hanson, MP
Personal Assistant to Prime Minister (Diary), Katie Kay
Director of Political Operations, Pat McFadden
Head of Policy, Geoff Mulgan
Policy Directorate, Carey Oppenheim; Simon Morys; Geoffrey Norris; Arnab Banerji; Sarah Hunter; Simon Stevens; Justin Russell; Clare Sumner; Alasdair McGowan; Matthew Elson; Martin Hurst; Matthew Taylor; Liz Lloyd
Foreign Policy, Matthew Rycroft; David Quarrey; Roger Liddle
Head of Delivery Unit, Prof. Michael Barber
Head of the Office of Public Services Reform, Wendy Thomson
Head of Strategy Unit, Geoff Mulgan

Research and Information Unit, Catherine Rimmer
Director of Communications and Strategy, David Hill
Strategic Communications Unit, Godric Smith
Direct Communications Unit, Jan Taylor
Prime Minister's Official Spokesman, Tom Kelly
Director of Events and Visits, Jo Gibbons
Director of Government Relations, The Baroness Margaret
    Morgan of Huyton
Secretary for Appointments, William Chapman
*Advisor on Education, Public Services and Constitutional
    Reform,* Andrew Adonis
*Advisor on Foreign Policy and Head of the Overseas and
    Defence Secretariat,* Nigel Sheinwald
*Advisor on European Union Affairs and Head of the
    European Secretariat,* Sir Stephen Wall
Parliamentary Clerk, Nicholas Howard

OFFICE OF THE DEPUTY PRIME MINISTER

26 Whitehall, London SW1A 2WH
T 020-7944 4400
W www.odpm.gov.uk

The Office of the Deputy Prime Minister (ODPM) was
created in May 2002 taking on responsibility for policy
areas from both the Department for Transport, Local
Government and the Regions and the Cabinet Office.
The ODPM brings together regional and local
government (including the Regional Government
Offices), housing, planning and regeneration, social
exclusion and neighbourhood renewal.

Regional and local government and the Government's
cross-cutting agenda for neighbourhood renewal and
social inclusion are administered by a single department
under the Deputy Prime Minister, who also has
responsibility for implementing regional government
and local government white papers. The Deputy Prime
Minister will continue to act as the Prime Minister's
deputy across the full range of domestic and international
business, chairing a range of key Cabinet committees.

Deputy Prime Minister and First Secretary of State, The Rt.
    Hon. John Prescott, MP
Private Secretary, Peter Betts
Minister of State, The Rt. Hon. Nick Raynsford, MP *(Local
    Government and the Regions)*
Private Secretary, Angela Kerr
Minister of State, The Rt. Hon. Lord Rooker *(Regeneration
    and Regional Development)*
Private Secretary, Jenny Mainland
Minister of State, Keith Hill, MP *(Housing and Planning)*
Private Secretary, Mark Livesey
Parliamentary Under-Secretary, Phil Hope, MP
Private Secretary, Karen Abbott
Parliamentary Under-Secretary, Yvette Cooper, MP
Private Secretary, Patrick Owen
Permanent Secretary, Mavis McDonald
Private Secretary, Andrew Vaughan
Chief Scientist, David Fisk

DIRECTORATE OF COMMUNICATION
Director of Communication Directorate, Derek Plews
Deputy Director of Communications, Jane Groom

CORPORATE STRATEGY AND RESOURCES GROUP
Director-General, Corporate Strategy and Resources Group,
    Peter Unwin
Director, Mike Bailey *(HR and Workplace Services)*;
    Andrew Lean *(Finance)*; Michael Kell *(Analysis and
    Research)*; vacant *(Business Change and Delivery)*

Heads of Departments, David Buttress; Caroline Cousin;
    Janet Fortune: Andree Kerr; David Smith; Helen
    Edwards; Su Bonfanti; Alan Beard; Amanda McFeeters;
    Steve Simmonds; Chris Smith; Jan White; Peter Capell;
    Andrew Morrison; Bruce Oelman; Shona Dunn; Steph
    Coster; Cath Shaw

LEGAL DIRECTORATE
Director of Legal Directorate, Sandra Unerman
Heads of Departments, Pamela Conlan; Fred Croft; Gloria
    Hedley-Dent; David Jordan; Judith-Anne MacKenzie;
    Donatella Phillips; John Wright

LOCAL GOVERNMENT AND FIRE GROUP
Director-General, Local Government and Fire Group, Neil
    Kinghan
Directors, Lindsay Bell *(Local Government Finance)*; Clive
    Norris *(Fire and Rescue Service)*; John O'Brien *(Local
    Government Performance and Practice)*; David Prout
    (Local Government Policy)
Heads of Departments, Pam Williams; Stephen Claughton;
    Robert Davies; Meg Green; Andrew Allberry; Terry
    Crossley; Richard Gibson; Kevin Lloyd; Paul Rowsell;
    Geoff Tierney; Paul Downie; Sarah Sturrock; Sir
    Graham Meldrum; Dr David Peace; Diana Kahn; Dave
    Lawrence; Marie Winckler; Shelagh Prosser; Mandy
    Skinner

REGIONAL DEVELOPMENT GROUP
Director-General, Regional Development Group,
    Rob Smith
Directors, Richard Allan *(Regional Policy)*; Andrew
    Campbell *(Regional Co-ordination Unit)*; Alun Evans
    (Civil Resilience)
Heads of Departments, Nick Dexter; Ian Jones; Julie
    Anderson; Vince Brady; Christopher Bowden; Mike
    Reed; Richard Bruce; Philip Cox; Ian Scotter; Mitesh
    Dhanak

SUSTAINABLE COMMUNITIES GROUP
Director-General, Sustainable Communities Group, Richard
    McCarthy
Directors, Jeff Channing *(Thames Gateway)*; Brian
    Hackland *(Planning)*; David Lunts *(Urban Policy)*; Neil
    McDonald *(Housing)*; Andrew Wells *(Sustainable
    Communities)*
Heads of Departments, Mark Coulshed; Henry Cleary;
    Duncan Campbell; Michelle Banks; Peter Ruback;
    David Liston-Jones; Peter Matthew; David Edwards;
    Keith Thorpe; Pam Temple; Paul Everall; Richard
    Footitt; Dawn Eastmead; Anne Kirkham; Carol
    Sweetenham; Hilary Bartle; Helen Giles; Mike Ash;
    Lester Hicks; Joan Bailey; John Stambollouian; Lisette
    Simcock; Bob Ledsome; Joanna Key

TACKLING DISADVANTAGE GROUP
Director-General, Tackling Disadvantage Group,
    Joe Montgomery
Directors, Terrie Alafat *(Homelessness and Housing Support)*;
    Alan Davis *(Neighbourhood Strategy)*; Alan Riddell
    (Neighbourhood Operations)
Director, Social Exclusion Unit, Claire Tyler
Heads of Departments, John Bright; Carol Hayden; Allan
    Bowman; Patrick Allen; Martin Joseph; Teresa Vokes;
    Gordon Campbell; Ashley Horsey; Neil O'Connor;
    Wendy Jarvis; Marcus Bell; Sally Burlington; Vanessa
    Scarborough; Bert Provan; Ruth Stainer; Rosie
    Seymour

REGIONAL CO-ORDINATION UNIT
River Walk House, Millbank, London SW1P 4RR
T 020-7217 3550
Director-General, Rob Smith
Director, Teresa Vokes

CIVIL RESILIENCE DIRECTORATE
Director-General, Rob Smith
Regional Directors, Caroline Bowdler *(Government Office for the East)*; Jane Todd *(Government Office for the East Midlands)*; Liz Meek *(Government Office for London)*; Jonathon Blackie *(Government Office for the North East)*; Keith Barnes *(Government Office for the North West)*; Paul Martin *(Government Office for the South East)*; Jane Henderson *(Government Office for the South West)*; Graham Garbutt *(Government Office for the West Midlands)*; Felicity Everiss *(Government Office for Yorkshire and the Humber)*

EXECUTIVE AGENCIES
FIRE SERVICE COLLEGE
Moreton-in-Marsh, Gloucestershire, GL56 0RH
T 01608-650831 F 01608-651788
W www.fireservicecollege.ac.uk
The Fire Service College provides unique facilities for both practical and theoretical fire fighting, fire safety and accident and emergency training, including urban search and rescue and community safety.
Acting Chief Executive, Anne Frost

ORDNANCE SURVEY
Romsey Road, Southampton SO16 4GU
T 08456-050505 F 023-8079 2615
W www.ordnancesurvey.co.uk
The Ordnance Survey department carries out official surveying and definitive mapping of Great Britain.
Chief Executive, V. Lawrence

PLANNING INSPECTORATE
Temple Quay House, 2 The Square, Temple Quay, Bristol BS1 6PN T 0117-372 6372
Crown Buildings, Cathays Park, Cardiff CF10 3NQ
T 029-2082 3866 F 029-2082 5150
W www.planning-inspectorate.gov.uk
The Inspectorate deals with appeals against the decisions of local authorities on planning applications and appeals against local authority enforcement notices. It also provides inspectors who hold inquiries into objections to local authority planning.
Chief Executive, Katrine Sporle

THE QUEEN ELIZABETH II CONFERENCE CENTRE
Broad Sanctuary, London SW1P 3EE
T 020-7222 5000 F 020-7798 4200
W www.qeiicc.co.uk
The Centre provides secure conference facilities for national and international government and private sector use.
Chief Executive, John McCarthy

THE RENT SERVICE
5 Welbeck Street, London W1G 9YQ
T 020-7023 6000 F 020-7023 6222
W www.therentservice.gov.uk
The Agency combines 77 independent units previously administered by local authorities.
Chief Executive, Ms C. Copeland

DEPARTMENT FOR CONSTITUTIONAL AFFAIRS (DCA)
Selbourne House, 54–60 Victoria Street, London SW1E 6QW
T 020-7210 8500
W www.dca.gov.uk
The Department for Constitutional Affairs was created on 12 June 2003, as part of the Government's drive to modernise the constitution. It brings together most of the Lord Chancellor's Department, the UK devolution settlements and, for administrative purposes only, the staff of the Scotland Office and the Wales Office. The new department is charged with building fair, effective and accessible justice services, which contribute towards a safe and secure society and protect the rights of citizens; and to modernise the law and constitution. Its principal responsibilities include: in partnership with the Home Office and the Crown Prosecution Service to deliver an effective criminal justice system; in partnership with the Home Office to improve the effectiveness of the asylum system; to reform the constitution, in particular establishing a Supreme Court, and a Judicial Appointments Commission; to effectively manage the courts and many tribunals; until the appointment of the Commission, to undertake the appointment and training of the judiciary; to provide legal aid and legal services to help tackle social exclusion; to oversee the legal services market, including regulation and competition; to reform and revise English civil law particularly in the fields of freedom of information, privacy and data sharing, human rights, reform of the House of Lords, the constitutional relationship with the Channel Islands and the Isle of Man, royal, church and hereditary issues, electoral law and policy, referenda and Party funding.

The department employs over 11,500 civil servants, over 10,000 of whom work in courts and tribunals throughout the country. It includes a number of related bodies: the Law Commission; the Judicial Studies Board; the Official Solicitor and Public Trustee; the Legal Services Ombudsman; the Judge Advocate General's Office; the Magistrates' Court Service Inspectorate; the Commission for Judicial Appointments; the Information Commissioner's Office and the Council on Tribunals. It is the sponsor department for the Legal Services Commission. The Secretary of State for Constitutional Affairs is also responsible for the Land Registry, the Public Record Office, and the Court Service in Northern Ireland. The Scotland and Wales Offices continue to exist under the umbrella of the Department for Constitutional Affairs but report to the Secretaries of State for Scotland and Wales respectively.

Secretary of State for Constitutional Affairs and Lord Chancellor, The Rt. Hon. The Lord Falconer of Thoroton, QC
Principal Private Secretary, Mike Anderson
Special Adviser, Philip Bassett
Parliamentary Clerk, Ann Nixon
Parliamentary Under-Secretary, David Lammy, MP
Private Secretary, Edward Bowles
Parliamentary Under-Secretary, Christopher Leslie, MP
Private Secretary, Grant Morris
Parliamentary Under-Secretary, Baroness Ashton of Upholland
Private Secretary, Nicola Westmore
Permanent Secretary, Alex Allan
Private Secretary, Jade Cortes

PERMANENT SECRETARY'S OFFICE
Permanent Secretary and Clerk of the Crown in Chancery,
    Alex Allan
Clerk of the Chamber and Head of the Crown Office, C. I. P.
    Denyer

COMMUNICATIONS GROUP
T 020-7210 2022
Head of Communications, Lucian Hudson
Head of Corporate Communications and Projects, Mike
    Wicksteed

CLIENTS AND POLICY GROUP
T 020-7210 2022
Director-General, Dr J. Spencer
Director, Civil Justice and Legal Services Directorate,
    A. Finlay
Director, Asylum and Diversity, N. Smedley
Director, Constitution, A. McDonald
Heads of Divisions, Kay Birch; Keith Budgen; Ms S. Field;
    Ms S. Johnson; Judith Simpson; E. Adams; John Sills;
    Edwin Kilby; Belinda Crowe; A. Frazer; A. Maultby;
    Ms M. Shaw

FINANCE
T 020-7210 2801
Director-General, S. Ball
Director of Facilities Management, C. Lyne
Principal Finance Officer, A. Cogbill
Head of Internal Audit, A. Rummins

LEGAL AND JUDICIAL SERVICES
T 020-7210 2810
Directors-General, John Lyon; P. Jenkins
Heads of Divisions, A. Shaw *(Courts Policy)*; J. Powell
    (Competitions (Courts)); P. Farmer *(Information and
    Planning)*; R. Sams *(Competitions, Tribunals)*; D. Staff
    (Pay, Pensions and Terms and Conditions); Ms M. Pigott
    and Ms J. Killick *(Policy and Correspondence)*; R. Heaton
    (The Legal Adviser); Ms C. Johnston *(Family and
    Criminal)*; E. Robinson *(Asylum, Civil and
    Administrative Justice and Public Legal Services)*; A.
    Wallace *(Civil Law, Legal Services, EU and
    Devolution)*

CHIEF EXECUTIVE OPERATIONS
T 020-7210 8001
Chief Executive Operations and Second Permanent Secretary,
    Ian Magee

CHIEF EXECUTIVE AND DIRECTOR FIELD
SERVICES
T 020-7210 1373
Acting Chief Executive, Sir Ron De Witt
Director, Kevin Pogson

ECCLESIASTICAL PATRONAGE
10 Downing Street, London SW1S 2AA
T 020-7930 4433

CROWN OFFICE
House of Lords, London SW1A 0PW
T 020-7219 4713

SUPREME COURT GROUP
Strand, London WC2A 2LL
T 020-7947 6000

EXECUTIVE AGENCIES
THE COURT SERVICE
Southside, 105 Victoria Street, London SW1E 6QT
T 020-7210 1646 F 020-7210 2059
W www.courtservice.gov.uk
The Court Service provides administrative support to the
Supreme Court, the Crown Court, county courts and a
number of tribunals in England and Wales.
Chief Executive (Acting), P. Handcock
Director of Human Resources (Acting), Ms H. Dudley
*Director of Information Services, Communications
    Technologies and e-Delivery,* Ms A. Vernon
Director of Programmes and Projects, D. Barr
Director of Purchasing and Contract Management, C. Lyne
Director of Tribunals, S. Smith
Head of Magistrates' Courts Administrative Division,
    N. Haighton
*Programme Director Magistrates' Courts IT Division and
    LIBRA Project,* N. Haighton

HM LAND REGISTRY
32 Lincoln Inn Fields, London WC2A 3PH
T 020-7917 8888

NATIONAL ARCHIVES
Ruskin Avenue, Kew, Surrey TW9 4DU
T 020-8876 3444

PUBLIC GUARDIANSHIP OFFICE
Archway Tower, 2 Junction Road, London N19 5SZ
T 0845-330 2900

DEPARTMENT FOR CULTURE, MEDIA AND SPORT
2–4 Cockspur Street, London SW1Y 5DH
T 020-7211 6200 F 020-7211 6032
W www.culture.gov.uk
The Department for Culture, Media and Sport was
established in July 1997 and is responsible for
Government policy relating to the arts, broadcasting,
press freedom and regulation, the film and music
industries, museums and galleries, libraries, architecture
and the historic environment, sport and recreation,
tourism, the National Lottery, gambling, and alcohol and
entertainment licensing.
Secretary of State for Culture, Media and Sport, The Rt.
    Hon. Tessa Jowell, MP
Principal Private Secretary, Heather Rogers
Special Advisers, Bill Bush; Nick Bent
Parliamentary Private Secretary, Gordon Marsden, MP
Minister of State, The Rt. Hon. Estelle Morris, MP *(Arts)*
Private Secretary, David McLaren
Parliamentary Private Secretary, Dr Howard Stoate, MP
Minister of State, The Rt. Hon. Richard Caborn, MP *(Sport
    and Tourism)*
Private Secretary, Graeme Cornell
Parliamentary Private Secretary, Ben Chapman, MP
Parliamentary Under-Secretary, The Rt. Hon. The Lord
    McIntosh of Haringey *(Media and Heritage)*
Private Secretary, Gareth Maybury
Permanent Secretary, Sue Street
Director-General, Children, Young People and Communities,
    Jeff Jacobs

STRATEGY AND COMMUNICATIONS DIRECTORATE
Head of Group, Siobhan Kenny
Head of News, Paddy Feeny
Head of Promotions and Publicity, Penny Dolby
Head of Strategy, Policy, and Delivery, David Roe

CORPORATE SERVICES DIRECTORATE
Head of Group, Nicholas Kroll
Head, Analytical Services, vacant
Head, Finance and Planning Division, Keith Smith
Head, Internal Audit, Michael Kirk
Head, Personnel and Central Services Division, Shaun Cove

ARTS AND CULTURE DIRECTORATE
Head of Group, Alan Davey
Director, Government Art Collection, Penny Johnson
Head, Architecture and Historic Environment Division, vacant
Head, Arts Division, Phil Clapp
Head, Museums and Cultural Property, Nigel Pittman
Head, Museums and Libraries Sponsorship, Richard Hartman
Head, Public Appointments, Honours and Modernisation, Janet Evans

CREATIVE INDUSTRIES, BROADCASTING, GAMBLING AND LOTTERY DIRECTORATE
Head of Group, Andrew Ramsay
Head, Broadcasting Division, Jon Zeff
Head, Creative Industries Division, Mark Ferrero
Head, Gambling and National Lottery Licensing, Elliot Grant
Head, National Lottery Distribution and Communities, Simon Broadley

TOURISM, LIBRARIES AND COMMUNITIES DIRECTORATE
Head of Group, Brian Leonard
Head, Alcohol and Entertainment Licensing, Andrew Cunningham
Head, Libraries and Communities, Vanessa Brand
Head, Tourism Division, Harry Reeves

SPORT DIRECTORATE
Head of Group, Nicky Roche
Head, Olympic Games Unit, Paul Bolt
Head, Sports Division, Paul Heron

EXECUTIVE AGENCY
ROYAL PARKS AGENCY
The Old Police House, Hyde Park, London W2 2UH
T 020-7298 2000 F 020-7298 2005
The agency is responsible for maintaining and developing the royal parks.
Chief Executive, William Weston, MVO

DEPARTMENT FOR EDUCATION AND SKILLS
Sanctuary Buildings, Great Smith Street, London SW1P 3BT
Caxton House, Tothill Street, London SW1H 9NA
Castle View House, East Lane, Runcorn, WA7 2GJ
Mowden Hall, Staindrop Road, Darlington DL3 9BG
Moorfoot, Sheffield S1 4PQ
T 08700-012345 **Public Enquiries** 08700-002288
E info@dfes.gsi.gov.uk W www.dfes.gov.uk
The Department for Education and Skills aims to help build a competitive economy and inclusive society by creating opportunities for everyone to develop their learning potential and achieve excellence in standards of education and levels of skills. The department's main objectives are to give children an excellent start in education and to enable young people and adults to develop and equip themselves with the skills, knowledge and personal qualities needed for life and work. The department also sponsors eleven non-departmental public bodies across a variety of professional disciplines and educational services.
Secretary of State for Education and Skills, The Rt. Hon. Charles Clarke, MP
Principal Private Secretary, Mela Watts
Private Secretary, Jenny Loosley
Special Advisers, Hannah Pawlby; Robert Hill
Parliamentary Private Secretary, Michael John Foster, MP
Minister of State for School Standards, David Miliband, MP
Private Secretary, Nick Carson
Parliamentary Private Secretary, Ian Cawsey, MP
Minister of State for Universities, Dr Kim Howells, MP
Private Secretary, Jo Ware
Parliamentary Private Secretary, David Borrow, MP
Minister of State for Children, The Rt. Hon. Margaret Hodge, MBE, MP
Private Secretary, Claire Carroll
Parliamentary Private Secretary, Meg Munn, MP
Parliamentary Under-Secretary of State for Schools, Stephen Twigg, MP
Private Secretary, Charles Deighton-Fox
Parliamentary Under-Secretary of State, The Lord Filkin, CBE
Private Secretary, Rebecca Beeton
Parliamentary Under-Secretary of State for Skills and Vocational Education, Ivan Lewis, MP
Private Secretary, Jo Bewley
Permanent Secretary, David Normington, CB
Private Secretary, Paul Price
Parliamentary Clerk, Jonathan Duff
Spokesman in the House of Lords, The Lord Filkin, CBE

STRATEGY AND COMMUNICATIONS DIRECTORATE
Director, Michael Stevenson
Heads of Divisions, Trevor Cook *(Press Office)*; D.-J. Collins *(News)*
Divisional Managers, Yasmin Diamond *(Corporate Communications)*; Mel Brown *(Marketing and Publicity)*; Mohammad Haroon *(Regions, Delivery Support and Regeneration)*; Diana Laurillard *(e-Learning Strategy Unit)*

SCHOOLS DIRECTORATE
Director-General, Peter Housden

SECONDARY EDUCATION GROUP
Director, Peter Wanless
Divisional Managers, Susanna Todd *(School Diversity)*; Neil Flint *(Academies Division)*; Barnaby Shaw *(School Improvement and Excellence)*; Jon Coles *(London Challenge Programme)*

STANDARDS AND EFFECTIVENESS UNIT
Directors, David Hopkins; Andrew McCully
Director of Innovation Unit, Mike Gibbons
Divisional Managers, Andrew McCully *(Pupil Standards)*; Hilary Emery *(Schools Directorate Adviser)*; Caroline Macready *(School Performance and Accountability)*
Leadership and Teacher Development, Richard Harrison

RESOURCES, INFRASTRUCTURE AND GOVERNANCE GROUP
Director, Stephen Crowne
Divisional Managers, Shan Scott (School Admissions, Organisation and Governance); Andrew Wye; Lorraine Chapman (School and LEA Funding); Sally Brooks (Schools Capital and Buildings); Mukund Patel (Schools Building and Design Unit); Penny Jones (School Transport, Safety and Independent Schools)

SCHOOL WORKFORCE UNIT
Director, Stephen Hillier
Deputy Directors, Stuart Edwards (SWU Infrastructure); Ian Whitehouse (SWU Pay and Performance Management); Heath Monk (School Workforce Remodelling)
SWU Team Leader, Pensions and Medical Fitness to Teach, Paul Bleasdale

PRIMARY EDUCATION AND E-LEARNING GROUP
Director, Helen Williams
Divisional Managers, Mela Watts (Curriculum); Doug Brown (ICT in Schools); Matthew Conway (PE and School Sport and Club Links Project, Joint with Department for Culture, Media and Sport); Annabel Burns (Ethnic Minority Achievement Project); Nick Baxter (Improving Behaviour and Attendance)

CHILDREN, YOUNG PEOPLE AND FAMILIES DIRECTORATE
Director-General, Tom Jeffery

SURE START UNIT
Director, Naomi Eisenstadt
Divisional Managers, David Jeffrey (Quality and Standards), Jackie Doughty (Programme Delivery); Nick Tooze (Infrastructure); Sue Lewis (Planning and Performance)

SAFEGUARDING CHILDREN AND SUPPORTING FAMILIES GROUP
Director, Althea Efunshile
Divisional Managers, Colin Green (Child Protection); David Holmes (Looked After Children); Bruce Clark (Vulnerable Children); Ann Gross (Special Educational Needs and Disability); Ruth Kennedy (Families)

SUPPORTING CHILDREN AND YOUNG PEOPLE GROUP
Chief Executive, Anne Weinstock
Divisional Managers, Gordon McKenzie (Cross Policy Group); Steve Jackson (Connexions and the Regions); Jane Haywood (Children and Youth); Marcus Bell (Cross Whitehall); Kathy Bundred (Children's Fund)

CHILDREN'S WORKFORCE UNIT
Director, Jeanette Pugh
Divisional Managers, Chris Wells (Children's Workforce Strategy); Peter Mucklow (Information Sharing and Assessment)

SCHOOLS DIRECTORATE AND CHILDREN, YOUNG PEOPLE AND FAMILIES DIRECTORATE JOINT COMMANDS
Divisional Manager, Policy and Performance, Christina Bienkowska

LOCAL TRANSFORMATION GROUP
Director, Sheila Scales
Divisional Managers, Robert Wood (Local Authority Performance); Andrew Sargent (Local Partnerships); Jenny Wright (Change and Innovation); Richard Blows (Local Implementation)

STRATEGY GROUP
Director, Anne Jackson
Divisional Managers, Janet Grauberg (Finance); Anne Jackson (Children's Bill and Strategy)

LIFELONG LEARNING DIRECTORATE
Director-General, Janice Shiner
Divisional Managers, Chris Barnham (Offenders Learning and Skills Unit); John Temple (Strategy and Funding)

ADULT BASIC SKILLS STRATEGY UNIT
Director, Susan Pember
Deputy Directors, Mark Dawe (Planning and Delivery); Barry Brooks (Standards and Achievement)

ADULT LEARNING GROUP
Director, Stephen Marston
Divisional Managers, Tim Down (Adult Learner Support); Margaret Bennett (Engaging Adults in Learning); Simon Perryman (Sector Skills); Hugh Tollyfield (Skills for Success); Madeleine Durie (Strategic Policy and Programme Support); Jane Mark-Lawson and Heidi Adcock (National and Regional Skills)

LEARNING DELIVERY AND STANDARDS GROUP
Director, Peter Lauener
Divisional Managers, Trevor Tucknutt (FE Strategy); James Turner (Learning and Skills Unit); Jon Ashe (Quality Improvement); Norman White (ILA Project)

STANDARDS UNIT
Director for Teaching and Learning, Jane Williams
Divisional Managers, David Taylor (Teaching and Learning); Barbara Roberts (Workforce Development)

QUALIFICATIONS AND YOUNG PEOPLE
Director, Rob Hull
Divisional Managers, Sara Marshall (Qualifications for Work); Celia Johnson (School and College Qualifications); Trevor Fellowes (Young People Learner Support); Alan Davies (Young People's Policy); Jane Benham (Examinations System); Carol Hunter (14–19 Programmes)

JOINT INTERNATIONAL UNIT
Director, Clive Tucker
Divisional Managers, Jane Evans (European Union); Gordon Pursglove (European Social Fund); Marie Niven (International Relations)

HIGHER EDUCATION DIRECTORATE
Director-General, Sir Alan Wilson
HE Adviser to Director-General, Nick Sanders
Head of HE Strategy Performance Unit, Elaine Hendry
Divisional Manager, HE Bill Team, Lesley Longstone

STRATEGY AND IMPLEMENTATION GROUP
Director, Ruth Thompson
Divisional Managers, Steve Geary *(Foundation Degrees, Employability and Progression Division);* Linda Dale *(Quality and Participation);* Rachel Green *(Funding and Research);* Martin Williams *(Access and Modernisation)*

STUDENT FINANCE GROUP
Director, Michael Hipkins
Divisional Managers, Peter Swift *(Student Finance Policy);* Ian Morrison *(Student Finance Delivery);* Noreen Graham *(Student Finance Modernisation)*

CORPORATE SERVICES AND DEVELOPMENT DIRECTORATE
Director-General, Susan Thomas
Divisional Managers, Graham Archer *(Leadership and Personnel);* Mike Daly *(Change);* Graham Holley *(Learning Academy);* Colin Moore *(Information Services);* Paul Neill *(Commercial Services);* Jan Stockwell and Dawn Jarvis *(Equality and Diversity Unit);* Katie Driver *(e-Delivery)*

LEGAL ADVISER'S OFFICE
Legal Adviser, Jonathan Jones
Divisional Managers, Dudley Aries *(Lifelong Learning and School Workforce);* Francis Clarke *(Effectiveness and Admissions);* Penny Halnan *(Governance and Finance);* Nic Ash *(Special Needs and Curriculum);* Carol Davies *(Equality, Establishment and European Commission);* Carola Geist-Divver *(Higher Education and Student Support);* Sandra Walker *(Children's Services)*

FINANCE AND ANALYTICAL SERVICES DIRECTORATE
Director-General, Peter Makeham
Divisional Managers, Suzanne Orr *(Internal Audit);* Ray Hinchcliffe *(Programme and Project Management Unit)*

FINANCE
Director, Stephen Kershaw
Divisional Managers, Peter Houten *(Finance Strategy);* Marion Maddox *(Corporate Planning and Performance);* Peter Connor, CBE *(Financial Accounting)*

ANALYTICAL SERVICES
Director, Paul Johnson
Divisional Managers, Audrey Brown *(Schools 1);* Richard Bartholomew *(Children and Families);* Tony Moody *(Youth);* Karen Hancock *(Higher Education);* Bob Butcher *(Adults);* John Elliot *(Central Economics and International);* Malcolm Britton *(Qualifications, Pupil Assessment and IT);* Alan Cranston *(Data Agency Project)*

DEPARTMENT FOR ENVIRONMENT, FOOD AND RURAL AFFAIRS
Nobel House, 17 Smith Square, London SW1P 3JR
T 020-7238 3000 F 020-7238 6591
W www.defra.gov.uk
The Department for Environment, Food, and Rural Affairs is responsible for Government policies on agriculture, horticulture and fisheries in England and for policies relating to the food chain. In association with

the agriculture departments of the Scottish Executive, the National Assembly for Wales and the Northern Ireland Office, and with the Intervention Board, the department is responsible for negotiations in the EU on the common agricultural and fisheries policies, and for single European market questions relating to its responsibilities. Its remit includes international agricultural and food trade policy.
The department exercises responsibilities for policies on climate change and international negotiations on sustainable development. It is also responsible for a range of pollution issues relating to waste and recycling, the protection and enhancement of the countryside and the marine environment, flood defence, GM crops, hunting, rural development and other rural issues. It is the licensing authority for veterinary medicines and the registration authority for pesticides. It administers policies relating to the control of animal, plant and fish diseases. It provides scientific, technical and professional services and advice to farmers, growers and ancillary industries, and commissions research to assist in the formulation and assessment of policy and to underpin applied research and development work done by industry. Responsibility for food safety and standards was transferred to the Food Standards Agency in April 2000.
Secretary of State for Environment, Food and Rural Affairs,
    The Rt. Hon. Margaret Beckett, MP
Principal Private Secretary, Gavin Ross
Private Secretaries, Robin Healey; Janice Kerr; Marianne Jenner
Special Advisers, Sheila Watson; Hazell Phillips
Minister of State (Environment and Agri-Environment), Elliot Morley, MP
Senior Private Secretary, Bradley Bates
Private Secretary, Emma Webbon
Minister of State (Rural Affairs and Urban Quality of Life),
    The Rt. Hon. Alun Michael, MP
Private Secretaries, Mike Burbridge; Rory Wallace
Assistant Private Secretaries, Louise Parry; Lewis Mortimer
Parliamentary Private Secretary, Peter Bradley, MP
Parliamentary Under-Secretary (Nature, Conservation and Fisheries), Ben Bradshaw, MP
Principal Private Secretary, Kathleen Cameron
Private Secretary, Jodie Tremelling
Parliamentary Under-Secretary (Farming, Food and Sustainable Energy), The Lord Whitty of Camberwell
Senior Private Secretary, Charlotte Middleton
Private Secretary, Emily Garner
Assistant Private Secretaries, Fiona Tranter; Mark Bainbridge
Permanent Secretary, Brian Bender, CB
Private Secretary, Claire Lewis
Assistant Private Secretary, Simon Huish

SUSTAINABLE FARMING, FOOD AND FISHERIES
T 020-7238 3000
Director-General, Andrew Lebrecht

FOOD CHAIN ANALYSIS AND FARMING
Director, vacant
Heads of Division, Ray Anderson; Andrea Young

EU AND INTERNATIONAL POLICY
Director, David Hunter
Heads of Division, Sarah Thomas; Andrew Lawrence

SUSTAINABLE AGRICULTURE AND LIVESTOCK
PRODUCTS DIRECTORATE
Director, Sonia Phippard
Heads of Division, Nigel Atkinson; Dr Mike Segal;
Andrew Slade

FOOD INDUSTRY AND CROPS DIRECTORATE
Director, John Robbs
Heads of Division, Andrew Perrins; Jeremy Cowper; David
Jones; Andrew Kuyk; Callton Young; Heather
Hamilton; Dr Stephen Hunter

FISHERIES DIRECTORATE
Fisheries Director, Rodney Anderson
Heads of Division, Peter Boyling; Richard Cowan;
Barry Edwards; Linsay Harris; Terence Ilott; James
Bradley
Chief Inspector, Sea Fisheries Inspectorate, Nigel
Gooding

ECONOMICS AND STATISTICS DIRECTORATE
East Block, Whitehall Place, London SW1A 2HH
T 020-7270 6000
Director, David Thompson
Heads of Division, Simon Harding; Peter Helm; Peter
Muriel; Stuart Platt; John Watson

NATURAL RESOURCES AND RURAL AFFAIRS
DIRECTORATE GENERAL
T 020-7238 3000
Director-General, Ursula Brennan

NATURAL RESOURCES RURAL AFFAIRS
Director, Jane Brown
Heads of Division, Martin Nesbit; John Osmond; Alan
Taylor; Mike Blackburn

RURAL POLICIES AND COMMUNITIES
Director, John Mills
Heads of Division, David Coleman; Graham Cory;
Katheryn Packer; Richard Pullen; Peter Cleasby; Robin
Mortimer

MODERNISING RURAL DELIVERY PROGRAMME
Director, Oona Muirhead
Heads of Division, Clare Hawley; Andrew Robinson

WILDLIFE, COUNTRYSIDE AND FLOOD MANAGEMENT
DIRECTORATE
Director, Brian Harding
Heads of Division, Martin Brasher; Martin Capstick; Susan
Carter; Linsay Harris; Terry Bird; Sheila McCabe; Peter
Costigan

ANIMAL HEALTH AND WELFARE DIRECTORATE
GENERAL
1A Page Street, London SW1P 4PQ T 020-7904 6000
Chief Veterinary Officer and Director-General, Debby
Reynolds
Deputy Chief Veterinary Officer, vacant
Heads of Division, Nigel Gibbens; Fred Landeg; Ruth
Lysons; David Pritchard; Alick Simmons; Peter Soul;
David Bench; Nick Coulson

ANIMAL HEALTH AND WELFARE DIRECTORATE
Director, David Dawson
Heads of Division, Malcolm Hunt; Diana Linksey; Alison
Reeves; John Bourne; Simon Hewitt

TSE GROUP
Director, Peter Nash
Heads of Division, Mandy Bailey; Catharine Boyle; Sue
Eades; Francis Marlow

ENVIRONMENT PROTECTION DIRECTORATE
GENERAL
Ashdown House, 123 Victoria Street, London SW1E 6DE
T 020-7238 6000
Director-General, Bill Stow, CB

ENVIRONMENT QUALITY AND WASTE
DIRECTORATE
Director, Neil Thornton
Heads of Division, Sue Ellis; Bob Ryder; Martin
Williams; Lindsay Cornish; Ivor Llewelyn;
John Burns

CLIMATE, ENERGY AND ENVIRONMENTAL RISK
DIRECTORATE
Director, Henry Derwent
Heads of Division, Colin Church; Jeremy Eppel; Sarah
Hendry; Chris Leigh; Chris De Grouchy; Stephen De
Souza

ENVIRONMENTAL PROTECTION STRATEGY
DIRECTORATE
Director, Robert Lowson
Heads of Division, Scott Ghagan; John Custance;
Bob Davies; Helen Marquard; Bob Davies;
Roy Hathaway

WATER AND LAND DIRECTORATE
Director, Richard Bird
Heads of Division, Daniel Instone; John Roberts; Prof. Jeni
Colbourne; Sarah Nason; Richard Wood

STRATEGY AND SUSTAINABLE DEVELOPMENT
Director, Jill Rutter
Heads of Division, Bronwen Jones; Andy Taylor

SOLICITOR AND LEGAL SERVICES DIRECTORATE
GENERAL
Solicitor and Director-General Legal Services, Donald
Macrae
Directors, Clare Sylvester; vacant
Heads of Division, Charles Allen; Chris Burke; Ian
Corbett; Peter Davis; Brian Dickinson; Nigel Lefton;
Alistair McGlone; Jonathan Robinson; Sue Spence;
Anne Werbicki; Gisela Davis; Anne Sachs;
Linda Dann
Chief Investigation Officer, Jan Panting

SCIENCE DIRECTORATE
Cromwell House, Dean Stanley Street, London SW1P 3JH
T 020-7238 6000
Chief Scientific Adviser and Head of Directorate, Prof.
Howard Dalton, FRS
Deputy Chief Scientific Adviser, Miles Parker
Heads of Division, Dr Tony Burne; Dr John Sherlock;
Michael Harrison

OPERATIONS AND SERVICE DELIVERY DIRECTORATE
GENERAL
T 020-7238 3000
Director-General, Mark Addison

VETERINARY SERVICES
1A Page Street, London SW1P 4PQ T 020-7904 6000
Deputy Chief Veterinary Officer (Services), Martin Atkinson
Heads of Veterinary Services, Linda Smith *(West)*; Robert
  Paul *(North)*; Gareth Jones *(East)*; Derick McIntosh
  (Scotland)
Chief Veterinary Officer (Scotland), Charles Milne
Assistant Veterinary Officer (Wales), Tony Edwards
Service Delivery, Richard Drummond
Contingency Planning, Ann Waters

CORPORATE SERVICES DIRECTORATE
East Block, Whitehall Place, London SW1A 2HH
T 020-7270 6000
Director, Richard Allen
Heads of Division, Wendy Cartwright; Neil MacIntosh;
  Tony Nickson; Caroline Smith; John Nodder; Mike
  Watkind

COMMUNICATIONS DIRECTORATE
Director of Communications, Lucian Hudson
Head of Corporate Communications, Kelly Freeman
Head of News, Martyn Smith

E-BUSINESS DIRECTORATE
Government Buildings, Epsom Road, Guildford, Surrey GU1 2LD
T 01483-568121
Director, David Myers
Director of IT, Shaun Soper
Heads of Division, Peter Barber; David Brown; Pearl
  Scrivener; Ray Boguslawski; Denise McDonagh

DELIVERY STRATEGY TEAM
1A Page Street, London SW1P 4PQ T 020-7904 6000
Head, George Trevelyan

GOVERNMENT OFFICES, RURAL DIRECTORS
East of England, Building A, Westbrook Centre, Milton Road,
  Cambridge, CB4 1YG T 01223-372759
Rural Director, J. Rabagliati
East Midlands, The Belgrave Centre, Talbot Street,
  Nottingham, NG1 5GG T 0115-971 9971
Rural Director, G. Norbury
North East, Welbar House, Gallowgate, Newcastle-upon-Tyne,
  NE1 4TD T 0191-201 3300
Rural Director, J. Bainton
North West, Sunley Tower, Piccadilly Plaza, Manchester, M1 4BE
  T 0161-952 4000
Regional Director, N. Cumberlidge
South East, Bridge House, 1 Walnut Tree Close, Guildford,
  Surrey, GU1 4GA T 01483-882255
Regional Director, Ms A. Parker
South West, 4th and 5th Floors, The Pithay, Bristol, BS1 2PB
  T 0117-900 1700
Regional Director, T. Render
West Midlands, 77 Paradise Circus, Queensway, Birmingham,
  B1 2DT T 0121-212 5000
Regional Director, B. Davies
Yorkshire and the Humberside, PO Box 213, City House, New
  Station Street, Leeds, LS1 4US T 0113-280 0600
Regional Director, G. Kingston

RURAL DEVELOPMENT SERVICE
T 020-7238 3000
Head of Group, John Adams
Head of Technical Advice, Alan Hooper
Business Process Director, Jeff Robinson
ERDPIT Programme Director, Ann Tarran
Strategy Delivery and Implementation, Paul Egginton

RURAL DEVELOPMENT CENTRES AND MANAGERS
East, Block B, Government Buildings, Brooklands Avenue,
  Cambridge, CB2 2DR T 01223-462727
Regional Manager, Martin Edwards
East Midlands, Block 7, Government Buildings, Chalfont
  Drive, Nottingham, NG8 3SN T 0115-929 1191
Regional Manager, Sue Buckenham
North East, Government Buildings, Kenton Bar, Newcastle-
  upon-Tyne, NE5 3EW T 0191-214 1800
Regional Manager, Fiona Gough
North West, Electra Way, Crewe Business Park, Crewe,
  Cheshire, CW1 6GJ T 01270-754000
Regional Manager, Tony Percival
South East, Block A, Government Buildings, Coley Park,
  Reading, Berkshire, RG1 6DT T 0118-958 1222
Regional Manager, Nick Beard
South West, Block 3, Government Buildings, Burghill Road,
  Westbury-on-Trym, Bristol, BS10 6NJ T 0117-959 1000
Regional Manager, David Sisson
West Midlands, Block C, Government Buildings, Whittington
  Road, Worcester, WR5 2LQ T 01905-763355
Regional Manager, Geoff Sansome
Yorkshire and The Humber, Government Buildings, Otley
  Road, Lawnswood, Leeds, LS16 5QT T 0113-230 3750
Regional Manager, Mark Watson

FINANCE, PLANNING AND RESOURCES DIRECTORATE
East Block, Whitehall Place, London SW1A 2HH
T 020-7270 6000
Finance Director, Andrew Burchell
Deputy Director, Ian Grattidge
Heads of Division, Roger Atkinson; Julie Flint; David
  Rabey; Richard Wilkinson; Andrew Cox; Lee
  McDonough; David Littler

IMPROVEMENT AND DELIVERY GROUP
Cromwell House, Dean Bradley Street, London SW1P 3JH
T 020-7238 6000
Director and Secretary to the Management Board, Francesca
  Okosi
Heads of Division, Marcus Nisbet; Angela Evans; Richard
  Chalk

EXECUTIVE AGENCIES
CENTRE FOR ENVIRONMENT, FISHERIES AND
AQUACULTURE SCIENCE
Pakefield Road, Lowestoft, Suffolk NR33 0HT
T 01502-562244 F 01502-513865
The Agency, established in April 1997, provides research
and consultancy services in fisheries science and
management, aquaculture, fish health and hygiene,
environmental impact assessment, and environmental
quality assessment.
Chief Executive, Dr P. Greig-Smith

CENTRAL SCIENCE LABORATORY (CSL)
Sand Hutton, York YO41 1LZ
T 01904-462000 F 01904-462111
The Central Science Laboratory (CSL) provides advice,
technical and enforcement support, underpinned by
appropriate research, to meet both the statutory and
policy objectives of DEFRA. It provides research and
development and advice on a commercial basis to other
government departments and to public and private sector
organisations both overseas and UK-based. CSL's main
work areas are: safeguarding food supplies through the
identification and control of invertebrate pests, plant pests
and diseases; the management of vertebrate wildlife, food

and consumer safety with the emphasis on the microbiological and chemical safety, and the quality and nutritional value of food. CSL is also concerned with environmental protection through the investigation of the impact of agriculture on the environment, and the promotion of biodiversity in agricultural habitats.
Chief Executive, Prof. M. Roberts

PESTICIDES SAFETY DIRECTORATE
Mallard House, Kings Pool, 3 Peasholme Green, York YO1 7PX
T 01904-640500 F 01904-455733
The Pesticides Safety Directorate is responsible for the evaluation and approval of agricultural pesticides and the development of policies relating to them, in order to protect consumers, users and the environment.
Chief Executive, Dr H. K. Wilson
Director (Approvals), R. Davis
Director (Finance, IT, and Corporate Services), Ms K. Dyson
Director (Policy), Dr S. Popple

RURAL PAYMENTS AGENCY
Kings House, 33 Kings Road, Reading RG1 3BU
T 0118-958 3626 F 0118-959 7736
The Rural Payments Agency (RPA) is an executive agency of the Department for Environment, Food and Rural Affairs. It is the single paying agency responsible for Common Agricultural Policy (CAP) schemes in England and for certain schemes throughout the UK.
Chief Executive, J. McNeill
Director (Business), S. Vry
Director (CAP), A. Sutton
Director (Finance), A. Kerr
Director (Human Resources), R. Gregg
Director (IS), A. McDermott
Director (Operations), H. MacKinnon

VETERINARY LABORATORIES AGENCY
Woodham Lane, New Haw, Addlestone, Surrey KT15 3NB
T 01932-341111 F 01932-347046
The Veterinary Laboratories Agency safeguards public and animal health through world class veterinary research and surveillance of farmed livestock and wildlife.
Chief Executive, Prof. S. Edwards
Director of Finance, C. Morrey
Director of Research (Acting), Prof. C. J. Thorns
Director of Science Strategy, Prof. J. A. Morris
Director of Surveillance and Laboratory Services, R. D. Hancock
Laboratory Secretary, C. Edwards

VETERINARY MEDICINES DIRECTORATE
Woodham Lane, New Haw, Addlestone, Surrey KT15 3LS
T 01932-336911 F 01932-336618
The Veterinary Medicines Directorate is responsible for all aspects of the authorisation and control of veterinary medicines, including post-authorisation surveillance of residues in animals and animal products, and the provision of policy advice to Ministers.
Chief Executive, S. Dean
Director (Corporate Business), C. Bean
Director (Licensing), J. O'Brien
Director (Policy), J. Fitzgerald

FOREIGN AND COMMONWEALTH OFFICE
King Charles Street, London SW1A 2AH
T 020-7008 1500 W www.fco.gov.uk
The Foreign and Commonwealth Office provides,

through its staff in the UK and through its diplomatic missions abroad, the means of communication between the British Government and other governments and international governmental organisations on all matters falling within the field of international relations.
It is responsible for alerting the British Government to the implications of developments overseas; for promoting British interests overseas; for protecting British citizens abroad; for explaining British policies to, and cultivating relationships with, governments overseas; for the discharge of British responsibilities to the overseas territories; for entry clearance UK Visas, with the Home Office and for promoting British business overseas (jointly with the Department of Trade and Industry through UK Trade and Investment).
Secretary of State for Foreign and Commonwealth Affairs, The Rt. Hon. Jack Straw, MP
Principal Private Secretary, Geoffrey Adams, CMG
Special Advisers, Dr Michael Williams; Ed Owen
Team Parliamentary Private Secretary, Roger Casale, MP
Minister of State, Dr Denis MacShane, MP *(Europe)*
Private Secretary, Peter Boxer
Parliamentary Private Secretary, Phyllis Starkey, MP
Minister of State, The Rt. Hon. The Baroness Symons of Vernham Dean *(Middle East)*
Private Secretary, Emma Wade
Parliamentary Private Secretary, Mark Todd, MP
Minister of State, Douglas Alexander, MP *(Trade, Investment and Foreign Affairs)*
Private Secretary, Peter Elder
Parliamentary Private Secretary, Lawrie Quinn, MP
Parliamentary Under-Secretary of State, Bill Rammell, MP
Private Secretary, David Whineray
Parliamentary Under-Secretary of State, Chris Mullin, MP
Private Secretary, Bharat Joshi
Permanent Under-Secretary of State and Head of HM Diplomatic Service, Sir Michael Jay, KCMG
Private Secretary, Menna Rawlings
Group Chief Executive, UK Trade and Investment, Sir Stephen Brown, KCVO
Directors-General, Dickie Stagg, CMG *(Corporate Affairs)*; John Sawers, CMG *(Political)*; Nicola Brewer, CMG *(EU Policy)*; William Ehrman, CMG *(Defence/Intelligence)*; Martin Donnelly *(Economic)*

DIRECTORS
Africa, James Bevan
Americas/Overseas Territories, Robert Culshaw, MVO
Asia Pacific, Nigel Cox
Chief Executive FCO Services, Stephen Sage
Communications, John Williams
Consular Services, Paul Sizeland
Finance, Ric Todd
EU Bilateral, Resources and Mediterranean, Dominick Chilcott
Global Issues, Philippa Drew
Human Resources, Darren Warren
International Security, David Richmond
Iraq, vacant
Middle East and North Africa, Simon Fraser
South Asia, Tom Phillips, CMG
Strategy and Information, Anne Pringle, CMG
UK Visas, Robin Barnett

SPECIAL REPRESENTATIVES
Afghanistan, Tom Phillips, CMG
Georgia, Sir Brian Fall, KCMG
Sudan, Alan Goulty, CMG

HEADS OF DEPARTMENTS
Afghanistan Unit, Jan Thompson
Africa Department (Equatorial), Tim Hitchens
Africa Department (Southern), Andrew Lloyd
Association of South East Asian Nations and Oceania Group, Michael Reilly
Commonwealth Co-ordination, Asif Ahmad
Consular Assistance Group, Janet Douglas
Consular Crisis Group, Ralph Publicover
Consular Resources Group, David Popplestone
Counter-Proliferation, David Landsman
Counter-Terrorism Policy Department, Philip Parham
Diplomatic Service Families Association, Emilie Salvesen
Drugs and International Crime Department, Lesley Pallett
Eastern Department, Simon Smith
Eastern Adriatic Department, Karen Pierce, CVO
Economic Policy, Creon Butler
Energy and Climate Change Group, Simon Banks (Deputy Head)
Environment Policy Department, Valerie Caton
Estate Strategy Unit, Julian Metcalfe
European Union Assistant Directorate (External), Tim Barrow, LVO, MBE
EU Common Foreign and Security Policy Team, James Morrison
EU Enlargement and Wider Europe Team, Charles Garrett
EU Northern Europe and International Team, Andrew Key
European Union Department (Internal), David Frost
European Union Mediterranean, Rob Fenn (Eastern); Wendy Wyver (Western)
Far East Group, Denis Keefe
Financial Planning and Performance Department, Tristan Price
FCO Services, Stephen Sage *(Chief Executive)*; Joy Herring *(Client Services)*; Nigel Morris *(Facilities Service Delivery)*; Patrick Cullen *(ICT Service Delivery)*; Dr Vanessa L. Davies *(People and Best Practice Service Delivery)*; John Elgie *(Positive Image UK Service Delivery)*; Rod Peters *(Supply Chain Service Delivery)*; Kerry Simmonds *(Finance)*; Elaine Kennedy *(Human Resources)*
Human Resources Directorate, David Warren *(Head of HR Directorate)*; Andrew Heyn *(HR Direct)*; Andrew George *(Health and Welfare Policy Team)*; Diane Corner; Carole Sweeney *(Legal Policy Team)*; David Powell *(Pay and Benefits Policy Team)*; Howard Drake *(Career Development and Senior Management)*; Richard Tauwhare *(Learning and Development)*; Gerry Reffo *(Performance Assessment and Development)*; Simon Pease *(Workforce Planning Team)*
Human Rights Policy, Jon Benjamin
Information Management, Heather Yasamee
Internal Audit (FCO/DFID), Jon Hews
IT Strategy Unit, Nick Westcott
Latin America and Caribbean Department, Stephen Williams
Legal Adviser, Sir Michael Wood, KCMG
Middle East Department, Charles Gray, CMG
Near East and North Africa Department, Nicholas Archer
North America Department, Martin Rickerd, OBE, MVO
Online Communications Department, Richard Codrington
Organisation for Security Co-operation in Europe and the Council of Europe Department, Peter January
Overseas Territories Department, Tony Crombie, OBE
Parliamentary Relations and Devolution, Matthew Hamlyn
Partnership and Networks Development Unit, Fraser Wheeler

Passports and Documentary Services Group, David Clegg, MVO
Policy, Communication and Training Group, Tim Flear, MVO
Press Office, John Williams *(Press Secretary)*; Peter Reid *(Head of News Room)*
Prism Programme, Andy Tucker
Procurement Policy, Michael Gower
Protocol Division, Charles de Chassiron, CVO
Public Diplomacy Policy Department, Paul Madden
Research Analysts, Robin Hoggard
Resource Accounting, Iain Morgan
Science and Technology Unit, Fiona Clouder Richards
Security Policy, Paul Johnston
Security Strategy Unit, Peter Millett
South Asian Department, Stephen Smith
Sudan Unit, Dr Alastair McPhail
Trade Union Side, Stephen Watson *(TUS Chair)*; Pam Chapman *(TUS Secretary)*
UK Visas (Joint FCO/Home Office Directorate), Robin Barnett
United Nations Department, Alistair Harrison, CVO
Whitehall Liaison Department, Matthew Kidd

UK TRADE AND INVESTMENT
Group Chief Executive, Sir Stephen Brown, KCVO
Deputy Group Chief Executive, Ian Jones

INTERNATIONAL SECTORS GROUP
Group Director, Peter Tibber

INTERNATIONAL TRADE DEVELOPMENT GROUP
Group Director, Ian Fletcher

STRATEGY AND COMMUNICATIONS GROUP
Group Director, John Reynolds

EXECUTIVE AGENCIES
CORPS OF QUEEN'S MESSENGERS
Support Group, Foreign and Commonwealth Office, London SW1A 2AH T 020-7270 2779
Superintendent of the Corps of Queen's Messengers, A. C. Brown
Queen's Messengers, P. Allen; R. Allen; Maj. A. N. D. Bols; Maj. P. C. H. Dening-Smitherman; Sqn. Ldr. J. S. Frizzell; Maj. D. A. Griffiths; Sqn Ldr A. Hill; R. Long; Maj. K. J. Rowbottom; Maj. M. R. Senior; Maj. J. E. A. Andre; W. Lisle; Maj. J. H. Steele; J. A. Hatfield; Sqn Ldr P. J. Hearn; S. J. Addy; Lt.-Col. R. I. S. Burgess

WILTON PARK CONFERENCE CENTRE
Wiston House, Steyning, W. Sussex BN44 3DZ
T 01903-815020 F 01903-816373
Wilton Park organises international affairs conferences and is hired out to Government departments and commercial users.
Chief Executive, Colin Jennings

DEPARTMENT OF HEALTH
Richmond House, 79 Whitehall, London SW1A 2NL
T 020-7210 3000
W www.doh.gov.uk
The Department of Health is responsible for the provision of the National Health Service in England and for social care. The department's aims are to support, protect, promote and improve the nation's health; to secure the provision of comprehensive, high quality care for all those who need it, regardless of their ability to pay, where they

live or their age; and to provide responsive social care and child protection for those who lack the support they need.

The Department of Health is responsible for setting health and social care policy in England. The department's work sets standards and drives modernisation across all areas of the NHS, social care and public health.

Secretary of State for Health, The Rt. Hon. Dr John Reid, MP

Principal Private Secretary, Dominic Hardy

Private Secretaries, Helena Feinstein; Nicola Hewer

Assistant Private Secretaries, Susanne Rowe; Rachel Robertson

Parliamentary Private Secretary, Mike Hall, MP

Minister of State for Health, The Rt. Hon. John Hutton, MP

Private Secretary, Sally Warren

Parliamentary Private Secretary, Claire Ward, MP

Minister of State, Rosie Winterton, MP

Private Secretary, Alistair Finney

Parliamentary Private Secretary, Jim Knight, MP

Parliamentary Under-Secretary of State (Community), Stephen Ladyman, MP

Private Secretary, Wendy Brown

Parliamentary Under-Secretary of State (Lords), Lord Warner of Brockley

Private Secretary, Frances Smethurst

Parliamentary Under-Secretary of State (Public Health), Melanie Johnson, MP

Acting Private Secretary, Anna Norris

Parliamentary Clerk, Neil Townley

Permanent Secretary, Sir Nigel Crisp, KCB

Head of Sir Nigel Crisp's Office, David McNeil

Private Secretaries, Yvonne Coghill; Andrew Larter

Assistant Private Secretaries, Lesley Whitehead; Clare Osborne

MANAGEMENT BOARD

Permanent Secretary and Chief Executive of the NHS, Sir Nigel Crisp KCB

Director of User Experience and Involvement and Chief Nursing Officer, Sarah Mullally

Group Director and Chief Medical Officer of Standards & Quality, Prof. Sir Liam Donaldson

Group Director of Delivery, John Bacon

Group Director, Strategy & Business Development, Hugh Taylor, CB

Director of Communications, Sian Jarvis

Director of Finance and Investment, Richard Douglas

Director of Strategy, Stephen O'Brien

HEALTH AND SOCIAL CARE STANDARDS AND QUALITY GROUP

Group Director, Prof. Sir Liam Donaldson

Director, Care Services Directorate, Anthony Sheehan

Director, Children and Mental Health, Mark Davies

Director, Group Business Team, Alan Doran

Director, Health Protection, International Health and Scientific Development, Dr David Harper, CB

Director, Older People & Disability, Craig Muir

Director, Regional Public Health, vacant

Director, Research and Development, Prof. Sir John Pattison

Deputy Director, Maggie King

Deputy Director, Delivery, Sally Davies

Deputy Director, Research Policy Strategy, Russell Hamilton

Division Head, Health Improvement & Prevention, Imogen Sharp

Division Head, Quality Strategy, Ron Cullen

Division Head, Sexual Health and Substance Misuse, Cathy Hamlyn

Division Head, Standards & Investigation, Ann Stephenson

Division Heads, Penny Bevan; Gerard Hetherington; Nick Boyd; Liz Woodeson Dr David Harper, CB

Chief Dental Officer, Professor Raman Bedi

Health Improvement, Deputy Chief Medical Officer, Dr Fiona Adshead

Healthcare Quality, Deputy Chief Medical Officer for Healthcare Quality, Prof. Aidan Halligan

STRATEGY AND BUSINESS DEVELOPMENT GROUP

Group Director, Hugh Taylor

Director of Development, Kate Barnard

Director, Communications, Sian Jarvis

Director, Corporate Management and Development, Hugh Taylor

Director, Strategy, Stephen O'Brien

Director, User Experience and Involvement, Sarah Mullally

Deputy Director, Flora Goldhill

Head of Campaign Management, Wynn Roberts

Head of News, Jon Hibbs

Head of Policy Unit, Tim Baxter

Head of Statistics, Dr John Fox

Head of Strategic Communications, John Worne

Head, Employee Reward, Sue Fathers

Head, Equality and Human Rights Group, Elisabeth Al-Khalifa

Head, Group Business Team, Peter Allanson

Head, Legislation, Richard Carter

Head, Operational Research for Leeds, Dr Geoff Royston

Head, Operational Research for London, Andre Hare

Head, Policy and Dissemination, Population and Lifestyles, Patsy Bailey *(Acting)*

Head, Social Care, Population Groups and Surveys, Anne Custance *(Acting)*

Branch Heads, Alan Angilley; Shaun Gallagher; Kevin Guinness; Mike Brownlee

Branch Heads, Equality and Human Rights Group, Melanie Field; Barry Mussenden; Lydia Yee

Branch Heads, Jim Allwood; Chris Horsey; Sue Lake; Linda Wishart; Judith Dainty; Adrian McNeil

Career Management, John Middleton

Change Management and Development, Anne Rainsberry

Change Management Team, Ruth Carnall

Chief Economic Adviser, Economics and Operational Research, Prof. Barry McCormick

Chief Health Professions Officer, Kay East

Chief Pharmaceutical Officer for England, Dr Jim Smith

Chief Scientific Officer, Sue Hill

Customer Services Centre, Linda Percival

Dental, Optical, Pharmacy and Prescription, Jim Stokoe

Deputy Chief Nursing Officer, Improving Patient Experience Programme, Kate Billingham

Deputy Chief Pharmacist, Jeanette Howe

DH Policy Collaborative Programme, Sue Gallagher

DH Security Unit, Joseph Neanor

Employee Relations and Support, vacant

Information Services, Dr Andrew Holt, CBE

Medicines, Pharmacy and Industry, Dr Felicity Harvey

NHS Workforce and General Practice, Andy Sutherland

Patients and the Public, Harry Cayton

Performance Management and Improvement, Marion Furr

Project Leader, Andrea Humphrey

Public Health, Disease, Hospital Care and Quality, Richard Willmer

Secretariat, Heather Gwynn, CBE

Senior Economic Advisers, Dr Donald Franklin; Richard Murray

Senior Medical Officer, Dr Peter Clappison

Strategic Human Resources, Pip Parr
System Reform Programme Manager, Steve Barnsley
Workstream Manager, Self Care, David Mowat

HEALTH AND SOCIAL CARE SERVICES DELIVERY
GROUP
Group Director, John Bacon
Director, Access, Margaret Edwards
Director, Counter Fraud and Security Management, Jim Gee
Director, Finance and Investment, Richard Douglas
Director, Programmes and Performance, Duncan Selbie
Director, Recovery and Support Unit, John Wilderspin
Director, Workforce, Andrew Foster
*Director-General, Information Systems and National
   Programme Delivery,* Richard Granger
Deputy Director, Accounting and Governance, Anne-Marie
   Miller
Deputy Director, Investment, Peter Coates
Deputy Director, NHS and Social Care, Phil Taylor
Deputy Director, Recovery and Support Unit, Richard
   Gleave
Deputy Director, Martin Staniforth
Head of Group Business Team, Julie Taylor
Head of Primary Care, Gary Belfield
Head of Secondary Care, Matthew Coats
Head, Business Improvement, Richard Mundon
Head, Delivery and Programmes, Ivan Ellul
Deputy Account Managers, Ian Dodge; Chris Garrett;
   Helen Robinson; Tim Young
Access Policy Development and Capacity Planning, Bob
   Ricketts
Branch Heads, Carl Vincent; Martin Campbell; Liz Eccles;
   Jeff Tomlinson; Peter Kendall; Alistair MacLellan; John
   Holden; Jeff Peers; Amanda Phillips; Keith Smith; Ben
   Dyson; Mike Walker; Andrew Griffiths; Pat Kelsey;
   Helen Pedley; Paul Loveland; Richard Armstrong;
   Debbie Mellor, OBE; Dean Royles; Steve Catling;
   Philip Leech
Chief Programme Officer, Gordon Hextall
Commercial Director, Ken Anderson
National Clinical Director of Primary Care, David
   Colin-Thome
Performance Policy and Delivery, Giles Wilmore
Workforce Capacity Portfolio Director, Rob Webster

MODERNISATION AGENCY
Director of Modernisation Agency, David Fillingham
Director, Corporate and External Affairs, Dr
   Valerie Day
Director, Finance, Martin Gore
Director, Health and Social Care Leadership Programmes,
   Penny Humphris
Director, Human Resources & Organisational Development,
   Caroline Corrigan
Director, Innovation and Knowledge, Pursuing Perfection,
   Helen Bevan
Director, New Ways of Working, Judy Hargadon
Director, Service Improvement, Michael Scott
Director, Strategic Communications, Jeremy Mooney
Director, Technologies in Health, Mark Outhwaite
Assistant Directors, Partnership Development, Tony
   Baldasera; Cathy Green; Jasbir Sunner; Anne O'Brien
Head, National Clinical Governance Support Team, Ron
   Cullen
*National Director, National Institute for Mental Health in
   England,* Philip Sculthorpe
Partnership Development Director, Prof. Christine
   Beasley

HER MAJESTY'S INSPECTOR OF ANATOMY
Branch Head, Dr Jeremy Metters, CB

SOLICITOR'S OFFICE, DEPARTMENT FOR WORK AND
PENSIONS
Solicitor, Ms Marilynne Morgan, CB
Director of Legal Services, Mrs Greer Kerrigan

ADVISORY COMMITTEES
ADVISORY COMMITTEE ON THE MICROBIOLOGICAL
SAFETY OF FOOD
Aviation House, 125 Kingsway, London WC2B 6NH
T 030-7276 8946

COMMITTEE ON THE SAFETY OF MEDICINES
Market Towers, 1 Nine Elms Lane, London SW8 5NQ
T 020-7084 2000 W www.mhra.gov.uk

SPECIAL HEALTH AUTHORITIES
DENTAL VOCATIONAL TRAINING AUTHORITY
Master's House, Temple Grove, Compton Place Road,
Eastbourne BN20 8AD T 01323-431189

FAMILY HEALTH SERVICES APPEAL AUTHORITY
30 Victoria Avenue, Harrogate HG1 5PR
T 01423-530280

HEALTH DEVELOPMENT AGENCY
Holborn Gate, 330 High Holborn, London WC1V 7BA
T 020-7430 0850

NATIONAL BLOOD SERVICE
Oak House, Reeds Crescent, Watford WD24 4QN
T 020-8258 2700 W www.blood.co.uk

NATIONAL INSTITUTE OF CLINICAL EXCELLENCE
71 High Holborn, London WC1V 6NA
T 020-7067 5800

NHS INFORMATION AUTHORITY
Aqueous II, Aston Cross, Rocky Lane, Birmingham B6 5RQ
T 0121-333 0333

NHS LITIGATION AUTHORITY
Napier House, 24 High Holborn, London WC1V 6AZ
T 020-7430 8700

PRESCRIPTION PRICING AUTHORITY
Bridge House, 152 Pilgrim Street, Newcastle-upon-Tyne
NE1 6SN T 0191-232 5371

UK TRANSPLANT
Fox Den Road, Stoke Gifford, Bristol BS34 8RR
T 0117-975 7575

EXECUTIVE AGENCIES
MEDICINES AND HEALTHCARE PRODUCTS
REGULATORY AGENCY (MHRA)
Market Towers, 1 Nine Elms Lane, London SW8 5NQ
T 020-7273 2000 F 020-7273 2353
The MHRA is responsible for protecting and promoting
public and patient safety by ensuring that medicines,
healthcare products and medical equipment meet
appropriate standards of safety, quality, performance and
effectiveness, and are used safely.

Chairman, Prof. Alasdair Breckenridge
Chief Executive, Prof. K. Woods

NHS ESTATES
1 Trevelyan Square, Boar Lane, Leeds LS1 6AE
T 0113-254 7000 F 0113-254 7299
NHS Estates provides advice and guidance in the area of health care estate and facilities management to the NHS and the health care industry.
Chief Executive, Peter Wearmouth

NHS PENSIONS AGENCY
Hesketh House, 200–220 Broadway, Fleetwood, Lancs FY7 8LG
T 01253-774774 F 01253-774860
NHS Pensions administers the NHS occupational pension scheme and the NHS Bursary Scheme for students.
Chief Executive, Alan Stuttard

NHS PURCHASING AND SUPPLY AGENCY
Premier House 60 Caversham Road, Reading, Berks RG1 7EB
T 0118-980 8600
The agency is responsible for ensuring that the NHS makes the most effective use of its resources by getting the best value for money possible when purchasing goods and services.
Chief Executive, Duncan Eaton

HOME OFFICE

Home Office, 50 Queen Anne's Gate, London SW1H 9AT
T 0870-000 1585 F 020-7273 2065
W www.homeoffice.gov.uk
The Home Office deals with those internal affairs in England and Wales which have not been assigned to other Government departments. The Home Secretary is the link between The Queen and the public and exercises certain powers on her behalf, including that of the royal pardon.
The Home Office's objectives are: to build a safe, just and tolerant society and to maintain and enhance public security and protection; to support and mobilise communities so that they are able to shape policy and improvement for their locality, overcome nuisance and anti-social behaviour, maintain and enhance social cohesion and enjoy their homes and public spaces peacefully; to deliver departmental policies and responsibilities fairly, effectively and efficiently; and to make the best use of resources. These objectives reflect the priorities of the Government and the Home Secretary in areas of crime, citizenship and communities, namely: to reduce crime and the fear of crime; to reduce organised and international crime; to combat terrorism and other threats to national security; to ensure the effective delivery of justice; to deliver effective custodial and community sentences; to reduce re-offending and protect the public; to reduce the availability and abuse of dangerous drugs; to regulate entry to, and settlement in, the UK in the interests of sustainable growth and social inclusion; and to support strong, active communities in which people of all races and backgrounds are valued and participate on equal terms.
The Home Office delivers these aims through the prison, probation and immigration services; its agencies and non-departmental public bodies, and by working with partners in private, public and voluntary sectors, individuals and communities. The Home Secretary is also the link between the UK Government and the governments of the Channel Islands and the Isle of Man.
Secretary of State for the Home Department, The Rt. Hon. David Blunkett, MP
Principal Private Secretary, Jonathan Sedgwick

Private Secretaries, Gareth Redmond; Kevin O'Connor; Nicola Thomas; Alice Reynolds; Dan Hartropp
Special Advisers, Katherine Raymond; Matthew Seward; Huw Evans; Matt Cavanagh
Minister of State, Hazel Blears, MP *(Crime Reduction, Policing, Community Safety)*
Private Secretary, Richard Austin
Minister of State, Des Browne, MP *(Citizenship, Immigration and Counter-Terrorism)*
Private Secretary, Neil Roberts
Minister of State, The Rt. Hon. Baroness Scotland of Asthal, QC *(Criminal Justice System and Law Reform)*
Private Secretary, Joanne Drean
Parliamentary Under-Secretary of State, Caroline Flint, MP *(Anti-Drugs Co-ordination and Organised and International Crime)*
Private Secretary, Jill Wanliss
Parliamentary Under-Secretary of State, Paul Goggins, MP *(Correctional Services and Reducing Re-Offending)*
Private Secretary, Dr Samantha Milton
Parliamentary Under-Secretary of State, Fiona Mactaggart, MP *(Race Equality, Community Policy, and Civil Renewal)*
Private Secretary, Graham Johnston
Permanent Secretary of State, John Gieve
Private Secretary, Diana Luchford
Parliamentary Clerk, Tony Strutt

COMMUNICATION DIRECTORATE
Director of Communications, Julia Simpson
Assistant Director and Head of Direct Communications Unit, Geoff Sampher
Customer Communications Manager, Katie Kerr
Deputy Director and Head of News (Press Office), John Toker
Deputy Director of Communications and Head of Marketing and Strategic Communications, Anne Nash
Head of Internal Communications Unit, Bill Reay
Head of Information Services Unit, Peter Griffiths

COMMUNITIES GROUP
Director-General, Helen Edwards
Director, Active Community Unit, vacant
Chairman, Commission for Racial Equality, Trevor Phillips
Heads of Units, Animal Procedures and Coroners Unit, Dr Jon Richmond; *Community Cohesion Unit*, Judith Lempriere; *Race Equality Unit*, Bruce Gill; *Regions and Renewals Unit*, Betty Moxon and John Curtis; *Identity Cards Programme Director*, Katherine Courtney; *Service Delivery Workstrand Assistant Director*, Richard Jenkins

CORPORATE DEVELOPMENT AND SERVICES DIRECTORATE
Director, Charles Everett
Heads of Units, Andrew Hyslop and David Palmer *(Agreement and Service Delivery)*; Tony Edwards *(Building and Estate Management)*; Nigel Arkle *(Commercial and Procurement Unit)*; Tony Fitzpatrick *(Home Office Pay and Pensions Service)*; Carol Anderson *(Programme Project Management Support Services)*; Peter Lowe *(Information Management Technology Unit)*
President of HO Sports and Social Association, John Gieve

CRIME REDUCTION AND COMMUNITY SAFETY GROUP
Director-General, Mark Neale
Directors, Margaret O'Mara *(Organised Crime)*; Peter Storr *(International)*; Sue Killen *(Drugs)*
Heads of Units, Vic Hogg *(Communities and Law Enforcement Drugs Unit)*; Paul Regan *(Extradition Bill*

Team); Lesley Pallett *(European and International Unit)*; Jim Bradley *(Financial Crime Team)*; Clive Welsh *(Judicial Co-operation Unit)*; Stephen Webb *(Policing and Organised Crime Unit)*; Judy Youell *(Strategic Co-ordination and Planning Unit)*; Judith Lempriere *(Treatment, Young People and Local Delivery Drugs Unit)*

CRIMINAL JUSTICE GROUP
Director-General, Moira Wallace, OBE
Director-General, Criminal Justice System IT, Jo Wright
Director, (Strategic Planning and Analysis)
Heads of Units, Anne Reece *(Claims Assessment Team)*; David Evans *(Confidence and Communications Team)*; David Reardon *(Criminal Justice System Race Unit)*; Deborah Grice *(Criminal Law Policy Unit)*; vacant *(Criminal Procedure and Evidence Unit)*; Catherine Lee *(Justice and Witnesses)*; Ann-Marie Field *(Local Performance and Delivery Support)*; Henry Cohen *(Programme Management)*; Paul A. David *(Resources, Planning and Communication)*; James Quinault *(Strategic Planning and Analysis)*; Frances Flaxington *(Victims Unit)*; *Chairman, Youth Justice Board,* Rod Morgan

HUMAN RESOURCES DIRECTORATE
Director, David Spencer
Personnel Director, Deborah Louden
Heads of Units, Tony Williams *(Human Resources Operations)*; Nigel Benger *(Corporate Support Services Unit)*; David McDonough *(Departmental Security Unit)*; Jill Douglas *(Personnel Management and Administration)*

IMMIGRATION AND NATIONALITY DIRECTORATE
Director-General, Bill Jeffrey
Senior Directors, Ken Sutton *(Asylum Support, Casework and Appeals)*; Mark Tanzer *(Change and Reform Strategy)*; David Stephens *(Finance and Services)*; Steven Barnett *(Human Resources)*; Paula Higson *(Managed Migration)*; Brodie Clark *(Operations and Projects)*; Nick Baird *(Policy)*
Directors, Joyce Irvine *(Appeals Directorate)*; Terry Neale *(Asylum Casework Directorate)*; Dave Roberts *(Border Control)*; Stephen Calvard *(Business Information Systems and Technology Directorate)*; Mary Shaw *(Department for Constitutional Affairs Asylum Division)*; Peter Topping *(Head of Correspondence Delivery Project)*; Brian Pollett *(Detention Services)*; Mark Goulding *(E-Border)*; Colin Allars *(Enforcement and Removals)*; Tony Arber *(Finance)*; Christina Parry *(General Group, Managed Migration)*; Ros McCool *(Human Resources Services)*; Lorraine Rogerson *(Immigration and Nationality Policy Directorate)*; Don Ingham *(Immigration Service Major Projects)*; Stacy Thornton *(Immigration Service Regions)*; David Wilson *(Intelligence)*; Susannah Simon *(International Policy Directorate)*; Emma de-la-Haye *(Joint Delivery Programme)*; Freda Chaloner *(National Asylum Support Service)*; Digby Griffith *(National Asylum Support Service: Accommodation)*; Jeremy Oppenheim *(National Asylum Support Service: Casework and Regions)*; Chris Hudson *(Operations Manager, Managed Migration)*

WORK PERMITS UK
Director, Kevin Faulkner
Heads of Units, Neil Hughes *(Customer Relations, Intelligence and Post Issue Checking)*; Roy Saxby *(Managed Migration)*; Steve Lamb *(Operations Manager)*; Mick Seals *(Policy, Reviews, Sector Schemes Evaluation)*

LEGAL ADVISORS' BRANCH
Senior Legal Advisor, David Seymour
Deputy Legal Advisor, Clive Osborne
Assistant Legal Advisors, Richard Clayton; Jim O'Meara; Anne Morris; Harry Carter; Sally Weston; Kevan Norris; Peter Fish; Rosemary Davies; Andrew Dodsworth; Robert Messenger; Sara Sternberg

PERFORMANCE AND FINANCE DIRECTORATE
Director, William Rye
Heads of Units, Tim Hurdle *(Audit and Assurance Unit)*; Carl Moynehan *(Accounting and Finance Unit)*; Alison Barnett *(Performance and Finance Support)*

RESEARCH, DEVELOPMENT AND STATISTICS DIRECTORATE
Director, Prof. Paul Wiles
Directors, Jon Simmons *(Analysing Crime Programme)*; Carol Hedderman *(Offending and Crime Justice Group)*
Assistant Directors, David Pyle; Carole F. Willis *(Crime and Policing Group)*; Gary Raw *(Immigration and Community Group)*
Heads of Units, Mark Greenhorn *(Corporate Management Unit)*

CENTRAL POLICE TRAINING AND DEVELOPMENT AUTHORITY (CENTREX)
Chief Executive, Chris Mould
Directors, Andy Humphreys *(Performance and Service Delivery)*; Valerie Vaughan-Dick *(Resources)*

EXECUTIVE AGENCIES
UK PASSPORT SERVICE
Globe House, 89 Ecclestone Square, London SW1V 1PN
Advice Line 0870-521 0410
Chief Executive, Bernard Herdan

CRIMINAL RECORDS BUREAU
Horton House, Exchange Flags, Liverpool L2 3YL
T 0870-909 0811
Chief Executive, Vincent Gaskill

FORENSIC SCIENCE SERVICE
Operational Headquarters, Priory House, Gooch Street North, Birmingham B5 6QQ T 0121-607 6800
Chief Executive, David Werrett

HM PRISON SERVICE
Cleland House, Page Street, London SW1P 4LN
Director-General, Phil Wheatley

PAROLE BOARD FOR ENGLAND AND WALES
see Prison Service section

PRISONS AND PROBATIONS OMBUDSMAN FOR ENGLAND AND WALES
see Prison Service section

DEPARTMENT FOR INTERNATIONAL DEVELOPMENT
1 Palace Street, London SW1 5HE
T 020-7023 0000 F 020-7023 0016
E enquiry@dfid.gov.uk
W www.dfid.gov.uk
Abercrombie House, Eaglesham Road, East Kilbride, Glasgow G75 8EA
T 01355-844000 F 01355-844099
Public Enquiries 0845-300 4100

The Department for International Development (DFID) is responsible for promoting sustainable development and reducing poverty. The central focus of the Government's policy, based on the 1997 and 2000 White Papers on International Development, is a commitment to the internationally agreed Millennium Development Goals, to be achieved by 2015. These seek to eradicate extreme poverty and hunger; achieve universal primary education; promote gender equality and empower women; reduce child mortality; improve maternal health; combat HIV/AIDS, malaria and other diseases; ensure environmental sustainability; and encourage a global partnership for development.

DFID's assistance is concentrated in the poorest countries of sub-Saharan Africa and Asia, but also contributes to poverty reduction and sustainable development in middle-income countries, including those in Latin America and Eastern Europe. DFID works in partnership with governments committed to the Millennium Development Goals, and with the private sector and the research community. It also works with multilateral institutions, including the World Bank, United Nations agencies, and the European Commission. DFID has headquarters in London and East Kilbride, offices in many developing countries, and staff based in British embassies and high commissions around the world.

Secretary of State for International Development, Hilary Benn, MP

Principal Private Secretary, Moazzam Malik

Private Secretary, Steven Sabey

Special Advisers, Alex Evans; Beatrice Stern

Parliamentary Private Secretaries, Tom Levitt, MP; Dr Ashok Kumar, MP

Parliamentary Clerk, Peter Gordon

Parliamentary Under-Secretary of State, Gareth R. Thomas, MP

Private Secretary, Alison Cochrane

Assistant Private Secretary, Hamid Kennedy

House of Lords Spokespeople, Baroness Amos; Lord Triesman

Liaison Peer, Baroness Whitaker

Permanent Secretary, Suma Chakrabarti

Private Secretary, Charlie Whetham

Director-General, Corporate Performance and Knowledge Sharing, Mark Lowcock

Director-General, Policy and International, Masood Ahmed

Director-General, Regional Programmes, Minouche Safix

Non-Executive Directors, Nemat Shafik; Bill Griffiths

REGIONAL PROGRAMMES

AFRICA DIVISION

Director of Division, Dave Fish

Director of Africa Policy, Graham Teskey

East and Central Africa, Heads of Departments, David Batt *(Deputy Director)*; Desmond Curran *(Africa Great Lakes and Horn)*

East and Central Africa, Heads of Offices, Peter Kerby *(Ethiopia)*; vacant *(Kenya)*; Dr Colin Kirk *(Rwanda)*; Caroline Sergeant *(Tanzania)*; Eric Hawthorne *(Uganda)*

East and Central Africa, Heads of Field Offices, Martin Johnston *(Angola)*; Georgina Yates *(Burundi)*; Paul Godfrey *(Democratic Republic of Congo)*; David Bell *(Somalia)*

Southern Africa, Head of Department, Anthony Smith *(Deputy Director)*

Southern Africa, Heads of Offices, Roger Wilson *(Malawi)*; Eamon Cassidy *(Mozambique)*; Helen Mealins *(Zambia)*; John Barrett *(Zimbabwe)*

Southern Africa, Heads of Field Offices, Sue Wardell *(South Africa, SACU, SADC)*; John Riley *(Botswana)*; Ish Thorn *(Lesotho)*; Kathy Wells *(Swaziland)*

West Africa, Sudan, Conflict and Humanitarian Policy, Heads of Departments, Brian Thomson *(Deputy Director)*

West Africa, Heads of Offices, John Winter *(Ghana)*; William Kingsmill *(Nigeria)*

West Africa, Heads of Field Offices, Jim Maund *(Sierra Leone)*; Louise Thomas *(Sudan)*; Rob Shooter *(West Africa, including Liberia)*; Bernard Harbone *(Conflict and Humanitarian Policy)*

ASIA AND PACIFIC DIVISION

Director of Division, Martin Dinham, CBE

Heads of Departments, Marcus Manuel *(Asia Directorate and Deputy Director, Asia and Pacific Division)*; Pam Jenkins *(Director's Cabinet)*; Howard Taylor *(County Programmes Unit)*; Jeremy Clarke *(Asia Policy and Strategy)*; John Gordon *(Regional Policy Unit)*; Joy Hutcheon *(Western Asia Department)*

Heads of Offices, Paul Ackroyd *(Bangladesh)*; Charlotte Seymour-Smith *(India)*; David Wood *(Nepal)*; Desmond Woode *(Pacific)*; Marshall Elliot *(South East Asia)*; Bela Bird *(Vietnam)*; Adrian Davis *(China)*; Dr Richard Hogg *(Afghanistan)*; Dr Daniel Arghiros *(Cambodia)*; vacant *(Indonesia)*; Penny Thorpe *(Sri Lanka)*; Gareth Aicken *(Pakistan)*

EUROPE, MIDDLE EAST AND AMERICAS DIVISION

Director of Division, Carolyn Miller

Heads of Departments, Brenda Killen *(Europe, Middle East and Americas)*; Jessica Irvine *(Europe and Central Asia)*; Richard Teuten *(Latin America)*; Alistair Fernie *(Middle East and North Africa)*; Clive Warren *(Overseas Territories)*

Heads of Offices, Sam Bickersteth *(Bolivia)*; vacant *(Brazil)*; Joanne Alston *(Caribbean)*; Gregory Briffa *(Guyana)*; Vic Heard *(Honduras)*; Elizabeth Carrire *(Jamaica)*; Georgia Taylor *(Nicaragua)*; Mark Lewis *(Peru)*; Simon Bland *(Russia)*; Doug Houston *(Ukraine)*

UK Delegation to the European Bank of Reconstruction and Development, Simon Ray

POLICY AND INTERNATIONAL

POLICY DIVISION

Director of Division, Sharon White

Deputy Directors, Marshall Elliott, Susanna Moorehead, Dr Michael Schultz

OFFICE OF THE CHIEF ADVISERS

Heads of Profession, Adrian Wood *(Economics)*; Roger Edmunds *(Statistics)*; Martin Sergeant *(Infrastructure and Urban Development)*; Jim Harvey *(Rural Livelihoods)*; John Warburton *(Environment)*; Desmond Bermingham *(Education)*

Chief Advisers, David Stanton *(Enterprise Development)*; Steve Bass *(Environment)*; Dr Julian Lob-Levyt *(Human Development)*; Sue Unsworth *(Governance)*; Dr Andrew Norton *(Social Development)*

Deputy Heads of Profession, John Burton *(Economics)*; Stewart Tyson *(Health)*; Max Everest-Phillips *(Governance)*; Pat Holden *(Social Development)*

INTERNATIONAL DIVISION
Director of Division, Peter Grant
Heads of Departments, Michael Mosselmans *(Conflict and Humanitarian Affairs)*; Nick Dyer *(European Union)*; Margaret Cund *(International Financial Institutions)*; Dianna Melrose *(International Trade)*; Carol Robson *(United Nations and Commonwealth)*
Team Leader, Rachel Turner *(International Division Advisory Team)*
UK Permanent Representative, Anthony Beattie *(FAO)*
UK Permanent Delegate, David Leslie Stanton *(UNESCO)*

CORPORATE PERFORMANCE AND
KNOWLEDGE SHARING

CORPORATE PERFORMANCE AND KNOWLEDGE
SHARING DIVISION
Heads of Departments, Mike Hammond *(Evaluation)*; Gavin McGillivray *(Private Sector Infrastructure/CDC)*; Paul Spray *(Policy Research)*

FINANCE AND CORPORATE PERFORMANCE
DIVISION
Director of Division, Richard Calvert
Heads of Departments, Kevin Sparkhall *(Strategy and Finance)*; Mike Smithson *(Accounts)*; Mike Noronha *(Internal Audit)*; Stephen Chard *(Programme Guidance and Support)*; Gordon Alexander *(ARIES)*

HUMAN RESOURCES DIVISION
Director, Liz Davies
Heads of Departments, John Anning *(Human Resources Operations)*; Ian McKendry *(Human Resources Policy)*; Peter Brough *(Overseas Pensions)*

INFORMATION, KNOWLEDGE AND
COMMUNICATIONS DIVISION
Director of Division, Owen Barder
Heads of Departments, Michael Green *(Information and Civil Society)*; Simon Jones *(Information Systems and Services)*; Gary James *(Office Services and Security)*; David Gillett *(Special Projects)*

OFFICE OF THE LEADER OF THE HOUSE OF COMMONS

2 Carlton Gardens, London SW1Y 5AA
W www.commonsleader.gov.uk
The Office of the Leader of the House of Commons is responsible for the arrangement of government business in the House of Commons and for planning and supervising the Government's legislative programme. The Leader upholds the rights and privileges of the House and acts as a spokesperson for the Government as a whole.

The Leader reports regularly to Cabinet on parliamentary business and the legislative programme. In his capacity as Leader of the House, he is a member of the Public Accounts Commission and of the House of Commons Commission, and also chairs the Select Committee on Modernisation of the House and the Electoral Policy Committee. As Lord Privy Seal, he is trustee of the Chevening Estate.

The Deputy Leader of the House of Commons supports the Leader in handling the Government's business in the House of Commons. He is responsible for monitoring MPs' and Peers' correspondence and is a member of several Committees including, the Cabinet Committee for the Legislative Programme, Parliamentary Modernisation,

Electoral Policy, Local Government Strategy, and the Criminal Justice Review Cabinet Committee.
Leader of the House of Commons, The Rt. Hon. Peter Hain, MP
Principal Private Secretary, Glynne Jones
Private Secretaries, Stephen Hillcoat; James Newman; Mike Newman
Deputy Leader of the House of Commons, Phil Woolas, MP
Private Secretary, Frances Slee

LORD CHANCELLOR'S DEPARTMENT
see Department for Constitutional Affairs

NORTHERN IRELAND OFFICE
11 Millbank, London SW1P 4PN
T 020-7210 3000
Castle Buildings, Stormont, Belfast BT4 3SG
T 028-9052 0700
W www.nio.gov.uk
The Northern Ireland Office was established in 1972, when the Northern Ireland (Temporary Provisions) Act transferred the legislative and executive powers of the Northern Ireland Parliament and Government to the UK Parliament and a Secretary of State.

The Northern Ireland Office is responsible primarily for security issues, law and order and prisons, and for matters relating to the political and constitutional future of the province. It also deals with international issues as they affect Northern Ireland.

Under the terms of the 1998 Good Friday Agreement, power was devolved to the Northern Ireland Assembly in 1999. The Assembly took on responsibility for all relevant areas of work previously undertaken by the departments of the Northern Ireland Office covering agriculture and rural development, the environment, regional development, social development, education, higher education, training and employment, enterprise, trade and investment, culture, arts and leisure, health, social services, public safety and finance and personnel. On 14 October 2002 the Northern Ireland Assembly was suspended and Northern Ireland returned to direct rule. For further details, *see* Regional Government section.
Secretary of State for Northern Ireland, The Rt. Hon. Paul Murphy, MP
Parliamentary Private Secretary, Gareth Thomas, MP
Minister of State, The Rt. Hon. John Spellar, MP
Parliamentary Private Secretary, Tom Harris, MP
Parliamentary Under-Secretaries of State, Ian Pearson, MP; Angela Smith, MP; Barry Gardiner, MP
Permanent Under-Secretary of State, Sir Joseph Pilling, KCB
Head of the Northern Ireland Civil Service, Nigel Hamilton

NORTHERN IRELAND INFORMATION SERVICE
Stormont Castle, Stormont Estate, Belfast BT4 3TT
T 028-9052 0700

EXECUTIVE AGENCIES
COMPENSATION AGENCY, Royston House, Upper Queen Street, Belfast BT1 6FD T 028-9024 9944
FORENSIC SCIENCE NORTHERN IRELAND, Seapark, 151 Belfast Road, Carrickfergus, Co. Antrim BT38 8PL
T 028-9036 5744
YOUTH JUSTICE AGENCY, Corporate Headquarters, 4143 Waring Street, Belfast BT1 2DY
T 028-9031 6 400
NORTHERN IRELAND PRISON SERVICE

SCOTLAND OFFICE

Dover House, Whitehall, London SW1A 2AU
T 020-7270 6754 F 020-7270 6812
1 Melville Crescent, Edinburgh, EH3 7HW
T 0131-244 9010 F 0131-244 9028
E scottish.secretary@scotland.gov.uk
W www.scottishsecretary.gov.uk

The Scotland Office is the department of the Secretary of State for Scotland, who represents Scottish interests in the Cabinet on matters reserved to the UK Parliament, i.e. constitutional matters, financial and economic matters, defence and international relations, immigration, social security, various matters relating to the single market with the UK (energy, transport, consumer protection) and employment. It also supports the Advocate-General, the legal adviser to the UK Government on Scottish law. *See* also Regional Government section and Department for Constitutional Affairs.

Secretary of State for Scotland, The Rt. Hon. Alistair Darling, MP
Private Secretary, Ms J. Colquhoun
Parliamentary Under-Secretary of State, Anne McGuire, MP
Private Secretary, Chloe Squires
Parliamentary Private Secretary, David Stewart, MP
Advocate-General for Scotland, Dr Lynda Clark, QC, MP
Private Secretary, James Johnston
Spokesperson in the House of Lords, Lord Evans of Temple Guiting, CBE

DEPARTMENT OF TRADE AND INDUSTRY

1 Victoria Street, London SW1H 0ET
T 020-7215 5000 F 020-7215 0105
W www.dti.gov.uk

The Department of Trade and Industry works with businesses, employees and consumers to increase UK productivity and competitiveness. The department's aim is to make the UK a more prosperous country and close the gap with its international competitors by making it easier and more attractive to start and grow new businesses in the UK. The DTI focuses on innovation to help more firms to grow and capture new markets, ensuring fair and open markets at home and overseas to support successful UK businesses and the creation of jobs, and better support for scientific excellence.

Secretary of State for Trade and Industry, Minister for Women and e-Minister, The Rt. Hon. Patricia Hewitt, MP
Principal Private Secretary, Matthew Hilton
Private Secretaries, Ian Gibbons; Shantha Shanmugalingam; Louise Proudlove; Joanne Edwards
Parliamentary Private Secretaries, Oona King, MP; Jackie Lawrence, MP
Minister of State, Douglas Alexander, MP *(Trade)*
Private Secretary, Peter Elder
Parliamentary Private Secretary, Lawrie Quinn, MP
Minister of State, Mike O'Brien, MP *(E-Commerce, Energy and Competitiveness)*
Private Secretary, Brian Payne
Parliamentary Private Secretary, Eric Joyce, MP
Minister of State, The Rt. Hon. Jacqui Smith, MP *(Industry, Regions, Deputy Minister for Women and Equality)*
Private Secretary, Spencer Mahoney
Parliamentary Private Secretary, Andy Love, MP
Parliamentary Under-Secretary of State, Gerry Sutcliffe, MP *(Employment Relations, Competition and Consumers)*
Private Secretary, Sam Myers

Parliamentary Under-Secretary of State, The Lord Sainsbury of Turville *(Science and Innovation)*
Private Secretary, Joe Burns
Parliamentary Under-Secretary of State, Nigel Griffiths, MP *(Small Business)*
Private Secretary, Claire Ball
Permanent Secretary, Sir Robin Young, KCB
Private Secretary, Tom Ridge
Parliamentary Clerk, Tim Williams
Chief Scientific Adviser and Head of Office of Science and Technology, Prof. Sir David King, KB
Director-General, Research Councils, Sir Keith O'Nions
Chief Executive UK Trade and Investment, Sir Stephen Brown, KCVO

STRATEGY UNIT
Director of Communications, Sheree Dodd
Director of Strategy Unit, Geoff Dart
Chief Economic Adviser, Vicky Pryce

INNOVATION GROUP
Director-General, David Hughes
Directors, Jonathan Startup *(Sustainable Development)*; Peter Burke *(Business Planning and Strategy)*; John Rhodes *(Facilitating Innovation)*; vacant *(Technical Innovation and Sustainable Development)*; David Reed *(Standards and Technical Regulations)*

BRITISH NATIONAL SPACE CENTRE
Director-General, Dr Colin Hicks
Deputy Director-General, David Leadbeater
Director, Space Applications and Programmes, Paula Freedman

NATIONAL WEIGHTS AND MEASURES LABORATORY
Director and Chief Executive, Jeffrey Llewellyn

PATENT OFFICE
Chief Executive, Ron Marchant

ENERGY GROUP
Director-General, Joan MacNaughton
Heads of Units, Jim Campbell *(Licensing and Consents Unit)*; Peter Waller *(Nuclear and Coal Liabilities Unit)*; Claire Durkin *(Energy Innovation and Business Unit)*; Neil Hirst *(Energy Markets Unit)*; Paul McIntyre *(British Energy Team)*; Rob Wright *(Energy Strategy Unit)*
Directors, Simon Toole *(Licensing Exploration and Development)*; Richard Mellish *(Electricity Consents and Agency Project Management)*; Alan Edwards *(Liabilities Management Unit)*; Stephen Spivey *(Nuclear Reform Bill)*; Ian Gregory *(Nuclear Business Relations)*; Ann Taylor *(Coal Health Claims)*; Iain Todd *(Energy Industries Business Unit and Oil and Gas Industry Development)*; Patrick Robinson *(Nuclear Safety and Security)*; Peter Fenwick *(Engineering Inspectorate)*; Ian Downing *(International Nuclear Policy and Programmes)*; Michael Buckland-Smith *(Civil Nuclear Security)*; Liz Baker *(Domestic and European Energy)*; Ann Eggington *(International and Infrastructure)*; Graham White *(Social Issues and Information)*; Ruth Hannant *(British Energy)*; David Hayes *(Strategic Issues)*; Adrian Gault *(Strategy Development, Research and Analysis)*; Rob Wright *(Energy MSU)*

BUSINESS GROUP
Director-General, Mark Gibson
Deputy Director-General, Regions, Katharine Elliott

BUSINESS RELATIONS
Director of Business Relations, John Alty
Directors, David Hendon *(Business Relations 2)*; David Saunders *(Business Support)*; Mark Higson *(Postal Services)*; Rachel Jenkinson *(Business Group, Change Management Team)*; Sheila Morris *(Business Relations Strategic Management)*; Rosa Wilkinson *(Policy, Business Relations)*; Martin Berry *(Industry Sponsorship Support)*

AEROSPACE AND DEFENCE INDUSTRIES TECHNOLOGY
Director, David Way

AUTOMOTIVE
Director, Sarah Chambers

BIOSCIENCE
Director, Monica Darnbrough

CHEMICALS
Director, Dr David Jennings

CONSTRUCTION INDUSTRIES
Director, Elizabeth Whatmore

CONSUMER GOODS AND SERVICES
Director, Jane Swift

MARINE UNIT
Director, Chris North

MATERIALS AND ENGINEERING
Director, Simon Edmonds

REGIONS
Directors, Tony Medawar *(RDA Sponsorship and Finance)*; Peter Bunn *(Regional Policy)*; John Neve *(Regional European Funds and Devolution)*; Andrew Steele *(Regional Assistance)*; vacant *(Social Enterprise Unit)*

SMALL BUSINESS SERVICE
Chief Executive, Martin Wyn-Griffith
Deputy Chief Executive, Stephen Lyle Smythe
Directors, Dr Ken Poulter *(Business Services)*; Mandy Mayer *(Strategy, Governance and Learning)*; Howard Capelin *(Channel Management)*; Peter Bentley *(Finance Director)*

SERVICES GROUP
Director-General, Dr Catherine Bell

EXPORT CONTROL AND NON PROLIFERATION
Director of Export Control and Non Proliferation, Mike O'Shea

FINANCE AND RESOURCE MANAGEMENT
Director of Finance and Resource Management, David Evans

HUMAN RESOURCES AND CHANGE MANAGEMENT
Director of Human Resources and Change Management, Shirley Pointer

INFORMATION AND WORKPLACE SERVICES
Director, Yvonne Gallagher
Directors, Jon Whitfield; David Evans *(Internal Audit)*; Peter Mason *(Finance)*; Curtis Juman *(Resource Accounting and Budgeting)*; Adam Jackson *(Business Planning and Performance Management)*; Tim Soane

(Change and Knowledge Management Unit); Rosemary Heyhoe *(HR Operations)*; Christine Hewitt, Jan Dixon *(HR Strategy and Terms of Employment)*; Howard Ewing *(People Deployment and Development)*; Andrew Matthew *(E-Strategy and Major Projects)*; Liz Maclachlan *(Information Policy and Services)*; Glyn Williams *(Export Control Organisation)*

FAIR MARKETS GROUP
Director-General, Stephen Haddrill

CORPORATE LAW AND GOVERNANCE
Director of Corporate Law and Governance, Bernadette Kelly
Directors, Robert Burns, Keith Masson, Rachel Clark, Richard Carter *(Company Law)*; John Grewe *(Financial Reporting Policy)*; Andrew Watchman *(Accountancy Advisor)*; Anne Willcocks *(Joint Head of Companies Bill Team)*; vacant *(Policy and Resources)*; Robert Burns *(Investigations and Inspector of Companies)*

CONSUMER AND COMPETITION POLICY
Director of Consumer and Competition Policy, Jonathan Rees
Directors, Pat Sellers *(Specific Market Interventions)*; Andrew Rees *(Research, Analysis and Evidence Database)*; Thoss Shearer *(Economic Regulation and Reform)*; Katherine Wright *(Strategy and Delivery)*; Tony Sims *(Europe and International)*; Adrian Walker-Smith *(Consumer Credit)*; Fiona Price *(Cross-Market Intervention)*

EMPLOYMENT RELATIONS
Director of Employment Relations, Janice Munday
Directors, Sarah Rhodes *(Dispute Resolution)*; Ros McCarthy-Ward *(Selected Employment Rights)*; Grant Fitzner *(Employment Market Analysis and Research)*; Jane Whewell *(European Strategy and Labour Market Flexibility)*; Julie Carney *(Participation and Skills)*

LOW PAY COMMISSION
Secretary, Kate Harre

WOMEN AND EQUALITY UNIT
35 Great Smith Street, London SW1P 3BJ
T 020-7273 8802
Director, Angela Mason
Directors, Liz Chennells *(Gender Equality and Social Justice)*; vacant *(Productivity and Diversity)*; Kate Allan *(Equality Co-Ordination)*

EUROPEAN AND WORLD TRADE POLICY
Director, World Trade, Edmund Hosker
Director, Europe, Jo Durning
Directors, Dr Elaine Drage *(EC Trade Policy)*; Julian Farrel *(EU Economic Reform)*; Tim Abraham *(Co-ordination World Trade)*; David Andrews *(Market Access)*; Matthew Cocks *(Future of Europe)*; Peter Dodd *(International Economies)*; vacant *(State Aid)*

LEGAL SERVICES GROUP
The Solicitor and Director-General, Anthony Inglese
Director of Legal Resource Management and Business Law, Carl Warren
Director of Legal Services A (Business and Consumers), Tessa Dunstan
Director of Legal Services B (Employment Discrimination, Equality and Intellectual Property), vacant

Director of Legal Services C (Energy, Communications, EC and Overseas Trade), Deborah Collins
Director of Legal Services D (Law Enforcement), Scott Milligan
Director of Legal Services E (Company Law and British Energy), Philip Bovey

UK TRADE AND INVESTMENT
Kingsgate House, 66–74 Victoria Street, London SW1E 6SW
T 020-7215 8000
UK Trade and Investment is the government organisation that supports both companies in the UK trading internationally and overseas enterprises seeking to locate in the UK. The organisation brings together the work of the DTI and the FCO.
Group Chief Executive, Sir Stephen Brown
Chief Executive, Inward Investment, William Pedder
Deputy Group Chief Executive, Director Corporate Resources, Susan Haird
Group Director, International Trade Development, David Warren
Group Director, Strategy and Communication, John Reynolds
Director, International Sectors Group, Peter Tibber

EXECUTIVE AGENCIES
COMPANIES HOUSE
Crown Way, Cardiff CF14 3UZ
T 0870-333 3636 F 029-2038 0900
E enquiries@companieshouse.gov.uk
W www.companieshouse.gov.uk
London Information Centre, 21 Bloomsbury Street, London WC1B 3XD T 0870-333 3636 F 029-2038 0517
Edinburgh, 37 Castle Terrace, Edinburgh EH1 2EB
T 0870-333 3636 F 0131-535 5820
Companies House incorporates companies, registers company documents and provides company information.
Registrar of Companies for England and Wales, Claire Clancy
Registrar for Scotland, Jim Henderson

EMPLOYMENT TRIBUNALS SERVICE
19–29 Woburn Place, London WC1H 0LU
T 020-7273 8666 F 020-7273 8686
The Service became an executive agency in 1997 and brought together the administrative support for the employment tribunals and the Employment Appeal Tribunal.
Chief Executive, Roger Heathcote

THE INSOLVENCY SERVICE
PO Box 203, 21 Bloomsbury Street, London WC1B 3QW
T 020-7637 1110 F 020-7291 6731
The Service administers and investigates the affairs of bankrupts and companies in compulsory liquidation; deals with the disqualification of directors in all corporate failures; regulates insolvency practitioners and their professional bodies; provides banking and investment services for bankruptcy and liquidation estates; and advises Ministers on insolvency policy issues.
Inspector-General and Chief Executive, Desmond Flynn
Deputy Inspectors-General, G. Horne; L. T. Cramp

NATIONAL WEIGHTS AND MEASURES LABORATORY
Stanton Avenue, Teddington, Middx TW11 0JZ
T 020-8943 7272 F 020-8943 7270
W www.nwml.gov.uk
The Laboratory administers weights and measures legislation, carries out type examination, calibration and testing, and runs courses on legal metrology.
Chief Executive, Dr Jeff Llewellyn

PATENT OFFICE
see Intellectual Property section

DEPARTMENT FOR TRANSPORT
Great Minster House, 76 Marsham Street, London SW1P 4DR
Ashdown House, 123 Victoria Street, London SW1E 6DE
T 020-7944 8300/020-7944 4873
W www.dft.gov.uk
The Department for Transport was established in May 2002 following the de-merger of the Department of Transport, Local Government and the Regions.
The department's main responsibilities are aviation, freight, health and safety, integrated and local transport, London Underground, maritime, mobility and inclusion, railways, roads and road safety, shipping and vehicles.
Secretary of State for Transport, The Rt. Hon Alistair Darling, MP
Principal Private Secretary, Scott McPherson
Minister of State, Tony McNulty, MP *(Transport)*
Private Secretary, Deborah Heenan
Parliamentary Under-Secretary of State, David Jamieson, MP *(Transport)*
Private Secretary, Naomi Hunt
Parliamentary Under-Secretary of State, Charlotte Atkins, MP *(Transport)*
Private Secretary, Emma Cliffe
Permanent Secretary, David Rowlands
Private Secretary, Dr Ben Still

BUSINESS DELIVERY SERVICES DIRECTORATE
Director, Michael Herron

DRIVER, VEHICLE AND OPERATOR GROUP
Director-General, Stephen Hickey

DRIVER, VEHICLE AND OPERATOR DIRECTORATE
Director, Andrew Stott

LEGAL SERVICES DIRECTORATE
Director, Christopher Muttukumaru
Divisional Managers, Alan Jones *(Aviation)*; Stephen Rock *(Driving and Road Safety)*; Hussein Kaya *(Highways)*; Elizabeth Walsh *(Railways, Operations and Construction)*; Robert Caune *(Railways, Track and Safety)*; Julie Murnane *(Road Vehicles)*; Martin Bedford *(Employment and Corporate Services)*; Ginny Harrison *(Marine)*; David Ingham *(Secondary Legislation)*

RAILWAYS, AVIATION, LOGISTICS, MARITIME AND SECURITY GROUP
Director-General, Sue Killen
Directors, David McMillan *(Aviation Directorate)*; Brian Wadsworth *(Logistics and Maritime Transport Directorate)*; Mark Lambirth *(Rail Directorate)*; Mike Fuhr *(Major Projects Directorate)*; Stephen Bligh *(Maritime and Coastguard Agency)*; Niki Tompkinson *(Transport Security Directorate)*; Vivien Bodnar *(Rail Performance Directorate)*
Deputy Director, John Grubb *(Transport Security Division)*
Chief Inspectors, Ken Smart *(Air Accidents Investigation Branch)*; Stephen Meyer *(Marine Accidents Investigation Branch)*
Principal Investigator of Rail Accidents, Carolyn Griffiths *(Rail Accidents Investigation Branch)*

ROADS, REGIONAL AND LOCAL TRANSPORT GROUP
Director-General, Robert Devereux
Directors, Bob Linnard *(Integrated and Local Transport Directorate)*; Steve Gooding *(Roads and Vehicle Directorate)*; Bronwyn Hill *(Regional Transport Directorate)*

STRATEGY, FINANCE AND DELIVERY GROUP
Director-General, Willy Rickett
Directors, Charles Skinner *(Communication Directorate)*; vacant *(Strategy and Delivery Directorate)*; Chris Riley *(Transport Analysis and Economics Directorate)*; Ken Beeton *(Transport Finance Directorate)*; Ann Frye *(Mobility and Inclusion Unit)*
Chair, Trade Union Side, Chris Hickey

EXECUTIVE AGENCIES
DRIVER AND VEHICLE LICENSING AGENCY
Longview Road, Morriston, Swansea SA6 7JL
T 01792-782341 F 01792-782793
W www.dvla.gov.uk
The Agency is responsible for registering and licensing drivers and vehicles, and the collection and enforcement of vehicle exercise duty.
Chief Executive, C. Bennett

DRIVING STANDARDS AGENCY
Stanley House, Talbot Street, Nottingham NG1 5GU
T 0115-901 2500 F 0115-901 2940
W www.dsa.gov.uk
The Agency is responsible for carrying out theory and practical driving tests for car drivers, motorcyclists, bus and lorry drivers and for maintaining the registers of Approved Driving Instructors and Large Goods Vehicle Instructors, as well as supervising Compulsory Basic Training (CBT) for learner motorcyclists. There are five area offices, which manage over 430 practical test centres across Britain.
Chief Executive, G. Austin

HIGHWAYS AGENCY
123 Buckingham Palace Road, London SW1W 9HA
T 08459-556575 F 020-7921 4592
W www.highways.gov.uk
The Agency is responsible for delivering the Transport Department's road programme and for maintaining the national road network in England.
Chief Executive, Archie Robertson

MARITIME AND COASTGUARD AGENCY
Spring Place, 105 Commercial Road, Southampton SO15 1EG
T 023-8032 9100 F 023-8032 9298
W www.mcga.gov.uk
The agency's aim is to prevent loss of life, continuously improve maritime safety and protect the marine environment.
Chief Executive, Capt. Stephen Bligh
Chief Coastguard, J. Astbury

VEHICLE CERTIFICATION AGENCY
1 Eastgate Office Centre, Eastgate Road, Bristol BS5 6XX
T 0117-951 5151 F 0117-952 4103
W www.vca.gov.uk
The agency is the UK authority responsible for ensuring that vehicles and vehicle parts have been designed and constructed to meet internationally agreed standards of safety and environmental protection.
Chief Executive, P. Markwick

VEHICLE AND OPERATOR SERVICES AGENCY
Berkeley House, Croydon Street, Bristol BS5 0DA
T 0117-954 3200 F 0117-954 3212
W www.vosa.gov.uk
The Vehicle and Operator Services Agency was formed on 1 April 2003 from the merger of the Vehicle Inspectorate and the Traffic Area Network. The agency is responsible for processing applications for licences to operate heavy goods and public service vehicles and registering bus services; operating and administering testing schemes for all vehicles including statutory annual testing of commercial vehicles, single vehicle approval of imported vehicles and vehicle identity checks; supervision of the MOT scheme; enforcement checks of vehicle safety, drivers' hours and emissions; supporting the independent Traffic Commissioners in carrying out their responsibilities for operator licensing, vocational drivers and bus registration; providing training and advice for commercial operators and MOT testers; investigating vehicle accidents, defects and recalls.
Chief Executive, Maurice R. Newey

HM TREASURY
1 Horse Guards Road, London SW1A 2HQ
T 020-7270 5000
E public.enquiries@hm-treasury.gov.uk
W www.hm-treasury.gov.uk
The Office of the Lord High Treasurer has been continuously in commission for well over 200 years. The Lord High Commissioners of HM Treasury are the First Lord of the Treasury (who is also the Prime Minister), the Chancellor of the Exchequer and five junior Lords. This Board of Commissioners is assisted at present by the Chief Secretary, the Parliamentary Secretary (who is also the Government Chief Whip in the House of Commons), the Paymaster-General, the Financial Secretary, and the Economic Secretary. The Prime Minister as First Lord is not primarily concerned with the day-to-day aspects of Treasury business; neither are the Parliamentary Secretary and the Junior Lords as Government Whips. Treasury business is managed by the Chancellor of the Exchequer and the other Treasury Ministers, assisted by the Permanent Secretary.

The Chief Secretary is responsible for public expenditure planning and control; public sector pay; value for money in the public services; public service agreements; public/private partnerships and procurement policy; strategic oversight of banking, financial services and insurance; departmental investment strategies; including the Capital Modernisation Fund and Invest to Save Budget; welfare reform; devolution; and resource accounting and budgeting.

The Paymaster-General is responsible for the Inland Revenue and the Valuation Office, with overall responsibility for the Finance Bill. She leads on personal taxation, business taxation, European and international tax issues.

The Economic Secretary is responsible for Customs and Excise; growth and productivity; science, research and development; competition and deregulation policy; export credit; VAT and road and fuel duties; and parliamentary financial business (Public Accounts Committee, National Audit Office).

The Financial Secretary is responsible for National Savings and Investments, the Debt Management Office, the Office of National Statistics, the Royal Mint, and the Government Actuary's Department; banking, financial services and insurance; foreign exchange reserves; debt management policy; financial services tax issues and charity taxation. She provides support to the Chancellor on EU issues.

Prime Minister and First Lord of the Treasury, The Rt. Hon. Tony Blair, MP
Chancellor of the Exchequer, The Rt. Hon. Gordon Brown, MP
Principal Private Secretary, Mark Bowman
Private Secretaries, Beth Russell; John-Christophe Gray
Parliamentary Private Secretary, Ann Keen, MP
Chief Economic Adviser to the Treasury, Michael Ellam
Special Advisers, Ian Austin; Spencer Livermore; Shriti Vadera; Stewart Wood; Paul Gregg; Chris Wales
Chief Secretary to the Treasury, The Rt. Hon. Paul Boateng, MP
Private Secretary, Dan Rosenfield
Parliamentary Private Secretary, Helen Southworth, MP
Special Adviser, Nicola Murphy
Paymaster-General, The Rt. Hon. Dawn Primarolo, MP
Private Secretary, Kathryn Morgan
Parliamentary Private Secretary, Chris Pond, MP
Financial Secretary to the Treasury, Stephen Timms, MP
Private Secretary, Guy Davison
Parliamentary Private Secretary, James Purnell, MP
Economic Secretary to the Treasury, John Healey, MP
Private Secretary, Sam Woods
Permanent Secretary to the Treasury, Gus O'Donnell, CB
Private Secretary, Cairan Martin
Parliamentary Secretary to the Treasury and Government Chief Whip, The Rt. Hon. Hilary Armstrong, MP
Private Secretary, Roy Stone, MP
Treasurer of HM Household and Deputy Chief Whip, Bob Ainsworth, MP
Comptroller of HM Household, The Rt. Hon. Thomas McAvoy, MP
Vice-Chamberlain of HM Household, Jim Fitzpatrick, MP
Lords Commissioners of HM Treasury (Whips), John Heppel, MP; Nick Ainger, MP; Jim Murphy, MP; Derek Twigg, MP; Joan Ryan, MP
Assistant Whips, Fraser Kemp, MP; Gillian Merron, MP; Charlotte Atkins, MP; Vernon Coaker, MP; Paul Clark, MP; Margaret Moran, MP; Bridget Prentice, MP; Tom Watson, MP

DIRECTORATES
Head of Ministerial Support Team, M. Bowman
Head of Communications and Strategy Team, M. Ellam

MACROECONOMIC POLICY AND INTERNATIONAL FINANCE
Managing Director, Jon Cunliffe
Directors, Simon Brooks; Stephen Pickford; Sue Owen; Melanie Dawes

BUDGET AND PUBLIC FINANCE
Managing Director, Nick Macpherson
Directors, Nick Holgate; Dave Ramsden; Edward Troup; Mike Williams

PUBLIC SERVICES
Managing Director, Jonathan Stephens
Directors, Ray Shostak; Paul Johnson; Anita Charlesworth

CORPORATE SERVICES AND DEVELOPMENT
Managing Director, Hilary Douglas

FINANCIAL MANAGEMENT, REPORTING AND AUDIT
Managing Director, Andrew Likierman
Director, Brian Glicksman

FINANCE, REGULATION AND INDUSTRY
Managing Director, James Sassoon
Directors, John Kingman; Phil Wynn Owen

EXECUTIVE AGENCIES
NATIONAL SAVINGS AND INVESTMENTS
see Finance section

OFFICE FOR NATIONAL STATISTICS
see Public Bodies section

ROYAL MINT
see Public Bodies section

UK DEBT MANAGEMENT OFFICE
Eastcheap Court, 11 Philpot Lane, London, EC3M 8UD
T 020-7862 6500 F 020-7862 6509
The UK Debt Management Office was launched as an executive agency of HM Treasury in April 1998. The office has two main functions: it is the Government's debt manager (issuing gilts, managing the gilt market); and the Government's cash manager (balancing the Exchequer's cash flow on a daily basis). On 1 July 2002 the operations of the Public Works Loan Board (PWLB), and the Commissioners for the Reduction of the National Debt (CRND) were integrated with the DMO.
Chief Executive, R. Stheeman

OTHER BODIES
OFFICE OF GOVERNMENT COMMERCE (OGC)
Trevelyan House, 26–30 Great Peter Street, London SW1P 2BY
T 0845-000 4999 W www.ogc.gov.uk
The Office of Government Commerce was set up on the 1 April 2000. It is a unique body within government, overseen by a supervisory board of Ministers and officials from across the departments of Government. Its aim is to achieve the best value for money for the Government's commercial relationships and coherence of purchasing activity across 200 Government departments, non-governmental bodies and agencies. The OGC is an office of HM Treasury.
Chief Executive, John Oughton

OGC BUYING SOLUTIONS

Royal Liver Building, Pier Head, Liverpool L3 1PE

T 0870-268 2222 F 0151-227 3315

W www.ogcbuyingsolutions.gov.uk

The Agency provides a professional purchasing service to Government departments and other public bodies. From April 2000 it became part of the Office of Government Commerce reporting to the Chief Secretary to the Treasury.

Chief Executive, Hugh Barrett

DEPARTMENT OF HM PROCURATOR-GENERAL AND TREASURY SOLICITOR

Queen Anne's Chambers, 28 Broadway, London SW1H 9JS

T 020-7210 3000 F 020-7210 3004

The Treasury Solicitor's Department, which became an executive agency in 1996, provides legal services for many Government departments. Those without their own lawyers are provided with legal advice, and both they and other departments are provided with litigation services. The Treasury Solicitor is also the Queen's Proctor, and is responsible for collecting Bona Vacantia on behalf of the Crown.

HM Procurator-General and Treasury Solicitor (SCS), Dame Juliet Wheldon, DCB, QC

LITIGATION DIVISION

Head of Division, D. Pearson

QUEEN'S PROCTOR DIVISION

Queen's Proctor, Juliet Wheldon

Assistant Queen's Proctor, Ravi Sampanthar

DIRECTORATE OF CORPORATE STRATEGY

Director of Corporate Strategy, Hilary Jackson

BONA VACANTIA DIVISION

Head of Division, Valerie Cain

EUROPEAN DIVISION

Legal Adviser, Frances Nash

CULTURE, MEDIA AND SPORT DIVISION

Head of Division, Ms I. Letwin

CABINET OFFICE AND CENTRAL ADVISORY DIVISION

Head of Division, Ms R. Jeffreys

MINISTRY OF DEFENCE ADVISORY DIVISION

Head of Division, M. J. Hemming

DEPARTMENT FOR EDUCATION AND SKILLS DIVISION

Head of Division, J. Jones

HM TREASURY ADVISORY DIVISION

Legal Adviser, S. Parker

WALES OFFICE

Gwydyr House, Whitehall, London SW1A 2ER

T 020-7270 0549 F 020-7270 0568

E walesoffice@walesoffice.gsi.gov.uk

W www.walesoffice.gov.uk

The Wales Office is the department of the Secretary of State for Wales, who represents Welsh interests in the Cabinet. *See* also Regional Government section and Department for Constitutional Affairs.

Secretary of State for Wales, The Rt. Hon. Peter Hain, MP

Principal Private Secretary, Simon Morris

Parliamentary Private Secretary, Chris Ruane, MP

Parliamentary Under-Secretary, Don Touhig, MP

Head of Office, Alison Jackson

DEPARTMENT FOR WORK AND PENSIONS

Richmond House, 79 Whitehall, London SW1A 2NS

T 020-7238 0800 F 020-7238 0763

E ministers@dwp.gsi.gov.uk

W www.dwp.gov.uk

The Department for Work and Pensions was formed on 8 June 2001 from parts of the former Department of Social Security and Department for Education and Employment and the Employment Service. The department helps unemployed people of working age into work, helps employers to fill their vacancies and provides financial support to people unable to help themselves through back to work programmes. The department also administers the Child Support system, social security benefits and the social fund. In addition, the department has reciprocal social security arrangements with other countries.

In April 2002 the Benefits Agency and the Employment Service was replaced by the Jobcentre Plus network (responsible for helping people to find jobs and paying benefits to people of working age), and the Pension Service which administers the Benefits Agency's pension-related services.

Secretary of State for Work and Pensions, The Rt. Hon. Alan Johnson, MP

Principal Private Secretary, Susan Park

Private Secretaries, Georgina Hill; Paul Todd; Matt Adams; Tammy Fevrier

Special Advisers, Chris Norton; Tom Clark

Parliamentary Private Secretary, Bob Laxton, MP

Minister of State, The Rt. Hon. Jane Kennedy, MP

Parliamentary Private Secretary, Kali Mountford, MP

Private Secretary, Caroline Crowther

Minister of State, Malcolm Wicks, MP *(Pensions)*

Private Secretary, Sara Protheroe

Assistant Private Secretary, Helen Hutchings

Parliamentary Private Secretary, David Cairns, MP

Parliamentary Under-Secretary of State, Chris Pond, MP

Private Secretary, Helen Daniels

Parliamentary Under-Secretary of State (Lords), The Rt. Hon. The Baroness Hollis of Heigham, DL

Private Secretary, Lucy Vause

Parliamentary Under-Secretary of State, Maria Eagle, MP *(Disabled People)*

Private Secretary, Paul McCourt

Permanent Secretary, Sir Richard Mottram, KCB

Private Secretary, Judith Tunstall

Parliamentary Clerk, Tim Elms

WORKING AGE AND CHILDREN GROUP

Group Director, Adam Sharples

Director, Fraud, Planning and Presentation Strategy, R. Clark

Director, National Employment Panel, Ms C. Stratton

Director, Work and Welfare Strategy, M. Richardson

Divisional Manager, Family Poverty and Employment Division, Julia Sweeney

PENSIONS AND DISABILITY GROUP
Managing Director, P. Gray
Director, Disability and Carers Service, Terry Moran
Director, Disability and Carers, Bruce Calderwood
Director, Information and Analysis Directorate, Robert Laslett
Director, Joint International Unit, C. Tucker
Director, Pensions Reform Division, Christopher Evans
Director, Pensions Stewardship Division, Richard d'Souza
Director, Private Pensions Centre, Policy Implementation Division, Charles Ramsden
Director, Private Pensions Policy Design Division, Tracy Gale
Director, Private Pensions Programme, Ms Hilary Reynolds
Divisional Manager, Pensions Strategy, Chris Capella
Head of Division, Private Pensions, Pension Protection Team, Charlie Massey

CORPORATE AND SHARED SERVICES GROUP FINANCE
Group Director and Principal Finance Officer, J. Codling
Director, Commercial, D. Smith
Director, Corporate Management Information, Sue Rice
Director, Financial Management, M. Davison
Director, Financial Services, P. Robinson
Director, Internal Assurance Services, C. Turner

PROGRAMME AND SYSTEMS DELIVERY GROUP
Group Director, Joe Harley
Head, Programme and Systems Delivery, Stephen Holt
Director, Digital Infrastructure, Debbie Heigh
Director, External Supply, John Priest
Director, Planning and Finance Strategy, Keith Palmer

HUMAN RESOURCES GROUP
Group Director, Kevin White
Diversity Director, Dr Barbara Burford
Head of Department, Development, Dawn Brodick
Head of Department, HR Services, G. Adey
Head of Department, Occupational Psychology, Dr M. Dalgliesh
Head of Department, Senior Civil Service, Kim Archer
Head of Department, Training Services, Mick Holbrook
Head of Department, Workforce Planning, Clarissa Poulson

MEDICAL POLICY AND CORPORATE MEDICAL GROUP
Chief Medical Adviser and Medical Director, Dr M. Aylward
Contractorisation of Medical Services (IMPACT) Project, Dr M. Henderson
EU of Medical Advisers in Social Security (UEMASS), Dr P. Stidolph
Policy Manager, Disability and Carer Benefits, Dr R. Thomas
Policy Manager, State Incapacity Benefits, Dr P. Sawney

LAW AND SPECIAL POLICY GROUP
Head of Group, Paul Jenkins
Director of Legal Services, J. Catlin
Assistant Director, Commercial Branch, R. Powell
Assistant Director, SOL Litigation, Ms A. James
Assistant Director, SOL Prosecutions, Amanda de Blaquiere

INFORMATION AND ANALYSIS DIRECTORATE
Director, Nick Dyson

Policy Manager, Ajudicational and Constitutional Reform, J. Griffiths
Policy Manager, Pension Provision Group, G. Fiegehen
Policy Manager, Welfare to Work Strategy, Jonathan Portes

COMMUNICATIONS DIRECTORATE
Group Director, Simon MacDowall
Head of Corporate Communications, Ken Young
Head of Marketing, Steve O'Neill
Head of Media Relations and News, Lindsey French

EXECUTIVE AGENCIES
APPEALS SERVICE AGENCY
see Tribunals Section

CHILD SUPPORT AGENCY
Long Benton, Benton Park Road, Newcastle upon Tyne NE98 1YX
CSA Helpline 08457-133133
The Agency was set up in April 1993. It is responsible for the administration of the Child Support Act and for the assessment, collection and enforcement of maintenance payments for all new cases.
Chief Executive, D. Smith
Non-Executive Directors, Dorit Braun; Mary Hay; Barbara Moorhouse; John Cross
Deputy Chief Executive and Director of Operations, M. Isaac
Directors, Ms E. Fox; John Oliver; Jim Edgar; Michael Foley; Sheila Bird; Ron Eagle

JOBCENTRE PLUS
Richmond House, 79 Whitehall, London SW1A 2NS
T 020-7238 0800 F 020-7238-0763
W www.jobcentreplus.gov.uk
Jobcentre Plus was formed in April 2002 following the merger of the Employment Service and some parts of the Benefits Agency. The agency administers claims for and payment of social security benefits to help people gain employment or improve their prospects for work as well as helping employers to fill their vacancies.
Chief Executive, D. Anderson

THE PENSION SERVICE
Trevelyan House, 30 Great Peter Street, London SW1P 2BY
Public Enquiries 0113-232 2414
The Pension Service was launched in April 2002 as an organisation dedicated to understanding the wishes and needs of today's and future pensioners, and providing State financial support for pensioners.
Chief Executive, Ms A. Cleveland

VETERANS AGENCY
Norcross, Blackpool, Lancs FY5 3WP
T 0800-169 2277
E help@veteransagency.gsi.gov.uk
W www.veteransagency.mod.uk
The Veterans Agency provides information and advice on issues of concern to veterans and their families. The Agency also administers the War Pension Scheme and provides welfare support to war pensioners and war widow(er)s and is responsible for the management of the Ilford Park Polish Home.
Chief Executive, A. Burnham

PUBLIC OFFICES

ADJUDICATOR'S OFFICE
Haymarket House, 28 Haymarket, London SW1Y 4SP
T 020-7930 2292 F 020-7930 2298
W www.adjucatorsoffice.gov.uk

The Adjudicator's Office opened in 1993 and investigates complaints about the way the Inland Revenue (including the Valuation Office Agency), Customs and Excise and the Public Guardianship Office have handled a person's affairs.
The Adjudicator, Dame Barbara Mills, DBE, QC
Head of Office, C. Gordon

ADVISORY, CONCILIATION AND ARBITRATION SERVICE
Brandon House, 180 Borough High Street, London SE1 1LW
T 020-7210 3613 F 020-7210 3708
W www.acas.org.uk

The Advisory, Conciliation and Arbitration Service (ACAS) was set up under the Employment Protection Act 1975 (the provisions now being found in the Trade Union and Labour Relations (Consolidation) Act 1992).

ACAS is directed by a Council consisting of a full-time chairman and part-time employer, trade union and independent members, all appointed by the Secretary of State for Trade and Industry. The functions of the Service are to promote the improvement of industrial relations in general, to provide facilities for conciliation, mediation and arbitration as means of avoiding and resolving industrial disputes, and to provide advisory and information services on industrial relations matters to employers, employees and their representatives.

ACAS has regional offices in Birmingham, Bury St Edmonds, Bristol, Cardiff, Glasgow, Kent, Leeds, Liverpool, London, Manchester, Newcastle upon Tyne and Nottingham.
Chair, R. Donaghy, OBE
Chief Executive, J. Taylor

ANCIENT MONUMENTS BOARD FOR WALES (CADW)
Crown Buildings, Cathays Park, Cardiff CF10 3NQ
T 029-2050 0200 F 029-2082 6375
E cadw@wales.gsi.gov.uk
W www.cadw.wales.gov.uk

The Ancient Monuments Board for Wales advises the Welsh Assembly on its statutory functions in respect of ancient monuments and historic buildings.
Chairman, Prof. R. R. Davies, CBE, FBA, DPHIL
Members, R. G. Keen; M. J. Garner; Prof. R. A. Griffiths, DLITT; R. Brewer, FSA; Prof. A. Whittle, FBA, DPHIL; C. Musson, MBE, FSA; Prof. M. Aldhouse-Green, FSA; Dr E. Plunkett Dillon; Dr N. Edwards
Secretary, Mrs J. Booker

ART GALLERIES

NATIONAL GALLERIES OF SCOTLAND
The Mound, Edinburgh EH2 2EL
T 0131-624 6200 F 0131-623 7126

The National Galleries of Scotland comprise the National Gallery of Scotland, the Scottish National Portrait Gallery, the Scottish National Gallery of Modern Art, the Dean Gallery and the Royal Scottish Academy Building. There are also outstations at Paxton House, Berwickshire, and Duff House, Banffshire. Total Government grant-in-aid for 2003–4 was £12.54 million.

TRUSTEES
Chairman of the Trustees, Mr B. Ivory, CBE
Trustees, Ms V. Atkinson; Ms A. Bonnar; Bailie E. Cameron; G. J. N. Gemmell, CBE; M. Ellington; Dr I. McKenzie Smith, OBE; Prof. R. Thomson; G. Weaver; Dr Ruth Wishart

OFFICERS
Director-General, Sir T. Clifford, FRSE
Director, National Gallery of Scotland, M. Clarke
Director, Scottish National Portrait Gallery, J. Holloway
Director, Scottish National Gallery of Modern Art and Dean Gallery, R. Calvocoressi

NATIONAL GALLERY
Trafalgar Square, London WC2N 5DN
T 020-7747 2885 F 020-7747 2423
W www.nationalgallery.org.uk

The National Gallery, which houses a permanent collection of western painting from the 13th to the 20th century, was founded in 1824, following a parliamentary grant of £60,000 for the purchase and exhibition of the Angerstein collection of pictures. The present site was first occupied in 1838; an extension to the north of the building with a public entrance in Orange Street was opened in 1975, and the Sainsbury wing was opened in 1991. Total Government grant-in-aid for 2004–5 is £21.227 million.

BOARD OF TRUSTEES
Chairman, P. Scott, QC
Trustees, Prof. D. Ades; S. Burke; J. Fenton; M. Getty; Prof. J. Higgins; Lady Hopkins; Sir John Kerr; J. Lessore; D. A. Moore; Lady Normanby; J. Snow; R. Sondhi; Sir Colin Southgate

OFFICERS
Director, Dr C. Saumarez Smith
Director of Administration, J. MacAuslan
Director of Conservation, M. H. Wyld, CBE
Director of Communications, Clare Gough
Director of Collections and Media, Dr S. Foister
Director of Education, K. Adler
Director of Scientific Research, Dr A. Roy
Senior Curator, D. Jaffé

NATIONAL PORTRAIT GALLERY

St Martin's Place, London WC2H 0HE
T 020-7306 0055 F 020-7306 0056
W www.npg.org.uk

A grant was made in 1856 to form a gallery of the portraits of the most eminent persons in British history. The present building was opened in 1896 and the Ondaatje Wing; including a new Balcony Gallery, Tudor Gallery, IT Gallery, Lecture Theatre and roof-top restaurant opened in May 2000. There are three regional partnerships displaying portraits at Montacute House, Beningbrough Hall and Bodelwyddan Castle. Total Government grant-in-aid for 2004-5 is £6.108 million.

BOARD OF TRUSTEES
Chairman, Sir David Scholey, CBE
Trustees, Prof. P. King, CBE, PRA; Ms F. Fraser; Sir M. Hastings; T. Phillips, CBE, RA; Prof. The Earl Russell, FBA; Mrs A. Shulman; Sir John Weston, KCMG; Baroness Willoughby de Eresby, DL; Prof. D. Cannadine; Prof. L. Jordanova; Dr C. Ondaatje, CBE, OC; Sara Selwood; Prof. R. Boucher, CBE, FRENG; Ms A. Fawcett, CBE; The Rt. Hon. Baroness Amos
Director, S. Nairne

ROYAL FINE ART COMMISSION FOR SCOTLAND

Bakehouse Close, 146 Canongate, Edinburgh EH8 8DD
T 0131-556 6699 F 0131-556 6633
W www.futurescotland.org

The Commission was established in 1927 and advises Ministers and local authorities on the visual impact and quality of design of construction projects. It is an independent body and gives its opinions impartially.
Chairman, The Rt. Hon. The Lord Cameron of Lochbroom, PC, FRSE
Commissioners, Ms J. Malvenan; R. G. Maund; M. Murray; D. Page; Ms B. Rae, CBE; Prof. R. Russell; M. Turnbull; A. Wright, OBE; Ms K. Anderson; Mrs M. Hickish; P. Stallan
Secretary, C. Prosser

TATE BRITAIN

Millbank, London SW1P 4RG
T 020-7887 8008 F 020-7887 8007
W www.tate.org.uk

Tate Britain displays the national collection of British art. The gallery opened in 1897, the cost of building (£80,000) being defrayed by Sir Henry Tate, who also contributed the nucleus of the present collection. The Turner wing was opened in 1910, and further galleries and a new sculpture hall followed in 1937. In 1979 a further extension was built, and the Clore Gallery, for the Turner collection, was opened in 1987. The Centenary Development was opened in 2001. There are four Tate galleries: Tate Britain and Tate Modern in London, Tate Liverpool and Tate St Ives.

BOARD OF TRUSTEES
Chairman, D. Verey
Trustees, Prof. D. Ades; Ms H. Alexander; Ms V. Barnsley; Prof. J. Latto; J. Snow; J. Studzinski; Ms G. Wearing; C. Ofili; J. Opie; Sir Howard Davies; P. Myners, CBE

OFFICERS
Director, Sir Nicholas Serota
Deputy Director, Alex Beard
Director of Collections, Jan Debbaut
Director, Tate Britain, S. Deuchar
Director, Tate Liverpool, C. Gruneberg
Director, Tate Modern, V. Todoli
Director, Tate St Ives, S. Daniel-McElvoy

TATE MODERN

Bankside, London SE1 9TG
T 020-7887 8008 Booking 020-7887 8888
W www.tate.org.uk

Opened on 11 May 2000, Tate Modern displays the Tate collection of international modern art dating from 1900 to the present day. It includes works by Dalí, Picasso, Matisse and Warhol as well as many contemporary works. It is housed in the former Bankside Power Station in London, which was redesigned by the Swiss architects Herzog & de Meuron.
Director, V. Todoli

WALLACE COLLECTION

Hertford House, Manchester Square, London W1M 3BN
T 020-7563 9500 F 020-7224 2155
W www.wallacecollection.org

The Wallace Collection was bequeathed to the nation by the widow of Sir Richard Wallace, in 1897, and Hertford House was subsequently acquired by the Government. Total Government grant-in-aid for 2003–4 was £2.2 million.
Director, Miss R. J. Savill
Head of Finance and Administration (acting), Simon Pink

ARTS COUNCILS

ARTS COUNCIL ENGLAND

14 Great Peter Street, London SW1P 3NQ
T 0845-300 6200 F 020-7973 6590
E enquiries@artscouncil.org.uk
W www.artscouncil.org.uk

Arts Council England is the national development agency for the arts in England, distributing public money from Government and the National Lottery. Between 2003 and 2006 Arts Council England will invest £2 billion of public funds in the arts in England. Arts Council Grants for the arts are for individuals, arts organisations, national touring and other people who use the arts in their work.

On 1 April 2002, the Arts Council of England and nine regional arts boards joined together to form a single development organisation for the arts. The nine regions are East, East Midlands, London, North East, North West, South East, South West, West Midlands and Yorkshire.
Chairman, Sir Christopher Frayling
Members, Sir Norman Adsetts, OBE; T. Bloxham, MBE; Ms D. Bull, CBE; P. Collard; Ms D. Grubb; Lady Sue Woodford Hollick; Prof. A. Livingston; S. Lowe; B. McMaster, CBE; Ms E. Owusu; W. Sieghart; Prof. S. Timperley; Ms D. Wilson
Chief Executive, P. Hewitt

ARTS COUNCIL OF NORTHERN IRELAND
MacNeice House, 77 Malone Road, Belfast BT9 6AQ
T 028-9038 5200 F 028-9066 1715
E publicaffairs@artscouncil-ni.org
W www.artscouncil-ni.org

The Arts Council of Northern Ireland is the prime distributor of Government funds in support of the arts in Northern Ireland. It is funded by the Department of Culture, Arts and Leisure, and the grant for 2003–4 was over £7 million.
Chair, Ms R. Kelly
Vice-Chair, M. Bradley
Members, Mrs E. M. Benson; Mrs K. Bond; W. Chamberlain; Ms L. Finnegan; Ms J. A. Holmes; A. Kennedy; T. Kerr; B. J. Milligan; W. H. C. Montgomery; Ms S. M. O'Connor; G. O'Heara; P. Spratt
Chief Executive, Ms R. McDonough

ARTS COUNCIL OF WALES
9 Museum Place, Cardiff CF10 3NX
T 029-2037 6500 F 029-2022 1447
E info@artswales.org.uk
W www.artswales.org.uk

The Arts Council of Wales is the development body for the arts in Wales. It funds arts organisations with funding from the National Assembly for Wales and is the distributor of National Lottery funds to the arts in Wales. The grant for 2003–4 was £34,445,801.
Chairman, Geraint Talfan Davies
Members, D. Davies; H. James; D. W. Walters; R. Till; S. Dancey; Dr F. Rhydderch; C. O'Neil; M. Elis; R. Wyn Hughes; D. Vokes; H. Roberts; J. Metcalf; J. Robert; Prof. D. Smith
Chief Executive, P. Tyndall

SCOTTISH ARTS COUNCIL
12 Manor Place, Edinburgh EH3 7DD
T 0131-226 6051 F 0131-225 9833
E help.desk@scottisharts.org.uk
W www.scottisharts.org.uk

The Scottish Arts Council is the main arts development agency in Scotland. It is a non-departmental public body, accountable to Scottish Ministers. The Scottish Arts Council investing funds from the Scottish Executive and National Lottery and working with partners to support and develop artistic excellence and creativity throughout Scotland.
Acting Chairman, D. Idiens
Members, Cllr E. Cameron; J. Scott Moncrieff; W. Speirs; Ms J. Baker; Ms L. Mitchell; J. Mulgrew; A. Cormack; S. Grimmond; Ms J. Hawksworth; A. Herman; R. McEwan; Ms A. Marrs; R. Smith; B. Twist
Director, G. Berry

ASSEMBLY OMBUDSMAN FOR NORTHERN IRELAND AND NORTHERN IRELAND COMMISSIONER FOR COMPLAINTS
Progressive House, 33 Wellington Place, Belfast BT1 6HN
T 028-9023 3821 F 028-9023 4912
E ombudsman@ni-ombudsman.org.uk
W www.ni-ombudsman.org.uk

The Ombudsman is appointed under legislation with powers to investigate complaints by people claiming to have sustained injustice in consequence of maladministration arising from action taken by a Northern Ireland Government department, or any other public body within his remit. Staff are presently seconded from the Northern Ireland Civil Service.
Ombudsman, T. Frawley
Deputy Ombudsman, J. MacQuarrie
Directors, C. O'Hare; R. Doherty; H. Mallon; P. Gibson

AUDIT COMMISSION FOR LOCAL AUTHORITIES AND THE NATIONAL HEALTH SERVICE IN ENGLAND AND WALES
1 Vincent Square, London SW1P 2PN
T 020-7828 1212 F 020-7976 6187
E enquiries@audit-commission.gov.uk
W www.audit-commission.gov.uk

The Audit Commission was set up in 1983 and is responsible for appointing external auditors to local authorities, including the Greater London Authority, and local National Health Service bodies in England and Wales. It is also responsible for promoting the proper stewardship of public finances and value for money in the services provided by local authorities and health bodies.
The Commission has a chairman, a deputy chairman and up to 18 members who are appointed by the Office of the Deputy Prime Minister in consultation with the Secretary of State for Wales and the Health Secretaries in England and Wales.
Chair, J. Strachan
Members, Dr. P. Lane; G. Lemos; D. Moss; J. Bowen; R. Hoyle; S. Bundred; Dr J. Dixon; Ms S. Drew Smith; P. Jones; Sir Michael Lyons; B. Pomeroy; Cllr. Baroness Scott; Prof. P. C. Smith
Chief Executive, Steve Bundred

AUDIT SCOTLAND
110 George Street, Edinburgh EH2 4LH
T 0131-477 1234 F 0131-477 4567
W www.audit–scotland.gov.uk

Audit Scotland was set up on 1 April 2000 to provide services to the Accounts Commission and the Auditor General for Scotland. Together they help to ensure that the Scottish Executive and public sector bodies in Scotland are held accountable for the proper, efficient and effective use of around £18 billion of public funds.
Audit Scotland's work covers over 200 bodies including local authorities, police and fire boards; NHS boards and trusts; further education colleges; the water authority; departments of the Scottish Executive; executive agencies such as the Prison Service and non-departmental public bodies such as Scottish Enterprise.
Audit Scotland carries out financial and regularity

audits to ensure that public sector bodies adhere to the highest standards of financial management and governance. It also performs audits to ensure that these bodies achieve the best value for money. All of Audit Scotland's work in connection with local authorities, fire and police boards is carried out for the Accounts Commission while its other work is undertaken for the Auditor General.

Auditor General, R. W. Black
Accounts Commission Chairman, A. MacNish
Secretary, W. F. Magee

BANK OF ENGLAND

Threadneedle Street, London EC2R 8AH
T 020-7601 4444 F 020-7601 4771
E enquiries@bankofengland.co.uk
W www.bankofengland.co.uk

The Bank of England was incorporated in 1694 under royal charter. It is the banker of the Government and it manages the issue of banknotes. Since May 1997 it has been operationally independent and its Monetary Policy Committee has had responsibility for setting short-term interest rates to meet the Government's inflation target. As the central reserve bank of the country, the Bank keeps the accounts of British banks, which maintain with it a proportion of their cash resources, and of most overseas central banks. The Bank has three main areas of activity: monetary stability, market operations and financial stability. Its responsibility for banking supervision has been transferred to the Financial Services Authority.

Governor, M. A. King
Deputy Governors, Sir Andrew Large; Ms R. Lomax
Non-Executive Directors, Sir David Cooksey; Sir Ian Gibson, CBE; Ms K. A. O'Donovan; Dr D. Julius, CBE; Sir. John Bond; Ms B. Blow; Sir Brian Moffat, OBE; Mrs L. Powers-Freeling; B. Barber; The Hon. Peter Jay; Dr D. Potter, CBE; Ms H. Rabbatts, CBE; Mrs M. Francis, LVO; Sir Graham Hall; C. McCarthy; Sir William Morris
Monetary Policy Committee, The Governor; the Deputy Governors; Prof. S. Nickell; C. Bean; Ms K. Barker; Ms M. Bell; P. Tucker; R. Lambert
Advisers to the Governor, M. Glover; C. Goodhart; A. Clark
Chief Cashier and Executive Director, Banking Services, A. Bailey
Chief Registrar, G. P. Sparkes
Secretary, A. Wardlow
The Auditor, Mrs C. Brady

BOUNDARY COMMISSIONS

The Commissions are constituted under the Parliamentary Constituencies Act 1986. The Speaker of the House of Commons is *ex officio* chairman of all four commissions in the UK. Each of the four commissions is required by law to keep the parliamentary constituencies in their part of the UK under review. The latest Boundary Commission report for England was completed in April 1995 and its proposals took effect at the 1997 general election. The next report must be submitted before April 2006. The latest Scottish report was completed in December 1994, with the European constituencies completed in April 1996.

ENGLAND

1 Drummond Gate, London SW1V 2QQ
T 020-7533 5177 F 020-7533 5176
Deputy Chairman, The Hon. Mr Justice Harrison
Joint Secretaries, R. Farrance; M. Barnett

WALES

1st Floor, Caradog House, 1–6 St Andrews Place, Cardiff CF10 3BE
T 029-2039 5031 F 029-2039 5250
Deputy Chairman, The Hon. Mr Justice Richards
Joint Secretaries, E. H. Lewis; M. Barnett

SCOTLAND

3 Drumsheugh Gardens, Edinburgh EH3 7QJ
T 0131-538 7200 F 0131-538 7240
Deputy Chairman, The Rt. Hon. Lady Cosgrove
Secretary, R. Smith

NORTHERN IRELAND

2nd Floor, Forestview, Purdy's Lane, Newtownbreda, Belfast BT8 7AR
T 028-9069 4800 F 028-9069 4801
Deputy Chairman, The Hon. Mr Justice Coghlin
Secretary, J. R. Fisher

BRITISH BROADCASTING CORPORATION

Broadcasting House, Portland Place, London W1A 1AA
T 020-7580 4468 BBC Information Line 0870-010 0222
W www.bbc.co.uk
Television Centre, Wood Lane, London W12 7RJ

The BBC was incorporated under royal charter in 1926 as successor to the British Broadcasting Company Ltd. The BBC's current charter came into force on 1 May 1996 and extends to 31 December 2006. The chairman, vice-chairman and other governors are appointed by The Queen-in-Council. The BBC is financed by revenue from receiving licences for the home services and by grant-in-aid from Parliament for the World Service (radio).

BOARD OF GOVERNORS
Chairman, M. Grade
Vice-Chairman, Anthony Salz
National Governors, Prof. F. Monds *(N. Ireland)*; Prof. M. Jones *(Wales)*; Sir Robert Smith *(Scotland)*; R. Sondhi, CBE
Governors, D. Gleeson; Dame Pauline Neville-Jones, DCMG; Dame Ruth Deech; Angela Sarkis, CBE; Deborah Bull, CBE; R.Tait

BOARD OF MANAGEMENT

EXECUTIVE COMMITTEE
Director-General and Editor-in-Chief, M. Thompson
Deputy Director-General, M. Byford
Directors, Ms J. Bennett *(Television)*; Ms J. Abramsky *(Radio and Music)*; Ms H. Boaden *(News)*; J. Willis *(Factual and Learning)*; A. Yentob *(Drama, Entertainment and Children)*; P. Loughrey *(Nations and Regions)*; J. Smith *(Chief Operating Officer)*; S. Dando *(Human Resources and Internal)*; A. Duncan *(Marketing, Communications and Audiences)*; P. Salmon *(Sport)*; Ms C. Thomson *(Policy and Legal)*; Ms C. Fairbairn *(Strategy and Distribution)*; A. Highfield *(New Media)*; vacant *(Chief Executive, BBC Worldwide)*

OTHER SENIOR STAFF
Controller, BBC1, L. Heggessey
Controller, BBC2, R. Keating
Controller, BBC3, S. Murphy
Controller, BBC4, R. Keating
Controller, Factual, G. Benson
Controller, BBC Daytime, Ms A. Sharman
Controller, Radio 1, A. Parfitt
Controller, Radio 2, L. Douglas
Controller, Radio 3, R. Wright
Controller, Radio 4, D. Damazer
Controller, Radio 5 Live, B. Shennan
*Controller, BBC Proms, Live Events and Television Classical
   Music*, N. Kenyon
Controller, Network Development, Nations and Regions,
   C. Cameron

BRITISH COUNCIL

10 Spring Gardens, London SW1A 2BN
T 020-7930 8466 F 020-7389 6347
Bridgewater House, 58 Whitworth Street, Manchester M1 6BB
T 0161-957 7000

The British Council was established in 1934,
incorporated by Royal Charter in 1940 and granted a
supplemental charter in 1993. It is an independent, non-
political organisation which promotes Britain abroad and
is the UK's international organisation for educational and
cultural relations. The British Council is represented in
216 towns and cities in 109 countries. Turnover in 2004–
5, including Foreign and Commonwealth Office grants
and contracted money, is expected to be £485.5 million.
Chairman, The Baroness Kennedy of The Shaws, QC
Director-General, D. Green, CMG

BRITISH FILM INSTITUTE

21 Stephen Street, London W1T 1LN
T 020-7255 1444 F 020-7436 0439
W www.bfi.org.uk

The British Film Institute (BFI) offers opportunities for
people throughout the UK to experience, learn and
discover more about the world of film and moving image
culture. The BFI incorporates the BFI National Library,
the monthly magazine *Sight and Sound*, the BFI National
Film Theatre, the annual London Film Festival and the
BFI London IMAX, and provides advice and support for
regional cinemas and film festivals across the UK. The BFI
also undertakes the preservation of, and promotes access
to films, television programmes, computer games, museum
collections, stills, posters and designs, and other special
collections.
Chairman, Anthony Minghella, CBE
Director, Amanda Nevill

BRITISH PHARMACOPOEIA COMMISSION

Market Towers, 1 Nine Elms Lane, London SW8 5NQ
T 020-7084 2561 F 020-7084 0566

The British Pharmacopoeia Commission sets standards
for medicinal products used in human and veterinary
medicines and is responsible for publication of the British
Pharmacopoeia (a publicly available statement of the
standard that a product must meet throughout its shelf-
life), the British Pharmacopoeia (Veterinary) and the
selection of British Approved Names. It has 15 members
who are appointed by the Secretary of State for Health,

the Minister for Environment, Food and Rural Affairs, the
Scottish Ministers, the National Assembly for Wales, and
the relevant Northern Ireland departments.
Chairman, Prof. D. Calam, OBE, DPHIL
Vice-Chairman, Prof. J. A. Goldsmith
Secretary and Scientific Director, Dr M. G. Lee

BRITISH STANDARDS INSTITUTION, BSI GROUP

389 Chiswick High Road, London W4 4AL
T 020-8996 9000 F 020-8996 7001
E cservices@bsi-global.com W www.bsi-global.com

British Standards – a part of the BSI Group – is the
recognised authority in the UK for the preparation and
publication of national standards, both for products and
the service sector. About 90 per cent of its standards work
is internationally linked. British Standards are issued
for voluntary adoption, though in some cases compliance
with a British Standard is required by legislation.
Industrial and consumer products and services certified as
complying with the relevant British Standard and
operating an assessed quality management system are
eligible to carry BSI's certification trade mark, known as
the 'Kitemark'.
Chairman, Sir David John, KCMG
Chief Executive, Stevan Breeze

BRITISH WATERWAYS

Willow Grange, Church Road, Watford, Herts WD17 4QA
T 01923-226422 F 01923-201400
E enquiries.hq@britishwaterways.co.uk
W www.britishwaterways.co.uk

British Waterways conserves and manages over 2,000
miles of canals and rivers in England, Scotland and Wales.
It is responsible to the Secretary of State for Environment,
Food and Rural Affairs.
   Its responsibilities include maintaining the waterways
and structures on and around them; looking after wildlife
and the waterway environment; and ensuring that canals
and rivers are safe and enjoyable places to visit.
Chairman, Dr G. Greener
Vice-Chairman of the Board, Sir P. Soulsby
Board Members, D. Langslow; I. Darling; Ms H. Gordon;
   C. Christie; Ms S. Achmatowicz; G. Fleming; Ms J.
   Lewis-Jones; Ms A. Malik; T. Tricker
Chief Executive, R. Evans

BROADS AUTHORITY

18 Colegate, Norwich NR3 1BQ
T 01603-610734 F 01603-765710
E broads@broads-authority.gov.uk
W www.broads-authority.gov.uk

The Broads Authority is a special statutory authority set
up under the Norfolk and Suffolk Broads Act 1988. The
functions of the Authority are to conserve and enhance
the natural beauty of the Broads; to provide integrated
management of the land and water space of the area; to
promote the enjoyment of the Broads by the public; and
to protect the interests of navigation. The Authority
comprises 35 members, appointed by the local authorities
in the area covered, environmental conservation bodies,
the Environment Agency, and the Great Yarmouth Port
Authority.
Chairman, Prof. K. Turner
Chief Executive, Dr J. Packman

CENTRAL ARBITRATION COMMITTEE
Third Floor, Discovery House, 28–42 Banner Street,
London, EC1Y 8QE
T 020-7251 9747 F 020-7251 3114
E enquiries@cac.gov.uk W www.cac.gov.uk

The Central Arbitration Committee is a permanent independent body which determines claims for statutory recognition and de-recognition of trade unions under the Employment Relations Act 1999, it also adjudicates on disclosure of information cases, issues relating to the European Works Council Directive and arbitrates on trade disputes.
Chairman, Sir Michael Burton
Secretary and Chief Executive, G. Charles

CERTIFICATION OFFICE FOR TRADE UNIONS AND EMPLOYERS' ASSOCIATIONS
Brandon House, 180 Borough High Street, London SE1 1LW
T 020-7210 3734/5 F 020-7210 3612
E info@certoffice.org W www.certoffice.org

The Certification Office is an independent statutory authority. The Certification Officer is appointed by the Secretary of State for Trade and Industry and is responsible for receiving and scrutinising annual returns from trade unions and employers' associations; for determining complaints concerning trade union elections, certain ballots and certain breaches of trade union rules; for ensuring observance of statutory requirements governing mergers between trade unions and employers' associations; for overseeing the political funds and finances of trade unions and employers' associations; and for certifying the independence of trade unions.
Certification Officer, David Cockburn

SCOTLAND
54–66 Frederick Street, Edinburgh EH2 1NB
T 0131-200 1200
Certification Officer for Scotland, Christine Stuart

CHARITY COMMISSION
Harmsworth House, 13–15 Bouverie Street, London EC4Y 8DP
T 0870-333 0123 F 020-7674 2310
2nd Floor, 20 King's Parade, Queen's Dock, Liverpool L3 4DQ
T 0870-333 0123 F 0151-703 1555
Woodfield House, Tangier, Taunton, Somerset TA1 4BL
T 0870-333 0123 F 01823-345003
W www.charitycommission.gov.uk

The Charity Commission for England and Wales is the Government Department whose aim is to give the public confidence in the integrity of charities. It also carries out the functions of the registration, monitoring and support of charities and the investigation of alleged wrong-doing. The Commission maintains a computerised register of some 187,000 charities. It is accountable to the courts and, for its efficiency, to the Home Secretary. There are five Commissioners appointed by the Home Office for a fixed term and the Commission has Offices in London, Liverpool, Taunton and Newport.
Chief Commissioner, J. Stoker
Acting Legal Commissioner, K. M. Dibble
Commissioners (part-time), D. Taylor; D. Unwin; Ms G. Peacock
Director of Operations, S. Gillespie

Heads of Legal Section, G. S. Goodchild; K. M. Dibble; J. Kilby
Head of Human Resources, Ms S. Bailey
Head of Policy Division, Ms R. Chapman
Information Systems Controller, K. Chown

REGIONAL OFFICES
SCOTLAND – Scottish Charities Office, Crown Office, 25 Chambers Street, Edinburgh EH1 1LA T 0131-226 2626
NORTHERN IRELAND – Department for Social Development, Charities Branch, 5th Floor, Churchill House, Victoria Square, Belfast BT1 4SD
WALES – 8th Floor, Clarence House, Clarence Place, Newport, South Wales NP19 7AA T 0870-333 0123

CHURCH COMMISSIONERS
1 Millbank, London SW1P 3JZ
T 020-7898 1000 F 020-7898 1131
E commissioners.enquiry@c-of-e.org
W www.churchcommissioners.org

The Church Commissioners were established in 1948 by the amalgamation of Queen Anne's Bounty (established 1704) and the Ecclesiastical Commissioners (established 1836). They are responsible for the management of the majority of the Church of England's assets, the income from which is predominantly used to help pay for the stipend and pension of the clergy. The Commissioners own over 120,000 acres of agricultural land, a number of residential estates in central London, and commercial property across Great Britain. They also carry out administrative duties in connection with pastoral reorganisation and redundant churches.

The Commissioners are: the Archbishops of Canterbury and of York; four bishops, three clergy and four lay persons elected by the respective houses of the General Synod; two deans or provosts elected by all the deans and provosts; three persons nominated by The Queen; three persons nominated by the Archbishops of Canterbury and York; three persons nominated by the Archbishops after consultation with others including the lord mayors of London and York and the vice-chancellors of the universities of Oxford and Cambridge; the First Lord of the Treasury; the Lord President of the Council; the Home Secretary; the Lord Chancellor; the Secretary of State for Culture, Media and Sport; and the Speaker of the House of Commons.

CHURCH ESTATES COMMISSIONERS
First, A. Whittam Smith
Second, Sir Stuart Bell, MP
Third, The Viscountess Brentford

OFFICERS
Secretary, A. C. Brown
Deputy Secretary (Finance and Investment), C. W. Daws

ASSISTANT SECRETARIES
Chief Surveyor, P. Clark
Chief Investments Manager, M. Chaloner
Pastoral and Redundant Churches, M. D. Elengorn
Official Solicitor, S. Jones

CIVIL AVIATION AUTHORITY
CAA House, 45–59 Kingsway, London WC2B 6TE
T 020-7379 7311
W www.caa.co.uk

The CAA is responsible for the economic regulation of UK airlines and for the safety regulation of UK civil aviation by the certification of airlines and aircraft and by licensing aerodromes, flight crew and aircraft engineers.

The CAA advises the Government on aviation issues, represents consumer interests, conducts economic and scientific research, produces statistical data, and provides specialist services and other training and consultancy services to clients world-wide. It also regulates UK airspace and runs the ATOL flight and air holiday protection scheme.

Chairman, Sir Roy McNulty
Secretary and Legal Adviser, R. J. Britton

COAL AUTHORITY
200 Lichfield Lane, Mansfield, Notts NG18 4RG
T 01623-427162 F 01623-622072
E thecoalauthority@coal.gov.uk
W www.coal.gov.uk

The Coal Authority was established under the Coal Industry Act 1994 to manage certain functions previously undertaken by British Coal, including ownership of unworked coal. It is responsible for licensing coal mining operations and for providing information on coal reserves and past and future coal mining. It settles subsidence claims not falling on coal mining operators. It deals with the management and disposal of property, and with surface hazards such as abandoned coal mine shafts.

Chairman, J. Harris
Chief Executive, Dr I. Roxburgh

COLLEGE OF ARMS (HERALDS' COLLEGE)
Queen Victoria Street, London EC4V 4BT
T 020-7248 2762 F 020-7248 6448
E enquiries@college-of-arms.gov.uk
W www.college-of-arms.gov.uk

The Sovereign's Officers of Arms (Kings, Heralds and Pursuivants of Arms) were first incorporated by Richard III. The powers vested by the Crown in the Earl Marshal (the Duke of Norfolk) with regard to state ceremonial are largely exercised through the College. The College is also the official repository of the arms and pedigrees of English, Welsh, Northern Irish and Commonwealth (except Canadian) families and their descendants, and its records include official copies of the records of Ulster King of Arms, the originals of which remain in Dublin. The 13 officers of the College specialise in genealogical and heraldic work for their respective clients.

Arms have always been, and still are, granted by letters patent from the Kings of Arms. A right to arms can only be established by the registration in the official records of the College of Arms of a pedigree showing direct male line descent from an ancestor already appearing therein as being entitled to arms, or by making application through the College of Arms for a grant of arms. Grants are made to corporations as well as to individuals.

Earl Marshal, The Duke of Norfolk

KINGS OF ARMS
Garter, P. L. Gwynn-Jones, CVO, FSA
Clarenceux, D. H. B. Chesshyre, LVO, FSA
Norroy and Ulster, T. Woodcock, LVO, FSA

HERALDS
Richmond (and Earl Marshal's Secretary), P. L. Dickinson
York, H. E. Paston-Bedingfeld
Chester (and Registrar), T. H. S. Duke
Lancaster, R. J. B. Noel
Windsor, W. G. Hunt, TD

PURSUIVANTS
Rouge Croix, D. V. White
Rouge Dragon, C. E. A. Cheesman

COMMISSION FOR ARCHITECTURE AND THE BUILT ENVIRONMENT
The Tower Building, 11 York Road, London SE1 7NX
T 020-7960 2400 F 020-7960 2444
E enquiries@cabe.org.uk W www.cabe.org.uk

The Commission for Architecture and the Built Environment (CABE) is responsible for promoting the importance of high quality architecture and urban design and encouraging the understanding of architecture through educational and regional initiatives. CABE offers free advice to local authorities, public sector clients and others embarking on building projects of any size or purpose.

Interim Chairman, Paul Finch
Chief Executive, R. Simmons

COMMISSION FOR INTEGRATED TRANSPORT
2nd Floor, 12 St James's Square, London SW1Y 4RB
E cfit@dft.gsi.gov.uk
W www.cfit.gov.uk

The Commission for Integrated Transport was proposed in the 1998 Transport White Paper and was set up in June 1999. Its role is to provide independent expert advice to the Government in order to achieve a transport system that supports sustainable development. Members of the Commission are appointed by the Secretary of State for Transport.

Chairman, Prof. D. Begg
Vice-Chairman, Sir Trevor Chinn
Members, L. Christensen, CBE; S. Francis; S. Joseph;
   D. Leeder; Ms L. Matson; W. Morris; Ms H. Holland;
   N. Scales; M. Parker; Baroness Scott; Sir Michael
   Hodgkinson; Sir Roy McNulty, CBE; R. Bowker;
   N. Betteridge; S. Hickey; M. Roberts

COMMISSION FOR LOCAL ADMINISTRATION IN ENGLAND
10th Floor, Millbank Tower, Millbank, London SW1P 4QP
T 020-7217 4620 F 020-7217 4621
Enquiry line 0845-602 1983

Local Commissioners (local government ombudsmen) are responsible for investigating complaints from members of the public against local authorities (but not town and parish councils); English Partnerships (planning matters only); Housing Action Trusts; education appeal panels; police authorities and certain other authorities. The Commissioners are appointed by the Crown on the recommendation of the Deputy Prime Minister.

Certain types of action are excluded from investigation, including personnel matters and commercial transactions unless they relate to the purchase or sale of land. Complaints can be sent direct to the Local Government Ombudsman or through a councillor, although the Local Government Ombudsman will not consider a complaint unless the council has had an opportunity to investigate and reply to a complainant.

A free leaflet *Complaint about the council? How to complain to the Local Government Ombudsman* is available from the Commission's offices.

Chairman and Chief Executive of the Commission and Local Commissioner (£147,198), T. Redmond
Vice-Chairman and Local Commissioner (£111,361), Mrs P. A. Thomas
Local Commissioner (£110,361), J. R. White
Member (*ex officio*), *The Parliamentary Commissioner for Administration*
Deputy Chief Executive and Secretary (£73,869), N. J. Karney

COMMISSION FOR RACIAL EQUALITY
St Dunstan's House, 201–211 Borough High Street, London SE1 1GZ
T 020-7939 0000 F 020-7939 0001
E info@cre.gov.uk W www.cre.gov.uk

The Commission for Racial Equality was set up under the 1976 Race Relations Act. It receives an annual grant from the Home Office but works independently of Government. The CRE is run by commissioners appointed by the Home Secretary, and has support from all the main political parties.

The CRE has three main duties: to work towards the elimination of racial discrimination and to promote equality of opportunity; to encourage good relations between people from different racial backgrounds; and to monitor the way the Race Relations Act is working and recommend ways in which it can be improved.

The CRE is the only Government-appointed body with statutory power to enforce the Race Relations Act. It also has a reference library which is open to the public (by appointment only).

Chairman, Trevor Phillips
Chief Executive, Sheila Rogers

COMMITTEE ON STANDARDS IN PUBLIC LIFE
35 Great Smith Street, London SW1P 3BQ
T 020-7276 2595 F 020-7276 2585
W www.public-standards.gov.uk

The Committee on Standards in Public Life was set up in October 1994. It is a standing body whose chairman and members are appointed by the Prime Minister; three members are nominated by the leaders of the three main political parties. The Committee's remit is to examine concerns about standards of conduct of all holders of public office, including arrangements relating to financial and commercial activities, and to make recommendations as to any changes in present arrangements which might be required to ensure the highest standards of propriety in public life. It is also charged with reviewing issues in relation to the funding of political parties. The Committee does not investigate individual allegations of misconduct.

Chair, Sir Alistair Graham
Members, The Rt. Hon. Chris Smith, MP; Rita Donaghy, OBE; Prof. Hazel Genn, CBE; Dame Patricia Hodgson,

DBE; Baroness Maddock; The Rt. Hon. Gillian Shephard, MP; Dr Elizabeth Vallance; Dr Brian Woods-Scawen
Secretary, Robert Behrens

COMMONWEALTH INSTITUTE
Kensington High Street, London W8 6NQ
T 020-7603 4535 F 020-7602 4525
E information@commonwealth.org.uk
W www.commonwealth.org.uk

The Commonwealth Institute is an educational trust. Its members are the member states of the Commonwealth who elect a Board of Trustees responsible to them. The Trustees have entered a joint venture with Cambridge University to create a Centre for Commonwealth Education.

Chairman, Miss J. Hanratty, OBE
Vice-Chairman, The Rt. Hon. Lord Fellowes, GCB, GCVO
Company Secretary, Ms J. Curry

COMMONWEALTH WAR GRAVES COMMISSION
2 Marlow Road, Maidenhead, Berks SL6 7DX
T 01628-634221 F 01628-771208
E general.enq@cwgc.org
W www.cwgc.org

The Commonwealth War Graves Commission (formerly Imperial War Graves Commission) was founded by royal charter in 1917. It is responsible for the commemoration of 1,694,783 members of the forces of the Commonwealth who lost their lives in the two world wars. More than one million graves are maintained in 23,292 burial grounds throughout the world. Over three-quarters of a million men and women who have no known grave or who were cremated are commemorated by name on memorials built by the Commission.

The funds of the Commission are derived from the six participating governments, i.e. the UK, Canada, Australia, New Zealand, South Africa and India.

President, HRH The Duke of Kent, KG, GCMG, GCVO, ADC
Chairman, The Secretary of State for Defence (UK)
Vice-Chairman, Gen. Sir John Wilsey, GCB, CBE, DL
Members, The High Commissioners in London for Australia, Canada, South Africa, New Zealand and India; Dame Susan Tinson, DBE; Sir John Keegan, OBE; Adm. Sir Peter Abbott, GBE, KCB; Alan Meale, MP; Ian Henderson, CBE, FRICS; Air Chief Marshal Sir Peter Squire, GCB, DFC, AFC, ADC; The Hon. Nicholas Soames, MP; Sir Rob Young, GCMG
Director-General and Secretary to the Commission, R. E. Kellaway
Deputy Director-General, M. S. Johnson, OBE
Legal Adviser and Solicitor, G. C. Reddie
Directors, D. R. Parker *(Information and Secretariat)*; B. Davidson, MBE *(Works)*; D. C. Parker *(Horticulture)*; Ms C. Cecil *(Personnel)*; P. J. Haysom *(Finance)*

IMPERIAL WAR GRAVES ENDOWMENT FUND
Trustees, A. C. Barker *(Chairman)*; C. G. Clarke; Gen. Sir John Wilsey, GCB, CBE
Secretary to the Trustees, P. J. Haysom

COMMUNITIES SCOTLAND

Thistle House, 91 Haymarket Terrace, Edinburgh EH12 5HE
T 0131-313 0044 F 0131-313 2680
W www.communitiesscotland.gov.uk

Communities Scotland is a Scottish Executive agency, reporting directly to Ministers. The agency's overall aim is to improve the quality of life for people in Scotland by working with others to create sustainable, healthy and attractive communities. They do this by regenerating neighbourhoods, empowering communities and improving the effectiveness of investment.
Chief Executive, Angiolina Foster

COMMUNITY FUND

1 Plough Place, London EC4A 1DE
T 020-7211 1800 Enquiries 020-7211 3737 F 020-7211 1750
W www.community-fund.org.uk

The Fund was set up under the National Lottery Act 1993 to distribute funds from the Lottery to support charitable, benevolent and philanthropic organisations. The chair and members are appointed by the Secretary of State for Culture, Media and Sport. The Fund's aim is to meet the needs of those at greatest disadvantage in society and also to improve the quality of life in the community.

It has UK-wide, county and regional priorities for its general grants programmes and runs two specialist programmes for research and international grants. So far the fund has distributed £2.4 billion to 54,000 charities and community groups.
Chair, Lady Brittan, CBE
Deputy Chairman, Dame Valerie Strachan, DCB
Members, E. Appelbee, MBE; S. Burkeman; J. Carroll;
P. Cavanagh; D. Graham; K. Hampton; Prof. J. Kearney, OBE; S. Malley; R. Martineau; Ms E. Watkins;
B. Whitaker, CBE; Ms C. Tongue; T. Idris
Director of Operations, Adrienne Kelbie
Director of Planning and Performance, Gerald Oppenheim

COMPETITION COMMISSION

Victoria House, Southampton Row, London WC1B 4AD
T 020-7271 0100 F 020-7271 0367
E info@competition-commission.gsi.gov.uk
W www.competition-commission.org.uk

The Commission was established in 1948 as the Monopolies and Restrictive Practices Commission (later the Monopolies and Mergers Commission); it became the Competition Commission in April 1999 under the Competition Act 1998. The Commission conducts in-depth inquiries into mergers (anticipated and completed); markets; and the regulation of major industries. Every inquiry the Commission undertakes is in response to a reference made to it by another authority, usually the Office of Fair Trading, but in certain circumstances by a Minister or by the regulators under sector-specific legislative provisions relating to regulated industries. The Commission has no power to conduct inquiries on its own initiative.

The Commission has a full-time chairman and three deputy chairmen. There are usually around 50 Commission members to carry out investigations. All are appointed by the Secretary of State for Trade and Industry for single eight-year terms.
Chairman, Prof P. A. Geroski
Deputy Chairman, P. J. Freeman

President, Appeal Tribunals, His Hon. Sir Christopher Bellamy, QC
Members, S. Ahmed; Prof. J. Baillie; R. D. D. Bertram; Mrs S. E. Brown, OBE; Miss L. I. Christmas; C. Clarke; Dr J. Collings; Dr D. Coyle; C. Darke; L. D. Elks; N. Garthwaite; W. Gibson; C. F. W. Goodall; Prof. C. Graham; Prof. A. Gregory; Mrs D. Guy; A. Hadfield; G. H. Hadley; Prof. A. Hamlin; Prof. J. Haskel; P. F. Hazell; C. E. Henderson, CB; G. L. Holbrook, MBE; R. N. Holroyd; Mrs M. J. Hopkirk; Prof. P. D. Klemperer; Prof. B. Lyons; N. C. L. Macdonald; Dame Barbara Mills, DBE, QC; Prof. P. Moizer; Dr E. M. Monck; Sir Derek Morris; Prof. D. Parker; Ms E. Pollard; R. A. Rawlinson; J. B. K. Rickford, CBE; E. J. Seddon; Dame Helena Shovelton, DBE; C. R. Smallwood; J. D. S. Stark; P. Stoddart; Prof. D. G. Trelford; R. Turgoose; Prof. C. Waddams; S. D. Walzer; M. R. Webster; Prof. S. R. M. Wilks; C. Wilson; A. M. Young
Non-Executive Directors, A. P. Foster; Dame Patricia Hodgson, DBE
Chief Executive and Secretary, R. Foster

COMPETITION SERVICE

Victoria House, Bloomsbury Place, London WC1A 2EB
T 020-7979 7979 F 020-7979 7978
E info@catribunal.org.uk
W www.catribunal.org.uk

The Enterprise Act 2002 created the Competition Service, a non-departmental public body whose purpose is to fund and provide support services to the Competition Appeal Tribunal. Support services include everything necessary to facilitate the carrying out by the Competition Appeal Tribunal of its statutory functions such as administration, accommodation and office equipment.
Director, Operations, Jeremy Straker

COUNCIL ON TRIBUNALS

81 Chancery Lane, London WC2A 1BQ
T 020-7855 5200 F 020-7855 5201
E enquiries@cot.gsi.gov.uk
W www.council-on-tribunals.gov.uk

The Council on Tribunals is an independent body that operates under the Tribunals and Inquiries Act 1992. It consists of 15 members appointed by the Lord Chancellor/Secretary of State for Constitutional Affairs and the Scottish Ministers; one member is appointed to represent the interests of people in Wales. The Scottish Committee of the Council generally considers Scottish tribunals and matters relating only to Scotland. The Parliamentary Commissioner for administration is an *ex officio* member of the Council and the Scottish Committee.

The Council advises on and keeps under review the constitution and working of the tribunals listed in the Tribunals and Inquiries Act, and considers and reports on administrative procedures relating to statutory inquiries. Some 80 tribunals are currently under the Council's supervision. It is consulted by and advises Government departments on a wide range of subjects relating to adjudicative procedures.
Chairman, The Rt. Hon. The Lord Newton of Braintree, OBE
Members, The Parliamentary Commissioner *(ex officio)*; J. Elliot, DKS *(Chairman of the Scottish Committee)*; Mrs C. Berkeley; Mrs E. C. Cameron; Miss J. C. Edwards; Ms Y. N. Genn; Mrs R. Hepplewhite; Mrs S. R. Howdle; Ms P.

Letts; B. Quoroll; Prof. G. Richardson; S. D. Mannion, QPM; A. W. Russell, CB; Dr A. V. Stokes; Ms H. Wilcox
Acting Secretary, R. B. Burningham

SCOTTISH COMMITTEE OF THE COUNCIL ON TRIBUNALS
44 Palmerston Place, Edinburgh EH12 5BJ
T 0131-220 1236 F 0131-225 4271
E sccot@gtnet.gov.uk
Chairman, R. J. Elliot, WS
Members, The Parliamentary Commissioner for Administration *(ex officio)*; Mrs B. Bruce; D. Graham; Mrs. M. Wood; Mrs E. Cameron; Mr S. Mannion; Mrs A. Watson
Secretary, Mrs E. M. MacRae

COUNTRYSIDE AGENCY
John Dower House, Crescent Place, Cheltenham, Glos GL50 3RA
T 01242-521381 F 01242-584270
W www.countryside.gov.uk

The Countryside Agency was set up in April 1999 by the merger of the Countryside Commission with parts of the Rural Development Commission. It is a statutory body which promotes the conservation and enhancement of the countryside in England and undertakes activities aimed at stimulating job creation and the provision of essential services in the countryside. The Agency is funded by an annual grant from the Department for Environment, Food and Rural Affairs and board members are appointed by the Secretary of State.
Chair, Ms P. Warhurst
Members, Ms K. Ashbrook; Rt. Revd Bishop of Norwich; Sir Martin Doughty; P. Fane; A. Hams, OBE; Prof. P. Lowe; Ms F. Rowe; J. Varley; Norman Glass; Dr Tayo Adebowale
Chief Executive, R. G. Wakeford
Directors, Miss M. A. Clark, OBE; Tim Lunel; S. Sleet; Tracey Slaven

COUNTRYSIDE COUNCIL FOR WALES/ CYNGOR CEFN GWLAD CYMRU
Maes y Ffynnon, Penrhosgarnedd, Bangor, Gwynedd LL57 2DW
T 0845-130 6229 F 01248-355782

The Countryside Council for Wales is the Government's statutory adviser on sustaining natural beauty, wildlife and the opportunity for outdoor enjoyment in Wales and its inshore waters. It is funded by the National Assembly for Wales and accountable to the First Secretary, who appoints its members.
Chairman, J. Lloyd Jones, OBE
Chief Executive, R. Thomas
Director, Corporate Services, L. Warmington
Director, Countryside Policy, Dr J. Taylor
Director of Science, Dr D. Parker

COURT OF THE LORD LYON
HM New Register House, Edinburgh EH1 3YT
T 0131-556 7255 F 0131-557 2148
W www.lyon-court.com

The Court of the Lord Lyon is the Scottish Court of Chivalry (including the genealogical jurisdiction of the *Ri-Sennachie* of Scotland's Celtic Kings). The Lord Lyon King of Arms has jurisdiction, subject to appeal to the Court of Session and the House of Lords, in questions of heraldry and the right to bear arms. The Court also administers the Scottish Public Register of All Arms and Bearings and the Public Register of All Genealogies. Pedigrees are established by decrees of Lyon Court and by letters patent. As Royal Commissioner in Armory, the Lord Lyon grants patents of arms (which constitute the grantee and heirs noble in the Noblesse of Scotland) to virtuous and well-deserving Scotsmen and to petitioners (personal or corporate) in The Queen's overseas realms of Scottish connection, and issues birthbrieves.
Lord Lyon King of Arms, R. O. Blair, LVO, WS

HERALDS
Albany, J. A. Spens, MVO, RD, WS
Rothesay, Sir Crispin Agnew of Lochnaw, BT, QC
Ross, C. J. Burnett, FSA SCOT

PURSUIVANTS
Unicorn, Alastair Campbell of Airds
Carrick, Mrs C. G. W. Roads, MVO, FSA SCOT
Bute, W. D. H. Sellar
Orkney Herald Extraordinary, Sir Malcolm Innes of Edinght, KCVO, WS
Linlithgow Pursuivant Extraordinary, J. C. G. George
Lyon Clerk and Keeper of Records, Mrs C. G. W. Roads, MVO, FSA SCOT
Procurator-Fiscal, George Way of Plean, SSC
Herald Painter, Mrs J. Phillips
Macer, H. M. Love

COVENT GARDEN MARKET AUTHORITY
Covent House, New Covent Garden Market, London SW8 5NX
T 020-7720 2211 F 020-7622 5307
E info@cgma.gov.uk
W www.cgma.gov.uk

The Covent Garden Market Authority is constituted under the Covent Garden Market Acts 1961 to 1977, the members being appointed by the Minister of Environment, Food and Rural Affairs. The Authority owns and operates the 56-acre New Covent Garden Markets (fruit, vegetables, flowers) which have been trading since 1974.
Chairman (part-time), L. Mills, CBE
General Manager, Dr P. M. Liggins
Secretary, C. Farey

CRIMINAL CASES REVIEW COMMISSION
Alpha Tower, Suffolk Street, Queensway, Birmingham B1 1TT
T 0121-633 1800 F 0121-633 1823/1804
E info@ccrc.gov.uk W www.ccrc.gov.uk

The Criminal Cases Review Commission is an independent body set up under the Criminal Appeal Act 1995. It is a non-departmental public body reporting to Parliament via the Home Secretary. It is responsible for investigating suspected miscarriages of justice in England, Wales and Northern Ireland, and deciding whether or not to refer cases back to an appeal court. Membership of the Commission is by royal appointment; the senior executive staff are appointed by the Commission.
Chairman, Prof. Graham Zellick
Members, B. Capon; L. Elks; A. Foster; I. Nicholl; D. Kyle; Prof. L. Leigh; J. MacKeith; K. Singh; B. Skitt; D. Jessel; M. Allen; M. Emerton; J. Weeden
Chief Executive, Ms J. Courtney
Director of Finance, C. Albert
Head of Human Resources, P. Wilkinson

Head of Communications, B. Worrall
Legal Advisers, J. Wagstaff; Ms F. Barrie
Police Adviser, R. Barrington

CRIMINAL INJURIES COMPENSATION APPEALS PANEL (CICAP)

11th Floor, Cardinal Tower, 12 Farringdon Road, London
EC1M 3HS
T 020-7549 4600 F 020-7549 4643
E info@cicap.gsi.gov.uk W www.cicap.gov.uk
Chairman, R. Goodier
Chief Executive and Secretary to the Panel, R. Burke

CRIMINAL INJURIES COMPENSATION AUTHORITY (CICA)

Morley House, 26–30 Holborn Viaduct, London EC1A 2JQ
T 020-7842 6800 F 020-7436 0804
W www.cica.gov.uk
Tay House, 300 Bath Street, Glasgow G2 4LN
T 0141-331 2726 F 0141-331 2287
Freephone 0800-358 3601

All applications for compensation for personal injury arising from crimes of violence in England, Scotland and Wales are dealt with at the above locations. (Separate arrangements apply in Northern Ireland.) Applications received up to 31 March 1996 are assessed on the basis of common law damages under the 1990 compensation scheme. Applications received on or after 1 April 1996 are assessed under a tariff-based scheme, made under the Criminal Injuries Compensation Act 1995, by the Criminal Injuries Compensation Authority (CICA). There is a separate avenue of appeal to the Criminal Injuries Compensation Appeals Panel (CICAP).
Chief Executive, Howard Webber
Deputy Chief Executive, Edward McKeown
Head of Legal Services, Anne Johnstone

CROFTERS COMMISSION

4–6 Castle Wynd, Inverness IV2 3EQ
T 01463-663450 F 01463-711820
E info@crofterscommission.org.uk
W www.crofterscommission.org.uk

The Crofters Commission, established in 1955 under the Crofters (Scotland) Act is a government funded organisation whose overall objective is the promotion of thriving and sustainable crofting communities. It works with communities to develop, reorganise and regulate crofting, and advises Scottish Ministers on crofting matters. The Commission administers the Crofting Counties Agricultural Grants Scheme, the Croft Entrant Scheme, the Livestock Improvement Schemes and the Crofting Community Development Scheme. It also provides a free enquiry service.
Chairman, David Green
Chief Executive, Shane Rankin

CROWN ESTATE

16 Carlton House Terrace, London SW1Y 5AH
T 020-7210 4377 F 020-7930 8187
W www.crownestate.co.uk

The Crown Estate includes substantial blocks of urban property, primarily in London, almost 120,000 hectares of agricultural land, almost half the foreshore, and the sea bed out to the twelve mile territorial limit throughout the United Kingdom. The Crown Estate is part of the hereditary possessions of the Sovereign 'in right of the Crown', managed under the provisions of the Crown Estate Act 1961 by the Crown Estate Commissioners who have a duty to maintain and enhance the capital value of estate and the income obtained from it.
Chairman, Ian Grant, CBE
Chief Executive, Roger Bright
Commissioners, Sir Donald Curry, KB, CBE; Hugh Duberly, CBE; Martin Moore; Dinah Nichols, CB; Ronald Spinney, FRICS; Jenefer Greenwood, FRICS
Director of Urban Estates, Tony Bickmore, FRICS

HEADS OF DEPARTMENTS
Asset Management, Dr Tony Murray
Communications, Irene Belcher
Corporate Planning and Human Resources, Martin Gravestock
Customer Management, Elspeth Miller
Development Management, Liam Colgan
Finance and Information Systems, John Lelliott
Internal Audit, John Ford
Legal Adviser and Head of Legal Services, David Harris
Marine Estates, Frank Parrish
Office Portfolio, Alan Meakin
Regional Portfolio, Mal Dillon
Residential Portfolio, Giles Clarke
Retail Portfolio, David Shaw
Rural Estates, Chris Bourchier
Valuation, Roland Spence

EDINBURGH OFFICE
6 Bell's Brae, Edinburgh EH4 3BJ
T 0131-260 6070 F 0131-260 6090
Edinburgh Office Manager, Ian Pritchard

WINDSOR ESTATE
The Crown Estate Office, The Great Park, Windsor, Berks SL4 2HT
T 01753-860222 F 01753-859617
Deputy Ranger, P. Everett

DEER COMMISSION FOR SCOTLAND

Knowsley, 82 Fairfield Road, Inverness IV3 5LH
T 01463-231751 F 01463-712931
E enquiries@deercom.com
W www.dcs.gov.uk

The Deer Commission for Scotland has the general functions of furthering the conservation and control of deer in Scotland. It has the statutory duty, with powers, to prevent damage to agriculture, forestry and the habitat by deer. It is funded by the Scottish Executive.
Chairman (part-time), A. Raven
Director, N. Reiter
Technical Director, D. Balharry

DESIGN COUNCIL

34 Bow Street, London WC2E 7DL
T 020-7420 5200 F 020-7420 5300

The Design Council is a campaigning and lobbying organisation which works with partners in business, education and Government to promote the effective use of good design. It is a registered charity with a Royal Charter and is funded by grant-in-aid from the Department of Trade and Industry.
Chairman, George Cox
Chief Executive, D. Kester

DISABILITY RIGHTS COMMISSION (DRC)
Stratford upon Avon CV37 9BR
T 0845-762 2633
W www.drc-gb.org

The Commission is an executive non-departmental public body established in April 2000. Its role is to advise Government on issues of discrimination against disabled people and the operation of the Disability Discrimination Act 1995. It promotes good practice to employers and service providers and provides advice, information and legal support to disabled people.
Chair, B. Massie, CBE
Chief Executive, B. Niven
Commissioners, S. Alam; M. Burton; Ms J. Campbell, MBE; Ms S. Daniels; M. Devenney; R. Exell, OBE; Dr K. Fitzpatrick; C. Holmes, MBE; Mrs E. Noad; Ms E. Rank-Petruzziello

DUCHY OF CORNWALL
10 Buckingham Gate, London SW1E 6LA
T 020-7834 7346 F 020-7931 9541
W www.princeofwales.gov.uk

The Duchy of Cornwall was created by Edward III in 1337 for the support of his eldest son Edward, later known as the Black Prince. It is the oldest of the English duchies. The duchy is acquired by inheritance by the sovereign's eldest son either at birth or on the accession of his parent to the throne, whichever is the later. The primary purpose of the estate remains to provide an income for the Prince of Wales. The estate is mainly agricultural and based in the south-west of England. A recent purchase has increased the landholding to approximately 150,000 acres in 26 counties. The duchy also has some residential property, a number of shops and offices, and a Stock Exchange portfolio. Prince Charles is the 24th Duke of Cornwall.

THE PRINCE'S COUNCIL
Chairman, HRH The Prince of Wales, KG, KT, GCB, OM
Lord Warden of the Stannaries, The Earl Peel
Receiver-General, The Rt. Hon. J. H. Leigh-Pemberton
Attorney-General to the Prince of Wales, N. Underhill, QC
Secretary and Keeper of the Records, W. R. A. Ross
Other members, R. Broadhurst; J. Coode; W. N. Hood, CBE; Sir Christopher Howes, CB; Sir Michael Peat; J. E. Pugsley; The Duke of Westminster

DUCHY OF LANCASTER
Lancaster Place, Strand, London WC2E 7ED
T 020-7269 1700 F 020-7267 1711
E info@duchyoflancaster.co.uk W www.duchyoflancaster.co.uk

The estates and jurisdiction known as the Duchy of Lancaster have belonged to the reigning monarch since 1399 when John of Gaunt's son came to the throne as Henry IV. As the Lancaster Inheritance it goes back as far as 1265 when Henry III granted his youngest son Edmund lands and possessions following the Baron's war. In 1267 Henry gave Edmund the County, Honor and Castle of Lancaster and created him the first Earl of Lancaster. In 1351 Edward III created Lancaster a County Palatine.

The Chancellor of the Duchy of Lancaster is responsible for the administration of the Duchy, the appointment of justices of the peace in Lancashire, Greater Manchester and Merseyside and ecclesiastical patronage in the Duchy gift.
Chancellor of the Duchy of Lancaster (and Minister for the Cabinet Office), D. G. Alexander, MP
Chairman of the Duchy Council, Sir Michael Bunbury, BT
Attorney-General, M. T. F. Briggs, QC
Receiver-General, A. Reid
Clerk of the Council and Chief Executive, P. R. Clarke

ECGD (EXPORT CREDITS GUARANTEE DEPARTMENT)
PO Box 2200, Exchange Tower, Harbour Exchange Square, London E14 9GS
T 020-7512 7000 F 020-7512 7649
W www.ecgd.gov.uk

ECGD, the Export Credits Guarantee Department is the UK's export credit agency. A separate government department reporting to the Secretary of State for Trade and Industry, it has more than 80 years' experience of working closely with exporters, project sponsors, banks and buyers to help UK exporters of capital equipment and project-related goods and services. ECGD does this by providing: help in arranging finance packages for buyers of UK goods by guaranteeing bank loans; insurance against non-payment to UK exporters; and, overseas investment insurance – a facility that gives UK investors up to 15 years' insurance against political risks such as war, expropriation and restrictions on remittances.

EXECUTIVE COMMITTEE
Chief Executive and Accounting Officer, P. Crawford
Group Directors, V. P. Lunn-Rockliffe *(Portfolio Asset Management)*; J. R. Weiss *(Business)*; T. M. Jaffray *(Risk Management Group)*; J. Ormerod *(Strategy and Communications Division)*; I. Dickson *(Finance Division)*; S. R. Dodgson *(Central Services Division)*; D. N. Ridley *(General Counsel)*

NON-EXECUTIVE DIRECTORS
D. Harrison; J. Wright; T. Davies

DIRECTORS
Business Divisions, G. G. Welsh; R. Gotts; M. D. Pentecost
Capital and Pricing Division, J. Croall
Country Risk and Economics Division, P. J. Radford
Operational Research and Portfolio Risk Analysis Division, Ms R. A. Kaufman
International Debt and Development Division, E. J. Walsby
Recovery Division, R. F. Lethbridge
Guarantee Management Division, A. C. Faulkner
Portfolio Management Division, J. Cross
Information Services Division Ms L. Woods
Internal Audit and Assurance, G. Cassell

EXPORT GUARANTEES ADVISORY COUNCIL
Chairman, E. P. Airey
Other Members, Sir S. Brown; J. Elkington; Prof. J. Kydd; A. Shepherd; Dr R. Thamotheram; M. Roberts; P. Talbot

ENGLISH HERITAGE (HISTORIC BUILDINGS AND MONUMENTS COMMISSION FOR ENGLAND)
23 Savile Row, London W1S 2ET
T 020-7973 3000 F 020-7973 3001
W www.english-heritage.org.uk

English Heritage was established under the National Heritage Act 1983. On 1 April 1999 it merged with the Royal Commission on the Historical Monuments of England to become the new lead body for England's historic environment. Its duties are to carry out and sponsor archaeological, architectural and scientific surveys and research designed to increase the understanding of England's past and its changing condition; to offer expert advice and skills and give grants to secure the preservation of listed buildings, cathedrals, churches, archaeological sites, ancient monuments and historic houses of England; to encourage the imaginative re-use of historic buildings to aid regeneration of the centres of cities, towns and villages; to manage the historic monuments and historic buildings in England; and to curate and make publicly accessible the National Monuments Record, whose records of over one million historic sites and buildings, and collections of more than 12 million photographs, maps, drawings and reports constitute the central database and archive of England's historic environment.
Chairman, Sir Neil Cossons, OBE
Commissioners, M. Cairns; Prof. D. Cannadine; Mrs G. Drummond; P. Gough, CBE; Ms J. Grenville; M. Jolly, CBE; The Earl of Leicester; R. Morris, OBE, FSA; L. Sparks, OBE; Miss M. Adebowale; Mrs J. Bridges, CBE; B. Bryson; M. Chande; Marquess of Douro, OBE; Hon. D. Des, FRSA; Ms E. Williamson
Chief Executive, Dr S. Thurley
NATIONAL MONUMENTS RECORD, National Monuments Record Centre, Kemble Drive, Swindon SN2 2GZ
T 01793-414600 F 01793-414606
LONDON SEARCH ROOM, 55 Blandford Street, London SW1H 3AF T 020-7208 8200 F 020-7224 5333

ENGLISH NATURE
Northminster House, Peterborough PE1 1UA
T 01733-455000 F 01733-568834
Enquiry Service 01733-455100
E enquiries@english-nature.org.uk
W www.english-nature.org.uk

English Nature was established in 1991 and is responsible for advising the Department of the Environment, Food and Rural Affairs on nature conservation in England. It promotes, directly and through others, the conservation of England's wildlife and natural features. It selects, establishes and manages National Nature Reserves and identifies and notifies Sites of Special Scientific Interest. It provides advice and information about nature conservation, and supports and conducts research relevant to these functions. Through the Joint Nature Conservation Committee, it works with its sister organisations in Scotland and Wales on UK and international nature conservation issues. Free publications are available by contacting the Enquiry Service.
Chairman, M. Doughty
Chief Executive, Dr A. Brown
Directors, Dr K. L. Duff; Miss C. E. M. Wood; Ms S. Collins; A. Clements; P. Newby

ENVIRONMENT AGENCY
Rio House, Waterside Drive, Aztec West, Almondsbury, Bristol BS32 4UD
T 01454-624400 F 01454-624409
E enquiries@environment-agency.gov.uk
W www.environment-agency.gov.uk

The Environment Agency was established in 1996 under the Environment Act 1995 and is a non-departmental public body sponsored by the Department of the Environment, Food and Rural Affairs and the National Assembly for Wales. The Agency is responsible for pollution prevention and control in England and Wales, and for the management and use of water resources, including flood defences, fisheries and navigation. It has head offices in London and Bristol and eight regional offices.

THE BOARD
Chairman, Sir John Harman
Members, T. Cantle; A. Dare, CBE; Prof. P. Matthews; Ms S. Parkin; Prof. D. Ritchie; Prof. L. Warren; K. Twitchen; P. Bye; J. Edmonds; Prof. R. Macrory; R. Percy; G. Wardell; Dr L. Stanton

THE EXECUTIVE
Chief Executive, B. Young
Director of Corporate Affairs, H. McCallum
Director of Environmental Protection, A. Skinner
Director of Finance, N. Reader
Director of Legal Services, R. Navarro
Director of Operations, Dr P. Leinster
Director of Personnel, G. Duncan
Director of Water Management, D. King

EQUAL OPPORTUNITIES COMMISSION
Arndale House, Arndale Centre, Manchester M4 3EQ
T 0845-601 5901 F 0161-838 1733
E info@eoc.org.uk
W www.eoc.org.uk
Media Enquiries, 36 Broadway, London SW1H 0BH
T 020-7222 0004
Other Offices, St Stephens House, 279 Bath Street, Glasgow G2 4JL
T 0845-601 5901
Windsor House, Windsor Lane, Cardiff CF10 3GE
T 029-2034 3552

The Equal Opportunities Commission was established under the Sex Discrimination Act in 1975. It was set up as an independent statutory body with the following powers: to work towards the elimination of discrimination on the grounds of sex or marriage; to promote equality of opportunity for women and men; to keep under review the Sex Discrimination Act and the Equal Pay Act; and to provide legal advice and assistance to individuals who have been discriminated against.
Chair, Ms J. Mellor
Deputy Chair, Ms J. Watson
Commissioners, Ms T. Akpeki; Ms S. Ashtiany; Ms K. Carberry; Ms F. Cannon; Ms J. Drake; Ms S. Pierce; S. Sharma; D. Smith; Ms T. Woodcraft; Ms D. Mattinson; Ms R. Arshad; N. Rhys Wooding
Chief Executive, C. Slocock

EQUALITY COMMISSION FOR NORTHERN IRELAND

Equality House, 7–9 Shaftesbury Square, Belfast, BT2 7DP
T 028-9050 0600 F 028-9024 8687
E information@equalityni.org
W www.equalityni.org

The Equality Commission was set up in 1999 under the Northern Ireland Act 1998 and is responsible for promoting equality, eliminating discrimination on the grounds of race, disability, gender, religion and political opinion and for overseeing the statutory duty on public authorities to promote equality of opportunity.
Chief Commissioner, Mrs J. Harbison
Deputy Chief Commissioner, Ms A. O'Reilly
Chief Executive, Ms E. Collins

FOOD STANDARDS AGENCY (UK)

Aviation House, 125 Kingsway, London, WC2B 6NH
T 020-7276 8000 F 020-7276 8004
W www.food.gov.uk

The Food Standards Agency (FSA) was established in April 2000 to protect public health from risks arising in connection with the consumption of food, and otherwise to protect the interests of consumers in relation to food. The Agency has the general function of developing policy in these areas and provides information and advice to the Government, other public bodies and consumers. It also sets standards for and monitors food law enforcement by local authorities. The Agency is a UK-wide non-ministerial Government body led by a board which has been appointed to act in the public interest. It has executive offices in Scotland, Wales and Northern Ireland. It is advised by advisory committees on food safety matters of special interest to each of these areas.
Chairman, Prof. Sir John Krebs, FRC
Deputy Chair, Julia Unwin, OBE
Chief Executive, Dr Jon Bell

EXECUTIVE AGENCY
MEAT HYGIENE SERVICE
Kings Pool, Peasholme Green, York YO1 7PR
T 01904-455500 F 01904-455502

The Meat Hygiene Service was launched on 1 April 1995 as an agency of the former Ministry of Agriculture, Fisheries and Food, and became an Executive Agency of the Food Standards Agency on 1 April 2000. It protects public health and animal welfare at slaughter through veterinary supervision and meat inspection in licensed fresh meat premises in Great Britain.
Chief Executive, C. J. Lawson

FOOD STANDARDS AGENCY NORTHERN IRELAND

10c Clarendon Road, Belfast, BT1 3BG
T 028-9041 7700 F 028-9041 7726
E infofsani@foodstandards.gsi.gov.uk
W www.food.gov.uk

FOOD STANDARDS AGENCY SCOTLAND

St Magnus House, 6th Floor, 25 Guild Street, Aberdeen, AB11 6NJ
T 01224-285100 F 01224-285167
E scotland@foodstandards.gsi.gov.uk
W www.food.gov.uk

FOOD STANDARDS AGENCY WALES

11th Floor, Southgate House, Wood Street, Cardiff CF10 1EW
T 029-2067 8999 F 029-2067 8919
E wales@foodstandards.gsi.gov.uk
W www.food.gov.uk

FOREIGN COMPENSATION COMMISSION

Room SG/111, Old Admiralty Building, Whitehall, London, SW1A 2PA
T 020-7008 1321 F 020-7008 0160

The Commission was set up by the Foreign Compensation Act 1950 primarily to distribute, under Orders in Council, funds received from other governments in accordance with agreements to pay compensation for expropriated British property and other losses sustained by British nationals.
Chairman, Dr John H. Bancer
Secretary, vacant

FORESTRY COMMISSION

Silvan House, 231 Corstorphine Road, Edinburgh EH12 7AT
T 0845-367 3787 F 0131-334 3047
E enquiries@forestry.gsi.gov.uk
W www.forestry.gov.uk

The Forestry Commission is the Government department responsible for forestry policy in Great Britain. It reports directly to forestry Ministers (i.e. the Minister of Environment, Food and Rural Affairs, the Scottish Ministers and the National Assembly for Wales), to whom it is responsible for advice on forestry policy and for the implementation of that policy.

The Commission's principal objectives are to protect Britain's forests and woodlands; expand Britain's forest area; enhance the economic value of forest resources; conserve and improve the biodiversity, landscape and cultural heritage of forests and woodlands; develop opportunities for woodland recreation; and increase public understanding of and community participation in forestry. Forest Enterprise, an executive agency of the Forestry Commission, ceased to exist on 1 April 2003. Three new bodies, one each for England, Scotland and Wales have been created in its place.
Chairman (part-time), The Rt. Hon. Lord Clark of Windermere
Director-General and Deputy Chairman, T. Rollinson

FORESTRY COMMISSION ENGLAND, Great Eastern House, Tenison Road, Cambridge CB1 2BU T 01223-314546
FORESTRY COMMISSION SCOTLAND, 231 Corstorphine Road, Edinburgh EH12 7AT T 9131-334 0303
FORESTRY COMMISSION WALES, Victoria Terrace, Aberystwyth, Ceredigion SY23 2DQ T 01970-625866
FOREST RESEARCH, Alice Holt Lodge, Wrecclesham, Farnham, Surrey GU10 4LU T 01420-222555
NORTHERN RESEARCH STATION, Roslin, Midlothian EH25 9SY T 0131-445 2176

GAMING BOARD FOR GREAT BRITAIN
Berkshire House, 168–173 High Holborn, London WC1V 7AA
T 020-7306 6200 F 020-7306 6266
E enqs@gbgb.org.uk
W www.gbgb.org.uk

The Board was established in 1968 and is responsible to the Secretary of State for Culture, Media and Sport. It is the regulatory body for casinos, bingo clubs, gaming machines and all local authority lotteries in Great Britain. Its functions are to ensure that those involved in organising gaming and lotteries are fit and proper to do so and to keep gaming free from criminal infiltration; to ensure that gaming and lotteries are run fairly and in accordance with the law; and to advise the Secretary of State on developments in gaming and lotteries.
Chairman, P. Dean, CBE
Secretary, T. Kavanagh, CBE

GOVERNMENT ACTUARY'S DEPARTMENT
Finlaison House, 15/17 Furnival Street, London EC4A 1AB
T 020-7211 2601 F 020-7211 2640/2650
E enquiries@gad.gov.uk
W www.gad.gov.uk

The Government Actuary's Department provides a consulting service to Government departments, the public sector, and overseas governments. The actuaries advise on social security schemes and superannuation arrangements in the public sector at home and abroad, on population and other statistical studies, and on supervision of insurance companies and pension funds.
Government Actuary, C. D. Daykin, CB
Directing Actuaries, A. G. Young; A. I. Johnston
Chief Actuaries, E. I. Battersby; I. A. Boonin;
   S. R. Humphrey; D. Lewis; G. T. Russell

GOVERNMENT HOSPITALITY
Lancaster House, Stable Yard, St James's, London SW1A 1BB
T 020-7008 8517 F 020-7008 8526

The Government Hospitality Fund was instituted in 1908 for the purpose of organising official hospitality on a regular basis with a view to the promotion of international goodwill.
   Government Hospitality is now incorporated as part of the Foreign and Commonwealth Office's Services Directorate.
Minister, B. Rammell
Manager of Government Hospitality, R. Alexander

GOVERNMENT OFFICES FOR THE REGIONS

The nine Government Offices for the Regions (GOs) are the primary means by which a wide range of Government policies are delivered in the English regions. The Government Offices bring together the activities and interests of ten 'sponsor' government departments: the Office of the Deputy Prime Minister; the Department for Education and Skills; the Department of Trade and Industry; the Department for Environment, Food and Rural Affairs; the Home Office; the Department for Culture, Media and Sport; the Department for Work and Pensions; the Department for Transport; the Department of Health; and the Cabinet Office.
   GOs contribute to the delivery of over forty Public Service Agreements (PSAs) on behalf of their sponsor departments. These PSAs cover a diverse range of tasks including regenerating communities, fighting crime, tackling housing needs, improving public health, raising standards in education and skills, tackling countryside issues, and reducing unemployment. GOs also manage European funds.
   GOs directly manage the spending programmes of the government departments listed above. They oversee budgets and contracts delegated to regional organisations, as well as carrying out regulatory functions and sponsoring Regional Development Agencies. As part of central government, their role also includes providing a regional perspective to inform the development and evaluation of policy. In 2002–3, the GOs were responsible for approximately £9 billion of government expenditure.
   The Government Office Network comprises the nine regional Government Offices, and the Regional Co-ordination Unit.

REGIONAL CO-ORDINATION UNIT
Riverwalk House, 157–161 Millbank, London SW1P 4RR
T 020-7217 3595 F 020-7217 3590
W www.rcu.gov.uk
Director-General, Rob Smith
Director, A. Campbell
Directors, Ian Jones *(Corporate Communications)*; Nick Dexter *(Strategy)*; Julie Anderson *(Business Development)*; Vince Brady *(Human Resources)*

EAST MIDLANDS
The Belgrave Centre, Stanley Place, Talbot Street, Nottingham NG1 5GG
T 0115-971 9971 F 0115-971 2404
E enquiries.goem@go-regions.gov.uk
W www.go-em.gov.uk
Regional Director, Jane Todd

EAST OF ENGLAND
Eastbrook, Shaftesbury Road, Cambridge CB2 2DF
T 01223-372500 F 01223-372501
W www.go-east.gov.uk
Regional Director, Caroline Bowdler

LONDON
Riverwalk House, 157–161 Millbank, London SW1P 4RR
T 020-7217 3111 F 020-7217 3450
W www.go-london.gov.uk
Regional Director, Liz Meek

NORTH-EAST
Citygate, Gallowgate, Newcastle upon Tyne NE1 4WH
T 0191-201 3300 F 0191-202 3998
W www.go-ne.gov.uk
Regional Director, Jonathan Blackie

NORTH-WEST
City Tower, Piccadilly Plaza, Manchester M1 4BE
T 0161-952 4000 F 0161-952 4099
W www.go-nw.gov.uk
Regional Director, Keith Barnes

SOUTH-EAST
Bridge House, 1 Walnut Tree Close, Guildford, Surrey GU1 4GA
T 01483-882255 F 01483-882259
W www.go-se.gov.uk
Regional Director, Paul Martin

SOUTH-WEST

2 Rivergate, Temple Quay, Bristol BS1 6ED
T 0117-900 1700 F 0117-900 1900
W www.gosw.gov.uk
Regional Director, Jane Henderson

WEST MIDLANDS

77 Paradise Circus, Queensway, Birmingham B1 2DT
T 0121-212 5050 F 0121-212 1010
E enquiries.gowm@go-regions.gsi.gov.uk
W www.go-wm.gov.uk
Regional Director, Graham Garbutt

YORKSHIRE AND THE HUMBER

PO Box 213, City House, New Station Street, Leeds LS1 4US
T 0113-283 8301 F 0113-283 6394
E enquiries.goyh@go-regions.gsi.gov.uk W www.goyh.gov.uk
Regional Director, Felicity Everiss

HEALTH AND SAFETY COMMISSION

Rose Court, 2 Southwark Bridge, London SE1 9HS
T 020-7717 6000 F 020-7717 6644
E hseinformationservices@natbrit.com
W www.hse.gov.uk

The Health and Safety Commission was created under the Health and Safety at Work etc. Act 1974, with duties to reform health and safety law, to propose new regulations, and generally to promote the protection of people at work and the public from hazards arising from industrial and commercial activity, including major industrial accidents and the transportation of hazardous materials.

Its members are nominated by organisations representing employers, employees, local authorities and others.

Chairman, B. Callaghan
Members, Ms J. Donovan; Ms J. Edmond-Smith;
    G. Brumwell; Ms M. Burns; A. Chowdry; J. Longworth;
    Ms J. Hackitt; H. Robertson; Ms E. Snape

HEALTH AND SAFETY EXECUTIVE

Rose Court, 2 Southwark Bridge, London SE1 9HS
T 020-7717 6000 F 020-7717 6717

The Health and Safety Executive is the Health and Safety Commission's major instrument. Through its inspectorates it enforces health and safety law in the majority of industrial premises. The Executive advises the Commission in its major task of laying down safety standards through regulations and practical guidance for many industrial processes. The Executive is also the licensing authority for nuclear installations, the reporting officer on the severity of nuclear incidents in Britain, and it is responsible for the Channel Tunnel Safety Authority.

Director-General, T. Walker
Deputy Director-General, Operations, J. McCracken
Deputy Director-General, Policy, K. Timms
*Director and HM Chief Inspector of the Nuclear
    Installations Inspectorate*, L. Williams
Director of Rail Safety, A. Sefton
*Director, Corporate Science and Analytical Service
    Directorate and Chief Scientist*, Dr P. Davies
Director, Field Operations Directorate, S. Caldwell
Director, Hazardous Installations Directorate, C. Willby
Director, Health Directorate, J. Willis
Director, Resource and Planning Directorate, V. Dews
Director, Safety Policy, N. Starling

HEALTH PROTECTION AGENCY

Central Office: Level 11, The Adelphi, 10–11 John Adam Street, London WC2N 6HT
T 020-7339 1300 F 020-7339 1302
E firstname.surname@ hpa.org.uk
W www.hpa.org.uk

The Health Protection Agency (HPA) was set up on 1 April 2003 to provide an integrated approach to protecting public health and reducing the impact of infections, chemicals, poisons and radiation hazards on human health. It brings together the functions and expertise from the Public Health Laboratory Service, including the Communicable Disease Surveillance Centre, the Centre for Applied Microbiology and Research, the National Focus for Chemical Incidents, the Regional Service Provider Units that support the management of chemical incidents, the National Poisons Information Service, and the NHS public health staff responsible for control of infectious disease, emergency planning and other protection support.

Chairman, Sir William Stewart
Chief Executive, Prof. Pat Troop
Directors, Prof. Roger Gilmour *(Business)*; Prof. Stephen
    Palmer *(Chemical Hazards and Poisons)*; Dr A. Nicoll
    (Communicable Disease Surveillance Centre); Dr Nigel
    Lightfoot *(Emergency Response)*; Dr Mary O'Mahony
    (Local and Regional Services); Prof. Pete Borriello
    (Specialist and Reference Microbiology)

HIGHLANDS AND ISLANDS ENTERPRISE

Cowan House, Inverness Retail and Business Park, Inverness, Scotland IV2 7GF
T 01463-234171 F 01463-244469
E hie.general@hient.co.uk
W www.hie.co.uk

Highlands and Islands Enterprise (HIE) was set up under the Enterprise and New Towns (Scotland) Act 1991. Its role is to design, direct and deliver enterprise development, training and environmental and social projects and services. HIE is made up of a strategic core body and ten Local Enterprise Companies (LECs) to which many of its individual functions are delegated.

Chairman, Dr J. Hunter
Chief Executive, I. J. R. S. Cumming

HISTORIC ENVIRONMENT ADVISORY COUNCIL FOR SCOTLAND

Longmore House, Salisbury Place, Edinburgh EH9 1SH
T 0131-668 8810 F 0131-668 8788
E heacs@scotland.gsi.gov.uk W www.heacs.org.uk

The Historic Environment Advisory Council for Scotland is the advisory body set up to provide Scottish Ministers with advice on issues affecting the historic environment and how the functions of the Scottish Ministers may be exercised effectively for the benefit of the historic environment. In this context the historic environment means any or all structures and places in Scotland of historical, archaeological or architectural interest or importance.

Chair, Mrs Elizabeth Burns, OBE
Secretary, Dr Malcolm Bangor-Jones

HISTORIC ROYAL PALACES
Hampton Court Palace, Surrey KT8 9AU
T 0870-751 5172 F 020-8781 9754
W www.hrp.org.uk

Historic Royal Palaces is a non-departmental public body with charitable status. The Secretary of State for Culture, Media and Sport is still accountable to Parliament for the care, conservation and presentation of the palaces, which are owned by the Sovereign in right of the Crown. The chairman of the trustees is appointed by The Queen on the advice of the Secretary of State. Historic Royal Palaces is responsible for the Tower of London, Hampton Court Palace, Kensington Palace State Apartments, the Royal Ceremonial Dress Collection, Kew Palace, Queen Charlotte's Cottage, and the Banqueting House, Whitehall.

TRUSTEES
Chairman, Sir Nigel Mobbs
Appointed by The Queen, A. Reid; Sir Hugh Roberts, KCVO, FSA; Field Marshal The Lord Inge, KG, GCB
Appointed by the Secretary of State, Ms A. Heylin, OBE; S. Jones, LVO; Mrs G. Woolfe, MBE; Dr B. Cherry, FSA
Ex officio, Sir Roger Wheeler, GCB, CBE *(Constable of the Tower of London)*

OFFICERS
Chief Executive, M. Day
Director of Conservation, J. Barnes
Director of Finance, Ms S. O'Neill
Director of Human Resources, G. Josephs
Director, Palaces Group, R. Giddins
Marketing Director, D. Homan
Resident Governor, HM Tower of London, Maj.-Gen. G. Field, CB, OBE
Retail Director, Ms A. Boyes

HOME-GROWN CEREALS AUTHORITY
Caledonia House, 223 Pentonville Road, London N1 9HY
T 020-7520 3904 F 020-7520 3954

Set up under the Cereals Marketing Act 1965, the HGCA Board consists of seven members representing UK cereal growers, seven representing dealers in, or processors of, grain and two independent members. HGCA's functions are to improve the production and marketing of UK-grown cereals and oilseeds through a research and development programme, to provide a market information service and to promote UK cereals in export markets.
Chairman, J. Page
Chief Executive, P. V. Biscoe

HONOURS SCRUTINY COMMITTEE
35 Great Smith Street, London SW1P 3BQ
T 020-7276 2770 F 020-7276 2766

The Honours Scrutiny Committee is a committee of Privy Counsellors. The Prime Minister submits certain particulars to the Committee about persons recommended for honour at any level other than a peerage for their political services, or for an honour at the level of Knight or Dame for non-political services. The Committee, after such enquiry as it thinks fit, reports to the Prime Minister whether, so far as it believes, the political candidates are fit and proper persons to be recommended and for any non-political candidate, who may have made a political donation, whether this was a

factor in the recommendation for an honour.
Chairman, The Lord Thomson of Monifieth, KT
Members, The Baroness Dean of Thornton-le-Fylde; The Lord Hurd of Westwell, CH, CBE
Secretary, Mrs P. G. W. Catto

HORSERACE TOTALISATOR BOARD
Tote House, 74 Upper Richmond Road, London SW15 2SU
T 020-8874 6411 F 020-8874 6107
W www.tote.co.uk

The Horserace Totalisator Board (the Tote) was established by the Betting, Gaming and Lotteries Act 1963. Its function is to operate totalisators on approved racecourses in Great Britain, and it also provides on and off-course cash and credit offices. Under the Horserace Totalisator and Betting Levy Board Act 1972, it is further empowered to offer bets at starting price (or other bets at fixed odds) on any sporting event, and under the Horserace Totalisator Board Act 1997 to take bets on any event, except the National Lottery. The chairman and members of the Board are appointed by the Secretary of State, Department of Culture, Media and Sport.

The Government announced in March 2001 that the Tote would eventually be sold to a racing trust, subject to the necessary legislation going through Parliament. The privatisation of the Tote was expected to be completed by the end of 2004.
Chairman, P. I. Jones
Chief Operating Officer, T. Phillips

HOUSING CORPORATION
Maple House, 149 Tottenham Court Road, London W1T 7BN
T 020-7393 2000 F 020-7393 2111
E enquiries@housingcorp.gsx.gov.uk
W www.housingcorp.gov.uk

Established by Parliament in 1964, the Housing Corporation regulates and funds registered social landlords which are non-profit making bodies run by voluntary committees. There are over 2,000 registered social landlords, most of which are housing associations, who provide homes for more than 1.5 million people. Under the Housing Act 1996, the Corporation's regulatory role was widened to embrace new types of landlords, in particular local housing companies. The Corporation is funded by the Office of the Deputy Prime Minister.
Chairman, Peter Dixon
Deputy Chairman, E. Armitage, OBE
Chief Executive, Jon Rouse

HOUSING OMBUDSMAN SERVICE
Norman House, 105–109 Strand, London WC2R 0AA
T 020-7836 3630 F 020-7836 3900
E ombudsman@ihos.org.uk
W www.ihos.org.uk

The Housing Ombudsman Service deals with complaints and disputes involving landlords and tenants. The Ombudsman has a statutory jurisdiction over all registered social landlords in England. Private and other landlords can join the Service on a voluntary basis.
Ombudsman, M. Biles
Chair of Board, G. Lewis
Director of Corporate Services, Wilma Jarvie

HUMAN FERTILISATION AND EMBRYOLOGY AUTHORITY

21 Bloomsbury Street, London WC1B 3HF
T 020-7291 8200 F 020-7291 8201
E admin@hfea.gov.uk
W www.hfea.gov.uk

The Human Fertilisation and Embryology Authority (HFEA) was established under the Human Fertilisation and Embryology Act 1990. Its function is to licence the following activities: the creation or use of embryos outside the body in the provision of infertility treatment services; the use of donated gametes in infertility treatment; the storage of gametes or embryos; and research on human embryos. It maintains a confidential database of all such treatments and of egg and sperm donors, and provides information to patients, clinics and the public. The HFEA also keeps under review information about embryos and, when requested to do so, gives advice to the Secretary of State for Health.

Chairman, S. Leather
Deputy Chairman, Prof. T. Baldwin
Members, Prof. D. Barlow; Prof. C. Barratt; Prof. P. Braude; I. Brecker; Ms C. Brown; Prof. I. Cameron; Prof. N. Haites; Dr M. Jamieson; S. Jenkins; W. Merricks; Ms S. Nathan; Ms S. Nebhrajani; The Right Hon. Bishop D. Harries; Ms E. Jackson; Ms J. Hunt
Director of Sub-Committees, Mrs J. Denton

HUMAN GENETICS COMMISSION

Area 652C, Skipton House, 80 London Road, London SE1 6LH
T 020-7972 1518 F 020-7972 1717
E hgc@doh.gov.uk
W www.hgc.gov.uk

The Human Genetics Commission was established in 1999, subsuming three previous advisory committees. Its remit is to give Ministers strategic advice on how developments in human genetics will impact on people and health care, focusing in particular on the special and ethical implications.

Chairman, Baroness H. Kennedy of the Shaws, QC
Members, Dr W. Albert, Prof. E. Anionwu; Dr S. Bain; Prof. J. Burn; Dr H. Harris; Prof. J. Harris; Ms S. Leather; Ms H. Newiss; Prof. M. Richards; Dr S. Singleton; Mr G. Watts; Mr P. Webb; Prof. V. van Heyningen; Dr Patrick Morrison; Dr R. Skinner; Emeritius Prof. Brenda Almond; Mrs C. Patch; P. Sayers; Sir John Sueston; Dr Celia Brazell; A. Kent
Head of Secretariat, M. Bale

INDEPENDENT INTERNATIONAL COMMISSION ON DECOMMISSIONING

Dublin Castle, Block M, Ship Street, Dublin 2
T 00 353 1-478 0111 F 00 353 1-478 0600
Rosepark House, Upper Newtownards Road, Belfast BT4 3NX
T 028-9048 8600 F 028-9048 8601

The Commission was established by agreement between the British and Irish Governments in August 1997. Its objective is to facilitate the decommissioning of illegally-held firearms and explosives in accordance with the relevant legislation in both jurisdictions. Its members are appointed jointly by the two Governments; staff are appointed by the Commission. All are drawn from countries other than the UK and the Republic of Ireland.

Commissioners, Gen. J. de Chastelain *(Chairman, Canada)*
    A. D. Sens *(USA)*

Staff Director, A. Suonio *(Finland)*
Admin/Finances, K. Juntunen; R. Schoen; J. Mladinich

INDEPENDENT POLICE COMPLAINTS COMMISSION (IPCC)

90 High Holborn, London WC1V 6BH
T 0845-300 2002 F 020-7404 0430
E enquiries@ipcc.gsi.gov.uk
W www.ipcc.gov.uk

The Independent Police Complaints Commission succeeded the Police Complaints Authority on 1 April 2004. It was established under the Police Reform Act 2002 following responses to the government document *Complaints against Police; Framework for a New System,* published in December 2000. The IPCC is an independent public body and is not part of any government department. The IPCC has teams of investigators headed by Regional Directors in each of its regions to assist with supervision and management of some police investigations. They also carry out independent investigations into serious incidents or allegations of misconduct by persons serving with the police. The 18 commissioners of the IPCC must not previously have worked for the police.

Chairman, N. Hardwick
Deputy Chairs, Ms C. Gilham; J. Wadham
Commissioners, I. Bynoe; J. Crawley; T. Davies; M. Franklin; G. Garland; Ms D. Glass; L. Jackson; N. Long; L. Lustgarten; N. Malik; Ms R. Marsh; D. Petch; M. Mian Pritchard; A. Somal; Ms N. Williams
Chief Executive, Susan Atkins

INDEPENDENT REVIEW SERVICE FOR THE SOCIAL FUND

4th Floor, Centre City Podium, 5 Hill Street, Birmingham B5 4UB
T 0845-300 1960 F 0121-606 2180
E sfc@irs-review.org.uk
W www.irs-review.org.uk

The Social Fund Commissioner is appointed by the Secretary of State for Work and Pensions. The Commissioner appoints Social Fund Inspectors, who provide an independent review of decisions made by Social Fund Officers in the Department of Work and Pensions.

Social Fund Commissioner, Sir Richard Tilt

INFORMATION COMMISSIONER'S OFFICE

Wycliffe House, Water Lane, Wilmslow, Cheshire SK9 5AF
T 01625-545745 F 01625-524510
E mail@ico.gsi.gov.uk
W www.informationcommissioner.gov.uk

The Information Commissioner Office oversees and enforces the Freedom of Information Act 2000 and the Data Protection Act 1998, with the objective of promoting public access to official information and protecting personal information.

The Data Protection Act 1998 sets out rules for the processing of personal information and applies to records held on computers and some paper files. It works in two ways; it dictates that those who record and use personal information (data controllers) must be open about how the information is used and must follow the eight principles of 'good information handling' and; it gives individuals certain rights to access their personal information.

The Freedom of Information Act 2000 is designed to help end the culture of unnecessary secrecy and open up the inner working of the public sector to citizens and businesses. Under the Freedom of Information Act, public authorities must publish a publication scheme that sets out what information the public authority is obliged publish by law.

The Information Commissioner reports annually to parliament on the performance of his functions under the Acts and has obligations to assess breaches of the Acts. *Commissioner*, Richard Thomas

INDUSTRIAL INJURIES ADVISORY COUNCIL

6th Floor, The Adelphi, 1–11 John Adam Street, London WC2N 6HT
T 020-7962 8066 F 020-7712 2255
E iiac@dial.pipex.com W www.iiac.org.uk

The Industrial Injuries Advisory Council was established under the Social Security Administration Act 1992, with statutory provisions governing its work set out in section 171 of the Act. The Council has three roles: to advise on the proscription of diseases; to advise on matters referred to the Council by the Secretary of State or proposals concerning the Industrial Injuries Benefit Scheme; and to advise on any other matter relating to industrial injuries benefit or its administration.
Chairman, Prof. A. J. Newman Taylor, OBE, FRCP
Administrative Secretary, N. Davidson

JOINT NATURE CONSERVATION COMMITTEE

Monkstone House, City Road, Peterborough PE1 1JY
T 01733-562626 F 01733-555948

The Committee was established under the Environmental Protection Act 1990. It advises the Government and others on UK and international nature conservation issues and disseminates knowledge on these subjects. It establishes common standards for the monitoring of nature conservation and research, and provides guidance to English Nature, Scottish Natural Heritage, the Countryside Council for Wales and the Department of the Environment for Northern Ireland.
Acting Chairman, Prof. David Ingram
Director of Resources and External Affairs, M. Yeo
Director of Science, Dr M. A. Vincent
Managing Director, D. Steer

LAND REGISTRIES

LAND REGISTRY

32 Lincoln's Inn Fields, London WC2A 3PH
T 020-7919 8888 F 020-7955 0110
E enquiries.pic@landregistry.gov.uk
W www.landregistry.gov.uk

The registration of title to land was first introduced in England and Wales by the Land Registry Act 1862; the Land Registry operates today under the Land Registration Acts 1925 to 2002. The object of registering title to land is to create and maintain a register of landowners whose title is guaranteed by the state and so to simplify the transfer, mortgage and other dealings with real property. Registration on sale is now compulsory throughout England and Wales. The register has been open to inspection by the public since 1990.

The Land Registry is an executive agency and Trading Fund administered by the Chief Land Registrar.

HEADQUARTERS OFFICE
Chief Land Registrar and Chief Executive, P. Collis
Director of Legal Services, J. V. Timothy
Director of Finance, Ms H. Jackson
Director of Business Development and Deputy Chief Executive, E. G. Beardsall
Director of Education and Training, Mrs L. Chamberlain
Director of Facilities, A. Elston
Director of Geographic Information, R. Ashwin
Director of Information Systems, I. Johnson
Director of Marketing and Communication, Mrs D. Reynolds
Director of Operations, A. Howarth
Director of Personnel, Mrs L. Daniels
Director of Service Development, P. Norman
Director of Strategy, A. Pemberton

INFORMATION SYSTEMS DIRECTORATE
Burrington Way, Plymouth PL5 3LP
T 01752-635600
Head of IT Services/Head of Strategy Division, P. A. Maycock/C. Bitton
Head of IT Development Division, J. Formby
Head of IT Directorate Services, K. Deards

LAND CHARGES CREDITS DEPARTMENT
Plumer House, Tailyour Road, Crownhill, Plymouth PL6 5HY
T 01752-636666
Superintendent, Ms M. Telfer

LAND REGISTRY OFFICES
BIRKENHEAD (OLD MARKET) – Old Market House, Hamilton Street, Birkenhead CH41 5FL T 0151-473 1110
  Land Registrar, P. J. Brough
BIRKENHEAD (ROSEBRAE) – Rosebrae Court, Woodside Ferry Approach, Birkenhead CH41 6DU T 0151-472 6666
  Land Registrar, M. J. Garwood
COVENTRY – Leigh Court, Torrington Avenue, Tile Hill, Coventry CV4 9XZ T 024-7686 0860 *Land Registrar*, Mrs D. M. Weaver
CROYDON – Sunley House, Bedford Park, Croydon CR9 3LE T 020-8781 9103 *Acting Land Registrar*, C. H. Johnson
DURHAM (BOLDON HOUSE) – Boldon House, Wheatlands Way, Pity Me, Durham DH1 5GJ T 0191-301 2345
  Land Registrar, R. B. Fearnley
DURHAM (SOUTHFIELD HOUSE) – Southfield House, Southfield Way, Durham DH1 5TR T 0191-301 3500
  Land Registrar, P. J. Timothy
GLOUCESTER – Twyver House, Bruton Way, Gloucester GL1 1DQ T 01452-511111 *Land Registrar*, Mrs J. Jenkins
HARROW – Lyon House, Lyon Road, Harrow, Middx HA1 2EU T 020-8235 1181 *Land Registrar*, C. Tate
KINGSTON UPON HULL – Earle House, Colonial Street, Hull HU2 8JN T 01482-223244 *Land Registrar*, S. R. Coveney
LANCASHIRE – Wrea Brook Court, Lytham Road, Warton, Preston, PR4 1TE T 01772-836700 *Land Registrar*, Mrs L. Wallwork
LEICESTER – Westbridge Place, Leicester LE3 5DR T 0116-265 4000 *Land Registrar*, Mrs J. A. Goodfellow
LYTHAM – Birkenhead House, East Beach, Lytham St Annes, Lancs FY8 5AB T 01253-849849 *Acting Land Registrar*, Mrs L. Wallwork
NOTTINGHAM (EAST) – Robins Wood Road, Nottingham NG8 3RQ T 0115-906 5353 *Land Registrar*, Ms A. M. Goss

NOTTINGHAM (WEST) – Chalfont Drive, Nottingham NG8 3RN T 0115-935 1166 *Land Registrar*, P. A. Brown

PETERBOROUGH – Touthill Close, City Road, Peterborough PE1 1XN T 01733-288288 *Land Registrar*, C. W. Martin

PLYMOUTH – Plumer House, Tailyour Road, Crownhill, Plymouth PL6 5HY T 01752-636000 *Land Registrar*, A. J. Pain

PORTSMOUTH – St Andrew's Court, St Michael's Road, Portsmouth PO1 2JH T 023-9276 8888 *Land Registrar*, S. R. Sehrawat

STEVENAGE – Brickdale House, Swingate, Stevenage, Herts SG1 1XG T 01438-788889 *Land Registrar*, M. Croker

SWANSEA – Tŷ Bryn Glas, High Street, Swansea SA1 1PW T 01792-458877 *Land Registrar*, G. A. Hughes

TELFORD – Parkside Court, Hall Park Way, Telford TF3 4LR T 01952-290355 *Land Registrar*, A. M. Lewis

TUNBRIDGE WELLS – Forest Court, Forest Road, Tunbridge Wells, Kent TN2 5AQ T 01892-510015 *Land Registrar*, G. R. Tooke

WALES – Tŷ Cwm Tawe, Phoenix Way, Llansamlet, Swansea SA7 9FQ T 01792-355000 *Land Registrar*, T. M. Lewis

WEYMOUTH – Melcombe Court, 1 Cumberland Drive, Weymouth, Dorset DT4 9TT T 01305-363636 *Land Registrar*, J. Pownall

YORK – James House, James Street, York YO10 3YZ T 01904-450000 *Land Registrar*, Mrs R. F. Lovel

REGISTERS OF SCOTLAND

Meadowbank House, 153 London Road, Edinburgh EH8 7AU
T 0131-659 6111 F 0131-479 3688
Customer Service Centre 0845-607 0161
E customer.services@ros.gov.uk
W www.ros.gov.uk

Registers of Scotland is the executive agency responsible for framing and maintaining records relating to property and other legal documents in Scotland. The agency holds 16 registers: two property registers (General Register of Sasines and Land Register of Scotland) and the remainder grouped under the Chancery and Judicial registers (Register of Deeds in the Books of Council and Session; Register of Protests; Register of Judgements; Register of Service of Heirs; Register of the Great Seal; Register of the Quarter Seal; Register of the Prince's Seal; Register of Crown Grants; Register of Sheriffs' Commissions; Register of the Cachet Seal; Register of Inhibitions and Adjudications; Register of Entails; Register of Hornings; and Register of Community Interests in Land).
Chief Executive and Keeper of the Registers of Scotland, J. Meldrum
Deputy Keeper, B. Beveridge
Managing Director, F. Manson

LAW COMMISSION

Conquest House, 37–38 John Street, London WC1N 2BQ
T 020-7453 1220 F 020-7453 1297
W www.lawcom.gov.uk

The Law Commission was set up in 1965, under the Law Commissions Act 1965, to make proposals to the Government for the examination of the law in England and Wales and for its revision where it is unsuited for modern requirements, obscure, or otherwise unsatisfactory. It recommends to the Lord Chancellor programmes for the examination of different branches of the law and suggests whether the examination should be carried out by the Commission itself or by some other body. The Commission is also responsible for the preparation of Consolidation and Statute Law (Repeals) Bills.
Chairman, The Hon. Mr Justice Toulson
Commissioners, Judge A. Wilkie, QC; Prof. H. Beale, QC; Prof. M. Partington, CBE; S. Bridge
Chief Executive, S. Humphreys

LAW OFFICERS' DEPARTMENTS

Legal Secretariat to the Law Officers, Attorney-General's Chambers, 9 Buckingham Gate, London SW1E 6JP
T 020-7271 2422 F 020-7271 2430
E lslo@gtnet.gov.uk
W www.lslo.gov.uk
Attorney-General's Chambers, Royal Courts of Justice, Belfast BT1 3JY
T 028-9054 6082 F 028-9054 6049

The Law Officers of the Crown for England and Wales are the Attorney-General and the Solicitor-General. The Attorney-General, assisted by the Solicitor-General, is the chief legal adviser to the Government and is also ultimately responsible for all Crown litigation. He has overall responsibility for the work of the Law Officers' Departments (the Treasury Solicitor's Department, the Crown Prosecution Service, the Serious Fraud Office and the Legal Secretariat to the Law Officers). He has a specific statutory duty to superintend the discharge of their duties by the Director of Public Prosecutions (who heads the Crown Prosecution Service) and the Director of the Serious Fraud Office. The Director of Public Prosecutions for Northern Ireland is also responsible to the Attorney-General for the performance of his functions. The Attorney-General has additional responsibilities in relation to aspects of the civil and criminal law.
Attorney-General, The Rt. Hon. The Lord Goldsmith, QC
Private Secretary, C. Bartlett
Parliamentary Private Secretary, M. Foster, MP
Solicitor-General, The Rt. Hon. Harriet Harman, QC, MP
Legal Secretary, D. Brummell
Deputy Legal Secretary, S. Parkinson

LEARNING AND SKILLS COUNCIL

Cheylesmore House, Quinton Road, Coventry, West Midlands, CV1 2WT
T 0845-019 4170 F 024-7649 3600
E info@lsc.gov.uk W www.lsc.gov.uk

The Learning and Skills Council (LSC) was established in April 2001 to replace the Further Education Funding and the Training and Enterprise Councils. It is a non-departmental public body responsible for the planning and funding of post-16 education and training. Its annual budget for 2003–4 was £8 billion. Its remit is to ensure that high quality post-16 provision is available to meet the needs of employers, individuals and communities. The LSC operates through a national office based in Coventry and 47 local departments, which work to promote the equality of opportunity in the workplace, aiming to ensure that the needs of the most disadvantaged people in the labour market are met. These local departments in most cases have coterminous boundaries with Small Business Service franchises.
Chairman, Chris Banks
Chief Executive, Mark Haysom

LEGAL SERVICES COMMISSION

85 Gray's Inn Road, London WC1X 8TX
T 020-7759 0000 **Directory Information line** 0845-608 1122
W www.legalservices.gov.uk

The Legal Services Commission was created under the Access to Justice Act 1999 and replaced the Legal Aid Board in April 2000. It is a non-departmental public body which is accountable to the Department for Constitutional Affairs.

The Commission's four core objectives are: to fund legal and advice services in England and Wales; to identify unmet legal needs; to develop those providing legal aid; and to develop innovative services to meet priority legal needs. It also runs the Community Legal Service which provides advice and legal representation for people involved in civil cases, and the Criminal Defence Service, which provides advice and legal representation for people facing criminal charges.

The Commission produces free information leaflets which are available from solicitors' and advisory offices and on the Commission's websites.

Chief Executive, Clare Dodgson
Members, A. Edwards; Ms J. Herzog; Ms Y. Mosquito; J. Shearer; Ms M. Richards; A. Andrew; D. Edmonds; T. Jones
Secretary, Anne-Marie Roberts

LIBRARIES

BRITISH LIBRARY

96 Euston Road, London NW1 2DB
T 020-7412 7000
E visitor-services@bl.uk W www.bl.uk

The British Library was established in 1973. It is the UK's national library and occupies a key position in the library and information network. The Library aims to serve scholarship, research, industry, commerce and all other major users of information. Its services are based on collections which include over 16 million volumes, 1 million discs, and 55,000 hours of tape recordings. The Library is now based at two sites: London (St Pancras and Colindale) and Boston Spa, W. Yorks. The Library's sponsoring department is the Department for Culture, Media and Sport.

Access to the reading rooms at St Pancras is limited to holders of a British Library Reader's Pass; information about eligibility is available from the Reader Admissions Office. The exhibition galleries and public areas are open to all, free of charge.

Opening hours of services vary and should be checked by telephone.

BRITISH LIBRARY BOARD

Chairman, Lord Eatwell of Stratton
Chief Executive and Deputy Chairman, Mrs L. Brindley
Members, H. Boyd-Carpenter, KCVO; S. Olswang; Prof. R. Burgess; Ms S. Forbes, CBE; D. Lewis; Sir Colin Lucas; Ms E. Mackay; R. S. Broadhurst, CBE; Dr G. W. Roberts

BRITISH LIBRARY, BOSTON SPA

Boston Spa, Wetherby, W. Yorks LS23 7BQ
T 01937-546000

BRITISH LIBRARY, ST PANCRAS

96 Euston Road, London NW1 2DB
T 020-7412 7000
Press and Public Relations, T 020-7412 7111
Visitor Services, T 020-7412 7332
Education Service, T 020-7412 7797

SCHOLARSHIP AND COLLECTIONS

Reader Services, T 020-7412 7676
Asia, Pacific and Africa Collections, T 020-7412 7873
British Collections, T 020-7412 7676
Western Manuscripts, T 020-7412 7513
Map Library, T 020-7412 7702
Music Library, T 020-7412 7772
Philatelic Collections, T 020-7412 7635
British Library Sound Archive, T 020-7412 7440
British Library Newspapers, Colindale Avenue, London NW9 5HE T 020-7412 7353
European and American Collections, T 020-7412 7676

OPERATIONS AND SERVICES

Reader Admissions, T 020-7412 7677

SCIENCE, TECHNOLOGY AND INNOVATION

Science and Technology, T 020-7412 7494/7289
Patents, T 020-7412 7919/7920
Business, T 020-7412 7454
Social Policy Information Service, T 020-7412 7536
National Preservation Office, T 020-7412 7612

NATIONAL LIBRARY OF SCOTLAND

George IV Bridge, Edinburgh EH1 1EW
T 0131-226 4531 F 0131-622 4803
E enquiries@nls.uk W www.nls.uk

The Library, which was founded as the Advocates' Library in 1682, became the National Library of Scotland in 1925. It is funded by the Scottish Executive. It contains about eight million books and pamphlets, 20,000 current periodicals, 350 newspaper titles and 120,000 manuscripts. It has an unrivalled Scottish collection.

The Reading Room is for reference and research which cannot conveniently be pursued elsewhere. Admission is by ticket.

Chairman of the Trustees, Prof. Michael Anderson, OBE, FBA, FRSE
National Librarian and Secretary to the Trustees, M. Wade
Director of Collection Development, C. Newton
Director of Corporate Services, D. Campbell
Director of Customer Services, G. Hunt
Director of Development and Marketing, A. Miller

NATIONAL LIBRARY OF WALES/ LLYFRGELL GENEDLAETHOL CYMRU

Aberystwyth SY23 3BU
T 01970-632800 F 01970-615709
W www.llgc.org.uk

The National Library of Wales was founded by royal charter in 1907, and is funded by the National Assembly for Wales. It contains about four million printed books, 40,000 manuscripts, four million deeds and documents, numerous maps, prints and drawings, and a sound and moving image collection. It specialises in manuscripts and books relating to Wales and the Celtic peoples. It is the repository for pre-1858 Welsh probate records, manorial records and tithe documents, and certain legal records. Admission is by reader's ticket to the Reading Rooms but

entry to the exhibition programme is free.
President, Dr R. Brinley Jones
Heads of Departments, M. W. Mainwaring *(Corporate Services)*; G. Jenkins *(Collection Services)*; Dr W. R. M. Griffiths *(Public Services)*
Librarian, A. M. W. Green

LIGHTHOUSE AUTHORITIES

CORPORATION OF TRINITY HOUSE

Trinity House, Tower Hill, London EC3N 4DH
T 020-7481 6900 F 020-7480 7662
W www.trinityhouse.co.uk

Trinity House, the first general lighthouse and pilotage authority in the kingdom, was granted its first charter by Henry VIII in 1514. The Corporation is the general lighthouse authority for England, Wales and the Channel Islands and maintains 72 lighthouses, 13 major floating aids to navigation (e.g. light vessels) and more than 420 buoys. The Corporation also has certain statutory jurisdiction over aids to navigation maintained by local harbour authorities and is responsible for dealing with wrecks dangerous to navigation, except those occurring within port limits or wrecks of HM ships.

The Trinity House Lighthouse Service is maintained out of the General Lighthouse Fund which is provided from light dues levied on ships calling at ports of the UK and the Republic of Ireland. The Corporation is also a deep-sea pilotage authority and a charitable organisation.

The affairs of the Corporation are controlled by a board of Elder Brethren and the Secretary. A separate board, which comprises Elder Brethren, senior staff and outside representatives, currently controls the Lighthouse Service. The Elder Brethren also act as nautical assessors in marine cases in the Admiralty Division of the High Court of Justice.

ELDER BRETHREN
Master, HRH The Prince Philip, Duke of Edinburgh, KG, KT, PC
Deputy Master and Executive Chairman, Rear-Adm. J. M. de Halpert, CB
Wardens, Capt. C. M. C. Stewart *(Rental)*; Cdre. P. J. Melson, CBE, RN; *(Nether)*
Elder Brethren, HRH The Prince of Wales, KG, KT; HRH The Duke of York, KCVO, ADC; Sir Brian Shaw; Capt. J. E. Bury; Capt. D. J. Cloke; Capt. Sir Miles Wingate, KCVO; The Rt. Hon. Sir Edward Heath, KG, MBE; Capt. P. F. Mason, CBE; Capt.T. Woodfield, OBE; The Rt. Hon. The Lord Simon of Glaisdale, DL; Capt. D. T. Smith, OBE, RN; Cdr. Sir Robin Gillett, BT, GBE, RD, RNR; Capt. Sir Malcolm Edge, KCVO; The Rt. Hon. The Lord Cuckney of Millbank; Capt. D. J. Orr; The Rt. Hon. The Lord Carrington, KG, GCMG, CH, MC, PC; The Rt. Hon. The Lord Mackay of Clashfern, KT; Sir Adrian Swire; CBE, GCVO; Cdr. M. J. Rivett-Carnac, RN, DL; Adm. Sir Jock Slater, GCB, LVO, DL; Capt. J. R. Burton-Hall, RD; Capt. I. Gibb; Capt. D. C. Glass; D. F. Potter; Capt. D. P. Richards, RD, RNR; S. P. Sherard; The Lord Brown of Madingley; The Rt. Hon. The Lord Robertson of Port Ellen, GCMG; Rear-Adm. Sir Patrick Rowe, KCVO, CBE; The Hon. C. C. Lyttelton; Capt. N. R. Pryke, MCIT

OFFICERS
Secretary, P. Galloway
Director of Finance, J. S. Wedge
Director of Operations and Asset Management, Cdre. P. J. Melson, CBE, RN
Head of Human Resources, P. F. Morgan
Legal and Risk Manager, J. D. Price
Navigation Manager, Mrs K. Hossain
Marketing and PR Manager , S. J. W. Dunning
Media and Communication Officer, H. L. Cooper

NORTHERN LIGHTHOUSE BOARD

84 George Street, Edinburgh EH2 3DA
T 0131-473 3100 F 0131-220 2093
E enquiries@nlb.org.uk W www.nlb.org.uk

The Lighthouse Board is the general lighthouse authority for Scotland and the Isle of Man and owes its origin to an Act of Parliament passed in 1786. At present there are 19 Commissioners who operate under the Merchant Shipping Act 1995.

The Commissioners control 199 lighthouses and many lighted and unlighted buoys and a DGPS system.

COMMISSIONERS
The Lord Advocate; the Solicitor-General for Scotland; the Lord Provosts of Edinburgh, Glasgow and Aberdeen; the Provost of Inverness; the Convener of Argyll and Bute Council; the Sheriffs-Principal of North Strathclyde, Tayside, Central and Fife, Grampian, Highlands and Islands, South Strathclyde, Dumfries and Galloway, Lothians and Borders and Glasgow and Strathkelvin; P. MacKay, CB; Capt. K. MacLeod; Dr A. Cubie, CBE; R. Quayle; A. Whyte

OFFICERS
Chief Executive, Capt. J. B. Taylor, RN
Director of Finance, D. Gorman
Director of Engineering, M. Waddell
Director of Operations and Navigational Requirements, G. Platten

LOCAL GOVERNMENT OMBUDSMAN FOR WALES

Derwen House, Court Road, Bridgend CF31 1BN
T 01656-661325 F 01656-673279
E enquiries@ombudsman-wales.org
W www.ombudsman-wales.org

The Local Government Ombudsman for Wales has similar powers to the Local Commissioners in England, but since the end of 2001 he has also had additional powers (similar to the Standards Board for England) to investigate allegations made against local authority members of misconduct. The Ombudsman is appointed by the Crown on the recommendation of the Secretary of State for Wales. A free leaflet *Your Local Government Ombudsman in Wales* is available from the Ombudsman's office.
Public Services and Local Government Ombudsman for Wales, Adam Peat
Member (ex officio), The Parliamentary Commissioner for Administration

LORD GREAT CHAMBERLAIN'S OFFICE

House of Lords, London SW1A 0PW
T 020-7219 3100 F 020-7219 2500

The Lord Great Chamberlain is a Great Officer of State, the office being hereditary since the grant of Henry I to the family of De Vere, Earls of Oxford. It is now a joint hereditary office rotating on the death of the Sovereign between the Cholmondeley, Carington and the Ancaster families. The Lord Great Chamberlain is responsible for the royal apartments in the Palace of Westminster, i.e. the Sovereign's Robing Room, the Royal Gallery, the administration of the Chapel of St Mary Undercroft and, in conjunction with the Lord Chancellor and the Speaker, Westminster Hall. The Lord Great Chamberlain has the right to perform specific services at a Coronation, he carries out ceremonial duties in the Palace of Westminster when the Sovereign visits the Palace and has particular responsibility for the internal administrative arrangements within the House of Lords for State Openings of Parliament.

Lord Great Chamberlain, The Marquess of Cholmondeley
Secretary to the Lord Great Chamberlain, Lt.-Gen. Sir
  Michael Willcocks, KCB
Clerks to the Lord Great Chamberlain, Ms J. Perodeau; Ms
  Rebecca Russel Ponte

LORD PRIVY SEAL'S OFFICE

Cabinet Office, 70 Whitehall, London SW1A 2AT
T 020-7270 3000
W www.cabinetoffice.gov.uk

The Lord Privy Seal is a member of the Cabinet and Leader of the House of Lords. He has no departmental portfolio, but is a member of a number of Cabinet committees. He is responsible to the Prime Minister for the organisation of Government business in the House and has a responsibility to the House itself to advise it on procedural matters and other difficulties which arise. He is the Lords' spokesperson on Northern Ireland issues.

Lord Privy Seal, Leader of the House of Lords, The Rt. Hon.
  Baroness Amos
Principal Private Secretary, Christopher Jacobs
Private Secretary (House of Lords), Andrew Makower

MENTAL HEALTH ACT COMMISSION

Maid Marian House, 56 Hounds Gate, Nottingham NG1 6BG
T 0115-943 7100 F 0115-943 7101
E chiefexec@mhac.trent.nhs.uk W www.mhac.trent.nhs.uk

The Mental Health Act Commission was established in 1983. Its functions are to keep under review the operation of the Mental Health Act 1983; to visit and meet patients detained under the Act; to investigate complaints falling within the Commission's remit; to operate the consent to treatment safeguards in the Mental Health Act; to publish a biennial report on its activities; to monitor the implementation of the Code of Practice; and to advise Ministers. Commissioners are appointed by the Secretary of State for Health.

Chairman, Prof. K. Patel
Vice-Chairman, Ms D. Jenkins
Chief Executive, C. Heginbotham

MILLENNIUM COMMISSION

Portland House, Stag Place, London SW1E 5EZ
T 020-7880 2001 F 020-7880 2000
E info@millennium.gov.uk

The Millennium Commission was established in February 1994 and is accountable to the Department for Culture, Media and Sport. It is an independent body which distributes money from National Lottery proceeds to projects to mark the millennium. The Commission expects all its grant-giving work to be complete by 2006.

Chair, The Rt. Hon. Tessa Jowell, MP
Members, Dr H. Couper, FRAS; Ms F. Benjamin, OBE; Lord
  Heseltine, MP, PC; Mrs J. Donovan, CBE; M. d'Ancona;
  Lord Glentoran, CBE; The Rt. Hon. R. Caborn, MP
Director, M. O'Connor, CBE

MUSEUMS

BRITISH MUSEUM

Great Russell Street, London WC1B 3DG
T 020-7323 8000 F 020-7323 8616
E information@thebritishmuseum.ac.uk
W www.thebritishmuseum.ac.uk

The British Museum houses the national collection of antiquities, ethnography, coins and paper money, medals, prints and drawings. The British Museum may be said to date from 1753, when Parliament approved the holding of a public lottery to raise funds for the purchase of the collections of Sir Hans Sloane and the Harleian manuscripts, and for their proper housing and maintenance. The building (Montagu House) was opened in 1759. The present buildings were erected between 1823 and the present day, and the original collection has increased to its present dimensions by gifts and purchases. Total government grant-in-aid for 2004–5 is £37,999 million.

BOARD OF TRUSTEES
Appointed by the Sovereign, HRH The Duke of Gloucester,
  KG, GCVO
Appointed by the Prime Minister, C. Allen-Jones; Hasan
  Askari; Nicholas Barber; Prof. Barry Cunliffe; The Rt.
  Hon. Countess of Dalkeith; Sir Michael Hopkins; Sir
  Joseph Hotung; Prof. Martin Kemp; David Lindsell;
  Christopher McCall; Tom Phillips; Anna Ritchie; Eric
  Salama; Prof. Jean Thomas; Sir Keith Thomas; Richard
  Lambert
Appointed by the Trustees of the British Museum, Sir John
  Boyd *(Chair)*; The Hon. Phillip Lader; Lord Powell of
  Bayswater, KCMG; J. Tusa *(Deputy Chair)*; Lord Browne
  of Madingley *(Deputy Chair)*

OFFICERS
Director, Neil MacGregor
Deputy Director, Andrew Burnett
Deputy Director, Dawn Austwick, OBE
Director of Marketing and Public Affairs, vacant
Director of Operations, Chris Rofe
Director of Resources, D. Austwick, OBE
Acting Head of Communications, Joanna Mackle
Head of Building and Estates, K. T. Stannard
Head of Education, J. F. Reeve
Head of Finance, Chris Herring
Head of Membership Development, Ms M. Fenn
Secretary, T. Doubleday
Visitor Operations Manager, Kerry Foster

KEEPERS
Keeper of Ancient Near East Antiquities, Dr John Curtis
Keeper of Coins and Medals, Andrew Burnett
Keeper of Department of Asia, Robert Knox
Keeper of Egyptian Antiquities, Vivian Davies
Keeper of Ethnography, John Mack
Keeper of Greek and Roman Antiquities, Dr Dyfri Williams
Keeper of Prehistory and Europe, Leslie Webster
Keeper, Presentation, Ian Jenkins
Keeper of Prints and Drawings, Antony Griffiths
Conservation, Documentation and Science, Sheridan Bowman

IMPERIAL WAR MUSEUM
Lambeth Road, London SE1 6HZ
T 020-7416 5320 F 020-7416 5374

The Museum, founded in 1917, illustrates and records all aspects of the two world wars and other military operations involving Britain and the Commonwealth since 1914. It was opened in its present home, formerly Bethlem Hospital, in 1936. The Museum is a multi-branch organisation which also includes: the Cabinet War Rooms in Whitehall, HMS Belfast in the Pool of London, Imperial War Museum Duxford in Cambridgeshire and Imperial War Museum North in Trafford.

The total grant-in-aid (including grants for special projects) for 2004–5 is £17.491 million.

OFFICERS
Chairman of Trustees, Adm. Sir Jock Slater, GCB, LVO
Director-General, R. W. K. Crawford, CBE
Director of Collections, M. Whitmore
Director of Corporate Services, A. Stoneman
Director of Development, Ms V. Cornwall
Director of HMS Belfast, B. King
Director of Public Services, Miss A. Godwin
Director, Cabinet War Rooms, P. Reed
Director, Imperial War Museum, Duxford, E. Inman, OBE
Director, Imperial War Museum, North, J. Forrester
Secretary and Director of Finance, J. Card

MUSEUM OF LONDON
London Wall, London EC2Y 5HN
T 0870-444 3852 F 0870-444 3853
E info@museumoflondon.org.uk
W www.museumoflondon.org.uk

The Museum of London illustrates the history of London from prehistoric times to the present day. It opened in 1976 and is based on the amalgamation of the former Guildhall Museum and London Museum. The Museum is controlled by a Board of Governors, appointed (nine each) by the Government and the Corporation of London. The Museum is currently funded by grants from the Department for Culture, Media and Sport and the Corporation of London. The total grant-in-aid for 2004–5 is £6.506 million.

Chairman of Board of Governors, R. Hambro
Director, Prof. J. Lohman

MUSEUMS, LIBRARIES AND ARCHIVES COUNCIL
16 Queen Anne's Gate, London SW1H 9AA
T 020-7273 1444 F 020-7273 1404
E info@mla.gov.uk W www.resource.gov.uk

The Museums, Libraries and Archives Council (MLA) was launched in April 2000 in order to provide strategic guidance, advice and advocacy across the whole of Government on museum, archive and library matters. It is a non-departmental public body sponsored by the Department for Culture, Media and Sport. The MLA replaced the Museums and Galleries Commission (MGC) and the Library and Information Commission (LIC), and now includes archives within its portfolio.

Chairman, Mark Wood
Chief Executive, C. Batt, OBE
Board Members, L. Grossman; V. Gray; A. Chowdhury; Dr M. Crozier; M. Jones; N. MacGregor; M. Stevenson; A. Watkin; D. Barrie; Ms L. Brindley; B. MacNaught; B. McKee; D. Henshaw; Sir Geoffrey Holland; N. Kingsley; Ms V. Tandy

NATIONAL ARMY MUSEUM
Royal Hospital Road, London SW3 4HT
T 020-7730 0717 F 020-7823 6573
E info@national-army-museum.ac.uk
W www.national-army-museum.ac.uk

The National Army Museum covers the history of five centuries of the British Army. It was established by royal charter in 1960.

Assistant Directors, D. K. Smurthwaite; Dr A. J. Guy; P. B. Boyden

NATURAL HISTORY MUSEUM
Cromwell Road, London SW7 5BD
T 020-7942 5000

The Natural History Museum originates from the natural history departments of the British Museum, which grew extensively during the 19th century; in 1860 the natural history collection was moved from Bloomsbury to a new location. Part of the site of the 1862 International Exhibition in South Kensington was acquired for the new museum, and the Museum opened to the public in 1881. In 1963 the Natural History Museum became completely independent with its own board of trustees. The Walter Rothschild Zoological Museum, Tring, bequeathed by the second Lord Rothschild, has formed part of the Museum since 1938. The Geological Museum merged with the Natural History Museum in 1985. Total Government grant-in-aid for 2004–5 is £39.367 million.

Trustees, Prof. Sir Keith O'Nions, FRS *(Chairman)*; Sir Richard Sykes, FRS; Dame Judith Mayhew, DBE; Prof. M. Hassell, CBE, FRS; O. Stocken; Prof. J. McGlade; Prof. Dianne Edwards, CBE, FRS, Prof. C. Leaver, CBE, FRS; The Lord Palumbo; Prof. Linda Partridge, FRS, FRSE; Prof. Georgina Mace, OBE; Sir William Castell

SENIOR STAFF
Director, Dr Michael Dixon
Director of Communications and Development, Ms S. Ament
Director of Estates, K. Rellis
Director of Finance, N. Greenwood
Director of Human Resources, D. Hill
Director of Science, R. Lane
Director, Tring Zoological Museum, Mrs T. Wild

Head of Audit and Review, D. Thorpe
Head of Library and Information Services, G. Higley
Head of Visitor and Operational Services, D. Candlin
Keeper of Botany, Dr J. Vogel
Keeper of Entomology, Dr R. Vane-Wright
Keeper of Mineralogy, Prof. A. Fleet
Keeper of Palaeontology, Dr N. MacLeod
Keeper of Zoology, Prof. P. Rainbow

NATIONAL MARITIME MUSEUM
Park Row, Greenwich, London SE10 9NF
T 020-8858 4422 F 020-8312 6632

Established by Act of Parliament in 1934, the National Maritime Museum illustrates the maritime history of Great Britain in the widest sense, underlining the importance of the sea and its influence on the nation's power, wealth, culture, technology and institutions. The Museum is in three groups of buildings in Greenwich Park the main building, the Queen's House (built by Inigo Jones, 1616–35) and the Royal Observatory (including Wren's Flamsteed House). In May 1999, a £20 million Heritage Lottery supported project opened 16 new galleries in a glazed courtyard in the Museum's west wing. Total Government grant-in-aid for 2004–5 is £15.731 million.
Director, R. Clare
Chairman, Sir David Hardy

NATIONAL MUSEUMS LIVERPOOL
PO Box 33, 127 Dale Street, Liverpool L69 3LA
T 0151-207 0001 F 0151-478 4790
W www.liverpoolmuseums.org.uk

The Board of Trustees of the National Museums Liverpool (formerly National Museums and Galleries on Merseyside) is responsible for the Liverpool Museum, the Merseyside Maritime Museum (incorporating HM Customs and Excise National Museum), the Museum of Liverpool Life, the Lady Lever Art Gallery, the Walker, Sudley House and the Conservation Centre. Total Government grant-in-aid for 2004–5 was £17.333 million.
Chairman of the Board of Trustees, D. McDonnell
Director, Dr David Fleming
Keeper of Art Galleries, J. Treuherz
Keeper of Conservation, A. Durham
Keeper, Liverpool Museum, J. Millard
Keeper, Merseyside Maritime Museum and Museum of Liverpool Life, T. Tibbles

NATIONAL MUSEUMS AND GALLERIES OF WALES
Cathays Park, Cardiff CF10 3NP
T 029-2039 7951 F 029-2057 3321
E post@nmgw.ac.uk W www.nmgw.ac.uk

The National Museums and Galleries of Wales comprise the National Museum and Gallery Cardiff, the Museum of Welsh Life, St Fagans, Big Pit National Museum of Wales, Blaenafon, the Roman Legionary Museum Caerleon, Turner House Gallery Penarth, the Welsh Slate Museum Llanberis, the Segontium Roman Museum Caernarfon and the Museum of the Welsh Woollen Industry Dre-fach, Felindre. Total funding from the Welsh Assembly Government for 2003–4 was £20.536 million.
President, Paul E. Loveluck, CBE
Vice-President, Dr Susan J. Davies
Treasurer, Gwyn Howells, ACIB

OFFICERS
Director-General, Michael Houlihan
Directors, Dr E. Wiliam *(Collections and Education and Deputy Director)*; J. Williams-Davies *(Museum of Welsh Life)*; M. Tooby *(National Museum and Gallery)*; R. Gwyn *(Strategic Communications)*; M. Richards *(Operations)*; J. Sheppard *(Finance and IT)*
Council Members, M.C. T. Prichard, CBE; Dr Brian Willott; M. A. J. Salter; J. E. Peirson Jones; Prof. Colin L. Jones, OBE; Dr Iolo ap Gwynn; D. Bowen Lewis; J. Wynford Evans, CBE; Dr Peter Warren, CBE; Prof. J. W. Last, CBE; Prof. D. Egan; H. R. C. Williams; Rhiannon Wyn Hughes, MBE

NATIONAL MUSEUMS OF SCOTLAND
Chambers Street, Edinburgh EH1 1JF
T 0131-247 4422 F 0131-220 4819
E info@nms.ac.uk W www.nms.ac.uk

The National Museums of Scotland comprise the Royal Museum of Scotland, the National War Museum of Scotland, the Museum of Scottish Country Life, the Museum of Flight, Shambellie House Museum of Costume and the Museum of Scotland. Total funding from the Scottish Executive is an annual grant of £16 million.

BOARD OF TRUSTEES
Chairman, The Lord Wilson of Tillyorn, KT, GCMG, PHD, FRSE
Members, G. S. Johnston, OBE, TD, KCSG, DL, CA; Ms C. Macaulay; Sir Neil McIntosh, CBE, DL; Mrs N. Mahal, DCG; Prof. A. Manning, OBE, DPHIL, FRSE, FIBIOL; Prof. J. Murray, CENG; I. Ritchie, CBE, FRENG, FRSE; A. J. C. Smith, FCIA; J. A. G. Fiddes, OBE; Prof. M. Lynch, PHD, FRSE, FSA (SCOT); Miss A. MacLean; Mrs L. Hart, MBE

OFFICERS
Director, Dr G. Rintoul, PHD
Director of Collections, Jane Carmichael
Director of Facilities Management and Projects, S. Elson, FSA SCOT
Director of Finance and Resources, A. Patience
Director of Marketing and Development, Catherine Holden
Director of Public Programmes, Mary Bryden, FRSA
Head of Corporate Policy and Performance, Sheila McClure
Managing Director of NMS Enterprises, P. Williamson

ROYAL AIR FORCE MUSEUM
Grahame Park Way, London NW9 5LL
T 020-8205 2266 F 020-8200 1751
W www.rafmuseum.com

Situated on the former airfield at RAF Hendon, the Museum illustrates the development of aviation from before the Wright brothers to the present-day RAF. Total Government grant-in-aid for 2003–4, including funding for the outstation at Cosford, is £6.798 million.
Director-General, Dr M. A. Fopp
Directors, J. Kitchen; S. Garman; K. Ifould
Senior Keeper, P. Elliott

SCIENCE MUSEUM
Exhibition Road, London SW7 2DD
T 0870-870 4868 F 020-7942 4447

The Science Museum, part of the National Museum of Science and Industry, houses the national collections of science, technology, industry and medicine. The Museum began as the science collection of the South Kensington Museum and first opened in 1857. In 1883 it acquired the collections of the Patent Museum and in 1909 the science collections were transferred to the new Science Museum, leaving the art collections with the Victoria and Albert Museum. The Wellcome Wing was opened in July 2000.

Some of the Museum's commercial aircraft, agricultural machinery, and road and rail transport collections are at Wroughton, Wilts. The National Museum of Science and Industry also incorporates the National Railway Museum, York, the National Museum of Photography, Film and Television, Bradford, and Locomotion: the National Railway Museum at Shildon.

Total Government grant-in-aid for 2004–5 is £32,494 million.

BOARD OF TRUSTEES
Chairman, The Rt. Hon. Lord Waldegrave of North Hill
Members, Prof. Sir Ron U. Cooke, DSC; Prof. A. Dowling, CBE, FRENG; G. Dyke; Dr A. Grocock; Dr D. Gurr; R. Haythornthwaite; D. E. Rayner, CBE; Prof. Sir Martin Rees; Dr Maggie Semple, OBE; S. Singh, MBE; M. G. Smith; Prof. R. A. Smith, PHD, FRENG; Prof. Kathy Sykes; Sir William Wells

OFFICERS
Director, Dr. L. Sharp
Head of Corporate Communications, M. Pudney
Head of Design, T. Molloy
Head of Estates, J. Bevin
Head of Finance, Ms A. Caine
Interim Head of Human Resources, Ms B. Halikowa
Head of IT, Ms M. Burns
Head of National Museum of Photography, Film and Television, C. Philpott
Managing Director, NMSI Trading Ltd, Ms M. Jackson
Head of National Railway Museum, A. Scott
Head of Planning and Development, A. Leitch
Head of Science Museum, J. Tucker
Head of Sustainable Development and Master Planning, C. Gordon

VICTORIA AND ALBERT MUSEUM
Cromwell Road, London SW7 2RL
T 020-7942 2000 W www.vam.ac.uk

The Victoria and Albert Museum is the national museum of fine and applied art and design. It descends directly from the Museum of Manufactures, which opened in Marlborough House in 1852 after the Great Exhibition of 1851. The Museum was moved in 1857 to become part of the South Kensington Museum. It was renamed the Victoria and Albert Museum in 1899. It also houses the National Art Library and Print Room.

The Museum administers two branch museums: the Museum of Childhood at Bethnal Green and the Theatre Museum in Covent Garden. The museum in Bethnal Green was opened in 1872 and the building is the most important surviving example of the type of glass and iron construction used by Paxton for the Great Exhibition.

Total Government grant-in-aid for 2004–5 is £36.1 million.

BOARD OF TRUSTEES
Chairman, Paula Ridley
Members, J. Altaras; Prof. M. Buck; R. Dickins; Prof. Sir Christopher Frayling, PHD; Prof. Lisa Jardine, PHD; Mrs J. Gordon Clark; R. Mather; P. Rogers; P. Ruddock; The Rt. Hon. Sir Timothy Sainsbury; Dame Marjorie Scardino, DBE
Secretary to the Board of Trustees, J. F. Rider

OFFICERS
Director, M. Jones
Director of Collections and Keeper of Asian Department, Dr D. Swallow
Director of Collections Services, N. Umney
Director of Finance and Resources, I. Blatchford
Director of Learning and Interpretation, D. Anderson, OBE
Director of Personnel and Visitor Services, L. Stracey
Director of Projects and Estate, Mrs G. F. Miles
Director of Public Affairs, D. Whitmore
Director of Development, J. McCaffrey
Director of the Museum of Childhood, Ms D. Lees
Director of the Theatre Museum, G. Marsh
Head of Conservation, Ms S. Smith
Head of Exhibitions, Mrs L. Lloyd Jones
Head of Photographic Services, J. Stevenson
Head of Records and Collections Services, A. Seal
Head of Regional Liaison and Purchase Grant Fund, Miss J. Davies
Head of Research Department, Ms C. Sargentson
Keeper of Furniture, Textiles and Fashion Department, C. Wilk
Keeper of Sculpture, Metalwork, Ceramics and Glass Department, Dr P. E. D. Williamson
Keeper of Word and Image Department, Ms S. B. Lambert
Managing Director of V&A Enterprises Ltd (Acting), Ms J. Prosser

NATIONAL AUDIT OFFICE
157–197 Buckingham Palace Road, London SW1W 9SP
T 020-7798 7000 F 020-7798 7070
3–4 Park Place, Cardiff CF10 3DP
T 029-2067 8500 F 029-2067 8501
E enquiries@nao.gsi.gov.uk
W www.nao.org.uk

The National Audit Office came into existence under the National Audit Act 1983 to replace and continue the work of the former Exchequer and Audit Department. The Act reinforced the Office's total financial and operational independence from the Government and brought its head, the Comptroller and Auditor-General, into a closer relationship with Parliament as an officer of the House of Commons.

The National Audit Office provides independent information, advice and assurance to Parliament and the public about all aspects of the financial operations of Government departments and many other bodies receiving public funds. It does this by examining and certifying the accounts of these organisations and by regularly publishing reports to Parliament on the results of its value for money investigations of the economy, efficiency and effectiveness with which public resources have been used. The National Audit Office is also the auditor by agreement of the accounts of certain international and other organisations. In addition, the Office authorises the issue of public funds to Government departments.

Comptroller and Auditor-General, Sir John Bourne, KCB
Private Secretary, N. Sayers
Deputy Comptroller and Auditor-General, T. Burr
Assistant Auditors-General, J. Colman; Miss C. Mawhood; M. Sinclair; Ms W. Kenway-Smith; M. Whitehouse; J. Rickleton

NATIONAL CONSUMER COUNCIL

20 Grosvenor Gardens, London SW1W 0DH
T 020-7730 3469 F 020-7730 0191
E info@ncc.org.uk W www.ncc.org.uk

The National Consumer Council (NCC) was set up by the Government in 1975 to give an independent voice to consumers in the UK. Its role is to advocate the consumer interest to decision-makers in national and local government, industry and regulatory bodies, business and the professions. It does this through a combination of research and campaigning. NCC is a non-profit making company limited by guarantee and is largely funded by grant-in-aid from the Department of Trade and Industry. The Council is not a consumer advice or complaints body.

Chair, Deirdre Hutton, CBE
Chief Executive, Ed Mayo

NATIONAL ENDOWMENT FOR SCIENCE, TECHNOLOGY AND THE ARTS (NESTA)

Fishmongers' Chambers, 110 Upper Thames Street, London EC4R 3TW
T 020-7645 9500 F 020-7645 9501
W www.nesta.org.uk

The National Endowment for Science, Technology and the Arts (NESTA) was established under the National Lottery Act 1998 with a £200 million endowment from the proceeds of the National Lottery. It runs four funding programmes: *Invention and Innovation* takes original ideas with commercial or social potential and helps them get to market; *Fellowship* supports exceptionally talented and innovative people, and enables them to pursue a tailor-made programme of personal creative development; *Learning* researches and pioneers initiatives, which will drive education and encourage public engagement with science, technology and the arts; and the *Graduate Pioneer Programme* supports recent graduates from the creative industries.

Chairman, Chris Powell
Chief Executive, J. Newton

NATIONAL HERITAGE MEMORIAL FUND

7 Holbein Place, London SW1W 8NR
T 020-7591 6000 F 020-7591 6001
W www.hlf.org.uk

The National Heritage Memorial Fund was set up under the National Heritage Act 1980 in memory of people who have given their lives for the United Kingdom. The Fund provides grants (and sometimes loans) to organisations based in the United Kingdom, mainly so they can buy items of outstanding interest and of importance to the national heritage. These must either be at risk or have a memorial character. The Fund is administered by 14 trustees who are appointed by the Prime Minister.

The National Lottery etc Act 1993 designated the Fund as distributor of the heritage share of proceeds from the National Lottery. As a result, the Fund now operates two funds: the National Heritage Memorial Fund and the Heritage Lottery Fund. The National Heritage Memorial Fund receives an annual grant from the Department for Culture, Media and Sport.

Chair, L. Forgan
Trustees, Prof. C. Baines; N. Dodd; Sir Angus Grossart, CBE; G. Waterfield; Ms P. Wilson; Earl of Dalkeith; Prof. T. Pritchard; J. Wright, CBE; Dr M. Phillips; Dr D. Langslow; Madhu Anjali; Catherine Graham-Harrison; M. Emmerich
Director, Ms C. Souter

NATIONAL LOTTERY COMMISSION

101 Wigmore Street, London W1U 1QU
T 020-7016 3400 F 020-7016 3401
W www.natlotcomm.gov.uk

The National Lottery Commission replaced the Office of the National Lottery (OFLOT) in April 1999 under the National Lottery Act 1998. The Commission is responsible for the granting, varying and enforcing of licences to run the National Lottery. Its duties are to ensure that the National Lottery is run with all due propriety, that the interests of players are protected, and, subject to these two objectives, that returns to the 'good causes' are maximised.

Gaming and lotteries in the UK are officially regulated and may only be run by licensed operators or in licensed premises.

The Department of Culture, Media and Sport is responsible for gaming and lottery policy and laws. The National Lottery is the most heavily regulated part of the gaming market. Empowered by the National Lottery Act 1993, the Department of Culture, Media and Sport directs the National Lottery Commission, who in turn regulates Camelot, the lottery operator. Camelot, a private company wholly owned by five shareholders, was granted a second seven-year licence to run the Lottery, which began on 27 January 2002. The main National Lottery draw was relaunched as Lotto in spring 2002. Total sales of Lottery products in 2002–3 were almost £4,600 million – this represented a fall of 5.4 per cent on the previous year. Lotto sales dropped by 12.1 per cent, making up just under 74 per cent of total sales revenue. A total of £3,387 million was spent on Lotto tickets alone during 2002–3, and £2,238 million was paid out in prizes.

Chair, Moira Black
Chief Executive, M. Harris
Commissioners, Ms H. Spicer; T. Hornsby; Ms J. Valentine; B. Pomeroy
Director of Compliance, Ms M. Phillips
Director of Licensing, K. Jones
Director of Performance and Communications, Ms C. Forrester
Director of Resources, Ms C. McCullough

NATIONAL PHYSICAL LABORATORY

Queens Road, Teddington, Middx TW11 0LW
T 020-8977 3222 F 020-8943 6458

The Laboratory is the UK's national standards laboratory. It develops, maintains and disseminates national measurement standards for physical quantities such as mass, length, time, temperature, voltage, force and

pressure. It also conducts underpinning research on engineering materials and information technology and disseminates good measurement practice. It is Government-owned but contractor-operated.
Managing Director, Dr B. McGuiness
Director of Business Development, D. C. Richardson

NATIONAL RADIOLOGICAL PROTECTION BOARD

Chilton, Didcot, Oxon OX11 0RQ
T 01235-831600 F 01235-833891
E nrpb@nrpb.org
W www.nrpb.org

The National Radiological Protection Board is an independent statutory body created by the Radiological Protection Act 1970. It is the national point of authoritative reference on radiological protection for both ionising and non-ionising radiations, and has issued recommendations on limiting human exposure to electromagnetic fields and radiation from a range of sources, including X-rays, the Sun, base stations and mobile phones. Its sponsoring department is the Department of Health. The National Radiological Protection Board also works in partnership with the Health Protection Agency.
Chairman, Sir William Stewart, FRS, FRSE
Director, Prof. R. Cox

NATIONAL SAVINGS AND INVESTMENTS

375 Kensington High Street, London W14 8SD
T 020-7348 9200 F 020-7048 9698
W www.nsandi.com

National Savings and Investments came into being in 1861 when the Palmerston government set up the Post Office Savings Bank, a savings scheme which aimed to encourage ordinary wage earners 'to provide for themselves against adversity and ill health'. National Savings and Investments was established as a Government department in 1969. It became an executive agency of the Treasury in 1996 and is responsible for the design, marketing and administration of savings and investment products for personal savers and investors. In April 1999 Siemens Business Services took over all the back office functions at National Savings and Investments.
Chief Executive, A. Cook
Finance Director, T. Bayley
Marketing Director, G. Cattanach
Partnerships and Operations Director, S. Owen
Sales Director, J. Prout

NEW OPPORTUNITIES FUND

1 Plough Place, London EC4A 1DE
T 020-7211 1800 F 020-7211 1750
E enquiries@nof.org.uk
W www.nof.org.uk

The New Opportunities Fund provides lottery funding for health, education and environment projects in order to help create lasting improvements to the quality of life, particularly in disadvantaged communities.
    The Fund works with national, regional and local partners from the public, private and voluntary sectors to fund initiatives, with particular focus on the needs of those who are most disadvantaged in society.
Chair of the Board, Sir Clive Booth

Members of the Board, G. Oppenheim *(Director, Performance and Planning)*; Ms V. Potter *(Director, Policy and External Relations)*; M. Cooke *(Director, Finance and Corporate Services)*; Ms A. Kelbie *(Director, Operations)*; W. Rader *(Director, Northern Ireland)*; Ms C. Doyle *(Director, Wales)*; vacant *(Director, Scotland)*
Chief Executive, S. Dunmore

NORTHERN IRELAND AUDIT OFFICE

106 University Street, Belfast BT7 1EU
T 028-9025 1000 F 028-9025 1106
E info@niauditoffice.gov.uk
W www.niauditoffice.gov.uk

The primary aim of the Northern Ireland Audit Office is to provide independent assurance, information and advice to the Northern Ireland Assembly on the proper accounting for Northern Ireland departmental and certain other public expenditure, revenue, assets and liabilities; on regularity and propriety; and on the economy, efficiency and effectiveness of the use of resources.
Comptroller and Auditor-General for Northern Ireland, J. M. Dowdall, CB

NORTHERN IRELAND AUTHORITY FOR ENERGY REGULATION

Brookmount Buildings, 42 Fountain Street, Belfast BT1 5EE
T 028-9031 1575 F 028-9031 1740
E ofreg@nics.gov.uk
W www.ofreg.nics.gov.uk

The Northern Ireland Authority for Energy Regulation operating as The Office for the Regulation of Electricity & Gas (Ofreg) is the regulatory body for the electricity and gas supply industries in Northern Ireland.
Chairman and Chief Executive, Douglas McIldoon

NORTHERN IRELAND HUMAN RIGHTS COMMISSION

Temple Court, 39 North Street, Belfast BT1 1NA
T 028-9024 3987 F 028-9024 7844
E information@nihrc.org
W www.nihrc.org

The Northern Ireland Human Rights Commission was set up in March 1999. Its main functions are to keep under review the law and practice relating to human rights in Northern Ireland, to advise the Government and to promote an awareness of human rights in Northern Ireland. It can also take cases to court. The Commission currently consists of one full-time commissioner and six part-time commissioners, all appointed by the Secretary of State for Northern Ireland.
Chief Commissioner, Prof. B. Dickson
Commissioners, Mrs M. A. Dinsmore, QC; T. Donnelly, MBE; Lady Christine Eames; Prof. T. Hadden; Ms P. Kelly; K. McLaughlin

OCCUPATIONAL PENSIONS REGULATORY AUTHORITY

Invicta House, Trafalgar Place, Brighton BN1 4DW
T 01273-627600 F 01273-627688
E helpdesk@opra.gov.uk
W www.opra.gov.uk

The Occupational Pensions Regulatory Authority (OPRA) was set up under the Pensions Act 1995 and became fully operational on 6 April 1997. It is the UK regulator of pension arrangements offered by employers. It maintains a register of stakeholder pensions and regulates payments into stakeholder and personal pensions.

Chairman, Harriet Maunsell, OBE

Chief Executive, Anthony Hobman

OFFICE FOR NATIONAL STATISTICS

1 Drummond Gate, London SW1V 2QQ
T 0845-601 3034
E info@statistics.gov.uk
W www.statistics.gov.uk

The Office for National Statistics was created in 1996 by the merger of the Central Statistical Office and the Office of Population Censuses and Surveys. It is both a Government department and an executive agency of the Treasury and is responsible for preparing, interpreting and publishing key statistics on the government, economy and society of the UK. Its key responsibilities include: the provision of population estimates and projections and statistics on health and other demographic matters in England and Wales; the production of the UK National Accounts and other key economic indicators; the organisation of population censuses in England and Wales and surveys for Government departments and public bodies; and the promotion of these functions within the UK, the European Union and internationally to provide a statistical service to meet European Union and international requirements.

The General Register Office is part of the ONS and is responsible for administering marriage laws, and for local registration of births, marriages and deaths in England and Wales.

The National Statistics initiative was launched in June 2000, headed by the National Statistician, with an independent Statistics Commission, providing assurance to Parliament about the integrity of official statistics and statistical practice. The National Statistics brand encompasses the statistical output of the ONS, plus many of the key public interest statistics produced by other Government departments.

National Statistician, Registrar General for England and Wales, Len Cook

Executive Directors, Karen Dunnell *(Surveys and Administrative Sources);* Colin Mowl *(Macroeconomics and Labour Market);* John Pullinger *(Economic and Social Reporting);* Peter Walton *(Organisational Development and Resources);* vacant *(Methodology);* Dennis Roberts *(Registration Services)*

Corporate Directors, Mike Hughes *(National Statistics and Planning);* Dayantha Joshua *(Information Management);* Peter Murphy *(Finance and Procurement);* Helena Rafalowska *(Communications);* Susan Young *(Human Resources)*

National Statistician's Private Office, Jackie Orme; Timothy Stamp; Brigid Keenan

Parliamentary Clerks, Robert Smith; Alex Elton-Wall

OFFICE FOR STANDARDS IN EDUCATION (OFSTED)

Alexandra House, 33 Kingsway, London WC2B 6SE
T 020-7421 6800 Early Years Helpline 0845-601 4771
F 020-7421 6707
E geninfo@ofsted.gov.uk
W www.ofsted.gov.uk

OFSTED is a non-ministerial Government department established under the Education (Schools Act) 1992.

Since April 2001 OFSTED has been responsible for inspecting all educational provision for 16–19 year olds to establish and monitor an independent inspection system for maintained schools in England. Its inspection role also includes the inspection of local education authorities, teacher training institutions and youth work. In September 2001, OFSTED took over the regulation of childcare providers, from 150 local authorities.

HM Chief Inspector, D. Bell

Directorate of Education, Ms M. Rosen

Director of Corporate Services, R. Knight

Director of Early Years, M. Smith

Director of Finance, P. Jolly

Director of Strategy and Resources, R. Green

OFFICE OF COMMUNICATIONS (OFCOM)

Riverside House, 2A Southwark Bridge Road, London, SE1 9HA
T 020-7981 3000 F 020-7981 3333
E wwwenq@ofcom.org.uk
W www.ofcom.org.uk

The Office of Communications (Ofcom) was established in 2003 under the Office of Communications Act 2002 as the independent regulator for the UK communications industries with responsibility for television, radio, telecommunications and wireless communications services. It merged the functions of five regulatory bodies: the Independent Television Commission (ITC), The Broadcasting Standards Commission (BSC), the Office of Telecommunications (Oftel), the Radio Authority (RAu) and the Radiocommunications Agency (RA). Ofcom's duties include: promoting choice, quality and value in electronic communications services; ensuring the most efficient use of the radiocommunications spectrum; ensuring a wide range of electronic communications services, including broadband, is available across the UK; ensuring the availability of a wide range of high quality TV and radio programmes; maintaining plurality in the media by ensuring a sufficiently broad range of ownership; and protecting audiences against offensive or harmful material, unfairness or the infringement of privacy on TV and radio. Members of the Board are appointed by the Secretaries of State for Trade and Industry and for Culture, Media and Sport.

Chief Executive, S. Carter

Chairman, D. Currie

Deputy Chairman, R. Hooper

Members, Ms M. Banerjee; D. Edmonds; I. Hargreaves; Ms K. Meek; Ms S. Nathan; E. Richards

OFFICE OF FAIR TRADING

Fleetbank House, 2–6 Salisbury Square, London EC4Y 8JX
T 020-7211 8000 F 020-7211 8800
E enquiries@oft.gov.uk
W www.oft.gov.uk

The Office of Fair Trading is a non-ministerial Government department established as a corporate body. It pursues its primary goal of making markets work better for consumers through enforcement of competition and consumer legislation, market studies and communication.

The Consumer Regulation Enforcement Division pursues the Office's consumer protection duties principally through the Enterprise Act 2002, the Consumer Credit Act 1974, the Estate Agents Act 1979, the Control of Misleading Advertisements Regulations

Act 1988, the Consumer Protection (Distance Selling) Regulations 2000 and the Unfair Terms in Consumer Contracts Regulations 1999.

The Competition Enforcement Division is responsible for investigating and taking action against agreements that restrict competition and conduct abusing a dominant position under both the UK Competition Act 1998, as amended by the Enterprise Act 2002, and European competition legislation. The Division also reviews mergers under the UK and EC merger control regimes. It has additional responsibilities for competition matters arising under other legislation, including the Financial Services and Markets Act 2000 and the Transport Act 2000.

The Markets and Policy Initiatives Division conducts market studies, which are made public, helping the Office assess whether action is needed to make markets work better for consumers. It negotiates and reviews undertakings following certain Competition Commission reports, provides advice to Government departments on the potential effects of new policy and legislation on competition and consumers, co-ordinates the Office's overall relationships with government departments, devolved administrations and other bodies, and leads on payment systems work.

The Communications Division's work entails the empowerment of consumers through campaigns, advice and education. It also informs businesses of their rights and duties under competition and consumer laws giving an opportunity for law-abiding businesses to complain about anti-competitive behaviour of others.

The Office of Fair Trading also liaises with the European Commission on competition and consumer protection initiatives.

Chairman, John Vickers
Executive Director, Penny Boys
Non-Executive Directors, Allan Asher, Lord Blackwell, Christine Farnish, Richard Whish, Rosalind Wright

COMMUNICATIONS DIVISION
Director of Communications, Mike Ricketts

COMPETITION ENFORCEMENT DIVISION
Divisional Director, Vincent Smith
Branch Directors, Ali Nikpay, Neil Feinson, Simon Priddis, Beckett McGrath, Justin Coombs, Alan Williams, Christiane Kent, Simon Williams

CONSUMER REGULATION ENFORCEMENT DIVISION
Divisional Director, Christine Wade
Branch Directors, Colin Brown, Steven Wood, Ray Hall, Ray Watson

LEGAL DIVISION
Solicitor , Brian McHenry
Branch Directors, Frances Barr, Simon Brindley, Louis Christofides, Jessica Farry, Paul Gurowich

MARKETS AND POLICIES INITIATIVES DIVISION
Divisional Director, Jonathan May
Branch Directors, Amelia Fletcher, Daniel Gordon, Chris Rawlins, Graham Winton

RESOURCES AND SERVICES
Director of Resources and Services, David Fisher

OFFICE OF GAS AND ELECTRICITY MARKETS (OFGEM)

9 Millbank, London, SW1P 3GE
T 020-7901 7000 F 020-7901 7066
Regents Court, 70 West Regent Street, Glasgow G2 2QZ
T 0141-331 2678 F 0141-331 2777
W www.ofgem.gov.uk

The Office of Gas and Electricity Markets (Ofgem) supports the Gas and Electricity Markets Authority, the regulator of the gas and electricity industries in Great Britain.

Ofgem aims to bring choice and value to all gas and electricity customers by promoting competition and regulating monopolies. The Authority's powers are provided for under the Gas Act 1986, the Electricity Act 1989 and the Utilities Act 2000.

Chief Executive, A. Buchanan
Managing Directors, J. Neilson *(Corporate Affairs);* Dr B. Moselle *(Corporate Strategy);* D. Gray *(Networks);* S. Smith *(Markets)*
Chief Operating Officer, R. Field

OFFICE OF THE LEGAL SERVICES OMBUDSMAN

3rd Floor, Sunlight House, Quay Street, Manchester M3 3JZ
T 0161-839 7262; 0845-601 0794 F 0161-832 5446
E lso@olso.gsi.gov.uk
W www.olso.org

The Legal Services Ombudsman is appointed by the Lord Chancellor under the Courts and Legal Services Act 1990 to oversee the handling of complaints against solicitors, barristers, licensed conveyancers, legal executives and patent agents by their professional bodies. A complainant must first complain to the relevant professional body before raising the matter with the Ombudsman. The Ombudsman is independent of the legal profession and her services are free of charge.

Legal Services Ombudsman, Ms Zahida Manzoor, CBE
Operations Director, S. Lees

OFFICE OF THE LEGAL SERVICES OMBUDSMAN (SCOTTISH)

17 Waterloo Place, Edinburgh, EH1 3DL
T 0131-556 9123 F 0131-556 9292
E ombudsman@slso.org.uk
W www.slso.org.uk

The Ombudsman investigates complaints about the way in which Scottish professional bodies have handled a complaint against a practitioner.

The Ombudsman also examines complaints about the unwillingness of a professional body to investigate a complaint against a practitioner.

Scottish Legal Services Ombudsman, Mrs L. Costelloe Baker

OFFICE OF THE LORD ADVOCATE

Crown Office, 25 Chambers Street, Edinburgh EH1 1LA
T 0131-226 2626 F 0131-226 6910
E scottish.ministers@scotland.gsi.gov.uk
W www.crownoffice.gov.uk

The Law Officers for Scotland are the Lord Advocate and the Solicitor-General for Scotland.

Lord Advocate, The Rt. Hon. Colin Boyd, QC
Solicitor-General for Scotland, Ms E. Angiolini, QC

Private Secretary to the Lord Advocate, Miss S. McGuire
Private Secretary to the Solicitor General, R. Kent
Assistant Private Secretary, C. Orman

OFFICE OF MANPOWER ECONOMICS

8th Floor, Oxford House, 76 Oxford Street, London W1D 1BS
T 020-7467 7244 F 020-7467 7248
W www.ome.uk.com

The Office of Manpower Economics was set up in 1971. It is an independent non-statutory organisation which is responsible for servicing independent review bodies which advise on the pay of various public service groups, the Pharmacists' Review Panel and the Police Negotiating and Police Advisory (England and Wales) Boards. The Office is also responsible for servicing *ad hoc* bodies of inquiry and for undertaking research into pay and associated matters as requested by the Government.

OME Director, Dr R. A. Wright
Director, Health Secretariats and OME Deputy Director, D. A. Miner
Director, Armed Forces' Secretariat, Mrs C. Haworth
Director, Senior Salaries Secretariat, N. D. Peace
Director, School Teachers' Secretariat, D. J. T. Wilson
Director, Prison Service Secretariat and Police Negotiating and Police Advisory (England and Wales) Boards Secretariat, M. C. Cahill
Press Liaison Officer, C. P. Jordan

OFFICE OF THE PENSIONS OMBUDSMAN

6th Floor, 11 Belgrave Road, London SW1V 1RB
T 020-7834 9144 F 020-7821 0065
E enquiries@pensions-ombudsman.org.uk
W www.pensions-ombudsman.org.uk

The Pensions Ombudsman is appointed under the Pension Schemes Act 1993 as amended by the Pensions Act 1995. He independently investigates and decides complaints and disputes concerning pension schemes.
Pensions Ombudsman, D. Laverick

OFFICE OF RAIL REGULATION

1 Waterhouse Square, 138–142 Holborn, London EC1N 2TQ
T 020-7282 2000 F 020-7282 2047
E orr@dial.pipex.com W www.rail-reg.gov.uk

The Office of the Rail Regulator was set up under the Railways Act 1993. It became the Office of Rail Regulation on 5 July 2004, under the provisions of the Railways and Transport Safety Act 2003. The Office's principal function is to regulate Network Rail's stewardship of the national network and to provide the economic regulation of the monopoly and dominant elements of the rail industry. The Office also licenses operators of railway assets, approves agreements for access by those operators to track, stations and light maintenance depots, and enforces domestic competition law. The International Rail Regulator is a statutory office separate from that of the Office of Rail Regulation. The International Rail Regulator licenses the operation of certain international rail services in the European Economic Area, and access to railway infrastructure in Great Britain for the purpose of the operation of such services. The Office of The International Rail Regulator is co-located with the Office of Rail Regulation, which fulfils both functions.
Chairman, C. Bolt

Chief Executive, Ms S. McCarthy
Director of Corporate Affairs, K. Webb
Director of Infrastructure and Economic Regulation, T. Martin

OFFICE OF WATER SERVICES

Centre City Tower, 7 Hill Street, Birmingham B5 4UA
T 0121-625 1300 F 0121-625 1400
E enquiries@ofwat.gsi.gov.uk
W www.ofwat.gov.uk

The Office of Water Services (Ofwat) was set up under the Water Act 1989 and is a non-ministerial Government department headed by the Director-General of Water Services. It is the independent economic regulator of the water and sewerage companies in England and Wales. Ofwat's main duties are to ensure that the companies can finance and carry out the functions specified in the Water Industry Act 1991 and to protect the interests of water customers. There are ten WaterVoice committees which are concerned solely with the interests of water customers. Representation of customer interests at national and European level is the responsibility of the WaterVoice Council.

Director-General of Water Services, P. Fletcher
Chairman, WaterVoice Council, M. Terry

ORDNANCE SURVEY

Romsey Road, Maybush, Southampton SO16 4GU
T 023-8030 5030 Helpline 0845-605 0505 F 023-8079 2615
E customerservices@ordnancesurvey.co.uk

Ordnance Survey is the national mapping agency for Great Britain. It is a Government department and executive agency operating as a Trading Fund and reporting to the Office of the Deputy Prime Minister.
Director-General and Chief Executive, Ms V. Lawrence

PARADES COMMISSION

Windsor House, 9–15 Bedford Street, Belfast BT2 7EL
T 028-9089 5900 F 028-9032 2988
E info@paradescommissionni.org
W www.paradescommission.org

The Parades Commission was set up under the Public Processions (Northern Ireland) Act 1998. Its function is to encourage and facilitate local accommodation on contentious parades; where this is not possible, the Commission is empowered to make legal determinations about such parades, which may include imposing conditions on aspects of the notified parade.

The chairman and members are appointed by the Secretary of State for Northern Ireland; the membership must, as far as is practicable, be representative of the community in Northern Ireland.
Chairman, Sir Anthony Holland
Members, J. Cousins; Revd R. Magee; W. Martin;
   P. Osborne; Sir John Pringle; P. Quinn

PARLIAMENTARY AND HEALTH SERVICE OMBUDSMAN

Millbank Tower, Millbank, London SW1P 4QP
T 0845-015 4033 F 020-7217 4160
E opca.enquiries@ombudsman.org.uk
W www.ombudsman.org.uk
Health Service Ombudsman T 0845-015 4033
F 020-7217 4000
E ohsc.enquiries@ombudsman.gsi.gov.uk

The Parliamentary Ombudsman (also known as the Parliamentary Commissioner for Administration) is independent of Government and is an officer of Parliament. She is responsible for investigating complaints referred to her by MPs from members of the public who claim to have sustained injustice in consequence of maladministration by or on behalf of Government departments and certain non-departmental public bodies. In March 1999 an additional 158 public bodies were brought within the jurisdiction of the Parliamentary Ombudsman. Certain types of action by Government departments or bodies are excluded from investigation. The Parliamentary Ombudsman is also responsible for investigating complaints, referred by MPs, alleging that access to official information has been wrongly refused under the Code of Practice on Access to Government Information 1994.

The Health Service Ombudsman (also known as the Health Service Commissioner) for England and for Wales is responsible for investigating complaints against National Health Service authorities and trusts that are not dealt with by those authorities to the satisfaction of the complainant. Complaints can be referred direct by the member of the public who claims to have sustained injustice or hardship in consequence of the failure in a service provided by a relevant body, failure of that body to provide a service or in consequence of any other action by that body. The Ombudsman's jurisdiction now covers complaints about family doctors, dentists, pharmacists and opticians, and complaints about actions resulting from clinical judgement.

The Health Service Ombudsman is also responsible for investigating complaints that information has been wrongly refused under the Code of Practice on Openness in the National Health Service 1995. The two offices are presently held by the Parliamentary Ombudsman.
Parliamentary Ombudsman and Health Service Ombudsman, Ms A. Abraham
Deputy Parliamentary Commissioner, Ms T. Longdon
Directors, Parliamentary Commissioner, Ms C. Corrigan; N. Jordan
Directors, Health Service Commissioners, D. R. G. Pinchin; L. Charlton
Finance and Establishment Officer, I. Walker

PARLIAMENTARY COMMISSIONER FOR STANDARDS

House of Commons, London SW1A 0AA
T 020-7219 0320 F 020-7219 0490

Following the recommendations of the Committee on Standards in Public Life, the House of Commons agreed to the appointment of an independent Parliamentary Commissioner for Standards with effect from November 1995. The Commissioner has responsibility for maintaining and monitoring the operation of the Register of Members' Interests; advising Members of Parliament and the Select Committee on Standards and Privileges;

interpreting the rules on disclosure and advocacy, and on other questions of propriety. The Commissioner also receives and investigates complaints about the conduct of MPs.
Parliamentary Commissioner for Standards, Sir Philip Mawer

PARLIAMENTARY COUNSEL

36 Whitehall, London SW1A 2AY
T 020-7210 6611 F 020-7210 6632
W www.parliamentary-counsel.gov.uk

Parliamentary Counsel draft all Government bills (i.e. primary legislation) except those relating exclusively to Scotland. They also advise on all aspects of parliamentary procedure in connection with such bills and draft Government amendments to them as well as any motions (including financial resolutions) necessary to secure their introduction into, and passage through, Parliament.
First Parliamentary Counsel, E. G. Bowman, CB
Counsel, Sir E. G. Caldwell; D. W. Saunders, CB; G. B. Sellers, CB; P. F. A. Knowles, CB; S. C. Laws, CB; R. S. Parker, CB; Miss C. E. Johnston, CB; P. J. Davies, CB; J. M. Sellers; A. J. Hogarth; Mrs H. J. Caldwell; D. I. Greenberg; Mrs E. A. F. Gardiner; D. J. Cook; Mrs L. A. McLaughlin; D. J. Ramsay

PAROLE BOARD FOR ENGLAND AND WALES

Abell House, John Islip Street, London SW1P 4LH
T 020-7217 5314 F 020-7217 5793
E info@paroleboard.gov.uk
W www.paroleboard.gov.uk

The duty of the Parole Board is to advise the Home Secretary with respect to matters referred to it by him which are connected with the early release or recall of prisoners. Its functions include giving directions concerning the release on licence of prisoners serving discretionary life sentences and of certain prisoners serving long-term determinate sentences.
Chairman, Prof. Sir Duncan Nichol, CBE
Vice-Chairman, The Hon. Mr Justice Gage
Chief Executive, C. Glenn

PAROLE BOARD FOR SCOTLAND

Saughton House, Broomhouse Drive, Edinburgh EH11 3XD
T 0131-244 8373 F 0131-244 6974

The Board directs and advises the Scottish Ministers on the release of prisoners on licence, and related matters.
Chairman, Prof. J. J. McManus
Vice-Chairman, Mrs M. Casserly
Secretary, H. P. Boyce

PATENT OFFICE

Concept House, Cardiff Road, Newport NP10 8QQ
T 0845-950 0505 F 01633-813600
E enquiries@patent.gov.uk
W www.patent.gov.uk

The Patent Office is an executive agency of the Department of Trade and Industry. The duties of the Patent Office are to administer the Patent Acts, the Registered Designs Act and the Trade Marks Act, and to deal with questions relating to the Copyright, Designs and Patents Act 1988. The Search and Advisory Service carries out commercial searches through patent information.

Comptroller-General and Chief Executive, R. Marchant
Director, Finance, Dr K. Woodrow
Director, Intellectual Property and Innovation, P. Lawrence
Director, IT and Corporate Services, Mrs C. Fullerton
Director, Patents, S. Dennehey
Director, Trade Marks and Designs, R. Webb

PENSIONS COMPENSATION BOARD
11 Belgrave Road, London SW1V 1RB
T 020-7828 9794 F 020-7931 7239

The Pensions Compensation Board was established under the Pensions Act 1995 and is funded by a levy paid by all eligible occupational pension schemes. Its function is to compensate occupational pension schemes for losses due to dishonesty where the employer is insolvent.

Chairman, Sir Bryan Carsberg
Secretary, M. Lydon

POLICE OMBUDSMAN FOR NORTHERN IRELAND
New Cathedral Buildings, St Anne's Square, Belfast BT1 1PG
T 028-9082 8600 F 028-9082 8659
E info@policeombudsman.org
W www.policeombudsman.org

Founded in November 2000 under the Police (Northern Ireland) Act 1998, the function of the Office of the Police Ombudsman for Northern Ireland is to investigate complaints against the police in an impartial, efficient, effective and (as far as is possible) transparent way, to win the confidence of the public and the police. It must report on trends in complaints and react to incidents involving the police, where it is in the public interest, even if no individual complaint has been made.

Police Ombudsman, N. O'Loan

PORT OF LONDON AUTHORITY
Bakers' Hall, 7 Harp Lane, London EC3R 6LB
T 020-7743 7900 F 020-7743 7999
W www.portoflondon.co.uk

The Port of London Authority (PLA) is the port authority for the 93 miles of the tidal River Thames from the Estuary to Teddington. It provides navigational and pilotage services for ships using the Port of London, including the maintenance of shipping channels. The PLA is also actively engaged in the promotion of the Port of London. The Port of London is one of the UK's main three ports, handling over 50 million tonnes of cargo each year. The port comprises over 80 independently owned terminals and port facilities, which handle a wide range of cargoes.

The PLA is a public trust constituted under the Port of London Act 1908 and subsequent legislation.

Chairman, S. P. Sherrard
Chief Executive, S. C. Cuthbert
Secretary, D. Cartlidge

POSTAL SERVICES COMMISSION
Hercules House, Hercules Road, London SE1 7DB
T 020-7593 2100

The Postal Services Commission (Postcomm) is an independent regulator set up by the Postal Services Act 2000 to ensure that postal operators, including Royal Mail, meet the needs of their customers throughout the UK. Postcomm monitors the network of post offices in the UK and makes annual reports to the DTI.

Chairman, Nigel Stapleton

PRISONS AND PROBATION OMBUDSMAN FOR ENGLAND AND WALES
Ashley House, 2 Monck Street, London SW1P 2BQ
T 020-7035 2876 F 020-7035 2860
E mail@ppo.gsi.gov.uk
W www.ppo.gov.uk

The Ombudsman is appointed by the Home Secretary. He provides a free and independent adjudication service for prisoners and those under probation supervision who have been unable to resolve their grievances with the Prison and Probation Services. He also conducts independent investigations into the deaths of prisoners, residents of probation hostels and people detained by the immigration authorities.

Ombudsman, S. Shaw

PRIVY COUNCIL OFFICE
2 Carlton Gardens, London SW1Y 5AA
T 020-7210 1033 F 020-7210 1071
W www.privycouncil.gov.uk

The Office is responsible for the arrangements leading to the making of all royal proclamations and Orders in Council; for certain formalities connected with ministerial changes; for considering applications for the granting (or amendment) of royal charters; for the scrutiny and approval of by-laws and statutes of chartered bodies; and for the appointment of high sheriffs and many Crown and Privy Council appointments to governing bodies.

Lord President of the Council (and Leader of the House of Lords), The Rt. Hon. Baroness Amos, PC
Principal Private Secretary, Chris Jacobs
Private Secretary, Nicki Daniels
Clerk of the Council, Alex Galloway
Deputy Clerk of the Council and Director of Corporate Services, Graham Donald
Senior Clerk, Meriel McCullagh
Registrar of the Judicial Committee, John Watherston

PUBLIC GUARDIANSHIP OFFICE
Archway Tower, 2 Junction Road, London N19 5SZ
T 020-7664 7000 F 020-7664 7705
E custserv@guardianship.gov.uk
W www.guardianship.gov.uk

The Public Guardianship Office (PGO) is the administrative arm of the Court of Protection and is part of the Department for Constitutional Affairs.

Established on the 1 April 2001, it has taken over the mental health functions previously undertaken by the Public Trust Office (PTO), which also provides services that promote the financial and social well-being of people with mental incapacity.

Acting Chief Executive and Director of Operations, D. Thompson
Acting Director of Finance, S. Taylor
Assistant Director of Client Services, G. Bradshaw
Assistant Director of Strategy and Finance, C. McIlwrath
Director of Business Strategy and Innovation, G. Dalton
Manager of Complaints Handling Team, N. Ross

RAIL SAFETY AND STANDARDS BOARD
Evergreen House, 160 Euston Road, London NW1 2DX
T 020-7904 7777 F 020-7557 7791
E enquiries@rssb.co.uk
W www.rssb.co.uk

The Rail Safety and Standards Board was established on 1 April 2003 to help focus the rail industry on the continuous improvement in the safety performance of Britain's railways through facilitating the reduction in risk to passengers and railway workers. Its objectives include: the development of a long-term industry safety strategy; the effective representation of the UK rail industry in the development of EU legislation and standards that impact on the safe interworking of trains and infrastructure; and the facilitation of a research and development programme, education and awareness of safety issues. The Rail Safety and Standards Board is a not-for-profit organisation.
Chief Executive, Len Porter

RECORD OFFICES

ADVISORY COUNCIL ON NATIONAL RECORDS AND ARCHIVES
Secretariat: The National Archives, Kew, Surrey TW9 4DU
T 020-8392 5381 F 020-8392 5286

Following the bringing together of the Public Record Office and the Historical Manuscripts Commission to form the National Archives, the Advisory Council advises on all matters relating to the preservation, use of, and access to historical manuscripts, records and archives of all kinds. The new Advisory Council on National Records and Archives encompasses the statutory Advisory Council on Public Records, and advises on public records issues as before.
Chairman, The Rt. Hon. Lord Phillips, Master of the Rolls
Secretary, T. R. Padfield

CORPORATION OF LONDON RECORDS OFFICE
PO Box 270, Guildhall, London EC2P 2EJ
T 020-7332 1251 F 020-7710 8682
E clro@corpoflondon.gov.uk
W www.cityoflondon.gov.uk/archives/clro

The Corporation of London Records Office contains the municipal archives of the City of London which are regarded as the most complete collection of ancient municipal records in existence. The collection includes charters of William the Conqueror, Henry II, and later kings and queens to 1957; ancient custumals: Liber Horn, Dunthorne, Custumarum, Ordinacionum, Memorandorum and Albus, Liber de Antiquis Legibus, and collections of statutes; continuous series of judicial rolls, books from 1252 and Council minutes from 1275; records of the Old Bailey and Guildhall sessions from 1603; financial records from the 16th century; the records of London Bridge from the 12th century; and numerous subsidiary series and miscellanea of historical interest.
Head Archivist, D. Jenkins, PHD
City Archives Manager, J. M. Bankes

HOUSE OF LORDS RECORD OFFICE (THE PARLIAMENTARY ARCHIVES)
House of Lords, London SW1A 0PW
T 020-7219 3074 F 020-7219 2570
E hlro@parliament.uk W www.parliament.uk

Since 1497, the records of Parliament have been kept within the Palace of Westminster. They are in the custody of the Clerk of the Parliaments. In 1946 the Record Office was established to supervise their preservation and their availability to the public.

Some three million documents are preserved, including Acts of Parliament from 1497, journals of the House of Lords from 1510, minutes and committee proceedings from 1610, and papers laid before Parliament from 1531. Amongst the records are the Petition of Right, the Death Warrant of Charles I, the Declaration of Breda, and the Bill of Rights. The House of Lords Record Office also has charge of the journals of the House of Commons (from 1547), and other surviving records of the Commons (from 1572), including documents relating to private bill legislation from 1818. Among other documents are the records of the Lord Great Chamberlain, the political papers of certain members of the two Houses, and documents relating to Parliament acquired on behalf of the nation. The Record Office makes the records available through a public search room and answers enquiries concerning the archives and history of Parliament.
Clerk of the Records, S. K. Ellison
Assistant Clerks of the Records, D. L. Prior; Dr C. Shenton; Ms F. P. Grey *(Freedom of Information Officer)*

NATIONAL ARCHIVES
Kew, Richmond, Surrey TW9 4DU
T 020-8876 3444 F 020-8878 8905
W www.nationalarchives.gov.uk

The National Archives, a government department and an executive agency reporting to the Lord Chancellor/ Secretary of State for Constitutional Affairs, was formed in April 2003 by bringing together the Public Record Office (founded in 1838) and the Historical Manuscripts Commission (founded in 1869).

The National Archives for England, Wales and the United Kingdom acts as the custodian of the nation's collective memory as revealed in the records of government. It also collects and disseminates information about archives relating to British history wherever they are held.

Its aims are: to assist and promote the study of the past through the public records and other archives in order to inform the present and the future; to act as chief source of authoritative advice and guidance on records management, archive policy and related information policy matters within government; to provide impartial advice to custodians of records and papers throughout public and private sectors on records and archives management.

The National Archives administers the UK's public records system under the Public Records Acts of 1958 and 1967. The records it holds span over 1,000 years – from the Domesday Book to the latest government papers to be released – and fill more than 100 miles of shelving. The records held by the National Archives are available to the public, without charge, in the reading rooms.

The National Archives also provides free expert advice to owners, custodians and users of archives throughout the UK. They include central and local government, universities, business and industry, many other individuals and institutions, and a range of public and private grant-awarding bodies.

Chief Executive, Mrs S. Tyacke, CB
Director of National Advisory and Public Services, Dr E. Hallam-Smith
Director of Government and Technology Group, Dr D. Thomas
Director of Strategy, Finance and Resources, Mrs W. Jones
Head of Online Services and Strategic Marketing, J. Strachan

NATIONAL ARCHIVES OF SCOTLAND

HM General Register House, Edinburgh EH1 3YY
T 0131-535 1314 F 0131-535 1360
E enquiries@nas.gov.uk W www.nas.gov.uk

The history of the national archives of Scotland can be traced back to the 13th century. The National Archives of Scotland (formerly the Scottish Record Office) is an executive agency of the Scottish Executive and keeps the administrative records of pre-Union Scotland, the registers of central and local courts of law, the public registers of property rights and legal documents, and many collections of local and church records and private archives. Certain groups of records, mainly the modern records of Government departments in Scotland, the Scottish railway records, the plans collection, and private archives of an industrial or commercial nature, are preserved in the branch repository at West Register House in Charlotte Square. The National Register of Archives for Scotland is based in the West Register House.

Keeper of the Records of Scotland, G. P. MacKenzie
Deputy Keepers, Dr P. D. Anderson; D. Brownlee

PUBLIC RECORD OFFICE OF NORTHERN IRELAND

66 Balmoral Avenue, Belfast BT9 6NY
T 028-9025 5905 F 028-9025 5999
E proni@dcalni.gov.uk W www.proni.gov.uk

The Public Record Office of Northern Ireland is responsible for identifying and preserving Northern Ireland's archival heritage and making it available to the public. It is an executive agency of the Department of Culture, Arts and Leisure.

Chief Executive, Dr G. Slater

REGISTRAR OF PUBLIC LENDING RIGHT

Richard House, Sorbonne Close, Stockton on Tees TS17 6DA
T 01642-604699 F 01642-615641
E jim.parker@plr.uk.com
W www.plr.uk.com

Under the Public Lending Right system, in operation since 1983, payment is made from public funds to authors whose books are lent out from public libraries. Payment is made once a year and the amount each author receives is proportionate to the number of times (established from a sample) that each registered book has been lent out during the previous year. The Registrar of PLR, who is appointed by the Secretary of State for Culture, Media and Sport, compiles the register of authors and books. Authors resident in all EC countries are eligible to apply. (The term 'author' covers writers, illustrators, translators, and some editors/compilers.)

A payment of 4.85 pence was made in 2003–4 for each estimated loan of a registered book, up to a top limit of £6,000 for the books of any one registered author; the money for loans above this level is used to augment the remaining PLR payments. In 2004, the sum of £6.4 million was paid out to 18,763 registered authors and assignees as the annual payment of PLR.

Registrar, Dr J. G. Parker
Chairman of Advisory Committee, S. Brett

SCOTTISH RECORDS ADVISORY COUNCIL

HM General Register House, Edinburgh EH1 3YY
T 0131-535 1403 F 0131-535 1430
W www.nas.gov.uk

The Council was established under the Public Records (Scotland) Act 1937. Its members are appointed by the First Minister and it may submit proposals or make representations to the First Minister, the Lord Justice General or the Lord President of the Court of Session on questions relating to the public records of Scotland.

Chairman, Prof. H. MacQueen
Secretary, Dr A. Rosie

HM REVENUE AND CUSTOMS

Board of Inland Revenue, Somerset House, Strand, London WC2R 1LB
T 020-7438 6622 F 020-7438 7562
E library.ir.sh@gtnet.gov.uk
W www.inlandrevenue.gov.uk
HM Customs and Excise, New King's Beam House, 5th Floor East, 22 Upper Ground, London SE1 9PJ
T 020-7620 1313 **National Advice Service** 0845-010 900
W www.hmce.gov.uk

The Board of Inland Revenue and HM Customs and Excise merged on 1 September 2004 to become HM Revenue and Customs. The Board of Inland Revenue was constituted under the Inland Revenue Board Act 1849. The Board administers and collects direct taxes – income tax, corporation tax, capital gains tax, inheritance tax, stamp duty, and petroleum revenue tax – and advises the Chancellor of the Exchequer on policy questions involving them.

The Valuation Office is an executive agency responsible for valuing property for tax purposes. The Contributions Agency of the Department for Work and Pensions which is responsible for the collection of contributions under the National Insurance scheme, became part of the Inland Revenue in April 1999 and is now an executive office called the National Insurance Contributions Office. The Contributions Unit of the Social Security Agency in Northern Ireland also transferred to the Inland Revenue in April 1999.

HM Customs and Excise is responsible for collecting and administering customs and excise duties and VAT, and advises the Chancellor of the Exchequer on any matters connected with them.

THE BOARD OF INLAND REVENUE
Chairman, David Varney
Deputy Chairman, Paul Gray
Head of Revenue Policy, D. Hartnett
Chief Executive, Valuation Office Agency, M. Johns

THE BOARD OF HM CUSTOMS AND EXCISE
Chairman, Mike Eland

VALUATION OFFICE AGENCY

New Court, 48 Carey Street, London WC2A 2JE
T 020-7506 1700 F 020-7506 1998
W www.voa.gov.uk
50 Frederick Street, Edinburgh EH2 1NG
T 0131-465 0700 F 0131-465 0799
Chief Executive, A. Hudson
Chief Valuer, Scotland, A. Ainslie
Chief Valuer, Wales, C. R. Danigls

REVIEW BODIES

The secretariat for these bodies is provided by the Office
of Manpower Economics

THE ARMED FORCES' PAY REVIEW BODY

The Review Body on Armed Forces Pay was appointed in
1971. It advises the Prime Minister and Government on
the pay and allowances of members of naval, military and
air forces of the Crown.
Chairman, Prof. D. Greenaway
Members, N. Sherlock; Vice-Adm. Sir Peter Woodhead; Dr
A. Wright; J. Davies; Prof. The Lord Patel of Dunkeld;
M. Ward; R. Burgin; Dr P. Knight

THE REVIEW BODY ON DOCTORS' AND DENTISTS' REMUNERATION

The Review Body on Doctors' and Dentists'
Remuneration was set up in 1971. It advises the Prime
Minister and the Secretaries of State for Health, Scotland
and Wales on the remuneration of doctors and dentists
taking any part in the National Health Service.
Chairman, M. Blair, QC
Members, Prof. F. Burchill; H. Donaldson; Dr G. Jones;
Prof. J. Beath; Dr M. Collingwood

THE REVIEW BODY FOR NURSING AND OTHER HEALTH PROFESSIONS

The Review Body for nursing staff, midwives, health
visitors and professions allied to medicine was set up in
1983. Following the Agenda for Change the review body
changed its name. It advises the Prime Minister and the
Secretaries of State for Health, Scotland and Wales on the
remuneration of nursing staff and other health professions
employed in the National Health Service.
Chairman, Prof. Sir C. Booth
Members, W. MacPherson; Prof. P. Weetman; Prof. R.
Disney; S. Whitlam

POLICE ADVISORY BOARD FOR ENGLAND AND WALES

The Police Advisory Board for England and Wales
provides advice to the Secretary of State on general
questions affecting the police in England and Wales and
considers draft regulations which the Secretary of State
proposes to make with respect to matters other than hours
of duty, leave, pay and allowances or the issue, use and
return of police clothing, personal equipment and other
effects.
Independent Chair, John Randall
Independent Deputy Chair, Mark Baker, CBE

POLICE NEGOTIATING BOARD

The Police Negotiating Board (PNB) was established by
Act of Parliament in 1980 to negotiate pay, allowances,
hours of duty, leave and pensions of United Kingdom
police officers and to make recommendations on these
matters to the Home Secretary, Secretary of State for
Northern Ireland, and Scottish Ministers.
Independent Chair, John Randall
Independent Deputy Chair, Mark Baker, CBE

THE PRISON SERVICE PAY REVIEW BODY

The Prison Service Pay Review Body (PSPRB) was set up
in 2001. It makes independent recommendations on the
pay of prison governors, prison officers and related grades
for the Prison Service in England and Wales and for the
Northern Ireland Prison Service.
Chairman, Sir Toby Frere, KCB
Members, J. Abrams; D. Bourn; B. Brewer; P. Heard; F.
Horisk; P. Tett

THE SCHOOL TEACHERS' REVIEW BODY

The School Teachers' Review Body (STRB) was set up
under the School Teachers' Pay and Conditions Act
1991. It is required to examine and report on such
matters relating to the statutory conditions of
employment of school teachers in England and Wales as
may be referred to it by the Secretary of State for
Education and Skills.
Chairman, W. Cockburn, CBE, TD
Members, R. Gardner; Dr B. Roberts; J. Singh; R. East; M.
Goodridge; J. Stephens; M. Chatterji; B. Warman

THE SENIOR SALARIES REVIEW BODY

The Senior Salaries Review Body (formerly the Top
Salaries Review Body) was set up in 1971 to advise the
Prime Minister on the remuneration of the judiciary,
senior civil servants and senior officers of the armed
forces. In 1993 its remit was extended to cover the pay,
pensions and allowances of MPs, Ministers and others
whose pay is determined by a Ministerial and Other
Salaries Order and the allowances of peers. It also advises
on the pay of officers and members of the devolved
Parliament and Assemblies.
Chairman, J. Baker, CBE
Members, D. Clayman; J. Rubin; M. Sim Lei; J. McKenna;
M. Galbraith; Prof. D. Greenaway; R. Pearson

ROYAL BOTANIC GARDEN EDINBURGH

20A Inverleith Row, Edinburgh EH3 5LR
T 0131-552 7171 F 0131-248 2901
E info@rbge.org.uk
W www.rbge.org.uk

The Royal Botanic Garden Edinburgh (RBGE)
originated as the Physic Garden, established in 1670
beside the Palace of Holyroodhouse. The Garden
moved to its present 28-hectare site at Inverleith,
Edinburgh, in 1821. There are also three Regional
Gardens: Benmore Botanic Garden, near Dunoon,
Argyll; Logan Botanic Garden, near Stranraer,
Wigtownshire; and Dawyck Botanic Garden, near Stobo,
Peeblesshire. Since 1986 RBGE has been administered by
a board of trustees established under the National
Heritage (Scotland) Act 1985. It receives an annual grant
from the Environment and Rural Affairs Department of
the Scottish Executive.

RBGE is an international centre for scientific research
on plant diversity and for horticulture education and
conservation. It has an extensive library, a herbarium with

over two million preserved plant specimens, and over 16,500 species in the living collections.
Chairman of the Board of Trustees, Dr P. Nicholson
Regius Keeper, Prof. S. Blackmore, FRSE

ROYAL BOTANIC GARDENS KEW
Richmond, Surrey TW9 3AB
T 020-8332 5000 F 020-8332 5197
Wakehurst Place, Ardingly, nr Haywards Heath, W. Sussex RH17 6TN
T 01444-89000 F 01444-894069
W www.kew.org

The Royal Botanic Gardens (RBG) Kew were originally laid out as a private garden for Kew House for George III's mother, Princess Augusta, in 1759. The gardens were much enlarged in the 19th century, notably by the inclusion of the grounds of the former Richmond Lodge. In 1965 the garden at Wakehurst Place was acquired; it is owned by the National Trust and managed by RBG Kew. Under the National Heritage Act 1983 a board of trustees was set up to administer the gardens, which in 1984 became an independent body supported by grant-in-aid from the Department of Environment, Food and Rural Affairs.

The functions of RBG Kew are to carry out research into plant sciences, to disseminate knowledge about plants and to provide the public with the opportunity to gain knowledge and enjoyment from the gardens' collections. There are extensive national reference collections of living and preserved plants and a comprehensive library and archive. The main emphasis is on plant conservation and bio-diversity.

BOARD OF TRUSTEES
Chairman, The Lord Selbourne
Members, Baroness Hayman; A. Cahn, CMG; Ms T. Burman; D. Norman; R. Lapthorne, CBE; I. Oag; Prof. C. Payne; Ms M. Regan; R. Deverell; D. Bradley; Sir Richard Sykes
Director, Prof. P. Crane, FRS

ROYAL COMMISSION FOR THE EXHIBITION OF 1851
Sherfield Building, Imperial College, London SW7 2AZ
T 020-7594 8790 F 020-7594 8794
E royalcom1851@ic.ac.uk
W www.royalcommission1851.org.uk

The Royal Commission was incorporated by supplemental charter as a permanent commission after winding up the affairs of the Great Exhibition of 1851. Its object is to promote scientific and artistic education by means of funds derived from its Kensington estate, purchased with the surplus left over from the Great Exhibition. Annual charitable expenditure on educational grants is about £1 million.
President, HRH The Prince Philip, Duke of Edinburgh, KG, KT, PC
Chairman, Board of Management, Sir Alan Rudge, CBE, FRS, FRENG
Secretary to Commissioners, M. C. Shirley

ROYAL COMMISSION ON ENVIRONMENTAL POLLUTION
3rd Floor, The Sanctuary, Westminster, London SW1P 3JS
T 020-7799 8970 F 020-7799 8971
E enquiries@rcep.org.uk W www.rcep.org.uk

The Commission was set up in 1970 to advise on national and international matters concerning the pollution of the environment.
Chairman, Prof. Sir Tom Blundell, FRS
Members, Dr I. Graham-Bryce, CBE; Prof. R. Clift, OBE, FRENG; Sir Brian Follett, FRS; Prof. B. Hoskins, CBE, FRS; Dr S. Owens, OBE; Prof. J. Plant, CBE; Prof. P. Ekins; Prof. S. Holgate; J. Speirs; Prof. J. Sprent; Prof. J. Jowell; Prof. S. Rayner
Secretary, T. Eddy

ROYAL COMMISSION ON THE ANCIENT AND HISTORICAL MONUMENTS OF SCOTLAND
John Sinclair House, 16 Bernard Terrace, Edinburgh EH8 9NX
T 0131-662 1456 F 0131-662 1499
E nmrs@rcahms.gov.uk W www.rcahms.gov.uk

The Royal Commission was established in 1908 and is appointed to provide for the survey and recording of ancient and historical monuments connected with the culture, civilisation and conditions of life of the people in Scotland from the earliest times. It is funded by the Scottish Executive. The Commission compiles and maintains the National Monuments Record of Scotland as the national record of the archaeological and historical environment.
Chairman, Mrs K. Dalyell
Commissioners, Dr B. E. Crawford, FSA; Miss A. C. Riches, OBE, FSA; J. W. T. Simpson; Dr M. A. Mackay; Dr J. Murray; Dr A. Macdonald; Prof. C. D. Morris, FSA, FRSE; Dr S. Nenadic; G. Masterton, CENG
Secretary, R. J. Mercer, FSA, FRSE

ROYAL COMMISSION ON THE ANCIENT AND HISTORICAL MONUMENTS OF WALES
Crown Building, Plas Crug, Aberystwyth SY23 1NJ
T 01970-621200 F 01970-627701
E nmr.wales@rcahmw.gov.uk
W www.rcahmw.org.uk

The Royal Commission was established in 1908 and is currently empowered by a Royal Warrant of 2001 to survey, record, publish and maintain a database of ancient and historical and maritime sites and structures, and landscapes in Wales. The Commission is funded by the National Assembly for Wales and is also responsible for the National Monuments Record of Wales, which is open daily for public reference, for the supply of archaeological information to the Ordnance Survey, for the co-ordination of archaeological aerial photography in Wales, and for sponsorship of the regional Sites and Monuments Records.
Chairman, Prof. R. A. Griffiths, DLITT
Commissioners, Prof. A. D. Carr, FSA; D. W. Crossley, FSA; N. Harries; J. W. Lloyd, CB; J. Newman, FSA; Prof. P. Sims-Williams, FBA; Dr L. O. W. Smith
Secretary, P. R. White, FSA

ROYAL MAIL GROUP PLC
148 Old Street, London EC1V 9HQ
T 020-7250 2888
W www.royalmailgroup.com

Crown services for the carriage of Government dispatches were set up in about 1516. The conveyance of public correspondence began in 1635 and the mail service was made a parliamentary responsibility with the setting up of a Post Office in 1657. Telegraphs came under Post Office control in 1870 and the Post Office Telephone Service began in 1880. The National Girobank service of the Post Office began in 1968. The Post Office ceased to be a Government department in 1969 when responsibility for the running of the postal, telecommunications, giro and remittance services was transferred to a public authority called The Post Office.

The 1981 British Telecommunications Act separated the functions of the Post Office, making it solely responsible for postal services and Girobank. Girobank was privatised in 1990. The Postal Services Act 2000 turned The Post Office into a wholly owned public limited company establishing a regulatory regime under the Postal Service Commission. The Post Office Group changed its name to Consignia plc on 26 March 2001 when its new corporate structure took effect. On 4 November the name was changed to Royal Mail Group plc.

The chairman, chief executive and members of the Board are appointed by the Secretary of State for Trade and Industry but responsibility for the running of Royal Mail Group plc as a whole rests with the Board in its corporate capacity.

BOARD
Chairman, A. Leighton
Chief Executive, A. Crozier
Members, M. Cassoni *(Group Finance Director)*; E. Toime *(Executive Deputy Chairman)*; T. McCarthy *(Group Director, People and Organisational Development)*; D. Mills *(Chief Executive, Post Office Ltd)*
Non Executive Directors, Ms R. Thorne; D. Fish; R. Handover; J. Neill; B. Wigley
Secretary, J. Evans

ROYAL MINT
Llantrisant, Pontyclun CF72 8YT
T 01443-222111 F 01443-623148
E information.office@royalmint.gov.uk
W www.royalmint.com

The prime responsibility of the Royal Mint is the provision of United Kingdom coinage but it actively competes in world markets for a share of the available circulating coin business and about half of the coins and blanks it produces annually are exported. The Mint also manufactures special proof and uncirculated quality coins in gold, silver and other metals; military and civil decorations and medals; commemorative and prize medals; and royal and official seals. It also markets a range of gifts and collectible items.

The Royal Mint became an executive agency of the Treasury in 1990. The Government announced in July 1999 that the Royal Mint would be given greater commercial freedom to expand its business into new areas and develop partnerships with the private sector.
Master of the Mint, The Chancellor of the Exchequer *(ex officio)*
Chief Executive, G. Sheehan

ROYAL NATIONAL THEATRE
South Bank, London, SE1 9PX
T 020-7452 3333 F 020-7452 3344
W www.nationaltheatre.org.uk
Chairman, Sir Christopher Hogg
Members, B. Okri; The Rt. Hon. Chris Smith, MP; E. Walker-Arnott; A. Ptaszynski; Ms R. Lomax; N. Wright; J. Hill; Ms N. Horlick; Ms C. Merrick; Ms C. Newling; G. Morris
Company Secretary, Mrs M. McGregor
Director, Nicholas Hytner
Executive Director, Nick Starr

RURAL PAYMENTS AGENCY (RPA)
Kings House, Kings Road, Reading, Berkshire RG1 3BU
T 0118-958 3626 F 0118-959 7736
E enquiries@rpa.gsi.gov.uk
W www.rpa.gov.uk

The Rural Payments Agency (RPA) is as an executive agency of the Department for Environment, Food and Rural Affairs. It is the single paying agency responsible for Common Agricultural Policy (CAP) schemes in England and for certain schemes throughout the UK.
Chief Executive, J. McNeill
Directors, H. MacKinnon *(Operations)*; A. Kerr, *(Finance)*; R. Gregg *(Human Resources)*; A. MacDermott *(Information Systems)*; S. Vry *(Business Development)*; I. Corbett *(Legal Director)*

SCOTTISH CRIMINAL CASES REVIEW COMMISSION
5th Floor, Portland House, 17 Renfield Street, Glasgow G2 5AH
T 0141-270 7030 F 0141-270 7040/23
E info@sccrc.org.uk
W www.sccrc.org.uk

The Commission is a non-departmental public body which started operating on 1 April 1999. It took over from the Secretary of State for Scotland powers to consider alleged miscarriages of justice in Scotland and refer cases meeting the relevant criteria to the High Court for determination. Members are appointed by Her Majesty The Queen on the recommendation of the First Minister; senior executive staff are appointed by the Commission.
Chairperson, The Very Revd G. Forbes, CBE
Members, Prof. P. Duff; Sir Gerald Gordon, CBE, QC; R. Anderson, QC; D. Belfall; J. Mackay, QPM; A. Wylie, QC; G. Bell, QC
Chief Executive, Gerard Sinclair

SCOTTISH ENTERPRISE
5 Atlantic Quay, 150 Broomielaw, Glasgow G2 8LU
T 0141-248 2700 Helpline 0845-607 8787 F 0141-221 3217
E network.helpline@scotent.co.uk
W www.scottish-enterprise.com

Scottish Enterprise was established in 1991 and its purpose is to create jobs and prosperity for the people of Scotland. It is funded largely by the Scottish Executive and is responsible to the Scottish Ministers. Working in partnership with the private and public sectors, Scottish Enterprise aims to further the development of Scotland's economy, to enhance the skills of the Scottish workforce and to promote Scotland's international competitiveness. Scottish Enterprise is concerned with attracting firms to Scotland and, through Scottish Trade International, it helps Scottish companies to compete in world export markets. Scottish Enterprise has a network of Local Enterprise Companies that deliver economic development services at local level.

Chairman, Sir John Ward, CBE

Chief Executive, Jack Perry

SCOTTISH ENVIRONMENT PROTECTION AGENCY

Erskine Court, The Castle Business Park, Stirling FK9 4TR
T 01786-457700 Hotline 0800 80 70 60
F 01786-446885 W www.sepa.org.uk

The Scottish Environment Protection Agency (SEPA) is the public body responsible for environmental protection in Scotland. It regulates potential pollution to land, air and water, the storage, transport and disposal of controlled waste and the safe keeping and disposal of radioactive materials. It does this within a complex legislative framework of Acts of Parliament, EC Directives and Regulations, granting licenses to operations of industrial processes and waste disposal. SEPA also operates Floodline, 0845-988 1188, a public service providing information on possible risk of flooding 24 hours a day, 365 days a year.

Chairman, Sir Ken Collins

Chief Executive, Campbell Gemmell

Director of Environmental Regulation and Improvement, Colin Bayes

Director of Environmental and Organisational Development, Calum MacDonald

Director of Environmental Science, Chris Spray

Head of Human Resources and Organisational Development, Richard Claughton

SCOTTISH LAW COMMISSION

140 Causewayside, Edinburgh EH9 1PR
T 0131-668 2131 F 0131-662 4900
E info@scotlawcom.gov.uk
W www.scotlawcom.gov.uk

The Commission keeps the law in Scotland under review and makes proposals for its development and reform. It is responsible to the Scottish Ministers through the Scottish Executive Justice Department.

Chairman (part-time), The Hon. Lord Eassie

Chief Executive, Miss J. McLeod

Commissioners, Prof. G. Maher, QC; Prof. K. G. C. Reid; Prof. J. M. Thomson; C. J. Tyre, QC

SCOTTISH LEGAL AID BOARD

44 Drumsheugh Gardens, Edinburgh EH3 7SW
T 0131-226 7061 F 0131-220 4878
E general@slab.org.uk
W www.slab.org.uk

The Scottish Legal Aid Board was set up under the Legal Aid (Scotland) Act 1986 to manage legal aid in Scotland. Board members are appointed by Scottish Ministers.

Chairman, Mrs J. Couper

Members, W. Gallagher; G. McKinstry; D. J. C. Nicol; Prof. J. P. Percy, CBE; Mrs Y. Osman; Mrs M. Scanlan; M. C. Thomson, QC; P. Gray, QC; Mrs E. Morton; S. Singh; Sheriff K. Ross

Chief Executive, L. Montgomery

SCOTTISH NATURAL HERITAGE

12 Hope Terrace, Edinburgh EH9 2AS
T 0131-447 4784 F 0131-446 2277
E enquiries@snh.gov.uk
W www.snh.org.uk

Scottish Natural Heritage was established in 1992 under the Natural Heritage (Scotland) Act 1991. It provides advice on nature conservation to all those whose activities affect wildlife, landforms and features of geological interest in Scotland, and seeks to develop and improve facilities for the enjoyment and understanding of the Scottish countryside. It is funded by the Scottish Executive.

Chairman, Dr J. Markland, CBE

Chief Executive, I. Jardine

Chief Scientific Adviser, C. Galbraith

Directors of Operations, J. Thomson *(West);* A. Bachell *(East);* J. Watson *(North)*

Director of Corporate Services, I. Edgeler

SCOTTISH PRISONS COMPLAINTS COMMISSION

Government Buildings, Broomhouse Drive, Edinburgh EH11 3XD
T 0131-244 8423 F 0131-244 8430
E spcc@scotland.gsi.gov.uk W www.scotland.gov.uk/spcc

The Commission was established in 1994. It is an independent body to which prisoners in Scottish prisons can make application in relation to any matter where they have failed to obtain satisfaction from the Scottish Prison Service's internal grievance procedures. Clinical judgements made by medical officers, matters which are the subject of legal proceedings and matters relating to sentence, conviction and parole decision-making are excluded from the Commission's jurisdiction. The Commissioner is appointed by the Scottish Ministers.

Commissioner, V. Barrett

SCOTTISH PUBLIC SERVICES OMBUDSMAN

4 Melville Street, Edinburgh, EH3 7NS
T 0870-011 5378 F 0870-011 5379
E enquiries@scottishombudsman.org.uk
W www.scottishombudsman.org.uk

The Scottish Public Services Ombudsman was established in 2002. The Ombudsman investigates complaints about Scottish government departments, councils, housing associations, the national health service and other public bodies. The public bodies which the Scottish Public Services Ombudsman may consider investigating are taken from a list of such bodies outlined in the Scottish Public Services Ombudsman Act 2002. Complaints considered by the Ombudsman can range from complaints about poor service, failure to provide a service, administrative failure and complaints about the NHS including hospital staff, GPs, dentists and other health professionals.

Scottish Public Services Ombudsman, Prof. A. Brown

SEAFISH INDUSTRY AUTHORITY

18 Logie Mill, Logie Green Road, Edinburgh EH7 4HG
T 0131-558 3331 F 0131-558 1442
E seafish@seafish.co.uk
W www.seafish.org.uk

Established under the Fisheries Act 1981, Seafish works with the seafood industry to satisfy consumers, raise standards, improve efficiency and secure a sustainable future. It is sponsored by the four UK fisheries departments.
Chairman, A. Dewar-Durie
Chief Executive, J. Rutherford

SECURITY AND INTELLIGENCE SERVICES

Under the Intelligence Services Act 1994, the Intelligence and Security Committee of Parliamentarians was established to oversee the work of GCHQ, MI5 and MI6; in 1999 an Investigator was appointed to the committee in order to reinforce the authority of its findings and establish public confidence in the system. The Act also established the Intelligence Services Tribunal, which hears complaints made against GCHQ and MI6. The Security Service Tribunal and Commissioner (*see* below) investigate complaints about MI5.

GOVERNMENT COMMUNICATIONS HEADQUARTERS (GCHQ)

Priors Road, Cheltenham, Glos GL52 5AJ
T 01242-221491 F 01242-574349

GCHQ produces signals intelligence in support of national security and the UK's economic wellbeing, and in the prevention or detection of serious crime. Additionally, GCHQ Communications-Electronics Security Group (CESG) provides advice and assistance to Government departments, the armed forces and other national infrastructure bodies on the security of their communications and information systems. GCHQ was placed on a statutory footing by the Intelligence Services Act 1994 and is headed by a director who is directly accountable to the Foreign Secretary.
Director, D. E. Pepper

INTELLIGENCE SERVICES COMMISSIONER

c/o PO Box 33220, London SW1H 9ZQ
T 020-7273 4514

The Commissioner is appointed by the Prime Minister. He keeps under review the issue of warrants by the Secretaries of State as detailed under the Regulation of Investigatory Powers Act (RIPA) 2000. The Commissioner is also required to submit an annual report on the discharge of his functions to the Prime Minister.
Commissioner, The Rt. Hon. Lord Justice Simon Brown
Private Secretary, D. Payne

INTERCEPTION OF COMMUNICATIONS COMMISSIONER

c/o PO Box 33220, London SW1H 9ZQ
T 020-7273 4514

The Interception of Communications Commissioner is appointed by the Prime Minister for a period of three years. The Commissioner's job is to keep under review the issue of interception warrants and the adequacy of the

arrangements for ensuring the product of interception is properly handled. He does this by reviewing the warrant applications that the intercepting agencies have made to the Secretary of State, in order to make sure that the Secretary of State was right to sign the warrants. He also visits the Security Service and other agencies to examine his selection of interception warrants with the officers responsible for the relevant investigations. At the end of each reporting year, the Commissioner submits a report to the Prime Minister which is subsequently laid before Parliament and published.
Commissioner, Sir Swinton Thomas
Private Secretary, D. Payne

INVESTIGATORY POWERS TRIBUNAL

PO Box 33220, London, SW1H 9ZQ
T 020-7273 4514

The Investigatory Powers Tribunal replaced the Interception of Communications Tribunal, the Intelligence Services Tribunal, the Security Services Tribunal and the complaints function of the Commissioner appointed under the Police Act 1997.

The Regulation of Investigatory Powers Act 2000 provides for a Tribunal made up of senior members of the legal profession, independent of the Government and appointed by The Queen, to consider all complaints against the intelligence services and those against public authorities in respect of powers covered by RIPA; and to consider proceedings brought under section 7 of the Human Rights Act 1998 against the intelligence services and law enforcement agencies in respect of these powers.
President, The Rt. Hon. Lord Justice John Mummery
Vice-President, Mr Justice Michael Burton
Members, W. Carmichael; Sir David Calcutt, QC; Sir Richard Gaskell; Sheriff Principal J. McInnes, QC; Sir John Pringle, QC; P. Scott, QC; R. Seabrook, QC
Secretary, Mr D. Payne

NCIS NATIONAL CRIMINAL INTELLIGENCE SERVICE

PO Box 8000, London SE11 5EN
T 020-7238 8000 W www.ncis.gov.uk

The National Criminal Intelligence Service (NCIS) provides intelligence about serious and organised crime to law enforcement, government and other relevant national and international agencies.
Director-General, P. Hampson, QPM, CBE
Deputy Director-General, D. Bolt
Director, Finance, Ms M. Ashworth
Director, Intelligence Services Division, N. Bailey
Director, International Division, R. Wainwright
Director, Resources Division, N. Beard
Director, UK Division, K. Bristow

SERVICE AUTHORITY

PO Box 2600, London SW1V 2WG
T 020-7238 2600

The Service Authority for NCIS is responsible for ensuring its effective operation. It operates with the Service Authority for the National Crime Squad. There are 26 members of the authorities, of whom the chairman and nine others serve as 'core members' on both authorities.
Chairman, D. Lock
Clerk, T. Simmons
Treasurer, P. Derrick

SECRET INTELLIGENCE SERVICE (MI6)
PO Box 1300, London SE1 1BD

The Secret Intelligence Service produces secret intelligence in support of the Government's security, defence, foreign and economic policies. It was placed on a statutory footing by the Intelligence Services Act 1994 and is headed by a chief, known as 'C', who is directly accountable to the Foreign Secretary.
Chief, J. M. Scarlett, OBE, CMG

SECURITY SERVICE (MI5)
PO Box 3255, London SW1P 1AE
T 020-7930 9000
W www.mi5.gov.uk

The Security Service is responsible for security intelligence work against covertly organised threats to the UK. These include terrorism, espionage and the proliferation of weapons of mass destruction. The Service also supports the police and other law enforcement agencies in their work against serious crime and provides security advice to a wide range of organisations to help reduce vulnerability to threats from individuals, groups or countries hostile to UK interests.
Director-General, Ms E. Manningham-Buller

SENTENCE REVIEW COMMISSIONERS
5th Floor, Windsor House, 12–16 Bedford Street,
Belfast BT2 7SR
T 028-9054 9412 F 028-9054 9427
E sentrev@belfast.org.uk
W www.sentencereview.org.uk

The Sentence Review Commissioners are appointed by the Secretary of State for Northern Ireland to consider applications from prisoners serving sentences in Northern Ireland for declarations that they are entitled to early release in accordance with the provisions of the Northern Ireland (Sentences) Act 1998. The commissioners have been appointed until 31 July 2005 and are served by staff seconded from the Northern Ireland Office.
Joint Chairmen, Sir John Belloch, KCB; B. Currin
Commissioners, Dr S. Casale; Dr P. Curran; I. Dunbar, CB; Mrs M. Gilpin; Dr A. Grounds; Ms C. McGrory; Dr D. Morrow
Secretary, Dr M. Power

SERIOUS FRAUD OFFICE
Elm House, 10–16 Elm Street, London WC1X 0BJ
T 020-7239 7272 F 020-7837 1689
E public.enquiries@sfo.gsi.gov.uk

The Serious Fraud Office is an independent government department that investigates and prosecutes serious or complex fraud. It is part of the UK Criminal Justice System. The Office is headed by the Director who is appointed by and accountable to the Attorney General. The SFO has jurisdiction over England, Wales and Northern Ireland but not Scotland, the Isle of Man or the Channel Islands.
Director, Robert Wardle

SMALL BUSINESS COUNCIL
6th Floor, Kingsgate House, 66–74 Victoria Street,
London SW1E 6SW
T 020-7215 8519
E sbcsecretariat@sbs.gsi.gov.uk
W www.sbs.gov.uk/sbc

The Small Business Council was set up in May 2000. It is a non-departmental public body reporting to the Secretary of State for Trade and Industry on the needs of small businesses.
Chairman, W. Sargent
Members, G. Burton; Ms E. Caleb; P. Donaldson; Ms L. Gradwell; Mrs T. Graham, OBE; P. Harrod; Ms C. Hughes; A. Ive; S. Johnson; Mrs S. Brownson, OBE; M. Robinson; S. Topman; Prof. M. Ram; Mrs L. Shafar; J. McLaren-Stewart; I. Patel; Ms S. Preston; Ms F. Price; Dr J. Reynolds; S. Taggart; Miss J. Ward; Mrs C. Whitmill

SMALL BUSINESS SERVICE
Kingsgate House, 66–74 Victoria Street, London SW1E 6SW
T 020-7215 5000 **Enquiries** 0845-001 0031
W www.sbs.gov.uk
Business Link T 0845-600 9006 W www.businesslink.gov.uk

The Small Business Service was set up in March 2000 as an agency of the Department of Trade and Industry. The Service works with the public, private and voluntary sectors. Working through the Business Link network, the Small Business Service provides information, advice or access to experts for small businesses.
Chairman, Nigel Griffiths, MP
Chief Executive, Martin Wyn Griffith
Strategy Board Members, M. Gibson; S. Haddrill; S. Lyle Smythe; R. Price; R. Buse; Ms T. Graham, OBE; A. Summers

STATISTICS COMMISSION
10 Great George Street, London SW1P 3AE
T 020-7273 8008
E statscom@statscom.org.uk
W www.statscom.org.uk

The Statistics Commission has been set up to advise on the quality, quality assurance and priority-setting for official statistics, and on the procedures designed to deliver statistical integrity, to help ensure official statistics are trustworthy and responsive to public needs. It is independent of both Ministers and the producers of National Statistics. It operates in a transparent way with the minutes of its meetings, correspondence and evidence it receives, and advice it gives, all normally publicly available for scrutiny.
Chairman, Prof. D. Rhind, CBE, FRS, FBA
Members, Miss C. Bowe; Sir Kenneth Calman, KCB; Ms P. Hodgson; Mrs J. Trewsdale; D. Wanless; M. Weale

STRATEGIC RAIL AUTHORITY
55 Victoria Street, London SW1H 0EU
T 020-7654 6000 F 020-7654 6010
W www.sra.gov.uk

The Strategic Rail Authority (SRA) formally came into being on 1 February 2001 following the introduction of the Transport Act 2000. On 14 January 2002 it published its Strategic Plan, setting out the strategic priorities for Britain's railways over the next ten years.

As well as providing overall strategic direction for Britain's railways, the SRA has responsibility for consumer protection, the development of rail freight and administering freight grants, and for steering forward investment projects aimed at opening up bottlenecks and expanding network capacity. It is directly responsible for letting and managing passenger rail franchises.

The SRA manages all public sector expenditure in the rail industry and operates under directions and guidance issued by the Secretary of State for Transport. In Scotland it is also subject to directions and guidance from the Scottish Minister for Transport, and to directions and guidance from the Mayor of London in respect of services operating within the capital.

In January 2004 the Secretary of State for Transport announced a fundamental review of the rail industry. In July 2004 a white paper was published highlighting the main proposals, one of which is that the SRA will eventually be wound up. Its strategic responsibilities and financial obligations will ultimately transfer to the Secretary of State for Transport.

Chairman and Chief Executive, R. Bowker
Non-executive members, L. D. Adams, OBE; D. A. Begg; W. Gallagher; D. Grayson, CBE; P. H. Kent, CBE; J. Mayhew; D. A. Quarmby, CBE; M. Banerjee, CBE; J. Lewis-Jones; D. Norgrove
Secretary, P. Trewin

TOURISM BODIES

Visit Britain, Visit Scotland, the Wales Tourist Board and the Northern Ireland Tourist Board are responsible for developing and marketing the tourist industry in their respective countries.

VISIT BRITAIN

Thames Tower, Black's Road, London W6 9EL **T** 020-8846 9000
F 020-8563-0302 **W** www.visitbritain.com
Chief Executive, T. Wright

VISIT SCOTLAND

23 Ravelston Terrace, Edinburgh EH4 3TP **T** 0131-332 2433
Thistle House, Beechwood Park North, Inverness IV2 3ED
T 01463-716996 **W** www.visitscotland.com
Chairman, P. Lederer; *Chief Executive,* P. Riddle

WALES TOURIST BOARD

Brunel House, 2 Fitzalan Road, Cardiff CF24 0UY
T 029-2049 9909 **F** 029-2048 5031
E info@tourism.wales.gov.uk **W** www.visitwales.com
Chief Executive, Jonathan Jones

NORTHERN IRELAND TOURIST BOARD

St Anne's Court, 59 North Street, Belfast BT1 1NB
T 028-9023 1221 **F** 028-9024 0960 **E** info@nitb.com
W www.discovernorthernireland.com
Chief Executive, A. Clarke

TRANSPORT FOR LONDON

Windsor House, 42–50 Victoria Street, London SW1H 0TL
T 020-7941 4500 **Travel Line** 020-7222 1234
E travinfo@tfl.gov.uk **W** www.tfl.gov.uk/tfl/

Transport for London (TfL) is responsible for the capital's transport system. Its role is to implement the Mayor of London's Transport Strategy and manage the transport services across London for which the Mayor has responsibility.
Chairman, Ken Livingstone
Vice-Chairman, Dave Wetzel
Commissioner of Transport for London, Bob Kiley

UK FILM COUNCIL

10 Little Portland Street, London W1W 7JG
T 020-7861 7861 **F** 020-7861 7862
E info@ukfilmcouncil.org.uk **W** www.ukfilmcouncil.org.uk

The Council was created in April 2000 by the Department for Culture, Media and Sport to develop a strategy for the development and leadership of film culture and the film industry. It is responsible for the majority of the Department for Culture, Media and Sport funding for film as well as lottery and grant-in-aid (with the exception of the National Film and Television School).
Chairman, A. Parker
Deputy Chairman, S. Till
Chief Executive, J. Woodward

UK FILM COUNCIL INTERNATIONAL

10 Little Portland Street, London W1W 7JG
T 020-7861 7860 **F** 020-7861 7864
E internationalinfo@ukfilmcouncil.org.uk
W www.ukfilmcouncil.org.uk

UK Film Council International (formerly the British Film Commission) was originally established in 1991. Its remit is to attract inward investment by promoting the UK as an international production centre to the film and television industries and encouraging the use of British locations, services, facilities and personnel. Working with the UK Screen Agencies, UK Film Council International also provides overseas producers with a bespoke information service and offers practical help and advice to those filming in the UK.
British Film Commissioner, S. Norris
Director, Ms C. Wise

UNITED KINGDOM SPORTS COUNCIL (UK SPORT)

40 Bernard Street, London WC1N 1ST
T 020-7211 5100 **F** 020-7211 5246
W www.uksport.gov.uk

The UK Sports Council (UK Sport) was established by Royal Charter in January 1997. Its role is to lead the UK to sporting excellence by supporting winning athletes, world class events, world class standards and ethically fair and drug-free sport.
Chairman, Sue Campbell, CBE
Acting Chief Executive, Liz Nicholl

UNRELATED LIVE TRANSPLANT REGULATORY AUTHORITY

c/o Department of Health, Room 339, Wellington House, 133–155 Waterloo Road, London SE1 8UG
T 020-7972 4812 **F** 020-7972 4852
E dhmail@doh.gsi.gov.uk/ultra
W www.advisorybodies.doh.gov.uk/ultra

The Unrelated Live Transplant Regulatory Authority (ULTRA) is a statutory body established in 1990. In every case where the transplant of an organ within the definition of the Human Organ Transplants Act 1989 is proposed between a living donor and a recipient who are not genetically related, the proposal must be referred to ULTRA. Applications must be made by registered medical practitioners.

The Authority comprises a chairman and ten members appointed by the Secretary of State for Health. The secretariat is provided by Department of Health officials.

Chairman, Prof. Sir Roddy MacSween
Members, Prof. J. A. Bradley; Ms D. Bowman; Dr J. F. Douglas; Dr S. Fuggle; Dr R. Gokal; A. J. Hooker; Ms A. Keogh; Prof. A. Rees; Mrs S. Roff; Mrs S. J. Sullivan
Administrative Secretary, E. Scarlett
Medical Secretary, Dr P. Doyle

UK ATOMIC ENERGY AUTHORITY

Harwell, Didcot, Oxon OX11 0RA
T 01235-820220 F 01235-436401
W www.ukaea.org.uk

The UKAEA was established by the Atomic Energy Authority Act 1954 and took over responsibility for the research and development of the civil nuclear power programme. The Authority's commercial arm, AEA Technology PLC, was privatised in 1996. UKAEA is now responsible for the safe management and decommissioning of its radioactive plant and for maximising the income from the buildings and land on its sites. UKAEA also undertakes the UK's contribution to the international fusion programme.

Acting Chairman, Hon Mrs Barbara Thomas
Chief Executive, Dipesh Shah

WALES YOUTH AGENCY

Leslie Court, Lon-y-Llyn, Caerphilly CF83 1BQ
T 029-2085 5700 F 029-2085 5701
E wya@wya.org.uk
W www.wya.org.uk

The Wales Youth Agency is an independent organisation funded by the National Assembly for Wales to support the youth service in Wales. Its functions include the encouragement and development of the partnership between statutory and voluntary agencies relating to young people; the promotion of staff development and training; and the extension of marketing and information services in the relevant fields. The board of directors does not receive a salary.

Acting Chairman of the Board of Directors, Dr H. William
Chief Executive, Huw Jones
Assistant Chief Executive, John Rose

WELSH ADMINISTRATION OMBUDSMAN

5th Floor, Capital Tower, Greyfriars Road, Cardiff CF10 3AG
T 0845-601 0987 F 029-2022 6909
E wao.enquiries@ombudsman.gsi.gov.uk
W www.ombudsman.org.uk

The Welsh Administration Ombudsman was appointed in July 1999 to investigate complaints by members of the public who have suffered an injustice through maladministration by the National Assembly for Wales and certain public bodies involved in devolved Welsh affairs.

Welsh Administration Ombudsman, Adam Peat

WELSH DEVELOPMENT AGENCY

Plas Glyndwr, Kingsway, Cardiff CF10 3AH
T 01443-845500 F 01443-845589
E enquiries@wda.co.uk W www.wda.co.uk

The Agency was established under the Welsh Development Agency Act 1975. Its remit is to help further the regeneration of the economy and improve the environment in Wales. Under the Government of Wales Act 1998, the Land Authority for Wales and the Development Board for Rural Wales merged with the Welsh Development Agency. The Agency is sponsored by the National Assembly for Wales.

The Agency's priorities are to create new businesses and to encourage existing small firms to grow. Its main activities include promoting Wales as a location for inward investment, helping to boost the growth, profitability and competitiveness of indigenous Welsh companies, providing investment capital for industry, encouraging investment by the private sector in property development, grant-aiding land reclamation, and stimulating quality urban and rural development.

Chairman, R. Jones, OBE
Chief Executive, G. Hawker, CBE

WOMEN'S NATIONAL COMMISSION

35 Great Smith Street, London SW1 3BQ
T 020-7276 2555 F 020-7276 2563
E wnc@dti.gsi.gov.uk
W www.thewnc.org.uk

The Women's National Commission was established in 1969 as an independent advisory committee to the Government. Its remit is to ensure that the informed opinions of women are given their due weight in the deliberations of the Government and in public debate on matters of public interest including those of special interest to women. The Commission is based within the Department of Trade and Industry alongside the Women and Equality Unit.

Chair, Baroness Margaret Prosser
Director, Ms J. Veitch

REGIONAL GOVERNMENT

LONDON

GREATER LONDON AUTHORITY (GLA)
City Hall, The Queen's Walk, London SE1 2AA
T 020-7983 4000
Press Office 020-7983 4071/4072/4090/4067/4228
E mayor@london.gov.uk W www.london.gov.uk

On 7 May 1998 London voted in favour of the formation of the Greater London Authority. The first elections to the GLA took place on 4 May 2000 and the new Authority took over its responsibilities on 3 July 2000. On 15 July 2002 the GLA moved to one of London's most spectacular buildings, built on a brownfield site on the south bank of the river Thames, adjacent to Tower Bridge. The second elections to the GLA took place on 10 June 2004.

The structure and objectives of the GLA stem from its eight main areas of responsibility. These are transport, planning, economic development and regeneration, the environment, police, fire and emergency planning, culture and health. The bodies that co-ordinate these functions and report to the GLA are: Transport for London (TfL), the London Development Agency (LDA), the Metropolitan Police Authority (MPA) and the London Fire and Emergency Planning Authority (LFEPA). The GLA also absorbed a number of other London bodies, such as the London Planning Advisory Committee, the London Ecology Unit and the London Research Centre.

The GLA consists of a directly elected Mayor, the Mayor of London, and a separately elected assembly, the London Assembly. The Mayor has the key role of decision making with the Assembly performing the tasks of regulating and scrutinising these decisions. In addition, the GLA has around 600 permanent staff to support the activities of the Mayor and the Assembly, which are overseen by a Head of Paid Service. The Mayor may appoint two political advisors but he may not appoint the Chief Executive, the Monitoring Officer or the Chief Finance Officer. These must be appointed by the Assembly.

Every aspect of the Assembly and its activities must be open to public scrutiny and therefore accountable. The Assembly holds the Mayor to account through scrutiny of his strategies, decisions and actions. This is carried out by direct questioning at Assembly meetings and by conducting detailed investigations in committee.

People's Question Time gives Londoners the chance to question the Mayor and the London Assembly about plans, priorities and policies for London. It is held twice a year in different areas of London. A People's Question Time meeting was scheduled to take place in October 2004.

The role of the Mayor can be broken down into a number of key areas: to represent and promote London at home and abroad and speak up for Londoners; to devise strategies and plans to tackle London-wide issues, such as transport, economic development and regeneration, air quality, noise, waste, bio-diversity, planning and culture; to set budgets for Transport for London, the London Development Agency, the Metropolitan Police Authority and the London Fire and Emergency Planning Authority; to control new transport and economic development bodies and appoint their members; to make appointments to the new police and fire authorities; and to publish regular reports on the state of the environment in London.

The role of the Assembly can be broken down into a number of key areas:
– to provide a check and balance on the Mayor
– to have the power to amend the Mayor's budget by a majority of two-thirds
– to investigate issues of London-wide significance and make proposals to the Mayor
– to provide the Deputy Mayor and the members serving on the police, fire and emergency planning authorities with advice

Mayor, Ken Livingstone
Deputy Mayor, Nicky Gavron
Chair of the London Assembly, Brian Coleman
Deputy Chair of the Assembly, Sally Hamwee

ELECTIONS AND THE VOTING SYSTEMS
The Assembly is elected every four years at the same time as the Mayor and consists of 25 members. There is one member from each of the 14 GLA constituencies topped up with 11 London members who are representatives of political parties or individuals standing as independent candidates. The next election will be in May 2008.

The GLA constituencies are: Barnet and Camden; Bexley and Bromley; Brent and Harrow; City and East, covering Barking and Dagenham, the City of London, Newham and Tower Hamlets; Croydon and Sutton; Ealing and Hillingdon; Enfield and Haringey; Greenwich and Lewisham; Havering and Redbridge; North East, covering Hackney, Islington and Waltham Forest; Lambeth and Southwark; West Central, covering Hammersmith and Fulham, Kensington and Chelsea and Westminster; South West, covering Hounslow, Kingston upon Thames and Richmond upon Thames; Merton and Wandsworth.

Two distinct voting systems are used to appoint the existing Mayor and the Assembly. The Mayor is elected using the Supplementary Vote System (SVS). With SVS electors have two votes; one to give a first choice for Mayor and one to give a second choice. Electors cannot vote twice for the same candidate. If one candidate gets more than half of all the first choice votes, he or she becomes Mayor. If no candidate gets more than half the first choice votes, the two candidates with the most first choice votes remain in the election and all the other candidates drop out. The second choice votes on the ballot papers of the candidates who drop out are then counted. Where these second choice votes are for the two remaining candidates they are added to the first choice votes these candidates already have. The candidate with the most first and second choice votes combined becomes the Mayor of London.

The Assembly is appointed using the Additional Member System (AMS). Under AMS, electors have two votes. The first vote is for a constituency candidate. The second vote is for a party list or individual candidate contesting the London-wide Assembly seats. The 14 constituency members are elected under the first-past-the-post system, the same system used in general and local elections. Electors vote for one candidate and the candidate with the most votes wins. The Additional (London) Members are drawn from party lists or are independent candidates who stand as London Members.

The Greater London Returning Officer (GLRO) is the independent official responsible for running the first election in London. The GLRO has overall responsibility for running a free, fair and efficient election. He is supported in this by Returning Officers in each of the 14 London Constituencies.

GLRO, Anthony Mayer
Deputy GLRO, John Bennett
Deputy Regional Returning Officer, David Weschler

TRANSPORT FOR LONDON (TfL)

TfL is the integrated body responsible for London's transport system. Its role is to implement the Mayor's transport strategy for London and manage transport services across the capital for which the Mayor has reponsibility. TfL is directed by a management board whose members are chosen for their understanding of transport matters and are appointed by the Mayor, who chairs the board. TfL's role is:
– to manage the Underground, buses, Croydon Tramlink and the Docklands Light Railway (DLR)
– to manage a 580 km network of main roads and all of London's 4,600 traffic lights
– to regulate taxis and minicabs
– to run the London River Services, Victoria Coach Station and London's Transport Museum
– to help to co-ordinate the Dial-a-Ride and Taxicard schemes for door-to-door services for transport users with mobility problems

The London Borough Councils maintain the role of highway and traffic authorities for 95 per cent of London's roads. A £5 congestion charge for motorists driving into central London between the hours of 7a.m. and 6.30p.m., Monday to Friday (excluding public holidays) was introduced on 17 February 2003.

Transport Commissioner for London, Robert Kiley

LONDON DEVELOPMENT AGENCY (LDA)

The LDA promotes economic development and regeneration. It is one of the nine regional development agencies set up around the country to perform this task. It is managed by a board of 14 members appointed by the Mayor.

The key aspects of the LDA's role are:
– to promote business efficiency, investment and competitiveness
– to promote employment
– to enhance the skills of local people
– to create sustainable development

The London Boroughs retain powers to promote economic development in their local areas.

Chair, Mary Reilly

THE ENVIRONMENT

The Mayor is required to formulate strategies to tackle London's environmental issues including the quality of water, air and land; the use of energy and London's contribution to climate change targets; ground water levels and traffic emissions; and municipal waste management.

METROPOLITAN POLICE AUTHORITY (MPA)

This body, which oversees the policing of London, consists of 12 members of the assembly, including the Deputy Mayor, four magistrates and seven independents. One of the independents is appointed directly by the Home Secretary. The role of the MPA is:
– to maintain an efficient and effective police force
– to publish an annual policing plan
– to set police targets and monitor performance
– to be part of the appointment, discipline and removal of senior officers
– to be responsible for the performance budget
– to oversee formal inquiries and the implementation of their recommendations

The boundaries of the metropolitan police districts have been changed to be in line with the 32 London boroughs. Areas beyond the GLA remit have been incorporated into the Surrey, Hertfordshire and Essex police areas. The City of London has its own police force.

Chair, Len Duvall

LONDON FIRE AND EMERGENCY PLANNING AUTHORITY (LFEPA)

On 3 July 2000 the London Fire and Civil Defence Authority became the London Fire and Emergency Planning Authority. It consists of 17 members, 9 drawn from the assembly and 8 from the London Boroughs. The role of LFEPA is:
– to set the strategy for the provision of fire services
– to ensure that the fire brigade can meet all the normal requirements efficiently
– to ensure that effective arrangements are made for the fire brigade to receive emergency calls and deal with them promptly
– to ensure that information useful to the development of the fire brigades is gathered
– to assist the boroughs with their emergency planning training and exercises

Chair, Valerie Shawcross

SALARIES *as at July 2004*

Mayor	£112,639
Deputy Mayor	£70,034
Assembly Member	£47,924

LONDON ASSEMBLY COMMITTEES

Chair, 2004 Elections Review Committee, Brian Coleman
Chair, Audit Panel, Peter Hulme Cross
Chair, Budget Committee, Andrew Pelling
Chair, Business Management and Appointments Committee, Sally Hamwee
Chair, Economic Development and Planning Committee, Dee Doocey
Chair, Environment Committee, Darren Johnson
Chair, Health and Public Services Committee, Joanne McCartney
Chair, Safer London Committee, Richard Barnes
Chair, Transport Committee, Lynne Featherstone
Commission on London Governance (Advisory Committee)
Standards Committee

LONDON ASSEMBLY ORGANISATIONAL STRUCTURE

MAYOR'S OFFICE

Public Affairs (International and European Relations, London Stakeholders, Government and Parliamentary Liaison, Public Consultation, Public Affairs Publications)
Best Value Partnership (Borough Liaison)

Economic and Business Policy (Private Sector, Strategic Evaluation Unit)
Equalities and Policing
Environment
Tourism and Creative Industries
London House (Brussels)
Administration Manager

SECRETARIAT
Assembly Support
Scrutiny and Investigations
Committee Services
Assembly's Media Relations

CHIEF EXECUTIVE'S OFFICE
Governance
Marketing
Mayor's Media Relations

POLICY AND PARTNERSHIPS
Spatial Development Strategy
Planning Decisions
Architecture and Urbanism Unit
Environment
Culture
Policy Support (Health, Housing and Homelessness, Social Inclusion, Sustainable Development)
Business Support

CORPORATE SERVICES
GLA Economics
Information and Communication Technology
Legal
HR and Administration (Facilities Management and Internal Communications)
Research Library
Data Management
Public Liaison
Business Support

FINANCE AND PERFORMANCE
Core Performance and Project Management
Strategic Performance
Core Finance
Strategic Finance

LONDON ASSEMBLY MEMBERS *as at 10 June 2004*
The Mayor, Ken Livingstone *(Lab.)*
Arbour, Anthony *(C.)*, *South West*, Maj. 4,067
Arnold, Jennette *(Lab.)*, *North East*, Maj. 13,338
Barnes, Richard Michael *(C.)*, *Ealing and Hillingdon*, Maj. 11,016
Biggs, John Robert *(Lab.)*, *City and East*, Maj. 14,336
Blackman, Robert *(C.)*, *Brent and Harrow*, Maj. 4,686
Bray, Angela Lavinia *(C.)*, *West Central*, Maj. 29,944
Coleman, Brian *(C.)*, *Barnet and Camden*, Maj. 11,519
Cross, Peter Kenneth Hulme *(UKIP)*, *London List*
Doocey, Dee *(LD)*, *London List*
Duvall, Leonard Lloyd *(Lab.)*, *Greenwich and Lewisham*, Maj. 14,083
Evans, Jeremy Roger *(C.)*, *Havering and Redbridge*, Maj. 16,706
Featherstone, Lynne Choona *(LD)*, *London List*
Gavron, Felicia Nicolette *(Lab.)*, *London List*
Hamwee, Sally Rachel *(LD)*, *London List*
Hockney, Nicholas Damian *(UKIP)*, *London List*
Howlett, Elizabeth *(C.)*, *Merton and Wandsworth*, Maj. 16,878
Johnson, Darren *(Green)*, *London List*

Jones, Jenny *(Green)*, *London List*
McCartney, Joanne *(Lab.)*, *Enfield and Haringey*, Maj. 1,574
Neill, Robert James Macgillivray *(C.)*, *Bexley and Bromley*, Maj. 34,254
Pelling, Andrew John *(C.)*, *Croydon and Sutton*, Maj. 23,694
Qureshi, Murad *(Lab.)*, *London List*
Shawcross, Valerie *(Lab.)*, *Lambeth and Southwark*, Maj. 5,475
Tope, Graham Norman *(LD)*, *London List*
Tuffrey, Michael William *(LD)*, *London List*

STATE OF THE PARTIES *as at 10 June 2004*

Party	Seats	Gain/Loss
Conservative	9	0
Labour	7	−2
Liberal Democrats	5	+1
Green	2	−1
UK Independence	2	+2

MAYORAL ELECTION RESULTS
10 June 2004
E. 5,197,647 T. 1,920,533 (36.95%)
Change in turnout from 2000: +2.52%
Good votes: 1st choice 1,863,671 (97.04%); 2nd choice 1,591,443 (82.86%)
Rejected votes: 1st choice 56,862 (2.96%); 2nd choice 329,090 (17.14%)

First Choice	Party	Votes	%
Ken Livingstone	Lab.	685,541	35.70
Steven Norris	C.	542,423	28.24
Simon Hughes	LD	284,645	14.82
Frank Maloney	UKIP	115,665	6.02
Lindsey German	Respect	61,731	3.21
Julian Leppert	BNP	58,405	3.04
Darren Johnson	Green	57,331	2.99
Ram Gidoomal	CPA	41,696	2.17
Lorna Reid Ind. Working Class		9,542	0.50
Tammy Nagalingam	Ind.	6,692	0.35

Second Choice	Party	Votes	%
Simon Hughes	LD	465,704	24.25
Ken Livingstone	Lab.	250,517	13.04
Steven Norris	C.	222,559	11.59
Darren Johnson	Green	208,686	10.87
Frank Maloney	UKIP	193,157	10.06
Julian Leppert	BNP	70,736	3.68
Lindsey German	Respect	63,294	3.30
Ram Gidoomal	CPA	56,721	2.95
Lorna Reid Ind. Working Class		39,678	2.07
Tammy Nagalingam	Ind.	20,391	1.06

LONDON ASSEMBLY ELECTION RESULTS
10 June 2004

CONSTITUENCIES

BARNET AND CAMDEN
E. 371,186, T. 38.41%

Brian Coleman, C.	47,640
Lucy Anderson, Lab.	36,121
Jonathan Simpson, LD	23,603
Miranda Dunn, Green	11,921
Magnus Nielsen, UKIP	8,685
Elisabeth Wheatley, Respect	5,150
Humberto Heliotrope, CPA	1,914

C. majority 11,519

BEXLEY AND BROMLEY
E. 397,075, *T.* 41.48%

Robert Neill, C.	64,246
Duncan Borrowman, LD	29,992
Heather Bennett, UKIP	26,703
Charles Mansell, Lab.	24,848
Ann Garrett, Green	8,069
Miranda Suit, CPA	3,397
Alun Morinan, Respect	1,673
C. majority 34,254	

BRENT AND HARROW
E. 332,723, *T.* 38.03%

Robert Blackman, C.	39,900
Toby Harris, Lab.	35,214
Havard Hughes, LD	20,782
Daniel Moss, UKIP	7,199
Mohammad Ali, Green	6,975
Albert Harriott, Respect	4,586
Gladstone Macaulay, CPA	2,734
C. majority 4,686	

CITY AND EAST
E. 437,298, *T.* 33.43%

John Biggs, Lab.	38,085
Shafi Choudhury, C.	23,749
Oliur Rahman, Respect	19,675
Guy Burton, LD	18,255
Christopher Pratt, UKIP	17,997
Terry McGrenera, Green	8,687
Christopher Gill, CPA	4,461
Lab. majority 14,336	

CROYDON AND SUTTON
E. 376,175, *T.* 37.82%

Andrew Pelling, C.	52,330
Steven Gauge, LD	28,636
Sean Fitzsimons, Lab.	25,861
James Feisenberger, UKIP	15,203
Shasha Khan, Green	6,175
David Campanale, CPA	4,234
Waqas Hussain, Respect	3,108
C. majority 23,694	

EALING AND HILLINGDON
E. 397,564, *T.* 37.28%

Richard Barnes, C.	45,230
Gurcharan Singh, Lab.	34,214
Michael Cox, LD	23,440
David Malindine, UKIP	14,698
Sarah Edwards, Green	9,395
Dalawar Chaudhry, Ind.	5,285
Salvinder Dhillon, Respect	4,229
Genevieve Hibbs, CPA	3,024
C. majority 11,016	

ENFIELD AND HARINGEY
E. 343,617, *T.* 36.14%

Joanne McCartney, Lab.	33,955
Peter Forrest, C.	32,381
Wayne Hoban, LD	19,720
Brian Hall, UKIP	10,652
Jayne Forbes, Green	10,310
Sait Akgul, Respect	6,855
Peter Wolstenholme, CPA	2,365
Lab. majority 1,574	

GREENWICH AND LEWISHAM
E. 329,450, *T.* 35.10%

Leonard Duvall, Lab.	36,251
Gareth Bacon, C.	22,168
Alexander Feakes, LD	19,183
Timothy Reynolds, UKIP	13,454
Susan Luxton, Green	11,271
Stephen Hammond, CPA	3,619
Ian Page, Respect/Soc. Alt.	2,825
Lab. majority 14,083	

HAVERING AND REDBRIDGE
E. 350,652, *T.* 38.96%

Jeremy Evans, C.	44,723
Keith Darvill, Lab.	28,017
Lawrence Webb, UKIP	18,297
Matthew Lake, LD	13,646
Malvin Brown, Residents Assn. of London	6,925
Ashley Gunstock, Green	6,009
Abdurahman Jafar, Respect	5,185
Juliet Hawkins, CPA	2,917
David Stephens, Third Way	2,031
Peter Thorogood, Ind.	1,597
C. majority 16,706	

LAMBETH AND SOUTHWARK
E. 373,293, *T.* 33.38%

Valerie Shawcross, Lab.	36,280
Caroline Pidgeon, LD	30,805
Bernard Gentry, C.	17,379
Shane Collins, Green	11,900
Frank Maloney, UKIP	8,776
Janet Noble, Respect	4,930
Simisola Lawanson, CPA	3,655
Navindh Baburam, Ind.	608
Lab. majority 5,475	

MERTON AND WANDSWORTH
E. 340,792, *T.* 38.55%

Elizabeth Howlett, C.	48,295
Kathryn Smith, Lab.	31,417
Andrew Martin, LD	17,864
Roy Vickery, Green	10,163
Adrian Roberts, UKIP	8,327
Ruairidh Maclean, Respect	4,291
Ellen Greco, CPA	2,782
Rathy Alagaratnam, Ind.	1,240
C. majority 16,878	

NORTH EAST
E. 410,719, *T.* 33.93%

Jennette Arnold, Lab.	37,380
Terry Stacy, LD	24,042
Andrew Boff, C.	23,264
Jon Nott, Green	16,739
Robert Selby, UKIP	11,459
Dean Ryan, Respect	11,184
Andrew Otchie, CPA	3,219
James Beavis, Comm.	1,378
Lab. majority 13,338	

SOUTH WEST	
E. 384,450, *T.* 40.31%	
Tony Arbour, C.	48,858
Dee Doocey, LD	44,791
Seema Malhotra, Lab.	25,225
Alan Hindle, UKIP	12,477
Judy Maciejowska, Green	9,866
Omar Waraich, Respect	3,785
Peter Flower, CPA	3,008
C. majority 4,067	

WEST CENTRAL	
E. 352,653, *T.* 35.28%	
Angela Bray, C.	51,884
Ansuya Sodha, Lab.	21,940
Francesco Fruzza, LD	17,478
Julia Stephenson, Green	10,762
Nicholas Hockney, UKIP	7,219
Kevin Cobham, Respect	4,825
Jillian McLachlan, CPA	1,993
C. majority 29,944	

WALES

NATIONAL ASSEMBLY FOR WALES
Cathays Park, Cardiff CF1 3NQ
T 029-2082 5111
National Assembly Information Line 029-2089 8200
E webmaster@wales.gov.uk
W www.wales.gov.uk

In July 1997 the Government announced plans to establish a National Assembly for Wales. In a referendum on 18 September 1997 about 50 per cent of the electorate voted, of whom 50.3 per cent voted in favour of the Assembly. Elections are to be held every four years. The first elections were held on 6 May 1999 when approximately 46 per cent of the electorate voted. On 1 May 2003 the second Welsh Assembly elections took place. The next election will take place in May 2007.

The Assembly has 60 members (including the Presiding Officer), comprising 40 constituency members and 20 additional regional members from party lists. It can introduce only secondary legislation and has no power to raise or lower income tax.

The National Assembly for Wales has responsibility in Wales for ministerial functions relating to health and personal social services; education, except for terms and conditions of service and student awards; training; the Welsh language, arts and culture; the implementation of the Citizen's Charter in Wales; local government; housing; water and sewerage; environmental protection; sport; agriculture and fisheries; forestry; land use, including town and country planning and countryside and nature conservation; new towns; non-departmental public bodies and appointments in Wales; ancient monuments and historic buildings and the Welsh Arts Council; roads; tourism; financial assistance to industry; the Strategic Development Scheme in Wales and the Programme for the Valleys; and the operation of the European Regional Development Fund in Wales and other European Union matters.

SALARIES *as at 1 April 2004*
†First Minister	£72,863
†Minister/Presiding Officer	£37,797
Assembly Members	£43,283*

* Reduced by two-thirds if the member is already an MP or an MEP
† First Minister, Ministers and Presiding Officer also receive the Assembly Member salary

THE PRESIDING OFFICER
Lord Daffydd Elis-Thomas

WELSH ASSEMBLY GOVERNMENT
First Minister of the Assembly, Rhodri Morgan, AM
Principal Private Secretary, Lawrence Conway
Special Advisers, Paul Griffiths; Mark Drakeford; Dr Rachel Jones; Cathy Owens; Martin Mansfield; Jane Runeckles
Minister for Business, Karen Sinclair, AM
Minister for Culture, Welsh Language and Sport, Alun Pugh, AM
Minister for Economic Development and Transport, Andrew Davies, AM
Minister for Education and Lifelong Learning, Jane Davidson, AM
Minister for Environment, Planning and Countryside, Carwyn Jones, AM
Minister for Finance, Local Government and Public Services, Sue Essex, AM
Minister for Health and Social Services, Jane Hutt, AM
Minister for Social Justice and Regeneration, Edwina Hart, AM
Deputy Minister for Communities, Huw Lewis
Deputy Minister for Older People, John Griffiths
Deputy Minister for Transport, Brian Gibbons
Permanent Secretary, Sir Jon Shortridge
Clerk to the Assembly, Paul Silk

EXECUTIVE BOARD
Senior Director, Policy, Derek Jones
Director, Business and Information Management, Bryan Mitchell
Director, Economic Development and Transport, David Pritchard
Director, Education and Training, Richard Davies
Director, Environment, Planning and Countryside, Gareth Jones
Director, Health and Social Care, Ann Lloyd
Director, Human Resources, Bernard Galton
Director, Local Government, Public Service and Culture, Hugh Rawlings
Director, Public Service Development, Barbara Wilson
Director, Regulation/Inspection Review, Helen Thomas
Director, Social Justice and Regeneration, John Bader
Director, Spending Review, Martin Evans
Director, Strategy and Communications, Huw Brodie
Chief Medical Officer, Dr Ruth Hall
Principal Finance Officer, David Richards
Non-executive Directors, Adrian Webb; Kathryn Bishop

DEPARTMENTS AND OFFICES
Agriculture and Rural Affairs Department
Communications Directorate
Economic Development Department
Finance Group
Health Protection and Improvement Directorate
Local Government Group
NHS Directorate
Office of the Counsel General
Office of the Presiding Officer
Social Services and Communities Group
Strategic Policy Unit
Training and Education Department
Transport, Planning and Environment Group

EXECUTIVE AGENCIES
Cadw: Welsh Historic Monuments
Planning Inspectorate
Welsh European Funding Office

COMMITTEES

SUBJECT COMMITTEES
Culture, Welsh Language and Sport
Economic Development and Transport
Education and Lifelong Learning
Environment, Planning and Countryside
Health and Social Services
Local Government and Public Services
Social Justice and Regeneration

STANDING COMMITTEES
Audit
Business
Equality of Opportunity
European and External Affairs
House
Legislation
Standards of Conduct

MEMBERS OF THE WELSH ASSEMBLY *as at July 2004*
Andrews, Leighton, *Lab., Rhondda*, Maj. 7,954
Barrett, Ms Lorraine Jayne, *Lab., Cardiff South and Penarth*, Maj. 4,114
Bates, Michael, *LD, Montgomeryshire*, Maj. 12,297
Black, Peter, *LD, South Wales West region*
Bourne, Prof. Nicholas, *C., Mid and West Wales region*
Burnham, Mrs Eleanor, *LD, North Wales region*
Butler, Mrs Rosemary Janet Mair, *Lab., Newport West*, Maj. 3,752
Cairns, Alun, *C., South Wales West region*
Chapman, Ms Christine, *Lab., Cynon Valley*, Maj. 7,117
Cuthbert, Jeffrey, *Lab., Caerphilly*, Maj. 4,974
Davidson, Ms Jane Elizabeth, *Lab., Pontypridd*, Maj. 6,920
Davies, Andrew David, *Lab., Swansea West*, Maj. 2,562
Davies, David Thomas Charles, *C., Monmouth*, Maj. 8,510
Davies, Edward, *C., Mid and West Wales region*
Davies, Ms Janet, *PC, South Wales West region*
Davies, Ms Jocelyn, *PC, South Wales East region*
Dunwoody-Kneafsey, Moyra Tamsin, *Lab., Preseli Pembrokeshire*, Maj. 1,326
Elis-Thomas, Lord Dafydd, *PC, Meirionnydd Nant Conwy*, Maj. 8,742
Essex, Ms Susan Linda, *Lab., Cardiff North*, Maj. 540
Francis, Elizabeth Ann (Lisa), *C., Mid and West Wales region*
German, Michael, *LD, South Wales East region*
Gibbons, Brian, *Lab., Aberavon*, Maj. 7,813
Graham, William, *C., South Wales East region*
Gregory, Ms Janice, *Lab., Ogmore*, Maj. 6,504
Griffiths, Albert John, *Lab., Newport East*, Maj. 3,464
Gwyther, Ms Christine Margery, *Lab., Carmarthen West and South Pembrokeshire*, Maj. 515
Hart, Ms Edwina, *Lab., Gower*, Maj. 5,688
Hutt, Ms Jane, *Lab., Vale of Glamorgan*, Maj. 2,653
Idris Jones, Ms Denise, *Lab., Conwy*, Maj. 72
Isherwood, Mark, *C., North Wales region*
James, Ms Irene, *Lab., Islwyn*, Maj. 7,320
Jones, Alun, *PC, Caernarfon*, Maj. 5,905
Jones, Carwyn Howell, *Lab., Bridgend*, Maj. 2,421
Jones, Ms Elin, *PC, Ceredigion*, Maj. 4,618
Jones, Ms Helen, *PC, Mid and West Wales region*
Jones, Ms Laura Anne, *C., South Wales East region*
Jones, Ms Margaret Ann (known as Ann), *Lab., Vale of Clwyd*, Maj. 3,341
Law, Peter, *Lab., Blaenau Gwent*, Maj. 11,736
Lewis, Huw, *Lab., Merthyr Tydfil and Rhymney*, Maj. 8,160
Lloyd, Dr David, *PC, South Wales West region*
Lloyd, Mrs Val, *Lab., Swansea East*, Maj. 3,997
Marek, Dr John, *Forward Wales, Wrexham*, Maj. 973
Melding, David, *C., South Wales Central region*
Mewies, Mrs Sandra Elaine, *Lab., Delyn*, Maj.1,624
Morgan, Hywel Rhodri, *Lab., Cardiff West*, Maj. 6,837
Morgan, Jonathan, *C., South Wales Central region*
Neagle, Mrs Lynne, *Lab., Torfaen*, Maj. 6,964
Pugh, Alun John, *Lab., Clwyd West*, Maj. 436
Randerson, Ms Jennifer Elizabeth, *LD, Cardiff Central*, Maj. 7,156

Ryder, Mrs Janet, *PC, North Wales region*
Sergeant, Carl, *Lab., Alyn and Deeside*, Maj. 3,503
Sinclair, Ms Karen, *Lab., Clwyd South*, Maj. 2,891
Thomas, Ms Catherine, *Lab., Llanelli*, Maj. 21
Thomas, Ms Gwenda, *Lab., Neath*, Maj. 4,946
Thomas, Owen, *PC, South Wales Central region*
Thomas, Rhodri, *PC, Carmarthen East and Dinefwr*, Maj. 4,614
Williams, Byrnle, *C., North Wales region*
Williams, Ms Kirsty, *LD, Brecon and Radnorshire*, Maj. 5,308
Wood, Ms Leanne, *PC, South Wales Central region*
Wyn Jones, Ieuan, *PC, Ynys Mon*, Maj. 2,255

STATE OF THE PARTIES *as at July 2004*

	Constituency AM	Regional AMs	AM Total
Labour	30	0	30
Plaid Cymru	4†	7	11†
Conservative	1	10	11
Liberal Democrats	3	3	6
Others	1	0	1
The Presiding Officer	1	0	1

† Excludes the Presiding Officer, who has no party allegiance while in post

WELSH ASSEMBLY ELECTION RESULTS
1 May 2003

CONSTITUENCIES

ABERAVON
(S. Wales West)
E. 50,208, T. 37.6%
Brian Gibbons, *Lab.*	11,137
Geraint Owen, *PC*	3,324
Ms Claire Waller, *LD*	1,840
Myr Boult, *C.*	1,732
Robert Williams, *Soc. Alt.*	608
Gwenno Saunders, *Ind. Wales*	114
Lab. majority 7,813	

ALYN AND DEESIDE
(Wales N.)
E. 60,518, T. 25.1%
Carl Sergeant, *Lab.*	7,036
Matthew Wright, *C.*	3,533
Paul Brighton, *LD*	2,509
Richard Coombs, *PC*	1,160
William Crawford, *UK Ind.*	826
Lab. majority 3,503	

BLAENAU GWENT
(S. Wales East)
E. 52,927, T. 37.8%
Peter Law, *Lab.*	13,884
Stephen Bard, *LD*	2,148
Rhys Ab Elis, *PC*	1,889
Barrie O'Keefe, *C.*	1,131
Roger Thomas, *UK Ind.*	719
Lab. majority 11,736	

BRECON AND RADNORSHIRE
(Wales Mid and W.)
E. 53,739, T. 50.0%

Ms Kirsty Williams, *LD*	13,325
Nicholas Bourne, *C.*	8,017
David Rees, *Lab.*	3,130
Brynach Parri, *PC*	1,329
Ms Elizabeth Phillips, *UK Ind.*	1,042

LD majority 5,308

BRIDGEND
(S. Wales West)
E. 62,540, T. 35.4%

Carwyn Howell Jones, *Lab.*	9,487
Alun Hugh Cairns, *C.*	7,066
Ms Cheryl Anne Green, *LD*	2,980
Keith Parry, *PC*	1,939
Timothy Charles Jenkins, *UK Ind.*	677

Lab. majority 2,421

CAERNARFON
(Wales N.)
E. 47,173, T. 45.0%

Alun Ffred Jones, *PC*	11,675
Martin Robert Eaglestone, *Lab.*	5,770
Goronwy Owen Edwards, *C.*	2,402
Stephen William Churchman, *LD*	1,392

PC majority 5,905

CAERPHILLY
(S. Wales East)
E. 68,152, T. 37.3%

Jeffrey Cuthbert, *Lab.*	11,893
Lindsay Whittle, *PC*	6,919
Ms Laura Jones, *C.*	2,570
Rob Roffe, *LD*	1,281
Ms Anne Blackman, *Ind.*	1,204
Revd Avril, Dafydd-Lewis, *Ind.*	930
Ms Brenda Vipass, *UK Ind.*	590

Lab. majority 4,974

CARDIFF CENTRAL
(S. Wales Central)
E. 62,470, T. 33.7%

Ms Jennifer Elizabeth Randerson, *LD*	11,256
Geoff Miles Mungham, *Lab.*	4,100
Craig Stuart Piper, *C.*	2,378
Owen John Thomas, *PC*	1,795
Raja Gul Raiz, *Soc. All.*	541
Captain Beany, *Bean*	289
Ms Madeleine Elise Jeremy, *ProLife,*	239

LD majority 7,156

CARDIFF NORTH
(S. Wales Central)
E. 64,528, T. 43.9%

Ms Susan Linda Essex, *Lab.*	10,413
Jonathan Morgan, *C.*	9,873
John Leslie Dixon, *LD*	3,474
Hewel William Wyn Jones, *PC*	2,679
Donald Edwin Hulston, *UK Ind.*	1,295

Lab. majority 540

CARDIFF SOUTH AND PENARTH
(S. Wales Central)
E. 65,505, T. 31.0%

Ms Lorraine Jayne Barrett, *Lab.*	8,978
Ms Dianne Elizabeth Rees, *C.*	4,864
Rodney Simon Berman, *LD*	3,154
Richard Rhys Grigg, *PC*	2,538
David Charles Bartlett, *Soc. Alt.*	585

Lab. majority 4,114

CARDIFF WEST
(S. Wales Central)
E. 60,523, T. 35.4%

Hywel Rhodri Morgan, *Lab.*	10,420
Ms Heather Douglas, *C.*	3,583
Ms Jacqueline-Anne Gasson, *LD*	2,914
Ms Eluned Mary Bush, *PC*	2,859
Frank Roger Wynne Hughes, *UK Ind.*	929

Lab. majority 6,837

CARMARTHEN EAST AND DINEFWR
(Wales Mid and W.)
E. 54,110, T. 49.5%

Rhodri Thomas, *PC*	12,969
Anthony Cooper, *Lab.*	8,355
Harri Lloyd-Davies, *C.*	3,576
Steffan John, *LD*	1,866

PC majority 4,614

CARMARTHEN WEST AND SOUTH PEMBROKESHIRE
(Wales Mid and W.)
E. 56,403, T. 43.0%

Ms Christine Margery Gwyther, *Lab.*	8,384
Llyr Hughes Griffiths, *PC*	7,869
David Nicholas Thomas, *C.*	4,917
Ms Mary Kathleen Megarry, *LD*	2,222
Arthur Ronald Williams, *Ind.*	580

Lab. majority 515

CEREDIGION
(Wales Mid and W.)
E. 52,940, T. 50.0%

Ms Elin Jones, *PC*	11,883
John Davies, *LD*	7,265
Ms Rhianon Passmore, *Lab.*	3,308
Owen Williams *C.*	2,923
Ian Sheldon, *UK Ind.*	940

PC majority 4,618

CLWYD SOUTH
(Wales N.)
E. 53,452, T. 35.1%

Ms Karen Sinclair, *Lab.*	6,814
Dyfed Edwards, *PC*	3,923
Albert Fox, *C.*	3,548
Marc Jones, *John Marek Ind.*	2,210
Derek Burnham, *LD*	1,666
Ms Edwina Theunissen, *UK Ind.*	501

Lab. majority 2,891

CLWYD WEST
(Wales N.)
E. 54,463, T. 40.6%

Alun John Pugh, *Lab.*	7,693
Brynle Williams *C.*	7,257
Ms Janet Ryder, *PC*	4,715
Ms Eleanor Burnham, *LD*	1,743
Peter Murray, *UK Ind.*	715

Lab. majority 436

CONWY
(Wales N.)
E. 54,443, T. 38.7%

Ms Denise Idris Jones, *Lab.*	6,467
Gareth Jones, *PC*	6,395
Guto ap Owain Bebb, *C.*	5,152
Graham Rees, *LD*	2,914
Lab. majority 72	

CYNON VALLEY
(S. Wales Central)
E. 44,473, T. 37.5%

Ms Christine Chapman, *Lab.*	10,841
David Alun Walters, *PC*	3,724
Robert Owen Humphreys, *LD*	1,120
Daniel Clive Byron Thomas, *C.*	984
Lab. majority 7,117	

DELYN
(Wales N.)
E. 54,426, T. 31.4%

Ms Sandra Elaine Mewies, *Lab.*	6,520
Mark Isherwood, *C.*	4,896
David Lloyd, *LD*	2,880
Paul Rowlinson, *PC*	2,588
Lab. majority 1,624	

GOWER
(S. Wales West)
E. 60,523, T. 39.9%

Ms Edwina Hart, *Lab.*	10,334
Stephen James, *C.*	4,646
Ms Sian Caiach, *PC*	3,502
Nicholas Tregoning, *LD*	2,775
Richard Lewis, *UK Ind.*	2,444
Lab. majority 5,688	

ISLWYN
(S. Wales East)
E. 51,170, T. 40.3%

Ms Irene James, *Lab.*	11,246
Brian Hancock, *PC*	3,926
Paul Taylor, *Tinker against the Assembly*	2,201
Ms Terri-Anne Matthews, *C.*	1,848
Huw Price, *LD*	1,268
Lab. majority 7,320	

LLANELLI
(Wales Mid and W.)
E. 57,428, T. 40.9%

Ms Catherine Thomas, *Lab.*	9,916
Ms Helen Mary Jones, *PC*	9,895
Gareth Jones, *C.*	1,712
Kenneth Rees, *LD*	1,644
Lab. majority 21	

MEIRIONYDD NANT CONWY
(Wales Mid and W.)
E. 33,742, T. 45.5%

Lord Dafydd Elis-Thomas, *PC*	8,717
Edwin Woodward, *Lab.*	2,891
Lisa Francis, *C.*	2,485
Kenneth Harris, *LD*	1,100
PC majority 5,826	

MERTHYR TYDFIL AND RHYMNEY
(S. Wales East)
E. 55,768, T. 33.5%

Huw Lewis, *Lab.*	11,148
Alun Cox, *PC*	2,988
John Prosser, *C.*	1,539
Neil Greer, *Ind.*	1,423
John Ault, *LD*	1,324
Lab. majority 8,160	

MONMOUTH
(S. Wales East)
E. 62,451, T. 44.9%

David Thomas Charles Davies, *C.*	15,989
Ms Sian Catherine James, *Lab.*	7,479
Ms Alison Leyland Willott, *LD*	2,973
Stephen Vaughan Thomas, *PC*	1,355
C. majority 8,510	

MONTGOMERYSHIRE
(Wales Mid and W.)
E. 45,598, T. 43.0%

Michael Bates, *LD*	7,869
Edward Davies, *C.*	5,572
Ms Rina Clarke, *Lab.*	2,039
David Senior, *PC*	1,918
David Rowlands, *UK Ind.*	1,107
Robert Mills, *Ind.*	985
LD majority 2,297	

NEATH
(S. Wales West)
E. 56,759, T. 39.4%

Ms Gwenda Thomas, *Lab.*	11,332
Alun Llewelyn, *PC*	6,386
Ms Helen Jones, *LD*	2,048
Chris Smart, *C.*	2,011
Huw Pudner, *WSA*	410
Lab. majority 4,946	

NEWPORT EAST
(S. Wales East)
E. 56,563, T. 30.4%

Albert John Griffiths, *Lab.*	7,621
Matthew Robert Hatton Evans, *C.*	4,157
Charles Edward Townsend, *LD*	2,768
Mohammad Asghar, *PC*	1,555
Neal John Reynolds, *UK Ind.*	987
Lab. majority 3,464	

NEWPORT WEST
(S. Wales East)
E. 61,238, T. 35.3%

Ms Rosemary Janet Mair Butler, *Lab.*	10,053
William Graham, *C.*	6,301
Phylip Andrew David Hobson, *LD*	2,094
Anthony Michael Salkeld, *PC*	1,678
Hugh Moelwyn Hughes, *UK Ind.*	1,102
Richard Morse, *WSA*	198
Lab. majority 3,752	

OGMORE
(S. Wales West)
E. 49,565, *T.* 34.3%

Ms Janice Gregory, *Lab.*	9,874
Ms Janet Marion Davies, *PC*	3,370
Ms Jacqueline Radford, *LD*	1,567
Richard John Hill, *C.*	1,532
Christopher Herriott, *Soc. Lab.*	410

Lab. majority 6,504

PONTYPRIDD
(S. Wales Central)
E. 63,204, *T.* 38.8%

Ms Jane Elizabeth Davidson, *Lab.*	12,206
Delme Ifor Bowen, *PC*	5,286
Michael John Powell, *LD*	3,443
Ms Jayne Louise Cowan, *C.*	2,438
Peter Manuel Gracia, *UK Ind.*	1,025

Lab. majority 6,920

PRESELI PEMBROKESHIRE
(Wales Mid and W.)
E. 55,195, *T.* 41.7%

Moyra Tamsin Dunwoody-Kneafsey, *Lab.*	8,067
Paul Windsor Davies, *C.*	6,741
Sion Tomos Jobbins, *PC*	5,227
Michael Ian Warden, *LD*	2,799

Lab. majority 1,326

RHONDDA
(S. Wales Central)
E. 50,463, *T.* 46.0%

Leighton Andrews, *Lab.*	14,170
Geraint Davies, *PC*	6,216
Jeff Gregory, *Ind.*	909
Ms Veronica Watkins, *LD*	680
Dr K. T. Rajan, *UK Ind.*	524
Paul Williams, *C.*	504

Lab. majority 7,954

SWANSEA EAST
(S. Wales West)
E. 57,252, *T.* 30.7%

Ms Val Lloyd, *Lab.*	8,221
Peter Black, *LD*	4,224
Dr Dewi Evans, *PC*	2,223
David Alan Robinson, *UK Ind.*	1,474
Peter Morris, *C.*	1,135
Alan Thomson, *WSA*	133

Lab. majority 3,997

SWANSEA WEST
(S. Wales West)
E. 58,749, *T.* 33.3%

Andrew David Davies, *Lab.*	7,023
Dr David Rees Lloyd, *PC*	4,461
Arthur Michael Day, *LD*	3,510
Dorian Rowbottom, *C.*	3,106
David Charles Evans, *UK Ind.*	1,040
David Leigh Richards, *WSA*	272

Lab. majority 2,562

TORFAEN
(S. Wales East)
E. 61,264, *T.* 32.1%

Ms Lynne Neagle, *Lab.*	10,152
Nicholas Ramsay, *C.*	3,188
Michael German, *LD*	2,746
Aneurin Preece, *PC*	2,092
David Rowlands, *UK Ind.*	1,377

Lab. majority 6,964

VALE OF CLWYD
(Wales N.)
E. 49,319, *T.* 36.5%

Ms Margaret Ann Jones, *Lab.*	8,256
Darren Millar, *C.*	5,487
Malcom Evans, *PC*	2,516
Ms Robina Feeley, *LD*	1,630

Lab. majority 2,769

VALE OF GLAMORGAN
(S. Wales Central)
E. 68,947, *T.* 40.7%

Ms Jane Hutt, *Lab.*	12,267
David Melding, *C.*	9,614
Christopher Franks, *PC*	3,921
Ms Nilmini de Silva, *LD*	2,049

Lab. majority 2,653

WREXHAM
(Wales N.)
E. 50,508, *T.* 34.5%

Dr John Marek, *John Marek Ind.*	6,539
Ms Susan Lesley Griffiths, *Lab.*	5,566
Ms Janet Finch-Saunders, *C.*	2,228
Tom Ripperth, *LD*	1,701
Peter Ryder, *PC*	1,329

John Marek Ind. majority 973

YNYS MON
(Wales N.)
E. 49,998, *T.* 51.0%

Ieuan Wyn Jones, *PC*	9,452
Peter Rogers, *C.*	7,197
William Jones, *Lab.*	6,024
Nicholas Bennett, *LD*	2,089
Francis Charles Wykes, *UK Ind.*	481

PC majority 2,255

REGIONS

MID AND WEST WALES
E. 409,155 *T.* 184,198

PC	51,874 (28.2%)
Lab.	46,451 (25.2%)
C.	35,566 (19.3%)
LD	30,119 (16.4%)
Green	7,794 (4.2%)
UK Ind.	5,945 (3.2%)
Mid and West Wales Pensioners	3,968 (2.2%)
Ind. Wales	1,324 (0.7%)
Vote 2 Stop The War	716 (0.4%)
ProLife	383 (0.2%)

PC majority 5,423
(May 1999 PC Majority 30,712)
Additional Members: Prof. N. Bourne, *C.*, G. Davies, *C.*, L. Francis, *C.*, H. Jones, *PC*

NORTH WALES
E. 474,300 T. 175,028

Lab.	55,250 (31.6%)
PC.	41,640 (23.8%)
C.	38,543 (22.0%)
LD	17,503 (10.0%)
John Marek Ind.	11,008 (6.3%)
UK Ind.	4,500 (2.6%)
Green	4,200 (2.4%)
Ind. Wales	1,552 (0.9%)
Comm.	522 (0.3%)
ProLife	310 (0.2%)

Lab. majority 13,610
(May 1999 Lab. Majority 4,155)
Additional Members: E. Burnham, *LD*, M. Isherwood, *C.*, J. Ryder, *PC*, B. Williams, *C.*

SOUTH WALES CENTRAL
E. 480,113 T. 181,047

Lab.	74,369 (41.1%)
C.	33,404 (18.5%)
PC	27,956 (15.4%)
LD	24,926 (13.8%)
UK Ind.	6,920 (3.8%)
Green	6,047 (3.3%)
Soc. Lab.	3,217 (1.8%)
Bean	1,027 (0.6%)
Ind. Wales	1,018 (0.6%)
Vote 2 Stop The War	1,013 (0.6%)
Comm.	577 (0.3%)
ProLife	573 (0.3%)

Lab. majority 40,965
(May 1999 Lab. Majority 21,484)
Additional Members: D. Melding, *C.*, J. Morgan, *C.*, O. Thomas, *PC*, L. Wood, *PC*

SOUTH WALES EAST
E. 469,533 T. 169,731

Lab.	76,522 (45.1%)
C.	34,231 (20.2%)
PC	21,384 (12.6%)
LD	17,661 (10.4%)
UK Ind.	5,949 (3.5%)
Green	5,291 (3.1%)
Soc. Lab.	3,695 (2.2%)
BNP	3,210 (1.9%)
Ind Wales	1,226 (0.7%)
ProLife	562 (0.3%)

Lab. majority 42,291
(May 1999 Lab. Majority 34,814)
Additional Members: J. Davies, *PC*, M. German, *LD*, W. Graham, *C.*, L. A. Jones, *C.*

SOUTH WALES WEST
E. 395,596 T. 23,541

Lab.	58,066 (41.6%)
PC	24,799 (17.8%)
C.	20,981 (15.0%)
LD	17,746 (12.7%)
Green	6,696 (4.8%)
UK Ind.	6,113 (4.4%)
Soc. Lab.	3,446 (2.5%)
Ind. Wales	1,346 (1.0%)
ProLife	355 (0.3%)

Lab. majority 33,267
(May 1999 Lab. Majority 19,868)
Additional Members: P. Black, *LD*, A. Cairns, *C.*, J. Davies, *PC*, D. Lloyd, *PC*

NORTHERN IRELAND

NORTHERN IRELAND ASSEMBLY

Parliament Buildings, Stormont, Belfast BT4 3XX
T 028-9052 1333 F 028-9052 1961
W www.ni-assembly.gov.uk

The Assembly was suspended from midnight on 14 October 2002 and was dissolved on 28 April 2003. On 26 November 2003 elections to the Assembly were held but the Assembly remains suspended at the time of going to press (August 2004). The Secretary of State assumed responsibility for the direction of the Northern Ireland departments. The following is an overview of the organisation and structure of the Assembly, which applied when it was operational. Talks to discuss the future of the Assembly are ongoing.

The Assembly has 108 members elected by single transferable vote (six from each of the 18 Westminster constituencies). The first elections took place on 25 June 1998 and members met for the first time on 1 July. Safeguards ensure that key decisions have cross-community support. The executive powers of the Assembly are discharged by an Executive Committee comprising a First Minister and Deputy First Minister (jointly elected by the Assembly on a cross-community basis) and up to ten ministers with departmental responsibilities. Ministerial posts are allocated on the basis of the number of seats each party holds. Ministers receive 70 per cent of full pay during suspension of the Assembly.

The Assembly met in shadow form, pending the establishment of an Executive and the transfer of powers from Parliament. Following devolution it has executive and legislative authority over those areas formerly the responsibility of the Northern Ireland government departments.

Power was initially due to be transferred to the new Executive on 10 March 1999, but disagreements emerged over whether Sinn Fein should be allowed to enter the Executive before IRA weapons had been decommissioned. Further deadlines of 2 April and 30 June were also missed. On 15 July the Assembly met to nominate ministers, with the transfer of power to follow on 18 July. However, as the decommissioning issue had still not been resolved, Unionists failed to nominate ministers (the UUP boycotting the meeting itself) and the process collapsed. On 20 July the two prime ministers announced a review of the implementation of the Good Friday Agreement to be facilitated by Senator George Mitchell. The timing of the review dove-tailed with the inevitably sensitive publication of the Patten Commission's report on policing.

Following a series of meetings involving the parties in London, Mitchell's interim report of 15 November stated that he was increasingly more confident that the parties could find a way through the impasse.

On 18 November, following statements from the UUP, Sinn Fein and the IRA, Senator Mitchell concluded the review indicating that he now believed there was a basis for devolution to occur, for the institutions to be established and for decommissioning to take place as soon as possible. He concluded that devolution should take effect, the Executive Committee should meet and paramilitary organisations should appoint their authorised representatives to the Independent International Commission on Decommissioning (IICD) in that order and all in the same day. On 20 November the Secretary of State announced support for the Mitchell proposals and stated that the Assembly should meet on 29 November for the purpose of running the d'Hondt procedure for appointing shadow ministers and devolution should take effect after the necessary Parliamentary procedures had been completed on 2 December 1999.

Powers were devolved to Assembly and other institutions established on 2 December on a basis agreed by the parties during the Mitchell review. The Mitchell review created the expectation that the establishment of the institutions and the appointment of authorised representatives produced conditions in which Sinn Fein could influence bringing about the start of decommissioning. But it was a matter of political reality that if decommissioning did not occur by the end of January it would be very difficult for David Trimble to continue as leader of the Ulster Unionist Party beyond this. In late November the Council of the UUP had endorsed the Mitchell outcome but, reflecting the political reality, also recommended that progress on the timing and modalities of decommissioning be reviewed at the end of January 2000 through reports presented to the two governments by the IICD.

Devolution and the institutions were able to flourish on the basis of sufficient cross-community support. Unfortunately that support began to ebb when the anticipated progress on decommissioning failed to materialise at the end of January. The two Governments took receipt of General de Chastelain's 31 January report but held back publication in order to explore any hope of credible progress on decommissioning. Both governments tried further efforts to gain clarity on the decommissioning issue.

The Secretary of State announced the suspension legislation on 3 February and warned publicly that it would come into effect on 11 February. On the morning of 11 February, there was some sign that a new IRA proposal was emerging. The Irish Government presented a new position from its leadership. There were still only words and no timescale, but it did include clearer and less equivocal words than before. Unfortunately this was not enough to avert the collapse of the institutions.

Suspension meant that the Assembly could not meet or conduct any business. Parliament Buildings remained open for use by Assembly Members for the purpose of carrying out constituency work and they continued to be paid salaries and allowances – set at the lower pre-devolution shadow rate to reflect the suspension of Assembly business.

Following a period of intensive discussions with pro-Agreement parties during 4 and 5 May at Hillsborough, the Prime Minister and Taoiseach issued a joint statement committing both Government's proposals. On May 6, the IRA responded with a significant and forthcoming statement in which they recognised that:

– the implementation of what the Governments had agreed would provide a new context in which Republicans could pursue their political objectives peacefully
– in that new context the IRA leadership would initiate a process that would completely and verifiably put arms beyond use
– the IRA would renew contact with the Decommissioning Commission
– agreed, as a confidence building measure, to open a number of arms dumps to independent inspectors reporting to the Decommissioning Commission on a regular basis to verify that arms remain secure

The pro-Agreement parties welcomed these developments. The UUP leader, David Trimble said that the IRA statement 'appeared to break new ground'. The Prime Minister and the Taoiseach announced on 8 May that they would ask the former Finnish President Martti Ahtisaari and Cyril Ramaphosa, the ANC negotiator, to become the independent inspectors. On 9 May, the Chief Constable of the RUC recognised that the IRA statement marked a significant reduction in the overall threat and announced a number of measures, spread across Northern Ireland, designed as a return to more normal policing.

The Government published the Police Bill on 16 May and gave assurances to Unionists that the legal description of the new police service would incorporate the RUC, while the operational and working name would change to Police Service of Northern Ireland. The Government also took an enabling power to resolve the flying of flags over Government buildings if the devolved Executive could not.

A week later than originally envisaged the Ulster Unionist Council endorsed the Government's proposals on 27 May and devolved government was restored to Northern Ireland with effect from midnight on 29 May 2000.

Following considerable political unrest, David Trimble resigned as Northern Ireland First Minister on 1 July 2001, followed on 18 October by other UUP Ministers. His resignation was an ultimatum to encourage the IRA to start decommissioning their weapons. The administrative elements of his post passed to Sir Reg Empey.

To allow time to resolve this situation the Secretary of State for Northern Ireland ordered 24-hour suspensions of the Assembly on 10 August and 22 September 2001. On 5 November 2001 this period was concluded when David Trimble was elected as First Minister and Mark Durkan was elected as Deputy First Minister to replace Seamus Mallon who had retired.

SALARIES *as at December 2003**
Assembly Member   £31,817
*In 2004 the salaries were frozen at 2003 level until the Assembly is reinstated.

NORTHERN IRELAND EXECUTIVE
Castle Buildings, Stormont, Belfast BT4 3SG
T 028-9052 0700 F 028-9052 8195
W www.northernireland.gov.uk

During suspension the following departments fall under the control of the Secretary of State for Northern Ireland and his Northern Ireland Office ministerial team.

Secretary of State for Northern Ireland, The Rt. Hon. Paul Murphy, MP
Under-Secretary of State, Ian Pearson *(Security and Policing, Finance and Personnel, Agriculture and Regional Development and Office of the First Minister and Deputy First Minister)*
Minister of State, John Spellar *(Social Development, Regional Development and Office of the First Minister and Deputy First Minister)*
Parliamentary Under-Secretary, Barry Gardiner *(Employment and Learning, Education and Enterprise, Trade and Investment)*
Parliamentary Under-Secretary, Angela Smith *(Health, Social Services and Public Safety, Environment and Culture, Arts and Leisure)*

OFFICE OF THE FIRST MINISTER AND DEPUTY MINISTER
Castle Buildings, Stormont Estate, Belfast BT4 3SR
T 028-9052 8400 W www.ofmdfmni.gov.uk

DEPARTMENT OF AGRICULTURE AND RURAL DEVELOPMENT
Dundonald House, Upper Newtownards Road, Belfast BT4 3SB
T 028-9052 4999 F 028-9052 5546 W www.dardni.gov.uk

EXECUTIVE AGENCIES
RIVERS AGENCY, 4 Hospital Road, Belfast BT8 8JP
  T 028-9025 3355
FOREST SERVICE, Dundonald House, Belfast BT4 3SB
  T 028-9052 4822

DEPARTMENT OF CULTURE, ARTS AND LEISURE
3rd Floor, Interpoint, 20–24 York Street, Belfast BT15 1AQ
T 028-9025 8825 F 028-9025 8906 W www.dcalni.gov.uk

EXECUTIVE AGENCIES
THE PUBLIC RECORD OFFICE OF NORTHERN IRELAND, 66 Balmoral Avenue, Belfast BT9 6NY T 028-9025 1318
  F 028-9025 5999
THE ORDNANCE SURVEY OF NORTHERN IRELAND, Colby House, Stranmillis Court, Belfast BT9 5BJ T 028-9025 5755
  F 028-9025 5700

DEPARTMENT OF EDUCATION
Rathgael House, 43 Balloo Road, Bangor, Co. Down BT19 7PR
T 028-9127 9279 F 028-9127 9100 W www.deni.gov.uk

DEPARTMENT FOR EMPLOYMENT AND LEARNING
39/49 Adelaide House, Adelaide Street, Belfast BT2 8FD
T 028-9025 7793 W www.delni.gov.uk

DEPARTMENT OF ENTERPRISE, TRADE AND INVESTMENT
Netherleigh, Massey Avenue, Belfast BT4 2JP T 028-9052 9900
F 028-9052 9550

DEPARTMENT OF THE ENVIRONMENT
Clarence Court, 10–18 Adelaide Street, Belfast BT2 8GB
T 028-9054 0540 W www.doeni.gov.uk

EXECUTIVE AGENCIES
Driver and Vehicle Licensing Agency (Northern Ireland)
Driver and Vehicle Testing Agency (Northern Ireland)
Environment and Heritage Service
Planning Service

DEPARTMENT OF FINANCE AND PERSONNEL
Rathgael House, Balloo Road, Bangor BT19 7NA
T 028-9127 9279 W www.dfpni.gov.uk

EXECUTIVE AGENCIES
BUSINESS DEVELOPMENT SERVICE, Craigantlet Buildings, Stoney Road, Belfast BT4 3SX T 028-9052 0444
LAND REGISTERS OF NORTHERN IRELAND, Lincoln Building, 27–45 Great Victoria Street, Belfast BT2 7SL T 028-9025 1515
NORTHERN IRELAND STATISTICS AND RESEARCH AGENCY*, McAuley House, 2–14 Castle Street, Belfast BT1 1SA
  T 028-9034 8100
RATE COLLECTION AGENCY, Oxford House, 49–55 Chichester Street, Belfast BT1 4HH T 028-9025 2252
VALUATION AND LANDS AGENCY, Queen's Court, 56–66 Upper Queen Street, Belfast BT1 6FD T 028-9025 0700
*Incorporates the General Register Office (Northern Ireland), Oxford House, 49–55 Chichester Street, Belfast BT1 4HH
T 028-9025 2000

DEPARTMENT OF HEALTH, SOCIAL SERVICES
AND PUBLIC SAFETY
Castle Buildings, Stormont, Belfast BT4 3SJ T 028-9052 0500
F 028-9052 0572 W www.dhsspsni.gov.uk

EXECUTIVE AGENCIES
Northern Ireland Health and Social Services Estates
Agency

DEPARTMENT FOR REGIONAL DEVELOPMENT
Clarence Court, 10–18 Adelaide Street, Belfast BT2 8GB
T 028-9054 0540 F 028-9054 0064 W www.drdni.gov.uk

DEPARTMENT FOR SOCIAL DEVELOPMENT
Churchill House, Victoria Square, Belfast BT1 4SD
T 028-9056 9100 W www.dsdni.gov.uk

NORTHERN IRELAND ASSEMBLY MEMBERS
 as at 2 August 2004
Adams, Gerry, *(SF), Belfast West*
Armstrong, Billy, *(UUP), Ulster Mid*
Attwood, Alex, *(SDLP), Belfast West*
*Beare, Norah, *(DUP), Lagan Valley*
Beggs, Roy, *(UUP), Antrim East*
Bell, Billy, *(UUP), Lagan Valley*
Bell, Eileen, *(All.), Down North*
Berry, Paul, *(DUP), Newry and Armagh*
Birnie, Dr Esmond, *(UUP), Belfast South*
Bradley, Dominic, *(SDLP), Newry and Armagh*
Bradley, Mary, *(SDLP), Foyle*
Bradley, P. J., *(SDLP), Down South*
Brolly, Francis, *(SF), East Londonderry*
Buchanan, Thomas, *(DUP), Tyrone West*
Burns, Thomas, *(SDLP), Antrim South*
Burnside, David, *(UUP), Antrim South*
Campbell, Gregory, *(DUP), Londonderry East*
Clarke, Willie, *(SF), Down South*
Close, Seamus, *(All.), Lagan Valley*
Clyde, Wilson, *(DUP), Antrim South*
Cobain, Fred, *(UUP), Belfast North*
Copeland, Michael, *(UUP), Belfast East*
Coulter, Revd Robert, *(UUP), Antrim North*
Cree, Leslie, *(UUP), Down North*
Dallat, John, *(SDLP), Londonderry East*
Dawson, George, *(DUP), Antrim East*
De Brun, Ms Bairbre, *(SF), Belfast West*
Deeny, Kieran, *(Ind.), Tyrone West*
Dodds, Diane, *(DUP), Belfast West*
Dodds, Nigel, *(DUP), Belfast North*
Doherty, Pat, *(SF), Tyrone West*
*Donaldson, Jeffrey, *(DUP), Lagan Valley*
Dougan, Geraldine, *(SF), Ulster Mid*
Durkan, Mark, *(SDLP), Foyle*
Easton, Alex, *(DUP), Down North*
Elliot, Tom, *(UUP), Fermanagh and South Tyrone*
Empey, Sir Reg, *(UUP), Belfast East*
Ennis, George, *(DUP), Strangford*
Ervine, David, *(PUP), Belfast East*
Farren, Dr Sean, *(SDLP), Antrim North*
Ferguson, Michael, *(SF), Belfast West*
Ford, David, *(All.), Antrim South*
*Foster, Arlene, *(DUP), Fermanagh and South Tyrone*
Gallagher, Tommy, *(SDLP), Fermanagh and South Tyrone*
Gardiner, Samuel, *(UUP), Upper Bann*
Gildernew, Michelle, *(SF), Fermanagh and South Tyrone*
Girvan, Paul, *(DUP), Antrim South*
Hanna, Carmel, *(SDLP), Belfast South*
Hay, William, *(DUP), Foyle*

Hilditch, David, *(DUP), Antrim East*
Hillis, Norman, *(UUP), Londonderry East*
Hussey, Derek, *(UUP), Tyrone West*
Hyland, Davy, *(SF), Newry and Armagh*
Kelly, Dolores, *(SDLP), Upper Bann*
Kelly, Gerry, *(SF), Belfast North*
Kennedy, Danny, *(UUP), Newry and Armagh*
Kilclooney, Lord, *(UUP), Strangford*
Lewsley, Patricia, *(SDLP), Lagan Valley*
Long, Naomi, *(All.), Belfast East*
Maginness, Alban, *(SDLP), Belfast North*
Maskey, Alex, *(SF), Belfast South*
McCann, Fra, *(SF), Belfast West*
McCarthy, Kieran, *(All.), Strangford*
†McCartney, Raymond, *(SF), Foyle*
McCartney, Robert, *(UKUP), Down North*
McCausland, Nelson, *(DUP), Belfast North*
McClarty, David, *(UUP), Londonderry East*
McCrea, Revd William, *(DUP), Ulster Mid*
McDonnell, Dr Alasdair, *(SDLP), Belfast South*
McElduff, Barry, *(SF), Tyrone West*
McFarland, Alan, *(UUP), Down North*
McGimpsey, Michael, *(UUP), Belfast South*
McGlone, Patsy, *(SDLP), Ulster Mid*
McGuigan, Philip, *(SF), Antrim North*
McGuinness, Martin, *(SF), Ulster Mid*
McLaughlin, Mitchel, *(SF), Foyle*
McMenamin, Eugene, *(SDLP), Tyrone West*
McNarry, David, *(UUP), Strangford*
Molloy, Francis, *(SF), Ulster Mid*
Morrow, Maurice, *(DUP), Fermanagh and South Tyrone*
Moutray, Stephen, *(DUP), Upper Bann*
Murphy, Conor, *(SF), Newry and Armagh*
Neeson, Sean, *(All.), Antrim East*
Nesbitt, Dermot, *(UUP), Down South*
Newton, Robin, *(DUP), Belfast East*
O'Dowd, John, *(SF), Upper Bann*
O'Rawe, Patricia, *(SF), Newry and Armagh*
O'Reilly, Tom, *(SF), Fermanagh and South Tyrone*
Paisley, Revd Dr Ian, *(DUP), Antrim North*
Paisley, Ian Jnr., *(DUP), Antrim North*
Poots, Edwin, *(DUP), Lagan Valley*
Ramsey, Pat, *(SDLP), Foyle*
Ritchie, Margaret, *(SDLP), Down South*
Robinson, George, *(DUP), East Londonderry*
Robinson, Iris, *(DUP), Strangford*
Robinson, Ken, *(UUP), Antrim East*
Robinson, Mark, *(DUP), Belfast South*
Robinson, Peter, *(DUP), Belfast East*
Ruane, Caitriona, *(SF), Down South*
Shannon, Jim, *(DUP), Strangford*
Simpson, David, *(DUP), Upper Bann*
Stanton, Kathy, *(SF), Belfast North*
Storey, Mervyn, *(DUP), Antrim North*
Trimble, The Rt. Hon. David, *(UUP), Upper Bann*
Weir, Peter, *(DUP), Down North*
Wells, Jim, *(DUP), Down South*
Wilson, Jim, *(UUP), Antrim South*
Wilson, Sammy, *(DUP), Antrim East*

* Elected as UUP candidate, became a member of the DUP with
effect from 15 January 2004
† Mrs Mary Nelis resigned from the Northern Ireland Assembly
and was replaced by Mr Raymond McCartney whose
appointment was notified by the Chief Electoral Officer with
effect from 15 July 2004

POLITICAL COMPOSITION

DUP	Democratic Unionist Party	33
SF	Sinn Fein	24
UUP	Ulster Unionist Party	24
SDLP	Social Democratic and Labour Party	18
All.	Alliance Party	6
PUP	Progressive Unionist Party	1
UKUP	UK Unionist Party	1
Ind.	Independent	1

NORTHERN IRELAND ASSEMBLY ELECTION RESULTS
26 November 2003
* Indicates those who were elected

ANTRIM EAST
E. 55,473, *T.* 56.50%
Total Valid Poll: 30,952
Quota: 4,422
*Roy Beggs, *UUP*
*Sammy Wilson, *DUP*
*George Dawson, *DUP*
*David Hilditch, *DUP*
Daniel O'Connor, *SDLP*
*Sean Neeson, *All.*
*Ken Robinson, *UUP*
Roy McCune, *UUP*
Jack McKee, *Ind.*
Stewart Dickson, *All.*
Roger Hutchinson, *Ind.*
Oliver McMullan, *SF*
Tom Robinson, *UKUP*
Carolyn Howarth, *PUP*
Robert Mason, *Ind.*
John Anderson, *Ind.*
Anne Monaghan, *NIWC*
Alan Greer, *C.*
Andrew Frew, *Green*

ANTRIM NORTH
E. 70,489, *T.* 63.32%
Total Valid Poll: 44,099
Quota: 6,300
*Revd Dr Ian Paisley, *DUP*
*Ian Paisley Jnr., *DUP*
*Revd Robert Coulter, *UUP*
*Philip McGuigan, *SF*
*Sean Farren, *SDLP*
*Mervyn Storey, *DUP*
James Currie, *UUP*
Declan O'Loan, *SDLP*
Jayne Dunlop, *All.*
Kane Gardiner, *Ind.*
Nathaniel Small, *UKUP*
Billy McCaughey, *PUP*

ANTRIM SOUTH
E. 63,640, *T.* 59.49%
Total Valid Poll: 37,421
Quota: 5,346
*David Burnside, *UUP*
*Wilson Clyde, *DUP*
*Paul Girvan, *DUP*
Martin Meehan, *SF*
*David Ford, *All.*
*Jim Wilson, *UUP*
*Thomas Burns, *SDLP*
Donovan McClelland, *SDLP*
John Smyth, *DUP*

Adrian Cochrane-Watson, *UUP*
Norman Boyd, *NIUP*
Joan Cosgrove, *NIWC*
Ken Wilkinson, *PUP*
Jason Docherty, *C.*

BELFAST EAST
E. 51,937, *T.* 60.70%
Total Valid Poll: 30,965
Quota: 4,424
*Peter Robinson, *DUP*
*Sir Reg Empey, *UUP*
*David Ervine, *PUP*
*Naomi Long, *All.*
*Michael Copeland, *UUP*
Jim Rodgers, *UUP*
*Robin Newton, *DUP*
Harry Toan, *DUP*
Joe O'Donnell, *SF*
Leo Van Es, *SDLP*
Terry Dick, *C.*
Thomas Black, *Soc.*
Joseph Bell, *WP*
John McBlain, *Ind.*
George Weiss, *VFY*

BELFAST NORTH
E. 51,353, *T.* 62.31%
Total Valid Poll: 31,532
Quota: 4,505
*Nigel Dodds, *DUP*
*Gerry Kelly, *SF*
*Alban Maginness, *SDLP*
*Kathy Stanton, *SF*
*Fred Cobain, *UUP*
Pat Convery, *SDLP*
*Nelson McCausland, *DUP*
William Hutchinson, *PUP*
Fraser Agnew, *UUC*
Frank McCoubrey, *Ind.*
Eliz Byrne McCullough, *NIWC*
Marjorie Hawkins, *All.*
Peter Emerson, *Green*
Raymond McCord, *Ind.*
Marcella Delaney, *WP*
John Gallagher, *VFYP*

BELFAST SOUTH
E. 50,707, *T.* 62.59%
Total Valid Poll: 31,330
Quota: 4,476
*Michael McGimpsey, *UUP*
*Mark Robinson, *DUP*
*Alex Maskey, *SF*
*Carmel Hanna, *SDLP*
*Alasdair McDonnell, *SDLP*
Ruth Patterson, *DUP*
*Esmond Birnie, *UUP*
Monica McWilliams, *NIWC*
Geraldine Rice, *All.*
John Hiddleston, *UUP*
Tom Ekin, *All.*
Thomas Morrow, *PUP*
John Wright, *Green*
James Barbour, *SP*
Roger Lomas, *C.*
Patrick Lynn, *WP*
Linsay Steven, *VFYP*

BELFAST WEST
E. 50,861, T. 65.92%
Total Valid Poll: 32,854
Quota: 4,694
*Gerry Adams, *SF*
*Fra McCann, *SF*
*Bairbre De Brun, *SF*
*Michael Ferguson, *SF*
*Alex Attwood, *SDLP*
Sue Ramsey, *SF*
Joe Hendron, *SDLP*
*Diane Dodds, *DUP*
Chris McGimpsey, *UUP*
Hugh Smyth, *PUP*
John Lowry, *WP*
John MacVicar, *Ind.*
Kathryn Ayers, *All.*
David Kerr, *Ulster Third Way*

DOWN NORTH
E. 57,422, T. 54.54%
Total Valid Poll: 30,835
Quota: 4,406
*Leslie Cree, *UUP*
*Peter Weir, *DUP*
*Alex Easton, *DUP*
*Alan McFarland, *UUP*
*Robert McCartney, *UKUP*
Diana Peacocke, *UUP*
*Eileen Bell, *All.*
Liam Logan, *SDLP*
Brian Wilson, *Ind.*
Jane Morrice, *NIWC*
Ann Chambers, *Ind. Unionist*
John Barry, *Green*
Stephen Farry, *All.*
Julian Robertson, *C.*
Alan Field, *Ind.*
David Rose, *PUP*
Maria George, *SF*
Tom Sheridan, *UKUP*
Chris Carter, *Ind.*

DOWN SOUTH
E. 70,149, T. 65.59%
Total Valid Poll: 45,346
Quota: 6,479
*Jim Wells, *DUP*
*Dermot Nesbitt, *UUP*
*P. J. Bradley, *SDLP*
*Catriona Ruane, *SF*
*Margaret Ritchie, *SDLP*
*Willie Clarke, *SF*
Eamonn O'Neill, *SDLP*
Jim Donaldson, *UUP*
Eamonn McConvey, *SF*
Marian Fitzpatrick, *SDLP*
Raymond Blaney, *Green*
Trudy Miller, *NIWC*
Neil Powell, *All.*
Nelson Wharton, *UKUP*
Malachi Curran, *Ind.*
Desmond O'Hagan, *WP*

FERMANAGH AND SOUTH TYRONE
E. 64,336, T. 72.86%
Total Valid Poll: 46,160
Quota: 6,595
*Michelle Gildernew, *SF*
*Tom Elliot, *UUP*
*Maurice Morrow, *DUP*
*Tom O'Reilly, *SF*
*Arlene Foster, *UUP†*
*Tommy Gallagher, *SDLP*
Gerry McHugh, *SF*
Bert Johnston, *DUP*
Frank Britton, *SDLP*
Robert Mulligan, *UUP*
Eithne McNulty, *NIWC*
Linda Cleland, *All.*
†elected as UUP candidate, became a member of the DUP
    with effect from 15 January 2004

FOYLE
E. 65,303, T. 63.45%
Total Valid Poll: 40,806
Quota: 5,830
*Mark Durkan, *SDLP*
*William Hay, *DUP*
*Mitchel McLaughlin, *SF*
Raymond McCartney, *SF*
*Mary Nelis, *SF†*
*Mary Bradley, *SDLP*
Mary Hamilton, *UUP*
*Pat Ramsey, *SDLP*
Eamonn McCann, *SEA*
Gerard Diver, *SDLP*
Annie Courtney, *Ind.*
Alan Castle, *All.*
Danny McBrearty, *Ind.*
†Mary Nelis resigned from the Northern Ireland
    Assembly and was replaced by Raymond McCartney
    whose appointment was notified by the Chief Electoral
    Officer with effect from 15 July 2004

LAGAN VALLEY
E. 67,910, T. 61.44%
Total Valid Poll: 41,254
Quota: 5,894
*Jeffrey Donaldson, *UUP†*
*Edwin Poots, *DUP*
*Seamus Close, *All.*
Andrew Hunter, *DUP*
Paul Butler, *SF*
*Patricia Lewsley, *SDLP*
*Billy Bell, *UUP*
Ivan Davis, *Ind.*
*Norah Beare, *UUP*
Jim Kirkpatrick, *UUP*
Joanne Johnston, *C.*
Andrew Park, *PUP*
Frances McCarthy, *WP*
†elected as UUP candidate, became a member of the DUP
    with effect from 15 January 2004

LONDONDERRY EAST
E. 56,203, T. 61.75%
Total Valid Poll: 34,273
Quota: 4,897
*Gregory Campbell, *DUP*
*David McClarty, *UUP*
*Francis Brolly, *SF*
*George Robinson, *DUP*
*John Dallat, *SDLP*
Maurice Bradley, *DUP*
Michael Coyle, *SDLP*
*Norman Hillis, *UUP*
Cliona O'Kane, *SF*
Boyd Douglas, *UUC*
Edwin Stevenson, *UUP*
Pauline Armitage, *UKUP*
Yvonne Boyle, *All.*
Marion Baur, *SEA*

NEWRY AND ARMAGH
E. 68,731, T. 70.18%
Total Valid Poll: 47,378
Quota: 6,769
* Paul Berry, *DUP*
* Conor Murphy, *SF*
* Danny Kennedy, *UUP*
* Davy Hyland, *SF*
* Patricia O'Rawe, *SF*
Jim Lennon, *SDLP*
* Dominic Bradley, *SDLP*
John Fee, *SDLP*
William Frazer, *Ind.*
Freda Donnelly, *DUP*
Peter Whitcroft, *All.*

STRANGFORD
E. 66,308, T. 57.06%
Total Valid Poll: 37,250
Quota: 5,322
*Iris Robinson, *DUP*
*Lord Kilclooney, *UUP*
*Jim Shannon, *DUP*
*George Ennis, *DUP*
*David McNarry, *UUP*
Joe Boyle, *SDLP*
*Kieran McCarthy, *All.*
Bob Little, *UUP*
Dermot Kennedy, *SF*
Cedric Wilson, *NIUP*
Colin Neill, *PUP*
Philip Orr, *Green*
Danny McCarthy, *Ind.*

TYRONE WEST
E. 57,795, T. 73.24%
Total Valid Poll: 41,729
Quota: 5,962
*Dr Kieran Deeny, *Ind.*
*Pat Doherty, *SF*
*Barry McElduff, *SF*
*Thomas Buchanan, *DUP*
Brian McMahon, *SF*
*Derek Hussey, *UUP*
*Eugene McMenamin, *SDLP*
Joe Byrne, *SDLP*
Derek Reaney, *DUP*
Bert Wilson, *UUP*
Roy Reid, *PUP*
Steven Alexander, *All.*

ULSTER MID
E. 60,095, T. 74.92%
Total Valid Poll: 44,362
Quota: 6,338
*Revd Dr William McCrea, *DUP*
*Martin McGuinness, *SF*
*Geraldine Dougan, *SF*
*Francie Molloy, *SF*
*Billy Armstrong, *UUP*
*Patsy McGlone, *SDLP*
Dennis Haughey, *SDLP*
Trevor Wilson, *UUP*
Alan Miller, *DUP*
Cora Groogan, *SF*
Francis Donnelly, *WP*
James Holmes, *All.*

UPPER BANN
E. 68,814, T. 64.15%
Total Valid Poll: 43,482
Quota: 6,212
*David Trimble, *UUP*
*David Simpson, *DUP*
*John O'Dowd, *SF*
*Stephen Moutray, *DUP*
Dara O'Hagan, *SF*
*Dolores Kelly, *SDLP*
Kieran Corr, *SDLP*
*Samuel Gardiner, *UUP*
Denis Watson, *DUP*
George Savage, *UUP*
David Jones, *Ind.*
Sidney Anderson, *Ind.*
Francis McQuaid, *All.*
Tom French, *WP*

SCOTLAND

SCOTTISH PARLIAMENT

Edinburgh EH99 1SP
T 0131-348 5000/0845-278 1999 F 0131-348 5601
Textphone 0131-348 5415/0845-270 0152
E sp.info@scottish.parliament.uk
W www.scottish.parliament.uk

In July 1997 the Government announced plans to establish a Scottish Parliament. In a referendum on 11 September 1997 about 60 per cent of the electorate voted. Of those who voted, 74.3 per cent voted in favour of the Parliament and 63.5 in favour of its having tax-raising powers. Elections are to be held every four years. The first elections were held on 6 May 1999 when about 59 per cent of the electorate voted. The first meeting was held on 12 May 1999 and the Scottish Parliament was officially opened on 1 July 1999 at the Assembly Hall, Edinburgh. A new building to house Parliament opened at Holyrood on 7 September 2004. On 1 May 2003 the second elections to the Scottish Parliament took place.

The Scottish Parliament has 129 members (including the Presiding Officer), comprising 73 constituency members and 56 additional regional members mainly from party lists. It can introduce primary legislation and has the power to raise or lower the basic rate of income tax by up to three pence in the pound.

The areas for which the Scottish Parliament is responsible include: education, health, law, environment, economic development, local government, housing, police, fire services, planning, financial assistance to industry, tourism, some transport, heritage and the arts, agriculture, forestry and food standards.

SALARIES *as at 1 April 2004*

First Minister	£72,862*
Ministers	£37,798*
Lord Advocate	£49,382*
Solicitor-General for Scotland	£35,707*
Junior Ministers	£23,675*
MSPs	£50,300†
Presiding Officer	£37,798*
Deputy Presiding Officers	£23,675*

* In addition to the MSP salary
† Reduced by two-thirds if the member is already an MP or an MEP

SCOTTISH EXECUTIVE

St Andrew's House, Regent Road,
Edinburgh EH1 3DG
T 0845-774 1741 Enquiry Line 0131-556 8400
E ceu@scotland.gov.uk
W www.scotland.gov.uk

The Scottish Executive is the devolved government for Scotland. It is responsible for most of the issues of day-to-day concern to the people of Scotland, including health, education, justice, rural affairs and transport, and manages an annual budget of around £20 billion.

The Executive was established in 1999, following the first elections to the Scottish Parliament. It is a coalition between the Scottish Labour Party and the Scottish Liberal Democrats.

The Executive is led by a First Minister who is nominated by the Parliament and in turn appoints the other Scottish Ministers.

Scottish Executive civil servants are accountable to Scottish Ministers, who are themselves accountable to the Scottish Parliament.

First Minister, The Rt. Hon. Jack McConnell, MSP *(Lab.)*
Deputy First Minister and Minister for Enterprise and Lifelong Learning, The Rt. Hon. Jim Wallace, QC, MSP *(LD)*
Minister for Communities, Margaret Curran, MSP *(Lab.)*
Minister for Education and Young People, Peter Peacock, MSP *(Lab.)*
Minister for Environment and Rural Development, Ross Finnie, MSP *(LD)*
Minister for Finance and Public Services, Andy Kerr, MSP *(Lab.)*
Minister for Health and Community Care, Malcolm Chisholm, MSP *(Lab.)*
Minister for Justice, Cathy Jamieson, MSP *(Lab.)*
Minister for Parliamentary Business, Patricia Ferguson, MSP *(Lab.)*
Minister for Tourism, Culture and Sport, Frank McAveety, MSP *(Lab.)*
Minister for Transport, Nicol Stephen, MSP *(LD)*
Lord Advocate, The Rt. Hon. Colin Boyd, QC

JUNIOR MINISTERS (NOT MEMBERS OF THE SCOTTISH EXECUTIVE)
Deputy Minister for Communities, Mary Mulligan, MSP *(Lab.)*
Deputy Minister for Education and Young People, Euan Robson, MSP *(LD)*
Deputy Minister for Enterprise, and Lifelong Learning, Lewis Macdonald, MSP *(Lab.)*
Deputy Minister for Environment and Rural Development, Allan Wilson, MSP *(Lab.)*
Deputy Minister for Finance and Parliamentary Business, Tavish Scott, MSP *(LD)*
Deputy Minister for Health and Community Care, Tom McCabe, MSP *(Lab.)*
Deputy Minister for Justice, Hugh Henry, MSP *(Lab.)*
Solicitor-General for Scotland, Elish Angiolini, QC

CHANGE AND CORPORATE SERVICES
Saughton House, Broomhouse Drive, Edinburgh EH11 3XD
T 0845-774 1741
Director of Change and Corporate Services, vacant

FINANCE AND CENTRAL SERVICES
DEPARTMENT (FCSD)
Victoria Quay, Edinburgh EH6 6QQ
T 0845-774 1741/0131-556 8400
Acting Head of Department, Dr A. Goudie

EXECUTIVE AGENCY
Scottish Public Pensions Agency

ENVIRONMENT AND RURAL AFFAIRS
DEPARTMENT
Pentland House, 47 Robb's Loan, Edinburgh EH14 1TY
T 0845-774 1741/0131-556 8400 F 0131 244 6116
Head of Department, J. S. Graham

EXECUTIVE AGENCIES
Animal Health Veterinary Unit
Fisheries Research Services
Scottish Agricultural Science Agency
Scottish Fisheries Protection Agency

DEVELOPMENT DEPARTMENT
Victoria Quay, Edinburgh EH6 6QQ
T 0131-244 0763
Head of Department, Mrs Nicola Munro

EXECUTIVE AGENCY
Communities Scotland

EDUCATION DEPARTMENT
Victoria Quay, Edinburgh EH6 6QQ
T 0845-774 1741/0131-556 8400
Head of Department, M. Ewart

EXECUTIVE AGENCIES
Historic Scotland
HM Inspectorate of Education

ENTERPRISE, TRANSPORT AND LIFELONG
LEARNING DEPARTMENT
Meridian Court, Cadogan Street, Glasgow G2 7AB
T 0131-556 8400 F 0131-244 8240
Head of Department, E. W. Frizzell, CB

EXECUTIVE AGENCY
Student Awards Agency for Scotland

HEALTH DEPARTMENT
St Andrew's House, Edinburgh EH1 3DG
T 0131-244 2440
Chief Executive, T. Jones

JUSTICE DEPARTMENT
St Andrew's House, Regent Road, Edinburgh EH1 3DG
T 0131-244 2120 F 0131-244 2121
Head of Department, J. D. Gallagher

EXECUTIVE AGENCIES
Accountant in Bankruptcy
General Register Office for Scotland
Registers of Scotland
Scottish Court Service
Scottish Prison Service

LEGAL AND PARLIAMENTARY SERVICES
25 Chambers Street, Edinburgh EH1 1LA
T 0845-774 1741 F 0131-225 7473
Head of Department, Robert Gordon

OFFICE OF THE PERMANENT SECRETARY
St Andrew's House, Regent Road, Edinburgh EH1 3DG
T 0131-244 2120 F 0131-244 2121
Head of Department, John Elvidge

MEMBERS OF THE SCOTTISH PARLIAMENT *as at*
August 2004
*Adam, Brian, *SNP, Glasgow, Aberdeen North*, Maj. 457
*Aitken, Bill, *C., Glasgow region*
*Alexander, Wendy, *Lab., Paisley North*, Maj. 4,310
*Baillie, Jackie, *Lab., Dumbarton*, Maj. 6,612
Baird, Shiona, *Green, North East Scotland region*
Baker, Richard, *Lab., North East Scotland region*
Ballance, Chris, *Green, South of Scotland region*
Ballard, Mark, *Green, Lothians region*
*Barrie, Scott, *Lab., Dunfermline West*, Maj. 4,080
*Boyack, Sarah, *Lab., Edinburgh Central*, Maj. 2,666
*Brankin, Rhona, *Lab. Co-op, Midlothian*, Maj. 5,542
Brocklebank, Ted, *C., Mid Scotland and Fife region*
*Brown, Robert E., *LD, Glasgow region*

*Butler, Bill, *Lab., Glasgow Anniesland*, Maj. 6,253
Byrne, Rosemary, *SSP, South of Scotland region*
*Canavan, Dennis, *Ind., Falkirk West*, Maj. 10,000
*Chisholm, Malcolm, *Lab., Edinburgh North and Leith*,
   Maj. 5,414
*Craigie, Cathie, *Lab., Cumbernauld and Kilsyth*, Maj. 520
*Crawford, Bruce, *SNP, Mid Scotland and Fife region*
*Cunningham, Roseanna, *SNP, Perth*, Maj. 727
Curran, Frances, *SSP, West of Scotland region*
*Curran, Margaret, *Lab., Glasgow Baillieston*, Maj. 6,178
*Davidson, David, *C., North East Scotland region*
*Deacon, Susan, *Lab., Edinburgh East and Musselburgh*,
   Maj. 6,158
*Douglas-Hamilton, James, *C., Lothians region*
*Eadie, Helen, *Lab. Co-op, Dunfermline East*, Maj. 7,290
*Ewing, Fergus, *SNP, Inverness East, Nairn and Lochaber*,
   Maj. 1,046
*Ewing, Margaret, *SNP, Moray*, Maj. 5,312
*Fabiani, Linda, *SNP, Central Scotland region*
*Ferguson, Patricia, *Lab., Glasgow Maryhill*, Maj. 5,368
*Fergusson, Alex, *C., Galloway and Upper Nithsdale*,
   Maj. 99
*Finnie, Ross, *LD, West of Scotland region*
Fox, Colin, *SSP, Lothians region*
*Fraser, Murdo, *C., Mid Scotland and Fife region*
*Gallie, Phil, *C., South of Scotland region*
Gibson, Rob, *SNP, Highlands and Islands region*
*Gillon, Karen, *Lab., Clydesdale*, Maj. 6,671
Glen, Marlyn, *Lab., North East Scotland region*
*Godman, Trish, *Lab., Renfrewshire West*, Maj. 2,492
*Goldie, Annabel, *C., West of Scotland region*
*Gorrie, Donald, *LD, Central Scotland region*
*Grahame, Christine, *SNP, South of Scotland region*
*Harper, Robin, *Green, Lothians region*
Harvie, Patrick, *Green, Glasgow region*
*Henry, Hugh, *Lab., Paisley South*, Maj. 2,453
*Home Robertson, John, *Lab., East Lothian*, Maj. 8,175
*Hughes, Janis, *Lab., Glasgow Rutherglen*, Maj. 6,303
*Hyslop, Fiona, *SNP, Lothians region*
*Ingram, Adam, *SNP, South of Scotland region*
*Jackson, Gordon, *Lab., Glasgow Govan*, Maj. 1,235
*Jackson, Dr Sylvia, *Lab., Stirling*, Maj. 2,880
*Jamieson, Cathy, *Lab. Co-op, Carrick, Cumnock and Doon
   Valley*, Maj. 7,454
*Jamieson, Margaret, *Lab., Kilmarnock and Loudoun*, Maj.
   1,210
*Johnstone, Alex, *C., North East Scotland region*
Kane, Rosie, *SSP, Glasgow region*
*Kerr, Andy, *Lab., East Kilbride*, Maj. 5,281
*Lamont, Johann, *Lab. Co-op, Glasgow Pollok*, Maj. 3,341
Leckie, Carolyn, *SSP, Central Scotland region*
*Livingstone, Marilyn, *Lab., Kirkcaldy*, Maj. 4,824
*Lochhead, Richard, *SNP, North East Scotland region*
*Lyon, George, *LD, Argyll and Bute*, Maj. 4,196
*MacAskill, Kenny, *SNP, Lothians region*
*Macdonald, Lewis, *Lab., Aberdeen Central*, Maj. 1,242
*MacDonald, Margo, *Ind., Lothians region*
*Macintosh, Kenneth, *Lab., Eastwood*, Maj. 3,702
*Maclean, Kate, *Lab., Dundee West*, Maj. 1,066
*Macmillan, Maureen, *Lab., Highlands and Islands region*
Martin, Campbell, *SNP, West of Scotland region*
*Martin, Paul, *Lab., Glasgow Springburn*, Maj. 8,007
*Marwick, Tricia, *SNP, Mid Scotland and Fife region*
Mather, Jim, *SNP, Highlands and Islands region*
*Matheson, Michael, *SNP, Central Scotland region*
Maxwell, Stewart, *SNP, West of Scotland*
May, Christine, *Lab. Co-op, Fife Central*, Maj. 2,762
*McAveety, Frank, *Lab., Glasgow Shettleston*, Maj. 6,347

*McCabe, Tom, *Lab., Hamilton South*, Maj. 4,824
*McConnell, Jack, *Lab., Motherwell and Wishaw*, Maj. 9,259
McFee, Bruce, *SNP, West of Scotland region*
*McGrigor, Jamie, *C., Highlands and Islands region*
*McLetchie, David, *C., Edinburgh Pentlands*, Maj. 2,111
*McMahon, Michael, *Lab., Hamilton North and Bellshill*, Maj. 7,905
*McNeil, Duncan, *Lab., Greenock and Inverclyde*, Maj. 3,009
*McNeill, Pauline, *Lab., Glasgow Kelvin*, Maj. 3,289
*McNulty, Des, *Lab., Clydebank and Milngavie*, Maj. 4,534
Milne, Nanette, *C., North East Scotland region*
Mitchell, Margaret, *C., Central Scotland region*
*Monteith, Brian, *C., Mid Scotland and Fife region*
*Morgan, Alasdair, *SNP, South of Scotland region*
*Morrison, Alasdair, *Lab., Western Isles*, Maj. 720
*Muldoon, Bristow, *Lab., Livingston*, Maj. 3,670
*Mulligan, Mary, *Lab., Linlithgow*, Maj. 1,970
*Mundell, David, *C., South of Scotland region*
Munro, John F., *LD, Ross, Skye and Inverness West*, Maj. 6,848
*Murray, Dr Elaine, *Lab., Dumfries*, Maj. 1,096
*Neil, Alex, *SNP, Central Scotland region*
*Oldfather, Irene, *Lab., Cunninghame South*, Maj. 6,076
*Peacock, Peter, *Lab., Highlands and Islands region*
*Peattie, Cathy, *Lab., Falkirk East*, Maj. 6,659
Pringle, Mike, *LD, Edinburgh South*, Maj. 158
Purvis, Jeremy, *LD, Tweeddale, Ettrick and Lauderdale*, Maj. 538
*Radcliffe, Nora, *LD, Gordon*, Maj. 4,071
*Raffan, Keith, *LD, Mid Scotland and Fife region*
*Reid, George, *SNP, Ochil*, Maj. 296
*Robison, Shona, *SNP, Dundee East*, Maj. 90
*Robson, Euan, *LD, Roxburgh and Berwickshire*, Maj. 2,490
*Rumbles, Mike, *LD, Aberdeenshire West Kincardine*, Maj. 5,399
Ruskell, Mark, *Green, Mid Scotland and Fife region*
*Scanlon, Mary, *C., Highlands and Islands region*
Scott, Eleanor, *Green, Highlands and Islands region*
*Scott, John, *C., Ayr*, Maj. 1,890
*Scott, Tavish, *LD, Shetland*, Maj. 2,260
*Sheridan, Tommy, *SSP, Glasgow region*
*Smith, Elaine, *Lab., Coatbridge and Chryston*, Maj. 8,571
*Smith, Iain, *LD, Fife North East*, Maj. 5,055
*Smith, Margaret, *LD, Edinburgh West*, Maj. 5,914
*Stephen, Nicol, *LD, Aberdeen South*, Maj. 8,016
*Stevenson, Stewart, *SNP, Banff and Buchan*, Maj. 8,364
*Stone, Jamie, *LD, Caithness, Sutherland and Easter Ross*, Maj. 2,092
*Sturgeon, Nicola, *SNP, Glasgow region*
Swinburne, John, *SSCUP, Central Scotland region*
*Swinney, John, *SNP, North Tayside*, Maj. 4,503
*Tosh, Murray, *C., West of Scotland region*
Turner, Dr Jean, *Ind., Strathkelvin and Bearsden*, Maj. 38
*Wallace, Jim, *LD, Orkney*, Maj. 1,755
*Watson, Mike (Lord Watson of Invergowrie), *Lab., Glasgow Cathcart*, Maj. 5,112
*Welsh, Andrew, *SNP, Angus*, Maj. 6,687
*White, Sandra, *SNP, Glasgow region*
*Whitefield, Karen, *Lab., Airdrie and Shotts*, Maj. 8,977
*Wilson, Allan, *Lab., Cunninghame North*, Maj. 3,387
*Sitting MSP

STATE OF THE PARTIES *as at August 2004†*

	Constituency MSPs	Regional MSPs	Total
Scottish Labour Party	46	4	50
Scottish National Party	9‡	18	27‡
Scottish Conservative and Unionist Party	3	15	18
Scottish Liberal Democrats	13	4	17
Scottish Green Party	0	7	7
Scottish Socialist Party	0	6	6
Scottish Senior Citizens' Unity Party	0	1	1
Independent†	2	1	3
Total	73	56	129

† Independents are: Dennis Canavan, Margo MacDonald and Dr Jean Turner
‡ The Presiding Officer was elected as a constituency member for the SNP but has no party allegiance while in post
The Presiding Officer, George Reid, MSP
Deputy Presiding Officers, Trish Godman, MSP *(Lab.)*; Murray Tosh, MSP *(C.)*

SCOTTISH PARLIAMENT ELECTION RESULTS
1 May 2003

ABERDEEN CENTRAL
(Scotland North East Region)
E. 49,477 T. 20,964 (42.37%)

Lewis Macdonald *(Lab.)*	6,835
Richard Lochhead *(SNP)*	5,593
Eleanor Anderson *(LD)*	4,744
Alan Butler *(C.)*	2,616
Andy Cumbers, *(SSP)*	1,176

Lab. Maj. 1,242 (5.92%)
2.13% swing Lab. to SNP

ABERDEEN NORTH
(Scotland North East Region)
E. 52,898 T. 25,027 (47.31%)

Brian Adam *(SNP)*	8,381
Elaine Thomson *(Lab.)*	7,924
John Reynolds *(LD)*	5,767
Jim Gifford *(C.)*	2,311
Katrine Trolle *(SSP)*	644

SNP Maj. 457 (1.83%)
1.63% swing Lab. to SNP

ABERDEEN SOUTH
(Scotland North East Region)
E. 58,204 T. 30,124 (51.76%)

Nicol Stephen *(LD)*	13,821
Richard Baker *(Lab.)*	5,805
Ian Duncan *(C.)*	5,230
Maureen Watt *(SNP)*	4,315
Keith Farnsworth *(SSP)*	953

LD Maj. 8,016 (26.61%)
10.77% swing Lab. to LD

ABERDEENSHIRE WEST AND KINCARDINE
(Scotland North East Region)
E. 62,542 T. 31,636 (50.58%)

Mike Rumbles *(LD)*	14,553
David Davidson *(C.)*	9,154
Ian Angus *(SNP)*	4,489
Kevin Hutchens *(Lab.)*	2,727
Alan Manley *(SSP)*	713

LD Maj. 5,399 (17.07%)
5.33% swing C. to LD

AIRDRIE AND SHOTTS
(Scotland Central Region)
E. 56,680 T. 25,086 (44.26%)

Karen Whitefield *(Lab.)*	14,209
Gil Paterson *(SNP)*	5,232
Alan Melville *(C.)*	2,203
Fraser Coats *(SSP)*	2,096
Kevin Lang *(LD)*	1,346

Lab. Maj. 8,977 (35.78%)
4.37% swing SNP to Lab.

ANGUS
(Scotland North East Region)
E. 60,608 T. 29,789 (49.15%)

Andrew Welsh *(SNP)*	13,251
Alex Johnstone *(C.)*	6,564
John Denning *(Lab.)*	4,871
Dick Speirs *(LD)*	3,802
Bruce Wallace *(SSP)*	1,301

SNP Maj. 6,687 (22.45%)
1.66% swing SNP to C.

ARGYLL AND BUTE
(Highlands and Islands Region)
E. 48,330 T. 27,948 (57.83%)

George Lyon *(LD)*	9,817
David Petrie *(C.)*	5,621
Jim Mather *(SNP)*	5,485
Hugh Raven *(Lab.)*	5,107
Des Divers *(SSP)*	1,667
David Walker *(SPA)*	251

LD Maj. 4,196 (15.01%)
1.68% swing LD to C.

AYR
(Scotland South Region)
E. 55,523 T. 31,591 (56.90%)

John Scott *(C.)*	12,865
Rita Miller *(Lab.)*	10,975
James Dornan *(SNP)*	4,334
Stuart Ritchie *(LD)*	1,769
James Stewart *(SSP)*	1,648

C. Maj. 1,890 (5.98%)
3.02% swing Lab. to C.

BANFF AND BUCHAN
(Scotland North East Region)
E. 55,358 T. 26,149 (47.24%)

Stewart Stevenson *(SNP)*	13,827
Stewart Whyte *(C.)*	5,463
Ian Brotchie *(Lab.)*	2,885
Debra Storr *(LD)*	2,227
Alan Buchan *(SPA)*	907
Alice Rowan *(SSP)*	840

SNP Maj. 8,364 (31.99%)
1.80% swing SNP to C.

CAITHNESS, SUTHERLAND AND EASTER ROSS
(Highlands and Islands Region)
E. 40,462 T. 21,127 (52.21%)

Jamie Stone *(LD)*	7,742
Deirdre Steven *(Lab.)*	5,650
Rob Gibson *(SNP)*	3,692
Alan McLeod *(C.)*	2,262
Gordon Campbell *(Ind.)*	953
Frank Ward *(SSP)*	828

LD Maj. 2,092 (9.90%)
3.48% swing LD to Lab.

CARRICK, CUMNOCK AND DOON VALLEY
(Scotland South Region)
E. 65,102 T. 34,366 (52.79%)

Cathy Jamieson *(Lab. Co-op)*	16,484
Phil Gallie *(C.)*	9,030
Adam Ingram *(SNP)*	5,822
Murray Steele *(SSP)*	1,715
Caron Howden *(LD)*	1,315

Lab. Co-op Maj. 7,454 (21.69%)
3.20% swing Lab. Co-op to C.

CLYDEBANK AND MILNGAVIE
(Scotland West Region)
E. 51,327 T. 26,514 (51.66%)

Des McNulty *(Lab.)*	10,585
Jim Yuill *(SNP)*	6,051
Rod Ackland *(LD)*	3,224
Mary Leishman *(C.)*	2,885
Dawn Brennan *(SSP)*	1,902
Danny McCafferty *(Ind.)*	1,867

Lab. Maj. 4,534 (17.10%)
1.49% swing SNP to Lab.

CLYDESDALE
(Scotland South Region)
E. 63,675 T. 32,442 (50.95%)

Karen Gillon *(Lab.)*	14,800
John Brady *(SNP)*	8,129
Alastair Campbell *(C.)*	5,174
Fraser Grieve *(LD)*	2,338
Owen Meharry *(SSP)*	1,422
David Morrison *(SPA)*	579

Lab. Maj. 6,671 (20.56%)
5.30% swing SNP to Lab.

COATBRIDGE AND CHRYSTON
(Scotland Central Region)
E. 51,521 T. 23,862 (46.32%)

Elaine Smith *(Lab.)*	13,422
James Gribben *(SNP)*	4,851
Donald Reece *(C.)*	2,041
Gordon Martin *(SSP)*	1,911
Doreen Nisbet *(LD)*	1,637

Lab. Maj. 8,571 (35.92%)
0.73% swing SNP to Lab.

CUMBERNAULD AND KILSYTH
(Scotland Central Region)
E. 48,667 T. 24,404 (50.14%)

Cathie Craigie *(Lab.)*	10,146
Andrew Wilson *(SNP)*	9,626
Kenny McEwan *(SSP)*	1,823
Hugh O'Donnell *(LD)*	1,264
Margaret McCulloch *(C.)*	978
Christopher Donohue *(Ind.)*	567

Lab. Maj. 520 (2.13%)
5.89% swing Lab. to SNP

CUNNINGHAME NORTH
(Scotland West Region)
E. 55,319 *T.* 28,631 (51.76%)

Allan Wilson *(Lab.)*	11,142
Campbell Martin *(SNP)*	7,755
Peter Ramsay *(C.)*	5,542
John Boyd *(LD)*	2,333
Sean Scott *(SSP)*	1,859

Lab. Maj. 3,387 (11.83%)
1.25% swing Lab. to SNP

CUNNINGHAME SOUTH
(Scotland South Region)
E. 49,877 *T.* 22,772 (45.66%)

Irene Oldfather *(Lab.)*	11,165
Michael Russell *(SNP)*	5,089
Rosemary Byrne *(SSP)*	2,677
Andrew Brocklehurst *(C.)*	2,336
Iain Dale *(LD)*	1,505

Lab. Maj. 6,076 (26.68%)
1.78% swing SNP to Lab.

DUMBARTON
(Scotland West Region)
E. 55,575 *T.* 28,823 (51.86%)

Jackie Baillie *(Lab.)*	12,154
Iain Docherty *(SNP)*	5,542
Eric Thompson *(LD)*	4,455
Murray Tosh *(C.)*	4,178
Les Robertson *(SSP)*	2,494

Lab. Maj. 6,612 (22.94%)
4.61% swing SNP to Lab.

DUMFRIES
(Scotland South Region)
E. 61,517 *T.* 32,110 (52.20%)

Elaine Murray *(Lab.)*	12,834
David Mundell *(C.)*	11,738
Andrew Wood *(SNP)*	3,931
Clare Hamblen *(LD)*	2,394
John Dennis *(SSP)*	1,213

Lab. Maj. 1,096 (3.41%)
3.05% swing Lab. to C.

DUNDEE EAST
(Scotland North East Region)
E. 53,876 *T.* 26,348 (48.90%)

Shona Robison *(SNP)*	10,428
John McAllion *(Lab.)*	10,338
Edward Prince *(C.)*	3,133
Clive Sneddon *(LD)*	1,584
James Gourlay *(Ind.)*	865

SNP Maj. 90 (0.34%)
4.68% swing Lab. to SNP

DUNDEE WEST
(Scotland North East Region)
E. 51,387 *T.* 25,003 (48.66%)

Kate McLean *(Lab.)*	8,234
Irene McGugan *(SNP)*	7,168
Ian Borthwick *(Ind.)*	4,715
Shona Ferrier *(LD)*	1,878
Jim McFarland *(SSP)*	1,501
Victoria Roberts *(C.)*	1,376
Morag MacLachlan *(SPA)*	131

Lab. Maj. 1,066 (4.26%)
1.92% swing SNP to Lab.

DUNFERMLINE EAST
(Scotland Mid and Fife Region)
E. 51,220 *T.* 23,154 (45.20%)

Helen Eadie *(Lab. Co-op)*	11,552
Janet Law *(SNP)*	4,262
Stuart Randall *(C.)*	2,485
Brian Stewart *(Local Hospital)*	1,890
Linda Graham *(SSP)*	1,537
Rodger Spillane *(LD)*	1,428

Lab. Co-op Maj. 7,290 (31.48%)
1.08% swing SNP to Lab. Co-op

DUNFERMLINE WEST
(Scotland Mid and Fife Region)
E. 53,915 *T.* 25,240 (46.81%)

Scott Barrie *(Lab.)*	8,664
David Wishart *(Local Hospital)*	4,584
Brian Goodall *(SNP)*	4,392
Jim Tolson *(LD)*	3,636
Jim Mackie *(C.)*	1,868
Andy Jackson *(SSP)*	923
Alastair Harper *(Ind.)*	714
Damien Quigg *(Ind. Q)*	459

Lab. Maj. 4,080 (16.16%)

EAST KILBRIDE
(Scotland Central Region)
E. 65,472 *T.* 34,087 (52.06%)

Andy Kerr *(Lab.)*	13,825
Linda Fabiani *(SNP)*	8,544
Grace Campbell *(C.)*	3,785
Carolyn Leckie *(SSP)*	2,736
Colin McCartney *(Ind.)*	2,597
Alex Mackie *(LD)*	2,181
John Houston *(Ind. Houston)*	419

Lab. Maj. 5,281 (15.49%)
0.08% swing Lab. to SNP

EAST LOTHIAN
(Scotland South Region)
E. 59,227 *T.* 31,204 (52.69%)

John Home Robertson *(Lab.)*	13,683
Judy Hayman *(LD)*	5,508
Stewart Thomson *(C.)*	5,459
Tom Roberts *(SNP)*	5,174
Hugh Kerr *(SSP)*	1,380

Lab. Maj. 8,175 (26.20%)
6.95% swing Lab. to LD

EASTWOOD
(Scotland West Region)
E. 67,051 *T.* 38,889 (58.00%)

Ken Macintosh *(Lab.)*	13,946
Jackson Carlaw *(C.)*	10,244
Allan Steele *(LD)*	5,056
Stewart Maxwell *(SNP)*	4,736
Margaret Hinds *(Local Health)*	3,163
Steve Oram *(SSP)*	1,504
Martyn Greene *(SPA)*	240

Lab. Maj. 3,702 (9.52%)
2.42% swing C. to Lab.

EDINBURGH CENTRAL
(Lothians Region)
E. 60,824 *T.* 28,014 (46.06%)

Sarah Boyack *(Lab.)*	9,066
Andy Myles *(LD)*	6,400
Kevin Pringle *(SNP)*	4,965
Peter Finnie *(C.)*	4,802
Catriona Grant *(SSP)*	2,552
James O'Neill *(SPA)*	229

Lab. Maj. 2,666 (9.52%)
5.98% swing Lab. to LD

EDINBURGH EAST AND MUSSELBURGH
(Lothians Region)
E. 57,704 *T.* 29,044 (50.33%)

Susan Deacon *(Lab.)*	12,655
Kenny MacAskill *(SNP)*	6,497
John Smart *(C.)*	3,863
Gary Peacock *(LD)*	3,582
Derek Durkin *(SSP)*	2,447

Lab. Maj. 6,158 (21.20%)
1.53% swing SNP to Lab.

EDINBURGH NORTH AND LEITH
(Lothians Region)
E. 60,501 *T.* 28,734 (47.49%)

Malcolm Chisholm *(Lab.)*	10,979
Anne Dana *(SNP)*	5,565
Ian Mowat *(C.)*	4,821
Sebastian Tombs *(LD)*	4,785
Bill Scott *(SSP)*	2,584

Lab. Maj. 5,414 (18.84%)
1.13% swing Lab. to SNP

EDINBURGH PENTLANDS
(Lothians Region)
E. 58,534 *T.* 33,382 (57.03%)

David McLetchie *(C.)*	12,420
Iain Gray *(Lab.)*	10,309
Ian McKee *(SNP)*	5,620
Simon Clark *(LD)*	3,943
Frank O'Donnell *(SSP)*	1,090

C. Maj. 2,111 (6.32%)
6.80% swing Lab. to C.

EDINBURGH SOUTH
(Lothians Region)
E. 60,366 *T.* 31,196 (51.68%)

Mike Pringle *(LD)*	10,005
Angus Mackay *(Lab.)*	9,847
Gordon Buchan *(C.)*	5,180
Alex Orr *(SNP)*	4,396
Shirley Gibb *(SSP)*	1,768

LD Maj. 158 (0.51%)
7.61% swing Lab. to LD

EDINBURGH WEST
(Lothians Region)
E. 60,136 *T.* 33,301 (55.38%)

Margaret Smith *(LD)*	14,434
James Douglas-Hamilton *(C.)*	8,520
Carol Fox *(Lab.)*	5,046
Alyn Smith *(SNP)*	4,133
Pat Smith *(SSP)*	993
Bruce Skivington *(SPA)*	175

LD Maj. 5,914 (17.76%)
3.37% swing C. to LD

FALKIRK EAST
(Scotland Central Region)
E. 56,175 *T.* 27,559 (49.06%)

Cathy Peattie *(Lab.)*	14,235
Keith Brown *(SNP)*	7,576
Thomas Calvert *(C.)*	2,720
Karen Utting *(LD)*	1,651
Mhairi McAlpine *(SSP)*	1,377

Lab. Maj. 6,659 (24.16%)
6.20% swing SNP to Lab.

FALKIRK WEST
(Scotland Central Region)
E. 52,122 *T.* 26,400 (50.65%)

Dennis Canavan *(Falkirk W)*	14,703
Michael Matheson *(SNP)*	4,703
Lee Whitehill *(Lab.)*	4,589
Iain Mitchell *(C.)*	1,657
Jacqueline Kelly *(LD)*	748

Falkirk W Maj. 10,000 (37.88%)
0.34% swing SNP to Falkirk W

FIFE CENTRAL
(Scotland Mid and Fife Region)
E. 57,633 *T.* 25,597 (44.41%)

Christine May *(Lab. Co-op)*	10,591
Tricia Marwick *(SNP)*	7,829
Andrew Rodger *(Ind.)*	2,258
James North *(C.)*	1,803
Elizabeth Riches *(LD)*	1,725
Morag Balfour *(SSP)*	1,391

Lab. Co-op Maj. 2,762 (10.79%)
7.81% swing Lab. Co-op to SNP

FIFE NORTH EAST
(Scotland Mid and Fife Region)
E. 58,695 *T.* 29,282 (49.89%)

Iain Smith *(LD)*	13,479
Ted Brocklebank *(C.)*	8,424
Capre Ross-Williams *(SNP)*	3,660
Gregor Poynton *(Lab.)*	2,353
Carlo Morelli *(SSP)*	1,366

LD Maj. 5,055 (17.26%)
1.59% swing C. to LD

GALLOWAY AND UPPER NITHSDALE
(Scotland South Region)
E. 51,651 *T.* 29,635 (57.38%)

Alex Fergusson *(C.)*	11,332
Alasdair Morgan *(SNP)*	11,233
Norma Hart *(Lab.)*	4,299
Neil Wallace *(LD)*	1,847
Joy Cherkaoui *(SSP)*	709
Graham Brockhouse *(SPA)*	215

C. Maj. 99 (0.33%)
4.70% swing SNP to C.

GLASGOW ANNIESLAND
(Glasgow Region)
E. 50,795 *T.* 22,165 (43.64%)

Bill Butler *(Lab. Co-op)*	10,141
Bill Kidd *(SNP)*	3,888
Bill Aitken *(C.)*	3,186
Charlie McCarthy *(SSP)*	2,620
Iain Brown *(LD)*	2,330

Lab. Co-op Maj. 6,253 (28.21%)
5.19% swing Lab. Co-op to SNP

GLASGOW BAILLIESTON
(Glasgow Region)
E. 46,346 *T.* 18,270 (39.42%)

Margaret Curran *(Lab.)*	9,657
Lachlan McNeill *(SNP)*	3,479
Jim McVicar *(SSP)*	2,461
Janette McAlpine *(C.)*	1,472
David Jackson *(LD)*	1,201

Lab. Maj. 6,178 (33.81%)
10.43% swing SNP to Lab.

GLASGOW CATHCART
(Glasgow Region)
E. 49,017 *T.* 22,307 (45.51%)

Mike Watson *(Lab.)*	8,742
David Ritchie *(SNP)*	3,630
Richard Cook *(C.)*	2,888
Malcolm Wilson *(SSP)*	2,819
Pat Lally *(Local Health)*	2,419
Tom Henery *(LD)*	1,741
Robert Wilson *(Parent Ex)*	68

Lab. Maj. 5,112 (22.92%)
1.50% swing SNP to Lab.

GLASGOW GOVAN
(Glasgow Region)
E. 48,635 *T.* 21,136 (43.46%)

Gordon Jackson *(Lab.)*	7,834
Nicola Sturgeon *(SNP)*	6,599
Jimmy Scott *(SSP)*	2,369
Faisal Butt *(C.)*	1,878
Paul Graham *(LD)*	1,807
Razaq Dean *(Ind.)*	226
John Foster *(CPPDS)*	215
Asif Nasir *(SPA)*	208

Lab. Maj. 1,235 (5.84%)
0.41% swing Lab. to SNP

GLASGOW KELVIN
(Glasgow Region)
E. 56,038 *T.* 22,080 (39.40%)

Pauline McNeill *(Lab.)*	7,880
Sandra White *(SNP)*	4,591
Douglas Herbison *(LD)*	3,334
Andy Harvey *(SSP)*	3,159
Gawain Towler *(C.)*	1,816
Alistair McConnachie *(Ind. Green)*	1,300

Lab. Maj. 3,289 (14.90%)
0.32% swing Lab. to SNP

GLASGOW MARYHILL
(Glasgow Region)
E. 49,119 *T.* 18,243 (37.14%)

Patricia Ferguson *(Lab.)*	8,997
Bill Wilson *(SNP)*	3,629
Donnie Nicolson *(SSP)*	2,945
Arthur Sanderson *(LD)*	1,785
Robert Erskine *(C.)*	887

Lab. Maj. 5,368 (29.42%)
5.31% swing SNP to Lab.

GLASGOW POLLOK
(Glasgow Region)
E. 47,134 *T.* 21,538 (45.70%)

Johann Lamont *(Lab. Co-op)*	9,357
Tommy Sheridan *(SSP)*	6,016
Kenneth Gibson *(SNP)*	4,118
Ashraf Anjum *(C.)*	1,012
Isabel Nelson *(LD)*	962
Robert Ray *(Parent Ex)*	73

Lab. Co-op Maj. 3,341 (15.51%)
3.35% swing Lab. Co-op to SSP

GLASGOW RUTHERGLEN
(Glasgow Region)
E. 49,512 *T.* 23,554 (47.57%)

Janis Hughes *(Lab.)*	10,794
Robert Brown *(LD)*	4,491
Anne McLaughlin *(SNP)*	3,511
Gavin Brown *(C.)*	2,499
Bill Bonnar *(SSP)*	2,259

Lab. Maj. 6,303 (26.76%)
0.21% swing LD to Lab.

GLASGOW SHETTLESTON
(Glasgow Region)
E. 46,730 *T.* 16,547 (35.41%)

Francis McAveety *(Lab. Co-op)*	9,365
Jim Byrne *(SNP)*	3,018
Rosie Kane *(SSP)*	2,403
Dorothy Luckhurst *(C.)*	982
Lewis Hutton *(LD)*	779

Lab. Co-op Maj. 6,347 (38.36%)
5.87% swing SNP to Lab. Co-op

GLASGOW SPRINGBURN
(Glasgow Region)
E. 49,551 *T.* 18,573 (37.48%)

Paul Martin *(Lab.)*	10,963
Frank Rankin *(SNP)*	2,956
Margaret Bean *(SSP)*	2,653
Alan Rodger *(C.)*	1,233
Charles Dundas *(LD)*	768

Lab. Maj. 8,007 (43.11%)
5.36% swing SNP to Lab.

GORDON
(Scotland North East Region)
E. 60,686 *T.* 28,798 (47.45%)

Nora Radcliffe *(LD)*	10,963
Nanette Milne *(C.)*	6,892
Alasdair Allan *(SNP)*	6,501
Ellis Thorpe *(Lab.)*	2,973
John Sangster *(SSP)*	780
Steven Mathers *(Ind.)*	689

LD Maj. 4,071 (14.14%)
1.48% swing LD to C.

GREENOCK AND INVERCLYDE
(Scotland West Region)
E. 46,045 *T.* 23,781 (51.65%)

Duncan McNeil *(Lab.)*	9,674
Ross Finnie *(LD)*	6,665
Tom Chalmers *(SNP)*	3,532
Tricia McCafferty *(SSP)*	2,338
Charles Dunlop *(C.)*	1,572

Lab. Maj. 3,009 (12.65%)
1.20% swing Lab. to LD

HAMILTON NORTH AND BELLSHILL
(Scotland Central Region)
E. 51,965 T. 24,195 (46.56%)

Michael McMahon *(Lab.)*	12,812
Alex Neil *(SNP)*	4,907
Charles Ferguson *(C.)*	2,625
Shareen Blackhall *(SSP)*	1,932
Siobhan Mathers *(LD)*	1,477
Gordon McIntosh *(SPA)*	442

Lab. Maj. 7,905 (32.67%)
7.36% swing SNP to Lab.

HAMILTON SOUTH
(Scotland Central Region)
E. 45,749 T. 20,518 (44.85%)

Tom McCabe *(Lab.)*	9,546
John Wilson *(SNP)*	4,722
Margaret Mitchell *(C.)*	2,601
Willie O'Neil *(SSP)*	1,893
John Oswald *(LD)*	1,756

Lab. Maj. 4,824 (23.51%)
2.09% swing Lab. to SNP

INVERNESS EAST, NAIRN AND LOCHABER
(Highlands and Islands Region)
E. 66,694 T. 34,795 (52.17%)

Fergus Ewing *(SNP)*	10,764
Rhoda Grant *(Lab.)*	9,718
Mary Scanlon *(C.)*	6,205
Patsy Kenton *(LD)*	5,622
Steve Arnott *(SSP)*	1,661
Thomas Lamont *(Ind.)*	825

SNP Maj. 1,046 (3.01%)
0.98% swing Lab. to SNP

KILMARNOCK AND LOUDOUN
(Scotland Central Region)
E. 61,055 T. 31,520 (51.63%)

Margaret Jamieson *(Lab.)*	12,633
Danny Coffey *(SNP)*	11,423
Robin Traquair *(C.)*	3,295
Ian Gibson *(LD)*	1,571
Colin Rutherford *(SSP)*	1,421
May Anderson *(Ind. Anderson)*	404
Matthew Donnelly *(Ind.)*	402
Lyndsay McIntosh *(SPA)*	371

Lab. Maj. 1,210 (3.84%)
1.59% swing Lab. to SNP

KIRKCALDY
(Scotland Mid and Fife Region)
E. 49,653 T. 21,939 (44.18%)

Marilyn Livingstone *(Lab. Co-op)*	10,235
Colin Welsh *(SNP)*	5,411
Alex Cole-Hamilton *(LD)*	2,417
Mike Scott-Hayward *(C.)*	2,332
Rudi Vogels *(SSP)*	1,544

Lab. Co-op Maj. 4,824 (21.99%)
3.10% swing SNP to Lab. Co-op

LINLITHGOW
(Lothians Region)
E. 54,113 T. 27,645 (51.09%)

Mary Mulligan *(Lab.)*	11,548
Fiona Hyslop *(SNP)*	9,578
Gordon Lindhurst *(C.)*	3,059
Martin Oliver *(LD)*	2,093
Steve Nimmo *(SSP)*	1,367

Lab. Maj. 1,970 (7.13%)
0.77% swing Lab. to SNP

LIVINGSTON
(Lothians Region)
E. 65,421 T. 30,557 (46.71%)

Bristow Muldoon *(Lab.)*	13,327
Peter Johnston *(SNP)*	9,657
Lindsay Paterson *(C.)*	2,848
Paul McGreal *(LD)*	2,714
Robert Richard *(SSP)*	1,640
Stephen Milburn *(SPA)*	371

Lab. Maj. 3,670 (12.01%)
0.67% swing SNP to Lab.

MIDLOTHIAN
(Lothians Region)
E. 48,319 T. 23,556 (48.75%)

Rhona Brankin *(Lab. Co-op)*	11,139
Graham Sutherland *(SNP)*	5,597
Jacqui Bell *(LD)*	2,700
Rosemary MacArthur *(C.)*	2,557
Bob Goupillot *(SSP)*	1,563

Lab. Co-op Maj. 5,542 (23.53%)
2.48% swing SNP to Lab. Co-op

MORAY
(Highlands and Islands Region)
E. 58,242 T. 26,981 (46.33%)

Margaret Ewing *(SNP)*	11,384
Tim Wood *(C.)*	6,072
Peter Peacock *(Lab.)*	5,157
Linda Gorn *(LD)*	3,283
Norma Anderson *(SSP)*	1,085

SNP Maj. 5,312 (19.69%)
3.24% swing C. to SNP

MOTHERWELL AND WISHAW
(Scotland Central Region)
E. 51,785 T. 25,388 (49.03%)

Jack McConnell *(Lab.)*	13,739
Lloyd Quinan *(SNP)*	4,480
Mark Nolan *(C.)*	2,542
John Milligan *(SSP)*	1,961
John Swinburne *(SSCUP)*	1,597
Keith Legg *(LD)*	1,069

Lab. Maj. 9,259 (36.47%)
9.92% swing SNP to Lab.

OCHIL
(Scotland Mid and Fife Region)
E. 55,596 T. 30,416 (54.71%)

George Reid *(SNP)*	11,659
Richard Simpson *(Lab.)*	11,363
Malcolm Parkin *(C.)*	2,946
Catherine Whittingham *(LD)*	2,536
Felicity Garvie *(SSP)*	1,102
Flash Gordon Approaching *(Loony)*	432
William Whyte *(ND)*	378

SNP Maj. 296 (0.97%)
2.25% swing Lab. to SNP

ORKNEY
(Highlands and Islands Region)
E. 15,487 T. 8,004 (51.68%)

Jim Wallace *(LD)*	3,659
Christopher Zawadski *(C.)*	1,904
John Mowat *(SNP)*	1,056
John Aberdein *(SSP)*	914
Richard Meade *(Lab.)*	471

LD Maj. 1,755 (21.93%)
14.93% swing LD to C.

PAISLEY NORTH
(Scotland West Region)
E. 44,999 *T.* 22,206 (49.35%)

Wendy Alexander *(Lab.)*	10,631
George Adam *(SNP)*	6,321
Allison Cook *(C.)*	1,871
Brian O'Malley *(LD)*	1,705
Sean Hurl *(SSP)*	1,678

Lab. Maj. 4,310 (19.41%)
1.39% swing SNP to Lab.

PAISLEY SOUTH
(Scotland West Region)
E. 49,818 *T.* 24,984 (50.15%)

Hugh Henry *(Lab.)*	10,190
Bill Martin *(SNP)*	7,737
Eileen McCartin *(LD)*	3,517
Mark Jones *(C.)*	1,775
Frances Curran *(SSP)*	1,765

Lab. Maj. 2,453 (9.82%)
2.42% swing Lab. to SNP

PERTH
(Scotland and Mid Fife Region)
E. 61,957 *T.* 31,614 (51.03%)

Roseanna Cunningham *(SNP)*	10,717
Alexander Stewart *(C.)*	9,990
Robert Ball *(Lab.)*	5,629
Gordon Campbell *(LD)*	3,530
Philip Stott *(SSP)*	982
Thomas Burns *(Ind.)*	509
Ken Buchanan *(SPA)*	257

SNP Maj. 727 (2.30%)
1.56% swing SNP to C.

RENFREWSHIRE WEST
(Scotland West Region)
E. 50,963 *T.* 28,302 (55.53%)

Trish Godman *(Lab.)*	9,671
Bruce McFee *(SNP)*	7,179
Annabel Goldie *(C.)*	6,867
Alison King *(LD)*	2,902
Gerry MaCartney *(SSP)*	1,683

Lab. Maj. 2,492 (8.81%)
0.15% swing SNP to Lab.

ROSS, SKYE AND INVERNESS WEST
(Highlands and Islands Region)
E. 55,777 *T.* 28,971 (51.94%)

John Farquhar Munro *(LD)*	12,495
David Thompson *(SNP)*	5,647
Maureen MacMillan *(Lab.)*	5,464
Jamie McGrigor *(C.)*	3,772
Anne McLeod *(SSP)*	1,593

LD Maj. 6,848 (23.64%)
6.66% swing SNP to LD

ROXBURGH AND BERWICKSHIRE
(Scotland South Region)
E. 45,625 *T.* 22,511 (49.34%)

Euan Robson *(LD)*	9,280
Sandy Scott *(C.)*	6,790
Roderick Campbell *(SNP)*	2,816
Sam Held *(Lab.)*	2,802
Graeme McIver *(SSP)*	823

LD Maj. 2,490 (11.06%)
0.90% swing LD to C.

SHETLAND
(Highlands and Islands Region)
E. 16,677 *T.* 8,645 (51.84%)

Tavish Scott *(LD)*	3,989
Willie Ross *(SNP)*	1,729
John Firth *(C.)*	1,281
Peter Hamilton *(Lab.)*	880
Peter Andrews *(SSP)*	766

LD Maj. 2,260 (26.14%)
7.00% swing LD to SNP

STIRLING
(Scotland and Mid Fife Region)
E. 52,087 *T.* 29,647 (56.92%)

Sylvia Jackson *(Lab.)*	10,661
Brian Monteith *(C.)*	7,781
Bruce Crawford *(SNP)*	5,645
Kenyon Wright *(LD)*	3,432
Margaret Stewart *(SSP)*	1,486
Keith Harding *(SPA)*	642

Lab. Maj. 2,880 (9.71%)
1.25% swing Lab. to C.

STRATHKELVIN AND BEARSDEN
(Scotland West Region)
E. 61,905 *T.* 35,736 (57.73%)

Jean Turner *(Ind.)*	10,988
Brian Fitzpatrick *(Lab.)*	10,950
Jo Swinson *(LD)*	4,950
Fiona McLeod *(SNP)*	4,846
Rory O'Brien *(C.)*	4,002

Ind. Maj. 38 (0.11%)

TAYSIDE NORTH
(Scotland Mid and Fife Region)
E. 62,697 *T.* 33,343 (53.18%)

John Swinney *(SNP)*	14,969
Murdo Fraser *(C.)*	10,466
Gordon MacRae *(Lab.)*	3,527
Bob Forrest *(LD)*	3,206
Rosie Adams *(SSP)*	941
George Ashe *(SPA)*	234

SNP Maj. 4,503 (13.51%)
1.24% swing C. to SNP

TWEEDDALE, ETTRICK AND LAUDERDALE
(Scotland South Region)
E. 50,912 *T.* 26,700 (52.44%)

Jeremy Purvis *(LD)*	7,197
Christine Grahame *(SNP)*	6,659
Catherine Maxwell Stuart *(Lab.)*	5,757
Derek Brownlee *(C.)*	5,686
Norman Lockhart *(SSP)*	1,055
Alex Black *(SPA)*	346

LD Maj. 538 (2.01%)
5.63% swing LD to SNP

WESTERN ISLES
(Highlands and Islands Region)
E. 21,205 *T.* 12,387 (58.42%)

Alasdair Morrison *(Lab.)*	5,825
Alasdair Nicholson *(SNP)*	5,105
Frank Warren *(C.)*	612
Conor Snowden *(LD)*	498
Joanne Telfer *(SSP)*	347

Lab. Maj. 720 (5.81%)
4.59% swing Lab. to SNP

REGIONS

GLASGOW
E. 492,877 T. 39.42%

Lab.	77,040	(39.65%)
SNP	34,894	(17.96%)
SSP	31,116	(16.02%)
C.	15,299	(7.87%)
LD	14,839	(7.64%)
Green	14,570	(7.50%)
SSCUP	4,750	(2.44%)
Soc. Lab.	3,091	(1.59%)
ProLife	2,477	(1.27%)
SUP	2,349	(1.21%)
BNP	2,344	(1.21%)
SPA	612	(0.32%)
UK Ind.	552	(0.28%)
CPPDS	345	(0.18%)
Lab. majority	42,146	(21.69%)

1.64% swing SNP to Lab.

ADDITIONAL MEMBERS

Bill Aitken	(C.)
Robert Brown	(LD)
Ms Sandra White	(SNP)
Ms Nicola Sturgeon	(SNP)
Patrick Harvie	(Green)
Tommy Sheridan	(SSP)
Ms Rosie Kane	(SSP)

HIGHLANDS AND ISLANDS
E. 322,874 T. 52.22%

SNP	39,497	(23.43%)
Lab.	37,605	(22.30%)
LD	31,655	(18.78%)
C.	26,989	(16.01%)
Green	13,935	(8.27%)
SSP	9,000	(5.34%)
UK Ind.	1,947	(1.15%)
SASSDR	1,822	(1.08%)
CPFRI	1,768	(1.05%)
Soc. Lab.	1,617	(0.96%)
PRSP	1,438	(0.85%)
SPA	793	(0.47%)
Ind.	353	(0.21%)
Rural	177	(0.10%)
SNP majority	1,892	(1.12%)

0.57% swing SNP to Lab.

ADDITIONAL MEMBERS

Jamie McGrigor	(C.)
Mrs Mary Scanlon	(C.)
Peter Peacock	(Lab.)
Ms Maureen MacMillan	(Lab.)
Jim Mather	(SNP)
Rob Gibson	(SNP)
Ms Eleanor Scott	(Green)

LOTHIANS
E. 525,918 T. 50.52%

Lab.	65,102	(24.50%)
SNP	43,142	(16.24%)
C.	40,173	(15.12%)
Green	31,908	(12.01%)
LD	29,237	(11.01%)
Ind.	27,144	(10.22%)
SSP	14,448	(5.44%)
PP	5,609	(2.11%)
Lib	2,573	(0.97%)
Soc. Lab.	2,181	(0.82%)
UK Ind.	1,057	(0.40%)
Witchery	964	(0.36%)
SPA	879	(0.33%)
ProLife	608	(0.23%)
Ind. C.	383	(0.14%)
Ind. A.	184	(0.07%)
Ind. Gatensbury	78	(0.03%)
Lab. majority	21,960	(8.27%)

1.89% swing SNP to Lab.

ADDITIONAL MEMBERS

Lord James Douglas-Hamilton	(C.)
Kenny MacAskill	(SNP)
Ms Fiona Hyslop	(SNP)
Robin Harper	(Green)
Mark Ballard	(Green)
Ms Margo MacDonald	(Ind.)
Colin Fox	(SSP)

SCOTLAND CENTRAL
E. 541,191 T. 48.61%

Lab.	106,318	(40.41%)
SNP	59,274	(22.53%)
C.	24,121	(9.17%)
SSP	19,016	(7.23%)
SSCUP	17,146	(6.52%)
LD	15,494	(5.89%)
Green	12,248	(4.66%)
Soc. Lab.	3,855	(1.47%)
SUP	2,147	(0.82%)
Ind.	1,265	(0.48%)
SPA	1,192	(0.45%)
UK Ind.	1,009	(0.38%)
Lab. majority	47,044	(17.88%)

3.19% swing SNP to Lab.

ADDITIONAL MEMBERS

Mrs Margaret Mitchell	(C.)
Donald Gorrie	(LD)
Alex Neil	(SNP)
Michael Matheson	(SNP)
Ms Linda Fabiani	(SNP)
John Swinburne	(SSCUP)
Ms Carolyn Leckie	(SSP)

SCOTLAND MID AND FIFE
E. 503,453 T. 49.68%

Lab.	63,239	(25.29%)
SNP	57,631	(23.04%)
C.	43,941	(17.57%)
LD	30,112	(12.04%)
Green	17,147	(6.86%)
SSP	11,401	(4.56%)
PP	8,380	(3.35%)
FHC	5,064	(2.02%)
SLH	4,662	(1.86%)
UK Ind.	2,355	(0.94%)
Soc. Lab.	2,273	(0.91%)
SPA	1,191	(0.48%)
Christian	1,064	(0.43%)
Ind. Gray	996	(0.40%)
Ind.	637	(0.25%)
Lab. majority	5,608	(2.24%)

1.22% swing Lab. to SNP

ADDITIONAL MEMBERS

Murdo Fraser	(C.)
Brian Monteith	(C.)
Ted Brocklebank	(C.)
Keith Raffan	(LD)
Bruce Crawford	(SNP)
Ms Tricia Marwick	(SNP)
Mark Ruskell	(Green)

SCOTLAND NORTH EAST
E. 505,036 T. 48.25%

SNP	66,463	(27.28%)
Lab.	49,189	(20.19%)
LD	45,831	(18.81%)
C.	42,318	(17.37%)
Green	12,724	(5.22%)
SSP	10,226	(4.20%)
PP	5,584	(2.29%)
Fishing	5,566	(2.28%)
Soc. Lab.	2,431	(1.00%)
UK Ind.	1,498	(0.61%)
SPA	941	(0.39%)
Ind.	902	(0.37%)
SNP majority	17,274	(7.09%)

0.10% swing Lab. to SNP

ADDITIONAL MEMBERS

David Davidson	(C.)
Alex Johnstone	(C.)
Mrs Nanette Milne	(C.)
Ms Marlyn Glen	(Lab.)
Richard Baker	(Lab.)
Richard Lochhead	(SNP)
Ms Shiona Baird	(Green)

SCOTLAND SOUTH
E. 503,109 T. 52.33%

Lab.	78,955	(29.99%)
C.	63,827	(24.24%)
SNP	48,371	(18.37%)
LD	27,026	(10.26%)
Green	15,062	(5.72%)
SSP	14,228	(5.40%)
PP	9,082	(3.45%)
Soc. Lab.	3,054	(1.16%)
UK Ind.	1,889	(0.72%)
SPA	1,436	(0.55%)
Rural	355	(0.13%)
Lab. majority	15,128	(5.75%)

1.83% swing Lab. to C.

ADDITIONAL MEMBERS

Phil Gallie	(C.)
David Mundell	(C.)
Ms Christine Grahame	(SNP)
Alasdair Morgan	(SNP)
Adam Ingram	(SNP)
Chris Ballance	(Green)
Ms Rosemary Byrne	(SSP)

SCOTLAND WEST
E. 483,002 T. 61.53%

Lab.	83,931	(28.24%)
LD	71,580	(24.09%)
SNP	50,387	(16.96%)
C.	40,261	(13.55%)
SSP	18,591	(6.26%)
Green	14,544	(4.89%)
SSCUP	7,100	(2.39%)
ProLife	3,674	(1.24%)
Soc. Lab.	3,155	(1.06%)
UK Ind.	1,662	(0.56%)
SUP	1,617	(0.54%)
SPA	674	(0.23%)
Lab. majority	12,351	(4.16%)

11.70% swing Lab. to LD

ADDITIONAL MEMBERS

Miss Annabel Goldie	(C.)
Murray Tosh	(C.)
Ross Finnie	(LD)
Campbell Martin	(SNP)
Bruce McFee	(SNP)
Stewart Maxwell	(SNP)
Ms Frances Curran	(SSP)

LOCAL GOVERNMENT

Major changes in local government were introduced in England and Wales in 1974 and in Scotland in 1975 by the Local Government Act 1972 and the Local Government (Scotland) Act 1973. Further significant alterations were made in England by the Local Government Acts of 1985, 1992 and 2000.

The structure in England was based on two tiers of local authorities (county councils and district councils) in the non-metropolitan areas; and a single tier of metropolitan councils in the six metropolitan areas of England and London borough councils in London.

Following reviews of the structure of local government in England by the Local Government Commission, 46 unitary (all-purpose) authorities were created between April 1995 and April 1998 to cover certain areas in the non-metropolitan counties. The remaining county areas continue to have two tiers of local authorities. The county and district councils in the Isle of Wight were replaced by a single unitary authority on 1 April 1995; the former counties of Avon, Cleveland, Humberside and Berkshire have been replaced by unitary authorities; and Hereford and Worcester was replaced by a new county council for Worcestershire (with district councils) and a unitary authority for Herefordshire.

The Local Government (Wales) Act 1994 and the Local Government etc. (Scotland) Act 1994 abolished the two-tier structure in Wales and Scotland with effect from 1 April 1996, replacing it with a single tier of unitary authorities.

ELECTIONS

Local elections are normally held on the first Thursday in May, although in 2004 they were held on the 10 June to coincide with the European Parliament elections. Generally, all British subjects, citizens of the Republic of Ireland, Commonwealth and other European Union citizens who are 18 years or over and resident on the qualifying date in the area for which the election is being held, are entitled to vote at local government elections. A register of electors is prepared and published annually by local electoral registration officers.

A returning officer has the overall responsibility for an election. Voting takes place at polling stations, arranged by the local authority and under the supervision of a presiding officer specially appointed for the purpose. Candidates, who are subject to various statutory qualifications and disqualifications designed to ensure that they are suitable persons to hold office, must be nominated by electors for the electoral area concerned.

In England, the Boundary Commission for England is responsible for carrying out periodic reviews of electoral arrangements and making recommendations to the Electoral Commission. Following the Deputy Prime Minister's announcement on 16 June 2003 that referendums would be held on the establishment of three elected regional assemblies in the North East, North West and Yorkshire and the Humber, the Boundary Committee for England commenced a major review of local government structure in these areas. Final recommendations were submitted to the Deputy Prime Minister on 25 May 2004 and provide for a minimum of two different options for the establishment of unitary authorities in each county area. A referendum in the North East region was set to be held on 4 November 2004.

In Wales and Scotland these matters are the responsibility of the Local Government Boundary Commission for Wales and the Boundary Commission for Scotland respectively. The Local Government Act 2000 provided for the Secretary of State to change the frequency and phasing of elections. *See* Public Offices section.

INTERNAL ORGANISATION

The council as a whole is the final decision-making body within any authority. Councils are free to a great extent to make their own internal organisational arrangements. The Local Government Act, given Royal assent on 28 July 2000, allows councils to adopt one of three broad categories of a new constitution which include a separate executive.

These three categories are:
– A directly elected mayor with a cabinet selected by that mayor
– A cabinet, either elected by the council or appointed by its leader
– A directly elected mayor and council manager

Normally, questions of policy are settled by the full council, while the administration of the various services is the responsibility of committees of councillors. Day-to-day decisions are delegated to the council's officers, who act within the policies laid down by the councillors.

FINANCE

Local government in England, Wales and Scotland is financed from four sources: the council tax, non-domestic rates, government grants, and income from fees and charges for services.

COUNCIL TAX
Under the Local Government Finance Act 1992, from 1 April 1993 the council tax replaced the community charge (which had been introduced in April 1989 in Scotland and April 1990 in England and Wales in place of domestic rates).

The council tax is a local tax levied by each local council. Liability for the council tax bill usually falls on the owner-occupier or tenant of a dwelling which is their sole or main residence. Council tax bills may be reduced because of the personal circumstances of people resident in a property, and there are discounts in the case of dwellings occupied by fewer than two adults.

In England, each county council, each district council and each police authority sets its own council tax rate. The district councils collect the combined council tax, and the county councils and police authorities claim their share from the district councils' collection funds. In Wales, each unitary authority and each police authority sets its own council tax rate. The unitary authorities collect the combined council tax and the police authorities claim their share from the funds. In Scotland, each local authority sets its own rate of council tax.

The tax relates to the value of the dwelling. Each dwelling is placed in one of eight valuation bands, ranging from A to H, based on the property's estimated market value as at 1 April 1991. Wales is currently undergoing a revaluation of bands based on the estimated market value of property as at 1 April 2003. The new band structure will take effect from 1 April 2005 and will be used to calculate council tax bills in Wales for the financial year 2005–6 onwards. The existing bands have been used to calculate council tax for 2004–5.

The valuation bands and ranges of values in England, Wales and Scotland are:

England

A	Up to £40,000	E	£88,001–£120,000
B	£40,001–£52,000	F	£120,001–£160,000
C	£52,001–£68,000	G	£160,001–£320,000
D	£68,001–£88,000	H	Over £320,000

Wales (up to 1 April 2005)

A	Up to £30,000	E	£66,001–£90,000
B	£30,001–£39,000	F	£90,001–£120,000
C	£39,001–£51,000	G	£120,001–£240,000
D	£51,001–£66,000	H	Over £240,000

Wales (from 1 April 2005)

A	Up to £44,000	F	£162,001–£223,000
B	£44,001–£65,000	G	£223,001–£324,000
C	£65,001–£91,000	H	£324,001–£424,000
D	£91,001–£123,000	I	Over £424,000
E	£123,001–£162,000		

Scotland

A	Up to £27,000	E	£58,001–£80,000
B	£27,001–£35,000	F	£80,001–£106,000
C	£35,001–£45,000	G	£106,001–£212,000
D	£45,001–£58,000	H	Over £212,000

The council tax within a local area varies between different bands according to proportions laid down by law. The charge attributable to each band as a proportion of the Band D charge set by the council is approximately:

A	67%	E	122%
B	78%	F	144%
C	89%	G	167%
D	100%	H	200%

The Band D rate is given in the tables on the following pages. There may be variations from the given figure within each district council area because of different parish or community precepts being levied.

NON-DOMESTIC RATES

Non-domestic (business) rates are collected by billing authorities; these are the district councils in those areas of England with two tiers of local government and unitary authorities in other parts of England, in Wales and in Scotland. In respect of England and Wales, the Local Government Finance Act 1988 provides for liability for rates to be assessed on the basis of a poundage (multiplier) tax on the rateable value of property (hereditaments). Separate multipliers are set by the Office of the Deputy Prime Minister in England, the National Assembly for Wales and the Scottish Executive, and rates are collected by the billing authority for the area where a property is located. Rate income collected by billing authorities is paid into a national non-domestic rating (NNDR) pool and redistributed to individual authorities on the basis of the adult population figure as prescribed by the Office of the Deputy Prime Minister, the National Assembly for Wales or the Scottish Executive. The rates pools are maintained separately in England, Wales and Scotland. Actual payment of rates in certain cases is subject to transitional arrangements, to phase in the larger increases and reductions in rates resulting from the effects of the latest revaluation.

Rates are levied in Scotland in accordance with the Local Government (Scotland) Act 1975. For 1995–6, the Secretary of State for Scotland prescribed a single non-domestic rates poundage to apply throughout the country at the same level as the uniform business rate (UBR) in England. Rate income is pooled and redistributed to local authorities on a per capita basis.

Rateable values for the 2005 rating lists come into effect on 1 April 2005. They are derived from the rental value of property as at 1 April 2003 and determined on certain statutory assumptions by the Valuation Office Agency in England and Wales, and by Regional Assessors in Scotland. New property which is added to the list, and significant changes to existing property, necessitate amendments to the rateable value on the same basis. Rating lists (valuation rolls in Scotland) remain in force until the next general revaluation. Such revaluations take place every five years, the next being in 2010. Certain types of property are exempt from rates, or benefit from a reduced rate.

COMPLAINTS

Local Government Ombudsmen are responsible for investigating complaints from members of the public who claim to have suffered as a consequence of maladministration in local government or in certain local bodies.

The Northern Ireland Commissioner for Complaints fulfils a similar function in Northern Ireland, investigating complaints about local authorities and certain public bodies.

Complaints are made to the relevant local authority in the first instance and complainants may approach the Ombudsmen or Commissioners if not satisfied. Complaints may also be made directly to the Ombudsmen or Commissioners.

The Local Government Act 2000 established a Standards Board and Adjudication Panel in England. The Standards Board investigates any allegations that councillors have breached the council's Code of Conduct and if there is evidence of wrongdoing the Adjudication Panel will consider the report of investigations and if it is upheld, impose a penalty. In Wales the Commission for Local Administration in Wales undertakes the role of the Standards Board.

THE QUEEN'S REPRESENTATIVES

The Lord-Lieutenant of a county is the permanent local representative of the Crown in that county. The appointment of Lords-Lieutenant is now regulated by the Lieutenancies Act 1997. They are appointed by the Sovereign on the recommendation of the Prime Minister.

The retirement age is 75. The office of Lord-Lieutenant dates from 1551, and its holder was originally responsible for the maintenance of order and for local defence in the county. The duties of the post include attending on royalty during official visits to the county, performing certain duties in connection with armed forces of the Crown (and in particular the reserve forces), and making presentations of honours and awards on behalf of the Crown. In England, Wales and Northern Ireland, the Lord-Lieutenant usually also holds the office of *Custos Rotulorum*. As such, he or she acts as head of the county's commission of the peace (which recommends the appointment of magistrates).

The office of Sheriff (from the Old English shire-reeve) of a county was created in the tenth century. The Sheriff was the special nominee of the Sovereign, and the office reached the peak of its influence under the Norman kings. The Provisions of Oxford (1258) laid down a yearly tenure of office. Since the mid-16th century the office has been purely civil, with military duties taken over by the Lord-Lieutenant of the county. The Sheriff (commonly known as 'High Sheriff') attends on royalty during official visits to the county, acts as the returning officer during parliamentary elections in county constituencies, attends the opening ceremony when a High Court judge goes on circuit, executes High Court writs, and appoints under-sheriffs to act as deputies. The appointments and duties of the High Sheriffs in England and Wales are laid down by the Sheriffs Act 1887.

The serving High Sheriff submits a list of names of possible future sheriffs to a tribunal which chooses three names to put to the Sovereign. The tribunal nominates the High Sheriff annually on 12 November and the Sovereign picks the name of the Sheriff to succeed in the following year. The term of office runs from 25 March to the following 24 March (the civil and legal year before 1752). No person may be chosen twice in three years if there is any other suitable person in the county.

CIVIC DIGNITIES

District councils in England may petition for a royal charter granting borough or 'city' status to the district. Local councils in Wales may petition for a royal charter granting county borough or 'city' status to the council.

In England and Wales the chairman of a borough or county borough council may be called a mayor, and the chairman of a city council may be called a Lord Mayor if Lord Mayoralty has been conferred on that city. Parish councils in England and community councils in Wales may call themselves 'town councils', in which case their chairman is the town mayor.

In Scotland the chairman of a local council may be known as a convenor; a provost is the equivalent of a mayor. The chairmen of the councils for the cities of Aberdeen, Dundee, Edinburgh and Glasgow are Lord Provosts.

ENGLAND

There are currently 34 counties; all are divided into districts. In addition, there are 46 unitary authorities and 238 district councils. The populations of most of the unitary authorities are in the range of 100,000 to 300,000. The district councils have populations broadly in the range of 60,000 to 100,000; some, however, have larger populations, because of the need to avoid dividing large towns, and some in mainly rural areas have smaller populations.

The main conurbations outside Greater London – Tyne and Wear, West Midlands, Merseyside, Greater Manchester, West Yorkshire and South Yorkshire – are divided into 36 metropolitan boroughs, most of which have a population of over 200,000.

There are also about 10,000 parishes, in 219 of the district councils and 18 of the metropolitan boroughs.

ELECTIONS

For districts, counties and for about 8,000 parishes, there are elected councils, consisting of directly elected councillors. The councillors elect annually one of their number as chairman.

Generally, councillors serve four years and there are no elections of district and parish councillors in county election years. In metropolitan boroughs, one-third of the councillors for each ward are elected each year except in the year when county elections take place elsewhere. District councils can choose whether to have elections by thirds or whole council elections. In the former case, one-third of the council, as nearly as may be, is elected in each year of metropolitan borough elections. If whole council elections are chosen, these are held in the year midway between county elections.

FUNCTIONS

In non-metropolitan areas, functions are divided between the districts and counties, those requiring the larger area or population are generally the responsibility of the county. The metropolitan councils, with the larger population in their areas, already had wider functions than non-metropolitan councils, and following abolition of the metropolitan county councils were also given most of their functions.

The allocation of functions is as follows:

County councils: education; strategic planning; traffic, transport and highways; fire service; consumer protection; refuse disposal; smallholdings; social services; libraries

District councils: local planning; housing; highways (maintenance of certain urban roads and off-street car parks); building regulations; environmental health; refuse collection; cemeteries and crematoria

Unitary and Metropolitan councils: their functions are all those listed above, except that the fire service is exercised by a joint body

Concurrently by county and district councils: recreation (parks, playing fields, swimming pools); museums; encouragement of the arts, tourism and industry

The Police and Magistrates Court Act 1994 set up police authorities in England and Wales separate from the local authorities.

PARISH COUNCILS

Parishes with 200 or more electors must generally have parish councils, which means that over three-quarters of the parishes have councils. A parish council comprises at least five members, the number being fixed by the district council. Elections are held every four years, at the time of the election of the district councillor for the ward including the parish. All parishes have parish meetings, comprising the electors of the parish. Where there is no council, the meeting must be held at least twice a year.

Parish council functions include: allotments; encouragement of arts and crafts; community halls, recreational facilities (e.g. open spaces, swimming pools), cemeteries and crematoria; and many minor functions. They must also be given an opportunity to comment on planning applications. They may, like county and district councils, spend limited sums for the general benefit of the parish. They levy a precept on the district councils for their funds.

FINANCE

Aggregate external finance for 2004–5 has been determined at £54,208 million. Of this, specific grants were estimated at £12,240 million; £26,964 million was in respect of Revenue Support Grant and £15,004 million was support from the national non-domestic rate pool.

In England, the average council tax per dwelling for 2004–5 is £967, an increase from £908 in 2003–4. The average council tax for 2004–5 is £1,005 in shire areas, £1,035 in London and £813 in metropolitan areas. In England, the average council tax bill for a band D dwelling (occupied by two adults) for 2004–5 is £1,167, an average increase of 5.9 per cent from 2003–4. The average band D council tax is £1,186 in shire areas, £1,119 in London and £1,143 in metropolitan areas. The assumed council tax yield for 2004–5 is £20,302 million.

The provisional amount estimated to be raised from national non-domestic rates from central and local lists is £17,400 million. The amount of national non-domestic rates to be redistributed to authorities from the pool in 2004–5 is £15,004 million. The national non-domestic rate multiplier, or poundage, for 2004–5 is 45.6p.

Under the Local Government and Housing Act 1989, local authorities have four main ways of paying for capital expenditure: borrowing and other forms of extended credit; capital grants from central government towards some types of capital expenditure; 'usable' capital receipts from the sale of land, houses and other assets; and revenue.

The amount of capital expenditure which a local authority can finance by borrowing (or other forms of credit) is effectively limited by the credit approvals issued to it by central government. Most credit approvals can be used for any kind of local authority capital expenditure; these are known as basic credit approvals. Others (supplementary credit approvals) can be used only for the kind of expenditure specified in the approval, and so are often given to fund particular projects or services.

Local authorities can use all capital receipts from the sale of property or assets for capital spending, except in the case of sales of council houses. Generally, the 'usable' part of a local authority's capital receipts consists of 25 per cent of receipts from the sale of council houses and 50 per cent of other housing assets such as shops or vacant land. The balance has to be set aside as provision for repaying debt and meeting other credit liabilities.

EXPENDITURE

Local authority budgeted net revenue expenditure for 2004–5 is:

Service	£m
Central services (including administration & emergency planning)	3,142
Education	32,509
Social Services	15,585
Police	9,739
Highways and Transport	5,367
Fire	2,025
Planning	1,532
Courts services	398
Mandatory rent allowances	6,642
Mandatory rent rebates	601
Non-housing revenue account housing	2,425
Rent rebates granted to housing revenue account tenants	2,895
Cultural services (including sport & recreation)	2,819
Environment	3,785
Other services	313
Net current expenditure	89,777
Capital financing	2,577
Capital expenditure charged to revenue account	524
Council tax benefit	2,747
Discretionary non-domestic rate relief	24
Flood defence payments to Environment Agency	28
Locally funded council tax discounts	1
Pension interest costs	57
Less interest receipts	(717)
Less specific grants outside AEF	(15,623)
Gross revenue expenditure	79,395
Less specific grants inside AEF	(12,240)
Net Revenue expenditure	67,155
Less appropriations from reserves	(589)
Less adjustments	(2)
BUDGET REQUIREMENT	66,564

AEF = aggregate external finance

LONDON

The Greater London Council was abolished in 1986 and London is divided into 32 borough councils, which have a status similar to the metropolitan borough councils in the rest of England, and the Corporation of the City of London.

In March 1998 the Government announced proposals for a Greater London Authority (GLA) covering the area of the 32 London boroughs and the City of London, which would comprise a directly elected mayor and a 25-member assembly. A referendum was held in London on 7 May 1998; the turnout was approximately 34 per cent, and 72 per cent of electors voted in favour of the GLA. The independent candidate for London Mayor, Ken Livingstone, was elected on 4 May 2000 and the Authority assumed its responsibilities on 3 July 2000. He was re-elected on 10 June 2004 as a Labour candidate.

The GLA is responsible for transport, economic development, strategic planning, culture, health, the environment, the police and fire and emergency planning. The separately elected assembly scrutinise the mayor's activities and approve plans and budgets. There are 14 Constituency Assembly members, each representing a separate area of London (each constituency is made up of two or three complete London boroughs). Eleven additional members, making up the total Assembly complement of 25 members, are elected on a London-wide basis, either as independents or from party political lists on the basis of proportional representation. Parties or independent candidates must secure at least five per cent of the vote to be entitled to additional seats.

LONDON BOROUGH COUNCILS

The London boroughs have whole council elections every four years, in the year immediately following the county council election year. The most recent elections took place on 2 May 2002.

The borough councils have responsibility for the following functions: building regulations; cemeteries and crematoria; consumer protection; education; youth employment; environmental health; electoral registration; food; drugs; housing; leisure services; libraries; local planning; local roads; museums; parking; recreation (parks, playing fields, swimming pools); refuse collection and street cleansing; social services; town planning; and traffic management.

CORPORATION OF LONDON

The Corporation of London is the local authority for the City of London. Its legal definition is 'The Mayor and Commonalty and Citizens of the City of London'. It is governed by the Court of Common Council, which consists of the Lord Mayor, 25 other aldermen, and about 100 common councilmen. The Lord Mayor and two sheriffs are nominated annually by the City guilds (the livery companies) and elected by the Court of Aldermen. Aldermen and councilmen are elected from the 25 wards into which the City is divided; councilmen must stand for re-election annually. The Council is a legislative assembly, and there are no political parties.

The Corporation has the same functions as the London borough councils. In addition, it runs the City of London Police; is the health authority for the Port of London; has health control of animal imports throughout Greater London, including at Heathrow airport; owns and manages public open spaces throughout Greater London; runs the Central Criminal Court; and runs Billingsgate, Smithfield and Spitalfields markets.

THE CITY GUILDS (LIVERY COMPANIES)

The livery companies of the City of London grew out of early medieval religious fraternities and began to emerge as trade and craft guilds, retaining their religious aspect, in the 12th century. From the early 14th century, only members of the trade and craft guilds could call themselves citizens of the City of London. The guilds began to be called livery companies, because of the distinctive livery worn by the most prosperous guild members on ceremonial occasions, in the late 15th century.

By the early 19th century the power of the companies within their trades had begun to wane, but those wearing the livery of a company continued to play an important role in the government of the City of London. Liverymen still have the right to nominate the Lord Mayor and sheriffs, and most members of the Court of Common Council are liverymen.

WALES

The Local Government (Wales) Act 1994 abolished the two-tier structure of eight county and 37 district councils which had existed since 1974, and replaced it, from 1 April 1996, with 22 unitary authorities. The new authorities were elected in May 1995. Each unitary authority has inherited all the functions of the previous county and district councils, except fire services (which are provided by three combined fire authorities, composed of representatives of the unitary authorities) and National Parks (which are the responsibility of three independent National Park Authorities).

COMMUNITY COUNCILS

In Wales community councils are the equivalent of parishes in England. Unlike England, where many areas are not in any parish, communities have been established for the whole of Wales, approximately 865 communities in all. Community meetings may be convened as and when desired.

Community councils exist in 737 communities and further councils may be established at the request of a community meeting.

FINANCE

Non-hypothecated funding for 2004–5 is £3,313.5 million. This comprises revenue support grant of £2,591 million, support from the national non-domestic rate pool of £672 million, Deprivation Grant of £20.5 million and Performance Incentive Grant of £30 million. The non-domestic rating multiplier or poundage for Wales for 2004–5 is 45.2p. The average Band D council tax levied in Wales for 2004–5 is £887, comprising unitary authorities £734, police authorities £133 and community councils £20.

EXPENDITURE

Local authority budgeted net revenue expenditure for 2004–5 is:

Service	£m
Education	2,005.1
Personal social services	1,014.5
Local Environmental services	298.6
Roads and transport	248.4
Libraries, culture, heritage, sport and recreation	161.2
Council tax benefit and administration	13.3
Non-housing revenue account housing, including housing benefit	372.8
Rent rebates granted to housing revenue account tenants	266.5
Debt financing costs	269.5
Other services	376.4
Police	548.5
Fire	126.7
Other law, order and protective services	30.1
National Parks	16.6
Gross Revenue Expenditure	5,748.0
Less specific government grants	(1,286.7)
Net revenue expenditure	4,461.4

SCOTLAND

The Local Government etc. (Scotland) Act 1994 abolished the two-tier structure of nine regional and 53 district councils which had existed since 1975 and replaced it, from 1 April 1996, with 29 unitary authorities on the mainland; the three islands councils remained. The new authorities were elected in April 1995.

In July 1999 the Scottish Parliament assumed responsibility for legislation on local government. The Government had established a Commission on Local Government and the Scottish Parliament (the McIntosh Commission) to make recommendations on the relationship between local authorities and the new Parliament and on increasing local authorities' accountability. The Commission published its reports in July 1999.

Following this report, the Scottish Executive established the 'Renewing Local Democracy' working group to consider ways in which to make council membership more attractive and councils more representative of their communities. The group would also advise on appropriate membership levels for each council, looking at modernising management practices and local concerns. They also investigated which method of election would be most appropriate, taking account of the following criteria; proportionality and the councillor-ward link, fair provision for independents, allowance for geographical diversity and a close fit between council wards and natural communities, and advise on an appropriate system of remuneration for councillors, taking account of available resources.

The Scottish Executive also set up the Leadership Advisory Panel in August 1999 following the recommendations of the McIntosh Report. The panel worked closely with Scottish local authorities helping them to conduct a self-review of their political management structures and to implement its recommendations.

The Local Government in Scotland Bill was introduced to the Scottish Parliament in May 2002. This Bill centres on three integrated core elements:
- A power for local authorities to promote and improve well-being of their area and/or persons in it
- Statutory underpinning for community planning through the introduction of a duty on local authorities and key partners, including police, health boards and enterprise agencies
- A duty to secure best value.

ELECTIONS

The unitary authorities consist of directly elected councillors. The Scottish Local Government (Elections) Act 2002 moved elections from a three-year to a four-year cycle; the last elections took place in May 2003. The 2004 register showed 3,857,997 electors in Scotland.

FUNCTIONS

The functions of the councils and islands councils are: education; social work; strategic planning; the provision of infrastructure such as roads; consumer protection; flood prevention; coast protection; valuation and rating; the police and fire services; civil defence; electoral registration; public transport; registration of births, deaths and marriages; housing; leisure and recreation; development and building control; environmental health; licensing; allotments; public conveniences; and the administration of district courts.

COMMUNITY COUNCILS

Scottish community councils differ from those in England and Wales. Their purpose as defined in statute is to ascertain and express the views of the communities they represent, and to take in the interests of their communities such action as appears to be expedient or practicable. Over 1,100 community councils have been established under schemes drawn up by local authorities in Scotland.

FINANCE

Budgeted aggregate external finance for 2004–5 is £7,669 million, comprising; £5,118 million revenue support grant, non-domestic rate income of £1,896 million and specific grants of £656 million. The non-domestic rate multiplier or poundage for 2004–5 is 48.8p. In 2003–4 a single owned property with a rateable value of £5,000 is eligible for 20 per cent small business rate relief. The average Band D council tax for 2004–5 is £1,053.

EXPENDITURE

The 2004–5 net expenditure budget estimates for local authorities in Scotland were:

Service	£m
Education	3,869.6
Cultural and related services	505.6
Social Work Services	1,867.1
Police	937.6
Roads and transport	496.9
Environmental services	441.4
Fire	248.6
Total planning and development services	146.0
Total	8,512.8

NORTHERN IRELAND

For the purpose of local government Northern Ireland has a system of 26 single-tier district councils.

ELECTIONS

Council members are elected for periods of four years at a time on the principle of proportional representation.

FUNCTIONS

The district councils have three main roles. These are:

Executive: responsibility for a wide range of local services including building regulations; community services; consumer protection; cultural facilities; environmental health; miscellaneous licensing and registration provisions, including dog control; litter prevention; recreational and social facilities; refuse collection and disposal; street cleansing; and tourist development

Representative: nominating representatives to sit as members of the various statutory bodies responsible for the administration of regional services such as drainage, education, fire, health and personal social services, housing, and libraries

Consultative: acting as the medium through which the views of local people are expressed on the operation in their area of other regional services, notably conservation (including water supply and sewerage services), planning and roads, provided by those departments of central government which have an obligation, statutory or otherwise, to consult the district councils about proposals affecting their areas

FINANCE

Local government in Northern Ireland is funded by a system of rates. The ratepayer receives a combined tax bill consisting of the Regional Rate and the District Rate, which is set by each district council. The Regional and District Rates are both collected by the Rate Collection Agency. The product of the District Rates is paid over to each council whilst the product of the Regional Rate supports expenditure by the departments of the Executive and Assembly. Rate bills are calculated by multiplying the property's Net Annual Value (NAV) by the Regional and District Rate poundages respectively. A general revaluation of non domestic properties became effective from 1 April 2003, based on 2001 rental values, however the values of domestic properties continue to be based on 1976 rental values.

For 2004–5 the overall average domestic poundage is 294.02p and the overall average non-domestic rate poundage is 43.94p.

POLITICAL COMPOSITION OF LOCAL COUNCILS

AS AT JUNE 2004

Abbreviations

All.	Alliance
BNP	British National Party
C.	Conservative
CU	Conservative and Unionist
DUP	Democratic Unionist
Green	Green
Ind.	Independent
Ind. All.	Independent Alliance
Ind. UU	Independent Unionist
IKHHC	Independent Kidderminster Hospital and Health Concern
IF	Island First
Lab.	Labour
LD	Liberal Democrat
Lib.	Liberal
NP	Non-Political/Non-Party
PC	Plaid Cymru
R.	Residents Association/Ratepayers
SD	Social Democrat
SDLP	Social Democratic and Labour Party
SF	Sinn Fein
SNP	Scottish National Party
Soc.	Socialist
Soc. Dem.	Social Democratic
SSP	Scottish Socialist Party
UKIP	UK Independence Party
UUP	Ulster Unionist Party
v.	Vacant

Total no. of seats is given in brackets after council name

ENGLAND

COUNTY COUNCILS

Bedfordshire (49)	C. 26; Lab. 13; LD 9; Ind. 1
Buckinghamshire (54)	C. 40; LD 9; Lab. 5
Cambridgeshire (59)	C. 34; LD 17; Lab. 8
Cheshire (51)	C. 28; Lab. 16; LD 6; Ind. 1
Cornwall (79)	LD 35; Ind. 25; C. 10; Lab. 9
Cumbria (84)	Lab. 38; C. 33; LD 11; Ind. 1; v. 1
Derbyshire (64)	Lab. 41; C. 13; LD 7; Other 2; Ind. 1
Devon (54)	LD 22; C. 22; Lab. 5; Ind. 5
Dorset (42)	C. 23; LD 13; Lab. 4; Ind. 1; v. 1
Durham (61)	Lab. 52; LD 4; Ind. 3; C. 2
East Sussex (44)	C. 24; LD 13; Lab. 7
Essex (79)	C. 49; Lab. 18; LD 10; Ind. 2
Gloucestershire (63)	C. 27; Lab. 19; LD 16; Ind. 1
Hampshire (74)	C. 46; LD 20; Lab. 8
Hertfordshire (77)	C. 41; Lab. 24; LD 11; Ind. 1
Kent (84)	C. 52; Lab. 22; LD 10
Lancashire (78)	Lab. 44; C. 27; LD 5; Green 1; Other 1
Leicestershire (54)	C. 29; Lab. 15; LD 10
Lincolnshire (77)	C. 48; Lab. 21; LD 4; Ind. 3; Other 1
Norfolk (84)	C. 47; Lab. 26; LD 11
North Yorkshire (74)	C. 42; LD 17; Lab. 12; Ind. 1; Other 2
Northamptonshire (73)	Lab. 39; C. 33; LD 1
Northumberland (67)	Lab. 38; C. 17; LD 9; Ind. 3
Nottinghamshire (63)	Lab. 39; C. 21; LD 3
Oxfordshire (69)	C. 24; Lab. 24; LD 20; Green 1; v. 1
Shropshire (44)	C. 19; Lab. 11; LD 8; Ind. Other 4; Ind. 2
Somerset (58)	LD 29; C. 24; Lab. 5
Staffordshire (62)	Lab. 36; C. 22; LD 4
Suffolk (80)	Lab. 33; C. 32; LD 12; Ind. 2; Other 1
Surrey (76)	C. 51; LD 13; Lab. 6; R. 4; Ind. 2
Warwickshire (62)	Lab. 27; C. 20; LD 13; Ind. 1; Other 1
West Sussex (71)	C. 41; LD 19; Lab. 11
Wiltshire (47)	C. 27; LD 13; Ind. 4; Lab. 3
Worcestershire (57)	C. 26; Lab. 14; LD 8; IKHHC 6; Lib. 2; Ind. 1

DISTRICT COUNCILS

Adur (29)	C. 24; Lab. 2; R. 2; LD 1
Allerdale (56)	Lab. 27; C. 16; LD 4; Other 6; Ind. 3
Alnwick (30)	Ind. 11; LD 10; Other 4; C. 3; Lab. 2
Amber Valley (45)	C. 24; Lab. 21
Arun (56)	C. 36; LD 11; Lab. 8; Ind. 1
Ashfield (33)	Lab. 18; Ind. 12; C. 1; Green 2
Ashford (43)	C. 25; Other 7; LD 5; Lab. 4; Ind. 2
Aylesbury Vale (59)	C. 30; LD 25; Ind. 4
Babergh (43)	LD 18; C. 11; Ind. 7; Lab. 6; Other 1
Barrow-in-Furness (38)	Lab. 24; C. 12; Ind. 2
Basildon (42)	C. 25; Lab. 14; LD 3
Basingstoke and Deane (60)	C. 28; LD 16; Lab. 12; Ind. 4
Bassetlaw (48)	C. 24; Lab. 18; Ind. 5; LD 1
Bedford (54)	C. 16; Lab. 15; LD 13; Ind. 10
Berwick-upon-Tweed (29)	C. 13; LD 8; Ind. 6; Other 2
Blaby (39)	C. 25; LD 9; Lab. 4; Ind. 1
Blyth Valley (50)	Lab. 35; LD 9; Ind. 3; C. 3
Bolsover (37)	Lab. 31; Ind. 4; R. 2
Boston (32)	C. 12; Lab. 11; Ind. 5; LD 4
Braintree (60)	C. 26; Lab. 20; Ind 7; LD 5; Green 2
Breckland (54)	C. 42; Lab. 8; Ind. 4
Brentwood (37)	C. 21; LD 13; Lab. 3
Bridgnorth (34)	C. 17; LD 8; Ind. 7; Lab. 2
Broadland (47)	C. 31; LD 11; Ind. 5
Bromsgrove (39)	C. 21; Lab. 8; Ind. 6; R. 4
Broxbourne (38)	C. 34; Lab. 2; Ind. 1; BNP 1
Broxtowe (44)	Lab. 15; C. 13; LD 13; Ind. 2; UKIP 1
Burnley (45)	Lab. 21; LD 11; BNP 6; C. 4; Ind. 3
Cambridge (42)	LD 28; Lab. 13; C. 1
Cannock Chase (41)	Lab. 17; LD 14; C. 10
Canterbury (50)	C. 24; LD 19; Lab. 7
Caradon (42)	Ind. 22; LD 14; C. 4; Lab. 1; v. 1
Carlisle (52)	Lab. 24; C. 20; LD 7; Ind. 1
Carrick (47)	LD 29; C. 11; Ind. 7

Castle Morpeth (33) — Lab. 10; C. 9; Ind. 7; LD 6; Green 1

Castle Point (41) — C. 35; R. 5; Ind. 1

Charnwood (52) — C. 24; Lab. 21; LD 7

Chelmsford (57) — C. 35; LD 20; Lab. 2

Cheltenham (40) — LD 18; C. 15; Ind. 5; Lab. 2

Cherwell (50) — C. 36; Lab. 10; LD 4

Chester (60) — LD 22; C. 20; Lab 17; Ind. 1

Chester-le-Street (32) — Lab. 27; Ind. 4; C. 1

Chesterfield (48) — LD 36; Lab. 12

Chichester (48) — C. 25; LD 21; Ind. 2

Chiltern (40) — C. 27; LD 12; R. 1

Chorley (47) — Lab. 21; C. 20; LD 3; Ind. 3

Christchurch (24) — C. 14; LD 8; Ind. 2

Colchester (60) — C. 28; LD 23; Lab. 6; Ind. 3

Congleton (48) — C. 25; LD 14; Ind. 7; Lab. 2

Copeland (51) — Lab. 30; C. 16; Ind. 4; LD 1

Corby (29) — Lab. 18; C. 9; LD 2

Cotswolds (44) — C. 26; Ind. 10; LD 8

Craven (30) — C. 13; Ind. 11; LD 6

Crawley (37) — Lab. 19; C. 16; LD 2

Crewe and Nantwich (56) — Lab. 22; C. 22; Ind. 6; LD 6

Dacorum (52) — C. 32; Lab. 14; LD 6

Dartford (44) — C. 21; Lab. 16; Other 7

Daventry (38) — C. 34; Lab. 3; LD 1

Derbyshire Dales (39) — C. 24; LD 9; Lab. 5; Ind. 1

Derwentside (55) — Lab. 38; Ind. 15; LD 1; Ind. Other 1

Dover (45) — C. 22; Lab. 20; LD 3

Durham (50) — LD 30; Lab. 17; Ind. 3

Easington (51) — Lab. 44; Ind. 5; LD 2

East Cambridgeshire (39) — LD 17; C. 15; Ind. 7

East Devon (59) — C. 35; LD 18; Ind. 6

East Dorset (36) — C. 24; LD 11; Ind. 1

East Hampshire (44) — C. 26; LD 17; v. 1

East Hertfordshire (50) — C. 41; LD 5; Ind. 4

East Lindsey (60) — Ind. 27; C. 14; Lab. 12; LD 6; Other 1

East Northamptonshire (36) — C. 33; Lab. 3

East Staffordshire (39) — C. 22; Lab. 16; LD 1

Eastbourne (27) — C. 14; LD 13

Eastleigh (44) — LD 32; C. 9; Lab. 3

Eden (38) — Ind. 27; C. 7; LD 4

Ellesmere Port and Neston (43) — Lab. 29; C. 12; LD 2

Elmbridge (60) — R. 31; C. 21; LD 8

Epping Forest (58) — C. 23; LD 15; R. 9; Lab. 4; Ind. 4; BNP 3

Epsom and Ewell (38) — R. 27; LD 6; Lab. 3; C. 2

Erewash (51) — C. 26; Lab. 19; LD 3; Ind. 2; v. 1

Exeter (40) — Lab. 19; LD 12; C. 5; Lib. 4

Fareham (31) — C. 22; LD 9

Fenland (40) — C. 35; Lab. 3; Ind. 1; v. 1

Forest Heath (27) — C. 22; Ind. 5

Forest of Dean (48) — C. 17; Lab. 16; Ind. 11; LD 4

Fylde (51) — C. 27; Ind. 11; R. 7; Ind. Other 4; LD 2

Gedling (50) — C. 21; Lab. 21; LD 7; Ind. 1

Gloucester (36) — C. 16; LD 12; Lab. 8

Gosport (34) — C. 15; Lab. 11; LD 6; Ind. 2

Gravesham (44) — Lab. 23; C. 21

Great Yarmouth (39) — C. 26; Lab. 13

Guildford (48) — C. 25; LD 20; Lab. 2; Ind. 1

Hambleton (44) — C. 36; Ind. 4; LD 3; Lab. 1

Harborough (37) — LD 18; C. 16; Ind. 2; Lab. 1

Harlow (33) — C. 13; Lab. 11; LD 9

Harrogate (54) — C. 29; LD 21; Ind. 4

Hart (35) — C. 18; LD 12; Ind. 3; R. 2

Hastings (32) — Lab 15; C. 13; LD 4

Havant (38) — C. 27; Lab 6; LD 5

Hertsmere (39) — C. 25; Lab. 7; LD 7

High Peak (43) — Lab. 18; C. 12; LD 7; Ind. 6

Hinckley and Bosworth (34) — C. 19; LD 8; Lab. 6; v. 1

Horsham (44) — C. 22; LD 19; Ind. 2; v. 1

Huntingdonshire (52) — C. 40; LD 10; Ind. 2

Hyndburn (35) — C. 20; Lab. 15

Ipswich (48) — Lab. 23; C. 18; LD 7

Kennet (43) — C. 27; Ind. 8; Other 4; LD 3; Lab. 1

Kerrier (44) — Ind. 21; LD 10; Lab. 5; C. 4; Other 4

Kettering (45) — C. 30; Lab. 13; Ind. 2

King's Lynn and West Norfolk (62) — C. 36; Lab. 14; LD 7; Ind. 5

Lancaster (60) — Lab. 20; Ind. 12; C. 11; LD 8; Green 7; Ind. Other 2

Lewes (41) — LD 27; C. 11; Ind. 3

Lichfield (56) — C. 35; Lab. 16; LD 5

Lincoln City (33) — Lab. 25; C. 7; LD 1

Macclesfield (60) — C. 35; LD 14; Lab. 6; R. 3; Ind. 2

Maidstone (55) — C. 23; LD 20; Lab. 9; Ind. 3

Maldon (31) — C. 21; Ind. 4; Other 4; Lab. 2

Malvern Hills (38) — LD 19; C. 13; Ind. 5; Green 1

Mansfield (46) — Ind. 26; Lab. 15; LD 4; C. 1

Melton (28) — C. 19; Ind. 5; Lab. 4

Mendip (46) — C. 31; LD 11; Ind. 4

Mid Bedfordshire (53) — C. 38; LD 11; Ind. 4

Mid Devon (42) — Ind. Other 20; C. 12; LD 8; Green 1; v. 1

Mid Suffolk (40) — C. 21; LD 11; Ind. 5; Lab. 2; Green 1

Mid Sussex (54) — C. 28; LD 24; Lab. 2

Mole Valley (41) — C. 19; LD 17; Ind. 5

New Forest (60) — C. 32; LD 27; Ind. 1

Newark and Sherwood (46) — C. 23; Lab. 12; Ind. 5; LD 4; Ind. Other 1; Other 1

Newcastle-under-Lyme (60) — Lab. 31; LD 14; C. 14; Ind 1

North Cornwall (36) — Ind. 19; LD 12; C. 3; Other 1; v. 1

North Devon (43) — LD 22; C. 10; Ind. 5; Ind. Other 4; Other 2

North Dorset (33) — C. 15; LD 12; Ind. 5; v. 1

North East Derbyshire (53) — Lab. 36; C. 9; LD 5; Ind. 3

North Hertfordshire (49) — C. 28; Lab. 14; LD 7

North Kesteven (40) — C. 17; UKIP 8; LD 5; Lab. 4; Ind. 3; Ind. Other 2; v. 1

North Norfolk (48) — LD 29; Other 16; Ind. 3

North Shropshire (40) — Ind. 21; C. 15; Lab. 4

North Warwickshire (35) — Lab. 16; C. 15; LD 4

North West Leicestershire (38) — Lab. 21; C. 12; LD 3; Ind. 2

North Wiltshire (53) — LD 26; C. 25; Lab. 1; Ind. 1

Northampton (47) — C. 19; LD 17; Lab. 11

Norwich (39) — LD 18; Lab. 15; Green 5; C. 1

Nuneaton and Bedworth (34) — Lab. 22; C. 11; LD 1

Oadby and Wigston (26) — LD 17; C. 9

Oswestry (29)   C. 10; Ind. Other 8; LD 7; Ind.
                        3; Lab. 1
Oxford (48)   Lab. 20; LD 18; Green 7; Ind. 3
Pendle (49)   LD 30; C. 11; Lab. 8
Penwith (35)   LD 14; C. 12; Ind. 8; Lab. 1
Preston (57)   Lab. 24; C. 18; LD 10; Ind. 4;
                        Soc. All. 1
Purbeck (24)   C. 13; LD 8; Ind. 3
Redditch (29)   Lab. 16; C. 10; LD 3
Reigate and Banstead   C. 37; R 6; LD 5; Lab. 3
  (51)
Restormel (45)   LD 22; Ind. 13; C. 9; Other 1
Ribble Valley (40)   C. 22; LD 15; Ind. 2; Lab. 1
Richmondshire (34)   C. 11; Ind. 9; LD 8;
                        Ind. Other 5; SD 1
Rochford (39)   C. 32; LD 4; Ind. 1; Lab. 1; R 1
Rossendale (36)   C. 25; Lab. 9; LD 1; Ind. 1
Rother (38)   C. 25; LD 7; Lab. 3; Ind. 3
Rugby (48)   C. 21; Lab. 14; LD 10; Ind. 3
Runnymede (42)   C. 33; Ind. 6; Lab. 3
Rushcliffe (50)   C. 34; LD 10; Lab. 4;
                        Ind. Other 1; Green 1
Rushmoor (42)   C. 24; LD 12; Lab. 5; Ind. 1
Ryedale (30)   C. 11; LD 8; Ind. 7; Lib. 2; Ind
                        Other 1; v. 1
St Albans (58)   LD 29; C. 17; Lab. 11; Ind. 1
St Edmundsbury (45)   C. 28; Lab. 12; Ind. 3; LD 2
Salisbury (55)   C. 31; LD 9; Lab. 11; Ind. 4
Scarborough (50)   C. 27; Ind. 14; Lab. 7; LD 2
Sedgefield (50)   Lab. 34; Ind. 7; LD 7; C. 1
Sedgemoor (50)   C. 35; Lab. 14; LD 1
Selby (41)   Lab. 14; C. 23; Ind. 3; LD 1
Sevenoaks (54)   C. 32; Lab. 10; LD 8; Ind. 3; v. 1
Shepway (46)   LD 26; C. 17; Lab. 1; Green 1;
                        Ind. 1
Shrewsbury and   C. 20; Lab. 10; LD 6; Ind. 3; v. 1
  Atcham (40)
South Bedfordshire   C. 34; LD 12; Lab. 4
  (50)
South Bucks (40)   C. 33; Ind. 6; LD 1
South Cambridgeshire   C. 23; LD 19; Ind. 13; Lab. 2
  (57)
South Derbyshire (36)   Lab. 21; C. 14; Ind. 1
South Hams (40)   C. 28; LD 7; Lab. 3; Ind. 2
South Holland (38)   C. 26; Ind. 11; Other 1
South Kesteven (58)   C. 30; Ind. 12; Lab. 10; LD 5; v. 1
South Lakeland (52)   LD 22; C. 20; Lab. 8; Ind. 2
South Norfolk (46)   LD 28; C. 18
South   C. 30; Ind. 8; Lab. 4
  Northants (42)
South Oxfordshire   C. 28; LD 9; Lab. 4; Other 4;
  (48)   Ind. 3
South Ribble (55)   C. 18; Lab. 16; LD 15; Other 3;
                        Ind. 2; v. 1
South Shropshire (34)   LD 14; C. 10; Ind. 8; Other 2
South Somerset (60)   LD 36; C. 17; Ind. 7
South Staffordshire   C. 35; Lab. 8; Ind. 4; Other 1;
  (49)   LD 1
Spelthorne (39)   C. 35; LD 4
Stafford (59)   C. 40; Lab. 14; LD 5
Staffordshire   C. 20; R. 13; LD 11; Lab. 7;
  Moorlands (56)   Ind. 4; v. 1
Stevenage (39)   Lab. 32; C. 3; LD 4
Stratford-on-Avon (53) C. 30; LD 20; Ind. 3
Stroud (51)   C. 27; Lab. 11; LD 6; Green 4;
                        Ind. 3
Suffolk Coastal (55)   C. 43; LD 10; Lab. 2
Surrey Heath (40)   C. 22; LD 13; Lab. 3; Ind. 2

Swale (47)   C. 26; Lab. 11; LD 10
Tamworth (30)   C. 16; Lab. 13; Ind. 1
Tandridge (42)   C. 28; LD 11; Lab. 2; Ind. 1
Taunton Deane (54)   C. 31; LD 15; Lab. 5; Ind. 3
Teesdale (32)   Ind. 12; Lab. 9; Ind. Other 8;
                        C. 3
Teignbridge (46)   LD 17; Ind. 15; C. 14
Tendring (60)   C. 25; LD 13; Lab. 11; Ind. 7;
                        Other 4
Test Valley (48)   C. 30; LD 16; Ind. 2
Tewkesbury (38)   C. 18; LD 9; Ind. Other 7; Lab.
                        3; Ind. 1
Thanet (56)   C. 30; Lab. 23; LD 1; Ind. 1; v. 1
Three Rivers (48)   LD 29; C. 12; Lab. 7
Tonbridge and   C. 33; LD 13; Lab. 7
  Malling (53)
Torridge (36)   Ind. 27; LD 7; Green 1; C. 1
Tunbridge Wells (48)   C. 35; LD 12; Lab. 1
Tynedale (52)   C. 27; LD 11; Lab. 9; Ind. 5
Uttlesford (44)   LD 31; C. 10; Ind. 3
Vale of White Horse   LD 29; C. 21; Ind. 1
  (51)
Vale Royal (57)   C. 22; Lab. 21; LD 12; Ind. 2
Wansbeck (45)   Lab. 37; LD 8
Warwick (46)   Lab. 14; C. 16; LD 10; Ind. 6
Watford (36)   LD 26; Lab. 4; C. 4; Green 2
Waveney (48)   C. 24; Lab. 14; Ind. 7; LD 3
Waverley (57)   C. 28; LD 29
Wealden (55)   C. 35; LD 13; Ind. 6; v. 1
Wear Valley (40)   Lab. 25; LD 9; Ind. 6
Wellingborough (36)   C. 26; Lab. 9; v. 1
Welwyn & Hatfield (48) C. 31; Lab. 15; LD 2
West Devon (31)   C. 12; Ind. 10; LD 8; UKIP 1
West Dorset (48)   C. 26; LD 12; Ind. 10
West Lancashire (54)   C. 29; Lab. 25
West Lindsey (37)   C. 19; LD 16; Ind. 2
West Oxfordshire (49)   C. 29; LD 13; Ind. 6; Lab. 1
West Somerset (31)   C. 18; Ind. 9; Lab. 2; LD 2
West Wiltshire (44)   LD 19; C. 18; Ind. 4; Lab. 3
Weymouth and   LD 14; Lab. 9; C. 8; Ind. 5
  Portland (36)
Winchester (58)   LD 26; C. 22; Ind. 5; Lab. 5
Woking (36)   C. 17; LD 15; Lab. 4
Worcester (35)   C. 18; Lab. 10; LD 3;
                        Ind. Other 3; Ind. 1
Worthing (37)   C. 26; LD 11
Wychavon (45)   C. 31; LD 12; Lab. 2
Wycombe (60)   C. 46; Lab. 9; LD 2;
                        Ind. 3
Wyre (55)   C. 33; Lab. 21; LD 1
Wyre Forest (42)   C. 19; IKHHC 8; Lib. 8; Lab. 4;
                        LD 2; Ind. 1

LONDON BOROUGH COUNCILS

Barking and   Lab. 42; R. 3; LD 3; C. 3
  Dagenham (51)
Barnet (63)   C. 33; Lab. 24; LD 6
Bexley (63)   Lab. 32; C. 30; LD 1
Brent (63)   Lab. 35; C. 18; LD 10
Bromley (60)   LD 41; C. 13; Lab. 6
Camden (54)   Lab. 35; C. 11; LD 8
Croydon (70)   Lab. 37; C. 31; LD 1; Ind. 1
Ealing (69)   Lab. 48; C. 17; LD 4
Enfield (63)   C. 39; Lab. 24
Greenwich (51)   Lab. 38; C. 9; LD 4
Hackney (57)   Lab. 45; C. 8; LD 3; v. 1
Hammersmith and   Lab. 29; C. 17
  Fulham (46)

Haringey (57)   Lab. 42; LD 15
Harrow (63)   Lab. 30; C. 28; LD 3; Ind. 2
Havering (53)   C. 26; R. 17; Lab. 10
Hillingdon (65)   C. 30; Lab. 27; LD 8
Hounslow (59)   Lab. 36; C. 14; LD 5; Ind. 4
Islington (48)   LD 36; Lab. 10; Ind. 2
Kensington and   C. 42; Lab. 12
  Chelsea (54)
Kingston upon   LD 30; C. 15; Lab. 3
  Thames (48)
Lambeth (63)   Lab. 28; LD 28; C. 7
Lewisham (54)   Lab. 42; LD 6; C. 2; Soc. 2;
                    Ind. 1; Green 1
Merton (60)   Lab. 33; C. 24; R. 3
Newham (60)   Lab. 59; Ind. 1
Redbridge (63)   C. 34; Lab. 20; LD 9
Richmond upon   C. 37; LD 16; v. 1
  Thames (54)
Southwark (63)   LD 29; Lab. 28; C. 6
Sutton (54)   LD 43; C. 8; Lab. 3
Tower Hamlets (51) Lab. 34; LD 16; Other 1
Waltham Forest (60) Lab. 27; C. 18; LD 15
Wandsworth (60)   C. 50; Lab. 10
Westminster (60)   C. 48; Lab. 12

METROPOLITAN BOROUGH COUNCILS

Barnsley (63)   Lab. 33; Ind. 22; C. 5; LD 3
Birmingham (120)   Lab. 53; C. 39; LD 28
Bolton (60)   LD 21; Lab. 20; C. 19
Bradford (90)   C. 38; Lab. 29; LD 15; BNP 4;
                    Green 4
Bury (51)   Lab. 27; C. 19; LD 5
Calderdale (51)   C. 21; LD 15; Lab. 9; Ind 3;
                    BNP 3
Coventry (54)   C. 27; Lab. 22; LD 3; Other 2
Doncaster (63)   Lab. Ind. 14; LD 13; C. 9
Dudley (72)   C. 40; Lab. 25; LD 7
Gateshead (66)   Lab. 43; LD 22; Lib. 1
Kirklees (69)   LD 25; C. 22; Lab. 17; Green 3;
                    Ind. 1; BNP 1
Knowsley (63)   Lab. 52; LD 11
Leeds (99)   Lab. 40; LD 26; C. 24; Green 3;
                    Ind. 6
Liverpool (90)   LD 60; Lab 27; Lib. 3
Manchester (96)   Lab. 56; LD 39; Green 1
Newcastle-upon-Tyne LD 48; Lab. 30
  (78)
North Tyneside (60) C. 27; Lab. 26; LD 7
Oldham (60)   Lab. 32; LD 25; C. 2; Ind. 1
Rochdale (60)   LD 25; Lab. 24; C. 11
Rotherham (63)   Lab. 53; C. 7; Ind. 3
St Helens (48)   Lab. 24; LD 18; C. 6
Salford (60)   Lab. 44; LD 8; C. 8
Sandwell (72)   Lab. 52; C. 13; LD 6; BNP 1
Sefton (66)   LD 27; Lab. 20; C. 19
Sheffield (84)   Lab. 44; LD 37; C. 2;
                    Green 1
Solihull (51)   C. 27; LD 15; Lab. 8; Ind 1
South Tyneside (54) Lab. 35; Ind. 12; LD 4; C. 3
Stockport (63)   LD 35; Lab. 14; C. 10; Ind. 4
Sunderland (75)   Lab. 61; C. 12; LD 2
Tameside (57)   Lab. 45; C. 7; LD 3; Ind. 2
Trafford (63)   C. 40; Lab. 20; LD 3
Wakefield (63)   Lab. 43; C. 11; Ind. 6; LD 3
Walsall (60)   C. 35; Lab. 18; LD 6; Other 1
Wigan (75)   Lab. 42; Ind. 18; LD 8; C. 7
Wirral (66)   Lab. 26; C. 21; LD 19
Wolverhampton (60) Lab. 41; C. 16; LD 3

UNITARY COUNCILS

Bath and North East   LD 29; C. 26; Lab. 6; Ind. 4
  Somerset (65)
Blackburn with   Lab. 33; C. 17; LD 12; v. 2
  Darwen (64)
Blackpool (42)   Lab. 25; C. 13; LD 4
Bournemouth (54)   LD 32; C. 17; Lab. 3; Ind. 2
Bracknell Forest (42) C. 34; Lab. 6; LD 1; Ind. 1
Brighton and Hove   Lab. 24; C. 20; Green 6; LD 3;
  (54)   Ind. 1
Bristol (70)   Lab. 31; LD 27; C. 11; Ind. 1
Darlington (53)   Lab. 35; C. 16; LD 2
Derby (51)   Lab. 24; LD 14; C. 11; UKIP 1;
                       v. 1
East Riding of   C. 28; LD 20; Lab. 8; Ind. 6;
  Yorkshire (64)   SDP 2
Halton (56)   Lab. 35; LD 14; C. 7
Hartlepool (46)   Lab. 25; LD 9; Ind. 9; C. 4
Herefordshire (58)   C. 21; Ind. 17; LD 16; Lab. 4
Isle of Wight (48)   IF 27; C. 13; Other 5;
                       Lab. 3
Kingston-upon-Hull   Lab. 27; LD 24; Ind. 5; C. 2;
  (59)   UKIP 1
Leicester (54)   LD 25; Lab. 20; C. 8; v. 1
Luton (48)   Lab. 23; LD 20; C. 4; Ind. 1
Medway (55)   C. 30; Lab. 17; LD 6; Ind. 2
Middlesbrough (48)   Lab. 32; C. 7; LD 5; Ind. 4
Milton Keynes (51)   LD 27; Lab. 16; C. 7; Ind. 1
North East   LD 16; C. 15; Lab. 7; Ind. 4
  Lincolnshire (42)
North Lincolnshire   Lab. 21; C. 22
  (43)
North Somerset (61)   C. 24; LD 23; Lab. 10; Ind. 3;
                       Green 1
Nottingham (55)   Lab. 36; LD 11; C. 8
Peterborough (57)   C. 33; Ind. 9; Lab. 7; Lib. 4;
                       LD 4
Plymouth (57)   Lab. 35; C. 19; LD 2; Ind. 1
Poole (42)   C. 26; LD 16
Portsmouth (42)   LD 20; C. 15; Lab. 7
Reading (46)   Lab. 35; C. 6; LD 5
Redcar and Cleveland   Lab. 22; LD 15; C. 13; Ind. 9
  (59)
Rutland (26)   C. 15; Ind. 6; LD 5
Slough (41)   Lab. 15; C. 8; Ind. 6; LD 6; R 3;
                       Lib. 3
South Gloucestershire LD 33; C. 21; Lab 16
  (70)
Southampton (48)   LD 19; Lab. 15; C. 14
Southend-on-Sea (51)   C. 33; Lab. 9; LD 7; Ind. 2
Stockton-on-Tees (55) Lab. 28; C. 13; Ind. 8; LD 6
Stoke-on-Trent (60)   Lab. 34; Ind. 13; LD 5; C. 5;
                       BNP 2; v. 1
Swindon (59)   C. 33; Lab. 19; LD 7
Telford and Wrekin   Lab. 29; C. 13; Ind. 6; LD 6
  (54)
Thurrock (49)   C. 28; Lab. 19; Ind. 2
Torbay (36)   LD 27; C. 9
Warrington (57)   Lab. 30; LD 21; C. 6
West Berkshire (52)   LD 26; C. 26
Windsor and   LD 34; C. 15; Ind 7; Lab. 1
  Maidenhead (57)
Wokingham (54)   C. 33; LD 20; v. 1
York (47)   Lab. 15; LD 29; Green 2;
                       Ind. 1

WALES

Blaenau Gwent (42)	Lab. 31; Ind. 8; LD 3
Bridgend (54)	Lab. 21; LD 13; Ind. 10; C. 8; PC 1; v. 1
Caerphilly (73)	Lab. 39; PC 26; Ind. 8
Cardiff (75)	LD 33; Lab. 27; C. 12; PC 3
Carmarthenshire (74)	Ind. 32; Lab. 25; PC 16; C. 1
Ceredigion (42)	Ind. 16; PC 16; LD 9; Lab. 1
Conwy (59)	Ind. 19; Lab. 12; C. 12; PC 9; LD 6; v. 1
Denbighshire (47)	Ind. 19; Lab. 8; C. 8; PC 7; Other 3; LD 2
Flintshire (70)	Lab. 37; Ind. 18; LD 10; C. 4; PC 1
Gwynedd (83)	PC 41; Ind. 17: Lab. 10; LD 7
Merthyr Tydfil (33)	Lab. 17; Ind. 16
Monmouthshire (43)	C. 24; Lab. 8; Ind. 5; LD 4; PC 2
Neath Port Talbot (64)	Lab. 36; PC 10; R 9; Ind. 7; LD 2
Newport (50)	Lab. 31; C. 11; LD 6; PC 1; Ind. 1
Pembrokeshire (60)	Ind. 40; Lab. 12; PC 5; LD 3
Powys (73)	Ind. 53; LD 16; Lab. 4
Rhondda Cynon Taff (75)	Lab. 57; PC 13; Ind. 3; LD 2
Swansea (72)	Lab. 32; LD 19; Ind. 12; PC 5; C. 4
Torfaen (44)	Lab. 34; Ind. 7; LD 2; C. 1
Vale of Glamorgan (47)	C. 20; Lab. 16; PC 8; Ind. 3
Wrexham (52)	Ind. 20; Lab. 19; LD 10; C. 3
Ynys Mon (Isle of Anglesey) (40)	Ind. 28; PC 8; C. 2; Lab. 1; LD 1

SCOTLAND

Aberdeen (43)	LD 20; Lab. 14; SNP 6; C. 3
Aberdeenshire (68)	LD 28; SNP 18; Ind. 11; C. 11
Angus (29)	SNP 17; Ind. 6; LD 3; C. 2; Lab. 1
Argyll and Bute (36)	Ind. 22; LD 8; SNP 3; C. 3
Clackmannanshire (18)	SNP 6; Lab. 10; C. 1; Ind. 1
Dumfries and Galloway (47)	Lab. 14; Ind. 12; CU 9; LD 5; SNP 5; v. 2
Dundee (29)	SNP 11; Lab. 10; C. 5; LD 2; Ind. 1
East Ayrshire (32)	Lab. 23; SNP 8; C. 1
East Dunbartonshire (24)	LD 12; Lab. 9; C. 3
East Lothian (23)	Lab. 16; C. 4; SNP 1; LD 1; Ind. 1
East Renfrewshire (20)	Lab. 8; C. 7; LD 3; Ind. 2
Edinburgh (58)	Lab. 30; LD 15; C. 13
Eilean Siar (Western Isles) (31)	Ind. 22; Lab. 5; SNP 3; v. 1
Falkirk (32)	Lab. 14; SNP 9; Ind. 7; C. 2
Fife (78)	Lab. 36; LD 23; SNP 11; Other 6; C. 2
Glasgow (79)	Lab. 71; SNP 3; LD 3; C. 1; SSP 1
Highland (80)	Ind. 57; LD 9; Lab. 8; SNP 6
Inverclyde (20)	LD 13; Lab. 6; Ind. 1
Midlothian (18)	Lab. 15; LD 2; Ind. 1
Moray (26)	Ind. 15; Lab. 5; SNP 3; CU 1; LD 1; v. 1

North Ayrshire (30)	Lab. 20; C. 5; SNP 3; Ind. 2
North Lanarkshire (70)	Lab. 54; SNP 11; Ind. 5
Orkney Islands (21)	Ind. 21
Perth and Kinross (41)	SNP 15; C. 10; LD 9; Lab. 5; Ind. 2
Renfrewshire (40)	Lab. 21; SNP 15; LD 3; C. 1
Scottish Borders (34)	CU 11; Ind. 11; LD 8; NP 3; SNP 1
Shetland Islands (22)	Ind. 17; LD 5
South Ayrshire (30)	Lab. 15; C. 15
South Lanarkshire (67)	Lab. 51; SNP 9; Ind. 3; C. 2; LD 2
Stirling (22)	Lab. 12; C. 10
West Dunbartonshire (22)	Lab. 17; SNP 3; SSP 1; Ind. 1
West Lothian (32)	Lab. 18; SNP 11; Ind. 2; C. 1

NORTHERN IRELAND

Antrim (19)	UUP 8; DUP 5; SDLP 4; SF 2
Ards (23)	DUP 9; UUP 8; All. 4; Ind. 2
Armagh City (22)	UUP 7; SDLP 6; SF 5; DUP 4
Ballymena (24)	DUP 11; UUP 7; SDLP 4; Ind. 2
Ballymoney (16)	DUP 8; UUP 5; SDLP 2; SF 1
Banbridge (17)	UUP 6; DUP 6; SDLP 3; All. 1; Ind. 1
Belfast (51)	SF 14; UUP 11; DUP 10; SDLP 9; Other 4; All. 3
Carrickfergus (17)	DUP 6; All. 5; UUP 4; Ind. 2
Castlereagh (24)	DUP 10; UUP 5; All. 4; SDLP 2; Ind. 2
Coleraine (22)	UUP 9; DUP 7; SDLP 3; Ind. 1; SF 1; Other 1
Cookstown (16)	SF 6; SDLP 4; UUP 3; DUP 2; Ind. 1
Craigavon (26)	UUP 7; SDLP 7; DUP 6; SF 4; Ind. UU 2
Derry City (30)	SDLP 13; SF 10; DUP 4; UUP 2; Ind. 1
Down (23)	SDLP 9; UUP 6; SF 4; DUP 2; Ind. 2
Dungannon and South Tyrone (22)	SF 8; UUP 6; SDLP 4; DUP 3; Ind. 1
Fermanagh (23)	UUP 9; SF 7; SDLP 4; DUP 2; Ind. 1
Larne (15)	DUP 5; UUP 4; All. 2; SDLP 2; Ind. 2
Limavady (15)	SDLP 4; SF 4; UUP 3; DUP 2; Other 2
Lisburn (30)	UUP 12; DUP 6; Other 5; SF 4; SDLP 3
Magherafelt (16)	SF 7; DUP 3; SDLP 3; UUP 2; Ind. 1
Moyle (15)	SDLP 5; Ind. 3; UUP 3; DUP 2; SF 2
Newry and Mourne (30)	SDLP 10; SF 13; UUP 4; Ind. 2; DUP 1
Newtownabbey (25)	UUP 9; DUP 7; Other 6; SDLP 2; SF 1
North Down (25)	UUP 8; Ind. 7; All 5; DUP 5
Omagh (21)	SF 8; SDLP 6; UUP 3; DUP 2; Ind. 2
Strabane (16)	SF 7; SDLP 4; DUP 3; UUP 2

ENGLAND

The Kingdom of England lies between 55° 46' and 49° 57' 30" N. latitude (from a few miles north of the mouth of the Tweed to the Lizard), and between 1° 46' E. and 5° 43' W. (from Lowestoft to Land's End). England is bounded on the north by the Cheviot Hills; on the south by the English Channel; on the east by the Straits of Dover (Pas de Calais) and the North Sea; and on the west by the Atlantic Ocean, Wales and the Irish Sea. It has a total area of 50,351 sq. miles (130,410 sq. km): land 50,058 sq. miles (129,652 sq. km); inland water 293 sq. miles (758 sq. km).

POPULATION
The population at the 2001 census was 49,138,831. The average density of the population in 2001 was 3.8 persons per hectare.

FLAG
The flag of England is the cross of St George, a red cross on a white field (cross gules in a field argent). The cross of St George, the patron saint of England, has been used since the 13th century.

RELIEF
There is a marked division between the upland and lowland areas of England. In the extreme north the Cheviot Hills (highest point, The Cheviot, 2,674 ft) form a natural boundary with Scotland. Running south from the Cheviots, though divided from them by the Tyne Gap, is the Pennine range (highest point, Cross Fell, 2,930 ft), the main orological feature of the country. The Pennines culminate in the Peak District of Derbyshire (Kinder Scout, 2,088 ft). West of the Pennines are the Cumbrian mountains, which include Scafell Pike (3,210 ft), the highest peak in England, and to the east are the Yorkshire Moors, their highest point being Urra Moor (1,490 ft).

In the west, the foothills of the Welsh mountains extend into the bordering English counties of Shropshire (the Wrekin, 1,334 ft; Long Mynd, 1,694 ft) and Hereford and Worcester (the Malvern Hills – Worcestershire Beacon, 1,394 ft). Extensive areas of highland and moorland are also to be found in the south-western peninsula formed by Somerset, Devon and Cornwall: principally Exmoor (Dunkery Beacon, 1,704 ft), Dartmoor (High Willhays, 2,038 ft) and Bodmin Moor (Brown Willy, 1,377 ft). Ranges of low, undulating hills run across the south of the country, including the Cotswolds in the Midlands and south-west, the Chilterns to the north of London, and the North (Kent) and South (Sussex) Downs of the south-east coastal areas.

The lowlands of England lie in the Vale of York, East Anglia and the area around the Wash. The lowest-lying are the Cambridgeshire Fens in the valleys of the Great Ouse and the River Nene, which are below sea-level in places. Since the 17th century extensive drainage has brought much of the Fens under cultivation. The North Sea coast between the Thames and the Humber, low-lying and formed of sand and shingle for the most part, is subject to erosion and defences against further incursion have been built along many stretches.

HYDROGRAPHY
The Severn is the longest river in Great Britain, rising in the north-eastern slopes of Plynlimon (Wales) and entering England in Shropshire with a total length of 220 miles (354 km) from its source to its outflow into the Bristol Channel, where it receives on the east the Bristol Avon, and on the west the Wye, its other tributaries being the Vyrnwy, Tern, Stour, Teme and Upper (or Warwickshire) Avon. The Severn is tidal below Gloucester, and a high bore or tidal wave sometimes reverses the flow as high as Tewkesbury (13½ miles above Gloucester). The scenery of the greater part of the river is very picturesque and beautiful, and the Severn is a noted salmon river, some of its tributaries being famous for trout. Navigation is assisted by the Gloucester and Berkeley Ship Canal (16¼ miles), which admits vessels of 350 tons to Gloucester. The Severn Tunnel was begun in 1873 and completed in 1886 at a cost of £2 million and after many difficulties caused by flooding. It is 4 miles 628 yards in length (of which 2¼ miles are under the river). The Severn road bridge between Haysgate, Gwent, and Almondsbury, Glos, with a centre span of 3,240 ft, was opened in 1966.

The longest river wholly in England is the Thames, with a total length of 215 miles (346 km) from its source in the Cotswold hills to the Nore, and is navigable by ocean-going ships to London Bridge. The Thames is tidal to Teddington (69 miles from its mouth) and forms county boundaries almost throughout its course; on its banks are situated London, Windsor Castle, Eton College and Oxford University. Of the remaining English rivers, those flowing into the North Sea are the Tyne, Wear, Tees, Ouse and Trent from the Pennine Range, the Great Ouse (160 miles), which rises in Northamptonshire, and the Orwell and Stour from the hills of East Anglia. Flowing into the English Channel are the Sussex Ouse from the Weald, the Itchen from the Hampshire Hills, and the Axe, Teign, Dart, Tamar and Exe from the Devonian hills. Flowing into the Irish Sea are the Mersey, Ribble and Eden from the western slopes of the Pennines and the Derwent from the Cumbrian mountains.

The English Lakes, noteworthy for their picturesque scenery and poetic associations, lie in Cumbria, the largest being Windermere (10 miles long), Ullswater and Derwent Water.

ISLANDS
The Isle of Wight is separated from Hampshire by the Solent. The capital, Newport, stands at the head of the estuary of the Medina, Cowes (at the mouth) being the chief port. Other centres are Ryde, Sandown, Shanklin, Ventnor, Freshwater, Yarmouth, Totland Bay, Seaview and Bembridge.

Lundy (the name means Puffin Island), 11 miles north-west of Hartland Point, Devon, is about three miles long and about half a mile wide on average, with a total area of about 1,116 acres, and a population of about 18. It became the property of the National Trust in 1969 and is now principally a bird sanctuary.

The Isles of Scilly consist of about 140 islands and skerries (total area, 6 sq. miles/10 sq. km) situated 28 miles south-west of Land's End in Cornwall. Only five are inhabited: St Mary's, St Agnes, Bryher, Tresco and St Martin's. The population at the 2001 census was 2,153. The entire group has been designated a Conservation Area, a Heritage Coast, and an Area of Outstanding Natural Beauty, and has been given National Nature

Reserve status by the Nature Conservancy Council because of its unique flora and fauna. Tourism and the winter/spring flower trade for the home market form the basis of the economy of the Isles. The island group is a recognised rural development area.

EARLY HISTORY

Archaeological evidence suggests that England has been inhabited since at least the Palaeolithic period, though the extent of the various Palaeolithic cultures was dependent upon the degree of glaciation. The succeeding Neolithic and Bronze Age cultures have left abundant remains throughout the country, the best-known of these being the henges and stone circles of Stonehenge (ten miles north of Salisbury, Wilts) and Avebury (Wilts), both of which are believed to have been of religious significance. In the latter part of the Bronze Age the Goidels, a people of Celtic race, and in the Iron Age other Celtic races of Brythons and Belgae, invaded the country and brought with them Celtic civilisation and dialects, place names in England bear witness to the spread of the invasion over the whole kingdom.

THE ROMAN CONQUEST
The Roman conquest of Gaul (57–50 BC) brought Britain into close contact with Roman civilisation, but although Julius Caesar raided the south of Britain in 55 BC and 54 BC, conquest was not undertaken until nearly 100 years later. In AD 43 the Emperor Claudius dispatched Aulus Plautius, with a well-equipped force of 40,000, and himself followed with reinforcements in the same year. Success was delayed by the resistance of Caratacus (Caractacus), the British leader from AD 48–51, who was finally captured and sent to Rome, and by a great revolt in AD 61 led by Boudicca (Boadicea), Queen of the Iceni; but the south of Britain was secured by AD 70, and Wales and the area north to the Tyne by about AD 80.

In AD 122, the Emperor Hadrian visited Britain and built a continuous rampart, since known as Hadrian's Wall, from Wallsend to Bowness (Tyne to Solway). The work was entrusted by the Emperor Hadrian to Aulus Platorius Nepos, legate of Britain from AD 122 to 126, and it was intended to form the northern frontier of the Roman Empire.

The Romans administered Britain as a province under a Governor, with a well-defined system of local government, each Roman municipality ruling itself and its surrounding territory, while London was the centre of the road system and the seat of the financial officials of the Province of Britain. Colchester, Lincoln, York, Gloucester and St Albans stand on the sites of five Roman municipalities, and Wroxeter, Caerleon, Chester, Lincoln and York were at various times the sites of legionary fortresses. Well-preserved Roman towns have been uncovered at or near Silchester *(Calleva Atrebatum)*, ten miles south of Reading, Wroxeter *(Viroconium Cornoviorum)*, near Shrewsbury, and St Albans *(Verulamium)* in Hertfordshire.

Four main groups of roads radiated from London, and a fifth (the Fosse) ran obliquely from Lincoln through Leicester, Cirencester and Bath to Exeter. Of the four groups radiating from London, one ran south-east to Canterbury and the coast of Kent, a second to Silchester and thence to parts of western Britain and south Wales, a third (later known as Watling Street) ran through Verulamium to Chester, with various branches, and the fourth reached Colchester, Lincoln, York and the eastern counties.

In the fourth century Britain was subject to raids along the east coast by Saxon pirates, which led to the establishment of a system of coastal defences from the Wash to Southampton Water, with forts at Brancaster, Burgh Castle (Yarmouth), Walton (Felixstowe), Bradwell, Reculver, Richborough, Dover, Lympne, Pevensey and Porchester (Portsmouth). The Irish (Scoti) and Picts in the north were also becoming more aggressive; from about AD 350 incursions became more frequent and more formidable. As the Roman Empire came under attack increasingly towards the end of the fourth century, many troops were removed from Britain for service in other parts of the empire. The island was eventually cut off from Rome by the Teutonic conquest of Gaul, and with the withdrawal of the last Roman garrison early in the fifth century, the Romano-British were left to themselves.

SAXON SETTLEMENT
According to legend, the British King Vortigern called in the Saxons to defend him against the Picts, the Saxon chieftains being Hengist and Horsa, who landed at Ebbsfleet, Kent, and established themselves in the Isle of Thanet; but the events during the one-and-a-half centuries between the final break with Rome and the re-establishment of Christianity are unclear. However, it would appear that in the course of this period the raids turned into large-scale settlement by invaders traditionally known as Angles (England north of the Wash and East Anglia), Saxons (Essex and southern England) and Jutes (Kent and the Weald), which pushed the Romano-British into the mountainous areas of the north and west. Celtic culture outside Wales and Cornwall survives only in topographical names. Various kingdoms established at this time attempted to claim overlordship of the whole country, hegemony finally being achieved by Wessex (capital, Winchester) in the ninth century. This century also saw the beginning of raids by the Vikings (Danes), which were resisted by Alfred the Great (871–899), who fixed a limit to the advance of Danish settlement in the Treaty of Wedmore (878), giving them the area north and east of Watling Street, on condition that they adopt Christianity.

In the tenth century the kings of Wessex recovered the whole of England from the Danes, but subsequent rulers were unable to resist a second wave of invaders. England paid tribute *(Danegeld)* for many years, and was invaded in 1013 by the Danes and ruled by Danish kings from 1016 until 1042, when Edward the Confessor was recalled from exile in Normandy. On Edward's death in 1066 Harold Godwinson (brother-in-law of Edward and son of Earl Godwin of Wessex) was chosen King of England. After defeating (at Stamford Bridge, Yorkshire, 25 September) an invading army under Harald Hadraada, King of Norway (aided by the outlawed Earl Tostig of Northumbria, Harold's brother), Harold was himself defeated at the Battle of Hastings on 14 October 1066, and the Norman conquest secured the throne of England for Duke William of Normandy, a cousin of Edward the Confessor.

CHRISTIANITY
Christianity reached the Roman province of Britain from Gaul in the third century (or possibly earlier); Alban, traditionally Britain's first martyr, was put to death as a Christian during the persecution of Diocletian (22 June 303), at his native town *Verulamium*; and the Bishops of

Londinium, Eboracum (York), and *Lindum* (Lincoln) attended the Council of Arles in 314. However, the Anglo-Saxon invasions submerged the Christian religion in England until the sixth century when conversion was undertaken in the north from 563 by Celtic missionaries from Ireland led by St Columba, and in the south by a mission sent from Rome in 597 which was led by St Augustine, who became the first archbishop of Canterbury. England appears to have been converted again by the end of the seventh century and followed, after the Council of Whitby in 663, the practices of the Roman Church, which brought the kingdom into the mainstream of European thought and culture.

PRINCIPAL CITIES

There are 50 cities in England and space constraints prevent us from including profiles of them all. The profiles below represent just a selection of England's principal cities (with date city status conferred). Other cities are: Brighton and Hove (2000), Chichester (pre-1900), Derby (1977), Ely (pre-1900), Gloucester (pre-1900), Hereford (pre-1900), Lichfield (pre-1900), London (pre-1900), Peterborough (pre-1900), Plymouth (1928), Portsmouth (1926), Preston (2002), Ripon (pre-1900), Salford (1926), Southampton (1964), Sunderland (1992), Truro (pre-1900), Wakefield (pre-1900), Wells (pre-1900), Westminster (pre-1900), Wolverhampton (2000) and Worcester (pre-1900).

Certain cities have also been granted a Lord Mayoralty – this grant confers no additional powers or functions and is purely honorific. Cities with Lord Mayors are: Birmingham, Bradford, Bristol, Canterbury, Chester, Coventry, Exeter, Kingston-upon-Hull, Leeds, Leicester, Liverpool, London, Manchester, Newcastle-upon-Tyne, Norwich, Nottingham, Oxford, Plymouth, Portsmouth, Sheffield and Stoke-on-Trent.

BATH (PRE-1900)

Bath stands on the River Avon between the Cotswold Hills to the North and the Mendips to the south. In the early eighteenth century, Bath became England's premier spa town where the rich and celebrated members of fashionable society gathered to 'take the waters' and enjoy the town's theatres and concert rooms. During this period the architect John Wood laid the foundations for a new Georgian city to be built using the honey-coloured stone that Bath is famous for today.

Today Bath is a thriving tourist destination and remains a leading cultural, religious and historical centre with many art galleries and historic sites including; the Pump Room (1790), The Royal Crescent (1767), the Circus (1754), the 18th-century Assembly Rooms (housing the Museum of Costume), Pulteney Bridge (1771), the Guildhall and the Abbey, now over 500 years old, which is built on the site of the Saxon monastery.

BIRMINGHAM (PRE-1900)

Birmingham is Britain's second largest city with a population of nearly one million. The generally accepted derivation of 'Birmingham' is the *ham* (dwelling-place) of the *ing* (family) of *Beorma*, presumed to have been Saxon. During the Industrial Revolution the town grew into a major manufacturing centre and in 1889 was granted city status.

Recent developments include the Millennium Point, incorporating the science museum, Thinktank and Brindleyplace. On 4 September 2003 the Bullring shopping centre was officially opened as part of the city's urban regeneration programme.

The principal buildings are the Town Hall (1834–50), the Council House (1879), Victoria Law Courts (1891), Birmingham University (1906–9), the 13th-century Church of St Martin-in-the-Bull-Ring (rebuilt 1873), Our Lady, Help of Christians Church, the Cathedral (formerly St Philip's Church) (1711), the Roman Catholic Cathedral of St Chad (1839–41), the assay office (1773) and the National Exhibition Centre (1976). There is also the Birmingham Museum and Art Gallery including the Waterhall Gallery which opened in 2001.

BRADFORD (PRE-1900)

During the Industrial Revolution of the 18th and 19th centuries Bradford expanded rapidly and a great deal of wealth was generated by the wool industry.

Bradford city centre has a host of buildings with historical and cultural interest, including: City Hall, with its 19th-century Lord Mayor's rooms and Victorian law court; Bradford Cathedral; The Priestly, a theatre and arts centre originally established as the Bradford Civic Playhouse by J. B. Priestly and friends; the Colour Museum; the National Museum of Photography, Film and Television which houses five floors of interactive displays and three cinemas; and Piece Hall Yard which incorporates the Bradford Club, a Victorian Gothic style club dating from 1837, and the Peace Museum.

BRISTOL (PRE-1900)

Bristol was a Royal Borough before the Norman Conquest. The earliest form of the name is *Bricgstow*. In 1373 Edward III granted Bristol county status.

The chief buildings include the 12th-century Cathedral (with later additions), with Norman chapter house and gateway, the 14th-century Church of St Mary Redcliffe, Wesley's Chapel, Broadmead, the Merchant Venturers' Almshouses, the Council House (1956), Guildhall, Exchange (erected from the designs of John Wood in 1743), Cabot Tower, the University and Clifton College. The Roman Catholic Cathedral at Clifton was opened in 1973.

The Clifton Suspension Bridge, with a span of 702 feet over the Avon, was projected by Brunel in 1836 but was not completed until 1864. Brunel's SS *Great Britain*, the first ocean-going propeller-driven ship, is now being restored in the City Docks from where she was launched in 1843. The docks themselves have been extensively restored and redeveloped; the 19th-century two-storey former tea warehouse is now the Arnolfini centre for contemporary arts, and an 18th-century sail loft houses the Architecture Centre. Behind the baroque-domed facade of the former 'E' Shed are shops, cafes, restaurants and the Watershed Media Centre, and on Princes Wharf disused transit sheds house the Industrial Museum.

CAMBRIDGE (1951)

Cambridge, a settlement far older than its ancient University, lies on the River Cam or Granta. The city is a county town and regional headquarters. Its industries include technology research and development, and biotechnology. Among its open spaces are Jesus Green, Sheep's Green, Coe Fen, Parker's Piece, Christ's Pieces, the University Botanic Garden, and the 'Backs' – lawns and gardens through which the Cam winds behind the principal line of college buildings. Historical sites east of the Cam include; King's Parade, Great St Mary's Church, Gibbs' Senate House and King's College Chapel.

University and college buildings provide the outstanding features of Cambridge's architecture but several churches (especially St Benet's, the oldest building in the city, and St Sepulchre's, the Round Church) are also notable. The Guildhall (1937) stands on a site of which at least part has held municipal buildings since 1224.

CANTERBURY (PRE-1900)

Canterbury, the Metropolitan City of the Anglican Communion, dates back to prehistoric times. It was the Roman *Durovernum Cantiacorum* and the Saxon *Cantwara-byrig* (stronghold of the men of Kent). Here in 597 St Augustine began the conversion of the English to Christianity, when Ethelbert, King of Kent, was baptised.

Of the Benedictine St Augustine's Abbey, burial place of the Jutish Kings of Kent, only ruins remain. St Martin's Church, on the eastern outskirts of the city, is stated by Bede to have been the place of worship of Queen Bertha, the Christian wife of King Ethelbert, before the advent of St Augustine.

In 1170 the rivalry of Church and State culminated in the murder in Canterbury Cathedral, by Henry II's knights, of Archbishop Thomas Becket. His shrine became a great centre of pilgrimage, as described in Chaucer's *Canterbury Tales*. After the Reformation pilgrimages ceased, but the prosperity of the city was strengthened by an influx of Huguenot refugees, who introduced weaving. The poet and playwright Christopher Marlowe was born and reared in Canterbury, and there are also literary associations with Defoe, Dickens, Joseph Conrad and Somerset Maugham.

The Cathedral, with architecture ranging from the 11th to the 15th centuries, is world famous. Modern pilgrims are attracted particularly to the Martyrdom, the Black Prince's Tomb, the Warriors' Chapel and the many examples of medieval stained glass.

The medieval city walls are built on Roman foundations and the 14th-century West Gate is one of the finest buildings of its kind in the country.

The 1,000-seat Marlowe Theatre is a centre for the Canterbury Arts Festival each autumn.

CARLISLE (PRE-1900)

Carlisle is situated at the confluence of the River Eden and River Caldew, 309 miles north-west of London and about ten miles from the Scottish border. It was granted a charter in 1158.

The city stands at the western end of Hadrian's Wall and dates from the original Roman settlement of *Luguvalium*. Granted to Scotland in the tenth century, Carlisle is not included in the Domesday Book. William Rufus reclaimed the area in 1092 and the castle and city walls were built to guard Carlisle and the western border; the citadel is a Tudor addition to protect the south of the city. Border disputes were common until the problem of the Debateable Lands was settled in 1552. During the Civil War the city remained Royalist; in 1745 Carlisle was besieged for the last time by the Young Pretender (Bonnie Prince Charlie).

The Cathedral, originally a 12th-century Augustinian priory, was enlarged in the 13th and 14th centuries after the diocese was created in 1133. To the south is a restored Tithe Barn and nearby the 18th-century church of St Cuthbert, the third to stand on a site dating from the seventh century.

Carlisle is the major shopping, commercial and agricultural centre for the area, and industries include the manufacture of metal goods, biscuits and textiles. However, the largest employer is the services sector, most notably in central and local government, retailing and transport. The city has an important communications position at the centre of a network of major roads, as a stage on the main west coast rail services, and with its own airport at Crosby-on-Eden.

CHESTER (PRE-1900)

Chester is situated on the River Dee. Its recorded history dates from the first century when the Romans founded the fortress of *Deva*. The city's name is derived from the Latin *castra* (a camp or encampment). During the Middle Ages, Chester was the principal port of north-west England but declined with the silting of the Dee estuary and competition from Liverpool. The city was also an important military centre, notably during Edward I's Welsh campaigns and the Elizabethan Irish campaigns. During the Civil War, Chester supported the King and was besieged from 1643 to 1646. Chester's first charter was granted *c.* 1175 and the city was incorporated in 1506. The office of Sheriff is the earliest created in the country (*c.* 1120s), and in 1992 the Mayor was granted the title of Lord Mayor. He/she also enjoys the title 'Admiral of the Dee'.

The city's architectural features include the city walls (an almost complete two-mile circuit), the unique 13th-century Rows (covered galleries above the street-level shops), the Victorian Gothic Town Hall (1869), the Castle (rebuilt 1788 and 1822) and numerous half-timbered buildings. The Cathedral was a Benedictine abbey until the Dissolution. Remaining monastic buildings include the chapter house, refectory and cloisters and there is a modern free-standing bell tower. The Norman church of St John the Baptist was a cathedral church in the early Middle Ages.

COVENTRY (PRE-1900)

Coventry is an important industrial centre, producing vehicles, machine tools, agricultural machinery, man-made fibres, aerospace components and telecommunications equipment. New investment has come from financial services, power transmission, professional services, leisure and education.

The city owes its beginning to Leofric, Earl of Mercia, and his wife Godiva who, in 1043, founded a Benedictine monastery. The guildhall of St Mary dates from the 14th century, three of the city's churches date from the 14th and 15th centuries, and 16th-century almshouses may still be seen. Coventry's first cathedral was destroyed at the Reformation, its second in the 1940 blitz (the walls and spire remain) and the new cathedral designed by Sir Basil Spence, consecrated in 1962, now draws numerous visitors.

Coventry is the home of the University of Warwick, Coventry University, the Westwood Business Park, the Cable and Wireless Technical Training College, the Museum of British Road Transport and the Skydome Arena.

DURHAM (PRE-1900)

The city of Durham is a major tourist attraction and its prominent Norman Cathedral and Castle are set high on a wooded peninsula overlooking the River Wear. The Cathedral was founded as a shrine for the body of St Cuthbert in 995. The present building dates from 1093 and among its many treasures is the tomb of the Venerable Bede (673–735). Durham's Prince Bishops had unique powers up to 1836, being lay rulers as well as religious leaders. As a palatinate, Durham could have its own army, nobility, coinage and courts. The Castle was the main seat of the Prince Bishops for nearly 800 years; it is now used as a college by the University. The University, founded on the initiative of Bishop William Van Mildert, is England's third oldest.

Among other buildings of interest is the Guildhall in the Market Place which dates originally from the 14th century. Work has been carried out to conserve this area as part of the city's contribution to the Council of Europe's Urban Renaissance Campaign. Annual events include Durham's Regatta in June (claimed to be the oldest rowing event in Britain) and the Annual Gala (formerly Durham Miners' Gala) in July.

The economy has undergone a significant change with the replacement of mining as the dominant industry by 'white collar' employment. Although still a predominantly rural area, the industrial and commercial sector is growing and a wide range of manufacturing and service industries are based on industrial estates in and around the city. A research and development centre, linked to the University, also plays an important role in the local economy.

EXETER (PRE-1900)

Exeter lies on the River Exe ten miles from the sea and was granted a charter by Henry II. The Romans founded *Isca Dumnoniorum* in the first century AD as a legionary fortress, and in the third century a stone wall (much of which remains) was built, providing protection against Saxon, and then Danish invasions. After the Conquest, the city led a resistance to William in the west until reduced by siege. The Normans built the ringwork castle of Rougemont, the gatehouse and towers remain, although the rest was pulled down in 1784. The first bridge across the Exe was built in the early 13th century. The city's main port was situated downstream at Topsham until the construction in the 1560s of the first true canal in England. The redevelopment of the canal in 1700 brought seaborne trade directly into the city. Exeter was the Royalist headquarters in the west during the Civil War.

The diocese of Exeter was established by Edward the Confessor in 1050, although a minster existed near the Cathedral site from the late seventh century. A new cathedral was built in the 12th century but the present building, incorporating the Norman Towers, was begun c. 1275 and completed about a century later. The Guildhall dates from the 12th century and there are many other medieval buildings in the city, as well as architecture in the Georgian and Regency styles, and the Custom House (1680). Damage suffered by bombing in 1942 led to the redevelopment of the city centre.

Exeter's prosperity from medieval times was based on trade in wool, commemorated by Tuckers Hall. The wool trade flourished until the late 18th century when export trade was hit by the French wars. Subsequently Exeter has developed as an administrative and commercial centre, notably in the distributive trades, light manufacturing industries and tourism.

KINGSTON-UPON-HULL (PRE-1900)

Hull (officially Kingston-upon-Hull) lies at the junction of the River Hull with the Humber, 22 miles from the North Sea. It is one of the major seaports of the United Kingdom. The port provides a wide range of cargo services, including ro-ro and container traffic, and handles an estimated million passengers annually on daily sailings to Rotterdam and Zeebrugge. There is a variety of manufacturing and service industries.

The city, restored after heavy air raid damage during the Second World War, has good educational facilities with both the University of Hull and the University of Lincoln being within its boundaries. Hull is home to the world's only submarium, The Deep, a £45.5 million project which opened in March 2002, and the Kingston Communications Stadium, with a seating capacity for 25,000, which was completed in December 2002. A £25 million BBC regional centre based at Queen's Gardens was due to open at the end of 2004.

Tourism is a major growth industry and the old town area has been renovated and includes Museums, a marina and shopping complex. Just west of the city is the Humber Bridge, until recently the world's longest single-span suspension bridge.

Kingston-upon-Hull was so named by Edward I. City status was accorded in 1897 and the office of Mayor, raised to the dignity of Lord Mayor in 1914.

LANCASTER (1937)

Lancaster was originally a Roman fort and in Anglo-Saxon times a church was built within the ruins of the fort.

In the late 17th century, Lancaster began to trade with the West Indies and the new American colonies. This trade meant the 18th century was an age of great prosperity for the city and there are many splendid buildings dating from this period, including the complete port facility of St George's Quay, with the Custom House and numerous warehouses.

In the Victorian age, Lancaster began to specialise in textiles and two major manufacturing firms, Storeys and Williamsons, dominated the industry, the latter having a world reputation for the production of linoleum.

Lancaster was originally a market town and a borough, gaining its first charter in 1193. In 1937 Lancaster was awarded city status on King George VI's Coronation Day. Today, Lancaster has mainly technology and service industries and is an important centre for education.

LEEDS (PRE-1900)

Leeds, situated in the lower Aire Valley, is a junction for road, rail, canal and air services and an important manufacturing and commercial centre.

The principal buildings are the Civic Hall (1933), the Town Hall (1858), the Municipal Buildings and Art Gallery (1884) with the Henry Moore Gallery (1982), the Corn Exchange (1863) and the University. The Parish Church (St Peter's) was rebuilt in 1841; the 17th-century St John's Church has a fine interior with a famous English Renaissance screen; the last remaining 18th-century church in the city is Holy Trinity in Boar Lane (1727). Kirkstall Abbey (about three miles from the centre of the city), founded by Henry de Lacy in 1152, is one of the most complete examples of Cistercian houses now remaining. Temple Newsam, birthplace of Lord Darnley, was acquired by the Council in 1922. The present house was largely rebuilt by Sir Arthur Ingram in about 1620. Adel Church, about five miles from the centre of the city, is a fine Norman structure. The new Royal Armouries Museum houses the collection of antique arms and armour formerly held at the Tower of London.

Leeds was first incorporated by Charles I in 1626. The earliest forms of the name are *Loidis* or *Ledes*, the origins of which are obscure.

LEICESTER (1919)

Leicester is situated geographically in the centre of England. The city was an important Roman settlement and also one of the five Danish boroughs of Danelaw. In 1485 Richard III was buried in Leicester following his death at the nearby Battle of Bosworth. In 1589 Queen Elizabeth I granted a charter to the city and the ancient title was confirmed by letters patent in 1919.

The textile industry, responsible for Leicester's early expansion, has declined in recent years, although the city still maintains a strong manufacturing base. Cotton mills and factories are now undergoing extensive regeneration and are being converted into offices, apartments, bars and restaurants. The principal buildings include the two universities, the University of Leicester and De Montfort University, as well as the Town Hall, the 13th-century Guildhall, De Montfort Hall, Leicester Cathedral, the Jewry Wall (the UK's highest standing Roman wall), St Nicholas Church and St Mary de Castro church. The motte and Great Hall of Leicester can be seen from the castle gardens, situated next to the ancient River Soar.

LINCOLN (PRE-1900)

Situated 40 miles inland on the River Witham, Lincoln derives its name from a contraction of *Lindum Colonia*, the settlement founded in AD 48 by the Romans to command the crossing of Ermine Street and Fosse Way. Sections of the third-century Roman city wall can be seen, including an extant gateway (Newport Arch), and excavations have discovered traces of a sewerage system unique in Britain. The Romans also drained the surrounding fenland and created a canal system, laying the foundations of Lincoln's agricultural prosperity and also the city's importance in the medieval wool trade as a port and Staple town.

As one of the Five Boroughs of Danelaw, Lincoln was an important trading centre in the ninth and tenth centuries and medieval prosperity from the wool trade lasted until the 14th century. This wealth enabled local merchants to build parish churches, of which three survive, and there are also remains of a 12th century Jewish community (Jew's House and Court, Aaron's House). However, the removal of the Staple to Boston in 1369 heralded a decline, from which the city only recovered fully in the 19th century, when improved drainage made Lincoln agriculturally important. Improved canal and rail links led to industrial development, mainly in the manufacture of machinery, components and engineering products.

The castle was built shortly after the Conquest and is unusual in having two mounds; on one motte stands a Keep (Lucy's Tower) added in the 12th century. It currently houses one of the four surviving copies of the Magna Carta. The Cathedral was begun c. 1073 when the first Norman bishop moved the see of Lindsey to Lincoln, but was mostly destroyed by fire and earthquake in the 12th century. Rebuilding was begun by St Hugh and completed over a century later. Other notable architectural features are the 12th-century High Bridge, the oldest in Britain still to carry buildings, and the Guildhall situated above the 15th–16th-century Stonebow gateway.

LIVERPOOL (PRE-1900)

Liverpool, on the north bank of the River Mersey, three miles from the Irish Sea, is the United Kingdom's foremost port for Atlantic trade. Tunnels link Liverpool with Birkenhead and Wallasey.

There are 2,100 acres of dockland on both sides of the river and the Gladstone and Royal Seaforth Docks can accommodate tanker-sized vessels. Liverpool Free Port was opened in 1984.

Liverpool was created a free borough in 1207 and a city in 1880. From the early 18th century it expanded rapidly with the growth of industrialisation and the Atlantic trade. Surviving buildings from this period include the Bluecoat Chambers (1717, formerly the Bluecoat School), the Town Hall (1754, rebuilt to the original design 1795), and buildings in Rodney Street, Canning Street and the suburbs. Notable from the 19th and 20th centuries are the Anglican Cathedral, built from the designs of Sir Giles Gilbert Scott (the foundation stone was laid in 1904, and the building was completed only in 1980); the Catholic Metropolitan Cathedral (designed by Sir Frederick Gibberd, consecrated 1967) and St George's Hall (1842), regarded as one of the finest modern examples of classical architecture. The refurbished Albert Dock (designed by Jesse Hartley) contains the Merseyside Maritime Museum and Tate Gallery, Liverpool.

In 1852 an Act was obtained for establishing a public library, museum and art gallery; as a result Liverpool had one of the first public libraries in the country. The Brown, Picton and Hornby libraries form one of the country's major collections. The Victoria Building of Liverpool University, the Royal Liver, Cunard and Mersey Docks & Harbour Company buildings at the Pier Head, the Municipal Buildings and the Philharmonic Hall are other examples of the city's fine architecture.

MANCHESTER (PRE-1900)

Manchester (the *Mamucium* of the Romans, who occupied it in AD 79) is a commercial and industrial centre with a population engaged in the engineering, chemical, clothing, food processing and textile industries and in education. Banking, insurance and a growing leisure industry are among the prime commercial activities. The city is connected with the sea by the Manchester Ship Canal, opened in 1894, 35.5 miles long, and accommodating ships up to 15,000 tons. In 2003 Manchester Airport handled just over 19.5 million terminal, transit, scheduled and charter passengers.

The principal buildings are: the Town Hall, erected in 1877 from the designs of Alfred Waterhouse, with a large extension of 1938; the Royal Exchange (1869, enlarged 1921); the Central Library (1934); Heaton Hall; the 17th-century Chetham Library; the Rylands Library (1900), which includes the Althorp collection; the University precinct; the 15th-century Cathedral (formerly the parish church) and G-MEX exhibition centre. Recent developments include the Manchester Arena, the largest indoor arena in Europe, and the Bridgewater Hall. Manchester is the home of the Hallé Orchestra, the Royal Northern College of Music, the Royal Exchange Theatre and seven public art galleries. Metrolink, the light rail system, opened in 1992.

To accommodate the Commonwealth Games held in Manchester in 2002, new sports facilities were built including a stadium, swimming pool complex and the National Cycling Centre.

The town received its first charter of incorporation in 1838 and was created a city in 1853.

NEWCASTLE UPON TYNE (PRE-1900)
Newcastle upon Tyne, on the north bank of the River Tyne, is eight miles from the North Sea. A cathedral and university city, it is the administrative, commercial and cultural centre for north-east England and the principal port. It is an important manufacturing centre with a wide variety of industries.

The principal buildings include the Castle Keep (12th century), Black Gate (13th century), Blackfriars (13th century), West Walls (13th century), St Nicholas's Cathedral (15th century, fine lantern tower), St Andrew's Church (12th–14th century), St John's (14th–15th century), All Saints (1786 by Stephenson), St Mary's Roman Catholic Cathedral (1844), Trinity House (17th century), Sandhill (16th-century houses), Guildhall (Georgian), Grey Street (1834–9), Central Station (1846–50), Laing Art Gallery (1904), University of Newcastle Physics Building (1962) and Medical Building (1985), Civic Centre (1963), Central Library (1969) and Eldon Square Shopping Development (1976). Open spaces include the Town Moor (927 acres) and Jesmond Dene. Ten bridges span the Tyne at Newcastle.

The city's name is derived from the 'new castle' (1080) erected as a defence against the Scots. In 1400 it was made a county, and in 1882 a city.

NORWICH (PRE-1900)
Norwich grew from an early Anglo-Saxon settlement near the confluence of the Rivers Yare and Wensum, and now serves as provincial capital for the predominantly agricultural region of East Anglia. The name is thought to relate to the most northerly of a group of Anglo-Saxon villages or *wics*. The city's first known charter was granted in 1158 by Henry II.

Norwich serves its surrounding area as a market town and commercial centre, banking and insurance being prominent among the city's businesses. From the 14th century until the Industrial Revolution, Norwich was the regional centre of the woollen industry, but now the biggest single industry is financial services and principal trades are engineering, printing, shoemaking, double glazing, the production of chemicals and clothing, food processing and technology. Norwich is accessible to seagoing vessels by means of the River Yare, entered at Great Yarmouth, 20 miles to the east.

Among many historic buildings are the Cathedral (completed in the 12th century and surmounted by a 15th-century spire 315 feet in height); the keep of the Norman castle (now a museum and art gallery); the 15th-century flint-walled Guildhall; some thirty medieval parish churches; St Andrew's and Blackfriars' Halls; the Tudor houses preserved in Elm Hill and the Georgian Assembly House. The University of East Anglia is on the city's western boundary.

NOTTINGHAM (PRE-1900)
Nottingham stands on the River Trent. *Snotingaham* or *Notingeham*, literally the homestead of the people of Snot, is the Anglo-Saxon name for the Celtic settlement of *Tigguocobauc*, or the house of caves. In 878, Nottingham became one of the Five Boroughs of Danelaw. William the Conqueror ordered the construction of Nottingham Castle, while the town itself developed rapidly under Norman rule. Its laws and rights were later formally recognised by Henry II's charter in 1155. The Castle became a favoured residence of King John. In 1642 King Charles I raised his personal standard at Nottingham Castle at the start of the Civil War.

Nottingham is home to Notts County FC (the world's oldest football league side), Nottingham Forest FC, Nottingham Racecourse, Trent Bridge cricket ground and the National Watersports Centre. The principal industries include textiles, pharmaceuticals, food manufacturing, engineering and telecommunications. There are two universities within the city boundaries.

Architecturally, Nottingham has a wealth of notable buildings, particularly those designed in the Victorian era by T. C. Hine and Watson Fothergill. The City Council owns the Castle, of Norman origin but restored in 1878, Wollaton Hall (1580–8), Newstead Abbey (home of Lord Byron), the Guildhall (1888) and Council House (1929). St Mary's, St Peter's and St Nicholas's Churches are of interest, as is the Roman Catholic Cathedral (Pugin, 1842–4). Nottingham was granted city status in 1897.

OXFORD (PRE-1900)
Oxford is a university city, an important industrial centre, and a market town. Industry played a minor part in Oxford until the motor industry was established in 1912.

Oxford is known for its architecture, its oldest specimens being the reputedly Saxon tower of St Michael's church, the remains of the Norman castle and city walls, and the Norman church at Iffley. It also has many Gothic buildings, such as the Divinity Schools, the Old Library at Merton College, William of Wykeham's New College, Magdalen College and Christ Church and many other college buildings. Later centuries are represented by the Laudian quadrangle at St John's College, the Renaissance Sheldonian Theatre by Wren, Trinity College Chapel, and All Saints Church, Hawksmoor's mock-Gothic at All Souls College, and the 18th-century Queen's College. In addition to individual buildings, High Street and Radcliffe Square both form interesting architectural compositions. Most of the Colleges have gardens, those of Magdalen, New College, St John's and Worcester being the largest.

ST ALBANS (PRE-1900)
The origins of St Albans, situated on the River Ver, stem from the Roman town of *Verulamium*. Named after the first Christian martyr in Britain, who was executed here, St Albans has developed around the Norman Abbey and Cathedral Church (consecrated 1115), built partly of materials from the old Roman city. The museums house Iron Age and Roman artefacts and the Roman Theatre, unique in Britain, has a stage as opposed to an amphitheatre. Archaeological excavations in the city centre have revealed evidence of pre-Roman, Saxon and medieval occupation.

The town's significance grew to the extent that it was a signatory and venue for the drafting of the Magna Carta. It was also the scene of riots during the Peasants' Revolt, the French King John was imprisoned there after the Battle of Poitiers, and heavy fighting took place there during the Wars of the Roses.

Previously controlled by the Abbot, the town achieved a charter in 1553 and city status in 1877. The street market, first established in 1553, is still an important feature of the city, as are many hotels and inns, surviving from the days when St Albans was an important coach stop. Tourist attractions include historic churches and houses, and a 15th-century clock tower.

The city is now home to a wide range of firms, with special emphasis on information and legal services. In addition, it is the home of the Royal National Rose Society, and of Rothamsted Park agricultural research centre.

SALISBURY (PRE-1900)

The history of Salisbury centres around the Cathedral and Cathedral Close. The city evolved from an Iron Age camp a mile to the north of its current position which was strengthened by the Romans and called *Serviodunum*. The Normans built a castle and cathedral on the site and renamed it Sarum. In AD 1220, Bishop Richard Poore and the architect Elias de Derham decided to build a new Gothic style cathedral. The cathedral was completed 38 years later and a community known as New Sarum, now called Salisbury, grew around it. Originally the cathedral had a squat tower. The 404 ft spire that makes the cathedral the tallest medieval structure in the world was added *c.* 1315. A walled Close with houses for the clergy was built around the cathedral, the Medieval Hall still stands today, alongside buildings dating from the 13th to the 20th century; including some designed by Sir Christopher Wren.

A prosperous wool and cloth trade allowed Salisbury to flourish until the 17th century. When the wool trade declined new crafts were established including cutlery, leather and basket work, saddlery, lacemaking, joinery and malting. By 1750 it had become an important road junction and coaching centre and in the Victorian era the railways created a new age of expansion and prosperity. Today Salisbury is a thriving tourist centre.

SHEFFIELD (PRE-1900)

Sheffield is situated at the junction of the Sheaf, Porter, Rivelin and Loxley valleys with the River Don. Though its cutlery, silverware and plate have long been famous, Sheffield has other and now more important industries: special and alloy steels, engineering, tool-making, medical equipment and media-related industries (in its new Cultural Industries Quarter). Sheffield has two universities and is an important research centre.

The parish church of St Peter and St Paul, founded in the 12th century, became the Cathedral Church of the Diocese of Sheffield in 1914. The Roman Catholic Cathedral Church of St Marie (founded 1847) was created Cathedral for the new diocese of Hallam in 1980. Parts of the present building date from *c.* 1435. The principal buildings are the Town Hall (1897), the Cutlers' Hall (1832), City Hall (1932), Graves Art Gallery (1934), Mappin Art Gallery, the Crucible Theatre and the restored 19th-century Lyceum theatre, which dates from 1897 and was reopened in 1990. Three major sports venues were opened in 1990 to 1991. These are Sheffield Arena, Don Valley Stadium and Pond's Forge. The Millennium Galleries opened in 2001. Sheffield was created a city in 1893.

STOKE-ON-TRENT (1925)

Stoke-on-Trent, standing on the River Trent and familiarly known as The Potteries, is the main centre of employment for the population of north Staffordshire. The city is the largest clayware producer in the world (china, earthenware, sanitary goods, refractories, bricks and tiles) and also has a wide range of other manufacturing industry, including steel, chemicals, engineering and tyres. Extensive reconstruction has been carried out in recent years.

The city was formed by the federation of the separate municipal authorities of Tunstall, Burslem, Hanley, Stoke, Fenton, and Longton in 1910 and received its city status in 1925.

WINCHESTER (PRE-1900)

Winchester, the ancient capital of England, is situated on the River Itchen. The city is rich in architecture of all types but the Cathedral takes pride of place. The cathedral was built in 1079–93 and exhibits examples of Norman, Early English and Perpendicular styles. The author Jane Austen is buried in the Cathedral. Winchester College, founded in 1382, is one of the most famous public schools, the original building (1393) remaining largely unaltered. St Cross Hospital, another great medieval foundation, lies one mile south of the city. The almshouses were founded in 1136 by Bishop Henry de Blois, and Cardinal Henry Beaufort added a new almshouse of 'Noble Poverty' in 1446. The chapel and dwellings are of great architectural interest, and visitors may still receive the 'Wayfarer's Dole' of bread and ale.

Excavations have done much to clarify the origins and development of Winchester. Part of the forum and several of the streets from the Roman town have been discovered. Excavations in the Cathedral Close have uncovered the entire site of the Anglo-Saxon cathedral (known as the Old Minster) and parts of the New Minster which was built by Alfred's son, Edward the Elder, and is the burial place of the Alfredian dynasty. The original burial place of St Swithun, before his remains were translated to a site in the present cathedral, was also uncovered.

Excavations in other parts of the city have thrown much light on Norman Winchester, notably on the site of the Royal Castle (adjacent to which the new Law Courts have been built) and in the grounds of Wolvesey Castle, where the great house built by Bishops Giffard and Henry de Blois in the 12th century has been uncovered. The Great Hall, built by Henry III between 1222 and 1236, survives and houses the Arthurian Round Table.

YORK (PRE-1900)

The city of York is an archiepiscopal seat. Its recorded history dates from AD 71, when the Roman Ninth Legion established a base under Petilius Cerealis later becoming the fortress of *Eboracum*. In Anglo-Saxon times the city was the royal and ecclesiastical centre of Northumbria, and after capture by a Viking army in AD 866 it became the capital of the Viking kingdom of Jorvik. By the 14th century the city had become a great mercantile centre, mainly because of its control of the wool trade, and was used as the chief base against the Scots. Under the Tudors its fortunes declined, though Henry VIII made it the headquarters of the Council of the North. Excavations on many sites, including Coppergate, have greatly expanded knowledge of Roman, Viking and medieval urban life.

With its development as a railway centre in the 19th century the commercial life of York expanded. The principal industries are the manufacture of chocolate, scientific instruments and sugar.

The city is rich in examples of architecture of all periods. The earliest church was built in AD 627 and, in the 12th to 15th centuries, the present Minster was built in a succession of styles. Other examples within the city are the medieval city walls and gateways, churches and guildhalls. Domestic architecture includes the Georgian mansions of The Mount, Micklegate and Bootham.

ENGLISH COUNTIES AND SHIRES

LORDS-LIEUTENANT AND HIGH SHERIFFS

County/Shire	Lord-Lieutenant	High Sheriff, 2004–5
Bedfordshire	S. C. Whitbread	C. Ibbett
Berkshire	P. L. Wroughton	J. West
Bristol	J. Tidmarsh	Lady Kingman
Cambridgeshire	Archibald Hugh Duberly	Sir Charles Chadwyck-Healey, Bt
Cheshire	W. A. Bromley-Davenport	S. Sherrard
Cornwall	Lady Mary Holborow	James Southwell
Cumbria	J. A. Cropper	Frederick Markham
Derbyshire	J. K. Bather	J. Olivier
Devon	E. Dancer, CBE	The Countess of Devon
Dorset	Capt. M. Fulford-Dobson	A. Simmons
Durham	Sir Paul Nicholson	Richard Coad
East Riding of Yorkshire	R. Marriott, TD	S. Booth
East Sussex	Mrs P. Stewart-Roberts	J. Avery
Essex	The Lord Petre	A. Streeter
Gloucestershire	H. W. G. Elwes	S. Preston
Greater London	The Lord Imbert, QPM	Frances Cairncross
Greater Manchester	Col. J. B. Timmins, OBE, TD	Robert Hough
Hampshire	Mrs F. M. Fagan	Sir James Scott, Bt.
Herefordshire	Sir Thomas Dunne, KCVO	James Nicholas
Hertfordshire	S. A. Bowes Lyon	Lady Nichols
Isle of Wight	C. D. J. Bland	A. Goddard
Kent	A. Willett, CBE	J. Loudon
Lancashire	The Lord Shuttleworth	Gail Stanley
Leicestershire	Lady Gretton	F. Hussain, MBE
Lincolnshire	Mrs B. K. Cracroft-Eley	C. Welby
Merseyside	A. W. Waterworth	Stuart Christie
Norfolk	Richard Jewson	J. Alston
North Yorkshire	The Lord Crathorne	Mrs C. Thornton-Berry
Northumberland	Sir John Riddell, CVO	Mrs S. Burnell
Nottinghamshire	Sir Andrew Buchanan, Bt.	H. Machin
Oxfordshire	H. L. J. Brunner	Mrs A. Kelaart
Rutland	Dr Laurence Howard	M. Taylor
Shropshire	A. E. H. Heber-Percy	H. Salwey
Somerset	Lady Gass	S. Evans
South Yorkshire	David Moody	Pamela Edwards Liversidge, OBE
Staffordshire	J. A. Hawley, TD	Mrs D. Carver
Suffolk	The Lord Tollemache	The Countess of Euston
Surrey	Mrs S. J. F. Goad	Dr G. Dowling
Tyne and Wear	N. Sherlock	Sir Neville Guthrie Trotter
Warwickshire	M. Dunne	Mrs G. Jefferson
West Midlands	R. R. Taylor, OBE	J. Andrews
West Sussex	H. Wyatt	R. Reed
West Yorkshire	Dr Ingrid Roscoe	J. Barker
Wiltshire	John Bush, OBE	Lt.-Col. J. Arkell, TD
Worcestershire	M. Brinton	James Nicholas

COUNTY COUNCILS: CONTACT DETAILS, AREA

Council	Administrative Headquarters	Telephone	Area (Hectares)
Bedfordshire	County Hall, Bedford	01234-363222	119,220
Buckinghamshire	County Hall, Aylesbury	01296-395000	156,509
Cambridgeshire	Shire Hall, Cambridge	01223-717111	304,357
Cheshire	County Hall, Chester	01244-602424	208,344
Cornwall	County Hall, Truro	01872-322000	354,810
Cumbria	The Courts, Carlisle	01228-606060	676,780
Derbyshire	County Hall, Matlock	01629-580000	255,000
Devon	County Hall, Exeter	01392-382000	656,085
Dorset	County Hall, Dorchester	01305-251000	254,181
Durham	County Hall, Durham	0191-383 3000	223,181
East Sussex	County Hall, Lewes	01273-481000	179,530
Essex	County Hall, Chelmsford	01245-492211	345,619
Gloucestershire	Shire Hall, Gloucester	01452-425000	279,875
Hampshire	The Castle, Winchester	01962-841841	367,896
Hertfordshire	County Hall, Hertford	01992-555555	163,416
Kent	County Hall, Maidstone	01622-671411	373,063
Lancashire	County Hall, Preston	01772-254868	289,780
Leicestershire	County Hall, Leicester	0116-232 3232	208,300
Lincolnshire	County Offices, Lincoln	01522-552222	591,470
Norfolk	County Hall, Norwich	0844-800 8020	537,234
Northamptonshire	County Hall, Northampton	01604-236236	235,966
Northumberland	County Hall, Morpeth	01670-533000	502,594
North Yorkshire	County Hall, Northallerton	01609-780780	803,741
Nottinghamshire	County Hall, Nottingham	0115-982 3823	208,519
Oxfordshire	County Hall, Oxford	01865-792422	260,595
Shropshire	The Shirehall, Shrewsbury	01743-251000	318,761
Somerset	County Hall, Taunton	01823-355455	345,233
Staffordshire	County Buildings, Stafford	01785-223121	262,355
Suffolk	County Hall, Ipswich	01473-583000	380,207
Surrey	County Hall, Kingston upon Thames	020-8541 8800	167,011
Warwickshire	Shire Hall, Warwick	01926-410410	197,854
West Sussex	County Hall, Chichester	01243-777100	198,936
Wiltshire	County Hall, Trowbridge	01225-713000	325,548
Worcestershire	County Hall, Worcester	01905-763763	173,529

COUNTY COUNCILS: POPULATION, BAND D COUNCIL TAX, CHIEF EXECUTIVES

Council	Population	Band D Charge*	Chief Executive
Bedfordshire	382,100	£943	Dick Wilkinson
Buckinghamshire	479,020	£858	Chris Williams
Cambridgeshire	556,800	£813	Ian Stewart
Cheshire	674,200	£887	Jeremy Taylor
Cornwall	502,000	£838	Peter Stethridge
Cumbria	488,513	£928	John Harwood
Derbyshire	739,300	£897	Nick Hodgson
Devon	710,500	£900	Philip Jenkinson
Dorset	391,517	£918	David Jenkins
Durham	489,700	£884	Kingsley Smith
East Sussex	498,800	£920	Cheryl Miller
Essex	1,310,922	£892	Stewart Ashurst
Gloucestershire	564,841	£889	Joyce Redfearn
Hampshire	1,244,400	£840	Peter Robertson
Hertfordshire	1,011,000	£895	Caroline Tapster
Kent	1,353,000	£846	Michael Pitt
Lancashire	1,429,400	£927	Chris Trinick
Leicestershire	610,300	£867	J. Sinnott
Lincolnshire	612,000	£858	David Bowles
Norfolk	797,900	£930	Tim Byles
North Yorkshire	570,100	£817	Jeremy Walker
Northamptonshire	629,676	£833	Peter Gould
Northumberland	307,000	£1,023	Mark Henderson
Nottinghamshire	748,800	£994	Roger Latham
Oxfordshire	607,500	£925	Richard Shaw
Shropshire	283,300	£848	Carolyn Downs
Somerset	503,400	£907	Alan Jones
Staffordshire	810,697	£823	N. Pursey
Suffolk	671,100	£924	Mike More
Surrey	1,059,500	£889	Paul Coen
Warwickshire	506,200	£922	Ian Caulfield
West Sussex	750,000	£910	Mark Hammond
Wiltshire	432,973	£852	Dr Keith Robinson
Worcestershire	542,238	£825	Rob Sykes

* Average Band D council tax in the county area exclusive of precepts for fire and police

DISTRICT COUNCILS

District Council	Telephone	Population	Band D Charge*	Chief Executive
Adur	01273-263000	59,627	£1,241	Ian Lowrie
Allerdale	01900-326333	93,000	£1,222	P. Leonard
Alnwick	01665-510505	31,400	£1,259	Bill Batey
Amber valley	01773-570222	118,000	£1,226	Peter Carney
Arun	01903-737500	140,759	£1,191	Ian Sumnall
Ashfield	01623-450000	109,800	£1,320	Alan Mellor
Ashford	01233-637311	102,661	£1,126	David Hill
Aylesbury vale	01296-585858	165,749	£1,172	Richard Carr
Babergh	01473-822801	82,310	£1,206	Patricia Rockall
Barrow-in-Furness	01229-894900	71,980	£1,259	Tom Campbell
Basildon	01268-533333	165,668	£1,256	John Robb
Basingstoke and Deane	01256-844844	152,800	£1,103	Gordon Hoadcroft
Bassetlaw	01909-533533	107,831	£1,319	James Molloy
Bedford	01234-267422	149,200	£1,263	Shaun Field
Berwick-upon-Tweed	01289-330044	27,000	£1,254	Jane Pannell
Blaby	0116-275 0555	91,600	£1,192	Philip Dolan
Blyth valley	01670-542322	80,000	£1,234	Geoff Paul
Bolsover	01246-240000	72,482	£1,272	W. Lumley
Boston	01205-314200	57,000	£1,124	Nicola Bulbeck
Braintree	01376-552525	132,468	£1,202	Allan Reid
Breckland	01362-695333	121,418	£1,165	Rob Garnett
Brentwood	01277-261111	71,502	£1,198	R. McLintock
Bridgnorth	01746-713100	52,497	£1,200	John Harmeston
Broadland	01603-431133	118,513	£1,206	Colin Bland
Bromsgrove	01527-873232	84,900	£1,183	Sue Nixon
Broxbourne	01992-785555	87,500	£1,098	Mike Walker
Broxtowe	0115-917 7777	108,000	£1,321	M. Brown
Burnley	01282-425011	89,000	£1,290	Dr Gillian Taylor
CAMBRIDGE CITY	01223-457000	120,650	£1,120	R. Hammond
Cannock Chase	01543-462621	92,127	£1,186	Stephen Brown
CANTERBURY CITY	01227-862000	165,000	£1,158	Colin Carmichael
Caradon	01579-341000	79,679	£1,135	B. Davies
CARLISLE CITY	01228-817000	100,734	£1,248	Peter Stybelski
Carrick	01872-224400	88,900	£1,136	John Winskill
Castle Morpeth	01670-535000	50,000	£1,292	Ken Dunbar
Castle Point	01268-882200	84,800	£1,237	B. Rollinson
Charnwood	01509-263151	158,300	£1,175	Brian Hayes
Chelmsford	01245-606606	157,072	£1,201	Steve Packham
Cheltenham	01242-262626	110,000	£1,201	Christine Laird
Cherwell	01295-252535	137,500	£1,215	G. Handley
CHESTER CITY	01244-324324	118,000	£1,198	Paul Durham
Chester-le-Street	0191-387 1919	55,000	£1,212	Roy Templeman
Chesterfield	01246-345345	100,000	£1,192	D. Shaw
Chichester	01243-785166	106,450	£1,159	John Marsland
Chiltern	01494-729000	71,013	£1,194	Alan Goodrum
Chorley	01257-515151	100,239	£1,244	Jeff Davies
Christchurch	01202-495000	44,908	£1,236	Mike Turvey
Colchester	01206-282222	159,600	£1,204	Adrian Pritchard
Congleton	01270-763231	90,758	£1,200	Glyn Chambers
Copeland	01946-852585	69,200	£1,241	J. Stanforth
Corby	01536-464000	52,000	£1,129	Chris Mallender
Cotswolds	01285-623000	81,402	£1,206	R. Austin
Craven	01756-700600	53,555	£1,199	Gill Dixon
Crawley	01293-438000	99,744	£1,178	Michael Coughlin
Crewe and Nantwich	01270-537777	114,900	£1,182	Alan Wenham
Dacorum	01442-228000	132,240	£1,149	Daniel Zammit
Dartford	01322-343434	85,911	£1,150	G. Harris
Daventry	01327-871100	73,521	£1,130	Steve Atkinson
Derbyshire Dales	01629-761100	69,469	£1,251	David Wheatcroft
Derwentside	01207-218000	85,065	£1,294	Mike Clark
Dover	01304-821199	104,566	£1,159	Nadeem Aziz

District Council	Telephone	Population	Band D Charge*	Chief Executive
DURHAM CITY	0191-386 6111	87,656	£1,235	B. Spears
Easington	0191-527 0501	93,981	£1,349	Janet Johnson
East Cambridgeshire	01353-665555	68,900	£1,138	John Hill
East Devon	01395-516551	125,520	£1,189	Mark Williams
East Dorset	01202-886201	83,788	£1,272	Alan Breakwell
East Hampshire	01730-266551	111,750	£1,161	Will Godfrey
East Hertfordshire	01279-655261	126,000	£1,174	Miranda Steward; Rachel Stopard
East Lindsey	01507-601111	130,500	£1,085	Rachel Mann, *acting*
East Northamptonshire	01832-742000	78,511	£1,132	Stephen Baker
East Staffordshire	01283-508000	103,000	£1,192	William Saunders
Eastbourne	01323-410000	89,800	£1,279	Martin Ray
Eastleigh	023-8068 8000	117,000	£1,163	Chris Tapp
Eden	01768-864671	49,880	£1,227	Ian Bruce
Ellesmere Port and Neston	0151-356 6789	81,400	£1,197	S. Ewbank
Elmbridge	01372-474474	124,300	£1,211	Michael Lockwood
Epping Forest	01992-564000	120,896	£1,217	John Burgess
Epsom and Ewell	01372-732000	66,800	£1,164	David Smith
Erewash	0115-907 2244	108,000	£1,215	John Rice
EXETER CITY	01392-277888	111,189	£1,172	Philip Bostock
Fareham	01329-236100	109,407	£1,123	A. Davies
Fenland	01354-654321	82,500	£1,210	Tim Pilsbury
Forest Heath	01638-719000	55,514	£1,212	David Burnip
Forest of Dean	01594-810000	80,000	£1,227	Tim Perrin
Fylde	01253-721222	73,217	£1,219	Ken Lee
Gedling	0115-901 3901	110,200	£1,300	Peter Murdoch
GLOUCESTER CITY	01452-522232	109,300	£1,198	Paul Smith
Gosport	023-9258 4242	76,415	£1,174	Malcolm Crocker
Gravesham	01474-564422	92,000	£1,138	David Williams
Great Yarmouth	01493-856100	89,900	£1,192	Richard Packham
Guildford	01483-505050	129,701	£1,180	David Willams
Hambleton	01609-779977	84,111	£1,128	P. Simpson
Harborough	01858-821100	75,200	£1,196	Michael Wilson
Harlow	01279-446611	83,000	£1,263	Malcolm Morley
Harrogate	01423-500600	150,588	£1,224	P. Walsh
Hart	01252-622122	87,806	£1,168	Jules Samuels
Hastings	01424-781066	84,000	£1,285	Roy Mawford
Havant	023-9247 4174	120,500	£1,152	Gwen Andrews
Hertsmere	020-8207 2277	94,947	£1,153	Ron Higgins
High Peak	0845-129 7777	89,300	£1,233	Peter Sloman
Hinckley and Bosworth	01455-238141	100,141	£1,146	*vacant*
Horsham	01403-215100	125,700	£1,158	Martin Pearson
Huntingdonshire	01480-388388	157,000	£1,133	David Monks
Hyndburn	01254-388111	81,800	£1,259	David Welsby
Ipswich	01473-432000	114,000	£1,313	J. Hehir
Kennet	01380-724911	74,833	£1,171	Mark Boden
Kerrier	01209-614000	90,990	£1,144	Barry Manning
Kettering	01536-410333	82,000	£1,140	David Cook
King's Lynn and West Norfolk	01553-616200	135,600	£1,203	Ray Harding, *acting*
LANCASTER CITY	01524-582000	133,914	£1,232	Mark Cullinan
Lewes	01273-471600	93,000	£1,292	John Crawford
Lichfield	01543-308000	93,835	£1,155	Nina Dawes
LINCOLN CITY	01522-881188	82,750	£1,154	Andrew Taylor
Macclesfield	01625-500500	150,144	£1,189	Vivien Horton
Maidstone	01622-602000	139,000	£1,198	David Petford
Maldon	01621-854477	57,300	£1,215	Avril Spencer, *acting*
Malvern Hills	01684-892700	72,182	£1,183	Chris Bocock
Mansfield	01623-463463	98,500	£1,337	Richard Goad
Melton	01664-502502	47,488	£1,185	Delwyn Burbidge
Mendip	01749-343399	103,865	£1,192	David Thomson
Mid Bedfordshire	01525-402051	121,300	£1,271	Jaki Salisbury
Mid Devon	01884-255255	69,883	£1,240	Paul Edwards
Mid Suffolk	01449-720711	86,000	£1,205	Andrew Good
Mid Sussex	01444-458166	127,400	£1,177	John Jory
Mole Valley	01306-885001	80,300	£1,165	Heather Kerswell
New Forest	02380-285000	172,319	£1,179	David Yates
Newark and Sherwood	01636-650000	105,800	£1,367	Richard Dix

District Council	Telephone	Population	Band D Charge*	Chief Executive
Newcastle-Under-Lyme	01782-717717	122,075	£1,164	Felix Harley
North Cornwall	01208-893333	81,000	£1,144	David Brown
North Devon	01271-327711	87,508	£1,234	John Sunderland
North Dorset	01258-454111	61,360	£1,223	Liz Goodall
North East Derbyshire	01246-231111	97,000	£1,273	Carole Gilby
North Hertfordshire	01462-474000	116,400	£1,175	John Campbell
North Kesteven	01529-414155	96,852	£1,128	Ruth Marlow
North Norfolk	01263-513811	100,500	£1,206	Philip Burton
North Shropshire	01939-232771	54,581	£1,228	R. Hughes
North Warwickshire	01827-715341	60,000	£1,263	Jerry Hutchinson
North West Leicestershire	01530-454545	88,800	£1,210	M. Diaper
North Wiltshire	01249-706111	125,370	£1,204	R. Marshall
Northampton	01604-837837	196,300	£1,158	Mairi McLean
NORWICH CITY	01603-622233	121,700	£1,251	Anne Seex
Nuneaton and Bedworth	02476-376376	119,132	£1,232	Christine Kerr
Oadby and Wigston	0116-288-8961	55,800	£1,197	R. Hyde
Oswestry	01691-671111	37,000	£1,266	Paul Shevlin
OXFORD CITY	01865-249811	134,248	£1,261	Caroline Bull
Pendle	01282-661661	89,248	£1,291	Stephen Barnes
Penwith	01736-362341	63,000	£1,101	J. McKenna
PRESTON CITY	01772-906000	135,000	£1,286	J. Carr
Purbeck	01929-556561	44,130	£1,260	P. Croft
Redditch	01527-64252	76,747	£1,192	Christopher Smith
Reigate and Banstead	01737-276000	119,000	£1,196	Nigel Clifford
Restormel	01726-223300	95,800	£1,104	P. Crowson
Ribble Valley	01200-425111	53,161	£1,206	David Morris
Richmondshire	01748-829100	47,846	£1,219	Harry Tabiner
Rochford	01702-546366	78,489	£1,229	Paul Warren
Rossendale	01706-217777	65,000	£1,296	O. Williams
Rother	01424-787878	85,000	£1,248	Derek Stevens
Rugby	01788-533533	88,900	£1,210	Diane Colley
Runnymede	01932-838383	78,048	£1,137	Tim Williams
Rushcliffe	0115-981 9911	106,301	£1,300	Keith Beaumont
Rushmoor	01252-398398	86,000	£1,152	Andrew Lloyd
Ryedale	01653-600666	50,800	£1,215	H. Mosley
ST ALBANS CITY	01727-866100	130,000	£1,184	Peter Learner
St Edmundsbury	01284-763233	98,000	£1,214	D. Cadman
SALISBURY	01722-336272	85,803	£1,155	Richard Sheard
Scarborough	01723-232323	108,000	£1,222	John Trebble
Sedgefield	01388-816166	87,206	£1,376	N. Vaulks
Sedgemoor	01278-435435	104,000	£1,160	Kerry Rickards
Selby	01757-705101	76,468	£1,207	M. Connor
Sevenoaks	01732-227000	109,305	£1,195	Robin Hales
Shepway	01303-850388	99,265	£1,230	R. Thompson
Shrewsbury and Atcham	01743-281000	95,425	£1,192	Robin Hooper
South Bedfordshire	01582-472222	111,100	£1,332	John Ruddick
South Bucks	01753-533333	61,945	£1,168	Chris Furness
South Cambridgeshire	01223-443000	132,000	£1,099	John Ballantyne
South Derbyshire	01283-221000	76,000	£1,208	Frank McArdle
South Hams	01803-861234	81,846	£1,207	Ruth Bagley
South Holland	01775-761161	79,125	£1,118	Terry Huggins
South Kesteven	01476-406080	120,000	£1,096	Duncan Kerr
South Lakeland	01539-733333	103,000	£1,237	Mike Jones, acting
South Norfolk	01508-533633	104,334	£1,221	Geoffrey Rivers
South Northamptonshire	01327-322322	79,293	£1,154	Rob Tinlin
South Oxfordshire	01491-823000	128,177	£1,213	David Buckle
South Ribble	01772-421491	103,900	£1,252	Jean Hunter
South Shropshire	01584-813000	40,000	£1,264	Graham Biggs
South Somerset	01935-462462	155,770	£1,200	Philip Dolan
South Staffordshire	01902-696000	105,600	£1,134	Les Barnfield
Spelthorne	01784-451499	89,600	£1,171	Karen Satterford
Stafford	01785-619000	120,000	£1,153	David Rawlings
Staffordshire Moorlands	01538-483483	94,390	£1,171	Simon Baker
Stevenage	01438-242242	79,177	£1,167	Ian Paske
Stratford-on-Avon	01789-267575	111,536	£1,190	Paul Lankester
Stroud	01453-766321	110,000	£1,247	David Hagg

District Council	Telephone	Population	Band D Charge*	Chief Executive
Suffolk Coastal	01394-383789	115,200	£1,193	Jan Ormodroyd
Surrey Heath	01276-707100	85,900	£1,198	Barry Catchpole
Swale	01795-424341	123,000	£1,143	J. Edwards
Tamworth	01827-709709	80,000	£1,129	David Weatherley
Tandridge	01883-722000	80,000	£1,198	Philip Thomas
Taunton Deane	01823-356356	100,800	£1,158	S. Fletcher
Teesdale	01833-690000	24,457	£1,242	Charles Anderson
Teignbridge	01626-361101	120,958	£1,222	Howard Davis
Tendring	01255-425501	138,555	£1,189	John Hawkins
Test Valley	01264-368000	113,352	£1,119	Roger Tetstall
Tewkesbury	01684-295010	77,321	£1,150	Teri Turner
Thanet	01843-577000	126,702	£1,182	Richard Samuel
Three Rivers	01923-776611	85,000	£1,181	S. Halls
Tonbridge and Malling	01732-844522	107,800	£1,167	David Hughes
Torridge	01237-428700	56,000	£1,203	Roger Heath, *acting*
Tunbridge Wells	01892-526121	103,000	£1,144	R. Stone
Tynedale	01434-652200	59,000	£1,268	Richard Robson
Uttlesford	01799-510510	70,300	£1,206	Alasdair Bovaird
Vale of White Horse	01235-520202	112,900	£1,173	Terry Stock
Vale Royal	01606-862862	122,300	£1,197	Anne Bingham-Holmes
Wansbeck	01670-532200	61,138	£1,249	R. Stephenson
Warwick	01926-450000	125,931	£1,178	Janie Barrett
Watford	01923-226400	80,400	£1,239	Alastair Robertson
Waveney	01502-562111	110,000	£1,173	*vacant*
Waverley	01483-523333	115,976	£1,202	Christine Pointer
Wealden	01892-653311	142,700	£1,286	Charles Lant
Wear Valley	01388-765555	61,339	£1,238	Iain Phillips
Wellingborough	01933-229777	70,000	£1,104	T. McArdle
Welwyn Hatfield	01707-357000	97,553	£1,201	Michel Saminaden
West Devon	01822-813600	50,689	£1,255	David Incoll
West Dorset	01305-251010	92,360	£1,254	David Clarke
West Lancashire	01695-577177	108,378	£1,246	William Taylor
West Lindsey	01427-676676	81,161	£1,152	Robert Nelsey
West Oxfordshire	01993-861000	99,000	£1,154	G. Bonner
West Somerset	01984-632291	35,075	£1,177	Tim Howes
West Wiltshire	01225-776655	112,000	£1,194	Andrew Pate
Weymouth and Portland	01305-838000	63,000	£1,315	Tom Grainger
WINCHESTER CITY	01962-840222	107,274	£1,147	S. Eden
Woking	01483-755855	89,431	£1,203	Paul Russell
WORCESTER CITY	01905-723471	95,363	£1,159	D. Wareing
Worthing	01903-239999	100,000	£1,185	Sheryl Grady
Wychavon	01386-565000	112,949	£1,146	Jack Hegarty
Wycombe	01494-461000	161,850	£1,163	Richard Cummins
Wyre	01253-891000	106,826	£1,224	Jim Corry
Wyre Forest	01562-820505	96,981	£1,200	W. Delin

*Average Band D council tax
Councils in CAPITAL LETTERS have city status

METROPOLITAN BOROUGH COUNCILS

Metropolitan Borough Councils	Telephone	Population	Band D Charge*	Chief Executive
Barnsley	01226-770770	218,000	£1,104	Phil Coppard
BIRMINGHAM CITY	0121-303 9944	977,000	£1,106	Lin Homer
Bolton	01204-333333	267,400	£1,162	B. Knight
BRADFORD CITY	01274-432001	467,665	£1,061	Philip Robinson, *acting*
Bury	0161-253 5000	181,000	£1,117	Mark Sanders
Calderdale	01422-357257	192,400	£1,181	Paul Sheehan
COVENTRY CITY	02476-833333	301,000	£1,210	Stella Manzie
Doncaster	01302-734444	289,897	£1,094	Susan Law
Dudley	01384-818181	305,155	£1,034	Andrew Sparke
Gateshead	0191-433 3000	200,000	£1,300	Roger Kelly
Kirklees	01484-221000	392,000	£1,134	A. Elson
Knowsley	0151-489 6000	153,094	£1,151	Steve Gallagher
LEEDS CITY	0113-247 4554	726,757	£1,040	P. Rogerson
LIVERPOOL CITY	0151-233 3000	439,476	£1,223	David Henshaw
MANCHESTER CITY	0161-234 5000	439,549	£1,133	Howard Bernstein
NEWCASTLE UPON TYNE CITY	0191-232 8520	283,000	£1,302	Ian Stratford
North Tyneside	0191-200 6565	192,000	£1,228	John Marsden
Oldham	0161-911 3000	218,680	£1,283	Andrew Kilburn
Rochdale	01706-647474	208,950	£1,152	Roger Ellis
Rotherham	01709-382121	253,706	£1,143	Mike Cuff
SALFORD CITY	0161-794 4711	220,000	£1,285	John Willis
Sandwell	0121-569 2200	282,900	£1,125	Nigel Summers
Sefton	0151-922 4040	287,700	£1,188	Graham Haywood
SHEFFIELD CITY	0114-272 6444	530,300	£1,216	Bob Kerslake
Solihull	0121-704 6000	205,600	£1,045	Katherine Kerswell
South Tyneside	0191-427 1717	152,710	£1,184	Irene Lucas
St Helens	01744-456000	178,854	£1,178	Carole Hudson
Stockport	0161-480 4949	291,500	£1,198	John Schultz
SUNDERLAND CITY	0191-553 1000	280,800	£1,101	Jed Fitzgerald
Tameside	0161-342 8355	213,043	£1,124	Janet Orchard
Trafford	0161-912 1212	225,000	£990	Dr Gary Pickering, *acting*
WAKEFIELD CITY	01924-306090	319,600	£1,048	John Foster
Walsall	01922-650000	261,599	£1,233	Anne Shepperd
Wigan	01942-244991	310,000	£1,136	Frank Costello
Wirral	0151-638 7070	312,289	£1,175	Stephen Maddox
WOLVERHAMPTON CITY	01902-556556	240,500	£1,174	D. Anderson

*Average Band D council tax
Councils in CAPITAL LETTERS have city status

UNITARY COUNCILS

Unitary Councils	Telephone	Population	Band D Charge*	Chief Executive
Bath and North East Somerset	01225-477000	165,000	£1,140	John Everitt
Blackburn with Darwen	01254-585585	137,600	£1,212	Philip Watson
Blackpool	01253-477477	153,600	£1,179	S. Weaver
Bournemouth	01202-451451	163,444	£1,186	Paul Godier
Bracknell Forest	01344-424642	109,617	£1,048	Timothy Wheadon
BRIGHTON AND HOVE CITY	01273-290000	247,817	£1,162	David Panter
BRISTOL CITY	0117-922 2000	380,615	£1,235	N. Gurney
Darlington	01325-380651	97,838	£1,099	Barry Keel
DERBY CITY	01332-293111	236,429	£1,079	Ray Cowlishaw
East Riding of Yorkshire	01482-887700	314,113	£1,183	D. Stephenson
Halton	0151-424 2061	118,200	£1,070	M. Cuff
Hartlepool	01429-266522	91,200	£1,297	Paul Walker
Herefordshire	01432-260000	167,000	£1,185	Neil Pringle
Isle of Wight	01983-821000	132,938	£1,195	M. Fisher
KINGSTON UPON HULL CITY	01482-609100	241,443	£1,094	Jan Didrichsen
LEICESTER CITY	0116-254 9922	296,000	£1,144	R. Green
Luton	01582-546000	184,356	£1,073	Darra Singh
Medway	01634-306000	249,502	£1,014	Judith Armitt
Middlesbrough	01642-245432	142,300	£1,173	Brian Dinsdale
Milton Keynes	01908-691691	210,980	£1,097	John Best
North East Lincolnshire	01472-313131	156,000	£1,265	Jim Leivers
North Lincolnshire	01724-296296	162,000	£1,237	Michael Garnett
North Somerset	01934-888888	188,500	£1,161	Graham Turner
NOTTINGHAM CITY	0115-915 5555	267,000	£1,259	Gordon Mitchell
PETERBOROUGH CITY	01733-563141	158,500	£1,117	Gillian Beasley
PLYMOUTH CITY	01752-668000	255,000	£1,121	Sohail Faruqi
Poole	01202-633633	140,940	£1,138	John McBride
PORTSMOUTH CITY	023-9282 2251	186,700	£1,070	N. Gurney
Reading	0118-939 0900	150,000	£1,212	Trish Haines
Redcar and Cleveland	01642-444000	139,200	£1,214	Colin Moore
Rutland	01572-722577	34,600	£1,344	K. Franklin
Slough	01753-552288	119,000	£1,055	Cheryl Coppell
South Gloucestershire	01454-868686	245,640	£1,193	Mike Robinson
SOUTHAMPTON CITY	023-8022 3855	216,000	£1,176	Brad Roynon
Southend-on-Sea	01702-215000	164,400	£1,016	J. Krawiec
Stockton-on-Tees	01642-393939	178,000	£1,165	George Garlick
STOKE-ON-TRENT CITY	01782-234567	253,200	£1,093	Ita O'Donovan
Swindon	01793-463000	182,600	£1,131	Simon Birch
Telford and Wrekin	01952-202100	158,285	£1,144	Michael Frater
Thurrock	01375-390000	134,806	£1,060	Eric Nath
Torbay	01803-201201	123,000	£1,168	R. Painter
Warrington	01925-444400	191,200	£1,053	Bernice Law
West Berkshire	01635-42400	144,483	£1,229	Jim Graham
Windsor and Maidenhead	01628-798888	133,626	£1,061	David Lunn
Wokingham	0118-974 6000	148,869	£1,195	Doug Patterson
YORK CITY	01904-613161	181,326	£1,078	David Atkinson

*Average Band D council tax

Councils in CAPITAL LETTERS have city status

1 Stockton-on-Tees
2 Middlesbrough
3 Blackpool
4 Blackburn
   with Darwen
5 Bolton
6 Bury
7 Rochdale
8 Salford
9 Oldham
10 Liverpool
11 Knowsley
12 St Helens
13 Halton
14 Warrington
15 Trafford
16 Manchester
17 Tameside
18 Stockport
19 Nottingham
20 Telford and
   Wrekin
21 Wolverhampton

22 Walsall
23 Sandwell
24 Dudley
25 Birmingham
26 Solihull
27 Coventry
28 Peterborough
29 South Glos
30 Bristol
31 Bath and
   NE Somerset
32 Windsor and
   Maidenhead
33 Slough
34 Reading
35 Wokingham
36 Bracknell Forest
37 Thurrock
38 Southend
39 Medway
40 Plymouth
41 Torbay

LONDON

1 Hillingdon
2 Harrow
3 Barnet
4 Enfield
5 Waltham Forest
6 Redbridge
7 Barking and Dagenham
8 Havering
9 Ealing
10 Brent
11 Camden
12 Haringey
13 Islington
14 Hackney
15 Newham
16 Hounslow
17 Hammersmith and Fulham

18 Kensington and Chelsea
19 City of Westminster
20 City of London
21 Tower Hamlets
22 Richmond upon Thames
23 Wandsworth
24 Lambeth
25 Southwark
26 Lewisham
27 Greenwich
28 Bexley
29 Kingston upon Thames
30 Merton
31 Sutton
32 Croydon
33 Bromley

LONDON

THE CORPORATION OF LONDON

The City of London is the historic centre at the heart of London known as 'the square mile' around which the vast metropolis has grown over the centuries. The City's residential population at census day 2001 was 7,186. The civic government is carried on by the Corporation of London through the Court of Common Council.

The City is an international financial centre, generating over £20 billion a year for the British economy. It includes the head offices of the principal banks, insurance companies and mercantile houses, in addition to buildings ranging from the historic Roman Wall and the 15th-century Guildhall, to the massive splendour of St Paul's Cathedral and the architectural beauty of Wren's spires.

The City of London was described by Tacitus in AD 62 as 'a busy emporium for trade and traders'. Under the Romans it became an important administration centre and hub of the road system. Little is known of London in Saxon times, when it formed part of the kingdom of the East Saxons. In 886 Alfred recovered London from the Danes and reconstituted it a burgh under his son-in-law. In 1066 the citizens submitted to William the Conqueror who in 1067 granted them a charter, which is still preserved, establishing them in the rights and privileges they had hitherto enjoyed.

THE MAYORALTY

The Mayoralty was probably established about 1189, the first Mayor being Henry Fitz Ailwyn who filled the office for 23 years and was succeeded by Fitz Alan (1212–14). A new charter was granted by King John in 1215, directing the Mayor to be chosen annually, which has been done ever since, though in early times the same individual often held the office more than once. A familiar instance is that of 'Whittington, thrice Lord Mayor of London' (in reality four times, 1397, 1398, 1406, 1419); and many modern cases have occurred. The earliest instance of the phrase 'Lord Mayor' in English is in 1414. It was used more generally in the latter part of the 15th century and became invariable from 1535 onwards. At Michaelmas the liverymen in Common Hall choose two Aldermen who have served the office of Sheriff for presentation to the Court of Aldermen, and one is chosen to be Lord Mayor for the following mayoral year.

LORD MAYOR'S DAY

The Lord Mayor of London was previously elected on the feast of St Simon and St Jude (28 October), and from the time of Edward I, at least, was presented to the King or to the Barons of the Exchequer on the following day, unless that day was a Sunday. The day of election was altered to 16 October in 1346, and after some further changes was fixed for Michaelmas Day in 1546, but the ceremonies of admittance and swearing-in of the Lord Mayor continued to take place on 28 and 29 October respectively until 1751. In 1752, at the reform of the calendar, the Lord Mayor was continued in office until 8 November, the 'new style' equivalent of 28 October. The Lord Mayor is now presented to the Lord Chief Justice at the Royal Courts of Justice on the second Saturday in November to make the final declaration of office, having been sworn in at Guildhall on the preceding day. The procession to the Royal Courts of Justice is popularly known as the Lord Mayor's Show.

REPRESENTATIVES

Aldermen are mentioned in the 11th century and their office is of Saxon origin. They were elected annually between 1377 and 1394, when an Act of Parliament of Richard II directed them to be chosen for life.

The Common Council, elected annually on the first Friday in December, was, at an early date, substituted for a popular assembly called the *Folkmote*. At first only two representatives were sent from each ward, but the number has since been greatly increased. The City of London (Ward Elections) Act gained Royal Assent in November 2002 and allowed for new voting arrangements. These include the introduction of periodic re-elections for the 25 Aldermen, a reduction in the number of Councilmen and a comprehensive review of the 25 electoral ward boundaries.

OFFICERS

Sheriffs were Saxon officers; their predecessors were the *wic-reeves* and *portreeves* of London and Middlesex. At first they were officers of the Crown, and were named by the Barons of the Exchequer; but Henry I (in 1132) gave the citizens permission to choose their own Sheriffs, and the annual election of Sheriffs became fully operative under King John's charter of 1199. The citizens lost this privilege, as far as the election of the Sheriff of Middlesex was concerned, by the Local Government Act 1888; but the liverymen continue to choose two Sheriffs of the City of London, who are appointed on Midsummer Day and take office at Michaelmas.

The office of Chamberlain is an ancient one, the first contemporary record of which is 1237. The Town Clerk (or Common Clerk) is first mentioned in 1274.

ACTIVITIES

The work of the Corporation is assigned to a number of committees which present reports to the Court of Common Council. These Committees are: Barbican Centre; Barbican Residential; Board of Governors of the City of London Freeman's School, the City of London School, London School for Girls, the Guildhall School of Music and Drama and the Museum of London; Bridge House Trust; City Lands and Bridge House Estates; Managers of West Ham Park; Community Services; Education; Epping Forest and Open Spaces; Establishment; Finance; Gresham (city side); Guildhall Yard East Building; Hampstead Heath Management; Libraries; Guildhall Art Galleries and Archives; Livery; Markets; Planning and Transportation; Police; Policy and Resources; Port Health and Environmental Services; Queen's Park and Highgate Wood Management and Standards Committees.

The City's estate, in the possession of which the Corporation of London differs from other municipalities, is managed by the City Lands and Bridge House Estates Committee, the chairmanship of which carries with it the title of Chief Commoner.

The Honourable the Irish Society, which manages the Corporation's estates in Ulster, consists of a Governor and five other Aldermen, the Recorder, and 19 Common Councilmen, of whom one is elected Deputy Governor.

THE LORD MAYOR 2004–5
The Rt. Hon. the Lord Mayor, Alderman Rt. Hon. Michael Savory
Private Secretary, P. Tribe

THE SHERIFFS 2004–5
David Bilsland; John Hughesdon *(Alderman Billingsgate)*

OFFICERS, ETC.
Town Clerk, Chris Duffield
Chamberlain, P. Derrick
Chief Commoner (2004), Tom Jackson
Clerk, The Honourable the Irish Society, S. Waley, 75 Watling Street, London EC4M 9BJ T 020-7489 7777

THE ALDERMEN
with office held and date of appointment to that office

Name and Ward	CC	Ald.	Shff	Lord Mayor
Sir Alan Towers-Traill, GBE, *Langbourn*	1970	1975	1982	1984
Sir David Rowe-Ham, GBE, *Bridge* and *Bridge Wt.*	–	1976	1984	1986
Sir Brian Jenkins, GBE, *Cordwainer*	–	1980	1987	1991
Sir Paul Newall, TD, *Walbrook*	1980	1981	1989	1993
Sir Richard Nichols, *Candlewick*	1983	1984	1994	1997
Lord Levene of Portsoken, KBE, *Portsoken*	1983	1984	1995	1998
Sir Clive Martin, OBE, *Aldgate*	–	1985	1996	1999
Sir David Howard, Bt.	1972	1986	1997	2000
Sir Michael Oliver, *Bishopsgate Out*	1980	1987	1997	2001
Gavyn Arthur, *Cripplegate*	1988	1991	1998	2002
Robert Finch, *Coleman Street*	–	1992	1999	2003

All the above have passed the Civic Chair

	CC	Ald.	Shff
Michael Savory, *Bread Street*	1980	1996	2001
Richard Agutter, *Castle Baynard*	–	1995	2000
David Brewer, *Bassishaw*	1992	1996	2002
Nicholas Anstee, *Aldersgate*	1987	1996	
John Hughesdon, *Billingsgate*	1991	1997	
Simon Walsh, *Farringdon Wt.*	1989	2000	
John Stuttard, *Lime Street*	–	2001	
Dr Andrew Parmley, *Vintry*	1992	2001	
David Lewis, *Broad Street*	–	2001	
Robert Hall, *Farringdon Wn.*	1995	2002	
Mrs Alison Gowman, *Dowgate*	1991	2002	
Richard Walduck, OBE, *Tower*	–	2003	
Gordon Haines, *Queenhithe*	–	2004	
Colin Hart, *Cheap*	–	2004	

THE COMMON COUNCIL
Deputy: Each Common Councilman so described serves as deputy to the Alderman of her/his ward.

Abrahams, G. (2000)	*Farringdon Wt.*
Absalom, J. D. (1994)	*Farringdon Wt.*
Altman, L. P., CBE (1996)	*Cripplegate Wn.*
Angell, E. H. (1991)	*Cripplegate Wt.*
Ayers, K. E. (1996)	*Bassishaw*
Barker, *Deputy* J. A. (1981)	*Cripplegate Wn.*
Beale, *Deputy* M. J. (1979)	*Lime Street*
Bear, M. D. (2003)	*Portsoken*
Bird, J. L., OBE (1977)	*Bridge*
Boleat, M. J. (2002)	*Cordwainer*
Bradshaw, D. J. (1991)	*Cripplegate Wn.*
Branson, N. A. C. (2002)	*Langbourn*
Brewster, J. W., OBE (1994)	*Bassishaw*
Caspi, D. R. (1994)	*Bridge*
Cassidy, *Deputy* M. J. (1989)	*Coleman Street*
Catt, R. M. (2004)	*Castle Baynard*
Cenci Di Bello, Mrs P. J. (2004)	*Farringdon Wn.*
Chadwick, R. A. H. (1994)	*Tower*
Cohen, Mrs C. M., OBE (1986)	*Lime Street*
Cotgrove, D. (1991)	*Lime Street*
Currie, *Deputy* Miss S. E. M. (1985)	*Cripplegate Wt.*
Dove, W. H., MBE (1993)	*Bishopsgate*
Duckworth, S. (2000)	*Bishopsgate*
Dudley, The Revd Dr M. R. (2002)	*Aldersgate*
Duffield, R. W. (2004)	*Farringdon Wn.*
Eskenzi, *Deputy* A. N., CBE (1970)	*Farringdon Wn.*
Eve, R. A. (1980)	*Cheap*
Everett, K. M. (1984)	*Candlewick*
Falk, F. A., TD (1997)	*Broad Street*
Farr, M. C. (1998)	*Walbrook*
Farrow, *Deputy* M. W. W. (1996)	*Farringdon Wt.*
Farthing, R. B. C. (1981)	*Aldgate*
FitzGerald, *Deputy* R. C. A. (1981)	*Bread Street*
Fraser, S. J. (1993)	*Coleman Street*
Fraser, *Deputy* W. B. (1981)	*Vintry*
Galloway, *Deputy* A. D. (1981)	*Broad Street*
Gillon, G. M. F. (1995)	*Cordwainer*
Ginsburg, S. (1990)	*Bishopsgate*
Graves, A. C. (1985)	*Bishopsgate*
Halliday, *Deputy* Mrs P. (1992)	*Walbrook*
Hardwick, Dr P. B. (1987)	*Aldgate*
Harris-Jones, Dr R. D. L. (2001)	*Farringdon Wt.*
Haynes, J. E. H. (1986)	*Cornhill*
Henderson-Begg, M. (1977)	*Coleman Street*
Hoffman, T. (2002)	*Vintry*
Holland, *Deputy* J., CBE (1972)	*Aldgate*
Hughes-Penney, R. C. (2004)	*Farringdon Wn.*
Hunt, W. G. (2004)	*Castle Baynard*
Jackson, L. St J. T. (1978)	*Bread Street*
Jones, H. L. M. (2004)	*Portsoken*
Kellett, Mrs M. W. F. (1986)	*Tower*
Kemp, D. L. (1984)	*Coleman Street*
King, A. (1999)	*Queenhithe*
Knowles, *Deputy* S. K. (1984)	*Candlewick*
Lawrence, G. A. (2003)	*Farringdon Wt.*
Leck, P. (1998)	*Aldersgate*
Lee, The Revd Dr B. J. (2001)	*Portsoken*
Lord, C. E. (2000)	*Coleman Street*
Luder, I. D. (1998)	*Castle Baynard*
McGuinness, C. (1997)	*Castle Baynard*
Malins, J. H., QC (1981)	*Farringdon Wt.*
Martinelli, *Deputy* P. J. (1994)	*Bassishaw*
Mayhew, J. P. (1996)	*Aldersgate*
Mead, Mrs W. (1997)	*Farringdon Wt.*
Millner, E. P. (2004)	*Portsoken*
Mitchell, *Deputy* C. R. (1971)	*Castle Baynard*
Mobsby, *Deputy* D. J. L. (1985)	*Billingsgate*
Mooney, B. D. F. (1998)	*Queenhithe*
Moss, A. D. (1989)	*Tower*
Moys, Mrs S. (2000)	*Aldgate*

Nash, *Deputy* Mrs J. C. (1983)	*Aldersgate*
Newman, Mrs P. B. (1989)	*Aldersgate*
Nove, P. R. (2004)	*Castle Baynard*
Owen, Mrs J. (1975)	*Langbourn*
Owen-Ward, J. R. (1983)	*Bridge*
Page, M. (2002)	*Farringdon Wn.*
Pembroke, *Deputy* Mrs A. M. F. (1978)	*Cheap*
Pointon, G. N. (2004)	*Billingsgate*
Pollard, J. H. G. (2002)	*Dowgate*
Price, E. E. (1996)	*Farringdon Wt.*
Pulman, *Deputy* G. A. G. (1983)	*Tower*
Punter, C. (1993)	*Cripplegate Wn.*
Quilter, S. D. (1998)	*Cripplegate Wt.*
Regan, R. D. (1998)	*Farringdon Wn.*
Robinson, Mrs D. C. (1989)	*Bishopsgate*
Roney, *Deputy* E. P. T., CBE (1974)	*Bishopsgate*
Scott, J. (1999)	*Broad Street*
Shalit, *Deputy* D. M. (1972)	*Farringdon Wn.*
Sherlock, *Deputy* M. R. C. (1992)	*Dowgate*
Simons, J. L. (2004)	*Castle Baynard*
Snyder, *Deputy* M. J. (1986)	*Cordwainer*
Spanner, J. H., TD (2001)	*Farringdon Wt.*
Stevenson, F. P. (1994)	*Cripplegate Wn.*
Streeter, P. T. (2004)	*Bishopsgate*
Thompson, D. J. (2004)	*Aldgate*
Tomlinson, J. (2004)	*Cripplegate*
Twogood, M. (2004)	*Farringdon Wt.*
Wang, Mrs C. A. M. (2004)	*Cornhill*
Willoughby, *Deputy* P. J. (1985)	*Bishopsgate*
Wooten, D. H. (2002)	*Farringdon Wn.*

THE CITY GUILDS (LIVERY COMPANIES)

The constitution of the livery companies has been unchanged for centuries. There are three ranks of membership: freemen, liverymen and assistants. A person can become a freeman by patrimony (through a parent having been a freeman); by servitude (through having served an apprenticeship to a freeman); or by redemption (by purchase).

Election to the livery is the prerogative of the company, who can elect any of its freemen as liverymen. Assistants are usually elected from the livery and form a Court of Assistants which is the governing body of the company. The Master (in some companies called the Prime Warden) is elected annually from the assistants.

The register for 2004–5 listed 24,336 liverymen of the guilds entitled to vote at elections at Common Hall.

The order of precedence, omitting extinct companies, is given in parenthesis after the name of each company in the list below. In certain companies the election of Master or Prime Warden for the year does not take place until the autumn. In such cases the Master or Prime Warden for 2003–4 is given.

THE TWELVE GREAT COMPANIES
In order of civic precedence

MERCERS *(1)*. *Hall,* Mercers' Hall, Ironmonger Lane, London EC2V 8HE *Livery,* 233. *Clerk,* C. H. Parker *Master,* C. C. Scott

GROCERS *(2)*. *Hall,* Grocers' Hall, Princes Street, London EC2R 8AD *Livery,* 323. *Clerk,* Brig. P. P. Rawlins, MBE *Master,* Vice-Adm. Sir Toby Frere, KCB

DRAPERS *(3)*. *Hall,* Drapers' Hall, Throgmorton Avenue, London EC2N 2DQ *Livery,* 282. *Clerk,* Rear-Adm. A. B. Ross, CB, CBE; *Master,* Martin Sankey

FISHMONGERS *(4)*. *Hall,* Fishmongers' Hall, London Bridge, London EC4R 9EL *Livery,* 353. *Clerk,* K. S. Waters *Prime Warden,* Sir Angus Stirling

GOLDSMITHS *(5)*. *Hall,* Goldsmiths' Hall, Foster Lane, London EC2V 6BN *Livery,* 275. *Clerk,* R. I. Talbot *Prime Warden,* B. E. Toye

SKINNERS *(6/7)*. *Hall,* Skinners' Hall, 8 Dowgate Hill, London EC4R 2SP *Livery,* 393. *Clerk,* Maj.-Gen. Brian Plummer, CBE; *Master,* A. B. E. Hudson, MBE

MERCHANT TAYLORS *(6/7)*. Hall, 30 Threadneedle Street, London EC2R 8JB *Livery,* 325. *Clerk,* D. A. Peck *Master,* M. W. G. Skinner

HABERDASHERS *(8)*. *Hall,* 18 West Smithfield, London EC1A 9HQ *Livery,* 288. *Clerk,* Capt. R. J. Fisher, RN *Master,* Julien Prevett

SALTERS *(9)*. *Hall,* Salters' Hall, 4 Fore Street, London EC2Y 5DE *Livery,* 168. *Clerk,* Col. M. P. Barneby *Master,* J. A. Goodeve

IRONMONGERS *(10)*. *Hall,* Ironmongers' Hall, Shaftesbury Place, Barbican, London EC2Y 8AA *Livery,* 133. *Clerk,* J. A. Oliver; *Master,* A. R. P. Carden

VINTNERS *(11)*. *Hall,* Vintners' Hall, Upper Thames Street, London EC4V 3BG *Livery,* 308. *Clerk,* Brig. M. Smythe, OBE, *Master,* F. J. Avery

CLOTHWORKERS *(12)*. *Hall,* Clothworkers' Hall, Dunster Court, Mincing Lane, London EC3R 7AH *Livery,* 215. *Clerk,* A. C. Blessley; *Master,* Peter Rawson

OTHER CITY GUILDS
In alphabetical order

ACTUARIES *(91)*. *Hall,* The Cote, Old Gloucester Road, Alveston, Bristol BS35 3LQ *Livery,* 200. *Clerk,* M. J. Turner *Master,* A. J. Frost

AIR PILOTS AND AIR NAVIGATORS *(81)*. *Hall,* Cobham House, 9 Warwick Court, Gray's Inn, London WC1R 5DJ *Livery,* 500. *Grand Master,* HRH The Duke of York, KCVO, ADC; *Clerk,* Paul Tacon *Master,* Capt. Richard Feux, LVO, FRAES

APOTHECARIES, SOCIETY OF *(58)*. *Hall,* Apothecaries' Hall, 14 Black Friars Lane, London EC4V 6EJ *Livery,* 1,758. *Clerk,* A. M. Wallington Smith; *Master,* W. S. Shand

ARBITRATORS *(93)*. 13 Hall Gardens, Colney Heath, St Albans, Herts AL4 0QF *Livery,* 150. *Clerk,* Mrs G. Duffy *Master,* A. W. Drysdale

ARMOURERS AND BRASIERS *(22)*. *Hall,* Armourers' Hall, 81 Coleman Street, London EC2R 5BJ *Livery,* 120. *Clerk,* Cdr. T. J. K. Sloane, OBE, RN; *Master,* A. M. R. Pontifex

BAKERS *(19)*. *Hall,* Bakers' Hall, Harp Lane, London EC3R 6DP *Livery,* 370. *Clerk,* J. W. Tompkins *Master,* Richard E. B. Sawyer

BARBERS *(17)*. *Hall,* Barber-Surgeons' Hall, Monkwell Square, Wood Street, London EC2Y 5BL *Livery,* 200. *Clerk,* Col. P. J. Durrant, MBE; *Master,* C. W. Sprague

BASKETMAKERS *(52)*. 29 Ingram House, Park Road, Hampton Wick, Surrey KT1 4BA *Livery,* 308. *Clerk,* R. de Pilkyngton; *Prime Warden,* R. Bartle

BLACKSMITHS *(40)*. 48 Upwood Road, London SE12 8AN *Livery,* 229. *Clerk,* C. Jeal; *Prime Warden,* John Shreeves

BOWYERS *(38)*. 5 Archer House, Vicarage Crescent, London SW11 3LF *Livery,* 102. *Clerk,* Richard Wilkinson *Master,* P. Seaton

BREWERS *(14)*. *Hall,* Brewers Hall, Aldermanbury Square, London EC2V 7HR *Livery,* 170. *Clerk,* Brig. D. J. Ross, CBE; *Master,* R. A. S. Everard

BRODERERS *(48)*. Ember House, 35–37 Creek Road, East Molesey, Surrey KT8 9BE *Livery,* 173. *Clerk,* P. J. C. Crouch; *Master,* M. A. Hissey

BUILDERS MERCHANTS *(88)*. 4 College Hill, London EC4R 2RB *Livery*, 200. *Clerk*, Miss S. M. Robinson, TD *Master*, S. J. Somerville

BUTCHERS *(24)*. *Hall*, Butchers' Hall, 87 Bartholomew Close, London EC1A 7EB *Livery*, 594. *Clerk*, A. J. C. Morrow, CVO; *Master*, Colin Cullimore, CBE

CARMEN *(77)*. 8 Little Trinity Lane, London EC4V 2AN *Livery*, 469. *Clerk*, Walter Gill; *Master*, R. N. Cullimore

CARPENTERS *(26)*. *Hall*, Carpenters' Hall, 1 Throgmorton Avenue, London EC2N 2JJ *Livery*, 150. *Clerk*, Maj.-Gen. P. T. Stevenson, OBE; *Master*, J. A. C. Wheeler

CHARTERED ACCOUNTANTS *(86)*. The Rustlings, Valley Close, Studham, Dunstable LU6 2QN *Livery*, 334. *Clerk*, C. Bygrave; *Master*, G. Acher, CBE, LVO

CHARTERED ARCHITECTS *(98)*. 82A Muswell Hill Road, London N10 3JR *Livery*, 172. *Clerk*, D. Cole-Adams *Master*, Nigel Thomson

CHARTERED SECRETARIES AND ADMINISTRATORS *(87)*. 3rd Floor, Saddlers' House, 40 Gutter Lane, London EC2V 6BR *Livery*, 224. *Clerk*, Col. M. J. Dudding, OBE, TD, FCIS; *Master*, D. H. Kirkham, CBE, FCIS

CHARTERED SURVEYORS *(85)*. 75 Meadway Drive, Horsell, Woking, Surrey GU21 4TF *Livery*, 350. *Clerk*, Mrs A. L. Jackson; *Master*, T. G. Knight

CLOCKMAKERS *(61)*. Salters' Hall, 4 Fore Street, London EC2Y 5DE *Livery*, 230. *Clerk*, Gp Capt. P. H. Gibson, MBE; *Master*, Mrs D. M. Uff

COACHMAKERS AND COACH-HARNESS MAKERS *(72)*. Woodlands House, The Clump, Chorleywood, Hertfordshire WD3 4BB *Livery*, 385. *Clerk*, Gp Capt. G. Bunn, CBE *Master*, Michael Limb, OBE

CONSTRUCTORS *(99)*. Forge Farmhouse, Glassenbury, Cranbrook, Kent TN17 2QE *Livery*, 130. *Clerk*, Tim Nicholson; *Master*, Peter Knight

COOKS *(35)*. Registry Chambers, The Old Deanery, Deans Court, London EC4V 5AA *Livery*, 75. *Clerk*, M. C. Thatcher; *Master*, G. A. V. Rees

COOPERS *(36)*. *Hall*, Coopers' Hall, 13 Devonshire Square, London EC2M 4TH *Livery*, 260. *Clerk*, A. G. R. Carroll *Master*, John Newton

CORDWAINERS *(27)*. 8 Warwick Court, Gray's Inn, London WC1R 5DJ *Livery*, 164. *Clerk*, Lt.-Col. J. R. Blundell, RM *Master*, L. J. E. Chamberlain

CURRIERS *(29)*. Hedgerley, 10 The Leaze, Ashton Keynes, Wiltshire SN6 6PE *Livery*, 88. *Clerk*, D. M. Moss *Master*, W. N. Bagshawe

CUTLERS *(18)*. *Hall*, Cutlers' Hall, Warwick Lane, London EC4M 7BR *Livery*, 100. *Clerk*, J. P. Allen *Master*, M. W. Roberts

DISTILLERS *(69)*. 71 Lincoln's Inn Fields, London WC2A 3JF *Livery*, 270. *Clerk*, C. V. Hughes *Master*, D. N. V. Churton, MBE

DYERS *(13)*. *Hall*, Dyers' Hall, 10 Dowgate Hill, London EC4R 2ST *Livery*, 127. *Clerk*, J. R. Chambers, FCA *Prime Warden*, M. Bird

ENGINEERS *(94)*. Wax Chandlers' Hall, Gresham Street, London EC2V 7AD *Livery*, 289. *Clerk*, Air Vice-Marshal G. Skinner, CBE *Master*, Maj.-Gen. E. G. Wilmott, CB, OBE

ENVIRONMENTAL CLEANERS *(97)*. 6 Grange Meadows, Elmswell, Bury St Edmunds, Suffolk IP30 9GE *Livery*, 258. *Clerk*, M. A. Bizley; *Master*, Paul R. Michael

FAN MAKERS *(76)*. Skinners' Hall, 8 Dowgate Hill, London EC4R 2SP *Livery*, 210. *Clerk*, K. J. Patterson *Master*, J. R. G. Thomas

FARMERS *(80)*. *Hall*, 3 Cloth Street, London EC1 *Livery*, 300. *Clerk*, Miss M. L. Winter *Master*, N. J. Fiske

FARRIERS *(55)*. 19 Queen Street, Chipperfield, Kings Langley, Herts WD4 9BT *Livery*, 345. *Clerk*, Mrs C. C. Clifford *Master*, Brig. P. G. H. Jepson

FELTMAKERS *(63)*. The Old Post House, Upton Grey, Basingstoke, Hampshire RG25 2RL *Livery*, 170. *Clerk*, Maj. J. T. H. Coombs *Master*, D. N. Bedford

FIREFIGHTERS *(103)*. The Insurance Hall, 20 Aldermanbury, London EC2V 7GF *Livery*, 65. *Clerk*, Mrs M. Holland Prior; *Master*, R. Dunley

FLETCHERS *(39)*. *Hall*, The Farmers' and Fletchers' Hall, 3 Cloth Street, London EC1A 7LD *Livery*, 140. *Clerk*, M. Johnson; *Master*, F. A. Neal, CMG

FOUNDERS *(33)*. *Hall*, Founders' Hall, Number One, Cloth Fair, London EC1A 7JQ *Livery*, 165. *Clerk*, A. J. Gillett *Master*, Richard J. Martin

FRAMEWORK KNITTERS *(64)*. 86 Park Drive, Upminster, Essex RM14 3AS *Livery*, 275. *Clerk*, A. J. Clark *Master*, D. A. Buswell

FRUITERERS *(45)*. Chapelstones, 84 High Street, Codford St Mary, Warminster BA12 0ND *Livery*, 284. *Clerk*, Lt.-Col. L. G. French; *Master*, H. H. Bryant

FUELLERS *(95)*. 26 Merrick Square, London SE1 4JB *Livery*, 95. *Clerk*, Sir W. Anthony J. Reardon Smith, Bt. *Master*, David Port

FURNITURE MAKERS *(83)*. Painters' Hall, 9 Little Trinity Lane, London EC4V 2AD *Livery*, 294. *Clerk*, Mrs J. A. Wright; *Master*, D. L. Burbidge, OBE

GARDENERS *(66)*. 25 Luke Street, London EC2A 4AR *Livery*, 269. *Clerk*, Col. N. G. S. Gray *Master*, C. R. G. Shewell-Cooper

GIRDLERS *(23)*. *Hall*, Girdlers' Hall, Basinghall Avenue, London EC2V 5DD *Livery*, 80. *Clerk*, Lt.-Col. R. Sullivan *Master*, O. C. S. Swann

GLASS-SELLERS *(71)*. 57 Witley Court, Coram Street, London WC1N 1MD *Livery*, 230. *Hon. Clerk*, A. J. Smith *Master*, Prof. J. R. Whiteman, PHD, FIMA, FRSA

GLAZIERS AND PAINTERS OF GLASS *(53)*. *Hall*, Glaziers' Hall, 9 Montague Close, London SE1 9DD *Livery*, 244. *Clerk*, Col. D. W. Eking *Master*, Ms P. Shaw

GLOVERS *(62)*. 73 Clapham Manor Street, London SW4 6DS *Livery*, 260. *Clerk*, Mrs M. Hood *Master*, William Loach

GOLD AND SILVER WYRE DRAWERS *(74)*. 'Twizzletwig', The Ballands South, Fetcham, Leatherhead, Surrey KT22 9EP *Livery*, 310. *Clerk*, T. J. Waller *Master*, Michael C. Roberts

GUNMAKERS *(73)*. The Proof House, 48–50 Commercial Road, London E1 1LP *Livery*, 265. *Clerk*, Col. W. F. Chesshyre; *Master*, C. D. Price

HACKNEY CARRIAGE DRIVERS *(104)*. 25 The Grove, Parkfield, Latimer, Buckinghamshire HP5 1UE *Livery*, 90. *Clerk*, Mary Whitworth; *Master*, John Rennie

HORNERS *(54)*. c/o Clergy House, Hide Place, London SW1P 4NJ *Livery*, 235. *Clerk*, A. R. Layard *Master*, I. A. McColl

INFORMATION TECHNOLOGISTS *(100)*. *Hall*, Information Technologists' Hall, 39A Bartholomew Close, London EC1A 7JN *Livery*, 293. *Clerk*, Mrs G. Wilson *Master*, Roger Graham, OBE

INNHOLDERS *(32)*. *Hall*, Innholders' Hall, 30 College Street, London EC4R 2RH *Livery*, 143. *Clerk*, D. E. Bulger *Master*, W. R. Spouse

INSURERS *(92)*. The Hall, 20 Aldermanbury, London EC2V 7HY *Livery*, 370. *Clerk*, L. J. Walters *Master*, M. K. Bewes

JOINERS AND CEILERS *(41)*. 75 Meadway Drive, Horsell, Woking, Surrey GU21 4TF *Livery*, 124. *Clerk*, Mrs A. L. Jackson; *Master*, John Christopher

LAUNDERERS *(89)*. *Hall*, Launderers Hall, 9 Montague Close, London Bridge, London SE1 9DD *Livery*, 250.
Clerk, Mrs J. Polek; *Master*, Alec Kennedy

LEATHERSELLERS *(15)*. *Hall*, Leathersellers' Hall, 15 St Helen's Place, London EC3A 6DQ *Livery*, 150. *Clerk*, Capt. J. G. F. Cooke, OBE, RN; *Master*, Tony Lister

LIGHTMONGERS *(96)*. Crown Wharf, 11a Coldharbour, Blackwall Reach, London E14 9NS *Livery*, 194.
Clerk, D. B. Wheatley; *Master*, Ian Crosby

LORINERS *(57)*. 8 Portland Square, London E1W 2QR *Livery*, 358. *Clerk*, G. B. Forbes; *Master*, John W. Owen, CMG, MBE

MAKERS OF PLAYING CARDS *(75)*. 42 Warnford Court, Throgmorton Street, London EC2N 2AT *Livery*, 147.
Clerk, Paul Bowen; *Master*, Graeme Living

MANAGEMENT CONSULTANTS *(105)*. Ladymead, 23 Hilltop Road, Earley, Reading RG6 1BY *Livery*, 150.
Clerk, Claire Dyer; *Master*, Alan Broomhead

MARKETORS *(90)*. 13 Hall Gardens, Colney Heath, St Albans, Herts AL4 0QF *Livery*, 240.
Clerk, Mrs G. Duffy; *Master*, David Hanger

MASONS *(30)*. 22 Cannon Hill, Southgate, London N14 6LG *Livery*, 122. *Clerk*, P. F. Clark; *Master*, M. J. Peachey

MASTER MARINERS *(78)*. *Hall*, HQS Wellington, Temple Stairs, Victoria Embankment, London WC2R 2PN *Livery*, 215. *Admiral*, HRH The Prince Philip, Duke of Edinburgh, KG, KT, OM, GBE, PC; *Clerk*, Cdr. I. S. Gregory, RN; *Master*, Capt. C. R. Smiley

MUSICIANS *(50)*. 6th Floor, 2 London Wall Building, London EC2M 5PP *Livery*, 374. *Clerk*, Col. T. P. B. Hoggarth *Master*, J. Rennert

NEEDLEMAKERS *(65)*. 5 Staple Inn, London WC1V 7QH *Livery*, 230. *Clerk*, M. G. Cook; *Master*, Graham Born

PAINTER-STAINERS *(28)*. *Hall*, Painters' Hall, 9 Little Trinity Lane, London EC4V 2AD *Livery*, 320. *Clerk*, Chris Twyman; *Master*, D. R. Clover

PATTENMAKERS *(70)*. 3 The High Street, Sutton Valence, Kent ME17 3AG *Livery*, 200. *Clerk*, Col. R. W. Murfin, TD; *Master*, Donald Newell

PAVIORS *(56)*. 3 Ridgemount Gardens, Enfield, Middx EN2 8QL *Livery*, 234. *Clerk*, J. L. White
Master, John Edward Mills

PEWTERERS *(16)*. *Hall*, Pewterers' Hall, Oat Lane, London EC2V 7DE *Livery*, 125. *Clerk*, Lt. Col. T. M. Reeve-Tucker, OBE; *Master*, R. G. Wildash

PLAISTERERS *(46)*. *Hall*, Plaisterers' Hall, 1 London Wall, London EC2Y 5JU *Livery*, 210. *Clerk*, Mrs. H. Machtus *Master*, D. R. Measom

PLUMBERS *(31)*. Wax Chandlers' Hall, 6 Greesham Street, London EC2V 7AD *Livery*, 332. *Clerk*, Lt.-Col. R. J. A. Paterson-Fox; *Master*, M. S. Samuel, CENG

POULTERS *(34)*. The Old Butchers, Station Road, Groombridge, Kent TN3 9QX *Livery*, 197. *Clerk*, Mrs G. W. Butcher; *Master*, R. G. T. Hulbert

SADDLERS *(25)*. *Hall*, Saddlers' Hall, 40 Gutter Lane, London EC2V 6BR *Livery*, 70. *Clerk*, Gp Capt. W. S. Brereton Martin, CBE; *Master*, H. S. Dyson-Laurie

SCIENTIFIC INSTRUMENT MAKERS *(84)*. 9 Montague Close, London SE1 9DD *Livery*, 240. *Clerk*, N. J. Watson *Master*, Prof. R. W. Hartley

SCRIVENERS *(44)*. HQS Wellington, Temple Stairs, Victoria Embankment, London WC2R 2PN *Livery*, 194. *Clerk*, A. Hill; *Master*, R. D. Millett

SHIPWRIGHTS *(59)*. Ironmongers Hall, Barbican, London EC2Y 8AA *Livery*, 414. *Grand Master*, HRH The Prince

Philip, Duke of Edinburgh, KG, KT, OM, GBE, PC *Clerk*, Rear Adm. Derek Anthony, MBE
Prime Warden, Peter Buckley

SOLICITORS *(79)*. 4 College Hill, London EC4R 2RB *Livery*, 354. *Clerk*, N. Cameron; *Master*, A. J. C. Collett

SPECTACLE MAKERS *(60)*. Apothecaries' Hall, Black Friars Lane, London EC4V 6EL *Livery*, 353. *Clerk*, Lt.-Col. J. A. B. Salmon, OBE, LLB; *Master*, N. H. Wingate

STATIONERS AND NEWSPAPER MAKERS *(47)*. *Hall*, Stationers' Hall, Ave Maria Lane, London EC4M 7DD *Livery*, 416. *Clerk*, Brig. D. G. Sharp, AFC; *Master*, J. G. Benn

TALLOW CHANDLERS *(21)*. *Hall*, Tallow Chandlers' Hall, 4 Dowgate Hill, London EC4R 2SH *Livery*, 200. *Clerk*, Brig. R. W. Wilde, CBE; *Master*, D. A. K. Simmonds

TIN PLATE WORKERS (ALIAS WIRE WORKERS) *(67)*. Bartholomew House, 66 Westbury Road, New Malden, Surrey KT3 5AS *Livery*, 200. *Clerk*, Michael Henderson-Begg; *Master*, Henry Edmonds

TOBACCO PIPE MAKERS AND TOBACCO BLENDERS *(82)*. Hackhurst Farm, Lower Dicker, Hailsham, E. Sussex BN27 4BP *Livery*, 153. *Clerk*, N. J. Hallings-Pott *Master*, D. Glynn-Jones

TURNERS *(51)*. 182 Temple Chambers, Temple Avenue, London EC4Y 0HP *Livery*, 169. *Clerk*, E. A. Windsor Clive *Master*, R. J. Levy

TYLERS AND BRICKLAYERS *(37)*. 30 Shelley Avenue, Tiptree CO5 0SF *Livery*, 150. *Clerk*, Barry Blumson *Master*, Sandy Angus

UPHOLDERS *(49)*. Hall in the Wood, 46 Quail Gardens, Selsdon Vale, Croydon CR2 8TF *Livery*, 210. *Clerk*, Mrs J. R. Cody; *Master*, M. A. Brecknell

WATER CONSERVATORS *(102)*. 22 Broadfields, Headstone Lane, Hatch End, Middlesex HA2 6NH *Livery*, 185. *Clerk*, R. A. Riley; *Master*, Dr Marion J. Carter

WAX CHANDLERS *(20)*. *Hall*, Wax Chandlers' Hall, 6 Gresham Street, London EC2V 7AD *Livery*, 129. *Clerk*, R. J. Percival; *Master*, A. G. McKay

WEAVERS *(42)*. Saddlers' House, Gutter Lane, London EC2V 6BR *Livery*, 125. *Clerk*, Mr. J. Snowdon
Upper Bailiff, J. F. M. Monkhouse

WHEELWRIGHTS *(68)*. Ember House, 35–37 Creek Road, East Molesey, Surrey KT8 9BE *Livery*, 217. *Clerk*, P. J. C. Crouch; *Master*, D. N. Legg

WOOLMEN *(43)*. 22 Broomfields, Headstone Lane, Hatch End, Middlesex HAZ 6WH *Livery*, 137. *Clerk*, Ralph Riley *Master*, John Townend

WORLD TRADERS *(101)*. 36 Ladbroke Grove, London W11 2PA *Livery*, 175. *Clerk*, N. R. Pullman
Master, Eric Stobart

INTERNATIONAL BANKERS *(No Livery)*. 1 Bengal Court, London EC3V 9DD *Freemen*, 502. *Clerk*, Tim Woods *Master*, Lord George of St Tudy, PC, GBE

TAX ADVISERS *(No Livery)*. 504 Bryer Court, Barbican, London EC2Y 8DE *Freemen*, 130. *Clerk*, John Jeffrey-Cook; *Master*, M. B. Squires

SECURITY PROFESSIONALS *(No Livery)*. 1 Wallis Mews, Guildford Road, Leatherhead, Surrey KT22 9DQ *Freemen*, 240 *Clerk*, John Maddock
Master, Wg Cdr. Michael Welply

PARISH CLERKS *(No Livery*)*. Acreholt, 33 Medstead Road, Beech, Alton, Hampshire GU34 4AD *Members*, 96. *Clerk*, Lt.-Col. B. J. N. Coombes; *Master*, M. R. C. Sherlock

WATERMEN AND LIGHTERMEN*(No Livery*)*. *Hall*, Watermen's Hall, 16 St Mary-at-Hill, London EC3R 8EF *Craft Owning Freemen*, 326. *Clerk*, C. Middlemiss
Master, Robert E. Lupton

* Parish Clerks and Watermen and Lightermen have requested to remain with no livery.

LONDON BOROUGH COUNCILS

Council	Administrative Headquarters	Telephone	Population	Band D charge *	Chief Executive
Barking and Dagenham	Dagenham, RM10 7BN	020-8592 4500	156,696	£1,110	Graham Farrant
Barnet	Hendon, NW4 4BG	020-8359 2000	314,564	£1,214	Leo Boland
Bexley	Bexleyheath, DA6 7LB	020-8303 7777	220,458	£1,186	Nick Johnson
Brent	Wembley, HA9 9HD	020-8937 1234	263,466	£1,141	Gareth Daniel
Bromley	Bromley, BR1 3UH	020-8464 3333	300,000	£1,040	David Bartlett
Camden	Judd Street, WC1H 9JE	020-7278 4444	210,000	£1,200	Moira Gibb
CORPORATION OF LONDON	Guildhall, EC2P 2EJ	020-7332 1902	6,700	£773	Chris Duffield
Croydon	Park Lane, Croydon, CR9 3JS	020-8686 4433	330,700	£1,165	David Wechsler
Ealing	New Broadway, W5 2BY	020-8825 5000	311,000	£1,192	Gillian Guy
Enfield	Silver Street, EN1 3XA	020-8379 1000	273,559	£1,193	Robert Leak
Greenwich	Wellington Street, SE18 6PW	020-8854 8888	214,403	£1,141	Mary Ney
Hackney	Mare Street, E8 1EA	020-8356 5000	202,824	£1,221	Max Caller
Hammersmith and Fulham	King Street, W6 9JU	020-8748 3020	157,470	£1,131	Geoff Alltimes
Haringey	High Road, N22 8LE	020-8489 0000	213,000	£1,259	David Warwick
Harrow	Harrow, HA1 2UJ	020-8863 5611	206,814	£1,275	Joyce Markham
Havering	Romford, RM1 3BD	01708-434343	224,250	£1,284	S. Evans
Hillingdon	Uxbridge, UB8 1UW	01895-250111	243,006	£1,215	Dorian Leatham
Hounslow	Lampton Road, TW3 4DN	020-8583 2000	240,397	£1,262	Mark Gilks
Islington	Upper Street, N1 2UD	020-7527 2000	175,797	£1,107	Helen Bailey
Kensington and Chelsea	Hornton Street, W8 7NX	020-7937 5464	190,300	£954	Derek Myers
Kingston upon Thames	Kingston upon Thames, KT1 1EU	020-8546 2121	147,273	£1,309	Bruce McDonald
Lambeth	Brixton, SW2 1RW	020-7926 1000	267,500	£1,050	Faith Boardman
Lewisham	Catford Road, SE6 4RU	020-8314 6000	250,000	£1,141	Barry Quirk
Merton	London Road, Morden SM4 5DX	020-8543 2222	179,000	£1,209	Ged Curran
Newham	Barking Road, East Ham, E6 2RP	020-8430 2000	254,041	£1,059	Dave Burbage
Redbridge	Ilford, IG1 1DD	020-8554 5000	238,635	£1,142	Roger Hampson
Richmond upon Thames	Twickenham, TW1 3BZ	020-8891 1411	182,766	£1,339	Gillian Norton
Southwark	Peckam Road, SE5 8UB	020-7525 5000	240,000	£1,071	Robert Coomber
Sutton	St. Nicholas Way, SM1 1EA	020-8770 5000	179,768	£1,180	Joanna Simons
Tower Hamlets	Clove Crescent, E14 2BG	020-7364 5000	181,251	£1,008	Christine Gilbert
Waltham Forest	Forest Road, E17 4JF	020-8496 4201	218,341	£1,245	Simon White
Wandsworth	Wandsworth High Street, SW18 2PU	020-8871 6000	266,600	£601	Gerald Jones
WESTMINSTER	Victoria Street, SW1E 6QP	020-7641 6000	181,000	£605	Peter Rogers

*Average Band D council tax
Councils in CAPITAL LETTERS have City Status

WALES

The Principality of Wales (Cymru) occupies the extreme west of the central southern portion of the island of Great Britain, with a total area of 8,015 sq. miles (20,758 sq. km): land 7,965 sq. miles (20,628 sq. km); inland water 50 sq. miles (130 sq. km). It is bounded on the north by the Irish Sea, on the south by the Bristol Channel, on the east by the English counties of Cheshire, Shropshire, Herefordshire and Gloucestershire, and on the west by St George's Channel.

Across the Menai Straits is the island of Anglesey (Ynys Môn) (276 sq. miles), communication with which is facilitated by the Menai Suspension Bridge (1,000 ft long) built by Telford in 1826, and by the tubular railway bridge (1,100 ft long) built by Stephenson in 1850. Holyhead harbour, on Holy Isle (north-west of Anglesey), provides accommodation for ferry services to Dublin (70 miles).

POPULATION
The population at the 2001 census was 2,903,085 (males 1,403,782; females 1,499,303). The average density of population in 2001 was 1.4 persons per hectare.

RELIEF
Wales is a country of extensive tracts of high plateau and shorter stretches of mountain ranges deeply dissected by river valleys. Lower-lying ground is largely confined to the coastal belt and the lower parts of the valleys. The highest mountains are those of Snowdonia in the north-west (Snowdon, 3,559 ft), Berwyn (Aran Fawddwy, 2,971 ft), Cader Idris (Pen y Gadair, 2,928 ft), Dyfed (Plynlimon, 2,467 ft), and the Black Mountain, Brecon Beacons and Black Forest ranges in the south-east (Carmarthen Van, 2,630 ft, Pen y Fan, 2,906 ft, Waun Fâch, 2,660 ft).

HYDROGRAPHY
The principal river in Wales is the Severn, which flows from the slopes of Plynlimon to the English border. The Wye (130 miles) also rises in the slopes of Plynlimon. The Usk (56 miles) flows into the Bristol Channel, through Gwent. The Dee (70 miles) rises in Bala Lake and flows through the Vale of Llangollen, where an aqueduct (built by Telford in 1805) carries the Pontcysyllte branch of the Shropshire Union Canal across the valley. The estuary of the Dee is the navigable portion, 14 miles in length and about five miles in breadth, and the tide rushes in with dangerous speed over the 'Sands of Dee'. The Towy (68 miles), Teifi (50 miles), Taff (40 miles), Dovey (30 miles), Taf (25 miles) and Conway (24 miles), the last named broad and navigable, are wholly Welsh rivers.

The largest natural lake is Bala (Llyn Tegid) in Gwynedd, nearly four miles long and about one mile wide. Lake Vyrnwy is an artificial reservoir, about the size of Bala, and forms the water supply of Liverpool; Birmingham is supplied from reservoirs in the Elan and Claerwen valleys.

WELSH LANGUAGE
According to the 2001 census results, the lowest estimate of percentage of persons aged three years and over able to speak Welsh is:

Blaenau Gwent	9.1	Neath Port Talbot	17.8
Bridgend	10.6	Newport	9.6
Caerphilly	10.9	Pembrokeshire	21.5
Cardiff	10.9	Powys	20.8
Carmarthenshire	50.1	Rhondda Cynon Taf	12.3
Ceredigion	51.8	Swansea	13.2
Conwy	29.2	Torfaen	10.7
Denbighshire	26.1	Vale of Glamorgan	11.1
Flintshire	14.1	Wrexham	14.4
Gwynedd	68.7	Ynys Mon (Isle of	59.8
Merthyr Tydfil	10.0	Anglesey)	
Monmouthshire	9.0		
Wales	20.5		

FLAG
The flag of Wales, the Red Dragon (Y Ddraig Goch), is a red dragon on a field divided white over green (per fess argent and vert a dragon passant gules). The flag was augmented in 1953 by a royal badge on a shield encircled with a riband bearing the words *Ddraig Goch Ddyry Cychwyn* and imperially crowned, but this augmented flag is rarely used.

EARLY HISTORY

The earliest inhabitants of whom there is any record appear to have been subdued or exterminated by the Goidels (a people of Celtic race) in the Bronze Age. A further invasion of Celtic Brythons and Belgae followed in the ensuing Iron Age. The Roman conquest of southern Britain and Wales was for some time successfully opposed by Caratacus (Caractacus or Caradog), chieftain of the Catuvellauni and son of Cunobelinus (Cymbeline). South-east Wales was subjugated and the legionary fortress at Caerleon-on-Usk established by about AD 75–77; the conquest of Wales was completed by Agricola about AD 78. Communications were opened up by the construction of military roads from Chester to Caerleon-on-Usk and Caerwent, and from Chester to Conwy (and thence to Carmarthen and Neath). Christianity was introduced during the Roman occupation, in the fourth century.

ANGLO-SAXON ATTACKS
The Anglo-Saxon invaders of southern Britain drove the Celts into the mountain stronghold of Wales, and into Strathclyde (Cumberland and south-west Scotland) and Cornwall, giving them the name of *Waelisc* (Welsh), meaning 'foreign'. The West Saxons' victory of Deorham (AD 577) isolated Wales from Cornwall and the battle of Chester (AD 613) cut off communication with Strathclyde and northern Britain. In the eighth century the boundaries of the Welsh were further restricted by the annexations of Offa, King of Mercia, and counter-attacks were largely prevented by the construction of an artificial boundary from the Dee to the Wye (Offa's Dyke).

In the ninth century Rhodri Mawr (844–878) united the country and successfully resisted further incursions of the Saxons by land and raids of Norse and Danish pirates by sea, but at his death his three provinces of Gwynedd (north), Powys (mid) and Deheubarth (south) were divided among his three sons, Anarawd, Mervyn and Cadell. Cadell's son Hywel Dda ruled a large part of Wales and codified its laws but the provinces were not united again until the rule of Llewelyn ap Seisyllt (husband of the heiress of Gwynedd) from 1018 to 1023.

THE NORMAN CONQUEST

After the Norman conquest of England, William I created palatine counties along the Welsh frontier, and the Norman barons began to make encroachments into Welsh territory. The Welsh princes recovered many of their losses during the civil wars of Stephen's reign and in the early 13th century Owen Gruffydd, prince of Gwynedd, was the dominant figure in Wales. Under Llewelyn ap Iorwerth (1194–1240) the Welsh united in powerful resistance to English incursions and Llywelyn's privileges and *de facto* independence were recognised in the Magna Carta. His grandson, Llywelyn ap Gruffydd, was the last native prince; he was killed in 1282 during hostilities between the Welsh and English, allowing Edward I of England to establish his authority over the country. On 7 February 1301, Edward of Caernarvon, son of Edward I, was created Prince of Wales, a title subsequently borne by the eldest son of the sovereign.

Strong Welsh national feeling continued, expressed in the early 15th century in the rising led by Owain Glyndwr, but the situation was altered by the accession to the English throne in 1485 of Henry VII of the Welsh House of Tudor. Wales was politically assimilated to England under the Act of Union of 1535, which extended English laws to the Principality and gave it parliamentary representation for the first time.

EISTEDDFOD

The Welsh are a distinct nation, with a language and literature of their own, and the national bardic festival (Eisteddfod), instituted by Prince Rhys ap Griffith in 1176, is still held annually. These *Eisteddfodau* (sessions) form part of the *Gorsedd* (assembly) and are believed to date from the time of Prydian, a ruling prince in an age many centuries before the Christian era.

PRINCIPAL CITIES

There are five cities in Wales (with date city status conferred); Bangor (pre-1900), Cardiff (1905), St David's (1994), Newport (2002) and Swansea (1969).

Cardiff and Swansea have also been granted Lord Mayoralities.

CARDIFF

Cardiff, at the mouth of the Rivers Taff, Rhymney and Ely, is the capital city of Wales and at the 2001 census had a population of 305,353. The city has changed dramatically in recent years following the regeneration of Cardiff Bay and construction of a barrage, which has created a permanent freshwater lake and waterfront for the city. As the capital city of Wales, Cardiff is home to the National Assembly for Wales and is a major administrative, retail, business and cultural centre.

The civic centre, is home to many fine buildings including, the City Hall, Castell Coch, Cardiff Castle, Llandaff Cathedral, the National Museum of Wales,

University Buildings, Law Courts and the Temple of Peace and Health. The Millennium Stadium opened in 1999.

SWANSEA

Swansea *(Abertawe)* is a city and a seaport and at the 2001 census had a population of 223,293. The Gower peninsula was brought within the city boundary under local government reform in 1974.

The principal buildings are the Norman Castle (rebuilt *c.* 1330), the Royal Institution of South Wales, founded in 1835 (including Library), the University of Wales Swansea at Singleton, and the Guildhall, containing Frank Brangwyn's British Empire panels. The Dylan Thomas Centre, formerly the old Guildhall, was restored in 1995. More recent buildings include the County Hall, the new Maritime Quarter Marina and leisure centre.

Swansea was chartered by the Earl of Warwick, *c.* 1158–84, and further charters were granted by King John, Henry III, Edward II, Edward III and James II, Cromwell (two) and the Marcher Lord William de Breos. It was formally invested with city status in 1969 by HRH The Prince of Wales.

LOCAL COUNCILS

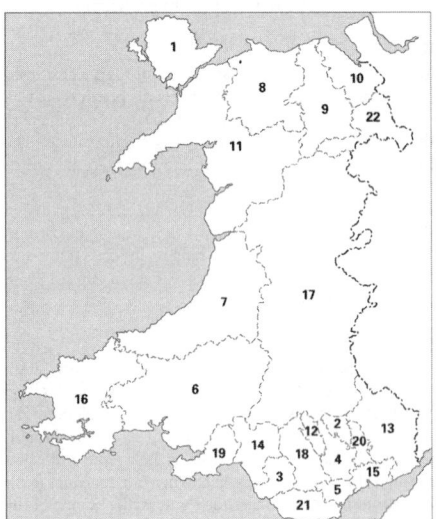

Key	County		
1	Anglesey	12	Merthyr Tydfil
2	Blaenau Gwent	13	Monmouthshire
3	Bridgend	14	Neath Port Talbot
4	Caerphilly	15	Newport
5	Cardiff	16	Pembrokeshire
6	Carmarthenshire	17	Powys
7	Ceredigion	18	Rhondda, Cynon, Taff
8	Conwy	19	Swansea
9	Denbighshire	20	Torfaen
10	Flintshire	21	Vale of Glamorgan
11	Gwynedd	22	Wrexham

LORDS-LIEUTENANT AND HIGH SHERIFFS

County/Shire	Lord-Lieutenant	High Sheriff, 2004–5
Clwyd	T. Jones, CBE	Dr J. O'Hara
Dyfed	The Rt. Hon. Baron Morris of Aberavon, QC	Mrs N. Drew
Gwent	S. Boyle	Brian Watkins, CMG
Gwynedd	Prof. E. Sunderland, OBE	J. Williams-Ellis
Mid Glamorgan	Kate Thomas	Mrs B. Williams
Powys	The Hon. Mrs E. S. Legge-Bourke, LVO	Lady Davies
S. Glamorgan	Capt. N. Lloyd-Edwards	Mrs F. Peel
W. Glamorgan	R. C. Hastie, CBE	David Lewis

LOCAL COUNCILS

Council	Administrative Headquarters	Telephone	Population	Band D charge*	Chief Executive
Blaenau Gwent	Ebbw Vale	01495-350555	73,000	£1,038	R. Morrison
Bridgend	Bridgend	01656-643643	129,000	£949	Keri Lewis
Caerphilly	Hengoed	01443-815588	170,000	£862	Malgwyn Davies
CARDIFF CITY	Cardiff	029-2087 2000	327,500	£872	Byron Davies
Carmarthenshire	Carmarthen	01267-234567	173,000	£907	Mark James
Ceredigion	Aberaeron	01545-570881	77,202	£883	Owen Watkin
Conwy	Conwy	01492-574000	110,500	£777	C. Barker
Denbighshire	Ruthin	01824-706000	93,065	£1,007	Ian Miller
Flintshire	Mold	01352-752121	148,565	£881	Philip McGreevy
Gwynedd	Caernarfon	01286-672255	116,000	£890	Harry Thomas
Merthyr Tydfil	Merthyr Tydfil	01685-725000	54,000	£1,049	Alistair Neill
Monmouthshire	Cwmbran	01633-644644	84,885	£917	Colin Berg *(Acting)*
Neath Port Talbot	Port Talbot	01639-763333	137,954	£1,087	Ken Sawyers
NEWPORT	Newport	01633-244491	138,500	£732	Chris Freegard
Pembrokeshire	Haverfordwest	01437-764551	114,700	£707	Bryn Parry-Jones
Powys	Llandrindod Wells	01597-826000	123,000	£868	Jacky Tonge
Rhondda Cynon Taff	Tonypandy	01443-424000	340,000	£955	Kim Ryley
SWANSEA	Swansea	01792-636000	231,180	£880	Tim Thorogood
Torfaen	Pontypool	01495-762200	90,500	£892	Meg Holborow
Vale of Glamorgan	Barry	01446-700111	119,281	£829	John Maitland-Evans
Wrexham	Wrexham	01978-292000	125,000	£911	I. Garner
Ynys Mon (Isle of Anglesey)	Ynys Mon	01248-750057	67,863	£843	Geraint Edwards

* Average Band D council tax rounded to the nearest £, without discounts and inclusive of precepts
Councils in CAPITAL LETTERS have City Status

SCOTLAND

The Kingdom of Scotland occupies the northern portion of the main island of Great Britain and includes the Inner and Outer Hebrides, Orkney, Shetland, and many other islands. It lies between 60° 51′ 30″ and 54° 38′ N. latitude and between 1° 45′ 32″ and 6° 14′ W. longitude, with England to the south, the Atlantic Ocean on the north and west, and the North Sea on the east.

The greatest length of the mainland (Cape Wrath to the Mull of Galloway) is 274 miles, and the greatest breadth (Buchan Ness to Applecross) is 154 miles. The customary measurement of the island of Great Britain is from the site of John o' Groats house, near Duncansby Head, Caithness, to Land's End, Cornwall, a total distance of 603 miles in a straight line and approximately 900 miles by road.

The total area of Scotland is 30,420 sq. miles (78,789 sq. km); land 29,767 sq. miles (77,097 sq. km), inland water 653 sq. miles (1,692 sq. km).

POPULATION
The population at the 2001 census was 5,062,011 (males 2,432,494; females 2,629,517). The average density of the population in 2001 was 0.65 persons per hectare.

RELIEF
There are three natural orographic divisions of Scotland. The southern uplands have their highest points in Merrick (2,766 ft), Rhinns of Kells (2,669 ft), and Cairnsmuir of Carsphairn (2,614 ft), in the west; and the Tweedsmuir Hills in the east (Hartfell 2,651 ft, Dollar Law 2,682 ft, Broad Law 2,756 ft).

The central lowlands, formed by the valleys of the Clyde, Forth and Tay, divide the southern uplands from the northern Highlands, which extend almost from the extreme north of the mainland to the central lowlands, and are divided into a northern and a southern system by the Great Glen.

The Grampian Mountains, which entirely cover the southern Highland area, include in the west Ben Nevis (4,406 ft), the highest point in the British Isles, and in the east the Cairngorm Mountains (Cairn Gorm 4,084 ft, Braeriach 4,248 ft, Ben Macdui 4,296 ft). The north-western Highland area contains the mountains of Wester and Easter Ross (Carn Eige 3,880 ft, Sgurr na Lapaich 3,775 ft).

Created, like the central lowlands, by a major geological fault, the Great Glen (60 miles long) runs between Inverness and Fort William, and contains Loch Ness, Loch Oich and Loch Lochy. These are linked to each other and to the north-east and south-west coasts of Scotland by the Caledonian Canal, providing a navigable passage between the Moray Firth and the Inner Hebrides.

HYDROGRAPHY
The western coast is fragmented by peninsulas and islands, and indented by fjords (sea-lochs), the longest of which is Loch Fyne (42 miles long) in Argyll. Although the east coast tends to be less fractured and lower, there are several great drowned inlets (firths), e.g. Firth of Forth, Firth of Tay, Moray Firth, as well as the Firth of Clyde in the west.

The lochs are the principal hydrographic feature. The largest in Scotland and in Britain is Loch Lomond (27 sq. miles), in the Grampian valleys; the longest and deepest is Loch Ness (24 miles long and 800 ft deep), in the Great Glen; and Loch Shin (20 miles long) and Loch Maree in the Highlands.

The longest river is the Tay (117 miles), noted for its salmon. It flows into the North Sea, with Dundee on the estuary, which is spanned by the Tay Bridge (10,289 ft) opened in 1887 and the Tay Road Bridge (7,365 ft) opened in 1966. Other noted salmon rivers are the Dee (90 miles) which flows into the North Sea at Aberdeen, and the Spey (110 miles), the swiftest flowing river in the British Isles, which flows into Moray Firth. The Tweed, which gave its name to the woollen cloth produced along its banks, marks in the lower stretches of its 96-mile course the border between Scotland and England.

The most important river commercially is the Clyde (106 miles), formed by the junction of the Daer and Portrail water, which flows through the city of Glasgow to the Firth of Clyde. During its course it passes over the picturesque Falls of Clyde, Bonnington Linn (30 ft), Corra Linn (84 ft), Dundaff Linn (10 ft) and Stonebyres Linn (80 ft), above and below Lanark. The Forth (66 miles), upon which stands Edinburgh, the capital, is spanned by the Forth Railway Bridge (1890), which is 5,330 ft long, and the Forth Road Bridge (1964), which has a total length of 6,156 ft (over water) and a single span of 3,000 ft.

The highest waterfall in Scotland, and the British Isles, is Eas a'Chùal Aluinn with a total height of 658 ft, which falls from Glas Bheinn in Sutherland. The Falls of Glomach, on a head-stream of the Elchaig in Wester Ross, have a drop of 370 ft.

GAELIC LANGUAGE
According to the 2001 census, 1.2 per cent of the population of Scotland, mainly in Western Isles, were able to speak the Scottish form of Gaelic.

LOWLAND SCOTTISH LANGUAGE
Several regional Lowland Scottish dialects, known variously as Scots, Scotch, Lallans or Doric, are widely spoken. The General Register Office (Scotland) estimated in 1996 that 1.5 million people, or 30 per cent of the population, are Scots speakers. A question on Scots was not included in the 2001 census.

FLAG
The flag of Scotland is known as the Saltire. It is a white diagonal cross on a blue field (saltire argent in a field azure) and represents St Andrew, the patron saint of Scotland.

THE SCOTTISH ISLANDS

ORKNEY
The Orkney Islands (total area 375.5 sq. miles) lie about six miles north of the mainland, separated from it by the Pentland Firth. Of the 90 islands and islets (holms and skerries) in the group, about one-third are inhabited.

The total population at the 2001 census was 19,245;

the 2001 populations of the islands shown here include those of smaller islands forming part of the same council district.

Mainland, 15,339	Rousay, 267
Burray, 357	Sanday, 478
Eday, 121	Shapinsay, 300
Flotta, 81	South Ronaldsay, 854
Hoy, 392	Stronsay, 358
North Ronaldsay, 70	Westray, 563
Papa Westray, 65	

The islands are rich in prehistoric and Scandinavian remains, the most notable being the Stone Age village of Skara Brae, the burial chamber of Maeshowe, the many brochs (towers) and the 12th-century St Magnus Cathedral. Scapa Flow, between the Mainland and Hoy, was the war station of the British Grand Fleet from 1914 to 1919 and the scene of the scuttling of the surrendered German High Seas Fleet (21 June 1919).

Most of the islands are low-lying and fertile, and farming (principally beef cattle) is the main industry. Flotta, to the south of Scapa Flow, is the site of the oil terminal for the Piper, Claymore and Tartan fields in the North Sea.

The capital is Kirkwall (population 6,206) situated on Mainland.

SHETLAND

The Shetland Islands have a total area of 551 sq. miles and a population at the 2001 census of 21,988. They lie about 50 miles north of the Orkneys, with Fair Isle about half-way between the two groups. Out Stack, off Muckle Flugga, one mile north of Unst, is the most northerly part of the British Isles (60° 51′ 30″ N. lat.).

There are over 100 islands, of which 16 are inhabited. Populations at the 2001 census were:

Mainland, 17,575	Muckle Roe, 104
Bressay, 384	Trondra, 133
East Burra, 66	Unst, 720
Fair Isle, 69	West Burra, 784
Fetlar, 86	Whalsay, 1,034
Housay, 76	Yell, 957

Shetland's many archaeological sites include Jarlshof, Mousa and Clickhimin, and its long connection with Scandinavia has resulted in a strong Norse influence on its place-names and dialect.

Industries include fishing, knitwear and farming. In addition to the fishing fleet there are fish processing factories, and the traditional handknitting of Fair Isle and Unst is supplemented now with machine-knitted garments. Farming is mainly crofting, with sheep being raised on the moorland and hills of the islands. Latterly the islands have become a centre of the North Sea oil industry, with pipelines from the Brent and Ninian fields running to the terminal at Sullom Voe, the largest of its kind in Europe. Lerwick is the main centre for supply services for offshore oil exploration and development.

The capital is Lerwick (population 6,830) situated on Mainland.

THE HEBRIDES

Until the late 13th century the Hebrides included other Scottish islands in the Firth of Clyde, the peninsula of Kintyre (Argyll), the Isle of Man, and the (Irish) Isle of Rathlin. The origin of the name is stated to be the Greek *Eboudai*, latinised as *Hebudes* by Pliny, and corrupted to its present form. The Norwegian name *Sudreyjar* (Southern Islands) was latinised as *Sodorenses*, a name that survives in the Anglican bishopric of Sodor and Man.

There are over 500 islands and islets, of which about 100 are inhabited, though mountainous terrain and extensive peat bogs mean that only a fraction of the total area is under cultivation. Stone, Bronze and Iron Age settlement has left many remains, including those at Callanish on Lewis, and Norse colonisation influenced language, customs and place-names. Occupations include farming (mostly crofting and stock-raising), fishing and the manufacture of tweeds and other woollens. Tourism is also an important factor in the economy.

The Inner Hebrides lie off the west coast of Scotland and relatively close to the mainland. The largest and best-known is Skye (area 643 sq. miles; pop. 9,251; chief town, Portree), which contains the Cuillin Hills (Sgurr Alasdair 3,257 ft), the Red Hills (Beinn na Caillich 2,403 ft), Bla Bheinn (3,046 ft) and The Storr (2,358 ft). Other islands in the Highland council area include Raasay (pop. 194), Rum, Eigg (pop. 131) and Muck.

Further south the Inner Hebridean islands include Arran (pop. 5,058) containing Goat Fell (2,868 ft); Coll and Tiree (pop. 934); Colonsay and Oronsay (pop. 113); Easdale (pop. 58); Gigha (pop. 110); Islay (area 235 sq. miles; pop. 3,457); Jura (area 160 sq. miles; pop. 188) with a range of hills culminating in the Paps of Jura (Beinn-an-Oir, 2,576 ft, and Beinn Chaolais, 2,477 ft); Lismore (pop. 146); Luing (pop. 220); and Mull (area 367 sq. miles; pop. 2,696; chief town Tobermory) containing Ben More (3,171 ft).

The Outer Hebrides, separated from the mainland by the Minch, now form the Eilean Siar Western Isles Islands Council area (area 1,119 sq. miles; population at the 2001 census 26,502). The main islands are Lewis with Harris (area 770 sq. miles, pop. 19,918), whose chief town, Stornoway, is the administrative headquarters; North Uist (pop. 1,320); South Uist (pop. 1,818); Benbecula (pop. 1,249) and Barra (pop. 1,078). Other inhabited islands include Bernera (233), Berneray (136), Eriskay (133), Grimsay (201), Scalpay (322) and Vatersay (94).

EARLY HISTORY

There is evidence of human settlement in Scotland dating from the third millennium BC, the earliest settlers being Middle Stone Age hunters and fishermen. Early in the second millennium BC, New Stone Age farmers began to cultivate crops and rear livestock; their settlements were on the west coast and in the north, and included Skara Brae and Maeshowe (Orkney). Settlement by the Early Bronze Age 'Beaker folk', so-called from the shape of their drinking vessels, in eastern Scotland dates from about 1800 BC. Further settlement is believed to have occurred from 700 BC onwards, as tribes were displaced from further south by new incursions from the Continent and the Roman invasions from AD 43.

Julius Agricola, the Roman governor of Britain AD 77–84, extended the Roman conquests in Britain by advancing into Caledonia, culminating with a victory at Mons Graupius, probably in AD 84; he was recalled to Rome shortly afterwards and his forward policy was not pursued. Hadrian's Wall, mostly completed by AD 30, marked the northern frontier of the Roman empire except for the period between about AD 144 and 190 when the frontier moved north to the Forth-Clyde isthmus and a turf wall, the Antonine Wall, was manned.

After the Roman withdrawal from Britain, there were centuries of warfare between the Picts, Scots, Britons, Angles and Vikings. The Picts, believed to be a non-Indo-European race, occupied the area north of the Forth. The Scots, a Gaelic-speaking people of northern Ireland, colonised the area of Argyll and Bute (the kingdom of Dalriada) in the fifth century AD and then expanded eastwards and northwards. The Britons, speaking a Brythonic Celtic language, colonised Scotland from the south from the first century BC; they lost control of south-eastern Scotland (incorporated into the kingdom of Northumbria) to the Angles in the early seventh century but retained Strathclyde (south-western Scotland and Cumbria). Viking raids from the late eighth century were followed by Norse settlement in the western and northern isles, Argyll, Caithness and Sutherland from the mid-ninth century onwards.

UNIFICATION
The union of the areas which now comprise Scotland began in AD 843 when Kenneth mac Alpin, king of the Scots from c.834, became also king of the Picts, joining the two lands to form the kingdom of Alba (comprising Scotland north of a line between the Forth and Clyde rivers). Lothian, the eastern part of the area between the Forth and the Tweed, seems to have been leased to Kenneth II of Alba (reigned 971–995) by Edgar of England c.973/4, and Scottish possession was confirmed by Malcolm II's victory over a Northumbrian army at Carham c.1016. At about this time Malcolm II (reigned 1005–34) placed his grandson Duncan on the throne of the British kingdom of Strathclyde, bringing under Scots rule virtually all of what is now Scotland.

The Norse possessions were incorporated into the kingdom of Scotland from the 12th century onwards. An uprising in the mid-12th century drove the Norse from most of mainland Argyll. The Hebrides were ceded to Scotland by the Treaty of Perth in 1266 after a Norwegian expedition in 1263 failed to maintain Norse authority over the islands. Orkney and Shetland fell to Scotland in 1468–9 as a pledge for the unpaid dowry of Margaret of Denmark, wife of James III, though Danish claims of suzerainty were relinquished only with the marriage of Anne of Denmark to James VI in 1590.

From the 11th century, there were frequent wars between Scotland and England over territory and the extent of England's political influence. The failure of the Scottish royal line with the death of Margaret of Norway in 1290 led to disputes over the throne which were resolved by the adjudication of Edward I of England. He awarded the throne to John Balliol in 1292 but Balliol's refusal to be a puppet king led to war. Balliol surrendered to Edward I in 1296 and Edward attempted to rule Scotland himself. Resistance to Scotland's loss of independence was led by William Wallace, who defeated the English at Stirling Bridge (1297), and Robert Bruce, crowned in 1306, who held most of Scotland by 1311 and routed Edward II's army at Bannockburn (1314). England recognised the independence of Scotland in the Treaty of Northampton in 1328. Subsequent clashes include the disastrous battle of Flodden (1513) in which James IV and many of his nobles fell.

THE UNION
In 1603 James VI of Scotland succeeded Elizabeth I on the throne of England (his mother, Mary Queen of Scots,

was the great-granddaughter of Henry VII), his successors reigning as sovereigns of Great Britain. Political union of the two countries did not occur until 1707.

THE JACOBITE REVOLTS
After the abdication (by flight) in 1688 of James VII and II, the crown devolved upon William III (grandson of Charles I) and Mary II (elder daughter of James VII and II). In 1689 Graham of Claverhouse roused the Highlands on behalf of James VII and II, but died after a military success at Killiecrankie.

After the death of Anne (younger daughter of James VII and II), the throne devolved upon George I (great-grandson of James VI and I). In 1715, armed risings on behalf of James Stuart (the Old Pretender, son of James VII and II) led to the indecisive battle of Sheriffmuir, and the Jacobite movement died down until 1745, when Charles Stuart (the Young Pretender) defeated the Royalist troops at Prestonpans and advanced to Derby (1746). From Derby, the adherents of 'James VIII and III' (the title claimed for his father by Charles Stuart) fell back on the defensive and were finally crushed at Culloden (16 April 1746).

PRINCIPAL CITIES

ABERDEEN
Aberdeen, 130 miles north-east of Edinburgh, received its charter as a Royal Burgh in 1124. Scotland's third largest city, Aberdeen lies between two rivers, the Dee and the Don facing the North Sea, the city has a strong maritime history and today is a main centre for offshore oil exploration and production. It is also an ancient university town and distinguished research centre. Other industries include engineering, food processing, textiles, paper manufacturing and chemicals.

Places of interest include King's College, St Machar's Cathedral, Brig o' Balgownie, Duthie Park and Winter Gardens, Hazlehead Park, the Kirk of St Nicholas, Mercat Cross, Marischal College and Marischal Museum, Provost Skene's House, Art Gallery, Gordon Highlanders Museum, Satrosphere Hands-On Discovery Centre, and Aberdeen Maritime Museum.

DUNDEE
The Royal Burgh of Dundee is situated on the north bank of the Tay estuary. The city's port and dock installations are important to the offshore oil industry and the airport also provides servicing facilities. Principal industries include textiles, biotechnology and digital media, lasers, printing, tyre manufacture, food processing, engineering, and tourism.

The unique City Churches – three churches under one roof, together with the 15th-century St Mary's Tower – are the most prominent architectural feature. Dundee has two historic ships: the Dundee-built RRS *Discovery* which took Capt. Scott to the Antarctic lies alongside Discovery Quay, and the frigate *Unicorn*, the only British-built wooden warship still afloat, is moored in Victoria Dock. Places of interest include Mills Public Observatory, the Tay road and rail bridges, Dundee Contemporary Arts Centre, McManus Galleries, Claypotts Castle, Broughty Castle, Verdant Works (Textile Heritage Centre) and the Sensation science centre.

EDINBURGH
Edinburgh is the capital city and seat of government in Scotland. The city is built on a group of hills and contains

in Princes Street one of the most beautiful thoroughfares in the world.

The principal buildings are the Castle, which now houses the Stone of Scone and also includes St Margaret's Chapel, the oldest building in Edinburgh, and near it, the Scottish National War Memorial; the Palace of Holyroodhouse; Parliament House, the present seat of the judicature; three universities (Edinburgh, Heriot-Watt, Napier); St Giles' Cathedral; St Mary's (Scottish Episcopal) Cathedral (Sir George Gilbert Scott); the General Register House (Robert Adam); the National and the Signet Libraries; the National Gallery of Scotland; the Royal Scottish Academy; the Scottish National Portrait Gallery; and the Edinburgh International Conference Centre.

GLASGOW

Glasgow, a Royal Burgh, is Scotland's largest city and its principal commercial and industrial centre. The city occupies the north and south banks of the Clyde, formerly one of the chief commercial estuaries in the world. The main industries include engineering, electronics, finance, chemicals and printing. The city is also a key tourist and conference destination.

The chief buildings are the 13th-century Gothic Cathedral, the University (Sir George Gilbert Scott), the City Chambers, the Royal Concert Hall, St Mungo Museum of Religious Life and Art, Pollok House, the School of Art (Mackintosh), Kelvingrove Art Galleries, the Gallery of Modern Art, the Burrell Collection museum and the Mitchell Library. The city is home to the Scottish National Orchestra, Scottish Opera, Scottish Ballet and BBC Scotland and Scottish Television.

INVERNESS

Inverness was granted city status in 2000. The city's name is derived from the Gaelic for 'the mouth of the Ness', referring to the river on which it lies. Inverness is recorded as being at the junction of the old trade routes since 565AD. Today the city is the main administrative centre for the north of Scotland and is the capital of the Highlands. Tourism is one of the city's main industries.

Among the city's most notable buildings is Abertarff House, built in 1593 and the oldest secular building remaining in Inverness. Balnain House, built as a town house in 1726 is a fine example of early Georgian architecture. Once a hospital for Hanoverian soldiers after the battle of Culloden and as billets for the Royal Engineers when completing the 1st Ordnance Survey, today Balnain House is the National Trust for Scotland's regional HQ. The Old High Church, on St Michael's Mount, is the original Parish Church of Inverness and is built on the sight of the earliest Christian church in the city. Parts of the church date back to the 14th century.

Stirling was granted city status in 2002. Aberdeen, Dundee, Edinburgh and Glasgow have also been granted Lord Mayoralty/Lord Provostship.

LORDS-LIEUTENANT

Stirling was granted city status in 2002. Aberdeen, Dundee, Edinburgh and Glasgow have also been granted Lord Mayoralty/Lord Provostship.

Title	Name
Aberdeenshire	A. D. M. Farquharson, OBE
Angus	Mrs G. L. Osborne
Argyll and Bute	K. A. Mackinnon
Ayrshire and Arran	Maj. R. Y. Henderson, TD
Banffshire	Mrs Clare Russell
Berwickshire	Maj. A. R. Trotter
Caithness	M. A. G. Dunnett
Clackmannan	Mrs S. C. Cruickshank
Dumfries	Capt. R. C. Cunningham-Jardine
Dunbartonshire	Brig. D. D. G. Hardie, TD
East Lothian	W. Garth Morrison, CBE
Eilean Siar/Western Isles	A. Matheson, OBE
Fife	Mrs C. M. Dean
Inverness	Donald Angus Cameron of Lochiel, KT, CVO
Kincardineshire	J. D. B. Smart
Lanarkshire	G. K. Cox, MBE
Midlothian	Patrick Robert Prenter, CBE

Title	Name
Moray	Air Vice-Marshal G. A. Chesworth, CB, OBE, DFC
Nairn	E. J. Brodie
Orkney	G. R. Marwick
Perth and Kinross	Sir David Montgomery, Bt.
Renfrewshire	C. H. Parker, OBE
Ross and Cromarty	Capt. R. W. K. Stirling of Fairburn, TD
Roxburgh, Ettrick and Lauderdale	Dr June Paterson-Brown, CBE
Shetland	J. H. Scott
Stirling and Falkirk	Lt.-Col. J. Stirling of Garden, CBE, TD
Sutherland	vacant
The Stewartry of Kirkcudbright	Lt.-Gen. Sir Norman Arthur, KCB
Tweeddale	Capt. D. Younger
West Lothian	Mrs I. G. Brydie, MBE
Wigtown	Maj. E. S. Orr-Ewing

The Lord Provosts of the four city districts of Aberdeen, Dundee, Edinburgh and Glasgow are Lords-Lieutenant for those districts *ex officio*.

LOCAL COUNCILS

Council	Administrative Headquarters	Telephone	Population	Band D charge *	Chief Executive
ABERDEEN	Aberdeen	01224-522000	211,250	£1,107	Douglas Paterson
Aberdeenshire	Aberdeen	01467-620981	226,940	£1,014	Alan Campbell
Angus	Forfar	01307-461460	109,000	£985	Sandy Watson
Argyll and Bute	Lochgilphead	01546-602127	89,000	£1,075	James McLellan
Clackmannanshire	Alloa	01259-452000	47,930	£1,043	Keir Bloomer
Dumfries and Galloway	Dumfries	01387-260000	147,000	£964	Philip Jones
DUNDEE	Dundee	01382-434000	145,663	£1,135	Alex Stephen
East Ayrshire	Kilmarnock	01563-576000	120,300	£1,064	Fiona Lees
East Dunbartonshire	Kirkintilloch	0141-578 8000	108,243	£1,033	Sue Bruce
East Lothian	Haddington	01620-827827	90,180	£1,042	John Lindsay
East Renfrewshire	Giffnock	0141-577 3000	89,790	£1,003	Peter Daniels
EDINBURGH	Edinburgh	0131-200 2000	444,020	£1,083	Tom Aitchison
Eilean Siar (Western Isles)	Stornoway	01851-703773	27,940	£911	Bill Howat
Falkirk	Falkirk	01324-506070	145,270	£951	Mary Pitcaithly
Fife	Glenrothes	01592-414141	349,200	£1,015	Douglas Sinclair
GLASGOW	Glasgow	0141-287 2000	609,370	£1,185	George Black
Highland	Inverness	01463-702000	208,900	£1,039	Arthur McCourt
Inverclyde	Greenock	01475-717171	82,930	£1,143	Robert Cleary
Midlothian	Dalkeith	0131-270 7500	82,200	£1,126	Trevor Muir
Moray	Elgin	01343-543451	86,940	£996	Alastair Keddie
North Ayrshire	Irvine	01294-324100	140,000	£1,025	Bernard Devine
North Lanarkshire	Motherwell	01698-302222	321,820	£1,006	Gavin Whitefield
Orkney	Kirkwall	01856-873535	19,245	£940	Alistair Buchan
Perth and Kinross	Perth	01738-475000	134,949	£1,037	Bernadette Malone
Renfrewshire	Paisley	0141-842 5000	172,867	£1,039	Tom Scholes
Scottish Borders	Melrose	01835-824000	106,764	£985	David Hume
Shetland	Lerwick	01595-744511	21,940	£936	Morgan Goodlad
South Ayrshire	Ayr	01292-612000	113,960	£1,012	Tom Cairns
South Lanarkshire	Hamilton	01698-454444	302,216	£1,005	Michael Docherty
STIRLING	Stirling	0845-277700	84,700	£1,105	Keith Yates
West Dumbarton	Dunbartonshire	01389-737000	93,378	£1,089	Tim Huntingford
West Lothian	Livingston	01506-777000	153,086	£1,028	Alex Linkston

* Average Band D council tax without discounts and inclusive of any precepts. Councils in CAPITAL LETTERS have City Status

Key	Council		
1	Aberdeen City	17	Inverclyde
2	Aberdeenshire	18	Midlothian
3	Angus	19	Moray
4	Argyll and Bute	20	North Ayrshire
5	City of Edinburgh	21	North Lanarkshire
6	Clackmannanshire	22	Orkney
7	Dumfries and Galloway	23	Perth and Kinross
8	Dundee City	24	Renfrewshire
9	East Ayrshire	25	Scottish Borders
10	East Dunbartonshire	26	Shetland
11	East Lothian	27	South Ayrshire
12	East Renfrewshire	28	South Lanarkshire
13	Falkirk	29	Stirling
14	Fife	30	West Dunbartonshire
15	Glasgow City	31	Western Isles (Eilean Siar)
16	Highland	32	West Lothian

NORTHERN IRELAND

Northern Ireland has a total area of 5,467 sq. miles (14,144 sq. km): land, 5,225 sq. miles (13,532 sq. km); inland water and tideways, 249 sq. miles (628 sq. km).

The population of Northern Ireland at the 2001 census was 1,685,267 (males, 821,449; females, 863,818).

In 2001 the number of persons in the various religious denominations (expressed as percentages of the total population) were: Catholic, 40.26; Presbyterian, 20.69; Church of Ireland, 15.30; Methodist Church in Ireland, 3.51; other Christian (including Christian related) 6.07; other religions and philosophies, 0.3; no religion or religion not stated, 13.88.

FLAG

The official national flag of Northern Ireland is now the Union Flag. The flag formerly in use (a white, six-pointed star in the centre of a red cross on a white field, enclosing a red hand and surmounted by a crown) has not been used since the imposition of direct rule.

PRINCIPAL CITIES

BELFAST

Belfast, the administrative centre of Northern Ireland, is situated at the mouth of the River Lagan at its entrance to Belfast Lough. The city grew, owing to its easy access by sea to Scottish coal and iron, to be a great industrial centre.

The principal buildings are of a relatively recent date and include the Parliament Buildings at Stormont, the City Hall, Waterfront Hall, the Law Courts, the Public Library and the Museum and Art Gallery.

Belfast received its first charter of incorporation in 1613 and was created a city in 1888; the title of Lord Mayor was conferred in 1892.

LONDONDERRY

Londonderry (originally Derry) is situated on the River Foyle, and has important associations with the City of London. The Irish Society was created by the City of London in 1610, and under its royal charter of 1613 it fortified the city and was for a long time closely associated with its administration. Because of this connection the city was incorporated in 1613 under the new name of Londonderry.

The city is famous for the great siege of 1688–9, when for 105 days the town held out against the forces of James II. The city walls are still intact and form a circuit of almost a mile around the old city.

Interesting buildings are the Protestant Cathedral of St Columb's (1633) and the Guildhall, reconstructed in 1912 and containing a number of beautiful stained glass windows, many of which were presented by the livery companies of London.

Three other places in Northern Ireland have been granted city status: Armagh (1994), Newry (2002) and Lisburn (2002).

CONSTITUTIONAL DEVELOPMENTS

Northern Ireland is subject to the same fundamental constitutional provisions which apply to the rest of the United Kingdom. It had its own parliament and government from 1921 to 1972, but after increasing civil unrest the Northern Ireland (Temporary Provisions) Act 1972 transferred the legislative and executive powers of the Northern Ireland parliament and government to the UK Parliament and a Secretary of State. The Northern Ireland Constitution Act 1973 provided for devolution in Northern Ireland through an assembly and executive, but a power-sharing executive formed by the Northern Ireland political parties in January 1974 collapsed in May 1974. Since then Northern Ireland has been governed by direct rule under the provisions of the Northern Ireland Act 1974. This allows Parliament to approve all laws for Northern Ireland and places the Northern Ireland department under the direction and control of the Secretary of State for Northern Ireland.

Attempts were made by successive governments to find a means of restoring a widely acceptable form of devolved government to Northern Ireland. In 1985 the governments of the United Kingdom and the Republic of Ireland signed the Anglo-Irish Agreement, establishing an intergovernmental conference in which the Irish government may put forward views and proposals on certain aspects of Northern Ireland affairs.

Discussions between the British and Irish governments and the main Northern Ireland parties began in 1991. It was agreed that any political settlement would need to address relationships within Northern Ireland, within the island of Ireland (north/south) and between the British and Irish governments (east/west). Although round table talks ended in 1992 the process continued from September 1993 as separate bilateral discussions with three of the Northern Ireland parties (the DUP declined to participate).

In December 1993 the British and Irish governments published the Joint Declaration complementing the political talks, and making clear that any settlement would need to be founded on principles of democracy and consent. The declaration also stated that all democratically mandated parties could be involved in political talks as long as they permanently renounced paramilitary violence.

The provisional IRA and loyalist paramilitary groups announced cease-fires on 31 August and 13 October 1994 respectively. The Government initiated exploratory meetings with Sinn Fein and loyalist representatives in December 1994.

In February 1995 the then Prime Minister (John Major) launched *A Framework for Accountable Government in Northern Ireland* and, with the Irish Prime Minister, *A New Framework for Agreement*. These outlined what a comprehensive political settlement might look like. The ideas were intended to facilitate multilateral dialogue involving the Northern Ireland parties and the British government.

In autumn 1995 the Prime Minister said that Sinn Fein would not be invited to all-party talks until the IRA had decommissioned its arms; the IRA ruled out any decommissioning of weapons in advance of a political settlement. An international body chaired by a former US senator, George Mitchell, reported in January 1996 that no weapons would be decommissioned before the start of all-party talks and that a compromise agreement was necessary under which weapons would be decommissioned during negotiations. The Prime Minister accepted the report and proposed the election of representatives to conduct all-party talks. On 9 February 1996 the IRA called off its cease-fire.

PEACE TALKS

Following elections on 30 May 1996, all-party talks opened at Stormont Castle on 10 June 1996 which included nine of the ten parties returned at the election; Sinn Fein representatives were turned away because the IRA had failed to reinstate its cease-fire. On 29 July 1996 the all-party talks were suspended after disagreements over the issue of decommissioning arms. An opening agenda for the talks was agreed in October 1996.

On 25 June 1997 the newly-elected Labour Government said that substantive negotiations should begin in September 1997 with a view to reaching conclusions by May 1998. The British and Irish governments issued a joint paper outlining their proposals for resolving the decommissioning issue. The Government also indicated that if the IRA were to call a cease-fire, it would assess whether it was genuine over a period of six weeks, and if satisfied that it was so, would then invite Sinn Fein to the talks. An IRA cease-fire was declared on 20 July 1997.

When the UK Government announced in August 1997 that Sinn Fein would be present when the substantive talks opened on 15 September, the unionist and loyalist parties, unhappy at the terms on which Sinn Fein had been admitted, boycotted the opening session. The Ulster Unionist Party, the Progressive Unionist Party and the Ulster Democratic Party re-entered the negotiations on 17 September. Full-scale peace talks began on 7 October. The parties had agreed to concentrate on constitutional issues, with the issue of decommissioning terrorist weapons to be handled by a new independent commission.

On 12 January 1998 the British and Irish governments issued a joint document, *Propositions on Heads of Agreement*, proposing the establishment of various new cross-border bodies; further proposals were presented on 27 January. A draft peace settlement was issued by the talks' chairman, Sen. George Mitchell, on 6 April 1998 but was rejected by the Unionists the following day. On 10 April agreement was reached between the British and Irish governments and the eight Northern Ireland political parties still involved in the talks (the Good Friday Agreement). The agreement provided for an elected New Northern Ireland Assembly; a North/South Ministerial Council, and a British-Irish Council comprising representatives of the British, Irish, Channel Islands and Isle of Man governments and members of the new assemblies for Scotland, Wales and Northern Ireland. Further points included the abandonment of the Republic of Ireland's constitutional claim to Northern Ireland; the decommissioning of weapons; the release of paramilitary prisoners; and changes in policing.

Referendums on the agreement were held in Northern Ireland and the Republic of Ireland on 22 May 1998. In Northern Ireland the turnout was 81 per cent, of which 71.12 per cent voted in favour of the agreement. In the Republic of Ireland, the turnout was about 55 per cent, of which 94.4 per cent voted in favour of both the agreement and the necessary constitutional change. In the UK, the Northern Ireland Act 1998, enshrining the provisions of the Agreement, received Royal Assent in November 1998.

For details of the Northern Ireland Assembly and further political developments in Northern Ireland, *see* the Regional Government section.

OTHER BODIES

Consultations between the First Minister and Deputy First Minister, the British and Irish Governments and the political parties concluded in early 1999 with an agreement to establish six areas for cross-border bodies and a further six areas for co-operation. Treaties between the British and Irish governments establishing the bodies and parallel domestic legislation to underpin them are now in place.

The Good Friday Agreement also provided for a British-Irish Intergovernmental Conference to promote bilateral co-operation at all levels on matters of mutual interest, with a particular focus on non-devolved Northern Ireland matters, and supported by a joint standing Secretariat.

The British-Irish Council operates on the basis of consensus and may reach agreements on common policies in areas of mutual interest. Since its formation in 1999, the Council has met five times at summit level. The last meeting was in Wales in November 2003.

FINANCE

Northern Ireland's expenditure is funded by the Northern Ireland Consolidated Fund (NICF). Up until devolution on 2 December 1999, the NICF was largely financed by Northern Ireland's attributed share of UK taxation and supplemented by a grant-in-aid. From devolution, these separate elements have been subsumed into a single Block Grant. The Northern Ireland Departmental Expenditure Limit for 2004–5 is £7,135.7 million.

LORDS-LIEUTENANT

County	Area (sq. miles)	Lord-Lieutenant
Antrim	1,093	The Lord O'Neill, TD
Armagh	484	The Earl of Caledon
Belfast City	25	Lady Carswell, OBE
Down	945	Maj. William Hall
Fermanagh	647	The Earl of Erne
Londonderry	798	Denis Desmond, CBE
Londonderry City	3.4	Dr Donal Keegan, OBE
Tyrone	1,211	The Duke of Abercorn

DISTRICT COUNCILS

Council	Telephone	Population	Chief Executive
Antrim, Co. Down	028-9446 3113	48,366	David McCammick
Ards, Co. Down	028-9182 4000	73,244	Ashley Boreland
ARMAGH CITY, Co. Armagh	028-3752 9600	54,263	Victor Brownlees
Ballymena, Co. Antrim	028-2566 0300	58,610	Mervyn Rankin
Ballymoney, Co. Antrim	028-2766 0200	26,894	John Dempsey
Banbridge, Co. Down	028-4066 0600	41,392	Robert Gilmore
BELFAST CITY, Co. Antrim and Co. Down	028-9032 0202	277,391	Peter McNaney
Carrickfergus, Co. Antrim	028-9335 1604	37,659	Alan Cardwell
Castlereagh, Co. Down	028-9049 4500	66,488	Adrian Donaldson
Coleraine, Co. Londonderry	028-7034 7034	56,315	Wavell Moore
Cookstown, Co. Tyrone	028-8676 2205	32,581	Michael McGuckin
Craigavon, Co. Armagh	028-3831 2400	80,671	Francis Rock
DERRY CITY, Co. Londonderry	028-7136 5151	105,066	Anthony McGurk
Down, Co. Down	028-4461 0800	63,828	John McGrillen
Dungannon, Co. Tyrone	028-8772 0300	47,735	William Beattie
Fermanagh, Co. Fermanagh	028-6632 5050	57,527	Rodney Connor
Larne, Co. Antrim	028-2827 2313	30,832	Colm McGarry
Limavady, Co. Londonderry	028-7772 2226	32,422	John Stevenson
LISBURN CITY, Co. Antrim	028-9250 9250	108,694	Norman Davidson
Magherafelt, Co. Londonderry	028-7939 7979	39,780	John McLaughlin
Moyle, Co. Antrim	028-2076 2225	15,933	Richard Lewis
NEWRY and Mourne, Co. Down and Co. Armagh	028-3031 3031	87,058	Thomas McCall
Newtownabbey, Co. Antrim	028-9034 0000	79,995	Norman Dunn
North Down, Co. Down	028-9127 0371	76,323	Trevor Polley
Omagh, Co. Tyrone	028-8224 5321	47,952	Daniel McSorley
Strabane, Co. Tyrone	028-7138 2204	38,248	Philip Faithfull

Councils in CAPITAL LETTERS have City Status

THE ISLE OF MAN
Ellan Vannin

The Isle of Man is an island situated in the Irish Sea, in latitude 54° 3'–54° 25' N. and longitude 4° 18'– 4° 47' W., nearly equidistant from England, Scotland and Ireland. Although the early inhabitants were of Celtic origin, the Isle of Man was part of the Norwegian Kingdom of the Hebrides until 1266, when this was ceded to Scotland. Subsequently granted to the Stanleys (Earls of Derby) in the 15th century and later to the Dukes of Atholl, it was brought under the administration of the Crown in 1765. The island forms the bishopric of Sodor and Man.

The total land area is 221 sq. miles (572 sq. km). The report on the 2001 census showed a resident population of 76,315. The main language in use is English. There are no remaining native speakers of Manx Gaelic but 1,527 people are able to speak the language.

CAPITAL ΨDouglas; population (2001), 25,347.

ΨCastletown (3,100) is the ancient capital; the other towns are ΨPeel (3,785) and ΨRamsey (7,322)

FLAG – A red flag charged with three conjoined armoured legs in white and gold

TYNWALD DAY – 5 July

GOVERNMENT
The Isle of Man is a self-governing Crown dependency, having its own parliamentary, legal and administrative system. The British Government is responsible for international relations and defence. Under the UK Act of Accession, Protocol 3, the island's relationship with the European Union is limited to trade alone and does not extend to financial aid. The Lieutenant-Governor is The Queen's personal representative on the island.

The legislature, Tynwald, is the oldest parliament in the world in continuous existence. It has two branches: the Legislative Council and the House of Keys. The Council consists of the President of Tynwald, the Bishop of Sodor and Man, the Attorney-General (who does not have a vote) and eight members elected by the House of Keys. The House of Keys has 24 members, elected by universal adult suffrage. The branches sit separately to consider legislation and sit together, as Tynwald Court, for most other parliamentary purposes.

The presiding officer of Tynwald Court is the President of Tynwald, elected by the members, who also presides over sittings of the Legislative Council. The presiding officer of the House of Keys is Mr Speaker, who is elected by members of the House.

The principal members of the Manx Government are the Chief Minister and nine departmental ministers, who comprise the Council of Ministers.

Lieutenant-Governor, HE Air-Marshal I. MacFadyen, CB, OBE

ADC to the Lieutenant-Governor, C. J. Tummon

President of Tynwald, The Hon. Noel Cringle

Speaker, House of Keys, The Hon. James Brown, SHK

The First Deemster and Clerk of the Rolls, John Michael Kerruish

Clerk of Tynwald, Secretary to the House of Keys and Counsel to the Speaker, Mr Malachy Cornwell-Kelly

Clerk of the Legislative Council and Deputy Clerk of Tynwald, Mrs M. Cullen

Attorney-General, W. J. H. Corlett, QC

Chief Minister, The Hon. Richard Corkill, MHK

Chief Secretary, Mrs M. Williams

ECONOMY
Most of the income generated in the island is earned in the services sector with financial and professional services accounting for just over half of the national income. Tourism and manufacturing are also major generators of income whilst the island's other traditional industries of agriculture and fishing now play a smaller role in the economy. Under the terms of Protocol 3, the island has tariff-free access to EU markets for its goods.

The island's unemployment rate is approximately 0.6 per cent and price inflation is around 3.6 per cent per annum.

FINANCE
The budget for 2004–5 provides for net revenue expenditure of £448 million. The principal sources of government revenue are taxes on income and expenditure. Income tax is payable at a rate of 10 per cent on the first £10,000 of taxable income for single resident individuals and 18 per cent on the balance, after personal allowances of £8,225. These bands are doubled for married couples. The rate of income tax is 10 per cent on the first £100 million of taxable income of trading companies, rising to 15 per cent on the balance. By agreement with the British Government, the island keeps most of its rates of indirect taxation (VAT and duties) the same as those in the United Kingdom. However, VAT on tourist accommodation, property, repairs and renovations is charged at 5 per cent. A reciprocal agreement on national insurance benefits and pensions exists between the governments of the Isle of Man and the United Kingdom. Taxes are also charged on property (rates), but these are comparatively low.

The major government expenditure items are health, social security and education, which account for 58 per cent of the government budget. The island makes an annual contribution to the United Kingdom for defence and other external services.

The island has a special relationship with the European Union and neither contributes money to nor receives funds from the EU budget.

THE ISLES OF SCILLY

The Isles of Scilly are a cluster of small islands, set 28 miles of the coast of Cornwall in the Atlantic Ocean. There are five inhabited islands; St Mary's, Tresco, St Martin's. Bryher and St. Agnes. The islands are administered by the Council of the Isles of Scilly; a 21-member body, of which 13 are elected by St Mary's residents and 2 by each of the remaining islands.

Administrative Headquarters, Town Hall, St Mary's, Isles of Scilly, TR21 0LW T 01720-422537

Chief Executive, Philip Hygate

THE CHANNEL ISLANDS

The Channel Islands, situated off the north-west coast of France (at distances from ten to 30 miles), are the only portions of the Dukedom of Normandy still belonging to the Crown, to which they have been attached since the Norman Conquest of 1066. They were the only British territory to come under German occupation during the Second World War, following invasion on 30 June to 1 July 1940. The islands were relieved by British forces on 9 May 1945, and 9 May (Liberation Day) is now observed as a bank and public holiday.

The islands consist of Jersey (28,717 acres/11,630 ha), Guernsey (15,654 acres/6,340 ha), and the dependencies of Guernsey: Alderney (1,962 acres/795 ha), Brecqhou (74/30), Great Sark (1,035/419), Little Sark (239/97), Herm (320/130), Jethou (44/18) and Lihou (38/15) – a total of 48,083 acres/19,474 ha, or 75 sq. miles/194 sq. km. The 2001 census showed the population of Jersey as 87,186; Guernsey, 59,807 and Alderney, 2,294. Sark did not complete the same census but a recent informal census gave its population figure as 591. The official languages are English and French.

GOVERNMENT

The islands are Crown dependencies with their own legislative assemblies (the States in Jersey, Guernsey and Alderney, and the Court of Chief Pleas in Sark), and systems of local administration and of law, and their own courts. Acts passed by the States require the sanction of The Queen-in-Council. The British Government is responsible for defence and international relations. The Channel Islands have trading rights alone within the European Union; these rights do not include financial aid.

In both Bailiwicks the Lieutenant-Governor and Commander-in-Chief, who is appointed by the Crown, is the personal representative of The Queen and the channel of communication between the Crown (via the Privy Council) and the island's government.

In 2001 the States of Jersey moved to a ministerial system of government combined with a system of scrutiny. This system is expected to be fully implemented by the end of December 2005. On 1 May 2004 Guernsey also introduced a ministerial governance system consisting of a Policy Council comprising a chief minister and ten departmental ministers. There are also five specialist committees. Justice is administered by the Royal Courts of Jersey and Guernsey, each consisting of the Bailiff and 12 elected Jurats. The Bailiffs of Jersey and Guernsey, appointed by the Crown, are President of the States and of the Royal Courts of their respective islands.

Each Bailiwick constitutes a deanery under the jurisdiction of the Bishop of Winchester.

ECONOMY

A mild climate and good soil have led to the development of intensive systems of agriculture and horticulture, which form a significant part of the economy. Equally important are invisible earnings, principally from tourism and banking and finance, the low rate of income tax (20p in the £ in Jersey and Guernsey; no tax of any kind in Sark) and the absence of super-tax and death duties, making the islands an important offshore financial centre.

Principal exports are agricultural produce and flowers; imports are chiefly machinery, manufactured goods, food, fuel and chemicals. Trade with the UK is regarded as internal.

JERSEY

Lieutenant-Governor and Commander-in-Chief of Jersey, Air Chief Marshal Sir John Cheshire, KBE, CB, *apptd* 2001
Secretary and ADC, Lt.-Col. A. J. C. Woodrow, OBE, MC
Bailiff of Jersey, Sir Philip Bailhache, Kt.
Deputy Bailiff, M. C. St J. Birt
Attorney-General, W. J. Bailhache, QC
Receiver-General, P. Lewin
Solicitor-General, Miss S. C. Nicolle, QC
Greffier of the States, M. N. de la Haye
States Treasurer, Mr I. Black

FINANCE

Year to 31 December	2002	2003
Revenue income	£572,179,000	£568,005,000
Revenue expenditure	£500,654,000	£526,837,000
Capital expenditure	£89,303,000	£62,730,000
Public debt	0	0

CHIEF TOWN – Ψ St Helier, on the south coast of Jersey
FLAG – A white field charged with a red saltire cross, and the arms of Jersey in the upper centre

GUERNSEY AND DEPENDENCIES

Lieutenant-Governor and Commander-in-Chief of the Bailiwick of Guernsey and its Dependencies, HE Lieutenant-General Sir John Foley, KCB, OBE, MC, *apptd* 2000
Secretary and ADC, Colonel R. H. Graham, MBE
Bailiff of Guernsey, Sir de Vic Graham Carey
Deputy Bailiff, G. R. Rowland, QC
HM Procureur and Receiver-General, J. N. van Leuven, QC
HM Comptroller, H. E. Roberts, QC
Chief Executive, States of Guernsey, M. J. Brown
Chief Minister, Deputy Laurie Morgan

FINANCE

Year to 31 Dec.	2002	2003
Revenue	£288,320,000	£287,969,000
Expenditure	£239,727,000	£254,390,000

CHIEF TOWNS – Ψ St Peter Port, on the east coast of Guernsey; St Anne on Alderney
FLAG – White, bearing a red cross of St George, with a gold cross overall in the centre

ALDERNEY
President of the States, Sir Norman Browse

SARK
Seigneur of Sark, J. M. Beaumont, OBE

OTHER DEPENDENCIES
Herm and Lihou are owned by the States of Guernsey; Herm is leased. Jethou is leased by the Crown to the States of Guernsey and is sub-let by the States. Brecqhou is within the legislative and judicial territory of Sark.

EUROPEAN PARLIAMENT

European Parliament elections take place at five-yearly intervals; the first direct elections to the Parliament were held in 1979. In mainland Britain MEPs were elected in all constituencies on a first-past-the-post basis until the elections of June 1999 when a regional system of proportional representation was introduced (*see* below); in Northern Ireland three MEPs have been elected by the single transferable vote system of proportional representation since 1979. From 1979 to 1994 the number of seats held by the UK in the European Parliament was 81. At the June 1994 election the number of seats increased to 87. Following EU enlargement in May 2004, the number of seats at the June 2004 election decreased to 78 (England 64, Wales 4, Scotland 7, Northern Ireland 3).

At the European Parliament elections held on 10 June 2004, all British MEPs were elected under a 'closed-list' regional system of proportional representation, with England being divided into nine regions and Scotland and Wales each constituting a region. Parties submitted a list of candidates for each region in their own order of preference. Voters voted for a party or an independent candidate, and the first seat in each region was allocated to the party or candidate with the highest number of votes. The rest of the seats in each region were then allocated broadly in proportion to each party's share of the vote. Each region returned the following number of members: East Midlands, 6; Eastern, 7; London, 9; North East, 3; North West, 9; South East, 10; South West, 7; West Midlands, 7; Yorkshire and the Humber, 6; Wales, 4; Scotland, 7.

If a vacancy occurs due to the resignation or death of an MEP, the vacancy is filled by the next available person on that party's list. If an independent MEP resigns or dies, a by-election is held. Where an MEP leaves the party on whose list he/she was elected, there is no requirement to resign and he/she can remain in office until the next election.

British subjects and nationals of member states of the European Union are eligible for election to the European Parliament provided they are 21 or over and not subject to disqualification. Since 1994, eligible citizens have had the right to vote in elections to the European Parliament in the UK as long as they are entered on the electoral register.

MEPs currently receive a salary from the parliaments or governments of their respective member states, set at the level of the national parliamentary salary and subject to national taxation. British MEPs receive a salary of £57,485. MPs who are also MEPs do not receive both salaries in full. Instead they receive the full MPs' salary plus a 'duality rate' equal to one third of the MEPs' salary. Thus their total salary is £76,646 (comprising £57,485 plus £19,161).

A proposal that all MEPs should be paid the same rate of salary out of the EU budget, and be subject to the EU tax rate, is under negotiation between the European Parliament and the Council of Ministers but has yet to be agreed.

The next elections to the European Parliament will take place in June 2009.

UK MEMBERS *as at 10 June 2004*

*Denotes membership of the last European Parliament
Allister, James (*b.* 1953), *DUP, Northern Ireland*
Ashworth, Richard (*b.* 1947), *C., South East*
***Atkins**, Rt. Hon. Sir Robert (*b.* 1946), *C., North West*
***Attwooll**, Ms Elspeth M. A. (*b.* 1943), *LD, Scotland*
Batten, Gerard (*b.* 1972), *UKIP, London*
***Beazley**, Christopher J. P. (*b.* 1952), *C., Eastern*
Bloom, Godfrey (*b.* 1949), *UKIP, Yorkshire and the Humber*
***Booth**, Graham (*b.* 1940), *UKIP, South West*
***Bowis**, John C., OBE (*b.* 1945), *C., London*
***Bradbourn**, Philip, OBE (*b.* 1951), *C., West Midlands*
***Bushill-Matthews**, Philip (*b.* 1943), *C., West Midlands*
***Callanan**, Martin (*b.* 1961), *C., North East*
***Cashman**, Michael (*b.* 1950), *Lab., West Midlands*
***Chichester**, Giles B. (*b.* 1946), *C., South West*
Clark, Derek (*b.* 1933), *UKIP, East Midlands*
***Corbett**, Richard (*b.* 1955), *Lab., Yorkshire and the Humber*
***Davies**, Christopher G. (*b.* 1954), *LD, North West*
de Brun, Bairbre Ms (*b.* 1954), *SF, Northern Ireland*
***Deva**, Niranjan J. A. (Nirj), FRSA (*b.* 1948), *C., South East*
***Dover**, Densmore (*b.* 1938), *C., North West*
***Duff**, Andrew N. (*b.* 1950), *LD, Eastern*
***Elles**, James E. M. (*b.* 1949), *C., South East*
***Evans**, Ms Jillian R. (*b.* 1959), *PC, Wales*
***Evans**, Jonathan P., FRSA (*b.* 1950), *C., Wales*
***Evans**, Robert J. E. (*b.* 1956), *Lab., London*
***Farage**, Nigel P. (*b.* 1964), *UKIP, South East*
***Ford**, Glyn J. (*b.* 1950), *Lab., South West*
***Gill**, Ms Neena (*b.* 1956), *Lab., West Midlands*
Hall, Fiona (*b.* 1955), *LD, North East*
***Hannan**, Daniel J. (*b.* 1971), *C., South East*
***Harbour**, Malcolm (*b.* 1947), *C., West Midlands*
***Heaton-Harris**, Christopher (*b.* 1967), *C., East Midlands*
***Helmer**, Roger (*b.* 1944), *C., East Midlands*
***Honeyball**, Mary Mrs (*b.* 1952), *Lab., London*
***Howitt**, Richard (*b.* 1961), *Lab., Eastern*
***Hudghton**, Ian (*b.* 1951), *SNP, Scotland*
***Hughes**, Stephen (*b.* 1952), *Lab., North East*
***Huhne**, Christopher M. P., OBE (*b.* 1954), *LD, South East*
***Jackson**, Mrs Caroline F., DPHIL (*b.* 1946), *C., South West*
Karim, Sajjad (*b.* 1970), *LD, North West*
Kilroy-Silk, Robert (*b.* 1942), *UKIP, East Midlands*
***Kinnock**, Mrs Glenys (*b.* 1944), *Lab., Wales*
***Kirkhope**, Timothy J. R. (*b.* 1945), *C., Yorkshire and the Humber*
Knapman, Roger (*b.* 1944), *UKIP, South West*
***Lambert**, Ms Jean D. (*b.* 1950), *Green, London*
***Lucas**, Dr Caroline (*b.* 1960), *Green, South East*
***Ludford**, Sarah Ms (*b.* 1951), *LD, London*
***Lynne**, Elizabeth Ms (*b.* 1948), *LD, West Midlands*
***McAvan**, Linda Ms (*b.* 1962), *Lab., Yorkshire and the Humber*
***McCarthy**, Arlene Ms (*b.* 1960), *Lab., North West*
***McMillan-Scott**, Edward H. C. (*b.* 1949), *C., Yorkshire and the Humber*
***Martin**, David W. (*b.* 1954), *Lab., Scotland*
***Moraes**, Claude (*b.* 1965), *Lab., London*
***Morgan**, Eluned Ms (*b.* 1967), *Lab., Wales*

Mote, Ashley (b. 1936), *UKIP, South East*
Nattrass, Mike (b. 1945), *UKIP, West Midlands*
*Newton Dunn, William F. (Bill) (b. 1941), *LD, East Midlands*
*Nicholson, Emma Ms (b. 1941), *LD, South East*
*Nicholson, James (b. 1945), *UUP, Northern Ireland*
*Parish, Neil (b. 1956), *C., South West*
*Purvis, John R., CBE (b. 1938), *C., Scotland*
*Skinner, Peter W. (b. 1959), *Lab., South East*
Smith, Alyn (b. 1973), *SNP, Scotland*
*Stevenson, Struan (b. 1948), *C., Scotland*
*Stihler, Catherine D. (b. 1973), *Lab., Scotland*
*Sturdy, Robert W. (b. 1944), *C., Eastern*

*Sumberg, David (b. 1941), *C., North West*
*Tannock, Dr Charles (b. 1957), *C., London*
*Titford, Jeffrey (b. 1933), *UKIP, Eastern*
*Titley, Gary (b. 1950), *Lab., North West,*
*van Orden, Geoffrey (b. 1945), *C., Eastern*
*Villiers, Theresa Ms (b. 1968), *C., London*
*Wallis, Diana Ms (b. 1954), *LD, Yorkshire and the Humber*
*Watson, Graham R. (b. 1956), *LD, South West*
*Whitehead, Phillip (b. 1937), *Lab., East Midlands*
Whittaker, John (b. 1945), *UKIP, North West*
Wise, Tom (b. 1948), *UKIP, Eastern*
*Wynn, Terence (Terry) (b. 1946), *Lab., North West*

UK REGIONS *as at 10 June 2004*

Abbreviations

AGS	Alliance for Green Socialism
Common	The Common Good
ED	English Democrats
EFP	English Freedom Party
FW	Forward Wales
OCV	Operation Christian Vote
Peace	Peace Party
PPBG	People's Party for Better Government
Respect	Respect – Unity Coalition
SEA	Socialist Environmental Alliance
Senior	Senior Citizens
Soc. All.	Socialist Alliance
SSP	Scottish Socialist Party
SWW	Scottish Wind Watch

For other abbreviations, *see* UK General Election Results

EASTERN

(Bedfordshire, Cambridgeshire, Essex, Hertfordshire, Luton, Norfolk, Peterborough, Southend-on-Sea, Suffolk, Thurrock)

E. 4,137,210	T. 36.63%
C.	465,526 (30.8%)
UKIP	296,160 (19.6%)
Lab.	244,929 (16.2%)
LD	211,378 (14.0%)
Ind.	93,028 (6.2%)
Green	84,068 (5.6%)
BNP	65,557 (4.3%)
ED	26,807 (1.8%)
Respect	13,094 (0.9%)
Ind.	5,137 (0.3%)
ProLife	3,730 (0.3%)
C. majority	169,366
(June 1999, C. maj. 174,959)	

MEMBERS ELECTED
*G. van Orden, *C.*
*J. Titford, *UKIP*
*R. Howitt, *Lab.*
*R. Sturdy, *C.*
A. Duff, *LD*
*C. Beazley, *C.*
T. Wise, *UKIP*

EAST MIDLANDS

(Derby, Derbyshire, Leicester, Leicestershire, Northamptonshire, Nottingham, Nottinghamshire, Rutland)

E. 3,220,019	T. 44.59%
C.	371,362 (26.4%)
UKIP	366,498 (26.1%)
Lab.	294,918 (21.0%)
LD	181,964 (12.9%)
BNP	91,860 (6.5%)
Green	76,633 (5.5%)
Respect	20,009 (1.4%)
Ind.	2,615 (0.2%)
Ind.	847 (0.1%)
C. majority	4,864
(June 1999, C. maj. 78,906)	

MEMBERS ELECTED
*R. Helmer, *C.*
R. Kilroy-Silk, *UKIP*
*P. Whitehead, *Lab.*
*C. Heaton-Harris, *C.*
D. Clark, *UKIP*
*W. Newton Dunn, *LD*

LONDON

E. 5,054,957	T. 37.65%
C.	504,941 (26.53%)
Lab.	466,584 (24.51%)
LD	288,790 (15.17%)
UKIP	232,633 (12.22%)
Green	158,986 (8.35%)
Respect	91,175 (4.79%)
BNP	76,152 (4.00%)
CPA	45,038 (2.37%)
ED	15,945 (0.84%)
PPBG	5,205 (0.27%)
C. majority	38,357
(June 1994, Lab. maj. 26,477)	

MEMBERS ELECTED
*Miss T. Villiers, *C.*
*C. Moraes, *Lab.*
*Ms S. Ludford, *LD*
*J. Bowis, *C.*
Ms M. Honeyball, *Lab.*
G. Batten, *UKIP*
*C. Tannock, *C.*
*Ms J. Lambert, *Green*
*R. Evans, *Lab.*

NORTH EAST

(Co. Durham, Darlington, Hartlepool, Middlesbrough, Northumberland, Redcar and Cleveland, Stockton-on-Tees, Tyne and Wear)

E. 1,905,132	T. 41.51%
Lab.	266,057 (34.1%)
C.	144,969 (18.6%)
LD	138,791 (17.8%)
UKIP	94,887 (12.2%)
BNP	50,249 (6.4%)
Ind.	39,658 (5.1%)
Green	37,247 (4.8%)
Respect	8,633 (1.1%)
Lab. majority	121,088
(June 1999, Lab. maj. 57,000)	

MEMBERS ELECTED
*S. Hughes, *Lab.*
*M. Callanan, *C.*
Ms F. Hall, *LD*

NORTHERN IRELAND

(Northern Ireland forms a three-member seat with a single transferable vote system)

E. 1,191,307	T. 46.53%
First Count	
Jim Allister, *DUP*	175,761 (31.9%)
Bairbre de Brun, *SF*	144,541 (26.3%)
Jim Nicholson, *UUP*	91,164 (16.6%)
Martin Morgan, *SDLP*	87,559 (15.9%)
John Gilliland, *Ind.*	36,270 (6.6%)
Eamonn McCann, *SEA*	9,172 (1.6%)
Lindsay Whitcroft, *Green*	4,810 (0.9%)

MEMBERS ELECTED
J. Allister, *DUP*
B. de Brun, *SF*
*J. Nicholson, *UUP*

NORTH WEST
(Blackburn-with-Darwen, Blackpool, Cheshire, Cumbria, Greater Manchester, Halton, Lancashire, Merseyside, Warrington)

E. 5,151,488	T. 41.46%
Lab.	576,388 (27.3%)
C.	509,446 (24.1%)
LD	335,063 (15.8%)
UKIP	257,158 (12.2%)
BNP	134,958 (6.4%)
Green	117,393 (5.6%)
Lib.	96,325 (4.6%)
ED	34,110 (1.6%)
Respect	24,636 (1.2%)
Country	11,283 (0.5%)
ProLife	10,084 (0.5%)
Ind.	8,318 (0.4%)
Lab. majority	66,942
(June 1999, C. maj. 9,516)	

MEMBERS ELECTED
*G. Titley, Lab.
*D. Dover, C.
*C. Davies, LD
*Ms A. McCarthy, Lab.
J. Whittaker, UKIP
*D. Sumberg, C.
*T. Wynn, Lab.
*Sir Robert Atkins, C.
S. Karim, LD

SCOTLAND

E. 3,807,521	T. 30.91%
Lab.	310,865 (26.40%)
SNP	231,505 (19.67%)
C.	209,028 (17.80%)
LD	154,178 (13.10%)
Green	79,695 (6.77%)
UKIP	78,828 (6.70%)
SSP	61,356 (5.20%)
OCV	21,056 (1.79%)
BNP	19,427 (1.65%)
SWW	7,255 (0.62%)
Ind.	3,624 (0.31%)
Lab. majority	79,360
(June 1999, Lab. maj. 14,962)	

MEMBERS ELECTED
*D. Martin, Lab.
*I. Hudghton, SNP
*S. Stevenson, C.
*Ms C. Stihler, Lab.
*Ms E. Attwooll, LD
A. Smith, SNP
*J. Purvis, C.

SOUTH EAST
(Bracknell Forest, Brighton and Hove, Buckinghamshire, East Sussex, Hampshire, Isle of Wight, Kent, Medway, Milton Keynes, Oxfordshire, Portsmouth, Reading, Slough, Southampton, Surrey, West Berkshire, West Sussex, Windsor and Maidenhead, Wokingham)

E. 6,048,349	T. 36.78%
C.	776,370 (35.2%)
UKIP	431,111 (19.5%)
LD	338,342 (15.3%)
Lab.	301,398 (13.7%)
Green	173,351 (7.9%)
BNP	64,877 (2.9%)
Senior	42,681 (1.9%)
ED	29,126 (1.3%)
Respect	13,426 (0.9%)
Peace	12,572 (0.6%)
CPA	11,733 (0.5%)
ProLife	6,579 (0.3%)
Ind.	5,671 (0.3%)
C. majority	345,259
(June 1999, C. maj. 369,785)	

MEMBERS ELECTED
*D. Hannan, C.
*N. Farage, UKIP
*N. Deva, C.
*C. Huhne, LD
*P. Skinner, Lab.
*J. Elles, C.
A. Mote, UKIP
R. Ashworth, C.
*Dr Caroline Lucas, Green
Ms E. Nicholson, LD

SOUTH WEST
(Bath and North East Somerset, Bournemouth, Bristol, Cornwall, Devon, Dorset, Gloucestershire, North Somerset, South Gloucestershire, Swindon, Torbay, Wiltshire)

E. 3,845,210	T. 44.59%
C.	457,371 (31.6%)
UKIP	326,684 (22.6%)
LD	265,619 (18.3%)
Lab.	209,908 (14.5%)
Green	103,821 (7.2%)
BNP	43,653 (3.0%)
Country	30,824 (2.1%)
Respect	10,437 (0.7%)
C. majority	130,687
(June 1999, C. maj. 246,283)	

MEMBERS ELECTED
*N. Parish, C.
G. Booth, UKIP
*G. Watson, LD
*Dr Caroline Jackson, C.
*G. Ford, Lab.
R. Knapman, UKIP
*G. Chichester, C.

WALES

E. 2,218,649	T. 41.9%
Lab.	297,810 (32%)
C.	177,771 (19%)
PC	159,888 (17%)
UKIP	96,677 (10.5%)
LD	96,116 (10%)
Green	32,761 (3.6%)
BNP	27,135 (3.0%)
FW	17,280 (1.9%)
Ch. D	6,821 (0.7%)
Respect	5,427 (0.6%)
Lab. majority	120,039
(June 1999, Lab. maj. 14,455)	

MEMBERS ELECTED
*Ms G. Kinnock, Lab.
*J. Evans, C.
*Ms J. Evans, PC
*Ms E. Morgan, Lab.

WEST MIDLANDS
(Herefordshire, Shropshire, Staffordshire, Stoke-on-Trent, Telford and Wrekin, Warwickshire, West Midlands Metropolitan area, Worcestershire)

E. 3,957,848	T. 36.63%
C.	392,937 (27.3%)
Lab.	336,613 (23.4%)
UKIP	251,366 (17.5%)
LD	197,479 (13.7%)
BNP	107,794 (7.5%)
Green	73,991 (5.2%)
Respect	34,704 (2.4%)
Pensioner	33,501 (2.3%)
Common	8,650 (0.6%)
C. majority	56,324
(June 1999, C. Maj. 84,048)	

MEMBERS ELECTED
*P. Bushill-Matthews, C.
*M. Cashman, Lab.
M. Nattrass, UKIP
*Ms E. Lynne, LD
*P. Bradbourn, C.
*Ms N. Gill, Lab.
*M. Harbour, C.

YORKSHIRE AND THE HUMBER

(East Riding of Yorkshire, Kingston upon Hull, North East Lincolnshire, North Lincolnshire, North Yorkshire, South Yorkshire, West Yorkshire, York)

E. 3,719,717		T. 42.93%
Lab.	413,213	(26.3%)
C.	387,369	(24.6%)
LD	244,607	(15.6%)
UKIP	228,666	(14.0%)
BNP	126,538	(8.0%)
Green	90,337	(5.7%)
Respect	29,865	(1.9%)
ED	24,068	(1.5%)
Ind.	14,762	(0.9%)
AGS	13,776	(0.9%)
Lab. majority		25,844

(June 1999, C. maj. 39,629)

MEMBERS ELECTED

*Ms Linda McAvan, Lab.
*T. Kirkhope, C.
*Ms D. Wallis, LD
G. Bloom, UKIP
*R. Corbett, Lab.
*E. McMillan-Scott, C.

For further information about the European Parliament, visit www.europarl.org.uk

The county and unitary authority areas listed after each European parliamentary constituency name are a guide to the areas covered by each constituency.

For detailed information about which areas of the country are covered by a particular region, please contact the Home Office.

LAW COURTS AND OFFICES

THE JUDICIAL COMMITTEE OF THE PRIVY COUNCIL

The Judicial Committee of the Privy Council is the final court of appeal for the United Kingdom overseas territories and Crown dependencies and those independent Commonwealth countries which have retained this avenue of appeal (Antigua and Barbuda, The Bahamas, Barbados, Belize, Brunei, Dominica, Grenada, Jamaica, Kiribati, Mauritius, St Christopher and Nevis, St Lucia, St Vincent and the Grenadines, Trinidad and Tobago, and Tuvalu). The Committee also hears appeals against pastoral schemes under the Pastoral Measure 1983.

Under the devolution legislation enacted in 1998, the Judicial Committee of the Privy Council is the final arbiter in disputes as to the legal competence of things done or proposed by the devolved legislative and Executive authorities in Scotland, Wales and Northern Ireland.

In 2003 the Judicial Committee dealt with a total of 99 appeals and 49 petitions for special leave to appeal.

The members of the Judicial Committee include past and present Lord Chancellors and Lords of Appeal in Ordinary, and other Privy Counsellors who hold or have held high judicial office in the United Kingdom and in certain designated courts of Commonwealth countries from which appeals lie to the Judicial Committee.

JUDICIAL COMMITTEE OF THE PRIVY COUNCIL
Downing Street, London SW1A 2AJ
T 020-7276 0483/5
Registrar of the Privy Council, J. A. C. Watherston
Chief Clerk, Mrs J. Lindsay

THE JUDICATURE OF ENGLAND AND WALES

The legal system of England and Wales is separate from those of Scotland and Northern Ireland and differs from them in law, judicial procedure and court structure, although there is a common distinction between civil law (disputes between individuals) and criminal law (acts harmful to the community).

The supreme judicial authority for England and Wales is the House of Lords, which is the ultimate court of appeal from all courts in Great Britain and Northern Ireland (except criminal courts in Scotland) for all cases except those concerning the interpretation and application of European Community law, including preliminary rulings requested by British courts and tribunals, which are decided by the European Court of Justice (*see* European Union section). Under the Human Rights Act 1998, which came into force on 2 October 2000, the European Convention on Human Rights is incorporated into British law; unresolved cases are still referred to the European Court of Human Rights. As a Court of Appeal the House of Lords consists of the Lord Chancellor and the Lords of Appeal in Ordinary (law lords).

SUPREME COURT OF JUDICATURE

The Supreme Court of Judicature comprises the Court of Appeal, the High Court of Justice and the Crown Court. The High Court of Justice is the superior civil court and is divided into three divisions. The Chancery Division is concerned mainly with equity, bankruptcy and contentious probate business. The Queen's Bench Division deals with commercial and maritime law, serious personal injury and medical negligence cases, cases involving a breach of contract and professional negligence actions. The Family Division deals with matters relating to family law. Sittings are held at the Royal Courts of Justice in London or at 126 District Registries outside the capital. High Court judges sit alone to hear cases at first instance. The Technology and Construction Court, which deals with cases that require expert evidence on technical and other issues concerning mainly the construction industry, is also currently part of the High Court. Appeals from the High Court are heard in the Court of Appeal (Civil Division), presided over by the Master of the Rolls, and may go on to the House of Lords.

In December 1999 the Lord Chancellor began a wide-ranging, independent review of the criminal courts in England and Wales. Lord Justice Auld lead the review into how the criminal courts work at every level. The report *Review of the Criminal Courts of England and Wales* was published in October 2001 and assesses what should be done to modernise and improve the criminal justice system so that its aims can be achieved more effectively.

CRIMINAL CASES

In criminal matters the decision to prosecute in the majority of cases rests with the Crown Prosecution Service, the independent prosecuting body in England and Wales. The Service is headed by the Director of Public Prosecutions, who works under the superintendence of the Attorney-General. Certain categories of offence continue to require the Attorney-General's consent for prosecution.

The Crown Court sits in about 90 centres, divided into six circuits, and is presided over by High Court judges, full-time circuit judges, and part-time recorders, sitting with a jury in all trials which are contested. Since 12 April 2000, the distinction between assistant recorders and recorders has changed. Consequently, there are now only full recorders. The post of assistant recorder remains on the statute book but appointments are no longer made. There were 1,325 full recorders at 1 June 2002. The Crown Court deals with trials of the more serious criminal offences, the sentencing of offenders committed for sentence by magistrates' courts (when magistrates consider their own power of sentence inadequate), and appeals from magistrates' courts. Magistrates usually sit with a circuit judge or recorder to deal with appeals and committals for sentence. Appeals from the Crown Court, either against sentence or conviction, are made to the Court of Appeal (Criminal Division), presided over by the Lord Chief Justice. A further appeal from the Court of Appeal to the House of Lords can be brought if a point of law of general public importance is considered to be involved.

Minor criminal offences (summary offences) are dealt with in magistrates' courts, which usually consist of three unpaid lay magistrates (justices of the peace) sitting without a jury, who are advised on points of law and procedure by a legally-qualified clerk to the justices. There were 24,520 justices of the peace at 1 April 2002. In busier courts a full-time, salaried and legally-qualified stipendiary magistrate presides alone. Cases involving people under 18 are heard in youth courts, specially constituted magistrates' courts. Preliminary proceedings in a serious case to decide whether there is evidence to justify committal for trial in the Crown Court are also dealt with in the magistrates' courts. Appeals from magistrates' courts against sentence or conviction are made to the Crown Court. Appeals upon a point of law are made to the High Court, and may go on to the House of Lords.

CIVIL CASES

Most minor civil cases are dealt with by the county courts, of which there are around 222 (see the Court Service website, www.courtservice.gov.uk for further details). Cases are heard by circuit judges, courts or district judges (magistrates' courts). There were 411 district judges and 107 District Judges (magistrates' courts) at 1 September 2003. For cases involving small claims there are special simplified procedures. Where there are financial limits on county court jurisdiction, claims which exceed those limits may be tried in the county courts with the consent of the parties, subject to the Court's agreement, or in certain circumstances on transfer from the High Court. Outside London, bankruptcy proceedings can be heard in designated county courts. Magistrates' courts can deal with certain classes of civil case and committees of magistrates license public houses, clubs and betting shops. For the implementation of the Children Act 1989, a new structure of hearing centres was set up in 1991 for family proceedings cases, involving magistrates' courts (family proceedings courts), divorce county courts, family hearing centres and care centres. Appeals in family matters heard in the family proceedings courts go to the Family Division of the High Court; affiliation appeals and appeals from decisions of the licensing committees of magistrates go to the Crown Court. Appeals from county courts may be heard in the High Court of Appeal (civil division) and may go on to the House of Lords.

CORONERS' COURT

Coroners' courts investigate violent and unnatural deaths or sudden deaths where the cause is unknown. Cases may be brought before a local coroner (a senior lawyer or doctor) by doctors, the police, various public authorities or members of the public. Where a death is sudden and the cause is unknown, the coroner may order a post-mortem examination to determine the cause of death rather than hold an inquest in court.

Judicial appointments are made by The Queen; the most senior appointments are made on the advice of the Prime Minister and other appointments on the advice of the Lord Chancellor.

Under the provisions of the Criminal Appeal Act 1995, a Commission was set up to direct and supervise investigations into possible miscarriages of justice and to refer cases to the courts on the grounds of conviction and

sentence; these functions were formerly the responsibility of the Home Secretary.

THE HOUSE OF LORDS
AS FINAL COURT OF APPEAL

The Lord High Chancellor and Secretary of State for Constitutional Affairs (£207,742, this is the statutory entitlement, however, Lord Falconer currently receives only a salary equivalent to that received by other Secretaries of State in the House of Lords), The Rt. Hon. the Lord Falconer of Thoroton, *born* 1951, *apptd* 2003

LORDS OF APPEAL IN ORDINARY *as at 26 August 2004* (each £179,431)
Style, The Rt. Hon. Lord/Lady–

Rt. Hon. Lord Bingham of Cornhill, *born* 1933, *apptd* 2000
Rt. Hon. Lord Nicholls of Birkenhead, *born* 1933, *apptd* 1994
Rt. Hon. Lord Steyn, *born* 1932, *apptd* 1995
Rt. Hon. Lord Hoffmann, *born* 1934, *apptd* 1995
Rt. Hon. Lord Hope of Craighead, *born* 1938, *apptd* 1996
Rt. Hon. Lord Saville of Newdigate, *born* 1936, *apptd* 1997
Rt. Hon. Lord Scott Foscote, *born* 1934, *apptd* 2000
Rt. Hon. Lord Rodger of Earlsferry, *born* 1944, *apptd* 2001
Rt. Hon. Lord Walker of Gestingthorpe, *born* 1938, *apptd* 2002
Lady Hale of Richmond, *born* 1945, *apptd* 2004
Lord Carswell, *born* 1934, *apptd* 2004
Lord Brown of Eaton-under-Heywood, *born* 1937, *apptd* 2004

JUDICIAL OFFICE OF THE HOUSE OF LORDS, House of Lords, London SW1A 0PW T 020-7219 3111
Registrar, The Clerk of the Parliaments

SUPREME COURT OF JUDICATURE

COURT OF APPEAL
The Master of the Rolls (£185,705), The Rt. Hon. Lord Phillips of Worth Matravers, *born* 1938, *apptd* 2000
Secretary, Mrs L. Francis
Clerk, Miss L. Turvey

LORDS JUSTICES OF APPEAL *as at 26 August 2004* (each £170,554)
Style, The Rt. Hon. Lord/Lady Justice [surname]

Rt. Hon. Sir Paul Kennedy, *born* 1935, *apptd* 1992
Rt. Hon. Sir Christopher Rose, *born* 1937, *apptd* 1992
Rt. Hon. Sir Peter Gibson, *born* 1934, *apptd* 1993
Rt. Hon. Sir Robin Auld, *born* 1937, *apptd* 1995
Rt. Hon. Sir Malcolm Pill, *born* 1938, *apptd* 1995
Rt. Hon. Sir Alan Ward, *born* 1938, *apptd* 1995
Rt. Hon. Sir Mathew Thorpe, *born* 1938, *apptd* 1995
Rt. Hon. Sir Mark Potter, *born* 1937, *apptd* 1996
Rt. Hon. Sir Henry Brooke, *born* 1936, *apptd* 1996
Rt. Hon. Sir Igor Judge, *born* 1941, *apptd* 1996
Rt. Hon. Sir George Waller, *born* 1940, *apptd* 1996
Rt. Hon. Sir John Mummery, *born* 1938, *apptd* 1996
Rt. Hon. Sir John Chadwick, ED, *born* 1941, *apptd* 1997
Rt. Hon. Sir Richard Buxton, *born* 1938, *apptd* 1997

Rt. Hon. Sir Anthony May, *born* 1940, *apptd* 1997
Rt. Hon. Sir Simon Tuckey, *born* 1941, *apptd* 1998
Rt. Hon. Sir Anthony Clarke, *born* 1943, *apptd* 1998
Rt. Hon. Sir John Laws, *born* 1945, *apptd* 1999
Rt. Hon. Sir Stephen Sedley, *born* 1939, *apptd* 1999
Rt. Hon. Sir Jonathan Mance, *born* 1943, *apptd* 1999
Rt. Hon. Sir David Latham, *born* 1942, *apptd* 2000
Rt. Hon. Sir Bernard Anthony Rix, *born* 1943, *apptd* 2000
Rt. Hon. Sir Jonathan Parker, *born* 1937, *apptd* 2000
Rt. Hon. Dame Mary Howarth Arden, DBE, *born* 1947, *apptd* 2000
Rt. Hon. Sir David Wolfe Keene, *born* 1941, *apptd* 2000
Rt. Hon. Sir John Anthony Dyson, *born* 1943, *apptd* 2001
Rt. Hon. Sir Andrew Centlivres Longmore, *born* 1944, *apptd* 2001
Rt. Hon. Sir Robert John Carnwath, CVO, *born* 1945, *apptd* 2002
Rt. Hon. Sir Thomas Baker, *born* 1937, *apptd* 2002
Rt. Hon. Dame Janet Hilary Smith, DBE, *born* 1940, *apptd* 2002
Rt. Hon. Sir Roger Laugharne Thomas, *born* 1947, *apptd* 2003
Rt. Hon. Sir Robin Jacob, *born* 1941, *apptd* 2003
Rt. Hon. Sir Nicholas Wall, *born* 1945, *apptd* 2004
Rt. Hon. Sir David Neuberger, *born* 1948, *apptd* 2004
Rt. Hon. Sir Maurice Ralph Kay, *born* 1942, *apptd* 2004
Rt. Hon. Sir Anthony Hooper, *born* 1937, *apptd* 2004

Ex officio Judges, The Lord High Chancellor and Secretary of State for Constitutional Affairs; the Lord Chief Justice of England and Wales; the Master of the Rolls; the President of the Family Division; and the Vice-Chancellor

COURT OF APPEAL (CIVIL DIVISION)
Vice-President, The Rt. Hon. Lord Justice Henry Brooke

COURT OF APPEAL (CRIMINAL DIVISION)
Vice-President, The Rt. Hon. Lord Justice Rose
Judges, The Lord Chief Justice of England; the Master of the Rolls; Lords Justices of Appeal; and Judges of the High Court of Justice

COURTS-MARTIAL APPEAL COURT
Judges, The Lord Chief Justice of England; the Master of the Rolls; Lords Justices of Appeal; and Judges of the High Court of Justice

HIGH COURT OF JUSTICE

CHANCERY DIVISION
President, The Lord High Chancellor and Secretary of State for Constitutional Affairs
The Vice-Chancellor (£179,431), The Rt. Hon. Sir Andrew Moritt, CVO, *born*, 1938 *apptd* 2000
Secretary, Miss E. Harbert
Clerk, Mrs A. Serfaty

JUDGES (each £150,878)
Style, The Hon. Mr/Mrs Justice [surname]

Hon. Sir John Lindsay, *born* 1935, *apptd* 1992
Hon. Sir Edward Evans-Lombe, *born* 1937, *apptd* 1993
Hon. Sir William Blackburne, *born* 1944, *apptd* 1993
Hon. Sir Gavin Lightman, *born* 1939, *apptd* 1994
Hon. Sir Colin Rimer, *born* 1944, *apptd* 1994

Hon. Sir Hugh Laddie, *born* 1946, *apptd* 1995
Hon. Sir Timothy Lloyd, *born* 1946, *apptd* 1996
Hon. Sir Andrew Park, *born* 1939, *apptd* 1997
Hon. Sir Nicholas Pumfrey, *born* 1951, *apptd* 1997
Hon. Sir Michael Hart, *born* 1948, *apptd* 1998
Hon. Sir Lawrence Collins, *born* 1941, *apptd* 2000
Hon. Sir Nicholas John Patten, *born* 1950, *apptd* 2000
Hon. Sir Terrence Michael Barnet Etherton, *born* 1951, *apptd* 2001
Hon. Sir Peter Winston Smith, *born* 1952, *apptd* 2002
Hon. Sir Kim Lewison, *born* 1952, *apptd* 2003
Hon. Sir David Richards, *born* 1951, *apptd* 2003
Hon. Sir George Anthony Mann, *born* 1951, *apptd* 2004

HIGH COURT OF JUSTICE IN BANKRUPTCY
Judges, The Vice-Chancellor and Judges of the Chancery Division of the High Court

COMPANIES COURT
Judges, The Vice-Chancellor and Judges of the Chancery Division of the High Court

PATENT COURT (APPELLATE SECTION)
Judge, The Hon. Mr Justice Jacob

QUEEN'S BENCH DIVISION
The Lord Chief Justice of England and Wales (£205,242)
The Rt. Hon. the Lord Woolf, *born* 1933, *apptd* 2000
Private Secretary, Miss M. Souris
Clerk, Ms J. Jones
Vice-President, The Rt. Hon. Lord Justice May, *born* 1940, *apptd* 2002

JUDGES *as at 26 August 2004* (each £150,878)
Style, The Hon. Mr/Mrs Justice [surname]

Hon. Sir Stuart McKinnon, *born* 1938, *apptd* 1988
Hon. Sir Douglas Dunlop Brown, *born* 1931, *apptd* 1996
Hon. Sir Roger Buckley, *born* 1939, *apptd* 1989
Hon. Sir Peter Cresswell, *born* 1944, *apptd* 1991
Hon. Sir Christopher Holland, *born* 1937, *apptd* 1992
Hon. Sir Richard Curtis, *born* 1933, *apptd* 1992
Hon. Sir Anthony Colman, *born* 1938, *apptd* 1992
Hon. Sir Thayne Forbes, *born* 1938, *apptd* 1993
Hon. Sir Rodger Bell, *born* 1939, *apptd* 1993
Hon. Sir Michael Harrison, *born* 1939, *apptd* 1993
Hon. Sir William Gage, *born* 1938, *apptd* 1993
Hon. Sir Thomas Morison, *born* 1939, *apptd* 1993
Hon. Sir Andrew Collins, *born* 1942, *apptd* 1994
Hon. Sir Alexander Butterfield, *born* 1942, *apptd* 1995
Hon. Sir George Newman, *born* 1941, *apptd* 1995
Hon. Sir David Poole, *born* 1938, *apptd* 1995
Hon. Sir Martin Moore-Bick, *born* 1946, *apptd* 1995
Hon. Sir Gordon Langley, *born* 1943, *apptd* 1995
Hon. Sir Robert Nelson, *born* 1942, *apptd* 1996
Hon. Sir Roger Toulson, *born* 1946, *apptd* 1996
Hon. Sir Michael Astill, *born* 1938, *apptd* 1996
Hon. Sir Alan Moses, *born* 1945, *apptd* 1996
Hon. Sir David Eady, *born* 1943, *apptd* 1997
Hon. Sir Jeremy Sullivan, *born* 1945, *apptd* 1997
Hon. Sir David Penry-Davey, *born* 1942, *apptd* 1997
Hon. Sir Stephen Richards, *born* 1950, *apptd* 1997
Hon. Sir David Steel, *born* 1943, *apptd* 1998
Hon. Sir Charles Gray, *born* 1942, *apptd* 1998
Hon. Sir Nicolas Bratza, *born* 1945, *apptd* 1998
Hon. Sir Michael Burton, *born* 1946, *apptd* 1998
Hon. Sir Rupert Jackson, *born* 1948, *apptd* 1999
Hon. Dame Heather Hallett, DBE, *born* 1949, *apptd* 1999

Hon. Sir Patrick Elias, *born* 1947, *apptd* 1999
Hon. Sir Richard Aikens, *born* 1948, *apptd* 1999
Hon. Sir Stephen Silber, *born* 1944, *apptd* 1999
Hon. Sir John Goldring, *born* 1944, *apptd* 1999
Hon. Sir Peter Crane, *born* 1940, *apptd* 2000
Hon. Dame Anne Rafferty, DBE, *born* 1950, *apptd* 2000
Hon. Sir Geoffrey Grigson, *born* 1944, *apptd* 2000
Hon. Sir Richard Gibbs, *born* 1941, *apptd* 2000
Hon. Sir Richard Henriques, *born* 1943, *apptd* 2000
Hon. Sir Stephen Tomlinson, *born* 1952, *apptd* 2000
Hon. Sir Andrew Smith, *born* 1947, *apptd* 2000
Hon. Sir Stanley Burnton, *born* 1942, *apptd* 2000
Hon. Sir Patrick Hunt, *born* 1943, *apptd* 2000
Hon. Sir Christopher Pitchford, *born* 1947, *apptd* 2000
Hon. Sir Brian Leveson, *born* 1949, *apptd* 2000
Hon. Sir Duncan Ouseley, *born* 1950, *apptd* 2000
Hon. Sir Raymond Jack, *born* 1942, *apptd* 2001
Hon. Sir Richard McCombe, *born* 1952, *apptd* 2001
Hon. Sir Robert Owen, *born* 1944, *apptd* 2001
Hon. Sir Colin Mackay, *born* 1943, *apptd* 2001
Hon. Sir John Mitting, *born* 1947, *apptd* 2001
Hon. Sir David Evans, *born* 1946, *apptd* 2001
Hon. Sir Nigel Davis, *born* 1951, *apptd* 2001
Hon. Sir Peter Gross, *born* 1952, *apptd* 2001
Hon. Sir Brian Keith, *born* 1944, *apptd* 2001
Hon. Sir Jeremy Cooke, *born* 1949, *apptd* 2001
Hon. Sir Richard Field, *born* 1947, *apptd* 2002
Hon. Sir Christopher Pitchers, *born* 1942, *apptd* 2002
Hon. Sir Adrian Fulford, *born* 1953, *apptd* 2002
Hon. Sir Colman Treacy, *born* 1949, *apptd* 2002
Hon. Sir Peregrine Simon, *born* 1950, *apptd* 2002
Hon. Sir Roger Royce, *born* 1944, *apptd* 2002
Hon. Dame Laura Cox, DBE, *born* 1951, *apptd* 2002
Hon. Sir Jack Beatson, *born* 1948, *apptd* 2003
Hon. Sir Michael Tugendhat, *born* 1944, *apptd* 2003
Hon. Sir David Clarke, *born* 1942, *apptd* 2003
Hon. Sir Richard Wakerley, *born* 1942, *apptd* 2003
Hon. Dame Elizabeth Gloster, DBE, *born* 1949, *apptd* 2004
Hon. Sir David Bean, *born* 1954, *apptd* 2004
Hon. Sir Anthony Hughes, *born* 1948, *apptd* 2004

FAMILY DIVISION
President (£179,431), The Rt. Hon. Dame Elizabeth Butler-Sloss, DBE, *born* 1933, *apptd* 1999
Secretary, Mrs S. Leung
Clerk, R. Smith

JUDGES *as at 26 August 2004* (each £150,878)
Style, The Hon. Mr/Mrs Justice [surname]

Hon. Dame Joyanne Bracewell, DBE, *born* 1934, *apptd* 1990
Hon. Sir Peter Singer, *born* 1944, *apptd* 1993
Hon. Sir Nicholas Wilson, *born* 1945, *apptd* 1993
Hon. Sir Andrew Kirkwood, *born* 1944, *apptd* 1993
Hon. Sir Hugh Bennett, *born* 1943, *apptd* 1995
Hon. Sir Edward Holman, *born* 1947, *apptd* 1995
Hon. Dame Mary Hogg, DBE, *born* 1947, *apptd* 1995
Hon. Sir Christopher Sumner, *born* 1939, *apptd* 1996
Hon. Sir Arthur Charles, *born* 1948, *apptd* 1998
Hon. Sir David Bodey, *born* 1947, *apptd* 1999
Hon. Dame Jill Black, DBE, *born* 1954, *apptd* 1999
Hon. Sir James Munby, *born* 1948, *apptd* 2000
Hon. Sir Paul Coleridge, *born* 1949, *apptd* 2000
Hon. Sir Mark Hedley, *born* 1946, *apptd* 2002
Hon. Dame Anna Hamilton Pauffley, DBE, *born* 1956, *apptd* 2003

Hon. Sir Roderic Wood, *born* 1951, *apptd* 2004
Hon. Dame Florence Baron, DBE, *born* 1952, *apptd* 2004
Hon. Sir Ernest Ryder, *born* 1957, *apptd* 2004

TECHNOLOGY AND CONSTRUCTION COURT
St Dunstan's House, 133–137 Fetter Lane, London EC4A 1HD
T 020-7947 6022

JUDGES (each £122,139, Presiding Judge, £150,878)
The Hon. Mr Justice Jackson *(Presiding Judge)*
His Hon. Judge Havery, QC
His Hon. Judge Lloyd, QC
His Hon. Judge Thornton, QC
His Hon. Judge Wilcox
His Hon. Judge Toulmin, CMG, QC
His Hon. Judge Seymour, QC
His Hon. Judge Coulson, QC

Court Manager, Kevin Johnson

LORD CHANCELLOR'S DEPARTMENT
see Government Departments section

SUPREME COURT DEPARTMENTS AND OFFICES
Royal Courts of Justice, London WC2A 2LL
T 020-7947 6000

DIRECTOR'S OFFICE
T 020-7947 6159
Director, Mark Camley
Group Manager and Deputy Director, J. Selch
Group Manager, Probate Service, R. P. Knight
Group Manager, Family Proceedings, J. Miller
Finance and Performance Officer, K. Richardson

ADMIRALTY AND COMMERCIAL REGISTRY AND MARSHAL'S OFFICE
T 020-7947 6112
Registrar, P. Miller
Admiralty Marshal and Court Manager, K. Houghton

BANKRUPTCY AND COMPANIES COURT
T 020-7947 6444
Chief Registrar, S. Baister
Bankruptcy Registrars, G. W. Jaques; J. A. Simmonds; P. J. S. Rawson; C. Derrett; W. Nicholls
Court Manager, Jane O'Connor

CENTRAL OFFICE OF THE SUPREME COURT
Senior Master of the Supreme Court (QBD), and Queen's Remembrancer, R. L. Turner
Masters of the Supreme Court (QBD), M. Tennant; P. Miller; I. H. Foster; G. H. Rose; P. G. A. Eyre; H. J. Leslie; J. G. G. Ungley; S. Whittaker; B. Yoxall; B. J. F. Fontaine
Court Manager, M. A. Brown

CHANCERY CHAMBERS
T 020-7947 7785
Chief Master of the Supreme Court, J. I. Winegarten
Masters of the Supreme Court, J. A. Moncaster; R. A. Bowman; N. W. Bragge; T. J. Bowles; N. S. Price
Court Manager, G. Robinson

COURT OF APPEAL CIVIL DIVISION
T 020-7947 6533
Head of the Civil Appeals Office, David Gladwell
Court Manager, Judy Anckorn

COURT OF APPEAL CRIMINAL DIVISION
T 020-7947 6011
Registrar, R. A. Venne
Deputy Registrar, Mrs L. G. Knapman
Group Manager, Helen Smith

ADMINISTRATIVE OFFICE OF THE SUPREME
COURT
T 020-7947 6655
*Master of the Crown Office, and Queen's Coroner and
Attorney,* R. A. Venne
Head of Crown Office, Mrs L. G. Knapman
Group Manager, Helen Smith

EXAMINERS OF THE COURT
Empowered to take examination of witnesses in all
Divisions of the High Court.
Examiners, A. G. Dyer; A. W. Hughes; Mrs G. M. Kenne;
R. M. Planterose; M. W. M. Chism

SUPREME COURT COSTS OFFICE
T 020-7947 7314
Senior Cost Judge, P. T. Hurst
Masters of the Supreme Court, T. H. Seager-Berry; C. C.
Wright; P. R. Rogers; J. E. O'Hare; C. D. N. Campbell;
J. Simons; A. Gordon-Saker
Court Manager, Geoff Waterhouse

COURT OF PROTECTION
Archway Towers, 11th Floor, 2 Junction Road,
London N19 5SZ
T 020-7664 7317
Master, D. A. Lush

ELECTION PETITIONS OFFICE
Room E113, Royal Courts of Justice, Strand,
London WC2A 2LL T 020-7947 6131
The office accepts petitions and deals with all matters
relating to the questioning of parliamentary, European
Parliament and local government elections, and with
applications for relief under the Representation of the
People legislation.
Prescribed Officer, R. L. Turner
Chief Clerk, Mrs A. J. Burns

OFFICE OF THE LORD CHANCELLOR'S VISITORS
Archway Towers, 11th Floor, 2 Junction Road,
London N19 5SZ T 020-7664 7317
Legal Visitor, A. R. Tyrrell
Medical Visitors, S. B. Mahapatra; A. Bailey; T. Heads; J.
Waite; P. Hettiaratchy; R. Lucas; N. Choudry; P.
Saleem

OFFICIAL RECEIVERS' DEPARTMENT
21 Bloomsbury Street, London WC1B 3QW
T 020-7637 1110
Inspector-General, D. Flynn
Deputies, L. Gramp; G. Horna

OFFICIAL SOLICITOR'S DEPARTMENT
81 Chancery Lane, London WC2B 6HD
T 020-7911 7127
Official Solicitor to the Supreme Court, L. C. Oates
Deputy Official Solicitor, E. Solomons
Chief Clerk, Edward Bloomfield

PRINCIPAL REGISTRY (FAMILY DIVISION)
First Avenue House, 42–49 High Holborn,
London WC1V 6NP
T 020-7947 6000
Senior District Judge, G. B. N. A. Angel
District Judges, A. R. S. Bassett-Cross; M. C. Berry; H.
Black; Miss S. M. Bowman; Miss H. C. Bradley; G. C.
Brasse; Miss P. Cushing; K. E. Green; R. Harper;
Maple; C. Million; Mrs K. T. Moorhouse; Redgrave;
Miss L. D. Roberts; Robinson; M. J. Segal; K. J. White;
P. Waller
Family and Probate Service Group Manager, R. P. Knight
District Probate Registrars:
Birmingham and Stoke-on-Trent, Miss P. Walbeoff
Brighton and Maidstone, P. Ellwood
Bristol, Exeter and Bodmin, R. H. P. Joyce
Cardiff, Bangor and Carmarthen, P. Curran (*Deputy*)
Ipswich, Norwich and Peterborough, Miss H. Whitby
Leeds, Lincoln and Sheffield, A. P. Dawson
Liverpool, Lancaster and Chester, C. Fox
Manchester and Nottingham, P. Burch
Newcastle, Carlisle, York and Middlesborough, P.
Sanderson
Oxford, Gloucester and Leicester, R. R. Da Costa
Winchester, A. K. Biggs

JUDGE ADVOCATES

THE JUDGE ADVOCATE OF THE FLEET
c/o Chichester Combined Court, Southgate, Chichester
PO19 1SX T 01243-520741

Judge Advocate of the Fleet (£113,000), His Hon. Judge
Sessions

OFFICE OF THE JUDGE ADVOCATE-GENERAL OF THE
FORCES
(*Joint Service for the Army and the Royal Air Force*)
81 Chancery Lane, London WC2A IBQ
T 020-7218 8089

Judge Advocate-General (£113,121), vacant
Vice-Judge Advocate-General (£108,850), E. G. Moelwyn-
Hughes
Judge Advocates *(£94,760), M. A. Hunter; J. P. Camp; C.
R. Burn; R. C. C. Seymour; I. H. Pearson; J. F. T.
Bayliss; M. R. Elsom
Style for Judge Advocates, Judge Advocate [surname]
*salary includes £4,000 inner London weighting

HIGH COURT AND CROWN COURT CENTRES

First-tier centres deal with both civil and criminal cases
and are served by High Court and circuit judges. Second-
tier centres deal with criminal cases only and are served
by High Court and circuit judges. Third-tier centres deal
with criminal cases only and are served only by circuit
judges.

MIDLAND CIRCUIT
First-tier – Birmingham, Lincoln, Nottingham, Stafford,
Warwick
Second-tier – Leicester, Northampton, Shrewsbury,
Worcester, Wolverhampton
Third-tier – Coventry, Derby, Hereford, Stoke-on-Trent
Circuit Administrator, Mrs D. Ponsonby, The Priory Courts,
6th Floor, 33 Bull Street, Birmingham B4 6DW
T 0121-681 3201

Group Managers: Mrs J. Grosvenor *(Acting)*, West Midlands; R. Perry *(Acting)*, Warwickshire Group; D. Bennett, *Staffordshire/West Mercia Group*; A. Phillips, *East Midlands Group*

NORTH-EASTERN CIRCUIT
First-tier – Leeds, Newcastle upon Tyne, Sheffield, Teesside
Second-tier – Bradford, York
Third-tier – Doncaster, Durham, Kingston-upon-Hull, Great Grimsby
Circuit Administrator, S. Proudlock, 18th Floor, West Riding House, Albion Street, Leeds LS1 5AA T 0113-251 1200
Group Managers: Linda Mayhew *(Acting)*, North and West Yorkshire Group; David Keane, *Tyne Tees Group*; Sarah Greenhough *(Acting)*, Humberside and South Yorkshire Group

NORTHERN CIRCUIT
First-tier – Carlisle, Liverpool, Manchester (Crown Square), Preston
Third-tier – Barrow-in-Furness, Bolton, Burnley, Lancaster; Manchester (Minshull Street)
Regional Director, North West, C. A. Mayer, 15 Quay Street, Manchester M60 9FD T 0161-833 1005
Group Managers: Miss G. Hague, *Lancashire Group*; R. Knott, *Greater Manchester Group*; S. McNally, *Merseyside Group*; S. Evans, *Cumbria Group*

SOUTH-EASTERN CIRCUIT
First-tier – Chelmsford, Lewes, Norwich
Second-tier – Ipswich, London (Central Criminal Court), Luton, Maidstone, Reading, St Albans
Third-tier – Aylesbury, Basildon, Bury St Edmunds, Cambridge, Canterbury, Chichester, Croydon, Guildford, King's Lynn, London (Blackfriars, Harrow, Inner London Sessions House, Isleworth, Kingston, Middlesex Guildhall, Snaresbrook, Southwark, Wood Green, Woolwich), Southend
Circuit Administrator, D. Ryan, CBE, New Cavendish House, 18 Maltravers Street, London WC2R 3EU T 020-7947 7232
Group Managers: D. Weston *(London Crown)*; L. Lennon *(London County)*; J. Cave *(Kent and Sussex)*; M. Littlewood *(East Anglia, Bedfordshire and Hertfordshire)*; S. Townley *(Thames Valley, Surrey and Oxford)*

The High Court in Greater London sits at the Royal Courts of Justice.

WALES AND CHESTER CIRCUIT
First-tier – Caernarfon, Cardiff, Chester, Mold, Swansea
Second-tier – Carmarthen, Merthyr Tydfil, Newport, Welshpool
Third-tier – Dolgellau, Haverfordwest, Knutsford, Warrington
Circuit Administrator, N. Chibnall, Churchill House, Churchill Way, Cardiff CF10 4HH T 029-2041 5500
Group Managers: G. Pickett, *South Wales Group*; G. Kenney, *North Wales and Cheshire Group*

WESTERN CIRCUIT
First-tier – Bristol, Exeter, Truro, Winchester
Second-tier – Dorchester, Gloucester, Plymouth, Weymouth
Third-tier – Barnstaple, Bournemouth, Newport (IOW), Portsmouth, Salisbury, Southampton, Swindon, Taunton

Circuit Administrator, Peter Risk, 5th Floor, Greyfriars, Lewins Mead, Bristol BS1 2NR T 0117-910 3600
Group Managers: N. Jeffery, *Wiltshire*; D. Gentry, *Devon and Cornwall*; R. White, *Avon and Somerset*; R. Brummitt, *Dorset*; M. Speller, *Gloucestershire*; S. Williamson, *Hampshire and Isle of Wight*; P. Downton, *Regional Transition Manager*

CIRCUIT JUDGES

*Senior Circuit Judges, each £122,139
Circuit Judges at the Central Criminal Court, London (Old Bailey Judges), each £122,139
Circuit Judges, each £113,121
Style, His/Her Hon. Judge [surname]
Senior Presiding Judge, The Rt. Hon. Lord Justice Judge

MIDLAND CIRCUIT
Presiding Judges, The Hon. Mr Justice Goldring; The Hon. Mr Justice Gibbs

I. D. G. Alexander, QC; Miss C. Alton; D. Bennett; R. Bray; D. Brunning; J. Burgess; Miss J. Butler, QC; J. Cavell; M. Challinor; *F. Chapman; P. Clark; M. Coates; R. Cole; N. B. Coles, QC; I. Collis; T. Corrie; P. De Mille (shared with South-Eastern Circuit); Miss P. Deeley; M. J. Dudley; M. R. Eades; P. Eccles, QC; T. Faber; Miss E. Fisher; J. Fletcher; A. Geddes; P. Glenn; J. Milmo, QC; R. Griffith-Jones; A. Hamilton; D. Hamilton; S. Hammond; Miss A. W. Hampton; C. Harris, QC (shared with South-Eastern Circuit); M. Heath; E. Hindley, QC; C. Hodson; H. Hughes; R. Inglis; R. Jenkins; F. Kirkham; A. MacDuff, QC; P. McCahill, QC; D. McCarthy; A. McCreath; D. McEvoy, QC; M. McKenna; J. Machin; W. D. Matthews; H. R. Mayor, QC; C. Metcalf; A. Mitchell; N. Mitchell; P. Morrell; I. Morris; M. Mott; A. H. Norris, QC; R. O'Rorke; S. Oliver-Jones, QC; R. Onions; R. Orme; J. Orrell; D. Perrett, QC; M. Pert, QC; *R. Pollard; D. Pugsley; J. Pyke; J. Rubery; R. Rundell; J. H. B. Saunders, QC *(Recorder of Birmingham)*; J. Shand; D. Stanley; M. Stokes, QC; G. Styler; A. Taylor; J. Teare; S. Tonking; S. Waine; J. Wait; J. Warner; N. Webb; C. Wide, QC; W. Wood, QC

NORTH-EASTERN CIRCUIT
Presiding Judges, The Hon. Mr Justice Henriques; The Hon. Mr Justice Andrew Smith

NORTH AND WEST YORKSHIRE GROUP
R. Adams; G. N. Barr Young; J. E. Barry; R. Bartfield; C. O. J. Behrens; P. Benson; B. Bush; G. Cliffe; P. J. Cockroft; J. Dobkin; A. C. Finnerty; R. A. Grant; S. P. Grenfell; S. J. Gullick; T. S. A. Hawkesworth, QC; P. M. L. Hoffman; P. Hunt; R. Ibbotson; N. H. Jones, QC; G. H. Kamil; T. D. Kent-Jones, TD; P. Langan, QC; K. M. P. Macgill; A. G. McCallum; R. M. Scott; J. Spencer, QC; S. M. Spencer, QC, J. S. H. Stewart, QC; L. Sutcliffe; T. Walsh; J. S. Wolstenholme

TYNE TEES GROUP
P. J. B. Armstrong; B. Bolton; P. H. Bowers; A. N. J. Briggs; D. M. A. Bryant; M. C. Carr; M. L. Cartlidge; E. J. Faulks; P. J. Fox, QC; T. Hewitt; D. Hodson; A. T. Lancaster; P. R. Lowden; J. T. Milford, QC; J. P. Moir; M. G. C. Moorhouse; L. Spittle; M. Taylor; C. T. Walton; J. De G. Walford; G. Whitburn, QC; D. R. Wood

HUMBERSIDE AND SOUTH YORKSHIRE GROUP
T. W. Barber; D. R. Bentley, QC; J. W. Bullimore; A. C. Carr; M. T. Cracknell; J. Davies; J. Dowse; A. R. Goldsack, QC; L. Hull; S. Jack; P. Jones; K. R. Keen, QC; S. W. Lawler, QC; M. K. Mettyear; R. J. Moore; M. J. A. Murphy, QC; J. H. Reddihough; P. E. Robertshaw; J. Shipley; J. A. Swanson

NORTHERN CIRCUIT
Presiding Judges, The Hon. Mr Justice McCombe; The Hon. Mr Justice Leveson

M. P. Allweis; J. M. Appleby; J. F. Appleton; E. K. Armitage, QC; R. K. Atherton; Miss P. H. Badley; S. W. Baker; P. Batty; R. C. W. Bennett; A. N. H. Blake; C. Bloom, QC; D. Boulton; L. F. M. Brown; R. Brown; J. K. Burke, QC; M. D. Byrne; B. I. Caulfield; D. Clark; G. M. Clifton; C. J. Cornwall; I. W. Crompton; Miss J. M. P. Daley; B. R. Duckworth; S. B. Duncan; Miss D. B. A. Forrester; J. R. Foster, QC; J. R. B. Geake; D. S. Gee; H. Gee, QC; W. George; A. J. Gilbart, QC; *J. A. D. Gilliland, QC; N. B. D. Gilmour, QC; *H. B. Globe, QC *(Recorder of Liverpool)*; C. L. Goldstone, QC; I. M. Hamilton; J. A. Hammond; D. Harris, QC; *T. B. Hegarty, QC; M. J. Henshell; F. R. B. Holloway; *R. C. Holman; A. D. Hope; *N. J. G. Howarth; C. James; *M. Kershaw, QC *(Commercial Circuit Judge)*; E. M. Knopf; Miss L. J. Kushner, QC; P. M. Lakin; B. L. Lever; B. Lewis; J. Lewis; A. C. Lowcock; D. Lynch; A. P. Lyon; D. I. Mackay; J. B. Macmillan; *D. G. Maddison *(Recorder of Manchester)*; *B. C. Maddocks; C. J. Mahon; W. P. Morris; T. J. Mort; L. A. Newton; *C. P. L. Openshaw, QC *(Recorder of Preston)*; F. D. Owen; J. A. Phillips; J. C. Phipps; P. R. Raynor, QC; J. H. Roberts; Miss M. Roddy; Miss G. D. Ruaux; M. W. Rudland; A. A. Rumbelow, QC; E. Slinger; A. Smith; P. Smith; Miss E. M. Steel; M. T. Steiger, QC; *S. Stewart, QC; D. R. Swift; P. Sycamore; C. B. Tetlow; I. J. C. Trigger; A. R. Warnock; Miss B. J. Watson; K. Wilkinson; B. Woodward

SOUTH-EASTERN CIRCUIT
Presiding Judges, The Hon. Mr Justice Aikens; The Hon. Mrs Justice Rafferty; The Hon. Mr Justice Bell

M. F. Addison; P. C. Ader; J. Altman; Mrs S. C. Andrew; A. R. L. Ansell; M. G. Anthony; S. A. Anwyl, QC; Charles Atkins; E. H. Bailey; F. Baker, QC; C. G. Ball, QC; A. F. Balston; G. S. Barham; B. J. Barker, QC; S. Barnes; W. E. Barnett, QC; R. A. Barratt, QC; *G. A. Bathurst-Norman; P. J. L. Beaumont, QC *(Common Serjeant)*; R. V. M. E. Behar; J. Bevan, QC; Mrs C. V. Bevington; N. C. van der Bijl; I. G. Bing; M. G. Binning; W. J. Birtles; B. M. B. Black; H. O. Blacksell, QC; J. G. Boal, QC; A. V. Bradbury; G. B. Breen; M. Brooke, QC; R. G. Brown; J. M. Bull, QC; J. P. Burke; L. S. Burn, QC; The Hon. C. W. Byers; D. Caddick; A. Campbell; Ms A. Campbell; J. Q. Campbell; J. Carey; M. J. Carroll; M. T. Catterson; R. Chapple; P. C. Clegg; Miss S. Coates; N. J. Coleman; S. H. Colgan; *P. H. Collins, CBE; S. S. Coltart; C. D. Compston; T. A. C. Coningsby, QC; J. G. Connor; R. D. Connor; R. A. Cooke; A. Cooper; P. E. Copley; T. G. E. Corrie; Dr E. Cotran; P. Coulson, QC; P. R. Cowell; K. Cox; R. C. Cox; M. L. S. Cripps; C. A. Critchlow; J. F. Crocker; D. L. Croft, QC; D. M. Cryan; P. Curl; Mrs P. M. T. Dangor; A. M. Darroch; M. Dean, QC; P. G. Dedman; J. E. Devaux; P. Dodgson; P. H. Downes; W. H. Dunn, QC; C. M. Edwards; D. R. Ellis; R. C. Elly; C. Elwen; Fabyan Evans; Miss D. Faber; J. D.

Farnworth; P. Fingret; P. E. J. Focke, QC; G. C. F. Forrester; R. Foster; Ms D. A. Freedman; M. Fysh, QC; C. A. H. Gibson; Miss A. F. Goddard, QC; A. Goldstaub, QC; D. N. Goodin; C. G. M. Gordon; J. B. Gosschalk; A. A. Goymer; C. Gratwicke; A. E. Greenwood; P. Grobel; TD, VRD; G. H. Gypps; J. Hall; Miss G. Hallon; J. Hamilton; Miss S. Hamilton, QC; C. R. H. Hardy; C. Harris, QC; M. F. Harris; W. G. Hawkesworth; R. G. Hawkins, QC; J. M. Haworth; R. J. Haworth; R. M. Hayward; R. Hayward-Smith, QC; D. E. A. Higgins; A. N. Hitching; H. E. G. Hodge, OBE; K. M. J. Hollis; J. F. Holt; K. A. D. Hornby; M. Horowitz, QC; M. Hucker; J. C. A. Hughes, QC; M. J. Hyam *(Recorder of London)*; D. A. Inman; A. B. Issard-Davies; Dr P. J. E. Jackson; G. Jones Nicholas; T. J. C. Joseph; I. G. F. Karsten, QC; S. S. Katkhuda; C. J. B. Kemp; W. A. Kennedy; G. M. P. F. Khayat, QC; A. W. P. King; T. R. King; B. J. Knight, QC; P. E. Knowles; Stephen Kramer; Capt. J. B. R. Langdon, RN; P. H. Latham; T. Lawrence; D. M. Levy, QC; C. C. D. Lindsay, QC; S. H. Lloyd; F. R. Lockhart; N. G. E. Loraine-Smith; J. A. M. Lowen; Mrs A. M. Ludlow; Capt. S. Lyons; A. G. McDowall; R. J. McGregor-Johnson; B. M. McIntyre; R. G. McKinnon; W. N. McKinnon; N. A. McKittrick; J. McMullen; D. Mackie, QC, CBE; K. C. Macrae; N. Madge; T. Maher; F. J. M. Marr-Johnson; D. N. N. Martineau; D. Matheson, QC; Ms S. Matthews, QC; V. Mayer; N. A. Medawar, QC; D. J. Mellor, QC; D. Mercer; P. N. De Mille; Miss A. E. Mitchell; C. R. Mitchell; D. C. Mitchell; F. I. Mitchell; H. M. Morgan; A. P. Morris; D. Morton Jack; C. J. Moss, QC; P. Moss; R. T. Moss; Miss M. J. S. Mowat; G. S. Murdoch, QC; T. M. E. Nash; M. H. D. Neligan; A. I. Niblett; Mrs M. F. Norrie-Walker; Brig. A. P. Norris, OBE; P. W. O'Brien; J. O'Mahony; M. A. Oppenheimer; M. O'Sullivan; D. Paget, QC; A. Pardoe, QC; A. Patience, QC; W. Pawlak; Mrs N. Pearce; Prof. D. S. Pearl; Miss V. A. Pearlman; N. A. J. Philpot; T. D. Pillay; A. B. Pitts; D. C. Pitman; J. R. Platt; J. R. Playford, QC; Miss I. M. Plumstead; T. G. Pontius; S. Pratt; R. J. C. V. Prendergast; J. Price; D. W. Radford; D. J. Rennie; J. R. Reid, QC; M. P. Reynolds; M. S. Rich, QC; J. Richards; D. J. Richardson; N. P. Riddell; G. Rivlin, QC; S. D. Robbins; J. Roberts, QC; J. M. Roberts; W. M. Rose; J. Rylance; T. R. G. Ryland; J. E. A. Samuels, QC; R. B. Sanders; A. R. G. Scott-Gall; J. S. Sennitt; D. Serota, QC; J. L. Sessions; A. G. Simmons; K. T. Simpson; P. R. Simpson; S. P. Sleeman; C. M. Smith, QC; S. A. R. Smith; Miss Z. P. Smith; E. Southwell; S. B. Spence; S. M. Stephens, QC; P. R. Statman; Mrs L. J. Stern, QC; N. A. Stewart; D. M. A. Stokes, QC; G. Stone, QC; T. M. F. Stow, QC; J. B. C. Tanzer, QC; A. M. Tapping; P. Testar; C. Thomas; P. J. Thompson; A. G. Y. Thorpe; C. H. Tilling; D. Turner; C. J. M. Tyrer; J. E. van der Werff; T. L. Viljoen; J. P. Wadsworth, QC; Miss A. P. Wakefield; R. Wakefield; R. Walker; S. P. Waller; A. R. Webb; C. S. Welchman; A. F. Wilkie, QC; S. R. Wilkinson; Miss J. A. Williams; Ms S. Williams; R. J. Winstanley; S. E. Woollam; D. Worsley; P. Wulwik; M. P. Yelton; M. K. Zeidman, QC; K. H. Zucker, QC

WALES AND CHESTER CIRCUIT
Presiding Judges, The Hon. Mr Justice Roderick Evans; The Hon. Mr Justice Pitchford

K. Barnett; M. R. Burr; J. R. Case; N. M. Chambers, QC; S. Clarke; J. Curran; D. L. Daniel; D. Davies; R. L. Denyer, QC; J. B. S. Diehl; R. Dutton; E. Edwards; G. O. Edwards; M. Farmer, QC; M. Furness; W. Gaskell; D. Halbert; D. Hale; J. D. Durham Hall, QC; G. R. Hickinbottom; S. Hopkins, QC; R. P. Hughes; T. M.

Hughes, QC; G. Jones; C. Llewellyn-Jones, QC; C. Masterman; D. W. Morgan; D. G. Morris; D. C. Morton; I. C. Parry; G. A. L. Price, QC; P. Price, QC; E. M. Rees; D. W. Richards; P. Richards; J. M. T. Rogers, QC; K. Thomas; *J. G. Williams, QC; W. Williams, QC; N. F. Woodward

WESTERN CIRCUIT
Presiding Judges, The Hon. Mrs Justice Hallett; The Hon. Mr Justice David Steel

P. R. Barclay; A. J. Barnett; J. F. Beashel; R. Bond; J. G. Boggis, QC; G. Boney, QC; J. Bonvin; *M. J. L. Brodrick; J. M. Burford, QC; *R. D. Bursell, QC; G. W. A. Cottle; M. G. Cotterill; T. G. Cowling; *T. Crowther, QC; K. C. Cutler; P. Darlow; Susan P. Darwall Smith; Mrs L. Davies; J. W. Dixon; J. Foley; F. Gilbert, QC; D. L. Griffiths; J. D. Griggs; C. M. A. Hagen; J. M. Harrow; A. M. Havelock-Allan, QC; P. J. Hooton; M. K. Harington; R. Rooke Hetherington; I. Hughes, QC; G. Hume Jones; J. R. Jarvis; P. Lambert; C. Leigh, QC; T. Longbotham; T. Mackean; I. S. McKintosh; J. G. McNaught; The Lord Meston, QC; T. J. Milligan; J. O. Neligan; S. K. O'Malley; S. K. Overend; R. Price; M. W. Roach; R. Rucker; J. Rudd; A. Rutherford; R. M. Shawcross; D. Smith, QC; G. Tabor, QC; W. E. M. Taylor; D. K. Ticehurst, QC; D. I. H. Tyzack, QC; N. Vincent; R. C. B. Wade; P. Wassall; J. H. Weeks, QC; J. S. Wiggs

DISTRICT JUDGES
District Judges (each £90,760)

MIDLAND CIRCUIT
M. Anson; S. W. Arnold; M. Asokan; P. Atkinson; C. Beale; A. Brown; A. Butler; M. Cardinal; D. Cernik; R. Chapman; A. Cleary; R. Cole; D. J. Cooke; T. Cotterill; T. Davies; E. Dickinson; D. D. Douce; P. Dowling; L. Eaton; M. Ellery; A. Elliott; S. Gailey; F. Goddard; R. Hearne; R. L. Hudson; J. Ilsley; J. Jack; A. Jenkins; A. Jones; P. Kesterton; K. Lacy; I. Lettall; D. Lipman; P. McHale; P. Mackenzie; A. Marston; A. Maw; R. Merriman; D. Millard; A. Mithani; R. J. Morton; D. O'Regan; B. Oliver; D. Owen; M. Parry; P. Rank; F. Reeson; P. Richmond; T. Ridgway; S. Rogers; P. Sanghera; R. Savage; L. H. Schroeder; V. Sedhev; S. C. W. Smith; V. Stamenkovich; A. F. Suckling; P. Thompson; R. J. Toombs; Ms K. A. Venables; W. A. Vincent; P. Waterworth; R. Whitehurst

NORTH-EASTERN CIRCUIT
S. T. Alderson; H. Anderson; C. A. Arkless; I. D. Atherton; A. M. Babbington; H. J. Bailey; R. Barraclough; C. W. Bellamy; I. P. Besford; C. M. Birkby; J. Bower; J. A. Buchan; P. E. Bullock; I. L. Buxton; S. Chesterfield; P. Cuthbertson; G. J. Edwards; I. S. Fairwood; J. Flanagan; P. R. Giles; M. M. Glentworth; N. W. Goudie; S. J. Greenwood; M. F. Handley; R. V. M. Hall; J. E. Harrison; H. F. Heath; N. G. Hickinbottom; R. N. Hill; T. W. Hill; J. R. A. Howard; R. A. Jordan; C. Khan; D. Kirkham; A. M. Large; D. E. Lascelles; P. E. Lawton; G. Y. Lingard; R. Loomba; G. Lord; J. E. Mainwaring-Taylor; G. M. Marley; P. C. Mort; D. A. Oldham; A. P. Powell; M. F. Rhodes; D. M. Robertson; J. S. Robinson; S. Rodgers; D. Scott-Phillips; I. F. Slim; S. E. Spencer; B. D. Stapely; D. M. Stocken; J. A. Taylor; P. W. J. Traynor; D. J. R. Weston; P. J. E. Wildsmith; J. S. Wilson; H. P. Wood; M. J. Young

NORTHERN CIRCUIT
G. R. Ashton; R. R. P. Ackroyd; I. Bennett; P. H. Berkson; Ms A. J. C. Brazier; R Bryce; M. E. Buckley; Ms V. Buckley; D. B. Chapman; J L. Clark; J. R. Clegg; J. F.

Coffey; P. St J. Dignan; E. Donnelly; J. F. Duerden; C. R. Fairclough; G. J. Fitzgerald; R. M. Forrester; C. R. Fox; C. E. Freeman; B. N. Gaunt; J. M. Geedes; M. Gosnell; M. J. Gregory; M. Griffiths; A. J. J. Harrison; N. Harrison; L. Henthorn; J. D. Heyworth; J. Horan; M. A. Hovington; G. A. Humphreys-Roberts; S. C. Jackson; J. A. James; E. Johnson; A. Jones; E. R. Jones; G. A. Needham; G. Nuttall; N. A. Law; R. A. McCullagh; B. V. McGrath; Ms M. A. Mornington; L. C. Osborne; J. K. Park; M. I. Peake; I. J. Pickup; J. J. B. Rawkins; A. M. Saffman; D. J. Shannon; Ms J. Shaw; M. J. Simpson; R. Smedley; G. D. Smith; W. H. Stansfield; L. S. Stephens; Ms P. S. Stockton; L. G. Sykes; C. M. Swindley; R. Talbot; B. W. Travers; M. W. Turner; M. J. Wilby; P. T. Wilby; S. Wright

SOUTH-EASTERN CIRCUIT
J. L. Allen; I. Avent; P. R. Ayers; J. D. Banks; S. Batcup; P. W. Bazley-White; J. L. Beattie; D. Beck; R. H. L. Blomfield; A. J. Blundson; M. Birchall; G. Brett; G. H. Burgess; L. M. Burgess; P. R. Carr; C. B. Chandler; J. H.G. Chrispin; E. Cohen; L. Cohen; J. I. Collier; B. R. J. Cole; A. J. Coni; C. N. Darbyshire; C. Dabezies; R. A. Davis; S. A. F. Davies; J. R. Davidson; I. M. Diamond; R. D. Dudley; C. M. Edwards; I. Evans; D. Eynon; M. Fawcett; G. B. Field; Ms R. Fine; S. H. D. Fink; N. G. Freeborough; J. M. Fortgang; V. W. Gatter; P. Gamba; S. M. Gerlis; M. C. Gilchrist; S. S. Gill; J. Gittens; P. M. L. Glover; S. G. Gold; G. A. Green; N. J. Gregory; E. J. Habershon; D. F. Hallett; C. Hamilton; S. Hasan; M. J. Haselgrove; D. N. Hayes; R. M. Henry; S. Henson; P. F. Hewetson-Brown; M. Hickman; R. S. Hicks; R. M. Jacey; N. E. Jackson; S. G. Jackson; W. Jackson; T. H. N. Jenkins; Ms H. Johns; S. V. Jones; J. I. Karet; J. L. C. Kirby; H. E. Kemp; D. C. Lamdin; M. Langley; I. H. Lay; Lee; C. J. Letham; H. A. J. Letts; A. Levey; S. E. Levinson; B. G. Lightman; W. N. McKinnon; H. L. Manners; M. J. Marin; R. Matthews; T. McLoughlin; J. S. Merrick; L. D. Millard; A. J. Mills; E. C. Millward; R. J. Mitchell; S. R. Mitchell; C. B. Molle; S. I. Morley; A. Morris; P. Mostyn; B. Mullis; R. M. Naqvi; M. J. Parker; T. Parker; M. J. Payne; G. L. Pearl; P. Pearl; P. H. Pelly; P. R. Pescod; S. Plaskow; Polden; K. A. Price; A. L. Raeside; M. A. Read; A. M. Rhodes; J. T. Robinson; P. Rogers; M. Royall; B. I. Rutland; S. Sethi; F. W. Shanks; I. Sheratte; G. Silverman; H. Silverman; M. N. Skerratt; E. J. Silverwood-Cope; M. M. Short; R. Southcombe; R. G. Sparrow; E. Stary; G. M. Stephenson; D. Steel; P. A. Sturdy; J. E. Taylor; J. R. K. Taylor; A. K. Taylor; E. R. W. Temple; R. C. Tetlow; A. D. Thomas; I. G. Tilbury; M. Trent; C. Vokes; M. Walker; A. S. Wharton; A. N. Wicks; G. K. Wilding; F. J. Wilkinson; E. Willers; J. E. Wright; A. J. Worthington; M. Zimmels

WALES AND CHESTER CIRCUIT
D. J. Asplin; C. F. Beattie; G. H. F. Carson; J. L. Davies; C. R. Dawson; Mrs H. Dawson; J. M. Doel; P. M. Evans; Miss R. Evans; Mrs J. E. Garland-Thomas; W. H. Godwin; S. G. Harrison; R. L. Hendicott; R. A. Hoffman; D. L. Hughes; D. P. Jenkins; T. A. John; T. J. Lewis; P. H. Llewellyn, OBE; C. W. Newman; A. T. North; Mrs C. E. O'Leary; C. G. Perry; D. Wyn Rees; V. Reeves; J. E. Regan; S. Rogers; R. Singh, CBE; J. G. Thomas; A. A. Wallace; A. J. P. Weaver; O. W. Williams

WESTERN CIRCUIT
C. M. Ackner; C. E. H. Ackroyd; R. D. I. Adam; J D. Ainsworth; R. C. Bird; D. Carney; B. R. Carron; G. F. Cawood; M. T. Cooper; P. W. Corrigan; J. P. Crosse; M. Dancey; M. P. H. Daniel; J. M. R. Dowell; Ms J. Exton; D.

J. Field; J. Freeman; J. W. Frenkel; C. Fuller; F. Goodard; R. A. F. Griggs; A. M. Harvey; J. Hurley; R. D. S. James; P. D. Jolly; B. G. Meredith; P. Mildred; P. Mitchell; A. D. Moon; N. J. Murphy; R. F. D. Naylor; M. Rutherford; A. L. Simons; P. N. Singleton; B. J. A. Smith; J. Sparrow; Mrs G. Stuart Brown; M. H. Tennant; A. B. Thomas; J. L. Thomas; C. J. Tromans; J. Turner; A. J. Wainwright; A. Walker; I. E. Weintroub; D. R. White; R. A. Wilson

DISTRICT JUDGES (MAGISTRATES' COURTS)

The Provisional and Metropolitan Division has been changed; all former Provincial and Metropolitan Stipendiary Magistrates can serve nationally within any district and are now called District Judges (Magistrates' Courts).

District Judges (each £94,760) salary includes £4,000 inner London weighting

M. A. Abelson; Mrs J. H. Alderson; R. W. Anderson; Mrs A. Arnold; G. B. Babington-Browne; A. Berg; J. S. Bennett; A. Bopa-Rai; J. A. Browne; P. H. R. Browning; N. R. Cadbury; A. L. Callaway; G. Chalk; J. J. Charles; T. M. Chatelier; D. J. Chinery; R. F. S. Clancy; D. A. Cooper; M. Cooper; S. N. Cooper; C. R. Darnton; Mrs S. E. Driver; S. Earl; R. Elsey; P. R. Farmer; J. Finestein; P. J. Firth; D. R. Fletcher; J. G. Foster; M. J. Friel; I. Gillespie; C. Goulborn; R. House; M. L. R. Harris; R. Holland; J. A. Jellema; R. D. Kitson; Ms B. A. Knight; N. Leigh-Smith; I. S. Lomax; C. M. McColl; D. V. Manning-Davies; D. M. Meredith; B. Morgan; Mrs L. Morgan; M. C. Morris; P. T. Nuttall; D. Parsons; J. B. Prowse; S. Qureshi; P. B. Richardson; P. G. G. Richards; M. A. Rosenberg; F. J. Rutherford; N. Sanders; A. Shaw; Mrs E. M. Shelvey; P. C. Tain; D. R. G. Tapp; D. L. Thomas; W. D. Thomas; M. J. Walker; P. Ward; G. R. Watkins; Miss P. J. Watkins; R. E. H. Williams; M. Wood; J. I. Woollard; R. J. Zara

METROPOLITAN DISTRICTS
Bow Street, T. H. Workman *(Senior District Judge)*; C. L. Pratt; H. N. Evans; Miss D. E. Wickham
Brent Magistrates' Court, Mrs K. J. Marshall
Camberwell Green, A. C. Baldwin; Miss S. V. Green; Ms A. L. Sawetz; P. Wain; J. A. Zani
Croydon Magistrates' Court, A. P. Carr; M. Hunter
East Central Division, Miss D. Quick; I. M. Baker; P. A. M. Clark; J. V. Perkins; R. A. McPhee
Essex, K. A. Gray
Greenwich/Woolwich, M. Kelly; H. C. F. Riddle; P. S. Wallis; D. Lynch
Feltham Magistrates' Court, S. N. Day
Hendon Magistrates' Court, C. S. Wiles
Highbury Corner, I. M. Baker; J. Henderson; R. A. McPhee; Miss D. Quick; J. V. Perkins; P. A. M. Clark
Horseferry Road, A. R. Davies; A. T. Evans; Miss C. S. R. Tubbs; Ms. Snow; Q. A. Purdy
Inner London and City, N. Crichton
Marylebone, Miss E. J. Roscoe; G. Parsons
Middlesex, S. N. Day; C. Wiles; K. Marshall; B. Barnes
North East London, G. E. Cawdron
South-Western, K. I. Grant; S. Bayne; P. M. Gillibrand
Stratford Magistrates' Court, H. Gott; Miss S. L. Sims; C. A. Dawson
Thames, Mrs J. R. Comyns; S. E. Dawson; Miss A. M. Rose; M. J. Read; Miss F. J. McIvor
Thames Valley, T. English; B. Loosley; A. Vickers
Tower Bridge, G. S. F. Black; S. Somjee; T. R. Stone

West London Magistrates' Court, J. B. Coleman; D. K. Lachlar; J. R. D. Philips; D. Simpson; Miss S. F. Williams; A. Sweet

GREATER LONDON MAGISTRATES' COURTS AUTHORITY
185 Marylebone Road, London, NW1 5QL T 0845 601 3600

Justices' Chief Executive and Clerk to the Committee (Acting), Michael Heap
Training Manager, Rosemary Marsh
Director of Human Resources, Sandra Campbell
Director of Finance, Tony Summers
Director of Legal Operations, Mark Eldridge

CROWN PROSECUTION SERVICE
50 Ludgate Hill, London EC4M 7EX
T 020-7796 8000
E enquiries@cps.gov.uk
W www.cps.gov.uk

The Crown Prosecution Service (CPS) is responsible for the independent review and conduct of criminal proceedings instituted by police forces in England and Wales, with the exception of cases conducted by the Serious Fraud Office and certain minor offences.
The Service is headed by the Director of Public Prosecutions (DPP), who works under the super-intendence of the Attorney General, and a Chief Executive. The Service comprises a headquarters and 42 areas, each area corresponding to a police area in England and Wales. Each area is headed by a Chief Crown Prosecutor, supported by an Area Business Manager.

Director of Public Prosecutions, Ken Macdonald, QC
Chief Executive , R. Foster
Directors, C. Newell *(Casework)*; G. Patten *(Policy)*; J. Graham *(Finance)*; Ms C. Hamon *(Business Information Systems)*; Ms A. O'Connor *(Human Resources)*
Head of Communications, Mrs S. Cunningham
Head of Management Audit Services, R. Capstick

CPS AREAS ENGLAND
AVON AND SOMERSET, 2nd Floor, Froomsgate House, Rupert Street, Bristol BS1 2QJ T 0117-930 2800
Chief Crown Prosecutor, D. Archer
BEDFORDSHIRE, Sceptre House, 7–9 Castle Street, Luton LU1 3AJ T 01582-816600
Chief Crown Prosecutor, R. Newcombe
CAMBRIDGESHIRE, Justinian House, Spitfire Close, Ermine Business Park, Huntingdon, Cambs PE29 6XY T 01480-825200
Chief Crown Prosecutor, R. Crowley
CHESHIRE, 2nd Floor, Windsor House, Pepper Street, Chester CH1 1TD T 01244-408600
Chief Crown Prosecutor, B. Hughes
CLEVELAND, 5 Linthorpe Road, Middlesbrough, Cleveland TS1 1TX T 01642-204500
Chief Crown Prosecutor, M. Goldman
CUMBRIA, 1st Floor, Stocklund House, Castle Street, Carlisle CA3 8SY T 01228-882900
Chief Crown Prosecutor, D. Farmer
DERBYSHIRE, 7th Floor, St Peter's House, Gower Street, Derby DE1 1SB T 01332-614000
Chief Crown Prosecutor, B. Gunn
DEVON AND CORNWALL, Hawkins House, Pynes Hill, Rydon Lane, Exeter EX2 5SS T 01392-288000
Chief Crown Prosecutor, A. Cresswell

DORSET, 1st Floor, Oxford House, Oxford Road, Bournemouth BH8 8HA T 01202-498700
Chief Crown Prosecutor, J. Revell

DURHAM, Elvet House, Hallgarth Street, Durham DH1 3AT T 0191-383 5800
Chief Crown Prosecutor, Ms P. Ragnauth

ESSEX, County House, 100 New London Road, Chelmsford CM2 0RG T 01245-455800
Chief Crown Prosecutor, J. Bell

GLOUCESTERSHIRE, 2 Kimbrose Way, Gloucester GL1 2DB T 01452-872400
Chief Crown Prosecutor, R. Coe Salazar

GREATER MANCHESTER, PO Box 237, 8th Floor, Sunlight House, Quay Street, Manchester M60 3PS T 0161-827 4700
Chief Crown Prosecutor, J. Holt

HAMPSHIRE AND ISLE OF WIGHT, 3rd Floor, Black Horse House, 8–10 Leigh Road, Eastleigh, Hants SO50 9FH T 02380-673800
Chief Crown Prosecutor, N. Hawkins

HERTFORDSHIRE, Queen's House, 58 Victoria Street, St Albans, Herts AL1 3HZ T 01727-798700
Chief Crown Prosecutor, C. Ingham

HUMBERSIDE, Citadel House, 58 High Street, Kingston-upon-Hull HU1 1QD T 01482-621000
Chief Crown Prosecutor, N. Cowgill

KENT, Priory Gate, 29 Union Street, Maidstone, Kent ME14 1PT T 01622-356300
Chief Crown Prosecutor, Ms E. Howe

LANCASHIRE, 1st Floor, Guildhall House, Guildhall Street, Preston PR1 3NU T 01772-208100
Chief Crown Prosecutor, R. Marshall

LEICESTERSHIRE, Princes Court, 34 York Road, Leicester LE1 5TU T 0116-204 6700
Chief Crown Prosecutor, M. Howard

LINCOLNSHIRE, Crosstrend House, 10A Newport, Lincoln LN1 3DF T 01522-585900
Chief Crown Prosecutor, Ms A. Kerr

LONDON, 7th Floor, CPS HQ, 50 Ludgate Hill, London EC4M 7EX T 020-7796 8000
Chief Crown Prosecutor, Ms D. Sharpling

MERSEYSIDE, 7th Floor (South), Royal Liver Building, Pier Head, Liverpool L3 1HN T 0151-239 6400
Chief Crown Prosecutor, J. Holt

NORFOLK, Haldin House, Old Bank of England Court, Queen Street, Norwich NR2 4SX T 01603-693000
Chief Crown Prosecutor, P. Tidey

NORTH YORKSHIRE, 6th Floor, Ryedale Building, 60 Piccadilly, York YO1 1NS T 01904-731700
Chief Crown Prosecutor, R. Turnbull

NORTHAMPTONSHIRE, Beaumont House, Cliftonville, Northampton NN1 5BE T 01604-823600
Chief Crown Prosecutor, C. Chapman

NORTHUMBRIA, St Ann's Quay, 122 Quayside, Newcastle upon Tyne NE1 3BD T 0191-260 4200
Chief Crown Prosecutor, Ms N. Reasbeck

NOTTINGHAMSHIRE, 2 King Edward Court, King Edward Street, Nottingham NG1 1EL T 0115-852 3300
Chief Crown Prosecutor, Ms K. Carty

SOUTH YORKSHIRE, Greenfield House, 32 Scotland Street, Sheffield S3 7DQ T 0114-229 8600
Chief Crown Prosecutor, Mrs J. Walker

STAFFORDSHIRE, 11a Princes Street, Stafford ST16 2EU T 01785-272200
Chief Crown Prosecutor, H. Ireland

SUFFOLK, Saxon House, 1 Cromwell Square, Ipswich IP1 1TS T 01473-282100
Chief Crown Prosecutor, C. Yule

SURREY, One Onslow Street, Guildford, Surrey GU1 4YA T 01483-468200
Chief Crown Prosecutor, Ms S. Hebblethwaite

SUSSEX, City Gates, 185 Dyke Road, Brighton BN3 1TL T 01273-765600
Chief Crown Prosecutor, Mrs S. J. Gallagher

THAMES VALLEY, The Courtyard, Lombard Street, Abingdon, Oxon OX14 5SE T 01235-551900
Chief Crown Prosecutor, B. Ubhey

WARWICKSHIRE, Rossmore House, 10 Newbold Terrace, Leamington Spa, Warks CV32 4EA T 01926-455000
Chief Crown Prosecutor, M. Lynn

WEST MERCIA, Artillery House, Heritage Way, Droitwich, Worcester WR9 8YB T 01905-825000
Chief Crown Prosecutor, J. England

WEST MIDLANDS, 14th Floor, Colmore Gate, 2 Colmore Row, Birmingham B3 2QA T 0121-262 1300
Chief Crown Prosecutor, D. Blundell

WEST YORKSHIRE, Oxford House, Oxford Row, Leeds LS1 3BE T 0113-290 2700
Chief Crown Prosecutor, N. Franklin

WILTSHIRE, 2nd Floor, Fox Talbot House, Bellinger Close, Malmesbury Road, Chippenham, Wilts SN15 1BN T 01249-766100
Chief Crown Prosecutor, Ms K. Harold

CPS AREAS WALES

DYFED POWYS, Heol Penlanffos, Tanerdy, Carmarthen, Dyfed SA31 2EZ T 01267-242100
Chief Crown Prosecutor, S. Rowlands

GWENT, 6th Floor, Chartist Tower, Upper Dock Street, Newport, Gwent NP20 1DW T 01633-261100
Chief Crown Prosecutor, vacant

NORTH WALES, Bromfield House, Ellice Way, Wrexham LL13 7YW T 01978-346000
Chief Crown Prosecutor, E. Beltrami

SOUTH WALES, 20th Floor, Capital House, Greyfriars Road, Cardiff CF1 3PL T 029-2080 3900
Chief Crown Prosecutor, C. Woolley

THE SCOTTISH JUDICATURE

Scotland has a legal system separate from and differing greatly from the English legal system in enacted law, judicial procedure and the structure of courts.

In Scotland the system of public prosecution is headed by the Lord Advocate and is independent of the police, who have no say in the decision to prosecute. The Lord Advocate, discharging his functions through the Crown Office in Edinburgh, is responsible for prosecutions in the High Court, sheriff courts and district courts. Prosecutions in the High Court are prepared by the Crown Office and conducted in court by one of the law officers, by an advocate-depute, or by a solicitor advocate. In the inferior courts the decision to prosecute is made and prosecution is preferred by procurators fiscal, who are lawyers and full-time civil servants subject to the directions of the Crown Office. A permanent legally-qualified civil servant known as the Crown Agent is responsible for the running of the Crown Office and the organisation of the Procurator Fiscal Service, of which he is the head.

Scotland is divided into six sheriffdoms, each with a full-time sheriff principal. The sheriffdoms are further divided into sheriff court districts, each of which has a legally-qualified resident sheriff or sheriffs, who are judges of the court.

In criminal cases sheriffs principal and sheriffs have the same powers; sitting with a jury of 15 members, they may try more serious cases on indictment, or, sitting alone, may try lesser cases under summary procedure. Minor summary offences are dealt with in district courts which are administered by the district and the islands local government authorities and presided over by lay justices of the peace (of whom there are about 4,000) and, in Glasgow only, by district judges (magistrates' courts). Juvenile offenders (children under 16) may be brought before an informal children's hearing comprising three local lay people. The superior criminal court is the High Court of Justiciary which is both a trial and an appeal court. Cases on indictment are tried by a High Court judge, sitting with a jury of 15, in Edinburgh and on circuit in other towns. Appeals from the lower courts against conviction or sentence are heard also by the High Court, which sits as an appeal court only in Edinburgh. There is no further appeal to the House of Lords in criminal cases.

In civil cases the jurisdiction of the sheriff court extends to most kinds of action. Appeal against decisions of the sheriff may be made to the sheriff principal and thence to the Court of Session, or direct to the Court of Session, which sits only in Edinburgh. The Court of Session is divided into the Inner and the Outer House. The Outer House is a court of first instance in which cases are heard by judges sitting singly, sometimes with a jury of 12. The Inner House, itself subdivided into two divisions of equal status, is mainly an appeal court. Appeals may be made to the Inner House from the Outer House as well as from the sheriff court. An appeal may be made from the Inner House to the House of Lords.

The judges of the Court of Session are the same as those of the High Court of Justiciary, the Lord President of the Court of Session also holding the office of Lord Justice General in the High Court. Senators of the College of Justice are Lords Commissioners of Justiciary as well as judges of the Court of Session. On appointment, a Senator takes a judicial title, which is retained for life. Although styled The Hon./Rt. Hon. Lord, the Senator is not a peer.

The office of coroner does not exist in Scotland. The local procurator fiscal inquires privately into sudden or suspicious deaths and may report findings to the Crown Agent. In some cases a fatal accident inquiry may be held before the sheriff.

COURT OF SESSION AND HIGH COURT OF JUSTICIARY

The Lord President and Lord Justice General (£185,705)
The Rt. Hon. the Lord Cullen of Whitekirk, *born* 1935, *apptd* 2001
Private Secretary, A. Maxwell

INNER HOUSE
Lords of Session (each £170,554)

FIRST DIVISION
The Lord President

Rt. Hon. Lord Marnoch (Michael Bruce), *born* 1938, *apptd* 1990
Rt. Hon. Lord Penrose, (George Penrose), *born* 1938, *apptd* 1990
Rt. Hon. Lord Hamilton (Arthur Hamilton), *born* 1942, *apptd* 1995
Rt. Hon. Lady Cosgrove (Hazel Aronson), *born* 1946, *apptd* 1996

SECOND DIVISION
Lord Justice Clerk (£179,431), The Rt. Hon. Lord Gill (Brian Gill), *born* 1942, *apptd* 2001
Rt. Hon. Lord Kirkwood (Ian Kirkwood), *born* 1932, *apptd* 1987
Rt. Hon. Lord MacLean (Ranald MacLean), *born* 1938, *apptd* 1990
Rt. Hon. Lord Osborne (Kenneth Osborne), *born* 1937, *apptd* 1990
Rt. Hon. Lord MacFadyen (Donald MacFadyen), *born* 1945, *apptd* 1995

OUTER HOUSE
Lords of Session (each £150,878)

Hon. Lord Abernethy (Alistair Cameron), *born* 1938, *apptd* 1992
Hon. Lord Johnston (Alan Johnston), *born* 1942, *apptd* 1994
Hon. Lord Dawson (Thomas Dawson), *born* 1948, *apptd* 1995
Hon. Lord Nimmo Smith (William Nimmo Smith), *born* 1942, *apptd* 1996
Hon. Lord Philip (Alexander Philip), *born* 1942, *apptd* 1996
Hon. Lord Kingarth (Derek Emslie), *born* 1949, *apptd* 1997
Hon. Lord Eassie (Ronald Mackay), *born* 1945, *apptd* 1997
Hon. Lord Reed (Robert Reed), *born* 1956, *apptd* 1998
Hon. Lord Wheatley (John Wheatley), *born* 1941, *apptd* 2000
Hon. Lady Paton (Ann Paton), *born* 1952, *apptd* 2000
Hon. Lord Carloway (Colin Sutherland), *born* 1954, *apptd* 2000
Hon. Lord Clarke (Matthew Clarke), *born* 1947, *apptd* 2000
Rt. Hon. The Lord Hardie (Andrew Hardie), *born* 1946, *apptd* 2000
Rt. Hon. The Lord Mackay of Drumadoon (Donald Mackay), *born* 1946, *apptd* 2000
Hon. Lord McEwan (Robin McEwan), *born* 1943, *apptd* 2000
Hon. Lord Menzies (Duncan Menzies), *born* 1953, *apptd* 2001
Hon. Lord Drummond Young (James Drummond Young), *born* 1950, *apptd* 2001
Hon. Lord Emslie (Nigel Emslie), *born* 1947, *apptd* 2001
Hon. Lady Smith (Anne Smith), *born* 1955, *apptd* 2001
Hon. Lord Brodie (Philip Brodie), *born* 1950, *apptd* 2002
Hon. Lord Bracadale (Alastair Campbell), *born* 1949, *apptd* 2003

COURT OF SESSION AND HIGH COURT OF JUSTICIARY
Parliament House, Parliament Square, Edinburgh EH1 1HQ
T 0131-225 2595

Principal Clerk of Session and Justiciary, J. L. Anderson
Deputy Principal Clerk of Justiciary, N. Dowie
Deputy Principal Clerk of Session and Principal Extractor, R. Cockburn
Deputy in Charge of Offices of Court, Y. Anderson
Deputy Principal Clerk (Keeper of the Rolls), A. Moffat
Deputy Clerks of Session and Justiciary, N. Dowie; I. Smith; Q. Oliver; W. Dunn; A. Finlayson; J. McLean; M. Weir; R. Sinclair; I. Martin; N. McGinley; J. Lynn; E. Dickson; Mr G. Combe; R. MacPherson; D. Bruton;

D. MacLeod; A. McKay; L. Maclachlan; A. Thompson; J. Moyes; J. O'Donnell; L. McFarlane; C. Reid; Mr T. Cruickshank

SCOTTISH EXECUTIVE JUSTICE DEPARTMENT
Hayweight House, 23 Lauriston Street, Edinburgh EH3 9DQ
T 0131-229 9200

The Judicial Appointments and Finance Division is responsible for the provision of sufficient Judges and Sheriffs to meet the needs of the business of the supreme and Sheriffs Court in Scotland. It is also responsible for providing the Secretariat for the independent Judicial Appointments Board for Scotland as well as providing resources for the efficient administration of a number of specialist courts and tribunals.
Head of Judicial Appointments and Finance Division, D. Stewart

SCOTTISH COURT SERVICE
Hayweight House, 23 Lauriston Street, Edinburgh EH3 9DQ
T 0131-229 9200

The Scottish Court Service is an executive agency within the Scottish Executive Justice Department. It is responsible to the Scottish Ministers for the provision of staff, court houses and associated services for the Supreme and Sheriff Courts.
Chief Executive, J. Ewing

SHERIFF COURT OF CHANCERY
27 Chambers Street, Edinburgh EH1 1LB
T 0131-225 2525

The Court deals with service of heirs and completion of title in relation to heritable property.
Sheriff of Chancery, I. D. Macphail, QC

HM COMMISSARY OFFICE
27 Chambers Street, Edinburgh EH1 1LB
T 0131-225 2525

The Office is responsible for issuing confirmation, a legal document entitling a person to execute a deceased person's will, and other related matters.
Commissary Clerk, David Shand

SCOTTISH LAND COURT
1 Grosvenor Crescent, Edinburgh EH12 5ER
T 0131-225 3595

The court deals with disputes relating to agricultural and crofting land in Scotland.
Chairman (£122,139), The Hon. Lord McGhie (James McGhie), QC
Members, D. J. Houston; A. Macdonald *(part-time)*; J. Kinloch *(part-time)*
Principal Clerk, K. H. R. Graham, WS

SHERIFFDOMS
SALARIES

Sheriff Principal	£122,139
Sheriff	£113,121
*Floating Sheriff	

GLASGOW AND STRATHKELVIN

Sheriff Principal, E. F. Bowen, QC
Area Director West, I. Scott

SHERIFFS AND SHERIFF CLERKS
Glasgow, B. Kearney; B. A. Lockhart; Mrs A. L. A. Duncan; A. C. Henry; J. K. Mitchell; A. G. Johnston; Miss S. A. O. Raeburn, QC; D. Convery; I. A. S. Peebles, QC; C. W. McFarlane, QC; H. Matthews, QC; J. A. Baird; *Mrs P. M. M. Bowman; Miss R. E. A. Rae, QC; A. W. Noble; J. D. Friel; Mrs D. M. MacNeill, QC; J. A. Taylor; C. A. L. Scott; S. Cathcart; *Ms L. M. Ruxton; I. H. L. Miller; Mrs F. L. Reith, QC; W. J. Totten; *M. G. O' Grady, QC; A. C. Normand; W. H. Holligan
Sheriff Clerk, C. Binning

GRAMPIAN, HIGHLANDS AND ISLANDS

Sheriff Principal, Sir Stephen S. T. Young, Bt., QC
Area Director North, J. Robertson

SHERIFFS AND SHERIFF CLERKS
Aberdeen and Stonehaven, A. S. Jessop; Mrs A. M. Cowan; C. J. Harris, QC; G. K. Buchanan; J. K. Tierney; K. A. Mchernan; D. J. Cusine; *P. P. Davies; *K. M. Stewart; *Sheriff Clerks*, Mrs E. Laing *(Aberdeen)*; A. Hempseed *(Stonehaven)*
Elgin, I. A. Cameron; *Sheriff Clerk*, M. McBey
Fort William, W. D. Small *(also Oban)*; *Sheriff Clerk Depute*, S. McKenna
Inverness, Portree, Stornoway, Dingwall, Tain, Wick and Dornoch, D. Booker-Milburn; A. Pollock; D. O. Sutherland; A. L. MacFadyen; *Sheriff Clerks*, A. Bayliss *(Inverness)*; M. McBey *(Dingwall)*; *Sheriff Clerks Depute*, Miss M. Campbell *(Lochmaddy and Portree)*; Miss A. B. Armstrong *(Stornoway)*; L. MacLachlan *(Tain)*; Mrs J. McEwan *(Wick)*; K. Kerr *(Dornoch)*
Kirkwall and Lerwick, G. Napier; *Sheriff Clerks Depute*, A. Moore *(Kirkwall)*; M. Flanagan *(Lerwick)*
Peterhead, *M. Garden; *Sheriff Clerk*, *(Peterhead)*; *Sheriff Clerk Depute*, Mrs F. L. MacPherson *(Banff)*
Lochmaddy/Banff, *P. P. Davies; A. L. MacFadyen

LOTHIAN AND BORDERS

Sheriff Principal, I. D. Macphail, QC
Area Director East, M. Bonar

SHERIFFS AND SHERIFF CLERKS
Edinburgh, R. G. Craik, QC *(also Peebles)*; Miss I. A. Poole; A. M. Bell; J. M. S. Horsburgh, QC; G. W. S. Presslie *(also Haddington)*; J. A. Farrell; A. Lothian; C. N. Stoddart; M. McPartlin; J. D. Allan; K. M. MacIver; N. M. P. Morrison, QC; G. W. M. Liddle; Miss M. M. Stephen; Mrs M. L. E. Jarvie, QC; *Mrs K. E. C. Mackie; *N. J. MacKinnon; *J. P. Scott; *D. W. M. McIntyre; *J. C. C. McSherry; *Sheriff Clerk*, J. Ross
Linlithgow, G. R. Fleming; P. Gillam; W. D. Muirhead; *M. G. R. Edington; *Sheriff Clerk*, R. D. Sinclair
Haddington, G. W. S. Presslie *(also Edinburgh)*; *Sheriff Clerk*, J. O'Donnell
Jedburgh and Duns, T. A. K. Drummond, QC; *Sheriff Clerk*, I. W. Williamson
Peebles, R. G. Craik, QC *(also Edinburgh)*; *Sheriff Clerk Depute*, M. L. Kubeczka
Selkirk, T. A. K. Drummond, QC; *Sheriff Clerk Depute*, L. McFarlane

NORTH STRATHCLYDE

Sheriff Principal, B. A. Kerr, QC
Area Director West, I. Scott

SHERIFFS AND SHERIFF CLERKS
Campbeltown, *W. Dunlop *(also Paisley)*; *Sheriff Clerk Depute*, Miss E. Napier
Dumbarton, J. T. Fitzsimons; T. Scott; S. W. H. Fraser; *Sheriff Clerk*, S. Bain
Dunoon, Mrs C. M. A. F. Gimblett; *Sheriff Clerk Depute*, J. McGraw
Greenock, J. Herald *(also Rothesay)*; V. J. Canavan; *Mrs R. Swanney; *Sheriff Clerk*, J. Tannahill
Kilmarnock, T. M. Croan; C. G. McKay; Mrs I. S. McDonald; *Sheriff Clerk*, G. Waddell
Oban, W. D. Small *(also Fort William)*; *Sheriff Clerk Depute*, D. Irwin
Paisley, J. Spy; N. Douglas; D. J. Pender; *W. Dunlop; *(also Campbeltown)* G. C. Kavanagh; Ms S. M. Sinclair; *C. W. Pettigrew; *Ms S. A. Waldron; *A. M. Cubie; *Sheriff Clerk*, Miss S. Hindes
Rothesay, J. Herald *(also Greenock)*; *Sheriff Clerk Depute*, Mrs C. K. McCormick

SOUTH STRATHCLYDE, DUMFRIES AND GALLOWAY

Sheriff Principal, J. C. McInnes, QC
Area Director West, I. Scott

SHERIFFS AND SHERIFF CLERKS
Airdrie, R. H. Dickson; J. C. Morris, QC; A. D. Vannet; Mrs M. M. Galbraith *(also Lanark)* *Sheriff Clerk*, D. Forrester
Ayr, N. Gow, QC; C. B. Miller; J. McGowan; *Sheriff Clerk*, Miss C. D. Cockburn
Dumfries, K. G. Barr; K. A. Ross; *Sheriff Clerk*, P. McGonigle
Hamilton, W. E. Gibson; J. H. Stewart; Miss J. Powrie; H. S. Neilson; T. Welsh, QC; D. M. Bicket; Mrs M. Smart; H. K. Small; *J. Montgomery; *Ms C. A. Kelly; *W. S. S. Ireland; *Sheriff Clerk*, P. Feeney
Lanark, Ms N. C. Stewart; Mrs M. M. Galbraith *(also Airdrie)*; *Sheriff Clerk*, Mrs M. McLean
Stranraer and Kirkcudbright, J. R. Smith; *Sheriff Clerks*, W. McIntosh *(Stranraer)*; B. Lindsay *(Kirkcudbright)*

TAYSIDE, CENTRAL AND FIFE

Sheriff Principal, R. A. Dunlop, QC
Area Director East, M. Bonar

SHERIFFS AND SHERIFF CLERKS
Alloa, W. M. Reid; *Sheriff Clerk*, R. G. McKeand
Arbroath, C. N. R. Stein; *Sheriff Clerks*, M. Herbertson *(Arbroath)*; S. Munro *(Forfar)*
Cupar, G. J. Evans; *Sheriff Clerk*, A. Nicol
Dundee, R. A. Davidson; I. D. Dunbar; F. R. Crowe; A. J. M. Duff; A. G. McCulloch; *L. Wood; *Sheriff Clerk*, D. Nicoll
Dunfermline, I. C. Simpson; Mrs I. G. McColl; *D. M. Mackie; *Sheriff Clerk*, W. McCulloch
Falkirk, A. V. Sheehan; A. J. Murphy; *C. Caldwell; *Sheriff Clerk*, R. McMillan
Forfar, K. A. Veal
Kirkcaldy, B. G. Donald; R. J. MacLeod; *Sheriff Clerk*, W. Jones
Perth, M. J. Fletcher; L. D. R. Foulis; R. A. McCreadie, QC; *D. C. W. Pyle; *Sheriff Clerk*, J. Murphy
Stirling, The Hon. R. E. G. Younger; A. W. Robertson

STIPENDIARY MAGISTRATES

GLASGOW
R. Hamilton, *apptd* 1984; J. B. C. Nisbet, *apptd* 1984; R. B. Christie, *apptd* 1985; Mrs J. A. M. MacLean, *apptd* 1990

CROWN OFFICE AND PROCURATOR FISCAL SERVICE

CROWN OFFICE
25 Chambers Street, Edinburgh EH1 1LA
T 0131-226 2626 W www.crownoffice.gov.uk

Crown Agent (£104,581), N. McFadyen
Deputy Crown Agent (£86,364), W. A. Gilchrist

PROCURATORS FISCAL

SALARIES
Area Fiscals   £53,451–£192,424
District Procurator Fiscal   £38,500–£56,600

GRAMPIAN AREA
Area Procurator Fiscal, J. Watt *(Aberdeen)*
Procurators Fiscal, Miss C. Frame; A. B. Hutchinson; S. Ralph

HIGHLAND AND ISLANDS AREA
Area Procurator Fiscal, A. Laing *(Inverness)*
Procurators Fiscal, R. W. Urquhart; Ms A. Wyllie; Ms S. Foard; D. S. Teale; G. Aitken; A. MacDonald

LANARKSHIRE AREA
Area Procurator Fiscal, J. Brisbane *(Hamilton)*
Procurators Fiscal, D. Spiers; Mrs A. C. Donaldson; S. Houston

CENTRAL AREA
Area Procurator Fiscal, Mrs G. M. Watt *(Stirling)*
Procurators Fiscal, R. McQuaid; M. Bell

TAYSIDE AREA
Area Procurator Fiscal, D. Howdle *(Dundee)*
Procurators Fiscal, J. I. Craigen; D. Griffiths; B. Bott

FIFE AREA
Area Procurator Fiscal, C. Ritchie *(Kirkcaldy)*
Procurators Fiscal, E. B. Russell; J. Robertson

LOTHIAN AND BORDERS AREA
Area Procurator Fiscal, D. Brown *(Edinburgh)*
Procurators Fiscal, A. R. G. Fraser; A. J. P. Reith; R. Stott; W. Gallacher; M. Paterson

AYRSHIRE AREA
Area Procurator Fiscal, Mrs J. E. Cameron *(Kilmarnock)*
Procurators Fiscal, I. L. Murray

ARGYLL AREA
Area Procurator Fiscal, J. Miller *(Paisley)*
Procurators Fiscal, D. L. Webster; W. S. Carnegie; B. R. Maguire; G. F. Williams; M. Ramage

DUMFRIES AND GALLOWAY
Area Procurator Fiscal, T. Dysart *(Dumfries)*
Procurators Fiscal, J. Service; N. Patrick

GLASGOW AREA
Area Procurator Fiscal, C. Dyer *(Glasgow)*

NORTHERN IRELAND JUDICATURE

In Northern Ireland the legal system and the structure of courts closely resemble those of England and Wales; there are, however, often differences in enacted law.

The Supreme Court of Judicature of Northern Ireland comprises the Court of Appeal, the High Court of Justice and the Crown Court. The practice and procedure of these courts is similar to that in England. The superior civil court is the High Court of Justice, from which an appeal lies to the Northern Ireland Court of Appeal; the House of Lords is the final civil appeal court.

The Crown Court, served by High Court and county court judges, deals with criminal trials on indictment. Cases are heard before a judge and, except those involving offences specified under emergency legislation, a jury. Appeals from the Crown Court against conviction or sentence are heard by the Northern Ireland Court of Appeal; the House of Lords is the final court of appeal.

The decision to prosecute in cases tried on indictment and in summary cases of a serious nature rests in Northern Ireland with the Director of Public Prosecutions, who is responsible to the Attorney-General. Minor summary offences are prosecuted by the police.

Minor criminal offences are dealt with in magistrates' courts by a legally qualified resident magistrate and, where an offender is under 17, by juvenile courts each consisting of a resident magistrate and two lay members specially qualified to deal with juveniles (at least one of whom must be a woman). On 19 August 2002 there were 878 justices of the peace in Northern Ireland. Appeals from magistrates' courts are heard by the county court, or by the Court of Appeal on a point of law or an issue as to jurisdiction.

Magistrates' courts in Northern Ireland can deal with certain classes of civil case but most minor civil cases are dealt with in county courts. Judgments of all civil courts are enforceable through a centralised procedure administered by the Enforcement of Judgments Office.

SUPREME COURT OF JUDICATURE

The Royal Courts of Justice, Belfast BT1 3JF
T 028-9023 5111
Lord Chief Justice of Northern Ireland (£185,705), The Rt.
  Hon. Sir Brian Kerr, *born* 1948, *apptd* 2004
Principal Secretary, S. T. A. Rogers

LORDS JUSTICES OF APPEAL (each £170,554)
Style, The Rt. Hon. Lord Justice [surname]

Rt. Hon. Sir Michael Nicholson, *born* 1933, *apptd* 1995
Rt. Hon. Sir William McCollum, *born* 1933, *apptd* 1997
Rt. Hon. Sir Anthony Campbell, *born* 1936, *apptd* 1998

PUISNE JUDGES (each £150,878)
Style, The Hon. Mr Justice [surname]

Hon. Sir John Sheil, *born* 1938, *apptd* 1989
Hon. Sir Brian Kerr, *born* 1948, *apptd* 1993
Hon. Sir Malachy Higgins, *born* 1944, *apptd* 1993

Hon. Sir Paul Girvan, *born* 1948, *apptd* 1995
Hon. Sir Patrick Coghlin, *born* 1945, *apptd* 1997
Hon. Sir John Gillen, *born* 1947, *apptd* 1998
Hon. Sir Richard McLaughlin, *born* 1947, *apptd* 1999
Hon. Sir Ronald Weatherup, *born* 1947, *apptd* June 2001
Hon. Sir Reginald Weir, *born* 1947, *apptd* 2003
Hon. Sir Declan Morgan, *born* 1952, *apptd* 2004

MASTERS OF THE SUPREME COURT (each £90,760)
Master, Queen's Bench and Appeals and Clerk of the Crown,
  J. W. Wilson, QC
Master, High Court, C. J. McCorry
Master, Office of Care and Protection, F. B. Hall
Master, Chancery Office, R. A. Ellison
Master, Bankruptcy and Companies Office, C. W. G.
  Redpath
Master, Probate and Matrimonial Office, Miss M.
  McReynolds
Master, Taxing Office, J. C. Napier

OFFICIAL SOLICITOR
Official Solicitor to the Supreme Court of Northern Ireland,
  Miss B. M. Donnelly

COUNTY COURTS

JUDGES (each £113,121)
Style, His/Her Hon. Judge [surname]

Judge Burgess, Judge Curran, QC; Judge Finnegan; Judge Gibson, QC; Judge Kennedy; Judge Lockie; Judge McFarland; Judge McKay, QC; Judge Markey, QC; Judge Marriman, QC; Judge Martin *(Chief Social Security and Child Support Commissioner)*; Judge Rodgers; Judge Smyth, QC

RECORDERS
Belfast (£131,910), Judge Hart, QC
Londonderry, Her Hon. Judge Philpott, QC

MAGISTRATES' COURTS

RESIDENT MAGISTRATES (each £90,760)
There are 19 resident magistrates in Northern Ireland.

CROWN SOLICITORS' OFFICE
PO Box 410, Royal Courts of Justice, Belfast BT1 3JY
T 028-9054 2555
Crown Solicitor, O. G. Paulin

DEPARTMENT OF THE DIRECTOR OF PUBLIC PROSECUTIONS
93 Chichester Street, Belfast BT1 3TR
T 028-9054 2444
Director of Public Prosecutions, Sir Alasdair Fraser, CB, QC
Deputy Director of Public Prosecutions, W. R. Junkin

NORTHERN IRELAND COURT SERVICE
Windsor House, Bedford Street, Belfast BT2 7LT
T 028-9032 8594
Director, D. A. Lavery

LORD CHANCELLORS SINCE 1900

Year appointed	Name
1895	Lord Halsbury
1905	Lord Loreburn
1912	Lord Haldane
1915	Lord Buckmaster
1916	Lord Finlay
1919	Lord Birkenhead
1922	Viscount Cave
1924 *Jan.*	Viscount Haldane
1924 *Nov.*	Viscount Cave
1928	Lord Hailsham
1929	Lord Sankey
1935	Viscount Hailsham
1938	Lord Maugham
1939	Viscount Caldecote
1940	Viscount Simon
1945	Lord Jowitt
1951	Lord Simonds
1954	Viscount Kilmuir
1962	Lord Dilhorne
1964	Lord Gardiner
1970	Lord Hailsham of St Marylebone
1974	Lord Elwyn-Jones
1979	Lord Hailsham of St Marylebone
1987 *June*	Lord Havers
1987 *Oct.*	Lord Mackay of Clashfern
1997	Lord Irvine of Lairg
2003	Lord Falconer of Thoroton

TRIBUNALS

AGRICULTURAL LAND TRIBUNALS

c/o DEFRA, Ergon House, Horseferry Road, London SW1P 2AL
T 020-7238 6523 F 020-7238 6553

Agricultural Land Tribunals settle disputes and other issues between agricultural landlords and tenants, and drainage disputes between neighbours.

There are seven tribunals covering England and one covering Wales. For each tribunal the Lord Chancellor* appoints a chairman and one or more deputies (barristers or solicitors of at least seven years standing). The Lord Chancellor also appoints lay members to three statutory panels: the 'landowners' panel, the 'farmers' panel and the 'drainage' panel.

Each tribunal is an independent statutory body with jurisdiction only within its own area. A separate tribunal is constituted for each case, and consists of a chairman and two lay members nominated by the chairman.
Chairmen (England), G. L. Newsom; W. D. M. Wood;
   P. A. de la Piquerie; N. Thomas; His Hon. Judge Robert
   Taylor; J. H. Weatherill; His Hon. Judge Machin, QC
Deputy Chairmen, Ms A. M. Seifert; T. D. Bowles;
   J. E. Mitting; P. Bleasdale; W. M. Kingston;
   M. E. Heywood; Mrs S. Evans; His Hon. Judge
   W. H. R. Crawford; M. O. Rodger; P. Morgan, QC;
   A. R. Gore; J. G. Orme, TD
Chairman (Wales), W. J. Owen
Deputy Chairman (Wales), B. L. Y. Richards

APPEALS SERVICE

14 Grays Inn Road, Fox Court, London WC1X 8HN
T 020-7712 2600
W www.appeals-service.gov.uk

The Appeals Service arranges and hears appeals on decisions concerned with social security, child support, housing benefit, council tax benefit, vaccine damage, tax credits and compensation recovery.

Judicial authority for the Service rests with the president, while administrative responsibility is exercised by the Appeals Service Agency, which is an executive agency of the Department for Work and Pensions.
President, His Hon. Judge Michael Harris
Chief Executive, Appeals Service Agency, Christina Townsend

CARE STANDARDS TRIBUNAL

18 Pocock Street, London SE1 0BW
T 020-7960 0660 F 020-7960 0661/0662
E cst@cst.gsi.gov.uk W www.carestandardstribunal.gov.uk

The Tribunal considers appeals in relation to decisions made about the inclusion of individuals' names on the list of those considered unsuitable to work with children, restrictions from teaching, and general registration decisions made about care homes, children's homes, nurses agencies, residential family centres and fostering agencies. The Tribunal's President appoints the panels for each case and each appeal is heard by a legally qualified chairman and two lay members with expertise in the field.
President, Judge David Pearl
Secretary to the Tribunal, Barbara Erne

COMMONS COMMISSIONERS

Room Zone 1/05b, Temple Quay House, 2 The Square, Temple Quay, Bristol BS1 6EB
T 0117-372 8973 F 0117-372 8250

The Commons Commissioners are responsible for deciding disputes arising under the Commons Registration Act 1965. They also enquire into the ownership of unclaimed common land and village greens. Commissioners are appointed by the Lord Chancellor*.
Chief Commons Commissioner (part-time), E. F. Cousins
Clerk, N. Wilson

COMPETITION APPEAL TRIBUNAL

Victoria House, Bloomsbury Place, London WC1A 2EB
T 020-7979 7979 F 020-7979 7978
E info@catribunal.org.uk
W www.catribunal.org.uk

The Competition Appeal Tribunal (CAT) is a specialist tribunal established to hear certain cases in the sphere of UK competition and economic regulatory law. The CAT hears appeals against decisions of the Office of Fair Trading and the regulators in the electricity, gas, water, railways and air traffic services sectors under the Competition Act 1998, and the Competition Commission under the merger control and market investigation provisions of the Enterprise Act 2002. The CAT also has jurisdiction under the Competition Act 1998 to award damages in respect of infringements of EC or UK competition law and to hear appeals against decisions of OFCOM under the Communications Act 2003. The CAT is headed by the President and has a panel of 19 members with backgrounds in law, economics, business, accountancy and regulation.
President, Sir Christopher Bellamy
Chairman, Marion Simmons, QC
Registrar, Charles Dhanowa
Members, Prof. A. Bain, OBE; M. Blair, QC; P. Clayton;
   B. Colgate; M. Davey; P. Grant-Hutchison; Prof.
   P. Grinyer; Ms S. Hewitt; Ms A. Kelly; Hon. A. Lewis;
   G. Mather; Prof. J. Pickering; R. Prosser, OBE;
   Dr A. Pryor, CB; Ms P. Quigley, WS; A. Scott, TD;
   Ms V. Smith-Hillman; Prof. P. Stoneman; D. Summers

COPYRIGHT TRIBUNAL

Harmsworth House, 13–15 Bouverie Street, London EC4Y 8DP
T 020-7596 6510 Minicom: 0845-922 2250 F 020-7596 6526
E copyright.tribunal@patent.gov.uk
W www.patent.gov.uk/copy/tribunal/index.htm

The Copyright Tribunal resolves disputes over copyright licences, principally where there is collective licensing.

The chairman and two deputy chairmen are appointed by the Lord Chancellor*. Up to eight ordinary members are appointed by the Secretary of State for Trade and Industry.
Chairman, C. P. Tootal
Secretary, Miss J. E. M. Durdin

EMPLOYMENT TRIBUNALS (ENGLAND AND WALES)
Ground Floor, 19–29 Woburn Place, London WC1H 0LU
T 020-7273 8603 Enquiry line 0845-795 9775
F 020-7273 8686
W www.employmenttribunals.gov.uk

Employment Tribunals for England and Wales sit in 12 regions. The tribunals deal with matters of employment law, redundancy, dismissal, contract disputes, sexual, racial and disability discrimination and related areas of dispute which may arise in the workplace. A public register of applications and decisions is held at Southgate Street, Bury St Edmunds, Suffolk IP33 2AQ. The tribunals are funded by the Department of Trade and Industry; administrative support is provided by the Employment Tribunals Service.
Chairmen, who may be full-time or part-time, are legally qualified. They are appointed by the Lord Chancellor*. Tribunal members are appointed by the Secretary of State for Trade and Industry.
President, G. Meeran

CENTRAL OFFICE OF THE EMPLOYMENT TRIBUNALS (SCOTLAND)
Eagle Building, 215 Bothwell Street, Glasgow G2 7TS
T 0141-204 0730 F 0141-204 0732

Tribunals in Scotland have the same remit as those in England and Wales. Chairmen are appointed by the Lord President of the Court of Session and lay members by the Secretary of State for Trade and Industry.
President, C. M. Milne
Regional Chairman, Shona Simon

EMPLOYMENT APPEAL TRIBUNAL
Central Office: Audit House, 58 Victoria Embankment, London EC4Y 0DS
T 020-7273 1040 F 020-7273 1045
Divisional Office: 52 Melville Street, Edinburgh EH3 7HS
T 0131-225 3963 F 0131-220 6694
W www.employmentappeals.gov.uk

The Employment Appeal Tribunal hears appeals on a question of law arising from any decision of an employment tribunal. A tribunal consists of a judge and two lay members. They are appointed by The Queen on the recommendation of the Lord Chancellor* and the Secretary of State for Trade and Industry. Administrative support is provided by the Employment Tribunals Service.
President, The Hon. Mr Justice Burton
Scottish Chairman, The Hon. Lord Johnson
Registrar, P. Donleavy

GENERAL COMMISSIONERS OF INCOME TAX
Department for Constitutional Affairs, Selborne House, 54–60 Victoria Street, London SW1E 6QW
T 020-7210 8990 F 020-7210 0660

General Commissioners of Income Tax operate under the Taxes Management Act 1970. They are unpaid judicial officers who sit in some 407 Divisions throughout the United Kingdom to hear appeals against decisions by the Inland Revenue on a variety of taxation matters. The Commissioners' jurisdiction was extended in 1999 to hear National Insurance appeals. The Lord Chancellor* appoints General Commissioners (except in Scotland, where they are appointed by the Scottish Executive).

There are approximately 2,300 General Commissioners appointed throughout the United Kingdom. In each Division, Commissioners appoint a Clerk, who is normally legally qualified, who makes the administrative arrangements for appeal hearings and advises the Commissioners on points of law and procedure. The Department for Constitutional Affairs pays the Clerks' remuneration. Appeals from the General Commissioners are by way of case stated, on a point of law, to the High Court (the Court of Session in Scotland or the Court of Appeal in Northern Ireland). In 2003, approximately 29,500 cases were listed before the General Commissioners.

IMMIGRATION APPELLATE AUTHORITY
Arnhem Support Centre, PO Box 6987, Leicester LE1 6ZX
T 0845-6000 877 W www.iaa.gov.uk

The Immigration Appellate Authority (IAA) is a tribunal which hears appeals against decisions made by the Home Secretary (and his officials) and its powers are derived from the Immigration and Asylum Act 1999. Immigration Adjudicators hear appeals from immigration decisions concerning the need for, and the refusal of, leave to enter or remain in the UK, refusals to grant asylum, decisions to make deportation orders and directions to remove persons subject to immigration control from the UK. An appeal against a decision by the Home Secretary will normally go to the first tier (the Immigration Adjudicators) where the person making the appeal, his/her representative and a representative from the Home Office will usually attend a hearing before an Immigration Adjudicator, who will determine whether or not to uphold the original Home Office decision.
The Immigration Appeal Tribunal provides a second appellate level for those dissatisfied with an Adjudicator's decision. Leave to appeal needs to be obtained. An appeal will usually require a hearing at which all sides attend before a panel of three people. The panel is normally comprised of a legally qualified chairman and two lay members, who decide whether to uphold or overturn the Adjudicator's determination. From the Tribunal there is an appeal to the Court of Appeal on a point of law only.

IMMIGRATION APPEAL TRIBUNAL
Field House, 15 Breams Buildings, Chancery Lane, London EC4A 1DZ T 020-7073 4200

The Immigration Appeal Tribunal comprises 26 full-time vice-presidents, 50 part-time legally qualified chairpersons and 60 lay members.
President, The Hon. Mr Justice Ouseley
Deputy President, C. M. G. Ockelton

IMMIGRATION APPEAL ADJUDICATORS
Chief Adjudicator, His Hon. Judge H. Hodge, OBE
Deputy Chief Adjudicator, E. Arfon-Jones

IMMIGRATION SERVICES TRIBUNAL
Procession House, 55 Ludgate Hill, London EC4M 7JW
T 020-7029 9780 F 020-7029 9782
E imset@dca.gsi.gov.uk
W www.immigrationservicestribunal.gov.uk

The Immigration Services Tribunal is an independent judicial body set up to provide a forum in which appeals against decisions of the Immigration Services Commissioner and complaints made by the Immigration

Services Commissioner can be heard and determined. The cases exclusively concern people providing advice and representation services in connection with immigration matters.

The Tribunal forms part of the Court Service. It is the responsibility of the Lord Chancellor*. There is a president, who is the judicial head; other judicial members, who must be legally qualified; lay members who must have substantial experience in immigration services or in the law and procedure relating to immigration; and a secretary who is responsible for administration. The tribunal can sit anywhere in the UK.

President, Hon. Judge Seddon Cripps

Judicial Members, D. Bean, QC; G. Marriott; Judge Burgess; B. Kennedy, QC; D. W. Hunter, QC

Members, P. Barnett; O. Conway; M. Hoare; S. Maguire; A. Montgomery; I. Newton; M. Quayum; S. Rowlands

Tribunal Manager, G. Evans

INDUSTRIAL TRIBUNALS AND THE FAIR EMPLOYMENT TRIBUNAL (NORTHERN IRELAND)

Long Bridge House, 20–24 Waring Street, Belfast BT1 2EB
T 028-9032 7666 F 028-9023 0184
W www.industrialfairemploymenttribunalsni.gov.uk

The industrial tribunal system in Northern Ireland was set up in 1965 and has a similar remit to the employment tribunals in the rest of the UK. There is also a Fair Employment Tribunal, which hears and determines individual cases of alleged religious or political discrimination in employment. Employers can appeal to the Fair Employment Tribunal if they consider the directions of the Equality Commission to be unreasonable, inappropriate or unnecessary, and the Equality Commission can make application to the Tribunal for the enforcement of undertakings or directions with which an employer has not complied.

The president, vice-president and part-time chairmen of the Fair Employment Tribunal are appointed by the Lord Chancellor*. The full-time chairman and the part-time chairmen of the industrial tribunals and the panel members to both the industrial tribunals and the Fair Employment Tribunal are appointed by the Department for Employment and Learning.

President of the Industrial Tribunals and the Fair Employment Tribunal, J. Maguire, CBE

Vice-President of the Industrial Tribunals and the Fair Employment Tribunal, Mrs M. P. Price

Secretary, Miss A. Loney

INFORMATION TRIBUNAL

Room 4.01, MWB Business Exchange, 10 Greycoat Place, London SW1P 1SB
T 020-7654 3465 F 020-7654 3583

The Information Tribunal determines appeals against notices issued by the Information Commissioner. The chairman and deputy chairman are appointed by the Lord Chancellor* and must be legally qualified. Lay members are appointed by the Lord Chancellor to represent the interests of data users or data subjects. A tribunal consists of a chairman sitting with equal numbers of the lay members. There is a separate panel of the tribunal which hears national security appeals; the president of this panel is the Rt. Hon. Sir Anthony Evans, RD.

Chairman, David Marks

Secretary, Charlotte Mercer

LANDS TRIBUNAL

Procession House, 55 Ludgate Hill, London EC4M 7JW
T 020-7029 9780 F 020-7029 9781
E lands@dca.gsi.gov.uk W www.landstribunal.gov.uk

The Lands Tribunal is an independent judicial body which determines questions relating to the valuation of land, rating appeals from valuation tribunals, appeals from leasehold valuation tribunals, the discharge or modification of restrictive covenants, and compulsory purchase compensation. The tribunal may also arbitrate under references by consent. The president and members are appointed by the Lord Chancellor*. Cases are usually heard by a single member but they may sometimes be heard by two members.

President, G. R. Bartlett, QC

Members, P. H. Clarke, FRICS; N. J. Rose, FRICS; P. R. Francis, FRICS

Member (part-time), His Hon. Judge Rich, QC

Tribunal Section Manager, J. Clottey

LANDS TRIBUNAL FOR SCOTLAND

1 Grosvenor Crescent, Edinburgh EH12 5ER
T 0131-225 7996 F 0131-226 4812
W www.lands-tribunal-scotland.org.uk

The Lands Tribunal for Scotland has the same remit as the tribunal for England and Wales but also covers questions relating to tenants' rights to buy their homes under the Housing (Scotland) Act 1987. The president is appointed by the Lord President of the Court of Session.

President, The Hon. Lord McGhie, QC

Members, A. R. MacLeary, FRICS

Members (part-time), J. N. Wright, QC, I. M. Darling, FRICS

Clerk, N. M. Tainsh

MENTAL HEALTH REVIEW TRIBUNALS

Secretariat: Health Service Directorate, Room LG02 Wellington House, 133–155 Waterloo Road, London SE1 8UG
T 020-7972 4577 F 020-7972 4884

The Mental Health Review Tribunals are independent judicial bodies which review the cases of patients compulsorily detained under the provisions of the Mental Health Act 1983. They have the power to discharge the patient, to recommend leave of absence, delayed discharge, transfer to another hospital or that a guardianship order be made, to reclassify both restricted and unrestricted patients, and to recommend consideration of a supervision application. There are four tribunals in England, each headed by a regional chairman who is appointed by the Lord Chancellor* on a part-time basis. Each tribunal is made up of at least three members, and must include a lawyer, who acts as president, a medical member and a lay member.

There are five regional offices:

LIVERPOOL, 3rd Floor, Cressington House, 249 St Mary's Road, Garston, Liverpool L19 0NF T 0151-728 5400

LONDON (NORTH), Spur 3, Block 1, Government Buildings, Honeypot Lane, Stanmore, Middx HA7 1AY
T 020-7972 1000

LONDON (SOUTH), Block 3, Crown Offices, Kingston Bypass Road, Surbiton, Surrey KT6 5QN T 020-8268 4549

NOTTINGHAM, Spur A, Block 5, Government Buildings, Chalfont Drive, Western Boulevard, Nottingham NG8 3RZ
T 0115-942 8308

WALES, 4th Floor, Crown Buildings, Cathays Park, Cardiff CF1 3NQ T 029-2082 5328

NATIONAL HEALTH SERVICE TRIBUNAL (SCOTLAND)
40 Craiglockhart Road North, Edinburgh EH14 1BT
T/F 0131-443 2575

The Scottish National Health Service Tribunal considers representations that the continued inclusion of a doctor, dentist, optometrist or pharmacist on a health board's list would be prejudicial to the efficiency of the service concerned. The tribunal sits when required and is composed of a chairman, one lay member, and one practitioner member drawn from a representative professional panel. The chairman is appointed by the Lord President of the Court of Session, and the lay member and the members of the professional panel are appointed by the Scottish Ministers.
Chairman, M. G. Thomson, QC
Lay member, J. D. M. Robertson, CBE
Clerk to the Tribunal, W. Bryden

PENSIONS APPEAL TRIBUNAL
Central Office (England and Wales), 55 Ludgate Hill, London EC4M 7JW
T 020-7029 9800 F 020-7029 9801
W www.pensionsappealtribunal.gov.uk

The Pensions Appeal Tribunals are responsible for hearing appeals from ex-servicemen or women and widows who have had their claims for a war pension rejected by the Secretary of State for Work and Pensions. The Entitlement Appeal Tribunals hear appeals in cases where the Secretary of State has refused to grant a war pension. The Assessment Appeal Tribunals hear appeals against the Secretary of State's assessment of the degree of disablement caused by an accepted condition. The tribunal members are appointed by the Secretary of State for Constitutional Affairs.
President, Dr H. M. G. Concannon
Tribunal Manager, Ms J. White

PENSIONS APPEAL TRIBUNALS FOR SCOTLAND
20 Walker Street, Edinburgh EH3 7HS
T 0131-220 1404
President, C. N. McEachran, QC

OFFICE OF THE SOCIAL SECURITY AND CHILD SUPPORT COMMISSIONERS
3rd Floor, Procession House, 55 Ludgate Hill, London EC4A 7JW
T 020-7029 9850 F 020-7029 9819
23 Melville Street, Edinburgh EH3 7PW
T 0131-225 2201
W www.osscsc.gov.uk

The Social Security Commissioners are the final statutory authority to decide appeals relating to entitlement to social security benefits. The Child Support Commissioners are the final statutory authority to decide appeals relating to child support. Appeals may be made in relation to both matters only on a point of law. The Commissioners' jurisdiction covers England, Wales and Scotland. There are 18 commissioners; they are all qualified lawyers.
Chief Social Security Commissioner and Chief Child Support Commissioner, His Hon. Judge Gary Hickinbottom
Secretary, Ms L. Armes *(London)*; S. Niven *(Edinburgh)*

OFFICE OF THE SOCIAL SECURITY COMMISSIONERS AND CHILD SUPPORT COMMISSIONERS FOR NORTHERN IRELAND
1st Floor, Headline Building, 10–14 Victoria Street, Belfast BT1 3GG
T 028-9033 2344 F 028-9031 3510
E socialsecuritycommissioners@courtsni.gov.uk
W www.courtsni.gov.uk

The role of Northern Ireland Social Security Commissioners and Child Support Commissioners is similar to that of the Commissioners in Great Britain. There are two commissioners for Northern Ireland.
Chief Commissioner, His Hon. Judge Martin, QC
Commissioner, Mrs M. F. Brown
Registrar of Appeals, W. R. Brown

SOLICITORS' DISCIPLINARY TRIBUNAL
3rd Floor, Gate House, 1 Farringdon Street, London EC4M 7NS
T 020-7329 4808 F 020-7329 4833
E enquiries@solicitorsdt.com
W www.solicitorstribunal.org.uk

The Solicitors' Disciplinary Tribunal is an independent statutory body whose members are appointed by the Master of the Rolls. The tribunal considers applications made to it alleging either professional misconduct and/or a breach of the statutory rules by which solicitors are bound against an individually named solicitor, former solicitor, registered foreign lawyer, or solicitor's clerk. The Tribunal has around 30 members, two thirds are solicitor members and one third lay members. The president and solicitor members do not receive remuneration and lay members are remunerated by the Department for Constitutional Affairs.
President, A. Isaacs
Clerk to the Tribunal, Mrs S. C. Elson

SOLICITORS' DISCIPLINE TRIBUNAL (SCOTTISH)
Unit 3.5, The Granary Business Centre, Coal Road, Cupar, Fife KY15 5YQ
T 01334-659088 F 01334-659099

The Scottish Solicitors' Discipline Tribunal is an independent statutory body with a panel of 18 members, ten of whom are solicitors; members are appointed by the Lord President of the Court of Session. Its principal function is to consider complaints of misconduct against solicitors in Scotland.
Chairman, G. F. Ritchie
Clerk, J. V. Lea, WS

SPECIAL COMMISSIONERS
15–19 Bedford Avenue, London WC1B 3AS
T 020-7612 9649 F 020-7436 4151
W www.financeandtaxtribunals.gov.uk

The Special Commissioners are an independent body appointed by the Lord Chancellor* to hear complex appeals against decisions of the Board of Inland Revenue and its officials.
Presiding Special Commissioner, His Hon. Stephen Oliver, QC
Clerk, R. P. Lester

SPECIAL EDUCATIONAL NEEDS AND DISABILITY TRIBUNAL

Central Office, Procession House, 55 Ludgate Hill,
London EC4M 7JW
T 0870-241 2555 F 020-7029 9726
Darlington Office, Ground Floor, Mowden Hall,
Staindrop Road DL3 9BG
W www.sendist.gov.uk

The Special Educational Needs and Disability Tribunal considers parents' appeals against the decisions of Local Education Authorities (LEAs) about children's special educational needs if parents cannot reach agreement with the LEA. The President and Chairmen are appointed by the Lord Chancellor* and the Secretaries of State for Education and Employment and Wales appoint the lay members.
President, Lady Rosemary Hughes
Tribunal Secretary, Kevin Mullany

SPECIAL IMMIGRATION APPEALS COMMISSION

15 Breams Buildings, London EC4A 1DZ
T 020-7073 4200

The Commission was set up under the Special Immigration Appeals Commission Act 1997. Its main function is to consider appeals against orders for deportations in cases which involve, in the main, considerations of national security. Members are appointed by the Lord Chancellor*.
Chairman, The Hon. Mr Justice Ouseley

TRAFFIC COMMISSIONERS

c/o Scottish Traffic Area, Argyle House, 3 Lady Lawson Street,
Edinburgh EH3 9SE
T 0131-200 4955 F 0131-229 0682
W www.vosa.gov.uk

The Traffic Commissioners are responsible for licensing operators of heavy goods and public service vehicles. There are seven Commissioners in the eight traffic areas covering Britain. Each Traffic Commissioner constitutes a tribunal for the purposes of the Tribunals and Inquiries Act 1992.
Traffic Commissioner, Miss J. N. Aitken

TRANSPORT TRIBUNAL

Procession House, 55 Ludgate Hill, London EC4M 7JW
T 020-7029 9780 F 020-7029 9782
E transport@dca.gsi.gov.uk
W www.transporttribunal.gov.uk

The Transport Tribunal has three jurisdictions; it hears appeals against decisions made by Traffic Commissioners at public inquiries as well as hearing appeals against decisions of the Registrar of Approved Driving Instructors and is able to resolve disputes under the Postal Services Act 2000. The tribunal consists of a legally qualified president, other judicial members, and lay members. The president and legal members are appointed by the Lord Chancellor* and the lay members by the Secretary of

State for Transport. Members of the Transport Tribunal also act as the London Service Permit Appeals Panel.
President, H. B. H. Carlisle, QC
Judicial members, His Hon. Judge Brodrick; J. Beech;
  F. Burton
Lay members, D. Yeomans; P. Steel; L. Milliken; G. Inch;
  S. James; J. Robinson
Tribunal Manager, E. Castle

VALUATION TRIBUNALS

Chief Executive's Office, Block 1, Angel Square, 1 Torrens Street,
London EC1V 1NY
T 020-7841 8700 F 020-7837 6131
W www.valuation-tribunals.gov.uk

The Valuation Tribunals hear appeals concerning the council tax, non-domestic rating and land drainage rates in England and Wales. There are 56 tribunals in England and four in Wales; those in England are funded by the Office of the Deputy Prime Minister and those in Wales by the National Assembly for Wales. A separate tribunal is constituted for each hearing, and normally consists of a chairman and two other members. Members are appointed by a representative of the local authorities and the Valuation Tribunal president and serve on a voluntary basis. The Valuation Tribunal Management Board considers all matters affecting valuation tribunals in England, and the Council of Wales Valuation Tribunals performs the same function in Wales.
Chairman, Valuation Tribunal Management Board,
  N. Galbraith
Valuation Tribunals Chief Executive Officer, Laurence
  Barnes
President, Council of Wales Valuation Tribunals, J. H.
  Owens

VAT AND DUTIES TRIBUNALS

15–19 Bedford Avenue, London WC1B 3AS
T 020-7612 9700 F 020-7436 4151
W www.financeandtaxtribunals.gov.uk

VAT and Duties Tribunals are administered by the Department for Constitutional Affairs in England and Wales, and by the First Minister in Scotland. They are independent and decide disputes between taxpayers and Customs and Excise. In England and Wales, the president and chairmen are appointed by the Lord Chancellor* and members by the Treasury. Chairmen in Scotland are appointed by the Lord President of the Court of Session.
President, His Hon. Stephen Oliver, QC
Vice-President, England and Wales, J. D. Demack
Vice-President, Scotland, T. G. Coutts, QC
Vice-President, Northern Ireland, His Hon. J. McKee, QC
Registrar, R. P. Lester

TRIBUNAL CENTRES

EDINBURGH, 44 Palmerston Place, Edinburgh EH12 5BJ
T 0131-226 3551
LONDON (including Belfast), 15–19 Bedford Avenue,
London WC1B 3AS T 020-7612 9700
MANCHESTER, 9th Floor, Westpoint, 501 Chester Road,
Manchester M16 5HU T 0161-868 6600

---

* The Lord Chancellor's Department was abolished and replaced with the Department for Constitutional Affairs in June 2003. The Secretary of State for Constitutional Affairs, the Rt. Hon. The Lord Falconer of Thoroton, is also the Lord Chancellor.

THE POLICE SERVICE

There are 52 police forces in the United Kingdom. Most forces' area is coterminous with one or more local authority areas. Policing in London is carried out by the Metropolitan Police and the City of London Police; in Northern Ireland by the Police Service of Northern Ireland; and by the Isle of Man, States of Jersey and Guernsey forces in their respective islands and bailiwicks. National services include the National Crime Squad and the National Criminal Intelligence Service (NCIS).

Police Authorities are independent bodies, responsible for the oversight of local policing. There are five police authorities in England and Wales, each with nineteen members comprising ten local councillors, three magistrates and six independent members. In Scotland, six of the forces are maintained by joint police boards, made up of local councillors from each council in the force area; the other two constabularies (Dumfries & Galloway and Fife) are directly administered by their respective local councils. In London the Metropolitan Police Authority oversees police operations and has twenty-three members; twelve drawn from the Greater London Authority (GLA), four magistrates and seven independent members. A committee of the Corporation of London including councillors and magistrates oversees the City of London Police. In Northern Ireland the policing board is made up of nineteen political and independent members.

Police authorities in England, Scotland and Wales are financed by central and local government grants and a precept on the council tax. The Northern Ireland Policing Board is wholly funded by central government. The police authorities, subject to the approval of the Home Secretary (in England and Wales), the Secretary of State for Northern Ireland and to regulations, are responsible for appointing the Chief Constable. In England and Wales they are responsible for publishing annual policing plans and reports, setting local objectives and a budget, and levying the precept. The police authorities in Scotland are responsible for setting a budget, providing the resources necessary to police the area adequately, appointing officers of the rank of Assistant Chief Constable and above, and determining the number of officers and civilian staff in the force. The Northern Ireland Policing Board exercises these functions in Northern Ireland.

The Home Secretary, the Secretary of State for Northern Ireland and the Scottish Executive are responsible for the organisation, administration and operation of the police service. They make regulations covering matters such as police ranks, discipline, hours of duty and pay and allowances. All police forces are subject to inspection by HM Inspectors of Constabulary, who report to the Home Secretary, Scottish Executive or Secretary of State for Northern Ireland.

COMPLAINTS

The Independent Police Complaints Commission (IPCC) has overall responsibility for the system for complaints against the police, taking over from the Police Complaints Authority (PCA) which ceased to exist on 31 March 2004. The IPCC has the power to initiate, carry out and oversee investigations and is also responsible for the way complaints are handled by local police forces. An officer who is dismissed, required to resign or reduced in rank, whether as a result of a complaint or not, may appeal to a police appeals tribunal established by the relevant police authority. In Scotland, Chief Constables are obliged to investigate a complaint against one of their officers; if there is a suggestion of criminal activity, the complaint is investigated by an independent public prosecutor. In Northern Ireland complaints are investigated by the Police Ombudsman.

RATES OF PAY

BASIC RATES OF PAY *at 1 April 2004*

Chief Constable of Police Service of Northern Ireland	
No fixed term	£123,660–£132,912
Fixed term appointment	£130,020–£139,740
Chief Constables of Greater Manchester, Strathclyde and West Midlands	£147,501–£150,000
Chief Constable	£105,000–£140,001
Deputy Chief Constable	£90,000–£115,002
Assistant Chief Constable	£75,000–£87,501
Chief Superintendent*	£59,988–£63,456
Superintendent*	£50,550–£58,965
Chief Inspector†	£42,810–£46,998
Inspector†	£38,679–£43,659
Sergeant	£30,186–£33,927
Constable	£19,227–£30,186

*The rank of Chief Superintendent was re-introduced on 1 January 2002. Superintendents who were not given the rank of Chief Superintendent on its re-introduction receive full protection of their existing Superintendent range 2 salary (£58,965–£62,751).
†Includes London salary range, applicable only to officers in the Metropolitan and City of London polices forces.

Metropolitan Police

Commissioner	£168,198–£180,777
Deputy Commissioner	£136,638–£146,853
Assistant Commissioner	£116,151–£130,020
Deputy Assistant Commissioner	£92,922–£104,016
Commander	£72,948–£83,736

City of London Police

Commissioner	£99,984–£116,151
Assistant Commissioner	80% of the basic salary of the commissioner or £83,736, whichever is higher

POLICE FORCES

Strength: size of force as known at February 2004
Source: Hazell & Co. Police and Constabulary Almanac 2004

ENGLAND

AVON AND SOMERSET CONSTABULARY, PO Box 37,
Portishead, Bristol BS20 8QJ T 01275-818181
Strength, 3,185
Chief Constable, S. Pilkington, QPM
BEDFORDSHIRE POLICE, Police Headquarters, Woburn Road,
Kempston, Bedford MK43 9AX T 01234-841212
Strength, 1,184
Chief Constable, P. Hancock, QPM
CAMBRIDGESHIRE CONSTABULARY, Hinchingbrooke Park,
Huntingdon PE29 6NP T 01480-456111
Strength, 1,415
Chief Constable, T. Lloyd, QPM
CHESHIRE CONSTABULARY, Clemonds Hey, Oakmere Road,
Winsford CW7 2UA T 01244-350000
Strength, 2,146
Chief Constable, P. Fahy, QPM
CLEVELAND POLICE, PO Box 70, Ladgate Lane,
Middlesbrough TS8 9EH T 01642-326326
Strength, 1,656
Chief Constable, Sean Price
CUMBRIA CONSTABULARY, Carleton Hall, Penrith, Cumbria
CA10 2AU T 01768-891999
Strength, 1,203
Chief Constable, Michael Baxter
DERBYSHIRE CONSTABULARY, Butterley Hall, Ripley,
Derbyshire DE5 3RS T 01773-570100
Strength, 2,118
Chief Constable, D. F. Coleman
DEVON AND CORNWALL CONSTABULARY, Middlemoor,
Exeter EX2 7HQ T 08452-777444
Strength, 3,287
Chief Constable, Maria Wallis, QPM
DORSET POLICE HEADQUARTERS, Winfrith, Dorchester,
Dorset DT2 8DZ T 01929-462727
Strength, 1,402
Chief Constable, Mrs J. Stichbury, QPM
DURHAM CONSTABULARY, Aykley Heads, Durham DH1 5TT
T 0191-386 4929 W www.durham.police.uk
Strength, 1,685
Chief Constable, P. Garvin
ESSEX POLICE, PO Box 2, Springfield, Chelmsford, Essex
CM2 6DA T 01245-491491 W www.essex.police.uk
Strength, 3,189
Chief Constable, D. F. Stevens, QPM
GLOUCESTERSHIRE CONSTABULARY, Holland House,
Lansdown Road, Cheltenham, Glos GL51 6QH
T 0845-0901234 W www.gloucestershire.police.uk
Strength, 1,174
Chief Constable, T. Brain, QPM, PHD
GREATER MANCHESTER POLICE, PO Box 22 (S West
PDO), Chester House, Boyer Street, Manchester M16 0RE
T 0161-872 5050
Strength, 7,111
Chief Constable, Michael J. Todd, QPM, MPHIL
HAMPSHIRE CONSTABULARY, West Hill, Winchester, Hants
SO22 5DB T 0845-045 4545
Strength, 3,500
Chief Constable, Paul Kernaghan, QPM
HERTFORDSHIRE CONSTABULARY, Stanborough Road,
Welwyn Garden City, Herts AL8 6XF T 01707-354200
Strength, 1,851
Chief Constable, Paul Acres, QPM

HUMBERSIDE POLICE, Priory Road Police Station, Priory Road,
Hull HU1 5SF T 01482-326111
Strength, 2,207
Chief Constable, D. Westwood, QPM, PHD
KENT CONSTABULARY, Sutton Road, Maidstone, Kent
ME15 9BZ T 01622-690690
Strength, 3,555
Chief Constable, M. Fuller
LANCASHIRE CONSTABULARY, PO Box 77, Hutton, Nr.
Preston, Lancs PR4 5SB
T 01772-614444 W www.lancashire.police.uk
Strength, 3,451
Chief Contstable, Paul Stephenson, QPM
LEICESTERSHIRE CONSTABULARY, St John's, Enderby,
Leicester LE19 2BX T 0116-222 2222
Strength, 2,211
Chief Constable, Matthew Baggott
LINCOLNSHIRE POLICE, PO Box 999, Lincoln LN5 7PH
T 01522-532222 W www.lincs.police.uk
Strength, 1,266
Chief Constable, Tony Lake
MERSEYSIDE POLICE, PO Box 59, Liverpool L69 1JD
T 0151-709 6010
Strength, 4,257
Chief Constable, N. Bettison, QPM
NORFOLK CONSTABULARY, Operations and
Communications Centre, Falconers Chase, Wymondham,
Norfolk NR18 0WW
T 01953-424242
Strength, 1,580
Chief Constable, A. Hayman
NORTHAMPTONSHIRE POLICE, Wootton Hall,
Northampton NN4 0JQ T 01604-700700
Strength, 1,258
Chief Constable, Peter Maddison
NORTHUMBRIA POLICE, Ponteland, Newcastle upon Tyne
NE20 0BL T 01661-872555
Strength, 4,031
Chief Constable, Crispian Strachan, QPM
NORTH YORKSHIRE POLICE, Newby Wiske Hall,
Northallerton, N. Yorks DL7 9HA
T 01609-783131 W www.northyorkshire.police.uk
Strength, 1,427
Chief Constable, Ms. D. Cannings
NOTTINGHAMSHIRE POLICE, Sherwood Lodge, Arnold,
Nottingham NG5 8PP T 0115-967 0999
Strength, 2,458
Chief Constable, S. Green, QPM
SOUTH YORKSHIRE POLICE, Snig Hill, Sheffield S3 8LY
T 0114-220 2020
Strength, 3,223
Chief Constable, M. Hedges, QPM
STAFFORDSHIRE POLICE, Cannock Road, Stafford ST17 0QG
T 01785-257717
Strength, 2,218
Chief Constable, John Giffard, CBE, QPM
SUFFOLK CONSTABULARY, Martlesham Heath, Ipswich
IP5 3QS T 01473-613500
Strength, 1,309
Chief Constable, A. McWhirter, QPM
SURREY POLICE, Mount Browne, Sandy Lane, Guildford, Surrey
GU3 1HG T 0845-125 2222 W www.surrey.police.uk
Strength, 1,995
Chief Constable, Denis O'Connor, CBE, QPM
SUSSEX POLICE, Malling House, Lewes, Sussex BN7 2DZ
T 0845-607 0999
Strength, 3,140
Chief Constable, Ken Jones, QPM

THAMES VALLEY POLICE, Kidlington, Oxon OX5 2NZ
T 0845-8505 505
Strength, 3,821
Chief Constable, Peter Neyroud, QPM
WARWICKSHIRE POLICE, Leek Wootton, Warwick CV35 7QB
T 01926-415000
Strength, 1,008
Chief Constable, John Burbeck, QPM
WEST MERCIA CONSTABULARY, Hindlip Hall, Hindlip,
PO Box 55, Worcester WR3 8SP
T 01905-723000 W www.westmercia.police.uk
Strength, 2,395
Chief Constable, P. West
WEST MIDLANDS POLICE, PO Box 52, Lloyd House, Colmore
Circus, Queensway, Birmingham B4 6NQ T 0845-113 5000
Strength, 7,573
Chief Constable, Paul Scott-Lee, QPM
WEST YORKSHIRE POLICE, PO Box 9, Wakefield, W. Yorks
WF1 3QP T 01924-375222
Strength, 4,927
Chief Constable, C. Cramphorn
WILTSHIRE CONSTABULARY, London Road, Devizes, Wilts
SN10 2DN T 01380-722341
Strength, 1,238
Chief Constable, Dame Elizabeth Neville, DBE, QPM, PHD

WALES

DYFED-POWYS POLICE, PO Box 99, Llangunnor, Carmarthen,
Carmarthenshire SA31 2PF T 01267-222020
Strength, 1,161
Chief Constable, T. Grange, QPM
GWENT POLICE, Croesyceiliog, Cwmbran, Torfaen NP44 2XJ
T 01633-838111 W www.gwent.police.uk
Strength, 1,261
Chief Constable, K. Turner, QPM
NORTH WALES POLICE, Colwyn Bay, Conwy LL29 8AW
T 01492-517171
Strength, 1,528
Chief Constable, R. Brunstrom
SOUTH WALES POLICE, Cowbridge Road, Bridgend
CF31 3SU T 01656-655555
Strength, 3,157
Chief Constable, Barbara Wilding, QPM

SCOTLAND

CENTRAL SCOTLAND POLICE, Police Headquarters,
Randolphfield, Stirling FK8 2HD
T 01786-456000 W www.centralscotland.police.uk
Strength, 751
Chief Constable, Andrew Cameron, QPM
DUMFRIES AND GALLOWAY CONSTABULARY, Police
Headquarters, Cornwall Mount, Dumfries DG1 1PZ
T 01387-252112 W www.dumfriesandgalloway.police.uk
Strength, 462
Chief Constable, D. Strang, QPM
FIFE CONSTABULARY, Detroit Road, Glenrothes, Fife KY6 2RJ
T 01592-418888 W www.fife.police.uk
Strength, 953
Chief Constable, Peter Wilson, QPM
GRAMPIAN POLICE, Queen Street, Aberdeen AB10 1ZA
T 0845-600 5700 W www.grampian.police.uk
Strength, 1,308
Chief Constable, Andrew Brown, CBE, QPM
LOTHIAN AND BORDERS POLICE, Fettes Avenue,
Edinburgh EH4 1RB T 0131-311 3131
Strength, 2,602
Chief Constable, Paddy Tomkins

NORTHERN CONSTABULARY, Old Perth Road, Inverness
IV2 3SY T 01463-715555
Strength, 680
Chief Constable, Ian Latimer
STRATHCLYDE POLICE, Police Headquarters, 173 Pitt Street,
Glasgow G2 4JS
T 0141-532 2000 W www.strathclyde.police.uk
Strength, 7,889
Chief Constable, William Rae, QPM
TAYSIDE POLICE, PO Box 59, West Bell Street, Dundee
DD1 9JU T 01382-223200 W www.tayside.police.uk
Strength, 1,161
Chief Constable, John Vine, QPM

NORTHERN IRELAND

POLICE SERVICE OF NORTHERN IRELAND, Brooklyn,
Knock Road, Belfast BT5 6LE
T 028-9065 0222 W www.psni.police.uk
Strength, 9,851
Chief Constable, H. Orde

ISLANDS

GUERNSEY POLICE, Police Headquarters, Hospital Lane, St
Peter Port, Guernsey GY1 2QN T 01481-725111
Strength, 177
Chief Officer, G. LePage
ISLE OF MAN CONSTABULARY, Police Headquarters,
Glencrutchery Road, Douglas, Isle of Man IM2 4RG
T 01624-631212
Strength, 236
Chief Constable, M. Culverhouse
STATES OF JERSEY POLICE, PO Box 789, St Helier, Jersey
JE4 3ZD T 01534-612612
Strength, 241
Chief Officer, Graham Power, QPM

METROPOLITAN POLICE SERVICE

NEW SCOTLAND YARD, 8–10 Broadway, London SW1H 0BG
T 020-7230 1212
Strength (February 2004), 28,477
Commissioner, Sir John Stevens, QPM, LLD
Deputy Commissioner, Sir Ian Blair, QPM
Chief of Staff, Deputy Assistant Commissioner, Carole
Howlett

TERRITORIAL POLICING
Assistant Commissioner, Tim Godwin, OBE
Deputy Assistant Commissioner, Stephen House

SPECIALIST OPERATIONS
Assistant Commissioner, David Veness, CBE, QPM
Deputy Assistant Commissioner, Peter Clarke, CVO, QPM

SPECIALIST CRIME
Assistant Commissioner, Tarique Ghaffur, QPM
Deputy Assistant Commissioners, Bill Griffiths; Mike Fuller

HUMAN RESOURCES
Assistant Commissioner, Bernard Hogan-Howe
Director, Martin Tiplady

CITY OF LONDON POLICE

37 Wood Street, London EC2P 2NQ
T 020-7601 2222
Strength (February 2004), 720

Though small, the City of London has one of the most
important financial centres in the world and the force has
particular expertise in areas such as fraud investigation as

well as the areas required of any police force. The force has a wholly elected police authority, the police committee of the Corporation of London, which appoints the Commissioner.

Commissioner, James Hart, QPM, PHD
Assistant Commissioner, Mike Bowron
Commander, Frank Armstrong

BRITISH TRANSPORT POLICE

15 Tavistock Place, London WC1H 9SJ T 020-7388 7541
Strength (February 2004), 2,206

British Transport Police is the national police force for the railways in England, Wales and Scotland, including the London Underground system, Docklands Light Railway, Midland Metro Tram system and Croydon Tramlink. The Chief Constable reports to the British Transport Police Authority. The members of the Authority are appointed by the Secretary of State for Transport and include representatives from the rail industry as well as independent members. Officers are paid the same as other police forces.

Chief Constable, Ian Johnston, CBE, QPM
Deputy Chief Constable, Andy Trotter, QPM

MINISTRY OF DEFENCE POLICE

MDP Wethersfield, Braintree, Essex CM7 4AZ T 01371-854000
Strength (March 2004), 3,281

The Ministry of Defence Police is a civilian police force with specific responsibility for meeting the requirements of the MOD and associated customers, including visiting forces and the Royal Mint. Other specialist services include marine policing, dogs, firearms and Police Search Teams. The Force also has its own Criminal Investigation Department with specialist officers working in the field of fraud investigation and can also offer crime prevention advice. MDP officers are also serving as a part of the British contingent of police officers supporting the United Nations policing operations.

Chief Constable, D. L. Clarke, QPM
Deputy Chief Constable, D. A. Ray, QPM, MA, LLM
Head of Secretariat, S. Beedle
Assistant Chief Constables, (Personnel & Training) vacant; *(Operational Support)* J. P. Bligh; *(Divisional Operations)* G. P. McAuley

ROYAL PARKS CONSTABULARY

Police Station, Hyde Park, London W2 2UH T 020-7298 2000
Strength (February 2004), 139

The Royal Parks Constabulary (RPC) is part of the Royal Parks, an executive agency of the Department for Culture, Media and Sport. It is responsible for policing 17 Royal Parks, Gardens and open spaces in and around London, comprising an area of around 6,000 acres. Officers of the force are appointed under the Parks Regulations Act 1872 (as amended).

On 1 April 2004 the RPC began a merger with the Metropolitan Police Service (MPS). The MPS established a Royal Parks Operational Command Unit and will co-police the Parks with the RPC until the two units become fully merged in 2005. The MPS Operational Command Unit is also based at Hyde Park Station.

Chief Officer RPC, Supt. D. Pollock
Deputy Chief Officer, Chief Inspector Kevin Quinn
Occupational Command Unit Commander MPS, Supt. H. Ball

UNITED KINGDOM ATOMIC ENERGY AUTHORITY CONSTABULARY

Building E6, Culham Science Centre, Abingdon, Oxon OX14 3DB
T 01235-463760
Strength (February 2004), 583

The Constabulary is responsible for policing the United Kingdom Atomic Energy Authority, URENCO (Uranium Enrichment Services Worldwide) and British Nuclear Fuels PLC establishments and for escorting nuclear material between establishments within the UK and worldwide. The Chief Constable is responsible, through the United Kingdom Atomic Energy Authority Police Authority, to the President of the Board of Trade.

Chief Constable, W. F. Pryke
Deputy Chief Constable, P. P. Crossan

NATIONAL POLICE BODIES

THE SPECIAL CONSTABULARY
Each police force has its own special constabulary, made up of volunteers who work in their spare time. Special Constables have full police powers. Visit www.specialconstables.gov.uk

NATIONAL CRIME SQUAD
Headquarters: PO Box 2500, London SW1V 2WF
T 020-7238 2500

The National Crime Squad was established on 1 April 1998, replacing the six regional crime squads in England and Wales. It investigates national and international organised and serious crime. It also supports police forces investigating serious crime. The Squad is accountable to the National Crime Squad Service Authority.

Director-General, William Hughes, QPM

NCS AND NCIS SERVICE AUTHORITIES
Headquarters: PO Box 2600, London SW1V 2WG
T 020-7238 2600

The Service Authorities are responsible for ensuring the effective operation of the National Crime Squad and National Criminal Intelligence Service. Each Authority has eleven members, of whom eight sit on both Authorities as core members. The Service Authorities are non-departmental public bodies.

Chairman, Paul Lever
Clerk, Andrew Mulholland

NATIONAL MISSING PERSONS BUREAU
Headquarters: New Scotland Yard, Broadway, London SW1H 0BG
T 0207-230 4029

The Police National Missing Persons Bureau (PNMPB) acts as a central clearing house of information, receiving reports about vulnerable missing persons that are still outstanding after 14 days and details of unidentified persons or remains within 48 hours of being found from all forces in England and Wales. Reports are also received from Scottish police forces, the Police Services of Northern Ireland and foreign police forces via Interpol. The Bureau also manages the Missing Kids website, http://uk.missingkids.com
Director, G. Pugh

NATIONAL INFORMATION TECHNOLOGY
ORGANISATION

Headquarters: New Kings Beam House, 22 Upper Ground, London SE1 9QY
T 020-8358 5555

The Police Information Technology Organisation (PITO) is a non-departmental public body funded by grant-in-aid from central Government and by charges from the services provided. It provides information technology, communications systems and services to the police and other criminal justice organisations in the UK and also has a role in the purchasing of goods and services for the police.

Chairman, Lt.-Gen. Sir Edmund Burton, KBE
Chief Executive, Phillip Webb

FORENSIC SCIENCE SERVICE

Headquarters: Trident Court, 2920 Solihull Parkway, Birmingham Business Park B37 3YN
T 0121-329 5200

The Forensic Science Service (FSS) is an executive agency of the Home Office providing forensic science services to the police forces in England and Wales. It employs over 2,500 people, including over 1,600 trained scientists and has seven laboratories throughout the country.

Chief Executive, David Werrett, PHD

STAFF ASSOCIATIONS

Police officers are not permitted to join a trade union or to take strike action. All ranks have their own staff associations.

ASSOCIATION OF CHIEF POLICE OFFICERS OF ENGLAND, WALES AND NORTHERN IRELAND, 7th Floor, 25 Victoria Street, London SW1H 0EX
T 020-7227 3434
Negotiating Secretary, N. Yeo

POLICE SUPERINTENDENTS' ASSOCIATION OF ENGLAND AND WALES, 67A Reading Road, Pangbourne, Reading RG8 7JD T 0118-984 4005
National Secretary, Chief Supt. Philip Aspey

POLICE FEDERATION OF ENGLAND AND WALES, 15–17 Langley Road, Surbiton, Surrey KT6 6LP
T 020-8335 1000
General Secretary, C. E. Elliott

ASSOCIATION OF CHIEF POLICE OFFICERS IN SCOTLAND, Police Headquarters, 173 Pitt Street, Glasgow G2 4JS T 0141-532 2052
Hon. Secretary, William Rae, QPM

ASSOCIATION OF SCOTTISH POLICE SUPERINTENDENTS, Secretariat, 173 Pitt Street, Glasgow G2 4JS T 0141-221 5796
General Secretary, Carol Forfar

SCOTTISH POLICE FEDERATION, 5 Woodside Place, Glasgow G3 7QF T 0141-332 5234
General Secretary, Douglas Keil, QPM

SUPERINTENDENTS' ASSOCIATION OF NORTHERN IRELAND, 77–79 Garnerville Road, Belfast BT4 2NX
T 028-909 22201
Hon. Secretary, Supt. M. L. Allen

POLICE FEDERATION FOR NORTHERN IRELAND, 77–79 Garnerville Road, Belfast BT4 2NX T 028-9076 4200
Secretary, T. Spence

THE PRISON SERVICE

The prison services in the United Kingdom are the responsibility of the Home Secretary, the Scottish Executive Justice Department and the Secretary of State for Northern Ireland. The chief director generals (Chief Executive in Scotland), officers of the Prison Service, the Scottish Prison Service and the Northern Ireland Prison Service are responsible for the day-to-day running of the system.

There are 139 prison establishments in England and Wales, 20 in Scotland and three in Northern Ireland. Convicted prisoners are classified according to their assessed security risk and are housed in establishments appropriate to that level of security. There are no open prisons in Northern Ireland. Female prisoners are housed in women's establishments or in separate wings of mixed prisons. Remand prisoners are, where possible, housed separately from convicted prisoners. Offenders under the age of 21 are usually detained in a young offender institution, which may be a separate establishment or part of a prison.

Eleven prisons are now run by the private sector, and in England and Wales all escort services have been contracted out to private companies. In Scotland, one prison (Kilmarnock) was built and financed by the private sector and is being operated by private contractors.

There are independent prison inspectorates in England and Wales and Scotland which report annually on conditions and the treatment of prisoners. HM Chief Inspector of Prisons for England and Wales also performs an inspectorate role for prisons in Northern Ireland. Every prison establishment also has an independent board of visitors or visiting committee made up of local volunteers.

Any prisoner whose complaint is not satisfied by the internal complaints procedures may complain to the Prisons Ombudsman for England and Wales or the Scottish Prisons Complaints Commission. There is no Prisons Ombudsman for Northern Ireland, but complaints by prisoners regarding maladministration may be made to the Parliamentary Commissioner for Administration.

From May 2003, the 11 private sector prisons in England and Wales became the direct responsibility of the Commissioner for Correctional Services, a new post in the Home Office with overall responsibility for HM Prison Service, the National Probation Service and the Youth Justice Board. The Commissioner also has responsibility for correctional services policy, the prisons and probation inspectorates, the Prisons Ombudsman and the Board of Visitors. Martin Narey was appointed Commissioner in March 2003, with Phil Wheatley taking over as Director-General of the Prison Service.

In January 2004, Martin Narey was appointed Chief Executive of the National Offender Management Service, a new service announced in the Government report, *Reducing Crime, Changing Lives*. This new service integrates prisons and probation in a system which will ensure end-to-end management of offenders and is expected to reduce re-offending and cut the rate of growth in the prison population.

AVERAGE PRISON POPULATION (UK)
as at March 2004

	Remand	Sentenced	Other
ENGLAND AND WALES			
Male	11,737	57,882	1,044
Female	1,019	3,562	51
Total	12,756	61,444	1,095
*SCOTLAND			
Male	—	—	—
Female	—	—	—
Total	1,018	5,168	—
N. IRELAND			
Male	443	818	—
Female	8	14	—
Total	451	832	—
UK TOTAL	27,432	129,720	2,190

The projected prison population for 2007 in England and Wales is 78,100 if custody rates and sentence lengths remain at 2001 levels.
*Figures for Scotland are for 2003
Sources: Home Office – *Research Development Statistics*; Scottish Prison Service – *Annual Report and Accounts*; Northern Ireland Prison Service – *Annual Report* 2003–4

SENTENCED PRISON POPULATION BY SEX AND OFFENCE (ENGLAND AND WALES)
as at 31 March 2004

	Male	Female
Violence against the person	13,305	578
Sexual offences	5,664	22
Burglary	8,543	251
Robbery	7,930	375
Theft, handling	4,382	513
Fraud and forgery	1,022	136
Drugs offences	9,069	1,262
Other offences	7,079	374
Offence not known	818	46
In default of payment of a fine	70	5
*Total	57,882	3,562

*Figures do not include civil (non-criminal) prisoners
Source: Home Office – *Research Development Statistics*

SENTENCED POPULATION BY LENGTH OF SENTENCE (ENGLAND AND WALES) *as at 31 March 2004*

	Adults	Young Offenders
Less than 12 months	6,660	2,019
12 months to less than 4 years	17,105	4,402
4 years to less than life	23,816	1,889
Life	5,393	160
*Total	52,974	8,470

*Figures include fine defaulters
Source: Home Office – *Research Development Statistics*

AVERAGE DAILY SENTENCED POPULATION BY LENGTH
OF SENTENCE 2002–3 (SCOTLAND)

	Adults	Young Offenders
Less than 4 years	2,120	433
4 years or over (including life)	2,506	169
Total	4,626	602

Source: Scottish Prison Service – Annual Report and Accounts 2002–3

PRISON SUICIDES APRIL 2003 – MARCH 2004
(ENGLAND AND WALES)

Males	83
Females	10
Total	93
Rate per 100,000 prisoners in custody	126

Source: Safer Custody Group

OPERATING COSTS OF PRISON SERVICE IN ENGLAND
AND WALES 2003–4

	£
Staff costs	1,364,193,000
Other administrative costs	969,138,000
Operating income	400,046,000
Net operating costs for the year	2,105,189,000
Average cost per prisoner place	27,320
(reflecting establishment costs only)	

Source: HM Prison Service – Annual Report and Accounts 2003–4

OPERATING COSTS OF SCOTTISH PRISON SERVICE
2002–3

	£
Total income	2,290,000
Total expenditure	20,214,000
Staff costs	121,912,000
Running costs	63,939,000
Other current expenditure	23,363,000
Operating cost	206,224,000
Cost of capital charges	23,264,000
Interest payable and similar charges	7,000
Interest receivable	68,000
Net operating costs for the year	229,427,000
Lockerbie Trial Costs	0
Cost for financial year	229,427,000

Source: Scottish Prison Service – Annual Report and Accounts 2002–3

OPERATING COSTS OF NORTHERN IRELAND PRISON
SERVICE 2003–4

	£
Income	187,000
Staff Costs	77,635,000
Depreciation and other charges	7,065,000
Other Operating Costs	20,817,000
Total Expenditure	105,677,000
Net operating costs for the year	112,461,000

Source: Northern Ireland Prison Service – Annual Report and Accounts 2003–4

THE PRISON SERVICES

HM PRISON SERVICE
Cleland House, Page Street, London SW1P 4LN
T 0870-000 1397 W www.hmprisonservice.gov.uk

SALARIES from 1 April 2004

Senior Manager A	£47,780–£69,455
Senior Manager B	£45,911–£66,406
Senior Manager C	£40,937–£59,803
Senior Manager D	£36,500–£54,667
Manager E	£25,873–£41,141
Manager F	£22,389–£34,898
Manager G	£20,159–£28,587

THE PRISON SERVICE MANAGEMENT BOARD
Director-General (SCS), P. Wheatley
Deputy Director-General (SCS), Director of High Security
  Prisons (SCS), P. Atherton
Director of Operations (SCS), M. Spurr
Director of Personnel (SCS), G. Hadley
Director of Finance (SCS), A. Beasley
Director of Corporate Affairs (SCS), M. Manisty
Director of Resettlement (SCS), P. Wrench
Head of the Prison Health Policy Unit (SCS), J. Boyington
Board Secretary and Head of Secretariat (SMB), K. Everett
Race Equality Advisor, B. Thompson
Legal Adviser, H. Carter

AREA MANAGERS
Eastern, D. McAllister; East Midlands (North), N. Clifford;
East Midlands (South), B. Perry; High Security Prisons, P.
Atherton; London, B. Duff; North East, M. Egan; North
West, I. Lockwood; South East (Thames Valley and
Hampshire), N. Pascoe; South East (Kent), A. Smith;
South West, J. Petherick; (Surrey and Sussex), S. Moore;
Wales, J. May; West Midlands, B.Payling; Yorkshire and
Humberside, S. Wagstaffe
Head of Women's Estate, N. Clifford
Operational Manager for Women's Estate, H. Banks
Operational Manager for Juvenile Estate, S. McEwan

PRISON ESTABLISHMENTS – ENGLAND AND
WALES
Prisoners as at 31 March 2004, 75,295
Adult Prisoners as at 31 March 2004, 64,211
Young Offenders as at 31 March 2004, 11,084

ACKLINGTON, Morpeth, Northumberland NE65 9XF
Prisoners, 869 Governor, N. Flinders
ALBANY, Newport, Isle of Wight PO30 5RS Prisoners, 512
Governor, M. Jones
†‡ALTCOURSE (private prison), Higher Lane, Fazakerley,
Liverpool L9 7LH Prisoners, 990 Director, W. MacGowan
†‡ASHFIELD (private prison), Shortwood Road,
Pucklechurch, Bristol BS16 9QT Prisoners, 289
Director, Ms V. O'Dea
ASHWELL, Oakham, Leics LE15 7LF Prisoners, 528
Governor, C. Di Paolo
*ASKHAM GRANGE, Askham Richard, York YO26 5RF
Prisoners, 134 Governor, Miss D. Elaine
†AYLESBURY, Bierton Road, Aylesbury, Bucks HP20 1EH
Prisoners, 359 Governor, D. Kennedy
†BEDFORD, St Loyes Street, Bedford MK40 1HG
Prisoners, 491 Governor, G. Baulf
†‡BELMARSH, Western Way, Thamesmead, London SE28 0EB
Prisoners, 909 Governor, G. Hughes

†BIRMINGHAM, Winson Green Road, Birmingham B18 4AS
Prisoners, 1,396 *Governor,* M. Shann

†BLAKENHURST, Hewell Lane, Redditch, Worcs B97 6QS
Prisoners, 873 *Governor,* F. Parker

BLANTYRE HOUSE, Goudhurst, Cranbrook, Kent TN17 2NH
Prisoners, 119 *Governor,* J. Wilson

BLUNDESTON, Lowestoft, Suffolk NR32 5BG
Prisoners, 457 *Governor,* Ms T. Clarke

†‡BRINSFORD, New Road, Featherstone, Wolverhampton
WV10 7PY *Prisoners,* 463 *Governor,* T. Watson

†BRISTOL, Cambridge Road, Bristol BS7 8PS *Prisoners,* 586
Governor, M. Bell

†BRIXTON, PO Box 369, Jebb Avenue, London SW2 5XF
Prisoners, 811 *Governor,* J. Podmore

*†‡BROCKHILL, Redditch, Worcester B97 6RD
Prisoners, 140 *Governor,* B. Treen

†BRONZEFIELD (private prison), Woodthorpe Road,
Ashford, Middlesex, TW15 3JX *Prisoners,* 450
Director, J. McDowell

*†‡BUCKLEY HALL (private prison), Buckley Farm Lane,
Rochdale, Lancs OL12 9DP *Prisoners,* 327
Governor, S. Morrison

†BULLINGDON, PO Box 50, Bicester, Oxon OX25 1WD
Prisoners, 953 *Governor,* S. Saunders

*‡BULLWOOD HALL, High Road, Hockley, Essex SS5 4TE
Prisoners, 155 *Governor,* T. Hassall

CAMP HILL, Newport, Isle of Wight PO30 5PB
Prisoners, 574 *Governor,* B. Bennett

CANTERBURY, 46 Longport, Canterbury CT1 1PJ
Prisoners, 309 *Governor,* H. Rinaldi

†CARDIFF, Knox Road, Cardiff CF24 1UG
Prisoners, 671 *Governor,* P. Tidball

‡CASTINGTON, Morpeth, Northumberland NE65 9XG
Prisoners, 313 *Governor,* M. Spencer

CHANNINGS WOOD, Denbury, Newton Abbott, Devon
TQ12 6DW *Prisoners,* 661 *Governor,* N. Evans

†‡CHELMSFORD, 200 Springfield Road, Chelmsford, Essex
CM2 6LQ *Prisoners,* 593 *Governor,* S. Rodford

COLDINGLEY, Bisley, Woking, Surrey GU24 9EX
Prisoners, 385 *Governor,* P. McDowell

*COOKHAM WOOD, Rochester, Kent ME1 3LU
Prisoners, 138 *Governor,* E. Tullet

DARTMOOR, Princetown, Yelverton, Devon PL20 6RR
Prisoners, 616 *Governor,* C. Sturt

‡DEERBOLT, Bowes Road, Barnard Castle, Co. Durham
DL12 9BG *Prisoners,* 479 *Governor,* A. Tallentire

†‡DONCASTER (private prison), Off North Bridge,
Marshgate, Doncaster DN5 8UX
Prisoners, 1,099 *Director,* R. MacFarquar

†DORCHESTER, North Square, Dorchester DT1 1JD
Prisoners, 234 *Governor,* S. Holland

DOVEGATE (Private prison), Uttoxeter, ST14 8XR
Prisoners, 858 *Director,* K. Rogers

§DOVER, The Citadel, Western Heights, Dover CT17 9DR
Prisoners, 280 *Governor,* V. Whitecross

*DOWNVIEW, Sutton Lane, Sutton, Surrey SM2 5PD
Prisoners, 220 *Governor,* P. Dawson

*DRAKE HALL, Eccleshall, Staffs ST21 6LQ
Prisoners, 300 *Governor,* J. Huntington

*†DURHAM, Old Elvet, Durham DH1 3HU
Prisoners, 729 *Governor,* M. Newell

*EAST SUTTON PARK, Sutton Valence, Maidstone, Kent
ME17 3DF *Prisoners,* 101 *Governor,* R. Carter

*†‡EASTWOOD PARK, Falfield, Wotton-under-Edge, Glos
GL12 8DB *Prisoners,* 336 *Governor,* T. Beeston

*EDMUNDS HILL, Stradishall, Newmarket, Suffolk CB8 9YG
Prisoners, 288 *Governor,* Sue Doolan

†‡ELMLEY, Church Road, Eastchurch, Sheerness, Kent
ME12 4DZ *Prisoners,* 986 *Governor,* C. Bartlett

ERLESTOKE, Devizes, Wilts SN10 5TU
Prisoners, 417 *Governor,* C. Broom

EVERTHORPE, Brough, E. Yorks HU15 1RB
Prisoners, 466 *Governor,* A. Rice

†EXETER, New North Road, Exeter EX4 4EX
Prisoners, 530 *Governor,* I. Mulholland

FEATHERSTONE, New Road, Wolverhampton WV10 7PU
Prisoners, 611 *Governor,* M. Bolton

†‡FELTHAM, Bedfont Road, Feltham, Middx TW13 4ND
Prisoners, 674 *Governor,* A. Cross

FORD, Arundel, W. Sussex BN18 0BX
Prisoners, 515 *Governor,* F. Radford

FOREST BANK (private prison), Agecroft Road, Pendlebury,
Manchester M27 8UE *Prisoners,* 991 *Governor,* I. Woods

*FOSTON HALL, Foston, Derbys DE65 5DN
Prisoners, 231 *Governor,* P. Scriven

FRANKLAND, Brasside, Durham DH1 5YD
Prisoners, 657 *Governor,* P. Copple

FULL SUTTON, Full Sutton, York YO41 1PS
Prisoners, 602 *Governor,* B. Mullen

GARTH, Ulnes Walton Lane, Leyland, Preston PR5 3NE
Prisoners, 662 *Governor,* B. McColm

GARTREE, Gallow Field Road, Market Harborough, Leics
LE16 7RP *Prisoners,* 412 *Governor,* R. Daly

†‡GLEN PARVA, Tigers Road, Wigston, Leicester LE18 4TN
Prisoners, 780 *Governor,* B. Edwards

†GLOUCESTER, Barrack Square, Gloucester GL1 2JN
Prisoners, 315 *Governor,* D. Chalmers

GRENDON, Grendon Underwood, Aylesbury, Bucks HP18 0TL
Prisoners, 225 *Governor,* P. Bennett

‡GUYS MARSH, Shaftesbury, Dorset SP7 0AH
Prisoners, 558 *Governor,* B. Greenbury

§HASLAR, Dolphin Way, Gosport, Hampshire, PO12 2AW
Prisoners, 116 *Manager,* C. Draper

‡HATFIELD, Thorne Road, Hatfield, Doncaster DN7 6EL
Prisoners, 180 *Governor,* T. Watson

HAVERIGG, Millom, Cumbria LA18 4NA
Prisoners, 555 *Governor,* S. McCullagh

HEWELL GRANGE, Redditch, Worcs B97 6QQ
Prisoners, 168 *Governor,* A. Gomme

†‡HIGH DOWN, Sutton Lane, Sutton, Surrey SM2 5PJ
Prisoners, 752 *Governor,* S. West

*†‡HIGHPOINT (NORTH AND SOUTH), Stradishall,
Newmarket, Suffolk CB8 9YG
Prisoners, 812 *Governor,* R. Haley

†HINDLEY, Gibson Street, Bickershaw, Wigan, Lancs WN2 5TH
Prisoners, 512 *Governor,* J. Blake

‡HOLLESLEY BAY COLONY, Woodbridge, Suffolk IP12 3JW
Prisoners, 299 *Governor,* M. Wood

*†‡HOLLOWAY, Parkhurst Road, London N7 0NU
Prisoners, 467 *Governor,* E. Willetts

HOLME HOUSE, Holme House Road, Stockton-on-Tees
TS18 2QU *Prisoners,* 968 *Governor,* M. Lees

†HULL, Hedon Road, Hull HU9 5LS
Prisoners, 1,078 *Governor,* M. Read

‡HUNTERCOMBE, Huntercombe Place, Nuffield, Henley-on-
Thames RG9 5SB *Prisoners,* 361 *Governor,* E. Jones

KINGSTON, 122 Milton Road, Portsmouth PO3 6AS
Prisoners, 137 *Governor,* J. Robinson

KIRKHAM, Freckleton Road, Preston PR4 2RN
Prisoners, 551 *Governor,* S. Lawrence

KIRKLEVINGTON GRANGE, Yarm, Cleveland TS15 9PA
Prisoners, 223 *Governor,* A. Richer

LANCASTER, The Castle, Lancaster LA1 1YL
Prisoners, 233 *Governor,* D. Harrison

‡LANCASTER FARMS, Far Moor Lane, Stone Row Head, off Quernmore Road, Lancaster LA1 3QZ
Prisoners, 510 *Governor*, T. Williams

LATCHMERE HOUSE, Church Road, Ham Common, Richmond, Surrey TW10 5HH
Prisoners, 197 *Governor*, T. Hinchliffe

†LEEDS, Armley, Leeds LS12 2TJ
Prisoners, 1,254 *Governor*, I. Blakeman

LEICESTER, Welford Road, Leicester LE2 7AJ
Prisoners, 379 *Governor*, S. Turner

†‡LEWES, Brighton Road, Lewes, E. Sussex BN7 1EA
Prisoners, 486 *Governor*, E. McLennan-Murray

LEYHILL, Wotton-under-Edge, Glos GL12 8BT
Prisoners, 499 *Governor*, R. Booty

†LINCOLN, Greetwell Road, Lincoln LN2 4BD
Prisoners, 460 *Governor*, L. Saunders

§LINDHOLME, Bawtry Road, Hatfield Woodhouse, Doncaster DN7 6EE *Prisoners*, 664 *Governor*, M. Ward

LITTLEHEY, Perry, Huntingdon, Cambs PE28 0SR
Prisoners, 698 *Governor*, J. Morgan

†LIVERPOOL, 68 Hornby Road, Liverpool L9 3DF
Prisoners, 1,427 *Governor*, C. James

LONG LARTIN, South Littleton, Evesham, Worcs WR11 8TZ
Prisoners, 434 *Governor*, N. Leader

LOWDHAM GRANGE (private prison), Lowdham, Notts NG14 7DA *Prisoners*, 519 *Director*, P. Wright

*†‡LOW NEWTON, Brasside, Durham DH1 5AD
Prisoners, 351 *Governor*, D. Thompson

MAIDSTONE, 36 County Road, Maidstone ME14 1UZ
Prisoners, 543 *Governor*, J. Glabally

MANCHESTER, Southall Street, Manchester M60 9AH
Prisoners, 1,223 *Governor*, C. Sheffield

‡MOORLAND CLOSED, Bawtry Road, Hatfield Woodhouse, Doncaster DN7 6BW *Prisoners*, 762 *Governor*, J. Tilley

‡MOORLAND OPEN, Thorne Road, Hatfield, Doncaster DN7 6EL *Prisoners*, 249 *Governor*, J. Tilley

*MORTON HALL, Swinderby, Lincoln LN6 9PT
Prisoners, 368 *Governor*, D. Evans

THE MOUNT, Molyneaux Avenue, Bovingdon, Hemel Hempstead HP3 0NZ *Prisoners*, 753 *Governor*, P. Wailen

*†‡NEW HALL, Dial Wood, Flockton, Wakefield WF4 4AX
Prisoners, 365 *Governor*, S. Snell

‡NORTHALLERTON, 15A East Road, Northallerton, N. Yorks DL6 1NW *Prisoners*, 216 *Governor*, B. Shaw

NORTH SEA CAMP, Freiston, Boston, Lincs PE22 0QX
Prisoners, 296 *Governor*, K. Beaumont

†NORWICH, Mousehold, Norwich NR1 4LU
Prisoners, 738 *Governor*, J. Knight

†NOTTINGHAM, Perry Road, Sherwood, Nottingham NG5 3AG *Prisoners*, 493 *Governor*, A. Beck

‡ONLEY, Willoughby, Rugby, Warks CV23 8AP
Prisoners, 490 *Governor*, A. Perry

†‡PARC (private prison), Heol Hopcyn John, Bridgend CF35 6AR *Prisoners*, 1,030 *Director*, R. Woolford

†PARKHURST, Newport, Isle of Wight PO30 5NX
Prisoners, 498 *Governor*, S. Metcalf

†PENTONVILLE, Caledonian Road, London N7 8TT
Prisoners, 1,190 *Governor*, R. Kringle

‡PORTLAND, Easton, Portland, Dorset DT5 1DL
Prisoners, 467 *Governor*, S. Twinn

†PRESTON, 2 Ribbleton Lane, Preston PR1 5AB
Prisoners, 674 *Governor*, A. Brown

RANBY, Ranby, Retford, Notts DN22 8EU
Prisoners, 858 *Governor*, P. Wragg

†‡READING, Forbury Road, Reading RG1 3HY
Prisoners, 263 *Governor*, P. Bryant

*RISLEY, Risley, Warrington WA3 6BP *Prisoners*, 1,059.
Governor, P. Norbury

†‡ROCHESTER, 1 Fort Road, Rochester, Kent ME1 3QS
Prisoners, 281 *Governor*, C. Kershaw

RYE HILL (private prison), Onley, Rugby CV23 8AM
Prisoners, 661 *Director*, S. Mitson

*SEND, Ripley Road, Send, Woking, Surrey GU23 7LJ
Prisoners, 211 *Governor*, B. Ritchie

SHEPTON MALLET, Cornhill, Shepton Mallet, Somerset BA4 5LU *Prisoners*, 186 *Governor*, S. Dymond-White

†SHREWSBURY, The Dana, Shrewsbury SY1 2HR
Prisoners, 329 *Governor*, M. Boulton

SPRING HILL, Grendon Underwood, Aylesbury, Bucks, HP18 0TH *Prisoners*, 330 *Governor*, P. Bennett

STAFFORD, 54 Gaol Road, Stafford ST16 3AW
Prisoners, 632 *Governor*, P. L. J. Taylor

STANDFORD HILL, Church Road, Eastchurch, Isle of Sheppey, Kent ME12 4AA
Prisoners, 453 *Governor*, T. Robson

STOCKEN, Stocken Hall Road, Stretton, nr Oakham, Leics LE15 7RD *Prisoners*, 619 *Governor*, M. Bartlett

‡STOKE HEATH, Stoke Heath, Market Drayton, Shropshire TF9 2JL *Prisoners*, 667 *Governor*, P. Small

*†‡STYAL, Wilmslow, Cheshire SK9 4HR
Prisoners, 408 *Governor*, S. Hall

SUDBURY, Ashbourne, Derbys DE6 5HW
Prisoners, 554 *Governor*, C. Davidson

SWALESIDE, Brabazon Road, Eastchurch, Isle of Sheppey, Kent ME12 4AX *Prisoners*, 771 *Governor*, M. Conway

†SWANSEA, 200 Oystermouth Road, Swansea SA1 3SR
Prisoners, 335 *Governor*, P. Taylor

‡SWINFEN HALL, Lichfield, Staffs WS14 9QS
Prisoners, 306 *Governor*, P. Knapton

‡THORN CROSS, Arley Road, Appleton Thorn, Warrington WA4 4RL *Prisoners*, 259 *Governor*, M. Moulden

‡USK, 47 Maryport Street, Usk, Gwent NP5 1XP
Prisoners, 248 *Governor*, P. Morgan

THE VERNE, Portland, Dorset DT5 1EQ
Prisoners, 582 *Governor*, M. Cook

WAKEFIELD, 5 Love Lane, Wakefield WF2 9AG
Prisoners, 559 *Governor*, J. Slater

†WANDSWORTH, Heathfield Road, London SW18 3HS
Prisoners, 1,431 *Governor*, J. Heavens

‡WARREN HILL, Hollesley, Woodbridge, Suffolk IP12 3JW
Prisoners, 202 *Governor*, S. Robinson

WAYLAND, Griston, Thetford, Norfolk IP25 6RL
Prisoners, 693 *Governor*, J. Shanley

WEALSTUN, Wetherby, W. Yorks LS23 7AZ
Prisoners, 593 *Governor*, S. Tilley

WEARE, Portland Dock, Castletown, Portland, Dorset DT5 1PZ
Prisoners, 380 *Governor*, D. Calvert

WELLINGBOROUGH, Millers Park, Doddington Road, Wellingborough, Northants NN8 2NH
Prisoners, 522 *Governor*, J. Lewis

‡WERRINGTON, Werrington, Stoke-on-Trent ST9 0DX
Prisoners, 137 *Governor*, F. Flynn

‡WETHERBY, York Road, Wetherby, W. Yorks LS22 5ED
Prisoners, 313 *Governor*, P. Foweather

WHATTON, 14 Cromwell Road, Nottingham NG13 9FQ
Prisoners, 351 *Governor*, V. Hart

WHITEMOOR, Longhill Road, March, Cambs PE15 0PR
Prisoners, 425 *Governor*, M. Lomas

*WINCHESTER, Romsey Road, Winchester SO22 5DF
Prisoners, 639 *Governor*, C. Allison

WOLDS (private prison), Everthorpe, Brough, E. Yorks HU15 2JZ *Prisoners*, 355 *Director*, D. McDonnell

†‡§WOODHILL, Tattenhoe Street, Milton Keynes MK4 4DA
Prisoners, 779 *Governor*, P. Haley

WORMWOOD SCRUBS, PO Box 757, Du Cane Road, London W12 0AE *Prisoners*, 1,227 *Governor*, K. Munns

WYMOTT, Ulnes Walton Lane, Leyland, Preston PR5 3LW
Prisoners, 906 *Governor*, A. Scott

SCOTTISH PRISON SERVICE

Calton House, 5 Redheughs Rigg, Edinburgh EH12 9HW
T 0131-556 8400 W www.sps.gov.uk

SALARIES 2003–4
The following pay bands have applied since 1 October 2002 and were scheduled for review by the end of 2004. Senior managers in the Scottish Prison Service, including governors and deputy governors of prisons, are paid across three pay bands:

Band I	£48,000–£58,000
Band H	£38,100–£48,100
Band G	£30,000–£40,000

STAFF
Chief Executive of Scottish Prison Service, T. Cameron
Director, Human Resources, B. Allison
Director, Finance and Information Systems, W. Pretswell
Director, Strategy and Business Performance, K. Thomson
Director, Rehabilitation and Care, A. Spencer
Director of Prisons, M. Duffy
Director of Prison Services, P. Withers
Head of Training, Scottish Prison Service College, W. Rattray
Head of Communications, T. Fox

PRISON ESTABLISHMENTS
Average prisoners numbers *as at 21 May 2004*
*ABERDEEN, Craiginches, 4 Grampian Place, Aberdeen AB1 8FN *Prisoners*, 223 *Governor*, A. Mooney
BARLINNIE, Barlinnie, Glasgow G33 2QX
Prisoners, 1,202 *Governor*, W. McKinlay
CASTLE HUNTLY, Castle Huntly, Longforgan, nr Dundee DD2 5HL *Prisoners*, 155 *Governor*, I. Whitehead
*†CORNTON VALE, Cornton Road, Stirling FK9 5NU
Prisoners, 247 *Governor*, S. Brookes
*DUMFRIES, Terregles Street, Dumfries DG2 9AX
Prisoners, 183 *Governor*, C. McGeever
EDINBURGH, 33 Stenhouse Road, Edinburgh EH11 3LN
Prisoners, 728 *Governor*, D. Croft
GLENOCHIL, King O'Muir Road, Tullibody, Clackmannanshire FK10 3AD *Prisoners*, 484 *Governor*, K. Donegan
GREENOCK, Gateside, Greenock PA16 9AH
Prisoners, 354 *Governor*, S. Swan

*INVERNESS, Porterfield, Duffy Drive, Inverness IV2 3HH
Prisoners, 142 *Governor*, A. MacDonald
KILMARNOCK (private prison), Bowhouse, Mauchline Road, Kilmarnock KA1 5JH
Prisoners, 588 *Governor*, N. Cameron
LOW MOSS, Low Moss, Bishopbriggs, Glasgow G64 2QB
Prisoners, 285 *Governor*, E. Fairbairn
NORANSIDE, Noranside, Fern, by Forfar, Angus DD8 3QY
Prisoners, 136 *Governor*, I. Whitehead
PERTH, 3 Edinburgh Road, Perth PH2 8AT
Prisoners, 704 *Governor*, W. Millar
PETERHEAD, Salthouse Head, Peterhead, Aberdeenshire AB42 2YY *Prisoners*, 295 *Governor*, I. Gunn
†POLMONT, Brightons, Falkirk, Stirlingshire FK2 0AB
Prisoners, 657 *Governor*, D. Gunn
SHOTTS, Shotts ML7 4LE *Prisoners*, 500 *Governor*, A. Park

NORTHERN IRELAND PRISON SERVICE

Dundonald House, Upper Newtownards Road, Belfast BT4 3SU
T 028-9052 2922 F 028-9052 5100
E info@niprisonservice.gov.uk
W www.niprisonservice.gov.uk

SALARIES 2004–5

Governor 1	£60,010–£64,673
Governor 2	£54,312–£57,950
Governor 3	£46,763–£50,145
Governor 4	£39,276–£42,962
Governor 5	£33,986–£38,501

A Northern Ireland allowance is also payable

PRISON ESTABLISHMENTS
Average number of prisoners/young offenders *as at September 2004*

‡HYDEBANK WOOD YOC, Hospital Road, Belfast BT8 8NA
Young Offenders, 238
*§MAGHABERRY, Old Road, Ballinderry Upper, Lisburn, Co. Antrim BT28 2PT *Prisoners*, 659
MAGILLIGAN, Point Road, Limavady, Co. Londonderry BT49 0LR *Prisoners*, 328

* Women's establishment or establishment with units for women
† Remand Centre or establishment with units for remand prisoners
‡ Young Offender Institution or establishment with units for young offenders
§ Immigration Removal Centre

DEFENCE

The armed forces of the United Kingdom comprise the Royal Navy, the Army and the Royal Air Force. The Queen is Commander-in-Chief of all the armed forces. The Secretary of State for Defence is responsible for the formulation and content of defence policy and for providing the means by which it is conducted. The formal legal basis for the conduct of defence in the UK rests on a range of powers vested by statute and Letters Patent in the Defence Council, chaired by the Secretary of State for Defence. Beneath the Ministers lies the top management of the Ministry of Defence, headed jointly by the Permanent Secretary and the Chief of Defence Staff. The Permanent Secretary is the Government's principal civilian adviser on defence and has the primary responsibility for policy, finance, management and administration. He is also personally accountable to Parliament for the expenditure of all public money voted for defence purposes. The Chief of the Defence Staff is the professional head of the Armed Forces in the UK and the principal military adviser to the Secretary of State and the Government.

The Defence Management Board (DMB) is the executive board of the Defence Council. Chaired by the Permanent Secretary, it acts as the main executive board of the Ministry of Defence, providing senior level leadership and strategic management of defence.

The Central Staff, headed by the Vice-Chief of the Defence Staff and the Second Permanent Under-Secretary of State is the policy core of the Department. The Defence Procurement Agency is responsible for purchasing equipment. The Defence Logistics Organisation has responsibility for logistic support.

A permanent Joint Headquarters for the conduct of joint operations was set up at Northwood in 1996. The Joint Headquarters connects the policy and strategic functions of the MoD Head Office with the conduct of operations and is intended to strengthen the policy/executive division.

Britain pursues its defence and security policies through its membership of NATO (to which most of its armed forces are committed), the European Union, the Organisation for Security and Co-operation in Europe and the UN (see International Organisations section).

ARMED FORCES STRENGTH as at 1 July 2004

All Services	205,140
Men	186,800
Women	18,340
Royal Naval Services	40,510
Army	111,500
Royal Air Force	53,130
Source: Ministry of Defence	

SERVICE PERSONNEL as at 1 July 2004

	Royal Navy	Army	RAF	All Services
1975 strength	76,200	167,100	95,000	338,300
1990 strength	63,210	152,810	89,680	305,700
1999 strength	43,700	109,720	55,210	208,630
2001 strength	42,420	109,530	53,700	205,650
2002 strength	41,630	110,050	53,000	204,680
2003 strength	41,550	112,130	53,240	206,920
2004 strength	40,510	111,500	53,130	205,140

Figures are for UK Regular Forces (including both trained and untrained personnel), and exclude Gurkhas, full-time Reserve Service personnel, the Home Service battalions of the Royal Irish Regiment, mobilised reservists and Naval Activated Reservists.
Source: Ministry of Defence

CIVILIAN PERSONNEL

1993 level	159,600
1999 level	123,000
2000 level	121,300
2001 level	118,200
2002 level	110,100
2003 level	107,600
2004 level	108,990

As of 1 April 2004 the definition of the civilian workforce changed to include permanent and casual personnel, Royal Fleet Auxiliaries, Trading Funds and Locally Engaged civilians. Figures above reflect the revised definition.
Source: UK Defence Statistics 2004

DEPLOYMENT OF UK PERSONNEL as at 1 July 2003*

	England	Wales	Scotland	N. Ireland	Other
All Services	139,010	2,100	13,870	5,160	8,580
Officers	23,380	300	1,850	580	1,270
Other Ranks	115,630	1,800	12,020	4,580	7,310
Army‡	69,950	920	3,040	4,620	4,710
Officers	9,770	110	550	490	380
Other Ranks	60,180	810	2,490	4,130	4,330
Navy†‡	31,950	20	4,890	150	660
Officers	6,310	10	570	10	160
Other Ranks	25,640	10	4,320	140	500
RAF‡	37,100	1,160	5,950	390	3,210
Officers	7,290	180	730	80	740
Other Ranks	29,810	980	5,220	310	2,470

*Figures are for UK Regular Forces, both Trained and Untrained, located in the UK. They exclude Gurkhas, full-time Reserve Service personnel, the Home Service battalions of the Royal Irish Regiment and mobilised reservists. These are the most recent figures available from the Ministry of Defence at the time of going to press.
† Naval Service personnel on sea service in home waters are included against the local authority containing the home port of their ship.
‡ The titles Naval Service, Army and Royal Air Force include nursing services.
Source: Ministry of Defence

SERVICE PERSONNEL OVERSEAS *as at 1 October 2002*

	Breakdown	Total
All Services		41,980
Officers	5,740	
Other Ranks	36,240	
Army		33,070
Officers	3,840	
Ranks	29,230	
Royal Navy		3,840
Officers	760	
Ranks	3,080	
RAF		5,080
Officers	1,140	
Ranks	3,940	

Source: Ministry of Defence. These are the most recent figures available at the time of going to press.

NUCLEAR FORCES

Britain's nuclear forces comprise four ballistic missile submarines carrying Trident missiles and equipped with nuclear warheads. All nuclear free-fall bombs have been taken out of service.

ARMS CONTROL

The 1990 Conventional Armed Forces in Europe (CFE) Treaty, which commits all NATO and former Warsaw Pact members to limiting their holdings of five major classes of conventional weapons, has been adapted to reflect the changed geo-strategic environment and negotiations continue for its implementation. The Open Skies Treaty, which the UK signed in 1992 and entered into force in 2002, allows for the overflight of States Parties by other States Parties using unarmed observation aircraft.

In 1968 the UK signed and ratified the Nuclear Non-Proliferation Treaty, which came into force in 1970 and was indefinitely and unconditionally extended in 1995. In 1996 the UK signed the Comprehensive Nuclear Test Ban Treaty and ratified it in 1998. The UK is a party to the 1972 Biological and Toxin Weapons Convention, which provides for a world-wide ban on biological weapons, and the 1993 Chemical Weapons Convention, which came into force in 1997 and provides for a verifiable world-wide ban on chemical weapons.

DEFENCE BUDGET (DEPARTMENTAL EXPENDITURE LIMIT PLANS)

Projection	£ billion
2003–4	30.8
2004–5	31.5
2005–6	32.3

Source: The Budget 2003

MINISTRY OF DEFENCE

Old War Office, Whitehall, London SW1A 2EU
T 020-7218 9000 **Public Enquiry Office** 020-7218 6645
W www.mod.uk

Officers promoted in an acting capacity to a more senior rank are listed under the more senior rank. Promotion to five-star rank is no longer usual in peacetime.

GRADE EQUIVALENTS

Grade 1 equivalents: (5*) Admiral of the Fleet, (5*) Field Marshal, (5*) Marshal of the RAF, (4*) Admiral, (4*) General, (4*) Air Chief Marshal
Grade 2 equivalents: (3*) Vice Admiral, (3*) Lieutenant-General, (3*) Air Marshal

Secretary of State for Defence, The Rt. Hon. Geoffrey Hoon, MP
Private Secretary, C. Baker
Special Advisers, R. Taylor; M. Dogher
Parliamentary Private Secretary, Liz Blackman, MP
Minister of State for the Armed Forces, The Rt. Hon. Adam Ingram, MP
Parliamentary Private Secretary, Alan Campbell, MP
Team PPS, Syd Rapson, MP
Private Secretary, G. Dean
Parliamentary Under-Secretary of State for Defence and Minister for Defence Procurement, Lord Bach
Private Secretary, B. Palmer
Parliamentary Under-Secretary of State for Defence and Minister for Veterans, Ivor Caplin, MP
Private Secretary, A. Cruttwell
Permanent Under-Secretary of State, Sir Kevin Tebbit, KCB, CMG
Chief of Defence Staff, Gen. Sir Michael Walker GCB, CMG, CBE, ADC, Gen
Second Permanent Under-Secretary, Ian Andrews, CBE, TD

THE DEFENCE COUNCIL

The Defence Council is the Senior Committee of the Ministry of Defence, which was established by Royal Prerogative under the Letters Patent in April 1964. The Letters Patent confer on the Defence Council the command over all of the Armed Forces and charge the Council with such matters relating to the administration of the Armed Forces as the Secretary of State for Defence should direct them to execute. It is chaired by the Secretary of State for Defence and consists of: the Minister of State for the Armed Forces, the Parliamentary Under-Secretary of State for Defence and Minister for Defence Procurement, the Parliamentary Under-Secretary of State for Defence and Minister for Veterans; the Permanent Under-Secretary of State, the Chief of the Defence Staff; the Chief of the Naval Staff and First Sea Lord, the Chief of the General Staff, the Chief of the Air Staff; the Vice-Chief of the Defence Staff, the Second Permanent Under-Secretary of State, the Chief Scientific Advisor, the Chief of Defence Procurement and the Chief of Defence Logistics.

CHIEFS OF STAFF

CHIEF OF THE NAVAL STAFF
First Sea Lord and Chief of the Naval Staff (4)*,
  Adm. Sir Alan West, GCB, DSC, ADC
Asst Chief of the Naval Staff (2)*,
  Rear-Adm. A. J. Johns, CBE

CHIEF OF GENERAL STAFF
Chief of the General Staff (4)*,
  Gen. Sir Mike Jackson, KCB, CBE, DSO, ADC
Asst Chief of the General Staff (2)*,
  Maj.-Gen. D. J. Richards, CBE, DSO

CHIEF OF THE AIR STAFF
Chief of the Air Staff (4)*,
  Air Chief Marshal Sir Jock Stirrup, KCB, AFC, ADC
Asst Chief of the Air Staff (2)*,
  Air Vice-Marshal, D. Walker, CBE, AFC

CENTRAL STAFFS

Vice-Chief of the Defence Staff, Air Chief Marshal Sir Anthony Bagnall, GBE, KCB
Second Permanent Under-Secretary, Ian Andrews, CBE, TD

DEFENCE INTELLIGENCE STAFF
Old War Office, Whitehall, London SW1A 2EU
T 020-7218 6645 F 020-7218 1562
Chief of Defence Intelligence (3*), Lt.-Gen. A. P. Ridgway, CBE
Deputy Chief of Defence Intelligence, Martin Howard

DEFENCE SCIENTIFIC STAFF
Chief Scientific Adviser, Prof. Sir Keith O'Nions, FRS
Science and Technology Director and Director-General of Research and Technology, M. Markin, OBE

COMMANDER-IN-CHIEF FLEET
C.-in-C. Fleet, Adm. Sir Jonathon Band, KCB
Deputy C.-in-C. Fleet, Vice-Adm. T. McClement, OBE

SECOND SEA LORD/COMMANDER-IN-CHIEF NAVAL HOME COMMAND
Second Sea Lord and C.-in-C. Naval Home Command, Vice-Adm. Sir James Burnell-Nugent, KCB, CBE, ADC
Chief of Staff to Second Sea Lord and C.-in-C. Naval Home Command, Rear-Adm. R. Melly

ADJUTANT-GENERAL'S DEPARTMENT
Adjutant-General, Lt.-Gen. Sir Alistair Irwin, KCB, CBE
Deputy Adjutant-General and Director-General Service Conditions, Maj.-Gen. Currie

COMMANDER-IN-CHIEF LAND COMMAND
C.-in-C., Land Command, Gen. Sir Timothy Granville-Chapman, KCB, CBE, ADC
Chief of Staff, HQ Land Command, Maj.-Gen. A. R. D. Shirreff, CBE

HQ STRIKE COMMAND
Air Officer Commanding-in-Chief, Air Chief Marshal Brian Burridge, KCB, CBE, ADC
Deputy Commander-in-Chief Strike Command, Air Marshal C. R. Loader, OBE

HQ PERSONNEL AND TRAINING COMMAND
Air Member for Personnel and Commander-in-Chief Personnel and Training Command, Air Marshal Sir Joe French, KCB, CBE
Chief of Staff and Deputy Commander-in-Chief Personnel and Training Command, Air Vice-Marshal J. A. Collier, CBE

DEFENCE PROCUREMENT AGENCY
215 MOD Abbey Wood, Bristol BS34 8JH
T 0117-913 0000 F 0117-913 0902
W www.mod.uk/dpa
Chief of Defence Procurement and Chief Executive, DPA, Vice-Adm. Sir Peter Spencer, KCB

EXECUTIVE AGENCIES

DEFENCE LOGISTICS ORGANISATION (DLO)
DLO Headquarters, Spur 4, E Block, Ensleigh, Bath BA1 5AB
Chief of Defence Logistics, Air Chief Marshal Sir Malcolm Pledger, KCB, OBE, AFC

DLO'S BUSINESS UNITS
ARMY BASE REPAIR ORGANISATION (ABRO), Building 203, Portway, Monxton Road, Andover, Hampshire SP11 8HT T 01264-383295
BRITISH FORCES POST OFFICE (BFPO), Inglis Barracks, Mill Hill, London NW7 1PX T 08457-697978
CORPORATE TECHNICAL SERVICES (CTS), DLO, Monxton Road, Andover SP11 8HT T 01264-382515
DEFENCE CATERING GROUP, Spur 12, Beckford, Ensleigh, Bath BA1 5AB T 01225-467943
DEFENCE COMMUNCATIONS SERVICES AGENCY (DCSA), Building 111, Basil Hill Site, Park Lane, Corsham, Wilts SN13 9NR T 01225-467733
DEFENCE FUELS GROUP, West Moors, Wimborne, Dorset BH21 6QS T 01202-654351
DEFENCE STORAGE AND DISTRIBUTION AGENCY, Ploughley Road, Lower Arncott, Bicester, Oxon OX25 2LD T 01869-256840
DEFENCE TRANSPORT AND MOVEMENTS AGENCY (DTMA), Building 400, DLO Andover, Monxton Road, Andover, Hampshire SP11 8HJ T 01264-381125
EQUIPMENT SUPPORT (AIR AND LAND), DLO Secretariat (Strike), Room J103, Cranswick House, RAF Wyton, Huntingdon, Cambs PE28 2EA T 01480-452451
PAYD PROJECT, Building 209, DLO Andover, Monxton Road, Andover, Hants SP11 8HT T 01264-348051
WARSHIP SUPPORT AGENCY, MOD Abbey Wood, Bristol BS34 8SH T 0117-913 7505

OTHER EXECUTIVE AGENCIES

ARMED FORCES PERSONNEL ADMINISTRATION AGENCY (AFPAA), Building 182, RAF Innsworth, Gloucester GL3 1HW T 01452-712612, ext. 7347
ARMY PERSONNEL CENTRE (APC), Kentigern House, 65 Brown Street, Glasgow G2 8EX T 0141-244 2023
ARMY TRAINING AND RECRUITING AGENCY, Building 370, Trenchard Lines, Upavon, Pewsey, Wilts SN9 6BE T 01980-618009
DEFENCE ANALYTICAL SERVICES AGENCY (DASA), Room 711 St Giles Court, 1–13 St Giles High Street, London WC2H 8LD T 020-7218 0390
DEFENCE AVIATION REPAIR AGENCY (DARA), Head Office, Building 145, St Athan, Barry, Vale of Glamorgan CF62 4WA T 01446-798834
DEFENCE BILLS AGENCY (DBA), Room 410, Mersey House, Drury Lane, Liverpool L2 7PX T 0151-242 2225
DEFENCE DENTAL AGENCY (DDA), RAF Halton, Aylesbury, Bucks HP22 5PG T 01296-623535
DEFENCE ESTATES, St George's House, Blakemore Drive, Sutton Coldfield, W. Midlands B75 7RL T 0121-311 2140
DEFENCE GEOGRAPHIC AND IMAGERY INTELLIGENCE AGENCY, Watson Building, Elmwood Avenue, Feltham TW13 7AH T 020-8818 2119
DEFENCE HOUSING EXECUTIVE, 6th Floor, Ibex House, 42–47 Minories, London EC3N 1DY T 020-7423 4815

DEFENCE INTELLIGENCE AND SECURITY CENTRE (DISC), Chicksands, Shefford, Beds SG17 5PR T 01462-752181

DEFENCE MEDICAL EDUCATION AND TRAINING AGENCY (DMETA), MacKenzie Building, Fort Blockhouse, Gosport, Hampshire PO12 2AB T 023-9276 5141

DEFENCE PROCUREMENT AGENCY (DPA), Maple 2120, MOD Abbey Wood, Bristol BS34 8JH T 0117-913 0000

DEFENCE SCIENCE AND TECHNOLOGY LABORATORY (DSTL), Porton Down, Salisbury, Wiltshire SP4 0JQ T 01980-613121

DEFENCE VETTING AGENCY, Building 107, Imphal Barracks, Fulford Road, York YO10 4AS T 01904-662444

DISPOSAL SERVICES AGENCY, St George's Court, 2–12 Bloomsbury Way, London WC1A 2SH T 020-7305 2588

THE DUKE OF YORK'S ROYAL MILITARY SCHOOL (DYRMS), Dover, Kent CT15 5EQ T 01304-245029

MEDICAL SUPPLIES AGENCY, Drummond Barracks, Ludgershall, Andover, Hants SP11 9RU T 01264-798622

MET OFFICE, Fitzroy Road, Exeter, EX1 3PB T 0870-900 0100

MINISTRY OF DEFENCE POLICE, Wethersfield, Braintree, Essex CM7 4AZ T 01371-854000

NAVAL MANNING AGENCY, Victory Building, HM Naval Base, Portsmouth PO1 3LS T 023-9272 7422

NAVAL RECRUITING AND TRAINING AGENCY (NRTA), Victory Building, HM Naval Base, Portsmouth PO1 3LS T 023-9272 7603

PAY AND PERSONNEL AGENCY, PO Box 99, Bath BA1 5AA T 01225-828105

QUEEN VICTORIA SCHOOL, Dunblane, Perthshire FK15 0JY T 01786-822288

QINETIQ, Ively Road, Farnborough, Hampshire GU14 0LX T 01980-613121

RAF PERSONNEL MANAGEMENT AGENCY, Building 248, RAF Innsworth, Gloucester GL3 1EZ T 01452-712612

RAF TRAINING GROUP DEFENCE AGENCY, RAF Innsworth, Gloucester GL3 1EZ T 01452-712612, ext. 5302

SERVICE CHILDREN'S EDUCATION, HQ UKSCE, Building 5, Wegberg Military Complex, BFPO 40

UNITED KINGDOM HYDROGRAPHIC OFFICE, Admiralty Way, Taunton, Somerset TA1 2DN T 01823-337900

VETERANS AGENCY, Tomlinson House, Norcross, Blackpool, FY5 3WP T 0800-169 2277

THE ROYAL NAVY

LORD HIGH ADMIRAL OF THE UNITED KINGDOM
HM The Queen

ADMIRALS OF THE FLEET
HRH The Prince Philip, Duke of Edinburgh, KG, KT, OM,
GBE, AC, QSO, PC, *apptd* 1953
Sir Michael Pollock, GCB, LVO, DSC, *apptd* 1974
Sir Edward Ashmore, GCB, DSC, *apptd* 1977
Sir Henry Leach, GCB, *apptd* 1982
Sir Julian Oswald, GCB, *apptd* 1993
Sir Benjamin Bathurst, GCB, *apptd* 1995

ADMIRALS
West, Sir Alan, GCB, DSC, ADC *(First Sea Lord and Chief of
Naval Staff)*
Garnett, Sir Ian, KCB *(Chief of Staff Supreme Headquarters
Allied Powers Europe)*
Forbes, Sir Ian, KCB, CBE *(Former Deputy Supreme Allied
Commander Transformation)*
Band, Sir Jonathon, KCB *(C.-in-C. Fleet, C.-in-C. East
Atlantic, and Commander Allied Naval Forces North)*
Stanhope, Sir Mark, KCB, OBE *(Deputy Supreme Allied
Commander Transformation)*

VICE-ADMIRALS
Haddacks, Sir Paul, KCB *(Director of International Military
Staff, NATO)*
Burnell-Nugent, Sir James Michael, KCB, CBE, ADC
(Second Sea Lord and C.-in-C. Naval Home Command)
Dunt, Peter Arthur, CB *(Chief Executive Defence Estate
Agency)*
McClement, Timothy, OBE *(Deputy C.-in-C. Fleet)*

REAR-ADMIRALS
HRH The Princess Royal, KG, KT, GCVO *(Chief
Commandant for Women in the Royal Navy)*
Stevens, Robert Patrick, CB *(Chief of Staff to Commander
Allied Naval Forces, Southern Europe)*
Ward, Rees Graham John, CB *(Chief Executive, Defence
Communications Services Agency)*
Guild, Nigel Charles Forbes, CB *(Director-General
Capability (Carrier Strike) Chief Naval Engineer Officer)*
Dymock, Anthony Knox, CB *(Head of British Defence
Staff, Washington)*
Reeve, Jonathon, CB *(Deputy Chief Executive, Warship
Support Agency and Navy Member for Logistics)*
Lockwood, Roger Graham *(Senior Naval Member of the
Directing Staff Royal College of Defence Studies)*
McLean, Rory Alistair Ian, CB, OBE *(Asst Chief of the
Defence Staff (Resources and Planning)*
Davies, Peter Roland, CBE *(Flag Officer Training and
Recruiting and Chief Executive, Naval Recruiting and
Training Agency)*
Kilgour, Niall Stuart Roderick *(Commander (Operations) to
C.-in-C. Fleet and Rear-Adm. Submarines)*
Style, Charles Rodney, CBE *(Commander, UK Maritime
Force)*
Kerr, Mark William Graham *(Naval Secretary and Chief
Executive, Naval Manning Agency)*
Boissier, Robin Paul *(Deputy Commander Strike Force
South)*
Cheadle, Richard Frank *(Defence Procurement Agency
Executive Director 4, Controller of the Navy)*
Goodall, Simon Richard James, CBE *(Director-General
Training and Education)*

Snelson, David George, CB *(Chief of Staff (Warfare) to
C.-in-C. Fleet)*
Harris, Nicholas Henry Linton, MBE *(Flag Officer Scotland,
N. England and N. Ireland, and Naval Base Commander
Clyde)*
Johns, Adrian James, CBE *(Assistant Chief of Naval
Staff)*
Chittenden, Timothy Clive *(Chief of Staff (Support) to
C.-in-C. Fleet)*
Spires, Trevor Allan *(Chief Executive Armed Forces
Personnel Administration Agency)*
Melly, Richard Graham *(Chief of Staff to Second Sea Lord
and Commander-in-Chief Naval Home Command)*
Wilcocks, Philip Lawrence *(Deputy Chief of Joint
Operations (Operational Support))*
Ainsley, Roger Stewart *(Flag Officer Sea Training)*
Soar, Trevor Alan, OBE *(Capability Manager (Precision
Attack))*
Lambert, Paul *(Commander (Operations) Fleet, Rear-Adm.
Submarines (as Head of Fighting ARM), Commander
Submarine Allied Naval Forces)*

HM FLEET *as at 1 September 2004*

SUBMARINES	
Vanguard Class	Vanguard, Vengeance, Victorious, Vigilant
Swiftsure Class	Sceptre, Sovereign, Spartan, Superb
Trafalgar Class	Talent, Tireless, Torbay, Trafalgar, Trenchant, Triumph, Turbulent
AIRCRAFT CARRIERS	Ark Royal, Illustrious, Invincible
AMPHIBIOUS ASSAULT SHIP	Ocean, Albion
DESTROYERS	
Type 42 Batch 1	Cardiff, Glasgow, Newcastle
Type 42 Batch 2	Exeter, Liverpool, Nottingham, Southampton
Type 42 Batch 3	Edinburgh, Gloucester, Manchester, York
FRIGATES	
Type 23	Argyll, Grafton, Iron Duke, Kent, Lancaster, Marlborough, Monmouth, Montrose, Norfolk, Northumberland, Portland, Richmond, St Albans, Somerset, Sutherland, Westminster
Type 22	Campbeltown, Chatham, Cornwall, Cumberland
MINEHUNTERS	
Hunt Class	Atherstone, Brecon, Brocklesby, Cattistock, Chiddingfold, Cottesmore, Dulverton, Hurworth, Ledbury, Middleton, Quorn
Sandown Class	Bangor, Blyth, Bridport, Grimsby, Inverness, Pembroke, Penzance, Ramsey, Sandown, Shoreham, Walney

PATROL CRAFT

Archer Class P2000 Fast Training Boats	Archer, Biter, Blazer, Charger, Dasher, Example, Exploit, Explorer, Express, Puncher, Pursuer, Raider, Smiter, Tracker, Ranger, Trumpeter
Gibraltar Squadron 16m Fast Patrol Class	Sabre, Scimitar
Castle Class Patrol Vessels	Leeds Castle, Dumbarton Castle
River Class Patrol Vessels	Tyne, Mersey, Severn

SURVEY VESSELS

Antarctic Patrol Ship	Endurance
Ocean Survey Vessels	Scott
Coastal Survey Vessels	Roebuck, Gleaner
Multi-Role Survey Vessels	HMS Echo, HMS Enterprise

OTHER PARTS OF THE NAVAL SERVICE

ROYAL MARINES

The Royal Marines were formed in 1664 and are part of the Naval Service. Their primary purpose is to conduct amphibious and land warfare. The principal operational units are 3 Commando Brigade Royal Marines, an amphibious all-arms brigade trained to operate in arduous environments, which is a core element of the UK's Joint Rapid Reaction Force; Fleet Protection Group Royal Marines, which is responsible for the security of nuclear weapon facilities; and Special Boat Service, the maritime special forces. The Royal Marines also provide detachments for warships and land-based naval parties as required. The headquarters of the Royal Marines is at Portsmouth and principal bases are at Plymouth, Arbroath, Poole, Taunton and Chivenor. The Corps of Royal Marines is about 6,500 strong.

Representative Colonel Commandant, Royal Marines, Lt.-Gen. R. H. G. Fulton

Deputy Commander, NATO Rapid Deployable Corps Italy, Maj.-Gen. R. G. T. Lane, CBE

Commandant-General, Royal Marines, Maj.-Gen. J. B. Dutton, CBE

ROYAL MARINES RESERVES (RMR)

The Royal Marines Reserve is a commando-trained volunteer force with the principal role, when mobilised, of supporting the Royal Marines. The current strength of the RMR is about 1,000.

Commanding Officer, RMR, Lt.-Col. E. C. Musto

ROYAL FLEET AUXILIARY SERVICE (RFA)

The Royal Fleet Auxiliary Service is a civilian-manned flotilla of 20 ships. Its primary role is to supply the Royal Navy at sea with fuel, ammunition, food and stores, enabling it to maintain operations away from its home ports. It also provides secure logistic support and amphibious operations for the Army and Royal Marines, and forward ship maintenance and repair and sea-borne aviation training facilities for the Royal Navy.

FLEET AIR ARM

The Fleet Air Arm (FAA) provides the Royal Navy with a multi-role aviation combat capability able to operate autonomously at short notice world-wide in all environments, over the sea and land. The FAA has some 6,200 people, which comprises 11.5 per cent of the total Royal Naval strength. It operates some 200 combat aircraft and more than 50 support/training aircraft.

ROYAL NAVAL RESERVE (RNR)

The Royal Naval Reserve is an integral part of the Naval Service. It comprises up to 3,850 men and women nation-wide who volunteer to train in their spare time to enable the Royal Navy to meet its operational commitments, at sea and ashore, in crisis or war.

The standard annual training commitment is 24 days, including 12 days' continuous operational training.

Director, Naval Reserves, Capt. S. J. Timms, OBE

QUEEN ALEXANDRA'S ROYAL NAVAL NURSING SERVICE

The first nursing sisters were appointed to naval hospitals in 1884 and the Queen Alexandra's Royal Naval Nursing Service (QARNNS) gained its current title in 1902. Nursing ratings were introduced in 1960 and men were integrated into the Service in 1982; QARNNS recruits qualified nurses as both officers and ratings and student nurse training can be undertaken in the Service.

Patron, HRH Princess Alexandra, the Hon. Lady Ogilvy, GCVO

Matron-in-Chief and Director of Naval Nursing Services, Capt. L. Gibbon

THE ARMY

THE QUEEN

FIELD MARSHALS
HRH The Prince Philip, Duke of Edinburgh, KG, KT, OM, GBE, AC, QSO, PC, apptd 1953
HRH The Duke of Kent, KG, GCMG, GCVO, ADC, apptd 1993
Sir Roland Gibbs, GCB, CBE, DSO, MC, apptd 1979
The Lord Bramall, KG, GCB, OBE, MC, apptd 1982
The Lord Vincent of Coleshill, GBE, KCB, DSO, apptd 1991
Sir John Stanier, GCB, MBE, apptd 1985
Sir John Chapple, GCB, CBE, apptd 1992
The Lord Inge, KG, GCB, DL, apptd 1994

GENERALS
Walker, Sir Michael, GCB, CMG, CBE, ADC, Gen (Chief of the Defence Staff)
Jackson, Sir Mike, KCB, CBE, DSO, ADC, Col. Cmdt. Parachute Regiment, Col. Cmdt. AG Corps, Hon. Col. The Rifle Volunteers (Chief of the General Staff)
Granville-Chapman, Sir Timothy, KCB, CBE, ADC, Gen (C-in-C. Land Command)

LIEUTENANT-GENERALS
Irwin, Sir Alistair, KCB, CBE, (Adjutant-General)
McColl, J. C., CBE, DSO (Senior British Military Representative – Iraq)
Delves, Sir Cedric, KBE, DSO (Held Strength)
O'Donoghue, K., CBE (Deputy Chief of the Defence Staff (Health))
Reith, Sir John, KCB, CBE (Chief of Joint Operations Permanent Joint Headquarters)
Kiszely, Sir John, KCB, MC (Commander Regional Forces Land Command)
Palmer, A. M. D., CBE (Deputy Chief of the Defence Staff (Personnel))
HRH The Prince of Wales, KG, KT, GCB and Great Master of the Order of the Bath, OM, QSO, PC, ADC(P)
Trousdell, P. C. C., KBE, CB (General Officer Commanding Northern Ireland)
Ridgway, A. P., CB, CBE (Chief of Defence Intelligence)
Dannatt, F. R., KCB, CBE, MC (Commander Allied Rapid Reaction Corps)
Watt, Sir Redmond, KVCO, CBE (Commander Field Army Land Command)
Judd, D. L., CB (Deputy Commander in Chief, North Europe)

MAJOR-GENERALS
Raper, A. J., CBE (Defence Logistics Transformation Team Leader/Quartermaster General)
Viggers, F. R., MBE (Military Secretary)
Moore-Bick, J. D., CBE, (GOC United Kingdom Support Command Germany)
Gordon, R. D. S., CBE (Force Commander UN Mission to Ethiopia and Eritrea)
Brims, R. V., CBE, (Deputy Chief Joint Operations (Operations) Permanent Joint Headquarters)
Gilchrist, P. (Technical Director, Defence Procurement Agency/Master General of the Ordnance)
Cross, T., CBE (End to End Implementation Team Leader)
Figgures, A. C., CBE (Technical Director, Defence Procurement Agency)

Gamon, J. A., CBE, QHDS (Chief Executive of the Defence Dental Agency)
Richards, D. J., CBE, DSO (Assistant Chief to the General Staff)
Shaw, J. M., MBE (GOC Theatre Troops Land Command)
Baxter, R., CBE (Commandant Royal Military College of Science)
Ritchie, A.S., CBE (Commandant Royal Military Academy, Sandhurst)
Bailey, J. B. A., MBE (Director-General Development and Doctrine)
Cima, K. H., (Senior Army Member, Royal College of Defence Studies)
Williams, P. G., OBE (Head of NATO Military Liaison Mission Moscow)
Short, J. H. T., OBE, (Chief of Staff Joint Headquarters (North)
Lamb, G. C. M., CMG, OBE, DSO (GOC 3rd (UK) Division)
Rollo, W. R., CBE (GOC (Designate) Multi-National Division (South East))
Leakey, A. D., CBE (Director-General Army Training and Recruiting)
Wood, M. D., CBE (Director-General Logistics (Supply Chain))
Huntley, M., (Director-General Logistics (Land))
Wall, P. A., CBE (GOC 1st (UK) Armoured Division)
Cottam, N. J., CBE (GOC 5th Division)
Shirreff, A. R. D., CBE (Chief of Staff HQ Land Command)
Duncan, A. D. A., DSO, OBE (Director-General Training Support (Land))
Houghton, J. N. R., CBE (Assistant Chief of the Defence Staff (Operations))
Pearson, P. T. C., CBE (Commander British Forces Cyprus)
Howell, D. M., OBE (Director Army Legal Services)
Lillywhite, L. P., MBE, QHS (Director-General Army Medical Services)
HRH The Duke of Westminster, KG, OBE, TD, DL (Assistant Chief of the Defence Staff (Reserves and Cadets))
Applegate, R. A. D., OBE (Capability Manager (Battlefield Manouvre))
Tyler, T. N. (Deputy Adjutant-General and Director-General Service Conditions (Army))
Loudon, W. E. B., OBE (GOC 2nd Division)
Kerr, J. S., CBE (GOC 4th Division)
Roberts, S. J. L., OBE (GOC London District)
Bill, D. R. (GOC United Kingdom Support Command (Germany))
Whitley, A. E., CBE, CMG (Senior British Loan Service Officer, Oman)
Fleet, A. R., OBE (Kosovo Protection Corps Co-ordinator)
Graham, A. J. N., CBE (Deputy Commanding General Multi-National Corps, Iraq)
Stewart, A. R. E. de C., CBE (GOC Multi-National Division (South-East))
Cooper, J., DSO (Deputy Commander Combined Force Command, Afghanistan)
Brown, C. C., OBE (Chief of Staff Allied Rapid Reaction Corps)
Wilkes, Revd D. E., QHC (Chaplain General)

CONSTITUTION OF THE ARMY

The regular forces include the following arms, branches and corps. They are listed in accordance with the order of precedence within the British Army. All enquiries with regard to records of serving personnel (Regular and Territorial Army) should be directed to: Relations with the Public, Army Personnel Office, Kentigern House, 65 Brown Street, Glasgow G2 8EX T 0141–224 2023/3303

THE ARMS
HOUSEHOLD CAVALRY – The Household Cavalry Regiment (The Life Guards and The Blues and Royals)
ROYAL ARMOURED CORPS – Cavalry Regiments: 1st The Queen's Dragoon Guards; The Royal Scots Dragoon Guards (Carabiniers and Greys); The Royal Dragoon Guards; The Queen's Royal Hussars (The Queen's Own and Royal Irish); 9th/12th Royal Lancers (Prince of Wales's); The King's Royal Hussars; The Light Dragoons; The Queen's Royal Lancers; Royal Tank Regiment, comprising two regular regiments
ARTILLERY – Royal Regiment of Artillery
ENGINEERS – Corps of Royal Engineers
SIGNALS – Royal Corps of Signals

THE INFANTRY
The Foot Guards and regiments of Infantry of the Line are grouped in divisions as follows:

GUARDS DIVISION – Grenadier, Coldstream, Scots, Irish and Welsh Guards. *Divisional Office*, HQ Infantry, Warminster Training Centre, Warminster, Wilts. *Training Centre*, Infantry Training Centre, Vimy Barracks, Catterick, N. Yorks
SCOTTISH DIVISION – The Royal Scots (The Royal Regiment); The Royal Highland Fusiliers (Princess Margaret's Own Glasgow and Ayrshire Regiment); The King's Own Scottish Borderers; The Black Watch (Royal Highland Regiment); The Highlanders (Seaforth, Gordons and Camerons); The Argyll and Sutherland Highlanders (Princess Louise's). *Divisional Office*, HQ Infantry, Warminster Training Centre, Warminster, Wilts. *Training Centre*, Infantry Training Centre, Vimy Barracks, Catterick, N. Yorks
QUEEN'S DIVISION – The Princess of Wales's Royal Regiment (Queen's and Royal Hampshire's); The Royal Regiment of Fusiliers; The Royal Anglian Regiment. *Divisional Office*, HQ Infantry, Warminster Training Centre, Warminster, Wilts. *Training Centre*, Infantry Training Centre, Vimy Barracks, Catterick, N. Yorks
KING'S DIVISION – The King's Own Royal Border Regiment; The King's Regiment; The Prince of Wales's Own Regiment of Yorkshire; The Green Howards (Alexandra, Princess of Wales's Own Yorkshire Regiment); The Queen's Lancashire Regiment; The Duke of Wellington's Regiment (West Riding). *Divisional Office*, HQ Infantry, Warminster Training Centre, Warminster, Wilts. *Training Centre*, Infantry Training Centre, Vimy Barracks, Catterick, N. Yorks
PRINCE OF WALES'S DIVISION – The Devonshire and Dorset Regiment; The Cheshire Regiment; The Royal Welch Fusiliers; The Royal Regiment of Wales (24th/41st Foot); The Royal Gloucestershire, Berkshire and Wiltshire Regiment; The Worcestershire and Sherwood Foresters Regiment (29th/45th Foot); The Staffordshire Regiment (The Prince of Wales's). *Divisional Office*, HQ Infantry, Warminster Training Centre, Warminster, Wilts. *Training Centre*, Infantry Training Centre, Vimy Barracks, Catterick, N. Yorks
LIGHT DIVISION – The Light Infantry; The Royal Green Jackets. *Divisional Office*, HQ Infantry, Warminster Training Centre, Warminster, Wilts. *Training Centre*, Infantry Training Centre, Vimy Barracks, Catterick, N. Yorks
THE ROYAL IRISH REGIMENT (one general service and three home service battalions) (27th (Inniskilling), 83rd, 87th and the Ulster Defence Regiment). *Regimental HQ* and *Training Centre*, St Patrick's Barracks, BFPO 808
BRIGADE OF GURKHAS – The Royal Gurkha Rifles; The Queen's Gurkha Engineers; Queen's Gurkha Signals; The Queen's Own Gurkha Logistic Regiment. *Regimental HQ*, Airfield Camp, Netheravon, Wilts. *Gurkha Company*, Infantry Training Centre, Vimy Barracks, Catterick, N. Yorks
THE PARACHUTE REGIMENT (three regular battalions) – *Regimental HQ*, Flagstaff House, Colchester, Essex. *Training Centre*, Infantry Training Centre, Vimy Barracks, Catterick, N. Yorks
SPECIAL AIR SERVICE REGIMENT – Stirling Lines, Hereford
ARMY AIR CORPS – *Regimental HQ* and *Training Centre*, Middle Wallop, Stockbridge, Hants

SERVICES
Royal Army Chaplains' Department – *Regimental HQ*, HQ AG, Upavon, Pewsey, Wilts. *Training Centre*, Armed Forces Chaplaincy Centre, Amport House, Amport, Andover, Hants
The Royal Logistic Corps – *Regimental HQ*, Blackdown Barracks, Deepcut, Camberley, Surrey. *Training Centre*, Princess Royal Barracks, Deepcut, Camberley, Surrey
Royal Army Medical Corps – *Regimental HQ*, former Army Staff College, Slim Road, Camberley, Surrey and *Training Centre*, Defence Medical Services Keogh Barracks, Ash Vale, Aldershot, Hants
Corps of Royal Electrical and Mechanical Engineers – *Regimental HQ* and *Training Centre*, Hazebrouck Barracks, Isaac Newton Road, Arborfield, Reading, Berks
Adjutant-General's Corps – Staff and Personnel Support Branch (SPS), Provost Branch (Royal Military Police and Military Provost Staff Corps (RMP and MPS), Educational and Training Services Branch (ETS), Army Legal Services Branch (ALS), Regimental HQ, Worthy Down, Winchester, Hants. *Training Centres*, SPS and ETS Worthy Down, Winchester, Hants; RMP and MPS, Roussillon Barracks, Chichester, West Sussex
Royal Army Veterinary Corps – *Regimental HQ*, former Army Staff College, Slim Road, Camberley, Surrey, *Training Centre*, Defence Animal Centre, Melton Mowbray, Leics
Royal Army Dental Corps – *Regimental HQ*, former Army Staff College, Slim Road, Camberley, Surrey, *Training Centre*, Evelyn Woods Road, Aldershot, Hants
Intelligence Corps – *Directorate HQ* and *Training Centre*, Chicksands, Shefford, Beds
Army Physical Training Corps – *Regimental HQ*, Trenchard Lines, Upavon, Pewsey, Wilts, *Training Centre*, Army School of Physical Training, Fox Lines, Queen's Avenue, Aldershot, Hants
Queen Alexandra's Royal Army Nursing Corps – *Regimental HQ*, former Army Staff College, Slim Road, Camberley, *Training Centres*, Army Nursing Training is

carried out at Universities of Birmingham and Portsmouth

Corps of Army Music – *Directorate HQ* and *Training Centre*, Army School of Music, Kneller Hall, Kneller Road, Twickenham, Middx

ARMY EQUIPMENT HOLDINGS *as at August 2003*

Tanks	560
Armoured combat vehicles	2,361
Artillery pieces	441
Combat Aircraft	502
Helicopters	254

THE TERRITORIAL ARMY (TA)

The Territorial Army provides formed units and individuals as an essential part of the Army's order of battle for operations across all military tasks in order to ensure that the Army is capable of mounting and sustaining operations at nominated states of readiness. It also provides a basis for regeneration, while at the same time maintaining links with the local community and society at large. Since 1 December 2002 its established strength has been 41,893.

Inspector-General, Lt.-Gen. Sir J. P. Kiszely, KCB, MC

QUEEN ALEXANDRA'S ROYAL ARMY NURSING CORPS

The Queen Alexandra's Royal Army Nursing Corps (QARANC) was founded in 1902 as Queen Alexandra's Imperial Military Nursing Service (QAIMNS) and gained its present title in 1949. The QARANC has trained nurses for the register since 1950 and also trains and employs Health Care Assistants to Level 3 NVQ. The Corps recruits qualified nurses as Officers and other ranks and in 1992 male nurses already serving in the Army were transferred to the QARANC.

Director of Army Nursing Services (DANS) and Matron in Chief Army, Col. K. George

THE ROYAL AIR FORCE

THE QUEEN

MARSHALS OF THE ROYAL AIR FORCE
HRH The Prince Philip, Duke of Edinburgh, KG, KT, OM, GBE, AC, QSO, PC, *apptd* 1953
Sir Michael Beetham, GCB, CBE, DFC, AFC, *apptd* 1982
Sir Keith Williamson, GCB, AFC, *apptd* 1985
The Lord Craig of Radley, GCB, OBE, *apptd* 1988

AIR CHIEF MARSHALS
HRH Princess Alice, Duchess of Gloucester, GCB, CI, GCVO, GBE
Stirrup, Sir Jock, KCB, AFC, ADC *(Chief of the Air Staff)*
Bagnall, Sir Anthony, KCB, GBE *(Vice-Chief of Defence Staff)*
Burridge, Sir Brian, KCB,CBE, ADC *(C.-in-C. RAF Strike Command)*
Pledger, Sir Malcolm, KCB, OBE, AFC *(Chief of Defence Logistics)*

AIR MARSHALS
French, Sir Joe, KCB, CBE *(Air Member for Personnel and C.-in-C. Personnel and Training Command)*
Loader, C. R., OBE *(Deputy C.-in-C. Strike Command)*
Miller, G. A., CBE *(Deputy Commander Joint Force Command, Naples)*
Sturley, P. O., CB, MBE *(Chief of Staff, HQ Component Command Air North)*
Torpy, G. L., CBE, DSO *(Chief of Joint Operations, JHQ)*
Wright, Sir Robert, KBE, AFC *(UK Military Representative to NATO and the EU)*
HRH The Prince of Wales, KG, KT, GCB and Great Master of the Order of the Bath, OM, QSO, PC, ADC(P)

AIR VICE-MARSHALS
Charles, R. A. *(Director Legal Services, RAF)*
Chisnall, S., *(Senior Directing Staff (Air), Royal College of Defence Studies)*
Cliffe, J. A., OBE *(Chief of Staff (Operations) Strike Command)*
Collier, J. A., CBE *(Chief of Staff to Air Member for Personnel and Deputy C.-in-C. Personnel and Training Command)*
Dalton, S. G. G. *(Capability Manager (Information Superiority), MOD)*
Dougherty, S. R. C., QHP *(Director-General, Medical Services (RAF))*
Heath, M. C., CBE *(Senior British Military Adviser, US Central Command)*
The Ven. Hesketh, R. D. *(Chaplain-in-Chief to the Royal Air Force) (Holds rank relative to Air Vice-Marshal)*
Jones, G., CBE, MBE *(Assistant Chief of Staff (Resources), Regional Headquarters, Allied Forces Southern Europe)*
Luker, P. D., OBE *(Commander Joint Helicopter Command)*
Maddox, N. D. A., CBE *(Air Officer Commanding No 2 Group)*
McNicoll, I. W., CBE *(Director-General Joint Doctrine and Concepts Centre)*
Moore, R. C., MBE *(Air Officer Administration and Air Officer Commanding Directly Administered Units)*
Moran, C. H., OBE, MVO *(Air Officer Commanding No 1 Group)*
Ness, C. W. *(Harrier Integrated Project Team Leader)*
Peach, S. W., CBE *(Director-General Intelligence Collection, MOD)*
Pocock, D. J. *(Defence Services Secretary)*

Rennison, D. R. G. *(Chief of Staff (Support) Strike Command)*
Ruddock, P. W. D., CBE *(Air Secretary)*
Smith, A. J., OBE *(Assistant Chief of the Defence Staff (Logistics Operations)*
Thompson, J. H., CB *(Director-General, Saudi Arabia Armed Forces Project)*
Thornton, B. M., CB *(Director-General Logistics (Strike))*
Thornton, E. J., QHP *(Director-General Healthcare)*
Vallance, A. G. B., CB, OBE *(Executive Assistant Chief of Staff Command Structure Implementation, SHAPE)*
Walker, D., CBE, AFC *(Assistant Chief of the Air Staff)*
Walker, D. A., OBE, MVO *(Air Officer Commanding Training Group)*
Walker, P. B., CBE *(Assistant Chief of Staff Policy and Requirements, SHAPE)*
White, A. D., CB *(Air Officer Commanding No 3 Group)*

CONSTITUTION OF THE ROYAL AIR FORCE

The RAF consists of two commands, Strike Command and Personnel and Training Command. Three RAF stations – Aldergrove, Benson and Odiham – are part of Joint Helicopter Command.

Strike Command's mission is to deliver, sustain and develop air power in the most effective manner to meet the UK's Foreign and Security Policy. Consisting of three groups, each organised around specific operational duties, the Command is responsible for all the RAF's front line forces. No 1 Group comprises the tactical fast-jet forces responsible for attack, offensive support and air defence operations. No 2 Group provides air combat support and includes enabling forces such as Air Transport and Air Refuelling, and the RAF Regiment. No 3 Group is the Air Battle management group and includes Airborne Early Warning, Maritime Patrol, and Search and Rescue aircraft.

Personnel and Training Command (PTC) is responsible for recruiting, training, supporting and retaining the servicemen and women needed to sustain the Royal Air Force. The Command consists of two agencies. The RAF Training Group Defence Agency deals with the recruitment and selection of all RAF personnel, as well as providing RAF non-operational flying and ground training. The RAF Personnel Management Agency (RAF PMA), is responsible for managing the careers of uniformed personnel serving in the Regular and Reserve Air Forces. It also assigns and deploys personnel to meet the military tasks in times of war, crisis and peace.

RAF EQUIPMENT *as at 1 February 2004**

AIRCRAFT	
BAe 125	5
BAe 146	2
Beech 200	7
Canberra	5
C17 Globemaster	4
Dominie	9
Harrier	60
Hawk	102
Hercules	50
Islander	1
Jaguar	46
Nimrod	23
Sentry E-3D	6

HELICOPTERS
Chinook	31
Griffin	9
Merlin	18
Puma	33
Sea King	21
Squirrel	26
Twin Squirrel	3

GLIDERS
Vigilant	61
Viking	87

BATTLE OF BRITAIN MEMORIAL FLIGHT
Chipmunk	2
Dakota	1
Hurricane	2
Lancaster	1
Spitfire	5

*All figures shown relate to the Required Operating Fleet. The actual number of aircraft will, in many cases, vary from the figure given due to reasons such as operational commitments and engineering programmes.

ROYAL AUXILIARY AIR FORCE (RAuxAF)

The Auxiliary Air Force was formed in 1924 to train an elite corps of civilians to serve their country in flying squadrons in their spare time. In 1947 the Force was awarded the prefix 'Royal' in recognition of its distinguished war service and The Sovereign's Colour for the Royal Auxiliary Air Force was presented in 1989. The RAuxAF continues to recruit civilians who undertake military training in their spare time to support the Royal Air Force in times of emergency or war.

Air Commodore-in-Chief, HM The Queen

Honorary Inspector-General Royal Auxiliary Air Force,
  AVM. B. H. Newton, CB, CVO, OBE

Inspector Royal Auxiliary Air Force, Gp. Capt. R. G. Kemp,
  QVRM, AE, ADC, FRIN, RAUXAF

PRINCESS MARY'S ROYAL AIR FORCE NURSING SERVICE

The Princess Mary's Royal Air Force Nursing Service (PMRAFNS) was formed on 1 June 1918 as the Royal Air Force Nursing Service. In June 1923, His Majesty King George V gave his Royal Assent for the Royal Air Force Nursing Service to be known as the Princess Mary's Royal Air Force Nursing Service. Men were integrated into the PMRAFNS in 1980 and now serve as officers and other ranks.

Patron and Air Chief Commandant, HRH Princess
  Alexandra, The Hon. Lady Ogilvy, GCVO

Director of Nursing Services and Matron-in-Chief, Gp Capt.
  R. A. Reid, OBE, ARRC, QHNS

SERVICE SALARIES

The following rates of pay apply from 1 April 2004.
  The pay rates shown are for Army personnel. The rates apply also to personnel of equivalent rank and pay band in the other services (see below for table of relative ranks).

Rank	Daily	Annual
SECOND LIEUTENANT	£56.66	£20,680.90
LIEUTENANT		
On appointment	£68.11	£24,860.15
After 1 year in rank	£69.90	£25,513.50
After 2 years in rank	£71.69	£26,166.85
After 3 years in rank	£73.48	£26,820.20
After 4 years in rank	£75.27	£27,473.55
CAPTAIN		
On appointment	£87.27	£31,853.55
After 1 year in rank	£89.61	£32,707.65
After 2 years in rank	£91.98	£33,572.70
After 3 years in rank	£94.35	£34,437.75
After 4 years in rank	£96.70	£35,295.50
After 5 years in rank	£99.07	£36,160.55
After 6 years in rank	£101.42	£37,018.30
After 7 years in rank	£102.61	£37,452.65
After 8 years in rank	£103.79	£37,883.35
MAJOR		
On appointment	£109.93	£40,124.45
After 1 year in rank	£112.65	£41,117.25
After 2 years in rank	£115.35	£42,102.75
After 3 years in rank	£118.08	£43,099.20
After 4 years in rank	£120.79	£44,088.35
After 5 years in rank	£123.51	£45,081.15
After 6 years in rank	£126.23	£46,073.95
After 7 years in rank	£128.94	£47,063.10
After 8 years in rank	£131.66	£48,055.90
LIEUTENANT-COLONEL		
On appointment	£154.29	£56,315.85
After 1 year in rank	£156.34	£57,064.10
After 2 years in rank	£158.37	£57,805.05
After 3 years in rank	£160.39	£58,542.35
After 4 years in rank	£162.42	£59,283.30
After 5 years in rank	£164.45	£60,024.25
After 6 years in rank	£166.48	£60,765.20
After 7 years in rank	£168.51	£61,506.15
After 8 years in rank	£170.56	£62,254.40
COLONEL		
On appointment	£178.68	£65,218.20
After 1 year in rank	£181.03	£66,075.95
After 2 years in rank	£183.38	£66,933.70
After 3 years in rank	£185.73	£67,791.45
After 4 years in rank	£188.08	£68,649.20
After 5 years in rank	£190.43	£69,506.95
After 6 years in rank	£192.77	£70,361.05
After 7 years in rank	£195.13	£71,222.45
After 8 years in rank	£197.49	£72,083.85
BRIGADIER		
On appointment	£214.32	£78,226.80
After 1 year in rank	£216.60	£79,059.00
After 2 years in rank	£218.88	£79,891.20
After 3 years in rank	£221.16	£80,723.40
After 4 years in rank	£223.46	£81,562.90

PAY SYSTEM FOR SENIOR OFFICERS

Revised pay rates effective from 1 April 2004 for all military officers of 2* rank and above (excluding medical and dental officers).

MAJOR-GENERAL (2*)

	Daily	Annual
Scale 1	£239.89	£87,559
Scale 2	£244.68	£89,310
Scale 3	£249.48	£91,060
Scale 4	£254.28	£92,812
Scale 5	£259.07	£94,562
Scale 6	£263.87	£96,313
Scale 7	£268.67	£98,063

LIEUTENANT-GENERAL (3*)

	Daily	Annual
Scale 1	£280.07	£102,227
Scale 2	£287.07	£104,781
Scale 3	£294.07	£107,336
Scale 4	£301.06	£109,888
Scale 5	£308.06	£112,442
Scale 6	£315.05	£114,995
Scale 7	n/a	n/a

GENERAL (4*)

	Daily	Annual
Scale 1	£344.88	£125,882
Scale 2	£353.82	£129,146
Scale 3	£362.77	£132,411
Scale 4	£371.71	£135,675
Scale 5	£380.66	£138,940
Scale 6	£389.60	£142,205
Scale 7	n/a	n/a

Field Marshal – appointments to this rank will not usually be made in peacetime. The salary for holders of the rank is equivalent to the salary of a 5-Star General, a salary created only in times of war. In peacetime, the equivalent rank to Field Marshal is the Chief of the Defence Staff. From 1 April 2004, the annual salary for the Chief of the Defence Staff is £189,000.

OFFICERS COMMISSIONED FROM THE SENIOR RANKS

Rank	Daily	Annual
Level 15	£116.66	£42,580.90
Level 14	£115.89	£42,299.85
Level 13	£115.09	£42,007.85
Level 12	£113.53	£41,438.45
Level 11	£111.99	£40,876.35
Level 10	£110.43	£40,306.95
Level 9	£108.87	£39,737.55
Level 8	£107.31	£39,168.15
Level 7*	£105.37	£38,460.05
Level 6	£104.17	£38,022.05
Level 5	£102.96	£37,580.40
Level 4**	£100.55	£36,700.75
Level 3	£99.36	£36,266.40
Level 2	£98.14	£35,821.10
Level 1***	£95.74	£34,945.10

*Minimum entry point for SUY, SCCs and LEs with over 15 years' service
**Minimum entry point for SUY, SCCs and LEs with between 12–15 years' service
***Minimum entry point for SUY, SCCs and LEs with under 12 years' service

SOLDIERS' SALARIES

The pay structure below officer level is divided into pay bands. Jobs at each rank are allocated to bands according to their score in the job evaluation system. Length of service is from age 18.

Scale A: committed to serve for less than 6 years, or those with less than 9 years' service who are serving on Open Engagement

Scale B: committed to serve for 6 years but less than 9 years

Scale C: committed to serve for 9 years or more, or those with more than 9 years' service who are serving on Open Engagement

Rates of pay effective from 1 April 2004 are:

	Lower Band		Higher Band	
	Daily	*Annual*	*Daily*	*Annual*
PRIVATE				
Level 1	£36.88	£13,461.20	£36.88	£13,461.20
Level 2	£39.05	£14,253.25	£42.22	£15,410.30
Level 3	£41.21	£15,041.65	£46.61	£17,012.65
Level 4	£44.83	£16,362.95	£50.12	£18,293.80
LANCE CORPORAL (levels 5–7 also applicable to Privates)				
Level 5	£47.23	£17,238.95	£55.42	£20,228.30
Level 6	£49.21	£17,961.65	£58.11	£21,210.15
Level 7	£51.32	£18,731.80	£60.78	£22,184.70
Level 8	£53.67	£19,589.55	£63.51	£23,181.15
Level 9	£55.61	£20,297.65	£66.61	£24,312.65

	Lower Band		Higher Band	
	Daily	*Annual*	*Daily*	*Annual*
CORPORAL				
Level 1	£60.78	£22,184.70	£63.51	£23,181.15
Level 2	£63.51	£23,181.15	£66.61	£24,312.65
Level 3	£66.61	£24,312.65	£69.87	£25,502.55
Level 4	£67.13	£24,502.45	£71.50	£26,097.50
Level 5	£67.65	£24,692.25	£73.23	£26,728.95
Level 6	£68.18	£24,885.70	£74.75	£27,283.75
Level 7	£68.69	£25,071.85	£76.38	£27,878.70

	Lower Band		Higher Band	
	Daily	*Annual*	*Daily*	*Annual*
SERGEANT				
Level 1	£69.09	£25,217.85	£75.40	£27,521.00
Level 2	£70.89	£25,874.85	£77.35	£28,232.75
Level 3	£72.67	£26,524.55	£79.31	£28,948.15
Level 4	£73.41	£26,794.65	£80.31	£29,313.15
Level 5	£75.32	£27,491.80	£81.87	£29,882.55
Level 6	£77.92	£28,440.80	£83.44	£30,455.60
Level 7	£78.51	£28,656.15	£85.00	£31,025.00

	Lower Band		Higher Band	
	Daily	*Annual*	*Daily*	*Annual*
STAFF SERGEANT				
Level 1	£76.48	£27,915.20	£85.06	£31,046.90
Level 2	£77.48	£28,280.20	£87.12	£31,798.80
Level 3	£79.99	£29,196.35	£89.19	£32,554.35
Level 4	£81.86	£29,878.90	£91.26	£33,309.90
WARRANT OFFICER II (levels 5–7 also applicable to staff Sergeants)				
Level 5	£82.98	£30,287.70	£93.34	£34,069.10
Level 6	£86.73	£31,656.45	£95.40	£34,821.00
Level 7	£88.06	£32,141.90	£96.78	£35,324.70
Level 8	£89.19	£32,554.35	£98.16	£35,828.40
Level 9	£91.21	£33,291.65	£99.55	£36,335.75

	Lower Band		Higher Band	
	Daily	*Annual*	*Daily*	*Annual*
WARRANT OFFICER I				
Level 1	£88.84	£32,426.60	£96.86	£35,353.90
Level 2	£90.57	£33,058.05	£98.77	£36,051.05
Level 3	£92.40	£33,726.00	£100.47	£36,671.55
Level 4	£94.23	£34,393.95	£102.31	£37,343.15
Level 5	£96.07	£35,065.55	£104.14	£38,011.10
Level 6	£98.77	£36,051.05	£105.99	£38,686.35
Level 7	£101.55	£37,065.75	£107.61	£39,277.65

RELATIVE RANK – ARMED FORCES

Royal Navy	*Army*	*Royal Air Force*
1 Admiral of the Fleet	1 Field Marshal	1 Marshal of the RAF
2 Admiral (Adm.)	2 General (Gen.)	2 Air Chief Marshal
3 Vice-Admiral (Vice-Adm.)	3 Lieutenant-General (Lt.-Gen.)	3 Air Marshal
4 Rear-Admiral (Rear-Adm.)	4 Major-General (Maj.-Gen.)	4 Air Vice-Marshal
5 Commodore (Cdre)	5 Brigadier (Brig.)	5 Air Commodore (Air Cdre)
6 Captain (Capt.)	6 Colonel (Col.)	6 Group Captain (Gp Capt.)
7 Commander (Cdr.)	7 Lieutenant-Colonel (Lt.-Col.)	7 Wing Commander (Wg Cdr.)
8 Lieutenant-Commander (Lt. Cdr.)	8 Major (Maj.)	8 Squadron Leader (Sqn Ldr)
9 Lieutenant (Lt.)	9 Captain (Capt.)	9 Flight Lieutenant (Flt. Lt.)
10 Sub-Lieutenant (Sub-Lt.)	10 Lieutenant (Lt.)	10 Flying Officer (FO)
11 Acting Sub-Lieutenant (Acting Sub-Lt.)	11 Second Lieutenant (2nd Lt.)	11 Pilot Officer (PO)

SERVICE RETIRED PAY
on compulsory retirement

Those who leave the services having served at least five years, but not long enough to qualify for the appropriate immediate pension, now qualify for a preserved pension and terminal grant, both of which are payable at age 60. The tax-free resettlement grants shown below are payable on release to those who qualify for a preserved pension and who have completed nine years service from age 21 (officers) or 12 years from age 18 (other ranks).

The annual rates for army personnel are given. The rates apply also to personnel of equivalent rank in the other services, including the nursing services.

OFFICERS
Applicable to officers who give full pay service on the active list on or after 31 March 2004. Pensionable earnings for senior officers (*) is defined as the total amount of basic pay received during the year ending on the day prior to retirement, or the amount of basic pay received during any 12 month period within 3 years prior to retirement, whichever is the higher. Figures for Senior Officers are percentage rates of pensionable earnings on final salary arrangements on or after 31 March 2004.

No. of years reckonable service over age 21	Capt. and below	Major	Lt.-Col.	Colonel	Brigadier	Major-General*	Lieutenant-General*	General*
16	£10,550	£12,565	£16,474	£19,076	£22,769	—	—	—
17	£11,036	£13,162	£17,237	£19,959	£23,657	—	—	—
18	£11,523	£13,759	£17,999	£20,841	£24,544	—	—	—
19	£12,009	£14,356	£18,761	£21,724	£25,432	—	—	—
20	£12,495	£14,952	£19,523	£22,606	£26,320	—	—	—
21	£12,981	£15,549	£20,285	£23,488	£27,207	—	—	—
22	£13,468	£16,146	£21,047	£24,371	£28,095	—	—	—
23	£13,954	£16,743	£21,810	£25,253	£28,983	—	—	—
24	£14,440	£17,339	£22,572	£26,136	£29,870	38.5%	—	—
25	£14,927	£17,936	£23,334	£27,018	£30,758	39.7%	—	—
26	£15,413	£18,533	£24,096	£27,901	£31,646	40.8%	—	—
27	£15,899	£19,130	£24,858	£28,783	£32,533	42.0%	42.0%	—
28	£16,385	£19,726	£25,620	£29,666	£33,421	43.1%	43.1%	—
29	£16,872	£20,323	£26,383	£30,548	£34,309	44.3%	44.3%	—
30	£17,358	£20,920	£27,145	£31,431	£35,197	45.4%	45.4%	45.4%
31	£17,844	£21,517	£27,907	£32,313	£36,084	46.6%	46.6%	46.6%
32	£18,330	£22,114	£28,669	£33,196	£36,972	47.7%	47.7%	47.7%
33	£18,817	£22,710	£29,431	£34,078	£37,860	48.9%	48.9%	48.9%
34	£19,303	£23,307	£30,193	£34,961	£38,747	50.0%	50.0%	50.0%

WARRANT OFFICERS, NCOS AND PRIVATES
(Applicable to soldiers who give full pay service on or after 31 March 2004)

No. of years reckonable service	Below Corporal	Corporal	Sergeant	Staff Sergeant	Warrant Officer Level II	Warrant Officer Level I
22	£6,235	£8,054	£8,829	£10,057	£10,581	£11,418
23	£6,452	£8,335	£9,138	£10,409	£10,950	£11,817
24	£6,670	£8,616	£9,446	£10,760	£11,320	£12,215
25	£6,888	£8,897	£9,754	£11,111	£11,689	£12,614
26	£7,105	£9,178	£10,062	£11,462	£12,058	£13,012
27	£7,323	£9,459	£10,370	£11,813	£12,428	£13,411
28	£7,541	£9,740	£10,678	£12,164	£12,797	£13,809
29	£7,758	£10,022	£10,987	£12,515	£13,166	£14,208
30	£7,976	£10,303	£11,295	£12,866	£13,535	£14,606
31	£8,193	£10,584	£11,603	£13,217	£13,905	£15,005
32	£8,411	£10,865	£11,911	£13,568	£14,274	£15,404
33	£8,629	£11,146	£12,219	£13,919	£14,643	£15,802
34	£8,846	£11,427	£12,528	£14,270	£15,013	£16,201
35	£9,064	£11,708	£12,836	£14,621	£15,382	£16,599
36	£9,282	£11,989	£13,144	£14,972	£15,751	£16,998
37	£9,499	£12,270	£13,452	£15,323	£16,121	£17,396

RESETTLEMENT GRANTS
Terminal grants are in each case three times the rate of retired pay or pension. There are special rates of retired pay for certain other ranks not shown above. Lower rates are payable in cases of voluntary retirement.

A gratuity of £3,590 is payable for officers with short service commissions for each year completed. Resettlement grants are: officers £12,339 non-commissioned ranks £8,433.

EDUCATION

Responsibility for education in England lies with the Secretary of State for Education and Skills; in Wales, with the Welsh Assembly; in Scotland, with the Scottish Executive; and in Northern Ireland with the Education Minister and the Minister for Employment and Learning.

The main concerns of the education departments are the formulation of national policies for education and the maintenance of consistency in educational standards. They are responsible for the broad allocation of revenue and capital resources for education, and for the supply and training of teachers. The Secretary of State is responsible for determining the rates of pay and conditions of employment of teachers in England and in Wales. In Scotland and Northern Ireland these are matters for the respective ministers. The Teacher Training Agency in England promotes teaching as a career on behalf of the Secretary of State and the Welsh Assembly.

EXPENDITURE

In the UK in 2002–3, total expenditure on education and training was:

	2002–3 outturn accruals £m	2003–4 estimated outturn accruals £m
Under fives	3,203	3,693
Primary schools	14,658	16,191
Secondary schools	15,870	17,479
Higher education	6,632	7,056
Further education	6,560	7,328
Student support	1,661	1,664
Training	1,496	1,527
Other education and training	5,232	6,098
Total education and training	55,312	61,036

Total managed expenditure on education and training in real terms from 1994–5 to 2003–4 in £ billion was:

	£bn		£bn
1994–5	44.7	1999–2000	45.4
1995–6	44.3	2000–1	48.6
1996–7	43.8	2001–2	52.7
1997–8	43.7	2002–3	55.3
1998–9	44.0	2003–4 (estimated)	59.4

Of which: education

	£bn		£bn
1994–5	43.1	1999–2000	43.9
1995–6	42.9	2000–1	47.1
1996–7	42.2	2001–2	51.4
1997–8	42.3	2002–3	53.8
1998–9	42.7	2003–4 (estimated)	57.9

Most of this expenditure, except that for higher and further education in England, Wales and Scotland (which is met by the respective funding agencies), is incurred by local authorities, which make their own expenditure decisions according to their local situations and needs. Expenditure on education by central government and local authorities in the UK in 2002–3 (£m) was:

	2002–3
Local education authorities	
Current	32,888
Capital	2,298
Total	35,186
Central government	
Current	17,490
Capital	1,140
Total	18,630
All public authorities	
Current	50,378
Capital	3,438
Total	53,816

The following table shows total managed expenditure on education and training as a percentage of GDP:

	2001–2 outturn	2002–3 outturn	2003–4 estimated outturn
Education and training	5.1	5.2	5.5
Of which: education	4.9	5.1	5.3

The bulk of direct expenditure by the Department for Education and Skills (DfES), the Welsh Assembly and the Scottish Executive is directed towards supporting post-16 education. Funding for higher education in universities and colleges is channelled through the Higher Education Funding Councils (HEFCs). Funding for further education, sixth form provision, and adult and community education is channelled through the funding councils for that sector and, in Wales, through the National Council for Education and Training (ELWA). In addition, the DfES currently funds student support in England and Wales (although Wales will be taking over responsibility for student support in Wales at a future date, still to be agreed), the City Technology Colleges, the City College for the Technology of the Arts, and pays grants under the specialist schools programme.

In Wales the Assembly also funds curriculum development, educational services and research. In Scotland the main elements of central government expenditure, in addition to those outlined above, are grant-aided special schools, student awards and bursaries (through the Student Awards Agency for Scotland), teachers, curriculum development, special educational needs and community education. In Northern Ireland the Department of Education also administers the teachers' superannuation scheme, pays teachers' salaries and funds grant-maintained integrated and voluntary grammar schools. The Department for Employment and Learning directly funds higher education, student awards and further education.

LOCAL EDUCATION ADMINISTRATION

In England and Wales the school education service is administered by Local Education Authorities (LEAs), which have day-to-day responsibility for providing most state primary and secondary education in their areas. They share with the appropriate funding bodies the duty to provide adult education to meet local needs. The LEAs own and maintain most schools and some colleges, build new ones and provide equipment. LEAs are financed largely from the council tax and aggregate external finance from the Office of the Deputy Prime Minister in England and the Welsh Assembly in Wales. LEA-maintained schools usually manage their own budgets. The LEA allocates funds to the school, largely on the basis of pupil numbers, and the school governing body is responsible for overseeing spending and for most aspects of staffing, including appointments and dismissals. LEAs also have intervention powers to add additional governors, take back a school's delegated budget or replace the governing body of a school with an interim executive when a school is placed in special measures, is judged to have serious weaknesses or is causing concern and has not complied with a formal warning from the LEA. The duty of providing education locally in Scotland rests with the education authorities. They are responsible for the construction of buildings, the employment of teachers and other staff, and the provision of equipment and materials. Devolved School Management is in place for all primary, secondary and special schools. Education authorities are required to establish school boards consisting of parents and teachers as well as co-opted members, responsible, among other things, for the appointment of staff.

Education, with the exception of further and higher education, is administered locally in Northern Ireland by five education and library boards, which fund controlled and maintained schools and whose costs are met in full by the Northern Ireland Executive. All grant-aided schools include elected parents and teachers on their boards of governors. Provision has been made for schools wishing to provide integrated education to have grant-maintained integrated status, funded directly by the Department of Education. All schools and colleges of further education have full responsibility for their own budgets, including staffing costs.

THE INSPECTORATE

ENGLAND

The Office for Standards in Education (Ofsted) is a non-ministerial government department in England headed by HM Chief Inspector of Schools (HMCI). Ofsted's remit is to help improve the quality and standards of childcare through regular independent inspection and regulation. It must also provide advice to the Secretary of State based on inspection evidence. Ofsted must report on all maintained schools in England, Local Education Authorities (supported by the Audit Commission), initial teacher training courses, the private, voluntary and independent nursery sector (including childminders and day-care establishments), independent schools, (including independent special schools), youth services, service children's education, and all education and training for people aged 16–19 in sixth form and further education colleges. Ofsted also reports on the impact of government initiatives such as the national numeracy and literacy strategies.

A new inspection framework, Framework 2003 – Inspecting Schools, came into effect in September 2003. Schools are inspected at least once every six years. There are 238 HMIs and 946 Childcare Inspectors on Ofsted's permanent staff. W www.ofsted.gov.uk

WALES

Estyn: Arolygiaeth Ei Mawrhydi dros Addysg a Hyfforddiant yng Nghymru (Her Majesty's Inspectorate for Education and Training in Wales) is responsible for inspecting early years provision in the non-maintained sector, primary schools, secondary schools, special schools (including independent special schools), pupil referral units, independent schools, further education, youth support services, local education authorities, teacher education and training, work-based learning, Careers Wales companies, the education, guidance and training elements of the New Deal, and adult community based learning. Its remit also includes providing advice to the Welsh Assembly on a wide range of education and training matters. W www.estyn.gov.uk

SCOTLAND

HM Inspectorate of Education (HMIE) is an executive agency of the Scottish Executive. HM Inspectors (HMI) inspect or review and report on education provision in primary, secondary and special schools, further education institutions (under contract to the Scottish Further Education Funding Council), initial teacher education, community learning and development, the care and welfare of pupils, the education functions of local authorities, prison education, children's services, and in other contexts as necessary. They work in collaboration with the Care Commission in integrated inspection of pre-school education centres and residential schools. They work with Audit Scotland on the inspection of education authorities and on behalf of the Scottish Further Education Funding Council in the review of Scotland's 43 further education colleges. HMIs work in teams alongside lay members (who are volunteer members of the public) and associate assessors (who are practising teachers or senior educationalists seconded for the inspection). HMIE is led by the senior chief inspector, supported by six chief inspectors (five of whom head inspectorates) and twelve assistant chief inspectors. There are approximately 80 HMI in Scotland. The inspection of higher education is the responsibility of inspectors appointed to the Higher Education Funding Council for Scotland. W www.hmie.gov.uk

NORTHERN IRELAND

Inspection is carried out in Northern Ireland by the Education and Training Inspectorate, which provides inspection services for the Department of Education, the Department for Employment and Learning and the Department of Culture, Arts and Leisure. Schools are currently inspected once every five to seven years. In further education and training, extended inspections are carried out once every eight years and focused inspections at least every four years. In addition, the Inspectorate provides evidence-based advice to ministers and departments to assist in the formulation and evaluation of policies in education, training and youth. The Inspectorate comprises one chief inspector, four assistant chief inspectors, 10 managing inspectors and 52 inspectors. W www.deni.gov.uk/inspection_services

SCHOOLS AND PUPILS

Full-time education is compulsory in Great Britain for all children between five and 16 years and between four and 16 years in Northern Ireland. About 93 per cent of children receive free education from public funds and the rest attend fee-paying schools or are educated at home. Provision is being increased for pre-school children and many pupils remain at school after the minimum leaving age. No fees are charged in any publicly maintained school in England, Wales or Scotland. In Northern Ireland, fees may be charged by voluntary schools and are paid by pupils in preparatory departments of grammar schools, but pupils admitted to the secondary departments of grammar schools, unless they come from outside Northern Ireland, do not pay fees. Students under 19 years of age attending courses at further education colleges are not charged course fees.

PUPIL NUMBERS
In the maintained sector in the UK in 2003 there were:

Primary pupils	5,178,200
Secondary pupils	3,995,000
Pupils in special schools	111,500
Pupils in pupil referral units	12,400
Total pupils in all maintained schools	10,100,400

ENGLAND AND WALES
There are two main types of school in England and Wales: schools maintained by the state, which charge no fees; and independent schools, which charge fees. Schools maintained by the state, with the exception in England of Academies and City Technology Colleges, are maintained by Local Education Authorities (LEAs).

Schools maintained by the state are classified as community, voluntary or foundation schools. Community schools are owned by LEAs and wholly funded by them (although sixth forms have separate funding arrangements). They are non-denominational and provide primary and secondary education. Schools in the voluntary category provide primary and secondary education and many have a particular religious ethos. Although the buildings are in many cases provided by the voluntary body, the LEA maintains them financially. There are two subdivisions in the voluntary category: voluntary controlled, and voluntary aided. In the case of voluntary controlled schools, the LEA bears all the costs. In voluntary aided schools, although the managers or governors are responsible for repairs, improvements and alterations to the building, central government may reimburse up to 90 per cent of approved capital expenditure (85 per cent in Wales), while the LEA pays for internal maintenance and other running costs. Foundation schools provide primary and secondary education. They can have a religious character, although most do not. They are funded by the LEA, and by the relevant funding bodies in respect of sixth form provision, although the land and buildings will be owned by a foundation or by the governors.

The number of schools by category in 2003 was:

	England	Wales
Maintained nursery schools (inc two Direct Grant for England)	477	37
Maintained primary and secondary schools: total	21,297	1,829
Of which:		
Community	13,401	1,544
Voluntary aided	4,280	162
Voluntary controlled	2,741	111
Foundation	875	12
Pupil Referral Units	360	29
Maintained special schools	1,088	43
Non-maintained special schools	72	–
CTCs and CCTAs (England only)	15	–
Academies	3	–
Independent schools	2,160	59
Total	25,472	1,997

LEAs are required to provide the schools that they maintain with a delegated budget to cover their running costs, including staffing costs. LEAs can retain funding of various centrally provided services, including transport and some special educational needs. The LEA acts as the admission authority for most community and some voluntary schools.

Governing bodies – All publicly maintained schools have a governing body, usually made up of a number of parent and local community representatives, governors appointed by the LEA if the school is LEA-maintained, the head teacher (unless he or she chooses otherwise), and serving teachers and other staff. Schools can appoint up to two sponsor governors; sponsor governors are persons who give substantial assistance to the school, financially or in kind, or who provide services to the school. Governing bodies are responsible for the overall policies of schools and their academic aims and objectives.

City Technology Colleges (CTCs) and City Colleges for the Technology of the Arts (CCTAs) are found in England only, and are state-aided but independent of LEAs. Their aim is to widen the choice of secondary education in disadvantaged urban areas and to teach a broad curriculum with an emphasis on science, technology, business understanding and arts technologies. Capital costs are shared by government and business sponsors, and running costs are covered by a per capita grant from the DfES in line with an average of the comparable costs in LEA-maintained schools in the areas where CTCs are located.

The Specialist Schools Programme is open to all state secondary schools, including special schools with secondary age pupils, in England that wish to develop a curriculum specialism in one of ten specialist areas: arts, business and enterprise, engineering, humanities, languages, mathematics and computing, music, science, sports, and technology. Schools can also combine two specialisms. Schools must raise £50,000 in unconditional private/business sponsorship, except smaller schools (schools with 500 pupils or fewer) which must raise at least £20,000 depending on pupil numbers. There are two application rounds a year. Schools must prepare four-year development plans. These must include measurable targets for how they intend to raise attainment and extend opportunities for pupils in the specialist area, improve teaching and learning and thereby secure improvement across the whole school. Schools must also share expertise, resources and good practice with other schools and the wider community. Specialist schools receive additional recurrent funding to support the targets within their plan. This is based on £129 for every additional pupil above 1,200 up to 1,400 pupils. In addition, specialist schools receive a one-off capital grant of £100,000 supplemented by sponsorship raised, to improve their specialist facilities. Specialist schools are encouraged to include sponsors and local businesses on their Governing Body. All maintained schools are able to appoint two sponsor governors, and specialist schools will be expected to appoint some sponsor/business/employer governors. Specialist schools can apply for redesignation at the end of the phase to extend the status for a further four-year period. In July 2004 there were 1,954 designated specialist schools.

Academies – Academies are schools open to all abilities. They are usually in disadvantaged areas and are established by sponsors from business or faith or voluntary groups. Sponsors and the DfES provide capital costs, and running costs are met in full by the DfES. Academies either replace seriously failing schools or are established to meet a demand for places. The first three academies opened in September 2002 and a further nine opened in September 2003. Five more academies were due to open in September 2004.

Excellence in Cities (EiC) is a programme of support designed to raise school standards and pupil expectations in disadvantaged urban communities. Excellence Clusters bring the core strands of the EiC programme to smaller pockets of deprivation elsewhere.

Federations are groups of two or more schools with a formal agreement to work together to raise standards.

The Beacon Schools programme was set up to help raise standards across primary and secondary education by sharing and spreading locally and nationally the good practice identified in successful schools. The programme is currently being phased out and the last contracts will end by August 2005. A new programme at secondary level, the *Leading Edge Partnership Programme*, builds on the success of the Beacon Schools programme and supports innovative approaches to addressing critical learning challenges; 103 partnerships began in September 2003 and a further 102 partnerships were announced in early 2004. In addition, a *Leading Practice* programme is currently being developed to recognise and spread best practice.

Independent/State School Partnerships were launched in 1998 and forge links between independent and state schools to enhance the opportunities on offer to pupils. From September 2004, a £1.4 million government package will fund 46 new partnership projects.

Education Action Zones (EAZs) were established from 1997 to develop local partnerships between schools, parents, the community, businesses and local authorities to find solutions to educational underachievement. They were set up as statutory bodies with a maximum five-year lifespan. After five years EAZs in rural areas will transform into Excellence Clusters and those in Excellence in Cities (EiC) areas will transform into EiC Action Zones. The last EAZs to transform will do so in May 2005.

SCOTLAND

Education authority schools (known as public schools) are financed by local government, partly through revenue support grants from central government, and partly from local taxation. Devolved management from the local authority to the school is in place for more than 88 per cent of all school-level expenditure. A small number of grant-aided schools, mainly in the special sector, are conducted by boards of managers and receive grants direct from the Scottish Executive Education Department. Independent schools charge fees and receive no direct grant, but are subject to inspection and registration. The number of schools by category in September 2003 was:

Publicly funded schools	2,826
Independent schools	150
Total	2,976

NORTHERN IRELAND

Controlled schools are managed by the Education and Library Boards (ELBs) through boards of governors consisting of representatives of transferors (mainly the Protestant churches), parents, teachers and the ELB. Within the controlled sector there is a small number of controlled integrated and Irish-medium schools. Voluntary maintained schools are managed by boards of governors consisting of members nominated by trustees (mainly Roman Catholic) with representatives of teachers,

parents and the ELB. Voluntary schools receive grants towards capital costs and running costs in whole or in part. A majority are entitled to capital grants at 100 per cent. Voluntary non-maintained schools are mainly voluntary grammar schools managed by boards of governors consisting of representatives of parents, teachers and, in most cases, the Department of Education and the ELB, as well as those appointed as provided in each school's scheme of management. Integrated schools exist to educate Protestant and Roman Catholic children, as well as those of other creeds, together. Latest figures show that there are currently 57 integrated schools, comprising 19 integrated second level colleges and 38 integrated primary schools. There are a number of schools and units that provide education entirely through the medium of the Irish language. Latest figures show that there are 16 Irish-medium schools and 12 Irish-medium units attached to schools in the English language sector. Of the 16 schools, 15 are Irish-medium primary schools. There are also 3 Irish-medium nursery units. The number of schools in Northern Ireland by type in 2003–4 was:

Grant Aided Mainstream		
Nursery*		100
Primary		892
Secondary: total		233
	grammar	70
	other	163
Non-maintained mainstream		17
Special (maintained)		47
Total		1,289

*Excludes voluntary and private pre-school education centres

THE STATE SYSTEM

SURE START

All early years services in England, including pre-school education, now come under the Sure Start banner. Sure Start programmes increase the availability of childcare for all children; improve health, education and emotional development for young people; and support parents in their role by increasing their opportunity to work, train and study. Its remit is usually confined to the under 5s, but in the case of childcare it is responsible for ensuring that accessible and affordable care is available for all children up to the age of 14, or 16 for children with a special need. W www.surestart.gov.uk

PRE-SCHOOL EDUCATION

Pre-school education is for children from three to five years. It is not compulsory, although a free place is available for every three and four-year-old whose parents want one. In Wales, a free part-time place in a maintained or non-maintained setting is available for each child from the term following their third birthday. The Early Years Advisory Panel is responsible for making recommendations to the Minister for Education and Lifelong Learning on the strategy for expanding early years provision in Wales. In Scotland, pre-school education places are available for all three- and four-year-olds whose parents want one. Northern Ireland has a compulsory school-starting age of four, and since March 2003 sufficient places have been available for each child in its' immediate pre-school year whose parents wish it.

Free, part-time, pre-school, or early education is funded by the Government via local authorities but takes place variously in nursery schools, nursery classes in primary schools, private schools, voluntary sector groups and some childminder networks in England. All providers, whatever their sector, can receive Government funding through local authorities to provide free places if they can show through Ofsted inspections that curricular goals are being met. In Northern Ireland approximately 30 per cent of pre-school education takes place in voluntary/private sector playgroups funded by the Department of Education. The proportion of all three- and four-year-olds in the UK enrolled in pre-school education as at January 2003, by sector, was:

	Public Sector %	Private and voluntary Sector %	All Providers %
UK	65	34	99
England	64	38	102
Wales	80	–	80
Scotland	65	26	91
Northern Ireland	59	13	71

PRIMARY EDUCATION

Primary education begins at five years of age in Great Britain and four years of age in Northern Ireland. In England, Wales and Northern Ireland the transfer to secondary school is generally made at 11 years of age. In Scotland, the primary school course lasts for seven years and pupils transfer to secondary courses at about the age of 12.

Primary schools consist mainly of infant schools for children aged five to seven, junior schools for those aged seven to 11, and combined junior and infant schools for both age groups. First schools in some parts of England cater for ages five to ten as the first stage of a three-tier system of first, middle and secondary schools. Scotland has only primary schools and not infant and junior schools.

PRIMARY SCHOOLS (UK) 2002–3
No. of primary schools	22,638
No. of pupils (including nursery classes)	5,178,200
No. of pupils (excluding nursery classes)	4,855,100

Pupil-teacher ratios in public sector mainstream primary schools were:

	2000–1	2001–2	2002–3
UK	22.3	22.0	22.0
England	22.9	22.5	22.6
Wales	21.5	21.0	21.0
Scotland	19.0	18.9	18.0
Northern Ireland	20.1	19.8	19.6

The average size of classes 'as taught' was 26.0 in 2002–3, the same as in 2001–2. (Figures refer to 'all classes' rather than 'one-teacher classes' only.)

MIDDLE SCHOOLS

Middle schools take children from first schools, mostly in England, cover varying age ranges between eight and 14 and usually lead on to comprehensive upper schools.

SECONDARY EDUCATION

Secondary schools are for children aged 11 to 16 and for those who choose to stay on to 18. At 16, many students prefer to move on to tertiary or sixth form colleges or into further education colleges or work-based training. Most secondary schools in England, Wales and Scotland are co-educational. The largest secondary schools have over 1,500 pupils, but only 5.2 per cent of schools in the United Kingdom take over 1,000 pupils.

SECONDARY SCHOOLS 2002–3
	England	Wales	Scotland	N. Ireland
No. of pupils (000s)	3,308.0	214.3	316.9	155.7
Average class size	21.9	20.5	n/a	n/a
Pupil–teacher ratio	17.0	16.4	12.7	14.4

In England and Wales the main types of maintained secondary schools are: comprehensive schools, whose admission arrangements are without reference to ability or aptitude; deemed middle schools, for children aged between eight and 14 years who then move on to senior comprehensive schools at 12, 13 or 14; and (in England) secondary grammar schools, with selective intake, providing an academic course from 11 to 16–18 years.

In Scotland all pupils in education authority secondary schools attend schools with a comprehensive intake. Most of these schools provide a full range of courses appropriate to all levels of ability from first to sixth year.

In most areas of Northern Ireland there is a selective system of secondary education with pupils transferring either to grammar schools (35 per cent of pupils in 2003) or secondary schools (65 per cent of pupils in 2003) at 10–11 years of age. Grammar schools provide an academic type of secondary education with A-levels at the end of the seventh year, while secondary non-grammar schools follow a curriculum suited to a wider range of aptitudes and abilities.

SPECIAL EDUCATION

Wherever possible, taking parents' wishes into account, children with special educational needs (SEN) are educated in ordinary schools, which are required to publish their policy for pupils with such needs. Local Education Authorities in England and Wales and Education and Library Boards in Northern Ireland are required to identify and secure provision for children with special educational needs and to involve the parents in any decision.

In Scotland, school placing is a matter of agreement between education authorities and parents. Parents have the right to say which school they want their child to attend, and a right of appeal if their wishes are not being met.

Maintained special schools are run by education authorities which pay all the costs of maintenance, but under the terms of local management, those able and wishing to manage their own budgets may choose to do so. Non-maintained special schools are run by voluntary bodies; they may receive some grant from central government for capital expenditure and for equipment but their current expenditure is met primarily from the fees charged to education authorities for pupils placed in the schools. Some independent schools provide education wholly or mainly for children with special educational needs. The number of pupils in maintained schools with statements of special needs in 2002–3 was:

	No.	%
UK	296,900	2.9
England	250,500	3.0
Wales	16,000	3.1
Scotland	20,000	2.3
Northern Ireland	10,300	3.0

ALTERNATIVE PROVISION

There is no legal obligation on parents in the UK to educate their children at school provided that the local education authority is satisfied that the child is receiving full-time education suited to its age, abilities and aptitudes. The education authority need not be informed that a child is being educated at home unless the child is already registered at a state school. In that case the parents must arrange for the child's name to be removed from the school's register (by writing to the head teacher) before education at home can begin. Failure to do so leaves the parents liable to prosecution for condoning non-attendance. There are no official figures on the numbers of pupils educated outside school but estimates suggest that between 100,000 and 170,000 children are being educated at home.

INDEPENDENT SCHOOLS

Independent schools charge fees and are owned and managed under special trusts, with profits being used for the benefit of the schools concerned. There are 2,300 independent schools in Britain, educating over 630,000 pupils, or seven per cent of the total school-age population. The number of pupils at independent schools in 2003 was:

UK	630,000
England	580,000
Wales	9,600
Scotland	31,400
Northern Ireland	9,200

The annual survey carried out by the Independent Schools Council (ISC) shows that 0.1 per cent more pupils were being educated in ISC accredited independent schools in 2004 than in 2003. The Independent Schools Council, formed in 1974, acts on behalf of seven independent schools' associations. These associations are: the Headmasters' and Headmistresses' Conference, the Girls' Schools Association, the Independent Schools Association, the Society of Headmasters and Headmistresses of Independent Schools, the Incorporated Association of Preparatory Schools, the Association of Governing Bodies of Independent Schools and the Independent Schools Bursars Association. There are 1,279 schools in membership of the ISC, responsible for 80 per cent of all children educated outside the state sector. Most of the schools outside ISC membership are likely to be privately owned. The ISC has overall responsibility for the Independent Schools Inspectorate (ISI), which works under a framework agreed with the DfES and Ofsted. A school must pass an ISI accreditation inspection to qualify for membership of an association within ISC. Schools are evaluated on their educational standards (including attainment, learning and behaviour), quality of teaching, assessment and recording, curriculum, staffing, premises and resources, links with parents and the community, pupils' personal development and pastoral care, management, efficiency, aims and ethos. ISC schools are subject to inspection every six years. In 2003 over half of the 11-year-olds who took national curriculum Key Stage 2 tests at preparatory schools achieved the level expected of 14-year-olds. At GCSE, 54.6 per cent of all exams taken by independent school candidates achieve either an A* or A grade (compared to the national average of 16.7 per cent) and at A-level, about 69 per cent of entries were awarded an A or B grade (national average,

44.5 per cent). In 2003, over 116,000 pupils at ISC schools received help with their fees in the form of bursaries and scholarships from the schools. In 2003, ISC member schools spent £523 million (an average of £1,034 per pupil) on new and improved buildings and equipment. W www.iscis.uk.net

THE CURRICULUM

ENGLAND

The national curriculum was introduced in primary and secondary schools between autumn 1989 and autumn 1996, for the period of compulsory schooling from five to 16. It is mandatory in all maintained schools. Following a review in 1999, a revised curriculum was introduced in schools from September 2000.

The Foundation Stage was introduced in September 2000 for children aged 3–5. It sets out six areas of learning:

- Personal, social and emotional development
- Communication
- Mathematical development
- Knowledge and understanding of the world
- Physical development
- Creative development

The Education Act 2002 extended the national curriculum to include the Foundation Stage. This Act also established a single national assessment system for the Foundation Stage called the Foundation Stage Profile.

The statutory subjects in the national curriculum are:

Core subjects	Foundation subjects
English	Design and Technology
Mathematics	Information and
Science	Communication Technology
	History
	Geography
	Art and Design
	Music
	Physical Education

At Key Stage 3 (11- to 14-year-olds) a modern foreign language is introduced. At Key Stage 4 (14- to 16-year-olds) pupils are required to continue to study the core subjects, plus physical education, design and technology, a modern foreign language, and information and communication technology. Citizenship is a compulsory subject for secondary pupils. Other foundation subjects are optional and other subjects, such as drama, dance and classical languages, are taught when the resources of individual schools permit. Religious education must be taught across all key stages.

Statutory assessment takes place on entry to primary school and national tests and tasks in English and mathematics at Key Stage 1 (five- to seven-year-olds), with the addition of science at Key Stages 2 (seven- to 11-year-olds) and 3 (11- to 14-year-olds), are in place. Teachers make their own assessments of their pupils' progress to set alongside the test results. At Key Stage 4, the GCSE and vocational equivalents are the main form of assessment.

The DfES in England publishes tables showing pupils' performance in A-level, AS-level, GCSE, GNVQ and Vocational A-level examinations school by school. LEAs are required to publish similar information in November each year showing the results of national curriculum tests and teacher assessments for seven, 11- and 14-year-olds.

The Qualifications and Curriculum Authority (QCA) is

an independent government agency funded by the DfES. It is responsible for ensuring that the curriculum and qualifications available to young people and adults are of high quality, coherent and flexible and its remit ranges from the under-fives to higher level vocational qualifications. W www.qca.org.uk

WALES

The national curriculum was introduced simultaneously in Wales and, although it is broadly similar, has separate and distinctive characteristics which are reflected, where appropriate, in the programmes of study. Following a review of the curriculum in Wales, changes were introduced from September 2000. Welsh is compulsory for pupils at all key stages, either as a first or as a second language. According to the January 2002 schools' census and the 2002 national curriculum assessment results, 20 per cent of primary school pupils are taught in classes where Welsh is used as a medium of teaching to some degree. In November 2002, additional funding of £9.5 million was announced for Welsh language education; £7 million will be used to support bilingual nursery education in 2004–6. The percentage of children speaking Welsh fluently in primary school has increased from 13.2 per cent in 1988 to 16.8 per cent in 2002.

Schools perform tests and tasks in all the national curriculum subjects except at Key Stage 1, where teacher assessment is the sole means of assessing attainment. Approximately 38,000 pupils in each of the Key Stages 2 and 3 take the tests each year.

In 2003, the percentage of pupils reaching or exceeding the expected standards at each key stage (teacher assessment results in parenthesis) in England and Wales were (figures for England are provisional):

	England		Wales	
	Boys	Girls	Boys	Girls
Key Stage 1				
7 year olds				
level 2 or above				
English				
Reading	80 (81)	88 (89)		
Writing	76 (78)	87 (87)		
Welsh	-	-	- (82)	- (91)
Reading	-	-	- (75)	- (85)
Writing	-	-	- (70)	- (82)
Maths	89 (87)	91 (90)	- (85)	-(89)
Science	- (88)	- (91)	- (86)	- (90)
Key Stage 2				
11 year olds				
level 4 or above				
English	70 (67)	80 (78)	74 (71)	84 (82)
Welsh	-	-	72 (70)	83 (81)
Maths	73 (74)	72 (75)	74 (75)	76 (78)
Science	86 (81)	87 (83)	87 (83)	88 (86)
Key Stage 3				
14 year olds				
level 5 or above				
English	61 (60)	75 (75)	55 (56)	72 (74)
Welsh	-	-	66 (65)	81 (81)
Maths	69 (70)	72 (74)	67 (67)	69 (70)

Awdurdod Cymwysterau, Cwricwlwm ac Asesu Cymru (ACCAC)/the Qualifications, Curriculum and Assessment Authority for Wales advises government on the matters within its remit. ACCAC is funded by the National Assembly for Wales. W www.accac.org.uk

SCOTLAND

The content and management of the curriculum in Scotland are not prescribed by statute but are the responsibility of education authorities and individual head teachers. Advice and guidance are provided by the Scottish Executive Education Department and Learning and Teaching Scotland, which also has a developmental role. These bodies have produced guidelines on the structure and balance of the curriculum as well as for each of five broad curriculum areas for the five to 14 age group. There are also guidelines on assessment across the whole curriculum, on reporting to parents, and on the use of national tests for reading, writing and mathematics at six levels. Testing is carried out by the school when the teacher judges that a pupil has completed a level; most pupils are expected to move from one level to the next at roughly 18-month to two-year intervals. Guidance on the curriculum for 14- to 16-year-olds recommends study within each of eight modes: language and communication; mathematical studies; science; technology; social studies; creative activities; physical education; and religious and moral education. There is also a recommended percentage of time to be devoted to each area over the two years. Provision is also made for teaching in Gaelic in many parts of Scotland and the number of pupils, at all levels from nursery to secondary, in Gaelic-medium education is growing. Local authorities must ensure that local education provision meets demand and consider whether they need a Gaelic-medium class, school or unit. For 16- to 18-year-olds, National Qualifications, a unified framework of courses and awards which brings together both academic and vocational courses, was introduced in 1999. The Scottish Qualifications Authority awards the certificates. W www.sqa.org.uk

NORTHERN IRELAND

The statutory Northern Ireland curriculum is made up of religious education and five broad areas of study at primary level and six at secondary level. Provided the requirements of the statutory curriculum are met, it is for each school to decide what additional subjects should be made available for pupils. Pupils at Key Stages 1 and 2 study religious education, English, mathematics, science, history and geography (known as the environment and society area of study), art and design, music and PE (the creative and expressive area of study), Irish (in Irish-speaking schools only) and four educational cross-curricular themes (education for mutual understanding, cultural heritage, health education and information technology). At Key Stage 3, pupils also study technology and design, plus a foreign language (pupils in Irish-speaking schools can study a foreign language or continue studying Irish) and two extra cross-curricular themes (economic awareness and careers education). At Key Stage 4, pupils can drop technology and design, art and design, and music and can choose one subject from history, geography, business studies, home economics, economics, political studies or social and environmental studies. The Northern Ireland Council for the Curriculum, Examinations and Assessment (CCEA) is currently reviewing the curriculum. The necessary legislation to implement the revised curriculum will be in place by September 2006, however, in practice the new curriculum will be phased in over a number of years to allow schools to plan for and implement the changes. Initially there is likely to be an increased level of piloting from September 2004. The assessment of pupils is broadly in line with

practice in England and Wales and takes place at the ages of eight, 11 and 14. The GCSE is used to assess 16-year-olds. The CCEA monitors and advises the Department of Education and teachers on all matters relating to the curriculum, assessment arrangements and examinations in grant-aided schools. It conducts GCSE, A- and AS-level examinations, pupil assessment at Key Stages 1, 2 and 3 and administers the transfer procedure tests.
W www.ccea.org.uk

PUBLIC EXAMINATIONS AND QUALIFICATIONS

ENGLAND, WALES AND NORTHERN IRELAND
In 1988 a single system of examinations, the General Certificate of Secondary Education (GCSE), which is usually taken after five years of secondary education was introduced. The GCSE is the main method of assessing the performance of pupils at age 16 in all national curriculum subjects required to be assessed at the end of compulsory schooling. The structure of the examination reflects national curriculum requirements where these apply. GCSE short-course qualifications are available in some subjects. As a rule the syllabus comprises half the content of a full GCSE course. In September 2002 eight GCSEs in vocational subjects were introduced and they are: applied art and design, applied business, engineering, health and social care, applied ICT, leisure and tourism, manufacturing, and applied science.

The GCSE differs from its predecessors in that there are syllabuses based on national criteria covering course objectives, content and assessment methods; differentiated assessment (i.e. different papers or questions for different ranges of ability) and grade-related criteria (i.e. grades awarded on absolute rather than relative performance). The GCSE certificates are awarded on an eight-point scale, A* to G. All GCSE syllabuses, assessments and grading procedures are monitored by the Qualifications and Curriculum Authority to ensure that they conform to the national criteria. In 2003, 52.9 per cent of 15 to 16-year olds gained at least five results at grade C or better at GCSE or General National Vocational Qualification (GNVQ) equivalent. Students are increasingly encouraged to continue their education post-16. For those who do so, in addition to the vocational qualifications outlined below, there are General Certificate of Education (GCE) and Vocational Certificate of Education (VCE) Advanced (A-level) examinations. A-level courses usually last two years and have traditionally provided the foundation for entry to higher education. Following extensive consultations in 1996 and 1997 which indicated the need to broaden the post-16 curriculum, new A-level qualifications were introduced in September 2000. The new Advanced Subsidiary (AS) level examinations represents the first half of a full A-level, and is assessed accordingly. The new A-level qualification consists of six units (three AS units and three A2 units). Students who go on to complete the full A-level will be assessed on their attainment in all six units, which may be taken either in stages or at the end of the course. A-levels and AS-levels are marked on a scale from A to E. There is also the opportunity for A-level candidates to take additional papers known as Advanced Extension Awards (which replaced Special papers). The awards are designed to stretch the most able A-level students. Many maintained schools offer BTEC Firsts and an increasing number offer BTEC Nationals. National Vocational

Qualifications (NVQs) in the form of General NVQs (GNVQs) are also available to students in schools. The Advanced Vocational Certificate of Education (AVCE) exists in three, six and 12-unit forms.

The City & Guilds Diploma of Vocational Education is intended for a wide ability range. Within guidelines and to meet specified criteria, schools and colleges design their own courses. These stress activity-based learning, core skills (which include application of number, communication and information technology), and work experience. The diploma is of value to those who want to find out what aptitudes they may have and to prepare themselves for work but who may not yet be committed to a particular occupation. It can be taken alongside GCSEs and can provide a context for the introduction of GNVQ units into the Key Stage 4 curriculum.

The various examining boards in England have combined into three unitary awarding bodies (UABs), which offer both academic and vocational qualifications: GNVQs, GCSEs, AS- and A-levels. The bodies are the Assessment and Qualifications Alliance (AQA), Edexcel, and Oxford, Cambridge and RSA Examinations (OCR). The Joint Council for General Qualifications (JCGQ) comprises the three English UABs, the Welsh Joint Education Committee and the Northern Ireland Council for the Curriculum, Examinations and Assessment.

SCOTLAND
Scotland has its own system of public examinations, and in 1999 a new system of National Qualifications was introduced. Five levels of study are offered: Access, Intermediate 1, Intermediate 2, Higher and Advanced Higher. The new Higher National course and Advanced Higher National course are direct replacements for the SCE Higher grade and the Certificate of Sixth Year Studies respectively. National Qualifications are included on the Scottish Credit and Qualifications Framework (see below), with Access equating to levels 1 to 3, Intermediate 1 to level 4, Intermediate 2 to level 5, Higher to level 6 and Advanced Higher to level 7.

National Courses consist of blocks of study called National Units. A unit usually consists of around 40 hours of study and there are three units in a course. Unit awards demonstrate that a learner has achieved competence in a particular area of study. National Course awards are graded by external assessment, which consists of an examination, coursework or performance, or a combination of two or more of these. National Course awards also require candidates to pass all unit assessments of the course. A typical National Course external assessment requires candidates to demonstrate long-term retention of knowledge, high levels of problem solving, integration of knowledge across a whole course and an ability to apply knowledge and skills in novel situations. The range of subjects has been expanded to include vocational qualifications.

A number of schools use the new National Qualifications system for pupils in their fourth year of secondary education, but the majority of this lower age group still take the traditional Standard Grade examinations take place at the end of a two-year course. Awards at Standard Grade are set at three levels: Credit (leading to awards at grade 1 or 2); General (leading to awards at grade 3 or 4); and Foundation (leading to awards at grade 5 or 6). Grade 7 is awarded to those who, although they have completed the course, have not attained any of these levels. Normally pupils will take examinations covering two pairs of grades, either grades 1–4 or grades 3–6. Most candidates take seven or eight Standard Grade examinations. The three levels of Standard Grade equate to levels 3 to 5 of the SCQF.

THE INTERNATIONAL BACCALAUREATE DIPLOMA

The International Baccalaureate Organisation is a non-profit, Swiss educational foundation established in 1968. The Diploma Programme for which it is best known was developed by a group of schools seeking to establish a common curriculum and a university entry credential for geographically mobile students. They believed that an education emphasising critical thinking and exposure to a variety of points of view would encourage intercultural understanding. Today the IBO offers three programmes to schools. The Diploma Programme is for students in the final two years of secondary school. The Middle Years Programme, adopted in 1994, is for students aged 11–16, and the Primary Years Programme, adopted in 1997, is for students aged 3–12. There are 59 schools in the UK offering the IB Diploma. W www.ibo.org

PROGRESS FILE

Progress File is the successor to the National Record of Achievement which ceased to be available in July 2004. Progress File is an interactive set of guides designed to help young people and adults identify their skills. It enables individuals to manage their learning through promoting ongoing reviewing, planning and development, and recording achievement as part of lifelong learning. The Progress File objectives are to equip people to plan and manage their learning and make effective transitions; to increase motivation and confidence to achieve; and to stimulate learning to gain knowledge and skills, including where these are not recognised in national qualifications. W www.dfes.gov.uk/progressfile/

TEACHERS

ENGLAND AND WALES

All teachers working in maintained primary, special and secondary schools, non-maintained special schools and pupil referral units are required to register with the General Teaching Council for England (GTCE) in England and the General Teaching Council for Wales (GTCW) in Wales. W www.gtce.org.uk and www.gtcw.org.uk

New entrants to the teaching profession in state primary and secondary schools are required to be graduates and to have Qualified Teacher Status (QTS). QTS is achieved by successfully completing a course of initial teacher training (ITT), traditionally either a Bachelor of Education (BEd) degree, BA with QTS, BSc with QTS or the Postgraduate Certificate of Education (PGCE) at an accredited institution. New entrants are statutorily required to serve a one-year induction period during which they will have a structured programme of support. All initial teacher training has a strong element of practical school-based work, with student teachers spending significant periods of their training in the classroom.

In addition to the traditional routes, in recent years various employment-based routes to QTS have been developed. The Graduate Teacher Programme (GTP) is designed for mature, well-qualified people who can quickly take on teaching responsibilities and who need to earn a living while they train. Trainees are paid a salary and undergo up to a year of school-based training. The Registered Teacher Programme (RTP) is designed for people without a degree or formal teaching qualification but with at least two years of higher education; entrants are paid a salary and complete a degree while undergoing training for up to two years. Employment-based training routes account for about 10 per cent of all teacher training places.

Teachers in further education are not required to have QTS, though roughly half have a teaching qualification and most have industrial, commercial or professional experience. As from July 2002, all new entrants to FE teaching in Wales are required to have, or to be working towards, a specified FE teaching qualification. A qualification for aspiring head teachers, the National Professional Qualification for Headship (NPQH), has been introduced. The National College for School Leadership administers this qualification and others and acts as a focus for development and support. In Wales, the NPQH and other headship programmes are administered by the Welsh Assembly Government and consideration is being given to establishing a similar scheme in respect of FE principals, in association with powers under the Education Act 2002 allowing the making of regulations requiring FE principals to have a specified qualification.

The Department for Education and Skills and the Welsh Assembly have introduced various financial incentives to encourage people to train as teachers. A tax-free training bursary of £6,000 is available to most people on post-graduate teacher training courses. Teachers who successfully gain QTS in a priority subject on a PGCE course and who then go on to teach that subject may receive a further £4,000 'Golden Hello' after completing their first year of work. The priority subjects are: English (including drama), Welsh (in Wales), design and technology, information technology, mathematics, modern foreign languages and science. In Wales a similar scheme operates, on a pilot basis, for those undertaking the full-time PGCE (FE) or PGCE (PcET) (Post-compulsory Education and Training). Eligible students receive a bursary of £6,000 (£7,000 for mathematics and science courses from September 2005), paid in instalments whilst studying. In England, other training awards may be available through the Secondary Shortage Subject Scheme (SSSS). This is an additional, means-tested hardship fund from the TTA. The subjects currently included are: design and technology, geography, information technology, mathematics, modern languages, music, religious education and science.

In Wales, placement grants supported by the Higher Education Funding Council for Wales (HEFCW) provide £1,000 per funded student on undergraduate priority courses – the same subjects that attract the £4,000 training grant – and £600 to students on other undergraduate courses.

The TTA administers a returners' programme for qualified teachers who wish to refresh their skills before returning to the profession. Participants are entitled to a bursary of up to £150 a week to a total of £1,500 and additional childcare support. The TTA supports the sharing of good practice in teacher training, encourages schools to offer placements for trainee teachers, and approves organisations to offer training and assessment for higher level teaching assistant (HLTA) status. The Secretary of State announced on 29 March 2004 that he is extending the TTA's remit to include training for school support staff, and aspects of continuing professional development for teachers.

The TTA funds all types of teacher training in England, whether run by universities, colleges or schools. In Wales funding is undertaken by the HEFCW. On an integrated England and Wales basis the TTA also acts as a central source of information and advice about entry to teaching. The General Teaching Council, an independent professional council, acts as a disciplinary body dealing with cases of misconduct and incompetence. It is also responsible for promoting the profession and professional standards and for advising the Secretary of State. The separate General Teaching Council for Wales operates on a similar basis.

The Specialist Teacher Assistant (STA) scheme provides trained support to qualified teachers in the teaching of reading, writing and arithmetic to young pupils. W   www.useyourheadteach.gov.uk   and   www.teachernet. gov.uk/management/professionaldevelopment/npqh

SCOTLAND

The General Teaching Council (GTC) for Scotland advises central government on matters relating to teacher supply and the professional suitability of all teacher training courses. The GTC is also the body responsible for disciplinary procedures in cases of professional misconduct. All teachers in maintained schools must be registered with the GTC. Only graduates are accepted as entrants to the profession; primary school teachers undertake either a four-year vocational degree course or a one-year postgraduate course, while teachers of academic subjects in secondary schools undertake the latter. There is also a combined degree sometimes known as a concurrent degree.

The Scottish Qualification for Headship has been introduced for aspiring head teachers. The colleges of education provide both in-service and pre-service training for teachers which is subject to inspection by HM Inspectorate of Education. The colleges are funded by the Scottish Higher Education Funding Council, which also sets intake levels for teacher education courses. W www.gtcs.org.uk and www.sqh.ed.ac.uk

NORTHERN IRELAND

All new entrants to teaching in grant-aided schools are graduates and hold an approved teaching qualification. A fully integrated programme of Initial Teacher Education (ITE), induction and early professional development as well as the Professional Qualification for Headship (PQH(NI)) programme, is in place in Northern Ireland. ITE is provided by Queen's University, Belfast, University of Ulster, Stranmillis University College, St Mary's University College and the Open University (NI). The university colleges are concerned with teacher education mainly for the primary school sector and the universities mainly for the post-primary sector. The General Teaching Council for Northern Ireland advises government on professional issues, maintains a register of professional teachers and acts as a disciplinary body.

QUALIFIED TEACHERS 2001–2
(full-time) (thousands)*

	E&W	Scotland	NI	Total UK
Maintained nursery and primary schools	181.5	21.5	8.6	211.6
Maintained secondary schools	194.2	22.7	9.7	226.6
Non-maintained mainstream schools	50.2	2.5	0.1	52.8
All special schools	13.5	2.1	0.8	16.3
Total	439.4	48.8	19.1	507.3

*Provisional

SALARIES

Qualified teachers in England, Wales and Northern Ireland, other than the leadership group (which includes head teachers, deputy head teachers and advanced skills teachers) are paid on a six point main pay scale. Good quality performers have the opportunity to be assessed against national standards and moving to the three point upper scale. An 'Excellent Teacher' scheme is being developed now which, subject to consideration by the School Teachers' review Body, would allow further salary progression. Entry points and placement depend on relevant experience. There are additional cash allowances for management responsibilities, special needs work and recruitment and retention factors which may be awarded at the discretion of the relevant body, i.e. the governing body or the LEA. The 'advanced skills teacher' grade was introduced to enhance prospects in the classroom for the most able teachers; this grade does not apply in Northern Ireland. Experienced teachers are assessed against national standards to move onto the upper pay scale, after which they receive performance-related pay increases. There is a statutory superannuation scheme. Teachers working in the London area are paid on separate pay scales. Salary scales for teachers in England, Wales and Northern Ireland as at 2004 are:

Head teacher	£36,432–£90,360+
Principal (Northern Ireland) (2003 figures)	£31,416–£88,155
Deputy head/Vice-principal (Northern Ireland) (2003 figures)	from £31,416
Advanced skills teacher	£30,501–£48,657
Teacher	£18,558–£31,602
Inner London	
Head teacher	£42,525–£96,450+
Deputy head teacher	from £38,292
Advanced skills teacher	£36,594–£54,747
Teacher	£22,059–£37,692

Teachers in Scotland are paid on a seven-point scale. The entry point depends on type of qualification and additional allowances are payable under a range of circumstances. Salary scales for teachers in Scotland from 1 August 2004 are:

Head teacher/Depute head teacher	£36,531–£71,310
Principal teacher	£32,208–£41,574
Chartered teacher	£30,459–£36,219
Main grade	£18,522–£29,541

POST-16 EDUCATION

In the United Kingdom in 2001–2, 79 per cent of 16-year-olds and 68 per cent of 17-year-olds were in post-compulsory education, either at school or in full-time further education or in Government supported training. There were over 5.3 million further education students in the UK during the academic year 2001–2, of which 80 per cent were part-time. The number of students by country of study in 2001–2 was (in thousands):

	Full-time	Part-time
UK	1,128.2	4,227.1
England	1,016.7	3,613.6
Wales	45.0	210.0
Scotland*	45.1	345.0
Northern Ireland†	21.4	58.4

* Enrolments, not head count
† Provisional

In 2002–3, there were 467 further education colleges in the UK of which 103 were sixth form colleges. In 2001–2, there were 57,000 full-time academic staff in further education institutions.

ENGLAND AND WALES

Further education and sixth form colleges are funded directly through the Learning and Skills Council in England, which operates through 47 local offices, and the National Council for Education and Training in Wales. Further education colleges are controlled by autonomous further education corporations, which include substantial representation from industry and commerce, and which own assets and employ staff. Their funding is determined in part by the number of students enrolled and their level of achievement.

Much further education tends to be broadly vocational in purpose and employers are often involved in designing courses. It ranges from lower-level technical and commercial courses and government-sponsored training, through courses for those aiming at higher-level posts in industry, commerce and administration, to professional courses. Facilities exist for GCE A- and AS-levels, GCSEs, GNVQs and a full range of vocational qualifications. These courses can form the foundation for progress to higher education qualifications. Many students attend part-time, either through day or block release from employment, or in the evenings. Adult learners usually form the largest proportion of students in further education colleges, often studying part-time in the evening or at weekends. The main courses and examinations in the vocational field, all of which link in with the National Vocational Qualification (NVQ) framework, are offered by the following bodies, but there are also many others. Edexcel resulted from the merger of the Business and Technology Education Council (BTEC) and London Examinations. It provides programmes of study across a wide range of subject areas. Qualifications offered include GNVQs, NVQs, GCSEs, AS- and A-levels, National and Higher National diplomas and certificates, and other BTEC qualifications. City & Guilds specialise in developing qualifications and assessments for work-related and leisure qualifications. They offer nationally and internationally recognised certificates in over 500 vocational qualifications. The progressive structure of awards spans seven levels, from foundation to the highest level of professional competence.

Oxford, Cambridge and RSA Examinations cover the full range of academic and vocational qualifications. The latter include accounting, business administration, customer service, management, language schemes, information technology and teaching qualifications. A wide range of NVQs and GNVQs are offered and a policy operates of credit accumulation, so that candidates can take a single unit or complete qualifications.
W www.lsc.gov.uk and www.elwa.ac.uk

WORK-BASED LEARNING

Apprenticeships are a way for young people aged 16–24 to get hands-on experience and on-the-job training while gaining nationally recognised qualifications. The Learning and Skills Council contributes towards the cost of training and assessment. The National Council for Education and Training Wales (ELWa) provides financial assistance in Wales. Apprenticeships normally last between one and three years and there are two levels: Apprenticeships and Advanced Apprenticeships at Levels 2 and 3 respectively. Both of these lead to:

– National Vocational Qualifications
– Key Skills qualifications – transferable work-related skills like IT and communication, problem solving, application of mathematics, improving learning, and performance and teamwork
– Technical certificates – vocationally related qualifications that provide the basic knowledge of the NVQ

There are approximately 255,500 young people aged between 16 to 24 on Apprenticeships in England alone, with similar programmes in place in Scotland, Northern Ireland and Wales.

From January 2004 the Apprenticeship programmes in Wales were opened to all people irrespective of age and who have left full-time statutory education.
W www.realworkrealpay.info

SCOTLAND

The Scottish Further Education Funding Council is the statutory body responsible for funding the 46 further education colleges. The Scottish Qualifications Authority (SQA) is the statutory awarding body for qualifications in the national education and training system in Scotland. It is both the main awarding body for qualifications for work including Scottish Vocational Qualifications (SVQs) and is also their accrediting body. The SQA is by statute required clearly to separate its awarding and accrediting functions. There are three main qualification 'families' in Scottish further education: National Qualifications; Higher National Qualifications (HNC and HND); and SVQs. In addition to Standard Grade qualifications, National Qualifications are available at five levels: Access, Intermediate 1, Intermediate 2, Higher and Advanced Higher. Another feature of the qualifications system is the Scottish Group Award (SGA). SGAs are built up unit by unit and allow opportunity for credit transfer from other qualifications (such as Standard Grade or SVQ), providing a further option for learners, especially adult learners. SVQs are competence-based qualifications suitable for work-place delivery but they can also be taken in further education colleges and other centres where work-place conditions can be simulated. The Scottish Credit and Qualifications Framework (SCQF) includes qualifications across academic and vocational sectors in a single credit-based framework. It comprises 12 levels, covering all mainstream qualifications from Access level in National Qualifications to postgraduate qualifications, and including SVQs. In the academic year 2001–2 there were 514,877 student enrolments on vocational and non-vocational courses in further education colleges. Of this total, higher educational courses accounted for 64,089 enrolments.
W www.sfefc.ac.uk and www.sqa.org.uk

NORTHERN IRELAND

All further education colleges are independent corporate bodies like their counterparts in the rest of the UK. Responsibility for the sector lies with the Department for Employment and Learning, which funds the colleges directly. The colleges own their own property, are responsible for their own services and employ their own staff.

The governing bodies of the colleges must include at least 50 per cent membership who are engaged or employed in business, industry, or any profession.

Northern Ireland has 16 institutions of further education, and in 2001–2 there were 21,422 full-time and 58,445 part-time enrolments on vocational further education courses.
W www.delni.gov.uk

STUDENT SUPPORT

Education Maintenance Allowance (EMA) is a means tested allowance to support young people in post-16 education. It became available across England from September 2004. It consists of a weekly payment of up to £30, plus periodic bonus payments. EMA is available to students who are 16 by 31 August and staying on at school or college (and to older students in EMA pilot areas for the academic year 2004–5). Also available to students in England in that age group are Learner Support Funds. These funds, which are targeted at those students in greatest need, have four separate strands: Transport, Childcare (Care2Learn), Residential and General funding. Whilst the funding for both transport and childcare is universal, the discretionary nature of the other funds allows local learning institutions to provide targeted help and support where it is most needed. In England, the Adult Learning Grant is currently being piloted in the North East and South East regions, plus a further nine Learning and Skills Council areas: Bedfordshire and Luton, Devon and Cornwall, Humberside, Lancashire, Leicestershire, London West, Shropshire, South Yorkshire, and the Black Country. It offers an allowance of up to £30 per week to adults on low incomes studying full time for a first full Level 2 qualification (five GCSEs or equivalent) or for young adults studying full time for a first Level 3 qualification (two A-levels or equivalent). Eligible Welsh-domiciled students aged over 18 on further education courses, whether full-time or part-time (subject to a minimum contact requirement), receive a means-tested non-repayable Assembly Learning Grant. The grant is administered by LEAs. Discretionary Financial Contingency Funds are also available to all students suffering hardship and are administered by the institutions themselves. In addition, Individual Learning Accounts are available in Wales, which provide adults with means-tested support of up to £200 to undertake a wide range of learning. Eligible Scottish-domiciled further education students can apply to their college for discretionary support in the form of bursaries. These can include allowances for maintenance, travel, study, two homes, dependants and special educational needs. College students receiving EMAs may also be eligible for the non-maintenance elements. In addition, colleges administer discretionary funds in the form of hardship, childcare and young students' retention funds.

Full-time students over 19 years of age and resident in Northern Ireland, on certain vocational courses, may benefit from discretionary non-repayable Access Bursaries. The bursaries are administered by the Education and Library Boards. Support for further education students in Northern Ireland includes free tuition to all full-time students up to age 18 and to all full-time students over 18 undertaking a vocational course at Level 3 or below. In addition, financial help is provided by colleges through a discretionary support fund for both full-time and part-time students whose access to and participation in further education is inhibited by financial considerations.

VOCATIONAL QUALIFICATIONS

National Vocational Qualifications (NVQs) are work-related competence-based qualifications. They are designed to reflect the skills and knowledge needed to do a job effectively, and represent national standards recognised by employers. General National Vocational Qualifications (GNVQs) provide a vocational alternative to academic qualifications in colleges and schools for 16–19 year olds. Each GNVQ is related to a broad area of work and is a unit-based qualification assessed through a combination of continuous assessment and short test papers. They are available in 14 vocational areas at two levels: Foundation and Intermediate.

The Vocational Certificate of Education (VCE), sometimes known as the Vocational A-level, replaced Advanced GNVQs. It is available in different forms: the three-unit VCE Advanced Subsidiary (equivalent to one GCE AS-level), the six-unit VCE Advanced Level (equivalent to one GCE A-level), and the 12-unit VCE Double Award (equivalent to two GCE A-levels). The timetable for the withdrawal of the individual six-unit GNVQ titles was issued by the Qualifications and Curriculum Authority in November 2003. The withdrawal is taking place in three stages from 2005 to 2007, starting with titles with extremely low numbers of candidate entries. The withdrawal of the six-unit GNVQ is the end of a process, first announced in 2000, whereby all elements of the GNVQ qualification (Part One, six-unit, and Advanced Level) were to be withdrawn. The QCA has identified and advised schools and colleges of alternative qualifications for each of the GNVQ subject areas.

HIGHER EDUCATION

The term higher education is used to describe education above A-level, Higher and Advanced Higher Grade and their equivalent, which is provided in universities, colleges of higher education and in some further education colleges.

A White Paper, *The Future of Higher Education*, published in January 2003, sets out the Government's plans for reform and investment in universities and higher education colleges, and includes proposals for changes in the student finance system.

STUDENT NUMBERS IN THE UK

Higher Education student numbers in the UK in 2002–3 were:

	Total	Full-time	Part-time
Total HE students in the UK	2,175,115	–	–
Total post-graduate students	497,500	206,755	290,745
Total undergraduate students	1,677,615	1,111,310	566,305

Higher Education qualifications obtained in the UK in 2002–3 were:

Total HE qualifications obtained	Total first degrees	Total higher degrees	Total other post-graduate	Total other under-graduate
Full-time	398,855	250,625	68,055	35,360	44,815
Part-time	158,935	31,755	30,830	30,105	66,245

Advice to government on matters relating to higher education is provided by the Higher Education Funding Councils for England, Wales and Scotland, and by the Higher Education Council in Northern Ireland. The former receive a block grant from central government which is allocated to the universities and colleges. In Northern Ireland the grant is allocated directly to institutions by the Department for Employment and Learning. W www.hefc.ac.uk, www.hefcw.ac.uk, www.shefc.ac.uk, www.delni.gov.uk

TYPES OF HIGHER EDUCATION INSTITUTION
The Further and Higher Education Act 1992 and parallel legislation in Scotland removed the distinction between higher education provided by the universities and that provided in England and Wales by the former polytechnics and colleges of higher education and in Scotland by the former central institutions and others. It allowed all polytechnics, and other higher education institutions which satisfy the necessary criteria, to award their own taught course and research degrees and to adopt the title of university. All the polytechnics, and some colleges of higher education have since done so. The change of name does not affect the legal constitution of the institutions. Funding is by the Higher Education Funding Councils for England, Wales and Scotland and directly by the Department for Employment and Learning in Northern Ireland. There are now 89 universities in the UK whereas only 48 existed prior to the Further and Higher Education Acts 1992. Of the 89, 72 are in England (including the University of London, which has a federal structure), two in Wales (one a federal institution comprising six constituent institutions and two university colleges), 14 in Scotland (15 including the Open University Scotland) and two in Northern Ireland. There are also 64 colleges of higher education, some of which are multidisciplinary while others specialise, for example, in teacher training.

GOVERNANCE OF UNIVERSITIES AND COLLEGES
The pre-1992 universities each have their own system of internal governance but broad similarities exist. Most are run by two main bodies: the senate, which deals primarily with academic issues and consists of members elected from within the university; and the council, which is the executive governing body and is responsible for all appointments and promotions, and bidding for and allocation of financial resources. At least half the members of the council are drawn from outside the university. Many of the council's functions are carried out through committees. Joint committees of senate and council are common. The 1992 Act, and the Education reform Act 1988, set out the system of governance for universities which were formerly polytechnics or other higher education institutions and for the colleges of higher education. Each institution also has articles of government that are approved by the Privy Council. These post-1992 institutions are run by boards of governors, which are responsible for the mission, finances and all appointments. Much of the board's business is delegated to committees. In particular, there is usually an academic board that deals with all matters related to teaching and research.

OPEN UNIVERSITY AND THE UNIVERSITY FOR INDUSTRY
The non-residential Open University provides a modular programme of courses throughout the UK leading to first and higher degrees, diplomas and certificates. Students are taught through distance learning, using written and audio-visual materials and the Internet, supported by tutorials and short residential courses. No qualifications are needed for entry. The Open University received £164.7 million in public funding 2002–3. In 2002–3, 158,000 undergraduates were registered. The University for Industry (Ufl) promotes learning ranging from basic skills to specialised technological and management skills. It aims to help individuals to improve their chances of employment, improve their career prospects and boost business competitiveness. It works as a public-private partnership in England, Wales and Northern Ireland. Ufl's services are delivered through Learndirect, which provides access to courses, over 80 per cent of which are online. There are over 2000 Learndirect centres. There is one private university in England, the University of Buckingham, which receives no public funding.

SCOTLAND
The Scottish Higher Education Funding Council (SHEFC) funds 20 institutions of higher education, including 14 universities. The universities are broadly managed as described above and the remaining colleges are managed by independent governing bodies which include representatives of industrial, commercial, professional and educational interests. Most of the courses outside the universities have a vocational orientation and a substantial number are sandwich courses.

NORTHERN IRELAND
In Northern Ireland higher education is provided in the 16 colleges of further education, the two universities and the two university colleges. These institutions offer a range of courses, including first and postgraduate degrees, PGCEs, undergraduate diplomas and certificates, and professional qualifications.

ACADEMIC STAFF
Each university and college appoints its own academic staff. The Universities and Colleges Employers Association (UCEA) is the employers' association for subscribing universities and other higher education institutions in the UK. It provides a framework within which representatives of institutions can discuss salaries, conditions of service, employee relations and all matters connected with the employment of staff and employees. The services of the UCEA include collective bargaining and an annual salary survey. Teaching staff in higher education require no formal teaching qualification. However, the Institute for Learning and Teaching in Higher Education, funded by the funding councils, was set up to establish an accreditation scheme and continuing professional development for higher education teachers and to encourage innovation in teaching and learning. The funding councils also fund the Learner and Teaching Support Network to develop and share good practice. In April 2004 both organisations were incorporated into a new national body: the Higher Education Academy.

Teacher trainers are required to spend a certain amount of time in schools to ensure that they have sufficient recent practical experience.

The number of full-time academic staff in all UK institutions in 2002–3 was:

	Total	Male	Female
UK	120,800	78,385	42,410
England	97,345	63,025	34,315
Wales	5,825	3,835	1,990
Scotland	14,585	9,545	5,040
Northern Ireland	3,045	1,980	1,065

Lecturers' Common Interest Group Higher Education Pay Scales effective from 1 August 2004 are given below. However, for many institutions these scales will be phased in between August 2004 and July 2006.

Grade Lecturer	£ p.a.
9	24,886
10	24,886
11	25,633
12	27,194
13	28,009
14	28,850
15	29,715
Senior lecturer	
0	28,850
1	29,715
2	30,607
3	31,544
4	32,471
5	33,445
6	34,448
7	35,482
8	36,546
Principal lecturer	
0	37,643
1	37,643
2	37,643
3	37,643
4	38,772
5	39,935
6	41,133
7	42,367
8	42,367
9	43,638
Researcher A	
1	12,987
2	14,192
3	15,056
4	15,973
5	16,946
6	17,978
Researcher B	
1	19,645
2	19,645
3	20,842
4	22,111
5	22,774
6	24,161
7	24,868
8	25,633
9	27,194
10	28,009
11	28,850

Part-time hourly rates	
I/II/III	32.42
IV	26.77
V	19.59

FINANCE

The total income of institutions of higher education in the UK in 2002–3 was:

	£	% of total
Funding Council grants	6,054,559	38.9
Tuition fees, education grants and contracts	3,743,094	24.1
Research grants and contracts	2,595,445	16.7
Other income	2,938,382	18.9
Endowment and investment income	230,491	1.5
Total	15,561,971	100

COURSES

In the UK all universities and some colleges award their own degrees and other qualifications and may act as awarding and validating bodies for colleges. The power to award degrees is regulated by law and it is an offence to purport to award a UK degree unless authorised to do so. The Quality Assurance Agency for Higher Education (QAA) advises government on applications for degree-awarding powers.

Facilities exist for full-time and part-time study, day release, sandwich or block release. Credit accumulation and transfer systems (CATS) allow a student to achieve a final qualification by accumulating credits for courses of study successfully achieved, or even professional experience, over a period.

Higher education courses comprise: first degree and postgraduate (including research); Diploma in Higher Education (DipHE); BTEC Higher National Diplomas (HND) and Higher National Certificates (HNC); and preparation for professional examinations.

The DipHE is commonly a two-year diploma usually intended to serve as a stepping stone to a degree course or other further study. The DipHE is awarded by the institution itself if it is accredited; by an accredited institution of its choice if not. The HNCs are awarded after two years' part-time study. The HNDs are awarded after two years' full-time, or three years' sandwich-course or part-time study.

The foundation degree, launched in 2001, is a two-year vocational higher education qualification which forms either a self-contained qualification or a basis for further study leading to an honours degree or further professional qualifications.

Undergraduate courses lead to the title of Bachelor, Bachelor of Arts (BA) and Bachelor of Science (BSc) being the most common, except in certain Scottish universities where Master is sometimes used for a first degree in arts subjects. For a higher degree the titles are Master of Arts (MA), Master of Science (MSc) and the research degrees of Master of Philosophy (MPhil) and Doctor of Philosophy (PhD or, at a few universities, DPhil).

Most undergraduate courses at universities and colleges of higher education run for three years, but some take four years or longer. Postgraduate studies vary in length.

Post-experience short courses form a significant part of higher education provision, reflecting the demand for

professional and technical training. Most of these courses fund themselves.
W www.qaa.ac.uk

ADMISSIONS

The target proportion of 18- to 30-year-olds entering full-time higher education by 2010 is set in England at 50 per cent. Institutions suffer financial penalties if the number of students laid down for them by the funding councils is exceeded, but the individual university or college decides which students to accept. The formal entry requirements to most degree courses are two or more A-levels at grade E or above (or equivalent), and to HND courses one A-level (or equivalent). In practice, most offers of places require qualifications in excess of this, higher requirements usually reflecting the popularity of a course or institution. These requirements do not, however, exclude applications from students with a variety of non-GCSE qualifications or unquantified experience and skills. For admission to a degree, DipHE or HND, potential students apply through the Universities and Colleges Admission Service (UCAS). UCAS operates an online application system. The aim is that by 2006, 100 per cent of applications will be received electronically. At present it is still possible to submit paper-based applications. Applicants can also fill in their applications using the CD-based electronic application system (EAS). UCAS handles over 450,000 applications a year as the UK's only central admissions service for full-time higher education courses. The only exception among universities is the Open University, which conducts its own admissions. Applications for undergraduate teacher training courses are made through UCAS and for postgraduate teacher training, through the Graduate Teacher Training Registry. Details of initial teacher training courses in Scotland can be obtained from colleges of education and those universities offering such courses, and from Universities Scotland. For 2005, applications for postgraduate social work will also be though UCAS. For admission as a postgraduate student, universities and colleges normally require a good first degree in a subject related to the proposed course of study or research. Most applications are made to individual institutions, except for teaching and social work. W www.ucas.ac.uk

FEES

Entrants to undergraduate courses domiciled in England, Wales and Northern Ireland pay, directly to the institution, an annual contribution to their fees (up to £1,150 in 2004–5) depending on their own level of income or that of their spouse or parents. Those whose parents' residual income is less than £21,475 pay nothing and those whose parents have a residual income of £31,973 or more pay the full £1,150. The fee contribution represents some 25 per cent of the average cost of a higher education course in the UK and the balance is paid by the student's LEA or, in Northern Ireland, by the student's regional Education and Library Board. Students from EU member countries pay fees at home student rates and, if studying at institutions in England, Wales and Northern Ireland, are liable to make an annual contribution to fees assessed against family income. Among the classes of students exempt from payment are: Scottish-domiciled and EU students at Scottish institutions; students from England, Wales and Northern Ireland in the fourth year of a four-year degree course at a Scottish institution; existing students with mandatory awards (see below), for whom the grant-

awarding body pays; students on certain courses of initial teacher training; medical students in the fifth year of their course; health professionals on National Health Service bursaries; and full-time or part-time students on benefit or low incomes. For students on an access course, fees start from about £200; financial help with this is available. For part-time or flexible learning tuition fees vary, and tuition is free for those on a low income or for those who receive certain benefits.

STUDENT SUPPORT

LOANS

Since September 1998, the means-tested loan has been the main form of support for most undergraduate students in the UK on full-time or sandwich undergraduate courses of higher education. Students apply through LEAs in England and Wales, education and library boards in Northern Ireland and the Students Awards Agency in Scotland. Of the maximum loan, 75 per cent is available to all eligible students regardless of income; the remaining 25 per cent is means tested by the LEA. The loan rates for 2004–5 are:

Living in college/lodgings in London area	£5,050
Living in college/lodgings elsewhere	£4,095
Living in parental home	£3,240

Extra income assessed loans are available to students whose courses last more than 30 term-time weeks or who need to study abroad in certain high-cost countries. Loans of up to £500 are available in 2003–4 to part-time students on low incomes or with dependent children.

Loans are available to students on designated courses. Certain residency conditions also apply. In 2002–3, 836,800 loans were taken up, to the value of £2,621.3 million.

Repayment of income contingent loans begins in the April following the end of the course. Those who pay tax through PAYE have repayments deducted from their salaries once they earn more than £10,000 a year. This amount will increase to £15,000 from April 2005. The self-employed make repayments through their tax returns. Repayments are calculated at 9 per cent of income over the threshold. If income falls below the threshold, repayments cease until income rises above it.

NON-REPAYABLE GRANTS AND ALLOWANCES

Eligible students, such as single parents, others with dependants or those leaving care, are entitled to apply for various additional means-tested supplementary grants for help in meeting certain living and other costs, for childcare and for each child at school. Disabled students are eligible for non means-tested Disabled Students' Allowances.

From the academic year 2004–5, Higher Education Grants of £1,000 will be available to students whose family income is £15,200 or less. Partial grants are available to those whose family income is between £15,201 and £21,185. Eligible Welsh-domiciled undergraduates from low-income families, whether on full-time or part-time courses, receive a means-tested non-repayable Assembly Learning Grant of up to £1,500 per year. The grant is administered by local education authorities. Eligible Scottish-domiciled students from low income families at institutions in Scotland may apply for a Young Students' Bursary. The maximum available in 2003–4 is £2,100. Full-time students on a low income who are resident in Northern Ireland may benefit from discretionary non-repayable Access Bursaries of up to £2,000. The award of a bursary carries a reduction in student loan entitlement. The bursaries are administered by the education and library boards.

LEARNER SUPPORT AND ACCESS FUNDS

Funds, variously known as hardship or access funds (Financial Contingency Funds in Wales and Support Funds in Northern Ireland) are allocated by central government to the appropriate funding councils in England and Wales and to the Student Awards Agency in Scotland, and are administered by further and higher education institutions. In Northern Ireland they are allocated by central government directly to the institution. Their purpose is to provide help for individual students facing financial difficulties. All students, whether full- or part-time, undergraduate or postgraduate, may apply. Universities and colleges set their own criteria and manage their own procedures within the national framework. The amount payable depends on individual circumstances and on the amount the institution has available. Some colleges offer non-repayable bursaries from hardship funds, i.e. a payment for each year of the course, to students who might be prevented from completing their studies due to financial problems. Individual colleges and universities may also offer emergency funds.

POSTGRADUATE AWARDS

Most postgraduates have to pay large contributions towards their tuition fees as the only mandatory funding for postgraduate study is for students taking the Postgraduate Certificate in Education (PGCE). Postgraduate students, with the exception of students in England, Wales and Northern Ireland on loan-bearing diploma courses such as teacher training, are not eligible to apply for student loans. The Research Councils and the Arts and Humanities Research Board are the biggest providers of postgraduate funding. Grants for postgraduate study are discretionary and competition for them is fierce. They comprise maintenance grants for students undertaking doctoral research or taught masters degrees, are not means-tested and are dependent on the class of first degree (especially for research degrees); and flat-rate maintenance grants. There are additional allowances for disabled students, those with dependants and for fieldwork expenses.

Awards are funded by the British Academy, the Higher Education Funding Councils for England and Wales, the Scottish Higher Education Funding Council and the Department for Employment and Learning for Northern Ireland, among others. Employers may also offer financial support.

ADULT AND CONTINUING EDUCATION

In the UK, the duty of securing adult and continuing education leading to academic or vocational qualifications is statutory. The Learning and Skills Council in England, the National Council for Education and Training in Wales and the Further Education Funding Council in Scotland are responsible for and fund those courses which take place in their sector and lead to academic and vocational

qualifications, prepare students to undertake further or higher education courses, or confer basic skills; the Higher Education Funding Councils fund advanced courses of continuing education. The LEAs have the power, although not the duty, to provide those courses which do not fall within the remit of the funding bodies. In Northern Ireland the Department for Employment and Learning is responsible for the funding of the statutory further education sector.

The involvement of universities in adult education and continuing education has diversified considerably. Birkbeck College in the University of London offers a range of degree and other courses designed specifically to meet the needs of mature students. The post-1992 universities and the colleges of higher education, because of their range of courses and flexible patterns of student attendance, provide opportunities in the field of adult and continuing education. The Forum for the Advancement of Continuing Education promotes collaboration between institutions of higher education active in this area. The Open University, in partnership with the BBC, provides distance teaching leading to first degrees, and also offers post-experience and higher degree courses. Of the voluntary bodies providing adult education, the biggest is the Workers' Educational Association (WEA), which operates throughout the UK and provides over 10,000 courses each year, reaching more than 110,000 adults. The WEA is a charity supported by funding from the Learning and Skills Council in England and by the Scottish Executive and local authorities in Scotland. NIACE, the National Institute of Adult Continuing Education, has a broad remit to promote lifelong learning opportunities for adults. NIACE works to develop increased participation in education and training in England and Wales, particularly for those currently under-represented. It does this through research and project work, conferences, publications and the provision of an information service to educational providers. NIACE and the Basic Skills Agency together manage the Community Learning Fund on behalf of the DfES. NIACE Dysgu Cymru, the Welsh committee, receives financial support from the National Assembly for Wales, support in kind from local authorities, and advises government, voluntary bodies and education providers on adult continuing education and training matters in Wales. In Scotland, advice on adult and community education, and promotion thereof, is provided by Community Learning Scotland; in April 2002 Community Learning Scotland ceased to be a non-departmental public body and some of its functions transferred to the Communities Scotland agency. In Northern Ireland, those functions are undertaken by the Department for Employment and Learning. W www.niace.org.uk

The Adult Learning Inspectorate (ALI) is a non-departmental government-funded public body established under the Learning and Skills Act 2000 with the responsibility of raising the standards of education and training for young people and adults in England. It inspects and reports on the quality of education and training and can also be commissioned to inspect private training provision in the UK. W www.ali.gov.uk

The Universities' Association for Continuing Education (UACE) represents and promotes the interests of continuing education and lifelong learning providers within higher education. W www.uace.org.uk

EDUCATION DIRECTORY

LOCAL EDUCATION AUTHORITIES

ENGLAND

COUNTY COUNCILS

BEDFORDSHIRE County Hall, Cauldwell Street, Bedford MK42 9AP T 01234-363222 W www.bedfordshire.gov.uk
Director, David Doran

BUCKINGHAMSHIRE County Hall, Walton Street, Aylesbury HP20 1UA T 01296-395000 W www.buckscc.gov.uk
Chief Education Officer, P. J. Mooney

CAMBRIDGESHIRE Box ELH 1505, Shire Hall, Castle Hill, Cambridge CB3 0AF T 01223-717111
W www.cambridgeshire.gov.uk
Director, A. Baxter

CHESHIRE County Hall, Chester CH1 1SQ T 01244-602424
W www.cheshire.gov.uk
Director of Education and Community, D. Cracknell

CORNWALL County Hall, Truro TR1 3AY T 01872-322000
W www.cornwall.gov.uk
Director, G. Aver

CUMBRIA 5 Portland Square, Carlisle CA1 1PU
T 01228-606877 W www.cumbria.gov.uk/education
Director of Education, V. Ashfield

DERBYSHIRE County Hall, Matlock DE4 3AG
T 01629-585814 W www.derbyshire.gov.uk
Chief Education Officer, R. V. Taylor

DEVON County Hall, Topsham Road, Exeter EX2 4QG
T 01392-382059 W www.devon.gov.uk
Director, P. Norrey

DORSET County Hall, Colliton Park, Dorchester DT1 1XJ
T 01305-224110 W www.dorsetcc.gov.uk
Director, D. Goddard

DURHAM County Hall, Durham DH1 5UJ T 0191-386 4411
W www.durham.gov.uk
Director, K. Mitchell

EAST SUSSEX PO Box 4, County Hall, St Anne's Crescent, Lewes BN7 1SG T 01273-481000
W www.eastsussexcc.gov.uk
Director of Education, Ms D. Stokoe

ESSEX PO Box 47, Chelmsford CM2 6WN T 01245-492211
W www.essexcc.gov.uk
Director of Learning Services, P. Lincoln

GLOUCESTERSHIRE Shire Hall, Westgate Street, Gloucester GL1 2TG T 01452-425302 W www.gloscc.gov.uk
Chief Education Officer, Roger Crouch

HAMPSHIRE County Office, Education Department, The Castle, Winchester SO23 8UG T 01962-846452
W www.hants.gov.uk/education
County Education Officer, A. J. Seber

HERTFORDSHIRE County Hall, Pegs Lane, Hertford SG13 8DE T 01438-737500 W www.hertsdirect.org
Director, J. Hariss

ISLE OF WIGHT County Hall, High Street, Newport PO30 1UD T 01983-823400 W www.iwight.com
Director of Education, D. Pettitt

KENT Sessions House, County Hall, Maidstone ME14 1XG
T 01622-671411 W www.kent.gov.uk
Strategic Director, Nick Henwood

LANCASHIRE PO Box 61, County Hall, Preston PR1 8RJ
T 01772-254868 W www.lancashire.gov.uk
Director, S. Mulvany

LEICESTERSHIRE County Hall, Glenfield, Leicester LE3 8RF
T 0116-265 6631 W www.leics.gov.uk
Director, Mrs J. A. M. Strong

LINCOLNSHIRE County Offices, Newland, Lincoln LN1 1YQ
T 01522-552222 W www.lincolnshire.gov.uk
Director, Dr C. Berry

NORFOLK County Hall, Martineau Lane, Norwich NR1 2DL
T 01603-222146 W www.norfolk.gov.uk
Director, Dr B. C. Slater

NORTHAMPTONSHIRE PO Box 216, John Dryden House, 8–10 The Lakes, Northampton NN4 7DD
T 01604-236252
W www.northamptonshire.gov.uk
Corporate Director, A. Sortwell

NORTHUMBERLAND County Hall, Morpeth NE61 2EF
T 01670-533001
Director, B. Edwards

NORTH YORKSHIRE County Hall, Northallerton, N. Yorks DL7 8AE T 01609-780780 W www.northyorks.gov.uk
Director, Cynthia Welbourn

NOTTINGHAMSHIRE County Hall, West Bridgford, Nottingham NG2 7QP T 0115-982 3823
W www.nottinghamshire.gov.uk
Director, P. Tulley

OXFORDSHIRE Macclesfield House, New Road, Oxford OX1 1NA T 01865-815449
W www.oxfordshire.gov.uk
Director for Learning and Culture, Keith Bartley

SHROPSHIRE The Shirehall, Abbey Foregate, Shrewsbury SY2 6ND T 01743-254307
W www.shropshireonline.gov.uk
Corporate Director, Mrs E. Nicholson

SOMERSET County Hall, Taunton TA1 4DY T 01823-355455
W www.somerset.gov.uk
Executive Director – Lifelong Learning, J. Rose *(acting)*

STAFFORDSHIRE Tipping Street, Stafford ST16 2DH
T 01785-223121
W www.staffordshire.gov.uk
Director, Peter Traves

SUFFOLK St Andrew House, County Hall, Ipswich IP4 1LJ
T 01473-584631
W www.suffolkcc.gov.uk
Director, D. J. Peachey

SURREY County Hall, Penrhyn Road, Kingston-upon-Thames KT1 2DJ T 0845-600 9009 W www.surreycc.gov.uk
Director, Dr P. Gray

WARWICKSHIRE 22 Northgate Street, Warwick CV34 4SP
T 01926-410410 W www.warwickshire.gov.uk
County Education Officer, E. Wood

WEST SUSSEX County Hall, Chichester PO19 1RF
T 01243-777750 W www.westsussex.gov.uk
Director, R. Back

WILTSHIRE County Hall, Bythesea Road, Trowbridge BA14 8JB T 01225-713000 W www.wiltshire.gov.uk
Director of Children, Education and Libraries,
R. W. Wolfson

WORCESTERSHIRE Educational Services Directorate, PO Box 73, Worcester WR5 2YA T 01905-766859
W www.worcestershire.gov.uk
Director, J. Kramer

UNITARY AND METROPOLITAN BOROUGH COUNCILS

BARNSLEY Berneslai Close, Barnsley S70 2HS
T 01226-773500 W www.barnsley.gov.uk
Executive Director, Education, E. Sutton
BATH AND NORTH EAST SOMERSET PO Box 25, Riverside, Temple Street, Keynsham, Bristol BS31 1DN
T 01225-477000 W www.bathnes.gov.uk
Education Director, M. Young
BIRMINGHAM Education Offices, Margaret Street, Birmingham B3 3BU T 0121-303 2550 W www.bgfl.org
Chief Education Officer, Tony Howell
BLACKBURN WITH DARWEN Town Hall, Blackburn BB1 7DY T 01254-477477 W www.blackburn.gov.uk
Director, Peter Morgan
BLACKPOOL Progress House, Clifton Road, Blackpool FY4 4US T 01253-477477
Director of Education, Leisure and Cultural Services,
   D. Lund
BOLTON Paderborn House, Civic Centre, Bolton BL1 1JW
T 01204-333333
Director, Mrs M. Blenkinsop
BOURNEMOUTH Dorset House, 20–22 Christchurch Road, Bournemouth BH1 3NL T 01202-456191
Director, P. Deshpande
BRACKNELL FOREST Seymour House, 38 Broadway, Bracknell, Berks RG12 1AU T 01344-424642
W www.bracknell-forest.gov.uk
Director of Education, T. Eccleston
BRADFORD Flockton House, Flockton Road, Bradford BD4 7EB
T 01274-751700 W www.educationbradford.com
Director of Education and Schools, P. Green
BRIGHTON AND HOVE PO Box 2503, Kings House, Grand Avenue, Hove BN3 2SU T 01273-290000
W www.brighton-hove.gov.uk
Strategic Director, David Hawker
BRISTOL The Council House, College Green, Bristol BS99 7EB
T 0117-903 7962 W www.bristol-lea.org.uk
Director of Education, Heather Tomlinson
BURY Athenaeum House, Market Street, Bury BL9 0BN
T 0161-253 5652
Chief Education Officer, H. Williams
CALDERDALE Northgate House, Northgate, Halifax HX1 1UN
T 01422-357257 W www.calderdale.gov.uk
Group Director, C. A. Gruen
COVENTRY Council Offices, Earl Street, Coventry CV1 5RS
T 024-7683 1511 W www.coventry.gov.uk
Strategic Director, Roger Edwardson
DARLINGTON Town Hall, Darlington DL1 5QT
T 01325-380651
W www.darlington.gov.uk
Director, G. Pennington
DERBY Middleton House, 27 St Mary's Gate, Derby DE1 3NN
T 01332-716924 W www.derby.gov.uk
Director, A. Flack
DONCASTER PO Box 266, The Council House, College Road, Doncaster DN1 3AD
T 01302-737103
Executive Director, M. Eales
DUDLEY Westox House, 1 Trinity Road, Dudley DY1 1JQ
T 01384-818181 W www.dudley.gov.uk
Director, John Freeman

EAST RIDING OF YORKSHIRE County Hall, Beverley HU17 9BA T 01482-392020
W www.eastriding.gov.uk
Director of Lifelong Learning, Jon Mager
GATESHEAD Civic Centre, Regent Street, Gateshead NE8 1HH
T 0191-433 3000 W www.gateshead.gov.uk
Director, Brian H. Edwards
HALTON Grosvenor House, Halton Lea, Runcorn WA7 2WD
T 0151-424 2061
Director, G. Talbot
HARTLEPOOL Civic Centre, Victoria Road, Hartlepool
TS24 8AY T 01429-266522 W www.hartlepool.gov.uk
Director, J. J. Fitt
HEREFORDSHIRE PO Box 185, Hereford HR4 9ZR
T 01432-260900
W www.education.herefordshire.gov.uk
Director, Dr E. Oram
KINGSTON UPON HULL Essex House, Manor Street, Kingston upon Hull HU1 1YD T 01482-613007
Corporate Director, Helen McMullen
KIRKLEES Oldgate House, 2 Oldgate, Huddersfield HD1 6QW
T 01484-225242 W www.kirkleesmc.gov.uk
Director of Lifelong Learning, G. Tonkin
KNOWSLEY Education Offices, Huyton Hey Road, Huyton, Knowsley L36 5YH T 0151-443 3232
W www.knowsley.gov.uk
Director, S. Munby
LEEDS Merrion House, 110 Merrion Centre, Leeds LS2 8DT
T 0113-247 5590 W www.educationleeds.co.uk
Chief Executive, Chris Edwards
LEICESTER Marlborough House, 38 Welford Road, Leicester LE2 7AA T 0116-252 7807 W www.leicester.gov.uk
Corporate Director of Education and Lifelong Learning,
   S. Andrews
LIVERPOOL 4th Floor, Lewis Buildings, 4 Renshaw Street, Liverpool L1 4AD T 0151-233 3006
W www.liverpool.gov.uk
Executive Director, Colin Hilton
LUTON Unity House, 111 Stuart Street, Luton LU1 5NP
T 01582-548001 W www.luton.gov.uk
Corporate Director Lifelong Learning, T. Dessent
MANCHESTER Overseas House, Quay Street, Manchester
M3 3BB T 0161-234 5000
Chief Education Officer, M. Waters
MEDWAY Civic Centre, Strood, Rochester, Kent ME2 4AY
T 01634-306000 W www.medway.gov.uk
Director of Education, R. Collinson
MIDDLESBROUGH PO Box 99, Town Hall, Middlesbrough
TS1 2QQ T 01642-245432
Corporate Director, Terry Redmayne
MILTON KEYNES Civic Offices, Saxon Court, 505 Avebury Boulevard, Milton Keynes MK9 3HS T 01908-691691
W www.mkweb.co.uk
Head of Education, J. McElligott
NEWCASTLE UPON TYNE Civic Centre, Newcastle upon Tyne NE1 8PU T 0191-232 8520 W www.newcastle.gov.uk
Director, P. Turner
NORTH EAST LINCOLNSHIRE 7 Eleanor Street, Grimsby
DN32 9DU T 01472-323021 W www.nelincs.gov.uk
Director, Geoff Hill
NORTH LINCOLNSHIRE PO Box 35, Hewson House, Station Road, Brigg DN20 8XJ T 01724-297240
W www.northlincs.gov.uk
Head of Education, Learning and Achievement, D. Lea
NORTH SOMERSET PO Box 51, Town Hall, Weston-super-Mare BS23 1ZZ T 01934-888888
W www.n-somerset.gov.uk
Director, Colin Diamond

NORTH TYNESIDE Stephenson House, Stephenson Street, North Shields NE30 1QA T 0191-200 6565 W www.northtyneside.gov.uk
Education Director, Gill Alexander

NOTTINGHAM Sandfield Centre, Sandfield Road, Lenton, Nottingham NG7 1QH T 0115-915 5555 W www.nottinghamschools.co.uk
Director, Heather Tomlinson

OLDHAM PO Box 40, Civic Centre, West Street, Oldham OL1 1XJ T 0161-911 4260 W www.oldham.gov.uk
Executive Director of Education and Culture (acting), P. Makin

PETERBOROUGH Bayard Place, Broadway, Peterborough PE1 1FB T 01733-748444 W www.peterborough.gov.uk
Director, J. Evans

PLYMOUTH Plymouth PL1 2AA T 01752-307400 W www.pgfl.plymouth.gov.uk
Director, Bronwen Lacey

POOLE Civic Centre, Poole, Dorset BH15 2RU T 01202-633633 W www.boroughofpoole.com
Policy Director – Education, John Nash

PORTSMOUTH Civic Offices, Guildhall Square, Portsmouth PO1 2AL T 023-9282 2251 W www.portsmouthcc.gov.uk
Director of Education and Lifelong Learning, Linda Fisher

READING Civic Centre, PO Box 2623, Reading RG1 7WA T 0118-939 0900 W www.reading.gov.uk
Director, Andrew Daykin

REDCAR AND CLEVELAND Council Offices, Kirkleatham Street, Redcar TS10 1YA T 01642-444121 W www.redcar-cleveland.gov.uk
Director, Jenny Lewis

ROCHDALE PO Box 70, Municipal Offices, Smith Street, Rochdale OL16 1YD T 01706-647474
Director of Education, T. Piggott

ROTHERHAM Education Office, Norfolk House, Walker Place, Rotherham S65 1AS T 01709-382121 W www.rotherham.gov.uk
Director of Education, A. Bedford *(acting)*

RUTLAND Catmose, Oakham, Rutland LE15 6HP T 01572-758481 W www.rutnet.co.uk
Director, Ms C. Chambers

SALFORD Minerva House, Pendlebury Road, Swinton, Manchester T 0161-778 0123 W www.salford.gov.uk
Director, Mrs J. Baker

SANDWELL PO Box 41, Shaftesbury House, 402 High Street, West Bromwich, West Midlands B70 9LT T 0121-569 2200 W www.lea.sandwell.gov.uk
Executive Director, E. Griffiths

SEFTON Town Hall, Oriel Road, Bootle, Merseyside L20 7AE T 0151-922 4040 W www.sefton.gov.uk/education
Strategic Director, Bryn Marsh

SHEFFIELD Education Directorate, Town Hall, Pinstone Street, Sheffield S1 2HH T 0114-273 5722 W www.sheffield.gov.uk
Executive Director, Jonathan Crossley-Holland

SLOUGH Town Hall, Bath Road, Slough SL1 3UQ T 01753-875700
Director of Learning and Cultural Services, Christopher Spencer

SOLIHULL PO Box 20, Council House, Solihull B91 3QU T 0121-704 6000 W www.solihull.gov.uk
Director of Education and Children's Services, K. Crompton

SOUTHAMPTON 5th Floor, Frobisher House, Nelson Gate, Southampton SO15 1BZ T 023-8083 2771 W www.southampton.gov.uk
Executive Director, I. Sandbrook

SOUTHEND Civic Centre, Victoria Avenue, Southend-on-Sea SS2 6ER T 01702-215000
Director, Lorraine O'Reilly

SOUTH GLOUCESTERSHIRE Bowling Hill, Chipping Sodbury, S. Glos BS37 6JX T 01454-868686 W www.southglos.gov.uk
Director of Education, Ms T. Gillespie

SOUTH TYNESIDE Town Hall and Civic Offices, Westoe Road, South Shields NE33 2RL T 0191-427 1717
Director, Barbara Hughes

ST HELENS Rivington Centre, Rivington Road, St Helens WA10 4ND T 01744-456000 W www.sthelens.gov.uk
Director, Mrs S. Richardson

STOCKPORT Town Hall, Stockport SK1 3XE T 0161-474 3813 W www.stockport.gov.uk
Director for Education, Ed Blundell

STOCKTON-ON-TEES Municipal Buildings, PO Box 228, Church Road, Stockton-on-Tees TS18 1XE T 01642-393939 W www.stockton.gov.uk
Director, S. T. Bradford

STOKE-ON-TRENT Floor 2, Civic Centre, Glebe Street, Stoke-on-Trent ST4 1HH T 01782-232014 W www.stoke.gov.uk/education
Director, N. Rigby

SUNDERLAND PO Box 101, Civic Centre, Sunderland SR2 7DN T 0191-553 1000 W www.sunderland.gov.uk
Director of Education, Barbara Comiskey

SWINDON Sanford House, Sanford Street, Swindon SN1 1QH T 01793-463069 W www.swindon.gov.uk
Director of Education, Hilary Pitts

TAMESIDE Council Offices, Wellington Road, Ashton under Lyne, Lancs OL6 6DL T 0161-342 8355 W www.tameside.gov.uk
Chief Education Officer, I. Smith

TELFORD AND WREKIN PO Box 440, Civic Offices, Telford, Shropshire TF3 4WF T 01952-202100 W www.telford.gov.uk
Corporate Director, Mrs C. Davies

THURROCK PO Box 118, Grays, Essex RM17 6GF T 01375-652652 W www.thurrock.gov.uk/education
Corporate Director – Education, Steve Beynon

TORBAY Oldway Mansion, Paignton, Devon TQ3 2TE T 01803-208208
Chief Executive of Children's Services, Frank Weeple

TRAFFORD PO Box 40, Trafford Town Hall, Talbot Road, Stretford, Trafford, Greater Manchester M32 OEL T 0161-912 2000 W www.trafford.gov.uk
Chief Executive, Chris Pratt

WAKEFIELD County Hall, Bond Street, Wakefield WF1 2QL T 01924-306090 W www.wakefield.gov.uk
Corporate Director (Education), J. McLeod

WALSALL Civic Centre, Darwall Street, Walsall WS1 1TP T 01922-652301 W www.walsall.gov.uk
Chief Education Officer, D. McNulty

WARRINGTON New Town House, Buttermarket Street, Warrington, Cheshire WA1 2NJ T 01925-444400
Director, M. L. Roxburgh

WEST BERKSHIRE Avonbank House, West Street, Newbury, Berks RG14 1BZ T 01635-42400 W www.westberks.gov.uk
Corporate Director, Richard Hubbard

WIGAN Gateway House, Standishgate, Wigan, Lancs WN1 1AE T 01942-828891 W www.wiganmbc.gov.uk
Director, G. Rowney

WINDSOR AND MAIDENHEAD Town Hall, St Ives Road, Maidenhead, Berks SL6 1RF T 01628-798888 W www.rbwm.gov.uk
Director, M. D. Peckham

WIRRAL Hamilton Building, Conway Street, Birkenhead, Wirral CH41 4FD **T** 0151-666 2121
Director, Howard Cooper
WOKINGHAM Shute End, Wokingham, Berks RG40 1WN
T 0118-974 6100
W www.wokingham.gov.uk
Assistant Chief Executive, Jackie Harrop
WOLVERHAMPTON St Peter's Square, Wolverhampton WV1 1RR **T** 01902-556556
W www.wolverhampton.gov.uk
Co-ordinating Director, Roy Lockwood
YORK Mill House, North Street, York YO1 6JD
T 01904-613161 **W** www.york.gov.uk
Director, Patrick Scott

LONDON
*Inner London borough
BARKING AND DAGENHAM Town Hall, Barking, Essex IG11 7LU **T** 020-8227 3181/3662 **W** www.bardaglea.org.uk
Director, R. Luxton
BARNET Building 4, North London Business Park, Oakleigh Road South, London N11 1NP **T** 020-8359 2000
W www.barnet.gov.uk
Director of Education, G. Palmer
BEXLEY Hill View, Hill View Drive, Welling, Kent DA16 3RY **T** 020-8303 7777 **W** www.bexley.gov.uk
Director of Education, D. Absalom
BRENT Chesterfield House, 9 Park Lane, Wembley, Middx HA9 7RW **T** 020-8937 3000 **W** www.brent.gov.uk
Director, John Christie
BROMLEY Civic Centre, Stockwell Close, Bromley BR1 3UH
T 020-8464 3333 **W** bk.bromley.gov.uk
Director, Ken Davis
*CAMDEN Crowndale Centre, 218–220 Eversholt Street, London NW1 1BD **T** 020-7911 1525
Director, R. Litchfield
*CITY OF LONDON PO Box 270, Guildhall, London EC2P 2EJ
T 020-7332 1750
City Education Officer, I. Canfort
*CITY OF WESTMINSTER City Hall, 64 Victoria Street, London SW1E 6QP **T** 020-7641 6000
W www.westminster.gov.uk
Director of Education, Mrs Phyl Crawford
CROYDON Taberner House, Park Lane, Croydon CR9 1TP
T 020-8760 5452 **W** www.croydon.gov.uk
Director, P. Wylie
EALING Perceval House, 14–16 Uxbridge Road, London W5 2HL **T** 020-8579 2424 **W** www.ealing.gov.uk
Director, Dr Caroline Whalley
ENFIELD PO Box 56, Civic Centre, Silver Street, Enfield, Middx EN1 3XQ **T** 020-8366 6565
Director, P. Lewis
*GREENWICH Riverside House, Woolwich High Street, London SE18 6DF **T** 020-8921 8238
W www.greenwich.gov.uk
Director, P. Burnett
*HACKNEY 1 Reading Lane, London E8 1GQ
T 020-8820 7000
W www.learningtrust.co.uk
Chief Executive, Alan Wood
*HAMMERSMITH AND FULHAM Town Hall, King Street, London W6 9JU **T** 020-8748 3020 **W** www.lbhf.gov.uk
Director, Sandy Adamson
HARINGEY Civic Centre, High Road, London N22 8LE
T 020-8489 0000 **W** www.haringey.gov.uk
Director of Education, D. Warwick

HARROW PO Box 22, Civic Centre, Station Road, Harrow HA1 2UW **T** 020-8863 5611 **W** www.harrow.gov.uk
Director of Learning and Community Development, Javed Khan
HAVERING Town Hall, Main Road, Romford RM1 3BC
T 01708-434343
Executive Director of Lifelong Learning, S. Evans
HILLINGDON Civic Centre, High Street, Uxbridge UB8 1UW
T 01895-250529
Corporate Director, P. O'Hear
HOUNSLOW Civic Centre, Lampton Road, Hounslow, Middx TW3 4DN **T** 020-8583 2000 **W** www.hounslow.gov.uk
Director, Robert Garnett
*ISLINGTON Laycock Street, Islington, London N1 1TH
T 020-7527 5566 **W** www.islington.gov.uk
Director of Regeneration and Education, Mohammed Mehmet
*KENSINGTON AND CHELSEA Town Hall, Hornton Street, London W8 7NX **T** 020-7361 3334
W www.rbkc.gov.uk
Executive Director, Jacky Griffin
KINGSTON UPON THAMES Guildhall 2, Kingston upon Thames KT1 1EU **T** 020-8546 2121
W www.kingston.gov.uk
Director, P. Leeson
*LAMBETH International House, Canterbury Crescent, London SW9 7QE **T** 020-7926 1000 **W** www.lambeth.gov.uk
Executive Director of Education, Phyllis Dunipace
*LEWISHAM 3rd Floor, Laurence House, 1 Catford Road, London SE6 4RU **T** 020-8314 6200
W www.lewisham.gov.uk
Executive Director, Ms F. Sulke
MERTON Civic Centre, London Road, Morden, Surrey SM4 5DX **T** 020-8543 2222 **W** www.merton.gov.uk
Director of Education, Leisure and Libraries, Mrs Sue Evans
NEWHAM Broadway House, 322 High Street, Stratford, London E15 1AJ **T** 020-8430 2000
Director of Education and Community Learning, Ms P. Maddison
REDBRIDGE Lynton House, 255–259 High Road, Ilford, Essex IG1 1NN **T** 020-8478 3020 **W** www.redbridge.gov.uk
Director, E. Grant
RICHMOND UPON THAMES 1st Floor, Regal House, London Road, Twickenham TW1 3QB
T 020-8891 1411
W www.richmond.gov.uk
Director of Education and Leisure Services, Anji Phillips
*SOUTHWARK John Smith House, 144–152 Walworth Road, London SE17 1JE **T** 020-7525 5050/5001
W www.southwark.lgfl.net
Director of Education and Culture, Dr Roger Smith
SUTTON The Grove, Carshalton, Surrey SM5 3AL
T 020-8770 5000 **W** www.sutton.gov.uk
Strategic Director, Dr I. Birnbaum
*TOWER HAMLETS Town Hall, Mulberry Place, 5 Clove Crescent, London E14 2BG **T** 020-7364 5000
W www.towerhamlets-pdc.org.uk
Corporate Director – Education, Stephen Grix
WALTHAM FOREST Education Centre, 97 Queens Road, Walthamstow, London E17 8QS **T** 020-8496 5900
Chief Executive, Graham Moss
*WANDSWORTH Town Hall, Wandsworth High Street, London SW18 2PU **T** 020-8871 8013
W www.wandsworth.gov.uk
Director, P. Robinson

WALES

ANGLESEY Ffordd Glanhwfa, Llangefni, Anglesey LL7 7EY
T 01248-752900 W www.ynysmon.gov.uk
Director, R. P. Jones
BLAENAU GWENT Festival House, Victoria Business Park,
Ebbw Vale, Blaenau Gwent NP23 6ER T 01495-355337
Director of Lifelong Learning and Strategic Partnerships, J.
Pearce
BRIDGEND Sunnyside, Bridgend CF31 4AR
T 01656-642600
W www.bridgend.gov.uk
Director, D. Matthews
CAERPHILLY Council Offices, Caerphilly Road, Ystrad
Mynach, Hengoed CF82 7EP T 01443-815588
Director, David Hopkins
CARDIFF County Hall, Atlantic Wharf, Cardiff CF10 4UW
T 029-2087 2700 W www.cardiff.gov.uk
Head of Service, H. Knight
CARMARTHENSHIRE Pibwrlwyd, Carmarthen SA31 2NH
T 01267-224532 W www.carmarthenshire.gov.uk
Director, Alun G. Davies
CEREDIGION Swyddfa'r Sir, Marine Terrace, Aberystwyth
SY23 2DE T 01970-633600
Director, R. J. Williams
CONWY Government Buildings, Dinerth Road, Colwyn Bay
LL28 4UL T 01492-575031 W www.conwy.gov.uk
Director, R. E. Williams
DENBIGHSHIRE Caledfryn, Smithfield Road, Denbigh,
Denbighshire LL16 3RJ T 01824-706777
W www.denbighshire.gov.uk
Director, S. Bowen
FLINTSHIRE County Hall, Mold CH7 6ND T 01352-704023
W www.flintshire.gov.uk
Director, John R. Clutton
GWYNEDD Cyngor Gwynedd, Council Offices, Caernarfon
LL55 1SH T 01286-679456 W www.gwynedd.gov.uk
Director, D. Whittall
MERTHYR TYDFIL Ty Keir Hardie, Riverside Court, Avenue
De Clichy, Merthyr Tydfil CF47 8XD T 01685-724600
W www.mnet2000.org.uk
Director of Integrated Children's Services, W. V. Morgan
MONMOUTHSHIRE Floor 5, County Hall, Cwmbran
NP44 2XH T 01633-644487
W www.monmouthshire.gov.uk
Director, P. Cooke
NEATH PORT TALBOT Civic Centre, Port Talbot SA13 1PJ
T 01639-763298 W www.neath-porttalbot.gov.uk
Director, K. Napieralla
NEWPORT Civic Centre, Newport NP20 4UR T 01633-232257
W www.newport.gov.uk
Chief Education Officer, D. Griffiths
PEMBROKESHIRE County Hall, Haverfordwest SA61 1TP
T 01437-764551 W www.pembrokeshire.gov.uk
Director, G. Davies
POWYS County Hall, Llandrindod Wells LD1 5LG
T 01597-826422 W www.education.powys.gov.uk
Group Director, M. Barker
RHONDDA CYNON TAFF Ty Trevithick, Abercynon,
Mountain Ash, CF45 4UQ T 01443-744000
Group Director, D. Jones
SWANSEA County Hall, Oystermouth Road, Swansea SA1 3SN
T 01792-636351 W www.swansea.gov.uk/education
Director, R. Parry
TORFAEN County Hall, Croesyceiliog, Cwmbran, Torfaen
NP44 2WN T 01495-762200 W www.torfaen.gov.uk
Director, M. de Val

VALE OF GLAMORGAN Civic Offices, Holton Road, Barry
CF63 4RU T 01446-709138
W www.valeofglamorgan.gov.uk
Director, B. Jeffreys
WREXHAM, Ty Henblas, Queen's Square, Wrexham LL13 8AZ
T 01978-297401
W www.wrexham.gov.uk
Director, Terry Garner

SCOTLAND

ABERDEEN Summerhill Education Centre, Stronsay Drive,
Aberdeen AB15 6JA T 01224-522000
W www.aberdeen-education.org.uk
Corporate Director, J. Stodter
ABERDEENSHIRE Woodhill House, Westburn Road,
Aberdeen AB16 5GJ T 01224-664630
W www.aberdeenshire.gov.uk
Director, H. Vernal
ANGUS County Buildings, Market Street, Forfar DD8 3WE
T 01307-461460 W www.angus.gov.uk
Director of Education, Jim Anderson
ARGYLL AND BUTE Argyll House, Alexandra Parade,
Dunoon, Argyll PA23 8AJ T 01369-704000
W www.argyll-bute.gov.uk
Strategic Director, A. Law
CLACKMANNANSHIRE Lime Tree House, Castle Street, Alloa
FK10 1EX T 01259-450000 W www.clacksweb.org.uk
Director, Dave Jones
DUMFRIES AND GALLOWAY Education Department, 30
Edinburgh Road, Dumfries DG1 1NW T 01387-260427
Director of Education and Community Services, F.
Sanderson
DUNDEE Floor 8, Tayside House, Crichton Street, Dundee
DD1 3RJ T 01382-433111 W www.dundeecity.gov.uk
Director of Education, Mrs A. Wilson
EAST AYRSHIRE Council Headquarters, London Road,
Kilmarnock KA3 7BU T 01563-576017
W www.east-ayrshire.gov.uk
Director, J. Mulgrew
EAST DUNBARTONSHIRE Boclair House, 100 Milngavie
Road, Bearsden, Glasgow G61 2TQ T 0141-578 8000
W www.eastdunbarton.gov.uk
Strategic Director - Community, Ms S. Bruce
EAST LOTHIAN John Muir House, Haddington EH413HA
T 01620-827827
W www.eastlothian.gov.uk
Director of Education and Community Services, A. Blackie
EAST RENFREWSHIRE Council Offices, Eastwood Park,
Rouken Glen Road, Giffnock G46 6UG T 0141-577 3000
W www.eastrenfrewshire.gov.uk
Director, John Wilson
EDINBURGH Wellington Court, 10 Waterloo Place, Edinburgh
EH1 3EG T 0131-469 3000
Director, Education, R. Jobson
EILEAN SIAR/WESTERN ISLES Council Offices, Sandwick
Road, Stornoway, Isle of Lewis HS1 2BW T 01851-703773
Director of Education, Murdo Macleod
FALKIRK McLaren House, Marchmont Avenue, Polmont,
Falkirk FK2 0NZ T 01324-506600 W www.falkirk.gov.uk
Director, Dr G. Young
FIFE Fife House, North Street, Glenrothes KY7 5PN
T 01592-414141 W www.fife.gov.uk
Head of Education, Roger Stewart
GLASGOW Nye Bevan House, 20 India Street, Glasgow G2 4PF
T 0141-287 6898 W www.glasgow.gov.uk
Director, Ronnie O'Connor

HIGHLAND Council Buildings, Glenurquhart Road, Inverness
IV3 5NX T 01463-702802 W www.highland.gov.uk
Director, B. Robertson
INVERCLYDE 105 Dalrymple Street, Greenock PA15 1HT
T 01475-712824
Director, B. McLeary
MIDLOTHIAN Fairfield House, 8 Lothian Road, Dalkeith
EH22 3ZG T 0131-270 7500 W www.midlothian.gov.uk
Director, D. MacKay
MORAY Council Offices, High Street, Elgin IV30 1BX
T 01343-563001 W www.moray.gov.uk
Director, Donald Duncan
NORTH AYRSHIRE Cunninghame House, Irvine KA12 8EE
T 01294-324100 W www.north-ayrshire.gov.uk
Corporate Director, J. Travers
NORTH LANARKSHIRE Municipal Buildings, Kildonan Street,
Coatbridge ML5 3BT T 01236-812222
W www.northlan.gov.uk
Director, Michael O'Neill
ORKNEY ISLANDS Council Offices, School Place, Kirkwall,
Orkney KW15 1NY T 01856-873535 W www.orkney.gov.uk
Director, Leslie Manson
PERTH AND KINROSS Pullar House, 35 Kinnoull Street, Perth
PH1 5GD T 01738-476200
Executive Director, George Waddell
RENFREWSHIRE Council Headquarters, South Building,
Cotton Street, Paisley PA1 1LE T 0141-8425663
W www.renfrewshire.gov.uk
Director of Education of Leisure, Ms S. Rae
SCOTTISH BORDERS Council Headquarters, Newtown St
Boswells, Melrose, Roxburghshire TD6 0SA
T 01835-824000
W www.scottishborders.gov.uk
Director, G. Roger
SHETLAND ISLANDS Hayfield House, Hayfield Lane,
Lerwick, Shetland ZE1 0QD T 01595-744000
W www.shetland.gov.uk
Head of Education, Alex Jamieson
SOUTH AYRSHIRE County Buildings, Wellington Square, Ayr
KA7 1DR T 01292-612201 W www.south-ayrshire.gov.uk
Director, Mike McCabe
SOUTH LANARKSHIRE Council Headquarters, Almada
Street, Hamilton ML3 0AE T 01698-454545
W www.southlanarkshire.gov.uk
Executive Director, Ms M. Allan
STIRLING Viewforth, Stirling FK8 2ET T 01786-442666
W www.stirling.gov.uk
Director, Gordon Jeyes
WEST DUNBARTONSHIRE Council Offices, Garshake Road,
Dumbarton G82 3PU T 01389-737301
Director, I. McMurdo
WEST LOTHIAN Lindsay House, South Bridge Street,
Bathgate EH48 1TS T 01506-776000
Director of Education and Cultural Services, Ms K. Reid

NORTHERN IRELAND

BELFAST 40 Academy Street, Belfast BT1 2NQ
T 028-9056 4000 W www.belb.org.uk
Chief Executive, David Cargo
NORTH EAST County Hall, 182 Galgorm Road, Ballymena,
Co. Antrim BT42 1HN T 028-2565 3333
W www.neelb.org.uk
Chief Executive, G. Topping
SOUTH 3 Charlemont Place, The Mall, Armagh BT61 9AX
T 028-3751 2200 W www.selb.org
Chief Executive, Mrs H. McClenagahan

SOUTH EAST Headquarters Offices, Grahamsbridge Road,
Dundonald, Belfast BT16 2HS T 028-9056 6200
W www.seelb.org.uk
Chief Executive, J. B. Fitzsimons
WEST 1 Hospital Road, Omagh, Co. Tyrone BT79 0AW
T 028-8241 1411 W www.welbni.org
Chief Executive, B. Mulholland

ISLANDS

GUERNSEY The Grange, St Peter Port, Guernsey GY1 1RQ
T 01481-710821
Director, D. T. Neale
ISLE OF MAN St. George's Court, Upper Church Street,
Douglas, Isle of Man IM1 2SG T 01624-685820
W www.gov.im
Director, John Cain
ISLES OF SCILLY Town Hall, St Mary's, Isles of Scilly TR21 0LW
T 01720-422537 W www.scilly.gov.uk
Secretary for Education, P. S. Hygate
JERSEY PO Box 142, Jersey JE4 8QJ T 01534-509500
Director of Education, Sport and Culture, T. W. McKeon

ADVISORY BODIES

SCHOOLS

BRITISH EDUCATIONAL COMMUNICATIONS AND
TECHNOLOGY AGENCY Milburn Hill Road, Science Park,
Coventry CV4 7JJ T 024-7641 6994 E becta@becta.org.uk
W www.becta.org.uk
Chief Executive, Owen Lynch
EDUCATION OTHERWISE PO Box 7420, London N9 9SG
T 0870-730 0074
E enquiries@education-otherwise.org
W www.education-otherwise.org
INTERNATIONAL BACCALAUREATE ORGANISATION
Peterson House, Malthouse Avenue, Cardiff Gate, Cardiff
CF23 8GL T 029-2054 7777 E ibca@ibo.org W www.ibo.org
Academic Director, Prof. Jeff Thompson
LEARNING AND SKILLS COUNCIL Cheylesmore House,
Quinton Road, Coventry CV1 2WT T 0845-019 4170
E info@lsc.gov.uk W www.lsc.gov.uk
Chief Executive, Mark Haysom
SPECIAL EDUCATIONAL NEEDS AND DISABILITY
TRIBUNAL 7th Floor, Windsor House, 50 Victoria Street,
London SW1H 0NW T 01325-392555
E tribunalqueries@sendist.gsi.gov.uk W www.sendist.gov.uk
President, Lady Rosemary Hughes

INDEPENDENT SCHOOLS

ASSOCIATION OF GOVERNING BODIES OF
INDEPENDENT SCHOOLS Field House, Newton Tony,
Salisbury, Wilts SP4 0HF W www.agbis.org.uk
Secretary, Shane Ruther-Jerome
INDEPENDENT SCHOOLS COUNCIL Grosvenor Gardens
House, 35–37 Grosvenor Gardens, London SW1W 0BS
T 020-7798 1500 E info@isis.org.uk W www.isis.org.uk
General Secretary, Jonathan Shephard
INDEPENDENT SCHOOLS EXAMINATIONS BOARD
Jordan House, Christchurch Road, New Milton, Hants
BH25 6QJ T 01425-621111 E ce@iseb.co.uk
W www.iseb.co.uk
General Secretary, Mrs J. Williams

FURTHER EDUCATION

ACER (ASSOCIATION OF COLLEGES IN THE EASTERN
REGION) Suite 1, Lancaster House, Meadow Lane, St Ives,
Huntingdon, Cambs PE27 4LG T 01480-468198
E general@acer.ac.uk W www.acer.ac.uk
Chief Executive, Veronica Windmill

AOSEC (ASSOCIATION OF SOUTH EAST COLLEGES)
Building 33, The University of Reading, London Road,
Reading RG1 5AQ T 0118-378 6319 W www.aosec.org.uk
Chief Executive, Breyan Knowles

CENTRA (EDUCATION AND TRAINING SERVICES) LTD
Duxbury Park, Duxbury Hall Road, Chorley, Lancs PR7 4AT
T 01257-241428 E enquiries@centra.org.uk
W www.centra.org.uk
Chief Executive, P. Wren

EMFEC (EAST MIDLAND FURTHER EDUCATION
COUNCIL) Robins Wood House, Robins Wood Road,
Aspley, Nottingham NG8 3NH T 0115-854 1616
E enquiries@emfec.co.uk W www.emfec.co.uk
Chief Executive, Ms J. Gardiner

LEARNING AND SKILLS DEVELOPMENT AGENCY
Regent Arcade House, 19–25 Argyll Street, London W1F 7LS
T 020-7297 9000 W www.lsda.org.uk
Chief Executive, Chris Hughes

LEARNING SOUTH WEST Bishops Hull House, Bishops Hull,
Taunton, Somerset TA1 5EP T 01823-335491
W www.learning-southwest.org.uk
Chief Executive, Liz McGrath

NCFE Citygate, St James Boulevard, Newcastle upon Tyne
NE1 4JE T 0191-239 8000 E info@ncfe.org.uk
W www.ncfe.org.uk
Chief Executive, Isabel Sutcliffe

WELSH JOINT EDUCATION COMMITTEE 245 Western
Avenue, Cardiff CF5 2YX T 029-2026 5000
E exams@wjec.co.uk W www.wjec.co.uk
Chief Executive, Wyn G. Roberts

HIGHER EDUCATION

ASSOCIATION OF COMMONWEALTH UNIVERSITIES
John Foster House, 36 Gordon Square, London WC1H 0PF
T 020-7380 6700 E info@acu.ac.uk W www.acu.ac.uk
Secretary-General, Prof. Michael Gibbons

NORTHERN IRELAND HIGHER EDUCATION COUNCIL
4th Floor, Room 407, Adelaide House, 39–49 Adelaide
Street, Belfast BT2 8FD T 02890-257400
E tony.hopkins@delni.gov.uk
Chairman, Tony Hopkins CBE

QUALITY ASSURANCE AGENCY FOR HIGHER
EDUCATION Southgate House, Southgate Street,
Gloucester GL1 1UB T 01452-557000 E comms@qaa.ac.uk
W www.qaa.ac.uk
Chief Executive, Peter Williams

UNIVERSITIES SCOTLAND 53 Hanover Street, Edinburgh
EH2 2PJ T 0131-226 1111
E info@universities-scotland.ac.uk
W www.universities-scotland.ac.uk
Director, David Caldwell

UNIVERSITIES UK Woburn House, 20 Tavistock Square,
London WC1H 9HQ T 020-7419 4111
E info@universitiesuk.ac.uk W www.universitiesuk.ac.uk
Chief Executive, Baroness Diana Warwick

CURRICULUM COUNCILS

ACCAC Castle Buildings, Womanby Street, Cardiff CF10 1SX
T 029-2037 5400 E info@accac.org.uk
W www.accac.org.uk
Chief Executive, John Valentine Williams

COUNCIL FOR THE CURRICULUM, EXAMINATIONS
AND ASSESSMENT 29 Clarendon Road, Clarendon Dock,
Belfast BT1 3BG T 028-9026 1200 E info@ccea.org.uk
W www.ccea.org.uk
Chief Executive, Gavin Boyd

LEARNING AND TEACHING SCOTLAND Gardyne Road,
Dundee DD5 1NY T 01382-443600
E enquiries@ltscotland.com W www.ltscotland.com
Chief Executive, M. Baughan

QUALIFICATIONS AND CURRICULUM AUTHORITY
83 Piccadilly, London W1Y 8QA T 020-7509 5555
E info@qca.org.uk W www.qca.org.uk
Chairman, Dr Ken Boston

EXAMINING BODIES

ENGLAND

ASSESSMENT AND QUALIFICATIONS ALLIANCE (AQA)
Devas Street, Manchester M15 6EX T 0161-953 1180
E mailbox@aqa.org.uk W www.aqa.org.uk
Director-General, Dr Mike Cresswell

EDEXCEL Stewart House, 32 Russell Square, London
WC1B 5DN T 0870-240 9800 E enquiries@edexcel.org.uk
W www.edexcel.org.uk
Chief Executive, John Kerr

OCR (OXFORD CAMBRIDGE AND RSA EXAMINATIONS)
Head Office, 1 Regent Street, Cambridge CB2 1GG
T 01223-552552 E helpdesk@ocr.org.uk W www.ocr.org.uk
Chief Executive, Greg Watson

SCOTLAND

SCOTTISH QUALIFICATIONS AUTHORITY Hanover
House, 24 Douglas Street, Glasgow G2 7NQ
T 0141-242 2214 E helpdesk@sqa.org.uk
W www.sqa.org.uk
Chief Executive, Anton Colella

WALES

WELSH JOINT EDUCATION COMMITTEE 245 Western
Avenue, Cardiff CF5 2YX T 029-2026 5000
E exams@wjec.co.uk W www.wjec.co.uk
Chief Executive, Wyn G. Roberts

NORTHERN IRELAND

NORTHERN IRELAND COUNCIL FOR THE
CURRICULUM, EXAMINATIONS AND ASSESSMENT
29 Clarendon Road, Belfast, County Antrim BT1 3BG
T 028-9026 1200 E info@ccea.org.uk W www.ccea.org.uk
Chief Executive, Gavin Boyd

GCSE AND A-LEVEL

See above: AQA, EDEXCEL, NORTHERN IRELAND COUNCIL FOR
THE CURRICULUM, EXAMINATIONS AND ASSESSMENT, WELSH
JOINT EDUCATION COMMITTEE

FURTHER EDUCATION
CITY & GUILDS 1 Giltspur Street, London EC1A 9DD
T 020-7294 2468 E enquiry@city-and-guilds.co.uk
W www.city-and-guilds.co.uk
Director-General, C. Humphries CBE
EDEXEL, OCR, *see above*

FUNDING COUNCILS

FURTHER EDUCATION
LEARNING AND SKILLS COUNCIL Cheylesmore House,
Quinton Road, Coventry CV1 2WT T 0845-019 4170
E info@lsc.gov.uk W www.lsc.gov.uk
Chief Executive, Mark Haysom
NATIONAL COUNCIL – ELWA Linden Court, The Orchards,
Ilex Close, Cardiff CF14 5DZ T 029-2076 1861
E info@elwa.org.uk W www.elwa.org.uk
Chief Executive, Elizabeth Raikes
SCOTTISH FUNDING COUNCILS FOR FURTHER AND
HIGHER EDUCATION Donaldson House, 97 Haymarket
Terrace, Edinburgh EH12 5HD T 0131-313 6500
E info@sfc.ac.uk W www.shefc.ac.uk
Chief Executive, Roger McClure

HIGHER EDUCATION
HIGHER EDUCATION COUNCIL – ELWA Linden Court, The
Orchards, Ilex Close, Cardiff CF14 5DZ T 029-2076 1861
E info@elwa.org.uk W www.elwa.org.uk
Chief Executive, S. Martin
HIGHER EDUCATION FUNDING COUNCIL FOR
ENGLAND Northavon House, Coldharbour Lane, Bristol
BS16 1QD T 0117-931 7317 E hefce@hefce.ac.uk
W www.hefce.ac.uk
Chief Executive, Sir Howard Newby
SCOTTISH FUNDING COUNCILS FOR FURTHER AND
HIGHER EDUCATION Donaldson House, 97 Haymarket
Terrace, Edinburgh EH12 5HD T 0131-313 6500
E info@sfc.ac.uk W www.sfc.ac.uk
Chief Executive, Roger McClure
STUDENT AWARDS AGENCY FOR SCOTLAND Gyleview
House, 3 Redheughs Rigg, Edinburgh EH12 9HH
T 0131-476 8212 E saas.geu@scotland.gov.uk
W www.saas.gov.uk
Chief Executive, D. Stephen
STUDENT LOANS COMPANY LTD 100 Bothwell Street,
Glasgow G2 7JD T 0141-306 2000 W www.slc.co.uk
Chief Executive, C. Ward
TEACHER TRAINING AGENCY Portland House, Stag Place,
London SW1E 5TT T 020-7925 3700
E enquiry@teach-tta.gov.uk W www.teach-tta.gov.uk
Chief Executive, R. Tabberer

ADMISSIONS AND COURSE INFORMATION

CAREERS RESEARCH AND ADVISORY CENTRE Sheraton
House, Castle Park, Cambridge CB3 0AX T 01223-460277
E enquiries@crac.org.uk W www.crac.org.uk
Chief Executive, David Thomas
GRADUATE TEACHER TRAINING REGISTRY Rosehill,
New Barn Lane, Cheltenham, Glos GL52 3LZ
T 0870-1122205 E enquiries@gttr.ac.uk W www.gttr.ac.uk
GTTR Unit Manager, Miss Houston
SOCIAL WORK ADMISSIONS SYSTEM Rosehill, New Barn
Lane, Cheltenham, Glos GL52 3LZ T 0870-112 2207
SWAS Unit Manager, Janet Pearce

UNIVERSITIES AND COLLEGES ADMISSIONS SERVICE
Rosehill, New Barn Lane, Cheltenham, Glos GL52 3LZ
T 01242-222444 E enquiries@ucas.ac.uk W www.ucas.com
Chief Executive, Anthony Maclaran
UNIVERSITIES SCOTLAND 53 Hanover Street, Edinburgh
EH2 2PJ T 0131-226 1111
E info@universities-scotland.ac.uk
W www.universities-scotland.ac.uk
Director, David Caldwell

UNIVERSITIES

The following is a list of universities which have been
granted degree awarding powers by either a Royal
Charter or an Act of Parliament. There are other
recognised bodies in the UK with degree awarding
powers, as well as institutions offering courses leading to
a degree of a recognised body. For further information
please visit www.dfes.gov.uk.

UNIVERSITY OF ABERDEEN (1495)
King's College, Aberdeen AB24 3FX T 01224-272000
E pubrel@abdn.ac.uk W www.abdn.ac.uk
Full-time students (2003–4), 10,727
Chancellor, Lord Wilson of Tillyhorn, KCMG
Vice-Chancellor and Principal, Prof. Duncan C Rice
Academic Registrar, Dr T. Webb

UNIVERSITY OF ABERTAY DUNDEE (1994)
Bell Street, Dundee DD1 1HG T 01382-308000
E sro@abertay.ac.uk W www.abertay.ac.uk
Full-time students (2003–4), 4,386
Chancellor, The Rt. Hon. Earl of Airlie, KT, GCVO, PC
Vice-Chancellor, Prof. Bernard King
Registrar, Philip Henry

ANGLIA POLYTECHNIC UNIVERSITY (1992)
Rivermead Campus, Bishop Hall Lane, Chelmsford, Essex
CM1 1SQ T 01245-493131 E info@anglia.ac.uk
W www.anglia.ac.uk
Full-time students (2003–4), 20,000
Chancellor, Lord Ashcroft, KCMG
Vice-Chancellor, Prof. David Tichmarsh
Secretary and Clerk, Stephen Bennett

ASTON UNIVERSITY (1895)
Aston Triangle, Birmingham B4 7ET T 0121-359 3611
W www.aston.ac.uk
Full-time students (2003–4), 5,657
Chancellor, Sir Adrian Cadbury
Vice-Chancellor, Prof. Mike Wright
Registrar, David Packham

UNIVERSITY OF BATH (1966)
Claverton Down, Bath BA2 7AY T 01225-388388
W www.bath.ac.uk
Full-time students (2003–4), 9,210
Chancellor, Lord Tugenhat
Vice-Chancellor, Prof. Glynis Breakwell
Registrar, Jonathan Bursey

UNIVERSITY OF BIRMINGHAM (1900)
Edgbaston, Birmingham BH15 2TT T 0121-414 3344
W www.bham.ac.uk
Full-time students (2003–4), 24,900
Chancellor, Sir Dominic Cadbury
Vice-Chancellor, Prof. Michael Sterling, FRENG
Registrar and Secretary, Jonathan Nicholls

BOURNEMOUTH UNIVERSITY (1992)
Fern Barrow, Poole, Dorset BH12 5BB T 01202-524111
E marketing@bournemouth.ac.uk W www.bournemouth.ac.uk
Full-time students (2003–4), 14,407
Chancellor, Lord John Taylor of Warwick
Vice-Chancellor, Prof. Gillian Slater
Registrar, Noel Richardson

UNIVERSITY OF BRADFORD (1966)
Richmond Building, Richmond Road, Bradford, W. Yorks
BD7 1DP T 01274-232323 W www.brad.ac.uk
Full-time students (2003–4), 7,816
Chancellor, Baroness Lockwood of Dewsbury
Vice-Chancellor, Prof. Chris Taylor
Registrar and Secretary, N. J. Andrew

UNIVERSITY OF BRIGHTON (1992)
Mithras House, Lewes Road, Brighton BN2 4AT
T 01273-600900 E postmaster@bton.ac.uk W www.bton.ac.uk
Full-time students (2003–4), 15,000
Chairman of the Board, Sir Michael Checkland
Director, Prof. Sir David Watson
Registrar and Secretary, Ms C. E. Moon

UNIVERSITY OF BRISTOL (1876)
Senate House, Tyndall Avenue, Bristol BS8 1TH
T 0117-928 9000 W www.bristol.ac.uk
Full-time students (2003–4), 14,500
Chancellor, Rt. Hon. Dame Brenda Hale, DBE, PC
Vice-Chancellor, Prof. Eric Thomas
Registrar, D. W. M. Pretty

BRUNEL UNIVERSITY (1966)
Uxbridge, Middx UB8 3PH T 01895-274000
W www.brunel.ac.uk
Full-time students (2003–4), 12,000
Chancellor, The Rt. Hon. Lord Wakeham, PC
Vice-Chancellor, Prof. Stephen Schwartz
Secretary and Registrar, Ms J. Weale

UNIVERSITY OF BUCKINGHAM (1983)
Buckingham MK18 1EG T 01280-814080
E reception@buckingham.ac.uk W www.buckingham.ac.uk
Full-time students (2003–4), 720
Chancellor, Sir Martin Jacomb
Vice-Chancellor, Dr Terence Kealey
Secretary, Prof. John Clarke

UNIVERSITY OF CAMBRIDGE (1209)
The Old Schools, Trinity Lane, Cambridge CB2 1TN
T 01223-337733 W www.cam.ac.uk
Undergraduates (2003–4), 17,600
Chancellor, HRH The Prince Phillip, Duke of Edinburgh,
  KG, KT, OM, GBE, PC (1977)
Vice-Chancellor, Prof. Alison Richard (Newnham) (2003)
Deputy High Steward, The Lord Richardson of
  Duntisbourne, MBE, TD, PC (1983)
Commissary, The Lord Mackay of Clashfern, KT, PC, FRSE
  (2002)
Orator, A. J. Bowen (Jesus) (1993)
Registrary, T. J. Mead, PHD (Wolfson) (1997)
Librarian, P. K. Fox (Selwyn) (1994)
Director of the Fitzwilliam Museum, D. D. Robinson
  (Magdalene) (1995)
High Steward, Dame Bridget Ogilvie FRS (Girton) (2001)
Academic Secretary, G. P. Allen (Wolfson)

COLLEGES AND HALLS *with dates of foundation*
CHRIST'S (1505) *Master,* Prof. Malcolm Bowie, DPHIL,
  FBA (2002)
CHURCHILL (1960) *Master,* Sir John Boyd, KCMG (1996)
CLARE (1326) *Master,* Prof. A. J. Badger, PHD (2003)
CLARE HALL (1966) *President,* Prof. E. Salje, PHD, FRS
  (2001)
CORPUS CHRISTI (1352) *Master,* Prof. H. Ahmed,
  FRENG (2000)
DARWIN (1964) *Master,* Prof. W. A. Brown, CBE
DOWNING (1800) *Master,* Prof. B. J. Everitt, PHD (2003)
EMMANUEL (1584) *Master,* Lord Wilson of Dinton, GCB,
  LLB (2002)
FITZWILLIAM (1966) *Master,* Prof. B. F. G. Johnson, PHD,
  FRS (1999)
GIRTON (1869) *Mistress,* Prof. Dame Marylin Strathern,
  PHD, FBA (1998)
GONVILLE AND CAIUS (1348) *Master,* N. McKendrick
  (1996)
HOMERTON (1824) *Principal,* Dr K. B. Pretty
HUGHES HALL (1985) *President,* Prof. P. Richards, MD,
  PHD (1998)
JESUS (1496) *Master,* Prof. R. Mair, PHD, FRENG (2001)
KING'S (1441) *Provost,* Prof. P. P. G. Bateson
LUCY CAVENDISH COLLEGE (1965) *President,* Dame
  Veronica Sutherland, CMG (2001)
MAGDALENE (1542) *Master,* D. D. Robinson (2002)
NEW HALL (1954) *President,* Mrs A. Lonsdale (1996)
NEWNHAM (1871) *Principal,* Baroness O'Neill of
  Bengarve, CBE (1992)
PEMBROKE (1347) *Master,* Sir Richard Dearlove, KCMG,
  OBE (2004)
PETERHOUSE (1284) *Master,* Lord Wilson of Tillyorn,
  KT, GCMG (2002)
QUEENS' (1448) *President,* Lord Eatwell, (1997)
ROBINSON (1977) *Warden,* A. D. Yates, (2001)
ST CATHARINE'S (1473) *Master,* Prof. D. S. Ingram,
  (2000)
ST EDMUND'S (1896) *Master,* Prof. Brian Heap, FRS
  (1996)
ST JOHN'S (1511) *Master,* Prof. R. N. Perham, SCD, FRS
  (2004)
SELWYN (1882) *Master,* Prof. R. J. Bowring, LITTD
  (2000)
SIDNEY SUSSEX (1596) *Master,* Prof. Dame Sandra
  Dawson, (1999)
TRINITY (1546) *Master,* Prof. Sir Martin Rees, FRS
  (2004)
TRINITY HALL (1350) *Master,* Prof. M. J. Daunton, FBA
  (2004)
WOLFSON (1965) *President,* Prof. G. Johnson, PHD
  (1994)

**UNIVERSITY OF CENTRAL ENGLAND IN
BIRMINGHAM (1992)**
Perry Barr, Birmingham B42 2SU T 0121-331 5000
E info@ucechoices.com W www.uce.ac.uk
Full-time students (2003–4), 24,000
Chancellor, Cllr John Alden
Vice-Chancellor, Dr Peter Knight
Secretary and Registrar, Maxine Penlington

UNIVERSITY OF CENTRAL LANCASHIRE (1992)
Preston PR1 2HE T 01772-201201 W www.uclan.ac.uk
Full-time students (2003–4), 34,000
Chancellor, Sir Richard Evans, CBE
Vice-Chancellor, Dr Malcolm McVicar
Director of Student Affairs, Ian McMillan

CITY UNIVERSITY (1966)
Northampton Square, London EC1V 0HB T 020-7040 5060
E registry@city.ac.uk W www.city.ac.uk
Full-time students (2003–4), 12,814
Chancellor, The Rt. Hon. Lord Mayor of London
Vice-Chancellor, Prof. D.W. Rhind, PHD, DSC
Registrar, Eamon Martin

COVENTRY UNIVERSITY (1992)
Priory Street, Coventry CV1 5FB T 024-7688 7688
E cor002@coventry.ac.uk W www.coventry.ac.uk
Full-time students (2003–4), 17,000
Chancellor, The Lord Plumb (1995)
Vice-Chancellor, Dr Michael Goldstein, CBE
Academic Registrar, Ms Kate Quantrell

CRANFIELD UNIVERSITY (1969)
Cranfield, Beds MK43 0AL T 01234-750111
E info@cranfield.ac.uk W www.cranfield.ac.uk
Full-time students (2003–4), 2,149
Chancellor, The Lord Vincent of Coleshill, GBE, KCB, DSO
Vice-Chancellor, Prof. Frank Hartley, DSC
Academic Registrar and Secretary, David Buck

DE MONTFORT UNIVERSITY (1992)
The Gateway, Leicester LE1 9BH T 08459-454647
E enquiry@dmu.ac.uk W www.dmu.ac.uk
Full-time students (2003–4), 17,000
Chancellor, The Baroness Usha Prasher of Runnymede, CBE
Chief Executive and Vice-Chancellor, Prof. Philip Turner, PHD
Registrar, Eugene Critchlow

UNIVERSITY OF DERBY (1992)
Kedleston Road, Derby DE22 1GB T 01332-590500
W www.derby.ac.uk
Full-time students (2003–4), 25,000
Chancellor, Sir Christopher Ball
Vice-Chancellor, Prof. Roger Waterhouse
Registrar, Jennifer Fry

UNIVERSITY OF DUNDEE (1967)
Dundee DD1 4HN T 01382-344000 E secretary@dundee.ac.uk
W www.dundee.ac.uk
Full-time students (2003–4), 9,271
Chancellor, Sir James Black, FRCP, FRS
Vice-Chancellor, Sir Alan Langlands
Academic Secretary, Dr David Duncan

UNIVERSITY OF DURHAM (1832)
The University Office, Durham DH1 3HP T 0191-334 2000
W www.dur.ac.uk
Full-time students (2003–4), 13,700
Chancellor, vacant
Vice-Chancellor and Warden, Prof. Sir Kenneth Calman, KCB, MD, PHD
Registrar and Secretary, L. Sanders

COLLEGES
COLLINGWOOD, *Principal,* Prof. Jane H. M. Taylor, DPHIL (2001)
GEORGE STEPHENSON, *Principal,* Prof. A. C. Darnell, (2001)
GREY, *Master,* Prof. J. M. Chamberlain, DPHIL (2004)
HATFIELD, *Acting Master,* Angel B. Scott, (2002)
JOHN SNOW, *Principal,* Prof. H. M. Evans, PHD (2002)
ST AIDAN'S, *Principal,* J. S. Ashworth, (1998)

ST CHAD'S, *Principal,* Revd J. P. M. Cassidy, PHD (1997)
ST CUTHBERT'S SOCIETY, *Principal,* Prof. R.D. Boyne, PHD (2004)
ST HILD AND ST BEDE, *Principal,* J. A. Pearson, PHD (2000)
ST JOHN'S, *Principal,* Rt. Revd Prof. S.W. Sykes, (1999)
ST MARY'S, *Principal,* Miss J. L. Hobbs, (1999)
TREVELYAN, *Principal,* N. Martin, PHD (2000)
UNIVERSITY, *Master,* Prof. M. E. Tucker, PHD (2000)
USHAW, *Rector,* Revd T. Drainey (2004)
USTINOV COLLEGE, *Principal,* Susan J. Scott (2003)
VAN MILDERT, *Principal,* G. Patterson (2000)

UNIVERSITY OF EAST ANGLIA (1963)
Norwich NR4 7TJ T 01603-456161 E press@uea.ac.uk
W www.uea.ac.uk
Full-time students (2003–4), 13,000
Chancellor, Sir Brandon Gough
Vice-Chancellor, Professor David Eastwood
Registrar and Secretary, Brian Summers

UNIVERSITY OF EAST LONDON (1898)
Longbridge Road, Dagenham, Essex RM8 2AS T 020-8223 3000
E publicity@uel.ac.uk W www.uel.ac.uk
Full-time students (2003–4), 15,000
Chancellor, Lord Rix
Vice-Chancellor, Prof. Michael Thorne
Registrar and Secretary, Alan Ingle

UNIVERSITY OF EDINBURGH (1583)
Old College, South Bridge, Edinburgh EH8 9YL
T 0131-650 1000 E communications.office@ed.ac.uk
W www.ed.ac.uk
Full-time students (2003–4), 20,000
Chancellor, HRH The Prince Philip, Duke of Edinburgh, KG, KT, OM
Principle and Vice-Chancellor, Prof. Tim O'Shea
Secretary, Melvyn Cornish

UNIVERSITY OF ESSEX (1964)
Wivenhoe Park, Colchester CO4 3SQ T 01206-873333
E admit@essex.ac.uk W www.essex.ac.uk
Full-time students (2003–4), 7,273
Chancellor, Lord Phillips of Sudbury
Vice-Chancellor, Prof. Ivor Crewe
Registrar and Secretary, Dr Tony Rich

UNIVERSITY OF EXETER (1955)
Northcote House, The Queen's Drive, Exeter EX4 4QJ
T 01392-661000 E s.d.franklin@exeter.ac.uk
W www.exeter.ac.uk
Full-time students (2003–4), 11,278
Chancellor, The Lord Alexander of Weedon
Vice Chancellor, Prof. Steve Smith
Registrar and Secretary, David J. Allen

UNIVERSITY OF GLAMORGAN (1992)
Pontypridd CF37 1DL
T 0800-716925
W www.glam.ac.uk
Full-time students (2003–4), 19,820
Chancellor, The Rt. Hon. Lord Morris of Aberavon
Vice-Chancellor, Sir Adrian Webb
Secretary, Leigh Bracegirdle

UNIVERSITY OF GLASGOW (1451)
Gilbert Scott Building, University Avenue, Glasgow G12 8QQ
T 0141-339 8855 E publicity.services@gla.ac.uk
W www.gla.ac.uk
Full-time students (2003–4), 19,521
Chancellor, Sir William Kerr Fraser, GCB, LLD
Vice-Chancellor, Sir Muir Russell, KCB, FRSE
Head of Registry, Christine Lowther

GLASGOW CALEDONIAN UNIVERSITY (1993)
City Campus, 70 Cowcaddens Road, Glasgow G4 0BA
T 0141-331 3000 E helpline@gcal.ac.uk
W www.caledonian.ac.uk
Full-time students (2003–4), 14,000
Chancellor, Magnus Magnusson, MBE
Vice-Chancellor, Dr Ian Johnston, CB
Secretary, Brian Murray

UNIVERSITY OF GLOUCESTERSHIRE (2001)
Cheltenham GL50 2QF T 01242-532700 W www.glos.ac.uk
Full-time students (2003–4), 6,063
Chancellor, Lord Carey of Clifton
Vice-Chancellor, Dame Janet Trotter
Academic Registrar, Peter Griffiths

UNIVERSITY OF GREENWICH (1992)
Old Royal Naval College, Park Row, Greenwich, London
SE10 9LS T 020-8331 8000 E courseinfo@gre.ac.uk
W www.gre.ac.uk
Full-time students (2003–4), 13,747
Chancellor, The Rt. Hon. Lord Holme of Cheltenham,
   CBE
Vice-Chancellor, Baroness Blackstone
Academic Registrar, Christine Rose

HERIOT-WATT UNIVERSITY (1966)
Edinburgh EH14 4AS T 0131-449 5111 W www.hw.ac.uk
Full-time students (2003–4) 6,300
Chancellor, The Lord Mackay of Clashfern, KT, PC
Vice-Chancellor, Prof. John Archer, FRENG
Secretary, P. L. Wilson

UNIVERSITY OF HERTFORDSHIRE (1992)
College Lane, Hatfield, Herts AL10 9AB T 01707-284000
W www.herts.ac.uk
Full-time students (2003–4), 16,656
Chancellor, Lord Maclaren of Knebworth
Vice-Chancellor, Prof. R. J. J. Wilson
Registrar and Secretary, P. E. Waters

UNIVERSITY OF HUDDERSFIELD (1992)
Queensgate, Huddersfield HD1 3DH T 01484-422288
E prospectus@hud.ac.uk W www.hud.ac.uk
Full-time students (2003–4), 18,432
Chancellor, Patrick Stewart
Vice-Chancellor, Prof. John Tarrant
Secretary, Tony Mears

UNIVERSITY OF HULL (1927)
Cottingham Road, Hull HU6 7RX T 01482-346311
W www.hull.ac.uk
Full-time students (2003–4), 10,390
Chancellor, Lord Armstrong of Ilminster
Vice-Chancellor, Prof. David Drewy
Registrar, David Lock

KEELE UNIVERSITY (1962)
Keele, Staffs ST5 5BG T 01782-621111 W www.keele.ac.uk
Full-time students (2003–4), 5,636
Chancellor, Prof. Sir David Weatherall, KT, DL, MB
Vice-Chancellor, Prof. Janet Finch, CBE
Secretary and Registrar, Simon Morris

UNIVERSITY OF KENT AT CANTERBURY (1965)
Canterbury, Kent CT2 7NZ T 01227-764000
W www.kent.ac.uk
Full-time students (2003–4), 8,411
Chancellor, Sir Crispin Tickle, GCMG, KCVO
Vice-Chancellor, Prof. David Melville
Registrar and Secretary, Nick McHard

KINGSTON UNIVERSITY (1992)
River House, 53–57 High Street, Kingston upon Thames, Surrey
KT1 1LQ T 020-8547 2000 E admissions-info@kingston.ac.uk
W www.kingston.ac.uk
Full-time students (2003–4), 12,776
Chancellor, Sir Peter Hall
Vice-Chancellor, Prof. Peter Scott
Senior Secretary, Ann Pohan

UNIVERSITY OF LANCASTER (1964)
Bailrigg, Lancaster LA1 4YW T 01524-65201
W www.lancs.ac.uk
Full-time students (2003–4), 9,386
Chancellor, HRH Princess Alexandra
Vice-Chancellor, Prof. Paul Wellings
Secretary, Fiona Aiken

UNIVERSITY OF LEEDS (1904)
Leeds LS2 9JT T 0113-243 1751 E pressoffice@leeds.ac.uk
W www.leeds.ac.uk
Full-time students (2003–4), 29,000
Chancellor, Lord Bragg of Wigton
Vice-Chancellor, Prof. Michael Arthur
Secretary, J. Roger Gair

LEEDS METROPOLITAN UNIVERSITY (1992)
City Campus, Leeds LS1 3HE T 0113-283 2600
E course-enquiries@lmu.ac.uk W www.lmu.ac.uk
Full-time students (2003–4), 15,505
Chancellor, Leslie Silver, OBE
Vice-Chancellor, Prof. Simon Lee
Secretary, Steve Denton

UNIVERSITY OF LEICESTER (1957)
University Road, Leicester LE1 7RH T 0116-252 2522
E pressoffice@le.ac.uk W www.le.ac.uk
Full-time students (2003–4), 10,462
Chancellor, Sir Michael Atiyah, OM, FRS, PHD
Vice-Chancellor, Prof. R. Burgess, PHD
Registrar and Secretary, K. J. Julian

UNIVERSITY OF LINCOLN (1992)
Brayford Pool, Lincoln, LN6 7TS T 01522-882000
E marketing@lincoln.ac.uk W www.ulh.ac.uk
Full-time students (2003–4), 7,531
Chancellor, Dame Elizabeth Esteve-Coll
Vice-Chancellor, Prof. David Chiddick
Registrar, Edmund Fitzpatrick

UNIVERSITY OF LIVERPOOL (1903)
Senate House, Abercromby Square, Liverpool L69 3BX
T 0151-794 2000 W www.liv.ac.uk
Full-time students (2003–4), 17,229
Chancellor, The Rt. Hon. Lord Owen, CH
Vice-Chancellor, Prof. J. D. Bone
Registrar and Secretary, M. D. Carr

LIVERPOOL JOHN MOORES UNIVERSITY (1992)
Egerton Court, 2 Rodaney Street, Liverpool L3 5UX
T 0151-231 2121 W www.livjm.ac.uk
Full-time students (2003–4), 14,623
Chancellor, Cherie Booth, QC
Vice-Chancellor, Prof. M. Brown
Registrar and Secretary, Alison Wild

UNIVERSITY OF LONDON (1836)
Senate House, Malet Street, London WC1E 7HU
T 020-7862 8000 E enquiries@lon.ac.uk
W www.lon.ac.uk
Full-time students (2003–4), 88,000
Visitor, HM the Queen in Council
Chancellor, HRH The Princess Royal, KG, GCVO, FRS
Vice-Chancellor, Prof. Sir Graeme Davies (2003)
Chairman of the Council, The Rt. Hon. The Lord Brooke
of Sutton Mandeville, CH, PC
Academic Registrar, Mrs G. F. Roberts
Director of Administration, Ms Catherine Swarbrick

COLLEGES AND INSTITUTES
BIRKBECK COLLEGE Malet Street, London WC1E 7HX
Master, Prof. D. Latchman (2003)
BRITISH INSTITUTE IN PARIS 9–11 rue de Constantine,
75340 Paris, Cedex 07
Director, Prof. Robert Lethbridge (2003)
COURTAULD INSTITUTE OF ART North Block, Somerset
House, Strand, London WC2R 0RN
Director, Prof. J. Cuno (2003)
GOLDSMITHS COLLEGE Lewisham Way, New Cross,
London SE14 6NW
Warden, Prof. B. Pimlott (1998)
HEYTHROP COLLEGE Kensington Square, London W8 5HQ
Principal, Revd Dr J. McDade, SJ, BD (1999)
IMPERIAL COLLEGE OF SCIENCE, TECHNOLOGY AND
MEDICINE (includes Imperial College Schools of Medicine
at Charing Cross, Hammersmith and St Mary's hospitals and
at the National Heart and Lung Institute), South Kensington,
London SW7 2AZ
Rector, Prof. Sir Richard Sykes, FRS (2001)
INSTITUTE OF CANCER RESEARCH Royal Cancer Hospital,
Chester Beatty Laboratories, 237 Fulham Road, London
SW3 6JB
Chief Executive, Prof. P. Rigby (1999)
INSTITUTE OF EDUCATION 20 Bedford Way, London
WC1H 0AL
Director, Prof. G. Whitty (2000)
KING'S COLLEGE LONDON (includes Guy's, King's and St
Thomas's Schools of Medicine, Dentistry and Biomedical
Sciences), Strand, London WC2R 2LS
Principal, Prof. R. Trainor (2004)
LONDON BUSINESS SCHOOL Sussex Place, Regent's Park,
London NW1 4SU
Principal, Prof. L. D'Andrea Tyson (2002)
LONDON SCHOOL OF ECONOMICS AND POLITICAL
SCIENCE Houghton Street, London WC2A 2AE
Director, Sir Howard Davies (2003)

LONDON SCHOOL OF HYGIENE AND TROPICAL
MEDICINE Keppel Street, London WC1E 7HT
Dean, Prof. A. Haines, 2001
QUEEN MARY AND WESTFIELD COLLEGE (incorporating
St Bartholomew's and the Royal London School of Medicine
and Dentistry), Mile End Road, London E1 4NS
Principal, Prof. A. Smith, FRS (1998)
ROYAL ACADEMY OF MUSIC Marylebone Road, London
NW1 5HT
Principal, Prof. Curtis Price (1995)
ROYAL HOLLOWAY Egham Hill, Egham, Surrey TW20 0EX
Principal, Prof. S. Hill, MPHIL (2002)
ROYAL VETERINARY COLLEGE Royal College Street,
London NW1 0TU
Principal and Dean, Prof. Q. McKellar (2004)
SCHOOL OF ADVANCED STUDY Senate House, Malet
Street, London WC1E 7HU
Dean, Prof. T. C. Daintith
INSTITUTE FOR THE STUDY OF THE AMERICAS
31 Tavistock Square, London WC1H 9HA
Director, Prof. J. Dunkerley (1998)
INSTITUTE OF ADVANCED LEGAL STUDIES Charles Clore
House, 17 Russell Square, London WC1B 5DR
Director, Prof. Avrom Sherr
INSTITUTE OF CLASSICAL STUDIES Senate House, Malet
Street, London WC1E 7HU
Director, Prof. G. B. Waywell, FSA (1996)
INSTITUTE OF COMMONWEALTH STUDIES 27–28
Russell Square, London WC1B 5DS
Director, Prof. T. Shaw (2001)
INSTITUTE OF ENGLISH STUDIES Senate House, Malet
Street, London WC1E 7HU
Director, Prof. W. Gould (2000)
INSTITUTE OF GERMANIC STUDIES 29 Russell Square,
London WC1B 5DP
Director, Prof. R. Görner, (1999)
INSTITUTE OF HISTORICAL RESEARCH Senate House,
Malet Street, London WC1E 7HU
Director, Prof. David Bates
INSTITUTE OF ROMANCE STUDIES Senate House, Malet
Street, London WC1E 7HU
Director, Prof. J. Still (2002)
WARBURG INSTITUTE Woburn Square, London WC1H 0AB
Director, Prof. C. Hope
SCHOOL OF ORIENTAL AND AFRICAN STUDIES
Thornhaugh Street, Russell Square, London WC1H1AX
Director, Prof. C. Bundy (2001)
SCHOOL OF PHARMACY 29–39 Brunswick Square, London
WC1N 1AX
Dean, Prof. A. T. Florence, CBE, PHD, FRSE (1989)
ST GEORGE'S HOSPITAL MEDICAL SCHOOL Cranmer
Terrace, London SW17 0RE
Principal, Prof. Michael Farthing (2003), FRCP
UNIVERSITY COLLEGE LONDON (including UCL Medical
School), Gower Street, London WC1E 6BT
Provost and President, Prof. Malcolm Grant (2003)
UNIVERSITY MARINE BIOLOGICAL STATION Millport,
Isle of Cumbrae KA28 0EG
Director, Dr Rupert Ormond
EXTERNAL PROGRAMME Senate House, Malet Street,
London WC1E 7HU
Director, Prof. J. M. McConnell (1992)
PHILOSOPHY PROGRAMME Senate House, Malet Street,
London WC1E 7HU
Director, Prof. T. Crane

LONDON METROPOLITAN UNIVERSITY (2002)
London City Campus, 31 Jewry Street, London EC3N 2EY
T 020-7320 1000 W www.londonmet.ac.uk
Full-time students (2003–4), 18,200
President, Prof. Roderick Floud
Vice-Chancellor and Chief Executive, Brian Roper
Secretary, John MacParland

LOUGHBOROUGH UNIVERSITY (1966)
Ashby Road, Loughborough, Leics LE11 3TU T 01509-263171
W www.lboro.ac.uk
Full-time students (2003–4), 12,000
Chancellor, Sir John Jennings, CBE
Vice-Chancellor, Prof. David Wallace, CBE, FRS, FRENG
Registrar and Secretary, John Town

UNIVERSITY OF LUTON (1993)
Park Square, Luton LU1 3JU T 01582-734111
E admissions@luton.ac.uk W www.luton.ac.uk
Full-time students (2003–4), 11,500
Chancellor, Sir Robin Biggam
Vice-Chancellor, Dr Dai John

UNIVERSITY OF MANCHESTER (1824)
Oxford Road, Manchester M13 9PL T 0161-275 2000
E enquiry@manchester.ac.uk W www.man.ac.uk
Full-time students (2003–4), 34,000
Co-Chancellors, Anna Ford and Sir Terry Leahy
Vice-Chancellor, Prof. Alan Gilbert
Registrar and Secretary, Dugald Mackie

MANCHESTER METROPOLITAN UNIVERSITY
(1992)
All Saints, Manchester M15 6BH T 0161-247 2000
E enquiries@mmu.ac.uk W www.mmu.ac.uk
Full-time students (2003–4), 26,000
Chancellor, Dame Janet Smith, OBE
Vice-Chancellor, Alexandra V. Burslem, OBE
Registrar, Janusz Karczewski-Slowikowski

MIDDLESEX UNIVERSITY (1992)
North London Business Park, Oakleigh Road, London N11 1QS
T 020-8411 5000 E admissions@mdx.ac.uk W www.mdx.ac.uk
Full-time students (2003–4), 25,000
Chancellor, The Rt. Hon. Lord Sheppard of Didgemere,
KCVO, KT
Vice-Chancellor, Prof. Michael Driscoll
Registrar, Colin Davis

NAPIER UNIVERSITY (1992)
Craighouse Campus, Craighouse Road, Edinburgh EH10 5LG
T 0500-353570 E info@napier.ac.uk W www.napier.ac.uk
Full-time students (2003–4), 12,000
Principal and Vice-Chancellor, Prof. Joan Stringer
Secretary, Dr Gerry Webby

UNIVERSITY OF NEWCASTLE UPON TYNE (1963)
6 Kensington Terrace, Newcastle upon Tyne NE17 7RU
T 0191-222 6000 W www.ncl.ac.uk
Full-time students (2003–4), 14,667
Chancellor, The Rt. Hon. Christopher Patten
Vice-Chancellor, Prof. Christopher Edwards
Registrar, Dr John Hogan

NORTHUMBRIA UNIVERSITY AT NEWCASTLE
(1992)
Ellison Building, Ellison Place, Newcastle upon Tyne NE1 8ST
T 0191-232 6002 E ca.marketing@northumbria.ac.uk
W www.northumbria.ac.uk
Full-time students (2003–4), 23,912
Chancellor, Lord Glenamara
Vice-Chancellor, Prof. Kel Fidler
Registrar, Mrs Cheryl Penna

UNIVERSITY OF NOTTINGHAM (1948)
University Park, Nottingham NG7 2RD T 0115-951 5151
E university-profile@nottingham.ac.uk
W www.nottingham.ac.uk
Full-time students (2003–4), 24,500
Chancellor, Prof. F. Yang, LITTD
Vice-Chancellor, Prof. Sir Colin Campbell
Registrar, K. H. Jones

NOTTINGHAM TRENT UNIVERSITY (1992)
Burton Street, Nottingham NG1 4BU T 0115-941 8418
E cor.web@ntu.ac.uk W www.ntu.ac.uk
Full-time students (2003–4), 18,546
Chairman, John Peace
Vice-Chancellor, Prof. Neil Gorman
Registrar, David Samson

OPEN UNIVERSITY (1969)
Walton Hall, Milton Keynes MK7 6AA T 01908-274066
E general-enquiries@open.ac.uk W www.open.ac.uk
Full-time students (2003–4), 79,262
Chancellor, Rt. Hon. Betty Boothroyd
Vice-Chancellor, Prof. Brenda Gourley
Registrar, Helen Niven

UNIVERSITY OF OXFORD (*c.* 12th century)
University Offices, Wellington Square, Oxford OX1 2JD
T 01865-270000 E information.officer@admin.ox.ac.uk
W www.ox.ac.uk
Students in residence 2003–4, 17,097
Chancellor, The Rt. Hon. Chris Patten, CH, elected
2003
High Steward, The Rt Hon. Lord Bingham of Cornhill
(Balliol, Nuffield), elected 2002
Vice-Chancellor, Dr J. A. Hood, elected 2004
Pro-Vice-Chancellors, Dr Bill Macmillan, Prof. Paul Slack,
Prof. Susan Iversen
Registrar, D. R. Holmes (St John's), elected 1998
Secretary of the Faculties and Academic Registrar, A. P. Weale
(Worcester), elected 1984
Proctors, Dr J. F. Wheater (University), Revd Dr J. D.
Maltby (Corpus Christi)
Assessor, Dr D. J. Walker (St Hugh's) elected 2004
Public Orator, R. H. A. Jenkyns
*Director of University Library Services and Bodley's
Librarian,* R. P. Carr (Balliol), appointed 1997
Director of the Ashmolean Museum, Dr C. Brown
(Worcester), elected 1998
Keeper of Archives, S. Bailey, appointed 2000
Surveyor to the University, Ms J. Wood, appointed 2004
Secretary of the Chest, J. R. Clements (Merton), elected
1995

COLLEGES AND HALLS *with dates of foundation*
ALL SOULS (1438) *Warden,* Prof. J. Davis, FBA, PHD
(1995)
BALLIOL (1263) *Master,* A. Graham (1998)
BLACKFRIARS (1221) *Regent,* Revd F. G. Kerr (1998)

BRASENOSE (1509) *Principal,* Prof. R. Cashmore, FRS (2003)

CAMPION HALL (1896) *Master,* Revd Dr G. J. Hughes (1998)

CHRIST CHURCH (1546) *Dean,* Very Revd C. A. Lewis (2003)

CORPUS CHRISTI (1517) *President,* Timothy Lankester, KCB (2001)

EXETER (1314) *Rector,* Ms Frances Cairncross, CBE (2004)

GREEN (1979) *Warden,* Sir John Hanson, KCMG, CBE (1997)

GREYFRIARS (1910) *Warden,* Revd Dr T. G. Weinandy (1996)

HARRIS MANCHESTER (1786) *Principal,* Revd R. Waller, PHD (1988)

HERTFORD (1974) *Principal,* Sir Walter Bodmer, FRS, FRCPATH (1996)

JESUS (1571) *Principal,* Sir Peter North, CBE, FBA (1984)

KEBLE (1868) *Warden,* Prof. A. Cameron, CBE, PHD, FBA (1994)

KELLOGG (1990) *President,* Dr G. P. Thomas (1990)

LADY MARGARET HALL (1878) *Principal,* Dr Frances Lannon, FRHIST (2002)

LINACRE (1962) *Principal,* Prof. P. A. Slack, FBA (1996)

LINCOLN (1427) *Rector,* Prof. P. Langford (2000)

MAGDALEN (1458) *President,* A. D. Smith, CBE (1998)

MANSFIELD (1886) *Principal,* Dr. D. Walford, FRCPATH, FRCP, FFPHM (1996)

MERTON (1264) *Warden,* Prof. Dame J. Rawson, CBE, FBA (1994)

NEW COLLEGE (1379) *Warden,* Prof. A. J. Ryan, FBA (1996)

NUFFIELD (1958) *Warden,* Sir Tony Atkinson, FBA (1994)

ORIEL (1326) *Provost,* Sir Derek Morris (2004)

PEMBROKE (1624) *Master,* Giles Henderson, CBE (2001)

QUEEN'S (1340) *Provost,* Sir Alan Budd (1999)

REGENT'S PARK (1820) *Principal,* Revd Dr P. S. Fiddes (1989)

ST ANNE'S (1952) *Principal,* vacant

ST ANTONY'S (1953) *Warden,* Sir Marrack Goulding, KCMG (1997)

ST BENET'S HALL (1897) *Master,* Father Leo Chamberlain (2004)

ST CATHERINE'S (1963) *Master,* Prof. Roger Ainsworth (2003)

ST CROSS (1965) *Master,* Prof. Andrew Goudie (2003)

ST EDMUND HALL (c.1278) *Principal,* Prof. D. M. P. Mingos, FRS, FRSC (1999)

ST HILDA'S (1893) *Principal,* Lady Judith English (2001)

ST HUGH'S (1886) *Principal,* A. Dilnot, CBE (2002)

ST JOHN'S (1555) *President,* Sir Michael Scholar, KCB (2001)

ST PETER'S (1929) *Master,* Prof. Bernard Silverman, FRS (2003)

SOMERVILLE (1879) *Principal,* Dame Fiona Caldicott, DBE, FRCP, FRCPSYCH (1996)

TEMPLETON (1965) *President,* Sir David Rowland (1998)

TRINITY (1554) *President,* The Hon. Michael J. Beloff, FRSA (1996)

UNIVERSITY (1249) *Master,* Lord Butler of Brockwell, GCB, CVO (1998)

WADHAM (1610) *Warden,* Sir Neil Chalmers, CBE (2003)

WOLFSON (1966) *President,* Prof. Sir Gareth Roberts, FRS, PHD (2000)

WORCESTER (1714) *Provost,* R. G. Smethurst (1991)

WYCLIFFE HALL (1877) *Principal,* Revd Dr A. E. McGrath (1995)

OXFORD BROOKES UNIVERSITY (1992)
Gipsy Lane, Oxford OX3 0BP T 01865-484848
E query@brookes.ac.uk W www.brookes.ac.uk
Full-time students (2003–4), 15,570
Chancellor, Jon Snow
Vice-Chancellor, Prof. Graham Upton
Academic Registrar, Stephen Marshall

UNIVERSITY OF PAISLEY (1992)
Paisley PA1 2BE T 0141-848 3000 E uni-direct@paisley.ac.uk
W www.paisley.ac.uk
Full-time students (2003–4), 7,500
Chancellor, Sir Robert Smith
Principal and Vice-Chancellor, Prof. John Macklin
Registrar, David Rigg

UNIVERSITY OF PLYMOUTH (1992)
Drake Circus, Plymouth PL4 8AA T 01752-600600
E admissions@plymouth.ac.uk W www.plymouth.ac.uk
Full-time students (2003–4), 17,328
Vice-Chancellor, Prof. R. Levinsky
Academic Registrar and Secretary, Miss J. Hopkinson

UNIVERSITY OF PORTSMOUTH (1992)
University House, Winston Churchill Avenue, Portsmouth
PO1 2UP T 023-9284 8484 E info.centre@port.ac.uk
W www.port.ac.uk
Full-time students (2003–4), 17,710
Chancellor, Lord Palumbo
Vice-Chancellor, Prof. John Craven
Registrar, Andy Rees

QUEEN'S UNIVERSITY OF BELFAST (1908)
Belfast BT7 1NN T 028-9024 5133 E comms.office@qub.ac.uk
W www.qub.ac.uk
Full-time students (2003–4), 16,000
Chancellor, Senator George Mitchell
Vice-Chancellor, Prof. Sir George Bain
Registrar, James O'Kane

UNIVERSITY OF READING (1926)
Whiteknights, PO Box 217, Reading RG6 6AH T 0118-987 5123
E communications@reading.ac.uk W www.reading.ac.uk
Full-time students (2003–4), 10,750
Chancellor, Lord Carrington, KG, GCMG, CH
Vice-Chancellor, Prof. R. G. Marshall, CBE
Director of Student Services, W.P. Watts

ROBERT GORDON UNIVERSITY (1992)
Schoolhill, Aberdeen AB10 1FR T 01224-262000
E admissions@rgu.ac.uk W www.rgu.ac.uk
Full-time students (2003–4), 8,230
Chancellor, Sir Bob Reid
Vice-Chancellor, Prof. William Stevely
Registrar, Hilary Douglas

UNIVERSITY OF ST ANDREWS (1411)
College Gate, St Andrews, Fife KY16 9AJ T 01334-476161
E secretary@st-and.ac.uk W www.st-and.ac.uk
Full-time students (2003–4), 6,700
Chancellor, Sir Kenneth Dover
Principal and Vice-Chancellor, Dr Brian Lang
Registrar, Alastair Work

UNIVERSITY OF SALFORD (1896)
Salford, Greater Manchester M5 4WT T 0161-295 5000
E marketing@salford.ac.uk W www.salford.ac.uk
Full-time students (2003–4), 15,000
Chancellor, Sir Walter Bodmer
Vice-Chancellor, Prof. Michael Harloe
Registrar, Dr Malcolm Winton

UNIVERSITY OF SHEFFIELD (1905)
Western Bank, Sheffield S10 2TN T 0114-222 2000
E proffice@sheffield.ac.uk W www.shef.ac.uk
Full-time students (2003–4), 21,403
Chancellor, Sir Peter Middleton
Vice-Chancellor, Prof. R. F. Boucher
Registrar and Secretary, Dr D. E. Fletcher

SHEFFIELD HALLAM UNIVERSITY (1992)
City Campus, Howard Street, Sheffield S1 1WB
T 0114-225 5555 W www.shu.ac.uk
Full-time students (2003–4), 21,000
Chancellor, Prof. The Lord Winston
Vice-Chancellor, Prof. Diana Green

UNIVERSITY OF SOUTHAMPTON (1952)
Highfield, Southampton SO17 1BJ T 023-8059 5000
E external@soton.ac.uk W www.soton.ac.uk
Full-time students (2003–4), 17,119
Chancellor, The Lord Selbourne
Vice-Chancellor, Prof. Bill Wakeham
Secretary and Registrar, John Lauwerys

SOUTH BANK UNIVERSITY (1992)
103 Borough Road, London SE1 0AA T 020-7928 8989
W www.sbu.ac.uk
Full-time students (2003–4), 15,940
Chancellor, Prof. Deian Hopkin
Vice-Chancellors, Dr Peter McCaffery, Dr Mike Wilkinson
Secretary, Dr Ruth Farwell

STAFFORDSHIRE UNIVERSITY (1992)
College Road, Stoke-on-Trent ST4 2DE T 01782-294000
E admissions@staffs.ac.uk W www.staffs.ac.uk
Full-time students (2003–4), 18,500
Chief Executive, Prof. Christine King
Dean of Students, Francesca Francis
Secretary, Ken Sproston

UNIVERSITY OF STIRLING (1967)
Stirling FK9 4LA T 01786-473171 E c&d@stir.ac.uk
W www.stir.ac.uk
Full-time students (2003–4), 6,800
Chancellor, Dame Diana Rigg
Vice-Chancellor (acting), Prof. Christine Hallet
Registrar, Douglas Wood

UNIVERSITY OF STRATHCLYDE (1796)
McCance Building, John Anderson Campus, Glasgow G1 1XQ
T 0141-552 4400 W www.strath.ac.uk
Full-time students (2003–4), 15,136
Chancellor, The Lord Hope of Craighead
Vice-Chancellor and Principal, Prof. Andrew Hamnett
Secretary, Dr Peter West

UNIVERSITY OF SUNDERLAND (1992)
Langham Tower, Ryhope Road, Sunderland SR2 7EE
T 0191-515 2000 E student-helpline@sunderland.ac.uk
W www.sunderland.ac.uk
Full-time students (2003–4), 8,500
Chancellor, The Lord Puttnam of Queensgate, CBE
Vice-Chancellor, Prof. P. Fidler, MBE
Secretary, J. D. Pacey

UNIVERSITY OF SURREY (1966)
Guildford, Surrey GU2 7XH T 01483-300800
E information@surrey.ac.uk W www.surrey.ac.uk
Full-time students (2003–4), 10,612
Chancellor, HRH The Duke of Kent, KG
Vice-Chancellor, Prof. P. J. Dowling, CBE, FRENG
Registrar, P. W. Beardsley

UNIVERSITY OF SUSSEX (1961)
Sussex House, Falmer, Brighton BN1 9RH T 01273-606755
E information@sussex.ac.uk W www.sussex.ac.uk
Full-time students (2003–4), 9,200
Chancellor, Lord Attenborough, CBE
Vice-Chancellor, Prof. Alasdair Smith
Registrar and Secretary, Neil Gershon

UNIVERSITY OF TEESSIDE (1992)
Middlesbrough, Tees Valley TS1 3BA T 01642-218121
E m.white@tees.ac.uk W www.tees.ac.uk
Full-time students (2003–4), 9,000
Chancellor, Lord Leon Brittan of Spennithorn
Vice-Chancellor, Prof. D. Fraser
University Secretary, J. M. McClintock

THAMES VALLEY UNIVERSITY (1992)
St Mary's Road, Ealing, London W5 5RF T 020-8579 5000
E learning.advice@tvu.ac.uk W www.tvu.ac.uk
Full-time students (2003–4), 12,948
Vice-Chancellor, Prof. Geoff Crispin
Secretary, Ann Marie Dalton

UNIVERSITY OF ULSTER (1984)
Cromore Road, Coleraine, Co. Londonderry BT52 1SA
T 08700 400 700 E online@ulster.ac.uk W www.ulster.ac.uk
Full-time students (2003–4), 16,479
Chancellor, Sir Richard Nichols, DCL, LLD
Vice-Chancellor, Prof. P. G. McKenna, PHD
Pro-Chancellor, Dr G. Butus

UNIVERSITY OF WALES (1893)
King Edward VII Avenue, Cathays Park, Cardiff CF10 3NS
T 029-2038 2656 E uniwales@wales.ac.uk W www.wales.ac.uk
Full-time students (2003–4), 62,000
Chancellor, HRH The Prince of Wales, KG, KT, GCB, OM,
  PC
Senior Vice-Chancellor, Prof. A. J. Chapman
Secretary-General, Dr L. E. Williams

MEMBER INSTITUTES
UNIVERSITY OF WALES, ABERYSTWYTH Old College,
  King Street, Aberystwyth SY23 2AX T 01970-623111
  Vice-Chancellor, Prof. N. G. Lloyd
UNIVERSITY OF WALES, BANGOR Bangor, Gwynedd
  LL57 2DG T 01248-351151
  Vice-Chancellor, Prof. R. M. Jones
UNIVERSITY OF WALES COLLEGE, NEWPORT Caerleon
  Campus, PO Box 179, Newport NP6 1YG T 01633-430088
  Vice-Chancellor, Prof. J. R. Lusty, PHD, FRSC (2002)

UNIVERSITY OF WALES INSTITUTE, CARDIFF Llandaff
Centre, Western Avenue, Cardiff CF5 2SG
T 01222-506070
Vice-Chancellor, A. J. Chapman
UNIVERSITY OF WALES, LAMPETER Lampeter SA48 7ED
T 01570-422351
Vice-Chancellor, Prof. R. A. Pearce
UNIVERSITY OF WALES, SWANSEA Singleton Park,
Swansea SA2 8PP T 01792-205678
Vice-Chancellor, Prof. R. B. Davies

UNIVERSITY OF WARWICK (1965)
Coventry CV4 7AL T 024-7652 3523 W www.warwick.ac.uk
Full-time students (2003–4), 15,536
Chancellor, Sir Nicholas Scheele
Vice-Chancellor, Prof. V. D. Vandelinde, FRS
Secretary, C. E. Charlton

UNIVERSITY OF WESTMINSTER (1992)
309 Regent Street, London W1B 2UW T 020-7911 5000
E admissions@wmin.ac.uk W www.wmin.ac.uk
Full-time students (2003–4), 12,647
Chairman of the Board of Governors, Sir Alan Thomas
Vice-Chancellor and Rector, Dr Geoffrey Copland
Academic Registrar, Evelyn Rugg

UNIVERSITY OF THE WEST OF ENGLAND (1992)
Frenchay Campus, Coldharbour Lane, Bristol BS16 1QY
T 0117-965 6261 E enquiries@uwe.ac.uk W www.uwe.ac.uk
Full-time students (2003—4), 18,519
Chancellor, The Rt. Hon. Dame Elizabeth Butler-Sloss,
DBE
Vice-Chancellor, A. C. Morris, CBE
Academic Secretary, Carole Webb

UNIVERSITY OF WOLVERHAMPTON (1992)
Wulfruna Street, Wolverhampton WV1 1SB T 01902-321000
W www.wlv.ac.uk
Full-time students (2003–4), 14,223
Chancellor, The Lord Paul of Marylebone
Vice-Chancellor, Prof. John Brooks, PHD, DSC
Registrar, J. Nelson

UNIVERSITY OF YORK (1963)
Heslington, York YO10 5DD T 01904-430000
W www.york.ac.uk
Full-time students (2003–4), 10,000
Chancellor, Dame Janet Barker, CH, DBE
Vice-Chancellor, Prof. B. Cantor, PHD, FRENG
Registrar and Secretary, D. J. Foster

PROFESSIONAL EDUCATION

The organisations listed below are those which, by
providing specialist training or conducting examinations,
control entry into a profession, or are responsible for
maintaining a register of those with professional
qualifications in their sector.

EU RECOGNITION
It is possible for those with professional qualifications
obtained in the UK to have these recognised in other
European Countries. A booklet, *Europe Open for
Professions,* is available at www.dfes.gov.uk/europeopen.
Further information can be obtained from:

DEPARTMENT FOR EDUCATION AND SKILLS Room E3B,
Moorfoot, Sheffield S1 4PQ T 0870-0012345 '
W www.dfes.gov.uk

ACCOUNTANCY
The main bodies granting membership on examination
after a period of practical work are:
ASSOCIATION OF CHARTERED CERTIFIED
ACCOUNTANTS (ACCA) 29 Lincoln's Inn Fields, London
WC2A 3EE T 020-7396 7000 W www.accaglobal.com
Chief Executive, Anthea Rose
CIMA (THE CHARTERED INSTITUTE OF MANAGEMENT
ACCOUNTANTS) 26 Chapter Street, London SW1P 4NP
T 020-7663 5441 W www.cimaglobal.com
Chief Executive, Charles Tilley
INSTITUTE OF CHARTERED ACCOUNTANTS IN
ENGLAND AND WALES Chartered Accountants' Hall, PO
Box 433, Moorgate Place, London EC2P 2BJ
T 020-7920 8100 W www.icaew.co.uk
Secretary-General, Peter Owen
INSTITUTE OF CHARTERED ACCOUNTANTS OF
SCOTLAND CA House, 21 Haymarket Yards, Edinburgh
EH12 5BH T 0131-347 0100 W www.icas.org.uk
Chief Executive, David Brew

ACTUARIAL SCIENCE
The UK actuarial profession is controlled by the Institute
of Actuaries in London and the Faculty of Actuaries in
Edinburgh. The Faculty and Institute together set
professional codes, disciplinary standards and
examinations continuing professional development. UK
qualified actuaries may be Fellows of either organisation.
Practising certificates are issued on certain actuaries for
their statutory role in the financial management of life
offices and most pension schemes.
FACULTY OF ACTUARIES IN SCOTLAND Maclaurin House,
18 Dublin Street, Edinburgh EH1 3PP T 0131-240 1300
W www.actuaries.org.uk
Secretary, Richard Machonachie
INSTITUTE OF ACTUARIES Staple Inn Hall, High Holborn,
London WC1V 7QJ T 020-7632 2100
W www.actuaries.org.uk
Secretary-General, Caroline Instance

ARCHITECTURE
The Education Committee of the Royal Institute of British
Architects sets standards and guides the whole system of
architectural education throughout the UK. The
Architects Registration Board is the independent
regulator for the architects' profession in the UK. It was
established to simultaneously protect the interests of
consumers and to safeguard the reputation of architects.
RIBA recognises courses at 36 schools of architecture in
the UK for exemption from their own examinations as
well as courses at 56 overseas schools.
ARCHITECTS REGISTRATION BOARD 8 Weymouth Street,
London W1W 5BU T 020-7580 5861 W www.arb.org.uk
Chief Executive and Registrar, Robin Vaughan
ARCHITECTURAL ASSOCIATION 34–36 Bedford Square,
London WC1B 3ES T 020-7887 4000
W www.aaschool.ac.uk
Chief Executive, Mohsen Mostafavi
ROYAL INSTITUTE OF BRITISH ARCHITECTS 66 Portland
Place, London W1N 4AD T 020-7580 5533
W www.architecture.com

BANKING

Professional organisations granting qualifications after examination are:

CHARTERED INSTITUTE OF BANKERS IN SCOTLAND Drumsheugh House, 38b Drumsheugh Gardens, Edinburgh EH3 7SW T 0131-473 7777 W www.ciobs.org.uk
Chief Executive, Prof. Charles Munn

INSTITUTE OF FINANCIAL SERVICES IFS House, 4/9 Burgate Lane, Canterbury CT1 2XJ T 01227-818609 W www.ifslearning.com
Chief Executive Officer, G. Shreeve

BUILDING

CHARTERED INSTITUTE OF BUILDING Englemere, Kings Ride, Ascot, Berks SL5 7TB T 01344-630700
W www.ciob.org.uk
Chief Executive, Chris Blythe

INSTITUTE OF CLERKS OF WORKS OF GREAT BRITAIN Equinox, 28 Commerce Road, Lynch Wood, Peterborough PE2 6LR T 01733-405160

RICS (ROYAL INSTITUTION OF CHARTERED SURVEYORS) 12 Great George Street, Parliament Square, London SW1P 3AD T 020-7222 7000 W www.rics.org.uk
Chief Executive, J. Armstrong

BUSINESS MANAGEMENT AND ADMINISTRATION

ASSOCIATION OF MBAS 25 Hosier Lane, London EC1A 9LQ T 020-7246 2686 W www.mba.org.uk
Director-General, M. A. Jones

CAM FOUNDATION Moor Hall, Cookham, Maidenhead, Berks SL6 9QH T 01628-427180
W www.camfoundation.com

CHARTERED INSTITUTE OF HOUSING Octavia House, Westwood Business Park, Westwood Way, Coventry CV4 8JP T 024-7685 1700 W www.cih.org
Chief Executive, D. Butler

CHARTERED INSTITUTE OF PERSONNEL AND DEVELOPMENT CIPD House, Camp Road, London SW19 4UX T 020-8971 9000 W www.cipd.co.uk
Director-General, G. Armstrong

CHARTERED INSTITUTE OF PURCHASING AND SUPPLY (1932) Easton House, Easton on the Hill, Stamford, Lincs PE9 3NZ T 01780-756777 W www.cips.org
Chief Executive, K. James

CHARTERED MANAGEMENT INSTITUTE Management House, Cottingham Road, Corby, Northants NN17 1TT T 01536-204222 W www.managers.org.uk
Chief Executive, Ms M. Chapman

HENLEY MANAGEMENT COLLEGE Greenlands, Henley on Thames, Oxon RG9 3AU T 01491-571454
W www.henleymc.ac.uk

INSTITUTE OF ADMINISTRATIVE MANAGEMENT 16 Park Crescent, London, W1B 1BA T 020-7612 7099
W www.instam.org
Chief Executive, David Woodgate

INSTITUTE OF CHARTERED SECRETARIES AND ADMINISTRATORS 16 Park Crescent, London W1B 1AH T 020-7580 4741 W www.icsa.org.uk
Chief Executive, M. J. Ainsworth

INSTITUTE OF CHARTERED SHIPBROKERS 85 Gracechurch Street London EC3V 0AA T 020-7623 1111 W www.ics.org.uk
Director-General, Alan Phillips

INSTITUTE OF EXPORT Export House, Minerva Business Park, Lynch Wood, Peterborough PE2 6FT T 01733-404400 W www.export.org.uk
Chief Executive, Hugh Allen

INSTITUTE OF HEALTHCARE MANAGEMENT 46 Grosvenor Gardens, London SW1W 0EB T 020-7881 9235 W www.ihm.org.uk
Chief Executive, Rosey Foster *(acting)*

INSTITUTE OF QUALITY ASSURANCE 12 Grosvenor Crescent, London SW1X 7EE T 020-7245 6722
W www.iqa.org

CHIROPRACTIC

The General Chiropractic Council (GCC) is the statutory regulatory body for chiropractors and its role and remit is defined in the Chiropractors Act 1994. It is illegal for anyone in the UK to use the title 'chiropractor' unless registered with the GCC.

BRITISH CHIROPRACTIC ASSOCIATION Blagrave House, Blagrave Street, Reading, Berks RG1 1QB T 0118-950 5950 W www.chiropractic-uk.co.uk

GENERAL CHIROPRACTIC COUNCIL 44 Wicklow Street, London WC1X 9HL T 020-7713 5155 W www.gcc-uk.org

SCOTTISH CHIROPRACTIC ASSOCIATION Laigh Hatton Farm, Old Greenock Road, Bishopton, Renfrewshire PA7 5PB T 01505-863151 W www.sca-chiropractic.org

DANCE

The Council for Dance Education and Training (CDET) accredits courses at the following: ArtsEdLondon; Arts Education Tring Park; Central School of Ballet; Bird College of Performing Arts; Elmhurst – The School for Dance and Performing Arts; The Hammond School; The Italia Conti Academy of Theatre Arts Limited; Laban; Laine Theatre Arts Ltd; London Contemporary Dance School; London Studio Centre; Midlands Academy of Dance and Drama Centre; Northern Ballet School; Performers College; Stella Mann College; Studios la Pointe; The Urdang Academy.

The accreditation of a course in a school does not neccessarily imply that other courses of a different type or duration in the same school are also accredited. CDET has approved the teacher registration systems of a number of other dance organisations in the UK. Contact CDET for further information.

CDET Toynbee Hall, 28 Commercial Street, London E1 6LS T 020-7247 4030 W www.cdet.org.uk

IMPERIAL SOCIETY OF TEACHERS OF DANCING Imperial House, 22–26 Paul Street, London EC2A 4QE T 020-7377 1577 W www.istd.org
Chief Executive, Michael J. Browne

INTERNATIONAL DANCE TEACHERS' ASSOCIATION International House, 76 Bennett Road, Brighton BN2 5JL T 01273-685652 W www.idta.co.uk

ROYAL ACADEMY OF DANCE 36 Battersea Square, London SW1 3RA T 020-7326 8000 W www.rad.org.uk
Chief Executive, L. Rittner

ROYAL BALLET SCHOOL 46 Floral Street, London WC2E 9DA T 020-7836 8899
W www.royalballetschool.co.uk
Director, Ms G. Stock, AM

DEFENCE

JOINT SERVICES COMMAND AND STAFF COLLEGE Faringdon Road, Watchfield, Swindon, Wilts SN6 8TS T 01793-788000 W www.jscsc.org.uk
Commandant, Maj.-Gen. J. C. McColl, CBE

ROYAL COLLEGE OF DEFENCE STUDIES Seaford House, 37 Belgrave Square, London SW1X 8NS T 020-7915 4800 W www.da.mod.uk/rcds
Commandant, Lt.-Gen. (Retd) Sir Christopher Wallace, KBE

ROYAL NAVAL COLLEGE
BRITANNIA ROYAL NAVAL COLLEGE Dartmouth, Devon
TQ6 0HJ T 01803-677108
Commodore, Cdre C. A. Johnstone-Burt, OBE, ADC

MILITARY COLLEGES
DIRECTORATE OF EDUCATIONAL AND TRAINING
SERVICES (ARMY) Trenchard Lines, Upavon, Pewsey, Wilts
SN9 6BE T 01980-618719/618701 W www.agc-ets.co.uk
Director, Brig. M. St. J. Filler
ROYAL MILITARY ACADEMY SANDHURST Camberley,
Surrey GU15 4PQ T 01276-63344
W www.sandhurst.mod.uk
Commandant, Maj.-Gen. A. S. Ritchie, CBE
ROYAL MILITARY COLLEGE OF SCIENCE Cranfield
University, RMCS Shrivenham, Swindon SN6 8LA
T 01793-782551 W www.rmcs.cranfield.ac.uk

ROYAL AIR FORCE COLLEGES
ROYAL AIR FORCE COLLEGE Cranwell, Sleaford, Lincs
NG34 8HB T 01400-261201 W www.cranwell.raf.mod.uk
Air Officer Commanding and Commandant,
TRAINING DEVELOPMENT WING RAF Halton, Aylesbury,
Bucks HP22 5PG T 01296-623535 ext. 6363

DENTISTRY
In order to practise in the UK, a dentist must be registered
with the General Dental Council. To be registered a
person must be qualified in one of the following ways:
hold the degree or diploma in dental surgery of a
university in the UK or hold the licentiate in dental
surgery awarded by one of the Royal Surgical Colleges in
the UK; have completed the Council's International
Qualifying Examination (IQE); be a European
Community or European Economic Area national holding
an appropriate European diploma; hold a registered
overseas diploma or be an EEA national holding a
primary dental qualification from outside the EEA but
having acquired the right to practise in the EEA. The
holder of a dental degree or diploma other than those
referred to above may be eligible for temporary
registration to enable him or her to practice dentistry in
the United Kingdom for a limited period and in
specificied posts without the need to take further
examinations. The Dentists Register and Rolls of Dental
Auxiliaries are maintained by:
GENERAL DENTAL COUNCIL 37 Wimpole Street, London
W1G 8DQ T 020-7887 3800 W www.gdc-uk.org

DIETETICS
The professional association is the British Dietetic
Association. Full membership is open to dieticians
holding a recognised qualification, who must also be
registered with the Health Professions Council (*see*
Professions Supplementary to Medicine).
BRITISH DIETETIC ASSOCIATION 5th Floor, Charles
House, 148–149 Great Charles Street Queensway,
Birmingham B3 3HT T 0121-200 8080 W www.bda.uk.com

DRAMA
The national validating body for courses providing
training in drama for the professional theatre is the
National Council for Drama Training (NCDT). NCDT
accredits courses at 21 drama schools in England,
Scotland and Wales. It also sponsers annual seminars on
graduate showcases, television training and skills needs in
the small sector. There are two useful guides for students
entering drama school: *A Practical Guide to Vocational
Training in Dance and Drama* and *An Applicant's Guide to
Auditioning and Interviewing at Dance and Drama.* These
publications and numerous information sheets and useful
links are available on the NCDT's website (*see* below).
NATIONAL COUNCIL FOR DRAMA TRAINING 1–7
Woburn Walk, London WC1H 0JJ T 020-7387 3650
W www.ncdt.co.uk

ENGINEERING
Engineering Council (UK) sets the standards for the
accreditation for academic courses in universities and
colleges and the practical training in industry. The
Council also runs the National Register of Chartered
Engineers, Incorporated Engineers and Engineering
Technicians.
The principal qualifying bodies are:
BRITISH COMPUTER SOCIETY 1 Sanford Street, Swindon
SN1 1HJ T 01793-417417 W www.bcs.org
Chief Executive, David Clarke
CHARTERED INSTITUTE OF BUILDING SERVICES
ENGINEERS 222 Balham High Road, London SW12 9BS
T 020-8675 5211 W www.cibse.org
Chief Executive, Julian Amey
ENGINEERING AND TECHNOLOGY BOARD 10
Maltravers Street, London WC2R 3ER T 020-7240 7333
W www.etechb.co.uk
INSTITUTE OF MARINE ENGINEERING, SCIENCE AND
TECHNOLOGY 80 Coleman Street, London EC2R 5BJ
T 020-7382 2600 W www.imarest.org
Director-General, K. F. Read
INSTITUTE OF MATERIALS, MINERALS AND MINING
1 Carlton House Terrace, London SW1Y 5DB
T 020-7451 7300 W www.iom3.org
Chief Executive, Dr B. Rickinson
INSTITUTE OF MEASUREMENT AND CONTROL 87
Gower Street, London WC1E 6AF T 020-7387 4949
W www.instmc.org.uk
Secretary, M. J. Yates
INSTITUTE OF PHYSICS 76 Portland Place, London
W1B 1NT T 020-7470 4800 W www.iop.org
Chief Executive, Julia King
INSTITUTION OF CHEMICAL ENGINEERS Davis Building,
165–189 Railway Terrace, Rugby, Warks CV21 3HQ
T 01788-578214 W www.icheme.org
Chief Executive, Dr Trevor Evans
INSTITUTION OF CIVIL ENGINEERS 1 Great George
Street, London SW1P 3AA T 020-7222 7722
W www.ice.org.uk
Acting Chief Executive, Amar Bhogal
INSTITUTION OF ELECTRICAL ENGINEERS Savoy Place,
London WC2R 0BL T 020-7240 1871 W www.iee.org.uk
Chief Executive, Dr Alf Roberts
INSTITUTION OF GAS ENGINEERS AND MANAGERS 12
York Gate, London NW1 4QG T 020-7487 0650
W www.igaseng.com
Chief Executive Officer, G. Davies

INSTITUTION OF MECHANICAL ENGINEERS 1 Birdcage Walk, London SW1H 9JJ T 020-7222 7899 W www.imeche.org.uk
Director-General, Sir Michael Moore, KBE, LVO
INSTITUTION OF STRUCTURAL ENGINEERS 11 Upper Belgrave Street, London SW1X 8BH T 020-7235 4535 W www.istructe.org.uk
Chief Executive and Secretary, Dr K. J. Eaton
INSTITUTION OF STRUCTURAL ENGINEERS (Scottish Branch), 15 Beresford Place, East Trinity Road, Edinburgh EH5 3SL T 0131-552 8852 W www.istructe.org.uk
Chief Executive and Secretary, Dr K. J. Eaton
ROYAL AERONAUTICAL SOCIETY 4 Hamilton Place, London W1J 7BQ T 020-7670 4300 W www.raes.org.uk
Director, K. Mans
ROYAL INSTITUTION OF NAVAL ARCHITECTS 10 Upper Belgrave Street, London SW1X 8BQ T 020-7235 4622 W www.rina.org.uk
Chief Executive, T. Blakeley

FILM AND TELEVISION

Postgraduate training for those intending to make a career in film, television and new media production is provided by the National Film and Television School, which offers MA courses in animation direction, documentary direction, fiction direction, producing, screenwriting, cinematography, production design, editing, sound post-production and composing for film and television. The school also offers a Diploma course in sound recording and a script development Executive Diploma, run in association with the Script Factory. Five-week feature development workshops run at intervals during the year. Short courses enabling professionals to update or expand their skills are run by the National Short Course Training Programme.
NATIONAL FILM AND TELEVISION SCHOOL Beaconsfield Studios, Station Road, Beaconsfield, Bucks HP9 1LJ T 01494-671234 W www.nftsfilm-tv.ac.uk
Director, Nick Powell

FORESTRY AND TIMBER STUDIES

Professional organisations include:
COMMONWEALTH FORESTRY ASSOCIATION PO 142, Bicester, Oxon OX26 6ZJ T 01865-271037 W www.cfa-international.org
Chairman, Dr J. S. Maini
INSTITUTE OF CHARTERED FORESTERS 7a St Colme Street, Edinburgh EH3 6AA T 0131-225 2705 W www.charteredforesters.org
Executive Director, Mrs M. W. Dick, FRSA, OBE
ROYAL FORESTRY SOCIETY OF ENGLAND, WALES AND NORTHERN IRELAND 102 High Street, Tring, Herts HP23 4AF T 01442-822028 W www.rfs.org.uk
Director, Dr J. E. Jackson
ROYAL SCOTTISH FORESTRY SOCIETY Hagg-on-Esk, Canonbie, Dumfriesshire DG14 0BE T 01387-371518 W www.rsfs.org
President, P. J. Fothergill

FUEL AND ENERGY SCIENCE

The principal professional body is:
INSTITUTE OF PETROLEUM 61 New Cavendish Street, London W1G 7AR T 020-7467 7100 W www.intertek-cb.com
Director-General, Mrs L. Kingham

HOTELKEEPING, CATERING AND INSTITUTIONAL MANAGEMENT

See also, DIETETICS
The qualifying professional body in these areas is:
HOTEL AND CATERING INTERNATIONAL MANAGEMENT ASSOCIATION Trinity Court, 34 West Street, Sutton, Surrey SM1 1SH T 020-8661 4900 W www.hcima.org.uk
Chief Executive, Philippe Rossiter

INSURANCE

Organisations conducting examinations and awarding diplomas are:
ASSOCIATION OF AVERAGE ADJUSTERS The Baltic Exchange, St Mary Axe, London EC3A 8BH T 020-7623 5501 W www.average-adjusters.com
Chairman, Tim Madge
CHARTERED INSTITUTE OF LOSS ADJUSTERS Peninsular House, 36 Monument Street, London EC3R 8LJ T 020-7337 9960 W www.cila.co.uk
Executive Director, Graham Cave
CHARTERED INSURANCE INSTITUTE 20 Aldermanbury, London EC2V 7HY T 020-8989 8464 W www.cii.co.uk
Director-General, Dr Sandy Scott

JOURNALISM

Courses for trainee newspaper journalists are available at 30 centres. One-year full time courses are available for selected students, three-year degree programmes and 18-week courses for graduates. Particulars for all these courses are available from the National Council for the Training of Journalists. Short courses for mid-career development are available, as are various distance learning courses.

For periodical journalists, there are twelve centres running courses approved by the Periodicals Training Council (PTC). The PTC also provides career information for people wishing to join the industry.
NATIONAL COUNCIL FOR THE TRAINING OF JOURNALISTS Latton Bush Centre, Southern Way, Harlow, Essex CM18 7BL T 01279-430009 W www.nctj.com
PERIODICALS TRAINING COUNCIL 28 Kingsway, London WC2B 6JR T 020-7404 4168 W www.ppa.co.uk/ptc

LAW

THE BAR
The governing body of the Bar of England and Wales is the General Council of the Bar (also known as the Bar Council). All practising barristers pay an annual subscription fee to support the Bar Council. Its functions include dealing with disciplinary matters, acting as the public voice of the profession, and regulating the education and training requirements for those wishing to enter the profession.

Those intending to practise at the Bar of England and Wales must complete three main stages of training: the academic stage (the law degree, or non-law degree plus conversion course), the vocational stage (the Bar Vocational Course/BVC), and pupillage (a period of in-service training). There are also Continuing Professional Development (CPD) requirements on barristers, and a minimum number of hours of CPD must be completed each year. Training at the vocational stage takes place at one of eight validated institutions around the country; pupillage can take place in any approved legal environment, usually a set of barristers' chambers, but it can also be in an employed legal environment, such as the government legal service. All barristers must be members of one of the four Inns of Court. Students are currently Called to the Bar by their Inn after completion of the vocational stage, but from 2008 Call will take place after a period of pupillage. Call to the Bar does not entitle a person to practise as a barrister, successful completion of pupillage is now a pre-requisite. Further information can be found on the Bar Council's website.

Admission to the Bar of Northern Ireland by the Honorable Society of the Inn of Court of Northern Ireland and admission as an Advocate of the Scottish Bar is controlled by the Faculty of Advocates.

BVCONLINE The General Council of the Bar, 2–3 Curistor Street, London EC4A 1NE T 020-7440 4000
W www.bvconline.co.uk
Chief Executive, N. Morison
FACULTY OF ADVOCATES Advocates Library, Parliament House, Edinburgh EH1 1RF T 0131-226 5071
W www.advocates.org.uk
Dean, G. N. H. Emslie, QC
GENERAL COUNCIL OF THE BAR 3 Bedford Row, London WC1R 4DB T 020-7242 0082 W www.barcouncil.org.uk
HONORABLE SOCIETY OF THE INN OF COURT OF NORTHERN IRELAND The Under-treasurer's Office, Royal Courts of Justice, Belfast BT1 3JF T 028-9072 4699
INNS OF COURT SCHOOL OF LAW 4 Gray's Inn Place, Gray's Inn, London WC1N 5DX T 020-7404 5787
W www.city.ac.uk/icsl

The Inns of Court
GRAY'S INN 8 South Square, London WC1R 5ET
T 020-7458 7800 W www.graysinn.org.uk
Treasurer, The Rt. Hon. Sir Paul Kennedy, QC
HONOURABLE SOCIETY OF LINCOLN'S INN Treasury Office, Lincoln's Inn, London WC2A 3TL T 020-7405 1393
W www.lincolnsinn.org.uk
Under-Treasurer, Col. D. Hills, MBE
INNER TEMPLE London EC4Y 7HL T 020-7797 8250
W www.innertemple.org.uk
Treasurer, Richard Southwell, QC
MIDDLE TEMPLE Middle Temple Lane, London EC4Y 9AT
T 020-7427 4800 W www.middletemple.org.uk
Treasurer, Rt. Hon. Lord Justice Rose, QC

SOLICITORS
The College of Law is the oldest and largest provider of vocational legal education and training for students wishing to become solicitors and barristers in England and Wales. It also offers training after qualification and a wide range of distance-learning courses. There are a number of other institutions offering the neccesary courses, namely the Legal Practice Course and the Common Professional Examination (conversion course for non-law graduates). The Law Society of England and Wales, the Law Society of Scotland and the Law Society of Northern Ireland control the education and examination of trainee solicitors and the admission of solicitors.

COLLEGE OF LAW Braboeuf Manor, Portsmouth Road, St Catherine's, Guildford, Surrey GU3 1HA T 01483-460200
W www.lawcol.org.uk
LAW SOCIETY OF ENGLAND AND WALES 113 Chancery Lane, London WC2A 1PL T 020-7242 1222
W www.lawsociety.org.uk
LAW SOCIETY OF NORTHERN IRELAND Law Society House, 98 Victoria Street, Belfast BT1 3JZ T 028-9023 1614
W www.lawsoc-ni.org
Chief Executive and Secretary, J. W. Bailie

LAW SOCIETY OF SCOTLAND 26 Drumsheugh Gardens, Edinburgh EH3 7YR T 0131-226 7411
W www.lawscot.org.uk

LIBRARIANSHIP AND INFORMATION SCIENCE
The Chartered Institute of Library and Information Professionals accredits degree and postgraduate courses in library and information science which are offered by 17 universities in the UK. A full list of accredited degree and postgraduate courses is available from the Institute's Membership, Careers and Qualifications Department and on its website.

CHARTERED INSTITUTE OF LIBRARY AND INFORMATION PROFESSIONALS 7 Ridgmount Street, London WC1E 7AE
T 020-7255 0500 Text phone 020-7255 0505
W www.cilip.org.uk

MEDICINE
All doctors must be registered with the General Medical Council (GMC), which is responsible for protecting the public by setting standards for professional practice, overseeing medical education, keeping a register of qualified doctors and taking action where a doctor's fitness to practice is in doubt. A doctor not registered with the GMC is not a 'legally qualified' medical practitioner for the purpose of the Medical Act 1983. In order to be eligible for registration, doctors must obtain a primary medical qualification recognised by the GMC and have satisfactorily completed a year of general medical training. Special arrangements apply to doctors qualified outside the UK. Once registered, doctors undertake general professional and basic specialist training as senior house officers. Further specialist training is provided by the royal colleges, faculties and societies listed below.

The United Examining Board holds qualifying examinations for candidates who have trained overseas. These candidates must also have spent a period at a UK medical school.

FACULTY OF PHARMACEUTICAL MEDICINE 1 St Andrew's Place, Regents Park, London NW1 4LB
T 020-7224 0343 W www.fpm.org.uk
Faculty Administrator, Mrs Kathryn Swanston
GENERAL MEDICAL COUNCIL 178 Great Portland Street, London W1N 6JE T 020-7580 7642 W www.gmc-uk.org
ROYAL COLLEGE OF GENERAL PRACTITIONERS 14 Princes Gate, London SW7 1PU T 020-7581 3232
W www.rcgp.org.uk
Hon. Secretary, Dr M. Baker
SCOTTISH COUNCIL FOR POSTGRADUATE MEDICAL AND DENTAL EDUCATION 2nd Floor, Hanover Buildings, 66 Rose Street, Edinburgh EH2 2NN T 0131-225 4365
UNITED EXAMINING BOARD Apothecaries Hall, Black Friars Lane, London EC4V 6EJ T 020-7236 1180
Chairman, Prof J. S. P. Lumley

COLLEGES/SOCIETIES HOLDING POSTGRADUATE MEMBERSHIP AND DIPLOMA
FACULTY OF ACCIDENT AND EMERGENCY MEDICINE 35–43 Lincoln's Inn Fields, London WC2A 3PE
T 020-7405 7071 W www.faem.org.uk
President, I. W. R. Anderson
FACULTY OF PUBLIC HEALTH MEDICINE 4 St Andrews Place, London NW1 4LB T 020-7935 0243
W www.fphm.org.uk
Faculty Secretary, P. Scourfield

ROYAL COLLEGE OF ANAESTHETISTS 48–49 Russell Square, London WC1B 4JY **T** 020-7813 1900 **W** www.rcoa.ac.uk
The College Secretary, Kevin Story
ROYAL COLLEGE OF OBSTETRICIANS AND GYNAECOLOGISTS 27 Sussex Place, Regent's Park, London NW1 4RG **T** 020-7772 6200 **W** www.rcog.org.uk
College Secretary, P. A. Barnett
ROYAL COLLEGE OF PAEDIATRICS AND CHILD HEALTH 50 Hallam Street, London W1W 6DE **T** 020-7307 5600 **W** www.rcpch.ac.uk
College Secretary, Len Tyler
ROYAL COLLEGE OF PATHOLOGISTS 2 Carlton House Terrace, London SW1Y 5AF **T** 020-7451 6700 **W** www.rcpath.org
Chief Executive, D. Ross
ROYAL COLLEGE OF PHYSICIANS 11 St Andrews Place, Regent's Park, London NW1 4LE **T** 020-7935 1174 **W** www.rcplondon.ac.uk
President, Prof. Sir George Alberti
ROYAL COLLEGE OF PHYSICIANS AND SURGEONS OF GLASGOW 232–242 St Vincent Street, Glasgow G2 5RJ **T** 0141-221 6072 **W** www.rcpsglasg.ac.uk
President, Prof. A. R. Lorimer
ROYAL COLLEGE OF PHYSICIANS OF EDINBURGH 9 Queen Street, Edinburgh EH2 1JQ **T** 0131-225 7324 **W** www.rcpe.ac.uk
President, Dr N. D. C. Finlayson, OBE
ROYAL COLLEGE OF PSYCHIATRISTS 17 Belgrave Square, London SW1X 8PG **T** 020-7235 2351 **W** www.rcpsych.ac.uk
President, Dr Mike Shooter
ROYAL COLLEGE OF RADIOLOGISTS 38 Portland Place, London W1B 1JQ **T** 020-7636 4432 **W** www.rcr.ac.uk
President, Dr Dan Ash
ROYAL COLLEGE OF SURGEONS OF EDINBURGH Nicolson Street, Edinburgh EH8 9DW **T** 0131-527 1600 **W** www.rcsed.ac.uk
Chief Executive, J. R. C. Foster
ROYAL COLLEGE OF SURGEONS OF ENGLAND 35–43 Lincoln's Inn Fields, London WC2A 3PE **T** 020-7405 3474 **W** www.rcseng.ac.uk
Chief Executive, Craig Duncan
SOCIETY OF APOTHECARIES OF LONDON 14 Black Friars Lane, London EC4V 6EJ **T** 020-7236 1189 **W** www.apothecaries.org
The Clerk, R. J. Stringer

PROFESSIONS SUPPLEMENTARY TO MEDICINE

The standard of professional education in art, drama and music therapies, biomedical sciences, chiropody, dietetics, occupational therapy, orthoptics, prosthetics, othotics, physiotherapy and radiography is regulated by the Health Professional Council. It also ensures that the registration of professionals is linked to continual professional development.
HEALTH PROFESSIONS COUNCIL TO MEDICINE Park House, 184 Kennington Park Road, London SE11 4BU **T** 020-7582 0866 **W** www.hpc-uk.org

ART, DRAMA AND MUSIC THERAPIES

A Postgraduate qualification in the relevant therapy is required. Details of accredited training programes in the UK can be obtained from the following organisations:
ASSOCIATION OF PROFESSIONAL MUSIC THERAPIES 26 Hamlyn Road, Glastonbury, Somerset BA6 8HT **T** 01458-834919 **W** www.apmt.org.uk
Administrator, Mrs D. Asbridge

BRITISH ASSOCIATION OF ART THERAPISTS Mary Ward House, 5 Tavistock Place, London WC1H 9SN **T** 020-7383 3774 **W** www.baat.org
BRITISH ASSOCIATION OF DRAMA THERAPISTS 41 Broomhouse Lane, London SW6 3DP **T** 020-7731 0160 **W** www.badth.demon.co.uk

BIOMEDICAL SCIENCES

Qualifications from higher education establishments and training in medical laboratories are required for membership of the Institute of Biomedical Science.
INSTITUTE OF BIOMEDICAL SCIENCE 12 Coldbath Square, London EC1R 5HL **T** 020-7713 0214 **W** www.ibms.org

CHIROPODY

Professional Recognition is granted by the Society of Chiropodists and Podiatrists to students who are awarded BSc degrees in Podiatry or Podiatric Medicine after attending a course of full-time training for three or four years at one of the 13 recognised schools in the UK (ten in England and Wales, two in Scotland and one in Northern Ireland). Qualifications granted and degrees recognised by the Society are approved for the purpose of State Registration, which is a condition of employment within the National Health Service.
SOCIETY OF CHIROPODISTS AND PODIATRISTS 1 Fellmongers Path, Tower Bridge Road, London SE1 3LY **T** 020-7234 8620 **W** www.feetforlife.org
Chief Executive, Ms Hilary De Lyon

COMPLEMENTARY MEDICINE

Professional courses are validated by:
INSTITUTE FOR COMPLEMENTARY MEDICINE PO Box 194, London SE16 7QZ **T** 020-7237 5165 **W** www.icmedicine.co.uk

OCCUPATIONAL THERAPY

The professional qualification and eligibility for registration may be obtained upon successful completion of a validated course in any of the institutions approved by the College of Occupational Therapists. The courses are normally degree-level courses based in higher education institutions. For further information please visit the websites below.
COLLEGE OF OCCUPATIONAL THERAPISTS 106–114 Borough High Street, London SE1 1LB **T** 020-7357 6480 **W** www.cot.org.uk
FACULTY OF OCCUPATIONAL MEDICINE 6 St Andrew's Place, London NW1 4LB **T** 020-7317 5890 **W** www.facoccmed.ac.uk
President, Dr W J Gunnyeon

ORTHOPTICS

Orthoptists undertake the diagnosis and treatment of all types of squint and other anomalies of binocular vision, working in close collaboration with ophthalmologists. The training and maintenance of professional standards are the responsibility of the Health Professions Council (*see* Professions Supplementary to Medicine). The professional body is the British and Irish Orthoptic Society and training is at degree level.
BRITISH AND IRISH ORTHOPTIC SOCIETY Tavistock House North, Tavistock Square, London WC1H 9HX **T** 020-7387 7992 **W** www.orthoptics.org.uk
Hon. Chairman, June Carpenter

PHYSIOTHERAPY
Full-time three- or four-year degree courses are available at 30 higher education institutions in the UK. Information about courses leading to eligibility for Membership of the Chartered Society of Physiotherapy and to State Registration is available from the Chartered Society of Physiotherapy.
CHARTERED SOCIETY OF PHYSIOTHERAPY 14 Bedford Row, London WC1R 4ED T 020-7306 6666
W www.csp.org.uk

PROSTHETICS AND ORTHOTICS
Prosthetists provide artificial limbs, while orthotists provide devices to support or control a part of the body. It is neccessary to obtain an honours degree to become a prosthetist or orthotist. Training is centred at two UK universities, University of Salford and University of Strathclyde.
BRITISH ASSOCIATION OF PROSTHETISTS AND ORTHOTISTS Sir James Clark Building, Abbey Mill Business Centre, Paisley PA1 1TJ T 0141-561 7217
W www.bapo.com

RADIOGRAPHY AND RADIOTHERAPY
In order to practise both diagnostic and therapeutic radiography in the UK, it is necessary to have successfully completed a course of education and training recognised by the Privy Council. Such courses are offered by universities throughout the UK and lead to the award of a degree in radiography. Further information is available from the Society and College of Radiographers.
SOCIETY AND COLLEGE OF RADIOGRAPHERS 207 Providence Square, Mill Street, London SE1 2EW
T 020-7740 7200 W www.sor.org

MERCHANT NAVY TRAINING
OFFICERS
WARSASH MARITIME CENTRE Southampton Institute, Newtown Road, Warsash, Southampton SO31 9ZL
T 01489-576161 W www.solent.ac.uk/wmc/
Head, John Milligan

SEAFARERS
NATIONAL SEA TRAINING CENTRE North West Kent College, Dering Way, Gravesend, Kent DA12 2JJ
T 01322-629600 W www.nwkcollege.ac.uk
Director of Faculty - NSTC, I. R. Goodwin

MUSIC
Education and training for a career in musical performance and composition are provided by the institutions and conservatoires listed below. Professional organisations granting qualifications after examination are the Associated Board of the Royal Schools of Music and the Trinity College Examination Board.
ASSOCIATED BOARD OF THE ROYAL SCHOOLS OF MUSIC 24 Portland Place, London W1B 1LU
T 020-7636 5400 W www.abrsm.org
BIRMINGHAM CONSERVATOIRE University of Central England in Birmingham, Paradise Place, Birmingham B3 3HG
T 0121-331 5901 W www.conservatoire.uce.ac.uk
Principal, Prof. George Caird
GUILDHALL SCHOOL OF MUSIC & DRAMA Silk Street, Barbican, London EC2Y 8DT T 020-7628 2571
W www.gsmd.ac.uk
Principal, Baroness McIntosh of Hudnall
LEEDS COLLEGE OF MUSIC 3 Quarry Hill, Leeds LS2 7PD
T 0113-222 3400 W www.lcm.ac.uk

LONDON COLLEGE OF MUSIC AND MEDIA Thames Valley University, St Mary's Road, London W5 5RF
T 020-8231 2304 W elgar.tvu.ac.uk
NATIONAL OPERA STUDIO 2 Chapel Yard, Wandsworth High Street, London SW18 4HZ T 0208-874 8811
W www.nationaloperastudio.org.uk
ROYAL ACADEMY OF MUSIC Marylebone Road, London NW1 5HT T 020-7873 7373 W www.ram.ac.uk
Principal, Prof. Curtis Price
ROYAL COLLEGE OF MUSIC Prince Consort Road, London SW7 2BS
Director, Ms J. Ritterman
ROYAL COLLEGE OF ORGANISTS 7 St Andrew Street, London EC4A 3LQ T 020-7936 3606 W www.rco.org.uk
The Registrar, Gordon St. J. Clarke
ROYAL NORTHERN COLLEGE OF MUSIC 124 Oxford Road, Manchester M13 9RD T 0161-907 5200
W www.rncm.ac.uk
Principal, Prof. E. Gregson
ROYAL SCOTTISH ACADEMY OF MUSIC AND DRAMA 100 Renfrew Street, Glasgow G2 3DB T 0141-332 4101
W www.rsamd.ac.uk
Principal, John Wallace, OBE
ROYAL WELSH COLLEGE OF MUSIC AND DRAMA Castle Grounds, Cathays Park, Cardiff CF10 3ER T 029-2034 2854
W www.rwcmd.ac.uk
TRINITY COLLEGE OF MUSIC King Charles Court, Old Royal Naval College, London SE10 9JF T 020-8305 4444
W www.tcm.ac.uk
Principal, G. Henderson

NURSING
All nurses and midwives must be registered with the Nursing and Midwifery Council (NMC). Courses leading to registration as a nurse or midwife are at least three years in length. Most courses are at diploma level, but some are at degree level. Students study in colleges of nursing or in institutions of higher education. Different courses lead to different types of registration, including Registered Nurse (RN), Registered Mental Nurse (RMN), Registered Learning Disability Nurse (RLDN), Registered Sick Children's Nurse (RSCN), Registered Midwife (RM) and Registered Health Visitor (RHV). The NMC is responsible for validating courses in nursing and midwifery.
The Royal College of Nursing is the largest professional union representing nurses and provides higher education through its Institute.
ROYAL COLLEGE OF NURSING 20 Cavendish Square, London W1G 0RN T 020-7409 3333
W www.rcn.org.uk
General Secretary, Dr Beverly Malone
UK CENTRAL COUNCIL FOR NURSING, MIDWIFERY AND HEALTH VISITING 23 Portland Place, London W1N 4JT T 020-7637 7181 W www.nmc-uk.org

OPHTHALMIC AND DISPENSING OPTICS
Professional bodies are:
ASSOCIATION OF BRITISH DISPENSING OPTICIANS Godmersham Park Mansion, Godmersham, Kent CT4 7DT
T 01227-738829 W www.abdo.org.uk
General Secretary, Sir Anthony Garrett, CBE
COLLEGE OF OPTOMETRISTS 42 Craven Street, London WC2N 5NG T 020-7839 6000
W www.college-optometrists.org
Chief Executive, P. D. Leigh

OSTEOPATHY

Osteopathy is the first of the professions previously outside conventional medical services to achieve statutory recognition under a new body the General Osteopathic Council (GOC). Since May 2000 all practising osteopaths have to be registered with the GOC and the title 'osteopath' is protected by law. To gain entry to the register, all newly qualified osteopaths have to be in possession of a recognised qualification from a course of training accredited by the GOC. The GOC is also responsible for the regulation, promotion and development of the profession.

GENERAL OSTEOPATHIC COUNCIL Osteopathy House, 176 Tower Bridge Road, London SE1 3LU T 020-7357 6655 W www.osteopathy.org.uk
Chief Executive & Registrar, Miss M. J. Craggs

PHARMACY

The Royal Pharmaceutical Society of Great Britain is the regulatory and professional body for pharmicists in all aspects of practice. It has a statutory duty to maintain the registers of pharmacists and pharmacy premises. In order to register students must have a degree in pharmacy followed by one year pre-registration training at a premises recognised by the Society and must pass an entrance examination.

ROYAL PHARMACEUTICAL SOCIETY OF GREAT BRITAIN 1 Lambeth High Street, London SE1 7JN T 020-7735 9141 W www.rpsgb.org.uk
Secretary and Registrar, Ms A. M Lewis

PHOTOGRAPHY

The professional body is:
BRITISH INSTITUTE OF PROFESSIONAL PHOTOGRAPHY Fox Talbot House, Amwell End, Ware, Herts SG12 9HN T 01920-464011 W www.bipp.com
Chief Executive, Alex Mair

PRINTING

Details of training courses in printing can be obtained from the Institute of Printing and the British Printing Industries Federation. Examinations are also held by various independent further education examining boards.
BRITISH PRINTING INDUSTRIES FEDERATION Farringdon Point, 29–35 Farringdon Rd, London EC1M 3JF T 020-7915 8300 W www.britishprint.com
Chief Executive, Michael Johnson
INSTITUTE OF PRINTING The Mews, Hill House, Clanricarde Road, Tunbridge Wells, Kent TN1 1PJ T 01892-538118 W www.instituteofprinting.org

SCIENCE

Professional qualifications are awarded by:
INSTITUTE OF BIOLOGY 20–22 Queensberry Place, London SW7 2DZ T 020-7581 8333 W www.iob.org
Chief Executive, Prof. Alan Malcolm
ROYAL SOCIETY OF CHEMISTRY Burlington House, Piccadilly, London W1J 0BA T 020-7437 8656 W www.rsc.org
Secretary-General and Chief Executive, Dr D. Giachardi

SPEECH AND LANGUAGE THERAPY

The Royal College of Speech and Language Therapists accredits education and training courses leading to qualification.

ROYAL COLLEGE OF SPEECH AND LANGUAGE THERAPISTS 2 White Hart Yard, London SE1 1NX T 020-7378 1200 W www.rcslt.org
Chief Executive, Kamini Gadhok

SURVEYING

The qualifying professional bodies include:
ASSOCIATION OF BUILDING ENGINEERS Lutyens House, Billing Brook Road, Weston Favell, Northampton NN3 8NW T 01604-404121 W www.abe.org.uk
Chief Executive, David Gibson
INSTITUTE OF REVENUES, RATING AND VALUATION 41 Doughty Street, London WC1N 2LF T 020-7831 3505 W www.irrv.org.uk
Director, David Magor
ROYAL INSTITUTION OF CHARTERED SURVEYORS 12 Great George Street, Parliament Square, London SW1P 3AD T 020-7222 7000 W www.rics.org
Chief Executive, J. H. A. J. Armstrong

TEACHING

To work as a qualified teacher in a school in England and Wales, Qualified Teacher Status (QTS) must be acquired by completing a programme of Initial Teacher Training. Teaching is an all-graduate profession. Those without a first degree may take a Bachelor of Education (BEd) or a Bachelor of Arts/Science (BA/BSc) with QTS, full-time for three or four years, depending on the programme followed. These degrees combine subject and professional studies with teaching practice.

For those who already have a first degree, the most common route is through a one-year Postgraduate Certificate in Education (PGCE). This may be taken full-time or part-time, or as a distance learning programme. Postgraduates may also gain QTS through training in a school (School-Centred Initial Teacher Training). Graduates aged 24 or above can apply to train through the Graduate Teacher Programme, which offers a salary while employed in a school as a trainee teacher, usually for one year.

Further information on how to become a teacher in England and Wales is available on the Teacher Training Agency's website (*see* below) or in *The Initial Teacher Training Handbook* (£9.99 plus p&p) available from UCAS on 01242-544610. Further personal advice is available from the Teaching Information Line, 0845-600 0991. The Higher Education Funding Council (ELWA) funds initial teacher training and accredits providers of initial teacher training in Wales. They also produce Performance Information on Initial Teacher Training Providers in Wales. Details on courses in Scotland can be obtained from universities and the Graduate Teacher Training Registry (GTTR). Details of the courses in Northern Ireland can be obtained from the Department of Education for Northern Ireland.

TEACHER TRAINING AGENCY Portland House, Stag Place, London SW1E 5TT T 020-7925 3700 W www.useyourheadteach.gov.uk

TEXTILES

TEXTILE INSTITUTE 1st Floor, St James's Buildings, Oxford Street, Manchester M1 6FQ T 0161-237 1188 W www.texi.org
Membership Director, Steven Kirkwood

VETERINARY MEDICINE

The regulatory body for veterinary medicine is the Royal College of Veterinary Surgeons, which keeps the register of those entitled to practice veterinary medicine. Holders of recognised degrees from any of the six UK university veterinary schools or from certain EU or overseas universities are entitled to be registered, and holders of certain other degrees may take a statutory membership examination.

The British Veterinary Association is the professional body representing veterinary surgeons. The British Veterinary Nursing Association is the professional body representing veterinary nurses.

BRITISH VETERINARY NURSING ASSOCIATION Level 15, Terminus House, Terminus Street, Harlow, Essex CM20 1XA
 T 01279-450567 **W** www.bvna.org.uk

ROYAL COLLEGE OF VETERINARY SURGEONS Belgravia House, 62–64 Horseferry Road, London SW1P 2AF
 T 020-7222 2001 **W** www.rcvs.org.uk

INDEPENDENT SCHOOLS

The following pages list those independent schools in the UK and Europe whose head is a member of the Headmasters' and Headmistresses' Conference (HMC), the Society of Headmasters and Headmistresses of Independent Schools (SHMIS) or the Girls' School Association (GSA). This list contains the name of the school, location, date founded, number of pupils, termly fees (day and board), the name of the head and details of which of the above associations the school is a member. This section has been compiled with the help of Klaus Boehm and Jenny Lees-Spalding, editors of the *Guide to Independent Schools 2005*.

School	Date founded	No. of pupils	Termly fees Day	Board	Head (with association affiliation)
ENGLAND					
The Abbey School, Reading	1887	990	£2,800	–	Mrs Barbara E. Stanley (GSA)
Abbey Gate College, Cheshire	1977	410	£2,393	–	Edward W. Mitchell (SHMIS)
Abbots Bromley School for Girls, Staffs	1921	285	£3,450	£5,915	Mrs Mary Steel (GSA)
Abbotsholme School, Uttoxeter	1889	252	£4,095	£5,995	Stephen Fairclough (SHMIS)
Abingdon School, Abingdon	1256	796	£3,354	£6,776	Mark Turner (HMC)
Ackworth School, Pontefract	1779	540	£2,971	£5,093	Martin Dickinson (HMC, SHMIS)
Aldenham School, Hertfordshire	1597	463	£4,484	£6,499	Richard Harman (HMC)
Alderley Edge School for Girls, Cheshire	1876	610	£2,268	–	Mrs Kathy Mills (GSA)
The Alice Ottley School, Worcester	1883	610	£2,731	–	Mrs Morag Chapman (GSA)
Alleyn's School, London	1619	942	£3,350	–	Colin Diggory (HMC)
Ampleforth College, York	1802	548	£3,650	£6,840	Revd Gabriel Everitt (HMC)
Ardingly College, Haywards Heath	1858	731	£4,880	£6,515	John Franklin (HMC)
Arnold School, Blackpool	1896	1,133	£2,200	–	Barry M. Hughes (HMC)
The Arts Educational School, Herts	1945	276	£5,850	£7,270	Stefan Anderson (SHMIS)
Ashford School, Kent	1898	575	£3,480	£6,043	Mrs Paula Holloway (GSA)
Ashville College, Harrogate	1877	840	£2,789	£5,229	A. Fleck (HMC)
The Atherley School Southampton	1926	450	£2,638	–	Mrs Maureen Bradley (GSA)
Austin Friars St Monica's, Cumbria	1951	471	£2,666	–	Christopher Lumb (SHMIS)
Bablake School, Coventry	1344	1,000	£2,212	–	Dr S. Nuttall (HMC)
Badminton School, Bristol	1858	399	£3,885	£6,910	Mrs Jan Scarrow (GSA)
Bancroft's School, Woodford Green	1737	965	£3,140	–	Dr Peter Scott (HMC)
Barnard Castle School, Durham	1883	691	£2,838	£4,795	David Ewart (HMC)
Batley Grammar School, W. Yorkshire	1612	407	£2,344	–	Brian Battye (HMC)
Battle Abbey School, E. Sussex	1912	287	£3,459	£5,557	Roger Clark (SHMIS)
Bearwood College, Wokingham	1827	342	£4,070	£6,315	S. G. G. Aiano (SHMIS)
Bedales School, Hampshire	1893	412	£5,698	£7,454	Keith Budge (HMC, SHMIS)
Bedford School, Bedford	1552	1,100	£4,010	£6,305	Dr I. Philip Evans OBE (HMC)
Bedford High School, Bedford	1882	874	£2,955	£5,417	Mrs Gina Piotrowska (GSA)
Bedford Modern School, Bedford	1566	1,170	£2,786	–	Stephen Smith (HMC)
Bedgebury School, Cranbrook, Kent	1860	350	£3,880	£6,245	Mrs Hilary Moriarty (GSA)
Bedstone College, Shropshire	1948	275	£3,090	£5,740	Michael S. Symonds (SHMIS)
Beechwood School, Tunbridge Wells	1915	350	£3,475	£5,625	Nicholas Beesley (GSA)
The Belvedere School GDST, Liverpool	1880	550	£2,310	–	Mrs Gillian Richards (GSA)
Benenden School, Kent	1923	470	–	£7,450	Mrs Claire Oulton (GSA)
Berkhamsted Collegiate School, Herts	1541	1,460	£3,939	£6,266	Dr P. Chadwick (HMC, GSA)
Bethany School, Kent	1866	340	£3,598	£5,597	Nicholas Dorey (SHMIS)
Birkdale School, Sheffield	1915	800	£2,577	–	Robert J. Court (HMC)
Birkenhead School, Wirral	1860	737	£2,339	–	John Clark (HMC)
Birkenhead High School GDST, Wirral	1901	830	£2,310	–	Mrs Carole Evans (GSA)
Bishop's Stortford College, Herts	1868	402	£3,804	£5,277	John G. Trotman (HMC)
Blackheath High School GDST, London	1880	590	£2,883	–	Mrs Elizabeth Laws (GSA)
Bloxham School, Oxfordshire	1860	410	£5,425	£6,995	Mark Allbrook (HMC)
Blundell's School, Devon	1604	553	£4,140	£6,485	Jonathan Leigh (HMC)
Bolton School Boys' Division, Lancs	1524	1,095	£2,498	–	Mervyn Brooker (HMC)
Bolton School Girls' Division, Lancs	1877	1,315	£2,498	–	Miss E. J. Panton (GSA)
Bootham School, York	1823	420	£3,660	£5,675	Jonathan Taylor (HMC)
Box Hill School, Dorking	1959	350	£3,520	£5,800	Mark Eagers (SHMIS)
Bradfield College, Reading	1850	600	£5,640	£7,050	Peter Roberts (HMC)
Bradford Girls' Grammar School, W. Yorks	1875	809	£2,643	–	Mrs L. J. Warrington (GSA)
Bradford Grammar School, W. Yorks	1548	1,077	£2,755	–	Stephen Davidson (HMC)

School	Date founded	No. of pupils	Termly fees Day	Board	Head (with association affiliation)
Brentwood School, Essex	1557	1,117	£3,482	£6,032	Ian Davies (HMC)
Brighton and Hove High School GDST, Brighton	1876	752	£2,310	–	Mrs Ann Greatorex (GSA)
Brighton College, E. Sussex	1845	700	£4,401	£6,822	Dr Anthony Seldon (HMC)
Brigidine School, Windsor	1948	274	£3,045	–	Mrs Janet Dunn (GSA)
Bristol Cathedral School, Bristol	1542	440	£2,496	–	K. J. Riley (HMC)
Bristol Grammar School, Bristol	1532	1,249	£2,505	–	David Mascord (HMC)
Bromley High School GDST, Kent	1883	912	£2,883	–	Mrs Lorna Duggleby (GSA)
Bromsgrove School, Worcestershire	1548	1,102	£3,415	£6,030	T. M. Taylor (HMC)
Bruton School for Girls, Somerset	1900	450	£2,985	£5,090	Mrs Barbara Bates (GSA)
Bryanston School, Dorset	1928	651	£5,815	£7,269	Tom Wheare (HMC)
Burgess Hill School for Girls, W. Sussex	1906	720	£3,170	£5,500	Mrs Susan Gorham (GSA)
Bury Grammar School, Lancashire	1726	826	£2,120	–	Keith Richards (HMC)
Bury Grammar School (Girls), Lancashire	1884	1,016	£2,120	–	Mrs R. S. Georghiou (GSA)
Canford School, Wimbourne	1923	600	£5,315	£7,085	John D. Lever (HMC)
Casterton School, Cumbria	1823	340	£3,308	£5,529	A. F. Thomas (GSA)
Caterham School, Surrey	1811	987	£3,469	£6,471	Rob Davey (HMC)
Central Newcastle High School GDST, Newcastle upon Tyne	1895	997	£2,310	–	Mrs Lindsey Jane Griffin (GSA)
Channing School, London	1885	536	£3,250	–	Mrs Elizabeth Radice (GSA)
Charterhouse, Godalming	1611	723	£6,112	£7,394	Revd John Witheridge (HMC)
Cheadle Hulme School, Cheshire	1855	1,394	£2,377	–	Paul Dixon (HMC)
Cheltenham College, Glos	1841	582	£5,360	£7,150	P. A. Chamberlain (HMC)
The Cheltenham Ladies' College, Glos	1853	867	£4,637	£6,906	Mrs Vicky Tuck (GSA)
Chetham's School of Music, Manchester	1653	292	£5,667	£7,321	Mrs Claire Moreland (HMC)
Chetwynde School, Barrow-in-Furness	1938	536	£1,533	–	Mrs I. Nixon (SHMIS)
Chigwell School, Essex	1629	726	£3,355	£5,099	David Gibbs (HMC)
Christ's Hospital, W. Sussex	1552	832	–	£5,966	Dr Peter Southern (HMC)
Churcher's College, Hampshire	1722	802	£2,795	–	J. M. L. Williams (HMC, SHMIS)
City of London School, London	1442	895	£3,507	–	David Levin (HMC)
City of London Freemen's School, Surrey	1854	840	£3,651	£5,805	D. C. Haywood (HMC)
City of London School for Girls, London	1894	668	£3,363	–	Dr Yvonne Burne (GSA)
Claremont Fan Court School, Surrey	1922	600	£3,285	–	Mrs Patricia Farrar (SHMIS)
Clayesmore School, Dorset	1896	340	£4,660	£6,459	Martin Cooke (SHMIS)
Clifton College, Bristol	1862	660	£4,500	£6,600	Stephen Spurr (HMC)
Clifton High School, Bristol	1877	740	£2,605	–	Mrs M. C. Culligan (GSA)
Cobham Hall School, Kent	1962	220	£4,450	£6,450	Helen Davy (GSA)
Cokethorpe School, Oxfordshire	1957	570	£3,750	–	Damian J. Ettinger (SHMIS)
Colfe's School, London	1652	1,078	£3,174	–	Andrew Chicken (HMC)
Colston's Collegiate School, Bristol	1710	929	£2,370	£5,015	D. G. Crawford (HMC, SHMIS)
Colston's Girls' School, Bristol	1891	443	£2,278	–	Mrs Lesley Jones (GSA)
Combe Bank School, Sevenoaks	1924	420	£3,720	–	Mrs Rosemary Martin (GSA)
Concord College, Shrewsbury	1949	326	£2,300	£6,068	Anthony Morris (SHMIS)
Cranleigh School, Surrey	1865	604	£5,700	£7,110	Guy Waller (HMC)
Croham Hurst School, Croydon	1899	558	£2,920	–	Miss Sue Budgen (GSA)
Croydon High School for Girls GDST, Croydon	1874	828	£2,883	–	Miss Lorna M. Ogilvie (GSA)
Culford School, Bury St Edmunds	1881	680	£4,095	£6,283	Julian Johnson-Munday (HMC)
The Dame Alice Harpur School, Bedford	1882	952	£2,767	–	Mrs Jill Berry (GSA)
Dame Allan's Boys' School, Newcastle upon Tyne	1705	470	£2,276	–	John Hind (HMC)
Dame Allan's Girls' School, Newcastle upon Tyne	1705	423	£2,276	–	John Hind (GSA)
Dauntsey's School, Wiltshire	1542	688	£3,790	£6,345	S. B. Roberts (HMC)
Dean Close School, Cheltenham	1886	466	£4,995	£7,095	Revd T. M. Hastie-Smith (HMC)
Denstone College, Uttoxeter	1868	456	£3,100	£4,863	David Derbyshire (HMC)
Derby High School, Derby	1892	600	£2,395	–	Colin Callaghan (GSA)
Dover College, Kent	1871	354	£2,995	£5,995	Howard Blackett (SHMIS)
Downe House, Newbury	1907	537	£5,210	£7,200	Mrs Emma McKendrick (GSA)
Downside School, Bath	1606	320	£3,230	£6,190	D. L. Maidlow Davis (HMC)
Duke of York Royal Military School, Dover	1803	500	–	£650	John Cummings (SHMIS)
Dulwich College, London	1619	1,450	£3,580	£7,210	Graham G. Able (HMC)
Dunottar School, Reigate	1926	425	£3,050	–	Mrs Jeanne Hobson (GSA)
Durham School, Durham	1414	360	£3,832	£5,832	N. G. Kern (HMC)

School	Date founded	No. of pupils	Termly fees Day	Board	Head (with association affiliation)
Durham High School for Girls, Durham	1884	578	£2,435	–	Mrs Ann J. Templeman (GSA)
Eastbourne College, E. Sussex	1867	580	£4,390	£6,695	Charles M. P. Bush (HMC)
Edgbaston High School for Girls, Birmingham	1876	930	£2,370	–	Miss E. Mullinger (GSA)
Ellesmere College, Shropshire	1884	482	£3,866	£4,995	B. J. Wignall (HMC)
Elmhurst in Association with Birmingham Royal Ballet, Birmingham	1910	186	£4,200	£5,400	John McNamara (SHMIS)
Eltham College, London	1842	785	£3,302	–	Paul Henderson (HMC)
Emanuel School, London	1594	692	£3,387	–	Mark Hanley-Browne (HMC)
Embley Park School, Romsey	1946	450	£3,280	£5,370	David Chapman (SHMIS)
Epsom College, Surrey	1855	680	£5,015	£7,108	Stephen Borthwick (HMC)
Eton College, Windsor	1440	1,287	–	£7,460	Anthony R. M. Little (HMC)
Ewell Castle School, Surrey	1926	510	£2,780	–	A. J. Tibble (SHMIS)
Exeter School, Devon	1633	850	£2,465	–	Bob Griffin (HMC)
Farlington School, W. Sussex	1896	478	£3,325	£5,105	Mrs Trina Mawer (GSA)
Farnborough Hill, Hampshire	1889	500	£2,640	–	Miss Jacqueline Thomas (GSA)
Farringtons and Stratford House, Kent	1911	502	£2,950	£5,420	Mrs Catherine James (GSA)
Felsted School, Essex	1564	450	£4,918	£6,615	Stephen Roberts (HMC)
Forest School, London	1834	1,175	£3,377	£5,294	A. G. Boggis (HMC)
Framlingham College, Suffolk	1864	710	£3,753	£5,839	Mrs Gwen Randall (HMC)
Francis Holland School, London NW1	1878	395	£3,450	–	Mrs Vivienne Durham (GSA)
Francis Holland School, London SW1	1881	480	£3,575	–	Miss S. Pattenden (GSA)
Frensham Heights School, Farnham	1925	480	£4,130	£6,460	Andrew Fisher (HMC)
Friends' School, Essex	1702	376	£3,428	£5,715	Andy Waters (SHMIS)
Fulneck School, W. Yorkshire	1753	426	£2,640	£4,850	T. Kernohan (SHMIS)
Gateways School, Leeds	1941	560	£2,463	–	Mrs Denise Davidson (GSA)
Giggleswick School, N. Yorkshire	1512	498	£4,400	£6,557	Geoffrey Boult (HMC)
The Godolphin School, Salisbury	1726	410	£3,995	£6,300	Miss Jill Horsburgh (GSA)
Godolphin and Latymer School, London	1905	700	£3,490	–	Miss Margaret Rudland (GSA)
The Grange School, Cheshire	1933	1,116	£2,100	–	Jennifer Stephen (HMC)
Greenacre School for Girls, Surrey	1933	430	£2,720	–	Mrs Pat Wood (GSA)
Grenville College, Devon	1954	410	£2,690	£5,432	Dr S. Wormleighton (SHMIS)
Gresham's School, Norfolk	1555	508	£5,045	£6,505	A. R. Clark (HMC)
Guildford High School, Guildford	1888	920	£3,117	–	Mrs Fiona Boulton (GSA)
The Haberdashers' Aske's Boys' School, Hertfordshire	1690	1,300	£3,420	–	Peter Hamilton (HMC)
The Haberdashers' Aske's School for Girls, Hertfordshire	1690	1,135	£2,800	–	Mrs Penelope Penney (GSA)
Haileybury, Hertfordshire	1862	720	£5,245	£6,985	Stuart Westley (HMC)
Halliford School, London	1921	350	£2,750	–	Philip V. Cottam (SHMIS)
Hampton School, Middlesex	1556	1,065	£3,330	–	Barry Martin (HMC)
Harrogate Ladies' College, N. Yorkshire	1893	360	£3,330	£5,600	Dr Margaret J. Hustler (GSA)
Harrow School, Middlesex	1572	785	–	£7,345	Barnaby Lenon (HMC)
Headington School, Oxford	1915	962	£3,060	£5,835	Mrs Anne Coutts (GSA)
Heathfield School, Ascot	1899	220	–	£7,270	Mrs Frances King (GSA)
Heathfield School GDST, Middlesex	1900	632	£2,883	–	Miss Christine Juett (GSA)
Hereford Cathedral School, Hereford	1384	900	£2,650	–	Dr Howard Tomlinson (HMC)
Hethersett Old Hall School, Norwich	1928	274	£2,785	£5,500	Mrs Janet Mark (GSA)
Highclare School, Birmingham	1934	866	£2,395	–	Mrs Margaret Viles (GSA)
Highgate School, London	1565	1,100	£4,035	–	Richard Kennedy (HMC)
Hipperholme Grammar School, Halifax	1648	300	£2,170	–	C. C. Robinson (SHMIS)
Holy Trinity College, Bromley	1886	520	£3,013	–	Mrs Pauline Lightfoot (GSA)
Holy Trinity School, Kidderminster	1903	406	£2,420	–	Mrs Y. Wilkinson (GSA)
Hull High School, Hull	1890	425	£2,240	–	Mrs A. V. Wood (GSA)
Hulme Grammar School for Boys, Oldham	1611	720	£2,099	–	Ken Jones (HMC)
Hulme Grammar School for Girls, Oldham	1895	598	£2,099	–	Miss M. S. Smolenski (GSA)
Hurstpierpoint College, W. Sussex	1849	385	£4,910	£6,340	Tim Manly (HMC)
Hymers College, Hull	1893	968	£2,151	–	John Morris (HMC)
Immanuel College, Hertfordshire	1990	545	£3,317	–	Philip Skelker (SHMIS)
Ipswich School, Suffolk	1390	703	£2,878	£5,007	Ian Galbraith (HMC)
Ipswich High School GDST, Suffolk	1878	700	£2,310	–	Miss Valerie MacCuish (GSA)
James Allen's Girls' School, London	1741	770	£3,275	–	Mrs Marion Gibbs (GSA)
The John Lyon School, Middlesex	1876	550	£3,395	–	Kevin Riley (HMC)
Kelly College, Devon	1877	360	£4,050	£6,600	Mark Steed (HMC)
Kent College, Canterbury	1885	680	£3,615	£6,175	G. G. Carminati (HMC)

School	Date founded	No. of pupils	Termly fees Day	Board	Head (with association affiliation)
Kent College, Tunbridge Wells	1886	575	£3,880	£6,265	Mrs Anne E. Upton (GSA)
Kimbolton School, Huntingdon	1600	1,111	£3,040	£5,140	Jonathan Belbin (HMC)
King Edward VII and Queen Mary School, Lytham St Anne's	1908	800	£2,115	–	Robert Karling (HMC)
King Edward's School, Bath	1552	990	£2,832	–	Miss C. Thompson (HMC)
King Edward's School, Birmingham	1552	860	£2,460	–	Roger Dancey (HMC)
King Edward VI High School for Girls, Birmingham	1883	550	£2,420	–	Miss Sarah Evans (GSA, SHMIS)
King Edward VI School, Southampton	1553	950	£2,807	–	Julian Thould (HMC)
King Edward's School, Surrey	1553	474	£4,150	£5,850	Kerr Fulton-Peebles (HMC)
King Henry VIII School, Coventry	1545	1,122	£2,212	–	G. Fisher (HMC, GSA)
King's School, Somerset	1519	343	£4,630	£6,230	N. M. Lashbrook (HMC)
The King's School, Canterbury	597	791	£5,420	£7,320	Keith Wilkinson (HMC)
The King's School, Chester	1541	746	£2,475	–	Timothy J. Turvey (HMC)
The King's School, Cambridgeshire	970	920	£4,295	£6,220	Mrs Susan Freestone (HMC)
The King's School, Gloucester	1541	515	£3,865	–	Peter Lacey (HMC)
The King's School in Macclesfield, Cheshire	1502	1,400	£2,332	–	S. Coyne (HMC)
King's School, Rochester	1541	720	£4,125	£6,850	Dr I. R. Walker (HMC)
King's College, Taunton	1522	420	£4,210	£6,320	Christopher Ramsey (HMC)
The King's School, Tynemouth	1860	850	£2,326	–	Philip Cantwell (HMC)
King's High School for Girls, Warwick	1879	550	£2,534	–	Elizabeth Surber (GSA)
The King's School, Worcester	1541	1,300	£2,906	–	T. H. Keyes (HMC)
King's College School, London	1829	762	£4,105	–	Tony Evans (HMC)
Kingham Hill School, Oxfordshire	1886	250	£4,131	£6,249	Martin J Morris (SHMIS)
The Kingsley School, Leamington Spa	1884	620	£2,530	–	Mrs Christine A. Mannion Watson (GSA)
Kingston Grammar School, Kingston upon Thames	1561	620	£3,376	–	C. D. Baxter (HMC)
Kingswood School, Bath	1748	636	£2,884	£6,109	Gary M. Best (HMC)
Kirkham Grammar School, Preston	1549	975	£2,065	£3,800	Douglas Walker (HMC) (SHMIS)
La Sagesse School, Newcastle upon Tyne	1912	260	£2,450	–	Miss Linda Clark (GSA)
The Lady Eleanor Holles School, Middlesex	1711	880	£3,224	–	Mrs Gillian Lowe (GSA)
Lancing College, W. Sussex	1848	488	£4,785	£6,880	P. M. Tinniswood (HMC)
Langley School, Norwich	1910	450	£2,725	£5,425	J. G. Malcolm (SHMIS)
Latymer Upper School, London	1624	970	£3,785	–	Peter Winter (HMC)
Lavant House Rosemead, Chichester	1919	150	£3,175	£5,030	Mrs M. Scott (GSA)
Leeds Grammar School, Leeds	1552	1,380	£2,685	–	Dr Mark Bailey (HMC)
Leeds Girls' High School, Leeds	1876	995	£2,602	–	Ms Sue Fishburn (GSA)
Leicester Grammar School, Leicester	1981	700	£2,510	–	Christopher King (HMC)
Leicester High School for Girls, Leicester	1906	435	£2,410	–	Mrs J. Burns (GSA)
Leighton Park School, Reading	1890	427	£4,484	£6,619	John Dunston (HMC, SHMIS)
The Leys School, Cambridge	1875	540	£4,260	£6,655	Mark Slater (HMC, GSA)
Licensed Victuallers' School, Ascot	1803	839	£3,390	£5,480	Ian Mullins (SHMIS)
Lincoln Minster School, Lincoln	1996	687	£2,675	£5,062	Clive Rickart (SHMIS)
Liverpool College, Liverpool	1840	920	£2,440	–	Brian Christian (HMC)
Lodge School, Surrey	1916	258	£2,750	–	Miss Pamela A. Maynard (GSA)
Longridge Towers School, Berwick upon Tweed	1983	322	£2,310	£4,750	Dr Michael Barron (SHMIS)
Lord Wandsworth College, Hants	1920	510	£4,545	£6,100	Ian Power (HMC, SHMIS)
Loughborough Grammar School, Loughborough	1495	1,040	£2,589	£4,626	Paul Fisher (HMC)
Loughborough High School, Loughborough	1849	605	£2,355	–	Miss Bridget O'Connor (GSA)
Luckley-Oakfield School, Wokingham	1918	350	£3,186	£5,438	Miss V. Davis (GSA)
Magdalen College School, Oxford	1480	630	£3,078	–	A. D. Halls (HMC)
Malvern College, Worcs	1865	539	£4,740	£7,330	Hugh Carson (HMC)
Malvern Girls' College, Worcs	1893	360	£4,800	£7,845	Mrs P. M. C. Leggate (GSA)
The Manchester Grammar School, Manchester	1515	1,440	£2,276	–	Dr Christopher Ray (HMC)
Manchester High School for Girls, Manchester	1874	920	£2,275	–	Mrs Christine Lee-Jones (GSA)
The Marist Senior School, Ascot	1870	308	£2,660	–	Karl McCloskey (GSA)
Marlborough College, Wilts	1843	860	£5,475	£7,300	Nicholas Sampson (HMC)

School	Date founded	No. of pupils	Termly fees Day	Board	Head (with association affiliation)
Marymount International School, Kingston upon Thames	1955	230	£4,317	£7,300	Cliff Canning (GSA)
The Maynard School, Exeter	1658	478	£2,544	–	Dr Daphne West (GSA)
Merchant Taylors' School, Liverpool	1620	850	£2,184	–	Simon Dawkins (HMC)
Merchant Taylors' School, Middlesex	1561	800	£3,755	–	Stephen Wright (HMC)
Merchant Taylors' School for Girls, Liverpool	1888	920	£2,052	–	Miss J. Brandreth (GSA)
Mill Hill School, London	1807	610	£4,195	£6,580	William R. Winfield (HMC)
Millfield School, Somerset	1935	1,253	£4,725	£7,145	Peter M. Johnson (HMC)
Milton Abbey School, Dorset	1954	225	£5,295	£7,060	W. J. Hughes-D'Aeth (SHMIS)
Moira House School, Eastbourne	1875	420	£3,455	£5,885	Mrs Ann Harris (GSA, SHMIS)
Monkton Combe School, Bath	1868	350	£4,635	£6,700	Michael Cuthbertson (HMC)
More House School, London	1953	220	£3,260	–	Mrs Lesley Falconer (GSA)
Moreton Hall, Oswestry	1913	310	£4,860	£6,650	J. Forster (GSA)
Mount School, London	1925	360	£2,493	–	Mrs J. Kirsten Jackson (GSA)
The Mount School, York	1785	463	£3,565	£5,535	Mrs Diana Gant (GSA)
Mount St Mary's College, Derbyshire	1842	321	£2,770	£4,995	Philip MacDonald (HMC)
New Hall School, Chelmsford	1642	700	£3,970	£5,970	Mrs K. A. Jeffrey (GSA)
Newcastle upon Tyne Church High School, Newcastle upon Tyne	1885	560	£2,400	–	Mrs Lesley Smith (GSA)
Newcastle-under-Lyme School, Staffordshire	1602	1,080	£2,136	–	Robert Dillow (HMC)
North Cestrian Grammar School, Altrincham	1951	320	£1,945	–	David G. Vanstone (SHMIS)
North London Collegiate School, Middlesex	1850	1009	£3,180	–	Mrs Bernice McCabe (GSA)
Northampton High School, Northampton	1878	844	£2,440	–	Mrs L. A. Mayne (GSA)
Northamptonshire Grammar School, Northampton	1989	360	£2,838	–	Simon Larter (SHMIS)
Northwood College, Middlesex	1878	770	£3,019	–	Mrs Ruth Mercer (GSA)
Norwich School, Norwich	1547	785	£2,667	–	J. B. Hawkins (HMC)
Norwich High School for Girls GDST, Norwich	1875	895	£2,310	–	Mrs Valerie Bidwell (GSA)
Notre Dame Senior School, Surrey	1937	375	£2,800	–	Mrs Bridget Williams (GSA)
Notting Hill and Ealing High School GDST, London	1873	830	£2,883	–	Mrs Susan Whitfield (GSA)
Nottingham High School for Girls GDST, Nottingham	1875	1,117	£2,310	–	Mrs Angela Rees (GSA)
Nottingham High School, Nottingham	1513	820	£2,690	–	C. Parker, CBE (HMC)
Oakham School, Rutland	1584	1,037	£4,040	£6,760	Dr Joseph A. F. Spence (HMC)
Ockbrook School, Derbyshire	1799	500	£2,246	£4,152	Denise P. Bolland (GSA)
Old Palace School of John Whitgift, Croydon	1889	850	£2,698	–	Mrs Joy Hancock (GSA)
The Oratory School, Woodcote, Reading	1859	400	£4,930	£6,835	Clive Dytor MC (HMC)
Oswestry School, Shropshire	1407	436	£3,310	£5,570	Paul Stockdale (SHMIS)
Oundle School, Peterborough	1556	1,067	£3,632	£6,632	Dr Ralph Townsend (HMC)
Our Lady of Sion School, Sussex	1862	520	£2,585	–	M. Scullion (SHMIS)
Our Lady's Convent Senior School, Oxon	1860	390	£2,380	–	Mrs Glynne Butt (GSA)
Oxford High School GDST, Oxford	1875	916	£2,310	–	Miss Felicity Lusk (GSA)
Pangbourne College, Berkshire	1917	362	£4,590	£6,545	Dr Kenneth Greig (HMC)
Parsons Mead School, Surrey	1897	302	£3,175	–	Mrs Patricia Taylor (GSA)
The Perse School, Cambridge	1615	650	£3,277	–	Nigel Richardson (HMC)
The Perse School for Girls, Cambridge	1881	680	£3,055	–	Miss Tricia Kelleher (GSA)
Peterborough High School, Peterborough	1895	370	£2,794	£5,090	Mrs Sarah Dixon (GSA)
Pipers Corner School, High Wycombe	1930	450	£3,215	£5,315	Mrs Valerie Stattersfield (GSA)
Plymouth College, Devon	1877	640	£2,711	£5,191	Alan Morsley (HMC, GSA)
Pocklington School, York	1514	622	£2,911	£5,073	Nicholas Clements (HMC)
Polam Hall School, Durham	1854	480	£2,690	£5,235	Miss Marie Green (GSA)
Portland Place School, London	1996	300	£3,550	–	Richard Walker (SHMIS)
The Portsmouth Grammar School, Hants	1732	940	£2,761	–	Dr Timothy Hands (HMC)
Portsmouth High School GDST, Hants	1882	629	£2,310	–	Miss P. Hulse (GSA)
The Princess Helena College, Herts	1820	190	£4,045	£5,895	Anne-Marie Hodgkiss (GSA)
Princethorpe College, Rugby	1958	655	£2,295	–	John M Shinkwin (SHMIS)
Prior Park College, Bath	1830	545	£3,310	£5,968	Giles Mercer (HMC)
Prior's Field School, Surrey	1902	310	£3,595	£5,695	Mrs Jenny Dwyer (GSA)
Priory School, Birmingham	1933	320	£2,415	–	Mrs Elaine Brook (GSA)

School	Date founded	No. of pupils	Termly fees Day	Board	Head (with association affiliation)
The Purcell School, Hertfordshire	1962	177	£6,434	£8,229	John Tolputt (SHMIS)
Putney High School GDST, London	1893	800	£2,883	–	Dr Denise V. Lodge (GSA)
Queen Anne's School, Reading	1894	332	£4,445	£6,580	Mrs Deborah Forbes (GSA)
Queen Elizabeth's Grammar School, Blackburn	1509	825	£2,445	–	Dr David Hempsall (HMC)
Queen Elizabeth Grammar School, Wakefield	1591	1,000	£2,497	–	Michael Gibbons (HMC)
Queen Elizabeth's Hospital, Bristol	1590	570	£2,444	£4,504	Stephen Holliday (HMC)
Queen Margaret's School, York	1901	369	£3,695	£5,831	Dr G. A. H. Chapman (GSA)
The Queen's School, Chester	1878	611	£2,495	–	Mrs C. M. Buckley (GSA)
Queen's College London, London	1848	380	£3,710	–	Miss M. M. Connell (GSA)
Queen's College, Somerset	1843	721	£3,597	£5,421	Christopher J. Alcock (HMC)
Queen's Gate School, London	1891	400	£3,250	–	Mrs Angela Holyoak (GSA)
Queenswood, Hertfordshire	1894	401	£5,120	£6,820	Clarissa Farr (GSA)
Radley College, Oxfordshire	1847	628	–	£7,120	Angus McPhail (HMC)
Ratcliffe College, Leicester	1847	616	£3,371	£5,077	Peter Farrar (HMC)
Read School, N. Yorkshire	1667	280	£2,125	£4,600	Richard Hadfield (SHMIS)
Reading Blue Coat School, Berkshire	1646	650	£3,085	–	S. J. W. McArthur (HMC, SHMIS)
The Red Maids' School, Bristol	1634	400	£2,340	–	Mrs Isobel Tobias (GSA)
Redland High School for Girls, Bristol	1882	672	£2,470	–	Dr Ruth A. Weeks (GSA)
Reed's School, Surrey	1813	460	£4,604	£6,090	D. W. Jarrett (HMC, SHMIS)
Reigate Grammar School, Surrey	1675	1,050	£3,085	–	David Thomas (HMC)
Rendcomb College, Cirencester	1920	350	£4,585	£5,787	Gerry Holden (HMC, SHMIS)
Repton School, Derby	1557	555	£4,955	£6,675	R. A. Holroyd (HMC)
Rishworth School, W. Yorkshire	1724	560	£2,645	£5,190	Richard Baker (SHMIS)
RNIB New College Worcester, Worcester	–	115	£8,450	£12,175	Nick Ratcliffe (HMC)
Roedean School, Brighton	1885	396	£4,130	£7,400	Mrs Carolyn Shaw (GSA)
Rossall School, Lancashire	1844	415	£2,782	£7,003	Tim Wilbur (HMC)
The Royal Ballet School, London	1929	205	£5,545	£7,639	Gailene Stock (SHMIS)
The Royal Grammar School, Guildford	1509	863	£3,305	–	Timothy Young (HMC)
Royal Grammar School, Newcastle upon Tyne	1510	1,135	£2,283	–	James F. X. Miller (HMC)
Royal Grammar School, Worcester	1291	1,069	£2,520	–	W. A. Jones (HMC)
The Royal High School GDST, Bath	1864	900	£2,310	£4,531	James Graham-Brown (GSA)
Royal Hospital School, Ipswich	1712	680	£3,380	£5,317	Howard Blackett (HMC, SHMIS)
The Royal Masonic School, Herts	1788	751	£2,947	£4,843	Mrs Diana Rose (GSA)
Royal Russell School, Croydon	1853	810	£3,220	£6,410	Dr John Jennings (HMC, SHMIS)
The Royal School Haslemere, Surrey	1840	356	£3,663	£5,816	Mrs L. Taylor-Gooby (GSA)
Royal Wolverhampton School, Wolverhampton	1850	310	£2,885	£5,940	T. Waters (SHMIS)
Rugby School, Warwickshire	1567	793	£4,600	£7,250	Patrick Derham (HMC)
Ryde School, Isle of Wight	1921	720	£2,470	£5,045	Dr Nick J. England (HMC, SHMIS)
Rye St Antony School, Oxford	1930	400	£2,885	£4,900	Miss Alison Jones (GSA)
St Albans School, Abbey Gateway, St Albans	1100	730	£3,331	–	Andrew Grant (HMC)
St Albans High School for Girls, St Albans	1889	950	£2,790	–	Mrs Carol Y. Daly (GSA)
St Antony's Leweston School, Dorset	1891	252	£3,925	£5,925	Henry J. MacDonald (GSA)
St Bede's Senior School, E. Sussex	1978	707	£3,860	£6,280	Stephen Cole (SHMIS)
St Bede's College, Manchester	1879	1,448	£2,028	–	John Byrne (HMC)
St Bees School, Cumbria	1583	300	£3,822	£6,377	Philip J. Capes (HMC)
St Benedict's School, London	1902	605	£3,040	–	Christopher J. Cleugh (HMC)
St Catherine's School, Guildford	1885	740	£3,465	£5,700	Mrs A. Phillips (GSA)
St Christopher School, Hertfordshire	1915	611	£3,585	£6,300	Donald Wilkinson (SHMIS)
St Columba's College, St Albans	1955	865	£2,570	–	D. S. Darlington (HMC)
St David's School, Middlesex	1716	437	£2,891	£5,341	Ms P. A. Bristow (GSA)
St Dominic's Priory School, Staffordshire	1934	300	£2,151	–	Andrew Egan (GSA)
St Dunstan's College, London	1446	925	£3,420	–	Fiona Cordeaux (HMC)
St Edmund's School, Canterbury	1749	561	£4,311	£6,677	A. Nicholas Ridley (HMC)
St Edmund's College, Hertfordshire	1568	680	£3,595	£5,825	Chris Long (HMC)
St Edward's School, Cheltenham	1987	450	£3,025	–	Dr Andrew J. Nash (SHMIS)
St Edward's School, Oxford	1863	640	£5,694	£7,208	Andrew Trotman (HMC)

School	Date founded	No. of pupils	Termly fees Day	Board	Head (with association affiliation)
St Elphin's School, Derbyshire	1844	210	£2,995	£4,985	Dr Deborah Mouat (GSA)
St Felix and St George's School, Suffolk	1897	340	£3,500	£5,500	David A. T. Ward (SHMIS)
St Francis' College, Hertfordshire	1933	500	£2,890	£5,685	Miss Mairin Hegarty (GSA)
St Gabriel's School, Newbury	1929	530	£2,950	–	Alun S. Jones (GSA)
St George's School, Ascot	1900	313	£4,350	£6,750	Mrs Joanna Grant-Peterkin (GSA)
St George's School, Birmingham	1999	380	£2,450	–	Miss Hilary Phillips (SHMIS)
St George's College, Surrey	1869	850	£3,540	–	Joseph A. Peake (HMC, SHMIS)
The School of St Helen and St Katharine, Abingdon	1903	616	£2,664	–	Mrs Cynthia Hall (GSA)
St Helen's School, Middlesex	1899	1,048	£3,040	£5,634	Mrs Mary Morris (GSA)
St James School, Grimsby	1880	235	£2,656	£4,431	Susan M. Isaac (SHMIS)
St James Independent School for Boys (Senior), Surrey	1975	295	£2,820	£3,920	David Boddy (SHMIS)
St James Independent School for Girls (Senior), London	1975	239	£2,820		Mrs L. Hyde (GSA)
St James's School, Worcestershire	1896	145	£3,998	£6,660	Rosalind Hayes (GSA)
St John's School, Surrey	1851	445	£4,650	£6,600	N. Haddock, MBE (HMC)
St John's College, Hampshire	1908	633	£2,260	£5,300	N. W. Thorne (SHMIS)
St Joseph's College, Ipswich	1937	588	£2,850	£4,895	Mrs S. Grant (SHMIS)
St Joseph's Convent School, Reading	1910	408	£2,700	–	Mrs M. Sheridan (GSA)
St Lawrence College, Kent	1879	482	£4,190	£6,780	Revd Mark Aitken (HMC)
St Leonards-Mayfield School, E. Sussex	1863	380	£4,020	£6,170	Mrs Julia Dalton (GSA)
St Margaret's School for Girls, Exeter	1902	386	£2,414	–	Miss R. Edbrooke (GSA)
St Margaret's School, Hertfordshire	1749	450	£3,395	£5,995	Miss Marlene de Villiers (GSA)
St Martin's, Malvern Hall, W. Midlands	1941	580	£2,510	–	Mrs Jennifer R. Taylor (GSA)
St Mary's School, Wiltshire	1873	290	£4,800	£7,100	Mrs Helen Wright (GSA)
St Mary's School, Cambridge	1898	485	£2,990	£5,990	Mrs Jayne Triffitt (GSA)
St Mary's College, Merseyside	1919	978	£2,113	–	Jean Marsh (HMC)
St Mary's School, Buckinghamshire	1872	300	£3,090	–	Mrs Fanny Balcombe (GSA)
St Mary's School, Dorset	1945	340	£4,105	£6,085	Mrs M. McSwiggan (GSA)
St Mary's School, Oxfordshire	1872	225	£4,650	£6,950	Mrs Susan Sowden (GSA)
St Mary's Convent School, Worcester	1934	330	£2,260	–	Mrs Susan Cookson (GSA)
St Mary's School Ascot, Berkshire	1885	360	£4,770	£6,900	Mrs Mary Breen (GSA)
St Mary's Hall, Brighton	1836	380	£3,369	£5,508	Mrs Susan M. Meek (GSA)
St Paul's School, London	1509	830	£4,500	£6,695	Dr. G. M. Stephen (HMC)
St Paul's Girls' School, London	1509	680	£3,724	–	Miss Elizabeth Diggory (GSA)
St Peter's School, York	627	500	£3,462	£5,813	Richard Smyth (HMC)
St Swithun's School, Winchester	1884	480	£3,760	£6,200	Dr Helen L. Harvey (GSA)
St Teresa's School, Surrey	1928	330	£3,455	£5,470	Mrs Mary Prescott (GSA)
Scarborough College, Scarborough	1898	530	£2,574	£3,833	T. L. Kirkup (SHMIS)
Seaford College, W. Sussex	1884	401	£3,955	£6,020	Toby J. Mullins (SHMIS)
Sedbergh School, Cumbria	1525	420	£4,900	£6,580	Christopher Hirst (HMC)
Sevenoaks School, Kent	1432	977	£4,179	£7,333	Mrs Katy Ricks (HMC)
Shebbear College, Devon	1841	290	£2,640	£4,930	R. S. Barnes (SHMIS)
Sheffield High School GDST, Sheffield	1878	962	£2,310	–	Mrs Valerie Dunsford (GSA)
Sherborne School, Dorset	1550	560	£5,635	£7,225	S. F. Eliot (HMC)
Sherborne School for Girls, Dorset	1899	360	£5,270	£7,195	Mrs G. Kerton-Johnson (GSA)
Shiplake College, Oxfordshire	1959	300	£4,235	£6,280	N. V. Bevan (HMC, SHMIS)
Shrewsbury School, Shrewsbury	1552	687	£5,045	£7,180	Jeremy Goulding (HMC)
Shrewsbury High School GDST, Shrewsbury	1885	647	£2,310	–	Mrs Marilyn Cass (GSA)
Sibford School, Banbury	1842	392	£2,817	£5,579	Michael Goodwin (SHMIS)
Sidcot School, Somerset	1808	484	£2,995	£6,525	John Walmsley (SHMIS)
Silcoates School, Wakefield	1820	750	£2,952	–	A. Paul Spillane (HMC)
Sir William Perkins's School, Surrey	1725	560	£2,838	–	Miss Susan Ross (GSA)
Solihull School, Solihull	1560	964	£2,515	–	John Claughton (HMC)
South Hampstead High School GDST, London	1876	907	£2,883	–	Jennifer Stephen (GSA)
Stafford Grammar School, Stafford	1982	363	£2,232	–	Michael R. Darley (SHMIS)
Stamford School, Lincolnshire	1532	648	£2,808	£5,328	Dr Peter Mason (HMC)
Stamford High School, Lincolnshire	1877	642	£2,808	£5,328	Dr Peter Mason (GSA)
Stanbridge Earls School, Hampshire	1952	199	£5,000	£6,745	Nicholas Hall (SHMIS)
Stockport Grammar School, Cheshire	1487	1,410	£2,205	–	I. Mellor (HMC)

School	Date founded	No. of pupils	Termly fees Day	Board	Head (with association affiliation)
Stonar School, Wiltshire	1895	450	£2,950	£5,250	Mrs Clare Osborne (GSA)
Stonyhurst College, Lancashire	1593	410	£3,844	£6,636	Adrian Aylward (HMC)
Stover School, Devon	1932	510	£2,495	£5,245	Thomas A. Packer (GSA, SHMIS)
Stowe School, Buckingham	1923	600	£5,445	£7,260	Dr A. Wallersteiner (HMC)
Streatham Hill and Clapham High School GDST, London	1887	830	£2,883	–	Mrs Susan Mitchell (GSA)
Sunderland High School, Sunderland	1884	600	£2,191	–	Dr Angela Slater (SHMIS)
Surbiton High School, Kingston upon Thames	1884	1,258	£2,987	–	Dr Jennifer Longhurst (GSA)
Sutton High School GDST, Surrey	1884	743	£2,883	–	Stephen Callaghan (GSA)
Sutton Valence School, Kent	1576	471	£4,220	£6,680	Joe Davies (HMC)
Sydenham High School for Girls GDST, London	1887	710	£2,883	–	Mrs Kathryn Pullen (GSA)
Talbot Heath, Bournemouth	1886	617	£2,750	£4,580	Mrs Christine Dipple (GSA)
Taunton School, Somerset	1850	480	£3,940	£6,130	Julian Whiteley (HMC)
Teesside High School, Stockton-on-Tees	1970	470	£2,412	–	Mrs Hilary French (GSA)
Tettenhall College, Wolverhampton	1863	492	£2,841	£4,937	Dr P. C. Bodkin (HMC, SHMIS)
Thetford Grammar School, Norfolk	1060	300	£2,455	–	J. R. Weeks (SHMIS)
Tonbridge School, Kent	1553	735	£5,210	£7,374	J. M. Hammond (HMC)
Tormead School, Guildford	1905	740	£2,900	–	Mrs Susan Marks (GSA)
Trent College, Nottingham	1866	1,030	£3,566	£5,375	Jonathan S. Lee (HMC)
Trinity School of John Whitgift, Croydon	1596	885	£3,175	–	Christopher Tarrant (HMC)
Truro School, Truro	1880	817	£2,678	£5,223	Paul K. Smith (HMC)
Truro High School, Truro	1880	450	£2,550	£4,785	Michael McDowell (GSA)
Tudor Hall School, Banbury	1850	275	£3,942	£6,117	Miss Wendy Griffiths (GSA)
University College School, London	1830	1,059	£4,015	–	Kenneth Durham (HMC)
Uppingham School, Rutland	1584	722	£4,972	£7,102	Dr Stephan Winkley (HMC)
Wakefield Girls' High School, Wakefield	1878	712	£2,497	–	Mrs Patricia Langham (GSA)
Walthamstow Hall, Sevenoaks	1838	450	£3,765	–	Mrs Jill Milner (GSA)
Warminster School, Wiltshire	1707	650	£3,045	£5,300	David Dowdles (SHMIS)
Warwick School, Warwick	c 914	1,086	£2,737	£5,841	Edward Halse (HMC)
Welbeck College, Loughborough	1953	220	–	£2,122	Tony Halliwell (SHMIS)
Wellingborough School, Northants	1595	836	£2,997	–	Garry Bowe (HMC)
Wellington College, Berkshire	1853	775	£5,840	£7,300	A. Hugh Munro (HMC)
Wellington School, Somerset	1837	800	£2,636	£4,910	A. J. Rogers (HMC)
Wells Cathedral School, Somerset	c 1150	713	£3,730	£6,230	Elizabeth Cairncross (HMC)
Wentworth College, Bournemouth	1871	235	£3,055	£4,920	Miss Sandra D. Coe (GSA)
West Buckland School, Devon	1858	700	£2,890	£5,040	John Vick (HMC)
Westfield School, Newcastle upon Tyne	1959	370	£2,385	–	Mrs Marion Farndale (GSA)
Westholme School, Lancashire	1923	1,095	£1,969	–	Mrs Lillian Croston (GSA)
Westminster School, London	1560	705	£5,068	£7,316	Tristram Jones-Parry (HMC)
Westonbirt School, Glos	1928	230	£4,470	£6,410	Mrs Mary Henderson (GSA)
Whitgift School, Croydon	1596	1,193	£3,574	–	Dr Christopher Barnett (HMC)
William Hulme's Grammar School, Manchester	1887	570	£2,372	–	Stephen R. Patriarca (HMC)
Wimbledon High School GDST, London	1880	900	£2,883	–	Mrs Pamela Wilkes (GSA)
Winchester College, Winchester	1382	700	£7,016	£7,385	Tommy Cookson (HMC)
Windermere St Anne's School, Cumbria	1863	405	£3,020	£5,460	Miss W. A. Ellis (SHMIS)
Wisbech Grammar School, Cambridgeshire	1379	720	£2,620	–	Robert S. Repper (HMC)
Wispers School, Surrey	1946	120	£3,700	£5,870	L. Henry Beltran (GSA)
Withington Girls' School, Manchester	1890	635	£2,215	–	Mrs Janet Pickering (GSA)
Woldingham School, Surrey	1842	530	£4,010	£6,710	Miss Diana Vernon (GSA)
Wolverhampton Grammar School, Wolverhampton	1512	730	£2,764	–	Dr Bernard Trafford (HMC)
Woodbridge School, Suffolk	1577	904	£3,264	£5,684	Stephen H. Cole (HMC)
Woodhouse Grove School, Bradford	1812	670	£2,760	£4,960	David Humphreys (HMC)
Worksop College, Nottinghamshire	1890	400	£3,945	£5,765	Roy A. Collard (HMC)
Worth School, W. Sussex	1933	440	£5,025	£6,783	Peter Armstrong (HMC)
Wrekin College, Shropshire	1880	450	£3,745	£6,195	Stephen Drew (HMC)
Wychwood School, Oxford	1897	150	£2,750	£4,480	S. Wingfield Digby (GSA)
Wycliffe College, Glos	1882	800	£4,415	£6,570	Dr Tony Collins (HMC)

School	Date founded	No. of pupils	Termly fees Day	Board	Head (with association affiliation)
Wycombe Abbey School, High Wycombe	1896	538	£5,475	£7,300	Mrs Pauline Davies (GSA)
Yarm School, Cleveland	1978	930	£2,666	–	David M. Dunn (HMC, SHMIS)
The Yehudi Menuhin School, Surrey	1963	61	£9,662	£9,924	Nicolas Chisholm (SHMIS)

WALES

School	Date founded	No. of pupils	Termly fees Day	Board	Head (with association affiliation)
Christ College, Brecon	1541	320	£4,350	£5,605	D. P. Jones (HMC)
Haberdashers' Monmouth School for Girls, Monmouth	1892	675	£2,940	£5,082	Dr Brenda Despontin (GSA)
Howell's School, Denbighshire	1540	340	£2,990	£4,590	Mrs Louise Robinson (GSA)
Howell's School GDST, Cardiff	1860	734	£2,310	–	Mrs Jane Fitz (GSA)
Llandovery College, Carmarthenshire	1847	312	£3,370	£5,085	Peter Hogan (HMC)
Monmouth School, Monmouth	1614	676	£2,989	£4,983	Tim Haynes (HMC)
Rougemont School, Gwent	1920	739	£2,373	–	Dr Jonathan Tribbick (HMC)
Ruthin School, North Wales	1284	245	£3,210	£5,170	John Rowlands (SHMIS)
Rydal Penrhos School, North Wales	1885	394	£3,541	£5,935	Michael S. James (HMC) (SHMIS)
St David's College, North Wales	1965	250	£3,384	£5,883	William G. Seymour (SHMIS)

SCOTLAND

School	Date founded	No. of pupils	Termly fees Day	Board	Head (with association affiliation)
Albyn School for Girls, Aberdeen	1867	390	£2,520	–	Dr John Halliday (GSA)
Craigholme School, Glasgow	1894	551	£2,380	–	Mrs Gillian Burt (GSA)
Dollar Academy, Dollar	1818	1,200	£2,412	£5,466	John Robertson (HMC)
High School of Dundee, Dundee	1239	1,042	£2,330	–	A. Michael Duncan (HMC)
The Edinburgh Academy, Edinburgh	1824	840	£2,901	£5,952	John Light (HMC)
Fernhill School, Glasgow	1972	165	£2,019	–	Mrs Louisa M. McLay (GSA)
Fettes College, Edinburgh	1870	581	£4,629	£6,733	Michael Spens (HMC)
George Heriot's School, Edinburgh	1628	1,547	£2,348	–	Alistair Hector (HMC)
George Watson's College, Edinburgh	1741	2,271	£2,496	–	Gareth Edwards (HMC)
The Glasgow Academy, Glasgow	1846	1,096	£2,460	–	David Comins (HMC)
The High School of Glasgow, Glasgow	1124	1,050	£2,502	–	Colin Mair (HMC)
Glenalmond College, Perthshire	1841	395	£4,575	£6,720	Gordon Woods (HMC)
Hutchesons' Grammar School, Glasgow	1641	2,086	£2,289	–	John Knowles (HMC)
Kelvinside Academy, Glasgow	1878	640	£2,673	–	John Broadfoot (HMC)
Kilgraston School, Perthshire	1920	225	£3,500	£5,930	Michael Farmer (GSA)
Lomond School, Argyll and Bute	1845	535	£2,446	£5,232	Angus Macdonald (SHMIS)
Loretto School, Midlothian	1827	416	£4,455	£6,676	Michael Mavor (HMC)
The Mary Erskine School, Edinburgh	1694	699	£2,418	£4,823	David Gray (GSA)
Merchiston Castle School, Edinburgh	1833	415	£4,690	£6,600	Andrew Hunter (HMC)
Morrison's Academy, Perthshire	1860	517	£2,427	£5,919	Simon Pengelley (HMC)
Robert Gordon's College, Aberdeen	1732	1,451	£2,410	–	Brian Lockhart (HMC)
St Aloysius' College, Glasgow	1859	1,300	£2,233	–	John Stoer (HMC)
St Columba's School, Renfrewshire	1897	720	£2,400	–	David G. Girdwood (HMC)
St George's School for Girls, Edinburgh	1888	1,020	£2,350	£5,075	Dr Judith McClure (GSA)
St Margaret's School for Girls, Aberdeen	1846	376	£2,409	–	Mrs Lyn McKay (GSA)
St Margaret's School, Edinburgh	1855	580	£2,327	£4,862	Mrs Eileen Davis (GSA)
Stewart's Melville College, Edinburgh	1832	710	£2,543	£4,823	David Gray (HMC)
Strathallan School, Perth	1913	450	£4,396	£6,504	Bruce K. Thompson (HMC)

NORTHERN IRELAND

School	Date founded	No. of pupils	Termly fees Day	Board	Head (with association affiliation)
Bangor Grammar School, Bangor	1856	1,010	£95	–	Stephen Connolly (HMC)
Belfast Royal Academy, Belfast	1785	1,566	£80	–	W. S. F. Young (HMC)
Campbell College, Belfast	1894	724	£575	£2,775	Dr Ivan Pollock (HMC)
Coleraine Academical Institution, Londonderry	1860	702	£75	–	Leonard F. Quigg (HMC)
The Methodist College, Belfast	1868	2,370	£27-£1,610	£3,663	Dr Wilfred Mulryne (HMC)
Portora Royal School, Enniskillen	1608	500	£25	–	J. Neill Morton (HMC)
The Royal Belfast Academical Institution, Belfast	1810	1,050	£230	–	Michael Ridley (HMC)
The Royal School, Dungannon	1614	660	£40	£3083	P. D. Hewitt (SHMIS)

BELGIUM

School	Date founded	No. of pupils	Termly fees Day	Board	Head (with association affiliation)
The British School of Brussels, 3080 Tervuren	1969	1,129	€7560	–	Roland S. Chant (HMC)

School	Date founded	No. of pupils	Termly fees Day	Board	Head (with association affiliation)
FRANCE					
International School of Paris, 75016 Paris	1964	450	€5,800	–	Gareth Jones (HMC)
ITALY					
St George's British International School, 00123 Rome	1958	610	€4,600	–	Nicholas Johnson (HMC)
Sir James Henderson School, 20134 Milan	1969	670	€3,100	–	Trevor Church (HMC)
NETHERLANDS					
The British School in the Netherlands, 2252 BG Voorschoten	1935	1,991	€4,300	–	Trevor Rowell (HMC)
PORTUGAL					
St Julian's School, 2776-601 Carcavelos	1932	914	€5,045	–	David Smith (HMC)
SPAIN					
King's College, 28761 Madrid	1969	1,352	€2,827	€4,963	Christopher T. Gill Leech (HMC)
SWITZERLAND					
Aiglon College, 1885 Chesieres-Villars	1949	333	14,167 SFr	21,467 SFr	Revd Dr Jonathan Long (HMC)
CHANNEL ISLANDS					
Elizabeth College, Guernsey	1563	740	£1,750	–	Dr N. D. Argent (HMC)
Ladies' College, Guernsey	1872	550	£1,170	–	Miss M. E. Macdonald (GSA)
Victoria College, Jersey	1852	900	£1,150	–	Robert Cook (HMC)

NATIONAL ACADEMIES OF SCHOLARSHIP

BRITISH ACADEMY (1902)
10 Carlton House Terrace, London SW1Y 5AH
T 020-7969 5200 F 020-7969 5300
W www.britac.ac.uk

The British Academy is an independent, self-governing learned society for the promotion of the humanities and social sciences. It supports advanced academic research and is a channel for the Government's support of research in those disciplines.

The Fellows are scholars who have attained distinction in one of the branches of study that the Academy exists to promote. Candidates must be nominated by existing Fellows. There are 770 Ordinary Fellows, 15 Honorary Fellows and 306 Corresponding Fellows overseas.

President, The Viscount Runciman, PBA
Treasurer, Prof. R. J. P. Kain, FBA
Foreign Secretary, Prof. C. N. J. Mann, FBA
Publications Secretary, Dr D. J. McKitterick, FBA
Secretary, P. W. H. Brown, CBE

ROYAL ACADEMY OF ARTS (1768)
Burlington House, Piccadilly, London W1J 0BD
T 020-7300 8000 F 020-7300 8001
W www.royalacademy.org.uk

The Royal Academy of Arts is an independent, self-governing society devoted to the encouragement and promotion of the fine arts.

Membership of the Academy is limited to 80 Royal Academicians, all being painters, engravers, sculptors or architects. Candidates are nominated and elected by the existing Academicians. There is also a limited class of honorary membership and there were 20 honorary members as at June 2004.

President, Prof. P. King, CBE, PRA
Treasurer, Prof. P. Huxley, RA
Keeper, Prof. B. Neiland, RA
Secretary, Miss L. Fitt

ROYAL ACADEMY OF ENGINEERING (1976)
29 Great Peter Street, London SW1P 3LW
T 020-7222 2688 F 020-7233 0054
W www.raeng.org.uk

The Royal Academy of Engineering was established as the Fellowship of Engineering in 1976. It was granted a royal charter in 1983 and its present title in 1992. It is an independent, self-governing body whose object is the pursuit, encouragement and maintenance of excellence in the whole field of engineering, in order to promote the advancement of the science, art and practice of engineering for the benefit of the public.

Election to the Fellowship is by invitation only, from nominations supported by the body of Fellows. At June 2004 there were 1,324 Fellows. The Duke of Edinburgh is the Senior Fellow and the Duke of Kent is a Royal Fellow.

President, Sir Alec Broers, FRS, FRENG
Senior Vice-President, Sir Duncan Michael, FRENG

Vice-Presidents, G. A. Campbell, FRENG; P. Saraga, OBE, FRENG; Dr S. E. Ion, OBE, FRENG; P. C. Ruffles, CBE, FRS, FRENG; Dr S. Steedman, FRENG; Sir Peter Williams, CBE, FRS, FRENG
Hon. Treasurer, C. Price, FRENG
Hon. Secretaries, P. Saraga, OBE, FRENG *(International Activities)*; Dr Julia King, CBE, FRENG *(Education and Training)*
Chief Executive, J. Burch

ROYAL SCOTTISH ACADEMY (1838)
The Mound, Edinburgh EH2 2EL
T 0131-225 6671 W www.royalscottishacademy.org

The Scottish Academy was founded in 1826 to arrange exhibitions of contemporary paintings and to establish a society of fine art in Scotland. The Academy was granted a royal charter in 1838.

Members are elected from the disciplines of painting, sculpture, architecture and printmaking. Elections are from nominations put forward by the existing membership. At mid-2004 there were four Senior Academicians, five Senior Associates, 36 Academicians, 46 Associates, four non-resident Associates and 20 Honorary Members.

President, I. McKenzie Smith, OBE, PRSA
Secretary, W. Scott, RSA
Treasurer, I. Metzstein, RSA
Administrative Secretary, B. Laidlaw, ACIS

ROYAL SOCIETY (1660)
6–9 Carlton House Terrace, London SW1Y 5AG
T 020-7839 5561 F 020-7930 2170
W www.royalsoc.ac.uk

The Royal Society is an independent academy promoting the natural and applied sciences. Founded in 1660, the Society has three roles, as the UK academy of science, as a learned Society and as a funding agency. It is an independent, self-governing body under a royal charter, promoting and advancing all fields of physical and biological sciences, of mathematics and engineering, medical and agricultural sciences and their application.

Fellows are elected for their contributions to science, both in fundamental research resulting in greater understanding, and also in leading and directing scientific and technological progress in industry and research establishments. A maximum of 42 new Fellows, who must be citizens or residents of the British Commonwealth countries or Ireland, may be elected annually.

Up to six Foreign Members, who are selected from those not eligible to become Fellows because of citizenship or residency, are elected annually for their contributions to science.

One Honorary Fellow may be elected each year from those not eligible for election as Fellows or Foreign members. There are approximately 1,300 Fellows and Foreign Members covering all scientific disciplines.

President, Lord May of Oxford, Kt., AC
Treasurer, Prof. D. Wallace, CBE, FRS
Biological Secretary, Prof. D. Read, FRS
Physical Secretary, Prof. J. Enderby, CBE, FRS

Foreign Secretary, Prof. Dame J. Higgins, DBE, FRS
Executive Secretary, S. Cox, CVO

ROYAL SOCIETY OF EDINBURGH (1783)

22–26 George Street, Edinburgh EH2 2PQ
T 0131-240 5000 F 0131-240 5024
W www.royalsoced.org.uk

The Royal Society of Edinburgh (RSE) is Scotland's National Academy. A wholly independent, non party-political body with charitable status, the RSE provides a forum for broadly-based interdisciplinary activity in Scotland. This includes organising conferences and lectures both for the specialist and for the general public; providing independent, expert advice to key decision making bodies, including Government and Parliament; strengthening links between academia and industry and boosting wealth generation at home. The Society's Research Awards programme annually awards nearly half a million pounds to exceptionally talented young academics and potential entrepreneurs in Scotland.

Fellows are elected by ballot after being nominated by at least four existing Fellows. Elections are held annually, on the first Monday in March.

At June 2004 there were 1,280 Ordinary Fellows, 71 Honorary Fellows and 24 Corresponding Fellows.
President, Lord Sutherland of Houndwood, Kt., FBA, FRSE
Vice-Presidents, Prof. J. Coggins, FRSE; Prof. A. C. Walker, FRSE; Prof. Gavin McCrone, CB, FRSE
Treasurer, Prof. Sir Laurence Hunter, CBE, FRSE
General Secretary, Prof. A. Miller, CBE, FRSE

THE RESEARCH COUNCILS

The Government funds basic and applied civil science research, mostly through the seven research councils, which are supported by the Department of Trade and Industry. The councils support research and training in universities and other higher education establishments. They also receive income for research commissioned by Government departments and the private sector. A total of £356 million of resource is being added to the science budget over three years from 2002 to increase basic research. Of this, £252 million, (including £12 million of capital) will be directed to cross-council research programmes in genomics, e-science and basic technology. The remaining £104 million of resource is added to the science budget, mainly to provide an uplift to existing council programmes. In July 2000, the Chancellor announced a further £1 billion of investment in science infrastructure over the years 2002–4, comprising £755 million from Government and £225 million from the Wellcome Trust.

The Government science budget for 2004–5 includes the following allocations:

	2004–5 £m
BBSRC	285.007
ESRC	102.694
EPSRC	490.519
MRC	435.088
NERC	266.687
PPARC	259.180
*CLRC	8.113
Pensions	31.140
Royal Society	31.045
Royal Academy of Engineering	5.600
Diamond	10.081
Higher Education Innovation Fund	60.305
Science Research Investment Fund	296.570
Cambridge/MIT	14.000
Exchange Rate and Contingency	25.000
OST Managed Funds	58.364
Exploitation of Discoveries at PSREs	4.655

*partially funded by the European Union

BIOTECHNOLOGY AND BIOLOGICAL SCIENCES RESEARCH COUNCIL (BBSRC)
Polaris House, North Star Avenue, Swindon SN2 1UH
T 01793-413200

The BBSRC promotes and supports research and postgraduate training relating to the understanding and exploitation of biological systems; advances knowledge and technology; provides trained scientists to meet the needs of biotechnological-related industries; and provides advice, disseminates knowledge, and promotes public understanding of biotechnology and the biological sciences.
Chairman, Dr P. Ringrose
Chief Executive, Prof. J. Goodfellow, CBE

INSTITUTES
BABRAHAM INSTITUTE, Babraham Hall, Babraham, Cambridge CB2 4AT T 01223-496000
Director, Dr R. G. Dyer,

INSTITUTE FOR ANIMAL HEALTH, Compton Laboratory, Compton, Newbury, Berks RG20 7NN T 01635-578411
Director, Prof. P. P. Pastoret

BBSRC/MRC NEUROPATHOGENESIS UNIT, Ogston Building, West Mains Road, Edinburgh EH9 3JF
T 0131-667 5204

PIRBRIGHT LABORATORY, Ash Road, Pirbright, Woking, Surrey GU24 0NF T 01483-232441
Director, Dr A. I. Donaldson

ROTHAMSTED RESEARCH, Rothamsted, Harpenden, Herts AL5 2JQ T 01582-763133 *Director*, Prof. I. R. Crute

BROOM'S BARN, Higham, Bury St Edmunds, Suffolk IP28 6NP
T 01284-812200 *Director*, Dr J. D. Pidgeon

INSTITUTE OF FOOD RESEARCH, Norwich Research Park, Colney Lane, Norwich NR4 7UA T 01603-255000
Director, Prof. D. White

INSTITUTE OF GRASSLAND AND ENVIRONMENTAL RESEARCH, Aberystwyth Research Centre, Plas Gogerddan, Aberystwyth, SY23 3EB
T 01970-823000 *Director*, Prof. C. Pollock, OBE

NORTH WYKE RESEARCH STATION, Okehampton, Devon EX20 2SB T 01837-883500 *Head*, Prof. S. Jarvis

JOHN INNES CENTRE, Norwich Research Park, Colney, Norwich NR4 7UH T 01603-452571
Director, Prof. C. Lamb

ROSLIN INSTITUTE, Roslin, Midlothian EH25 9PS
T 0131-527 4200 *Director*, Prof. John Clarke

SILSOE RESEARCH INSTITUTE, Wrest Park, Silsoe, Bedford MK45 4HS T 01525-860000 *Director*, Prof. B. Day

SCOTTISH EXECUTIVE ENVIRONMENT AND RURAL AFFAIRS DEPARTMENT

BIOMATHEMATICS AND STATISTICS SCOTLAND BioSS (administered by SCRI), University of Edinburgh, James Clerk Maxwell Building, The King's Buildings, Mayfield Road, Edinburgh EH9 3JZ T 0131-650 4900
Acting Director, David Elstan
HANNAH RESEARCH INSTITUTE, Hannah Research Park, Ayr KA6 5HL T 01292-674000
Director, Prof. Chris Knight
MACAULAY LAND USE RESEARCH INSTITUTE, Craigiebuckler, Aberdeen AB15 8QH T 01224-498200
Director, Prof. E. M. Gill
MOREDUN RESEARCH INSTITUTE, Pentlands Science Park, Bush Loan, Penicuik, Midlothian EH26 0PZ
T 0131-445 5111 *Director*, Prof. Julie Fitzpatrick

ROWETT RESEARCH INSTITUTE, Greenburn Road, Bucksburn, Aberdeen AB21 9SB T 01224-712751 *Director,* Prof. P. J. Morgan
SCOTTISH CROP RESEARCH INSTITUTE (SCRI), Invergowrie, Dundee DD2 5DA T 01382-562731 *Director,* Prof. J. Hillman, FRSE

COUNCIL FOR THE CENTRAL LABORATORY OF THE RESEARCH COUNCILS (CCLRC)

Rutherford Appleton Laboratory, Chilton, Didcot, Oxon OX11 0QX
T 01235-445553 F 01235-446665
W www.cclrc.ac.uk

The CCLRC is a non-departmental body of the Office of Science and Technology, which is part of the Department of Trade and Industry. It is the national portal and centre for key, large-scale research facilities in support of science and engineering research. In particular, the CCLRC has strategic and operational roles in respect of neutron scattering, synchrotron radiation and high power laser facilities. These will enable UK researchers to carry out world-leading science. As well as providing strategic advice, the CCLRC also provides facilities for scientists to research a broad spectrum of applications, from the molecular structure of drugs enabling them to be targeted to maximise efficiency and minimise side effects, to the discovery of planets in distant galaxies.

The CCLRC operates the Rutherford Appleton Laboratory in Oxfordshire, the Daresbury Laboratory in Cheshire and the Chilbolton Observatory in Hampshire.
Chairman, Prof. Sir Graeme Davies
Chief Executive, Prof. J. Wood

CHILBOLTON OBSERVATORY, Stockbridge, Hampshire SO20 6BJ T 01264-860391
DARESBURY LABORATORY, Daresbury, Warrington, Cheshire WA4 4AD T 01925-603000
RUTHERFORD APPLETON LABORATORY, Chilton, Didcot, Oxon OX11 0QX T 01235-445000

ECONOMIC AND SOCIAL RESEARCH COUNCIL (ESRC)

Polaris House, North Star Avenue, Swindon SN2 1UJ
T 01793-413000
E comms@esrc.ac.uk W www.esrc.ac.uk

The purpose of the ESRC is to promote and support research and postgraduate training in the social sciences; to advance knowledge and provide trained social scientists; to provide advice on, and disseminate knowledge and promote public understanding of the social sciences.
Chairman, F. Cairncross, CBE
Chief Executive, I. Diamond

RESEARCH CENTRES
CENTRE FOR ANALYSIS OF RISK AND RELEGATION, London School of Economics and Political Science, Houghton Street, London WC2A 2AE T 020-7955 6577 *Directors,* Prof. M. Power; Prof. B. Hutter
CENTRE FOR THE ANALYSIS OF SOCIAL EXCLUSION, London School of Economics, Houghton Street, London WC2A 2AE T 020-7955 7419 *Director,* Prof. J. Hills
CENTRE FOR BUSINESS RELATIONSHIPS, ACCOUNTABILITY, SUSTAINABILITY AND SOCIETY, Cardiff University, 54 Park Place, Cardiff CF10 3AT T 029-7955 6577, *Director,* Prof. K. Peattie

CENTRE FOR BUSINESS RESEARCH, Department of Applied Economics, University of Cambridge, Sidgwick Avenue, Cambridge CB3 9DE T 01223-335248 *Director,* Prof. A. Hughes
CENTRE FOR ECONOMIC AND SOCIAL ASPECTS OF GENOMICS, Lancaster University, Furness College, Lancaster, RA1 4YG T 01524-592503 *Director,* Prof. R. Chadwick
CENTRE FOR ECONOMIC LEARNING AND SOCIAL EVOLUTION, Department of Economics, University College London, Gower Street, London WC1E 6BT T 020-7387 7050 *Research Director,* Prof. T. Börgers
CENTRE FOR ECONOMIC PERFORMANCE, London School of Economics, Houghton Street, London WC2A 2AE T 020-7955 7048 *Directors,* Prof. R. Layard; Prof. R. Freeman
CENTRE FOR GENOMICS IN SOCIETY, University of Exeter, Amory Building, Rennes Drive, Exeter, Devon, EX4 4RJ T 01392-262053 *Director,* J. Dupré
CENTRE FOR MICROECONOMIC ANALYSIS OF PUBLIC POLICY (CMAPP), Institute for Fiscal Studies, 7 Ridgmount Street, London WC1E 7AE T 020-7636 3784 *Director,* Prof. R. Blundell
CENTRE FOR ORGANISATION AND INNOVATION, Institute of Work Psychology, University of Sheffield, Sheffield S10 2TN T 0114-222 3287 *Director,* Prof. T. Wall
CENTRE FOR RESEARCH ON INNOVATION AND COMPETITION, Faculty of Economic and Social Studies, University of Manchester M13 9PL T 0161-275 2000 *Directors,* Prof. S. Metcalfe; Prof. R. Coombs
CENTRE FOR SKILLS, KNOWLEDGE AND ORGANISATIONAL PERFORMANCE (SKOPE), University of Oxford, Department of Economics, Manor Road, Oxford, OX1 3UP T 01865-271087 *Director,* K. Mayhews
CENTRE FOR SOCIAL AND ECONOMIC RESEARCH ON INNOVATION IN GENOMICS, The University of Edinburgh, Old Surgeon's Hall, High School Yards, Edinburgh, EH1 1LZ T 0131-650 9113 *Director,* Prof. J. Tait
CENTRE FOR SOCIAL AND ECONOMIC RESEARCH ON THE GLOBAL ENVIRONMENT, School of Environmental Sciences, University of East Anglia, Norwich NR4 7TJ T 01603-593176 *Director,* Prof. R. K. Turner
CENTRE FOR THE STUDY OF GLOBALISATION AND REGIONALISATION, Department of Political Science, University of Warwick, Coventry CV4 7AL T 024-7652 3916 *Directors,* Prof. R. Higgott; J. Whalley
CENTRE ON MICRO-SOCIAL CHANGE, University of Essex, Wivenhoe Park, Colchester, Essex CO4 3SQ T 01206-872957 *Director,* Prof. J. Ermisch
CENTRE ON MIGRATION, POLICY AND SOCIETY, University of Oxford, 58 Banbury Road, Oxford OX2 6QS T 01865-274711, *Director,* Dr S. Vertovec
COMPLEX PRODUCT SYSTEMS INNOVATION CENTRE, SPRU, Mantell Building, University of Sussex, Brighton BN1 9RF T 01273-686758 *Director,* Prof. M. Hobday
FINANCIAL MARKETS CENTRE, London School of Economics, Houghton Street, London WC2A 2AE T 020-7955 7002 *Director,* Prof. D. Webb
TRANSPORT STUDIES UNIT, Centre for Transport Studies, University College London, Gower Street, London WC1E 6BT T 020-7380 7009 *Director,* Prof. P. Goodwin

RESOURCE CENTRES
CENTRE FOR APPLIED SOCIAL SURVEYS, Social and Community Planning Research, 35 Northampton Square, London EC1V 0AX T 020-7250 1866 *Director,* R. Thomas

CENTRE FOR ECONOMIC POLICY RESEARCH, 90–98
Goswell Road, London EC1V 7DB T 020-7878 2900
Director, Prof. R. Portes

ESRC DATA ARCHIVE, University of Essex, Wivenhoe Park,
Colchester, Essex CO4 3SQ T 01206-872001
Director, K. Schurer

ESRC UK CENTRE FOR EVIDENCE BASED POLICY,
Queen Mary and Westfield College, Department of Politics,
Mile End Road, London E1 4NS
Director, Prof. K. Young

INTERNATIONAL BIBLIOGRAPHY OF THE SOCIAL
SCIENCES, British Library of Political and Economic Science,
London School of Economics, Houghton Street, London
WC2A 2AE T 020-7955 7000
Director, Ms J. Sykes

INTERNATIONAL BIBLIOGRAPHY OF THE SOCIAL
SCIENCES: ON-LINE RESOURCE CENTRE, LSE, 10
Portugal Street, London WC2A 2HD T 020-7955 7455
Director, Ms. L. Brindley

QUALITATIVE DATA ARCHIVAL RESOURCE CENTRE,
Department of Sociology, University of Essex, Colchester,
Essex CO4 3SQ T 01206-873058
Director, Prof. P. Thompson

RESOURCE CENTRE FOR ACCESS TO DATA IN EUROPE,
Department of Geography, University of Durham, Durham
DH1 3HP T 0191-374 7350 *Director*, Prof. R. Hudson

ENGINEERING AND PHYSICAL SCIENCES RESEARCH COUNCIL (EPSRC)

Polaris House, North Star Avenue, Swindon SN2 1ET
T 01793-444000 W www.epsrc.ac.uk

The EPSRC is the largest of the UK Research Councils and funds research and postgraduate training in engineering, the physical sciences and basic technology in universities and other organisations throughout the UK. It also provides advice, disseminates knowledge and promotes public understanding in these areas.
Chairman, Prof. Dame Julia Higgins, FRS, FRENG
Chief Executive, Prof. J. O'Reilly, FRENG, CENG

MEDICAL RESEARCH COUNCIL (MRC)

20 Park Crescent, London W1B 1AL
T 020-7636 5422 F 020-7436 2663 W www.mrc.ac.uk

The purpose of the MRC is to promote medical and related biological research. The council employs its own research staff and funds research by other institutions and individuals, complementing the research resources of the universities and hospitals.
Chairman, Sir Anthony Cleaver
Chief Executive, Prof. Colin Blakemore
Chairman, Neurosciences and Mental Health Board,
Prof. A. North
Chairman, Molecular and Cellular Medicine Board,
Prof. M. Wakelam
Chairman, Infections and Immunity Board,
Prof. A. McMichael
Chairman, Health Services and Public Health Research Board,
Dr D. Armstrong
Chairman, Physiological and Clinical Sciences Board,
Prof. John Savill

MRC RESEARCH CENTRES

Biostatistics Unit W www.mrc-bsu.cam.ac.uk
Cambridge Centre for Behavioural and Clinical Neuroscience
T 01223-333558
Cancer Cell Unit W www.hutchison-mrc.cam.ac.uk

Cell Biology Unit W www.ucl.ac.uk/lmcb
MRC/UCl Centre Development for Medical Molecular Virology
T 020-7679 9119
W www.ucl.ac.uk/windeyer-institute/institute/mrc.htm
MRC/University of Newcastle Centre Development in Clinical Brain Ageing
W www.ncl.ac.uk/iah/cdcba.htm
Centre for Developmental Neurobiology
W www.kcl.ac.uk/depsta/biomedical/mrcdevbiol
MRC/University of Edinburgh Centre for Inflammation Research
W www.med.ed.ac.uk/idg/inflamrs.htm
Centre for Protein Engineering
W www.mrc-cpe.cam.ac.uk
MRC/University of Bristol Centre for Synaptic Plasticity
W www.bris.ac.uk/depts/synaptic
Clinical Sciences Centre W www.csc.mrc.ac.uk
Clinical Trials Unit W www.ctu.mrc.ac.uk
Cognition and Brain Sciences Unit
W www.mrc-cbu.cam.ac.uk
Dunn Human Nutrition Unit
W www.mrc-dunn.cam.ac.uk
Epidemiology Unit T 01223-330315
Epidemiology Resource Centre T 023-8077 7624
Functional Genetics Unit W www.mrcfgu.ox.ac.uk
MRC/University of Sussex Genome Damage and Stability Centre
W www.biols.susx.ac.uk/gdsc/frameset
Health Services Research Collaboration
W www.hsrc.ac.uk
Human Genetics Unit W www.hgu.mrc.ac.uk
Human Immunology Unit
W www.jr2.ox.ac.uk/mrc-hiu/pages.home.htm
Human Reproductive Sciences Unit
W www.hrsu.mrc.ac.uk
Immunochemistry Unit
W www.bioch.ox.ac.uk/immunoch
MRC/University of Birmingham Centre for Immune Regulation
W www.bham.ac.uk/mrcbcir/home.htm
Institute for Environment and Health
W www.le.ac.uk/ieh
Institute of Hearing Research
W www.ihr.mrc.ac.uk
Laboratories Fajara, The Gambia
W www.extra.mrc.ac.uk/gambia
Laboratory of Molecular Biology
T 01223-248011 W www2.mrc-lmb.cam.ac.uk
MRC/UCL Laboratory for Molecular Virology
T 020-7679 9119
Mammalian Genetics Unit
T 01235-841000 W www.mgu.har.mrc.ac.uk
Molecular Haemotology Unit T 01865-222443
W www.imm.ox.ac.uk/groups/mrc_molhaem
National Institute for Medical Research
W www.nimr.mrc.ac.uk
Prion Unit W www.prion.ucl.ac.uk
Protein Phosphorylation Unit
W www.dundee.ac.uk/lifesciences/mrcppu
Radiation and Genome Stability Unit
W www.ragsu.har.mrc.ac.uk
Resource Centre for Human Nutrition Research
W www.mrc-hnr.cam.ac.uk
Rosalind Franklin Centre for Genomics Research
W www.hgmp.mrc.ac.uk
Social and Public Health Sciences Unit
W www.msoc-mrc.gla.ac.uk

Social, Genetic and Developmental Psychiatry Centre
  W www.iop.kcl.ac.uk/iopweb/departments/home/
  default.aspx?locator=10
Toxicology Unit W www.le.ac.uk/cmht
Virology Unit W www.vir.gla.ac.uk

NATURAL ENVIRONMENT RESEARCH COUNCIL (NERC)
Polaris House, North Star Avenue, Swindon SN2 1EU
T 01793-411500 F 01793-411501
W www.nerc.ac.uk

The UK's Natural Environment Research Council (NERC) funds and carries out impartial scientific research in the sciences of the environment. Its work covers the full range of atmospheric, earth, terrestrial and aquatic sciences, from the depth of the oceans to the upper atmosphere. Its mission is to gather and apply knowledge, create understanding and predict the behaviour of the natural environment and its resources.
Chairman, R. Margetts, CBE, FRENG
Chief Executive, Prof. J. Lawton, CBE, FRS

RESEARCH CENTRES
BRITISH ANTARCTIC SURVEY, High Cross, Madingley
  Road, Cambridge, CB3 OET T 01223-221400
  Director, Prof. C. Rapley
BRITISH GEOLOGICAL SURVEY, Kingsley Dunham Centre,
  Keyworth, Nottingham, NG12 5GG
  T 0115-936 3100 *Executive Director*, Dr D. Falvey
CENTRE FOR ECOLOGY AND HYDROLOGY (CEH),
  Corporate Planning Office, Polaris House, North Star
  Avenue, Swindon, SN2 1EU T 01793-442524
  Director, Prof. P. Nuttall, OBE
PROUDMAN OCEANOGRAPHIC LABORATORY, Joseph
  Proudman Building, 6 Brownlow Street, Liverpool L3 5DA
  T 0151-795 4800 *Director*, Dr E. Hill

COLLABORATIVE CENTRES
CENTRE OF OBSERVATION OF AIR-SEA INTERACTIONS
  AND FLUXES, PLYMOUTH MARINE LABORATORY,
  Prospect Place, Plymouth, PL1 3DH *Director*, Prof. J. Aiken
CENTRE FOR OBSERVATION AND MODELLING OF
  EARTHQUAKES AND TECTONICS, COMET Centre of
  Excellence, Department of Earth Sciences, University of
  Oxford, Parks Road, Oxford OX1 3PR T 01865-272030
  Head of Department, Prof. J. Woodhouse
CENTRE FOR POLAR OBSERVATION AND MODELLING,
  Department of Space and Climate Physics, Pearson Building,
  University College London, Gower Street, London WC1E
  6BT T 020-7679 3031 *Director*, Prof. Duncan Wingham
CENTRE FOR POPULATION BIOLOGY, Imperial College,
  Silwood Park, Ascot, SL5 7PY T 0200-7594 2474
  Director, Prof. J. Godfray
CLIMATE AND LAND SURFACE SYSTEMS INTERACTION
  CENTRE, University of Wales Swansea, Singleton Park,
  Swansea, SA2 8PP T 01792-295647
  Director, Prof. M. Barnsley
DATA ASSIMILATION RESEARCH CENTRE, Department of
  Meteorology, University of Reading, Reading RG6 6BB
  T 0118-931 6981 *Director*, Prof. A. O'Neill
ENVIRONMENTAL SYSTEMS SCIENCE CENTRE,
  University of Reading, PO Box 238, Reading, RG6 6AL
  T 0118-931 8741 *Director*, Prof. R. Gurney

NATIONAL INSTITUTE FOR ENVIRONMENTAL
  E-SCIENCE, Centre for Mathematical Science, Wilberforce
  Road, Cambridge, CB3 0WA T 01223-764289
  Director, Dr M. Dove
NERC CENTRES FOR ATMOSPHERIC SCIENCE, University
  of Reading, Earley Gate, PO Box 243, Reading RG6 6BB
  T 0118-378 6452 *Director*, Prof. A. Thorpe
NCAS ATMOSPHERIC CHEMISTRY MODELLING
  SUPPORT UNIT, Dept of Chemistry, University of
  Cambridge, Lensfield Road, Cambridge CB2 1EW
  T 01223-336473 *Director*, Prof. J. Pyle
NCAS BRITISH ATMOSPHERIC DATA CENTRE,
  Rutherford Appleton Laboratory, Chilton, Didcot, OX11 0QX
  T 01235-446432 *Director*, Dr B. Lawrence
NCAS CENTRE FOR GLOBAL ATMOSPHERIC
  MODELLING, Department of Meteorology, University of
  Reading, PO Box 243, Earley Gate, Reading, RG6 6BB
  T 0118-378 8315 *Director*, Prof. J. Slingo
NCAS DISTRIBUTED INSTITUTE FOR ATMOSPHERIC
  COMPOSITION, School of Chemistry, University of Leeds,
  Leeds, LS2 9JT T 0113-343 6450 *Director*, Prof. M. Pilling
NCAS FACILITY FOR AIRBORNE ATMOSPHERIC
  MEASUREMENTS, Physics Dept, UMIST, PO Box 88,
  Manchester, M60 1QD T 0161-200 3936
  Director, Prof. P. Jonas
NCAS UNIVERSITIES FACILITY FOR ATMOSPHERIC
  MEASUREMENTS, School of Environment, University of
  Leeds, Leeds, LS2 9JT T 0113-343 1632
  Director, Dr A. Blyth
NCAS UNIVERSITIES WEATHER RESEARCH NETWORK,
  Dept of Meteorology, University of Reading, PO Box 243,
  Earley Gate, Reading, RG6 6BB T 0118-931 6311
  Director, Prof. P. Mason
NERC CENTRE FOR TERRESTRIAL CARBON
  DYNAMICS, University of Sheffield, Hicks Building,
  Hounsfield Road, Sheffield S3 7RH T 0114-222 3803
PLYMOUTH MARINE LABORATORY, Prospect Place, West
  Hoe, Plymouth, PL1 3DH T 01752-633100
  Director, Prof. N. Owens
SCOTTISH ASSOCIATION FOR MARINE SCIENCE,
  Dunstaffnage Marine Laboratory, by Dunbeg, Oban, Argyll,
  PA37 1QA T 01631-559000 *Director*, Prof. G. Shimmield
SEA MAMMAL RESEARCH UNIT, Gatty Marine Laboratory,
  University of St Andrews, Fife, KY16 8LB T 01334-462630
  Director, Prof. I. Boyd
SOUTHAMPTON OCEANOGRAPHY CENTRE, University
  of Southampton, European Way, Southampton, SO14 3ZH
  T 023-8059 6666 *Director*, Prof. H. Roe
TYNDALL CENTRE, School of Environmental Sciences,
  University of East Anglia, Norwich, Norfolk NR4 7TJ
  T 01603-593900 *Director*, Dr M. Hulme

PARTICLE PHYSICS AND ASTRONOMY RESEARCH COUNCIL (PPARC)
Polaris House, North Star Avenue, Swindon SN2 1SZ
T 01793-442000 F 01793-442125
E pr.pus@pparc.ac.uk

The Particle Physics and Astronomy Research Centre (PPARC) is the UK's strategic science investment agency. It funds research, education and public understanding in four broad areas of science – particle physics, astronomy, cosmology and space sciences.
  PPARC is government funded and provides research grants and studentships to scientists in British universities, gives researchers access to world-class facilities and funds the UK membership of international bodies such as the European Laboratory for Particle Physics (CERN), the

European Space Agency (ESA) and The European Southern Observatory (ESO). It also contributes money to the UK telescopes overseas on La Palma, Hawaii, Australia and in Chile, the UK Astronomy Technology Centre at the Royal Observatory, Edinburgh and the MERLIN/ VLBI National Facility.
Chairman, P. Warry
Chief Executive, Prof. I. Halliday, FRSE, FINSTP

ISAAC NEWTON GROUP OF TELESCOPES, Apartado de Coreos 321, Santa Cruz de la Palma, Tenerife 38780, Canary Islands T +34 922-42500 *Director,* R. Rutten
JOINT ASTRONOMY CENTRE, 660 N A'ohoku Place, University Park, Hilo, Hawaii, USA T +808 96720 *Director,* Prof. G. Davies
UK ASTRONOMY TECHNOLOGY CENTRE, Blackford Hill, Edinburgh EH9 3HJ T 0131-668 8100 *Director,* Dr A. Russell

RESEARCH AND TECHNOLOGY ORGANISATIONS

The following industrial and technological research bodies are members of the Applied Industrial Research Trading Organisations (AIRTO). Members' activities span a wide range of disciplines from life sciences to engineering. Their work includes basic research, development and design of innovative products or processes, instrumentation testing and certification, and technology and management consultancy. AIRTO publishes a directory to help clients identify the organisations that might be able to assist them.

AIRTO, c/o CCFRA, Station Road, Chipping Campden, Gloucestershire, GL55 6LD T 01386-842247
President, Prof. R. Brook
ADVANCED MANUFACTURING TECHNOLOGY RESEARCH INSTITUTE, Hulley Road, Macclesfield, Cheshire SK10 2NE T 01625-425421
Managing Director, P. Sholl
AIRCRAFT RESEARCH ASSOCIATION LTD, Manton Lane, Bedford MK41 7PF T 01234-350681
Chief Executive, B. Timmins
BLC (THE LEATHER TECHNOLOGY CENTRE), Leather Trade House, Kings Park Road, Moulton Park, Northants NN3 6JD T 01604-679999 *Chief Executive,* M. Parsons
BRE (BUILDING RESEARCH ESTABLISHMENT), Garston, Watford, Hertfordshire WD2 7JR T 01923-664000
Chief Executive, Dr M. Wyatt
BREWING RESEARCH INTERNATIONAL,
Lyttel Hall, Coopers Hill Road, Nutfield, Surrey RH1 4HY T 01737-822272
Director-General, Dr M. Kierstan
BRITISH MARITIME TECHNOLOGY LTD, Orlando House, 1 Waldegrave Road, Teddington, Middx TW11 8LZ T 020-8943 5544 *Chief Executive,* R. Swann
BRITISH TEXTILE TECHNOLOGY GROUP, Wira House, West Park Ring Road, Leeds LS16 6QL T 0113-259 1999; Shirley House, Wilmslow Road, Didsbury, Manchester M20 2RB T 0161-445 8141 *Chief Executive,* A. King
BUILDING SERVICES RESEARCH AND INFORMATION ASSOCIATION, Old Bracknell Lane West, Bracknell, Berks RG12 7AH T 01344-465526 *Chief Executive,* A. Eastwell
CAMPDEN AND CHORLEYWOOD FOOD RESEARCH ASSOCIATION, Chipping Campden, Glos GL55 6LD T 01386-842000 *Director-General,* Prof. C. Dennis

CENTRAL LABORATORY OF THE RESEARCH COUNCILS, Chilton, Didcot, Oxfordshire, OX11 0QX T 01235-821900 *Chief Executive,* Prof. J. Wood
CERAM RESEARCH (BRITISH CERAMIC RESEARCH LTD), Queen's Road, Penkhull, Stoke-on-Trent ST4 7LQ T 01782-764444 *Chief Executive,* Dr N. E. Sanderson
CIRIA (CONSTRUCTION INDUSTRY RESEARCH AND INFORMATION ASSOCIATION), Classic House, 174–180 Old St., London EC1V 9BP T 020-7549 3300 *Director-General,* Dr T. Broyd
CRL (Specialist products, technology licences, research and development), Dawley Road, Hayes, Middx UB3 1HH T 020-8848 9779 *Managing Director,* Dr B. Holcroft
FIRA INTERNATIONAL LTD (FURNITURE INDUSTRY RESEARCH ASSOCIATION), Maxwell Road, Stevenage, Herts SG1 2EW T 01438-777700
Managing Director, H. Davies
HR WALLINGFORD GROUP LTD (Hydroinformatics and engineering), Howbery Park, Wallingford, Oxon OX10 8BA T 01491-835381 *Chief Executive,* Dr S. W. Huntington
ITRI LIMITED (Tin and chemicals), Kingston Lane, Uxbridge, Middlesex UB8 3PJ T 01895-272 406
Chief Executive, D. Bishop
LGC, Queens Road, Teddington, Middx TW11 0LY T 020-8943 7000
Chief Executive and Government Chemist, Dr R. Worswick
LEATHERHEAD FOOD INTERNATIONAL, Randalls Road, Leatherhead, Surrey KT22 7RY T 01372-376761
Director, J. Bevington
MATERIALS ENGINEERING RESEARCH LABORATORY LTD, Tamworth Road, Hertford SG13 7DG T 01992-500120 *Managing Director,* Dr. R. H. Martin
MOTOR INDUSTRY RESEARCH ASSOCIATION, Watling Street, Nuneaton, Warks CV10 0TU T 024-7635 5000 *Managing Director,* J. R. Wood
MOTOR INSURANCE REPAIR RESEARCH CENTRE, Colthorp Lane, Thatcham, Berks RG19 4NP T 01635-868855 *Chief Executive,* P. Roberts
NATIONAL COMPUTING CENTRE LTD, Oxford House, Oxford Road, Manchester M1 7ED T 0161-242 2499
Chief Executive, M. Gough
NATIONAL PHYSICAL LABORATORY, Queens Road, Teddington, Middx TW11 0LW T 020-8977 3222
Chief Executive, Dr B. McGuiness
NCIMB LIMITED (Microbiological supply and bacterial culture collection), 23 St Machar Drive, Aberdeen, AB24 3RY T 01224-273332 *Chief Executive,* Dr A. Syms
PAINT RESEARCH ASSOCIATION, 8 Waldegrave Road, Teddington, Middx TW11 8LD T 020-8614 4800
Acting Managing Director, Company Secretary and Finance Director, J. Marshall
PERA GROUP (Multi-disciplinary research, design, development and consultancy), Pera Innovation Park, Melton Mowbray, Leicestershire LE13 0PB T 01664-501501 *Chief Executive,* Dr P. Davies, CBE
QINETIQ (Science Consultancy), Cody Building, Ively Road, Farnborough, Hants GU14 0LX T 08700-100942
Chief Executive, Sir John Chisholm, FENG
RAPRA TECHNOLOGY LTD (Rubber and plastics), Shawbury, Shrewsbury SY4 4NR T 01939-250383; North East Centre, 18 Belasis Court, Belasis Technology Park, Billingham TS23 4AZ T 01642-370406
Managing Director, A. Ward
SATRA TECHNOLOGY CENTRE (Footwear, apparel, safety products and furniture), Satra House, Rockingham Road, Kettering, Northants NN16 9JH T 01536-410000 *Chief Executive,* Dr R. E. Whittaker

SCOTCH WHISKY RESEARCH INSTITUTE, The Robertson Trust Building, Research Park North, Riccarton, Edinburgh, EH14 4AP T 0131 449-8900 *Director*, Dr G. M. Steele

SIRA LTD (Measurement, instrumentation, control and optical systems technology), South Hill, Chislehurst, Kent BR7 5EH T 020-8467 2636
Managing Director, Prof. R. A. Brook

SMITH INSTITUTE (Mathematics and computing), PO Box 183, Guildford, Surrey GU2 5GG T 01483-579108
Chairman of the Council, Dr B. Smith, CBE

SPORTS TURF RESEARCH INSTITUTE, St Ives Estate, Bingley, W. Yorks BD16 1AU T 01274-565131
Chief Executive, Dr G. McKillop

STEEL CONSTRUCTION INSTITUTE, Silwood Park, Ascot, Berks SL5 7QN T 01344-623345 *Director*, Dr G. Owens

TNO BIBRA INTERNATIONAL LTD, Woodmansterne Road, Carshalton, Surrey SM5 4DS T 020-8652 1000
Director, Dr G. van der Veek

TRADA TECHNOLOGY LTD (Timber and wood-based products), Chiltern House, Stocking Lane, Hughenden Valley, High Wycombe, Bucks HP14 4ND T 01494-563091
Managing Director, A. Abbott

TWI, Abington Hall, Abington, Cambridge CB1 6AL T 01223-891162
Chief Executive, A. B. M. Braithwaite, OBE

SOCIAL WELFARE

NATIONAL HEALTH SERVICE

The National Health Service (NHS) came into being on 5 July 1948 under the National Health Service Act 1946, covering England and Wales and, under separate legislation, Scotland and Northern Ireland. The NHS is now administered by the Secretary of State for Health (in England), the National Assembly for Wales, the Scottish Executive and the Secretary of State for Northern Ireland.

The function of the NHS is to provide a comprehensive health service designed to secure improvement in the physical and mental health of the people and to prevent, diagnose and treat illness. It was founded on the principle that treatment should be provided according to clinical need rather than ability to pay, and should be free at the point of delivery.

Hospital, mental, dental, nursing, ophthalmic and ambulance services and facilities for the care of expectant and nursing mothers and young children are provided by the NHS to meet all reasonable requirements. Rehabilitation services such as occupational therapy, physiotherapy, speech therapy and surgical and medical appliances are supplied where appropriate. Specialists and consultants who work in NHS hospitals can also engage in private practice, including the treatment of their private patients in NHS hospitals.

STRUCTURE

The structure of the NHS remained relatively stable for the first 30 years of its existence. In 1974, a three-tier management structure comprising Regional Health Authorities, Area Health Authorities and District Management Teams was introduced in England, and the NHS became responsible for community health services. In 1979 Area Health Authorities were abolished and District Management Teams were replaced by District Health Authorities.

The National Health Service and Community Care Act 1990 provided for more streamlined Regional Health Authorities and District Health Authorities, and for the establishment of Family Health Services Authorities (FHSAs) and NHS Trusts. The concept of the 'internal market' was introduced into health care, whereby care was provided through NHS contracts where health authorities or boards and GP fundholders (the purchasers) were responsible for buying health care from hospitals, non-fundholding GPs, community services and ambulance services (the providers). The Act also paved the way for the Community Care reforms, which were introduced in April 1993, and changed the way care is administered for older people, the mentally ill, the physically handicapped and people with learning disabilities.

ENGLAND

Regional Health Authorities in England were abolished in April 1996 and replaced by eight regional offices which, together with the headquarters in Leeds, formed the NHS Executive (which has since been merged with the Department of Health). In April 2002, as an interim arrangement, the eight regional offices were replaced by

four Directorates of Health and Social Care (DsHSC). In April 2003, the DsHSCs were abolished.

STRATEGIC HEALTH AUTHORITIES

In April 1996 the District Health Authorities and Family Health Service Authorities were merged to form 100 unified Health Authorities (HAs) in England. In April 2002, 28 new health authorities were formed from the existing HAs. In October 2002, as part of the new arrangements set out in the NHS Reform and Health Care Professions Act 2002, these new health authorities were renamed Strategic Health Authorities (SHAs) and charged with creating a strategic framework for managing the performance of Primary Care Trusts and building the capacity of health services locally.

PRIMARY CARE TRUSTS

The first 17 Primary Care Trusts (PCTs) became operational in England on 1 April 2000. As at 1 April 2004 a total of 304 PCTs covered all areas of England. PCTs were created to give primary care professionals greater control over how resources are best used to benefit patients. PCTs are responsible for tackling health inequalities, developing primary and community health services and commissioning secondary care services. They are free-standing statutory bodies undertaking many of the functions previously exercised by former Health Authorities, such as securing the provision of services and integrating health and social care.

Each PCT is overseen by a lay board, comprising a chairman and non-executive directors who are appointed by the NHS Appointments Commission and who are members of the local community to be served by the PCT. The Board's role is to provide strategic oversight and verification to the work of the Executive, which is made up of health professionals.

FOUNDATION TRUSTS

The first ten NHS foundation trusts were established on 1 April 2004 with a further ten established on 1 July 2004. NHS foundation trusts are NHS hospitals, they are part of the NHS but have their own accountabilty and governance systems, which function outside of the Department of Health's framework, giving them greater freedom to run their own affairs. NHS foundation trusts treat patients according to NHS principles and standards and are inspected by the Healthcare Commission. The Government's aim is that by 2008, all NHS trusts will have reached a standard which will enable them to apply for NHS foundation trust status.

Contact details for all the SHAs, PCTs and other NHS organisations in England can be found in the *NHS England, Authorities and Trusts* section on the NHS website: www.nhs.uk or by calling the Department of Health Public Enquiry Office on 020-7210 4850.

WALES

In Wales there were five HAs which replaced the former 17 HAs and FHSAs in April 1996. The HAs set up 22 Local Health Groups (LHGs), coterminous with local authority areas (*see* Local Government Section), which began work in April 1999. Originally they advised HAs, but in March 2003 the five HAs were abolished and the LHGs, were renamed Local Health Boards (LHBs) and took up a role similar to PCTs; assuming responsibility for commissioning services and devising strategies for improving health. They also integrate the delivery of primary and community care. Each Local Health Board has a governing body made up of local doctors, a nurse, other health professionals, members of the local authority and voluntary organisations and others to represent the interests of patients. There is also a small executive team to take action on decisions and provide services for the public.

Contact details for the LHBs and other NHS organisations in Wales are available in the *NHS Wales Directory* section on the Welsh NHS website. W www.wales.nhs.uk

SCOTLAND

In Scotland, the Scottish Executive Health Department leads the central management of the NHS, heading a Management Executive which oversees the work of 15 area Health Boards responsible for planning health services for their area, and 28 self-governing NHS Trusts responsible for providing services to patients and the community. At a local level there are currently Local Health Care Co-operatives (LHCCs) which are voluntary associations of primary health care professionals and local authority representatives. There are plans to replace the LHCCs with Community Health Partnerships (CHPs) to give more consistency to the planning, development and delivery of local services across Scotland.

FOUNDATION TRUSTS

ARGYLL AND CLYDE, Ross House, Hawkhead Road, Paisley PA2 7BN T 0141-842 7200 W www.show.scot.nhs.uk/achb
AYRSHIRE AND ARRAN, Boswell House, 10 Arthur Street, Ayr KA7 1QJ T 01292-611040 W www.nhsayrshireandarran.com
BORDERS, Newstead, Melrose, Roxburghshire TD6 9BD T 01896-825500 W www.nhsborders.org.uk
DUMFRIES AND GALLOWAY, Mid North, The Crichton, Glencaple Road, Dumfries DG1 4TG T 01387-272700 W www.show.scot.nhs.uk/dghb
FIFE, Springfield House, Cupar KY15 5UP T 01334-656200 W www.show.scot.nhs.uk/fhb
FORTH VALLEY, 33 Spittal Street, Stirling FK8 1DX T 01786-463031 W www.show.scot.nhs.uk/nhsfv
GRAMPIAN, Summerfield House, 2 Eday Road, Aberdeen AB15 6RE T 01224-663456 W www.ghb.uk.com
GREATER GLASGOW, Dalian House, 350 St Vincent Street, Glasgow G3 8YZ T 0141-201 4444 W www.nhsgg.org.uk
HIGHLAND, Assynt House, Beechwood Park, Inverness IV2 3HG T 01463-717123 W www.show.scot.nhs.uk/hhb
LANARKSHIRE, 14 Beckford Street, Hamilton, Lanarkshire ML3 0TA T 01698-281313 W www.show.scot.nhs.uk/nhslanarkshire
LOTHIAN, Deaconess House, 148 Pleasance, Edinburgh EH8 9RS T 0131-536 9000 W www.nhslothian.scot.nhs.uk
ORKNEY, Garden House, New Scapa Road, Kirkwall, Orkney KW15 1BQ T 01856-885400 W www.show.scot.nhs.uk/ohb
SHETLAND, Brevik House, South Road, Lerwick ZE1 0TG T 01595-696767 W www.show.scot.nhs.uk/shb
TAYSIDE, Kings Cross, Clepington Road, Dundee DD3 8EA T 01382-818479 W www.nhstayside.scot.nhs.uk
WESTERN ISLES, 37 South Beach Street, Stornoway, Isle of Lewis HS1 2BB T 01851-702997 W www.show.scot.nhs.uk/wihb

NORTHERN IRELAND

In Northern Ireland there are four Health and Social Services Boards responsible for commissioning services to meet the needs of their respective populations. They are also responsible for assessing the needs of that population, establishing objectives and developing policies and priorities to meet these objectives. There are 15 Local Health and Social Care Groups (LHSCGs) responsible for the planning and delivery of primary and community care and to represent local interests to their respective Health and Social Services Board.

EASTERN, Champion House, 12–22 Linenhall Street, Belfast BT2 8BS T 028-9032 1313 W www.ehssb.n-i.nhs.uk
NORTHERN, County Hall, 182 Galgorm Road, Ballymena BT42 1QB T 028-2565 3333 W www.nhssb.n-i.nhs.uk
SOUTHERN, Tower Hill, Armagh BT61 7DR T 028-3741 0041 W www.shssb.n-i.nhs.uk
WESTERN, 15 Gransha Park, Clooney Road, Londonderry BT47 6FN T 028-7186 0086 W www.whssb.n-i.nhs.uk

PATIENT AND PUBLIC INVOLVEMENT FORUMS

There are Patient and Public Involvement (PPI) Forums throughout the UK; their role is to represent the interests of the public to NHS Trusts, PCTs and SHAs and their equivalents in Wales and Scotland.

There is a PPI Forum for every NHS Trust and PCT in England. PPI Forums are made up of local people and play an active role in health-related decision-making within their communities. They have a number of primary roles which include:

– Obtaining views from local communities on the range and day to day delivery of health services and making recommendations and reports
– Influencing the design of and access to NHS services
– Providing advice and information to patients and their carers about services
– Monitoring the effectiveness of local Patient Advice and Liaison Services (PALS)

THE NHS PLAN

In July 2000 the government launched the NHS Plan, a ten year strategy to modernise the health service. In June 2004 the Government launched the NHS Improvement Plan, which set out the next stage of NHS reform, moving the focus from access to services towards the broader issues of public health and chronic disease management. The core aims are to sustain increased levels of investment in the NHS and to continue to focus on the improvements outlined in the NHS Plan, while delivering greater levels of choice and information to patients. In July 2004, the Department of Health published *National Standards, Local Action: Health and Social Care Standards and Planning Framework 2005/6–2007/8* which cut the number of national targets that NHS providers must comply from 62 to 20. These national targets, which cover areas such as waiting times for accident and emergency treatment, will become national core standards which all providers of care must maintain from April 2005. Alongside, NHS providers will be given power to set more locally relevant targets.

FINANCE

The NHS is still funded mainly through general taxation, although in recent years more reliance has been placed on the NHS element of National Insurance contributions, patient charges and other sources of income.

In the April 2002 Budget, the Chancellor announced a five-year spending plan for the NHS. Over the years 2003–4 to 2007–8, these plans mean that expenditure on the NHS in the UK will increase on average by 7.2 per cent a year over and above inflation, 7.4 per cent a year for England. The spending plans are set out in the table below:

£ millions	UK	% real terms increase*	England	% real terms increase*
2003–4	74,800	7.0	61,300	7.1
2004–5	82,200	7.1	67,400	7.2
2005–6	90,500	7.4	74,400	7.6
2006–7	99,400	7.2	81,800	7.3
2007–8	109,400	7.4	90,200	7.5

* calculated using GDP deflator at 27 June 2003
Source: Department of Health

NATIONAL HEALTH SERVICE EXPENDITURE 2002–3 OUTTURN (ENGLAND)

	£ million
Hospitals, community health, family health (discretionary) and related services and NHS Trusts	51,053
Family health services (non-discretionary)	2,023
Central and other services*	966
Total	54,042

* includes: environmental health, health promotion, support to the voluntary sector and expenditure on the administration of the Department of Health
Source: Department of Health

GOVERNMENT EXPENDITURE ON WELFARE SERVICES 2001–2

	£ million
Central government	52
Local authorities running expenses	13,279
Capital expenditure	137
Total	13,472

Source: The Stationery Office – Annual Abstract of Statistics 2004 (Crown copyright)

PRIVATE FINANCE INITIATIVE
The Private Finance Initiative (PFI) was launched in 1992, and involves the private sector in designing, building, financing and operating new hospitals and primary care premises, which are then leased to the NHS. The NHS Plan committed the NHS to entering into a new public private partnership, Partnerships for Health, a joint venture between the Department of Health and Partnerships UK plc (PUK) established in September 2001. Its role is to support the development of NHS Local Improvement Finance Trusts (LIFT) by implementing a standard approach to procurement as well as providing some equity. LIFTs are set up as limited companies with the local NHS, Partnerships for Health and the private sector as shareholders. LIFT schemes build and refurbish primary care premises, which the schemes own and then rent to GPs on a lease basis (as well as other parties such as chemists, opticians, dentists etc). There are 42 LIFT schemes covering more than 100 PCTs, with up to £1,000 million investment supported by £195 million of public money.

EMPLOYEES AND SALARIES

EMPLOYEES

NHS HOSPITAL AND COMMUNITY HEALTH SERVICE STAFF (Great Britain) 2002
Full-time equivalent

Hospital medical staff	76,122
Community health medical staff	1,902
Hospital dental staff	1,944
Community health dental staff	1,413
Nursing and midwifery staff	455,361
General medical practitioners	38,649
General dental practitioners	22,194

Source: National Statistics – Annual Abstract of Statistics 2004 (Crown copyright)

SALARIES
General Practitioners (GPs), dentists, optometrists and pharmacists are self-employed, and are employed by the NHS under contract. On 20 June 2003 GPs accepted a new practice-based contract which rewards practices for delivering quality and a wider range of services. Dentists receive payment for items of treatment for individual adult patients and, in addition, a continuing care payment for those registered with them. Optometrists receive approved fees for each sight test they carry out. Pharmacists receive professional fees from the NHS and are refunded the cost of prescriptions supplied. Doctors in training receive additional supplements reflecting the intensity and out-of-hours elements of their duties, these can range from 20–100 per cent of the basic salary.

SALARIES
As at 1 April 2004 for Hospital Medical and Dental Staff and Nurses (these figures do not include merit awards, discretionary points or banding supplements):

Consultant	£55,699–£72,483
Specialist Registrar	£27,483–£41,733
Registrar	£27,483–£33,337
Senior House Officer	£24,587–£34,477
House Officer	£19,703–£22,240
Nursing Grades H–I (Modern Matron)	£26,650–£34,920
Nursing Grades G–I (Senior Ward Sister)	£23,860–£34,920
Nursing Grade F (Ward Sister)	£20,220–£25,250
Nursing Grade E (Senior Staff Nurse)	£18,230–£22,015
Nursing Grade D (Staff Nurse)	£17,060–£18,830
Nursing Grade C (Enrolled Nurse and some Nursing auxiliary staff)	£13,900–£17,060
Nursing Grades A–B	£10,375–£13,025

HEALTH SERVICES

PRIMARY AND COMMUNITY HEALTH CARE
Primary and community health care services comprise the family health services (i.e. the general medical, personal medical, pharmaceutical, dental, and ophthalmic services) and community services (including preventive activities such as vaccination, immunisation and fluoridation). Nursing services including practice nurses, community nurses and health visitors and ante- and post-natal care.

PRIMARY MEDICAL SERVICES

In England, Primary Medical Services are the responsibility of Primary Care Trusts (PCTs) who contract with GPs to provide the service to the NHS. They do so in one of two ways: by providing general medical services (GMS) under national rules or by successfully applying to become a personal medical service (PMS) pilot, with a contract that is largely locally determined. As at 1 October 2003, just over 40 per cent of GPs were in PMS.

In Wales, responsibility for primary medical services rests with Local Health Boards (LHBs) and in Scotland with the NHS Trusts (*see* Structure section).

Any vocationally trained doctor may provide general or personal medical services. The average number of patients on a doctor's list in the UK as at September 2002 was 1,838. GPs may also have private fee-paying patients, but not if that patient is already an NHS patient on that doctor's patient list.

A person who is ordinarily resident in the UK is eligible to register with a GP (or PMS provider) for free primary care treatment. Should a patient have difficulty in registering with a doctor, he or she should contact the local PCT for help. When a person is away from home he/she can still access primary care treatment from a GP if they ask to be treated as a temporary resident. In an emergency any doctor in the service will give treatment and advice.

GPs are responsible for the care of their patients 24 hours a day, seven days a week, but can fulfil the terms of their contract by delegating or transferring responsibility for out-of-hours (OOH) care to an accredited provider. Under the new GMS contract, practices will be able to opt out of responsibility for patient care during the OOH period. When they do so, it will become a Primary Care Trust (PCT) responsibility. PCTs will be able to provide the OOH cover themselves or commission the service from an OOH provider.

Increasingly, some secondary care services, such as minor operations and consultations can be provided in a primary care setting. The number of such practitioners is growing and the new GMS contract provides a platform for further expansion.

In addition, drop-in services are being developed. A total of 42 NHS Walk-in Centres are operational across the country, with further centres planned to open over the next few years. They are nurse-led and provide treatment for minor ailments and injuries, health information and self-help advice with extended opening hours (normally every day of the year from 7a.m.-10p.m. Monday to Friday, and 9a.m.-10p.m. Saturday and Sunday).

HEALTH COSTS

Some people are exempt or entitled to help with health costs such as prescription charges, ophthalmic and dental costs, and in some cases help towards travel costs to and from hospital.

The following list is intended as a general guide to those who are entitled to help or are exempt:
– children under 16 and young people in full time education who are under 19
– people aged 60 or over
– pregnant women and women who have had a baby in the last 12 months
– people receiving Income Support and/or Jobseeker's Allowance
– people receiving Tax Credits
– people with a specified medical condition
– people with impaired hearing
– patients of a genito-urinary medicine clinic
– people who need help to go out or live in residential care or a nursing home
– people supported by a Local Authority after leaving care
– NHS in-patients
– NHS out-patients for all medication given at the hospital
– patients of the Community Dental Service
– people registered blind or partially sighted
– people who need complex lenses
– war pensioners

People in other circumstances may also be eligible for help; Booklet HC11, available from main post offices or local social security offices, gives further details. Or visit: www.dh.gov.uk

PHARMACEUTICAL SERVICES

Patients may obtain medicines and appliances under the NHS from any pharmacy whose owner has entered into arrangements with the PCT to provide this service; the number of these pharmacies in England and Wales as at March 2003 was 10,452. There are also some suppliers who only provide special appliances. In rural areas, where access to a pharmacy may be difficult, patients may be able to obtain medicines, etc., from a dispensing doctor.

Except for contraceptives (for which there is no charge), a charge of £6.40 is payable for each item supplied unless the patient is exempt and the declaration on the back of the prescription form is completed. Prepayment certificates (£33.40 valid for four months, £91.80 valid for a year) may be purchased by those patients not entitled to exemption who require frequent prescriptions.

DENTAL SERVICES

Dentists, like doctors, may take part in the NHS and also have private patients. Over 18,000 dentists in England provide NHS general dental services. They are responsible to the PCTs in whose areas they provide services. Patients may go to any dentist who is taking part in the NHS and is willing to accept them. Patients are required to pay 80 per cent of the cost of NHS dental treatment. Since 1 April 2003 the maximum charge allowed for an NHS course of treatment has been £372. There is no charge for arrest of bleeding or repairs to dentures; home visits by the dentist or re-opening a surgery in an emergency are charged for as treatment given in the normal way.

In July 2004 the government announced a £368 million funding injection for NHS dentistry. The Department of Health plans to recruit the equivalent of an extra 1,000 dentists by October 2005, of which around 650 will be new recruits. This funding was accompanied by a package of reforms to modernise the dentistry profession and ensure continued local expenditure on dentistry through PCTs.

GENERAL DENTAL SERVICE 2002–3 (ENGLAND)

Number of dentists	18,500
Number of patients registered	
Adults	16,600,000
Children	6,700,000
Number of courses of treatment	
Adults	26,300,000
Expenditure (£ million)	
Gross expenditure	1,770
Paid by patients	500
Paid out of public funds	1,270

Source: Department of Health

GENERAL OPHTHALMIC SERVICES
General Ophthalmic Services are administered by PCTs. Testing of sight may be carried out by any ophthalmic medical practitioner or ophthalmic optician (optometrist). The optician must give the prescription to the patient, who can take this to any supplier of glasses to have them dispensed. Only registered opticians can supply glasses to children and to people registered as blind or partially sighted. At the end of December 2002 there were 8,096 ophthalmic practitioners under contract to provide NHS sight tests. An estimated 16.9 million sight tests were carried out in 2002–3 in Great Britain.

The NHS sight test costs £16.72. Free eyesight tests and help towards the cost are available to people in certain circumstances. Help is also available for the purchase of glasses. (*see* Health Costs section or booklet HC11)

COMMUNITY CHILD HEALTH SERVICE
Pre-school services at GP surgeries or child health clinics provide regular monitoring of children's physical, mental and emotional health and development, and advice to parents on their children's health and welfare.

The School Health Service provides for the medical and dental examination of schoolchildren, and advises the local education authority, the school, the parents and the pupil of any health factors which may require special consideration during the pupil's school life. GPs are increasingly undertaking child health monitoring in order to improve the preventive health care of children.

All Primary Care Trusts (PCTs) are working with Local Authorities under accredited local health and education partnerships to recruit more schools into the Healthy Schools Programme which was established in 1999 as a joint initiative between the Department of Health and the Department for Education and Skills.

NHS DIRECT
NHS Direct is a telephone service staffed by nurses which gives patients advice on how to look after themselves as well as directing them to the appropriate part of the NHS for treatment if necessary. T 0845-4647

SECONDARY CARE AND OTHER SERVICES

HOSPITALS
NHS hospitals provide acute and specialist care services, treating conditions which normally cannot be dealt with by primary care specialists and medical emergencies.

NUMBER OF BEDS AND PATIENT ACTIVITY 2002

	England	Wales
In-patients:		
Average daily available beds	184,000	14,300
Average daily occupation of beds	157,000	11,800
Persons waiting for admission at 31 March	992,000	74,600
Day-case admissions	3,592,000*	109,400
Ordinary admissions	8,761,000*	493,000
Out-patient attendances:		
New patients	13,032,000	747,300
Total attendances	44,598,000	2,842,500
Accident and emergency:		
New cases	12,945,000	888,700
Total attendances	14,046,000	1,004,700
Ward attendances	1,179,000	–
* 2001 figures		

SCOTLAND

In-patients:	
Average available staffed beds	30,900
Average occupied beds	25,100
Out-patient attendances:	
New patients	2,743,000
Total attendances	6,291,000

NORTHERN IRELAND

In-patients:	
Beds available	8,301
Average daily occupation of beds	6,973
Out-patients:	
New cases	992,000
Total attendances	2,122,000

Source: The Stationery Office – *Annual Abstract of Statistics 2004* (Crown copyright)

CHARGES
NHS trusts can provide accommodation in single rooms or small wards, if not required for patients who need privacy for medical reasons. The patient is still an NHS patient, but there may be a charge for these additional facilities. NHS trusts can charge for certain patient services that are considered to be additional treatments over and above the normal service provision. There is no blanket policy to cover this and each case is considered in the light of the patient's clinical need. However, if an item or service is considered to be an integral part of a patient's treatment by their clinician, then a charge should not be made.

In some NHS hospitals, accommodation and services are available for the treatment of private patients where it does not interfere with care for NHS patients. Income generated by treating private patients is then put back into the local NHS services. Private patients undertake to pay the full costs of medical treatment, accommodation, medication and other related services. Charges for private patients are set locally.

WAITING LISTS
At the end of March 2004 the total number of patients waiting to be admitted to NHS hospitals in England was 906,000, a decrease of 8.7 per cent on the previous year. The number of patients in England and Wales who had been waiting more than nine months was 48, a decrease of 99.9 per cent on the previous year, when the total was 53,183. No patients had been waiting longer than 12 months at the end of March 2004 and the average wait was 10.2 weeks. Under the charter *Your Guide to the NHS*, patients are guaranteed admission within 18 months of being placed on a waiting list. In July 2004 a new target was set of an 18 week maximum wait from start time (i.e. seeing a GP) to treatment by 2008.

AMBULANCE SERVICE
The NHS provides emergency ambulance services free of charge via the 999 emergency telephone service. Air ambulances, provided through local charities and partially funded by the NHS, are used throughout the UK. They assist with cases where access may be difficult or heavy traffic could hinder road progress. Non-emergency ambulance services are provided free of charge to patients who are deemed to require them on medical grounds.

In 2003–4 in England approximately 5.3 million emergency calls were made to the ambulance service, an increase of 8 per cent on the previous year. There were about 3.4 million emergency patient journeys. Since 1

April 2001 all services have had a system of call prioritisation. The prioritisation procedures require all emergency calls to be classified as either immediately life threatening (category A) or other emergency (category B/C). Services are expected to reach 75 per cent of Category A (life threatening) calls within eight minutes and 95 per cent of category B/C calls within 19 minutes in rural areas and 14 minutes in urban areas. In 2003–4, 75.7 per cent of life threatening calls resulted in emergency response arriving at the scene of the incident within 8 minutes (74.6 per cent in 2002–3). Twenty-two services met or exceeded the 75 per cent target. For category B/C calls, 11 services responded to 95 per cent or more calls within 14 or 19 minutes.

BLOOD SERVICES

There are four national bodies which co-ordinate the blood donor programme in the UK. Donors give blood at local centres on a voluntary basis.

NATIONAL BLOOD SERVICE, Oak House, Reeds Crescent, Watford, Herts WD24 4QN T 01923-486800 W www.blood.co.uk

SCOTTISH NATIONAL BLOOD TRANSFUSION SERVICE, 21 Ellens Glen Road, Edinburgh EH17 7QT T 0131-536 5700 W www.scotblood.co.uk

WELSH BLOOD SERVICE, Ely Valley Road, Talbot Green, Pontyclun CF72 9WB T 01443-622000 W www.welsh-blood.org.uk

NORTHERN IRELAND BLOOD TRANSFUSION SERVICE, Belfast City Hospital Complex, Lisburn Road, Belfast BT9 7TS T 028-9032 1414 W www.nibts.org

HOSPICES

Hospice or palliative care may be available for patients with life-threatening illnesses. It may be provided at the patient's home or in a voluntary or NHS hospice or in hospital, and is intended to ensure the best possible quality of life for the patient during their illness, and to provide help and support to both the patient and the patient's family. The National Council for Hospices and Specialist Palliative Care Services co-ordinates NHS and voluntary services in England, Wales and Northern Ireland; the Scottish Partnership Agency for Palliative and Cancer Care performs the same function in Scotland.

NATIONAL COUNCIL FOR HOSPICE AND SPECIALIST PALLIATIVE CARE SERVICES, 1st Floor, 34–44 Britannia Street, London WC1X 9JG T 020-7520 8299 W www.hospiceinformation.info

SCOTTISH PARTNERSHIP FOR PALLIATIVE CARE, 1A Cambridge Street, Edinburgh EH1 2DY T 0131-229 0538 W www.palliativecarescotland.org.uk

NHS CHARTERS

The original Patient's Charter was published in 1991 and came into force in 1992; an expanded version was published in 1995. The Charter set out the rights of patients in relation to the standards of service they should expect to receive at all times and standards of service that the NHS aimed to provide.

The Patient's Charter was replaced nationally in 2001 with *Your Guide to the NHS,* which provided information on how to get treatment and gave specific details on minimum standards for patients, targets for the NHS and improvements in the NHS Plan. It also detailed what patients had a right to expect from the NHS and what is expected from patients.

Information for patients about all aspects of the NHS has now been reorganised and is available on the NHS website. W www.nhs.uk

COMPLAINTS

There are three levels to the NHS complaints procedure: the first level involves resolution of a complaint locally, following a direct approach to the Patients Advice and Liaison Service (PALS) at the relevant NHS service provider; the second level involves an independent review procedure by the local PCT if the complaint is not resolved locally. As a final resort, patients may approach the Health Service Ombudsman (in Northern Ireland, the Commissioner for Complaints) if they are dissatisfied with the response of the NHS to a complaint.

RECIPROCAL ARRANGEMENTS

Citizens of countries in the European Economic Area (EEA – *see* European Union section) who are resident in the UK are entitled to receive emergency health care either free of charge or for a reduced charge when they are temporarily visiting other member states of the EEA. Form E111, available at post offices, should be obtained before travelling (to be replaced by the European Health Insurance Card from December 2005). There are also bilateral agreements with several other countries, including Australia and New Zealand, for the provision of urgent medical treatment free of charge.

EEA nationals visiting the UK and visitors from other countries with which the UK has bilateral health care agreements, are entitled to receive emergency health care on the NHS on the same terms as it is available to UK residents.

PERSONAL SOCIAL SERVICES

The Secretary of State for Health (in England), the National Assembly for Wales, the Scottish Executive and the Secretary of State for Northern Ireland are responsible, under the Local Authority Social Services Act 1970, for the provision of social services for older people, disabled people, families and children, and those with mental disorders. Personal Social Services are administered by local authorities according to policies with standards set by central and devolved government. Each authority has a Director of Social Services and a Social Services Committee responsible for the social services functions placed upon them. Local authorities provide, enable and commission care after assessing the needs of their population. The private and voluntary sectors also play an important role in the delivery of social services, and an estimated six million people in Great Britain provide substantial regular care for a member of their family.

Under the Care Standards Act 2000, the National Care Standards Commission (NCSC) was set up on 1 April 2002 to regulate social, private and voluntary care services throughout England. In April 2004, under the Health and Social Care (Community Health and Standards) Act 2003, the NCSC was replaced by the Commission for Social Care Inspection (CSCI). The CSCI was established as a single, regulatory authority, incorporating the work formerly carried out by the the Social Services Inspectorate (SSI), the SSI/Audit Commission Joint Review Team and the NCSC. Services such as care homes and children's homes managed by local authorities, domiciliary care services, independent fostering agencies and residential family centres, that were previously regulated by the NCSC, are now registered and inspected by the CSCI. The CSCI ensures that care services are run in accordance with national minimum standards and regulations that have been set by the Government. As well as regulating care services, the CSCI assesses all areas of care services provided by the 150 local authorities in England against a national agenda, ensuring they meet their social services responsibilities through a system of inspections and self-assessment. The CSCI collates information on local services from May to July each year and makes this information available to the public.

COMMISSION FOR SOCIAL CARE INSPECTION (CSCI), 33 Greycoat Street, London SW1P 2QF T 020-7979 2000 W www.csci.org.uk

FINANCE

The Personal Social Services programme is financed partly by central government, with decisions on expenditure allocations being made at local authority level. Spending on personal social services in 2001–2 by central government was £52 million with £13,416 million allocated by local authorities.

STAFF

PERSONAL SOCIAL SERVICES STAFF 2002 (ENGLAND)
Full-time equivalent

Home help service	37,300
Field social workers	35,800
Residential care staff	51,400
Day care establishments staff	29,300
All other staff (including management and administration and ancillary staff)	54,500
Total staff	208,300

Source: National Statistics – Annual Abstract of Statistics 2004 (Crown copyright)

OLDER PEOPLE

Services for older people are designed to enable them to remain living in their own homes for as long as possible. Local authority services include advice, domestic help, meals in the home, alterations to the home to aid mobility, emergency alarm systems, day and/or night attendants, laundry services and the provision of day centres and recreational facilities. Charges may be made for these services. Respite care may also be provided in order to allow carers temporary relief from their responsibilities.

Local authorities and the private sector also provide 'sheltered housing' for older people, sometimes with resident wardens.

If an older person is admitted to a residential home, charges are made according to a means test; if the person cannot afford to pay, the costs are met by the local authority.

In March 2001 a National Service Framework for Older People was published. The framework set national standards and service models of care across health and social service for older people whether they live at home, in residential care or are being cared for in hospital.

DISABLED PEOPLE

Services for disabled people are designed to enable them to remain living in their own homes wherever possible. Local authority services include advice, adaptations to the home, meals in the home, help with personal care, occupational therapy, educational facilities and recreational facilities. Respite care may also be provided in order to allow carers temporary relief from their responsibilities.

Special housing may be available for disabled people who can live independently, and residential accommodation for those who cannot.

FAMILIES AND CHILDREN

Local authorities are required to provide services aimed at safeguarding the welfare of children in need and, wherever possible, allowing them to be brought up by their families. Services include advice, counselling, help in the home and the provision of family centres. Many authorities also provide short-term refuge accommodation for women and children.

DAY CARE

In allocating day care places to children, local authorities give priority to children with special needs, whether in terms of their health, learning abilities or social needs. Since September 2001 the Office for Standards in Education (OFSTED) has been responsible for the regulation and registration of all early years childcare and education provision in England (previously the responsibility of the local authorities). All day care and childminding services which care for children under 8 years of age for more than two hours a day must register with OFSTED and are inspected at least every two years. In March 2003 there were over 1.3 million childcare places and almost 100,000 childcare providers in England.

In Wales, Scotland and Northern Ireland local authorities have responsibility for registration and inspection of day care facilities.

CHILD PROTECTION

Children considered to be at risk of physical injury, neglect or sexual abuse are placed on the local authority's child protection register. Local authority social services staff, schools, health visitors and other agencies work together to prevent and detect cases of abuse. In England as of 31 March 2003 there were 26,600 children on child protection registers, a 3.5 per cent increase from March 2002. Of the children registered during 2002–3, 11,700 were at risk of neglect, 5,700 of physical abuse, 3,000 of sexual abuse and 5,400 of emotional abuse. On 31 March 2003 there were 2,239 children on child protection registers in Wales and 1,608 in Northern Ireland. In Scotland as of 31 March 2002*, there were 2,018 children on local child protection registers.
* 2003 figures for Scotland were not available at the time of going to press.

LOCAL AUTHORITY CARE

Local authorities are required to provide accommodation for children who have no parents or guardians or whose parents or guardians are unable or unwilling to care for them. A family proceedings court may also issue a care order where a child is being neglected or abused, or is not attending school; the court must be satisfied that this would positively contribute to the well-being of the child.

The welfare of children in local authority care must be properly safeguarded. Children may be placed with foster families, who receive payments to cover the expenses of caring for the child or children, or in residential care.

Children's homes may be run by the local authority or by the private or voluntary sectors; all homes are subject to inspection procedures. In England as of 31 March 2002,

59,700 children were in the care of local authorities. Of these, 39,200 were in foster placements.

ADOPTION

Local authorities are required to provide an adoption service, either directly or via approved voluntary societies. In the UK, in 2002, 6,239 children (under 18 years of age) were entered onto the Adopted Children Register; 5,680 in England and Wales, 385 in Scotland and 174 in Northern Ireland.

PEOPLE WITH LEARNING DISABILITIES

Services for people with learning disabilities are designed to enable them to remain living in the community wherever possible. Local authority services include short-term care, support in the home, the provision of day care centres, and help with other activities outside the home. Residential care is provided for the severely or profoundly disabled.

MENTALLY ILL PEOPLE

Under the Care Programme Approach, mentally ill people should be assessed by specialist services and receive a care plan, and a key worker should be appointed for each patient. Regular reviews of the patient's progress should be conducted. Local authorities provide help and advice to mentally ill people and their families, and places in day centres and social centres. Social workers can apply for a mentally disturbed person to be compulsorily detained in hospital. Where appropriate, mentally ill people are provided with accommodation in special hospitals, local authority accommodation, or homes run by private or voluntary organisations. Patients who have been discharged from hospitals may be placed on a supervision register. A Mental Health National Service Framework was published in September 1999 setting national standards on how to prevent and treat mental illness.

NATIONAL INSURANCE

The National Insurance (NI) scheme operates under the Social Security Contributions and Benefits Act 1992 and the Social Security Administration Act 1992, and orders and regulations made thereunder. The scheme is financed by contributions payable by earners, employers and others (*see* below) and by a Treasury grant. Money collected under the scheme is used to finance the National Insurance Fund (from which contributory benefits are paid) and to contribute to the cost of the National Health Service.

NATIONAL INSURANCE FUND

Estimated receipts and payments of the National Insurance Fund for 2004–5:

Receipts	*£000s*
Net National Insurance contributions	62,239,000
Compensation from Consolidated Fund for	
Statutory Sick Pay and Statutory	
Maternity Pay recoveries	1,284,000
Income from investments	1,375,000
State scheme premiums	149,000
Other receipts	68,000
Total receipts	65,115,000

Payments	*£000s*
Benefits	55,290,000
Benefits increase due to proposed changes	1,536,000

Personal and stakeholder pensions	
contracted-out rebates	3,793,000
Age-related rebates for contracted-out	
money purchase schemes	295,000
Transfers to Northern Ireland	255,000
Administration	1,321,000
Redundancy fund payments (net)	248,000
Other payments	20,000
Total receipts	62,759,000

Balances	*£000s*
Opening balance	27,264,000
Excess of receipts over payments	2,369,000
Balance at end of year	29,633,000

CONTRIBUTIONS

There are six classes of National Insurance contributions (NICs):

Class 1	paid by employees and their employers
Class 1A	paid by employers who provide employees with certain benefits in kind for private use, such as company cars
Class 1B	paid by employers who enter into a Pay As You Earn (PAYE) Settlement Agreement with the Inland Revenue
Class 2	paid by self-employed people
Class 3	voluntary contributions paid to protect entitlement to the State Pension and who do not pay enough NI contributions in another class
Class 4	paid by the self-employed on their taxable profits over a set limit. These are normally paid by self-employed people in addition to Class 2 contributions. Class 4 contributions do not count towards benefits.

The lower and upper earnings limits and the percentage rates referred to below apply from April 2004 to April 2005.

CLASS 1

Class 1 contributions are paid where a person:

– is an employed earner (employee), office holder (e.g. company director) or employed under a contract of service in Great Britain or Northern Ireland
– is 16 or over and under state pension age
– earns at or above the earnings threshold of £91.00 per week (including overtime pay, bonus, commission, etc., without deduction of superannuation contributions)

Class 1 contributions are made up of primary and secondary contributions. Primary contributions are those paid by the employee and these are deducted from earnings by the employer. Since 6 April 2001 the employee's and employer's earnings thresholds have been the same and are referred to as the earnings threshold. Primary contributions are not paid on earnings below the earnings threshold of £91.00. Contributions are payable at the rate of eleven per cent on earnings between the earnings threshold and the upper earnings limit of £610.00 per week (9.4 per cent for contracted-out employment). Above the upper earnings limit one per cent is payable.

Some married women or widows pay a reduced rate of 4.85 per cent on earnings between the earnings threshold and upper earnings limits and one per cent above this. It is no longer possible to elect to pay the reduced rate but those who had reduced liability before 12 May 1977 may retain it so long as certain conditions are met. *See* leaflet CA09 (widows) or leaflet CA13 (married women).

Secondary contributions are paid by employers of employed earners at the rate of 12.8 per cent on all earnings above the earnings threshold of £91.00 per week. There is no upper earnings limit for employers' contributions. Employers operating contracted-out salary related schemes pay reduced contributions of 9.3 per cent; those with contracted-out money-purchase schemes pay 11.8 per cent. The contracted-out rate applies only to that portion of earnings between the earnings threshold and the upper earnings limits. Employers' contributions below and above those respective limits are assessed at the appropriate not contracted-out rate.

CLASS 2

Class 2 contributions are paid where a person is self-employed and is 16 or over and under state pension age. Contributions are paid at a flat rate of £2.05 per week regardless of the amount earned. However, those with earnings of less than £4,215 a year can apply for Small Earnings Exception, e.g. exemption from liability to pay Class 2 contributions. Those granted exemption from Class 2 contributions may pay Class 2 or Class 3 contributions voluntarily. Self-employed earners (whether or not they pay Class 2 contributions) may also be liable to pay Class 4 contributions based on profits. There are special rules for those who are concurrently employed and self-employed.

Married women and widows can no longer choose not to pay Class 2 contributions but those who elected not to pay Class 2 contributions before 12 May 1977 may retain the right so long as certain conditions are met.

Class 2 contributions are collected by the National Insurance Contributions Office (NICO), an executive agency of the Inland Revenue, by direct debit or quarterly bills. *See* leaflets CWL2 and CA02.

CLASS 3

Class 3 contributions are voluntary flat-rate contributions of £7.15 per week payable by persons over the age of 16 who would otherwise be unable to qualify for retirement pension and certain other benefits because they have an insufficient record of Class 1 or Class 2 contributions. This may include those who are not working, those not liable for Class 1 or Class 2 contributions or those excepted from Class 2 contributions. Married women and widows who on or before 11 May 1977 elected not to pay Class 1 (full rate) or Class 2 contributions cannot pay Class 3 contributions while they retain this right. Class 3 contributions are collected by the NICO by quarterly bills or direct debit. *See* leaflet CA08.

CLASS 4

Self-employed people whose profits and gains are over £4,745 a year pay Class 4 contributions in addition to Class 2 contributions. This applies to self-employed earners over 16 and under the state pension age. Class 4 contributions are calculated at eight per cent of annual profits or gains between £4,745 and £31,720 and one per cent above. Class 4 contributions are assessed and collected by the Inland Revenue together with Schedule D tax. It is possible, in some circumstances, to apply for exceptions from liability to pay Class 4 contributions or to have the amount of contribution reduced (where Class 1 contributions are payable on earnings assessed for Class 4 contributions). *See* leaflet CWL2.

PENSIONS

The Social Security Pensions Act (1975) came into force in 1978. It aimed to:
- reduce reliance on means-tested benefit in old age, widowhood and chronic ill-health
- ensure that occupational pension schemes which are contracted out of the state scheme fulfil the conditions of a good scheme
- ensure that pensions are adequately protected against inflation
- ensure that men and women are treated equally in State and occupational schemes

Legislation and regulations introduced since 1978 go further towards fulfilling these aims and more changes came into effect in April 1997. One of the changes is to equalise the state pension age for men (currently 65 years) and women (currently 60 years) from 6 April 2020. The change will be phased in over the ten years leading up to 6 April 2020. As a result the state pension age is as follows:
- the pension age for men remains at 65
- the pension age for women born on or before 5 October 1950 remains at 60
- the pension age for women born on or between 6 October 1950 and 5 October 1951 is 61
- the pension age for women born on or between 6 October 1951 and 5 October 1952 is 62
- the pension age for women born on or between 6 October 1952 and 5 October 1953 is 63
- the pension age for women born on or between 6 October 1953 and 5 October 1954 is 64
- the pension age for women born on 6 October 1954 or later is 65

STATE PENSION SCHEME

The state pension scheme consists of the basic State Pension and the State Second Pension, also known as the Additional Pension, which reformed the State Earnings-Related Pension Scheme (SERPS) from 6 April 2002.

The amount of basic State Pension paid is dependent on the number of 'qualifying years' a person has in their 'working life'. A 'qualifying year' is a tax year in which a person pays enough Class 1 National Insurance contributions (NICs) at the standard rate or class 2 or 3 NICs for the whole year (*see* National Insurance section) for it to count towards their basic State Pension. Those in receipt of Carer's Allowance, Working Tax Credit (with a disability element), Jobseeker's Allowance, Incapacity Benefit, Statutory Sick Pay or Statutory Maternity Pay may have Class 1 NICs credited to them. Persons undertaking certain training courses or jury service or who have been wrongly imprisoned for a conviction which is quashed on appeal may also get class 1 credits for each week they receive benefit or fulfil certain conditions. Class 1 credits count toward all future contributory benefits. A Class 3 credit for basic State Pension and bereavement benefit purposes is awarded, where required, for each week the Working Tax Credit (without a disability element) has been received.

'Working life' is counted from the start of the tax year in which a person reaches 16 to the end of the tax year before the one in which they reach pensionable age: for men this is normally 49 years and for women this varies between 44 and 49 years depending on birth date (*see above*). To get the full rate (100 per cent) basic pension a person must have qualifying years for about 90 per cent of their working life. To get the minimum basic pension (25 per cent) a person will need ten or eleven qualifying years. Married women who are not entitled to a pension on their own NICs may get a pension on their husband's NICs. It is possible for people who are unable to work because they care for children or a sick or disabled person at home to reduce the number of qualifying years required. This is called home responsibilities protection (HRP) and can be given for any tax year since April 1978; the number of years for which HRP is given is deducted from the number of qualifying years needed. From April 2002, HRP may also qualify the recipient for additional State Pension through the State Second Pension.

The amount of Additional Pension paid depends on the amount of earnings a person has, or is treated as having, between the lower and upper earnings limits for each complete tax year between 6 April 1978 (when the scheme started) and the tax year before they reach state pension age. The right to Additional Pension does not depend on the person's right to basic State Pension. The amount of additional State Pension paid also depends on when a person reaches state pension age; changes phased in from 6 April 1999 mean that pensions are calculated differently from that date. Men or women widowed before 6 October 2002 inherit all their late spouse's additional State Pension. From 6 October 2002, the maximum percentage of SERPS that a person can inherit from a late spouse will depend on their late spouse's date of birth:

Maximum %
SERPS
entitlement for

surviving spouse	d.o.b (men)	d.o.b (women)
100%	5/10/37 or earlier	5/10/42 or earlier
90%	6/10/37 to 5/10/39	6/10/42 to 5/10/44
80%	6/10/39 to 5/10/41	6/10/44 to 5/10/46
70%	6/10/41 to 5/10/43	6/10/46 to 5/10/48
60%	6/10/43 to 5/10/45	6/10/48 to 5/7/50
50%	6/10/45 or later	6/7/50 or later

The maximum State Second Pension a person can inherit from a late spouse is 50 per cent.

There are four categories of State Pension provided under the Social Security Contributions and Benefits Act 1992:
– Category A, a contributory pension made up of a basic State Pension dependent on the number of qualifying years in one's working life and an additional State Pension dependent on earnings since April 1978
– Category B, a contributory pension made up of basic and additional elements, payable to married women, widows and widowers based on their spouse's qualifying years and earnings. From 6 April 2010 both men and women will be able to get a basic State Pension based on their spouse's NICs, if this is better than the pension based on their own NIC record
– Category C, this pension is now obsolete
– Category D, a non-contributory State Pension for those aged 80 and over. Graduated Retirement Benefit is also available to those who paid graduated NICs into the scheme when it existed between April 1961 and April 1975

The Pension Service provides a State Pension forecasting service. T 0845-300 0168

From 1978 to 2002, additional pension was called the State Earnings-Related Pension Scheme (SERPS). SERPS covered all earnings by employees from 6 April 1978 to 5 April 1997 on which standard rate class 1 National Insurance had been paid and earnings between 6 April

1997 and 5 April 2002 if the standard rate class 1 contributions had been contracted-in.

In 2002 The Welfare Reform and Pensions Act 1999 replaced SERPS with State Second Pension, targeted at low and moderate earners and certain carers and people with long-term illness or disability. If earnings on which Class 1 NICs have been paid or can be treated as paid are above the annual National Insurance Lower Earnings Limit (£4,108 for 2004–5) but below the new Low Earnings Threshold (£11,600 for 2004–5), the State Second Pension regards this as earnings of £11,600 and it is treated equivalently. Certain carers and people with long term illness and disability will be considered as at the Low Earnings Threshold for each complete tax year even if they do not work at all, or earn less than the annual Lower Earnings Limit.

CONTRACTED-OUT PENSION SCHEMES
Personal Pension Schemes
Since July 1988, an employee has been able to start a personal pension which, if it meets certain conditions, can be used in place of additional State Pension. These pensions are known as Appropriate Personal Pensions (APPs). That part of an APP derived from the protected rights (rights comprising mainly the NIC rebate and its investment return) is intended to provide benefits broadly equivalent to those given up in the additional State Pension. At retirement, a contracted-out deduction will be made from additional State Pension built up from 6 April 1987 to 5 April 1997. The reduction may be more or less than that part of the pension derived from the protected right. From 6 April 1997 to 5 April 2002, members of an APP scheme will not have built up any entitlement to additional State Pension during the period of their membership. From 6 April 2002, employees contracted-out into a personal pension and earning between the lower earnings limit and the low earnings threshold (£4,108 and £11,600 in 2004–5) will be entitled to a reduced amount of State Second Pension.

Stakeholder Pension Schemes
Introduced in 2001, Stakeholder pensions are available to everyone but are principally for moderate earners who do not have access to a good value company pension scheme. Stakeholder pensions must meet a number of minimum standards to make sure they are flexible and not expensive (the annual management charge is capped). The minimum contribution is £20 per month.

As with personal pensions it is possible to invest up to £3,600 (including tax relief) into stakeholder pensions each year without evidence of earnings. Contributions can be made on someone else's behalf, for example, a non-working partner. Some people who are already members of occupational pension schemes can also contribute to a stakeholder pension scheme. If it meets certain conditions, it can be used to contract out of the State Second Pension (formerly SERPS). When someone contracts out of the State scheme with either an APP or a Stakeholder Pension, both the employee and their employers pay NICs at the full not contracted out rate. At the end of the tax year to which those NICs relate, the Inland Revenue pays an age-related rebate (which increases with age) and tax relief on the employee's share of the rebate directly into to the scheme for investment on behalf of the employee.

OCCUPATIONAL PENSION SCHEMES
Contracted-Out Salary-Related (COSR) Scheme
– this scheme provides a pension related to earnings
– any notional additional pension built up from 6 April 1978 to 5 April 1997 will be reduced by the amount of Guaranteed Minimum Pension (GMP) built up during that period (the contracted-out deduction)
– from 6 April 1997 these schemes no longer provide a GMP. Instead, as a condition of contracting out they have to satisfy a reference scheme test to ensure that the benefits provided are at least as good as a prescribed standard
– when someone contracts out of the additional State Pension through a COSR scheme, both the scheme member and the employer pay a reduced rate of NICs (known as the rebate) to compensate for the State Pension given up

Contracted-Out Money Purchase (COMP) Scheme
– this scheme provides a pension based on the value of the fund at retirement i.e. the money paid in, along with the investment return
– that part of the COMP fund derived from protected rights is intended to provide benefits broadly equivalent to those given up in the additional State Pension
– a contracted-out deduction, which may be more or less than that part of the pension derived from the protected rights will be made from any additional pension built up from 6 April 1988 to 5 April 1997. Between 6 April 1997 and 5 April 2002 members of a COMP scheme will not have built up any entitlement to additional State Pension during the period of their membership
– as with a COSR scheme, when someone contracts out of the additional State Pension through a COMP scheme, both the scheme member and the employer pay a reduced rate of NICs to compensate for the State Pension given up. In addition, at the end of the tax year to which the NICs relate, the Inland Revenue pays an additional age-related rebate direct to the scheme for investment on behalf of the employer

Contracted-Out Mixed Benefit (COMB) Scheme
A mixed benefit scheme has two active sections, one salary related and the other money purchase. Scheme rules set out which section individual employees may join and the circumstances (if any), in which members may move between sections. Each section must satisfy the respective contracting-out conditions for COSR and COMP schemes.

From April 2002, members of contracted-out occupational schemes earning between £4,108 and £26,600 (in 2004–5) may build up entitlement to a reduced amount of State Second Pension as well as that built up in their occupational pension.

COMPLAINTS
The Pensions Advisory Service (OPAS) gives free help and advice to people who have problems with occupational or personal pensions. There are two bodies for pension complaints. The Financial Ombudsman Service deals with complaints which predominantly concern the sale and marketing of occupational, stakeholder and personal pensions. The Pensions Ombudsman deals with complaints which predominantly concern the management (after sale or marketing) of occupational, stakeholder and personal pensions. The Occupational Pensions Regulatory Authority (OPRA) was set up by parliament to help make sure occupational pension

schemes are safe and well run, it can impose penalties where there are breaches of the law.

TAX CREDITS

From April 2003 Working Families' Tax Credit, Disabled Person's Tax Credit and the Children's Tax Credit were replaced with Working Tax Credit and Child Tax Credit. Tax Credits are administered by the Inland Revenue and are awarded for up to 12 months, although they can be adjusted during the year to reflect changes of income or circumstances.

WORKING TAX CREDIT
Working Tax Credit is made up of a basic payment with additional payments for couples, lone parents, people working over 30 hours a week, disabled workers and people aged 50 or over returning to work after a period of benefits. The tax credit will be paid with wages to people who are employed and directly to the self-employed. It is available to:
– People with dependant children and/or a disability, working at least 16 hours a week
– People aged 25 or over and working at least 30 hours a week

The aim of the tax credit system is to provide a guaranteed income from full-time work for those aged 25 or over without children or a disability, of £193 a week for couples, and £164 a week for single people.

WORKING TAX CREDIT 2004–5

Annual Income/status*	Tax Credit per annum
£5,000	
Single	–
Couple	–
Single adult with a disability	£3,675
£8,000	
Single	£1,125
Couple	£2,675
Single adult with a disability	£3,230
£10,000	
Single	£385
Couple	£1,935
Single adult with a disability	£2,490
£15,000	
Single	–
Couple	–
Single adult with a disability	£640

* Those with incomes of £5,000 a year are assumed to work part-time (working between 16 and 30 hours a week). In families with an income of £8,000 a year or more, at least one adult is assumed to be working 30 or more hours a week.

CHILD CARE
In families where a lone parent or both partners in a couple work for at least 16 hours a week, or where one partner works and the other is disabled, the family is entitled to child care payments. This payment can contribute up to £135 a week to the cost of child care for one child and up to £200 a week for two or more children. Families can only claim if they use an approved child care provider.

CHILD TAX CREDIT
Child Tax Credit combines all income-related support for children and is paid direct to the main carer. The credit is made up of a main 'family' payment with additional payments for each extra child in the household, for

children with a disability and an extra payment for children who are severely disabled. Child Tax Credit is available to households where:

– There is at least one dependant child under 16 years old
– There is at least one dependant young person under 19 years old and in full-time non-advanced education or registered with the Careers or Connexions Service (does not include Scotland or Northern Ireland)

CHILD TAX CREDIT 2004–5
(£ per year)

	One Child		Two Children	
Annual Income	No Childcare	Maximum Childcare	No Childcare	Maximum Childcare
0	2,175	2,175	3,800	3,800
5,000	5,295	10,220	6,920	14,225
8,000	4,850	9,775	6,475	13,780
10,000	4,110	9,035	5,735	13,040
15,000	2,260	7,185	3,885	11,190
20,000	545	5,335	2,035	9,340
25,000	545	3,485	545	7,490
30,000	545	1,635	545	5,640
35,000	545	545	545	3,790
40,000	545	545	545	1,940
45,000	545	545	545	545
50,000	545	545	545	545
60,000	–	–	–	–

BENEFITS

Leaflets relating to the various benefits and contribution conditions for different benefits are available from local social security offices; leaflet GL23 *Social Security Benefit Rates* is a general guide to benefit rates and contributions.

CONTRIBUTORY BENEFITS
Entitlement to contributory benefits depends on contribution conditions being satisfied either by the claimant or by some other person (depending on the kind of benefit). The class or classes of contribution which for this purpose are relevant to each benefit are:

Jobseeker's Allowance (contribution-based)	Class 1
Incapacity Benefit	Class 1 or 2
Maternity Allowance	Class 1 or 2
Widow's Benefit and Bereavement Benefit	Class 1, 2 or 3
State Pensions, categories A and B	Class 1, 2 or 3

The system of contribution conditions relates to yearly levels of earnings on which contributions have been paid.

JOBSEEKER'S ALLOWANCE
Jobseeker's allowance (JSA) replaced unemployment benefit and income support for unemployed people under pension age from 7 October 1996. There are two routes of entitlement. Contribution-based JSA is paid as a personal rate (i.e. additional benefit for dependants is not paid) to those who have made sufficient NI contributions in two particular tax years. Savings and partner's earnings are not taken into account and payment can be made for up to six months. Rates of JSA correspond to income support rates.

Claims for this benefit are made through Jobcentre Plus offices and Jobcentres. A person wishing to claim JSA must be unemployed, capable of work and available for any work which they can reasonably be expected to do, usually for at least 40 hours per week. They must agree

and sign a 'jobseeker's agreement', which will set out each claimant's plans to find work, and must actively seek work. If they refuse work or training their benefit may be sanctioned for between one and 26 weeks.

A person will be sanctioned from JSA for up to 26 weeks if they have left a job voluntarily without just cause or through misconduct. In these circumstances, it may be possible to receive hardship payments, particularly where the claimant or their family is vulnerable, e.g. if sick or pregnant, or for those with children or caring responsibilities. See leaflet JSAL5.

INCAPACITY BENEFIT
Incapacity Benefit is available to those who are incapable of work but cannot get statutory sick pay from their employer. It is not payable to those over State Pension age. However, people who are already in receipt of short-term Incapacity Benefit when they reach State Pension age may continue to receive this benefit for up to 52 weeks. Apart from those people who qualify under the special provisions for people incapacitated in youth, entitlement is based on a person's National Insurance Contribution record. In order to qualify for Incapacity Benefit, two contribution conditions, based on the last three tax years before the year in which benefit is claimed, must be satisfied. The amount of Incapacity Benefit payable may be reduced where a claimant receives more than a specified amount of occupational or personal pension. Severely disabled people aged between 16 and 19 should receive Incapacity Benefit without meeting the national insurance contribution conditions. There are three rates of Incapacity Benefit:

– short-term lower rate for the first 28 weeks of sickness
– short-term higher rate from weeks 29 to 52
– long-term rate from week 53 onwards

The terminally ill and those entitled to the highest rate care component of disability living allowance are paid the long-term rate after 28 weeks. Incapacity benefit is taxable after 28 weeks.

Two rates of age addition are paid with long-term benefit based on the claimant's age when incapacity started. The higher rate is payable where incapacity for work commenced before the age of 35; and the lower rate where incapacity commenced before the age of 45. Increases for dependants are also payable with short and long-term incapacity benefit.

There are two medical tests of incapacity: the 'own occupation' test and the 'personal capability' assessment. Those who worked before becoming incapable of working will be assessed, for the first 28 weeks of incapacity, on their ability to do their own job. After 28 weeks (or from the start of incapacity for those who were not working) claimants are assessed on their ability to carry out a range of work-related activities. See leaflets IB1 and IB214. Since October 2001 all new benefit claimants in the 51 Jobcentre Plus areas receive a service combining jobs and benefits advice and support. The government plans to extend this as Jobcentre Plus is rolled out nationally. New Incapacity Benefit claimants will be invited back for work-focused interviews at intervals of not longer than three years. The interviews do not include medical tests, but if the claimant is due for a medical test around the same time, their local office will aim to schedule both together. People who are severely disabled and those who are terminally ill will not be asked to attend these interviews.

BEREAVEMENT BENEFITS

Bereavement benefits replaced widow's benefit on 9 April 2001. Those claiming widow's benefit before this date will continue to receive them under the old scheme for as long as they qualify. The new system provides bereavement benefits for widows and widowers providing that their deceased spouse paid National Insurance contributions. The new system offers benefits in three forms:

Bereavement Payment – may be received by a man or woman who is under the state pension age at the time of their spouse's death, or whose husband or wife was not entitled to a Category A retirement pension when he or she died. It is a single tax-free lump sum of £2,000 payable immediately on becoming a widow or widower

Widowed Parent's Allowance – a taxable benefit payable to the surviving partner if he or she is entitled or treated as entitled to child benefit, or to a widow if she is expecting her husband's baby

Bereavement Allowance – a taxable weekly benefit paid for 52 weeks after the spouse's death. A widow or widower may receive this pension if aged 45 or over at the time of his or her spouse's death or if his or her Widowed Parent's Allowance ends before 52 weeks. If aged 55 or over he or she will receive the full Bereavement Allowance

It is not possible to receive Widowed Parent's Allowance and Bereavement Allowance at the same time. Bereavement benefits and widow's benefit, in any form, cease upon remarriage or are suspended during a period of cohabitation as man and wife without being legally married. *See* leaflet GL14, D49 (D49S for deaths that occur in Scotland).

STATE PENSION: CATEGORIES A AND B

Category A pension is payable for life to men and women who reach State Pension age and who satisfy the contributions conditions. Category B pension is payable for life to married women, widows and widowers and is based on their wife or husband's contributions. It is payable to a married woman only when the wife and husband have claimed their State Pension and they have both reached State Pension age. From April 2010, a married man will be able to qualify for a Category B pension from his wife's contributions providing she was born on or after 6 April 1950. A Category B pension is also payable on widowhood after the State Pension age. This is payable to widows regardless of the age of their husband when he died. At present it is paid to widowers only if their wife had reached State Pension age when she died. Widowers who reach State Pension age on or after 6 April 2010 will be able to get a Category B pension on the same terms as widows. There are special rules for those who are widowed before reaching State Pension age.

Where a person is entitled to both a Category A and Category B pension then only one can be paid. The person can choose which to get. If no choice is made, the most favourable one will be paid.

A person may defer claiming their pension for five years after State Pension age. In doing so they may earn increments which will increase the weekly amount paid when they claim their State Pension. If a married man defers his Category A pension, his wife cannot claim a Category B pension on his contributions but she may earn increments on her State Pension during this time. A woman can defer her Category B pension, and earn increments, even if her husband is claiming his Category A pension.

The basic State Pension is £79.60 per week plus any additional (earnings-related) State Pension the person may be entitled to. An increase of £47.65 is paid for an adult dependant, providing the dependant's earnings do not exceed the rate of Jobseeker's Allowance for a single person (*see* below) and the couple are living together. If the couple are not living together an increase is payable of the dependant's earnings are not above £47.65. Before April 2003 it was also possible to get an increase of Category A and B pensions for a child or children. Since April 2003 provision for children has been made through Child Tax Credits. An age addition of 25p per week is payable with a State Pension if a pensioner is aged 80 or over.

Since 1989 pensioners have been allowed to have unlimited earnings without affecting their State Pension. Income support can be paid where a person's income is below a set level and pensioners may also be entitled to housing and council tax benefits.

GRADUATED RETIREMENT BENEFIT

Graduated NI contributions were first payable from 1961 and were calculated as a percentage of earnings between certain bands. They were discontinued in 1975. Graduated Retirement Benefit is paid in addition to any State Pension. A husband or wife can only get a graduated pension in return for his/her own graduated contributions, but not for his/her spouse's.

Graduated Retirement Benefit is at a weekly rate for each 'unit' of graduated contributions paid by the employee (half a unit or more counts as a whole unit); the rate varies from person to person. A unit of graduated Retirement Benefit can be calculated by adding together all graduated contributions and dividing by 7.5 (men) or 9.0 (women). If a person defers making a claim beyond 65 (60 for a woman), entitlement may be increased by one seventh of a penny per £1 of its weekly rate for each complete week of deferred retirement, as long as the retirement is deferred for a minimum of seven weeks.

In April 2002 the Pension Service, part of the Department for Work and Pensions was set up to provide an improved service for pensioners, through its network of pension centres and local services.

WEEKLY RATES OF BENEFIT *from April 2004*
Jobseeker's Allowance (JSA) (contribution-based)

Person under 18	£33.50
Person aged 18–24	£44.05
Person aged 25 to State Pension age	£55.65

From October 2003 people between 60 and State Pension age can choose to claim Pension Credits instead of JSA.

Short-term Incapacity Benefit

Person under State Pension age – lower rate	£55.90
Person under State Pension age – higher rate	£66.15
Increase for adult dependant	£34.60
Person over State Pension age	£71.15
Person over State Pension age – higher rate	£74.15
Increase for adult dependant	£42.65

Long-term Incapacity Benefit

Person under State Pension age	£74.15
Increase for adult dependant	£44.35
Age addition – lower rate	£7.80
Age addition – higher rate	£15.55

Widow's Benefit (from April 2004)

Widowed mother's allowance	£79.60
Widow's pension, full entitlement	
(aged 55 and over at time of spouse's death)	£79.60

Amount of widow's pension by age of widow at spouse's death (for deaths occurring before 11 April 1988 refer to the age-points in brackets):

aged 54 (49)	£74.03
aged 53 (48)	£68.46
aged 52 (47)	£62.88
aged 51 (46)	£57.31
aged 50 (45)	£51.74
aged 49 (44)	£46.17
aged 48 (43)	£40.60
aged 47 (42)	£35.02
aged 46 (41)	£29.45
aged 45 (40)	£23.88

Bereavement Benefit (from April 2003)

Bereavement Payment (lump sum)	£2,000.00
Widowed Parent's Allowance	£79.60
Bereavement Allowance, full entitlement	
(aged 55 and over at time of spouse's death)	£79.60

Amount of Bereavement Allowance by age of widow/widower at spouse's death:

aged 54	£74.03
aged 53	£68.46
aged 52	£62.88
aged 51	£57.31
aged 50	£51.74
aged 49	£46.17
aged 48	£40.60
aged 47	£35.02
aged 46	£29.45
aged 45	£23.88

State Pension: categories A and B

Single person	£79.60
Increase for adult dependant	£47.65

NON-CONTRIBUTORY BENEFITS

These benefits are paid from general taxation and are not dependent on NI contributions. Unless otherwise stated, a benefit is tax-free and is not means tested.

JOBSEEKER'S ALLOWANCE (INCOME-BASED)

Those who do not qualify for contribution-based Jobseeker's Allowance (JSA(c)), those who have exhausted their entitlement to contribution-based JSA or those for whom contribution-based JSA provides insufficient income may qualify for income-based JSA. The amount paid depends on age, number of dependants, amount of income and savings. Income-based JSA comprises of three parts:

– A personal allowance for the jobseeker and his/her partner and an allowance for each child or young person for whom they are responsible (*see* below)
– Premiums for people with special needs
– Premiums for housing costs

The rules of entitlement are the same as for contribution-based JSA.

If one person in a couple was born after 28 October 1957 and neither person in the couple has responsibility for a child or children, then the couple will have to make a joint claim for JSA if they wish to receive income-based JSA.

Since April 2003 claimants have had the option to choose to claim Child Tax Credit instead of an increase of JSA for children.

MATERNITY ALLOWANCE

Maternity Allowance (MA) covers women who are self-employed or otherwise do not qualify for Statutory Maternity Pay (SMP). In order to qualify for payment, a woman must have been employed and/or self-employed for at least 26 weeks in the 66 week period up to and including the week before the baby is due (test period). She must also have average weekly earning of at least £30 (Maternity Allowance Threshold) in any 13 weeks of the test period. Women who are self-employed will be deemed to have earnings at or above the Maternity Allowance Threshold. A woman can choose to start receiving MA from the 11th week before the week in which the baby is due up to the day following the day of birth. This will depend on when the woman stops work to have her baby or if the baby is born before she stops work. However, where the woman is absent from work for pregnancy related illness on or after the Sunday of the 4th week before the baby is due to be born, MA will start the day following the first day of absence from work for a pregnancy related illness. MA is paid up to 26 weeks and is only paid while the woman is not working.

CHILD BENEFIT

Child Benefit is payable for virtually all children aged under 16, and for those aged 16 to 18 who are studying full-time up to and including A-level or equivalent standard. It is also payable for a short period if the child has left school recently and is registered for work or work-based training for young people at a careers office or with the Connexions Service (in Northern Ireland, Training and Employment Agency).

GUARDIAN'S ALLOWANCE

Where the parents of a child are dead, the person who has the child in his/her family may claim a Guardian's Allowance in addition to Child Benefit. In specified circumstances the allowance is payable on the death of only one parent. *See* leaflet NI14.

CARER'S ALLOWANCE

Carer's Allowance (CA) is a benefit payable to people who spend at least 35 hours per week caring for a severely disabled person. To qualify for CA a person must be caring for someone in receipt of one of the following benefits:

– the middle or highest rate of disability living allowance care component
– either rate of attendance allowance
– constant attendance allowance, paid at not less than the normal maximum rate, under the industrial injuries or war pension schemes

See leaflets SD1 and SD4.

SEVERE DISABLEMENT ALLOWANCE

Since April 2001 Severe Disablement Allowance (SDA) has not been available to new claimants. Those claiming SDA before that date will continue to receive it for as long as they qualify. *See* leaflet NI252.

ATTENDANCE ALLOWANCE

This is payable to disabled people who claim after the age of 65 and who need a lot of care or supervision because of physical or mental disability for a period of at least six months. Attendance Allowance has two rates: the lower rate is for day or night care, and the higher rate is for day and night care. People not expected to live for more than six months because of an illness can receive the highest rate of Attendance Allowance straight away. *See* leaflets DS702 and SD1.

DISABILITY LIVING ALLOWANCE
This is payable to disabled people who claim before the age of 65 who have personal care and/or mobility needs because of an illness or disability for a period of at least three months and are likely to have those needs for a further six months or more. The allowance has two components: the care component, which has three rates, and the mobility component, which has two rates. The rates depend on the care and mobility needs of the claimant. People not expected to live for more than six months because of an illness will automatically receive the highest rate of the care component. *See* leaflets DS704 and SD1.

STATE PENSION: CATEGORY D
Category D pension is provided for people aged 80 and over if they are not entitled to another category of pension or are entitled to less than the Category D rate. The person must also normally live in Great Britain and have done so for a continuous period of ten years within any 20-year period since their 60th birthday.

WEEKLY RATES OF BENEFIT *from April 2004*
Jobseeker's Allowance (income-based)

Person under 18, living with family	£33.50
Person under 18, living away from home	£44.05
Person aged 18–24	£44.05
Person aged 25 to state pension age	£55.65
Couple with one or both under 18	£33.50–£87.30
	(depending on circumstances)
Couple aged 18 to state pension age	£87.30
Dependant children and young persons premium	
up to 16	£42.27
16–19 years	£42.27
Family premium	£15.95
Family premium (lone parent)	£15.95

Maternity Allowance

Standard rate	£100 or 90% of the women's average weekly earnings if less than £100
Increase for adult dependant	£34.60

Child Benefit

Eldest child	£16.50
Each subsequent child	£11.05

Guardian's allowance

Each child	£11.85

Carer's Allowance

	£44.35
Increase for dependant adult	£26.50

Severe Disablement Allowance

*Basic rate	£44.80
Age related addition:	
Under 40	£15.55
40–49	£10.00
50–59	£5.00

Additions may be payable for dependant adults

Attendance allowance

Higher rate	£58.80
Lower rate	£39.35

Disability living allowance
Care component

Higher rate	£58.80
Middle rate	£39.35
Lowest rate	£15.55
Mobility component	
Higher rate	£41.05
Lower rate	£15.55

State Pension: category D

Single person	£47.65
Increase for wife/other adult dependant	£28.50
Age addition to State Pension at age 80	£0.25

* The age addition applies to the age when incapacity began

INCOME SUPPORT
Income Support is a benefit for those aged 16 and over whose income is below a certain level. It can be paid to people who are not expected to sign on as unemployed (Income Support for unemployed people was replaced by Jobseeker's Allowance in October 1996) and who are:
– incapable of work due to sickness or disability
– bringing up children alone
– looking after a person who has a disability
– registered blind
Pension Credit replaced Income Support for people aged 60 or over on 6 October 2003. Some people who are not in these categories may also be able to claim income support.

Income Support is also payable to people who work for less than 16 hours a week on average (or 24 hours for a partner). Some people can claim Income Support if they work longer hours.

Income Support is not payable if the claimant, or claimant and partner, have capital or savings in excess of £8,000. For capital and savings in excess of £3,000, a deduction of £1 is made for every £250 or part of £250 held. Different limits apply to people permanently in residential care and nursing homes: the upper limit is £16,000 and deductions apply for capital in excess of £10,000.

Sums payable depend on fixed allowances laid down by law for people in different circumstances. If both partners are entitled to Income Support, either may claim it for the couple. People receiving Income Support may be able to receive Housing Benefit, help with mortgage or home loan interest and help with health care. They may also be eligible for help with exceptional expenses from the Social Fund. Special rates may apply to some people living in residential care or nursing homes. Leaflet IS20 gives a detailed explanation of income support.

In October 1998 the Government's voluntary New Deal for Lone Parents programme became available throughout the UK. All lone parents receiving Income Support are assigned a personal adviser at a Jobcentre who will provide guidance and support with a view to enabling the claimant to find work.

INCOME SUPPORT PREMIUMS
Income Support premiums are additional weekly payments for those with special needs. People qualifying for more than one premium will normally only receive the highest single premium for which they qualify. However,

family premium, disabled child premium, severe disability premium and carer premium are payable in addition to other premiums.

People with children may qualify for:
– the family premium if they have at least one child (a higher rate is paid to lone parents, although from 6 April 1998 it has not been available to new claimants)
– the disabled child premium if they have a child who receives Disability Living Allowance or is registered blind

Carers may qualify for:
– the carer premium if they or their partner are in receipt of Carer's Allowance

Long-term sick or disabled people may qualify for:
– the disability premium if they or their partner are receiving certain benefits because they are disabled or cannot work; are registered blind; or if the claimant has been incapable of work or receiving Statutory Sick Pay for at least 364 days (196 days if the person is terminally ill), including periods of incapacity separated by eight weeks or less
– the severe disability premium if the person lives alone and receives Attendance Allowance or the middle or higher rate of Disability Living Allowance care component and no one receives Carer's Allowance for caring for that person. This premium is also available to couples where both partners meet the above conditions

WEEKLY RATES OF BENEFIT *from April 2004*
Income Support
Single person

under 18	£33.50
under 18 (higher)	£44.05
aged 18–24	£44.05
aged 25 and over	£55.65
aged under 18 and a single parent (lower)	£33.50
aged under 18 and a single parent (higher)	£44.05
aged 18 and over and a single parent	£55.65

Couples	
Both under 18	£66.50
One or both aged 18 or over	£87.30
For each child in a family from birth to day before 19th birthday	£42.27

Premiums	
Family premium	£15.95
Family (lone parent) premium	£15.95
Disabled child premium	£42.49
Carer premium	£25.55
Disability premium	
Single	£23.70
Couple	£33.85
Enhanced disability premium	
Single	£11.60
Enhanced disabled child premium	£17.08
Severe disability premium	
Lower rate (single person and some couples)	£44.15
Higher rate (couples)	£88.30

PENSION CREDIT
Pension Credit was introduced on 6 October 2003 and replaces Income Support for those aged 60 and over.

There are two elements to Pension Credit:

The Guarantee Credit
The guarantee credit provides a guaranteed minimum income, with additional elements for people who have:
– relevant housing costs
– severe disabilities
– caring responsibilities

Income from State Pension, private pensions, income from capital, earnings and certain benefits are taken into account when calculating the guarantee credit. For savings and capital in excess of £6,000 a deduction of £1 is made for every £500 or part of £500 held.

People receiving the guarantee credit element of Pension Credit may be able to receive Housing Benefit, Council Tax Benefit and help with health care.

The Savings Credit
Single people aged 65 or over (and couples where one member is 65 or over) may be entitled to a Savings Credit which will reward pensioners who have modest income or savings. The Savings Credit is calculated by taking into account any qualifying income above the Savings Credit threshold. For 2004–5 the threshold is £79.60 for single people and £127.25 for couples. The Savings Credit gives pensioners a cash addition calculated at 60p for every pound of qualifying income they have between the Savings Credit threshold and the Guarantee Credit. After this, the maximum reward will be reduced by 40p for every pound of income above the guarantee level. The maximum Savings Credit is £15.51 per week (£20.22 a week for couples).

Income that qualifies towards the Savings Credit includes state pensions, earnings, second pensions and capital above £6,000.

Where only the Savings Credit is in payment, people need to claim standard Housing Benefit or Council Tax Benefit. Although local authorities take any Savings Credit into account in the Housing Benefit/Council Tax Benefit assessment. The Housing Benefit/Council Tax Benefit applicable amount for people aged 65 and over is enhanced to ensure that gains in Pension Credit are not depleted.

WEEKLY RATES OF BENEFIT *from April 2004*

Standard minimum guarantee:	
Single	£105.45
Couple	£160.95
Additional amount for:	
Severe disability	£44.15
Carers	£25.55
Savings Credit threshold	
Single	£79.60
Couple	£127.25

HOUSING BENEFIT
Housing Benefit is designed to help people with rent (including rent for accommodation in guesthouses, lodgings or hostels). It does not cover mortgage payments. The amount of benefit paid depends on:
– the income of the claimant, and partner if there is one, including earned income, unearned income (any other income including some other benefits) and savings
– number of dependants
– certain extra needs of the claimant, partner or any dependants
– number and gross income of people sharing the home who are not dependent on the claimant
– how much rent is paid

Housing Benefit is not payable if the claimant, or claimant and partner, have savings of over £16,000. The amount of benefit is affected if savings held exceed £3,000 (£6,000 for pensioners and £10,000 for people living in care homes). Housing Benefit is not paid for meals, fuel or certain service charges that may be included in the rent. Deductions are also made for most non-dependants who live in the same accommodation as the claimant (and their partner).

The maximum amount of benefit (which is not necessarily the same as the amount of rent paid) may be paid where the claimant is in receipt of Income Support or income-based Jobseeker's Allowance or where the claimant's income is less than the amount allowed for their needs. Any income over that allowed for their needs will mean that their benefit is reduced. See leaflets GL16 and RR2.

COUNCIL TAX BENEFIT

Nearly all the rules which apply to Housing Benefit apply to Council Tax Benefit, which helps people on low incomes to pay council tax bills. The amount payable depends on how much council tax is paid and who lives with the claimant. The benefit may be available to those receiving Income Support or income-based Jobseeker's Allowance or to those whose income is less than that allowed for their needs. Any income over that allowed for their needs will mean that their Council Tax Benefit is reduced. Deductions are made for non-dependants.

The maximum amount that is payable for those living in properties in council tax bands A to E is 100 per cent of the claimant's council tax liability. This also applies to those living in properties in bands F to H who were in receipt of the benefit at 31 March 1998 if they have remained in the same property. From 1 April 1998 council tax benefit for new claimants living in property bands F to H (or existing claimants moving into these bands) was restricted to the level payable for band E.

If a person shares a home with one or more adults (not their partner) who are on a low income, it may be possible to claim a second adult rebate. Those who are entitled to both Council Tax Benefit and second adult rebate will be awarded whichever is the greater. Second adult rebate may be claimed by those not in receipt of Council Tax Benefit.

ONE-OFF 70+ PAYMENT

In 2004 the Government made a one-off payment of up to £100 to each household with one occupier aged 70 or over to help them with living expenses, including council tax bills. To be eligible for the payment, the person had to reside in the UK on any day of the week between 20–26 September 2004 and have reached the age of 70 on or before 26 September 2004. The payment was a tax-free lump sum that did not affect any state pensions or benefits received. The One-off 70+ Payment was paid automatically with the Winter Fuel Payment.

THE SOCIAL FUND

REGULATED PAYMENTS

Sure Start Maternity Grant

The Sure Start Maternity Grant (SSMG) is a one-off payment of £500 for parents on low incomes to buy essential items for new babies. To qualify, mothers and expectant mothers must also receive health and welfare advice for themselves and their child from an approved health professional. SSMG can be claimed any time from the 29th week of pregnancy until the child is three months old. Those eligible are mothers or their partners in receipt of Income Support, income-based Jobseeker's Allowance, Child Tax Credit at a rate higher than the family element or Working Tax Credit where a disability or severe disability element is in payment.

Funeral Payments

Payable for the necessary cost of burial or cremation, plus other funeral expenses reasonably incurred up to £700, to people receiving Income Support, income-based Jobseeker's Allowance, Child Tax Credit at a higher rate than the family element, Working Tax Credit where a disability or severe disability element is in payment, Council Tax Benefit or Housing Benefit who have good reason for taking responsibility for the funeral expenses. These payments are recoverable from any estate of the deceased.

Cold Weather Payments

A payment of £8.50 when the average temperature over seven consecutive days is recorded at or forecast to be 0°C or below in the qualifying person's area. Payments are made to people on Income Support or income-based Jobseeker's Allowance and those who have a child under five or whose benefit includes a pensioner or disability premium. Payments do not have to be repaid.

Winter Fuel Payments

An annual payment of £200 per household paid to most people aged 60 or over. The majority of eligible people are paid automatically before Christmas, although a few need to claim. Payments do not have to be repaid.

DISCRETIONARY PAYMENTS

Community Care Grants

These are intended to help people on Income Support or income-based Jobseeker's Allowance or receiving payments on account of such benefits (or those likely to receive these benefits on leaving residential or institutional accommodation) to live as independently as possible in the community; ease exceptional pressures on families; care for a prisoner or young offender released on temporary licence; help people set up home as part of a resettlement programme and/or assist with certain travelling expenses. They do not have to be repaid.

Budgeting Loans

These are interest-free loans to people who have been receiving Income Support or income-based Jobseeker's Allowance, or payments on account of such benefits for at least 26 weeks, for intermittent expenses that may be difficult to budget for.

Crisis Loans

These are interest-free loans to anyone, whether receiving benefits or not, who is without resources in an emergency, where there is no other means of preventing serious damage or serious risk to their health or safety.

SAVINGS

Savings over £500 (£1,000 for people aged 60 or over) are taken into account for Community Care Grants and Budgeting Loans. All savings are taken into account for Crisis Loans. Savings are not taken into account for Sure Start Maternity Grants, Funeral Payments, Cold Weather or Winter Fuel Payments.

INDUSTRIAL INJURIES AND DISABLEMENT BENEFITS

The industrial injuries scheme, administered under the Social Security Contributions and Benefits Act 1992, provides a range of benefits designed to compensate for disablement resulting from an industrial accident (i.e. an accident arising out of and in the course of an employed earner's employment) or from a prescribed disease due to the nature of a person's employment. Those who are self-employed are not covered by this scheme.

INDUSTRIAL INJURIES DISABLEMENT BENEFIT

A person must be at least 14 per cent disabled (except for certain respiratory diseases) in order to qualify for this benefit. The amount paid depends on the degree of disablement:

- those assessed as 14–19 per cent disabled are paid at the 20 per cent rate
- those with disablement of over 20 per cent will have the percentage rounded up or down to the nearest ten per cent, e.g. a disablement of 44 per cent will be paid at the 40 per cent rate while a disablement of 45 per cent will be paid at the 50 per cent rate

Benefit is payable 15 weeks (90 days) after the date of the accident or onset of the disease and may be payable for a limited period or for life. The benefit is payable whether the person works or not and those who are incapable of work are entitled to draw statutory sick pay or incapacity benefit in addition to industrial injuries disablement benefit. It may also be possible to claim the following allowances:

- reduced earnings allowance for those who are unable to return to their regular work or work of the same standard and who had their accident (or whose disease started) before 1 October 1990
- retirement allowance for those who were entitled to reduced earnings allowance who have reached State Pension age
- constant attendance allowance for those with a disablement of 100 per cent who need constant care. There are four rates of allowance depending on how much care the person needs
- exceptionally severe disablement allowance for those who are entitled to constant care attendance allowance at one of the higher rates and who need constant care permanently

See leaflets SD6, SD7 and SD8.

OTHER BENEFITS

People who are disabled because of an accident or disease that was the result of work that they did before 5 July 1948 are not entitled to industrial injuries disablement benefit. They may, however, be entitled to payment under the workmen's compensation scheme or the pneumoconiosis, byssinosis and miscellaneous diseases benefit scheme. See leaflet GL23. People who suffer from certain industrial diseases caused by dust, or their dependants, can make a claim for an additional payment under the Pneumoconiosis etc. (Workers' Compensation) Act 1979 if they are unable to get damages from the employer who caused or contributed to the disease.

WEEKLY RATES OF BENEFIT *from April 2004*
*Disablement benefit/pension
Degree of disablement:

100 per cent	£120.10
90	£108.09
80	£96.08
70	£84.07
60	£72.06
50	£60.05
40	£48.04
30	£36.03
20	£24.02
Unemployability supplement	£74.15
Addition for adult dependant (subject to earnings rule)	£44.35
Reduced earnings allowance (maximum)	£48.04
Retirement allowance (maximum)	£12.01
Constant attendance allowance (normal maximum rate)	£48.10
Exceptionally severe disablement allowance	£48.10

* There is a weekly benefit for those under 18 with no dependants which is set at a lower rate

CLAIMS AND QUESTIONS

Entitlement to benefit and regulated Social Fund payments is determined by a decision maker on behalf of the Secretary of State for the Department of Work and Pensions. A claimant who is dissatisfied with that decision can ask for an explanation. They can dispute the decision by applying to have it revised or, in particular circumstances, superseded. If they are still dissatisfied they can go to the Appeals Service where it will be heard by an independent tribunal. There is a further right of appeal to a Social Security Commissioner against the tribunal's decision but this is on a point of law only and leave to appeal must first be obtained.

Decisions on claims and applications for Housing Benefit and Council Tax Benefit are made by Local Authority decision makers. The explanation, dispute and appeals process is the same as for other benefits. See leaflets GL24 and NI260DMA.

Decisions on applications to the discretionary Social Fund are made by Social Fund Officers. Applicants can ask for a review within 28 days of the date on the decision letter. The Social Fund Review Officer will review the case and there is a further right of review by an independent Social Fund Inspector.

EMPLOYER PAYMENTS

STATUTORY MATERNITY PAY

Employers pay Statutory Maternity Pay (SMP) to pregnant women who have been employed by them full or part-time for at least 26 weeks into the 15th week before the week the baby is due, and whose earnings on average at least equal the lower earnings limit applied to NI contributions (£79 per week from April 2004). All women who meet these conditions receive payment of 90 per cent of their average earnings for the first six weeks, followed by a maximum of 20 weeks at £102.80 or 90 per cent of the woman's average weekly earnings if this is less than £102.80. SMP can be paid, at the earliest, 11 weeks before the week in which the baby is due, up to the day following the birth. Women can decide when they wish their maternity leave to start and can work until the baby is born. However, where the woman is absent from work for a pregnancy related illness on or after the

Sunday of the 4th week before the baby is due to be born, SMP will start the day following the first day of absence from work for the pregnancy related illness. SMP is not payable for any week in which the woman works. Employers are reimbursed for 92 per cent of the SMP they pay. Small employers with annual gross NI payments of £45,000 or less recover 100 per cent of the SMP paid out plus 4.5 per cent in compensation for the secondary National Insurance Contributions paid on SMP. *See* Leaflet NI17A and Inland Revenue guide for employers E15.

STATUTORY PATERNITY PAY

Employers pay Statutory Paternity Pay (SPP) to employees who are taking leave when a child is born or placed for adoption. To qualify the employee must:
– have responsibility for the child's upbringing
– be the biological father of the child (or the child's adopter), or the husband/partner of the mother or adopter
– be taking time off work to care for the child and/or support the mother or adopter
– have been employed by the same employer for at least 26 weeks ending with the 15th week before the baby is due (or the week in which the adopter is notified of having been matched with a child)
– continue working for the employer up to the child's birth (or placement for adoption)
– have earnings on average at least equal to the lower earnings limit applied to NI contributions (£79 per week from April 2004)
Employees who meet these conditions receive payment of £102.80 or 90 per cent of the employee's average weekly earnings if this is less than £102.80. The employee can choose to be paid for one or two consecutive weeks. The earliest the SPP period can begin is the date of the child's birth or placement for adoption. The SPP period must be completed within eight weeks of that date. SSP is not payable for any week in which the employee works. Employers are reimbursed in the same way as for Statutory Maternity Pay. *See* Department of Trade and Industry leaflet PL514 and PL515.

STATUTORY ADOPTION PAY

Employers pay Statutory Adoption Pay (SAP) to employees taking adoption leave from their employers. To qualify for SAP the employee must:
– be newly matched with a child by an adoption agency
– have been employed by the same employer for at least 26 weeks ending the week in which they have been notified of being matched with a child
– have earnings at least equal to the lower earnings limit applied to NI contributions (£79 per week from April 2004)
Employees who meet these conditions receive payment of £102.80 or 90 per cent of their average weekly earnings if this is less than £102.80 for up to 26 weeks. The SAP period can start from the date of the child's placement. SAP is not payable for any week in which the employee works. Where a couple adopt a child only one of them may receive SAP, the other may be able to receive Statutory Paternity Pay (SPP) if they meet the eligibility criteria. Employers are reimbursed in the same way as for Statutory Maternity Pay. *See* Department of Trade and Industry leaflet PL515.

STATUTORY SICK PAY

Employers pay Statutory Sick Pay (SSP) for up to 28 weeks to any employee incapable of work for four or more consecutive days. SSP is payable to employees between the ages of 16 and 65 who have average earnings at or above the point at which earnings become relevant for NI purposes (£79 from April 2004) in a specified period. SSP is paid at £66.15 per week and is subject to PAYE and NI contributions. Employees who cannot obtain SSP may be able to claim Incapacity Benefit. Employers may be able to recover some SSP costs. *See* Inland Revenue Leaflets CA86 *Employees* and CA30 *Employer Manual.*

WAR PENSIONS

The Veteran's Agency (originally known as The War Pensions Agency) became an executive agency of the Ministry of Defence in June 2001. The Agency awards war pensions under the Naval, Military and Air Forces, Etc. (Disablement and Death) Service Pensions Order 1983 to members of the armed forces in respect of disablement or death due to service. There is also a scheme for civilians and civil defence workers in respect of the 1939–45 war, and other schemes for groups such as merchant seamen and Polish armed forces who served under British command during World War II.

PENSIONS

War disablement pension is awarded for the disabling effects of any injury, wound or disease which is the result of, or has been aggravated by, conditions of service in the armed forces. Claims can only be considered once the person has left the armed forces. The amount of pension paid depends on the severity of disablement, which is assessed by comparing the health of the claimant with that of a healthy person of the same age and sex. The person's earning capacity or occupation are not taken into account in this assessment. A pension is awarded if the person has a disablement of 20 per cent or more and a lump sum is usually payable to those with a disablement of less than 20 per cent. No award is made for noise-induced sensorineural hearing loss where the assessment of disablement is less than 20 per cent.

War widow/widower's pension is payable where the spouse's death was due to, or hastened by, service in the armed forces or where the spouse was in receipt of a war disablement pension constant attendance allowance (or would have been if not in hospital) at the time of death. A war widow/widower's pension is also payable if the spouse was getting War Disablement Pension at the 80 per cent rate or higher and was receiving unemployability supplement at the time of death. War widows/widowers receive a standard rank-related rate but a lower weekly rate is payable to war widows/widowers of personnel below the rank of Major who are under the age of 40, without children and capable of maintaining themselves. This is increased to the standard rate at age 40. Allowances are paid for children (in addition to child benefit) and adult dependants. An age allowance is automatically given when the widow/widower reaches 65 and increased at ages 70 and 80.

All war pensions and war widow/widower's pensions are tax-free and pensioners living overseas receive the same amount as those resident in the UK.

SUPPLEMENTARY ALLOWANCES

A number of supplementary allowances may be awarded to a war pensioner which are intended to meet various needs which may result from disablement or death and take account of its particular effect on the pensioner or spouse. The principal supplementary allowances are unemployability supplement, allowance for lowered standard of occupation and constant attendance allowance. Others include exceptionally severe disablement allowance, severe disablement occupational allowance, treatment allowance, mobility supplement, comforts allowance, clothing allowance, age allowance and widow/widower's age allowance. Rent and children's allowances are also available on war widow/widower's pensions.

DEPARTMENT FOR WORK AND PENSIONS BENEFITS

Most benefits are paid in addition to the basic war disablement pension or war widow/widower's pension, but may be affected by supplementary allowances in payment. Any State Pension for which a war widow/widower qualifies on their own NI contribution record can be paid in addition to war widow/widower's pension.

CLAIMS AND QUESTIONS

To claim a war pension it is necessary to contact the nearest war pensioners' welfare service office, the address of which is available from local social security offices, or to write to the Veteran's Agency, Norcross, Blackpool FY5 3WP. Claims can also be made through authorised agents, usually ex-service organisations such as the RBL, BLESMA etc. General advice on any war pensions matter can be obtained by ringing the War Pensions Freeline (UK only) on 0800-169 2277. If living overseas, call T (+44) (125) 386-6043 E help@veteransagency.mod.uk W www.veteransagency.mod.uk

THE WATER INDUSTRY

ENGLAND AND WALES

The water industry supplies around 18,000 million litres of water every day. In 2002 water companies in England and Wales carried out around 2.9 million tests on drinking water samples of which 99.87 per cent met all British and European standards. In England and Wales the Secretary of State for Environment, Food and Rural Affairs and the National Assembly for Wales have overall responsibility for water policy and oversee environmental standards for the water industry.

THE WATER COMPANIES

Until 1989 nine regional water authorities in England and the Welsh Water Authority in Wales were responsible for water supply and the development of water resources, sewerage and sewage disposal, pollution control, freshwater fisheries, flood protection, water recreation and environmental conservation. The Water Act 1989 provided for the creation of a privatised water industry under public regulation. The functions of the regional water authorities were taken over by ten holding companies and the regulatory bodies and have since been consolidated into the Water Industry Act 1991.

Water UK is the industry association that represents all UK water and wastewater service suppliers at national and European level. Water UK provides a framework for the water industry to engage with government, regulators, stakeholder organisations and the public. Water UK is funded directly by its members who are the service suppliers for England, Scotland, Wales and Northern Ireland; every member has a seat on the Water UK Council.

WATER UK, 1 Queen Anne's Gate, London SW1H 9BT
T 020-7344 1844 W www.water.org.uk
Chief Executive, Pamela Taylor

WATER SERVICE COMPANIES

ANGLIAN WATER SERVICES LTD, Anglian House, Ambury Road, Huntingdon, Cambs PE29 3NZ T 01480-323000
W www.anglianwater.co.uk

BOURNEMOUTH & WEST HAMPSHIRE WATER PLC, George Jessel House, Francis Avenue, Bournemouth, Dorset BH11 8NB T 01202-591111
W www.bwhwater.co.uk

BRISTOL WATER PLC, PO Box 218, Bridgwater Road, Bristol BS99 7AU T 0117-966 5881
W www.bristolwater.co.uk

CAMBRIDGE WATER PLC, 41 Rustat Road, Cambridge CB1 3QS T 01223-403000
W www.cambridge-water.co.uk

CHOLDERTON & DISTRICT WATER COMPANY, Estate Office, Cholderton, Salisbury, Wiltshire SP4 0DR
T 01980-629203

DEE VALLEY WATER PLC, Packsaddle, Wrexham Road, Rhostyllen, Wrexham LL14 4EH T 01978-846946

DWR CYMRU CYFYNGEDIG (WELSH WATER), Pentwyn Road, Nelson, Treharris, Mid Glamorgan CF46 6LY
T 01443-452300
W www.dwrcymru.co.uk

ESSEX & SUFFOLK WATER PLC (subsidiary of Northumbrian Water Ltd), Hall Street, Chelmsford, Essex CM2 0HH T 01245-491234
W www.eswater.co.uk

FOLKSTONE & DOVER WATER SERVICES LTD, Cherry Garden Lane, Folkestone, Kent CT19 4QB T 01303-298800

MID KENT WATER PLC, Snodland, Kent ME6 5AH
T 01634-873111
W www.midkentwater.co.uk

NORTHUMBRIAN WATER LTD, Abbey Road, Pity Me, Durham DH1 5FJ T 0191-383 2222 W www.nwl.co.uk

PORTSMOUTH WATER PLC, PO Box 8, West Street, Havant, Hampshire PO9 1LG T 02392-499888
W www.portsmouthwater.co.uk

SEVERN TRENT PLC, 2297 Coventry Road, Birmingham B26 3PU T 0121-722 4000 W www.severn-trent.com

SOUTH EAST WATER PLC, 3 Church Road, Haywards Heath, West Sussex RH16 3NY T 01444-448200
W www.southeastwater.co.uk

SOUTH STAFFORDSHIRE WATER PLC, Green Lane, Walsall, West Midlands WS2 7PD T 01922-638282
W www.south-staffs-water.co.uk

SOUTH WEST WATER LTD, Peninsula House, Rydon Lane, Exeter EX2 7HR T 01392-446688 W www.swwater.co.uk

SOUTHERN WATER, Southern House, Yeoman Road, Worthing, W. Sussex BN13 3NX T 01903-264444
W www.southernwater.co.uk

SUTTON AND EAST SURREY WATER PLC, London Road, Redhill, Surrey RH1 1LY T 01737-772000
W www.waterplc.com

TENDRING HUNDRED WATER SERVICES LTD, Mill Hill, Manningtree, Essex CO11 2AZ T 01206-399200
W www.thws.co.uk

THAMES WATER UTILITIES LTD, 14 Cavendish Place, London W1M 0NU T 020-7636 8686
W www.thameswater.com

THREE VALLEYS WATER PLC, PO Box 48, Bishops Rise, Hatfield, Hertfordshire AL10 9HL T 01707-268111
W www.3valleys.co.uk

UNITED UTILITIES WATER PLC, Dawson House, Liverpool Road, Great Sankey, Warrington WA5 3LW
T 01925-234000
W www.unitedutilities.com

WESSEX WATER SERVICES LTD, Claverton Down, Bath BA2 7WW T 01225-526000 W wessexwater.co.uk

YORKSHIRE WATER SERVICES LTD, Western House, Western Way, Halifax Road, Bradford BD6 2LZ
T 01274-600111 W www.yorkshirewater.com

ISLAND WATER AUTHORITIES (NOT MEMBERS OF WATER UK)

COUNCIL OF THE ISLES OF SCILLY, Town Hall, St Mary's, Isles of Scilly TR21 0LW T 01720-422902

ISLE OF MAN WATER AUTHORITY, Drill House, Tromode Road, Isle of Man IM2 5PA T 01624-624414

JERSEY NEW WATERWORKS COMPANY LTD, Mulcaster House, Westmount Road, St Helier, Jersey JE1 1DG T 01534-509999

STATES OF GUERNSEY WATER BOARD, PO Box 30, South Esplanade, St Peter Port, Guernsey GY1 3AS
T 01481-724552 W www.gov.gg

WATER SUPPLY AND CONSUMPTION 2002–3

	Supply		Consumption			
	Supply from Treatment Works (Ml/day)	Total Leakage (Ml/day)	Household (l/head/day) Unmetered	Metered	Non-household (l/prop/day) Unmetered	Metered
WATER AND SEWERAGE COMPANIES						
Anglian	1,150	192	159	123	254	3,003
Dwr Cymru	883	234	151	140	705	2,409
Northumbrian	736	153	146	128	831	4,355
Severn Trent	1,929	514	129	132	600	2,185
South West	447	84	159	138	1,481	1,614
Southern	595	92	162	148	550	2,631
Thames	2,842	943	165	149	962	3,334
United Utilities	1,952	465	149	128	759	2,642
Wessex	368	75	147	129	2,636	2,393
Yorkshire	1,299	296	146	137	123	2,879
Total	12,201	3,048	—	—	—	—
Average	—	—	150	135	771	2,702
WATER ONLY COMPANIES						
Total	3,203	559	—	—	—	—
Average	—	—	153	137	885	2,701

Source: Office of Water Services

REGULATORY BODIES

The Office of Water Services (Ofwat) was set up under the Water Act 1989 and is the independent economic regulator of the water and sewerage companies in England and Wales. Overall responsibility for water policy and overseeing environmental standards for the water industry lies with the Department for Environment, Food and Rural Affairs and the Welsh Assembly. Ofwat's main duty is to ensure that the companies can finance and carry out their statutory functions and to protect the interests of water customers. Ofwat is a non-ministerial government department headed by the Director-General of Water Services.

Under the Competition Act 1998, from 1 March 2000 the Competition Appeal Tribunal has heard appeals against the regulator's decisions regarding anti-competitive agreements and abuse of a dominant position in the marketplace. The 2003 Water Bill placed a new duty on Ofwat to have regard to sustainable development.

The Environment Agency was set up by the 1995 Environment Act as a non-departmental public body and is sponsored largely by the Department for Environment, Food and Rural Affairs and the Welsh Assembly. The Environment Agency has statutory duties and powers in relation to water resources, pollution control, flood defence, fisheries, recreation, conservation and navigation in England and Wales. They are also responsible for issuing permits, licences, consents and registrations such as industrial licences to abstract water and fishing licences.

The Drinking Water Inspectorate (DWI) is the drinking water quality regulator for England and Wales, responsible for assessing the quality of the drinking water supplied by the water companies and investigating any incidents affecting drinking water quality, initiating prosecution where necessary. The DWI also provides scientific advice on drinking water policy issues to the Department of the Environment, Food and Rural Affairs and the Welsh Assembly.

OFWAT, Centre City Tower, 7 Hill Street, Birmingham, B5 4UA
T 0121-625 1300 E enquiries@ofwat.gsi.gov.uk
W www.ofwat.gov.uk
Director-General: Philip Fletcher

METHODS OF CHARGING

In England and Wales, most domestic customers still pay for domestic water supply and sewerage services through charges based on the old rateable value of their property. It is expected that by March 2005 about 26 per cent of householders will be charged according to consumption, which is recorded by meter. Industrial and most commercial customers are charged according to consumption.

Under the Water Industry Act 1999, water companies can continue basing their charges on the old rateable value of property. Domestic customers can continue paying on an unmeasured basis unless they choose to pay according to consumption. After having a meter installed (which is free of charge), a customer can revert to unmeasured charging within 12 months. Domestic, school and hospital customers cannot be disconnected for non-payment.

Price Limits for the period 2000–5 were set by Ofwat in November 1999. Price limits for the period 2005–10 will be finalised by Ofwat in December 2004.

AVERAGE HOUSEHOLD WATER BILLS 2004–5

	Unmetered (£)	Metered (£)
Water	122	101
Sewerage	136	121
Combined	258	222

SCOTLAND

Overall responsibility for national water policy in Scotland rested with the Secretary of State for Scotland until July 1999 when it was devolved to the Scottish Ministers. Until The Local Government (Scotland) Act 1994, water supply and sewerage services were local authority responsibilities. The Central Scotland Water Development Board had the function of developing new sources of water supply for the purpose of providing water in bulk to water authorities whose limits of supply were within the Board's area. Under the Act, three new public water authorities, covering the north, east and west of Scotland respectively, took over the provision of water and sewerage services from April 1996. The Central Scotland Water Development Board was then abolished. The Act also established the Scottish Water and Sewerage Customers Council representing consumer interests. It monitored the performance of the authorities; approved charges schemes; investigated complaints; and advised the Secretary of State. The Water Industry Act 1999, whose Scottish provisions were accepted by the Scottish Executive, abolished the Scottish Water and Sewerage Customers Council and replaced it in November 1999 by a Water Industry Commissioner.

The Water Industry (Scotland) Act 2002 resulted from the Scottish Executive's proposal that a single authority was better placed than three separate authorities to harmonise changes across the Scottish water industry. In 2002 the three existing water authorities, East of Scotland Water, North of Scotland Water and West of Scotland Water merged to form Scottish Water. Scottish Water is a public sector company, structured and managed like a private company, but remains answerable to the Scottish Parliament. Scottish Water is regulated by the Water Industry Commissioner for Scotland, the Scottish Environment Protection Agency (SEPA), and the Drinking Water Quality Regulator for Scotland. The Water Industry Commissioner is responsible for regulating all aspects of economic and customer service performance, including water and sewerage charges and SEPA is responsible for environmental issues, including controlling pollution and promoting the cleanliness of Scotland's rivers, lochs and coastal waters.

SCOTTISH WATER, 26 Castle Drive, Carnegie Campus, Dunfermline KY11 8GG T 01383-848200
  W www.scottishwater.co.uk
SCOTTISH ENVIRONMENT PROTECTION AGENCY, Erskine Court, Castle Business Park, Stirling FK9 4TR
  T 01786-457700 W www.sepa.org.uk
WATER INDUSTRY COMMISSIONER FOR SCOTLAND, Ochil House, Springkerse Business Park, Stirling, FK7 7XE
  T 01786-430200 W www.watercommissioner.co.uk

METHODS OF CHARGING

Scottish Water sets charges for domestic and non-domestic water and sewerage provision through charges schemes which are regulated by the Water Industries Commissioner for Scotland. In February 2004 the harmonisation of all household charges across the country was completed following the merger of the separate authorities under Scottish Water.

NORTHERN IRELAND

In Northern Ireland ministerial responsibility for water services lies with The Minister of the Department for Regional Development. The Water Service, which is an executive agency of the Department for Regional Development, is responsible for policy and co-ordination with regard to supply, distribution and cleanliness of water, and the provision and maintenance of sewerage services.

The Water Service comprises four Divisions: Eastern, Northern, Western and Southern. The main divisional offices are based in Belfast, Ballymena, Londonderry and Craigavon.

METHODS OF CHARGING

The Water service is currently funded from public funds and direct charges. The department's policy is to meter all properties that are not exclusively domestic. They are, however, granted an allowance of 200 cubic metres per annum to reflect domestic usage – this is known as the domestic usage allowance. Customers are charged only for water used in excess of the domestic usage allowance together with a standing charge, which is intended to cover the costs of meter provision, maintenance, reading and billing. This allowance is not granted if rates are not paid on the property. Traders operating from de-rated, rate exempt or rate rebated premises are required to pay for the treatment and disposal of trade effluent which they discharge into the public sewer.

In December 2002, the Northern Ireland Office announced that water and sewerage services would become self-financed by 2006. Domestic customers would be charged directly for water and sewerage services, currently a proportion of the rates paid on domestic properties. Following a major public consultation on *The Reform of the Water and Sewerage Services In Northern Ireland* the initial conclusions from the Department for Regional Development was that the new domestic charge would included a fixed element and a variable element, the latter determined by property value or consumption.

NORTHERN IRELAND WATER SERVICE, Northland House, 3 Frederick Street, Belfast, BT1 2NR T 028-90 244711
  W www.waterni.gov.uk

ENERGY

The main primary sources of energy in Britain are oil, natural gas, coal, nuclear power and water power. The main secondary sources (e.g. sources derived from the primary sources) are electricity, coke and smokeless fuels and petroleum products. The Department for the Environment, Food and Rural Affairs (DEFRA) is responsible for promoting energy efficiency.

INDIGENOUS PRODUCTION OF PRIMARY FUELS
Million tonnes of oil equivalent

	2003
Coal	19.3
Petroleum	116.2
Natural gas	103.9
Primary electricity	20.9
Nuclear	20.5
Natural flow hydro	0.4
Total	260.4

Source: Department of Trade and Industry

INLAND ENERGY CONSUMPTION BY PRIMARY FUEL
Million tonnes of oil equivalent, seasonally adjusted

	2003
Coal	42.7
Petroleum	74.9
Natural gas	98.0
Primary electricity	21.1
Nuclear	20.5
Natural flow hydro	0.4
Net Imports	0.2
Total	236.7

Source: Department of Trade and Industry

TRADE IN FUELS AND RELATED MATERIALS 2003

	Quantity*	Value†
Imports		
Coal and other solid fuel	22.5	994
Crude petroleum	48.7	5,954
Petroleum products	25.0	3,874
Natural gas	1.0	137
Electricity	0.4	170
Total	97.6	11,129
Total ‡	—	10,318
Exports		
Coal and other solid fuel	0.6	53
Crude petroleum	75.9	9,236
Petroleum products	35.6	5,158
Natural gas	7.3	968
Electricity	0	181
Total	119.4	15,596
Total ‡	—	6,260

* Million tonnes of oil equivalent
† £ million
‡ Adjusted to exclude estimated costs of insurance, freight, etc.
Source: HM Customs & Excise

OIL

Until the 1960s Britain imported almost all its oil supplies. In 1969 oil was discovered in the Arbroath field of the UK Continental Shelf (UKCS). The first oilfield to be brought into production was the Argyll field in 1975, and since the mid-1970s Britain has been a major producer of crude oil.

Licences for exploration and production are granted to companies by the Department of Trade and Industry; the leading British oil companies are BP and Shell. At the end of 2003, 1,155 Seaward Production Licences and 132 onshore Petroleum Exploration and Development Licences had been awarded, and there were a total of 259 offshore oil and gas fields in production. In 2002 there were 9 oil refineries and three smaller refining units processing crude and process oils. There are estimated to be reserves of 1,300 million tonnes of oil remaining in the UKCS. Royalties are payable on fields approved before April 1982 and petroleum revenue tax is levied on fields approved between 1975 and March 1993.

DRILLING ACTIVITY 2003

Number of wells started	Offshore	Onshore
Exploration and appraisal	45	4
Exploration	26	3
Appraisal	19	1
Development	204	17

VALUE OF UKCS OIL AND GAS PRODUCTION AND INVESTMENT
£ million

	2001	2002
Total income	24,074	24,143
Operating costs	4,347	4,596
Gross trading profits*	19,794	19,460
Percentage contribution to GVA	2.3	2.2
Exploration expenditure	420	389
Other Capital investment	3,570	3,598
Percentage contribution to industrial investment	15	16

* Net of stock appreciation
Source: Department of Trade and Industry

INDIGENOUS PRODUCTION AND REFINERY RECEIPTS

	2002	2003
Indigenous production		
(thousand tonnes)	115,944	106,073
Crude oil	107,430	97,835
NGLs*	8,514	8,238
Refinery receipts (thousand tonnes)		
Indigenous	28,556	30,794
Other†	2,333	2,315
Net foreign imports	54,114	52,721

* Natural Gas Liquids: condensates and petroleum gases derived at onshore treatment plants
† Mainly recycled products
Source: Department of Trade and Industry

DELIVERIES OF PETROLEUM PRODUCTS FOR INLAND CONSUMPTION BY ENERGY USE
Thousand tonnes

	2002	2003
Industry	6,126	6,597
Transport	48,803	47,933
Domestic	3,260	3,239
Other	1,684	1,275
Total	59,873	59,044

Source: Department of Trade and Industry

COAL

Coal has been mined in Britain for centuries and the availability of coal was crucial to the industrial revolution of the 18th- and 19th-centuries. Mines were in private ownership until 1947 when they were nationalised and came under the management of the National Coal Board, later the British Coal Corporation. In addition to producing coal at its own deep-mine and opencast sites, of which there were 850 in 1955, British Coal was responsible for licensing private operators.

Under the Coal Industry Act 1994, the Coal Authority was established to take over ownership of coal reserves and to issue licences to private mining companies as part of the privatisation of British Coal. The Coal Authority also deals with the physical legacy of mining, e.g. subsidence damage claims, and is responsible for holding and making available all existing records. The mines were sold as five separate businesses in 1994 and coal production in the UK is now undertaken entirely in the private sector.

The main UK customer for coal is the electricity supply industry. A review of energy policy was undertaken in 1998 and the Government announced measures in its October 1998 Energy White Paper which included a freeze on new applications to build gas-fired power stations in order to increase opportunities for coal-fired power stations. The moratorium on new gas-fired power stations was lifted in 2000 in the light of two measures to improve the competitiveness of coal-fired generation. Firstly, the Government reached an agreement with the European Commission to make available temporary state aid for the coal industry with such aid to end with the termination of the European Coal and Steel Community Treaty in 2002. The second measure was the reform of the electricity wholesale market and the replacement of the Electricity Pool with the New Electricity Trading Arrangement (NETA) which took effect from 27 March 2001. In 2003, the Government launched Coal Investment Aid with a budget of up to £60 million to be allocated between 2003–5 to coal producers for projects that maintain access to coal reserves. An Energy White Paper published on 24 February 2003 stated that coal generation still provides around a third of the UK's power output but recognised that for a low-carbon economy the development of cleaner coal technologies is required. By 2020 coal generation's contribution to the UK's power output is likely to be significantly lower than today.

COAL PRODUCTION AND FOREIGN TRADE
Thousand tonnes

	2002	2003p
Total production	29,991	28,234
Deep-mined	16,391	15,635
Opencast	13,149	12,126
Imports*	28,686	32,141
Exports†	537	543

* Includes an estimate for slurry
† As recorded in the Overseas Trade Statistics of the United Kingdom, although these are based on estimates from extra-EC trade until monthly statistics for intra-EC trade become available from HM Customs and Excise
p provisional
Source: Department of Trade and Industry

INLAND COAL USE
Thousand tonnes

	2002	2003p
Fuel producers		
Collieries	9	5
Electricity generators	47,712	53,252
Heat generation*	712	547
Coke ovens and blast furnaces	6,533	6,614
Other conversion industries†	436	396
Final users		
Industry‡	1,324	543
Domestic	1,803	1,183
Public administration, commerce		
and agriculture	65	72
Total	58,641	62,615

* Generation of heat for sale under the provision of a contract
† Low temperature carbonisation and patent fuel plants
‡ Includes estimates of imports
p provisional
Source: Department of Trade and Industry

GAS

From the late 18th-century gas in Britain was produced from coal. In the 1960s town gas began to be produced from oil-based feedstocks using imported oil. In 1965 gas was discovered in the North Sea in the West Sole field, which became the first gasfield in production in 1967, and from the late 1960s natural gas began to replace town gas. Britain is now the world's fourth largest producer of gas and in 1998 only 1.5 per cent of gas available for consumption in the UK was imported. From October 1998 Britain was connected to the continental European gas system via a pipeline from Bacton, Norfolk to Zeebrugge, Belgium. There are 275,000km of mains pipeline including 6,400km of high pressure gas pipelines owned and operated in the UK by National Grid Transco.

The gas industry in Britain was nationalised in 1949 and operated as the Gas Council. The Gas Council was replaced by the British Gas Corporation in 1972 and the industry became more centralised. The British Gas Corporation was privatised in 1986 as British Gas plc.

In 1993 the Monopolies and Mergers Commission found that British Gas's integrated business in Great Britain as a gas trader and the owner of the gas transportation system could operate against the public interest. In February 1997, British Gas demerged its trading arm to become two separate companies, BG plc and Centrica plc. BG Group, as the company is now known, is an international natural gas company whose principal business is finding and developing gas reserves and building gas markets. Its core operations are located in the UK, South America, Egypt, Trinidad & Tobago, Kazakhstan and India. Centrica runs the trading and services operations under the British Gas brand name in Great Britain. In October 2000 BG demerged its pipeline business, Transco, which became part of Lattice Group, finally merging with the National

Grid Group in 2002 to become National Grid Transco plc.

Competition was gradually introduced into the industrial gas market from 1986. Supply of gas to the domestic market was opened to companies other than British Gas, starting in April 1996 with a pilot project in the West Country and Wales. From early 1997 competition was progressively introduced throughout the rest of Britain in stages which were completed in May 1998.

BG GROUP PLC, 100 Thames Valley Park Drive, Reading RG6 1PT T 0118-935 3222 W www.bg-group.com
Chairman, Sir Robert Wilson
Chief Executive, Frank Chapman

CENTRICA PLC, Millstream, Maidenhead Road, Windsor, Berkshire, SL4 5GD T 01753-494000 W www.centrica.co.uk
Chief Executive, Sir Roy Gardner

NATIONAL GRID TRANSCO PLC, 1–3 Strand, London, WC2N 5EH T 020-7004 3000 W www.ngtgroup.com
Chairman, Sir John Parker
Chief Executive, Roger Urwin

UK NATURAL GAS PRODUCTION
GWh

	2001	2002
Power stations	309,732	326,220
Coal extraction and manufacture of solid fuels	4	—
Coke ovens	—	—
Petroleum Refineries	4,192	3,240
Nuclear fuel production	1,210	402
Production and distribution of other energy	451	709
Total final producers	315,589	330,571

Source: The Stationery Office: *Annual Abstract of Statistics 2004* (Crown copyright)

NATURAL GAS CONSUMPTION
GWh

	2001	2002
Iron and steel industry	20,969	19,533
Other industries	16,585	16,433
Domestic	379,163	376,327
Public administration	46,121	43,715
Agriculture	1,623	1,509
Miscellaneous	65,046	56,080
Total final users	529,507	513,597

Source: The Stationery Office: *Annual Abstract of Statistics 2004* (Crown copyright)

ELECTRICITY

The first power station in Britain generating electricity for public supply began operating in 1882. In the 1930s a national transmission grid was developed and it was reconstructed and extended in the 1950s and 1960s. Power stations were operated by the Central Electricity Generating Board.

Under the Electricity Act 1989, 12 regional electricity companies (RECs), which were responsible for the distribution of electricity from the national grid to consumers, were formed from the former area electricity boards in England and Wales. Four companies were formed from the Central Electricity Generating Board: three generating companies (National Power plc, Nuclear Electric plc and PowerGen plc) and the National Grid Company plc, which owned and operated the transmission system. National Power and PowerGen were floated on the stock market in 1991. National Power was demerged in October 2000 to form two separate companies: International Power plc and Innogy plc, which manages the bulk of National Power's UK assets. Nuclear Electric was split into two parts in 1996 British Energy (*see* Nuclear Energy) and Magnox Electric, which owns the magnox nuclear reactors, remained in the public sector and was integrated into British Nuclear Fuels (BNFL) in 1998. The National Grid Company was floated on the stock market in 1995 and formed a new holding company, National Grid Group. National Grid Group completed a merger with Lattice in 2002 to form National Grid Transco, a public limited company.

NATIONAL GRID TRANSCO PLC, 1–3 Strand, London, WC2N 5EH T 020-7004 3000 W www.ngtgroup.com

Generators and suppliers participate in a competitive wholesale trading market known as NETA (New Electricity Trading Arrangements) which began in March 2001, replacing the Electricity Pool. The introduction of competition into the domestic electricity market was completed in May 1999. With the gas market also open, most suppliers now offer their customers both gas and electricity.

In Scotland, three new companies were formed under the Electricity Act 1989: Scottish Power plc and Scottish Hydro-Electric plc, which are responsible for generation, transmission, distribution and supply; and Scottish Nuclear Ltd. Scottish Power and Scottish Hydro-Electric were floated on the stock market in 1991. Scottish Hydro-Electric merged with Southern Electric in 1998 to become Scottish and Southern Energy plc. Scottish Nuclear Ltd. was incorporated into British Energy in 1996.

In Northern Ireland, Northern Ireland Electricity plc was set up in 1993 under a 1991 Order in Council. In 1993 it was floated on the stock market and in 1998 it became part of the Viridian Group and is responsible for distribution and supply.

On 30 September 2003 the Electricity Association, the industry's main trade association, was replaced by three separate trade bodies:

ASSOCIATION OF ELECTRICITY PRODUCERS (AEP), First Floor, 17 Waterloo Place, London, SW1Y 4AR T 020-7930 9390 W www.aepuk.com
Promotes the interests of members who generate electricity
ENERGY NETWORKS ASSOCIATION (ENA), 18 Stanhope Place, London, W2 2HH T 020-7706 5100 W www.energynetworks.org
Represents UK gas and electricity transmission and distribution licence holders
ENERGY RETAIL ASSOCIATION, 2nd Floor, 17 Waterloo Place, London, SW1Y 4AR T 020-7747 2932 W www.energy-retail.org.uk
Represents the main suppliers operating in the UK energy market

ELECTRICITY GENERATION, SUPPLY AND
CONSUMPTION
GWh

Electricity generated	2001	2002
Major power producers: total	352,770	354,208
Conventional thermal and other*	138,626	134,933
Combined cycle gas turbine stations	117,966	123,893
Nuclear stations	89,870	88,043
Hydro-electric stations		
Natural flow	3,215	3,925
Pumped storage	2,356	2,652
Renewables other than hydro	737	762
Other generators: total	31,913	32,934
Electricity used on works: total	17,114	17,360
Major generating companies	15,779	15,960
Other generators	1,335	1,400
Electricity supplied (gross)		
Major power producers: total	336,991	338,248
Conventional thermal and other*	131,885	128,105
Combined cycle gas turbine stations	115,894	121,886
Nuclear stations	82,985	81,090
Hydro-electric stations:		
Natural flow	3,204	3,914
Pumped storage	2,340	2,562
Renewables other than hydro	683	691
Other generators: total	30,578	31,534
Electricity used in pumping		
Major power producers	3,210	3,463
Electricity supplied (net): total	364,359	366,318
Major power producers	333,781	334,785
Other generators	30,578	31,534
Net Imports	10,399	8,414
Electricity available	374,758	374,733
Losses in Transmission	31,980	30,902
Electricity consumption: Total	342,778	343,831
Fuel industries	8,625	9,977
Final users: total	334,153	333,854
Industrial sector	112,867	112,823
Domestic sector	115,336	114,535
Other sectors	105,950	106,496

* Includes electricity supplied by gas turbines, oil engines and plants producing electricity from renewable resources other than hydro.
Source: The Stationery Office – *Annual Abstract of Statistics 2004* (Crown copyright)

GAS AND ELECTRICITY SUPPLIERS

Now that the gas and electricity markets are open, most suppliers now offer their customers both gas and electricity. The majority of gas/electricity companies have become part of larger multi-utility companies, often operating internationally. The following list comprises a selection of some of the suppliers offering gas and electricity. Organisations in italics are subsidiaries of the companies listed in capital letters directly above.

ENGLAND, SCOTLAND AND WALES

CE ELECTRIC UK W www.ce-electricuk.com
Northern Electric Distribution Ltd (NEDL), Manor House, Station Road, New Penshaw, Houghton-le-Spring DH4 7LA T 0845-070 7172
Yorkshire Electricity Distribution (YEDL), 161 Gelderd Road, Leeds LS1 1QZ T 0845-602 4454
CENTRICA PLC, Millstream, Maidenhead Road, Windsor, Berkshire SL4 5GD T 01753-494000 W www.centrica.com
British Gas/Scottish Gas, T 0845-070 9010 W www.house.co.uk
EDF ENERGY, 40 Grosvenor Place, London SW1X 4EN T 020-7242 9050 W www.edfenergy.com
London Energy, 40 Grosvenor Place, London SW1X 4EN T 0800-096 9000 W www.london-energy.com
Seeboard Energy, 40 Grosvenor Place, London SW17 4EN T 0800-096 9696 W www.seeboard-energy.com
SWEB Energy, Osprey Road, Exeter EX2 7HZ T 0800-365000 W www.sweb-energy.com
Virgin Home Energy, Freepost LON14908, Exeter EX2 7BF T 0800-028 8269 W www.virginhome.co.uk
NPOWER, PO Box 93, Tyne House, Birchwood Drive, Peterlee SR8 2XX T 0800-389 2388 W www.npower.com
POWERGEN, PO Box 7750, Nottingham NG1 6WR T 0800-015 2029 W www.powergen.co.uk
SCOTTISH AND SOUTHERN ENERGY PLC, Inveralmond House, 200 Dunkeld Road, Perth PH1 3AQ W www.scottish-southern.co.uk
Scottish Hydro Electric, PO Box 7506, Perth PH1 3QR T 0845-300 2141 W www.hydro.co.uk
Southern Electric, PO Box 7506, Perth PH1 3QR T 0845-744 4555 W www.southern-electric.
SWALEC, PO Box 7506, Perth PH1 3QR T 0800-052 5252 W www.swalec.co.uk
SCOTTISHPOWER, Cathcart House, Cathcart Business Park, Spean Street, Glasgow G44 4BE T 0845-2700 700 W www.scottishpower.co.uk

NORTHERN IRELAND

VIRIDIAN GROUP PLC, 120 Malone Road, Belfast BT9 5HT T 028-9066 8416 W www.viridiangroup.co.uk
Energia, Energia House, 62 Newforge Lane, Belfast BT9 5NF T 028-9068 5900 W www.viridian energia.co.uk
Northern Ireland Electricity, 120 Malone Road, Belfast BT9 5HT T 028-9066 1100 W www.nie.co.uk

REGULATION OF THE GAS AND ELECTRICITY INDUSTRIES

The Office of the Gas and Electricity Markets (Ofgem) supports the Gas and Electricity Markets Authority, the regulator of the gas and electricity industries in Great Britain. Ofgem's aim is to bring choice and value to all gas and electricity customers by promoting competition and regulating monopolies. The Authority's powers are provided for under the Gas Act 1986, the Electricity Act 1989 and the Utilities Act 2000.
OFGEM, 9 Millbank, London SW1P 3GE T 020-7901 7000 W www.ofgem.gov.uk

NUCLEAR POWER

Nuclear reactors began to supply electricity to the national grid in 1956. It is generated at six magnox reactors, seven advanced gas-cooled reactors (AGRs) and one pressurised water reactor (PWR), Sizewell 'B' in Suffolk. In 1989 nuclear stations were withdrawn from privatisation. In 1996 Nuclear Electric Ltd and Scottish

Nuclear Ltd became operating subsidiaries of British Energy and the magnox stations were transferred to Nuclear Electric which became Magnox Electric, later part of British Nuclear Fuels Ltd (BNFL). In September 2002 the Government stepped in to provide a loan facility to British Energy which was facing insolvency and a major financial restructuring package was announced in November 2002. In March 2003 British Energy received formal approvals for loan standstill agreements from its creditors and the Government agreed to extend the loan facility until September 2004.

The UK Atomic Energy Authority (UKAEA) is responsible for the decommissioning of nuclear reactors and other nuclear facilities used in research and development. UKAEA is a non-departmental public body, funded mainly by the Department of Trade and Industry. UK Nirex, which was set up by the nuclear generating companies with the agreement of the Government, is responsible for the disposal of intermediate and some low-level nuclear waste. The Nuclear Safety Directorate of the Health and Safety Executive is the nuclear industry's regulator.

RENEWABLE SOURCES

Renewable sources of energy principally include biofuels, hydro, wind and solar. Renewable sources accounted for 3.2 million tonnes of oil equivalent of primary energy use in 2002; of this, about 2.5 million tonnes was used to generate electricity and 0.7 million tonnes to generate heat.

The Non-Fossil Fuel Obligation (NFFO) Renewables Orders have been the Government's principal mechanism for developing renewable energy sources. NFFO Renewables Orders require the regional electricity companies to buy specified amounts of electricity from specified non-fossil fuel sources.

In January 2000 the government announced a target for renewables to supply 10 per cent of UK electricity by 2010, which would require about 10,000 megawatts of renewables to be installed. A new renewables obligation was introduced in England and Wales in April 2002 to give incentives to generators to supply progressively higher levels of renewable energy over time. These measures included:

– the exemption of renewable electricity sources from the Climate Change Levy
– the creation of a renewables support programme worth £250 million from 2002–5
– the creation of a strategic framework for a major expansion of offshore wind generation
– the formation of a new organisation within the Government (Renewables UK) to help the industry grow and compete internationally

In July 2003 the DTI announced that the world's biggest wind farms will be built in three sites off the English coast (the Thames Estuary, the Wash on the east coast and from Morecambe Bay to north Wales), providing enough power for one in six British homes.

RENEWABLE ENERGY SOURCES 2002

	Percentages
Biofuels and wastes	83.2
Landfill gas	27.9
Sewage gas	5.7
Wood combustion	14.7
Straw combustion	2.2
Waste combustion	22.7
Other biofuels	10.0
Hydro	12.9
Large-scale	12.3
Small-scale	0.6
Wind and wave	3.4
Geothermal and active solar	
heating	0.5
Total	100

Source: Department of Trade and Industry

TRANSPORT

CIVIL AVIATION

Since the privatisation of British Airways in 1987, UK airlines have been operated entirely by the private sector. In 2003, total capacity of British airlines amounted to 43 billion tonne-km, of which 31 billion tonne-km was on scheduled services. In 2003 British airlines carried 110 million passengers, 76 million on scheduled services and 34 million on charter flights. Overall, passenger traffic grew by six per cent in 2003. In 2003, traffic at the five main London airports grew by 3 per cent over 2002 and regional airlines saw a growth of 11 per cent in 2003, largely due to the expansion of no-frills airlines. The number of passengers is estimated to be growing at 6 per cent each year. Leading British airlines include British Airways, Britannia Airways, BMI British Midland, Air 2000, My Travel, Thomas Cook Airlines, Monarch, Virgin Atlantic and easyJet. Irish airline Ryanair also operates frequent flights from Britain.

There are around 140 licensed civil aerodromes in Britain, with Heathrow and Gatwick handling the highest volume of passengers. BAA PLC owns and operates the seven major airports: Heathrow, Gatwick, Stansted, Southampton, Glasgow, Edinburgh and Aberdeen, which between them handle about 70 per cent of air passengers and a high percentage of air cargo traffic in Britain. Other airports are controlled by local authorities or private companies.

The Civil Aviation Authority (CAA), an independent statutory body, is responsible for the regulation of UK airlines. This includes economic and airspace regulation, air safety, consumer protection and environmental research and consultancy. All commercial airline companies must be granted an Air Operator's Certificate, which is issued by the CAA to operators meeting the required safety standards. The CAA issues airport safety licences, which must be obtained by any airport used for public transport and training flights. All British-registered aircraft must be granted an airworthiness certificate, and the CAA issues professional licences to pilots, flight crew, ground engineers and air traffic controllers. The CAA also manages the Air Travel Organiser's Licence (ATOL), the UK's principal travel protection scheme. The CAA's costs are met entirely from charges on those whom it regulates; there is no direct Government funding of the CAA's work.

The Transport Act, passed by Parliament on 29 November 2000, separated the CAA from its subsidiary, National Air Traffic Services (NATS), which provides air traffic control services to aircraft flying in UK airspace, over the eastern part of the North Atlantic and at 14 of Britain's major airports. In 2003 a total of 2,078,207 flights used UK airspace, an increase of 3.9 per cent on 2002 and 2.8 per cent on 2001. In March 2001, the Airline Group, a consortium of seven UK airlines (British Airways, BMI British Midland, Virgin Atlantic, Britannia, Monarch, easyJet and My Travel), was selected by the government as its strategic partner for NATS. Financial restructuring of NATS was completed in March 2003 with additional equity investment of £65 million each from BAA and the government. The new structure has enabled NATS to begin its £1 billion investment programme to run over the next ten years. NATS is a public private partnership between the Airline Group which holds 42 per cent of the shares, NATS staff who hold 5 per cent, BAA which holds 4 per cent and the government which holds 49 per cent and a golden share.

AIR PASSENGERS 2003*

ALL UK AIRPORTS: TOTAL	199,950,353
LONDON AREA AIRPORTS: TOTAL	118,606,029
Metro London Heliport	0
Heathrow (BAA)	63,208,042
Gatwick (BAA)	29,893,288
Luton	6,785,732
Southend	2,702
Stansted (BAA)	18,716,265
OTHER UK AIRPORTS: TOTAL	81,344,324
Aberdeen (BAA)	2,507,878
Barra (HIAL)†	8,318
Barrow-in-Furness	0
Belfast City	1,974,036
Belfast International	3,954,432
Benbecula (HIAL)†	31,914
Biggin Hill	683
Birmingham	8,923,902
Blackpool	186,604
Bournemouth	460,872
Bristol	3,886,740
Cambridge	2,485
Campbeltown (HIAL)†	8,268
Cardiff	1,899,971
Carlisle	0
City of Derry (Eglinton)	205,505
Coventry	2,429
Dundee	51,734
East Midlands	4,253,684
Edinburgh (BAA)	7,476,357
Exeter	378,010
Glasgow (BAA)	8,115,476
Gloucestershire	0
Hawarden	6,666
Humberside	517,171
Inverness (HIAL)†	434,644
Islay (HIAL)†	21,422
Isle of Man	742,590
Isles of Scilly (St Mary's)	138,466
Isles of Scilly (Tresco)	43,612
Kent International	3,256
Kirkwall (HIAL)†	102,716
Lands End (St Just)	24,751
Leeds Bradford	2,015,320
Lerwick (Tingwall)	2,056
Liverpool	3,175,343
London City	1,470,576
Lydd	4,498
Manchester	19,520,062
Newcastle	3,903,340
Norwich	447,112
Penzance Heliport	130,643
Plymouth	69,928
Prestwick	1,854,484

Scatsta	229,558
Sheffield City	0
Shoreham	263
Southampton (BAA)	1,217,891
Stornoway (HIAL)†	106,233
Sumburgh (HIAL)†	110,482
Teesside	699,838
Tiree (HIAL)†	5,293
Unst	0
Wick (HIAL)†	16,812
CHANNEL ISLANDS AIRPORTS: TOTAL	2,397,339
Alderney	72,075
Guernsey	861,275
Jersey	1,463,989

*Total terminal, transit, scheduled and charter passengers. Passengers carried on air taxi services are excluded
†Highlands and Islands Airports Ltd (HIAL)
Source: Civil Aviation Authority

CAA, CAA House, 45–59 Kingsway, London, WC2B 6TE
  T 020-7379 7311 W www.caa.co.uk
BAA PLC, 130 Wilton Road, London, SW1V 1LQ
  T 020-7834 9449 W www.baa.co.uk
  Heathrow Airport   T 0870-000 0123
  Gatwick Airport   T 0870-000 2468
  Stansted Airport   T 0870-000 0303
  Glasgow Airport   T 0870-040 0008
  Edinburgh Airport   T 0870-040 0007
  Aberdeen Airport   T 0870-040 0006
  Southampton Airport   T 0870-040 0009

BMI BRITISH MIDLAND, Donington Hall, Castle Donington, Derby, DE74 2SB T 01332-854000 W www.flybmi.com
BRITANNIA AIRWAYS, Britannia House, London Luton International Airport, Luton, Bedfordshire, LU2 9ND
  T 01582-424155 W www.britanniaairways.com
BRITISH AIRWAYS, Waterside, PO Box 365, Harmondsworth, UB7 0G T 0870-850 9850 W www.britishairways.com
EASYJET, London Luton Airport, LU2 9LS T 0871-7500 100
  W www.easyjet.com
FIRST CHOICE AIRWAYS (previously known as Air 2000) Commonwealth House, Chicago Avenue, Manchester Airport, M90 3DP T 0870-850 3999
  W www.firstchoice.co.uk
MONARCH, Prospect House, Prospect Way, London Luton Airport, LU2 9NU T 01582-400000
  W www.monarch-airlines.com
MY TRAVEL, Parkway One, Parkway Business Centre, 300 Princess Road, Manchester, M14 7QU T 0870-238 7777
  W www.mytravel.com
THOMAS COOK AIRLINES, Thomas Cook Business Park, Coningsby Road, Peterborough, PE3 8XP T 0870-750 5711
  W www.thomascook.cm
VIRGIN ATLANTIC, Manor Royal, Crawley, West Sussex RH10 9NU T 01293-562345 W www.virgin-atlantic.com

RAILWAYS

Britain pioneered railways and a railway network was developed across Britain by private companies in the 19th century. In 1948 the main railway companies were nationalised and were run by a public authority, the British Transport Commission. The Commission was replaced by the British Railways Board in 1963, operating as British Rail. On 1 April 1994, responsibility for managing the track and railway infrastructure passed to a newly-formed company, Railtrack plc. In October

2001 Railtrack was put into administration under the Railways Act 1993 and Ernst and Young was appointed as administrator. In October 2002 Railtrack was taken out of administration and replaced by the not-for-profit company Network Rail. The British Railways Board continued as operator of all train services until 1996–7 when they were sold or franchised to the private sector.

On 15 July 2004 the Government announced a new structure for the rail industry in the white paper, *The Future of Rail*. The Strategic Rail Authority will be abolished (*see* below), the number of rail franchises will be reduced, and devolved governments in Scotland and Wales will have more say in decisions at a local level. The Office of Rail Regulation will also regulate safety, currently the responsibility of the Health and Safety Executive.

OTHER RAIL SYSTEMS

Plans for a public-private partnership (PPP) for London Underground were pushed through by the Government in February 2002 despite opposition from the Mayor of London and a range of transport organisations. Under the PPP, long-term contracts with private companies are estimated to enable around £16 billion to be invested in renewing and upgrading the Underground's infrastructure over 15 years. Responsibility for stations, trains, operations, signalling and safety will remain in the public sector. In 2002–3 there were 942 million passenger journeys on the London Underground, down 1.2 per cent on the previous year.

Britain has seven other light rail systems; Croydon Tramlink, Docklands Light Railway (DLR), Manchester Metrolink, Midland Metro, the Nottingham Express Transit (NET), Sheffield Supertram and Tyne and Wear Metro. Most recently opened was the Nottingham Express Transit in March 2004.

Light rail and metro systems in Great Britain contributed to the growth in public transport, with 136 million passenger journeys in 2002–3, up seven per cent on the previous year. The Government's 10-year Transport Plan target is to double light rail use in England by 2010.

OFFICE OF RAIL REGULATION (ORR)

Under the Railways Act 1993 the Rail Regulator was created with responsibility for the regulation of the monopoly of the railways and the network infrastructure operator, now known as Network Rail (formerly Railtrack). The Transport Act 2000 enabled the Regulator to direct enhancement of a network facility, expand an operator's existing rights, and under the Competition Act 1998, prevent anti-competitive practices. Tom Winsor's five-year appointment as Rail Regulator ended on 4 July 2004 and under the Railways and Transport Safety Bill 2003 he was replaced by a regulatory board. The re-named Office of Rail Regulation consists of a board of nine members headed by a chairman, who is appointed by the Secretary of State for Transport, and a chief executive.

STRATEGIC RAIL AUTHORITY (SRA)

The Strategic Rail Authority (SRA) was created to provide strategic leadership to the rail industry and formally came into being on 1 February 2001 following the passing of the Transport Act 2000. In January 2002 it published its first Strategic Plan, setting out the strategic priorities for Britain's railways over the next ten years. In addition to its coordinating role, the SRA is responsible for allocating Government funding to the railways, awarding and monitoring the franchises for operating rail services, as well as a number of other statutory functions; particularly relating to customer protection. On 15 July 2004 a white paper, *The Future of Rail*, was published which announced that the SRA would be abolished, its strategic functions and financial obligations passing to the Department for Transport. Network Rail will have full responsibility for industry planning and timetables.

For privatisation, domestic passenger services were divided into 25 train operating units, which were franchised to private sector operators via a competitive tendering process overseen by the SRA. The majority of the original franchises were let on a seven-year term, consequently there are now a large number of franchises to be let over the next few years. The SRA has devised a long-term programme to enable a steady state replacement of franchises of approximately three per annum. In November 2002 the SRA issued a franchising policy statement specifying that new franchises should set service levels and quality standards and the private sector should be charged with delivering the standards set. This led to the development of a new standard form of Franchise Agreement, which incorporates rewards and penalties for standards of train and station cleanliness, security and passenger information. It also contains guidelines and incentives for customer services and business priorities such as short and long-term costs. The first franchise to be let under this new agreement was the Greater Anglia franchise (One Railway), incorporating: Anglia; Great Eastern; West Anglia and Stansted Express train services, on 1 April 2004, and operated by the National Express Group plc.

SERVICES

As at March 2004 there were 23 train operating companies (TOCs): Arriva Trains Northern; Arriva Trains Wales; c2c; Central Trains; Chiltern; First Great Western; First Great Western Link; First North Western Trains; Gatwick Express; Great North Eastern Railways; Island Line (Isle of Wight); Midland Mainline; One Railway; ScotRail; Silverlink; South Central; South Eastern Trains; South West Trains; ThamesLink; Virgin Trains (CrossCountry Trains Ltd); Virgin Trains (West Coast Trains Ltd); WAGN and Wessex Trains.

In addition, Eurostar and Merseyrail provide services, but are not subject to the franchise process. The Heathrow Express service is a subsidiary of the airports group BAA.

Network Rail publishes a national timetable which contains details of rail services operated over the network, coastal shipping information and connections with Ireland, the Isle of Man, the Isle of Wight, the Channel Islands and some European destinations.

The national rail enquiries service offers information about train times and fares for any part of the country:

NATIONAL RAIL ENQUIRIES T 08457-484950
  W www.nationalrail.co.uk
TRANSPORT FOR LONDON T 020-7941 4500
  W www.transportforlondon.gov.uk
EUROSTAR T 08705-186186 W www.eurostar.com

Rail Users' Consultative Committees (RUCCs) were set up under the Railways Act 1993 to protect the interests of users of the services and facilities provided on Britain's rail network. The Transport Act 2000 changed their name to the Rail Passenger Committees (RPCs) and transferred sponsorship from the Rail Regulator to the SRA. There are nine RPCs nationwide, seven for England and one

each for Scotland and Wales. They are statutory bodies and have a legal right to make recommendations for changes. The London Transport Users' Committee represents users of buses, the Underground and rail services in and around London, including Eurostar and Heathrow Express, Croydon Tramlink and the Docklands Light Railway. The interests of pedestrians, cyclists and motorists are also represented, as are those of taxi users. Transport for London was established by the Greater London Assembly and the Mayor in 2000.

On privatisation, British Rail's bulk freight haulage companies and Rail Express Systems, which carried Royal Mail traffic, were sold to English, Welsh and Scottish Railways (EWS), which also purchased Railfreight Distribution (international freight) in 1997. At the end of 2003 18.6 billion-tonne-kilometres of freight was transported by EWS and other freight companies. In 2003 Royal Mail announced it would phase out its use of rail for postal distribution by the end of March 2004.

NETWORK RAIL

Network Rail owns and maintains 21,000 miles of track, owns and provides access to 2,500 stations and operates and maintains more than 9,000 level crossings and 40,000 bridges and tunnels. In addition to providing the timetables for the passenger and freight operators Network Rail is also responsible for all the signalling and electrical control equipment needed to operate the rail network.

Network Rail is run as a commercial business but has members instead of shareholders. The members have similar rights to those of shareholders in a public company except they do not receive dividends or share capital and thereby having no financial or economic interest in Network Rail. All of Network Rail's profits are reinvested into maintaining and upgrading the rail infrastructure.

ASSOCIATION OF TRAIN OPERATING COMPANIES
  (ATOC), 3rd Floor, 40 Bernard Street, London WC1N 1BY
  T 020-7841 8000 W www.atoc.org
OFFICE OF RAIL REGULATION, 1 Waterhouse Square,
  138–142 Holborn, London EC1N 2TQ T 020-7282 2000
  W www.rail-reg.gov.uk
  Chairman, Chris Bolt
NETWORK RAIL, 40 Melton Street, London NW1 2EE
  T 020-7557 8000 W www.networkrail.co.uk
RAIL PASSENGERS COUNCIL (RPC), Whittles House, 14
  Pentonville Road, London, N1 9HF T 020-7713 2700
  W www.railpassengers.org.uk
STRATEGIC RAIL AUTHORITY, 55 Victoria Street, London,
  SW1H 0EU T 020-7654 6000 W www.sra.gov.uk
  Chairman and Chief Executive, Richard Bowker

RAIL SAFETY

The Railways (Safety Case) Regulations 2000 came into force on 31 December 2000 and transferred responsibility for safety cases from Railtrack to HM Railway Inspectorate, part of the Health and Safety Executive (HSE). The regulations demand that rail operators such as Network Rail, London Underground, the station and train operators must prepare a comprehensive safety case and have it accepted by HSE before being allowed to operate their business. The Office of Rail Regulation will not grant a licence to a railway operator without an accepted safety case or an exemption being in place.

Amendments to railway safety case regulations were

announced in March 2003 and came into force on 1 April 2003. The requirement for infrastructure controllers to obtain an independent assessment of safety cases in addition to the Health and Safety Executive's acceptance was removed and the requirement to obtain annual independent health and safety audits of train and station operations was transferred from HSE to individual operators. The Rail Safety and Standards Board (RSSB) was established on 1 April 2003 as a new industry body to provide health and safety leadership for the railway industry.

ACCIDENTS ON RAILWAYS

	2001–2	2002–3
Train accidents: total	1,704	1,421
Persons killed: total	5	10
Passengers	0	6
Railway staff	0	1
Others	5	3
Persons injured: total	52	106
Passengers	21	128
Railway staff	23	23
Others	8	15
Other accidents through movement of railway vehicles		
Persons killed	21	32
Persons injured	909	908
Other accidents on railway premises		
Persons killed	6	8
Passengers	3	3
Railway staff	1	4
Others	2	1
Persons injured	3,906	3,983
Trespassers and suicides		
Persons killed	275	256
Persons injured	179	137

Source: Department for Transport

THE CHANNEL TUNNEL
The earliest recorded scheme for a submarine transport connection between Britain and France was in 1802. Tunnelling has begun simultaneously on both sides of the Channel three times: in 1881, in the early 1970s, and on 1 December 1987, when construction workers began to bore the first of the three tunnels which form the Channel Tunnel. They 'holed through' the first tunnel (the service tunnel) on 1 December 1990 and tunnelling was completed in June 1991. The tunnel was officially inaugurated by The Queen and President Mitterrand of France on 6 May 1994.
The submarine link comprises three tunnels. There are two rail tunnels, each carrying trains in one direction, which measure 24.93 ft (7.6 m) in diameter. Between them lies a smaller service tunnel, measuring 15.75 ft (4.8 m) in diameter. The service tunnel is linked to the rail tunnels by 130 cross-passages for maintenance and safety purposes. The tunnels are 31 miles (50 km) long, 24 miles (38 km) of which is under the sea-bed at an average depth of 132 ft (40 m). The rail terminals are situated at Folkestone and Calais, and the tunnels go underground at Shakespeare Cliff, Dover, and Sangatte, west of Calais.
Eurostar is the high speed passenger train connecting London with Paris in three hours and Brussels in two hours 40 minutes, via the Channel Tunnel. Some trains stop en route at Ashford (Kent) and Calais, Disneyland Paris and Lille in France.

RAIL LINKS
The route for the British Channel Tunnel Rail Link will run from Folkestone to a new terminal at St Pancras station, London, with new intermediate stations at Ebbsfleet, Kent, and Stratford, east London; at present services run into a terminal at Waterloo station, London.
Construction of the rail link is being financed by the private sector with a substantial government contribution. A private sector consortium, London and Continental Railways Ltd (LCR), is responsible for the design, construction and ownership of the rail link, and comprises Union Railways and the UK operator of Eurostar. Construction was expected to be completed in 2003, but on 28 January 1998 LCR informed the Government that it was unable to fulfil its obligations. On 3 June 1998 the Government announced a new funding agreement with LCR. The rail link will be constructed in two phases: phase one, from the Channel Tunnel to Fawkham Junction, North Kent began in October 1998 and opened to fare paying passengers on 28 September 2003; phase two, from Southfleet Junction to St Pancras, is due to be completed in 2007. Infrastructure developments in France have been completed and high-speed trains run from Calais to Paris and from Lille to the south of France.

ROADS

HIGHWAY AUTHORITIES
The powers and responsibilities of highway authorities in England and Wales are set out in the Highways Act 1980; for Scotland there is separate legislation.
Responsibility for trunk road motorways and other trunk roads in Great Britain rests in England with the Secretary of State for Transport, in Scotland with the Scottish Executive, and in Wales with the Welsh Assembly. The costs of construction, improvement and maintenance are paid for by central government in England and by the Welsh Assembly in Wales. The highway authority for non-trunk roads in England, Wales and Scotland is, in general, the local authority in whose area the roads lie. With the establishment of the Greater London Authority in July 2000, Transport for London became the highway authority for roads in London.
In Northern Ireland the Department of Regional Development is the statutory road authority responsible for public roads and their maintenance and construction; the Roads Service executive agency carries out these functions on behalf of the Department.

FINANCE
In England all aspects of trunk road and motorway funding are provided directly by the Government to the Highways Agency which operates, maintains and improves around 5,878 miles of motorways and trunk roads on behalf of the Secretary of State. For the financial year 2004–5 the Highways Agency was allocated £1.7 billion, of which £730 million was for maintenance, £508 million for major new roads including private finance payments and £231 million on smaller improvements and traffic management measures.
Government support for local authority capital expenditure on roads and other transport infrastructure is provided through grant and credit approvals as part of the Local Transport Plan (LTP). Local Authorities bid for resources on the basis of a five-year programme built around delivering integrated transport strategies. As well

as covering the structural maintenance of local roads and the construction of major new road schemes, LTP funding also includes smaller-scale safety and traffic management measures with associated improvements for public transport, cyclists and pedestrians.

For the financial year 2004–5 local authorities received a total of £1.9 billion in the form of a Local Transport Plan budget. This includes £657 million for small-scale integrated transport measures, £651 million for road maintenance and £459 million for new and existing major projects.

Total expenditure by Welsh Assembly on trunk roads, motorways and transport services (including grants to local authorities and credit approvals) in 2003–4 was £243 million. Forecast expenditure for 2004–5 is £326 million.

Until 1999 the Scottish Office received a block vote from Parliament and the Secretary of State for Scotland determined how much was spent on roads. Since 1 July 1999 all decisions on transport expenditure have been devolved to the Scottish Executive. Total planned expenditure on motorways and trunk road in Scotland during 2003–4 including depreciation and cost of capital charge was £631.2 million. Planned expenditure for 2004–5 is £643.47 million.

In Northern Ireland total expenditure by the Roads Service on trunk roads and motorways for 2003–4 was £84.5 million and £96.5 million has been allocated for expenditure in 2004–5.

The Transport Act 2000 gave English and Welsh local authorities (outside London) powers to introduce road user charging or workplace parking levy schemes. The Act requires that the net revenue raised is used to improve local transport services and facilities for at least ten years. The aim is to reduce congestion and encourage greater use of alternative modes of transport. Schemes developed by local authorities require Government approval. The Government's Ten Year Plan for Transport assumes that eight large road user charging schemes and 12 large workplace parking levy schemes will be developed by 2010. Charging schemes in London are allowed under the 1999 Greater London Authority Act. The Central London Congestion Charge Scheme began on 17 February 2003.

TARGETED PROGRAMME OF IMPROVEMENT

The 1998 Roads Review increased the emphasis given to making better use of the existing road network and improving road maintenance. In addition a carefully targeted programme of major trunk road improvements was announced which initially consisted of 37 schemes. The current programme contains 78 schemes, funded conventionally or through public-private partnerships. A series of 22 studies were announced in March 1999 to look at transport problems across all modes. Based on these studies the Government announced a major national road expansion programme on 10 July 2003.

ROAD LENGTHS (IN KILOMETRES) 2002

	England	Wales	Scotland	Great Britain
Motorways	2,949	141	386	3,477
Dual Carriageway	6,522	543	766	7,831
Single carriageway	25,668	3,634	9,533	38,834
B roads	19,871	2,985	7,336	30,192
C roads	64,720	9,822	10,315	84,857
Unclassified roads	179,436	15,957	31.069	226,462
Total	299,166	33,082	59,405	391,653

MOTORWAYS

ENGLAND AND WALES

M1	London to Yorkshire
M2	London to Faversham
M3	London to Southampton
M4	London to South Wales
M5	Birmingham to Exeter
M6	Catthorpe to Carlisle
M6	Toll Birmingham bypass*
M10	St Albans spur
M11	London to Cambridge
M18	Rotherham to Goole
M20	London to Folkestone
M23	London to Gatwick
M25	London orbital
M26	M20 to M25 spur
M27	Southampton bypass
M32	M4 to Bristol spur
M40	London to Birmingham
M42	South-west of Birmingham to Measham
M45	Dunchurch spur
M48	M4 to South Wales
M49	M4 to M5
M50	Ross spur
M53	Chester to Birkenhead
M54	M6 to Telford
M55	Preston to Blackpool
M56	Manchester to Chester
M57	Liverpool outer ring
M58	Liverpool to Wigan
M60	Manchester ring road
M61	Manchester to Preston
M62	Liverpool to Hull
M65	Calder Valley
M66	Manchester Whitefield to Ramsbottom
M67	Manchester Hyde to Denton
M69	Coventry to Leicester
M180	South Humberside
M181	M180 to Scunthorpe
M271	West of Southampton
M275	M27 to Portsmouth
M602	Eccles to Salford
M606	M62 to Bradford
M621	M1 to M62

SCOTLAND

M8	Edinburgh–Newhouse (Glasgow)
M9	Edinburgh to Dunblane and M9 Spur to A8000
M73	Jn. 4 of M74 to A80 (Mollinsburn)
M74	Glasgow–Gretna
M77	Jn. 22 of M8 to Malletsheugh (Ayr Road)
M80	Jn. 9 of M9 (Stirling) to Jn. 4 of M80/A80 (Haggs) and M80 Stepps Bypass
M90	Forth Bridge Road/Inverkeithing to Perth
M876	Kincardine Bridge to Jn. 5 of M80
M898	Jn. 30 of M8 to Erskine Bridge
A823(M)	Jn. 2 of M90 to A823 (Dunfermline)

* The UK's first toll motorway opened on 9 December 2003

NORTHERN IRELAND

M1	Belfast to Dungannon
M2	Belfast to Antrim
M2	Ballymena bypass
M3	Belfast Cross Harbour Bridge
M5	M2 to Greencastle
M12	M1 to Craigavon
M22	Antrim to Randalstown

ROAD USE

ESTIMATED TRAFFIC ON ALL ROADS (GREAT BRITAIN) 2002

Million vehicle kilometres

All motor vehicles	485,900
Cars and taxis	392,400
Two-wheeled motor vehicles	5,100
Buses and coaches	5,200
Light vans	55,000
Other goods vehicles	28,300
Pedal cycles	4,400

Source: Department for Transport

ROAD GOODS TRANSPORT (GREAT BRITAIN) 2003
Analysis by mode of working and by gross weight of vehicle

Estimated tonne kilometres (thousand million)	151.7
Own account	37.4
Public haulage	114.3
By gross weight of vehicle (billion tonne kilometres)	
Estimated tonnes lifted (millions)	1,643
Own account	590
Public haulage	1,053
By gross weight of vehicle (million tonnes)	
Not over 25 tonnes	265
Over 25 tonnes	1,378

Source: Department for Transport

BUSES

Nearly all bus and coach services in Great Britain are provided by private sector companies. The Transport Act 2000 outlines a 10-year transport plan intended to promote bus use, through agreements between local authorities and bus operators and to improve the standard and efficiency of services. The 10-year plan sets targets for bus patronage and reliability of services. There are a number of ways in which the Government supports bus services:
– Bus Service Operators Grant (BSOG) is paid directly to bus operators and reimburses 80 per cent of fuel duty and 100 per cent of duty for some 'clean' fuels
– Local authorities outside London have a duty to secure socially necessary bus services not provided commercially. Services are tendered and let to commercial operators in return for payment from the local authority
– Rural Bus Challenge supports innovative and flexible rural transport solutions, such as taxi-bus services and awarded £20 million to 42 projects in 2003
– Rural Bus subsidy grant was £48.5 million in 2003–4 and supported some 21,000 services
– Urban Bus Challenge aims to improve transport in deprived urban areas and awarded £19.6 million to 40 projects in 2003
Since June 2001 it has been a statutory minimum requirement for all local authorities to provide at least half fares and a free bus pass to pensioners and disabled people in the area. Local authorities recompense operators for the reduced fare revenue.

In London, Transport for London (TfL) has overall responsibility for setting routes, service standards and fares for the bus network. Almost all routes are competitively tendered to commercial operators. TfL

budget for buses in 2004–5 is £229 million, in addition London also benefits from a share of the funding schemes listed above.

In Northern Ireland, passenger transport services are provided by Ulsterbus Limited and Citybus Limited, two wholly owned subsidiaries of the Northern Ireland Transport Holding Company. Along with Northern Ireland Railways, Ulsterbus and Citybus operate under the brand name of Translink and are publicly owned. Ulsterbus is responsible for virtually all bus services in Northern Ireland except Belfast city services which are operated by Citybus.

BUSES AND COACHES (GREAT BRITAIN) 2001–2

Vehicle kilometres (millions)	4,226
Local bus services passenger journeys (millions)	4,347
Passenger receipts (£ million)	4,625

Source: Department for Transport

TAXIS

A taxi is a public transport vehicle with fewer than nine passenger seats, which is licenced to 'ply for hire'. This distinguishes taxis from private hire vehicles which must be booked in advance through an operator.

In London, taxis and their drivers are licensed by The Public Carriage Office (PCO) which is part of Transport for London (TfL). At the end of December 2001 there were 59,682 licensed taxis in England, of which 20,500 were in London. At the end of 2001, 3,381 taxis were licensed in Wales and 9,343 in Scotland.

AVERAGE TAXI FARE FOR A FOUR-MILE JOURNEY BY REGION 2002

Region	*Fare in £*
London (Transport for London)	9.10
North East	5.64
North West	5.96
Yorkshire & the Humber	5.85
East Midlands	6.09
West Midlands	6.14
East	6.58
South East	6.87
South West	7.14
Wales	6.07

ROAD SAFETY

In March 2000, the Government published a new road safety strategy, *Tomorrow's Roads – Safer for Everyone*, which set new casualty reduction targets for 2010. The new targets include a 40 per cent reduction in the overall number of people killed or seriously injured in road accidents, a 50 per cent reduction in the number of children killed or seriously injured and a 10 per cent reduction in the slight casualty rate, all compared with the average for 1994–8.

There were 290,607 reported casualties on roads in Great Britain in 2003, 4 per cent less than in 2002. Road traffic levels were estimated to be 1 per cent higher than in 2002, consequently the casualty rate per 100 million vehicle kilometres was five per cent lower. Child casualties fell by eight per cent with 171 child fatalities, 4 per cent less than in 2002. Car user casualties decreased by 5 per cent on the 2002 level to 188,342, although fatalities were one per cent higher. Pedestrian casualties were

36,405 in 2003, 6 per cent less than 2002 and pedal cyclist casualties fell marginally to 17,033.

ROAD ACCIDENT CASUALTIES 2003

	Fatal	Serious	Slight	All Severities
England	3,004	29,292	225,603	257,899
Wales	173	1,482	12,381	14,036
Scotland	331	2,933	15,408	18,672
Great Britain	3,508	33,707	253,392	290,607

	Killed	Injured
1965	7,952	389,985
1970	7,499	355,869
1975	6,366	318,584
1980	6,010	323,000
1985	5,165	312,359
1990	5,217	335,924
1995	3,621	306,885
1996	3,598	316,704
1997	3,599	323,945
1998	3,421	321,791
1999	3,423	316,887
2000	3,409	316,872
2001	3,450	313,309
2002	3,431	302,605
2003	3,508	290,607

Source: Department for Transport

DRIVING LICENCES
It is necessary to hold a valid full licence in order to drive unaccompanied on public roads in the UK. Learner drivers must obtain a provisional driving licence before starting to learn to drive and must then pass theory and practical tests to obtain a full driving licence.

There are separate tests for driving motor cycles, cars, passenger-carrying vehicles (PCVs) and large goods vehicles (LGVs). Drivers must hold full car entitlement before they can apply for PCV or LGV entitlements.

The Driver and Vehicle Licensing Agency (DVLA) ceased the issue of paper licences in March 2000, however, those currently in circulation will remain valid until they expire or the details on them change. The photocard driving licence was introduced to comply with the second EC directive on driving licences. This requires a photograph of the driver to be included on all UK licences issued from July 2001.

To apply for a first photocard driving licence, individuals are required to complete the forms *Application for a Driving Licence* (D1) and *Application for a Photocard Driving Licence* (D750). Application forms are available from post offices.

The minimum age for driving motor cars, light goods vehicles up to 3.5 tonnes and motor cycles is 17 (moped, 16). Since June 1997, drivers who collect six or more penalty points within two years of qualifying lose their licence and are required to take another test. A leaflet, *What You Need to Know About Driving Licences* (form D100), is available from post offices.

The DVLA is responsible for issuing driving licences, registering and licensing vehicles, and collecting excise duty in Great Britain. In Northern Ireland the Driver and Vehicle Licensing Agency (Northern Ireland) has similar responsibilities.

DRIVING LICENCE FEES *as at 1 April 2004*

First provisional licence	
Car, motorcycle or moped	£38.00
Bus or lorry	Free
Changing a car, motorcycle or moped provisional licence to a full licence	
If first provisional licence issued before 1 March 2004	£9.00
If first provisional licence issued after 1 March 2004	Free
Changing a bus or lorry provisional licence to a full licence	Free
Licence renewal	
At age 70 and over	Free
For medical reasons	Free
Bus or lorry	Free
After disqualification	£50.00
After disqualification for some drink driving offences*	£75.00
After revocation	£38.00
Replacing a lost or stolen licence	£19.00
Adding an entitlement to a full licence	Free
Removing expired endorsements	£19.00
Exchanging	
a paper licence for a photocard licence	£19.00
for a full Northern Ireland car licence	Free
for a full EC/EEA or other foreign licence (including Channel Islands and Isle of Man)	£38.00
Change of name or address (existing licence must be surrendered)	Free

* For an alcohol related offence where the DVLA needed to arrange medical enquiries.

DRIVING TESTS
The Driving Standards Agency is responsible for carrying out driving tests and approving driving instructors in Great Britain. In Northern Ireland the Driver and Vehicle Testing Agency (Northern Ireland) is responsible for testing drivers and vehicles.

DRIVING TESTS TAKEN/PERCENTAGE PASSED
April 2003–March 2004

Type of Test	Number Taken	Percentage Passed
Practical Tests		
Car	1,399,115	43%
Motorcycle	83,428	64%
Large goods vehicle	61,594	49%
Passenger carrying vehicle	9,373	46%
Theory Tests		
Car	1,297,635	57%
Motorcycle	81,879	77%
Large goods vehicle	44,067	64%
Passenger carrying vehicle	10,542	61%

The theory and practical driving tests can be booked by postal application, online at www.dsa.gov.uk or by telephoning 0870-010 1372.

DRIVING TEST FEES (weekday rate/evening and Saturday rate) *effective from 1 September 2003**

For cars	£39.00/£48.00
For motor cycles	£48.00/£57.00
For lorries, buses	£76.00/£94.00
Extended Test for cars (after disqualification)	£78.00/£96.00
Extended Test for motorcycles (after disqualification)	£96.00/£114.00
Motorcycle Compulsory Basic Training Certificate (CBT)	£8.00
Theory Test for all categories	£20.50

* Correct at the time of going to press – see DSA website for further information: www.dsa.gov.uk

MOTOR VEHICLES

Vehicles must be licensed by the DVLA or the DVLNI before they can be driven on public roads. They must also be approved as roadworthy by the Vehicle Certification Agency. The Vehicle Inspectorate carries out annual testing and inspection of goods vehicles, buses and coaches.

There were 31,207 thousand vehicles licensed at the DVLA at the end of 2003.

VEHICLE LICENCES

Registration and first licensing of vehicles is through local offices of the Driver and Vehicle Licensing Agency in Swansea. Local facilities for relicensing are available at any post office which deals with vehicle licensing. Applicants will need to take their vehicle registration document; if this is not available the applicant must complete form V62 which is held at post offices. Postal applications can be made to the post offices shown in the V100 booklet, available at any post office. This V100 also provides guidance on registering and licensing vehicles.

Details of the present duties chargeable on motor vehicles are available at post offices and Local Offices. The Vehicle Excise and Registration Act 1994 provides *inter alia* that any vehicle kept on a public road but not used on roads is chargeable to excise duty as if it were in use. All non-commercial vehicles constructed before 1 January 1973 are exempt from vehicle excise duty. Any vehicle licensed on or after 31 January 1998, not in use and not kept on public roads must be registered as SORN (Statutory Off Road Notification) to be exempted from vehicle excise duty. From 1 January 2004 the registered keeper of a vehicle remains responsible for licensing a vehicle or making a SORN declaration until that liability is formally transferred to a new keeper.

MOTOR VEHICLES CURRENTLY LICENSED BY BODY TYPE 2003 (GREAT BRITAIN)

Thousands

All Cars (including exempt)	26,240
All company cars	2,212
Taxis (black cabs only)	39
Motor cycles, Scooters and Mopeds	1,135
Tricycles	19
Light goods vehicles	2,434
Goods vehicles	639
Buses and coaches	175
Other vehicles	526
Total	31,207

Source: Department for Transport: *Vehicle Licensing Statistics 2003*

VEHICLE EXCISE DUTY RATES *from 1 March 2004*
REGISTERED BEFORE 1 MARCH 2001

	Twelve Months £	Six Months £		Twelve Months £	Six Months £
Motor Cars			*Tricycles*		
Light vans, cars, taxis, etc.			Not over 150 cc	15.00	–
Under 1549cc	110.00	60.50	All Others	60.00	33.00
Over 1549cc	165.00	90.75	*Buses* (excluding driver)*		
Motor Cycles (with or			Seating 9–16 persons	165.00 (165.00)	90.75 (90.75)
without sidecar)			Seating 17–35 persons	220.00 (165.00)	121.00 (90.75)
Not over 150 cc	15.00	–	Seating 36–60 persons	330.00 (165.00)	181.50 (90.75)
151–400 cc	30.00	–	Seating over 61 persons	500.00 (165.00)	275.00 (90.75)
401–600 cc	45.00	–			
All other motorcycles	60.00	33.00	* Figures in parentheses refer to reduced pollution vehicles.		

REGISTERED ON OR AFTER 1 MARCH 2001

Band	CO^2 Emissions (g/km)	Diesel Car 12 month rate £	6 month rate £	Petrol Car 12 month rate £	6 month rate £	Alternative Fuel Car 12 month rate £	6 month rate £
AAA	Up to 100	75.00	41.25	65.00	35.75	55.00	30.25
AA	101–120	85.00	46.75	75.00	41.25	65.00	35.75
A	121–150	115.00	63.25	105.00	57.75	95.00	52.25
B	151–165	135.00	74.25	125.00	68.75	115.00	63.25
C	166–185	155.00	85.25	145.00	79.75	135.00	74.25
D	Over 185	165.00	90.75	160.00	88.00	155.00	85.25

MOT TESTING

Cars, motor cycles, motor caravans, light goods and dual-purpose vehicles more than three years old must be covered by a current MOT test certificate. However, some vehicles i.e. minibuses may require a certificate at one year old. All certificates must be renewed annually. The MOT testing scheme is administered by the Vehicle and Operator Services Agency (VOSA) on behalf of the Secretary of State for Transport.

A fee is payable to MOT testing stations, which must be authorised to carry out tests. The maximum fees, which are prescribed by regulations, are:

For cars and light vans	£40.75	
For solo motor cycles	£15.20	
For motor cycle combinations	£24.85	
For three-wheeled vehicles	£29.00	
Motor caravans	£40.75	
Dual purpose vehicles	£40.75	
Public service vehicles		
(up to 8 seats)	£40.75	
Ambulances and Taxis	£40.75	
Private passenger vehicles and		
ambulances		
With 9–12 passenger seats	£42.65	£47.85*
13–16 passenger seats	£45.70	£61.80*
Over 16 passenger seats	£61.95	£95.65*
For light goods vehicles between		
3,000 and 3,500 kg	£44.40	

*Including seatbelt installation check

METHOD OF TRAVEL TO WORK, GREAT BRITAIN
(percentage)*

	1997	2002
Car, van, minibus, works van	71	70
Bus, coach, private bus	8	8
Train (incl. Underground and light rail)	6	7
Walk	11	11
Other	5	5
All	100	100

* All figures are rounded
Source: DfT/The Stationery Office – *Transport Statistics Great Britain* (Crown copyright)

SHIPPING AND PORTS

Since earliest times sea trade has played a central role in Britain's economy. By the 17th century Britain had built up a substantial merchant fleet and by the early 20th century it dominated the world shipping industry. Until the late 1990s the size and tonnage of the UK-registered trading fleet had been steadily declining. In December 1998 the Government published, *British Shipping: Charting a New Course*, which outlined strategies to promote the long-term interests of British shipping. By the end of 2003 the number of ships in the UK fleet had increased by 55 per cent whilst tonnage more than tripled; and the UK-flagged merchant fleet now constitutes over 1 per cent of the world fleet.

Freight is carried by liner and bulk services, almost all scheduled liner services being containerised. About 95 per cent by weight of Britain's overseas trade is carried by sea; this amounts to 75 per cent of its total value. Passengers and vehicles are carried by roll-on, roll-off ferries, hovercraft, hydrofoils and high-speed catamarans.

There were about 51 million ferry passengers a year in 2002, of whom 29 million travelled internationally. The leading British operators of passenger services are P&O Ferries and Stena Line (which has a Swedish parent company).

Lloyd's of London provides the most comprehensive shipping intelligence service in the world. *Lloyd's Shipping Index*, published daily, lists some 25,000 ocean-going vessels and gives the latest known report of each.

PORTS

There are about 100 commercially significant ports in Great Britain, including such ports as London, Dover, Forth, Tees and Hartlepool, Grimsby and Immingham, Sullom Voe, Milford Haven, Southampton, Felixstowe and Liverpool. Belfast is the principal freight port in Northern Ireland.

Broadly speaking, ports are owned and operated by private companies, local authorities or trusts. The largest operator is Associated British Ports which owns 21 ports. Total freight traffic through UK ports in 2002 amounted to 558 million tonnes, a decrease of 1 per cent on the previous year's figure of 566 million tonnes.

MARINE SAFETY

From 1 October 2002 all roll-on, roll-off ferries operating to and from the UK are required to meet the new international safety standards on stability established by the Stockholm Agreement.

The Maritime and Coastguard Agency (MCA) was established on 1 April 1998 by the merger of the Coastguard Agency and the Marine Safety Agency. It is an executive agency of the Department for Transport. The Agency's aims are to reduce accidents and deaths at sea and minimise pollution in UK waters. HM Coastguard co-ordinates all civil maritime Search and Rescue around the UK and over a large part of the eastern Atlantic. There are about 560 full-time Coastguard Officers and a further 3,100 Auxiliary Coastguards. Each year HM Coastguard responds to around 13,000 incidents of which 7,500 are accidents to which search and rescue resources are deployed.

Locations hazardous to shipping in coastal waters are marked by lighthouses and other lights and buoys. The lighthouse authorities are the Corporation of Trinity House (for England, Wales and the Channel Islands), the Northern Lighthouse Board (for Scotland and the Isle of Man), and the Commissioners of Irish Lights (for Northern Ireland and the Republic of Ireland). Trinity House maintains 72 lighthouses, 11 major floating aids to navigation, 412 buoys, 19 beacons and 7 DGPS (Differential Positioning System) beacons*. The Northern Lighthouse Board maintains 198 lighthouses and 131 buoys; and Irish Lights 80 lighthouses and 145 buoys.

Harbour authorities are responsible for pilotage within their harbour areas; and the Ports Act 1991 provides for the transfer of lights and buoys to harbour authorities where these are used for mainly local navigation.

* DGPS is a satellite based navigation system provided under the three Lighthouse Authorities' Marine Navigation Plan and became operational on 1 July 2002

UK OWNED TRADING VESSELS OF 100 GROSS TONS AND OVER *as at end 2002*

Type of vessel	No.	Gross tonnage
Tankers	140	2,628,000
Bulk carriers	35	1,772,000
Specialised carriers	14	101,000
Fully cellular container	72	2,509,000
Ro-Ro (passenger & cargo)	140	1,432,000
Other general cargo	149	580,000
Passenger	40	730,000
Total	590	9,752,000

Source: Department for Transport

UK INTERNATIONAL PASSENGER MOVEMENTS BY SEA 2002*

All passenger movements†	29,295,000
Irish Republic, European continent and Mediterranean Sea area	28,726,000
Rest of the World	32,000
Pleasure cruises†	537,000

* Passengers are included at both departure and arrival if their journeys begin and end at a UK seaport
† provisional figures
Source: The Stationery Office – *Annual Abstract of Statistics 2004* (Crown copyright)

MARINECALL WEATHER FORECAST SERVICE

Marinecall provides information for coastal, inshore and offshore UK sea areas by telephone. Forecasts include gale and strong wind warnings, the general situation, wind speed and direction, probability and strength of gusts, developing weather conditions, visibility and sea state and can vary in format from current observations to six-hour summaries, to 48-hour and five-day forecasts.

	By Phone 6-hour coastal location and 5-day outlook forecast	By Fax 6-hour coastal location and 48-hour outlook forecasts
COASTAL/INSHORE AREA	09014-737 4+	09065-300 2+
National inshore waters (3–5 day outlook only)	60	–
Cape Wrath – Rattray Head	61	51
Rattray Head – Berwick	62	52
Berwick – Whitby	63	53
Whitby – The Wash	64	54
The Wash – North Foreland	65	55
North Foreland – Selsey Bill	66	56
Selsey Bill – Lyme Regis	67	57
Lyme Regis – Hartland Point	68	58
Hartland Point – St David's Head	69	59
St David's Head – Colwyn Bay	70	60
Colwyn Bay – Mull of Galloway	71	61
Mull of Galloway – Mull of Kintrye	72	62
Mull of Kintrye – Ardnamurchan	73	63
Ardnamurchan – Cape Wrath*	74	64
Lough Foyle – Carlingford Lough*	75	65
Channel Islands*	76	66
OFFSHORE AREA		
English Channel	41	70
Southern North Sea	42	71
Irish Sea	43	73
Biscay	44	74
North-west Scotland	45	75
Northern North Sea	46	76

* Localised 6-hour forecasts are unavailable for these areas
Based upon calls from a BT landline. Marinecall by telephone is charged at 60p per minute. Marinecall by fax is charged at £1.50 per minute.

UK SHIPPING FORECAST AREAS

Weather bulletins for shipping are broadcast daily on BBC Radio 4 at the following times: 0048 and 0535 (long wave and FM), 1200 and 1755 (normally long wave only). The bulletins consist of a gale warning summary, general synopsis, sea-area forecasts and coastal station reports. In addition, gale warnings are broadcast at the first available programme break after receipt. If this does not coincide with a news bulletin, the warning is repeated after the next news bulletin.

RELIGION IN THE UK

The 2001 census included a voluntary question on religion for the first time (although the question had been included in previous censuses in Northern Ireland); 92 per cent of people chose to answer the question. In the UK, 71.6 per cent of people in Britain identified themselves as Christian (42.1 million people). After Christianity, the next most prevalent faith was Islam with 2.7 per cent describing their religion as Muslim (1.6 million people). The next largest religious groups were Hindus (559,000), followed by Sikhs (336,000), Jews (267,000), Buddhists (152,000) and people from other religions (179,000). Together, these groups accounted for less than 3 per cent of the total UK population. People in Northern Ireland were most likely to say that they identified with a religion (86 per cent) compared with 77 per cent in England and Wales and 67 per cent in Scotland. About 16 per cent of the UK population stated that they had no religion. This category included those who identified themselves as agnostics, atheists, heathens and Jedi Knights.

CENSUS 2001 RESULTS – RELIGIONS IN THE UK
(thousands)

Christian	42,079	71.6%
Buddhist	152	0.3%
Hindu	559	1.0%
Jewish	267	0.5%
Muslim	1,591	2.7%
Sikh	336	0.6%
Other religion	179	0.3%
All religions	45,163	76.8%
No religion	9,104	15.5%
Not stated	4,289	7.3%
All no religion/not stated	13,626	23.2%
Total	58,789	100%

Source: Census 2001

ADHERENTS TO RELIGIONS IN THE UK
(millions)

	1975	1985	1995	2000
Christian (Trinitarian)	40.2	39.1	38.1	37.5
Non-Trinitarian	0.7	1.0	1.3	1.3
Hindu	0.3	0.4	0.4	0.5
Jew	0.4	0.3	0.3	0.3
Muslim	0.4	0.9	1.2	1.4
Sikh	0.2	0.3	0.6	0.6
Other	0.1	0.3	0.3	0.4
Total	42.3	42.3	42.2	42.0

Source: Christian Research – *UK Christian Handbook Religious Trends No. 3 2002–3*

INTER-CHURCH AND INTER-FAITH CO-OPERATION

The main umbrella body for the Christian churches in the UK is the Churches Together in Britain and Ireland. There are also ecumenical bodies in each of the constituent countries of the UK: Churches Together in England, Action of Churches Together in Scotland, CYTUN (Churches Together in Wales), and the Irish Council of Churches. The Free Churches' Council comprises most of the Free Churches in England and Wales, and the Evangelical Alliance represents evangelical Christians.

The Inter Faith Network for the United Kingdom promotes co-operation between faiths, and the Council of Christians and Jews works to improve relations between the two religions. Churches Together in Britain and Ireland also has a Commission on Inter-Faith Relations.

ACTION OF CHURCHES TOGETHER IN SCOTLAND,
Scottish Churches House, Kirk Street, Dunblane, Perthshire
FK15 0AJ T 01786-823588 F 01786-825844
E ecumenical@acts-scotland.org W www.acts-scotland.org
General Secretary, Revd Dr Kevin Franz
CHURCHES TOGETHER IN BRITAIN AND IRELAND,
Bastille Court, 2 Paris Garden, London SE1 8ND
T 020-7654 7254 F 020-7654 7222 E info@ctbi.org.uk
W www.ctbi.org.uk
General Secretary, Dr David Goodbourn
CHURCHES TOGETHER IN ENGLAND, 27 Tavistock
Square, London WC1H 9HH T 020-7529 8141
F 020-7529 8134 W www.churches-together.org.uk
General Secretary, Revd Bill Snelson
COUNCIL OF CHRISTIANS AND JEWS, Camelford House,
87–89 Albert Embankment, London, SE1 7TP
T 020-7820 0090 F 020-7820 0504 E cjrelations@ccj.org.uk
W www.ccj.org.uk
Director, Sister Margaret Shepherd
CYTUN (CHURCHES TOGETHER IN WALES),
58 Richmond Road, Cardiff CF24 3UR T 029-2046 4204
F 029-2045 5427 E post@cytun.org.uk
W www.cytun.org.uk
General Secretary, Revd Gethin Abraham-Williams
EVANGELICAL ALLIANCE, Whitefield House,
186 Kennington Park Road, London SE11 4BT
T 020-7207 2100 F 020-7207 2150 E london@eauk.org
W www.eauk.org
General Director, Revd Joel Edwards
INTER FAITH NETWORK FOR THE UNITED KINGDOM,
8A Lower Grosvenor Place, London SW1W 0EN
T 020-7931 7766 F 020-7931 7722
E ifnet@interfaith.org.uk W www.interfaith.org.uk
Director, Brian Pearce, OBE
IRISH COUNCIL OF CHURCHES, Inter-Church Centre,
48 Elmwood Avenue, Belfast BT9 6AZ T 028-9066 3145
F 028-9066 4160 E icpep@email.com
W www.irishchurches.org
General Secretary, Michael Earle

CHRISTIANITY

Christianity is a monotheistic faith based on the person and teachings of Jesus Christ and all Christian denominations claim his authority. Central to its teaching is the concept of God and his son Jesus Christ, who was crucified and resurrected in order to enable mankind to attain salvation. The Jewish scriptures predicted the coming of a *Messiah*, an 'anointed one', who would bring salvation. To Christians, Jesus of Nazareth, a Jewish rabbi (teacher), who was born in Palestine, was the promised Messiah. Jesus' birth, teachings, crucifixion and subsequent resurrection are recorded in the *Gospels*, which, together with other scriptures that summarise Christian belief, form the *New Testament*. This, together with the Hebrew scriptures, entitled the *Old Testament* by Christians, makes up the *Bible*, the sacred texts of Christianity.

BELIEFS

Christians believe that sin distanced mankind from God, and that Jesus was the Son of God, sent to redeem mankind from that sin by his death. In addition, many believe that Jesus will return again at some future date, triumph over evil and establish a kingdom on earth, thus inaugurating a new age. The Gospel assures Christians that those who believe in Jesus and obey his teachings will be forgiven their sins and will be resurrected from the dead.

PRACTICES

Christian practices vary widely between different Christian churches, but prayer is universal to all, as is charity, giving for the maintenance of the church buildings, for the work of the church, and to the poor and needy. In addition, certain days of observance, i.e. the *Sabbath, Easter* and *Christmas,* are celebrated by most Christians. The Orthodox, Roman Catholic and Anglican churches celebrate many more days of observance, based on saints and significant events in the life of Jesus. The belief in sacraments, physical signs believed to have been ordained by Jesus Christ to symbolise and convey spiritual gifts, varies greatly between Christian denominations; *Baptism* and the *Eucharist* are practised by most Christians. Baptism, symbolising repentance and faith in Jesus is an act marking entry into the Christian community; the Eucharist, the ritual re-enactment of the Last Supper, Jesus' final meal with his disciples, is also practised by most denominations. Other sacraments, such as anointing the sick, the laying on of hands to symbolise the passing on of the office of priesthood or to heal the sick and speaking in tongues, where it is believed that the person is possessed by the Holy Spirit, the Spirit of God, are less common. In denominations where infant baptism is practised, confirmation is common, where the person repeats the commitments made for him or her at infancy. Matrimony and the ordination of priests are also widely believed to be sacraments. Many Protestants only view baptism and the Eucharist as sacraments; the Quakers and the Salvation Army reject the use of sacraments. Most Christians believe that God actively guides the Church.

THE EARLY CHURCH

The apostles were Jesus' first converts and are recognised by Christians as the founders of the Christian community. The new faith spread rapidly throughout the eastern provinces of the Roman Empire. Early Christianity was subject to great persecution until 313 AD, when Emperor Constantine's Edict of Toleration confirmed its right to exist and it became established as the religion of the Roman Empire in 381 AD.

The Christian faith was slowly formulated in the first millennium of the Christian era. Between AD 325 and 787 there were seven Oecumenical Councils at which bishops from the entire Christian world assembled to resolve various doctrinal disputes. The estrangement between East and West began after Constantine moved the centre of the Roman Empire from Rome to Constantinople, and it grew after the division of the Roman Empire into eastern and western halves. Linguistic and cultural differences between Greek East and Latin West served to encourage separate ecclesiastical developments which became pronounced in the tenth and early 11th centuries.

Administration of the church was divided between five ancient patriarchates: Rome and all the West, Constantinople (the imperial city – the 'New Rome'), Jerusalem and all Palestine, Antioch and all the East, and Alexandria and all Africa. Of these, only Rome was in the Latin West and after the schism in 1054, Rome developed a structure of authority centralised on the Papacy, while the Orthodox East maintained the style of localised administration. Papal authority over the doctrine and jurisdiction of the Church in western Europe was unrivalled after the split with the Eastern Orthodox Church until the Protestant Reformation in the 16th century.

CHRISTIANITY IN BRITAIN

An English Church already existed when Pope Gregory sent Augustine to evangelise the English in AD 596. Conflicts between Church and State during the Middle Ages culminated in the Act of Supremacy in 1534, which repudiated papal supremacy and declared King Henry VIII to be the supreme head of the Church in England. Since 1559 the English monarch has been termed the Supreme Governor of the Church of England. In 1560 the jurisdiction of the Roman Catholic Church in Scotland was abolished and the first assembly of the Church of Scotland ratified the Confession of Faith, drawn up by a committee including John Knox. In 1592 Parliament passed an Act guaranteeing the liberties of the Church and its presbyterian government. King James VI (James I of England) and later Stuart monarchs attempted to reintroduce episcopacy, but a presbyterian church was finally restored in 1690 and secured by the Act of Settlement (1690) and the Act of Union (1707).

PORVOO DECLARATION

The Porvoo Declaration was drawn up by representatives of the British and Irish Anglican churches and the Nordic and Baltic Lutheran churches and was approved by the General Synod of the Church of England in July 1995. Churches that approve the Declaration regard baptised members of each other's churches as members of their own, and allow free interchange of episcopally ordained ministers within the rules of each church.

NON-CHRISTIAN RELIGIONS AND BELIEFS

BAHÁ'Í FAITH

Mirza Husayn-'Ali, known as *Bahá'u'lláh* (Glory of God) was born in Iran in 1817 and became a follower of the *Báb*, a religious reformer and prophet who was imprisoned for his beliefs and executed on the grounds of heresy in 1850. *Bahá'u'lláh* was himself imprisoned in 1852, and in 1853 he had a vision that he was the Promised One foretold by the *Báb*. He was exiled after his release from prison and eventually arrived in Acre, now in Israel, where he continued to compose the Bahá'í sacred scriptures. He died in 1892 and was succeeded by his son, Abdu'l-Bahá, as spiritual leader, under whose guidance the faith spread to Europe and North America. He was followed by Shoghi Effendi, his grandson, who translated many of *Bahá'u'lláh*'s works into English. Upon his death in 1957, a democratic system of leadership was brought into operation. The Bahá'í faith recognises the unity and relativity of religious truth and teaches that there is only one God, whose will has been revealed to mankind by a series of messengers, such as Zoroaster, Abraham, Moses, Buddha, Krishna, Christ, Muhammad, the Báb and Bahá'u'lláh, who were seen as the founders of separate religions, but whose common purpose was to bring God's message to mankind. It teaches that all races and both sexes are equal and deserving of equal opportunities and treatment, that education is a fundamental right and encourages a fair distribution of wealth. In addition, mankind is exhorted to establish a world federal system to promote peace and tolerance.

A Feast is held every 19 days, which consists of prayer and readings of Bahá'í scriptures, consultation on community business, and social activities. Music, food and beverages usually accompany the proceedings. There is no clergy; each local community elects a local assembly, which co-ordinates community activities, enrols new members, counsels and assists members in need, and conducts Bahá'í marriages and funerals. A national assembly is elected annually by locally elected delegates, and every five years the national spiritual assemblies meet together to elect the Universal House of Justice, the supreme international governing body of the Bahá'í Faith. World-wide there are over 13,000 local spiritual assemblies; there are around five million members residing in about 235 countries, of which 182 have national organisations.

THE BAHÁ'Í OFFICE OF PUBLIC INFORMATION, 27 Rutland Gate, London SW7 1PD T 020-7584 2566 F 020-7584 9402 E nsa@bahai.org.uk W www.bahai.org.uk
Secretary of the National UK Spiritual Assembly, The Hon. Barnabus Leith

BUDDHISM

Buddhism originated in northern India, in the teachings of Siddharta Gautama, who was born near Kapilavastu about 560 BC and became the *Buddha* (Enlightened One).

Fundamental to Buddhism is the concept of rebirth. Each life carries with it the consequences of the conduct of earlier lives (known as the law of *karma*). This cycle of death and rebirth is broken only when the state of *nirvana* has been reached. Buddhism steers a middle path between belief in personal immortality and belief in death as the final end.

The Four Noble Truths of Buddhism (*dukkha*, suffering; *tanha*, a thirst or desire for continued existence which causes dukkha; *nirvana*, the final liberation from desire and ignorance; and *ariya*, the path to nirvana) are all held to be universal and to sum up the *dhamma* or true nature of life. Necessary qualities to promote spiritual development are *sila* (morality), *samadhi* (meditation) and *panna* (wisdom).

There are two main schools of Buddhism: *Theravada* Buddhism, the earliest extant school, which is more traditional, and *Mahayana* Buddhism, which began to develop about 500 years after the Buddha's death and is more liberal; it teaches that all people may attain Buddhahood. Important schools that have developed within Mahayana Buddhism are *Zen* Buddhism, *Nichiren* Buddhism and Pure Land Buddhism or *Amidism*. There are also distinctive Tibetan forms of Buddhism. Buddhism began to establish itself in the West in the early 20th century. The scripture of Theravada Buddhism is the *Pali Canon*, which dates from the first century BC. Mahayana Buddhism uses a Sanskrit version of the Pali Canon but also has many other works of scripture.

There is no set time for Buddhist worship, which may take place in a temple or in the home. Worship centres around meditation, acts of devotion centring on the image of the Buddha, and, where possible, offerings to a relic of the Buddha. Buddhist festivals vary according to local traditions and within Theravada and Mahayana Buddhism. For religious purposes Buddhists use solar and lunar calendars, the New Year being celebrated in April. Other festivals mark events in the life of the Buddha.

There is no supreme governing authority in Buddhism. In the United Kingdom communities representing all schools of Buddhism have developed and operate independently. The Buddhist Society was established in 1924; it runs courses and lectures, and publishes books about Buddhism. It represents no one school of Buddhism.

There are estimated to be at least 300 million Buddhists world-wide, and more than 500 groups and centres and up to 20 temples or monasteries in the UK.

THE BUDDHIST SOCIETY, 58 Eccleston Square, London SW1V 1PH T 020-7834 5858 F 020-7976 5238 E info@thebuddhistsociety.org.uk W www.thebuddhistsociety.org.uk
FRIENDS OF THE WESTERN BUDDHIST ORDER, FWBO Communications Office, 59 Roman Road, E2 0QN T 020-8981 8000 W www.lbc.org.uk
THE NETWORK OF BUDDHIST ORGANISATIONS, 6 Tyne Road, Bishopston, Bristol BS7 8EE T 0845-345 8978 E secretary@nbo.org.uk W www.nbo.org.uk
OFFICE OF TIBET, Tibet House, 1 Culworth Street, London NW8 7AF T 020-7722 5378
SOKA GAKKAI UK, Taplow Court, Taplow, Maidenhead, Berkshire SL6 0ER T 01628-773163 W www.sgi-uk.org

HINDUISM

Hinduism has no historical founder but had become highly developed in India by about 1200 BC. Its adherents originally called themselves Aryans; Muslim invaders first called the Aryans 'Hindus' (derived from 'Sindhu', the name of the river Indus) in the eighth century.

Most Hindus hold that *satya* (truthfulness), *ahimsa* (non-violence), honesty, sincerity and devotion to God are essential for good living. They believe in one supreme spirit *(Brahman)*, and in the transmigration of *atman* (the soul). Most Hindus accept the doctrine of *karma* (consequences of actions), the concept of *samsara* (successive lives) and the possibility of all atmans achieving *moksha* (liberation from samsara) through *jnana* (knowledge), *yoga* (meditation), *karma* (work or action) and *bhakti* (devotion).

Most Hindus offer worship to *murtis* (images of deities) representing different incarnations or aspects of Brahman, and follow their *dharma* (religious and social duty) according to the traditions of their *varna* (social class), *ashrama* (stage in life), *jati* (caste) and *kula* (family).

Hinduism's sacred texts are divided into *shruti* ('that which is heard'), including the *Vedas*; or *smriti* ('that which is remembered'), including the *Ramayana*, the *Mahabharata*, the *Puranas* (ancient myths), and the sacred law books. Most Hindus recognise the authority of the *Vedas*, the oldest holy books, and accept the philosophical teachings of the *Upanishads*, the *Vedanta Sutras* and the *Bhagavad-Gita*.

Brahman is omniscient, omnipotent, limitless and all-pervading, and is usually worshipped in His deity form. Brahma, Vishnu and Shiva are the most important gods worshipped by Hindus; their respective consorts are

Saraswati, Lakshmi and Durga or Parvati, also known as Shakti. There are believed to have been ten *avatars* (incarnations) of Vishnu, of whom the most important are Rama and Krishna. Other popular gods are Ganesha, Hanuman and Subrahmanyam. All gods are seen as aspects of the supreme God, not as competing deities.

Orthodox Hindus revere all gods and goddesses equally, but there are many denominations, including the Hare-Krishna movement (ISKCon), the Arya Samaj, the Swami Narayan Hindu mission and the Satya Sai-Baba movement, in which worship is concentrated on one deity. The *guru* (spiritual teacher) is seen as the source of spiritual guidance.

Hinduism does not have a centrally-trained and ordained priesthood. The pronouncements of the *shankaracharyas* (heads of monasteries) of Shringeri, Puri, Dwarka and Badrinath are heeded by the orthodox but may be ignored by the various sects.

The commonest form of worship is a *puja*, in which offerings of water, flowers, food, fruit, incense and light are made to a deity. Puja may be done either in a home shrine or a *mandir* (temple). Many British Hindus celebrate *samskars* (purification rites) to name a baby, the sacred thread (an initiation ceremony), marriage and cremation.

The largest communities of Hindus in Britain are in Leicester, London, Birmingham and Bradford, and developed as a result of immigration from India, eastern Africa and Sri Lanka.

There are an estimated 800 million Hindus world-wide; there are about 500,000 adherents, according to the 2001 UK census, and over 150 temples in the UK.

ARYA PRATINIDHI SABHA (UK) AND ARYA SAMAJ
LONDON, 69A Argyle Road, London W13 0LY
T 020-8991 1732
BHARATIYA VIDYA BHAVAN, Institute of Indian Art and
Culture, 4A Castletown Road, London W14 9HE
T 020-7381 3086 E info@bhavan.net W www.bhavan.net
Executive Director, Dr M. N. Nandakumara
INTERNATIONAL SOCIETY FOR KRISHNA
CONSCIOUSNESS (ISKCON), Bhaktivedanta Manor,
Dharam Marg, Hilfield Lane, Aldenham, Watford, Herts
WD2 8EZ T 01923-857244 W www.krishnatemple.com
Temple President, Gauri Das
NATIONAL COUNCIL OF HINDU TEMPLES (UK),
Bhakrivedanta Manor, Letchmore Heath, Watford WD2 8EP
T 01923-856269
Secretary, Bimal Krishna Das
SWAMINARAYAN HINDU MISSION (SHRI
SWAMINARAYAN MANDIR), 105–119 Brentfield Road,
London NW10 8LD T 020-8965 2651 F 020 8965 6313
E admin@mandir.org W www.mandir.org
VISHWA HINDU PARISHAD (UK), 48 Wharfedale Gardens,
Thornton Heath, Surrey CR7 6LB T 020-8684 9716
General Secretary, Kishor Ruparelia

HUMANISM

Humanism traces its roots back to ancient times, with Indian, Chinese, Greek and Roman philosophers expressing Humanist ideas some 2,500 years ago. Confucius, the Chinese philosopher who lived around 500 BC, believed that religious observances should be replaced with moral values as the basis of social and political order and that 'the true way' is based on reason and humanity. He also stressed the importance of benevolence, respect for others and believed that the individual situation should be considered rather than the global application of traditional rules. Humanists believe that there is no God or other supernatural beings and that humans have only one life within the material universe (Humanists do not believe in an after-life or reincarnation). Humanists believe that humans can live ethical and fulfilling lives without religious beliefs through a moral code derived from the lessons of history, personal experience and thought. Particular emphasis is placed on science as the only reliable source of knowledge of the universe. Humanists have a positive outlook on life believing that the world's problems can be solved through co-operation and mutual respect and that personal inspiration can be gained from life, especially art, culture and the natural world. There are no sacred Humanist texts. Humanists believe in ceremonies to mark important occasions in life and the British Humanist Association has a network of accredited officials and celebrants who are qualified to conduct baby namings, weddings and funerals.

BRITISH HUMANIST ASSOCIATION, 1 Gower Street,
London, WC1E 6HD T 020-7079 3580
F 020-7079 3588 E info@humanism.org.uk
W www.humanism.org.uk

ISLAM

Islam (which means 'peace arising from submission to the will of Allah' in Arabic) is a monotheistic religion which was taught in Arabia by the Prophet Muhammad, who was born in Mecca (Al-Makkah) in 570 CE. Islam spread to Egypt, North Africa, Spain and the borders of China in the century following the Prophet's death, and is now the predominant religion in Indonesia, the Near and Middle East, northern and parts of western Africa, Pakistan, Bangladesh, Malaysia and some of the former Soviet republics. There are also large Muslim communities in other countries.

For Muslims (adherents of Islam), there is one God (*Allah*), who holds absolute power. His commands were revealed to mankind through the prophets, who include Abraham, Moses and Jesus, but his message was gradually corrupted until revealed finally and in perfect form to Muhammad through the angel *Jibril* (Gabriel) over a period of 23 years. This last, incorruptible message has been recorded in the *Qur'an* (Koran), which contains 114 divisions called *surahs*, each made up of *ayahs*, and is held to be the essence of all previous scriptures. The *Ahadith* are the records of the Prophet Muhammad's deeds and sayings (the *Sunnah*) as recounted by his immediate followers. A culture and a system of law and theology gradually developed to form a distinctive Islamic civilisation. Islam makes no distinction between sacred and worldly affairs and provides rules for every aspect of human life. The *Shari'ah* is the sacred law of Islam based upon prescriptions derived from the Qur'an and the *Sunnah* of the Prophet.

The 'five pillars of Islam' are *shahadah* (a declaration of faith in the oneness and supremacy of Allah and the messengership of Muhammad); *salat* (formal prayer, to be performed five times a day facing the *Ka'bah* (sacred house in the holy city of Al-Makkah)); *zakat* (welfare due); *sawm* (fasting during the month of Ramadan); and *hajj* (pilgrimage to Al-Makkah); some Muslims would add *jihad* (striving for the cause of good and resistance to evil).

Two main groups developed among Muslims. Sunni Muslims accept the legitimacy of Muhammad's first four *caliphs* (successors as head of the Muslim community) and of the authority of the Muslim community as a whole. About 90 per cent of Muslims are Sunni Muslims.

Shi'ites recognise only Muhammad's son-in-law Ali as his rightful successor and the *Imams* (descendants of Ali, not to be confused with *imams* (prayer leaders or religious teachers)) as the principal legitimate religious authority. The largest group within Shi'ism is *Twelver Shi'ism*, which has been the official school of law and theology in Iran since the 16th century; other subsects include the *Ismailis,* the *Druze* and the *Alawis,* the latter two differing considerably from the main body of Muslims. The *Ibadhis* of Oman are neither Sunni nor Shi'a, deriving from the strictly observant *Khariji* (Seceeders). There is no organised priesthood, but learned men such as *ulama, imams* and *ayatollahs* are accorded great respect. The *Sufis* are the mystics of Islam. Mosques are centres for worship and teaching and also for social and welfare activities.

Islam was first known in western Europe in the eighth century AD when 800 years of Muslim rule began in Spain. Later, Islam spread to eastern Europe. More recently, Muslims came to Europe from Africa, the Middle East and Asia in the late 19th century. Both the Sunni and Shi'a traditions are represented in Britain, but the majority of Muslims in Britain adhere to Sunni Islam. Efforts to establish a representative central organisation recognised by all Muslims in Britain are beginning to yield results with the emergence of the Muslim Council of Britain. In addition, there are many other Muslim organisations in Britain. There are about 1,000 million Muslims world-wide, with nearly two million adherents and about 1,200 mosques in Britain.

IMAMS AND MOSQUES COUNCIL, 20–22 Creffield Road, London W5 3RP T 020-8992 6636
  Chairman of the Council and Principal of the Muslim College, Dr M. A. Z. Badawi
ISLAMIC CULTURAL CENTRE, 146 Park Road, London NW8 7RG T 020-7724 3363 F 020-7724 0493
  E islamic200@aol.com W www.islamicculturalcentre.co.uk
  Director, Dr A. Al-Dubayan
MUSLIM COUNCIL OF BRITAIN, Suite 5, Boardman House, 64 Broadway, Stratford, London E15 1NT T 020-8432 0585
  F 020-8432 0587 E admin@mcb.org.uk
  W www.mcb.org.uk
  Secretary-General, Iqbal Sacranie
MUSLIM WORLD LEAGUE, 46 Goodge Street, London W1P 1FJ T 020-7636 7568 E mwlgb@btconnect.com
  Secretary, Ghulamur Rahman
UNION OF MUSLIM ORGANISATIONS OF THE UK AND EIRE, 109 Campden Hill Road, London W8 7TL
  T 020-7229 0538/7221 6608
  Secretary-General, Dr Syed A. Pasha

JAINISM

Jainism traces its history to Vardhamana Jnatiputra, known as *Tirthankara Mahavira* (The Great Hero) whose traditional dates were 599–527 BC. He was the last of a series of 24 *Jinas* (those who overcome all passions and desires) or *Tirthankaras* (those who show a way across the ocean of life) stretching back to remote antiquity. Born to a noble family in north-eastern India, he renounced the world for the life of a wandering ascetic and after 12 years of austerity and meditation he attained enlightenment. He then preached his message until, at the age of 72, he passed away and reached *moksha,* total liberation from the cycle of death and rebirth.

Jains deny the authority of the *Vedas,* the Hindu sacred scriptures. They recognise some of the minor deities of the Hindu pantheon, but the supreme objects of worship are the *Tirthankaras.* The pious Jain does not ask favours from the *Tirthankaras,* but seeks to emulate their example in his or her own life.

Jains believe that the universe is eternal and self-subsisting: there is no omnipotent creator God ruling it and the destiny of the individual is in his or her own hands. *Karma,* the fruit of past actions, determines the place of every living being and rebirth may be in the heavens, on earth as a human, an animal or other lower being, or in the hells. The ultimate goal of existence is *moksha* or *nirvana,* a state of perfect knowledge and tranquility for each individual soul, which can be achieved only by gaining enlightenment.

The path to liberation is defined by the Three Jewels, *samyak darsana* (right thought), *samyak jnana* (right knowledge) and *samyak charitra* (right conduct).

There are about 25,000 Jains in Britain, sizeable communities in North America and East Africa and smaller groups in many other countries.

INSTITUTE OF JAINOLOGY, Unit 18, Silicon Business Centre, 28 Wadsworth Road, Greenford, Middx, UB6 7JZ
  T 020-8997 2300 W www.jainology.org
  Chairman, Ratilal P. Chandaria

JUDAISM

Judaism is the oldest monotheistic faith. The primary authority of Judaism is the Hebrew Bible or *Tanakh,* which records how the descendants of Abraham were led by Moses out of their slavery in Egypt to Mount Sinai where God's law *(Torah)* was revealed to them as the chosen people. The *Talmud,* which consists of commentaries on the *Mishnah* (the first text of rabbinical Judaism), is also held to be authoritative, and may be divided into two main categories: the *halakah* (dealing with legal and ritual matters) and the *Aggadah* (dealing with theological and ethical matters not directly concerned with the regulation of conduct). The *Midrash* comprises rabbinic writings containing biblical interpretations in the spirit of the Aggadah. The *halakah* has become a source of division; Orthodox Jews regard Jewish law as derived from God and therefore unalterable; Reform and Liberal Jews seek to interpret it in the light of contemporary considerations; and Conservative Jews aim to maintain most of the traditional rituals but to allow changes in accordance with tradition. Reconstructionist Judaism, a 20th-century movement, regards Judaism as a culture rather than a theological system and accepts all forms of Jewish practice.

The family is the basic unit of Jewish ritual, with the synagogue playing an important role as the centre for public worship and religious study. A synagogue is led by a group of laymen who are elected to office. The Rabbi is primarily a teacher and spiritual guide. The Sabbath is the central religious observance. Most British Jews are descendants of either the *Ashkenazim* of central and eastern Europe or the *Sephardim* of Spain, Portugal and the Middle East.

The Chief Rabbi of the United Hebrew Congregations of the Commonwealth is appointed by a Chief Rabbinate Conference, and is the rabbinical authority of the mainstream Orthodox sector of the Ashkenazi Jewish community, the largest body of which is the United Synagogue. His formal ecclesiastical authority is not recognised by the Reform Synagogues of Great Britain (the largest progressive group), the Union of Liberal and

Progressive Synagogues, the Sephardi community, or the Assembly of Masorti Synagogues. He is, however, generally recognised both outside the Jewish community and within it as the public religious representative of the totality of British Jewry. The Chief Rabbi is President of the London *Beth Din*. *Beth Din* (Court of Judgement) is a rabbinic court. The *Dayanim* (Assessors) adjudicate in disputes or on matters of Jewish law and tradition; they also oversee dietary law administration.

The Board of Deputies of British Jews, established in 1760, is the representative body of British Jewry. The basis of representation is mainly synagogal, but communal organisations are also represented. It watches over the interests of British Jewry, acts as the central voice of the community and seeks to counter anti-Jewish discrimination and antisemitic activities. In November 1998 a Consultative Committee was established comprising representatives of the Assembly of Masorti Synagogues, Reform Synagogues of Great Britain, Union of Liberal and Progressive Synagogues and the United Synagogue. The Committee holds discussions to further communal harmony and development.

There are over 12.5 million Jews world-wide; in Great Britain and Ireland there are an estimated 285,000 adherents and about 365 synagogues. Of these, 191 congregations and about 175 rabbis and ministers are under the jurisdiction of the Chief Rabbi; 99 orthodox congregations have a more independent status; and 79 congregations are outside the jurisdiction of the Chief Rabbi.

CHIEF RABBINATE, Adler House, 735 High Road, London N12 0US T 020-8343 6301 F 020-8343 6310
E info@chiefrabbi.org W www.chiefrabbi.org
Chief Rabbi, Dr Jonathan Sacks
Executive Director, Syma Weinberg
BETH DIN (COURT OF THE CHIEF RABBI), 735 High Road, London N12 0US T 020-8343 6270 F 020-8343 6257
E info@bethdin.org.uk
Registrar, D. Frei; *Dayanim*, Rabbi Chanoch Ehrentreu; Ivan Binstock; Menachem Gelley; Yonason Abraham; I. Berger
BOARD OF DEPUTIES OF BRITISH JEWS, 6 Bloomsbury Square, London WC1A 2LP T 020-7543 5400
F 020-7543 0010 E info@bod.org.uk W www.bod.org.uk
President, Henry Grunwald, QC
ASSEMBLY OF MASORTI SYNAGOGUES, 1097 Finchley Road, London NW11 0PU T 020-8201 8772
F 020-8201 8917 E office@masorti.org.uk
W www.masorti.org.uk
Executive Director, Michael Gluckman
FEDERATION OF SYNAGOGUES, 65 Watford Way, London NW4 3AQ T 020-8202 2263 F 020-8203 0610
Chief Executive, G. D. Coleman
BETH DIN OF THE FEDERATION OF SYNAGOGUES, 65 Watford Way, London NW4 3AQ T 020-8202 2263
Registrar, Rabbi Zalman Unsdorfer; *Dayanim*, Yisroel Lichtenstein; Berel Berkovits; M. D. Elzas
LIBERAL JUDAISM, The Montagu Centre, 21 Maple Street, London W1T 4BE T 020-7580 1663 F 020-7631 9838
E montagu@liberaljudaism.org
W www.liberaljudaism.org
REFORM SYNAGOGUE OF GREAT BRITAIN, The Sternberg Centre for Judaism, 80 East End Road, London N3 2SY T 020-8349 5640 F 020-8349 5699
E admin@reformjudaism.org.uk
W www.reformjudaism.org.uk
Chief Executive, Rabbi Tony Bayfield

SPANISH AND PORTUGUESE JEWS' CONGREGATION, 2 Ashworth Road, London W9 1JY T 020-7289 2573
F 020-7289 2709 E howardmiller@spsyn.org.uk
W www.sandp.org
Chief Executive, Howard Miller
UNION OF ORTHODOX HEBREW CONGREGATIONS, 140 Stamford Hill, London N16 6QT T 020-8802 6226
Principal Rabbinical Authority, Rabbi Ephraim Padwa
UNITED SYNAGOGUE HEAD OFFICE, Adler House, 735 High Road, London N12 0US T 020-8343 8989
F 020-8343 6262 E info@unitedsynagogue.org.uk
W www.unitedsynagogue.org.uk
Chief Executive, Rabbi Saul Zneimer

PAGANISM

Paganism draws on the ideas of the Celtic people of pre-Roman Europe and is closely linked to Druidism. The first historical record of Druidry comes from classical Greek and Roman writers of the 3rd century BC, who noted the existence of Druids among a people called the Keltoi who inhabited central and southern Europe. The word druid may derive from the Indo-European 'dreo-vid', meaning 'one who knows the truth'. In practice it was probably understood to mean something like 'wise-one' or 'philospher-priest'. Pagans place much emphasis on the natural world and the ongoing cycle of life and death is central to Pagan beliefs. Most Pagans are eco-friendly and seek to live in a way that minimises harm to the natural environment. Pagans worship many different forms. The most important and widely recognised of these are the God and Goddess whose annual cycle of procreation, birth and dying defines the Pagan year. Paganism strongly emphasises the equality of the sexes with women playing a prominent role in the modern Pagan movement and Goddess worship featuring in most ceremonies. Paganism is not based on doctrine and many pagans follow the code 'if it harms none, do what you will'.

The Pagan Federation was founded in 1971 to provide information on Paganism and publishes a quarterly journal, *Pagan Dawn,* and other publications. It arranges members-only and public events and maintains personal contact by letter with individual members and the wider Pagan community. An annual conference is held at the end of each November and there are regional gatherings throughout the year. The aims of the Pagan Federation are to provide contact between national and international Pagan organisations.

THE PAGAN FEDERATION, BM Box 7097, London, WC1N 3XX

SIKHISM

The Sikh religion dates from the birth of Guru Nanak in the Punjab in 1469. 'Guru' means teacher but in Sikh tradition has come to represent the divine presence of God giving inner spiritual guidance. Nanak's role as the human vessel of the divine guru was passed on to nine successors, the last of whom (Guru Gobind Singh) died in 1708. The immortal guru is now held to reside in the sacred scripture, *Guru Granth Sahib*, and so to be present in all Sikh gatherings.

Guru Nanak taught that there is one God and that different religions are like different roads leading to the same destination. He condemned religious conflict, ritualism and caste prejudices. The fifth Guru, Guru Arjan Dev, largely compiled the Sikh Holy Book, a collection of hymns *(gurbani)* known as the *Adi Granth*. It includes the writings of the first five Gurus and the ninth Guru, and selected writings of Hindu and Muslim saints whose views are in accord with the Gurus' teachings. Guru Arjan Dev also built the Golden Temple at Amritsar, the centre of Sikhism. The tenth Guru, Guru Gobind Singh, passed on the guruship to the sacred scripture, Guru Granth Sahib. He also founded the *Khalsa*, an order intended to fight against tyranny and injustice. Male initiates to the order added 'Singh' to their given names and women added 'Kaur'. Guru Gobind Singh also made five symbols obligatory: *kaccha* (a special undergarment), *kara* (a steel bangle), *kirpan* (a small sword), *kesh* (long unshorn hair, and consequently the wearing of a turban), and *kangha* (a comb). These practices are still compulsory for those Sikhs who are initiated into the Khalsa (the *Amritdharis*). Those who do not seek initiation are known as *Sehajdharis*.

There are no professional priests in Sikhism; anyone with a reasonable proficiency in the Punjabi language can conduct a service. Worship can be offered individually or communally, and in a private house or a *gurdwara* (temple). Sikhs are forbidden to eat meat prepared by ritual slaughter; they are also asked to abstain from smoking, alcohol and other intoxicants. Such abstention is compulsory for the *Amritdharis*.

There are about 20 million Sikhs world-wide and about 500,000 adherents and 250 gurdwaras in Great Britain. Every gurdwara manages its own affairs and there is no central body in the UK. The Sikh Missionary Society provides an information service.

SIKH MISSIONARY SOCIETY UK, 10 Featherstone Road, Southall, Middx UB2 5AA T 020-8574 1902
Hon. General Secretary, M. S. Chahal
WORLD SIKH FOUNDATION (THE SIKH COURIER INTERNATIONAL), 33 Wargrave Road, South Harrow, Middx HA2 8LL T 020-8864 9228
Managing Editor, Mrs H. B. Bharara

ZOROASTRIANISM

Zoroastrianism was founded by Zarathushtra (or Zoroaster in its hellenised form) in Persia. Linguistic analysis of the earliest extant Zoroastrian texts suggests that he lived around 1500 BC. Zarathushtra's words are recorded in five poems called the *Gathas*, which, together with other scriptures, forms the *Avesta*.

Zoroastrianism teaches that there is one God, *Ahura Mazda* (the Wise Lord), and that all creation stems ultimately from God; the Gathas teach that human beings have free will, are responsible for their own actions and can choose between good and evil: Choosing *Asha* (truth or righteousness), with the aid of *Vohu Manah* (good mind), leads to happiness for the individual and society, whereas choosing evil leads to unhappiness and conflict. The *Gathas* also encourage hard work, good deeds and charitable acts. Zoroastrians believe that after death, the immortal soul is judged by God, and is then sent to paradise or hell, where it will stay until the end of time. It will be resurrected for the final judgement.

In Zoroastrian places of worship, an urn containing fire is the central feature; the fire symbolises purity, light, and truth and is a visible symbol of the *Fravashi* or *Farohar*, the presence of *Ahura Mazda* in every human being.

Zoroastrians respect nature and much importance is attached to cultivating land and protecting the air, the earth and water. The practice of leaving corpses on mountain tops or towers developed to avoid pollution.

Zoroastrians were persecuted in Iran following the Arab invasion of Persia in the seventh century AD, which also brought Islam and a group migrated to India in the tenth century AD, who are known as Parsis, to avoid harassment and persecution; there are fewer than 150,000 Zoroastrians world-wide, of which 7,000 reside in Britain, mainly in London and the south east.

ZOROASTRIAN TRUST FUNDS OF EUROPE, 88 Compayne Gardens, London NW6 3RU T 020-7328 6018
E secretary@ztfe.com W www.ztfe.com
President, Dorab E. Mistry

CHURCHES

There are two established, i.e. state, churches in the United Kingdom: the Church of England and the Church of Scotland. There are no established churches in Wales or Northern Ireland, though the Church in Wales, the Scottish Episcopal Church and the Church of Ireland are members of the Anglican Communion.

THE CHURCH OF ENGLAND

The Church of England is the established (i.e. national) church in England and seeks to serve the nation through its dioceses and parishes. It traces its life back to the first coming of Christianity to England. Its position is defined by the ancient creeds of the Church and by the 39 Articles of Religion (1571), the Book of Common Prayer (1662) and the Ordinal. The Church of England is thus both catholic and reformed. It is the mother church of the Anglican Communion.

THE ANGLICAN COMMUNION
The Anglican Communion consists of 38 independent provincial or national Christian churches throughout the world, many of which are in Commonwealth countries and originated from missionary activity by the Church of England. Every ten years all the bishops in the Communion meet at the Lambeth Conference, convened by the Archbishop of Canterbury. The Conference has no policy-making authority but is an important forum for discussing and forming consensus around issues common concern. The Anglican Consultative Council was set up in 1968 to liaise between the member churches and provinces of the Anglican Communion. It meets every three years. Meetings of the Anglican primates have taken place every two years since 1979.

There are about 70 million Anglicans organised into 500 dioceses and 64,000 individual congregations world-wide.

STRUCTURE
The Church of England is divided into the two provinces of Canterbury and York, each under an archbishop. The two provinces are subdivided into 44 dioceses.

Legislative provision for the Church of England is made by the General Synod, established in 1970. It also discusses and expresses opinion on any other matter of religious or public interest. The General Synod has 580 members in total, divided between three houses: the House of Bishops, the House of Clergy and the House of Laity. It is presided over jointly by the Archbishops of Canterbury and York and normally meets twice a year. The Synod has the power, delegated by Parliament, to frame statute law (known as a Measure) on any matter concerning the Church of England. A Measure must be laid before both Houses of Parliament, who may accept or reject it but cannot amend it. Once accepted the Measure is submitted for royal assent and then has the full force of law. In addition to the General Synod, there are Synods at diocesan level.

The Archbishops' Council was established in January 1999. Its creation was the result of changes to the Church of England's national structure proposed in 1995 and subsequently approved by the Synod and Parliament. The Council's purpose, set out in the National Institutions Measure 1998, is 'to co-ordinate, promote and further the work and mission of the Church of England'. It reports to the General Synod. The Archbishops' Council comprises the Archbishops of Canterbury and York, ex officio, the Prolocutors elected by the Convocations of Canterbury and York, the Chairman and Vice-Chairman of the House of Laity, elected by that House, two bishops, two clergy and two lay persons elected by their respective Houses of the General Synod, and up to six persons appointed jointly by the two Archbishops with the approval of the General Synod.

There are also a number of national Boards, Councils and other bodies working on matters such as social responsibility, mission, Christian unity and education which report to the General Synod through the Archbishops' Council.

GENERAL SYNOD OF THE CHURCH OF ENGLAND, Church House, Great Smith Street, London SW1P 3NZ T 020-7898 1000
Joint Presidents, The Archbishops of Canterbury and York
HOUSE OF BISHOPS: *Chairman,* The Archbishop of Canterbury; *Vice-Chairman,* The Archbishop of York
HOUSE OF CLERGY: *Chairmen (alternating),* Canon Bob Baker; Canon Glyn Webster
HOUSE OF LAITY: *Chairman,* Dr Christina Baxter; *Vice-Chairman,* Brian McHenry
ARCHBISHOPS' COUNCIL, Church House, Great Smith Street, London SW1P 3NZ T 020-7898 1000
Joint Presidents, The Archbishops of Canterbury and York; *Secretary-General,* William Fittall

THE ORDINATION OF WOMEN
The canon making it possible for women to be ordained to the priesthood was promulgated in the General Synod in February 1994 and the first 32 women priests were ordained on 12 March 1994.

MEMBERSHIP
In 2001, 153,000 people were baptised, the Church of England had an electoral roll membership of 1.4 million, and each week about 1.2 million people attended services. As at December 2002 there were over 16,000 churches and places of worship. At December 2002 there were 370 dignitaries (including bishops, archdeacons and cathedral clergy); 8,712 parochial stipendiary clergy; 399 non parochial stipendiary clergy; 1,159 chaplains etc; 35 lay workers and Church Army evangelists; 8,384 licensed readers and 1,900 readers with permission to officiate and active emeriti; and approximately 4,600 active retired ordained clergy.

FULL-TIME DIOCESAN CLERGY AND CHURCH
ELECTORAL ROLL 2002

| | Clergy | | |
	Male	Female	Membership
Bath and Wells	202	31	38,000
Birmingham	160	26	18,200

Blackburn	217	17	34,300
Bradford	103	12	12,300
Bristol	121	25	16,600
Canterbury	143	18	21,000
Carlisle	133	20	20,600
Chelmsford	347	53	48,600
Chester	230	35	45,700
Chichester	321	10	51,800
Coventry	120	23	16,300
Derby	156	18	20,700
Durham	192	27	24,000
Ely	122	26	19,100
Europe	98	1	9,300
Exeter	243	24	30,500
Gloucester	128	19	23,600
Guildford	153	36	29,500
Hereford	83	22	18,100
Leicester	136	28	17,000
Lichfield	293	51	45,000
Lincoln	166	38	27,800
Liverpool	197	34	28,800
London	464	60	59,600
Manchester	244	42	34,500
Newcastle	128	22	16,700
Norwich	181	21	23,900
Oxford	338	72	54,600
Peterborough	132	22	18,000
Portsmouth	100	12	27,500
Ripon and Leeds	112	29	17,600
Rochester	190	29	29,900
St Albans	216	55	39,400
St Edmundsbury and Ipswich	139	23	24,100
Salisbury	193	33	40,500
Sheffield	157	28	18,600
Sodor and Man	19	0	2,400
Southwark	295	63	44,200
Southwell	137	29	18,300
Truro	114	12	16,900
Wakefield	141	28	20,300
Winchester	221	25	38,500
Worcester	125	28	20,300
York	210	35	33,400
Total	7,920	1,262	1,206,000

STIPENDS 2004–5

Archbishop of Canterbury	£62,520
Archbishop of York	£54,770
Bishop of London	£51,080
Other diocesan bishops	£33,930
Suffragan bishops	£27,850
Assistant bishops (full-time)	£26,740
Deans and provosts	£27,850
Archdeacons (recommended)	£27,660
Residentiary canons	£22,690
Incumbents and clergy of similar status	£18,480*

*National Stipends Benchmark

CANTERBURY

104th ARCHBISHOP AND PRIMATE OF ALL ENGLAND
Most Revd and Rt. Hon. Rowan Williams, *cons.* 1992, *apptd* 2002; Lambeth Palace, London SE1 7JU
Signs Rowan Cantuar

BISHOPS SUFFRAGAN
Dover, Rt. Revd Stephen Venner, *cons.* 1994, *apptd* 1999; Upway, St Martin's Hill, Canterbury, Kent CT1 1PR
Maidstone, Rt. Revd Graham Cray, *cons.* 2001, *apptd*

2001, Bishop's House, Pett Lane, Charing, Ashford, Kent TN27 0DL
Ebbsfleet, Rt. Revd Andrew Burnham, *cons.* 2001, *apptd* 2001 (provincial episcopal visitor); Bishop's House, Dry Sandford, Oxon OX13 6JP
Richborough, Rt. Revd Keith Newton, *cons.* 2002, *apptd* 2002 (provincial episcopal visitor); 6 Mellis Gardens, Woodford Green, Essex IG8 0BH

DEAN
Very Revd Robert Willis, *apptd* 2001

CANONS RESIDENTIARY
Edward Condry, *apptd* 2002; Richard Marsh, *apptd* 2001

Organist, D. Flood, FRCO, *apptd* 1988

ARCHDEACONS
Canterbury, Ven. Patrick Evans, *apptd* 2002
Maidstone, Ven. Philip Down, *apptd* 2002

Vicar-General of Province and Diocese, Chancellor Sheila Cameron, QC
Commissary-General, His Hon. Judge Richard Walker
Joint Registrars of the Province, F. E. Robson, OBE; B. J. T. Hanson, CBE
Diocesan Registrar and Legal Adviser, Richard Sturt
Diocesan Secretary, David Kemp, Diocesan House, Lady Wootton's Green, Canterbury CT1 1NQ T 01227-459401

YORK

96th ARCHBISHOP AND PRIMATE OF ENGLAND
Most Revd and Rt. Hon. David M. Hope, KCVO, DPHIL., LLD, *cons.* 1985, *trans.* 1995; Bishopthorpe, York YO23 2GE
Signs David Ebor

BISHOPS SUFFRAGAN
Hull, Rt. Revd Richard M. C. Frith, *cons.* 1998, *apptd* 1998; Hullen House, Woodfield Lane, Hessle, Hull HU13 0ES
Selby, Rt. Revd Martin Wallace, *cons.* 2003, *apptd* 2003; Bishop's House, Barton le Street, Malton, York YO17 6PL
Whitby, Rt. Revd Robert S. Ladds, *cons.* 1999, *apptd* 1999; 60 West Green, Stokesley, Middlesbrough TS9 5BD
Beverley, Rt. Revd Martyn Jarrett, *cons.* 1994, *apptd* 2000 (provincial episcopal visitor); 3 North Lane, Roundhay, Leeds LS8 2QJ

DEAN
Very Revd Keith Jones, *apptd* 2004

CANONS RESIDENTIARY
Edward Norman, PHD, *apptd* 1999; Glyn Webster, *apptd* 1999; Jonathan Draper, *apptd* 2000; Jeremy Fletcher, *apptd* 2002

CANONS LAY
Lindsay Mackinlay, *apptd* 2000; Carol Rymer, *apptd* 2000; Dr Allen Warren, *apptd* 2000; Brig. Peter Lyddon (as Chapter Steward), *apptd* 2000; Peter Collier, QC, *apptd* 2001

Organist, Philip Moore, FRCO, *apptd* 1983

ARCHDEACONS
Cleveland, Ven. Paul Ferguson, *apptd* 2001
East Riding, Ven. Peter Harrison, *apptd* 1998
York, Ven. Richard Seed, *apptd* 1999

Official Principal and Auditor of the Chancery Court, Sir
   John Owen, QC
Chancellor of the Diocese, His Hon. Judge Coningsby, QC,
   apptd 1977
*Vicar-General of the Province and Official Principal of the
   Consistory Court*, His Hon. Judge Coningsby, QC
Registrar and Legal Secretary, Lionel Lennox
Diocesan Secretary, Colin Sheppard, Diocesan House,
   Aviator Court, Clifton Moor, York YO30 4WJ
   T 01904-699500

LONDON *(Province of Canterbury)*
132nd BISHOP
Rt. Revd and Rt. Hon Richard J. C. Chartres, *cons.* 1992,
   apptd. 1995; The Old Deanery, Dean's Court, London
   EC4V 5AA
   Signs Richard Londin

AREA BISHOPS
Edmonton, Rt. Revd Peter W. Wheatley, *cons.* 1999, *apptd*
   1999; 27 Thurlow Road, London NW3 5PP
Kensington, Rt. Revd Michael J. Colclough, *cons.* 1996,
   apptd 1996; Dial House, Riverside, Twickenham, Middx
   TW1 3DT
Stepney, Rt. Revd Canon Stephen J. Oliver, *cons.* 2003,
   apptd 2003; 63 Coborn Road, London E3 2DB
Willesden, Rt. Revd Peter Broadbent, *cons.* 2001, *apptd*
   2001; 173 Willesden Lane, London NW6 7YN

BISHOP SUFFRAGAN
Fulham, Rt. Revd John C. Broadhurst, *cons.* 1996, *apptd*
   1996; 26 Canonbury Park South, London N1 2FN

DEAN OF ST PAUL'S
Very Revd John H. Moses, PHD, *apptd* 1996

CANONS RESIDENTIARY
Philip Buckler, *apptd* 1999; Peter Chapman, *apptd* 2001;
   Edmund Newall, *apptd* 2001; Martin Warner, *apptd*
   2003; Lucy Winckett, *apptd* 2003

Registrar and Receiver of St Paul's, Maj.-Gen. John Milne

Organist, John Scott, FRCO, *apptd* 1990

ARCHDEACONS
Charing Cross, Ven. Dr William Jacob, *apptd* 1996
Hackney, Ven. Lyle Dennen, *apptd* 1999
Hampstead, Ven. Michael Lawson, *apptd* 1999
London, Ven. Peter Delaney, *apptd* 1999
Middlesex, Ven. Malcolm Colmer, *apptd* 1996
Northolt, Ven. Christopher Chessun, *apptd* 2001

Chancellor, Nigel Seed, QC, *apptd* 2002
Registrar and Legal Secretary, Paul Morris
Diocesan Secretary, Keith Robinson, London Diocesan
   House, 36 Causton Street, London SW1P 4AU
   T 020-7932 1226

DURHAM *(Province of York)*
71st BISHOP
Rt. Revd Dr N. Thomas Wright, *cons.* 2003, *apptd* 2003;
   Auckland Castle, Bishop Auckland DL14 7NR
   Signs Thomas Dunelm

BISHOP SUFFRAGAN
Jarrow, Rt. Revd John Pritchard, *cons.* 2002, *apptd* 2002;
   Bishop's House, Ivy Lane, Low Fell, Gateshead NE9 6QD

DEAN
Very Revd Michael Sadgrove, *apptd* 2003

CANONS RESIDENTIARY
Prof David Brown, *apptd* 1990; Stephen Conway, *apptd*
   2002; David Kennedy, *apptd* 2001; Martin Kitchen,
   apptd 1997

Organist, James Lancelot, FRCO, *apptd* 1985

ARCHDEACONS
Auckland, Ven. Ian Jagger, *apptd* 2001
Durham, Ven. Stephen Conway, *apptd* 2002
Sunderland, Ven. Stuart Bain, *apptd* 2002

Chancellor, Revd Canon Rupert Bursell, QC, *apptd* 1989
Registrar and Legal Secretary, A. N. Fairclough
Diocesan Secretary, Jonathan Cryer, Auckland Castle, Bishop
   Auckland, Co. Durham DL14 7QJ T 01388-604515

WINCHESTER *(Canterbury)*
96th BISHOP
Rt. Revd Michael C. Scott-Joynt, *cons.* 1987, *trans.* 1995;
   Wolvesey, Winchester SO23 9ND
   Signs Michael Winton

BISHOPS SUFFRAGAN
Basingstoke, Rt. Revd Trevor Willmott, *cons.* 2002, *apptd*
   2002; Bishopswood End, Kingswood Rise, Four Marks,
   Alton, Hants GU34 5BD
Southampton, Rt. Revd Paul Butler, *cons.* 2004, *apptd*
   2004; Ham House, The Crescent, Romsey SO51 7NG

DEAN
Very Revd Michael Till, *apptd* 1996

Dean of Jersey (A Peculiar), Very Revd John Seaford, *apptd*
   1993
Dean of Guernsey (A Peculiar), Very Revd K. Paul Mellor,
   apptd 2003

CANONS RESIDENTIARY
Keith Anderson, *apptd* 2003; Ven. John Guille, *apptd*
   1998; Charles Stewart, *apptd* 1997; Flora Winfield,
   apptd 2002

Organist, Andrew Lumsden, *apptd* 2002

ARCHDEACONS
Bournemouth, Ven. Adrian Harbidge, *apptd* 1998
Winchester, Ven. John Guille, *apptd* 1998

Chancellor, Christopher Clark, *apptd* 1993
Registrar and Legal Secretary, Peter White
Diocesan Secretary, Ray Anderton, Church House,
   9 The Close, Winchester, Hants SO23 9LS
   T 01962-844644

BATH AND WELLS *(Canterbury)*
78th BISHOP
Rt. Revd Peter Price, *cons.* 1997, *apptd* 2002; The Palace,
   Wells BA5 2PD
   Signs Peter Bath & Wells

BISHOP SUFFRAGAN
Taunton, Rt. Revd Andrew John Radford, *cons.* 1998,
   apptd 1998; The Bishop's Lodge, Monkton Heights,
   West Monkton, Taunton, Somerset TA2 8LU

DEAN
Very Revd John Clarke *apptd* 2004

CANONS RESIDENTIARY
Russell Bowman-Eadie, *apptd* 2002; Melvyn Matthews, *apptd* 1997; Peter Maurice, *apptd* 2003; Patrick Woodhouse, *apptd* 2000

Organist, Malcolm Archer, *apptd* 1996

ARCHDEACONS
Bath, vacant
Taunton, Ven. John Reed, *apptd* 1999
Wells, Ven. Peter Maurice, *apptd* 2003
Chancellor, Timothy Briden, *apptd* 1993
Registrar and Legal Secretary, Tim Berry
Diocesan Secretary, Nicholas Denison, The Old Deanery, Wells, Somerset BA5 2UG T 01749-670777

BIRMINGHAM *(Canterbury)*
8th BISHOP
Rt. Revd Dr John Sentamu, *cons.* 1996, *apptd* 2002; Bishop's Croft, Harborne, Birmingham B17 0BG
Signs Sentamu Birmingham

BISHOP SUFFRAGAN
Aston, Rt. Revd John Austin, *cons.* 1992, *apptd* 1992; Strensham House, 8 Strensham Hill, Moseley, Birmingham B13 8AG

PROVOST
The Very Revd Gordon Mursell, *apptd* 2000

CANON RESIDENTIARY
Revd Gary O'Neill, *apptd* 1997

Organist, Marcus Huxley, FRCO, *apptd* 1986

ARCHDEACONS
Aston, vacant
Birmingham, Ven. Hayward Osborne, *apptd* 2001

Chancellor, vacant
Vice-Chancellor, David Pittaway
Registrar and Legal Secretary, Hugh Carslake
Diocesan Secretary, Jim Drennan, 175 Harborne Park Road, Harborne, Birmingham B17 0BH T 0121-426 0400

BLACKBURN *(York)*
8th BISHOP
Rt. Revd Nicholas Reade, *apptd* 2003, *cons.* March 2004; Bishop's House, Ribchester Road, Blackburn BB1 9EF
Signs Nicholas Blackburn

BISHOPS SUFFRAGAN
Burnley, Rt. Revd John Goddard, *cons.* 2000, *apptd* 2000; Dean House, 449 Padiham Road, Burnley BB12 6TE
Lancaster, Rt. Revd Stephen Pedley, *cons.* 1998, *apptd* 1998; Shireshead Vicarage, Whinneybrow, Forton, Preston PR3 0AE

DEAN
Very Revd Christopher Armstrong, *apptd* 2001

CANONS RESIDENTIARY
Peter Ballard, *apptd* 1998; Andrew Clitherow, *apptd* 2000; Andrew Hindley, *apptd* 1996

Organist, Richard Tanner, *apptd* 1998

ARCHDEACONS
Blackburn, Ven. John Hawley, *apptd* 2002
Lancaster, Ven. Colin Williams, *apptd* 1999

Chancellor, John Bullimore, *apptd* 1990
Registrar and Legal Secretary, Thomas Hoyle
Diocesan Secretary, Revd Canon Michael Wedgeworth, Diocesan Office, Cathedral Close, Blackburn BB1 5AA
T 01254-54421

BRADFORD *(York)*
9th BISHOP
Rt. Revd David James, *apptd* 2002; Bishopscroft, Ashwell Road, Heaton, Bradford BD9 4AU
Signs David Bradford

DEAN
Very Revd Dr Christopher David Hancock, *apptd* 2002

CANON RESIDENTIARY
vacant

Organist, Andrew Teague, FRCO, *apptd* 2003

ARCHDEACONS
Bradford, Ven. David Lee, *apptd* 2004
Craven, Ven. Malcolm Grundy, *apptd* 1994

Chancellor, John de G. Walford, *apptd* 1999
Registrar and Legal Secretary, Peter Foskett
Diocesan Secretary, Malcolm Halliday, Kadugli House, Elmsley Street, Steeton, Keighley BD20 6SE T 01535-650555

BRISTOL *(Canterbury)*
55th BISHOP
Rt. Revd Michael Hill, *cons.* 1998, *apptd* 2003; Wethered House, 11 The Avenue, Clifton, Bristol BS8 3HG
Signs Michael Bristol

BISHOP SUFFRAGAN
Swindon, vacant

DEAN
Very Revd Robert W. Grimley, *apptd* 1997

CANONS RESIDENTIARY
Brendan Clover, *apptd* 1999; Douglas Holt, *apptd* 1998; Peter Johnson, *apptd* 1990

Organist, Mark Lee, *apptd* 1998

ARCHDEACONS
Bristol, Ven. Tim McClure, *apptd* 1999
Malmesbury, Ven. Alan Hawker, *apptd* 1998

Chancellor, Sir David Calcutt, QC, *apptd* 1971
Registrar and Legal Secretary, Tim Berry
Diocesan Secretary, Lesley Farrall, Diocesan Church House, 23 Great George Street, Bristol, Avon BS1 5QZ
T 0117-906 0100

CARLISLE *(York)*
66th BISHOP
Rt. Revd Graham Dow, *cons.* 1985, *apptd* 2000; Rose Castle, Dalston, Carlisle CA5 7BZ
Signs Graham Carlisle

BISHOP SUFFRAGAN
Penrith, Rt. Revd James Newcome, *cons.* 2002, *apptd*
2002; Holm Croft, Castle Road, Kendal, Cumbria LA9 7AU

DEAN
Very Revd Mark Boyling, *apptd* 2004

CANONS RESIDENTIARY
David Jenkins, *apptd* 2004; David Weston, *apptd* 1994

Organist, Jeremy Suter, FRCO, *apptd* 1991

ARCHDEACONS
Carlisle, Ven. David Thomson, *apptd* 2002
West Cumberland, Ven. Colin Hill *apptd* 2004
Westmorland and Furness, Ven. George Howe, *apptd* 2000

Chancellor, Geoffrey Tattersall, QC, *apptd* 2003
Registrar and Legal Secretary, Susan Holmes
Diocesan Secretary, vacant, Church House, West Walls,
Carlisle CA3 8UE T 01228-522573

CHELMSFORD *(Canterbury)*
9th BISHOP
Rt. Revd John Warren Gladwin, *cons.* 1994, *apptd* 2003,
trans. 2004; Bishopscourt, Margaretting, Ingatestone
CM4 0HD *Signs* John Chelmsford

BISHOPS SUFFRAGAN
Barking, Rt. Revd David Hawkins, *apptd* 2002
Bradwell, Rt. Revd Laurence Green, *cons.* 1993, *apptd*
1993; The Vicarage, Orsett Road, Horndon-on-the-Hill,
Stanford-le-Hope, Essex SS17 8NS
Colchester, Rt. Revd Christopher Morgan, 1 Fitzwalter
Road, Colchester, Essex CO3 3SS

DEAN
Very Revd Peter S. M. Judd, *apptd* 1997

CANONS RESIDENTIARY
Walter King, *apptd* 2001; Andrew Knowles, *apptd* 1998;
Genny Tunbridge, *apptd* 2002

Master of Music, Peter Nardone, *apptd* 2000

ARCHDEACONS
Colchester, Ven. Annette Cooper, *apptd* 2004
Harlow, Ven. Peter Taylor, *apptd* 1996
Southend, Ven. David Lowman, *apptd* 2001
West Ham, Ven. Michael Fox, *apptd* 1996

Chancellor, George Pulman, *apptd* 2001
Registrar and Legal Secretary, Brian Hood
Diocesan Secretary, David Phillips, 53 New Street,
Chelmsford, Essex CM1 1AT T 01245-294400

CHESTER *(York)*
40th BISHOP
Rt. Revd Peter R. Forster, PHD, *cons.* 1996, *apptd* 1996;
Bishop's House, Chester CH1 2JD *Signs* Peter Cestr

BISHOPS SUFFRAGAN
Birkenhead, Rt. Revd David A. Urquhart, *cons.* 2000, *apptd*
2000; Bishop's Lodge, 67 Bidston Road, Oxton, Birkenhead
CH43 6TR
Stockport, Rt. Revd Nigel Stock, *cons.* 2000, *apptd* 2000;
Bishop's Lodge, Back Lane, Dunham Town, Altrincham,
Cheshire WA14 4SG

DEAN
Very Revd Dr Gordon McPhate

CANONS RESIDENTIARY
Christopher Burkett, *apptd* 2000; Trevor Dennis, *apptd*
1994; Judy Hunt, *apptd* 2002; John Roff, *apptd* 2000

Organist and Director of Music, David Poulter, FRCO,
apptd 1997

ARCHDEACONS
Chester, Ven. Donald Allister, *apptd* 2002
Macclesfield, Ven. Richard Gillings, *apptd* 1994

Chancellor, David Turner, QC, *apptd* 1998
Registrar and Legal Secretary, Alan McAllester
Diocesan Secretary, Stephen P. A. Marriott, Church House,
Lower Lane, Aldford, Chester CH3 6HP T 01244-620444

CHICHESTER *(Canterbury)*
102nd BISHOP
Rt. Revd John Hind, *cons.* 1991, *apptd* 2001; The Palace,
Chichester PO19 1PY *Signs* John Cicestr

BISHOPS SUFFRAGAN
Horsham, Rt. Revd Lindsay G. Urwin, *cons.* 1993, *apptd*
1993; Bishop's House, 21 Guildford Road, Horsham,
W. Sussex RH12 1LU
Lewes, Rt. Revd Wallace P. Benn, *cons.* 1997, *apptd* 1997;
Bishop's Lodge, 16A Prideaux Road, Eastbourne, E. Sussex
BN21 2NB

DEAN
Revd Nicholas Frayling, *apptd* 2002

CANONS RESIDENTIARY
Peter Atkinson, *apptd* 1997; John Ford, *apptd* 2000; Peter
Kefford, *apptd* 2001

Organist, Alan Thurlow, FRCO, *apptd* 1980

ARCHDEACONS
Chichester, Ven. Douglas McKittrick, *apptd* 2002
Horsham, Ven. Roger Combes, *apptd* 2003
Lewes and Hastings, vacant

Chancellor, Mark Hill
Registrar and Legal Secretary, Tim Gleeson
Diocesan Secretary, Jonathan Prichard, Diocesan Church
House, 211 New Church Road, Hove, E. Sussex BN3 4ED
T 01273-421021

COVENTRY *(Canterbury)*
8th BISHOP
Rt. Revd Colin J. Bennetts, *cons.* 1994, *apptd* 1997; The
Bishop's House, 23 Davenport Road, Coventry CV5 6PW
Signs Colin Coventry

BISHOP SUFFRAGAN
Warwick, vacant

DEAN
Very Revd John Irvine, *apptd* 2001

CANONS RESIDENTIARY
Stuart Beake, *apptd* 2000; Adrian Daffern, *apptd* 2003;
Justin Welby, *apptd* 2002; Andrew White, *apptd* 1998

Director of Music, Rupert Jeffcoat, *apptd* 1997

ARCHDEACONS
Coventry, Ven. Mark Bryant, *apptd* 2001
Warwick, Ven. Michael Paget-Wilkes, *apptd* 1990

Chancellor, Sir William Gage, *apptd* 1980
Registrar and Legal Secretary, David Dumbleton
Diocesan Secretary, Isobel Chapman, Church House,
 Palmerston Road, Coventry CV5 6FJ T 024-7671 0500

DERBY *(Canterbury)*
6th BISHOP
Rt. Revd Jonathan S. Bailey, *cons.*1992, *apptd* 1995; Derby
 Church House, Full Street, Derby DE1 3DR
 Signs Jonathan Derby

BISHOP SUFFRAGAN
Repton, Rt. Revd David C. Hawtin, *cons.* 1999, *apptd*
 1999; Repton House, Lea, Matlock, Derbys DE4 5JP

DEAN
vacant

CANONS RESIDENTIARY
Andrew Brown, *apptd* 2003; Barrie Gauge, *apptd* 1999;
 Nicholas Henshall, *apptd* 2002; Elaine Jones, *apptd*
 2004

Organist, Peter Gould, *apptd* 1982

ARCHDEACONS
Chesterfield, Ven. David Garnett, *apptd* 1996
Derby, Ven. Ian Gatford, *apptd* 1992

Chancellor, His Hon. Judge John Bullimore, *apptd* 1981
Registrar and Legal Secretary, Mrs Nadine Waldron
Diocesan Secretary, Bob Carey, Derby Church House, Full
 Street, Derby DE1 3DR T 01332-388650

ELY *(Canterbury)*
68th BISHOP
Rt. Revd Dr Anthony Russell, *cons.* 1988, *apptd* 2000;
 The Bishop's House, Ely, Cambs CB7 4DW
 Signs Anthony Ely

BISHOP SUFFRAGAN
Huntingdon, Rt. Revd Dr John Inge, *cons.* 2003, *apptd*
 2003; 14 Lynn Road, Ely, Cambs CB6 1DA

DEAN
Very Revd Dr Michael Chandler, *apptd* 2003

CANONS RESIDENTIARY
Dr Alan Hargrave, *apptd* 2004; Dr Peter Sills, *apptd* 2000

CANON PRECENTOR
Revd David Pritchard, *apptd* 2004

Organist, Paul Trepte, FRCO, *apptd* 1991

ARCHDEACONS
Ely, vacant
Huntingdon Wisbech, Ven. John Beer, *apptd* 1997

Chancellor, William Gage, QC
Registrar, Peter Beesley
Diocesan Secretary, Dr Matthew Lavis, Bishop Woodford
 House, Barton Road, Ely, Cambs CB7 4DX T 01353-652701

EXETER *(Canterbury)*
70th BISHOP
Rt. Revd Michael L. Langrish, *cons.* 1993, *apptd* 2000;
 The Palace, Exeter, EX1 1HY
 Signs Michael Exon

BISHOPS SUFFRAGAN
Crediton, Rt. Revd Robert Evens, *cons.* 2004, *apptd* 2004;
 10 The Close, Exeter EX1 1EZ
Plymouth, Rt. Revd John Garton, *cons.* 1996, *apptd* 1996;
 31 Riverside Walk, Tamerton Foliot, Plymouth PL5 4AQ

DEAN
vacant

CANONS RESIDENTIARY
Neil Collings, *apptd* 1999; David Ison, *apptd* 1997; Carl
 Turner, *apptd* 2001

Director of Music, Andrew Millington, *apptd* 1999

ARCHDEACONS
Barnstaple, Ven. David Gunn-Johnson, *apptd* 2003
Exeter, Ven. Dr Paul Gardner, *apptd* 2003
Plymouth, Ven. Tony Wilds, *apptd* 2001
Totnes, Ven. Richard Gilpin, *apptd* 1996

Chancellor, Sir David Calcutt
Registrar and Legal Secretary, R. Wheeler
Diocesan Secretary, Mark Beedell, Diocesan House, Palace
 Gate, Exeter, Devon EX1 1HX T 01392-272686

GIBRALTAR IN EUROPE *(Canterbury)*
BISHOP
Rt. Revd Dr Geoffrey Rowell, *cons.* 1994, *apptd* 2001;
 Bishop's Lodge, Church Road, Worth, Crawley, West Sussex,
 RH10 7RT

BISHOP SUFFRAGAN
In Europe, Rt. Revd David Hamid, *cons.* 2002, *apptd* 2002;
 14 Tufton Street, London SW1P 3QZ
Dean, Cathedral Church of the Holy Trinity, Gibraltar, Very
 Revd Alan Woods

Chancellor, Pro-Cathedral of St Paul, Valletta, Malta,
 Canon Thomas Mendel
Chancellor, Pro-Cathedral of the Holy Trinity, Brussels,
 Belgium, Canon Nigel Walker

ARCHDEACONS
Eastern, Ven. Patrick Curran
North-West Europe, Ven. Geoffrey Allen
France, Ven. Anthony Wells
Gibraltar, Ven. Howell Sasser
Italy, Rt. Revd David Hamid *(Acting)*
Scandinavia and Germany, Ven. David Ratcliff
Switzerland, Ven. John Williams

Chancellor, Sir David Calcutt, QC
Registrar and Legal Secretary, John Underwood
Diocesan Secretary, Adrian Mumford, 14 Tufton Street,
 London SW1P 3QZ T 020-7898 1155

GLOUCESTER *(Canterbury)*
40th BISHOP
Rt. Revd Michael Perham, *cons.* 2004, *apptd* 2004;
 Bishopscourt, Pitt Street, Gloucester GL1 2BQ
 Signs Michael Gloucestr

BISHOP SUFFRAGAN
Tewkesbury, Rt. Revd John S. Went, *cons.* 1995, *apptd*
1995; Bishop's House, Staverton, Cheltenham GL51 0TW

DEAN
Very Revd Nicholas Bury, *apptd* 1997

CANONS RESIDENTIARY
Guy Bridgewater, *apptd* 2002; Neil Heavisides, *apptd*
1993; David Hoyle, *apptd* 2002; Celia Thomson, *apptd*
2003

Director of Music, Andrew Nethsingha, *apptd* 2002

ARCHDEACONS
Cheltenham, Ven. Hedley Ringrose, *apptd* 1998
Gloucester, Ven. Geoffrey Sidaway, *apptd* 2000

Chancellor and Vicar-General, June Rodgers, *apptd* 1990
Registrar and Legal Secretary, Chris Peak
Diocesan Secretary, Michael Williams, Church House,
College Green, Gloucester GL1 2LY T01452-410022

GUILDFORD *(Canterbury)*
9th BISHOP
vacant; Willow Grange, Woking Road, Guildford GU4 7QS

BISHOP SUFFRAGAN
Dorking, Rt. Revd Ian Brackley, *cons.* 1996, *apptd* 1995;
Dayspring, 13 Pilgrims Way, Guildford GU4 8AD

DEAN
Very Revd Victor Stock, *apptd* 2002

CANONS RESIDENTIARY
Jonathan Frost, *apptd* 2002; Julian Hubbard, *apptd* 1999;
Dr Maureen Palmer, *apptd* 1996; Dr Nicholas
Thistlethwaite, *apptd* 1999

Organist, Stephen Farr, FRCO, *apptd* 1999

ARCHDEACONS
Dorking, Ven. Mark Wilson, *apptd* 1996
Surrey, Ven. Robert Reiss, *apptd* 1996

Chancellor, The Worshipful Andrew Jordan
Registrar and Legal Secretary, Peter Beesley
Diocesan Secretary, Stephen Marriott

HEREFORD *(Canterbury)*
105th BISHOP
Rt. Revd Anthony Priddis, *cons.* 2004, *apptd* 2004; The
Palace, Hereford HR4 9BN

BISHOP SUFFRAGAN
Ludlow, Ven. Michael Wrenford Hooper, *cons.* 2002,
apptd 2002; Bishop's House, Halford, Craven Arms,
Shropshire SY7 9BT

DEAN
Very Revd Michael Tavinor, *apptd* 2002

CANONS RESIDENTIARY
Val Hamer, *apptd* 2002; Andrew Piper, *apptd* 2002; John
Tiller, *apptd* 1984

Organist, Geraint Bowen, FRCO, *apptd* 2001

ARCHDEACONS
Hereford, Ven. John Tiller, *apptd* 2002
Ludlow, Michael Wrenford Hooper, *apptd* 2002

Chancellor, Val Hamer
Joint Registrars and Legal Secretaries, Tom Jordan; Peter
Beesley
Diocesan Secretary, John Clark, The Palace, Hereford HR4 9BL
T 01432-373300

LEICESTER *(Canterbury)*
6th BISHOP
Rt. Revd Timothy J. Stevens, *cons.* 1995, *apptd* 1999;
Bishop's Lodge, 10 Springfield Road, Leicester LE2 3BD
Signs Timothy Leicester

DEAN
Very Revd Vivienne F. Faull, *apptd* 2000

CANONS RESIDENTIARY
Stephen Foster, *apptd* 2004; Michael Wilson, *apptd* 1988

Master of Music, Jonathan Gregory, *apptd* 1994

ARCHDEACONS
Leicester, Ven. Richard Atkinson, *apptd* 2002
Loughborough, Ven. Ian Stanes, *apptd* 1992

Chancellor, James Behrens
Registrar and Legal Secretary, Trevor Kirkman
Diocesan Secretary, Jane Easton, Church House,
3–5 St Martin's East, Leicester LE1 5FX
T 0116-248 7400

LICHFIELD *(Canterbury)*
98th BISHOP
Rt. Revd Jonathan Gledhill, *cons.* 1996, *apptd* 2003;
Bishop's House, The Close, Lichfield WS13 7LG

BISHOPS SUFFRAGAN
Shrewsbury, Rt. Revd Alan Smith, *cons.* 2001, *apptd* 2002;
68 London Road, Shrewsbury SY2 6PG
Stafford, Rt. Revd Christopher J. Hill, *cons.* 1996, *apptd*
1996; Ash Garth, Broughton Crescent, Barlaston, Staffs
ST12 9DD
Wolverhampton, Rt. Revd Michael G. Bourke, *cons.* 1993,
apptd 1993; 61 Richmond Road, Wolverhampton WV3 9JH

DEAN
Very Revd Michael Yorke, *apptd* 1999

CANONS RESIDENTIARY
A. Barnard, *apptd* 1977; Ven. Christopher Liley, *apptd*
2001; C. Taylor, *apptd* 1995

Organist, Philip Scriven, *apptd* 2002

ARCHDEACONS
Lichfield, Ven. Christopher Liley, *apptd* 2001
Salop, Ven. John Hall, *apptd* 1998
Stoke-on-Trent, Ven. Godfrey Owen Stone, *apptd* 2002
Walsall, Revd Robert Jackson, *apptd* 2004

Chancellor, His Hon. Judge John Shand
Joint Registrars and Legal Secretaries, J. P. Thorneycroft;
N. Blackie
Diocesan Secretary, D. R. Taylor, St Mary's House, The Close,
Lichfield, Staffs WS13 7LD T 01543-306030

LINCOLN (Canterbury)
71st BISHOP
Rt. Revd Dr John Saxbee, cons. 1994, apptd 2002;
   Bishop's House, Eastgate, Lincoln LN2 1QQ
   Signs John Lincoln

BISHOPS SUFFRAGAN
Grantham, Rt. Revd Alastair L. J. Redfern, cons. 1997,
   apptd 1997; Fairacre, 234 Barrowby Road, Grantham, Lincs
   NG31 8NP
Grimsby, Rt. Revd David D. J. Rossdale, cons. 2000, apptd
   2000; Bishop's House, Church Lane, Irby-upon-Humber,
   Grimsby DN37 7JR

DEAN
Very Revd Alexander Knight, apptd 1998

CANONS RESIDENTIARY
Gavin Kirk, apptd 2003; Alan Nugent, apptd 2003;
   Michael West, apptd 2003

Director of Music, A. Prentice, apptd 2003

ARCHDEACONS
Lincoln, Ven. Arthur Hawes, apptd 1995
Lindsey and Stow, Ven. Dr Timothy Ellis, apptd 2001
Chancellor, Peter N. Collier, QC, apptd 1999
Registrar and Legal Secretary, Derek Wellman
Diocesan Secretary, Max Manin, The Old Palace, Lincoln
   LN2 1PU T 01522-529241

LIVERPOOL (York)
7th BISHOP
Rt. Revd James Jones, cons. 1994, apptd 1998; Bishop's
   Lodge, Woolton Park, Liverpool L25 6DT
   Signs James Liverpool

BISHOP SUFFRAGAN
Warrington, Rt. Revd David Jennings, cons. 2000, apptd
   2000; 34 Central Avenue, Eccleston Park, Prescot,
   Merseyside L34 2QP

DEAN
Rt. Revd Dean Dr Rupert W. N. Hoare, apptd 2000

CANON RESIDENTIARY
Anthony Hawley, apptd 2002

Organist, Prof. Ian Tracey, apptd 1980

ARCHDEACONS
Liverpool, Ven Richard Panter, apptd 2002
Warrington, Ven. Peter Bradley, apptd 2001

Chancellor, Hon. Sir Mark Hedley
Registrar and Legal Secretary, Roger Arden
Diocesan Secretary, Mike Eastwood, Church House,
   1 Hanover Street, Liverpool L1 3DW T 0151-709 9722

MANCHESTER (York)
11th BISHOP
Rt. Revd Nigel McCulloch, cons. 1986, apptd 2002, trans.
   2002; Bishopscourt, Bury New Road, Manchester M7 4LE
   Signs Nigel Manchester

BISHOPS SUFFRAGAN
Bolton, Rt. Revd David K. Gillett, cons. 1999, apptd 1999;
   4 Bishop's Lodge, Bolton Road, Hawkshaw, Bury BL8 4JN

Hulme, Rt. Revd Stephen R. Lowe, cons. 1999, apptd.
   1999; 14 Moorgate Avenue, Withington, Manchester
   M20 1HE
Middleton, Rt. Revd Michael A. O. Lewis, cons. 1999,
   apptd 1999; The Hollies, Manchester Road, Rochdale
   OL11 3QY

DEAN
Very Revd Kenneth Riley, apptd 1993

CANONS RESIDENTIARY
Paul Denby, apptd 1995; Robin Gamble, apptd 2002;
   Andrew Shanks, apptd 2004

Organist, Christopher Stokes, apptd 1992

ARCHDEACONS
Bolton, John Applegate, apptd 2002
Manchester, vacant
Rochdale, Ven. Andrew Ballard, apptd 2000

Chancellor, G. F. Tattersall
Registrar and Legal Secretary, Michael Darlington
Diocesan Secretary, Nigel Spraggins, 1st Floor, Diocesan
   Church House, 90 Deansgate, Manchester M3 2GH
   T 0161-833 9521

NEWCASTLE (York)
11th BISHOP
Rt. Revd J. Martin Wharton, cons. 1992, apptd 1997;
   Bishop's House, 29 Moor Road South, Gosforth, Newcastle
   upon Tyne NE3 1PA Signs Martin Newcastle

STIPENDIARY ASSISTANT BISHOP
Rt. Revd Paul Richardson, cons. 1987, apptd 1999

HON. ASSISTANT BISHOP
Rt. Revd K. E. Gill, cons. 1972, apptd 1998

DEAN
Very Revd Christopher C. Dalliston, apptd 2003

CANONS RESIDENTIARY
David Elkington, apptd 2002; Ven. Peter Elliott, apptd
   1993; Geoffrey Miller, apptd 1999; Peter Strange,
   apptd 1986

Director of Music, Scott Farrell, apptd 2002

ARCHDEACONS
Lindisfarne, Ven. Robert Langley, apptd 2001
Northumberland, Ven. Peter Elliott, apptd 1993

Chancellor, Prof. David McClean, apptd 1998
Registrar and Legal Secretary, Jane Lowdon
Diocesan Secretary, Philip Davies, Church House, St John's
   Terrace, North Shields, NE29 6HS T 0191-270 4100

NORWICH (Canterbury)
71st BISHOP
Rt. Revd Graham R. James, cons. 1993, apptd 2000;
   Bishop's House, Norwich NR3 1SB Signs Graham Norvic

BISHOPS SUFFRAGAN
Lynn, Rt. Revd James Langstaff, cons. 2004, apptd 2004;
   The Old Vicarage, Castle Acre, King's Lynn PE32 2AA
Thetford, Rt. Revd David J. Atkinson, cons. 2001, apptd
   2001; Rectory Meadow, Bramerton, Norwich NR14 7DW

DEAN
Very Revd Graham Smith, apptd 2004

CANONS RESIDENTIARY
Michael Kitchener, *apptd* 1999; Richard Hanmer, *apptd* 1994; Jeremy Haselock, *apptd* 1998; Ven. Clifford Offer, *apptd* 1994

Organist, David Dunnett, *apptd* 1996

ARCHDEACONS
Lynn, Ven. Martin Gray, *apptd* 1999
Norfolk, Ven. David Hayden, *apptd* 2002
Norwich, Ven. Clifford Offer, *apptd* 1994

Chancellor, The Hon. Mr Justice Blofeld, *apptd* 1998
Registrar and Legal Secretary, John Herring
Diocesan Secretary, Revd Richard Bowett, Diocesan House, 109 Dereham Road, Easton, Norwich, Norfolk NR9 5ES T 01603-880853

OXFORD *(Canterbury)*
41st BISHOP
Rt. Revd Richard D. Harries, *cons.* 1987, *apptd* 1987; Diocesan Church House, North Hinksey Lane, Oxford OX2 0NB *Signs* Richard Oxon

AREA BISHOPS
Buckingham, Rt. Revd Alan Wilson *cons.* 2003, *apptd* 2003; Sheridan, Grimms Hill, Great Missenden, Bucks HP16 9BD
Dorchester, Rt. Revd Colin Fletcher, *cons.* 2000, *apptd* 2000; Arran House, Sandy Lane, Yarnton, Oxon OX5 1PB
Reading, Rt. Revd Stephen Cottrell, *cons.* 2004, *apptd* 2004; Bishop's House, Tidmarsh Lane, Tidmarsh, Reading RG8 8HA

DEAN OF CHRIST CHURCH
Very Revd Christopher Lewis, *apptd* 2003

CANONS RESIDENTIARY
Marilyn McCord Adams, *apptd* 2004; Nicholas Coulton, *apptd* 2002; Ven. John Morrison, *apptd* 1998; Oliver O'Donovan, *apptd* 1982; Marilyn Parry, *apptd* 2001; George Pattison, *apptd* 2004

Organist, Stephen Darlington, FRCO, *apptd* 1985

ARCHDEACONS
Berkshire, Ven. Norman Russell, *apptd* 1998
Buckingham, Ven. Sheila Watson, *apptd* 2002
Oxford, Ven. John Morrison, *apptd* 1998

Chancellor, Revd Dr Rupert Bursell, *apptd* 2001
Registrars and Legal Secretaries, Dr F. E. Robson and Revd. Canon John Rees
Diocesan Secretary, Rosemary Pearce, Diocesan Church House, North Hinksey, Oxford OX2 0NB T 01865-208202

PETERBOROUGH *(Canterbury)*
37th BISHOP
Rt. Revd Ian P. M. Cundy, *cons.* 1992, *apptd* 1996; Bishop's Lodging, The Palace, Peterborough PE1 1YA *Signs* Ian Petriburg

BISHOP SUFFRAGAN
Brixworth, Rt. Revd Frank White, *cons.* 2002, *apptd* 2002; 4 The Avenue, Dallington, Northampton NN1 4RZ

DEAN
Very Revd Michael Bunker, *apptd* 1992

CANONS RESIDENTIARY
Jonathan Baker, *apptd* 2004; David Painter, *apptd* 2000; Bruce Ruddock, *apptd* 2004
Organist, Andrew Reid, *apptd* 2004

ARCHDEACONS
Northampton, vacant
Oakham, Ven. David Painter, *apptd* 2000

Chancellor, Thomas Coningsby, QC, *apptd* 1989
Registrar and Legal Secretary, Canon Raymond Hemingray
Diocesan Secretary, Richard Pestell, Diocesan Office, The Palace, Peterborough, Cambs PE1 1YB T 01733-887000

PORTSMOUTH *(Canterbury)*
8th BISHOP
Rt. Revd Dr Kenneth Stevenson, *cons.* 1995, *apptd* 1995; Bishopsgrove, 26 Osborn Road, Fareham, Hants PO16 7DQ *Signs* Kenneth Portsmouth

DEAN
Very Revd David Brindley, *apptd* 2002

CANONS RESIDENTIARY
Nicholas Ash, *apptd* 2003; David Isaac, *apptd* 1990; Michael Tristram *apptd* 2003

Organist, David Price, *apptd* 1996

ARCHDEACONS
Isle of Wight, Ven. Trevor Reader, *apptd* 2003
Portsdown, Ven. Christopher Lowson, *apptd* 1999
The Meon, Ven. Peter Hancock, *apptd* 1999

Chancellor, C. Clark, QC
Registrar and Legal Secretary, Hilary Tyler
Diocesan Secretary, Michael Jordan, Cathedral House, St Thomas's Street, Portsmouth, Hants PO1 2HA T 023-9282 5731

RIPON AND LEEDS *(York)*
12th BISHOP
Rt. Revd John R. Packer, *cons.* 1996, *apptd* 2000; Bishop Mount, Ripon HG4 5DP *Signs* John Ripon and Leeds

BISHOP SUFFRAGAN
Knaresborough, Rt. Revd James Bell, *cons.* 2004, *apptd* 2004; Thistledown, Main Street, Exelby, Bedale DL8 2HD

DEAN
Very Revd John Methuen, *apptd* 1995

CANONS RESIDENTIARY
Michael Glanville-Smith, *apptd* 1990; Keith Punshon, *apptd* 1996

Organist, Simon Morley *apptd* 2003

ARCHDEACONS
Leeds, Ven. John Oliver, *apptd* 1992
Richmond, Ven. Kenneth Good, *apptd* 1993

Chancellor, His Hon. Judge Grenfell, *apptd* 1992
Registrars and Legal Secretaries, Christopher Tunnard, Nichola Harding
Diocesan Secretary, Philip Arundel, Diocesan Office, St Mary's Street, Leeds LS9 7DP T 0113-200 0540

ROCHESTER *(Canterbury)*
106th BISHOP
Rt. Revd Dr Michael Nazir-Ali, *cons.* 1984, *apptd* 1994;
Bishopscourt, Rochester ME1 1TS *Signs* Michael Roffen

BISHOP SUFFRAGAN
Tonbridge, Rt. Revd Dr Brian C. Castle, *cons.* 2002, *apptd* 2002; Bishop's Lodge, 48 St Botolph's Road, Sevenoaks TN13 3AG

DEAN
Adrian Newman, *apptd* 2004

CANONS RESIDENTIARY
Canon Ralph Godsall, *apptd* 2001; Jonathan Meyrick, *apptd* 1998

Director of Music, Roger Sayer, FRCO, *apptd* 1995

ARCHDEACONS
Bromley, Ven. Paul Wright, *apptd* 2003
Rochester, Ven. Peter Lock, *apptd* 2000
Tonbridge, Ven. Clive Mansell, *apptd* 2002

Chancellor, His Hon. Judge Michael Goodman, *apptd* 1971
Registrar and Legal Secretary, Michael Thatcher
Diocesan Secretary, Mrs Louise Gilbert, St Nicholas Church, Boley Hill, Rochester ME1 1SL T 01634-830333

ST ALBANS *(Canterbury)*
9th BISHOP
Rt. Revd Christopher W. Herbert, *cons.* 1995, *apptd* 1995; Abbey Gate House, St Albans AL3 4HD
Signs Christopher St Albans

BISHOPS SUFFRAGAN
Bedford, Rt. Revd Richard N. Inwood, *apptd* 2002
Hertford, Rt. Revd Christopher R. J. Foster, *cons.* 2001, *apptd* 2001; Hertford House, Abbey Mill Lane, St Albans AL3 4HE

DEAN
Very Revd Jeffrey John, *apptd* 2004

CANONS RESIDENTIARY
Stephen Lake, *apptd* 2001; Iain Lane, *apptd* 2000; Michael Sansom, *apptd* 1988; Dennis Stamps, *apptd* 2002; Richard Wheeler, *apptd* 2001

Organist, Andrew Lucas, *apptd* 1998

ARCHDEACONS
Bedford, Ven. Paul Hughes, *apptd* 2004
Hertford, Ven. Trevor Jones, *apptd* 1997
St Albans, Ven. Helen Cunliffe, *apptd* 2003

Chancellor, Roger Kaye, *apptd* 2002
Registrar and Legal Secretary, David Cheetham
Diocesan Secretary, Susan Pope, Holywell Lodge, 41 Holywell Hill, St Albans AL1 1HE T 01727-854532

ST EDMUNDSBURY AND IPSWICH *(Canterbury)*
9th BISHOP
Rt. Revd J. H. Richard Lewis, *cons.* 1992, *apptd* 1997;
Bishop's House, 4 Park Road, Ipswich IP1 3ST
Signs Richard St Edmundsbury and Ipswich

BISHOP SUFFRAGAN
Dunwich, Rt. Revd Clive Young, *cons.* 1999, *apptd* 1999; 28 Westerfield Road, Ipswich IP4 2UJ

DEAN
Very Revd James Atwell, *apptd* 1995

CANONS RESIDENTIARY
Peter Barham, *apptd* 2003; Andrew Todd, *apptd* 2001

Organist, James Thomas, *apptd* 1997

ARCHDEACONS
Ipswich, Ven. Terry Gibson, *apptd* 1987
Sudbury, Ven. John Cox, *apptd* 1995
Suffolk, Ven. Geoffrey Arrand, *apptd* 1994

Chancellor, The Hon. Mr Justice Blofeld, *apptd* 1974
Registrar and Legal Secretary, James Hall
Diocesan Secretary, Nicholas Edgell, Churchgates House, Cutler Street, Ipswich IP1 1QU T 01473-298500

SALISBURY *(Canterbury)*
77TH BISHOP
Rt. Revd David S. Stancliffe, *cons.* 1993, *apptd* 1993;
South Canonry, The Close, Salisbury SP1 2ER
Signs David Sarum

BISHOPS SUFFRAGAN
Ramsbury, Rt. Revd Peter F. Hullah, *cons.* 1999, *apptd* 1999
Sherborne, Rt. Revd Timothy M. Thornton, *cons.* 2001, *apptd* 2001

DEAN
Very Revd. June Osborne, *apptd* 2004

CANONS RESIDENTIARY
Mark Bonney, *apptd* 2004; Jeremy Davies, *apptd* 1985; Edward Probert, *apptd* 2004

Organist, Simon Lole, *apptd* 1997

ARCHDEACONS
Dorset, Ven. Alistair Magowan, *apptd* 2000
Sherborne, Ven. Paul Taylor, *apptd* 2004
Wilts, Ven. John Wraw, *apptd* 2004
Sarum, Ven. Alan Jeans, *apptd* 2003

Chancellor, His Hon. Judge Samuel Wiggs, *apptd* 1997
Registrar and Legal Secretary, Andrew Johnson
Diocesan Secretary, Lucinda Herklots, Church House, Crane Street, Salisbury SP1 2QB T 01722-411922

SHEFFIELD *(York)*
6th BISHOP
Rt. Revd John (Jack) Nicholls, *cons.* 1990, *apptd* 1997;
Bishopscroft, Snaithing Lane, Sheffield S10 3LG
Signs Jack Sheffield

BISHOP SUFFRAGAN
Doncaster, Rt. Revd Cyril Guy Ashton, *cons.* 2000, *apptd* 2000; Bishop's House, 3 Farrington Court, Wickersley, Rotherham S66 1JQ

DEAN
Very Revd Peter Bradley, *apptd* 2003

CANONS RESIDENTIARY
Ven. Richard Blackburn, *apptd* 1999; Revd Canon Nick Howe, *apptd* 2003; Revd Canon Paul Shackerley, *apptd* 2002; Revd Canon Howard Such, *apptd* 2003

Master of Music, Neil Taylor, *apptd* 1997

ARCHDEACONS
Doncaster, Ven. Robert Fitzharris, *apptd* 2001
Sheffield, Ven. Richard Blackburn, *apptd* 1999

Chancellor, Prof. David McClean, *apptd* 1992
Registrar and Legal Secretary, Mrs Miranda Myers
Diocesan Secretary, Tony Beck, FCIS, Diocesan Church House, 95–99 Effingham Street, Rotherham S65 1BL
T 01709-309100

SODOR AND MAN *(York)*
80th BISHOP
Rt. Revd Graeme Knowles, *cons.* 2003, *apptd* 2003; Bishop's House, The Falls, Tromode Road, Cronkbourne, Douglas, Isle of Man IM4 4PZ
Signs Graeme Sodor and Man

CANONS
Malcolm Convery, *apptd* 1999; Duncan Whitworth, *apptd* 1996

ARCHDEACON
Isle of Man, vacant

Vicar-General and Chancellor, Clare Faulds
Registrar and Legal Secretary, Christopher Callow
Diocesan Secretary, Christine Roberts, Holly Cottage, Ballaughton Meadows, Douglas, Isle of Man IM2 1JG
T 01624-626994

SOUTHWARK *(Canterbury)*
9TH BISHOP
Rt. Revd Dr Tom F. Butler, *cons.* 1985, *apptd* 1998; Bishop's House, 38 Tooting Bec Gardens, London SW16 1QZ
Signs Thomas Southwark

AREA BISHOPS
Croydon, Rt. Revd Nicholas Baines, *cons.* 2003, *apptd* 2003
Kingston upon Thames, Rt. Revd Richard Cheetham, *cons.* 2002, *apptd* 2002
Woolwich vacant

DEAN
Very Revd Colin B. Slee, OBE, *apptd* 1994

CANONS RESIDENTIARY
Andrew Nunn, *apptd* 1999; Stephen Roberts, *apptd* 2000; Bruce Saunders, *apptd* 1997

Organist, Peter Wright, FRCO, *apptd* 1989

ARCHDEACONS
Croydon, Ven. Tony Davies, *apptd* 1994
Lambeth, Ven. Christopher Skilton, *apptd* 2004
Lewisham, Ven. Christine Hardman, *apptd* 2001
Reigate, Ven. Daniel Kajumba, *apptd* 2001
Southwark, Revd Dr Michael Ipgrave, *apptd* 2004
Wandsworth, Ven. David Gerrard, *apptd* 1989

Chancellor, Charles George, QC
Registrar and Legal Secretary, Paul Morris
Diocesan Secretary, Simon Parton, Trinity House, 4 Chapel Court, Borough High Street, London SE1 1HW
T 020-7939 9400

SOUTHWELL *(York)*
10th BISHOP
Rt. Revd George H. Cassidy, *cons.* 1999, *apptd* 1999; Bishop's Manor, Southwell NG25 0JR *Signs* George Southwell

BISHOP SUFFRAGAN
Sherwood, Rt. Revd Alan W. Morgan, *cons.* 1989, *apptd* 1989; Dunham House, Westgate, Southwell, Notts NG25 0JL

DEAN
Very Revd David Leaning, *apptd* 1991

CANON RESIDENTIARY
Jacqueline Jones, *apptd* 2003

Organist, Paul Hale, *apptd* 1989

ARCHDEACONS
Newark, Ven. Nigel Peyton, *apptd* 1999
Nottingham, Ven. Gordon Ogilvie, *apptd* 1996

Chancellor, John Shand, *apptd* 1981
Registrar and Legal Secretary, Christopher Hodson
Diocesan Secretary, Dunham House, Westgate, Southwell, Notts NG25 0JL T 01636-817204

TRURO *(Canterbury)*
14th BISHOP
Rt. Revd William Ind, *cons.* 1987, *apptd* 1997; Lis Escop, Truro TR3 6QQ *Signs* William Truro

BISHOP SUFFRAGAN
St Germans, Revd Royden Screech, *cons.* 2000, *apptd* 2000

DEAN
Very Revd Michael A. Moxon, LVO, *apptd* 1998

CANONS RESIDENTIARY
Roger Bush, *apptd* 2004; Perran Gay, *apptd* 1994; Peter Walker, *apptd* 2001

Organist, Robert Sharpe, *apptd* 2002

ARCHDEACONS
Cornwall, Ven. Rodney Whiteman, *apptd* 2000
Bodmin, Ven. Clive Cohen, *apptd* 2000

Chancellor, Timothy Briden, *apptd* 1998
Registrar and Legal Secretary, Michael Follett
Diocesan Secretary, Sheri Sturgess, Diocesan House, Kenwyn, Truro TR1 1JQ T 01872-274351

WAKEFIELD *(York)*
12th BISHOP
Rt. Revd Stephen Platten, *cons.* 2003, *apptd* 2003; Bishop's Lodge, Woodthorpe Lane, Wakefield, WF2 6JL
Signs Stephen Wakefield

BISHOP SUFFRAGAN
Pontefract, Rt. Revd Anthony William Robinson, *cons.* 2003, *apptd* 2002; Pontefract House, 181A Manygates Lane, Wakefield WF2 7DR

DEAN
Very Revd George P. Nairn-Briggs, *apptd* 1997

CANONS RESIDENTIARY
Richard Capper, *apptd* 1997; Robert Gage, *apptd* 1997;
   Ian Gaskell, *apptd* 1998; John Holmes, *apptd* 1998

Organist, Jonathan Bielby, FRCO, *apptd* 1972

ARCHDEACONS
Halifax, Ven. Robert Freeman, *apptd* 2003
Pontefract, Ven. Jonathan Greener, *apptd* 2003

Chancellor, Peter Collier, QC, *apptd* 1992
Registrar and Legal Secretary, Linda Box
Diocesan Secretary, Ashley Ellis, Church House, 1 South
   Parade, Wakefield WF1 1LP T 01924-371802

WORCESTER *(Canterbury)*
112th BISHOP
Rt. Revd Dr Peter S. M. Selby, *cons.* 1984, *apptd* 1997;
   The Bishop's House, Hartlebury Castle, Kidderminster
   DY11 7XX *Signs* Peter Wigorn

SUFFRAGAN BISHOP
Dudley, Rt. Revd Dr David S. Walker, *cons.* 2000, *apptd*
   2000; The Bishop's House, Bishop's Walk, Cradley Heath
   B64 7JF

DEAN
Very Revd Peter J. Marshall, *apptd* 1997

CANONS RESIDENTIARY
Alvyn Pettersen, *apptd* 2002; Ven. Joy Tetley, *apptd* 1999

Organist, Adrian Lucas, *apptd* 1996

ARCHDEACONS
Dudley, Ven. Fred Trethewey, *apptd* 2001
Worcester, Ven. Dr Joy Tetley

Chancellor, Charles Mynors, *apptd* 1999
Registrar and Legal Secretary, Michael Huskinson
Diocesan Secretary, Robert Higham, The Old Palace,
   Deansway, Worcester WR1 2JE T 01905-20537

ROYAL PECULIARS
WESTMINSTER

The Collegiate Church of St Peter

Dean, Very Revd Dr Wesley Carr, *apptd* 1997
Sub Dean and Archdeacon, David Hutt, *apptd* 1995
Canons of Westminster, David Hutt, *apptd* 1995; Michael
   Middleton, *apptd* 1997; Nicholas Sagovsky, *apptd*
   2004; Robert Wright, *apptd* 1998; Dr Tom Wright,
   apptd 1999
Chapter Clerk and Receiver-General, Maj.-Gen. David
   Burden, CB, CBE, Chapter Office, 20 Dean's Yard, London
   SW1P 3PA
Organist, James O'Donnell, *apptd* 1999
Registrar, Stuart Holmes, MVO
Legal Secretary, Christopher Vyse, *apptd* 2000

WINDSOR

*The Queen's Free Chapel of St George within Her Castle of
   Windsor*

Dean, Rt. Revd David Conner, *apptd* 1998
Canons Residentiary, Laurence Gunner, *apptd* 1996; John
   Ovenden, *apptd* 1998; John White, *apptd* 1982
Chapter Clerk, Charlotte Manley, LVO, OBE, *apptd* 2003,
   Chapter Office, The Cloisters, Windsor Castle, Windsor,
   Berks SL4 1NJ
Director of Music, Timothy Byram-Wigfield, *apptd* 2004

OTHER ANGLICAN CHURCHES

THE CHURCH IN WALES
The Anglican Church was the established church in Wales
from the 16th century until 1920, when the estrangement
of the majority of Welsh people from Anglicanism
resulted in disestablishment. Since then the Church in
Wales has been an autonomous province consisting of six
sees. The bishops are elected by an electoral college
comprising elected lay and clerical members, who also
elect one of the diocesan bishops as Archbishop of Wales.
   The legislative body of the Church in Wales is the
Governing Body, which has 350 members divided
between the three orders of bishops, clergy and laity. Its
President is the Archbishop of Wales and it meets twice
annually. Its decisions are binding upon all members of
the Church. The Church's property and finances are the
responsibility of the Representative Body. There are about
84,000 members of the Church in Wales, with 648
stipendiary clergy and 1,020 parishes.

THE GOVERNING BODY OF THE CHURCH IN WALES,
   39 Cathedral Road, Cardiff CF1 9XF T 029-2034 8200
   Lay Secretary, John Shirley
12th ARCHBISHOP OF WALES, The Most Revd Dr Barry
   C. Morgan (Bishop of Llandaff), *elected* 2003
   Signs Barry Cambrensis
BISHOPS
Bangor (80th), Rt. Revd Anthony Crockett, *b.* 1946, *cons.*
   2004, *elected* 2004; Ty'r Esgob, Bangor, Gwynedd LL57 2SS
   Signs Anthony Bangor. *Stipendiary clergy,* 71
Llandaff (102nd), The Most Revd Dr Barry C. Morgan, *b.*
   1947, *cons.* 1993, *trans.* 1999; Llys Esgob, The Cathedral
   Green, Llandaff, Cardiff CF5 2YE
   Signs Barry Landav. *Stipendiary clergy,* 146
Monmouth (9th), Rt. Revd Dominic Walker, *b.* 1948, *cons.*
   1997, *elected* 2003; Bishopstow, Stow Hill, Newport
   NP20 4EA
   Signs, Dominic Monmouth. *Stipendiary clergy,* 104
St Asaph (74th), Rt. Revd John S. Davies, *b.* 1943, *cons.*
   1999, *elected* 1999; Esgobty, St Asaph, Denbighshire
   LL17 0TW *Signs* John St Asaph. *Stipendiary clergy,* 116
St David's (127th), Rt. Revd Carl N. Cooper, *b.* 1960,
   cons. 2002, *elected* 2002; Llys Esgob, Abergwili,
   Carmarthen SA31 2JG
   Signs Carl St Davids. *Stipendiary clergy,* 126
Swansea and Brecon (8th), Rt. Revd Anthony E. Pierce, *b.*
   1941, *cons.* 1999, *elected* 1999; Ely Tower, Brecon, Powys
   LD3 9DE *Signs* Anthony Swansea & Brecon. *Stipendiary
   clergy,* 85

The stipend for a diocesan bishop of the Church in Wales
is £32,005 a year for 2004–5.

THE SCOTTISH EPISCOPAL CHURCH
The Scottish Episcopal Church was founded after the Act
of Settlement (1690) established the presbyterian nature
of the Church of Scotland. The Scottish Episcopal Church
is a member of the world-wide Anglican Communion.
The governing authority is the General Synod, an elected
body of approximately 140 members which meets once a
year. The diocesan bishop who convenes and presides at
meetings of the General Synod is called the Primus and is
elected by his fellow bishops.
   There are 44,280 members of the Scottish Episcopal
Church, of whom 29,251 are communicants. There are
seven bishops, approximately 482 serving clergy, and 313
churches and places of worship.

THE GENERAL SYNOD OF THE SCOTTISH EPISCOPAL CHURCH, 21 Grosvenor Crescent, Edinburgh EH12 5EE T 0131-225 6357 W www.scottishepiscopal.com
Secretary-General, J. F. Stuart
PRIMUS OF THE SCOTTISH EPISCOPAL CHURCH, Most Revd A. Bruce Cameron (Bishop of Aberdeen and Orkney), *elected* 2000

BISHOPS
Aberdeen and Orkney, A. Bruce Cameron, *b.* 1941, *cons.* 1992, *elected* 1992. *Clergy*, 54
Argyll and the Isles, Martin Shaw, *b.* 1944, *cons.* 2004, *elected* 2004. *Clergy*, 22
Brechin, Neville Chamberlain, *b.* 1939, *cons.* 1997, *elected* 1997. *Clergy*, 35
Edinburgh, Brian Smith, *b.* 1943, *cons.* 1993, *elected* 2001. *Clergy*, 162
Glasgow and Galloway, Idris Jones, *b.* 1943, *cons.* 1998, *elected* 1998. *Clergy*, 99
Moray, Ross and Caithness, John Crook, *b.* 1940, *cons.* 1999, *elected* 1999. *Clergy*, 31
St Andrews, Dunkeld and Dunblane, vacant. *Clergy*, 86

The minimum stipend of a diocesan bishop of the Scottish Episcopal Church for 2004–5 is £27,540 (i.e. 1.5 times the minimum clergy stipend of £18,360)

THE CHURCH OF IRELAND

The Anglican Church was the established church in Ireland from the 16th century but never secured the allegiance of the majority and was disestablished in 1871. The Church of Ireland is divided into the provinces of Armagh and Dublin, each under an archbishop. The provinces are subdivided into 12 dioceses.

The legislative body is the General Synod, which has 660 members in total, divided between the House of Bishops and the House of Representatives. The Archbishop of Armagh is elected by the House of Bishops; other episcopal elections are made by an electoral college.

There are about 375,000 members of the Church of Ireland, with two archbishops, ten bishops, about 600 clergy and about 1,100 churches and places of worship.

CENTRAL OFFICE, Church of Ireland House, Church Avenue, Rathmines, Dublin 6 T (00 353) (1) 4978422
Chief Officer and Secretary of the Representative Church Body, D. C. Reardon

PROVINCE OF ARMAGH
ARCHBISHOP OF ARMAGH, PRIMATE OF ALL IRELAND AND METROPOLITAN, Most Revd Robert H. A. Eames, PHD, *b.* 1937, *cons.* 1975, *trans.* 1986. *Clergy*, 55

BISHOPS
Clogher, Michael G. Jackson, PHD, DPHIL, *b.* 1956, *cons.* 2002, *apptd* 2002. *Clergy*, 32
Connor, Alan E. T. Harper, OBE, *b.* 1944, *cons.* 2002, *apptd* 2002. *Clergy*, 106
Derry and Raphoe, Kenneth R. Good, *b.* 1952, *cons.* 2002, *apptd* 2002. *Clergy*, 51
Down and Dromore, Harold C. Miller, *b.* 1950, *cons.* 1997, *apptd* 1997. *Clergy*, 116
Kilmore, Elphin and Ardagh, Kenneth H. Clarke, *b.* 1949, *cons.* 2001, *apptd* 2001. *Clergy*, 21
Tuam, Killala and Achonry, Richard C. A. Henderson, DPHIL, *b.* 1957, *cons.* 1998, *apptd* 1998. *Clergy*, 13

PROVINCE OF DUBLIN
ARCHBISHOP OF DUBLIN, BISHOP OF GLENDALOUGH, PRIMATE OF IRELAND AND METROPOLITAN, Most Revd John R. W. Neill, *b.* 1945, *apptd* 2002. *Clergy*, 86

BISHOPS
Cashel and Ossory, Peter F. Barrett, *b.* 1956, *cons.* 2003, *apptd* 2003. *Clergy*, 42
Cork, Cloyne and Ross, W. Paul Colton, *b.* 1960, *cons.* 1999, *apptd* 1999. *Clergy*, 30
Limerick and Killaloe, Michael H. G. Mayes, *b.* 1941, *cons.* 1993, *trans.* 2000. *Clergy*, 19
Meath and Kildare, (Most Revd) Richard L. Clarke, PHD, *b.* 1949, *cons.* 1996, *apptd* 1996. *Clergy*, 26

OVERSEAS

PRIMATES
PRIMATE AND PRESIDING BISHOP OF AOTEAROA, NEW ZEALAND AND POLYNESIA, Most Revd Whakahuihui Vercoe
PRIMATE OF AUSTRALIA, Most Revd Peter Carnley
PRIMATE OF BRAZIL, Most Revd Orlando Santos de Oliveira
ARCHBISHOP OF THE PROVINCE OF BURUNDI, Most Revd Samuel Ndayisenga
ARCHBISHOP AND PRIMATE OF CANADA, Most Revd Andrew Sandford Hutchison
ARCHBISHOP OF THE PROVINCE OF CENTRAL AFRICA, Most Revd Bernard Amos Malango
PRIMATE OF THE CENTRAL REGION OF AMERICA, Most Revd Martin de Jesus Barahona
ARCHBISHOP OF THE PROVINCE OF CONGO, Most Revd Dr Dirokpa Balufuga Fidèle
PRIMATE OF THE PROVINCE OF HONG KONG SHENG KUNG HUI, Most Revd Peter Kwong
ARCHBISHOP OF THE PROVINCE OF THE INDIAN OCEAN, Most Revd Remi Rabenirina
PRESIDENT-BISHOP OF JERUSALEM AND THE MIDDLE EAST, Most Revd George Handford
ARCHBISHOP OF THE PROVINCE OF KENYA, Most Revd Benjamin M. P. Nzimbi
ARCHBISHOP OF THE PROVINCE OF KOREA, Most Revd Dr Matthew Chul Bum Chung
ARCHBISHOP OF THE PROVINCE OF MELANESIA, Most Revd Sir Ellison L. Pogo, KBE
ARCHBISHOP OF MEXICO, Most Revd Carlos Touche-Porter
ARCHBISHOP OF THE PROVINCE OF MYANMAR, Most Revd Samuel Si Htay
ARCHBISHOP OF THE PROVINCE OF NIGERIA, Most Revd Peter Akinola
PRIMATE OF NIPPON SEI KO KAI, Most Revd James Toru Uno
ARCHBISHOP OF PAPUA NEW GUINEA, Most Revd James Ayong
PRIME BISHOP OF THE PHILIPPINES, Most Revd Ignacio C. Soliba
ARCHBISHOP OF THE PROVINCE OF RWANDA, Most Revd Emmanuel Musaba Kolini
PRIMATE OF THE PROVINCE OF SOUTH EAST ASIA, Most Revd Datuk Yong Ping Chung
METROPOLITAN OF THE PROVINCE OF SOUTHERN AFRICA, Most Revd Njongonkulu W. H. Ndungane
PRESIDING BISHOP OF THE SOUTHERN CONE OF AMERICA, Most Revd Gregory James Venables
ARCHBISHOP OF THE PROVINCE OF THE SUDAN, Most Revd Joseph Marona

ARCHBISHOP OF THE PROVINCE OF TANZANIA, Most Revd Donald L. Mtetemela

ARCHBISHOP OF THE PROVINCE OF UGANDA, Most Revd Henry Luke Orombi

PRESIDING BISHOP AND PRIMATE OF THE USA, Most Revd Frank T. Griswold

ARCHBISHOP OF THE PROVINCE OF WEST AFRICA, Most Revd Justice Ofei Akrofi

ARCHBISHOP OF THE PROVINCE OF THE WEST INDIES, Most Revd Drexel Gomez

OTHER CHURCHES AND EXTRA-PROVINCIAL DIOCESES

ANGLICAN CHURCH OF BERMUDA, *extra-provincial to Canterbury*

Bishop of Bermuda, Rt. Revd Ewen Ratteray

CHURCH OF CEYLON, *extra-provincial to Canterbury*

Bishop of Colombo, Rt. Revd Duleep de Chickera

Bishop of Kurunagala, Rt. Revd Kumara Illangasinghe

EPISCOPAL CHURCH OF CUBA, Rt. Revd Jorge Perera Hurtado

LUSITANIAN CHURCH (*Portuguese Episcopal Church*), *extra-provincial to Canterbury*

Bishop of Lustanian Church, Rt. Revd Fernando Soares

SPANISH REFORMED EPISCOPAL CHURCH, Rt. Revd Carlos López-Lozano

MODERATION OF CHURCHES IN FULL COMMUNION WITH THE ANGLICAN COMMUNION

CHURCH OF BANGLADESH, Rt. Revd Michael Baroi

CHURCH OF NORTH INDIA, Most Revd Zechariah J. Terom

CHURCH OF SOUTH INDIA, Most Revd Badda Peter Sugandhar

CHURCH OF PAKISTAN, Rt. Revd Dr Alexander John Malik

THE CHURCH OF SCOTLAND

The Church of Scotland is the established (i.e. national) church of Scotland. The Church is Reformed in doctrine, and presbyterian in constitution, i.e. based on a hierarchy of councils of ministers and elders and, since 1990, of members of a diaconate. At local level the Kirk Session consists of the parish minister and ruling elders. At district level the presbyteries, of which there are 44 in Britain, consist of all the ministers in the district, one ruling elder from each congregation, and those members of the diaconate who qualify for membership. The General Assembly is the supreme authority, and is presided over by a Moderator chosen annually by the Assembly. The Sovereign, if not present in person, is represented by a Lord High Commissioner who is appointed each year by the Crown.

The Church of Scotland has about 550,000 members, 1,100 ministers and 1,500 churches. There are about 100 ministers and other personnel working overseas.

Lord High Commissioner (2004), The Rt. Hon. Lord Steel of Aikwood

Moderator of the General Assembly (2004), Dr Alison J. Elliot

Principal Clerk, Very Revd Dr F. A. J. Macdonald

Depute Principal Clerk, Revd. Dr M. A. MacLean

Procurator, P. S. Hodge

Law Agent and Solicitor of the Church, Mrs J. S. Wilson

Parliamentary Agent, I. McCulloch *(London)*

General Treasurer, D. F. Ross

Secretary, Church and Nation Committee, Revd Dr D. Sinclair

CHURCH OFFICE, 121 George Street, Edinburgh EH2 4YN
T 0131-225 5722

PRESBYTERIES AND CLERKS

Edinburgh, Revd W. P. Graham

West Lothian, Revd D. Shaw

Lothian, J. D. McCulloch, DL

Melrose and Peebles, Revd A. J. Morton

Duns, J. Watson

Jedburgh, Revd N. R. Combe

Annandale and Eskdale, Revd C. B. Haston

Dumfries and Kirkcudbright, Revd G. M. A. Savage

Wigtown and Stranraer, Revd D. W. Dutton

Ayr, Revd J. Crichton

Irvine and Kilmarnock, Revd C. G. G. Brockie

Ardrossan, Revd J. Mackay

Lanark, Revd M. Frew

Greenock and Paisley, Revd David Kay

Glasgow, Revd D. W. Lunan

Hamilton, Revd S. Paterson

Dumbarton, Revd D. P. Munro

Argyll, I. MacLagan

Falkirk, Revd I. W. Black

Stirling, Revd M. MacCormick

Dunfermline, Revd W. E. Farquhar

Kirkcaldy, A. Moore

St Andrews, Revd Dr D. Sinclair

Dunkeld and Meigle, Revd J. Russell

Perth, Revd D. G. Lawson

Dundee, Revd J. A. Roy

Angus, Revd M. I. G. Rooney

Aberdeen, Revd I. MacLean

Kincardine and Deeside, Revd J. Holt

Gordon, Revd E. Glen

Buchan, George Barston

Moray, Revd G. M. Wood

Abernethy, Revd J. A. I. MacEwan

Inverness, Revd A. S. Younger

Lochaber, Revd D. M. Anderson

Ross, Revd T. M. McWilliam

Sutherland, Revd J. L. Goskirk

Caithness, Mrs M. Gillies, MBE

Lochcarron-Skye, Revd A. I. MacArthur

Uist, Revd M. Smith

Lewis, Revd T. S. Sinclair

Orkney, Revd T. G. Hunt

Shetland, Revd C. H. M.Greig

England, Revd W. A. Cairns

Europe, Revd J. A. Cowie

The stipends for ministers in the Church of Scotland in 2004 range from £20,090–£24,659, depending on length of service. In addition, congregations can make extra payments.

THE ROMAN CATHOLIC CHURCH

The Roman Catholic Church is one world-wide Christian Church acknowledging as its head the Bishop of Rome, known as the Pope (Father). He leads a communion of followers of Christ, who believe they continue his presence in the world as servants of faith, hope and love to all society. The Pope is held to be the successor of St Peter and thus invested with the power which was entrusted to St Peter by Jesus Christ. A direct line of succession is therefore claimed from the earliest Christian communities. With the fall of the Roman Empire the Pope also became an important political leader. His territory is now limited to the 107 acres of the Vatican City State, created to provide some independence to the Pope from Italy and other nations.

The Pope exercises spiritual authority over the Church with the advice and assistance of the Sacred College of Cardinals, the supreme council of the Church. He is also advised by bishops in communion with him, by a group of officers which form the Roman Curia and by his ambassadors, called Apostolic Nuncios, who liaise with the Bishops' Conference in each country.

Those members of the College of Cardinals who are under the age of 80 elect a successor of the Pope following his death. The assembly of the Cardinals called to the Vatican for the election of a new Pope is known as the Conclave. In complete seclusion the Cardinals vote by a secret ballot; a two-thirds majority is necessary before the vote can be accepted as final. When a Cardinal receives the necessary number of votes, the Dean of the Sacred College formally asks him if he will accept election and the name by which he wishes to be known. On his acceptance of the office of Supreme Pontiff, the Conclave is dissolved and the first Cardinal Deacon announces the election to the assembled crowd in St Peter's Square.

The number of cardinals was fixed at 70 by Pope Sixtus V in 1586 but has been steadily increased since the pontificate of John XXIII and at the end of October 2003 stood at 194, plus two cardinals created 'in pectore' (their names being kept secret by the Pope for fear of persecution; they are thought to be Chinese).

The Pope has full legislative, judicial and administrative power over the whole church. He is aided in his administration by the Curia, which is made up of a number of departments. The Secretariat of State is the central office for carrying out the Pope's instructions and is presided over by the Cardinal Secretary of State. It maintains relations with the departments of the Curia, with the episcopate, with the representatives of the Holy See in various countries, governments and private persons. The congregations and pontifical councils are the Pope's ministries and include departments such as the Congregation for the Doctrine of Faith, whose field of competence concern faith and morals; the Congregation for the Clergy and the Congregation for the Evangelisation of Peoples, the Pontifical Council for the Family and the Pontifical Council for the Promotion of Christian Unity.

The Vatican State does not have diplomatic representatives. The Holy See, composed of the Pope and those who help him in his mission for the Church, is recognised by the Conventions of Vienna as an International Moral Body. The representatives of the Holy See are known as Apostolic Nuncio's. Where representation is only to the local churches and not to the government of a country, the Papal representative is known as an apostolic delegate. The Roman Catholic Church has an estimated 840 million adherents under the care of some 2,500 diocesan bishops world-wide.

SOVEREIGN PONTIFF

His Holiness Pope John Paul II (Karol Wojtyla), *born* Wadowice, Poland, 18 May 1920; *ordained priest* 1946; *appointed Archbishop* of Kraków 1964; *created Cardinal* 1967; *assumed pontificate* 16 October 1978

SECRETARIAT OF STATE

Secretary of State, HE Cardinal Angelo Sodano
First Section (General Affairs), Archbishop Leonardo Sandri (Titular Archbishop of Cittanova)
Second Section (Relations with other states), Most Revd Giovanni Lajolo (Titular Archbishop of Cesariana)

BISHOPS' CONFERENCE

The Roman Catholic Church in England and Wales consists of a total of 22 dioceses and is governed by the Bishops' Conference, membership of which includes the Diocesan Bishops, the Apostolic Exarch of the Ukrainians, the Bishop of the Forces and the Auxiliary Bishops. The Conference is headed by the President *(HE Cardinal Cormac Murphy-O'Connor, Archbishop of Westminster)* and Vice-President *(The Most Revd Patrick Kelly, Archbishop of Liverpool)*. There are five departments, each with an episcopal chairman: the Department for Christian Life and Worship (the Bishop of Menevia), the Department for Mission and Unity (the Bishop of Portsmouth), the Department for Catholic Education and Formation (the Archbishop of Birmingham), the Department for Christian Responsibility and Citizenship (the Archbishop of Cardiff), and the Department for International Affairs (the Bishop of Leeds).

The Bishops' Standing Committee, made up of all the Archbishops and the chairman of each of the above departments, has general responsibility for continuity of policy between the plenary sessions of the Conference. It prepares the Conference agenda and implements its decisions. It is serviced by a General Secretariat. There are also agencies and consultative bodies affiliated to the Conference.

The Bishops' Conference of Scotland is the permanently constituted assembly of the Bishops of Scotland. The Conference is headed by the President *(HE Cardinal Keith Patrick O'Brien, Archbishop of St Andrews and Edinburgh)*. To promote its work, the Conference establishes various agencies which have an advisory function in relation to the Conference. The more important of these agencies are called Commissions and each one has a Bishop President who, with the other members of the Commissions, are appointed by the Conference.

The Irish Episcopal Conference has as its president Archbishop Brady of Armagh. Its membership comprises all the Archbishops and Bishops of Ireland and it appoints various Commissions to assist it in its work. There are three types of Commissions: (a) those made up of lay and clerical members chosen for their skills and experience, and staffed by full-time expert secretariats; (b) Commissions whose members are selected from existing institutions and whose services are supplied on a part-time basis; and (c) Commissions of Bishops only.

The Roman Catholic Church in the UK has an estimated 1,631,449 members, 6,583 priests and 4,475 churches. Bishops' Conferences secretariats:

ENGLAND AND WALES, 39 Eccleston Square, London SW1V 1BX T 020-7630 8220 F 020 7901 4821 E secretariat@cbcew.org.uk W www.catholic-ew.org.uk
General Secretary, Mgr Andrew Summersgill

SCOTLAND, 64 Aitken Street, Airdrie, Lanarkshire ML6 6LT
General Secretary, Rt. Revd Mgr Henry Docherty
IRELAND, Columba Centre, Maynooth, County Kildare.
Secretary, The Most Revd William Lee (Bishop of
Waterford and Lismore); *Executive Secretary*, Revd
Aidan O'Boyle

GREAT BRITAIN

APOSTOLIC NUNCIO TO GREAT BRITAIN
The Most Revd Pablo Puente, 54 Parkside, London
SW19 5NE **T** 020-8944 7189

ENGLAND AND WALES
THE MOST REVD ARCHBISHOPS
Westminster, HE Cardinal Cormac Murphy-O'Connor,
cons. 1977, *apptd* 2000. *Auxiliaries*, James J. O'Brien,
cons. 1977; George Stack, *cons.* 2001; Bernard Longley
cons. 2003; Alan Hopes *cons.* 2003. *Clergy*, 779.
Archbishop's Residence, Archbishop's House, Ambrosden
Avenue, London SW1P 1QJ **T** 020-7798 9033
Birmingham, Vincent Nichols, *cons.* 1992, *apptd* 2000.
Auxiliaries, Philip Pargeter, *cons.* 1990. *Clergy*, 443.
Diocesan Curia, Cathedral House, St Chad's Queensway,
Birmingham B4 6EX **T** 0121-236 5535
Cardiff, Peter Smith, *cons.* 1995, *apptd* 2001. *Clergy*, 126.
Diocesan Curia, Archbishop's House, 41–43 Cathedral
Road, Cardiff CF11 9HD **T** 029-2022 0411
Liverpool, Patrick Kelly, *cons.* 1984, *apptd* 1996.
Auxiliaries, Vincent Malone, *cons.* 1989; Thomas
Williams, *cons.* 2003. *Clergy*, 486. *Diocesan Curia*,
Archdiocese of Liverpool, Centre for Evangelisation,
Croxteth Drive, Sefton Park, Liverpool L17 1AA
T 0151-522 1000
Southwark, Kevin McDonald, *cons.* 2001, *apptd* 2003.
Auxiliary, John Hine, *cons.* 2001. *Clergy*, 498. *Diocesan
Curia*, Archbishop's House, 150 St George's Road, London
SE1 6HX **T** 020-7928 5592

THE RT. REVD BISHOPS
Arundel and Brighton, Kieran Conry, *cons.* 2001, *apptd*
2001. *Clergy*, 111. *Diocesan Curia*, Bishop's House, The
Upper Drive, Hove, E. Sussex BN3 6NE **T** 01273-506387
Brentwood, Thomas McMahon, *cons.* 1980, *apptd* 1980.
Clergy, 175. *Bishop's Office*, Cathedral House, Ingrave
Road, Brentwood, Essex CM15 8AT **T** 01277-232266
Clifton, Declan Lang, *cons.* 2001, *apptd* 2001.
Clergy, 251. *Bishop's House*, St Ambrose, North Road,
Leigh Woods, Bristol BS8 3PW **T** 0117-973 3072
East Anglia, Michael Evans, *cons.* 2003, *apptd* 2003. *Clergy*,
129. *Diocesan Curia*, The White House, 21 Upgate,
Poringland, Norwich NR14 7SH **T** 01508-492202
Hallam, John Rawsthorne, *cons.* 1981, *apptd* 1997.
Clergy, 75. *Bishop's House*, 75 Norfolk Road, Sheffield
S2 2SZ **T** 0114-278 7988
Hexham and Newcastle, Kevin Dunn, *cons.* 2004, *apptd*
2004. *Clergy*, 214. *Diocesan Curia*, Bishop's House, East
Denton Hall, 800 West Road, Newcastle upon Tyne NE5 2BJ
T 0191-228 0003
Lancaster, Patrick O'Donoghue, *cons.* 1993, *apptd* 2001.
Clergy, 248. *Bishop's Residence*, Bishop's Apartment,
Cathedral House, Balmoral Road, Lancaster LA1 3BT
T 01524-596050
Leeds, Arthur Roche, *cons.* 2001, *apptd* 2004. *Clergy*, 226.
Diocesan Curia, Hinsley Hall, 62 Headingley Lane, Leeds
LS6 2BU **T** 0113-261 8000
Menevia (Wales), Mark Jabalé, *cons.* 2001, *apptd* 2001.
Clergy, 60. *Diocesan Curia*, 27 Convent Street, Greenhill,
Swansea SA1 2BX **T** 01792-644017

Middlesbrough, John Crowley, *cons.* 1986, *apptd* 1992.
Clergy, 113. *Diocesan Curia*, 50a The Avenue, Linthorpe,
Middlesbrough, Cleveland TS5 6QT **T** 01642-850505
Northampton, vacant. *Clergy*, 159. *Diocesan Curia*, Bishop's
House, Marriott Street, Northampton NN2 6AW
T 01604-715635
Nottingham, Malcolm McMahon, *cons.* 2000, *apptd* 2000.
Clergy, 214. *Bishop's House*, 27 Cavendish Road East, The
Park, Nottingham NG7 1BB **T** 0115-947 4786
Plymouth, Christopher Budd, *cons.* 1986, *apptd* 1985.
Clergy, 125. *Diocesan Curia*, Bishop's House, 31
Wyndham Street West, Plymouth PL1 5RZ **T** 01752-224414
Portsmouth, F. Crispian Hollis, *cons.* 1987, *apptd* 1989.
Clergy, 282. *Bishop's Residence*, Bishop's House,
Edinburgh Road, Portsmouth, Hants PO1 3HG
T 023-9282 0894
Salford, Terence J. Brain, *cons.* 1991, *apptd* 1997. *Clergy*,
346. *Diocesan Curia*, 5 Gerald Road, Pendleton, Salford
M6 6DL **T** 0161-736 1421
Shrewsbury, Brian Noble, *cons.* 1995, *apptd* 1995. *Clergy*
180. *Diocesan Curia*, 2 Park Road South, Prenton, Wirral
CH43 4UX **T** 0151-652 9855
Wrexham (Wales), Edwin Regan, *cons.* 1994, *apptd* 1994.
Clergy, 83. *Diocesan Curia*, Bishop's House, Sontley Road,
Wrexham LL13 7EW **T** 01978-262726

SCOTLAND

THE MOST REVD ARCHBISHOPS
St Andrews and Edinburgh, HE Cardinal Keith Patrick
O'Brien, *cons.* 1985, *apptd* 1985, *elevated* 2003. *Clergy*,
160. *Archbishop's House*, 42 Greenhall Gardens, Edinburgh
EH10 4BJ **T** 0131-447 3337
Glasgow, Mario Joseph Conti, *cons.* 1977, *apptd* 2002.
Clergy, 252. *Diocesan Curia*, 196 Clyde Street, Glasgow
G1 4JY **T** 0141-226 5898

THE RT. REVD BISHOPS
Aberdeen, Peter Moran, *cons.* 2003, *apptd* 2003. *Clergy*,
46. *Diocesan Curia*, Bishop's House, 3 Queen's Cross,
Aberdeen AB15 4XU **T** 01224-319154
Argyll and the Isles, Ian Murray, *cons.* 1999, *apptd* 1999.
Clergy, 26. *Bishop's House*, Esplanade, Oban, Argyll
PA34 5AB **T** 01631-571395
Dunkeld, Vincent Logan, *cons.* 1981. *Clergy*, 44. *Diocesan
Curia*, 24–28 Lawside Road, Dundee DD3 6XY
T 01382-225453
Galloway, John Cunningham, *cons.* 2004, *apptd* 2004.
Clergy, 61. *Diocesan Curia*, 8 Corsehill Road, Ayr KA7 2ST
T 01292-266750
Motherwell, Joseph Devine, *cons.* 1977, *apptd* 1983.
Clergy, 129. *Diocesan Curia*, Coursington Road,
Motherwell ML1 1PP **T** 01698-269114
Paisley, John A. Mone, *cons.* 1984, *apptd* 1988. *Clergy*,
56. *Diocesan Curia*, Diocesan Centre, Cathedral Precincts,
Incle Street, Paisley PA1 1HR **T** 0141-847 6130

BISHOPRIC OF THE FORCES
Rt. Revd Thomas Matthew Burns, *cons.* 2002, *apptd*
2002. *Administration*, Bishopric of the Forces, Middle Hill,
Aldershot, Hants GU11 1PP **T** 01252-349004

IRELAND

There is one hierarchy for the whole of Ireland. Several of
the dioceses have territory partly in the Republic of
Ireland and partly in Northern Ireland.

APOSTOLIC NUNCIO TO IRELAND
Most Revd Giuseppe Lazzarotto (Titular Archbishop of Numana), 183 Navan Road, Dublin 7
T (00 353) (1) 838 0577 F (00 353) (1) 838 0276

THE MOST REVD ARCHBISHOPS
Armagh, Sean Brady, *cons.* 1995, *apptd* 1996. *Auxiliary*, Gerard Clifford, *cons.* 1991. *Clergy*, 183. *Diocesan Curia*, Ara Coeli, Armagh BT61 7QY T 028-3752 2045
Cashel and Emly, Dermot Clifford, *cons.* 1986, *apptd* 1988. *Clergy*, 128. *Archbishop's Residence*, Archbishop's House, Thurles, Co. Tipperary T (00 353) (504) 21512
Dublin, HE Cardinal Desmond Connell, *cons.* 1988, *apptd* 1988, *elevated* 2001. *Coadjutor Archbishop*, Diarmuid Martin, *apptd* 2003. *Auxiliaries*, Eamonn Walsh, *cons.* 1990; Fiachra O'Ceallaigh, *cons.* 1994; Martin Drennan, *cons.* 1997; Raymond Field, *cons.* 1997. *Clergy*, 994. *Archbishop's Residence*, Archbishop's House, Dublin 9 T (00 353) (1) 836 0723
Tuam, Michael Neary, *cons.* 1992, *apptd* 1995. *Clergy*, 141. *Archbishop's Residence*, Archbishop's House, Tuam, Co. Galway T (00 353) (93) 24166

THE MOST REVD BISHOPS
Achonry, Thomas Flynn, *cons.* 1975, *apptd* 1977. *Clergy*, 62. *Bishop's Residence*, Bishop's House, Ballaghaderreen, Co. Roscommon T (00 353) (9498) 60021
Ardagh and Clonmacnois, Colm O'Reilly, *cons.* 1983, *apptd* 1983. *Clergy*, 64. *Bishop's Residence*, St Michael's, Longford, Co. Longford T (00 353) (43) 46432
Clogher, Joseph Duffy, *cons.* 1979, *apptd* 1979. *Clergy*, 108. *Bishop's Residence*, Bishop's House, Monaghan T (00 353) (47) 81019
Clonfert, John Kirby, *cons.* 1988. *Clergy*, 71. *Bishop's Residence*, St Brendan's, Coorheen, Loughrea, Co. Galway T (0 353) (91) 841560
Cloyne, John Magee, *cons.* 1987, *apptd* 1987. *Clergy*, 153. *Diocesan Centre*, Cobh, Co. Cork T (00 353) (21) 4811430
Cork and Ross, John Buckley, *cons.* 1984, *apptd* 1998. *Clergy*, 153. *Diocesan Office*, Cork and Ross Offices, Redemption Road, Cork T (00 353) (21) 4301717
Derry, Seamus Hegarty, *cons.* 1982, *apptd* 1994. *Clergy*, 138. *Bishop's Residence*, Bishop's House, St Eugene's Cathedral, Derry BT48 9AP T 028-7126 2302.
Auxiliary, Francis Lagan, *cons.* 1988
Down and Connor, Patrick J. Walsh, *cons.* 1983, *apptd* 1991. *Clergy*, 240. *Bishop's Residence*, Lisbreen, 73 Somerton Road, Belfast, Co. Antrim BT15 4DE T 028-9077 6185. *Auxiliaries*, Anthony Farquhar, *cons.* 1983; Donal McKeown, *cons.* 2001
Dromore, John McAreavey, *cons.* 1999, *apptd* 1999. *Clergy*, 78. *Bishop's Residence*, Bishop's House, 44 Armagh Road, Newry, Co. Down BT35 6PN T 028-3026 2444
Elphin, Christopher Jones, *cons.* 1994, *apptd* 1994. *Clergy*, 70. *Bishop's Residence*, St Mary's, Sligo T (00 353) (71) 9162670
Ferns, Éamonn Walsh, *cons.* 1990, *apptd* 2002. *Clergy*, 138. *Bishop's Residence*, Bishop's House, Summerhill, Wexford T (00 353) (53) 22177
Galway and Kilmacduagh, James McLoughlin, *cons.* 1993, *apptd* 1993. *Clergy*, 87. *Diocesan Office*, The Cathedral, Galway T (00 353) (91) 563566
Kerry, William Murphy, *cons.* 1995, *apptd* 1995. *Clergy*, 126. *Bishop's Residence*, Bishop's House, Killarney, Co. Kerry T (00 353) (64) 31168
Kildare and Leighlin, James Moriarty, *apptd* 2002. *Clergy*, 127. *Bishop's Residence*, Bishop's House, Carlow T (00 353) (59) 917 6725

Killala, John Fleming, *cons.* 2002, *apptd* 2002. *Clergy*, 52. *Bishop's Residence*, Bishop's House, Ballina, Co. Mayo T (00 353) (96) 21518
Killaloe, William Walsh, *cons.* 1994. *Clergy*, 149. *Bishop's Residence*, Westbourne, Ennis, Co. Clare T (00 353) (65) 6828638
Kilmore, Leo O'Reilly, *cons.* 1997, *apptd* 1998. *Clergy*, 98. *Bishop's Residence*, Bishop's House, Cullies, Co. Cavan T (00 353) (49) 4331496
Limerick, Donal Murray, *cons.* 1982, *apptd* 1996. *Clergy*, 110. *Diocesan Offices*, 66 O'Connell Street, Limerick T (00 353) (61) 315856
Meath, Michael Smith, *cons.* 1984, *apptd* 1990. *Clergy*, 141. *Bishop's Residence*, Bishop's House, Dublin Road, Mullingar, Co. Westmeath T (00 353) (44) 48841
Ossory, Laurence Forristal, *cons.* 1980, *apptd* 1981. *Clergy*, 91. *Bishop's Residence*, Sion House, Kilkenny T (00 353) (56) 7762448
Raphoe, Philip Boyce, *cons.* 1995, *apptd* 1995. *Clergy*, 90. *Bishop's Residence*, Ard Adhamhnáin, Letterkenny, Co. Donegal T (00 353) (74) 9121208
Waterford and Lismore, William Lee, *cons.* 1993, *apptd* 1993. *Clergy*, 114. *Bishop's Residence*, John's Hill, Waterford T (00 353) (51) 874463

OTHER CHURCHES IN THE UK

AFRICAN AND AFRO-CARIBBEAN CHURCHES

There are more than 160 Christian churches or groups of African or Afro-Caribbean origin in the UK. These include the Apostolic Faith Church, the Cherubim and Seraphim Church, the New Testament Church Assembly, the New Testament Church of God, the Wesleyan Holiness Church and the Aladura Churches. The Afro-West Indian United Council of Churches and the Council of African and Afro-Caribbean Churches UK (which was initiated as the Council of African and Allied Churches in 1979 to give one voice to the various Christian churches of African origin in the UK) are the media through which the member churches can work jointly to provide services they cannot easily provide individually.

There are about 70,000 adherents of African and Afro-Caribbean churches in the UK, and over 1,000 congregations. The Council of African and Afro-Caribbean Churches UK has about 17,000 members, 250 ministers and 125 congregations.

COUNCIL OF AFRICAN AND AFRO-CARIBBEAN CHURCHES UK , 31 Norton House, Sidney Road, London SW9 0UJ T 020-7274 5589
Chairman, His Grace The Most Revd Father Olu A. Abiola, OBE

ASSOCIATED PRESBYTERIAN CHURCHES OF SCOTLAND

The Associated Presbyterian Churches came into being in 1989 as a result of a division within the Free Presbyterian Church of Scotland. Following two controversial disciplinary cases, the culmination of deepening differences within the Church, a presbytery was formed calling itself the Associated Presbyterian Churches (APC). The Associated Presbyterian Churches has about 900 members, 9 ministers and 16 churches.

Clerk of the Scottish Presbytery, Revd A. N. McPhail, Fernhill, Polvinster Road, Oban PA34 5TN T 01631-567076

THE BAPTIST CHURCH

Baptists trace their origins to John Smyth, who in 1609 in Amsterdam reinstituted the baptism of conscious believers as the basis of the fellowship of a gathered church. Members of Smyth's church established the first Baptist church in England in 1612. They came to be known as 'General' Baptists and their theology was Arminian, whereas a later group of Calvinists who adopted the baptism of believers came to be known as 'Particular' Baptists. The two sections of the Baptists were united into one body, the Baptist Union of Great Britain and Ireland, in 1891. In 1988 the title was changed to the Baptist Union of Great Britain.

Baptists emphasise the complete autonomy of the local church, although individual churches are linked in various kinds of associations. There are international bodies (such as the Baptist World Alliance) and national bodies, but some Baptist churches belong to neither. However, in Great Britain the majority of churches and associations belong to the Baptist Union of Great Britain. There are also Baptist Unions in Wales, Scotland and Ireland which are much smaller than the Baptist Union of Great Britain, and there is some overlap of membership.

There are over 40 million Baptist church members world-wide; in the Baptist Union of Great Britain there are 139,028 members, 1,917 pastors and 2,099 churches. In the Baptist Union of Scotland there are 14,002 members, 120 pastors and 176 churches. In the Baptist Union of Wales (Undeb Bedyddwyr Cymru) there are about 15,073 members, 100 pastors and 443 churches. In the Association of Baptist Churches in Ireland (formerly the Baptist Union of Ireland) there are 8,251 members, 85 pastors and 111 churches.

President of the Baptist Union of Great Britain (2004–5), Revd Peter Manson

General Secretary, Revd David Coffey, Baptist House, PO Box 44, 129 Broadway, Didcot, Oxon OX11 8RT
T 01235-517700 E info@baptist.org.uk
W www.baptist.org.uk

General Director of the Baptist Union of Scotland, Revd William Slack, 14 Aytoun Road, Glasgow G41 5RT
T 0141-423 6169 F 0141-424 1422
E admin@scottishbaptist.org.uk

President of the English Assembly of the Baptist Union of Wales (2004–5), Revd Keith Fantham

President of the Welsh Assembly of the Baptist Union of Wales (2004–5), Revd Idris Hughes

General Secretaries of the Baptist Union of Wales, Revd Peter Thomas and Revd W. O. Meredith Powell, 94 Mansel Street, Swansea SA1 5TZ T 01792-655468

Secretary of the Association of Baptist Churches in Ireland, Revd W. Colville, The Baptist Centre, 19 Hillsborough Road, Moira BT67 0HG T 028-9261 9267
E abc@thebaptistcentre.org

THE CONGREGATIONAL FEDERATION

The Congregational Federation was founded by members of Congregational churches in England and Wales who did not join the United Reformed Church in 1972. There are also churches in Scotland and France affiliated to the Federation. The Federation exists to encourage congregations of believers to worship in free assembly, but it has no authority over them and emphasises their right to independence and self-government.

The Federation has 10,058 members, 59 accredited ministers and 294 churches in England, Wales and Scotland.

President of the Federation (2004–5), Val Price
General Secretary, Revd. M. Heaney, 4 Castle Gate, Nottingham NG1 7AS T 0115-911 1460
E admin@congregational.org.uk

THE FREE CHURCH OF ENGLAND

The Free Church of England is a union of two bodies in the Anglican tradition, the Free Church of England, founded in 1844 as a protest against the Oxford Movement in the established Church, and the Reformed Episcopal Church, founded in America in 1873 but which also had congregations in England. As both Churches sought to maintain the historic faith, tradition and practice of the Anglican Church since the Reformation, they decided to unite as one body in England in 1927. The historic episcopate was conferred on the English Church in 1876 through the line of the American bishops, who had pioneered an open table Communion policy towards members of other denominations.

The Free Church of England has 1,300 members, 45 ministers and 30 churches in England. It also has three house churches and three ministers in New Zealand and one church and one minister in St Petersburg, Russia.

General Secretary, Revd Paul Hunt, 329 Wolverhampton Road West, Willen Hall WV13 2RL T 01902-607335

THE FREE CHURCH OF SCOTLAND

The Free Church of Scotland was formed in 1843 when over 400 ministers withdrew from the Church of Scotland as a result of interference in the internal affairs of the church by the civil authorities. In 1900, all but 26 ministers joined with others to form the United Free Church (most of which rejoined the Church of Scotland in 1929). In 1904 the remaining 26 ministers were recognised by the House of Lords as continuing the Free Church of Scotland.

The Church maintains strict adherence to the Westminster Confession of Faith (1648) and accepts the Bible as the sole rule of faith and conduct. Its General Assembly meets annually. It also has links with Reformed Churches overseas. In January 2000, a division occurred within the church, the larger body retains the name of the Free Church of Scotland with the smaller body known as the Free Church of Scotland (Continuing) and has around 2,000 members. The Free Church of Scotland has about 11,500 members, 82 ministers and 162 churches.

General Treasurer, I. D. Gill, The Mound, Edinburgh EH1 2LS
T 0131-226 5286 E offices@freechurchofscotland.org.uk

THE FREE PRESBYTERIAN CHURCH OF SCOTLAND

The Free Presbyterian Church of Scotland was formed in 1893 by two ministers of the Free Church of Scotland who refused to accept a Declaratory Act passed by the Free Church General Assembly in 1892. The Free Presbyterian Church of Scotland is Calvinistic in doctrine and emphasises observance of the Sabbath. It adheres strictly to the Westminster Confession of Faith of 1648.

The Church has about 3,000 members in Scotland and about 4,000 in overseas congregations. It has 16 ministers and 50 churches in the UK.

Moderator, Revd R. MacLeod, 4 Laurel Park Close, Glasgow G13 1RD

Clerk of Synod, Revd J. MacLeod, 16 Matheson Road, Stornoway, Isle of Lewis HS1 2LA T 01851-702755

THE HOLY APOSTOLIC CATHOLIC ASSYRIAN CHURCH OF THE EAST

The Holy Apostolic Catholic Assyrian Church of the East traces its beginnings to the middle of the first century. It spread from Upper Mesopotamia throughout the territories of the Persian Empire. The Assyrian church of the East became theologically separated from the rest of the Christian community following the Council of Ephesus in 431. The Church is headed by the Catholicos Patriarch and is episcopal in government. The liturgical language is Syriac (Aramaic). The Assyrian Church of the East and the Roman Catholic Church agreed a common Christological declaration in 1994 and a process of dialogue between the Assyrian Church of the East and the Chaldean Catholic Church, which is in communion with Rome but shares the Syriac liturgy, was instituted in 1996.

The Church numbers about 400,000 members in the Middle East, India, Europe, North America and Australasia. There are around 600 members in the UK.

The Church in Great Britain forms part of the diocese of Europe under Mar Odisho Oraham.

Representative in Great Britain, Very Revd Younan Y.
    Younan, 66 Montague Road, London W7 3PQ
    T 020-8579 7259

THE INDEPENDENT METHODIST CHURCHES

The Independent Methodist Churches were formed in 1805 and remained independent when the Methodist Church in Great Britain was formed in 1932. They are mainly concentrated in the industrial areas of the north of England.

The churches are Methodist in doctrine but their organisation is congregational. All the churches are members of the Independent Methodist Connexion of Churches. The controlling body of the Connexion is the Annual Meeting, to which churches send delegates. The Connexional President is elected annually. Between annual meetings the affairs of the Connexion are handled by departmental committees. Ministers are appointed by the churches and trained through the Connexion. The ministry is open to both men and women and is unpaid.

There are 2,108 members, 90 ministers and 89 churches in Great Britain.

Connexional President (2003–5), Geoffrey Lomas
General Secretary, W. C. Gabb, 66 Kirkstone Drive,
    Loughborough LE11 3RW T 01942-223526

THE LUTHERAN CHURCH

Lutheranism is based on the teachings of Martin Luther, the German leader of the Protestant Reformation. The authority of the scriptures is held to be supreme over Church tradition. The teachings of Lutheranism are explained in detail in 16th century confessional writings, particularly the Augsburg Confession. Lutheranism is one of the largest Protestant denominations and it is particularly strong in northern Europe and the USA. Some Lutheran churches are episcopal, while others have a synodal form of organisation; unity is based on doctrine rather than structure. Most Lutheran churches are members of the Lutheran World Federation, based in Geneva.

Lutheran services in Great Britain are held in 18 languages to serve members of different nationalities. Services usually follow ancient liturgies. English-language congregations are members either of the Lutheran Church in Great Britain, or of the Evangelical Lutheran Church of England. The Lutheran Church in Great Britain and other Lutheran churches in Britain are members of the Lutheran Council of Great Britain, which represents them and co-ordinates their common work.

There are over 70 million Lutherans world-wide; in Great Britain there are about 100,000 members, 50 clergy and 100 congregations.

General Secretary of the Lutheran Council of Great Britain,
    Revd T. Bruch, 30 Thanet Street, London WC1H 9QH
    T 020-7554 2900 F 020-7383 3081
    E enquiries@lutheran.org.uk W www.lutheran.org.uk

THE METHODIST CHURCH

The Methodist movement started in England in 1729 when the Revd John Wesley, an Anglican priest, and his brother Charles met with others in Oxford and resolved to conduct their lives and study by 'rule and method'. In 1739 the Wesleys began evangelistic preaching and the first Methodist chapel was founded in Bristol in the same year. In 1744 the first annual conference was held, at which the Articles of Religion were drawn up. Doctrinal emphases included repentance, faith, the assurance of salvation, social concern and the priesthood of all believers. After John Wesley's death in 1791 the Methodists withdrew from the established Church to form the Methodist Church. Methodists gradually drifted into many groups, but in 1932 the Wesleyan Methodist Church, the United Methodist Church and the Primitive Methodist Church united to form the Methodist Church in Great Britain as it now exists.

The governing body and supreme authority of the Methodist Church is the Conference, but there are also 33 district synods, consisting of all the ministers and selected lay people in each district, and circuit meetings of the ministers and lay people of each circuit. There are over 60 million Methodists world-wide; in Great Britain in 2001 there were 327,724 members, 3,626 ministers, 9,951 lay preachers and 6,378 churches.

President of the Conference in Great Britain (2004–5), Revd
    W. Morrey
Vice-President of the Conference (2004–5), Deacon M.
    Poxon
Secretary of the Conference, Revd David G. Deeks,
    Methodist Church, 25 Marylebone Road, London NW1 5JR
    T 020-7486 5502 F 020-7467 5226
    E generalsecretary@methodistchurch.org.uk
    W www.methodist.org.uk

THE METHODIST CHURCH IN IRELAND

The Methodist Church in Ireland is autonomous but has close links with British Methodism. It has a community roll of 53,829, 15,800 members, 203 ministers, 287 lay preachers and 223 churches.

President of the Methodist Church in Ireland (2004–5),
    Revd Dr W. Brian Fletcher, 33a Arderlee Avenue, Belfast
    BT9 0AA T 028-9045 1521
Secretary of the Methodist Church in Ireland, Revd W.
    Winston Graham, 1 Fountainville Avenue, Belfast BT9 6AN
    T 028-9032 4554

THE (EASTERN) ORTHODOX CHURCH

The Eastern (or Byzantine) Orthodox Church is a communion of self-governing Christian churches recognising the honorary primacy of the Oecumenical Patriarch of Constantinople.

The position of Orthodox Christians is that the faith was fully defined during the period of the Oecumenical Councils. In doctrine it is strongly trinitarian, and stresses the mystery and importance of the sacraments. It is episcopal in government. The structure of the Orthodox Christian year differs from that of western Churches.

Orthodox Christians throughout the world are estimated to number about 300 million; there are an estimated 284,298 in the UK.

EASTERN ORTHODOX CHURCHES IN THE UK
THE PATRIARCHATE OF ANTIOCH
There are ten parishes served by 15 clergy. In Great Britain the Patriarchate is represented by the Revd Fr Samir Gholam, St George's Cathedral, 1A Redhill Street, London NW1 4BG T 020-7383 0403

THE GREEK ORTHODOX CHURCH (PATRIARCHATE OF CONSTANTINOPLE)
The presence of Greek Orthodox Christians in Britain dates back at least to 1677 when Archbishop Joseph Geogirenes of Samos fled from Turkish persecution and came to London. The present Greek cathedral in Moscow Road, Bayswater, was opened for public worship in 1879 and the Diocese of Thyateira and Great Britain was established in 1922. There are now 121 parishes and other communities (including monasteries) in the UK, served by five bishops, 110 clergy, nine cathedrals and about 93 churches.

In Great Britain the Patriarchate of Constantinople is represented by Archbishop Gregorios of Thyateira and Great Britain, Thyateira House, 5 Craven Hill, London W2 3EN T 020-7723 4787 F 020-7224 9301

THE RUSSIAN ORTHODOX CHURCH (PATRIARCHATE OF MOSCOW) AND THE RUSSIAN ORTHODOX CHURCH OUTSIDE RUSSIA
The records of Russian Orthodox Church activities in Britain date from the visit to England of Tsar Peter I in the early 18th century. Clergy were sent from Russia to serve the chapel established to minister to the staff of the Imperial Russian Embassy in London.

In Great Britain the Patriarchate of Moscow is represented by Bishop Basil of Sergievo, 94a Banbury Road, Oxford OX2 6JT. He is assisted by one bishop and 30 clergy. There are 30 parishes and smaller communities. The Russian Orthodox Church Outside Russia is represented by Archbishop Mark of Berlin, Germany and Great Britain, c/o *Dean of English-Language Parishes*, Very Revd Archimandrite Alexis, Saint Edward Brotherhood, St Cyprian's Avenue, Brookwood, Surrey GU24 0BL T 01483-487763 W www.rocorbritishisles.org.

There are eight communities, including two monasteries in England and one mission in Northern Ireland.

THE SERBIAN ORTHODOX CHURCH (PATRIARCHATE OF SERBIA)
There are 33 parishes and smaller communities in Great Britain served by 11 clergy. The Patriarchate of Serbia is represented by the Episcopal Vicar, the Very Revd Milenko Zebic, 131 Cob Lane, Bournville, Birmingham B30 1QE T 0121-458 5273

OTHER NATIONALITIES
Most of the Ukrainian parishes in Britain have joined the Patriarchate of Constantinople, leaving a small number of Ukrainian parishes in Britain under the care of other patriarchates (not all of which are recognised by the other Orthodox Churches). The Latvian, Polish and some Belarusian parishes are also under the care of the Patriarchate of Constantinople. The Patriarchate of

Romania has one parish served by two clergy. The Patriarchate of Bulgaria has one parish served by one priest. The Belarusian Autocephalous Orthodox Church has five parishes served by two priests.

THE ORIENTAL ORTHODOX CHURCHES
The term 'Oriental Orthodox Churches' is now generally used to describe a group of six ancient eastern churches which reject the Christological definition of the Council of Chalcedon (AD 451) and use Christological terms in different ways from the Eastern Orthodox Church. There are about 34 million members world-wide of the Oriental Orthodox Churches and about 22,020 in the UK.

ORIENTAL ORTHODOX CHURCHES IN THE UK
THE ARMENIAN ORTHODOX CHURCH (PATRIARCHATE OF ETCHMIADZIN)
The Armenian Orthodox Church is the longest-established Oriental Orthodox community in Great Britain. It is represented by the Rt. Revd Bishop Nathan Hovhannisian, Armenian Primate of Great Britain, Armenian Vicarage, Iverna Gardens, London W8 6TP T 020-7937 0152 E armchurchlondon@aol.com

THE COPTIC ORTHODOX CHURCH
The Coptic Orthodox Church is the largest Oriental Orthodox community in Great Britain.

Coptic Orthodox Church, Bishop Angaelos, Coptic Orthodox
  Church Centre, Shephalbury Manor, Broadhall Way,
  Stevenage, Herts SG2 8RH T 01438-748473
  F 01438-313879 E angaelos@copticcentre.com
  W www.copticcentre.com
The British Orthodox Church, Metropolitan Seraphim,
  10 Heathwood Gardens, Charlton, London SE7 8EP
  T 020-8854 3090 E boc@nildram.co.uk
  W www.britishorthodox.org

THE ERITREAN ORTHODOX CHURCH
In Great Britain the Eritrean Orthodox Church is represented by Bishop Markos, 78 Edmund Street, Camberwell, London SE5 7NR

THE MALANKARA ORTHODOX SYRIAN CHURCH
The Malankara Orthodox Syrian Church is part of the Diocese of Europe, UK and Canada under Metropolitan Thomas Mar Makarios. The church in Great Britain can be contacted via Fr Abraham Thomas, St Gregorios Indian Orthodox Church, Cranfield Road, Brockley, London SE4 1UF T 020-8691 9456

THE SYRIAN ORTHODOX CHURCH
The Syrian Orthodox Church in Great Britain comes under the Patriarchal Vicar, whose representative is Fr Touma Hazim Dakkama, Antiochian, 5 Canning Road, Croydon CR0 6QA T 020-8654 7531

THE COUNCIL OF ORIENTAL ORTHODOX CHURCHES, *Secretary*, Deacon Aziz M. A. Nour, 34 Chertsey Road, Church Square, Shepperton, Middlesex TW17 9LF T 020-8368 8447 *President*, Rt. Revd Bishop Nathan Hovhannisian

PENTECOSTAL CHURCHES
Pentecostalism is inspired by the descent of the Holy Spirit upon the apostles at Pentecost. The movement began in Los Angeles, USA, in 1906 and is characterised by baptism with the Holy Spirit, divine healing, speaking in tongues (glossolalia), and a literal interpretation of the scriptures. The Pentecostal movement in Britain dates from 1907. Initially, groups of Pentecostalists were led by

laymen and did not organise formally. However, in 1915 the Elim Foursquare Gospel Alliance (more usually called the Elim Pentecostal Church) was founded in Ireland by George Jeffreys and in 1924 about 70 independent assemblies formed a fellowship, the Assemblies of God in Great Britain and Ireland. The Apostolic Church grew out of the 1904–5 revivals in South Wales and was established in 1916, and the New Testament Church of God was established in England in 1953. In recent years many aspects of Pentecostalism have been adopted by the growing charismatic movement within the Roman Catholic, Protestant and Eastern Orthodox churches. There are about 105 million Pentecostalists world-wide, with about 280,260 adherents in Great Britain and Ireland.

THE APOSTOLIC CHURCH, International Administration Offices, PO Box 389, 24–27 St Helens Road, Swansea SA1 1ZH T 01792-473992 *National Leader*, Warren Jones
The Apostolic Church has about 106 churches, 4,481 adherents and 77 ministers

THE ASSEMBLIES OF GOD INCORPORATED, PO Box 7634, Nottingham NG11 6ZY T 0115-921 7272 F 0115-921 7273 E info@aog.org.uk *General Superintendent*, P. C. Weaver
The Assemblies of God has 640 churches, about 60,000 adherents (including children) and 1,039 accredited ministers

THE ELIM PENTECOSTAL CHURCH, PO Box 38, Cheltenham, Glos GL50 3HN T 01242-519904 E info@elimhq.com
General Superintendent, Revd J. J. Glass
The Elim Pentecostal Church has 600 churches, 68,500 adherents and 650 accredited ministers

THE NEW TESTAMENT CHURCH OF GOD, Main House, Overstone Park, Overstone, Northampton NN6 0AD T 01604-643311 *National Overseer*, Bishop Eric Arthur Brown
The New Testament Church of God has about 120 organised congregations, about 21,540 members and 280 accredited ministers

PLYMOUTH BRETHREN

The Brethren was founded in Dublin in 1827–28. It rejected denominationalism and clericalism and based itself on the structures and practices of the early Church. Many groups sprang up and that at Plymouth became the best known, which resulted in the designation by others as Plymouth Brethren. Other groups are based in Ireland, USA, Burma and Guyana.

Early worship had a prescribed form but quickly assumed an unstructured, non-liturgical format. There were services devoted to worship, usually involving the breaking of bread, and separate preaching meetings. There was no salaried ministry.

A theological dispute led in 1848 to schism between the Open Brethren and the Closed or Exclusive Brethren, each branch later suffering further divisions.

Open Brethren churches are completely independent, but freely co-operate with each other. Churches are run by appointed elders. Exclusive Brethren churches believe in a universal fellowship between congregations. They do not have elders, but appoint respected members of their congregation to perform certain administrative functions.

The Brethren are established throughout the UK, Ireland, Europe, India, Africa and Australasia. Total membership in the UK is 80,210.

GOSPEL TRACT PUBLICATIONS, 7 Beech Avenue, Dumbreck, Glasgow G41 5BY T 0141-427 4661

CHAPTER TWO, Fountain House, Conduit Mews, London SE18 7AP T 020-8316 5389

THE PRESBYTERIAN CHURCH IN IRELAND

The Presbyterian Church in Ireland is Calvinistic in doctrine and presbyterian in constitution. Presbyterianism was established in Ireland as a result of the Ulster plantation in the early 17th century, when English and Scottish Protestants settled in the north of Ireland.

There are 21 presbyteries and five regional synods under the chief court known as the General Assembly. The General Assembly meets annually and is presided over by a Moderator who is elected for one year. The ongoing work of the Church is undertaken by 18 boards under which there are a number of specialist committees.

There are about 179,549 Presbyterians in Ireland, mainly in the north, in 460 congregations and with 370 ministers.

Moderator (2004–5), Rt. Revd Ken Newell
Clerk of Assembly and General Secretary, Revd Dr Donald Watts, Church House, Belfast BT1 6DW T 028-9032 2284

THE PRESBYTERIAN CHURCH OF WALES

The Presbyterian Church of Wales or Calvinistic Methodist Church of Wales is Calvinistic in doctrine and presbyterian in constitution. It was formed in 1811 when Welsh Calvinists severed the relationship with the established church by ordaining their own ministers. It secured its own confession of faith in 1823 and a Constitutional Deed in 1826, and since 1864 the General Assembly has met annually, presided over by a Moderator elected for a year. The doctrine and constitutional structure of the Presbyterian Church of Wales was confirmed by Act of Parliament in 1931–2.

The Church has about 31,970 members, 93 ministers and 762 churches.

Moderator (2004–5), Revd W. G. Edwards
General Secretary, Revd Ifan Roberts, Tabernacle Chapel, 81 Merthyr Road, Whitchurch, Cardiff CF14 1DD T 029-2062 7465

THE RELIGIOUS SOCIETY OF FRIENDS (QUAKERS)

Quakerism is a movement, not a church, which was founded in the 17th century by George Fox and others in an attempt to revive what they saw as 'primitive Christianity'. The movement was based originally in the Midlands, Yorkshire and north-west England, but there are now Quakers in 36 countries around the world. The colony of Pennsylvania, founded by William Penn, was originally Quaker.

Emphasis is placed on the experience of God in daily life rather than on sacraments or religious occasions. There is no church calendar. Worship is largely silent and there are no appointed ministers; the responsibility for conducting a meeting is shared equally among those present. Social reform and religious tolerance have always been important to Quakers, together with a commitment to non-violence in resolving disputes.

There are 213,800 Quakers world-wide, with over 16,000 in Great Britain and Ireland. There are about 500 meetings in Great Britain.

CENTRAL OFFICES: (GREAT BRITAIN) Friends House, 173–177 Euston Road, London NW1 2BJ T 020-7663 1000 F 020-7663 1001 W www.quaker.org.uk

THE SALVATION ARMY

The Salvation Army was founded by a Methodist minister, William Booth, in the east end of London in 1865, and has since become established in 108 countries worldwide. In 1878 it adopted a quasi-military command structure intended to inspire and regulate its endeavours and to reflect its view that the Church was engaged in spiritual warfare. Salvationists emphasise evangelism and the provision of social welfare. World-wide there are about 26,000 active officers (full-time ordained ministers) and 15,500 worship centres and outposts. In Great Britain and Ireland there are 45,000 members, 1,400 active officers and 800 worship centres.

International Leader, Gen. John Larsson
UK Leader, Commissioner Alex Hughes
TERRITORIAL HEADQUARTERS, 101 Newington Causeway, London SE1 6BN T 020-7367 4500
E thq@salvationarmy.org.uk
W www.salvationarmy.org.uk

THE SEVENTH-DAY ADVENTIST CHURCH

The Seventh-day Adventist Church was founded in 1863 in the USA and the first church in the UK was established in 1886. Its members look forward to the second coming of Christ and observe the Sabbath (the seventh day) as a day of rest, worship and ministry. The Church bases its faith and practice wholly on the Bible and has developed 27 core beliefs. The World Church is divided into 13 divisions, each made up of unions of churches. The Seventh-day Adventist Church in the British Isles is known as the British Union Conference of Seventh-day Adventists and is a member of the Trans-European Division. In the British Isles the administrative organisation of the church is arranged in three tiers: the local churches; the regional conferences for south England, north England, Wales, Scotland and Ireland; and the national headquarters. There are over 12 million members and 53,500 churches in 203 countries. In the UK and Ireland there are 22,205 members and 249 churches.

President of the British Union Conference, Cecil Perry
BRITISH ISLES HEADQUARTERS, Stanborough Park, Watford WD25 9JZ T 01923-672251

THE (SWEDENBORGIAN) NEW CHURCH

The New Church is based on the teachings of the 18th century Swedish scientist and theologian Emanuel Swedenborg (1688–1772), who believed that Jesus Christ appeared to him and instructed him to reveal the spiritual meaning of the Bible. He claimed to have visions of the spiritual world, including heaven and hell, and conversations with angels and spirits. He published several theological works, including descriptions of the spiritual world and a Bible commentary.

The Second Coming of Jesus Christ is believed to have already taken place and is still taking place, being not an actual physical reappearance of Christ, but rather His return in spirit. It is also believed that concurrent with our life on earth is life in a parallel spiritual world, of which we are usually unconscious until death. There are around 30,000 Swedenborgians world-wide, with 1,130 members, 27 Churches and 10 ministers in the UK.
THE GENERAL CONFERENCE OF THE NEW CHURCH, Swedenborg House, 20 Bloomsbury Way, London WC1A 2TH T 020-7229 9340

UNDEB YR ANNIBYNWYR CYMRAEG

Undeb Yr Annibynwyr Cyraeg, the Union of Welsh Independents was formed in 1872 and is a voluntary association of Welsh Congregational Churches and personal members. It is mainly Welsh-speaking. Congregationalism in Wales dates back to 1639 when the first Welsh Congregational Church was opened in Gwent. Member churches are Calvinistic in doctrine, although a wide range of interpretations are permitted, and congregationalist in organisation. Each church has complete independence in the government and administration of its affairs.

The Union has 32,500 members, 220 ministers and 500 member churches.
President of the Union (2004–5), Dr Hefin Jones
General Secretary, Revd D. Myrddin Hughes, Ty John Penry, 11 Heol Sant Helen, Swansea SA1 4AL T 01792-652542
F 01792-650647

THE UNITED REFORM CHURCH

The United Reformed Church was first formed by the union of most of the Congregational churches in England and Wales with the Presbyterian Church of England in 1972. Congregationalism dates from the mid 16th century. It is Calvinistic in doctrine, and its followers form independent self-governing congregations bound under God by covenant, a principle laid down in the writings of Robert Browne (1550–1633). From the late 16th century the movement was driven underground by persecution, but the cause was defended at the Westminster Assembly in 1643 and the Savoy Declaration of 1658 laid down its principles. Congregational churches formed county associations for mutual support and in 1832 these associations merged to form the Congregational Union of England and Wales.

Presbyterianism in England also dates from the mid 16th century, and was Calvinistic and evangelical in its doctrine. It was governed by a hierarchy of courts.

In the 1960s there was close co-operation locally and nationally between Congregational and Presbyterian Churches. This led to union negotiations and a Scheme of Union, supported by Act of Parliament in 1972. In 1981 a further unification took place, with the Reformed Association of Churches of Christ becoming part of the URC. In 2000 a third union took place, with the Congregational Union of Scotland. In its basis the United Reformed Church reflects local church initiative and responsibility with a conciliar pattern of oversight. The General Assembly is the central body, and is made up of equal numbers of ministers and lay members.

The United Reformed Church is divided into 13 Synods, each with a Synod Moderator, and 78 Districts. There are 87,732 members, 628 full-time stipendiary ministers, 83 part-time stipendiary ministers, 173 non-stipendiary ministers, 16 active church related community workers and 1,719 local churches.
General Secretary, Revd Dr David C. Cornick, 86 Tavistock Place, London WC1H 9RT T 020-7916 2020 F 7916 2021
E david.cornick@urc.org.uk

THE WESLEYAN REFORM UNION

The Wesleyan Reform Union was founded by Methodists who left or were expelled from Wesleyan Methodism in 1849 following a period of internal conflict. Its doctrine is conservative evangelical and its organisation is congregational, each church having complete independence in the government and administration of its affairs. The Union has 1,947 members, 17 ministers, 131 lay preachers and 108 churches.

President (2004–5), Revd R. Brindley
General Secretary, Revd A. J. Williams, Wesleyan Reform
Church House, 123 Queen Street, Sheffield S1 2DU
T 0114-272 1938

NON-TRINITARIAN CHURCHES

CHRISTADELPHIANISM
Christadelphians believe that the Bible is the word of God and that it reveals both God's dealing with mankind in the past and his plans for the future. These plans centre on the work of Jesus Christ, who is believed shortly to return to earth to establish God's kingdom. Christadelphians have existed since the 1850s, beginning in the USA through the work of an Englishman, Dr John Thomas.
THE CHRISTADELPHIANISM MAGAZINE AND
   PUBLISHING ASSOCIATION, 404 Shaftmoor Lane,
   Birmingham B28 8SZ T 0121-777 6324 F 0121-778 5024

THE CHURCH OF CHRIST, SCIENTIST
The Church of Christ, Scientist was founded by Mary Baker Eddy in the USA in 1879 to 'reinstate primitive Christianity and its lost element of healing'. Christian Science teaches the need for spiritual regeneration and salvation from sin, but is best known for its reliance on prayer alone in the healing of sickness. Adherents believe that such healing is a law, or Science, and is in direct line with that practised by Jesus Christ (revered, not as God, but as the Son of God) and by the early Christian Church.

The denomination consists of The First Church of Christ, Scientist, in Boston, Massachusetts, USA (the Mother Church) and its branch churches in over 80 countries world-wide. The Bible and Mary Baker Eddy's book, *Science and Health with Key to the Scriptures*, are used at services; there are no clergy. Those engaged in full-time healing are called practitioners, of whom there are 3,500 world-wide.

No membership figures are available, since Mary Baker Eddy felt that numbers are no measure of spiritual vitality and ruled that such statistics should not be published. There are over 2,000 branch churches world-wide, including nearly 120 in the UK.
CHRISTIAN SCIENCE COMMITTEE ON PUBLICATION,
   Claridge House, 29 Barnes High Street, London SW13 9LW
   T 020-8282 1645 F 020-8487 1566 E londoncs@csps.com
District Manager for the UK and the Republic of Ireland,
   Tony Lobl

THE CHURCH OF JESUS CHRIST OF LATTER-DAY SAINTS
The Church (often referred to as 'the Mormons') was founded in New York State, USA, in 1830, and came to Britain in 1837. The oldest continuous branch in the world is to be found in Preston, Lancs. Mormons are Christians who claim to belong to the 'Restored Church' of Jesus Christ. They believe that true Christianity died when the last original apostle died, but that it was given back to the world by God and Christ through Joseph Smith, the Church's founder and first president. They accept and use the Bible as scripture, but believe in continuing revelation from God and use additional scriptures, including *The Book of Mormon: Another Testament of Jesus Christ*. The importance of the family is central to the Church's beliefs and practices. Church members set aside Monday evenings as Family Home Evenings when Christian family values are taught. Polygamy was formally discontinued in 1890. The

Church has no paid ministry; local congregations are headed by a leader chosen from amongst their number. The world governing body, based in Utah, USA, is the three-man First Presidency, assisted by the Quorum of the Twelve Apostles. There are more than 11 million members world-wide, with about 178,000 adherents in Britain in 371 congregations.
BRITISH HEADQUARTERS, Church Offices, 751 Warwick
   Road, Solihull, W. Midlands B91 3DQ T 0121-712 1207

JEHOVAH'S WITNESS
The movement now known as Jehovah's Witnesses grew from a Bible study group formed by Charles Taze Russell in 1872 in Pennsylvania, USA. In 1896 it adopted the name of the Watch Tower Bible and Tract Society, and in 1931 its members became known as Jehovah's Witnesses. Jehovah's (God's) Witnesses believe in the Bible as the word of God, and consider it to be inspired and historically accurate. They take the scriptures literally, except where there are obvious indications that they are figurative or symbolic, and reject the doctrine of the Trinity. Witnesses also believe that the earth will remain for ever and that all those approved of by Jehovah will have eternal life on a cleansed and beautified earth; only 144,000 will go to heaven to rule with Christ. They believe that the second coming of Christ began in 1914 and his thousand-year reign on earth is imminent, and that Armageddon (a final battle in which evil will be defeated) will precede Christ's rule of peace. They refuse to take part in military service, and do not accept blood transfusions. The 10-member world governing body is based in New York, USA. There is no paid ministry, but each congregation has elders assigned to look after various duties and every Witness is assigned homes to visit in their congregation. There are over 6 million Jehovah's Witnesses world-wide, with 130,000 Witnesses in the UK organised into over 1,400 congregations.
BRITISH ISLES HEADQUARTERS, Watch Tower House, The
   Ridgeway, London NW7 1RN T 020-8906 2211
   F 020-8371 0051 E pr@wtbts.org.uk
   W www.watchtower.org

UNITARIAN AND FREE CHRISTIAN CHURCHES
Unitarianism has its historical roots in the Judaeo-Christian tradition but rejects the deity of Christ and the doctrine of the trinity. It allows the individual to embrace insights from all the world's faiths and philosophies, as there is no fixed creed. It is accepted that beliefs may evolve in the light of personal experience.

Unitarian communities first became established in Poland and Transylvania in the 16th century. The first avowedly Unitarian place of worship in the British Isles opened in London in 1774. The General Assembly of Unitarian and Free Christian Churches came into existence in 1928 as the result of the amalgamation of two earlier organisations.

There are about 4,400 Unitarians in Great Britain and Ireland and about 72 Unitarian ministers. Nearly 200 self-governing congregations and fellowship groups, including a small number overseas, are members of the General Assembly.
GENERAL ASSEMBLY OF UNITARIAN AND FREE
   CHRISTIAN CHURCHES, Essex Hall, 1–6 Essex Street,
   London WC2R 3HY T 020-7240 2384 F 020-7240 3089
   E ga@unitarian.org.uk W www.unitarian.org.uk
President 2004–5, Dawn Buckle

COMMUNICATIONS

POSTAL SERVICES

The Royal Mail Group plc operates Parcelforce, Post Office and Royal Mail, which handles over 82 million items of mail each day. The Postal Services Commission (Postcomm), an independent regulator accountable to parliament, oversees postal operations in the UK and is tasked with the gradual introduction of competition into postal services.

POSTCOMM, 6 Hercules Road, London SE1 7DB
T 020-7593 2100 W www.postcomm.gov.uk
POSTWATCH, 28 Grosvenor Gardens, London SW1W 0TT
T 08456-013265 E info@postwatch.co.uk

Postwatch is the consumer organisation responsible for postal services and takes up complaints on behalf of consumers against any licensed provider of postal services. Below are details of a number of popular postal services along with prices correct as at July 2004. For further details please contact the relevant service provider, i.e. Royal Mail or Parcelforce.

INLAND POSTAL SERVICES AND REGULATIONS

INLAND LETTER POST RATES

Weight up to	1st class	2nd class†
60g	£0.28	£0.21
100g	£0.42	£0.35
150g	£0.60	£0.47
200g	£0.75	£0.58
250g	£0.88	£0.71
300g	£1.01	£0.83
350g	£1.15	£0.94
400g	£1.33	£1.14
450g	£1.50	£1.30
500g	£1.68	£1.48
600g	£2.03	£1.75
700g	£2.38	£2.00
750g	£2.55	£2.12
800g	£2.73	(not
900g	£3.10	admissible
1kg	£3.45	over 750 g)

Costs for first class items over 1kg are £3.45 and then £0.89 for each extra 250g or part thereof.
*Postcards travel at the same rates as letter post
† First class letters are normally delivered the following day and second class post within three days

UK PARCEL RATES

Standard Tariff
Weight up to

1kg	£3.46
1.5kg	£4.45
2kg	£4.78
4kg	£7.20
6kg	£7.86
8kg	£8.96
10kg	£9.62

OVERSEAS POSTAL SERVICES AND REGULATIONS

Royal Mail divides the world into three zones: **Europe** (Albania, Andorra, Armenia, Austria, Azerbaijan, Azores, Balearic Islands, Belarus, Belgium, Bosnia-Hercegovina, Bulgaria, Canary Islands, Corsica, Croatia, Cyprus, Czech Republic, Denmark, Estonia, Faroe Islands, Finland, France, Georgia, Germany, Gibraltar, Greece, Greenland, Hungary, Iceland, Ireland, Italy, Kazakhstan, Kyrgystan, Latvia, Liechtenstein, Lithuania, Luxembourg, Macedonia, Madeira, Malta, Modova, Monaco, Netherlands, Norway, Poland, Portugal, Romania, Russia, San Marino, Serbia and Montenegro, Slovakia, Slovenia, Spain, Spitzbergen, Sweden, Switzerland, Tajikistan, Turkey, Turkmenistan, Ukraine, Uzbekistan, Vatican City State); **Zone 1** (USA, Canada, South America, the Middle East, Africa, parts of Asia and the Indian sub-continent, most of south east Asia and Hong Kong); **Zone 2** (American Samoa, Australia, China, East Timor, Fiji, French Southern and Antarctic Territories, French Polynesia, Guam, Japan, Kiribati, Korea, Marshall Islands, Micronesia, Mongolia, Nauru, New Caledonia, New Zealand & Territories, Norfolk Island, North Mariana Island, Palau, Papua New Guinea, Philippines, Pitcairn Islands, Samoa, Solomon Islands, Taiwan, Tonga, Tuvalu, Vanuatu, Wake Island, Wallis and Futuna Island, Western Samoa).

OVERSEAS SURFACE MAIL RATES (WORLD ZONES 1 & 2)

Letters

Weight not over		Weight not over	
20g*	£0.39	450g	£3.52
60g	£0.66	500g	£3.89
100g	£0.93	750g	£5.74
150g	£1.30	1,000g	£7.59
200g	£1.67	1,250g	£9.44
250g	£2.04	1,500g	£11.29
300g	£2.41	1,750g	£13.14
350g	£2.78	2,000g	£14.99
400g	£3.15		

* Including postcards

AIRMAIL LETTER RATES

Europe: Letters

Weight not over		Weight not over	
20g	£0.40	280g	£2.54
40g	£0.57	300g	£2.70
60g	£0.74	320g	£2.86
80g	£0.91	340g	£3.02
100g	£1.08	360g	£3.18
120g	£1.25	380g	£3.34
140g	£1.42	400g	£3.50
160g	£1.58	420g	£3.66
180g	£1.74	440g	£3.82
200g	£1.90	460g	£3.98
220g	£2.06	480g	£4.14
240g	£2.22	500g	£4.30
260g	£2.38	1,000g	£8.30
		*2,000g	£16.30

* Max. 2kg

Zones 1 & 2: Letters

Postcards	Not over 10g	Not over 20g	Over 20g
43p	47p	68p	price varies

SPECIAL DELIVERY SERVICES

ROYAL MAIL SPECIAL DELIVERY

A guaranteed next working day delivery service by noon to most UK destinations for first class letters and packets. Prices start at £3.75. There is also a service which guarantees delivery by 9 a.m. Prices start at £6.95. Compensation of up to £2,500 is available for lost or damaged items.

INTERNATIONAL SIGNED FOR AND AIRSURE

Express airmail services. The fee for International Signed For is £3.30 plus airmail postage. The fee for Airsure is £4.00 plus airmail postage.

RECORDED MAIL (SIGNED FOR)

Provides a record of posting and delivery of letters and ensures a signature on delivery. This service is recommended for items of little or no monetary value. All packets must be handed to the post office and a certificate of posting issued. Charges: 65p plus the standard first or second class postage.

OTHER SERVICES

BUSINESS SERVICES

A range of postal services are available to businesses including business collection, freepost, business reply services, business packaging for special deliveries and international mailing options.

COMPENSATION

Compensation for loss or damage to an item sent varies according to the service used to send the item. Royal Mail does not accept responsibility for loss or damage arising from faulty packing.

PASSPORT APPLICATIONS

Around 2,000 post offices process passport applications. To find out your nearest office, and for further information, *see* contact details below.

TRACK AND TRACE

This service enables customers to track the progress of items sent using selected delivery services. *See* below for contact details.

REDIRECTION

A printed form obtainable from the Post Office must be signed by the person to whom the letters are to be addressed. A fee is payable for each different surname on the application form. Charges: 1 month, £6.55 (abroad via airmail, £13.15); 3 months, £14.30 (£28.60); 6 months, £22.00 (£44.05); 12 months, £33.00 (£66.05).

INTERNATIONAL PREPAID PRODUCTS

Prepaid products are a secure way of packaging items that are to be sent overseas. There are a number of different types of prepaid products to choose from, depending on the weight of the article to be sent, ranging in price up to £6.99.

KEEPSAFE

Mail is held for up to two months while the addressee is away and is delivered when the addressee returns. Prices start at £5.25. Perishable items are returned to the sender. Recorded items are held for a week and Special Delivery items are held for three weeks before being returned to the sender.

POST OFFICE BOX

A PO Box provides a short and easy-to-remember alternative address. Mail is held at a local delivery office until the addressee is ready to collect it. Prices start at £43.00.

SMALL PACKETS AND PRINTED PAPERS (INTERNATIONAL)

Weight not over		Weight not over	
100g	£0.64	450g	£2.11
150g	£0.85	500g	£2.32
200g	£1.06	750g	£3.37
250g	£1.27	1,000g	£4.42
300g	£1.48	1,500g	£6.52
350g	£1.69	2,000g	£8.62
400g	£1.90		

CONTACT DETAILS

Royal Mail general enquiries: T 08457-740740
Royal Mail business enquiries: T 08457-950950
Postcode enquiry line: T 08457-111222 **or** 0906-302 1222
Online shop: T 08457-641641
Parcelforce Worldwide: T 08708-501150
Post Office enquires: T 08457-223344
Track and Trace: T 08457-001200
W www.royalmail.com

IDD CODES

INTERNATIONAL DIRECT DIALLING (IDD)

International dialling codes are composed of four elements which are dialled in sequence:

(i)   the international code
(ii)   the country code
(iii)   the area code
(iv)   the telephone number

Calls to some countries must be made via the international operator.

*Can vary depending on area and/or carrier

Country	IDD from UK	IDD to UK
Afghanistan	00 93	00 44
Albania	00 355	00 44
Algeria	00 213	00 44
Andorra	00 376	00 44
Angola	00 244	00 44
Anguilla	00 1 264	11 44
Antigua and Barbuda	00 1 268	011 44
Argentina	00 54	00 44
Armenia	00 374	810 44
Aruba	00 297	00 44
Ascension Island	00 247	00 44
Australia	00 61	00 11 44
Austria	00 43	00 44
Azerbaijan	00 994	810 44
Azores	00 351	00 44
Bahamas	00 1 242	11 44
Bahrain	00 973	0 44
Bangladesh	00 880	00 44
Barbados	00 1 246	11 44
Belarus	00 375	810 44
Belgium	00 32	00 44
Belize	00 501	00 44
Benin	00 229	00 44
Bermuda	00 1 441	11 44
Bhutan	00 975	00 44
Bolivia	00 591	00 44
Bosnia-Hercegovina		
Muslim-Croat		
Federation	00 387	00 44
Republika Srpska	00 381	00 44
Botswana	00 267	00 44
Brazil	00 55	00 44
British Virgin Islands	00 1 284	11 44
Brunei	00 673	00 44
Bulgaria	00 359	00 44
Burkina Faso	00 226	00 44
Burundi	00 257	90 44
Cambodia	00 855	00 44
Cameroon	00 237	00 44
Canada	00 1	011 44
Canary Islands	00 34	00 44
Cape Verde	00 238	0 44
Cayman Islands	00 1 345	11 44
Central African		
Republic	00 236	19 44
Chad	00 235	15 44
Chile	00 56	00 44
China	00 86	00 44
Hong Kong	00 852	1 44
Macao	00 853	00 44
Colombia	00 57	9 44

Country	IDD from UK	IDD to UK
Comoros	00 269	00 44
Congo, Dem. Rep. of	00 243	00 44
Congo, Republic of	00 242	00 44
Cook Islands	00 682	00 44
Costa Rica	00 506	00 44
Côte d'Ivoire	00 225	00 44
Croatia	00 385	00 44
Cuba	00 53	119 44
Cyprus	00 357	00 44
Czech Republic	00 420	00 44
Denmark	00 45	00 44
Djibouti	00 253	00 44
Dominica	00 1 767	11 44
Dominican Republic	00 1 809	11 44
East Timor	00 670	00 44
Ecuador	00 593	00 44
Egypt	00 20	00 44
El Salvador	00 503	0 44
Equatorial Guinea	00 240	00 44
Eritrea	00 291	00 44
Estonia	00 372	800 44
Ethiopia	00 251	00 44
Falkland Islands	00 500	0 44
Faroe Islands	00 298	9 44
Fiji	00 679	5 44
Finland	00 358	00 44*
France	00 33	00 44
French Guiana	00 594	00 44
French Polynesia	00 689	00 44
Gabon	00 241	00 44
Gambia	00 220	00 44
Georgia	00 995	810 44
Germany	00 49	00 44
Ghana	00 233	00 44
Gibraltar	00 350	00 44
Greece	00 30	00 44
Greenland	00 299	99 44
Grenada	00 1 473	11 44
Guadeloupe	00 590	00 44
Guam	00 1 671	1 44
Guatemala	00 502	00 44
Guinea	00 224	00 44
Guinea-Bissau	00 245	99 44
Guyana	00 592	1 44
Haiti	00 509	00 44
Honduras	00 504	00 44
Hungary	00 36	00 44
Iceland	00 354	00 44
India	00 91	00 44
Indonesia	00 61	008 44*
Iran	00 98	00 44
Iraq	00 964	00 44
Ireland, Republic of	00 353	00 44
Israel	00 972	00 44*
Italy	00 39	00 44
Jamaica	00 1 876	11 44
Japan	00 81	001 44*
		0041 44*
		0061 44*
Jordan	00 962	00 44*
Kazakhstan	00 7	810 44
Kenya	00 254	00 44
Kiribati	00 686	00 44
Korea, North	00 850	00 44
Korea, South	00 82	001 44*
Kuwait	00 965	00 44
Kyrgyzstan	00 996	00 44

Country	IDD from UK	IDD to UK	Country	IDD from UK	IDD to UK
Laos	00 856	00 44	Romania	00 40	00 44
Latvia	00 371	00 44	Russia	00 7	810 44
Lebanon	00 961	00 44	Rwanda	00 250	00 44
Lesotho	00 266	00 44	St Christopher and Nevis	00 1 869	11 44
Liberia	00 231	00 44	St Helena	00 290	00 44
Libya	00 218	00 44	St Lucia	00 1 758	11 44
Liechtenstein	00 423	00 44	St Pierre and Miquelon	00 508	00 44
Lithuania	00 370	810 44	St Vincent and the		
Luxembourg	00 352	00 44	Grenadines	00 1 784	1 44
Macedonia	00 389	99 44	Samoa	00 685	0 44
Madagascar	00 261	00 44	Samoa, American	00 684	00 44
Madeira	00 351	00 44*	San Marino	00 378	00 44
Malawi	00 265	00 44	Sao Tomé and Principe	00 239	00 44
Malaysia	00 60	00 44	Saudi Arabia	00 966	00 44
Maldives	00 960	00 44	Senegal	00 221	00 44
Mali	00 223	00 44	Serbia & Montenegro	00 381	99 44
Malta	00 356	00 44	Seychelles	00 248	00 44
Mariana Islands,			Sierra Leone	00 232	00 44
Northern	00 1 670	11 44	Singapore	00 65	1 44
Marshall Islands	00 692	11 44	Slovakia	00 421	00 44
Martinique	00 596	00 44	Slovenia	00 386	00 44
Mauritania	00 222	00 44	Solomon Islands	00 677	00 44
Mauritius	00 230	00 44	Somalia	00 252	16 44
Mayotte	00 269	10 44	South Africa	00 27	09 44
Mexico	00 52	98 44	Spain	00 34	00 44
Micronesia, Federated	00 691	11 44	Sri Lanka	00 94	00 44
States of			Sudan	00 249	00 44
Moldova	00 373	810 44	Suriname	00 597	00 44
Monaco	00 377	00 44	Swaziland	00 268	00 44
Mongolia	00 976	00 44	Sweden	00 46	00 44
Montenegro	00 381	99 44	Switzerland	00 41	00 44
Montserrat	00 1 664	11 44	Syria	00 963	00 44
Morocco	00 212	00 44	Taiwan	00 886	2 44
Mozambique	00 258	00 44	Tajikistan	00 992	810 44
Myanmar	00 95	00 44	Tanzania	00 255	00 44
Namibia	00 264	00 44	Thailand	00 66	1 44
Nauru	00 674	00 44	Tibet	00 86	00 44
Nepal	00 977	00 44	Togo	00 228	00 44
Netherlands	00 31	00 44	Tonga	00 676	00 44
Netherlands Antilles	00 599	00 44	Trinidad and Tobago	00 1 868	11 44
New Caledonia	00 687	00 44	Tunisia	00 216	00 44
New Zealand	00 64	00 44	Turkey	00 90	00 44
Nicaragua	00 505	00 44	Turkmenistan	00 993	810 44
Niger	00 227	00 44	Turks and Caicos Islands	00 1 649	00 44
Nigeria	00 234	9 44	Tuvalu	00 688	00 44
Niue	00 683	00 44	Uganda	00 256	00 44
Norfolk Island	00 672	101 44	Ukraine	00 380	810 44
Norway	00 47	00 44	United Arab Emirates	00 971	00 44
Oman	00 968	00 44	Uruguay	00 598	00 44
Pakistan	00 92	00 44	USA	00 1	011 44
Palau	00 680	011 44	Alaska	00 1 907	011 44
Panama	00 507	00 44	Hawaii	00 1 808	011 44
Papua New Guinea	00 675	5 44	Uzbekistan	00 998	810 44
Paraguay	00 595	002 44	Vanuatu	00 678	00 44
Peru	00 51	00 44	Vatican City State	00 390 66982	00 44
Philippines	00 63	00 44	Venezuela	00 58	00 44
Poland	00 48	00 44	Vietnam	00 84	00 44
Portugal	00 351	00 44	Virgin Islands (US)	00 1 340	11 44
Puerto Rico	00 1 787	11 44	Yemen	00 967	00 44
Qatar	00 974	00 44	Zambia	00 260	00 44
Réunion	00 262	00 44	Zimbabwe	00 263	00 44

MOBILE COMMUNICATIONS

CURRENT NETWORK OPERATOR MARKET SHARES

January 2004	O_2	Vodafone	T-Mobile	Orange	Hutchison
Current Subscriber Base	10,897,740	16,773,480	9,190,260	13,358,520	n/a
Total Market Share	21.7%	33.4%	18.3%	26.6%	n/a

5-YEAR SUBSCRIBER GROWTH

Date	Jan 1999	Jan 2000	Jan 2001	Jan 2002	Jan 2003	Jan 2004
Subscriber Base	13,001,000	23,944,000	40,057,300	45,677,600	46,922,000	50,220,000
Penetration Rate	22.3%	41%	67.2%	76.6%	78.8%	84.4%

The UK mobile communications industry is continuing to be dominated by the introduction of new technologies. This has led to an increasing emphasis on expanding the traditional mobile operator services as well as encouraging consumer use of more expensive handset devices. The push towards new technology and enhanced service offerings is due to the near to saturation point of the mobile market and the need to increase revenues through other means. The combination of fewer 'new' customers, heavy licence fees for mobile Network Operators, the government having sold the 3G operating licences at a great profit and the costs associated with technology upgrades have left the Network Operators with financial holes to fill.

INDUSTRY PLAYERS

The mobile communications industry has a number of players: Network Operators who own the infrastructure and provide services; Service Providers and MVNOs who do not own infrastructure but have commercial agreements with the Network Operators; and the Regulator, who is responsible for setting the controls of the mobile market, implementing EU-wide legislation and ensuring that industry players do not behave anti-competitively.

NETWORK OPERATORS
Competition was introduced into the UK's mobile market at an early stage. Until recently there were only four network operators rolling out their mobile networks and actively offering mobile services. A fifth, Hutchison 3G, was launched in March 2003. The licensed Network Operators in the UK are detailed in the table below. Network Operators are responsible for setting tariffs, billing, offering services and maintaining the network infrastructure.

UK MOBILE NETWORK OPERATORS

Operator	Ownership	Licence	Launch Date
O_2	Formerly BT Cellnet	Tacs-900	January 1985
	100% O_2	GSM	January 1994
Vodafone	100% Vodafone	Tacs-900	January 1985
		GSM	July 1992
T-Mobile	Formerly One2One	GSM 1800	September 1993
	100% – Deutsche Telekom		
Orange	100% – France Telecom	GSM 1800	April 1994
Hutchison 3G	65% – Hutchison Whampoa	UMTS	March 2003
	20% – DoCoMo		
	15% – KPN Mobile		

ALTERNATIVE SERVICE PROVIDERS
Service Providers were introduced into the UK market from its inception as a means to stimulate competition. Service Providers buy airtime wholesale from the Network Operators and sell it on to end users. This agreement means that they can set their own tariff structures and have a direct billing relationship with customers. O_2 and Vodafone have an obligation under the terms of their licences to offer wholesale minutes of airtime to Service Providers while Orange and T-Mobile have not been subject to this condition. There are said to be around 50 Service Providers operating in the UK market and in order to maintain a viable business operation many of these have diversified their product offering away from pure mobile services to other telecommunication or Internet based services.

The newest players in the mobile market offering mobile services are MVNOs, Mobile Virtual Network Operators. Whereas a number of the Network Operators are obliged to open their networks to Service Providers, none of the Network Operators are currently obliged to open their networks to MVNOs. That they choose to do so, is purely a commercial agreement between the MVNO and Network Operator.

The main difference between Service Providers and MVNOs is the degree of ownership over the equipment used. A true MVNO has its own mobile network code, issues its own SIM cards (Subscriber Identity Module card – the 'brain' of a handset), operates its own mobile switching centre and has a pricing structure fully independent from the Network Operator. MVNOs include Virgin Mobile and FT Mobile, a joint venture between the Financial Times and the Carphone Warehouse.

TYPES OF MOBILE SERVICE
Network Operators, Service Providers and MVNOs offer two basic types of service, contract and pre-paid (pay-as-you-go). Contracts (generally paid on a monthly basis though fixed to a minimum contract term) mean that the end user pays a fixed subscription fee each month that entitles them to a number of services (for example voicemail, SMS text messaging, downloadable games, access to news and other information updates) and gives them a certain amount of 'free' airtime/access to services each month. Pre-paid subscribers have access to the same services but pay in advance and simply top up their account when it is running low. The introduction of pre-paid services has allowed industry players to target additional consumer segments, in particular the youth market and customers who do not have an acceptable credit rating for a contract service. Pre-paid has proven to be a very popular option as it allows customers to control their spend. For the first half of 2004, the split between pre-paid and contract customers in the UK remained constant at around 68:32.

NETWORK TECHNOLOGY

DEVELOPMENT OF MOBILE INFRASTRUCTURE

The first technology introduced into the UK was an analogue technology called TACS which was adopted in 1985. In 1992 Vodafone launched a new digital GSM network, usually referred to as 2G or second generation. BT Cellnet (now O_2) and two more entrants launched GSM services in the following two years making the UK one of Europe's most competitive markets.

More recently, GSM networks have been modified to enable them to transfer packet-switch data and this technology is known as GPRS (General Packet Radio Service). GPRS is not a completely new network – rather it is an upgrade from the existing GSM infrastructure and is also referred to as 2.5G. The main difference between GSM and GPRS technology is the ability to transmit data as well as voice across the network. This is a result of higher bandwidth and with GPRS.

The industry is still waiting for the fully-fledged delivery of next generation mobile services, 3G or UMTS (Universal Mobile Telecommunications System). The main difference between GPRS and UMTS lies with the capacity of UMTS to offer even faster data transmission speeds, therefore allowing expanded data facilities and access to the internet. Additionally, UMTS has the potential to offer further advantages over GSM/GPRS such as international roaming, whereas at present, despite GSM's widespread presence, other mobile technologies used in other parts of the world are incompatible with GSM handsets, for instance in parts of Asia and in America.

As 3G or UMTS technology is an entirely new network, Network Operators must hold a licence to deploy it. The UK was the third European country to licence 3G operators after Finland and Spain but was the first to auction its licences. Auctions are not new to the European communications industry – many of the second and third entrants to Europe's communications markets had to bid for their licences – but what was spectacular about the UK's 3G auction was the size of the bids. While industry observers had speculated that the auction might reach £4 billion, a total of £22 billion was raised from the sale of the spectrum.

DATA SERVICES

GSM from analogue brought clearer voice quality, while the upgrade from GSM through GPRS to UMTS has brought not only improved voice quality but also new services, primarily data-based services as seen in the table below.

DATA SERVICES MIGRATION PATH

Mobile Infrastructure	Data Services available
GSM (2G)	Phone calls
Speed:	Voice mail
10kb/sec	Receipt of simple email messages
GPRS (2.5G)	Phone calls/fax
Speed:	Voice mail
64–144kb/sec	Receipt and transmission of large emails
	Web browsing
	Navigation/maps
UMTS (3G)	Phone calls/fax
Speed:	Global roaming
144kb–2mb/sec	Receipt and transmission of large emails
	High speed web
	Navigation/maps
	Video-conferencing
	TV Streaming
	Electronic agenda meeting reminder

The provision of improved and new services is crucially important for the industry as it reaches saturation point. In order to maintain revenues, Network Operators have had to change focus from customer acquisition strategies to increasing customer service usage levels, as well as encouraging more frequent handset renewal.

2G & 2.5G DATA SERVICES

To date, the most popular and readily available data service has been SMS (Short Messaging Service). SMS or 'text messaging' allows consumers to send and receive text messages up to 160 characters long on their mobile phones. Due to its simplicity and popularity, particularly among young users, the number of SMS messages being sent has increased dramatically. In 2003 approximately 1.75 billion SMS messages were sent per month compared with 271 million per month in 1999. In the last few years, SMS has helped boost revenues for network operators through integrated use with interactive TV – for example, during Channel 4's *Big Brother* in 2003 over 10m text alerts and 5.5m votes were recorded.

WAP, Wireless Application Protocol, is a software language that allows Internet-style data to be downloaded and viewed on a mobile phone. WAP was billed as 'mobile internet' – that consumers could access content from mobile portals which, like traditional Internet portals, aggregate and display mobile Internet content in an accessible manner. WAP has been generally used by consumers to obtain travel information, sports headlines, financial news and emails. Mobile operators such as Vodafone, Orange, T-Mobile, and O_2 all launched pan-European portals which allowed customers to have very similar – if not the same – services around their different countries of operations. However, WAP mobile portals have been characterised by their poor usability and the limited online experience offered to end-users. Many factors have been responsible for this, including unreliable early handsets, limited content, slow connections, and poor portal navigation.

Many of the factors that made WAP so cumbersome have been largely solved by improved handsets, better content and high-speed infrastructure. Portal navigation remains a problem though, with users routinely expected to make perhaps 20–25 'clicks' on their mobile handset in order to locate content, thus greatly limiting accessibility.

With increased consumer familiarity and accessibility of SMS technology, network operators have re-positioned their service offerings from an emphasis on mobile phones being billed as 'mobile internet' to other new services (sending logos, basic pictures and downloading personal ring-tones) that have proved to be very popular. These types of services are referred to as EMS, Enhanced Messaging Services. In late 2002, Vodafone launched its 'Live!' service which offered mobile users access to multimedia services, including the taking, sending and receiving of photos with an integrated camera, Java games, email, polyphonic ring-tones, chat, SMS and mobile phone calls. Vodafone Live! has been popular with over 2 million customers subscribing to the service in its first year.

Consumers are clearly attracted to enhanced data-services as well as the colour screens, improved quality in sound and more intuitive user interfaces that have been introduced in parallel with operator branded initiatives. Both T-Mobile and O_2 have followed suit by launching similar services called T-Zone and Active respectively.

3G DATA SERVICES

The main difference between UMTS and GPRS/GSM from the customer's viewpoint is the extension of data services that are accessible through one's mobile. All operators have launched 3G style services over their GPRS networks though these services will be further enhanced (for example by the introduction of video messaging) once the move to the 3G network has taken place. Hutchison 3G was the first to launch its highly advertised '3' service which offers video calling, content browsing, interactive games and location based services which took place in March 2003. The uptake of '3' to date has been disappointing, with only 361,000 subscribers by March 2004 compared with an initial target of 1 million.) The slowness of up-take and launch of 3G has been exacerbated by delays in handset availability (leading to high handset prices), network teething problems – including many reports of 'lost' calls, and the reticence by the mobile consumer market to upgrade to a new technology.

Vodafone officially launched its 3G service in the UK at the start of April 2004, though at this stage, the 3G service is accessible only with laptop 3G data cards, not handsets. Vodafone's services are aimed mainly at business users. Currently, the service works in the UK, Sweden, Italy, Spain, the Netherlands, Japan and Portugal. Both T-Mobile and Orange have launched similar initiatives. Vodafone has not yet revealed when 3G services will be made available to mobile phone users.

REGULATION

Until July 2003, the industry was regulated by two government bodies; Oftel, a government department independent of ministerial control, headed by the Director General of Telecommunications; and the Radiocommunications Agency, which was the part of the Department of Trade and Industry (DTI). The greater part of regulatory control was assumed by Oftel; it had authority over licensing procedures, tariffing, interconnection issues (where one operator has access to another's infrastructure), and acted as arbitrator in operator disputes. The Radiocommunications Agency was responsible for radio frequency allocation.

In July 2003, the regulation of the mobile industry changed significantly, with the passing of a Communications Bill in the UK and the implementation of new EU framework for the regulation of electronic communications networks and service providers. The aim of the EU framework is to set out a technology-neutral regime for the regulation of communications companies across the EU. This technology neutral regime is based on EU directives that cover interconnections and access, data protection, universal services, authorisation of electronic communications networks and services and a common regulatory framework.

The Communications Bill in the UK took forward four of the Directives and following its enactment has changed the UK's regulatory structure by creating a new regulatory body for the whole communications industry – Ofcom (the Office of Communications). Ofcom has replaced the existing communications and broadcasting regulators, including Oftel and the Radiocommunications Agency and has a different funding structure to Oftel – while Oftel was funded by licence fees, Ofcom levies administration charges. Ofcom is responsible for furthering the interests of the users of television, radio, telecommunications and wireless communications services.

Key features of the 2003 Communications Act are:

– *The abolition of licensing requirements* – With the removal of licensing requirements, Ofcom has drawn up a set of conditions for providers in the areas of universal service, significant market power, access and privileged supplier obligations – these conditions are effectively regulations but are much more flexible than the previous system
– *The provision for spectrum trading* – Previously, when an operator was awarded a mobile licence, the allocated spectrum could only be used by that named company; under the new Bill, licencees are able to transfer the entitlement to use the spectrum to another player
– *New enforcement provisions for dealing with anti-competitive behaviour* – Ofcom has the power to levy a fine of up to 10 per cent of turnover (or suspend a licence in extreme cases) should a mobile operator breach the conditions of its authorisation instead of having to refer cases to the Competition Authority

CONTACTS

DEPARTMENT OF TRADE AND INDUSTRY (DTI)
1 Victoria Street, London SW1H 0ET
T 020-7215 5000 F 020-7215 2909
W www.dti.gov.uk

OFCOM
Riverside House, 2A Southwark Bridge Road, London SE1 9HA
T 020-7981 3000 F 020-7981 3333 W www.ofcom.org.uk

O_2
260 Bath Road, Slough, Berkshire SL1 4DX
T 01753-565000 F 01753-565010 W www.O2.co.uk

HUTCHISON 3G UK
43 New Bond Street, London W1Y 9HB
T 020-7499 1886 F 020-7491 7266
W www.three.co.uk

ORANGE PLC
50 George Street, London W1U 7DZ
T 020-7984 1600 F 020-7984 1601
W www.orange.co.uk

T-MOBILE
Imperial Place, Maxwell Road, Borehamwood WD6 1EA
T 020-8214 2121 F 020-8214 3601
W www.t-mobile.co.uk

VODAFONE GROUP
The Courtyard, 2–4 London Road, Newbury RG14 1JX
T 01635-33251 F 01635-45713
W www.vodafone.co.uk

INFORMATION TECHNOLOGY

ANCESTRY

The ancestors of the modern computer are the Difference Engine and the Analytical Engine devised by mathematician Charles Babbage. Designed in 1820 to automatically compute mathematical tables, Babbage abandoned construction of his mechanical, clockwork-like Difference Engine in the 1840s for personal and financial reasons. In 1834 he began work on his Analytical Engine. Unlike the Difference Engine, the Analytical Engine was designed as a general-purpose tool with a store to hold information.

Babbage's work relied heavily on mechanics and physical machinery. It was not until the twentieth century invention of the electrical vacuum tube, and then the transistor, that computers became a feasible means to solving problems.

FIRST GENERATION

War has been a significant factor in the development of the computer. In 1943, during World War II, the British and Americans developed electro-mechanical computers. Colossus, a British effort, was specifically developed to crack German coding ciphers, whilst an American effort, Harvard Mark I, was developed as a more general-purpose electro-mechanical programmable computer (partly for atom bomb research). Regarded as early first generation computers, these machines primarily comprised wired circuits and vacuum valves. Punched cards and paper tape were largely employed as the input, output and main storage systems. ENIAC (Electronic Numerical Integrator and Computer) was completed in 1946 at the University of Pennsylvania, USA. Capable of carrying out 100,000 calculations a second, it was remarkable for its day despite weighing thirty tons.

SECOND GENERATION

Similar to light bulbs, valves were prone to failure, requiring tedious checks to resolve problems (ENIAC alone contained 18,000 vacuum valves). In 1947, the transistor was invented. Performing the same role as a vacuum valve but less prone to failure, smaller and more efficient, the transistor allowed smaller 'second generation' computers to be developed throughout the 1950s and early 1960s.

THIRD GENERATION

In 1958 Jack St Claire Kilby produced the first integrated circuit 'microchip'. A microchip is comprised of a large number of transistors and other components bonded to a wafer ('chip') of silicon, interconnected by a surface film of conductive material rather than by wires. By reducing distance between components, savings are made in both size and electricity. In 1963 the first 'third generation' computers based on microchip technology appeared.

FOURTH GENERATION

In 1971 Intel produced the first 'microprocessor' heralding a 'fourth generation' of computers. The Intel 4004 (capable of 60,000 instructions per second) grouped much of the processing functions onto a single microchip. Around the same time, Intel invented the RAM (random access memory) chip which grouped significant amounts of memory onto a single chip. Supercomputers and mainframes, utilising scores of microprocessors, had terrific power in the order of 150 million instructions per second. Developments such as multi-layer circuits, and the use of copper instead of gold in microchips, yielded improvements in size and performance through miniaturisation. The size of the transistor was scaled down from thumb size to far smaller than the thickness of a human hair, allowing for greater density and thus exponentially increasing the total power of the computer.

NEXT GENERATION

Most modern computers are still regarded as 'fourth generation' as they use essentially the same technology, albeit highly miniaturised. The future of computer technology is widely thought to be dependent on the physics of light. Already used extensively in the computer industry for high-speed communications, light offers future possibilities for both calculation and storage.

Gordon Moore, co-founder of Intel, observed in 1965 that the number of transistors per square inch had doubled every 12 months since the inception of the integrated circuit. The pace of development has slowed somewhat. The widely recognised current definition of the so-called 'Moore's Law' is that data density doubles every 18 months and is likely to do so for the next few decades.

PROGRAMMING LANGUAGES

Numerous programming languages have been adopted with the common purpose of devising a program of instructions for computers to follow to achieve a task. The languages are categorised by generation:

1GL or first-generation language is the machine language that the processor chips execute in raw binary form (strings of zeros and ones).

2GL or second-generation language. Assembly language is a human-understandable language insofar as it uses names as well as numbers. An assembler program takes assembly language and turns it into a machine code program. Very common in early systems where resources (speed, storage) were at a premium, it is typically only used today as an output from 3GL and higher systems.

3GL or third-generation language is a 'high-level' programming language typically more readable and concise than assembly language.

4GL or fourth generation language is designed to be closer to natural language than a 3GL language.

5GL or fifth-generation programming uses graphical development environments to create source language to be compiled with a 3GL or 4GL language compiler. Often a mix of generations is used, with a high level language (4 or 5GL) used to produce interface elements and a lower level language used to provide the processing power.

OPERATING SYSTEMS

An operating system (OS) is a set of utility programs that acts as the liaison between the computer user, the hardware (processor unit, memory) and its peripherals (disk, mouse, display, printer, network, etc.) and the program that the user is running (e.g. a word processor). The first computers had no operating system, and each program had to directly control the hardware on its own, adding greatly to the burden of programming. Early operating systems were hardware and manufacturer-specific with assembly language or machine code as the programming language. Each computer model or series tended to have its own specific operating system. UNIX was one of the first operating systems that could be ported (converted) to a variety of system hardware. This ability was enabled largely through the use of the 'C' programming language.

PERSONAL COMPUTER OPERATING SYSTEMS
Since the 1990s, the personal computer world has been dominated by Microsoft Corporation. Although not a significant manufacturer of computer equipment, the Microsoft Corporation has built on its market share secured in the 1980s with MS-DOS to become the market leading operating system provider. Microsoft's MS Windows personal computer operating systems are installed on more computers than any other commercial operating system. Microsoft's main personal computer rival is Apple which was established in the 1970s.

THE INTERNET
Prior to the Internet ('the Net' or 'the Web') computers tended to be connected together by hardware and protocols that were specific to each particular connection. Typically, links were point-to-point (a link had to be directly and physically established between the two computers). In 1969 ARPANET was formed by the US Department of Defence to establish a way for the computer capability of the military to be dispersed so that no one centre was critical to the operation of the network as a whole. This was achieved by interconnecting computers both directly and by way of other intermediary computers; thus if one computer was hit by a nuclear bomb, other pathways of communication could be established. The interconnections, when drawn, appeared as a mesh, or net or web. ARPANET was extended to non-military users such as universities early in the 1970s, with initial international links appearing in 1972.

The introduction of domain names (e.g. www.whitakersalmanack.com) in 1984 offered an easier means of using the Web. Prior to domain names one had to remember IP numbers (e.g.192.168.1.100) for accessing destination computers. However, before 1989 the Internet was still primarily limited to government agencies, the military, academic and research organisations and some big businesses.

In 1989, what most people perceive as 'the Net' was born. It was effectively invented at CERN (the European Particle Physics Laboratory) by Tim Berners-Lee as a way for scientists to share information by placing it in a prescribed format on a server. Initially text only, development of computer capability allowed inclusion of images.

By 1993 a whole new industry of ISPs (Internet Service Providers) had begun, allowing computer users to dial up via a modem and access the Internet and to view the Web through a browser (see glossary). Developments throughout the late 1990s (such as the widespread introduction of 'broadband') have allowed music, video, games, text, graphics and telephone calls to travel the Internet in much greater quantities and speeds than ever before. The future is likely to see the majority of telephone calls, and probably video, being transmitted over the Internet for at least part of their journey. Expansion of fibre-optic cable networks to homes and businesses will underpin this.

INTERNET STATISTICS
• 19% of households had access to the Internet in 1998 compared with 40% of households in 2001/2 and approximately 48% in 2003
• 32% of UK homes access the Internet via dial-up/ narrowband
• 15% of UK homes access the Internet via broadband
• 33% of businesses with between 1 and 250 employees access the Internet via dial-up/narrowband

• 32% of businesses with between 1 and 250 employees access the Internet via broadband

Sources: Oftel 2003; UK 2004 published by TSO; Office for National Statistics Expenditure and Food Survey

COUNTRIES WITH THE HIGHEST NUMBER OF BROADBAND SUBSCRIBERS

Global Ranking	Country	Broadband subscribers as at 31 December 2003
1	China	10,950,000
2	Japan	10,272,052
3	USA	9,119,000
4	South Korea	6,435,955
5	Germany	4,500,000
6	France	3,262,700
7	Taiwan	2,800,000
8	Italy	2,280,000
9	Canada	2,170,243
10	UK	1,820,230

Source: www.dslforum.org

GLOSSARY OF TERMS
The following is a selected list of modern computing terms. It is by no means exhaustive but is intended to cover those that the average computer user might encounter.

3G: Third Generation wireless – a popular term commonly used to describe high bandwidth (2 Mbps) wireless technologies for mobile phones. 3G is still in its infancy but will offer high speed and capacity transmission of sound, vision and data to and from wireless devices and networks.

ADSL: Asymmetric Digital Subscriber Line – high speed Internet connection, four or more times faster than a modem, but using the same standard cables as regular telephone. Faster at downloading than uploading.

BLOG: A blog (short for weblog) is an online personal journal that is frequently updated and intended to be read by the public. Blogs are kept by 'bloggers'.

BLUETOOTH: Standard for short-range (10 metre) wireless connectivity between devices such as laptops, mobile telephones and printers to interact without cables. Bluetooth typically operates at speeds of up to 2Mbps.

BROADBAND: Generic term to describe high speed Internet access technologies such as ADSL, cable etc. as opposed to narrowband connections via modem.

BROWSER: Typically referring to a 'web browser' program that allows a computer user to view web page content on their computer, e.g. Microsoft Explorer, Netscape Navigator, AOL, etc.

BURN: To 'burn' a file or files to a CD-ROM or similar media means to copy the files to the media from hard disk (or other source). Derived from the fact that CD-ROMs are burnt by a laser during the process of writing to the disk.

C: A 3GL programming language developed in the late 1960s in parallel with the UNIX operating system. Primarily limited to UNIX until the mid-1980s when standards such as POSIX emerged, allowing C to be widely adopted on many operating systems. UNIX used C as its core programming language.

CACHING: In order to provide enhanced response times or to reduce the demands on computer resources, a *cache* is often employed to hold copies of recently or frequently accessed content (e.g. web pages). The cache (stored on a user's machine, or on a *proxy server)* is searched for the requested item. If a sufficiently fresh copy is not available it is retrieved from the remote server, a copy stored in the cache and another supplied to the requesting machine. If for example ten users request the same page it is only retrieved from the remote server once if a *caching proxy* is used. If a user requests the same page multiple times it can be downloaded once and retrieved from the cache many times. Hard disk drives and computer memory employ similar caching techniques to optimise performance.

CAT-5: An electrical performance and cable quality standard prescribed to support high-speed Ethernet networks. There are higher category and capability specifications denoted by higher numbers but Cat-5 is the most commonly installed today.

CD: Compact Disc – a digital disk format capable of storing 650 megabytes of information per side. A laser head detects pits etched into the substrate of the spinning disk and interprets them as information. Widely used in an audio format for storing recorded music. The computer format CD-ROM is likely to be superceded by the higher capacity DVD in the next few years. CD-RAM/CD-RW and CD-R are modifiable versions that use lasers to alter the disk substrate to make the pits interpreted later as information. *See also* DVD.

DNS: Domain Name Server – a server that translates domain names into the IP numbers used by programs to directly access computers on the Internet. Each server has an IP number and a name. DNS is analogous to the telephone directory enquiry service, providing a means of looking up and locating a computer connected to the Internet.

DOMAIN: A set of words, numbers and letters separated by dots used to identify an Internet server or group of servers, e.g. www.whitakersalmanack.co.uk, where 'www' denotes a web (http) server, 'whitakersalmanack' denotes the organisation name, 'co' denotes that the organisation is a company and 'uk' denotes United Kingdom (there are alternatives for every country but 'us' is typically omitted for the United States).

DVD: Digital Versatile Disc – DVD-ROM is a high capacity (read only) disk format that has the same form factor as CD-ROM but can store several gigabytes of information on each surface and can have four readable surfaces (through laser focusing technology). DVD-RAM is a modifiable version. Various formats are available, the most common being that used to store high-quality digital video, an alternative to the laser disk or videotape. *See also* CD.

EMAIL: Electronic mail – an email message is a document that is addressed to one or more persons from an individual address. Usually containing a message, it can also include other documents. The advent of the Internet has seen an explosion in the use of email in modern life. Without encryption or digital signature, an Internet email is not secure.

ETHERNET: Utilising simple, standard and relatively cheap cable and connectors, Ethernet has become the standard for local area networks. Ethernet employs a system whereby each computer listens for information addressed to its own unique address. Before transmitting, each computer waits for silence on the line; if multiple computers start transmitting simultaneously, they each detect the 'collision' and each wait a random period of time before trying again, thus allowing communications to proceed politely.

EXTRANET: An extranet is a secure and private subset of the Internet, protected by security protocols and typically used for exchanging information and services between a specific group.

FILE SERVER: A computer on a network that stores computer files that users can access from other computers on the network. Popular modern systems include Microsoft Windows, UNIX, Linux, and MacOS Server.

FIREWALL: Computer or device to protect a network from security risks posed by the Internet. Just as a firewall protects parts of a building from a fire raging on the other side, a network firewall stops risks posed by the Internet from egressing into a private network.

FIREWIRE: Apple Computer's implementation of IEEE 1394. *See also* IEEE 1394.

FTP: File Transfer Protocol – an Internet protocol whereby an FTP client program can exchange files with a remote server.

GBPS: Giga bits per second – denoting 1,000 million bits transmitted per second.

GIF: Graphics Interchange Format – compressed graphic format suitable for logos and non-photographic images. Invented by Unisys to allow images to be sent electronically in an efficient manner.

GPRS: General Packet Radio Services – a service for continuous wireless communication over the Internet from mobile phones and computers. Presently available in data rates of between 56 and 114K Bps, GPRS is normally charged by volume of information transferred rather than by time connected.

HTML: HyperText Mark-up Language – a small programming language used to denote or mark-up how an Internet page should be presented to a user from an HTTP server via a web browser. HTML is an evolving standard that has grown greatly from its first version to accommodate new types of web content and features provided by the different web browsers.

HTTP: HyperText Transfer Protocol – an Internet protocol whereby a web server sends web pages, images and files to a web browser.

IEEE 1394: High-speed serial (400 Mbps) connection standard for hard disks, digital video cameras and other multimedia devices. Popularised as iLink (Sony) and FireWire (Apple).

iLINK: Sony's implementation of IEEE 1394. *See also* IEEE 1394.

IMAP: Internet Mail Access Protocol – an Internet protocol IMAP allows a user to review, manipulate and store email on a central server from one or more workstations without necessitating message removal from the server.

INTERNET: An abstract concept applied to describe the global network of INTER-connected computer NET-works of computers. *See* body of article.

INTRANET: Subset of the Internet, using Internet protocols over a local area network, common today for publishing information and services within an organisation.

iPOD: Market leading high capacity personal MP3 player marketed by Apple Computer.

IRC: Internet Relay Chat – protocol that allows users to 'chat' online with other users using their keyboards. Under IRC a user can log into various chat rooms under their own name or an alias and have a text 'conversation' in real time with other users.

ISDN: Integrated Services Digital Network – widely adopted in the United Kingdom and Europe but not North America, ISDN allows both digital computer data and voice telephony to exist simultaneously on the same cable circuits. Data can be digitally exchanged at 64 Kbps per circuit. Used for file transfer of large documents and on-demand Internet access, it is increasingly being replaced by broadband connections such as ADSL.

JPEG: Joint Photographic Experts Group – compressed graphic format suitable for compression of photographic images, losing some detail in the process.

KBPS: Kilo bits per second – measure of transmission speed, denoting approximately 1,000 bits of information transmitted per second.

LINUX: A UNIX-like operating system first developed as a free or low cost system for personal computers. Linux was first developed by Linus Torvalds but its source code is now in the public domain and there are many distributions (versions) available. It is increasingly popular for business enterprise applications, highly scalable and can be used for anything from running a vehicles engine managementsystem to controlling a supercomputing cluster. *See also* UNIX.

MACOS: Operating system developed by Apple Computer for use on their own Macintosh computers.

MBPS: Mega bits per second – denoting approximately 1 million bits of information transmitted per second.

MODEM: A device that modulates digital signals from a computer into analogue signals for transmission over a standard telephone line and demodulates an incoming analogue signal and converts it to a digital signal for the computer.

MP3: Popular format for compressing audio information for transmission over the Internet for later playback on personal computers, music players and other devices.

MPEG: Motion Picture Encoding Group – popular format standard for compressing video and audio information for transmission over the Internet for later playback on personal computers and other players.

MS-DOS: Microsoft Corporation's Disk Operating System – an early OS commercially developed, but not invented, by Microsoft for use on early Intel-based personal computers. *See also* Operating System.

NNTP: Network News Transfer Protocol – an Internet protocol that implements a bulletin board on a global scale. Using a NNTP browser one can subscribe and contribute to one or more news groups covering a large variety of topics.

OPERATING SYSTEM (OS): Computer software developed to provide computer programs with standard facilities to interact with users and with computer hardware (via drivers). *See also* MS-DOS, UNIX, MacOS.

PNG: An improved royalty-free graphics file replacement for GIF.

POP3: Post Office Protocol 3 – an Internet protocol whereby email can be collected from a personal mailbox on an email server and moved off the server to a user's own computer.

PROXY (SERVER): A computer or device that transparently accepts Internet requests from a users computer and forwards them on to the required destination, providing enhanced performance (through caching) and/or enhanced security (by isolating the user computer from the Internet. *See* CACHING.

PRINT SERVER: A computer or device on a network that manages the sharing of one or more printers between multiple computers over a network. Many modern printers have a print server built in.

ROUTER: Where multiple networks are joined together, a router acts like a fast sorting office, examining the destination address of each information packet and passing or routing it to the appropriate network. Routers can select the most efficient route for packets.

SMTP: Simple Mail Transfer Protocol – an Internet protocol whereby a workstation can send email to a server or whereby two servers can exchange email.

SNMP: Simple Network Management Protocol – widely used protocol for remotely monitoring and managing network device status and function.

SPAM: A term used for unsolicited, generally junk, email. To spam someone is to send them (multiple) junk emails. Spam is becoming a major Internet problem with many estimates indicating that spam is becoming more prevalent than legitimate email. Most spam contains offers of pornography, get-rich schemes, prescription drugs, low cost finance or discount goods or services. Many legislatures around the globe are taking steps to ban or regulate spam.

TAR: Compression – a common mechanism on UNIX and Linux operating systems to compress information in order to save resources.

TCP/IP: Transmission Control Protocol/Internet Protocol – a protocol which is the lifeblood of the Internet, TCP/IP defines how information and requests generated by all other protocols are transmitted over the Internet. Information on the Internet is chopped up into small chunks or packets which are addressed with a destination and origination address. It sometimes happens that a packet gets lost and TCP/IP dictates how such a loss is handled.

UNIX: See body of article. Modern derivative versions include Linux, MacOS X, Solaris, BSD.

USB: Universal Serial Bus – standard for connecting serial devices such as scanners, mice, keyboards, modems and printers to computers. With USB, speeds of up to 10 Mbps are possible. USB2 is a revised, higher performance version of USB provides speeds up to 480 Mbps.

URL: Uniform Resource Locator – address of an Internet file or resource accessible on the Internet, e.g. http://www.whitakersalmanack.co.uk.

VIRUS: A computer program or script written for the express purpose of replicating itself onto as many machines as possible (much like its biological namesake) often with negative side effects to the host computer and computer network. Such effects vary from harmless screen messages to corruption of document integrity, network overload or compromising data security or privacy. Historically transmitted slowly by floppy disk and over networks within offices, the prevalence of Internet access allows viruses to spread globally within minutes.

WAP: Wireless Application Protocol – a set of standards to define how portable devices connected via radio waves (such as mobile telephones) can access Internet services.

WARCHALKING: To 'warchalk' is to mark an open or security-exposed Wi-Fi or other wireless network by writing symbols on or outside the relevant buildings in chalk.

WAR DRIVING: The activity of locating and exploiting security exposed Wi-Fi and other wireless networks to gain access to the network resource or information on or accessible to that network.

WI-FI: Industry brand name for the increasingly popular high frequency wireless local area Ethernet networking technology specification IEEE 802.11. Most prevalent is the 802.11b specification offering speeds of up to 11 Mps.

WLAN: Wireless local area network where information is transferred by radio frequency rather than wires between computers and base stations. As radio waves can pass through objects such as walls, it is becoming increasingly important for WLANs to be secured by encryption against unauthorised access.

XML: Extensible Mark-up Language, similar to HTML but more powerful, XML allows information to be encoded or tagged in a manner that is both human and computer readable.

ZIP: Compression – a popular mechanism on PCs to compress to compress information in order to save resources.

THE ENVIRONMENT

Europe's environment has improved in several respects over the last decade but further progress is needed to manage the environmental impacts of agriculture, transport and energy, according to the European Environment Agency.

Emissions from transport are a growing concern throughout the EU. In the accession and candidate countries, carbon dioxide emissions from transport decreased 19 per cent between 1990 and 1995 but rose afterwards and in 2001 were 4 per cent higher than 1990 levels. In the previously existing member states (EU-15) transport emissions increased by nearly 21 per cent between 1990–2001. Environmental policies are developed at several levels – international conventions and protocols (of which there are over 50), European Directives (of which there are over 300), and national legislation and strategies.

EUROPEAN UNION MEASURES

The European Union is developing an interlinked set of policies – the sixth Environmental Action Programme, the Cardiff process for the integration of environment into other policies and the EU sustainable development strategy – which form the framework for more detailed strategies. The Commission is also diversifying the instruments it uses in particular to include market-based instruments such as environmental taxes, and voluntary measures.

The Environmental Action Programme began in the 1970s. The Sixth Environmental Action Programme, *Environment 2010: Our Future, Our Choice*, was adopted in January 2001 and sets the programme to 2010. It proposes five priority areas: improving the implementation of existing legislation; integrating environmental concerns into other policies; working more closely with the market; empowering private citizens and helping them to change behaviour; and taking account of the environment in land-use planning and management decisions. The programme focuses on four topics: climate change, nature and biodiversity, environment and health, and natural resources and waste.

Much European Union environmental legislation is based around the principle that the polluter pays. The Environmental Liability Directive, agreed in February this year, will be used to hold polluters financially liable for damage they cause. It is due to enter into force in 2007.

ENLARGEMENT

Ten countries (EU-10) joined the EU in May 2004 – Cyprus, the Czech Republic, Estonia, Hungary, Latvia, Lithuania, Malta, Poland, Slovenia and Slovakia. The new member states have been granted transition measures, in particular for investment-heavy sectors such as waste water treatment. These measures vary from country to country and include extensions for meeting the targets and legally binding intermediate targets.

In general, most countries are on track to implement legislation. However, some countries have significant work to do in waste management and industrial pollution. Also, there are some worrying trends, such as a decline in rail transport for freight, and a 73 per cent increase in car ownership.

It is estimated that to achieve full implementation the new member states will have to spend on average 2–3 per cent of GDP on the environment in the coming years. Current expenditure is generally well below this target. Financial assistance was given through a variety of EU programmes in the lead up to accession. Following accession, this will almost treble. Until the end of the EU's budgetary period in 2006, the new states will receive some €8 billion, which equates to more than 10 per cent of the total investment requirements.

SUSTAINABLE DEVELOPMENT

The environmental agenda is increasingly becoming part of a wider move to address sustainability which incorporates social, environmental and economic development. In 2002, the World Summit on Sustainable Development was held in Johannesburg. Governments agreed on a series of commitments in five priority areas – water and sanitation, energy, health, agriculture, and biodiversity. Targets and timetables agreed include halving the number of people who lack access to clean water or proper sanitation by 2015 and reducing biodiversity loss by 2010.

Following the summit, the United Nations Commission on Sustainable Development has agreed its programme for the next 15 years. It will work in two-year cycles, with the first (2004–5) focusing on water, sanitation and human settlements. This will be followed by energy, climate change, atmosphere and industrial development in 2006–7. The EU's sustainable development strategy, adopted in May 2001, sets out long-term objectives, such as limiting major threats to public health and breaking the link between economic growth and transport growth.

In April 2004, a consultation was launched to develop a new UK sustainable development strategy. The three-month consultation asks for views on a wide range of issues from what should be in a UK vision of sustainable development to how to tackle unsustainable consumption patterns. The new framework is to be in place by early 2005. It will provide the background for separate strategies and plans by each administration.

The existing UK strategy *A Better Quality of Life* was published in May 1999. It provides a framework for integrating social, environmental and economic policies to meet four objectives: social progress, protection of the environment, prudent use of natural resources, and to maintain high and stable levels of economic growth and employment. The latest annual progress report highlighted areas of particular concern, such as the levels of waste generated and rising road traffic volumes, although the weakening in the link between road traffic and economic growth is encouraging.

The government has also developed a strategy on sustainable consumption and production. Key proposals include breaking the link between economic growth and environmental pollution, examining the whole life-cycle of products, and improving resource efficiency.

Local authorities also have a role to play in sustainable development. Under Local Agenda 21, which came out of the UN Conference on Environment and Development in Rio, Brazil in 1992, local authorities have an obligation to draw up sustainable development strategies for their areas. Regional Development Agencies take Local Agenda 21 strategies into account in sustainable development frameworks for each English region. At the World

Summit, the UK government committed itself to taking further action towards the implementation of Agenda 21 and achieving the Millennium Development Goals which have grown out of agreements and declarations at UN Conferences.

Many businesses are also working towards sustainable development and some are assessing and reporting their own progress with initiatives, such as the Global Reporting Initiative.

WASTE

Waste policy in the UK follows a number of principles: the hierarchy of reduce, reuse, recycle, dispose; the proximity principle of disposing of waste close to its generation; and national self sufficiency. Directives from Europe are playing an increasingly important role in driving UK policy, particularly regarding commercial and industrial waste. For instance, the Landfill Directive, which was adopted in July 1999, sets stringent targets for reducing the amount of waste sent to landfill and the technical requirements for landfill sites.

The proposed European integrated products policy aims to internalise the environmental costs of products throughout their life-cycle through market forces, by focusing on eco-design and incentives to ensure increased demand for greener products. The policy will culminate in 2007 with the identification of a first set of products with the greatest potential for environmental improvement and the beginning of action to tackle them.

Greater responsibility for end-of-life products is already being addressed by the EU's producer responsibility directives for packaging waste, which came into force in the UK in 1997 and for which the EU has recently set new more stringent targets: the end-of-life-vehicle directive, which entered into force in December 2001; and the directives on waste from electrical and electronic equipment and on the restriction of the use of certain hazardous substances in such equipment which came into effect in February. A new directive concerning the collection and recycling of batteries has also been adopted.

In addition to meeting EU directives, the UK also has its own targets. To meet these the public and local authorities will have to vastly increase their current recycling rates. In 2002–3, 15.6 per cent of household waste was recycled and composted, up from 13.6 per cent in 2001–2. Scotland and Northern Ireland also have national waste strategies.

CLIMATE CHANGE AND AIR POLLUTION

The UK's response to climate change is driven by the international Framework Convention on Climate Change. This is a binding agreement that has been signed and ratified by 189 countries. It was ratified in the UK in December 1993 and came into force in March 1994. It is intended to reduce the risks of global warming by limiting 'greenhouse' gas emissions.

Progress towards the convention's targets are assessed at regular conferences. At Kyoto in 1997, a protocol (the Kyoto Protocol) to the convention was adopted. It covers the six main greenhouse gases – carbon dioxide, methane, nitrous oxide, hydrofluorocarbons (HFCs), perfluorocarbons (PFCs) and sulphur hexafluoride. Under the protocol industrialised countries agreed to legally binding targets for cutting emissions of greenhouse gases by 5.2 per cent below 1990 levels by 2008–12. EU members agreed to an 8 per cent reduction and the UK's target is a 12.5 per cent cut. The ten accession (EU-10) countries have all ratified the Kyoto protocol and have their own targets of between 6 per cent and 8 per cent. The EU's 8 per cent target now only refers to the previous 15 member states (EU-15).

The latest data from the European Environment Agency, published in December 2003, shows that emissions of greenhouse gases from the EU have decreased by 2.3 per cent between 1990 and 2001, just over one quarter of the way towards the target. Ten of the EU-15 member states (Austria, Belgium, Denmark, Finland, Greece, Ireland, Italy, the Netherlands, Portugal and Spain) are not on track to meet their targets. Seven of the ten accession countries are on track to achieve their target under Kyoto, with only Slovenia expecting to miss its target.

The Kyoto Protocol will enter into force 90 days after it has been ratified by 55 governments, including developed countries representing at least 55 per cent of that group's carbon dioxide emissions. It had been expected to enter into force in early 2003. This has not happened as ratification by either the US or Russia is still needed. The US has stated that it will not ratify the treaty. Russia has recently pledged to ratify, having been reluctant to do so because of the perceived negative economic impact of such a move. Despite the Government's positive stance, a number of key Russian organisations are lobbying against the move.

In November 2000, a UK climate change programme was published which sets out how the UK intends to meet its Kyoto target and progress towards its domestic goal of a 20 per cent cut in carbon dioxide emissions by 2010.

The European Commission also set up a European Climate Change Programme in 2000 to identify measures to meet the Kyoto target and will introduce a mandatory emissions trading scheme at company level for carbon dioxide in the European Union beginning in January 2005. The companies covered by the scheme account for almost half of the EU's total carbon dioxide emissions. The EU has also indicated that it is willing to link the scheme to trading schemes in other countries that have ratified the Kyoto Protocol. Under the scheme, member states will set limits on carbon dioxide emissions from energy-intensive companies by issuing allowances according to how much they are allowed to emit. Reductions below these limits will be tradable.

Member states are required to submit national allocation plans setting out how they will issue allowances to companies. The deadline for plans was 31 March for the EU-15 and 1 May for the EU-10. In May, the Commission had received just nine from the EU-15 and three from the EU-10 and infringement proceedings have started against those that have not submitted.

The EU's national emission ceilings directive sets upper limits for each member state for the total emissions in 2010 of the four pollutants responsible for acidification, eutrophication and ground-level ozone pollution (sulphur dioxide, nitrogen oxides, volatile organic compounds and ammonia), but leaves it largely to the member states to decide which measures to take in order to comply. For emissions of ground-level ozone, only the UK, Germany, the Netherlands and Finland are below the target path to meet their obligations under the directive. Emissions of Portugal, Spain, Greece, Ireland and Belgium are significantly above their target paths while of the accession countries, Slovenia, Hungary, Poland and the Czech Republic will need significant reductions to meet their 2010 targets.

At a European level, air pollutant emissions show a general decreasing trend. Between 1990 and 2000, emissions of acidifying pollutants and ozone precursor gases decreased by 40 per cent and 29 per cent respectively. The European Integrated Pollution Prevention and Control (IPPC) Directive regulates emissions to any environmental medium from certain industrial and includes returning sites to a satisfactory state on closure, using energy efficiently and noise and vibration regulation. IPPC has been implemented in the UK through the Pollution Prevention and Control regulations 2000. Also, the UK's National Air Quality Strategy sets air quality objectives for the main pollutants (benzene, 1-3, butadiene, carbon monoxide, lead, nitrogen dioxide, sulphur dioxide, ozone, and particulates) to be met by 2003–8.

WATER

Water quality targets are set at both EU and UK level for drinking water sources, waste water discharges, rivers, coastal water and bathing water. The EU's water framework directive, which entered into force in December 2000, has an objective to achieve 'good water status' throughout the EU by 2015. In response to the requirements of the framework directive, the Commission has proposed a new directive to protect groundwater from pollution. The UK's Water Act was granted royal assent late last year.

The Water Environment and Water Services Bill for Scotland completed its passage through the Scottish parliament in early 2003. It establishes, for the first time, a source-to-sea planning framework for river basin management. Meanwhile, proposals for amending the regulatory framework for water and sewerage services were published for consultation late last year.

The EC Bathing Water Directive sets standards for bathing waters. This applies to 391 coastal and nine inland bathing waters in the UK. This directive is over 25 years old. The commission adopted a proposal for a new directive in October 2002 which would set a much tighter bathing water quality standard than the existing Directive.

The Environment Agency sets river quality objectives for each stretch of river. Water quality is currently protected through licensing abstraction and regulating discharges. Consents to discharge sewage and industrial effluent are regulated under the Water Resources Act 1991 and the IPPC regime. Discharge consents are based on the river quality objectives and relevant EU directives and specify the concentration and quantity permitted.

The European Urban Waste Water Treatment Directive sets minimum standards for sewage treatment before discharge into coastal waters with the levels of treatment needed depending on the sensitivity of the receiving water. In 1999 the government set more stringent UK targets for all significant coastal discharges to have a minimum of secondary treatment by 2005.

ENERGY

In February 2003, the UK government published a White Paper setting out a long-term strategy for UK Energy policy to 2050 combining environmental, security of supply, competitiveness and social goals. It builds on the Performance and Innovation Unit's (now the Prime Minister's Strategy Unit) Energy Review, published a year earlier.

In April 2004, the UK government published its first annual report on implementation of the white paper. A total of 112 milestones had been set as a first step towards achieving the long-term commitments, 56 have been met. An energy bill was also introduced in November 2003.

ENVIRONMENT AND HEALTH

In October 2003, the European Commission put forward a proposal for a new chemicals policy under which industry will have to provide information on the effects of chemicals on human health and the environment as well as on safe ways of handling them. The proposal has been met with stiff opposition and still has a long way to go before it is implemented. The Commission has also launched a strategy that will tackle environmental risks for human health in a broader sense. The strategy on science, children, awareness, legislation and evaluation, known as Scale, was launched in June 2003. Apart from aiming to reduce diseases caused by environmental factors in Europe, it aims to strengthen the EU's capacity for policy making in the area.

The first cycle of the strategy, running from 2004 to 2010, will focus on four health effects – childhood respiratory diseases, asthma and allergies; neuro-development disorders; childhood cancer; and endocrine disrupting effects.

SELECTED UK TARGETS

Global atmosphere
- Reduce greenhouse gas emissions to 12.5 per cent below 1990 levels by 2010
- Reduce carbon dioxide emissions to 20 per cent below 1990 levels by 2010, and by 60 per cent by 2050

Air quality
- Reduce sulphur dioxide emissions by 63 per cent based on 1990 levels by 2010
- Reduce emissions of nitrogen oxides by 41 per cent based on 1990 levels by 2010
- Reduce emissions of volatile organic compounds by 40 per cent based on 1990 levels by 2010

Fresh water and sea
- 97 per cent of bathing waters to meet European directive standards consistently by 2005
- Provide secondary treatment for all significant coastal discharges (over 2,000 population equivalent) by 2005

Waste
- Reduce industrial and commercial waste going to landfill by 85 per cent of 1998 levels by 2005
- Recover 40 per cent of municipal waste by 2005, 45 per cent by 2010 and 67 per cent by 2015
- Recycle or compost 25 per cent of household waste by 2005, 30 per cent by 2010 and 33 per cent by 2015
- Reduce biodegradable municipal waste sent to landfill by 75 per cent of 1995 levels by 2010
- Ensure 65 per cent of UK newspaper feedstock content is waste paper by end of 2003 and 70 per cent by end of 2006
- Proposed re-use and recovery of 85 per cent of the mass of end-of-life vehicles with a minimum of 80 per cent recycling by 2006, 95 per cent and 85 per cent by 2015
- EU target to reduce the amount of waste going to final disposal by 20 per cent by 2010 and 50 per cent by 2050
- Collect 4kg of household waste electrical and electronic equipment per head of population per year by 31 December 2006
- Provide segregated kerbside waste collection to over 90 per cent of households in Scotland by 2020

Land
- Ensure 60 per cent of all new housing is built on re-used sites

Energy
- Provide 10.4 per cent of electricity from renewable sources by 2010 in UK and Scotland

CONSERVATION AND HERITAGE

NATIONAL PARKS

ENGLAND AND WALES

The ten National Parks of England and Wales were set up under the provisions of the National Parks and Access to the Countryside Act 1949 to conserve and protect scenic landscapes from inappropriate development and to provide access to the land for public enjoyment.

The Countryside Agency (established on 1 April 1999 from the merger of the Countryside Commission and the Rural Development Commission) is the statutory body which has the power to designate National Parks in England, and the Countryside Council for Wales is responsible for National Parks in Wales. Designations in England are confirmed by the Secretary of State for Environment, Food and Rural Affairs and those in Wales by the National Assembly for Wales. The designation of a National Park does not affect the ownership of the land or remove the rights of the local community. The majority of the land in the National Parks is owned by private landowners (74 per cent) or by bodies such as the National Trust (7 per cent) and the Forestry Commission (7 per cent). The National Park Authorities own only 2.3 per cent of the land.

The Environment Act 1995 replaced the existing National Park boards and committees with free-standing National Park Authorities (NPAs). NPAs are the sole local planning authorities for their areas and as such influence land use and development, and deal with planning applications. Their duties include conserving and enhancing the natural beauty, wildlife and cultural heritage of the National Parks; promoting opportunities for public understanding and enjoyment of the National Parks; and fostering the economic and social well-being of the communities within National Parks. The NPAs publish management plans as statements of their policies and appoint their own officers and staff.

Membership of the NPAs differs slightly between England and Wales. In England, those local authorities that have land in the Parks appoint one half of the members of the National Parks Authorities plus one other person. Of the remaining members, one half minus one person are parish representatives who are elected through a process of local democracy while the rest are appointed by the Secretary of State to represent the national interest. In Wales two-thirds of NPA members are appointed by the constituent local authorities and one-third by the National Assembly for Wales, advised by the Countryside Council for Wales.

Since April 2004 the Department for Environment, Food and Rural Affairs has provided 100 per cent of the funding for the parks in England through the National Park and Broads Authority Grant; a total of £35.76 million in 2004–5. In Wales, National Parks are funded via a grant from the National Assembly and levies raised from participating local authorities. In addition, all NPAs and the Broads Authority can take advantage of grants from other bodies including lottery and European grants.

The National Parks (with date designation confirmed) are:

BRECON BEACONS (1957), Powys (66 per cent)/Carmarthenshire/Rhondda, Cynon and Taff/Merthyr Tydfil/Blaenau Gwent/Monmouthshire, 1,349sq. km/519 sq. miles – The park is centred on the Beacons, Pen y Fan, Corn Du and Cribyn, but also includes the valley of the Usk, the Black Mountains to the east and the Black Mountain to the west. There are information centres at Brecon, Craig-y-nos Country Park, Abergavenny and Llandovery, a study centre at Danywenallt and a day visitor centre near Libanus.
Information Office, Plas y Ffynnon, Cambrian Way, Brecon, Powys LD3 7HP T 01874-624437
E enquiries@breconbeacons.org
National Park Officer, Christopher Gledhill

DARTMOOR (1951 and 1994), Devon, 954 sq. km/368 sq. miles – The park consists of moorland and rocky granite tors, and is rich in prehistoric remains. There are information centres at Haytor, Newbridge, Princetown and Postbridge.
Information Office, Parke, Bovey Tracey, Devon TQ13 9JQ T 01626-832093 E hq@dartmoor-npa.gov.uk
Chief Executive, Dr Nick Atkinson

EXMOOR (1954), Somerset (71 per cent)/Devon, 693 sq. km/268 sq. miles – Exmoor is a moorland plateau inhabited by wild ponies and red deer. There are many ancient remains and burial mounds. There are information centres at Lynmouth, County Gate, Dulverton and Combe Martin.
Information Office, Exmoor House, Dulverton, Somerset TA21 9HL T 01398-323665
E info@exmoor-nationalpark.gov.uk
National Park Officer, Dr Nigel Stone

LAKE DISTRICT (1951), Cumbria, 2,292 sq. km/885 sq. miles – The Lake District includes England's highest mountains (Scafell Pike, Helvellyn and Skiddaw) but it is most famous for its glaciated lakes. There are information centres at Broughton, Keswick, Waterhead, Hawkshead, Seatoller, Bowness, Grasmere, Coniston, Glenridding and Pooley Bridge and a park centre at Brockhole, Windermere.
Information Office, Murley Moss, Oxenholme Road, Kendal, Cumbria, LA9 7RL T 01539-724555
E hq@lake-district.gov.uk
National Park Officer, Paul Tiplady

NORTH YORK MOORS (1952), North Yorkshire (96 per cent)/Redcar and Cleveland, 1,432 sq. km/554 sq. miles – The park consists of woodland and moorland, and includes the Hambleton Hills and the Cleveland Way. There are information centres at Danby, Sutton Bank and at The Old Coastguard Station in Robin Hood's Bay.
Information Office, The Old Vicarage, Bondgate, Helmsley, York YO6 5BP T 01439-770657
E general@northyorkmoors-npa.gov.uk
National Park Officer, Andrew Wilson

NORTHUMBERLAND (1956), Northumberland, 1,049 sq. km/405 sq. miles – The park is an area of hill country stretching from Hadrian's Wall to the Scottish Border. There are information centres at Ingram, Once Brewed and Rothbury.

Information Office, Eastburn, South Park, Hexham, Northumberland NE46 1BS T 01434-605555
E admin@nnpa.org.uk
National Park Officer, Graham Taylor
PEAK DISTRICT (1951), Derbyshire (64 per cent)/ Staffordshire/South Yorkshire/Cheshire/West Yorkshire/Greater Manchester, 1,438 sq. km/555 sq. miles – The Peak District includes the gritstone moors of the 'Dark Peak' and the limestone dales of the 'White Peak'. There are information centres at Bakewell, Edale, Castleton and Upper Derwent.
Information Office, Aldern House, Baslow Road, Bakewell, Derbyshire DE45 1AE T 01629-816200
E aldern@peakdistrict-npa.gov.uk
National Park Officer, Jim Dixon
PEMBROKESHIRE COAST (1952 and 1995), Pembrokeshire, 620 sq. km/240 sq. miles – The park includes cliffs, moorland and a number of islands, including Skomer. There are information centres at St David's and Newport.
Information Office, Llanion Park, Pembroke Dock, Pembrokeshire SA72 6DF T 0845-345 7275
E pcnp@pembrokeshirecoast.org.uk
National Park Officer, Nic Wheeler
SNOWDONIA/ERYRI (1951), Gwynedd/Conwy, 2,171 sq. km/835 sq. miles – Snowdonia is an area of deep valleys and rugged mountains. There are information centres at Aberdyfi, Beddgelert, Betws y Coed, Blaenau Ffestiniog, Conwy, Dolgellau and Harlech.
Information Office, Penrhyndeudraeth, Gwynedd LL48 6LF T 01766-770274 E parc@eryri-npa.gov.uk
Chief Executive, Aneurin Phillips
YORKSHIRE DALES (1954), North Yorkshire (88 per cent)/Cumbria, 1,769 sq. km/683 sq. miles – The Yorkshire Dales are composed primarily of limestone overlaid in places by millstone grit. The three peaks of Ingleborough, Whernside and Pen-y-Ghent are within the park. There are information centres at Grassington, Hawes, Aysgarth Falls, Malham, Reeth and Sedbergh.
Information Office, Yorebridge House, Bainbridge, Leyburn, N. Yorks DL8 3EE T 01969-650456
E info@yorkshiredales.org.uk
Chief Executive, David Butterworth

Two other areas considered to have equivalent status to the National Parks are the Broads and the New Forest. The Broads Authority was established in 1989 under separate legislation to develop, conserve and manage the Norfolk and Suffolk Broads. In 1999 the Countryside Agency began the process of designating the New Forest and the South Downs (within the Sussex Downs and East Hampshire 'Areas of Outstanding Natural Beauty') as National Parks. On 28 June 2004 the Government announced that, following the finalisation of the boundary, the New Forest will become a National Park.

THE BROADS (1989), Norfolk, 303 sq. km/117 sq. miles – The Broads are located between Norwich and Great Yarmouth on the flood plains of the five rivers flowing through the area to the sea. The area is one of fens, winding waterways, woodland and marsh. The 40 or so broads are man-made, and are connected to the rivers by dikes, providing over 200 km of navigable waterways. There are information centres at Beccles, Hoveton, North West Tower (Yarmouth), Potter Heigham, Ranworth and Toad Hole.

The Broads Authority, 18 Colegate, Norwich NR3 1BQ T 01603 610734 E broads@broads-authority.gov.uk
Chief Executive, Dr John Packman
THE NEW FOREST Hampshire, 580 sq. km/224 sq. miles – The forest has been protected since 1079 when it was declared a royal hunting forest. The area consists of forest, ancient woodland and heathland. Much of the Forest is managed by the Forestry Commission, which provides several camp-sites. The main villages are Brockenhurst, Burley and Lyndhurst, which has a visitor centre.
The New Forest Committee, 4 High Street, Lyndhurst, Hants SO43 7BD T 023-8028 4144
E office@newforestcommittee.org.uk
Chairman, Ted Johnson, FRICS, *Committee Officer*, Maddy Jago
THE SOUTH DOWNS, West Sussex/Hampshire,1,637 sq. km/632 sq. miles – The South Downs contains a diversity of natural habitats, including flower-studded chalk grassland, ancient woodland, flood meadow, lowland heath and rare chalk heathland.
Sussex Downs Conservation Board, Victorian Barn, Victorian Business Centre, Ford Lane, Ford, Arundel, West Sussex, BN18 0EF T 01234-558700
E info@southdowns-aonb.gov.uk
Chief Officer, Martin Beaton

SCOTLAND
On 9 August 2000 The National Parks (Scotland) Bill received Royal Assent, providing the Parliament with the ability to create National Parks in Scotland. The first two Scottish National Parks, *Loch Lomond and the Trossachs* and the *Cairngorms*, became operational in 2002 and 2003 respectively. The Act gives Scottish Parks wider powers than in England and Wales, including statutory responsibilities for the economy and rural communities. Membership of the two NPAs in Scotland consists of 20 per cent directly elected members. The remaining 80 per cent are chosen by the Secretary of State, 40 per cent of which are nominated by the constituent Local Authorities. In Scotland, the National Parks are central Government bodies and wholly funded by the Scottish Executive.

CAIRNGORMS (2003), Morayshire, 3,800 sq. km/1,461 sq. miles – The Cairngorms National Park is the largest in the UK. It displays a vast collection of landforms and includes four of Scotland's highest mountains.
Information Office, 14 The Square, Grantown-on-Spey, Morayshire, PH26 3HG T 01479-873535
E mainoffice@cairngorms.co.uk
Chief Executive, Jane Hope
LOCH LOMOND AND THE TROSSACHS (2002), Argyll and Bute/Stirling/West Dunbartonshire, 1,865 sq. km/720 sq. miles – The park boundaries encompass lochs, rivers, forests, 20 mountains above 3,000 ft including Ben Moore and a further 20 mountains between 2,500 ft and 3,000 ft.
Information Office, The Old Station, Balloch Road, Balloch G83 8SS T 01389-722600 E info@lochlomond-trossachs.org
Chief Executive, Bill Dalrymple

NORTHERN IRELAND
There is power to designate National Parks in Northern Ireland under the Amenity Lands Act 1965 and the Nature Conservation and Amenity Lands Order (Northern Ireland) 1985.

AREAS OF OUTSTANDING NATURAL BEAUTY

ENGLAND AND WALES

Under the National Parks and Access to the Countryside Act 1949, provision was made for the designation of Areas of Outstanding Natural Beauty (AONBs) by the Countryside Commission. The Countryside Agency is now responsible for AONBs in England and since April 1991 the Countryside Council for Wales has been responsible for the Welsh AONBs. Designations in England are confirmed by the Secretary of State for Environment, Food and Rural Affairs and those in Wales by the National Assembly for Wales. The Countryside and Rights of Way Act 2000 provided for the creation of conservation boards for individual AONBs and placed greater responsibility on local authorities to protect them.

Although less emphasis is placed upon the provision of open-air enjoyment for the public than in the national parks, AONBs are areas which require the same degree of protection to conserve and enhance the natural beauty of the countryside. This includes protecting flora and fauna, geological and other landscape features. Overall responsibility for AONBs lies with the relevant local authorities, however, most fall within more than one local authority area. To co-ordinate planning and management responsibilities, AONBs are overseen by a Joint Advisory Committee (or similar body) which includes representatives from the local authorities, landowners, farmers, residents and conservation and recreation groups. In addition, an AONB officer is appointed to oversee matters. All AONBs also have to prepare Statements of Intent (or Commitment) and Management Plans. Since April 2002, 75 per cent of core funding for AONBs has been provided by central government through the Countryside Agency and Countryside Council for Wales.

The 41 Areas of Outstanding Natural Beauty (with date designation confirmed) are:

ANGLESEY (1967), Anglesey, 221 sq. km/85 sq. miles
ARNSIDE AND SILVERDALE (1972), Cumbria/Lancashire, 75 sq. km/29 sq. miles
BLACKDOWN HILLS (1991), Devon/Somerset, 370 sq. km/143 sq. miles
CANNOCK CHASE (1958), Staffordshire, 68 sq. km/26 sq. miles
CHICHESTER HARBOUR (1964), Hampshire/West Sussex, 74 sq. km/29 sq. miles
CHILTERNS (1965; extended 1990), Bedfordshire/Buckinghamshire/Herefordshire/Oxfordshire, 833 sq. km/322 sq. miles
CLWYDIAN RANGE (1985), Denbighshire/Flintshire, 157 sq. km/60 sq. miles
CORNWALL (1959; Camel estuary 1983), 958 sq. km/370 sq. miles
COTSWOLDS (1966; extended 1990), Gloucestershire/Oxfordshire/Wiltshire/Warwickshire/Worcestershire, 2,038 sq. km/787 sq. miles
CRANBORNE CHASE AND WEST WILTSHIRE DOWNS (1983), Dorset/Hampshire/Somerset/Wiltshire, 983 sq. km/379 sq. miles
DEDHAM VALE (1970; extended 1978, 1991), Essex/Suffolk, 90 sq. km/35 sq. miles
DORSET (1959), 1,129 sq. km/436 sq. miles
EAST DEVON (1963), 268 sq. km/103 sq. miles
EAST HAMPSHIRE (1962), 383 sq. km/148 sq. miles
FOREST OF BOWLAND (1964), Lancashire/North Yorkshire, 802 sq. km/310 sq. miles
GOWER (1956), Swansea, 188 sq. km/73 sq. miles
HIGH WEALD (1983), Kent/East Sussex/Surrey/West Sussex, 1,460 sq. km/564 sq. miles
HOWARDIAN HILLS (1987), North Yorkshire, 204 sq. km/79 sq. miles
ISLE OF WIGHT (1963), 189 sq. km/73 sq. miles
ISLES OF SCILLY (1976), 16 sq. km/6 sq. miles
KENT DOWNS (1968), 878 sq. km/339 sq. miles
LINCOLNSHIRE WOLDS (1973), 558 sq. km/215 sq. miles
LLEYN (1957), Gwynedd, 161 sq. km/62 sq. miles
MALVERN HILLS (1959), Gloucestershire/Worcestershire, 150 sq. km/58 sq. miles
MENDIP HILLS (1972; extended 1989), Somerset, 198 sq. km/76 sq. miles
NIDDERDALE (1994), North Yorkshire, 603 sq. km/233 sq. miles
NORFOLK COAST (1968), 451 sq. km/174 sq. miles
NORTH DEVON (1960), 171 sq. km/66 sq. miles
NORTH PENNINES (1988), Cumbria/Durham/Northumberland, 1,983 sq. km/766 sq. miles
NORTH WESSEX DOWNS (1972), Hampshire/Oxfordshire/Wiltshire, 1,730 sq. km/668 sq. miles
NORTHUMBERLAND COAST (1958), 135 sq. km/52 sq. miles
QUANTOCK HILLS (1957), Somerset, 99 sq. km/38 sq. miles
SHROPSHIRE HILLS (1959), 804 sq. km/310 sq. miles
SOLWAY COAST (1964), Cumbria, 115 sq. km/44 sq. miles
SOUTH DEVON (1960), 337 sq. km/130 sq. miles
SOUTH HAMPSHIRE COAST (1967), 77 sq. km/30 sq. miles
SUFFOLK COAST AND HEATHS (1970), 403 sq. km/156 sq. miles
SURREY HILLS (1958), 419 sq. km/162 sq. miles
SUSSEX DOWNS (1966), 983 sq. km/379 sq. miles
TAMAR VALLEY (1995), Cornwall/Devon, 195 sq. km/115 sq. miles
WYE VALLEY (1971), Gloucestershire/Herefordshire/Monmouthshire, 326 sq. km/126 sq. miles

NORTHERN IRELAND

The Department of the Environment for Northern Ireland, with advice from the Council for Nature Conservation and the Countryside, designates Areas of Outstanding Natural Beauty in Northern Ireland. At present there are nine and these cover a total area of approximately 284,948 hectares (704,103 acres). Dates given are those of designation.

ANTRIM COAST AND GLENS (1988), Co. Antrim, 70,600 ha/174,452 acres
CAUSEWAY COAST (1989), Co. Antrim, 4,200 ha/10,378 acres
LAGAN VALLEY (1965), Co. Down, 2,072 ha/5,119 acres
LECALE COAST (1967), Co. Down, 3,108 ha/7,679 acres
MOURNE (1986), Co. Down, 57,012 ha/140,876 acres
NORTH DERRY (1966), Co. Londonderry, 12,950 ha/31,999 acres
RING OF GULLION (1991), Co. Armagh, 15,353 ha/37,938 acres
SPERRIN (1968), Co. Tyrone/Co. Londonderry, 101,006 ha/249,585 acres

STRANGFORD LOUGH (1972), Co. Down, 18,647 ha/
46,077 acres

NATIONAL SCENIC AREAS

In Scotland, National Scenic Areas have a broadly equivalent status to AONBs. Scottish Natural Heritage recognises areas of national scenic significance. At the end of June 2004 there were 40, covering a total area of 1,001,800 hectares (2,475,448 acres).

Development within National Scenic Areas is dealt with by local authorities, who are required to consult Scottish Natural Heritage concerning certain categories of development. Disagreements between Scottish Natural Heritage and local authorities are referred to the Scottish Executive. Land management uses can also be modified in the interest of scenic conservation.

ASSYNT-COIGACH, Highland, 90,200 ha/222,884 acres
BEN NEVIS AND GLEN COE, Highland, 101,600 ha/
251,053 acres
CAIRNGORM MOUNTAINS, Highland/Aberdeenshire/
Moray, 67,200 ha/166,051 acres
CUILLIN HILLS, Highland, 21,900 ha/54,115 acres
DEESIDE AND LOCHNAGAR, Aberdeenshire, 40,000 ha/
98,840 acres
DORNOCH FIRTH, Highland, 7,500 ha/18,532 acres
EAST STEWARTRY COAST, Dumfries and Galloway,
4,500 ha/11,119 acres
EILDON AND LEADERFOOT, The Borders, 3,600 ha/
8,896 acres
FLEET VALLEY, Dumfries and Galloway, 5,300 ha/
13,096 acres
GLEN AFFRIC, Highland, 19,300 ha/47,690 acres
GLEN STRATHFARRAR, Highland, 3,800 ha/9,390 acres
HOY AND WEST MAINLAND, Orkney Islands, 14,800
ha/36,571 acres
JURA, Argyll and Bute, 21,800 ha/53,868 acres
KINTAIL, Highland, 15,500 ha/38,300 acres
KNAPDALE, Argyll and Bute, 19,800 ha/48,926 acres
KNOYDART, Highland, 39,500 ha/97,604 acres
KYLE OF TONGUE, Highland, 18,500 ha/45,713 acres
KYLES OF BUTE, Argyll and Bute, 4,400 ha/10,872 acres
LOCH NA KEAL, MULL, Argyll and Bute, 12,700 ha/
31,382 acres
LOCH LOMOND, Argyll and Bute, 27,400 ha/67,705
acres
LOCH RANNOCH AND GLEN LYON, Perthshire and
Kinross, 48,400 ha/119,596 acres
LOCH SHIEL, Highland, 13,400 ha/33,111 acres
LOCH TUMMEL, Perthshire and Kinross, 9,200 ha/
22,733 acres
LYNN OF LORN, Argyll and Bute, 4,800 ha/11,861 acres
MORAR, MOIDART AND ARDNAMURCHAN, Highland,
13,500 ha/33,358 acres
NORTH-WEST SUTHERLAND, Highland, 20,500 ha/
50,655 acres
NITH ESTUARY, Dumfries and Galloway, 9,300 ha/
22,980 acres
NORTH ARRAN, North Ayrshire, 23,800 ha/58,810
acres
RIVER EARN, Perthshire and Kinross, 3,000 ha/7,413
acres
RIVER TAY, Perthshire and Kinross, 5,600 ha/13,838
acres
ST KILDA, Western Isles, 900 ha/2,224 acres
SCARBA, LUNGA AND THE GARVELLACHS, Argyll and
Bute, 1,900 ha/4,695 acres

SHETLAND, Shetland Isles, 11,600 ha/28,664 acres
SMALL ISLANDS, Highland, 15,500 ha/38,300 acres
SOUTH LEWIS, HARRIS AND NORTH UIST, Western
Isles, 109,600 ha/270,822 acres
SOUTH UIST MACHAIR, Western Isles, 6,100 ha/15,073
acres
THE TROSSACHS, Stirling, 4,600 ha/11,367 acres
TROTTERNISH, Highland, 5,000 ha/12,355 acres
UPPER TWEEDDALE, The Borders, 10,500 ha/25,945
acres
WESTER ROSS, Highland, 145,300 ha/359,036 acres

THE NATIONAL FOREST

The National Forest is being planted across 200 square miles of Derbyshire, Leicestershire and Staffordshire. Nearly six million trees, of mixed species but mainly broadleaved, have been planted, with the aim being to eventually cover about one-third of the designated area. The project is funded by the Department for Environment, Food and Rural Affairs. It was developed in 1992–5 by the Countryside Commission and is now run by the National Forest Company, which was established in April 1995. Under the National Forest Tender Scheme, anybody wishing to undertake a woodland creation project can submit a competitive bid to the National Forest Company.

NATIONAL FOREST COMPANY, Enterprise Glade, Bath
Lane, Moira, Swadlincote, Derbyshire DE12 6BD
T 01283-551211 W www.nationalforest.org
Chief Executive, Miss S. Bell, OBE

SITES OF SPECIAL SCIENTIFIC INTEREST

Site of Special Scientific Interest (SSSI) is a legal notification applied to land in England, Scotland or Wales which English Nature (EN), Scottish Natural Heritage (SNH) or the Countryside Council for Wales (CCW) identifies as being of special interest because of its flora, fauna, geological or physiographical features. In some cases, SSSIs are managed as nature reserves.

EN, SNH and CCW must notify the designation of an SSSI to the local planning authority, every owner/occupier of the land, and the Secretary of State for Environment, Food and Rural Affairs, the Scottish Ministers or the National Assembly for Wales. Forestry and agricultural departments and a number of other bodies are also informed of this notification.

Objections to the notification of an SSSI can be made and ultimately considered at a full meeting of the Council of EN or CCW. In Scotland an objection will be dealt with by the appropriate area board or the main board of SNH, depending on the nature of the objection. Unresolved objections on scientific grounds must be referred to the Advisory Committee on SSSI.

The protection of these sites depends on the co-operation of individual landowners and occupiers. Owner/occupiers must consult EN, SNH or CCW and, in England and Wales, gain written consent before they can undertake certain listed activities on the site. In Scotland, owner/occupiers can carry out a listed operation four months after consultation, unless SNH obtains a Nature Conservation Order from Scottish Ministers. Funds are available through management agreements and grants to assist owners and occupiers in conserving sites' interests. As a last resort a site can be purchased.

The number and area of SSSIs in Britain as at May 2004 was:

	No.	Hectares	Acres
England	4,111	1,076,704	2,660,536
Scotland	1,451	1,005,152	2,482,725
Wales*	1,021	264,354	652,954

* Some sites in Wales amalgamated 2002–3

NORTHERN IRELAND

In Northern Ireland 208 Areas of Special Scientific Interest (ASSIs) have been declared by the Department of the Environment for Northern Ireland.

NATIONAL NATURE RESERVES

National Nature Reserves are defined in the National Parks and Access to the Countryside Act 1949 as land designated for the study and preservation of flora and fauna, or of geological or physiographical features.

English Nature (EN), Scottish Natural Heritage (SNH) or the Countryside Council for Wales (CCW) can designate as a National Nature Reserve land which is being managed as a nature reserve under an agreement with one of the statutory nature conservation agencies; land held and managed by EN, SNH or CCW; or land held and managed as a nature reserve by another approved body. EN, SNH or CCW can make by-laws to protect reserves from undesirable activities; these are subject to confirmation by the Secretary of State for Environment, Food and Rural Affairs, the National Assembly for Wales or the Scottish Ministers in Scotland.

The number and area of National Nature Reserves in Britain as at May 2004 was:

	No.	Hectares	Acres
England	215	87,917	217,242
Scotland	66	117,228	289,612
Wales	67	24,123	59,584

NORTHERN IRELAND

National Nature Reserves are established and managed by the Department of the Environment for Northern Ireland, with advice from the Council for Nature Conservation and the Countryside. There are 48 National Nature Reserves covering 4,746.3 hectares (11,723 acres).

LOCAL NATURE RESERVES

Local Nature Reserves are defined in the National Parks and Access to the Countryside Act 1949 as land designated for the study and preservation of flora and fauna, or of geological or physiographical features. The Act gives local authorities in England, Scotland and Wales the power to acquire, declare and manage local nature reserves in consultation with English Nature, Scottish Natural Heritage and the Countryside Council for Wales. Other organisations, including wildlife trusts, may manage local nature reserves, providing that a local authority has a legal interest in the land.

The number and area of designated Local Nature Reserves in Britain as at May 2004 was:

	No.	Hectares	Acres
England	947	31,012	76,631
Scotland	36	9,410	23,252
Wales	54	4,890	12,078

FOREST NATURE RESERVES

In 1999 responsibility for forestry was transferred to Scottish Ministers and the National Assembly for Wales. Westminster retained responsibility for forestry in England and for international issues. In April 2003 Forest Enterprise, an executive agency of the Forestry Commission, ceased to exist as a single agency. Three new bodies for England, Scotland and Wales were created in its place. The Forest Enterprise manages 665,000 hectares in Scotland, 258,500 hectares in England and 130,000 hectares in Wales.

Forest Nature Reserves extend in size from under 50 hectares (124 acres) to over 500 hectares (1,236 acres). The largest include the Black Wood of Rannoch, by Loch Rannoch; Cannop Valley Oakwoods, Forest of Dean; Culbin Forest, near Forres; Glen Affric, near Fort Augustus; Kylerhea, Skye; Pembrey, Carmarthen Bay; Starr Forest, in Galloway Forest Park; and Wyre Forest, near Kidderminster.

NORTHERN IRELAND

There are 34 Forest Nature Reserves in Northern Ireland, covering 1,512 hectares (3,736 acres). They are designated and administered by the Forest Service, an agency of the Department of Agriculture and Rural Development for Northern Ireland. There are also 16 National Nature Reserves on Forest Service-owned property.

MARINE NATURE RESERVES

The Secretary of State for Environment, Food and Rural Affairs, the National Assembly for Wales and the Scottish Executive have the power to designate Marine Nature Reserves. English Nature, Scottish Natural Heritage and the Countryside Council for Wales select and manage these reserves. Marine Nature Reserves may be established in Northern Ireland under a 1985 Order.

Marine Nature Reserves provide protection for marine flora and fauna, and geological and physiographical features on land covered by tidal waters or parts of the sea in or adjacent to the UK. Reserves also provide opportunities for study and research.

The three statutory Marine Nature Reserves are:

LUNDY (1986), Bristol Channel
KOMER (1990), Dyfed
STRANGFORD LOUGH (1995), Northern Ireland

Non-statutory marine reserves have also been set up by conservation groups.

EUROPEAN MARINE SITES

The 1992 EC Habitats Directive and the 1979 Birds Directive allow the UK government to establish Special Areas of Conservation (SACs) or Special Protection Areas (SPAs) for animals and birds on land and at sea. Where the designated area includes sea or seashore it is described as a European marine site. The 1998–2002 UK Marine SACs project formed a demonstration initiative, funded partly by the EU, to establish management schemes for twelve of the marine SACs in the UK. In England, a further 11 management schemes have been published and five are being developed.

WORLD HERITAGE SITES

The Convention Concerning the Protection of the World Cultural and Natural Heritage was adopted by the United Nations Educational, Scientific and Cultural Organisation (UNESCO) in 1972 and ratified by the UK in 1984. As at 1 May 2004 the convention had been ratified by 178 states. The convention provides for the identification, protection and conservation of cultural and natural sites of outstanding universal value.

Cultural sites may be:
– monuments
– groups of buildings
– sites of historic, aesthetic, archaeological, scientific, ethnologic or anthropologic value
– historic areas of towns
– 'cultural landscapes', i.e. sites whose characteristics are marked by significant interactions between human populations and their natural environment

Natural sites may be:
– those with remarkable physical, biological or geological formations
– those with outstanding universal value from the point of view of science, conservation or natural beauty
– the habitat of threatened species and plants

Governments which are party to the convention nominate sites in their country for inclusion in the World Cultural and Natural Heritage List. Nominations are considered by the World Heritage Committee, an inter-governmental committee composed of 21 representatives of the parties to the convention. The committee is advised by the International Council on Monuments and Sites (ICOMOS), the International Centre for the Study of the Preservation and Restoration of Cultural Property (ICCROM) and the World Conservation Union (IUCN). ICOMOS evaluates and reports on proposed cultural sites, ICCROM provides expert advice and training on how to conserve the listed sites and IUCN advises on proposed natural sites. The Department for Culture, Media and Sport represents the UK government in matters relating to the convention.

A prerequisite for inclusion in the World Cultural and Natural Heritage List is the existence of an effective legal protection system in the country in which the site is situated (e.g. listing, conservation areas and planning controls in the United Kingdom) and a detailed management plan to ensure the conservation of the site. Inclusion in the list does not confer any greater degree of protection on the site than that offered by the national protection framework.

If a site is considered to be in serious danger of decay or damage the committee may add it to a complementary list, the World Heritage in Danger List. Sites on this list may benefit from particular attention or emergency measures.

Financial support for the conservation of sites on the World Cultural and Natural Heritage List is provided by the World Heritage Fund. This is administered by the World Heritage Committee, which determines the financial and technical aid to be allocated. The fund's income is derived from contributions of the parties to the convention, voluntary contributions from other States, other United Nations and intergovernmental organisations, public or private bodies and individuals, through interest due on the fund and from events organised for the benefit of the fund.

DESIGNATED SITES

As at 3 July 2004 there were 788 sites in 134 countries on the World Cultural and Natural Heritage List. Of these, 23 are in the United Kingdom and three in British overseas territories; 20 are listed for their cultural significance (†) and six for their natural significance (*). The year in which sites were designated appears in parentheses.

UNITED KINGDOM
†Bath – the city (1987)
†Blaenarvon, Wales (2000)
†Blenheim Palace and Park, Oxfordshire (1987)
†Canterbury Cathedral, St Augustine's Abbey, St Martin's Church, Kent (1988)
†Castle and town walls of King Edward I, north Wales – Beaumaris, Anglesey, Caernarfon Castle, Conwy Castle, Harlech Castle (1986)
†Derwent Valley Mills, Derbyshire (2001)
*Dorset and East Devon Coast (2001)
†Durham Cathedral and Castle (1986)
†Edinburgh Old and New Towns (1995)
*Giant's Causeway and Causeway coast, Co. Antrim (1986)
†Greenwich, London – maritime Greenwich, including the Royal Naval College, Old Royal Observatory, Queen's House, town centre (1997)
†Hadrian's Wall, northern England (1987)
†Heart of Neolithic Orkney (1999)
†Ironbridge Gorge, Shropshire – the world's first iron bridge and other early industrial sites (1986)
†Liverpool – six areas of the Maritime Mercantile City (2004)
†New Lanark, South Lanarkshire, Scotland (2001)
†Royal Botanic Gardens, Kew (2003)
*St Kilda, Western Isles (1986)
†Saltaire, West Yorkshire (2001)
†Stonehenge, Avebury and related megalithic sites, Wiltshire (1986)
†Studley Royal Park, Fountains Abbey, St Mary's Church, N. Yorkshire (1986)
†Tower of London (1988)
†Westminster Abbey, Palace of Westminster, St Margaret's Church, London (1987)

BRITISH OVERSEAS TERRITORIES
*Henderson Island, Pitcairn Islands, South Pacific Ocean (1988)
*Gough Island wildlife reserve (part of Tristan da Cunha), South Atlantic Ocean (1995)
*St George town and related fortifications, Bermuda (2000)

CONTACTS
ARCHITECTURE AND HISTORIC ENVIRONMENT DIVISION, Department for Culture, Media and Sport, Queen's Yard, 179a Tottenham Court Road, London W1T 7PA T 020-7211 2330
WORLD HERITAGE CENTRE, UNESCO, 7 Place de Fontenoy, 75007 Paris, France W www.unesco.org
INTERNATIONAL CENTRE FOR THE STUDY OF THE PRESERVATION AND RESTORATION OF CULTURAL PROPERTY (ICCROM), Via di San Michele 13, I-00153 Rome, Italy T (+ 39) (06) 585 531 W www.iccrom.org
INTERNATIONAL COUNCIL ON MONUMENTS AND SITES (ICOMOS), 70 Cowcross Street, London EC1M 6EJ T 020-7566 0031 W www.icomos.org
WORLD CONSERVATION UNION (IUCN), Rue Mauverney 28, 1196 Gland, Switzerland T (+ 41) (22) 999 0000 W www.iucn.org

CONSERVATION OF WILDLIFE AND HABITATS

The UK is party to a number of international conventions.

RAMSAR CONVENTION

The 1971 Ramsar Convention on Wetlands of International Importance especially as Waterfowl Habitat, entered into force in the UK in May 1976. As at May 2004, 138 countries were party to the convention.

The aim of the convention is the conservation and wise use of wetlands and their flora and fauna. Governments that are party to the convention must designate wetlands and include wetland conservation considerations in their land-use planning. A total of 1,364 wetland sites, totalling 121 million hectares have been designated for inclusion in the List of Wetlands of International Importance. The UK currently has 159* designated sites covering 849,106 hectares. The member countries meet every three years to assess the progress of the convention and the next meeting is scheduled for November 2005.

The UK has set targets under the Ramsar Strategic Plan, 2003–8. Progress towards these is monitored by the UK Ramsar Committee, known as the Joint Working Party. The UK and the Republic of Ireland have established a formal protocol to ensure common monitoring standards for waterbirds in the two countries.
* The UK government consolidated a number of overlapping sites in 2004, resulting in a lower total compared with 2003.
RAMSAR CONVENTION BUREAU, Rue Mauverney 28, CH-1196 Gland, Switzerland T (+41) (22) 999 0170 W www.ramsar.org

BIODIVERSITY

There is much synergy between the Ramsar Convention and the 1992 Convention on Biological Diversity. In 1996 the Ramsar Secretariat became a lead partner in implementing activities under the Convention on Biological Diversity with joint work plans. The UK ratified the Convention on Biological Diversity in June 1994. As at May 2004 there were 188 parties to the convention.

The objectives are the conservation of biological diversity, the sustainable use of its components and the fair and equitable sharing of the benefits arising out of the use of genetic resources. There are thematic work programmes addressing marine and coastal, forest, inland waters, dry land and sub-humid land. The Conference of the Parties to the Convention on Biological Diversity adopted a supplementary agreement to the Convention known as the *Cartagena Protocol on Biosafety* on 29 January 2000. The protocol seeks to protect biological diversity from potential risks that may be posed by introducing modified living organisms, resulting from modern biotechnology, into the environment. As at May 2004 101 countries were party to the protocol. The UK became party to the protocol on 17 February 2004.

The UK published its own Biodiversity Action Plan in 1994. A report from the UK Biodiversity Steering Group, published in 1995, proposed monitoring a list of 1,252 species to check on biodiversity within the UK.

A report, *Sustaining the Variety of Life: 5 years of the UK Biodiversity Action Plan*, was published in March 2001 and made a number of recommendations including to support actions for the conservation of species and habitats at UK, county and local levels. There are around 391 Species Action Plans, 45 Habitat Action Plans and 162 Local Biodiversity Action Plans. There are four country groups: England Biodiversity Group, Scotland Biodiversity Forum, Northern Ireland Biodiversity Group and Wales Biodiversity Partnership. These are involved in implementing the action plans at national level. In October 2002, the England Biodiversity Group, DEFRA and the Biodiversity Policy Unit jointly launched a *Biodiversity Strategy for England* as part of the UK Biodiversity Action Plan.
BIODIVERSITY POLICY UNIT, Zone 1/10b, Temple Quay House, 2 The Square, Temple Quay, Bristol BS1 6EB T 0117-372 6276 E admin@ukbap.org.uk W www.ukbap.org.uk

CITES

The 1973 Convention on International Trade in Endangered Species of Wild Fauna and Flora (CITES) came into force in the UK in July 1975. Currently 166 countries are members. The countries party to the convention ban commercial international trade in an agreed list of endangered species and regulate and monitor trade in others species that might become endangered. The convention covers approximately 5,000 species of animals and 28,000 species of plants.

The Conference of the Parties to CITES meets every two to three years to review the convention's implementation. The Global Wildlife Division at the Department for Environment, Food and Rural Affairs carries out the government's responsibilities under CITES and the Bonn Convention on the Conservation of Migratory Species of Wild Animals.
CITES SECRETARIAT, International Environment House, Chemin des Anémones, CH-1219 Châtelaine, Geneva, Switzerland T (+41) (22) 917 8139/8140 E cites@unep.ch W www.cites.org

BONN CONVENTION

The 1979 Convention on Conservation of Migratory Species of Wild Animals came into force in the UK in October 1979. As at 1 June 2004, 86 countries were party to the convention.

It requires the protection of listed endangered migratory species and encourages international agreements covering these and other threatened species. International agreements can range from legally binding treaties to less formal memoranda of understanding. Six agreements have been concluded to date under the convention. They aim to conserve: seals in the Wadden Sea; bat populations in Europe; small cetaceans of the Baltic and North Seas; African-Eurasian migratory waterbirds; cetaceans of the Mediterranean and Black Seas; and albatrosses and petrels. A further seven memorandums of understanding have been agreed for the Siberian Crane, Slender-billed Curlew, marine turtles of the Atlantic coast of Africa, Indian Ocean and South-East Asia, the middle-European population of the Great Bustard, Bukhara Deer and the Aquatic Warbler.
UNEP/CMS SECRETARIAT, Martin-Luther-King-Str. 8, D-53175, Bonn, Germany T (+49) (228) 81 2401/2 E secretariat@cms.int W www.cms.int

BERN CONVENTION

The 1979 Bern Convention on the Conservation of European Wildlife and Natural Habitats came into force in the UK in June 1982. Currently there are 45 Contracting Parties and a number of other states attend meetings as observers.

The aims are to conserve wild flora and fauna and their natural habitats, especially where this requires the co-operation of several countries, and to promote such co-operation. The convention gives particular emphasis to endangered and vulnerable species.

All parties to the convention must promote national conservation policies and take account of the conservation of wild flora and fauna when setting planning and development policies. Reports on contracting parties' conservation policies must be submitted to the Standing Committee every four years.

SECRETARIAT OF THE BERN CONVENTION STANDING COMMITTEE, Council of Europe, 67075 Strasbourg-Cedex, France T (+33) (3) 8841 2000 W www.coe.int

EUROPEAN WILDLIFE TRADE REGULATION

The Council (EC) Regulation on the Protection of Species of Wild Fauna and Flora by Regulating Trade Therein came into force in the UK on 1 June 1997. It is intended to standardise wildlife trade regulations across Europe and to improve the application of CITES.

UK LEGISLATION

The Wildlife and Countryside Act 1981 gives legal protection to a wide range of wild animals and plants. Subject to parliamentary approval, the Secretary of State for Environment, Food and Rural Affairs may vary the animals and plants given legal protection. The most recent variation of Schedules 5 and 8 came into effect in March and April 1998.

Under Section 9 of the Act it is an offence to kill, injure, take, possess or sell (whether alive or dead) any wild animal included in Schedule 5 of the Act and to disturb its place of shelter and protection or to destroy that place.

Under Section 13 of the Act it is illegal without a licence to pick, uproot, sell or destroy plants listed in Schedule 8. Since January 2001, under the Countryside and Rights of Way Act 2000, persons found guilty of an offence under part 1 of the Wildlife and Countryside Act 1981 face a maximun penalty of up to £5,000 and/or up to six months custodial sentence per specimen.

The Act lays down a close season for wild birds (other than game birds) from 1 February to 31 August inclusive, each year. Exceptions to these dates are made for:

Capercaillie and (except Scotland) Woodcock – 1 February to 30 September

Snipe – 1 February to 11 August

Birds listed on Schedule 2, part 1 (see below) (below high water mark) – 21 February to 31 August

Birds listed on Schedule 2, Part 1, which may be killed or taken outside the close season (except on Sundays and on Christmas Day in Scotland, and on Sundays in prescribed areas of England and Wales) are capercaille, coot, certain wild duck (gadwall, goldeneye, mallard, pintail, pochard, shoveler, teal, tufted duck, wigeon), certain wild geese (Canada, greylag, pink-footed, white-fronted (in England and Wales only)), moorhen, golden plover and woodcock.

Section 16 of the 1981 Act allows licences to be issued on either an individual or general basis, to allow the killing, taking and sale of certain birds for specified reasons such as public health and safety. All other British birds are fully protected by law throughout the year.

ANIMALS PROTECTED BY SCHEDULE 5

Adder *(Vipera berus)*
Allis shad *(Alosa alosa)*
Atlantic Stream Crayfish *(Austropotomobius pallipes)*
Anemone, Ivell's Sea *(Edwardsia ivelli)*
Anemone, Starlet Sea *(Nematosella vectensis)*
Apus, Tadpole shrimp *(Triops cancriformis)*
Bat, Horseshoe *(Rhinolophidae,* all species*)*
Bat, Typical *(Vespertilionidae,* all species*)*
Beetle *(Graphoderus zonatus)*
Beetle *(Hypebaeus flavipes)*
Beetle, Lesser Silver Water *(Hydrochara caraboides)*
Beetle, Mire Pill *(Curimopsis nigrita)*
Beetle, Rainbow Leaf *(Chrysolina cerealis)*
Beetle, Stag *(Lucanus cervus)*
Beetle, Violet Click *(Limoniscus violaceus)*
Beetle, Water *(Paracymus aeneus)*
Burbot *(Lota lota)*
Butterfly, Adonis Blue *(Lysandra bellargus)*
Butterfly, Black Hairstreak *(Strymonidia pruni)*
Butterfly, Brown Hairstreak *(Thecla betulae)*
Butterfly, Chalkhill Blue *(Lysandra coridon)*
Butterfly, Chequered Skipper *(Carterocephalus palaemon)*
Butterfly, Duke of Burgundy Fritillary *(Hamearis lucina)*
Butterfly, Glanville Fritillary *(Melitaea cinxia)*
Butterfly, Heath Fritillary *(Mellicta athalia* (or *Melitaea athalia))*
Butterfly, High Brown Fritillary *(Argynnis adippe)*
Butterfly, Large Blue *(Maculinea arion)*
Butterfly, Large Copper *(Lycaena dispar)*
Butterfly, Large Heath *(Coenonympha tullia)*
Butterfly, Large Tortoiseshell *(Nymphalis polychloros)*
Butterfly, Lulworth Skipper *(Thymelicus acteon)*
Butterfly, Marsh Fritillary *(Eurodryas aurinia)*
Butterfly, Mountain Ringlet *(Erebia epiphron)*
Butterfly, Northern Brown Argus *(Aricia artaxerxes)*
Butterfly, Pearl-bordered Fritillary *(Boloria euphrosyne)*
Butterfly, Purple Emperor *(Apatura iris)*
Butterfly, Silver Spotted Skipper *(Hesperia comma)*
Butterfly, Silver-studded Blue *(Plebejus argus)*
Butterfly, Small Blue *(Cupido minimus)*
Butterfly, Swallowtail *(Papilio machaon)*
Butterfly, White Letter Hairstreak *(Stymonida w-album)*
Butterfly, Wood White *(Leptidea sinapis)*
Cat, Wild *(Felis silvestris)*
Cicada, New Forest *(Cicadetta montana)*
Cricket, Field *(Gryllus campestris)*
Cricket, Mole *(Gryllotalpa gryllotalpa)*
Damselfly, Southern *(Coenagrion mercuriale)*
Dolphin *(Cetacea)*
Dormouse *(Muscardinus avellanarius)*
Dragonfly, Norfolk Aeshna *(Aeshna isosceles)*
Frog, Common *(Rana temporaria)*
Goby, Couch's *(Gobius couchii)*
Goby, Giant *(Gobius cobitis)*
Grasshopper, Wart-biter *(Decticus verrucivorus)*
Hatchet Shell, Northern *(Thyasira gouldi)*
Hydroid, Marine *(Clavopsella navis)*
Lagoon Snail *(Paludinella littorina)*
Lagoon Snail, De Folin's *(Caecum armoricum)*
Lagoon Worm, Tentacled *(Alkmaria romijni)*

Leech, Medicinal *(Hirudo medicinalis)*
Lizard, Sand *(Lacerta agilis)*
Lizard, Viviparous *(Lacerta vivipara)*
Marten, Pine *(Martes martes)*
Mat, Trembling Sea *(Victorella pavida)*
Moth, Barberry Carpet *(Pareulype berberata)*
Moth, Black-veined *(Siona lineata* (or *Idaea lineata))*
Moth, Essex Emerald *(Thetidia smaragdaria)*
Moth, Fiery clearwing *(Bembecia chrysidiformis)*
Moth, Fisher's estuarine *(Gortyna borelii)*
Moth, New Forest Burnet *(Zygaena viciae)*
Moth, Reddish Buff *(Acosmetia caliginosa)*
Moth, Sussex Emerald *(Thalera fimbrialis)*
Mussel, Fan *(Atrina fragilis)*
Mussel, Freshwater Pearl *(Margaritifera margaritifera)*
Newt, Great Crested (or Warty) *(Triturus cristatus)*
Newt, Palmate *(Triturus helveticus)*
Newt, Smooth *(Triturus vulgaris)*
Otter, Common *(Lutra lutra)*
Porpoise *(Cetacea)*
Sandworm, Lagoon *(Armandia cirrhosa)*
Sea Fan, Pink *(Eunicella verrucosa)*
Sea Slug, Lagoon *(Tenellia adspersa)*
Shad, Twaite *(alosa fallax)*
Shark, Basking *(Cetorhinus maximus)*
Shrimp, Fairy *(Chirocephalus diaphanus)*
Shrimp, Lagoon Sand *(Gammarus insensibilis)*
Slow-worm *(Anguis fragilis)*
Snail, Glutinous *(Myxas glutinosa)*
Snail, Sandbowl *(Catinella arenaria)*
Snake, Grass *(Natrix natrix (Natrix helvetica))*
Snake, Smooth *(Coronella austriaca)*
Spider, Fen Raft *(Dolomedes plantarius)*
Spider, Ladybird *(Eresus niger)*
Squirrel, Red *(Sciurus vulgaris)*
Sturgeon *(Acipenser sturio)*
Toad, Common *(Bufo bufo)*
Toad, Natterjack *(Bufo calamita)*
Turtle, Marine *(Dermochelyidae* and *Cheloniidae, all species)*
Vendace *(Coregonus albula)*
Vole, Water *(Arvicola terrestris)*
Walrus *(Odobenus rosmarus)*
Whale *(Cetacea)*
Whitefish *(Coregonus lavaretus)*

PLANTS PROTECTED BY SCHEDULE 8

Adder's tongue, Least *(Ophioglossum lusitanicum)*
Alison, Small *(Alyssum alyssoides)*
Anomodon, Long leaved *(Anomodon longifolius)*
Beech-lichen, New Forest *(Enterographa elaborata)*
Blackwort *(Southbya nigrella)*
Bluebell *(Hyacinthoides non-scripta)*
Bolete, Royal *(Boletus regius)*
Broomrape, Bedstraw *(Orobanche caryophyllacea)*
Broomrape, Oxtongue *(Orobanche loricata)*
Broomrape, Thistle *(Orobanche reticulata)*
Cabbage, Lundy *(Rhynchosinapis wrightii)*
Calamint, Wood *(Calamintha sylvatica)*
Caloplaca, Snow *(Caloplaca nivalis)*
Catapyrenium, Tree *(Catapyrenium psoromoides)*
Catchfly, Alpine *(Lychnis alpina)*
Catillaria, Laurer's *(Catellaria laureri)*
Centaury, Slender *(Centaurium tenuiflorum)*
Cinquefoil, Rock *(Potentilla rupestris)*
Cladonia, Convoluted *(Cladonia convoluta)*
Cladonia, Upright Mountain *(Cladonia stricta)*
Clary, Meadow *(Salvia pratensis)*
Club-rush, Triangular *(Scirpus triquetrus)*

Colt's-foot, Purple *(Homogyne alpina)*
Cotoneaster, Wild *(Cotoneaster integerrimus)*
Cottongrass, Slender *(Eriophorum gracile)*
Cow-wheat, Field *(Melampyrum arvense)*
Crocus, Sand *(Romulea columnae)*
Crystalwort, Lizard *(Riccia bifurca)*
Cudweed, Broad-leaved *(Filago pyramidata)*
Cudweed, Jersey *(Gnaphalium luteoalbum)*
Cudweed, Red-tipped *(Filago lutescens)*
Cut-grass *(Leersia oryzoides)*
Deptford Pink (England and Wales only) *(Dianthus armeria)*
Diapensia *(Diapensia lapponica)*
Dock, Shore *(Rumex rupestris)*
Earwort, Marsh *(Jamesoniella undulifolia)*
Eryngo, Field *(Eryngium campestre)*
Feather-moss, Polar *(Hygrohypnum polare)*
Fern, Dickie's bladder *(Cystopteris dickieana)*
Fern, Killarney *(Trichomanes speciosum)*
Flapwort, Norfolk *(Leiocolea rutheana)*
Fleabane, Alpine *(Erigeron borealis)*
Fleabane, Small *(Pulicaria vulgaris)*
Frostwort, Pointed *(Gymnomitrion apiculatum)*
Fungus, Hedgehog *(Hericium erinaceum)*
Galingale, Brown *(Cyperus fuscus)*
Gentian, Alpine *(Gentiana nivalis)*
Gentian, Dune *(Gentianella uliginosa)*
Gentian, Early *(Gentianella anglica)*
Gentian, Fringed *(Gentianella ciliata)*
Gentian, Spring *(Gentiana verna)*
Germander, Cut-leaved *(Teucrium botrys)*
Germander, Water *(Teucrium scordium)*
Gladiolus, Wild *(Gladiolus illyricus)*
Goblin Lights *(Catolechia wahlenbergii)*
Goosefoot, Stinking *(Chenopodium vulvaria)*
Grass-poly *(Lythrum hyssopifolia)*
Grimmia, Blunt-leaved *(Grimmia unicolor)*
Gyalecta, Elm *(Gyalecta ulmi)*
Hare's-ear, Sickle-leaved *(Bupleurum falcatum)*
Hare's-ear, Small *(Bupleurum baldense)*
Hawk's-beard, Stinking *(Crepis foetida)*
Hawkweed, Northroe *(Hieracium northroense)*
Hawkweed, Shetland *(Hieracium zetlandicum)*
Hawkweed, Weak-leaved *(Hieracium attenuatifolium)*
Heath, Blue *(Phyllodoce caerulea)*
Helleborine, Red *(Cephalanthera rubra)*
Helleborine, Young's *(Epipactis youngiana)*
Horsetail, Branched *(Equisetum ramosissimum)*
Hound's-tongue, Green *(Cynoglossum germanicum)*
Knawel, Perennial *(Scleranthus perennis)*
Knotgrass, Sea *(Polygonum maritimum)*
Lady's-slipper *(Cypripedium calceolus)*
Lecanactis, Churchyard *(Lecanactis hemisphaerica)*
Lecanora, Tarn *(Lecanora archariana)*
Lecidea, Copper *(Lecidea inops)*
Leek, Round-headed *(Allium sphaerocephalon)*
Lettuce, Least *(Lactuca saligna)*
Lichen, Arctic kidney *(Nephroma arcticum)*
Lichen, Ciliate strap *(Heterodermia leucomelos)*
Lichen, Coralloid rosette *(Heterodermia propagulifera)*
Lichen, Ear-lobed dog *(Peltigera lepidophora)*
Lichen, Forked hair *(Bryoria furcellata)*
Lichen, Golden hair *(Teloschistes flavicans)*
Lichen, Orange fruited Elm *(Caloplaca luteoalba)*
Lichen, River jelly *(Collema dichotomum)*
Lichen, Scaly breck *(Squamarina lentigera)*
Lichen, Stary breck *(Buellia asterella)*
Lily, Snowdon *(Lloydia serotina)*

Liverwort *(Petallophyllum ralfsi)*
Liverwort, Lindenberg's Leafy *(Adelanthus lindenbergianus)*
Marsh-mallow, Rough *(Althaea hirsuta)*
Marshwort, Creeping *(Apium repens)*
Milk-parsley, Cambridge *(Selinum carvifolia)*
Moss *(Drepanocladius vernicosus)*
Moss, Alpine copper *(Mielichoferia mielichoferi)*
Moss, Baltic bog *(Sphagnum balticum)*
Moss, Blue dew *(Saelania glaucescens)*
Moss, Blunt-leaved bristle *(Orthotrichum obtusifolium)*
Moss, Bright green cave *(Cyclodictyon laetevirens)*
Moss, Cordate beard *(Barbula cordata)*
Moss, Cornish path *(Ditrichum cornubicum)*
Moss, Derbyshire feather *(Thamnobryum angustifolium)*
Moss, Dune thread *(Bryum mamillatum)*
Moss, Flamingo *(Desmatodon cernuus)*
Moss, Glaucous beard *(Barbula glauca)*
Moss, Green shield *(Buxbaumia viridis)*
Moss, Hair silk *(Plagiothecium piliferum)*
Moss, Knothole *(Zygodon forsteri)*
Moss, Large yellow feather *(Scorpidium turgescens)*
Moss, Millimetre *(Micromitrium tenerum)*
Moss, Multifruited river *(Cryphaea lamyana)*
Moss, Nowell's limestone *(Zygodon gracilis)*
Moss, Rigid apple *(Bartramia stricta)*
Moss, Round-leaved feather *(Rhyncostegium rotundifolium)*
Moss, Schleicher's thread *(Bryum schleicheri)*
Moss, Triangular pygmy *(Acaulon triquetrum)*
Moss, Vaucher's feather *(Hypnum vaucheri)*
Mudwort, Welsh *(Limosella australis)*
Naiad, Holly-leaved *(Najas marina)*
Naiad, Slender *(Najas flexilis)*
Orache, Stalked *(Halimione pedunculata)*
Orchid, Early spider *(Ophrys sphegodes)*
Orchid, Fen *(Liparis loeselii)*
Orchid, Ghost *(Epipogium aphyllum)*
Orchid, Lapland marsh *(Dactylorhiza lapponica)*
Orchid, Late spider *(Ophrys fuciflora)*
Orchid, Lizard *(Himantoglossum hircinum)*
Orchid, Military *(Orchis militaris)*
Orchid, Monkey *(Orchis simia)*
Pannaria, Caledonia *(Panneria ignobilis)*
Parmelia, New Forest *(Parmelia minarum)*
Parmentaria, Oil stain *(Parmentaria chilensis)*
Pear, Plymouth *(Pyrus cordata)*
Penny-cress, Perfoliate *(Thlaspi perfoliatum)*
Pennyroyal *(Mentha pulegium)*
Pertusaria, Alpine moss *(Pertusaria bryontha)*
Physcia, Southern grey *(Physcia tribacioides)*
Pigmyweed *(Crassula aquatica)*
Pine, Ground *(Ajuga chamaepitys)*
Pink, Cheddar *(Dianthus gratianopolitanus)*
Pink, Childing *(Petroraghia nanteuilii)*

Plantain, Floating water *(Luronium natans)*
Polypore, Oak *(Buglossoporus pulvinus)*
Pseudocyphellaria, Ragged *(Pseudocyphellaria lacerata)*
Psora, Rusty Alpine *(Psora rubiformis)*
Puffball, Sandy Stilt *(Battarraea phalloides)*
Ragwort, Fen *(Senecio paludosus)*
Ramping-fumitory, Martin's *(Fumaria martinii)*
Rampion, Spiked *(Phyteuma spicatum)*
Restharrow, Small *(Ononis reclinata)*
Rock-cress, Alpine *(Arabis alpina)*
Rock-cress, Bristol *(Arabis stricta)*
Rustwort, Western *(Marsupella profunda)*
Sandwort, Norwegian *(Arenaria norvegica)*
Sandwort, Teesdale *(Minuartia stricta)*
Saxifrage, Drooping *(Saxifraga cernua)*
Saxifrage, Marsh *(Saxifrage hirulus)*
Saxifrage, Tufted *(Saxifraga cespitosa)*
Solenopsora, Serpentine *(Solenopsora liparina)*
Solomon's-seal, Whorled *(Polygonatum verticillatum)*
Sow-thistle, Alpine *(Cicerbita alpina)*
Spearwort, Adder's-tongue *(Ranunculus ophioglossifolius)*
Speedwell, Fingered *(Veronica triphyllos)*
Speedwell, Spiked *(Veronica spicata)*
Spike rush, Dwarf *(Eleocharis parvula)*
Stack Fleawort, South *(Tephroseris integrifolia (ssp maritima))*
Star-of-Bethlehem, Early *(Gagea bohemica)*
Starfruit *(Damasonium alisma)*
Stonewort, Bearded *(Chara canescens)*
Stonewort, Foxtail *(Lamprothamnium papulosum)*
Strapwort *(Corrigiola litoralis)*
Sulphur-tresses, Alpine *(Alectoria ochroleuca)*
Threadmoss, Long-leaved *(Bryum neodamense)*
Turpswort *(Geocalyx graveolens)*
Violet, Fen *(Viola persicifolia)*
Viper's-grass *(Scorzonera humilis)*
Water-plantain, Ribbon-leaved *(Alisma gramineum)*
Wood-sedge, Starved *(Carex depauperata)*
Woodsia, Alpine *(Woodsia alpina)*
Woodsia, Oblong *(Woodsia ilvenis)*
Wormwood, Field *(Artemisia campestris)*
Woundwort, Downy *(Stachys germanica)*
Woundwort, Limestone *(Stachys alpina)*
Yellow-rattle, Greater *(Rhinanthus serotinus)*

MOST UNDER THREAT

The animals and birds considered to be most under threat in Great Britain by the Joint Nature Conservation Committee are the high brown fritillary butterfly; violet click beetle; new forest burnet moth; corncrake; aquatic warbler; tree sparrow; wryneck; water vole; red squirrel; allis shad; and twaite shad.

HISTORIC BUILDINGS AND MONUMENTS

Under the Planning (Listed Buildings and Conservation Areas) Act 1990, the Secretary of State for Culture, Media and Sport has a statutory duty to compile lists of buildings or groups of buildings in England which are of special architectural or historic interest. Under the Ancient Monuments and Archaeological Areas Act 1979 as amended by the National Heritage Act 1983, the Secretary of State is also responsible for compiling a schedule of ancient monuments. Decisions are taken on the advice of English Heritage.

Listed buildings are classified into Grade I, Grade II* and Grade II. There are currently about 370,000 individual listed buildings in England, of which about 92 per cent are Grade II listed. Almost all pre-1700 buildings are listed, and most buildings of 1700 to 1840. English Heritage carries out thematic surveys of particular types of buildings with a view to making recommendations for listing, and members of the public may propose a building for consideration. The main purpose of listing is to ensure that care is taken in deciding the future of a building. No changes which affect the architectural or historic character of a listed building can be made without listed building consent (in addition to planning permission where relevant). Applications for listed building consent are normally dealt with by the local planning authority, although English Heritage is always consulted about proposals affecting Grade I and Grade II* properties. It is a criminal offence to demolish a listed building, or alter it in such a way as to affect its character, without consent.

There are currently about 18,300 scheduled monuments in England. English Heritage is carrying out a Monuments Protection Programme assessing archaeological sites with a view to making recommendations for scheduling, and members of the public may propose a monument for consideration. All monuments proposed for scheduling are considered to be of national importance. Where buildings are both scheduled and listed, ancient monuments legislation takes precedence. The main purpose of scheduling a monument is to preserve it for the future and to protect it from damage, destruction or any unnecessary interference. Once a monument has been scheduled, scheduled monument consent is required before any works can be carried out. The scope of the control is more extensive and more detailed than that applied to listed buildings, but certain minor works, as detailed in the Ancient Monuments (Class Consents) Order 1994, may be carried out without consent. It is a criminal offence to carry out unauthorised work to scheduled monuments.

Under the Planning (Listed Buildings and Conservation Areas) Act 1990 and the Ancient Monuments and Archaeological Areas Act 1979, the Secretary of State for Wales is responsible for listing buildings and scheduling monuments in Wales on the advice of CADW, the Historic Buildings Council for Wales and the Royal Commission on the Ancient and Historical Monuments of Wales. The criteria for evaluating buildings are similar to those in England and the same listing system is used. There are approximately 26,400 listed buildings and approximately 3,500 scheduled monuments in Wales.

Under the Planning (Listed Buildings and Conservation Areas) (Scotland) Act 1997 and the Ancient Monuments and Archaeological Areas Act 1979, Scottish Ministers are responsible for listing buildings and scheduling monuments in Scotland on the advice of Historic Scotland, the Historic Buildings Council for Scotland and the Royal Commission on the Ancient and Historical Monuments of Scotland. The criteria for evaluating buildings are similar to those in England but an A, B, C categorisation is used. There are approximately 46,000 listed buildings and 6,500 scheduled monuments in Scotland.

Under the Planning (Northern Ireland) Order 1991 and the Historic Monuments and Archaeological Objects (Northern Ireland) Order 1995, the Department of the Environment of the Northern Ireland Executive is responsible for listing buildings and scheduling monuments in Northern Ireland on the advice of the Historic Buildings Council for Northern Ireland and the Historic Monuments Council for Northern Ireland. The criteria for evaluating buildings are similar to those in England but no statutory grading system is used. There are approximately 8,500 listed buildings and 1,500 scheduled monuments in Northern Ireland.

OPENING TO THE PUBLIC
The following is a selection of the many historic buildings and monuments open to the public. Admission charges and opening hours vary. Many properties are closed in winter (usually November–March) and some are also closed in the mornings. Most properties are closed on Christmas Eve, Christmas Day, Boxing Day and New Year's Day, and many are closed on Good Friday. During the winter season, many English Heritage monuments are closed on Mondays and Tuesdays and monuments in the care of CADW are closed on Sunday mornings. In Northern Ireland many monuments are closed on Mondays except on bank holidays. Information about a specific property should be checked by telephone or online.

ENGLAND

For more information on any of the English Heritage properties listed below, the official website is:
www.english-heritage.org.uk
For more information on any of the National Trust properties listed below, the official website is:
www.nationaltrust.org.uk
EH English Heritage property
NT National Trust property

A LA RONDE (NT), Summer Lane, Exmouth, Devon EX8 5BD
  T 01395-265514
  Unique 16-sided house completed c.1796
ALNWICK CASTLE, Northumberland NE66 1NQ
  T 01665-510777 W www.alnwickcastle.com
  Seat of the Dukes of Northumberland since 1309; Italian Renaissance-style interior. Gardens with spectacular water features
ALTHORP, Northants NN7 4HQ T 0870-167 9000
  W www.althorp.com
  Spencer family seat. Diana, Princess of Wales memorabilia
ANGLESEY ABBEY (NT), Cambridge CB5 9EJ
  T 01223-810080

House built c.1600. Houses many paintings and a unique clock collection. Gardens and Lode Mill

APSLEY HOUSE, London W1J 7NT T 020-7499 5676
W www.apsleyhouse.org.uk
Built by Robert Adam 1771–8, home of the Dukes of Wellington since 1817 and known as 'No. 1 London'. Collection of fine and decorative arts

ARUNDEL CASTLE, W. Sussex BN18 9AB T 01903-883173
W www.arundelcastle.org
Castle dating from the Norman Conquest. Seat of the Dukes of Norfolk

AVEBURY (NT), Wilts SN8 1RF T 01672-539250
Remains of stone circles constructed 4,000 years ago surrounding the later village of Avebury

BANQUETING HOUSE, Whitehall, London SW1A 2ER
T 0870-751 5178 W www.hrp.org.uk
Designed by Inigo Jones; ceiling paintings by Rubens. Site of the execution of Charles I

BASILDON PARK (NT), Reading RG8 9NR T 0118-984 3040
Palladian house built in 1776–83 by John Carr

BATTLE ABBEY (EH), E. Sussex T 01424-773792 Remains of the abbey founded by William the Conqueror on the site of the Battle of Hastings

BEAULIEU, Hants SO42 7ZN T 01590-612345
W www.beaulieu.co.uk
House and gardens, Beaulieu Abbey and exhibition of monastic life, National Motor Museum

BEESTON CASTLE (EH), Cheshire CW6 9TX
T 01829-260464. Thirteenth-century inner ward with gatehouse and towers, and remains of outer ward built by Ranulf sixth Earl of Chester

BELTON HOUSE (NT), Leics NG32 2LS T 01476-566116
Fine 17th-century house, formal gardens in landscaped park

BELVOIR CASTLE, Leics NG32 1PD T 01476-871000
W www.belvoircastle.com.
Seat of the Dukes of Rutland; 19th-century Gothic-style castle

BERKELEY CASTLE, Glos GL13 9BQ T 01453-810332
Completed 1153; site of the murder of Edward II (1327)

BLENHEIM PALACE, Woodstock, Oxon OX20 1PX
T 0870-060 2080 W www.blenheimpalace.com
Seat of the Dukes of Marlborough and Winston Churchill's birthplace; designed by Vanbrugh

BLICKLING HALL (NT), Norwich NR11 6NF
T 01263-738030
Jacobean house with state rooms, temple and 18th-century orangery

BODIAM CASTLE (NT), E. Sussex TN32 5UA
T 01580-830436
Well-preserved medieval moated castle, built 1385

BOLSOVER CASTLE (EH), Derbys S44 6PR T 01246-822844
Notable 17th-century buildings

BOSCOBEL HOUSE (EH), Shropshire T 01902-850244
Timber-framed 17th-century hunting lodge, refuge of fugitive Charles II

BOUGHTON HOUSE, Northants NN14 1BJ T 01536-515731
W www.boughtonhouse.org.uk
A 17th-century house with French-style additions. Home of the Dukes of Buccleuch and Queensbury

BOWOOD HOUSE, Wilts SN11 0PQ T 01249-812102
W www.bowood-house.co.uk
An 18th-century house in Capability Brown park, with lake, temple and arboretum

BROADLANDS, Hants SO51 9ZD T 01794-505010
W www.broadlands.net
Palladian mansion in Capability Brown parkland. Mountbatten exhibition

BRONTË PARSONAGE, Haworth, W. Yorks BD22 8DR
T 01535-642323 W www.bronte.org,uk
Home of the Brontë sisters; museum and memorabilia

BUCKFAST ABBEY, Devon TQ11 0EE T 01364-642500
W www.buckfast.org.uk
Benedictine monastery on medieval foundations

BUCKINGHAM PALACE, London SW1A 1AA
T 020-7839 1377 W www.royal.gov.uk
Purchased by George III in 1762, the Sovereign's official London residence since 1837. Eighteen state rooms, including the Throne Room, and Picture Gallery

BUCKLAND ABBEY (NT), Devon PL20 6EY T 01822-853607
A 13th-century Cistercian monastery. Home of Sir Francis Drake

BURGHLEY HOUSE, Stamford, Lincs T 01780-752451
W www.burghley.co.uk
Late Elizabethan house built by William Cecil, first Lord Burghley

CALKE ABBEY (NT), Derbys DE73 1LE T 01332-863822
Baroque 18th-century mansion

CARISBROOKE CASTLE (EH), Isle of Wight PO30 1XY
T 01983-522107 W www.carisbrookecastlemuseum.org.uk
Norman castle; prison of Charles I 1647–8

CARLISLE CASTLE (EH), Cumbria CA3 8UR T 01228-591922
Medieval castle, prison of Mary Queen of Scots

CARLYLE'S HOUSE (NT), Cheyne Row, London SW3 5HL
T 020-7352 7087
Home of Thomas Carlyle

CASTLE ACRE PRIORY (EH), Norfolk T 01760-755394
Remains include 12th-century church and prior's lodgings

CASTLE DROGO (NT), Devon EX6 6PB T 01647-433306
Granite castle designed by Lutyens

CASTLE HOWARD, N. Yorks YO60 7DA T 01653-648444
W www.castlehoward.co.uk
Designed by Vanbrugh 1699–1726; mausoleum designed by Hawksmoor

CASTLE RISING (EH), Norfolk T 01553-631330
A 12th-century keep in a massive earthwork with gate-house and bridge

CHARTWELL (NT), Kent TN16 1PS T 01732-868381
Home of Sir Winston Churchill

CHATSWORTH, Derbys DE45 1PP T 01246-582204
W www.chatsworth-house.co.uk
Tudor mansion in magnificent parkland

CHESTERS ROMAN FORT (EH), Northumberland
T 01434-681379
Roman cavalry fort

CHYSAUSTER ANCIENT VILLAGE (EH), Cornwall
T 07831-757934 Remains of Celtic settlement. Eight stone-walled homesteads

CLIFFORD'S TOWER (EH), York T 01904-646940
A 13th-century tower built on a mound

CLIVEDEN (NT), Maidenhead SL6 0JA T 01628-605069
Former home of the Astors, now a hotel set in garden and woodland

CORBRIDGE ROMAN SITE (EH), Northumberland
T 01434-632349
Excavated central area of a Roman town and successive military bases

CORFE CASTLE (NT), Wareham BH20 5EZ T 01929-481294
Ruined former royal castle dating from 11th-century

CROFT CASTLE (NT), Herefordshire HR6 9PW
T 01568-780246
Pre-Conquest border castle with Georgian-Gothic interic

DEAL CASTLE (EH), Kent T 01304-372762
Largest of the coastal defence forts built by Henry VIII

DICKENS'S HOUSE, 48 Doughty Street, London WC1N 2LX
T 020-7405 2127 W www.dickensmuseum.com
House occupied by Charles Dickens 1837–9; manu-
scripts, furniture and portraits

DOVE COTTAGE, Grasmere, Cumbria LA22 9SH
T 01539-435544 W www.wordsworth.org.uk
Wordsworth's home 1799–1808; museum

DOVER CASTLE (EH), Kent CT16 1HU T 01304-201628
Castle with Roman, Saxon and Norman features; wartime
operations rooms

DR JOHNSON'S HOUSE, 17 Gough Square, London EC4A
3DE T 020-7353 3745 W www.drjh.dircon.co.uk
Home of Samuel Johnson

DUNSTANBURGH CASTLE (EH), Northumberland
T 01665-576231
A 14th-century castle on a cliff, with a substantial gate-
house-keep

ELTHAM PALACE (EH), Court Yard, Eltham, London SE9 5QE
T 020-8294 2548
Combines an Art Deco country house and remains of
medieval palace set in moated gardens.

FARLEIGH HUNGERFORD CASTLE (EH), Somerset BA2
7RS T 01225-754026
Late 14th-century castle with two courts; chapel with
tomb of Sir Thomas Hungerford

FARNHAM CASTLE KEEP (EH), Surrey GU9 0AG
T 01252-713393
Large 12th-century Motte and Bailey

FOUNTAINS ABBEY (NT), nr Ripon, N. Yorks HG4 3DY
T 01765-608888 W www.fountainsabbey.org.uk
Deer park, visitor centre and St Church. Ruined
Cistercian monastery; 18th-century landscaped gardens
of Studley Royal estate

FRAMLINGHAM CASTLE (EH), Suffolk T 01728-724189
W www.framlingham.com
Castle (c.1200) with high curtain walls enclosing an
almshouse (1639)

FURNESS ABBEY (EH), Cumbria T 01229-823420
Remains of church and conventual buildings founded
in 1123

GLASTONBURY ABBEY, Somerset BA6 9EL T 01458-832267
W www.glastonburyabbey.com
Ruins of a 12th-century abbey rebuilt after fire. Site of an
early Christian settlement

GOODRICH CASTLE (EH), Herefordshire T 01600-890538
Remains of 13th- and 14th-century castle with 12th-
century keep

GREENWICH, London SE10 T 020-8858 6565
W www.rog.nmm.ac.uk
Former Royal Observatory (founded 1675) housing the
time ball and zero meridian of longitude. The Queen's
House. T 020-8858 4422. Designed for Queen Anne,
wife of James I, by Inigo Jones. Painted Hall and
Chapel (Royal Naval College)

GRIMES GRAVES (EH), Norfolk T 01842-810656
Neolithic flint mines. One shaft can be descended

GUILDHALL, London EC2P 2EJ T 020-7606 3030
Centre of civic government of the City. Built c.1441;
facade built 1788–9

HADDON HALL, Derbys DE45 1LA T 01629-812855
W www.haddonhall.co.uk
Well-preserved 12th-century manor house

HAILES ABBEY (EH), Glos GL54 5PB T 01242-602398
Ruins of a 13th-century Cistercian monastery

HAM HOUSE (NT), Richmond, Surrey TW10 7RS
T 020-8940 1950
Stuart house with fine interiors

HAMPTON COURT PALACE, East Molesey, Surrey KT8 9AU
T 0870-752 7777 W www.hrp.org.uk
A 16th-century palace with additions by Wren. Gardens
with maze; Tudor tennis court (summer only)

HARDWICK HALL (NT), Derbys S44 5QJ T 01246-850430
Built 1591–7 for Bess of Hardwick; notable furnishings

HARDY'S COTTAGE (NT), Dorset DT2 8QJ T 01305-262366
Birthplace and home of Thomas Hardy

HAREWOOD HOUSE, W. Yorks LS17 9LQ T 0113-218 1010
An 18th-century house designed by John Carr and
Robert Adam; park by Capability Brown

HATFIELD HOUSE, Herts AL9 5NQ T 01707-287000
W www.hatfield-house.co.uk
Jacobean house built by Robert Cecil; surviving wing of
Royal Palace of Hatfield (1497)

HELMSLEY CASTLE (EH), N. Yorks YO62 5AB T 01439-770442
A 12th-century keep and curtain wall with 16th-century
buildings. Spectacular earthwork defences

HEVER CASTLE, Kent TN8 7NG T 01732-865224
W www.hevercastle.co.uk
A 13th-century double-moated castle, childhood home
of Anne Boleyn

HOLKER HALL, Cumbria LA11 7PL T 01539-558328
W www.holker-hall.co.uk
Former home of the Dukes of Devonshire; award-
winning gardens

HOLKHAM HALL, Norfolk NR23 1AB T 01328-710227
W www.holkham.co.uk
Fine Palladian mansion

HOUSESTEADS ROMAN FORT (EH), Northumberland.
T 01434-344363 W www.hadrians-wall.org
Excavated infantry fort on Hadrian's Wall with extra-
mural civilian settlement

HUGHENDEN MANOR (NT), High Wycombe HP14 4LA
T 01494-755565
Home of Disraeli; small formal garden

JANE AUSTEN'S HOUSE, Chawton, Hants GU34 1SD
T 01420-83262 Jane Austen's home 1809–17

KEDLESTON HALL (NT), Derby DE22 5JH T 01332-842191
A classical Palladian mansion built 1759–65; complete
Robert Adam interiors.

KELMSCOTT MANOR, nr Lechlade, Glos GL7 3HJ
T 01367-252486 W www.kelmscottmanor.co.uk
Summer home of William Morris, with products of
Morris and Co.

KENILWORTH CASTLE (EH), Warks CV8 1NE
T 01926-852078 Largest castle ruin in England

KENSINGTON PALACE, London W8 4PX T 0870-751 5170
W www.hrp.org.uk
Built in 1605 and enlarged by Wren; bought by William
and Mary in 1689. Birthplace of Queen Victoria. Royal
Ceremonial Dress Collection

KENWOOD HOUSE (EH), Hampstead Lane, London NW3 7JR
T 020-8348 1286
Adam villa housing the Iveagh bequest of paintings and
furniture

KEW, Surrey TW9 3AB T 020-8332 5655
W www.rbgkew.org.uk Queen Charlotte's Cottage

KINGSTON LACY (NT), Dorset BH21 4EA T 01202-882402
A 17th-century house with 19th-century alterations;
important art collection

KNEBWORTH HOUSE, Herts SG3 6PY T 01438-812661
W www.knebworthhouse.com
Tudor manor house concealed by 19th-century Gothic
decoration; Lutyens gardens

KNOLE (NT), Kent TN15 0RP T 01732-450608
House dating from 1456 set in parkland; fine art
treasures

LAMBETH PALACE, London SE1 7JU T 020-7898 1200
W www.archbishopofcanterbury.org. Official residence of
the Archbishop of Canterbury. A 19th-century house
with parts dating from the 12th-century

LANERCOST PRIORY (EH), Cumbria CA8 2HQ
T 01697-73030
The nave of the Augustinian priory church, c.1166, is still
used; remains of other claustral buildings

LANHYDROCK (NT), Cornwall PL30 5AD T 01208-265950
House dating from the 17th-century; 45 rooms,
including kitchen and nursery

LEEDS CASTLE, Kent ME17 1PL T 01622-765400
W www.leeds-castle.com
Castle dating from 9th-century, on two islands in lake

LEVENS HALL, Cumbria LA8 0PD T 01539-560321
W www.levenshall.co.uk
Elizabethan house with unique topiary garden (1694).
Steam engine collection

LINCOLN CASTLE LN1 3AA T 01522-511068
Built by William the Conqueror in 1068

LINDISFARNE PRIORY (EH), Northumberland.
T 01289-389200
Founded in AD 635; re-established in the 12th-century
as a Benedictine priory, now ruined

LITTLE MORETON HALL (NT), Cheshire CW12 4SD
T 01260-272018 Timber-framed moated manor house
with knot garden

LONGLEAT HOUSE, Wilts BA12 7NW T 01985-844400
W www.longleat.co.uk
Elizabethan house in Italian Renaissance style

LULLINGSTONE ROMAN VILLA (EH), Kent.
T 01322-863467
Large villa occupied for much of the Roman period; fine
mosaics

MANSION HOUSE, London EC4N 8BH T 020-7626 2500
W www.cityoflondon.gov.uk
The official residence of the Lord Mayor of London

MARBLE HILL HOUSE (EH), Twickenham, Middx TW1 2NL
T 020-8892 5115 English Palladian villa with Georgian
paintings and furniture

MICHELHAM PRIORY, E. Sussex T 01323-844224
Tudor house built onto an Augustinian priory

MIDDLEHAM CASTLE (EH), N. Yorks DL8 4QR
T 01969-623899
A 12th-century keep within later fortifications.
Childhood home of Richard III

MONTACUTE HOUSE (NT), Somerset TA15 6XP
T 01935-823289
Elizabethan house with National Portrait Gallery.
Portraits from the period

MOUNT GRACE PRIORY (EH), N. Yorks DL6 3JG
T 01609-883494. Carthusian monastery, with remains of
monastic buildings

NETLEY ABBEY (EH), Hants SO31 5GA T 023-9258 1059
Remains of 13th-century Cistercian abbey, used as house
in Tudor period

OLD SARUM (EH), Wilts. T 01722-335398
Earthworks enclosing remains of the castle and the 11th-
century cathedral

ORFORD CASTLE (EH), Suffolk. T 01394-450472
Circular keep of c.1170 and remains of coastal defence
castle built by Henry II

OSBORNE HOUSE (EH), Isle of Wight. T 01983-200022
Queen Victoria's seaside residence

OSTERLEY PARK HOUSE (NT), Isleworth, Middx TW7 4RB
T 020-8232 5050 W www.osterleypark.org.uk
Elizabethan mansion set in parkland

PENDENNIS CASTLE (EH), Cornwall. T 01326-316594
Well-preserved 16th-century coastal defence castle

PENSHURST PLACE, Kent TN11 8DG T 01892-870307
W www.penhurstplace.com
House with medieval Baron's Hall and 14th-century
gardens

PETWORTH (NT), W. Sussex GU28 0AE T 01798-343929
Late 17th-century house set in Capability Brown
landscaped park

PEVENSEY CASTLE (EH), E. Sussex. T 01323-762604
Walls of a 4th-century Roman fort; remains of an
11th-century castle

PEVERIL CASTLE (EH), Derbys S33 8WQ T 01433-620613
A 12th-century castle defended on two sides by precipit-
ous rocks

POLESDEN LACEY (NT), Surrey RH5 6BD T 01372-458203
Regency villa remodelled in the Edwardian era. Fine
paintings and furnishings

PORTCHESTER CASTLE (EH), Hants PO3 5LY
T 023-9237 8291 Walls of a late Roman fort enclosing a
Norman keep and an Augustinian priory church

POWDERHAM CASTLE, Devon EX6 8JQ T 01626-890243
W www.powderham.co.uk
Medieval castle with 18th- and 19th-century alterations.
Historic home of the Earl of Devon

RABY CASTLE, Co. Durham DL2 3AH T 01833-660202
W www.rabycastle.com
A 14th-century castle with walled gardens

RAGLEY HALL, Warks B49 5NJ T 01789-762090
W www.ragleyhall.com
A 17th-century house with gardens, park and lake

RICHBOROUGH ROMAN FORT (EH), Kent.
T 01304-612013. Landing-site of the Claudian invasion
in AD 43

RICHMOND CASTLE (EH), N. Yorks. T 01748-822493
A 12th-century keep with 11th-century curtain wall and
domestic buildings

RIEVAULX ABBEY (EH), N. Yorks YO6 5LB T 01439-798228
Remains of a Cistercian abbey founded c.1132

ROCHESTER CASTLE (EH), Kent ME1 1SX T 01634-402276
An 11th-century castle partly on the Roman city wall,
with a square keep of c.1130

ROCKINGHAM CASTLE, Leics LE16 8TH T 01536-770240
W www.rockinghamcastle.com
Built by William the Conqueror

ROYAL PAVILION, Brighton BN1 1EE T 01273-290900
Palace of George IV, in Chinese style with Indian exterior
and Regency gardens

RUFFORD OLD HALL (NT), Lancs L40 1SG T 01704-821254
A 16th-century hall with unique screen

ST AUGUSTINE'S ABBEY (EH), Kent T 01227-767345
Remains of Benedictine monastery, with Norman church,
on site of abbey founded AD 597 by St Augustine

ST MAWES CASTLE (EH), Cornwall TR2 3AA
T 01326-270526. Coastal defence castle built by Henry
VIII

ST MICHAEL'S MOUNT (NT), Cornwall TR17 0EF
T 01736-710265
A 12th-century castle with later additions, off the coast at
Marazion

SANDRINGHAM, Norfolk PE35 6EN T 01553-772675
W www.sandringhamestate.co.uk
The Queen's private residence; a neo-Jacobean house
built in 1870

SCARBOROUGH CASTLE (EH), N. Yorks T 01723-372451
Remains of 12th-century keep and curtain walls

SHERBORNE CASTLE, Dorset DT9 3PY T 01935-813182
W www.sherbornecastle.com. Sixteenth-century castle
built by Sir Walter Raleigh set in landscaped gardens

SHUGBOROUGH (NT), Staffs ST17 0XB T 01889-881388
House set in 18th-century park with monuments,
temples and pavilions in the Greek Revival style. Seat of
the Earls of Lichfield

SKIPTON CASTLE, N. Yorks BD23 1AQ T 01756-792442
W www.skiptoncastle.co.uk
D-shaped castle with six round towers and beautiful
inner courtyard

SMALLHYTHE PLACE (NT), Kent TN30 7NG
T 01580-762334 Half-timbered 16th-century house;
home of Ellen Terry 1899–1928. Barn Theatre

STANFORD HALL, Leics LE17 6DH T 01788-860250
W www.stanfordhall.co.uk William and Mary house with
Stuart portraits. Motorcycle museum

STONEHENGE (EH), Wilts T 01980-624715
Prehistoric monument consisting of concentric stone
circles surrounded by a ditch and bank

STONOR PARK, Oxon RG9 6HF T 01491-638587
W www.stonor.com
Medieval house with Georgian facade. Centre of Roman
Catholicism after the Reformation

STOURHEAD (NT), Wilts BA12 6QD T 01747-841152
English Palladian mansion with famous gardens

STRATFIELD SAYE HOUSE, Hants RG7 2BT T 01256-882882
W www.stratfield-saye.co.uk House built 1630–40; home
of the Dukes of Wellington since 1817

STRATFORD-UPON-AVON, Warks. Shakespeare's
Birthplace Trust with Shakespeare Centre; Anne
Hathaway's Cottage, home of Shakespeare's wife; Mary
Arden's House, home of Shakespeare's mother; Nash's
House and New Place, where Shakespeare died; and
Hall's Croft, home of Shakespeare's daughter.
T 01789-204016 W www.shakespeare.org.uk Also
Grammar School attended by Shakespeare, Holy
Trinity Church, where Shakespeare is buried, Royal
Shakespeare Theatre (burnt down 1926, rebuilt 1932)
and Swan Theatre (opened 1986)

SUDELEY CASTLE, Glos GL54 5JD T 01242-602308
W www.sudeleycastle.co.uk
Castle built in 1442; restored in the 19th-century

SULGRAVE MANOR, nr Banbury OX17 2SD T 01295-760205
W www.sulgravemanor.org.uk
Home of George Washington's family

SYON HOUSE, Brentford, Middx TW8 8JF T 020-8560 0881
W www.syonhouse.co.uk
Built on the site of a former monastery; Adam interior;
Capability Brown parkland

TILBURY FORT (EH), Essex RM18 7NR T 01375-858489
A 17th-century coastal fort

TINTAGEL CASTLE (EH), Cornwall T 01840-770328
A 12th-century cliff-top castle and Dark Age settlement
site; linked with Arthurian legend

TOWER OF LONDON, London EC3N 4AB T 0870-756 6060
W www.hrp.org.uk. Royal palace and fortress begun by
William the Conqueror in 1078. Houses the Crown
Jewels

TRERICE (NT), Cornwall TR8 4PG T 01637-875404
Elizabethan manor house

TYNEMOUTH PRIORY AND CASTLE (EH), Tyne and Wear.
T 0191-257 1090.
Remains of a Benedictine priory, founded c.1090, on
Saxon monastic site

UPPARK (NT), W. Sussex GU31 5QR T 01730-825857
Late 17th-century house, completely restored after fire.
Fetherstonhaugh art collection

WALMER CASTLE (EH), Kent T 01304-364288
One of Henry VIII's coastal defence castles, now the
residence of the Lord Warden of the Cinque Ports

WALTHAM ABBEY (EH), Essex. T 01992-702200
Ruined abbey including the nave of the abbey church,
'Harold's Bridge' and late 14th-century gatehouse.
Traditionally the burial place of Harold II (1066)

WARKWORTH CASTLE (EH), Northumberland
T 01665-711423
A 15th-century keep amidst earlier ruins, with 14th-
century hermitage upstream

WARWICK CASTLE Warks CV34 4QU T 0870-442 200
W www.warwick-castle.co.uk
Medieval castle with Madame Tussaud's waxworks, in
Capability Brown parkland

WHITBY ABBEY (EH), N. Yorks T 01947-603568
Remains of Norman church on the site of a monastery
founded in AD 657

WILTON HOUSE, Wilts SP2 0BJ T 01722-746720
W www.wiltonhouse.co.uk
A 17th-century house on the site of a Tudor house and
9th Century nunnery

WINDSOR CASTLE, Berks SL4 1NJ T 020-7321 2233
W www.royal.gov.uk
Official residence of The Queen; oldest royal residence
still in regular use. Also *St George's Chapel*

WOBURN ABBEY, Beds MK17 9WA T 01525-290666
W www.woburnabbey.co.uk
Built on the site of a Cistercian abbey; seat of the
Dukes of Bedford. Important art collection; antiques
centre

WROXETER ROMAN CITY (EH), Shropshire T 01743-761330
Second-century public baths and part of the forum of the
Roman town of Viroconium

WALES

For more information on any of the National Trust properties
listed below, the official website is:
www.nationaltrust.org.uk
For more information on any of the CADW properties listed
below, the official website is:
www.cadw.wales.gov.uk
(C) Property of CADW: Welsh Historic Monuments
(NT) National Trust property

BEAUMARIS CASTLE (C), Anglesey T 01248-810361
Concentrically-planned castle, still almost intact

CAERLEON ROMAN BATHS AND AMPHITHEATRE (C),
nr Newport T 01633-422518
Rare example of a legionary bath-house and late 1st-
century arena surrounded by bank for spectators

CAERNARFON CASTLE (C). T 01286-677617
Important Edwardian castle built, with the town wall,
between 1283 and 1330

CAERPHILLY CASTLE (C) CF83 1JD T 029-2088 3143
Concentrically-planned castle (c.1270) notable for its
scale and use of water defences

CARDIFF CASTLE CF10 3RB T 029-2087 8100
W www.cardiffcastle.com.
Castle built on the site of a Roman fort; spectacular
towers and rich interior

CASTELL COCH (C), nr Cardiff CF15 7JS
T 029-2081 0101 'Fairy Castle' rebuilt 1875–90 on
medieval foundations

CHEPSTOW CASTLE (C) NP16 5EY T 01291-624065
Rectangular keep amid extensive fortifications

CONWY CASTLE (C) LL32 8LD T 01492-592358
Built by Edward I, 1283–7

CRICCIETH CASTLE (C) Gwynedd LL52 0DP
T 01766-522227
Native Welsh 13th-century castle, altered by Edward I

DENBIGH CASTLE (C) LL16 3NB T 01745-813385
Remains of the castle (begun 1282), including triple-towered gatehouse

HARLECH CASTLE (C) LL46 2YH T 01766-780552
Well-preserved Edwardian castle, constructed 1283–90, on an outcrop above the former shoreline

PEMBROKE CASTLE SA71 4LA T 01646-681510
W www.pembrokecastle.co.uk
Castle founded in 1093; Great Tower built 1200; birthplace of King Henry VII

PENRHYN CASTLE (NT), Bangor LL57 4HN T 01248-353084
Neo-Norman castle built in the 19th-century. Industrial railway museum

PORTMEIRION, Gwynedd LL48 6ET T 01766-770000
W www.portmeirion-village.com
Village in Italianate style

POWIS CASTLE (NT), Welshpool SY21 8RF T 01938-551944
Medieval castle with interior in variety of styles; 17th-century gardens and Clive of India museum

RAGLAN CASTLE (C) NP15 2BT T 01291-690228
Remains of 15th-century castle with moated hexagonal keep

ST DAVIDS BISHOP'S PALACE (C), St Davids SA62 6PE
T 01437-720517
Remains of residence of Bishops of St Davids built 1328–47

TINTERN ABBEY (C), nr Chepstow T 01291-689251
Remains of 13th-century church and conventual buildings of a Cistercian monastery

TRETOWER COURT AND CASTLE (C), nr Crickhowell NP8 2RF T 01874-730279
Medieval house with remains of 12th-century castle nearby

SCOTLAND

For more information on any of the Historic Scotland properties listed below, the official website is:
www.historic-scotland.gov.uk
For more information on any of the National Trust For Scotland properties listed below, the official website is:
www.nts.org.uk
(HS) Historic Scotland property
(NTS) National Trust for Scotland property

ABBOTSFORD HOUSE, Melrose, Scottish Borders TD6 9BQ
T 01869-752043
Home of Sir Walter Scott

ANTONINE WALL, between the Clyde and the Forth.
Built about AD 142, consists of ditch, turf rampart and road, with forts every two miles

BALMORAL CASTLE, nr Braemar AB35 5TB T 01339-742534
W www.balmoralcastle.com Baronial-style castle built for Victoria and Albert. The Queen's private residence

BLACKHOUSE, ARNOL (HS), Lewis, Western Isles
T 01851-710395
Traditional Lewis thatched house

BLAIR CASTLE, Blair Atholl PH18 5TL T 01796-481207
W www.blair-castle.co.uk
Mid 18th-century mansion with 13th-century tower; seat of the Dukes of Atholl

BONAWE IRON FURNACE (HS), Argyll and Bute PA35 1JQ
T 01866-822432
Charcoal-fuelled ironworks founded in 1753

BOWHILL, Selkirk TD7 5ET T 01750-22204
Seat of the Dukes of Buccleuch and Queensberry; fine collection of paintings, including portrait miniatures

BROUGH OF BIRSAY (HS), Orkney T 01856-841815
Remains of Norse church and village on the tidal island of Birsay.

CAERLAVEROCK CASTLE (HS), nr Dumfries DG1 4RN
T 01387-770244
Fine early classical Renaissance building

CAIRNPAPPLE HILL (HS), West Lothian T 01506-634622
Neolithic and Bronze age burial chambers and henge

CALANAIS STANDING STONES (HS), Lewis, Western Isles
T 01851-621422 Standing stones in a cross-shaped setting, dating from 2900–2600 BC

CATERTHUNS (BROWN AND WHITE) (HS), nr Brechin
Two large Iron Age hill forts

CAWDOR CASTLE, Inverness IV12 5RD T 01667-404401
W www.cawdorcastle.com
A 14th-century keep with 15th- and 17th-century additions

CLAVA CAIRNS (HS), Highlands T 01667-460232
Late Neolithic or early Bronze Age cairns

CRATHES CASTLE (NTS), nr Banchory AB31 5QJ
T 01330-844525
A 16th-century baronial castle in woodland, fields and gardens

CULZEAN CASTLE (NTS), S. Ayrshire KA19 8LE
T 01655-884455
An 18th-century Adam castle with oval staircase and circular saloon

DUNFERMLINE ABBEY AND PALACE (HS), Fife
T 01383-739026 W www.dunfabbey.freeserve.co.uk
Remains of Abbey and Royal Palace

DRYBURGH ABBEY (HS), Scottish Borders T 01835-822381
A 12th-century abbey containing tomb of Sir Walter Scott

DUNVEGAN CASTLE, Skye IV55 8WF T 01470-521206
W www.dunvegancastle.com
A 13th-century castle with later additions; home of the chiefs of the Clan MacLeod; trips to seal colony

EDINBURGH CASTLE (HS) EH1 2NG T 0131-225 9846
Includes the Scottish Crown Jewels, Scottish National War Memorial, Scottish United Services Museum and historic apartments

EDZELL CASTLE (HS), nr Brechin DD9 7UE T 01356-648631
Medieval tower house; unique walled garden

EILEAN DONAN CASTLE, Wester Ross IV40 8DX
T 01599-555202
A 13th-century castle with Jacobite relics

ELGIN CATHEDRAL (HS), Moray T 01343-547171
A 13th-century cathedral with fine chapterhouse

FLOORS CASTLE, Kelso T 01573-223333
W www.floorscastle.com
Largest inhabited castle in Scotland; seat of the Dukes of Roxburghe. Built 1721 by William Adam.

FORT GEORGE (HS), Highlands T 01667-462777
An 18th-century fort

GLAMIS CASTLE, Angus T 01307-840393
W www.strathmore-estates.co.uk
Seat of the Lyon family (later Earls of Strathmore and Kinghorne) since 1372

GLASGOW CATHEDRAL (HS). T 0141-552 6891
Medieval cathedral with elaborately vaulted crypt

GLENELG BROCHS (HS), Highlands T 01667-460232
Two broch towers with well-preserved structural features

HILL HOUSE, Helensburgh G84 9AJ T 01436-673900
  House and furnishings designed by Charles Rennie
  Macintosh
HOPETOUN HOUSE, nr Edinburgh EH30 9SL
  T 0131-331 2451 W www.hopetounhouse.com
  House designed by Sir William Bruce, enlarged by
  William Adam
HUNTLY CASTLE (HS) Aberdeenshire T 01466-793191
  Ruin of a 16th- and 17th-century house
INVERARAY CASTLE, Argyll T 01499-302203
  W www.inveraray-castle.com Gothic-style 18th-century
  castle; seat of the Dukes of Argyll
IONA ABBEY (HS), Inner Hebrides
  Monastery founded by St Columba in AD 563
JARLSHOF (HS), Shetland T 01950-460112 Prehistoric and
  Norse settlement
JEDBURGH ABBEY (HS), Scottish Borders T 01835-863925
  Romanesque and early Gothic church founded c.1138
KELSO ABBEY (HS), Scottish Borders.
  Remains of great abbey church founded 1128 by David I
KISIMUL CASTLE (HS), Barra, Hebrides T 01871-810313
  Historic home of clan MacNeill
LINLITHGOW PALACE (HS) EH49 7AL T 01506-842896
  Ruin of royal palace in park setting. Birthplace of Mary,
  Queen of Scots
MAES HOWE (HS), Orkney T 01856-761606
  Neolithic tomb
MEIGLE SCULPTURED STONES (HS), Angus
  T 01828-640612
  Twenty six Celtic Christian stones
MELROSE ABBEY (HS), Scottish Borders T 01896-822562
  Ruin of Cistercian abbey founded c.1136 by David I
MOUSA BROCH (HS), Shetland T 01466-793191
  Finest surviving Iron Age broch tower
NEW ABBEY CORN MILL (HS), nr Dumfries
  T 01387-850260
  Water-powered mill
PALACE OF HOLYROODHOUSE, Edinburgh
  T 0131-556 5100 W www.royal.gov.uk
  The Queen's official Scottish residence. Main part of the
  palace built 1671–9
RING OF BROGAR (HS), Orkney T 01865-841815
  Neolithic circle of upright stones with an enclosing ditch
ROSSLYN CHAPEL, Midlothian EH25 9PU
  W www.rosslynchapel.org.uk
  Historic church with unique stone carvings
RUTHWELL CROSS (HS), Dumfries and Galloway
  T 01387-870249
  Seventh-century Anglian cross
ST ANDREWS CASTLE AND CATHEDRAL (HS), Fife KY16
  9AR T 01334-477196 (castle); 01334-472563 (cathedral)
  Ruins of 13th-century castle and remains of the largest
  cathedral in Scotland
SCONE PALACE, Perth PH2 6BD T 01738-552300
  W www.scone-palace.co.uk
  House built 1802–13 on the site of a medieval palace.
  Home of the Earls of Mansfield
SKARA BRAE (HS), Orkney T 01856-841815
  Prehistoric village with adjacent 17th-century house
SMAILHOLM TOWER (HS), Scottish Borders
  T 01573-460365
  Well-preserved tower-house

STIRLING CASTLE (HS) FK8 1EJ T 01786-450000
  Great Hall and gatehouse of James IV, palace of James V,
  Chapel Royal remodelled by James VI
TANTALLON CASTLE (HS), E. Lothian EH39 5PN
  T 01620-892727 Fortification with earthwork defences
  and a 14th-century curtain wall with towers
THREAVE CASTLE (HS), Dumfries and Galloway
  Late 14th-century tower on an island; reached by boat,
  long walk to castle
URQUHART CASTLE (HS), Loch Ness IV63 6XJ
  T 01456-450551 Castle remains with well-preserved
  tower

NORTHERN IRELAND

For more information on any of the National Trust properties
listed below, the official website is:
www.nationaltrust.org.uk
For the Northern Ireland Environment and Heritage Service, the
official website is:
www.ehsni.gov.uk
EHS Property in the care of the Northern Ireland Environment
and Heritage Service
NT National Trust property

CARRICKFERGUS CASTLE (EHS), Co. Antrim BT38 7BG
  T 028-9335 1273 Castle begun in 1180 and garrisoned
  until 1928
CASTLE COOLE (NT), Co. Fermanagh BT74 6JY
  T 028-6632 2690
  An 18th-century mansion by James Wyatt in parkland
CASTLE WARD (NT), Co. Down BT30 7LS T 028-4488 1204
  An 18th-century house with Classical and Gothic
  facades
DEVENISH ISLAND (EHS), Co. Fermanagh T 028-6862 1588
  Island monastery founded in the 6th century by St
  Molaise
DOWNHILL CASTLE (NT), Co. Londonderry T 028-7084
  8728 Ruins of palatial house in landscaped estate
  including Mussenden Temple.
DUNLUCE CASTLE (EHS), Co. Antrim T 028-2073 1938
  Ruins of 16th-century stronghold of the MacDonnells
FLORENCE COURT (NT), Co. Fermanagh BT92 1DB
  T 028-6634 8249
  Mid-18th-century house with rococo decoration
GREY ABBEY (EHS), Co. Down T 028-9181 1491
  Substantial remains of a Cistercian abbey founded in
  1193
HILLSBOROUGH FORT (EHS), Co. Down T 028-9268 3285
  Built in 1650
MOUNT STEWART (NT), Co. Down BT22 2AD
  T 028-4278 8387
  An 18th-century house, childhood home of Lord
  Castlereagh
NENDRUM MONASTERY (EHS), Mahee Island, Co. Down
  T 028-9181 1491
  Founded in the 5th century by St Machaoi
TULLY CASTLE (EHS), Co. Fermanagh T 028-6862 1588
  Fortified house and bawn built in 1613
WHITE ISLAND (EHS), Co. Fermanagh
  Tenth-century monastery and 12th-century church.
  Access by ferry

MUSEUMS AND GALLERIES

There are over 2,500 museums and galleries in the United Kingdom. Around 1,800 are registered with the Museums, Libraries and Archives Council (MLA), which indicates that they have an appropriate constitution, are soundly financed, have adequate collection management standards and public services, and have access to professional curatorial advice. Museums must achieve full or provisional registration status in order to be eligible for grants from MLA and from Area Museums Councils. Many registered museums are run by a local authority.

The national museums and galleries receive direct government grant-in-aid. These are: British Museum; Imperial War Museum; National Army Museum; National Galleries of Scotland; National Gallery; National Maritime Museum; National Museums and Galleries on Merseyside; National Museum of Wales; National Museums of Scotland; National Portrait Gallery; Natural History Museum; RAF Museum; Royal Armouries; Science Museum; Tate Gallery; Ulster Folk and Transport Museum; Ulster Museum; Victoria and Albert Museum; Wallace Collection. An online art museum (www.24hourmuseum.org.uk) has also been awarded national collection status.

ENGLAND

BARNARD CASTLE, Co. Durham – *The Bowes Museum*, Westwick Road DL12 8NP **T** 01833-690606
W www.bowesmuseum.org.uk
European art from the late medieval period to the 19th-century; music and costume galleries; English period rooms from Elizabeth I to Victoria; local archaeology

BATH – *American Museum*, Claverton Manor BA2 7BD
T 01225-460503 **W** www.americanmuseum.org
American decorative arts from the 17th- to 19th-century

Museum of Costume, Bennett Street BA1 2QH **T** 01225-477789
W www.museumofcostume.co.uk
Fashion from the 16th-century to the present day

Roman Baths Museum, Pump Room, Stall Street BA1 1LZ
T 01225-477785 **W** www.romanbaths.co.uk
Museum adjoins the remains of a Roman baths and temple complex

Victoria Art Gallery, Bridge Street BA2 4AT **T** 01225-477772
W www.victoriagal.org.uk
European Old Masters and British art since the 18th-century

BEAMISH, Co. Durham – *Beamish, The North of England Open Air Museum*, DH9 0RG **T** 0191-370 4000
W www.beamish.org.uk
Recreated northern town *c.*1900, with rebuilt and furnished local buildings, colliery village, farm, railway station, tramway, Pockerley Manor and horse-yard (set *c.*1800)

BEAULIEU, Hants – *National Motor Museum*, SO42 7ZN
T 01590-612345 **W** www.beaulieu.co.uk
Displays of over 250 vehicles dating from 1895 to the present day

BIRMINGHAM – *Aston Hall*, Trinity Road, B6 6JD
T 0121-327 0062 **W** www.bmag.org.uk/aston_hall
Jacobean House containing paintings, furniture and tapestries from the 17th- to 19th-century

Barber Institute of Fine Arts, off Edgbaston Park Road, B15 2TS
T 0121-414 7333 **W** www.barber.org.uk
Fine arts, including Old Masters

Birmingham Nature Centre, Pershore Road, Edgbaston, B5 7RL
T 0121-472 7775
Indoor and outdoor enclosures displaying wildlife, especially British and European

City Museum and Art Gallery, Chamberlain Square B3 3DH
T 0121-303 2834
W www.bmag.org.uk/museum_and_art_gallery
Includes notable collection of Pre-Raphaelite art

Museum of the Jewellery Quarter, Vyse Street, Hockley B18 6HA
T 0121-554 3598 **W** www.bmag.org.uk/jewellery_quarter
Built around a real jewellery workshop

Soho House, Soho Avenue B18 5LB **T** 0121-554 9122
W www.bmag.org.uk/soho_house
Eighteenth-century home of industrialist Matthew Boulton

BOVINGTON CAMP, Dorset – *Tank Museum BH20 6JG*
T 01929-405096 **W** www.tankmuseum.co.uk
Collection of 300 tanks from the earliest days of tank warfare to the present

BRADFORD – *Cartwright Hall Art Gallery*, Lister Park BD9 4NS
T 01274-751212
British 19th- and 20th-century fine art

Industrial Museum and Horses at Work, Moorside Road BD2 3HP
T 01274-631756
Engineering, textiles, transport and social history exhibits, including recreated back-to-back cottages, shire horses and horse tram-rides

National Museum of Photography, Film and Television, Bradford BD1 1NQ **T** 0870-701 0200 **W** www.nmpft.org.uk
Photography, film and television interactive exhibits. Features the UK's first IMAX cinema and the only public Cinerama screen in the world

BRIGHTON – *Booth Museum of Natural History*, Dyke Road BN1 5AA **T** 01273-292777 **W** www.booth.virtualmuseum.info
Zoology, botany and geology collections; British birds in recreated habitats

Brighton Museum and Gallery, Royal Pavilion Gardens, BN1 1EE
T 01273-290900 **W** www.brighton.virtualmuseum.info
Includes fine art and design, fashion, non-Western art, Brighton history

BRISTOL – *Arnolfini*, Narrow Quay BS1 4QA **T** 0117-917 2303
W www.arnolfini.demon.co.uk
Contemporary visual arts, dance, performance, music, talks and workshops

Blaise Castle House Museum, Henbury BS10 7QS
T 0117-903 9818 **W** www.bristol-city.gov.uk/museums
Agricultural and social history collections in an 18th-century mansion

Bristol Industrial Museum, Princes Wharf BS1 4RN
T 0117-925 1470 **W** www.bristol-city.gov.uk/museums
Industrial, maritime and transport collections

British Empire and Commonwealth Museum, Temple Meads BS1 6QH **T** 0117-925 4980 **W** www.empiremuseum.co.uk

City Museum and Art Gallery, Queen's Road BS8 1RL
T 0117-922 3571 **W** www.bristol-city.gov.uk
Includes fine and decorative art, oriental art, Egyptology and Bristol ceramics and paintings

CAMBRIDGE – *Duxford Imperial War Museum*, Duxford CB2 4QR **T** 01223-835000 **W** www.iwm.org.uk

Displays of military and civil aircraft, tanks, guns and naval exhibits

Fitzwilliam Museum, Trumpington Street CB2 1RB
T 01223-332900 W www.fitzmuseum.cam.ac.uk
Antiquities, fine and applied arts, clocks, ceramics, manuscripts, furniture, sculpture, coins and medals, temporary exhibitions

Sedgwick Museum of Earth Sciences, Downing Street, CB2 3EQ
T 01223-333456 W www.sedgwickmuseum.org
Extensive geological collection

University Museum of Archaeology and Anthropology, Downing Street CB2 3DZ T 01223-333516
Archaeology and anthropology from all parts of the world

University Museum of Zoology, Downing Street CB2 3EJ
T 01223-336650 W www.zoo.cam.ac.uk
Extensive zoological collection

Whipple Museum of the History of Science, Free School Lane CB2 3RH T 01223-330906 W www.hps.cam.ac.uk/whipple
Scientific instruments from 14th-century to the present

CARLISLE - *Tullie House Museum and Art Gallery,* Castle Street CA3 8TP T 01228-534781 W www.tulliehouse.co.uk
Prehistoric archaeology, Hadrian's Wall, Viking and medieval Cumbria, and the social history of Carlisle; also British 19th- and 20th-century art and English porcelain

CHATHAM — *World Naval Base* ME4 4TZ T 01634-823800
W www.chdt.org.uk
Maritime attractions including HMS Cavalier, the UK's last World War II destroyer

Royal Engineers Museum of Military Engineering, Prince Arthur Road ME4 4UG T 01634-822839
W www.army.mod.uk/royalengineers
Regimental history, ethnography, decorative art and photography

CHELTENHAM — *Art Gallery and Museum* Clarence Street GL50 3JT T 01242-237431
W www.cheltenhammuseum.org.uk
Paintings, arts and crafts

CHESTER - *Grosvenor Museum,* Grosvenor Street CH1 2DD
T 01244-402008
W www.chesterccc.gov.uk/heritage/museum/home
Roman collections, natural history, art, Chester silver, local history and costume

CHICHESTER - *Weald and Downland Open Air Museum,* Singleton PO18 0EU T 01243-811363
W www.wealddown.co.uk
Rebuilt vernacular buildings from south-east England; includes medieval houses, agricultural and rural craft buildings and a working watermill

COLCHESTER - *Colchester Castle Museum,* Castle Park CO1 1TJ T 01206-282939 W www.colchestermuseums.org.uk
Largest Norman keep in Europe standing on foundations of Roman Temple of Claudius; tours of the Roman vaults, castle walls and chapel with medieval and prison displays

COVENTRY - *Herbert Art Gallery and Museum,* Jordan Well CV1 5QP T 024-7683 2381 W www.coventrymuseum.org.uk
Local history, archaeology and industry, and fine and decorative art

Museum of British Road Transport, Hales Street CV1 1PN
T 024-7683 2425 W www.mbrt.co.uk
Hundreds of motor vehicles and bicycles

CRICH, nr Matlock, Derbys – *Crich Tramway Museum* DE4 5DP
T 0870-758 7267 W www.tramway.co.uk
Open-air working museum with tram rides

DERBY - *Derby Museum and Art Gallery,* The Strand DE1 1BS
T 01332-716659 W www.derby.gov.uk/museums
Includes paintings by Joseph Wright of Derby and Derby porcelain

Industrial Museum, off Full Street DE1 3AR T 01332-255308
W www.derby.gov.uk/museums
Rolls-Royce aero engine collection and a railway engineering gallery

Pickford's House Museum, Friar Gate DE1 1DA T 01332-255363
W www.derby.gov.uk/museums
Georgian Town House by architect Joseph Pickford; reconstructed period rooms and garden

DEVIZES - *Wiltshire Heritage Museum,* Long Street SN10 1NS
T 01380-727369 W www.wiltshireheritage.org.uk
Natural and local history, art gallery, archaeological finds from Bronze Age, Iron Age, Roman and Saxon sites

DORCHESTER - *Dorset County Museum,* High West Street, DT1 1XAT 01305-262735 W www.dorsetcountymuseum.org
Includes a collection of Thomas Hardy's manuscripts, books, notebooks and drawings

DOVER — *Dover Museum,* Market Square CT16 1PB
T 01304-201066 W www.dovermuseum.co.uk
Contains Dover Bronze Age Boat Gallery and archaeological finds from Bronze Age, Roman and Saxon sites.

ELLESMERE PORT — *Boat Museum,* South Pier Road CH65 4FW T 0151-355 5017 W www.boatmuseum.org.uk
Craft and boating history

EXETER — *Royal Albert Memorial Museum and Art Gallery,* Queen Street EX4 3RX T 01392-665858
W www.exeter.gov.uk/museums
Natural history, archaeology, worldwide fine and decorative art including Exeter silver

GATESHEAD — *Shipley Art Gallery,* Prince Consort Road NE8 4JB T 0191-477 1495
Contemporary crafts

Baltic Centre for Contemporary Art, South Shore Road, Gateshead, NE8 3BA T 0191-478 1810 W www.balticmill.com
Presents a constantly changing programme of contemporary art exhibitions and events

GAYDON, Warwick – *British Motor Industry Heritage Trust,* Heritage Motor Centre, Banbury Road CV35 0BJ
T 01926-641188 W www.heritage.org.uk
History of British motor industry from 1895 to present; classic vehicles; engineering gallery; Corgi and Lucas collections

GLOUCESTER - *National Waterways Museum,* Llanthony Warehouse, Gloucester Docks GL1 2EH T 01452-318200
W www.nwm.org.uk
Two-hundred-year history of Britain's canals and inland waterways

GOSPORT, Hants – *Royal Navy Submarine Museum,* Haslar Jetty Road PO12 2AS T 023-9252 9217 W www.rnsubmus.co.uk
Underwater warfare, including the submarine Alliance; historical and nuclear galleries; and first Royal Navy submarine

GRASMERE, Cumbria – *Dove Cottage* and the *Wordsworth Museum* LA22 9SH T 01539-433554
W www.wordsworth.org.uk

HALIFAX – *Eureka! The Museum for Children,* Discovery Road HX1 2NE T 01422-330069 W www.eureka.org.uk
Hands-on museum designed for children up to age 12

HULL - *Ferens Art Gallery,* Queen Victoria Square HU1 3RA
T 01482-613902 W www.hullcc.gov.uk/museums
European art, especially Dutch 17th-century paintings, British portraits from 17th- to 20th-century, and marine paintings

Hull Maritime Museum, Queen Victoria Square HU1 3DX
T 01482-613902 W www.hullcc.gov.uk/museums
Whaling, fishing and navigation exhibits

HUNTINGDON - *Cromwell Museum*, Grammar School Walk PE29 3LF **T** 01480-375830 **W** www.edweb.camcnty.gov.uk/cromwell
Portraits and memorabilia relating to Oliver Cromwell

IPSWICH - *Christchurch Mansion and Wolsey Art Gallery*, Christchurch Park IP4 2BE **T** 01473-433554
Tudor house with paintings by Gainsborough, Constable and other Suffolk artists; furniture and 18th-century ceramics. Art gallery for temporary exhibitions

LEEDS — *City Art Gallery*, The Headrow LS1 3AA **T** 0113-247 8248 **W** www.leeds.gov.uk/artgallery
British and European paintings including English watercolours, modern sculpture, Henry Moore gallery, print room

Leeds Industrial Museum at Armley Mills, Canal Road, Armley LS12 2QF **T** 0113-263 7861 **W** www. leeds.gov.uk/armleymills
Largest woollen mill in world

Lotherton Hall, Aberford LS25 3EB **T** 0113-281 3259 **W** www.leeds.gov.uk/lothertonhall
Costume and oriental collections in furnished Edwardian house; deer park and bird garden

Royal Armouries Museum, Armouries Drive LS10 1LT **T** 0113-220-1916 **W** www.armouries.org.uk
National collection of arms and armour from BC to present; demonstrations of foot combat in museum's five galleries; falconry and mounted combat in the tiltyard

Temple Newsam House LS15 0AE **T** 0113-264 7321 **W** www.leeds.gov.uk/templenewsam
Old Masters and 17th- and 18th-century decorative art in furnished Jacobean/Tudor house

LEICESTER - *Jewry Wall Museum*, St Nicholas Circle LE1 4LB **T** 0116-225 4971 **W** www.leicestermuseums.ac.uk
Archaeology, Roman Jewry Wall and baths, and mosaics

New Walk Museum and Art Gallery, New Walk LE1 7EA **T** 0116-255 4900 **W** www.leicestermuseums.ac.uk
Natural history, geology, ancient Egypt gallery, European art and decorative arts

Snibston Discovery Park, Coalville LE67 3LN **T** 01530-278444
Open-air science and industry museum on site of a coal mine; country park with nature trail

LINCOLN - *Museum of Lincolnshire Life*, Burton Road LN1 3LY **T** 01522-528448
Social history and agricultural collection

Usher Gallery, Lindum Road LN2 1NN **T** 01522-527980
Watches, miniatures, porcelain, silver; collection of Peter de Wint works; Lincolnshire topography and Royal Lincs Regiment memorabilia

LIVERPOOL - *Lady Lever Art Gallery*, Wirral CH62 5EQ **T** 0151-478 4136 **W** www.ladyleverartgallery.org.uk
Paintings, furniture and porcelain

Liverpool Museum, William Brown Street L3 8EN **T** 0151-478 4399 **W** www.nmgm.org.uk
Includes Egyptian mummies, weapons and classical sculpture; planetarium, aquarium, vivarium and natural history centre

Merseyside Maritime Museum, Albert Dock L3 4AQ **T** 0151-478 4499 **W** www.liverpoolmuseums.org.uk
Floating exhibits, working displays and craft demonstrations; incorporates HM Customs and Excise National Museum

Museum of Liverpool Life, Pier Head, Albert Dock L3 1QA **T** 0151-478 4080 **W** www.nmgm.org.uk
The history of Liverpool

Sudley House, Mossley Hill Road L18 8BX **T** 0151-724 3245
Late 18th- and 19th-century British paintings in former shipowner's home

Tate Gallery Liverpool, Albert Dock L3 4BB **T** 0151-702 7400 **W** www.tate.org.uk/liverpool
Twentieth-century painting and sculpture

Walker Art Gallery, William Brown Street L3 8EL **T** 0151-478 4199 **W** www.nmgm.org.uk
Paintings from the 14th- to 20th-century

LONDON: GALLERIES - *Barbican Art Gallery*, Barbican Centre EC2Y 8DS **T** 020-7638 8891 **W** www.barbican.org.uk
Temporary exhibitions

Courtauld Gallery, Somerset House, Strand, WC2R 0RN **T** 020-7848 2526 **W** www.courtauld.ac.uk
The University of London galleries

Dulwich Picture Gallery, Gallery Road, SE21 7AD **T** 020-8693 5254 **W** www.dulwichpicturegallery.org.uk
Built by Sir John Soane to house 17th- and 18th-century paintings

Hayward Gallery, Belvedere Road, SE1 8XZ **T** 020-7921 0830 **W** www.hayward.org.uk
Temporary exhibitions

National Gallery, Trafalgar Square, WC2N 5DN **T** 020-7747 2885 **W** www.nationalgallery.org.uk
Western painting from the 13th- to 20th-century; early Renaissance collection in the Sainsbury wing

National Portrait Gallery, St Martin's Place, WC2H 0HE **T** 020-7306 0055 **W** www.npg.org.uk
Portraits of eminent people in British history

Percival David Foundation of Chinese Art, Gordon Square, WC1H 0PD **T** 020-7387 3909 **W** www.pdfmuseum.org.uk
Chinese ceramics from 10th- to 18th-century

Photographers' Gallery, Great Newport Street, WC2H 7HY **T** 020-7831 1772 **W** www.photonet.org.uk
Temporary exhibitions

The Queen's Gallery, Buckingham Palace, SW1A 1AA **T** 020-7766 7301 **W** www.royal.gov.uk
Art from the Royal Collection

Royal Academy of Arts, Piccadilly, W1J 0BD **T** 020-7300 8000 **W** www.royalacademy.org.uk
British art since 1750 and temporary exhibitions; annual Summer Exhibition

Saatchi Gallery, County Hall, South Bank SE1 7PB **T** 020-7928 8195 **W** www.saatchi-gallery.co.uk
Contemporary art including paintings, photographs, sculpture and installations

Serpentine Gallery, Kensington Gardens, W2 3XA **T** 020-7402 6075 **W** www.serpentinegallery.org
Temporary exhibitions of British and international contemporary art

Tate Britain, Millbank SW1P 4RG **T** 020-7887 8000 **W** www.tate.org.uk
British painting and 20th-century painting and sculpture

Tate Modern, Bankside, SE1 9TG **T** 020-7887 8000 **W** www.tate.org.uk
International modern art from 1900 to the present

Wallace Collection, Manchester Square, W1U 3BN **T** 020-7563 9500 **W** www.twallacecollection.org.uk
Paintings and drawings, French 18th-century furniture, armour, porcelain, clocks and sculpture

Whitechapel Art Gallery, Whitechapel High Street, E1 7QX **T** 020-7522 7888 **W** www.whitechapel.org
Temporary exhibitions of modern art

LONDON: MUSEUMS - *Bank of England Museum*, Threadneedle Street, EC2R 8AH (entrance from Bartholomew Lane). **T** 020-7601 5491 **W** www.bankofengland.co.uk
History of the Bank since 1694

Bethnal Green Museum of Childhood, Cambridge Heath Road, E2 9PA **T** 020-8983 2415 **W** www.museumofchildhood.org.uk

Toys, games and exhibits relating to the social history of childhood

British Museum, Great Russell Street, WC1B 3DG

T 020-7323 8299 W www.thebritishmuseum.ac.uk

Antiquities, coins, medals, prints and drawings

Cabinet War Rooms, King Charles Street, SW1A 2AQ

T 020-7930 6961 W www.iwm.org.uk/cabinet

Underground rooms used by Churchill and the Government during the Second World War

Cutty Sark, Greenwich, SE10 9HT T 020-8858 3445

W www.cuttysark.org.uk

Restored and re-rigged tea clipper with exhibits on board.

Design Museum, Shad Thames, SE1 2YD T 020-7378 6055

W www.designmuseum.org

The development of design and the mass-production of consumer objects

Estorick Collection, Canonbury Square, N1 2AN

T 020-7704 9522 W www.estorickcollection.com

Stages the main Estorick Collection of modern Italian art together with temporary loan exhibitions

Firepower! The Royal Artillery Museum, Royal Arsenal, Woolwich, SE18 6ST T 020-8855 7755 W www.firepower.org.uk

The history and development of artillery over the last 700 years including the collections of the Royal Regiment of Artillery

Geffrye Museum, Kingsland Road, E2 8EA T 020-7739 9893

W www.geffrye-museum.org.uk

English urban domestic interiors from 1600 to present day; also paintings, furniture, decorative arts, walled herb garden and period garden rooms

Gilbert Collection, Somerset House WC2R 1LA T 020-7420 9400

W www.gilbert-collection.org.uk

The collection comprises some 800 works of art including European silver, gold snuff boxes and Italian mosaics

HMS Belfast, Morgan's Lane, Tooley Street, SE1 2JH

T 020-7940 6300 W www.iwm.org.uk/belfast

Life on a World War II warship

Horniman Museum and Gardens, London Road SE23 3PQ

T 020-8699 1872 W www.horniman.ac.uk

Museum of ethnography, musical instruments, natural history and aquarium; reference library; sunken, water and flower gardens

Imperial War Museum, Lambeth Road SE1 6HZ T 020-7416 5320

W www.iwm.org.uk

All aspects of the two world wars and other military operations involving Britain and the Commonwealth since 1914

Jewish Museum, Camden Town, Albert Street NW1 7NB

T 020-7284 1997 W www.jewishmuseum.org.uk

Jewish life, history and religion

Jewish Museum, Finchley, East End Road N3 2SY

T 020–8349 1143 W www.jewishmuseum.org.uk

Jewish life in London and Holocaust education

London's Transport Museum, Covent Garden WC2E 7BB

T 020-7379 6344 W www.ltmuseum.co.uk

Vehicles, photographs and graphic art relating to the history of transport in London

MCC Museum, Lord's NW8 8QN T 020-7616 8595

W www.mcc.org.uk

Cricket museum. Conducted tours by appointment with Tours Manager

Museum in Docklands, West India Quay, Hertsmere Road E14 4AL

T 0870-444 3856 W www.museumindocklands.org.uk

Explores the story of London's river, port and people over 2,000 years; from Roman times through to the recent regeneration of London's Docklands

Museum of Garden History, Lambeth Palace Road SE1 7LB

T 020-7401 8865

W www.museumgardenhistory.org

Exhibition of aspects of garden history and re-created 17th-century garden

Museum of London, London Wall, EC2Y 5HN T 020-7600 3699

W www.museumoflondon.org.uk

History of London from prehistoric times to present day

National Army Museum, Royal Hospital Road SW3 4HT

T 020-7730 0717 W www.national-army-museum.ac.uk

Five-hundred-year history of the British soldier; exhibits include model of the Battle of Waterloo and Army for Today gallery

Natural History Museum, Cromwell Road SW7 5BD

T 020-7942 5000 W www.nhm.ac.uk

Natural history collections

National Maritime Museum, Greenwich SE10 9NF

T 020-8858 4422 W www.nmm.ac.uk

Comprises the main building, the Royal Observatory and the Queen's House. Maritime history of Britain; collections include globes, clocks, telescopes and paintings

Petrie Museum of Egyptian Archaeology, University College London, Malet Place WC1E 6BT T 020-7679 2884

W www.petrie.ucl.ac.uk

Egyptian archaeology collection

Royal Air Force Museum, Hendon, NW9 5LL T 020-8205 2266

W www.rafmuseum.org

National museum of aviation with over 70 full-size aircraft; aviation from before the Wright brothers to the present-day RAF; flight simulator

Royal Mews, Buckingham Palace SW1A 1AA T 020-7766 7302

W www.royal.gov.uk

Carriages, coaches, stables and horses

Science Museum, Exhibition Road, SW7 2DD T 0870-870 4868

W www.sciencemuseum.org.uk

Science, technology, industry and medicine collections

Shakespeare Globe Theatre and Exhibition, Bankside SE1 9DT

T 020-7902 1500 W www.shakespeares-globe.org

Recreation of Elizabethan theatre using 16th-century techniques

Sherlock Holmes Museum, Baker Street NW1 6XE

T 020-7935 8866 W www.sherlock-holmes.co.uk

Recreated rooms of the fictional detective

Sir John Soane's Museum, Lincoln's Inn Fields WC2A 3BP

T 020-7405 2107 W www.soane.org

Art and antiques

Theatre Museum, Russell Street WC2E 7PR T 020-7943 4700

W www.theatremuseum.org

History of the performing arts

Tower Bridge Experience, SE1 2UP T 020-7403 3761

W www.towerbridge.org.uk

History of the bridge and display of Victorian steam machinery; panoramic views from walkways

Victoria and Albert Museum, Cromwell Road SW7 2RL

T 020-7942 2000 W www.vam.ac.uk

Includes National Art Library and Print Room. Fine and applied art and design, including furniture, glass, textiles, dress collections

Wellington Museum, Apsley House, W1J 7NT T 020-7499 5676

W www.apsleyhouse.org.uk

Wimbledon Lawn Tennis Museum, Church Road SW19 5AE

T 020-8946 6131 W www.wimbledon.org/museum

Tennis trophies, fashion and memorabilia; view of Centre Court

MANCHESTER - *Gallery of Costume*, Rusholme M14 5LL

T 0161-224 5217 W www.manchestergalleries.org

Exhibits from the 16th- to 20th-century

Imperial War Museum North, Trafford Wharf Road, Trafford Park, Manchester, M17 1TZ **T** 0161-836 4000
W www.iwm.org.uk/north

Manchester Art Gallery, Mosley Street M2 3JL **T** 0161-235 8888
W www.manchestergalleries.org

Manchester Museum, Oxford Road M13 9PL **T** 0161-275 2634
W www.museum.man.ac.uk.
Archaeology, archery, botany, Egyptology, entomology, ethnography, geology, natural history, numismatics, oriental and zoology collections

Museum of Science and Industry, Castlefield M3 4FP
T 0161-832 2244 **W** www.msim.org.uk
On site of world's oldest passenger railway station; galleries relating to space, energy, power, transport, aviation, textiles and social history; interactive science centre

People's History Museum, Pump House, Bridge Street M3 3ER
T 0161-839 6061 **W** www.peopleshistorymuseum.org.uk
Political and working life history

Whitworth Art Gallery, Oxford Road M15 6ER **T** 0161-275 7450
W www.whitworth.man.ac.uk
Watercolours, drawings, prints, textiles, wallpapers and 20th-century British art

MILTON KEYNES - Bletchley Park, Bucks
W www.bletchleypark.org.uk
Enigma codebreaking and other WW2 collections

MONKWEARMOUTH – *Monkwearmouth Station Museum*
North Bridge Street SR5 1AP **T** 0191-567 7075
W www.twmuseums.org.uk/monkwearmouth
Victorian train station

NEWCASTLE UPON TYNE - *Hancock Museum*, Barras Bridge
NE2 4PT **T** 0191-222 6765 **W** www.twmuseums.org.uk
Natural history. Egyptology

Laing Art Gallery, New Bridge Street NE1 8AG **T** 0191-232 7734
W www.twmuseums.org.uk
British and European art, ceramics, glass, silver, textiles and costume; *Art on Tyneside* display

Discovery Museum, Blandford Square NE1 4JA **T** 0191-232 6789
W www.twmuseums.org.uk
Science and industry, local history, fashion and Tyneside's maritime history; *Turbinia* (first steam-driven vessel) gallery

NEWMARKET - *National Horseracing Museum*, High Street
CB8 8JL **T** 01638-667333 **W** www.nhrm.co.uk
The Essential Horse Millennium Exhibition, horseracing exhibits and tours of local trainers' yards and studs

NORTHAMPTON – *Central Museum and Art Gallery*, Guildhall
Road NN1 1DP **T** 01604-238548
W www.northampton.gov.uk/museums
Boot and shoe collection

NORTH SHIELDS - *Stephenson Railway Museum*, Middle
Engine Lane NE29 8DX **T** 0191-200 7146
W www.twmuseums.org.uk/stephenson
Locomotive engines and rolling stock

NOTTINGHAM - *Brewhouse Yard Museum*, Castle Boulevard
NG7 1FB **T** 0115-915 3600
Daily life from the 17th- to 20th-century

Castle Museum and Art Gallery NG1 6EL **T** 0115-915 3700
Paintings, ceramics, silver and glass; history of Nottingham

Industrial Museum, Wollaton Park NG8 2AE **T** 0115-915 3900
Lacemaking machinery, steam engines and transport exhibits

Museum of Costume and Textiles, Castle Gate NG1 6AF
T 0115-915 3500
Costume displays from 1790 to the mid-20th century in period rooms

Natural History Museum, Wollaton Park NG8 2AE
T 0115-915 3900
Local natural history and wildlife dioramas

OXFORD - *Ashmolean Museum*, Beaumont Street OX1 2PH
T 01865-278000 **W** www.ashmol.ox.ac.uk
European and Oriental fine and applied arts, archaeology, Egyptology and numismatics

Museum of Modern Art, Pembroke Street OX1 1BP
T 01865-722733 **W** www.modernartoxford.org.uk
Temporary exhibitions

Museum of the History of Science, Broad Street OX1 3AZ
T 01865-277280 **W** www.mhs.ox.ac.uk
Displays include early scientific instruments, chemical apparatus, clocks and watches

Oxford University Museum of Natural History, Parks Road OX1
3PW **T** 01865-272950 **W** www.oum.ox.ac.uk
Entomology, geology, mineralogy and zoology

Pitt Rivers Museum, South Parks Road OX1 3PP **T** 01865-270927
W www.prm.ox.ac.uk
Ethnographic and archaeological artefacts

PLYMOUTH - *City Museum and Art Gallery*, Drake Circus PL4
8AJ **T** 01752-304774 **W** www.plymouthmuseum.gov.uk
Local and natural history, ceramics, silver, Old Masters, temporary exhibitions

The Dome, The Hoe PL1 2NZ **T** 01752-603300
W www.plymouthdome.info
Maritime history museum

PORTSMOUTH - *Charles Dickens Birthplace Museum*, Old
Commercial Road PO1 4QL **T** 023-9282 7261
W www.charlesdickensbirthplace.co.uk
Dickens memorabilia

D-Day Museum, Clarence Esplanade PO5 3NT **T** 023-9282 7261
W www.ddaymuseum.co.uk
Includes the Overlord Embroidery

Flagship Portsmouth, HM Naval Base (**W** www.flagship.org.uk).
Incorporates the *Royal Naval Museum* (**T** 023-9272 7562
W www.royalnavalmuseum.org), HMS *Victory* (**T** 023-9286
1512 **W** www.hms-victory.com), HMS *Warrior* (**T** 023-9286
1512 **W** www.hmswarrior.org), the *Mary Rose* (**T** 023-9286
1512 **W** www.maryrose.org) and the *Dockyard Museum*.
History of the Royal Navy and of the dockyard and the trades in it

PRESTON - *Harris Museum and Art Gallery*, Market Square PR1
2PP **T** 01772-258248
British art since the 18th-century, ceramics, glass, costume and local history; also contemporary exhibitions

READING – *Rural History Centre*, University of Reading,
Whiteknights RG6 6AG **T** 0118-931 8660
W www.ruralhistory.org
History of farming and the countryside over the last 200 years

ST ALBANS - *Verulamium Museum*, St Michael's AL3 4SW
T 01727-751810 **W** www.stalbansmuseums.org.uk
Iron Age and Roman Verulamium, including wall plasters, jewellery, mosaics and room reconstructions

ST IVES, Cornwall – *Tate Gallery St Ives*, Porthmeor Beach
TR26 1TG **T** 01736-796226 **W** www.tate.org.uk/stives
Modern art, much by artists associated with St Ives. Includes the Barbara Hepworth Museum and Sculpture Garden

SALISBURY – *Salisbury and South Wiltshire Museum*, The Close
SP1 2EN **T** 01722-332151 **W** www.salisburymuseum.org.uk
Archaeology collection

SHEFFIELD - *City Museum and Mappin Art Gallery*, Weston
Park S10 2TP **T** 0114-278 2600
W www.sheffieldgalleries.org.uk
Includes applied arts, natural history, Bronze Age archaeology and ethnography, 19th- and 20th-century art

Graves Art Gallery, Surrey Street S1 1XZ **T** 0114-278 2600
20th-century British art, Grice Collection of Chinese
ivories

Kelham Island Industrial Museum, Alma Street. **T** 0114-272 2106
Local industrial and social history

Ruskin Gallery and Ruskin Craft Gallery, Arundle Gate S1 2PP
T 0114-278 2600

SOUTHAMPTON – *City Art Gallery*, Commercial Road SO14
7LP **T** 023-8083 2277 **W** www.southampton.gov.uk/art
Fine art, especially 20th-century British

Maritime Museum, Town Quay SO14 2AR **T** 023-8063 5904
Southampton maritime history

Museum of Archaeology, Town Quay SO14 2NY **T** 023-8063 5904
Roman, Saxon and medieval archaeology

Tudor House Museum and Garden, Bugle Street SO14 2AD
T 023-8063 5904
Restored 16th-century garden; social history exhibitions

SOUTH SHIELDS – *Arbeia Roman Fort*, Baring Street NE33
2BB **T** 0191-456 1369 **W** www.twmuseums.org.uk/arbeia
Excavated ruins

South Shields Museum and Art Gallery, Ocean Road NE33 2JA
T 0191-456 8740 **W** www.twmuseums.org.uk/southshields
South Tyneside history, including reconstructed street

STOKE-ON-TRENT - *Etruria Industrial Museum*, Etruria ST4
7AF **T** 01782-233144
Britain's sole surviving steam-powered potter's mill

Gladstone Pottery Museum, Longton ST3 1PQ **T** 01782-319232
A working Victorian pottery

Potteries Museum and Art Gallery, Hanley ST1 3DE
T 01782-232323
Pottery, china and porcelain collections and a Mark XVI
Spitfire. Pottery factory tours are available by
arrangement, at the following: *Royal Doulton*, Burslem;
Spode, Stoke; *Wedgwood*, Barlaston; *W. Moorcroft*,
Cobridge; H & R Johnson Tiles, Tunstall; *Staffordshire
Enamels*, Longton; *Royale Stratford China*, Fenton

STYAL, Cheshire – *Quarry Bank Mill SK9 4LA* **T** 01625-527468
W www.quarrybankmill.org.uk
Working mill illustrating history of cotton industry;
costumed guides at restored Apprentice House

SUNDERLAND – *Sunderland Museum and Winter Gardens*,
Sunderland SR1 1PP **T** 0191-553 2323
W www.twmuseums.org.uk/sunderland
Fine and decorative art, local history and gardens

TELFORD - *Ironbridge Gorge Museums TF8 7DQ*
T 01952-884391 **W** www.ironbridge.org.uk
Includes first iron bridge; Blists Hill (late Victorian
working town); Museum of Iron; Jackfield Tile Museum;
Coalport China Museum; Tar Tunnel; Broseley
Pipeworks

WAKEFIELD - *Yorkshire Sculpture Park*, West Bretton WF4 4LG
T 01924-830302 **W** www.ysp.co.uk
Open-air sculpture gallery including works by Moore,
Hepworth, Frink and others in 300 acres of parkland

WASHINGTON – *Washington 'F' Pit Museum* Albany Way,
NE37 1BJ
Colliery-related collection

WEYBRIDGE - Brooklands Motorsport and Aviation Museum
KT13 0QN **T** 01932-857381
W www.brooklandsmuseum.com
Birthplace of British Motorsport

WORCESTER - *City Museum and Art Gallery*, Foregate Street
WR1 1DT **T** 01905-25371
W www.worcestercitymuseums.org.uk
Includes a military museum, River Severn Gallery and
changing art exhibitions

*Museum of Worcester Porcelain and Royal Worcester Visitor
Centre*, Severn Street WR1 2NE **T** 01905-746000

WROUGHTON, nr Swindon, Wilts – *Science Museum*,
Wroughton Airfield. **T** 01793-846200
W www.sciencemuseum.org.uk
Aircraft displays and some of the Science Museum's
transport and agricultural collection

YEOVIL, Somerset – *Fleet Air Arm Museum*, Royal Naval Air
Station, Yeovilton BA22 8HT **T** 01935-840565
W www.fleetairarm.com
History of naval aviation; historic aircraft, including
Concorde 002

YORKSHIRE - *Beningbrough Hall*, Beningbrough YO30 1DD
T 01904-470666
Portraits from the National Portrait Gallery

Castle Museum, Eye of York YO1 9RY **T** 01904-650333
W www.york.castle.museum
Reconstructed streets; costume and military collections

City Art Gallery, Exhibition Square YO1 7EW
T 01904-697979 **W** www.york.art.museum
European and British painting spanning seven centuries;
modern pottery

Eden Camp, Malton, North Yorkshire **W** www.edencamp.co.uk
Restored POW camp and WW2 memorabilia

Jorvik – The Viking City, Coppergate YO1 9WT **T** 01904-543403
W www.jorvik-viking-centre.co.uk
Reconstruction of Viking York

National Railway Museum, Leeman Road YO26 4XJ
T 01904-621261 **W** www.nrm.org.uk
Includes locomotives, rolling stock and carriages

Yorkshire Museum, Museum Gardens YO1 7FR **T** 01904-687687
W www.york.yorkshire.museum
Yorkshire life from Roman to medieval times; geology
gallery

WALES

BLAENAFON, Torfaen – *Big Pit National Mining Museum* NP4
9XP **T** 01495-790311 **W** www.nmgw.ac.uk/bigpit
Colliery with underground tour

BODELWYDDAN, Denbighshire – *Bodelwyddan Castle* LL18
5YA **T** 01745-584060 **W** www.bodelwyddan-castle.co.uk
Portraits from the National Portrait Gallery, furniture
from the Victoria and Albert Museum and sculptures
from the Royal Academy

CAERLEON - *Roman Legionary Museum* NP6 1AE
T 01633-423134 **W** www.nmgw.ac.uk/rlm
Material from the site of the Roman fortress of Isca and
its suburbs

CARDIFF - *National Museum and Gallery Cardiff*, Cathays Park
CF10 3NP **T** 029-2039 7951
W www.nmgw.ac.uk/nmgc
Includes natural sciences, archaeology and Impressionist
paintings

Museum of Welsh Life, St Fagans CF5 6XB **T** 029-2057 3500
W www.nmgw.ac.uk/mwl
Open-air museum with re-erected buildings, agricultural
equipment and costume

DRE-FACH FELINDRE, nr Llandysul – *Museum of the Welsh
Woollen Industry SA44 5UP*
T 01559-370929 **W** www.nmgw.ac.uk/mwwi
Exhibitions, a working woollen mill and craft workshops

LLANBERIS, nr Caernarfon – *Welsh Slate Museum LL55 4TY*
T 01286-870630 **W** www.nmgw.ac.uk/wsm
Former slate quarry with original machinery and plant;
slate crafts demonstrations

LLANDRINDOD WELLS – *National Cycle Collection*,
Automobile Palace, Temple Street LD1 5DL **T** 01597-825531
W www.cyclemuseum.org.uk.

Over 200 bicycles on display, from 1818 to the present day

SWANSEA - *Glynn Vivian Art Gallery and Museum*, Alexandra Road SA1 5DZ **T** 01792-655006
W www.swansea.gov.uk/glynnvivian
Paintings, ceramics, Swansea pottery and porcelain, clocks, glass and Welsh art

Swansea Museum, Victoria Road SA1 1SN
T 01792-653763
W www.swansea.gov.uk
Archaeology, social history, Swansea pottery

SCOTLAND

ABERDEEN – *Aberdeen Art Gallery*, Schoolhill AB10 1FQ
T 01224-523700 **W** www.aagm.co.uk
Art from the 18th- to 20th-century

Aberdeen Maritime Museum, Shiprow AB11 5BY
T 01224-337700 **W** www.aagm.co.uk
Maritime history, incl. shipbuilding and North Sea oil

EDINBURGH - *Britannia*, Leith docks EH6 6JJ
T 0131-555 5566 **W** www.royalyachtbritannia.co.uk
Former royal yacht with royal barge and royal family picture gallery. Tickets must be pre-booked

City Art Centre, Market Street EH1 1DE **T** 0131-529 3993
W www.cac.org.uk
Late 19th- and 20th-century art and temporary exhibitions

Museum of Childhood, High Street EH1 1TG
T 0131-529 4142
W www.cac.org.uk
Toys, games, clothes and exhibits relating to the social history of childhood

Museum of Edinburgh, Canongate EH8 8DD
T 0131-529 4143
W www.cac.org.uk
Local history, silver, glass and Scottish pottery

Museum of Flight, East Fortune Airfield, East Lothian EH39 5LF
T 01620-880308
Display of aircraft

Museum of Scotland, Chambers Street EH1 1JF
T 0131-247 4422 **W** www.nms.ac.uk
Scottish history from prehistoric times to the present

Museum of Scottish Country Life, East Kilbride G76 9HR
T 0131-247 4377
W www.nms.ac.uk
History of rural life and work

National Gallery of Scotland, The Mound EH2 2EL
T 0131-624 6200 **W** www.nationalgalleries.org
Paintings, drawings and prints from the 16th- to 20th- century, and the national collection of Scottish art

National War Museum of Scotland, Edinburgh Castle EH1 2NG
T 0131-225 7534 **W** www.nms.ac.uk
History of Scottish military and conflicts

The People's Story, Canongate EH8 8BN **T** 0131-529 4057
W www.cac.org.uk
Edinburgh life since the 18th-century

Royal Museum of Scotland, Chambers Street EH1 1JF
T 0131-247 4219 **W** www.nms.ac.uk
Scottish and international collections from prehistoric times to the present

Scottish National Gallery of Modern Art, Belford Road EH4 3DR
T 0131-624 6200 **W** www.nationalgalleries.org
20th-century painting, sculpture and graphic art

Scottish National Portrait Gallery, Queen Street EH2 1JD
T 0131-624 6200 **W** www.nationalgalleries.org
Portraits of eminent people in Scottish history, and the national collection of photography

The Writers' Museum, Lawnmarket EH1 2PA **T** 0131-529 4901
W www.cac.org.uk
Robert Louis Stevenson, Walter Scott and Robert Burns exhibits

FORT WILLIAM - *West Highland Museum*, Cameron Square PH33 6AJ **T** 01397-702169 **W** www.fort-william.net/museum
Includes tartan collections and exhibits relating to 1745 uprising

GLASGOW - *Burrell Collection*, Pollokshaws Road G43 1AT
T 0141-287 2550 **W** www.glasgowmuseums.com
Paintings, textiles, furniture, ceramics, stained glass and silver from classical times to the 19th-century

Gallery of Modern Art, Queen Street G1 3AH **T** 0141-229 1996
W www.glasgowmuseums.com
Collection of contemporary Scottish and world art

Hunterian Art Gallery, Hillhead Street G12 8QQ
T 0141-330 4221
W www.hunterian.gla.ac.uk
Rennie Mackintosh and Whistler collections; Old Masters, Scottish paintings and modern paintings, sculpture and prints

Kelvingrove Art Gallery and Museum G3 8AG
T 0141-287 2699
W www.glasgowmuseums.com
Includes Old Masters, 19th-century French paintings and armour collection. Closed until 2006 for refurbishment

McLellan Galleries, Sauchiehall Street G2 3EH **T** 0141-331 1854
W www.glasgowmuseums.com
Temporary exhibitions

Museum of Transport, Bunhouse Road G3 8DP
T 0141-287 2720
W www.glasgowmuseums.com
Includes a reproduction of a 1938 Glasgow street, cars since the 1930s, trams and a Glasgow subway station

People's Palace Museum, Glasgow Green G40 1AT
T 0141-554 0223 **W** www.glasgowmuseums.com
History of Glasgow since 1175

St Mungo Museum of Religious Life and Art, Castle Street G4 0RH
T 0141-553 2557 **W** www.glasgowmuseums.com
Explores universal themes through objects of all the main world religions

ST ANDREWS - British Golf Museum, Bruce Embankment KY16 9AB **T** 01334-460046
W www.british golfmuseum.com
History of golf

NORTHERN IRELAND

BELFAST – *Ulster Museum*, Botanic Gardens BT9 5AB
T 028-9038 3000
W www.ulstermuseum.org.uk
Irish antiquities, natural and local history, fine and applied arts

HOLYWOOD, Co. Down – *Ulster Folk and Transport Museum*, Cultra BT18 0EU
Open-air museum with original buildings from Ulster town and rural life *c*.1900; indoor galleries including Irish rail and road transport and *Titanic* exhibitions

LONDONDERRY - *The Tower Museum*, Union Hall Place BT48 6LU **T** 028-7137 2411
Tells the story of Ireland through the history of Londonderry

OMAGH, Co. Tyrone – *Ulster American Folk Park*, Castletown BT78 5QY **T** 028-8224 3292 **W** www.folkpark.com
Open-air museum telling the story of Ulster's emigrants to America; restored or recreated dwellings and workshops; ship and dockside gallery

SIGHTS OF LONDON

For historic buildings, museums and galleries in London, see the Historic Buildings and Monuments and Museums and Galleries sections.

BRIDGES

The bridges over the Thames (from east to west) are:

The Queen Elizabeth II Bridge, opened 1991, from Dartford to Thurrock

Tower Bridge, opened 1894

London Bridge, opened after rebuilding by Rennie, 1831; the new London Bridge opened 1973

Alexandra Bridge (railway bridge), built 1863–6

Southwark Bridge (Rennie), built 1814–19; rebuilt 1912–21

Millennium Bridge, opened June 2000; reopened after modification February 2002

Blackfriars Railway Bridge, completed 1864

Blackfriars Bridge, built 1760–9; rebuilt 1860–9; widened 1907–10

Waterloo Bridge (Rennie), opened 1817; rebuilt 1937–42

Hungerford Footbridge, opened 2002

Hungerford Railway Bridge (Brunel), suspension bridge built 1841–5; replaced by present railway and footbridge 1863

Westminster Bridge, opened 1750; rebuilt 1854–62

Lambeth Bridge, built 1862; rebuilt 1929–32

Vauxhall Bridge, built 1811–16; rebuilt 1895–1906

Grosvenor Bridge (railway bridge), built 1859–60; rebuilt 1963–7

Chelsea Bridge, built 1851–8; replaced by suspension bridge 1934; widened 1937

Albert Bridge, opened 1873; restructured (Bazalgette) 1884; strengthened 1971–3

Battersea Bridge (Holland), opened 1772; rebuilt (Bazalgette) 1890

Battersea Railway Bridge, opened 1863

Wandsworth Bridge, opened 1873; rebuilt 1940

Putney Railway Bridge, opened 1889

Putney Bridge, built 1727–9; rebuilt (Bazalgette) 1882–6; starting point of Oxford and Cambridge Boat Race

Hammersmith Bridge, built 1824–7; rebuilt (Bazalgette) 1883–7; closed 1997–9 for safety work

Barnes Railway Bridge (also pedestrian), built 1846–9; restructured 1893

Chiswick Bridge, opened 1933

Kew Railway Bridge, opened 1869

Kew Bridge, built 1758–9; rebuilt and renamed King Edward VII Bridge 1903

Richmond Lock, lock, weir and footbridge opened 1894

Twickenham Bridge, opened 1933

Richmond Railway Bridge, opened 1848; restructured 1906–8

Richmond Bridge, built 1774–7; widened 1937

Teddington Lock, footbridge opened 1889; marks the end of the tidal reach of the Thames

Kingston Bridge, built 1825–8; widened 1914

Hampton Court Bridge, built 1753; replaced by iron bridge 1865; present bridge built 1933

CEMETERIES

Abney Park, Stamford Hill, N16 (35 acres), tomb of General Booth, founder of the Salvation Army, and memorials to many Nonconformist divines. *Brompton*, Old Brompton Road, SW10 (40 acres), graves of Sir Henry Cole, Emmeline Pankhurst, John Wisden. *City of London Cemetery and Crematorium*, Aldersbrook Road, E12 (200 acres). *Golders Green Crematorium*, Hoop Lane, NW11 (12 acres), with Garden of Rest and memorials to many famous men and women. *Hampstead*, Fortune Green Road, NW6 (36 acres), graves of Kate Greenaway, Lord Lister, Marie Lloyd. *Highgate*, Swains Lane, N6 (38 acres), tombs of George Eliot, Faraday and Marx; guided tours only, west side. *Kensal Green*, Harrow Road, W10 (70 acres), tombs of Thackeray, Trollope, Sydney Smith, Wilkie Collins, Tom Hood, George Cruikshank, Leigh Hunt, I. K. Brunel and Charles Kemble. Churchyard of the former *Marylebone Chapel*, Marylebone High Street, W1, Charles Wesley and his son Samuel Wesley buried; chapel demolished in 1949, now Garden of Rest. *Nunhead*, Linden Grove, SE15 (26 acres), closed in 1969, subsequently restored and opened for burials. *St Marylebone Cemetery and Crematorium*, East End Road, N2 (47 acres). *West Norwood Cemetery and Crematorium*, Norwood High Street, SE27 (42 acres), tombs of Sir Henry Bessemer, Mrs Beeton, Sir Henry Tate and Joseph Whitaker *(Whitaker's Almanack)*.

MARKETS

The London markets are mostly administered by the Corporation of London. *Billingsgate* (fish), Thames Street site dating from 1875, a market site for over 1,000 years, moved to the Isle of Dogs in 1982. *Borough,* SE1 (vegetables, fruit, flowers, etc.), established on present site 1756, privately owned and run. *Covent Garden* (vegetables, fruit, flowers, etc.), established in 1661 under a charter of Charles II, moved in 1973 to Nine Elms, SW8. *Leadenhall*, EC3 (meat, poultry, fish, etc.), built 1881, part recently demolished. *London Fruit Exchange*, Brushfield Street, built by Corporation of London 1928–9 as buildings for Spitalfields market; not connected with the market since it moved in 1991. *Petticoat Lane*, Middlesex Street, E1, a market has existed on the site for over 500 years, now a Sunday morning market selling almost anything. *Portobello Road*, W11, originally for herbs and horse-trading from 1870; became famous for antiques after the closure of the Caledonian Market in 1948. *Smithfield, Central Meat, Fish, Fruit, Vegetable and Poultry Markets*, built 1851–66, the site of St Bartholomew's Fair from 12th- to 19th-century, new hall built 1963, market refurbished 1993–4. *Spitalfields*, E1 (vegetables, fruit, etc.), established 1682, modernised 1928, moved to Leyton in 1991. A much smaller market still exists on the original site on Commercial Street, selling arts, crafts, books, clothes and antiques on Sundays.

MONUMENTS

CENOTAPH, Whitehall, London SW1. The word 'cenotaph' means 'empty tomb'. The monument, erected 'To the Glorious Dead', is a memorial to all ranks of the sea, land and air forces who gave their lives in the service of the Empire during the First World War. Designed by Sir Edwin Lutyens and erected as a temporary memorial in 1919, it was replaced by a permanent structure unveiled by George V on Armistice Day

1920. An additional inscription was made after the Second World War to commemorate those who gave their lives in that conflict.

LONDON MONUMENT, (commonly called The Monument), Monument Street, EC3. Built from designs of Wren, 1671–7, to commemorate the Great Fire of London, which broke out in Pudding Lane on 2 September 1666. The fluted Doric column is 120 ft high; the moulded cylinder above the balcony supporting a flaming vase of gilt bronze is an additional 42 ft; and the column is based on a square plinth 40 ft high (with fine carvings on the west face) making a total height of 202 ft. Splendid views of London from gallery at top of column (311 steps).

OTHER MONUMENTS, (sculptor's name in parenthesis). *Albert Memorial* (Durham), Kensington Gore; *Royal Air Force* (Blomfield), Victoria Embankment; *Viscount Alanbrooke,* Whitehall; *Beaconsfield,* Parliament Square; *Beatty* (Macmillan), Trafalgar Square; *Belgian Gratitude* (setting by Blomfield, statue by Rousseau), Victoria Embankment; *Boadicea* (or Boudicca), Queen of the Iceni (Thornycroft), Westminster Bridge; *Brunel* (Marochetti), Victoria Embankment; *Burghers of Calais* (Rodin), Victoria Tower Gardens, Westminster; *Burns* (Steel), Embankment Gardens; *Canada Memorial* (Granche), Green Park; *Carlyle* (Boehm), Chelsea Embankment; *Cavalry* (Jones), Hyde Park; *Edith Cavell* (Frampton), St Martin's Place; *Cenotaph* (Lutyens), Whitehall; *Charles I* (Le Sueur), Trafalgar Square; *Charles II* (Gibbons), South Court, Chelsea Hospital; *Churchill* (Roberts-Jones), Parliament Square; *Cleopatra's Needle,* (38.5 ft high, *c.*1500 BC, erected in 1877–8; the sphinxes are Victorian), Thames Embankment; *Clive* (Tweed), King Charles Street; *Captain Cook* (Brock), The Mall; *Crimean,* Broad Sanctuary; *Oliver Cromwell* (Thornycroft), outside Westminster Hall; *Cunningham* (Belsky), Trafalgar Square; *Gen. Charles de Gaulle,* Carlton Gardens; *Lord Dowding* (Faith Winter), Strand; *Duke of Cambridge* (Jones), Whitehall; *Duke of York* (124 ft), Carlton House Terrace; *Edward VII* (Mackennal), Waterloo Place; *Elizabeth I* (1586, oldest outdoor statue in London; from Ludgate), Fleet Street; *Eros* (Shaftesbury Memorial) (Gilbert), Piccadilly Circus; *Marechal Foch* (Mallisard, copy of one in Cassel, France), Grosvenor Gardens; *Charles James Fox* (Westmacott), Bloomsbury Square; *George III* (Cotes Wyatt), Cockspur Street; *George IV* (Chantrey), Trafalgar Square; *George V* (Reid Dick), Old Palace Yard; *George VI* (Macmillan), Carlton Gardens; *Gladstone* (Thornycroft), Strand; *Guards'* (Crimea) (Bell), Waterloo Place; *(Great War)* (Ledward, figures, Bradshaw, cenotaph), Horse Guards' Parade; *Haig* (Hardiman), Whitehall; *Sir Arthur (Bomber) Harris* (Faith Winter), Strand; *Irving* (Brock), north side of National Portrait Gallery; *James II* (Gibbons and/or pupils), Trafalgar Square; *Jellicoe* (Wheeler), Trafalgar Square; *Samuel Johnson* (Fitzgerald), opposite St Clement Danes; *Kitchener* (Tweed), Horse Guards' Parade; *Abraham Lincoln* (Saint-Gaudens, copy of one in Chicago), Parliament Square; *Milton* (Montford), St Giles, Cripplegate; *Mountbatten,* Foreign Office Green; *Nelson* (170 ft 2 in), Trafalgar Square, with Landseer's lions (cast from guns recovered from the wreck of the *Royal George*); *Florence Nightingale* (Walker), Waterloo Place; *Palmerston* (Woolner), Parliament Square; *Peel* (Noble), Parliament Square; *Pitt* (Chantrey), Hanover Square; *Portal* (Nemon), Embankment Gardens; *Prince Consort* (Bacon), Holborn Circus; *Queen Elizabeth Gate,* Hyde Park Corner; *Raleigh* (Macmillan), Whitehall; *Richard I (Coeur de Lion)* (Marochetti), Old Palace Yard; *Roberts* (Bates), Horse Guards' Parade; *Franklin D. Roosevelt* (Reid Dick), Grosvenor Square; *Royal Artillery* (South Africa) (Colton), The Mall; (Great War), Hyde Park Corner; *Captain Scott* (Lady Scott), Waterloo Place; *Shackleton* (Sarjeant Jagger), Kensington Gore; *Shakespeare* (Fontana, copy of one by Scheemakers in Westminster Abbey), Leicester Square; *Smuts* (Epstein), Parliament Square; *Sullivan* (Goscombe John), Victoria Embankment; *Trenchard* (Macmillan), Victoria Embankment; *Victoria Memorial,* in front of Buckingham Palace; *Raoul Wallenberg* (Phillip Jackson), Great Cumberland Place; *George Washington* (Houdon copy), Trafalgar Square; *Wellington* (Boehm), Hyde Park Corner, (Chantrey), outside Royal Exchange; *John Wesley* (Adams Acton), City Road; *William III* (Bacon), St James's Square; *Wolseley* (Goscombe John), Horse Guards' Parade.

PARKS, GARDENS AND OPEN SPACES

CORPORATION OF LONDON OPEN SPACES
Ashtead Common (500 acres), Surrey
Burnham Beeches and *Fleet Wood* (540 acres), Bucks. Purchased by the Corporation for the benefit of the public in 1880, Fleet Wood (65 acres) being presented in 1921.
Coulsdon Common (133 acres), Surrey
Epping Forest (6,000 acres), Essex. Purchased by the Corporation and opened to the public in 1882. The present forest is 12 miles long by 1 to 2 miles wide, about one-tenth of its original area.
Farthing Downs (121 acres), Surrey
Hampstead Heath (789 acres), NW3. Including: Golders Hill (36 acres) and Parliament Hill (271 acres)
Highgate Wood (70 acres), N6/N10
Kenley Common (138 acres), Surrey
Queen's Park (30 acres), NW6
Riddlesdown (90 acres), Surrey
Spring Park (51 acres), Kent
West Ham Park (77 acres), E15
West Wickham Common (25 acres), Kent
Woodredon and Warlies Park Estate (740 acres), Waltham Abbey.
Also smaller open spaces within the City of London, including *Finsbury Circus Gardens.*

OTHER PARKS AND GARDENS
CHELSEA PHYSIC GARDEN, 66 Royal Hospital Road, SW3 4HS T 020-7352 5646 W www.chelseaphysicgarden.co.uk. A garden of general botanical research and education, maintaining a wide range of rare and unusual plants. The garden was established in 1673 by the Society of Apothecaries.

ROYAL PARKS
W www.royalparks.gov.uk

Bushy Park (1,099 acres), Middx. Adjoining Hampton Court, contains avenue of horse-chestnuts enclosed in a fourfold avenue of limes planted by William III.
Green Park (40 acres), W1. Between Piccadilly and St James's Park, with Constitution Hill leading to Hyde Park Corner.
Greenwich Park (183 acres), SE10
Hyde Park (350 acres), W1/W2. From Park Lane to Kensington Gardens, containing the Serpentine lake. Fine gateway at Hyde Park Corner, with Apsley House, the Achilles Statue, Rotten Row and the Ladies' Mile. To the north-east is the Marble Arch, originally erected

by George IV at the entrance to Buckingham Palace and re-erected in the present position in 1851.

Kensington Gardens (275 acres), W2/W8. From the western boundary of Hyde Park to Kensington Palace, containing the Albert Memorial, Serpentine Gallery and Peter Pan statue.

Kew, Royal Botanic Gardens Richmond, Surrey, TW9 3AB T 020-8332 5655 E info@kew.org W www.rbgkew.org.uk. Officially inscribed on the UNESCO list of World Heritage Sites in July 2003.

Regent's Park and *Primrose Hill* (487 acres), NW1. From Marylebone Road to Primrose Hill surrounded by the Outer Circle and divided by the Broad Walk leading to the Zoological Gardens.

Richmond Park (2,500 acres), Middlesex

St James's Park (93 acres), SW1. From Whitehall to Buckingham Palace. Ornamental lake of 12 acres. The original suspension bridge built in 1857 was replaced in 1957. The Mall leads from the Admiralty Arch to Buckingham Palace, Birdcage Walk from Storey's Gate to Buckingham Palace.

Hampton Court Park and Gardens (669 acres), Surrey

PLACES OF HISTORICAL AND CULTURAL INTEREST

ALEXANDRA PALACE, Alexandra Palace Way, Wood Green, N22 7AY T 020-8365 2121 W www.alexandrapalace.com The Victorian palace was severely damaged by fire in 1980 but was restored, and reopened in 1988. Alexandra Palace now provides modern facilities for exhibitions, conferences, banquets and leisure activities. There is an ice rink, a boating lake, the Phoenix Bar and a conservation area.

BARBICAN CENTRE, Silk Street, EC2Y 8DS T 020-7638 4141 W www.barbican.org.uk Owned, funded and managed by the Corporation of London, the Barbican Centre opened in 1982 and houses the Barbican Theatre, a studio theatre called The Pit, the Barbican Hall and is home to the London Symphony Orchestra. There are also three cinemas, six conference rooms, two art galleries, a sculpture court, a lending library, trade and banqueting facilities, a conservatory, shops, restaurants, cafes and bars.

CHARTERHOUSE, Charterhouse Square, EC1M 6AN T 020-7253 9503 A Carthusian monastery from 1371 to 1537, purchased in 1611 by Thomas Sutton, who endowed it as a residence for aged men 'of gentle birth' and a school for poor scholars (removed to Godalming in 1872).

DOWNING STREET, SW1 Number 10 Downing Street is the official town residence of the Prime Minister, No. 11 to the Chancellor of the Exchequer and No. 12 is the office of the Government Whips. The street was named after Sir George Downing, Bt., soldier and diplomat, who was MP for Morpeth from 1660 to 1684.

GEORGE INN, Borough High Street, SE1 1NH The last galleried inn in London, built in 1677. Now run as an ordinary public house.

GREENWICH, SE10. The Royal Naval College, T 020-8269 4747, was until 1873 the Greenwich Hospital. It was built by Charles II, largely from designs by John Webb, and by Queen Mary II and William III, from designs by Wren. It stands on the site of an ancient abbey, a royal house and Greenwich Palace which was constructed by Henry VII. Henry VIII, Mary I and Elizabeth I were born in the royal palace and Edward VI died there.

Greenwich Park (196.5 acres), T 020-8858 2608, was enclosed by Humphrey, Duke of Gloucester, and laid out by Charles II from the designs of Le Nôtre. On a hill in Greenwich Park is the *Royal Observatory* (founded 1675). Its buildings are now managed by the *National Maritime Museum*, T 020-8858 4422 and the earliest building is named Flamsteed House, after John Flamsteed (1646–1719), the first Astronomer Royal. *The Cutty Sark*, T 020-8858 3445 The last of the famous tea clippers was moved into a specially constructed dry dock in 1954 and opened to the public in 1957. Sir Francis Chichester's round-the-world yacht, *Gipsy Moth IV*, can also be seen.

HORSE GUARDS, Whitehall, SW1 Archway and offices built about 1753. The changing of the guard takes place at 11a.m. (10a.m. on Sundays) and the dismounted inspection at 4p.m. Only those with the Queen's permission may drive through the gates and archway into *Horse Guards' Parade*, where the Colour is 'trooped' on The Queen's official birthday.

HOUSE OF COMMONS, Westminster, London, SW1A 0AA T 020-7219 4272 E hcinfo@parliament.uk

HOUSE OF LORDS, Westminster, London, SW1A 0PW T 020-7219 3107 E hlinfo@parliament.uk The royal palace of Westminster, originally built by Edward the Confessor, was the normal meeting place of Parliament from about 1340. St Stephen's Chapel was used from about 1550 for the meetings of the House of Commons, which had previously been held in the Chapter House or Refectory of Westminster Abbey. The House of Lords met in an apartment of the royal palace. The fire of 1834 destroyed much of the palace and the present Houses of Parliament were erected on the site from the designs of Sir Charles Barry and Augustus Welby Pugin between 1840 and 1867. The chamber of the House of Commons was destroyed by bombing in 1941 and a new Chamber designed by Sir Giles Gilbert Scott was used for the first time in 1950. *Westminster Hall and the Crypt Chapel* was the only part of the old palace of Westminster to survive the fire of 1834. It was built by William Rufus (1097–9) and altered by Richard II (1394–9). The hammerbeam roof of carved oak dates from 1396–8. The Hall was the scene of the trial of Charles I. *The Victoria Tower* of the House of Lords is about 330 ft high, and when Parliament is sitting the Union flag flies by day from its flagstaff. *The Clock Tower* of the House of Commons is about 320 ft high and contains 'Big Ben', the hour bell said to be named after Sir Benjamin Hall, First Commissioner of Works when the original bell was cast in 1856. This bell, which weighed 16 tons 11 cwt, was found to be cracked in 1857. The present bell (13.5 tons) is a recasting of the original and was first brought into use in 1859. The dials of the clock are 23 ft in diameter, the hands being 9 ft and 14 ft long (including balance piece). A light is displayed from the Clock Tower at night when Parliament is sitting. During session tours of the Houses of Parliament are only available to UK residents who have made advance arrangements through an MP or peer. Overseas visitors are no longer provided with permits to tour the Houses of Parliament during session, although they can tour during the summer opening and attend debates for both houses in the Strangers' Galleries (*see* below). During the summer recess tickets for tours of the Houses of Parliament can be booked by T 0870-906 3773 or bought on site at the ticket office on Abingdon Green opposite Parliament and the Victoria Tower Gardens. The Strangers' Gallery of the House of Commons is open to the public when the house is sitting. To acquire tickets in advance UK residents should write to their local MP and overseas visitors should apply to their Embassy or High Commission in the UK for a permit. If none of these arrangements have been made, visitors should join the public queue outside St Stephen's Entrance, where there is also a queue for entry to the House of Lords Gallery.

INNS OF COURT The Inns of Court are ancient unincorporated bodies of lawyers which for more than five centuries have had the power to call to the Bar those of their members who have qualified for the rank or degree of Barrister-at-Law. There are four Inns of Court as well as many lesser inns.

Lincoln's Inn, Chancery Lane/Lincoln's Inn Fields, WC2 T 020-7405 1393 W www.lincolnsinn.org.uk The most ancient of the inns with records dating back to 1422. The hall and library buildings are of 1845, although the library is first mentioned in 1474; the old hall (late 15th-century) and the chapel were rebuilt c. 1619–23.

Inner Temple, King's Bench Walk, EC4 T 020-7797 8208 W www.innertemple.org.uk

Middle Temple, Fleet Street/Victoria Embankment, EC4 T 020-7427 4800 W www.middletemple.org.uk

Records for the Middle and Inner temple date back to the beginning of the 16th century. The site was originally occupied by the Order of Knights Templars c.1160–1312. The two inns have separate halls thought to have been formed c. 1350. The division between the two societies was formalised in 1732 with Temple Church and the Masters house remaining in common. The Inner Temple Garden is normally open to the public on weekdays between 12.30p.m. and 3p.m.

Temple Church, EC4 T 020-7353 3470 The nave forms one of five remaining round churches in England. *Master of the Temple,* Revd Robin Griffith-Jones.

Gray's Inn, South Square, WC1 T 020-7458 7900 W www.graysinn.org.uk Founded early 14th-century; Hall 1556–8.

No other 'Inns' are active, but there are remains of *Staple Inn,* a gabled front on Holborn (opposite Gray's Inn Road). *Clement's Inn* (near St Clement Danes Church), *Clifford's Inn,* Fleet Street, and *Thavies Inn,* Holborn Circus, are all rebuilt. *Serjeants' Inn,* Fleet Street, and another (demolished 1910) of the same name in Chancery Lane, were composed of Serjeants-at-Law, the last of whom died in 1922.

LLOYD'S, One Lime Street, EC3M 7HA T 020-7327 1000 W www.lloydsoflondon.com International insurance market which evolved during the 17th-century from Lloyd's Coffee House. The present building was opened for business in May 1986, and houses the Lutine Bell. Underwriting is on three floors with a total area of 114,000 sq. ft. The Lloyd's building is not open to the general public.

LONDON EYE, The Thames South Bank, SE1 T 0870-500 0600 W www.londoneye.com Opened in February 2000 as London's millennium landmark, this 450ft observation wheel is the capital's fourth largest structure. The wheel provides a 30 minute ride offering spectacular panoramic views of the capital.

LONDON ZOO, Regent's Park, NW1 T 020-7722 3333 W www.londonzoo.org

MADAME TUSSAUD'S AND THE LONDON PLANETARIUM, Marylebone Road, NW1 5LR T 0870-400 3000 W www.madame-tussauds.co.uk Waxwork exhibition and interactive star show

MARLBOROUGH HOUSE, Pall Mall, SW1A 5HX Built by Wren for the first Duke of Marlborough and completed in 1711, the house reverted to the Crown in 1835. In 1863 it became the London house of the Prince of Wales and was the London home of Queen Mary until her death in 1953. In 1959 Marlborough House was given by The Queen as the headquarters for the Commonwealth Secretariat and it was opened as such in 1965. The Queen's Chapel, Marlborough Gate was begun in 1623 from the designs of Inigo Jones for the Infanta Maria of Spain, and completed for Queen Henrietta Maria.

PORT OF LONDON, Port of London Authority, Bakers' Hall, 7 Harp Lane, EC3R 6LB T 020-7743 7900 W www.portoflondon.co.uk The Port of London covers the tidal section of the River Thames from Teddington to the seaward limit (the outer Tongue buoy and the Sunk light vessel), a distance of 150km. The governing body is the Port of London Authority (PLA). Cargo is handled at privately operated riverside terminals between Fulham and Canvey Island, including the enclosed dock at Tilbury, 40km below London Bridge. Passenger vessels and cruise liners can be handled at moorings at Greenwich, Tower Bridge and Tilbury.

ROMAN REMAINS, The city wall of Roman *Londinium* was largely rebuilt during the medieval period but sections may be seen near the White Tower in the Tower of London; at Tower Hill; at Coopers' Row; at All Hallows, London Wall, its vestry being built on the remains of a semi-circular Roman bastion; at St Alphage, London Wall, showing a succession of building repairs from the Roman until the late medieval period; and at St Giles, Cripplegate. Sections of the great forum and basilica, more than 165m^2, have been encountered during excavations in the area of Leadenhall, Gracechurch Street and Lombard Street. Traces of Roman activity along the river include a massive riverside wall built in the late Roman period, and a succession of Roman timber quays along Lower and Upper Thames Street. Finds from these sites can be seen at the Museum of London.

Other major buildings are the amphitheatre at Guildhall; remains of bath-buildings in Upper and Lower Thames Street; and the temple of Mithras in Walbrook.

ROYAL ALBERT HALL, Kensington Gore, SW7 2AP T 020-7589 8212 W www.royalalberthall.com The elliptical hall, one of the largest in the world, was completed in 1871, and since 1941 has been the venue each summer for the Promenade Concerts founded in 1895 by Sir Henry Wood. Other events include pop and classical music concerts, dance, opera, sporting events, conferences and banquets.

ROYAL HOSPITAL, CHELSEA, Royal Hospital Road, SW3 4SR T 020-7881 5204 W www.chelsea-pensioners.co.uk Founded by Charles II in 1682, and built by Wren; opened in 1692 for old and disabled soldiers. The extensive grounds include the former Ranelagh Gardens and are the venue for the Chelsea Flower Show each May. *Governor,* Gen. Sir Jeremy Mackenzie, GCB, OBE.

ROYAL OPERA HOUSE, Covent Garden, WC2E 9DD T 020-7304 4000 W www.royalopera.org Home of The Royal Ballet (1931) and The Royal Opera (1946). The Royal Opera House is the third theatre to be built on the site, opening 1858; the first was opened in 1732.

ST JAMES'S PALACE, Pall Mall, SW1A 1BP T 020-7930 4832 W www.royal.gov.uk Built by Henry VIII; the Gatehouse and Presence Chamber remain; later alterations were made by Wren and Kent. Representatives of foreign powers are still accredited 'to the Court of St James's'. *Clarence House* (1825), the official London residence of the Prince of Wales and his sons, stands within the St James's Palace environs.

ST PAUL'S CATHEDRAL, St Paul's Churchyard, EC4M 8AD T 020-7236 4128 E chapter@stpaulscathedral.org.uk W www.stpauls.co.uk Built 1675–1710, cost £747,660. The cross on the dome is 365 ft above the ground level, the inner cupola 218 ft above the floor. 'Great Paul' in the south-west tower weighs nearly 17 tons. The organ by Father Smith (enlarged by Willis and rebuilt by Mander) is in a case carved by Grinling Gibbons, who also carved the choir stalls.

SOMERSET HOUSE, Strand and Victoria Embankment, WC2 The river façade (600 ft long) was built in 1776–86 from the designs of Sir William Chambers; the eastern extension, which houses part of King's College, was built by Smirke in 1829. Somerset House was the property of Lord Protector Somerset, at whose attainder in 1552 the palace passed to the Crown, and it was a royal residence until 1692. Somerset House has recently undergone extensive renovation and is home to the Gilbert Collection, Hermitage Rooms and the Courtauld Institute Gallery. Open-air concerts and ice-skating (Nov–Jan) are held in the courtyard

SOUTH BANK, SE1 The arts complex on the south bank of the River Thames which consists of the *Royal Festival Hall* T 020-7921 0600 W www.rfh.org.uk (opened in 1951 for the Festival of Britain), the adjacent 1,056-seat *Queen Elizabeth Hall*, the *Purcell Room*, and the *Voice Box*.

The *National Film Theatre* (Opened 1952) T 020-7928 3232 W www.bfi.org.uk Administered by the British Film Institute, has three auditoria showing over 2,000 films a year. The London Film Festival is held here every November. There is also an IMAX cinema with 500 seats.

The *Royal National Theatre* T 020-7452 3000 W www.nationaltheatre.org.uk Opened in 1976 and stages classical, modern, new and neglected plays in its three auditoria: the Olivier theatre, the Lyttelton theatre and the Cottesloe theatre.

SOUTHWARK CATHEDRAL, London Bridge, SE1 9DA T 020-7367 6700 E cathedral@dswark.org.uk W www.dswark.org Mainly 13th-century, but the nave is largely rebuilt. The tomb of John Gower (1330–1408) is between the Bunyan and Chaucer memorial windows in the north aisle; Shakespeare's effigy, backed by a view of Southwark and the Globe Theatre, is in the south aisle; the tomb of Bishop Andrewes (died 1626) is near the screen. The lady chapel was the scene of the consistory courts of the reign of Mary (Gardiner and Bonner) and is still used as a consistory court. John Harvard, after whom Harvard University is named, was baptised here in 1607, and the chapel by the north choir aisle is his memorial chapel.

THAMES EMBANKMENTS. The *Victoria Embankment*, on the north side from Westminster to Blackfriars, was constructed by Sir Joseph Bazalgette (1819–91) for the Metropolitan Board of Works, 1864–70; the seats, of which the supports of some are a kneeling camel, laden with spicery, and of others a winged sphinx, were presented by the Grocers' Company and by W. H. Smith, MP, in 1874; the *Albert Embankment*, on the south side from Westminster Bridge to Vauxhall, 1866–9; the *Chelsea Embankment*, 1871–4. The total cost exceeded £2,000,000. Bazalgette also inaugurated the London main drainage system, 1858–65. A medallion (*Flumini vincula posuit*) has been placed on a pier of the *Victoria Embankment* to commemorate the engineer.

THAMES FLOOD BARRIER. Officially opened in May 1984, though first used in February 1983, the barrier consists of ten rising sector gates which span 570 yards from bank to bank of the Thames at Woolwich Reach. When not in use the gates lie horizontally, allowing shipping to navigate the river normally; when the barrier is closed, the gates turn through 90 degrees to stand vertically more than 50 feet above the river bed. The barrier took eight years to complete and can be raised within about 30 minutes.

THAMES TUNNELS. The *Rotherhithe Tunnel*, opened 1908, connects Commercial Road, E14, with Lower Road, Rotherhithe SE16; it is 1 mile 332 yards long, of which 525 yards are under the river. The first *Blackwall Tunnel* (northbound vehicles only), opened 1897, connects East India Dock Road, Poplar, with Blackwall Lane, East Greenwich. The height restriction on the northbound tunnel is 13ft 4in. A second tunnel (for southbound vehicles only) opened 1967. The lengths of the tunnels measured from East India Dock Road to the Gate House on the south side are 6,215 ft (old tunnel) and 6,152 ft. *Greenwich Tunnel* (pedestrians only), opened 1902, connects the Isle of Dogs, Poplar, with Greenwich; it is 406 yards long. The *Woolwich Tunnel* (pedestrians only), opened 1912, connects North and South Woolwich below the passenger and vehicular ferry from North Woolwich Station, E6, to High Street, Woolwich, SE18; it is 552 yards long.

WALTHAM CROSS, Herts. One of the crosses (partly restored) erected by Edward I to mark a resting place of the corpse of Queen Eleanor on its way to Westminster Abbey. Ten crosses were erected, but only those at Geddington, Northampton and Waltham survive; 'Charing' Cross originally stood near the spot now occupied by the statue of Charles I at Whitehall.

WESTMINSTER ABBEY, Broad Sanctuary, SW1P 3PA T 0207-7222 5152 E info@westminster-abbey.org W www. westminster-abbey.org
Founded as a Benedictine monastery over 1,000 years ago, the Church was rebuilt by Edward the Confessor in 1065 and again by Henry III in the 13th-century. The Abbey is the resting place for monarchs including Edward I, Henry III, Henry V, Henry VII, Elizabeth I, Mary I and Mary Queen of Scots, and has been the setting of coronations since that of William the Conqueror in 1066. In Poets' Corner there are memorials to many literary figures, and many scientists and musicians are also remembered here. The grave of the Unknown Warrior is to be found in the nave.

WESTMINSTER CATHEDRAL, 42 Francis Street, SW1P 1QW T 020-7798 9055 W www.westminstercathedral.org.uk Roman Catholic cathedral built 1895–1903 from the designs of J. F. Bentley. The campanile is 283 feet high.

THEATRES

ADELPHI THEATRE, Strand, WC2E 7NA
Tube: Charing Cross T 020-7344 0055
ALBERY THEATRE, St Martin's Lane, WC2N 4AH
Tube: Leicester Square T 020-7369 1740
ALDWYCH THEATRE, Aldwych, WC2B 4DF
Tube: Covent Garden T 020-7379 3367
ALMEIDA THEATRE, Almeida Street, N1 1TA
Tube: Highbury & Islington T 020-7359 4404
APOLLO THEATRE, Shaftesbury Avenue, W1V 7HD
Tube: Piccadilly Circus T 020-7494 5070
APOLLO VICTORIA THEATRE, Wilton Road, SW1V 1LL
Tube: Victoria T 0870-400 0650
ARCOLA THEATRE, Arcola Street, E8 2DJ
Tube: Highbury & Islington T 020-7503 1645
ARTS THEATRE, Great Newport Street, WC2H 7JB
Tube: Leicester Square T 020-7836 3334
BARBICAN THEATRE, Barbican Centre, EC2Y 8BQ
Tube: Barbican T 020-7638 8891
BATTERSEA ARTS CENTRE, Lavender Hill, SW11 5TN
Tube: Clapham Common T 020-7223 6557
BRIDEWELL THEATRE, Bride Lane EC4Y 8EQ
Tube: Blackfriars T 020-7353 0259
CAMBRIDGE THEATRE, Earlham Street, WC2 9HH
Tube: Covent Garden T 020-7494 5549
COLISEUM, St. Martin's Lane WC2
Tube: Charing Cross T 020-7836 0111
COMEDY THEATRE, Panton Street, SW1Y 4DN
Tube: Leicester Square T 020-7369 1731
CRITERION THEATRE, Piccadilly Circus, W1V 9LB
Tube: Piccadilly Circus T 020-7413 1437
DOMINION THEATRE, Tottenham Court Road, W1P 0AG
Tube: Tottenham Court Road T 020-7413 3546
DONMAR WAREHOUSE, Earlham Street, WC2H 9LX
Tube: Covent Garden T 020-7240 4882
DRURY LANE, Theatre Royal, Catherine Street, WC2B 5JF
Tube: Covent Garden T 020-7494 5000
DUCHESS THEATRE, Catherine Street, WC2B 5LA
Tube: Covent Garden T 020-7494 5075
DUKE OF YORK'S THEATRE, St Martin's Lane, WC2H 4BG
Tube: Leicester Square T 020-7369 1791
FORTUNE THEATRE, Russell Street, WC2B 5HH
Tube: Covent Garden T 020-7369 1737
GARRICK THEATRE, Charing Cross Road, WC2H 0HH
Tube: Charing Cross T 020-7494 5080
GLOBE THEATRE, New Globe Walk, SE1 9DT
Tube: Mansion House T 020-7902 1400
GIELGUD THEATRE, Shaftesbury Avenue, W1V 8AR
Tube: Piccadilly Circus T 020-7494 5065
HACKNEY EMPIRE, Mare Street, E8 1EJ
Tube: Bethnal Green T 020-8510 4500
HAYMARKET THEATRE, Haymarket, SW1Y 4HT
Tube: Piccadilly Circus T 020-7930 8800
HER MAJESTY'S THEATRE, Haymarket, SW1Y 4QL
Tube: Piccadilly Circus T 020-7494 5400
LONDON PALLADIUM, Argyll Street, W1A 3AB
Tube: Oxford Circus T 020-7494 5570
LYCEUM THEATRE, Wellington Street, WC2E 7DA
Tube: Covent Garden T 0870-243 9000

LYRIC THEATRE, Shaftesbury Avenue, W1V 7HA
Tube: Piccadilly Circus T 020-7494 5045
NATIONAL THEATRE, South Bank, SE1 9PX
Tube: Waterloo T 020-7452 3000
NEW AMBASSADORS THEATRE, West Street, WC2H 9ND
Tube: Leicester Square T 020-7369 1761
NEW LONDON THEATRE, Drury Lane, WC2B 5PW
Tube: Holborn T 0870-890 0141
OLD VIC THEATRE, Waterloo Road, SE1 8NB
Tube: Waterloo T 020-7369 1722
OPEN AIR THEATRE, Regent's Park NW1 4NR
Tube: Regent's Park T 020-7935 5756
PALACE THEATRE, Shaftesbury Avenue, W1V 8AY
Tube: Leicester Square T 020-7434 0909
PHOENIX THEATRE, Charing Cross Road, WC2H 0JP
Tube: Tottenham Court Road T 020 7369 1733
PICCADILLY THEATRE, Denman Street, W1V 8DY
Tube: Piccadilly Circus T 020-7369 1734
PLAYHOUSE THEATRE, Northumberland Avenue, WC2N
5DE Tube: Embankment T 020-7839 4401
PRINCE EDWARD THEATRE, Old Compton Street,
W1V 6HS Tube: Leicester Square/Tottenham Court Road
T 020-7447 5400
PRINCE OF WALES THEATRE, Coventry Street, W1V 8AS
Tube: Piccadilly Circus T 020-7839 5972
QUEENS THEATRE, Shaftesbury Avenue, W1V 8BA
Tube: Piccadilly Circus T 020-7494 5040
ROYAL ALBERT HALL, Kensington Gore, SW7 2AP
Tube: South Kensington T 020-7589 8212
ROYAL COURT THEATRE, Sloane Square, SW1W 8AS
Tube: Sloane Square T 020-7565 5000
ROYAL FESTIVAL HALL, South Bank SE1 8XX
Tube: Waterloo T 020-7921 0600
SADLER'S WELLS, Rosebery Avenue, EC1R 4TN
Tube: Angel T 020-7863 8198
SAVOY THEATRE, Strand, WC2R 0ET
Tube: Charing Cross T 0870-166 7372
SOHO THEATRE, Dean Street, W1D 3NE
Tube: Tottenham Court Road T 020-7287 5060
SHAFTESBURY THEATRE, Shaftesbury Avenue, WC2H 8DP
Tube: Holborn T 0870-906 3798
ST MARTIN'S THEATRE, West Street, WC2H 9NH
Tube: Leicester Square T 020-7836 1443
STRAND THEATRE, Strand, WC2B 5LD
Tube: Charing Cross T 0870-060 2335
VAUDEVILLE THEATRE, Strand, WC2R 0NH
Tube: Charing Cross T 0870-890 0511
THE VENUE (NOTRE DAME HALL), Leicester Place, WC2H
7BP Tube: Leicester Square T 0870-899 3335
VICTORIA PALACE THEATRE, Victoria Street, SW1E 5EA
Tube: Victoria T 020-7834 1317
WHITEHALL THEATRE, Whitehall, SW1X 2DY
Tube: Charing Cross T 0870-060 6632
WYNDHAM'S THEATRE, Charing Cross Road, WC2H 0DA
Tube: Leicester Square T 020-7369 1736
YOUNG VIC, The Cut, SE1 8LZ
Tube: Waterloo T 020-7928 6363

HALLMARKS

Hallmarks are the symbols stamped on gold, silver or platinum articles to indicate that they have been tested at an official Assay Office and that they conform to one of the legal standards. With certain exceptions, all gold, silver or platinum articles are required by law to be hallmarked before they are offered for sale. Hallmarking was instituted in England in 1300 under a statute of Edward I.

MODERN HALLMARKS

Since 1 January 1999, UK hallmarks have consisted of three compulsory symbols – the sponsor's mark, the fineness (purity) mark and the assay office mark. Traditional marks such as the year date letter, the Britannia for 958 silver, the lion passant for 925 silver (lion rampant in Scotland) and the orb for 950 platinum may be added voluntarily. The distinction between UK and foreign articles has been removed, and more finenesses are now legal, reflecting the more common finenesses elsewhere in Europe.

SPONSOR'S MARK
Instituted in England in 1363, the sponsor's mark was originally a device such as a bird or fleur-de-lis. Now it consists of the initial letters of the name or names of the manufacturer or firm. Where two or more sponsors have the same initials, there is a variation in the surrounding shield or style of letters.

FINENESS (PURITY) MARK
The fineness (purity) mark indicates that the content of the precious metal in the alloy from which the article is made, is not less than the legal standard. The legal standard is the minimum content of precious metal by weight in parts per thousand, and the standards are:

Gold	999	
	990	
	916.6	(22 carat)
	750	(18 carat)
	585	(14 carat)
	375	(9 carat)
Silver	999	
	958.4	(Britannia)
	925	(sterling)
	800	
Platinum	999	
	950	
	900	
	850	

ASSAY OFFICE MARK
This mark identifies the particular assay office at which the article was tested and marked. The British assay offices are:

LONDON, Goldsmiths' Hall, Gutter Lane, London EC2V 8AQ
T 020-7606 8971 W www.thegoldsmiths.co.uk

BIRMINGHAM, PO Box 151, Newhall Street, Birmingham
B3 1SB T 0121-236 6951 W www.theassayoffice.co.uk

SHEFFIELD, Guardian's Hall, 137 Portobello Street, Sheffield
S1 4DS T 0114-275 5111 W www.assayoffice.co.uk

EDINBURGH, Goldsmiths' Hall, 24a Broughton Street, Edinburgh EH1 3RH T 0131-556 1144
W www.assayofficescotland.com

Assay offices formerly existed in other towns, e.g. Chester, Exeter, Glasgow, Newcastle, Norwich and York, each having its own distinguishing mark.

DATE LETTER
The date letter shows the year in which an article was assayed and hallmarked. Each alphabetical cycle has a distinctive style of lettering or shape of shield. The date letters were different at the various assay offices and the particular office must be established from the assay office mark before reference is made to tables of date letters. Date letter marks became voluntary from 1 January 1999.

The table below shows specimen shields and letters used by the London Assay Office on silver articles in each period from 1498. The same letters are found on gold articles but the surrounding shield may differ. Since 1 January 1975, each office has used the same style of date letter and shield for all articles.

OTHER MARKS

FOREIGN GOODS
Foreign goods imported into the UK are required to be hallmarked before sale, unless they already bear a convention mark (*see* below) or a hallmark struck by an independent assay office in the European Economic Area which is deemed to be equivalent to a UK hallmark.

The following are the assay office marks used for gold until the end of 1998. For silver and platinum the symbols remain the same but the shields differ in shape.

 London

 Sheffield

 Birmingham

 Edinburgh

CONVENTION HALLMARKS

Special marks at authorised assay offices of the signatory countries of the International Convention on Hallmarking (Austria, the Czech Republic, Denmark, Finland, Ireland, the Netherlands, Norway, Portugal, Sweden, Switzerland and the UK) are legally recognised in the United Kingdom as approved hallmarks. These consist of a sponsor's mark, a common control mark, a fineness mark (arabic numerals showing the standard in parts per thousand), and an assay office mark. There is no date letter.

The common control marks are:

Gold (18 carat)

Silver

Platinum

COMMEMORATIVE MARKS

There are three other marks to commemorate special events: the silver jubilee of King George V and Queen Mary in 1935, the coronation of Queen Elizabeth II in 1953, and her silver jubilee in 1977. During 1999 and 2000 there was a voluntary additional Millennium Mark. A mark to commemorate the golden jubilee of Queen Elizabeth II was available during 2002.

LONDON (GOLDSMITHS' HALL) DATE LETTERS FROM 1498

Black letter, small	1498–9	1517–8
Lombardic	1518–9	1537–8
Roman and other capitals	1538–9	1557–8
Black letter, small	1558–9	1577–8
Roman letter, capitals	1578–9	1597–8
Lombardic. external cusps	1598–9	1617–8
Italic letter, small	1618–9	1637–8
Court hand	1638–9	1657–8
Black letter, capitals	1658–9	1677–8
Black letter, small	1678–9	1696–7
Court hand	1697	1715–6
Roman letter, capitals	1716–7	1735–6
Roman letter, small	1736–7	1738–9
Roman letter, small	1739–40	1755–6
Old English, capitals	1756–7	1775–6
Roman letter, small	1776–7	1795–6
Roman letter, capitals	1796–7	1815–6
Roman letter, small	1816–7	1835–6
Old English, capitals	1836–7	1855–6
Old English, small	1856–7	1875–6
Roman letter, capitals [A to M *square* shield N to Z as shown]	1876–7	1895–6
Roman letter, small	1896–7	1915–6
Black letter, small	1916–7	1935–6
Roman letter, small	1936–7	1955–6
Italic letter, small	1956–7	1974
Italic letter, capitals	1975	

EVENTS OF THE YEAR

BRITISH AFFAIRS

SEPTEMBER 2003

4. In Birmingham, the Bullring shopping centre was officially opened after 2½ years of construction and a total cost of £550 million, as part of the city's urban regeneration programme. The first phase of the Hutton Inquiry closed. **7.** A mock chemical attack was carried out at Bank underground station in London as a training exercise for the emergency services. **8.** Defence Secretary Geoff Hoon announced that 1,200 extra British troops would be sent to the south of Iraq. **9.** The Government published a White Paper on the future constitution of Europe which supported the appointment of a full-time chairman for the Council of Ministers and the use of Qualified Majority Voting (QMV) for EU business. **11.** Commander Richard Farrington and his officers were reprimanded after pleading guilty at a court martial in Portsmouth to a range of charges relating to £39 million of damage caused to *HMS Nottingham* when it ran aground on Wolf Rock, off the coast of Australia, in 2002. **14.** An investigation started on 30 June by the Office of Fair Trading (OFT) into alleged fee-fixing among four leading public schools was extended to include a further 700 independent schools. **15.** The Hutton Inquiry started a second round of witness-calling with Sir Richard Dearlove, the chief of MI6, and Greg Dyke, Director-General of the BBC, giving evidence. **16.** Six platforms at King's Cross station had to be closed during the morning rush hour after a train derailed at low speed in the station; no one was injured. **18.** *The Times* reported that the headmaster of Winchester College had admitted in a letter to parents that exchanging information on fees had been standard practice throughout the independent schools sector for many years, in a possible infringement of the 1998 Competition Act. Andrew Gilligan, the BBC reporter who interviewed Dr Kelly, was called to give further evidence to the Hutton Inquiry. **20.** Lord Williams of Mostyn, life peer, privy councillor and leader of the House of Lords died unexpectedly at his Gloucestershire home of a heart attack aged 62. **22.** The Liberal Democrat Party began its annual conference in Brighton. **23.** The Office of the Rail Regulator (ORR) approved a revised budget submitted by Network Rail to spend £24.5 billion over the next five years on the rail network. **25.** The Hutton Inquiry completed its main public proceedings. **30.** Tony Blair addressed the Labour Party Conference in Bournemouth, stating that there would be no reversal on the Party's schedule of reforms, including policies on foundation hospitals and tuition fees, and that he had no regrets over the conflict in Iraq.

OCTOBER 2003

1. A high court judge ruled that under European Law NHS patients on waiting lists could have surgery in European hospitals, refunded by the NHS, if they had faced an 'undue delay' receiving treatment in the UK. **2.** The Qualifications and Curriculum Authority announced major reforms for secondary education, including tailoring education to each individual's aptitude and ability and allowing pupils to study at their own speed, with courses such as GCSEs not having a pre-determined time span. **4.** Pope John Paul II held his first private audience with the Archbishop of Canterbury, Dr Rowan Williams, at the Vatican. The Strategic Rail Authority admitted that up to 500 new railway carriages, commissioned after legislation insisted on safer carriages, would have to be held in storage as there was not enough power to run them on the network. **5.** Allegations were made throughout the media that the Conservative leader Iain Duncan Smith improperly claimed allowances for 15 months for his wife, Betsy, after he became party leader. **10.** John Armitt, the Chief Executive of Network Rail, announced that it would take control of all three maintenance contracts surrendered by Jarvis, one of the main contractors used by Network Rail, effectively putting 40 per cent of the country's track back under public control. Lord Bach, Minister of Defence Procurement, admitted in a written parliamentary answer, that on 21 December 1990, three-and-a-half weeks before the 1991 Gulf War began, the MoD was told that tests on mice had produced serious side effects when anthrax and whooping cough vaccines were given together. Since the war thousands of soldiers had reported suffering from 'Gulf War Syndrome', believed to be caused by the vaccination programme. **15.** Parliamentary Standards Commissioner Sir Philip Mawer began a formal investigation into Iain Duncan Smith's employment of his wife as diary secretary. **19.** *The Times* reported a study by Datamonitor which found that 500 call centres in Britain had installed technology that filtered customers according to whether their postcodes represented 'poor' or 'wealthy' areas. The Prime Minister, Tony Blair, was admitted to Hammersmith Hospital in west London suffering from an irregular heartbeat, he was later discharged and returned home to rest. The second London underground derailment in 48 hours happened when a Northern Line train derailed at Camden station injuring seven passengers. **20.** NHS hospital consultants voted in favour of a new contract under which they would work a 40-hour week and receive a 20 per cent pay rise. **21.** The House of Lords again overturned the Government's attempt to ban fox hunting, with Peers voting 261 to 49 for a regulated system. Private correspondence of the late Diana, Princess of Wales, was published in *The Mirror*, the letters were obtained by the newspaper after it bought the serialisation rights to a book written by Paul Burrell, Diana's former butler. **22.** New guidelines were published by the National Institute for Clinical Excellence (NICE) on antenatal healthcare, aiming to standardise care across the country and offer earlier scans and Down's Syndrome screening to all pregnant women. **23.** The MP for Glasgow Kelvin, George Galloway, was expelled from the Labour Party after he was found guilty of four out of five charges of bringing the party into disrepute; including inciting British troops to disobey orders in Iraq. Dame Brenda Hale was appointed to Britain's highest court becoming the first female judge to be made a law lord, or *Lord of Appeal in Ordinary*. **24.** Concorde flew its last flight after being decommissioned by British Airways. Network Rail announced that it planned to take all remaining contracted-out track maintenance work back in-house by mid 2004. Prince William issued a statement asking Paul Burrell, the former butler to his late mother, to bring an end to the revelations regarding her private life. **29.** Iain Duncan Smith resigned as leader of the

Conservative Party after losing a vote of confidence by 90 votes to 75. **30**. Eighteen-year-old paratrooper, Christopher Finney, became the youngest serviceman to be awarded the George Cross for saving a comrade in a 'friendly-fire' incident in the war in Iraq. The MoD's annual report and accounts were published revealing losses of £1.7 billion; the Auditor-General, Sir John Bourne, stated that the losses were significant.

NOVEMBER 2003
1. Fifteen out of 73 postal areas in Britain were closed due to unofficial strike action by 30,000 members of the Communication Workers Union (CWU). **2**. Despite formal complaints and threats of schism within the Church, the consecration of the first openly gay bishop in the Anglican Communion took place in the US when Gene Robinson became Bishop of New Hampshire. **3**. At Durham Castle the Deputy Prime Minister, John Prescott, launched a Labour campaign to encourage electors to participate in three referendums to create three new regional assemblies for the North-East, the North-West and Yorkshire and Humberside. **5**. Michael Howard was elected leader of the Conservative Party. **6**. The House of Lords voted 150 to 100 against Labour plans to create Foundation Hospitals. **8**. The Countess of Wessex gave birth to a baby girl, Lady Louise Alice Windsor, eighth in line to the throne, at the NHS Frimley Park Hospital in Surrey. **18**. The US President, George W. Bush, arrived to begin his four-day state visit, the first state visit by a US President since Woodrow Wilson in 1918. **20**. Roger Short, the UK consul general in Turkey, was killed in a terrorist bomb blast at the UK consulate in Istanbul. **26**. The Government's 2003–4 legislative programme was delivered in the Queen's speech at the state opening of Parliament.

DECEMBER 2003
3. The Queen arrived in Nigeria to attend the Commonwealth summit, her first visit to the country since it became independent. **5**. The Independent Schools Council (ISC) issued a code of practice to all its 1,280 members banning the exchange of information on fees and costs between schools. **9**. Britain's first toll motorway, running for 27 miles around the edge of Birmingham, was officially opened to vehicles. **22**. Mark Henderson, a British tourist, was released alongside four Israelis, after being held hostage for 102 days in the Colombian jungle by Marxist guerrillas. The world's biggest passenger liner, the Queen Mary 2, set sail from its French shipyard after being handed over to its British owners, Cunard Line. **25**. Princess Alice, the Queen's aunt and oldest member of the British Royal family, celebrated her 102nd birthday. **26**. The Health Secretary John Reid announced that an additional £12 million was to be allocated to train medical staff working with the terminally ill. **28**. The Department for Transport made a joint announcement with the Home Office that armed, plain-clothes agents, or 'sky marshals', were to be deployed on British flights for the first time. **31**. British Airways flight 223 from Heathrow was escorted by fighter jets to a remote area of tarmac when it came to land at Dulles Airport in Washington following a security alert.

JANUARY 2004
1. New rules were introduced allowing the Driver and Vehicle Licensing Agency (DVLA) to automatically fine car owners who fail to renew their car tax within 6 weeks of date of expiry of their tax disc. British Airways flight 223 to Washington was cancelled as a security measure after British and US security forces received intelligence of a plot to hijack a BA airliner. **4**. On his way home from his Christmas break Tony Blair made a surprise visit to British forces stationed in Basra in southern Iraq; during his address he stated that it was expected that several thousand soldiers would remain in Iraq until at least 2006. **5**. A report published by the European Commission showed that more Britons were working longer than the weekly maximum of 48 hours than when the EU legislation was introduced 11 years ago. **6**. The Royal Coroner, Michael Burgess, opened two separate inquests into the deaths of Diana, Princess of Wales, and Dodi Fayed in a car crash on 31 August 1997 and asked the Metropolitan Police Commissioner Sir John Stevens to make enquiries into the incident. Two MPs, David Chidgey and Richard Ottaway, were cleared of contempt of Parliament after being accused of using prompts from a witness when questioning Dr Kelly at the Foreign Affairs Committee. Downing Street named Canon Stephen Cottrell as the Bishop of Reading after Canon Jeffrey John stood down in 2003 following objections within the church concerning his homosexuality. The National Executive Committee voted 22 to 2 in favour of re-admitting Ken Livingstone, Mayor of London, to the Labour Party so that he could become the party's official candidate for the Mayoral elections in June. **7**. US Officials announced that all British travellers to the USA with passports issued after 26 October 2004 would need a visa under new security measures imposed by the US Congress. **8**. It was announced in The Times that the Ministry of Defence had paid out its first compensation awards to the families of three men in Iraq who died after British troops allegedly tortured them whilst held in custody in Iraq. Pierre-Richard Prosper, the US Ambassador at Large for War Crimes, agreed that the nine British terrorist suspects held in Cuba could be repatriated, as long as they were 'managed' by British authorities. A new Higher Education Bill was published which would abolish the £1,125-a-year advance tuition fee by 2006 and allow universities to set their own fees of up to £3,000 a year. Students from the poorest 20 per cent of homes would be exempt from paying the first £1,200 of their fees and would also qualify for bursaries of at least £300 at universities charging the full £3,000. **12**. The Health Secretary John Reid announced that seven private companies had been awarded contracts to run 24 mobile specialist treatment centres in England; the centres would offer a limited range of treatments, including ophthalmology units offering cataract operations, and would travel to areas where waiting lists are longest. **22**. Steve Gough, also known as the 'naked rambler', completed his Land's End to John o' Groats solo nude hike; he was arrested 15 times and spent nearly five months in prison. The National Audit Office revealed that four defence projects, including the construction of three Astute submarines, the Eurofighter aircraft, Brimstone anti-armour missiles and 18 Nimrod MRAs, were running so late and over-budget that the total cost for the projects had risen by £2.7 billion. **23**. Charles Kennedy, leader of the Liberal Democrats, formally dismissed Dr Jenny Tonge from her position as party spokeswoman for international development, after she expressed sympathy to terrorists at a pro-Palestinian lobby on 21 January; she will stand down as MP for Richmond Park at the next election. The Health Secretary John Reid announced that patients infected with hepatitis C after receiving blood from the NHS would be eligible for compensation of

£20,000, with a further £25,000 available to patients with the more advanced stage of the disease. **27.** At a second reading, the Higher Education Bill was passed by the House of Commons by a majority of just five votes. **28.** Lord Hutton's report on the death of Dr David Kelly was published clearing Tony Blair and the Government of behaving duplicitously in revealing Dr Kelly's name to the media. The report strongly criticised BBC governance, stating that editorial control and complaints procedures were defective. It criticised the MoD for not informing Dr Kelly that he had been identified as the 'source' prior to publication and stated that BBC allegations that Downing Street had knowingly doctored an intelligence dossier were unfounded. The report concluded that Dr Kelly had killed himself after a 'severe loss of self esteem'. Gavyn Davies resigned as BBC chairman following the findings of the Hutton report. Snow fell throughout Britain with temperatures reaching −15°C in some parts of the country. **29.** Greg Dyke, the director-general of the BBC, resigned from his position following the results of the Hutton Inquiry. **30.** Andrew Gilligan, the journalist who originally made the claims on the BBC *Today* programme that the Government had 'sexed-up' a dossier on weapons of mass destruction resigned from the BBC, stating that the BBC had been served a grave injustice by the Hutton Inquiry.

FEBRUARY 2004

3. The Prime Minister, Tony Blair, set up an inquiry, to be led by Lord Butler of Brockwell, into the reliability of pre-war intelligence on Iraq's weapons of mass destruction. **6.** Nineteen Chinese migrant workers drowned while picking cockles at night in Morecambe Bay, 16 workers were rescued but it was not known how many were still missing. The RMT transport union voted 42 to 8 in favour of allowing union branches to affiliate to other parties if they felt they better represented their interests; five branches had already affiliated to the Scottish Socialist Party and two more had requested to do so. **7.** Labour took the unprecedented step of expelling the RMT transport union from the party following the union's decision to allow branches to affiliate to other political parties. **9.** The government announced plans for the formation of a new FBI-style police force combining the functions of the National Crime Squad (NCS), the National Criminal Intelligence Service (NCIS), the investigative arm of Customs and Excise and the Home Office's Immigration Service into one body: the Serious Organised Crime Agency. The Queen approved reforms put forward by Lord Falconer, the Lord Chancellor, to appoint a moderator and an additional body made up of three privy councillors to oversee Westminster Abbey and the five other *Royal Peculiars*, distancing the monarch from the role as sole authority. **10.** The Prime Minister, Tony Blair, met the Libyan Foreign Minister, Abdul Rahman Mohammad Shalgam, at Downing Street. **12.** The Health Minister, Rosie Winterton, announced that the cost of a NHS prescription would rise by 10p to £6.40 in England from 1 April 2004. **17.** All SAS One-Step pregnancy testing kits used by the NHS were recalled by the Medicines Healthcare Products Regulatory Agency (MHRA) after the Co. Durham and Darlington NHS Trust discovered abnormally high false negative readings during a routine quality control check. Estimates suggested that between 15,000 and 20,000 women could have been affected. **18.** The Chancellor Gordon Brown unveiled a national voluntary work scheme for young people which would allow school leavers to take a gap

year to help their local communities; participants would receive help with basic living expenses and a possible contribution towards university or college fees. **19.** The Foreign Secretary Jack Straw announced that five British men held for more than two years without trial at Guantanamo Bay camp in Cuba would be flown back to the UK. **23.** The Home Secretary David Blunkett announced that citizens of countries joining the EU on 1 May 2004 would be free to work in Britain, provided they registered their employment, but would not be eligible for benefits, apart from tax credits and housing benefit, until they had worked for at least a year. **25.** The Home Secretary David Blunkett announced that MI5's budget would rise by 50 per cent to £300 million to support a recruitment drive to expand staff numbers to around three thousand. **26.** The former International Development Secretary, Clare Short, alleged on the Radio 4 *Today* programme that Britain had spied on Kofi Annan, the Secretary-General of the UN prior to the war in Iraq. **27.** Snow and extreme temperatures spread across the country forcing more than 1,000 schools to close.

MARCH 2004

9. Five Britons arrived in Britain after being released from Camp X-Ray in Guantanamo Bay. The five men were taken to Paddington Green high-security police station and one man was released immediately after questioning. **10.** The remaining four detainees who arrived back in Britain from Guantanamo Bay were released without charge. **17.** In the 2004 Budget the Chancellor Gordon Brown announced detailed proposals based on Sir Michael Lyons' report of 15 March to cut 54,000 posts by 2008 from the Department for Work and Pensions, Inland Revenue and Customs and Excise in a move to reduce administration costs. During an adventure-training exercise in Mexico partly funded by the Armed Forces, 13 British cavers, including nine military personnel, became trapped 120ft underground by unseasonable floodwater. **25.** The Prime Minister, Tony Blair, met with Libyan leader Colonel Gaddafi in Libya after a 20-year deadlock in diplomatic relations between the two countries. In a six-hour operation, a team of British cavers were rescued, after being trapped underground by floodwater for eight days in Mexico. **26.** The Prime Minister, Tony Blair, called for the new constitution for Europe to be agreed within three months and, if possible, prior to the European elections on 10 June. **28.** It was announced that Network Rail, the not-for-profit company that owns and manages the UK's railways, had submitted a proposal to the Transport Secretary Alistair Darling requesting direct operational control of the train operating companies (TOCs). **29.** Iain Duncan Smith, the former Conservative leader, was cleared of deliberately misusing parliamentary funds to employ his wife as diary secretary in a report published by the Parliamentary Commissioner for Standards Sir Philip Mawer. **30.** The Home Secretary, David Blunkett, suspended all immigration applications from Romania and Bulgaria and promised an inquiry, following allegations that immigration officials were allowing bogus claims to be processed from these areas. **31.** The Higher Education Bill passed through to the House of Lords by a majority of 28 after a Labour back bench amendment to strike out the principle of varying fees was defeated by 316 votes to 288 in the House of Commons. The Civil Partnerships Bill was published to enable homosexual couples to register their partnerships in a civil ceremony and receive legal rights similar to those of a married couple. The first ten hospitals; Basildon and Thurrock; Bradford Teaching Hospital; Countess of Chester; Doncaster and Bassetlaw; Homerton University; Moorfields Eye Hospital; Peterborough & Stamford; Stockport; Royal Devon and Exeter and Royal Marsden assumed their status as Foundation Hospitals.

APRIL 2004
1. The Immigration Minister Beverley Hughes resigned after admitting that she had been warned over a year previously by Labour Deputy Chief Whip Bob Ainsworth that the Home Office was approving visa claims from eastern Europe backed by forged documents. The Prime Minister replaced Ms Hughes with Work and Pensions Minister Des Browne. 5. Thames Trains was fined a record £2 million for its part in the 1999 Paddington rail disaster in which 31 people died. The judge ruled that the company had failed to limit the risk to passengers by not correcting faults with its driver-training programme. 17. Research by the Audit Commission found there were at least 3.5 million excess names on GP lists in England alone, as practices receive NHS funds based on the number of patients registered, doctors were warned that they would face prosecution if they had deliberately failed to strike-off names. 19. Tony Blair announced in the House of Commons that the British people would be given the chance to vote on whether to adopt a European constitution. 22. On security advice from MI5, MPs voted in favour of spending £1.3 million on a permanent glass security barrier to be erected in the House of Commons between the public gallery and the rest of the chamber. 23. Universities such as Durham, Nottingham, Warwick, Edinburgh, London and Bristol warned that thousands of candidates would face rejection due to unprecedented pressure on places due to an increase in the number of students achieving high grades. 25. The car of French National Front leader, Jean-Marie Le Pen was pelted with eggs and rubbish by protesters after he left the launch of the British National Party's European election campaign at a hotel in Altrincham. 26. A letter signed by 52 signatories including former ambassadors, high commissioners and governors was sent to the Prime Minister, Tony Blair, expressing concern regarding foreign policy on the Middle East and Iraq. 27. Market analysts Mintel published figures showing that a quarter of seven to ten-year olds own mobile phones. The rail maintenance company Jarvis admitted joint liability with Network Rail for the Potters Bar rail crash, enabling compensation claims to proceed. 28. New NHS guidelines developed in consultation with the National Institute for Clinical Excellence and the Collaborating Centre for Women's and Children's Health recommended that NHS doctors should not automatically arrange caesareans on request without legitimate medical reasons.

MAY 2004
2. Senior investigators from the Royal Military Police flew to Cyprus to interview soldiers from the Queen's Lancashire Regiment following claims that members of the regiment had been involved in mistreating Iraqi prisoners. 6. The Government announced that John Scarlett, an MI6 intelligence officer and former head of the Joint Intelligence Committee, was to be the next chief of MI6 on the retirement of Sir Richard Dearlove in July 2004. Dr Jeffrey John was installed as the Dean of St Albans following his withdrawal from the post of Bishop of Reading in 2003 after protests concerning his homosexuality. 9. Prime Minister, Tony Blair, apologised for the abuse of Iraqi prisoners in British custody and stated that those responsible would be punished according to Army disciplinary rules. 11. Eight people were killed and more than 40 injured in Glasgow when a plastics factory collapsed following a huge explosion on the ground floor. A report leaked from the International Red Cross stated that officials within the US and UK armed forces had ignored its repeated and detailed complaints, regarding the abuse of prisoners held in custody in Iraq, throughout a period of many months. Figures published by Christian Research compiled on rural ministries showed that attendance at Anglican churches in the countryside had decreased by more than a third in the last ten years. 19. Prime Minister Tony Blair was hit by a missile made of purple flour during Question Time in the House of Commons; the missile was thrown by two protesters in the public gallery who were there at the invitation of Lady Golding. A review of Commons security already underway by MI5 and Scotland Yard was accelerated following the incident. 24. Britain and the USA tabled a draft United Nations Security Council resolution outlining their plans for the transfer of responsibility for all aspects of statehood in Iraq, excluding security, to an interim Iraqi government on 30 June. 29. Some 20,000 people living in caravans on local authority sites won the same tenancy rights as council house tenants after a European court in Strasbourg ruled that summary evictions, without justification or the right to appeal, were against their human rights.

JUNE 2004
3. More than a thousand flights were delayed or cancelled when the computer system at West Drayton air traffic control centre failed. 6. A BBC cameraman was killed and the BBC's security correspondent, Frank Gardner, was seriously injured in an attack blamed on islamist extremists in the Saudi Arabian capital, Riyadh. 10. European parliamentary, local and London mayoral elections took place. In the London mayoral elections, Labour candidate Ken Livingstone, was re-elected for a second term, having completed his first term as an independent candidate. 11. With three-quarters of the results declared in the local authority elections Labour had lost more than 400 seats with the Conservatives and the Liberal Democrats gaining more than 200 and 100 seats respectively. Turnout for the local elections was at 40 per cent, an increase from 31 per cent in 2003. 12. The Queen's 2004 Birthday Honours List was published. Among those recognised were newsreader and presenter, Angela Rippon, who was awarded an OBE alongside bestselling author Jilly Cooper, poets Pam Ayres and Roger McGough and weather forecaster Michael Fish were awarded MBEs. 15. Lord Goldsmith, the Attorney General, announced that four soldiers from the Royal Regiment of Fusiliers were to face a court martial on charges of abusing and sexually assaulting Iraqi civilians. 17. The Fire Brigades Union (FBU) voluntarily disaffiliated from the Labour Party following a vote in which 250 delegates voted 35,105 to 14,611 in favour of leaving the Party. 23. The Higher Education Minister, Alan Johnson, told the House of Commons that the Higher Education Bill, passed in January by five votes, would be amended to protect students opting for a gap year in 2005. Students completing their A-levels in 2005 who decided to take a gap year would pay the existing £1,125-a-year fee, capped for the duration of their studies. 24. The Government announced, as part of its

draft manifesto for the health service, that it would cut hospital waiting times (the time from GP referral to receiving hospital treatment) from 13 months to 18 weeks by 2008. The results of the first national education assessments for five-year-olds were published; the assessments known as Foundation Stage profile became compulsory in state schools in 2003. The tests had been widely criticised by teaching unions as well as the Chief Inspector of Schools, David Bell, as unreliable, unhelpful and time-consuming for teachers; initial results showed that more girls than boys were reaching or working beyond early learning goals. 29. The RMT union began a 24-hour London Underground strike over pay; the union wanted a 35-hour, 4-day week and a minimum of £22,000 pa for all station staff. 30. The London Underground strike continued; five tube lines were operating but with severe delays, many major roads were gridlocked.

JULY 2004

6. Prime Minister Tony Blair conceded for the first time, during a biannual appearance before the Commons Liaison Committee, that weapons of mass destruction might never be found in Iraq. 7. The Times reported that doctors were treating record numbers of teenagers and young adults for mumps; the Health Protection Agency recorded 578 cases in the first three months of 2004, a 75 per cent increase over the first quarter in 2003. The UK was hit by severe storms with winds of up to 60mph recorded in some exposed places, an inch of rain fell across the Solent and 25ft-high waves were recorded in the English Channel forcing freighters to take shelter in emergency anchorages and ferries to be cancelled. 8. Ian Gibson, Chairman of the Commons Science and Technology Committee, proposed that a joint committee of peers and MPs should be formed to re-consider the 1967 Abortion Act and the 1990 amendment, under which a foetus can be legally aborted for social reasons up to 24-weeks gestation. The Government's five-year plan for Education was published; the main reforms included the expansion of popular schools to increase admissions, financial independence for all schools from local authorities, the closure of failing schools and the introduction of more personalised learning for all children, such as the opportunity to learn a musical instrument or a foreign language at primary school level. 9. The Department of Health announced that pilot 'fee-for-service' schemes would be introduced in 32 trusts in England in which doctors and other NHS staff will receive bonus payments for carrying out extra operations and treatments. 14. Lord Butler of Brockwell's report into the reliability and quality of intelligence used to support the case for war with Iraq was published. Lord Butler surmised that the intelligence reports used to support the conflict were 'seriously flawed' although he cleared the Prime Minister Tony Blair of deliberately attempting to mislead the public and Parliament about the intelligence, finding no evidence to question Mr Blair's faith in the information he was given. Lord Butler reported that the Joint Intelligence Committee's warnings on the limitations of the intelligence were not made sufficiently clear in the dossier and that language used in the dossier and by the Prime Minister may have left readers with the impression that there was firmer intelligence than was the case. 15. A new White Paper for the Rail Industry outlined proposals to abolish the Strategic Rail Authority and transfer its responsibilities to the Department for Transport. 16. Health Secretary John Reid unveiled a plan to rescue NHS dentistry, promising to spend an extra £368 million on the

service and recruit 1,000 extra dentists by October 2005. 19. The Home Secretary David Blunkett announced plans for a five-year anti-crime drive, initiatives included on-the-spot fines for anti-social behaviour, the use of satellite tracking technology to keep track of offenders with an increase in the use of electronic tagging. Plans also included new border controls that would help to track criminals and terrorists, such as the introduction of photographic records for every traveller entering or leaving the UK. 20. Transport Secretary Alistair Darling announced that the long-awaited £10 billion Crossrail scheme linking east and west London would go ahead. 22. Culture Secretary Tessa Jowell, said in a statement to Parliament that the date for switching off analog television could be postponed until 2012; ministers had maintained that a 2010 deadline was possible but broadcasters said that not enough people would have access to digital television by then. 29. Metropolitan Police, in partnership with Westminster Council, banned unaccompanied children under 16 from the West End of London after 9 p.m. 30. The Home Office announced measures to increases police powers when dealing with animal rights extremists who orchestrate attacks on those working in the biotechnology and pharmaceutical industries.

AUGUST 2004

3. Severe flooding in London shut parts of the Underground and major road routes out of the capital. 12. A human skeleton from the Iron Age was discovered almost intact on the island of Orkney; the body appeared to have been ritualistically buried with a set of antlers resting on its chest and a toe ring on each foot. 13. The General Secretary of the train drivers' union ASLEF was dismissed for gross misconduct for allegedly failing to co-operate with an independent inquiry into the union's affairs. 15. The Information Commissioner Richard Thomas voiced concerns over Government plans to introduce an identity card scheme and proposals by the Office for National Statistics for a population register, warning that civil liberties could be infringed. 16. Torrential rain in Cornwall caused the River Valency to burst its banks resulting in a 10ft wall of water flooding the village of Boscastle. In total 108 people were rescued by the emergency services; there were no fatalities. 19. A-level results showed that students gained a record 171,639 A-grades in the 2004 exams, representing 22.4 per cent of the total entry of 766,247. The overall pass rate increased for the 22nd consecutive year to 96 per cent. Scotland was hit by 24-hours of torrential rain, causing widespread flooding and mudslides. 22. Paul Miller, chairman of the British Medical Consultants' Committee, warned that there could be a mass exodus of experienced consultants from the NHS due to the introduction of a new pension scheme. 25. The 2004 GCSE exam results were published. The overall pass rate remained unchanged from 2003 with 97.6 per cent awarded A* to G grades with the proportion of entries awarded A* or A rising from 16.7 to 17.4 per cent.

NORTHERN IRELAND AFFAIRS

SEPTEMBER 2003

2. Sean Hoey, an alleged Real IRA bomb-maker, was arrested in Jonesborough, south Armagh, in connection with the 1998 Omagh bombing, and another man was arrested on suspicion of designing the 500lb car bomb. 4.

Northern Ireland Secretary Paul Murphy announced the formation of the International Monitoring Commission, set up to monitor paramilitary cease-fires in Northern Ireland and to try and restore the Northern Ireland Assembly. 5. Sean Hoey was charged with conspiracy to cause an explosion, possessing explosive substances with intent to endanger life, and membership of the Real IRA and was due to appear in court on 6 September. 8. It was announced that paramilitaries being held in Northern Ireland's Maghaberry prison would be segregated to avoid attacks on prison officers and fights between republican and loyalist prisoners. 9. Shadow Defence Minister Gerald Howarth called for a halt to the five-year Bloody Sunday inquiry due to it having cost £113 million. It was not due to reach a conclusion for 12 months. 10. Paddy Ward, a former member of the IRA's youth wing, told the Saville inquiry that Martin McGuinness had arranged the supply of 16 detonators for nail bombs which the IRA had planned to use on Bloody Sunday. 18. Four men and a woman were arrested in Strabane, Co Tyrone, after several Roman Catholic members of Northern Ireland's community policing boards received death threats; two members had their cars set alight and one member was sent a hoax bomb. 25. General Sir Mike Jackson, the Chief of the General Staff, was recalled for further questioning by the Bloody Sunday inquiry to answer questions after it emerged that he was in possession of documents containing interviews with some of the soldiers who had fired shots on Bloody Sunday. 29. Our Lady of Mercy Roman Catholic girls' secondary school in North Belfast was attacked by Protestants who set six cars on fire.

OCTOBER 2003
1. A former paratrooper, known as 'Soldier F' during the Saville Inquiry, who had been shown by forensic scientific evidence to have shot dead Michael Kelly on Bloody Sunday, told the Inquiry that he had complete memory loss about his actions on the day in 1972. He had previously admitted that he had shot three men during the demonstration in Londonderry. 2. Northern Ireland Secretary Paul Murphy announced that a new law would be introduced by ministerial order to enable people to be more effectively prosecuted for committing 'hate crime', and would include a clause aimed specifically at dealing with anti-gay bigotry. 'Soldier F' admitted at the Saville Inquiry that he had shot dead Bernard McGuigan as he attempted to go to the aid of a dying man during the civil rights march on 30 January 1972. 7. Martin McGuinness issued a statement to the Saville Inquiry denying that he had planned an IRA nail bomb attack hours before 13 people were shot dead on Bloody Sunday. 12. Residents in Roslea, Co Fermanagh, were evacuated while army bomb experts carried out a controlled explosion on a crude car bomb containing 59kg of explosives, which had been left outside a police station. 17. Five former members of the Provisional IRA submitted statements to the Saville inquiry in which they said that Martin McGuinness had not distributed nail bombs during the Londonderry peace march. 21 The Bloody Sunday inquiry moved from London to Londonderry after the total bill for its time in London came to £120 million. 24. The IRA issued an apology to the families of the 'disappeared' men and women who were abducted and killed by the IRA in the 1970s and 80s, and said that they had begun an inquiry to locate the remains of those still missing.

NOVEMBER 2003
4. Seven suspected members of the Real IRA were arrested in a joint operation by Irish and French police in Dublin and Brittany after automatic weapons and ammunition were found in a forest near Dieppe. 5. Martin McGuinness was threatened with legal action for refusing to co-operate with the Saville inquiry after he refused to reveal the names of IRA colleagues. 12. A former member of the IRA, known as OIRA1, told the Saville Inquiry that he had shot at a soldier on Bloody Sunday and claimed that the soldier had previously wounded two civilians. 28. The Revd Ian Paisley's Democratic Unionist Party won 30 seats in the elections to the National Assembly, the Ulster Unionist Party won 27 seats and Sinn Fein won 24 seats. The Democratic Unionist Party had previously promised to abolish the Good Friday agreement if it won the election.

DECEMBER 2003
1. The Revd Ian Paisley met the Northern Ireland Secretary Paul Murphy and told him that his party would not deal with republicans. 12. Mitchell B. Reiss, a US government official, was selected as the special envoy to Northern Ireland in order to focus on issues of IRA decommissioning. 16. Prime Minister Tony Blair held talks with the leader of the Democratic Unionist Party, Revd Ian Paisley, to attempt to break the political deadlock in Northern Ireland; Revd Paisley said there was 'no way' his party would share power with Sinn Fein. 17. Charges against Fiona Farrelly, who had been accused of being part of an IRA spy ring that led to the collapse of the power-sharing Executive at Stormont, were dropped without explanation. 18. Jeffrey Donaldson resigned from David Trimble's Ulster Unionist Party, saying that the party had 'abandoned its principles'.

JANUARY 2004
4. A 16-year-old boy was shot in both legs by three men who broke into a house in east Belfast and another 17-year-old youth was shot in both ankles by a man who broke into his home in west Belfast. 9. Police in Northern Ireland published figures which showed that racist crimes in the predominantly loyalist areas of Belfast had soared from 25 in 1998 to 223 a year. 19. The Police Ombudsman Nuala O'Loan announced that an investigation into the murder of Roman Catholic Sean Brown in 1997 had found that there had been 'significant failures' by the Royal Ulster Constabulary at the time. 25. Around 100 former members of the Parachute Regiment were issued with handguns in Northern Ireland after police obtained information about the Provisional IRA gathering intelligence from the Bloody Sunday inquiry and other sources in order to kill those that gave evidence at the inquiry. 26. Education Minister Jane Kennedy announced that all 71 grammar schools in Northern Ireland would be abolished and that the last 11-plus examinations would be held in 2008. 27. It was announced that the Bloody Sunday Inquiry only had until 13 February 2004 to hear the evidence of around 900 witnesses, and that lawyers had a deadline of 12 March to hand in their written submissions. 29. The Irish Prime Minister Bertie Ahern met Revd Ian Paisley, the leader of the Democratic Unionist Party, for talks at the Irish Embassy in London, a week before the opening of a review designed to revive the Good Friday agreement.

FEBRUARY 2004

4. Jaybe Ofrasio was arrested in Belfast on charges of making money and property available to terrorists in the Far East; he is believed to have links to the Bali nightclub bombing in October 2002. **17.** The funeral of 18-year-old Barney Cairns took place in the Ardoyne area of Belfast after he committed suicide as a result of being shot in the legs in 2002 for 'squaring up' to the Irish National Liberation Army; his friend Anthony O'Neill had committed suicide a week earlier after also being a victim of a 'punishment attack'. **22.** Alasdair McDonnell, a GP from south Belfast, was elected the new deputy leader of the nationalist SDLP party, replacing Brid Rodgers. **27.** The Police Service of Northern Ireland announced that punishment attacks had risen to a record high with 51 beatings and shootings carried out in 2004 by republican and loyalist groups who claim to be helping their communities to combat antisocial behaviour.

MARCH 2004

2. Seamus Daly, one of the leading suspects in the 1998 Omagh bombing, was jailed for three-and-a-half years at the Special Criminal Court in Dublin for being a member of the Real IRA. The Ulster Unionist leader, David Trimble, walked out on talks in Belfast aimed at restoring devolved government to Northern Ireland, in protest at the British government's failure to exclude Sinn Fein from the talks following the alleged abduction of dissident republican Bobby Tohill. **11.** The British government secured the right to prevent new investigations into alleged 'shoot to kill' deaths by security forces in Northern Ireland, after five Law Lords ruled that investigations into killings that occurred before the Human Rights Act 2002 came into force did not fall under the Act. **22.** A 46-year-old man was arrested in England and taken to Belfast in connection with the murder of 10-year-old Brian McDermott whose torso was found in the River Lagan in 1973. **27.** Ulster Unionist leader David Trimble urged his opponents to unite behind him after he secured a majority 448 votes during a leadership contest at a party meeting in Belfast.

APRIL 2004

8. Arthur Templeton, a member of the Democratic Unionists, was suspended by the Party after being found guilty at Belfast Magistrates' Court of harassing a gay colleague. **13.** A man was being questioned by police in connection with the murder of 16-year-old Megan McAlorum, whose body was found in woodland close to a quarry in west Belfast. **17.** Five prison officers, including one woman, were suspended after it was alleged that they had 'improper relations' with inmates at Maghaberry Prison in Co Antrim. **20.** The Independent Monitoring Commission in Northern Ireland issued a report condemning the Sinn Fein leaders, Gerry Adams and Martin McGuinness, for failing to use their influence to end violence by the IRA, which the commission claimed was still linked to the political party.

MAY 2004

12. Chief Constable Hugh Orde told the Northern Ireland Policing Board that loyalist and republican paramilitaries had carried out 1,700 punishment attacks in Northern Ireland since 1998. **26.** At Belfast Crown Court, Mr Justice Girvan ruled that the Real IRA could not be described as a proscribed group because the British Government had failed to list the organisation in the Terrorism Act 2000.

JUNE 2004

3. Kevin McAlorum, a former member of the Irish National Liberation Army, was shot dead outside Oakwood integrated primary school in Derriaghy, Belfast. **17.** Lt.-Gen. Sir Philip Trousdell, the General Officer Commanding Northern Ireland, announced that 1,200 members of the Devon and Dorset Regiment and the Queen's Dragoon Guards would leave Northern Ireland and revert to mainland command. **25.** Tony Blair announced that the IRA had until September 2004 to end its paramilitary activities and decommission its weapons, otherwise plans to reinstate the Northern Ireland Assembly could be abandoned. **29.** Donald Mullan, Brendan O'Connor, Sean Dillon and Kevin Murphy were cleared of plotting to murder police and troops in Northern Ireland at Belfast Crown Court after they were found with a rocket launcher outside Dungannon in 2002. **30.** The High Court in Belfast overturned the ruling by Justice Paul Girvan that the Real IRA is not an illegal terrorist organisation.

JULY 2004

12. Paratroopers came under attack after loyalists on the Orange Parade march were forbidden from returning along a route through the contentious Ardoyne area; it was reported that both republicans and loyalists were involved in the rioting. **22.** Mohammad Hossain, his wife and their five-year-old daughter escaped serious injury when their house in the Lisburn Road area, was petrol bombed. **27.** Workers at Belfast City Council went on strike in support of an ongoing civil service dispute over pay. **31.** Eight suspicious packages were discovered by Royal Mail staff at Mallusk. The packages were addressed to members of the Police Ombudsman and police board.

AUGUST 2004

1. The police ombudsman Nuala O'Loan announced that a report into a police raid on the Stormont offices of Sinn Fein in October 2002 found that it was not politically motivated, but a complaint from Sinn Fein that the scale of the search was excessive and disproportionate was upheld. **15.** Rita Restorick made a complaint to the Defence Secretary Geoff Hoon after the Northern Ireland police ombudsman Nuala O'Loan accused the Ministry of Defence of 'frustrating' her inquiry into the death of Mrs Restorick's son Stephen, who was shot dead in Ulster in 1997 whilst serving as a lance-bombardier in the Royal Horse Artillery. **29.** A memorial to 18 soldiers killed by the IRA 25 years ago at Narrow Water, Co Down, was vandalised two days after being unveiled.

ARTS AND THE MEDIA

SEPTEMBER 2003

2. ITN reported that Neil Armstrong's first steps on the moon was the most popular and frequently requested piece of news footage. **4.** The winners of the James Tait Black Memorial Prize were announced as Jonathan Franzen for his novel *The Corrections* in the fiction category, and *The Lunar Men: The Friends Who Made the Future* by Jenny Uglow, in the biography category. Anne Jones from Leicestershire won the title of the world's fastest reader after she read a 300-page novel in 47 minutes. **5.** Simon Beaufoy's budget film *This Is Not A Love Song* became the first to be officially premiered on the internet after it was released online. **7.** The director Andrey Zvyagintsev won the Venice Film Festival's

Golden Lion award for his film *The Return*. **8**. Religious groups objected to Damien Hirst's new exhibition *Romance in the Age of Uncertainty*, which contains reinterpretations of biblical themes using cows' heads and bloodied medical instruments. **9**. The 19-year-old rap artist Dizzee Rascal won the £20,000 Mercury Music Prize for his debut record *Boy In Da Corner*. **10**. The travel writer Bill Bryson was appointed a commissioner of English Heritage. It was reported that the opera *Carmen* would be performed outside the bullring and cigarette factory in Seville where the story of the opera unfolds. **16**. The Man Booker Prize shortlist was announced with the highest number of women novelists and the most debut novels in its history, only one well-known author, Margaret Atwood, was shortlisted. **17**. A pair of paintings by Robert Dodd, believed to be some of the earliest depictions of Lord Nelson's victory at Trafalgar, sold for a record sum of £270,650 at Bonhams. **18**. Dame Shirley Bassey was at Christie's in London for the sale of 50 of her gowns, which she had worn throughout her career; the sale raised £250,000 for charity and the highest price paid for one dress was £35,000. **21**. Hayley Westenra's classical album *Pure* set the record for being the fastest-selling debut album in the history of the British classical charts when it went straight to number one. **22**. Alexander McCall Smith, 55, won the £20,000 Saga Award for Wit, which rewards the most amusing book by an author over 50, for his detective thriller *The Full Cupboard of Life*. **24**. A signed copy of the Beatles *Revolver* album sold for £21,600 at Sotheby's in London. Six thousand stuffed animals were sold at Bonhams for £529,000; they had previously made up the Walter Potter Museum of Curiosities. **25**. It was reported that Damien Hirst had made £11 million within 15 days of the opening of his *Romance in the Age of Uncertainty* exhibition through sales of works on-show. Alexander McQueen was named the British Style Awards Designer of the Year. *The English Roses*, the debut children's novel by the singer Madonna, became the fastest-selling hardback children's picture book in British history after it sold more than 8,500 copies in its first week of release. **29**. The Royal Navy paid the Saatchi and Saatchi advertising agency £100,000 to 'refresh' their logo. **30**. A man found a small Roman vessel believed to date from the 2nd century AD in the Staffordshire Moorlands – it was valued at £100,000.

OCTOBER 2003

1. During a pop memorabilia sale at Christie's in London, a sculpture by John Lennon sold for £28,200, and a note from Lennon to his publicist Tony Bramwell telling him to keep quiet about the recording of *The Ballad of John and Yoko* until its release, sold for £19,975. A survey revealed that 71 per cent of Britons were not able to name Monet as the creator of the painting *Water Lilies*, 49 per cent could not name the painter of the *Mona Lisa*, and 85 per cent of respondents were unable to identify Edvard Munch as the artist who painted *The Scream*. **2**. The South African writer J. M. Coetzee was named the winner of the 2003 Nobel Prize for Literature, worth £900,000. The rock band *Radiohead* was voted the Best Act in the World by readers of Q music magazine. **7**. Students from Camberwell College of Art in London earned a place in *The Guinness Book of Records* after they assembled a 13ft statue of King Kong using 480,000 pieces of popcorn, in honour of the film's 70th anniversary. **8**. Ciaran Carson won the £10,000 Forward Poetry Prize for his work *Breaking*

News. **9**. The actor Roger Moore was knighted by the Queen for his charity work. **10**. Ms Lesley Douglas was named as the new controller of BBC Radio 2, and was due to take over the £220,000 position in January 2004. One of the first coins minted in colonial America in the 17th century was found in the home of a deceased collector and was expected to fetch up to £25,000 at auction. **12**. The Zehetmair Quartet won the Record of the Year prize at the *Gramophone* Awards for its recording of String Quartets Number 1 and Number 3 by Schumann. **13**. The rap singer Ms Dynamite won the Capital Big Voice award at the Women of the Year Awards for speaking out against gun crime in urban areas. **14**. The £50,000 Man Booker Prize was awarded to DBC Pierre for his debut novel *Vernon God Little*. Philip Larkin's *The Whitsun Weddings* was voted Britain's favourite poem by over 800 visitors to poetry festivals; the top ten also included poems by Carol Ann Duffy, Seamus Heaney and Sylvia Plath. **15**. The Prince of Wales attended the Fashion Rocks event at the Albert Hall, which involved performances by key figures in the fashion and music industries in order to raise funds for the Prince's Trust charity. Gerhard Schulz was named Wildlife Photographer of the Year for his picture of a young boy watching a gorilla watching a photographer at Miami Metrozoo in Florida. **16**. The Channel 4 comedy sitcom *Peter Kay's Phoenix Nights* became the fastest-selling television DVD in Britain when it sold 160,000 copies in one week. **20**. Dame Diana Rigg won £38,000 for libel and breach of privacy after the *Daily Mail* and *Evening Standard* newspapers published articles claiming she had retired and was an 'embittered woman'. The *Saved!* exhibition containing 400 works of art by artists such as Picasso and Michelangelo, which were kept in Britain through the efforts of the National Art Collections Fund, opened at the Hayward Gallery in London. **22**. The London Film Festival opened with the British premiere of *In the Cut*, an erotic thriller starring Meg Ryan. Five police officers resigned after Mark Daly, an undercover reporter for the BBC, secretly filmed the officers making racist remarks and praising the Ku Klux Klan and Hitler as well as admitting to treating ethnic minorities differently whilst performing police duties. **27**. Elvis Presley was named as the highest earning dead celebrity in the Forbes rich list after the singer's estate made £24 million in the last year. **28**. Tony Blair presented Sir Trevor McDonald with a Special Recognition Award at the National Television Awards in honour of his 30 years in broadcasting. **29**. One of the largest dolls houses in Britain, Victorian Dingley Hall, was sold for £124,750 at Christie's to a toy museum near Hamburg.

NOVEMBER 2003

1. The creator of the Harry Potter novels, J. K. Rowling, became the highest-paid author in history after it was revealed that she earned £125 million in the past year, equivalent to receiving £388 for every word of her latest book *Harry Potter and the Order of the Phoenix*. **3**. The Independent Television Commission rejected complaints about a homosexual kiss that appeared in the soap *Coronation Street* and ruled that it had been suitable for family viewing. **4**. Stephen Frears's film *Dirty Pretty Things*, about asylum-seekers in London, won the Best British Film, Best Director and Best Actor awards at the British Independent Film Awards. **5**. A Victoria Cross, which had been awarded to Commander Daniel Beak for several acts of heroism on the Western Front during the First World War, sold at auction in London for a world record £178,250. Modigliani's *Reclining Nude (On Her Left Side)* was sold by the billionaire Steve Wynn for a record £16 million in New York. **9**. The Walt Disney Company paid £2.1 million for the rights to the unpublished novel *A Stolen Smile* by Jimmy Boyle, a former gangster from Glasgow who was jailed in 1967 for the murder of a rival. **12**. A plaque carrying William Wordsworth's poem *Composed Upon Westminster Bridge* was unveiled on London's Westminster Bridge, near the Houses of Parliament. **13**. Two cargo handlers at New York's John F. Kennedy airport were arrested for stealing *Painter's Garden* by Lucian Freud, worth £890,000. **14**. A Damien Hirst work entitled *Something Solid Beneath the Surface of All Creatures Great and Small*, consisting of animal skeletons, was sold to an anonymous bidder for a record price of £700,000 at a contemporary art auction in New York. **17**. *The Engagement between the Spanish Armada and the English Fleet off Calais*, the earliest known painting of Sir Francis Drake's fleet defeating the Spanish Armada, was discovered at Bonhams auction house when the owner of the painting took it to be valued; the owner's father paid £20 for the painting by an anonymous Dutch artist and it was valued at between £30,000 and £50,000. **19**. Lyrics to the Beatles song *Nowhere Man* in John Lennon's handwriting sold for £268,000 at a Christie's auction in New York. **21**. George Harrison's first guitar, given to him by his parents, sold at the annual Cooper Owen's Beatles sale for £276,000. **24**. *Jerry Springer – The Opera* won the Best Musical of the Year award at the *Evening Standard* Theatre awards. **26**. The poet Benjamin Zephaniah rejected an invitation to receive an OBE in protest at the Government's policies on the Iraq war and because of the order's 'legacy of colonialism'. **27**. The British Museum acquired a Babylonian terracotta relief of a naked woman for £1.5 million; it was thought to have hung as a sign outside a brothel 4,000 years ago. **30**. The low-budget New Zealand film *Whale Rider* won the Best Film award at the BAFTA Children's Awards, beating both *Harry Potter* and *Lord of the Rings*.

DECEMBER 2003

1. David Almond's *The Fire Eaters* was voted by 9 to 11-year-olds as their favourite novel and awarded the Nestle Smarties Book Prize Gold Medal. **2**. An unpublished account of the sinking of the *Titanic* by Second Officer Charles Lightoller was sold for £8,400 and a lunch menu from the ship was sold for £28,800 at an auction in London. **5**. Sir Christopher Frayling was appointed the new chairman of the Arts Council. Thirty-five Aboriginal stencils and paintings believed to be 11,000 years old, were discovered in a cave near Sydney, Australia. The handwritten manuscript of Beethoven's *Scherzo* from the String Quartet Op.127 in E Flat Major was sold for £1,181,600 at auction at Sotheby's in London. **7**. Transvestite artist Grayson Perry, whose work depicts images of child abuse scratched into the surfaces of ceramic vases, won the £20,000 Turner Prize. **9**. *Eats, Shoots and Leaves (The Zero Tolerance to Punctuation)* by Lynne Truss, became the fastest-selling book in Britain after it sold 67,287 copies in one week. **10**. At the British Comedy Awards Steve Coogan won the Best Comedy Actor award, David Walliams the Best Newcomer award, and Lenny Henry was given a Lifetime Achievement award. The father of the author

J. K. Rowling sold four first editions of the Harry Potter books for £50,600, which had been inscribed by her and given to him as a Father's Day present. **11**. A Renaissance bronze roundel was sold for £7 million at auction in London after it was found in a cupboard under a staircase in Devon and thought to be worth only a few thousand pounds. **13**. *The Lord of the Rings* by J. R. R. Tolkien was voted Britain's favourite book after the BBC carried out a poll for its television programme *The Big Read*. **15**. Prime Minister Tony Blair announced that the British Museum would receive a grant of £500,000 in order to fund a five-year project aimed at building new links with African institutions. **18**. The pop star Michael Jackson was formally charged by prosecutors in California with performing lewd acts with a young boy. **19**. *The Return of the King*, the final film in the *Lord of the Rings* trilogy, recorded the biggest opening in British box office history after it made £3,029,176 in the first three days. **25**. *Gone With The Wind* was voted the greatest epic film by a poll of 6,500 customers of the *Blockbuster* video chain. **27**. *Grease* was voted the best musical in a poll for the Channel 4 programme, *100 Greatest Musicals*.

JANUARY 2004

5. It was reported by the Mobile Data Association that a record 111 million text messages were sent in Britain on New Year's Day. **8**. Mark Haddon won the Whitbread Novel Award 2004 for his book *The Curious Incident of the Dog in the Night-Time*, a popular children's book about an autistic boy. **9**. Michael Dixon was appointed the new director of the Natural History Museum and was due to take up the post in October 2004. **12**. The research company BLM reported that children watched an average of two-and-a-half hours of television every day while adults watched just over four hours per day. **14**. The British Museum paid £150,000 for a Roman drinking cup made from the mineral fluorspar; the Emperor Nero reportedly paid the equivalent of the wages of 830 soldiers for a year for one such fluorspar cup. The American company Kodak announced that it would halt production of traditional cameras in Europe and America and would only continue to produce digital cameras. **15**. The National Heritage Memorial Fund gave the Bodleian Library in Oxford £3 million to purchase a collection of Mary Shelley's manuscripts which include the original draft of *Frankenstein*. **16**. The BBC announced that the television presenter Robert Kilroy-Silk had left his morning chat-show 'Kilroy' after he had been suspended over an article he had written for the *Sunday Express* newspaper, expressing derogatory views about Arabs. **18**. Barry Joule, a friend of the late artist Francis Bacon, made a donation of more than 1,200 sketches by Bacon to the Tate Gallery, they were believed to be worth around £20 million. **19**. Don Paterson was awarded the T. S. Eliot Prize, worth £10,000, for his new collection of poetry *Landing Light*. **26**. Ricky Gervais, the British comedian who starred as David Brent in the comedy series *The Office*, was named Best Comedy Actor, and the programme Best TV Comedy, at the American Golden Globe awards. **27**. Mark Haddon's *The Curious Incident of the Dog in the Night-Time* was awarded the overall Whitbread prize; he received £25,000. **28**. The Culture Secretary Tessa Jowell announced that a greater role for 'decoding the media' would be introduced into the national curriculum so that children would be more 'active and informed' in decoding merchandising tie-ins in films.

FEBRUARY 2004
2. The Saudi Arabian Jameels family gave the Victoria and Albert Museum a donation of £5 million to house the museum's collection of Islamic art. 3. One of Degas's 27 bronze sculptures belonging to his *Little Dancers* collection, was sold at Sotheby's for £5.04 million; it was the only sculpture exhibited by the artist during his lifetime. 6. Frances Partridge, the last remaining member of the Bloomsbury set, died aged 103; she was best known for keeping journals in which she recounted conversations between people such as Virginia Woolf and E. M. Forster. 9. A poll commissioned by the Mayor of London, Ken Livingstone, found that the nurse Mary Seacole was considered the greatest black Briton. The British rock band Coldplay won the Record of the Year prize at the Grammy Awards for their single *Clocks*. 13. The National Gallery paid £35 million to the Duke of Northumberland, the owner of the Raphael masterpiece *Madonna of the Pinks*, in order to keep the painting in Britain. 15. The final film in the *Lord of the Rings* trilogy, *The Return of the King*, was given the Best Film award at the BAFTA ceremony, while Bill Murray and Scarlett Johansson won Best Actor and Best Actress prizes for their respective roles in *Lost in Translation*. 16. The Scottish Executive announced the appointment of Edwin Morgan as 'The Scots Makar', the Scottish equivalent of the English Poet Laureate. 17. The British band *The Darkness* won three awards, Best British Album, Best British Group and Best British Rock Act, at the Brit Awards. 22. At the Olivier Awards, Matthew Kelly was awarded the Best Actor prize for his role as Lenny in *Of Mice and Men* and *Jerry Springer – The Opera* was awarded three prizes including Best New Musical. 24. A three-volume set of the first edition of *The Lord of the Rings* signed by J. R. R. Tolkien sold for more than £31,000 at Bonhams in London. 27. T. E. Lawrence's working copy of *The Seven Pillars of Wisdom* was sold for a world record £51,400 at Christie's in New York.

MARCH 2004
1. Scottish Culture Minister Frank McAveety announced that the Scottish Executive would contribute £6.5 million to the National Library of Scotland to aid its bid to buy the John Murray Archive which contains 150,000 pieces of writing by authors including Jane Austen, Lord Byron and Charles Dickens. *The Lord of the Rings* films won 11 awards at the Oscars ceremony, including the Best Picture award; Sean Penn was awarded the Best Actor prize and Charlize Theron won Best Actress. 3. The Film Distributors' Association released figures showing that only four out of the top 100 film successes of 2003 were British films. Letters from Robert Browning to Julia Wedgwood were sold for £83,650 at Christie's in London. 7. The John Lennon album *Double Fantasy*, signed by him for his killer Mark Chapman, went on sale on the internet for £290,000. 8. The Spitz Gallery in east London removed photographs of a naked five-year-old girl which formed part of an exhibit by the artist Betsy Schneider following an investigation by the Obscene Publications Unit and fears over paedophilia. 9. The Archbishop of Canterbury, Dr Rowan Williams, recommended that school children study Philip Pullman's *His Dark Materials* trilogy to counter the 'inadequacies' of religious education. 11. Five million people tuned in to hear the first gay kiss on long-running radio show *The Archers*. 12. The Rijksmuseum in Amsterdam made its most expensive purchase ever when it paid £8.1 million for *The Burghermaster of Delft and his Daughter* by 17th

century master Jan Steen. 14. Disney paid £557,000 to supermarket manager Clive Woodall for the rights to his unpublished novel *One for Sorrow*, and planned to produce an animated film version of the story. 15. Charles Saatchi purchased a portrait of schoolgirl Rachel Whitear, who died of a suspected heroin overdose and whose picture was used as part of an anti-drugs campaign, planning to display it as part of the *New Blood* show at the Saatchi Gallery. A panel acting for the Greater London Authority decided that a marble sculpture of an armless, naked pregnant woman by Marc Quinn and a 21-storey perspex tower entitled *Hotel for the Birds* by Thomas Schutte, would occupy the fourth plinth in Trafalgar Square. 16. A survey of more than 400 people by the Mothers' Union found that the majority named Marge Simpson from *The Simpsons* cartoon as the best mother in public life. 19. The BBC announced that the actor Christopher Eccleston would play the ninth Doctor Who in a new series of the television show. 22. Emap, the publishers of *Just 17* magazine for teenage girls, announced that the magazine would be closed down and that the last edition would be published on 8 April. 25. The British Museum and the Victoria and Albert Museum jointly paid £850,000 to acquire a 7th century Indian standing figure of the Buddha Sakyamuni from a European private collection. The Danish artist Marco Evaristti unveiled a red iceberg as his latest work of art off the coast of western Greenland. Sir Michael Atiyah and Professor Isadore Singer won the £475,000 Abel Prize for mathematics for developing the 'Atiyah-Singer index theorem'. 27. Kate Long's debut novel *The Bad Mother's Handbook*, sold 18,000 copies in its first three weeks, outselling novels by established authors including John Grisham and Joanna Trollope. The British comedy *Only Fools and Horses*, was voted the best British sitcom in a poll commissioned by the BBC. 29. Mel Gibson's *The Passion of the Christ*, became the fastest grossing subtitled film in Britain after making £2 million in its opening weekend. 30. The Victoria and Albert Museum launched its biggest exhibition of the work of a British designer with its retrospective of the work of Vivienne Westwood. 31. A 16th century coin featuring the face of Henry VIII was sold for a world record £34,500 at the coin auction specialist Spink in London. Linguistics experts at a conference at the University of Newcastle, announced that dialects in Britain are developing at record speed, mainly due to new immigrants to the country mixing the language of their host country with their native tongue.

APRIL 2004
1. Michael Grade was appointed Chairman of the BBC. 2. It was announced that all 112,000 tickets for the Glastonbury music festival in June had sold out in 17 hours. 6. The Royal Opera House announced that 100 of its most expensive seats would be available for £10 instead of £175 if bought 90 minutes before a performance on Monday; this had been made possible through a donation of £1 million from the foreign exchange specialist, Travelex. 7. Canterbury City Council bought a £1 million portrait of Sir Basil Dixwell by Flemish painter Van Dyck to display at Canterbury's Royal Museum, after receiving more than £800,000 in lottery funding. The Royal Shakespeare Company announced that its new base would be the Whitehall Theatre following the company's controversial decision to leave the Barbican Centre. 11. A survey for tesco.com found that men voted *Star Wars* their favourite film of all

time and women preferred the 1987 film *Dirty Dancing*. **12.** Rachmaninov's Piano Concerto No 2 was voted Britain's favourite piece of classical music for the fourth consecutive year by listeners of Classic FM. **15.** A collection of 41 perforated snail shells, believed to have been strung together about 75,000 years ago, were discovered at Blombos Cave in South Africa, making them the oldest known example of jewellery. Sir Tim Berners-Lee, the inventor of the world wide web, won the €1 million Millennium Technology Prize, presented by the Finnish Technology Award Foundation. **16.** Deaf Jam, the first club night for deaf people, was held at Plastic People nightclub in east London. **18.** Julie Walters was named Best Actress for her role in BBC1s *The Wife of Bath* at the BAFTA awards and comedian Ricky Gervais won the Comedy Performance Prize for the third consecutive year for his performance in *The Office Christmas Special*. **19.** *The Singing Butler*, a painting by Jack Vettriano, fetched a record price for the Scottish painter of £750,000 at Sotheby's. **22.** A diary kept by Captain Scott's deputy, Captain Albert Armitage, was sold at Bloomsbury Auctions for £36,000 to a private collector. Andrew O'Hagan won the £3,000 James Tait Black Memorial Prize for Fiction for his second novel *Personality*. **25.** The founder of DreamWorks, David Geffen, bought the painting *Gray Numbers* by Jasper Johns for $40 million (£22.5 million), making it the most expensive picture by a living artist. **27.** Saskia Olde Wolbers won the £24,000 Beck's Futures Prize for *Interloper*, a video installation featuring a comatose hospital patient. **28.** The National Heritage Memorial Fund granted £1 million towards the erection of a 22ft high bronze sculpture by John Mills in remembrance of the seven million British women who contributed to the Second World War effort.

MAY 2004
5. Pablo Picasso's *Garcon à la pipe* fetched $93 million (£56 million) at Sotheby's in New York, making it the most expensive picture ever sold at auction. A signed copy of the 1962 contract between the Beatles and their manager Brian Epstein was sold for £122,850 at Christie's in London. The release of the film *Fahrenheit 9/11* by American documentary-maker Michael Moore, was blocked by Walt Disney, its American distributor because the company felt uncomfortable about the film linking President Bush with prominent Saudi families including that of Osama bin Laden. **10.** The European Audiovisual Observatory reported that screenings of European films beyond national boundaries attracted only 6.3 per cent of their total audience, down from 10 per cent the previous year. Jonny Hurst, a Birmingham City football club supporter, was awarded a bursary of £10,000 after he was picked to become the Premier League's first official Chant Laureate. **12.** Radio 4 was named Station of the Year at the Sony Radio Academy Awards in London. **14.** The editor of the *Daily Mirror* newspaper, Piers Morgan, was dismissed from his job after it was found that pictures printed in the newspaper alleged to have been of British soldiers abusing Iraqi prisoners, were fake. **16.** *The Poseidon Adventure* was voted the best disaster movie by film fans in a poll carried out by UCI Cinemas. **20.** *Total Film* magazine voted Janet Leigh's shower scene in Hitchcock's *Psycho* as the 'best movie death'; Slim Pickens' descent to atomic armageddon in *Dr Strangelove* came second. **23.** At the Cannes Film Festival, the Palme d'Or prize was awarded to *Fahrenheit 9/11*. **25.** A fire at a warehouse in Leyton,

east London, destroyed numerous artworks worth millions of pounds including those belonging to Charles Saatchi: Tracey Emin's tent *Everyone I Have Ever Slept With* and *Hell* by Jake and Dinos Chapman. **26.** Daniel Hope was named Young British Classical Performer of the Year at the Classical Brit Awards in London. **28.** A dozen paintings by the Scottish artist Jack Vettriano sold at auction in Edinburgh for almost £1 million.

JUNE 2004
2. A new literary prize worth £60,000 was announced by John Carey, professor of English at Oxford University; the Man Booker International Prize is designed to 'celebrate English language fiction as a major cultural force in the modern world'. A 1940 photograph by Herbert Mason, of St Paul's Cathedral during the Blitz, was voted the most inspirational photograph of all time. **3.** Leontia Flynn, a post-graduate student at Queen's University, was picked by a panel chaired by Andrew Motion, the Poet Laureate, as one of the '20 most exciting poets of their generation' for her collection *These Days*. **8.** Andrea Levy won the £30,000 Orange Prize for Fiction for her novel *Small Island*. **10.** A 23-year-old man was arrested in connection with the east London warehouse fire which destroyed £20 million worth of art works. **14.** Bill Bryson won the £10,000 Aventis Prize for science books with his work *A Short History of Nearly Everything*. **15.** Anna Funder won the £30,000 Samuel Johnson Prize for non-fiction for her debut *Stasiland: Stories from Behind the Berlin Wall*. **17.** Richard Wallace, the former deputy editor of the *Sunday Mirror* was appointed editor of the *Daily Mirror* newspaper. *Two Figures Lying on a Bed with Attendants*, a painting worth around £5 million, by Francis Bacon, was put on display at Tate Britain after it had been locked away in the vaults of Teheran's Museum of Contemporary Art for 30 years; it was loaned to Tate Britain by the Iranian Museum. **21.** Stephen Shankland won the National Portrait Gallery's £25,000 BP Portrait Award for his painting of his wife and son *The Miracle*. **24.** Charles Saatchi paid £28,000 for *Beneath the Stride of Giants*, a 40ft boat by artist Brian Griffiths, made from bric-a-brac and waste items. **25.** Eric Clapton raised more than £4 million for a drugs and alcohol rehabilitation centre in the Caribbean after he auctioned 79 guitars at Christie's in New York – one of which became the most expensive guitar auctioned when it fetched £527,198. **29.** A 1795 letter written by Admiral Nelson, in which he offered to resign over accusations of bad leadership, fetched £7,170 at Bonhams.

JULY 2004
1. The painting *Portrait of Mrs Baldwin* by Joshua Reynolds became the most expensive work of art bought by the charitable foundation Littlewoods Pools when it was sold for £3,365,600 at Sotheby's in London. **6.** David Miliband, the School Standards Minister, announced the launch of the Government's 'Music Manifesto' which aimed to provide every child with the chance to learn a musical instrument. **7.** The painting *A Young Woman Seated at the Virginals* was sold for £16.2 million at a Sotheby's auction after only recently having been recognised as a work by the Dutch painter Johannes Vermeer. **8.** *Head of a Child*, a drawing by Raphael, fetched £179,200 at Sotheby's in London when it was bought by the millionaire Leon Black. An erotic letter from the writer James Joyce to his girlfriend Nora Barnacle was bought for £240,800 at Sotheby's in London. **9.** The American author Jennifer Donnelly won

the Carnegie Medal for Children's Literature for her debut novel *A Gathering Light*. **12.** *Spider-Man 2* premiered in London after it was announced that it had already made £22 million in its first day in the USA, making it the highest-grossing opening in Hollywood history. **14.** A BBC documentary *The Secret Agent* claimed to expose racist behaviour within the British National Party (BNP) and had secretly recorded Nick Griffin, BNP chairman, telling supporters that their 'women' were under threat from Muslims and Islam. **25.** John Constable's great-great-great-granddaughter, Sasha Constable, presented her 'Peace of Art' project in Cambodia which involved sculptures made from weapons used during the Khmer Rouge genocide of the 1970s. **30.** It was announced that the Grade I listed West Pier in Brighton would be demolished after English Heritage reported that the structure was beyond repair.

AUGUST 2004

3. Cadbury's became the first company to give homeless *Big Issue* sellers a permanent pitch at its offices in Birmingham. English Heritage announced that it was searching for the first state jester since the post was abolished 350 years ago after the execution of Charles I. **5.** It was reported that Pink Floyd's 1979 album *The Wall* was being developed into a Broadway musical. **8.** *Portrait of a Londoner*, a lost essay by Virginia Woolf, was discovered by publisher Emma Cahill in a Bloomsbury antiquarian bookshop; the essay had never before been published and Ms Cahill planned to publish it alongside Woolf's five other essays on London, previously collected in the book *London Scene*. **12.** It was reported that Channel 4 had overtaken BBC2 in ratings for the first time in 10 years – this was largely due to BBC2's loss of the television show *The Simpsons*, which was bought by Channel 4 for £600,000 per episode. **16.** The singer Billy Bragg announced that he was rewriting the words to the hymn *I Vow To Thee My Country* after it was also criticised by the Right Revd Stephen Lowe, the suffragan Bishop of Hulme for being heretical with racist undertones. **21.** The Royal Shakespeare Company voted *Hamlet* the best play by William Shakespeare – *King Lear* came second and *Antony and Cleopatra* third. **22.** Armed robbers stole Edvard Munch's *The Scream* and *Madonna* paintings from the Munch Museum in Oslo. **24.** The former editor of the *Daily Mirror* Piers Morgan received £1.7 million in compensation from the newspaper after he was sacked for refusing to apologise for publishing pictures which purported to show British soldiers abusing Iraqi prisoners. **26.** A cleaner at Tate Britain mistook a bag of rubbish that was designed to be part of the 'recreation of the first public demonstration of auto-destructive art' for a bag of rubbish and threw it away.

CRIMES AND LEGAL AFFAIRS

OCTOBER 2003

1. A judge at the High Court in London ruled that the frozen embryos of Natallie Evans and Lorraine Hadley should be destroyed on the grounds that their former partners, who had fertilised the embryos but did not want the women to use them in future IVF treatment, had rights that should be respected. **5.** Eight police officers were suspended after an inquest into the death of Roger Sylvester in January 1999 found that he had been unlawfully killed. Mr Sylvester had been restrained by six police officers in a hospital and as a result slipped

into a coma and died seven days later. **7.** Legal history was made when Margaret McTear began legal action against Imperial Tobacco for failing to warn her late husband, who died of lung cancer, of the dangers of smoking. She became the first person in Britain to bring a damages case against a cigarette manufacturer. The boy known as Boy C when he gave evidence at the Damilola Taylor murder trial was sentenced to 18 months in a young offenders institute for burglary. **8.** Audrey Hingston, 81, was charged with the murder of her husband Eric, who was found with a neck wound at their home on 29 August 2003. **9.** William Horncy and Peter Rees appeared at the Central Criminal Court charged with murdering the millionaire businessman Amarjit Chohan; both men denied the charges and were remanded in custody. A man and a woman were arrested by police in connection with the murder of seven-year-old Toni-Ann Byfield. **12.** Solicitor-General Harriet Harman made a plea to the Court of Appeal against a five-year jail sentence given to a man who regularly raped his sister-in-law over 18 months. The jail sentence was doubled to 10 years after the court found the original sentence to be 'unduly lenient'. **13.** More than 50 disabled people won the right to receive damages of more than £1 million from Buckinghamshire County Council after it was found that they were physically abused throughout the 1980s and 90s while resident at two care homes for people with learning difficulties. The police force in England was given the right to use anti-social behaviour orders to ban prostitutes from residential areas after two High Court judges overturned a ruling by a District judge who had refused to grant such an order against a prostitute operating in Preston. **15.** It was announced that Winston Silcott, the man convicted and later cleared on appeal of the murder of PC Keith Blakelock during riots on the Broadwater Farm Estate in 1985, would be released from prison after serving 17 years for the murder of another man, Anthony Smith, for which he had originally received a 14-year prison term. **16.** Five Law Lords ordered an independent public inquiry into the death of Zahid Mubarek after an independent hearing requested by Mr Mubarek's family was refused by the Home Office. Mr Mubarek was placed in a cell with a known racist at Feltham Young Offenders' Institute and was beaten to death by him on the day he was due to be released. Detectives investigating the murder of the boy code-named 'Adam', whose torso was found in the Thames in 2001, announced that traces of the poisonous calaber bean had been found in the boy's lower intestine; the bean is alleged to have been used in witchcraft rituals. **20.** Rafaqat and Tafarak Hussain were jailed for life for the 'honour killing' of their cousin, Sahjda Bibi, whom they stabbed to death on her wedding day because they disagreed with her marrying a divorcee. **21.** Twelve men were jailed at Liverpool Crown Court for smuggling more than £100 million worth of Class A drugs into Britain after the drugs ring was broken when a £15 million consignment was seized in the Channel Tunnel in May. **23.** Zhang Yong Hui, who headed an £11 million operation which smuggled more than 700 illegal immigrants into Britain, was jailed for seven years after it was found that he was torturing the immigrants and blackmailing their families in China in order to receive more money. **28.** The Court of Appeal quashed the conviction of George Kelly, who was executed in March 1950 after being found guilty for the murder of Leonard Thomas, on the grounds that police officers had withheld crucial evidence, including the fact that another man, Donald Johnson, had confessed to the crime. **30.** Michael Little was convicted of murdering Rachel Moran on 1 January 2003 after her body was found in a cupboard in his home with at least 20 stab wounds; he was sentenced to life imprisonment at Hull Crown Court.

NOVEMBER 2003

3. Mohammed Dica became the first person to be convicted of the crime of inflicting 'biological' grievous bodily harm after he knowingly infected two women with HIV by insisting on having unprotected sexual intercourse with them; he was jailed for eight years at the Inner London Crown Court. It was reported that a six-year-old girl, Makada Weaver, became one of the youngest victims of gun crime when she was shot on 2 November as she opened the door of her house in Liverpool to a gunman who then shot her brother and mother before a ricocheting bullet hit Makada in the arm; it was thought that the attack was connected to the murder of Clay Benjamin three years ago. **13.** Four men were charged with the murders of Charlene Ellis and Letisha Shakespeare, who were shot dead at a New Year party in Aston, Birmingham on 2 January 2003; one of the men charged with murder was Ms Ellis's half-brother Marcus Ellis. **14.** Benjamin Lewis and Scott Bower became the first people in Britain to be jailed for religious harassment after they were found guilty of conducting a three-month campaign of harassment against the Revd Christopher Rowberry and his family. A fifth man, Tafarwa Beckford, was charged with the murders of Charlene Ellis and Letisha Shakespeare. **16.** Lee Holbrook was charged with the murder of 18-year-old Alicia Eborne, whose body was found near Dartmoor. She had gone missing on 7 November from her home in Plymouth. **17.** A gang of five men known as the 'Prada Boys' were jailed at Harrow Crown Court for between seven and nine years after being found guilty of stealing more than £2 million of jewellery and cash from wealthy victims whom they targeted in the West End of London. **19.** Colin Waite, 42, was convicted of the rape and murder of 17-year-old Nicola Dixon, whose body was found on New Year's Day in 1997; Mr Waite was jailed for life at Warwick Crown Court. **20.** The Queen won a landmark ruling against a tabloid paper when the High Court imposed a temporary injunction on the *Daily Mirror* banning it from publishing photographs of private royal apartments taken by one of their reporters who had obtained a job as a footman at Buckingham Palace. **24.** Abdul Baset Ali al-Megrahi was sentenced at the High Court in Glasgow to at least 27 years in prison after he was convicted of killing 259 people in 1988 when a bomb went off on Pan Am flight 103 over Lockerbie, in Scotland. **25.** Anthony Hardy was given three life sentences at the Central Criminal Court after he was convicted of the murders of Sally Rose White, Elizabeth Valad and Brigitte Maclennan, whom he had strangled and dismembered. **27.** Police in London and the south-east of England arrested 11 Colombians suspected of controlling the distribution of £650 million worth of cocaine smuggled into Britain over the last four years. **30.** Cdr Janet Williams was appointed leader of Scotland Yard's Special Branch, becoming the first woman to lead the Branch in its 120-year history.

DECEMBER 2003

1. At the High Court in London, the Revd Joanna Jepson won the right to challenge West Mercia police force's decision not to prosecute doctors who aborted a 24-week-old baby with a cleft palate, an abortion which would normally be illegal unless there was a risk of 'serious handicap'. **3.** Police announced that they had opened a new investigation into the death of PC Keith Blakelock, who was hacked to death during the Broadwater Farm riots in 1985. **7.** Police announced that a woman jogger had been stabbed by a man on 5 December in Clissold Park in north east London; police believe she was attacked by the same man who murdered Margaret Muller while she was jogging in an east London park in February. **8.** Multimillionaire Nicholas van Hoogstraten was freed at the Central Criminal Court after serving 13 months of a 10-year prison sentence for the manslaughter of a business rival who was shot and stabbed on his doorstep. **10.** At the Court of Appeal, Angela Cannings had her conviction for murdering her three children quashed and was set free after spending 20 months in prison; she was the third woman in 11 months to have her conviction overturned after it was found that a key witness, the paediatrician Professor Sir Roy Meadow, had given 'wrong' evidence in many similar cases. Police found guns, machetes and drugs and 12 people were arrested in north London after one of the biggest co-ordinated armed raids was carried out to clamp down on organised crime gangs in the Turkish and Kurdish communities. **15.** Police arrested a 24-year-old man and a 15-year-old boy in connection with the murder of Margaret Muller and the stabbing of a female jogger on 5 December. **17.** Ian Huntley was convicted of the murders of Holly Wells and Jessica Chapman and was sentenced to two life sentences at the Central Criminal Court in London, while Maxine Carr was cleared of two charges of aiding an offender but convicted of conspiring to pervert the course of justice. **19.** Eight-year-old Matthew King was awarded £5.75 million in damages after an obstetric emergency at his birth was not dealt with properly; it was the highest award given for a child suffering from cerebral palsy. **31.** In Gateshead, police arrested an American man, David Francis Bieber, also known as Nathan Wayne Coleman, on suspicion of the murder of PC Ian Broadhurst and the attempted murder of PC Neil Roper after he shot the policemen on 26 December in the Oakwood area of Leeds.

JANUARY 2004

2. Paul Smith, 17, was arrested and charged with the murder of 10-year-old Rosie May Storrie after she was found dead by her parents at a family party on 28 December; she had been strangled. **7.** Two men aged 19 and 20 were arrested in connection with the death of Michael Howard on 6 January. Mr Howard was run over at Liverpool John Lennon Airport after thieves tried to steal his car as he was unpacking suitcases. **11.** Lincolnshire police announced that they would reinvestigate the death of 60-year-old Hugh Wallace, who was found dead in October 1999 by Ian Huntley, the man convicted of murdering Holly Wells and Jessica Chapman. **12.** Delroy 'the King' Lewis, also known as Antonio Kidd, who ran one of the biggest crack and heroin rings in Britain, was jailed for 16 years after being convicted of conspiracy to supply class A drugs and possessing a prohibited weapon. **13.** The serial killer Harold Shipman was found dead in his cell at Wakefield prison after hanging himself with his bed sheets. He had been convicted of the murder of 15 of his patients in January 2000 but was believed to have murdered at least 215 people during his 20 years as a doctor in Manchester. Gordon Park was arrested in connection with the murder of his wife, Carol Park, in 1976, who was known as 'The Lady in the Lake' after she was discovered in 1997 in Cumbria's Coniston Water. **16.** A 15-year-old boy was arrested and charged with the attempted murder of a female jogger who was stabbed on 5 December in Clissold Park, north London. **19.** Attorney-General Lord Goldsmith announced that the convictions of 258 parents charged with killing their children would be reviewed, making it the biggest inquiry into potential miscarriages of justice in British legal history. **28.** A 42-year-old man and his 41-year-old wife were arrested in Droitwich, Worcestershire, on suspicion of the murder of a six-month-old girl, whose body was found in a block of concrete 12 years ago. **29.** Cannabis was downgraded from a class B to a class C drug. **30.** The Crown Prosecution Service announced that the charge of rape against the Leeds United footballer Jody Morris and his friend Kristofer Dickie had been dropped as there was no 'realistic prospect' of securing a conviction.

FEBRUARY 2004

3. An appeal tribunal in Edinburgh decided that the Gulf War veteran Corporal Kenny Duncan would be awarded a pension for suffering from depleted uranium poisoning, making him the first person to receive such compensation. **4.** Graham Coutts was jailed for life at Lewes Crown Court for the murder of Jane Longhurst on 14 March 2003, whose body he had kept in a cardboard box for five weeks before he set it on fire in woodland near Pulborough in West Sussex. **6.** PCs Mark Witcher and Andrew Lang were arrested and charged with raping a 23-year-old woman whilst on duty. **7.** Police arrested five men in connection with a raid on the Menzies World Cargo depot at Heathrow airport, during which eight men stole £1.75 million after they tied up 15 workers on 6 February. **13.** Police smashed an international drugs ring after they raided an illegal drugs factory in Ovingdean near Brighton, and seized equipment and chemicals for making up to £4 million worth of amphetamines and LSD. **18.** Police charged Peter Bryan with murder after the dismembered body of a 45-year-old man was found in a flat in Walthamstow in London; police believe there may have been traces of human tissue in a frying pan at the property. **23.** Zaheer Ahmed was charged with murdering his wife Adeeba at Horseferry Road Magistrates' Court after her body was found in a suitcase on the banks of the River Thames. **24.** Stephen Soans-Wade was jailed for life at the Central Criminal court in London after he was found guilty of murdering Christophe Duclos on 13 September 2002 when he pushed Mr Duclos in front of a tube train at Mile End station in east London in order to be admitted to a psychiatric hospital; he had previously been told he was not mentally ill and turned away from various institutions by doctors. **27.** John Bale was jailed for five years at Taunton Crown Court after being found guilty of committing more than 320 burglaries and stealing cash and jewellery worth £260,000. **28.** Melanie Horridge, 25, was stabbed to death near her home in Chorley, Lancashire, as she was walking in an alleyway with her four-month-old son Oliver.

MARCH 2004

1. The Home Office released figures showing that police numbers in England and Wales had reached a record high of 138,000, with an addition of 6,000 new officers in 12 months being the largest yearly increase ever recorded. Thomas Titley was jailed for life at Wolverhampton Crown Court for sex attacks on two boys aged seven after he had previously served four-and-a-half years for similar offences. **2.** Sean Brown was sentenced to a minimum of 19 years in prison at Preston Crown Court after he pleaded guilty to the murder of his daughter Carry Ann – he deliberately crashed the car they were both in following revelations that he had impregnated her at the age of 13 and then made her abort the baby. **3.** PC Ian Tolmaer was jailed for 12 years after admitting to raping an 18-year-old woman and also filming and photographing her as she lay unconscious. **4.** Antoni Imiela was sentenced to seven life sentences at Maidstone Crown Court after he was convicted of raping four women and three girls between November 2001 and October 2002 in the south east of England. **8.** Peers in the House of Lords voted by 216 to 183 to block the Government's Constitutional Reform Bill, so that it would have to go before a select committee before it could be passed by the House of Commons. The Minister for Prisons, Paul Goggins, urged courts to make greater use of non-custodial sentences as the prisons population in England and Wales exceeded 75,000 for the first time. **12.** Audrey Hingston 81 became the oldest woman to be jailed in Britain after she was found guilty of stabbing her husband to death because she was unable to cope with his illness; she was jailed for two years at Plymouth Crown Court. **15.** The government announced the introduction of on-the-spot fines to be imposed on brewers, licensees and bar staff who serve alcohol to under-18s and drunks. **16.** Stephen King was jailed for seven years at Middlesex Guildhall Crown Court in London after admitting to 21 charges of paedophilia, including sex with a girl under the age of 13 and ten counts of indecent assault. **18.** The Court of Appeal ordered the release of a Libyan asylum seeker known as 'M' from prison after he had been detained for 16 months without being charged; the court ruled that the evidence against him was unfounded and rejected a Home Office appeal to keep him in jail. **19.** Police in Hertfordshire arrested a man in his sixties in connection with the murder of Colonel Robert Workman who was shot on his doorstep in January. **24.** Sallie-Anne Loughran was cleared of drowning her son at her home in 1991 after it was found that the police investigation drew on work by Sir Roy Meadow, whose evidence had in the past been successfully discredited in a number of court cases. **26.** A High Court judge in London ruled that families of children whose organs were removed after their death without their families' consent, had the right to seek compensation from the NHS. The Home Office announced that the number of England football fans subject to banning orders had risen to 2,083 and was expected to reach 2,100 by the start of the European 2004 Championship in June. **27.** Six men were arrested after police seized 200lb of heroin valued at £5 million in a lorry load of charcoal in Walthamstow, east London. **30.** Eight British men were arrested by MI5 agents and anti-terrorist officers after half a tonne of fertiliser was found in a west London storage unit; it was believed that the men planned to use the fertiliser to make a bomb and use it on a 'soft target' such as a shopping centre. All visa applications from Bulgarian and Romanian migrants wanting to enter Britain, were halted by the Home Secretary David Blunkett, following reports from embassy staff that many of the applicants were using forged papers. Following an appeal by John Hirst, serving a life sentence for manslaughter in Britain, the European Court of Human Rights ruled that a ban on convicted prisoners voting in local and general elections was a breach of their human rights. **31.** A survey by the charity Drugscope showed that one in five 11- to 15-year-olds had taken drugs during 2003.

APRIL 2004

1. A 22-year-old man was charged with the murder of Charlotte Pinkney, who was last seen near her home in Devon on 28 February 2004. **2.** Toby Studabaker, the former US Marine who groomed a 12-year-old British girl over the internet, was jailed by Manchester Crown Court for four-and-a-half years after he pleaded guilty to child abduction and to inciting a child to commit gross indecency. **6.** A third man, Kenneth Regan, was charged with the murder of the millionaire Amarjit Chohan after his body was found in the sea near Bournemouth and his wife's body was found in Poole Bay. **7.** A 15-year-old schoolboy was sentenced to six years in a young offenders' institution after being found guilty of raping two girls aged 15 and 17 near their school in Eastbourne. **8.** Anthony Garcia, Jawad Akbar, Omar Khyam, Waheed Mahmoud and Nabeel Hussain were charged with plotting to cause a terrorist explosion after homemade explosives were found in a storage Unit in Hanwell, west London. **13.** The senior Home Office pathologist, Michael Heath, was facing a disciplinary tribunal over alleged flaws in his work after independent experts reviewed two of his murder cases and told the Crown Prosecution Service of their concerns; if the tribunal were to find that Mr Heath had made errors, hundreds of criminal cases in which he was involved would be reviewed. **15.** A teenage boy appeared at Edinburgh Sheriff Court charged with the murder of Jodi Jones, who was stabbed to death in June 2003; the 15-year-old boy did not enter a plea. Ken Ralphs won £134,000 in compensation for a police blunder which resulted in his name being leaked after he had assisted detectives investigating a gangland killing. **16.** The body of Amanda Edwards was found buried at a building site in Wiltshire a week after she went missing and police had suspected she had been kidnapped; the body of the suspected kidnapper, Ian Cortis was also found dead – it was believed he had committed suicide. **17.** Daniel Archer was charged with the murder of Nasra Ismail, whose torso was found in a suitcase in a canal on 12 April in London. **21.** Brett Osborn was jailed for five years at Woolwich Crown Court for the manslaughter of Wayne Halling, who had forced his way into a flat and confronted Osborn in August 2003. Emma Last, Kerry Bauer and Steven Wood were jailed at Chelmsford Crown Court for the murder of Debra Carne after they were found guilty of setting Ms Carne alight in July 2002; Ms Last was ordered to be detained at Her Majesty's pleasure for a minimum of 20 years, Ms Bauer was jailed for life with a recommendation that she serve at least 17 years, and Mr Wood was jailed for eight years. **22.** Guy Beckett admitted that he had killed Laura Torn, whose body was found in Nottinghamshire in April 2003; he pleaded not guilty to murder but guilty to manslaughter at Hull Crown Court. A report by the TUC showed that unemployment among black and Asian people was two-and-a-half times worse than rates for whites. **23.** Gary Seabrook, a plumber, was jailed at Lewes Crown Court, for 30 months, for charging a 73-year-old woman £5,000 for unblocking a drain, which would normally cost around £107. Curtis Rowe was jailed for seven years at the Central Criminal Court after he was found guilty of killing his neighbour, Peter King, by stabbing him and setting him alight because he had 'made too much noise'. **28.** Lincoln White was jailed for 25 years at Kingston Crown Court for running an international drugs operation worth around £170 million.

MAY 2004

1. The new Sexual Offences Act came into force which allows juries to assume there was no consent if a rape victim was asleep, unconscious or disabled and also repeals offences of buggery and indecency between men which had previously criminalised certain homosexual activity. **2.** A survey carried out by the Local Authorities Co-ordinators of Regulatory Services showed that one in 29 civil weddings in Britain were fraudulent and a result of a multimillion-pound black market weddings industry. **4.** Brian Braker and Keith Hill were jailed for 11 and seven years respectively after police found 650,000 ecstasy pills with a street value of £2 million in their possession. **5.** Steven Poole, Daniel Poole and Richard Greyham from Derbyshire were all found guilty of murder at Nottingham Crown Court after they beat to death Matthew Murray because they believed him to be a paedophile. **14.** Feston Konzani was jailed for 10 years at Teesside Crown Court after he was found guilty on three counts of causing grievous bodily harm by attempting to deliberately infect three women with the HIV virus. **17.** Six men were arrested at Heathrow airport after an attempted armed robbery at a warehouse containing £40 million in gold bullion as well as £40 million in cash. The Constitutional Affairs Minister, David Lammy, announced a Criminal Defence Service Bill that outlined a £70 million decrease in the criminal legal aid budget; the Bill also proposed that the power to grant legal aid be taken from magistrates' courts and given to the Legal Services Commission. Nigel Da Costa was jailed for 20 years at Chelmsford Crown Court for the rape of two women after convincing them he was a member of the SAS and pretending to arrest them for being a 'security risk'. **18.** Humberside Police closed an inquiry into the death of the skydiver Stephen Hilder, after forensic evidence showed that he almost certainly killed himself. **21.** Moira Greenslade was jailed for two years at Leeds Crown Court for selling her unborn baby over the internet to three childless couples. **23.** A 48-year-old man was charged with the murder of Detective Constable Michael Swindells who was killed on 21 May in Birmingham whilst on duty. **24.** Six companies were fined £75,000 each for tricking people into ringing premium rate telephone numbers by sending unsolicited text messages logging a 'missed call'. **25.** Mahmood Siddiqui was awarded £178,000 in compensation for racial discrimination after hidden cameras proved that he routinely suffered racial abuse and bullying from colleagues at the Royal Mail sorting office in Harlow, Essex. **26.** Animal rights activists were barred for life from protesting outside Huntingdon Life Science laboratories at the High Court in London. **28.** Jason Ward was sentenced to life imprisonment at Nottingham Crown Court after raping and battering to death 87-year-old Gladys Godfrey at her home in Mansfield.

JUNE 2004

1. Douglas Mullings was shot dead during a dispute over parking in Tottenham, north London. **2.** The concert pianist Brian Parnell was jailed for two years after becoming the first person to be convicted under Britain's 'sex tourism' laws. **3.** Former police officer David Nutton was jailed for 18 months at Winchester Crown Court for gross misconduct in office after he passed on details from a police computer to a paedophile which enabled the man to continue abusing children. Scotland Yard announced that four men had been arrested in connection with the shooting of Douglas Mullings on 1 June. **4.** Iain Davis was found guilty of killing Ashley Keaton and Wayne Mowatt with one bullet at a New Year's Day party in 2002 and was sentenced to life imprisonment. **7.** Two 18-year-old men were arrested in Leeds for raping a woman and assaulting her boyfriend in the city's Chapel Allerton Park. **8.** A police doctor, Robert Wells, was jailed for 15 years at Winchester Crown Court for two rapes and three indecent assaults of an 11-year-old. **15.** Jonathan Rees-Williams, the Queen's former choirmaster was convicted at Reading Crown Court of 13 charges of indecent assault against children over a 14-year period. Shabina Begum, 15, lost her application for judicial review at the High Court in London following a decision that her human rights had not been infringed by Denbigh High School, after it refused to allow her to wear her jilbab, an Islamic gown covering her whole body except her hands and face. **18.** Barbara Salisbury, a nurse at Leighton Hospital in Crewe, was jailed for five years at Chester Crown Court for the attempted murder of two of her patients, May Taylor and Frank Owen. **21.** Law Lords ruled by a majority of four to one that the Human Rights Act required courts to read the phrase 'surviving spouse' in the Rent Act as including the survivor of a homosexual couple. **22.** Paul Dalton was charged with murder after the dismembered body of his wife, Tae Hui, was found at their home in London. **26.** Two 16-year-old boys and one 17-year-old boy were arrested in connection with the murder of 15-year-old Kieran Rodney-Davis, who was stabbed in the chest by three youths whilst on an errand for his mother near their home in Fulham, London, on 23 June.

JULY 2004

5. The House of Lords voted by 250 to 75 to reject an attempt to outlaw physical punishment of children by parents but backed a compromise proposal which removed the defence of 'reasonable chastisement' but still allowed parents to administer moderate punishment, as long as it did not result in visible marking on the skin for several hours afterwards. Dale Whittington was sentenced to eight years in prison at Southampton Crown Court after he was found guilty of arson with intent to endanger life when he was found to have disconnected three smoke alarms at a property housing asylum seekers before setting it alight. **6.** Kingsley Ojo from Nigeria admitted to six identity and trafficking offences at Southwark Crown Court and was due to be questioned by police in connection with the ritual killing of the boy known as 'Adam', whose torso was found in the River Thames in 2001. The first public inquiry into Gulf War Syndrome opened in London but the Ministry of Defence refused to co-operate with the investigation. **7.** Karen Parlour, the former wife of footballer Ray Parlour, won a landmark ruling at the High Court which secured her right to a third of Mr Parlour's future income. **8.** Bernard

Heginbotham, 100, became the oldest man in Britain to be convicted of murder after he killed his wife, Ida, to spare her from dementia; he pleaded guilty to manslaughter on the grounds of diminished responsibility at Preston Crown Court and was ordered to complete a 12-month community rehabilitation order. **9.** Richard Jan was jailed for life at Middlesex Guildhall Crown Court for stalking around 200 people over a seven-year period between 1996 and 2003. **13.** The Court of Appeal ruled that nine Afghans who hijacked an airliner and forced it to land at Stansted Airport in 2000 could not be deported from the UK as their human rights would be infringed. The House of Lords voted by 240 to 208 to keep the post of Lord Chancellor; the government said it would use its majority to reinstate the measure into the Constitutional Reform Bill. **15.** Police launched an investigation after Noel White jumped from the top of a multi-storey car park with his five-year-old daughter Shanice in Wolverhampton – both were killed instantly. **16.** Sion Jenkins won a retrial after he was convicted in June 1998 of the murder of his step-daughter Billie-Jo; his conviction was quashed as unsafe due to scientific evidence being unavailable at his original trial. **21.** Nebojsa Denic was jailed for 15 years at the Central Criminal Court for conspiracy to rob and possessing a gun and using it to resist arrest after he helped steal £23 million worth of diamonds from Graff jewellers in Mayfair, London. **22.** The Department of Trade and Industry announced a new obligatory scheme for estate agents which would make it compulsory for all agents to sign up to an ombudsman scheme which would adjudicate on complaints from the public. Police announced a search for Mark Hobson as the main suspect for the murders of his girlfriend Claire Sanderson, her twin sister Diane Sanderson, and an elderly couple, James and Joan Britton, all of whom were found dead after having suffered violent deaths between 10 and 17 July. **23.** Dean Taylor and Craig Abbott were sentenced to seven-and-a-half-years in jail for the manslaughter of Michael Howard at Liverpool's John Lennon Airport on 6 January. **25.** Mark Hobson was captured by police at a petrol station on the A19 in Shipton, near York; he was first taken to a police station before being taken to Harrogate District Hospital. **26.** Andrew Wragg was arrested by Sussex police on suspicion of the murder of his son, Jacob, who had been suffering from Hunter syndrome and whose condition had deteriorated considerably; he died on 24 July at the family home. Kingsley Ojo was sentenced to four-and-a-half years in prison at Southwark Crown Court for running a trafficking ring thought to have brought the boy known as 'Adam' whose torso was found in the Thames, into Britain. **27.** The Association of Chief Police Officers announced that anyone working for the police force who chose to join the British National Party (BNP) would face dismissal. Alan Pennell was convicted of the murder of Luke Walmsley at Nottingham Crown Court and sentenced to a minimum of 12 years in prison after he was found guilty of stabbing him in the chest at Birkbeck School in Lincolnshire in November 2003. **28.** Shahajan Kabir was jailed for life at Carlisle Crown Court for slitting the throat of his one-year-old son Hassan Martin in October 2003 in front of Hassan's mother and grandmother because he faced being deported to Bangladesh. **30.** Figures published by the Department for Education and Skills showed that more than 10 children a day were expelled from schools in England for assaulting staff or fellow pupils during the summer term in 2003.

AUGUST 2004

2. Lee Holbrook was jailed for life at Plymouth Crown Court for the murder on 7 November 2003 of Alicia Eborne. 4. A senior al-Qa'eda suspect was arrested followed by the arrest of a dozen other men on 13 August, suspected of plotting a terrorist attack in Britain. 5. A 16-year-old boy was convicted of stabbing Monica Watts while she was jogging in Clissold Park in north London in December 2003. 6. Mark Smith, a youth worker at Hammersmith and Fulham council, was jailed for eight years at the Central Criminal Court for conspiracy to sell or transfer prohibited weapons and of possessing them. Professor David Southall was banned by a General Medical Council tribunal from child protection work for three years for 'abusing his professional position' by accusing a father of murdering his two infant sons based on a 50-minute television documentary he had seen on the case. 9. The Premiership footballer Lee Hughes was sentenced to six years in prison at Coventry Crown Court for killing Douglas Graham in a car crash in November 2003. 10. George and Gwendoline Elliott, 75 and 72 respectively, were sentenced to one year in jail at Norwich Crown Court for allowing their son to hide heroin in their home. 13. A 17-year-old boy, believed to be Britain's most prolific graffiti vandal, was sentenced to a 12-month referral order at Bath Youth Court after he admitted 10 counts of criminal damage. 15. It was reported that MPs would be forced to declare their expense claims worth more than £100,000 a year when parliamentary accounts are published in order to comply with the Freedom of Information Act. Robert Boyer was arrested on suspicion of murdering Keith Frogson after Boyer was found hiding in Nottinghamshire woodland during a police search which involved 620 officers. 16. Terry Rodgers was arrested for the murder of his daughter Chanel, who was found dead by her husband on 30 July. 17. Joseph Mansoor was jailed for life at the Central Criminal Court for battering his wife, Yona, to death. 19. James Raven, a 'covert operative' employed by the BBC and Channel 4, was jailed for life at Chester Crown Court for the murder of Brian Waters. 20. Amelia Delagrange was murdered in Twickenham, south London; police believed she was the second victim of a serial killer after Marsha McDonnell was murdered in a similar way in the same area in February 2003. 22. Tom Brown, a BBC archivist, was stabbed to death in an unprovoked attack in Southgate, north London.

ECONOMIC AND BUSINESS AFFAIRS

SEPTEMBER 2003

4. The Bank of England kept the base interest rate on hold at 3.5 per cent and the European Central Bank kept its key interest rate at 2 per cent. 8. The Inland Revenue announced new legislation barring companies from claiming backdated tax refunds extending back more than six years with immediate effect. The new legislation was introduced after Deutsche Morgan Grenfell, part of Deutsche Bank, won the right in the High Court to seek a refund of tax payments made a decade ago. 9. The Office of Fair Trading (OFT) announced that it was launching an inquiry into store cards offered by high street retailers, after MPs on the Commons Treasury Select Committee complained that research showed that the consumer arm of General Electric could own 70 per cent of the market share. 17. Dick Grasso resigned as head of the New York Stock Exchange (NYSE) after a public outcry concerning his $187.5 million pay deal. He had previously returned

$48 million, but in an emergency meeting the board of the NYSE voted 13 to 7 in favour of a motion proposing his resignation. 18. The annual report of National Savings and Investments, the fundraising arm of the Treasury, revealed that funds had risen by £784 million to £63.1 billion due to record sales of premium bonds; sales topped £4.75 billion compared to £3.8 billion in 2002. 22. A sharp fall in the value of the US dollar sparked a 2.5 per cent rise in the price of gold, which finished the day on the London market at $386 (£234) per troy ounce, continuing a three-year upward trend. 26. Levi Strauss & Co, the American jeans label, announced it was to close its remaining US production plants and move its operation to South America and Asia making 2,000 employees redundant. 30. Official figures published by the Office for National Statistics showed that inflation in the public sector was at its highest for 13 years: an average of 7.9 per cent over the first half of 2003. In a major cross-border deal in European aviation Air France agreed to an all-share takeover of Dutch airline KLM.

OCTOBER 2003

1. British Energy avoided bankruptcy after its creditors agreed to forfeit the £1.3 billion they were owed in return for £425 million worth of bonds and 97.5 per cent of the restructured energy company's equity. 2. At the Labour Party conference the unions voted unanimously to make it compulsory for employers to contribute to employee pension schemes; Andrew Smith, Secretary of State for Work and Pensions, responded by saying that the Pension Commission would consider the case for greater compulsion. In his conference speech Mr Smith announced a pilot scheme with cash incentives to help single parents get back to work and plans for a more flexible state pension offering lump sums of up to £30,000 for people who defer their state pension for five years. 3. The first UK outlet for the US brand Krispy Kreme doughnuts officially opened at Harrods. 6. The Pension Credit replaced the pension Minimum Income Guarantee (MIG); the new system intended to ensure a minimum weekly income for everyone aged over 60 in the UK and was designed to reward those that had saved for their retirement via a system of monetary-linked credits. Robert Wiseman, managing director of Robert Wiseman Dairies, won the Ernst and Young UK Entrepreneur of the Year competition for his transformation of the company from a door step supplier to the country's third largest milk supplier with an annual turnover of £390 million. 7. The two television companies Carlton and Granada merged in a £4 billion deal creating a single ITV. 8. A British academic, Prof. Clive Granger from the University of California at San Diego was awarded the Nobel Economics Prize for his research techniques which have been used by the Bank of England and the Treasury for forecasting and monitoring the UK economy. 10. The first week of electronic trading at the International Petroleum Exchange (IPE) in London ended with only 57 lots traded electronically compared to 147,000 lots traded traditionally on the floor by 'open outcry' after traders boycotted the new electronic system. 13. Share prices surged to a 13-month high with the FTSE 100 index closing at 4431.6 points, its highest level since August 2002. 16. Eddie Stobart announced that he was selling his haulage company to WA Developments, a real estate and railway infrastructure business, part-owned by his brother William Stobart. HSBC confirmed it would be moving 4,000 jobs to India, China and Malaysia. 19. The British Retail Consortium reported the fourth consecutive

month of solid sales growth in September, with like-for-like sales up 2.6 per cent and total sales up 5.5 per cent. A Valuation Tribunal ruled that individuals working from home would not have to pay business property rates on top of council tax after Eileen Tully who works for the Inland Revenue mounted a successful challenge against her employer's policy.

NOVEMBER 2003

3. Figures published by the Bank of England showed that during the first three-quarters of the year the number of businesses becoming bankrupt had increased by 11.1 per cent compared to the same period in 2002. **6.** The Bank of England's monetary policy committee raised the base interest rate by a quarter per cent to 3.75 per cent. **7.** Figures from the Department of Trade and Industry (DTI) showed that more than 9,000 Britons became bankrupt in the three months leading up to 30 September 2003; an increase of 17 per cent compared to the same period in 2002 and the highest number for 10 years. **13.** The price of gold soared to its highest level since March 1996, closing up $3 at $394 per troy ounce in London. **14.** The media group Hollinger International, the American parent company of the *Daily Telegraph* Group, revealed $32.5 million in payments to Hollinger executives had not been approved by the full board of directors or the audit committee. **19.** An 18-month joint undercover operation by the FBI, US Securities and Exchange Commission (SEC) and the US Attorney for the Southern District for New York into alleged fraudulent foreign exchange activities resulted in the arrests of 48 traders on Wall Street. Lord Black of Crossharbour announced his resignation as the chief executive of Hollinger International following the revelations concerning payments to Hollinger executives on the 14 November.

DECEMBER 2003

10. Chancellor Gordon Brown delivered his pre-budget report to the House of Commons in which he revealed that borrowing of up to £37.4 billion would be required in 2003–6 to meet government spending commitments. The price of platinum soared above $800 an ounce, the highest for 23-years, as concerns grew that not enough was being produced to satisfy demand. **18.** The price of platinum continued to rise closing at $840 an ounce, an all-time high. **31.** The US Securities and Exchange Commission started legal proceedings against Parmalat in a New York Court and sent investigators to Italy to liaise with prosecutors. Two executives at the Italian branch of Grant Thornton, auditors for Parmalat, were arrested on suspicion of fraudulent accounting practices. The FTSE 100 index of leading companies finished the year up for the first time since 1999 and the pound gained more than a cent against the dollar to finish at $1.7904.

JANUARY 2004

1. Citibank and HSBC Holdings became the first foreign bank to win approval to issue credit cards in China. The aerospace group Boeing was awarded a $1.6 billion (£900 million) extension from NASA to its contract to supply the International Space Station. **9.** Royal Dutch/Shell, the Anglo-Dutch oil company, revealed that it had overstated its oil and gas reserves by 20 per cent resulting in a drop in oil stocks world-wide. **12.** Figures from the Office of the Deputy Prime Minister showed that house price inflation was back into single figures after house

prices dropped by 1.1 per cent in November 2003. **13.** Standard Life, one of the largest mutual insurance companies in Europe, stated that it was considering a stock market listing. **15.** The retailer Boots plc confirmed that it would be cutting 900 jobs at its head office in Nottingham. **18.** Sir David and Sir Frederick Barclay launched a bid to buy Lord Black of Crossharbour's 78 per cent stake in the Canadian-listed Hollinger Incorporated, which owns 30 per cent of the New York-listed Hollinger International's equity and controls 73 per cent of the voting shares. **19.** A resurgence in the stock market due to gains in insurance and oil shares raised the FTSE 100 index to its highest level for 18 months, closing up 30.2 points (0.7 per cent), at 4,518.1. **26.** The New York law firm, Milberg Weiss Bershad Hynes & Lerach, launched a lawsuit against Shell, the Anglo-Dutch oil company, on behalf of investors after the company's admission on 9 January that it had overstated its proven oil reserves by 20 per cent. Hollinger International filed a lawsuit to prevent the former chairman, Lord Black of Crossharbour, selling his controlling stake in the company to brothers Sir David and Sir Frederick Barclay. **27.** The media regulator Ofcom ruled that the operator of the *118 118* directory enquiry service had used the 'trademark' long hair, drooping moustache and red socks of the former 10,000-metre world record holder, David Bedford, without his permission in its £16 million advertising campaign. The Barclay brothers tabled a formal tender offer to buy Lord Black of Crossharbour's 30 per cent stake in Hollinger International for £259 million.

FEBRUARY 2004

3. The European Commission ruled that the Ryanair airline should repay more than £2 million in unlawful subsidies given by the Walloon regional government as an incentive for the airline to fly from Charleroi airport near Brussels. **5.** The Bank of England raised the base interest rate by 0.25 per cent to 4.0 per cent. **6.** Figures released by the Department of Trade and Industry showed the number of personal bankruptcies had risen by 29 per cent in the last four months of 2003 compared to the same period in 2002. A total of 36,328 people in England and Wales declared themselves personally insolvent in 2003, the highest figure for a decade. **7.** Tickets went on sale for a new European lottery organised and run by Camelot in partnership with its French and Spanish counterparts. **9.** The Treasury's annual assessment of European economic reform stated that EU spending should be capped at one per cent of gross national income and subjected to the same value-for-money assessment as spending by member states. **10.** The US dollar dropped to $1.86 against the pound sterling; its lowest level since Black Wednesday. **17.** The latest UK inflation data was published showing that the Consumer Prices Index was rising by an annual 1.4 per cent in January 2004, an increase from 1.3 per cent in December 2003. Italian police arrested the son and a daughter of Calisto Tanzi, founder of Parmalat, and six others, in connection with the investigation into suspected fraud and misappropriation of funds within the Parmalat group. **18.** The dollar continued to fall against the pound sterling, closing at $1.91 against the pound. **25.** Figures released by the Office for National Statistics showed an unchanged rate of economic expansion of 0.9 per cent for the fourth quarter, equivalent to a year-on-year 2.8 per cent increase in GDP for 2003. **26.** Lord Black of Crossharbour had his proposal to sell his controlling stake in Hollinger International to the Barclay brothers blocked after a judge in Delaware, USA, ruled that he had breached company law.

MARCH 2004

1. *The Times* newspaper reported that the Inland Revenue had written off more than £750 million in unpaid national insurance contributions after attempts to recover the money failed; the shortfall arose after the Inland Revenue failed to send out reminders for the five years (1996–2002) to those whose contributions fell short. The British retailer Marks & Spencer said that it would raise £400 million by issuing bonds to fund a £1 billion shortfall in its pension scheme funds. HSBC, the high-street bank announced record pre-tax profits of £7.8 billion, the biggest profit ever recorded by a British bank in a single year. **8.** Lord Penrose's report on the near-collapse of Equitable Life was published after two-and-a-half years. The report found that regulators failed to monitor the company adequately but blamed the company's former management as the direct cause of the losses suffered by policyholders, thereby ruling out the possibility of government compensation for the one million investors. **17.** The Chancellor Gordon Brown delivered the 2004 Budget to the House of Commons. Many taxes and duties were frozen but beer went up 1p a pint, wine up 4p a bottle and tax on cigarettes increased in-line with inflation. The inheritance tax threshold was increased to £263,000 and a £3,000 fine for late filing was introduced. Individual pension allowances were capped at £1.5 million under a new scheme to be introduced in 2006 with the allowance scheduled to rise to £1.8 million by 2010. Public spending plans included an annual 7.2 per cent increase in NHS funding until 2008 and an additional £6 billion allocated to fight terrorism. Overall the economy grew by 2.3 per cent in 2003, meeting Treasury forecasts, and growth forecasts remained at 3–3.5 per cent for 2004–5 and at 2.5–3 per cent for 2006. **18.** In Milan, prosecutors called for 29 people to strand trial in connection with the collapse of the Italian dairy firm, Parmalat. These included the company's founder, Calisto Tanzi, his son Stephano and his former financial chief, Fausto Tonna. The Anglo-Dutch business Shell admitted that revised figures issued in January for its proven oil and gas reserves, following revelations that it had overestimated stocks for 2003 by 20 per cent, were also too high. **22.** The European Commission fined Microsoft a record €497 million after ruling that Microsoft had abused its market position by not making its operating systems compatible with rival software. **24.** Figures published by the National Audit Office (NAO) showed that the Inland Revenue failed to collect £14 billion of tax for the financial year 2002–3; the missing debt included £4.9 billion in PAYE, £4.5 billion in self-assessment, £3.1 billion in corporation tax and £1.8 billion in other taxes. **29.** A survey published by Hometrack stated that house prices were continuing to rise at a high rate forecasting an eight per cent rise in 2004. The Post Office launched the first of a wide range of low-cost financial services products in collaboration with the Bank of Ireland.

APRIL 2004

8. The Bank of England kept the base interest rate on hold at four per cent despite much speculation that it would be raised by a quarter of a percentage point. **13.** The HSBC bank launched a new pension fund compliant with Shari'ah or Islamic law. **18.** *The Sunday Times Rich List* reported that Britain's richest people had seen their wealth increase by almost 30 per cent in the past 12 months, an increase of 15 times the rate of inflation. **19.** An investigation carried out on behalf of Royal Dutch Shell by US law firm, Davis, Polk and Wardwell, reported that former executives at the company had knowingly lied to investors about the true level of the company's oil and gas reserves for a number of years. **23.** Figures released by the Office for National Statistics showed that the UK economy grew by its fastest annual rate in almost three-and-a-half years in the first quarter of 2004, the growth was mainly from rapid expansion in the retailing, hotels and leisure sectors. The Financial Services Authority (FSA) confirmed that it had launched a formal investigation into Royal Dutch Shell, following the conclusion by its internal investigation. **26.** The US aerospace company, Boeing, announced it would start production of its new 7E7 *Dreamliner* jet after the Japanese airline All Nippon Airways ordered 50 of the jets in a deal worth about $6 billion. **29.** Figures released by the Nationwide Building Society showed that the value of the average home went up by almost £3,400 in a month to £145,918; overall, house prices had climbed seven per cent since January and 18.9 per cent in the past 12 months.

MAY 2004

2. Between 750 and 1,000 passengers were left stranded when a new airline, Duo, went into administration after only operating for seven months. **6.** The Bank of England raised the base interest rate by 0.25 per cent to 4.25 per cent. **10.** The FTSE-100 index dropped by 2.3 per cent, its sharpest one-day decline for a year, closing down 103.2 points at a five-week low of 4,395.2, amid fears of surging oil prices and a possible increase in US interest rates. **12.** From midnight British Airways added a £5 surcharge to its non-European fares due to an increase in oil prices. **16.** The Office of Fair Trading announced that British credit card companies were over-charging retailers for processing card payments and these costs were eventually borne by consumers. **24.** Oil prices continued to rise with the cost of a barrel of crude oil reaching $41.80, close to a 21-year high, on the New York Stock Exchange.

JUNE 2004

8. Carl Cushnie and Fred Clough, the former chairman and finance director of Versailles, the trade finance house which collapsed in 2000, were both convicted of conspiracy to defraud; Cushnie was convicted of defrauding £23 million from investors and Clough £19 million. **10.** The Bank of England raised the base interest rate by a quarter percentage point to 4.5 per cent. **16.** It was reported that UK inflation reached 1.5 per cent in May 2004, its highest level for more than one year. **21.** The Barclay twins, Sir David and Sir Frederick were successful, subject to regulatory approval, in their £665 million bid for the ownership of *The Daily Telegraph*.

JULY 2004

12. Chancellor Gordon Brown unveiled his 2004 Spending Review; public spending by government departments was forecast to rise from £279.3 billion in 2004–5 to £340.5 billion in 2007–8. NHS funding was to be increased from £69 to £92 billion by 2008, security spending to increase by 10 per cent annually (real-terms rise) with the Armed Forces budget to increase from £29.7 billion to £33.4 billion by 2008. Cutbacks included the loss of 84,150 civil service posts and plans to raise £30 billion from the sale of Government assets. **16**. Martha Stewart, former chief executive of Martha Stewart Living Omnimedia, was sentenced to five months in jail followed by five months house arrest, after being found guilty on 1 March of lying to the FBI and securities regulators; she was granted bail pending appeal. **22**. The British high street had its longest run of retail sales growth in at least two decades when sales rose for the thirteenth consecutive month in June. A warning from the Russian oil company Yukos, that a liquidity crisis could force it to cease export operations increased American crude oil prices to above $41 per barrel on the New York stock exchange. **25**. The board of Abbey agreed in principle to sell the high street bank to Santander Central Hispano, Spain's biggest finance group, for an estimated £8.5 billion. **28**. The price of American crude oil reached a 21-year high of $43.05 a barrel and London Brent oil reached a 14-year high of $39.60, after Siberian oil company Yukos received an order from the Russian Justice Ministry to halt all sales. Oil analysts believed the order to be a restraint aimed at stopping the company selling or changing the status of its assets, however, the Russian Justice Ministry failed to clarify the meaning of the order, resulting in shares in Yukos falling by 20 per cent.

AUGUST 2004

5. The Bank of England raised interest rates to 4.75 per cent, the highest level for almost three years. **6**. Analysts' concerns over the crude oil market subsided after the Moscow Arbitration Court ruled that seizure of a key production subsidiary of Russian oil company, Yukos, was illegal. **8**. Figures from the Land Registry showed that house prices in the three months to June were 17 per cent higher than in the same period in 2003; taking the average house price from just under £150,000 to more than £175,000 within a 12-month period. **20**. As the price of American crude oil reached nearly $50 a barrel and London Brent oil above $40 a barrel, fuel retailers across the UK began to raise prices with Total becoming the first chain to confirm a forecourt price increase of 0.6p a litre for petrol and diesel. **24**. Britain's largest gas and electricity supplier, British Gas, announced its highest single price increase since privatisation in 1996; gas would rise by 12.4 per cent and electricity by 9.4 per cent from 20 September 2004. British Gas blamed rises in the prices of wholesale energy and oil for the increase.

ENVIRONMENT AND SCIENCE

SEPTEMBER 2003

3. Scientists from the Weizmann Institute of Science in Israel developed a test to measure the activity of 8-oxoguanine DNA N-glycosylase (OGG), an enzyme responsible for DNA repair, and discovered that some people are better at repairing smoking-related damage to their DNA. **7**. NASA announced that Galileo space probe's 14-year mission to explore Jupiter and its moons would be brought to a close as the craft had run low on fuel; technicians put Galileo on course to disintegrate in the Jovian atmosphere. **10**. The Institute of Child Health in London identified a small fraction of the human genetic code that affects the part of the brain implicated in autism. Lord Winston warned of the possible long-term dangers of IVF treatment, stating that poorly researched fertility

treatments were being used as a matter of course. He was particularly concerned with the long-term effects of freezing embryos and the use of intra-cytoplasmic sperm injection (ICSI), which involves directly injecting a sperm into an egg, increasing the risk of genetic defects being passed on. **15**. Prof. Alex Markham, chief executive of Cancer Research UK, said that a national screening programme for bowel cancer could save 5,000 lives a year but could not be implemented because the NHS did not have the capacity to treat the number of patients that such a programme would identify. **19**. It was reported in *The Times* that a complete fossil of a giant guinea-pig type creature, *Phoberomys pattersoni*, had been unearthed at Urumaco in Venezuela. The creature lived in South America eight million years ago and would have weighed about 700kg (110st), was 3m long and 1.3m high at the shoulder. **24**. Scientists reported that the largest ice shelf in the Arctic, the Ward Hunt ice shelf on the north coast of Ellesmere Island in Canada, had split into two main parts, each of which had cracked into many smaller pieces. Researchers stated that local warming of the climate was responsible. **30**. Cancer Research UK launched a 10-year study to test if the drug Arimidex anastrozole can reduce the risk of post-menopausal women developing breast cancer; initial studies had suggested that it could reduce the risk by up to 70 per cent.

OCTOBER 2003

1. The Met Office announced that September 2003 had been the sunniest September since sunshine records began in 1961, with an average of just over six hours of sunshine each day across England and Wales. **3**. Provisional figures released by the Office for National Statistics showed that the summer's exceptionally hot weather caused 2,045 more deaths compared to the averages for the previous five years. **6**. The Central Science Laboratory announced that wild boar were again breeding in the south east of England; government scientists estimated the numbers to be about 200, although farmers believed the numbers to be much higher. British physicist Sir Peter Mansfield and American scientist Paul Lauterbur from the University of Illinois jointly won the Nobel Prize for Medicine for developing magnetic resonance imaging (MRI), a technique for producing images of internal organs without using X-rays. **7**. Anthony Leggett, a British scientist and Professor of Physics at the University of Illinois, was honoured with the Nobel Prize for Physics for his work on superfluidity. **9**. A study by the Zoological Society of London and the University of Las Palmas in Gran Canaria reported that military sonar is confusing whales and dolphins by causing them to surface too quickly and suffer fatal attacks of decompression sickness. **14**. A team of scientists from Duke University in Durham, North Carolina reported they had successfully taught two rhesus macaque monkeys to control a cursor on screen via electrodes planted in the frontal and parietal lobes of their brains. **15**. The European Food Safety Authority confirmed its scientists had discovered the toxin semicarbazide, which can damage DNA and has been linked to a range of cancers in a variety of jarred food products, including baby food. China became the third nation to send a man into space after Lieutenant-Colonel Yang Liwei completed his mission. **21**. Microsoft launched a new range of software which allows users to send emails that can be ordered to 'self-destruct' at a date set by the sender. **23**. The first three-year phase of the 10-year marine life census recorded 15,304 species of fish and 210,000 marine species of all types. **29**. One of the most powerful solar storms on record hit Earth's atmosphere resulting in problems with aircraft navigational systems and a spectacular display of Northern Lights; the storm resulted from a massive gas cloud which erupted from the sun two days previously. **30.** The British award winning wildlife film-maker, Michael Linley, pleaded guilty in a Perth court to smuggling protected reptiles out of Australia; he was caught in October at Perth airport as he tried to leave with the protected species.

NOVEMBER 2003

4. A run of wild salmon were rescued from the waterfall at Cargill's Leap on the river Ericht in Perthshire after becoming too exhausted to leap upstream in shallow water. They were transported upstream to their spawning ground by the Tay District Salmon Fisheries. A new osteoporosis drug, the hormone derivative teriparatide, which increases the number of bone forming cells, was licensed for use in Britain for post-menopausal women. **14.** A possible new planet, named *Sedna*, located eight billion miles away from the sun, was sighted from the Palomar Observatory in California.

DECEMBER 2003

19. The *Beagle 2* Mars probe was successfully released from the nose cone of the European Space Agency's *Mars Express* spacecraft for the final part of its journey to the red planet where it was due to land on 25 December. **26.** The Jodrell Bank Radio Observatory in Cheshire failed to pick up a signal from the *Beagle 2* lander for a second night, the failure followed a second unsuccessful attempt at contact by the NASA *Mars Odyssey* orbiter.

JANUARY 2004

2. NASA successfully flew the *Stardust* space probe through the tail of the *Wild 2* comet where it took pictures of the comet's nucleus and was hoped to have successfully gathered a sample of comet dust. **4.** The first of two NASA exploration rovers successfully landed on Mars to begin a 90-day mission to establish if Mars was capable of sustaining life. **5.** The World Health Organisation confirmed that a new case of SARS had been identified in Guangdong, in south China. **7.** The *Mars Express* passed the landing site for the *Beagle 2*, but failed to pick up any radio signal from the missing probe. **12.** Research carried out by a team of scientists led by Philippa Darbre, a lecturer in cellular and molecular biology at Reading University, established the possibility of a link between the parabens contained in some anti-perspirants and breast cancer. **15.** The NASA *Spirit* rover successfully left its landing platform on Mars and drove three metres across the planet's surface. **21.** NASA lost contact with the *Spirit* Mars rover after it failed to send back expected scientific data and sent a simple signal instead. **22.** The Big Bird Race (The Ultimate Flutter) was launched in London by David Bellamy to raise money for the Conservation Foundation's work on seabird protection; gamblers could place bets on which one of 18 electronically tagged Tasmanian shy albatrosses would finish first on their 6,000-mile annual migration from Tasmania to South Africa. **23.** The European *Mars Express* transmitted a spectrometer image providing the first direct evidence that the Martian South Pole contained deposits of frozen water. **25.** NASA's second Mars rover *Opportunity* touched down in a shallow meteorite crater. **26.** The *Beagle 2* team announced that they accepted that the probe was probably lost and commenced an

evaluation of what could have gone wrong. **29.** NASA re-established partial contact with the *Spirit* Mars rover which successfully transmitted an image back to Earth.

FEBRUARY 2004

11. A study published by the British Medical Association (BMA) aiming to consolidate medical evidence on the effects of smoking on fertility, pregnancy and childhood health concluded that smoking causes early menopause and reduces the chances of conceiving by approximately 40 per cent. **12.** The journal *Science* reported that a team of South Korean scientists had successfully produced human stem cells from cloned embryos as part of their research into therapeutic cloning. **13.** Microsoft called in the FBI to investigate the alleged theft of a 660-megabyte portion of the source code for the Windows 2000 and Windows NT 4 operating systems after they discovered the code was being traded over the internet. **16.** A study for the Global Initiative for Asthma reported that the asthma rate for British teenagers aged 13 to 14 years was the highest in the world, with 33.6 per cent suffering from the condition. **17.** A study reported in *The Times*, conducted by scientists at the University of Washington in Seattle, showed that long-term and regular users of antibiotics increased their risk of developing breast cancer by one-and-a-half times compared to those who had never taken antibiotics. **22.** The General Medical Council announced it was to investigate allegations that research by Dr Andrew Wakefield published in *The Lancet* in 1998, linking the MMR vaccine with autism, was fundamentally flawed due to a conflict of interests between Dr Wakefield's research projects at the time. **23.** The British Medical Association stated that if current trends in childhood weight gain and obesity continued, three million Britons would suffer from diabetes by 2010; twice the number recorded four years ago.

MARCH 2004

2. The European Space Agency's *Rosetta* spacecraft began a 12-year mission to land on Comet 67P/Churyumov-Gerasimenko in 2014 after an *Ariane-5* rocket carrying the probe was launched successfully from the Kourou spaceport in French Guiana. **3.** Ten of the 12 authors of the 1998 paper which linked autism with the MMR vaccine issued a retraction statement stating that while no causal link was established between the MMR vaccine and autism, the possibility of such a link had been raised. **9.** A study was published in the medical journal *The Lancet*, which announced that scientists at the Cornell University, New York, had for the first time successfully managed to conceive an embryo using tissue from a frozen human ovary. **24.** The Health Secretary John Reid announced a £1 million project to look into providing a 24-hour angioplasty service across the country, with the aim of offering patients the procedure, which unblocks arteries, within two hours of a heart attack. **28.** The world's first working 'scramjet', built by NASA, reached 5,000 mph (seven times the speed of sound) in its test flight; the flight lasted just 11 seconds and ended with a planned splashdown into the pacific ocean.

APRIL 2004

6. *The Times* reported that a study conducted by scientists in America and published in the US journal *Pediatrics* found that for every hour of television watched daily, children under two faced a 10 per cent increased risk of having attention problems by the age of seven. **16.** A team of scientists lead by Ian Bond of the Institute of Astronomy in Edinburgh announced the discovery of a planet 17,000 light years away orbiting a dwarf star in the constellation Sagittarius. **18**. A study by researchers from the University of Catania in Italy and the New York Medical College showed high concentrations of curcumin, which is present in tumeric, protected the brain against the progression of neurodegenerative diseases, such as Alzheimer's. **29**. Scientists at the Weizmann Institute in Israel, announced that they had built the world's smallest biological computer measuring just 100 nanometres across.

MAY 2004

3. Japanese car company Honda unveiled its new eco-friendly concept-car: the FCX car, which runs entirely on water-generated hydrogen gas and is completely soundless; the car looked like an ordinary car and had a top speed of 100mph. **7**. A report by Dutch scientist Jan Andries van Franeker concluded that the deaths of hundreds of seabirds on beaches along the North Norfolk coast in February were due to food shortages several months earlier; the bodies of up to 250 seabirds had been found daily mainly between Holkham and Cromer. **20**. A government-funded study published in the *Journal of Pathology* predicted that 3,800 people might be infected with vCJD. Pathologists found three cases of the prion protein responsible for vCJD in 12,500 specimens of tonsils and appendices and concluded that if this proportion was repeated throughout the country, about 3,800 people would be carrying the infective agent. **27**. It was reported in *The Times*, that a golden eagle had been successfully bred from frozen sperm via artificial insemination; the technique could be used to safeguard rare birds of prey.

JUNE 2004

1. Figures presented to Parliament by the Health Protection Agency indicated that the amount of teenagers with sexually transmitted diseases had increased. Cases of gonorrhoea in boys aged 13 to 19 more than tripled between 1995 and 2002, while cases in girls increased at almost the same rate. **8**. Between 6.19 a.m. and 12.23 p.m. the planet Venus could be seen moving across the face of the sun; the first visible 'transit' made by the planet since 6 December 1882. **9**. A well-preserved embryo of a pterosaur, dating back 121 million years, was discovered in a fossilised egg in north-eastern China. **11**. The first close-up pictures of Phoebe, one of Saturn's moons, were taken by the *Cassini* spacecraft when it flew within 2,000 km (1,240 miles) of the satellite. **18**. The first pictures of a comet taken by the *Stardust* probe, which passed within 149 miles of the nucleus of comet *Wild 2* on 2 January 2004, were published in the journal *Science*; the images showed the comet to be a rounded chunk of rock and ice, unexpectedly covered with craters, flat-topped hills and canyons. **21**. *SpaceShipOne* became the world's first manned vehicle to free itself from the Earth's gravitational pull and return to Earth immediately after it climbed to 340,000ft on gained momentum, before being steered back to Earth by 62-year old test pilot, Michael Mevill. **28**. The Government designated the New Forest as a National Park, covering an area of 220 sq. miles (571 sq. km) and with an estimated population of 38,000 it became England's first new National Park for almost half a century. **30**. It was reported in *The Times* that a 32-year old woman was 24-weeks pregnant after successfully undergoing a procedure to re-implant ovarian tissue removed and frozen prior to chemotherapy treatment for cancer which had rendered her infertile.

JULY 2004

1. The *Cassini* space probe successfully entered into a four-year orbit of Saturn. **12**. Six young red kites were freed in Tyneside as part of the £1 million Northern Kites project, led by the RSPB, to bring rare birds of prey into an urban environment. **19**. Following encouraging results from an initial clinical trial in Australia, a vaccine to treat melanoma was to be tested in Britain after the US Cancer Research Institute awarded a grant of $600,000 (£320,000) for trials to be carried out in Australia, New Zealand and Britain. **21**. At the International Conference on General Relativity and Gravitation held in Dublin Professor Stephen Hawking presented new calculations that suggest black holes are able to cast out their contents. Figures released by the Department of Health showed that abortions in England and Wales increased by 3.2 per cent in 2003 compared to 2002 figures; there were 181,600 terminations of which the majority (87 per cent) were carried out before 13 weeks. **27**. Figures released by the Health Protection Agency showed that cases of chlamydia rose by nine per cent between 2002 and 2003 while syphilis showed a 28 per cent increase, overall sexually transmitted infections rose by four per cent.

AUGUST 2004

11. The Human Fertilisation and Embryology Authority (HFEA) granted a one-year licence to a team of scientists at the University of Newcastle upon Tyne to enable them to clone human embryos for medical research into the use of embryonic stem cells for the treatment of disease. **19**. A team of scientists from the Royal Botanic Gardens at Kew and the Earthwatch Institute in Oxford published the findings of their 10-year project to catalogue and classify plant species in the forests of Cameroon. The scientists said the study had identified as many as 150 new species of which 50 had been independently scrutinised. The Government announced that an inquiry would be conducted by the Office for National Statistics in conjunction with the confidential inquiry into maternal and child health to establish why the number of stillbirths had risen for two years running after decades of decline. **26**. *The Lancet* reported that doctors at a hospital in Germany had successfully created a new jaw bone for a man – during a unique procedure. A titanium mesh was constructed from a mould of the patient's jaw and filled with bone minerals, protein and patient bone marrow which was then implanted under the patient's shoulder blade and left to grow for seven weeks.

SPORT

SEPTEMBER 2003

4. The International Skating Union (ISU) introduced a new scoring system at the annual Nebelhorn International in Oberstdorf, Germany; the new system used anonymous judging and each element of a skater's programme was scored against a base rate of difficulty. **6**. In football, England secured a 2–1 victory over Macedonia in the Euro 2004 qualifying tie, with Wayne Rooney becoming the youngest player, at 17 years and 317 days, to score a goal for England during a senior match. In tennis, Justine Henin-Hardenne reached the final of the US Open after defeating Jennifer Capriati, 4–6, 7–5, 7–6, in a gruelling three-hour match after which Henin-Hardenne was placed on a drip to recover. **8**. In cricket, England had a nine-wicket victory over South Africa at the Oval; the game was the last Test match for Alec Stewart who retired from Test cricket after the game. **9**. In athletics, Kelli White (US) was stripped of her 100 m and 200 m gold medals and $120,000 in prize-money after the International Association of Athletics Federations (IAAF) rejected her evidence in defence of a failed drugs test at the World Championships in August. **14**. Yetunde Price, the sister and personal assistant of tennis stars Venus and Serena Williams, was shot dead whilst driving through the suburb of Compton in Los Angeles. **18**. In cricket, Sussex won the county championships for the first time since the formal organisation of the championship by a governing body in 1890. **26**. Keith Mills, who devised the Air Miles programme and the Nectar loyalty card, was appointed chief executive of London's bid to host the 2012 Olympic Games. **28**. Paul Tergat (Kenya) set a new world record for the marathon when he won the Berlin Marathon in 2 hr 4 min 55 sec, taking 43 seconds off the previous record set by Khalid Khannouchi (USA) at the London Marathon in April 2002.

OCTOBER 2003

4. In horseracing, *Chivalry*, ridden by George Duffield and owned by Sir Mark Prescott, became the first horse this century to win the Tote Cambridgeshire without a previous run during the season. Paula Radcliffe won the World Half-Marathon at Vilamoura in Portugal after completing the 13.1-mile race in 1hr 7 min 35 sec; 51 seconds outside South African Elana Meyer's world best. **5**. In golf, Tiger Woods regained his position as top of the standings in the American Express World Championship after winning the final round in Atlanta, USA. **7**. In athletics, heptathlon champion Denise Lewis confirmed that she had dropped her controversial coach Dr Ekkart Arbeit, who was the lead athletics coach for East Germany during the 1970s and 80s when the state practised systematic doping of its athletes. She reinstated her former coach Charles van Commence. **10**. The Rugby Union World Cup opened in Sydney, Australia. **11**. In football, England secured a place in the Euro 2004 finals in Portugal after winning a single point for a nil-nil draw with Turkey. **12**. England beat Georgia in their opening match in the Rugby World Cup. In motor racing, Michael Schumacher won the Formula One Driver's World Championship for a record-breaking sixth time, despite finishing eighth in the Japanese Grand Prix in Suzuka. **15**. Arsenal football club and five of its players pleaded guilty to Football Association misconduct charges relating to a game played against Manchester United on 21 September 2003. **19**. In golf, Ernie Els (Australia) won the World Matchplay Championship title for the fifth time at Wentworth. **20**. In football, Sir Alex Ferguson, the manager of Manchester United, received a touchline ban for two matches and a £10,000 fine from the Football Association after he was found guilty of two charges of improper conduct and insulting or abusing match officials. **22**. British sprinter Dwain Chambers was suspended pending a hearing by UK Athletics after it was alleged that he had tested positive for the banned steroid THG. In the Rugby Union World Cup in Australia, Scottish player Martin Leslie was banned from playing for 12 weeks after being found guilty of kneeing an opponent in the head during Scotland's game against the USA two days previously. **23**. In the Rugby Union World Cup England accidentally sent on Dan Luger as a substitute back for the injured Mike Tindall who had not left the field, resulting in 16 men being present for about 30 seconds during their 35–22 victory over Samoa. **30**. After a Rugby World Cup disciplinary hearing in Sydney the England team were fined £10,000 and received a two-match touchline ban for fitness coach Dave Reddin, who was found responsible for illegally substituting Dan Luger, causing England to play with 16 men in their match against Samoa on 23 October.

NOVEMBER 2003

2. Sir Ranulph Fiennes and Mike Stroud became the first men to run seven marathons in seven days when they both finished the New York Marathon in 5 hr 25 min. In tennis, Tim Henman won the Masters Series, placing him 14th in the Association of Tennis Professionals' world rankings. **3**. Frank Bruno made his first public appearance since being released from hospital after being sectioned under the Mental Health Act on 22 September, when he led out the 10-strong England amateur boxing team for their match against the United States at York Hall in Bethnal Green, London. **8**. The 37-time champion jockey Pat Eddery retired after 37 years race-riding. **9**. The Norwegian rally driver Peter Solberg, driving a Subaru, won the World Rally Championship after taking first place in the final placings for the Wales Rally. **11**. Keith Mills, the chief executive officer for London's 2012 bid to host the Olympic Games announced that the games would be centred on a 500-acre area near Stratford in east London. **22**. England beat Australia 20–17 in the Rugby Union World Cup final in Sydney, with fly-half Jonny Wilkinson winning the match with a drop goal in the last minute of extra time.

DECEMBER 2003

8. The England rugby team celebrated its World Cup win with a victory parade in central London attended by approximately three quarters of a million people. The team attended a private reception with the Queen at Buckingham Palace in the afternoon. **14**. England rugby fly-half, Jonny Wilkinson, won the 50th BBC Sports Personality of the Year, second place went to the England rugby captain, Martin Johnson, and the 2002 winner, runner Paula Radcliffe, took third place. Rower Sir Steve Redgrave won the BBC Golden Personality award. Twenty-five-year-old Georgina Harland secured her first gold medal in a world cup final, after winning the Pentathlon world cup final in Athens. **16**. The Premiership football league agreed a deal with competition regulators in Brussels which would allow Premiership football to be screened live on terrestrial television for the first time in 10 years ending BSkyB's exclusivity deal. **19**. The Manchester United and England footballer Rio Ferdinand was given an eight-month suspension and fined £50,000 by the Football Association for failing to attend a routine drugs test on 23 September 2003. **26**. In horse racing, Jim Culloty won the Boxing Day King George VI Chase at Kempton Park on *Edredon Bleu* against odds of 25–1. **31**. In the New Year's Honours list the England Rugby coach Clive Woodward was awarded a knighthood with the rest of the team awarded MBEs; the captain, Martin Johnson, was promoted from OBE to CBE and Jonny Wilkinson, the record point-scoring fly-half, was awarded an OBE in addition to his MBE received on 10 December. The former boxer, Michael Watson, was also recognised with an MBE.

JANUARY 2004

1. Paula Radcliffe's times on road for the 10km, 20km and the London marathon in April 2003 were officially recognised as world records by the International Association of Athletics Federations. **2.** England cricketer Robert Croft announced his retirement from international cricket. **6.** The final Test match of the series between Australia and India was drawn, with Steve Waugh, Australia's captain, who retired from test cricket after the game, scoring 80 of the 357 runs of Australia's second innings. **8.** British tennis player Greg Rusedski confirmed that a sample he had provided for the Association of Tennis Professionals (ATP) had tested positive for a low concentration of nandrolone, a banned steroid. **11.** Fiona Thornewill, a 37-year-old recruitment consultant from Nottingham, completed the fastest unaided trek to the South Pole, becoming the first British woman to complete the journey alone. **13.** Former England goalkeeper David Seaman announced his retirement from football after 22 years in the game and stated that he would be leaving Manchester City immediately rather than at the end of the season due to a shoulder injury. **16.** London presented its bid to hold the 2012 Olympic Games. **17.** The England rugby captain, Martin Johnson, announced his retirement from international rugby with immediate effect; he confirmed that he would continue to play at club level for Leicester. **28.** Leeds United Football Club accepted an immediate payment of £1.5 million from Manchester United Football Club as final settlement on Rio Ferdinand's transfer, instead of £3.25 million in instalments, towards the £5 million needed by 5 p.m. on 30 January to satisfy creditors until the end of the season. **29.** Players at Leeds United Football Club agreed to have payment of 25 per cent of their wages deferred until the end of the season, raising £2.5 million towards a £5 million payment needed to stop the club from going into administration. Simon Murray, a 63-year-old British businessman became the oldest person to walk unaided to the South Pole. **31.** Belgian tennis player Justine Henin-Hardenne won the Australian Open title, her third Grand Slam title in seven months, beating Kim Clijsters 6–3, 4–6, 6–3.

FEBRUARY 2004

1. Swiss tennis player Roger Federer beat unseeded Russian, Marat Safin, in the final of the Australian Open, 7–6, 6–4, 6–2. **6.** Heavyweight boxer, Lennox Lewis, announced his retirement after 14 years in the game. **14.** The Italian former world cycling champion, 34-year-old Marco Pantani, was found dead in his hotel room in Rimini after a heart attack. **16.** The champion jockey, Tony McCoy, fractured his cheekbone in three places after a fall from his mount *Polar Red* in a novice chase at Plumpton. **20.** At the Norwich Union athletics Grand Prix in Birmingham, Kelly Holmes won the 1,000 metres, setting a new British and European record of 2 min 32.96 sec. **22.** In the football Premiership, Liverpool was defeated 1–0 by Portsmouth in their fifth round replay, forfeiting their chance to go through to the FA Cup quarter-finals. **23.** Arsenal Football Club announced that it had secured the funds to build a new £357 million, 60,000-seat stadium at Ashburton Grove. **24.** Sprinter Dwain Chambers was banned from competing for two years after he was found guilty by a UK Athletics disciplinary hearing of failing a drugs test; he tested positive for the banned steroid THG at a training camp in Germany on 1 August 2003 while preparing for the World Championships. **29.** In football,

Middlesbrough won the Carling Cup beating Bolton Wanderers 2–1.

MARCH 2004

3. Nine Leicester City footballers on a five-day training break were arrested in Spain following allegations of sexual assault made by three German women; six were later released, three without charge and three on bail, while three were detained. **6.** In the rugby union Six Nations Tournament Ireland beat world champions England, 19–13 at Twickenham, ending England's 22-match winning run at the ground. **8.** Jockey Kieren Fallon received a 21-day suspension from the Jockey Club after being found guilty for failing to ride out for first place at Lingfield Park on 29 February. **10.** The tennis player Greg Rusedski was cleared of deliberately taking the banned stimulant nandrolone after he proved before a tribunal appointed by the Association of Tennis Professionals (ATP), that the drug was contained in supplements supplied by ATP trainers. In badminton, Briton Richard Vaughan, who had recently had a hip operation, produced the best win of his career when he beat the world champion, Xia Xuanze, at the Yonex All-England Open, 15–9, 7–15, 15–10. **12.** Three Leicester City footballers, Keith Gillespie, Frank Sinclair and Paul Dickov, arrested in Spain on 3 March, flew back to Britain on bail after spending seven nights in a Spanish jail on charges of serious sexual assault. **18.** In horse racing, *Best Mate* ridden by Jim Culloty won the Cheltenham Gold Cup for the third consecutive time matching *Arkle's* 1966 record. An appeal by footballer Rio Ferdinand to reduce his eight-month ban for failing to attend a routine drugs test was rejected by the Football Association. **23.** The British adventurer David Hempleman-Adams landed in a field in Colorado, USA, and claimed a new world altitude record of ascending more than eight miles (43,000 ft) in an open basket hot air balloon. **27.** In rugby union, France won a grand slam victory in the six nations championship following their defeat of England 24–21 in Paris. In swimming, the Australian 400-metre world champion, Ian Thorpe, considered an almost certain winner at the 2004 Athens Olympics, ruled himself out of the race under the international one-start rule after a false start at the Australian Olympic trials. **28.** The 150th University Boat Race was won by Cambridge: Oxford took an early lead in the race but a clash of oars with Cambridge which momentarily unseated their bow man allowed Cambridge to establish their lead. **29.** Sven-Goran Eriksson, the England Football coach, agreed a two-year contract extension until 2008 with the Football Association.

APRIL 2004

3. In horse racing, *Amberleigh House* with odds of 16–1, ridden by Graham Lee, won the Grand National making it the fourth time trainer Ginger McCain had won the event. **5.** American Steve Fossett and his multinational 12-man crew circumnavigated the globe in 58 days 9 hr 32 min 45 sec becoming the first sailors to complete the feat in less than 60 days. **11.** In golf, Phil Mickelson won the Masters championship by one stroke from Ernie Els. **12.** Brian Lara made cricketing history during the Fourth West Indies Test against England when he declared at 400 runs not out, reclaiming the record from Matthew Hayden (Australia) for the highest amount of runs scored in a test game. **14.** In cricket, England won the final match in Antigua in the four-match Test series against the West Indies, winning the series 3–0. **18.** In the London

Marathon, Tracey Morris, a 36-year optician from Leeds, who had never completed a marathon before, qualified for the Athens Olympics after completing the course in 2 hr 33 min 52 sec, coming 10th in the London women's race and the first British woman to finish. **21.** Ron Atkinson, the former Manchester United manager, sports broadcaster and newspaper columnist, resigned from ITV after a racist remark made following the European Cup semi-final between Chelsea and Monaco, was broadcast in parts of the Middle East from ITV footage not aired in the UK. **25.** In motor racing Jenson Button finished second at the San Marino Grand Prix, after losing his pole position to Michael Schumacher. **27.** Des Wilson resigned from the England and Wales Cricket Board after disagreeing with colleagues over the apolitical line taken by the International Cricket Council to the sport in Zimbabwe.

MAY 2004

2. William Fox-Pitt qualified his horse *Tamarillo* for the Olympic Games in Athens after taking first place at the Badminton Horse Trials. **3.** In snooker, Ronnie O'Sullivan won the £250,000 first prize in the Embassy World Championship at Sheffield's Crucible Theatre after defeating Graeme Dott 18–8. **4.** In Formula One motor racing, 10 team principals voted unanimously in favour of new rules put forward by the FIA, the sport's governing body, to outlaw high-technology cars by the beginning of the 2006 season; the move was expected to save the sport at least £300 million a year. **9.** In motor-racing, Michael Schumacher won the Spanish Grand Prix, his fifth successive victory of the season. **10.** The Zimbabwe Cricket Union (ZCU) terminated the contracts of 15 of its white cricketers following a disciplinary hearing regarding their protests against the political regime in Zimbabwe during the cricket World Cup in 2003. **15.** In football, Arsenal beat Leicester 2–1 completing an entire league season unbeaten. **18.** The International Olympic Committee announced that five cities, London, Madrid, Moscow, New York and Paris, had been short-listed to host the 2012 Olympic Games. **22.** In football, Manchester United won the FA Cup, their 11th FA Cup triumph. **21.** In cricket, Andrew Strauss scored a century in his Test debut at Lord's against New Zealand, becoming one of four batsmen in world cricket to achieve the feat. **25.** In the French Open, Fabrice Santoro defeated Arnaud Clément, 6–4, 6–3, 6–7, 3–6, 16–14, in six hours and 33 minutes, setting a record for the longest tennis match ever played. **26.** In football, Porto beat Monaco 3–0 to win the Champions League. **27.** The former England cricket captain, Nasser Hussain, announced his retirement from Test and first class cricket just three days after scoring a match winning century in the first Test against New Zealand at Lord's.

JUNE 2004

4. In tennis, Tim Henman reached the semi-final of the French Open where he was beaten 3–6, 6–4, 6–0, 7–5 by Argentinean Guilermo Coria. **6.** Guilermo Coria was defeated in the final of the French Open by fellow Argentinean Gaston Gaudio, ranked at number 44 in the world. **10.** The England Cricket Board (ECB) announced that England would go ahead with its one-day series against Zimbabwe in the autumn, despite the indefinite postponement of its Test matches. Failure to fulfil the three limited-overs matches would leave the ECB open to a fine of about £1.1 million and the

possibility of suspension from the international game. **12.** In football, Greece beat host nation Portugal 2–1 in the opening game of the Euro 2004 championship. **14.** In England, more than 100 football fans were arrested and eight police forces had to call out reserve officers to curb rioting in towns and cities throughout England following England's defeat by France in the Euro 2004 championship; Portugese police reported no incidents. **16.** Eleven England football fans appeared in court in Albufeira, Portugal, after violent clashes between fans broke-out in the region. **17.** Ten England football fans arrived back in the UK after being voluntarily deported from Portugal following their court appearances on 16 June. In England's second match of the Euro 2004 championship, Wayne Rooney scored two goals for England resulting in a 3–0 win over Switzerland. **20.** Long-distance runner, Paula Radcliffe, returned to the track for the first time in almost two years in the European Cup women's 5,000 metres, winning the race in 14 min 29.11 sec; breaking her own British and Commonwealth record. **21.** England qualified for the quarter-finals of the Euro 2004 championship in Portugal after it beat Croatia 4–2. In tennis, Martina Navratilova, aged 47, beat Colombian, Catalina Castrano, 6–0, 6–1, on the first day of the Wimbledon tournament. **24.** England went out of the Euro 2004 championship defeated in extra time on penalties by the host nation Portugal; final score 2–2 (1–1 after 90 minutes, 6–5 on penalties). **30.** Tim Henman was defeated 7–6, 6–4, 6–2 in his eighth quarter-final of nine Wimbledon championship attempts by Croatian Mario Ancic.

JULY 2004

1. In football, a goal by Traianos Dellas in the first period of extra time secured a 1–0 win by Greece over the Czech Republic in the semi-final of the Euro 2004 Championship and took Greece into the final against the host nation Portugal. **3.** Maria Sharapova (Russia), beat Serena Williams (USA) to win the Wimbledon women's singles final, 6–1, 6–4, to become the second youngest winner of the championship. **4.** Greece won the Euro 2004 Football Championship, its first win in an international competition, beating favourites Portugal 1–0. In tennis, Roger Federer (Switzerland) defeated Andy Roddick (US) in four sets; 4–6, 7–5, 7–6, 6–4, to take his second Wimbledon men's title. **6.** Roads in Central London were closed to allow Formula One cars to race through the streets, an estimated 300,000 people turned out to watch the event and police had to turn away thousands more. The Mayor of London, Ken Livingstone announced a £20 million bid to stage the British Formula One Grand Prix in London in place of Silverstone in Northampton. **14.** St Lucia won the right to hold England's first-round matches in the 2007 Cricket World Cup; the England management team had identified St Lucia as its first choice to host the tournament because of its impressive facilities. **18.** In golf, Todd Hamilton (USA) won the Open Championship at Royal St George's, beating the world no. 2 and pre-tournament favourite, Ernie Els. **25.** Lance Armstrong set a new record when he rode into Paris to claim his sixth Tour de France victory.

AUGUST 2004

1. Mark Palios resigned as chief executive of the Football Association (FA) following allegations that he had a relationship with FA secretary Faria Alam and then had tried to cover-up the affair. In golf, Karen Stupples won her first major championship at the Weetabix Women's British Open at Sunningdale. **3.** Manchester United midfielder Paul Scholes announced his retirement from international football; he won 66 caps for England and scored 14 goals. **7.** The Irish Sports Council confirmed that distance runner, Cathal Lombard, who had qualified for the men's 5,000m and 10,000m at the Athens Olympics, had tested positive for the banned substance EPO. **8.** Six days away from completing a transatlantic crossing by rowing boat, four British oarsmen had to abandon ship when a rogue wave split their boat in half; the crew were rescued six hours later from their life-raft by a Danish cargo ship. The former French rugby captain, Marc Cécillon, was taken into custody after allegedly shooting his wife dead at a party attended by about 60 people at St Savin in central France. **14.** On the first day of the Olympic Games Britain's first medal was won by Leon Taylor and Peter Waterfield who took silver in the 10m synchronised diving. **18.** At the Olympics Great Britain's Helen Reeves won bronze in the canoeing, Alison Williamson became the first woman archer to win a medal since 1908, taking bronze and the Great Britain Equestrian team won a bronze medal in the three-day event. **19.** Great Britain won its first gold medal in the Olympic Games for sailing; Shirley Robertson's team won the title in the Yngling keelboat class. **20.** Chris Hoy secured Great Britain's second Olympic gold medal in the 1km cycling time trial. **21.** At the Olympics, Great Britain won four gold medals in eight hours; Matthew Pinsent's team took the rowing, Ben Ainslie Finn class sailing, Bradley Wiggins the 4,000 m cycling pursuit and Leslie Law in the individual equestrian competition after an appeal committee upheld penalties against Germany's Bettina Hoy. **22.** Runner Paula Radcliffe, Britain's favourite for a gold medal, failed to complete the Women's Olympic marathon after collapsing at 36 km. **23.** Kelly Holmes won the Olympic women's 800 m gold medal by five hundredths of a second, beating defending champion Maria Mutola. Amir Khan, aged 17, guaranteed himself and Britain a bronze medal in the Olympic lightweight boxing division after reaching the semi-finals in Athens. **27.** For the second time at the Olympic Games, runner Paula Radcliffe dropped out of a race when she failed to complete the 10,000 metres. **28.** Kelly Holmes secured her second Olympic Gold medal for Great Britain in the 1500 metres and became the third woman in Olympic history to win gold in both events. **29.** Britain's Amir Khan won Olympic Boxing silver after losing 30–22 to Cuban Mario Kindelan in the lightweight final on the final day of the 2004 Olympic Games in Athens.

INTERNATIONAL EVENTS

AFRICA

SEPTEMBER 2003
1. In Kenya, an estimated 300 tourists were evacuated from four blazing hotels in Mombasa. **2.** 243 Moroccan soldiers captured by the Polisario Front in the mid-1970s, were released. Zimbabwe's opposition Movement for Democratic Change (MDC) won a victory in local elections. **13.** At least 18 Somali asylum seekers drowned and 27 were missing after they were forced from their ship when it arrived off the coast of Yemen. **18.** The president of Guinea Bissau, Kumba Yala, resigned from

his position. **26.** In Morocco, twin sisters aged 14 appeared in court charged with planning attacks against the king and royal family and of plotting to blow up parliament and a supermarket. **27.** In Côte d'Ivoire, at least 23 people were shot dead during a raid on a bank in the rebel stronghold of Bouake. It was unclear as to whether the dead were civilians or soldiers. It was announced that Algerian armed forces had killed 150 Islamic rebels during a two-week crackdown on the GSPC which is blamed for the kidnap of western tourists.

OCTOBER 2003
7. The United Nations announced that its peacekeeping troops in the north-eastern region of the Congo had uncovered a mass grave containing the bodies of 65 people, including 40 children. The victims were all from the Hema tribe and the UN believed that the rival Lendu tribe were behind the attack. A bush fire, believed to have been started by poachers, destroyed three quarters of Zimbabwe's Matopos National Park. **8.** Riot police arrested 40 trade unionists, including Lovemore Matombo, the president of the Zimbabwe Congress of Trade Unions, for demonstrating against high taxation and human rights abuses under President Robert Mugabe. **14.** South Africa's Constitutional Court passed a landmark judgement to restore ownership of ancestral lands and award compensation to the Richtersveld people, who were forcibly removed from their land by British colonial authorities; the diamond-rich territory is worth almost £1 billion.

NOVEMBER 2003
8. Maaoya Sid'Ahmed Ould Taya was re-elected president of Mauritania. **9.** The Sudanese army, also known as the Sudan Liberation Movement, announced that it had killed more than 60 people in attacks in the Darfur region of the country. **10.** Zimbabwe's first black president, Canaan Banana, died aged 67 after a long illness; he ruled the country between 1980 and 1987. **12.** Eugene Terre'Blanche, the leader of the South African white supremacist organisation, the Afrikaner Resistance Movement, was convicted of political crimes after he admitted ordering five bombings in the run-up to the first post-apartheid elections. **17.** Thirteen people were killed when a cargo plane exploded in the air near the city of Wau in southern Sudan. **25.** President Obasanjo of Nigeria announced that Zimbabwe's President Mugabe would not be allowed to attend the Commonwealth summit in Nigeria between 5–8 December. **27.** In the Congo, 163 people drowned after the *Dieu Merci* capsized during a storm on Lake Mai-Ndombe.

DECEMBER 2003
4. Interpol issued an international arrest warrant for the former Liberian President, Charles Taylor, on charges related to his support in the 1990s for the Sierra Leone rebels. **7.** President Mugabe of Zimbabwe announced that the country had unilaterally withdrawn from the Commonwealth after Commonwealth officials requested that Mr Mugabe's Zanu (PF) Party hold talks with the opposition Movement for Democratic Change Party. In Cairo, a western Sudanese rebel group claimed they had killed about 700 government troops in the Darfur region of the country. **16.** In Mogadishu, Somalia, around 34 people were killed and 80 wounded in clashes between the rival Dir and Marehan clans. **19.** Colonel Gaddafi signed an agreement that Libya would disclose and dismantle all weapons of mass destruction. **25.** Official

results were published showing that President Conte of Guinea won 95.63 per cent of the vote and was elected for a third term following presidential elections on 21 December. In Benin, at least 82 people died when a passenger aircraft clipped a building after take-off and crashed into the sea. **28.** The former president of Mauritania, Mohamed Khouna Ould Haidallah, was given a five-year suspended jail sentence and fined £1,250 for plotting a coup to overthrow President Maaoya Sid'Ahmed Ould Taya during the elections.

JANUARY 2004

3. A Boeing 737, which had just taken off from the resort of Sharm el-Sheikh in Egypt, crashed into the Red Sea a few minutes after take-off, killing all 148 passengers and crew. **9.** Libya agreed to pay £1 million to each of the families of the people who died in 1989 when a bomb planted on a French airliner killed 170 people. **22.** Jean de Dieu Kamuhanda, a minister of the Rwandan Government during the 1994 ethnic genocide, was sentenced to life imprisonment by a UN court in Tanzania after he was found guilty of charges of crimes against humanity. **30.** South Africa's President Thabo Mbeki approved the new Land Rights Amendments Act, which allows the government to seize the land of white farmers from which black people were forcibly evicted by the former colonial and apartheid authorities. **31.** A ferry was destroyed by fire and 200 people were feared dead 280 miles from Kinshasa on the Congo River.

FEBRUARY 2004

3. Forty people drowned in western Uganda after a boat capsized on Lake Albert because of bad weather and overcrowding. **22.** In Uganda, the Lord's Resistance Army (LRA) from southern Sudan killed 192 people at a camp for displaced civilians in Ogur. **23.** Military officials from the Democratic Republic of Congo announced that around 100 civilians had been killed since January by peasant Mai Mai fighters. **24.** An earthquake killed around 600 people and injured around 300 more when it hit near the Moroccan city of al-Hoceima. **25.** Religious violence broke out in the town of Yelwa in central Nigeria and 48 Christians were killed by Muslims.

MARCH 2004

5. In Rwanda, nine people were sentenced to death and one to life in jail for the murder of Emile Ntahimana, who was killed to prevent him from giving evidence against suspects of the 1994 genocide. **6.** The White House announced that Libya had sent all its remaining nuclear arms equipment to the USA. **8.** Eighteen people died and around 50,000 were made homeless after cyclone Gafilo struck Madagascar. **21.** In Sudan, an Arab militia group executed 49 residents of the town of Korma in the Darfur region; 100 people died in a separate incident when rebels from the Sudan Liberation Movement fought with militia groups known as Janjaweed fighters. The Ugandan army announced that it had killed 52 Lord's Resistance Army rebels who had been killing and torturing civilians in northern Uganda. **25.** Tony Blair was the first British Prime Minister since Winston Churchill to visit Libya when he met Colonel Muammar Gaddafi in Tripoli to discuss the agreement to exchange intelligence information on terrorism. **28.** It was announced that more than 300 people had died in clashes between protesters and security forces during a rally against President Gbagbo in Cote d'Ivoire. Government forces defeated a

coup by fighters loyal to Mobutu Sese Seko, against President Kabila of the Democratic Republic of Congo in Kinshasa, where fighting broke out at military bases and television headquarters.

APRIL 2004

8. It was reported that 63 people had died of starvation in one month in Zimbabwe's second largest city, Bulawayo. A cease-fire agreement was signed between representatives of the Sudanese government and rebel fighters from the western Darfur region of the country, allowing humanitarian agencies 45 days to reach a peace agreement. **9.** In Algeria, President Abdelaziz Bouteflika received 83 per cent of the vote during national elections and was given a second five-year term in office. **14.** In Zanzibar, parliament unanimously passed a bill to outlaw homosexuality, with jail terms of up to 25 years being passed on anyone involved in a gay male relationship. **27.** In South Africa, President Thabo Mbeki was sworn in for a second five-year term after his African National Congress party won its biggest ever landslide. The former prime minister of Guinea, Sidya Touré, was arrested for allegedly plotting to kill President Conté and overthrow the country's parliament. **30.** It was reported that around 120 Muslims and Christians had died in fighting in six farming villages in Nigeria.

MAY 2004

6. Kenya's police commissioner removed 57 senior officers from their positions following accusations of crime and corruption in the force; it was the largest reform of the police force since Kenya gained independence in 1963. **13.** In the northern Nigerian city of Kano, around 600 people were killed in riots between Christians and Muslims. **18.** The Ugandan army reported that its helicopter gunships had killed 54 members of the rebel Lord's Resistance Army.

JUNE 2004

1. At least 20 people were killed and 50 others wounded as clan militias fought for control of Beledhawo, a town on the border between Somalia and Kenya. **11.** In the Democratic Republic of Congo, Major Eric Lenge led a failed coup to overthrow President Kabila. **13.** The newly elected president of Malawi, Bingu wa Mutharika, appointed 20 ministers to his Cabinet, including members of opposition parties. **17.** At the United Nations International Criminal Tribunal for Rwanda in Tanzania, Sylvestre Gacumbitsi, a former district mayor in Rwanda, was sentenced to 30 years in jail for ordering the slaughter of 20,000 Tutsis during the 1994 Rwandan genocide.

JULY 2004

2. The Zimbabwean opposition leader, Morgan Tsvangirai, was attacked by supporters of President Robert Mugabe while he was giving a speech north of Harare. **18.** It was reported that around 1 million people had been displaced and at least 30,000 killed in the Darfur region of Sudan – pro-government Arab militias were being accused of ethnic cleansing and genocide in the region. **28.** The African Union announced that it planned to send peacekeeping troops into the Darfur region of Sudan.

AUGUST 2004

2. Sudan refused to co-operate with the UN's 30-day deadline for disarming the Janjaweed militia and announced that it would fight any foreign forces entering the country. **6.** Sudan's foreign minister Mustapha Osman Ismail announced that the country had accepted the United Nations resolution on Darfur to curb gunmen from the Janjaweed militia within 30 days. **8.** South Africa's National Party leader Marthinus van Schalkwyk announced that he would apply to join the African National Congress and that all other party members should do the same. **10.** Around 480 people in the Darfur refugee camps in Sudan were reported to have contracted hepatitis E. **14.** It was reported that around 159 Tutsi men, women and children were murdered during a raid on Gatumba refugee camp in Burundi – the country's Hutu rebel National Liberation Forces claimed responsibility. **15.** In Sudan, 150 Rwandans arrived as part of the African Union's mission to keep the peace in the Darfur region. **25.** Sir Mark Thatcher, the son of former prime minister Margaret Thatcher, was arrested at his home in Cape Town, South Africa, on suspicion of helping to fund a coup attempt in the state of Equatorial Guinea. **30.** In Somalia, the last 258 members of a new national assembly were sworn in.

THE AMERICAS

SEPTEMBER 2003

5. Hurricane Fabian battered Bermuda in the worst storm to hit the country in 50 years. **7.** A tape aired on Arabic television stated that there would be attacks on the US or US interests abroad on a more destructive scale than those of 11 September 2001. **11.** The names of people that died in the World Trade Centre on 11 September 2001 were read out by children who had lost a parent in the attacks, during a ceremony held at Ground Zero in Manhattan, New York. **14.** In Colombia, eight foreign tourists were kidnapped by left-wing rebels in a mountainous region in the north of the country. **17.** In Seattle, residents voted against a 10 per cent rise in tax on coffee. The tax was to be used to fund better child day-care for poor families. **21.** Seven people were killed near the Grand Canyon after their helicopter crashed. **24.** Matthew Scott, a Briton kidnapped in Colombia by anti-government forces, escaped and was taken to safety after wandering through rain forest for 12 days. Seven hostages remained in captivity.

OCTOBER 2003

2. A court in Alexandria, Virginia, ruled that Zacarias Moussaoui, the only person charged with being involved in the terrorist attacks of 11 September 2001, may not be executed. **8.** Arnold Schwarzenegger was elected governor of California after he received 48 per cent of the vote; the previous governor, Gray Davis received 45 per cent of the vote. The White House announced that it would be imposing economic and diplomatic sanctions on Syria after President George Bush said that the country was 'on the wrong side in the war on terrorism'. **9.** The US under-secretary of state, John Bolton, extended the members of America's 'axis of evil' to include Syria, Libya and Cuba, stating that all three countries were intent on developing weapons of mass destruction and were a threat to America and its allies. **12.** Twelve people were killed in Bolivia during riots in El Alto over the export of natural gas to Chile. **15.** Ten people were killed and dozens injured after a ferry smashed into the pier at Staten Island harbour in New York as it was docking; the boat's pilot had to undergo surgery after he fled to his home immediately after the

crash and slit his wrists. **17.** The President of Bolivia, Sanches de Lozada, agreed to resign after weeks of protests over plans to sell natural gas to the US led to violence in La Paz and more than 80 people died in riots; Vice-President Mesa was sworn in as the new president. **19.** Foreign ministers at the Asia-Pacific Economic Co-operation forum meeting in Bangkok agreed to President Bush's plea to impose stricter controls on portable surface-to-air missiles, which are hampering the coalition reconstruction efforts in Iraq. **21.** The United States senate voted 64 to 34 in favour of banning a form of late-term abortion. **26.** Fires in southern California destroyed at least 650 homes and killed 11 people after powerful winds stoked a string of blazes across the state. **28.** Iyman Faris was jailed for 20 years at a court in Virginia for planning terrorist acts, including a plot to cut through cables supporting the Brooklyn Bridge.

NOVEMBER 2003

5. Gary Ridgway became America's most prolific serial killer after he pleaded guilty to the murders of 48 women between 1982 and 1998; he had originally pleaded not guilty to seven counts of murder but changed his plea after making a deal with prosecutors to escape the death penalty in return for guiding investigators to the remains of other victims. **12.** Five of Colombia's top policemen, including Teodoro Campo, the chief of Colombia's national police, lost their jobs after it was found that they had used government money to buy watches, works of art and other luxuries over a period of three years. **16.** The democrat Kathleen Babineaux Blanco was elected as the governor of Louisiana and became the first female governor of the state after she beat her Republican opponent Bobby Jindal. **25.** In Colombia, 850 members of the paramilitary group Bloque Cacique Nutibara surrendered their weapons to Luis Carlos Restrepo, the government's peace commissioner.

DECEMBER 2003

2. President Chavez of Venezuela rejected the results of a four-day petition by opposition leaders, which called for a recall referendum to remove him from power. **7.** In Managua, the former Nicaraguan President, Arnoldo Aleman, was jailed for 20 years after being found guilty of money-laundering, fraud, embezzlement and electoral crimes. **12.** Canadian Prime Minister Jean Chretien stepped down from his post after 10 years; the former finance minister Paul Martin was appointed to take over. **23.** In Virginia, Lee Malvo, 18, the accomplice of the 'Washington Sniper' John Muhammad, was sentenced to life imprisonment after being convicted of one charge of terrorism, one of murdering two people and one firearm charge. **29.** Oscar Berger of the Grand National Alliance won Guatemala's presidential elections with 54.1 per cent of the vote.

JANUARY 2004

4. In Quito, Ecuador, the senior commander in the Revolutionary Armed Forces of Colombia, Ricardo Palmera, was captured and charged with 59 crimes including kidnapping and murder. **12.** In Haiti, parliament was forced to close down after the mandate of MPs expired and government failed to hold new elections; President Jean-Bertrand Aristide refused calls to stand down.

FEBRUARY 2004

9. In Haiti, 40 people were killed as armed rebels belonging to the Artibonite Resistance Front took over nine towns in an attempt to drive out President Aristide. **19.** Argentina was brought to a standstill by more than 50,000 protesters who took to the country's main highways to demand the repudiation of the country's foreign debt after its economy collapsed in December 2001. The Canadian government agreed to pay £20 million compensation to 2,000 former soldiers exposed to mustard gas and other chemical weapons during the Second World War. **22.** In Haiti, more than 200 anti-government rebels captured the second largest city in the country, Cap-Haitien. Forty-two people died in north-eastern Brazil when the bus they were on veered off the road and plunged into a reservoir. **24.** The United States charged two men held at its Guantanamo Bay prison camp with conspiracy to commit war crimes; Ali Hamza Ahmed Sulayman al-Bahlul and Ibrahim Ahmed Mahmoud al-Qosi were the first men from the camp to be formally charged and were expected to be the first prisoners to face the special military tribunals created by President Bush. **26.** The United States lifted its ban on Americans travelling to Libya after Tripoli reaffirmed its guilt over the Lockerbie bombing. **29.** In Haiti, President Aristide fled the country after he resigned following violent civil unrest in the country; Louis Jodel Chamblain and his Rebel Army took control of most cities and towns in the country and President Bush announced that 500 US Marines were being sent to keep the peace.

MARCH 2004

2. Violent protests erupted across cities in Venezuela after the National Electoral Council announced that President Chavez would not be forced to submit to a referendum over his rule. **4.** Haiti's former President, Jean-Bertrand Aristide, was offered permanent asylum by the Central African Republic. **9.** The Washington sniper, John Allen Muhammad, was sentenced to death for the killing of Dean Harold Meyers on 9 October 2002. **10.** Lee Boyd Malvo, the teenager involved in the Washington sniper shootings, was sentenced to life imprisonment in court in Chesapeake, Virginia. **12.** Chile's parliament voted in favour of legalising divorce, making it the last country in the Western world to do so. **14.** Police in California announced that they had discovered nine dead bodies, eight of them children aged between 1 and 17, after searching the home of 57-year-old Marcus Wesson, who was believed to have fathered two of the victims with another of his daughters. **17.** Haiti's new government was sworn in by President Boniface Alexandre at Haiti's National Palace; Gerard Latortue was appointed Prime Minister. **24.** Baldwin Spencer became the new Prime Minister of Antigua and Barbuda following a landslide victory in elections for his United Progressive Party.

APRIL 2004

6. In Mexico, President Fox declared a state of emergency after flash floods in the town of Piedras Negras killed 31 people and left dozens more missing and without homes. **12.** The Canadian government approved the killing of 350,000 harp seals off the northern coast of Newfoundland after years of reduced quotas lead to an increase in the seal population of over 5 million; the cull was given backing in order to restore the cod population and to provide income to one of Canada's poorest regions.

MAY 2004

3. Martin Torrijos won Panama's first presidential election since the handover of the Panama Canal and the withdrawal of US troops in December 1999. **11.** A film was broadcast on the internet which showed Nick Berg, an American, identifying himself before being executed by militants with links to al-Qa'eda. **17.** Marriages between same-sex couples became legal in the American state of Massachusetts, the only US state to have introduced such legislation. A fire at a jail in San Pedro Sula, Honduras, killed 101 prisoners and injured 27 others. **26.** Terry Nichols was convicted of the murder of 161 people in the Oklahoma City bombing in April 1995 by a court in Oklahoma; he had previously been convicted of involuntary manslaughter and conspiracy in the deaths of eight federal law enforcement officials. Around 579 people were killed and 3,000 more left homeless in Haiti and the Dominican Republic after 10 days of flash floods.

JUNE 2004

1. Inmates at the Benfica Penitentiary in Rio de Janeiro murdered around 50 fellow prisoners following a week-long rebellion demanding increased visiting rights. **3.** The former prime minister of the Ukraine, Pavlo Lazarenko, was convicted by a court in San Francisco of using his position to extort money and launder it through Californian banks. **11.** The state funeral of former US president Ronald Reagan took place in Washington National Cathedral and was attended by Mikhail Gorbachev and Baroness Thatcher amongst others. **13.** Two shanty-town fires in Sao Paulo, Brazil, destroyed around 177 shacks and left 600 people homeless. **15.** In French Polynesia, the pro-independence Oscar Temaru, was elected leader of the island, replacing the conservative Gaston Flosse, who had held the position for 20 years. **29.** In Canada, the Liberals won 134 seats, while the Conservatives won 99 seats in the general election, leaving the Bloc Quebecois Party and the New Democratic Party as the ruling parties in parliament.

JULY 2004

14. The US Senate rejected President George W. Bush's appeal for constitutional amendment to ban same-sex marriage. **22.** The 9/11 Commission published its report into the September 11 attacks after 20 months of investigations. The report criticised both Bill Clinton's and George W. Bush's administrations for failing to combat the threat of terrorism as well as highlighting 10 missed opportunities to detect the September 11 plot, and concluded that there was no 'collaborative link' between Iraq and al-Qa'eda. **23.** The United States Congress declared that the killings in the Darfur region of Sudan were genocide stating that Khartoum's Arab regime was carrying out a genocidal campaign against the black African population; Congress also urged President George W. Bush to send military troops to the region.

AUGUST 2004

1. At least 236 people died and dozens were injured when a fire broke out in a supermarket in the Paraguayan capital of Asuncion. **3.** Lynndie England appeared before a military court in Fort Bragg, North Carolina on charges of abusing Iraqi prisoners in the Abu Ghraib prison in Baghdad – if convicted she faced up to 38 years in prison. **4.** Richard Smith pleaded guilty to manslaughter and to lying about his medical history after the Staten Island ferry he was operating hit a pier and killed 11 people in

October 2003. **12**. California's supreme court voided 4,000 same-sex marriages sanctioned by the mayor of San Francisco after it declared that legislation defined marriage as a union between man and woman. **13**. It was announced that President George W. Bush would order the withdrawal of 170,000 US troops and military staff from Europe and Asia. **14**. President George W. Bush declared a state of emergency in Florida after Hurricane Charley left at least 15 people dead and hundreds more missing and homeless. **16**. In Venezuela, President Hugo Chavez won more than 58 per cent of a ballot in a referendum on his rule. **22**. International observers endorsed the referendum results that gave Venezuelan President Hugo Chavez a victory following allegations that the elections were rigged. **26**. Chile's Supreme Court voted by nine to eight to lift General Augusto Pinochet's immunity from prosecution allowing victims of repression to take him to court. **29**. In New York, more than 120,000 protesters took part in demonstrations against President George W. Bush and his Republican Party who were arriving in the city for the Republican convention.

ASIA

SEPTEMBER 2003

3. In Afghanistan, an alleged al-Qa'eda suspect believed to be responsible for the suicide bombing of a German army bus, was captured in Kabul. **6**. In two incidents in Kashmir, at least six people died after a car bomb exploded at a market in Srinagar. **10**. More than 1,000 Nepalese pro-democracy protesters, including a former prime minister, were arrested in Kathmandu as police broke up a demonstration against the King. **18**. Ali Imron, responsible for the bombings in Bali of October 2002, was sentenced to life imprisonment. **22**. In India, Dara Singh, a Hindu extremist accused of killing an Australian missionary and his two young children in 1999, was sentenced to death by a court in Orissa. **25**. Two huge earthquakes hit northern Japan causing widespread damage and raised fears of tsunami. **27**. Aung San Suu Kyi, the Burmese opposition leader, was returned to house arrest after being discharged from hospital where she had undergone surgery. **29**. The world's oldest man died in southern Japan, aged 114.

OCTOBER 2003

2. Heavy fighting erupted in Afghanistan and Pakistan as Pakistan launched its largest offensive to date against al-Qa'eda near the Afghan border. The last of four main suspects in the Bali nightclub bombings of October 2002, Ali Ghufron, was sentenced to death. North Korea claimed that it had finished reprocessing 8,000 plutonium fuel rods. **7**. North Korea announced that it would bar Japan from any future negotiations on its nuclear programme in a move that threatened to undermine months of work aimed at disarming the country. **9**. In Indonesia, around 54 schoolchildren died when their coach crashed into a lorry in East Java. **12**. Families gathered on Kuta beach in Bali to mark the first anniversary of the terrorist attacks that killed 202 people. **15**. China became the third nation to send a man into space when the *Shenzhou 5* spacecraft lifted off from the Gobi Desert base at 9 a.m. and orbited the Earth 14 times in 21 hours before landing in Inner Mongolia. **17**. The world's tallest building, the Taipei 101 tower, was unveiled in Taiwan. Its full height is 1,671 ft (509 metres). **18**. Three people were jailed for 10 years in Karachi for carrying out an assassination attempt on

President Pervez Musharraf. **22**. India announced that it would reverse its Kashmir policy and hold talks with the separatists for the first time in 13 years. **29**. Tomomasa Nakagawa, a senior member of the Aum Shinrikyo cult, was sentenced to death for his part in the murder of 24 people. **30**. Javed Hashmi, the leader of the Alliance for the Restoration of Democracy in Pakistan, was arrested on a charge of treason after he criticised the Pakistani military for failing to restore democracy. 'Tohir', one of the men wanted for the Bali bombing, was arrested by a police near Jakarta in Cirebon as he was preparing to carry out another two suicide bombings. Prime Minister Datuk Seri Dr Mahathir Mohamad of Malaysia retired after 22 years in the post.

NOVEMBER 2003

3. A flash flood in Bukit Lawang, northern Sumatra, killed 71 people and 98 others were missing, feared dead. **5**. Sri Lankan President Chandrika Kumaratunga imposed a state of emergency after she suspended parliament and sacked the defence, interior and information ministers from the cabinet. **8**. In Myanmar, the pro-democracy campaigner Aung San Suu Kyi was released from house arrest but refused to accept liberty until 35 of her colleagues were released. **9**. In Japan, the governing coalition party, the Democratic Party of Japan, won the most votes in the general election and Junichiro Koizumi was re-elected Prime Minister. **14**. Norway pulled out of efforts to revive peace talks in Sri Lanka and said they would not be involved until the Sri Lankan Prime Minister and President settled their political differences. A gas explosion in a mine in Jiangxi province in eastern China killed 48 miners, bringing the death toll in Chinese mines up to 4,000 for the year. **23**. Zafarullah Khan Jamali, the Prime Minister of Pakistan, announced a cease-fire with India on the Line of Control, which separates the Himalayan region of Kashmir. **27**. In Taiwan, Parliament approved legislation to allow referendums to be held on constitutional change.

DECEMBER 2003

4. India's ruling party, the Bharatiya Janata Party, won over the Hindi states of Madhya Pradesh, Rajasthan and Chattisgarh from the Congress Party in state legislative elections. **9**. Japanese Prime Minister Junichiro Koizumi announced that 1,000 Japanese troops would be dispatched to Iraq making it the first military deployment since the Second World War. **14**. President Pervez Musharraf of Pakistan escaped an assassination attempt after a bomb exploded under a bridge over which his car had just passed. **25**. It was reported that 190 people had died in a natural gas explosion in south-western China on 23 December. President Pervez Musharraf of Pakistan survived a second assassination attempt after two trucks packed with explosives drove into the President's motorcade in Rawalpindi. **29**. In Pakistan, the Lower House approved constitutional changes to give the president the power to disband parliament and dismiss the prime minister.

JANUARY 2004

6. Sixteen people were killed in Afghanistan when two bombs exploded in the city of Kandahar near an army barracks. **14**. The World Health Organisation announced that avian flu could become deadlier than SARS after three people died from it in Vietnam and a further five possible cases were discovered. **22**. The Indian Deputy

Prime Minister, Lal Krishna Advani, and the Kashmiri separatist coalition, the All Party Hurriyat Conference, agreed that all violence in Kashmir should end and pledged to meet in March to agree terms. **25.** Indonesia reported cases of avian flu, making it the seventh country in Asia to have been infected; other countries that had confirmed the existence of avian flu included Thailand, Vietnam, Cambodia, Taiwan, South Korea and Japan. **26.** Afghanistan's new constitution became law, making it a democratic Islamic state with a two-chamber parliament. **27.** Indian Prime Minister Atal Behari Vajpayee and his Cabinet asked for parliament to be dissolved on 6 February in preparation for an early national election. **28.** In southern Thailand, more than 1,000 schools were closed and Buddhist monks evacuated temples after attacks by Muslim extremists left eight people dead.

FEBRUARY 2004

12. Kasitah Gaddam, Malaysia's Land Minister, was arrested on charges of corruption after he had been accused of accepting bribes in multimillion share deals. **15.** Fifty-three people died and more than 60 were injured in a fire at the Zhongbai Commercial Plaza in Jilin, and a further 39 people died in a fire at a Buddhist temple at Haining in Zhejiang province. **16.** In Bangladesh, violent clashes between the opposition Awami League and the government over crime control and allegedly looted public money, lead to 140 people being injured. **23.** The Indonesian Health Ministry announced that 227 people had died since the beginning of an outbreak of dengue fever on 1 January. **24.** In India, more than 2 million workers in banks and state-owned companies went on strike in protest at a Supreme Court order banning strikes. **27.** Shoko Asahara, the founder of the Aum Shinrikyo cult which carried out the sarin nerve gas attack on the Tokyo subway in 1995, was sentenced to death for multiple charges of murder at Tokyo District Court. In the Philippines, a ferry travelling from Manila to Bacolod caught fire following several explosions; 110 people were missing, feared dead.

MARCH 2004

2. In the Pakistani city of Quetta, armed men opened fire on hundreds of Shia worshippers taking part in a procession, and riots broke out after 40 people were killed and more than 150 wounded. **9.** Pakistan test-fired its long-range ballistic missile, Shaheen II. **12.** President Roh Moo Hyun of South Korea was voted out of power after deputies voted by 193 to 2 to impeach him. **16.** Pakistani troops killed 24 Islamic militants on the border with Afghanistan; eight Pakistani soldiers were killed and 15 wounded. **19.** Taiwan's President Chen Shui-bian and Vice-President Annette Lu were shot during an attempted assassination. **20.** Taiwan's President Chen Shui-bian was re-elected to government. **21.** More than 100 people were killed during fighting in western Afghanistan following the assassination of Mirwais Sadiq, the Aviation Minister. In Malaysia, Abdullah Badawi of the National Front coalition won the general election, driving the Pan-Malaysian Islamic Party from power in its heartland regional assemblies. The Nepalese military claimed to have killed 500 Maoist rebels during a 12-hour battle at Beni Bazar in the Mygdi district. **23.** President Chen of Taiwan agreed to a recount of all ballots cast in the election following protests held by more than 10,000 opposition supporters, who accused the ruling party of interfering with the vote count. **26.** The Niigata District Court in

Japan ordered the Japanese government to compensate Chinese Second World War slave labourers. **28.** President Karzai of Afghanistan announced that national elections would be delayed until September 2004 in order to give the United Nations more time to organise the poll. **29.** In Uzbekistan, two female suicide bombers set off a series of explosions in a crowded bazaar in Tashkent, killing 19 people.

APRIL 2004

4. The Sri Lankan government suffered a defeat at the country's elections as the opposition alliance, lead by President Kumaratunga, won a majority of 105 seats in parliament. **5.** In Indonesia, the country's second democratic elections resulted in the ruling Indonesian Democratic Party of Struggle being given only 15 per cent of the 600 million votes, with the new Democratic Party winning the majority of votes in President Megawati Sukarnoputri's own ward. **9.** In Nepal, 25,000 protesters from a coalition of five political parties held a rally in Kathmandu against King Gyanendra, in protest at his dismissal of the elected government a year earlier. **13.** Aung Shwe and U Lwin of Burma's opposition party, the National League for Democracy, were released from house arrest; it was hoped that the party leader, Aung San Suu Kyi, would also be released. **15.** Hong Kong's Chief Executive, Tung Chee-hwa, ruled out full elections to choose his successor. A tornado destroyed several villages in northern Bangladesh, killing more than 70 people and injuring nearly 1,000. **16.** The Uri Party of South Korea won the national parliamentary election; the party supported President Roh Moo Hyun when the Grand National Party tried to impeach him. Police detained more than 1,000 pro-democracy protesters in the Nepalese capital Kathmandu, including the former prime minister, Sher Bahadur Deuba. **22.** North Korea declared a state of emergency after two fuel trains collided at Ryongchon station, 30 miles south of the border with China, killing up to 3,000 people. **25.** Japan's ruling Liberal Democratic Party retained all three seats contested in by-elections. **28.** Thai troops killed 34 militants and 132 Muslims died following a day of fighting in the southern provinces of Pattani, Yala and Songkhla.

MAY 2004

5. In Indonesia, a coalition government was planned after the Golkar party of former President Suharto won the election with 21.6 per cent of the vote while the ruling Indonesian Democratic Party of Struggle received 18.5 per cent of the vote. **9.** In Nepal, 34 people died and 22 Maoist rebels were shot in around four clashes between the rebels and police following the resignation of Prime Minister Surya Bahadur Thapa a week before. **13.** In the general election in India, the opposition Congress party, lead by Sonia Gandhi, won 217 seats and the governing Bharatiya Janata Party won 187. **14.** Roh Moo Hyun, the impeached South Korean President, regained power after a court overturned a vote to unseat him. **18.** Sonia Gandhi refused the post of prime minister of India after her Congress Party won the general election. **19.** Dr Manmohan Singh was appointed prime minister of India. **23.** The Commonwealth Secretary-General, Don McKinnon, announced the readmission of Pakistan into the Commonwealth after it had been suspended for five years following a coup.

JUNE 2004

2. King Gyanendra of Nepal re-appointed Sher Bahadur Deuba to the position of prime minister after his dismissal from the post in 2002. **9.** Twenty thousand people were evacuated after two volcanoes erupted in east Java province, near Jakarta, Indonesia. **14.** In Pakistan, at least 72 people were killed near the Afghan border following a five-day assault on al-Qa'eda hideouts. **20.** President Gloria Macapagal Arroyo of the Philippines was re-elected following a six-week count of votes; she had beaten Fernando Poe by 1.1 million votes. **24.** North Korea threatened to test a nuclear weapon despite an offer of aid from the US if it promised to scrap its weapons programme; North Korea demanded energy aid up front in exchange for freezing its nuclear programme. **26.** Chaudhry Shujaat Hussain was named as Pakistan's new prime minister after the resignation of Zafarullah Khan Jamali. **28.** The governing party of Mongolia, the Mongolian People's Revolutionary Party, lost its majority during elections, winning only 36 of 76 seats – the opposition Motherland Democratic Coalition also won 36 seats.

JULY 2004

11. Japan's ruling Liberal Democrat Party lost half of the 242 seats in the upper house of parliament to the opposition Democratic Party in elections. **15.** Maninder Pal Singh Kohli was arrested in Kalimpong in India on suspicion of raping and murdering the British teenager Hannah Foster in March 2003 near her home in Hampshire. Sultan Hassanal Bolkiah of Brunei announced that he would reconvene parliament – it had been 20 years since it last met. Cambodia's government was officially approved after more than 11 months of negotiations following a general election. **20.** The New York think tank Freedom House published its 2004 Freedom in the World survey which ranked Burma's regime as the worst in the world; Cuba and North Korea were also ranked as two of the worst regimes. **23.** The Constitutional Court in Jakarta declared that the terrorism legislation used to convict the 29 people involved in the Bali bombing was invalid as it was only passed into law months after the bombings. **25.** Severe monsoon floods across Bangladesh and parts of India and Nepal killed around 570 people in one month, forced millions from their homes and caused at least 10,000 Bangladeshis to suffer from various diseases. **26.** In Indonesia, it was announced that following a presidential election, Susilo Yudhoyono had received 33.5 per cent of the vote and the incumbent Megawati Sukarnoputri 26.6 per cent of the vote. **29.** Ahmed Khalfan Ghailani, one of the most-wanted leaders of al-Qa'eda, was arrested in the Pakistani city of Gujrat following a 12-hour gun battle with security forces.

AUGUST 2004

3. Pakistani authorities arrested eight al-Qa'eda terrorist suspects in the Punjab province. **10.** In Singapore, it was announced that the son of Prime Minister Lee Kuan Yew, Lee Hsien Loong would be sworn in as the new prime minister following his father's resignation. **25.** Thousands of people were evacuated from their homes in south-east China as Typhoon Aere approached the Fujian province – it had already killed at least 14 people in Taiwan and Japan and caused serious flooding. **27.** Shaukat Aziz was elected prime minister of Pakistan following Chaudhry Shujaat Hussain resignation on 26 June after having been in the post for only two months. **29.** The defence ministry

in India said it had successfully tested a long-range missile capable of carrying a nuclear warhead off its eastern coast. In Thailand, the democrat Apirak Kosayodhin was elected governor of Bangkok.

AUSTRALASIA AND THE PACIFIC

SEPTEMBER 2003

2. The Australian government announced that a four-year jail sentence imposed on Abu Bakar Bashir, leader of Islamist group, Jemaah Islamiah was too lenient. **5.** The theft of two computers from an intelligence area at Sydney International Airport raised fears of terrorist interference as the 2nd anniversary of the attacks in New York and Washington drew close. **8.** Two men were jailed for life in Australia's worst serial murder case. John Bunting was found guilty of 11 and Robert Wagner of seven murders. **18.** A 1,800-mile railway line between Adelaide and Darwin was completed.

OCTOBER 2003

14. MPs in New Zealand voted to establish a Supreme Court of New Zealand, thereby abolishing appeals to the Privy Council in London and severing the last judicial link with Britain. **22.** Per Johan Adolfsson, a Swedish tourist, was jailed for two months at a court in Sydney after he had tried to smuggle eight baby snakes into Australia by strapping them to his legs on a flight from Bangkok to Sydney.

NOVEMBER 2003

5. The Australian government retrospectively removed Melville Island from the country's migration zone in order to prevent 14 Kurdish people, who arrived on the island in an Indonesian boat, from seeking asylum on the mainland; Australian law states that migrants are allowed to apply for refugee status once they have reached Australian mainland. **6.** Pauline Hanson, the former leader of the One Nation nationalist party in Australia, was released from jail after her conviction for electoral fraud was overturned by the Queensland Court of Appeal; her colleague David Ettridge was also freed. **10.** Bradley Murdoch was arrested at the South Australian District Court in Adelaide, after having been acquitted of separate rape and abduction charges, for the murder of the British tourist Peter Falconio and the unlawful detention of Joanne Lees, in the Northern Territory in July 2001.

DECEMBER 2003

1. Australia's opposition Labor Party voted in favour of Mark Latham taking over as leader of the party from Kim Beazley. **10.** The High Court in Canberra, Australia, ruled by a 4 to 3 majority that long-term British residents who have committed a crime in Australia can be deported back to Britain. **11.** Australia announced that it would be sending at least 230 armed police officers and 70 officials to Papua New Guinea in order to combat terrorism and criminal activity.

JANUARY 2004

30. The acclaimed British cosmologist, Will Saunders, was sentenced to nine months' weekend detention along with the Australian David Burgess, after they painted the words 'No War' in red paint across the highest 'sail' of the Sydney Opera House in protest at the war in Iraq.

FEBRUARY 2004

1. *The Ghan*, the first passenger train to run between the north and south of Australia, set off on its first journey between Adelaide and Darwin. **15.** Four people were arrested and 50 police officers were hurt during a nine-hour riot which broke out in the Aboriginal Redfern district of Sydney after 17-year-old Thomas Hickey died whilst allegedly being chased by police. **20.** The New Zealand Immigration Minister, Lianne Dalziel, resigned after it was found she had lied when she initially denied knowing how a letter about a Sri Lankan teenager, who was refused refugee status and deported, reached the media, but later admitted approving its release. **23.** Twenty-nine people died in Brisbane following a heatwave in Australia where temperatures reached 44.4C in Queensland and humidity rates rose to 70 per cent.

MARCH 2004

17. A plague of locusts devastated an area twice the size of England in eastern Australia as they devoured crops over 745 miles from south-west Queensland to central New South Wales; the infestation was a result of two years of drought followed by heavy rains. **25.** The leader of the Australian opposition Labor Party, Mark Latham, pledged to withdraw all 850 military personnel from Iraq if he were to win the next general election. David Kemp, the Australian Environment Minister, announced that from July 2004 fishing would be banned in 44,000 sq. miles of the coral reef along the coast of Queensland. **29.** In New Zealand, Maori Television (MT), set up to promote the Maori language and culture, went on air for the first time.

APRIL 2004

15. The Australian Prime Minister, John Howard, announced that he would be abolishing the country's Aboriginal and Torres Strait Islander Commission, and planned to appoint a panel of 'distinguished indigenous people' to advise on how to replace the Commission. **20.** Australia's leader of the opposition Labor Party, Mark Latham, announced that if his party won the upcoming elections, they would give Australians the opportunity to vote again on whether the country should become a republic.

MAY 2004

27. The Australian Prime Minister, John Howard, announced his intention to amend the 1961 Marriage Act in order to ban same-sex marriages and same-sex couples adopting children from overseas.

JUNE 2004

16. In Australia, the Human Rights and Equal Opportunity Commission reported that 99 per cent of Muslim women had suffered racist abuse or violence since the September 11 attacks in the US.

JULY 2004

1. The Great Barrier Reef became the world's largest protected marine reserve after the Australian government banned commercial fishermen from a third of the World Heritage listed site. **19.** Ivens Buffett, the deputy chief minister of Norfolk Island, was found shot dead in his office – it was only the second murder committed on the island in 150 years. **27.** The Australian government announced that it would send 300 police and officials to take up posts in the government of Papua New Guinea in order to stamp out corruption.

AUGUST 2004

8. The South Pacific nation of Tokelau announced that it would hold a referendum in 2005 on independence from New Zealand. **11.** In Australia, the New South Wales Farmers' Association released a warning to hikers about an aggressive new breed of half-dingo wild dog after the new 'super-dingoes' were found to have killed livestock and attacked walkers, horse riders and campers along the Great Dividing Range from Queensland through to Victoria. **29.** Australia's Prime Minister John Howard announced that the next general election would be held on 9 October 2004.

EUROPE

SEPTEMBER 2003

1. The Netherlands became the first country to introduce legislation permitting the medical use of cannabis when prescribed by a doctor as a painkiller. **2.** In Russia, President Vladimir Putin announced that elections for the *State Duma*, the lower chamber of the federal legislature, would be conducted on 7 December 2003. The Congress for Freedom and Democracy in Kurdistan (Kadek), the main militant Kurdish group in Turkey, announced they were ending their four-year unilateral cease-fire. **3.** In Stavropol, southern Russia, six people died and more than 40 were injured when two bombs exploded simultaneously beneath a crowded commuter train. **4.** In Spain, Prime Minister Jose Maria Aznar announced his successor of the right-wing People's Party (PP), with immediate effect, as the Deputy Prime Minister Mariano Rajoy Brey. **5.** In Italy, riot police used batons to beat back anti-globalisation protesters who tried to disrupt a meeting of EU foreign ministers. A riot took place in Kosovo's largest prison, killing five prisoners and injuring sixteen. **9.** In Slovenia, Prime Minister Anton Rop announced the abolition of obligatory military service stating that recruits would no longer be called-up. **10.** Swedish Foreign Minister Anna Lindh was stabbed and killed in a department store in central Stockholm by an unknown assailant. **16.** In Sweden, 35 year-old Per Olof Svensson was arrested on suspicion of the murder of Swedish Foreign minister Anna Lindh. In the Netherlands, the centre-right coalition government announced an austerity budget, which included cutting welfare benefits and increasing workers' premiums in a bid to comply with EU budget deficit guidelines. **18.** In France, new measures were announced giving the government the power to close mosques connected with fundamental islamicism and expel extremist Imams. **21.** In Germany, Chancellor Gerhard Schröder's Social Democrat Party was defeated in the Bavarian elections with the conservative Christian Socialist Union gaining the majority of seats in the state parliament. **23.** In Azerbaijan, a memorial to British servicemen who died defending the country's oilfields during the First World War was vandalised one week after it was erected. **24.** The Danish royal family announced that Crown Prince Frederick of Denmark would marry Australian estate agent, Mary Donaldson. Per Olof Svensson was cleared of all charges of the murder of Swedish Foreign Minister, Anna Lindh. **25.** Italian Prince Emmanuel-Filiberto, second in line to the Italian throne, married French actress, Clotilde Courau. **26.** In Germany, police claimed to have uncovered one of the world's biggest pornography rings: 530 men, including police officers and teachers had been identified as suspects. In France, a severely handicapped 22 year-old man at the centre of a debate over euthanasia died after his mother gave him an overdose. **28**. In Italy, a power cut plunged almost the entire country into darkness. Chechen Prime Minister Anatoli Povov was taken to hospital after what was believed to be an attempted assassination using poison. **30**. A member of al-Qa'eda, Nizar Trabelsi, was jailed for ten years by a Belgian court for planning to carry out a suicide bombing in the country just days after the terrorist attacks in America on 11 September 2001.

OCTOBER 2003
3. France's right-wing ruling party announced its intention to revoke the maximum 35-hour working week, following the suggestion by Economic Minister, Alain Lambert, that it was costing the state £11 billion per year. Lilla Freivalds was appointed as Sweden's new Foreign Minister. **5**. In southern Russia, the graves of 185 German soldiers who died during fighting with the Soviet Red Army between October and December 1942 were discovered in Diagara. **7**. Akhmed Kadyrov was elected president of Chechnya following a ballot that was widely believed to have been fixed. **12**. In the Ukraine, 30 people died at a mental hospital in Kozlovichi, when a man started a fire in the building. **15**. In Azerbaijan, Ilham Aliyev, won an overwhelming victory in the presidential elections. **17**. The lower house of the German parliament voted 306 to 291 in favour of new welfare reforms aimed at reviving the economy; the changes included cutting unemployment benefit and introducing legislation to make it compulsory for the long-term unemployed claiming benefits to accept any legal job offer. **19**. German Chancellor Gerhard Schröder ordered the first cut in pension benefits since the end of the Second World War; the cut was one of five measures agreed as a strategy to overcome an estimated €8 billion (£5.5 billion) shortfall in the state pay-as-you-go pension schemes. In Switzerland, the right-wing Swiss People's Party won a landslide victory in the general election. **23**. Hans Eichel, Germany's Finance Minister announced that Germany's public deficit had soared to €43 billion, its highest level since 1945, and warned that Germany was likely to breach the European single currency's Stability and Growth Pact for the third year in a row in 2004. **25**. In Russia, 33 of the 46 men trapped in the flooded Zapadnaya coal mine in Novoshakhtinsk were rescued. **27**. Russia's stock market plunged by 10 per cent (the RTS index of Russia's biggest stocks fell 59.86 points to 535.05) after the arrest of Russian oil billionaire Mikhail Khodorkovsky sparked fears amongst traders about the Government's commitment to economic reform. **29**. A further 11 of the 13 miners trapped in a deep shaft in the Zapadnaya coal mine in Russia were found alive after rescuers dug a 200ft tunnel from a neighbouring coal mine to get to the trapped men. **30**. Russian state prosecutors froze 44 per cent of shares in the country's leading oil company Yukos, following the arrest of its major shareholder, Mikhail Khodorkovsky. **31**. Ilham Aliyev was inaugurated as the new president of Azerbaijan replacing his father, Geider Aliyev, who had stood down due to serious illness after serving in the post since 1993.

NOVEMBER 2003
2. In Georgia parliamentary elections were held, the results were widely believed to have been rigged in favour of the President, Eduard Shevardnadze, who had been in office as President since 1992. **3**. Mikhail Khodorkovsky resigned as head of the Russian oil company Yukos following his detainment on tax evasion charges. In Lithuania, a special commission was established to investigate alleged links between President Rolandas Paksas and organised crime in Russia and a separate criminal investigation of Yuri Borisov, the Lithuanian-based Russian businessman at the centre of the allegations, began. **4**. In Azerbaijan, the Milli Majlis (the unicameral legislature) approved President Aliyev's proposal to appoint Artur Rasizade as prime minister. **11**. On the fourth day of protests in the Georgian capital Tbilisi, against the results of the parliamentary election, opposition leaders announced that they would not allow the new parliament to convene unless elections were re-held. **13**. In Germany, the Christian Democratic Union/Christian Social Union (CDU/CSU) coalition voted 195 to 28 in favour of the expulsion of CDU party member Martin Hohman, after he made anti-Semitic comments in October. **16**. In Serbia, presidential election results were declared null and void as turnout was below the required 50 per cent. **19**. In Serbia, the ruling coalition, the Democratic Opposition of Serbia (DOS), announced that the coalition would split up prior to the 28 December elections. **20**. In Turkey, two separate truck bombs exploded within five minutes of each other outside the headquarters of the HSBC bank and the UK consulate in Istanbul, the explosions killed at least 31 people, including the UK Consul-General Roger Short, and injured over 450 others. **23**. In Georgia, President Shevardnadze signed a statement of resignation in return for immunity from prosecution. Nino Burdjanadze, Speaker of the parliament, assumed all presidential powers pending fresh presidential and legislative elections. In Croatia, elections to the 152-seat Chamber of Representatives (the lower chamber of the bicameral legislature) the right-wing Croatian Democratic Union (HDZ) won a decisive victory, winning 66 seats. **29**. In Bulgaria, five defendants accused of the assassination of former prime minister Andrei Lukanov in 1996, were convicted and sentenced to life imprisonment in a court in Sofia.

DECEMBER 2003
2. Following heavy rainfall, southern France experienced extensive flooding which killed five people and forced the evacuation of more than 7,000 others; roads and rail lines were cut-off and the state electricity supplier was obliged to shut down four nuclear reactors. **4**. Ibon Fernandez, the alleged leader of the Basque separatist movement ETA, was rearrested in France near the border with Spain following his escape from prison in December 2002. In Poland, Prime Minister Leszek Miller was admitted to hospital with two fractured vertebrae after the helicopter in which he was travelling carried out an emergency landing near the town of Piaseczno, south of Warsaw. **5**. Thirty-two people were reported dead and dozens injured in an explosion on a commuter train between the towns of Mineralnye Vody and Kislovodsk in southern Russia near the Chechnya region; the Russian Ministry of Emergencies believed it was the result of a terrorist act. **7**. In Russia, President Putin's Unified Russia Party won nearly 38 per cent of the vote in the general election, resulting in a nearly two-thirds majority of the 300 seats in the State Duma (lower house). **11**. In France, a report by the commission on state secularism was published which recommended that the wearing of overt religious symbols in state educational institutions and public buildings should be banned. **12**. Geidar Aliyev, the

former president of Azerbaijan, died aged 80 in Ohio, USA, where he had been undergoing treatment for heart and kidney problems. **19.** In Germany, Chancellor Gerhard Schröder secured parliamentary support for his Agenda 2010 package of economic and social reforms aimed at reviving the German economy. **23.** Turkey and Greece signed a deal in Ankara to build a gas pipeline between the two countries that would also carry gas to other parts of Europe; the project was expected to be completed in 2006 at a cost of £53.8 million. **24.** Spanish police foiled an attempt by Basque separatists to detonate two bombs at Madrid's main railway station; one man was arrested as he unloaded a suitcase containing 28kg of chemical explosives from his car and a further 20kg of explosives were found aboard a train en route to Madrid. **26.** In Serbia, the Bosnian Serb government set up a commission to investigate the 1995 Srebrenica massacre. In Turkey, the city governor for Istanbul announced that a cell of Turkish nationals linked to the al-Qa'eda network had orchestrated the November bombings of the UK Consulate, HSBC bank and two synagogues; 35 people had been charged in connection with the attacks. **28.** In Serbia, the Serbian Radical Party (SRS), whose leader was on trial for alleged atrocities committed in the Balkan wars of the 1990s, won the parliamentary elections taking 27.5 per cent of the vote and gaining 82 seats in the 250-member parliament.

JANUARY 2004
2. In Russia, the Defence Minister Sergei Ivanov approved President Putin's plans to end conscription and fill more than half of its one million-strong army with professional soldiers by 2007. **4.** In Georgia, Mikhail Saakashvili won a landslide victory in the presidential elections. **5.** In Lithuania, President Rolandas Paksas, stated that he would not appear before a parliamentary committee to consider whether he should be impeached as he had not been provided with full information on the charges against him. **7.** In Sweden, Mijailo Mijailovic was arrested in conjunction with the murder of Anna Lindh, the Swedish Foreign Minister who died after being stabbed in a Stockholm department store in September 2003. In Greece, Prime Minister, Kostas Simitis, announced his resignation as leader of the ruling party, the Panhellenic Socialist Movement (Pasok), and called for an early general election to be held on 7 March. **9.** In Spain, Prime Minister, José María Aznar, called a general election for 14 March. **11.** In the Turkish Republic of Northern Cyprus, Mehmet Ali Talat, leader of the pro-EU Republican Turkish Party agreed to form a coalition government with the anti-EU Democrat Party led by Serdar Denktash. **12.** In Russia, a Moscow court sentenced Adam Dekkushev and Yusef Krymshamkhalov to life imprisonment for their part in the 1999 Moscow and Volgodonsk bombings that killed 246 people. **14.** In the Turkish Republic of Northern Cyprus, President Serdar Denktash, leader of the Democrat Party approved the new cabinet, naming Ali Talat, leader of the Republican Turkish Party, as Prime Minister, with himself as Deputy Prime Minister and Foreign Minister. **15.** In Russia, former chief executive of the Yukos oil company, Mikhail Khodorkovsky, lost his appeal against continued detention in Moscow's Matrosskaya Tishina prison following the ruling on 23 December that he should stay in pre-trial detention until at least 25 March. **19.** A Norwegian cargo ship capsized in the Raune Fjord, just off the island of Bjoroey, 12 crew members were rescued, three bodies were recovered and the remaining 15

missing crew members were presumed dead. **25.** The new president of Georgia, Mikhail Saakashvili, was inaugurated on the steps of the parliament building in the capital Tibilisi. **28.** In France, the Cabinet approved a bill banning the wearing in state schools of symbols and clothing, which conspicuously display the religious affiliation of pupils; no banned items were specified in the bill which was left to the discretion of the teacher. In Turkey, the Grand National Assembly approved the proposal by Economy Minister, Ali Babacan to eliminate six zeros from the Turkish lira and rename it the 'new Turkish lira'; the old currency would remain in circulation, alongside the new currency, until its withdrawal on 30 December 2005.

FEBRUARY 2004
2. In the central Turkish city of Konya more than 100 people were feared dead after an 11-storey building collapsed. **3.** In France, Alain Juppé announced that he would remain Mayor of Bordeaux, an MP and president of the UMP despite being convicted on 30 January of organising illegal party funding; his prison sentence was suspended pending appeal. **6.** In Russia, a bomb was detonated on Moscow's underground rail system at 8:30 a.m. At least 39 people died and more than 120 were injured in the incident, which was believed to have been carried out by Chechyen separatists. German Chancellor Gerhard Schröder resigned as leader of the Social Democratic Party after internal criticism over his economic reform programme Agenda 2010. Herr Schröder stated that he would continue as chancellor and head of government but would hand the party leadership to the party's parliamentary group leader, Franz Münterfering. **10.** The Netherlands Government issued a deportation order for approximately 26,000 failed asylum-seekers that had arrived before the introduction of a new asylum regime in April 2001; the order constituted one of the biggest mass deportations in modern European history. **17.** The Dutch parliament voted in favour of the mass deportation of failed asylum seekers announced by the Government on 10 February 2004. **18.** In Lithuania, a parliamentary panel concluded that there were sufficient legal grounds for the impeachment of President Rolandas Paksas. In France, Jean-Marie Le Pen, the leader of France's far-right party was refused his application to stand in the April regional elections after election officials stated that he had not provided the necessary tax records to stand as a candidate in southern France. **21.** In France the terrorist group AZF directed French police to a bomb hidden beneath a railway line in Limoges after threatening that ten other such bombs hidden beneath railway lines throughout France would be detonated unless they received a £2.8 million ransom from the French government. **24.** In Russia, President Putin dismissed Prime Minister Mikhail Kasyanov and his entire Cabinet prior to the presidential election on 14 March 2004. **26.** Boris Trajkovski, President of Macedonia since 1999, died in an air crash in Bosnia. **29.** A terrorist attack on the Spanish capital, Madrid, was foiled when police intercepted a van containing more than 1,000lbs of explosives. In Germany, Chancellor Gerhard Schröder suffered a defeat when his party, the Social Democrats, took only 32 per cent of the vote in the Hamburg city-state elections; the Christian Democrats took the majority (46 per cent) and were set to secure 62 seats in the Hamburg State Parliament.

MARCH 2004

3. France's Senate voted 276 to 20 in favour of a law banning the wearing of overt religious symbols in state schools. In Belgrade, the new Serbian parliament voted in an 18-member, Conservative-led coalition cabinet led by Vojislav Kostunica, the former Yugoslav President and leader of the Democratic Party of Serbia (DSS). **4.** In France, more than 10,000 railway workers were deployed to search all 20,000 miles of railway track for bombs following the threat made by the terrorist group AZF on 21 February. **11.** In Spain, ten bombs exploded during the morning rush hour in Madrid; six bombs exploded on trains approaching central stations, three exploded at the Atocha terminus and one exploded at Santa Eugenia station. In total around 1,400 people were injured and 198 people killed in one of the worst terrorist attacks in Spain. Spanish Foreign Minister Ana Palacio said evidence appeared to indicate ETA as responsible for the attacks, although a London-based Arabic newspaper, Al-Quds, said it had received an email in which a group linked to al-Qae'da, the Abu Hafs al-Masri Brigades, claimed to have carried out the attacks. **13.** Spain's interior minister announced that al-Qa'eda had claimed responsibility for the terrorist attacks in Madrid, the claim was made on a video tape which had yet to be authenticated. **14.** In Russia, President Putin was re-elected for a second four-year term winning 71.2 per cent of the vote in the presidential elections. In the Spanish general election the Socialist Party won by a margin of 5 percent, winning 43 per cent of the votes. **17.** In the Serbian province of Kosovo ethnic Albanians carried out co-ordinated attacks against the Serbian minority; 14 people were killed and about 250 injured in the worst spate of violence seen in the region since the 1999 war. **18.** In Georgia, President Saakashvili, announced he was lifting the economic blockade imposed on the Adjaria region on 14 March following talks with the region's leader, Aslan Abashidze. **23.** In Sweden, Mijailo Mijailovic, was sentenced to life imprisonment for the murder of Anna Lindh, the Swedish Foreign Minister, after judges rejected his plea of insanity. **28.** In Georgia, President Saakashvili's National-Movement Democratic Party won 78.6 per cent of the vote in the parliamentary elections. **29.** In the Republic of Ireland, a smoking ban came into force in all places of work and public areas, including bars and restaurants. **31.** In Russia, the State Duma passed a government-drafted bill (294 votes for and 137 votes against) banning public protests near official buildings and pipelines and rallies that threaten 'public morality'.

APRIL 2004

1. The German state of Baden-Württemberg, led by a coalition of the Christian Democratic Union and the liberal Free Democrats, became the first German state to ban the wearing of headscarves by Muslim teachers in schools. **2.** In Spain, a 26 lb bomb was found under a railway track at Mocejon near Toledo, the device was connected to a detonator but had not been fully assembled. **3.** In Spain, security forces traced the whereabouts of a terrorist cell linked to the 11 March Madrid bombings to a flat in the Madrid suburbs. While residents were being evacuated a gunman opened fire resulting in a two-hour siege which ended when the suspects detonated explosives killing themselves, a special forces police officer and injuring 11 officers from Spain's specialist anti-terrorist unit. **5.** Police in France broke up a suspected Islamic terrorist cell on the outskirts of Paris,

arresting 15 people in connection with the suicide-bomb attacks in Morocco in 2003. **25.** In Austria, Heinz Fischer won the presidential elections with more than 53 per cent of the vote ahead of his Conservative rival Benita Ferrero-Waldner. In Rome, the Pope appointed Sister Enrica Rosanna, a Salesian nun, as under-secretary of the Congregation for the Consecrated Life, the highest appointment ever bestowed on a woman in the Roman Catholic Church. **30.** Macedonian police acknowledged that the killing of seven alleged Pakistani terrorists in March 2002 was staged to win US support and promote Macedonia as a player in the global fight against terrorism and admitted that the victims were actually illegal immigrants. Three former police commanders, two special officers and a businessman were charged with murder in connection with the incident.

MAY 2004

3. In Turkey, police foiled a plot by terrorists to assassinate President Bush at the NATO summit to be held in Istanbul in June; in total 24 suspected members of a militant group linked to al-Qa'eda were detained and guns, explosives and detonators seized. **5.** President Mikhail Saakashvili of Georgia arrived in Adjaria's regional capital Batumi and assumed direct rule of the province. In Greece, three bombs exploded outside a police station in the Kallithea area of Athens, injuring a policeman and damaging buildings and cars. **6.** Turkish Prime Minister Tayyip Erdogan visited Greece for talks with Greek Prime Minister Kostas Karamanlis. **7.** In Germany, Sven Jaschen, 18, was arrested and admitted responsibility for the 'sasser' internet worm; Jaschen was traced after acquaintances gave information to Microsoft's German office in return for a £139,000 reward. **9.** Chechen President, Akhmed Kadyrov, was killed and at least 30 others injured when a bomb exploded under the VIP stand at Grozny Dinamo Stadium where the President was attending a Victory Day parade marking the anniversary of the end of the Second World War. **23.** In France, five people were killed and four others injured, one seriously, when a large part of the roof of Terminal 2E at Charles de Gaulle Airport in Paris collapsed onto a waiting area just before 7a.m. In Germany, Horst Koehler, joint candidate of the Christian Democratic Union/Christian Social Union and the Free Democratic Party was elected for the post of Federal President, defeating Gesine Schwan, the candidate of the ruling coalition of the Social Democratic Party and the Greens.

JUNE 2004

1. Spanish newspaper *El Mundo* published letters between two senior members of terrorist groups, al-Qa'eda and ETA, dating back to 2001. **8.** Italy announced that anti-terrorist police in Milan had arrested Osman Sayed Ahmed, who was believed to have played a key role in the 11 March Madrid bombings. **9.** Turkish state television made its first broadcast in the once banned language of Kurdish, the language of Turkey's largest minority. In Turkey, four former MPs, Leyla Zana, Orhan Dogan, Hatip Dicle and Selim Sadek, were released after 10 years following a ruling by the Turkish court of appeal that the State Security Court, which twice tried them for alleged membership of an armed separatist group, failed to give them a fair hearing at their original trial. **22.** In the Russian autonomous region of Ingushetia bordering Chechnya, insurgents seized an Interior Ministry building and attacked police posts throughout the region; 57 people were killed including the Interior Minister, Abukar

Kostoyev. **24**. In Turkey, three people were killed and more than a dozen injured when a bomb exploded on a busy Istanbul bus just two days prior to the arrival of world leaders for the NATO summit in the city. **30**. In Bosnia, Lord Ashdown of Norton-sub-Hamdon, the Chief International Envoy to Bosnia, sacked 60 senior Bosnian Serb officials, including Dragan Kalinic, Speaker of the Bosnian Serb parliament, and Zoran Djeric, the Bosnian Serb Interior Minister, for allegedly helping Radovan Karadzic and other indicted war criminals to evade capture.

JULY 2004

5. Italian Prime Minister, Silvio Berlusconi presented a package of expenditure reforms and special tax measures worth €4.5 billion (£5.25 billion) to ensure that Italy kept within the European single currency country deficit regulations. Prime Minister Silvio Berlusconi made the announcement in place of former Economy Minister, Giulio Tremonti, who resigned over the weekend. **19**. In Turkey, a taxi driver was jailed for 36 years for the murder of a British child who was caught in crossfire during a gunfight in the resort of Foca in July 2003. **20**. In Russia the Justice Ministry announced that bailiffs were to sell off the Yukos subsidiary, Yuganskneftegaz, to cover a £1.8 billion bill for back taxes from 2000 that Yukos failed to pay in June. **22**. In Turkey, at least 36 people were killed when a train travelling from Istanbul to the Turkish capital Ankara derailed.

AUGUST 2004

1. Italian police working undercover arrested three Italians and three Bulgarians after discovering a baby-selling ring in which Bulgarian women were brought to Italy to give birth and their children sold. One woman was arrested on leaving the hospital where she had just given birth and two infants were taken into care. **10**. In Austria, a tourist coach carrying mainly British passengers came off a road near the village of Bad Dürnberg and rolled 100ft down a mountain into a field, five passengers died and 20 were seriously injured in the accident. **10**. In Turkey two people died and eleven people were injured in simultaneous explosions in two hotels in Istanbul; the Islamic Abu Hafs al-Masri Brigades claimed responsibility for the blasts. **18**. Italian police discovered a bomb close to the Italian Prime Minister Silvio Berlusconi's villa in Sardinia just hours after Prime Minister Tony Blair and his wife Cherie had left following a private visit to Mr Berluscconi's Sardinian home. **22**. Russian president Vladimir Putin made a surprise visit to the region of Chechnya where he visited the grave of the late Chechen president Akhmed Kadyrov assassinated on 9 May. **24**. Two Russian airliners carrying more than 80 people simultaneously disappeared from Russian air traffic control radar screens. The first aircraft was en route from Moscow to Volgograd and wreckage was found near the village of Buchalki with no reports of survivors. The other aircraft remained missing after disappearing near the city of Rostov-on-Don about 600 miles south of Moscow en route from Moscow to the Black Sea resort of Sochi. **25**. The wreckage of the second plane that went missing in Russia on 24 August was discovered. **28**. The Russian Federal Security Service confirmed that traces of explosives had been found in the wreckage of both planes concluding that it was an act of terrorism that caused the destruction of the planes and the death of all passengers and crew.

EUROPEAN UNION

SEPTEMBER 2003

2. The European Commission rejected US demands for airlines to reveal passenger information as an anti-terrorist measure. **11**. The EU added Hamas to its blacklist of terrorist organisations in an attempt to reduce the flow of funds that support the group's campaign of suicide bombings against Israelis. **14**. A Swedish referendum voted overwhelmingly against joining the European single currency. Estonia voted to join the EU in a referendum. **18**. The International Monetary Fund criticised the economic performance of the countries in the European single currency. **20**. Latvia voted for EU membership during a referendum; 67 per cent of the 72.5 per cent turnout voted in favour of accession on 1 May 2004.

OCTOBER 2003

16. Twenty-eight European leaders met in Brussels to discuss a new constitution for Europe. It was envisaged that the constitution would create a full-time European president and foreign minister, make majority voting the norm in EU business and put the European Commission in charge of justice and home affairs. Britain ruled out holding a referendum on the new EU constitution, several other nations, including Spain, Portugal, the Netherlands, Denmark, Ireland and Luxembourg stated they were almost certain to hold referendums, whilst France, Italy and the Czech Republic were among those still considering the idea. **31**. Wim Duisenberg stepped down after five years in charge of the European Central Bank and handed over to his successor, Jean-Claude Trichet.

NOVEMBER 2003

25. EU finance ministers meeting in Brussels decided by a majority not to impose sanctions on France and Germany for breaching Euro budget deficit rules; effectively breaking the Stability and Growth Pact governing participation in the Euro single currency.

DECEMBER 2003

27. The President of the European Union, Romano Prodi, received a letter bomb, which he opened, at his home in Bologna, Italy. No-one was injured in the blast. **30**. A letter bomb was intercepted in the post room of Eurojust, an EU agency situated in the Hague, Netherlands; the bomb was the fourth device in as many days to be received by an EU institution.

JANUARY 2004

1. Irish Prime Minister, Bertie Ahern, assumed the EU's rotating presidency for a six-month term. **12**. In Rome, Italian police found a package containing bullet casings and firecrackers at the Bologna home of the European Commission President, Romano Prodi, the package contained a threatening letter claiming to be from an anarchist group in Sardinia. **13**. The European Commission announced that it would take legal action in the European Court of Justice to challenge the decision by EU finance Ministers on 25 November 2003 to suspend the rules of the Stability and Growth Pact governing participation in the euro single currency. **23**. The European Union imposed a ban on the import of all Thai chicken slaughtered after 1 January 2004 after an outbreak of avian flu in Thailand.

FEBRUARY 2004

18. German Chancellor Gerhard Schröder hosted a trilateral summit in Berlin attended by French President Jacques Chirac and Prime Minister Tony Blair to establish a joint line on key policy issues in an enlarged European Union.

MARCH 2004

23. Talks on a new constitution for the European Union were revived in Warsaw after Germany and Poland paved the way for an agreement to be reached by the end of June.

APRIL 2004

27. Libyan leader, Colonel Gaddafi, made his first visit to Europe for 15 years.

MAY 2004

1. Membership of the EU increased from 15 to 25 states with the formal admission of Cyprus, the Czech Republic, Estonia, Hungary, Latvia, Lithuania, Malta, Poland, Slovakia and Slovenia.

JUNE 2004

1. The Dutch Prime Minister, Jan Peter Balkenende, began the first day of his sixth-month EU presidency. **10.** European parliamentary elections took place across Europe. **11.** As part of the ongoing negotiations to create a European constitution, EU member states agreed to go ahead with the creation of a European Union diplomatic service, the *European External Action Service*, serving under an EU Foreign Minister. **15.** Final results for the UK in the European parliamentary elections showed that the Liberal Democrats increased their number of seats from 10 to 12, the UK Independence Party (UKIP) from 3 to 12 with Labour and the Conservatives losing ten and nine seats respectively. **17/18.** During a summit in Brussels European leaders agreed on a constitution for Europe which had to be ratified by all 25 member states within two years, either by parliamentary vote or national referendum; at least eight countries, including Britain, were set to hold referendums. **18.** EU Member States appointed José Manuel Barroso to take office as European Commission President on 1 November 2004, replacing Romano Prodi.

JULY 2004

14. In France, President Jacques Chirac announced that France would hold a national referendum on the new constitution of the European Union, qualifying that the vote will take place in the second half of 2005.

AUGUST 2004

12. President of the European Commission, José Manuel Barroso, named Hartlepool MP and former cabinet minister, Peter Mandelson, as the next European Union Trade Commissioner. **20.** The incoming 25-member European Commission held its first informal session under new president José Manuel Barroso.

INTERNATIONAL RELATIONS

SEPTEMBER 2003

4. The UN was forced to shut down all its famine relief field offices in Zimbabwe by the government. **12.** The UN Security Council voted to lift sanctions against Libya. **22.** In an attack on the UN offices in Baghdad one policeman was killed and 19 people were injured. **14.** The World Trade Organisation talks to further the Doha round of trade negotiations in Cancún, Mexico, collapsed after some 90 developing countries walked out following a late demand by the EU and Japan for immediate negotiations to take place on investment, competition rules, trade facilitation and transparency in Government procurement. **23.** The new president of the UN, Julian Hunte of St Lucia, opened the 58th session of the General Assembly of the UN.

OCTOBER 2003

3. The UN Secretary-General Kofi Annan challenged the draft US-British plan for Iraq stating that the occupation might not be sustainable for long enough to prepare a new constitution; he outlined a rival UN blueprint that would transfer sovereignty to the Iraqi people in three months. **23.** The UN General Assembly elected five non-permanent members to the Security Council for a two-year term; the new members are Algeria, Benin, Brazil, the Philippines and Romania. **24.** At the close of an international donor conference in Madrid, $33.75 billion (£20 billion) was pledged towards the reconstruction of Iraq; the amount fell short of the $56 billion (£33 billion) target.

NOVEMBER 2003

4. A new 16-member UN group was formed to review the role of the UN in the wake of the diplomatic failures in the run-up to the war against Iraq. The UN's envoy in Iraq and its global security chief were suspended pending the outcome of an investigation into the lapses of security that had preceded the bombing of the UN offices in Baghdad, Iraq on 19 August 2003. **15.** After two days of intensive talks with the US-appointed Iraqi governing council, US Ambassador Paul Bremer appeared to have reached an agreement for transferring power in Iraq to an elected Iraqi government by the end of 2005.

DECEMBER 2003

14. The US Army released photographs of Saddam Hussein's arrest and medical examination. **19.** Libya announced its decision to abandon its programme to develop weapons of mass destruction.

JANUARY 2004

5. The former Dutch Foreign Minister, Jaap de Hoop Scheffer, took up his post as NATO Secretary-General succeeding Lord Robertson of Port Ellen. **8.** The UN launched a multimillion dollar appeal to help fund relief efforts and reconstruction in Bam, south east Iran, after earthquake devastated the area on 26 December 2003. **16–21.** Some 100,000 activists from around the world attended the anti-corporate globalisation World Social Forum (WSF) in Bombay, India. **21–25.** The World Economic Forum (WEF) took place in Davos, Switzerland and was attended by some 2,100 people from 94 countries. **23.** Dr David Kay, head of the Iraq survey group searching for Saddam Hussein's weapons of mass destruction for eight months, resigned saying that he believed Saddam Hussein had not possessed any such weapons for at least a decade. **28.** Milan Babic, a former Croatian Serb leader, was convicted of persecuting Croats between 1991–2 by the war crimes tribunal at The Hague. **30.** The UN Security Council adopted Resolution 1526 (2004), proposed by Chile, Russia and the USA, outling tougher sanctions and controls over people and entities associated with the al-Qa'eda network and the former ruling Afghan Taliban group.

FEBRUARY 2004

9–20. The seventh ordinary meeting of the Conference of the Parties to the UN Convention on Biological Diversity was held in Kuala Lumpur, Malaysia; 123 member states signed an agreement to ensure 'a significant' reduction of biodiversity loss by 2010. **15.** In Cyprus, decisive negotiations began in Nicosia on a UN blueprint to unite the island as a federation with a central government overseeing two largely autonomous areas. **25.** The UN General Assembly approved the nomination by UN Secretary-General, Kofi Annan of Canadian Louise Arbour as the new UN High Commissioner for Human Rights; Arbour was expected to begin her four-year term of office in June following her retirement from the Canadian Supreme Court.

MARCH 2004

4. In Germany, Mounir el Motassadeq, the only person to be convicted of involvement in the 11 September suicide hijackings won his appeal for a retrial. **15.** The new Spanish Prime Minister Jose Rodriguez Zapatero accused Tony Blair and President George W. Bush of dishonesty over the war in Iraq during a radio interview, and pledged to withdraw his country's 1,300 troops from Iraq. **18.** NATO made a request for 825 reserve troops from Britain, Italy and the US to reinforce the 17,500 German-led NATO force in Kosovo following fighting between ethnic Albanians and Serbs in the Serbian province on 17 March. **24.** UK Chancellor Gordon Brown used new anti-terrorist powers introduced after 11 September attacks in the US to freeze all assets held in British banks in the name of the new Hamas leader in Gaza, Abdel Aziz Rantisi. **31.** Kofi Annan, the UN Secretary-General, handed his final plan for the reunification of Cyprus to Greek, Turkish and Cypriot officials.

APRIL 2004

13. A number of European countries instructed their civilian workers to leave Iraq after a spate of civilian kidnappings in the country; Russia prepared to evacuate all of its 500 citizens while the French Foreign Ministry and the Czech Republic formally advised all non- military personnel to leave. **24.** In Cyprus, Greek Cypriots overwhelmingly rejected UN proposals to reunify the island, 75.8 per cent voted against the plan in a referendum, while in a separate poll the Turkish Cypriot community backed the proposals with 64.9 per cent voting in favour of the UN reunification plan.

MAY 2004

4. The UN Economic and Social Council elected 14 countries to serve on the 53-member UN Human Rights Commission for three-year terms starting from January 2005.

JUNE 2004

11. Turkish security services admitted bugging the telephone of the British Ambassador in Ankara in 2002; the admission was made in a letter submitted to a court by the Turkish National Intelligence Organisation as evidence in a trial of a journalist who published a transcript of a conversation between the ambassador and a senior EU official. **28/29.** The NATO summit took place in Istanbul, Turkey, amid tight security. **30.** In Qatar, two Russian intelligence agents were convicted of murdering former Chechen President Zelimkham Yandarbiyev and were sentenced to life imprisonment.

JULY 2004

1. In Iraq, the trial of former President Saddam Hussein for alleged crimes against humanity began.

AUGUST 2004

1. German Chancellor Gerhard Schröder marked the 60th anniversary of the start of the 1944 Warsaw Uprising by visiting the square where the rebellion began. **9.** In Afghanistan, Canada handed over control of the NATO force to Europe's five-nation defence force, Eurocorps, for a sixth month period. It was the Eurocorps first deployment outside Europe.

THE MIDDLE EAST

SEPTEMBER 2003

1. Iraq's Governing Council named the 25 ministers of the new cabinet that would form an interim administration. **3.** Polish forces took command of a multi-national coalition division in Iraq, becoming the only nation apart from the US and Britain to assume control of a sector of the country. **6.** Palestinian Prime Minister, Mahmoud Abbas, resigned from his position. One of the reasons he gave was the apparent lack of Israeli willingness to adhere to the 'roadmap to peace process'. **8.** Ahmed Qureia became Prime Minister of Palestine, having earlier demanded guarantees of American and European support in negotiations with Israel. **9.** Two Palestinian suicide attacks took place within five hours of each other. The first bomb killed at least seven Israeli soldiers and wounded dozens more at a crowded bus stop near Tel Aviv and the second took place in a café in the German Colony neighbourhood, killing at least six more people. **10.** A suicide bomber killed himself and an Iraqi child and wounded more than 50 people in a car-bomb attack in the northern Kurdish city of Arbil. Israel launched an airstrike against the home of a leading Hamas member in response to the double suicide bombings of the day before. **20.** A leading Iranian cleric called for his country to consider withdrawing from the nuclear non-proliferation treaty which raised fresh fears that Iran would ignore an international deadline to curb its nuclear ambitions. **29.** Jordan announced that it would train 30,000 Iraqi police and troops in the first such pledge of aid from an Arab country in support of the American-led reconstruction effort in Iraq.

OCTOBER 2003

1. The Israeli cabinet announced that it had decided to go ahead with the building of a security fence around Jewish settlements in the West Bank. The fence was designed to keep Palestinian suicide bombers out of Jewish areas. **4.** A female suicide bomber detonated a bomb in a crowded restaurant in the Israeli city of Haifa, killing at least 19 people and wounding more than 40. **5.** Israel attacked what was believed to be a terrorist training camp for Islamic Jihad in Syria in response to the suicide bombing in Israel of the previous day. **6.** The Palestinian terrorist group Hamas vowed to take revenge against Israel for the militant attack in Syria against the group. **9.** Israel stated that it would call up 800 reserve soldiers in readiness for increased operations in the West Bank and Gaza Strip following the suicide bombing that killed 19 people on 4 November. **10.** Seven Palestinians were killed when Israeli tanks entered the Rafah refugee camp in southern Gaza. Some 10,000 Shia Muslim demonstrators congregated on the streets of Baghdad in protest against the US after a night of violence that left two Americans and two Iraqis dead. The lawyer and democracy activist Shirin Ebadi was named as the first Iranian and Muslim woman winner of the £800,000 Nobel Peace Prize. She had previously been imprisoned by the Iranian regime for representing certain clients in human rights cases. **12.** According to reports from the *Los Angeles Times*, Israel had acquired the capability of launching a nuclear strike from submarines. **13.** Saudi Arabia announced it would hold its first elections for municipal councils. **14.** Israel ordered the expulsion of 15 Palestinian prisoners from the West Bank to Gaza. The prisoners were being held without trial or charges and human rights groups claimed that the army was violating international law. A gun battle broke out in Karbala and at least one person was killed as followers of the cleric Moqtada al-Sadr fought for control of the Imam Hussein mosque, which is run by the cleric Ayatollah Ali al-Sistani. **15.** Thousands of people demonstrated against a rigged presidential election in Azerbaijan's capital Baku, after Ilham Aliyev, the son of the previous president, was declared the winner before the counting of votes had been completed. **19.** Three Israeli soldiers were shot dead east of Ramallah; the Al-Aqsa Martyrs' Brigades claimed responsibility for the killings. **20.** Ten people were killed and almost 100 injured after Israeli aircraft carried out five raids in Gaza. **21.** Iran announced that it would meet all of the key demands of the International Atomic Energy Agency in order to prove to the United Nations that it did not have plans to develop nuclear weapons under cover of a civil nuclear power project. **26.** Eight rockets were fired at the al-Rasheed hotel in Baghdad where coalition troops were staying; one American colonel died and 15 other soldiers were injured. Israeli forces demolished three tower blocks in the Gaza Strip and ordered 2,000 Palestinians out of their homes claiming that the towers had been used by militants planning attacks on nearby Jewish settlements. **27.** Suicide bombers in Baghdad killed 35 people and injured around 230 after car bombs were driven into the headquarters of the International Committee of the Red Cross and three separate police stations.

NOVEMBER 2003

2. A surface-to-air missile shot down a US Chinook helicopter near Baghdad; 15 American soldiers, about to take leave after months of serving in Iraq, were killed. **8.** Three bombs exploded in the Saudi capital Riyadh; 28 people were killed and around 100 more were injured. **9.** Iran announced that it was suspending uranium enrichment 'within days' to prove that it was not trying to make nuclear weapons. **9.** The Israeli cabinet voted 12 to 11 in favour of freeing 400 Palestinian and 20 Lebanese prisoners in exchange for the kidnapped Israeli businessman Elhanan Tannenbaum. Syria's former president, General Amin al-Hafez, returned to the country after spending 36 years in exile in Iraq. **12.** In Israel, the Palestinian Legislative Council ratified the new Palestinian cabinet 48 to 13, and Ahmed Qureia was announced as the new Palestinian Prime Minister. **15.** Twelve US servicemen were killed and nine injured after two American Black Hawk helicopters crashed into each other over the Iraqi city of Mosul. **17.** Six people were killed when American troops fired a 500 lb satellite-guided missile at a suspected guerrilla hideout south of Tikrit in Iraq. **22.** Two bombs were set off by suicide bombers outside police stations in Baghdad; 18 people were killed. **30.** A US military convoy was attacked in Samarra, Iraq, resulting in 46 Iraqis being killed by US tank fire.

DECEMBER 2003

9. Two suicide bombers blew themselves up at the gates of an American army base near the town of Fallujah in Iraq, wounding 58 soldiers. **13.** Economic and diplomatic sanctions were imposed on Syria by the US. In al-Maabar near Tikrit, American forces captured the former Iraqi leader Saddam Hussein; he had been hiding in a tiny underground shaft, known as a 'spider hole'. **15.** In Baku, thousands of people gathered for the funeral of the former President of Azerbaijan Heydar Aliyev; his son Ilham Aliyev took over the presidency. **18.** Iran signed an agreement to allow United Nations inspectors to make surprise visits to its atomic facilities. **26.** In Iran, an earthquake measuring 6.3 on the Richter scale killed an estimated 50,000 people and destroyed the city of Bam.

JANUARY 2004

9. Saddam Hussein was formally declared an enemy prisoner of war by Pentagon spokesman, Major Michael Shavers. **18.** Twenty people died and many people were injured when a suicide bomber detonated half a ton of explosives outside the headquarters of the coalition troops in Baghdad. **28.** Eight Palestinians were killed by Israeli troops when fighting broke out between them and around 200 Palestinian gunmen near the Jewish settlement of Netzarim in Israel.

FEBRUARY 2004

1. In Saudi Arabia, 244 people were trampled to death during the annual muslim pilgrimage to the Jamarat Bridge near Mecca for the stoning ritual which is part of the Eid al-Adha feast day of sacrifice. Two suicide bombers blew themselves up in the Kurdish city of Arbil in Iraq, killing 57 people, including the deputy governor of Arbil province and the city police chief. In Iran, 100 reformist MPs resigned in protest at the disqualification by the ruling Guardian Council of hundreds of reformist candidates from upcoming parliamentary elections. **2.** Israeli Prime Minister Ariel Sharon announced his intention to begin the evacuation of 17 Jewish settlements in the Gaza Strip and said that he was working on the assumption that in the future there would be no Jews in Gaza. **10.** In Iraq, 55 people were killed near Baghdad after a 500 lb bomb exploded outside a police station; it was believed that al-Qa'eda had planted the bomb in order to provoke tensions between the majority Shia population and the Sunni minority. **18.** A train carrying fuel and chemicals derailed in north-east Iran, killing 295 people. **22.** The European Union and the US Administration criticised Iran's general election as 'undemocratic' after the Traditionalists won the election; 2,500 Reformists had been barred from standing at the election and many voters boycotted the elections.

MARCH 2004

2. Around 150 Shia muslims were killed and many more injured as five bombs exploded in Karbala and Baghdad. **15.** The International Atomic Energy Agency chief, Mohamed ElBaradei, announced that Iran had lifted its freeze on nuclear inspections and that they would resume on 27 March. **22.** In Israel, the founder of Hamas, Sheikh Ahmed Yassin, was assassinated outside his mosque by Israeli troops during a dawn missile attack, leading to 200,000 Palestinians protesting in the streets of Gaza City.

APRIL 2004

4. In Baghdad, nine American soldiers were killed and more than 24 wounded in fighting with Shia Muslims loyal to the radical Shia cleric, Hojatoleslam Moqtada al-Sadr; there was fighting in cities across Iraq in protest at the presence of the coalition forces in the country, resulting in more than 20 Iraqi deaths. **17.** The newly-appointed leader of the Palestinian group Hamas, Abdel Aziz al-Rantissi, was assassinated by Israeli forces after two Israeli helicopters fired rockets at his car. **18.** Hamas announced that the physician, Mahmoud Zahar, had been appointed as its new leader. **20.** In Iraq, a multiple mortar attack on the Abu Ghraib prison, west of Baghdad, killed 22 Iraqi inmates and injured almost 100 more. **21.** Four co-ordinated suicide bombings in the Iraqi city of Basra killed at least 68 people, including 17 schoolchildren, and injured a further 100 people. **27.** Two bombs exploded in the Syrian Capital Damascus and security forces fought gunmen in the Mezze suburb of the city; the attack was believed to have been carried out by a militant Muslim group. US forces in the Iraqi city of Najaf killed 64 Shia militiamen after they opened fire on an American patrol on the edge of the Kufa suburb. **29.** The American CBS television channel broadcast pictures taken in the Abu Ghraib prison outside Baghdad which depicted US troops abusing and humiliating Iraqi inmates; six soldiers faced charges of conspiracy, dereliction of duty, cruelty and maltreatment, assault and indecent acts and 11 others were suspended.

MAY 2004

4. An internal investigation by the US army reported that two Iraqi prisoners had been murdered by American soldiers and that there had been 35 criminal investigations into claims of prisoner abuse and deaths in Iraq and Afghanistan. **16.** The Kuwaiti cabinet approved a Bill to grant women the right to vote and stand for parliament. **17.** Abdel-Zahraa Othman, the president of the Iraqi Governing Council, was assassinated in Baghdad by a suicide car bomber at the headquarters of the American military. **19.** In Israel, 10 Palestinians were killed and more than 50 wounded when an Israeli tank fired into a crowd of unarmed demonstrators in the Gaza Strip. In Iraq, the US army killed around 40 members of a wedding party in the village of Maker al-Theeb after mistaking them for foreign fighters. **28.** An earthquake in the Mazandaran province of Iran killed 20 and injured 80 people. **30.** In Saudi Arabia, at least 22 people died after al-Qa'eda members launched kidnappings and attacks on Western targets.

JUNE 2004

6. Marwan Barghouti, the leader of the Palestinian intifada, was jailed by an Israeli court for attempted murder and membership of a terrorist organisation; he was sentenced to five life terms and 40 years in jail. **8.** Effi Eitam, the Israeli housing minister, and Yitzhak Levy, a deputy minister, resigned from Arial Sharon's coalition in protest at plans to withdraw from the Gaza Strip. **12.** Bassam Qubba, the Iraqi Deputy Foreign Minister was killed by gunmen while driving to work. **13.** In Iraq, the Cultural Affairs Officer, Kamal al-Jarrah, was shot dead outside his home. **17.** At least 35 Iraqis were killed and more than 130 wounded when a suicide bomber blew up a car outside the Iraqi army recruiting centre in Baghdad. **18.** Security officials in Saudi Arabia announced that they

had killed three of the most-wanted al-Qa'eda members after they had made a broadcast on the internet claiming to have tortured and beheaded Paul Johnson, an aeronautical engineer from New Jersey. **22.** Iran state television showed three British servicemen blindfolded and apologising for their 'big mistake' after their patrol vessels strayed off course into Tehran's territorial waters. **24.** In Iraq, at least 62 people died and 220 were injured in car bombings in the northern city of Mosul. **27.** Israeli paratroopers killed six Palestinian militant leaders in a secret tunnel beneath a house in the city of Nablus, including Nayef Abu Sharkh, the commander of the militant group the Al-Aqsa Martyrs Brigades. **28.** The US and Britain handed over sovereignty to Iraq and officially ended the 15-month occupation two days earlier than expected. Iyad Allawi was named as the new Prime Minister of Iraq and a document containing the transfer of power was handed to him by Paul Bremer, the head of the Coalition Provisional Authority. **30.** In Israel, the Supreme Court ordered the Government to change the route of its security fence in the West Bank and to rip up a section already built in north Jerusalem as it caused unjustified hardship to around 35,000 Palestinians. Saudi Arabian security forces killed Abdullah al-Rooshood, believed to be al-Qa'eda's spiritual leader in the country, following a car chase in Riyadh.

JULY 2004

7. Iraq's prime minister Iyad Allawi signed in the new National Safety Law which would allow the interim government to declare an emergency in any area of the country deemed under threat from terrorism and would give security forces the power to search houses and detain suspects without an arrest warrant. **9.** Israel rejected a demand from the International Court of Justice to dismantle its security fence being built through occupied Palestinian territory after 14 out of 15 judges in the Hague voted that it breached international law. **13.** Khaled al-Harbi, a leading member of al-Qa'eda, gave himself up to Saudi Arabian authorities as part of a Saudi government amnesty which had recently been extended to terrorists. **22.** American marines in Iraq reported that they had killed 25 insurgents, wounded 17 and captured another 25 in a battle in the city of Ramadi after a US patrol came under attack from militants. **28.** At least 129 people were killed in Iraq by suicide bomb attacks in Baghdad, Ramadi, Fallujah and Balad-Ruz.

AUGUST 2004

6. Three hundred militants loyal to the cleric Moqtada al-Sadr were killed by US marines following fighting to regain control of the Iraqi city of Najaf. **8.** Palestine's justice minister, Nahed al-Reyes, and Nabil Qasis, the planning minister, announced their resignation from the Palestinian cabinet. **18.** The Iranian defence minister Ali Shamkhani warned America and Israel that it was ready to launch pre-emptive strikes to stop them attacking its nuclear facilities. In Israel, Prime Minister Ariel Sharon's Likud Party rejected proposals to enter a coalition with the Labour Party.

OBITUARIES

Aiken, Joan, children's author, aged 79 – d. 4 January 2004, b. 4 September 1924

Ainley, Anthony, actor, gained cult status for his role in Dr Who, the television series, aged 66 – d. 3 May 2004, b. 30 August 1937

Alcock, Vivien, children's author, aged 79 – d. 12 October 2003, b. 23 September 1924

Alison, Michael, Conservative MP for Barkston Ash (1964–83) and Selby (1983–97), minister of state at the Northern Ireland Office (1979–83) and parliamentary private secretary to Margaret Thatcher (1983–7), aged 77 – d. 28 May 2004, b. 27 June 1926

Aliyev, Heydar, president of Azerbaijan (1993–2003), aged 80 – d. 12 December 2003, b. 10 May 1923

Atkins, Babs, conservationist, owner and last inhabitant of the 22-acre St George's Island, Looe, aged 86 – d. 30 March 2004, b. 3 June 1917

Baldock, John, MBE, VRD, businessman, MP and founder of the Hollycombe Steam Collection, aged 87 – d. 3 October 2003, b. 19 November 1915

Bates, Sir Alan, actor, aged 69 – d. 27 December 2003, b. 17 February 1934

Batty, Sir William, former chairman and managing director of Ford in Britain, aged 90 – d. 31 October 2003, b. 15 May 1913

Berger, Vice-Adm. Sir Peter, KCB, LVO, DSC, aged 78 – d. 19 October 2003, b. 11 February 1925

Bertram, Elsie, MBE, book wholesaler, aged 91 – d. 26 October 2003, b. 2 June 1912

Blake, Lord, FBA, life peer, historian and provost of Queen's College, Oxford (1968–87), aged 86 – d. 20 September 2003, b. 23 December 1916

Blankers-Koen, Fanny, Dutch athlete who won four gold medals at the 1948 London Olympics and was voted the greatest female athlete of the 20th century by the IAAF in 1999, aged 85 – d. 25 January 2004, b. 26 April 1918

Blow, Prof. David, FRS, biophysicist, aged 72 – d. 8 June 2004, b. 27 June 1931

Boreham, Sir Leslie, High Court judge (1972–), aged 85 – d. 2 May 2004, b. 19 October 1918

Boyd, Prof. Sir Robert, CBE, FRS, space research scientist, professor of physics at the University of London (1962–83), aged 81 – d. 5 February 2004, b. 19 October 1922

Brando, Marlon, American actor, aged 80 – d. 1 July 2004, b. 3 April 1924

Brockhouse, Bertram, Canadian physicist, winner of the Nobel Prize for Physics (1994), aged 85 – d. 13 October 2003, b. 15 July 1918

Brown, Iona, violinist and conductor, aged 63 – d. 5 June 2004, b. 7 January 1941

Buck, Sir Antony, QC, Conservative MP for Colchester (1961–83) and for Colchester North (1983–92), aged 74 – d. 6 October 2003, b. 19 December 1928

Buckeridge, Anthony, OBE, schoolmaster and author of the 'Jennings' stories, aged 92 – d. 28 June 2004, b. 20 June 1912

Bullock, Lord, historian, founder of St Catherine's College, Oxford, created a life peer in 1976, aged 89 – d. 2 February 2004, b. 13 December 1914

Cameron of Lochiel, Col. Sir Donald, KT, CVO, TD, clan chief, appointed Knight of the Thistle in 1973, aged 93 – d. 26 May 2004, b. 12 September 1910

Campbell/Birkin, Judy, actress, aged 88 – d. 6 June 2004, b. 31 May 1916

Carr, Joe, golfer, aged 82 – d. 3 June 2004, b. 18 February 1922

Carrington, Joanna, artist, aged 72 – d. 13 November 2003, b. 6 November 1931

Cartier-Bresson, Henri, French photographer, aged 95 – d. 2 August 2004, b. 22 August 1908

Cartwright, Stephen, children's book illustrator, aged 57 – d. 12 February 2004, b. 28 December 1947

Cash, Johnny, country music singer, aged 71 – d. 12 September 2003, b. 26 February 1932

Causley, Charles, CBE, poet, aged 86 – d. 4 November 2003, b. 24 August 1917

Cavenagh, Prof. Winifred, OBE, criminologist, aged 95 – d. 7 May 2004, b. 12 November 1908

Charles, Pierre, prime minister of Dominica (2000–4), aged 49 – d. 6 January 2004 of a heart attack, b. 30 June 1954

Charles, John, CBE, Welsh footballer, aged 72 – d. 21 February 2004, b. 27 December 1931

Charles, Ray, American musician, aged 73 – d. 10 June 2004, b. 23 September 1930

Chilcott, Susan, opera singer, aged 40 – d. 4 September 2003, b. 8 July 1963

Coldstream, Sir George, KCB, KCVO, permanent secretary to the Lord Chancellor (1954–68), aged 96 – d. 19 April 2004, b. 20 December 1907

Constantine of Stanmore, Lord, CBE, AE, business and political activist, created a life peer in 1981, aged 93 – d. 13 February 2004, b. 15 March 1910

Cooke, Alistair, journalist and broadcaster, aged 95 – d. 29 March 2004, b. 20 November 1908

Crick, Francis, OM, FRS, biologist, joint recipient of the Nobel Prize for Medicine (1962) for the discovery of the structure of DNA, aged 88 – d. 28 July 2004, b. 8 June 1916

Daly, Lt.-Gen. Sir Tom, KBE, CB, DSO, Australia's chief of general staff (1966–71), aged 90 – *d.* 5 January 2004 in Sydney, Australia, *b.* 19 March 1913

Darling (2nd), Lord, aged 84 – *d.* 16 October 2003, *b.* 15 May 1919

Davis, Richard, cricketer, aged 37 – *d.* 29 December 2003, *b.* 18 March 1966

Devonshire (11th), Duke of, KG, MC, aged 84 – *d.* 3 May 2004, *b.* 2 January 1920

Diamond, Lord, PC, QC, former Labour MP, chief secretary to the Treasury (1964–70) and SDP leader in House of Lords (1982–8), aged 96 – *d.* 3 April 2004, *b.* 30 April 1907

Donaldson, Dame Mary, GBE, philanthropist, first woman to hold the office of Lord Mayor of London (1983–4), aged 82 – *d.* 4 October 2003, *b.* 29 August 1921

Doniach, Prof. Deborah, clinical immunologist, aged 91 – *d.* 1 January 2004, *b.* 6 April 1912

Dormand of Easington, Lord, MP for Easington (1970–87) and chairman of the Parliamentary Labour Party (1981–7), created a life peer in 1987, aged 84 – *d.* 18 December 2003, *b.* 27 August 1919

Downshire (8th), The Marquess of, aged 74 – *d.* 18 December 2003, *b.* 10 May 1929

Duffen, Leslie, teacher and pioneer in the teaching of Down's syndrome children, aged 79 – *d.* 8 May 2004, *b.* 14 November 1924

Dugdale, Lady, DCVO, lady-in-waiting to the Queen (1955–2002), aged 80 – *d.* 4 November 1923, *b.* 12 March 2004

Dumas, Charles, American athlete who became the first man to clear 7ft in the high jump in 1956, aged 66 – *d.* 5 January 2004, *b.* 12 February 1937

Dunboyne (28th), Lord, judge, aged 87 – *d.* 19 May 2004, *b.* 27 January 1917

Dunn, Air Marshal Sir Patrick, KBE, CB, DFC, aged 91 – *d.* 17 June 2004, *b.* 31 December 1912

Dunne, John Gregory, American journalist, novelist and screenwriter, aged 71 – *d.* 30 December 2003, *b.* 25 May 1932

Durkin, Air Marshal Sir Herbert, KBE, CB, aged 82 – *d.* 12 April 2004, *b.* 31 March 1922

Ederle, Gertrude, American swimmer, the first woman to swim the English Channel, aged 97 – *d.* 30 November 2003, *b.* 23 October 1906

Esher (4th), Viscount, CBE, architect and town planner, aged 90 – *d.* 9 July 2004, *b.* 18 July 1913

Fiennes, Lady Virginia, explorer, aged 56 – *d.* 20 February 2004, *b.* 9 July 1947

Fluss, Elfrieda, milliner, aged 89 – *d.* 8 January 2004, *b.* 16 November 1914

Foot, Paul, author and journalist, aged 66 – *d.* 18 July 2004, *b.* 8 November 1937

Forest, Antonia, children's author, aged 88 – *d.* 28 November 2003, *b.* 26 May 1915

Friedlander, Rabbi Dr Albert, spiritual leader and interfaith worker, aged 77 – *d.* 8 July 2004, *b.* 10 May 1927

Frost, Sir Terry, RA, artist, aged 87 – *d.* 1 September 2003, *b.* 13 October 1915

Fry, Tim, car designer and engineer, aged 68 – *d.* 17 May 2004, *b.* 25 August 1935

Geraint, Lord, Welsh politician, leader of the Welsh Liberal party (1979–85), created a life peer in 1992, aged 79 – *d.* 17 April 2004, *b.* 15 April 1925

Getting, Ivan, American scientist, aged 91 – *d.* 11 October 2003, *b.* 18 January 1912

Gibson, Sir Ralph, PC, QC, chairman of the Law Commission (1981–5) and Lord Justice of Appeal (1985–94), aged 81 – *d.* 30 October 2003, *b.* 17 October 1922

Gibson, Lord, chairman of the Arts Council (1972–7), the National Trust (1977–86) and the Pearson Group (1978–83), aged 88 – *d.* 20 April 2004, *b.* 5 February 1916

Gilmour, Sally, ballerina, aged 82 – *d.* 23 May 2004, *b.* 2 November 1921

Ginsberg, Jean, doctor and specialist in women's health, aged 77 – *d.* 8 April 2004, *b.* 19 October 1926

Golub, Leon, artist, aged 82 – *d.* 8 August 2004, *b.* 23 January 1922

Gordon, Nick, wildlife cameraman and film producer, aged 51 – *d.* 25 April 2004, *b.* 9 May 1952

Grandy, Marshal of the RAF Sir John, GCB, GCVO, KBE, DSO, chief of the Air Staff (1967–71), appointed Marshal of the Royal Air Force on his retirement in 1971, aged 90 – *d.* 2 January 2004, *b.* 8 February 1913

Grant Duff, Shiela, writer and reporter, aged 90 – *d.* 19 March 2004, *b.* 11 May 1913

Greene of Harrow Weald, Lord, CBE, life peer, general secretary of the National Union of Railwaymen (1957–75), aged 94 – *d.* 26 July 2004, *b.* 12 February 1910

Gregg, Hubert, composer, actor and broadcaster, aged 89 – *d.* 29 March 2004, *b.* 19 July 1914

Gunn, Thom, poet, aged 74 – *b.* 29 August 1929, *d.* 25 April 2004

Hampshire, Prof. Sir Stuart, philosopher and warden of Wadham College, Oxford (1970–84), aged 89 – *d.* 13 June 2004, *b.* 1 October 1914

Hardinge (6th), Viscount, of, aged 47 – *d.* 18 January 2004, *b.* 25 August 1956

Hardy of Wath, Lord, Labour MP for Rother Valley (1970–83) and Wentworth (1983–97), created a life peer in 1997, aged 72 – *d.* 16 December 2003, *b.* 17 July 1931

Hayter (3rd), Lord, last family chairman of Chubb & Sons, Locksmiths, aged 92 – *d.* 2 September 2003, *b.* 25 April 1911

Hemmings, David, actor, director and producer, aged 62 – *d.* 3 December 2003, *b.* 18 November 1941

Henley, Sir Douglas, KCB, 14th comptroller and auditor-general at the Treasury (1976–81), aged 84 – d. 1 October 2003, b. 5 April 1919

Henniker (8th), Lord, KCMG, CMG, CVO, MC, diplomat, aged 88 – d. 29 April 2004, b. 19 February 1916

Hill-Norton, Admiral of the Fleet, Lord, GCB, GCVO, KBE, DSO, chief of Defence Staff (1971–3), chairman of the Military Committee of NATO (1974–7), aged 89 – d. 16 May 2004, b. 8 February 1915

Hobhouse of Woodborough, Lord, PC, QC, Lord of Appeal (1998–2004), created a life peer in 1998, aged 72 – d. 15 March 2004, b. 31 January 1932

Holland, Mary, journalist, aged 67 – d. 7 June 2004, b. 19 June 1936

Hounsfield, Sir Godfrey, CBE, FRS, scientist, winner of the Nobel Prize for Medicine (1979) for inventing the CAT (computerised axial tomography) scanner, aged 84 – d. 12 August 2004, b. 29 August 1919

Hurley, Denis, Archbishop of Durban (1952–92), aged 88 – d. 13 February 2004, b. 9 November 1915

Hurley, Dame Rosalinde, DBE, microbiologist and pathologist, chairman of the Medicines Commission (1982–93), aged 74 – d. 30 June 2004, b. 30 December 1929

Ishihara, Takashi, president (1977–85) and chairman (1985–92) of Nissan Motor Co., aged 91 – d. 31 December 2003, b. 3 March 1912

Islwyn, Lord, Labour MP for Newport (1966–83) and Newport East (1983–97), created a life peer in 1997, aged 78 – d. 19 December 2003, b. 9 June 1925

Izetbegovic, Alija, Bosnian politician, Muslim member of the joint presidency of Bosnia Hercegovina (1996–2000), aged 78 – d. 19 October 2003, b. 8 August 1925

Jenkins, Vivien, rugby player for Wales in the 1930s and later, sports journalist who retired in 1976, aged 92 – d. 5 January 2004, b. 2 November 1911

Jenkins of Putney, Lord, Labour MP for Wandsworth, Putney (1964–79), created a life peer in 1981, aged 95 – d. 26 January 2004, b. 27 July 1908

Jennings, Sir Robert, international lawyer, president of the International Court of Justice (1982–96), aged 90 – d. 4 August 2004, b. 19 October 1913

Jupp, Sir Kenneth, MC, judge of the High Court, Queen's Bench Division (1975–90), aged 86 – d. 15 March 2004, b. 2 June 1917

Kadyrov, Akhmad, president of Chechnya (2003–4), aged 53 – d. assassinated 9 May 2004, b. 23 August 1950

Kay, Sir John, PC, QC, Lord Justice of Appeal (2000–4), aged 60 – d. 2 July 2004, b. 13 September 1943

Keating, Caron, television presenter, aged 41 – d. 13 April 2004, b. 5 October 1962

Keith of Castleacre, Lord, merchant banker and industrialist, chairman of Rolls-Royce (1972–80), created a life peer in 1980, aged 88 – d. 1 September 2004, b. 30 August 1916

Kessel, Barney, American jazz guitarist, aged 80 – d. 6 May 2004, b. 17 October 1923

Landen, Dinsdale, actor, aged 71 – d. 29 December 2003, b. 4 September 1932

Langman, Mary, MBE, organic farmer, founder member of the Soil Association, aged 95 – d. 31 March 2004, b. 6 August 1908

Lauder, Estée, founder of the Estée Lauder cosmetics company, aged 97 – d. 24 April 2004, b. 1 July 1906

Leask, Lt.-Gen. Sir Henry, KCB, DSO, OBE, GOC, aged 90 – d. 10 January 2004, b. 30 June 1913

Lee, Air Chief Marshal Sir David, GBE, CB, military representative to NATO (1968–71), aged 91 – d. 13 February 2004, b. 4 September 1912

Lee, Anna, actress, aged 91 – d. 14 May 2004, b. 2 January 1913

Levin, Bernard, CBE, journalist, aged 75 – d. 7 August 2004, b. 19 August 1928

Lindh, Anna, Swedish politician and Foreign Minister, aged 46 – d. 11 September 2003, b. 19 June 1957

Livesay, Adm. Sir Michael, KCB, head of the Naval Advisory Group during the Falklands war, aged 67 – d. 6 October 2003, b. 5 April 1936

Lodge, David, actor, aged 82 – d. 18 October 2003, b. 19 August 1921

MacDougall, Sir Donald, CBE, economist, aged 91 – d. 22 March 2004, b. 26 October 1912

May, Sir Richard, presiding judge of the International Criminal Tribunal for the former Yugoslavia (1997–2004), aged 65 – d. 1 July 2004, b. 12 November 1938

Maynard Smith, John, FRS, biologist, aged 84 – d. 19 April 2004, b. 6 January 1920

McKechnie, Dame Sheila, DBE, director of Shelter, the housing charity, (1985–94) and the Consumers' Association (1995–2003), aged 55 – d. 2 January 2004 of cancer, b. 3 May 1948

McWhirter, Norris, CBE, co-founder of the *Guinness Book of Records* and contributor to *Whitaker's Almanack*, aged 78 – d. 19 April 2004, b. 12 August 1925

Mercer, The Rt. Revd Eric, Bishop of Exeter (1973–85), aged 85 – d. 8 November 2003, b. 6 December 1917

Metcalfe, Ben, journalist and founding member of Greenpeace, aged 84 – d. 16 October 2003, b. 27 November 1918

Monkhouse, Bob, entertainer, aged 75 – d. 29 December 2003, b. 1 June 1928

Morgan, Peter, sports car manufacturer, aged 83 – d. 20 October 2003, b. 3 November 1919

Mountgarret (17th), Viscount, aged 67 – d. 7 February 2004, b. 8 November 1936

Murray of Epping Forest, Lord, OBE, PC, trades unionist, general secretary of the TUC (1973–84), aged 81 – d. 20 May 2004, b. 2 August 1922

Neagu, Paul, Romanian sculptor, aged 66 – d. 16 June 2004, b. 22 February 1938

Newton, Helmut, photographer, aged 83 – *d.* 23 January 2004 in Los Angeles, USA, *b.* 31 October 1920

Nuttall, Jeff, painter, poet, author and performance artist, aged 70 – *d.* 4 January 2004, *b.* 8 July 1933

Palmer, Robert, rock singer, aged 53 – *d.* 25 September 2003, *b.* 19 January 1949

Pantani, Marco, former world cycling champion, aged 34 – *d.* 14 February 2004, Rimini, Italy, *b.* 13 January 1970

Partridge, Frances, CBE, author and last survivor of the 'Bloomsbury set', aged 103 – *d.* 5 February 2004, *b.* 15 March 1990

Paul, Sir John, GCMG, MC, governor-general of the Gambia (1961–6), the Bahamas (1972–3) and lieutenant-governor of the Isle of Man (1974–80), aged 88 – *d.* 31 March 2004, *b.* 29 March 1916

Pearce, Sir Austen, chairman of British Aerospace (1980–7), aged 82 – *d.* 21 March 2004, *b.* 1 September 1921

Pembroke (17th) and Montgomery (18th), Earl of, film and television director, aged 64 – *d.* 7 October 2003, *b.* 19 May 1939

Pike, Baroness Mervyn, DBE, Conservative MP for Melton (1956–74), chairman of the Women's Royal Voluntary Service (1974–81) and life peer, aged 85 – *d.* 11 January 2004, *b.* 16 September 1918

Pople, Anthony, musicologist, aged 48 – *d.* 10 October 2003, *b.* 18 January 1955

Pople, Sir John, KBE, FRS, quantum chemist, winner of the Nobel Prize for Chemistry in 1998, aged 78 – *d.* 15 March 2004, *b.* 31 October 1925

Quilley, Denis, actor, aged 75 – *d.* 5 October 2003, *b.* 26 December 1927

Ravensworth (8th), Lord, aged – *d.* 28 March 2004, *b.* 25 July 1924

Rayne, Lord, QC, property developer and philanthropist, made a life peer in 1976, aged 85 – *d.* 10 October 2003, *b.* 8 February 1918

Reagan, Ronald, actor and politician, president of the USA (1980–89), aged 93 – *d.* 5 June 2004, *b.* 6 February 1911

Reid, Gordon, television and theatre actor, aged 64 – *d.* 26 November 2003, *b.* 8 June 1939

Resnick, Milton, artist, aged 87 – *d.* 12 March 2004, *b.* 8 January 1917

Richardson, Lord, LVO, physician, president of the General Medical Council (1973–80), the British Medical Association (1970–1) and the Royal Society of Medicine (1969–71), created a life peer in 1979, aged 94 – *d.* 8 August 2004, *b.* 16 June 1910

Rossiter, Nick, BBC documentary-maker, aged 43 – *d.* 23 July 2004, *b.* 17 July 1961

Roxburgh, Vice-Adm. Sir John, KCB, CBE, DSO, DSC and Bar, aged 84 – *d.* 13 April 2004, *b.* 29 June 1919

Sackville (6th), Lord, aged 90 – *d.* 27 March 2004, *b.* 30 May 1913

Said, Edward, literary and political commentator, aged 67 – *d.* 24 September 2003, *b.* 1 November 1935

Sandilands, John, journalist, aged 72 – *d.* 15 March 2004, *b.* 19 July 1931

Scanlon, Lord, trade union leader, created a life peer in 1979, aged 90 – *d.* 27 January 2004, *b.* 26 October 1913

Scarbrough (12th), Earl of, aged 71 – *d.* 23 March 2004, *b.* 5 December 1932

Schott, Alberic, Belgian cyclist, aged 84 – *d.* 4 April 2004, *b.* 7 September 1919

Shapiro, Isaac Avi, literary scholar, aged 99 – *d.* 14 March 2004, *b.* 7 November 1904

Shenfield, Dame Barbara, DBE, sociologist, aged 85 – *d.* 17 June 2004, *b.* 9 March 1919

Shoenberg, Prof. David, MBE, physicist known for his work in the field of superconductivity, aged 93 – *d.* 10 March 2004, *b.* 4 January 1911

Short, Roger, diplomat, UK consul-general in Turkey, aged 58 – *d.* 20 November 2003, killed in a terrorist bombing, *b.* 9 December 1944

Skeet, Trevor, Conservative MP for Willesden East (1959–64) and Bedford, later Bedfordshire North (1970–97), aged 86 – *d.* 14 August 2004, *b.* 28 January 1918

Smart, Prof. Sir George, physician, endocrinologist and Director of the British Postgraduate Medical Federation (1971–8), aged 89 – *d.* 1 November 2003, *b.* 16 December 1913

Squire, Raglan, architect, aged 92 – *d.* 18 May 2004, *b.* 30 January 1912

Stacey, Margaret, sociologist, aged 81 – *d.* 10 February 2004, *b.* 27 March 1922

Stamper, John, aeronautical engineer and chief designer of the Buccaneer strike aircraft (1961), aged 77 – *d.* 15 November 2003, *b.* 12 October 1926

Stanbrook, Ivor, Conservative MP (1970–92), aged 80 – *d.* 18 February 2004, *b.* 13 January 1924

Steel, Sir David, DSO, MC, chairman of BP (1975–81), aged 87 – *d.* 9 August 2004, *b.* 29 November 1916

Steig, William, American cartoonist and children's author, aged 95 – *d.* 3 October 2003, *b.* 17 November 1907

Stockdale, Sir Noel, founding chairman of the ASDA supermarket chain, aged 83 – *d.* 2 February 2004, *b.* 25 December 1920

Tanner, John, CBE, director, RAF Museum (1963–88), aged 77 – *d.* 18 May 2004, *b.* 2 January 1927

Taylor, Lt.-Gen. Sir Allan, KBE, MC, deputy commander-in-chief, UK Land Forces (1973–6), aged 85 – *d.* 13 June 2004, *b.* 26 March 1919

Tidsdale, Bob, Irish athlete, gold medallist at the 1932 Los Angeles Olympics, aged 97 – *d.* 28 July 2004, *b.* 16 May 1916

Trajkovski, Boris, president of Macedonia (1999–2004), aged 47 – *d.* 26 February 2004, killed in an air crash in Bosnia, *b.* 25 June 1956

Trevor-Roper, Patrick, ophthalmologist and art historian, aged 87 – *d.* 22 April 2004, *b.* 7 June 1916

Tumim, Sir Stephen, lawyer and prison reformer, aged 73 – *d.* 8 December 2003, *b.* 15 August 1930

Ustinov, Sir Peter, actor, director and writer, aged 82 – *d.* 28 March 2004, *b.* 16 April 1921

Venables, Clare, theatre director, aged 60 – *d.* 17 October 2003, *b.* 17 March 1943

Vladimov, Georgi, Russian writer and political dissident, aged 72 – *d.* 19 October 2003, *b.* 19 February 1931

Walker of Doncaster, Lord, PC, Labour MP for 33 years, knighted in 1992 and created a life peer in 1997, aged 76 – *d.* 11 November 2003, *b.* 12 July 1927

Wallace of Coslany, Lord, Labour politician, aged 97 – *d.* 11 November 2003, *b.* 18 April 1906

Watson, Willie, cricketer, aged 84 – *d.* 24 April 2004, *b.* 7 March 1920

Wickham, Glynne, academic and drama teacher, aged 81 – *d.* 27 January 2004, *b.* 15 May 1922

Wigoder, Lord, QC, lawyer and Liberal peer, Liberal chief whip in the Lords (1977–84), aged 83 – *d.* 12 August 2004, *b.* 12 February 1921

Williams of Mostyn, Lord, PC, QC, barrister and politician, Lord President of the Privy Council and leader of the House of Lords, aged 62 – *d.* 20 September 2003, *b.* 5 February 1941

Wilson, Sir Geoffrey, KCB, CMG, lawyer and diplomat, vice-president of the World Bank (1961–6), aged 94 – *d.* 11 July 2004, *b.* 7 April 1910

Winter, Fred, CBE, jump jockey and trainer, aged 77 – *d.* 5 April 2004, *b.* 20 September 1926

Woodin, Michael, principal speaker of the Green Party (2001 and 2003–4), aged 38 – *d.* 9 July 2004, *b.* 6 November 1965

Ziegler, Anne, 1940s concert and variety performance singer, aged 93 – *d.* 13 October 2003, *b.* 22 June 1910

THE WORLD

TIME ZONES

Standard time differences from the
Greenwich meridian

+   hours ahead of GMT
−   hours behind GMT
*   may vary from standard time at
    some part of the year (Summer
    Time or Daylight Saving Time)
‡   some areas may keep another
    time zone
h   hours
m   minutes

	h	*m*
Afghanistan	+ 4	30
*Albania	+ 1	
Algeria	+ 1	
*Andorra	+ 1	
Angola	+ 1	
Anguilla	− 4	
Antigua and Barbuda	− 4	
Argentina	− 3	
*Armenia	+ 4	
Aruba	− 4	
Ascension Island	0	
*Australia		
ACT, NSW (except Broken		
Hill area) Qld, Tas., Vic,		
Whitsunday Islands	+10	
*Broken Hill area	+ 9	30
(NSW)		
*Lord Howe Island	+10	30
Northern Territory	+ 9	30
*South Australia	+ 9	30
Western Australia	+ 8	
*Austria	+ 1	
*Azerbaijan	+ 4	
*Bahamas	− 5	
Bahrain	+ 3	
Bangladesh	+ 6	
Barbados	− 4	
*Belarus	+ 2	
*Belgium	+ 1	
Belize	− 6	
Benin	+ 1	
*Bermuda	− 4	
Bhutan	+ 6	
Bolivia	− 4	
*Bosnia-Hercegovina	+ 1	
Botswana	+ 2	
Brazil		
western states	− 5	
central states	− 4	
N. and NE coastal		
states	− 3	
*S. and E. coastal states,		
including Brasilia	− 3	
Fernando de Noronha		
Island	− 2	
British Antarctic Territory	− 3	
British Indian Ocean		
Territory	+ 5	
Diego Garcia	+ 6	

	h	*m*
British Virgin Islands	− 4	
Brunei	+ 8	
*Bulgaria	+ 2	
Burkina Faso	0	
Burundi	+ 2	
Cambodia	+ 7	
Cameroon	+ 1	
Canada		
*Alberta	− 7	
*‡British Columbia	− 8	
*‡Labrador	− 4	
*Manitoba	− 6	
*New Brunswick	− 4	
*Newfoundland	− 3	30
*Northwest Territories		
east of 85° W.	− 5	
85° W. − 102° W.	− 6	
*Nunavut	− 7	
*Nova Scotia	− 4	
Ontario		
*east of 90° W.	− 5	
west of 90° W.	− 5	
*Prince Edward Island	− 4	
Québec		
east of 63° W.	− 4	
*west of 63° W.	− 5	
‡Saskatchewan	− 6	
*Yukon	− 8	
Cape Verde	− 1	
Cayman Islands	− 5	
Central African Republic	+ 1	
Chad	+ 1	
*Chatham Islands	+12	45
*Chile	− 4	
China (inc. Hong Kong		
and Macao)	+ 8	
Christmas Island (Indian		
Ocean)	+ 7	
Cocos (Keeling) Islands	+ 6	30
Colombia	− 5	
Comoros	+ 3	
Congo (Dem. Rep.)		
Haut-Zaïre, Kasai, Kivu,		
Shaba	+ 2	
Kinshasa, Mbandaka	+ 1	
Congo-Brazzaville	+ 1	
Costa Rica	− 6	
Côte d'Ivoire	0	
*Croatia	+ 1	
*Cuba	− 5	
*Cyprus	+ 2	
*Czech Republic	+ 1	
*Denmark	+ 1	
*Færøe Islands	0	
*Greenland	− 3	
Danmarkshavn, Mesters		
Vig	0	
*Scoresby Sound	− 1	
*Thule area	− 4	
Djibouti	+ 3	
Dominica	− 4	
Dominican Republic	− 5	

	h	*m*
East Timor	+ 9	
Ecuador	− 5	
Galápagos Islands	− 6	
*Egypt	+ 2	
El Salvador	− 6	
Equatorial Guinea	+ 1	
Eritrea	+ 3	
Estonia	+ 2	
Ethiopia	+ 3	
*Falkland Islands	− 4	
Fiji	+12	
*Finland	+ 2	
*France	+ 1	
French Guiana	− 3	
French Polynesia	−10	
Guadeloupe	− 4	
Martinique	− 4	
Réunion	+ 4	
Marquesas Islands	− 9	30
Gabon	+ 1	
Gambia	0	
*Georgia	+ 3	
*Germany	+ 1	
Ghana	0	
*Gibraltar	+ 1	
*Greece	+ 2	
Grenada	− 4	
Guam	+10	
Guatemala	− 6	
Guinea	0	
Guinea-Bissau	0	
Guyana	− 4	
Haïti	− 5	
Honduras	− 6	
*Hungary	+ 1	
Iceland	0	
India	+ 5	30
Indonesia		
Java, Kalimantan (west		
and central), Madura,		
Sumatra	+ 7	
Bali, Flores, Kalimantan		
(south and east),		
Lombok, Sulawesi,		
Sumbawa, West Timor	+ 8	
Irian Jaya, Maluku,	+ 9	
*Iran	+ 3	30
*Iraq	+ 3	
*Ireland, Republic of	0	
*Israel	+ 2	
*Italy	+ 1	
Jamaica	− 5	
Japan	+ 9	
*Jordan	+ 2	
*Kazakhstan		
western	+ 4	
central	+ 5	
eastern	+ 6	
Kenya	+ 3	
Kiribati	+12	
Line Islands	+14	
Phoenix Islands	+13	

	h	m		h	m		h	m
Korea, North	+ 9		*Portugal	0		United Arab Emirates	+ 4	
Korea, South	+ 9		*Azores	− 1		*United Kingdom	0	
Kuwait	+ 3		*Madeira	0		*United States of America		
*Kyrgyzstan	+ 5		Puerto Rico	− 4		Alaska	− 9	
Laos	+ 7		Qatar	+ 3		Aleutian Islands, east	− 9	
Latvia	+ 2		Réunion	+ 4		of 169° 30′ W.		
*Lebanon	+ 2		*Romania	+ 2		Aleutian Islands, west	−10	
Lesotho	+ 2		*Russia			of 169° 30′ W.		
Liberia	0		Zone 1	+ 2		eastern time	− 5	
Libya	+ 2		Zone 2	+ 3		central time	− 6	
*Liechtenstein	+ 1		Zone 3	+ 4		Hawaii	−10	
Line Islands not part of	−10		Zone 4	+ 5		mountain time	− 7	
Kiribati			Zone 5	+ 6		Pacific time	− 8	
Lithuania	+ 2		Zone 6	+ 7		Uruguay	− 3	
*Luxembourg	+ 1		Zone 7	+ 8		Uzbekistan	+ 5	
*Macedonia	+ 1		Zone 8	+ 9		Vanuatu	+11	
Madagascar	+ 3		Zone 9	+10		*Vatican City State	+ 1	
Malawi	+ 2		Zone 10	+11		Venezuela	− 4	
Malaysia	+ 8		Zone 11	+12		Vietnam	+ 7	
Maldives	+ 5		Rwanda	+ 2		Virgin Islands (US)	− 4	
Mali	0		St Helena	0		Yemen	+ 3	
*Malta	+ 1		St Christopher and Nevis	− 4		Zambia	+ 2	
Marshall Islands	+12		St Lucia	− 4		Zimbabwe	+ 2	
Ebon Atoll	−12		*St Pierre and Miquelon	− 3				
Mauritania	0		St Vincent and the					
Mauritius	+ 4		Grenadines	− 4				
*Mexico	− 6		Samoa	−11				
*Nayarit, Sinaloa,			Samoa, American	−11				
S. Baja California	− 7		*San Marino	+ 1				
Sonora	− 7		São Tomé and Princípe	0				
N. Baja California	− 8		Saudi Arabia	+ 3				
Micronesia			Senegal	0				
Caroline Islands	+10		Serbia & Montenegro	+ 1				
Kosrae, Pingelap,			Seychelles	+ 4				
Pohnpei	+11		Sierra Leone	0				
*Moldova	+ 2		Singapore	+ 8				
*Monaco	+ 1		*Slovakia	+ 1				
Mongolia	+ 8		*Slovenia	+ 1				
Montserrat	− 4		Solomon Islands	+11				
Morocco	0		Somalia	+ 3				
Mozambique	+ 2		South Africa	+ 2				
Myanmar	+ 6	30	South Georgia	− 2				
*Namibia	+ 1		*Spain	+ 1				
Nauru	+12		*Canary Islands	0				
Nepal	+ 5	45	Sri Lanka	+ 6				
*Netherlands	+ 1		Sudan	+ 3				
Netherlands Antilles	− 4		Suriname	− 3				
New Caledonia	+11		Swaziland	+ 2				
*New Zealand	+12		*Sweden	+ 1				
*Cook Islands	−10		*Switzerland	+ 1				
Nicaragua	− 6		*Syria	+ 2				
Niger	+ 1		Taiwan	+ 8				
Nigeria	+ 1		Tajikistan	+ 5				
Niue	−11		Tanzania	+ 3				
Norfolk Island	+11	30	Thailand	+ 7				
Northern Mariana Islands	+10		Togo	0				
*Norway	+ 1		*Tonga	+13				
Oman	+ 4		Trinidad and Tobago	− 4				
Pakistan	+ 5		Tristan da Cunha	0				
Palau	+ 9		Tunisia	+ 1				
Panama	− 5		*Turkey	+ 2				
Papua New Guinea	+10		Turkmenistan	+ 5				
*Paraguay	− 4		*Turks and Caicos Islands	− 5				
Peru	− 5		Tuvalu	+12				
Philippines	+ 8		Uganda	+ 3				
*Poland	+ 1		*Ukraine	+ 2				

CURRENCIES AND EXCHANGE RATES

AGAINST £ STERLING

COUNTRY/TERRITORY	MONETARY UNIT	AVERAGE RATE TO £1 29 August 2003	AVERAGE RATE TO £1 27 August 2004
Afghanistan	Afghani (Af) of 100 puls	Af 67.87	Af 77.16
Albania	Lek (Lk) of 100 qindraka	Lk 196.37	Lk 186.10
Algeria	Algerian dinar (DA) of 100 centimes	DA 121.55	DA 129.69
American Samoa	Currency is that of the USA	US$1.58	US$1.79
Andorra	Euro (€) of 100 cents	€1.45	€1.48
Angola	Readjusted kwanza (Krzl) of 100 lwei	Kzrl 125.89	Kzrl 145.95
Anguilla	East Caribbean dollar (EC$) of 100 cents	EC$4.21	EC$4.84
Antigua and Barbuda	East Caribbean dollar (EC$) of 100 cents	EC$4.21	EC$4.84
Argentina	Peso of 10,000 australes	Pesos 4.70	Pesos 5.37
Armenia	Dram of 100 louma	Dram 880.91	Dram 926.93
Aruba	Aruban florin	Florins 2.83	Florins 3.21
Ascension Island	Currency is that of St Helena	at parity with £ sterling	
Australia	Australian dollar ($A) of 100 cents	$A2.47	$A2.55
Norfolk Island	Currency is that of Australia	$A2.47	$A2.55
Austria	Euro (€) of 100 cents	€1.45	€1.48
Azerbaijan	Manat of 100 gopik	Manat 7757.35	Manat 8813.53
The Bahamas	Bahamian dollar (B$) of 100 cents	B$1.58	B$1.79
Bahrain	Bahraini dinar (BD) of 1,000 fils	BD 0.60	BD 0.67
Bangladesh	Taka (Tk) of 100 poisha	Tk 92.20	Tk 106.486
Barbados	Barbados dollar (BD$) of 100 cents	BD$3.14	BD$3.58
Belarus	Belarusian rouble of 100 kopeks	BYR 3311.27	BYR 3883.62
Belgium	Euro (€) of 100 cents	€1.45	€1.48
Belize	Belize dollar (BZ$) of 100 cents	BZ$3.11	BZ$3.55
Benin	Franc FCA	Francs 949.21	Francs 973.63
Bermuda	Bermuda dollar of 100 cents	$1.58	$1.79
Bhutan	Ngultrum of 100 chetrum (Indian currency is also legal tender)	Ngultrum 72.39	Ngultrum 83.09
Bolivia	Boliviano ($b) of 100 centavos	$b12.20	$b14.27
Bosnia-Hercegovina	Convertible marka	Marka 2.83	Marka 2.83
Botswana	Pula (P) of 100 thebe	P 7.69	P 8.64
Brazil	Real of 100 centavos	Real 4.67	Real 5.29
Brunei	Brunei dollar (B$) of 100 sen (fully interchangeable with Singapore currency)	B$2.77	B$3.07
Bulgaria	Lev of 100 stotinki	Leva 2.82	Leva 2.90
Burkina Faso	Franc CFA	Francs 949.21	Francs 973.63
Burundi	Burundi franc of 100 centimes	Francs 1696.67	Francs 1902.34
Cambodia	Riel of 100 sen	Riel 6052.78	Riel 6900.43
Cameroon	Franc CFA	Francs 949.21	Francs 973.63
Canada	Canadian dollar (C$) 100 cents	C$2.20	C$2.35
Cape Verde	Escudo Caboverdiano of 100 centavos	Esc 171.96	Esc 164.56
Cayman Islands	Cayman Islands dollar (CI$) of 100 cents	CI$1.29	CI$1.48
Central African Republic	Franc CFA	Francs 949.21	Francs 973.63
Chad	Franc CFA	Francs 949.21	Francs 973.63
Chile	Chilean peso of 100 centavos	Pesos 1104.57	Pesos 1126.95
China	Renminbi Yuan of 10 jiao or 100 fen	Yuan 13.06	Yuan 14.85
Hong Kong	Hong Kong (HK$) of 100 cents	HK$12.31	HK$13.99
Macao	Pataca of 100 avos	Pataca 12.68	Pataca 14.41
Colombia	Colombian peso of 100 centavos	Pesos 4493.58	Pesos 4611.76
Comoros	Comorian franc (KMF) of 100 centimes	Francs 717.06	Francs 730.221
Congo, Rep. of	Franc CFA	Francs 949.21	Francs 973.63
Congo, Dem. Rep. of	Congolese franc	CFr 681.83	CFr 698.5
Costa Rica	Costa Rican colón (₡) of 100 céntimos	₡639.56	₡797.05
Cote d'Ivoire	Franc CFA	Francs 949.21	Francs 973.63
Croatia	Kuna of 100 lipa	Kuna 10.81	Kuna 10.97

Cuba	Cuban peso of 100 centavos	Pesos 33.14	Pesos 37.56
Cyprus	Cyprus pound (C£) of 100 cents	C£0.85	C£0.85
Czech Republic	Koruna (Kčs) of 100 haléřu	Kčs 46.96	Kčs 47.35
Denmark	Danish krone of 100 øre	Kroner 10.75	Kroner 11.03
Faroe Islands	Currency is that of Denmark	Kroner 10.75	Kroner 11.03
Dijbouti	Dijbouti franc of 100 centimes	Francs 276.20	Francs 305.53
Dominica	East Caribbean dollar (EC$) of 100 cents	EC$4.21	EC$4.84
Dominican Republic	Dominican Republic peso (RD$) of 100 centavos	RD$52.24	RD$69.09
East Timor	Currency is that of the USA	US$1.58	US$1.79
Ecuador	Currency is that of the USA (formerly sucre of 100 centavos)	US$1.58	US$1.79
Egypt	Egyptian pound (£E) of 100 piastres or 1,000 millièmes	£E9.71	£E11.12
El Salvador	Currency is that of the USA	US$1.58	US$1.79
Equatorial Guinea	Franc CFA	Francs 949.21	Francs 973.63
Eritrea	Nakfa	—	Nafka 24.22
Estonia	Kroon of 100 sents	Kroons 22.64	Kroons 23.22
Ethiopia	Ethiopian birr (EB) of 100 cents	EB 13.49	EB 15.43
Falkland Islands	Falkland pound of 100 pence	at parity with £ sterling	
Fiji	Fiji dollar (F$) of 100 cents	F$3.03	F$ 3.19
Finland	Euro (€) of 100 cents	€1.45	€1.48
France	Euro (€) of 100 cents	€1.45	€1.48
French Guiana	Euro (€) of 100 cents	€1.45	€1.48
French Polynesia	Franc CFP	Francs 167.95	Francs 177.00
Gabon	Franc CFA	Francs 949.21	Francs 973.63
Gambia	Dalasi (D) of 100 butut	D 46.56	D 52.04
Georgia	Laria of 100 tetri	Laria 3.33	Laria 3.91
Germany	Euro (€) of 100 cents	€1.45	€1.48
Ghana	Cedi of 100 pesewas	Cedi 13739.1	Cedi 16196.7
Gibraltar	Gibraltar pound of 100 pence	at parity with £ sterling	
Greece	Euro (€) of 100 cents	€1.45	€1.48
Greenland	Currency is that of Denmark	Kroner 10.75	Kroner 11.30
Grenada	East Caribbean dollar (EC$) of 100 cents	EC$4.21	EC$4.84
Guadeloupe	Euro (€) of 100 cents	€1.45	€1.48
Guam	Currency is that of the USA	US$1.58	US$1.79
Guatemala	Quetzal (Q) of 100 centavos	Q 12.54	Q 14.18
Guinea	Guinea franc of 100 centimes	Francs 3156.60	Francs 4585.33
Guinea-Bissau	Franc CFA	Francs 949.21	Francs 973.63
Guyana	Guyana dollar (G$) of 100 cents	G$ 282.52	G$321.24
Haiti	Gourde of 100 centimes	Gourdes 60.92	Gourdes 61.1
Honduras	Lempira of 100 centavos	Lempiras 27.45	Lempiras 32.94
Hungary	Forint of 100 fillér	Forints 371.98	Forints 370.58
Iceland	Icelandic króna (Kr) of 100 aurar	Kr 126.40	Kr 129.215
India	Indian rupee (Rs) of 100 paisa	Rs 72.39	Rs 83.09
Indonesia	Rupiah (Rp) of 100 sen	Rp 13439.2	Rp 16699.2
Iran	Rial	Rials 13123.6	Rials 15663.7
Iraq	New Iraqi dinar (NID)	—	NID 2624.67
Ireland, Republic of	Euro (€) of 100 cents	€1.45	€1.48
Israel	Shekel of 100 agora	Shekels 7.03	Shekels 8.15
Italy	Euro (€) of 100 cents	€1.45	€1.48
Jamaica	Jamaican dollar (J$) of 100 cents	J$92.33	J$109.72
Japan	Yen	Yen 185.36	Yen 196.64
Jordan	Jordanian dinar (JD) of 1,000 fils	JD 1.12	JD 1.27
Kazakhstan	Tenge	Tenge 232.43	Tenge 245.13
Kenya	Kenya shilling (Ksh) of 100 cents	Ksh 121.14	Ksh 145.54
Kiribati	Australian dollar ($A) of 100 cents	$A2.47	$A2.55
Korea, Dem. People's Rep. Of	Won of 100 chon	—	Won 1615.18
Korea, Republic of	Won	Won 1860.03	Won 2070.13
Kuwait	Kuwaiti dinar (KD) of 1,000 fils	KD 0.47	KD 0.52
Kyrgyzstan	Som	Som 67.23	Som 75.67
Laos	Kip (K) of 100 at	K 11995.1	K 14071.8
Latvia	Lats of 100 santims	Lats 0.91	Lats 0.97
Lebanon	Lebanese pound (L£) of of 100 piastres	L£2389.74	L£2718.00
Lesotho	Loti (M) of 100 lisente	M 11.60	M 11.84

Country	Currency		
Liberia	Liberian dollar (L$) of 100 cents	L$1.58	L$1.50
Libya	Libyan dinar (LD) of 1,000 dirhams	LD 2.19	LD 2.35
Liechtenstein	Swiss franc of 100 rappen (or centimes)	Francs 2.23	Francs 2.28
Lithuania	Litas of 100 centas	Litas 4.99	Litas 5.12
Luxembourg	Euro (€) of 100 cents	€1.45	€1.48
Macedonia	Denar of 100 deni	Den 89.23	Den 90.28
Madagascar	Franc malgache (FMG) of 100 centimes	FMG 9390.89	FMG 18260.6
Malawi	Kwacha (K) of 100 tambala	MK 166.51	MK 195.25
Malaysia	Malaysian dollar (ringgit) (M$) of 100 sen	M$5.99	M$6.81
Maldives	Rufiyaa of 100 laaris	Rufiyaa 20.20	Rufiyaa 22.97
Mali	Franc CFA	Francs 949.21	Francs 973.63
Malta	Maltese lira (LM) of 100 cents of 1,000 mils	LM 0.61	LM 0.63
Marshall Islands	Currency is that of the USA	US$1.58	US$1.79
Martinique	Currency is that of France	€1.45	€1.48
Mauritania	Ouguiya (UM) of 5 khoums	UM 420.22	UM 477.37
Mauritius	Mauritius rupee of 100 cents	Rs 45.69	Rs 50.96
Mayotte	Euro (€) of 100 cents	€1.45	€1.48
Mexico	Peso of 100 centavos	Pesos 17.35	Pesos 20.40
Micronesia, Federated States of	Currency is that of the USA	US$1.58	US$1.79
Moldova	Moldovan leu of 100 bani	MDL 21.94	MDL 21.57
Monaco	Euro (€) of 100 cents	€1.45	€1.48
Mongolia	Tugrik of 100 möngö	Tugriks 1777.17	Tugriks 2141.2
Montserrat	East Caribbean dollar (EC$) of 100 cents	EC$4.21	EC$4.84
Morocco	Dirham (DH) of 100 centimes	DH 15.54	DH 16.28
Mozambique	Metical (MT) of 100 centavos	MT 36814.6	MT 39502.8
Myanmar	Kyat (K) of 100 pyas	K 9.79	K 11.52
Namibia	Namibian dollar of 100 cents	at parity with SA Rand	
Nauru	Australian dollar ($A) of 100 cents	$A2.47	$A2.55
Nepal	Nepalese rupee of 100 paisa	Rs 117.74	Rs 132.94
The Netherlands	Euro (€) of 100 cents	€1.45	€1.48
Netherlands Antilles	Netherlands Antilles guilder of 100 cents	Guilders 2.81	Guilders 3.21
New Caledonia	Franc CFP	Francs 167.95	Francs 191.04
New Zealand	New Zealand dollar (NZ$) of 100 cents	NZ$2.77	NZ$2.75
Cook Islands	Currency is that of New Zealand	NZ$2.77	NZ$2.75
Niue	Currency is that of New Zealand	NZ$2.77	NZ$2.75
Tokelau	Currency is that of New Zealand	NZ$2.77	NZ$2.75
Nicaragua	Córdoba (C$) of 100 centavos	C$23.94	C$28.60
Niger	Franc CFA	Francs 949.21	Francs 973.63
Nigeria	Naira (N) of 100 kobo	N 207.23	N 239.22
Northern Mariana Islands	Currency is that of the USA	US$1.58	US$1.79
Norway	Krone of 100 øre	Kroner 11.99	Kroner 12.37
Oman	Rial Omani (OR) of 1,000 baisas	OR 0.61	OR 0.69
Pakistan	Pakistan rupee of 100 paisa	Rs 91.08	Rs 105.301
Palau	Currency is that of the USA	US$1.58	US$1.79
Panama	Balboa of 100 centésimos (US notes are also in circulation)	Balboa 1.58	Balboa 1.79
Papua New Guinea	Kina (K) of 100 toea	K 5.35	K 5.48
Paraguay	Guarani (Gs) of 100 céntimos	Gs 9903.83	Gs 10615.4
Peru	New Sol of 100 cénts	New Sol 5.49	New Sol 6.05
The Philippines	Philippine peso (P) of 100 centavos	P 86.65	P 100.55
Pitcairn Islands	Currency is that of New Zealand	NZ$2.77	NZ$2.75
Poland	Zloty of 100 groszy	Zlotych 6.30	Zlotych 6.66
Portugal	Euro (€) of 100 cents	€1.45	€1.48
Puerto Rico	Currency is that of the USA	US$1.58	US$1.79
Qatar	Qatar riyal of 100 dirhams	Riyals 5.75	Riyals 6.53
Réunion	Euro (€) of 100 cents	€1.45	€1.48
Romania	Leu of 100 bani	Lei 53574.6	Lei 60900.3
Russia	Rouble of 100 kopeks	Rbl 48.13	Rbl 52.43
Rwanda	Rwanda franc of 100 centimes	Francs 845.65	Francs 1012.00
St Christopher and Nevis	East Caribbean dollar (EC$) of 100 cents	EC$4.21	EC$4.84
St Helena	St Helena pound (£) of 100 pence	at parity with £ sterling	

St Lucia	East Caribbean dollar (EC$) of 100 cents	EC$4.21	EC$4.84
St Pierre and Miquelon	Euro (€) of 100 cents	€1.45	€1.48
St Vincent and the Grenadines	East Caribbean dollar (EC$) of 100 cents	EC$4.21	EC$4.84
Samoa	Tala (S$) of 100 sene	S$4.66	S$5.07
San Marino	Euro (€) of 100 cents	€1.45	€1.48
São Tomé and Princípe	Dobra of 100 centavos	Dobra 13731.2	Dobra 15818.0
Saudi Arabia	Saudi riyal (SR) of 20 qursh or 100 halala	SR 5.92	SR 6.73
Senegal	Franc CFA	Francs 949.21	Francs 973.63
Serbia and Montenegro	New dinar of 100 paras	New Dinars 94.88	New Dinars 99.00
Seychelles	Seychelles rupee of 100 cents	Rs 8.80	Rs 9.90
Sierra Leone	Leone (Le) of 100 cents	Le 3712.95	Le 4405.89
Singapore	Singapore dollar (S$) of 100 cents	S$2.77	S$3.07
Slovakia	Koruna (Sk) of 100 halierov	Kčs 60.77	Kčs 59.75
Slovenia	Tolar (SIT) of 100 stotin	Tolars 340.22	Tolars 356.19
Solomon Islands	Solomon Islands dollar (SI$) of 100 cents	SI$11.89	SI$13.34
Somalia	Somali shilling of 100 cents	Shillings 4135.15	Shillings 4886.83
South Africa	Rand (R) of 100 cents	R 11.60	R 11.84
Spain	Euro (€) of 100 cents	€1.45	€1.48
Sri Lanka	Sri Lankan rupee of 100 cents	Rs 152.57	Rs 184.84
Sudan	Sudanese dinar (SD) of 100 piastres	SD 412.41	SD 464.85
Suriname	Surinamese guilder of 100 cents	Guilders 3969.43	Guilders 4476.29
Swaziland	Lilangeni (E) of 100 cents (South African currency is also in circulation)	at parity with SA Rand	
Sweden	Swedish krona of 100 öre	Kronor 13.35	Kronor 13.55
Switzerland	Swiss franc of 100 rappen (or centimes)	Francs 2.23	Francs 2.28
Syria	Syrian pound (S£) of 100 piastres	S£72.60	S£92.71
Taiwan	New Taiwan dollar (NT$) of 100 cents	NT$53.98	NT$60.88
Tajikistan	Somoni (TJS) of 100 dirams	—	—
Tanzania	Tanzanian shilling of 100 cents	Shillings 1650.11	Shillings 1948.99
Thailand	Baht of 100 satang	Baht 64.95	Baht 74.75
Togo	Franc CFA	Francs 949.21	Francs 973.63
Tonga	Pa'anga (T$) of 100 seniti	T$2.47	T$3.57
Trinidad and Tobago	Trinidad and Tobago dollar (TT$) of 100 cents	TT$9.70	TT$11.17
Tristan da Cunha	Currency is that of the UK	—	—
Tunisia	Tunisian dinar of 1,000 millimes	Dinars 2.08	Dinars 2.27
Turkey	Turkish lira (TL) of 100 kurus	TL 2214355	TL 2711717
Turkmenistan	Manat of 100 tenge	—	—
Turks and Caicos Islands	US dollar (US$)	US$1.58	US$1.79
Tuvalu	Australian dollar ($A) of 100 cents	$A2.47	$A2.55
Uganda	Uganda shilling of 100 cents	Shillings 3154.23	Shillings 3073.34
Ukraine	Hryvna of 100 kopiykas	UAH 8.42	UAH 9.55
United Arab Emirates	UAE dirham (Dh) of 100 fils	Dirham 5.80	Dirham 6.59
United States of America	US dollar (US$) of 100 cents	US$1.58	US$1.79
Uruguay	Uruguayan peso of 100 centésimos	Pesos 43.99	Pesos 52.10
Uzbekistan	Sum of 100 tiyin	Sum 1536.46	Sum 1849.53
Vanatu	Vatu of 100 centimes	Vatu 194.54	Vatu 206.04
Vatican City State	Euro (€) of 100 cents y	€1.45	€1.48
Venezuela	Bolívar (Bs) of 100 céntimos	Bs 2522.12	Bs 4711.75
Vietnam	Dông of 10 hào or 100 xu	Dông 24501.5	Dông 28309.7
Virgin Islands, British	US dollar (US$) (£ sterling and EC$ also circulate)	US$1.58	US$1.79
Virgin Islands, US	Currency is that of the USA	US$1.58	US$1.79
Wallis and Futuna Islands	Franc CFP	Francs 167.95	Francs 191.04
Yemen	Riyal of 100 fils	Riyals 280.95	Riyals 331.68
Zambia	Kwacha (K) of 100 ngwee	K 7346.99	K 8524.60
Zimbabwe	Zimbabwe dollar (Z$) of 100 cents	Z$1300.52	Z$10068.8

†The euro is also legal tender in Kosovo and Serbia and Montenegro

THE WORLD IN FIGURES

The total population of the world in mid-2003 was estimated at 6,301 million, compared with 5,292 million in 1990 and 3,019 million in 1960.

Continent, etc.	Area Sq. miles 000s	Sq. km 000s	Estimated population mid-2003
Africa	11,704	30,313	850,558,000
North America[1]	8,311	21,525	325,698,000
Latin America[2]	7,933	20,547	543,246,000
Asia[3]	10,637*	27,549*	3,823,390,000
Europe[4]	1,915†	4,961†	726,338,000
Oceania[5]	3,286	8,510	32,234,000
Former USSR	8,649	22,402	–
Total	52,435	135,807	6,301,463,000

[1] Includes Greenland and Hawaii
[2] Mexico, the Caribbean and the remainder of the Americas south of the USA
[3] Includes European Turkey
[4] Excludes European Turkey
[5] Includes Australia, New Zealand and the islands inhabited by Micronesian, Melanesian and Polynesian peoples
* Figure includes some former USSR countries
† Figure excludes some former USSR countries
Source: UN Population Division; Department of Economic and Social Affairs (2003)

The population forecast for the years 2025 and 2050 is:

Estimated population (million)

Continent	2025	2050
Africa	1,292,085	1,803,298
North America[1]	394,312	447,931
Latin America[2]	686,857	767,685
Asia	4,742,232	5,222,058
Europe	696,036	631,938
Oceania	39,933	45,815
Total	7,851,455	8,918,725

[1] Includes Bermuda, Greenland, and St Pierre and Miquelon
[2] Mexico, the Caribbean and the remainder of the Americas south of the USA

GLOBAL STATISTICS
The following tables are intended to provide a 'snapshot' of world-wide socio-economic and environmental trends.

WORLD COMPETITIVENESS SCOREBOARD 2001*

Rank	Country	Score
1	United States	100.00
2	Singapore	87.66
3	Finland	83.38
4	Luxembourg	82.81
5	Netherlands	81.46
6	Hong Kong	79.55
7	Ireland	79.20
8	Sweden	77.86
9	Canada	76.94
10	Switzerland	76.81
11	Australia	75.87
12	Germany	74.04
13	Iceland	73.75
14	Austria	72.54
15	Denmark	71.79
16	Israel	67.92
17	Belgium	66.03
18	Taiwan	64.84
19	United Kingdom	64.78
20	Norway	63.10
21	New Zealand	61.73
22	Estonia	60.20
23	Spain	60.14
24	Chile	59.84
25	France	59.56
26	Japan	57.52
27	Hungary	55.64
28	South Korea	51.08
29	Malaysia	50.03
30	Greece	49.96
31	Brazil	49.66
32	Italy	49.58
33	China	49.53
34	Portugal	48.36
35	Czech Republic	46.68
36	Mexico	43.67
37	Slovakia	43.59
38	Thailand	42.67
39	Slovenia	42.48
40	Philippines	40.60
41	India	40.41
42	South Africa	38.61
43	Argentina	37.51
44	Turkey	35.44
45	Russia	34.57
46	Colombia	32.84
47	Poland	32.01
48	Venezuela	30.66
49	Indonesia	28.26

Source: The Business, Bloomsbury Publishing plc

* Calculated using four basic categories: economic performance, Government efficiency, business efficiency and infrastructure

CREDIT CARD TRANSACTIONS*

Country	Credit card transactions (US$ million) 2000
United States	1,233,500
United Kingdom	267,950
France	169,700
China	156,270
South Korea	127,270
Japan	114,340
Canada	87,940
Brazil	69,630
Spain	67,380
Australia	50,390
Mexico	44,840
Argentina	33,160
Sweden	30,450
Germany	27,140
Turkey	26,810
Taiwan	23,890
Norway	22,400
Italy	22,340
Portugal	18,780
Hong Kong	18,310
Israel	17,270
Saudi Arabia	11,990
Denmark	10,650
Switzerland	10,560
Poland	9,810
South Africa	9,670
Finland	6,780
Kuwait	6,560
Netherlands	6,540
Colombia	6,380
Belgium	5,950
New Zealand	5,050
Singapore	4,740
Ireland	4,720
Peru	4,620
Thailand	4,500
United Arab Emirates	4,390
Malaysia	4,340
Chile	4,120
Venezuela	4,010
Iceland	3,990
Hungary	3,960
Czech Republic	3,490
Austria	3,250
Greece	2,840
Puerto Rico	2,290
Costa Rica	1,740
Russia	1,670
Dominican Republic	1,560
Luxembourg	1,530

Source: The Business, Bloomsbury Publishing plc

* Visa and Mastercard

COUNTRIES WITH THE MOST BILLIONAIRES 2001

Country	No. of billionaires
United States	265
Germany	57
France	31
Japan	29
United Kingdom	29
Italy	19
Switzerland	19
Canada	16
Hong Kong	14
Mexico	13
World total	620

Source: The Business, Bloomsbury Publishing plc

HUMAN DEVELOPMENT INDEX (HDI) (2003)*

Ten highest ranking countries

Country
Norway
Iceland
Sweden
Australia
Netherlands
Belgium
United States
Canada
Japan
Switzerland

Ten lowest ranking countries

Country
Sierra Leone
Niger
Burkina Faso
Mali
Burundi
Mozambique
Ethiopia
Central African Republic
Democratic Republic of Congo
Guinea-Bissau

*The HDI is an index that measures a country's average achievements in three basic aspects of human development: longevity (life expectancy), knowledge (adult literacy rate) and standard of living (GDP per capita).

CANCER PREVALENCE AND CARDIOVASCULAR
DEATHS*

Country	Cancer deaths (per 100,000) 2000	Cardiovascular deaths (per 100,000) 1994–98
Hungary	420	1,725
Czech Republic	350	1,392
Croatia	335	–
Denmark	329	1,150
Slovakia	327	1,464
Uruguay	324	–
Slovenia	319	–
Poland	317	1,442
Russia	312	1,961
Belgium	312	1,001
Estonia	306	–
Kazakhstan	304	–
Netherlands	302	979
Luxembourg	300	–
France	300	831
Latvia	299	–
United Kingdom	299	958
New Zealand	298	–
Ireland	298	1,109
Germany	294	987

Source: The Business, Bloomsbury Publishing plc

HIGHEST PER CAPITA CARBON EMISSIONS

Country	CO_2 emissions per capita (tonnes) 1999	Growth in CO_2 emissions (%) 1990–99
Australia	28.0	6
Canada	23.1	30
United States	21.5	21
Ireland	17.6	25
Belgium	14.7	7
New Zealand	14.0	3
Czech Republic	13.9	−25
Netherlands	13.6	3
Russia	13.5	−35
Luxembourg	13.0	−57
Denmark	12.7	−1
Greece	12.6	26
Finland	12.0	16
Germany	11.9	−18
United Kingdom	11.0	−13
Iceland	10.0	0
Japan	10.0	10
Italy	9.2	7
Austria	8.9	6
Bulgaria	8.9	−53

Source: The Business, Bloomsbury Publishing plc

HIGHEST DENSITY OF PCs 2001

Country	PCs (per 100 people)
United States	62.5
Sweden	56.1
Australia	51.6
Luxembourg	51.5
Norway	50.8
Singapore	50.8
Switzerland	50.0
Bermuda	49.5
Denmark	43.2
Netherlands	42.8

Source: The Business, Bloomsbury Publishing plc

GREATEST ACCESS TO TV

Country	TV sets (per 100 people) 1999
United States	84.4
Latvia	74.1
Japan	71.9
Canada	71.5
Australia	70.6
United Kingdom	65.2
Norway	64.8
Finland	64.3
France	62.3
Denmark	62.1

Source: The Business, Bloomsbury Publishing plc

GREATEST ACCESS TO MAINLINE TELEPHONES 2001

Country	Main telephone lines (per 100 people)	Mobile subscribers (per 100 people)
Bermuda	87.2	20.6
Luxembourg	78.3	96.7
Sweden	73.9	79.0
Denmark	72.3	73.8
Norway	72.0	82.5
Switzerland	71.8	72.4
United States	66.5	45.1
Iceland	66.4	82.0
Canada	65.5	36.2
Cyprus	64.3	45.6

Source: The Business, Bloomsbury Publishing plc

DISTANCES FROM LONDON BY AIR

This list details the distances in miles from London, Heathrow, to various cities (airports) abroad.

To	Miles
Abidjan	3,197
Abu Dhabi (International)	3,425
Addis Ababa	3,675
Adelaide (International)	10,111
Aden	3,670
Algiers	1,035
'Amman (Queen Alia)	2,287
Amsterdam (Schiphol)	230
Ankara (Esenboga)	1,770
Athens	1,500
Atlanta	4,198
Auckland	11,404
Baghdad (International)	2,551
Bahrain	3,163
Baku	2,485
Bangkok	5,928
Barbados (Grantley Adams)	4,193
Barcelona (Muntadas)	712
Basel-Mulhouse	447
Beijing (Capital)	5,063
Beirut	2,161
Belfast (Aldergrove)	325
Belgrade	1,056
Berlin (Tegel)	588
Bermuda	3,428
Bern	476
Bogotá	5,262
Bombay (Mumbai)	4,478
Boston	3,255
Brasília	5,452
Bratislava	817
Brisbane (Eagle Farm)	10,273
Brussels	217
Bucharest (Otopeni)	1,307
Budapest (Ferihegy)	923
Buenos Aires	6,915
Cairo (International)	2,194
Calcutta	4,958
Calgary	4,357
Canberra	10,563
Cape Town	6,011
Caracas	4,639
Casablanca (Mohamed V)	1,300
Chicago (O'Hare)	3,941
Cologne	331
Colombo (Katunayake)	5,411
Copenhagen	608
Dakar	2,706
Dallas (Fort Worth)	4,736
Dallas (Lovefield)	4,732
Damascus (International)	2,223
Dar-es-Salaam	4,662
Darwin	8,613
Delhi	4,180
Denver	4,655
Detroit (Metropolitan)	3,754

Dhahran	3,143
Dhaka	4,976
Doha	3,253
Dubai	3,414
Dublin	279
Durban	5,937
Düsseldorf	310
Entebbe	4,033
Frankfurt (Main)	406
Freetown	3,046
Geneva	468
Gibraltar	1,084
Gothenburg (Landvetter)	664
Hamburg (Fuhlsbüttel)	463
Harare	5,156
Havana	4,647
Helsinki (Vantaa)	1,148
Hobart	10,826
Ho Chi Minh City	6,345
Hong Kong	5,990
Honolulu	7,220
Houston (Intercontinental)	4,821
Houston (William P. Hobby)	4,837
Islamabad	3,767
Istanbul (Atatürk)	1,560
Jakarta (Halim Perdanakusuma)	7,295
Jeddah	2,947
Johannesburg	5,634
Kabul	3,558
Karachi	3,935
Kathmandu	4,570
Khartoum	3,071
Kiev (Borispol)	1,357
Kiev (Julyany)	1,337
Kingston, Jamaica	4,668
Kuala Lumpur (Subang)	6,557
Kuwait	2,903
Lagos	3,107
Larnaca	2,036
Lima (Callao)	6,303
Lisbon	972
Lomé	3,129
Los Angeles (International)	5,439
Madras	5,113
Madrid (Barajas)	773
Malta	1,305
Manila (Ninoy Aquino)	6,685
Marseille (Provence)	614
Mauritius	6,075
Melbourne (Essendon)	10,504
Melbourne (Tullamarine)	10,499
Mexico City	5,529
Miami	4,414
Milan (Linate)	609
Minsk	1,176
Montego Bay	4,687
Montevideo	6,841
Montreal (Dorval)	3,241
Moscow (Sheremetyevo)	1,557
Munich (Franz Josef Strauss)	584

Muscat	3,621
Nairobi (Jomo Kenyatta)	4,248
Naples	1,011
Nassau	4,333
New York (J. F. Kennedy)	3,440
Nice (Côte d'Azur)	645
Oporto	806
Oslo (Gardermoen)	722
Ottawa	3,321
Palma, Majorca (Son San Juan)	836
Paris (Charles de Gaulle)	215
Paris (Le Bourget)	215
Paris (Orly)	227
Perth, Australia	9,008
Port of Spain	4,404
Prague (Ruzine)	649
Pretoria	5,602
Reykjavík (Domestic)	1,167
Reykjavík (Keflavík)	1,177
Rhodes	1,743
Rio de Janeiro (Galeão)	5,745
Riyadh (King Khaled) International	3,067
Rome (Leonardo da Vinci)	895
St John's, Newfoundland	2,308
St Petersburg	1,314
Salzburg (Mozart)	651
San Francisco	5,351
São Paulo (Guarulhos)	5,892
Sarajevo	1,017
Seoul (Kimpo)	5,507
Shanghai	5,725
Shannon	369
Singapore (Changi)	6,756
Sofia	1,266
Stockholm (Arlanda)	908
Suva	10,119
Sydney (Kingsford Smith)	10,568
Tangier	1,120
Tehran	2,741
Tel Aviv	2,227
Tokyo (Narita)	5,956
Toronto	3,544
Tripoli (International)	1,468
Tunis	1,137
Turin (Caselle)	570
Ulaanbaatar	4,340
Valencia	826
Vancouver	4,707
Venice (Marco Polo)	715
Vienna (Schwechat)	790
Vladivostok	5,298
Warsaw	912
Washington (Dulles)	3,665
Wellington	11,692
Yangon/Rangoon	5,582
Yokohama (Aomori)	5,647
Zagreb	848
Zürich	490

TIME AND SPACE

ASTRONOMY

TIME MEASUREMENT AND CALENDARS

TIDAL PREDICTIONS

ASTRONOMY

The following pages give astronomical data for each month of the year 2005. There are four pages of data for each month. All data are given for 0h Greenwich Mean Time (GMT), i.e. at the midnight at the beginning of the day named. This applies also to data for the months when British Summer Time is in operation (for dates, see below).

The astronomical data are given in a form suitable for observation with the naked eye or with a small telescope. These data do not attempt to replace the *Astronomical Almanac* for professional astronomers.

A fuller explanation of how to use the astronomical data is given on pages 667–71.

CALENDAR FOR EACH MONTH

The calendar for each month comprises dates of general interest plus the dates of birth or death of well-known people. For key religious, civil and legal dates see page 9. For details of flag-flying days see page 23. For royal birthdays see pages 23 and 24–5. Public holidays are given in italics. See also pages 10 and 11.

Fuller explanations of the various calendars can be found under Time Measurement and Calendars (pages 677–92).

The zodiacal signs through which the Sun is passing during each month are illustrated. The date of transition from one sign to the next, to the nearest hour, is given under Astronomical Phenomena.

JULIAN DATE

The Julian date on 2005 January 0.0 is 2453370.5. To find the Julian date for any other date in 2005 (at 0h GMT), add the day-of-the-year number on the extreme right of the calendar for each month to the Julian date for January 0.0.

SEASONS

The seasons are defined astronomically as follows:

Spring from the vernal equinox to the summer solstice
Summer from the summer solstice to the autumnal equinox
Autumn from the autumnal equinox to the winter solstice
Winter from the winter solstice to the vernal equinox

The seasons in 2005 are:

Northern Hemisphere

Vernal equinox	March 20d 13h GMT
Summer solstice	June 21d 07h GMT
Autumnal equinox	September 22d 23h GMT
Winter solstice	December 21d 19h GMT

Southern Hemisphere

Autumnal equinox	March 20d 13h GMT
Winter solstice	June 21d 07h GMT
Vernal equinox	September 22d 23h GMT
Summer solstice	December 21d 19h GMT

The longest day of the year, measured from sunrise to sunset, is at the summer solstice. The longest day in the United Kingdom will fall on 21 June in 2005.

The shortest day of the year is at the winter solstice. The shortest day in the United Kingdom will fall on 21 December in 2005.

The equinox is the point at which day and night are of equal length all over the world.

In popular parlance, the seasons in the northern hemisphere comprise the following months:

Spring	March, April, May
Summer	June, July, August
Autumn	September, October, November
Winter	December, January, February

BRITISH SUMMER TIME

British Summer Time is the legal time for general purposes during the period in which it is in operation (*see also* page 669). During this period, clocks are kept one hour ahead of Greenwich Mean Time. The hour of changeover is 01h Greenwich Mean Time. The duration of Summer Time in 2005 is from March 27 01h GMT to October 30 01h GMT.

JANUARY 2005

FIRST MONTH, 31 DAYS. *Janus*, god of the portal, facing two ways, past and future

| 1 | Saturday | John Le Carré b. 1931. King John of England d. 1216 | 1 |
| 2 | Sunday | David Bailey b. 1938. Ovid d. AD17 | 2 |

3	Monday	J. R. R. Tolkien b. 1892. Pierre Larousse d. 1875	week 1 day 3
4	Tuesday	Augustus John b. 1878. T. S. Eliot d. 1965	4
5	Wednesday	Juan Carlos, King of Spain b. 1938. Catherine de Medici, Queen of France d. 1589	5
6	Thursday	Richard II b. 1367. Rudolf Nureyev d. 1993	6
7	Friday	Gerald Durrell b. 1925. Catherine of Aragon, d. 1536	7
8	Saturday	Wilkie Collins b. 1824. Paul Verlaine d. 1896	8
9	Sunday	The ocean liner Queen Elizabeth destroyed by fire 1972	9

10	Monday	Dame Barbara Hepworth b. 1903. Sinclair Lewis d. 1951	week 2 day 10
11	Tuesday	James Earl Jones b. 1931. Thomas Hardy d. 1928	11
12	Wednesday	John Singer Sargent b. 1856. Dame Agatha Christie d. 1976	12
13	Thursday	Jan van Goyen b. 1656. James Joyce d. 1941	13
14	Friday	Sir Cecil Beaton b. 1904. Lewis Carroll d. 1898	14
15	Saturday	The coronation of Queen Elizabeth I 1559	15
16	Sunday	Diane Fossey b. 1932. Léo Delibes d. 1891	16

17	Monday	Anne Brontë b. 1820. Ruskin Spear d. 1990	week 3 day 17
18	Tuesday	A. A. Milne b. 1882. Rudyard Kipling d. 1936	18
19	Wednesday	Paul Cézanne b. 1839. Patricia Highsmith, b. 1951	19
20	Thursday	Sir John Soane d. 1837. George V d. 1936	20
21	Friday	George Orwell d. 1950. Louis XVI, King of France d. 1793	21
22	Saturday	Lord Byron b. 1788. Queen Victoria d. 1901	22
23	Sunday	Édouard Manet b. 1832. Anna Pavlova d. 1931	23

24	Monday	Frederick the Great, King of Prussia b. 1712. Amadeo Modigliani d. 1920	week 4 day 24
25	Tuesday	Henry VIII and Anne Boleyn married in secret 1533	25
26	Wednesday	Mary Mapes Dodge b. 1831. Nelson Rockefeller d. 1979	26
27	Thursday	Wolfgang Amadeus Mozart b. 1756. Giuseppe Verdi d. 1901	27
28	Friday	Jackson Pollock b. 1912. Henry VIII d. 1547	28
29	Saturday	Germaine Greer b. 1939. George III d. 1820	29
30	Sunday	Anton Chekhov b. 1860. Charles I d. 1649	30

| 31 | Monday | Franz Schubert b. 1797. A. A. Milne d. 1956 | week 5 day 31 |

ASTRONOMICAL PHENOMENA

d	h	
2	00	Earth at perihelion (147 million km.)
4	01	Jupiter in conjunction with Moon. Jupiter 0°.3 N.
7	19	Mars in conjunction with Moon. Mars 3° N.
9	02	Mercury in conjunction with Moon. Mercury 5° N.
9	03	Venus in conjunction with Moon. Venus 5° N.
13	23	Saturn at opposition
14	03	Venus in conjunction with Mercury. Venus 0°.4 N.
19	23	Sun's longitude 300° ♒
24	09	Saturn in conjunction with Moon. Saturn 5° S.
31	10	Jupiter in conjunction with Moon. Jupiter 0°.8 N.

MINIMA OF ALGOL

d	h	d	h	d	h
1	07.6	12	18.8	24	06.1
4	04.4	15	15.7	27	02.9
7	01.2	18	12.5	29	23.8
9	22.0	21	09.3		

CONSTELLATIONS

The following constellations are near the meridian at

	d	h		d	h
December	1	24	January	16	21
December	16	23	February	1	20
January	1	22	February	15	19

Draco (below the Pole), Ursa Minor (below the Pole), Camelopardus, Perseus, Auriga, Taurus, Orion, Eridanus and Lepdus

THE MOON

Phases, Apsides and Node	d	h	m
☾ Last Quarter	3	17	46
● New Moon	10	12	03
☽ First Quarter	17	06	57
○ Full Moon	25	10	32
Perigee (356,569 km)	10	10	00
Apogee (406,458 km)	23	18	38

Mean longitude of ascending node on January 1, 28°

THE SUN

s.d. 16′.3

Day	Right Ascension h	m	s	Dec. – °	′	Equation of time m	s	Rise 52° h	m	Rise 56° h	m	Transit h	m	Set 52° h	m	Set 56° h	m	Sidereal time h	m	s	Transit of first point of Aries h	m	s
1	18	46	24	23	01	−3	26	8	08	8	31	12	04	15	59	15	36	6	42	58	17	14	12
2	18	50	49	22	56	−3	54	8	08	8	31	12	04	16	00	15	38	6	46	55	17	10	16
3	18	55	13	22	50	−4	22	8	08	8	31	12	05	16	02	15	39	6	50	51	17	06	20
4	18	59	37	22	44	−4	49	8	08	8	30	12	05	16	03	15	40	6	54	48	17	02	24
5	19	04	01	22	38	−5	16	8	07	8	30	12	05	16	04	15	42	6	58	45	16	58	28
6	19	08	24	22	31	−5	43	8	07	8	29	12	06	16	05	15	43	7	02	41	16	54	32
7	19	12	47	22	23	−6	09	8	06	8	28	12	06	16	07	15	45	7	06	38	16	50	36
8	19	17	09	22	15	−6	35	8	06	8	28	12	07	16	08	15	46	7	10	34	16	46	40
9	19	21	31	22	07	−7	00	8	05	8	27	12	07	16	09	15	48	7	14	31	16	42	44
10	19	25	52	21	58	−7	25	8	05	8	26	12	08	16	11	15	49	7	18	27	16	38	49
11	19	30	13	21	49	−7	49	8	04	8	25	12	08	16	12	15	51	7	22	24	16	34	53
12	19	34	33	21	40	−8	13	8	03	8	24	12	08	16	14	15	53	7	26	20	16	30	57
13	19	38	53	21	30	−8	36	8	03	8	23	12	09	16	15	15	55	7	30	17	16	27	01
14	19	43	12	21	19	−8	58	8	02	8	22	12	09	16	17	15	56	7	34	14	16	23	05
15	19	47	30	21	09	−9	20	8	01	8	21	12	10	16	18	15	58	7	38	10	16	19	09
16	19	51	47	20	57	−9	41	8	00	8	20	12	10	16	20	16	00	7	42	07	16	15	13
17	19	56	04	20	46	−10	01	7	59	8	19	12	10	16	22	16	02	7	46	03	16	11	17
18	20	00	20	20	34	−10	21	7	58	8	17	12	11	16	23	16	04	7	50	00	16	07	21
19	20	04	36	20	22	−10	39	7	57	8	16	12	11	16	25	16	06	7	53	56	16	03	25
20	20	08	50	20	09	−10	57	7	56	8	15	12	11	16	27	16	08	7	57	53	15	59	29
21	20	13	04	19	56	−11	15	7	55	8	13	12	11	16	28	16	10	8	01	50	15	55	34
22	20	17	17	19	42	−11	31	7	54	8	12	12	12	16	30	16	12	8	05	46	15	51	38
23	20	21	30	19	28	−11	47	7	53	8	10	12	12	16	32	16	14	8	09	43	15	47	42
24	20	25	41	19	14	−12	02	7	51	8	09	12	12	16	34	16	16	8	13	39	15	43	46
25	20	29	52	18	59	−12	16	7	50	8	07	12	12	16	35	16	18	8	17	36	15	39	50
26	20	34	02	18	44	−12	29	7	49	8	06	12	13	16	37	16	20	8	21	32	15	35	54
27	20	38	11	18	29	−12	42	7	47	8	04	12	13	16	39	16	22	8	25	29	15	31	58
28	20	42	19	18	14	−12	54	7	46	8	02	12	13	16	41	16	25	8	29	25	15	28	02
29	20	46	27	17	58	−13	05	7	44	8	00	12	13	16	43	16	27	8	33	22	15	24	06
30	20	50	33	17	41	−13	15	7	43	7	58	12	13	16	44	16	29	8	37	19	15	20	10
31	20	54	39	17	25	−13	24	7	41	7	57	12	13	16	46	16	31	8	41	15	15	16	14

DURATION OF TWILIGHT (in minutes)

Latitude	52°	56°	52°	56°	52°	56°	52°	56°
	1 January		11 January		21 January		31 January	
Civil	41	47	40	45	38	43	37	41
Nautical	84	96	82	93	80	90	78	87
Astronomical	125	141	123	138	120	134	117	130

THE NIGHT SKY

Mercury, magnitude −0.3, is visible as a morning object for the first week of the month. It is very close to Venus which should make the location of Mercury much easier. On the 1st Mercury will be 1.1 degrees above and 0.2 degrees to the right of Venus, while by the 7th these figures have changed gradually to 0.6 degrees above and 0.6 degrees to the right of Venus. If visibility is poor the glare from Venus may overpower the light from the much fainter innermost planet.

Venus is a brilliant object in the early morning sky, magnitude −3.9, and at the beginning of the month is visible very low in the east-south-eastern sky for nearly an hour before dawn.

Mars, magnitude +1.5, although technically a morning object, is continuing to move slowly southwards in declination, and this means that it will be a very difficult object to detect even with very clear conditions. It will be barely 10 degrees above the horizon one hour before sunrise for observers in southern England. Measured in ecliptic longitude Mars is 15 degrees from Venus at the beginning of the month: this distance increases to 32 degrees by the end of January.

Jupiter is a brilliant object in the morning sky, magnitude −2.1. By the end of the month it is visible in the east-south-eastern sky before midnight. Jupiter is in the constellation of Virgo. On the night of the 3rd–4th the Moon, at Last Quarter, passes about 1 degree south of the planet.

Saturn, magnitude −0.4, reaches opposition on the 13th, and therefore is visible throughout the hours of darkness, crossing the meridian around midnight. Saturn is retrograding slowly in the constellation of Gemini, some 7 degrees south of Pollux. The Full Moon will be seen near the planet around the 23rd–25th.

THE MOON

Day	RA h	RA m	Dec. °	Hor. par. '	Semi-diam. '	Sun's Co-long. °	PA of Br. Limb °	Ph. %	Age d	Rise 52° h	Rise 52° m	Rise 56° h	Rise 56° m	Transit h	Transit m	Set 52° h	Set 52° m	Set 56° h	Set 56° m
1	10	49	+11.6	54.9	15.0	154	110	76	19.9	22	10	22	05	4	14	11	12	11	20
2	11	34	+6.2	55.4	15.1	166	112	67	20.9	23	24	23	24	4	55	11	23	11	26
3	12	18	+0.3	56.1	15.3	179	113	58	21.9	—	—	—	—	5	37	11	33	11	31
4	13	04	−5.6	56.9	15.5	191	113	47	22.9	0	41	0	46	6	20	11	45	11	37
5	13	52	−11.6	57.8	15.8	203	111	37	23.9	2	01	2	12	7	06	11	58	11	45
6	14	43	−17.2	58.8	16.0	215	107	27	24.9	3	27	3	45	7	57	12	16	11	56
7	15	40	−22.0	59.7	16.3	227	101	17	25.9	4	57	5	23	8	54	12	41	12	14
8	16	41	−25.7	60.5	16.5	239	93	9	26.9	6	27	7	01	9	56	13	20	12	45
9	17	48	−27.7	61.1	16.7	252	80	4	27.9	7	47	8	26	11	03	14	20	13	41
10	18	57	−27.6	61.5	16.7	264	51	1	28.9	8	47	9	23	12	11	15	41	15	06
11	20	05	−25.5	61.4	16.7	276	293	1	0.5	9	28	9	55	13	16	17	15	16	49
12	21	09	−21.5	61.1	16.6	288	265	4	1.5	9	54	10	13	14	16	18	51	18	33
13	22	08	−16.1	60.4	16.5	300	255	9	2.5	10	13	10	25	15	10	20	22	20	12
14	23	02	−10.0	59.6	16.2	312	250	17	3.5	10	27	10	33	15	59	21	48	21	44
15	23	53	−3.6	58.6	16.0	325	248	27	4.5	10	39	10	40	16	45	23	09	23	11
16	0	41	+2.8	57.6	15.7	337	247	37	5.5	10	50	10	46	17	30	—	—	—	—
17	1	28	+8.8	56.7	15.5	349	248	47	6.5	11	02	10	52	18	14	0	28	0	36
18	2	15	+14.3	55.9	15.2	1	251	57	7.5	11	16	11	00	18	59	1	46	1	59
19	3	03	+19.1	55.3	15.1	13	254	67	8.5	11	33	11	11	19	46	3	02	3	23
20	3	52	+23.0	54.7	14.9	25	259	76	9.5	11	55	11	27	20	35	4	18	4	45
21	4	43	+25.9	54.4	14.8	38	266	83	10.5	12	26	11	52	21	25	5	29	6	02
22	5	36	+27.5	54.1	14.7	50	273	90	11.5	13	08	12	30	22	16	6	33	7	10
23	6	30	+27.9	54.0	14.7	62	282	95	12.5	14	02	13	25	23	07	7	24	8	01
24	7	23	+27.1	53.9	14.7	74	295	98	13.5	15	07	14	35	23	57	8	03	8	36
25	8	15	+24.9	54.0	14.7	86	329	100	14.5	16	19	15	53	—	—	8	31	8	58
26	9	05	+21.7	54.2	14.8	98	69	100	15.5	17	33	17	14	0	45	8	52	9	12
27	9	52	+17.6	54.4	14.8	110	96	98	16.5	18	47	18	34	1	30	9	07	9	22
28	10	38	+12.7	54.7	14.9	123	105	94	17.5	20	01	19	53	2	13	9	20	9	29
29	11	23	+7.3	55.1	15.0	135	109	89	18.5	21	14	21	12	2	54	9	31	9	35
30	12	07	+1.6	55.6	15.1	147	112	82	19.5	22	28	22	32	3	35	9	41	9	40
31	12	51	−4.3	56.2	15.3	159	112	73	20.5	23	46	23	55	4	17	9	51	9	46

MERCURY

Day	RA h	RA m	Dec. °	Diam. "	Phase %	Transit h	Transit m	5° high 52° h	5° high 52° m	5° high 56° h	5° high 56° m
1	17	10	−21.3	6	69	10	28	7	10	7	41
3	17	20	−21.8	6	72	10	30	7	16	7	48
5	17	31	−22.2	6	76	10	32	7	23	7	56
7	17	42	−22.6	6	79	10	36	7	29	8	03
9	17	53	−22.9	6	81	10	39	7	36	8	11
11	18	05	−23.2	5	83	10	43	7	42	8	18
13	18	17	−23.4	5	85	10	48	7	48	8	25
15	18	30	−23.5	5	87	10	53	7	54	8	31
17	18	42	−23.6	5	89	10	57	7	59	8	37
19	18	55	−23.6	5	90	11	03	8	04	8	41
21	19	08	−23.5	5	91	11	08	8	08	8	45
23	19	22	−23.3	5	93	11	13	8	12	8	48
25	19	35	−23.0	5	94	11	19	8	15	8	50
27	19	48	−22.6	5	95	11	24	8	17	8	51
29	20	02	−22.2	5	96	11	30	8	19	8	51
31	20	16	−21.6	5	96	11	36	8	20	8	50

VENUS

Day	RA h	RA m	Dec. °	Diam. "	Phase %	Transit h	Transit m	5° high 52° h	5° high 52° m	5° high 56° h	5° high 56° m
1	17	13	−22.3	11	93	10	30	7	21	7	54
6	17	40	−22.8	11	94	10	38	7	33	8	08
11	18	07	−23.1	11	95	10	45	7	43	8	19
16	18	34	−23.1	10	95	10	53	7	50	8	26
21	19	02	−22.8	10	96	11	00	7	55	8	29
26	19	29	−22.2	10	97	11	08	7	57	8	30
31	19	55	−21.3	10	97	11	15	7	57	8	27

MARS

Day	RA h	RA m	Dec. °	Diam. "	Phase %	Transit h	Transit m	5° high 52° h	5° high 52° m	5° high 56° h	5° high 56° m
1	16	10	−20.9	4	96	9	26	6	06	6	35
6	16	24	−21.5	4	96	9	21	6	06	6	37
11	16	39	−22.1	4	96	9	16	6	05	6	38
16	16	54	−22.6	4	95	9	11	6	05	6	39
21	17	09	−23.0	4	95	9	07	6	04	6	39
26	17	24	−23.3	5	95	9	02	6	02	6	38
31	17	39	−23.5	5	94	8	58	5	59	6	37

SUNRISE AND SUNSET

	London 0° 05′ 51° 30′		Bristol 2° 35′ 51° 28′		Birmingham 1° 55′ 52° 28′		Manchester 2° 15′ 53° 28′		Newcastle 1° 37′ 54° 59′		Glasgow 4° 14′ 55° 52′		Belfast 5° 56′ 54° 35′	
	h m	h m	h m	h m	h m	h m	h m	h m	h m	h m	h m	h m	h m	h m
1	8 06	16 02	8 16	16 12	8 18	16 05	8 25	16 01	8 31	15 49	8 47	15 54	8 46	16 09
2	8 06	16 03	8 16	16 13	8 18	16 06	8 25	16 02	8 31	15 50	8 47	15 55	8 46	16 10
3	8 06	16 04	8 16	16 15	8 18	16 07	8 24	16 03	8 31	15 52	8 47	15 57	8 46	16 11
4	8 05	16 06	8 15	16 16	8 18	16 08	8 24	16 04	8 30	15 53	8 46	15 58	8 45	16 13
5	8 05	16 07	8 15	16 17	8 17	16 09	8 24	16 05	8 30	15 54	8 46	15 59	8 45	16 14
6	8 05	16 08	8 15	16 18	8 17	16 11	8 23	16 07	8 29	15 56	8 45	16 01	8 44	16 15
7	8 04	16 09	8 14	16 19	8 16	16 12	8 23	16 08	8 29	15 57	8 45	16 02	8 44	16 17
8	8 04	16 11	8 14	16 21	8 16	16 13	8 22	16 10	8 28	15 59	8 44	16 04	8 43	16 18
9	8 03	16 12	8 13	16 22	8 15	16 15	8 22	16 11	8 27	16 00	8 43	16 06	8 42	16 20
10	8 03	16 13	8 13	16 24	8 15	16 16	8 21	16 13	8 27	16 02	8 42	16 07	8 42	16 21
11	8 02	16 15	8 12	16 25	8 14	16 18	8 20	16 14	8 26	16 03	8 41	16 09	8 41	16 23
12	8 02	16 16	8 11	16 26	8 13	16 19	8 20	16 16	8 25	16 05	8 40	16 11	8 40	16 25
13	8 01	16 18	8 11	16 28	8 13	16 21	8 19	16 17	8 24	16 07	8 39	16 12	8 39	16 26
14	8 00	16 19	8 10	16 29	8 12	16 22	8 18	16 19	8 23	16 09	8 38	16 14	8 38	16 28
15	7 59	16 21	8 09	16 31	8 11	16 24	8 17	16 21	8 22	16 10	8 37	16 16	8 37	16 30
16	7 58	16 22	8 08	16 33	8 10	16 26	8 16	16 22	8 21	16 12	8 36	16 18	8 36	16 32
17	7 57	16 24	8 07	16 34	8 09	16 27	8 15	16 24	8 20	16 14	8 35	16 20	8 35	16 33
18	7 56	16 26	8 06	16 36	8 08	16 29	8 14	16 26	8 19	16 16	8 34	16 22	8 34	16 35
19	7 55	16 27	8 05	16 37	8 07	16 31	8 13	16 27	8 17	16 18	8 32	16 24	8 33	16 37
20	7 54	16 29	8 04	16 39	8 06	16 32	8 11	16 29	8 16	16 20	8 31	16 26	8 31	16 39
21	7 53	16 31	8 03	16 41	8 05	16 34	8 10	16 31	8 15	16 22	8 30	16 28	8 30	16 41
22	7 52	16 32	8 02	16 42	8 03	16 36	8 09	16 33	8 13	16 23	8 28	16 30	8 29	16 43
23	7 51	16 34	8 01	16 44	8 02	16 38	8 08	16 35	8 12	16 25	8 27	16 32	8 27	16 45
24	7 50	16 36	8 00	16 46	8 01	16 39	8 06	16 37	8 10	16 27	8 25	16 34	8 26	16 47
25	7 48	16 38	7 58	16 48	7 59	16 41	8 05	16 38	8 09	16 29	8 23	16 36	8 24	16 48
26	7 47	16 39	7 57	16 49	7 58	16 43	8 03	16 40	8 07	16 31	8 22	16 38	8 23	16 50
27	7 46	16 41	7 56	16 51	7 57	16 45	8 02	16 42	8 06	16 33	8 20	16 40	8 21	16 52
28	7 44	16 43	7 54	16 53	7 55	16 47	8 00	16 44	8 04	16 36	8 18	16 42	8 20	16 54
29	7 43	16 45	7 53	16 55	7 54	16 49	7 59	16 46	8 02	16 38	8 17	16 44	8 18	16 56
30	7 42	16 46	7 51	16 56	7 52	16 50	7 57	16 48	8 01	16 40	8 15	16 46	8 16	16 59
31	7 40	16 48	7 50	16 58	7 51	16 52	7 56	16 50	7 59	16 42	8 13	16 49	8 15	17 01

JUPITER

Day	RA		Dec.		Transit		5° high			
							52°		56°	
	h	m	°	′	h	m	h	m	h	m
1	13	05.7	−5	36	6	22	1	25	1	33
11	13	08.8	−5	52	5	46	0	50	0	58
21	13	10.9	−6	02	5	08	0	13	0	22
31	13	11.8	−6	04	4	30	23	31	23	40

Diameters – equatorial 38″ polar 35″

SATURN

Day	RA		Dec.		Transit		5° high			
							52°		56°	
	h	m	°	′	h	m	h	m	h	m
1	7	47.5	+21	08	1	04	8	23	8	39
11	7	44.1	+21	18	0	22	7	42	7	57
21	7	40.6	+21	27	23	35	7	00	7	16
31	7	37.3	+21	36	22	52	6	18	6	34

Diameters –equatorial 20″ polar 19″
Rings – major axis 46″ minor axis 18″

URANUS

Day	RA		Dec.		Transit		10° high			
							52°		56°	
	h	m	°	′	h	m	h	m	h	m
1	22	24.3	−10	46	15	39	19	30	19	11
11	22	25.9	−10	37	15	01	18	54	18	35
21	22	27.7	−10	26	14	24	18	17	17	59
31	22	29.7	−10	14	13	46	17	41	17	23

Diameter 4″

NEPTUNE

Day	RA		Dec.		Transit		10° high			
							52°		56°	
	h	m	°	′	h	m	h	m	h	m
1	21	05.4	−16	46	14	20	17	28	16	58
11	21	06.7	−16	40	13	42	16	51	16	21
21	21	08.2	−16	33	13	04	16	14	15	44
31	21	09.7	−16	27	12	26	15	37	15	08

Diameter 2″

FEBRUARY 2005

SECOND MONTH, 28 or 29 DAYS. *Februa*, Roman festival of Purification

1	*Tuesday*	Mary Shelley b. 1851. Piet Mondrian d. 1944	32
2	*Wednesday*	James Joyce b. 1882. James Joyce's *Ulysses* published in Paris 1922	33
3	*Thursday*	Felix Mendelssohn b. 1809. Buddy Holly d. 1959	34
4	*Friday*	Jaques Prévert b. 1900. Patricia Highsmith d. 1995	35
5	*Saturday*	Marquise de Sévigné b. 1626. Marianne Moore d. 1972	36
6	*Sunday*	Christopher Marlowe b. 1564. Gustav Klimt d. 1918	37

7	*Monday*	Charles Dickens b. 1812. King Hussein of Jordan d. 1999	week 6 day 38
8	*Tuesday*	John Ruskin b. 1819. Dame Iris Murdoch d. 1999	39
9	*Wednesday*	Alice Walker b. 1944. Fyodor Dostoevsky, d. 1881	40
10	*Thursday*	Berthold Brecht b. 1898. Aleksandr Pushkin d. 1837	41
11	*Friday*	William Henry Fox Talbot b. 1800. Sylvia Plath d. 1963	42
12	*Saturday*	Anna Pavlova b. 1881. Lady Jane Grey d. 1554	43
13	*Sunday*	Georges Simenon b. 1903. Richard Wagner d. 1883	44

14	*Monday*	Richard II d. 1400. P. G. Wodehouse d. 1975	week 7 day 45
15	*Tuesday*	Jeremy Bentham b. 1748. Mikhail Glinka d. 1857	46
16	*Wednesday*	Iain Banks b. 1954. Pierre-Paul Prud'hon d. 1823	47
17	*Thursday*	Ruth Rendell b. 1930. Molière d. 1673	48
18	*Friday*	Henri Laurens b. 1885. Balthus d. 2001	49
19	*Saturday*	Duke of York b. 1960. Georg Büchner d. 1837	50
20	*Sunday*	Dame Marie Rambert b. 1888. James I d. 1437	51

21	*Monday*	W. H. Auden b. 1907. Dame Margot Fonteyn d. 1991	week 8 day 52
22	*Tuesday*	Eric Gill b. 1872. Andy Warhol d. 1987	53
23	*Wednesday*	George Frideric Handel b. 1685. John Keats d. 1821	54
24	*Thursday*	Wilhelm Grimm b. 1786. Bobby Moore d. 1993	55
25	*Friday*	Anthony Burgess b. 1917. Tennessee Williams d. 1983	56
26	*Saturday*	Victor Hugo b. 1802. Frank Bridge b. 1879	57
27	*Sunday*	John Steinbeck b. 1902. John Evelyn d. 1706	58

28	*Monday*	Sir Stephen Spender b. 1909. Henry James d. 1916	week 9 day 59

ASTRONOMICAL PHENOMENA

d h
2 02 Jupiter at stationary point
3 19 Neptune in conjunction
5 13 Mars in conjunction with Moon. Mars 4° N.
8 01 Venus in conjunction with Moon. Venus 4° N.
8 15 Mercury in conjunction with Moon.
Mercury 3° N.
14 11 Mercury in superior conjunction
18 14 Sun's longitude 330° ♓
20 12 Saturn in conjunction with Moon. Saturn
5° S.
25 07 Uranus in conjunction
27 14 Jupiter in conjunction with Moon. Jupiter
1° N.

MINIMA OF ALGOL

d	h	d	h	d	h
1	20.6	10	11.1	19	01.5
4	17.4	13	07.9	21	22.3
7	14.2	16	04.7	24	19.2

CONSTELLATIONS

The following constellations are near the meridian at

	d	h		d	h
January	1	24	February	15	21
January	16	23	March	1	20
February	1	22	March	16	19

Draco (below the Pole), Camelopardus, Auriga, Taurus, Gemini, Orion, Canis Minor, Monoceros, Lepus, Canis Major and Puppis

THE MOON

Phases, Apsides and Node	d	h	m
☾ Last Quarter	2	07	27
● New Moon	8	22	28
☽ First Quarter	16	00	16
○ Full Moon	24	04	54

Perigee (358,556 km)	7	22	05
Apogee (405,833 km)	20	04	51

Mean longitude of ascending node on February 1, 27°

THE SUN

s.d. 16′.2

Day	Right Ascension			Dec. −		Equation of time		Rise 52°		Rise 56°		Transit		Set 52°		Set 56°		Sidereal time			Transit of first point of Aries		
	h	m	s	°	′	m	s	h	m	h	m	h	m	h	m	h	m	h	m	s	h	m	s
1	20	58	44	17	08	−13	33	7	40	7	55	12	14	16	48	16	33	8	45	12	15	12	18
2	21	02	49	16	51	−13	41	7	38	7	53	12	14	16	50	16	35	8	49	08	15	08	23
3	21	06	52	16	33	−13	47	7	37	7	51	12	14	16	52	16	38	8	53	05	15	04	27
4	21	10	55	16	16	−13	54	7	35	7	49	12	14	16	54	16	40	8	57	01	15	00	31
5	21	14	57	15	58	−13	59	7	33	7	47	12	14	16	55	16	42	9	00	58	14	56	35
6	21	18	58	15	39	−14	04	7	32	7	45	12	14	16	57	16	44	9	04	54	14	52	39
7	21	22	58	15	21	−14	07	7	30	7	43	12	14	16	59	16	46	9	08	51	14	48	43
8	21	26	58	15	02	−14	10	7	28	7	41	12	14	17	01	16	49	9	12	48	14	44	47
9	21	30	57	14	43	−14	13	7	26	7	39	12	14	17	03	16	51	9	16	44	14	40	51
10	21	34	55	14	23	−14	14	7	24	7	36	12	14	17	05	16	53	9	20	41	14	36	55
11	21	38	52	14	04	−14	15	7	23	7	34	12	14	17	07	16	55	9	24	37	14	32	59
12	21	42	48	13	44	−14	15	7	21	7	32	12	14	17	09	16	57	9	28	34	14	29	03
13	21	46	44	13	24	−14	14	7	19	7	30	12	14	17	10	17	00	9	32	30	14	25	08
14	21	50	39	13	03	−14	12	7	17	7	27	12	14	17	12	17	02	9	36	27	14	21	12
15	21	54	33	12	43	−14	10	7	15	7	25	12	14	17	14	17	04	9	40	23	14	17	16
16	21	58	26	12	22	−14	06	7	13	7	23	12	14	17	16	17	06	9	44	20	14	13	20
17	22	02	19	12	01	−14	03	7	11	7	21	12	14	17	18	17	08	9	48	17	14	09	24
18	22	06	11	11	40	−13	58	7	09	7	18	12	14	17	20	17	11	9	52	13	14	05	28
19	22	10	02	11	19	−13	53	7	07	7	16	12	14	17	22	17	13	9	56	10	14	01	32
20	22	13	53	10	58	−13	47	7	05	7	13	12	14	17	23	17	15	10	00	06	13	57	36
21	22	17	43	10	36	−13	40	7	03	7	11	12	14	17	25	17	17	10	04	03	13	53	40
22	22	21	32	10	14	−13	33	7	01	7	09	12	13	17	27	17	19	10	07	59	13	49	44
23	22	25	21	9	52	−13	25	6	59	7	06	12	13	17	29	17	21	10	11	56	13	45	48
24	22	29	09	9	30	−13	16	6	57	7	04	12	13	17	31	17	24	10	15	52	13	41	53
25	22	32	56	9	08	−13	07	6	54	7	01	12	13	17	33	17	26	10	19	49	13	37	57
26	22	36	43	8	46	−12	57	6	52	6	59	12	13	17	34	17	28	10	23	46	13	34	01
27	22	40	29	8	23	−12	47	6	50	6	56	12	13	17	36	17	30	10	27	42	13	30	05
28	22	44	15	8	01	−12	36	6	48	6	54	12	13	17	38	17	32	10	31	39	13	26	09

DURATION OF TWILIGHT (in minutes)

Latitude	52°	56°	52°	56°	52°	56°	52°	56°
	1 February		11 February		21 February		31 February	
Civil	37	41	35	39	34	38	34	37
Nautical	77	86	75	83	74	81	73	80
Astronomical	117	130	114	126	113	124	112	124

THE NIGHT SKY

Mercury passes through superior conjunction on the 14th and is unsuitably placed for observation throughout the month.

Venus remains too close to the Sun for observation throughout the month.

Mars, magnitude +1.3, reaches its greatest southerly declination of −23.7 degrees during this month and despite its increasing elongation from the Sun observers in these latitudes will continue to have great difficulty in locating the planet. Observers in southern England may possibly be able to detect it as a difficult morning object low in the south-eastern sky, though only for a short while before the morning twilight inhibits observation, and only under exceptionally clear conditions.

Jupiter, magnitude −2.3, continues to be visible as a brilliant morning object, rising above the east-south-eastern horizon well before midnight. Jupiter reaches its first stationary point on the 2nd and then begins its slow retrograde motion, west of Spica, in the constellation of Virgo.

Saturn continues to be visible as a bright object in the southern sky in the evenings and in fact, for most of the night, magnitude −0.2. It is retrograding slowly in the constellation of Gemini, south of Castor and Pollux. On the 20th the waxing gibbous Moon passes 4 degrees north of the planet. The rings of Saturn present a beautiful spectacle to the observer with a small telescope. The rings were at their maximum opening in 2002. They will next appear edge-on in 2009. The diameter of the minor axis is now 18 arcseconds, almost exactly the same as the polar diameter of the planet itself.

Zodiacal Light. The evening cone may be observed stretching up from the western horizon, along the ecliptic, after the end of twilight, from the beginning of the month until the 10th and again after the 26th. This faint phenomenon is only visible under good conditions and in the absence of both moonlight and artificial lighting.

THE MOON

Day	RA h	RA m	Dec. °	Hor. par. '	Semi-diam. '	Sun's Co-long. °	PA of Br. Limb °	Ph. %	Age d	Rise 52° h	Rise 52° m	Rise 56° h	Rise 56° m	Transit h	Transit m	Set 52° h	Set 52° m	Set 56° h	Set 56° m
1	13	37	−10.2	56.8	15.5	171	111	64	21.5	—	—	—	—	5	01	10	03	9	52
2	14	26	−15.8	57.6	15.7	183	109	53	22.5	1	07	1	22	5	49	10	19	10	01
3	15	19	−20.7	58.4	15.9	195	105	43	23.5	2	32	2	55	6	41	10	39	10	15
4	16	17	−24.7	59.2	16.1	208	99	32	24.5	4	00	4	31	7	39	11	10	10	38
5	17	20	−27.3	60.0	16.3	220	91	22	25.5	5	23	6	01	8	41	11	58	11	19
6	18	26	−28.1	60.6	16.5	232	82	13	26.5	6	31	7	09	9	47	13	06	12	29
7	19	34	−26.8	61.0	16.6	244	71	6	27.5	7	20	7	52	10	53	14	34	14	03
8	20	39	−23.5	61.2	16.7	256	55	1	28.5	7	52	8	16	11	55	16	10	15	48
9	21	41	−18.7	61.0	16.6	269	330	0	0.1	8	14	8	30	12	53	17	46	17	32
10	22	38	−12.8	60.5	16.5	281	262	1	1.1	8	31	8	40	13	46	19	17	19	10
11	23	31	−6.2	59.8	16.3	293	252	6	2.1	8	44	8	47	14	35	20	43	20	43
12	0	21	+0.4	58.9	16.0	305	249	13	3.1	8	56	8	53	15	22	22	06	22	12
13	1	10	+6.9	57.9	15.8	317	248	21	4.1	9	07	9	00	16	07	23	27	23	38
14	1	58	+12.8	57.0	15.5	330	249	30	5.1	9	20	9	07	16	53	—	—	—	—
15	2	47	+18.0	56.1	15.3	342	252	40	6.1	9	36	9	17	17	41	0	47	1	05
16	3	37	+22.2	55.4	15.1	354	257	50	7.1	9	57	9	31	18	29	2	05	2	29
17	4	29	+25.4	54.8	14.9	6	262	60	8.1	10	24	9	52	19	20	3	19	3	51
18	5	22	+27.4	54.4	14.8	18	268	69	9.1	11	02	10	25	20	11	4	26	5	03
19	6	15	+28.2	54.1	14.7	30	275	77	10.1	11	53	11	15	21	02	5	22	6	00
20	7	09	+27.6	54.0	14.7	42	282	85	11.1	12	55	12	21	21	53	6	05	6	39
21	8	01	+25.7	54.1	14.7	55	289	91	12.1	14	05	13	38	22	41	6	36	7	04
22	8	51	+22.7	54.2	14.8	67	296	95	13.1	15	20	14	59	23	27	6	58	7	20
23	9	40	+18.8	54.5	14.8	79	307	98	14.1	16	35	16	20	—	—	7	15	7	31
24	10	26	+14.0	54.8	14.9	91	351	100	15.1	17	49	17	40	0	11	7	28	7	39
25	11	11	+8.6	55.2	15.0	103	94	99	16.1	19	04	19	00	0	53	7	39	7	45
26	11	56	+2.9	55.6	15.2	115	108	97	17.1	20	18	20	20	1	35	7	49	7	50
27	12	41	−3.1	56.1	15.3	127	111	92	18.1	21	35	21	43	2	17	8	00	7	55
28	13	26	−9.1	56.6	15.4	140	112	86	19.1	22	55	23	09	3	00	8	11	8	01

MERCURY

Day	RA h	RA m	Dec. °	Diam. "	Phase %	Transit h	Transit m	5° high 52° h	5° high 52° m	5° high 56° h	5° high 56° m
1	20	22	−21.3	5	97	11	39	8	20	8	50
3	20	36	−20.6	5	97	11	44	8	20	8	48
5	20	50	−19.8	5	98	11	50	8	20	8	46
7	21	04	−18.9	5	99	11	56	8	19	8	44
9	21	17	−18.0	5	99	12	02	15	48	15	25
11	21	31	−16.9	5	100	12	08	16	02	15	41
13	21	45	−15.7	5	100	12	14	16	16	15	56
15	21	59	−14.4	5	100	12	20	16	30	16	13
17	22	13	−13.1	5	100	12	26	16	45	16	29
19	22	27	−11.6	5	99	12	32	17	00	16	46
21	22	41	−10.1	5	98	12	38	17	15	17	03
23	22	54	−8.5	5	97	12	44	17	30	17	20
25	23	08	−6.8	5	95	12	50	17	45	17	36
27	23	21	−5.0	5	92	12	55	18	00	17	53
29	23	34	−3.3	6	88	13	00	18	15	18	09
31	23	47	−1.5	6	83	13	05	18	28	18	24

VENUS

Day	RA h	RA m	Dec. °	Diam. "	Phase %	Transit h	Transit m	5° high 52° h	5° high 52° m	5° high 56° h	5° high 56° m
1	20	01	−21.1	10	97	11	16	7	56	8	26
6	20	27	−19.9	10	98	11	23	7	53	8	20
11	20	53	−18.5	10	98	11	29	7	49	8	13
16	21	18	−16.8	10	98	11	34	7	43	8	04
21	21	43	−15.0	10	99	11	39	7	35	7	54
26	22	07	−12.9	10	99	11	44	7	27	7	43
31	22	31	−10.8	10	99	11	48	7	18	7	31

MARS

Day	RA h	RA m	Dec. °	Diam. "	Phase %	Transit h	Transit m	5° high 52° h	5° high 52° m	5° high 56° h	5° high 56° m
1	17	42	−23.6	5	94	8	57	5	59	6	36
6	17	58	−23.7	5	94	8	52	5	56	6	33
11	18	13	−23.7	5	94	8	48	5	52	6	30
16	18	29	−23.7	5	93	8	44	5	47	6	25
21	18	44	−23.5	5	93	8	40	5	41	6	18
26	19	00	−23.3	5	92	8	36	5	35	6	11
31	19	15	−23.0	5	92	8	31	5	28	6	03

SUNRISE AND SUNSET

	London 0° 05′ 51° 30′				Bristol 2° 35′ 51° 28′				Birmingham 1° 55′ 52° 28′				Manchester 2° 15′ 53° 28′				Newcastle 1° 37′ 54° 59′				Glasgow 4° 14′ 55° 52′				Belfast 5° 56′ 54° 35′			
	h	m	h	m	h	m	h	m	h	m	h	m	h	m	h	m	h	m	h	m	h	m	h	m	h	m	h	m
1	7	39	16	50	7	48	17	00	7	49	16	54	7	54	16	52	7	57	16	44	8	11	16	51	8	13	17	03
2	7	37	16	52	7	47	17	02	7	47	16	56	7	52	16	54	7	55	16	46	8	09	16	53	8	11	17	05
3	7	35	16	54	7	45	17	04	7	46	16	58	7	50	16	56	7	53	16	48	8	07	16	55	8	09	17	07
4	7	34	16	55	7	44	17	06	7	44	17	00	7	49	16	58	7	52	16	50	8	05	16	57	8	07	17	09
5	7	32	16	57	7	42	17	07	7	42	17	02	7	47	17	00	7	50	16	52	8	03	16	59	8	05	17	11
6	7	30	16	59	7	40	17	09	7	41	17	04	7	45	17	02	7	48	16	54	8	01	17	02	8	03	17	13
7	7	29	17	01	7	39	17	11	7	39	17	05	7	43	17	04	7	46	16	56	7	59	17	04	8	02	17	15
8	7	27	17	03	7	37	17	13	7	37	17	07	7	41	17	06	7	44	16	58	7	57	17	06	8	00	17	17
9	7	25	17	05	7	35	17	15	7	35	17	09	7	39	17	08	7	42	17	01	7	55	17	08	7	58	17	19
10	7	23	17	06	7	33	17	17	7	33	17	11	7	38	17	10	7	40	17	03	7	53	17	10	7	56	17	21
11	7	22	17	08	7	32	17	18	7	31	17	13	7	36	17	12	7	37	17	05	7	51	17	13	7	53	17	23
12	7	20	17	10	7	30	17	20	7	30	17	15	7	34	17	14	7	35	17	07	7	48	17	15	7	51	17	25
13	7	18	17	12	7	28	17	22	7	28	17	17	7	32	17	16	7	33	17	09	7	46	17	17	7	49	17	27
14	7	16	17	14	7	26	17	24	7	26	17	19	7	30	17	18	7	31	17	11	7	44	17	19	7	47	17	30
15	7	14	17	16	7	24	17	26	7	24	17	21	7	27	17	20	7	29	17	13	7	42	17	21	7	45	17	32
16	7	12	17	17	7	22	17	27	7	22	17	23	7	25	17	22	7	27	17	15	7	39	17	23	7	43	17	34
17	7	10	17	19	7	20	17	29	7	20	17	24	7	23	17	24	7	24	17	17	7	37	17	26	7	41	17	36
18	7	08	17	21	7	18	17	31	7	18	17	26	7	21	17	26	7	22	17	20	7	35	17	28	7	38	17	38
19	7	06	17	23	7	16	17	33	7	16	17	28	7	19	17	28	7	20	17	22	7	32	17	30	7	36	17	40
20	7	04	17	25	7	14	17	35	7	13	17	30	7	17	17	29	7	18	17	24	7	30	17	32	7	34	17	42
21	7	02	17	26	7	12	17	37	7	11	17	32	7	15	17	31	7	15	17	26	7	28	17	34	7	32	17	44
22	7	00	17	28	7	10	17	38	7	09	17	34	7	12	17	33	7	13	17	28	7	25	17	36	7	29	17	46
23	6	58	17	30	7	08	17	40	7	07	17	36	7	10	17	35	7	11	17	30	7	23	17	39	7	27	17	48
24	6	56	17	32	7	06	17	42	7	05	17	38	7	08	17	37	7	08	17	32	7	20	17	41	7	25	17	50
25	6	54	17	34	7	04	17	44	7	03	17	39	7	06	17	39	7	06	17	34	7	18	17	43	7	22	17	52
26	6	52	17	35	7	02	17	45	7	01	17	41	7	04	17	41	7	04	17	36	7	16	17	45	7	20	17	54
27	6	50	17	37	7	00	17	47	6	58	17	43	7	01	17	43	7	01	17	38	7	13	17	47	7	18	17	56
28	6	48	17	39	6	58	17	49	6	56	17	45	6	59	17	45	6	59	17	40	7	11	17	49	7	15	17	58

JUPITER

Day	RA		Dec.		Transit		5° high			
							52°		56°	
	h	m	°	′	h	m	h	m	h	m
1	13	11.8	−6	04	4	26	23	27	23	36
11	13	11.4	−5	59	3	46	22	47	22	56
21	13	09.8	−5	47	3	05	22	05	22	13
31	13	07.2	−5	28	2	23	21	21	21	29

Diameters – equatorial 41″ polar 38″

SATURN

Day	RA		Dec.		Transit		5° high			
							52°		56°	
	h	m	°	′	h	m	h	m	h	m
1	7	37.0	+21	37	22	48	6	14	6	30
11	7	34.0	+21	45	22	05	5	32	5	49
21	7	31.5	+21	51	21	24	4	51	5	08
31	7	29.7	+21	56	20	43	4	11	4	27

Diameters – equatorial 20″ polar 18″
Rings – major axis 46″ minor axis 18″

URANUS

Day	RA		Dec.		Transit		10° high			
							52°		56°	
	h	m	°	′	h	m	h	m	h	m
1	22	29.9	−10	13	13	43	17	37	17	20
11	22	32.0	−10	01	13	05	17	02	16	44
21	22	34.1	−9	48	12	28	16	26	16	08
31	22	36.3	−9	35	11	51	15	50	15	33

Diameter 4″

NEPTUNE

Day	RA		Dec.		Transit		10° high			
							52°		56°	
	h	m	°	′	h	m	h	m	h	m
1	21	09.8	−16	26	12	23	9	12	9	41
11	21	11.4	−16	20	11	45	8	33	9	02
21	21	12.9	−16	13	11	07	7	55	8	23
31	21	14.3	−16	07	10	29	7	16	7	44

Diameter 2″

 **MARCH 2005** ♈

THIRD MONTH, 31 DAYS. *Mars*, Roman god of battle

1	*Tuesday*	Frédéric Chopin b. 1810. Girolamo Frescobaldi d. 1643	60
2	*Wednesday*	Horace Walpole d. 1797. D. H. Lawrence d. 1930	61
3	*Thursday*	Sir Henry J. Wood b. 1869. Robert Adam d. 1792	62
4	*Friday*	Antonio Vivaldi b. 1678. Nikolai Gogol d. 1852	63
5	*Saturday*	Henry II b. 1133. Sergey Prokofiev d. 1953	64
6	*Sunday*	Savinien Cyrano de Bergerac b. 1619. Elizabeth Barrett Browning b. 1806	65

7	*Monday*	Piet Mondrian b. 1872. Stevie Smith d. 1971	week 10 day 66
8	*Tuesday*	Kenneth Grahame b. 1859. Dame Ninette de Valois d. 2001	67
9	*Wednesday*	David Riccio, secretary to Mary Queen of Scots murdered d. 1566	68
10	*Thursday*	Earl of Wessex b. 1964. Mikhail Bulgakov d. 1940	69
11	*Friday*	Douglas Adams b. 1952. Erle Stanley Gardner d. 1970	70
12	*Saturday*	Vaslav Nijinsky b. 1890. Anne Frank d. 1945	71
13	*Sunday*	Sir Hugh Walpole b. 1884. John Middleton Murry d. 1957	72

14	*Monday*	Johann Strauss b. 1804. Karl Marx d. 1883	week 11 day 73
15	*Tuesday*	H. P. Lovecraft d. 1937. Dame Rebecca West d. 1983	74
16	*Wednesday*	Bernardo Bertolucci b. 1941. Aubrey Beardsley d. 1898	75
17	*Thursday*	Rudolf Nureyev b. 1938. Harold I (Harefoot) d. 1046	76
18	*Friday*	Nikolay Rimsky-Korsakov b. 1844. Wilfred Owen d. 1893	77
19	*Saturday*	Glenn Close b. 1947. Edgar Rice Burroughs d. 1950	78
20	*Sunday*	Henrik Ibsen b. 1828. Henry IV d. 1413	79

21	*Monday*	Johann Sebastian Bach b. 1685. Phyllis McGinley b. 1925	week 12 day 80
22	*Tuesday*	Sir Anthony Van Dyck b. 1599. Thomas Hughes d. 1896	81
23	*Wednesday*	Princess Eugenie of York b. 1990. Stendhal d. 1842	82
24	*Thursday*	William Morris b. 1834. Elizabeth I d. 1603	83
25	*Friday*	Béla Bartók b. 1881. Claude Debussy d. 1918	84
26	*Saturday*	Tennessee Williams b. 1911. Sir Noel Coward d. 1973	85
27	*Sunday*	Sir George Gilbert Scott b. 1878. James I (IV of Scotland) d. 1625	86

28	*Monday*	Maxim Gorky b. 1868. Virginia Woolf d. 1941	week 13 day 87
29	*Tuesday*	Sir William Walton b. 1902. George Seurat d. 1891	88
30	*Wednesday*	Anna Sewell b. 1820. Paul Verlaine d. 1844	89
31	*Thursday*	John Constable d. 1837. Charlotte Brontë d. 1855	90

ASTRONOMICAL PHENOMENA

d h
6 07 Mars in conjunction with Moon. Mars 4° N.
10 00 Venus in conjunction with Moon. Venus 2° N.
11 18 Mercury in conjunction with Moon. Mercury 3° N.
12 18 Mercury at greatest elongation E.18°
19 18 Saturn in conjunction with Moon. Saturn 5° S.
20 00 Mercury at stationary point
20 13 Sun's longitude 0° ♈
22 03 Saturn at stationary point
26 15 Jupiter in conjunction with Moon. Jupiter 0°.9 N.
27 02 Pluto at stationary point
29 16 Mercury in inferior conjunction
29 20 Venus in conjunction with Mercury. Venus 4° S.
31 03 Venus in superior conjunction

MINIMA OF ALGOL

d	h	d	h	d	h
2	12.8	14	00.1	25	11.4
5	09.6	16	20.9	28	08.2
8	06.5	19	17.7	31	05.0
11	03.3	22	14.6		

CONSTELLATIONS

The following constellations are near the meridian at

	d	h		d	h
February	1	24	March	16	21
February	15	23	April	1	20
March	1	22	April	15	19

Cepheus (below the Pole), Camelopardus, Lynx, Gemini, Cancer, Leo, Canis Minor, Hydra, Monoceros, Canis Major and Puppis

THE MOON

Phases, Apsides and Node		*d*	*h*	*m*
☾	Last Quarter	3	17	36
●	New Moon	10	09	10
☽	First Quarter	17	19	19
○	Full Moon	25	20	58

	d	h	m
Perigee (363,215 km)	8	03	32
Apogee (404,883 km)	19	22	50

Mean longitude of ascending node on March 1, 25°

THE SUN

s.d. 16′.1

Day	Right Ascension			Dec.		Equation of time		Rise 52°		Rise 56°		Transit		Set 52°		Set 56°		Sidereal time			Transit of first point of Aries		
	h	m	s	°	′	m	s	h	m	h	m	h	m	h	m	h	m	h	m	s	h	m	s
1	22	48	00	−7	38	−12	25	6	46	6	51	12	12	17	40	17	34	10	35	35	13	22	13
2	22	51	45	−7	15	−12	13	6	44	6	49	12	12	17	42	17	36	10	39	32	13	18	17
3	22	55	29	−6	52	−12	01	6	41	6	46	12	12	17	43	17	38	10	43	28	13	14	21
4	22	59	13	−6	29	−11	48	6	39	6	44	12	12	17	45	17	41	10	47	25	13	10	25
5	23	02	56	−6	06	−11	35	6	37	6	41	12	11	17	47	17	43	10	51	21	13	06	29
6	23	06	39	−5	43	−11	21	6	35	6	39	12	11	17	49	17	45	10	55	18	13	02	33
7	23	10	22	−5	19	−11	07	6	32	6	36	12	11	17	51	17	47	10	59	15	12	58	38
8	23	14	04	−4	56	−10	53	6	30	6	34	12	11	17	52	17	49	11	03	11	12	54	42
9	23	17	45	−4	33	−10	38	6	28	6	31	12	11	17	54	17	51	11	07	08	12	50	46
10	23	21	27	−4	09	−10	23	6	26	6	28	12	10	17	56	17	53	11	11	04	12	46	50
11	23	25	08	−3	46	−10	07	6	23	6	26	12	10	17	58	17	55	11	15	01	12	42	54
12	23	28	49	−3	22	−9	51	6	21	6	23	12	10	17	59	17	57	11	18	57	12	38	58
13	23	32	29	−2	58	−9	35	6	19	6	21	12	09	18	01	17	59	11	22	54	12	35	02
14	23	36	09	−2	35	−9	19	6	17	6	18	12	09	18	03	18	02	11	26	50	12	31	06
15	23	39	49	−2	11	−9	02	6	14	6	15	12	09	18	05	18	04	11	30	47	12	27	10
16	23	43	29	−1	47	−8	45	6	12	6	13	12	09	18	06	18	06	11	34	44	12	23	14
17	23	47	08	−1	24	−8	28	6	10	6	10	12	08	18	08	18	08	11	38	40	12	19	18
18	23	50	48	−1	00	−8	11	6	07	6	07	12	08	18	10	18	10	11	42	37	12	15	23
19	23	54	27	−0	36	−7	54	6	05	6	05	12	08	18	12	18	12	11	46	33	12	11	27
20	23	58	06	−0	12	−7	36	6	03	6	02	12	07	18	13	18	14	11	50	30	12	07	31
21	0	01	44	+0	11	−7	18	6	00	6	00	12	07	18	15	18	16	11	54	26	12	03	35
22	0	05	23	+0	35	−7	00	5	58	5	57	12	07	18	17	18	18	11	58	23	11	59	39
23	0	09	01	+0	59	−6	42	5	56	5	54	12	07	18	18	18	20	12	02	19	11	55	43
24	0	12	40	+1	22	−6	24	5	53	5	52	12	06	18	20	18	22	12	06	16	11	51	47
25	0	16	18	+1	46	−6	06	5	51	5	49	12	06	18	22	18	24	12	10	12	11	47	51
26	0	19	56	+2	09	−5	47	5	49	5	46	12	06	18	24	18	26	12	14	09	11	43	55
27	0	23	35	+2	33	−5	29	5	46	5	44	12	05	18	25	18	28	12	18	06	11	39	59
28	0	27	13	+2	56	−5	11	5	44	5	41	12	05	18	27	18	30	12	22	02	11	36	04
29	0	30	51	+3	20	−4	53	5	42	5	38	12	05	18	29	18	32	12	25	59	11	32	08
30	0	34	30	+3	43	−4	34	5	39	5	36	12	04	18	30	18	34	12	29	55	11	28	12
31	0	38	08	+4	06	−4	16	5	37	5	33	12	04	18	32	18	36	12	33	52	11	24	16

DURATION OF TWILIGHT (in minutes)

Latitude	52°	56°	52°	56°	52°	56°	52°	56°
	1 March		11 March		21 March		31 March	
Civil	34	37	34	37	34	37	34	38
Nautical	73	80	73	80	74	81	75	84
Astronomical	112	124	113	125	115	128	120	135

THE NIGHT SKY

Mercury is at greatest eastern elongation (18 degrees) on the 12th and thus is visible in the evenings low in the western sky around the end of evening civil twilight during the first half of the month. It is best seen (because it is brighter) near the beginning of the month: by the 18th its magnitude has faded to +1.1. On the evening of the 11th, the New Moon, barely 1.5 days old, passes 4 degrees south of the planet. This evening apparition is the most suitable one of the year for observers in northern temperate latitudes, and, in fact, the only evening apparition for observers in the latitudes of the British Isles.

Venus passes through superior conjunction on the last day of the month and therefore remains too close to the Sun for observation.

Mars continues to be visible as a very difficult morning object, low above the south-eastern horizon for a short while before twilight renders observation impossible. Its magnitude is +1.1.

Jupiter, magnitude −2.4, continues to be visible as a brilliant object in the night sky, and by the end of the month may be seen rising above the east-south-eastern horizon soon after sunset. The Moon, near Full, will be seen close to the planet between the 25th and 27th.

Saturn continues to be visible as an evening object, magnitude 0.0. It reaches its second stationary point on the 22nd, and then resumes its direct motion, in the constellation of Gemini. On the early evening of the 19th the waxing gibbous Moon passes 4 degrees north of the planet.

Zodiacal Light. The evening cone may be observed, stretching up from the western horizon, along the ecliptic, after the end of twilight, from the beginning of the month until the 11th, and again after the 27th.

THE MOON

Day	RA h	RA m	Dec. °	Hor. par. ′	Semi-diam. ′	Sun's Co-long. °	PA of Br. Limb °	Ph. %	Age d	Rise 52° h	Rise 52° m	Rise 56° h	Rise 56° m	Transit h	Transit m	Set 52° h	Set 52° m	Set 56° h	Set 56° m
1	14	15	−14.7	57.1	15.6	152	110	78	20.1	—	—	—	—	3	46	8	24	8	09
2	15	06	−19.8	57.7	15.7	164	107	69	21.1	0	18	0	39	4	36	8	43	8	20
3	16	02	−24.0	58.3	15.9	176	102	58	22.1	1	44	2	13	5	31	9	09	8	39
4	17	01	−26.9	58.9	16.0	188	96	47	23.1	3	08	3	44	6	30	9	48	9	11
5	18	05	−28.2	59.4	16.2	200	88	36	24.1	4	20	5	00	7	33	10	46	10	06
6	19	10	−27.6	59.9	16.3	213	80	25	25.1	5	14	5	50	8	36	12	04	11	29
7	20	14	−25.1	60.2	16.4	225	72	16	26.1	5	51	6	19	9	38	13	35	13	09
8	21	15	−21.0	60.4	16.4	237	65	8	27.1	6	17	6	36	10	36	15	09	14	52
9	22	13	−15.5	60.3	16.4	249	57	3	28.1	6	35	6	47	11	31	16	42	16	31
10	23	07	−9.2	60.0	16.3	261	35	0	29.1	6	49	6	55	12	21	18	10	18	07
11	23	59	−2.4	59.4	16.2	274	261	1	0.6	7	01	7	01	13	09	19	36	19	39
12	0	49	+ 4.2	58.7	16.0	286	249	3	1.6	7	12	7	07	13	56	21	00	21	08
13	1	38	+10.6	57.9	15.8	298	248	9	2.6	7	25	7	14	14	43	22	22	22	37
14	2	28	+16.2	57.0	15.5	310	250	16	3.6	7	39	7	23	15	31	23	44	—	—
15	3	19	+21.0	56.2	15.3	322	253	24	4.6	7	58	7	35	16	21	—	—	0	06
16	4	11	+24.7	55.5	15.1	335	258	33	5.6	8	22	7	52	17	11	1	02	1	32
17	5	04	+27.1	54.9	15.0	347	264	42	6.6	8	56	8	20	18	03	2	14	2	50
18	5	58	+28.2	54.5	14.8	359	270	52	7.6	9	43	9	04	18	55	3	16	3	55
19	6	52	+28.0	54.2	14.8	11	276	61	8.6	10	41	10	05	19	46	4	04	4	41
20	7	45	+26.6	54.2	14.8	23	283	70	9.6	11	49	11	19	20	35	4	39	5	10
21	8	36	+23.9	54.2	14.8	36	288	79	10.6	13	03	12	39	21	22	5	04	5	28
22	9	25	+20.2	54.5	14.8	48	293	86	11.6	14	18	14	01	22	07	5	22	5	40
23	10	12	+15.6	54.8	14.9	60	297	92	12.6	15	33	15	22	22	50	5	36	5	49
24	10	58	+10.4	55.3	15.1	72	301	96	13.6	16	48	16	43	23	32	5	48	5	55
25	11	43	+ 4.6	55.8	15.2	84	307	99	14.6	18	04	18	04	—	—	5	58	6	00
26	12	28	−1.4	56.3	15.3	96	69	100	15.6	19	21	19	27	0	14	6	08	6	05
27	13	14	−7.5	56.8	15.5	109	111	99	16.6	20	41	20	53	0	57	6	19	6	11
28	14	02	−13.4	57.3	15.6	121	112	95	17.6	22	05	22	24	1	43	6	32	6	18
29	14	53	−18.8	57.8	15.7	133	110	89	18.6	23	32	23	58	2	33	6	48	6	28
30	15	48	−23.3	58.2	15.9	145	105	82	19.6	—	—	—	—	3	26	7	11	6	44
31	16	48	−26.5	58.6	16.0	157	99	72	20.6	0	57	1	32	4	24	7	46	7	11

MERCURY

Day	RA h	RA m	Dec. °	Diam. ″	Phase %	Transit h	Transit m	5° high 52° h	5° high 52° m	5° high 56° h	5° high 56° m
1	23	34	−3.3	6	88	13	00	18	15	18	09
3	23	47	−1.5	6	83	13	05	18	28	18	24
5	23	59	+0.2	6	77	13	09	18	41	18	39
7	0	10	+1.9	6	69	13	12	18	53	18	51
9	0	20	+3.5	7	61	13	14	19	02	19	02
11	0	29	+4.9	7	53	13	14	19	09	19	10
13	0	36	+6.2	7	44	13	13	19	14	19	16
15	0	42	+7.2	8	35	13	10	19	15	19	18
17	0	45	+8.0	8	27	13	05	19	14	19	17
19	0	47	+8.4	9	20	12	58	19	08	19	12
21	0	46	+8.6	9	14	12	49	19	00	19	04
23	0	44	+8.5	10	8	12	39	18	48	18	52
25	0	41	+8.1	10	4	12	27	18	34	18	37
27	0	36	+7.5	11	2	12	15	18	17	18	20
29	0	31	+6.6	11	1	12	01	17	59	18	01
31	0	25	+5.7	11	1	11	48	5	54	5	52

VENUS

Day	RA h	RA m	Dec. °	Diam. ″	Phase %	Transit h	Transit m	5° high 52° h	5° high 52° m	5° high 56° h	5° high 56° m
1	22	22	−11.7	10	99	11	46	7	22	7	36
6	22	45	−9.4	10	99	11	50	7	13	7	24
11	23	09	−7.1	10	100	11	54	7	03	7	13
16	23	32	−4.6	10	100	11	57	6	53	7	00
21	23	55	−2.1	10	100	12	00	6	43	6	48
26	0	17	+0.4	10	100	12	03	6	33	6	36
31	0	40	+2.9	10	100	12	07	6	23	6	24

MARS

Day	RA h	RA m	Dec. °	Diam. ″	Phase %	Transit h	Transit m	5° high 52° h	5° high 52° m	5° high 56° h	5° high 56° m
1	19	09	−23.1	5	92	8	33	5	31	6	06
6	19	24	−22.7	5	92	8	29	5	23	5	57
11	19	40	−22.2	5	91	8	24	5	14	5	47
16	19	55	−21.7	5	91	8	20	5	05	5	37
21	20	10	−21.0	6	90	8	16	4	56	5	25
26	20	25	−20.3	6	90	8	11	4	45	5	13
31	20	40	−19.5	6	90	8	06	4	34	5	00

SUNRISE AND SUNSET

	London 0° 05' 51° 30'		Bristol 2° 35' 51° 28'		Birmingham 1° 55' 52° 28'		Manchester 2° 15' 53° 28'		Newcastle 1° 37' 54° 59'		Glasgow 4° 14' 55° 52'		Belfast 5° 56' 54° 35'	
	h m	h m	h m	h m	h m	h m	h m	h m	h m	h m	h m	h m	h m	h m
1	6 45	17 41	6 55	17 51	6 54	17 47	6 57	17 47	6 56	17 42	7 08	17 51	7 13	18 00
2	6 43	17 42	6 53	17 53	6 52	17 49	6 54	17 49	6 54	17 44	7 06	17 54	7 11	18 02
3	6 41	17 44	6 51	17 54	6 50	17 51	6 52	17 51	6 51	17 46	7 03	17 56	7 08	18 04
4	6 39	17 46	6 49	17 56	6 47	17 52	6 50	17 53	6 49	17 48	7 01	17 58	7 06	18 06
5	6 37	17 48	6 47	17 58	6 45	17 54	6 47	17 54	6 47	17 50	6 58	18 00	7 03	18 08
6	6 35	17 49	6 45	18 00	6 43	17 56	6 45	17 56	6 44	17 52	6 55	18 02	7 01	18 10
7	6 32	17 51	6 42	18 01	6 40	17 58	6 43	17 58	6 42	17 54	6 53	18 04	6 58	18 12
8	6 30	17 53	6 40	18 03	6 38	18 00	6 40	18 00	6 39	17 56	6 50	18 06	6 56	18 14
9	6 28	17 55	6 38	18 05	6 36	18 01	6 38	18 02	6 37	17 58	6 48	18 08	6 54	18 16
10	6 26	17 56	6 36	18 06	6 34	18 03	6 36	18 04	6 34	18 00	6 45	18 10	6 51	18 18
11	6 23	17 58	6 33	18 08	6 31	18 05	6 33	18 06	6 32	18 02	6 43	18 12	6 49	18 20
12	6 21	18 00	6 31	18 10	6 29	18 07	6 31	18 08	6 29	18 04	6 40	18 14	6 46	18 22
13	6 19	18 02	6 29	18 12	6 27	18 09	6 28	18 10	6 27	18 06	6 37	18 16	6 44	18 24
14	6 17	18 03	6 27	18 13	6 24	18 10	6 26	18 11	6 24	18 08	6 35	18 19	6 41	18 26
15	6 14	18 05	6 24	18 15	6 22	18 12	6 24	18 13	6 21	18 10	6 32	18 21	6 39	18 28
16	6 12	18 07	6 22	18 17	6 20	18 14	6 21	18 15	6 19	18 12	6 30	18 23	6 36	18 30
17	6 10	18 08	6 20	18 18	6 17	18 16	6 19	18 17	6 16	18 14	6 27	18 25	6 34	18 32
18	6 08	18 10	6 18	18 20	6 15	18 17	6 16	18 19	6 14	18 16	6 24	18 27	6 31	18 34
19	6 05	18 12	6 15	18 22	6 13	18 19	6 14	18 21	6 11	18 18	6 22	18 29	6 29	18 35
20	6 03	18 14	6 13	18 24	6 10	18 21	6 11	18 22	6 09	18 20	6 19	18 31	6 26	18 37
21	6 01	18 15	6 11	18 25	6 08	18 23	6 09	18 24	6 06	18 22	6 16	18 33	6 24	18 39
22	5 58	18 17	6 08	18 27	6 06	18 25	6 07	18 26	6 04	18 24	6 14	18 35	6 21	18 41
23	5 56	18 19	6 06	18 29	6 03	18 26	6 04	18 28	6 01	18 26	6 11	18 37	6 19	18 43
24	5 54	18 20	6 04	18 30	6 01	18 28	6 02	18 30	5 59	18 28	6 09	18 39	6 16	18 45
25	5 52	18 22	6 02	18 32	5 58	18 30	5 59	18 32	5 56	18 30	6 06	18 41	6 13	18 47
26	5 49	18 24	5 59	18 34	5 56	18 32	5 57	18 33	5 53	18 32	6 03	18 43	6 11	18 49
27	5 47	18 25	5 57	18 35	5 54	18 33	5 54	18 35	5 51	18 34	6 01	18 45	6 08	18 51
28	5 45	18 27	5 55	18 37	5 51	18 35	5 52	18 37	5 48	18 36	5 58	18 47	6 06	18 53
29	5 43	18 29	5 53	18 39	5 49	18 37	5 50	18 39	5 46	18 38	5 55	18 49	6 03	18 55
30	5 40	18 30	5 50	18 40	5 47	18 39	5 47	18 41	5 43	18 40	5 53	18 51	6 01	18 57
31	5 38	18 32	5 48	18 42	5 44	18 40	5 45	18 43	5 41	18 42	5 50	18 53	5 58	18 59

JUPITER

Day	RA		Dec.		Transit		5° high 52°		56°	
	h	m	°	'	h	m	h	m	h	m
1	13	07.8	-5	33	2	32	21	30	21	38
11	13	04.4	-5	10	1	49	20	45	20	53
21	13	00.2	-4	43	1	06	19	59	20	07
31	12	55.6	-4	13	0	22	19	13	19	20

Diameters – equatorial 44" polar 41"

SATURN

Day	RA		Dec.		Transit		5° high 52°		56°	
	h	m	°	'	h	m	h	m	h	m
1	7	30.0	+21	55	20	51	4	19	4	35
11	7	28.8	+21	59	20	10	3	39	3	55
21	7	28.3	+22	01	19	31	2	59	3	16
31	7	28.6	+22	01	18	52	2	20	2	37

Diameters – equatorial 19" polar 18"
Rings – major axis 44" minor axis 18"

URANUS

Day	RA		Dec.		Transit		10° high 52°		56°	
	h	m	°	'	h	m	h	m	h	m
1	22	35.9	-9	38	11	58	8	00	8	17
11	22	38.0	-9	25	11	21	7	21	7	38
21	22	40.1	-9	13	10	44	6	43	6	59
31	22	42.1	-9	01	10	07	6	04	6	21

Diameter 4"

NEPTUNE

Day	RA		Dec.		Transit		10° high 52°		56°	
	h	m	°	'	h	m	h	m	h	m
1	21	14.0	-16	08	10	37	7	24	7	52
11	21	15.4	-16	02	9	59	6	45	7	13
21	21	16.6	-15	57	9	21	6	06	6	34
31	21	17.7	-15	52	8	42	5	27	5	55

Diameter 2"

APRIL 2005

FOURTH MONTH, 30 DAYS. *Aperire*, to open; Earth opens to receive seed.

1	*Friday*	Eleanor of Aquitaine d. 1204. Max Ernst d. 1976	91
2	*Saturday*	Hans Christian Andersen b. 1805. C. S. Forester d. 1966	92
3	*Sunday*	Johannes Brahms d. 1897. Graham Greene d. 1991	93

4	*Monday*	Maya Angelou b. 1928. Oliver Goldsmith d. 1774	week 14 day 94
5	*Tuesday*	Jean-Baptiste Rousseau b. 1671. Allen Ginsberg, poet d. 1997	95
6	*Wednesday*	Andre Previn b. 1929. Igor Stravinsky d. 1971	96
7	*Thursday*	William Wordsworth b. 1770. El Greco d. 1614	97
8	*Friday*	Vaslav Nijinsky d. 1950. Pablo Picasso d. 1973	98
9	*Saturday*	François-Rabelais d. 1553. Dante Gabriel Rosetti d. 1882	99
10	*Sunday*	Joseph Pulitzer b. 1847. Evelyn Waugh d. 1966	100

11	*Monday*	John O'Hara d. 1970. Jaques Prévert d. 1977	week 15 day 101
12	*Tuesday*	Alan Ayckbourn b. 1939. William Kent d. 1748	102
13	*Wednesday*	Samuel Beckett b. 1906. Sir William Orchardson d. 1910	103
14	*Thursday*	George Frideric Handel d. 1759. Simone de Beauvoir d. 1986	104
15	*Friday*	Leonardo da Vinci b. 1452. Jean Paul Sartre d. 1980	105
16	*Saturday*	Sir Kingsley Amis b. 1922. Francisco de Goya d. 1828	106
17	*Sunday*	Nick Hornby b. 1957. Marquise de Sévigné d. 1696	107

18	*Monday*	Leopold Stokowski b. 1882. Dame Elizabeth Frink d. 1993	week 16 day 108
19	*Tuesday*	Richard Hughes b. 1900. Dame Daphne du Maurier d. 1989	109
20	*Wednesday*	Canaletto d. 1768. Bram Stoker d. 1912	110
21	*Thursday*	Elizabeth II b. 1926. Mark Twain d. 1910	111
22	*Friday*	Henry Fielding b. 1707. Vladimir Nabokov b. 1899	112
23	*Saturday*	J. M. W. Turner b. 1775. William Shakespeare d. 1616	113
24	*Sunday*	Anthony Trollope b. 1815. Daniel Defoe d. 1731	114

25	*Monday*	Walter de la Mare b. 1873. Anna Sewell d. 1878	week 17 day 115
26	*Tuesday*	Edward II b. 1284. Eugène Delacroix b. 1798	116
27	*Wednesday*	Cecil Day Lewis b. 1904. Mary Wollstonecraft Godwin b. 1759	117
28	*Thursday*	Edward IV b. 1442. Francis Bacon d. 1992	118
29	*Friday*	Jean-George Naverre b. 1727. Sir Thomas Beecham b. 1879	119
30	*Saturday*	Jaroslav Hašek b. 1883. Édouard Manet d. 1883	120

ASTRONOMICAL PHENOMENA

d h
3 16 Jupiter at opposition
4 00 Mars in conjunction with Moon. Mars 4° N.
7 16 Mercury in conjunction with Moon. Mercury 3° N.
8 21 Annular-Total eclipse of Sun
9 01 Venus in conjunction with Moon. Venus 1° S.
12 08 Mercury at stationary point
16 03 Saturn in conjunction with Moon. Saturn 5° S.
20 00 Sun's longitude 30° ♉
22 17 Jupiter in conjunction with Moon. Jupiter 0°.5 N.
26 16 Mercury at greatest elongation W.27°

MINIMA OF ALGOL

d	*h*	*d*	*h*	*d*	*h*
3	01.8	14	13.1	26	00.4
5	22.7	17	09.9	28	21.2
8	19.5	20	06.8		
11	16.3	23	03.6		

CONSTELLATIONS

The following constellations are near the meridian at

	d	*h*		*d*	*h*
March	1	24	April	15	21
March	16	23	May	1	20
April	1	22	May	16	19

Cepheus (below the Pole), Cassiopeia (below the Pole), Ursa Major, Leo Minor, Leo, Sextans, Hydra and Crater

THE MOON

Phases, Apsides and Node		*d*	*h*	*m*
☾	Last Quarter	2	00	50
●	New Moon	8	20	32
☽	First Quarter	16	14	37
○	Full Moon	24	10	06

Perigee (368,462 km)	4	11	02
Apogee (404,344 km)	16	18	40
Perigee (368,995 km)	29	10	20

Mean longitude of ascending node on April 1, 24°

THE SUN

s.d. 16′.0

Day	Right Ascension			Dec. +		Equation of time		Rise 52°		Rise 56°		Transit		Set 52°		Set 56°		Sidereal time			Transit of First point of Aries		
	h	m	s	°	′	m	s	h	m	h	m	h	m	h	m	h	m	h	m	s	h	m	s
1	0	41	47	4	30	−3	58	5	35	5	31	12	04	18	34	18	38	12	37	48	11	20	20
2	0	45	26	4	53	−3	41	5	33	5	28	12	04	18	36	18	40	12	41	45	11	16	24
3	0	49	04	5	16	−3	23	5	30	5	25	12	03	18	37	18	42	12	45	41	11	12	28
4	0	52	43	5	39	−3	05	5	28	5	23	12	03	18	39	18	44	12	49	38	11	08	32
5	0	56	23	6	02	−2	48	5	26	5	20	12	03	18	41	18	46	12	53	35	11	04	36
6	1	00	02	6	24	−2	31	5	23	5	18	12	02	18	42	18	49	12	57	31	11	00	40
7	1	03	42	6	47	−2	14	5	21	5	15	12	02	18	44	18	51	13	01	28	10	56	44
8	1	07	21	7	10	−1	57	5	19	5	12	12	02	18	46	18	53	13	05	24	10	52	49
9	1	11	02	7	32	−1	41	5	17	5	10	12	02	18	48	18	55	13	09	21	10	48	53
10	1	14	42	7	54	−1	24	5	14	5	07	12	01	18	49	18	57	13	13	17	10	44	57
11	1	18	22	8	16	−1	09	5	12	5	05	12	01	18	51	18	59	13	17	14	10	41	01
12	1	22	03	8	38	−0	53	5	10	5	02	12	01	18	53	19	01	13	21	10	10	37	05
13	1	25	44	9	00	−0	37	5	08	5	00	12	00	18	54	19	03	13	25	07	10	33	09
14	1	29	26	9	22	−0	22	5	06	4	57	12	00	18	56	19	05	13	29	04	10	29	13
15	1	33	08	9	44	−0	08	5	03	4	54	12	00	18	58	19	07	13	33	00	10	25	17
16	1	36	50	10	05	+0	07	5	01	4	52	12	00	19	00	19	09	13	36	57	10	21	21
17	1	40	32	10	26	+0	21	4	59	4	49	12	00	19	01	19	11	13	40	53	10	17	25
18	1	44	15	10	47	+0	35	4	57	4	47	11	59	19	03	19	13	13	44	50	10	13	29
19	1	47	58	11	08	+0	48	4	55	4	44	11	59	19	05	19	15	13	48	46	10	09	34
20	1	51	42	11	29	+1	01	4	53	4	42	11	59	19	06	19	17	13	52	43	10	05	38
21	1	55	26	11	49	+1	13	4	50	4	40	11	59	19	08	19	19	13	56	39	10	01	42
22	1	59	10	12	09	+1	26	4	48	4	37	11	58	19	10	19	21	14	00	36	9	57	46
23	2	02	55	12	30	+1	37	4	46	4	35	11	58	19	11	19	23	14	04	33	9	53	50
24	2	06	41	12	49	+1	48	4	44	4	32	11	58	19	13	19	25	14	08	29	9	49	54
25	2	10	26	13	09	+1	59	4	42	4	30	11	58	19	15	19	27	14	12	26	9	45	58
26	2	14	13	13	29	+2	09	4	40	4	28	11	58	19	17	19	29	14	16	22	9	42	02
27	2	18	00	13	48	+2	19	4	38	4	25	11	58	19	18	19	31	14	20	19	9	38	06
28	2	21	47	14	07	+2	28	4	36	4	23	11	57	19	20	19	33	14	24	15	9	34	10
29	2	25	35	14	26	+2	37	4	34	4	21	11	57	19	22	19	35	14	28	12	9	30	14
30	2	29	23	14	44	+2	45	4	32	4	18	11	57	19	23	19	37	14	32	08	9	26	19

DURATION OF TWILIGHT (in minutes)

Latitude	52°	56°	52°	56°	52°	56°	52°	56°
	1 April		11 April		21 April		31 April	
Civil	34	38	35	39	37	42	39	44
Nautical	76	84	79	89	83	96	89	106
Astronomical	120	136	127	147	137	165	152	204

THE NIGHT SKY

Mercury is too close to the Sun for observation throughout the month, despite the facts that it (a) reaches greatest western elongation on the 26th, and (b) reaches aphelion only 5 days earlier.

Venus is not suitably placed for observation at first, but becomes visible during the last few days of the month as a brilliant object in the evening sky, magnitude −3.9. It may be seen low above the western horizon for a very short while just after sunset.

Mars is visible as a difficult morning object, low in the south-eastern sky for a short while before sunrise. Its magnitude brightens slowly during the month from +0.9 to +0.6. The slight reddish tinge in its colour is an aid to its identification.

Jupiter, magnitude −2.5, reaches opposition on the 3rd, and is visible throughout the hours of darkness. Jupiter is retrograding slowly in the constellation of Virgo. The nearly Full Moon is near the planet on the 21st to the 23rd. The four Galilean satellites are readily observable with a small telescope or even a good pair of binoculars provided that they are held rigidly. Time of eclipses and shadow transits of these satellites are given on page 666.

Saturn, magnitude +0.2, continues to be visible as an evening object in the constellation of Gemini. The Moon, at First Quarter, is in the vicinity of the planet on the evenings of the 15th and 16th. The rings of Saturn present a beautiful spectacle to the observer with a small telescope. The rings were at their maximum opening in 2002. They will next appear edge-on in 2009. The diameter of the minor axis is now the same as the polar diameter of the planet itself (17 arcseconds).

THE MOON

Day	RA h	RA m	Dec. °	Hor. par. ′	Semi-diam. ′	Sun's Co-long. °	PA of Br. Limb °	Ph. %	Age d	Rise 52° h	Rise 52° m	Rise 56° h	Rise 56° m	Transit h	Transit m	Set 52° h	Set 52° m	Set 56° h	Set 56° m
1	17	50	−28.2	58.9	16.1	169	92	62	21.6	2	13	2	53	5	26	8	37	7	57
2	18	54	−28.1	59.2	16.1	182	85	51	22.6	3	12	3	50	6	28	9	48	9	11
3	19	57	−26.1	59.4	16.2	194	78	39	23.6	3	53	4	24	7	29	11	13	10	44
4	20	57	−22.5	59.5	16.2	206	71	28	24.6	4	21	4	44	8	27	12	44	12	23
5	21	55	−17.5	59.5	16.2	218	66	18	25.6	4	40	4	56	9	21	14	15	14	02
6	22	48	−11.5	59.3	16.2	230	63	10	26.6	4	55	5	04	10	11	15	43	15	36
7	23	39	−5.1	59.1	16.1	243	61	4	27.6	5	07	5	10	10	59	17	08	17	08
8	0	29	+1.6	58.6	16.0	255	60	1	28.6	5	19	5	16	11	46	18	32	18	37
9	1	18	+8.1	58.1	15.8	267	253	0	0.1	5	31	5	23	12	32	19	55	20	07
10	2	08	+14.1	57.4	15.6	279	246	2	1.1	5	44	5	30	13	20	21	18	21	37
11	2	58	+19.3	56.7	15.5	291	249	5	2.1	6	00	5	40	14	10	22	39	23	05
12	3	51	+23.4	56.0	15.3	304	254	11	3.1	6	22	5	55	15	01	23	56	—	—
13	4	45	+26.4	55.4	15.1	316	259	18	4.1	6	52	6	18	15	53	—	—	0	30
14	5	39	+28.1	54.9	15.0	328	265	26	5.1	7	33	6	55	16	46	1	04	1	42
15	6	34	+28.3	54.5	14.9	340	272	35	6.1	8	27	7	49	17	38	1	58	2	37
16	7	28	+27.2	54.3	14.8	353	278	44	7.1	9	32	8	59	18	28	2	38	3	12
17	8	19	+24.9	54.2	14.8	5	284	54	8.1	10	44	10	17	19	15	3	07	3	35
18	9	09	+21.6	54.4	14.8	17	288	63	9.1	11	59	11	39	20	00	3	27	3	49
19	9	56	+17.3	54.6	14.9	29	292	72	10.1	13	13	13	00	20	44	3	43	3	58
20	10	42	+12.3	55.1	15.0	41	295	80	11.1	14	28	14	20	21	26	3	55	4	05
21	11	27	+6.7	55.6	15.2	54	296	88	12.1	15	43	15	41	22	08	4	06	4	10
22	12	12	+0.7	56.3	15.3	66	297	94	13.1	17	00	17	03	22	51	4	16	4	16
23	12	58	−5.4	56.9	15.5	78	295	98	14.1	18	20	18	29	23	36	4	26	4	21
24	13	46	−11.5	57.6	15.7	90	285	100	15.1	19	44	20	00	—	—	4	38	4	27
25	14	37	−17.2	58.2	15.9	102	121	100	16.1	21	12	21	36	0	25	4	54	4	36
26	15	32	−22.1	58.7	16.0	114	112	97	17.1	22	41	23	13	1	19	5	15	4	50
27	16	31	−25.8	59.1	16.1	127	105	92	18.1	—	—	—	—	2	17	5	45	5	12
28	17	34	−27.9	59.3	16.2	139	97	84	19.1	0	03	0	42	3	18	6	32	5	52
29	18	39	−28.2	59.4	16.2	151	89	75	20.1	1	09	1	48	4	22	7	37	6	59
30	19	43	−26.7	59.4	16.2	163	82	65	21.1	1	55	2	28	5	24	9	00	8	28

MERCURY

Day	RA h	RA m	Dec. °	Diam. ″	Phase %	Transit h	Transit m	5° high 52° h	5° high 52° m	5° high 56° h	5° high 56° m
1	0	22	+5.1	11	1	11	41	5	50	5	49
3	0	17	+4.1	11	3	11	28	5	42	5	42
5	0	13	+3.0	11	5	11	16	5	35	5	36
7	0	09	+2.1	11	9	11	06	5	29	5	31
9	0	07	+1.3	11	12	10	56	5	23	5	26
11	0	07	+0.7	11	16	10	48	5	18	5	21
13	0	07	+0.2	10	20	10	41	5	13	5	16
15	0	09	−0.1	10	24	10	35	5	09	5	12
17	0	12	−0.2	10	28	10	30	5	04	5	08
19	0	16	−0.2	9	31	10	26	5	00	5	04
21	0	21	0.0	9	35	10	24	4	56	5	00
23	0	27	+0.3	9	38	10	22	4	52	4	55
25	0	33	+0.8	8	42	10	20	4	49	4	51
27	0	40	+1.4	8	45	10	20	4	45	4	47
29	0	48	+2.1	8	48	10	20	4	41	4	43
31	0	57	+2.9	7	51	10	21	4	38	4	39

VENUS

Day	RA h	RA m	Dec. °	Diam. ″	Phase %	Transit h	Transit m	5° high 52° h	5° high 52° m	5° high 56° h	5° high 56° m
1	0	45	+3.4	10	100	12	07	17	54	17	54
6	1	07	+5.9	10	100	12	10	18	10	18	12
11	1	30	+8.3	10	100	12	14	18	26	18	29
16	1	54	+10.7	10	100	12	17	18	41	18	47
21	2	17	+12.9	10	100	12	21	18	57	19	05
26	2	41	+15.0	10	99	12	25	19	13	19	22
31	3	05	+17.0	10	99	12	30	19	28	19	40

MARS

Day	RA h	RA m	Dec. °	Diam. ″	Phase %	Transit h	Transit m	5° high 52° h	5° high 52° m	5° high 56° h	5° high 56° m
1	20	43	−19.3	6	90	8	05	4	32	4	58
6	20	58	−18.4	6	89	8	00	4	21	4	45
11	21	13	−17.4	6	89	7	55	4	09	4	31
16	21	28	−16.4	6	88	7	50	3	57	4	17
21	21	42	−15.3	6	88	7	45	3	44	4	03
26	21	56	−14.2	7	88	7	40	3	32	3	49
31	22	10	−13.0	7	87	7	34	3	19	3	35

SUNRISE AND SUNSET

	London 0°05' 51°30'		Bristol 2°35' 51°28'		Birmingham 1°55' 52°28'		Manchester 2°15' 53°28'		Newcastle 1°37' 54°59'		Glasgow 4°14' 55°52'		Belfast 5°56' 54°35'	
	h m	h m	h m	h m	h m	h m	h m	h m	h m	h m	h m	h m	h m	h m
1	5 36	18 34	5 46	18 44	5 42	18 42	5 42	18 44	5 38	18 44	5 48	18 55	5 56	19 00
2	5 33	18 35	5 43	18 45	5 40	18 44	5 40	18 46	5 36	18 46	5 45	18 57	5 53	19 02
3	5 31	18 37	5 41	18 47	5 37	18 45	5 38	18 48	5 33	18 47	5 42	18 59	5 51	19 04
4	5 29	18 39	5 39	18 49	5 35	18 47	5 35	18 50	5 31	18 49	5 40	19 01	5 48	19 06
5	5 27	18 40	5 37	18 50	5 33	18 49	5 33	18 52	5 28	18 51	5 37	19 03	5 46	19 08
6	5 24	18 42	5 34	18 52	5 30	18 51	5 30	18 54	5 26	18 53	5 35	19 05	5 43	19 10
7	5 22	18 44	5 32	18 54	5 28	18 52	5 28	18 55	5 23	18 55	5 32	19 07	5 41	19 12
8	5 20	18 45	5 30	18 55	5 26	18 54	5 26	18 57	5 21	18 57	5 29	19 09	5 39	19 14
9	5 18	18 47	5 28	18 57	5 24	18 56	5 23	18 59	5 18	18 59	5 27	19 11	5 36	19 16
10	5 16	18 49	5 26	18 59	5 21	18 58	5 21	19 01	5 16	19 01	5 24	19 13	5 34	19 18
11	5 13	18 50	5 23	19 00	5 19	18 59	5 19	19 03	5 13	19 03	5 22	19 15	5 31	19 20
12	5 11	18 52	5 21	19 02	5 17	19 01	5 16	19 04	5 11	19 05	5 19	19 17	5 29	19 21
13	5 09	18 54	5 19	19 04	5 15	19 03	5 14	19 06	5 08	19 07	5 17	19 19	5 26	19 23
14	5 07	18 55	5 17	19 05	5 12	19 05	5 12	19 08	5 06	19 09	5 14	19 21	5 24	19 25
15	5 05	18 57	5 15	19 07	5 10	19 06	5 09	19 10	5 03	19 11	5 12	19 24	5 22	19 27
16	5 03	18 59	5 13	19 09	5 08	19 08	5 07	19 12	5 01	19 13	5 09	19 26	5 19	19 29
17	5 00	19 00	5 10	19 10	5 06	19 10	5 05	19 14	4 59	19 15	5 07	19 28	5 17	19 31
18	4 58	19 02	5 08	19 12	5 03	19 12	5 02	19 15	4 56	19 17	5 04	19 30	5 14	19 33
19	4 56	19 04	5 06	19 14	5 01	19 13	5 00	19 17	4 54	19 19	5 02	19 32	5 12	19 35
20	4 54	19 05	5 04	19 15	4 59	19 15	4 58	19 19	4 51	19 21	4 59	19 34	5 10	19 37
21	4 52	19 07	5 02	19 17	4 57	19 17	4 56	19 21	4 49	19 23	4 57	19 36	5 07	19 39
22	4 50	19 09	5 00	19 19	4 55	19 19	4 53	19 23	4 47	19 25	4 54	19 38	5 05	19 41
23	4 48	19 10	4 58	19 20	4 53	19 20	4 51	19 24	4 44	19 26	4 52	19 40	5 03	19 43
24	4 46	19 12	4 56	19 22	4 51	19 22	4 49	19 26	4 42	19 28	4 50	19 42	5 01	19 44
25	4 44	19 14	4 54	19 24	4 49	19 24	4 47	19 28	4 40	19 30	4 47	19 44	4 58	19 46
26	4 42	19 15	4 52	19 25	4 46	19 26	4 45	19 30	4 37	19 32	4 45	19 46	4 56	19 48
27	4 40	19 17	4 50	19 27	4 44	19 27	4 43	19 32	4 35	19 34	4 43	19 48	4 54	19 50
28	4 38	19 19	4 48	19 29	4 42	19 29	4 41	19 34	4 33	19 36	4 40	19 50	4 52	19 52
29	4 36	19 20	4 46	19 30	4 40	19 31	4 39	19 35	4 31	19 38	4 38	19 52	4 49	19 54
30	4 34	19 22	4 44	19 32	4 38	19 32	4 36	19 37	4 29	19 40	4 36	19 54	4 47	19 56

JUPITER

Day	RA h m	Dec. ° '	Transit h m	5° high 52° h m	5° high 56° h m
1	12 55.2	−4 10	0 17	5 22	5 15
11	12 50.4	−3 41	23 29	4 41	4 34
21	12 45.9	−3 13	22 45	3 59	3 53
31	12 41.9	−2 49	22 02	3 18	3 12

Diameters – equatorial 44" polar 41"

SATURN

Day	RA h m	Dec. ° '	Transit h m	5° high 52° h m	5° high 56° h m
1	7 28.7	+22 01	18 48	2 16	2 33
11	7 29.9	+21 59	18 10	1 38	1 54
21	7 31.8	+21 56	17 32	1 00	1 17
31	7 34.4	+21 51	16 56	0 23	0 39

Diameters – equatorial 18" polar 17"
Rings – major axis 41" minor axis 17"

URANUS

Day	RA h m	Dec. ° '	Transit h m	10° high 52° h m	10° high 56° h m
1	22 42.3	−9 00	10 03	6 00	6 17
11	22 44.1	−8 49	9 25	5 22	5 38
21	22 45.7	−8 40	8 48	4 43	4 59
31	22 47.1	−8 32	8 10	4 04	4 20

Diameter 4"

NEPTUNE

Day	RA h m	Dec. ° '	Transit h m	10° high 52° h m	10° high 56° h m
1	21 17.8	−15 51	8 39	5 23	5 51
11	21 18.7	−15 47	8 00	4 44	5 12
21	21 19.4	−15 44	7 22	4 05	4 33
31	21 19.9	−15 42	6 43	3 26	3 54

Diameter 2"

MAY 2005

FIFTH MONTH, 31 DAYS. *Maia*, goddess of growth and increase

1	*Sunday*	Queen Victoria opened the Great Exhibition in Hyde Park 1851	121
2	*Monday*	Catherine II of Russia (The Great) b. 1729. Leonardo da Vinci d. 1519	week 18 day 122
3	*Tuesday*	Dodie Smith b. 1896. Thomas Hood d. 1845	123
4	*Wednesday*	Audrey Hepburn b. 1929. Sir Osbert Sitwell d. 1969	124
5	*Thursday*	Karl Marx b. 1818. Edward Young d. 1765	125
6	*Friday*	Henry David Thoreau d. 1862. Edward VII d. 1910	126
7	*Saturday*	Johannes Brahms b. 1833. Pyotr Ilyich Tchaikovsky b. 1840	127
8	*Sunday*	Francis Quarles b. 1592. Henri Laurens d. 1954	128
9	*Monday*	Sir James M. Barrie b. 1860. Alan Bennett b. 1934	week 19 day 129
10	*Tuesday*	Fred Astaire b. 1899. Hokusai d. 1849	130
11	*Wednesday*	Salvador Dalí b. 1904. Douglas Adams d. 2001	131
12	*Thursday*	Dante Gabriel Rosetti b. 1828. John Dryden d. 1700	132
13	*Friday*	Dame Daphne du Maurier b. 1907. John Nash d. 1835	133
14	*Saturday*	Thomas Gainsborough b. 1727. Jean Rhys d. 1979	134
15	*Sunday*	Mikhail Bulgakov b. 1891. Joseph Whitaker d. 1895	135
16	*Monday*	John Sell Cotman b. 1782. Charles Perrault d. 1703	week 20 day 136
17	*Tuesday*	Dennis Potter b. 1935. Sandro Botticelli d. 1510	137
18	*Wednesday*	Nicholas II, Tzar of Russia b. 1868. George Meredith d. 1909	138
19	*Thursday*	Ogden Nash d. 1971. Sir John Betjeman d. 1984	139
20	*Friday*	Honoré de Balzac b. 1799. Dame Barbara Hepworth d. 1975	140
21	*Saturday*	King Philip II of Spain b. 1527. Mikhail Glinka b. 1804	141
22	*Sunday*	Sir Arthur Conan Doyle b. 1859. Victor Hugo d. 1885	142
23	*Monday*	Edmund Rubbra b. 1901. Henrik Ibsen d. 1906	week 21 day 143
24	*Tuesday*	William Byrd b. 1543. Queen Victoria b. 1819	144
25	*Wednesday*	Sir Ian McKellen b. 1939. Gustav Holst d. 1934	145
26	*Thursday*	Isadora Duncan b. 1877. Samuel Pepys d. 1706	146
27	*Friday*	Julia Ward Howe b. 1819. John Calvin d. 1564	147
28	*Saturday*	Ian Fleming b. 1908. Anne Brontë d. 1849	148
29	*Sunday*	Charles II b. 1630. Sir W. S. Gilbert d. 1911	149
30	*Monday*	Christopher Marlowe d. 1593. Voltaire d. 1778	week 22 day 150
31	*Tuesday*	Walt Whitman b. 1819. Joseph Haydn d. 1809	151

ASTRONOMICAL PHENOMENA

d h
2 17 Mars in conjunction with Moon. Mars 2° N.
6 08 Mercury in conjunction with Moon. Mercury 3° S.
9 05 Venus in conjunction with Moon. Venus 3° S.
13 15 Saturn in conjunction with Moon. Saturn 5° S.
19 22 Jupiter in conjunction with Moon. Jupiter 0°.3 N.
20 00 Neptune at stationary point
20 23 Sun's longitude 60° ♊
31 10 Mars in conjunction with Moon. Mars 0°.5 N.

MINIMA OF ALGOL

Algol is inconveniently situated for observation during May

CONSTELLATIONS

The following constellations are near the meridian at

	d	h		d	h
April	1	24	May	16	21
April	15	23	June	1	20
May	1	22	June	15	19

Cepheus (below the Pole), Cassiopeia (below the Pole), Ursa Minor, Ursa Major, Canes Venatici, Coma Berenices, Bootes, Leo, Virgo, Crater, Corvus and Hydra

THE MOON

Phases, Apsides and Node		d	h	m
☾	Last Quarter	1	06	24
●	New Moon	8	08	45
☽	First Quarter	16	08	57
○	Full Moon	23	20	18
☾	Last Quarter	30	11	47

Apogee (404,638 km)	14	13	44
Perigee (364,219 km)	26	10	50

Mean longitude of ascending node on May 1, 22°

THE SUN

s.d. 15'.8

Day	Right Ascension h	m	s	Dec. + °	'	Equation of time m	s	Rise 52° h	m	Rise 56° h	m	Transit h	m	Set 52° h	m	Set 56° h	m	Sidereal time h	m	s	Transit of first point of Aries h	m	s
1	2	33	12	15	02	+2	53	4	30	4	16	11	57	19	25	19	39	14	36	05	9	22	23
2	2	37	01	15	21	+3	00	4	28	4	14	11	57	19	27	19	41	14	40	02	9	18	27
3	2	40	51	15	38	+3	07	4	26	4	12	11	57	19	28	19	43	14	43	58	9	14	31
4	2	44	42	15	56	+3	13	4	25	4	09	11	57	19	30	19	45	14	47	55	9	10	35
5	2	48	33	16	13	+3	18	4	23	4	07	11	57	19	32	19	47	14	51	51	9	06	39
6	2	52	25	16	30	+3	23	4	21	4	05	11	57	19	33	19	49	14	55	48	9	02	43
7	2	56	17	16	47	+3	27	4	19	4	03	11	57	19	35	19	51	14	59	44	8	58	47
8	3	00	10	17	03	+3	31	4	17	4	01	11	56	19	36	19	53	15	03	41	8	54	51
9	3	04	04	17	20	+3	34	4	16	3	59	11	56	19	38	19	55	15	07	37	8	50	55
10	3	07	58	17	35	+3	36	4	14	3	57	11	56	19	40	19	57	15	11	34	8	46	59
11	3	11	52	17	51	+3	38	4	12	3	55	11	56	19	41	19	59	15	15	31	8	43	04
12	3	15	47	18	06	+3	40	4	11	3	53	11	56	19	43	20	01	15	19	27	8	39	08
13	3	19	43	18	21	+3	41	4	09	3	51	11	56	19	44	20	03	15	23	24	8	35	12
14	3	23	39	18	36	+3	41	4	08	3	49	11	56	19	46	20	05	15	27	20	8	31	16
15	3	27	36	18	50	+3	41	4	06	3	47	11	56	19	48	20	07	15	31	17	8	27	20
16	3	31	34	19	04	+3	40	4	05	3	45	11	56	19	49	20	09	15	35	13	8	23	24
17	3	35	31	19	18	+3	38	4	03	3	43	11	56	19	51	20	10	15	39	10	8	19	28
18	3	39	30	19	32	+3	36	4	02	3	42	11	56	19	52	20	12	15	43	06	8	15	32
19	3	43	29	19	45	+3	34	4	00	3	40	11	56	19	54	20	14	15	47	03	8	11	36
20	3	47	28	19	57	+3	31	3	59	3	38	11	57	19	55	20	16	15	51	00	8	07	40
21	3	51	29	20	10	+3	28	3	58	3	37	11	57	19	56	20	18	15	54	56	8	03	44
22	3	55	29	20	22	+3	24	3	56	3	35	11	57	19	58	20	19	15	58	53	7	59	48
23	3	59	30	20	33	+3	19	3	55	3	34	11	57	19	59	20	21	16	02	49	7	55	53
24	4	03	32	20	45	+3	14	3	54	3	32	11	57	20	01	20	23	16	06	46	7	51	57
25	4	07	34	20	56	+3	08	3	53	3	31	11	57	20	02	20	24	16	10	42	7	48	01
26	4	11	37	21	06	+3	02	3	52	3	29	11	57	20	03	20	26	16	14	39	7	44	05
27	4	15	40	21	17	+2	56	3	51	3	28	11	57	20	04	20	27	16	18	35	7	40	09
28	4	19	43	21	27	+2	49	3	50	3	27	11	57	20	06	20	29	16	22	32	7	36	13
29	4	23	47	21	36	+2	41	3	49	3	25	11	57	20	07	20	30	16	26	29	7	32	17
30	4	27	52	21	45	+2	33	3	48	3	24	11	58	20	08	20	32	16	30	25	7	28	21
31	4	31	57	21	54	+2	25	3	47	3	23	11	58	20	09	20	33	16	34	22	7	24	25

DURATION OF TWILIGHT (in minutes)

Latitude	52°	56°	52°	56°	52°	56°	52°	56°
	1 May		11 May		21 May		31 May	
Civil	39	44	41	48	44	53	46	57
Nautical	89	106	97	120	106	141	115	187
Astronomical	152	204	176	TAN	TAN	TAN	TAN	TAN

THE NIGHT SKY

Mercury is too close to the Sun to be visible in either the early evenings or early mornings during the month.

Venus, magnitude −3.9, is slowly beginning to move out of the long evening twilight, becoming a brilliant object. It may be seen low above the western horizon for a very short time after sunset.

Mars continues to brighten slowly during the month, its magnitude changing from +0.6 to +0.3. Mars is now moving northwards in declination and thereby slowly improving its visibility prospects, despite the lengthening twilight. By the end of the month it may be detected low above the east-south-eastern horizon by about 02h. Mars is in the constellation of Aquarius. On the last day of the month the Moon, just after Last Quarter, passes 1 degree south of the planet.

Jupiter, magnitude −2.3, continues to be visible as a brilliant object in the evening skies, and even at the end of the month can be seen in the south-western sky until well after midnight. Jupiter is in the constellation of Virgo. The waxing gibbous Moon passes 1 degree south of the planet on the evening of the 19th.

Saturn is still visible in the western sky in the evenings, magnitude +0.3, though no longer visible after midnight. Saturn passes 7 degrees south of Pollux at the end of the month. On the 13th the waxing crescent Moon will be seen in the vicinity of the planet.

THE MOON

Day	RA h	RA m	Dec. °	Hor. par.	Semi-diam. '	Sun's Co-long. °	PA of Bright Limb °	Ph. %	Age d	Rise 52° h	Rise 52° m	Rise 56° h	Rise 56° m	Transit h	Transit m	Set 52° h	Set 52° m	Set 56° h	Set 56° m
1	20	44	−23.4	59.3	16.2	175	75	53	22.1	2	26	2	51	6	22	10	29	10	06
2	21	41	−18.7	59.1	16.1	188	70	42	23.1	2	47	3	05	7	17	11	59	11	43
3	22	35	−13.1	58.9	16.0	200	67	31	24.1	3	03	3	14	8	07	13	26	13	17
4	23	25	−6.9	58.5	16.0	212	65	21	25.1	3	15	3	21	8	54	14	49	14	47
5	0	14	−0.4	58.2	15.8	224	65	13	26.1	3	27	3	26	9	40	16	11	16	15
6	1	02	+6.0	57.7	15.7	236	66	6	27.1	3	38	3	32	10	26	17	33	17	42
7	1	51	+12.1	57.2	15.6	249	72	2	28.1	3	50	3	39	11	12	18	55	19	10
8	2	40	+17.5	56.7	15.4	261	95	0	29.1	4	05	3	48	12	00	20	16	20	39
9	3	32	+22.1	56.1	15.3	273	235	0	0.6	4	24	4	00	12	51	21	36	22	06
10	4	25	+25.5	55.6	15.1	285	250	3	1.6	4	50	4	19	13	43	22	48	23	25
11	5	20	+27.6	55.1	15.0	298	259	7	2.6	5	27	4	50	14	36	23	49	—	—
12	6	15	+28.3	54.7	14.9	310	266	13	3.6	6	16	5	37	15	29	—	—	0	28
13	7	10	+27.7	54.4	14.8	322	273	20	4.6	7	17	6	42	16	20	0	35	1	11
14	8	02	+25.8	54.2	14.8	334	279	28	5.6	8	27	7	58	17	08	1	08	1	38
15	8	52	+22.7	54.2	14.8	347	285	37	6.6	9	41	9	18	17	54	1	31	1	55
16	9	40	+18.8	54.4	14.8	359	289	47	7.6	10	55	10	39	18	38	1	49	2	06
17	10	26	+14.0	54.7	14.9	11	292	56	8.6	12	08	11	58	19	20	2	02	2	14
18	11	11	+8.7	55.2	15.0	23	294	66	9.6	13	22	13	17	20	01	2	13	2	20
19	11	55	+2.9	55.8	15.2	35	295	75	10.6	14	37	14	38	20	43	2	23	2	25
20	12	40	−3.1	56.6	15.4	48	294	83	11.6	15	55	16	01	21	27	2	33	2	30
21	13	27	−9.2	57.4	15.6	60	292	90	12.6	17	17	17	29	22	14	2	44	2	36
22	14	16	−15.0	58.2	15.9	72	286	96	13.6	18	44	19	03	23	06	2	58	2	43
23	15	11	−20.3	58.9	16.1	84	273	99	14.6	20	14	20	42	—	—	3	16	2	55
24	16	09	−24.6	59.5	16.2	96	160	100	15.6	21	42	22	18	0	03	3	43	3	13
25	17	13	−27.4	60.0	16.3	108	110	98	16.6	22	57	23	37	1	05	4	23	3	46
26	18	19	−28.3	60.2	16.4	121	97	93	17.6	23	52	—	—	2	10	5	23	4	44
27	19	25	−27.2	60.2	16.4	133	87	86	18.6	—	—	0	28	3	15	6	43	6	08
28	20	29	−24.3	60.0	16.3	145	79	77	19.6	0	29	0	56	4	16	8	13	7	47
29	21	28	−19.8	59.6	16.2	157	73	67	20.6	0	53	1	13	5	13	9	45	9	27
30	22	23	−14.3	59.1	16.1	169	69	56	21.6	1	10	1	23	6	05	11	13	11	03
31	23	14	−8.2	58.6	16.0	182	67	44	22.6	1	24	1	30	6	53	12	38	12	33

MERCURY

Day	RA h	RA m	Dec. °	Diam. "	Phase %	Transit h	Transit m	5° high 52° h	5° high 52° m	5° high 56° h	5° high 56° m
1	0	57	+2.9	7	51	10	21	4	38	4	39
3	1	06	+3.8	7	54	10	22	4	34	4	35
5	1	15	+4.8	7	57	10	24	4	31	4	30
7	1	25	+5.8	7	60	10	26	4	28	4	26
9	1	36	+7.0	6	63	10	29	4	25	4	23
11	1	47	+8.2	6	67	10	33	4	22	4	19
13	1	59	+9.4	6	70	10	37	4	20	4	15
15	2	11	+10.7	6	73	10	41	4	17	4	12
17	2	24	+12.1	6	77	10	46	4	15	4	09
19	2	38	+13.4	6	80	10	52	4	14	4	06
21	2	52	+14.8	6	84	10	59	4	13	4	04
23	3	07	+16.2	5	87	11	06	4	12	4	02
25	3	23	+17.6	5	91	11	14	4	13	4	01
27	3	39	+18.9	5	94	11	23	4	14	4	01
29	3	56	+20.1	5	97	11	32	4	16	4	01
31	4	14	+21.3	5	99	11	42	4	19	4	03

VENUS

Day	RA h	RA m	Dec. °	Diam. "	Phase %	Transit h	Transit m	5° high 52° h	5° high 52° m	5° high 56° h	5° high 56° m
1	3	05	+17.0	10	99	12	30	19	28	19	40
6	3	30	+18.8	10	99	12	35	19	43	19	57
11	3	56	+20.3	10	98	12	41	19	58	20	13
16	4	21	+21.7	10	98	12	47	20	12	20	28
21	4	47	+22.8	10	97	12	53	20	25	20	43
26	5	14	+23.6	10	97	13	00	20	37	20	55
31	5	40	+24.1	10	96	13	07	20	47	21	06

MARS

Day	RA h	RA m	Dec. °	Diam. "	Phase %	Transit h	Transit m	5° high 52° h	5° high 52° m	5° high 56° h	5° high 56° m
1	22	10	−13.0	7	87	7	34	3	19	3	35
6	22	24	−11.8	7	87	7	28	3	05	3	20
11	22	38	−10.5	7	86	7	22	2	52	3	05
16	22	52	−9.3	7	86	7	16	2	39	2	50
21	23	05	−8.0	7	86	7	10	2	25	2	36
26	23	19	−6.6	8	86	7	04	2	12	2	21
31	23	32	−5.3	8	85	6	57	1	58	2	06

SUNRISE AND SUNSET

	London 0° 05' 51° 30'		Bristol 2° 35' 51° 28'		Birmingham 1° 55' 52° 28'		Manchester 2° 15' 53° 28'		Newcastle 1° 37' 54° 59'		Glasgow 4° 14' 55° 52'		Belfast 5° 56' 54° 35'	
	h m	h m	h m	h m	h m	h m	h m	h m	h m	h m	h m	h m	h m	h m
1	4 32	19 24	4 42	19 34	4 36	19 34	4 34	19 39	4 26	19 42	4 33	19 56	4 45	19 58
2	4 30	19 25	4 40	19 35	4 34	19 36	4 32	19 41	4 24	19 44	4 31	19 58	4 43	20 00
3	4 28	19 27	4 39	19 37	4 33	19 38	4 30	19 42	4 22	19 46	4 29	20 00	4 41	20 01
4	4 27	19 29	4 37	19 38	4 31	19 39	4 28	19 44	4 20	19 48	4 27	20 02	4 39	20 03
5	4 25	19 30	4 35	19 40	4 29	19 41	4 26	19 46	4 18	19 50	4 25	20 04	4 37	20 05
6	4 23	19 32	4 33	19 42	4 27	19 43	4 25	19 48	4 16	19 51	4 23	20 06	4 35	20 07
7	4 21	19 33	4 31	19 43	4 25	19 44	4 23	19 50	4 14	19 53	4 20	20 08	4 33	20 09
8	4 20	19 35	4 30	19 45	4 23	19 46	4 21	19 51	4 12	19 55	4 18	20 10	4 31	20 11
9	4 18	19 37	4 28	19 46	4 22	19 48	4 19	19 53	4 10	19 57	4 16	20 12	4 29	20 13
10	4 16	19 38	4 26	19 48	4 20	19 49	4 17	19 55	4 08	19 59	4 14	20 14	4 27	20 14
11	4 15	19 40	4 25	19 50	4 18	19 51	4 15	19 56	4 06	20 01	4 12	20 16	4 25	20 16
12	4 13	19 41	4 23	19 51	4 17	19 52	4 14	19 58	4 04	20 03	4 10	20 17	4 23	20 18
13	4 12	19 43	4 22	19 53	4 15	19 54	4 12	20 00	4 02	20 04	4 08	20 19	4 22	20 20
14	4 10	19 44	4 20	19 54	4 13	19 56	4 10	20 01	4 01	20 06	4 07	20 21	4 20	20 21
15	4 08	19 46	4 19	19 56	4 12	19 57	4 09	20 03	3 59	20 08	4 05	20 23	4 18	20 23
16	4 07	19 47	4 17	19 57	4 10	19 59	4 07	20 05	3 57	20 10	4 03	20 25	4 16	20 25
17	4 06	19 49	4 16	19 59	4 09	20 00	4 05	20 06	3 55	20 11	4 01	20 27	4 15	20 27
18	4 04	19 50	4 14	20 00	4 07	20 02	4 04	20 08	3 54	20 13	3 59	20 28	4 13	20 28
19	4 03	19 52	4 13	20 02	4 06	20 03	4 02	20 10	3 52	20 15	3 58	20 30	4 12	20 30
20	4 02	19 53	4 12	20 03	4 04	20 05	4 01	20 11	3 51	20 16	3 56	20 32	4 10	20 32
21	4 00	19 54	4 10	20 04	4 03	20 06	4 00	20 13	3 49	20 18	3 54	20 34	4 08	20 33
22	3 59	19 56	4 09	20 06	4 02	20 08	3 58	20 14	3 48	20 20	3 53	20 35	4 07	20 35
23	3 58	19 57	4 08	20 07	4 01	20 09	3 57	20 16	3 46	20 21	3 51	20 37	4 06	20 36
24	3 57	19 59	4 07	20 08	3 59	20 11	3 56	20 17	3 45	20 23	3 50	20 39	4 04	20 38
25	3 55	20 00	4 06	20 10	3 58	20 12	3 54	20 18	3 43	20 24	3 48	20 40	4 03	20 39
26	3 54	20 01	4 05	20 11	3 57	20 13	3 53	20 20	3 42	20 26	3 47	20 42	4 02	20 41
27	3 53	20 02	4 03	20 12	3 56	20 15	3 52	20 21	3 41	20 27	3 46	20 43	4 00	20 42
28	3 52	20 04	4 03	20 13	3 55	20 16	3 51	20 23	3 39	20 29	3 44	20 45	3 59	20 44
29	3 51	20 05	4 02	20 15	3 54	20 17	3 50	20 24	3 38	20 30	3 43	20 46	3 58	20 45
30	3 50	20 06	4 01	20 16	3 53	20 18	3 49	20 25	3 37	20 32	3 42	20 48	3 57	20 46
31	3 50	20 07	4 00	20 17	3 52	20 19	3 48	20 26	3 36	20 33	3 41	20 49	3 56	20 48

JUPITER

Day	RA		Dec.		Transit		5° high 52°		56°	
	h	m	°	'	h	m	h	m	h	m
1	12	41.9	−2	49	22	02	3	18	3	12
11	12	38.7	−2	31	21	19	2	37	2	32
21	12	36.4	−2	19	20	38	1	57	1	51
31	12	35.2	−2	14	19	58	1	17	1	11

Diameters – equatorial 42" polar 39"

SATURN

Day	RA		Dec.		Transit		5° high 52°		56°	
	h	m	°	'	h	m	h	m	h	m
1	7	34.4	+21	51	16	56	0	23	0	39
11	7	37.6	+21	44	16	20	23	42	0	02
21	7	41.3	+21	36	15	44	23	06	23	22
31	7	45.5	+21	27	15	09	22	30	22	46

Diameters – equatorial 17" polar 16"
Rings – major axis 39" minor axis 16"

URANUS

Day	RA		Dec.		Transit		10° high 52°		56°	
	h	m	°	'	h	m	h	m	h	m
1	22	47.1	−8	32	8	10	4	04	4	20
11	22	48.3	−8	25	7	32	3	26	3	41
21	22	49.2	−8	20	6	53	2	47	3	02
31	22	49.8	−8	17	6	14	2	08	2	23

Diameter 4"

NEPTUNE

Day	RA		Dec.		Transit		10° high 52°		56°	
	h	m	°	'	h	m	h	m	h	m
1	21	19.9	−15	42	6	43	3	26	3	54
11	21	20.3	−15	41	6	04	2	47	3	15
21	21	20.3	−15	40	25	2	2	08	2	35
31	21	20.2	−15	41	4	45	1	29	1	56

Diameter 2"

JUNE 2005

SIXTH MONTH, 30 DAYS. *Junius*, Roman gens (family)

1	*Wednesday*	Sir David Wilkie d. 1841. Sir Hugh Walpole d. 1941	152
2	*Thursday*	Sir Edward Elgar b. 1857. Vita Sackville-West d. 1962	153
3	*Friday*	George V b. 1865. Georges Bizet d. 1875	154
4	*Saturday*	George III b. 1738. Kaiser Wilhelm II d. 1941	155
5	*Sunday*	Margaret Drabble b. 1939. Sir David Hare d. 1947	156
6	*Monday*	Aleksandr Pushkin b. 1799. Jeremy Bentham d. 1832	week 23 day 157
7	*Tuesday*	Paul Gauguin b. 1848. E. M. Forster d. 1970	158
8	*Wednesday*	Frank Lloyd Wright b. 1867. Thomas Paine d. 1809	159
9	*Thursday*	Peter I (The Great), Tzar of Russia 1682–1725 b. 1672. Charles Dickens d. 1870	160
10	*Friday*	Duke of Edinburgh b. 1921. Frederick Delius d. 1934	161
11	*Saturday*	John Constable b. 1776. Catherine Cookson d. 1998	162
12	*Sunday*	Anne Frank b. 1929. Dame Marie Rambert d. 1982	163
13	*Monday*	William Butler Yeats b. 1865. Alexander the Great d. 332BC	week 24 day 164
14	*Tuesday*	Maxim Gorky d. 1938. Henry Mancini d. 1994	165
15	*Wednesday*	Edward the Black Prince b. 1330. Edward Grieg b. 1843	166
16	*Thursday*	Russian ballet dancer Rudolf Nureyev defects to the West 1961	167
17	*Friday*	Edward I (Longshanks) b. 1239. Joseph Addison d. 1719	168
18	*Saturday*	Sir Paul McCartney b. 1942. Samuel Butler d. 1902	169
19	*Sunday*	Salman Rushdie b. 1947. Sir William Golding d. 1993	170
20	*Monday*	Catherine Cookson b. 1906. William IV d. 1908	week 25 day 171
21	*Tuesday*	Ian McEwan b. 1948. Prince William of Wales b. 1982	172
22	*Wednesday*	Jaques Delille b. 1738. Walter de la Mare d. 1956	173
23	*Thursday*	Anna Akhmatova b. 1889. Jean Anouilh b. 1910	174
24	*Friday*	Mary Tudor d. 1533. Warner d. 1986	175
25	*Saturday*	John Marston d. 1634. Margaret Oliphant d. 1897	176
26	*Sunday*	Laurie Lee b. 1914. Ford Madox Ford d. 1939	177
27	*Monday*	Louis XII, King of France b. 1462. Helen Keller b. 1880	week 26 day 178
28	*Tuesday*	Henry VIII b. 1491. Archduke Franz Ferdinand assassinated d. 1914	179
29	*Wednesday*	Elizabeth Barrett Browning d. 1861. Paul Klee d. 1940	180
30	*Thursday*	George Duhamel b. 1884. Nancy Mitford d. 1973	181

ASTRONOMICAL PHENOMENA

d h
3 09 Mercury in superior conjunction
5 07 Jupiter at stationary point
7 08 Mercury in conjunction with Moon. Mercury 3° S.
8 13 Venus in conjunction with Moon. Venus 4° S.
10 04 Saturn in conjunction with Moon. Saturn 5° S.
14 03 Pluto at opposition
14 23 Uranus at stationary point
16 07 Jupiter in conjunction with Moon. Jupiter 0°.4 N.
21 07 Sun's longitude 90° ♋
26 03 Saturn in conjunction with Venus. Saturn 1° S.
26 11 Saturn in conjunction with Mercury. Saturn 1° S.
27 19 Venus in conjunction with Mercury. Venus 0°.01 N.
29 02 Mars in conjunction with Moon. Mars 2° S.

MINIMA OF ALGOL

Algol is inconveniently situated for observation during June

CONSTELLATIONS

The following constellations are near the meridian at

	d	*h*		*d*	*h*
May	1	24	June	15	21
May	16	23	July	1	20
June	1	22	July	16	19

Cassiopeia (below the Pole), Ursa Minor, Draco, Ursa Major, Canes Venatici, Bootes, Corona, Serpens, Virgo and Libra

THE MOON

Phases, Apsides and Node		*d*	*h*	*m*
●	New Moon	6	21	55
☽	First Quarter	15	01	22
○	Full Moon	22	04	14
☾	Last Quarter	28	18	23
Apogee (405,534 km)		11	06	18
Perigee (359,661 km)		23	11	53

Mean longitude of ascending node on June 1, 20°

THE SUN

Day	Right Ascension h	m	s	Dec. + °	′	Equation of time m	s	Rise 52° h	m	56° h	m	Transit h	m	Set 52° h	m	56° h	m	Sidereal time h	m	s	Transit of first point of Aries h	m	s
1	4	36	02	22	02	+2	16	3	46	3	22	11	58	20	10	20	35	16	38	18	7	20	29
2	4	40	08	22	10	+2	07	3	45	3	21	11	58	20	11	20	36	16	42	15	7	16	33
3	4	44	14	22	18	+1	57	3	44	3	20	11	58	20	13	20	37	16	46	11	7	12	38
4	4	48	21	22	25	+1	47	3	44	3	19	11	58	20	14	20	38	16	50	08	7	08	42
5	4	52	28	22	32	+1	36	3	43	3	18	11	58	20	14	20	40	16	54	04	7	04	46
6	4	56	35	22	38	+1	26	3	42	3	17	11	59	20	15	20	41	16	58	01	7	00	50
7	5	00	43	22	44	+1	15	3	42	3	17	11	59	20	16	20	42	17	01	58	6	56	54
8	5	04	51	22	50	+1	03	3	41	3	16	11	59	20	17	20	43	17	05	54	6	52	58
9	5	08	59	22	55	+0	51	3	41	3	15	11	59	20	18	20	44	17	09	51	6	49	02
10	5	13	08	23	00	+0	40	3	41	3	15	11	59	20	19	20	45	17	13	47	6	45	06
11	5	17	16	23	05	+0	27	3	40	3	14	12	00	20	19	20	45	17	17	44	6	41	10
12	5	21	25	23	09	+0	15	3	40	3	14	12	00	20	20	20	46	17	21	40	6	37	14
13	5	25	34	23	12	+0	03	3	40	3	14	12	00	20	21	20	47	17	25	37	6	33	18
14	5	29	43	23	16	−0	10	3	40	3	13	12	00	20	21	20	48	17	29	34	6	29	23
15	5	33	53	23	18	−0	23	3	39	3	13	12	00	20	22	20	48	17	33	30	6	25	27
16	5	38	02	23	21	−0	35	3	39	3	13	12	01	20	22	20	49	17	37	27	6	21	31
17	5	42	12	23	23	−0	48	3	39	3	13	12	01	20	23	20	49	17	41	23	6	17	35
18	5	46	21	23	24	−1	01	3	39	3	13	12	01	20	23	20	50	17	45	20	6	13	39
19	5	50	31	23	25	−1	14	3	39	3	13	12	01	20	23	20	50	17	49	16	6	09	43
20	5	54	40	23	26	−1	27	3	40	3	13	12	02	20	24	20	50	17	53	13	6	05	47
21	5	58	50	23	26	−1	40	3	40	3	13	12	02	20	24	20	50	17	57	09	6	01	51
22	6	02	59	23	26	−1	53	3	40	3	13	12	02	20	24	20	51	18	01	06	5	57	55
23	6	07	09	23	26	−2	06	3	40	3	14	12	02	20	24	20	51	18	05	03	5	53	59
24	6	11	18	23	25	−2	19	3	41	3	14	12	02	20	24	20	51	18	08	59	5	50	03
25	6	15	27	23	24	−2	32	3	41	3	14	12	03	20	24	20	51	18	12	56	5	46	07
26	6	19	36	23	22	−2	44	3	41	3	15	12	03	20	24	20	51	18	16	52	5	42	12
27	6	23	46	23	20	−2	57	3	42	3	15	12	03	20	24	20	50	18	20	49	5	38	16
28	6	27	54	23	17	−3	09	3	42	3	16	12	03	20	24	20	50	18	24	45	5	34	20
29	6	32	03	23	14	−3	21	3	43	3	17	12	03	20	24	20	50	18	28	42	5	30	24
30	6	36	12	23	11	−3	33	3	44	3	18	12	04	20	23	20	49	18	32	38	5	26	28

DURATION OF TWILIGHT (in minutes)

Latitude	52°	56°	52°	56°	52°	56°	52°	56°
	1 June		11 June		21 June		31 June	
Civil	46	58	48	61	49	63	48	61
Nautical	116	TAN	124	TAN	127	TAN	124	TAN
Astronomical	TAN	TAN	TAN	TAN	TAN	TAN	TAN	TAN

THE NIGHT SKY

Mercury remains too close to the Sun for observation throughout June as it passes through superior conjunction on the 3rd.

Venus, magnitude −3.9, is a brilliant object in the evening sky, though only visible low above the west-north-western horizon for about half an hour after sunset.

Mars continues to be visible as a morning object in the south-eastern sky, its magnitude brightening during the month from +0.3 to 0.0. Mars is moving northeastwards, starting the month in Aquarius and ending it in Pisces, having passed through the extreme northwestern portion of Cetus on the way. On the morning of the 29th the Moon, at Last Quarter, passes 1 degree north of the planet.

Jupiter, magnitude −2.1, continues to be visible as an evening object in the south-western quadrant of the sky, though by the end of the month it is lost to view over the western horizon before midnight. It reaches its second stationary point on the 5th and then resumes its direct eastward motion towards Spica. The Moon, around First Quarter, is near Jupiter on the evenings of the 15th and 16th.

Saturn, magnitude +0.3, is a difficult object to detect, low above the west-north-western horizon, in the evenings. By the middle of the month it is lost to view in the long twilight. On the evenings of the 9th and 10th the waxing crescent Moon is near the planet.

THE MOON

Day	RA h	RA m	Dec. °	Hor. par. '	Semi-diam. '	Sun's Co-long. °	PA of Br. Limb °	Ph. %	Age d	Rise 52° h	Rise 52° m	Rise 56° h	Rise 56° m	Transit h	Transit m	Set 52° h	Set 52° m	Set 56° h	Set 56° m
1	0	03	−1.8	58.1	15.8	194	66	34	23.6	1	35	1	36	7	38	13	59	14	01
2	0	50	+4.6	57.5	15.7	206	67	24	24.6	1	46	1	42	8	23	15	19	15	26
3	1	38	+10.6	57.0	15.5	218	69	15	25.6	1	58	1	48	9	09	16	39	16	53
4	2	26	+16.2	56.5	15.4	231	74	9	26.6	2	11	1	56	9	55	18	00	18	20
5	3	17	+20.9	56.0	15.2	243	81	4	27.6	2	29	2	07	10	44	19	19	19	46
6	4	09	+24.6	55.5	15.1	255	98	1	28.6	2	52	2	24	11	35	20	34	21	08
7	5	03	+27.0	55.1	15.0	267	188	0	0.1	3	24	2	50	12	28	21	39	22	17
8	5	58	+28.2	54.7	14.9	280	249	1	1.1	4	09	3	30	13	21	22	30	23	07
9	6	53	+27.9	54.4	14.8	292	264	4	2.1	5	06	4	29	14	13	23	08	23	40
10	7	46	+26.3	54.2	14.8	304	273	9	3.1	6	13	5	42	15	02	23	34	—	—
11	8	37	+23.6	54.1	14.7	316	280	15	4.1	7	26	7	01	15	49	23	53	0	00
12	9	26	+19.9	54.1	14.7	329	285	22	5.1	8	39	8	21	16	33	—	—	0	13
13	10	12	+15.4	54.3	14.8	341	289	31	6.1	9	52	9	40	17	15	0	08	0	22
14	10	56	+10.3	54.6	14.9	353	292	40	7.1	11	05	10	58	17	56	0	20	0	28
15	11	39	+4.8	55.1	15.0	5	293	50	8.1	12	17	12	16	18	37	0	30	0	34
16	12	23	−1.1	55.8	15.2	17	294	59	9.1	13	32	13	36	19	18	0	40	0	38
17	13	08	−7.0	56.6	15.4	30	292	69	10.1	14	50	15	00	20	03	0	50	0	44
18	13	56	−12.9	57.5	15.7	42	290	78	11.1	16	13	16	29	20	52	1	02	0	50
19	14	47	−18.3	58.4	15.9	54	285	87	12.1	17	41	18	05	21	46	1	18	1	00
20	15	44	−23.0	59.3	16.2	66	277	93	13.1	19	11	19	44	22	46	1	40	1	14
21	16	46	−26.4	60.1	16.4	78	264	98	14.1	20	35	21	14	23	50	2	13	1	39
22	17	52	−28.1	60.6	16.5	91	209	100	15.1	21	41	22	19	—	—	3	04	2	25
23	19	00	−27.7	60.9	16.6	103	107	99	16.1	22	26	22	57	0	57	4	18	3	40
24	20	06	−25.4	60.9	16.6	115	88	95	17.1	22	56	23	18	2	02	5	48	5	18
25	21	09	−21.2	60.6	16.5	127	78	88	18.1	23	16	23	30	3	03	7	23	7	02
26	22	07	−15.8	60.1	16.4	139	72	80	19.1	23	31	23	39	3	59	8	56	8	43
27	23	00	−9.6	59.5	16.2	152	69	70	20.1	23	43	23	46	4	49	10	24	10	17
28	23	51	−3.1	58.7	16.0	164	67	59	21.1	23	54	23	51	5	36	11	47	11	47
29	0	39	+3.3	58.0	15.8	176	67	48	22.1	—	—	23	58	6	22	13	08	13	14
30	1	27	+9.5	57.2	15.6	188	68	37	23.1	0	06	—	—	7	07	14	28	14	40

MERCURY

Day	RA h	RA m	Dec. °	Diam. "	Phase %	Transit h	Transit m	5° high 52° h	5° high 52° m	5° high 56° h	5° high 56° m
1	4	23	+21.9	5	99	11	48	4	21	4	04
3	4	42	+22.8	5	100	11	58	4	25	4	08
5	5	01	+23.7	5	100	12	09	19	49	20	08
7	5	20	+24.3	5	98	12	21	20	04	20	24
9	5	39	+24.8	5	96	12	32	20	18	20	38
11	5	57	+25.1	5	93	12	42	20	30	20	51
13	6	16	+25.2	5	89	12	53	20	40	21	01
15	6	33	+25.2	5	86	13	02	20	49	21	09
17	6	50	+24.9	6	82	13	11	20	56	21	16
19	7	06	+24.6	6	78	13	19	21	01	21	21
21	7	22	+24.1	6	74	13	27	21	05	21	24
23	7	36	+23.5	6	70	13	33	21	07	21	25
25	7	50	+22.8	6	66	13	39	21	08	21	25
27	8	03	+22.0	6	62	13	43	21	08	21	24
29	8	15	+21.2	7	59	13	47	21	06	21	21
31	8	26	+20.3	7	55	13	50	21	04	21	18

VENUS

Day	RA h	RA m	Dec. °	Diam. "	Phase %	Transit h	Transit m	5° high 52° h	5° high 52° m	5° high 56° h	5° high 56° m
1	5	46	+24.2	10	96	13	08	20	49	21	08
6	6	13	+24.4	10	95	13	15	20	57	21	16
11	6	40	+24.3	10	95	13	23	21	03	21	22
16	7	06	+23.9	11	94	13	30	21	07	21	25
21	7	33	+23.2	11	93	13	36	21	08	21	26
26	7	59	+22.2	11	92	13	42	21	08	21	25
31	8	24	+21.0	11	91	13	48	21	06	21	21

MARS

Day	RA h	RA m	Dec. °	Diam. "	Phase %	Transit h	Transit m	5° high 52° h	5° high 52° m	5° high 56° h	5° high 56° m
1	23	35	−5.1	8	85	6	56	1	55	2	03
6	23	48	−3.7	8	85	6	49	1	42	1	48
11	0	01	−2.4	8	85	6	43	1	28	1	33
16	0	14	−1.1	9	84	6	36	1	14	1	18
21	0	26	+0.2	9	84	6	29	1	00	1	04
26	0	39	+1.5	9	84	6	22	0	47	0	49
31	0	51	+2.8	9	84	6	14	0	33	0	34

SUNRISE AND SUNSET

	London 0°05' 51°30'		Bristol 2°35' 51°28'		Birmingham 1°55' 52°28'		Manchester 2°15' 53°28'		Newcastle 1°37' 54°59'		Glasgow 4°14' 55°52'		Belfast 5°56' 54°35'	
	h m	h m	h m	h m	h m	h m	h m	h m	h m	h m	h m	h m	h m	h m
1	3 49	20 08	3 59	20 18	3 51	20 21	3 47	20 28	3 35	20 34	3 40	20 51	3 55	20 49
2	3 48	20 09	3 58	20 19	3 50	20 22	3 46	20 29	3 34	20 35	3 39	20 52	3 54	20 50
3	3 47	20 10	3 57	20 20	3 49	20 23	3 45	20 30	3 33	20 37	3 38	20 53	3 53	20 51
4	3 47	20 11	3 57	20 21	3 49	20 24	3 44	20 31	3 32	20 38	3 37	20 54	3 52	20 53
5	3 46	20 12	3 56	20 22	3 48	20 25	3 44	20 32	3 32	20 39	3 36	20 56	3 51	20 54
6	3 45	20 13	3 56	20 23	3 47	20 26	3 43	20 33	3 31	20 40	3 35	20 57	3 51	20 55
7	3 45	20 14	3 55	20 24	3 47	20 27	3 42	20 34	3 30	20 41	3 35	20 58	3 50	20 56
8	3 44	20 15	3 55	20 25	3 46	20 27	3 42	20 35	3 30	20 42	3 34	20 59	3 49	20 57
9	3 44	20 16	3 54	20 25	3 46	20 28	3 41	20 36	3 29	20 43	3 33	21 00	3 49	20 57
10	3 44	20 16	3 54	20 26	3 46	20 29	3 41	20 36	3 28	20 44	3 33	21 01	3 48	20 58
11	3 43	20 17	3 54	20 27	3 45	20 30	3 41	20 37	3 28	20 45	3 32	21 01	3 48	20 59
12	3 43	20 18	3 53	20 27	3 45	20 30	3 40	20 38	3 28	20 45	3 32	21 02	3 48	21 00
13	3 43	20 18	3 53	20 28	3 45	20 31	3 40	20 38	3 27	20 46	3 31	21 03	3 47	21 01
14	3 43	20 19	3 53	20 29	3 44	20 32	3 40	20 39	3 27	20 47	3 31	21 04	3 47	21 01
15	3 43	20 19	3 53	20 29	3 44	20 32	3 40	20 40	3 27	20 47	3 31	21 04	3 47	21 02
16	3 42	20 20	3 53	20 30	3 44	20 33	3 39	20 40	3 27	20 48	3 31	21 05	3 47	21 02
17	3 42	20 20	3 53	20 30	3 44	20 33	3 39	20 41	3 27	20 48	3 31	21 05	3 47	21 03
18	3 42	20 21	3 53	20 30	3 44	20 33	3 39	20 41	3 27	20 49	3 31	21 06	3 47	21 03
19	3 43	20 21	3 53	20 31	3 44	20 34	3 39	20 41	3 27	20 49	3 31	21 06	3 47	21 03
20	3 43	20 21	3 53	20 31	3 44	20 34	3 40	20 42	3 27	20 49	3 31	21 06	3 47	21 04
21	3 43	20 21	3 53	20 31	3 45	20 34	3 40	20 42	3 27	20 49	3 31	21 06	3 47	21 04
22	3 43	20 21	3 53	20 31	3 45	20 34	3 40	20 42	3 27	20 50	3 31	21 07	3 47	21 04
23	3 43	20 22	3 54	20 31	3 45	20 35	3 40	20 42	3 28	20 50	3 32	21 07	3 48	21 04
24	3 44	20 22	3 54	20 31	3 45	20 35	3 41	20 42	3 28	20 50	3 32	21 07	3 48	21 04
25	3 44	20 22	3 54	20 31	3 46	20 35	3 41	20 42	3 28	20 50	3 32	21 07	3 48	21 04
26	3 45	20 22	3 55	20 31	3 46	20 34	3 42	20 42	3 29	20 50	3 33	21 06	3 49	21 04
27	3 45	20 22	3 55	20 31	3 47	20 34	3 42	20 42	3 29	20 49	3 33	21 06	3 49	21 04
28	3 46	20 21	3 56	20 31	3 47	20 34	3 43	20 42	3 30	20 49	3 34	21 06	3 50	21 04
29	3 46	20 21	3 56	20 31	3 48	20 34	3 43	20 41	3 31	20 49	3 35	21 06	3 51	21 03
30	3 47	20 21	3 57	20 31	3 49	20 34	3 44	20 41	3 31	20 48	3 35	21 05	3 51	21 03

JUPITER

Day	RA h m	Dec. ° '	Transit h m	5° high 52° h m	5° high 56° h m
1	12 35.2	-2 14	19 54	1 13	1 07
11	12 35.2	-2 17	19 14	0 33	0 28
21	12 36.3	-2 27	18 36	23 50	23 45
31	12 38.4	-2 43	17 59	23 11	23 06

Diameters – equatorial 38" polar 36"

SATURN

Day	RA h m	Dec. ° '	Transit h m	5° high 52° h m	5° high 56° h m
1	7 46.0	+21 26	15 05	22 26	22 42
11	7 50.6	+21 14	14 31	21 51	22 06
21	7 55.5	+21 02	13 56	21 15	21 30
31	8 00.7	+20 48	13 22	20 39	20 54

Diameters – equatorial 17" polar 15"
Rings – major axis 38" minor axis 14"

URANUS

Day	RA h m	Dec. ° '	Transit h m	10° high 52° h m	10° high 56° h m
1	22 49.9	-8 16	6 11	2 04	2 19
11	22 50.2	-8 15	5 32	1 24	1 40
21	22 50.1	-8 16	4 52	0 45	1 01
31	22 49.8	-8 18	4 13	0 06	0 21

Diameter 4"

NEPTUNE

Day	RA h m	Dec. ° '	Transit h m	10° high 52° h m	10° high 56° h m
1	21 20.2	-15 41	4 41	1 25	1 52
11	21 19.8	-15 43	4 01	0 45	1 13
21	21 19.3	-15 46	3 22	0 06	0 33
31	21 18.6	-15 49	2 42	23 22	23 50

Diameter 2"

JULY 2005

SEVENTH MONTH, 31 DAYS. *Julius* Caesar, formerly *Quintilis*, fifth month of Roman pre-Julian calendar

1	*Friday*	Harriet Beecher Stowe b. 1896. Erik Satie d. 1925	182
2	*Saturday*	Ernest Hemingway d. 1961. Vladimir Nabokov d. 1977	183
3	*Sunday*	Robert Adam b. 1728. Tom Stoppard b. 1937	184
4	*Monday*	Samuel Richardson d. 1761. Georgette Heyer d. 1974	week 27 day 185
5	*Tuesday*	Jean Cocteau b. 1889. Max Klinger d. 1920	186
6	*Wednesday*	Henry II d. 1189. Kenneth Grahame d. 1932	187
7	*Thursday*	Edward I (Longshanks) d. 1307. Sir Arthur Conan Doyle d. 1930	188
8	*Friday*	Percy Grainger b. 1882. Percy Bysshe Shelley d. 1822	189
9	*Saturday*	Dame Barbara Cartland b. 1901. David Hockney b. 1937	190
10	*Sunday*	Marcel Proust b. 1871. George Stubbs d. 1806	191
11	*Monday*	Robert I of Scotland (Bruce) b. 1274. George Gershwin d. 1937	week 28 day 192
12	*Tuesday*	Henry David Thoreau b. 1817. Amadeo Modigliani b. 1884	193
13	*Wednesday*	Sir George Gilbert Scott b. 1811. David Storey d. 1933	194
14	*Thursday*	Gustav Klimt b. 1862. Alphonse Mucha d. 1939	195
15	*Friday*	Inigo Jones b. 1573. Dame Iris Murdoch b. 1919	196
16	*Saturday*	Tsar Nicholas II d. 1918. Sir Stephen Spender d. 1995	197
17	*Sunday*	Erle Stanley Gardner b. 1889. James McNeill Whistler d. 1903	198
18	*Monday*	William Makepeace Thackeray b. 1811. Jane Austen d. 1817	week 29 day 199
19	*Tuesday*	Edgar Degas b. 1834. A. J. Cronin b. 1896	200
20	*Wednesday*	Erik Karlfeldt b. 1864. Bruce Lee d. 1973	201
21	*Thursday*	Ernest Hemingway b. 1899. Robert Burns d. 1796	202
22	*Friday*	James Whale b. 1893. Carl Sandburg d. 1967	203
23	*Saturday*	Raymond Chandler b. 1888. Domenico Scarlatti d. 1757	204
24	*Sunday*	Alphonse Mucha b. 1860. John Sell Cotman d. 1842	205
25	*Monday*	Eric Hoffer b. 1902. Samuel Taylor Coleridge d. 1834	week 30 day 206
26	*Tuesday*	George Bernard Shaw b. 1856. Aldous Huxley b. 1894	207
27	*Wednesday*	Alexandre Dumas fils b. 1824. Sir Anton Dolin b. 1904	208
28	*Thursday*	Beatrix Potter b. 1866. Johann Sebastian Bach d. 1750	209
29	*Friday*	Robert Schumann d. 1856. Vincent van Gogh d. 1890	210
30	*Saturday*	Emily Brontë b. 1818. Henry Moore b. 1898	211
31	*Sunday*	J. K. Rowling b. 1965. Franz Liszt d. 1886	212

ASTRONOMICAL PHENOMENA

d	h	
5	05	Earth at aphelion (152 million km.)
7	17	Saturn in conjunction with Moon. Saturn 5° S.
8	21	Venus in conjunction with Moon. Venus 3° S.
8	22	Mercury in conjunction with Moon. Mercury 5° S.
9	03	Mercury at greatest elongation E.26°
9	10	Venus in conjunction with Mercury . Venus 2° N.
13	18	Jupiter in conjunction with Moon. Jupiter 0°.7 N.
22	18	Sun's longitude 120° ♌
23	03	Mercury at stationary point
23	17	Saturn in conjunction
27	17	Mars in conjunction with Moon. Mars 4° S.

MINIMA OF ALGOL

d	h	d	h	d	h
3	19.9	15	07.2	26	18.4
6	16.7	18	04.0	29	15.2
9	13.6	21	00.8		
12	10.4	23	21.6		

CONSTELLATIONS

The following constellations are near their meridian at

	d	h		d	h
June	1	24	July	16	21
June	15	23	August	1	20
July	1	22	August	16	19

Ursa Minor, Draco, Coruna, Hercules, Lyra, Serpens, Ophiuchus, Libra, Scorpius and Sagittarius

THE MOON

Phases, Apsides and Node		d	h	m
●	New Moon	6	12	02
☽	First Quarter	14	15	20
○	Full Moon	21	11	00
☾	Last Quarter	28	03	19
Apogee (406,379 km)		8	17	52
Perigee (357,154 km)		21	19	50

Mean longitude of ascending node on July 1, 19°

THE SUN

s.d. 15′.8

Day	Right Ascension			Dec. +		Equation of time		Rise 52°		56°		Transit		Set 52°		56°		Sidereal time			Transit of first point of Aries		
	h	m	s	°	′	m	s	h	m	h	m	h	m	h	m	h	m	h	m	s	h	m	s
1	6	40	20	23	07	−3	45	3	44	3	18	12	04	20	23	20	49	18	36	35	5	22	32
2	6	44	28	23	03	−3	57	3	45	3	19	12	04	20	23	20	48	18	40	32	5	18	36
3	6	48	36	22	58	−4	08	3	46	3	20	12	04	20	22	20	48	18	44	28	5	14	40
4	6	52	44	22	53	−4	19	3	47	3	21	12	04	20	22	20	47	18	48	25	5	10	44
5	6	56	51	22	48	−4	30	3	47	3	22	12	05	20	21	20	46	18	52	21	5	06	48
6	7	00	58	22	42	−4	40	3	48	3	23	12	05	20	21	20	46	18	56	18	5	02	52
7	7	05	05	22	36	−4	50	3	49	3	24	12	05	20	20	20	45	19	00	14	4	58	57
8	7	09	11	22	29	−5	00	3	50	3	25	12	05	20	19	20	44	19	04	11	4	55	01
9	7	13	17	22	22	−5	09	3	51	3	27	12	05	20	19	20	43	19	08	07	4	51	05
10	7	17	22	22	15	−5	18	3	52	3	28	12	05	20	18	20	42	19	12	04	4	47	09
11	7	21	27	22	07	−5	26	3	53	3	29	12	06	20	17	20	41	19	16	01	4	43	13
12	7	25	31	21	59	−5	34	3	54	3	31	12	06	20	16	20	40	19	19	57	4	39	17
13	7	29	35	21	51	−5	42	3	56	3	32	12	06	20	15	20	39	19	23	54	4	35	21
14	7	33	39	21	42	−5	49	3	57	3	33	12	06	20	14	20	37	19	27	50	4	31	25
15	7	37	42	21	33	−5	55	3	58	3	35	12	06	20	13	20	36	19	31	47	4	27	29
16	7	41	44	21	23	−6	01	3	59	3	36	12	06	20	12	20	35	19	35	43	4	23	33
17	7	45	46	21	13	−6	06	4	00	3	38	12	06	20	11	20	33	19	39	40	4	19	37
18	7	49	48	21	03	−6	11	4	02	3	39	12	06	20	10	20	32	19	43	37	4	15	41
19	7	53	49	20	52	−6	15	4	03	3	41	12	06	20	09	20	30	19	47	33	4	11	46
20	7	57	49	20	41	−6	19	4	04	3	43	12	06	20	08	20	29	19	51	30	4	07	50
21	8	01	49	20	30	−6	22	4	06	3	44	12	06	20	06	20	27	19	55	26	4	03	54
22	8	05	48	20	18	−6	25	4	07	3	46	12	06	20	05	20	26	19	59	23	3	59	58
23	8	09	46	20	06	−6	27	4	08	3	48	12	06	20	04	20	24	20	03	19	3	56	02
24	8	13	44	19	54	−6	29	4	10	3	49	12	06	20	02	20	22	20	07	16	3	52	06
25	8	17	42	19	41	−6	29	4	11	3	51	12	07	20	01	20	21	20	11	12	3	48	10
26	8	21	39	19	28	−6	30	4	13	3	53	12	07	19	59	20	19	20	15	09	3	44	14
27	8	25	35	19	14	−6	29	4	14	3	55	12	06	19	58	20	17	20	19	06	3	40	18
28	8	29	31	19	01	−6	29	4	16	3	56	12	06	19	56	20	15	20	23	02	3	36	22
29	8	33	26	18	47	−6	27	4	17	3	58	12	06	19	55	20	13	20	26	59	3	32	26
30	8	37	20	18	32	−6	25	4	19	4	00	12	06	19	53	20	11	20	30	55	3	28	31
31	8	41	14	18	18	−6	23	4	20	4	02	12	06	19	51	20	09	20	34	52	3	24	35

DURATION OF TWILIGHT (in minutes)

Latitude	52°	56°	52°	56°	52°	56°	52°	56°
	1 July		11 July		21 July		31 July	
Civil	48	61	47	58	44	53	42	49
Nautical	124	TAN	117	TAN	107	146	98	123
Astronomical	TAN	TAN	TAN	TAN	TAN	TAN	182	TAN

THE NIGHT SKY

Mercury reaches greatest eastern elongation on the 9th but the long duration of twilight means that it is unsuitably placed for observation throughout the month.

Venus, magnitude −3.9, is a brilliant object in the evening sky, but only visible low above the western horizon for about half an hour after sunset. Under good conditions the thin crescent Moon, just over 2 days old, may be glimpsed nearly 3 degrees above Venus on the evening of the 8th.

Mars continues to brighten during the month, its magnitude changing from −0.1 to −0.5. Although technically a morning object, by the end of July it is visible low in the eastern sky before midnight, and will be seen high in the southern sky before dawn. Mars is moving east-north-eastwards in the constellation of Pisces. The Moon, at Last Quarter, passes 3 degrees north of the planet on the 27th.

Jupiter, magnitude −1.9, continues to be visible as a brilliant evening object in the south-western sky, in the constellation of Virgo. The Moon, near First Quarter, passes 1 degree south of Jupiter on the 13th.

Saturn passes through conjunction on the 23rd and therefore remains too close to the Sun for observation throughout the month.

Twilight. Reference to the section above shows that astronomical twilight lasts all night for a period around the summer solstice (i.e. in June and July), even in southern England. Under these conditions the sky never gets completely dark as the Sun is always less than 18 degrees below the horizon.

THE MOON

Day	RA h m	Dec. °	Hor. par. '	Semi-diam. '	Sun's Co-long. °	PA of Br. Limb °	Ph. %	Age d	Rise 52° h m	Rise 56° h m	Transit h m	Set 52° h m	Set 56° h m
1	2 15	+15.1	56.5	15.4	201	71	27	24.1	0 18	0 05	7 53	15 48	16 07
2	3 05	+20.0	55.9	15.2	213	76	19	25.1	0 34	0 15	8 41	17 07	17 33
3	3 56	+23.9	55.4	15.1	225	82	11	26.1	0 55	0 29	9 31	18 23	18 56
4	4 49	+26.6	55.0	15.0	237	91	6	27.1	1 24	0 52	10 23	19 31	20 09
5	5 44	+28.0	54.6	14.9	250	103	2	28.1	2 05	1 27	11 15	20 27	21 05
6	6 38	+28.1	54.3	14.8	262	135	0	29.1	2 58	2 20	12 07	21 08	21 42
7	7 32	+26.8	54.1	14.7	274	237	0	0.5	4 02	3 29	12 58	21 38	22 05
8	8 23	+24.3	54.0	14.7	286	268	2	1.5	5 14	4 47	13 45	21 59	22 20
9	9 12	+20.9	54.0	14.7	299	279	6	2.5	6 27	6 07	14 30	22 14	22 30
10	9 59	+16.5	54.0	14.7	311	285	11	3.5	7 40	7 26	15 13	22 27	22 37
11	10 43	+11.6	54.3	14.8	323	289	17	4.5	8 52	8 44	15 53	22 37	22 42
12	11 26	+6.2	54.6	14.9	335	292	25	5.5	10 04	10 01	16 33	22 47	22 47
13	12 09	+0.5	55.1	15.0	347	293	34	6.5	11 16	11 18	17 14	22 56	22 52
14	12 53	−5.3	55.7	15.2	360	293	44	7.5	12 31	12 38	17 56	23 07	22 58
15	13 39	−11.1	56.5	15.4	12	291	54	8.5	13 49	14 03	18 41	23 21	23 05
16	14 27	−16.6	57.4	15.6	24	288	64	9.5	15 13	15 33	19 31	23 39	23 17
17	15 21	−21.5	58.3	15.9	36	283	74	10.5	16 41	17 09	20 27	— —	23 35
18	16 19	−25.3	59.3	16.2	49	276	83	11.5	18 07	18 44	21 29	0 05	— —
19	17 23	−27.7	60.2	16.4	61	267	91	12.5	19 22	20 01	22 35	0 46	0 09
20	18 30	−28.2	60.8	16.6	73	254	97	13.5	20 17	20 52	23 41	1 49	1 09
21	19 38	−26.6	61.3	16.7	85	223	99	14.5	20 54	21 20	— —	3 12	2 38
22	20 43	−23.1	61.4	16.7	97	106	99	15.5	21 18	21 36	0 46	4 49	4 24
23	21 44	−17.9	61.2	16.7	110	81	96	16.5	21 35	21 46	1 45	6 26	6 10
24	22 41	−11.8	60.6	16.5	122	72	90	17.5	21 49	21 54	2 39	7 59	7 51
25	23 34	−5.1	59.9	16.3	134	68	82	18.5	22 01	22 00	3 30	9 28	9 26
26	0 24	+1.6	59.0	16.1	146	67	73	19.5	22 12	22 06	4 17	10 52	10 56
27	1 13	+8.1	58.1	15.8	158	68	62	20.5	22 25	22 13	5 04	12 15	12 25
28	2 02	+14.0	57.2	15.6	171	70	52	21.5	22 40	22 22	5 50	13 37	13 53
29	2 52	+19.1	56.4	15.4	183	74	41	22.5	22 59	22 35	6 38	14 57	15 21
30	3 44	+23.3	55.7	15.2	195	78	31	23.5	23 26	22 54	7 28	16 15	16 45
31	4 37	+26.2	55.1	15.0	207	85	23	24.5	— —	23 25	8 19	17 25	18 02

MERCURY

Day	RA h m	Dec. °	Diam. ''	Phase %	Transit h m	5° high 52° h m	5° high 56° h m
1	8 26	+20.3	7	55	13 50	21 04	21 18
3	8 36	+19.4	7	52	13 53	21 01	21 14
5	8 46	+18.5	7	49	13 54	20 56	21 09
7	8 55	+17.6	8	46	13 54	20 51	21 03
9	9 02	+16.6	8	42	13 54	20 46	20 56
11	9 09	+15.7	8	39	13 52	20 39	20 49
13	9 15	+14.8	9	36	13 50	20 32	20 41
15	9 19	+14.0	9	32	13 47	20 24	20 32
17	9 23	+13.2	9	29	13 42	20 16	20 23
19	9 26	+12.6	10	25	13 36	20 06	20 13
21	9 27	+12.0	10	22	13 30	19 56	20 03
23	9 27	+11.5	10	18	13 21	19 46	19 52
25	9 26	+11.1	11	14	13 12	19 35	19 41
27	9 24	+10.9	11	11	13 02	19 23	19 29
29	9 20	+10.8	11	8	12 50	19 12	19 17
31	9 16	+10.9	11	5	12 37	19 00	19 05

VENUS

Day	R.A. h m	Dec. °	Diam. ''	Phase %	Transit h m	5° high 52° h m	5° high 56° h m
1	8 24	+21.0	11	91	13 48	21 06	21 21
6	8 49	+19.5	11	90	13 54	21 03	21 16
11	9 14	+17.8	11	89	13 58	20 57	21 09
16	9 38	+15.9	12	88	14 02	20 51	21 01
21	10 01	+13.8	12	86	14 06	20 43	20 51
26	10 24	+11.6	12	85	14 09	20 35	20 40
31	10 47	+9.3	12	84	14 12	20 25	20 29

MARS

Day	RA h m	Dec. °	Diam. ''	Phase %	Transit h m	5° high 52° h m	5° high 56° h m
1	0 51	+2.8	9	84	6 14	0 33	0 34
6	1 04	+4.0	10	84	6 07	0 19	0 19
11	1 16	+5.2	10	84	5 59	0 06	0 05
16	1 28	+6.3	10	84	5 51	23 49	23 47
21	1 39	+7.4	11	84	5 43	23 36	23 33
26	1 51	+8.4	11	84	5 35	23 22	23 18
31	2 02	+9.4	11	84	5 26	23 08	23 04

SUNRISE AND SUNSET

	London 0°05′	51°30′	Bristol 2°35′	51°28′	Birmingham 1°55′	52°28′	Manchester 2°15′	53°28′	Newcastle 1°37′	54°49′	Glasgow 4°14′	55°52′	Belfast 5°56′	54°35′
	h m	h m	h m	h m	h m	h m	h m	h m	h m	h m	h m	h m	h m	h m
1	3 47	20 21	3 58	20 30	3 49	20 33	3 45	20 41	3 32	20 48	3 36	21 05	3 52	21 03
2	3 48	20 20	3 58	20 30	3 50	20 33	3 45	20 40	3 33	20 48	3 37	21 04	3 53	21 02
3	3 49	20 20	3 59	20 30	3 51	20 33	3 46	20 40	3 34	20 47	3 38	21 04	3 54	21 02
4	3 50	20 19	4 00	20 29	3 52	20 32	3 47	20 39	3 35	20 46	3 39	21 03	3 55	21 01
5	3 50	20 19	4 01	20 29	3 52	20 32	3 48	20 39	3 36	20 46	3 40	21 02	3 56	21 00
6	3 51	20 18	4 02	20 28	3 53	20 31	3 49	20 38	3 37	20 45	3 41	21 02	3 57	21 00
7	3 52	20 18	4 02	20 28	3 54	20 30	3 50	20 37	3 38	20 44	3 42	21 01	3 58	20 59
8	3 53	20 17	4 03	20 27	3 55	20 30	3 51	20 37	3 39	20 44	3 43	21 00	3 59	20 58
9	3 54	20 16	4 04	20 26	3 56	20 29	3 52	20 36	3 40	20 43	3 45	20 59	4 00	20 57
10	3 55	20 16	4 05	20 25	3 57	20 28	3 53	20 35	3 41	20 42	3 46	20 58	4 01	20 56
11	3 56	20 15	4 06	20 25	3 58	20 27	3 54	20 34	3 42	20 41	3 47	20 57	4 02	20 55
12	3 57	20 14	4 07	20 24	4 00	20 26	3 55	20 33	3 44	20 40	3 48	20 56	4 04	20 54
13	3 58	20 13	4 09	20 23	4 01	20 25	3 57	20 32	3 45	20 39	3 50	20 55	4 05	20 53
14	4 00	20 12	4 10	20 22	4 02	20 24	3 58	20 31	3 46	20 37	3 51	20 53	4 06	20 52
15	4 01	20 11	4 11	20 21	4 03	20 23	3 59	20 30	3 48	20 36	3 53	20 52	4 07	20 51
16	4 02	20 10	4 12	20 20	4 04	20 22	4 00	20 29	3 49	20 35	3 54	20 51	4 09	20 50
17	4 03	20 09	4 13	20 19	4 06	20 21	4 02	20 28	3 51	20 34	3 56	20 49	4 10	20 49
18	4 04	20 08	4 15	20 18	4 07	20 20	4 03	20 26	3 52	20 32	3 57	20 48	4 12	20 47
19	4 06	20 07	4 16	20 17	4 08	20 19	4 05	20 25	3 54	20 31	3 59	20 47	4 13	20 46
20	4 07	20 06	4 17	20 15	4 10	20 17	4 06	20 24	3 55	20 29	4 00	20 45	4 15	20 44
21	4 08	20 04	4 18	20 14	4 11	20 16	4 07	20 22	3 57	20 28	4 02	20 43	4 16	20 43
22	4 10	20 03	4 20	20 13	4 13	20 15	4 09	20 21	3 58	20 26	4 04	20 42	4 18	20 41
23	4 11	20 02	4 21	20 12	4 14	20 13	4 10	20 20	4 00	20 25	4 05	20 40	4 19	20 40
24	4 12	20 00	4 23	20 10	4 15	20 12	4 12	20 18	4 02	20 23	4 07	20 39	4 21	20 38
25	4 14	19 59	4 24	20 09	4 17	20 11	4 13	20 16	4 03	20 22	4 09	20 37	4 23	20 37
26	4 15	19 58	4 25	20 07	4 18	20 09	4 15	20 15	4 05	20 20	4 11	20 35	4 24	20 35
27	4 17	19 56	4 27	20 06	4 20	20 07	4 17	20 13	4 07	20 18	4 12	20 33	4 26	20 33
28	4 18	19 55	4 28	20 04	4 21	20 06	4 18	20 12	4 08	20 16	4 14	20 31	4 28	20 32
29	4 20	19 53	4 30	20 03	4 23	20 04	4 20	20 10	4 10	20 15	4 16	20 30	4 29	20 30
30	4 21	19 51	4 31	20 01	4 24	20 03	4 21	20 08	4 12	20 13	4 18	20 28	4 31	20 28
31	4 22	19 50	4 33	20 00	4 26	20 01	4 23	20 07	4 14	20 11	4 20	20 26	4 33	20 26

JUPITER

Day	RA		Dec.		Transit		5° high 52°		56°	
	h	m	°	′	h	m	h m		h m	
1	12	38.4	−2	43	17	59	23 11		23 06	
11	12	41.5	−3	05	17	23	22 33		22 27	
21	12	45.5	−3	33	16	48	21 56		21 49	
31	12	50.3	−4	06	16	13	21 18		21 11	

Diameters – equatorial 35″ polar 33″

SATURN

Day	RA		Dec.		Transit		5° high 52°		56°	
	h	m	°	′	h	m	h m		h m	
1	8	00.7	+20	48	13	22	20 39		20 54	
11	8	06.0	+20	34	12	48	20 04		20 19	
21	8	11.4	+20	18	12	14	19 28		19 43	
31	8	16.8	+20	02	11	40	18 53		19 07	

Diameters – equatorial 16″ polar 15″
Rings – major axis 37″ minor axis 13″

URANUS

Day	RA		Dec.		Transit		10° high 52°		56°	
	h	m	°	′	h	m	h m		h m	
1	22	49.8	−8	18	4	13	0 06		0 21	
11	22	49.2	−8	22	3	33	23 22		23 38	
21	22	48.4	−8	27	2	52	22 43		22 58	
31	22	47.3	−8	34	2	12	22 03		22 19	

Diameter 4″

NEPTUNE

Day	RA		Dec.		Transit		5° high 52°		56°	
	h	m	°	′	h	m	h m		h m	
1	21	18.6	−15	69	2	42	23 22		23 50	
11	21	17.8	−15	53	2	01	22 42		23 10	
21	21	16.8	−15	58	1	21	22 03		22 31	
31	21	15.8	−16	03	0	41	21 23		21 51	

Diameter 2″

AUGUST 2005

EIGHTH MONTH, 31 DAYS. *Augustus*, formerly *Sextilis*, sixth month of Roman pre-Julian calendar

1	*Monday*	Herman Melville b. 1819. Queen Anne d. 1714	week 31 day 213
2	*Tuesday*	Thomas Gainsborough d. 1788. Carlos Chavez d. 1978	214
3	*Wednesday*	Sir Joseph Paxton b. 1801. P. D. James b. 1920	215
4	*Thursday*	Percy Bysshe Shelley b. 1792. Hans Christian Andersen d. 1874	216
5	*Friday*	Guy de Maupassant b. 1850. Friedrich Engels d. 1895	217
6	*Saturday*	Alfred, Lord Tennyson b. 1809. Ben Jonson d. 1637	218
7	*Sunday*	Emil Nolde b. 1867. Rabindranath Tagore d. 1941	219
8	*Monday*	Princess Beatrice of York b. 1988. James Tissot d. 1902	week 32 day 220
9	*Tuesday*	Ruggero Leoncavallo d. 1919. Dmitry Shostakovich d. 1975	221
10	*Wednesday*	Ferdinand VI d. 1759. Alan Ramsay d. 1784	222
11	*Thursday*	Enid Blyton b. 1897. Jackson Pollock d. 1956	223
12	*Friday*	William Blake d. 1827. Ian Fleming d. 1964	224
13	*Saturday*	H. G. Wells b. 1866. Sir John Everett Millais d. 1896	225
14	*Sunday*	John Galsworthy b. 1867. Bertolt Brecht d. 1956	226
15	*Monday*	Sir Walter Scott b. 1771. The Princess Royal b. 1950	week 33 day 227
16	*Tuesday*	Ted Hughes b. 1930. Margaret Mitchell d. 1946	228
17	*Wednesday*	Frederick the Great d. 1786. Ludwig Mies van der Rohe d. 1969	229
18	*Thursday*	William Henry Hudson d. 1922. Honoré de Balzac d. 1850	230
19	*Friday*	John Dryden b. 1631. Sergey Diaghilev d. 1929	231
20	*Saturday*	H. P. Lovecraft b. 1890. Leon Trotsky, d. 1940	232
21	*Sunday*	William IV b. 1765. Aubrey Beardsley b. 1872	233
22	*Monday*	Claude Debussy b. 1862. Richard III d. 1485	week 34 day 234
23	*Tuesday*	Louis XVI, King of France b. 1754. Willy Russell b. 1947	235
24	*Wednesday*	George Stubbs b. 1724. Jean Rhys b. 1890	236
25	*Thursday*	Leonard Bernstein b. 1918. Frederick Forsyth b. 1938	237
26	*Friday*	Albert, Prince Consort to Queen Victoria b. 1819	238
27	*Saturday*	C. S. Forester b. 1899. Le Corbusier d. 1965	239
28	*Sunday*	Johann Wolfgang von Goethe b. 1749. Leigh Hunt d. 1859	240
29	*Monday*	Jean Ingres b. 1780. Joseph Wright d. 1797	week 35 day 241
30	*Tuesday*	Mary Shelley b. 1797. Cleopatra d. 30BC	242
31	*Wednesday*	Henry V d. 1422. Henry Moore d. 1986	243

ASTRONOMICAL PHENOMENA

d	h	
4	06	Saturn in conjunction with Moon. Saturn 5° S.
5	06	Mercury in conjunction with Moon. Mercury 9° S.
6	00	Mercury in inferior conjunction
8	05	Venus in conjunction with Moon. Venus 1° S.
8	16	Neptune at opposition
10	07	Jupiter in conjunction with Moon. Jupiter 1° N.
16	04	Mercury at stationary point
23	01	Sun's longitude 150° ♍
23	23	Mercury at greatest elongation W.18°
25	04	Mars in conjunction with Moon. Mars 5° S.
31	19	Saturn in conjunction with Moon. Saturn 4° S.

MINIMA OF ALGOL

d	h	d	h	d	h
1	12.0	12	23.3	24	10.5
4	08.8	15	20.1	27	07.3
7	05.7	18	16.9	30	04.1
10	02.5	21	13.7		

CONSTELLATIONS

The following constellations are near their meridian at

	d	h		d	h
July	1	24	August	16	21
July	16	23	September	1	20
August	1	22	September	15	19

Draco, Hercules, Lyra, Cygnus, Sagitta, Ophiuchus, Serpens, Aquila and Sagittarius

THE MOON

Phases, Apsides and Node	d	h	m
● New Moon	5	03	05
☽ First Quarter	13	02	39
○ Full Moon	19	17	53
☾ Last Quarter	26	15	18
Apogee (406,630 km)	4	22	04
Perigee (357,398 km)	19	05	43

Mean longitude of ascending node on August 1, 17°

THE SUN

s.d. 15'.8

Day	Right Ascension			Dec. +		Equation of time		Rise 52°		Rise 56°		Transit		Set 52°		Set 56°		Sidereal time			Transit of first point of Aries		
	h	m	s	°	'	m	s	h	m	h	m	h	m	h	m	h	m	h	m	s	h	m	s
1	8	45	08	18	03	−6	19	4	22	4	04	12	06	19	50	20	07	20	38	48	3	20	39
2	8	49	01	17	48	−6	16	4	23	4	06	12	06	19	48	20	05	20	42	45	3	16	43
3	8	52	53	17	32	−6	11	4	25	4	08	12	06	19	46	20	03	20	46	41	3	12	47
4	8	56	44	17	16	−6	06	4	26	4	10	12	06	19	45	20	01	20	50	38	3	08	51
5	9	00	35	17	00	−6	01	4	28	4	11	12	06	19	43	19	59	20	54	35	3	04	55
6	9	04	26	16	44	−5	55	4	30	4	13	12	06	19	41	19	57	20	58	31	3	00	59
7	9	08	15	16	27	−5	48	4	31	4	15	12	06	19	39	19	55	21	02	28	2	57	03
8	9	12	05	16	10	−5	40	4	33	4	17	12	06	19	37	19	53	21	06	24	2	53	07
9	9	15	53	15	53	−5	32	4	34	4	19	12	05	19	36	19	50	21	10	21	2	49	11
10	9	19	41	15	36	−5	24	4	36	4	21	12	05	19	34	19	48	21	14	17	2	45	16
11	9	23	29	15	18	−5	15	4	38	4	23	12	05	19	32	19	46	21	18	14	2	41	20
12	9	27	15	15	00	−5	05	4	39	4	25	12	05	19	30	19	44	21	22	10	2	37	24
13	9	31	02	14	42	−4	55	4	41	4	27	12	05	19	28	19	41	21	26	07	2	33	28
14	9	34	47	14	24	−4	44	4	42	4	29	12	05	19	26	19	39	21	30	04	2	29	32
15	9	38	32	14	05	−4	32	4	44	4	31	12	04	19	24	19	37	21	34	00	2	25	36
16	9	42	17	13	46	−4	20	4	46	4	33	12	04	19	22	19	34	21	37	57	2	21	40
17	9	46	01	13	27	−4	08	4	47	4	35	12	04	19	20	19	32	21	41	53	2	17	44
18	9	49	44	13	08	−3	55	4	49	4	37	12	04	19	18	19	29	21	45	50	2	13	48
19	9	53	27	12	49	−3	41	4	50	4	39	12	04	19	16	19	27	21	49	46	2	09	52
20	9	57	10	12	29	−3	27	4	52	4	41	12	03	19	13	19	25	21	53	43	2	05	56
21	10	00	52	12	09	−3	12	4	54	4	43	12	03	19	11	19	22	21	57	39	2	02	01
22	10	04	33	11	49	−2	57	4	55	4	45	12	03	19	09	19	20	22	01	36	1	58	05
23	10	08	15	11	29	−2	42	4	57	4	47	12	03	19	07	19	17	22	05	33	1	54	09
24	10	11	55	11	09	−2	26	4	59	4	49	12	02	19	05	19	15	22	09	29	1	50	13
25	10	15	36	10	48	−2	10	5	00	4	50	12	02	19	03	19	12	22	13	26	1	46	17
26	10	19	15	10	27	−1	53	5	02	4	52	12	02	19	00	19	10	22	17	22	1	42	21
27	10	22	55	10	06	−1	36	5	04	4	54	12	01	18	58	19	07	22	21	19	1	38	25
28	10	26	34	9	45	−1	19	5	05	4	56	12	01	18	56	19	05	22	25	15	1	34	29
29	10	30	13	9	24	−1	01	5	07	4	58	12	01	18	54	19	02	22	29	12	1	30	33
30	10	33	51	9	03	−0	43	5	08	5	00	12	01	18	52	19	00	22	33	08	1	26	37
31	10	37	30	8	41	−0	25	5	10	5	02	12	00	18	49	18	57	22	37	05	1	22	41

DURATION OF TWILIGHT (in minutes)

Latitude	52°	56°	52°	56°	52°	56°	52	56°
	1 August		11 August		21 August		31 August	
Civil	41	49	39	45	37	42	35	40
Nautical	97	121	90	107	84	97	79	90
Astronomical	179	TAN	154	210	139	168	128	148

THE NIGHT SKY

Mercury is unsuitably placed for observation at first, since it passes through inferior conjunction on the 5th. For the last ten days in the month it may be seen as a morning object, magnitude +0.5 to −0.9, low above the east-north-east horizon at the beginning of morning civil twilight.

Venus, magnitude −4.0, continues to be visible as a brilliant object in the evening skies, though only visible for about half an hour after sunset, low above the western horizon. Under good conditions the thin crescent Moon may be seen about 4 degrees to the right of Venus on the evening of the 7th and 8th. On the following evening the Moon will be seen about 6 degrees to the left of the planet.

Mars has now become a conspicuous object in the night sky, its magnitude brightening during the month from −0.5 to −1.0. By the end of August it is easily located in the eastern sky before 22h. Mars is in the constellation of Aries. During the night of the 24th–25th the gibbous Moon passes about 5 degrees north of the planet.

Jupiter is still a bright evening object, magnitude −1.8. It is moving towards the Sun and only visible for a short time in the south-western sky before it sets. By the end of the month it is a difficult object to detect in the gathering twilight. The waxing crescent Moon is in the vicinity of the planet on the evenings of the 9th and 10th.

Saturn, magnitude +0.3, slowly becomes visible during the second half of the month, low above the eastern horizon in the early mornings before it is lost in the pre-dawn twilight. The waning crescent Moon will be seen about 8 degrees above the planet on the morning of the 31st.

Neptune is at opposition on the 8th, in the constellation of Capricornus. It is not visible to the naked-eye since its magnitude is +7.8.

Meteors. The maximum of the famous Perseid meteor shower occurs on the 12th, and will be best seen from the late evening onwards.

THE MOON

Day	RA h	RA m	Dec. °	Hor. par. '	Semi-diam. '	Suns Co-long. °	PA of Br. Limb °	Ph. %	Age d	Rise 52° h	Rise 52° m	Rise 56° h	Rise 56° m	Transit h	Transit m	Set 52° h	Set 52° m	Set 56° h	Set 56° m
1	5	31	+27.9	54.7	14.9	219	92	15	25.5	0	02	—	—	9	11	18	24	19	03
2	6	25	+28.3	54.3	14.8	232	100	9	26.5	0	51	0	13	10	03	19	09	19	45
3	7	19	+27.3	54.1	14.7	244	109	4	27.5	1	53	1	18	10	54	19	42	20	12
4	8	11	+25.1	54.0	14.7	256	124	1	28.5	3	03	2	34	11	43	20	05	20	28
5	9	00	+21.8	53.9	14.7	268	179	0	29.5	4	16	3	54	12	28	20	22	20	39
6	9	47	+17.6	54.0	14.7	281	267	1	0.9	5	30	5	14	13	12	20	35	20	46
7	10	32	+12.7	54.1	14.7	293	283	3	1.9	6	42	6	32	13	53	20	45	20	52
8	11	16	+7.4	54.4	14.8	305	289	7	2.9	7	54	7	49	14	33	20	55	20	57
9	11	58	+1.7	54.7	14.9	317	292	13	3.9	9	06	9	06	15	13	21	04	21	01
10	12	41	−4.0	55.2	15.0	330	293	20	4.9	10	18	10	24	15	53	21	14	21	07
11	13	26	−9.8	55.7	15.2	342	292	29	5.9	11	34	11	46	16	37	21	26	21	13
12	14	12	−15.3	56.4	15.4	354	290	39	6.9	12	54	13	12	17	24	21	41	21	22
13	15	03	−20.2	57.2	15.6	6	286	49	7.9	14	18	14	44	18	15	22	03	21	36
14	15	58	−24.3	58.1	15.8	19	281	60	8.9	15	43	16	17	19	12	22	36	22	01
15	16	58	−27.2	59.0	16.1	31	274	70	9.9	17	02	17	41	20	15	23	26	22	46
16	18	02	−28.4	59.8	16.3	43	266	80	10.9	18	05	18	43	21	20	—	—	—	—
17	19	09	−27.7	60.6	16.5	55	257	89	11.9	18	49	19	20	22	24	0	39	0	01
18	20	14	−24.9	61.1	16.6	67	247	95	12.9	19	18	19	40	23	26	2	09	1	39
19	21	17	−20.4	61.3	16.7	79	230	99	13.9	19	38	19	53	—	—	3	47	3	26
20	22	16	−14.5	61.3	16.7	92	113	100	14.9	19	54	20	01	0	23	5	24	5	11
21	23	12	−7.9	60.8	16.6	104	75	98	15.9	20	06	20	08	1	17	6	57	6	52
22	0	04	−0.9	60.2	16.4	116	69	93	16.9	20	18	20	14	2	07	8	26	8	27
23	0	55	+5.9	59.3	16.2	128	67	85	17.9	20	30	20	21	2	55	9	52	10	00
24	1	46	+12.3	58.4	15.9	140	68	77	18.9	20	44	20	29	3	43	11	17	11	31
25	2	36	+17.8	57.4	15.6	153	71	67	19.9	21	02	20	40	4	32	12	41	13	02
26	3	29	+22.4	56.5	15.4	165	75	57	20.9	21	26	20	57	5	22	14	02	14	31
27	4	22	+25.8	55.7	15.2	177	81	46	21.9	21	59	21	23	6	14	15	17	15	52
28	5	17	+27.8	55.1	15.0	189	87	37	22.9	22	45	22	06	7	06	16	20	17	00
29	6	12	+28.5	54.6	14.9	201	94	28	23.9	23	43	23	06	7	59	17	10	17	48
30	7	06	+27.8	54.3	14.8	214	100	20	24.9	—	—	—	—	8	51	17	46	18	18
31	7	58	+25.8	54.1	14.7	226	107	13	25.9	0	51	0	19	9	40	18	11	18	37

MERCURY

Day	RA h	RA m	Dec. °	Diam. "	Phase %	Transit h	Transit m	5° high 52° h	5° high 52° m	5° high 56° h	5° high 56° m
1	9	13	+11.0	11	4	12	31	18	54	19	00
3	9	08	+11.4	11	2	12	17	18	42	18	48
5	9	02	+11.8	11	1	12	04	18	31	18	38
7	8	56	+12.4	11	1	11	50	5	20	5	13
9	8	50	+13.0	11	2	11	37	5	04	4	56
11	8	46	+13.7	10	5	11	25	4	48	4	40
13	8	43	+14.4	10	8	11	15	4	34	4	25
15	8	42	+15.0	10	12	11	06	4	21	4	12
17	8	42	+15.5	9	18	10	59	4	11	4	01
19	8	44	+16.0	9	24	10	54	4	04	3	53
21	8	49	+16.3	8	31	10	51	3	59	3	48
23	8	55	+16.5	8	39	10	50	3	57	3	46
25	9	04	+16.4	7	47	10	51	3	57	3	47
27	9	14	+16.2	7	55	10	53	4	01	3	50
29	9	25	+15.8	6	64	10	57	4	07	3	57
31	9	38	+15.2	6	71	11	02	4	15	4	06

VENUS

Day	RA h	RA m	Dec. °	Diam. "	Phase %	Transit h	Transit m	5° high 52° h	5° high 52° m	5° high 56° h	5° high 56° m
1	10	51	+8.8	12	83	14	13	20	23	20	27
6	11	13	+6.3	13	82	14	15	20	13	20	14
11	11	35	+3.8	13	81	14	17	20	02	20	01
16	11	56	+1.3	13	79	14	19	19	50	19	48
21	12	18	−1.3	14	78	14	20	19	39	19	34
26	12	39	−3.9	14	76	14	22	19	27	19	20
31	13	00	−6.4	15	75	14	23	19	15	19	05

MARS

Day	RA h	RA m	Dec. °	Diam. "	Phase %	Transit h	Transit m	5° high 52° h	5° high 52° m	5° high 56° h	5° high 56° m
1	2	04	+9.6	11	84	5	25	23	06	23	01
6	2	15	+10.5	12	85	5	16	22	52	22	46
11	2	25	+11.4	12	85	5	06	22	38	22	32
16	2	35	+12.2	13	85	4	56	22	24	22	17
21	2	44	+12.9	13	86	4	46	22	09	22	02
26	2	52	+13.6	13	86	4	35	21	55	21	47
31	3	00	+14.2	14	87	4	23	21	39	21	31

SUNRISE AND SUNSET

	London 0°05'	51°30'	Bristol 2°35'	51°28'	Birmingham 1°55'	52°28'	Manchester 2°15'	53°28'	Newcastle 1°37'	54°59'	Glasgow 4°14'	55°52'	Belfast 5°56'	54°35'
	h m	h m	h m	h m	h m	h m	h m	h m	h m	h m	h m	h m	h m	h m
1	4 24	19 48	4 34	19 58	4 27	19 59	4 25	20 05	4 15	20 09	4 21	20 24	4 34	20 24
2	4 25	19 47	4 36	19 56	4 29	19 58	4 26	20 03	4 17	20 07	4 23	20 22	4 36	20 23
3	4 27	19 45	4 37	19 55	4 31	19 56	4 28	20 01	4 19	20 05	4 25	20 20	4 38	20 21
4	4 29	19 43	4 39	19 53	4 32	19 54	4 30	19 59	4 21	20 03	4 27	20 18	4 40	20 19
5	4 30	19 41	4 40	19 51	4 34	19 52	4 31	19 57	4 22	20 01	4 29	20 15	4 41	20 17
6	4 32	19 40	4 42	19 50	4 35	19 50	4 33	19 55	4 24	19 59	4 31	20 13	4 43	20 15
7	4 33	19 38	4 43	19 48	4 37	19 49	4 35	19 54	4 26	19 57	4 33	20 11	4 45	20 13
8	4 35	19 36	4 45	19 46	4 39	19 47	4 36	19 52	4 28	19 55	4 35	20 09	4 47	20 11
9	4 36	19 34	4 46	19 44	4 40	19 45	4 38	19 50	4 30	19 53	4 37	20 07	4 49	20 08
10	4 38	19 32	4 48	19 42	4 42	19 43	4 40	19 48	4 32	19 51	4 39	20 05	4 51	20 06
11	4 39	19 30	4 50	19 40	4 44	19 41	4 42	19 46	4 34	19 48	4 41	20 02	4 52	20 04
12	4 41	19 29	4 51	19 38	4 45	19 39	4 43	19 43	4 35	19 46	4 42	20 00	4 54	20 02
13	4 43	19 27	4 53	19 36	4 47	19 37	4 45	19 41	4 37	19 44	4 44	19 58	4 56	20 00
14	4 44	19 25	4 54	19 35	4 49	19 35	4 47	19 39	4 39	19 42	4 46	19 55	4 58	19 58
15	4 46	19 23	4 56	19 33	4 50	19 33	4 49	19 37	4 41	19 40	4 48	19 53	5 00	19 55
16	4 47	19 21	4 57	19 31	4 52	19 31	4 50	19 35	4 43	19 37	4 50	19 51	5 01	19 53
17	4 49	19 19	4 59	19 29	4 54	19 29	4 52	19 33	4 45	19 35	4 52	19 48	5 03	19 51
18	4 51	19 17	5 01	19 27	4 55	19 27	4 54	19 31	4 47	19 33	4 54	19 46	5 05	19 49
19	4 52	19 15	5 02	19 24	4 57	19 24	4 55	19 28	4 48	19 30	4 56	19 44	5 07	19 46
20	4 54	19 12	5 04	19 22	4 59	19 22	4 57	19 26	4 50	19 28	4 58	19 41	5 09	19 44
21	4 55	19 10	5 05	19 20	5 00	19 20	4 59	19 24	4 52	19 26	5 00	19 39	5 11	19 42
22	4 57	19 08	5 07	19 18	5 02	19 18	5 01	19 22	4 54	19 23	5 02	19 36	5 12	19 39
23	4 59	19 06	5 09	19 16	5 04	19 16	5 02	19 19	4 56	19 21	5 04	19 34	5 14	19 37
24	5 00	19 04	5 10	19 14	5 05	19 14	5 04	19 17	4 58	19 18	5 06	19 31	5 16	19 35
25	5 02	19 02	5 12	19 12	5 07	19 11	5 06	19 15	5 00	19 16	5 08	19 29	5 18	19 32
26	5 03	19 00	5 13	19 10	5 09	19 09	5 08	19 13	5 02	19 14	5 10	19 26	5 20	19 30
27	5 05	18 58	5 15	19 08	5 10	19 07	5 09	19 10	5 03	19 11	5 12	19 24	5 22	19 27
28	5 06	18 55	5 17	19 05	5 12	19 05	5 11	19 08	5 05	19 09	5 14	19 21	5 23	19 25
29	5 08	18 53	5 18	19 03	5 14	19 02	5 13	19 06	5 07	19 06	5 16	19 19	5 25	19 23
30	5 10	18 51	5 20	19 01	5 15	19 00	5 15	19 03	5 09	19 04	5 18	19 16	5 27	19 20
31	5 11	18 49	5 21	18 59	5 17	18 58	5 16	19 01	5 11	19 01	5 19	19 14	5 29	19 18

JUPITER

Day	RA h m	Dec. ° '	Transit h m	5° high 52° h m	56° h m
1	12 50.8	−4 09	16 10	21 14	21 08
11	12 56.4	−4 46	15 36	20 37	20 30
21	13 02.6	−5 26	15 03	20 01	19 53
31	13 09.3	−6 09	14 30	19 24	19 15

Diameters – equatorial 33" polar 31"

SATURN

Day	RA h m	Dec. ° '	Transit h m	5° high 52° h m	56° h m
1	8 17.3	+20 00	11 37	4 24	4 10
11	8 22.6	+19 44	11 03	3 52	3 38
21	8 27.8	+19 27	10 29	3 19	3 06
31	8 32.7	+19 11	9 54	2 47	2 33

Diameters – equatorial 16" polar 15"
Rings – major axis 37" minor axis 13"

URANUS

Day	RA h m	Dec. ° '	Transit h m	5° high 52° h m	56° h m
1	22 47.2	−8 35	2 08	21 59	22 15
11	22 45.9	−8 43	1 27	21 19	21 35
21	22 44.5	−8 52	0 47	20 39	20 56
31	22 43.0	−9 01	0 06	20 00	20 16

Diameter 4"

NEPTUNE

Day	RA h m	Dec. ° '	Transit h m	5° high 52° h m	56° h m
1	21 15.6	−16 03	0 37	3 50	3 22
11	21 14.6	−16 08	23 52	3 09	2 41
21	21 13.5	−16 13	23 12	2 28	2 00
31	21 12.5	−16 18	22 32	1 47	1 18

Diameter 2"

SEPTEMBER 2005

NINTH MONTH, 30 DAYS. *Septem* (seven), seventh month of Roman pre-Julian calendar

1	Thursday	Edgar Rice Burroughs b. 1875. Francois Mauriac d. 1970	244
2	Friday	Henri Rousseau d. 1910. J. R. R. Tolkien d. 1973	245
3	Saturday	Joseph Wright b. 1734. E. E. Cummings d. 1962	246
4	Sunday	Edvard Grieg d. 1907. Georges Simenon d. 1989	247

5	Monday	Louis XIV b. 1638. Victorien Sardou b. 1831	week 36 day 248
6	Tuesday	James II d. 1701. John Clavell d. 1994	249
7	Wednesday	Elizabeth I b. 1533. Dame Edith Sitwell b. 1887	250
8	Thursday	Richard I (The Lionheart) b. 1157. Antonín Dvořák b. 1841	251
9	Friday	Leo Tolstoy b. 1828. William I (The Conqueror) d. 1087	252
10	Saturday	Sir John Soane b. 1753. Mary Wollstonecraft Godwin d. 1797	253
11	Sunday	D. H. Lawrence b. 1885. Jessica Tandy d. 1994	254

12	Monday	Louis MacNeice b. 1907. Peter Mark Roget d. 1869	week 37 day 255
13	Tuesday	Dante Alighieri d. 1321. Leopold Stokowski d. 1977	256
14	Wednesday	Princess Grace of Monaco d. 1982. Isadora Duncan d. 1927	257
15	Thursday	Dame Agatha Christie b. 1890. Prince Henry of Wales b. 1984	258
16	Friday	Henry V b. 1387. Louis XVIII, King of France d. 1824	259
17	Saturday	Sir Frederick Ashton b. 1904. William Henry Fox Talbot d. 1871	260
18	Sunday	Dr Samuel Johnson b. 1709. William Hazlitt d. 1830	261

19	Monday	Sir William Golding b. 1911. Jeremy Irons b. 1948	week 38 day 262
20	Tuesday	Stevie Smith b. 1902. Jean Sibelius d. 1957	263
21	Wednesday	H. G. Wells b. 1866. Sir Walter Scott d. 1832	264
22	Thursday	Fay Weldon b. 1931. Irving Berlin d. 1989	265
23	Friday	Ferdinand VI, King of Spain b. 1713. Pablo Neruda d. 1973	266
24	Saturday	Horace Walpole b. 1717. F. Scott Fitzgerald b. 1896	267
25	Sunday	Mark Rothko b. 1903. Dimitry Shostakovich b. 1906	268

26	Monday	George Gershwin b. 1898. Béla Bartók d. 1945	week 39 day 269
27	Tuesday	Ariel Sharon b. 1928. Edgar Degas d. 1917	270
28	Wednesday	Herman Melville d. 1891. Sir Robert Helpman d. 1986	271
29	Thursday	W. H. Auden d. 1973. Roy Lichtenstein d. 1997	272
30	Friday	Truman Capote b. 1924. Patrick White d. 1990	273

ASTRONOMICAL PHENOMENA

d	h	
1	03	Uranus at opposition
2	00	Jupiter in conjunction with Venus. Jupiter 1° N.
2	11	Pluto at stationary point
2	12	Mercury in conjunction with Moon. Mercury 3° S.
6	22	Jupiter in conjunction with Moon. Jupiter 2° N.
7	09	Venus in conjunction with Moon. Venus 0°.6 N.
18	03	Mercury in superior conjunction
22	04	Mars in conjunction with Moon. Mars 6° S.
22	22	Sun's longitude 180° ♎
28	08	Saturn in conjunction with Moon. Saturn 4° S.

MINIMA OF ALGOL

d	h	d	h	d	h
2	00.9	13	12.2	24	23.4
4	21.8	16	09.0	27	20.2
7	18.6	19	05.8	30	17.0
10	15.4	22	02.6	17	

CONSTELLATIONS

The following constellations are near their meridian at

	d	h		d	h
August	1	24	September	15	21
August	16	23	October	1	20
September	1	22	October	16	19

Draco, Cepheus, Lyra, Cygnus, Vulpecula, Sagitta, Delphinus, Equuleus, Aquila, Aquarius and Capricornus

THE MOON

Phases, Apsides and Node	d	h	m
● New Moon	3	18	45
☽ First Quarter	11	11	37
○ Full Moon	18	02	01
☾ Last Quarter	25	06	41

Apogee (406,192 km)	1	02	46
Perigee (360,418 km)	16	13	59
Apogee (405,275 km)	28	15	26

Mean longitude of ascending node on September 1, 15°

THE SUN

s.d. 15′.9

Day	Right Ascension			Dec.		Equation of time		Rise 52°		Rise 56°		Transit		Set 52°		Set 56°		Sidereal time			Transit of first point of Aries		
	h	m	s	°	′	m	s	h	m	h	m	h	m	h	m	h	m	h	m	s	h	m	s
1	10	41	07	+8	19	−0	06	5	12	5	04	12	00	18	47	18	54	22	41	02	1	18	46
2	10	44	45	+7	58	+0	13	5	13	5	06	12	00	18	45	18	52	22	44	58	1	14	50
3	10	48	22	+7	36	+0	33	5	15	5	08	11	59	18	43	18	49	22	48	55	1	10	54
4	10	51	59	+7	14	+0	52	5	17	5	10	11	59	18	40	18	47	22	52	51	1	06	58
5	10	55	36	+6	51	+1	12	5	18	5	12	11	59	18	38	18	44	22	56	48	1	03	02
6	10	59	12	+6	29	+1	32	5	20	5	14	11	58	18	36	18	41	23	00	44	0	59	06
7	11	02	49	+6	07	+1	52	5	21	5	16	11	58	18	33	18	39	23	04	41	0	55	10
8	11	06	25	+5	44	+2	13	5	23	5	18	11	58	18	31	18	36	23	08	37	0	51	14
9	11	10	01	+5	22	+2	33	5	25	5	20	11	57	18	29	18	33	23	12	34	0	47	18
10	11	13	36	+4	59	+2	54	5	26	5	22	11	57	18	26	18	31	23	16	31	0	43	22
11	11	17	12	+4	36	+3	15	5	28	5	24	11	57	18	24	18	28	23	20	27	0	39	26
12	11	20	47	+4	13	+3	36	5	30	5	26	11	56	18	22	18	26	23	24	24	0	35	31
13	11	24	23	+3	50	+3	57	5	31	5	28	11	56	18	19	18	23	23	28	20	0	31	35
14	11	27	58	+3	27	+4	19	5	33	5	30	11	56	18	17	18	20	23	32	17	0	27	39
15	11	31	33	+3	04	+4	40	5	35	5	32	11	55	18	15	18	18	23	36	13	0	23	43
16	11	35	08	+2	41	+5	02	5	36	5	34	11	55	18	12	18	15	23	40	10	0	19	47
17	11	38	43	+2	18	+5	23	5	38	5	35	11	54	18	10	18	12	23	44	06	0	15	51
18	11	42	18	+1	55	+5	45	5	39	5	37	11	54	18	08	18	10	23	48	03	0	11	55
19	11	45	53	+1	32	+6	06	5	41	5	39	11	54	18	05	18	07	23	52	00	0	07	59
20	11	49	29	+1	08	+6	27	5	43	5	41	11	53	18	03	18	04	23	55	56	0	04	03
21	11	53	04	+0	45	+6	49	5	44	5	43	11	53	18	01	18	02	23	59	53	0	00	07
22	11	56	39	+0	22	+7	10	5	46	5	45	11	53	17	58	17	59	0	03	49	23	56	11
																				23	52	16
23	12	00	15	−0	02	+7	31	5	48	5	47	11	52	17	56	17	56	0	07	46	23	48	20
24	12	03	50	−0	25	+7	52	5	49	5	49	11	52	17	54	17	54	0	11	42	23	44	24
25	12	07	26	−0	48	+8	13	5	51	5	51	11	52	17	51	17	51	0	15	39	23	40	28
26	12	11	02	−1	12	+8	34	5	53	5	53	11	51	17	49	17	48	0	19	35	23	36	32
27	12	14	38	−1	35	+8	54	5	54	5	55	11	51	17	47	17	46	0	23	32	23	32	36
28	12	18	14	−1	58	+9	14	5	56	5	57	11	51	17	44	17	43	0	27	28	23	28	40
29	12	21	51	−2	22	+9	34	5	57	5	59	11	50	17	42	17	40	0	31	25	23	24	44
30	12	25	27	−2	45	+9	54	5	59	6	01	11	50	17	40	17	38	0	35	22	23	20	48

DURATION OF TWILIGHT (in minutes)

Latitude	52°	56°	52°	56°	52°	56°	52°	56
	1 September		11 September		21 September		31 September	
Civil	35	39	34	38	34	37	34	37
Nautical	79	89	76	85	74	82	73	80
Astronomical	127	147	120	136	116	129	113	125

THE NIGHT SKY

Mercury continues to be visible in the mornings but only for the first 4 or 5 days of the month, magnitude −1.1, low above the east-north-eastern horizon, around the time of beginning of morning civil twilight. On the morning of the 2nd the old crescent Moon, barely 1.5 days before New, passes 2 degrees north of the planet.

Venus, magnitude −4.1, is a brilliant object in the early evening sky, but still only visible for about half an hour after sunset, low above the south-western horizon. Under good conditions the four-day old crescent Moon will be seen about 5 degrees to the left of Venus on the evening of the 7th.

Mars is a conspicuous object, its magnitude brightening from −1.0 to −1.7 during the month. By the end of September it becomes visible low in the eastern sky shortly after the end of evening astronomical twilight. During the month Mars moves from Aries into Taurus.

During the night of the 21st–22nd the waning gibbous Moon passes 5 degrees north of the planet.

Jupiter, although technically an evening object, is lost in the gathering twilight and will not be seen again until it reappears in the morning skies in November.

Saturn, magnitude +0.3, continues to be visible as a morning object in the south-eastern quadrant of the sky. Saturn is in the constellation of Gemini. On the morning of the 1st the thin, waning crescent Moon, less than 3 days before New, may be detected about 6 degrees to the left of, and 2 degrees lower than the planet.

Uranus is at opposition on the 1st, in the constellation of Aquarius. Uranus is barely visible to the naked eye as its magnitude is +5.7, but it is readily located with only small optical aid.

Zodiacal Light. The morning cone may be seen reaching up from the eastern horizon along the ecliptic, before the beginning of morning twilight, from the 3rd to the 16th.

THE MOON

Day	RA h	RA m	Dec. °	Hor. par. ′	Semi-diam. ′	Sun's Co-long. °	PA of Br. Limb °	Ph. %	Age d	Rise 52° h	Rise 52° m	Rise 56° h	Rise 56° m	Transit h	Transit m	Set 52° h	Set 52° m	Set 56° h	Set 56° m
1	8	48	+22.8	54.0	14.7	238	113	7	26.9	2	04	1	39	10	26	18	30	18	49
2	9	36	+18.7	54.0	14.7	250	120	3	27.9	3	18	3	00	11	10	18	43	18	57
3	10	21	+14.0	54.2	14.8	263	133	1	28.9	4	31	4	20	11	52	18	54	19	03
4	11	05	+8.7	54.4	14.8	275	246	0	0.2	5	44	5	38	12	33	19	04	19	08
5	11	48	+3.0	54.7	14.9	287	287	1	1.2	6	56	6	55	13	13	19	13	19	12
6	12	31	−2.8	55.0	15.0	299	292	5	2.2	8	09	8	13	13	53	19	23	19	17
7	13	15	−8.6	55.5	15.1	312	293	10	3.2	9	24	9	34	14	36	19	34	19	22
8	14	01	−14.2	56.0	15.3	324	292	16	4.2	10	42	10	58	15	21	19	48	19	30
9	14	50	−19.2	56.6	15.4	336	289	25	5.2	12	04	12	27	16	10	20	06	19	42
10	15	43	−23.5	57.2	15.6	348	284	34	6.2	13	27	13	59	17	04	20	34	20	01
11	16	40	−26.7	57.9	15.8	0	278	45	7.2	14	47	15	26	18	03	21	15	20	36
12	17	42	−28.4	58.7	16.0	13	271	56	8.2	15	55	16	35	19	05	22	17	21	36
13	18	46	−28.3	59.4	16.2	25	264	67	9.2	16	44	17	19	20	08	23	38	23	04
14	19	50	−26.3	60.0	16.3	37	256	77	10.2	17	18	17	44	21	09	—	—	—	—
15	20	52	−22.5	60.5	16.5	49	249	86	11.2	17	41	17	59	22	07	1	11	0	45
16	21	51	−17.2	60.8	16.6	61	243	94	12.2	17	58	18	09	23	01	2	47	2	30
17	22	47	−10.9	60.8	16.6	74	237	98	13.2	18	11	18	16	23	53	4	21	4	12
18	23	41	−4.0	60.6	16.5	86	190	100	14.2	18	23	18	22	—	—	5	52	5	50
19	0	33	+3.0	60.0	16.4	98	69	99	15.2	18	35	18	28	0	42	7	21	7	25
20	1	24	+9.8	59.3	16.2	110	66	95	16.2	18	49	18	36	1	31	8	48	8	59
21	2	16	+15.9	58.4	15.9	122	68	89	17.2	19	05	18	45	2	21	10	15	10	33
22	3	09	+21.0	57.5	15.7	134	72	81	18.2	19	26	19	00	3	12	11	40	12	06
23	4	04	+24.9	56.6	15.4	147	77	72	19.2	19	56	19	22	4	04	13	01	13	34
24	4	59	+27.4	55.8	15.2	159	83	63	20.2	20	37	19	58	4	58	14	11	14	50
25	5	55	+28.5	55.2	15.0	171	89	53	21.2	21	32	20	53	5	52	15	07	15	46
26	6	50	+28.2	54.7	14.9	183	96	43	22.2	22	37	22	03	6	45	15	48	16	22
27	7	43	+26.6	54.3	14.8	195	102	34	23.2	23	49	23	22	7	35	16	16	16	44
28	8	34	+23.8	54.1	14.7	208	107	25	24.2	—	—	—	—	8	23	16	37	16	58
29	9	23	+20.0	54.1	14.7	220	112	17	25.2	1	04	0	43	9	07	16	52	17	07
30	10	09	+15.4	54.2	14.8	232	115	11	26.2	2	18	2	04	9	50	17	03	17	14

MERCURY

Day	RA h	RA m	Dec. °	Diam. ″	Phase %	Transit h	Transit m	5° high 52° h	5° high 52° m	5° high 56° h	5° high 56° m
1	9	44	+14.8	6	75	11	05	4	20	4	11
3	9	58	+13.9	6	82	11	11	4	31	4	23
5	10	12	+12.8	6	87	11	17	4	44	4	36
7	10	27	+11.5	5	91	11	24	4	57	4	51
9	10	41	+10.2	5	95	11	30	5	11	5	06
11	10	56	+8.8	5	97	11	37	5	25	5	21
13	11	10	+7.3	5	99	11	43	5	39	5	36
15	11	24	+5.7	5	99	11	49	5	53	5	51
17	11	38	+4.2	5	100	11	55	6	06	6	07
19	11	51	+2.6	5	100	12	00	17	39	17	37
21	12	04	+1.0	5	100	12	06	17	36	17	33
23	12	17	−0.6	5	99	12	10	17	32	17	28
25	12	29	−2.1	5	99	12	15	17	29	17	23
27	12	42	−3.7	5	98	12	19	17	25	17	18
29	12	54	−5.2	5	97	12	24	17	21	17	13
31	13	06	−6.7	5	96	12	28	17	17	17	07

VENUS

Day	RA h	RA m	Dec. °	Diam. ″	Phase %	Transit h	Transit m	5° high 52° h	5° high 52° m	5° high 56° h	5° high 56° m
1	13	05	−6.9	15	74	14	24	19	12	19	02
6	13	26	−9.4	15	73	14	26	19	00	18	48
11	13	48	−11.8	16	71	14	27	18	48	18	33
16	14	09	−14.2	16	70	14	30	18	36	18	18
21	14	32	−16.3	17	68	14	32	18	24	18	03
26	14	54	−18.4	17	66	14	35	18	12	17	48
31	15	17	−20.3	18	64	14	38	18	02	17	33

MARS

Day	RA h	RA m	Dec. °	Diam. ″	Phase %	Transit h	Transit m	5° high 52° h	5° high 52° m	5° high 56° h	5° high 56° m
1	3	02	+14.3	14	87	4	20	21	36	21	28
6	3	09	+14.8	15	88	4	07	21	21	21	12
11	3	15	+15.3	15	89	3	54	21	04	20	55
16	3	19	+15.7	16	90	3	39	20	47	20	37
21	3	23	+16.0	17	91	3	23	20	29	20	19
26	3	25	+16.3	17	92	3	05	20	10	20	00
31	3	26	+16.5	18	93	2	47	19	50	19	40

SUNRISE AND SUNSET

	London 0°05′ 51°30′		Bristol 2°35′ 51°28′		Birmingham 1°55′ 52°28′		Manchester 2°15′ 53°28′		Newcastle 1°37′ 54°59′		Glasgow 4°14′ 55°52′		Belfast 5°56′ 54°35′	
	h m	h m	h m	h m	h m	h m	h m	h m	h m	h m	h m	h m	h m	h m
1	5 13	18 47	5 23	18 57	5 19	18 56	5 18	18 59	5 13	18 59	5 21	19 11	5 31	19 15
2	5 14	18 44	5 25	18 54	5 20	18 53	5 20	18 56	5 15	18 56	5 23	19 08	5 33	19 13
3	5 16	18 42	5 26	18 52	5 22	18 51	5 22	18 54	5 16	18 54	5 25	19 06	5 34	19 10
4	5 18	18 40	5 28	18 50	5 24	18 49	5 23	18 51	5 18	18 51	5 27	19 03	5 36	19 08
5	5 19	18 38	5 29	18 48	5 25	18 46	5 25	18 49	5 20	18 49	5 29	19 01	5 38	19 05
6	5 21	18 35	5 31	18 45	5 27	18 44	5 27	18 47	5 22	18 46	5 31	18 58	5 40	19 03
7	5 22	18 33	5 32	18 43	5 29	18 42	5 29	18 44	5 24	18 44	5 33	18 55	5 42	19 00
8	5 24	18 31	5 34	18 41	5 30	18 39	5 30	18 42	5 26	18 41	5 35	18 53	5 44	18 58
9	5 26	18 29	5 36	18 38	5 32	18 37	5 32	18 39	5 28	18 39	5 37	18 50	5 45	18 55
10	5 27	18 26	5 37	18 36	5 34	18 35	5 34	18 37	5 30	18 36	5 39	18 48	5 47	18 53
11	5 29	18 24	5 39	18 34	5 35	18 32	5 36	18 34	5 31	18 33	5 41	18 45	5 49	18 50
12	5 30	18 22	5 40	18 32	5 37	18 30	5 37	18 32	5 33	18 31	5 43	18 42	5 51	18 48
13	5 32	18 19	5 42	18 29	5 39	18 27	5 39	18 30	5 35	18 28	5 45	18 40	5 53	18 45
14	5 34	18 17	5 44	18 27	5 40	18 25	5 41	18 27	5 37	18 26	5 47	18 37	5 55	18 43
15	5 35	18 15	5 45	18 25	5 42	18 23	5 43	18 25	5 39	18 23	5 49	18 34	5 56	18 40
16	5 37	18 12	5 47	18 22	5 44	18 20	5 44	18 22	5 41	18 21	5 51	18 32	5 58	18 38
17	5 38	18 10	5 48	18 20	5 45	18 18	5 46	18 20	5 43	18 18	5 52	18 29	6 00	18 35
18	5 40	18 08	5 50	18 18	5 47	18 16	5 48	18 17	5 44	18 16	5 54	18 26	6 02	18 33
19	5 42	18 06	5 52	18 16	5 49	18 13	5 49	18 15	5 46	18 13	5 56	18 24	6 04	18 30
20	5 43	18 03	5 53	18 13	5 50	18 11	5 51	18 12	5 48	18 10	5 58	18 21	6 06	18 27
21	5 45	18 01	5 55	18 11	5 52	18 08	5 53	18 10	5 50	18 08	6 00	18 18	6 07	18 25
22	5 46	17 59	5 56	18 09	5 54	18 06	5 55	18 08	5 52	18 05	6 02	18 16	6 09	18 22
23	5 48	17 56	5 58	18 06	5 55	18 04	5 56	18 05	5 54	18 03	6 04	18 13	6 11	18 20
24	5 50	17 54	6 00	18 04	5 57	18 01	5 58	18 03	5 56	18 00	6 06	18 11	6 13	18 17
25	5 51	17 52	6 01	18 02	5 59	17 59	6 00	18 00	5 57	17 58	6 08	18 08	6 15	18 15
26	5 53	17 49	6 03	17 59	6 00	17 57	6 02	17 58	5 59	17 55	6 10	18 05	6 17	18 12
27	5 54	17 47	6 04	17 57	6 02	17 54	6 04	17 55	6 01	17 52	6 12	18 03	6 18	18 10
28	5 56	17 45	6 06	17 55	6 04	17 52	6 05	17 53	6 03	17 50	6 14	18 00	6 20	18 07
29	5 58	17 43	6 08	17 53	6 05	17 49	6 07	17 50	6 05	17 47	6 16	17 57	6 22	18 05
30	5 59	17 40	6 09	17 50	6 07	17 47	6 09	17 48	6 07	17 45	6 18	17 55	6 24	18 02

JUPITER

Day	RA	Dec.	Transit	5° high 52°	56°
	h m	° ′	h m	h m	h m
1	13 10.0	−6 14	14 27	19 21	19 12
11	13 17.2	−6 59	13 55	18 44	18 35
21	13 24.7	−7 45	13 23	18 08	17 58
31	13 32.6	−8 32	12 52	17 32	17 21

Diameters – equatorial 31″ polar 29″

SATURN

Day	RA	Dec.	Transit	5° high 52°	56°
	h m	° ′	h m	h m	h m
1	8 33.2	+19 09	9 51	2 43	2 30
11	8 37.8	+18 53	9 16	2 10	1 57
21	8 42.0	+18 39	8 41	1 36	1 23
31	8 45.8	+18 25	8 05	1 02	0 49

Diameters – equatorial 17″ polar 15″
Rings – major axis 38″ minor axis 12″

URANUS

Day	RA	Dec.	Transit	10° high 52°	56°
	h m	° ′	h m	h m	h m
1	22 42.8	−9 02	0 02	4 04	3 48
11	22 41.3	−9 10	23 17	3 22	3 06
21	22 39.9	−9 19	22 36	2 41	2 24
31	22 38.6	−9 27	21 56	1 59	1 42

Diameter 4″

NEPTUNE

Day	RA	Dec.	Transit	10° high 52°	56°
	h m	° ′	h m	h m	h m
1	21 12.4	−16 18	22 28	1 43	1 14
11	21 11.5	−16 22	21 47	1 03	0 33
21	21 10.7	−16 26	21 07	0 22	23 49
31	21 10.0	−16 29	20 27	23 38	23 08

Diameter 2″

OCTOBER 2005

TENTH MONTH, 31 DAYS. *Octo* (eighth), eighth month of Roman pre-Julian calendar

1	*Saturday*	Henry III b. 1207. Sir Edwin Landseer d. 1873	274
2	*Sunday*	Richard III b. 1452. Graham Greene b. 1904	275
3	*Monday*	William Morris d. 1896. Jean Anouilh d. 1987	week 40 day 276
4	*Tuesday*	Jean Francois Millet b. 1814. Rembrandt d. 1669	277
5	*Wednesday*	Václav Havel b. 1936. Joachim Patinir d. 1524	278
6	*Thursday*	Le Corbusier b. 1887. Lord Tennyson d. 1862	279
7	*Friday*	James Whitcomb Riley b. 1849. Edgar Allen Poe d. 1849	280
8	*Saturday*	John Cowper Powys b. 1872. Henry Fielding d. 1754	281
9	*Sunday*	Giuseppe Verdi b. 1813. André Maurois d. 1967	282
10	*Monday*	James Clavell b. 1924. Harold Pinter b. 1930	week 41 day 283
11	*Tuesday*	Francois Mauriac b. 1885. Jean Cocteau d. 1963	284
12	*Wednesday*	Edward VI b. 1537. Ralph Vaughan Williams b. 1872	285
13	*Thursday*	Alan Ramsay b. 1713. Margaret Thatcher b. 1925	286
14	*Friday*	Harold II d. 1066. Leonard Bernstein d. 1990	287
15	*Saturday*	Sir P. G. Wodehouse b. 1881. James Tissot b. 1836	288
16	*Sunday*	Oscar Wilde b. 1854. Marie-Antoinette d. 1793	289
17	*Monday*	Georg Büchner b. 1813. Frédéric Chopin d. 1849	week 42 day 290
18	*Tuesday*	Canaletto b. 1697. Charles Babbage d. 1871	291
19	*Wednesday*	Leigh Hunt b. 1784. Jean-George Navarre d. 1810	292
20	*Thursday*	Sir Christopher Wren b. 1632. Thomas Hughes b. 1822	293
21	*Friday*	Samuel Taylor Coleridge b. 1772. Jack Kerouac d. 1969	294
22	*Saturday*	Franz Liszt b. 1811. Paul Cézanne d. 1906	295
23	*Sunday*	Robert Bridges b. 1844. Michael Crichton b. 1942	296
24	*Monday*	Luciano Berio b. 1925. Jane Seymour d. 1537	week 43 day 297
25	*Tuesday*	Pablo Picasso b. 1881. Geoffrey Chaucer d. 1400	298
26	*Wednesday*	Domenico Scarlatti b. 1685. William Hogarth d. 1764	299
27	*Thursday*	Dylan Thomas b. 1914. Sylvia Plath b. 1932	300
28	*Friday*	Francis Bacon b. 1909. Ted Hughes d. 1998	301
29	*Saturday*	Joseph Pulitzer d. 1911. Sir Kenneth Macmillan d. 1992	302
30	*Sunday*	Ezra Pound b. 1885. Robert Volkmann d. 1883	303
31	*Monday*	John Evelyn b. 1626. Augustus John d. 1961	week 44 day 304

ASTRONOMICAL PHENOMENA

d	h	
1	22	Mars at stationary point
3	10	Annular eclipse of Sun
4	11	Mercury in conjunction with Moon.
		Mercury 0°.8 N.
4	15	Jupiter in conjunction with Moon. Jupiter 2° N.
5	22	Jupiter in conjunction with Mercury. Jupiter 1° N.
7	06	Venus in conjunction with Moon. Venus 1° N.
17	12	Partial eclipse of Moon
19	11	Mars in conjunction with Moon. Mars 5° S.
22	13	Jupiter in conjunction
23	08	Sun's longitude 210° ♏.
25	19	Saturn in conjunction with Moon. Saturn 4° S.
26	23	Neptune at stationary point

MINIMA OF ALGOL

d	h	d	h	d	h
3	13.9	15	01.1	26	12.4
6	10.7	17	21.9	29	09.2
9	07.5	20	18.7		
12	04.3	23	15.5		

CONSTELLATIONS

The following constellations are near their meridian at

	d	h		d	h
September	1	24	October	16	21
September	15	23	November	1	20
October	1	22	November	15	19

Ursa Major (below the Pole), Cepheus, Cassiopeia, Cygnus, Lacerta, Andromeda, Pegasus, Capricornus, Aquarius and Piscis Austrinus

THE MOON

Phases, Apsides and Node	d	h	m
● New Moon	3	10	28
☽ First Quarter	10	19	01
○ Full Moon	17	12	14
☾ Last Quarter	25	01	17
Perigee (365,473 km)	14	14	07
Apogee (404,455 km)	26	09	35

Mean longitude of ascending node on October 1, 14°

THE SUN

s.d. 16′.1

Day	Right Ascension h	m	s	Dec. − °	′	Equation of time m	s	Rise 52° h	m	56° h	m	Transit h	m	Set 52° h	m	56° h	m	Sidereal time h	m	s	Transit of first point of Aries h	m	s
1	12	29	04	3	08	+10	14	6	01	6	03	11	50	17	37	17	35	0	39	18	23	16	52
2	12	32	42	3	32	+10	33	6	03	6	05	11	49	17	35	17	33	0	43	15	23	12	56
3	12	36	19	3	55	+10	52	6	04	6	07	11	49	17	33	17	30	0	47	11	23	09	01
4	12	39	57	4	18	+11	10	6	06	6	09	11	49	17	30	17	27	0	51	08	23	05	05
5	12	43	36	4	41	+11	29	6	08	6	11	11	48	17	28	17	25	0	55	04	23	01	09
6	12	47	14	5	04	+11	46	6	09	6	13	11	48	17	26	17	22	0	59	01	22	57	13
7	12	50	54	5	27	+12	04	6	11	6	15	11	48	17	24	17	20	1	02	57	22	53	17
8	12	54	33	5	50	+12	21	6	13	6	17	11	48	17	21	17	17	1	06	54	22	49	21
9	12	58	13	6	13	+12	38	6	14	6	19	11	47	17	19	17	14	1	10	51	22	45	25
10	13	01	53	6	36	+12	54	6	16	6	21	11	47	17	17	17	12	1	14	47	22	41	29
11	13	05	34	6	59	+13	10	6	18	6	23	11	47	17	15	17	09	1	18	44	22	37	33
12	13	09	15	7	21	+13	25	6	20	6	25	11	46	17	12	17	07	1	22	40	22	33	37
13	13	12	57	7	44	+13	40	6	21	6	27	11	46	17	10	17	04	1	26	37	22	29	41
14	13	16	39	8	06	+13	54	6	23	6	29	11	46	17	08	17	02	1	30	33	22	25	46
15	13	20	22	8	28	+14	08	6	25	6	31	11	46	17	06	16	59	1	34	30	22	21	50
16	13	24	05	8	50	+14	21	6	26	6	33	11	46	17	04	16	57	1	38	26	22	17	54
17	13	27	49	9	12	+14	34	6	28	6	35	11	45	17	02	16	54	1	42	23	22	13	58
18	13	31	33	9	34	+14	46	6	30	6	38	11	45	16	59	16	52	1	46	20	22	10	02
19	13	35	19	9	56	+14	58	6	32	6	40	11	45	16	57	16	49	1	50	16	22	06	06
20	13	39	04	10	18	+15	09	6	33	6	42	11	45	16	55	16	47	1	54	13	22	02	10
21	13	42	51	10	39	+15	19	6	35	6	44	11	45	16	53	16	45	1	58	09	21	58	14
22	13	46	38	11	00	+15	28	6	37	6	46	11	44	16	51	16	42	2	02	06	21	54	18
23	13	50	25	11	22	+15	37	6	39	6	48	11	44	16	49	16	40	2	06	02	21	50	22
24	13	54	14	11	43	+15	45	6	41	6	50	11	44	16	47	16	37	2	09	59	21	46	26
25	13	58	03	12	03	+15	53	6	42	6	52	11	44	16	45	16	35	2	13	55	21	42	31
26	14	01	53	12	24	+15	59	6	44	6	54	11	44	16	43	16	33	2	17	52	21	38	35
27	14	05	43	12	44	+16	05	6	46	6	56	11	44	16	41	16	30	2	21	49	21	34	39
28	14	09	34	13	05	+16	11	6	48	6	59	11	44	16	39	16	28	2	25	45	21	30	43
29	14	13	27	13	25	+16	15	6	49	7	01	11	44	16	37	16	26	2	29	42	21	26	47
30	14	17	19	13	44	+16	19	6	51	7	03	11	44	16	35	16	24	2	33	38	21	22	51
31	14	21	13	14	04	+16	22	6	53	7	05	11	44	16	33	16	21	2	37	35	21	18	55

DURATION OF TWILIGHT (in minutes)

Latitude	52°	56°	52°	56°	52°	56°	52°	56
	1 October		11 October		21 October		31 October	
Civil	34	37	34	37	34	38	35	39
Nautical	73	80	73	80	74	81	75	83
Astronomical	113	125	112	124	113	124	114	126

THE NIGHT SKY

Mercury remains too close to the Sun for observation throughout the month.

Venus, magnitude −4.3, continues to be a brilliant object in the early evenings, low above the south-western horizon for a short while after sunset. This interval increases slightly during October so that by the end of the month Venus is visible for almost an hour. Under good conditions the waxing crescent Moon will be seen about 6 degrees to the left of the planet on the evening of the 7th.

Mars reaches its first stationary point on the 1st, and then moves retrograde from Taurus back into Aries during the month. Its magnitude is still brightening (from −1.7 to −2.3) during October as it approaches opposition next month. Due to the eccentricity of its orbit the closest approach of Mars to the Earth during this apparition (69 million kilometres) occurs on the last day of October, one week before opposition. Mars is already visible for most of the night and by the end of the month may be seen rising in the east about an hour after sunset. The Moon, just past Full, is near the planet around the 19th–20th.

Jupiter passes through conjunction on the 22nd and thus remains too close to the Sun for observation throughout the month.

Saturn, magnitude +0.3, continues to be visible in the eastern sky in the early mornings. It is noticeably brighter than the nearby bright stars in Gemini, Castor and Pollux, which are of magnitude +1.9 and +1.1 respectively. The Moon, around Last Quarter, is near the planet on the mornings of the 25th and 26th.

THE MOON

Day	RA h	RA m	Dec. °	Hor. par. ′	Semi-diam. ′	Sun's Co-long. °	PA of Br. Limb °	Ph. %	Age d	Rise 52° h	Rise 52° m	Rise 56° h	Rise 56° m	Transit h	Transit m	Set 52° h	Set 52° m	Set 56° h	Set 56° m
1	10	53	+10.3	54.5	14.8	244	118	6	27.2	3	31	3	22	10	31	17	13	17	18
2	11	36	+4.6	54.8	14.9	256	120	2	28.2	4	43	4	40	11	11	17	23	17	23
3	12	19	−1.2	55.2	15.0	269	123	0	29.2	5	56	5	59	11	52	17	32	17	27
4	13	03	−7.1	55.6	15.2	281	296	0	0.6	7	11	7	19	12	34	17	42	17	33
5	13	49	−12.9	56.1	15.3	293	295	3	1.6	8	30	8	44	13	19	17	55	17	40
6	14	38	−18.1	56.6	15.4	305	292	7	2.6	9	51	10	13	14	07	18	12	17	50
7	15	31	−22.7	57.1	15.6	318	288	13	3.6	11	15	11	45	15	00	18	37	18	06
8	16	27	−26.1	57.6	15.7	330	282	21	4.6	12	37	13	14	15	57	19	13	18	35
9	17	27	−28.2	58.1	15.8	342	275	31	5.6	13	48	14	29	16	57	20	07	19	26
10	18	29	−28.5	58.6	16.0	354	268	41	6.6	14	42	15	20	17	59	21	20	20	43
11	19	32	−27.1	59.0	16.1	6	261	52	7.6	15	20	15	49	18	59	22	47	22	18
12	20	33	−23.9	59.5	16.2	18	254	64	8.6	15	45	16	07	19	56	—	—	23	59
13	21	32	−19.2	59.8	16.3	31	249	75	9.6	16	03	16	17	20	50	0	19	—	—
14	22	27	−13.4	60.0	16.3	43	245	84	10.6	16	17	16	25	21	41	1	51	1	39
15	23	20	−6.8	60.0	16.3	55	243	92	11.6	16	30	16	31	22	30	3	21	3	16
16	0	11	+0.1	59.8	16.3	67	244	97	12.6	16	41	16	37	23	18	4	49	4	50
17	1	02	+7.0	59.4	16.2	79	250	100	13.6	16	54	16	44	—	—	6	16	6	24
18	1	54	+13.4	58.8	16.0	91	56	100	14.6	17	08	16	52	0	08	7	44	7	58
19	2	47	+19.0	58.1	15.8	104	65	97	15.6	17	27	17	04	0	58	9	11	9	33
20	3	41	+23.5	57.4	15.6	116	71	92	16.6	17	53	17	22	1	51	10	36	11	06
21	4	38	+26.6	56.6	15.4	128	77	86	17.6	18	30	17	52	2	46	11	53	12	30
22	5	35	+28.3	55.8	15.2	140	84	78	18.6	19	19	18	40	3	41	12	57	13	37
23	6	31	+28.5	55.2	15.0	152	91	69	19.6	20	22	19	45	4	35	13	45	14	22
24	7	26	+27.3	54.7	14.9	164	97	60	20.6	21	33	21	03	5	27	14	18	14	49
25	8	18	+24.8	54.4	14.8	177	103	51	21.6	22	47	22	24	6	16	14	41	15	05
26	9	07	+21.3	54.2	14.8	189	108	41	22.6	—	—	23	44	7	02	14	58	15	16
27	9	54	+17.0	54.2	14.8	201	111	32	23.6	0	01	—	—	7	45	15	11	15	23
28	10	39	+12.0	54.4	14.8	213	114	24	24.6	1	14	1	03	8	27	15	22	15	29
29	11	22	+6.5	54.7	14.9	225	115	16	25.6	2	26	2	21	9	07	15	31	15	33
30	12	05	+0.7	55.2	15.0	238	115	9	26.6	3	39	3	39	9	48	15	40	15	38
31	12	49	−5.2	55.7	15.2	250	113	4	27.6	4	54	4	59	10	29	15	50	15	43

MERCURY

Day	RA h	RA m	Dec. °	Diam. ″	Phase %	Transit h	Transit m	5° high 52° h	5° high 52° m	5° high 56° h	5° high 56° m
1	13	06	−6.7	5	96	12	28	17	17	17	07
3	13	18	−8.1	5	95	12	32	17	13	17	02
5	13	29	−9.5	5	94	12	35	17	09	16	56
7	13	41	−10.9	5	93	12	39	17	05	16	51
9	13	52	−12.2	5	92	12	42	17	00	16	45
11	14	04	−13.5	5	91	12	46	16	56	16	39
13	14	15	−14.7	5	89	12	49	16	52	16	33
15	14	26	−15.9	5	88	12	53	16	47	16	27
17	14	37	−17.0	5	86	12	56	16	43	16	21
19	14	49	−18.0	5	85	12	59	16	39	16	15
21	15	00	−19.0	5	83	13	02	16	35	16	09
23	15	10	−20.0	6	81	13	05	16	31	16	03
25	15	21	−20.8	6	79	13	08	16	27	15	58
27	15	32	−21.6	6	76	13	11	16	24	15	52
29	15	42	−22.3	6	73	13	13	16	20	15	47
31	15	52	−22.9	6	70	13	15	16	17	15	41

VENUS

Day	RA h	RA m	Dec. °	Diam. ″	Phase %	Transit h	Transit m	5° high 52° h	5° high 52° m	5° high 56° h	5° high 56° m
1	15	17	−20.3	18	64	14	38	18	02	17	33
6	15	40	−21.9	19	62	14	41	17	51	17	19
11	16	03	−23.4	20	60	14	44	17	42	17	05
16	16	26	−24.6	21	58	14	48	17	35	16	53
21	16	50	−25.6	22	56	14	52	17	29	16	41
26	17	13	−26.4	23	54	14	55	17	25	16	32
31	17	36	−26.9	24	51	14	59	17	23	16	27

MARS

Day	RA h	RA m	Dec. °	Diam. ″	Phase %	Transit h	Transit m	5° high 52° h	5° high 52° m	5° high 56° h	5° high 56° m
1	3	26	+16.5	18	93	2	47	19	50	19	40
6	3	26	+16.6	18	95	2	26	19	29	19	18
11	3	23	+16.6	19	96	2	04	19	07	18	56
16	3	20	+16.6	19	97	1	41	18	43	18	33
21	3	15	+16.6	20	98	1	16	18	19	18	08
26	3	09	+16.4	20	99	0	51	17	54	17	43
31	3	02	+16.2	20	100	0	24	17	28	17	18

SUNRISE AND SUNSET

	London 0°05′	51°30′	Bristol 2°35′	51°28′	Birmingham 1°55′	52°28′	Manchester 2°15′	53°28′	Newcastle 1°37′	54°59′	Glasgow 4°14′	55°52′	Belfast 5°56′	54°35′
	h m	h m	h m	h m	h m	h m	h m	h m	h m	h m	h m	h m	h m	h m
1	6 01	17 38	6 11	17 48	6 09	17 45	6 11	17 46	6 09	17 42	6 20	17 52	6 26	18 00
2	6 03	17 36	6 13	17 46	6 10	17 42	6 12	17 43	6 11	17 40	6 22	17 50	6 28	17 57
3	6 04	17 33	6 14	17 43	6 12	17 40	6 14	17 41	6 13	17 37	6 24	17 47	6 30	17 55
4	6 06	17 31	6 16	17 41	6 14	17 38	6 16	17 38	6 15	17 35	6 26	17 44	6 32	17 52
5	6 08	17 29	6 18	17 39	6 16	17 35	6 18	17 36	6 16	17 32	6 28	17 42	6 33	17 50
6	6 09	17 27	6 19	17 37	6 17	17 33	6 20	17 34	6 18	17 30	6 30	17 39	6 35	17 47
7	6 11	17 24	6 21	17 34	6 19	17 31	6 21	17 31	6 20	17 27	6 32	17 37	6 37	17 45
8	6 13	17 22	6 23	17 32	6 21	17 29	6 23	17 29	6 22	17 25	6 34	17 34	6 39	17 42
9	6 14	17 20	6 24	17 30	6 23	17 26	6 25	17 27	6 24	17 22	6 36	17 31	6 41	17 40
10	6 16	17 18	6 26	17 28	6 24	17 24	6 27	17 24	6 26	17 20	6 38	17 29	6 43	17 37
11	6 18	17 16	6 28	17 26	6 26	17 22	6 29	17 22	6 28	17 17	6 40	17 26	6 45	17 35
12	6 19	17 13	6 29	17 23	6 28	17 20	6 30	17 20	6 30	17 15	6 42	17 24	6 47	17 33
13	6 21	17 11	6 31	17 21	6 30	17 17	6 32	17 17	6 32	17 12	6 44	17 21	6 49	17 30
14	6 23	17 09	6 33	17 19	6 31	17 15	6 34	17 15	6 34	17 10	6 46	17 19	6 51	17 28
15	6 24	17 07	6 34	17 17	6 33	17 13	6 36	17 13	6 36	17 08	6 48	17 16	6 53	17 25
16	6 26	17 05	6 36	17 15	6 35	17 11	6 38	17 10	6 38	17 05	6 50	17 14	6 55	17 23
17	6 28	17 03	6 38	17 13	6 37	17 08	6 40	17 08	6 40	17 03	6 52	17 11	6 56	17 21
18	6 29	17 01	6 39	17 11	6 38	17 06	6 42	17 06	6 42	17 00	6 54	17 09	6 58	17 18
19	6 31	16 59	6 41	17 09	6 40	17 04	6 43	17 04	6 44	16 58	6 56	17 07	7 00	17 16
20	6 33	16 56	6 43	17 07	6 42	17 02	6 45	17 01	6 46	16 56	6 58	17 04	7 02	17 14
21	6 35	16 54	6 45	17 05	6 44	17 00	6 47	16 59	6 48	16 53	7 00	17 02	7 04	17 11
22	6 36	16 52	6 46	17 02	6 46	16 58	6 49	16 57	6 50	16 51	7 02	16 59	7 06	17 09
23	6 38	16 50	6 48	17 00	6 47	16 56	6 51	16 55	6 52	16 49	7 05	16 57	7 08	17 07
24	6 40	16 48	6 50	16 58	6 49	16 54	6 53	16 53	6 54	16 46	7 07	16 55	7 10	17 05
25	6 42	16 46	6 51	16 56	6 51	16 52	6 55	16 51	6 56	16 44	7 09	16 52	7 12	17 02
26	6 43	16 44	6 53	16 55	6 53	16 50	6 57	16 48	6 58	16 42	7 11	16 50	7 14	17 00
27	6 45	16 43	6 55	16 53	6 55	16 48	6 59	16 46	7 00	16 40	7 13	16 48	7 16	16 58
28	6 47	16 41	6 57	16 51	6 57	16 46	7 00	16 44	7 02	16 38	7 15	16 45	7 18	16 56
29	6 49	16 39	6 59	16 49	6 58	16 44	7 02	16 42	7 04	16 35	7 17	16 43	7 20	16 54
30	6 50	16 37	7 00	16 47	7 00	16 42	7 04	16 40	7 06	16 33	7 19	16 41	7 22	16 52
31	6 52	16 35	7 02	16 45	7 02	16 40	7 06	16 38	7 08	16 31	7 21	16 39	7 24	16 50

JUPITER

Day	RA		Dec.		Transit		5° high			
							52°		56°	
	h	m	°	′	h	m	h	m	h	m
1	13	32.6	−8	32	12	52	8	11	8	22
11	13	40.7	−9	19	12	20	7	44	7	56
21	13	48.9	−10	06	11	49	7	17	7	30
31	13	57.2	−10	52	11	18	6	51	7	04

Diameters – equatorial 31″ polar 29″

SATURN

Day	RA		Dec.		Transit		5° high			
							52°		56°	
	h	m	°	′	h	m	h	m	h	m
1	8	45.8	+18	25	8	05	1	02	0	49
11	8	49.0	+18	14	7	29	0	27	0	15
21	8	51.7	+18	05	6	53	23	48	23	35
31	8	53.7	+17	58	6	15	23	11	22	59

Diameters – equatorial 18″ polar 16″
Rings – major axis 40″ minor axis 12″

URANUS

Day	RA		Dec.		Transit		10° high			
							52°		56°	
	h	m	°	′	h	m	h	m	h	m
1	22	38.6	−9	27	21	56	1	59	1	42
11	22	37.5	−9	33	21	15	1	18	1	01
21	22	36.5	−9	38	20	35	0	37	0	20
31	22	35.9	−9	42	19	55	23	53	23	36

Diameter 4″

NEPTUNE

Day	RA		Dec.		Transit		10° high			
							52°		56°	
	h	m	°	′	h	m	h	m	h	m
1	21	10.0	−16	29	20	27	23	38	23	08
11	21	09.6	−16	31	19	48	22	58	22	28
21	21	09.3	−16	32	19	08	22	18	21	48
31	21	09.3	−16	32	18	29	21	39	21	09

Diameter 2″

NOVEMBER 2005

ELEVENTH MONTH, 30 DAYS. *Novem* (nine), ninth month of Roman pre-Julian calendar

1	Tuesday	Naomi Mitchison b. 1897. Ezra Pound d. 1972	305
2	Wednesday	Marie-Antoinette b. 1755. George Bernard Shaw d. 1950	306
3	Thursday	Karl Baedeker b. 1801. Henri Matisse d. 1954	307
4	Friday	Felix Mendelssohn d. 1847. Wilfred Owen d. 1918	308
5	Saturday	Sam Shepard b. 1943. Maurice Utrillo d. 1955	309
6	Sunday	Pyotr Ilyich Tchaikovsky d. 1893. Kate Greenaway d. 1901	310

7	Monday	Albert Camus b. 1913. Steve McQueen d. 1980	week 45 day 311
8	Tuesday	Margaret Mitchell b. 1900. John Milton d. 1674	312
9	Wednesday	Edward VII b. 1841. Dylan Thomas d. 1953	313
10	Thursday	William Hogarth b. 1697. Oliver Goldsmith b. 1730	314
11	Friday	Fyodor Dostoevsky b. 1821. Sir Edward German d. 1936	315
12	Saturday	Auguste Rodin b. 1840. Cnut the Great d. 1035	316
13	Sunday	Robert Louis Stevenson b. 1850. Camile Pissarro d. 1903	317

14	Monday	Dame Elizabeth Frink b. 1930. Prince of Wales b. 1948	week 46 day 318
15	Tuesday	Marianne Moore b. 1887. George Romney d. 1802	319
16	Wednesday	Clarke Gable d. 1960. Henry III d. 1272	320
17	Thursday	Catherine II (The Great) of Russia d. 1796. Auguste Rodin d. 1917	321
18	Friday	Sir David Wilkie b. 1785. Marcel Proust d. 1922	322
19	Saturday	Charles I b. 1600. Franz Schubert d. 1828	323
20	Sunday	Leo Tolstoy d. 1910. Queen Alexandra d. 1925	324

21	Monday	Voltaire b. 1694. Henry Purcell d. 1695	week 47 day 325
22	Tuesday	Benjamin Britten b. 1913. C. S. Lewis d. 1963	326
23	Wednesday	James Thomson b. 1834. Roald Dahl d. 1990	327
24	Thursday	Laurence Sterne b. 1713. Henri de Toulouse-Lautrec b. 1864	328
25	Friday	Upton Sinclair d. 1968. Sir Anton Dolin d. 1983	329
26	Saturday	Tina Turner b. 1939. Isabella I d. 1504	330
27	Sunday	Alexander Dumas d. 1895. Eugene O'Neill d. 1953	331

28	Monday	Nancy Mitford b. 1904. Enid Blyton d. 1968	week 48 day 332
29	Tuesday	Louisa May Alcott b. 1832. Giacomo Puccini d. 1924	333
30	Wednesday	Mark Twain b. 1835. Oscar Wilde d. 1900	334

ASTRONOMICAL PHENOMENA

d h
1 10 Jupiter in conjunction with Moon. Jupiter 3° N.
3 16 Mercury at greatest elongation E.24°
3 19 Venus at greatest elongation E.47°
3 23 Mercury in conjunction with Moon. Mercury 1° N.
5 19 Venus in conjunction with Moon. Venus 1° N.
7 08 Mars at opposition
14 06 Mercury at stationary point
15 05 Mars in conjunction with Moon. Mars 3° S.
16 00 Uranus at stationary point
22 05 Saturn in conjunction with Moon. Saturn 4° S.
22 05 Sun's longitude 240° ♐
22 09 Saturn at stationary point
24 16 Mercury in inferior conjunction
29 06 Jupiter in conjunction with Moon. Jupiter 3° N.
30 15 Mercury in conjunction with Moon. Mercury 6° N.

MINIMA OF ALGOL

d	h	d	h	d	h
1	06.0	12	17.2	24	04.5
4	02.8	15	14.1	27	01.3
6	23.6	18	10.9	29	22.1
9	20.4	21	07.7		

CONSTELLATIONS

The following constellations are near their meridian at

	d	h		d	h
October	1	24	November	15	21
October	16	23	December	1	20
November	1	22	December	16	19

Ursa Major (below the Pole), Cepheus, Cassiopeia, Andromeda, Pegasus, Pisces, Acquarius and Cetus

THE MOON

Phases, Apsides and Node	d	h	m
● New Moon	2	01	25
☽ First Quarter	9	01	57
○ Full Moon	16	00	58
☾ Last Quarter	23	22	11
Perigee (370,046 km)	10	00	28
Apogee (404,331 km)	23	06	16

Mean longitude of ascending node on November 1, 12°

THE SUN

s.d. 16'.2

Day	Right Ascension			Dec. −	Equation of time		Rise 52°		Rise 56°		Transit		Set 52°		Set 56°		Sidereal time			Transit of first point of Aries		
	h	m	s	°	m	s	h	m	h	m	h	m	h	m	h	m	h	m	s	h	m	s
1	14	25	08	14	23	+16	24	6	55	7	07	11	44	16	32	16	19	2	41	31	21	14	59
2	14	29	03	14	43	+16	25	6	57	7	09	11	44	16	30	16	17	2	45	28	21	11	03
3	14	32	59	15	01	+16	26	6	59	7	11	11	44	16	28	16	15	2	49	24	21	07	07
4	14	36	56	15	20	+16	25	7	00	7	13	11	44	16	26	16	13	2	53	21	21	03	11
5	14	40	54	15	39	+16	24	7	02	7	16	11	44	16	24	16	11	2	57	18	20	59	16
6	14	44	52	15	57	+16	22	7	04	7	18	11	44	16	23	16	09	3	01	14	20	55	20
7	14	48	51	16	15	+16	19	7	06	7	20	11	44	16	21	16	07	3	05	11	20	51	24
8	14	52	52	16	32	+16	16	7	08	7	22	11	44	16	19	16	05	3	09	07	20	47	28
9	14	56	53	16	49	+16	11	7	09	7	24	11	44	16	18	16	03	3	13	04	20	43	32
10	15	00	54	17	07	+16	06	7	11	7	26	11	44	16	16	16	01	3	17	00	20	39	36
11	15	04	57	17	23	+16	00	7	13	7	28	11	44	16	15	15	59	3	20	57	20	35	40
12	15	09	01	17	40	+15	53	7	15	7	30	11	44	16	13	15	57	3	24	53	20	31	44
13	15	13	05	17	56	+15	45	7	16	7	32	11	44	16	12	15	55	3	28	50	20	27	48
14	15	17	10	18	12	+15	37	7	18	7	35	11	44	16	10	15	54	3	32	47	20	23	52
15	15	21	16	18	27	+15	27	7	20	7	37	11	45	16	09	15	52	3	36	43	20	19	56
16	15	25	23	18	42	+15	17	7	22	7	39	11	45	16	07	15	50	3	40	40	20	16	01
17	15	29	30	18	57	+15	06	7	23	7	41	11	45	16	06	15	49	3	44	36	20	12	05
18	15	33	39	19	12	+14	54	7	25	7	43	11	45	16	05	15	47	3	48	33	20	08	09
19	15	37	48	19	26	+14	41	7	27	7	45	11	45	16	03	15	45	3	52	29	20	04	13
20	15	41	58	19	40	+14	27	7	29	7	47	11	46	16	02	15	44	3	56	26	20	00	17
21	15	46	09	19	53	+14	13	7	30	7	49	11	46	16	01	15	43	4	00	22	19	56	21
22	15	50	21	20	06	+13	58	7	32	7	51	11	46	16	00	15	41	4	04	19	19	52	25
23	15	54	34	20	19	+13	42	7	33	7	53	11	46	15	59	15	40	4	08	16	19	48	29
24	15	58	47	20	31	+13	25	7	35	7	54	11	47	15	58	15	38	4	12	12	19	44	33
25	16	03	01	20	43	+13	07	7	37	7	56	11	47	15	57	15	37	4	16	09	19	40	37
26	16	07	16	20	55	+12	49	7	38	7	58	11	47	15	56	15	36	4	20	05	19	36	41
27	16	11	32	21	06	+12	30	7	40	8	00	11	48	15	55	15	35	4	24	02	19	32	46
28	16	15	49	21	17	+12	10	7	41	8	02	11	48	15	54	15	34	4	27	58	19	28	50
29	16	20	06	21	27	+11	49	7	43	8	04	11	48	15	54	15	33	4	31	55	19	24	54
30	16	24	24	21	37	+11	28	7	44	8	05	11	49	15	53	15	32	4	35	52	19	20	58

DURATION OF TWILIGHT (in minutes)

Latitude	52°	56°	52°	56°	52°	56°	52°	56
	1 November		11 November		21 November		31 November	
Civil	36	40	37	41	38	43	40	45
Nautical	75	84	78	87	80	90	82	93
Astronomical	115	127	117	130	120	134	123	138

THE NIGHT SKY

Mercury, although it reaches greatest eastern elongation on the 3rd and later passes through inferior conjunction on the 24th, is unsuitably placed for observation throughout the month.

Venus, magnitude −4.5, is still visible as a brilliant object in the early evenings, low above the south-western horizon after sunset. Under good conditions the four-day old crescent Moon will be seen nearly 3 degrees below the planet on the evening of the 5th. Venus is at greatest eastern elongation (47 degrees) on the 3rd and during the month is gradually becoming visible for a little longer each evening until by the end of the month it may be seen for almost two hours after sunset, from southern England, and for about an hour and a half from Scotland.

Mars reaches opposition on the 7th, and is visible throughout the hours of darkness. Its magnitude then is −2.3, and for a few weeks around opposition is actually brighter than Jupiter. Mars is in the constellation of Aries. The Full Moon is in the vicinity of the planet on the 15th and 16th.

Jupiter, magnitude −1.7, becomes visible as a bright morning object after the first week of the month, low above the south-eastern horizon for a short while before sunrise. Jupiter is moving slowly eastwards, a few degrees east of Spica, in Virgo. On the morning of the 29th, the thin waning crescent Moon, only 2 days before New, passes 4 degrees south of the planet.

Saturn, magnitude +0.2, is moving very slowly direct in the constellation of Cancer: it reaches its first stationary point on the 22nd, when it starts to retrograde. It is now rising in the east about three hours before midnight. The gibbous Moon, just before Last Quarter, is near the planet around the 21st to the 23rd.

Meteors. Although the Leonids do not usually produce a brilliant display there has been considerable activity during the last few years. The peak of any activity will occur around the 17th but is not likely to produce a spectacular display.

THE MOON

Day	RA h	m	Dec. °	Hor. par. '	Semi-diam. '	Sun's Co-long. °	PA of Br. Limb °	Ph. %	Age d	Rise 52° h	m	Rise 56° h	m	Transit h	m	Set 52° h	m	Set 56° h	m
1	13	35	−11.1	56.3	15.3	262	106	1	28.6	6	11	6	23	11	14	16	02	15	49
2	14	23	−16.6	56.9	15.5	274	36	0	29.6	7	33	7	52	12	01	16	18	15	58
3	15	16	−21.5	57.4	15.6	286	301	1	0.9	8	58	9	25	12	54	16	40	16	13
4	16	12	−25.3	57.9	15.8	299	290	4	1.9	10	23	10	58	13	51	17	13	16	37
5	17	12	−27.8	58.3	15.9	311	281	10	2.9	11	40	12	20	14	51	18	02	17	21
6	18	15	−28.5	58.7	16.0	323	273	18	3.9	12	40	13	19	15	53	19	10	18	31
7	19	18	−27.5	58.9	16.1	335	265	27	4.9	13	22	13	54	16	54	20	33	20	02
8	20	20	−24.7	59.1	16.1	347	258	38	5.9	13	50	14	14	17	51	22	03	21	41
9	21	18	−20.3	59.2	16.1	360	252	49	6.9	14	10	14	26	18	45	23	33	23	19
10	22	13	−14.9	59.3	16.1	12	248	61	7.9	14	25	14	34	19	35	—	—	—	—
11	23	05	−8.7	59.2	16.1	24	246	71	8.9	14	37	14	41	20	23	1	01	0	53
12	23	55	−2.0	59.1	16.1	36	245	81	9.9	14	48	14	47	21	10	2	27	2	25
13	0	44	+4.7	58.8	16.0	48	247	89	10.9	15	00	14	53	21	58	3	51	3	56
14	1	35	+11.1	58.5	15.9	60	251	95	11.9	15	13	15	00	22	47	5	17	5	28
15	2	26	+16.9	58.0	15.8	72	261	99	12.9	15	30	15	10	23	38	6	43	7	01
16	3	20	+21.8	57.5	15.7	85	337	100	13.9	15	52	15	25	—	—	8	08	8	35
17	4	16	+25.5	56.9	15.5	97	61	99	14.9	16	24	15	50	0	32	9	30	10	04
18	5	13	+27.7	56.2	15.3	109	75	96	15.9	17	08	16	29	1	27	10	41	11	20
19	6	10	+28.5	55.6	15.2	121	84	91	16.9	18	06	17	28	2	23	11	36	12	15
20	7	06	+27.7	55.1	15.0	133	92	84	17.9	19	15	18	42	3	17	12	16	12	49
21	8	00	+25.7	54.7	14.9	145	98	76	18.9	20	29	20	03	4	08	12	44	13	10
22	8	51	+22.5	54.4	14.8	157	104	68	19.9	21	43	21	24	4	55	13	03	13	23
23	9	38	+18.4	54.2	14.8	170	108	59	20.9	22	56	22	44	5	40	13	17	13	31
24	10	23	+13.6	54.3	14.8	182	111	49	21.9	—	—	—	—	6	22	13	29	13	38
25	11	07	+8.3	54.5	15.0	194	113	40	22.9	0	08	0	01	7	02	13	38	13	43
26	11	49	+2.7	54.9	15.0	206	114	31	23.9	1	20	1	18	7	42	13	48	13	47
27	12	32	−3.1	55.4	15.1	218	113	22	24.9	2	33	2	36	8	22	13	57	13	52
28	13	17	−9.0	56.1	15.3	230	111	15	25.9	3	48	3	57	9	05	14	08	13	57
29	14	04	−14.6	56.8	15.5	243	107	8	26.9	5	08	5	23	9	51	14	22	14	05
30	14	56	−19.8	57.5	15.7	255	99	3	27.9	6	32	6	55	10	42	14	41	14	17

MERCURY

Day	RA h	m	Dec. °	Diam. "	Phase %	Transit h	m	5° high 52° h	m	5° high 56° h	m
1	15	57	−23.2	6	68	13	16	16	15	15	39
3	16	06	−23.7	7	65	13	17	16	12	15	34
5	16	14	−24.1	7	60	13	17	16	09	15	30
7	16	22	−24.4	7	55	13	16	16	06	15	26
9	16	28	−24.5	7	49	13	14	16	03	15	22
11	16	33	−24.5	8	43	13	11	16	00	15	19
13	16	36	−24.4	8	36	13	05	15	56	15	16
15	16	36	−24.1	9	28	12	57	15	51	15	13
17	16	34	−23.6	9	20	12	46	15	45	15	09
19	16	29	−22.9	9	12	12	32	15	38	15	04
21	16	21	−22.0	10	5	12	16	15	30	14	59
23	16	11	−20.9	10	1	11	58	8	37	9	05
25	16	00	−19.7	10	0	11	40	8	09	8	35
27	15	50	−18.5	10	3	11	22	7	43	8	07
29	15	41	−17.6	9	8	11	06	7	21	7	43
31	15	36	−16.9	9	16	10	53	7	03	7	24

VENUS

Day	RA h	m	Dec. °	Diam. "	Phase %	Transit h	m	5° high 52° h	m	5° high 56° h	m
1	17	40	−26.9	24	51	14	59	17	23	16	26
6	18	03	−27.1	26	48	15	02	17	24	16	26
11	18	25	−27.0	27	46	15	04	17	27	16	31
16	18	45	−26.7	29	43	15	05	17	32	16	39
21	19	05	−26.1	31	40	15	04	17	38	16	48
26	19	22	−25.4	33	36	15	02	17	44	16	59
31	19	38	−24.5	36	33	14	58	17	48	17	08

MARS

Day	RA h	m	Dec. °	Diam. "	Phase %	Transit h	m	5° high 52° h	m	5° high 56° h	m
1	3	00	+16.2	20	100	0	19	7	09	7	19
6	2	53	+16.0	20	100	23	46	6	40	6	51
11	2	45	+15.7	20	100	23	19	6	12	6	22
16	2	39	+15.5	19	100	22	53	5	45	5	55
21	2	33	+15.3	18	99	22	28	5	18	5	28
26	2	28	+15.2	18	98	22	04	4	53	5	03
31	2	25	+15.1	17	97	21	41	4	30	4	40

SUNRISE AND SUNSET

	London 0°05'	51°30'	Bristol 2°35'	51°28'	Birmingham 1°55'	52°28'	Manchester 2°15'	53°28'	Newcastle 1°37'	54°59'	Glasgow 4°14'	55°52'	Belfast 5°56'	54°35'
	h m	h m	h m	h m	h m	h m	h m	h m	h m	h m	h m	h m	h m	h m
1	6 54	16 33	7 04	16 43	7 04	16 38	7 08	16 36	7 10	16 29	7 24	16 37	7 26	16 48
2	6 56	16 31	7 06	16 42	7 06	16 36	7 10	16 34	7 12	16 27	7 26	16 35	7 28	16 46
3	6 57	16 30	7 07	16 40	7 08	16 34	7 12	16 32	7 14	16 25	7 28	16 32	7 30	16 44
4	6 59	16 28	7 09	16 38	7 09	16 32	7 14	16 31	7 16	16 23	7 30	16 30	7 32	16 42
5	7 01	16 26	7 11	16 36	7 11	16 31	7 16	16 29	7 18	16 21	7 32	16 28	7 34	16 40
6	7 03	16 25	7 13	16 35	7 13	16 29	7 18	16 27	7 20	16 19	7 34	16 26	7 36	16 38
7	7 04	16 23	7 14	16 33	7 15	16 27	7 20	16 25	7 22	16 17	7 36	16 24	7 38	16 36
8	7 06	16 21	7 16	16 31	7 17	16 25	7 21	16 23	7 24	16 15	7 38	16 22	7 40	16 34
9	7 08	16 20	7 18	16 30	7 19	16 24	7 23	16 22	7 27	16 13	7 41	16 20	7 42	16 32
10	7 10	16 18	7 20	16 28	7 20	16 22	7 25	16 20	7 29	16 12	7 43	16 18	7 44	16 30
11	7 12	16 17	7 21	16 27	7 22	16 21	7 27	16 18	7 31	16 10	7 45	16 17	7 46	16 29
12	7 13	16 15	7 23	16 25	7 24	16 19	7 29	16 17	7 33	16 08	7 47	16 15	7 48	16 27
13	7 15	16 14	7 25	16 24	7 26	16 18	7 31	16 15	7 35	16 06	7 49	16 13	7 50	16 25
14	7 17	16 12	7 27	16 22	7 28	16 16	7 33	16 14	7 36	16 05	7 51	16 11	7 52	16 24
15	7 18	16 11	7 28	16 21	7 29	16 15	7 35	16 12	7 38	16 03	7 53	16 10	7 54	16 22
16	7 20	16 10	7 30	16 20	7 31	16 13	7 36	16 11	7 40	16 01	7 55	16 08	7 56	16 20
17	7 22	16 08	7 32	16 18	7 33	16 12	7 38	16 09	7 42	16 00	7 57	16 06	7 58	16 19
18	7 23	16 07	7 33	16 17	7 35	16 11	7 40	16 08	7 44	15 58	7 59	16 05	8 00	16 17
19	7 25	16 06	7 35	16 16	7 36	16 09	7 42	16 06	7 46	15 57	8 01	16 03	8 02	16 16
20	7 27	16 05	7 37	16 15	7 38	16 08	7 44	16 05	7 48	15 56	8 03	16 02	8 04	16 15
21	7 28	16 04	7 38	16 14	7 40	16 07	7 45	16 04	7 50	15 54	8 05	16 00	8 05	16 13
22	7 30	16 02	7 40	16 13	7 41	16 06	7 47	16 03	7 52	15 53	8 07	15 59	8 07	16 12
23	7 32	16 01	7 42	16 12	7 43	16 05	7 49	16 01	7 54	15 52	8 09	15 57	8 09	16 11
24	7 33	16 00	7 43	16 11	7 45	16 04	7 51	16 00	7 56	15 50	8 11	15 56	8 11	16 10
25	7 35	15 59	7 45	16 10	7 46	16 03	7 52	15 59	7 57	15 49	8 13	15 55	8 13	16 08
26	7 36	15 59	7 46	16 09	7 48	16 02	7 54	15 58	7 59	15 48	8 14	15 54	8 14	16 07
27	7 38	15 58	7 48	16 08	7 50	16 01	7 56	15 57	8 01	15 47	8 16	15 53	8 16	16 06
28	7 39	15 57	7 49	16 07	7 51	16 00	7 57	15 56	8 03	15 46	8 18	15 51	8 18	16 05
29	7 41	15 56	7 51	16 06	7 53	15 59	7 59	15 55	8 04	15 45	8 20	15 50	8 19	16 04
30	7 42	15 55	7 52	16 06	7 54	15 58	8 00	15 55	8 06	15 44	8 21	15 49	8 21	16 04

JUPITER

Day	RA		Dec.		Transit		5° high	
							52°	56°
	h	m	°	′	h	m	h m	h m
1	13	58.0	−10	57	11	15	6 48	7 02
11	14	06.3	−11	41	10	44	6 21	6 36
21	14	14.4	−12	23	10	13	5 54	6 10
31	14	22.4	−13	03	9	41	5 27	5 43

Diameters – equatorial 31″ polar 29″

SATURN

Day	RA		Dec.		Transit		5° high	
							52°	56°
	h	m	°	′	h	m	h m	h m
1	8	53.9	+17	57	6	11	23 07	22 55
11	8	55.2	+17	54	5	33	22 29	22 17
21	8	55.7	+17	56	4	55	21 50	21 38
31	8	55.4	+17	56	4	15	21 10	20

Diameters – equatorial 19″ polar 17″
Rings – major axis 42″ minor axis 13″

URANUS

Day	RA		Dec.		Transit		10° high	
							52°	56°
	h	m	°	′	h	m	h m	h m
1	22	35.8	−9	42	19	51	23 49	23 32
11	22	35.5	−9	43	19	11	23 09	22 52
21	22	35.5	−9	43	18	32	22 30	22 13
31	22	35.8	−9	41	17	53	21 51	21 34

Diameter 4″

NEPTUNE

Day	RA		Dec.		Transit		10° high	
							52°	56°
	h	m	°	′	h	m	h m	h m
1	21	09.3	−16	32	18	25	21 35	21 05
11	21	09.6	−16	31	17	46	20 56	20 26
21	21	10.0	−16	29	17	07	20 17	19 48
31	21	10.7	−16	26	16	28	19 39	19 10

Diameter 2″

DECEMBER 2005

TWELFTH MONTH, 31 DAYS. *Decem* (ten), tenth month of Roman pre-Julian calendar

1	*Thursday*	Queen Alexandra b. 1844. Henry I d. 1135	335
2	*Friday*	George Seurat b. 1859. Marquis de Sade d. 1814	336
3	*Saturday*	Robert Louis Stevenson d. 1894. Pierre Renoir d. 1919	337
4	*Sunday*	Wassily Kandinsky b. 1866. Benjamin Britten d. 1976	338
5	*Monday*	Wolfgang Amadeus Mozart d. 1791. Claude Monet d. 1926	week 49 day 339
6	*Tuesday*	Sir Osbert Sitwell b. 1892. Anthony Trollope d. 1882	340
7	*Wednesday*	Lord Darnley b. 1545. Robert Graves d. 1985	341
8	*Thursday*	Mary Queen of Scots b. 1542. Jean Sibelius b. 1865	342
9	*Friday*	John Milton b. 1608. Sir Anthony Van Dyck d. 1641	343
10	*Saturday*	Emily Dickinson b. 1830. Otis Redding d. 1967	344
11	*Sunday*	Hector Berlioz b. 1803. Sir Kenneth Macmillan d. 1992	345
12	*Monday*	Edvard Munch b. 1863. Robert Browning d. 1889	week 50 day 346
13	*Tuesday*	Dr Samuel Johnson b. 1784. Wassily Kandinsky d. 1944	347
14	*Wednesday*	George VI b. 1895. Albert, Prince Consort to Queen Victoria d. 1861	348
15	*Thursday*	George Romney b. 1734. Johannes Vermeer d. 1851	349
16	*Friday*	Sir Arthur C. Clarke b. 1917. Wilhelm Grimm d. 1859	350
17	*Saturday*	Ford Madox Ford b. 1873. Dorothy L. Sayers d. 1957	351
18	*Sunday*	Archduke Franz Ferdinand of Austria-Hungary b. 1863. Paul Klee b. 1879	352
19	*Monday*	Emily Brontë d. 1848. J. M. W. Turner d. 1851	week 51 day 353
20	*Tuesday*	James Hilton d. 1954. John Steinbeck d. 1968	354
21	*Wednesday*	Dame Rebecca West b. 1892. F. Scott Fitzgerald d. 1940	355
22	*Thursday*	Giacomo Puccini b. 1858. Samuel Becket d. 1989	356
23	*Friday*	Alexander I, Tsar of Russia b. 1777. Peggy Guggenheim d. 1979	357
24	*Saturday*	CHRISTMAS EVE. William Makepeace Thackeray d. 1863	358
25	*Sunday*	CHRISTMAS DAY. Maurice Utrillo b. 1883	359
26	*Monday*	BOXING DAY. Thomas Gray b. 1716	week 52 day 360
27	*Tuesday*	Marlene Dietrich b. 1901. Charles Lamb d. 1834	361
28	*Wednesday*	Mary II d. 1694. Maurice Ravel d. 1937	362
29	*Thursday*	Thomas Becket is killed by soldiers in Canterbury Cathedral 1170	363
30	*Friday*	Rudyard Kipling b. 1865. Richard Rogers, American composer d. 1979	364
31	*Saturday*	John Denver b. 1943. Henri Matisse b. 1869	365

ASTRONOMICAL PHENOMENA

d h
4 02 Mercury at stationary point
4 19 Venus in conjunction with Moon. Venus 2° N.
9 13 Venus at greatest brilliancy
10 04 Mars at stationary point
12 05 Mars in conjunction with Moon. Mars 1° S.
12 13 Mercury at greatest elongation W.21°
16 04 Pluto in conjunction
19 12 Saturn in conjunction with Moon. Saturn 4° S.
21 19 Sun's longitude 270° ♑
24 10 Venus at stationary point
27 01 Jupiter in conjunction with Moon. Jupiter 4° N.
29 23 Mercury in conjunction with Moon. Mercury 5° N.

MINIMA OF ALGOL

d	h	d	h	d	h
2	19.0	14	06.2	25	17.5
5	15.8	17	03.0	28	14.3
8	12.6	19	23.9	31	11.1
11	09.4	22	20.7		

CONSTELLATIONS

The following constellations are near their meridian at

	d	h		d	h
November	1	24	January	1	20
December	16	21	December	1	22
November	15	23	January	16	19

Ursa Major (below the Pole), Ursa Minor (below the Pole), Cassiopeia, Andromeda, Perseus, Triangulum, Aries, Taurus, Cetus and Eridanus

THE MOON

Phases, Apsides and Node	d	h	m
● New Moon	1	15	01
☽ First Quarter	8	09	36
○ Full Moon	15	16	16
☾ Last Quarter	23	19	36
● New Moon	31	03	12
Perigee (367,392 km)	5	04	24
Apogee (404,978 km)	21	02	45

Mean longitude of ascending node on December 1, 11°

THE SUN

Day	Right Ascension h	m	s	Dec. − °	′	Equation of time m	s	Rise 52° h	m	56° h	m	Transit h	m	Set 52° h	m	56° h	m	Sidereal time h	m	s	Transit of first point of Aries h	m	s
1	16	28	42	21	47	+11	06	7	46	8	07	11	49	15	52	15	31	4	39	48	19	17	02
2	16	33	02	21	56	+10	43	7	47	8	09	11	49	15	51	15	30	4	43	45	19	13	06
3	16	37	22	22	05	+10	20	7	48	8	10	11	50	15	51	15	29	4	47	41	19	09	10
4	16	41	42	22	13	+9	56	7	50	8	12	11	50	15	50	15	29	4	51	38	19	05	14
5	16	46	03	22	21	+9	31	7	51	8	13	11	51	15	50	15	28	4	55	34	19	01	18
6	16	50	25	22	29	+9	06	7	52	8	15	11	51	15	50	15	27	4	59	31	18	57	22
7	16	54	47	22	36	+8	41	7	54	8	16	11	52	15	49	15	27	5	03	27	18	53	26
8	16	59	09	22	42	+8	15	7	55	8	17	11	52	15	49	15	26	5	07	24	18	49	30
9	17	03	32	22	48	+7	48	7	56	8	19	11	52	15	49	15	26	5	11	21	18	45	35
10	17	07	56	22	54	+7	21	7	57	8	20	11	53	15	49	15	26	5	15	17	18	41	39
11	17	12	20	22	59	+6	54	7	58	8	21	11	53	15	48	15	25	5	19	14	18	37	43
12	17	16	44	23	04	+6	26	7	59	8	22	11	54	15	48	15	25	5	23	10	18	33	47
13	17	21	08	23	08	+5	58	8	00	8	23	11	54	15	48	15	25	5	27	07	18	29	51
14	17	25	33	23	12	+5	30	8	01	8	24	11	55	15	48	15	25	5	31	03	18	25	55
15	17	29	58	23	16	+5	02	8	02	8	25	11	55	15	49	15	25	5	35	00	18	21	59
16	17	34	24	23	19	+4	33	8	03	8	26	11	56	15	49	15	25	5	38	56	18	18	03
17	17	38	49	23	21	+4	04	8	03	8	27	11	56	15	49	15	25	5	42	53	18	14	07
18	17	43	15	23	23	+3	34	8	04	8	28	11	57	15	49	15	25	5	46	50	18	10	11
19	17	47	41	23	25	+3	05	8	05	8	29	11	57	15	50	15	26	5	50	46	18	06	15
20	17	52	08	23	26	+2	35	8	05	8	29	11	58	15	50	15	26	5	54	43	18	02	20
21	17	56	34	23	26	+2	05	8	06	8	30	11	58	15	50	15	27	5	58	39	17	58	24
22	18	01	00	23	26	+1	36	8	06	8	30	11	59	15	51	15	27	6	02	36	17	54	28
23	18	05	27	23	26	+1	06	8	07	8	31	11	59	15	52	15	28	6	06	32	17	50	32
24	18	09	53	23	25	+0	36	8	07	8	31	12	00	15	52	15	28	6	10	29	17	46	36
25	18	14	19	23	24	+0	06	8	07	8	31	12	00	15	53	15	29	6	14	25	17	42	40
26	18	18	46	23	22	−0	24	8	08	8	32	12	01	15	54	15	30	6	18	22	17	38	44
27	18	23	12	23	20	−0	53	8	08	8	32	12	01	15	54	15	31	6	22	19	17	34	48
28	18	27	38	23	17	−1	23	8	08	8	32	12	02	15	55	15	32	6	26	15	17	30	52
29	18	32	04	23	14	−1	52	8	08	8	32	12	02	15	56	15	33	6	30	12	17	26	56
30	18	36	30	23	11	−2	21	8	08	8	32	12	03	15	57	15	34	6	34	08	17	23	00
31	18	40	55	23	06	−2	50	8	08	8	31	12	03	15	58	15	35	6	38	05	17	19	04

DURATION OF TWILIGHT (in minutes)

Latitude	52°	56°	52°	56°	52°	56°	52°	56
	1 December		11 December		21 December		31 December	
Civil	40	45	41	47	41	47	41	47
Nautical	82	93	84	96	85	97	84	96
Astronomical	123	138	125	141	126	142	125	141

THE NIGHT SKY

Mercury is at its greatest western elongation (21 degrees) on the 12th and thus is visible in the mornings for about 12 days either side of that date, magnitude +0.9 to −0.5. It may be seen low above the east-south-eastern horizon around the time of beginning of morning civil twilight. This morning apparition is the most suitable one of the year for observers in the latitudes of the British Isles.

Venus is still a magnificent object in the early evening sky, reaching its greatest brilliancy, magnitude −4.7, on the 9th. It is visible low above the south-western horizon for about two hours after sunset. On the evening of the 4th the three-day old crescent Moon will be seen about 4 degrees below the planet. Observers with telescopes can witness the decreasing crescent phase during the month (falling from 33 to 6 per cent illuminated) while the apparent diameter increases from 36 to 57 arcseconds.

Mars reaches its second stationary point on the 10th, when it resumes its direct motion, in the constellation of Aries. Its brightness decreases noticeably during the month, from a magnitude of −1.6 to −0.6, though still noticeably brighter than Aldebaran, some 30 degrees to the east. The waxing gibbous Moon is near the planet on the 11th and 12th.

Jupiter, magnitude −1.8, is a brilliant morning object, in the south-eastern sky. By the end of the month it is crossing the meridian at about the same time as sunrise. On the morning of the 27th the waning crescent Moon, 4 days before New, passes 5 degrees south of the planet. Jupiter moves from Virgo into Libra early in the month.

Saturn, magnitude 0.0, is now well placed for observation as it becomes visible in the eastern sky from the latter part of the evening onwards. Saturn is in the constellation of Cancer. The waning gibbous Moon will be seen near the planet around the 18th to the 20th.

Meteors. The maximum of the well-known Geminid meteor shower occurs on the late evening of the 13th though observation will be seriously affected by bright moonlight.

THE MOON

Day	RA		Dec.	Hor. par.	Semi- diam.	Sun's Co- long.	PA of Br. Limb	Ph.	Age	Rise				Transit		Set			
										52°		56°				52°		56°	
	h	m	°	'	'	°	°	%	d	h	m	h	m	h	m	h	m	h	m
1	15	51	−24.1	58.2	15.9	267	77	1	28.9	7	59	8	30	11	38	15	10	14	38
2	16	52	−27.1	58.8	16.0	279	319	0	0.4	9	22	10	00	12	39	15	53	15	14
3	17	55	−28.4	59.3	16.2	291	285	3	1.4	10	31	11	11	13	43	16	56	16	17
4	19	00	−27.8	59.6	16.2	304	272	8	2.4	11	20	11	55	14	46	18	18	17	44
5	20	04	−25.4	59.7	16.3	316	263	15	3.4	11	53	12	19	15	46	19	48	19	24
6	21	04	−21.3	59.6	16.2	328	256	24	4.4	12	16	12	34	16	41	21	20	21	04
7	22	00	−16.0	59.5	16.2	340	251	34	5.4	12	32	12	43	17	33	22	49	22	39
8	22	53	−9.9	59.2	16.1	352	248	46	6.4	12	45	12	50	18	21	—	—	—	—
9	23	43	−3.4	58.8	16.0	4	246	57	7.4	12	56	12	56	19	08	0	14	0	11
10	0	32	+3.2	58.5	15.9	17	247	68	8.4	13	07	13	02	19	54	1	37	1	40
11	1	21	+9.6	58.0	15.8	29	249	77	9.4	13	20	13	09	20	41	3	00	3	09
12	2	11	+15.4	57.6	15.7	41	253	86	10.4	13	35	13	17	21	30	4	24	4	40
13	3	03	+20.5	57.1	15.6	53	259	92	11.4	13	55	13	30	22	22	5	48	6	11
14	3	57	+24.4	56.6	15.4	65	269	97	12.4	14	22	13	50	23	17	7	10	7	41
15	4	53	+27.1	56.2	15.3	77	293	99	13.4	15	01	14	23	—	—	8	25	9	02
16	5	50	+28.3	55.7	15.2	89	37	100	14.4	15	54	15	15	0	12	9	26	10	05
17	6	47	+28.0	55.2	15.0	102	77	98	15.4	16	59	16	24	1	07	10	12	10	47
18	7	42	+26.3	54.8	14.9	114	90	95	16.4	18	11	17	43	1	59	10	44	11	13
19	8	34	+23.5	54.5	14.8	126	98	89	17.4	19	26	19	05	2	48	11	06	11	29
20	9	22	+19.6	54.2	14.8	138	104	83	18.4	20	40	20	25	3	34	11	22	11	39
21	10	08	+15.0	54.1	14.8	150	109	75	19.4	21	52	21	43	4	17	11	35	11	46
22	10	52	+9.9	54.2	14.8	162	111	67	20.4	23	03	22	59	4	57	11	45	11	51
23	11	34	+4.4	54.4	14.8	174	113	58	21.4	—	—	—	—	5	37	11	54	11	55
24	12	16	−1.3	54.8	14.9	187	113	48	22.4	0	14	0	15	6	16	12	03	12	00
25	13	00	−7.0	55.4	15.1	199	112	39	23.4	1	26	1	33	6	57	12	13	12	05
26	13	45	−12.6	56.1	15.3	211	110	29	24.4	2	43	2	55	7	41	12	26	12	12
27	14	34	−17.9	56.9	15.5	223	106	20	25.4	4	03	4	22	8	28	12	42	12	21
28	15	27	−22.5	57.8	15.8	235	100	13	26.4	5	29	5	56	9	21	13	05	12	37
29	16	25	−26.0	58.7	16.0	247	91	6	27.4	6	54	7	29	10	20	13	41	13	05
30	17	28	−28.1	59.5	16.2	260	76	2	28.4	8	11	8	51	11	23	14	35	13	55
31	18	34	−28.2	60.1	16.4	272	17	0	29.4	9	11	9	48	12	29	15	51	15	14

MERCURY

Day	RA		Dec.	Diam.	Phase	Transit		5° high			
								52°		56°	
	h	m	°	"	%	h	m	h	m	h	m
1	15	36	−16.9	9	16	10	53	7	03	7	24
3	15	33	−16.5	9	25	10	43	6	50	7	11
5	15	33	−16.4	8	34	10	36	6	43	7	03
7	15	35	−16.5	8	43	10	31	6	39	7	00
9	15	40	−16.9	7	51	10	28	6	38	7	00
11	15	46	−17.4	7	58	10	27	6	41	7	03
13	15	54	−18.0	7	64	10	27	6	45	7	08
15	16	03	−18.7	6	69	10	28	6	51	7	16
17	16	12	−19.3	6	74	10	30	6	58	7	24
19	16	23	−20.0	6	78	10	33	7	06	7	33
21	16	34	−20.7	6	81	10	36	7	14	7	43
23	16	45	−21.3	6	84	10	40	7	23	7	54
25	16	57	−21.9	5	86	10	44	7	32	8	04
27	17	09	−22.5	5	88	10	48	7	41	8	14
29	17	22	−22.9	5	90	10	53	7	49	8	25
31	17	35	−23.4	5	91	10	58	7	58	8	35

VENUS

Day	RA		Dec.	Diam.	Phase	Transit		5° high			
								52°		56°	
	h	m	°	"	%	h	m	h	m	h	m
1	19	38	−24.5	36	33	14	58	17	48	17	08
6	19	52	−23.5	39	29	14	51	17	51	17	15
11	20	03	−22.4	42	25	14	42	17	52	17	19
16	20	10	−21.3	46	20	14	30	17	48	17	19
21	20	14	−20.1	50	16	14	13	17	41	17	14
26	20	14	−19.0	54	11	13	53	17	28	17	04
31	20	09	−18.0	57	7	13	28	17	11	16	48

MARS

Day	RA		Dec.	Diam.	Phase	Transit		5° high			
								52°		56°	
	h	m	°	"	%	h	m	h	m	h	m
1	2	25	+15.1	17	97	21	41	4	30	4	40
6	2	23	+15.2	16	96	21	19	4	09	4	18
11	2	22	+15.3	15	95	20	59	3	49	3	59
16	2	23	+15.5	14	94	20	41	3	31	3	41
21	2	25	+15.8	14	93	20	23	3	15	3	25
26	2	28	+16.1	13	93	20	07	3	00	3	11
31	2	32	+16.5	12	92	19	51	2	47	2	58

SUNRISE AND SUNSET

	London 0°05′	51°30′	Bristol 2°35′	51°28′	Birmingham 1°55′	52°28′	Manchester 2°15′	53°28′	Newcastle 1°37′	54°59′	Glasgow 4°14′	55°52′	Belfast 5°56′	54°35′
	h m	h m	h m	h m	h m	h m	h m	h m	h m	h m	h m	h m	h m	h m
1	7 44	15 55	7 54	16 05	7 56	15 58	8 02	15 54	8 07	15 43	8 23	15 49	8 23	16 03
2	7 45	15 54	7 55	16 04	7 57	15 57	8 03	15 53	8 09	15 42	8 25	15 48	8 24	16 02
3	7 46	15 54	7 56	16 04	7 58	15 56	8 05	15 53	8 11	15 42	8 26	15 47	8 26	16 01
4	7 48	15 53	7 58	16 03	8 00	15 56	8 06	15 52	8 12	15 41	8 28	15 46	8 27	16 01
5	7 49	15 53	7 59	16 03	8 01	15 55	8 08	15 51	8 14	15 40	8 29	15 46	8 28	16 00
6	7 50	15 52	8 00	16 03	8 02	15 55	8 09	15 51	8 15	15 40	8 31	15 45	8 30	16 00
7	7 51	15 52	8 01	16 02	8 04	15 55	8 10	15 51	8 16	15 39	8 32	15 44	8 31	15 59
8	7 53	15 52	8 02	16 02	8 05	15 54	8 11	15 50	8 18	15 39	8 34	15 44	8 32	15 59
9	7 54	15 52	8 04	16 02	8 06	15 54	8 13	15 50	8 19	15 39	8 35	15 44	8 34	15 58
10	7 55	15 51	8 05	16 02	8 07	15 54	8 14	15 50	8 20	15 38	8 36	15 43	8 35	15 58
11	7 56	15 51	8 06	16 01	8 08	15 54	8 15	15 50	8 21	15 38	8 37	15 43	8 36	15 58
12	7 57	15 51	8 07	16 01	8 09	15 54	8 16	15 50	8 22	15 38	8 38	15 43	8 37	15 58
13	7 58	15 51	8 08	16 01	8 10	15 54	8 17	15 49	8 23	15 38	8 39	15 43	8 38	15 58
14	7 59	15 51	8 09	16 01	8 11	15 54	8 18	15 49	8 24	15 38	8 40	15 43	8 39	15 58
15	8 00	15 51	8 09	16 02	8 12	15 54	8 19	15 50	8 25	15 38	8 41	15 43	8 40	15 58
16	8 00	15 52	8 10	16 02	8 13	15 54	8 20	15 50	8 26	15 38	8 42	15 43	8 41	15 58
17	8 01	15 52	8 11	16 02	8 13	15 54	8 20	15 50	8 27	15 38	8 43	15 43	8 42	15 58
18	8 02	15 52	8 12	16 02	8 14	15 54	8 21	15 50	8 28	15 39	8 44	15 43	8 42	15 58
19	8 02	15 52	8 12	16 03	8 15	15 55	8 22	15 51	8 28	15 39	8 45	15 44	8 43	15 59
20	8 03	15 53	8 13	16 03	8 15	15 55	8 22	15 51	8 29	15 39	8 45	15 44	8 44	15 59
21	8 04	15 53	8 13	16 04	8 16	15 56	8 23	15 51	8 30	15 40	8 46	15 44	8 44	15 59
22	8 04	15 54	8 14	16 04	8 16	15 56	8 23	15 52	8 30	15 40	8 46	15 45	8 45	16 00
23	8 05	15 54	8 14	16 05	8 17	15 57	8 24	15 53	8 30	15 41	8 47	15 46	8 45	16 01
24	8 05	15 55	8 15	16 05	8 17	15 57	8 24	15 53	8 31	15 41	8 47	15 46	8 46	16 01
25	8 05	15 56	8 15	16 06	8 18	15 58	8 24	15 54	8 31	15 42	8 47	15 47	8 46	16 02
26	8 06	15 56	8 15	16 07	8 18	15 59	8 25	15 55	8 31	15 43	8 48	15 48	8 46	16 03
27	8 06	15 57	8 16	16 07	8 18	16 00	8 25	15 55	8 31	15 44	8 48	15 49	8 46	16 04
28	8 06	15 58	8 16	16 08	8 18	16 00	8 25	15 56	8 32	15 45	8 48	15 50	8 46	16 04
29	8 06	15 59	8 16	16 09	8 18	16 01	8 25	15 57	8 32	15 46	8 48	15 51	8 46	16 05
30	8 06	16 00	8 16	16 10	8 18	16 02	8 25	15 58	8 32	15 47	8 48	15 52	8 46	16 06
31	8 06	16 01	8 16	16 11	8 18	16 03	8 25	15 59	8 31	15 48	8 48	15 53	8 46	16 08

JUPITER

Day	RA		Dec.		Transit		5° high			
							52°		56°	
	h	m	°	′	h	m	h	m	h	m
1	14	22.4	−13	03	9	41	5	27	5	43
11	14	30.1	−13	40	9	10	4	59	5	16
21	14	37.4	−14	19	8	38	4	31	4	48
31	14	44.1	−14	44	8	05	4	01	4	19

Diameters – equatorial 32″ polar 30″

SATURN

Day	RA		Dec.		Transit		5° high			
							52°		56°	
	h	m	°	′	h	m	h	m	h	m
1	8	55.4	+17	56	4	15	21	10	20	58
11	8	54.4	+18	02	3	35	20	30	20	17
21	8	52.7	+18	10	2	54	19	48	19	35
31	8	50.4	+18	21	2	12	19	05	18	53

Diameters – equatorial 20″ polar 18″
Rings – major axis 45″ minor axis 14″

URANUS

Day	RA		Dec.		Transit		10° high			
							52°		56°	
	h	m	°	′	h	m	h	m	h	m
1	22	35.8	−9	41	17	53	21	51	21	34
11	22	36.4	−9	37	17	14	21	13	20	56
21	22	37.4	−9	31	16	36	20	35	20	18
31	22	38.6	−9	23	15	58	19	58	19	41

Diameter 4″

NEPTUNE

Day	RA		Dec.		Transit		10° high			
							52°		56°	
	h	m	°	′	h	m	h	m	h	m
1	21	10.7	−16	26	16	28	19	39	19	10
11	21	11.6	−16	22	15	50	19	01	18	32
21	21	12.6	−16	18	15	12	18	23	17	54
31	21	13.8	−16	12	14	33	17	46	17	17

Diameter 2″

RISING AND SETTING TIMES

TABLE 1. SEMI-DIURNAL ARCS (HOUR ANGLES AT RISING/SETTING)

Dec.	Latitude 0°	10°	20°	30°	40°	45°	50°	52°	54°	56°	58°	60°	Dec.
	h m	h m	h m	h m	h m	h m	h m	h m	h m	h m	h m	h m	
0°	6 00	6 00	6 00	6 00	6 00	6 00	6 00	6 00	6 00	6 00	6 00	6 00	0°
1°	6 00	6 01	6 01	6 02	6 03	6 04	6 05	6 05	6 06	6 06	6 06	6 07	1°
2°	6 00	6 01	6 03	6 05	6 07	6 08	6 10	6 10	6 11	6 12	6 13	6 14	2°
3°	6 00	6 02	6 04	6 07	6 10	6 12	6 14	6 15	6 17	6 18	6 19	6 21	3°
4°	6 00	6 03	6 06	6 09	6 13	6 16	6 19	6 21	6 22	6 24	6 26	6 28	4°
5°	6 00	6 04	6 07	6 12	6 17	6 20	6 24	6 26	6 28	6 30	6 32	6 35	5°
6°	6 00	6 04	6 09	6 14	6 20	6 24	6 29	6 31	6 33	6 36	6 39	6 42	6°
7°	6 00	6 05	6 10	6 16	6 24	6 28	6 34	6 36	6 39	6 42	6 45	6 49	7°
8°	6 00	6 06	6 12	6 19	6 27	6 32	6 39	6 41	6 45	6 48	6 52	6 56	8°
9°	6 00	6 06	6 13	6 21	6 31	6 36	6 44	6 47	6 50	6 54	6 59	7 04	9°
10°	6 00	6 07	6 15	6 23	6 34	6 41	6 49	6 52	6 56	7 01	7 06	7 11	10°
11°	6 00	6 08	6 16	6 26	6 38	6 45	6 54	6 58	7 02	7 07	7 12	7 19	11°
12°	6 00	6 09	6 18	6 28	6 41	6 49	6 59	7 03	7 08	7 13	7 20	7 26	12°
13°	6 00	6 09	6 19	6 31	6 45	6 53	7 04	7 09	7 14	7 20	7 27	7 34	13°
14°	6 00	6 10	6 21	6 33	6 48	6 58	7 09	7 14	7 20	7 27	7 34	7 42	14°
15°	6 00	6 11	6 22	6 36	6 52	7 02	7 14	7 20	7 27	7 34	7 42	7 51	15°
16°	6 00	6 12	6 24	6 38	6 56	7 07	7 20	7 26	7 33	7 41	7 49	7 59	16°
17°	6 00	6 12	6 26	6 41	6 59	7 11	7 25	7 32	7 40	7 48	7 57	8 08	17°
18°	6 00	6 13	6 27	6 43	7 03	7 16	7 31	7 38	7 46	7 55	8 05	8 17	18°
19°	6 00	6 14	6 29	6 46	7 07	7 21	7 37	7 45	7 53	8 03	8 14	8 26	19°
20°	6 00	6 15	6 30	6 49	7 11	7 25	7 43	7 51	8 00	8 11	8 22	8 36	20°
21°	6 00	6 16	6 32	6 51	7 15	7 30	7 49	7 58	8 08	8 19	8 32	8 47	21°
22°	6 00	6 16	6 34	6 54	7 19	7 35	7 55	8 05	8 15	8 27	8 41	8 58	22°
23°	6 00	6 17	6 36	6 57	7 23	7 40	8 02	8 12	8 23	8 36	8 51	9 09	23°
24°	6 00	6 18	6 37	7 00	7 28	7 46	8 08	8 19	8 31	8 45	9 02	9 22	24°
25°	6 00	6 19	6 39	7 02	7 32	7 51	8 15	8 27	8 40	8 55	9 13	9 35	25°
26°	6 00	6 20	6 41	7 05	7 37	7 57	8 22	8 35	8 49	9 05	9 25	9 51	26°
27°	6 00	6 21	6 43	7 08	7 41	8 03	8 30	8 43	8 58	9 16	9 39	10 08	27°
28°	6 00	6 22	6 45	7 12	7 46	8 08	8 37	8 52	9 08	9 28	9 53	10 28	28°
29°	6 00	6 22	6 47	7 15	7 51	8 15	8 45	9 01	9 19	9 41	10 10	10 55	29°
30°	6 00	6 23	6 49	7 18	7 56	8 21	8 54	9 11	9 30	9 55	10 30	12 00	30°
35°	6 00	6 28	6 59	7 35	8 24	8 58	9 46	10 15	10 58	12 00	12 00	12 00	35°
40°	6 00	6 34	7 11	7 56	8 59	9 48	12 00	12 00	12 00	12 00	12 00	12 00	40°
45°	6 00	6 41	7 25	8 21	9 48	12 00	12 00	12 00	12 00	12 00	12 00	12 00	45°
50°	6 00	6 49	7 43	8 54	12 00	12 00	12 00	12 00	12 00	12 00	12 00	12 00	50°
55°	6 00	6 58	8 05	9 42	12 00	12 00	12 00	12 00	12 00	12 00	12 00	12 00	55°
60°	6 00	7 11	8 36	12 00	12 00	12 00	12 00	12 00	12 00	12 00	12 00	12 00	60°
65°	6 00	7 29	9 25	12 00	12 00	12 00	12 00	12 00	12 00	12 00	12 00	12 00	65°
70°	6 00	7 56	12 00	12 00	12 00	12 00	12 00	12 00	12 00	12 00	12 00	12 00	70°
75°	6 00	8 45	12 00	12 00	12 00	12 00	12 00	12 00	12 00	12 00	12 00	12 00	75°
80°	6 00	12 00	12 00	12 00	12 00	12 00	12 00	12 00	12 00	12 00	12 00	12 00	80°

TABLE 2. CORRECTION FOR REFRACTION AND SEMI-DIAMETER

	m	m	m	m	m	m	m	m	m	m	m	m	
0°	3	3	4	4	4	5	5	5	6	6	6	7	0°
10°	3	3	4	4	4	5	5	6	6	6	7	7	10°
20°	4	4	4	4	5	5	6	7	7	8	8	9	20°
25°	4	4	4	4	5	6	7	8	8	9	11	13	25°
30°	4	4	4	5	6	7	8	9	11	14	21	—	30°

NB: Regarding Table 1. If latitude and declination are of the same sign, take out the respondent directly. If they are of opposite signs, subtract the respondent from 12h.

Table 1 gives the complete range of declinations in case any user wishes to calculate semi-diurnal arcs for bodies other than the Sun and Moon.

Example:

Lat.	Dec.	Semi-diurnal arc
+52°	+20°	7h 51m
+52°	−20°	4h 09m

SUNRISE AND SUNSET

The local mean time of sunrise or sunset may be found by obtaining the hour angle from Table 1 and applying it to the time of transit. The hour angle is negative for sunrise and positive for sunset. A small correction to the hour angle, which always has the effect of increasing it numerically, is necessary to allow for the Sun's semi-diameter (16′) and for refraction (34′); it is obtained from Table 2. The resulting local mean time may be converted into the standard time of the country by taking the difference between the longitude of the standard meridian of the country and that of the place, adding it to the local mean time if the place is west of the standard meridian, and subtracting it if the place is east.

Example – Required the New Zealand Mean Time (12h fast on GMT) of sunset on May 23 at Auckland, latitude 36° 50′ S. (or minus), longitude 11h 39m E. Taking the declination as +20°.6 (page 629), we find

	h	m
New Zealand Standard Time	+ 12	00
Longitude	− 11	39
Longitudinal Correction	+ 0	21
Tabular entry for Lat. 30° and Dec. 20°, opposite signs	+ 5	11
Proportional part for 6° 50′ of Lat.	−	15
Proportional part for 0°.6 of Dec.	−	2
Correction (Table 2)	+	4
Hour angle	4	58
Sun transits (page 1235)	11	57
Longitudinal correction	+	21
New Zealand Mean Time	17	16

MOONRISE AND MOONSET

It is possible to calculate the times of moonrise and moonset using Table 1, though the method is more complicated because the apparent motion of the Moon is much more rapid and also more variable than that of the Sun.

TABLE 3. LONGITUDE CORRECTION

X A h	40m	45m	50m	55m	60m	65m	70m
	m	m	m	m	m	m	m
1	2	2	2	2	3	3	3
2	3	4	4	5	5	5	6
3	5	6	6	7	8	8	9
4	7	8	8	9	10	11	12
5	8	9	10	11	13	14	15
6	10	11	13	14	15	16	18
7	12	13	15	16	18	19	20
8	13	15	17	18	20	22	23
9	15	17	19	21	23	24	26
10	17	19	21	23	25	27	29
11	18	21	23	25	28	30	32
12	20	23	25	28	30	33	35
13	22	24	27	30	33	35	38
14	23	26	29	32	35	38	41
15	25	28	31	34	38	41	44
16	27	30	33	37	40	43	47
17	28	32	35	39	43	46	50
18	30	34	38	41	45	49	53
19	32	36	40	44	48	51	55
20	33	38	42	46	50	54	58
21	35	39	44	48	53	57	61
22	37	41	46	50	55	60	64
23	38	43	48	53	58	62	67
24	40	45	50	55	60	65	70

The parallax of the Moon, about 57′, is near to the sum of the semi-diameter and refraction but has the opposite effect on these times. It is thus convenient to neglect all three quantities in the method outlined below.

Notation

ϕ	= latitude of observer
λ	= longitude of observer (measured positively towards the west)
T_{-1}	= time of transit of Moon on previous day
T_0	= time of transit of Moon on day in question
T_1	= time of transit of Moon on following day
δ_0	= approximate declination of Moon
δ_R	= declination of Moon at moonrise
δ_S	= declination of Moon at moonset
h_0	= approximate hour angle of Moon
h_R	= hour angle of Moon at moonrise
h_S	= hour angle of Moon at moonset
t_R	= time of moonrise
t_S	= time of moonset

Method

1. With arguments ϕ, δ_0 enter Table 1 on page 1266 to determine h_0 where h_0 is negative for moonrise and positive for moonset.

2. Form approximate times from
$$t_R = T_0 + \lambda + h_0$$
$$t_S = T_0 + \lambda + h_0$$

3. Determine δ_R, δ_S for times t_R, t_S respectively.

4. Re-enter Table 1 on page 1266 with
   (*a*) arguments ϕ, δ_R to determine h_R
   (*b*) arguments ϕ, δ_S to determine h_S

5. Form $t_R = T_0 + \lambda + h_R + AX$
$$t_S = T_0 + \lambda + h_S + AX$$

where $A = (\lambda + h)$

and $X = (T_0 - T_{-1})$ if $(\lambda + h)$ is negative
$X = (T_1 - T_0)$ if $(\lambda + h)$ is positive

AX is the respondent in Table 3.

Example – To find the times of moonrise and moonset at Vancouver ($\phi = +49°$, $\lambda = +8h\ 12m$) on 2005 August 24. The starting data (page 1248) are

T_{-1}	= 2h 55m
T_0	= 3h 43m
T_1	= 4h 32m
δ_0	= +15°

1. h_0 = 7h 12m
2. Approximate values
   t_R = 24d 03h 43m + 8h 12m + (−7h 12m)
   = 24d 04h 43m
   t_S = 24d 03h 43m + 8h 12m + (+7h 12m)
   = 24d 19h 07m
3. δ_R = +13°.4
   δ_S = +16°.7
4. h_R = −7h 04m
   h_S = +7h 20m
5. t_R = 24d 03h 43m + 8h 12m + (−7h 04m) + 2m
   = 24d 04h 53m
   t_S = 24d 03h 43m + 8h 12m + (+7h 20m) + 31m
   = 24d 19h 46m

To get the LMT of the phenomenon the longitude is subtracted from the GMT thus:

Moonrise = 8d 06h 40m − 8h 12m = 7d 22h 28m
Moonset = 8d 22h 29m − 8h 12m = 8d 14h 17m

ECLIPSES AND OCCULTATIONS 2005

ECLIPSES

During 2005 there will be three eclipses, two of the Sun and one of the Moon. (Penumbral eclipses are not mentioned in this section as they are so difficult to observe).

1. An annular-total eclipse of the Sun on April 8 is visible as a partial eclipse from North Island (New Zealand), the Pacific Ocean, southern North America, Central America, South America (except for eastern Brazil and south of about S.35), the Caribbean and Bermuda. The partial phase begins at 17h 51m and ends at 23h 20m. The path of the central line is annular at the beginning of the track, but is total over most of the Pacific Ocean. It again becomes annular before crossing Panama and Columbia. The annular eclipse ends in Venezuela. Annularity begins at 18h 53m and ends at 22h 18m. The maximum duration of totality (42 seconds) occurs in the middle of the Pacific Ocean.

2. An annular eclipse of the Sun on October 3 is visible as a partial eclipse from the Arctic Ocean, Greenland, Iceland, the eastern North Atlantic Ocean, Africa (except the southern tip), Europe (including the British Isles), west and south Asia, and the Indian Ocean, including Madagascar. The partial phase begins at 07h 35m and ends at 13h 28m. The path of annularity starts in the eastern North Atlantic Ocean, crosses northern Portugal, Spain, northern Algeria, Tunisia, Libya, north-east Chad, Sudan, south-west Ethiopia, north-east Kenya, and the extreme south of Somalia before ending in the Indian Ocean. Totality begins at 08h 41m and ends at 12h 23m. The maximum duration is 4m 31s. At Greenwich the partial phase begins at 7h 49m and ends at 10h 18m, with 66 per cent of the Sun obscured at maximum. From Edinburgh the corresponding times are 7h 53m and 10h 13m, with a maximum obscuration of the Sun of 58 per cent.

3. A partial eclipse of the Moon on the October 17 is visible from the Arctic Ocean, North and Central America, western South America, the Pacific Ocean, Asia, Australasia, the Indian Ocean and the Southern Ocean. The eclipse begins at 11h 34m and ends at 12h 32m. At maximum only 7 per cent of the moon is obscured.

LUNAR OCCULTATIONS

Observations of the times of occultations are made by both amateur and professional astronomers. Such observations are later analysed to yield accurate positions of the Moon; this is one method of determining the difference between terrestrial time and universal time.

Many of the observations made by amateurs are obtained with the use of a stop-watch which is compared with a time-signal immediately after the observation. Thus an accuracy of about one-fifth of a second is obtainable, though the observer's personal equation may amount to one-third or one-half of a second.

The list on page 663 includes most of the occultations visible under favourable conditions in the British Isles. No occultation is included unless the star is at least 10° above the horizon and the Sun sufficiently far below the horizon to permit the star to be seen with the naked eye or with a small telescope. The altitude limit is reduced from 10° to 2° for stars and planets brighter than magnitude 2.0 and such occultations are also predicted in daylight.

The column Phase shows (i) whether a disappearance (D) or reappearance (R) is to be observed; and (ii) whether it is at the dark limb (D) or bright limb (B). The column

headed 'El. of Moon' gives the elongation of the Moon from the Sun, in degrees. The elongation increases from 0° at New Moon to 180° at Full Moon and on to 360° (or 0°) at New Moon again. Times and position angles (P), reckoned from the north point in the direction north, east, south, west, are given for Greenwich (lat. 51° 30′, long. 0°) and Edinburgh (lat. 56° 00′, long. 3° 12′ west).

The coefficients a and b are the variations in the GMT for each degree of longitude (positive to the west) and latitude (positive to the north) respectively; they enable approximate times (to within about 1m generally) to be found for any point in the British Isles. If the point of observation is $\Delta\lambda$ degrees west and $\Delta\phi$ degrees north, the approximate time is found by adding $a.\Delta\lambda + b.\Delta\phi$ to the given GMT.

Example: the disappearance of ZC465 on March 14 at Coventry, found from both Greenwich and Edinburgh.

	Greenwich	Edinburgh
	°	°
Longitude	0.0	+3.2
Long. of Coventry	+1.5	+1.5
$\Delta\lambda$	+1.5	−1.7
Latitude	+51.5	+56.0
Lat. of Coventry	+52.4	+52.4
$\Delta\phi$	+0.9	−3.6

	h	m	h	m
GMT	21	32.4	21	22.3
$a.\Delta\lambda$		+0.3		+0.2
$b.\Delta\phi$		−2.3		+7.6
	21	30.4	21	30.1

If the occultation is given for one station but not the other, the reason for the suppression is given by the following code:

N = star not occulted
A = star's altitude less than 10° (2° for bright stars and planets)
S = Sun not sufficiently below the horizon
G = occultation is of very short duration

In some cases the coefficients a and b are not given; this is because the occultation is so short that prediction for other places by means of these coefficients would not be reliable.

LUNAR OCCULTATIONS 2005

Date		ZC	Mag.	Phase	El. of Moon	GREENWICH UT h	m	a m	b m	P °	EDINBURGH UT h	m	a m	b m	P °
Jan.	17	319	7.6	DD	97	22	10.1	−0.9	−2.8	111	21	57.5	−0.9	−1.7	92
	18	325	7.4	DD	98	0	18.2	G		5	N				
	18	416	5.4	DD	106	16	50.9	+0.2	+3.2	5	N				
	18	429	6.9	DD	108	20	18.6	G		129	20	01.7	−1.7	−1.1	102
	18	433	5.6	DD	108	21	11.3	−1.5	−1.4	95	21	02.8	−1.3	−0.5	78
	18	432	5.9	DD	108	21	24.0	G		7	N				
	19	563	6.9	DD	120	23	28.2	−1.0	−0.3	57	23	24.8	−1.0	+0.3	42
	19	566	5.9	DD	121	23	43.0	−0.4	−4.4	135	23	25.8	−0.8	−2.7	115
	20	582	5.8	DD	122	N					3	11.5	G		155
	20	703	6.3	DD	131	22	16.8	−1.5	−1.5	104	22	07.3	−1.4	−0.6	88
	22	844	5.7	DD	143	1	12.4	−0.2	−3.5	141	0	57.2	−0.5	−2.8	127
Feb.	13	264	7.0	DD	64	18	46.3	−1.4	−1.9	101	18	36.1	−1.2	−0.9	82
	19	1067	7.2	DD	132	20	15.3	−1.7	−3.7	153	20	00.4	−1.5	−1.1	130
	20	1088	5.6	DD	134	2	02.5	−0.2	−1.8	104	1	53.4	−0.4	−1.8	100
	20	1105	6.5	DD	136	A					4	32.3	+0.1	−1.3	68
	21	1206	5.9	DD	145	0	30.5	−2.2	+0.5	53	0	28.0	G		39
	21	1211	6.2	DD	145	0	54.5	−0.8	−1.9	113	0	43.6	−0.9	−1.7	107
Mar.	14	465	4.5	DD	57	21	32.4	+0.2	−2.5	116	21	22.3	−0.1	−2.1	103
	15	611	7.0	DD	70	A					23	44.0	+0.2	−1.4	87
	17	890	4.5	DD	91	22	28.3	−0.4	−2.0	109	22	18.0	−0.5	−1.9	101
	18	909	6.1	DD	93	A					1	47.8	+0.2	−1.3	80
	18	1035	6.8	DD	102	21	19.2	−1.2	−1.6	102	21	09.4	−1.2	−1.1	92
	19	1056	7.0	DD	104	2	23.3	+0.3	−1.2	82	2	18.1	+0.2	−1.4	80
	20	1169	5.4	DD	114	0	29.3	+0.2	−2.5	144	0	18.5	0.0	−2.5	140
	20	1270	6.1	DD	123	19	53.6	−2.1	+2.2	62	20	02.7	G		37
	22	1393	6.7	DD	136	0	31.3	G		37	N				
	22	1479	6.3	DD	145	19	45.5	−1.1	−0.9	142	19	40.0	−1.0	−0.1	128
Apr.	12	683	7.3	DD	48	19	29.5	G		146	S				
	12	698	7.6	DD	49	21	52.5	−0.7	+0.4	26	21	53.7	G		10
	13	812	7.8	DD	59	19	31.8	G		17	N				
	14	979	7.7	DD	71	20	44.6	−1.4	−0.1	51	20	40.7	−1.6	+0.6	39
	15	1108	6.9	DD	82	20	58.4	−0.4	−2.6	134	20	45.9	−0.6	−2.3	127
	16	1131	7.2	DD	84	A					1	05.3	+0.7	−1.9	152
	17	1251	5.9	DD	95	1	22.8	+0.4	−1.6	111	1	16.3	+0.2	−1.7	111
	17	1348	7.7	DD	104	21	09.7	−1.3	−1.4	103	20	59.9	−1.3	−1.1	97
	19	1462	7.4	DD	117	1	30.2	−0.4	−1.5	71	1	21.6	−0.5	−1.6	71
	20	1645	6.6	DD	137	20	44.7	−0.8	−1.6	155	20	36.1	−0.8	−1.1	147
	20	1648	7.0	DD	138	21	43.1	−1.7	−0.5	100	21	36.5	−1.6	−0.1	95
May	10	780	6.8	DD	30	A					21	26.5	+0.9	−2.4	146
	12	1067	7.2	DD	52	20	54.6	0.0	−1.9	114	S				
Jun.	19	2237	5.1	DD	149	22	26.0	−1.3	−0.6	126	22	20.0	−1.1	−0.4	126
Jul.	2	465	4.5	RD	310	2	47.5	0.0	1.7	254	S				
	11	1644	4.1	DD	59	21	53.3	−0.1	−1.6	82	21	45.1	−0.2	−1.8	81
Sep.	14	3032	7.2	DD	135	21	44.3	−0.9	+0.3	41	A				
	15	3175	4.8	DD	148	20	06.5	G		349	N				
	22	472	5.0	RD	233	3	17.2	−1.6	+0.1	265	3	11.4	−1.7	−0.4	283
	24	890	4.5	RD	266	22	39.9	+0.7	+2.0	218	22	50.5	+0.6	+1.8	228
Oct.	12	3130	5.5	DD	117	20	41.3	−1.5	−0.3	84	20	36.3	−1.2	−0.1	75
	14	3421	5.1	DD	146	22	55.9	−0.5	+1.1	20	23	00.8	0.0	+1.5	2
Nov.	9	3228	6.5	DD	99	19	10.1	−1.5	0.0	80	19	06.1	−1.2	+0.2	71
	12	81	6.6	DD	139	20	20.3	−0.6	+1.8	21	20	27.5	−0.2	+2.0	8
Dec.	5	3032	7.2	DD	54	16	36.5	−1.7	−0.6	101	A				
	6	3191	7.6	DD	69	18	39.2	−1.4	−1.0	92	18	31.6	−1.1	−0.6	79
	7	3327	6.8	DD	82	18	31.5	−1.5	−0.3	82	18	26.6	−1.2	0.0	70
	9	38	7.9	DD	107	16	42.7	−1.0	+1.5	64	16	46.8	−0.8	+1.6	57
	9	50	6.0	DD	109	21	21.8	−0.5	+1.2	21	21	28.1	0.0	+2.2	359
	11	309	7.9	DD	135	22	18.7	−1.1	+0.8	46	22	20.4	−0.8	+1.4	28
	12	326	6.0	DD	137	1	55.8	−0.4	−0.5	56	1	52.8	−0.5	−0.2	41

MEAN PLACES OF STARS 2005.5

Name	Mag.	RA h m	Dec. ° '	Spectrum	Name	Mag.	RA h m	Dec. ° '	Spectrum
α And *Alpheratz*	2.1	0 08.7	+29 07	A0p	γ Corvi	2.6	12 16.1	−17 34	B8
β Cassiopeiae *Caph*	2.3	0 09.5	+59 11	F5	α Crucis	1.0	12 26.9	−63 08	B1
γ Pegasi *Algenib*	2.8	0 13.5	+15 13	B2	γ Crucis	1.6	12 31.5	−57 09	M3
β Mensae	2.9	0 26.0	−77 13	G0	γ Centauri	2.2	12 41.8	−48 59	A0
α Phoenicis	2.4	0 26.6	−42 17	K0	γ Viriginis	2.7	12 41.9	−1 29	F0
α Cassiopeiae *Schedar*	2.2	0 40.8	+56 34	K0	β Crucis	1.3	12 48.0	−59 43	B1
β Ceti *Diphda*	2.0	0 43.9	−17 57	K0	ε Ursae Majoris *Alioth*	1.8	12 54.3	+55 56	A0p
γ Cassiopeiae*	Var.	0 57.0	+60 45	B0p	α Canum *Venaticorum*	2.9	12 56.3	+38 17	A0p
β Andromedae *Mirach*	2.1	1 10.0	+35 39	M0	ζ Ursae Majoris *Mizar*	2.1	13 24.1	+54 54	A2p
δ Cassiopeiae	2.7	1 26.2	+60 16	A5	α Virginis *Spica*	1.0	13 25.5	−11 11	B2
α Eridani *Achernar*	0.5	1 37.9	−57 13	B5	ε Centauri	2.6	13 40.2	−53 30	B1
β Arietis *Sheratan*	2.6	1 54.9	+20 50	A5	η Ursae Majoris *Alkaid*	1.9	13 47.8	+49 17	B3
γ Andromedae *Almak*	2.3	2 04.2	+42 21	K0	β Centauri *Hadar*	0.6	14 04.2	−60 24	B1
α Arietis *Hamal*	2.0	2 07.5	+23 29	K2	θ Centauri	2.1	14 07.0	−36 24	K0
α Ursae Minoris *Polaris*	2.0	2 38.2	+89 17	F8	α Bootis *Arcturus*	0.0	14 15.9	+19 09	K0
β Persei *Algol**	Var.	3 08.5	+40 59	B8	α Centauri *Rigil Kent*	0.1	14 40.0	−60 51	G0
α Persei *Mirfak*	1.8	3 24.7	+49 53	F5	ε Bootis	2.4	14 45.2	+27 03	K0
η Tauri *Alcyone*	2.9	3 47.8	+24 07	B5p	β UMi *Kochab*	2.1	14 50.7	+74 08	K5
α Tauri *Aldebaran*	0.9	4 36.2	+16 31	K5	γ Ursae Minoris	3.1	15 20.7	+71 49	A2
β Orionis *Rigel*	0.1	5 14.8	−8 12	B8p	α CrB *Alphecca*	2.2	15 34.9	+26 42	A0
α Aurigae *Capella*	0.1	5 17.1	+46 00	G0	β Trianguli *Australis*	3.0	15 55.6	−63 27	F0
γ Orionis *Bellatrix*	1.6	5 25.4	+6 21	B2	δ Scorpii	2.3	16 00.7	−22 38	B0
β Tauri *Elnath*	1.7	5 26.6	+28 37	B8	β Scorpii	2.6	16 05.8	−19 49	B1
δ Orionis	2.2	5 32.3	−0 18	B0	α Scorpii *Antares*	1.0	16 29.7	−26 27	M0
α Leporis	2.6	5 33.0	−17 49	F0	α Trianguli Australis	1.9	16 49.3	−69 02	K2
ε Orionis	1.7	5 36.5	−1 12	B0	ε Scorpii	2.3	16 50.5	−34 18	K0
ζ Orionis	1.8	5 41.0	−1 56	B0	α Herculis†	Var.	17 14.9	+14 23	M3
κ Orionis	2.1	5 48.0	−9 40	B0	λ Scorpii	1.6	17 34.0	−37 06	B2
α Orionis *Betelgeuse**	Var.	5 55.5	+7 24	M0	α Ophiuchi *Rasalhague*	2.1	17 35.2	+12 33	A5
β Aurigae *Menkalinan*	1.9	5 59.9	+44 57	A0p	θ Scorpii	1.9	17 37.7	−43 00	F0
β CMa *Mirzam*	2.0	6 22.9	−17 58	B1	κ Scorpii	2.4	17 42.9	−39 02	B2
α Carinae *Canopus*	−0.7	6 24.1	−52 42	F0	λ Draconis	2.2	17 56.7	+51 29	K5
γ Geminorum *Alhena*	1.9	6 38.0	+16 24	A0	ε Sgr Kaus *Australis*	1.9	18 24.5	−34 23	A0
α Canis Majoris *Sirius*	−1.5	6 45.4	−16 43	A0	α Lyrae *Vega*	0.0	18 37.1	+38 47	A0
ε Canis Majoris	1.5	6 58.8	−28 59	B1	σ Sagittarii	2.0	18 55.6	−26 17	B3
δ Canis Majoris	1.9	7 08.6	−26 24	F8p	β Cygni *Albireo*	3.1	19 30.9	+27 58	K0
α Germinorum *Castor*	1.6	7 35.0	+31 53	A0	α Aquilae *Altair*	0.8	19 51.1	+8 53	A5
α CMi *Procyon*	0.4	7 39.6	+5 13	F5	α Capricorni	3.8	20 18.4	−12 32	G5
β Geminorum *Pollux*	1.1	7 45.7	+28 01	K0	γ Cygni	2.2	20 22.4	+40 16	F8p
ζ Puppis	1.7	8 03.8	−40 01	Od	α Pavonis	1.9	20 26.1	−56 43	B3
γ Velorum	1.8	8 09.7	−47 21	Oap	α Cygni *Deneb*	1.3	20 41.6	+45 18	A2p
ε Carinae	1.9	8 22.6	−59 32	K0	α Cephei *Alderamin*	2.4	21 18.7	+62 37	A5
δ Velorum	2.0	8 44.9	−54 44	A0	ε Pegasi	2.4	21 44.5	+9 54	K0
λ Velorum *Suhail*	2.2	9 08.2	−43 27	K5	δ Capricorni	2.9	21 47.3	−16 06	A5
β Carinae	1.7	9 13.3	−69 44	A0	α Gruis	1.7	22 08.6	−46 56	B5
ι Carinae	2.2	9 17.2	−59 18	F0	δ Cephei†	3.7	22 29.4	+58 27	†
κ Velorum	2.6	9 22.3	−55 02	B3	β Gruis	2.1	22 43.0	−46 51	M3
α Hydrae *Alphard*	2.0	9 27.9	−8 41	K2	α PsA *Fomalhaut*	1.2	22 58.0	−29 36	A3
α Leonis *Regulus*	1.3	10 08.7	+11 56	B8	β Pegasi *Scheat*	2.4	23 04.0	+28 07	M0
γ Leonis *Algeiba*	1.9	10 20.3	+19 49	K0	α Pegasi *Markab*	2.5	23 05.0	+15 14	A0
β Ursae Majoris *Merak*	2.4	11 02.2	+56 21	A0					
α Ursae Majoris *Dubhe*	1.8	11 04.1	+61 43	K0					
δ Leonis	2.6	11 14.4	+20 30	A3					
β Leonis *Denebola*	2.1	11 49.3	+14 32	A2					
γ Ursae Majoris *Phecda*	2.4	11 54.1	+53 40	A0					

*γ Cassiopeiae, 2004 mag. 2.6. β Persei, mag. 2.1 to 3.4.
α Orionis, mag. 0.1 to 1.2.
†α Herculis, mag. 3.1 to 3.9.
δ Cephei, mag. 3.7 to 4.4, spectrum F5 to G0.

The positions of heavenly bodies on the celestial sphere are defined by two co-ordinates, right ascension and declination, which are analogous to longitude and latitude on the surface of the Earth. If we imagine the plane of the terrestrial equator extended indefinitely, it will cut the celestial sphere in a great circle known as the celestial equator. Similarly the plane of the Earth's orbit, when extended, cuts in the great circle called the ecliptic. The two intersections of these circles are known as the First Point of Aries and the First Point of Libra. If from any star a perpendicular is drawn to the celestial equator, the length of this perpendicular is the star's declination. The arc, measured eastwards along the equator from the First Point of Aries to the foot of this perpendicular, is the right ascension. An alternative definition of right ascension is that it is the angle at the celestial pole (where the Earth's axis, if prolonged, would meet the sphere) between the great circles to the First Point of Aries and to the star.

The plane of the Earth's equator has a slow movement, so that our reference system for right ascension and declination is not fixed. The consequent alteration in these quantities from year to year is called precession. In right ascension it is an increase of about 3 seconds a year for equatorial stars, and larger or smaller changes in either direction for stars near the poles, depending on the right ascension of the star. In declination it varies between +20″ and −20″ according to the right ascension of the star.

A star or other body crosses the meridian when the sidereal time is equal to its right ascension. The altitude is then a maximum, and may be deduced by remembering that the altitude of the elevated pole is numerically equal to the latitude, while that of the equator at its intersection with the meridian is equal to the co-latitude, or complement of the latitude.

Thus in London (lat. 51° 30′) the meridian altitude of Sirius is found as follows:

	°	′
Altitude of equator	38	30
Declination south	16	43
Difference	21	47

The altitude of Capella (Dec. +46° 00′) at lower transit is:

	°	′
Altitude of pole	51	30
Polar distance of star	44	00
Difference	7	30

The brightness of a heavenly body is denoted by its magnitude. Omitting the exceptionally bright stars Sirius and Canopus, the twenty brightest stars are of the first magnitude, while the faintest stars visible to the naked eye are of the sixth magnitude. The magnitude scale is a precise one, as a difference of five magnitudes represents a ratio of 100 to 1 in brightness. Typical second magnitude stars are Polaris and the stars in the belt of Orion. The scale is most easily fixed in memory by comparing the stars with Norton's *Star Atlas*. The stars Sirius and Canopus and the planets Venus and Jupiter are so bright that their magnitudes are expressed by negative numbers. A small telescope will show stars down to the ninth or tenth magnitude, while stars fainter than the twentieth magnitude may be photographed by long exposures with the largest telescopes.

MEAN AND SIDEREAL TIME

Acceleration						Retardation					
h	m	s	m	s	s	h	m	s	m	s	s
1	0	10	0	00	0	1	0	10	0	00	0
2	0	20	3	02	1	2	0	20	3	03	1
3	0	30	9	07	2	3	0	29	9	09	2
4	0	39	15	13	3	4	0	39	15	15	3
5	0	49	21	18	4	5	0	49	21	21	4
6	0	59	27	23	5	6	0	59	27	28	5
7	1	09	33	28	6	7	1	09	33	34	6
8	1	19	39	34	7	8	1	19	39	40	7
9	1	29	45	39	8	9	1	28	45	46	8
10	1	39	51	44	9	10	1	38	51	53	9
11	1	48	57	49	10	11	1	48	57	59	10
12	1	58	60	00		12	1	58	60	00	
13	2	08				13	2	08			
14	2	18				14	2	18			
15	2	28				15	2	27			
16	2	38				16	2	37			
17	2	48				17	2	47			
18	2	57				18	2	57			
19	3	07				19	3	07			
20	3	17				20	3	17			
21	3	27				21	3	26			
22	3	37				22	3	36			
23	3	47				23	3	46			
24	3	57				24	3	56			

The length of a sidereal day in mean time is 23h 56m 04s.09. Hence 1h MT = 1h+9s.86 ST and 1h ST = 1h−9s.83 MT.

To convert an interval of mean time to the corresponding interval of sidereal time, enter the acceleration table with the given mean time (taking the hours and the minutes and seconds separately) and add the acceleration obtained to the given mean time. To convert an interval of sidereal time to the corresponding interval of mean time, take out the retardation for the given sidereal time and subtract.

The columns for the minutes and seconds of the argument are in the form known as critical tables. To use these tables, find in the appropriate left-hand column the two entries between which the given number of minutes and seconds lies; the quantity in the right-hand column between these two entries is the required acceleration or retardation. Thus the acceleration for 11m 26s (which lies between the entries 9m 07s and 15m 13s) is 2s. If the given number of minutes and seconds is a tabular entry, the required acceleration or retardation is the entry in the right-hand column above the given tabular entry, e.g. the retardation for 45m 46s is 7s.

Example – Convert 14h 27m 35s from ST to MT

	h	m	s
Given ST	14	27	35
Retardation for 14h		2	18
Retardation for 27m 35s			5
Corresponding MT	14	25	12

For further explanation, *see* pages 669–70.

ECLIPSES AND SHADOW TRANSITS OF JUPITER'S SATELLITES 2005

GMT d	h	m	Sat.	Phen.
January				
1	07	04	II	Sh.I
3	02	05	II	Ec.D
7	06	15	I	Sh.I
8	03	22	I	Ec.D
9	01	59	III	Sh.E
9	02	55	I	Sh.E
10	04	40	II	Ec.D
12	01	35	II	Sh.E
15	05	15	I	Ec.D
16	02	36	I	Sh.I
16	03	08	III	Sh.I
16	04	48	I	Sh.E
16	05	55	III	Sh.E
17	07	15	II	Ec.D
19	01	27	II	Sh.I
19	04	08	II	Sh.E
22	07	08	I	Ec.D
23	04	29	I	Sh.I
23	06	42	I	Sh.E
23	07	05	III	Sh.I
24	01	37	I	Ec.D
25	01	10	I	Sh.E
26	04	01	II	Sh.I
26	06	41	II	Sh.E
30	06	23	I	Sh.I
31	03	30	I	Ec.D
February				
1	00	51	I	Sh.I
1	03	03	I	Sh.E
2	06	34	II	Sh.I
3	01	07	III	Ec.D
3	03	54	III	Ec.R
4	01	42	II	Ec.D
7	05	23	I	Ec.D
8	02	44	I	Sh.I
8	04	56	I	Sh.E
8	23	51	I	Ec.D
9	23	24	I	Sh.E
10	05	04	III	Ec.D
11	04	17	II	Ec.D
13	01	06	II	Sh.E
15	04	37	I	Sh.I
15	06	49	I	Sh.E
16	01	44	I	Ec.D
16	23	06	I	Sh.I
17	01	18	I	Sh.E
18	06	51	II	Ec.D
20	00	59	II	Sh.I
20	03	40	II	Sh.E
20	22	56	III	Sh.I
21	01	39	III	Sh.E
22	06	31	I	Sh.I
23	03	37	I	Ec.D
24	00	59	I	Sh.I
24	03	11	I	Sh.E
27	03	34	II	Sh.I
27	06	15	II	Sh.E
28	02	53	II	Sh.I
28	05	36	III	Sh.E
28	22	43	II	Ec.D
March				
2	05	31	I	Ec.D
3	02	52	I	Sh.I
3	05	04	I	Sh.E
3	23	59	I	Ec.D
4	23	33	I	Sh.E
6	06	08	II	Ec.D
8	01	17	II	Ec.D
9	22	07	II	Sh.E
10	04	46	I	Sh.I
11	01	53	I	Ec.D
11	23	14	I	Sh.I
12	01	26	I	Sh.E
15	03	52	II	Ec.D
16	22	00	II	Sh.I
17	00	42	II	Sh.E
18	00	55	III	Ec.D
18	03	47	I	Ec.D
19	01	07	I	Sh.I
19	03	19	I	Sh.E
19	22	15	I	Ec.D
20	21	48	I	Sh.E
24	00	36	II	Sh.I
24	03	17	II	Sh.E
25	04	53	III	Ec.D
25	05	41	I	Ec.D
26	03	01	I	Sh.I
26	05	13	I	Sh.E
27	00	09	I	Ec.D
27	21	29	I	Sh.I
27	23	41	I	Sh.E
28	21	23	III	Sh.E
31	03	11	II	Sh.I
April				
1	22	17	II	Ec.D
2	04	55	I	Sh.I
3	02	03	I	Ec.D
3	04	16	I	Ec.R
3	23	23	I	Sh.I
4	01	35	I	Sh.E
4	22	43	III	Sh.I
4	22	44	I	Ec.R
5	01	20	III	Sh.E
5	20	04	I	Sh.E
9	03	32	II	Ec.R
10	21	47	II	Sh.E
11	01	17	I	Sh.I
11	03	29	I	Sh.E
12	00	39	I	Ec.R
12	02	42	III	Sh.I
12	19	46	I	Sh.I
12	21	57	I	Sh.E
17	21	42	II	Sh.I
18	00	23	II	Sh.E
18	03	11	I	Sh.I
19	02	33	I	Ec.R
19	21	40	I	Sh.I
19	23	51	I	Sh.E
20	21	02	I	Ec.R
22	23	23	III	Ec.R
25	00	19	II	Sh.I
25	03	00	II	Sh.E
26	21	57	II	Ec.R
26	23	34	I	Sh.I
27	01	45	I	Sh.E
27	22	56	I	Ec.R
28	20	14	I	Sh.E
30	03	21	III	Ec.R
May				
2	02	55	II	Sh.I
4	00	31	II	Ec.R
4	01	28	I	Sh.I
5	00	51	I	Ec.R
5	22	08	I	Sh.E
10	21	08	III	Sh.E
12	21	31	II	Sh.I
12	21	51	I	Sh.I
13	00	02	I	Sh.E
13	21	15	I	Ec.R
17	22	35	III	Sh.I
18	01	06	III	Sh.E
19	21	28	II	Sh.I
19	23	45	I	Sh.I
20	00	08	II	Sh.E
20	01	56	I	Sh.E
20	23	10	I	Ec.R
27	00	05	II	Sh.I
27	01	40	I	Sh.I
28	01	05	I	Ec.R
28	21	31	II	Ec.R
28	22	19	I	Sh.E
June				
4	22	03	I	Sh.I
4	23	12	III	Ec.R
5	00	05	II	Ec.R
5	00	13	I	Sh.E
5	21	29	I	Ec.R
11	23	57	I	Sh.I
12	23	24	I	Ec.R
13	21	18	II	Sh.E
20	21	17	II	Sh.I
20	22	31	I	Sh.I
20	23	55	II	Sh.E
27	22	15	I	Sh.I
28	21	43	I	Ec.R
29	22	30	III	Sh.I
July				
15	21	05	II	Sh.E
21	21	57	I	Ec.R
22	21	05	II	Sh.I
31	20	40	II	Ec.R
November				
24	06	26	II	Sh.I
26	06	05	I	Ec.D
December				
4	07	19	I	Sh.E
8	06	22	III	Ec.R
10	05	56	II	Ec.D
11	07	02	I	Sh.I
19	05	57	II	Sh.E
19	06	13	I	Ec.D
20	05	34	I	Sh.E
26	05	56	II	Sh.I
27	05	18	I	Sh.I
27	07	28	I	Sh.E

Jupiter's satellites transit across the disk from east to west, and pass behind the disk from west to east. The shadows that they cast also transit across the disk. With the exception at times of Satellite IV, the satellites also pass through the shadow of the planet, i.e. they are eclipsed. Just before opposition the satellite disappears in the shadow to the west of the planet and reappears from occultation on the east limb. Immediately after opposition the satellite is occulted at the west limb and reappears from eclipse to the east of the planet. At times approximately two to four months before and after opposition, both phases of eclipses of Satellite III may be seen. When Satellite IV is eclipsed, both phases may be seen.

The times given refer to the centre of the satellite. As the satellite is of considerable size, the immersion and emersion phases are not instantaneous. Even when the satellite enters or leaves the shadow along a radius of the shadow, the phase can last for several minutes. With Satellite IV, grazing phenomena can occur so that the light from the satellite may fade and brighten again without a complete eclipse taking place.

The list of phenomena gives most of the eclipses and shadow transits visible in the British Isles under favourable conditions.

Ec. = Eclipse   R = Reappearance
Sh. = Shadow transit I = Ingress
D = Disappearance   E = Egress

EXPLANATION OF ASTRONOMICAL DATA

Positions of the heavenly bodies are given only to the degree of accuracy required by amateur astronomers for setting telescopes, or for plotting on celestial globes or star atlases. Where intermediate positions are required, linear interpolation may be employed.

Definitions of the terms used cannot be given here. They must be sought in astronomical literature and textbooks.

A special feature has been made of the times when the various heavenly bodies are visible in the British Isles. Since two columns, calculated for latitudes 52° and 56°, are devoted to risings and settings, the range 50° to 58° can be covered by interpolation and extrapolation. The times given in these columns are Greenwich Mean Times for the meridian of Greenwich. An observer west of this meridian must add his/her longitude (in time) and vice versa.

In accordance with the usual convention in astronomy, + and − indicate respectively north and south latitudes or declinations.

All data are, unless otherwise stated, for 0h Greenwich Mean Time (GMT), i.e. at the midnight at the beginning of the day named. Allowance must be made for British Summer Time during the period that this is in operation.

PAGE ONE OF EACH MONTH

The calendar for each month is explained on page 611.

Under the heading Astronomical Phenomena will be found particulars of the more important conjunctions of the Sun, Moon and planets with each other, and also the dates of other astronomical phenomena of special interest.

Times of Minima of Algol are approximate times of the middle of the period of diminished light.

The Constellations listed each month are those that are near the meridian at the beginning of the month at 22h local mean time. Allowance must be made for British Summer Time if necessary. The fact that any star crosses the meridian 4m earlier each night or 2h earlier each month may be used, in conjunction with the lists given each month, to find what constellations are favourably placed at any moment. The table preceding the list of constellations may be extended indefinitely at the rate just quoted.

The principal phases of the Moon are the GMTs when the difference between the longitude of the Moon and that of the Sun is 0°, 90°, 180° or 270°. The times of perigee and apogee are those when the Moon is nearest to, and farthest from, the Earth, respectively. The nodes or points of intersection of the Moon's orbit and the ecliptic make a complete retrograde circuit of the ecliptic in about 19 years. From a knowledge of the longitude of the ascending node and the inclination, whose value does not vary much from 5°, the path of the Moon among the stars may be plotted on a celestial globe or star atlas.

PAGE TWO OF EACH MONTH

The Sun's semi-diameter, in arc, is given once a month.

The right ascension and declination (Dec.) is that of the true Sun. The right ascension of the mean Sun is obtained by applying the equation of time, with the sign given, to the right ascension of the true Sun, or, more easily, by applying 12h to the Sidereal Time. The direction in which the equation of time has to be applied in different problems is a frequent source of confusion and error. Apparent Solar Time is equal to the Mean Solar Time plus the Equation of Time. For example, at 12h GMT on August 8 the Equation of Time is −5m 36s and thus at 12h Mean Time on that day the Apparent Time is 12h − 5m 36s = 11h 54m 24s.

The Greenwich Sidereal Time at 0h and the Transit of the First Point of Aries (which is really the mean time when the sidereal time is 0h) are used for converting mean time to sidereal time and vice versa.

The GMT of transit of the Sun at Greenwich may also be taken as the local mean time (LMT) of transit in any longitude. It is independent of latitude. The GMT of transit in any longitude is obtained by adding the longitude to the time given if west, and vice versa.

LIGHTING-UP TIME

The legal importance of sunrise and sunset is that the Road Vehicles Lighting Regulations 1989 (SI 1989 No. 1796) make the use of front and rear position lamps on vehicles compulsory during the period between sunset and sunrise. Headlamps on vehicles are required to be used during the hours of darkness on unlit roads or whenever visibility is seriously reduced. The hours of darkness are defined in these regulations as the period between half an hour after sunset and half an hour before sunrise.

In all laws and regulations 'sunset' refers to the local sunset, i.e. the time at which the Sun sets at the place in question. This common-sense interpretation has been upheld by legal tribunals. Thus the necessity for providing for different latitudes and longitudes, as already described, is evident.

SUNRISE AND SUNSET

The times of sunrise and sunset are those when the Sun's upper limb, as affected by refraction, is on the true horizon of an observer at sea-level. Assuming the mean refraction to be 34′, and the Sun's semi-diameter to be 16′, the time given is that when the true zenith distance of the Sun's centre is 90°+34′+16′ or 90° 50′, or, in other words, when the depression of the Sun's centre below the true horizon is 50′. The upper limb is then 34′ below the true horizon, but is brought there by refraction. An observer on a ship might see the Sun for a minute or so longer, because of the dip of the horizon, while another viewing the sunset over hills or mountains would record an earlier time. Nevertheless, the moment when the true zenith distance of the Sun's centre is 90° 50′ is a precise time dependent only on the latitude and longitude of the place, and independent of its altitude above sea-level, the contour of its horizon, the vagaries of refraction or the small seasonal change in the Sun's semi-diameter; this moment is suitable in every way as a definition of sunset (or sunrise) for all statutory purposes. (For further information, see footnote on page 668.)

TWILIGHT

Light reaches us before sunrise and continues to reach us for some time after sunset. The interval between darkness and sunrise or sunset and darkness is called twilight. Astronomically speaking, twilight is considered to begin or end when the Sun's centre is 18° below the horizon, as no light from the Sun can then reach the observer. As thus defined twilight may last several hours; in high latitudes at the summer solstice the depression of 18° is not reached, and twilight lasts from sunset to sunrise.

The need for some sub-division of twilight is met by dividing the gathering darkness into four stages.

(1) *Sunrise or Sunset*, defined as above
(2) *Civil twilight*, which begins or ends when the Sun's centre is 6° below the horizon. This marks the time when operations requiring daylight may commence or

must cease. In England it varies from about 30 to 60 minutes after sunset and the same interval before sunrise

(3) *Nautical twilight*, which begins or ends when the Sun's centre is 12° below the horizon. This marks the time when it is, to all intents and purposes, completely dark

(4) *Astronomical twilight*, which begins or ends when the Sun's centre is 18° below the horizon. This marks theoretical perfect darkness. It is of little practical importance, especially if nautical twilight is tabulated

To assist observers the durations of civil, nautical and astronomical twilights are given at intervals of ten days. The beginning of a particular twilight is found by subtracting the duration from the time of sunrise, while the end is found by adding the duration to the time of sunset. Thus the beginning of astronomical twilight in latitude 52°, on the Greenwich meridian, on March 11 is found as 06h 23m − 113m = 04h 30m and similarly the end of civil twilight at 17h 58m +34m = 18h 32m. The letters TAN (twilight all night) are printed when twilight lasts all night.

Under the heading The Night Sky will be found notes describing the position and visibility of the planets and other phenomena.

PAGE THREE OF EACH MONTH
The Moon moves so rapidly among the stars that its position is given only to the degree of accuracy that permits linear interpolation. The right ascension (RA) and declination (Dec.) are geocentric, i.e. for an imaginary observer at the centre of the Earth. To an observer on the surface of the Earth the position is always different, as the altitude is always less on account of parallax, which may reach 1°.

The lunar terminator is the line separating the bright from the dark part of the Moon's disk. Apart from irregularities of the lunar surface, the terminator is elliptical, because it is a circle seen in projection. It becomes the full circle forming the limb, or edge, of the Moon at New and Full Moon. The selenographic longitude of the terminator is measured from the mean centre of the visible disk, which may differ from the visible centre by as much as 8°, because of libration.

Instead of the longitude of the terminator the Sun's selenographic co-longitude (Sun's co-long.) is tabulated. It is numerically equal to the selenographic longitude of the morning terminator, measured eastwards from the mean centre of the disk. Thus its value is approximately 270° at New Moon, 360° at First Quarter, 90° at Full Moon and 180° at Last Quarter.

The Position Angle (PA) of the Bright Limb is the position angle of the midpoint of the illuminated limb, measured eastwards from the north point on the disk. The Phase column shows the percentage of the area of the Moon's disk illuminated; this is also the illuminated percentage of the diameter at right angles to the line of cusps. The terminator is a semi-ellipse whose major axis is the line of cusps, and whose semi-minor axis is determined by the tabulated percentage; from New Moon to Full Moon the east limb is dark, and vice versa.

The times given as moonrise and moonset are those when the upper limb of the Moon is on the horizon of an observer at sea-level. The Sun's horizontal parallax (Hor. par.) is about 9″, and is negligible when considering sunrise and sunset, but that of the Moon averages about 57′. Hence the computed time represents the moment when the true zenith distance of the Moon is 90° 50′ (as for the Sun) minus the horizontal parallax. The time required for the Sun or Moon to rise or set is about four minutes (except in high latitudes). *See also* page 661 and footnote below.

The GMT of transit of the Moon over the meridian of Greenwich is given; these times are independent of latitude but must be corrected for longitude. For places in the British Isles it suffices to add the longitude if west, and vice versa. For other places a further correction is necessary because of the rapid movement of the Moon relative to the stars. The entire correction is conveniently determined by first finding the west longitude λ of the place. If the place is in west longitude, λ is the ordinary west longitude; if the place is in east longitude λ is the complement to 24h (or 360°) of the longitude and will be greater than 12h (or 180°). The correction then consists of two positive portions, namely λ and the fraction λ/24 (or λ°/360) multiplied by the difference between consecutive transits. Thus for Christchurch, New Zealand, the longitude is 11h 31m east, so λ = 12h 29m and the fraction λ/24 is 0.52. The transit on the local date 31 May 2005 is found as follows:

		d	h	m
GMT of transit at Greenwich	May	30	06	05
λ			12	29
0.52 × (6h 53m − 6h 05m)				25
GMT of transit at Christchurch		30	18	59
Corr. to NZ Standard Time			12	00
Local standard time of transit	May	31	06	59

As is evident, for any given place the quantities λ and the correction to local standard time may be combined permanently, being here 24h 29m.

Positions of Mercury are given for every second day, and those of Venus and Mars for every fifth day; they may be interpolated linearly. The diameter (Diam.) is given in seconds of arc. The phase is the illuminated percentage of the disk. In the case of the inner planets this approaches 100 at superior conjunction and 0 at inferior conjunction. When the phase is less than 50 the planet is crescent-shaped or horned; for greater phases it is gibbous. In the case of the exterior planet Mars, the phase approaches 100 at conjunction and opposition, and is a minimum at the quadratures.

Since the planets cannot be seen when on the horizon, the actual times of rising and setting are not given; instead, the time when the planet has an apparent altitude of 5° has been tabulated. If the time of transit is between 00h and 12h the time refers to an altitude of 5° above the eastern horizon; if between 12h and 24h, to the western horizon. The phenomenon tabulated is the one that occurs between sunset and sunrise. The times given may be interpolated for latitude and corrected for longitude, as in the case of the Sun and Moon.

SUNRISE, SUNSET, MOONRISE AND MOONSET
The tables have been constructed for the meridian of Greenwich and for latitudes 52° and 56°. They give Greenwich Mean Time (GMT) throughout the year. To obtain the GMT of the phenomenon as seen from any other latitude and longitude in the British Isles, first interpolate or extrapolate for latitude by the usual rules of proportion. To the time thus found, the longitude (expressed in time) is to be added if west (as it usually is in Great Britain) or subtracted if east. If the longitude is expressed in degrees and minutes of arc, it must be converted to time at the rate of 1° = 4m and 15′ = 1m. A method of calculating rise and set time for other places in the world is given on pages 660 and 661

The GMT at which the planet transits the Greenwich meridian is also given. The times of transit are to be corrected to local meridians in the usual way, as already described.

PAGE FOUR OF EACH MONTH

The GMTs of sunrise and sunset for seven cities, whose adopted positions in longitude (W.) and latitude (N.) are given immediately below the name, may be used not only for these phenomena, but also for lighting-up times (*see* page 667 for a fuller explanation).

The particulars for the four outer planets resemble those for the planets on Page Three of each month, except that, under Uranus and Neptune, times when the planet is 10° high instead of 5° high are given; this is because of the inferior brightness of these planets. The diameters given for the rings of Saturn are those of the major axis (in the plane of the planet's equator) and the minor axis respectively. The former has a small seasonal change due to the slightly varying distance of the Earth from Saturn, but the latter varies from zero when the Earth passes through the ring plane every 15 years to its maximum opening half-way between these periods. The rings were last open at their widest extent (and Saturn at its brightest) in 2002; this will occur again in 2017. The Earth passed through the ring plane in 1995–6 and will do so again in 2009.

TIME

From the earliest ages, the natural division of time into recurring periods of day and night has provided the practical time-scale for the everyday activities of the human race. Indeed, if any alternative means of time measurement is adopted, it must be capable of adjustment so as to remain in general agreement with the natural time-scale defined by the diurnal rotation of the Earth on its axis. Ideally the rotation should be measured against a fixed frame of reference; in practice it must be measured against the background provided by the celestial bodies. If the Sun is chosen as the reference point, we obtain Apparent Solar Time, which is the time indicated by a sundial. It is not a uniform time but is subject to variations which amount to as much as a quarter of an hour in each direction. Such wide variations cannot be tolerated in a practical time-scale, and this has led to the concept of Mean Solar Time in which all the days are exactly the same length and equal to the average length of the Apparent Solar Day.

The positions of the stars in the sky are specified in relation to a fictitious reference point in the sky known as the First Point of Aries (or the Vernal Equinox). It is therefore convenient to adopt this same reference point when considering the rotation of the Earth against the background of the stars. The time-scale so obtained is known as Apparent Sidereal Time.

GREENWICH MEAN TIME

The daily rotation of the Earth on its axis causes the Sun and the other heavenly bodies to appear to cross the sky from east to west. It is convenient to represent this relative motion as if the Sun really performed a daily circuit around a fixed Earth. Noon in Apparent Solar Time may then be defined as the time at which the Sun transits across the observer's meridian. In Mean Solar Time, noon is similarly defined by the meridian transit of a fictitious Mean Sun moving uniformly in the sky with the same average speed as the true Sun. Mean Solar Time observed on the meridian of the transit circle telescope of the Royal Observatory at Greenwich is called Greenwich Mean Time (GMT). The mean solar day is divided into 24 hours and, for astronomical and other scientific purposes, these are numbered 0 to 23, commencing at midnight. Civil

time is usually reckoned in two periods of 12 hours, designated a.m. (*ante meridiem*, i.e. before noon) and p.m. (*post meridiem*, i.e. after noon), although the 24 hour clock is increasingly being used.

UNIVERSAL TIME

Before 1925 January 1, GMT was reckoned in 24 hours commencing at noon; since that date it has been reckoned from midnight. To avoid confusion in the use of the designation GMT before and after 1925, since 1928 astronomers have tended to use the term Universal Time (UT) or Weltzeit (WZ) to denote GMT measured from Greenwich Mean Midnight.

In precision work it is necessary to take account of small variations in Universal Time. These arise from small irregularities in the rotation of the Earth. Observed astronomical time is designated UT0. Observed time corrected for the effects of the motion of the poles (giving rise to a 'wandering' in longitude) is designated UT1. There is also a seasonal fluctuation in the rate of rotation of the Earth arising from meteorological causes, often called the annual fluctuation. UT1 corrected for this effect is designated UT2 and provides a time-scale free from short-period fluctuations. It is still subject to small secular and irregular changes.

APPARENT SOLAR TIME

As mentioned above, the time shown by a sundial is called Apparent Solar Time. It differs from Mean Solar Time by an amount known as the Equation of Time, which is the total effect of two causes which make the length of the apparent solar day non-uniform. One cause of variation is that the orbit of the Earth is not a circle but an ellipse, having the Sun at one focus. As a consequence, the angular speed of the Earth in its orbit is not constant; it is greatest at the beginning of January when the Earth is nearest the Sun.

The other cause is due to the obliquity of the ecliptic; the plane of the equator (which is at right angles to the axis of rotation of the Earth) does not coincide with the ecliptic (the plane defined by the apparent annual motion of the Sun around the celestial sphere) but is inclined to it at an angle of 23° 26′. As a result, the apparent solar day is shorter than average at the equinoxes and longer at the solstices. From the combined effects of the components due to obliquity and eccentricity, the equation of time reaches its maximum values in February (−14 minutes) and early November (+16 minutes). It has a zero value on four dates during the year, and it is only on these dates (approximately April 15, June 14, September 1 and December 25) that a sundial shows Mean Solar Time.

SIDEREAL TIME

A sidereal day is the duration of a complete rotation of the Earth with reference to the First Point of Aries. The term sidereal (or 'star') time is a little misleading since the time-scale so defined is not exactly the same as that which would be defined by successive transits of a selected star, as there is a small progressive motion between the stars and the First Point of Aries due to the precession of the Earth's axis. This makes the length of the sidereal day shorter than the true period of rotation by 0.008 seconds. Superimposed on this steady precessional motion are small oscillations (nutation), giving rise to fluctuations in apparent sidereal time amounting to as much as 1.2 seconds. It is therefore customary to employ Mean Sidereal Time, from which these fluctuations have been removed. The conversion of GMT to Greenwich sidereal time (GST) may be performed by adding the value of the GST at 0h on the day in question (page two of each month) to the GMT converted to sidereal time using the table on page 665.

Example – To find the GST at August 8d 02h 41m 11s GMT

	h	m	s
GST at 0h	21	06	24
GMT	2	41	11
Acceleration for 2h			20
Acceleration for 41m 11s			7
Sum = GST =	23	48	02

If the observer is not on the Greenwich meridian then his/her longitude, measured positively westwards from Greenwich, must be subtracted from the GST to obtain Local Sidereal Time (LST). Thus, in the above example, an observer 5h east of Greenwich, or 19h west, would find the LST as 4h 48m 59s.

EPHEMERIS TIME
An analysis of observations of the positions of the Sun, Moon and planets taken over an extended period is used in preparing ephemerides. (An ephemeris is a table giving the apparent position of a heavenly body at regular intervals of time, e.g. one day or ten days, and may be used to compare current observations with tabulated positions.) Discrepancies between the positions of heavenly bodies observed over a 300-year period and their predicted positions arose because the time-scale to which the observations were related was based on the assumption that the rate of rotation of the Earth is uniform. It is now known that this rate of rotation is variable. A revised time-scale, Ephemeris Time (ET), was devised to bring the ephemerides into agreement with the observations.

The second of ET is defined in terms of the annual motion of the Earth in its orbit around the Sun (1/31556925.9747 of the tropical year for 1900 January 0d 12h ET). The precise determination of ET from astronomical observations is a lengthy process as the requisite standard of accuracy can only be achieved by averaging over a number of years.

In 1976 the International Astronomical Union adopted Terrestrial Dynamical Time (TDT), a new dynamical time-scale for general use whose scale unit is the SI second (*see* Atomic Time, below). TDT was renamed Terrestrial Time (TT) in 1991. ET is now of little more than historical interest.

TERRESTRIAL TIME
The uniform time system used in computing the ephemerides of the solar system is Terrestrial Time (TT), which has replaced ET for this purpose. Except for the most rigorous astronomical calculations, it may be assumed to be the same as ET. During 2005 the estimated difference TT − UT is about 65 seconds.

ATOMIC TIME
The fundamental standards of time and frequency must be defined in terms of a periodic motion adequately uniform, enduring and measurable. Progress has made it possible to use natural standards, such as atomic or molecular oscillations. Continuous oscillations are generated in an electrical circuit, the frequency of which is then compared or brought into coincidence with the frequency

characteristic of the absorption or emission by the atoms or molecules when they change between two selected energy levels. The National Physical Laboratory (NPL) routinely uses clocks of high stability produced by locking a quartz oscillator to the frequencies defined by caesium or hydrogen atoms.

International Atomic Time (TAI), established through international collaboration, is formed by combining the readings of many caesium clocks and was set close to the astronomically-based Universal Time (UT) near the beginning of 1958. It was formally recognised in 1971 and since 1988 January 1 has been maintained by the International Bureau of Weights and Measures (BIPM). The second markers are generated according to the International System (SI) definition adopted in 1967 at the 13th General Conference of Weights and Measures: 'The second is the duration of 9,192,631,770 periods of the radiation corresponding to the transition between the two hyperfine levels of the ground state of the caesium-133 atom.'

Civil time in almost all countries is now based on Co-ordinated Universal Time (UTC), which was adopted for scientific purposes on 1972 January 1. UTC differs from TAI by an integer number of seconds (determined from studies of the rate of rotation of the Earth) and was designed to make both atomic time and UT accessible with accuracies appropriate for most users. The UTC time-scale is adjusted by the insertion (or, in principle, omission) of leap seconds in order to keep it within ±0.9 s of UT. These leap seconds are introduced, when necessary, at the same instant throughout the world, either at the end of December or at the end of June. All leap seconds so far have been positive, with 61 seconds in the final minute of the UTC month. The time 23h 59m 60s UTC is followed one second later by 0h 0m 00s of the first day of the following month. Notices concerning the insertion of leap seconds are issued by the International Earth Rotation Service (IERS) at the Observatoire de Paris.

RADIO TIME-SIGNALS
UTC is made generally available through time-signals and standard frequency broadcasts such as MSF in the UK, CHU in Canada and WWV and WWVH in the USA. These are based on national time-scales that are maintained in close agreement with UTC and provide traceability to the national time-scale and to UTC. The markers of seconds in the UTC scale coincide with those of TAI.

To disseminate the national time-scale in the UK, special signals are broadcast on behalf of the National Physical Laboratory from the BT radio station at Rugby (call-sign MSF). The signals are controlled from a caesium beam atomic frequency standard and consist of a precise frequency carrier of 60 kHz which is switched off, after being on for at least half a second, to mark every second. The first second of the minute begins with a period of 500 ms with the carrier switched off, to serve as a minute marker. In the other seconds the carrier is always off for at least one tenth of a second at the start and then it carries an on-off code giving the British clock time and date, together with information identifying the start of the next minute. Changes to and from summer time are made following government announcements. Leap seconds are inserted as announced by the IERS and information provided by them on the difference between UTC and UT is also signalled. Other broadcast signals in the UK include the BBC six pips signal, the BT Timeline ('speaking clock'), the NPL Truetime service for computers, and a coded time-signal on the BBC 198 kHz transmitters which is used for timing in the electricity supply industry. From 1972 January 1 the six pips on the BBC have consisted of five short pips from second 55 to second 59 (six pips in the case of a leap second) followed by one lengthened pip, the start of which indicates the exact minute. From 1990 February 5 these signals have been controlled by the BBC with seconds markers referenced to the satellite-based US navigation system GPS (Global Positioning System) and time and day referenced to the MSF transmitter. Formerly they were generated by the Royal Greenwich Observatory. The BT Timeline is compared daily with the National Physical Laboratory caesium beam atomic frequency standard at the Rugby radio station. The NPL Truetime service is directly connected to the national time scale.

Accurate timing may also be obtained from the signals of international navigation systems such as the ground-based Omega, or the satellite-based American GPS or Russian GLONASS systems.

STANDARD TIME

Since 1880 the standard time in Britain has been Greenwich Mean Time (GMT); a statute that year enacted that the word 'time' when used in any legal document relating to Britain meant, unless otherwise specifically stated, the mean time of the Greenwich meridian. Greenwich was adopted as the universal meridian on 13 October 1884. A system of standard time by zones is used world-wide, standard time in each zone differing from that of the Greenwich meridian by an integral number of hours, either fast or slow. The large territories of the USA and Canada are divided into zones approximately 7.5° on either side of central meridians.

Variations from the standard time of some countries occur during part of the year; they are decided annually and are usually referred to as Summer Time or Daylight Saving Time.

At the 180th meridian the time can be either 12 hours fast on Greenwich Mean Time or 12 hours slow, and a change of date occurs. The internationally recognised date or calendar line is a modification of the 180th meridian, drawn so as to include islands of any one group on the same side of the line, or for political reasons. The line is indicated by joining up the following co-ordinates:

Lat.	Long.	Lat.	Long.
60° S.	180°	48° N.	180°
51° S.	180°	53° N.	170° E.
45° S.	172.5° W.	65.5° N.	169° W.
15° S.	172.5° W.	75° N.	180°
5° S.	180°		

Changes to the date line would require an international conference.

BRITISH SUMMER TIME

In 1916 an Act ordained that during a defined period of that year the legal time for general purposes in Great Britain should be one hour in advance of Greenwich Mean Time. The Summer Time Acts 1922 and 1925 defined the period during which Summer Time was to be in force, stabilising practice until the Second World War.

During World War 2 the duration of Summer Time was extended and in the years 1941 to 1945 and in 1947 Double Summer Time (two hours in advance of Greenwich Mean Time) was in force. After the war,

Summer Time was extended each year in 1948–52 and 1961–4 by Order in Council.

Between 1968 October 27 and 1971 October 31 clocks were kept one hour ahead of Greenwich Mean Time throughout the year. This was known as British Standard Time.

The most recent legislation is the Summer Time Act 1972, which enacted that 'the period of summer time for the purposes of this Act is the period beginning at two o'clock, Greenwich mean time, in the morning of the day after the third Saturday in March or, if that day is Easter Day, the day after the second Saturday in March, and ending at two o'clock, Greenwich mean time, in the morning of the day after the fourth Saturday in October.'

The duration of Summer Time can be varied by Order in Council and in recent years alterations have been made to bring the operation of Summer Time in Britain closer to similar provisions in other countries of the European Union; for instance, since 1981 the hour of changeover has been 01h Greenwich Mean Time.

The duration of Summer Time in 2005 is:

March 27 01h GMT to October 30 01h GMT

MEAN REFRACTION

Alt.	Ref.		Alt.	Ref.		Alt.	Ref.	
°	′	′	°	′	′	°	′	′
1	20	21	3	12	13	7	54	6
1	30	20	3	34	12	9	27	5
1	41	19	4	00	11	11	39	4
1	52	18	4	30	10	15	00	3
2	05	17	5	06	9	20	42	2
2	19	16	5	50	8	32	20	1
2	35	15	6	44	7	62	17	0
2	52	14	7	54		90	00	
3	12							

The refraction table is in the form of a critical table (*see* page 665)

ASTRONOMICAL CONSTANTS

Solar parallax	8″.794
Astronomical unit	149597870 km
Precession for the year 2005	50″.291
Precession in right ascension	3^s.075
Precession in declination	20″.043
Constant of nutation	9″.202
Constant of aberration	20″.496
Mean obliquity of ecliptic (2005)	23° 26′ 20″
Moon's equatorial hor. parallax	57′ 02″.70
Velocity of light in vacuo per second	299792.5 km
Solar motion per second	20.0 km
Equatorial radius of the Earth	6378.140 km
Polar radius of the Earth	6356.755 km
North galactic pole (IAU standard)	
	RA 12h 49m (1950.0). Dec. +27°.4 N.
Solar apex	RA 18h 06m Dec. + 30

Length of year (in mean solar days)

Tropical	365.24219
Sidereal	365.25636
Anomalistic (perihelion to perihelion)	365.25964
Eclipse	346.62000

Length of month (mean values)	d	h	m	s
New Moon to New	29	12	44	02.9
Sidereal	27	07	43	11.5
Anomalistic (perigee to perigee)	27	13	18	33.2

ELEMENTS OF THE SOLAR SYSTEM

Orb	Mean distance from Sun (Earth = 1)	km 10⁶	Sidereal period days	Synodic period days	Incl. of orbit to ecliptic ° ′	Diameter km	Mass (Earth = 1)	Period of rotation on axis days
Sun	—	—	—	—	—	1,392,530	332,946	25–35*
Mercury	0.39	58	88.0	116	7 00	4,879	0.0553	58.646
Venus	0.72	108	224.7	584	3 24	12,104	0.8150	243.019r
Earth	1.00	150	365.3	—	—	12,756e	1.0000	0.997
Mars	1.52	228	687.0	780	1 51	6,794e	0.1074	1.026
Jupiter	5.20	778	4,332.6	399	1 18	142,984e 133,708p	317.89	0.410e
Saturn	9.54	1427	10,759.2	378	2 29	120,536e 108,728p	95.18	0.426e
Uranus	19.18	2870	30,684.6	370	0 46	51,118e	14.54	0.718r
Neptune	30.06	4497	60,191.0	367	1 46	49,528e	17.15	0.671
Pluto	39.80	5954	91,708.2	367	17 09	2,302	0.002	6.387

e equatorial, p polar, r retrograde, * depending on latitude

THE SATELLITES

Name	Star mag.	Mean distance from primary km	Sidereal period of revolution d	Name	Star mag.	Mean distance from primary km	Sidereal period of revolution d
EARTH				**SATURN**			
I Moon	—	384,400	27.322	VII Hyperion	14	1,481,100	21.277
				VIII Iapetus	11	3,561,300	79.330
MARS				IX Phoebe	16	12,952,000	550.48r
I Phobos	11	9,378	0.319				
II Deimos	12	23,459	1.262	**URANUS**			
				VI Cordelia	24	49,750	0.335
JUPITER				VII Ophelia	24	53,760	0.376
XVI Metis	17	127,960	0.295	VIII Bianca	23	59,170	0.435
XV Adrastea	19	128,980	0.298	IX Cressida	22	61,780	0.464
V Amalthea	14	181,300	0.498	X Desdemona	22	62,660	0.474
XIV Thebe	16	221,900	0.675	XI Juliet	21	64,360	0.493
I Io	5	421,600	1.769	XII Portia	21	66,100	0.513
II Europa	5	670,900	3.552	XIII Rosalind	22	69,930	0.558
III Ganymede	5	1,070,000	7.155	XIV Belinda	22	75,260	0.624
IV Callisto	6	1,883,000	16.689	XV Puck	20	86,000	0.762
XIII Leda	20	11,165,000	240.92	V Miranda	16	129,900	1.413
VI Himalia	15	11,460,000	250.57	I Ariel	14	190,900	2.520
X Lysithea	18	11,717,000	259.20	II Umbriel	15	266,000	4.144
VII Elara	17	11,741,000	259.64	III Titania	14	426,300	8.706
XII Ananke	19	21,276,000	629.77r	IV Oberon	14	583,600	13.463
XI Carme	18	23,404,000	734.17r	XVI Caliban	22	7,231,000	579.93
VIII Pasiphae	17	23,624,000	743.68r	XX Stephano	24	9,608,400	677.36
IX Sinope	18	23,939,000	758.90r	XVII Sycorax	21	12,179,000	1,288.30
				XVIII Prospero	23	16,256,000	1,978.29
SATURN				XIX Setebos	23	17,418,000	2,225.21
XVIII Pan	20	133,583	0.575				
XV Atlas	18	137,640	0.602	**NEPTUNE**			
XVI Prometheus	16	139,353	0.613	III Naiad	25	48,230	0.294
XVII Pandora	16	141,700	0.629	IV Thalassa	24	50,070	0.311
XI Epimetheus	15	151,422	0.695	V Despina	23	52,530	0.335
X Janus	14	151,472	0.695	VI Galatea	22	61,950	0.429
I Mimas	13	185,520	0.942	VII Larissa	22	73,550	0.555
II Enceladus	12	238,020	1.370	VIII Proteus	20	117,650	1.122
III Tethys	10	294,660	1.888	I Triton	13	354,760	5.877
XIII Telesto	19	294,660	1.888	II Nereid	19	5,513,400	360.136
XIV Calypso	19	294,660	1.888				
IV Dione	10	377,400	2.737	**PLUTO**			
XII Helene	18	377,400	2.737	I Charon	17	19,600	6.387
V Rhea	10	527,040	4.518				
VI Titan	8	1,221,850	15.945				

Currently the total number of satellites of the outer planets are: Jupiter 63, Saturn 31, Uranus 28, Neptune 13, Pluto 1.

THE EARTH

The shape of the Earth is that of an oblate spheroid or solid of revolution whose meridian sections are ellipses not differing much from circles, whilst the sections at right angles are circles. The length of the equatorial axis is about 12,756 km, and that of the polar axis is 12,714 km. The mean density of the Earth is 5.5 times that of water, although that of the surface layer is less. The Earth and Moon revolve about their common centre of gravity in a lunar month; this centre in turn revolves round the Sun in a plane known as the ecliptic, that passes through the Sun's centre. The Earth's equator is inclined to this plane at an angle of 23.4°. This tilt is the cause of the seasons. In mid-latitudes, and when the Sun is high above the Equator, not only does the high noon altitude make the days longer, but the Sun's rays fall more directly on the Earth's surface; these effects combine to produce summer. In equatorial regions the noon altitude is large throughout the year, and there is little variation in the length of the day. In higher latitudes the noon altitude is lower, and the days in summer are appreciably longer than those in winter.

The average velocity of the Earth in its orbit is 30 km a second. It makes a complete rotation on its axis in about 23h 56m of mean time, which is the sidereal day. Because of its annual revolution round the Sun, the rotation with respect to the Sun, or the solar day, is more than this by about four minutes (*see* page 669). The extremity of the axis of rotation, or the North Pole of the Earth, is not rigidly fixed, but wanders over an area roughly 20 metres in diameter.

TERRESTRIAL MAGNETISM

The Earth's main magnetic field corresponds approximately to that of a very strong small bar magnet near the centre of the Earth, but with appreciable smooth spatial departures. The origin of the main field is generally ascribed to electric currents associated with fluid motions in the Earth's core. As a result not only does the main field vary in strength and direction from place to place, but also with time. Superimposed on the main field are local and regional anomalies whose magnitudes may in places approach that of the main field; these are due to the influence of mineral deposits in the Earth's crust. A small proportion of the field is of external origin, mostly associated with electric currents in the ionosphere. The configuration of the external field and the ionisation of the atmosphere depend on the incident particle and radiation flux from the Sun. There are, therefore, short-term and non-periodic as well as diurnal, 27-day, seasonal and 11-year periodic changes in the magnetic field, dependent upon the position of the Sun and the degree of solar activity.

A magnetic compass points along the horizontal component of a magnetic line of force. These lines of force converge on the 'magnetic dip-poles', the places where the Earth's magnetic field is vertical. These poles move with time, and their present approximate adopted mean positions are 83.3° N., 118.7° W. and 64.5° S., 137.8° E.

There is also a 'magnetic equator', at all points of which the vertical component of the Earth's magnetic field is zero and a magnetised needle remains horizontal. This line runs between 2° and 12° north of the geographical equator in Asia and Africa, turns sharply south off the west African coast, and crosses South America through Brazil, Bolivia and Peru; it re-crosses the geographical equator in mid-Pacific.

Reference has already been made to secular changes in the Earth's field. The following table indicates the changes in magnetic declination (or variation of the compass). Declination is the angle in the horizontal plane between the direction of true north and that in which a magnetic compass points. Similar, though much smaller, changes have occurred in 'dip' or magnetic inclination. Secular changes differ throughout the world. Although the London observations suggest a cycle with a period of several hundred years, an exact repetition is unlikely.

London				Greenwich			
1580	11°	15'	E.	1900	16°	29'	W.
1622	5°	56'	E.	1925	13°	10'	W.
1665	1°	22'	W.	1950	9°	07'	W.
1730	13°	00'	W.	1975	6°	39'	W.
1773	21°	09'	W.	1998	3°	32'	W.
1850	22°	24'	W.				

In order that up-to-date information on declination may be available, many governments publish magnetic charts on which there are lines (isogonic lines) passing through all places at which specified values of declination will be found at the date of the chart.

In the British Isles, isogonic lines now run approximately north-east to south-west. Though there are considerable local deviations due to geological causes, a rough value of magnetic declination may be obtained by assuming that at 50° N. on the meridian of Greenwich, the value in 2005 is 1° 45' west and allowing an increase of 14' for each degree of latitude northwards and one of 27' for each degree of longitude westwards. For example, at 53° N., 5° W., declination will be about 1°45' + 42' + 135', i.e. 4° 42' west. The average annual change at the present time is about 11' decrease.

The number of magnetic observatories is about 180, irregularly distributed over the globe. There are three in Great Britain, run by the British Geological Survey: at Hartland, north Devon; at Eskdalemuir, Dumfries and Galloway; and at Lerwick, Shetland Islands. The following are some recent annual mean values of the magnetic elements for Hartland.

Year	Declination West ° '		Dip or inclination ° '		Horizontal intensity nanoTesla (nT)	Vertical intensity nT
1960	9	58.8	66	43.9	18707	43504
1965	9	30.1	66	34.0	18872	43540
1970	9	06.5	66	26.1	19033	43636
1975	8	32.3	66	17.0	19212	43733
1980	7	43.8	66	10.3	19330	43768
1985	6	56.1	66	07.9	19379	43796
1990	6	15.0	66	09.7	19539	43896
1995	5	33.2	66	07.3	19457	43951
2000	4	43.6	66	06.9	19508	44051
2003	4	14.4	66	06.8	19545	44134

As well as navigation at sea, in the air and on land by compass the oil industry depends on the Earth's magnetic field as a directional reference. They use magnetic survey tools when drilling well-bores and require accurate estimates of the local magnetic field, taking into account the crustal and external fields.

MAGNETIC STORMS

Occasionally, sometimes with great suddenness, the Earth's magnetic field is subject for several hours to marked disturbance. During a severe storm in October 2003 the declination at Eskdalemuir changed by over 5° in six minutes. In many instances such disturbances are accompanied by widespread displays of aurorae, marked changes in the incidence of cosmic rays, an increase in the reception of 'noise' from the Sun at radio frequencies, and rapid changes in the ionosphere and induced electric currents within the Earth which adversely affect satellite operations, telecommunications and electric power transmission systems. The disturbances are caused by changes in the stream of ionised particles which emanates from the Sun and through which the Earth is continuously passing. Some of these changes are associated with visible eruptions on the Sun, usually in the region of sun-spots. There is a marked tendency for disturbances to recur after intervals of about 27 days, the apparent period of rotation of the Sun on its axis, which is consistent with the sources being located on particular areas of the Sun.

ARTIFICIAL SATELLITES

Since the beginning of the Space Age, *Whitaker's Almanack* has given details of every successful satellite launch. This edition gives details of all successful launches that have taken place since the last edition. To consider the orbit of an artificial satellite, it is best to imagine that one is looking at the Earth from a distant point in space. The Earth would then be seen to be rotating about its axis inside the orbit described by the rapidly revolving satellite. The inclination of a satellite orbit to the Earth's equator (which generally remains almost constant throughout the satellite's lifetime) gives at once the maximum range of latitudes over which the satellite passes. Thus a satellite whose orbit has an inclination of 53° will pass overhead all latitudes between 53° S. and 53° N., but would never be seen in the zenith of any place nearer the poles than these latitudes. If we consider a particular place on the earth, whose latitude is less than the inclination of the satellite's orbit, then the Earth's rotation carries this place first under the northbound part of the orbit and then under the southbound part of the orbit, these two occurrences being always less than 12 hours apart for satellites moving in direct orbits (i.e. to the east). (For satellites in retrograde orbits, the words 'northbound' and 'southbound' should be interchanged in the preceding statement.) As the value of the latitude of the observer increases and approaches the value of the inclination of the orbit, so this interval gets shorter until (when the latitude is equal to the inclination) only one overhead passage occurs each day.

OBSERVATION OF SATELLITES

The regression of the orbit around the Earth causes alternate periods of visibility and invisibility, though this is of little concern to the radio or radar observer. To the visual observer the following cycle of events normally occurs (though the cycle may start in any position): invisibility, morning observations before dawn, invisibility, evening observations after dusk, invisibility, morning observations before dawn, and so on. With reasonably high satellites and for observers in high latitudes around the summer solstice, the evening observations follow the morning observations without interruption as sunlight passing over the polar regions can still illuminate satellites which are passing over temperate latitudes at local midnight. At the moment all satellites rely on sunlight to make them visible, though a satellite with a flashing light has been suggested for a future launching. The observer must be in darkness or twilight in order to make any useful observations. (For durations of twilight, and sunrise and sunset times, *see* page two of each month.)

Some of the satellites are visible to the naked eye and much interest has been aroused by the spectacle of a bright satellite disappearing into the Earth's shadow. The event is even more interesting telescopically as the disappearance occurs gradually as the satellite traverses the Earth's penumbral shadow, and during the last few seconds before the eclipse is complete the satellite may change colour (in suitable atmospheric conditions) from yellow to red. This is because the last rays of sunlight are refracted through the denser layers of our atmosphere before striking the satellite.

Some satellites rotate about one or more axes so that a periodic variation in brightness is observed. This was particularly noticeable in several of the Soviet satellites.

Satellite research has provided some interesting results, including a revised value of the Earth's oblateness (1/298.2), and the discovery of the Van Allen radiation belts.

LAUNCHINGS

Apart from their names, e.g. Cosmos 6 Rocket, the satellites are also classified according to their date of launch. Thus 1961 α refers to the first satellite launching of 1961. A number following the Greek letter indicated the relative brightness of the satellites put in orbit. From the beginning of 1963 the Greek letters were replaced by numbers and the numbers by roman letters e.g. 1963–01A. For all satellites successfully injected into orbit the following table gives the designation and names of the main objects, the launch date and some initial orbital data. These are the inclination to the equator (i), the nodal period of revolution (P), and the apogee and perigee heights.

Although most of the satellites launched are injected into orbits less than 1,000 km high, there are an increasing number of satellites in geostationary orbits, i.e. where the orbital inclination is zero, the eccentricity close to zero, and the period of revolution is 1436.1 minutes. Thus the satellite is permanently situated over the equator at one selected longitude at a mean height of 35,786 km. This geostationary band is crowded. In one case there are six television satellites (Astra 2, 5, 6, 7, 1H and 2C) orbiting within a few tens of kilometres of each other. In the sky they appear to be separated by only a few arcminutes.

In 1997 a number of *Iridium* satellites were launched into high inclination orbits. These are owned by the mobile telephone company Cellnet. For visual observers, these satellites have the interesting characteristic that the large aerials they carry can, when in exactly the right orientation with respect to the Sun and the observer, give off a 'flare' in brightness which can on occasion attain a magnitude of −6, much brighter than Venus. The flare can be visible to the naked eye for nearly a minute.

The Russian Space Station, Mir, 1986–17A, which was launched in 1986 was successfully de-orbited on March 23 2001. The re-entry was carried out in several stages, the first small burn to lower the orbit occurring at 00h 33m. The main de-orbit burn began at 05h 07m, which lowered the perigee height to <80km. At 05h 50m observers in Fiji saw multiple bright re-entry bodies in the sky. The impact area was at about W. 160°, S. 40°. During its 15 years in orbit it had been visited by 111 spacecraft. The record for the longest spaceflight was set by Valeriy Polyakov in 1994–5 who spent 437 days in Mir.

The new International Space Station ISS, 1998–67A, is currently being assembled in an orbit of similar size and inclination to Mir. It will become even brighter as more parts are added to it. When passing over Britain it can appear to be almost as bright as Jupiter on favourable transits, though only visible for four or five minutes on each pass.

ARTIFICIAL SATELLITE LAUNCHES

Desig-nation	Satellite	Launch date	P	i	Apogee	Perigee
2003–			m	°	km	km
001	CORIOLIS, rocket	Jan. 6	95.9	98.7	841	279
002	ICESAT, CHIPSAT, rocket, DPAF	Jan. 13	96.5	94.0	594	586
003	STS 107	Jan. 16	90.1	39.0	287	271
004	SORCE, rocket	Jan. 25	97.3	40.0	649	609
005	NAVSTAR 51 (USA 166), rocket, rocket XSS 10	Jan. 29	720.7	55.1	20345	20155
006	PROGRESS M-47, rocket	Feb. 2	92.3	51.6	390	382
007	INTELSAT 907, rocket	Feb. 15	1431.2	0.1	35748	35634
008	USA 167, rocket, IABS	Mar. 11	No elements available			
009	IGS 1A, IGS 1B	Mar. 28	94.3	97.3	490	484
010	NAVSTAR 52 (USA 168), rocket, rocket	Mar. 31	717.9	55.0	20376	19984
011	MOLNIYA 1–92, platform, rocket, rocket	Apr. 2	736.4	62.9	40643	625
012	USA 169, rocket	Apr. 8	1436.1	4.2	35774	35759
013	INSAT 3A, Galaxy XII, rocket	Apr. 9	645.9	2.0	35881	867
014	ASIASAT 4, rocket	Apr. 12	871.3	27.3	47506	174
015	CONGLOMERATE, rocket, platform	Apr. 24	1443.0	2.3	35927	35917
016	SOYUZ TMA-2, rocket	Apr. 26	90.6	51.6	358	254
017	GALEX, rocket	Apr. 28	98.7	29.0	699	691
018	GSAT 2, rocket	May 8	626.6	19.2	35601	157
019	MUSES C, rocket	May 9	No elements available			
020	HELLAS-SAT 2, rocket	May 13	1793.9	17.0	84650	404
021	BEIDOU 1C, rocket	May 24	1436.1	0.3	35822	35752
022	MARS EXPRESS, rocket	June 2	88.0	51.8	177	177
023	COSMOS 2398, rocket	June 5	105.0	83.0	1015	971
024	AMC-9, BREEZE M	June 6	1334.4	0.8	35690	31852
025	PROGRESS M1–10, rocket	June 8	90.8	51.6	319	305
026	THURAYA 2, rocket	June 10	650.5	6.3	35777	1203
027	MARS EXPLORER ROVER A, rocket, rocket	June 10	No elements available			
028	B-SAT 2C, OPTUS C1, rocket	June 11	1427.2	0.0	35796	35430
029	MOLNIYA 3–53, rocket, platform, rocket	June 19	736.3	62.9	40635	629
030	ORBVIEW 3, rocket	June 26	92.5	97.3	429	365
031	MONITOR-E/SL-19, MIMOSA, DTUSAT, MOST, CUTE-1, QUAKESAT, AAU CUBESAT, CANX-1, CUBESAT XI-IV	June 30	100.1	98.7	834	694
032	MARS EXPLORER ROVER B, rocket, rocket	July 8	87.8	29.4	175	155
033	RAINBOW 1, rocket	July 17	1436.2	0.0	35796	35782
034	ECHOSTAR 9 (TELSTAR 13), rocket	Aug. 8	1436.1	0.0	35810	35764
035	COSMOS 2399, rocket	Aug. 12	89.8	64.9	326	202
036	SCISAT 1, rocket	Aug. 13	97.7	73.9	655	641
037	COSMOS 2400, COSMOS 2401, rocket	Aug. 19	115.6	82.5	1501	1469
038	SIRTF, rocket	Aug. 25	87.7	31.5	163	161
039	PROGRESS-M 48, rocket	Aug. 28	92.2	51.6	387	377
040	USA 170, rocket, IABS	Aug. 29	No elements available			
041	USA 171, rocket	Sep. 9	No elements available			
042	MOZHAYETS 2, RUBIN 4/SL-8 NIGERIASAT 1, UK-DMC BILSAT 1, LARETS, KAISTSAT, rocket	Sep. 27	98.5	98.2	696	676
043	ARIANE 5 rocket, E-BIRD, SMART 1, INSAT 1E	Sep. 27	644.4	7.1	36006	666
044	HORIZONS 1 (GALAXY 13), rocket	Oct. 1	673.5	0.0	35751	2397
045	SHENZHOU 5, rocket, module	Oct. 15	91.2	42.4	336	332
046	IRS P6, rocket	Oct. 17	101.7	98.7	875	803
047	SOYUZ, rocket	Oct. 18	89.9	51.6	274	268
048	DMSP-16	Oct. 18	101.9	98.9	852	844
049	OBJECTS A,B,C, rocket	Oct. 21	99.9	98.5	765	739
050	UNK, rocket	Oct. 30	105.1	99.5	1016	984
051	FSW-3 1, rocket	Nov. 3	88.9	62.9	265	177

ARTIFICIAL SATELLITE LAUNCHES

Desig-nation	Satellite	Launch date	P	i	Apogee	Perigee
2003–			m	°	km	km
052	ZHONGXING 20, rocket	Nov. 14	1436.0	0.3	35797	35771
053	CONGLOMERATE, platform, rocket	Nov. 24	649.8	49.3	36736	208
054	USA 137, rocket	Dec. 2	107.5	63.4	1209	1011
055	GRUZOMAKET, rocket	Dec. 5	93.7	67.1	461	453
056	COSMOS 2402–4, rocket	Dec. 10	672.0	65.1	19104	18970
057	UFO 11 (USA 174), rocket	Dec. 18	No elements available			
058	NAVSTAR 53, rocket, rocket	Dec. 21	356.1	39.0	20349	181
059	AMOS-2, rocket	Dec. 27	714.4	23.6	35778	4410
060	EXPRESS AM-22, rocket platform	Dec. 28	633.4	48.6	35863	243
061	?	Dec. 29	No elements available			
2004–						
001	ESTRELA DU SOL-TELSTAR14, rocket	Jan. 11	641.1	0.1	35757	747
002	PROGRESS-M1 11, rocket	Jan. 29	88.6	51.7	234	178
003	AMC-10 (GE-10)	Feb. 5	858.2	4.0	35710	11364
004	USA 176, rocket, rocket, rocket	Feb. 14	No elements available			
005	COSMOS 2405, rocket, rocket, platform	Feb. 18	735.5	62.8	40600	624
006	ROSETTA, rocket	Mar. 2	No elements available			

TIME MEASUREMENT AND CALENDARS

MEASUREMENTS OF TIME

Measurements of time are based on the time taken by the earth to rotate on its axis (day); by the moon to revolve round the earth (month); and by the earth to revolve round the sun (year). From these, which are not commensurable, certain average or mean intervals have been adopted for ordinary use.

THE DAY

The day begins at midnight and is divided into 24 hours of 60 minutes, each of 60 seconds. The hours are counted from midnight up to 12 noon (when the sun crosses the meridian), and these hours are designated a.m. *(ante meridiem)*; and again from noon up to 12 midnight, which hours are designated p.m. *(post meridiem)*, except when the 24-hour reckoning is employed. The 24-hour reckoning ignores a.m. and p.m., numbering the hours 0 to 23 from midnight.

Colloquially the 24 hours are divided into day and night, day being the time while the sun is above the horizon (including the four stages of twilight defined in the Astronomy section). Day is subdivided into morning, the early part of daytime, ending at noon; afternoon, from noon to about 6 p.m.; and evening, which may be said to extend from 6 p.m. until midnight. Night begins at the close of astronomical twilight (*see* the Astronomy section) and extends beyond midnight to sunrise the next day.

The names of the days are derived from Old English translations or adaptations of the Roman titles.

Sunday	Sun	Sol
Monday	Moon	Luna
Tuesday	Tiw/Tyr (god of war)	Mars
Wednesday	Woden/Odin	Mercury
Thursday	Thor	Jupiter
Friday	Frigga/Freyja	Venus
	(goddess of love)	
Saturday	Saeternes	Saturn

THE MONTH

The month in the ordinary calendar is approximately the twelfth part of a year, but the lengths of the different months vary from 28 (or 29) days to 31.

THE YEAR

The equinoctial or tropical year is the time that the earth takes to revolve round the sun from equinox to equinox, i.e. 365.24219 mean solar days, or 365 days 5 hours 48 minutes and 45 seconds.

The calendar year usually consists of 365 days but a year containing 366 days is called bissextile (*see* Roman calendar) or leap year, one day being added to the month of February so that a date 'leaps over' a day of the week. In the Roman calendar the day that was repeated was the sixth day before the beginning of March, the equivalent of 24 February.

A year is a leap year if the date of the year is divisible by four without remainder, unless it is the last year of the century. The last year of a century is a leap year only if its number is divisible by 400 without remainder, e.g. the years 1800 and 1900 had only 365 days but the year 2000 has 366 days.

THE SOLSTICE

A solstice is the point in the tropical year at which the sun attains its greatest distance, north or south, from the Equator. In the northern hemisphere the furthest point north of the Equator marks the summer solstice and the furthest point south the winter solstice.

The date of the solstice varies according to locality. For example, if the summer solstice falls on 21 June late in the day by Greenwich time, that day will be the longest of the year at Greenwich though it may be by only a second, but it will fall on 22 June, local date, in Japan, and so 22 June will be the longest day there. The date of the solstice is also affected by the length of the tropical year, which is 365 days 6 hours less about 11 minutes 15 seconds. If a solstice happens late on 21 June in one year, it will be nearly six hours later in the next (unless the next year is a leap year), i.e. early on 22 June, and that will be the longest day.

This delay of the solstice does not continue because the extra day in leap year brings it back a day in the calendar. However, because of the 11 minutes 15 seconds mentioned above, the additional day in leap year brings the solstice back too far by 45 minutes, and the time of the solstice in the calendar is earlier, in a four-year pattern, as the century progresses. The last year of a century is in most cases not a leap year, and the omission of the extra day puts the date of the solstice later by about six hours too much. Compensation for this is made by the fourth centennial year being a leap year. The solstice has become earlier in date throughout the last century and, because the year 2000 was a leap year, the solstice will get earlier still throughout the 21st century.

The date of the winter solstice, the shortest day of the year, is affected by the same factors as the longest day.

At Greenwich the sun sets at its earliest by the clock about ten days before the shortest day. The daily change in the time of sunset is due in the first place to the sun's movement southwards at this time of the year, which diminishes the interval between the sun's transit and its setting. However, the daily decrease of the Equation of Time causes the time of apparent noon to be continuously later day by day, which to some extent counteracts the first effect. The rates of the change of these two quantities are not equal or uniform; their combination causes the date of earliest sunset to be 12 or 13 December at Greenwich. In more southerly latitudes the effect of the movement of the sun is less, and the change in the time of sunset depends on that of the Equation of Time to a greater degree, and the date of earliest sunset is earlier than it is at Greenwich, e.g. on the Equator it is about 1 November.

THE EQUINOX

The equinox is the point at which the sun crosses the Equator and day and night are of equal length all over the world. This occurs in March and September.

DOG DAYS

The days about the heliacal rising of the Dog Star, noted from ancient times as the hottest period of the year in the northern hemisphere, are called the Dog Days. Their incidence has been variously calculated as depending on the Greater or Lesser Dog Star (Sirius or Procyon) and their duration has been reckoned as from 30 to 54 days. A generally accepted period is from 3 July to 15 August.

CHRISTIAN CALENDAR

In the Christian chronological system the years are distinguished by cardinal numbers before or after the birth of Christ, the period being denoted by the letters BC (Before Christ) or, more rarely, AC *(Ante Christum)*, and AD *(Anno Domini –* In the Year of Our Lord). The correlative dates of the epoch are the fourth year of the 194th Olympiad, the 753rd year from the foundation of Rome, AM 3761 in Jewish chronology, and the 4714th year of the Julian period. The actual date of the birth of Christ is somewhat uncertain.

The system was introduced into Italy in the sixth century. Though first used in France in the seventh century, it was not universally established there until about the eighth century. It has been said that the system was introduced into England by St Augustine (AD 596), but it was probably not generally used until some centuries later. It was ordered to be used by the Bishops at the Council of Chelsea (AD 816).

THE JULIAN CALENDAR

In the Julian calendar (adopted by the Roman Empire in 45 BC) all the centennial years were leap years, and for this reason towards the close of the 16th century there was a difference of ten days between the tropical and calendar years; the equinox fell on 11 March of the calendar, whereas at the time of the Council of Nicaea (AD 325), it had fallen on 21 March. In 1582 Pope Gregory ordained that 5 October should be called 15 October and that of the end-century years only the fourth should be a leap year.

THE GREGORIAN CALENDAR

The Gregorian calendar was adopted by Italy, France, Spain and Portugal in 1582, by Prussia, the Roman Catholic German states, Switzerland, Holland and Flanders on 1 January 1583, by Poland in 1586, Hungary in 1587, the Protestant German and Netherland states and Denmark in 1700, and by Great Britain and Dominions (including the North American colonies) in 1752, by the omission of eleven days (3 September being reckoned as 14 September). Sweden omitted the leap day in 1700 but observed leap days in 1704 and 1708, and reverted to the Julian calendar by having two leap days in 1712; the Gregorian calendar was adopted in 1753 by the omission of eleven days (18 February being reckoned as 1 March). Japan adopted the calendar in 1872, China in 1912, Bulgaria in 1915, Turkey and Soviet Russia in 1918, Yugoslavia and Romania in 1919, and Greece in 1923.

In the same year that the change was made in England from the Julian to the Gregorian calendar, the beginning of the new year was also changed from 25 March to 1 January.

THE ORTHODOX CHURCHES

Some Orthodox Churches still use the Julian reckoning but the majority of Greek Orthodox Churches and the Romanian Orthodox Church have adopted a modified 'New Calendar', observing the Gregorian calendar for fixed feasts and the Julian for movable feasts.

The Orthodox Church year begins on 1 September. There are four fast periods and, in addition to Pascha (Easter), twelve great feasts, as well as numerous commemorations of the saints of the Old and New Testaments throughout the year.

THE DOMINICAL LETTER

The dominical letter is one of the letters A–G which are used to denote the Sundays in successive years. If the first day of the year is a Sunday the letter is A; if the second, B; the third, C; and so on. A leap year requires two letters, the first for 1 January to 29 February, the second for 1 March to 31 December.

EPIPHANY

The feast of the Epiphany, commemorating the manifestation of Christ, later became associated with the offering of gifts by the Magi. The day was of great importance from the time of the Council of Nicaea (AD 325), as the primate of Alexandria was charged at every Epiphany feast with the announcement in a letter to the churches of the date of the forthcoming Easter. The day was also of importance in Britain as it influenced dates, ecclesiastical and lay, e.g. Plough Monday, when work was resumed in the fields, fell on the Monday in the first full week after Epiphany.

LENT

The Teutonic word *Lent*, which denotes the fast preceding Easter, originally meant no more than the spring season; but from Anglo-Saxon times at least it has been used as the equivalent of the more significant Latin term Quadragesima, meaning the 'forty days' or, more literally, the fortieth day. Ash Wednesday is the first day of Lent, which ends at midnight before Easter Day.

PALM SUNDAY

Palm Sunday, the Sunday before Easter and the beginning of Holy Week, commemorates the triumphal entry of Christ into Jerusalem and is celebrated in Britain (when palm is not available) by branches of willow gathered for use in the decoration of churches on that day.

MAUNDY THURSDAY

Maundy Thursday is the day before Good Friday, the name itself being a corruption of *dies mandati* (day of the mandate) when Christ washed the feet of the disciples and gave them the mandate to love one another.

EASTER DAY

Easter Day is the first Sunday after the full moon which happens on, or next after, the 21st day of March; if the full moon happens on a Sunday, Easter Day is the Sunday after.

This definition is contained in an Act of Parliament (24 Geo. II c. 23) and explanation is given in the preamble to the Act that the day of full moon depends on certain tables that have been prepared. These tables are summarised in the early pages of the Book of Common Prayer. The moon referred to is not the real moon of the heavens, but a hypothetical moon on whose 'full' date of Easter depends, and the lunations of this 'calendar' moon consist of twenty-nine and thirty days alternately, with certain necessary modifications to make the date of its full agree as nearly as possible with that of the real moon, which is known as the Paschal Full Moon.

A FIXED EASTER

In 1928 the House of Commons agreed to a motion for the third reading of a bill proposing that Easter Day shall, in the calendar year next but one after the commencement of the Act and in all subsequent years, be the first Sunday after the second Saturday in April. Easter would thus fall on the second or third Sunday in April, i.e. between 9 and 15 April (inclusive). A clause in the Bill provided that before it shall come into operation, regard shall be had to any opinion expressed officially by the various Christian churches. Efforts by the World Council of Churches to secure a unanimous choice of date for Easter by its member churches have so far been unsuccessful.

ROGATION DAYS
Rogation Days are the Monday, Tuesday and Wednesday preceding Ascension Day and from the fifth century were observed as public fasts with solemn processions and supplications. The processions were discontinued as religious observances at the Reformation, but survive in the ceremony known as 'beating the parish bounds'. Rogation Sunday is the Sunday before Ascension Day.

EMBER DAYS
The Ember Days at the four seasons are the Wednesday, Friday and Saturday (a) before the third Sunday in Advent, (b) before the second Sunday in Lent, and (c) before the Sundays nearest to the festivals of St Peter and of St Michael and All Angels.

TRINITY SUNDAY
Trinity Sunday is eight weeks after Easter Day, on the Sunday following Pentecost (Whit Sunday). Subsequent Sundays are reckoned in the Book of Common Prayer calendar of the Church of England as 'after Trinity'.

Thomas Becket (1118–70) was consecrated Archbishop of Canterbury on the Sunday after Whit Sunday and his first act was to ordain that the day of his consecration should be held as a new festival in honour of the Holy Trinity. This observance spread from Canterbury throughout the whole of Christendom.

MOVABLE FEASTS TO THE YEAR 2035

Year	Ash Wednesday	Easter	Ascension	Pentecost (Whit Sunday)	Advent Sunday
2005	9 February	27 March	5 May	15 May	27 November
2006	1 March	16 April	25 May	4 June	3 December
2007	21 February	8 April	17 May	27 May	2 December
2008	6 February	23 March	1 May	11 May	30 November
2009	25 February	12 April	21 May	31 May	29 November
2010	17 February	4 April	13 May	23 May	28 November
2011	9 March	24 April	2 June	12 June	27 November
2012	22 February	8 April	17 May	27 May	2 December
2013	13 February	31 March	9 May	19 May	1 December
2014	5 March	20 April	29 May	8 June	30 November
2015	18 February	5 April	14 May	24 May	29 November
2016	10 February	27 March	5 May	15 May	27 November
2017	1 March	16 April	25 May	4 June	3 December
2018	14 February	1 April	10 May	20 May	2 December
2019	6 March	21 April	30 May	9 June	1 December
2020	26 February	12 April	21 May	31 May	29 November
2021	17 February	4 April	13 May	23 May	28 November
2022	2 March	17 April	26 May	5 June	27 November
2023	22 February	9 April	18 May	28 May	3 December
2024	14 February	31 March	9 May	19 May	1 December
2025	5 March	20 April	29 May	8 June	30 November
2026	18 February	5 April	14 May	24 May	29 November
2027	10 February	28 March	6 May	16 May	28 November
2028	1 March	16 April	25 May	4 June	3 December
2029	14 February	1 April	10 May	20 May	2 December
2030	6 March	21 April	30 May	9 June	1 December
2031	26 February	13 April	22 May	1 June	30 November
2032	11 February	28 March	6 May	16 May	28 November
2033	2 March	17 April	26 May	5 June	27 November
2034	22 February	9 April	18 May	28 May	3 December
2035	7 February	25 March	3 May	13 May	2 December

NOTES
Ash Wednesday (first day in Lent) can fall at earliest on 4 February and at latest on 10 March

Mothering Sunday (fourth Sunday in Lent) can fall at earliest on 1 March and at latest on 4 April

Easter Day can fall at earliest on 22 March and at latest on 25 April

Ascension Day is forty days after Easter Day and can fall at earliest on 30 April and at latest on 3 June

Pentecost (Whit Sunday) is seven weeks after Easter and can fall at earliest on 10 May and at latest on 13 June

Trinity Sunday is the Sunday after Whit Sunday

Corpus Christi falls on the Thursday after Trinity Sunday

Sundays after Pentecost – there are not less than 18 and not more than 23

Advent Sunday is the Sunday nearest to 30 November

EASTER DAYS AND DOMINICAL LETTERS 1500 TO 2035

Dates up to and including 1752 are according to the Julian calendar. For dominical letters in leap years, *see* note below

			1500–1599	1600–1699	1700–1799	1800–1899	1900–1999	2000–2035
March								
d	22		1573	1668	1761	1818		
e	23		1505/16	1600	1788	1845/56	1913	2008
f	24			1611/95	1706/99		1940	
g	25		1543/54	1627/38/49	1722/33/44	1883/94	1951	2035
A	26		1559/70/81/92	1654/65/76	1749/58/69/80	1815/26/37	1967/78/89	
b	27		1502/13/24/97	1608/87/92	1785/96	1842/53/64	1910/21/32	2005/16
c	28		1529/35/40	1619/24/30	1703/14/25	1869/75/80	1937/48	2027/32
d	29		1551/62	1635/46/57	1719/30/41/52	1807/12/91	1959/64/70	
e	30		1567/78/89	1651/62/73/84	1746/55/66/77	1823/34	1902/75/86/97	
f	31		1510/21/32/83/94	1605/16/78/89	1700/71/82/93	1839/50/61/72	1907/18/29/91	2002/13/24
April								
g	1		1526/37/48	1621/32	1711/16	1804/66/77/88	1923/34/45/56	2018/29
A	2		1553/64	1643/48	1727/38	1809/20/93/99	1961/72	
b	3		1575/80/86	1659/70/81	1743/63/68/74	1825/31/36	1904/83/88/94	
c	4		1507/18/91	1602/13/75/86/97	1708/79/90	1847/58	1915/20/26/99	2010/21
d	5		1523/34/45/56	1607/18/29/40	1702/13/24/95	1801/63/74/85/96	1931/42/53	2015/26
e	6		1539/50/61/72	1634/45/56	1729/35/40/60	1806/17/28/90	1947/58/69/80	
f	7		1504/77/88	1667/72	1751/65/76	1822/33/44	1901/12/85/96	
g	8		1509/15/20/99	1604/10/83/94	1705/87/92/98	1849/55/60	1917/28	2007/12
A	9		1531/42	1615/26/37/99	1710/21/32	1871/82	1939/44/50	2023/34
b	10		1547/58/69	1631/42/53/64	1726/37/48/57	1803/14/87/98	1955/66/77	
c	11		1501/12/63/74/85/96	1658/69/80	1762/73/84	1819/30/41/52	1909/71/82/93	2004
d	12		1506/17/28	1601/12/91/96	1789	1846/57/68	1903/14/25/36/98	2009/20
e	13		1533/44	1623/28	1707/18	1800/73/79/84	1941/52	2031
f	14		1555/60/66	1639/50/61	1723/34/45/54	1805/11/16/95	1963/68/74	
g	15		1571/82/93	1655/66/77/88	1750/59/70/81	1827/38	1900/06/79/90	2001
A	16		1503/14/25/36/87/98	1609/20/82/93	1704/75/86/97	1843/54/65/76	1911/22/33/95	2006/17/28
b	17		1530/41/52	1625/36	1715/20	1808/70/81/92	1927/38/49/60	2022/33
c	18		1557/68	1647/52	1731/42/56	1802/13/24/97	1954/65/76	
d	19		1500/79/84/90	1663/74/85	1747/67/72/78	1829/35/40	1908/81/87/92	
e	20		1511/22/95	1606/17/79/90	1701/12/83/94	1851/62	1919/24/30	2003/14/25
f	21		1527/38/49	1622/33/44	1717/28	1867/78/89	1935/46/57	2019/30
g	22		1565/76	1660	1739/53/64	1810/21/32	1962/73/84	
A	23		1508	1671		1848	1905/16	2000
b	24		1519	1603/14/98	1709/91	1859		2011
c	25		1546	1641	1736	1886	1943	

No dominical letter is placed against the intercalary day 29 February but since it is still counted as a weekday and given a name, the series of letters moves back one day every leap year after intercalation. Thus, a leap year beginning with the dominical letter C will change to a year with the dominical letter B on 1 March

HINDU CALENDAR

The Hindu calendar is a luni-solar calendar of twelve months, each containing 29 days, 12 hours. Each month is divided into a light fortnight (Shukla or Shuddha) and a dark fortnight (Krishna or Vadya) based on the waxing and waning of the moon. In most parts of India the month starts with the light fortnight, i.e. the day after the new moon, although in some regions it begins with the dark fortnight, i.e. the day after the full moon.

The new year begins in the month of Chaitra (March/ April) and ends in the month of Phalgun (March). The twelve months, Chaitra, Vaishakh, Jyeshtha, Ashadh, Shravan, Bhadrapad, Ashvin, Kartik, Margashirsh, Paush, Magh and Phalgun, have Sanskrit names derived from twelve asterisms (constellations). There are regional variations to the names of the months but the Sanskrit names are understood throughout India.

Every lunar month must have a solar transit and is termed pure (shuddha). The lunar month without a solar transit is impure (mala) and called an intercalary month. An intercalary month occurs approximately every 32 lunar months, whenever the difference between the Hindu year of 360 lunar days (354 days 8 hours solar time) and the 365 days 6 hours of the solar year reaches the length of one Hindu lunar month (29 days 12 hours).

The leap month may be added at any point in the Hindu year. The name given to the month varies according to when it occurs but is taken from the month immediately following it. There is no leap month in 2005.

The days of the week are called Raviwar (Sunday), Somawar (Monday), Mangalwar (Tuesday), Budhawar (Wednesday), Guruwar (Thursday), Shukrawar (Friday) and Shaniwar (Saturday). The names are derived from the Sanskrit names of the Sun, the Moon and five planets, Mars, Mercury, Jupiter, Venus and Saturn.

Most fasts and festivals are based on the lunar calendar but a few are determined by the apparent movement of the Sun, e.g. Sankranti and Pongal (in southern India), which are celebrated on 14/15 January to mark the start of the Sun's apparent journey northwards and a change of season.

Festivals celebrated throughout India are Chaitra (the New Year), Raksha-bandhan (the renewal of the kinship bond between brothers and sisters), Navaratri (a nine-night festival dedicated to the goddess Parvati), Dasara (the victory of Rama over the demon army), Diwali (a festival of lights), Makara Sankranti, Shivaratri (dedicated to Shiva), and Holi (a spring festival).

Regional festivals are Durga-puja (dedicated to the goddess Durga (Parvati)), Sarasvati-puja (dedicated to the goddess Sarasvati), Ganesh Chaturthi (worship of Ganesh on the fourth day (Chaturthi) of the light half of Bhadrapad), Ramanavami (the birth festival of the god Rama) and Janmashtami (the birth festival of the god Krishna).

The main festivals celebrated in Britain are Navaratri, Dasara, Durga-puja, Diwali, Holi, Sarasvati-puja, Ganesh Chaturthi, Raksha-bandhan, Ramanavami and Janmashtami.

For dates of the main festivals in 2005, see page 9.

JEWISH CALENDAR

The story of the Flood in the Book of Genesis indicates the use of a calendar of some kind and that the writers recognised thirty days as the length of a lunation. However, after the diaspora, Jewish communities were left in considerable doubt as to the times of fasts and festivals. This led to the formation of the Jewish calendar as used today. It is said that this was done in AD 358 by Rabbi Hillel II, though some assert that it did not happen until much later.

The calendar is luni-solar, and is based on the lengths of the lunation and of the tropical year as found by Hipparchus (c.120 BC), which differ little from those adopted at the present day. The year AM 5765 (2004–2005) is the 8th year of the 304th Metonic (Minor or Lunar) cycle of 19 years and the 25th year of the 206th Solar (or Major) cycle of 28 years since the Era of the Creation. Jews hold that the Creation occurred at the time of the autumnal equinox in the year known in the Christian calendar as 3760 BC (954 of the Julian period). The epoch or starting point of Jewish chronology corresponds to 7 October 3761 BC. At the beginning of each solar cycle, the Tekufah of Nisan (the vernal equinox) returns to the same day and to the same hour.

The hour is divided into 1080 minims, and the month between one new moon and the next is reckoned as 29 days, 12 hours, 793 minims. The normal calendar year, called a Regular Common year, consists of 12 months of 30 days and 29 days alternately. Since 12 months such as these comprise only 354 days, in order that each of them shall not diverge greatly from an average place in the solar year, a 13th month is occasionally added after the fifth month of the civil year (which commences on the first day of the month Tishri), or as the penultimate month of the ecclesiastical year (which commences on the first day of the month Nisan). The years when this happens are called Embolismic or leap years.

Of the 19 years that form a Metonic cycle, seven are leap years; they occur at places in the cycle indicated by the numbers 3, 6, 8, 11, 14, 17 and 19, these places being chosen so that the accumulated excesses of the solar years should be as small as possible.

A Jewish year is of one of the following six types:

Minimal Common	353 days
Regular Common	354 days
Full Common	355 days
Minimal Leap	383 days
Regular Leap	384 days
Full Leap	385 days

The Regular year has alternate months of 30 and 29 days. In a Full year, whether common or leap, Marcheshvan, the second month of the civil year, has 30 days instead of 29; in Minimal years Kislev, the third month, has 29 instead of 30. The additional month in leap years is called Adar I and precedes the month called Adar in Common years. Adar II is called Adar Sheni in leap years, and the usual Adar festivals are kept in Adar Sheni. Adar I and Adar II always have 30 days, but neither this, nor the other variations mentioned, is allowed to change the number of days in the other months, which still follow the alternation of the normal twelve.

These are the main features of the Jewish calendar, which must be considered permanent because as a Jewish law it cannot be altered except by a great Sanhedrin.

The Jewish day begins between sunset and nightfall. The time used is that of the meridian of Jerusalem, which is 2h 21m in advance of Greenwich Mean Time. Rules for the beginning of sabbaths and festivals were laid down for the latitude of London in the 18th century and hours for nightfall are now fixed annually by the Chief Rabbi.

JEWISH CALENDAR 5765–6

AM 5765 (765) is a Minimal Leap year of 13 months, 55 sabbaths and 383 days.

Month (first day)	AM 5765	AM 5766
Tishri 1	16 September 2004	4 October 2005
Marcheshvan 1	16 October	3 November
Kislev 1	14 November	2 December
Tebet 1	13 December	
Shebat 1	11 January 2005	
*Adar 1	9 February	
†Adar II	11 March	
Nisan 1	10 April	
Iyar 1	9 May	
Sivan 1	8 June	
Tammuz 1	7 July	
Ab 1	6 August	
Elul 1	4 September	

*Known as Adar Rishon in leap years
†Known as Adar Sheni in leap years

JEWISH FASTS AND FESTIVALS

For dates of principal festivals in 2005, see page 9.

Tishri 1–2	Rosh Hashanah (New Year)
Tishri 3	*Fast of Gedaliah
Tishri 10	Yom Kippur (Day of Atonement)
Tishri 15–21	Succoth (Feast of Tabernacles)
Tishri 21	Hoshana Rabba
Tishri 22	Shemini Atseret (Solemn Assembly)
Tishri 23	Simchat Torah (Rejoicing of the Law)
Kislev 25	Chanucah (Dedication of the Temple) begins
Tebet 10	Fast of Tebet
†Adar 13	§Fast of Esther
†Adar 14	Purim
†Adar 15	Shushan Purim
Nisan 15–22	Pesach (Passover)
Sivan 6–7	Shavuot (Feast of Weeks)
Tammuz 17	*Fast of Tammuz
Ab 9	*Fast of Ab

*If these dates fall on the sabbath the fast is kept on the following day
†Adar Sheni in leap years
§This fast is observed on Adar 11 (or Adar Sheni 11 in leap years) if Adar 13 falls on a Sabbath

THE MUSLIM CALENDAR

The Muslim era is dated from the *Hijrah,* or flight of the Prophet Muhammad from Mecca to Medina, the corresponding date of which in the Julian calendar is 16 July AD 622. The lunar *hijri* calendar is used principally in Iran, Egypt, Malaysia, Pakistan, Mauritania, various Arab states and certain parts of India. Iran uses the solar *hijri* calendar as well as the lunar *hijri* calendar. The dating system was adopted about AD 639, commencing with the first day of the month Muharram.

The lunar calendar consists of twelve months containing an alternate sequence of 30 and 29 days, with the intercalation of one day at the end of the twelfth month at stated intervals in each cycle of 30 years. The object of the intercalation is to reconcile the date of the first day of the month with the date of the actual new moon.

Some adherents still take the date of the evening of the first physical sighting of the crescent of the new moon as that of the first of the month. If cloud obscures the moon the present month may be extended to 30 days, after which the new month will begin automatically regardless of whether the moon has been seen. (Under religious law a month must have less than 31 days.) This means that the beginning of a new month and the date of religious festivals can vary from the published calendars.

In each cycle of 30 years, 19 years are common and contain 354 days, and 11 years are intercalary (leap years) of 355 days, the latter being called *kabisah*. The mean length of the Hijrah years is 354 days 8 hours 48 minutes and the period of mean lunation is 29 days 12 hours 44 minutes.

To ascertain if a year is common or kabisah, divide it by 30: the quotient gives the number of completed cycles and the remainder shows the place of the year in the current cycle. If the remainder is 2, 5, 7, 10, 13, 16, 18, 21, 24, 26 or 29, the year is kabisah and consists of 355 days.

MUSLIM CALENDAR 1425–26
Hijrah 1425 AH (remainder 15) is a common year, 1426 AH (remainder 16) is a kabisah year. Calendar dates below are estimates based on calculations of moon phases.

Month Length	1426 *(1425)* AH
Dhu'l-Qa'da (30)	13 December
Dhu'l-Hijjah (29 or 30)	12 January
Muharram (30)	10 February
Safar (29)	12 March
Rabi' I (30)	10 April
Rabi' II (29)	10 May
Jumada I (30)	8 June
Jumada II (29)	8 July
Rajab (30)	6 August
Sha'ban (29)	5 September
Ramadán (30)	4 October
Shawwál (29)	3 November

MUSLIM FESTIVALS
Ramadan is a month of fasting for all Muslims because it is the month in which the revelation of the *Qur'an* (Koran) began. During Ramadan Muslims abstain from food, drink and sexual pleasure from dawn until after sunset throughout the month.

The two major festivals are Id al-Fitr and Id al-Adha. Id al-Fitr marks the end of the Ramadan fast and is celebrated on the day after the sighting of the new moon of the following month. Id al-Adha, the festival of sacrifice (also known as the great festival), celebrates the submission of the Prophet Ibrahim (Abraham) to God. Id al-Adha falls on the tenth day of Dhul-Hijjah, coinciding with the day when those on *hajj* (pilgrimage to Mecca) sacrifice animals.

Other days accorded special recognition are:

Muharram 1	New Year's Day
Muharram 10	Ashura (the day Prophet Noah left the Ark and Prophet Moses was saved from Pharaoh (Sunni), the death of the Prophet's grandson Husain (Shi'ite))
Rabi'u-l-Awwal (Rabi' I) 12	Mawlid al-Nabi (birthday of the Prophet Muhammad)
Rajab 27	Laylat al-Isra' wa'l-Mi'raj (The Night of Journey and Ascension)
Ramadán One of the odd-numbered nights in the last 10 of the month	Laylat al-Qadr (Night of Power)
Dhu'l-Hijjah 10	Id al-Adha (Festival of Sacrifice)

THE SIKH CALENDAR

The Sikh calendar is a lunar calendar of 365 days divided into 12 months. The length of the months varies between 29 and 32 days.

There are no prescribed feast days and no fasting periods. The main celebrations are Baisakhi Mela (the new year and the anniversary of the founding of the Khalsa), Diwali Mela (festival of light), Hola Mohalla Mela (a spring festival held in the Punjab), and the Gurupurabs (anniversaries associated with the ten Gurus).

For dates of the major celebrations in 2005, *see* page 9.

THAI CALENDAR

Thailand adopted the Suriyakati calendar, a modified version of the Gregorian calendar (Suriyakati) during the reign of King Rama V in 1888, using 1 April as the first day of the year. In 1940, the date of the new year was changed to 1 January. The years are counted from the beginning of the Buddhist era (BE), which is calculated to have commenced upon the death of the Lord Buddha, which is taken to have occurred in BC 543, so AD 2005 is BE 2548. The Chinese system of associating years with one of twelve animals is also in use in Thailand. The Chantarakati lunar calendar is used to determine religious holidays; the new year begins on the first day of the waxing moon in November or, if there is a leap month, in December.

CIVIL AND LEGAL CALENDAR

THE HISTORICAL YEAR
Before 1752, two calendar systems were used in England. The civil or legal year began on 25 March and the historical year on 1 January. Thus the civil or legal date 24 March 1658 was the same day as the historical date 24 March 1659; a date in that portion of the year is written as 24 March 165 8/9, the lower figure showing the historical year.

THE NEW YEAR
In England in the seventh century, and as late as the 13th, the year was reckoned from Christmas Day, but in the 12th century the Church in England began the year with the feast of the Annunciation of the Blessed Virgin ('Lady Day') on 25 March and this practice was adopted generally in the 14th century. The civil or legal year in the British Dominions (exclusive of Scotland) began with Lady Day until 1751. But in and since 1752 the civil year

has begun with 1 January. New Year's Day in Scotland was changed from 25 March to 1 January in 1600.

Elsewhere in Europe, 1 January was adopted as the first day of the year by Venice in 1522, German states in 1544, Spain, Portugal and the Roman Catholic Netherlands in 1556, Prussia, Denmark and Sweden in 1559, France in 1564, Lorraine in 1579, the Protestant Netherlands in 1583, Russia in 1725, and Tuscany in 1751.

REGNAL YEARS

Regnal years are the years of a sovereign's reign and each begins on the anniversary of his or her accession, e.g. regnal year 54 of the present Queen begins on 6 February 2005.

The system was used for dating Acts of Parliament until 1962. The Summer Time Act 1925, for example, is quoted as 15 and 16 Geo. V c. 64, because it became law in the parliamentary session which extended over part of both of these regnal years. Acts of a parliamentary session during which a sovereign died were usually given two year numbers, the regnal year of the deceased sovereign and the regnal year of his or her successor, e.g. those passed in 1952 were dated 16 Geo. VI and 1 Elizabeth II. Since 1962 Acts of Parliament have been dated by the calendar year.

QUARTER AND TERM DAYS

Holy days and saints days were the usual means in early times for setting the dates of future and recurrent appointments. The quarter days in England and Wales are the feast of the Nativity (25 December), the feast of the Annunciation (25 March), the feast of St John the Baptist (24 June) and the feast of St Michael and All Angels (29 September).

The term days in Scotland are Candlemas (the feast of the Purification), Whitsunday, Lammas (Loaf Mass), and Martinmas (St Martin's Day). These fell on 2 February, 15 May, 1 August and 11 November respectively. However, by the Term and Quarter Days (Scotland) Act 1990, the dates of the term days were changed to 28 February (Candlemas), 28 May (Whitsunday), 28 August (Lammas) and 28 November (Martinmas).

RED-LETTER DAYS

Red-letter days were originally the holy days and saints days indicated in early ecclesiastical calendars by letters printed in red ink. The days to be distinguished in this way were approved at the Council of Nicaea in AD 325.

These days still have a legal significance, as judges of the Queen's Bench Division wear scarlet robes on red-letter days falling during the law sittings. The days designated as red-letter days for this purpose are:

Holy and saints days
The Conversion of St Paul, the Purification, Ash Wednesday, the Annunciation, the Ascension, the feasts of St Mark, SS Philip and James, St Matthias, St Barnabas, St John the Baptist, St Peter, St Thomas, St James, St Luke, SS Simon and Jude, All Saints, St Andrew.

Civil calendar (for dates, *see* page 9)
The anniversaries of The Queen's accession, The Queen's birthday and The Queen's coronation, The Queen's official birthday, the birthday of the Duke of Edinburgh, the birthday of the Prince of Wales, St David's Day and Lord Mayor's Day.

PUBLIC HOLIDAYS

Public holidays are divided into two categories, common law and statutory. Common law holidays are holidays 'by habit and custom'; in England, Wales and Northern Ireland these are Good Friday and Christmas Day.

Statutory public holidays, known as bank holidays, were first established by the Bank Holidays Act 1871. They were, literally, days on which the banks (and other public institutions) were closed and financial obligations due on that day were payable the following day. The legislation currently governing public holidays in the UK, which is the Banking and Financial Dealings Act 1971, stipulates the days that are to be public holidays in England, Wales, Scotland and Northern Ireland.

Certain holidays (indicated by * below) are granted annually by royal proclamation, either throughout the UK or in any place in the UK. The public holidays are:

England and Wales
*New Year's Day
Good Friday
Easter Monday
*The first Monday in May
The last Monday in May
The last Monday in August
26 December, if it is not a Sunday
27 December when 25 or 26 December is a Sunday

Scotland
New Year's Day, or if it is a Sunday, 2 January
2 January, or if it is a Sunday, 3 January
Good Friday
The first Monday in May
*The last Monday in May
The first Monday in August
Christmas Day, or if it is a Sunday, 26 December
*Boxing Day – if Christmas Day falls on a Sunday, 26 December is given in lieu and an alternative day is given for Boxing Day

Northern Ireland
*New Year's Day
17 March, or if it is a Sunday, 18 March
Easter Monday
*The first Monday in May
The last Monday in May
*12 July, or if it is a Sunday, 13 July
The last Monday in August
26 December, if it is not a Sunday
27 December if 25 or 26 December is a Sunday

For dates of public holidays in 2005 and 2006, *see* pages 10–11.

CHRONOLOGICAL CYCLES AND ERAS

SOLAR (OR MAJOR) CYCLE
The solar cycle is a period of twenty-eight years in any corresponding year of which the days of the week recur on the same day of the month.

METONIC (LUNAR, OR MINOR) CYCLE
In 432 BC, Meton, an Athenian astronomer, found that 235 lunations are very nearly, though not exactly, equal in duration to 19 solar years and so after 19 years the phases of the Moon recur on the same days of the month (nearly). The dates of full moon in a cycle of 19 years were inscribed in figures of gold on public monuments in Athens, and the number showing the position of a year in the cycle is called the golden number of that year.

JULIAN PERIOD
The Julian period was proposed by Joseph Scaliger in 1582. The period is 7980 Julian years, and its first year coincides with the year 4713 BC. The figure of 7980 is

the product of the number of years in the solar cycle, the Metonic cycle and the cycle of the Roman indiction ($28 \times 19 \times 15$).

ROMAN INDICTION

The Roman indiction is a period of fifteen years, instituted for fiscal purposes about AD 300.

EPACT

The epact is the age of the calendar Moon, diminished by one day, on 1 January, in the ecclesiastical lunar calendar.

CHINESE CALENDAR

A lunar calendar was the sole calendar in use in China until 1911, when the government adopted the new (Gregorian) calendar for official and most business activities. The Chinese tend to follow both calendars, the lunar calendar playing an important part in personal life, e.g. birth celebrations, festivals, marriages; and in rural villages the lunar calendar dictates the cycle of activities, denoting the change of weather and farming activities.

The lunar calendar is used in Hong Kong, Singapore, Malaysia, Tibet and elsewhere in south-east Asia. The calendar has a cycle of 60 years. The new year begins at the first new moon after the sun enters the sign of Aquarius, i.e. the new year falls between 21 January and 19 February in the Gregorian calendar.

Each year in the Chinese calendar is associated with one of 12 animals: the rat, the ox, the tiger, the rabbit, the dragon, the snake, the horse, the goat or sheep, the monkey, the chicken or rooster, the dog, and the pig.

The date of the Chinese new year and the astrological sign for the years 2005–2008 are:

2005	9 February	Chicken or Rooster
2006	29 January	Dog
2007	18 February	Pig
2008	7 February	Rat

COPTIC CALENDAR

In the Coptic calendar, which is used in parts of Egypt and Ethiopia, the year is made up of 12 months of 30 days each, followed, in general, by five complementary days. Every fourth year is an intercalary or leap year and in these years there are six complementary days. The intercalary year of the Coptic calendar immediately precedes the leap year of the Julian calendar. The era is that of Diocletian or the Martyrs, the origin of which is fixed at 29 August AD 284 (Julian date).

INDIAN ERAS

In addition to the Muslim reckoning, other eras are used in India. The Saka era of southern India, dating from 3 March AD 78, was declared the national calendar of the Republic of India with effect from 22 March 1957, to be used concurrently with the Gregorian calendar. As revised, the year of the new Saka era begins at the spring equinox, with five successive months of 31 days and seven of 30 days in ordinary years, and six months of each length in leap years. The year AD 2005 is 1927 of the revised Saka era.

The year AD 2005 corresponds to the following years in other eras:

Year 2062 of the Vikram Samvat era
Year 1412 of the Bengali San era
Year 1181 of the Kollam era
Vedanga Jyotisa year 1 of the five-yearly cycle (387th cycle of Paitamah Siddhanta)

Year 6006 of the Kaliyuga era
Year 2547 of the Buddha Nirvana era

JAPANESE CALENDAR

The Japanese calendar is essentially the same as the Gregorian calendar, the years, months and weeks being of the same length and beginning on the same days as those of the Gregorian calendar. The numeration of the years is different, based on a system of epochs or periods, each of which begins at the accession of an Emperor or other important occurrence. The method is not unlike the British system of regnal years, except that each year of a period closes on 31 December. The Japanese chronology begins about AD 650 and the three latest epochs are defined by the reigns of Emperors, whose actual names are not necessarily used:

Epoch
Taishō 1 August 1912 to 25 December 1926
Shōwa 26 December 1926 to 7 January 1989
Heisei 8 January 1989

The year Heisei 17 begins on 1 January 2005.

The months are known as First Month, Second Month, etc., First Month being equivalent to January. The days of the week are Nichiyōbi (Sun-day), Getsuyōbi (Moon-day), Kayōbi (Fire-day), Suiyōbi (Water-day), Mokuyōbi (Wood-day), Kinyōbi (Metal-day), Doyōbi (Earth-day).

THE MASONIC YEAR

Two dates are quoted in warrants, dispensations, etc., issued by the United Grand Lodge of England, those for the current year being expressed as *Anno Domini* 2005– *Anno Lucis* 6005. This *Anno Lucis* (year of light) is based on the Book of Genesis 1:3, the 4000-year difference being derived, in modified form, from *Ussher's Notation*, published in 1654, which places the Creation of the World in 4004 BC.

OLYMPIADS

Ancient Greek chronology was reckoned in Olympiads, cycles of four years corresponding with the periodic Olympic Games held on the plain of Olympia in Elis once every four years. The intervening years were the first, second, etc., of the Olympiad, which received the name of the victor at the Games. The first recorded Olympiad is that of Choroebus, 776 BC.

ZOROASTRIAN CALENDAR

Zoroastrians, followers of the Iranian prophet Zarathushtra (known to the Greeks as Zoroaster) are mostly to be found in Iran and in India, where they are known as Parsees.

The Zoroastrian era dates from the coronation of the last Zoroastrian Sasanian king in AD 631. The Zoroastrian calendar is divided into twelve months, each comprising 30 days, followed by five holy days of the Gathas at the end of each year to make the year consist of 365 days.

In order to synchronise the calendar with the solar year of 365 days, an extra month was intercalated once every 120 years. However, this intercalation ceased in the 12th century and the New Year, which had fallen in the spring, slipped back to August. Because intercalation ceased at different times in Iran and India, there was one month's difference between the calendar followed in Iran (Kadmi calendar) and that followed by the Parsees (Shenshai calendar). In 1906 a group of Zoroastrians decided to bring the calendar back in line with the seasons again and restore the New Year to 21 March each year (Fasli calendar).

The Shenshai calendar (New Year in August) is mainly used by Parsees. The Fasli calendar (New Year, 21 March) is mainly used by Zoroastrians living in Iran, in the Indian subcontinent, or away from Iran.

THE ROMAN CALENDAR

Roman historians adopted as an epoch the foundation of Rome, which is believed to have happened in the year 753 BC. The ordinal number of the years in Roman reckoning is followed by the letters AUC *(ab urbe condita)*, so that the year 2005 is 2758 AUC (MMDCCLVIII). The calendar that we know has developed from one said to have been established by Romulus using a year of 304 days divided into ten months, beginning with March. To this Numa added January and February, making the year consist of 12 months of 30 and 29 days alternately, with an additional day so that the total was 355. It is also said that Numa ordered an intercalary month of 22 or 23 days in alternate years, making 90 days in eight years, to be inserted after 23 February.

However, there is some doubt as to the origination and the details of the intercalation in the Roman calendar. It is certain that some scheme of this kind was inaugurated and not fully carried out, for in the year 46 BC Julius Caesar found that the calendar had been allowed to fall into some confusion. He sought the help of the Egyptian astronomer Sosigenes, which led to the construction and adoption (45 BC) of the Julian calendar, and, by a slight alteration, to the Gregorian calendar now in use. The year 46 BC was made to consist of 445 days and is called the Year of Confusion.

In the Roman (Julian) calendar the days of the month were counted backwards from three fixed points, or days, and an intervening day was said to be so many days before the next coming point, the first and last being counted. These three points were the Kalends, the Nones, and the Ides. Their positions in the months and the method of counting from them will be seen in the table below. The year containing 366 days was called *bissextillis annus*, as it had a doubled sixth day *(bissextus dies)* before the March Kalends on 24 February – *ante diem sextum Kalendas Martias*, or a.d. VI Kal. Mart.

Present days of the month	*March, May, July, October have thirty-one days*		*January, August, December have thirty-one days*		*April, June, September, November have thirty days*		*February has twenty-eight days, and in leap year twenty-nine*	
1	Kalendis		Kalendis		Kalendis		Kalendis	
2	VI		IV ⎱ ante		IV ⎱ ante		IV ⎱ ante	
3	V	ante	III ⎰ Nonas		III ⎰ Nonas		III ⎰ Nonas	
4	IV	Nonas	pridie Nonas		pridie Nonas		pridie Nonas	
5	III		Nonis		Nonis		Nonis	
6	pridie Nonas		VIII		VIII		VIII	
7	Nonis		VII		VII		VII	
8	VIII		VI	ante	VI	ante	VI	ante
9	VII		V	Idus	V	Idus	V	Idus
10	VI	ante	IV		IV		IV	
11	V	Idus	III		III		III	
12	IV		pridie Idus		pridie Idus		pridie Idus	
13	III		Idibus		Idibus		Idibus	
14	pridie Idus		XIX		XVIII		XVI	
15	Idibus		XVIII		XVII		XV	
16	XVII		XVII		XVI		XIV	
17	XVI		XVI		XV		XIII	
18	XV		XV		XIV		XII	
19	XIV		XIV		XIII		XI	
20	XIII		XIII		XII	ante Kalendas	X	ante Kalendas
21	XII		XII	ante Kalendas	XI	(of the month	IX	Martias
22	XI	ante Kalendas	XI	(of the month	X	following)	VIII	
23	X	(of the month	X	following)	IX		VII	
24	IX	following)	IX		VIII		*VI	
25	VIII		VIII		VII		V	
26	VII		VII		VI		IV	
27	VI		VI		V		III	
28	V		V		IV		pridie Kalendas	
29	IV		IV		III		Martias	
30	III		III		pridie Kalendas			
31	pridie Kalendas (Aprilis, Iunias, Sextilis, Novembris)		pridie Kalendas (Februarias, Septembris, Ianuarias)		(Maias, Quinctilis, Octobris, Decembris)		* (repeated in leap year)	

CALENDAR FOR ANY YEAR 1780–2040

To select the correct calendar for any year between 1780 and 2040, consult the index below

*leap year

1780 N*	1813 K	1846 I	1879 G	1912 D*	1945 C	1978 A	2011 M
1781 C	1814 M	1847 K	1880 J*	1913 G	1946 E	1979 C	2012 B*
1782 E	1815 A	1848 N*	1881 M	1914 I	1947 G	1980 F*	2013 E
1783 G	1816 D*	1849 C	1882 A	1915 K	1948 J*	1981 I	2014 G
1784 J*	1817 G	1850 E	1883 C	1916 N*	1949 M	1982 K	2015 I
1785 M	1818 I	1851 G	1884 F*	1917 C	1950 A	1983 M	2016 L*
1786 A	1819 K	1852 J*	1885 I	1918 E	1951 C	1984 B*	2017 A
1787 C	1820 N*	1853 M	1886 K	1919 G	1952 F*	1985 E	2018 C
1788 F*	1821 C	1854 A	1887 M	1920 J*	1953 I	1986 G	2019 E
1789 I	1822 E	1855 C	1888 B*	1921 M	1954 K	1987 I	2020 H*
1790 K	1823 G	1856 F*	1889 E	1922 A	1955 M	1988 L*	2021 K
1791 M	1824 J*	1857 I	1890 G	1923 C	1956 B*	1989 A	2022 M
1792 B*	1825 M	1858 K	1891 I	1924 F*	1957 E	1990 C	2023 A
1793 E	1826 A	1859 M	1892 L*	1925 I	1958 G	1991 E	2024 D*
1794 G	1827 C	1860 B*	1893 A	1926 K	1959 I	1992 H*	2025 G
1795 I	1828 F*	1861 E	1894 C	1927 M	1960 L*	1993 K	2026 I
1796 L*	1829 I	1862 G	1895 E	1928 B*	1961 A	1994 M	2027 K
1797 A	1830 K	1863 I	1896 H*	1929 E	1962 C	1995 A	2028 N*
1798 C	1831 M	1864 L*	1897 K	1930 G	1963 E	1996 D*	2029 C
1799 E	1832 B*	1865 A	1898 M	1931 I	1964 H*	1997 G	2030 E
1800 G	1833 E	1866 C	1899 A	1932 L*	1965 K	1998 I	2031 G
1801 I	1834 G	1867 E	1900 C	1933 A	1966 M	1999 K	2032 J*
1802 K	1835 I	1868 H*	1901 E	1934 C	1967 A	2000 N*	2033 M
1803 M	1836 L*	1869 K	1902 G	1935 E	1968 D*	2001 C	2034 A
1804 B*	1837 A	1870 M	1903 I	1936 H*	1969 G	2002 E	2035 C
1805 E	1838 C	1871 A	1904 L*	1937 K	1970 I	2003 G	2036 F*
1806 G	1839 E	1872 D*	1905 A	1938 M	1971 K	2004 J*	2037 I
1807 I	1840 H*	1873 G	1906 C	1939 A	1972 N*	2005 M	2038 K
1808 L*	1841 K	1874 I	1907 E	1940 D*	1973 C	2006 A	2039 M
1809 A	1842 M	1875 K	1908 H*	1941 G	1974 E	2007 C	2040 B*
1810 C	1843 A	1876 N*	1909 K	1942 I	1975 G	2008 F*	
1811 E	1844 D*	1877 C	1910 M	1943 K	1976 J*	2009 I	
1812 H*	1845 G	1878 E	1911 A	1944 N*	1977 M	2010 K	

A

	January	February	March
Sun.	1 8 15 22 29	5 12 19 26	5 12 19 26
Mon.	2 9 16 23 30	6 13 20 27	6 13 20 27
Tue.	3 10 17 24 31	7 14 21 28	7 14 21 28
Wed.	4 11 18 25	1 8 15 22	1 8 15 22 29
Thur.	5 12 19 26	2 9 16 23	2 9 16 23 30
Fri.	6 13 20 27	3 10 17 24	3 10 17 24 31
Sat.	7 14 21 28	4 11 18 25	4 11 18 25

	April	May	June
Sun.	2 9 16 23 30	7 14 21 28	4 11 18 25
Mon.	3 10 17 24	1 8 15 22 29	5 12 19 26
Tue.	4 11 18 25	2 9 16 23 30	6 13 20 27
Wed.	5 12 19 26	3 10 17 24 31	7 14 21 28
Thur.	6 13 20 27	4 11 18 25	1 8 15 22 29
Fri.	7 14 21 28	5 12 19 26	2 9 16 23 30
Sat.	1 8 15 22 29	6 13 20 27	3 10 17 24

	July	August	September
Sun.	2 9 16 23 30	6 13 20 27	3 10 17 24
Mon.	3 10 17 24 31	7 14 21 28	4 11 18 25
Tue.	4 11 18 25	1 8 15 22 29	5 12 19 26
Wed.	5 12 19 26	2 9 16 23 30	6 13 20 27
Thur.	6 13 20 27	3 10 17 24 31	7 14 21 28
Fri.	7 14 21 28	4 11 18 25	1 8 15 22 29
Sat.	1 8 15 22 29	5 12 19 26	2 9 16 23 30

	October	November	December
Sun.	1 8 15 22 29	5 12 19 26	3 10 17 24 31
Mon.	2 9 16 23 30	6 13 20 27	4 11 18 25
Tue.	3 10 17 24 31	7 14 21 28	5 12 19 26
Wed.	4 11 18 25	1 8 15 22 29	6 13 20 27
Thur.	5 12 19 26	2 9 16 23 30	7 14 21 28
Fri.	6 13 20 27	3 10 17 24	1 8 15 22 29
Sat.	7 14 21 28	4 11 18 25	2 9 16 23 30

EASTER DAYS

March 26	1815, 1826, 1837, 1967, 1978, 1989
April 2	1809, 1893, 1899, 1961
April 9	1871, 1882, 1939, 1950, 2023, 2034
April 16	1786, 1797, 1843, 1854, 1865, 1911
	1922, 1933, 1995, 2006, 2017
April 23	1905

B (LEAP YEAR)

	January	February	March
Sun.	1 8 15 22 29	5 12 19 26	4 11 18 25
Mon.	2 9 16 23 30	6 13 20 27	5 12 19 26
Tue.	3 10 17 24 31	7 14 21 28	6 13 20 27
Wed.	4 11 18 25	1 8 15 22 29	7 14 21 28
Thur.	5 12 19 26	2 9 16 23	1 8 15 22 29
Fri.	6 13 20 27	3 10 17 24	2 9 16 23 30
Sat.	7 14 21 28	4 11 18 25	3 10 17 24 31

	April	May	June
Sun.	1 8 15 22 29	6 13 20 27	3 10 17 24
Mon.	2 9 16 23 30	7 14 21 28	4 11 18 25
Tue.	3 10 17 24	1 8 15 22 29	5 12 19 26
Wed.	4 11 18 25	2 9 16 23 30	6 13 20 27
Thur.	5 12 19 26	3 10 17 24 31	7 14 21 28
Fri.	6 13 20 27	4 11 18 25	1 8 15 22 29
Sat.	7 14 21 28	5 12 19 26	2 9 16 23 30

	July	August	September
Sun.	1 8 15 22 29	5 12 19 26	2 9 16 23 30
Mon.	2 9 16 23 30	6 13 20 27	3 10 17 24
Tue.	3 10 17 24 31	7 14 21 28	4 11 18 25
Wed.	4 11 18 25	1 8 15 22 29	5 12 19 26
Thur.	5 12 19 26	2 9 16 23 30	6 13 20 27
Fri.	6 13 20 27	3 10 17 24 31	7 14 21 28
Sat.	7 14 21 28	4 11 18 25	1 8 15 22 29

	October	November	December
Sun.	7 14 21 28	4 11 18 25	2 9 16 23 30
Mon.	1 8 15 22 29	5 12 19 26	3 10 17 24 31
Tue.	2 9 16 23 30	6 13 20 27	4 11 18 25
Wed.	3 10 17 24 31	7 14 21 28	5 12 19 26
Thur.	4 11 18 25	1 8 15 22 29	6 13 20 27
Fri.	5 12 19 26	2 9 16 23 30	7 14 21 28
Sat.	6 13 20 27	3 10 17 24	1 8 15 22 29

EASTER DAYS

April 1	1804, 1888, 1956, 2040
April 8	1792, 1860, 1928, 2012
April 22	1832, 1984

C

	January	February	March
Sun.	7 14 21 28	4 11 18 25	4 11 18 25
Mon.	1 8 15 22 29	5 12 19 26	5 12 19 26
Tue.	2 9 16 23 30	6 13 20 27	6 13 20 27
Wed.	3 10 17 24 31	7 14 21 28	7 14 21 28
Thur.	4 11 18 25	1 8 15 22	1 8 15 22 29
Fri.	5 12 19 26	2 9 16 23	2 9 16 23 30
Sat.	6 13 20 27	3 10 17 24	3 10 17 24 31

	April	May	June
Sun.	1 8 15 22 29	6 13 20 27	3 10 17 24
Mon.	2 9 16 23 30	7 14 21 28	4 11 18 25
Tue.	3 10 17 24	1 8 15 22 29	5 12 19 26
Wed.	4 11 18 25	2 9 16 23 30	6 13 20 27
Thur.	5 12 19 26	3 10 17 24 31	7 14 21 28
Fri.	6 13 20 27	4 11 18 25	1 8 15 22 29
Sat.	7 14 21 28	5 12 19 26	2 9 16 23 30

	July	August	September
Sun.	1 8 15 22 29	5 12 19 26	2 9 16 23 30
Mon.	2 9 16 23 30	6 13 20 27	3 10 17 24
Tue.	3 10 17 24 31	7 14 21 28	4 11 18 25
Wed.	4 11 18 25	1 8 15 22 29	5 12 19 26
Thur.	5 12 19 26	2 9 16 23 30	6 13 20 27
Fri.	6 13 20 27	3 10 17 24 31	7 14 21 28
Sat.	7 14 21 28	4 11 18 25	1 8 15 22 29

	October	November	December
Sun.	7 14 21 28	4 11 18 25	2 9 16 23 30
Mon.	1 8 15 22 29	5 12 19 26	3 10 17 24 31
Tue.	2 9 16 23 30	6 13 20 27	4 11 18 25
Wed.	3 10 17 24 31	7 14 21 28	5 12 19 26
Thur.	4 11 18 25	1 8 15 22 29	6 13 20 27
Fri.	5 12 19 26	2 9 16 23 30	7 14 21 28
Sat.	6 13 20 27	3 10 17 24	1 8 15 22 29

EASTER DAYS
March 25   1883, 1894, 1951, 2035
April 1   1866, 1877, 1923, 1934, 1945, 2018, 2029
April 8   1787, 1798, 1849, 1855, 1917, 2007
April 15   1781, 1827, 1838, 1900, 1906, 1979, 1990, 2001
April 22   1810, 1821, 1962, 1973

E

	January	February	March
Sun.	6 13 20 27	3 10 17 24	3 10 17 24 31
Mon.	7 14 21 28	4 11 18 25	4 11 18 25
Tue.	1 8 15 22 29	5 12 19 26	5 12 19 26
Wed.	2 9 16 23 30	6 13 20 27	6 13 20 27
Thur.	3 10 17 24 31	7 14 21 28	7 14 21 28
Fri.	4 11 18 25	1 8 15 22	1 8 15 22 29
Sat.	5 12 19 26	2 9 16 23	2 9 16 23 30

	April	May	June
Sun.	7 14 21 28	5 12 19 26	2 9 16 23 30
Mon.	1 8 15 22 29	6 13 20 27	3 10 17 24
Tue.	2 9 16 23 30	7 14 21 28	4 11 18 25
Wed.	3 10 17 24	1 8 15 22 29	5 12 19 26
Thur.	4 11 18 25	2 9 16 23 30	6 13 20 27
Fri.	5 12 19 26	3 10 17 24 31	7 14 21 28
Sat.	6 13 20 27	4 11 18 25	1 8 15 22 29

	July	August	September
Sun.	7 14 21 28	4 11 18 25	1 8 15 22 29
Mon.	1 8 15 22 29	5 12 19 26	2 9 16 23 30
Tue.	2 9 16 23 30	6 13 20 27	3 10 17 24
Wed.	3 10 17 24 31	7 14 21 28	4 11 18 25
Thur.	4 11 18 25	1 8 15 22 29	5 12 19 26
Fri.	5 12 19 26	2 9 16 23 30	6 13 20 27
Sat.	6 13 20 27	3 10 17 24 31	7 14 21 28

	October	November	December
Sun.	6 13 20 27	3 10 17 24	1 8 15 22 29
Mon.	7 14 21 28	4 11 18 25	2 9 16 23 30
Tue.	1 8 15 22 29	5 12 19 26	3 10 17 24 31
Wed.	2 9 16 23 30	6 13 20 27	4 11 18 25
Thur.	3 10 17 24 31	7 14 21 28	5 12 19 26
Fri.	4 11 18 25	1 8 15 22 29	6 13 20 27
Sat.	5 12 19 26	2 9 16 23 30	7 14 21 28

EASTER DAYS
March 24   1799
March 31   1782, 1793, 1839, 1850, 1861, 1907
            1918, 1929, 1991, 2002, 2013
April 7   1822, 1833, 1901, 1985
April 14   1805, 1811, 1895, 1963, 1974
April 21   1867, 1878, 1889, 1935, 1946, 1957, 2019, 2030

D (LEAP YEAR)

	January	February	March
Sun.	7 14 21 28	4 11 18 25	3 10 17 24 31
Mon.	1 8 15 22 29	5 12 19 26	4 11 18 25
Tue.	2 9 16 23 30	6 13 20 27	5 12 19 26
Wed.	3 10 17 24 31	7 14 21 28	6 13 20 27
Thur.	4 11 18 25	1 8 15 22 29	7 14 21 28
Fri.	5 12 19 26	2 9 16 23	1 8 15 22 29
Sat.	6 13 20 27	3 10 17 24	2 9 16 23 30

	April	May	June
Sun.	7 14 21 28	5 12 19 26	2 9 16 23 30
Mon.	1 8 15 22 29	6 13 20 27	3 10 17 24
Tue.	2 9 16 23 30	7 14 21 28	4 11 18 25
Wed.	3 10 17 24	1 8 15 22 29	5 12 19 26
Thur.	4 11 18 25	2 9 16 23 30	6 13 20 27
Fri.	5 12 19 26	3 10 17 24 31	7 14 21 28
Sat.	6 13 20 27	4 11 18 25	1 8 15 22 29

	July	August	September
Sun.	7 14 21 28	4 11 18 25	1 8 15 22 29
Mon.	1 8 15 22 29	5 12 19 26	2 9 16 23 30
Tue.	2 9 16 23 30	6 13 20 27	3 10 17 24
Wed.	3 10 17 24 31	7 14 21 28	4 11 18 25
Thur.	4 11 18 25	1 8 15 22 29	5 12 19 26
Fri.	5 12 19 26	2 9 16 23 30	6 13 20 27
Sat.	6 13 20 27	3 10 17 24 31	7 14 21 28

	October	November	December
Sun.	6 13 20 27	3 10 17 24	1 8 15 22 29
Mon.	7 14 21 28	4 11 18 25	2 9 16 23 30
Tue.	1 8 15 22 29	5 12 19 26	3 10 17 24 31
Wed.	2 9 16 23 30	6 13 20 27	4 11 18 25
Thur.	3 10 17 24 31	7 14 21 28	5 12 19 26
Fri.	4 11 18 25	1 8 15 22 29	6 13 20 27
Sat.	5 12 19 26	2 9 16 23 30	7 14 21 28

EASTER DAYS
March 24   1940
March 31   1872, 2024
April 7   1844, 1912, 1996
April 14   1816, 1968

F (LEAP YEAR)

	January	February	March
Sun.	6 13 20 27	3 10 17 24	2 9 16 23 30
Mon.	7 14 21 28	4 11 18 25	3 10 17 24 31
Tue.	1 8 15 22 29	5 12 19 26	4 11 18 25
Wed.	2 9 16 23 30	6 13 20 27	5 12 19 26
Thur.	3 10 17 24 31	7 14 21 28	6 13 20 27
Fri.	4 11 18 25	1 8 15 22 29	7 14 21 28
Sat.	5 12 19 26	2 9 16 23	1 8 15 22 29

	April	May	June
Sun.	6 13 20 27	4 11 18 25	1 8 15 22 29
Mon.	7 14 21 28	5 12 19 26	2 9 16 23 30
Tue.	1 8 15 22 29	6 13 20 27	3 10 17 24
Wed.	2 9 16 23 30	7 14 21 28	4 11 18 25
Thur.	3 10 17 24	1 8 15 22 29	5 12 19 26
Fri.	4 11 18 25	2 9 16 23 30	6 13 20 27
Sat.	5 12 19 26	3 10 17 24 31	7 14 21 28

	July	August	September
Sun.	6 13 20 27	3 10 17 24 31	7 14 21 28
Mon.	7 14 21 28	4 11 18 25	1 8 15 22 29
Tue.	1 8 15 22 29	5 12 19 26	2 9 16 23 30
Wed.	2 9 16 23 30	6 13 20 27	3 10 17 24
Thur.	3 10 17 24 31	7 14 21 28	4 11 18 25
Fri.	4 11 18 25	1 8 15 22 29	5 12 19 26
Sat.	5 12 19 26	2 9 16 23 30	6 13 20 27

	October	November	December
Sun.	5 12 19 26	2 9 16 23 30	7 14 21 28
Mon.	6 13 20 27	3 10 17 24	1 8 15 22 29
Tue.	7 14 21 28	4 11 18 25	2 9 16 23 30
Wed.	1 8 15 22 29	5 12 19 26	3 10 17 24 31
Thur.	2 9 16 23 30	6 13 20 27	4 11 18 25
Fri.	3 10 17 24 31	7 14 21 28	5 12 19 26
Sat.	4 11 18 25	1 8 15 22 29	6 13 20 27

EASTER DAYS
March 23   1788, 1856, 2008
April 6   1828, 1980
April 13   1884, 1952, 2036
April 20   1924

G

	January	February	March
Sun.	5 12 19 26	2 9 16 23	2 9 16 23 30
Mon.	6 13 20 27	3 10 17 24	3 10 17 24 31
Tue.	7 14 21 28	4 11 18 25	4 11 18 25
Wed.	1 8 15 22 29	5 12 19 26	5 12 19 26
Thur.	2 9 16 23 30	6 13 20 27	6 13 20 27
Fri.	3 10 17 24 31	7 14 21 28	7 14 21 28
Sat.	4 11 18 25	1 8 15 22	1 8 15 22 29

	April	May	June
Sun.	6 13 20 27	4 11 18 25	1 8 15 22 29
Mon.	7 14 21 28	5 12 19 26	2 9 16 23 30
Tue.	1 8 15 22 29	6 13 20 27	3 10 17 24
Wed.	2 9 16 23 30	7 14 21 28	4 11 18 25
Thur.	3 10 17 24	1 8 15 22 29	5 12 19 26
Fri.	4 11 18 25	2 9 16 23 30	6 13 20 27
Sat.	5 12 19 26	3 10 17 24 31	7 14 21 28

	July	August	September
Sun.	6 13 20 27	3 10 17 24 31	7 14 21 28
Mon.	7 14 21 28	4 11 18 25	1 8 15 22 29
Tue.	1 8 15 22 29	5 12 19 26	2 9 16 23 30
Wed.	2 9 16 23 30	6 13 20 27	3 10 17 24
Thur.	3 10 17 24 31	7 14 21 28	4 11 18 25
Fri.	4 11 18 25	1 8 15 22 29	5 12 19 26
Sat.	5 12 19 26	2 9 16 23 30	6 13 20 27

	October	November	December
Sun.	5 12 19 26	2 9 16 23 30	7 14 21 28
Mon.	6 13 20 27	3 10 17 24	1 8 15 22 29
Tue.	7 14 21 28	4 11 18 25	2 9 16 23 30
Wed.	1 8 15 22 29	5 12 19 26	3 10 17 24 31
Thur.	2 9 16 23 30	6 13 20 27	4 11 18 25
Fri.	3 10 17 24 31	7 14 21 28	5 12 19 26
Sat.	4 11 18 25	1 8 15 22 29	6 13 20 27

EASTER DAYS

March 23	1845, 1913
March 30	1823, 1834, 1902, 1975, 1986, 1997
April 6	1806, 1817, 1890, 1947, 1958, 1969
April 13	1800, 1873, 1879, 1941, 2031
April 20	1783, 1794, 1851, 1862, 1919, 1930, 2003, 2014, 2025

I

	January	February	March
Sun.	4 11 18 25	1 8 15 22	1 8 15 22 29
Mon.	5 12 19 26	2 9 16 23	2 9 16 23 30
Tue.	6 13 20 27	3 10 17 24	3 10 17 24 31
Wed.	7 14 21 28	4 11 18 25	4 11 18 25
Thur.	1 8 15 22 29	5 12 19 26	5 12 19 26
Fri.	2 9 16 23 30	6 13 20 27	6 13 20 27
Sat.	3 10 17 24 31	7 14 21 28	7 14 21 28

	April	May	June
Sun.	5 12 19 26	3 10 17 24 31	7 14 21 28
Mon.	6 13 20 27	4 11 18 25	1 8 15 22 29
Tue.	7 14 21 28	5 12 19 26	2 9 16 23 30
Wed.	1 8 15 22 29	6 13 20 27	3 10 17 24
Thur.	2 9 16 23 30	7 14 21 28	4 11 18 25
Fri.	3 10 17 24	1 8 15 22 29	5 12 19 26
Sat.	4 11 18 25	2 9 16 23 30	6 13 20 27

	July	August	September
Sun.	5 12 19 26	2 9 16 23 30	6 13 20 27
Mon.	6 13 20 27	3 10 17 24 31	7 14 21 28
Tue.	7 14 21 28	4 11 18 25	1 8 15 22 29
Wed.	1 8 15 22 29	5 12 19 26	2 9 16 23 30
Thur.	2 9 16 23 30	6 13 20 27	3 10 17 24
Fri.	3 10 17 24 31	7 14 21 28	4 11 18 25
Sat.	4 11 18 25	1 8 15 22 29	5 12 19 26

	October	November	December
Sun.	4 11 18 25	1 8 15 22 29	6 13 20 27
Mon.	5 12 19 26	2 9 16 23 30	7 14 21 28
Tue.	6 13 20 27	3 10 17 24	1 8 15 22 29
Wed.	7 14 21 28	4 11 18 25	2 9 16 23 30
Thur.	1 8 15 22 29	5 12 19 26	3 10 17 24 31
Fri.	2 9 16 23 30	6 13 20 27	4 11 18 25
Sat.	3 10 17 24 31	7 14 21 28	5 12 19 26

EASTER DAYS

March 22	1818
March 29	1807, 1891, 1959, 1970
April 5	1795, 1801, 1863, 1874, 1885, 1931, 1942, 1953, 2015, 2026, 2037
April 12	1789, 1846, 1857, 1903, 1914, 1925, 1998, 2009
April 19	1829, 1835, 1981, 1987

H (LEAP YEAR)

	January	February	March
Sun.	5 12 19 26	2 9 16 23	1 8 15 22 29
Mon.	6 13 20 27	3 10 17 24	2 9 16 23 30
Tue.	7 14 21 28	4 11 18 25	3 10 17 24 31
Wed.	1 8 15 22 29	5 12 19 26	4 11 18 25
Thur.	2 9 16 23 30	6 13 20 27	5 12 19 26
Fri.	3 10 17 24 31	7 14 21 28	6 13 20 27
Sat.	4 11 18 25	1 8 15 22 29	7 14 21 28

	April	May	June
Sun.	5 12 19 26	3 10 17 24 31	7 14 21 28
Mon.	6 13 20 27	4 11 18 25	1 8 15 22 29
Tue.	7 14 21 28	5 12 19 26	2 9 16 23 30
Wed.	1 8 15 22 29	6 13 20 27	3 10 17 24
Thur.	2 9 16 23 30	7 14 21 28	4 11 18 25
Fri.	3 10 17 24	1 8 15 22 29	5 12 19 26
Sat.	4 11 18 25	2 9 16 23 30	6 13 20 27

	July	August	September
Sun.	5 12 19 26	2 9 16 23 30	6 13 20 27
Mon.	6 13 20 27	3 10 17 24 31	7 14 21 28
Tue.	7 14 21 28	4 11 18 25	1 8 15 22 29
Wed.	1 8 15 22 29	5 12 19 26	2 9 16 23 30
Thur.	2 9 16 23 30	6 13 20 27	3 10 17 24
Fri.	3 10 17 24 31	7 14 21 28	4 11 18 25
Sat.	4 11 18 25	1 8 15 22 29	5 12 19 26

	October	November	December
Sun.	4 11 18 25	1 8 15 22 29	6 13 20 27
Mon.	5 12 19 26	2 9 16 23 30	7 14 21 28
Tue.	6 13 20 27	3 10 17 24	1 8 15 22 29
Wed.	7 14 21 28	4 11 18 25	2 9 16 23 30
Thur.	1 8 15 22 29	5 12 19 26	3 10 17 24 31
Fri.	2 9 16 23 30	6 13 20 27	4 11 18 25
Sat.	3 10 17 24 31	7 14 21 28	5 12 19 26

EASTER DAYS

March 29	1812, 1964
April 5	1896
April 12	1868, 1936, 2020
April 19	1840, 1908, 1992

J (LEAP YEAR)

	January	February	March
Sun.	4 11 18 25	1 8 15 22 29	7 14 21 28
Mon.	5 12 19 26	2 9 16 23	1 8 15 22 29
Tue.	6 13 20 27	3 10 17 24	2 9 16 23 30
Wed.	7 14 21 28	4 11 18 25	3 10 17 24 31
Thur.	1 8 15 22 29	5 12 19 26	4 11 18 25
Fri.	2 9 16 23 30	6 13 20 27	5 12 19 26
Sat.	3 10 17 24 31	7 14 21 28	6 13 20 27

	April	May	June
Sun.	4 11 18 25	2 9 16 23 30	6 13 20 27
Mon.	5 12 19 26	3 10 17 24 31	7 14 21 28
Tue.	6 13 20 27	4 11 18 25	1 8 15 22 29
Wed.	7 14 21 28	5 12 19 26	2 9 16 23 30
Thur.	1 8 15 22 29	6 13 20 27	3 10 17 24
Fri.	2 9 16 23 30	7 14 21 28	4 11 18 25
Sat.	3 10 17 24	1 8 15 22 29	5 12 19 26

	July	August	September
Sun.	4 11 18 25	1 8 15 22 29	5 12 19 26
Mon.	5 12 19 26	2 9 16 23 30	6 13 20 27
Tue.	6 13 20 27	3 10 17 24 31	7 14 21 28
Wed.	7 14 21 28	4 11 18 25	1 8 15 22 29
Thur.	1 8 15 22 29	5 12 19 26	2 9 16 23 30
Fri.	2 9 16 23 30	6 13 20 27	3 10 17 24
Sat.	3 10 17 24 31	7 14 21 28	4 11 18 25

	October	November	December
Sun.	3 10 17 24 31	7 14 21 28	5 12 19 26
Mon.	4 11 18 25	1 8 15 22 29	6 13 20 27
Tue.	5 12 19 26	2 9 16 23 30	7 14 21 28
Wed.	6 13 20 27	3 10 17 24	1 8 15 22 29
Thur.	7 14 21 28	4 11 18 25	2 9 16 23 30
Fri.	1 8 15 22 29	5 12 19 26	3 10 17 24 31
Sat.	2 9 16 23 30	6 13 20 27	4 11 18 25

EASTER DAYS

March 28	1880, 1948, 2032
April 4	1920
April 11	1784, 1852, 2004
April 18	1824, 1976

K

	January	February	March
Sun.	3 10 17 24 31	7 14 21 28	7 14 21 28
Mon.	4 11 18 25	1 8 15 22	1 8 15 22 29
Tue.	5 12 19 26	2 9 16 23	2 9 16 23 30
Wed.	6 13 20 27	3 10 17 24	3 10 17 24 31
Thur.	7 14 21 28	4 11 18 25	4 11 18 25
Fri.	1 8 15 22 29	5 12 19 26	5 12 19 26
Sat.	2 9 16 23 30	6 13 20 27	6 13 20 27

	April	May	June
Sun.	4 11 18 25	2 9 16 23 30	6 13 20 27
Mon.	5 12 19 26	3 10 17 24 31	7 14 21 28
Tue.	6 13 20 27	4 11 18 25	1 8 15 22 29
Wed.	7 14 21 28	5 12 19 26	2 9 16 23 30
Thur.	1 8 15 22 29	6 13 20 27	3 10 17 24
Fri.	2 9 16 23 30	7 14 21 28	4 11 18 25
Sat.	3 10 17 24	1 8 15 22 29	5 12 19 26

	July	August	September
Sun.	4 11 18 25	1 8 15 22 29	5 12 19 26
Mon.	5 12 19 26	2 9 16 23 30	6 13 20 27
Tue.	6 13 20 27	3 10 17 24 31	7 14 21 28
Wed.	7 14 21 28	4 11 18 25	1 8 15 22 29
Thur.	1 8 15 22 29	5 12 19 26	2 9 16 23 30
Fri.	2 9 16 23 30	6 13 20 27	3 10 17 24
Sat.	3 10 17 24 31	7 14 21 28	4 11 18 25

	October	November	December
Sun.	3 10 17 24 31	7 14 21 28	5 12 19 26
Mon.	4 11 18 25	1 8 15 22 29	6 13 20 27
Tue.	5 12 19 26	2 9 16 23 30	7 14 21 28
Wed.	6 13 20 27	3 10 17 24	1 8 15 22 29
Thur.	7 14 21 28	4 11 18 25	2 9 16 23 30
Fri.	1 8 15 22 29	5 12 19 26	3 10 17 24 31
Sat.	2 9 16 23 30	6 13 20 27	4 11 18 25

EASTER DAYS
March 28	1869, 1875, 1937, 2027
April 4	1790, 1847, 1858, 1915, 1926, 1999, 2010, 2021
April 11	1819, 1830, 1841, 1909, 1971, 1982, 1993
April 18	1802, 1813, 1897, 1954, 1965
April 25	1886, 1943, 2038

M

	January	February	March
Sun.	2 9 16 23 30	6 13 20 27	6 13 20 27
Mon.	3 10 17 24 31	7 14 21 28	7 14 21 28
Tue.	4 11 18 25	1 8 15 22	1 8 15 22 29
Wed.	5 12 19 26	2 9 16 23	2 9 16 23 30
Thur.	6 13 20 27	3 10 17 24	3 10 17 24 31
Fri.	7 14 21 28	4 11 18 25	4 11 18 25
Sat.	1 8 15 22 29	5 12 19 26	5 12 19 26

	April	May	June
Sun.	3 10 17 24	1 8 15 22 29	5 12 19 26
Mon.	4 11 18 25	2 9 16 23 30	6 13 20 27
Tue.	5 12 19 26	3 10 17 24 31	7 14 21 28
Wed.	6 13 20 27	4 11 18 25	1 8 15 22 29
Thur.	7 14 21 28	5 12 19 26	2 9 16 23 30
Fri.	1 8 15 22 29	6 13 20 27	3 10 17 24
Sat.	2 9 16 23 30	7 14 21 28	4 11 18 25

	July	August	September
Sun.	3 10 17 24 31	7 14 21 28	4 11 18 25
Mon.	4 11 18 25	1 8 15 22 29	5 12 19 26
Tue.	5 12 19 26	2 9 16 23 30	6 13 20 27
Wed.	6 13 20 27	3 10 17 24 31	7 14 21 28
Thur.	7 14 21 28	4 11 18 25	1 8 15 22 29
Fri.	1 8 15 22 29	5 12 19 26	2 9 16 23 30
Sat.	2 9 16 23 30	6 13 20 27	3 10 17 24

	October	November	December
Sun.	2 9 16 23 30	6 13 20 27	4 11 18 25
Mon.	3 10 17 24 31	7 14 21 28	5 12 19 26
Tue.	4 11 18 25	1 8 15 22 29	6 13 20 27
Wed.	5 12 19 26	2 9 16 23 30	7 14 21 28
Thur.	6 13 20 27	3 10 17 24	1 8 15 22 29
Fri.	7 14 21 28	4 11 18 25	2 9 16 23 30
Sat.	1 8 15 22 29	5 12 19 26	3 10 17 24 31

EASTER DAYS
March 27	1785, 1842, 1853, 1910, 1921, 2005
April 3	1825, 1831, 1983, 1994
April 10	1803, 1814, 1887, 1898, 1955, 1966, 1977, 2039
April 17	1870, 1881, 1927, 1938, 1949, 2022, 2033
April 24	1791, 1859, 2011

L (LEAP YEAR)

	January	February	March
Sun.	3 10 17 24 31	7 14 21 28	6 13 20 27
Mon.	4 11 18 25	1 8 15 22 29	7 14 21 28
Tue.	5 12 19 26	2 9 16 23	1 8 15 22 29
Wed.	6 13 20 27	3 10 17 24	2 9 16 23 30
Thur.	7 14 21 28	4 11 18 25	3 10 17 24 31
Fri.	1 8 15 22 29	5 12 19 26	4 11 18 25
Sat.	2 9 16 23 30	6 13 20 27	5 12 19 26

	April	May	June
Sun.	3 10 17 24	1 8 15 22 29	5 12 19 26
Mon.	4 11 18 25	2 9 16 23 30	6 13 20 27
Tue.	5 12 19 26	3 10 17 24 31	7 14 21 28
Wed.	6 13 20 27	4 11 18 25	1 8 15 22 29
Thur.	7 14 21 28	5 12 19 26	2 9 16 23 30
Fri.	1 8 15 22 29	6 13 20 27	3 10 17 24
Sat.	2 9 16 23 30	7 14 21 28	4 11 18 25

	July	August	September
Sun.	3 10 17 24 31	7 14 21 28	4 11 18 25
Mon.	4 11 18 25	1 8 15 22 29	5 12 19 26
Tue.	5 12 19 26	2 9 16 23 30	6 13 20 27
Wed.	6 13 20 27	3 10 17 24 31	7 14 21 28
Thur.	7 14 21 28	4 11 18 25	1 8 15 22 29
Fri.	1 8 15 22 29	5 12 19 26	2 9 16 23 30
Sat.	2 9 16 23 30	6 13 20 27	3 10 17 24

	October	November	December
Sun.	2 9 16 23 30	6 13 20 27	4 11 18 25
Mon.	3 10 17 24 31	7 14 21 28	5 12 19 26
Tue.	4 11 18 25	1 8 15 22 29	6 13 20 27
Wed.	5 12 19 26	2 9 16 23 30	7 14 21 28
Thur.	6 13 20 27	3 10 17 24	1 8 15 22 29
Fri.	7 14 21 28	4 11 18 25	2 9 16 23 30
Sat.	1 8 15 22 29	5 12 19 26	3 10 17 24 31

EASTER DAYS
March 27	1796, 1864, 1932, 2016
April 3	1836, 1904, 1988
April 17	1808, 1892, 1960

N (LEAP YEAR)

	January	February	March
Sun.	2 9 16 23 30	6 13 20 27	5 12 19 26
Mon.	3 10 17 24 31	7 14 21 28	6 13 20 27
Tue.	4 11 18 25	1 8 15 22 29	7 14 21 28
Wed.	5 12 19 26	2 9 16 23	1 8 15 22 29
Thur.	6 13 20 27	3 10 17 24	2 9 16 23 30
Fri.	7 14 21 28	4 11 18 25	3 10 17 24 31
Sat.	1 8 15 22 29	5 12 19 26	4 11 18 25

	April	May	June
Sun.	2 9 16 23 30	7 14 21 28	4 11 18 25
Mon.	3 10 17 24	1 8 15 22 29	5 12 19 26
Tue.	4 11 18 25	2 9 16 23 30	6 13 20 27
Wed.	5 12 19 26	3 10 17 24 31	7 14 21 28
Thur.	6 13 20 27	4 11 18 25	1 8 15 22 29
Fri.	7 14 21 28	5 12 19 26	2 9 16 23 30
Sat.	1 8 15 22 29	6 13 20 27	3 10 17 24

	July	August	September
Sun.	2 9 16 23 30	6 13 20 27	3 10 17 24
Mon.	3 10 17 24 31	7 14 21 28	4 11 18 25
Tue.	4 11 18 25	1 8 15 22 29	5 12 19 26
Wed.	5 12 19 26	2 9 16 23 30	6 13 20 27
Thur.	6 13 20 27	3 10 17 24 31	7 14 21 28
Fri.	7 14 21 28	4 11 18 25	1 8 15 22 29
Sat.	1 8 15 22 29	5 12 19 26	2 9 16 23 30

	October	November	December
Sun.	1 8 15 22 29	5 12 19 26	3 10 17 24 31
Mon.	2 9 16 23 30	6 13 20 27	4 11 18 25
Tue.	3 10 17 24 31	7 14 21 28	5 12 19 26
Wed.	4 11 18 25	1 8 15 22 29	6 13 20 27
Thur.	5 12 19 26	2 9 16 23 30	7 14 21 28
Fri.	6 13 20 27	3 10 17 24	1 8 15 22 29
Sat.	7 14 21 28	4 11 18 25	2 9 16 23 30

EASTER DAYS
March 26	1780
April 2	1820, 1972
April 9	1944
April 16	1876, 2028
April 23	1848, 1916, 2000

GEOLOGICAL TIME

The earth is thought to have come into existence approximately 4,600 million years ago, but for nearly half this time, the Archean era, it was uninhabited. Life is generally believed to have emerged in the succeeding Proterozoic era. The Archean and the Proterozoic eras are often together referred to as the Precambrian.

Although primitive forms of life, e.g. algae and bacteria, existed during the Proterozoic era, it is not until the strata of Palaeozoic rocks is reached that abundant fossilised remains appear.

Since the Precambrian, there have been three great geological eras:

PALAEOZOIC ('ancient life')
c. 550–c. 248 million years ago
Cambrian – Mainly sandstones, slate and shales; limestones in Scotland. Shelled fossils and invertebrates, e.g. trilobites and brachiopods appear, as do the earliest known vertebrates (jawless fish)
Ordovician – Mainly shales and mudstones, e.g. in north Wales; limestones in Scotland. First fishes
Silurian – Shales, mudstones and some limestones, found mostly in Wales and southern Scotland
Devonian – Old red sandstone, shale, limestone and slate, e.g. in south Wales and the West Country
Carboniferous–Coal-bearing rocks, millstone grit, limestone and shale. First traces of land-living life
Permian – Marls, sandstones and clays. First reptile fossils

There were two great phases of mountain building in the Palaeozoic era: the Caledonian, characterised in Britain by NE–SW lines of hills and valleys; and the later Hercynian, widespread in west Germany and adjacent areas, and in Britain exemplified in E.–W. lines of hills and valleys.

The end of the Palaeozoic era was marked by the extensive glaciations of the Permian period in the southern continents and the decline of amphibians. It was succeeded by an era of warm conditions.

MESOZOIC ('middle forms of life')
c. 245–c. 65 million years ago
Triassic – Mostly sandstone, e.g. in the West Midlands; primitive mammals appear
Jurassic–Mainly limestones and clays, typically displayed in the Jura mountains, and in England in a NE–SW belt from Lincolnshire and the Wash to the Severn and the Dorset coast
Cretaceous – Mainly chalk, clay and sands, e.g. in Kent and Sussex

Giant reptiles were dominant during the Mesozoic era, but it was at this time that marsupial mammals first appeared, as well as *Archaeopteryx lithographica*, the earliest known species of bird. Coniferous trees and flowering plants also developed during the era and, with the birds and the mammals, were the main species to survive into the Cenozoic era. The giant reptiles became extinct.

CENOZOIC ('recent life')
from c. 65 million years ago
Palaeocene ⎤   The emergence of new forms of life,
Eocene   ⎦   including existing species; primates appear
Oligocene – Fossils of a few still existing species
Miocene – Fossil remains show a balance of existing and extinct species

Pliocene – Fossil remains show a majority of still existing species
Pleistocene – The majority of remains are those of still existing species
Holocene–The present, post-glacial period. Existing species only, except for a few exterminated by man.

In the last 25 million years, from the Miocene through the Pliocene periods, the Alpine-Himalayan and the circum-Pacific phases of mountain building reached their climax. During the Pleistocene period ice-sheets repeatedly locked up masses of water as land ice; its weight depressed the land, but the locking-up of the water lowered the sea-level by 100–200 metres. The glaciations and interglacials of the Ice Age are difficult to date and classify, but recent scientific opinion considers the Pleistocene period to have begun approximately 1.64 million years ago. The last glacial retreat, merging into the Holocene period, was 10,000 years ago.

HUMAN DEVELOPMENT

Any consideration of the history of mankind must start with the fact that all members of the human race belong to one species of animal, i.e. *Homo sapiens*, the definition of a species being in biological terms that all its members can interbreed. As a species of mammal it is possible to group man with other similar types, known as the primates. Amongst these is found a sub-group, the apes, which includes, in addition to man, the chimpanzees, gorillas, orang-utans and gibbons. All lack a tail, have shoulder blades at the back, and a Y-shaped chewing pattern on the surface of their molars, as well as showing the more general primate characteristics of four incisors, a thumb which is able to touch the fingers of the same hand, and finger and toe nails instead of claws. The factors available to scientific study suggest that human beings have chimpanzees and gorillas as their nearest relatives in the animal world. However, there remains the possibility that there once lived creatures, now extinct, which were closer to modern man than the chimpanzees and gorillas, and which shared with modern man the characteristics of having flat faces (i.e. the absence of a pronounced muzzle), being bipedal, and possessing large brains.

There are two broad groups of extinct apes recognised by specialists. The ramapithecines, the remains of which, mainly jaw fragments, have been found in east Africa, Asia, and Turkey. They lived about 14 to 8 million years ago, and from the evidence of their teeth it seems they chewed more in the manner of modern man than the other presently living apes. The second group, the australopithecines, have left more numerous remains amongst which sub-groups may be detected, although the geographic spread is limited to south and east Africa. Living between 5 and 1.5 million years ago, they were closer relatives of modern man to the extent that they walked upright, did not have an extensive muzzle and had similar types of pre-molars. The first australopithecine remains were recognised at Taung in South Africa in 1924 and named *Australopithecus africanus*, dating to 2.8 to 2.3 million years ago. The most impressive discovery was made at Hadar, Ethiopia, in 1974 when about half a skeleton of *Australopithecus afarensis*, known as 'Lucy', was found. Some 3.2 million years ago, 'Lucy' certainly walked upright.

Also in east Africa, especially at Olduvai Gorge in Tanzania, between 1.9 and 1.8 million years ago, lived a hominid group which not only walked upright, had a flat face, and a large brain case, but also made simple pebble and flake stone tools. On present evidence these habilines seem to have been the first people to make tools, however crude. This facility is related to the larger brain size and human beings are the only animals to make implements to be used in other processes. These early pebble tool users, because of their distinctive characteristics, have been grouped as a separate sub-species, now extinct, of the genus *Homo* and are known as *Homo habilis.*

The use of fire, again a human characteristic, is associated with another group of extinct hominids whose remains, about a million years old, are found in south and east Africa, China, Indonesia, north Africa and Europe. Mastery of the techniques of making fire probably helped the colonisation of the colder northern areas and in this respect the site of Vertesszollos in Hungary is of particular importance. *Homo ergaster* in Africa and *Homo erectus* in Asia are the names given to this group of fossils and they relate to a number of famous individual discoveries, e.g. Solo Man, Heidelberg Man, and especially Peking Man who lived at the cave site at Choukoutien which has yielded evidence of fire and burnt bone.

The well-known group Neanderthal Man, or *Homo neanderthalensis*, is an extinct form of man who lived between about 230,000 and 28,000 years ago, thus spanning the last Ice Age. Indeed, its ability to adapt to the cold climate on the edge of the ice-sheets is one of its characteristic features, the remains being found only in Europe, Asia and the Middle East. Complete neanderthal skeletons were found during excavations at Tabun in Israel, together with evidence of tool-making and the use of fire. Distinguished by very large brains, it seems that neanderthal man was the first to develop recognisable social customs, especially deliberate burial rites. Why the neanderthals became extinct is not clear but it may be connected with the climatic changes at the end of the Ice Ages, which would have seriously affected their food supplies; possibly they became too specialised for their own good.

The shin bone of Boxgrove Man found in 1993 – *Homo heidelbergensis* – and the Swanscombe skull are the best known human fossil remains found in England. Some specialists see Swanscombe Man (or, more probably, woman) as best grouped together with the Steinheim skull from Germany, seeing both as a separate sub-species. There is too little evidence as yet on which to form a final judgement.

Modern Man, *Homo sapiens* had evolved to our present physical condition and had colonised much of the world by about 40,000 years ago. There are many previously distinguished individual specimens, e.g. Cromagnon Man, which may now be grouped together as *Homo sapiens*. It was modern man who spread to the American continent by crossing the landbridge between Siberia and Alaska and thence moved south through North America and into South America. Equally it is modern man who over the last 40,000 years has been responsible for the major developments in technology, art and civilisation generally.

One of the problems for those studying fossil man is the lack in many cases of sufficient quantities of fossil bone for analysis. It is important that theories should be tested against evidence, rather than the evidence being made to fit the theory. The Piltdown hoax of 1912 (and not fully exposed until the 1970s) is a well-known example of 'fossils' being forged to fit what was seen in some quarters as the correct theory of man's evolution.

The discovery of the structure of DNA in 1953 has come to have a profound effect upon the study of human evolution. For example, it was claimed in 1987 that a common ancestor of all human beings was a person who lived in Africa some 200,000 years ago, thus encouraging the 'out of Africa' theory of hominid migration from east Africa to the Middle East and then throughout the world. There is no doubt that the studies based on DNA have vast potential to elucidate further the course of human evolution.

CULTURAL DEVELOPMENT

The Eurocentric bias of early archaeologists meant that the search for a starting point for the development and transmission of cultural ideas, especially by migration, trade and warfare, concentrated unduly on Europe and the Near East. The Three Age system, whereby pre-history was divided into a Stone Age, a Bronze Age and an Iron Age, was devised by Christian Thomsen, curator of the National Museum of Denmark in the early 19th century, to facilitate the classification of the museum's collections. The descriptive adjectives referred to the materials from which the implements and weapons were made and came to be regarded as the dominant features of the societies to which they related. The refinement of the Three Age system once dominated archaeological thought and remains a generally accepted concept in the popular mind. However, it is now seen by archaeologists as an inadequate model for human development.

Common sense suggests that there were no complete breaks between one so-called Age and another, any more than contemporaries would have regarded 1485 as a complete break between medieval and modern English history. Nor can the Three Age system be applied universally. In some areas it is necessary to insert a Copper Age, while in Africa south of the Sahara there would seem to be no Bronze Age at all; in Australia, Old Stone Age societies survived, while in South America, New Stone Age communities existed into modern times. The civilisations in other parts of the world clearly invalidate a Eurocentric theory of human development.

The concept of the 'Neolithic revolution', associated with the domestication of plants and animals, was a development of particular importance in the human cultural pattern. It reflected change from the primitive hunter/gatherer economies to a more settled agricultural way of life and therefore, so the argument goes, made possible the development of urban civilisation. However, it can no longer be argued that this 'revolution' took place only in one area from which all development stemmed. Though it appears that the cultivation of wheat and barley was first undertaken, together with the domestication of cattle and goats/sheep in the Fertile Crescent (the area bounded by the rivers Tigris and Euphrates), there is evidence that rice was first deliberately planted and pigs domesticated in south-east Asia, maize first cultivated in Central America and llamas first domesticated in South America. It has been recognised in recent years that cultural changes can take place independently of each other in different parts of the world at different rates and different times. There is no need for a general diffusionist theory.

Although scholars will continue to study the particular societies which interest them, it may be possible to obtain a reliable chronological framework, against which the cultural development of any particular area may be set. The development and refinement of radio-carbon dating and other scientific methods of producing absolute chronologies is enabling the cross-referencing of societies to be undertaken. As the techniques of dating become more rigorous in application and the number of scientifically obtained dates increases, the attainment of an absolute chronology for prehistoric societies throughout the world comes closer to being achieved.

GEOLOGICAL TIME

Era	Period	Epoch	Date began*	Evolutionary stages
Cenozoic	Quaternary	Holocene	0.01	Man
Cenozoic	Quaternary	Pleistocene	1.64	Man
Cenozoic	Tertiary	Pliocene	5.2	Man
Cenozoic	Tertiary	Miocene	23.3	Man
Cenozoic	Tertiary	Oligocene	35.4	Man
Cenozoic	Tertiary	Eocene	56.5	Man
Cenozoic	Tertiary	Palaeocene	65.0	Man
Mesozoic	Cretaceous		145.6	
Mesozoic	Jurassic		208.0	First birds
Mesozoic	Triassic		248.0	First mammals
Palaeozoic	Permian		290.0	First reptiles
Palaeozoic	Carboniferous		362.5	First amphibians and insects
Palaeozoic	Devonian		408.5	
Palaeozoic	Silurian		439.0	
Palaeozoic	Ordovician		510.0	First fishes
Palaeozoic	Cambrian		550.0	First invertebrates
Precambrian			4,600.0	First primitive life forms e.g. algae and bacteria

* Millions of years ago

TIDAL PREDICTIONS

CONSTANTS

The constant tidal difference may be used in conjunction with the time of high water at a standard port shown in the predictions data below to find the time of high water at any of the ports or places listed.

These tidal differences are very approximate and should be used only as a guide to the time of high water at the places below. More precise local data should be obtained for navigational and other nautical purposes.

All data allow high water time to be found in Greenwich Mean Time: this applies to data for the months when British Summer Time is in operation and the hour's time difference should be allowed for. Ports marked * are in a different time zone and the standard time zone difference also needs to be added/subtracted to give local time.

EXAMPLE

Required time of high water at Stranraer at 2 January 2005

Appropriate time of high water at Greenock

Afternoon tide 2 January	1633hrs
Tidal difference	– 0020hrs
High water at Stranraer	1613hrs

The columns headed 'Springs' and 'Neaps' show the height, in metres, of the tide above datum for mean high water springs and mean high water neaps respectively.

Port		Diff. h	m	Springs m	Neaps m
Aberdeen	Leith	-1	19	4.4	3.4
*Antwerp (Prosperpolder)	London	+0	50	5.8	4.8
Ardrossan	Greenock	-0	15	3.2	2.6
Avonmouth	London	-6	45	12.2	9.8
Ayr	Greenock	-0	25	3.0	2.5
Barrow (Docks)	Liverpool	0	00	9.3	7.1
Belfast	London	-2	47	3.5	3.0
Blackpool	Liverpool	-0	10	8.9	7.0
*Boulogne	London	-2	44	8.9	7.2
*Calais	London	-2	04	7.2	5.9
*Cherbourg	London	-6	00	6.4	5.0
Cobh	Liverpool	-5	55	4.2	3.2
Cowes	London	-2	38	4.2	3.5
Dartmouth	London	+4	25	4.9	3.8
*Dieppe	London	-3	03	9.3	7.3
Douglas, IoM	Liverpool	-0	04	6.9	5.4
Dover	London	-2	52	6.7	5.3
Dublin	London	-2	05	4.1	3.4
Dun Laoghaire	London	-2	10	4.1	3.4
*Dunkirk	London	-1	54	6.0	4.9
Fishguard	Liverpool	-4	01	4.8	3.4
Fleetwood	Liverpool	0	00	9.2	7.3
*Flushing	London	-0	15	4.7	3.9
Folkestone	London	-3	04	7.1	5.7
Galway	Liverpool	-6	08	5.1	3.9
Glasgow	Greenock	+0	26	4.7	4.0
Harwich	London	-2	06	4.0	3.4
*Le Havre	London	-3	55	7.9	6.6
Heysham	Liverpool	+0	05	9.4	7.4

Holyhead	Liverpool	-0	50	5.6	4.4
*Hook of Holland	London	-0	01	2.1	1.7
Hull (Albert Dock)	London	-7	40	7.5	5.8
Immingham	London	-8	00	7.3	5.8
Larne	London	-2	40	2.8	2.5
Lerwick	Leith	-3	48	2.2	1.6
Londonderry	London	-5	37	2.7	2.1
Lowestoft	London	-4	25	2.4	2.1
Margate	London	-1	53	4.8	3.9
Milford Haven	Liverpool	-5	08	7.0	5.2
Morecambe	Liverpool	+0	07	9.5	7.4
Newhaven	London	-2	46	6.7	5.1
Oban	Greenock	+5	43	4.0	2.9
*Ostend	London	-1	32	5.1	4.2
Plymouth	London	+4	05	5.5	4.4
Portland	London	+5	09	2.1	1.4
Portsmouth	London	-2	38	4.7	3.8
Ramsgate	London	-2	32	5.2	4.1
Richmond Lock	London	+1	00	4.9	3.7
Rosslare Harbour	Liverpool	-5	24	1.9	1.4
Rosyth	Leith	+0	09	5.8	4.7
*Rotterdam	London	+1	45	2.0	1.7
St Helier	London	+4	48	11.0	8.1
St Malo	London	+4	27	12.2	9.2
St Peter Port	London	+4	54	9.3	7.0
Scrabster	Leith	-6	06	5.0	4.0
Sheerness	London	-1	19	5.8	4.7
Shoreham	London	-2	44	6.3	4.9
Southampton (1st high water)	London	-2	54	4.5	3.7
Spurn Head	London	-8	25	6.9	5.5
Stornoway	Liverpool	-4	16	4.8	3.7
Stranraer	Greenick	-0	20	3.0	2.4
Stromness	Leith	-5	26	3.6	2.7
Swansea	London	-7	35	9.5	7.2
Tees (River Entrance)	Leith	+1	09	5.5	4.3
Tilbury	London	-0	49	6.4	5.4
Tobermory	Liverpool	-5	11	4.4	3.3
Tyne River (North Shields)	London	-10	30	5.0	3.9
Ullapool	Leith	-7	40	5.2	3.9
Walton-on-the-Naze	London	-2	10	4.2	3.4
Wick	Leith	-3	26	3.5	2.8
Zeebrugge	London	-0	55	4.8	3.9

PREDICTIONS

The following data are daily predictions of the time and height of high water at London Bridge, Liverpool, Greenock and Leith. The time of the data is Greenwich Mean Time; this applies also to data for the months when British Summer Time is in operation and the hour's time difference should be allowed for. The datum of predictions for each port shows the difference of height, in metres from Ordnance data (Newlyn).

JANUARY 2005   *High Water*   GMT

	LONDON BRIDGE *Datum of Predictions 3.20m below*						LIVERPOOL *Datum of Predictions 4.93m below*						GREENOCK *Datum of Predictions 1.62m below*						LEITH *Datum of Predictions 2.90m below*					
	hr	m	ht	hr	m	ht	hr	m	ht	hr	m	ht	hr	m	ht	hr	m	ht	hr	m	ht	hr	m	ht
SA 1	04	41	6.4	17	23	6.4	02	19	8.3	14	36	8.5	03	58	3.0	15	52	3.4	05	58	4.8	18	06	4.9
SU 2	05	20	6.3	18	05	6.4	03	01	8.0	15	19	8.3	04	41	3.0	16	33	3.4	06	41	4.7	18	48	4.8
M 3	06	03	6.2	18	52	6.2	03	47	7.8	16	08	8.1	05	27	2.9	17	18	3.3	07	29	4.6	19	37	4.7
TU 4	06	54	6.1	19	46	6.1	04	42	7.6	17	05	7.9	06	16	2.8	18	09	3.2	08	23	4.5	20	36	4.6
W 5	07	55	5.9	20	49	5.9	05	46	7.6	18	10	7.9	07	10	2.8	19	08	3.1	09	24	4.6	21	45	4.6
TH 6	09	06	5.9	21	59	6.0	06	54	7.7	19	17	8.1	08	17	2.8	20	19	3.1	10	29	4.6	22	55	4.7
FR 7	10	19	6.0	23	07	6.2	08	00	8.1	20	23	8.4	09	34	2.9	21	37	3.1	11	32	4.8	—	—	
SA 8	11	29	6.3	—	—		09	01	8.6	21	26	8.8	10	37	3.1	22	43	3.2	00	01	5.0	12	30	5.0
SU 9	00	08	6.5	12	31	6.7	09	56	9.1	22	23	9.1	11	29	3.3	23	42	3.3	01	02	5.2	13	24	5.3
M 10	01	03	6.7	13	28	6.9	10	48	9.5	23	17	9.4	—	—		12	16	3.5	01	57	5.5	14	13	5.5
TU 11	01	54	6.9	14	22	7.1	11	39	9.7	—	—		00	38	3.4	13	03	3.6	02	48	5.7	15	01	5.7
W 12	02	43	6.9	15	14	7.2	00	08	9.5	12	29	9.9	01	33	3.4	13	49	3.8	03	38	5.8	15	49	5.7
TH 13	03	31	6.9	16	05	7.2	00	59	9.5	13	18	9.9	02	25	3.4	14	34	3.8	04	27	5.8	16	37	5.7
FR 14	04	18	6.9	16	54	7.1	01	47	9.4	14	05	9.7	03	14	3.4	15	18	3.8	05	17	5.6	17	26	5.6
SA 15	05	04	6.8	17	42	7.0	02	33	9.1	14	52	9.4	04	00	3.3	16	03	3.8	06	08	5.3	18	18	5.4
SU 16	05	49	6.7	18	30	6.7	03	19	8.7	15	39	9.0	04	44	3.3	16	49	3.6	07	00	5.0	19	12	5.2
M 17	06	34	6.5	19	19	6.4	04	07	8.2	16	29	8.4	05	28	3.2	17	37	3.5	07	55	4.8	20	11	4.9
TU 18	07	24	6.3	20	11	6.1	05	01	7.7	17	27	7.9	06	13	3.1	18	29	3.2	08	52	4.5	21	13	4.7
W 19	08	22	6.1	21	09	5.8	06	05	7.4	18	36	7.6	07	02	3.0	19	30	3.0	09	53	4.4	22	19	4.5
TH 20	09	29	5.9	22	10	5.7	07	20	7.3	19	50	7.5	08	03	2.9	21	08	2.9	10	58	4.4	23	28	4.5
FR 21	10	38	5.8	23	13	5.8	08	28	7.6	20	54	7.7	09	31	2.9	22	28	2.9	—	—		12	04	4.5
SA 22	11	42	6.0	—	—		09	22	7.9	21	46	8.0	10	36	3.1	23	22	3.0	00	34	4.5	13	01	4.7
SU 23	00	11	6.0	12	40	6.2	10	07	8.3	22	30	8.3	11	24	3.2	—	—		01	27	4.7	13	46	4.9
M 24	01	02	6.2	13	28	6.4	10	47	8.6	23	08	8.5	00	08	3.0	12	06	3.3	02	09	4.8	14	24	5.0
TU 25	01	45	6.4	14	10	6.5	11	23	8.8	23	44	8.6	00	49	3.0	12	42	3.4	02	45	5.0	14	58	5.1
W 26	02	21	6.5	14	46	6.6	11	57	8.9	—	—		01	26	3.0	13	14	3.4	03	17	5.1	15	29	5.2
TH 27	02	53	6.4	15	19	6.5	00	17	8.7	12	31	9.0	01	59	3.0	13	45	3.5	03	48	5.1	16	01	5.3
FR 28	03	23	6.4	15	51	6.5	00	50	8.7	13	04	9.0	02	29	3.0	14	18	3.5	04	21	5.1	16	32	5.3
SA 29	03	52	6.4	16	25	6.6	01	23	8.7	13	37	9.0	03	00	3.0	14	52	3.5	04	55	5.1	17	04	5.2
SU 30	04	23	6.5	17	00	6.6	01	57	8.7	14	12	8.9	03	32	3.0	15	29	3.5	05	31	5.0	17	37	5.1
M 31	04	58	6.5	17	39	6.6	02	32	8.5	14	48	8.7	04	06	3.0	16	06	3.4	06	09	4.9	18	14	5.0

FEBRUARY 2005   *High Water*   GMT

	LONDON BRIDGE						LIVERPOOL						GREENOCK						LEITH					
TU 1	05	38	6.5	18	21	6.4	03	10	8.3	15	30	8.5	04	41	3.0	16	45	3.3	06	51	4.8	18	56	4.9
W 2	06	24	6.4	19	10	6.2	03	57	8.0	16	22	8.1	05	20	2.9	17	29	3.2	07	38	4.6	19	48	4.7
TH 3	07	19	6.1	20	07	5.9	04	57	7.7	17	28	7.8	06	05	2.8	18	22	3.0	08	35	4.5	20	57	4.5
FR 4	08	26	5.9	21	15	5.7	06	11	7.5	18	44	7.7	07	06	2.7	19	30	2.9	09	46	4.4	22	24	4.5
SA 5	09	43	5.8	22	34	5.7	07	31	7.7	20	05	7.9	08	50	2.7	21	10	2.9	11	01	4.5	23	45	4.7
SU 6	11	07	5.9	23	49	6.0	08	46	8.2	21	18	8.4	10	19	2.9	22	36	3.0	—	—		12	12	4.8
M 7	—	—		12	21	6.4	09	47	8.9	22	18	8.9	11	16	3.2	23	40	3.1	00	54	5.1	13	13	5.1
TU 8	00	51	6.4	13	22	6.8	10	40	9.4	23	10	9.4	—	—		12	05	3.4	01	50	5.4	14	04	5.5
W 9	01	44	6.8	14	14	7.1	11	29	9.9	23	58	9.9	00	35	3.2	12	53	3.6	02	39	5.7	14	50	5.7
TH 10	02	31	7.0	15	03	7.3	—	—		12	15	10.1	01	27	3.3	13	38	3.8	03	25	5.8	15	34	5.9
FR 11	03	16	7.1	15	49	7.3	00	42	9.7	13	00	10.1	02	14	3.4	14	21	3.8	04	10	5.8	16	19	5.9
SA 12	03	58	7.1	16	32	7.3	01	25	9.6	13	42	10.0	02	55	3.4	15	02	3.9	04	54	5.6	17	03	5.8
SU 13	04	38	7.1	17	13	7.1	02	06	9.3	14	23	9.6	03	32	3.4	15	42	3.8	05	39	5.4	17	48	5.5
M 14	05	16	7.0	17	52	6.8	02	44	8.9	15	04	9.1	04	07	3.3	16	20	3.7	06	23	5.0	18	35	5.2
TU 15	05	53	6.8	18	28	6.5	03	23	8.4	15	45	8.4	04	43	3.3	17	00	3.4	07	10	4.7	19	25	4.8
W 16	06	32	6.5	19	05	6.1	04	06	7.8	16	34	7.7	05	22	3.1	17	42	3.1	08	01	4.4	20	25	4.5
TH 17	07	19	6.1	19	51	5.7	05	01	7.2	17	41	7.1	06	05	3.0	18	31	2.9	09	00	4.2	21	33	4.2
FR 18	08	23	5.6	20	57	5.3	06	23	6.9	19	13	6.9	06	58	2.8	19	38	2.6	10	08	4.1	22	52	4.1
SA 19	09	58	5.4	22	32	5.3	07	57	7.1	20	33	7.2	08	11	2.8	22	20	2.6	11	28	4.2	—	—	
SU 20	11	19	5.6	23	44	5.6	09	01	7.6	21	29	7.7	10	12	2.9	23	12	2.8	00	16	4.3	12	41	4.5
M 21	—	—		12	19	6.0	09	49	8.1	22	13	8.1	11	06	3.1	23	54	2.9	01	14	4.5	13	29	4.7
TU 22	00	39	6.1	13	08	6.4	10	29	8.5	22	51	8.5	11	47	3.2	—	—		01	55	4.8	14	07	5.0
W 23	01	24	6.4	13	49	6.6	11	05	8.8	23	25	8.6	00	33	3.0	12	23	3.3	02	27	5.0	14	39	5.1
TH 24	02	02	6.5	14	25	6.7	11	38	9.0	23	57	8.9	01	09	3.0	12	53	3.3	02	56	5.1	15	09	5.3
FR 25	02	35	6.5	14	57	6.7	—	—		12	10	9.1	01	40	3.0	13	22	3.4	03	26	5.2	15	39	5.4
SA 26	03	05	6.5	15	29	6.6	00	28	8.9	12	41	9.2	02	07	3.0	13	54	3.4	03	56	5.3	16	08	5.4
SU 27	03	32	6.5	16	01	6.6	00	59	9.0	13	13	9.2	02	32	3.0	14	29	3.4	04	29	5.3	16	38	5.4
M 28	04	02	6.6	16	35	6.7	01	31	9.0	13	45	9.1	03	00	3.1	15	04	3.5	05	03	5.2	17	11	5.3

MARCH 2005   *High Water*   GMT

	LONDON BRIDGE *Datum of Predictions 3.20m below						LIVERPOOL *Datum of Predictions 4.93m below						GREENOCK *Datum of Predictions 1.62m below						LEITH *Datum of Predictions 2.90m below					
	hr	*m*	*ht*	*hr*	*m*	*ht*	*hr*	*m*	*ht*	*hr*	*m*	*ht*	*hr*	*m*	*ht*	*hr*	*m*	*ht*	*hr*	*m*	*ht*	*hr*	*m*	*ht*
TU 1	04	37	6.7	17	12	6.6	02	03	8.9	14	21	9.0	03	30	3.1	15	40	3.4	05	39	5.1	17	48	5.2
W 2	05	17	6.7	17	53	6.5	02	39	8.6	15	01	8.6	04	02	3.0	16	17	3.3	06	19	4.9	18	31	5.0
TH 3	06	02	6.5	18	38	6.2	03	23	8.2	15	51	8.1	04	37	2.9	16	59	3.1	07	04	4.7	19	24	4.7
FR 4	06	54	6.2	19	31	5.8	04	21	7.7	16	59	7.5	05	20	2.8	17	51	2.9	07	59	4.5	20	36	4.5
SA 5	07	59	5.8	20	39	5.4	05	42	7.3	18	28	7.3	06	19	2.7	19	00	2.7	09	15	4.3	22	10	4.4
SU 6	09	21	5.5	22	10	5.4	07	16	7.4	20	03	7.6	08	16	2.6	21	11	2.7	10	43	4.4	23	39	4.7
M 7	11	02	5.7	23	38	5.8	08	38	8.1	21	16	8.2	10	06	2.9	22	39	2.9	—	—		12	01	4.7
TU 8	—	—		12	17	6.3	09	38	8.8	22	10	8.9	11	03	3.2	23	36	3.1	00	48	5.1	13	02	5.1
W 9	00	40	6.3	13	13	6.9	10	27	9.5	22	56	9.4	11	51	3.4	—	—		01	40	5.4	13	50	5.5
TH 10	01	30	6.8	14	01	7.3	11	13	9.9	23	39	9.7	00	26	3.2	12	37	3.6	02	25	5.7	14	32	5.8
FR 11	02	13	7.1	14	45	7.4	11	55	10.1	—	—		01	11	3.3	13	21	3.7	03	06	5.7	15	14	5.9
SA 12	02	54	7.2	15	26	7.4	00	19	9.7	12	36	10.1	01	51	3.3	14	02	3.8	03	46	5.7	15	55	5.9
SU 13	03	32	7.2	16	04	7.2	00	58	9.6	13	15	9.8	02	26	3.4	14	40	3.8	04	27	5.5	16	37	5.7
M 14	04	09	7.2	16	39	7.0	01	34	9.3	13	53	9.4	02	58	3.4	15	16	3.7	05	07	5.3	17	19	5.5
TU 15	04	44	7.1	17	11	6.8	02	09	8.9	14	29	8.9	03	30	3.4	15	51	3.5	05	47	5.0	18	02	5.1
W 16	05	19	6.9	17	43	6.5	02	43	8.4	15	07	8.2	04	04	3.3	16	28	3.3	06	29	4.7	18	50	4.7
TH 17	05	58	6.5	18	17	6.2	03	21	7.9	15	50	7.5	04	40	3.2	17	08	3.0	07	16	4.4	19	45	4.3
FR 18	06	42	6.0	18	59	5.7	04	09	7.3	16	52	6.9	05	23	3.0	17	56	2.7	08	12	4.2	20	50	4.1
SA 19	07	38	5.5	19	54	5.3	05	27	6.8	18	36	6.6	06	14	2.8	19	00	2.5	09	21	4.0	22	07	4.0
SU 20	09	08	5.2	21	38	5.1	07	19	6.8	20	04	6.9	07	22	2.7	22	00	2.5	10	42	4.1	23	44	4.1
M 21	10	50	5.4	23	12	5.5	08	30	7.3	21	01	7.5	09	33	2.7	22	48	2.7	—	—		12	06	4.3
TU 22	11	52	5.9	—	—		09	20	7.9	21	45	8.0	10	36	2.9	23	28	2.8	00	47	4.4	12	59	4.6
W 23	00	10	6.0	12	40	6.4	10	01	8.4	22	22	8.4	11	17	3.1	—	—		01	26	4.7	13	37	4.9
TH 24	00	56	6.3	13	20	6.7	10	37	8.7	22	56	8.7	00	05	2.9	11	52	3.2	01	58	5.0	14	09	5.1
FR 25	01	34	6.5	13	56	6.8	11	10	9.0	23	28	8.9	00	39	3.0	12	21	3.2	02	27	5.1	14	40	5.3
SA 26	02	08	6.6	14	29	6.7	11	41	9.1	23	59	9.1	01	09	3.0	12	53	3.3	02	56	5.3	15	09	5.4
SU 27	02	38	6.5	15	02	6.7	—	—		12	13	9.2	01	34	3.0	13	27	3.3	03	27	5.4	15	40	5.5
M 28	03	08	6.6	15	35	6.7	00	31	9.1	12	47	9.3	02	00	3.1	14	04	3.4	04	00	5.4	16	13	5.5
TU 29	03	41	6.7	16	11	6.7	01	04	9.1	13	22	9.2	02	28	3.1	14	41	3.4	04	35	5.3	16	50	5.4
W 30	04	19	6.8	16	48	6.6	01	39	9.0	14	00	9.0	02	59	3.2	15	18	3.4	05	12	5.2	17	31	5.2
TH 31	05	01	6.7	17	29	6.4	02	18	8.7	14	43	8.5	03	32	3.2	15	57	3.2	05	54	5.0	18	19	5.0

APRIL 2005   *High Water*   GMT

	LONDON BRIDGE						LIVERPOOL						GREENOCK						LEITH					
FR 1	05	47	6.5	18	14	6.1	03	04	8.2	15	36	7.9	04	09	3.0	16	41	3.0	06	41	4.7	19	17	4.7
SA 2	06	42	6.1	19	07	5.7	04	05	7.7	16	50	7.3	04	54	2.9	17	37	2.8	07	39	4.5	20	34	4.4
SU 3	07	50	5.7	20	21	5.3	05	32	7.3	18	28	7.1	06	00	2.7	19	03	2.6	09	02	4.3	22	06	4.5
M 4	09	23	5.5	22	02	5.4	07	08	7.5	19	58	7.6	08	16	2.6	21	21	2.6	10	32	4.4	23	30	4.7
TU 5	10	58	5.9	23	21	5.9	08	23	8.1	21	02	8.3	09	48	2.9	22	30	2.9	11	47	4.8	—	—	
W 6	—	—		12	03	6.5	09	20	8.8	21	51	8.9	10	43	3.2	23	21	3.1	00	34	5.1	12	44	5.2
TH 7	00	19	6.5	12	55	7.1	10	07	9.4	22	35	9.3	11	30	3.4	—	—		01	23	5.4	13	29	5.5
FR 8	01	06	6.9	13	39	7.3	10	51	9.7	23	15	9.5	00	05	3.2	12	15	3.5	02	04	5.5	14	10	5.7
SA 9	01	48	7.2	14	20	7.4	11	31	9.8	23	52	9.5	00	45	3.2	12	58	3.6	02	42	5.6	14	51	5.8
SU 10	02	28	7.2	14	59	7.2	—	—		12	10	9.7	01	21	3.3	13	38	3.6	03	20	5.5	15	32	5.7
M 11	03	06	7.2	15	34	7.0	00	28	9.3	12	47	9.5	01	53	3.3	14	15	3.5	03	59	5.4	16	13	5.5
TU 12	03	42	7.1	16	05	6.8	01	02	9.1	13	23	9.1	02	25	3.4	14	50	3.5	04	37	5.2	16	54	5.3
W 13	04	17	6.9	16	35	6.6	01	36	8.8	13	58	8.6	02	57	3.4	15	25	3.3	05	15	5.0	17	36	5.0
TH 14	04	54	6.7	17	07	6.5	02	09	8.4	14	34	8.1	03	31	3.4	16	02	3.1	05	54	4.7	18	22	4.6
FR 15	05	33	6.4	17	43	6.2	02	46	7.9	15	17	7.4	04	07	3.2	16	44	2.9	06	38	4.5	19	13	4.3
SA 16	06	17	6.0	18	26	5.8	03	32	7.4	16	13	6.9	04	48	3.0	17	35	2.6	07	32	4.2	20	12	4.1
SU 17	07	10	5.6	19	18	5.4	04	38	6.9	17	48	6.6	05	41	2.8	18	41	2.5	08	39	4.1	21	21	4.0
M 18	08	22	5.3	20	34	5.2	06	28	6.8	19	20	6.8	06	47	2.7	20	31	2.4	09	54	4.1	22	38	4.1
TU 19	10	04	5.4	22	25	5.4	07	45	7.2	20	20	7.3	08	11	2.7	22	04	2.6	11	10	4.2	23	51	4.3
W 20	11	10	5.8	23	29	5.8	08	38	7.7	21	05	7.9	09	41	2.8	22	48	2.8	—	—		12	09	4.5
TH 21	—	—		12	01	6.3	09	21	8.2	21	44	8.3	10	29	3.0	23	25	2.9	00	38	4.6	12	53	4.8
FR 22	00	17	6.2	12	43	6.6	09	58	8.6	22	19	8.7	11	06	3.1	—	—		01	15	4.9	13	30	5.1
SA 23	00	57	6.4	13	21	6.8	10	33	8.9	22	53	8.9	00	00	3.0	11	42	3.2	01	49	5.1	14	04	5.3
SU 24	01	34	6.6	13	58	6.8	11	08	9.1	23	27	9.1	00	31	3.0	12	20	3.2	02	23	5.3	14	38	5.4
M 25	02	09	6.7	14	34	6.8	11	44	9.2	—	—		01	01	3.1	13	00	3.3	02	57	5.4	15	13	5.5
TU 26	02	45	6.8	15	11	6.8	00	03	9.2	12	23	9.2	01	31	3.2	13	41	3.3	03	32	5.4	15	52	5.5
W 27	03	24	6.8	15	50	6.7	00	41	9.2	13	04	9.1	02	03	3.3	14	22	3.3	04	10	5.4	16	34	5.4
TH 28	04	07	6.8	16	31	6.6	01	22	9.1	13	48	8.8	02	38	3.3	15	03	3.3	04	51	5.2	17	21	5.2
FR 29	04	53	6.7	17	14	6.3	02	07	8.7	14	37	8.4	03	14	3.3	15	47	3.1	05	36	5.0	18	14	5.0
SA 30	05	44	6.4	18	02	6.0	02	59	8.3	15	36	7.8	03	55	3.1	16	39	2.9	06	28	4.8	19	17	4.7

MAY 2005   *High Water*   GMT

		LONDON BRIDGE				LIVERPOOL				GREENOCK				LEITH			
		* Datum of Predictions 3.20m below				* Datum of Predictions 4.93m below				* Datum of Predictions 1.62m below				* Datum of Predictions 2.90m below			
		hr	m (ht)	hr	m (ht)	hr	m (ht)	hr	m (ht)	hr	m (ht)	hr	m (ht)	hr	m (ht)	hr	m (ht)
SU	1	06 44	6.1	19 01	5.7	04 05	7.9	16 52	7.4	04 46	3.0	17 50	2.7	07 33	4.6	20 34	4.6
M	2	07 58	5.8	20 23	5.5	05 28	7.6	18 20	7.4	06 04	2.8	19 29	2.6	08 56	4.5	21 55	4.6
TU	3	09 24	5.9	21 46	5.7	06 49	7.8	19 36	7.8	08 01	2.8	21 03	2.7	10 16	4.6	23 09	4.8
W	4	10 37	6.3	22 53	6.2	07 57	8.3	20 35	8.3	09 21	3.0	22 05	2.9	11 24	4.9	—	—
TH	5	11 36	6.7	23 49	6.6	08 53	8.8	21 25	8.7	10 16	3.2	22 53	3.0	00 09	5.0	12 19	5.1
FR	6	—	—	12 27	7.1	09 42	9.1	22 08	9.0	11 05	3.3	23 36	3.1	00 58	5.2	13 06	5.3
SA	7	00 37	6.9	13 12	7.2	10 26	9.3	22 48	9.1	11 50	3.4	—	—	01 39	5.3	13 48	5.4
SU	8	01 22	7.1	13 53	7.1	11 07	9.3	23 25	9.1	00 14	3.2	12 33	3.4	02 18	5.4	14 30	5.5
M	9	02 03	7.1	14 32	7.0	11 45	9.2	—	—	00 50	3.2	13 13	3.3	02 56	5.3	15 12	5.4
TU	10	02 43	6.9	15 06	6.7	00 00	9.0	12 22	9.0	01 24	3.3	13 51	3.3	03 34	5.3	15 53	5.3
W	11	03 21	6.8	15 37	6.6	00 34	8.9	12 57	8.7	01 57	3.4	14 28	3.2	04 11	5.1	16 34	5.1
TH	12	03 58	6.6	16 07	6.5	01 08	8.7	13 32	8.4	02 31	3.4	15 04	3.1	04 48	5.0	17 15	4.9
FR	13	04 35	6.5	16 41	6.4	01 43	8.4	14 10	8.0	03 05	3.4	15 43	3.0	05 26	4.8	17 57	4.6
SA	14	05 14	6.3	17 18	6.2	02 22	8.0	14 53	7.6	03 41	3.3	16 28	2.8	06 08	4.6	18 44	4.4
SU	15	05 58	6.0	18 00	6.0	03 07	7.6	15 44	7.1	04 22	3.1	17 20	2.7	06 58	4.4	19 36	4.3
M	16	06 46	5.8	18 49	5.7	04 03	7.3	16 51	6.9	05 11	2.9	18 21	2.6	07 57	4.2	20 34	4.2
TU	17	07 44	5.6	19 52	5.4	05 18	7.1	18 15	6.9	06 11	2.8	19 28	2.5	09 04	4.2	21 37	4.2
W	18	08 55	5.5	21 13	5.4	06 38	7.2	19 22	7.2	07 19	2.8	20 42	2.6	10 09	4.3	22 40	4.3
TH	19	10 09	5.8	22 29	5.7	07 40	7.6	20 14	7.7	08 28	2.8	21 47	2.7	11 09	4.5	23 37	4.6
FR	20	11 10	6.1	23 27	6.0	08 29	8.0	20 58	8.2	09 29	2.9	22 36	2.8	12 00	4.7	—	—
SA	21	12 00	6.5	—	—	09 13	8.4	21 39	8.6	10 20	3.0	23 17	2.9	00 26	4.8	12 46	5.0
SU	22	00 15	6.4	12 45	6.7	09 55	8.7	22 18	8.9	11 05	3.1	23 54	3.0	01 09	5.1	13 28	5.2
M	23	01 00	6.6	13 28	6.9	10 37	9.0	22 58	9.1	11 50	3.2	—	—	01 49	5.2	14 09	5.3
TU	24	01 42	6.8	14 09	6.9	11 20	9.1	23 40	9.3	00 31	3.1	12 36	3.3	02 29	5.4	14 52	5.5
W	25	02 26	6.9	14 52	6.9	—	—	12 05	9.2	01 09	3.2	13 23	3.3	03 09	5.4	15 37	5.5
TH	26	03 12	6.9	15 36	6.7	00 25	9.3	12 53	9.1	01 47	3.3	14 10	3.3	03 52	5.4	16 24	5.5
FR	27	04 00	6.9	16 21	6.6	01 13	9.1	13 44	8.8	02 26	3.4	14 59	3.2	04 37	5.3	17 15	5.4
SA	28	04 52	6.8	17 09	6.4	02 04	8.9	14 37	8.5	03 08	3.4	15 52	3.1	05 26	5.2	18 11	5.2
SU	29	05 47	6.5	18 02	6.2	03 00	8.6	15 36	8.1	03 54	3.3	16 53	2.9	06 22	5.0	19 13	4.9
M	30	06 47	6.3	19 02	6.0	04 02	8.3	16 43	7.8	04 52	3.1	18 02	2.8	07 27	4.9	20 22	4.8
TU	31	07 55	6.2	20 11	6.0	05 10	8.2	17 54	7.7	06 05	3.0	19 14	2.8	08 41	4.8	21 32	4.7

JUNE 2005   *High Water*   GMT

		LONDON BRIDGE				LIVERPOOL				GREENOCK				LEITH			
W	1	09 03	6.3	21 18	6.1	06 19	8.1	19 02	7.8	07 30	3.0	20 24	2.8	09 51	4.8	22 38	4.8
TH	2	10 06	6.5	22 19	6.3	07 24	8.2	20 02	8.0	08 45	3.1	21 26	2.9	10 54	4.9	23 38	4.9
FR	3	11 03	6.7	23 16	6.6	08 23	8.4	20 55	8.3	09 46	3.2	22 18	3.0	11 52	5.0	—	—
SA	4	11 55	6.8	—	—	09 15	8.6	21 41	8.5	10 39	3.2	23 04	3.0	00 30	5.0	12 43	5.1
SU	5	00 08	6.7	12 44	6.9	10 02	8.7	22 23	8.7	11 27	3.2	23 46	3.1	01 16	5.1	13 30	5.1
M	6	00 57	6.8	13 28	6.8	10 45	8.7	23 01	8.8	—	—	12 13	3.1	01 57	5.1	14 14	5.1
TU	7	01 43	6.8	14 09	6.7	11 24	8.7	23 37	8.7	00 24	3.2	12 54	3.1	02 36	5.2	14 56	5.1
W	8	02 27	6.7	14 45	6.5	—	—	12 02	8.6	01 00	3.3	13 34	3.0	03 14	5.1	15 37	5.1
TH	9	03 07	6.6	15 18	6.4	00 12	8.7	12 38	8.5	01 35	3.3	14 12	3.0	03 50	5.1	16 16	5.0
FR	10	03 45	6.4	15 49	6.4	00 48	8.6	13 14	8.3	02 10	3.4	14 50	2.9	04 26	5.0	16 54	4.9
SA	11	04 21	6.4	16 22	6.3	01 25	8.4	13 52	8.1	02 45	3.4	15 30	2.9	05 04	4.9	17 33	4.7
SU	12	04 58	6.3	16 58	6.3	02 04	8.2	14 32	7.9	03 21	3.3	16 14	2.8	05 43	4.8	18 15	4.6
M	13	05 38	6.2	17 38	6.1	02 46	8.0	15 16	7.6	04 00	3.2	17 01	2.7	06 27	4.6	19 01	4.5
TU	14	06 21	6.1	18 22	6.0	03 33	7.8	16 06	7.4	04 44	3.1	17 52	2.7	07 15	4.5	19 50	4.4
W	15	07 10	5.9	19 13	5.8	04 26	7.6	17 05	7.3	05 34	2.9	18 43	2.7	08 10	4.4	20 46	4.4
TH	16	08 06	5.8	20 16	5.7	05 27	7.5	18 10	7.3	06 31	2.9	19 37	2.6	09 10	4.4	21 44	4.4
FR	17	09 10	5.8	21 26	5.7	06 29	7.6	19 12	7.6	07 31	2.8	20 37	2.7	10 11	4.5	22 43	4.5
SA	18	10 17	6.0	22 34	5.9	07 30	7.9	20 09	8.0	08 36	2.9	21 41	2.7	11 09	4.6	23 39	4.7
SU	19	11 18	6.3	23 35	6.2	08 26	8.2	21 00	8.4	09 39	3.0	22 37	2.9	—	—	12 05	4.8
M	20	—	—	12 12	6.6	09 20	8.5	21 49	8.8	10 35	3.1	23 25	3.0	00 32	4.9	12 58	5.1
TU	21	00 30	6.6	13 02	6.8	10 12	8.8	22 36	9.1	11 28	3.2	—	—	01 21	5.1	13 48	5.3
W	22	01 22	6.8	13 50	6.9	11 04	9.0	23 25	9.3	00 10	3.2	12 20	3.2	02 07	5.3	14 38	5.5
TH	23	02 12	7.0	14 37	6.9	11 55	9.1	—	—	00 54	3.3	13 13	3.2	02 52	5.4	15 27	5.6
FR	24	03 03	7.1	15 25	6.8	00 15	9.4	12 47	9.1	01 37	3.4	14 07	3.2	03 39	5.5	16 16	5.6
SA	25	03 55	7.0	16 14	6.8	01 06	9.4	13 39	9.1	02 21	3.5	15 02	3.2	04 27	5.5	17 08	5.5
SU	26	04 47	7.0	17 03	6.7	01 58	9.4	14 31	8.9	03 06	3.5	15 56	3.1	05 17	5.4	18 01	5.4
M	27	05 40	6.9	17 53	6.6	02 50	9.2	15 23	8.6	03 54	3.5	16 50	3.1	06 11	5.3	18 58	5.1
TU	28	06 35	6.7	18 45	6.5	03 44	8.9	16 17	8.2	04 46	3.4	17 44	3.0	07 10	5.2	19 58	4.9
W	29	07 32	6.6	19 42	6.4	04 40	8.5	17 16	7.9	05 44	3.2	18 36	2.9	08 13	5.0	20 59	4.7
TH	30	08 31	6.4	20 41	6.3	05 41	8.2	18 21	7.7	06 48	3.1	19 30	2.9	09 18	4.9	22 01	4.6

JULY 2005   *High Water*   GMT

	LONDON BRIDGE *Datum of Predictions 3.20m below				LIVERPOOL *Datum of Predictions 4.93m below				GREENOCK *Datum of Predictions 1.62m below				LEITH *Datum of Predictions 2.90m below			
	hr	m	hr	m (ht)	hr	m	hr	m (ht)	hr	m	hr	m (ht)	hr	m	hr	m (ht)
FR 1	09 30	6.3	21 42	6.3	06 46	8.0	19 25	7.7	08 01	3.0	20 32	2.8	10 22	4.8	23 02	4.6
SA 2	10 27	6.3	22 42	6.2	07 50	7.9	20 25	7.8	09 15	3.0	21 38	2.9	11 24	4.7	—	—
SU 3	11 23	6.3	23 42	6.3	08 50	8.0	21 18	8.1	10 18	3.0	22 35	2.9	00 01	4.7	12 25	4.8
M 4	—	—	12 17	6.4	09 43	8.2	22 04	8.3	11 12	3.0	23 23	3.0	00 55	4.8	13 18	4.8
TU 5	00 38	6.4	13 07	6.5	10 29	8.3	22 45	8.5	12 00	3.0	—	—	01 41	4.9	14 05	4.9
W 6	01 29	6.5	13 52	6.5	11 11	8.4	23 22	8.6	00 05	3.2	12 45	2.9	02 22	5.0	14 46	5.0
TH 7	02 15	6.6	14 31	6.5	11 49	8.4	23 58	8.7	00 44	3.2	13 26	2.9	03 00	5.1	15 23	5.0
FR 8	02 56	6.5	15 05	6.4	—	—	12 24	8.4	01 20	3.3	14 04	2.9	03 35	5.1	15 58	5.0
SA 9	03 32	6.5	15 36	6.4	00 33	8.7	12 59	8.4	01 53	3.3	14 40	2.8	04 09	5.1	16 33	5.0
SU 10	04 05	6.4	16 07	6.4	01 09	8.6	13 34	8.3	02 27	3.3	15 16	2.8	04 43	5.1	17 09	4.9
M 11	04 38	6.4	16 39	6.4	01 45	8.5	14 10	8.2	03 01	3.3	15 53	2.8	05 19	5.0	17 46	4.8
TU 12	05 14	6.4	17 14	6.3	02 22	8.4	14 47	8.1	03 37	3.3	16 31	2.8	05 56	4.9	18 27	4.7
W 13	05 52	6.3	17 53	6.3	03 01	8.2	15 27	7.9	04 16	3.2	17 12	2.8	06 36	4.8	19 10	4.6
TH 14	06 35	6.2	18 36	6.1	03 44	8.1	16 14	7.7	04 58	3.1	17 55	2.8	07 19	4.7	19 58	4.5
FR 15	07 24	6.0	19 30	6.0	04 35	7.9	17 10	7.5	05 46	3.0	18 41	2.7	08 10	4.6	20 53	4.5
SA 16	08 23	5.9	20 34	5.8	05 35	7.7	18 16	7.5	06 41	2.9	19 36	2.6	09 13	4.5	21 55	4.5
SU 17	09 29	5.8	21 46	5.8	06 41	7.7	19 24	7.7	07 48	2.8	20 49	2.7	10 23	4.5	22 59	4.6
M 18	10 39	6.0	23 00	6.0	07 50	7.9	20 30	8.1	09 04	2.9	22 05	2.8	11 33	4.7	—	—
TU 19	11 44	6.3	—	—	08 57	8.2	21 29	8.6	10 15	3.0	23 04	3.0	00 02	4.8	12 38	5.0
W 20	00 08	6.4	12 43	6.6	09 58	8.6	22 23	9.1	11 16	3.1	23 54	3.2	01 00	5.0	13 36	5.3
TH 21	01 08	6.8	13 35	6.8	10 54	9.0	23 14	9.5	—	—	12 13	3.1	01 52	5.3	14 28	5.6
FR 22	02 02	7.1	14 25	7.0	11 47	9.2	—	—	00 42	3.4	13 10	3.2	02 40	5.5	15 16	5.8
SA 23	02 54	7.2	15 13	7.0	00 04	9.7	12 38	9.4	01 28	3.5	14 04	3.2	03 26	5.7	16 04	5.8
SU 24	03 44	7.3	16 00	7.0	00 54	9.8	13 26	9.4	02 14	3.6	14 55	3.2	04 13	5.8	16 52	5.7
M 25	04 33	7.2	16 45	7.0	01 42	9.8	14 12	9.2	02 58	3.7	15 42	3.2	05 01	5.8	17 41	5.5
TU 26	05 21	7.1	17 30	6.9	02 29	9.6	14 57	8.9	03 41	3.7	16 25	3.2	05 50	5.6	18 31	5.2
W 27	06 08	6.9	18 13	6.8	03 16	9.2	15 43	8.5	04 25	3.6	17 06	3.2	06 41	5.4	19 24	5.0
TH 28	06 56	6.6	19 00	6.6	04 04	8.7	16 32	8.0	05 11	3.4	17 48	3.1	07 38	5.1	20 20	4.7
FR 29	07 48	6.3	19 53	6.3	04 58	8.1	17 30	7.5	06 02	3.2	18 33	2.9	08 41	4.8	21 20	4.5
SA 30	08 45	6.0	20 57	6.0	06 03	7.6	18 43	7.3	07 00	2.9	19 24	2.8	09 47	4.6	22 24	4.4
SU 31	09 47	5.8	22 09	5.8	07 19	7.4	19 58	7.4	08 36	2.7	20 41	2.8	10 58	4.4	23 33	4.5

AUGUST 2005   *High Water*   GMT

	LONDON BRIDGE				LIVERPOOL				GREENOCK				LEITH			
M 1	10 51	5.8	23 20	5.9	08 31	7.5	20 59	7.7	10 11	2.8	22 11	2.9	—	—	12 10	4.5
TU 2	11 53	6.0	—	—	09 28	7.7	21 49	8.1	11 08	2.8	23 06	3.0	00 38	4.6	13 11	4.6
W 3	00 22	6.2	12 48	6.3	10 16	8.1	22 32	8.5	11 55	2.9	23 51	3.2	01 29	4.8	13 57	4.8
TH 4	01 15	6.5	13 35	6.5	10 58	8.3	23 09	8.7	—	—	12 37	2.9	02 10	5.0	14 34	5.0
FR 5	02 00	6.6	14 15	6.6	11 34	8.5	23 44	8.8	00 30	3.2	13 17	2.9	02 46	5.1	15 07	5.0
SA 6	02 39	6.7	14 50	6.6	—	—	12 08	8.5	01 03	3.3	13 52	2.9	03 18	5.2	15 37	5.1
SU 7	03 13	6.6	15 20	6.5	00 17	8.9	12 40	8.6	01 35	3.3	14 23	2.9	03 48	5.3	16 08	5.1
M 8	03 43	6.5	15 48	6.4	00 49	8.8	13 11	8.6	02 05	3.3	14 52	2.9	04 20	5.3	16 41	5.1
TU 9	04 13	6.5	16 16	6.4	01 21	8.8	13 42	8.5	02 37	3.3	15 21	2.9	04 51	5.2	17 16	5.0
W 10	04 45	6.5	16 46	6.5	01 53	8.7	14 14	8.4	03 11	3.3	15 53	3.0	05 24	5.1	17 53	4.9
TH 11	05 20	6.5	17 22	6.5	02 27	8.6	14 49	8.3	03 47	3.3	16 27	2.9	05 59	5.0	18 32	4.8
FR 12	05 59	6.4	18 04	6.4	03 05	8.4	15 31	8.0	04 24	3.2	17 03	2.9	06 39	4.9	19 16	4.7
SA 13	06 44	6.1	18 53	6.2	03 53	8.0	16 23	7.7	05 06	3.1	17 45	2.8	07 26	4.7	20 08	4.5
SU 14	07 38	5.9	19 55	5.9	04 54	7.7	17 32	7.4	05 57	2.9	18 39	2.7	08 29	4.5	21 13	4.4
M 15	08 44	5.6	21 08	5.7	06 07	7.4	18 53	7.5	07 05	2.8	20 00	2.6	09 51	4.4	22 28	4.5
TU 16	10 03	5.6	22 33	5.8	07 30	7.6	20 12	7.9	08 40	2.7	21 44	2.8	11 14	4.6	23 42	4.7
W 17	11 23	5.9	23 56	6.2	08 49	8.0	21 18	8.6	10 10	2.9	22 50	3.0	—	—	12 27	5.0
TH 18	—	—	12 28	6.4	09 52	8.6	22 13	9.2	11 15	3.1	23 41	3.3	00 46	5.1	13 26	5.4
FR 19	00 59	6.7	13 22	6.8	10 45	9.1	23 02	9.7	—	—	12 10	3.2	01 39	5.4	14 15	5.7
SA 20	01 52	7.2	14 10	7.1	11 34	9.5	23 49	10.0	00 28	3.5	13 02	3.3	02 24	5.7	15 01	5.9
SU 21	02 40	7.4	14 54	7.2	—	—	12 19	9.6	01 14	3.7	13 50	3.3	03 08	5.9	15 45	5.9
M 22	03 26	7.5	15 37	7.3	00 34	10.1	13 03	9.6	01 58	3.8	14 34	3.4	03 52	6.0	16 29	5.8
TU 23	04 10	7.4	16 18	7.3	01 18	10.0	13 45	9.4	02 40	3.8	15 12	3.4	04 37	6.0	17 13	5.6
W 24	04 52	7.2	16 58	7.2	02 01	9.7	14 25	9.0	03 19	3.8	15 48	3.4	05 23	5.8	17 59	5.3
TH 25	05 32	6.9	17 37	7.0	02 42	9.2	15 04	8.5	03 58	3.6	16 23	3.3	06 10	5.4	18 46	4.9
FR 26	06 11	6.6	18 16	6.7	03 25	8.5	15 47	8.0	04 37	3.4	17 01	3.2	07 02	5.0	19 38	4.6
SA 27	06 50	6.1	19 01	6.2	04 14	7.8	16 38	7.4	05 20	3.1	17 44	3.1	08 04	4.6	20 38	4.4
SU 28	07 37	5.7	20 03	5.7	05 19	7.2	17 57	7.0	06 10	2.8	18 33	2.9	09 13	4.3	21 46	4.3
M 29	08 52	5.4	21 37	5.4	06 53	6.9	19 33	7.1	07 21	2.6	19 38	2.8	10 30	4.2	23 03	4.3
TU 30	10 19	5.4	23 00	5.6	08 14	7.1	20 41	7.6	10 09	2.7	21 49	2.9	11 56	4.3	—	—
W 31	11 29	5.7	—	—	09 11	7.6	21 31	8.1	11 00	2.8	22 48	3.1	00 18	4.5	12 59	4.6

SEPTEMBER 2005   *High Water*   GMT

	LONDON BRIDGE * Datum of Predictions 3.20m below				LIVERPOOL * Datum of Predictions 4.93m below				GREENOCK * Datum of Predictions 1.62m below				LEITH * Datum of Predictions 2.90m below			
	hr m	ht	hr m	ht	hr m	ht	hr m	ht	hr m	ht	hr m	ht	hr m	ht	hr m	ht
TH 1	00 03	6.1	12 25	6.2	09 57	8.0	22 12	8.5	11 41	3.0	23 32	3.2	01 11	4.8	13 41	4.8
FR 2	00 54	6.5	13 11	6.5	10 36	8.4	22 49	8.8	—	—	12 18	3.0	01 51	5.0	14 14	5.0
SA 3	01 37	6.8	13 51	6.7	11 11	8.6	23 22	9.0	00 09	3.3	12 55	3.0	02 23	5.2	14 43	5.1
SU 4	02 14	6.8	14 25	6.6	11 43	8.7	23 53	9.0	00 42	3.3	13 27	3.0	02 53	5.3	15 11	5.2
M 5	02 46	6.7	14 55	6.5	—	—	12 13	8.8	01 10	3.3	13 55	3.0	03 22	5.4	15 40	5.3
TU 6	03 15	6.6	15 21	6.4	00 22	9.0	12 42	8.8	01 39	3.4	14 19	3.1	03 51	5.4	16 11	5.3
W 7	03 44	6.6	15 47	6.5	00 51	9.0	13 11	8.8	02 10	3.4	14 45	3.1	04 22	5.4	16 44	5.2
TH 8	04 14	6.6	16 18	6.6	01 22	8.9	13 42	8.7	02 44	3.4	15 14	3.1	04 54	5.3	17 20	5.1
FR 9	04 48	6.6	16 55	6.6	01 55	8.8	14 16	8.5	03 19	3.4	15 46	3.1	05 30	5.1	17 58	5.0
SA 10	05 26	6.4	17 37	6.5	02 33	8.5	14 56	8.2	03 55	3.3	16 20	3.0	06 11	5.0	18 41	4.8
SU 11	06 09	6.2	18 27	6.2	03 21	8.0	15 50	7.7	04 34	3.1	16 59	2.9	07 02	4.7	19 34	4.6
M 12	07 00	5.8	19 28	5.8	04 25	7.5	17 04	7.3	05 24	2.9	17 54	2.8	08 08	4.5	20 42	4.4
TU 13	08 06	5.5	20 43	5.5	05 51	7.2	18 37	7.3	06 36	2.7	19 26	2.7	09 36	4.4	22 09	4.5
W 14	09 33	5.4	22 22	5.6	07 27	7.4	20 04	7.9	08 40	2.7	21 31	2.9	11 04	4.7	23 28	4.7
TH 15	11 08	5.8	23 49	6.2	08 45	8.0	21 07	8.7	10 14	2.9	22 34	3.2	—	—	12 17	5.1
FR 16	—	—	12 13	6.4	09 41	8.8	21 58	9.4	11 11	3.1	23 24	3.4	00 31	5.2	13 12	5.5
SA 17	00 47	6.9	13 04	6.9	10 29	9.3	22 44	9.9	11 59	3.3	—	—	01 21	5.6	13 57	5.8
SU 18	01 35	7.3	13 48	7.2	11 13	9.6	23 27	10.2	00 10	3.6	12 44	3.4	02 04	5.9	14 39	5.9
M 19	02 19	7.5	14 29	7.4	11 55	9.7	—	—	00 54	3.8	13 25	3.4	02 45	6.1	15 20	5.9
TU 20	03 01	7.5	15 09	7.4	00 09	10.2	12 35	9.6	01 37	3.8	14 03	3.5	03 28	6.1	16 01	5.8
W 21	03 41	7.4	15 48	7.3	00 51	9.9	13 13	9.4	02 16	3.8	14 37	3.5	04 11	6.0	16 43	5.5
TH 22	04 18	7.1	16 26	7.2	01 30	9.5	13 50	9.0	02 54	3.8	15 10	3.5	04 56	5.7	17 26	5.3
FR 23	04 53	6.8	17 03	7.0	02 08	9.0	14 26	8.5	03 30	3.6	15 45	3.5	05 42	5.3	18 10	4.9
SA 24	05 25	6.5	17 42	6.6	02 48	8.3	15 04	8.0	04 07	3.4	16 22	3.4	06 32	4.9	18 59	4.6
SU 25	05 59	6.1	18 26	6.1	03 33	7.6	15 52	7.4	04 47	3.1	17 04	3.2	07 30	4.5	19 58	4.4
M 26	06 38	5.7	19 22	5.6	04 37	6.9	17 10	6.9	05 37	2.8	17 55	3.0	08 39	4.2	21 08	4.2
TU 27	07 35	5.3	21 04	5.2	06 25	6.6	19 02	6.9	06 47	2.6	19 00	2.9	09 56	4.1	22 27	4.3
W 28	09 44	5.2	22 33	5.5	07 48	7.0	20 12	7.4	09 52	2.7	21 06	2.9	11 27	4.3	23 46	4.5
TH 29	10 58	5.6	23 34	6.0	08 44	7.5	21 02	8.0	10 36	2.9	22 18	3.1	—	—	12 31	4.6
FR 30	11 54	6.1	—	—	09 28	8.0	21 43	8.5	11 13	3.1	23 02	3.2	00 39	4.8	13 12	4.8

OCTOBER 2005   *High Water*   GMT

	LONDON BRIDGE				LIVERPOOL				GREENOCK				LEITH			
SA 1	00 24	6.5	12 40	6.5	10 06	8.5	22 19	8.8	11 49	3.1	23 38	3.3	01 19	5.1	13 43	5.1
SU 2	01 06	6.8	13 19	6.6	10 40	8.7	22 52	9.0	—	—	12 22	3.2	01 51	5.3	14 11	5.2
M 3	01 41	6.8	13 53	6.6	11 11	8.9	23 21	9.1	00 08	3.3	12 54	3.2	02 21	5.4	14 39	5.3
TU 4	02 13	6.8	14 23	6.6	11 41	9.0	23 51	9.1	00 38	3.4	13 20	3.2	02 51	5.5	15 09	5.4
W 5	02 43	6.7	14 51	6.5	—	—	12 10	9.0	01 09	3.4	13 44	3.2	03 21	5.5	15 40	5.4
TH 6	03 13	6.7	15 21	6.6	00 21	9.1	12 41	9.0	01 43	3.4	14 12	3.3	03 53	5.5	16 14	5.4
FR 7	03 45	6.6	15 56	6.6	00 55	9.0	13 15	8.9	02 19	3.5	14 42	3.3	04 29	5.4	16 50	5.3
SA 8	04 20	6.6	16 36	6.7	01 32	8.8	13 52	8.6	02 56	3.4	15 15	3.3	05 09	5.2	17 30	5.1
SU 9	04 59	6.5	17 21	6.5	02 14	8.4	14 36	8.2	03 33	3.3	15 50	3.2	05 56	5.0	18 16	4.9
M 10	05 43	6.2	18 13	6.2	03 05	7.9	15 34	7.8	04 15	3.1	16 32	3.1	06 51	4.8	19 11	4.6
TU 11	06 34	5.8	19 16	5.8	04 15	7.3	16 52	7.4	05 08	2.9	17 31	2.9	08 01	4.6	20 26	4.5
W 12	07 42	5.4	20 38	5.5	05 48	7.1	18 28	7.5	06 35	2.7	19 19	2.8	09 29	4.5	21 55	4.6
TH 13	09 21	5.4	22 19	5.8	07 22	7.5	19 48	8.1	08 47	2.8	21 11	3.0	10 52	4.8	23 11	4.9
FR 14	10 48	5.9	23 32	6.4	08 30	8.2	20 48	8.8	10 03	3.0	22 13	3.2	12 00	5.2	—	—
SA 15	11 48	6.5	—	—	09 22	8.9	21 37	9.4	10 53	3.2	23 01	3.6	00 10	5.3	12 52	5.5
SU 16	00 26	7.0	12 37	7.0	10 07	9.3	22 22	9.8	11 37	3.4	23 47	3.7	00 58	5.6	13 35	5.7
M 17	01 12	7.4	13 21	7.3	10 48	9.6	23 04	10.0	—	—	12 17	3.5	01 41	5.9	14 15	5.8
TU 18	01 54	7.5	14 02	7.4	11 28	9.6	23 44	9.9	00 30	3.8	12 55	3.5	02 22	6.0	14 54	5.8
W 19	02 33	7.4	14 42	7.3	—	—	12 05	9.5	01 13	3.8	13 30	3.6	03 05	5.9	15 34	5.7
TH 20	03 11	7.2	15 21	7.2	00 23	9.6	12 42	9.3	01 52	3.7	14 04	3.6	03 48	5.8	16 14	5.5
FR 21	03 45	6.9	15 59	7.0	01 01	9.2	13 17	8.9	02 29	3.7	14 38	3.7	04 33	5.5	16 55	5.2
SA 22	04 17	6.7	16 38	6.7	01 38	8.7	13 53	8.5	03 05	3.5	15 14	3.6	05 18	5.2	17 37	5.0
SU 23	04 48	6.4	17 18	6.4	02 17	8.1	14 31	8.0	03 43	3.3	15 51	3.5	06 06	4.8	18 24	4.7
M 24	05 22	6.2	18 02	6.0	03 01	7.5	15 17	7.5	04 25	3.1	16 33	3.4	07 00	4.5	19 21	4.4
TU 25	06 02	5.8	18 55	5.6	03 59	6.9	16 23	7.1	05 17	2.8	17 24	3.2	08 01	4.2	20 29	4.3
W 26	06 54	5.4	20 10	5.3	05 38	6.6	18 11	7.0	06 28	2.6	18 27	3.0	09 10	4.1	21 41	4.3
TH 27	08 27	5.2	21 47	5.4	07 05	6.9	19 37	7.5	08 56	2.7	19 49	3.0	10 26	4.2	22 53	4.4
FR 28	10 12	5.4	22 52	5.8	08 03	7.4	20 21	7.8	09 52	2.9	21 22	3.1	11 37	4.5	23 51	4.7
SA 29	11 11	5.8	23 43	6.2	08 49	7.9	21 04	8.3	10 33	3.1	22 15	3.2	—	—	12 24	4.7
SU 30	11 59	6.2	—	—	09 28	8.4	21 41	8.6	11 10	3.2	22 54	3.3	00 35	5.0	13 00	5.0
M 31	00 25	6.5	12 40	6.5	10 03	8.7	22 15	8.9	11 45	3.3	23 29	3.3	01 12	5.2	13 32	5.2

NOVEMBER 2005   *High Water*   GMT

	LONDON BRIDGE * Datum of Predictions 3.20m below				LIVERPOOL * Datum of Predictions 4.93m below				GREENOCK * Datum of Predictions 1.62m below				LEITH * Datum of Predictions 2.90m below			
	hr	m	hr	m	hr	m	hr	m	hr	m	hr	m	hr	m	hr	m
TU 1	01 03	6.7	13 16	6.6	10 36	8.9	22 47	9.1	—	—	12 16	3.3	01 46	5.3	14 04	5.3
W 2	01 38	6.8	13 50	6.6	11 08	9.1	23 21	9.2	00 03	3.4	12 45	3.3	02 19	5.5	14 37	5.4
TH 3	02 12	6.8	14 24	6.7	11 41	9.2	23 57	9.2	00 41	3.4	13 14	3.4	02 54	5.5	15 12	5.5
FR 4	02 47	6.8	15 01	6.7	—	—	12 17	9.1	01 20	3.5	13 46	3.5	03 31	5.5	15 48	5.4
SA 5	03 23	6.7	15 42	6.8	00 36	9.1	12 57	9.0	02 00	3.5	14 20	3.5	04 12	5.4	16 27	5.3
SU 6	04 01	6.6	16 27	6.7	01 19	8.8	13 41	8.8	02 40	3.4	14 56	3.5	04 57	5.3	17 10	5.2
M 7	04 43	6.4	17 16	6.5	02 07	8.4	14 30	8.4	03 22	3.3	15 35	3.4	05 47	5.1	18 00	5.0
TU 8	05 28	6.2	18 11	6.2	03 03	8.0	15 31	8.1	04 11	3.1	16 22	3.3	06 46	4.9	18 59	4.8
W 9	06 22	5.8	19 17	5.9	04 13	7.6	16 45	7.8	05 15	2.9	17 29	3.1	07 56	4.7	20 14	4.7
TH 10	07 36	5.6	20 38	5.8	05 38	7.4	18 08	7.9	06 48	2.8	19 08	3.1	09 16	4.7	21 37	4.8
FR 11	09 07	5.7	21 58	6.1	06 58	7.7	19 20	8.3	08 25	2.9	20 39	3.2	10 30	4.9	22 46	5.0
SA 12	10 18	6.1	23 02	6.5	08 03	8.2	20 20	8.8	09 33	3.1	21 43	3.4	11 34	5.1	23 44	5.3
SU 13	11 16	6.6	23 56	6.9	08 56	8.7	21 12	9.2	10 24	3.3	22 35	3.5	—	—	12 26	5.3
M 14	—	—	12 07	6.9	09 41	9.1	21 58	9.4	11 08	3.4	23 23	3.6	00 34	5.5	13 11	5.5
TU 15	00 44	7.2	12 54	7.1	10 23	9.3	22 41	9.5	11 48	3.5	—	—	01 20	5.6	13 51	5.5
W 16	01 27	7.2	13 38	7.2	11 03	9.3	23 22	9.4	00 08	3.6	12 26	3.5	02 03	5.7	14 31	5.6
TH 17	02 07	7.1	14 20	7.1	11 40	9.3	—	—	00 51	3.6	13 02	3.6	02 47	5.6	15 11	5.5
FR 18	02 45	6.9	15 01	6.9	00 00	9.2	12 16	9.1	01 31	3.5	13 38	3.7	03 31	5.5	15 51	5.4
SA 19	03 19	6.7	15 42	6.7	00 38	8.9	12 52	8.9	02 10	3.5	14 14	3.7	04 15	5.3	16 30	5.2
SU 20	03 50	6.5	16 21	6.5	01 15	8.6	13 29	8.6	02 47	3.3	14 50	3.7	04 58	5.0	17 10	5.0
M 21	04 21	6.4	17 01	6.3	01 54	8.2	14 09	8.3	03 27	3.2	15 28	3.6	05 42	4.8	17 53	4.8
TU 22	04 57	6.2	17 42	6.1	02 37	7.7	14 53	7.9	04 11	3.1	16 09	3.5	06 29	4.6	18 43	4.6
W 23	05 37	6.0	18 29	5.8	03 27	7.3	15 47	7.5	05 03	2.9	16 56	3.3	07 21	4.4	19 43	4.4
TH 24	06 24	5.7	19 22	5.6	04 32	7.0	16 55	7.3	06 04	2.8	17 52	3.1	08 19	4.3	20 47	4.4
FR 25	07 24	5.5	20 27	5.5	05 53	6.9	18 15	7.3	07 11	2.8	18 54	3.1	09 20	4.3	21 50	4.4
SA 26	08 47	5.4	21 40	5.6	07 04	7.2	19 20	7.6	08 27	2.8	20 01	3.1	10 22	4.4	22 48	4.6
SU 27	10 06	5.6	22 44	5.9	07 58	7.6	20 11	7.9	09 33	3.0	21 07	3.1	11 17	4.6	23 41	4.8
M 28	11 05	5.9	23 36	6.3	08 43	8.1	20 55	8.3	10 23	3.1	22 02	3.2	—	—	12 07	4.8
TU 29	11 54	6.2	—	—	09 23	8.5	21 36	8.7	11 04	3.2	22 49	3.3	00 27	5.0	12 51	5.0
W 30	00 22	6.6	12 39	6.5	10 01	8.8	22 16	8.9	11 40	3.3	23 33	3.3	01 11	5.2	13 32	5.2

DECEMBER 2005   *High Water*   GMT

	LONDON BRIDGE				LIVERPOOL				GREENOCK				LEITH			
TH 1	01 05	6.8	13 21	6.7	10 40	9.1	22 58	9.1	—	—	12 15	3.4	01 52	5.3	14 10	5.4
FR 2	01 46	6.9	14 03	6.8	11 20	9.2	23 41	9.2	00 17	3.4	12 51	3.5	02 33	5.4	14 49	5.5
SA 3	02 27	6.9	14 48	6.9	—	—	12 02	9.3	01 02	3.4	13 28	3.6	03 16	5.5	15 29	5.5
SU 4	03 08	6.8	15 34	6.9	00 26	9.1	12 48	9.3	01 48	3.4	14 07	3.6	04 01	5.5	16 12	5.4
M 5	03 51	6.7	16 24	6.8	01 15	8.9	13 37	9.1	02 34	3.4	14 48	3.6	04 49	5.4	16 59	5.3
TU 6	04 37	6.5	17 16	6.6	02 06	8.7	14 29	8.9	03 23	3.3	15 32	3.6	05 41	5.3	17 50	5.2
W 7	05 25	6.3	18 12	6.4	03 01	8.4	15 26	8.7	04 18	3.1	16 24	3.5	06 37	5.1	18 47	5.1
TH 8	06 20	6.1	19 13	6.3	04 02	8.1	16 28	8.4	05 21	3.0	17 26	3.4	07 41	4.9	19 55	5.0
FR 9	07 27	6.0	20 20	6.2	05 10	7.8	17 35	8.3	06 30	3.0	18 39	3.3	08 51	4.8	21 08	4.9
SA 10	08 38	6.1	21 26	6.3	06 21	7.8	18 44	8.3	07 40	3.0	19 57	3.3	09 59	4.8	22 15	5.0
SU 11	09 43	6.2	22 28	6.4	07 28	8.0	19 48	8.5	08 48	3.1	21 09	3.3	11 02	4.9	23 17	5.1
M 12	10 43	6.4	23 24	6.6	08 27	8.3	20 46	8.7	09 48	3.2	22 10	3.4	11 58	5.0	—	—
TU 13	11 38	6.6	—	—	09 18	8.6	21 38	8.8	10 38	3.3	23 03	3.4	00 13	5.2	12 49	5.1
W 14	00 15	6.7	12 31	6.7	10 03	8.8	22 24	8.9	11 23	3.4	23 51	3.4	01 05	5.2	13 34	5.2
TH 15	01 03	6.7	13 20	6.8	10 44	9.0	23 06	8.9	—	—	12 03	3.5	01 52	5.3	14 16	5.3
FR 16	01 47	6.7	14 06	6.7	11 23	9.0	23 45	8.8	00 37	3.3	12 42	3.6	02 37	5.3	14 56	5.3
SA 17	02 27	6.6	14 50	6.6	12 00	9.0	—	—	01 20	3.3	13 20	3.6	03 20	5.2	15 35	5.3
SU 18	03 02	6.5	15 31	6.5	00 23	8.7	12 37	8.9	02 00	3.2	13 56	3.7	04 00	5.1	16 12	5.2
M 19	03 33	6.4	16 08	6.4	01 00	8.5	13 14	8.8	02 38	3.2	14 33	3.7	04 39	5.0	16 49	5.1
TU 20	04 05	6.3	16 44	6.3	01 38	8.3	13 52	8.6	03 17	3.1	15 10	3.6	05 18	4.9	17 27	5.0
W 21	04 39	6.3	17 21	6.3	02 17	8.1	14 32	8.3	03 57	3.1	15 48	3.5	05 59	4.7	18 09	4.8
TH 22	05 16	6.2	18 00	6.2	02 58	7.8	15 15	8.1	04 41	3.0	16 29	3.4	06 42	4.6	18 55	4.7
FR 23	05 57	6.1	18 44	6.0	03 44	7.6	16 03	7.8	05 28	2.9	17 14	3.3	07 29	4.5	19 47	4.5
SA 24	06 44	5.9	19 33	5.9	04 38	7.3	16 59	7.6	06 18	2.9	18 04	3.2	08 22	4.4	20 44	4.5
SU 25	07 40	5.7	20 31	5.8	05 41	7.2	18 01	7.5	07 11	2.8	18 59	3.1	09 19	4.4	21 45	4.5
M 26	08 49	5.6	21 37	5.8	06 47	7.4	19 05	7.7	08 12	2.8	20 01	3.0	10 18	4.4	22 46	4.5
TU 27	10 01	5.7	22 44	6.0	07 49	7.7	20 05	8.0	09 21	2.9	21 10	3.0	11 16	4.6	23 45	4.7
W 28	11 07	6.0	23 44	6.3	08 43	8.1	21 01	8.3	10 21	3.0	22 14	3.1	—	—	12 12	4.8
TH 29	—	—	12 06	6.4	09 32	8.6	21 52	8.7	11 10	3.2	23 09	3.2	00 40	4.9	13 03	5.0
FR 30	00 37	6.6	12 59	6.7	10 19	9.0	22 42	9.0	11 53	3.3	—	—	01 32	5.2	13 50	5.2
SA 31	01 26	6.8	13 49	6.9	11 06	9.3	23 32	9.2	00 01	3.3	12 35	3.5	02 20	5.4	14 34	5.4

INDEX

STOP-PRESS

CHANGES SINCE PAGES WENT TO PRESS

PARLIAMENT
A by-election for Hartlepool was held on 30 September 2004 following the resignation of Peter Mandelson. Labour candidate Iain Wright won with 12,752 votes, a majority of 2,033.

PUBLIC OFFICES

HM REVENUE AND CUSTOMS
3 September 2004 – Steve Lamey was appointed as Chief Information Officer.

REGIONAL GOVERNMENT

NORTHERN IRELAND
16–18 September, Leeds Castle – Talks between British Prime Minister Tony Blair and Irish Prime Minister Bertie Ahern on the re-wording of the Good Friday Agreement, to ensure full decommissioning of IRA weapons, ended without a deal being reached.

21–22 September, Stormont – Northern Ireland Secretary Paul Murphy and Irish Minister of State Tom Kitt met with representatives of Northern Ireland's political parties, however the talks broke down on 22 September.

POLICE
5 July 2004 – Sir John Stevens confirmed he would retire as Commissioner of the Metropolitan Police on 31 January 2005.

EVENTS OF THE YEAR – SEPTEMBER 2004

BRITISH AFFAIRS
13. A *Fathers 4 Justice* protester trespassed the perimeter walls of Buckingham Palace and climbed up the front of the building. Metropolitan Police Commissioner, Sir John Stevens, demanded a full report into the security breach. 15. A pro-hunting demonstration in Parliament Square ended in violent clashes between protesters and police. Five protesters managed to enter the House of Commons during a debate of the Hunting Bill.

ENVIRONMENT AND SCIENCE
8. A £153 million NASA mission to collect particles of the sun ended in disaster when the probe carrying the samples crashed into the Utah desert after two parachutes failed to open; scientists hoped that some of the sample could still be salvaged if the pod remained sealed.

THE AMERICAS
12. Hurricane Ivan passed directly over the Cayman Islands, causing flash flooding and mudslides. Across the Caribbean sixty people had already been killed as a result of the storm. 19. Floodwaters tore through Haiti in the wake of tropical storm Jeanne, submerging the entire northern coastal city of Gonaives and killing at least 250 people.

ASIA
9. A British couple was shot dead by an off-duty policeman in Thailand following an argument in a restaurant near the River Kwai. 12. It was reported that a large explosion causing a two-mile-wide mushroom cloud had occurred in North Korea near the Chinese border.

EUROPE
1. Twenty Chechen terrorists took hundreds of adults and children hostage in a school in Beslan, southern Russia, as the children returned after the summer break. The terrorists threatened to blow-up the school if the Russian Government did not withdraw its troops from Chechnya and release prisoners captured after recent Chechen attacks on the neighbouring region of Ingushetia. 2. The siege of the school in Beslan continued; fifteen children and eleven women were released following negotiations. 3. The siege of the school in Beslan ended after two explosions, followed by gunfire from within the school, forced Russian special forces to storm the building. 4. Official figures were released stating that 323 people had died during the Beslan school siege. More than 600 people were injured.

THE MIDDLE EAST
18. In Iraq, terrorists from the Tawhid wal Jihad group released video footage of three hostages (a British engineer and two Americans) stating that they would be beheaded unless demands for the release of Iraqi women prisoners were met within 48 hours. 20. Video footage was released by Tawhid wal Jihad showing that one of the American hostages had been beheaded. 21. The Tawhid wal Jihad group announced that the second American hostage had been killed. 22. Baghdad police retrieved the body of the second American hostage. A video of the final hostage, Briton Kenneth Bigley, was released in which he made a direct plea to Prime Minister Tony Blair to intervene and requested him to meet the demands of the hostage-takers and free the female prisoners held in Iraqi jails.

OBITUARIES
Ramone, Johnny (John Cummings), guitarist, aged 55 – d. 15 September 2004, b. 8 October 1948
Clough, Brian, footballer and manager, aged 69 – d. 20 September 2004, b. 21 March 1935